PRINCIPLES

OF THE

LAW OF SCOTLAND

George Joseph Bell

(1770-1843)

From a portrait by Sir Henry Raeburn

Principles
of the
Law of Scotland

BY

GEORGE JOSEPH BELL
PROFESSOR OF THE LAW OF SCOTLAND IN THE UNIVERSITY OF EDINBURGH

The Tenth Edition, Revised and Enlarged

BY

WILLIAM GUTHRIE, ADVOCATE, LL.D. EDIN.
1899

THE 1989 REPRINT
INTRODUCTION BY PROFESSOR WILLIAM M. GORDON

THE LAW SOCIETY OF SCOTLAND
BUTTERWORTHS

EDINBURGH

The Law Society of Scotland
The Law Society's Hall, 26 Drumsheugh Gardens, EDINBURGH EH3 7YR

Butterworths

United Kingdom	Butterworth & Co (Publishers) Ltd, 88 Kingsway, LONDON WC2B 6AB and 4 Hill Street, EDINBURGH EH2 3JZ
Australia	Butterworths Pty Ltd, SYDNEY, MELBOURNE, BRISBANE, ADELAIDE, PERTH, CANBERRA and HOBART
Canada	Butterworth & Co (Canada) Ltd, TORONTO and VANCOUVER
Ireland	Butterworth (Ireland) Ltd, DUBLIN
Malaysia	Malayan Law Journal Sdn Bhd, KUALA LUMPUR
New Zealand	Butterworths of New Zealand Ltd, WELLINGTON and AUCKLAND
Singapore	Butterworth & Co (Asia) Pte, Ltd, SINGAPORE
USA	Butterworth Legal Publishers, ST PAUL, Minnesota, SEATTLE, Washington, BOSTON, Massachusetts, AUSTIN, Texas and D & S Publishers, CLEARWATER, Florida

ISBN 0 406 179034

INTRODUCTION

TO THE 1989 REPRINT

BELL'S LIFE[1]

George Joseph Bell was born on 26 March 1770, the third son of an Episcopalian clergyman. His father died in 1779 and in a memoir written in his later years Bell says that his formal schooling could not continue after his eleventh year because the fees were beyond the family means. However, in his short monograph on Bell, Wilton states that Bell's memory must have played him false because he is shown as a pupil of the High School of Edinburgh for the years 1784 to 1788.[2] According to Wilton, Bell also attended the lectures on moral philosophy of Dugald Stewart at Edinburgh University, although he never graduated in arts, and Bell himself says that he attended Hume's lectures on Scots law there.[3] As he speaks of attending Hume's 'first course' this would put his attendance in the session 1787–88 which was Hume's first full session as professor.[4] All this creates an inconsistency with the dates given by Wilton for his attendance at the High School and, if these were correct, Bell might have meant that he attended a first course of lectures in one of the years in which Hume gave a second course devoted to criminal law.[5] But in a history of the High School of Edinburgh[6] both Bell and his younger brother Charles, who became a distinguished surgeon, are said to have attended the High School in the same years (1784–1788) and under the same masters and some confusion between the two brothers seems likely.

Bell's immediately elder brother, Robert, the author of *Bell on Leases* and other works, had become a Writer to the Signet in 1784 and it seems probable that he encouraged Bell to enter the legal profession. Bell himself sought a career at the bar and he passed advocate on 19 November 1791. As he was a Whig in politics his early years at the bar may have been particularly difficult but his decision to write the work on bankruptcy which became the *Commentaries*, the work which made his reputation, was not necessarily taken because he had time on his hands. In the Spring of 1797 he and his brother Charles, to whom he was very close,[7] both decided to write a book, each on his own area of expertise. It was presumably the Bankruptcy (Scotland) Act 1772 which turned Bell's thoughts to bankruptcy as his topic. Because it had been found useful the Act had been renewed in 1793 for the third time, this time for five years, and in 1799 it was continued in force until 1804. However, it is tempting to think that he may have had other inspiration as it is said of his elder brother John, another eminent surgeon, that 'Although his income was large, it was not sufficient for his style of living; hence he was sometimes placed in circumstances of great embarrassment.'[8] The first volume of Bell's work appeared in 1800; a second volume dedicated to the Lord Chancellor, Lord Thurlow, appeared in 1804 and the whole work was issued under the title of *Commentaries on the Municipal and Mercantile Law of Scotland considered in relation to the subject of Bankruptcy* in that year.[9]

By 1806 Bell was sufficiently established in practice to marry and on 22 October 1806 he took as his wife Barbara Shaw, eldest daughter of Charles Shaw, a solicitor in Ayr. There were five daughters of the marriage, which ended with the death of his wife on 28 March 1827. He continued with his writing and produced the second edition of the *Commentaries* in 1810 and the first volume of a third edition in 1816 but the appearance of the second volume of the third edition was delayed until 1819. Between 1816 and 1818, by arrangement with the Society of Writers to the Signet, Bell delivered lectures on conveyancing at the University of Edinburgh in place of his brother Robert who had died in 1816. The arrangement continued until the appointment of McVey Napier who subsequently became the first professor of conveyancing and Bell paid the stipend to Robert's widow who had not been well provided for.[10] When Hume demitted office as Professor of Scots Law on his appointment as a Baron of Exchequer in 1821, Bell, who had produced a fourth edition of the *Commentaries* in that year, was proposed as his successor by the Dean of Faculty John Clerk of Eldin, seconded by Sir Walter Scott. The proposal was accepted by the Town Council on 27 February 1822 and Bell was admitted to the Senate of the University on 9 March of that year. On 23 January 1822 he had been made an honorary member of the Juridical Society along with Hume, who was the first such member to be granted that honour,[11] and on 3 June 1822 he became a Fellow of the Royal Society of Edinburgh.[12]

Anderson[13] states that 'As a lecturer on Scots Law he was unsurpassed. His style was terse and lucid in a remarkable degree' but, although one might easily form such a judgment on the basis of the *Principles*, taking them as typical of his style, not all the students of his early years would have shared it. One of them reports[14] that Bell came ill-prepared to his lectures and was considered much inferior to Napier as a lecturer. He may have improved in time and his own evidence to the Royal Commission on the Universities of Scotland is that he spoke from a detailed text[15]. At the same time it is clear from the preface to the first edition of the *Principles* addressed to his students, that he expected them to play an active part in the learning process, and he may not have been as methodical in presenting material for their digestion as he suggested to the commission[16].

One reason why he may not have given his full attention to his early lectures is that he was appointed in 1823 to the first of the commissions on law reform on which he served. This commission was the Royal Commission on the courts which was set up under the Act 4 Geo 4 c 85. The commission reported in March 1824 (C 241) and Bell evidently played a substantial part in its work as well as in the drafting of the bill which followed. He was congratulated on behalf of the House of Lords for his assistance. However the bill did not have an easy passage. When first presented it met with opposition. The WS Society, the SSC Society and the noblemen, freeholders, JPs and Commissioners of Supply of the county of Edinburgh all presented petitions to the House of Lords.[17] They also presented petitions to the House of Commons along with the magistrates and town council of the Royal burgh of Irvine, the Dean of the Faculty of Advocates and the Keepers, Commissioners and Clerks of HM Signet.[18] Bell wrote an *Examination of Objections to the Bill* which appeared in 1825. His work apparently helped to allay opposition. The bill was reintroduced in that year and became the Court of Session Act 1825. Bell was also working at this time on the fifth edition of his *Commentaries*, the last which he himself prepared, which appeared in 1826.

Unlike his predecessor Hume, Bell never reached the Bench. Cockburn[19] has a somewhat mysterious reference to his exclusion from the Bench 'because he would not be dishonest' which suggests that his political views may have affected his prospects. However he did receive a salaried post in the Court of Session in late December 1831 when he was appointed a Principal Clerk of Session.[20] Bell remained in demand for work on law reform. In 1833 he was made chairman of a Royal Commission which among other things was asked to look at the fees charged to suitors in the Court of Session and the possibility of reducing them by reducing the court staff. One of the recommendations of the commission's first report, which appeared in 1834, was that the number of Principal Clerks, which had already been reduced in 1830, be reduced still further. No doubt it would have been difficult for Bell to dissent. The commission was renewed and extended in 1834 and a second report appeared in 1835. It was renewed again in 1837 and still further extended but finally expired in 1839. By this time a third report had been produced in 1838, dealing with conveyancing, and while further material was published late in 1839 after expiry of the commission, there was no fourth report as such. In all, the commission met on 303 occasions.[21] That it proceeded no further may have been connected with Bell's health.

His labours on the commission did not prevent him from working on the *Principles*, of which the fourth edition appeared in 1839, and he brought out between 1836 and 1838 three volumes of *Illustrations* to supplement them for his students by giving short accounts of leading cases. In the preface to the fourth edition he refers to this as completing his original design, along with the *Principles* themselves. This edition was the last which he was to produce and, as already mentioned, he completed no further edition of the *Commentaries*, although his brother-in-law and literary executor Patrick Shaw says in the prefatory note in his edition of the *Principles* that Bell worked on the *Commentaries* in all the time he could spare thereafter, and he did publish supplementary studies, for example, on sale. In his last years Bell suffered from poor health and in particular from an affliction of the eyes which led to blindness or near blindness. Even in 1838 Charles Sumner[22] refers to him as 'quite weak, even for his years'. He was eventually unable to carry out his duties as Clerk of Session and he died in relatively poor circumstances on 23 September 1843, and was buried with his wife in St John's Episcopal Church. He left most of his estate to his second daughter Barbara in token of the care she had shown for her mother. Wilton[23] notes also that his death merited only a few lines in the current newspapers although they do record that 'a very eminent lawyer' had passed away.

The Principles

As the full title, 'Principles of the Law of Scotland for the use of students in the University of Edinburgh', and the prefatory remarks addressed to his students show, Bell intended the first edition of the *Principles* in 1829 as a guide for his students, for their studies in the first place and for the emergencies of practice thereafter. The later editions were all dedicated to Jeffrey, first as Dean of Faculty, then as Lord Advocate and Member of Parliament for Edinburgh and finally as Judge of the Supreme Court of Scotland and Senator of the College of Justice. If it be true that Jeffrey failed to take an opportunity to have Bell raised to the Bench when his politics would no longer have been an obstacle – other Whigs were so honoured[24] – there is no sign that Bell felt any grudge. In the last edition he still refers to a 'long-cherished friendship' and there may have been no ulterior motive behind the assiduous dedication. In this last edition Bell says that 'the former editions' have all been dedicated to Jeffrey which suggests that he regarded the first one as what might now be called an exposure draft. Although it is sometimes said that it grew out of outlines of his lectures issued soon after he took up office, Bell's own evidence to the Scottish Universities' Commission was that he had never been able to prepare a syllabus of his lectures[25] and this was said in 1826. He may have been stimulated to put the substance of his lectures in published form by the questions of the commissioners as he certainly was moved to reconsider his position on examinations – after consultation with his brother Charles.[26] In the Report by the Law Faculty on the commission's provisional proposals the appearance of the *Principles* is cited as evidence that 'new means of study have been furnished' for the students showing that reform could be achieved without the changes suggested.[27]

However the first appearance of the book may be explained, it underwent considerable changes in the three further editions by Bell which came out in 1830, 1833 and 1839. Over these three editions it increased in length by some 50 per cent and the number of paragraphs increased from 896 to 2351 (having reached a high point of 2439 in the third edition). Not all of the increase in numbered paragraphs reflects increase in length. The structure of the book was set in the first edition and the most considerable changes made thereafter were made in the final sections. The largest increase in numbered paragraphs in fact took place between the first and second editions (from 896 to 2435) and, while the treatment of topics in the second edition is generally fuller than in the first, much of the increase reflects sub-division of the original paragraphs rather than the addition of new topics. By the time Bell begins to deal with property, for example, para 151 has become para 636 and para 241 on nuisance becomes paras 973 and 974, with little increase in content.

After para 886 the changes are more radical. First of all, Bell adds a long section (paras 2129 to 2213) on the rights of persons in their public relations, covering, among other things, voting rights and public corporations such as burghs. Then he inserts a new Part V on actions and diligence. In the first edition this had consisted of no more than a short 'Conclusion' (paras 887 to 896) giving a 'general view of actions and diligence'. It explained the types of action possible, mainly petitory, possessory and declaratory (para 888); gave a short but clear statement of the function of pleading and the distinction of the issue to be resolved into questions of law and questions of fact (paras 889 to 891); and then listed the forms of diligence available, ending with a paragraph on insolvency. In the new Part V Bell added a 'general view of the courts of justice in Scotland' (remarking *inter alia* at para 2225 that the House of Lords sits as a Scottish court of justice when dealing with a Scottish case). He also extended his account of actions (paras 2232 to 2270) and of the principles of pleading and issues and other procedural questions (paras 2271 to 2350), explaining the objects of pleading (paras 2272 to 2274) in a way well worth reading even today. A new feature was an account of the law of evidence (paras 2279 to 2328) and he expanded his treatment of diligence (paras 2351 to 2435). All these features were then kept in the third edition, where he covers much the same ground, but in the fourth he abandoned the treatment of the courts and procedure, explaining in an introductory note to Part V that the law had become too complex and the number of recent decisions too great to be accommodated in the *Principles*. The account of evidence and diligence remained, with a fuller account of the recently reformed law of mercantile sequestration (paras 2341 to 2351), a reform in which Bell himself and his commission had had a hand.[28]

A new edition had to wait for some time after Bell's death and was produced, as already mentioned, by Bell's brother-in-law Patrick Shaw, who is also the Shaw of the reports of Session Cases. He was inclined to meddle more than was really necessary with Bell's text and introduced the division into books and chapters (which goes unnoticed in citation – as indeed do the divisions of the French civil code). There was again a considerable interval before the sixth edition in 1872 which was produced by William Guthrie, who became a Sheriff Substitute of Lanarkshire in 1874 and was later Sheriff Principal.[29] David Murray, who was to attain distinction not only in his profession of solicitor but as an antiquary and book collector,[30] assisted him in its preparation. He received a complimentary copy which is still in the Murray Collection which he donated to Glasgow University Library – along with an interleaved copy of the fourth edition containing a note by Murray that this was the only law book which Sheriff Henry Glassford Bell[31] (no relative of Bell) possessed. In the sixth edition Guthrie reverted to the text of the fourth edition, marking additions by square brackets, but he kept the division into books and chapters. He was also responsible for all subsequent editions from the seventh of 1876 to the tenth and last of 1899, which might be regarded as providing, for lawyers at least, a fitting conclusion to the century. The policy of adhering substantially to Bell's text but making and marking additions was maintained. Although the number of paragraphs found in the fourth edition was retained, many new paragraphs were added with alphabetical suffixes in order to cope with topics such as the Companies Acts (paras 403A to 403U in the tenth edition) without disturbing the arrangement left by Bell. Essentially, therefore, Bell's work is still there in the edition now reproduced despite the extensive additions made by Guthrie. The experiment of dividing the work into two volumes in the editions of 1885 and 1889 was given up in the last edition. The problem of including the large accretion of material which occurred over the years as new statutes and decisions were incorporated was solved by adopting a double column text and a larger format.

The *Principles* has never been a discursive text. Bell's skill as displayed in it lay in compressing an enormous amount of information into relatively small space. The range of material included is indeed quite astonishing. There are few topics which are not at least touched on in the text or in the notes and it is little wonder that Bell was called on to serve on the wide-ranging law reform commissions of which he was chairman. At the same time the range of material which he had covered posed for the editor Guthrie an increasing problem in updating the content while retaining as much as possible of Bell's own text. It is not surprising that there were eventually no new editions and that in 1903 Frank Halley Morrison, a solicitor in Dundee, who had himself recently qualified,[32] published a *Synopsis* for the benefit of students.

IMPORTANCE OF THE PRINCIPLES

The function of providing a succinct account of the most important provisions of Scots law in a single volume 'for the use of students, and for the sudden occasions of practice', as Bell himself put it in the preface to his last edition (p iv), is now fulfilled by Gloag and Henderson's *Introduction to the Law of Scotland*. The first edition of that work was produced, as its authors said in their Preface, specifically to replace the updated, but increasingly dated, versions of the *Principles* of Bell and Erskine which still served as basic student textbooks in Glasgow and Edinburgh. Even the tenth edition of Bell's *Principles* cannot be relied on to provide an answer, or the starting-point for an immediate answer, to many of the new problems which confront the practitioner in his daily practice. It cannot be a guide to the detail of the latest additions to the statutory jungle. But the function of an institutional treatise, in the sense of a work of recognised authority, which Bell's *Principles* has become,[33] has not been to provide simply a guide to the current law, however works which are now institutional may have been conceived by their authors. One very important function has been to provide a coherent and structured account of the law which provides a foundation of principle for subsequent development. That function Bell's *Principles* continues to fulfil. There are always questions to which an answer must be sought by starting from basic principles. On such questions Bell, author of many now classic definitions, such as the definitions of common interest (para 1086 of the 10th edition) or of nuisance (para 974), is and will remain one of the indispensable guides.

WILLIAM M GORDON
Douglas Professor of Civil Law
University of Glasgow

April 1989

NOTES

1. The fullest biography of Bell is G W Wilton, *George Joseph Bell* (1929). In biographical dictionaries, such as *Dictionary of National Biography* and W Anderson, *The Scottish Nation* (3 vols 1865), Bell comes a poor second in length of entry to his brothers John and Charles who both achieved distinction as surgeons. D M Walker, *The Scottish Jurists* (1985) pp 337ff, with notes at pp 352ff, adds recent references but, not unnaturally, he tends to concentrate on Bell's *Commentaries*. The present account is based on published sources in which some inaccuracies have been noted and corrected.
2. Wilton, *op cit*, pp 5–6.
3. *Evidence . . . taken . . . by the Commissioners . . . for visiting the Universities of Scotland*. Vol I (University of Edinburgh) (1837), p 186.
4. G C H Campbell, ed, *Baron Humes's Lectures 1786–1822. Biography of Baron Hume*, Vol VI (Stair Society Publications, Vol 19, 1958), pp 327ff at p 336; *cf* also *Evidence, cit, Appendix*, p 285, where Hume says that he held examinations in his first two sessions as professor; Bell says that he recollected that there were examinations when he attended.
5. Campbell, *Biography, cit*, p 408.
6. W Steven, *History of the High School of Edinburgh* (1849), Appendix No XI at p 204.
7. See note in *Journal of Jurisprudence*, 16 (1872) 428.
8. Anderson, *op cit,* Vol I, p 277.
9. See title page of copy in Glasgow University Library.
10. *History of the Society of Writers to H. M. Signet* (1890) p cxvii; Wilton, *op cit*, pp 11–12. Napier's appointment as professor is recorded at p cxxi of the *History*. At p cxix it is noted that Bell was one of a minority of the Faculty of Advocates who had favoured the creation of the chair.
11. Campbell, *op cit*, p 378.
12. See entry in H Frew, ed, *Index of Fellows of the Royal Society of Edinburgh Elected Nov. 1783 to July 1883* (1984).
13. Anderson, *op cit,* Vol I, p 278.
14. T St J N Bates, 'Mr McConnachie's Notes and Mr Fraser's Confessional' 1980 JR 166 at pp 176–177, with reference there to an earlier article in a student magazine. Student expectations of him were higher on his appointment – see J T D Hall, ed, *The Tounis College. An Anthology of Edinburgh University Student Journals* (1985) p 13, quoting a piece from January 1823 – although even there there is perhaps a hint of reservation in the statement, 'Of Mr Bell . . . it would be premature, at present, to offer any criticism . . .', unless 'criticism' is to be read in the sense of 'critique'.
15. *Evidence, cit*, p 188.
16. Preface to 1st edition (1829) p iv, addressed 'To the Students of the Law of Scotland in the University of Scotland'.
17. *House of Lords Journals*, Vol 56 (1824), pp 396, 405, 428.
18. *House of Commons Journals*, Vol 79 (1824), p 507.
19. *Circuit Journeys*, (1889), p 203.
20. The number of Principal Clerks has been reduced by the Court of Session Act 1830, providing Sir Walter Scott with an occasion for resignation – J G Lockhart, *Life of Sir Walter Scott* (1896), pp 704–706. Bell was not his immediate successor as is suggested in the *Journal of Jurisprudence, cit*.
21. For the various reports, see *House of Commons Papers,* 1834, xxvi, 163; 1835, xxxv, 463; 1837–38, xxix, 1; 1840, xx, 15; and the returns by the clerk to the commission 1837–38, xliv, 421; 1840, xli, 473.
22. K H Nadelman, 'Joseph Story and George Joseph Bell' 1959 JR 31 at p 37.
23. Wilton, *op cit*, p 17–18. Much of his estate consisted of life policies, valued at £12,000; he left debts of £9,000.
24. See Walker, *op cit*, at p 338 and n 12.
25. *Evidence, cit*, p 188.
26. *Evidence, cit, Appendix*, p 285.
27. *Evidence, cit, Appendix*, p 257. It is also noted that Bell had provided a library for his students, which he did at his own expense – see his own evidence at p 56.
28. See the Bankruptcy (Scotland) Act 1839 (2 & 3 Vict c 41) and the earlier Cessio (Scotland) Act 1836 (6 and 7 Will 4 c 56).
29. See entry in *DNB, Second Supplement*, vol 2, (1912), p 179. Guthrie (1835–1908) became Sheriff Principal in 1903. He was an active editor and translator. As well as his editions of Bell's *Principles*, he produced, among other things, three editions of Erskine's *Principles*, two series of *Select Cases in the Sheriff Courts* and a translation of Savigny's *Private International Law*. He also edited the *Journal of Jurisprudence* from 1867 to 1874 and he received an LLD from the University of Edinburgh.
30. See entry in *Who Was Who*, Vol 2 (1916–1928) (1947), p 764, Murray (1842–1928) was a partner in the well-known firm of Maclay, Murray and Spens and he served as Dean of the Royal Faculty of Procurators in

Glasgow from 1895 to 1898. He was rector's assessor on Glasgow University Court from 1896 to 1899 and he received an LLD from Glasgow University.

31. See entry in *DNB*, Vol 4 (1885), pp 160–61. Bell (1803–1874) passed advocate in 1832, became a Sheriff-Substitute of Lanarkshire in 1839 and Sheriff Principal in 1867. He was a man of letters before turning to the law and the entry in the *DNB* refers to his reputation as 'the last of the literary sheriffs' and 'the best judge that ever sat in the Sheriff Court of Glasgow'. In the note referred to, Murray also gives him high praise as a judge and acknowledges that he borrowed other books as required from the agents who appeared before him or from the library.

32. *Scottish Law List* – he was admitted in 1901.

33. J W G Blackie, 'Stair's Later Reputation as a Jurist' in D M Walker, ed, *Stair Tercentenary Studies* (Stair Society Publications, Vol 33, 1981) 207, especially at pp 208ff and 218ff, and J W Cairns, 'Institutional Writings in Scotland Reconsidered' in A Kiralfy and H L MacQueen, eds, *New Perspectives in Scottish Legal History* (1984) (reprinted from Vol 4, part 3 of the *Journal of Legal History*) 76, especially at p 94 and pp 98ff.

JURISPERITORUM PRINCIPI

JOANNI INGLIS

SACRUM

AB ILLO LAUDATUM

OPUS

PRAEMIO ORNATUM GRATISSIMO

PREFACE TO THE TENTH EDITION

THE general plan remains as stated in the Preface to the Eighth Edition. Only a few modifications have to be noticed.

Many friends advised me to abandon the device of marking the additions to Professor Bell's text by square brackets, and, following the Editors of Blackstone, Smith's Leading Cases, and other English books of authority, to make no distinction between what is old and what is new. I have not thought it right to do this; but in the text I have substituted single inverted commas for square brackets, and in the notes no distinction is now made between Professor Bell's citations and remarks and mine. Where in the notes it is desired to distinguish, the internal evidence of dates, or of the matter itself, in most cases sufficiently informs the intelligent reader.

I have attempted, though not so completely as I wished, to help the reader by subdividing the longer sections by paragraphs and further sub-titles; and I have begun, what I hope my successors in editing may fully accomplish, to print the names of leading cases in blacker type. To select all the leading cases for this purpose, and thoroughly to weed out, as I also proposed to do, the references which have become useless, involved more labour and delay than could be allowed. For the present edition has been loudly demanded for several years, and I regret that even after I realised this, several unfortunate circumstances have delayed the completion of the work.

In this edition I have been greatly helped, as in the ninth, by Mr. George Guthrie, LL.B., Glasgow, for whose ability and accuracy I can securely vouch. He has almost entirely revised the portions of the book which deal with Stamp Duties, Feudal Conveyancing, Heritable Securities, Leases, Marriage, Marriage Contracts, Legacy Duty, Estate Duty; and he has also read the proof-sheets and otherwise assisted me.

W. GUTHRIE.

GLASGOW, *August* 1899.

PREFACE TO THE EIGHTH EDITION

In preparing for the third time an edition of Bell's Principles of the Law of Scotland, I have adhered to the plan pursued in my former editions. I have preserved the original text, and put all additions within square brackets. There are, however, some differences in this edition which it is proper to mention.

I have endeavoured to remedy the anomaly and inconvenience of stating in the text, in the words of Professor Bell, propositions which are immediately contradicted in the notes, by turning the original into the past tense when it has been altered by subsequent legislation or decisions, or into oblique narration, when Mr. Bell's view has to be corrected. The statement of the law and its changes thus become continuous, and more easily read; and the text itself is made to show in almost all cases the present state of the law. I have thus endeavoured to make the text such a synopsis or code of the principles of the law of Scotland as the author would have given if he had been writing at the present day, and according to his original plan; or, rather, if he still survived, and were himself re-editing the book. I have, however, made fewer changes in the old text than he would probably have done.

This edition also differs from those which preceded it in the greater bulk of the additions. The 768 pages of the volume now issued correspond with 477 pages of Mr. Shaw's edition of 1860, and 473 pages of the author's last edition of 1839; being an increase of 291 and 295 pages respectively. As, however, each of these 768 pages has a line more than each page in the edition of 1860, the actual increase is equal to 309 pages. If we count in the same way, this volume exceeds by 199 pages the same portion of the last edition—that of 1876.

In the second volume the additions to the text will probably be somewhat less bulky; but it will contain a list of authorities and reports cited, and for the first time a full index of the cases cited, besides a very large number of additional entries in the index of matters.

The careful and competent reader cannot fail to observe that Professor Bell left many passages of the text in an imperfect state, and passed over, or but slightly touched on, many subjects which he would undoubtedly have desired to treat more fully in the finished work. I cannot say that I have filled up many such blanks; but the cases cited by Mr. Bell, which are not always authorities for the text, but landmarks for tracing the development of the law as it may be more fully seen in the three volumes of the Illustrations of the Law of Scotland, have in many instances been more carefully verified than in former editions, and many errors of reference have been corrected. My chief endeavour has been to present the most important results of later legislation and litigation in a convenient and accurate form, with ample reference to the authorities which students or practising lawyers may require for the fuller examination of the questions which lie within the scope of the book.

Examples of passages which have been written with difficulty and labour out of all proportion to their length, abound in the first two chapters treating of the *generalia* of Obligations and of Sale, as well as in subsequent chapters; *e.g.* the sections on Error and Fraud, Homologation and Personal Exception, Impossible and Illegal Contracts, the Measure of Damages, the Computation of Time, the Wrongful Use of Diligence, Restrictions on Buildings in Feu-Contracts, Obligations to Relieve of Public Burdens, and many other subjects; while in the incorporation of the Bills of Exchange Act and the late Conveyancing Acts, and of the great mass of recent decisions on the Law of Companies, Shipping, and other branches of Mercantile Law, I cannot hope altogether to have overcome the difficulty of giving a correct summary of what is new, and at the same time making it harmonise in some degree with the original arrangement.

No one, indeed, can be more aware than I am of many omissions and defects; but only those who have been engaged in work of the same kind can rightly estimate the labour and difficulty with which the shortest statements of the law in such a book are frequently attended; and the sense of responsibility with which, in a new issue of the most familiar handbook of every Scots lawyer, such statements are submitted to the public.

For such labour and responsibility there is in general, as the life of Professor Bell himself proved, no adequate reward, except those which grow out of the work itself, and such as may be found in the indulgent appreciation of the learned and liberal profession for whose use the book is mainly intended.

W. G.

GLASGOW, *Dec.* 1884.

PREFATORY NOTE TO MR. SHAW'S EDITION

George Joseph Bell was born in Edinburgh on the 26th of March 1770. He was the third son of the Reverend William Bell, a clergyman of the Episcopal communion. He was educated in Edinburgh, or, more correctly, was to a great extent self-taught. On the 19th of November 1791 he was admitted to the Bar, and in 1805 he married the eldest daughter of Charles Shaw, Esq., Ayr (*a*). He was unanimously elected by the Faculty of Advocates, on the 2nd of February 1822, Professor of the Law of Scotland in the University of Edinburgh. The motion was made by John Clerk of Eldin, then Leader of the Bar, and was seconded by Sir Walter Scott.

Soon afterwards, he issued, for the use of the Students, "Outlines" of his lectures. In 1829 he was induced to give them more extensive circulation, by publishing them under the title of "Principles of the Law of Scotland." He dedicated the book to the Students, expressing a "hope that it would render their study of a very difficult science more easy, by supplying them with a brief statement of the leading rules and exceptions, and a correct list of the authorities relied on in support of the several propositions, or useful in illustrating them" (*b*). This, which forms the first edition of the work, contained only about nine hundred sections; but it was greatly enlarged in the second edition, published in 1830, which embraced upwards of two thousand four hundred sections, and a large additional number of authorities. The popularity and the utility of the work were shown by a new edition being called for in three years thereafter; and this was followed by the publication, in 1839, of a fourth edition.

Still more to aid the studies of his pupils, Mr. Bell published, in 1836 and 1838, "Illustrations of the Principles of the Law of Scotland," in three volumes,—a work of much labour and of great utility.

He died in September 1843. In the interval, he had devoted all the time he could spare from the performance of public duties to the preparation of a new edition of his "Commentaries on the Laws of Scotland." On that work he had made large alterations, which are embodied in the edition which I lately published (*c*). He had, however, left untouched the

(*a*) His youngest brother, Sir Charles Bell, the well-known anatomist, married the second daughter of Mr. Shaw.

(*b*) In consulting the authorities, the origin and object of the work should be kept in view. Sometimes they appear adverse to the doctrine in the text; but this was pointed out and formed the subject of comment in the Lectures.

(*c*) From my connection with Mr. Bell (brother-in-law), I was on the most intimate and confidential footing with him. I assisted him in carrying through the press the fifth edition of his "Commentaries," and the later editions of the "Principles." On his death, his manuscripts were entrusted to me.

"Principles"; and in this edition the text stands as in the last. The only alterations are, that the work is now divided into books and chapters; that many of the divisions and subdivisions in the sections (which tended somewhat to perplex) have been omitted; and that a few of the sections have been thrown together, in order to bring similar or analogous doctrines into immediate juxtaposition (*a*).

(*a*) These may be seen in the table of corresponding sections at the end of the work, marked by a circumflex. It became necessary, for that and other reasons, to make some alteration on the numbers of the sections. These are shown in the table.

CHARLOTTE SQUARE, *April* 1860.

[*Note.*—An interesting notice of Professor Bell by the late Lord Justice-Clerk Moncreiff may be found in the "Edinburgh Review" for April 1872, and is quoted in the "Journal of Jurisprudence," vol. xvi. p. 428.]

ADVERTISEMENT TO THE FOURTH EDITION

I HAVE made important additions to the text of this edition. Since the former edition was published, many decisions have been pronounced, both here and in England, greatly affecting the doctrines and rules of Law; and several statutes have been passed, by which changes have been made both in legal doctrine and in matters of form. I have endeavoured, in a careful revisal, to incorporate this new matter in the present edition, in fulfilment of that duty which is most especially necessary in what is meant for Students and the younger part of the profession.

In this work, and in three volumes of Illustrations, I have completed my original design. My purpose was to exhibit for the use of Students, and for the sudden occasions of practice, a concise and clear statement of the principles and rules of the Law, with proofs and illustrations from decided cases of their practical application in the actual business of the Bar. And I am happy to learn that, in the opinion of the profession, I have in some measure accomplished my object.

UNIVERSITY OF EDINBURGH,
1*st November* 1839.

CONTENTS

BOOK FIRST

OF RIGHTS PERSONAL; ARISING FROM OBLIGATION OR CONTRACT, EXPRESS OR IMPLIED

PART I

RIGHTS ARISING FROM EXPRESS OBLIGATIONS AND CONTRACTS

PART II

OF RIGHTS ARISING FROM IMPLIED OBLIGATIONS INDEPENDENT OF CONVENTION (§ 525)

PART III

OF EXTINCTION OF OBLIGATIONS (§ 555)

BOOK SECOND

OF REAL RIGHTS IN PROPERTY HERITABLE AND MOVEABLE

PART I

REAL RIGHTS IN HERITABLE PROPERTY (§§ 636, 637)

PART II

REAL RIGHTS OF PROPERTY AND POSSESSION IN MOVEABLES (§§ 1283, 1284)

BOOK THIRD

OF RIGHTS ARISING FROM MARRIAGE AND CONSTITUTION OF A FAMILY; AND OF THE LAWS OF SUCCESSION

PART I

OF MARRIAGE; AND PARENT AND CHILD

PART II

OF THE LAWS OF SUCCESSION

BOOK FOURTH

OF RIGHTS OF THE PERSON

BOOK FIFTH

OF THE EVIDENCE AND ENFORCEMENT OF RIGHTS

LIST OF AUTHORITIES AND ABBREVIATIONS

The dates are those of the period included in reports or collections of the cases, and those of the publication of text-books.

A

A. & E.—Adolphus & Ellis's King's Bench Reports, 12 vols., ... 1834-41
Abbott—Abbott (Lord Tenterden) on the Law of Merchant Ships and Seamen, 12th ed., 1 vol., ... 1881
Act. Ass.—Acts of the General Assembly of the Church of Scotland from 1638 to 1842, . 1843
Act. Parl.—Acts of the Parliaments of Scotland, Thomson's edition, 12 vols., . . 1814-44
Ad. & El.—Adolphus & Ellis's King's Bench Reports, 12 vols., ... 1834-41
Adam on Jury Trial in Civil Causes, 1 vol., . . . 1836
Addam's Ecclesiastical Reports, 3 vols., . . . 1823-6
Addison Contr. — Addison on the Law of Contracts, 8th ed., 1 vol., ... 1883
Addison on the Law of Torts, 5th ed., 1 vol., . . . 1879
Adm. D.—Admiralty Division (Law Reports), . . 1875-
Agnew on the Law and Practice relating to Letters Patent for Inventions, 1 vol., . . 1874
Alison's Practice of the Criminal Law of Scotland, 1 vol., . 1833
Ambler — Ambler's Chancery Reports, 2 vols., . . 1737-84
Angell on the Law of Carriers of Goods and Passengers, 1 vol., ... 1849
Anst.—Anstruther's Exchequer Reports, 3 vols., . . 1792-7
App. Ca.—Appeal Cases (Law Reports), . . . 1875-
Arkley—Arkley's Justiciary Reports, 1 vol., . . . 1846-8
Arnould—Arnould on the Law of Marine Insurance, 5th ed., 2 vols., ... 1877
Atk.—Atkyns's Chancery Reports, 3 vols., . . 1736-54
Austin's Lectures on Jurisprudence, 5th ed. by Campbell, 2 vols., . . . 1879

B

B. & Ad.—Barnewall & Adolphus's King's Bench Reports, 5 vols., ... 1830-4
B. & Ald.—Barnewall & Alderson's King's Bench Reports, 5 vols., . . . 1817-22
B. & B.—Broderip & Bingham's Common Pleas Reports, 3 vols., ... 1819-22
B. & Cr.—Barnewall & Cresswell's King's Bench Reports, 10 vols., . . . 1822-30
B. & L.—Browning & Lushington's Admiralty Reports, 1 vol., ... 1864-5
B. Moo.—Bayly Moore's Common Pleas Reports, 12 vols., 1817-27
B. & P.—Bosanquet & Puller's Common Pleas Reports, 5 vols., . . . 1796-1803
B. & P. N. S., or N. R.—Bosanquet & Puller's Common Pleas Reports, new series, 2 vols., 1804-7
B. & S.—Best & Smith's Queen's Bench Reports, 10 vols., 1860-70
B. S. or B. Sup. — Brown's Supplement to Morison's Dictionary of Decisions, 5 vols., 1622-1794
Baily on General Average, 2nd ed., 1 vol., ... 1856
Balf. — Balfour's Practicks, 1 vol., ... 1754
Ball & B.—Ball & Beatty's Irish Chancery Reports, 2 vols., 1807-14
Bankt.—Lord Bankton's (And. M'Douall) Institute of the Law of Scotland, 3 vols., 1753
Bar on Private International Law (trans. Gillespie), 1 vol., 1883
Barclay's Digest of the Law of Scotland, 4th ed., 1 vol., . 1880
Baring on Orders in Council.
Barnard.—Barnardiston's Chancery Reports, 1 vol., . 1740-1
Bayley on Bills of Exchange, 6th ed., 1 vol., . . . 1849
Beav.—Beavan's Rolls Court Reports, 36 vols., . 1838-66
Beawes, Lex Mercatoria (1720), 6th ed. by Chitty, 2 vols., . 1813
Begg's Conveyancing Code, . 1879
Begg on Law Agents in Scotland, 2nd ed., 1 vol., . . 1883
Bell's Ap.—Bell's (S.S.) House of Lords (Scots) Reports, 7 vols., ... 1843-52
Bell's Com.—Bell's (G. J.) Commentaries on the Law of Scotland, 6th ed. by Shaw, 1858
Bell's Com. (M'L.'s ed.)—7th ed. edited by M'Laren, 2 vols., ... 1870
Bell's Convg.—A. Montgomerie Bell's Lectures on Conveyancing, 3rd ed., 2 vols., . . 1882
Bell (Robert, Advocate) on Conveyance of Land to a Purchaser, 2nd ed., 1 vol., . 1828
Bell's (William) Dictionary of the Law of Scotland, 7th ed. by Geo. Watson, 1 vol., . 1890
Bell (Robert) on the Completion of Title, 3rd ed., . . . 1830
Bell (Robert, W.S.) on the Election Law relating to Scotland, 1 vol., . . . 1812
Bell (Robert) on the Forms of Deeds used in Scotland, 3rd ed., 7 vols., . . 1811-17
Bell's fo. ca.—Robert Bell's (folio) Cases in the Court of Session, 1 vol., . . 1794-5
Bell's 8vo Ca.—Robert Bell's (octavo) Cases in the Court of Session, 1 vol., . . 1790-2
Bell (John Montgomerie) on the Laws of Arbitration in Scotland, 2nd ed., . . . 1877
Bell (Geo. Joseph) on Sale—Inquiries into the Contract of Sale of Goods and Merchandise, ... 1844
Bell (Robert) on Leases, 4th ed., 2 vols., ... 1825
Bell (Robert, Advocate), Report of a Case of Putative Marriage in 1811, ... 1825
Bell (Rob.) on the Testing of Deeds, 1 vol., . . . 1795
Benecke on Idemnity in Marine Insurance and Bottomry, 1 vol., ... 1824
Benjamin on Sales—Benjamin

on the Law of Sale of Personal Property, 3rd ed., . . 1883
Best on the Principles of Evidence, 8th ed., 1 vol., . . 1893
Beveridge's (Thomas, A.C.S.) Forms of Process, 3 vols. (including Bill Chamber), 1826-8
Bing. — Bingham's Common Pleas Reports, 10 vols., 1822-33
Bing. N. C. or N.S.—Bingham's Common Pleas Reports, new series, 6 vols., . . 1834-40
Birnie (J. B. L.) on Issues in Jury Trials, 1 vol., . . 1881
Bishop on the Law of Marriage and Divorce (American), 6th ed., 2 vols., . . . 1882
Blackburn on the Contract of Sale, 2nd ed., 1 vol., . . 1885
Blackst. — W. Blackstone's King's Bench Reports, 2 vols., ... 1746-80
Blackst. Com. — Blackstone's Commentaries, 18th ed., 4 vols., ... 1829
Blair on Justices of the Peace—Blair's Scottish Justice's Manual, 1 vol., ... 1834
Bligh—Bligh's House of Lords Reports, 4 vols., . . 1819-21
Bligh, N. S.—Bligh's House of Lords Reports, new series, 11 vols., ... 1827-37
Book of Discipline of the General Assembly of the Church of Scotland, ... 1638
Boulay-Paty, Cours de Droit Commercial Maritime, 4 vols., 1834
Br. Ch. Ca.—Brown's Chancery Reports, 4 vols., . 1788-94
Br. Par. Ca.—Brown's Parliamentary Cases, 8 vols., 1702-1800
Br. Sup.—Brown's Supplement to Morison's Dictionary of Decisions, 5 vols., . 1622-1794
Br. & L.—Browning & Lushington's Admiralty Reports, 1 vol., ... 1864-5
Brod. & Bing. — Broderip & Bingham's Common Pleas Reports, 3 vols., . . 1819-22
Brodie's Stair—Stair's Institutions of the Law of Scotland, the 4th ed. by Brodie, 2 vols., ... 1827
Brown's Justiciary Reports, 2 vols., ... 1842-5
Brown (M. P.) on the Law of Sale, 1 vol., ... 1821
Brown (Rich.), Notes and Commentaries on the Sale of Goods Act, 1893, 1 vol., . 1895
Brown's Synopsis of the Decisions of the Court of Session, 4 vols., ... 1532-1827
Buchanan (Wm.) on Teinds, 1 vol., ... 1862
Buch. Rep. or Cases—Buchanan's Reports of certain Remarkable Cases and Trials, 1 vol., 1813
Buck's Bkr. Ca.—Buck's Bankruptcy Reports, 1 vol., 1816-20
Buckley on the Companies Acts, 7th ed., 1 vol., . . . 1897
Bunyon on Fire Insurance, 2nd ed., 1 vol., ... 1875
Bunyon on Life Insurance, 2nd ed., 1 vol., ... 1868
Burn on the Poor Law—Burn's Justice of the Peace and Parish Officer — title *Poor*, 30th ed., 5 vols., . . 1869
Burnet on the Criminal Law in Scotland, ... 1811
Burr.—Burrow's King's Bench Reports, 5 vols., . . 1756-72
Byles on Bills of Exchange, 6th ed., 1 vol., ... 1851
Bynkershoek, Quaestiones Juris Publici, 1 vol., . . . 1737

C

C. B.—Common Bench (Manning Granger & Scott's Common Pleas) Reports, 19 vols., 1845-56
C. B., N. S.—Common Bench Reports, new series, 20 vols., ... 1856-66
C. & J.—Crompton & Jervis's Exchequer Reports, 2 vols., 1830-2
C. & K.—Carrington & Kirwan's Nisi Prius Reports, 3 vols., 1843-50
C. & M.—Crompton & Meeson's Exchequer Reports, 2 vols., 1832-4
C. M. & R.—Crompton, Meeson, & Roscoe's Exchequer Reports, 2 vols., . . . 1835-6
C. & P.—Carrington & Payne's Nisi Prius Reports, 9 vols., 1823-41
C. P. D.—Common Pleas Division (Law Reports), . 1875-
C. Rob.—Sir C. Robinson's Admiralty Reports, 6 vols., 1799-1808
Camp.—Campbell's Nisi Prius Reports, 4 vols., . . 1807-16
Campbell on Humfrey *v.* Dale.
Canons of Perth, in vol. iii. of Hailes's Annals, ed. 1819; and Concilia Scotiæ, Bannatyne Club, 2 vols., . . 1866
Car. & M.—Carrington & Marshman's Nisi Prius Reports, 1 vol., ... 1840-2
Car. & P.—Carrington & Payne's Nisi Prius Reports, 9 vols., 1823-41
Carthew's King's Bench Reports, 1 vol., ... 1686-1701
Casaregis, Discursus Legales de Commercio, etc., 3 vols., 1719-29
Ch. D. — Chancery Division (Law Reports), . . 1875-
Chabot sur la Loi de Succession.
Chalmers's Digest of the Law of Bills of Exchange, etc., 5th ed., 1 vol., ... 1896
Chalmers's Sale of Goods Act, including the Factors' Acts, 2nd ed., Lond., . . . 1894
Chitty on Bills, 11th ed., 1 vol., 1878
Chitty, Com. Law—Chitty on the Laws of Commerce and Manufacture, 4 vols., . . 1824
Chitty Rep.—Chitty's Bail Court Reports, 2 vols., . . 1819-20
Cl. & F.—Clark & Finelly's House of Lords Reports, 12 vols., ... 1831-46
Clark's Cabinet Library of Scarce and Celebrated Tracts, 8 vols., ... 1838
Clark (F. W.) on Partnership and Joint-Stock Companies according to the Law of Scotland, 2 vols., ... 1866
Code Civil des Français, 8 vols., 1807
Code de Commerce, 2 vols., . 1807
Codex—Divi Justiniani Codicis libri duodecim; in the Corpus Juris Civilis.
Coke—Coke's King's Bench Reports, 6 vols., . . 1572-1616
Coke on Littleton, Hargreave & Butler's ed. (the 19th), 2 vols., ... 1832
Collyer — Collyer's Vice-Chancellor's Court Reports, 2 vols., ... 1844-5
Collyer on Partnership, 2nd ed., 1 vol., ... 1840
Colquhoun's (Ludovic) Report of the Case of Duncan *v.* Yoolow, 1 vol., ... 1837
Comyns's (Sir John) Digest of the Laws of England, 5th ed., 8 vols., ... 1822
Comyns's Reports — Comyns's King's Bench, etc., Cases, 2 vols., ... 1792
Connell (Sir John) on Parishes, 1 vol., ... 1818
Connell's Supplement to his Treatise on the Law of Scotland respecting Parishes, 1 vol., ... 1823
Connell on Teinds—Connell on the Law of Scotland respecting Tithes, 2nd ed., 2 vols., . 1830
Connell (Arthur, Advocate) on the Election Laws in Scotland, 1 vol., ... 1827
Cons. del Mare—Consolato del Mare. See Pardessus, Collection de Lois Maritimes, ii. 338; Ortolan Dip. de la Mer, ii. 68.
Convention of Holyrood, see 4 Act. Parl. c. 184, 237.
Cook's Styles of Writs and Forms of Procedure in the Church Courts of Scotland, 5th ed., ... 1882
Cooke B. L.—Cooke on the Bankruptcy Law, 7th ed., 2 vols., ... 1817
Copinger on Copyright, 3rd ed., 1 vol., ... 1893
Coryton on Patents, 1 vol., . 1855
Couper's Justiciary Reports, 1868-85
Coventry on the Stamp Laws, 1 vol., ... 1833
Cowp.—Cowper's King's Bench Reports, 1 vol., . . . 1774-8
Cox C. C. or Cr. Ca.—Cox's Criminal Law Cases, 9 vols., 1843-64
Cr. & St.—Craigie & Stewart's House of Lords (Scots) Reports, 1 vol., . . 1726-57
Cr. St. & P.—Craigie Stewart & Paton's House of Lords (Scots) Reports, 6 vols., 1726-1821
Craig, or Craig Jus Feudale, or Craig de Feudis — Craig's Jus Feudale, 3rd ed., . . 1732
Cran. — Cranch's American Supreme Court Reports, 9 vols., ... 1801-15
Crichton (David, Advocate), Analysis of the Ballot Act as applicable to Scotland, 1 vol., 1873
Cromp. & J. — Crompton & Jervis's Exchequer Reports, 2 vols., ... 1830-2
Cromp. & M. — Crompton & Meeson's Exchequer Reports, 2 vols., ... 1832-4

Cromp. M. & R.—Crompton, Meeson, & Roscoe's Exchequer Reports, 2 vols., . 1834–6
Curtis—Curtis's Reports of Decisions in the Supreme Court of the United States, 22 vols., 1781–1854; Boston, 1855–6
Curtis on Patents (American), 1 vol., 4th ed., Boston, . . 1873

D

D.—Dunlop's Court of Session Reports (the 2nd series), 24 vols., ... 1838–62
D. & A.—Deas & Anderson's Court of Session Cases, 5 vols., 1829–32
D. H. L.—Dunlop's Court of Session Reports (the 2nd series), House of Lords part, in vols. 17–24, . . 1854–62
D. & E.—Durnford & East's King's Bench Reports (Term Reports), 8 vols., . 1785–1800
D. & R.—Dowling & Rylands's King's Bench Reports, 9 vols., ... 1821–27
Dallas — Dallas's American Supreme Court Reports, 4 vols., ... 1790–1800
Dallas's Styles of Writs, 2nd ed., 2 vols., ... 1774
Dan. & Ll.—Danson & Lloyd's Mercantile Cases, 1 vol., 1828–9
Davies's Patent Cases, 1 vol., . 1816
Deas on the Law of Railways applicable to Scotland, 3rd ed., 1 vol., . . . 1897
Decretal. — Nova Decretalium Compilatio Gregorii, . . 1475
De G. & S.—De Gex & Smale's Vice-Chancellor's Court Reports, 5 vols., . . 1846–52
De G. M. & G.—De Gex Macnaghten & Gordon's Chancery Appeal Reports, 8 vols., ... 1851–57
De G. & J.—De Gex & Jones's Chancery Appeal Reports, 4 vols., ... 1857–9
De G. J. & S.—De Gex Jones & Smith's Chancery Appeal Reports, 4 vols., . . 1863–65
De G. F. & J.—De Gex Fisher & Jones's Chancery Appeal Reports, 4 vols., . 1859–62
Demaimbry's Precedents in Chancery.
De Morgan on Probabilities, 1 vol., ... 1841
Dicey (Professor Albert) on the Law of Domicil, 1 vol., . 1879
Dicey, Conflict of Laws, 1 vol., 1896
Dick.—Dickens's Chancery Reports, 2 vols., . . 1559–1798
Dickson (W. Gillespie) on the Law of Evidence in Scotland, 2nd ed., 2 vols., . . . 1864
Dig. — Justiniani Digestorum seu Pandectarum libri quinquaginta; in Corpus Juris Civilis.
Directory for Worship, . 1644
Dirleton's Doubts and Questions in the Law, especially of Scotland, folio, . . 1698
Dix's Report of The Queen *v.* Mills (Q.B. Ireland), 1 vol., 1842
Dixon on the Adjustment of General Average, 1 vol., . 1867
Dods. or Dods. Ad.—Dodson's Admiralty Reports, 2 vols., 1811–22
Dodson's Report of Sir Wm. Scott's Judgment in Dalrymple *v.* Dalrymple, 1 vol., 1811
Domat, Les Loix Civiles dans leur Ordre Naturel, 5 vols., 1695–9
Domat's Civil Law, trans. by Strahan, 2 vols., ... 1722
Donell.—Donelli Hugonis Commentarii de Jure Civili, . 1596
Donellus, Tractatus de Evictionibus.
Doug.—Douglas's King's Bench Reports, 4 vols., . 1778–84
Dow—Dow's House of Lords Reports, 6 vols., . 1812–18
Dow & C.—Dow & Clark's House of Lords Reports, 2 vols., 1827–32
Dow. & Ry. — Dowling & Ryland's King's Bench Reports, 9 vols., ... 1821–7
Dowl. or Dowl. P. C.—Dowling's Queen's Bench Practice Court Reports, 9 vols., 1830–41
Dowl. P. C. N. S.—Dowling's Queen's Bench Practice Court Reports, new series, 2 vols., 1841–3
Dr. & Sm.—Drewry & Smale's Chancery Reports, 2 vols., 1860–1
Drew. — Drewry's Vice-Chancellor's Court Reports, 4 vols., ... 1852–9
Duer on Marine Insurance (American), 2 vols., . 1845
Duff on Deeds chiefly affecting Moveables, 1 vol., . . 1840
Duff's Commentary on Entails, 1 vol., ... 1848
Duff on Feudal Conveyancing, 1 vol., ... 1838
Duff on Feudal Conveyancing, Supplement, 1 vol., . . 1848
Duncan's Manual of Entail Procedure, 1 vol., . . 1858
Duncan on Parochial Law, 2nd ed., 1 vol., ... 1869
Dunlop on Parochial Law, 2nd ed., 1 vol., ... 1835
Dunlop on the Poor Law, 3rd ed., 1 vol., ... 1854

E

E. & B.—Ellis & Blackburn's Queen's Bench Reports, 8 vols., ... 1852–8
E. B. & E.—Ellis, Blackburn, & Ellis's Queen's Bench Reports, 1 vol., . . 1859
E. & E.—Ellis & Ellis's Queen's Bench Reports, 1 vol., . 1859
E. Jur.—English Jurist Reports, 55 vols., . . . 1837–66
E. Jur. N. S.—English Jurist Reports, new series, . 1855–66
East—East's King's Bench Reports, 16 vols., . 1800–12
Ecc. & Ad.—Ecclesiastical and Admiralty Reports. See Notes of Cases. . . . 1841–50
Edinburgh Medical and Surgical Journal, 82 vols., . . 1805–55
Edw.—Edwards's Admiralty Reports, 1 vol., . . 1808–11
El. & El.—Ellis & Ellis's Queen's Bench Reports, 1 vol., . . 1859
Elch.—Lord Elchies' Court of Session Decisions (and in vol. xxiv. of Morison's Dictionary), 2 vols., ... 1733–54
Elchies' Annot. or Notes — Elchies' Annotations on Stair's Institutions, 1 vol., . . 1824
Elliot (Nenion, S.S.C.) on the Position of Fiars Prices, 1 vol., ... 1879
Emerigon's Traité des Assurances et des Contrats à la Grosse, 2 vols., ... 1783
Erle—Sir W. Erle, C.J., on the Law relating to Trades Unions, 1869
Ersk. — Erskine's Institute of the Law of Scotland, 1st ed., 2 vols., ... 1773
Erskine's Institute, by Ivory, 6th ed., 2 vols., . . 1824–8
Erskine's Institute, by J. B. Nicolson, Advocate, 2 vols., . 1871
Ersk. Prin. — Erskine's Principles of the Law of Scotland, 16th ed., 1 vol., . . . 1881
Esp. — Espinasse's Nisi Prius Reports, 6 vols., . . 1793–1807
Ex.—Exchequer Reports (Welsby, Hurlston, & Gordon), 11 vols., ... 1847–56
Ex. Ch.—Exchequer Chamber case.
Ex. D. — Exchequer Division (Law Reports), . . 1875–

F

F. C.—Faculty (of Advocates) Collection of Court of Session Cases, 38 vols., . . 1752–1841
Fearne (Charles) on Contingent Remainders and Executory Devises, 10th ed., 2 vols., . 1844
Ferg. Cons. Law — Ferguson's Treatise on Consistorial Law in Scotland, with Reports of Cases, 1 vol., ... 1829
Ferg. Cons. Ca. or Cons. R.—Ferguson's Consistorial Reports, 1 vol., ... 1823
Folkard on the Law of Slander and Libel, 4th ed., 1 vol., . 1876
Foote Pr. Int. Law—Foote on Private International Jurisprudence, 1 vol., ... 1878
Foster's Crown Law — Sir M. Foster's Report of the Trial of the Rebels in 1746, etc., Oxford, 1746; 3rd ed. by Dodson, ... 1809
Fount. — Lord Fountainhall's Court of Session, etc., Cases, 2 vols., ... 1678–1712
Fraser on the Conflict of Laws in Cases of Divorce, 1 vol., . 1860
Fraser on the Law of Guardian and Ward. See Fraser, P. & C.
Fraser, H. & W.—Fraser on Husband and Wife according to the Law of Scotland, 2nd ed., 2 vols., ... 1876
Fraser, M. & S.—Fraser on Master and Servant according to the Law of Scotland, 3rd ed., 1 vol., ... 1882

Fraser, P. & C.—Fraser on the Law of Scotland relative to Parent and Child, Guardian and Ward, 2nd ed., 1 vol., . 1866
Friedberg, Das Recht der Eheschliessung, 1 vol., . . . 1865

G

G. & D. — Gale & Davison's Queen's Bench Reports, 3 vols., . . . 1841–3
Gale. See G. & D.
Giff.—Giffard's Vice-Chancellor's Court Reports, 5 vols., . 1856–64
Gluck Com.—Gluck's Ausführliche Erläuterung der Pandekten, 44 vols., . . 1797–1851
Glyn & Jam.—Glyn & Jameson's Bankruptcy Reports, 2 vols., 1821–8
Godefroi & Shortt's Law of Railway Companies, 1 vol., . 1869
Godson on Patents and Copyright, 2nd ed., 1 vol., . . 1840
Goudy, Prof. Henry, Law of Bankruptcy in Scotland, 2nd ed., 1 vol., ... 1895
Gow's Cases—Gow's Nisi Prius Reports, 1 vol., . . 1818–20
Gow on Partnership, 3rd ed., 1 vol., ... 1830
Grant on Banking, 4th ed., 1 vol., 1882
Grant on the Law of Corporations, 1 vol., . . . 1850
Griffith's Married Women's Property Act, 5th ed. by Bromfield, 1 vol., . . . 1883
Grotius, De jure belli ac pacis (Whewell's ed.), 4 vols., . 1853
Guthrie on Bank Monopoly, 1 vol., ... 1864
Guthrie's Erskine's Principles of the Law of Scotland, 14th ed., 1 vol., ... 1870
Guthrie on the Law of Trade Unions, 1 vol., . . . 1873
Guthrie's Sel. Sh. Ct. Ca.—Guthrie's Select Sheriff Court Cases, 1st series, 1 vol., . 1879
Guthrie's Sel. Sh. Ct. Ca.—Guthrie's Select Sheriff Court Cases, 2nd series, 1 vol., . 1894
Guthrie's Savigny on Private International Law, 2nd ed., . 1880
Guthrie Smith's Digest of the Poor Law, 3rd ed., 1 vol., . 1878
Guthrie Smith on Damages, 2nd ed., 1 vol., ... 1889
Gwynne's (Thomas) Law of Duties on Probates, Legacies, etc., 3rd ed., . . . 1841

H

H. Bl.—Henry Blackstone's Common Pleas Reports, 2 vols., 1788–96
H. & C.—Hurlston & Coltman's Exchequer Reports, 4 vols., 1862–6
H. & G.—Hurlston & Gordon's Exchequer Reports, 2 vols., 1854–6
H. L. or H. of L.—House of Lords.
H. L. Ca.—House of Lord's Cases (Clark's), 12 vols., 1847–66
H. & M.—Hemming & Miller's Vice-Chancellor's Court Reports, 2 vols., . . 1862–5
H. & N.—Hurlston & Norman's Exchequer Reports, 7 vols., 1856–62
H. & T.—Hall & Twells's Chancery Reports, 2 vols., . 1849–50
Hag. or Hag. Ad.—Haggard's Admiralty Reports, 3 vols., 1822–38
Hag. Cons. — Haggard's Consistorial Reports, 2 vols., 1789–1821
Hag. Ec.—Haggard's Ecclesiastical Reports, 4 vols., . 1827–33
Hailes—Lord Hailes's (Sir David Dalrymple) Court of Session Decisions, 2 vols., . 1766–91
Hailes's Annals of Scotland, 1797, and 3 vols., . . . 1819
Hanson on the Probate, Legacy, and Succession Duty Acts, 4th ed., ... 1897
Hare—Hare's Vice-Chancellor's Court Reports, 11 vols., 1841–53
Harrison's Analysis of the Valuation Acts.
Hector's Memorandum on Fiars Prices, 1 vol., . . . 1878
Hendry's Manual of Conveyancing, 4th ed., 1 vol., . . 1888
Hendry's Styles of Deeds, 3rd ed., 1 vol., ... 1878
Hertius de Collisione Legum, in his Commentationes et Opuscula, ... 1688
Hindmarch on Patents, 1 vol., 1846
History of the Exchequer, by Barons Clerk and Scrope, 1 vol., ... 1820
Hodges on Railways, 7th ed., 2 vols., ... 1889
Holt or Holt N. P.—Holt's Nisi Prius Reports, 1 vol., . 1815–17
Hope's Major Practicks, 1 vol. See List of Authors in Fraser's P. & C., p. xxv.
Hope's Minor Practicks, 1 vol., Spottiswood's ed., . . . 1734
Hopkin's (Manley) on Average, 4th ed., 1 vol., ... 1884
Hopkin's (Manley) Manual of Marine Insurance, 1 vol., . 1867
Hopw. & C. — Hopwood and Coltman's Registration Cases (England), 2 vols., . 1869–77
Horne on Captures.
Hort on Apportionment of Losses.
Houard, Anciennes Loix des François, 2 vols., Rouen, . 1776
Howell's State Trials—Cobbett's Collection of State Trials, etc., compiled by Howell, 33 vols., ... 1809–26
Huber de Conflictu Legum, in his Prælectiones Juris Civilis, 1707 See Guthrie's Savigny, Appendix iv.
Hume—Baron Hume's Court of Session Decisions, 1 vol., 1781–1822
Hume's Com. or Hume's Crim. Law—Baron Hume's Commentaries on the Law of Scotland respecting Crimes, 3rd ed., 2 vols., . . . 1829
Hunter, L. & T.—Hunter on Landlord and Tenant, 4th ed., 2 vols., ... 1876
Hutchison, Justice of the Peace, 3rd ed., 4 vols., . . . 1815
Hy. Bl. — Henry Blackstone's Common Pleas Reports, 2 vols., ... 1788–96

I

I. or Inst.—Institutes of Justinian.
Ill.—George Joseph Bell's Illustrations of the Law of Scotland from Cases, 3 vols., . 1838
Impey's Commentaries on the Stamp Act, 55 Geo. III., . 1839
Ingram on Compensation, 2nd ed., 1 vol., ... 1869
Innes's Scottish Legal Antiquities, 1 vol., ... 1872
Instructions to the Commissaries (see the Acts of Sederunt), 1563–1688
Ir. R. Eq. — Irish Reports, Equity;
Ir. L. R.—Irish Common Law Reports; and
Ir. Ch. or Ir. Ch. R.—Irish Chancery Reports, in 60 vols., ... 1838–66
Ir. Jur.—Irish Jurist, 7 vols., 1849–55
Ir. Jur. N. S.—Irish Jurist, new series, 11 vols., . . . 1855–66
Irv. — Irvine's Justiciary Reports, 5 vols., . . . 1852–67
Irvine on the Game Laws, 3rd ed., 1 vol., ... 1883
Ivory's Ersk.—Erskine's Institute of the Law of Scotland, 6th ed. by Ivory, 2 vols., 1824–8

J

J. & H.—Johnson & Hemming's Vice-Chancellor's Court Reports, 2 vols., . . . 1860–2
J. of J.—Journal of Jurisprudence, Edinburgh, 35 vols., 1857–91
J. Shaw Justy.—John Shaw's Justiciary Reports, 1 vol., 1848–52
Jac. & W.—Jacob & Walker's Chancery Reports, 2 vols., 1819–21
Jacob — Jacob's Chancery Reports, 1 vol., . . . 1821–2
Jarman (Thomas) on Wills, 5th ed., 2 vols., ... 1893
Jeremy on the Law of Carriers, etc., 1 vol., ... 1815
Johns. — Johnson's Vice-Chancellor's Court Reports, 1 vol., ... 1858–60
Jones (Sir William) on Bailments, 6th ed., 1 vol., . . 1833
Journals of House of Lords from 1509 to 1833, 31 vols.
Jugemens d'Oleron. See Pardessus, Collection de Lois Maritimes, vol. i.
Jur.—Scottish Jurist, 46 vols., 1829–73
Jur. N. S.—English Jurist, new series, 12 vols., . . 1855–60
Juridical Styles, 3 vols. (vols. 1 and 2, 5th ed., 1881–3; vol. 3, 3rd ed., 1888).

K

K. & J.—Kay & Johnson's Vice-Chancellor's Ct. Reports, 4 vols., ... 1854–8
Kames's (Henry Home, Lord) Elucidations respecting the Law of Scotland, 1 vol., . 1777
Kames's Gentleman Farmer, 6th ed., ... 1815

Kames's Historical Law Tracts, 1761

Kames Pr. of Eq. — Kames's Principles of Equity, 3rd ed., 1778

Kames Rem. Dec.—Kames's Remarkable Decisions of the Court of Session, 2 vols. (in Morison's Dictionary), . 1716–52

Kames's Statute Law of Scotland, 1757

Kent Com.—Kent's Commentaries on American Law, 11th ed., 4 vols., ... 1867

Kilk.—Lord Kilkerran's Court of Session Decisions (in Morison's Dict.), 1 vol., 1738–52

Kinnear (J. Boyd) on Bankruptcy, 2nd ed., 1 vol., . 1862

Knapp P. C.—Knapp's Privy Council Reports, 3 vols., 1826–36

Kuricke, Jus Maritimum Hanseaticum, ... 1667

L

L. J. Ad.—Law Journal Admiralty Reports, . . 1822–

L. J. Bankr. — Law Journal Bankruptcy Reports, . 1822–

L. J. C. P.—Law Journal Common Pleas Reports, . 1822–

L. J. Ch.—Law Journal Chancery Reports, . . 1822–

L. J. Ex.—Law Journal Exchequer Reports, . . 1822–

L. J. K. B.—Law Journal King's Bench Reports, . . 1822–

L. J. Mag. Ca.—Law Journal Magistrates' Cases, 1822–

L. J. (O.S.) K. B.—Law Journal (old series), King's Bench, 1822–31

L. J. P. C.—Law Journal Privy Council Reports, . . 1822–

L. J. Pr.—Law Journal Probate Reports, . . . 1822–

L. J. Pr. and Mat.—Law Journal Probate and Matrimonial Reports, ... 1822–

L. J. Q. B. — Law Journal Queen's Bench Reports, 1822–

L. R. Ad. and E.—Law Reports, Admiralty and Ecclesiastical Reports, ... 1865–75

L. R. Ch. App.—Law Reports, Chancery Appeal Reports, 1865–75

L. R. C. C.—Law Reports, Crown Cases, . . 1865–75

L. R. C. P.—Law Reports, Common Pleas Reports, 1865–75

L. R. E. and I. App.—Law Reports, English and Irish Appeals Reports, . . 1865–75

L. R. Eq.—Law Reports, Equity Reports, . . . 1865–75

L. R. Ex.—Law Reports, Exchequer Reports, . . 1865–75

L. R. H. L.—Law Reports, House of Lords Reports (English and Irish Appeals), 1865–75

L. R. P. C.—Law Reports, Privy Council Reports, . 1865–75

L. R. P. & D.—Law Reports, Probate and Divorce Reports, 1865–75

L. R. Q. B.—Law Reports, Queen's Bench Reports, 1865–75

L. R. Sc. Ap.—Law Reports, Scottish and Divorce Appeals Reports, . . . 1865–75

L. T. R. or L. T.—Law Times Reports, . . . 1843–

L. T., N. S.—Law Times Reports, new series, . . 1859–

Ld. Raym.—Lord Raymond's King's Bench Reports, 3 vols., ... 1694–1734

Leg. Burg.—Leges et Consuetudines Quatuor Burgorum, in Acta Parl.

Le Marchant's Report of the Banbury Peerage Case ; Apx. E. of his Gardner Peerage Report.

Le Marchant's Report of the Gardner Peerage Case, 1 vol., 1828

Lib. Feud.—Consuetudines Feudorum, at the end of Corpus Juris Civilis Amstel., . 1681

Lindley on Partnership, 6th ed., 2 vols., ... 1893

Lloyd on Compensation under the Lands Clauses, etc., Acts, 5th ed., 1 vol., ... 1882

Lush. or Lush. Adm.—Lushington's Admiralty Reports, 1 vol., ... 1860–3

Lush on the Practice of the Superior Courts of Common Law, 3rd ed., . . . 1865

M

M. — Morison's Dictionary of Decisions in the Court of Session, 27 vols., . . 1532–1816

M. Apx. *Ins.*—Morison's Dictionary, Appendix to the title "Insurance."

M. & G. or M. & Gr.—Manning & Granger's Common Pleas Reports, 7 vols., . . 1840–4

M. Bell's Convg.—Montgomerie Bell's Lectures on Conveyancing, 3rd ed., 2 vols., 1882

M. & M.—Moody and Malkin's Nisi Prius Reports, 1 vol., 1826–30

M. & P.—Moore and Payne's Common Pleas Reports, 5 vols., ... 1828–31

M. & R.—Manning and Ryland's King's Bench Reports, 5 vols., ... 1827–30

M. & R. or M. & Rob.—Moody & Robinson's Nisi Prius Reports, 2 vols., . . 1830–44

M. & S.—Maule and Selwyn's King's Bench Reports, 6 vols., ... 1813–17

M. & S.—Moore and Scott's Common Pleas Reports, 4 vols., ... 1831–4

M. & W.—Meeson & Welsby's Exchequer Reports, 17 vols., 1836–47

M'F. Jur. Ca. — Macfarlane's Jury Court Reports, 1 vol., 1838–9

M'Glashan on Sheriff Court Practice, 3rd ed., 1 vol., 1854

Mackay (Æneas J. G., Advocate) on Court of Session Practice, 2 vols., ... 1877–9

Mackay's (Æneas J. G., Advocate) Manual of Court of Session Practice, 1 vol., . . . 1893

M'Kenzie — M'Kenzie's (Sir George) Institutions of the Law of Scotland, 7th ed., 1730

M'Kenzie's Crim. Law, etc., 1 vol., ... 1699

M'Kenzie's Observations on the Acts of Parliament from James I. to Charles II., 1 vol., . 1686

M'Kenzie's (Sir George) Works 2 vols., ... 1716–22

Maclachlan on Merchant Shipping, 4th ed., 1 vol., . 1892

M'Laren (Lord) on Wills and Succession, 3rd ed., 2 vols., . 1894

M'Laren's Bell's Commentaries, the 7th ed., 2 vols., . . 1870

M'Laur.—Maclaurin's Justiciary Cases, 1 vol., . . . 1774

M'Lean—U. S. Circuit Court Reports, 6 vols., . . 1829–54

Macl. & Rob.—Maclean & Robinson's House of Lords Reports, 1 vol., ... 1839

Macn. & G.—Macnaghten & Gordon's Chancery Reports, 3 vols., . . . 1849–51

Macph.—Macpherson's Court of Session Reports (the 3rd series), 11 vols., . . 1862–73

Macph. H. L.—Macpherson's Reports, House of Lords part.

Macq. — Macqueen's House of Lords Reports, 4 vols., 1851–65

Madd.—Maddock's Vice-Chancellor's Court Reports, 6 vols., ... 1815–22

Maddock on Chancery Principles and Practice, 2nd ed., 2 vols., 1820

Man. & Ry.—Manning & Ryland's King's Bench Reports, 5 vols., ... 1827–44

Manley Hopkins on Average, 4th ed., 1 vol., . . . 1884

Manley Hopkin's Manual of Marine Insurance, 1 vol., . 1867

Mar. Law Ca.—Maritime Law Cases, 3 vols., . . 1861–70

Mar. Law Ca.—New series by Aspinall, 7 vols., . . 1871–95

Marsden on the Law of Collision at Sea, 3rd ed., 1 vol., . 1891

Marsh. — Marshall's Common Pleas Reports, 2 vols., . 1813–16

Marsh. Ins. — Marshall on Marine Insurance, 5th ed., 1 vol., ... 1865

Marshall's Analysis of the Titles to Land Consolidation (Scotland) Act, 1868, 1 vol., . 1869

Marwick (Sir J. D., S.S.C., LL.D., Town-Clerk of Glasgow) on the Law and Practice of Municipal Elections in Scotland, etc., 1 vol., . . 1879

Mayne on Dam.—Mayne on the Law of Damages, 1 vol., 5th ed., ... 1894

Menzies' Lectures on Conveyancing, 3rd ed., 1 vol., . 1856

Mer. or Meriv. — Merivale's Chancery Reports, 3 vols., 1815–17

Merlin, Répertoire de Jurisprudence, 4th ed., 18 vols., 1812–25

Millar on Insurance, 1 vol., . 1787

Mod. — Modern Reports in King's Bench, 12 vols., 1669–1732

Montagu — Montagu's Bankruptcy Reports, 1 vol., . 1829–32

Montagu on Lien, 1 vol., . 1821

Montagu & Macarthur's Bankruptcy Reports, 1 vol., . 1826–30

Montagu on Partnership, 2 vols., 2nd ed., ... 1822

Monypenny (Lord Pitmilly) on

the Poor Laws, 2nd ed., 1 vol., ... 1831
Moo. & Mal.—Moody and Malkin's Nisi Prius Reports, 1 vol., ... 1826–30
Moo. P.C.—Moore's Privy Council Reports, 15 vols., . 1836–62
Moo. P. C., N. S.—Moore's Privy Council Reports, new series, 9 vols., . . . 1862–8
Moo. & Rob.—Moody & Robinson's Nisi Prius Reports, 2 vols., ... 1830–44
Moore—Moore's Common Pleas Reports, 12 vols., . 1817–27
Moore & P.—Moore & Payne's Common Pleas Reports, 5 vols., ... 1828–31
More's Notes, or More's Stair, or More's Supplement to Stair, or More on Stair — More's edition of Stair's Institutions of the Law of Scotland, 2 vols., ... 1832
Mowbray's (John T., W.S.) Analysis of the Conveyancing Act, 1874, 1 vol., . . . 1874
Mowbray's Hendry's Manual of Conveyancing, 4th ed. by J. P. Wood, ... 1888
Mowbray's Hendry's Styles of Writs (the 3rd ed.), 1 vol., . 1878
Mur.—Murray's Jury Court Reports, 5 vols., . . . 1815–30
Murdoch's (James) Manual of the Law of Insolvency and Bankruptcy, 5th ed., 1 vol., . 1886
My. & Cr.—Mylne & Craig's Chancery Reports, 5 vols., 1835–40
My. & K.—Mylne & Keene's Chancery Reports, 3 vols., 1833–5

N

N. & M.—Neville & Manning's King's Bench Reports, 6 vols., ... 1832–6
N. R.—New Reports (Bosanquet & Puller's Common Pleas), 2 vols., ... 1804–7
Napier on Prescription, 1 vol., 1839, completed . . . 1854
Nicolas on Adulterine Bastardy, and Report of Banbury Peerage Case, 1 vol., . . . 1836
Nicolson's Ersk. Inst. — Erskine's Institute of the Law of Scotland (Nicolson's edition), 2 vols., ... 1871
Nicolson (J. Badenach, Advocate) on the Law of Parliamentary Elections in Scotland, 2nd ed., 1 vol., . . 1879
Nicolson de Nuptiis (1 Stair 4, § 6).
Noodt ad Pandectas; Opera Omnia, 2 vols., . . . 1724
Notes of Cases in Ecclesiastical and Maritime Courts, 7 vols., 1841–50

O

Oliphant on the Law of Horses, Innkeepers, etc., 1 vol., 4th ed., ... 1882

P

P. D.—Probate Division (Law Reports), . . . 1875–
P. W.—Peere Williams's Chancery Reports, 3 vols., . 1695–1735
Paley on Principal and Agent, 3rd ed., 1 vol., . . . 1833
Pardessus, Cours de Droit Commercial, 5 vols., . 1825–6
Park on Marine Insurance, 8th ed., 2 vols., ... 1842
Parker's Exchequer Cases, 1 vol., ... 1743–67
Parker's (John) Styles of Summonses, 2nd ed., . . 1853
Parsons on Bills (American), 2 vols., ... 1874
Parsons on Contracts, 8th ed., 3 vols., ... 1893
Parsons on Marine Insurance, 2 vols., ... 1868
Parsons on Shipping, 2 vols., . 1869
Pat.—Paton's House of Lords Reports, 6 vols., . . 1726–1821
Paterson's House of Lords Reports, 2 vols., . . 1851–73
Peake, or Peake N. P.—Peake's Nisi Prius Reports, 2 vols., 1790–1812
Peckius ad Leges Rhodias, cum notis Vinnii, 1 vol., . . 1661
Peere Williams's Chancery Reports, 3 vols., . . 1695–1735
Pet.—Peters's (American) Supreme Court Reports, 9 vols., 1820–35
Peterkin's Notes on Orkney—Peterkin's Rentals, etc., of Orkney, 1 vol., . . . 1820
Ph.—Phillips's Chancery Reports, 2 vols., . . 1841–9
Phillimore's Ecclesiastical Cases, 3 vols., . . . 1809–21
Phillimore on Licenses.
Phillips on Evidence, 10th ed. 2 vols., ... 1852
Phillips on Insurance (American), 5th ed., 2 vols., . . 1867
Plowden's Reports, reigns Ed. VI. to Eliz., 2 vols., pub. 1816
Pollock on Contracts, 6th ed., 1 vol., ... 1894
Pollock on Partnership, 4th ed., 1 vol., ... 1888
Prin. of Eq. See Kames.
Pothier, Traités sur différentes Matières de Droit Civil, 2nd ed., 4 vols., ... 1781
Pothier on Obligations, translated by Evans, 3rd ed., 2 vols., ... 1853
Pothier, Œuvres, edited by Bugnet, 2nd ed., 10 vols., . . 1860
Pothier, Pandectae Justiniani, 4th ed., 3 vols., . . . 1818
Pothier on Partnership, translated by Tudor, 1 vol., . 1854
Pothier on Sale, translated by Cushing (American), 1 vol., ... 1839
Powell on Devises, 1 vol., . 1788
Pozzo (Chev. dal), Observations sur la Régime Hypothécaire.
Price—Price's Exchequer Reports, 13 vols., . . 1814–24
Pritchard's Digest of Admiralty Cases, 1 vol., . . . 1847
Pulling on the Law and Practice relating to Attorneys, 3rd ed., 1 vol., ... 1862

Q

Q. B.—Queen's Bench Reports (Adolphus & Ellis, new series), 18 vols., ... 1841–52
Q. B. D.—Queen's Bench Division (Law Reports), . 1875–
Quon. Att.—Quoniam Attachiamenta, in Acta Parl.

R

R.—Rettie's Court of Session Reports (the 4th series), 25 vols., ... 1873–98
R. H. L.—Rettie's Reports, House of Lords part, . 1873–98
R. Just.—Rettie's Reports, Justiciary Court Cases, . 1873–98
R. & M.—Russell & Mylne's Chancery Reports, 2 vols., 1829–31
R. & R. C. C.—Russell & Ryan's Crown Cases, 1 vol., . 1799–1823
R. R.—The Revised Reports.
Rankine on Land Ownership, 3rd ed., 1 vol., . . . 1891
Raym. — Raymond's King's Bench, etc., Reports, 1 vol., 1660–84
Redfield on Carriers (American), 1 vol., ... 1869
Reid (J. A., Advocate), Digest of Decisions relating to the Poor Law of Scotland, 1 vol., 1880
Reg. Maj. — Regiam Majestatem; in Acta Parl., and in Skene's Scotiæ Veteres Leges, etc., ... 1609
Renouard, Traité de Brevet d'Invention, 2 vols., . . . 1839
Report of the Committee of the House of Commons on Patents, June 12, . . . 1829
Report of the Law Commissioners, 2 vols., . . . 1838
Report of the Royal Commission on the Laws of Marriage, . 1868
Rob. — Robinson's House of Lords Reports, 1 vol., . 1707–27
Rob. or Rob. Adm.—C. Robinson's Admiralty Reports, 6 vols., ... 1798–1808
Roberts (William) on Wills and Codicils, 3rd ed., 2 vols., . 1837
Robertson's Ap. — Robertson's House of Lords Reports, 1 vol., ... 1707–27
Robertson (David) on Personal Succession, 1 vol., . . 1836
Robertson's (William) Proceedings relating to the Peerage of Scotland from 1707 to 1788, 1790
Roccus de Navibus et Naulo, 1 vol., ... 1708
Roccus on Maritime Law, trans. by Ingersoll, 1 vol., . . 1809
Rose—Rose's Bankruptcy Reports, 2 vols., . . 1810–16
Ross, L. C.—George Ross's Leading Cases in the Law of Scotland, 3 vols., . . 1849–51
Ross, L. C.—George Ross's Leading Cases in Commercial Law, 3 vols., ... 1857

Ross's (Walter) Lectures on the Law of Scotland, 2 vols., . 1822
Rules of the Supreme Court of Judicature in England; Weekly Notes, Aug. 4, . 1883
Russ., or Russ. Ch. C.—Russell's Chancery Reports, 5 vols., ... 1826–9
Russ. & My.—Russell & Mylne's Chancery Reports, 2 vols., 1829–31
Ry. & Moo.—Ryan & Moody's Nisi Prius Reports, 1 vol., 1823–6

S

S.—Shaw's Court of Session Reports (the first series), 16 vols., ... 1822–38
S. App.—Shaw's House of Lords Reports, 2 vols., . . 1821–4
S. Apx.—Shaw's Court of Session Reports, Appendix.
S. Jur.—Scottish Jurist, 46 vols., ... 1829–73
S.L.R.—Scottish Law Reporter, 1865–
S. & M'L.—Shaw & M'Lean's House of Lords Reports, 3 vols., ... 1835–8
S. N. E.—Shaw's Reports, new edition of first 5 volumes.
S. & T.—Swabey & Tristram's Probate and Divorce Reports, 4 vols., ... 1858–66
S. T. C.—Shaw's Teind Cases, 1 vol., ... 1821–31
Sacrosancta Concilia, in Hailes's Annals.
Salk.—Salkeld's King's Bench Reports, 3 vols., . . 1689–1712
Sande Dec. Fris.—Sande's Decisiones Frisicae, 1 vol., . . 1656
Sandford (Erskine Douglas, Advocate) on Entails, 2nd ed., 1 vol., ... 1842
Sandford Her. Suc.—Sandford on the Law of Heritable Succession in Scotland, 2 vols., . 1830
Savigny, System des Heutigen Römischen Rechts, 8 vols., 1840–51
Savigny Obl.—Savigny, Das Obligationenrecht, 2 vols., 1851–3
Savigny on Private International Law, translated by Guthrie, 2nd ed., . . . 1880
Sc.—Scott's Common Pleas Reports, 8 vols., . . 1834–40
Sc. Jur.—Scottish Jurist, 46 vols., ... 1829–73
Scott N. R., or N. C.—Scott's New Reports (Common Pleas), 8 vols., ... 1840–5
Scottish Law Review, began 1885.
Scottish Provincial Councils at Perth, 1269 and 1420, in Hailes's Annals, vol. iii.; and in Concilia Scotiæ, Bannatyne Club, ... 1866
Sebastian on Trade Marks, 3rd ed., 1 vol., ... 1890
Sel. Sh. Ct. Ca.—Guthrie's (W.) Select Sheriff Court Cases, 1st series pub. 1879; 2nd series pub. 1894.
Selw. Nisi Pr.—Selwyn on the Law of Nisi Prius, 11th ed., 2 vols., ... 1845
Sess. Pa.—Session Papers.
Sh. Ct. R.—Scottish Law Review and Sheriff Court Reports, ... 1885–
Sh. Justy.—John Shaw's Justiciary Court Reports, 1 vol., 1848–52
Sh. T. C.—Shaw's Teind Cases, 1 vol., ... 1821–31
Shaw's Bell's Commentaries on the Law of Scotland (the 6th ed.), 2 vols., . . . 1858
Shearman on Negligence (American), 4th ed., 2 vols., . 1888
Shortt on the Law of Works of Literature and Art, 2nd ed., 1 vol., ... 1884
Sim.—Simon's Chancery Reports, 17 vols., . . 1826–49
Sim. N. S.—Simon's Chancery Reports, new series, 2 vols., 1850–2
Skene, de Verborum Significatione (subjoined to his edition of Acta Parl.), . . 1597
Sm. L. C.—Smith's Leading Cases, 8th ed., 2 vols., 1879, and 10th ed., . . . 1896
Sm. Merc. Law—Smith on Mercantile Law, 10th ed., . . 1890
Smith on Chancery Practice, 12th ed., 1 vol., . . . 1878
Smith (Horace) on Negligence, 1880
Snell on Principles of Equity, 6th ed., ... 1882
Spinks—Spinks's Ecclesiastical and Admiralty Reports, 2 vols., ... 1853–5
Spottiswood's Notes — Sir Robert Spottiswood's Practicks of the Law of Scotland, 1 vol., ... 1706
Sprague—Sprague's (American) Admiralty Cases, 2 vols., 1841–64
Stair—Stair's Institutions of the Law of Scotland, 2nd ed., 1693; More's edition, . . 1832
Stark.—Starkie's Nisi Prius Reports, 3 vols., . . 1814–22
Starkie on Evidence, 4th ed., 1 vol., ... 1853
Stephen's Commentaries on the Law of England, 10th ed., 4 vols., ... 1886
Steuart's Answers to Dirleton's Doubts, 2nd ed., 1 vol., . 1762
Stevens on Average, 5th ed., 1 vol., ... 1835
Stewart on Rights of Fishing, 2nd ed., 1 vol., . . . 1892
Story's Abbott on Merchant Shipping and Seamen, American ed. by Judge Story.
Story on Agency, 9th ed., 1 vol., 1882
Story on Bailments, 9th ed., 1 vol., ... 1878
Story on Bills, 4th ed., 1 vol., . 1860
Story on the Conflict of Laws, 8th ed., 1 vol., . . . 1883
Story on Contracts, 3rd ed., 1 vol., ... 1851
Story on Equity Jurisprudence, 12th ed., 2 vols., . . . 1877
Story on Partnership, 7th ed., 1 vol., ... 1881
Story on Promissory Notes, 7th ed., 1 vol., ... 1878
Story's R.—Story's U. S. Circuit Court Reports, 3 vols., 1839–45
Straccha; see Zilettus, Tractatus universi Juris, vol. vi.
Str.—Strange's King's Bench Reports, 2 vols., . . 1716–49
Stu.—Stuart's (Sir Robert) Court of Session, etc., Reports, 2 vols., . . 1851–3
Sugden (Lord St. Leonards) on Vendors and Purchasers of Estates, 14th ed., 1 vol., . 1862
Sw. & T.—Swabey & Tristram's Probate and Divorce Reports, 4 vols., ... 1858–66
Swa. Adm.—Swabey's Admiralty Reports, 1 vol., . . 1858–9
Swan.—Swanston's Chancery Reports, 3 vols., . . 1818–9
Swin.—Swinton's Justiciary Court Reports, 2 vols., . 1835–41
Syme—Syme's Justiciary Court Reports, 1 vol., . . 1826–9

T

T. R.—Term Reports in King's Bench (Durnford & East), 8 vols., ... 1785–1800
Tait on Evidence, 3rd ed., 1 vol., 1834
Tait, J. P.—Tait on Justices of the Peace, 4th ed., 1 vol., . 1828
Taunt.—Taunton's Common Pleas Reports, 8 vols., . 1807–19
Taylor on the Law of Evidence, 9th ed., 2 vols. . . . 1895
Thomasius de usu practico doctrinae de culparum præstatione in contractibus.
Thoms on Judicial Factors, 2nd ed., 1 vol., ... 1881
Thomson on Bills of Exchange, 3rd ed., by Dove Wilson, 1 vol., ... 1865
Thorburn on the Bills of Exchange Act, 1882, 1 vol., . 1882
Throop on the Validity of Verbal Agreements (American), . 1870
Tidd on the Practice of the King's Bench and Common Pleas, 7th ed., 2 vols., . 1821
Toullier, Le Droit Civil Français, 21 vols., . . 1830–43
Tudor's L. C.—Tudor's Leading Cases in Mercantile and Maritime Law, 3rd ed., 1 vol., ... 1884
Turn. & R.—Turner & Russell's Chancery Reports, 1 vol., 1822–24
Tyr.—Tyrwhitt's Exchequer Reports, 5 vols., . . 1830–35

U

Upper Canada Law Journal, 28 vols., ... 1855–82

V

Valin, Nouveau Commentaire sur l'Ordonnance de la Marine, 2 vols., ... 1766
Van Leeuwen, Censura Forensis 1 vol., ... 1662
Van Leeuwen's Commentaries translated into English, 1 vol., 1820
Vattel, Le Droit de Gens (new ed.), 3 vols., . . 1835–38
Vattel's Law of Nations (Chitty's ed.), 1 vol., ... 1834

Vent.—Ventris's King's Bench Reports, 1 vol., . . . 1726
Vern.—Vernon's Chancery Reports, 2 vols., . . 1681–1720
Ves. & B.—Vesey & Beames's Chancery Reports, 2 vols., 1812–14
Ves., or Ves. Sen. — Vesey's Chancery Reports, 2 vols., 1746–55
Ves. Jr.—Vesey Junior's Chancery Reports, 17 vols., 1789–1811
Vinnii Commentarii in Institutiones Imperiales, 1 vol., . . 1726
Vinnii Quaestiones Selectae, Rotterdam, ... 1664
Voet (John), Commentarii ad Pandectas, 2 vols., . . 1707
Voet (Paul) de Statutis (see Guthrie's Savigny, Appendix iii.), Amstel., . . . 1661

W

W. Bl.—W. Blackstone's King's Bench Reports, 2 vols., 1746–80
W. H. & G.—Welsby, Hurlston, & Gordon's Exch. Rep., 1847–54
W. N.—Weekly Notes (English Law Rep.), . . . 1866–
W. R.—Weekly Reporter, 1852–
W. Rob.—W. Robinson's Admiralty Reports, 3 vols., 1838–50
W. & S.—Wilson & Shaw's House of Lords Reports, 7 vols., 1825–34
Wallace's (George, Advocate) Principles of the Law of Scotland, 1 vol., ... 1760
Warnkoenig, Commentarii Juris Romani Privati, 3 vols., 1825–29
Webs. P. R.—Webster's Patent Cases, 1 vol., . . . 1844
West on the Law and Practice of Extents, 1 vol., . . 1817
Westlake Pr. Int. Law—Westlake on Private International Law, 3rd ed., 1 vol., . . 1890
Wh. & Tud. L. C.—White & Tudor's Leading Cases in Equity, 6th ed., 2 vols., . 1886
Wheaton's Digest of the Law of Maritime Capture, 1 vol., ... 1815
Wheaton—Wheaton's (American) Supreme Court Reports, 12 vols., ... 1816–27
Wight on Elections—Wight's (Alexander, Advocate) Inquiry into the Rise and Progress of Parliament, chiefly in Scotland, new ed., 2 vols., . . 1806
Wigram on Extrinsic Evidence, 4th ed., 1 vol., . . . 1858
Willes—Willes's Common Pleas Reports, 1 vol., . . 1737–58
Wils.—Wilson's King's Bench Reports, 3 vols., . . 1742–74
Wilson's Sh. Ct. Pr.—Dove Wilson on Sheriff Court Practice, 4th ed., 1 vol., . . 1891
Wilson's Thomson on Bills of Exchange (the 3rd ed.), 1 vol., ... 1865
Wms. Saunders — Saunders' King's Bench Reports (by Williams), 3 vols., . 1666–73
Woodman's Precedents in Chancery.
Wright (Robert S.) on the Law of Criminal Conspiracies, 1 vol., ... 1873

Y

Y. & Coll.—Younge & Collyer's Exchequer Reports, 4 vols., 1834–41
You. & C. C. C. — Younge & Collyer's Vice-Chancellor's Court Reports, 2 vols., . 1841–43

INDEX OF CASES

The references are to the sections. The figures in brackets after some cases indicate the year in which they were decided.

E

F

H

L

M

Q

S

T

U

X

Y

Z

INTRODUCTION

1. The object of Jurisprudence is the protection and enforcement of Civil Rights; and the system is perfect or imperfect, in proportion as the doctrine of Rights is regulated on sound principles and enlarged views of the happiness of men, and as the means of protecting and vindicating them are well or ill provided.

The Civil Jurisprudence of Scotland comprehends, first, a knowledge of the rules and exceptions relative to Civil Rights, with the grounds on which they rest; and secondly, the application of those rules and exceptions to judicial determinations for the protection or enforcement of right.

2. Right, in Jurisprudence, differs from Right in Morals, in so far as the latter term is used to express what ought to be; while the former expresses that which, as belonging to a person, he may vindicate by judicial aid.

Rights of this latter species may be distinguished into—1. Those which relate to Property or Things external,—as land, moveables, goods, money, debts, estates, and effects of all kinds; and, 2. Those which relate to the Person,—the safety, liberty, and reputation of men.

3. Of the Rights relative to Property, another division has been made by lawyers,—into those which depend upon the engagement or obligation of the person to give the thing, or to make it available to another, in perpetual or temporary use; and those in which, by immediate connection with the thing itself, without the intervention of another, it is said to belong to the person. Rights of the former kind are sometimes termed Personal Rights relative to things, being available only by demand against a particular person. Rights of the latter kind are called Real Rights, and are available against the thing itself, in whose hands soever it may be found. The former the Roman lawyers called 'Jura ad Rem,' the latter 'Jura in Re'; and the distinction is very important in practical jurisprudence (*a*).

(*a*) 2 Stair, 1. § 1. 3 Ersk. 1. § 2. Pothier, Tr. de Propriété, § 245. 7.

4. The doctrine of Rights may be explained in the following order:—

Book I. Rights Personal; arising from Obligation or Contract Express or Implied.

Book II. Rights Real; in Property, Heritable and Moveable.

Book III. Rights arising from Marriage and the Constitution of a family; with the laws of Succession.

Book IV. Rights relative to the Person.

Book V. The Evidence and Enforcement of these Rights.

BOOK FIRST

OF RIGHTS PERSONAL; ARISING FROM OBLIGATION OR CONTRACT, EXPRESS OR IMPLIED

PART I

RIGHTS ARISING FROM EXPRESS OBLIGATIONS AND CONTRACTS

CHAPTER I

OF CONVENTIONAL OBLIGATIONS

5. Nature and Kinds of Obligations.—One has a Right to demand of another person a thing or the use of it, or the services of that other person, in virtue of an engagement to deliver the thing or to perform the service. The counterpart of rights thus derived through personal engagement is OBLIGATION. Such obligations are either unilateral or mutual; the former being strictly called OBLIGATIONS, the latter CONTRACTS. The peculiarities of mutual obligations will be explained hereafter (*a*); but whether the right in question arises from a unilateral or from a mutual agreement, Obligation or Engagement is the essential point (*b*).

(*a*) See below, § 70. (*b*) 3 Ersk. 1. § 2.

6. Obligation is express or implied; the former being Conventional, the latter what some lawyers have called Obediential.

7. Definition of Conventional Obligation.—A Conventional Obligation is an engagement or undertaking to deliver, or to pay, or to do, or to abstain from doing, something; conferring on him to whom the engagement is undertaken, a right to demand performance of it (*a*).

Three separate acts of the will, terminating in such engagement, have been distinguished: deliberation; resolution; engagement. It is the Engagement only which law will enforce (*b*).

(*a*) 1 Stair, 10. § 1, 2. 3 Ersk. 2. § 3. Pothier, Tr. des Oblig. p. 2. Toullier, tom. 6. p. 1 et seq. See Instit. de Oblig. lib. 3. tit. 14.

(*b*) Kincaid *v.* Dickson, 1673; M. 12,143; 1 Ill. 1. Kennedy *v.* Kennedy, 1723; M. 9441. Tunno *v.* Tunno, 1681; M. 9438. Reoch *v.* Crawford, 1712; M. 9440. Paterson *v.* Inglis, 1717; M. 9441. Kerr *v.* Kerr, 1751; M. 9442. M'Queen *v.* M'Tavish, March 3, 1812; F. C. M'Lachlan *v.* M'Lachlan, 1821; 1 S. 49. Fair *v.* Hunter, 1861; 24 D. 1. Scott *v.* Dawson, 1862; 24 D. 440. As to certainty, see § 524, *ad init.*

8. Promise and Offer.—A promise is an engagement (to which no preceding consideration is, by the law of Scotland, essential) to give, or deliver, or pay, or do, or abstain (*a*). It may be either absolute or conditional (*b*). It is binding if undertaken as a final engagement; but not if mentioned only as a probable intention (*c*). It may be proved by writing; or by oath (*d*); or even by witnesses, when followed by *rei interventus*, or 'except in the case of cautionry,' when forming part of a bargain of moveables (*e*). But a promise may be discharged by rejection express or implied; or by the failure of any annexed condition (*f*).

(*a*) The law of Scotland does not, on the one hand, follow the Roman law of *nudum pactum* (Pand. Justin. Pothier, lib. 2. tit. 14); nor recognise the subtilties of the English and American law, on the other. 1 Plowden, 308. 2 Blackst. 445. Rann *v.* Hughes, 7 Term Rep. 350, note. Pillans *v.* Mierop, 3 Burr. 1663; 1 Ross' L. C. 464. 1 Illus. 3 and 4. 2 Kent, Com. 464. Stephen's Com. 2. 59. Pollock on Contracts, 246 sqq. 1 Smith's L. C. 136 sqq. (Lampleigh *v.* Brathwaite). See below, § 64.

(*b*) 1 Stair, 10. § 4. 3 Ersk. 3. § 88. So one may be presently and irrevocably bound by a delivered document to pay an annuity or legacy after the promisor's death. Duguid *v.* Caddell's Trs., 1831; 9 S. 844. Miller *v.* Milne's Trs., 1859; 21 D. 377. 3 Ersk. 9. § 6. 3 Stair, 8. § 27. Johnston *v.* Goodlet, 1868; 6 Macph. 1067. *Infra*, § 64.

(*c*) Kintore *v.* Sinclair, 1623; M. 9425; 1 Ill. 2. Clackmannan *v.* Nisbet, 1624; Spottiswoode, 248; 1 B. Sup. 130. Gordon *v.* Cunningham, 1740; M. 9425; and cases, *sup.* § 7 (*b*). Macfarlan *v.* Johnston, 1864; 2 Macph. 1210.

(*d*) Deuchar *v.* Brown, 1672; M. 12,387 (cautionry). Harvie *v.* Crawford, 1732; M. 12,388 (marriage).

(*e*) Grant *v.* Macdonald, 1827; 5 S. 317. See below, § 249. See § 26, 1518; Dickson on Evid. § 593–595. See Chaplin *v.* Allan, 1842; 4 D. 616. Millar *v.* Tremamondo, 1771; M. 12,395; Hailes, 409.

(*f*) 1 Stair, 10. § 4. Allan *v.* Colzier, 1664, M. 9428; 1 Ill. 82.

9. A promise differs from an offer, as being a unilateral engagement, to which acceptance is presumed; while an offer is always and *in terminis* conditional, raised into an obligation only by acceptance (*a*).

(*a*) 1 Stair, 10. § 4. 3 Ersk. 3. § 88. See below, § 73.

10. Nature and Requisites of Consent.—To a perfect obligation (besides the proof requisite), it is necessary that there shall be a deliberate and voluntary consent and purpose to engage; excluding, on the one hand, Incapacity by nonage, disease, or imbecility (*a*); and, on the other, Error, Force, and Fraud.

(*a*) See as to this below, § 2065–2113.

11. (1.) *Error* 'has in itself no legal effect. It becomes operative on a man's legal position only in exceptional cases (*a*). If, for example, he buys too dear or sells too cheap, he is not by reason of his mistake protected from loss (*b*). Hence, in written agreements, where consent is not doubtful or disputed, obvious mistakes and omissions are to be corrected from the general meaning or context, and even more serious mistakes may be set right if the instrument itself afford the means of doing so; or, being latent or mere clerical errors, by the appropriate extrinsic evidence (*c*). Error is operative only when it prevents an act or deed from being done or executed, or an agreement from being concluded, according to the true intention of the actor or granter or contracting parties. The effects in such cases are: that obligations and contracts are annulled or dissolved on the ground either of essential error (§ 11), or of error produced by misrepresentation or fraud (§ 13 sqq.); testamentary writings are avoided on like grounds (§ 1864); and what has actually been paid or delivered in error may be recovered back (§ 531).'

Error in substantials, whether in fact or in law, invalidates consent, 'or rather excludes real consent,' where reliance is placed on the thing mistaken (*d*). Such error in substantials may be—1. In relation to the *subject* of the contract or obligation; as when one commodity is mistaken for another (*e*); 2. In relation to the *person* who undertakes the engagement, or to whom it is supposed to be undertaken, wherever personal identity is essential (*f*); 3. In relation to the *price* or consideration for the undertaking (*g*); 4. In relation to the *quality*, '*quantity*, or *extent*' of the thing engaged for, if expressly or tacitly essential to the bargain (*h*); or 5. In relation to the *nature* of the contract itself supposed to be entered into, 'as, for example, if one sign a conveyance believing it to be a bond or security or a testamentary deed (*i*), or a bill believing it to be a guarantee (*k*), or even a deed under the mistaken belief induced by the other party that it contains material clauses which were in the draft (*l*), or does not contain clauses which are concealed or improperly added afterwards (*m*), or has a legal effect different from that which it really has (*n*).

'It is an important question not yet fully answered by decisions how far an error of one party only will give him a right to rescind a contract or onerous unilateral obligation. It has been laid down in the House of Lords that, in the case of an onerous contract reduced to writing, the erroneous belief of one of the contracting parties in regard to the nature of the obligations which he has undertaken, does not give him this right, unless it has been induced by the representations, whether fraudulent or not, of the other party (*n*).

'The legal effect of *ignorance* and error is the same, ignorance being in truth the generic term and including error (*o*). In a narrower sense, ignorance excludes the idea of reliance on the thing mistaken, and may go rather to affect the construction of an obligation than to invalidate it; *e.g.* a general discharge does not include claims competent to the granter, of which he was ignorant at the time. (See below, § 584, note.) And where the intention is to sell the whole interest under a succession, or all the stock in certain premises, the seller has no redress (both parties having been in ignorance) if he afterwards find that there were claims as to which he was ignorant (*p*), or that certain boxes forming one of the lots put up to auction contained valuable commodities (*q*).'

Although error in *law* as well as error in *fact* will invalidate a contract, it will not always entitle to restitution after the contract is fulfilled or money paid (*r*). 'There is no Scots authority impugning the proposition, that a mistake of law invalidates a contract when its existence excludes real consent. But it has been held in England that the rule *ignorantia juris neminem excusat* applies to cases of error in contracts as well as to payments of money in error (*s*). The application of the general rule, however, has, in practice, been much restricted; and it may almost be said that the preceding proposition is practically in harmony with English law, as now explained. It is held that the principle "*ignorantia*," etc., applies only to ignorance of the general law of the country, and not to ignorance or error as to private rights, or mistake as to the mutual and respective rights of the parties to a contract: all mistakes, in short, as to the application of the law to particular circumstances being regarded, when they are an essential element in an apparent agreement or contract, as errors of fact (*t*).'

(*a*) Savigny, System, § 115; and Beylage, viii. No. 6, vol. iii. p. 113, 340. Bennie's Trs. *v.* Couper, 1890, 17 R. 782. Pollock on Contracts, p. 420.

(*b*) *Infra*, § 96, 97A. United Mut. Mining Ass. *v.* Murray, 1860; 23 D. 69.

(*c*) See *e.g.* Wilson *v.* Wilson, 5 H. L. Ca. 40. Greenwood *v.* Greenwood, 5 Ch. D. 954; 47 L. J. Ch. 298. Fitch *v.* Jones, 5 E. and B. 238; 24 L. J. Q. B. 293. Boddan *v.* Moore, 1823; 2 S. 583. N. B. Ins. Co. *v.* Tunnock, 1864; 3 Macph. 1. Coutts & Co. *v.* Allan, 1758, M. 11,549. Johnston *v.* Pettigrew, 1865, 3 Macph. 954. 1 Smith's L. C. 302; 2 *ib.* 392. Pollock, Contracts, p. 467. Errors of this kind belong to the subject of Construction; § 524. See also § 68 (*f*). As to *error calculi* in docqueted accounts, etc., see M'Laren *v.* Liddell's Trs., 1860; 22 D. 373; 1862, 24 D. 577, and below, § 535 (*b*); in a decree, Brown *v.* Graham, 1848, 10 D. 867; 1849, 11 D. 1330; in a building schedule, Jamieson *v.* M'Innes, 1887; 15 R. 17.

(*d*) 1 Stair, 10. § 13. 3 Ersk. 1. § 16. Dig. lib. 50. de Reg. Juris. 1. 116. § 2. and lib. 44. tit. 7. de Oblig. et Act. 1. 57. Pothier, Tr. des Oblig. § 17 et seq. 6 Toullier, Dr. Civil Francais, 43. See § 14. Purdon *v.* Rowatt's Trs., 1856; 19 D. 206, 220, 223. Kennedy *v.* Panama Mail Co., L. R. 2 Q. B. 580; 36 L. J. Q. B. 260 (*per* Blackburn, J.). Dick & Stevenson *v.* Mackay, 1881; 8 R. H. L. 37, 42. In pleading it is necessary to specify the nature of the error alleged. Ritchie *v.* Ritchie's Trs., 1866; 4 Macph. 292. Yeatman *v.* Proctors, 1877; 5 R. 179. Johnston *v.* Goodlet, 1868; 6 Macph. 1067. The definition of error in this section is approved and adopted by L.-P. Inglis and Lord Watson, in Stewart *v.* Kennedy, *infra* (*n*).

(*e*) Stair and Ersk. *ut sup.* Hepburn *v.* Campbell, 1781; M. 14,168; 1 Ill. 4. Grieve *v.* Wilson, 1828; 6 S. 454; aff. 1833, 6 W. & S. 543. Thornton *v.* Kempster, 5 Taunton, 786; 15 R. R. 658. Adamson *v.* Glasgow Water Comrs., 1859; 21 D. 1012. Wilson *v.* Cal. Ry. Co., 1860; 22 D. 1408. Hamilton *v.* Western Bank, 1861; 23 D. 1033. E. Wemyss *v.* Campbell, 1858; 29 D. 1090. Raffles *v.* Wichelhaus, 2 H. & C. 906; 33 L. J. Ex. 160. Calverley *v.* Williams, 1 Ves. 210; 1 R. R. 118. It is a mistake of this kind avoiding the contract if the subject of the contract does not exist, or has ceased to exist when the bargain is made. **Couturier *v.* Hastie**, 5 H. L. Ca. 673; 25 L. J. Ex. 253 (specific cargo lost at sea). See § 29. Strickland *v.* Turner, 7 Ex. 208. Cochrane *v.* Willis, L. R. 1 Ch. App. 58; 35 L. J. Ch. 36 (cases of rights dependent on lives expired at the time of bargain); or if one in ignorance bargains to buy what proves to be his own already. Bingham *v.* Bingham, 1 Ves. J. 126. Jones *v.* Clifford, 3 Ch. Div. 779; 45 L. J. Ch. 809. Cochrane, *cit.* **Cooper *v.* Phibbs**, L. R. 2 H. L. 149. Scrabster Harb. Trs. *v.* Sinclair, 1864; 2 Macph. 884.

(*f*) Christie *v.* Fairholmes, 1748; M. 4897; 1 Ill. 5. Dunlop *v.* Crookshanks, 1752; M. 4879. Love *v.* Kemp's Crs., 1786; M. 4948. Mitchell *v.* Lepage, Holt's Rep. 253. Fellowes *v.* L. Gwydir, 1 Russ. & My. 83. Boulton *v.* Jones, 2 H. & N. 564; 27 L. J. Ex. 117. Hardman *v.* Booth, 1 H. & C. 103; 32 L. J. Ex. 105. Hunter *v.* Humble, 12 Q. B. 310. Lindsay *v.* Cundy, 2 Q. B. D. 96; aff. 2 App. Ca. 459; 47 L. J. Q. B. 481. See Waddell *v.* Waddell, 1863; 1 Macph. 635, a particular case of a bond taken in favour of the wrong person as creditor.

(*g*) See Christie, *supra* (*f*). Sword *v.* Sinclairs, 1771; M. 14,241. Hogg *v.* Campbell, 1864; 2 Macph. 848. Stewart's Trs. *v.* Hart, 1875; 3 R. 192. Wardlaw *v.* Mackenzie, 1859; 21 D. 940. Clason *v.* Stewart, 1844; 6 D. 1201.

(*h*) Adamson *v.* Smith, 1799; M. 14,244 (seeds). Dickson *v.* Kincaid, Dec. 15, 1808; F. C. (seeds). Baird *v.* Pagan, 1765; M. 14,240 (ale for export). See Coutts & Co. *v.* Allan & Co., 1758; M. 11,549. Johnston *v.* Johnston, 1857; 19 D. 706; aff. 1860, 3 Macq. 619. Mortimer *v.* Mitchell, 1850; 23 S. Jur. 64. Morton, *cit.* (*q*). Broughton *v.* Hutt, 3 De G. & J. 501. According to Savigny (Syst. § 137, vol. iii. 283), an error in quality, the specific thing being agreed on, must in order to annul the contract be such as to make a difference in kind, according to the ordinary use of language and understanding in business. It is here necessary to distinguish a fundamental error from a mistake as to a collateral fact, or mistake in motive on the part of one of the parties, which has no effect, but must be made the subject of warranty. Hardy *v.* Austin & M'Aslan, 1870; 8 Macph. 798. But if it be a condition of the contract, express or implied, that the subject of the contract shall be of a certain kind or quality, then the condition failing (*i.e.* a mistake having been made by both parties), the contract is void. See below, § 95, 98. Smith *v.* Hughes, L. R. 6 Q. B. 597; 40 L. J. Q. B. 221. Azemar *v.* Casella, L. R. 2 C. P. 431, 677; 36 L. J. C. P. 124, 263. 2 Smith's L. C. 28.

(*i*) M'Connechy *v.* M'Indoe, 1853; 16 D. 315. Priestnell *v.* Hutcheson, 1857; 19 D. 495. Maclaurin *v.* Stafford, 1875; 3 R. 265. Kennedy *v.* Green, 3 My. & K. 699.

(*k*) Foster *v.* Mackinnon, L. R. 4 C. P. 704; 38 L. J. C. P. 310.

(*l*) Hogg *v.* Campbell, 1864; 2 Macph. 848. See § 14 (*h*).

(*m*) Couston *v.* Miller, 1862; 24 D. 607. Munro *v.* Strain, 1874; 1 R. 527. Swan *v.* N. B. Australasian Co., 2 H. & C. 175; 32 L. J. Ex. 273. See below, § 14 (*h*), and as to effect of negligence, § 13 (*d*), 14 (*c*) (*f*).

(*n*) **Stewart** *v.* **Kennedy**, 1889, 16 R. 857; 1890, 15 App. Ca. 108; 17 R. H. L. 25 (*per* L. Herschell, p. 119, and L. Watson, 121).

(*o*) Donellus, 1 Com. 19. § 5. Savigny, Syst. § 115, and Beyl. viii. vol. iii. p. 111, 326.

(*p*) Hawkins *v.* Jackson, 19 L. J. Ch. 451.

(*q*) Dawson *v.* Muir, 1831; 13 D. 851. Morton *v.* Smith, 1877; 5 R. 83. See the converse case of the buyer in Lamert *v.* Heath, 15 M. & W. 487. Lawes *v.* Purser, 6 E. & B. 930; 26 L. J. Q. B. 25.

(*r*) 1 Pothier, Pand. Justin. 645, No. 2. Domat, l. 1. tit. 18. § 14. Cod. Civ. No. 1109. See the distinction in Herbert *v.* Champion, 1 Camp. 134; 1 Ill. 7. Sinclair *v.* Wilson & M'Lellan, 4 W. & S. 398; 1 Ill. 328. See below, § 534.

(*s*) See Pollock on Contracts, 423, 435. Snell's Prin. of Eq. 429 sqq. Benjamin on Sales, 392.

(*t*) **Cooper** *v.* **Phibbs**, L. R. 2 H. L. 149. E. Beauchamp *v.* Winn, L. R. 6 H. L. 223. Daniel *v.* Sinclair, 6 App. Ca. 180. Comp. Baird's Trs. *v.* Baird & Co., 1877; 4 R. 1005. And see as to Scots law on this point, Mercer's Trs. *v.* Anstruther, 1871; 9 Macph. 618, esp. p. 628, 652 (on appeal the H. of L. went rather on undue influence as between parent and child; 10 Macph. H. L. 39). Dickson *v.* Halbert, 1854; 16 D. 586. Inglis's Trs. *v.* Inglis, 1887; 14 R. 740.

12. (2.) *Force and Fear* ('Anglice, *Duress*') annul engagement, when not vain or foolish fear, but such as to overpower a mind of ordinary firmness (*a*); or such as, applied to a person of weaker age, sex, or condition, will produce the effect of overpowering violence on a firmer mind (*b*). Among the instruments of force and fear which have been held to annul engagement, are, threats and terror of death; pain to oneself, or parent, or child (*c*); infamy and disgrace; imprisonment, when employed to obtain an advantage beyond the lawful object of it (*d*); and even loss of property (*e*). But mere vexation and inconvenience (as the threat of a lawsuit), 'or fear of the lawful consequences of refusing to do what is asked, *e.g.* of imprisonment (*f*),' will not be sufficient.

(*a*) 1 Stair, 9. § 8. 3 Ersk. 1. § 16, and 4. 1. § 26. Domat, 138. Pothier, des Obligations, § 25. 6 Toullier, 81. See 1 Bell's Com. 295 (314, M'L.'s ed.); and the cases cited in previous editions in 1 Ill. 8 et seq., from Cassie to Kerr, chiefly as showing the state of Scotland in the 17th century. Peel, 16 Ves. 157. Woodman, Prec. in Chanc. 266. See § 14. Gelot *v.* Stewart, 1870; 8 Macph. 649; 1871, 9 Macph. 957.

(*b*) Alexander *v.* Hamilton, 1694; 4 B. Sup. 186. Johnston *v.* Napier, 1708; 5 B. Sup. 50. Cairns *v.* Marianski, 1850; 12 D. 919, 1286; H. L. 1852, 2 Macq. 212, 766. Intimidation, combined with fraud or circumvention, in order to influence a person of facile disposition, is a ground of reduction. See Love *v.* Marshall, 1870: 9 Macph. 291. Cairns, *cit.*

(*c*) Dig. lib. 4. t. 2. c. 8. Stair, *sup.* (*a*). M'Intosh *v.* Farquharson, 1671; M. 16,485; 2 B. Sup. 634; 1 Ill. 9. See in further illustration, the King *v.* Southerton, 6 East, 126. See Priestnell, *infra* (*f*).

(*d*) Blair *v.* Blair, 1673; 2 B. Sup. 170. Herriot *v.* Bird, 1681; M. 16,496. Lutwidge *v.* Murray, 1706; 4 B. Sup. 652. Nisbet *v.* Stewart, 1706; M. 16,512. Arrat *v.* Wilson, 1718–19; Robertson's App. Ca. 234. Munro *v.* Bruce, 1721; *ib.* 387. Bell *v.* Thomson, 1762; M. 16,515. Willocks *v.* Callender, 1776; M. 1519; Hailes, 724. Wightman *v.* Graham, 1787; M. 1521. Fraser *v.* Black, Dec. 13, 1810; F. C. See Canison *v.* Marshall, 1764; 6 Pat. Ap. 759. Dickie *v.* Gutzmer, 1829; 8 S. 147. Priestnell and Craig, *infra.* M'Intosh *v.* Chalmers, 1883; 11 R. 8. Williams *v.* Bayley, L. R. 1 H. L. 200; 35 L. J. Ch. 717. As to threats of confinement in a lunatic asylum, see Cumming *v.* Ince, 11 Q. B. 112; 17 L. J. Q. B. 105. Biffin *v.* Bignell, 7 H. & N. 877; 31 L. J. Ex. 189.

(*e*) Wiseman *v.* Logie, 1700; M. 16,505. Dundas *v.* Hardie, 1700; M. 16,506. Forman *v.* Sheriff, 1791; M. 16,515. See Skeate *v.* Beale, 11 A. & E. 983. Atlee *v.* Backhouse, 3 M. & W. 633. Wakefield *v.* Newbon, 6 Q. B. 276. Liverpool Mar. Cred. Co. *v.* Hunter, 37 L. J. Ch. 386; L. R. 3 Ch. 487 (compulsion by legal proceedings abroad). Qu. whether the remedy in these cases (duress of goods) is given on the ground of coercion alone? Pollock on Contracts, 576–8, and 2 Smith's L. C. 419.

(*f*) Priestnell *v.* Hutcheson. 1857; 19 D. 495. Craig *v.* Paton, 1865; 4 Macph. 192. Nisbet and Arrat, *cit.* (*d*).

13. (3.) *Fraud* is a machination or contrivance to deceive, and annuls (*a*) obligations induced by it (*b*). There is in such obligations apparently consent and engagement, but not such as the party defrauding is entitled to rely upon (*c*). Fraud is either such as gives *rise*, or *leads*, to the engagement; without which the engagement would not have taken place: Or such as is only *incident* to or an accompaniment of a contract, in which, independently of it, the parties were engaged (*d*). Error by fraud of the former kind, though not in substantials (*e*), if induced by stratagem sufficient to deceive a person of ordinary capacity; or accompanied by imbecility and loss on the part of the obligor (*f*); or induced in a case in which the obligor relies on the obligee for his information, as in insurance contracts (*g*); will ground an action for reducing the contract, or an exception in defence against an action grounded on it: 'while, the author wrote,' error by fraud of the latter kind will give relief by damages only. 'Yet, in general there must be material fraud (*dans locum contractui*) even to found an action for damages, so that the distinction, if it be at all recognised in modern practice, is of little moment, except as indicating that fraud of the latter kind has no effect (*h*).'

There is an important distinction between fraud of the contracting party, and fraud of a third party, in which the contracting party does not participate. The former entitles the obligor to redress by exception or by reduction; the latter directs his remedy against the third party (*i*).

(*a*) See § 13A.

(*b*) 1 Stair, 9. § 9. 3 Ersk. 1. § 16. Sanderson *v.* Carnie, 1821; 1 S. 149; 1 Ill. 10. M'Neil *v.* M'Neil's Trs., 1824; 2 S. Ap. 206. Power *v.* Barham, 4 Ad. & Ell. 473; 3 Ill. 101. See Chesterfield *v.* Jansen, 2 Ves. 155, for Lord Hardwicke's classification of frauds.

(*c*) 1 Stair, 9. § 9, 15. 3 Ersk. 1. § 16; and 4. 1. § 27. 6 Toullier, 88.

(*d*) Huber, in Dig. lib. 4. tit. 3. § 4. Voet. 1. 4. tit. 3. § 3. 4. 6 Toullier, 91. Ewen *v.* Mags. of Montrose, 1824; 2 S. 612; 1830, 4 W. & S. 346; 1 Ill. 10. Keith *v.* Smart, 1832; 10 S. 514. Nat. Exch. Co. *v.* Drew, 1850; 12 D. 950; aff. 1855, 2 Macq. 103. Burnes *v.* Pennell (Forth Marine Ins. Co. *v.* Burnes), 1848; 10 D. 689; aff. 1849, 6 Bell's Ap. 541. Ehrenbacher *v.* Kennedy, 1874; 1 R. 1131. **Attwood *v.* Small**, 6 Cl. and Fin. 305. It is not fraud *dans locum contractui* if the party said to be deceived relies on his own judgment, or sees the deceit and nevertheless agrees to the bargain. M'Lellan *v.* Gibson, 1843; 5 D. 1032. Kirkpatrick *v.* Irvine, 1850; 7 Bell's Ap. 186, 237; below, § 14 (*f*).

(*e*) That is to say, though in order to have this effect, the fraudulent representation or concealment must be *primâ facie material*, in the sense that it was likely to induce the person deceived to enter into the contract and was followed by his doing so; yet when such an unfair statement or suppression has been proved, it is not necessary to show what precise effect it had in producing the agreement, or what the result might have been if the whole truth had been known. Pulsford *v.* Richards, 17 Beav. 94. Reynell *v.* Sprye, 1 De G. M. & G. 660; 21 L. J. Ch. 663. Smith *v.* Kay, 30 L. J. Ch. 61; 7 H. L. Ca. 775. Watson *v.* Charlemont, 12 Q. B. 856. Kintrea's Case, 39 L. J. Ch. 193; L. R. 5 Ch. 95. Redgrave v. Hurd, 20 Ch. D. 1. Smith *v.* Land & Prop. Corpn., 28 Ch. D. 7.

(*f*) See § 14A. *Facility and Circumvention.*

(*g*) See § 14, 474, 514, 522.

(*h*) Attwood *v.* Small, *cit.* (*d*). M'Laren's Bell's Com. i. 263. Gillespie *v.* Russel, 1856; 18 D. 677, 686 (*per* L. Curriehill).

(*i*) Webster *v.* Christie, 1813: 1 Dow, 247; 5 Pat. 705. Masters *v.* Ibberson, 8 C. B. 100. Cf. Ehrenbacher, *cit.* Reese River Mining Co. *v.* Smith, 36 L. J. Ch. 618; L. R. 2 Ch. 604 (*per* Cairns, L. J.). Wheelton *v.* Hardisty, 8 E. & B. 232; 27 L. J. Q. B. 241. Young *v.* Clydesdale Bank, 1889, 17 R. 231 (fraud of principal debtor as against cautioner). The text here refers to frauds not committed by an agent of the contracting party, and by which he has taken no benefit. See § 224B. Taylor *v.* Tweedie, 1865; 3 Macph. 925.

13A. 'An obligation induced by fraud (in the absence of essential error) is not void, but only voidable in the election of the party (*a*) defrauded, provided (1) that he is able to restore the party against whom he seeks relief to the same position in which he was at the time of the transaction challenged, (2) that no third parties have in good faith and for value acquired rights under the contract, and (3), in some cases, that the position of the wrong-doer himself has not been materially changed by delay in challenging the contract (*b*). If it is impossible to restore things to their original condition, the party defrauded, instead of rescinding the contract, may obtain relief in damages (*c*). It is a result of the rule, that an obligation originating in or tainted by fraud is valid till reduced, that innocent third parties may, while it is unchallenged, acquire for onerous causes rights in regard to it which cannot be set aside (*d*). But even third parties cannot take benefit from a fraudulent transaction if they have acquired their rights gratuitously (*quod nemo debet locupletari jacturâ alienâ*), or with notice of the fraud (*e*), or if they represent the fraudulent bankrupt (*f*).'

(*a*) Edin. United Breweries *v.* Molleson, 1892; 20 R. 581; aff. on different grounds, 1894, A. C. 96; 21 R. H. L. 10.

(*b*) Clough *v.* London and N. W. Ry. Co., 41 L. J. Ex. 17; L. R. 7 Ex. 26. Morrison *v.* Univ. Mar. Ins. Co., 42 L. J. Ex. 17, 115; L. R. 8 Ex. 40, 197. Clarke *v.* Dickson, E. B. & E. 148; 27 L. J. Q. B. 223. Addie, *infra* (*b*). Adam *v.* Newbigging, 13 App. Ca. 308.

(*c*) **Addie *v.* Western Bank**, 1864; 2 Macph. 809; 3 Macph. 899; rev. 1867, 5 Macph. H. L. 81; L. R. 1 Sc. Ap. 156. M'Laren's Bell's Com. i. 262, 466. Tulloch *v.* Davidson's Trs., 1858; 20 D. 1045; aff. 3 Macq. 783. Jardine's Trs. *v.* Carron Co., 1864; 2 Macph. 639, 1101. Graham *v.* Western Bank, 1865; 3 Macph. 617. As to the liability of principals for the fraud of their agents, see below, § 224B.

(*d*) **Oakes *v.* Turquand**, L. R. 2 App. Ca. 325, 375; 36 L. J. Ch. 949. Pease *v.* Gloahec, L. R. 1 P. C. 219. Henderson *v.* Royal Br. Bank, 7 E. & B. 356; 26 L. J. Q. B. 112. Benjamin on Sales, 392 sqq. Wardlaw *v.* Mackenzie, 1859; 21 D. 940. Tennent *v.* City of Glasgow Bank, 1879; 6 R. 554; aff. *ib.* H. L. 69; 4 App. Ca. 615. Babcock *v.* Lawson, 5 Q. B. D. 284; 49 L. J. Q. B. 408. Burgess's Case, 15 Ch. D. 507; 49 L. J. Ch. 541. Comp. Brown *v.* Marr, 1880; 7 R. 427, with Moyce *v.* Newington, 4 Q. B. D. 32; 48 L. J. Q. B. 125; and see York Buildings Co. *v.* Mackenzie, 1795; 3 Pat. 378, 579. Fraser *v* Hankey, 1847, 9 D. 415. See below, § 403B, 403P. And see the cases as to sale by insolvents, § 14 (*g*), and in 1 Ill. 12–16.

(*e*) Bridgman *v.* Green, 2 Ves. 626. **Huguenin *v.* Baseley**, 14 Ves. 289; 2 Wh. & Tud. L. C. 504; 9 R. R. 148, 276. Topham *v.* D. Portland, 1 De G. J. & S. 517, 569. Scholefield *v.* Templer, Johns. 155; 4 De G. & J. 429; 28 L. J. Ch. 452. M'Cowan *v.* Wright, 1853; 15 D. 494. Kames's Princ. of Eq. 107 (ed. 1825). Wardlaw, *cit.* In this and other cases "notice" to third parties includes knowledge of such facts and circumstances as ought to have made them inquire into their author's title. Cooke *v.* Eshelby, 12 App. Ca. 271. E. of Sheffield *v.* London Jt. St. Bank, 13 App. Ca. 333. Dunlop's Trs. (Thomson, etc.) *v.* Clydesdale Bk. 1891; 18 R. 757; aff. 1893, A. C. 282; 20 R. H. L. 59.

(*f*) See the cases as to creditors affected by fraud of bankrupt in § 14 (*e*). Molleson *v.* Challis, 1873; 11 Macph. 510. 1 Bell's Com. 297 (316, M'L.'s ed.).

14. Fraud may be by false representation (*a*) 'made to another, or to the public, with the intention that it shall be acted upon, and so as to cause damage to be incurred (*b*), of material facts (*c*) known by the party making it to be untrue, or not believed by him to be true, *i.e.* with reckless ignorance whether it is true or false (*d*); but not of matters honestly believed by the party making the statements to be true (*e*), or of matters as to which the person said to be misled could and did exercise his own judgment (*f*)'; or by concealment of material circumstances (*g*) 'provided that by the nature of the contract and the position of the parties, a duty of communication is incumbent on the creditor, or the concealment is active and industrious'; or by underhand dealing (*h*); or by means of intoxication (*i*); or of imbecility (*k*).

'*Duty of Disclosure.*—There is a duty of disclosure, varying in degree according to circumstances, in insurance contracts (*infra*, § 474, 514, 522), in cautionry or suretyship (*infra*, § 251, 289, 291, 301), in contracts to take shares in companies (*infra*, § 403B), in family settlements and arrangements (*l*). It is sometimes a difficult question whether mere silence as to an error of the other party is sufficient to avoid a contract. If it be not an essential error making the contract void *ab initio* (*m*), and if the parties are treating at arms' length as in ordinary sales (see § 96, etc.), it is held that there is no duty of disclosure, no obligation on the one party to correct a mistake of the other to which he has not contributed (*n*). "Either party may be innocently silent as to grounds open to both to exercise their judgment upon" (*o*).

'"*Active Concealment*" is virtually misrepresentation, as when one uses devices to conceal the defects of articles sold (*p*), or having innocently caused a misapprehension, fails to correct it when he discovers the error (*q*), or keeps silence as to facts which if disclosed would alter the whole effect of what he has stated (*r*).'

NOTE relative to sections 11, 12, and 13.—The want of consent where the obligation proceeds from error or force annuls the contract; but the nullity must be declared judicially. The contract ostensibly is valid and regular, and—1. It subsists till it be reduced; 'and the Court will not reform the contract in accordance with the real intention of the parties, but will reduce it, subject, it may be, to conditions as to restitution or recompense (*s*).' 2. 'The objection on the ground of error or force (*t*)' will be effectual against third parties without notice; under the exception of land or heritable securities acquired on the faith of the records, moveables corporeal, and bills and notes.

A distinction has been taken in the case of fraud, that it will not be effectual as a ground of reduction against third parties; seeing there is here consent, though proceeding on a false ground. 'The author asked,' is there any real ground for such a distinction? 'But as it is a fixed principle that a contract obtained by fraud is not void, but voidable, and so is valid till rescinded, it is now settled that a contract cannot be rescinded for fraud after innocent third parties have acquired rights under it for value (*u*).'

(*a*) 1 Bell's Com. 242 (263, M'L.'s ed.). 1 Stair, 9. § 1. See Scott *v.* Christy and other cases in 1 Ill. 11. Dunlop and Love, *sup.* § 11 (*f*). Hill *v.* Grey, 1814; 2 Dow, 263. Gillespie *v.* Russel, 1856; 18 D. 677, 686.

(*b*) Pollock on Contr. 534. Addison on Torts, 732. Addie *v.* Western Bank, § 13A. Peek *v.* Gurney, L. R. 6 H. L. 377; 43 L. J. Ch. 19 (where it was held that the prospectus of a company, being intended only to induce persons to apply to the company for shares, and not being addressed to those who buy shares in the market, only original allottees, and not purchasers from them in the market, have a remedy against the promoters for falsehoods contained in it).

(*c*) This includes misrepresentations known to be untrue as to matters of law (at least within the limits now settled in regard to error, § 11); and the cases sometimes supposed to exclude such misrepresentations from the ordinary rule only show that fraud is there less easily established, because it is generally the business of one party as much as of the other to know the law; *e.g.* if a man be acquainted with the contents of a writing, it will require pregnant proof of fraud to show that he has been misled as to its legal effect. Rashdall *v.* Ford, L. R. 2 Eq. 750; 35 L. J. Ch. 769. Beattie *v.* Ebury, 41 L. J. Ch. 393, 804; 44 *ib.* 20; L. R. 7 Ch. 777; 7 H. L. 102. Weeks *v.* Propert, L. R. 8 C. P. 427; 42 L. J. C. P. 127. Hirschfeld *v.* Lon. B. and S. C. Ry., 2 Q. B. D. 1; 46 L. J. Q. B. D. 94. Lewis *v.* Jones, 4 B. & C. 506. Brownlie *v.* Miller, *infra* (*d*). Drummond's Trs. *v.* Melville, 1861; 23 D. 450, 462. See above, § 11 *fin.*

(*d*) Oliver *v.* Suttie, 1840; 2 D. 514. Campbell *v.* Boswell, 1841; 3 D. 639. City of Edin. Brewery Co. *v.* Gibsons, 1869; 7 Macph. 886. **Brownlie** *v.* **Miller**, 1878; 5 R. 1076, 1091; aff. 1880, 5 App. Ca. 925; 7 R. H. L. 66, 79 sqq. (*per* L. Blackburn). Reese River Ming. Co. *v.* Smith, L. R. 4 H. L. 64; 39 L. J. Ch. 849 (*per* L. Cairns). Evans *v.* Edmonds, 13 C. B. 777. See 1 Smith's L. C., notes to Chandelor *v.* Lopus; 2 *ib.*, notes to Pasley *v.* Freeman. Smith *v.* Chadwick, 20 Ch. D. 87; 51 L. J. Ch. 597. Peek *v.* Derry, 37 Ch. D. 541; revd. 14 App. Ca. 337. It has been said that a false statement of material facts is fraud if the person making it had no reasonable grounds to believe it to be true. But it is more correct to say that there must be an absence of belief, of which the absence of reasonable grounds for believing is evidence. Peek *v.* Derry, *cit.* *Per* L. Cranworth in Addie *v.* Western Bk. *sup.* § 13A. Brownlie *v.* Miller, *cit.* Kelly *v.* Solari, 9 M. & W. 54; 11 L. J. Ex. 10. Lees *v.* Tod, 1882; 9 R. 807 (esp. *per* L. Pres. Inglis, p. 854—a case which shows how the duty of inquiry may differ according to the position of the speaker, *e.g.* according as he is manager or director of a company in which a person is induced by false reports to take shares).

(*e*) *I.e.* an innocent misrepresentation (not leading to essential error and not being a warranty) does not invalidate a contract; in other words, a representation, false in fact but not known to be so by the party making it, who honestly believes it to be true, is not fraud in law. Brownlie *v.* Miller, *cit.* (p. 1092). Dunnett *v.* Mitchell, 1887; 15 R. 131. Evans *v.* Collins, 5 A. & E. 804; 13 L. J. Q. B. 180. Ormrod *v.* Huth, 14 M. & W. 651; 14 L. J. Ex. 366. Kennedy *v.* Panama Mail Co. L. R. 2 Q. B. 580; 36 L. J. Q. B. 260. Joliffe *v.* Baker, 11 Q. B. D. 255. Benjamin on Sales, 394, 445.

(*f*) Cases cited above, § 13, note (*d*) *ad fin.* Jennings *v.* Broughton, 5 De G. M. & G. 126. Dyer *v.* Hargrave, 10 Ves. 505. Attwood *v.* Small, 6 Cl. & Fin. 232. Horsfall *v.* Thomas, 1 H. & C. 90; 31 L. J. Ex. 322 (as to which, however, see Smith *v.* Hughes, *infra* (*n*). But where there is active misrepresentation, it is not enough that the party misled could have made inquiries and found out the truth. One cannot complain that another has too implicitly relied on the truth of what he himself has represented. Dobell *v.* Stevens, 3 B. & C. 623. Reynell *v.* Sprye, 1 De G. M. & G. 660; 21 L. J. Ch. 663. Central Ry. Co. of Venezuela *v.* Kisch, L. R. 2 H. L. 99; 36 L. J. Ch. 849 (*per* L. Chelmsford, C.). Scot. Widows Fund *v.* Buist, 1876; 3 R. 1078, 1083 (*per* Inglis, L. Pres.). Redgrave *v.* Hurd, 20 Ch. D. 1; 51 L. J. Ch. 113.

(*g*) 1 Stair, 9. § 9. Kennedy *v.* Blackbarony, 1687; M. 4858. Wood *v.* Baird 1696; M. 4860. Taylor *v.* Crop, 1821; 1 S. 68; 1824, 2 S. App. 233. Prince *v.* Pallet, 1680; M. 4932; see 5 B. Sup. 194 (concealment of bankruptcy or insolvency); and see many other cases on this ground in 1 Ill. 12–16. Allan & Stewart *v.* Stein's Crs., 1788; M. 4949; Hailes, 1059, 1071; 1 Bell's Com. 246; 1 Ill. 15; 3 Pat. 191. Smith *v.* Bank of Scotland, 1 Dow, 272, and 7 S. 244. Brown *v.* Syme, 1834; 12 S. 536. Comp. Edin. United Breweries, *supra*, 13A. Fraser *v.* Fraser's Trs., 1834; 13 S. 703. Hill *v.* Gray, 1 Starkie, 434; 18 R. R. 802. Hamilton *v.* Watson, 1842; 5 D. 280; aff. 4 Bell's App. 67 (cf. Lee *v.* Jones, 17 C. B. N. S. 482; 34 L. J. C. P. 131). Railton *v.* Matthews, 1843; 6 D. 1348; rev. 3 Bell's App. 56; see 7 D. 748; 8 D. 747. Kirkpatrick *v.* Irvine, 1848; 10 D. 367; rev. 1850, 7 Bell's App. 186. Oakes *v.* Turquand, L. R. 2 H. L. 325, 342; 36 L. J. Ch. 949. Davies *v.* Lond. Ins. Co., 8 Ch. D. 469; 47 L. J. Ch. 511.

(*h*) Campbell *v.* Moir, 1681; M. 4889. Ballantyne *v.* Watson, 1682; M. 4891. Walker *v.* Young, 1695; 4 B. Sup. 290 (see these cases, 1 Ill. 17). Cockshot *v.* Bennett, 2 T. R. 765; 1 R. R. 617. Dougall *v.* Marshall, 1833; 11 S. 1028. Gourlay *v.* Watt, 1870; 9 Macph. 107. M'Neillie *v.* Cowie, 1858; 20 D. 1229 (falsification of writing after execution).

(*i*) 3 Ersk. 1. § 16. Pothier, Oblig. No. 49. (See the cases in 1 Ill. 17, including Johnston *v.* Brown, 1823; 2 S. 495. Cook *v.* Clayworth, 18 Ves. 16; 11 R. R. 37. Pitt *v.* Smith, 3 Camp. 34; 13 R. R. 1141. Johnston *v.* Clark, 1854; 17 D. 229. Couston *v.* Miller, 1862; 24 D. 607. Taylor *v.* Provan, 1864; 2 Macph. 1226. Pollok *v.* Burns, 1875; 2 R. 497. Jardine *v.* Elliot, 1803; Hume, 684. Hunter *v.* Stevenson, 1804; Hume 686. Molton *v.* Camroux, 2 Ex. 487; 4 Ex 17; 18 L. J. Ex. 68, 256. Matthews *v.* Baxter, 42 L. J. Ex 73; L. R. 8 Ex. 132. 56 & 57 Vict. c. 71, s. 2 (Sale of Goods Act, 1893). No case appears to have decided that a contract made in a state of complete incapacity from drunkenness is *ab initio* void, and the opinions in Matthews *v.* Baxter, and perhaps in Pollok *v.* Burns, indicate that it is only voidable. It is difficult to suppose a case of intoxication avoiding a deed without some degree of fraud, but such cases may occur, especially if both parties are the worse of drink, where there is such a degree of intoxication as to make one utterly incapable of entering into business transactions (see Johnston *v.* Clark and Taylor *v.* Provan, *citt.*). In all cases the party seeking relief will be barred from pleading his intoxication, unless he makes his challenge as soon as he comes to his senses and knows what he is said to have done (Pollok *v.* Burns, *cit.*). It seems that he may ratify the agreement, and that the other party who contracted with him, knowing his condition, may be held to his bargain (Pollock on Contr. 90). But if both were drunk, *quære?* The cases of Jardine and Hunter, *citt.*, show that drunkenness may merely be an element in proving that the parties did not really intend to make a serious bargain.

(*k*) Maitland *v.* Ferguson, 1729; M. 4956; aff. Cr. & S. 73. Gordon *v.* Crawford, 1730; Cr. & St. 47. Cowper *v.* Grant, 1740; Elch. *Fraud*, 10. Irvine *v.* Ramsay Irvine, 1753; Elch. *Fraud*, 32; Elch. Notes, 168; rev. Cr. & S. 547. M'Ilwham v. Kerr, 1823; 2 S. 240 (and other cases in 1 Ill. 18). M'Neill *v.* Moir, 1824; 2 S. App. 206. M'Diarmid *v.* M'Diarmid, 1826; 4 S. 583; aff. 1828, 3 W. & S. 37. Tosh *v.* Ogilvy, 1873; 1 R. 254.

(*l*) Kirkpatrick, *cit.* (*g*); Gray *v.* Binny, Cunningham *v.* Anstruther, and Mercer *v.* Anstruther (*infra*, § 14B (*c*)), etc.

(*m*) As in Steuart's Trs. *v.* Hart, 1875; 3 R. 192; see § 11.

(*n*) **Smith *v.* Hughes**, L. R. 6 Q. B. 597; 40 L. J. Q. B. 221. **Gillespie *v.* Russel**, 1856; 18 D. 677, 686; 1857, 19 D. 904, 911. Brownlie *v.* Miller (*d*). Broatch *v.* Jenkins, 1866; 4 Macph. 1030. Davidson *v.* Dalziel, 1881; 8 R. 990. Paterson *v.* Allan, 1801; Hume, 681. Morrison *v.* Boswell, 1801, *ib.* 679; 5 Pat. App. 649. New Brunswick, etc., Co. *v.* Conybeare, 9 H. L. Ca. 711, 742; 31 L. J. Ch. 297. Fletcher *v.* Krell, 42 L. J. Q. B. 55. Baker *v.* Cartwright, 10 C. B. N. S. 124; 30 L. J. C. P. 364. Benjamin on Sales, 387, 404, 471.

(*o*) Carter *v.* Boehm, 1 Sm. L. C. 474–8; 3 Burr. 1905. Ward *v.* Hobbs, 4 App. Ca. 13. Turner *v.* Green, 1895; 2 Ch. 205. In Smith *v.* Soeder, 1895, 23 R. 60, a lawyer selling for a client a house to one who had no agent, was held bound to inform the buyer of serious building restrictions; but perhaps the case falls within the rule in § 11 (4), and see § 893 (*c*). Many cases as to concealment relate to concealment of insolvency. See cases in note (*g*) and 1 Bell's Com. 243 sqq. (264, M'L.'s ed.). See also M'L.'s note, p. 316.

(*p*) Schneider *v.* Heath, 3 Camp. 506; 14 R.R. 825. Hill *v.* Gray, *cit.* (*g*). Keates *v.* E. Cadogan, 10 B. & C. 591; 20 L. J. C. P. 76.

(*q*) Reynell *v.* Sprye, 1 De G. M. & G. 680.

(*r*) **Peek *v.* Gurney**, L. R. 6 H. L. 337; 43 L. J. Ch. 19.

(*s*) Steuart's Trs. *v.* Hart, 1875; 3 R. 192.

(*t*) This is substituted for "It," which stood in the original text; and seems to give the true meaning of a hastily written note.

(*u*) See above, § 13A.

14A. '*Facility and Circumvention.* Contracts and deeds are reduced on the ground of "facility and fraud or circumvention," when they have been obtained by artifice or fraud practised upon persons, who though not insane or even (strictly speaking) imbecile, are of a weak and facile disposition by reason of age, disease, or congenital infirmity (*a*). Circumvention and fraud seem to be just two shades of the same thing (*b*). Facility and lesion (*i.e.* damage) without fraud or circumvention, are not grounds for setting aside obligations (*c*).

(*a*) Cases in § 14, note (*k*). 1 Bell's Com. 141 (136, M'L.'s ed.). Cairns *v.* Marianski, *sup.* § 12 (*b*). Chiene *v.* Stirling, 1854; 17 D. 15. Gall *v.* Bird, 1855; 17 D. 1027. Morrison *v.* M'Lean's Trs., 1862; 24 D. 625. Mann *v.* Smith, 1861; 23 D. 435. Taylor *v.* Tweedie, 1865; 3 Macph. 928. Liston *v.* Cowan, *ib.* 1041. Munro *v.* Strain, 1874; 1 R. 522.

(*b*) Unless it be held that circumvention implies a course of deception, "being fraud in grain, but not fraud perpetrated by a single specific act." *Per* L. Kinloch in Love *v.* Marshall, 1870; 9 Macph. 291. See Chiene and Mann (*a*). Gray *v.* Binnie, 1879; 7 R. 332, 347.

(*c*) Scott *v.* Wilson, 1825; 3 Mur. 526. M'Kirdy *v.* Anstruther, 1839; 1 D. 855. Tennent *v.* Tennent's Trs., *infra*. As to the combination of circumvention and fraud with intimidation, see § 12 (*b*).

14B. '*Undue Influence* as a ground for setting aside deeds and agreements borders closely on facility and circumvention. In England, Courts of equity give relief in all cases where advantages have been procured by one party by the use of influence of any kind, which appears to be inconsistent with the exercise of free and deliberate judgment by the other. It has been said that "the principle applies to every case where influence is acquired and abused, and where confidence is reposed and betrayed" (*a*). In Scotland, it has been held that undue influence invalidates deeds and contracts where a relation exists which imports confidence or imposes a duty of protection. Perhaps it might be correctly said that the existence of such a relation only operates, where there is no facility, to create a presumption of fraud or unfairness (or error?) (*b*). To support this ground of reduction, there must be not only inadequacy of consideration, but subjection to a dominant influence and abuse of confidence; and it is often of importance that the person seeking relief had no independent legal adviser (*c*).'

(*a*) *Per* Lord Kingsdown in Smith *v.* Kay, 7 H. L. C. 750, 759. See also as to the law of England, Huguenin *v.* Baseley, 14 Ves. 273; 2 Wh. & T. L. C. 504; 9 R. R. 148, 276. Hunter *v.* Atkins, 3 My. & K. 113. Williams *v.* Bayley, *sup.* § 12 (*d*). And the cases in Pollock on Contr. 579 sqq.

(*b*) See 4 Ersk. Inst. 1. 27, and Pr. 4. 1. 11. Johnston *v.* Goodlet, 1868; 6 Macph. 1061.

(*c*) *Parents and Children.*—Ewen *v.* Ewen's Trs., and Ewen *v.* Mags. of Montrose, 1824; 2 S. 612; rev. 1 W. & S. 595; 1828, 6 S. 478; rev. 4 W. & S. 346. Cunningham *v.* Anstruther's Trs. and Mercer *v.* Eosd., 1872; 10 Macph. H. L. 39, 48; L. R. 2 Sc. Ap. 223. Tennent *v.* Tennent's Trs., 1868; 6 Macph. 840; aff. 1870, 8 Macph. H. L. 10. Gray *v.* Binny, 1879; 7 R. 332.

Agents and Clients.—Walker's Exrs. *v.* Lewis's Trs., 1833; 12 S. 44. Anstruther *v.* Wilkie, 1856; 18 D. 405. Harris *v.* Robertson, 1864; 2 Macph. 664. Grieve *v.* Cunningham, 1869; 8 Macph. 317. Cleland *v.* Morrison, 1878; 6 R. 156. Comp. Watt *v.* M'Pherson's Trs., 1877; 4 R. 601; rev. 5 R. H. L. 9. See below, § 36 (2).

Spiritual Adviser.—Monro *v.* Strain, 1874; 1 R. 522. See L. Shand in Gray *v.* Binny, *cit.* Allcard *v.* Skinner, 36 Ch. D. 145.

15. Proof of Consent.—In order to distinguish the requisites of final and conclusive engagement in different situations, contracts have been arranged into Consensual; Real; Written.

16. (1.) *Consensual Contracts*, strictly speaking, are those in which mere consent proved by writing, by witnesses, or by confession, is sufficient to establish the obligation; as sale, barter, or location of moveables; mandate; and partnership. But every obligation to which writing is not indispensable, is effectual where consent is proved (*a*).

(*a*) 1 Stair, 10. § 11. 3 Ersk. 3. § 1.

17. (2.) *Real Contracts* require to their completion as such, an act of delivery or possession; as, loan, commodate, deposit, pledge. But the consent alone will bind the party to complete the contract (*a*).

(*a*) 1 Stair, 10. § 11. 3 Ersk. 1. § 17.

18. Written Contracts, in strict technical language, are those to which authentic written evidence is required, not merely in proof, but in solemnity; as, obligations relative to land; or obligations agreed to be reduced to writing; or those required by statute to be in writing. On other occasions, writing is required only in evidence; as in promises to pay money, or 'formerly' in cautionary obligations, and so may be supplied by oath, or admission of the party (*a*).

(*a*) 1 Stair, 10. § 11; also § 9. 3 Ersk. 2. § 1, 2. See below, § 249A, as to cautionary obligations.

19. Written obligations and contracts may be distinguished into three classes: Attested, Holograph, and Privileged (*a*).

(1.) *Attested Writings* are subscribed by the granter, either in presence of two witnesses, or acknowledged to them by him: Or if the granter cannot write, by two notaries subscribing for him, duly authorised so to do (orally and symbolically) before four witnesses, 'but since 1st Oct. 1874, by one notary before two witnesses.' The witnesses subscribe, adding the word "witness" in attestation of the party's subscription, or of that of the notaries as duly authorised by the party. The writing bears a clause attesting the fact of the subscription of the party (or notaries) and witnesses, and expressly 'mentioned until 1st Oct. 1874' the name and designation of the writer of the deed, and of the witnesses; and the parties and witnesses are by their subscription held to attest the contents of this clause (*b*).

(*a*) These will be hereafter more particularly discussed as part of the Law of Evidence (see below, § 2225 et seq.); at present a general statement is sufficient.

(*b*) See below, § 2226, and 37 and 38 Vict. c. 94, § 39–41 (Conveyancing Act, 1874).

20. (2.) *Holograph Writings* are wholly or in the essential parts (*a*) written by the party, and subscribed by him (*b*). 'The privileges of a holograph writing are extended to documents which though not holograph are clearly adopted by, or by reference imported into, a holograph writing (*c*). Writing in a firm's name holograph of a partner is holograph of the firm (*d*).' They are held equivalent to attested writings, in affording proof at once of authenticity and of deliberate engagement. But they are probative only during twenty years (*e*). They do not at any time prove their own date, 'except against the party issuing them (*f*)'; but to that effect must be attested by instrumentary witnesses (*g*). 'The burden of proving that a writing is holograph of the alleged granter lies on the person who founds on it (*h*). It is said that a statement in the writing itself that it is holograph, is *primâ facie* evidence of the fact, and throws the onus on the party challenging it (*i*). But such a presumption can be of little value, and is important chiefly in non-contentious cases in the Commissary Court (*k*).'

(*a*) 4 Stair, 42. § 6. Lawrie *v.* Lawrie, 1859; 21 D. 240.

(*b*) But see 4 Stair, 42. § 16. M. Bell's Convg. i. 82, and Currence *v.* Hacket, and other cases cited below, § 1868. Writings subscribed by two or more persons, but holograph only of one of them, are obligatory only against the writer. Miller *v.* Farquharson, 1835; 13 S. 838. Sproul *v.* Wilson, 1809; Hume, 920.

(*c*) Christie's Trs. *v.* Muirhead, 1870; 8 Macph. 461. Bryson *v.* Crawford, 1833; 12 S. 39, 937. Alexander *v.* Alexander, 1830; 8 S. 602. Young's Trs. *v.* Ross, 1864; 3 Macph. 10. Gavine's Tr. *v.* Lee, 1883; 10 R. 448; and cases in § 1868, *infra*.

(*d*) Buchanan *v.* Dennistoun's Trs., 1835; 13 S. 841. Nisbet *v.* Neil's Trs., 1869; 7 Macph. 1097. M'Laren *v.* Law, 1871; 44 S. Jur. 17. Writings holograph of an authorised agent are of course binding. Whyte *v.* Lee, 1879; 6 R. 699.

(*e*) See below, § 590.

(*f*) Dunfermline *v.* Callander, 1674; 1 B. S. 703. M. Bell's Convg. i. 80. Purvis *v.* Dowie, 1869; 7 Macph. 764. As to testamentary writings, see 37 and 38 Vict. c. 94, § 40; *infra*, § 1868.

(*g*) See below, § 2231, 1465, 1868.

(*h*) Anderson *v.* Gill, 1850: 20 D. 1326; 22 S. Jur. 478; aff. 1858, 3 Macq. 180. M'Laren *v.* Howie, 1870; 8 Macph. 106 (discharge of legacy or bequest).

(*i*) 3 Ersk. 2. § 22. Turnbull *v.* Doods, 1844; 6 D. 896. Robertson *v.* Ogilvie's Trs., 1844: 7 D. 236.

(*k*) Cranston, 1890; 17 R. 410. See Duff's Feud. Convg. § 17. Anderson, *cit.*

21. (3.) *Privileged Writings* are such as law sanctions, although defective in some of the proofs or solemnities necessary in attested or holograph writings. So Last Wills, from peculiar favour, and from respect to the tranquillity of dying persons, are sustained, although subscribed only by one notary (or a 'parish' clergyman acting as such) and two witnesses (*a*); and Mercantile Writings are effectual, although neither attested nor holograph, on account of the rapidity which may be necessary in preparing them, the immediate use to which they are to be applied, and the interests of merchants, who are often unacquainted with the peculiar usages of Scotland. Bills, notes, bank-cheques, orders, mandates, guarantees, 'receipts, fitted accounts,' and letters *in re mercatoria*, fall under this rule (*b*). 'The privilege does not extend to writings unconnected or but remotely connected with trade (*c*). Landlord's discharges for rent are valid by usage if only subscribed by the landlord or his factor (*d*).'

(*a*) See below, § 1868, 2232.

(*b*) 3 Ersk. 2. § 24. 1 Bell's Com. 324 (342, M'L.'s ed.). Paterson *v.* Wright, Jan. 31, 1810; 15 F. C. 545; aff. 1814, 6 Pat. 38. Robertson *v.* Galloway, 1821; 1 S. 204. Gilkison *v.* Thomson, 1831; 9 S. 520. Buchanan, *supra*, § 20 (*d*). Bovill *v.* Dixon, 1854; 16 D. 619; 19 D. H. L. 9; 28 Sc. Jur. 684. Dimmack *v.* Dixon, 1856; 18 D. 428. Rhind *v.* Comml. Bk., 1857; 19 D. 519; rem. 1860, 3 Macq. 643. Comml. Bk. *v.* Kennard, 1859; 21 D. 864. Thoms *v.* Thoms, 1867; 6 Macph. 184 (letter relative to bill). Dykes *v.* Roy, 1869; 7 Macph. 357 (award). Fell *v.* Rattray, 1869; 41 Sc. Jur. 236 (fitted account). Purvis *v.* Dowie, 1869; 7 Macph. 764 (receipt for loan does not prove date in bankruptcy).

(*c*) Fell, Purvis, *citt.*; M'Laren, *cit.* § 20 (*h*). Hamilton's Exrs. *v.* Struthers, 1858; 21 D. 51. Stewart *v.* M'Call, 1869; 7 Macph. 544 (contract of service to warehouseman). Paterson *v.* Edington, 1830; 8 S. 931 (ditto).

(*d*) 3 Ersk. 2. § 23. Boyd *v.* Stone, 1674; M. 12,456. Hunter, L. & T. ii. 440. As to other receipts, see below, § 565.

22. (4.) *The Stamp Laws*, of which the primary object is revenue, although not intended to regulate the proof of contracts and obligations, indirectly affect it; and in questions of evidence as to the authenticity of writings, the chronology of the Stamp Acts (as well as the paper mark) may be of importance (*a*). The general rules 'given in former editions are much modified by legislation, the whole system of stamp laws having been revised and consolidated by the Act of 1870, which again has been superseded by the Act of 1891 (*b*); and in revising this section it has appeared expedient to omit some of the general rules taken from earlier statutes.

'The rules' are—1. A stamp is required in all agreements, 'except those' which admit of pecuniary estimation, 'and relate to matters not of the value of £5'; not being for the hire of a labourer, 'artificer, manufacturer, or menial' servant (*c*); nor a memorandum, letter, or agreement for or relating to the sale of goods, 'wares, or merchandise (*d*); nor an agreement or memorandum between masters and mariners for wages on a coasting voyage from port to port in the United Kingdom (*e*); nor an instrument of apprenticeship of a poor child by the parish or a public charity, or under any statute for regulating parish apprentices (*f*); nor a special pawn ticket (*g*). The Act, under special heads, expressly exempts from duty certain bank-notes, drafts, warrants, coupons, etc. (*h*); excise bonds for drawback on goods to be exported (*i*); receipts for money not amounting to £2; and certain receipts by bankers and public officers; receipts by seamen, soldiers, etc., for State pay; receipts for the price of and dividends on public stock, or for the contents of exchequer bills, etc.; receipts for the contents endorsed on duly stamped instruments, etc. (*k*); receipts for goods by inland carriers, and weight-notes issued with duly stamped warrants and relating solely to the same goods (*l*). The following instruments fall under the express general exemptions from stamp duty—transfers of shares in the Government or Parliamentary stocks or funds; dispositions or mortgages of ships, or shares therein; agreements made in the United Kingdom for service as artificer, clerk, domestic servant, handicraftsman, mechanic, gardener, servant in husbandry, or labourer, in any British colony or possession abroad; testaments and dispositions *mortis causa* in Scotland (*m*).'

2. 'Unstamped or insufficiently stamped instruments may (unless express provision to the contrary is made by the Stamp Act) be stamped on payment of the unpaid duty and a penalty of £10, and also, where the unpaid duty exceeds £10, interest at 5 per cent.; but the Commissioners of Inland Revenue have power at any time to mitigate or remit the penalty. Deeds first executed abroad are, for thirty days after receipt in the United Kingdom, stamped on payment of the unpaid duty only; and certain instruments liable to *ad valorem* duty may be afterstamped, without penalty, within thirty days after their first execution (*n*). Policies of sea insurance may be afterstamped on payment of a penalty of £100 (*o*). Inland' bills and notes, and 'bills of lading' require a stamp so absolutely, that it cannot afterwards be supplied (*p*). 3. No stamp duty is imposed unless the words of the Act clearly apply to the specific description of transaction (*q*). 'And the question whether any and what stamp duty is chargeable is determined by the real substance and effect of the deed, and not by a critical view of its particular words, or even by the description given of it in the instrument by the parties themselves (*r*).' 4. Stamps of a denomination applicable to the particular instrument shall be effectual though of greater value than required; 'but a stamp which, by any word on the face of it, is appropriated to any particular description of instrument, is not available for an instrument of any other description. And an instrument to which a particular stamp it appropriated is not duly stamped unless it has such a stamp (*s*). Stamp duties and postage duties to the extent of 2s. 6d. may, however, be denoted by the same stamps, when unappropriated adhesive stamps are allowed (*t*).'

5. The agreement duty is sufficiently complied with if affixed to any one of a series of letters making the contract (*u*). 6. However numerous the parties, one stamp is sufficient when the instrument relates to one subject-matter, as to a security by several co-obligants for all the debts of a bankrupt (*v*); but where the transactions are different, the stamp will validate only one of them (*w*). 'Several instruments upon the same paper must be separately stamped (*x*).'

7. An action raised on an unstamped instrument, which may by the Act be stamped *ex post facto*, 'may be' sisted till the stamp be procured (*y*); 'and in any case upon the production of such a deed in a civil action or submission, the stamp duty and penalty, with £1 further, may be paid to the clerk of Court

or arbiter (*z*), and' when 'the stamp is' adhibited, 'or such payment made,' the whole proceedings on the instrument are held to be retrospectively rendered unexceptionable (*aa*). 'It is *pars judicis* to notice the omission of a stamp (*bb*). 8. When secondary evidence of the contents of a lost document is admissible, there is a presumption *omnia rite esse acta*, and therefore that the deed was stamped, unless evidence be given to the contrary; but if it is proved to have been unstamped at any time after execution, the onus is shifted, and the party who relies on it must prove that it was stamped at some future time (*cc*). 9. The stamp duties apply to instruments executed in the United Kingdom, or relating, wheresoever executed, to any property situate, or to any matter or thing done or to be done, in any part of the United Kingdom. But unstamped or insufficiently stamped deeds are admissible in criminal proceedings (*dd*), or for a collateral purpose, such as to prove a fraud (*ee*). And it seems the better opinion, that when a deed is excluded by the Stamp Acts, parole evidence, if otherwise competent, may be admitted to prove the agreement or facts to which it referred, just as if it did not exist (*ff*). An unstamped document which combines two characters or purposes, requiring a stamp in regard to one and not in regard to the other, is admissible in evidence in the latter character for any purpose unconnected with the first (*gg*). 10. It has been held in various matters that our Courts do not take notice of the revenue laws of foreign countries, so that writings executed abroad, and void there for want of stamps, are admissible in our Courts (*hh*); yet where the local law is not a mere law of procedure, but makes the stamp necessary to the validity of the instrument, our Courts will give effect to the foreign law, if it be the law of the contract (*ii*). 11. Bare offers and proposals not accepted in writing and not proving a concluded contract are generally admissible in evidence without being stamped, such as estimates for work, the prospectus of a school, unsigned conditions of lease, offers of salary, or payment for work or services, though acted upon (*kk*). Mere admissions or acknowledgments, or authorities not themselves amounting to evidence of a contract, are also admitted in evidence although unstamped (*ll*).'

(*a*) 44 Geo. III. c. 98; 48 Geo. III. c. 149; 55 Geo. III. c. 184; and Schedule of Duties. Impey's Com. on the Stamp Act. Coventry, Tr. on the Stamp Laws. Alpe's Law of Stamp Duties. 1 and 2 Geo. IV. c. 55; 3 Geo. IV. c. 117; 6 Geo. IV. c. 41; 9 Geo. IV. c. 13, c. 23, c. 27, c. 49; 3 Will. IV. c. 23, c. 97; 4 and 5 Will. IV. c. 97; 5 and 6 Will. IV. c. 64. The chief recent enactments (of which those marked r. are repealed in whole) are—13 and 14 Vict. c. 97, r.; 16 and 17 Vict. c. 59; 17 and 18 Vict. c. 83; 28 and 29 Vict. c. 96; 30 and 31 Vict. c. 23, r.; 33 and 34 Vict. c. 97 (Stamp Act, 1870, consolidating and amending the law, r.); 33 and 34 Vict. c. 98 (Stamp Duties Management Act, 1870, r.); 33 and 34 Vict. c. 99 (repealing many former Acts—spent); 34 Vict. c. 4 (foreign securities, mortgages, proxies, r.); 35 and 36 Vict. c. 20, § 7 (navy bills, r.); 37 and 38 Vict. c. 19 (admission of advocates and barristers, r.); c. 26 (Canadian Stock, r.); 40 and 41 Vict. c. 13 (Inventories—Scotland—Ecclesiastical Benefices); 40 and 41 Vict. c. 59 (colonial stock); 39 and 40 Vict. c. 6 (afterstamping marine policies, r.); 39 and 40 Vict. c. 16, § 11 (leases increasing rent, r.); 41 and 42 Vict. c. 15, § 26 (contract notes by brokers, r.); 43 and 44 Vict. c. 20, § 53 sq. (municipal stock, etc.—letters of renunciation, r.); 44 and 45 Vict. c. 12, § 26–47 (inventories of moveable estate, etc.); 45 and 46 Vict. c. 72, § 8 sqq. (various amendments, r.); 48 and 49 Vict. c. 51, § 21 (securities to bearer and foreign securities, r.); 50 and 51 Vict. c. 15, § 5 sqq. (sea policies—transfers—compositions by companies); 51 and 52 Vict. c. 8, § 10 sqq. (limited companies' capital—foreign share certificates, securities, mortgages and contract notes—assignments of life policies, etc., r.); 54 and 55 Vict. c. 38 (Stamp Duties Management Act, 1891); 54 and 55 Vict. c. 39 (Stamp Act, 1891); 56 and 57 Vict. c. 7, § 3, 4 (contract notes—marketable securities); 57 and 58 Vict. c. 30, § 39, 40 (composition for duties—coupons); 58 Vict. c. 16, § 9–15 (amendments on Stamp Act, 1891); 59 and 60 Vict. c. 28, § 12, 13 (companies—compositions).

(*b*) The principal Act, 54 and 55 Vict. c. 39.

(*c*) The principal Act, 54 and 55 Vict. c. 39, Sched. 1, *v.* Agreement. Firemen and stokers in merchant steamers are artificers and labourers (not seamen) in the sense of this Act. Wilson *v.* Zulueta, 14 Q. B. 405; 19 L. J. Q. B. 49. See Fraser, M. & S. 34.

(*d*) The Act, *l.c.* Addison, Contr. 1081. This exemption includes guarantees for the price of goods sold. Addison, *l.c.*

(*e*) The Act, *l.c.*

(*f*) The Act, Sched. 1, *v.* Apprenticeship.

(*g*) 35 and 36 Vict. c. 93, § 24.

(*h*) The Act, Sched. 1, *v.* Bill of Exch., and see *ib.* § 29 to 39. 57 and 58 Vict. c. 30, § 40.

(*i*) The Act, Sched. 1, *v.* Bond.

(*k*) The Act, Sched. 1, *v.* Receipt.

(*l*) The Act, Sched. 1, *v.* Warrant for Goods.

(*m*) The Act, Sched. 1, *fin. v.* General Exemptions. A receipt or acknowledgment of money paid by way of gift or gratuity is not within the statute. Boyle *v.* Brandon, 13 M. & W. 738. Deeds relating solely to the sequestrated estate of a bankrupt are exempt from stamp duty (19 and 20 Vict. c. 79, § 184); and so is the disposition operating a *cessio bonorum* (16 and 17 Will. IV. c. 56, § 20); as also various documents exempted by the Acts relating to Friendly and Building Societies, Savings Banks, the Mercantile Marine, the Post-Office, Truck, Drill Grounds, Public Health, and other like matters.

(*n*) The Act, § 15. 58 Vict. c. 16, § 15.

(*o*) The Act, § 95 (2). See § 466, *infra.*

(*p*) The Act, § 37–40. Vallance *v.* Forbes, 1879; 6 R. 1099. As to stamps on bills and notes, see below, § 323.

(*q*) Warrington *v.* Furbor, 8 East, 244; 1 Ill. 19. Lawrie *v.* Ogilvie, Feb. 6, 1810; F. C. Phillips *v.* Morrison, 12 M. & W. 740; 13 L. J. Ex. 212. Glas. and S.-W. Ry. Co. *v.* Inland Rev., 1886; 13 R. 480; rev. 1887, 12 App. Ca. 315; 14 R. H. L. 33.

(*r*) Belch *v.* Comrs. of Inland Rev., 1877; 4 R. 592. Limmer Asphalte Co. *v.* Comrs. of Inl. Rev., L. R. 7 Ex. 211; 41 L. J. Ex. 106. Gibb *v.* Comrs. of Inl. Rev., 1880; 8 R. 120. Comrs. of Inl. Rev. *v.* City of Glas. Bk., 1881; 8 R. 389. Hutton *v.* Lippert, 8 App. Ca. 309 (P.C.). Mortgage Ins. Corp. *v.* Comrs., 21 Q. B. D. 352; 57 L. J. Q. B. 630.

(*s*) The Act, § 7. (*t*) The Act, § 10.

(*u*) Grant *v.* Maddox, 15 M. & W. 737; 15 L. J. Ex. 104.

(*v*) Johnston *v.* Attwell, 1801; M. *Writ*, App. 5. Ramsbottom *v.* Davis, 4 M. & W. 584; 7 Dowl. 175. Comp. Wilson *v.* Smith, 12 M. & W. 401; 13 L. J. Ex. 113. Rushbrook *v.* Hood, 17 L. J. C. P. 58. Croft *v.* Tidbury, 14 C. B. 304; 23 L. J. C. P. 57.

(*w*) The Act, § 4 (*a*). Parry *v.* Boucher, 1814; 4 Camp. 80. Lovelock *v.* Frankland, 8 Q. B. 379; 16 L. J. Q. B. 182. Watling *v.* Horwood, 12 E. Jur. 48. Wharton *v.* Walton, 7 Q. B. 474. So with several contracts in one broker's note; the Act, § 52 (2).

(*x*) The Act, § 3.

(*y*) Hatton *v.* Richard, 1833; 11 S. 727.

(*z*) The Act, § 14. 31 and 32 Vict. c. 100, § 40, 41. Wilson's Sheriff Ct. Pr. 260.

(*aa*) Kingstorie's Crs., 1743; Elch. *Writ.* 14. Lamont *v.* Lamont's Crs., 1789; M. 5494. Rob *v.* Forrest, 1831; 5 W. & S. 740. Davidson *v.* Douglas, 1838; 1 D. 10. Wood *v.* Ker, 1838; 1 D. 14. Morris *v.* Glen, 1843; 6 D. 97. King *v.* Baillie, 1844; 7 D. 228. Ivison *v.* Edinburgh Silk Yarn Co., 1845; 8 D. 236.

(*bb*) Nixon *v.* Albion Marine Ins. Co., L. R. 2 Ex. 388; 36 L. J. Ex. 180. Cowan *v.* Stewart, 1872; 10 Macph. 735. 1 Bell's Com. 322.

(*cc*) Taylor on Evid. § 145, 148; 1 Bell's Com. 322. Marine Investment Co. *v.* Haviside, H. L. 42 L. J. Ch. 173; L. R. 5 H. L. 624. Dickson on Ev. § 978.

(*dd*) The Act, § 14.

(*ee*) Matheson *v.* Ross, 1849; 6 Bell's App. 374; 2 H. L. Ca. 300. Henning *v.* Hewatson, 1852; 4 D. 1084. Bannatyne *v.* Wilson, 1855; 18 D. 230. Durie's Exrs. *v.* Fielding, 1893; 20 R. 295. Evans *v.* Prothero, 2 Macn. & G. 319; 15 E. Jur. 113. Bethell *v.* Blencowe, 3 M. & Gr. 119; Addison, Contr. 1218. Taylor on Evid. § 405. Dickson on Evid. § 987 sq.

(*ff*) Hutchinson *v.* Ferrier, 1851; 13 D. 837. Cooper *v.* Smillie, 1880; 2 Guthrie's Sh. Ct. Ca. 26. Taylor on Evid. § 1411 sq. Dickson on Evid. § 993. 1 Bell's Com. 322.

(*gg*) Matheson *v.* Ross, *cit.* Adams *v.* Morgan, 12 I. L. R. Ex. 1.

(*hh*) Stewart *v.* Gelot, 1871; 9 Macph. 1057. James *v.* Catherwood, 3 D. & R. 190. Valery, *infra.* Westlake, Pr. Int. Law, § 145, 199. Guthrie's Savigny, § 372, note (*a*).

(*ii*) Bristow *v.* Sequeville, 5 Ex. 279; 19 L. J. Ex. 289. Westlake and Savigny, *cit.* See Valery *v.* Scott, 1876; 3 R. 965.

(*kk*) Clay *v.* Crofts, 20 L. J. Ex. 361. Hudspeth *v.* Yarnold, 9 C. B. 625; 19 L. J. C. P. 321; and see Addison, Contr. 1247, 1250.

(*ll*) Goodyear *v.* Simpson, 15 M. & W. 16 (statement of accounts admitting a balance). See Addison, *l.c.*, and cases as to acknowledgment of debt and I O U's, *infra*, § 202A.

23. (5.) *Delivery of Written Deed.*—The general rule is, that an obligation in writing, in order to be effectual, must be delivered to the obligee, or a third party for him, in token of complete engagement (*a*). Questions of delivery of writings occur chiefly in relation to deeds of succession and provision. In ordinary contracts and obligations there is seldom room for the question, unless in those cases in which several obligants are concerned. Delivery does not (as in England) require any ceremony; the fact of the deed being in the obligee's or in neutral custody, or recorded in a public register, or followed by sasine, being sufficient in the ordinary case to infer delivery (*b*). In doubtful cases, one's agent is as himself; so possession by the granter's agent is not delivery (*c*). Possession by the grantee's agent is; and if he be agent for both, the presumption is for delivery (*d*). A neutral person is presumed to hold for the *creditor*, when the bond is for a consideration given; for the *debtor*, when the bond is gratuitous (*e*). The presumption as to time is, that delivery took place at the date (*f*).

(*a*) 3 Ersk. 2. § 43. Fisher *v.* Campbell, 1736; Elch. *Presumption*, 7; 1 Ill. 19. See § 84. Anderson *v.* Robertson, 1867; 5 Macph. 503. Tennent *v.* Tennent's Trs., 1869; 7 Macph. 936. See below, § 1994 *fin.*, as to delivery to trustees for grantees or beneficiaries.

(*b*) 4 Stair, 42. § 8. 3 Ersk. 2. § 43, 44. Tait on Evidence, 147. Bruce *v.* Bruce, 1675; M. 11,156. Stamfield's Crs. *v.* Scott, 1696; 4 B. Sup. 344. Comp. with this case Crawford *v.* Kerr. 1807; M. App. *Moveables*, 2. Leckie *v.* Leckies, 1776; M. 11,581, and App. *Presumption*, 1; Hailes, 721; 5 B. Sup. 432; and other cases in 1 Ill. 19, 20. The statement in the text is recognised as correct (Tennent *v.* Tennent's Trs. (*a*)), although it has been questioned whether registration in a public register is sufficient in all conceivable cases to infer delivery. See Leckie, *cit.* Burnet *v.* Morrow, 1864; 2 Macph. 929. Downie *v.* M'Killop, 1843; 6 D. 180. Stewart *v.* Rae, 1883; 10 R. 463. Dunlop *v.* M'Crae, 1884; 11 R. 1104.

(*c*) Life Assoc. of Scot. *v.* Douglas, 1886; 13 R. 910 (bond by several co-obligants, one dying after signing it).

(*d*) 3 Ersk. 2 § 43. Byres *v.* Johnson, 1626; M. 16,990; 1 Ill. 20. Irvine *v.* Irvine, 1738; M. 11,576. Logan *v.* Logan, 1823; 2 S. 253. Maule *v.* Ramsay, 1828; 6 S. 343; 4 W. & S. 58. In such a case, it is rather a question of intention to be proved as a matter of fact whether there is delivery or not. Spence *v.* Ross, 1826; 5 S. 17; aff. 1829, 3 W. & S. 380. Lady Ramsay *v.* Cowan, 1833; 11 S. 967. Stewart *v.* Stewart, 1842; 1 Bell's Ap. 796. Collie *v.* Pirie, 1851; 13 D. 506. Maiklem *v.* M'Gruthar, 1842; 4 D. 1182. Mair & Sons *v.* Thom's Trs., 1850; 12 D. 748 (bond held delivered as to part of the sum only). M'Creath *v.* Borland, 1860; 22 D. 1551. Geddes *v.* Geddes, 1862; 24 D. 794. See *infra*, § 24 (*c*).

(*e*) Stair, as corrected by 3 Ersk. 2. § 43. Sinclair *v.* Purves, 1707; M. 11,572; 1 Ill. 21. Holwell *v.* Cuming, 1796; M. 11,583. See 1 Ill. 22. Maule, *sup.* (*d*).

(*f*) Gordon *v.* Maitland, 1757; M. 11,161; and Maitland *v.* Forbes, 1767; 1 Br. S. 431.

24. The general rule suffers exception in testaments; in mutual contracts (*a*); where, by a clause in the deed, delivery is dispensed with (*b*); where the granter is the natural custodier for the obligee, as parents for their children (*c*). And where the granter is himself interested to detain the deed, it is 'if onerous' good without delivery (*d*). The presumption 'arising from the grantee's possession of the writ' may be overcome by evidence; 'or rather, in most cases, delivery is a fact to be proved by evidence such as will satisfy a jury (*e*).'

(*a*) See below, § 84. 3 Ersk. 2. § 44, and cases there cited. Crauford *v.* Vallance, 1625 ; M. 12,304.

(*b*) Ellis *v.* Ingliston, 1669 ; M. 16,999. A. *v.* B., 1683 ; M. 17,005.

(*c*) Hamilton *v.* Hamilton, 1741 ; M. 11,576 ; Elch. *Prov. to Heirs*, 5.

(*d*) Ersk. *l.c.* Cormack *v.* Anderson, 1829 ; 7 S. 868. See below, § 1692. Comp. Gilpin *v.* Martin, 1869 ; 7 Macph. 807.

(*e*) See M'Aslan *v.* Glen, 1859 ; 21 D. 511. Martini & Co. *v.* Steel & Craig, 1878 ; 6 R. 342 ; and *supra*, § 23 (*d*).

25. Locus Pœnitentiæ (a corollary to the rule of final engagement) is a power of resiling from an incomplete engagement ; from an unaccepted offer (*a*) ; from a mutual contract to which all have not assented (*b*) ; from an obligation to which writing is requisite (*c*), or has been stipulated (*d*), and has not yet been adhibited in an authentic shape (*e*) ; from a marriage which, by marriage-contract, is agreed to be afterwards solemnised (*f*).

The principle is, that the final assent is not yet given, so that a reference to oath is no answer to the plea of *locus pœnitentiæ* (*g*). But it is necessary, where writing is stipulated, to distinguish whether it be the intention of parties thereby to *suspend* the engagement, or to bind the parties in the meanwhile: There is *locus pœnitentiæ* in the former case ; not in the latter (*h*). 'It is a matter of construction in the circumstances of each case whether there is a final agreement ; and while the mere reference in letters to a future formal agreement does not necessarily prevent these letters from constituting a final bargain (*i*), it is generally evidence tending to show that the parties did not yet intend to be bound (*k*).' In marriage - contracts, although there is *locus pœnitentiæ* from the *marriage*, the obligation is so far binding as to give action for damage if not fulfilled (*l*).

(*a*) 1 Stair, 10. § 3. 3 Ersk. Inst. 2. § 2 *fin.* *Infra*, § 72 sqq.

(*b*) 1 Stair, 10. § 9. 3 Ersk. Pr. 2. § 2, 3. Edinham *v.* Stirling, 1634 ; M. 8408 ; 1 Ill. 23. Hope *v.* Cleghorn, 1727 ; M. 8409. York Buildings Co. *v.* Baillie, 1724 ; M. 8435. Paterson *v.* Bonar, 1844 ; 6 D. 987. *Infra*, § 250 and § 71.

(*c*) 1 Stair, 10. § 9. More's Notes, p. lxv. 3 Ersk. 2. § 3. Keith *v.* Johnson, 1636 ; M. 8400 ; 1 Ill. 23. Skene *v.* ——, 1637 ; M. 8401. Hope, and York Buildings Co., *sup.* (*b*). Oliphant *v.* Monorgan, 1628 ; M. 8400. Montgomery *v.* Brown, 1663 ; M. 8411. Barron *v.* Petrie, 1736 ; Elch. *Loc. Pœn.* 2. Christie *v.* Christie, 1745 ; M. 8437. Buchanan *v.* Baird, 1773 ; M. 8478. Maitland *v.* Neilson, 1779 ; M. 8459 ; Hailes, 840. Edmonston *v.* Edmonston, 1861 ; 23 D. 995 ; and authorities in § 889, *infra*.

(*d*) Campbell *v.* Douglas, 1676 ; M. 8470. Ogilvie *v.* Stuart, 1700 ; 4 B. Sup. 373. Wallace & Co. *v.* Miller, 1766 ; M. 8475 ; Hailes, 27.

(*e*) Park *v.* M'Kenzie, 1764 ; M. 8449 ; 5 B. Sup. 539 ; 1 Ill. 24. Stewart *v.* Bisset, 1765 ; 5 B. Sup. 902 ; 1 Ill. 25 ; and other cases in 1 Ill. 25. Muir *v.* Wallace, 1770 ; M. 8457 ; Hailes, 340 ; 5 B. Sup. 639. Grieve *v.* Macfarlane, 1790 ; M. 8459 ; Hailes, 1080. Paterson *v.* Edington, 1830 ; 8 S. 931 (contract of service). Stewart *v.* M'Call, 1869 ; 7 Macph. 544. Sinclair *v.* Weddell, 1868 ; 41 S. Jur. 121. See § 889.

(*f*) 1 Ersk. 6. § 3. Fraser, Hd. and Wife, 489.

(*g*) Barron and Grieve's Cases, *sup.* (*c*) and (*e*).

(*h*) 3 Ersk. 2. § 4. Campbell, *cit.* Wallace & Co., and Paterson, *sup.* Broomfield *v.* Young, 1757 ; M. 9446. Rutherford *v.* Feuars of Bowden, 1748 ; M. 8443. Chalmers *v.* Muirhead, 1759 ; M. 8444. See below, § 71. Smeaton *v.* St. Andrews Pol. Comrs., 1868 ; 7 Macph. 206 ; revd. 1871, 9 Macph. H. L. 24 ; L. R. 2 H. L. 107.

(*i*) Erskine *v.* Glendinning, 1871 ; 9 Macph. 656.

(*k*) Chinnock *v.* Marss. of Ely, 2 De G. J. & S. 638 ; 34 L. J. Ch. 399. Ridgway *v.* Wharton, 6 H. L. Ca. 238 ; 27 L. J. Ch. 46. Rossiter *v.* Miller, 46 L. J. Ch. 737 ; 48 *ib.* 10 ; L. R. 5 Ch. D. 648 ; 3 App. Ca. 1124. Bonnewell *v.* Jenkins, 8 Ch. D. 70 ; 47 L. J. Ch. D. 758. Lewis *v.* Brass, 3 Q. B. D. 667.

(*l*) See below, § 1514.

26. Rei Interventus raises a personal exception, which excludes the plea of *locus pœnitentiæ* (*a*). It is inferred from any proceedings not unimportant on the part of the obligee, known to and permitted by the obligor to take place on the faith of the contract as if it were perfect (*b*) ; provided they are unequivocally referable to the agreement, and productive of alteration of circumstances, loss, or inconvenience, though not irretrievable (*c*). 'This sentence has been repeatedly recognised as a correct statement of the law (*d*) ; but it must be added that the knowledge or permission of the obligor is not necessarily actual knowledge or express permission, for one who signs and gives forth an imperfect contract knowing that the other party relies on it, must be held to have assented to his acting upon it in the way contemplated (*e*).'

(*a*) 3 Ersk. 2. § 3. See cases in 2 Ill. 92 et seq. Hamilton *v.* Wright, 1836 ; 14 S. 323 ; 3 Ill. 101 ; aff. 1838, 3 S. & M'L. 127.

(*b*) See cases in 1 Ill. 27 et seq. Moodie *v.* Moodie, 1745 ; M. 8439 ; Elch. *Rei In.* 7. Wemyss *v.* Wemyss, 1768 ; M. 9174. Ctess. of Moray *v.* Stewart, 1773 ; M. 4392 ; rev. 2 Paton, 317. Rymer *v.* M'Intyre, 1781 ; M. 5726 ; Hailes, 887 (apprenticeship). Grieve *v.* Pringle, 1797 ; M. 5951. M'Rory (Mackenzie) *v.* M'Whirter, Dec. 18, 1810 ; F. C. Bill's Crs. *v.* Dunbar, June 14, 1810 ; 16 F. C. 170, n. Paterson *v.* Wright, Jan. 31, 1810 ; F. C. ; 1 Ill. 176 ; 6 Paton, 38 (cautionry). Gibb *v.* Ogg, 1835 ; 13 S. 612. Parker *v.* Isat, 1803 ; Hume, 915. Napier *v.* Dick, 1805 ; Hume, 388 (service). Forbes *v.* Wilson, 1873 ; 11 Macph. 454. Wark *v.* Bargaddie Coal Co., 1856 ; 18 D. 556 ; rev. 1859, 3 Macq. 467. Kirkpatrick *v.* Allanshaw Coal Co., 1880 ; 8 R. 327. Brogden *v.* Metr. Ry. Co., 2 App. Ca. 666 (acting on approved draft).

(*c*) Correct Kilkerran's rule (M. 8439 ; 1 Ill. 29) by Dunmore Coal Co. *v.* Young, Feb. 1, 1811 ; F. C. ; 1 Ill. 30. Keith *v.* Johnson, 1636 ; M. 8400 ; 1 Ill. 23. Buchanan *v.* Baird, 1773 ; M. 8478 ; 1 Ill. 30. M'Pherson *v.* M'Pherson, May 12, 1815 ; F. C. Cairns *v.* Gerrard, 1833 ; 11 S. 737. Hamilton *v.* Wright, *cit.* (*a*). Taylor *v.* Simson, 1836 ; 14 S. 935 ; 3 Ill. 102. Colquhoun *v.* Wilson's Trs., 1860 ; 22 D. 1035. See § 27A.

(*d*) Even in England : Maddison *v.* Alderson, 1883 ; 8 App. Ca. 467, 476.

(*e*) Hamilton *v.* Wright, *cit.* (*a*). Ballantyne *v.* Carter, 1842 ; 4 D. 419. Johnston *v.* Grant, 1844 ; 6 D. 875 ; 1845, 7 D. 390. Church of Engl. Ass. Co. *v.* Wink, 1857 ; 19 D. 415, 1079. Gardner *v.* Lucas, 1877 ; 5 R. 638. Natl. Bank *v.* Campbell, 1892 ; 19 R. 885. As to *rei interventus*, see further in § 889, 946, 1189, 2257.

27. Homologation (in principle similar to *rei interventus*) is an act 'of the obligor or his legal representative (*a*)' approbatory of a preceding engagement, which in itself is defective or informal 'or unauthorised,' either confirming or adopting it as binding. It may be express, or inferred from circumstances (*b*). It must be absolute, and not compulsory, nor proceeding on error or fraud, and unequivocally referable to the engagement; and must imply assent to it, with full knowledge of its extent (*c*), and of all the relative interests of the homologator (*d*). It establishes the engagement 'not' as if granted at the date of the homologation, 'but from the beginning (*e*).' Homologation may be by the obligor, otherwise imperfectly bound (*f*); or by another having an interest adverse to the obligation (*g*). It sanctions the whole obligation (unless fairly divisible into parts), according to its true nature and meaning (*h*); and bars the homologator and his representatives, not third parties in competition (*i*). It may be effectual to sanction even deeds which are null by defect in form, provided they have been granted by persons not incapable (*k*); and it may operate as a bar against 'or imply waiver of' a claim of damage for breach of contract (*l*). 'When *rei interventus* is founded upon as varying a formal written deed, it operates by showing that a contravention of it has been permitted ; and thus, as in a lease, excludes an action of damages for breach of contract or a decree for specific performance. It may be, strictly speaking, that it does not in any case abrogate a condition of the written deed, though in some cases the effect is practically the same. The permitted deviation infers discharge of a condition of the lease, only so far as it unequivocally requires such an inference ;—a licence to a tenant to do certain things forbidden by his lease does not *necessarily* imply, even when long continued, consent to his continuing to do them all through the lease (*m*).

'*Adoption of Null Deeds.*—When a deed or obligation is intrinsically null ; *e.g.* if it be granted by a pupil or insane person, or be forged, homologation or subsequent approbation operates only as the adoption of what is reduced to an intelligible and precise shape, and its binding effect has in this case no retrospect (*n*). But there is no reason why adoption should not be so conceived as to be retrospective.'

(*a*) M'Calman *v.* M'Arthur, 1864 ; 2 Macph. 678. Mitchell *v.* Scott's Trs., 1874 ; 2 R. 162. See below (*g*).

(*b*) 1 Stair, 10. § 11 ; Elchies' Notes on Stair, 58 ; More's Notes, p. lxvii ; 3 Ersk. Pr. 3. § 15. Stein's Assignees *v.* Gibson-Craig, 1829 ; 7 S. 686 ; rev. 1831, 5 W. & S. 47 ; 1 Ill. 30. Grant *v.* Baillie, 1830 ; 8 S. 606. Keith's Trs. *v.* Keith, 1857 ; 19 D. 1040.

(*c*) Rires *v.* Rires, 1663 ; M. 5619 ; 1 Ill. 31. Linton *v.* Dundas, 1729 ; M. 5624. Brown *v.* Gardner, 1739 ; M. 5659, 8474 (arbitration). See also Elgin Lun. Bd. *v.* Bremner, 1874 ; 1 R. 1155 ; aff. 1875, 2 R. H. L. 136 ; L. R. 2 H. L. Sc. 535 (Elgin *v.* Rathven). M'Naughton *v.* Murray, 1792 ; Bell's Ca. 253 (do.). Hamilton *v.* Cardross, 1712 ; Robertson's Ap. 37. King *v.* Durward, 1776 ; M. 5672. Home *v.* L. Justice-Clerk, 1671 ; M. 5688. Sinclair *v.* Sinclair, 1715 ; M. 5654. Telford *v.* Hamilton, 1735 ; M. 5647 (arbitration).

As to the effect of signing as a witness, see Walwood *v.* Taylor, 1625 ; M. 5630 ; 1 Ill. 32. Veitch *v.* Pallet, 1676 ; M. 5646. Dallas *v.* Paul, 1704 ; M. 5677. Davidson *v.* Davidson, 1714 ; M. 5652. Johnstone *v.* Berry, 1725 ; M. 5657. Riddel *v.* Scott, 1728 ; M. 5681. Bothwell *v.* E. of Home, 1748 ; M. 5662.

As to the effect of ignorance of rights, see Johnston *v.* Paterson, 1825 ; 4 S. 237 ; 1 Ill. 32. Gardner *v.* Gardner, 1830 ; 9 S. 138. See Brown *v.* Perthshire Rd. Trs., 1832 ; 10 S. 667. Drummond *v.* Hunter, 1834 ; 12 S. 620. Keith's Trs. *v.* Keith, 1857 ; 19 D. 1040. Shaw *v.* Shaw, 1851 ; 13 D. 877.

(*d*) Brown and Johnstone, *sup.* (*c*). Hope *v.* Dickson, 1833 ; 12 S. 222 ; 1 Ill. 34. Douglas *v.* Douglas' Trs., 1859 ; 21 D. 1066. Keith's Trs., *cit.* Stewart *v.* Baillie, 1841 ; 3 D. 463. Paterson *v.* Moncrieff, 1866 ; 4 Macph. 706. L. Panmure *v.* Crokat, 1854 ; 17 D. 85. Wemyss' Trs. *v.* L. Adv., 1896 ; 24 R. 216. See § 11 *ad fin.*

(*e*) Mitchel *v.* Cunningham, 1672 ; M. 5711 ; 1 Ill. 35. Harvie *v.* Gordon, 1726 ; M. 5712. Gordon *v.* Farquhar, 1766 ; 5 B. Sup. 932. The cases cited refer to deeds granted by incapable persons, and do not support the proposition for which they were cited by the author. The correct rule is given in the Com. i. 145. See M. Bell's Conveyancing, 192–3. Haswell *v.* Fortune, 1852 ; 24 Jur. 555. Elgin Lunacy Board *v.* Bremner, *supra* (*c*).

(*f*) Christies *v.* Christie, 1745 ; M. 8437 ; 1 Ill. 35. See Lady Bute's Chaplain *v.* the Earl, 1666 ; 2 B. Sup. 423. Robertson *v.* Boyd and Winans, 1885 ; 12 R. 419.

(*g*) Riddel *v.* Scott, 1728 ; M. 5681 ; 1 Ill. 33. It seems an impropriety of language to say that an imperfect deed or contract is homologated or ratified by a stranger. One cannot make or confirm an obligation for another except as his agent or factor (see *e.g.* Grants *v.* Shepherd, 1847 ; 6 Bell's App. 153, 173 ; *supra* (*a*)) ; and the so-called homologation by "one having an adverse interest" falls more correctly under the head of subsequent adoption or confirmation of an agent's act (see *e.g.* Grant *v.* Baillie, 1830 ; 8 S. 606) ; or of personal exception, see § 27A ; and comp. 1 Bell's Com. 145 (140, M'L.'s ed.).

(*h*) Erskine *v.* Erskine, 1682 ; M. 5703 ; 1 Ill. 36. Steel *v.* Steel, 1774 ; 5 B. Sup. 471 ; M. 5600. Primrose *v.* Duie, 1662 ; M. 5702. Dow *v.* Beith, 1856 ; 18 D. 820.

(*i*) Liddel *v.* Dick's Crs., 1744 ; M. 5721 ; Elchies' Notes, 185. Harkness *v.* Graham, 1833 ; 11 S. 760. Mansfield *v.* Walker's Trs., 1833 ; 11 S. 813.

(*k*) 3 Ersk. 3. § 47. Lady Bute's Chaplain, *sup.* (*f*). Wemyss *v.* Wemyss, 1768 ; M. 9174 ; 1 Ill. 29. Christies, *sup.* (*f*). See Armstrong *v.* Monro, 1833 ; 12 S. 61. Robertson *v.* Ogilvie's Trs., 1844 ; 7 D. 236 (deed containing erasures *in substantialibus*). Fraser *v.* L. Lovat, 1850 ; 7 Bell's App. 171 (arbitration). Elgin Lunacy Board, *sup.* (*c*).

(*l*) Graham *v.* Muir, 1833 ; 11 S. 308 ; 3 Ill. 102. Hunter *v.* Fleming, 1829 ; 8 S. 234. Barclay *v.* G. N. of Scotl. Ry. Co., 1882 ; 10 R. 144.

(*m*) Wark *v.* Bargaddie Coal Co., *cit.* § 26 (*b*). Carron Co. *v.* Henderson's Trs., 1896 ; 23 R. 1042.

(*n*) 1 Bell's Com. 145 (140, M'L.'s ed.). Gall *v.* Bird. 1855 ; 17 D. 1027. More's Notes, 68. Dickson on Evid. § 856. As to forged writings, Maiklem *v.* Walker, 1833 ; 12 S. 53. Frost. *v.* N. of S. Bkg. Co., 1858 ; 20 D. 1135. Warden *v.* B. L. Bank, 1863 ; 1 Macph. 402. M'Kenzie *v.* B. L. Co., 1880 ; 7 R. 836 ; rev. 1881, 8 R. H. L. 8 ; 6 App. Ca. 82, where the other cases on this point are cited. See § 27A and § 1868.

27A. 'There is no authority for saying that in the law of Scotland the acts from which homologation is inferred must be such as to prejudice the party pleading it, or to lead him to alter his position. On the contrary, they are such acts of the obligor as imply distinct and unequivocal consent; and, it may perhaps be said, such as make it unfair or contrary to good conscience to hold that he is not bound. *Rei interventus*, however, indicates a change of the obligee's position, made by him upon the faith of the obligation, raising a personal exception (*a*).

'*Personal Exception.*—The principle of *personal bar*, personal objection, or personal exception, like homologation, acquiescence, or waiver, from which in numerous cases it can hardly be distinguished, operates beyond the domain of contracts. And although it is constantly pleaded and enforced in practice (*b*), it is difficult to find in the law of Scotland any precise statement of its meaning and effect except in the form and application in which it occurs here. It may not be incorrect to say that *Rei interventus*, *i.e.* the occurrence of a real change of position, is in all cases the foundation of the plea or defence known as personal bar or personal exception, which closely corresponds with the English Estoppel *in pais* (*c*).

'A personal exception may be pleaded successfully against anyone who, either by words or conduct (including culpable neglect in the transaction itself of some duty owing to the other party or the public (*d*)),—which words or conduct are such as to warrant a reasonable man in inferring the existence of a certain state of facts upon which he is expected to act,—has wilfully caused another to believe in the existence of that state of things, and so (*e*) induced him to alter his position to his prejudice. The effect of the personal exception is, that the party against whom it is pleaded is not permitted to gainsay the reasonable inference to be drawn from his words or conduct (*f*). The principle has been briefly explained thus, that "whatever a man's real intention may be, if he manifests an intention to another party so as to induce him to act upon it, he will be barred from denying that the intention as manifested was his real intention" (*g*). But, of course, where the representation is not of existing facts, but of a mere intention, *i.e.* a statement of something which the party intends or does not intend to do, and where he does not bind himself by a promise or contract, such a representation will not found a personal exception (*h*). And no one is to be prevented from asserting a just demand or averring the truth unless his conduct has caused the party pleading personal bar to alter his position (*i*).'

(*a*) See above, § 26. M'Calman *v.* M'Arthur, 1864 ; 2 Macph. 678. Lord Blackburn in Burkinshaw *v.* Nicholls, cited below (*g*), uses homologation and estoppel as equivalent terms.

(*b*) See Mor. Dict. *s.vv.* Homolgation, Locus Pœnitentiæ, Personal Objection. Shaw's Dig. *s.vv.* Acquiescence, Homologation, Personal Objection, Obligations, etc. 1 Bell's Com. 144 (139, M'L.'s ed.). 2 Bell's Com. 499 sqq. (393, M'L.'s ed.), where it is dealt with in regard to accession of creditors to trust-deeds. 1 Stair, 10. § 11 ; 4. 40. § 29. M. Bell's Convg. 195. Rankine on Landownership, 347.

(*c*) See 1 Smith's L. C. 879-912 (2 do. 808-840, 10th ed.) ; and cf. 775, 801 sq. The following statement in the text of the rules common to English and Scotch law is founded on the dicta of English judges. The most explicit statement in a Scotch case is this by Lord Cranworth, C., in **Cairncross** *v.* **Lorimer**, 1860 ; 3 Macq. 827 : "The doctrine will apply which is to be found, I believe, in the laws of all civilised nations, that, if a man, either by words or by conduct, has intimated that he consents to an act which has been done, and that he will offer no opposition to it, although it could not have been lawfully done without his consent, and he thereby induces others to do that from which they otherwise might have abstained,—he cannot question the legality of the act he had so sanctioned, to the prejudice of those who have so given faith to his words or to the fair inference to be drawn from his conduct." Hunter *v.* Falconer, 1835 ; 13 S. 252 (delegation—discharge). M'Intosh & Son *v.* Ainslie, 1872 ; 10 Macph. 304).

(*d*) Swan *v.* N. B. Australasian Co., 2 H. & C. 175 ; 32

L. J. Ex. 273. Johnson *v.* Lyonnais Credit Co., 3 C. P. D. 32; 47 L. J. C. P. 241. Baxendale *v.* Bennett, 3 Q. B. D. 525; 47 L. J. Q. B. 624 (stolen bank-bill). Dixon *v.* Reuter's Telegr. Co., 3 C. P. D. 1; 47 L. J. C. P. 1 (claim by receiver of telegram for mistake). Arnold *v.* Cheque Bank, 1 C. P. D. 578; 45 L. J. C. P. 562. See as to these cases, and others as to forged bills, below, § 328.

(*e*) The negligence or statement must be the *real* or *proximate cause* of the other party's loss. Swan *v.* N. B. Austr. Co., *cit.*, and cases in note (*d*). Seton *v.* Lafone, 19 Q. B. D. 68.

(*f*) Cairncross *v.* Lorimer, *cit.* Pickard *v.* Sears, 6 A. & E. 475. Freeman *v.* Cooke, 2 Ex. 654; 18 L. J. Ex. 114. Cornish *v.* Abington, 4 H. & N. 549; 28 L. J. Ex. 262. Carr *v.* L. and N.-W. Ry. Co., L. R. 10 C. P. 307; 44 L. J. C. P. 109. Simm *v.* Anglo-Amer. Tel. Co., 49 L. J. Ch. 392. Robson *v.* Bywater, 1870; 8 Macph. 757. Irvine *v.* Hart & Son, 1869; 7 Macph. 723. Allhusen & Sons *v.* Mitchell & Co., 1870; 8 Macph. 600. Shepherd *v.* Reddie, *ib.* 619. Dunlop & Co. *v.* Meiklem, 1876; 4 R. 11. Ewing *v.* Campbell, 1877; 5 R. 230. B. L. Co. *v.* Mackenzie, 1880; 7 R. 836; rev. 1881, 8 R. H. L. 8; 6 App. Ca. 82. Scott *v.* Hatton, 1827; 6 S. 233. Aytoun *v.* Dundee Bkg. Co., 1844; 6 D. 1409.

(*g*) Freeman *v.* Cooke, *cit.*, *per* L. Wensleydale. Burkinshaw *v.* Nicholls, 3 App. Ca. 1004; 48 L. J. Ch. 179, *per* L. Blackburn. See Walker *v.* Milne, and cases in § 29, note (*s*); and also § 2226 *fin.* (*p*). *Qu.* Whether Muldoon *v.* Pringle, 1882, 9 R. 915, *as reported*, is consistent with this or the statement above? There the inspector's negligence could hardly raise in the defaulting contractor a belief that his employer was intentionally acquiescing in his breach of contract.

(*h*) Jorden *v.* Money, 5 H. L. Ca. 185; 23 L. J. Ch. 865. Citizens' Bank of Louisiana *v.* Bk. of New Orleans, L. R. 6 H. L. 352; 43 L. J. Ch. 269. Mitchell *v.* Heys & Sons, 1894; 21 R. 600 (owner of articles hired not affected by statements of hirer). *Qu.* Whether Donnison *v.* Employers' Acct., etc., Insur. Co., 1897, 24 R. 681, is quite consistent with this doctrine. Maunsell *v.* White, 4 H. L. Ca. 1039. Pollock on Contracts, 506, 711. See above, § 8.

(*i*) *Ex p.* Adamson, *in re* Collie, 8 Ch. D. 817; 47 L. J. Bkr. 106. M'Kenzie *v.* B. L. Co., *supra* (*f*). Thew & Co. *v.* Sinclair & Co., 1881; 8 R. 467. For further examples of personal bar, see cases in the Digest, which are too numerous to classify or refer to. But these cases are less valuable, and, it may be feared, are sometimes ill-decided, by reason of the failure to distinguish between *rei interventus* and acquiescence, and indeed to state any general rules whatever. See the remark of Lord Blackburn, 8 R. H. L. 16. And see a case in which the want of a solemnity of diligence was obviated by personal exception, Taylor *v.* Macknight, 1882; 9 R. 857.

28. Effect of Obligations.—The essence of an obligation consists in the obligor being so bound to give, or do, or abstain, as to entitle the obligee to rely on fulfilment. The *jus exigendi* is the right conferred, and forms part of the *universitas* of the creditor's estate. The necessity of fulfilment is the obligation imposed, and forms a charge upon the debtor's funds. The effect of the obligation is to confer the right, and to impose the duty which the engagement fairly and equitably imports. Dismissing all distinction (as in the Roman law) between "contractus stricti juris" and "contractus bonæ fidei," the subject of obligations may be either general or specific; present, future, or contingent (*a*).

(*a*) 1 Stair, 10. § 2 et seq. 3 Ersk. 1. § 2, 3, and t. 3. § 83.

29. If the obligation be *general*, not confined to a specific thing, the engagement is absolute; provided the object of it be intelligible (*a*). If the object be some *specific* thing, the obligation is so far conditional that it may be defeated by extinction of the thing. 'That is to say, when by the nature of the contract its performance depends on the existence of a particular thing or state of things, the failure or destruction of that thing or state of things, without default on either side (*b*), liberates both parties. Thus if the parties contemplate as the foundation of their bargain a particular building on which work is to be done (*c*), or in which an entertainment is to be given (*d*), and it is destroyed by accidental fire; or if they contract for the sale of the corn or potatoes of a particular field and season which perish by blight (*e*); or of a certain quantity of grain or oil or other goods forming an undivided portion of a specific bulk, and the whole bulk is destroyed by accident (*f*); or if the performance of personal services which cannot be done by deputy is prevented by the promisor's death or incapacity from temporary or permanent illness (*g*), the contract is at an end. In such cases impossibility of performance dissolves or determines the contract, because as a matter of construction ability to do what is promised is an implied condition (*h*). But in general, practical impossibility of performance (such as extreme cost or difficulty) is no excuse for the non-performance of a contract (*i*), unless (1) the thing stipulated for is according to the existing state of knowledge so absurd, that a reasonable man would not have contemplated it (*k*); or (2) it is unlawful, or impossible by law (*l*).'

A pecuniary obligation may be enforced by execution against the estate, and, 'but now only in exceptional cases (*m*),' against the person.

An obligation to perform an act (*ad factum præstandum*) has been held in England not to ground an action at law, but only a remedy in equity (*n*). Such contracts may in Scotland be specifically enforced where the act can be performed 'by the defender, or, failing him' by another, and the action, 'if it is not desired or is incompetent to enforce specific performance by imprisonment,' may be laid alternatively for performance or for damages (*o*).

Where the obligor is *himself* to perform the act and refuses, or where the act becomes impossible (*p*), damages are substituted for specific performance, 'if the obligation be in form and substance sufficiently definite to be specifically performed (*q*).' The imprisonment of workmen for non-performance of their engagement rests now entirely on the statutes relative to workmen (*r*). 'A promise to marry, or a contract of service or of partnership, will not be specifically enforced, yet damages are given for their breach. And in certain cases, one who has induced another in bad faith or negligently to act upon an informal or legally incomplete agreement, which cannot be enforced by specific implement, has been held bound to recoup specific loss or expenditure so incurred (*s*).'

An obligation to abstain may be enforced by interdict.

(*a*) As to certainty, see below, § 524 *init.*

(*b*) See below, § 571; and see for the rule when there is fault impeding the execution of a contract, below, § 50 *fin.*, § 88.

(*c*) Appleby *v.* Myers, L. R. 2 C. P. 651; 36 L. J. C. P. 331. Comp. below, § 152, 1208.

(*d*) Taylor *v.* Caldwell, 3 B. & S. 826; 32 L. J. Q. B. 164.

(*e*) Howell *v.* Coupland, L. R. 9 Q. B. 462; 43 L. J. Q. B. 201; L. R. 1 Q. B. D. 258; 46 L. J. Q. B. 147. See below, § 87, 91, 116.

(*f*) This case seems to belong to this place, though it is treated in the notes to Lord M'Laren's ed. of Bell's Com. (vol. i. 461 and 473) as a case of completed sale, in which the buyer is liable for the price. See Warnkoenig, Com. ii. 28. Toullier, vi. Nos. 444 sq., and § 88, below.

(*g*) Fraser, M. & S. p. 316 sqq. (3rd ed.), and *infra*, § 179 *fin.* Boast *v.* Firth, L. R. 4 C. P. 8; 38 L. J. C. P. 1. Robinson *v.* Davison, L. R. 6 Ex. 269; 40 L. J. Ex. 172. Poussard *v.* Spiers & Pond, L. R. 1 Q. B. D. 410; 45 L. J. Q. B. 621.

(*h*) L. 31 Dig. *Obl. et Act.* (44. 7); l. 107 Dig. *de Solut.* (46. 3); Savigny, Obl. § 37 (vol. ii. 381 sqq.); Syst. § 121–124 (vol. iii. 126 sqq.). 1 Stair, 10. § 13; 2. 3. 56. 3 Ersk. 3. § 84. Pollock on Contracts, chap. vii. Clifford *v.* Watts, L. R. 5 C. P. 577; 40 L. J. C. P. 36. Gowans *v.* Christie, 1871; 9 Macph. 485; aff. 1873, 11 Macph. H. L. 1. N. B. Ry. Co. *v.* Benhar Coal Co., 1886; 14 R. 141. See below, § 116, § 431 (*h*). But the dissolution of the contract does not affect rights already acquired under it, *e.g.* payments made or right to payment of an instalment become due. Constable *v.* Robinson's Trs., June 1, 1808; F. C. Stubbs *v.* Holywell Ry. Co., 36 L. J. Ex. 166; L. R. 2 Ex. 311. Whincup *v.* Hughes, L. R. 6 C. P. 78; 40 L. J. C. P. 104. Anglo-Egyp. Nav. Co. *v.* Rennie, L. R. 10 C. P. 271, 571; 44 L. J. C. P. 130.

(*i*) Ersk. *l.c.* M'Elroy *v.* Tharsis Sulphur Co., 1877; 5 R. 161; rev. 1878, *ib.* H. L. 171; 1 App. Ca. 1040. Gillespie *v.* Howden, 1885; 12 R. 800. Jones *v.* St. John's Coll., L. R. 6 Q. B. 115; 40 L. J. Q. B. 80. Thorn *v.* Mayor of London, L. R. 9 Ex. 163; 10 Ex. 112; 1 App. Ca. 120; 43 L. J. Ex. 115; 44 *ib.* 62; 45 *ib.* 487. Hills *v.* Sughrue, 15 M. & W. 253. Kearon *v.* Pearson, 7 H. & N. 386; 31 L. J. Ex. 1. Brown *v.* Royal Ins. Co., 1 E. & E. 853; 28 L. J. Q. B. 275; Mennie *v.* Blair, 1852; 14 D. 359 (strike—see Budgett *v.* Binnington, 1891; 1 Q. B. 35). Roberts *v.* Bury Comrs., L. R. 5 C. P. 325; 39 L. J. C. P. 129. See Robertson *v.* Driver's Trs., 1881; 8 R. 555 (penalty), and Moore *v.* Paterson, 1881; 9 R. 337 (damages or specific implement). Wilkie *v.* Bethune, 1848, 11 D. 132, is a remarkable and exceptional case of supervening difficulty, in which the Court modified the terms of the contract.

(*k*) Clifford *v* Watts, *cit.*

(*l*) Stair and Ersk. *cit.* Brown *v.* Mayor of London, 30 L. J. C. P. 225; 31 *ib.* 280; 9 C. B. N. S. 726; 13 *ib.* 828. Baily *v.* De Crespigny, L. R. 4 Q. B. 180; 38 L. J. Q. B. 98. Dunbar *v.* Scott's Trs., 1872; 10 Macph. 982.

(*m*) See § 2311, *infra.*

(*n*) 1 Maddock on Chancery, 360. Snell's Prin. of Equity, 519 sq. Fry on Specific Performance. A decree of consignation has been held to be a decree *ad f. pr.* Mackenzie *v.* Balerno Paper Co., 1883; 10 R. 1147.

(*o*) 1 Stair, 17. § 16. 3 Ersk. 3. § 86 and § 62. The distinction in the text is taken from the Civilians; but it scarcely affords an adequate explanation of the principles on which an order for specific performance will be granted. The subject has been illustrated by almost no decisions; and it is familiar chiefly where the obligant is required to make delivery of something. See discussions in Glasgow and Inveraray Steamb. Co. *v.* Henderson, 1877; 1 Guthrie's Sel. Sh. Ct. Ca. 184. Fraser, M. & S. 101 sq. (3rd ed.). Winans *v.* Mackenzie, 1883; 10 R. 941 (*per* L. Kinnear). Seaforth's Trs. *v.* Macaulay, 1844; 7 D. 180. Millat *v.* Marshall, 2 Guthrie's Sel. Sh. Ct. Ca. 226.

(*p*) See Moore *v.* Paterson (*i*).

(*q*) M'Arthur *v.* Lawson, 1877; 4 R. 1134. See Clark *v.* City of Glasgow Ass. Co., 1850; 12 D. 1047; rev. 1854, 1 Macq. 668; 26 Sc. Jur. 638.

(*r*) Murray *v.* Bisset, May 15, 1810; F. C.; 1 Ill. 36. Raeburn *v.* Reid, 1824; 3 S. 69. Gentle *v.* M'Lellan, 1825; 4 S. 165. Campbell *v.* Anderson, 1825; 4 S. 476. See Bookless *v.* Normand, 1832; 11 S. 50; also below, § 190 et seq. 4 Geo. IV. c. 34, § 3. Haig *v.* Buchanan, 1823; 2 S. 412. Morrison *v.* Cuthbert, 1835; 13 S. 772. 30 and 31 Vict. c. 141 (Master and Servant Act, 1867), repealed by 38 and 39 Vict. c. 86. See 38 and 39 Vict. c. 90. There was at common law, under certain limitations, a power in the Judge Ordinary to imprison summarily workmen who desert service upon which they have entered. Cameron *v.* Murray, 1866; 4 Macph. 547. Raeburn, *cit.* But it is thought that since the Act of 1875 this remedy is incompetent. Fraser on Master and Servant, pp. 101–111, 382 sq., 3rd ed.

(*s*) Walker *v.* Milne, 1823; 2 S. 361. Bell *v.* Bell, 1841; 3 D. 1201. Allan *v.* Gilchrist, 1875; 2 R. 587. Dobie *v.* Lauder's Trs., 1873; 11 Macph. 749. But it may be doubted whether these ought not to be regarded as cases of contract perfected by *rei interventus.* See § 26, 27A. Pollock on Contracts, 507, 711.

30. Damages.—An obligation may ground a claim of damages either tacitly or expressly.

31. The general rule is, that if one bound absolutely (§ 29) become, without fraud or fault (*a*), unable to fulfil his engagement, damages are due: the damage being indemnification for that which, by the breach of engagement, the obligee has directly lost or been prevented from gaining, with the expense of the proceedings for obtaining reparation (*b*). 'Whenever a breach of contract is proved, damages follow, although if no loss or inconvenience be proved the damages will be nominal (*c*).'

Under such claim of damage will fall lawful interest in pecuniary obligations, as the damage for money not paid (*d*): the loss sustained on the thing itself (*propter rem ipsam non habitam*); or foreseen, or naturally in the contemplation of the parties, 'as the natural result or consequence to be reasonably expected from a breach' (*e*): But not collateral or consequential damage (*f*); unless either such damage has, by special stipulation of the parties, been brought into view (*g*); or unless it be a loss on the *thing itself*, as by rise or fall of markets (*h*).

(*a*) See below, § 33.

(*b*) 1 Stair, 17. § 16. 3 Ersk. 3. § 75, 86. Brown on Sale, 211–26. Pothier, Oblig. § 159 et seq. Strachan & Gavin *v.* Paton, 1828; 3 W. & S. 19; 1 Ill. 37. See for the distinction of damage for delict, below, § 545 and 553. As to damages for delay, see § 115.

(*c*) Meikle *v.* Sneddon, 1862; 24 D. 720. Webster *v.* Cramond Iron Co., 1875; 2 R. 752. Kinninmont *v.* Paxton, 1892; 20 R. 128. But see Murdison *v.* Scot. Football Club, 1896; 23 R. 449, 466 (*per* L. Kinnear), and *qu.* See Mayne on Damages, 5, etc.

(*d*) 1 Ill. 38. 3 Ersk. 3. § 75 et seq. *Infra*, § 32.

(*e*) Anderson *v.* Goddard & Co., Feb. 21, 1809; F. C. See Mansfield *v.* Campbell, 1836; 14 S. 585; 3 Ill. 102. Downe *v.* Mackinlay, 1834; 12 S. 528. Houldsworth *v.* Brit. Linen Co., 1850; 13 D. 376. See the note of the Sheriff (Fraser) in Ovington *v.* M'Vicar, 1864; 2 Macph. 1066. Webster *v.* Cramond Iron Co., *cit.* Houldsworth *v.* Brand's Trs., 1877; 4 R. 369. The principles stated here, and more fully in the Com. i. 448 sqq. (478, M'L.'s ed.), do not differ materially from what is called in England "the rule in Hadley *v.* Baxendale." See **Hadley** *v.* **Baxendale,** 9 Ex. 341; 23 L. J. Ex. 179. Cory *v.* Thames Iron Works Co., L. R. 3 C. P. 181; 37 L. J. C. P. 235. France *v.* Gaudet, L. R. 6 Q. B. 199; 40 L. J. Q. B. 121. Horne *v.* Midland Ry. Co., 42 L. J. C. P. 59; L. R. 8 C. P. 131. Macmahon *v.* Field, 50 L. J. Ex. 311, 552; L. R. 7 Q. B. D. 591. Burrows *v.* March Gas Co., L R. 7 Ex. 96; 41 L. J. Ex. 46. Le Blanche *v.* L. and N.-W. Ry., 45 L. J. C. P. 521; L. R. 1 C. P. D. 286 (cost of special train when train too late). Brit. Columbia Sawmill Co. *v.* Nettleship, L. R. 3 C. P. 499; 37 L. J. C. P. 235. Addison on Contracts, 259, 989. Mayne on Damages, ch. ii. and x. 2 Smith's L. C. 568 sqq. (552 sq., 10th ed.). *Infra*, § 33. As to infection conveyed by animals sold or admitted to stable or grazing fields, see Robertson *v.* Connolly, 1851; 13 D. 779. Hill *v.* Balls, 2 H. & N. 299; 27 L. J. Ex. 45. Smith *v.* Green, 45 L. J. C. P. 29; 1 C. P. D. 92. 2 Smith's L. C. 534–37.

(*f*) Dunlop *v.* M'Kellar, May 31, 1815; F. C. Walton *v.* Fothergill, 7 Carr. & P. 392.

(*g*) So, a seller failing to deliver the goods sold is liable for loss by the buyer on a subsale, if and so far as such subsale, or the purpose to make it, was disclosed. Elbinger Actiengesellschaft *v.* Armstrong, 43 L. J. Q. B. 211; L. R. 9 Q. B. 473. Grebert-Borgnis *v.* Nugent, 15 Q. B. D. 85. See below, § 33 (*e*) (*f*) (*h*).

(*h*) Hadley, *supra*. Engell *v.* Fitch, L. R. 4 Q. B. 659; 38 L. J. Q. B. 304. Godwin *v.* Francis, L. R. 5 C. P. 121; 39 L. J. C. P. 121. Williams *v.* Reynolds, 6 B. & S. 495; 34 L. J. Q. B. 221. Wilson *v.* Lanc. Ry. Co., 30 L. J. C. P. 232; 9 C. B. N. S. 632. Prehn *v.* Royal Bank of Liverpool 39 L. J. Ex. 41; L. R. 5 Ex. 92 (contract to accept bills).

32. (1.) *Damage in Pecuniary Obligations—Interest.*—Here interest is the damage due. It is due by law on bills and notes from the date of the bill, in case of non-acceptance; from the day of payment of a note or of an accepted bill; from the date of presentment, if payable on demand; and from the date of acceptance—or if the acceptance is not dated, from the date of the bill—if drawn at sight (*a*). After denunciation, 'adjudication or decree of sale,' interest is due on the whole sum as accumulated in the diligence (*b*). 'It is due on all sums (including expenses of process) constituted by decree (*c*).' It is due on sums paid by a cautioner for the principal debtor (*d*). By agreement, interest 'might' be stipulated not to exceed five per cent. on a British debt, 'but since the repeal of the usury laws there is no limitation' (*e*). On a foreign debt, the rate 'will, in the absence of express stipulation (*f*),' be according to the law 'and market' of the place 'where payment is to be made' (*g*); but 'formerly' it 'could' not be continued beyond five per cent. after the debt 'became' British by judgment or novation (*h*). Interest is due as damage from delay raised by a judicial demand or protest (*i*); or from the rendering of accounts (*k*); or by duty under trust to pay money. 'Arrears of feu-duties do not bear interest, nor arrears of ground-annuals (*l*).' Where money has been improperly obtained, and is detained against the will of the owner, interest is due at the full legal rate, not the current rate merely (*m*). By implied agreement, interest is due in all cases of intromission, possession, loan, and the enjoyment of the use of money after it ought to have been paid (*n*), 'or where it has been overpaid or wrongly paid and a claim of repetition arises (*o*), "unless from the circumstances of the case there is ground in equity to hold that interest was not meant to be demanded" (*p*).'

Compound Interest.—'As a general rule, compound interest is not due (*q*); but' interest is given, by decree of the House of Lords, on the interest included in judicial accumulations (*r*). Accumulation of interest also is allowed on bankers' accounts periodically settled, and the interest added to the principal; on writers' accounts of cash transactions, settled annually like bankers'; on accounts of judicial factors; and on India accounts by usage; 'and where there is a fixed usage in commercial or other transactions' (*s*): And the law agent and cashier of tutors and curators (himself being one of them, liable for interest) has been held bound to settle yearly, and to lend out the balance or pay bank interest on it till lent out (*t*). 'Judicial factors, tutors at law, and similar guardians, are bound to lay out and accumulate annually the funds under their management (*u*).'

(*a*) 1681, c. 20. 1696, c. 36. 12 Geo. III. c. 72. 3 Ersk. 3. § 77 ; 45 and 46 Vict. c. 61, § 57.

(*b*) 1621, c. 20, and 1 and 2 Vict. c. 114, § 5. 19 and 20 Vict. c. 91, § 4. Findlay *v.* Donaldson's Trs., 1849 ; 11 D. 569. Gordon *v.* Buchanan, 1848 ; 10 D. 751.

(*c*) Dalmahoy & Wood *v.* Magis. of Brechin, 1859 ; 21 D. 210 ; and cases there cited. Bell's Com. i. 649 (693, M'L.'s ed.).

(*d*) 1 Bell's Com. 652 (696, M'L.'s ed.). 3 Ersk. 3. § 78.

(*e*) 17 and 18 Vict. c. 90 ; *infra*, § 36 (3). In the absence of stipulation or special circumstances, five per cent. is still the rate allowed. See Smith *v.* Barlas, 1857 ; 19 D. 267. Wauchope *v.* N. B. Ry. Co., 1863 ; 2 Macph. 326. Douglas *v.* Douglas's Trs., 1867 ; 5 Macph. 827. But the Courts may fix a lower rate. As to interest on bonds stipulated to be at the market rate, see Field *v.* Watt's Trs., 1863 ; 2 Macph. 33.

(*f*) In the original text, "may be."

(*g*) Haviland *v.* Bowerbanks, 1 Camp. 50 ; 1 Ill. 38. Gordon *v.* Swan, 12 East, 419. Marshall *v.* Poole, 13 East, 98. Calton *v.* Bragg, 15 East, 223. These cases cited by Professor Bell relate generally to the English law as to interest, and are not authorities for the statement in the text. Gillow & Co. *v.* Burgess, 1824 ; 3 S. 45. Campbell *v.* Ramsay, Feb. 15, 1809 ; F. C. Graham *v.* Keble, 1820 ; 2 Bligh, 127 ; 6 Pat. 616, and 6 S. 119. Wilkinson *v.* Monies, June 28, 1821 ; F. C. Palmer & Co. *v.* Glass's Trs., 1835 ; 13 S. 308 ; 1 Ill. 41. Fyffe *v.* Fergusson, 1838 : 16 S. 1038 ; H. L. 2 Rob. 267 ; 8 Cl. & Fin. 121. See Cochrane *v.* Gilkison, 1857 ; 20 D. 213. Price & Logan *v.* Wise, 1862 ; 24 D. 491. See Guthrie's Savigny's Priv. Int. Law, 118, 245, 257. Westlake's Priv. Int. Law, § 211.

(*h*) Graham, *sup.* (*g*).

(*i*) Jolly *v.* M'Neill, 1829 ; 7 S. 666. Goldie *v.* Napier, 1830 ; 8 S. 357 ; aff. 1831 ; 5 W. & S. 745. Maclean *v.* Campbell, 1856 ; 18 D. 609.

(*k*) See Bremner *v.* Mabon, 1837 ; 16 S. 213. Cardno & Darling *v.* Stewart, 1869 ; 7 Macph. 1026 ; 6 S. L. R. 670 (as discussed in Aberdeen Com. Co. *v.* Gordon ; Macfarlan *v.* M'Leod, 1875 ; Benhar Coal Co. *v.* Henderson, 1876 ; 1 Guthrie's Sel. Sh. Ct. Ca. 227, 230, 234 ; Macrae *v.* Macrae, 2 Guthrie's Sh. Ct. Ca. 221. Comp. Bald *v.* Miller's Trs., 1870 ; 1 *ib.* 582). The question whether interest is exigible upon open accounts except from the date of citation is not authoritatively settled (unless Blair's Trs. *v.* Payne, 1884 ; 12 R. 104, following upon Cardno, *cit.*, be thought to do so) ; but the preponderance of principle and practice (notwithstanding the dictum in the text) is in favour of applying the general rule that in such cases (apart from usage or stipulation) interest is due only from the date of citation, or from a year after the date of the last item (see 3 Ersk. 3. § 80). Interest is, however, in the discretion of the Court, which would probably allow it from the time when, an account being rendered with notice that interest would be claimed, it ought to have been paid. The case of Bremner *v.* Mabon was very special, and related besides to a law agent's accounts, consisting partly of outlays, on which interest has generally been allowed after a year from the date of rendering.

(*l*) Napier *v.* Spiers, 1831 ; 9 S. 655. Wallace *v.* Eglinton, 1835 ; 13 S. 564 ; 1838, 1 D. 162. See Mags. of Edin. *v.* Horsburgh, 1835 ; 13 S. 571. M. of Tweeddale *v.* Aytoun, 1842 ; 4 D. 862. Pollock *v.* Mags. of Edin., 1862 ; 24 D. 371. And as to stipends and teind duties, see Drummond *v.* Montgomerie, 1842 ; 5 D. 277. Ld. Advocate *v.* Sinclair's Trs., 1855 ; 17 D. 290. Preston *v.* Mags. of Edin., 1870 ; 8 Macph. 502. Glasg. Univ. *v.* Pollok, 1868 ; 6 Macph. 878. C. of Cromertie (*n*). Haldane *v.* Ogilvie, 1871 ; 10 Macph. 62. And as to ground-annuals, Moncrieff *v.* Dundas, 1835 ; 14 S. 61.

(*m*) Duncan *v.* Bruce, 1836 ; 14 S. 583. See M'Neill, *infra* (*q*), and cases in (*n*).

(*n*) See More's Notes on Stair, lxxviii. D. of Queensberry's Trs. *v.* Tait, 1822 ; 1 S. 398. Jolly *v.* M'Neill, 1829 ; 7 S. 666 ; 1 Ill. 41. Brown's Trs. *v.* Brown, 1830 ; 4 W. & S. 28. Darling *v.* Adamson, 1834 ; 12 S. 598. Howden *v.* Porterfield, 1836 ; 14 S. 828. Cunninghame *v.* Boswell, 1868 ; 8 Macph. 890 (and cases as to loan there cited). Carmichael *v.* Union Canal Co., 1842 ; 1 Bell's App. 316. Sinclair *v.* Sinclair, 1847 ; 10 D. 190. Forbes *v.* Forbes, 1869 ; 8 Macph. 85. C. of Cromertie *v.* L. Adv., 1871 ; 9 Macph. 988.

(*o*) Glasg. Gaslight Co. *v.* Barony Par., 1868 ; 6 Macph. 406. See, however, as to negligence on the part of the true creditor, C. of Cromertie, *sup.* (*n*).

(*p*) This addition to the text is taken from 1 Bell's Com. 647 (692, M'L.'s ed.), and is illustrated by the cases cited in note (*n*) and in the Com. See Durie's Trs. *v.* Ayton, 1894 ; 22 R. 34.

(*q*) 3 Ersk. 3. § 81, 82. Pr. 3. 3. § 33. Macneill *v.* Macneill, 1830 ; 4 W. & S. 455 ; 1 Ill. 40. Graham's Exrs. *v.* Fletcher's Exrs., 1870 ; 9 Macph. 298.

(*r*) 48 Geo. III. c. 151, § 19. 2 Bligh, 145. Napier *v.* Gordon, 1829 ; 8 S. 149 ; aff. 5 W. & S. 745 ; 1 Ill. 39. 1 Bell's Com. 651 (695, M'L.'s ed.).

(*s*) D. of Queensberry *v.* Tait, 1826 ; 5 S. 167 ; 1 Ill. 40. Graham and Palmer's cases, *sup.* (*g*). Fyffe, *sup.* (*g*). Lambe *v.* Ritchie, 1837 ; 16 S. 219. Campbell *v.* Keith, 1840 ; 2 D. 1367. Findlay, Bannatyne, & Co.'s Assignee *v.* Donaldson, 1864 ; 2 Macph. H. L. 86. Douglas *v.* Douglas's Trs., 1867 ; 5 Macph. 827. Bell's Com. *cit.*

(*t*) Lady Montgomerie *v.* Wauchope, 4 Dow, 110 ; 1822, 1 S. 421 ; 1 Ill. 40. Ralston *v.* Eaton, 1826 ; 4 S. 42. Blair *v.* Murray, 1843 ; 5 D. 1315.

(*u*) 12 and 13 Vict. c. 51, § 4, 5, 37. See as to trustees, testamentary tutors, factors, etc., Montgomerie, *cit.* Campbell *v.* Keith, 1840 ; 2 D. 1367. Wellwood's Trs. *v.* Boswell, 1856 ; 19 D. 187. M'Laren on Wills, etc., ii. 1211 sqq.

33. (2.) *Damage in Obligations not Pecuniary.*—To the above general rule as to damage, it is 'said by the author to be' an exception, that if the failure to fulfil the engagement be fraudulent or wilful, damage both direct and collateral is demandable ; 'but while it is true that the rules for assessing damages in actions for wrongs or *quasi* delicts, such as slander, assault, etc., are much wider, there is little or no authority (except perhaps in actions for breach of promise of marriage) for admitting the motives or conduct of a party breaking a contract, or any circumstances not arising from the breach itself, as elements in estimating the measure of damages (*a*).'

In England a distinction has been made, in awarding damages for not delivering goods, between that case and the failure to restore stock lent, on the ground that, in the case of lent stock, the borrower has the lender's means in his hand ; whereas in the non-delivery of goods the vendee has still his money with which to buy, and so may 'in general' indemnify himself by going to market on or about the stipulated day of delivery; and so in that case the damage is calculated according to the price at or about the day when the goods should have been delivered (*b*). In Scotland, the course has been, 'or rather was,' to take either the highest price which might have been got for the goods at any time after the day of sale, or the average value between the stipulated day of delivery and the date of the action (*c*); but the fair criterion seems to be that of the English practice—namely, the price at which the buyer could procure the goods in market at the stipulated time of delivery. 'It has been indeed repeatedly laid down in Scotland that there is no absolute rule to this effect, and that in each case the whole circumstances are to be looked at so as to give the pursuer fair compensation for his loss (*d*). But this proposition is not to be taken as negativing the fitness of the criterion suggested for the general run of cases in which no special damage is proved. It is true that a jury, or a judge who has to deal with the facts in evidence, is not to be tied down by a hard and fast rule to give as damages for a seller's breach of contract only the difference between the contract price and the market value at the date of the breach, and is bound to consider all the facts proved. But if there be no evidence of other loss, that is the obvious and natural measure of damages in such a case.

'And it may be laid down as a rule of law and good sense in Scotland as well as in England, that the damages to be given for breach of contract are such "as may fairly and reasonably be considered either as arising naturally, *i.e.* according to the usual course of things, from the breach of contract itself; or such as may reasonably be supposed to have been in contemplation of both parties at the time when they made the contract as the probable result of the breach of it" (*e*). But under the latter alternative mere knowledge of the surrounding circumstances, such *e.g.* as the other party's purpose in making the contract, does not impose upon the party breaking the contract liability for all the results, natural and proximate, or indirect and remote: the knowledge must be so brought home to him as to imply that he accepted the circumstances founded on as the basis of the contract, his knowledge that the person he contracts with reasonably believes that he accepts the contract with the special condition being sufficient to raise this inference (*f*). Thus a seller is liable for a reasonable sum for loss of profit, if he knew that the goods were for resale, and if such goods cannot be had at any price at the place of delivery (*g*). In short, the damages are to be what would be the natural consequences of a breach under circumstances which both parties were aware of and contemplated as the foundation of their dealing at the time of the contract (*h*). Accordingly damages for the loss of goods under contracts for carriage are measured by their market value (if the owner can go into the market and supply himself) at the place of delivery, independently of any circumstances peculiar to the owner, such as a contract for the sale of the goods on arrival (*i*).' Damage is to be given as at the stipulated *place* of delivery (*k*).

(*a*) Mayne on Dams. p. 43 sqq. M'Dowall *v.* Stewart, 1871; 10 Macph. 193. When a jury or judge has to consider the amount of damages in the nature of solatium, there is of necessity a more arbitrary estimate of what is due, and the practice of judges and juries has not been subjected to strict rules. See below, § 545, 2029, 2032 sqq.

(*b*) Leigh *v.* Paterson, 8 Taunt. 540; 1 Ill. 42. Gainsford *v.* Carroll, 2 B. & Cr. 624. Howie *v.* Anderson, 1848; 10 D. 355, and cases below. Williams and Wilson, *supra*, § 31 (*h*). Ogle *v.* Vane, L. R. 3 Q. B. 272; 7 B. & S. 855; 36 L. J. Q. B. 175; 37 *ib.* 77. Josling *v.* Irvine, 6 H. & N. 512; 30 L. J. Ex. 78. Brown *v.* Muller, 41 L. J. Ex. 214; L. R. 7 Ex. 319 (delivery by instalments). Roper *v.* Johnston, L. R. 8 C. P. 167; 42 L. J. C. P. 165.

(*c*) Morrison *v.* Boswell, 1806; M. *Damages*, Apx. 1; aff. 5 Pat. 649; 1 Ill. 41. Shirra *v.* Harvie, Dec. 11, 1807; F. C. Robinson & Co. *v.* M'Culloch, Dec. 23, 1808; F. C. Taylor & Co. *v.* Morrison, June 17, 1809; F. C.

(*d*) Watt *v.* Mitchell, 1839; 1 D. 1157. Howie *v.* Anderson, 1848; 10 D. 355. **Higgins** *v.* **Dunlop**, 1847; 9 D. 1407; aff. 6 Bell's App. 195; 1 H. L. Ca. 381. Baird *v.* Reilly, 1856; 18 D. 734. See Dickson *v.* Henderson, 1849; 12 D. 306; and Warin & Craven *v.* Forrester, 1876; 4 R. 190; *ib.* H. L. 90.

(*e*) **Hadley** *v.* **Baxendale**, 9 Ex. 341; 23 L. J. Ex. 179. See above, § 31. Wilson *v.* Newport Dock Co., L. R. 1 Ex. 177; 35 L. J. Ex. 97. Simpson *v.* L. and N.-W. Ry. Co., 1 Q. B. D. 274; 45 L. J. Q. B. 182. Hydraulic Engineering Co. *v.* M'Haffie, 4 Q. B. D. 670.

(*f*) British Columbia Sawmill Co. *v.* Nettleship, L. R. 3 C. P. 509; 37 L. J. C. P. 235. Horne, § 31 (*e*), and cases in § 31 (*g*). Keddie, Gordon, & Co. *v.* N. B. Ry. Co., 1886; 14 R. 233. Schulze *v.* G. E. Ry. Co., 19 Q. B. D. 30 (carriage of "samples"). The costs of defending an action for breach of contract at the instance of a sub-purchaser may be recovered. See Hammond *v.* Bussey & Co., 20 Q. B. D. 79.

(*g*) Watt *v.* Mitchell, and Higgins *v.* Dunlop, *citt.* (*d*). Duff & Co. *v.* Iron, etc., Fencing and Building Co., 1891 19 R. 199.

(*h*) See *per* Blackburn, J., in Cory *v.* Thames I. W. Co.,

§ 31 (*e*). The doctrine comes very near to holding that parties make the results of the breach a term of the contract. It will of course be more easy to infer that parties contemplated all the results, and accepted liability, in some kinds of contracts than others; *e.g.* responsibility for loss of profits upon the working of a machine will be more readily fixed on a maker who fails to have it ready by the stipulated time, than on a carrier who fails to deliver a necessary part of it. Comp. Smeed *v.* Foord, 1 E. & E. 602; Cory, *cit.*, etc., with British Col. Co., *cit.* Horne, *cit.*, and other cases in 2 Smith's L. C. 523 sqq.

(*i*) G. W. Ry. Co. *v.* Redmayne, L. R. 1 C. P. 329. Rodocanachi *v.* Milburn, 18 Q. B. D. 67. Schulze, *cit.* As to damages for breach by the merchant of a running contract for carriage, see Dunn & Co. *v.* Anderston Foundry Co., 1894; 21 R. 880.

(*k*) Anderson *v.* Goddard, Feb. 21, 1809; F. C.; 1 Ill. 37.

34. (3.) *Stipulated Damages.*—In relation to stipulated damages, these points are to be marked: 1. That the parties may fix the amount of loss resulting, or likely to result, from the breach of engagement, as *estimated damages*; in which case no inquiry into the actual damage seems competent (*a*), 'unless the sum assessed is exorbitant and unconscionable, when the Court will modify the penalty on equitable grounds (*b*)'; 2. That the obligation may be fortified by a penalty, which is held to cover but not to assess the damage, to entitle the 'Court, with, if necessary, the aid of a' jury, to find under it the true amount of damage, not exceeding the penalty (*c*); and 3. That the stipulation of a penalty (unless when expressly so declared) is not alternative, and does not discharge the obligation on payment of the penalty (*d*). 'The words "*liquidated damages*" or "*penalty*" are not conclusive as to the character of the sum stipulated to be paid. This is to be gathered from the matter of agreement (*e*).'

(*a*) Craig *v.* Sinclair, 1628; M. 10,034; 1 B. Sup. 227; 1 Ill. 42. Skene, 1637; M. 8401; 1 Ill. 23. M'Intosh *v.* M'Donnell, 1798; M. *Tack*, Apx. 5. Henderson *v.* Maxwell, 1802; M. 10,054. Frazer *v.* Ewart, Feb. 25, 1813; F. C. Graham *v.* Straiton, 1789; 15 F. C. 423; 3 Pat. 119. Morrison *v.* Blair, 1823; 2 S. 241. Miller *v.* L. Gwydir, 1824; 3 S. 65; aff. 1826, 2 W. & S. 52. See below, § 1221. **Johnston** *v.* **Robertson,** 1861; 23 D. 646. Lawson *v.* Ogilvie, 1833; 10 S. 531; aff. 7. W. & S. 397. **Barton** *v.* **Glover,** Holt's Cases, 43; 17 R. R. 601, and cases cited, 1 Ill. 44. Rolfe *v.* Paterson, 2 Br. Parl. Ca. 436. Lowe *v.* Peers, 4 Burr. 2225. Smith *v.* Dickinson, 3 B. & P. 630.

(*b*) **Forrest & Barr** *v.* **Henderson, Coulborn, & Co.,** 1869; 8 Macph. 187. See Craig, *infra* (*c*); 1 Bell's Com. 655 (679, M'L.'s ed.). In many cases the unreasonableness of the stipulated damages has been held as an element in the construction of agreements to show that the stipulated sum is not really damages but a penalty; see English cases in (*e*), and Addison on Contracts, pp. 267–270; and it must be confessed that the judgments in Forrest & Barr tend to pare away the distinction between penalties and liquidated damages. See also Robertson *v.* Driver's Trs., 1881; 8 R. 555. The impossibility of performing a contract within the stipulated time is in general no defence to a claim for pactional damages, for if persons bind themselves to impossibilities, *sibi imputent.* Jones *v.* St. John's Coll., 40 L. J. Q. B. 80; L. R. 6 Q. B. 115, and cases, *supra*, § 29, *infra*, § 49.

(*c*) Johnston *v.* Forbes, 1639; M. 10,037; 1 Ill. 42. Pollock *v.* Paton, 1777; M. *Tack*, Apx. 4; Hailes, 766. Muir M'Kenzie *v.* Craigies, June 18, 1811; F. C. Wortley M'Kenzie *v.* Gilchrist, Dec. 13, 1811; F. C. Wright *v.* M'Gregor, 1826; 4 S. 440. Johnstone's Trs. *v.* Johnstone, Jan. 19, 1819; F. C. (limits the amount of damages). Craig *v.* Macbeath, 1863; 1 Macph. 1020. Cf. Watson *v.* Noble, 1885; 13 R. 347. Wilbeam *v.* Ashton, 1 Camp. 78. See Holt's Cases, 45, note. Astley *v.* Weldon, 2 B. & P. 346; 1 Ill. 46. Smith, *sup.* (*a*).

(*d*) Beattie *v.* Lambie, 1695; M. 10,039; 1 Ill. 47. Clark *v.* Cairncross, 1632; M. 10,036. Crichton *v.* Pirie, 1630; M. 10,035. Broomfield *v.* Young, 1753; M. 9446. Muir M'Kenzie and Wortley M'Kenzie, *sup.* (*c*). See Elch. *Alternative*, notes, p. 23. See below, § 36, 1221. Curtis *v.* Sandison, 1831; 10 S. 72. Howard *v.* Woodward, 34 L. J. Ch. 47. French *v.* Macale, 2 Drew. & W. 274. Gold *v.* Houldsworth, 1870; 8 Macph. 1006. Dalrymple *v.* Henderson, 1878; 5 R. 847.

(*e*) Johnston *v.* Robertson (*a*). **Forrest & Barr** and Robertson *v.* Driver's Trs. (*b*). Elphinston *v.* Monkland Iron Co., 1886; 11 App. Ca. 332; 13 R. H. L. 99. Comml. Bk. *v.* Beal, 1890; 18 R. 80. Betts *v.* Burch, 28 L. J. Ex. 267; 4 H. & N. 506. Magee *v.* Lavell, 43 L. J. C. P. 131; L. R. 9 C. P. 107. Kemble *v.* Farren, 3 M. & P. 440; 6 Bing. 141; 7 L. J. C. P. 258. Thompson *v.* Hudson, 38 L. J. Ch. 431; L. R. 4 H. L. 1. Dimech *v.* Corlett, 12 Moore's P. C. 299. **Wallis** *v.* **Smith,** 21 Ch. D. 243. Mayne on Dams., chap. iii.

35. Illegal and Immoral Contracts.—No obligation is recognised as a ground of action which is derived from an illegal or immoral contract. In such a case, "melior est conditio possidentis vel defendentis" (*a*). 'Illegality or Immorality in the obligation itself, as in its consideration or counterpart, makes the whole agreement void; but where the unlawful can be severed from the lawful part of a contract, and probably where the illegal part of a consideration can be apportioned, the remaining untainted portion of the contract may be enforced (*b*). When the obligation, though not illegal or immoral in itself, is entered into with an unlawful purpose or intention, it is void if that purpose was common to both parties, or even if it was known to both (*c*). If one of them was ignorant of the unlawful purpose of the other, and discovers it, he may and ought to refuse performance (*d*); and if the contract has already been executed, he may probably obtain restitution or repetition on equitable grounds (*e*). The maxim, "in pari casu potior est conditio defendentis" (also "ex turpi causa non oritur actio"), rests on the principle that "no Court will lend its aid to a man who founds his cause on an immoral or illegal act" (*f*); and it further follows from that principle, not only that there is no repetition of money paid or property handed over in furtherance of an unlawful contract or agreement (*g*), but that a completed transfer of property or of an interest in property for an unlawful consideration cannot be set aside (*h*). The taint of illegality extends to avoid a subsequent security for the payment of money due under an illegal contract (*i*). The cases both in England and Scotland hold that an insolvent purchasing by a preference a particular creditor's assent to his discharge upon a composition is not *in pari delicto* with the creditor extorting it, and may recover back money so paid; but if, after the arrangement is complete, the debtor voluntarily pays a bill so obtained, this is a voluntary payment of which there is no repetition (*k*).'

(*a*) Benyon *v.* Nettleford, 3 Macn. & G. 94; 20 L. J. Ch. 186. Ayerst *v.* Jenkins, 42 L. J. Ch. 690; L. R. 16 Eq. 275. *Infra*, § 37.

(*b*) Hamilton *v.* De Gares, 1756; M. 9471. Hamilton *v.* Main, 1823; 2 S. 356. Hamilton *v.* Waring, *infra*, § 37 (*d*). Blair *v.* Allen, 1858; 21 D. 15. Cases below, § 36 (6) (*c*). Gaskell *v.* King, 11 East, 165; 10 R. R. 462. **Pickering *v.* Ilfracombe Ry. Co.,** L. R. 3 C. P. 235; 37 L. J. C. P. 118. Price *v.* Green, 16 M. & W. 346; 16 L. J. Ex. 108. *In re* Burdett, 20 Q. B. D. 310. See Young *v.* Johnson & Wright, 1880; 7 R. 760, and 1 Sm. L. C. 371 sqq.

(*c*) **Cannan *v.* Bryce,** § 36 (*c*). Smith *v.* White and Pearce *v.* Brooks, § 37 (*e*).

(*d*) Cowan *v.* Milbourn, L. R. 2 Ex. 230; 36 L. J. Ex. 124.

(*e*) Feret *v.* Hill, 15 C. B. 207; 23 L. J. C. P. 185, is not an authority to the contrary.

(*f*) *Per* L. Mansfield in Holman *v.* Johnson, Cowp. 341.

(*g*) Holman *v.* Johnson, *cit.* Taylor *v.* Chester, L. R. 4 Q. B. 309; 38 L. J. Q. B. 225. Tyndal Bruce *v.* Grant, 1839; 1 D. 583. It has been held that money paid for an illegal purpose may be recovered before the agreement is performed. Taylor *v.* Bowers, 1 Q. B. D. 291; 45 L. J. Q. B. 163, and cases there cited. Herman *v.* Jeuchner, 15 Q. B. D. 561. See below, § 490.

(*h*) Ayerst *v.* Jenkins, *cit.* (*a*). Hamilton *v.* Waring, § 37 (*d*). The case of Cuthbertson *v.* Lowes, 1870, 8 Macph. 1070, appears to show that when a statutory nullity is enacted, not on the ground of turpitude or on account of any inherent vice in the nature of the contract prohibited, but merely to enforce a measure of public policy, *e.g.* the nullity of contracts made according to prohibited weights and measures, the Court, while it cannot enforce such a contract, will not allow either party to take unfair advantage of the nullity, but if the contract has been partly performed will require restitution or payment of *quantum meruit* or market price, as the circumstances require.

(*i*) Fisher *v.* Bridges, 2 E. & B. 118; 3 *ib.* 642; 23 L. J. Q. B. 276. Geere *v.* Mare, 2 H. & C. 339; 33 L. J. Ex. 50. Att.-Gen. *v.* Hollingsworth, 2 H. & N. 416. (See 1 Smith's L. C. 377 sq.) Strachan *v.* Graham, 1823; 2 S. 391. Russell *v.* Liston's Trs., 1844; 6 D. 1138.

(*k*) Arroll *v.* Montgomerie, 1826; 4 S. 499. Macfarlan *v.* Nicoll, 1864; 3 Macph. 237. Atkinson *v.* Denby, 6 H. & N. 778; 7 *ib.* 934; 30 L. J. Ex. 361; 31 *ib.* 362. See 2 Smith's L. C. 385 sqq., 443, 548, and below, § 37.

36. Contracts Illegal by Statute.—No obligation to give, do, or abstain, against the express (*a*) prohibition of a statute, will sustain an action (*b*). A penalty imposed by statute is for punishment, not to give licence; and it implies prohibition (*c*). 'But when a duty is imposed by statute and a penalty annexed for its violation or neglect, it depends on the purview and terms of the statute whether the penalty is the sole remedy, or the administrators of the statute and persons injured have also remedies by action of damages or interdict (*d*).' In contracts, by force of stipulation the penalty may discharge the obligation (*e*).

(*a*) No contract can be held immoral or illegal upon a conjectural view of the construction of a statute; there must be no doubt as to its construction and effect. Barton *v.* Muir, 44 L. J. P. C. 19; L. R. 6 P. C. 134.

(*b*) A stipulation that an annuity shall be paid free of income tax is void by statute. Blair *v.* Allen, 1858; 21 D. 15. Rodger's Trs. *v.* Rodger, 1875; 2 R. 294. Mackie's Trs. *v.* Mackie, *ib.* 312. Kinloch's Trs. *v.* Kinloch, 1880; 7 R. 596.

(*c*) 1 Ersk. 1. § 59, 60. **Bartlet *v.* Viner,** Carthew, 252; 1 Ill. 47. Law *v.* Hodson, 11 East, 300; 2 Camp. 147; 10 R. R. 513. **Cannan *v.* Bryce,** 2 B. & Ald. 179; 22 R. R. 342. Foster *v.* Taylor, 5 B. & Ad. 887. De Begnis *v.* Armistead, 10 Bing. 110. Taylor *v.* Crowland Gas Co., 10 Ex. 293; 23 L. J. Ex. 294 (penalty on unqualified persons acting as conveyancers; see now 54 and 55 Vict. c. 39, § 44). Cope *v.* Rowlands, 2 M. & W. 149. Bensley *v.* Bignold, *infra*, § 36 (7). Chambers *v.* Manchr. and Milford Ry. Co., 33 L. J. Q. B. 268; 5 B. & S. 588. *Re* Cork and Youghal Ry. Co., 39 L. J. Ch. 277; L. R. 4 Ch. 748. Gordon *v.* Howden, 1843; 5 D. 698; rev. 1845, 4 Bell's App. 254; 12 Cl. & F. 237. Fraser *v.* Hill, 1852; 14 D. 335; rev. 1 Macq. 392 (see 16 D. 789). Swan *v.* Bank of Scotland, 1835; 2 S. & M'L. 67, 95. Glasg. City and D. Ry. Co. *v.* Mags. of Glasgow, 1884; 11 R. 1110.

(*d*) Atkinson *v.* Newcastle Waterworks Co., 2 Ex. D. 441; 46 L. J. Ex. 775 (questioning Couch *v.* Steel, 3 E. & B. 402; 23 L. J. Q. B. 121). **Wolverhampton Waterworks Co. *v.* Hawksford,** 28 L. J. C. P. 242; 6 C. B. N. S. 336; 1 Smith's L. C. 285. Tay Dist. Fishery Bd. *v.* Robertson, 1887; 15 R. 40. See Carruthers *v.* Cal. Ry. Co., 1853; 15 D. 591; 1854, 16 D. 425. Wilson *v.* Merry & Cunningham, 1868; 6 Macph. H. L. 84, 92; L. R. 1 Sc. App. 326 (*per* L. Chelmsford). Institute of Patent Agents *v.* Lockwood, 1893; 20 R. 319, 332. Kelly *v.* Glebe Sugar Co., 1893; 20 R. 833. Blamires *v.* L. & Y. Ry. Co., L. R. 8 Ex. 283; 42 L. J. Ex. 182. See below, § 548.

(*e*) See § 34, and below, § 548.

(1.) *Purchase of Heritage, while it is the subject of a depending lawsuit,* is forbidden to any member of the College of Justice, or any inferior Court, directly or indirectly; 'it subjects the buyer to deprivation, but' the contract is 'not' null (*a*). In construction this is extended to all matters in depending suits (*b*). But security for the costs may be taken on the subject of the lawsuit (*c*).

(*a*) The original text had it by mistake that the contract

is null. See Purves and Home, *infra*, and 2 Ersk. Inst. 3. § 16; Pr. 2. 3. § 6.

(*b*) 1594, c. 216. Sir G. M'Kenzie, Obs., James VI. Par. 14, c. 116. Mowat *v.* M'Lellan, 1625; M. 9496; 1 Ill. 48. Purves *v.* Keith, 1683; M. 9500. Home *v.* E. Home, 1713; M. 9502. Richardson *v.* Sinclair, 1635; M. 9496. E. Home *v.* Home, 1678; M. 9498.

(*c*) Forbes *v.* Blair, 1774; 5 B. Sup. 530.

(2.) *Pactum de quota litis*, or a bargain by an advocate or law agent to receive, in remuneration of his professional services, a share of the subject in contest, is unlawful at common law, and according to the spirit of the statute 1594 (*a*). The principle of the rule has been applied to an agreement by a country writer to employ an Edinburgh agent, and make advances of money, on condition of receiving a share of the profits (*b*). 'But now by statute agreements between law agents acting for the same client to share fees or profits are lawful (*c*).' It was even held an agreement to be discouraged in general (though in some cases allowable), for an agent to stipulate for remuneration only on success (*d*).

'An obligation by a client to pay to his agent a sum of money as a gift in addition to his ordinary business charges, or a gift by the client not unequivocally confirmed after the relation of agent and client has ceased, is ineffectual, and may be reduced (*e*). So, if a law agent or solicitor purchases or obtains a benefit from a client, the contract will, unless so confirmed, be set aside if it is connected with the business or matters to which the agent's employment extends, unless he discharges the burden of showing not only that the bargain is as good as could with due diligence have been obtained from any other purchaser, but also (apart from all questions of value and undue influence) that the client knew that he was the purchaser (*f*).'

(*a*) 1594, c. 216. 1 Stair, 10. § 8. Hume *v.* Nisbet, 1675; M. 9496; 1 Ill. 49. Ruthven *v.* Weir, 1680; M. 9499. M'Kenzie *v.* Forbes, 1774; 5 B. Sup. 528. Acts of Sed. p. 585. Glasford *v.* Morrison, 1823; 2 S. 372. Rucker *v.* Fischer, 1826; 4 S. 443. Johnston *v.* Rowe, 1831; 9 S. 364. Wood *v.* Downes, 18 Ves. 120. Simpson *v.* Lamb, 7 E. & B. 84; 26 L. J. Q. B. 121. See Pollock, Contr. 321. 330.

(*b*) **Gilfillan** *v.* **Henderson**, 1832; 10 S. 523; aff. 1833, 6 W. & S. 489. See Pattison, 1845; 18 Jur. 88.

(*c*) 36 and 37 Vict. c. 63, § 21.

(*d*) Clyne *v.* Swanson, 1830; 8 S. 391. Swanson *v.* Robertson, 1833; 11 S. 718. See Bolden *v.* Foggo, 1850; 12 D. 798. **Taylor** *v.* **Forbes**, 1853; 24 D. 19. Bell *v.* Ogilvie, 1863; 2 Macph. 336. Scotland *v.* Henry, 1865; 3 Macph. 1125. Moscrip *v.* O'Hara, 1880; 8 R. 360.

(*e*) **Anstruther** *v.* **Wilkie**, 1856; 18 D. 405. Logan's Trs. *v.* Reid, 1885; 12 R. 1094. O'Brien *v.* Lewis, 32 L. J. Ch. 569. Morgan *v.* Minett, 6 Ch. D. 638.

(*f*) Gourlay's Trs. *v.* Kerr, 1856; 19 D. 135. M'Pherson's Trs. *v.* Watt, 1877; 4 R. 601; rev. 5 R. H. L. 9; 3 App. Ca. 254. Cleland *v.* Morrison, 1878; 6 R. 156. Tyrrell *v.* Bk. of London, 10 H. L. Ca. 26; 31 L. J. Ch. 369. Lewis *v.* Hillman, 3 H. L. Ca. 607. Savery *v.* King, 5 H. L. Ca. 627; 25 L. J. Ch. 482. Pisani *v.* Att.-Gen. of Gibraltar, L. R. 5 P. C. 516. Masons' Hall Tavern Co. *v.* Nokes, 22 L. T. 503.

(3.) *Usury*, forbidden by early Scottish statutes, and by an Act in Queen Anne's reign, is the taking or contracting, in the loan of money, wares, or commodities, for more than the value of £5 for the forbearance of £100 for a year; or after that rate for a greater or lesser sum, or longer or shorter time. The contract 'was' annulled if usury 'were' taken, or if it 'were' stipulated (*a*); but the penalties 'were' incurred only by the actual taking of the usurious interest. Where there 'was' risk in the contract beyond that of insolvency, it legalised a greater rate of interest, as in bottomry (*b*). The annulling of the bond or contract 'did' not annihilate the debt, if it 'could' be proved otherwise (*c*). By statute it 'was' provided that in the hand of an indorsee for value, a bill, though given on a usurious bargain, 'should' not be null without notice of the usury (*d*); and that no bill of exchange or promissory note payable within twelve months from the date, or not having more than twelve months to run, 'should' be null on usury (*e*). 'The laws against usury are repealed by 17 and 18 Vict. c. 90.'

(*a*) 1597, c. 247; 1621, c. 28. 12 Anne, c. 16. 31 Eliz. c. 5. See the cases cited in former editions, and in 1 Ill. 50–56.

(*b*) See § 452.

(*c*) Gray *v.* Fowler, 1 H. Black. 460.

(*d*) 58 Geo. III. c. 93, and 5 and 6 Will. IV. c. 41.

(*e*) 3 and 4 Will. IV. c. 98, § 7, and 1 Vict. c. 80.

(4.) *Gaming, and Betting on the Game*, are forbidden both in Scotland and in England, to the effect of entitling the poor of the parish in Scotland to all winnings within twenty-four hours above 100 merks; and in both countries of annulling notes and other securities for gaming debts; entitling the loser of money above £10 at a sitting, or £20 within twenty-four hours, to recover it from the winner; and giving action to common informers for the winnings and triple value, one-half to himself and the other to the poor of the parish. But, by statute, bills, notes, and mortgages in the hands of purchasers for value shall not be void, but only held as for an illegal consideration, '*i.e.* "whenever such note, etc., shall be in the hands of a *bonâ fide* holder for value, and without notice, they shall be effectual" (*a*)'; and if on such instruments the granter or maker shall pay to the holder the money so secured, he shall be entitled to recover it as money paid to the original payee on an illegal consideration (*b*).

(*a*) Prof. Bell in 1 Ill. 488. So in Bills of Exch. Act (45 and 46 Vict. c. 61), § 29, 30.

(*b*) 1621, c. 14. 9 Anne, c. 14, § 1, 2. 13 Geo. II. c. 19. 18 Geo. II. c. 34 and 114. 5 and 6 Will. IV. c. 41; 1 Ill. 487. Neilson *v.* Bruce, 1740; M. 9507; 1 Ill. 56. Pringle *v.* Biggar, 1700; M. 9505. Stewart *v.* Hyslop, 1741; M. 9510. M'Coull *v.* Braidwood, 1767; M. 9518. Bruce *v.* Ross, 1787; M. 9523; aff. 3 Pat. 107. Wordsworth *v.* Pettigrew, 1799; M. 9524. Ferrier *v.* Graham's Trs., 1828; 6 S. 818; 5 Mur. 92. Hamilton *v.* Russel, 1832; 10 S. 549. Edwards *v.* Dick, 4 B. & Ald. 212; and other English cases in 1 Ill. 57-58. See below, § 37 *fin.*, § 325, and cases there cited. The Act 1621 is not in desuetude. Maxwell *v.* Blair, 1774; M. 9522. O'Connell *v.* Russel, 1864; 3 Macph. 89. See as to penalties on betting houses and advertisements, 16 and 17 Vict. c. 119; 37 and 38 Vict. c. 15.

(5.) *Sale of Offices* of public trust, and those connected with the receipt of the revenue or administration of justice, or the public departments of Government at home or in the colonies, is prohibited by statutes grounded on the policy of the common law. This extends to the right of appointing deputies (*a*).

(*a*) 5 and 6 Edw. VI. c. 16. 49 Geo. III. c. 126. 2 Blackst. 36. 2 Stephen's Com. 642. 3 Kent's Com. 454. See Young *v.* Thomson, 1759; M. 9525. Dalrymple *v.* Shaw, 1786; M. 9531; Hailes, 989. Dove *v.* Thomson, Feb. 16, 1811; F. C. Haldane *v.* De Maria, March 6, 1812; F. C. Gardiner *v.* Grant, 1835; 13 S. 664. Tyndall Bruce *v.* Grant, 1839; 1 D. 583. See Mason *v.* Wilson, 1844; 7 D. 160. Ord *v.* Hill, 1847; 9 D. 118. Graeme *v.* Wroughton, 11 Ex. 146; 24 L. J. Ex. 265. Eicke *v.* Jones, 11 C. B. N. S. 631. Eyre *v.* Forbes, 12 C. B. N. S. 191. Sterry *v.* Clifton, 9 C. B. 110. Blackford *v.* Preston, 8 T. R. 89; 1 Ill. 62. Benjamin on Sales, 529 sqq.

(6.) *Liquor Act.*—No one may sue for the price of spirituous liquors (*a*) unless the debt shall have been *bonâ fide* contracted to the amount of twenty shillings at one time, 'or have been contracted for spirituous liquors sold to be consumed elsewhere than on the premises where sold, and delivered at the residence of the purchaser in quantities not less than a reputed quart at once (*b*). The statement that' this does not apply to liquor sold for resale 'is negatived by an authoritative English case (*c*). The true construction of the statute appears to make all sales of spirits by retail on credit illegal, so that a creditor receiving an indefinite payment to account of a claim consisting partly of items falling within the Act, cannot appropriate it to them so as to preserve entire his right of action for the remainder (*d*); and that a bill granted for an account part of which is for tippling is wholly vitiated (*e*). It seems that the Act does not apply to cases where spirits are supplied to guests lodging in the inn (*f*).'

(*a*) It was held that this enactment does not apply to wine. Alexander *v.* Boyd, 1824; 2 S. 788 f. n. But it includes grog, or spirits mixed with water. Scott *v.* Gillmore, 3 Taunt. 226; 12 R. R. 641.

(*b*) 24 Geo. II. c. 40. Burnyeat *v.* Hutchinson, 5 B. & Ald. 241; 24 R. R. 325; 1 Ill. 58. Alexander & Co. *v.* Boyd, 1824; 2 S. 788 f. n. 25 and 26 Vict. c. 38.

(*c*) Hughes *v.* Doane, 1 Q. B. 294; 10 L. J. Q. B. 65.

(*d*) Johnston *v.* Law, 1843; 5 D. 1372. Maitland *v.* Rattray, 1848; 11 D. 71. See Wright *v.* Laing, 3 B. & C. 165. A different view prevails in England, founded on a faulty construction of the Act. Philpott *v.* Jones, 2 Ad. & E. 41. Cruickshanks *v.* Rose, 5 C. & P. 19. Pollock on Contr. 654. Benjamin on Sales, 529, 748.

(*e*) Maitland *v.* Rattray, *cit.* Scott *v.* Gillmore, *cit.* Gaitskill *v.* Greathead, 1 Dow. & R. 359. Dawson *v.* Remnant, 6 Esp. 24.

(*f*) Procter *v.* Nicolson, 7 C. & P. 67. Guthrie *v.* Ireland, 1891; 28 S. L. R. 641.

(7.) *The Printer's Name and Residence* is by statute required, under high penalties, on the first and last leaf of each book or paper which he prints; and he will not be allowed to sue for the price of printing if he neglect these orders (*a*).

(*a*) 39 Geo. III. c. 79, § 27. Bensley *v.* Bignold, 5 B. & Ald. 335; 1 Ill. 58. See 2 and 3 Vict. c. 12, and 32 and 33 Vict. c. 24, sched. 2. See Addison, Contr. 101, 9th ed.

(8.) 'Sales or other contracts made according to illegal weights or measures (*a*); sales by lottery, and contracts regarding lotteries (*b*); and contracts for the payment of wages of artisans of certain kinds otherwise than in money (*c*), are void. Coal may be sold by weight only, unless by written consent it is sold by boatload, or by waggons or tubs from the colliery into the buyer's works (*d*). No one can recover charges for medical or surgical attendance or advice unless he is registered as a medical practitioner (*e*); nor for legal proceedings in a court of law unless he is at the time of the proceedings duly certificated (*f*).'

(*a*) Below, § 91 (3).

(*b*) 10 Will. III. c. 23. 9 Anne, c. 6, § 56. 12 Geo. II. c. 28. 42 Geo. III. c. 119. 4 Geo. IV. c. 60. 6 and 7 Will. IV. c. 66 (foreign lotteries). See M'Allister *v.* Douglas, 1878; 5 R. Just. 30. Sykes *v.* Beadon, 11 Ch. D. 170; 48 L. J. Ch. 522. Christison *v.* M'Bride, 1881; 9 R. 34. 9 and 10 Vict. c. 48 (exemption for art unions).

(*c*) Below, § 192.

(*d*) 52 and 53 Vict. c. 21, § 20, 31.

(*e*) 21 and 22 Vict. c. 90, § 32; 49 and 50 Vict. c. 48, etc.

(*f*) See Begg on Law Agents, 51; 54 and 55 Vict. c. 39, § 43.

37. Contracts void at Common Law.—Obligations or Contracts immoral, or *contra bonos mores*, are ineffectual (*a*). Such are: An 'obligation amounting to an' incentive or encouragement to crime, 'or a bribe to procure a pardon or stifle a prosecution' (*b*); but with us the sale of an expected inheritance is not so considered; though it was so in the Roman law (*c*): The price of prostitution 'or illicit intercourse,' from which, however, is to be distinguished a compensation for injury already sustained (*d*): Contracts for indecent or mischievous purposes or considerations (*e*), or prejudicial or offensive to the public or to third parties (*f*), or inconsistent with public law or arrangements (*g*), are invalid, and ground no action.

And wagers and *sponsiones ludicræ* (*h*) 'will not be enforced, on the ground that "courts of justice were instituted to enforce the rights of parties arising from serious transactions, and can pay no regard to *sponsiones ludicræ*" (*i*). But this rule does not extend so far as to prevent the Court from adjudicating on any collateral or connected matter of contract or property not involving the determination of a mere question of sport (*k*). A bargain for the purchase or sale of shares or goods, under which neither party has an action to compel the other to deliver or accept them, but which is in fact a mere agreement to pay the differences according to the rise or fall of the market, is not enforceable between the parties, and it is a jury question whether such a contract is a mere betting contract (*l*). But a broker who pays for another according to custom or by request the amount of such differences, and a turf commission agent who pays for an employer money lost on bets, have been held entitled to recover upon contracts really made for the principal (*m*). It is always necessary for a broker suing his principal for monies expended on such contracts or commission to prove that he has made contracts which his principal can enforce.'

(*a*) 1 Stair, 10. § 8. More's Notes, lxii. 3 Ersk. 1. § 10. Toullier, tom. 6, p. 123. *Sup.* § 35.

(*b*) Stewart *v.* E. Galloway, 1752; M. 9466; 1 Ill. 59. Grant *v.* Davidson, 1786; M. 9571; Hailes, 100. *Infra*, § 41. Kerr *v.* Leeman, 6 Q. B. 108. Williams *v.* Bayley, L. R. 1 H. L. 200; 1 Sm. L. C. 364.

(*c*) 1 Stair, 10. § 8. Aikenhead *v.* Bothwell, 1630; M. 9491. Ragg *v.* Brown, 1708; M. 9492. Cook *v.* Field, 15 Q. B. 460; 19 L. J. Q. B. 441.

(*d*) Durham *v.* Blackwood, 1622; M. 9469; 1 Ill. 59. Ross *v.* Robertson, 1642; M. 9470. Sir W. Hamilton *v.* De Gares, 1765; M. 9471. See Webster *v.* Webster's Tr., *infra.* D. of Hamilton *v.* Waring, March 21, 1816; F. C.; 2 Bligh, 197; 6 Pat. 644. Marchs. of Annandale *v.* Harris, 2 Peere W. 432. Johnstone *v.* M'Kenzie's Trs., 1835; 14 S. 106; 3 Ill. 103. Priest *v.* Parrot, 2 Ves. jun. 160. Hamilton *v.* Main, 1823; 2 S. 356. Walker *v.* Perkins, 3 Burr. 1568. Hill *v.* Spencer, 2 Amb. 641; 1 Ill. 61. Gibson *v.* Dickie, 3 M. & S. 463. Nye *v.* Moseley, 6 B. & C. 133. Friend *v.* Harrison, 2 C. & P. 534. Young *v.* Johnson & Wright, 1880; 7 R. 760. It has been contended that there is a sub-exception, restoring the general rule, where the obligee is a prostitute, or is aware of the connection being adulterous. It was so held in Scotland in Durham's case, and in England in Priest's. But this has been denied in Nye's case. In England the rule that a past executed consideration is no consideration, has been established since the cases cited were decided, and as such contracts not under seal are void on that ground, questions of character and history are now immaterial. Pollock on Contr. 288. See on the whole subject, and as to contracts upon marriage with a deceased wife's sister, **Ayerst** *v.* **Jenkins**, L. R. 16 Eq. 275; 42 L. J. Ch. 690. Pawson *v.* Brown, 49 L. J. Ch. 193; 13 Ch. D. 202. Hall *v.* Palmer, 3 Hare, 532. Williams *v.* Bullmore, 33 L. J. Ch. 462. Webster *v.* Webster's Tr., 1886; 14 R. 90.

(*e*) Du Bost *v.* Beresford, 2 Camp. 511. Poplett *v.* Stockdale, Ry. & M. 337. Smith *v.* White, 35 L. J. Ch. 454; L. R. 1 Eq. 626 (lease of house to be used as a brothel). Pearce *v.* Brooks, 35 L. J. Ex. 134; L. R. 1 Ex. 213 (brougham jobbed to a harlot for purposes of "display").

(*f*) Da Costa *v.* Jones, Cowper, 729. Gilbert & Sykes, 16 East, 150. Such are, *e.g.*, agreements in which a creditor in fraud of an agreement to accept a composition stipulates for a preference to himself. 2 Bell's Com. 370, 395, 399 (M'L.'s ed.). 19 and 20 Vict. c. 79, § 150. Pendreigh's Tr. *v.* M'Laren, 1869; 8 Macph. 64; rev. 1871, 9 Macph. H. L. 49. Thomas *v.* Sandeman, 1872; 11 Macph. 81. Mallalieu *v.* Hodson, 16 Q. B. 689; 20 L. J. Q. B. 339. Dauglish *v.* Tenant, 36 L. J. Q. B. 10; L. R. 2 Q. B. 49. See above, § 35 *fin.*; also, dealings by an agent or partner on his own account in the matter of his agency, *infra*, § 222.

(*g*) Blackford *v.* Preston, 8 T. R. 89. Glen *v.* Dundas, 1822; 1 S. 222. Coppock *v.* Bower, 4 M. & W. 361. Hoggan *v.* Wardlaw, 1735; 1 Pat. 148. See below, § 41, and Egerton *v.* E. Brownlow, 4 H. L. Ca. 1, 235; 18 E. Jur. 71; 23 L. J. Ch. 328.

(*h*) Bruce *v.* Ross, 1787; Hailes, 1816; aff. 3 Pat. 107. See 2 T. R. 616, and 3 T. R. 697. Wordsworth *v.* Pettigrew, 1799; M. 9254. See above, § 36 (4). Gordon *v.* Campbell, 1804; M. *Pact. Ill.* 3.

(*i*) Wordsworth, *cit.* Bruce, *cit.* It seems that the statute 8 and 9 Vict. c. 109, § 18, which enacts a similar rule for England, does not extend to Scotland. See Foulds, O'Connell, Calder, *citt. infra.* See also 55 Vict. c. 9 (Gaming Act, 1892), which makes it desirable that the question whether the earlier Act applies in Scotland should be decided.

(*k*) Graham *v.* Pollok, 1848; 10 D. 646. Calder *v.* Stevens, 1871; 9 Macph. 1074. O'Connell *v.* Russell, 1864; 3 Macph. 89. See Hampden *v.* Walsh, 45 L. J. Q. B. 238; L. R. 1 Q. B. D. 183. Diggle *v.* Higgs, 46 L. J. Ex. 721; L. R. 2 Ex. D. 422. It has been held that money unfairly won at cards cannot be recovered back. Paterson *v.* Macqueen, 1866; 4 Macph. 602. But this case does not absolutely exclude all remedy for fraud and circumvention by means of gambling.

(*l*) Grizewood *v.* Blane, 11 C. B. 538. Rourke *v.* Short, 25 L. J. Q. B. 196; 5 E. & B. 504. Newton *v.* Cribbes, 1884; 11 R. 554. Heimann *v.* Hardie & Co., 1885; 12 R. 406. Shaw *v.* Cal. Ry. Co., 1890; 17 R. 466. Univ. Stock Exch. Co. *v.* Howat, 1891; 19 R. 128. If there be an enforceable obligation to take and give delivery, the fact that both parties "expected" the transaction to be "financed" by a resale does not avoid it. Cases cited. See Benjamin on Sales, 82, 526.

(*m*) Foulds *v.* Thomson, 1857; 19 D. 803. Risk *v.* Auld & Guild, 1881; 8 R. 729. Rosewarne *v.* Billing, 15 C. B. N. S. 316; 33 L. J. C. P. 55. Thacker *v.* Hardy, 4 Q. B. D. 685; 48 L. J. Q. B. 289. Read *v.* Anderson, 13 Q. B. D. 779. Gillies *v.* M'Lean, 1885; 13 R. 12. Maffett *v.* Stewart, 1887; 14 R. 506. Knight & Co. *v.* Stott, 1892; 19 R. 959. Conversely, such a broker or agent may be sued for monies had and received for his principal on such transactions. Bridger *v.* Savage, 15 Q. B. D. 363. As to the reasonableness of a custom, see Perry *v.* Barnet, 15 Q. B. D. 388 (custom of Stock Exch. to disregard Leeman's Act), and below, § 219.

38. Contracts inconsistent with Public Policy are void (*a*).—Of these the following are remarkable:—

(*a*) As to the question whether contracts contrary to public policy in the view of the Court are void, although not violating any known rule of law, see 1 Smith's L. C. 377. Farrar *v.* Close, L. R. 4 Q. B. 602; 38 L. J. Mag. Ca. 132; esp. *per* Hannen, J. Mogul Co. *v.* M'Gregor, Gow, & Co., 1892; A. C. 25. Nordenfelt *v.* Maxim-Nordenfelt Guns, etc., Co., 1894; A. C. 535, 554 (*per* L. Watson) (rules of policy vary with changes of times). Sir W. Erle, Law relating to Trade Unions (1869).

39. (1.) *Contracts against the Policy of the Domestic Relations.*—A bond imposing a restraint on marriage (not to marry at all, or not to marry a particular person (*a*)) is ineffectual. And the exception contended for, where the person imposing it has an interest in the prohibition, seems not to be law; the party being left to make effectual, judicially or otherwise, any right existing independently of the forfeiture (*b*). When an engagement to marry is fortified by a bond in case of marrying another, the engagement may ground an action of damages for breach of promise; but no action will lie on the bond on account of marrying another (*c*). 'So, while a voluntary contract of separation between spouses is not now regarded as null, but is only revocable (*d*), it receives effect only upon the ground that immediate separation, a state of things which the law discourages, has become inevitable; and accordingly, it seems that a contract providing for future separation is invalid (*e*), and even that a contract of separation once avoided by reconciliation will not revive on a second *de facto* separation, and a stipulation to that effect is void (*f*).' Marriage brocage bonds, or obligations to give a reward for influence exerted for bringing about a marriage, are void from their pernicious tendency (*g*).

(*a*) But see M'Laren on Wills, i. 601. Notes to Scott *v.* Tyler in 2 White & Tud. L. C.

(*b*) Key *v.* Bradshaw, 2 Vern. 105; 1 Ill. 63. Baker *v.* White, 2 Vern. 215. Cock *v.* Richards, 10 Ves. 429. See below as to Impossible Conditions, § 49; Conditions annexed to Settlements, § 1785; and to Legacies, § 1883.

(*c*) Lowe *v.* Peers, 4 Bur. 2225. Gibson *v.* Dickie, 3 M. & S. 463; 1 Ill. 64. See Calder *v.* Provan, 1743; Elch. *Bill*, 25; M. 9511; 1 Pat. 359.

(*d*) See below, § 1541, 1544.

(*e*) Fraser, H. & W. 911. M. Westmeath *v.* Mss. Westmeath, 1 Dow & C. 519. Cartwright *v.* Cartwright, 3 De G. M. & G. 982; 22 L. J. Ch. 841. Anonymous, 3 Kay & J. 382.

(*f*) Hindley *v.* Westmeath, 6 B. & C. 200; see 5 Bligh N. S. 339, 395; 30 R. R. 290.

(*g*) 2 Comyn's Digest, 631. Campbell *v.* Burns & Stewart, 1678; M. 9505. E. of Buchan *v.* Cochran, 1698; M. 9507. Thomson *v.* M'Kail, 1770; M. 9519; Hailes, 339; 5 B. Sup. 532. Stribblehill *v.* Brett, 2 Vern. 406. Keat *v.* Allen, 2 Vern. 588. D. of Hamilton *v.* Mohun, 2 Vern. 652. Cock *v.* Richards, 10 Ves. 429; 8 R. R. 23. Smith *v.* Aikwell, 3 Atk. 567. Cole *v.* Gibson, 1 Ves. 583.

40. (2.) *Obligations in Restraint of the Liberty of the Person*, if absolute and unqualified (or virtually so), are void (*a*). But contracts for service during a certain time (*b*), or obligations in restriction of the exercise of trade to particular districts, and for protection by reasonable restraint of a fair interest, are good (*c*): it has even been held that a restraint on trade for the lifetime of the parties is binding (*d*). 'It is laid down in many cases, and is the general rule, that a contract not to carry on any trade or not to carry on a particular trade, if it be unlimited in regard to time and space, or be without consideration, is invalid (*e*); but it is now settled that there is merely a presumption that unlimited restrictions are unreasonable and therefore invalid, which may be rebutted, all the circumstances of each case being considered; and the general principle is that covenants in restraint of trade are invalid, "unless they are natural and not unreasonable for the protection of the parties in dealing with the particular trade or business" (*f*).

'Contracts of association for determining the conditions of employment in any trade (*i.e.* rules of trade unions) are held to be illegal at common law, in the sense that they are void and incapable of being enforced by courts of law (*g*); and while it is now enacted by the Trade Union Act, 1871, that "the purposes of any trade union shall not, by reason merely that they are in restraint of trade, be deemed to be unlawful, so as to render" its members "liable to criminal prosecution for conspiracy or otherwise," or "so as to render void or voidable any agreement or trust" (*h*); yet, as it is provided that nothing in the Act shall enable any Court to enforce the ordinary rules and agreements of trade unions (*i*), and as such associations are unlawful at common law, it seems that no condition or stipulation, however laudable in itself, which forms one of the terms of membership of a trade union, can be directly (*k*) enforced in a court of law, except those expressly permitted by the Trade Union Act, 1871 (*l*). Where, however, it is not the general object of the society to fetter the course of trade, though certain rules have such a tendency, the latter only are invalid and the others may be enforced (*m*).'

(*a*) 1 Ersk. 7. § 62. Allan *v.* Skene, 1728; M. 9454; 1 Ill. 64. Wedderburn *v.* Monorgan, 1612; M. 9453. Ld. of Caprington *v.* Geddew, 1632; M. 9454. Reid *v.* Scott, 1687; M. 9505. Younge *v.* Timmins, 1 Tyrwh. 226; 1 C. & J. 331; and cases in 1 Smith's L. C. 402 sqq.

(*b*) As to the validity of contracts to serve for life, see below, § 174 (*i*).

(*c*) **Stalker** *v.* **Carmichael**, 1735; M. 9455. **Mitchell** *v.* **Reynolds**, 1 P. W. 181; 1 Sm. L. C. 391. Chesman *v.* Nainby, 2 Strange, 739; 1 Bro. Parl. Ca. 234. Davis *v.* Masson, 5 T. R. 118. Homer *v.* Ashford, 3 Bing. 322. Horner *v.* Graves, 7 Bing. 735. Curtis *v.* Sandison, 1831; 10 S. 72. Watson *v.* Neuffert, 1863; 1 Macph. 1110. M'Intyre *v.* M'Raild, 1866; 4 Macph. 571. Pilkington *v.* Scott, 15 M. & W. 657. Harms *v.* Parsons, 32 L. J. Ch. 247; 32 Beav. 328. Jones *v.* Lees, 1 H. & N. 189. Mallan *v.* May, 14 L. J. Ex. 48; 11 M. & W. 653. Mumford *v.* Gething, 7 C. B. N. S. 305. Leather Cloth Co. *v.* Lorsont, L. R. 9 Eq. 345; 39 L. J. Ch. 86. Allsop *v.* Wheatcroft, 42 L. J. Ch. 12; L. R. 15 Eq. 64. In the absence of any prescribed mode of measuring the distance in such a stipulation, it is to be measured as the crow flies. Moufflet *v.* Cole, 41 L. J. Ex. 28; 42 *ib.* 8; L. R. 7 Ex. 70; *ib.* 8 Ex. 32.

(*d*) Hitchcock *v.* Coker, 6 Ad. & El. 438; 3 Ill. 103.

(*e*) Watson *v.* Neuffert, and cases cited in note (*c*). The Court does not inquire into the sufficiency of the consideration. Hitchcock, *cit.* Davies, *infra.*

(*f*) **Nordenfelt** *v.* **Maxim Nordenfelt Guns, etc., Co.**, 1894; A. C. 535. Leather Cloth Co. *v.* Lorsont, L.R. 9 Eq. 345; 39 L. J. Ch. 86. Printing and Numerical Co. *v.* Sampson, L. R. 19 Eq. 462; 44 L. J. Ch. 705. Rousillon *v.* Rousillon, 14 Ch. D. 351; 49 L. J. Ch. 338. Collins *v.* Locke, L. R. 4 App. Ca. 674; 48 L. J. P. C. 38. Davies *v.* Davies, 36 Ch. D. 359.

(*g*) Hilton *v.* Eckersley, 6 E. & B. 47; 24 L. J. Q. B. 359. Hornby *v.* Close, L. R. 2 Q. B. 153; 36 L. J. Mag. Ca. 43. Farrar *v.* Close, L. R. 4 Q. B. 602; 38 L. J. Mag. Ca. 132. Mineral Water, etc., Protection Soc. *v.* Booth, 36 Ch. D. 465. Barr *v.* Carr, 1766; M. 9564. P. F. *v.* Woolcombers in Aberdeen, 1762; M. 1961. Tailors of Edinr. v. Journeymen, 1762; M. 7862. See Erle on Trade Unions. Wright's Law of Criminal Conspiracies.

(*h*) 34 and 35 Vict. c. 31, § 2, 3.

(*i*) *Ib.* § 4.

(*k*) Wolfe *v.* Mathews, 21 Ch. D. 194; 51 L. J. Ch. 833.

(*l*) 34 and 35 Vict. c. 31, § 5. M'Kernan *v.* United Operative Masons, 1874; 1 R. 453. Shanks *v.* do., 1874; 1 R. 823. Rigby *v.* Connol, 14 Ch. D. 482; 49 L. J. Ch. 328. Duke *v.* Littleboy, 49 L. J. Ch. 802. Maclean *v.* Pickett, 1895; 11 Sh. Ct. Rep. 191. See conflicting decisions in England and Scotland as to competency of interdict, Amalg. Ry. Servts. *v.* Motherwell Branch, 1880; 7 R. 867; and Duke *v.* Littleboy, *cit.*

(*m*) Collins *v.* Locke, L. R. 4 App. Ca. 674; 48 L. J. P. C. 38. Swaine *v.* Wilson, 24 Q. B. D. 252.

41. (3.) *Contracts tending to disturb Public Arrangements, or to impede the course of Justice*, are void,—as when a parochial schoolmaster agreed to hold his office at pleasure (*a*), 'or a minister engages not to ask a second augmentation of his stipend (*b*)'; or simoniacal pactions (*c*); 'contracts' for restraining witnesses from giving testimony, 'or for compromising an indictment or prosecution for matters which are of public concern' (*d*); 'for forbearing to expose adultery or sue for divorce (*e*)'; for preventing a bankrupt from making a full disclosure (*f*); for compromising felony, or procuring pardon (*g*); for securing indemnification to a magistrate or jailer against the escape of a prisoner (*h*); for defeating the laws against slavery (*i*).

(*a*) Duff *v.* Grant, 1799; M. 9576; 1 Ill. 66. Gardner *v.* Grant, 1835; 13 S. 664; 3 Ill. 103. See Ramsay *v.* Brewster, 1859; 21 D. 1367 (bursary—condition inconsistent with terms of foundation).

(*b*) E. of Kellie *v.* Brodie, 1803; M. 15,710.

(*c*) Steven *v.* Lyall, 1759; M. 9578; 1 Ill. 66. Maxwell *v.* E. Galloway, 1775; M. 9580.

(*d*) Pool *v.* Bousfield, 1 Camp. 55; 10 R. R. 633. Keir *v.* Leeman, 6 Q. B. 108; 9 Q. B. 371; 15 L. J. Q. B. 360. Windhill Local Bd. *v.* Vint, 45 Ch. D. 351.

(*e*) Gipps *v.* Hume, 2 J. & H. 517; 31 L. J. Ch. 37. Brown *v.* Brine, 1 Ex. D. 5; 45 L. J. Ex. 129.

(*f*) Nerot *v.* Wallace, 3 T. R. 17.

(*g*) Stewart *v.* E. of Galloway, 1752; M. 9465; 1 Ill. 59; (correct the Faculty Report by that of the Select Decisions). Grant *v.* Davidson, 1786; M. 9571. Collins *v.* Blantern, 2 Wils. 349; 1 Sm. L. C. 355. M'Leod *v.* Fraser, 1758; M. 9563. Lee *v.* Watson's Exrs., 1795; Bell's Ca. 176. Kennedy *v.* Cameron, 1823; 2 S. 192. See Wallace *v.* Hardacre, 1 Camp. 44; 10 R. R. 629. Edgecombe *v.* Rood, 5 East, 294; 7 R. R. 700. Keir *v.* Leeman, *cit.*, and cases in § 37 (*b*).

(*h*) Shoolbred *v.* Osborn, 1789; M. 9468. *Sed quære?* 1 Ill. 67. See 2 and 3 Vict. c. 42; and Lamb *v.* Mags. of Jedburgh, 1865; 3 Macph. 1105.

(*i*) Gibson *v.* Stewart, 1828; 6 S. 733, and 12 S. 683; aff. 1 Rob. 260; see 1835, 14 S. 166; 1 Ill. 69; 3 Ill. 103. See Santos *v.* Illidge, 8 C. B. N. S. 861; 29 L. J. C. P. 348, a questionable decision, affirming that a British Court may enforce a contract by a British subject for the sale of slaves in Brazil, where slavery was lawful. (Comp. Guthrie's Savigny, 85. Pollock, Contracts, 372. Tudor's L. C. 639. Westlake, 239. Foote's Pr. Int. Law, 294.) Payments made or promised in consideration of withdrawing opposition to private bills in Parliament are not illegal. Simpson *v.* Ld. Howden, 10 A. & E. 793; 9 Cl. & F. 61. Scottish N.-E. Ry. Co. *v.* Stewart, 1859; 3 Macq. 382. Taylor *v.* Chichester, etc., Ry. Co., 36 L. J. Ex. 201; 39 L. J. Ex. 217 (H. of L.); L. R. 2 Ex. 356.

42. (4.) *Contracts for defeating the Revenue Laws* are void, and action is denied, according to the maxim, "Potior est conditio possidentis vel defendentis" (*a*). This rule holds in contracts for *smuggling*, action being denied if the party who brings the action is aware of the design to defraud the revenue: as, for example, when he is a native of this country (*b*); or when, although a foreigner, he engages for or knows of the goods being packed in the way necessary to evade the revenue laws; or is participant in preparing false papers; or active in planning, forwarding, or giving aid in the scheme of evasion; or in actually landing the goods in this country (*c*). The same rule applies to contracts *relative to contraband goods*, which are known to be or purchased *as* contraband, being either absolutely prohibited or manifestly smuggled with the duty unpaid (*d*). But the rule does not hold where the goods are only *sold* abroad (*e*), or where they have been *bought* fairly in the market of this country (*f*).

(*a*) 3 Ersk. 3. § 3. Story's Conflict of Laws, § 246–259. 6 Geo. IV. c. 108; 3 and 4 Will. IV. c. 53; 4 and 5 Will. IV. c. 13, for the prevention of smuggling. 8 and 9 Vict. c. 87; 13 and 14 Vict. c. 95; 23 and 24 Vict. c. 114; 39 and 40 Vict. c. 36, etc.; 44 and 45 Vict. c. 3, § 11. Russel *v.* Liston's Trs., 1844; 6 D. 1138. Greig *v.* Conacher, 1876; 4 R. 187.

(*b*) M'Master *v.* Forsyth, 1775; 5 B. Sup. 530; 1 Ill. 67. Duncan *v.* Thomson, 1776; M. 9546; *Pact. Ill.* Apx. 1; 5 B. Sup. 531; Hailes, 683. Malcolm *v.* Morgan, 1780; 5 B. Sup. 583; Hailes, 859. Mitchell *v.* Morgan, 1780; 5 B. Sup. 533; Hailes, 859. Cantley *v.* Robertson, 1790; M. 9550; Hailes, 1077. Young & Co. *v.* Imlach, 1790; M. 9553.

(*c*) Nisbet's Crs. *v.* Robertson, 1791; M. 9554; Bell's Ca. 349. Cullen & Co. *v.* Phillips, 1793; M. 9554. Reid & Parkinson *v.* Macdonald, 1793; M. 9555. Stoddart *v.* M'Queen, 1779; 5 B. Sup. 533.

(*d*) Scougall *v.* Gilchrist, 1736; M. 9536; Elch. *Pact. Ill.* 7. Cockburn *v.* Grant, 1741; M. 9539; 5 B. Sup. 714. M'Lure & M'Cree *v.* Paterson, 1775 and 1779; 5 B. Sup. 532; M. 9546; Hailes, 829. Duncan, *sup.* (*b*). Gibson *v.* Stewart, 1828; 6 S. 733 (*sup.* § 41 (*i*)). Brown *v.* Limond, 1791; Hume, 672.

(*e*) Holman *v.* Johnston, Cowper, 341; 1 Ill. 69. Biggs *v.* Lawrence, 3 T. R. 454; 1 R. R. 740. Clugas *v.* Penaluna, 4 T. R. 466. Maxwell *v.* Reid, 5 T. R. 599. Hodgson *v.* Temple, 5 Taunt. 181. Isaacson *v.* Wiseman, 1806; Hume, 714. See Tudor's L. C. 634.

(*f*) Wilkie *v.* M'Neil, 1740; M. 9538; Elch. *Pact. Ill.* 11; 5 B. Sup. 217; 1 Ill. 67. M'Lean *v.* Sword, 1780; M. 9549.

43. (5.) *Contracts inconsistent with the national War Policy* are void (*a*); for war is an instrument of national justice under the direction of Government, and is not to be interfered with by individuals (*b*). There is no war for arms, and peace for commerce; and the hands of the enemy are not to be strengthened. Therefore the subjects or citizens of the belligerent States are enemies, and cannot lawfully trade with each other. When war intervenes, payment of debt 'and performance of contracts' due by the subjects of the one State to those of the other cannot be exacted during hostilities; but by the practice and public law of Europe the debt is not forfeited, payment being only suspended, and the debt 'or contract' reviving on the termination of hostilities (*c*); 'unless the nature and objects of the contract be inconsistent with suspension, when the contract is dissolved and the parties absolved from further performance (*d*).'

There are two exceptions to the general rule of non-intercourse during war: *First*, Neutrals may trade with either belligerent; and, indirectly, even between the belligerents (*e*). But this neutral trade is liable to these interruptions:—The right of searching private neutral merchant vessels during war to detect any breach of neutrality (*f*): the necessity of being furnished with neutral documents, register, passport, sea-letter, muster-roll, log-book, charter-party, invoice, and bill of lading—the want of which will strongly infer a breach of neutrality; and, much more, the destruction of papers (*g*): the prohibition of contraband of war—as ammunition, arms, artillery, timber for ships, naval stores, tar, pitch, hemp, sail-cloth; and also provisions going to a besieged port or country, or in circumstances indicating aid to hostilities—as to a naval and military, not a mercantile port (*h*): interruption by blockade, by which is meant an actual existing siege or blocking up of a city, port, or coast, known and enforced by a present and effectual force (*i*), although by accident or storm the blockading power may be removed for a time (*k*). *Second*, Licences by authority of Government may open, to the persons to whom they are granted, the whole or certain parts of the prohibited trade, so far as the Government which grants it is concerned; but the use of this privilege to trade with the enemy is an act of hostility (*l*). Licence has of late years been freely granted, and liberally construed (*m*).

(*a*) 1 Bell's Com. 303. And see on the whole subject, the Reports of Lord Stowell's Judgments in Admiralty, by Robinson, 1798–1808. Edwards, 1808–1811. Dodson, 1811–1822. Horne on Captures. Baring on Orders in Council. Wheaton's Digest of Law of Maritime Captures and Prizes. Dr. Phillimore on Licences. And below, of Prizes and Captures, § 1295 et seq. Tudor's L. C. 867 sqq.

(*b*) 2 Stair, 2. § 10 et seq. 3 Vattel, 5. § 70.

(*c*) 3 Vattel, 7. In America, however, the severe rule of an immediate confiscation of property and of debts on the breaking out of a war has been judicially declared, after very learned discussion, and by two judges whose names are among the highest of judicial authorities, Marshall and Story; leaving the hardship to be relieved by the discretionary act of Congress. Brown *v.* United States, 8 Cranch, 10. Ware *v.* Hylton, 3 Dallas, 199. See also 1 Kent, Com. 55 et seq. Potts *v.* Bell, 8 T. R. 548; 5 R. R. 452.

Clementson *v.* Blessig, 11 Ex. 135. *Ex p.* Boussmaker, 13 Ves. 71; 9 R. R. 142.

(*d*) Esposito *v.* Bowden, 7 E. & B. 763; 27 L. J. Q. B. 17.

(*e*) 3 Vattel, 4. § 63. 1 Emerigon, 567. *Ex p.* Chavasse, 4 De G. J. & S. 655. By the Treaty of Paris, April 1856, the neutral flag covers enemy's goods, with the exception of contraband of war; and neutral goods, with the same exception, although under the enemy's flag, are not liable to capture.

(*f*) The Maria, 1 Rob. 287. Tudor's L. C. 889. The Mariana Flora (American), 11 Wheaton's Rep. 42. 1 Kent, Com. 153.

(*g*) Bernardi *v.* Matheaux, Dougl. 581. The Hunter, 1 Dods. Adm. 480. The Pizarro, 2 Wheat. 277 (American).

(*h*) 2 Valin, 264. Pothier, Tr. de Propriété, § 9. 3 Vattel, 7. § 112. The Jonge Margaretha, 1 Rob. Adm. Rep. 189. The Commerce (American), 1 Wheaton, 382. Tudor's L. C. 981 sqq. Seymour *v.* London and Prov. M. I. Co., 41 L. J. C. P. 193.

(*i*) The Mercurius, 1 Rob. Ad. Rep. 80. The Betsy, *ib.* 93. The Stert, 4 Rob. 65. Tudor's L. C. 1013 sqq. The Franciska, Spinks, 115; 10 Moore, 46. The Circassian, 2 Wall. 150, and other American cases.

(*k*) The Frederick Molke, 1 Rob. 86. The Hoffnung, 6 Rob. 112. Vos & Graves *v.* Un. Ins. Co., 2 Johns. 187. Radcliffe *v.* Un. Ins. Co., 7 Johns. 53.

(*l*) The Elizabeth, 5 Rob. 2. The Julia (American), 8 Cranch, 181. The Caledonia (American), 4 Wheaton, 100. See Tudor's L. C. 921 sqq., 942 sqq.

(*m*) See the Goede Hoope, Edw. Ad. Rep. 327, for Lord Stowell's exposition of the rules of construction of licences. By the Treaty of Paris, blockades, to be effective, must be maintained by a force actually sufficient to prevent access to the coast of the enemy; and privateering by the contracting parties is abolished.

44. (6.) *Sunday Trading.*—Bargains or engagements made on Sunday are not null in Scotland (*a*), though forbidden in England (*b*); nor are they void at common law even in England (*c*).

(*a*) Thomson on Bills, 79. See 1579, c. 70; 1690, c. 21. Oliphant *v.* Douglas, 1662; M. 1500; 1 Ill. 70. Philips *v.* Innes, 1837; 2 S. & M'L. 465; 3 Ill. 104. Elliot & Son, *infra.* By statute a bill is not invalid by reason merely that it bears date on Sunday. 45 and 46 Vict. c. 61, § 13.

(*b*) Bloxham *v.* Williams, 3 B. & Cr. 232. Fennel *v.* Ridler, 5 *ib.* 406. Smith *v.* Sparrow, 4 Bing. 84. See Elliot & Son *v.* Faulke & Shute, 1844; 6 D. 411.

(*c*) Drury *v.* Defontaine, 1 Taunt. 135. Fennel, *sup.* (*b*). Williams *v.* Paul, 6 Bing. 655. Addison on Contr. 100.

45. Pure or Simple Obligations are debts presently due, and for which execution may immediately proceed (*a*).

(*a*) 1 Stair, 3. § 7. 3 Ersk. Pr. 1. § 3. 3 Ersk. Inst. 1. § 6, 7.

46. Future Obligations.—A debt payable on a future day certain, or an event that must arrive, is improperly termed "future." It is *debitum in præsenti solvendum in futuro*: "Dies cedit etsi nondum venerit." A proper debt exists from the moment of completion of the engagement: the execution only is suspended till the arrival of the appointed day (*a*). 'So claims depending on the event of a suit are not future debts, for the judgment admitting the claim draws back to the time when the debts first became due (*b*); *e.g.* the expenses of establishing a claim against a bankrupt are due (to the effect of ranking), even when his trustee refuses to sist himself in an action raised to constitute it before the sequestration' (*c*). But at common law, where the debtor, whose solvency is relied on in the contract, is *vergens ad inopiam*, or when he is diminishing a security relied on, 'but only in these or similar circumstances,' diligence for *security* may proceed, but not for payment (*d*); and so retention may be competent, but not compensation (*e*). By statute in the case of bankruptcy, and in contemplation of a division of funds, a creditor may claim in a sequestration, with abatement of interest to the day of payment for a debt payable at a future day (*f*). 'Where a term of credit is allowed for paying the price of goods, it is incompetent to raise action for the price before the term expires, unless the debtor be *vergens ad inopiam*' (*g*).

The creditor cannot be compelled to take payment before the term, especially of large sums lent out at interest (*h*).

The term of payment which suspends the demand in favour of the debtor, may be fixed by the original obligation, or by subsequent agreement, or by *supersedere* sometimes made a part of an arrangement with creditors (*i*). The day of payment appointed makes part of the time of suspension; so that execution cannot proceed till the following day (*k*). When the term is fixed by the lapse of a certain space (as to pay in ten days), the day on which the obligation is made is not included, but the term begins to run with the next day (*l*). Where a large sum is payable by instalments, the failure to pay one of them does not infer a power to demand the whole as a pure debt; but only to proceed to diligence in execution for what is due, and diligence in security for the rest. But it may be stipulated, that failure in one or more instalments will justify a demand for the whole; and in such a case (as when the failure of three terms is stipulated as making the whole a present debt) the debtor may avoid the penalty by requiring the creditor to receive payment of the first instalment when two are due and the third current, leaving the second unpaid (*m*).

(*a*) 2 Voet. 4. § 20; 5 Voet. 1. § 28. Pothier, Tr. des Oblig. No. 228 et seq. 6 Toullier, 675. Dirl. and Stewart, voce *Debitum in diem.* 3 Stair, 1. § 46. See Brodie's note, p. 429. 3 Ersk. Inst. 6. § 10, 18, and 2. 12. § 42. See below, § 69.

(*b*) Ersk. iii. 6. 8.

(*c*) Miller *v.* M'Intosh, 1884; 11 R. 729.

(*d*) Dove *v.* Henderson, 1865; 3 Macph. 339. Symington *v.* Symington, 1875; 3 R. 205. Bennett *v.* Fraser, 1834; 12 S. 760. M'Donald *v.* M'Leod, Jan. 15, 1811; F. C. See Ersk. and Stair, *citt.* (*a*). 1 Bell's Com. 316 (333, M'L.'s ed.); and as to diligence for annuities, 1 Bell's Com. 336 seq. (353, M'L.'s ed.).

(*e*) Pothier, Tr. des Obl. No. 234. 6 Toullier, 690.

(*f*) 19 and 20 Vict. c. 79, § 52.

(*g*) Crear *v.* Morrison, 1882; 9 R. 890. The rule, that diligence is not available for future debts, has been relaxed in the discretion of the Court where the reason on which it rests was inapplicable. Smith *v.* Cameron, 1880; 6 R. 1107.

(*h*) 6 Toullier, 706.

(*i*) 4 Ersk. 3. § 24. 1 Bell's Com. 574, 600.

(*k*) Instit. de Verb. Oblig. § 2.

(*l*) 6 Toullier, 711.

Note on the Computation of Time.—As to the computation of time in general, see 1 Stair, 17. § 18, and More's Notes, 257. 2 Ersk. Inst. 6. § 46; 3. 8. § 96, and 4. 1. § 41 (in the Notes). 1 Bell's Com. 88 (84, M'L.'s ed.); 2 *ib.* 178, 179 (167–68, M'L.'s ed.). 2 Hunter, Landl. & T. 48 (4th ed.). *Infra*, § 326, 327, 344, 349 (bills), 1578, 1789, etc. 19 and 20 Vict. c. 79, § 5 (Bankruptcy Act); 13 and 14 Vict. c. 21, § 4 (Lord Romilly's Act, re-enacted, 52 and 53 Vict. c. 63, § 3—Month in statutes passed after 1850 = calendar months). See as to lunar or calendar months, Smith *v.* Roberton & Jeffrey, 1826; 4 S. 442. Mackenzie *v.* Liddell, 1883; 10 R. 705 (charter-party). Campbell's Trs. *v.* Cazenove, 1880; 8 R. 21 (will). Farquharson *v.* Whyte, 1886; 13 R. Just. 29; 45 and 46 Vict. c. 61, § 14 (bills). Ogilvie *v.* Mercer, 1793; M. 3336, 3343; aff. 1796, 3 Pat. 434. M'Neill *v.* M'Murchie, 1841; 3 D. 554. Thom *v.* Steuart, 1842; 5 D. 369. Scott *v.* Rutherford, 1839; 2 D. 269. Lindsay *v.* Giles, 1844; 6 D. 771. Lawford or Davies *v.* Davies, 4 P. D. 61; 47 L. J. Pr. 38 (21 days' residence under 19 and 20 Vict. c. 96—Marriage Act). Blackie *v.* Cleggs, Jan. 21, 1809; F. C. Anderson *v.* Fletcher, March 2, 1813; F. C. Addison on Contr. 55. Benjamin on Sales, 686 sq. Isaacs *v.* Royal Ins. Co., L. R. 5 Ex. 296; 39 L. J. Ex. 189. Savigny, Syst. vol. iv. 297 sqq. § 177–188, and App. xi. As to Sundays in calculations as to steps of judicial procedure, see Macvean *v.* Jamieson, 1896; 23 R. Just. 25, and below, § 327 *fin.* In computing time under contracts the Courts are inclined to regard the intention of the parties in construing doubtful or ambiguous stipulations or conditions. (See a remarkable instance, in regard to a will, in Campbell's Trs. *v.* Cazenove, 1880; 8 R. 21.) It is, however, a general rule that time is calculated not *de momento in momentum* (*naturalis computatio*), but *de die in diem* (*civilis computatio*), *i.e.* that fractions of days are not to be reckoned, but computation is to the midnight following or preceding the last day of the specified term. Comp. L. Pres. Campbell, 3 Pat. 437, with Savigny, § 182; and see Pugh *v.* D. of Leeds, 2 Cowp. 714, 720. Lester *v.* Garland, 12 M. & W. 2. *In re* Railway Sleepers Co., 29 Ch. D. 205. Commentators on the Roman law have gathered from the instances which occur in the law sources the further rule, that when, as in usucapion, a right is acquired by the lapse of a period of time, the preceding midnight is to be taken as its termination (*dies inceptus pro completo habetur*), because the person acquiring is entitled at any moment of the calendar day to regard the acquisition as completed; but that if, as in the prescription of actions, a right is lost by the lapse of the period, the following midnight is the end of the term, because the person who has the right of action may assert, by reason of the uncertainty inherent in the limitation put upon his right, that he can still bring his action at any moment of the last day. This holds, it is said, in ordinary cases where the lapse of a period of time is made the condition of a change in the rights of a party; but if the condition expressly requires the period of time to be completed and overpassed, then even in regard to the acquisition of a right, the following midnight is the limit, because, as the calendar day is indivisible, it can only be said on the next day that the period has been exceeded. Savigny, Syst. iv. 352–53. This distinction is not expressly recognised in our law; but the principle receives effect in computing the induciæ of summonses and terms appointed by law or by Courts for complying with judicial orders, in which the term runs till the midnight following the last day. The rule that fractions of a day are disregarded has no place in diligence and competitions of rights depending on it, where all depends on the arithmetical reckoning of time (*naturalis computatio*). See Digests, *voce* Arrestment, and *e.g.* Wilson, etc., Ptrs., 1891; 19 R. 219. And a fraction of a day is also considered when the good sense of the matter or the intention of parties requires it. Chick *v.* Smith, 8 Dowl. P. C. 337. Reg. *v.* Middlesex Justices, 14 L. J. M. C. 139. Campbell *v.* Strangeways, 47 L. J. M. C. 6; 3 Q. B. D. 105.

(*m*) Pothier, *ut sup.* 6 Toullier, 719. See § 33 (*b*) and § 108 as to the converse case of delivery by instalments.

47. Contingent and Conditional Obligations. —An obligation, of which the efficacy depends on an event which must *certainly* happen, is properly a future debt; but one which depends on an *uncertain future event* is properly contingent. The contingency operates either in suspending the debt or in dissolving it. In either case, the engagement or obligation is independent of the event; the existence or discharge of the debt rests on it entirely. Under a suspensive condition, there is no debt till the event exists (*dies nec cedit nec venit*), and yet the engagement cannot be defeated otherwise than by failure of the condition. When the condition is fulfilled, the debt becomes perfect. If the condition be resolutive, the debt at once ceases on the event stipulated (*a*). Conditions must be lawful in order to receive effect. What conditions are so to be regarded will be discussed hereafter (*b*). They may be not only express, but implied. Thus, an obligation to pay a tocher implies marriage as a condition (*c*).

(*a*) It may be doubted whether future and contingent estates coming to a bankrupt can be regarded as funds of his, which his creditors can attach by diligence of adjudication or arrestment in security. Aitkenhead *v.* Bothwell, 1630; M. 9491; 1 Ill. 59, 93. Ragg *v.* Brown, 1708; M. 9492. Beaton, Jan. 7, 1821; F. C. This case is not reported. See 19 and 20 Vict. c. 79, § 103, 53, 54, as to claiming for contingent debts in sequestrations.

(*b*) See § 1783 et seq., 49, 109 et seq.

(*c*) 1 Stair, 3. § 7. 3 Ersk. 1. § 6, 7, and 3. § 85. Pothier, Tr. des Obl. § 99. 6 Toullier, 501 et seq. 2 Dig. 14. 4. § 2, 3. Paterson *v.* Patersons, 1849; 11 D. 441. See § 93 sqq., 98, 250, etc.

48. As a creditor in a future debt may insist for additional security should the credit fail on which he had relied, so a contingent creditor may, for the protection of his right, follow a similar course (*a*). In the case of a suspensive condition, the creditor is in bankruptcy not admitted to draw a dividend, but only to have one set aside to abide the event. Under a resolutive condition, the obligee is creditor *de præsenti*, and entitled to claim for the computed value (*b*).

(*a*) 1 Pothier, Tr. des Obl. 99.
(*b*) 19 and 20 Vict. c. 79, § 53.

49. (1.) *Possible or Impossible Conditions.*—The latter (including unlawful conditions) annul the obligation to which they are annexed, as not being seriously intended, nor relied on (*a*). 'A condition makes the existence of an obligation depend on a future contingent event: but if the obligation be dependent on an event which is either necessary or impossible, there is obviously no contingency. In the former case there is no condition, and the contract is pure: in the latter, what is, *ex figura verborum*, an obligation, is in substance none, being negatived by the condition (*b*).' But an important distinction is to be marked in deeds of settlement, and in obligations and provisions to which the granter is naturally bound (*c*).

(*a*) 1 Stair, 3. § 7, 8. 3 Ersk. Pr. 3. § 34, 35. 3 Ersk. Inst. 3. § 84, 85. 3 Bankt. 45. 185. See above, § 29, 34, note (*b*). Ramsay *v.* Brewster, 1859; 21 D. 1367.
(*b*) Savigny, Syst. § 121 (vol. iii. p. 156 sqq.). Dig. 45. 1. 7 (*de verb. obl.*); 44. 7. 31 (*de obl. et act.*); 46. 2. 9. § 1 (*de nov.*). 3 Inst. 19. § 11 (*de inut. stip.*), etc.
(*c*) Of these notice will be taken hereafter, § 1785 and 1883.

50. (2.) *Potestative, Casual, or Mixed Conditions.*—Potestative depend on an act which is in the power of one or other of the parties (*a*): Casual depend on mere accident, or the will of a third party: Mixed partake of both.

If time be annexed to the condition (as the arrival or non-arrival of a ship (*b*)), the expiration of the time, the happening of the event, or the impossibility of it, terminate the contingency, and, as lawyers term it, purify the condition (*c*). If there be no time annexed, the contract is pendent while the condition is possible. The condition may be precedent or subsequent; which nearly corresponds with the condition suspensive or resolutive. In the former, as in a conditional bond, *dies nec cedit nec venit* till the event; in the latter, as in an annuity bond, the obligation ceases on the event.

If the debtor, bound under a certain condition, have impeded or prevented the event, it is held as accomplished. If 'in such circumstances' the creditor have done all that he can to fulfil a condition which is incumbent on himself, it is held sufficient implement (*d*). 'So also if the person in whose favour the condition is conceived has waived or renounced its fulfilment (*e*).'

(*a*) Philip *v.* Edin. P. & D. Ry. Co., 1854; 16 D. 1065; 1857, 2 Macq. 514.
(*b*) See below, § 108.
(*c*) Colvin *v.* Short & Co., 1857; 19 D. 890.
(*d*) 3 Ersk. Pr. 3. § 35. Pothier, Tr. des Obl. No. 198 et seq. Hunter *v.* E. Hopetoun, 1863; 1 Macph. 1074; rev. 1865, 3 Macph. H. L. 50; 4 Macq. 972. Pirie *v.* Pirie, 1872; 11 Macph. 941. Dick & Stevenson *v.* Mackay, 1880; 7 R. 788; aff. 1881, 8 R. H. L. 37. Savigny, Syst. § 119, vol. iii. p. 140. See Roberts *v.* Bury Comrs. § 29 (*i*), and Pollock on Contr. 410 sq., and Addison on Contr. 131, 811, 840. In Paterson *v.* M'Ewan's Trs., 1881, 8 R. 646, which properly, however, was a question as to an alleged implied obligation, the opinions show that one does not impede or prevent a condition from being fulfilled in the sense of this rule, who merely exercises a separate and independent right, provided (it would seem) that that right has not been subsequently acquired with the wrongful purpose of defeating the condition or preventing the performance of the contract; and (it may be added) provided that the existence of the right has not been unfairly concealed from the other party. The principle in the text also applies where the performance of a contract becomes impossible by the act or wilful default of one of the parties. That is a breach of contract entitling the other to damages or to enforce his rights under the contract, as the case may be. Cases cited above and in (*e*); and cf. Kinninmont *v.* Paxton, 1892; 20 R. 128. See below, § 910A.
(*e*) Savigny, Syst. iii. 138. Hay *v.* M'Tier, 1806; Hume, 836. Wark *v.* Bargaddie Coal Co., 1859; 3 Macq. 467, etc. Addison on Contr. 154. Benjamin on Sales, 547 sqq.

51. Joint and Several Obligations.—Obligations may be viewed as joint or several, either as in relation to the creditors or to the debtors. The general rule and presumption is, that each co-obligant is concerned to the extent of his own share only, not for the whole. And this applies equally to creditors and to debtors (*a*).

(*a*) 1 Stair, 17. § 20. 3 Ersk. Pr. 3. § 29. 3 Ersk. Inst. 3. § 74. See Voet. lib. 45. tit. 2. Vinnius, lib. 3. t. 20. § 4, No. 9, 10. Alexander *v.* Scott, 1827; 6 S. 151; 1 Ill. 71. Campbell *v.* Farquhar, 1724; M. 14,626. M'Arthur & Weddell *v.* Scott, 15 S. 270; 3 Ill. 104. M'Laren's Bell's Com. i. 361. Savigny, Obligationenrecht, i. 136 sqq.

52. (1.) *Co-Creditors.*—When a bond or bill is granted to two or more persons, or when two or more succeed to a debt (as, for example, heirs-portioners), their right is *pro rata*, each for a share. The entire debt cannot be sued for, or assigned, or fully discharged, but by them all; though each co-creditor may assign his individual share, or sue for it separately, or grant an effectual discharge for it (*a*). But a right may be established *in solidum* in each, by convention, as where the obligation is taken to them jointly and severally, in which case a mandate is held as given to each co-creditor; or by partnership express or tacit (*b*). Under such a right each may sue or discharge the debt; and judicial proceedings taken by one will, in a question of prescription, be available to all.

(*a*) Pothier, Tr. des Obl., No. 258. Fergusson *v.* Link, 1671; 1 B. Sup. 623. Robertson *v.* Forbes, 1695; M. 14,674. Carrick *v.* Vickery, Douglas, 653. Lawson *v.* Leith and Newcastle St. Packet Co., 1850; 13 D. 175. Detrick & Webster *v.* Laing's Sewing Mach. Co., 1885; 12 R. 416. Shaw *v.* Gibb's Trs., 1893; 20 R. 718.

(*b*) See below, § 354. Lord Lyon *v.* Ardoch, 1744; M. 14,676.

53. (2.) *Co-Debtors.*—The general rule and presumption holds with regard to debtors, whether bound simply in a bond or bill (*a*), or becoming liable as heirs-portioners (*b*). The rule is confirmed when the obligant is taken bound for his own share only, as in a policy of insurance.

(*a*) This seems to be a mistake. See § 61.

(*b*) 3 Stair, 5. § 14. Home *v.* Home, 1632; M. 14,678. Duncan *v.* Ogilvie, 1635; M. 14,680. Jordanhill *v.* Edmiston, 1687; M. 14,682. See Lockhart *v.* Shiells, 1770; M. 7244.

54. Exceptions are admitted to the rule either on express or on implied agreement.

If the obligation bear the money to be "for the use of one," or if the obligants are bound for a town or corporation (*a*), all are held as cautioners, and liable each for the whole (*b*).

(*a*) *Quære?* See Menzies' Lect. 203. 2 Jur. Styles, 314. The case cited (Inverness) was decided on the simple ground that the obligants were *cautioners*.

(*b*) Grant *v.* Strachan, 1721; M. 14,633; 1 Ill. 71. Provost of Inverness *v.* the Town, 1631; M. 14,628. See below, § 245 et seq.

55. If the obligants are taken bound as "co-principals and full debtors," each is bound for the whole (*a*).

(*a*) Cloberhill *v.* Ladyland, 1631; M. 14,623; 1 Ill. 71. Dunbar *v.* E. Dundee, 1665; M. 3584; 1 Ill. 72. Cleghorn *v.* Yorkston, 1707; M. 14,624.

56. If they are bound "jointly and severally," each is liable for the whole, or for a share, at the option of the creditor (*a*).

(*a*) 3 Ersk. 3. § 74. Richmond *v.* Grahame, 1847; 9 D. 633. If the obligation be illiquid, and the creditor has to constitute his claim, he must call all the *correi* within Scotland. Zuill *v.* M'Murchy, Ralston, & Co., 1842; 4 D. 871. Muir *v.* Collett, 1862; 24 D. 1119. Neilson *v.* Wilson, 1890; 17 R. 608; but the opinions of the minority in this case show that the rule of procedure is contrary to principle, if not to authority. It ought not to be applied where the debt is less than £25, and so cannot be sued for in the Court of Session. Comp. § 550.

57. If they are bound "conjunctly," each is liable for the whole, though at first this point was doubted (*a*); and they are held to be so liable, if such be the fair import of the obligation taken in all its parts (*b*). But any one called on to pay, is 'in general (*c*)' entitled to have the others also called before he is forced to pay.

(*a*) Campbell *v.* Farquhar, 1724; M. 14,626; 1 Ill. 72. M'Millan *v.* Sloan, 1751; Elch. *Sol. et Pro Rata*, 1; Notes, 431. M'Kellar *v.* Campbell, June 7, 1811; F. C. It rather seems that the word "conjunctly" does not import a liability *in solidum.* See Campbell, *cit.* 1 Stair, 17. § 20. M'Kellar *v.* Campbell, June 7, 1811; F. C.; except in the event pointed out by Parke, B., in King *v.* Hoare, 13 M. & W. 505; *i.e.* where a party sued severally does not plead in abatement. See below, § 62. The other cases cited refer to cautionary obligations, and therefore do not support the text. See M'Laren's Bell's Com. i. 362 (345, 5th ed.). Montgomerie Bell's Conveyancing, 248. Duff on Moveable Deeds, p. 20. Menzies' Lect. 211. See below, § 62.

(*b*) Boyd *v.* Peter, 1649; 1 B. Sup. 403. Wallace *v.* Cossar, 1671; 1 B. Sup. 635.

(*c*) The plea that all parties interested are not called is equitable and subject to the discretion of the Court. Mackay's Practice, i. 351, 353. Muir *v.* Collett, *sup.* § 56.

58. If the subject of the obligation be indivisible, or the obligation *ad factum præstandum*, each is bound for the whole, though the words "jointly" etc., be not used (*a*). But the liability is only *pro rata*, according to the general rule and natural construction, where the obligation is alternative (one divisible, the other not), and the indivisible alternative becomes imprestable. The obligation for the divisible alternative binds the debtors *pro rata*. The mere resolving into a claim of damages does not alter the obligation *in solidum* to an obligation *pro rata* (*b*).

(*a*) 1 Stair, 17. § 20. 3 Ersk. 3. § 74. Grott *v.* Sutherland, 1672; M. 14,631; 1 Ill. 72. Urie *v.* Cheyne, 1630; M. 14,626. Comp. Crant, *supra*, § 54.

(*b*) Correct Ersk. *ut sup.* by Denniston *v.* Semple, 1669; M. 14,630. Darlington *v.* Gray, 1836; 15 S. 197; 3 Ill. 104. See M'Laren's Bell's Com. i. 362. The true distinction is rather this: indivisible obligations involving liability *in solidum* are only those in which the stipulation or promise itself is directed to the doing or giving of something indivisible; but when such prestations are not *in obligatione*, but *in conditione*, as when a pecuniary penalty is stipulated in the event of failure in an act or omission promised, the obligation becomes one for payment of money, and such obligations are always divisible. Savigny, Obligationenrecht, § 31, 34, vol. i. p. 326, 367.

59. Partners in trade (*a*), or joint adventures (*b*), or joint purchasers (*c*), or even joint pursuers in an action in which expenses are found due to the defender, 'or joint delinquents (*d*),' are each *in solidum* bound for the whole (*e*).

(*a*) *Infra*, § 356, 371.

(*b*) *Infra*, § 395.

(*c*) See 2 Bell's Com. 654 (544, M'L.'s ed.); and Neilson *v.* M'Dougall, 1682; M. 14,551.

(*d*) See below, § 550.

(c) 3 Ersk. 3. § 74. Mushet v. Harvey, 1710; M. 14,636; 1 Ill. 73. Ctss. of Sutherland v. Cuthbert, 1776; 5 B. Sup. 439. Gibson v. Lupton, 9 Bing. 297. See Reid v. Lamond, 1856; 19 D. 265. Ramsay v. Smail, 1840; 2 D. 1336 (society—expenses).

60. Parties jointly interested in any employment, the prosecution or accomplishment of which they have authorised, are held each *in solidum* bound for the whole debt incurred by such employment (*a*). But this may be counteracted by an express stipulation to the contrary (*b*). The rule formerly applied in sequestration is altered, and the claim of an agent restricted to the amount of the funds, 'and the personal liability of the trustee employing him (*c*),' or the express engagement of individual creditors (*d*).

(*a*) Anderson v. Sinclair, 1726; M. 14,706; 1 Ill. 74. Chalmers v. Ogilvie, 1730; M. 14,706. French v. E. Galloway, 1730; M. 14,706. Walker v. Brown, 1803; M. *Sol. et Pro Rata*, Apx. 1. Wilsons, Petrs., July 10, 1813; F. C. Wilson v. Mags. of Dunfermline, 1822; 1 S. 389. Comml. Bk. v. Sprot, 1841; 3 D. 939 (loan to trustees). Webster v. M'Lellan, 1852; 14 D. 932. *Infra*, § 448, as to ship-owners.

(*b*) Murdoch v. Hunter, Feb. 15, 1815; F. C.

(*c*) See below, § 2000.

(*d*) 19 and 20 Vict. c. 79, § 57. Goudy on Bankr. 230.

61. Bills and promissory-notes, by usage, bind the drawers or acceptors jointly and severally, without the use of these words (*a*); nay, even where it is otherwise expressed (*b*).

(*a*) 3 Ersk. 3. § 74. MacMorland v. Maxwell, 1675; M. 14,673; 1 Ill. 74. Rutherford v. Donaldson, 1707; M. 14,675. Gordon v. Sutherland, 1761; M. 14,677. M'Kellar v. Campbell, June 7, 1811; F. C.; 1 Ill. 72. See below, § 349c.

(*b*) Alexander v. Scott & Wilson, 1742; M. 14,675. Sharp v. Harvey, 1808; M. *Bill*, Apx. 22 (signing as cautioner).

62. (3.) *Relief inter se.*—But co-obligants, even when bound *in solidum* to the creditor, are, in relation to each other, liable only *pro rata* in relief or indemnification to those of their number who shall have paid more than their share (*a*).

The right to relief is regulated by these rules:—If bound "each for his share," although no one can be called upon by the creditor to pay more, yet if he should pay more, he becomes the creditor of the co-obligants whose shares are thus paid. A co-obligant bound "jointly" may refuse to pay till each co-obligant shall be called: If bound "jointly and severally," any one may be selected by the creditor for payment of the whole. In either of these cases, the person who shall pay the portion of another will be entitled to relief to that extent, without an assignation (*b*). The insolvency of a joint obligant lays on the rest *pro rata* the burden of his share. If the obligation be "indivisible," or expressly "several," there is no relief but against the principal debtor. A co-obligant making payment of the debt, is bound, in claiming relief, to communicate the benefit of any deduction or "ease" (as it is sometimes called) which he may receive at settling, or which may accrue from the funds of insolvent co-obligants (*c*). 'There is no right of relief in respect of payment of a debt which the alleged debtor was only under a moral obligation to pay (*d*); or of one which the pursuer claiming relief was under no legal obligation to pay, and did not pay as agent of the defender, such as damages for injury sued for but paid by way of compromise before judgment (*e*).'

(*a*) As to relief in obligations arising from delict, see § 550, *infra*.

(*b*) See Erskine v. Cormack, 1842; 4 D. 1478.

(*c*) 3 Ersk. Pr. 3. § 29. Craigie v. Graham, 1720; M. 14,649. Muir v. Chalmers, 1682; M. 14,654. Lamberton v. E. Annandale, 1683; M. 14,655. Lillie v. Crawford, 1705; M. 14,655. Ledingham v. M'Kenzie, 1824; 3 S. 74. See below, § 270. 1 Stair, 8. § 9; 2. 17. § 13. Brodie's Notes, 942-44.

(*d*) Henderson v. Paul, 1867; 5 Macph. 628.

(*e*) Gardiner v. Main, 1894; 22 R. 100. Clarke v. Scott, 1896; 23 R. 442.

63. Unilateral Obligations may be either gratuitous or for valuable consideration. It is not necessary that an obligation shall proceed upon a valuable consideration, adequate or inadequate. It is effectual if an engagement (§ 7) be proved by such evidence as law requires in the special case (§ 15, etc.). But still there is a distinction of importance, in some respects, between obligations with or without consideration.

64. (1.) *Gratuitous.*—Obligations which are, as free gifts, voluntarily undertaken, or at least without an adequate consideration, are called gratuitous, and are effectual. Donations once made, otherwise than by last Will, 'or *mortis causa* (*a*),' are not revocable (*b*), except between husband and wife (*c*). 'Donation may be proved by parole (*d*); but there is a strong presumption against it, which can be overcome only by strong and unimpeachable evidence (*e*).'

But although gratuitous obligations are effectual against the obligor and his heirs, they are by statute liable to be declared void at the suit of a prior creditor, if the granter is already insolvent, and the grantee is a near relation or confidant (*f*).

In England, obligations without consideration are *nuda pacta* (*g*), 'and although it had been thought that' a moral cause is a good consideration, 'that view has been negatived, and it has been settled that a mere moral obligation is not a sufficient foundation for a binding promise (*h*). As the practical use of the English doctrine of consideration is to provide evidence and guard against inconsiderate and improvident engagements, it has come to be a rule that, in the absence of fraud, there can be no inquiry as to the adequacy of the consideration (*i*); yet in questions as to the validity of contracts, the insufficiency of the consideration or counterpart is important though not conclusive evidence of error or fraud (*k*). Accordingly,' if the consideration be inadequate, 'and' the obligation fraudulent, it will not be admitted into competition with creditors who have given value for the debt on which they make their demand (*l*); and the existence of debt at the time of granting is of importance, as grounding a presumption of fraud (*m*).

(*a*) See below, § 1874.
(*b*) Warnoch *v.* Murdoch, 1759; M. 7730; 1 Ill. 75. Duguid *v.* Caddel's Trs., 1831; 9 S. 844. M'Gibbon *v.* M'Gibbon, 1852; 14 D. 605. 3 Ersk. Inst. 3. § 91. Campbell *v.* Glasgow Pol. Commrs., 1895; 22 R. 621 ("gratuity" by public commissioners under statute).
(*c*) See below, § 1616.
(*d*) Wright's Exrs. *v.* City of Glasgow Bank, 1880; 7 R. 527. Sharp *v.* Paton, 1883; 10 R. 1000. Anderson's Trs. *v.* Webster, 1883; 11 R. 35. L. Adv. *v.* M'Court, 1893; 20 R. 488. Cases in § 1874, *infra.* 18 Journ. of Jur. 289, 345.
(*e*) Sharp *v.* Paton, *cit.* Dawson *v.* M'Kenzie, 1891; 19 R. 261. As to the necessity and effect of delivery of the thing given, or of a writing making the gift, see Smith *v.* Smith's Trs., 1884; 12 R. 186. Thomson's Exrs. *v.* Thomson, 1882; 9 R. 211. Shaw *v.* Muir's Exx., 1892; 19 R 997.
(*f*) 1621, c. 18. E. of Queensberry *v.* Mouswell, 1677; M. 936; 1 Ill. 75; 2 Bell's Com. 205. Cult's Crs. *v.* His Children, 1783; M. 974. Grierson *v.* Wallace, 1821; 1 S. 9. Remington & Co. *v.* Bruce, 1821; 8 S. 215; **Bruce** *v.* **Bruce**, 1831; 9 S. 695. Geddes *v.* Waddell, 1836; 14 S. 1084; 3 Ill. 104. See below, § 2324.
(*g*) Pillans *v.* Mierop, 3 Burr. 1663; 1 Ill. 4. Rann v. Hughes, 7 T. R. 350; 1 Ill. 31. See Williamson *v.* Taylor, 1845: 8 D. 156; and above, § 8.
(*h*) Eastwood *v.* Kenyon, 11 A. & E. 452. See 1 Smith's L. C. 143. Addison on Contr. 10. Pollock on Contr. 167.
(*i*) Austin on Jurispr. p. 940 (Fragm. on Contracts). Pollock on Contr. 169, 173, 596. Addison, 2, 111. 1 Smith's L. C 141, 404 sq. *et al*
(*k*) Pollock on Contr. 596. 1 Smith's L. C. 29.
(*l*) 13 Eliz. c. 5, § 2; 29 Eliz. c. 5. Smith, *ex parte*, 1 Rose, 208; 1 Ill. 76. See Lord Mansfield's argument in Doe *v.* Routledge, Cowper, 710.
(*m*) Ld. Townsend *v.* Wyndham, 1 Vesey, sen., 11. Battersbee *v.* Farrington, 1 Swanst. 113. Kidney *v.* Cousmaker, 12 Ves. 155. Montague *v.* Lord Sandwich, 12 Ves. 148, note.

65. Of gratuitous obligations, alimentary provisions are among the most frequent. They are, in relation to the debtor and his creditors, under the same rules as other obligations. But the nature of the right conferred on the creditor is very different, and especially considered as a fund attachable for his debts (*a*).

(*a*) See 1 Bell's Com. 128; below, § 2276.

66. (2.) *Onerous* obligations are such as are granted for a valuable consideration (*a*); to which, however, by the law of Scotland, something more is necessary than a mere obligation in morality (*b*). Every obligation is *presumed* to be for an adequate consideration.

(*a*) The word *Onerous*, in contradistinction to *Gratuitous*, is used in the law of Scotland as synonymous with the English phrase, "for a valuable consideration."
(*b*) See Henderson *v.* Paul, § 62 (*d*).

67. Money obligations are required to be in writing; the essential and indispensable part of which is the personal engagement to pay. And this may either be by formal bond, or by simple engagement to pay the sum, as in a promissory-note.

68. (3.) *Enforcement.*—A formal bond has, added to the obligation or engagement, a consent to the registration of the bond in the books of a competent court, and to a summary warrant for execution being issued, as if decree were pronounced on the bond. On such registration, at any time of the year (Session or Vacation), execution may proceed (*a*). A similar expedient for saving the delay and expense of an action was, without the necessity of any express consent, adopted by statute in the case of promissory-notes and bills of exchange (*b*). 'All bonds taken to Her Majesty, though not having a clause of registration, may be registered for execution (*c*).'

In every bond there must be an obligor, an obligee, and a sum engaged to be paid, or act to be performed.

It is important to observe the distinction between a bond as the groundwork of summary execution, and as the groundwork of an action. The difference of effect practically is, that summary execution, besides avoiding delay and expense, cannot be questioned or suspended without finding caution; while there is no such necessity in defending against an action. For summary execution, the obligation must be so certain and precise, that it may at once be enforced without further inquiry. But this, in bank bonds for cash accounts, or suretyship for bank agents, is sufficiently complied with, if the sum for which execution is to proceed is fixed by reference to an account from the bank books, to be signed by the accountant or some other officer of the bank (*d*). A bond not in itself clear and conclusive, but indefinite, or requiring something to be ascertained judicially before it can be put to execution, must be followed by an action, in order to obtain a warrant for diligence (*e*). But though defective in the expression of the obligatory clause, if from other parts of the instrument the obligation is clear, the bond will be effectual (*f*).

(*a*) 2 Ersk. 5. § 54. 1 Ross, 192. See the analogous remedy in England, 3 Blackst. 395; 1 Tidd's Pract. of K. B. 490. 3 Stephen's Com. 684. Lush's Pract. 800 sqq. (3rd ed.). 32 and 33 Vict. c. 62, § 24 sqq. (Debtors Act). A Scottish decree of registration has also execution in England and Ireland under the Judgments Extension Act, 1868; 31 and 32 Vict. c. 54, § 3. See also below, § 2270 et seq. Menzies' Lect. 160 sqq. M. Bell's Lect. 219 sqq. Duff, Mov. Deeds, § 15. 31 and 32 Vict. c. 101, § 138 (short statutory clause of consent to registration). By 1693, c. 15, and 1696, c. 39, registration is competent even after the death of the creditor, or of the debtor, in a bond containing such clause of consent. See 1 and 2 Vict. c. 114, § 1, etc. (Personal Diligence Act).

(*b*) See below, § 343.

(*c*) 19 and 20 Vict. c. 56, § 38, 39.

(*d*) Forrester *v.* Walker & Hunt, June 27, 1815; F. C.; 1 Ill. 77. Smith *v.* Drummond, 1829; 7 S. 792. Paisley Bank *v.* Hamilton, 1831; 9 S. 488. See below, § 302.

(*e*) Hamilton *v.* Ormiston, 1708; M. 5909, 9436.

(*f*) Cochrane *v.* Bryson, 1713; M. 11,627. Coult *v.* Angels, 1749; M. 17,040. Coles *v.* Hulme, 8 B. & Cr. 568. Waugh *v.* Russell, 1 Marsh. 214. See Hamilton's Exrs. *v.* Hope, 1853; 15 D. 594, and above, § 11 (*c*).

69. Execution of the obligation is to be enforced according to its terms and extent, express or implied; and so execution may at once proceed for a pure debt. If payable at a future term, no proceedings can be taken upon it, unless the debtor be *vergens ad inopiam*; in which case diligence *for security*, 'or retention,' is permitted. If the debt be contingent, proceedings to the same effect may be taken where the debtor is *vergens ad inopiam* (*a*).

(*a*) See above, § 45–8. 3 Ersk. 6. § 18. 2 Ersk. 12. § 4. Linton *v.* Sutherland, 1889; 17 R. 213.

70. Mutual Obligations or Contracts.—A mutual contract is the reciprocal undertaking or engagement of two or more persons, whereby something is to be given, or done, or abstained from, on the one side, for a valuable consideration or counter-engagement on the other: "Duorum pluriumve in idem placitum consensus et conventio"; each being bound, and each acquiring a right, by the convention.

71. Those engagements are either strictly reciprocal, or with a difference in time or place. Hence arise these important consequences,—that both are bound, or neither (*a*); that where the obligations are strictly reciprocal, if one refuse, or delay performance 'of a material part of the contract (*b*),' the other whose part is still unfulfilled is entitled to refuse 'performance' or retain (*c*); that where the obligations are not strictly reciprocal in point of time, the anterior obligation may be suspended, if the party whose performance is postponed be *vergens ad inopiam*, 'or at all events if he be openly insolvent' (*d*); and that, if the one party cannot fulfil his part, the other may be free, or may insist for damages (*e*). 'As a pursuer in an action upon a mutual contract must show that he has performed or offered to perform his part of the contract, it is open to the defender to plead and prove that he has not done so, not merely to the effect of relieving himself from the fulfilment of the counterpart so far as unperformed, but of retaining or appropriating monies due under the contract in payment of damages arising from the other party's breach. And, as this rests upon the general law of contracts, and not upon the statute as to compensation (see below, § 572 sqq.), it is not required that the damages shall be liquidated or ascertained, or that they shall be sued for in a separate action; but the claim may be pleaded in defence (*f*).'

(*a*) 1 Stair, 10. § 16. 3 Ersk. 3. § 86–90.

(*b*) Turnbull and other cases in (*c*). It has in England been held that this failure must be one "going to the root of the matter," *i.e.* amounting to a virtual rescission or refusal of performance. It does not appear this means much more than to emphasise the word material. Mersey Iron and Steel Co. *v.* Naylor & Co., 9 App. Ca. 434. See Sale of Goods Act, 1893 (56 and 57 Vict. c. 71), § 11, 31. Livingston, Conner, & Co. *v.* Calder & Co., 1891; 2 Sel. Sh. Ct. Ca. 546. *Infra*, § 108 (*f*).

(*c*) Selkrig *v.* Selkrig, 1721; M. 9167; 1 Ill. 79. Woollen Manuf. of Haddington *v.* Grey, 1781; M. 9144. Buchanan *v.* Speirs & Boyle, 1787; M. 9201. Shaw *v.* M'Donnell, 1786; M. 9185, and other cases as to retention of tocher in 1 Ill. 79, 80. Barclay *v.* Anderston Foundry Co., 1856; 18 D. 1190. Johnston *v.* Robertson, 1861; 23 D. 646. Boswell *v.* Miller, 1846; 8 D. 430 (see below, § 1944, note). Turnbull *v.* M'Lean, 1874; 1 R. 730. Macbride *v.* Hamilton, 1875; 2 R. 775. Gibson & Stewart *v.* Brown & Co., 1876; 3 R. 328. Davie *v.* Stark, 1876, *ib.* 1114. (See below, § 1231, as to leases.) Pegler *v.* Northern Agric. Co., 1877; 4 R. 435. Kelman *v.* Barr's Tr., 1878; 5 R. 816. Meikle & Wilson *v.* Pollard, 1880; 8 R. 70. Miller *v.* Learmonth, *infra*, § 1944. Lovie *v.* Baird's Trs., 1895; 23 R. 1 (claim under lease fixed by arbitration as against claim for arrears, interest, etc., under lease; comp. with Sutherland *v.* Urquhart, 1895; 23 R. 284). And as to the mutuality of covenants, see 1 Bell's Com. 431 (454, and Lord M'Laren's note on p. 455).

(*d*) Carmichael *v.* Dempster, 1776; M. 9163. See above, § 46; below, § 100.

(*e*) Raith *v.* Wolmett, 1670; M. 9154-55. Maitland *v.* L. Gight, 1675; M. 9158. Drummond *v.* Crs. of Daes, 1729; M. 9168. Jordanhill's Crs. *v.* Garnock, 1747; M. 9170. Constable *v.* Robinson's Trs., June 1, 1808; M. *Mut. Cont.* Apx. 12. More's Notes, 70. "Mr. More questions this decision; but it seems to me sound on this point, that the death of the author must have been in contemplation, and the risk of it before the bookseller when he made the contract."—Author's note in 1 Ill. 81, 82. Hunter *v.* Carson, 1822; 1 S. 235; 1 Ill. 82. As to impossibility of performance, see above, § 29.

(*f*) Johnston *v.* Robertson and other cases in note (*c*). It has been suggested (see Macbride and Pegler (*c*) that this rule applies only where the damages are claimed for violation of an *express* term of the contract; but such a view is not consistent either with the fair application of the admitted principle, or with the decision of the same eminent judges in Gibson & Stewart (*c*). Pegler's case was decided on the pleadings, and can hardly be held as fixing a general rule.

72. Offer and Acceptance.—A mutual contract may commence by offer, and be completed by acceptance (*a*).

(*a*) 1 Stair 3. § 9. 3 Ersk. 3. § 88. Pothier, Tr. du Cont. de Vente, No. 32. 6 Toullier, 26. 1 Bell's Com. 326 (343, M'L.'s ed.). Addison, Contr. 17. Pollock on Contr. ch. i. Bell on Sale, pp. 32-38.

73. (1.) *Offer.*—An offer is an obligation provisional on acceptance. It is presumed to be continued till acceptance (*a*); but 'a simple offer' may, before acceptance, be recalled. 'In England an offer, being without consideration, may be revoked at any time before acceptance, even if the offerer has promised to keep it open for a certain time (*b*); but by the law of Scotland it is a question of intention or construction in each case whether an offer does or does not amount to a promise (§ 8, 9, *supra*) binding the offerer for a reasonable time, or until a specified time. If it does not, there is *locus pœnitentiæ* (§ 25); if it does, the offeree duly accepting it may claim performance of the completed contract, or damages for its breach (*c*); but if there be no such promise, no obligation exists, and it is not correct to say that the withdrawal takes effect only' under the burden of making reparation for any loss fairly occasioned by the offer (*d*). 'But the recall of an offer has no effect unless it be communicated to the other party before acceptance (*e*).'

(*a*) 1 Stair, 10. § 3. 3 Ersk. 3. § 88. Allan *v.* Colzier, 1664; M. 9428; 1 Ill. 82. M'Iver *v.* Richardson, 1 M. & S. 557. Gaunt *v.* Hill, 1 Starkie, 10. Pothier, Vente, No. 32 and 475. 1 Pardessus, 252. 6 Toullier, 26. See above, § 9.

(*b*) Cooke *v.* Oxley, 3 T. R. 653; 1 R. R. 783. G. N. Ry. *v.* Whitham, L. R. 9 C. P. 16; 44 L. J. C. P. 1. Dickinson *v.* Dodds, 2 Ch. D. 463; 45 L. J. Ch. 777. Benjamin on Sales, 47, 56 sqq.

(*c*) See § 8, 9. Possibly in some cases special damage arising from the revocation may be given even where there has not been acceptance; see Walker *v.* Milne, and Allan *v.* Gilchrist, *supra*, § 29 (*s*). See below, § 79.

(*d*) Pothier and Pardessus, *ut sup.*; 6 Toullier, 27. The authority for the above modification of the text is chiefly Thomson *v.* James, 1855; 18 D. 1, the opinions in which anticipate many of the English decisions referred to below, § 78.

(*e*) Thomson *v.* James, *cit.* Byrne *v.* Tienhoven, 49 L. J. C. P. 316. Stevenson *v.* M'Lean, 5 Q. B. D. 346; 49 L. J. Q. B. 701. See below, § 78.

74. An offer may be made by parole; by letter; or even tacitly, as when goods are sent without an order or contrary to order, in which cases acquiescence is acceptance (*a*). 'It may be made by advertisement or circular addressed to the public or to a class of persons; and then, in the absence of wilful misrepresentation, it is a question of interpretation whether it is (1) an offer which becomes a contract with any one who, before it is retracted, fulfils the conditions mentioned in it; as in offers of reward for the detection of criminals (*b*), some unqualified statements in railway time-tables (*c*), the advertisement of a general ship (*d*), and perhaps in advertisements of sales "without reserve" (*e*); or (2) merely a declaration that the advertiser will do a certain kind of business, or enter into a particular dealing, and an invitation to the world to make offers; as, *e.g.*, in a simple advertisement of a sale by auction or by tender, which does not imply any contract that all the goods mentioned shall be actually exposed (*f*), or that the highest tender shall be accepted (*g*).'

(*a*) Lombe *v.* Scott, 1779; M. 5627; 1 Ill. 84. 1 Pardessus, 256, No. 253. See Benjamin on Sales, 57. Addison on Contr. 21, 1042, 1054.

(*b*) Williams *v.* Carwardine, 4 B. & Ad. 621. Comp., however, M'Kune *v.* Joynson, 5 C. B. N. S. 218; 28 L. J. C. P. 133 (advance note), and Bovill *v.* Dixon, 1856; 3 Macq. 1. Taylor *v.* Coml. Bk., 1838; M'F. Jur. Ca. 61.

(*c*) Denton *v.* G. N. Ry. Co., 5 E. & B. 568; 25 L. J. Q. B. 129. Campbell *v.* Kerr & Co., Feb. 24, 1810; F. C.

(*d*) See below, § 412.

(*e*) Warlow *v.* Harrison, 1 E. & E. 295; 28 L. J. Q. B. 18; 29 *ib.* 14. See Harris *v.* Nickerson, *infra.* Carlill *v.* Carbolic Smoke Ball Co., 1893; 1 Q. B. 256 (advertisement offering payment on certain conditions).

(*f*) Harris *v.* Nickerson, 42 L. J. Q. B. 171; L. R. 8 Q. B.

286. See Richardson *v.* Sylvester, 43 L. J. Q. B. 1 ; L. R. 9 Q. B. 34.

(*g*) Spencer *v.* Harding, 39 L. J. C. P. 332 ; L. R. 5 C. P. 561. See § 80. See as to an advertisement of a competition for bursaries, Martins *v.* M'Dougall's Trs., 1885 ; 13 R. 274.

75. (2.) *Acceptance.*—Acceptance is either Tacit or Express.

76. Tacit acceptance may be inferred from silence, where the proposal is so put as to require rejection if the party do not mean to assent (*a*); as when a merchant writes to another that he is against a certain day to send him a certain commodity at a certain price, unless he shall previously forbid (*b*). An offer may be tacitly accepted by immediate compliance in sending the goods, for then the execution is the acceptance; or by proceeding on the offer to transact with third parties when a mandate to that effect is implied in the offer (*c*); or by a demand or action for implement before the offer is withdrawn (*d*).

(*a*) Pardessus, p. 256. See Ballantine *v.* Stevenson, 1881 ; 8 R. 959 (retention by landlord of lease signed by tenant in possession).

(*b*) Pierson *v.* Balfour, Dec. 1, 1812 ; F. C. ; 1 Ill. 82. Jaques Serruys *v.* Watt & Co., Feb. 12, 1817 ; F. C. ; 1 Ill. 84. M'Neill *v.* Cameron, 1830 ; 8 S. 362. Harford Brothers & Co. *v.* Robertson, 1831 ; 9 S. 352 ; rev. 6 W. & S. 1. Wylie & Lochead *v.* M'Elroy, 1873 ; 1 R. 41. As to telegrams, see below, § 82.

(*c*) Tweedie *v.* M'Intyre, 1823 ; 2 S. 361 ; 1 Ill. 84. Comp. Kinninmont *v.* Paxton, 1892 ; 20 R. 128.

(*d*) M'Duff *v.* M'Culloch, 1627 ; M. 8406 ; 1 Ill. 85.

77. Express acceptance must precisely meet the offer. If it substantially differ from the offer, the alteration is equivalent to a new offer, which requires acceptance (*a*).

(*a*) 3 Inst. t. 20. De inutil. Stip. § 5. 6 Toullier, 28 et seq. Champion *v.* Short, 1 Camp. 53 ; 1 Ill. 83 ; 10 R. R. 631. Richardson *v.* Roscoe & Rigg, 1837 ; 15 S. 952 ; 3 Ill. 105. Smith *v.* Surman, 9 B. & Cr. 569. Routledge *v.* Grant, 4 Bing. 660. Johnstone *v.* Clark, 1855 ; 18 D. 70. Jack *v.* Roberts & Gibson, 1865 ; 3 Macph. 554. Erskine *v.* Glendinning, 1871 ; 9 Macph. 656. Dickson *v.* Blair, 1871 ; 10 Macph. 41. Wylie & Lochead *v.* M'Elroy, 1873 ; 1 R. 41. Nelson *v.* Assets Co., 1889 ; 16 R. 898. Hutchison *v.* Bowker, 5 M. & W. 535. Engl. and For. Credit Co. *v.* Arduin, 40 L. J. Ex. 108 ; L. R. 5 H. L. 64.

78. The acceptance completes the contract 'if it be despatched before receipt of a retractation of the offer (*a*) within any time that may be stated in the offer as a limit, or if there be no such limited time, while no such change of circumstances has taken place as makes the tender unsuitable and absurd (*b*).' The agreement is not suspended till the offerer has received notice of the acceptance (*c*), though contended for by some commentators (*d*); but this is under the qualification that there shall be no undue delay in notifying the acceptance. 'It is settled that the contract is completed by despatch of the acceptance by the usual or intended method of transmission (generally the post-office) (*e*), even if it should never reach the offerer (*f*); but it seems also that the acceptance may be annulled by revocation, *e.g.* by telegram which reaches the offerer before or simultaneously with it (*g*).'

(*a*) **Thomson** *v.* **James,** 1855 ; 18 D. 1 ; and cases under § 71, *supra.* See Alexander *v.* Ctss. of Dunmore, 1830 ; 9 S. 190. Wylie & Lochead, *cit.* **Higgins** *v.* **Dunlop,** 1847 ; 9 D. 1407 ; 6 Bell's App. 195. Murray *v.* Rennie & Angus, 1897 ; 24 R. 965.

(*b*) Macrae *v.* Edin. Tramways Co., 1885 ; 13 R. 265 (*per* Inglis, L. Pres.). See § 79.

(*c*) 1 Stair, 10. § 3. 3 Ersk. 3. § 88. 1 Pardessus, 254. Adams *v.* Lindsell, 1 B. & Ald. 681 ; 19 R. R. 415 ; 1 Ill. 86. **Higgins** *v.* **Dunlop,** *cit.* See Imperial Land Co. of Marseilles (Harris's case), L. R. 7 Ch. 587 ; 41 L. J. Ch. 198, 621. Deas on Railways, p. 3. Wall's case, L. R. 15 Eq. 18. Jacobsen *v.* Underwood, 1894 ; 21 R. 654. Henthorn *v.* Fraser, 1892 ; 2 Ch. 27.

(*d*) 6 Toullier, No. 29.

(*e*) As to the post-office, see discussions in Household Fire, etc., Ins. Co., below, and Pollock on Contr. 32. But the manner of transmission is immaterial, the true theory being that of Savigny (Syst. viii. 235, § 371 ; Priv. Internl. Law, p. 214) and Lord Ivory (Thomson *v.* James, *cit.*), viz. that "a contract by correspondence is in some sort *ad longum manum,*" *i.e.* that "the sender of the first letter is to be regarded as if he had gone to meet the other, and had received his assent," at the destination of his letter. Revocation is exceptional, and "when it does happen the question can only be decided by taking into account a multitude of particular circumstances, so that the arbitrary rule proposed by our opponents is not sufficient."—Savigny, *l.c.*

(*f*) **Higgins** *v.* **Dunlop,** *cit.* Household Fire, etc., Ins. Co. *v.* Grant, 4 Ex. D. 216 ; 48 L. J. Ex. 577, overruling Brit. and Amer. Tel. Co. *v.* Colson, L. R. 6 Ex. 108 ; 40 L. J. Ex. 97. See, however, *per* Lord Shand in Mason *v.* Benhar Coal Co., 1882 ; 9 R. 883, 890.

(*g*) Alexander *v.* C. Dunmore, *cit.* Pollock on Contr. 34 ; below, § 79 *fin.* See Benjamin on Sales, 4th ed., p. 56.

79. The provisional engagement of an offer may become ineffectual by the death of the offerer, or by his bankruptcy before acceptance; there being no final consent or contract on the part of the offerer till acceptance (*a*). It is 'not' held to be withdrawn by an alteration of circumstances before acceptance (*b*) 'unless the continuance of a particular state of circumstances is a condition of the offer expressed or implied.' If a time be limited for acceptance, the offer is held to subsist, and not to be revocable during that time (*c*); and to be withdrawn by the expiration of that time without acceptance; and the return of post is, in mercantile cases, *presumed* to be the time limited (*d*). If, under such limitation of time, the delay in the acceptance beyond the time allowed have been occasioned by the offerer himself (as by a wrong address of the offer), the mere expiration of the time mentioned in the original offer, or implied in it, will not discharge the offer (*e*). If the offer be accompanied by a recall sent by the same post, it is not binding (*f*).

(*a*) 6 Toullier, 34. See Dickinson *v.* Dodds, § 73 (*b*). Pollock on Contr. 37.

(*b*) Allan *v.* Colzier, 1664; M. 9428; 1 Ill. 82. I do not know of any authority for the modification which I have here made; but it does not seem to need authority. See, however, above, § 78 (*c*).

(*c*) See above, § 73.

(*d*) Farries *v.* Stein, 1799; M. 8482; rev. 1800, 4 Pat. 131; 1 Bell's Com. 326. Jaffray *v.* Boag, 1824; 3 S. 266. Watson & Co. *v.* O'Reilly & Co., 1826; 4 S. 480. Felthouse *v.* Bindley, 11 C. B. N. S. 869; 31 L. J. C. P. 204. Mere continued negotiations will not keep an offer open. Glasgow, etc., Steam Shipping Co. *v.* Watson, 1873; 1 R. 89. As to the effect of silence, see Wylie & Lochead *v.* M'Elroy, *supra*, § 77.

(*e*) Adams, *supra*, § 78 (*c*).

(*f*) Alexander *v.* Ctss. of Dunmore, 1830; 9 S. 190. Pothier, Tr. de Vente, No. 32. 6 Toullier, p. 32, No. 29. Merlin Répertoire, tom. 14, p. 494 et seq. Thomson *v.* James, 1855; 18 D. 1. *Supra*, § 73, 78.

80. Order in Trade.—An order must be distinguished from an offer. It is a part of the law of mandate; and acceptance is presumed from the undertaking which one in trade is held to profess, that he will answer any orders in the line of his trade, or immediately intimate his refusal; and more especially when the dealer has circulated current price lists of goods to be sold by him.

81. An order in trade must be absolute, and neither uncertain, conditional, nor alternative, otherwise it becomes a mere offer. An order may be rejected, but does not require acceptance to bind the person who gives the order. It will bind also the person to whom it is addressed, if strictly in his line of trade, unless refused in course of post,—as an order for goods to a dealer; for insurance to an insurance broker; for carriage of goods to a public carrier (*a*).

(*a*) Pierson *v.* Balfour, Dec. 1, 1812; F. C.; 1 Ill. 82. Bell on Sale, 38.

82. An order may, by the law of Scotland, be in writing or parole (*a*). It is otherwise in England, by the Statute of Frauds; and this must be attended to in making use of English cases and authorities on this point (*b*). 'When an order is sent by telegram, the sender is not responsible for a mistake made by the telegraph clerk in transmitting it; and there is no contract unless the message be correctly delivered (*c*).'

An order must be executed in the terms in which it is given, and is not otherwise binding on the person who gives it (*d*); but acquiescence in the mode of execution followed may make an effectual agreement (*e*).

(*a*) Milne *v.* Harris, James, & Co., 1803; M. 8493; 1 Ill. 83.

(*b*) 39 Ch. II. c. 3, § 17. Price *v.* Lee, 1 B. & Cr. 156. See below, § 89.

(*c*) Verdin Bros. *v.* Robertson, 1871; 10 Macph. 35. Henkel *v.* Pape, L. R. 6 Ex. 7; 40 L. J. Ex. 15.

(*d*) Richardson *v.* Roscoe & Rigg, 1837; 15 S. 952. Van Oppen *v.* Arbuckle, 1855; 18 D. 113.

(*e*) Champion *v.* Short, 1 Camp. 53; 1 Ill. 83; 10 R. R. 631. Lombe *v.* Scott, 1779; M. 5627. Leather Cloth Co. *v.* Hieronymus, 44 L. J. Q. B. 54; L. R. 10 Q. B. 140.

83. Interpretation of Contracts. — Mercantile usage, when general, consistent with law, and not departed from by express contract, is held and read as a part of every mercantile bargain (*a*).

(*a*) *Per* Holt in Blunt *v.* Cumyns, 2 Vesey, senior, 38. Newman *v.* Cazalet, *per* Buller, J.; Park, Insur. 900; 1 Ill. 326. Robertson *v.* French, *per* Lord Ellenborough; 4 East, 135; 3 Ill. 145; 7 R. R. 535. See below, § 524, for a fuller exposition of the rules as to the construction of contracts. Calder *v.* Aitchison, 1831; 9 S. 777; aff. 5 W. & S. 410. Mackenzie *v.* Dunlop, 1853; 16 D. 129; aff. 1856, 3 Macq. 22. Athya & Co. *v.* Rowell, 1856; 18 D. 1299. Armstrong & Co. *v.* M'Gregor & Co., 1875; 2 R. 339; and below, § 101. Proof of what generally happens is not necessarily proof of a usage. *Per* L. Gifford in Brown *v.* M'Connell, 1876; 3 R. 788.

84. Delivery of Contracts.—Mutual contracts in writing, 'unless contained in a unilateral deed, as a feu charter or policy of insurance,' do not require delivery, but are completed by the subscription of all the parties (*a*).

(*a*) Crawford *v.* Vallance, 1625; M. 12,304; 1 Ill. 22. Lockhart *v.* Baillie, 1709; M. 8430. See above, § 23, 24; and as to Extinction of Obligations, below, § 555 et seq. Robertson's Trs. *v.* Lindsay, 1874; 1 R. 323.

'**Particular Contracts.**—In the fourth edition (1839) the author thus introduces the subject of Particular Contracts:'—

The main objects of contracts are—1. The transferring and disposing of property, by sale, or location, or loan, or deposite, or pledge; 2. The employment of manufacturers and workmen whose labours are used in the common intercourse of life, or the engaging of professional aid in law, medicine, etc.; 3. The carrying trade of the country by land and sea; 4. The administering of affairs during absence, by means of factors or mandatories, 5. The insuring of property against perils by sea, fire, etc.; 6. The combination in partnership of the capital, skill, and industry of several in one common concern; or finally, the circulating of money and credit by means of notes and bills negotiable. In considering these several contracts and forms of engagement, they may be reduced to these four classes: *First*, The Contract of Sale, by which goods and commodities are transferred. *Secondly*, Those Contracts in the course and existence of which the property of one is necessarily entrusted to the care or custody of another. *Thirdly*, Those in which personal credit is more immediately the object of convention; and, *Fourthly*, Those by which maritime concerns are carried on or made safe.

CHAPTER II

OF THE CONTRACT OF SALE OF GOODS

85. Nature of the Contract of Sale (*a*).—The contract of sale is a mutual consensual contract, for the transference of property, in consideration of a price; the seller binding himself to deliver and transfer the thing; the buyer to pay the price.

(*a*) 1 Stair, 14. 3 Ersk. by Ivory, 3. § 2–13. 3 Ersk. Pr. 3. § 2–4. 1 Bell's Com. 166 sqq., 434 sqq. M. P. Brown on Sale. 2 Kent, Com. 468. Pothier, Tr. du Cont. de Vente. 1 Domat, tit. 79. Code Civ. § 1582–83. 4 Van Leeuwin, c. 17. See also the Author's Inquiries into the Law of Sale of Goods and Merchandise, Edin. 1844. Blackburn, Contr. of Sale. Benjamin, Sales of Pers. Prop.

86. (1.) Sale, as a *contract*, is contradistinguished from sale as a *transference*. The contract of sale, when completed, is, in the law of Scotland, nothing more than the *titulus transferendi dominii*, with obligations on either part to pay the price and to deliver the thing sold (*a*). No property passes till delivery; nothing but the *jus ad rem specificam* (*b*).

'(2.) **Sale of Goods Act, 1893.**—This codifying and assimilating statute has materially, in regard to goods, altered the principles of law stated in the foregoing paragraph, and more fully treated of below in § 1299 sqq. By the new law, "a contract of sale of goods (*i.e.* all corporeal moveables except money) is a contract whereby the seller transfers or agrees to transfer the property in goods to the buyer for a money consideration called the price" (*c*).

'When under a contract of sale the property in the goods is transferred from the seller to the buyer (which in the case of specific or ascertained goods depends on the intention of the parties (*d*)), the contract is called a *sale*; but when the transfer of the property is to take place at a future time or subject to a condition thereafter to be fulfilled, the contract is called an *agreement to sell*. An *agreement to sell* becomes *a sale* when the time elapses or the conditions are fulfilled subject to which the property is to be transferred (*e*).

'Thus an agreement to sell (or executory contract of sale) is a contract pure and simple; a sale is a contract plus a conveyance, and the distinction involves important differences in regard to the remedies available to buyer and seller respectively in case of breach, as well as in regard to risk (*f*).

'In this matter property means "general" or absolute property, not *special* property such as that of a bailee or custodier (*g*), and in that respect Prof. Bell's note to this section is erroneous (*h*).'

(*a*) A distinction is to be observed between the language of the English law and that of the Scottish in this respect; for much confusion has arisen from this source, in running the analogy between the laws of the two countries (Brown on Sale; Introductory discourse). The English lawyers say that, the contract of sale being completed, the property is passed (2 Blackst. 448). They do not, however, mean by this that the absolute property, the proprietary right or dominium, is thenceforward with the buyer; but only that a special property, *jus ad rem specificam*, has passed. There is still with the seller a right to retain the thing sold for the price. The English law in this respect is law in America (2 Kent, Com. 498); and by the Code Civil of France, the rule which formerly prevailed there, according to the principle of the civil law, has been abandoned, and the property held to pass with the completion of the contract (Cod. Civ. No. 938; 1583. 6 Toullier, 213). In Holland the property is not passed till delivery on credit, or payment of the price (4 Van Leeuwin, c. 17. § 3. 4 Dig. lib. 18. t. 1. c. 19. Voet. lib. 6. t. 1: De rei vind. § 20).

(*b*) This chapter treats of Sale as a personal contract, or *jus ad rem*. Separately it is considered as constituting a real right, or *jus in re*. See § 1299 et seq.

(*c*) 56 and 57 Vict. c. 71, § 1 (1), § 62 (1).

(*d*) *Ib.* § 17 (1).

(*e*) *Ib.* § 1 (3), (4).

(*f*) Chalmers, Sale of Goods Act, p. 6.

(*g*) 56 and 57 Vict. c. 71, § 62 (1).

(*h*) The law of England is more correctly stated in Bell on Sale, p. 15. R. Brown, Sale of G. Act, p. 5.

87. Risk.—(1.) The risk of the thing sold is, 'by the common law of Scotland,' on the buyer, according to the maxim, "Periculum rei venditæ nondum traditæ est emptoris" (*a*); and this 'was' strengthened if the goods 'were' deposited, or placed (as on shipboard) at the buyer's desire (*b*). 'Professor Bell went on to say,' This, in the law of Scotland, does not, as in England, proceed on the ground that the property is transferred; but the engagement of the seller being to deliver the thing sold, and the right of the buyer being *ad rem specificam*, the engagement is discharged, and the right extinguished by the thing perishing without fault. On the other hand, the engagement of the buyer is to pay the price; against which it is no answer that the thing has not been delivered, if it have perished without fault of the seller (*c*). In order to transfer the risk to the buyer, the thing must be specifically appropriated as under the contract, '*i.e.* the thing sold must be ascertained and identified so that the buyer is creditor for delivery of a specific thing (*d*).

'(2.) *General Rule.*—The law is now assimilated to that of England, which rests on the general rule "*res perit domino*," to which in the civil law and our own the maxim "*periculum rei venditæ*," etc., was an exception. The alteration in the law of risk, however, is probably not great, as we in Scotland formerly reached the same result by a different road. The general rule as to risk of ascertained and identified goods is contained in the Sale of Goods Act, viz.: Unless otherwise agreed, the goods remain at the seller's risk, until the property therein is transferred to the buyer, but when the property is transferred to the buyer, the goods are at the buyer's risk, whether delivery has been made or not (*e*).

'Variations on this general rule, as on other rules in the statute, may be freely made by the agreement of parties expressed or implied (*f*). And it applies of course only to sales, not to agreements to sell, *i.e.* not to contracts for the sale of unascertained goods (*g*).

'(3.) It is further provided that "where delivery has been delayed through the fault of either buyer or seller, the goods are at the risk of the party in fault, as regards any loss which might not have occurred but for that fault"; and that "nothing in this section (Act, § 20) shall affect the duties or liabilities of either seller or buyer as a bailee or custodier of the goods of the other party" (*h*).

'(4.) Where, on the other hand, the agreement is to deliver any goods of a certain description,—*venditio generis* (as opposed to *venditio speciei* or *v. corporis*), similar to the executory contract for a sale of goods in the law of England (*i*), or the "agreement to sell" of the Sale of Goods Act,—the buyer has no right to demand delivery of a specific thing, and the seller fulfils his obligation by delivering any goods answering to the description. The seller's obligation cannot therefore be discharged by any *damnum fatale* affecting any goods which he may hold, for the risk, in the sense in which the word is here used, can only attach to an ascertained subject. *Genus nunquam perit* (*k*).'

(*a*) 1 Stair, 14. § 1 and 7. 3 Ersk. 3. § 7. Brown on Sale, 2 et seq., 31, 355. 2 Blackst. 448. Voet. lib. 18. t. 6. § 1. Noodt ad Pand. l. 18. t. 6. Code Civil, art. 1138; 1 Pardessus, 282. Pothier, Oblig. No. 115; Vente, No. 56, 69. M'Donald *v.* Hutchison, 1744; M. 10,070; Elch. *Sale*, No. 5; 1 Ill. 86. Campbell *v.* Barry, 1768; M. 10,071. See Milne & Co. *v.* Miller, Feb. 1, 1809; F. C. And § 91, 116–7.

(*b*) M'Laren *v.* Barclay, 1777; 5 B. Sup. 506. Hall & Co. *v.* Armstrong, 1823; 2 S. 358.

(*c*) M'Donald, *sup.* (*a*). Hinde *v.* Whitehouse, 7 East, 558; 8 R. R. 678. Phillimore *v.* Barry, 1 Camp. 513; 10 R. R. 742. Tarling *v.* Baxter, 6 B. & Cr. 360; 2 Ross' L. C. 1. Anderson *v.* Scott, 1 Camp. 235, note. See above, § 29.

(*d*) Hinde, *sup.* (*c*). Green *v.* Haythorn, 1 Starkie, 447. Hodgson *v.* Le Bret, 1 Camp. 233. Anderson, *sup.* (*c*). Hansen *v.* Craig & Rose, 1859; 21 D. 432. Anderson & Crompton *v.* Walls & Co., 1870; 9 Macph. 122.

(*e*) 56 and 57 Vict. c. 71, § 20.

(*f*) See the Act, § 55. Martineau *v.* Kitching, L. R. 7 Q. B. 736; 41 L. J. Q. B. 22. Castle *v.* Playford, L. R. 5 Ex. 165; 7 Ex. 98; 39 L. J. Ex. 33; 41 *ib.* 44. Anderson *v.* Morice, 46 L. J. Q. B. 11; L. R. 10 C. P. 58, 609; 1

App. Ca. 719. Dunlop & Co. *v.* Lambert, *cit.* § 88 (*d*). Brewer & Co. *v.* Duncan & Co., 1892; 20 R. 230 (express stipulation).

(*g*) The Act, § 16. *Supra*, § 86 (2); *infra*, § 91 (1), 116.

(*h*) See next section.

(*i*) Benjamin on Sales, 5, 273, 318.

(*k*) Pothier, Vente, No. 179. It would seem, though it was not expressly decided, that, in the common law of Scotland, on a sale of a definite and ascertained mass or bulk at a price depending on weight or measurement, the risk did not pass to the buyer until the price was ascertained. *Per* L. J.-C. Inglis in Hansen *v.* Craig & Rose, *cit.* See below, § 88 (*e*). There is little doubt that our Courts would practically have reached the same result as those of England (see Busk *v.* Davis, 2 M. & S. 397. Campbell *v.* Mersey Docks Co., 14 C. B. N. S. 412, and others in Benjamin on Sales, 311 sqq.), which is now our law also under the Act, § 18 (2), (3), in regard to the sale of an undivided and unascertained portion of a specific mass or bulk (*e.g.* oil in tanks, or corn in a store, or sheep by number out of a flock), viz. that the buyer has no *jus ad rem* (in England no property), and therefore no risk, till his portion is measured, weighed, or counted and separated (see Hansen *v.* Craig, *cit.*, and Anderson & Crompton *v.* Walls & Co., *cit.*—*per* L. Cowan). The argument in the learned notes in the last edition of 1 Bell's Com. 461 sq., 473, fails to notice that in such a sale the buyer whose portion has not been separated cannot have a *jus ad rem specificam* in any usual and proper sense of the words. Hence, where it is a term of the contract that the subject sold is to be furnished out of a particular mass, which totally perishes by accident, the performance of the contract becomes impossible, and neither party is bound. See § 29, *supra*.

88. But the risk is continued on the seller, where there is undue delay in making delivery without fault on the buyer's part (*a*); 'where the vendor neglects to give timeous notice of shipment so as to enable the buyer to insure (*b*), or fails to put the goods in such a course of conveyance as to give the buyer indemnity against the carriers in case of loss (*c*)'; where there is an express or implied undertaking of the risk by the seller, as to deliver at a certain place (*d*); or where anything remains to be done in completing, ascertaining, or identifying the thing to be delivered (*e*), 'or fixing its price (*f*). The matter may be stated thus: under the former law the risk passed to the buyer when he acquired by the contract a *jus ad rem*, or special right to have delivery, as against the seller (*g*), of a specific thing, and it now passes to him with the transference of the property, unless it is continued with the seller either (1) by *mora* or other fault on his part (notes (*a*), (*b*), (*c*)); or (2) by the intention of the parties expressed in the bargain, or implied in its terms (*h*).'

(*a*) 1 Stair, 14. § 7. 3 Ersk. 3. § 7; 4 Domat, 2. § 7. 1 Ill. 98. Sale of Goods Act, § 20, *supra*, § 87 (3).

(*b*) Andrew *v.* Ross, Dec. 6, 1810; F. C. Fleet *v.* Morrison, 1845; 16 D. 1122. See § 118. Hastie *v.* Campbell, 1857; 19 D. 557. 1 Bell's Com. 445 (475, M'L.'s ed.). Sale of Goods Act, § 32 (3).

(*c*) Clark *v.* Hutchins, 14 East, 475. 1 Bell's Com. 445 (474, M'L.'s ed.). Benjamin on Sales, 703. Sale of Goods Act, § 32 (2).

(*d*) Pothier, Tr. des Obl. No. 663; Tr. du Vente, No. 58. 1 Pardessus, 282. Spence *v.* Ormiston, 1687; M. 3153. Melville & Riddell *v.* Robertson, 1749; M. 10,072, corrected by Milne & Co., *sup.* § 87 (*a*). Rugg *v.* Minett (2 Ross' L. C. 30), 11 East, 210. See **Dunlop & Co.** *v.* **Lambert,** 1837; 15 S. 884, 1232; rev. 1839, Macl. & Rob. 663; 6 Cl. & F. 600; *infra*, § 117, 118. Walker *v.* Langdales Chemical Co., 1873; 11 Macph. 906. Du Buisson & Co. *v.* Swan & Co., 1889; 17 R. 252. Brodie's Stair, 857. Sale of Goods Act, § 20.

(*e*) 3 Ersk. 3. § 7. Hanson *v.* Meyer, 6 East, 614; 1 Ill. 90; 2 Ross' L. C. 20. Simmons *v.* Swift, 5 B. & Cr. 857 (2 Ross' L. C. 37). Pothier, Tr. du Vente, No. 309. Voet. lib. 18. t. 5. § 4. Hansen *v.* Craig & Rose, 1859; 21 D. 432. Anderson & Crompton, *sup.* § 87 (*d*).

(*f*) Walker *v.* Langdales Co., *cit.* The Act, § 18 (3).

(*g*) In English law the completion of the contract passed the absolute property, when the specific goods to be sold were agreed on, unless it could be shown that such was not the intention of the parties. Gilmour *v.* Supple, 11 Moo. P. C. 566. Calcutta Co. *v.* De Mattos, 32 L. J. Q. B. 322; 33 L. J. Q. B. 214. Turley *v.* Bates, 2 H. & C. 200; 33 L. J. Ex. 43. Young *v.* Matthews, L. R. 2 C. P. 127; 36 L. J. C. P. 61.

(*h*) See Benjamin on Sales, 287. Above, § 87, especially cases in note (*f*).

89. Completion and Evidence.—(1.) The contract of sale is complete when the parties are agreed, the one to pay a certain price, and the other to sell for that price a certain subject. There is then *consensus in idem placitum et conventio* (*a*). Written evidence of the consent is required in Scotland to complete the contract of sale of land, of copyright, of ships, and of goods bonded for duties in the warehouse of the importer (*b*). But the sale of goods and merchandise in general is effectually proved by evidence *prout de jure*; parole, written, or confession (*c*). When the bargain is made by the principals without writing, the evidence of two witnesses, or one corroborated by circumstances, is necessary; or the letters of the parties, holograph, or signed by them, are good proof (*d*). 'The Sale of Goods Act provides as follows: Subject to the provisions of this Act, and of any statute in that behalf (*e*), a contract of sale may be made in writing (either with or without seal), or by word of mouth, or partly in writing and partly by word of mouth, or may be implied from the conduct of the parties (*f*).' Where a factor or broker makes the bargain, his authority must be proved. Where, as in England, and in great mercantile cities, brokers are employed, a *bought and sold note*, signed by him, completes the bargain (*g*): Or, where he acts for both, the entry of the sale in his book, accompanied by the notes sent to the parties, completes the contract in England (*h*); though there is not in Scotland any necessity, as by the practice of England (*i*), for a signed note to be entered in the broker's book (*k*). If, in a sale by intervention of a broker, the buyer's name be not previously communicated by the broker, there is a power of rejection within a reasonable time, on disclosure of the name (*l*).

(*a*) See above, § 73 sqq., as to Offer and Acceptance, etc.
(*b*) See below, § 889, 1330, 1361, 1378.
(*c*) 4 Ersk. 2. § 20. Hamilton *v.* Richard, 1698; M. 12,412; 1 Ill. 88. Gibb *v.* Walker, 1751; Elch. *Caut.* No. 19. See also Carruthers *v.* Bell, Nov. 13, 1812; F. C.; 1 Ill. 176. Pollock & Dickson *v.* M'Andrew, 1828; 7 S. 189. Wilson *v.* Walker, 1856; 18 D. 673.
(*d*) See below, § 2232. The proof of this contract in England is regulated by the Statute of Frauds (29 Ch. II. c. 3, § 17), and a supplementary Act (9 Geo. IV. c. 14): the former requiring in sales for £10 or upwards, either a note in writing, signed by the parties; or something given in earnest to bind the bargain; or part payment of the price; or delivery and acceptance of part of the goods sold; the latter supplying a defect in the older statute, by providing that the same rule shall apply to executory sales; *i.e.* where the goods are to be delivered at some future period, or are not yet made, or provided, or ready for delivery. See Smith's Mercantile Law, 615 et seq., 10th ed.; and 1 Starkie on Evidence, 353, 868. Addison on Contr. 21. Blackburn on Sale, 81–119. Benjamin on Sales, 93, 179, etc.
The United States of America have adopted the English Statute of Frauds; 2 Kent, Com. 493 et seq. Parsons on Contracts. Throop's Treatise on the Validity of Verbal Agreements, Albany, 1870.
In France, the law of this contract is not very different from that of Scotland. Parole evidence is admitted, but with strong injunctions to jealousy and caution. Code de Com. No. 109; 9 Toullier, 367.
The law of Holland seems most nearly to resemble that of Scotland; 4 Van Leeuwin, 17. § 7, and 5. 20. § 12; 14, 22.
(*e*) See the Act, § 4, re-enacting for England the Statute of Frauds, and the cases indicated above at (*b*).
(*f*) 56 and 57 Vict. c. 71, § 3. See Brogden *v.* Metr. Ry. Co., 2 App. Ca. 666, and above, § 27.
(*g*) The bought and sold note is in this form:—"Sold for A B, to C D, 250 firkins butter, at 100s. Shipped in the month of July, and payable by bill at two months." See § 219. It requires no stamp in the case of goods; 54 and 55 Vict. c. 39, *v.* Agreement, exemp. 3. Blackburn, Sale, 81 sq. Benjamin, Sales, 205 sqq. Towill & Co. *v.* Br. Agricl. Assn., 1875; 3 R. 117.
(*h*) Hayman *v.* Neale, 2 Camp. 337. Cumming *v.* Roebuck, Holt's Cases, 172. Sievewright *v.* Archibald, 17 Q. B. 103; 20 L. J. Q. B. 259. Magee *v.* Atkinson, 2 M. & W. 440.
(*i*) In England, where no entry has been made in the broker's books, the bought and sold notes seem to complete the contract, but only if they correspond in their terms. Goom *v.* Aflalo, 6 B. & Cr. 117. Short *v.* Spackman, 2 B. & Ad. 962. Maclean *v.* Dunn, 1 Moo. & P. 778. Sievewright, *cit.* See Heyworth *v.* Knight, 5 Moo. P. C. 232.
(*k*) Grant *v.* Fletcher, 5 B. & Cr. 436. Hawes *v.* Foster, 1 M. & R. 368. Thornton *v.* Charles, 9 M. & W. 802.
(*l*) Hodgson *v.* Davies, 2 Camp. 530; 11 R. R. 789; 1 Ill. 104. See below, § 105.

90. Essentials of Sale.—It is essential in 'a contract of' sale that there shall be a determinate subject and a price; but it is not necessary that the subject should be identified, or the price a certain definite sum; 'but till the subject is identified there can be only an agreement to sell, not a sale (*a*).'

In relation to the subject, sale may be of three several kinds:—1. Of a certain specific thing, clearly distinguished in description, or set apart for the buyer; or 2. Of a determinate quantity, or number, or weight, of a commodity, described generically,—as cattle, or corn, or wine; or 3. Of a commodity or thing to be prepared or provided for delivery at some future time, 'now called in the Sale of Goods Act, 1893, "future goods," whether they are to be manufactured or merely acquired by the seller (*b*),'—as a ship to be built; or provisions to be furnished for a voyage, or an hospital, or an army. This last is in England called an "executory sale," though, properly speaking, there are combined with the contract of sale other contracts,—as *locatio operis*, mandate, etc. (*c*). 'The second also is in England an executory agreement, but capable of being converted into an actual sale (bargain and sale) by specific appropriation of goods to the contract (*d*).

'If the specific goods sold or agreed to be sold have perished without the knowledge of the seller at the time when the contract is made, the contract is void (*e*). This may be referred in principle, either to mutual error (§ 11 (*d*)), or impossibility of performance (§ 29).'

(*a*) *i.e.* The identification of the subject is not necessary to the completion of the contract, though it is necessary to the passing of property and the risk. See above, § 86, 88. 1 Bell's Com. 437; *infra*, § 91 (2), and § 92 (*c*).
(*b*) 56 and 57 Vict. c. 71, § 5, Sale of Goods Act.
(*c*) See below, § 147.
(*d*) Benjamin on Sales, pp. 318, 342.
(*e*) Sale of Goods Act, 57 and 58 Vict. c. 71, § 6. **Couturier *v.* Hastie**, 5 H. L. Ca. 673; 25 L. J. Ex. 253. See above, § 11 (*d*); § 29.

91. *Subject or Thing Sold.*—(1.) In proper sale, a certain specific commodity capable of identification is sold; and as soon as it is so, it lies for delivery to the buyer at his risk. The property is passed in England; in Scotland, 'formerly only' the *jus ad rem specificam*; 'but since Jan. 1, 1894, the property also passes at the making of the contract, or at such time as the parties intend it to pass (*a*).' In a sale of a certain number, or quantity, or weight of a commodity, described generically, until the stipulated quantity is separated from the mass, or weighed or measured off, neither the property in England nor the specific right in Scotland 'was' passed, nor 'is' the risk laid on the buyer; and yet the contract is 'and was' obligatory, and will ground an action for fulfilment 'as an agreement to sell' (*b*). In the executory sale also, 'of a thing to be made or provided by the seller,' the same distinction and effect take place (*c*). If the thing to be furnished is specific, and capable of identification, as the very thing to be furnished, it will be at the buyer's risk; if indefinite, the risk will remain with the seller (*d*).

(2.) If the sale be indefinite, as of a quantity of goods, no part of that species of goods in the dealer's warehouse being specifically the buyer's, a duty on such goods unsold will fall on the buyer (*e*). A mere *spes* may be sold, as the cast of a net (*jactus retis*); a hope of succession (*f*); the goodwill of a trade or shop (*g*). 'The application of the Sale of Goods Act to contracts of sale of such subjects as a *spes* or chance is excluded by the definition of "goods" (§ 62); but the terms of the contract may, as they have usually been held to do in English cases, apply to the subject of the *spes*, and to be conditional or contingent sales of it, or sometimes, as would be the case in the Civil Law illustration of *jactus retis*, contracts for work and labour (*h*).'

(3.) A commodity sold by measurement or weight may be very different, according to the standard used in different countries; and either the standard or the place should be fixed (*i*). 'If the intention of the parties with regard to weight, measure, coinage, etc., is left in doubt (*i.e.* is not to be ascertained from the terms of the contract, or the circumstances, or from usage), the presumption is that the weight, etc., of the place of fulfilment is intended, not only because that is what the parties most probably had in view, but because adjustment by those weights, etc., will generally be more easily effected (*k*).'

(4.) All British contracts are ruled by the imperial standard; the Winchester bushel, Scottish ell, and all other local and customary measures being abolished (*l*). 'All contracts and dealings in the United Kingdom are deemed to be made and had according to one of the imperial weights or measures or to some multiple or aliquot part thereof, and if not so made or had, are void (*m*). The nullity and penalties of the Act do not apply to the sale of an article in a vessel not represented as containing any amount of imperial measure, nor to the possession of a vessel not used or intended for use as a measure (*n*). So it has been held that the sale of spirits by the "threepence worth" or by the "glass" (*o*), or by a pewter measure not of the name or denomination of an imperial measure, though containing a certain proportion of such a measure (*p*), is not within the 24th section of the Act, which imposes a penalty on the use of weights or measures not of the denomination of a Board of Trade standard.'

(5.) *Rules as to Quantity*.—If the quantity be vaguely expressed (as *about* 300 quarters of corn), a disproportioned excess is not to be held as sold, 'but the vendor is allowed a certain moderate and reasonable latitude in the performance (*q*).' (6.) If an order be given for several articles, the buyer is entitled to consider it as one order, and to refuse to accept any one article unless the whole be sent (*r*). 'But the rule is different if the nature of the contract contemplates the possible delivery of a part only, or the buyer acquiesces in the delivery of a part as fulfilment of the contract to that extent (*s*).

'The rules as to delivery of the wrong quantity are now as follows:—(1) Where the seller delivers a quantity of goods less than he contracted to sell, the buyer may reject them; but if the buyer accepts the goods so delivered, he must pay for them at the contract rate. (2) Where the seller delivers a quantity of goods larger than he contracted to sell, the buyer may accept the goods included in the contract and reject the rest, or he may reject the whole. If the buyer accepts the whole of the goods so delivered, he must pay at the contract rate. (3) Where the seller delivers the goods he contracted to sell mixed with goods of a different description not included in the contract, the buyer may accept the goods which are in accordance with the contract and reject the rest, or he may reject the whole.

(4) These provisions are subject to any usage of trade, special agreement, or course of dealing between the parties (*t*).'

(*a*) Sale of Goods Act, § 1, 17, 18, etc.

(*b*) 3 Ersk. 3. § 3. Brown on Sale, 44. Pothier, Vente, No. 6, 7. Rugg *v.* Minett, 11 East, 210; 1 Ill. 89; 10 R. R. 475; 2 Ross' L. C. 30. Buck *v.* Davis, 2 M. & S. 397; 2 Ross' J. C. 187. Zagury *v.* Furnell, 2 Camp. 240; 11 R. R. 704. Wallace *v.* Breeds, 13 East, 322; 12 R. R. 423. White *v.* Willis, 1 Marsh. 2. Hanson *v.* Meyer, 6 East, 614; 8 R. R. 672; 2 Ross' L. C. 20. Simmons *v.* Swift, 5 B. & Cr. 857; 2 Ross' L. C. 37.

(*c*) See § 90 *fin.*

(*d*) See § 87, 88.

(*e*) Haig *v.* Napier, 1805, 1813; 1 Dow, 255; 1 Ill. 94. The author's statement is not very clear. The case, which is one rather of construction than of principle, decided that a seller of a quantity of spirits, not separated or appropriated in his store at the date of the incidence of a new duty, was entitled to the benefit of a clause in the statute imposing it (43 Geo. III. c. 31), which authorised sellers under previous contracts to add the amount of the duty to the price of undelivered goods.

(*f*) See above, § 37. 3 Ersk. 3. § 3. Pothier, Vente, No. 6. Aikenhead *v.* Bothwell, 1630; M. 9491; 1 Ill. 93. Ragg *v.* Brown, 1708; M. 9492.

(*g*) See as to goodwill, below, § 379, 1361c.

(*h*) *Per* Benjamin on Sale, p. 87. See the distinction of *spes* and *emptio rei speratæ; ib.* p. 82.

(*i*) See Schuurmans *v.* Stephen, 1833; 11 S. 779; and below, § 117.

(*k*) Savigny, Priv. Int. Law, § 374, p. 245, and cases cited there. Bar, Int. Law, § 66, 70 (p. 269, etc., Gillespie's Transl.). Schuurmanns *v.* Stephen, *cit.* Rossetter *v.* Cahlmann, 8 Ex. 361. Ainslie *v.* Murray, 1881; 8 R. 636. Miller *v.* Mair, 1860; 22 D. 660. As to British coinage, see § 92 *fin.*

(*l*) 5 Geo. IV. c. 75, § 15; 6 Geo. IV. c. 12; 5 and 6 Will. IV. c. 63. Watts *v.* Friend, 10 B. & Cr. 446. See Thomsons *v.* Garioch, 1841; 3 D. 625. Alexander *v.* M'Gregor, 1845; 7 D. 915. Davie *v.* Robertson, 1847; Arkley's Crim. Ca. 336. Handyside *v.* Pringle, 1863; 1 Macph. 1164.

(*m*) 41 and 42 Vict. c. 49, consolidating previous Acts, and amended as to verification of weighing instruments, etc., sale of coal, bread, etc., by 52 and 53 Vict. c. 21. As to sales by multiples or parts of legal measures, see Jones *v.* Giles, 10 Ex. 119; 11 Ex. 393; 23 L. J. Ex. 292; 24 L. J. Ex. 259. Hughes *v.* Humphries, 3 E. & B. 954; 23 L. J. Q. B. 356. Robertson *v.* Gow, 1858; 20 D. 1170. Miller *v.* Mair, 1860; 22 D. 660. Lang *v.* Cameron, 1894; 21 R. 337. Melvin *v.* Skene, 1878; 2 Sel. Sh. Ct. Ca. 596, and cases there noted. By § 21 of this Act, re-enacting 27 and 28 Vict. c. 117, and 60 and 61 Vict. c. 46, contracts may lawfully be made according to the metric system of weights and measures. See Cuthbertson, § 92 (*c*).

(*n*) 41 and 42 Vict. c. 49, § 22.

(*o*) Craig *v.* M'Phee, 1883; 10 R. Just. 51.

(*p*) Ross *v.* Johnston, 1886; 13 R. Just. 73.

(*q*) Cross *v.* Eglin, 2 B. & Ad. 106; 1 Ill. 94, and other cases in Benjamin on Sales, 699 sqq.

(*r*) Champion *v.* Short, 1 Camp. 53; 1 Ill. 83; 10 R. R. 631. See also Baldy *v.* Parker, 2 B. & Cr. 37; 1 Ill. 95; 26 R. R. 260. Richardson *v.* Roscoe, 1837; 15 S. 952. Jaffé *v.* Ritchie, 1860; 23 D. 242, 249.

(*s*) Bell on Sale, 83. See Hall & Sons, and Linn, below, § 100, and see § 108 *fin.* Smith *v.* Napier, 1804; Hume, 338.

(*t*) Sale of Goods Act, 1893, § 30.

92. Price.—The rule 'in Scotland was': No price, no sale. There 'might' be donation, transference, engagement, but no sale without a price stipulated (*a*). If there be a material error as to the price, it is no sale (*b*). 'Yet, where the contract had been conclusively settled by delivery of the goods sold, the parties were presumed in law to have had in contemplation the reasonable value of the thing sold (*c*).'

(1.) The price must, 'prior to 1894,' be certain, or, 'but both formerly and under the Sale of Goods Act it may by the contract be,' referred to such standard or criterion as to fix it beyond question (*d*); as to the Sheriff-fiars fixing the price of grain (*e*); or the award of a third party (*f*); or even of one of the parties, subject to the control of equity (*g*); or the market or current price at a particular time or place; and if no place or time be fixed, the price at the time and place of receiving the order or settling the bargain will be presumed (*h*). The price may by the bargain be made to vary according to events (*i*).

'The result of these qualifications of the rule that there is no contract unless the price can be made certain was to make the rule of little practical importance where delivery had taken place. And in this way our law hardly differed from the law of England. But in the case of goods to be acquired or manufactured by the seller (future goods—executory contracts) a contract of sale could not exist unless a price were fixed. The Sale of Goods Act has now assimilated our law to the law of England, enacting as follows:—(1) The price may be fixed by the contract, or may be left to be fixed in some manner thereby agreed, or may be determined by the course of dealing between the parties. (2) Where the price is not so determined, the buyer must pay a reasonable price; and that is a question of fact dependent on the circumstances of each particular case (*k*). (3) When the price is to be fixed by the valuation of a third party, and he cannot or does not make such valuation, the agreement is avoided; but the buyer must pay a reasonable price for any part of the goods that have been delivered and appropriated. If the valuation is prevented by the fault of the buyer or seller, the other party may maintain an action for damages (*l*).

'Unless a different intention appears from

the terms of the contract, stipulations as to time of payment are not of the essence of a contract of sale (*m*).'

(2.) The price must not be illusory, for that is donation (*n*).

(3.) The price must be in money, or what passes as such, otherwise it is barter, not sale (*o*). Between these two contracts, however, there is no essential distinction (*p*). 'All contracts and dealings relating to money, or involving payment of or liability to pay money, must be made according to the coins which are current and legal tender under the Coinage Act, 1870, and not otherwise, unless made according to the currency of some British possession (*q*).'

(*a*) 1 Stair, 10. § 13, and 9. § 14. 3 Ersk. 3. § 4. Pothier, Tr. du Vente, No. 18, 20 See below, § 103, 127. See Anderson *v.* Wilson, 1856; 19 D. 39.

(*b*) Sword *v.* Sinclairs, 1771; M. 14,241; 1 Ill. 6.

(*c*) Bell on Sale, p. 19, referring to Acebal *v.* Levy, 10 Bing. 382; Hoadley *v.* M'Laine (*h*); Leslie, *infra* (*h*). *Infra*, § 1227. So goods delivered under a misconception on both sides as to the price (Wilson *v.* M. of Breadalbane, 1859; 21 D. 957. Stuart & Co. *v.* Kennedy, 1885; 13 R. 221), or at a price fixed according to an illegal measure (Cuthbertson *v.* Lowes, 1870; 8 Macph. 1073—see above, § 35 (*h*)), are to be paid for by the purchaser at the market price.

(*d*) 2 Vinnius, lib. 3. c. 24, p. 613. Voet. lib. 18. tit. 1. § 23. 2 Noodt, p. 388. Pothier, Vente, No. 18. 1 Stair, 10. § 13; 9. § 13; 9. § 14; 14. § 1. 3 Ersk. 3. § 4. E. of Selkirk *v.* Nasmith, 1778; M. 627; 1 Ill. 96. Hunter *v.* Duff, 1831; 9 S. 703; 1 Ill. 95. *Infra*, § 524 (*b*). It was held that when a definite mass had been sold at a price according to measure, and the measurement of the mass had still to be ascertained, the contract was not complete, so as to pass the risk to the buyer. *Per* Inglis, J.-C., in Hansen *v.* Craig & Rose, 1859; 21 D. 432. See Tudor's L. C. in Comm. Law, p. 619. See *contra*, 1 Bell's Com. 437, and above. § 87 (*d*).

(*e*) Act of Sederunt, Dec. 21, 1723. Treasurer of Aberdeen *v.* Gordon, 1760; M. 4415.

(*f*) 1 Stair, 14. § 1. E. Montrose *v.* Scot, 1639; M. 14,155. E. Selkirk (*d*). 3 Inst. 24. § 1. 4 Cod. 1. 38. 1. 15. Pothier, Vente, No. 24. Comyn's Dig. tit., *Agree.*, l. 4.

(*g*) 1 Stair, 14. § 1. 3 Ersk. 3. § 4. E. of Montrose, *supra* (*f*). Lavaggi *v.* Pirie & Sons, 1872; 10 Macph. 312.

(*h*) Leslie *v.* Miller, 1714; M. 14,197; 1 Ill. 95. 2 Blackst. 30. Hoadley *v.* M'Laine, 10 Bing. 487; 1 Ill. 95. Champion *v.* Milne, Jan. 14, 1811; F. C. Malloch *v.* Hodghton, 1849; 12 D. 215 (contract for work to be done). Wilson, *supra* (*c*).

(*i*) Smith *v.* Brown, Dec. 12, 1735; Elch. *Sale*, No. 1; Cuthbertson, *supra* (*c*).

(*k*) 56 and 57 Vict. c. 71, § 8.

(*l*) *Ib.* § 9.

(*m*) Sale of Goods Act, § 10 (1). Martindale *v.* Smith, 1 Q. B. 389. Benjamin on Sale, 290, 304.

(*n*) 1 Stair, 10. § 14. 3 Ersk. 3. § 4.

(*o*) 1 Stair, 14. § 1. 3 Ersk. 3. § 4, 13. Sale of Goods Act, § 1.

(*p*) 3 Ersk. 3. § 4. Brown on Sale, 151, objects to this, but he proceeds on a distinction peculiar to excambion of land. See below, § 894.

(*q*) 33 Vict. c. 10, § 6. See below, § 1333 sqq.

93. Implied Conditions in Sale.—Conditions in sale are—1. Implied, from the nature of the contract, as part of the agreement, if not otherwise stipulated; or 2. Express, or Special, introducing by stipulation some point of agreement not naturally arising from the sale.

94. (1.) *Implied Condition as to Quality; and Warranty* (*a*).—The implied conditions may relate either to the quality and state of the goods, or to the mode and terms of payment of the price.

(*a*) See further, § 111 and 121.

94A. 'The fundamental undertaking (*a*) in a contract of sale is that "the goods shall correspond with the description" (*b*), *i.e.* the description contained in the contract. This, of course, will generally apply to executory contracts, and not often to sales of specific goods. But the statute adds, "If the sale be by sample, as well as by description, it is not sufficient that the bulk of the goods corresponds with the sample, if the goods do not also correspond with the description" (*c*).'

(*a*) *Per* Lord Esher in Randall *v.* Newson, 2 Q. B. D. 102; 46 L. J. Q. B. 209.

(*b*) Sale of Goods Act, § 13. See below, § 97 (*c*).

(*c*) Benjamin on Sale, 595 sqq.

95. It is a condition implied, that the goods shall be fit for the purpose for which they are bought (*a*), and such as they are represented or taken to be, according to the fair understanding of the parties (*b*). In applying this principle, two cases are to be distinguished,—one where the thing bought is produced to the buyer, and under his examination; the other where it is not seen or examined by the buyer.

(*a*) 1 Stair, 9. § 5, 10, 11. 3 Ersk. 3 § 10. 1 Pardessus, 291. See § 97A. Cooper & Aves *v.* Clydesdale Shg. Co., 1863; 1 Macph. 677. Edin. Brewery Co. *v.* Reid, 1866; 24 D. 26. Stewart *v.* Jamieson, 1863; 1 Macph. 525. Hutchison & Co. *v.* Henry & Corrie, 1867; 6 Macph. 57. Campbell *v.* Mason, 1801; Hume, 678. Below, § 97B.

(*b*) Ralston *v.* Robb, 1808; M. *Sale*, Apx. 6; 1 Ill. 114. Baird *v.* Pagan, 1765; M. 14,240; 1 Ill. 7. Adamson *v.* Smith, 1797; M. 14,244. Dickson *v.* Kincaid, Dec. 15, 1808; F. C. Fisher *v.* Samuda, 1 Camp. 193; 1 Ill. 96. Kerr & Sons *v.* M'Dowall, 1828; 6 S. 1029. Jones *v.* Bright, 5 Bing. 533; 30 R. R. 728; 1 Ill. 101. Okill *v.* Small, 1 Starkie, 108. Gray *v.* Cox, 4 B. & Cr. 108; 1 Ill. 99. See Poulton *v.* Latimer, 9 B. & Cr. 259; 32 R. R. 603; 1 Ill. 97. Roberts & Co. *v.* Yule, 1896; 23 R. 855. See above, § 94A.

96. *Caveat Emptor.*—Where the buyer has himself seen and examined the 'specific' goods, the *general* rule (and it is so in England as well as in Scotland) is, *Caveat emptor*—the buyer's eye is his merchant; once approved, the subject is held unexceptionable, unless fraud shall be proved against the seller (*a*). But to this rule there are exceptions:—

The rule does not apply if the 'specific' commodity have not been seen, or an opportunity given to the buyer of satisfying himself; or if the seller knew of any material defect not obvious, and concealed it; or if any misrepresentation have been made, or statement framed to mislead (*b*). 'On the sale of specific goods, whether by sample or in bulk, the purchaser must take the goods though they do not possess some quality which he thought they possessed, unless either there was a warranty that they had that quality, or being specifically described, they do not on trial answer the description in the contract (§ 97), or the mistake was induced by the active fraud (not the mere silence) of the seller, or the defect is of the kind mentioned in § 98, *infra* (*c*).'

(*a*) 1 Stair, 9. § 11; and 10. § 14. Parkinson *v.* Lee, 2 East, 314; 1 Ill. 97. 2 Ross' L. C. 327. La Neuville *v.* Nourse, 3 Camp. 351. Bluett *v.* Osborne, 1 Starkie, 384. Power *v.* Barham, 4 Ad. & El. 473. Hill *v.* Gray, 1 Starkie, 435; 1 Ill. 16. Pilmore *v.* Hood, 5 Bing. N. C. 97. Muil *v.* Gibb, 1840; 2 D. 1227.

(*b*) Stair, *ut sup.* Gardiner *v.* Gray, 4 Camp. 144; 16 R. R. 764; 1 Ill. 98. Laing *v.* Fidgeon, 6 Taunt. 108; 4 Camp. 169; 16 R. R. 589. Duthie *v.* Carnegie, Jan. 12, 1815; F. C. Mellish *v.* Motteux, Peake, 115; 3 Ill. 195 (disapproved, Baglehole *v.* Walters, 3 Camp. 154; 13 R. R. 778). Jones *v.* Bowden, 4 Taunt. 847; 14 R. R. 683. Rain *v.* Old, 2 B. & Cr. 627; 26 R. R. 497. Freeman *v.* Baker, 5 B. & Ad. 797.

(*c*) Smith *v.* Hughes, 40 L. J. Q. B. 221; L. R. 6 Q. B. 597; and above, § 11 (*h*).

97. If the fault be latent, although the buyer should see the commodity, there 'was,' by the law of Scotland, an implied warranty (*a*); the goods 'might,' on discovery of the fault, be rejected; and if the article 'perished' by such latent fault, the buyer 'was' relieved from payment, or entitled to have back the price (*b*). 'It was, however, and still is, the law of Scotland, that specific goods sold by description may be rejected even when the buyer has seen and examined them, if they turn out to be different in kind from those described, provided that the difference was not apparent on inspection, *e.g.* when one sells flax yarn, and delivers yarn partly consisting of jute. In such a case the vendor does not fulfil the terms of his contract (*c*).'

The English rule formerly was, that a sound price implies the warranty of sound goods; but this is now departed from, as too elusory; and in all defects, even latent, the buyer is 'now' held 'in the law of England and also of Scotland' to be aware of the possibility of their existence, and to take the risk, unless either an express warranty is taken, or there is fraud on the part of the seller. 'In short, there is no implied warranty against latent defects in the sale of a definite existing article, the actual condition of which may be ascertained by either party (*d*).'

(*a*) 1 Stair, 10. § 15. Reid *v.* Steele, 1824; 3 S. 141. Whealler *v.* Methuen, 1843; 5 D. 402. Paterson *v.* Dickson, 1850; 12 D. 402.

(*b*) Gilmer *v.* Galloway, 1830; 8 S. 420.

(*c*) **Jaffé** *v.* **Ritchie,** 1860; 23 D. 242. Carter & Co. *v.* Campbell, 1885; 12 R. 1075. Josling *v.* Kingford, 13 C. B. N. S. 447; 32 L. J. C. P. 94. Barr *v.* Gibson, 3 M. & W. 390. The same principle applies to sales by sample, see § 98, and is embodied in § 13 of the Act of 1893; see above, § 94A.

(*d*) **Jones** *v.* **Just**, L. R. 3 Q. B. 197; 37 L. J. Q. B. 89. Barr *v.* Gibson, 3 M. & W. 390. Emmerton *v.* Matthews, 7 H. & N. 586; 31 L. J. Ex. 139. Cf. Mody *v.* Gregson, L. R. 4 Ex. 49; 38 L. J. Ex. 12. Jaffé *v.* Ritchie, *cit.* Baglehole *v.* Walters, *cit.*, § 96. Ward *v.* Hobbs, 4 App. Ca. 13; 47 L. J. Q. B. 90.

97A. '*Mercantile Law Amendment Act,* 1856.—An attempt was made to assimilate the law of Scotland to that of England by 19 and 20 Vict. c. 60, § 5, now repealed (*a*), by which it was enacted, that "where goods (*b*) shall, after the passing of this Act, be sold, the seller, if at the time of the sale he was without knowledge (*c*) that the same were defective or of bad quality, shall not be held to have warranted their quality or sufficiency; but the goods, with all faults, shall be at the risk of the purchaser, unless the seller shall have given an express warranty (*d*) of the quality or sufficiency of such goods, or unless the goods have been expressly sold for a specified and particular purpose (*e*), in which case the seller shall be considered, without such warranty, to warrant that the same are fit for such purpose."'

(*a*) Sale of Goods Act, 1893, § 60 and Sch.

(*b*) Under the term "goods," horses are included. Young *v.* Giffen, 1858; 21 D. 87. This statutory rule, as well as the rule of the English law which it was intended to embody, applied only to sales of a specific *corpus*, or definite part of a *corpus*, which is at the risk of the buyer after the sale, not to the sale of a quantity of goods by measure and weight, the specific goods not being pointed out; nor did it apply to a case where the goods are of a different description from those about which the parties contracted (*supra*, § 97). Jaffé *v.* Ritchie, 1860; 23 D. 242. Hutchison & Co. *v.* Henry & Corrie, 1867; 6 Macph. 57. See below, § 98 (*a*). Stewart *v.* Jamieson, 1863, 1 Macph. 525, and Edinr. etc. Brewing Co. *v.* Keith, 1861, 24 D. 26, though there are some loose and inaccurate expressions in the reports, are decisions under the common law. See § 95, 111. So the Lord Chancellor (Cairns), in Taylor *v.* Macfarlane & Co., 1868, 6 Macph. H. L. 1, L. R. 1 Sc. Ap. 245, seems, unless the cases cited are wrongly decided, to have unnecessarily founded his judgment on the statute instead of the common law.

(*c*) Rough *v.* Moir, 1875 ; 2 R. 528. Robeson (*d*).

(*d*) If an express warranty not in writing is alleged, there must be satisfactory evidence specifying the terms in which it was granted. Robeson *v.* Waugh, 1874 ; 2 R. 63. Mackie *v.* Riddell, *ib.* 115. Rough, *cit.* Rose *v.* Johnston, 1877 ; 5 R. 600.

(*e*) Hardie *v.* Austin & M'Aslan, 1870 ; 8 Macph. 798. Taylor *v.* Macfarlane, *cit.* Rough, *supra* (*c*). Hamilton *v.* Robertson, 1878 ; 5 R. 839. Dunlop *v.* Crawford, 1886 ; 13 R. 973. Randall *v.* Newsom, 2 Q. B. D. 102 ; 46 L. J. Q. B. 259. Adams *v.* Pattison & Co., 1884 ; 2 Sel. Sh. Ct. Ca. 526. See above, § 95. If the buyer rely on his own judgment, the purchase of a known, defined, and described article, although known to be for a particular purpose, does not necessarily imply a warranty that it is fit for that purpose, the thing being actually supplied. Chanter *v.* Hopkins, 4 M. & W. 399 ; 2 Ross' L. C. 368. **Jones** *v.* **Just,** *sup.* § 97 (*d*). Kerr *v.* M'Dowall, 1828 ; 6 S. 1029. Ollivant *v.* Bayley, 5 Q. B. 288 ; 13 L. J. Q. B. 34. Rowan *v.* Coats Iron Co., 1885 ; 12 R. 395.

97B. *Sale of Goods Act,* 1893, *on the Rule of Caveat Emptor and Exceptions.*—'The fourteenth clause of this Act sets forth the present law. Subject to the provisions of this Act and of any statute on that behalf, there is no implied warranty or condition as to the quality or fitness for any particular purpose of goods supplied under a contract of sale (*a*), except as follows :—

'(1) Where the buyer, expressly or by implication makes known to the seller the particular purpose for which the goods are required, so as to show that the buyer relies on the seller's skill or judgment, and the goods are of a description (*i.e.* kind) which it is in the course of the seller's business to supply (whether he be the manufacturer or not),—there is an implied condition that the goods shall be reasonably fit for such purpose (*b*). But when an article is sold under its patent or other trade name, there is no such implied condition (*c*).

'(2) When goods are bought by description from a seller who deals in goods of that description (*i.e.* kind), whether he be the manufacturer or not, there is an implied condition that they shall be of merchantable quality (*d*). If, however, the buyer has examined them, there is no implied condition as regards defects which such examination ought to have revealed.

'(3) An implied warranty or condition as to quality or fitness for a particular purpose may be annexed by usage of trade (*e*).

'(4) An express warranty or condition does not negative a warranty or condition implied by the Act, unless inconsistent therewith.'

(*a*) Jones *v.* Just, Ward *v.* Hobbs, and other cases in § 97 (*d*).

(*b*) Jones *v.* Bright, and other cases in § 95 (*b*), and § 97A (*e*).

(*c*) Gillespie Bros. *v.* Cheney & Co., 1896 ; 2 Q. B. 259.

(*d*) **Jones** *v.* **Just**, and cases in § 98 (*a*) (*b*).

(*e*) Jones *v.* Bowden, 4 Taunt. 847 ; 14 R. R. 683.

98. When the goods are afterwards to be furnished or sent to the buyer, they may be rejected on implied warranty: either where they are not merchantable according to the denomination of the commodity (*a*); or where, sold by sample, they do not, when sent in bulk, correspond with the sample (*b*). 'When a manufacturer or dealer supplies an article which he makes or produces, to be applied to a particular purpose, or which the buyer cannot see, so that in either case the buyer trusts to his judgment, there is an implied warranty that it shall be reasonably fit for that purpose or merchantable (*c*). When goods are bought without inspection from a manufacturer who does not hold himself out as dealing in such goods otherwise than as a manufacturer, and whose goods have no special brand or character, it has been held in England that it is, and in Scotland that it is not, an implied term in the contract that the seller shall furnish goods manufactured by himself (*d*). And it is thought, and certainly was intended by the Legislature, that the effect of the Sale of Goods Act, 1893, was to make the Scotch rule generally applicable (*e*).'

In order to raise this implied warranty by sample, it is not sufficient that a part of the goods shall have been drawn and exhibited; unless it is expressly referred to in the bargain as such, and due precaution taken for identifying the sample. But although the sale be not properly by sample, a specimen produced to the buyer, as indicating the quality, may be referred to as evidence of deceit or error (*f*).

(*a*) Gardiner and Laing, *supra*, § 96 (*b*). Tyre *v.* Fynmore, 3 Camp. 461 ; 1 Ill. 95. Bridge *v.* Wain, 1 Starkie, 504. Parker *v.* Palmer, 4 B. & Ald. 387. See Whealler *v.* Methuen, 1843 ; 5 D. 402. Jones *v.* Just, 37 L. J. Q. B. 89 ; L. R. 3 Q. B. 197. Jaffé *v.* Ritchie, 1860 ; 23 D. 242. Cooper and Aves *v.* Clydesdale Shipping Co., 1863 ; 1 Macph. 677. Chitty on Contracts, 419, 9th ed.

(*b*) Hibbert *v.* Shee, 1 Camp. 113 ; 10 R. R. 649. 1 Pardessus, 293. Watt *v.* Glen, 1829 ; 7 S. 372 ; 1 Ill. 103. See Padgett and Melville, below, § 99 (*d*). Jowitt *v.* Stead, 1860 ; 22 D. 1400. Chapman, *infra*, § 99 (*a*). Meyer *v.* Everth, 4 Camp. 22 ; 1 Ill. 101 ; 15 R. R. 722. Whether goods are sold by sample or even after inspection in bulk, it is an implied term in the contract that they shall reasonably answer the specified description, *i.e.* "be merchantable according to the denomination of the commodity"; *supra* (*a*); and § 97B. Nicholls *v.* Godts, 10 Ex. 191. Josling *v.* Kingford, 13 C. B. N. S. 447. Mody *v.* Gregson, L. R. 4 Ex. 49; 38 L. J. Ex. 12. Drummond *v.* Van Ingen, 12 App. Ca. 284 (latent defect in sample repeated in goods delivered). Jones *v.* Padgett, 24 Q. B. D. 650. *Supra*, § 95, 96.

(*c*) Jones *v.* Just, *cit.* Campbell *v.* Mason, 1801; Hume, 678. Brown *v.* Edgington, 2 M. & G. 279; 2 Ross' L. C. 375. Jones *v.* Bright, 5 Bing. 533; 2 Ross, 343. Laing, *supra*, § 96 (*b*). Shepherd *v.* Pybus, 3 M. & G. 368. Macfarlane *v.* Taylor, 1868; 6 Macph. H. L. 1. Van Oppen *v.* Arbuckle, 1855; 18 D. 113. Fleming & Co. *v.* Airdrie Iron Co., 1882; 9 R. 473. Douglas & Co. *v.* Milne, 1895; 23 R. 163.

(*d*) Johnson & Reay *v.* Raylton, Dixon, & Co., 7 Q. B. D. 438; 50 L. J. Q. B. 753. West Stockton Iron Co. *v.* Nielson & Maxwell, 1880; 7 R. 1055. Johnson & Reay *v.* Nicoll, 1881; 8 R. 437.

(*e*) 57 and 58 Vict. c. 71, § 13, 14.

(*f*) Meyer *v.* Everth, *sup.* (*b*). White & Co. *v.* Dougherty, 1891; 18 R. 972. See below, as to Special Warranties, § 111.

99. In order to avail himself of warranty, the buyer must make his challenge instantly, or without unreasonable delay, otherwise he is liable for the full price. 'He is not bound actually to return the goods, or even to place them in neutral custody, but only to make an unequivocal rejection (*a*).' (1.) Where the fault is known or manifest, if the challenge be not immediate 'and distinct,' the legal inference is that the buyer is satisfied (*b*). (2.) Where the fault is not manifest at first sight, but easily discoverable by such examination as a merchant skilled in the commodity naturally bestows in buying, he must immediately investigate and determine (*c*); and if he break bulk, or make use of the article, 'or do anything which infers an election to accept the goods,' he is barred from objecting to it (*d*). 'In every case the right of rejecting the goods and rescinding the contract must be exercised "within a reasonable time." What is a reasonable time is a question of fact (*e*). But a buyer is not barred from rejecting goods as disconform to order by the mere fact that he has sold or used part of them before discovery of the defect (*f*).' (3.) Sometimes there is a certain time allowed by custom for examination (*g*). 'Indeed, in all cases the buyer must have a fair opportunity of examining the articles furnished to him (*h*); and he may even experiment on a small quantity, if no more than absolutely necessary, for the purpose of testing their quality (*i*). And in some executory contracts, as in the case of machinery to be erected on the premises of the buyer, a reasonable time must be allowed for trial (*k*).' (4.) Immediate inspection is more especially required when the commodity may alter by keeping (*l*). (5.) When in an executory contract goods have been returned as disconform to order, proof of conformity is necessary to sustain action by the seller (*m*). 'In an executory contract in which payment is made by instalments, and constructive delivery and appropriation take place as the work proceeds, the purchaser may claim damages for breach of contract even after he has taken full possession and without rejecting the article (*n*).'

(*a*) **Chapman** *v.* **Couston, Thomson, & Co.**, 1871; 9 Macph. 675; aff. 1872, 10 Macph. H. L. 74; L. R. 2 Sc. App. 250, explained as to this point in Grimoldby *v.* Wells, 44 L. J. C. P. 203; L. R. 10 C. P. 391. Lucy *v.* Moufflet, 5 H. & N. 229; 29 L. J. Ex. 110. See Jowitt *v.* Stead, 1860, 22 D. 1400, and the cases in following notes, and Cal. Ry. Co. *v.* Rankin, 1882; 11 R. 64.

(*b*) 1 Stair, 10. § 15. 3 Ersk. 3. § 10. Paton *v.* Lockhart, 1675; M. 14,232; 1 Ill. 101. Seaton *v.* Carmichael, 1680; M. 14,234. Brisbane *v.* Glasgow Merchants, 1684; M. 12,328. Mitchell *v.* Bisset, 1694; M. 14,236. Murdoch *v.* Richardson, 1776; 5 B. Sup. 583. Gordon *v.* Scott, 1773; *ib.* 585. Stevenson *v.* Dalrymple, 1808; M. *Sale*, Apx. 5. Bennoch *v.* M'Kail, Jan. 27, 1820; F. C.; 1 Ill. 104. Cossar *v.* Marjoribanks, 1826; 4 S. 685. **M'Cormick** *v.* **Rittmeyer**, 1869; 7 Macph. 854. Edin. Brewing Co. *v.* Reid, 1861; 24 D. 26. **Chapman** *v.* **Couston & Co.**, 1871; *supra.* Carter & Co. *v.* Campbell, 1885; 12 R. 1075 (seed oats free of barley). Fisher *v.* Samuda, 1 Camp. 193; 1 Ill. 96. Hopkins *v.* Appleby, *ib.* 477. Groning *v.* Mendham, 1 Starkie, 257; 1 Ill. 100. Parker *v.* Palmer, 4 B. & Ald. 387; 23 R. R. 313. Rowe *v.* Osborne, 1 Starkie, 140; 18 R. R. 574.

(*c*) Yeats *v.* Pym, Holt's Cases, 95; 6 Taunt. 446; 16 R. R. 653. See Street *v.* Blay, 2 B. & Ald. 456. Smart *v.* Begg, 1852; 14 D. 912. Smith Brothers *v.* Scott, 1875; 2 R. 601.

(*d*) Murdoch and Gordon, *supra* (*b*). Jeffrey *v.* Boag, 1824; 3 S. 375. See below, § 118B. Ransan *v.* Mitchell, 1845; 7 D. 813. Ramsay *v.* M'Lellan, 1845; 8 D. 142. Smith Brothers, *cit.* Chapman *v.* Morton, 11 M. & W. 534, and other cases in Benjamin on Sales, 711. Carter & Co. *v.* Campbell, *cit.* (*b*). It was held that a purchaser cannot both object to goods delivered, and retain them in security of a claim of damages. Padgett *v.* M'Nair, 1852; 15 D. 76. Melville *v.* Critchley, 1856; 18 D. 643. Comp. Laing *v.* Westren, 1858; 20 D. 519. Pearce, *infra* (*k*). In the sale of seed where the quality and description can be ascertained only after the crop has grown, an action of damages is admitted. 1 Bell's Com. 438 (463, 464, M'L.'s ed.). Dickson *v.* Kincaid, Dec. 15, 1808; F. C.; 2 Ross' L. C. 833. Baird *v.* Aitken, 1788; M. 14,243; and comp. **Hardie** *v.* **Austin & M'Aslan**, 1870; 8 Macph. 798. Hardie *v.* Smith & Simons, 1870; 42 Sc. Jur. 454. Carter & Co. *v.* Campbell, *cit.* (*b*). Smith & Son *v.* Waite, Nash, & Co., 1888; 15 R. 533. Poulton *v.* Lattimore, 9 B. & C. 259. Randall *v.* Raper, E. B. & E. 84; 27 L. J. Q. B. 266. Allan *v.* Leake, 18 Q. B. 567. See the Scotch cases classified in R. Brown's Sale of Goods Act, p. 54, note.

(*e*) Sale of Goods Act, § 11 (2), 56.

(*f*) M'Cormick *v.* Rittmeyer, *cit.* (*b*). M'Caw, Stevenson, & Orr *v.* M'Laren & Sons, 1893; 20 R. 437.

(*g*) Yeats, *supra* (*c*).

(*h*) See Isherwood *v.* Whitmore, 12 L. J. Ex. 318; 11 M. & W. 347.

(i) Baird v. Pagan, 1765; M. 14,240. Hunt v. Hecht, 8 Ex. 817. Heilbutt v. Hickson, L. R. 7 C. P. 438; 41 L. J. C. P. 228. Castle v. Sworder, 30 L. J. Ex. 310.

(k) **Pearce Brothers v. Irons**, 1869; 7 Macph. 571. See Morson & Co. v. Burns, 1866; 5 Macph. 99. Fleming & Co. v. Airdrie Iron Co., 1882; 9 R. 473. Bradley & Co. v. Dollar, 1886; 13 R. 893. Morrison & Mason v. Clarkson Brothers, 1898; 25 R. 427.

(l) Yeats, *sup.* (c), and Stevenson (b).

(m) Haydon v. Hayward, 1 Camp. 180; 1 Ill. 101.

(n) Spencer & Co. v. Dobie & Co., 1879; 7 R. 396. Gillespie v. Howden, 1885; 12 R. 800. Dick & Stevenson v. Woodside Iron Co., 1888; 16 R. 242. See below, § 1303.

99A. 'Until 1892 there was by the law of Scotland no right to retain the goods and claim an abatement of the price as in the *actio quanti minoris* of the Roman law, unless in the case of fraud (a), or of a special bargain or usage (b). But it is now enacted "that in Scotland failure by the seller to perform any material part of the contract of sale is a breach of contract, and entitles the buyer either within a reasonable time after delivery to reject the goods and treat the contract as repudiated, or to retain the goods and treat the failure to perform such material part as a breach which may give rise to a claim for compensation or damages" (c). A purchaser who elects to reject must not break bulk or use or consume the goods, but must act in accordance with the rules stated above (§ 99 (f)) in regard to rejection (d). If the rejection when made was justified by the seller's breach of contract, but the buyer by his subsequent conduct is barred from availing himself of it, he is not entitled to claim damages under this alternative clause (e). But if it is found in legal proceedings, or afterwards appears, that the rejection was not originally justified by the seller's breach of contract, then, as there was really no valid rejection, the buyer may still elect to claim damages (f).'

(a) 1 Stair, 9. § 10–14, 10. § 14, 15. 3 Ersk. Inst. 3. 10. 1 Bankt. 19. 3. Gray v. Hamilton, 1800; M. Apx. *Sale*, 2. Watt v. Glen, 1829; 7 S. 372; 1 Ill. 103. Amaan v. Handyside & Henderson, 1865; 3 Macph. 526. Latta v. Park & Co., *ib.* 508. Dobbie v. Duncanson, 1872; 10 Macph. 810. Houldsworth v. City of Glasgow Bank, 1879; 6 R. 1164; aff. 1880, 7 R. H. L. 53. See further, § 893, *infra.*

(b) *Per* Inglis, J.-C., in Hansen v. Craig & Rose, 1859; 21 D. 441. M'Cormick v. Rittmeyer, 1869; 7 Macph. 854. A course of dealing or usage between the parties may also create an exception to the rule that challenge and rejection must be immediate. M'Carter v. Stewart & M'Kenzie, 1877; 4 R. 890.

(c) 56 and 57 Vict. c. 71, § 11 (2), and see § 35, 53, and 62.

(d) Electric Construction Co. v. Hurry & Young, 1896; 24 R. 312.

(e) Electric Construction Co., *cit.*; and § 35 of the Act.

(f) Paton & Sons v. Payne & Co., 1897; 35 S. L. R. 112; cf. Morrison & Mason v. Clarkson Brothers, 1898; 25 R. 427.

100. (2.) *Implied Conditions as to Payment of the Price.*—'"When the bargain is simple and without special stipulation, the buyer's obligation is to pay immediately, and the seller is entitled to demand and have action for payment on offering delivery of the thing, or proving the delivery made, or on showing that the thing has perished by accident" (a). By the Sale of Goods Act, "it is the duty of the seller to deliver the goods, and of the buyer to accept and pay for them, in accordance with the terms of the contract of sale" (b). Unless otherwise agreed, delivery of the goods and payment of the price are concurrent conditions, *i.e.* the seller must be ready and willing to give possession of the goods to the buyer in exchange for the price, and the buyer must be ready and willing to pay the price in exchange for the possession of the goods (c). And where the property has passed and the buyer wrongly neglects or refuses to pay in terms of the contract, the seller has an action for the price (d). If the property has not passed, the seller has an action of damages; the measure of damages is the estimated loss directly and naturally resulting in the ordinary course of events from the buyer's breach of contract (e); and where there is an available market, that is *primâ facie* the difference between the market price at the time or times when the goods ought to have been accepted, or if there was no fixed time at the time of refusal (f).'

Sale on Credit — Insolvency of Buyer.—Where the sale is on credit, solvency is an implied condition; and if the buyer fail, or be *vergens ad inopiam*, the seller may refuse to proceed (g). 'In the case of declared insolvency, the seller's right to retain (h) or to stop *in transitu* (i) is clear; but in modern practice the question has not been raised with one alleged to be *vergens ad inopiam* (k). The mere insolvency of the buyer does not rescind the contract. His creditors (or trustee) may still, on fulfilling his obligations under the contract, obtain delivery of the goods (l). The rule settled in England is, that if one who has become openly insolvent, or his creditors, or trustee, fail within a reasonable time to intimate their intention to carry out a current contract, the other party may treat it as rescinded (m).,

(*a*) Bell on Sale, p. 103; cf. pp. 20, 78. Hall & Sons *v.* Scott, 1860; 22 D. 413. Linn *v.* Shield, 1863; 2 Macph. 88. Benjamin on Sales, 717 sqq. *Infra*, § 127, 128.
(*b*) Act, § 27.
(*c*) Act, § 28.
(*d*) Act, § 49 (1).
(*e*) Act, § 50 (1) (2). See below, § 128.
(*f*) Act, § 50 (3). See below, § 128.
(*g*) See above, § 71 and 46. It would seem that a seller may claim restitution of his goods if inadvertently delivered without payment, unless he is barred by delay, or by giving credit. Richmond *v.* Railton, 1854; 16 D. 403.
(*h*) See § 116, 1300 sqq., below.
(*i*) See § 1303, 1307 sqq.
(*k*) See 1 Bell's Com. 223 (242, M'L.'s ed.). *In re* Phœnix Bessemer Steel Co., *infra*.
(*l*) 1 Bell's Com. 442 (471, M'L.'s ed.). *Ex p.* Lambton (*m*).
(*m*) Bloxam *v.* Sanders, 4 B. & C. 951; 28 R. R. 519; 2 Ross' L. C. 47; 1 Smith's L. C. 720. Wentworth *v.* Outhwaite, 10 M. & W. 436; 12 L. J. Ex. 172. Griffiths *v.* Perry, 1 E. & E. 680; 28 L. J. Q. B. 204. *Ex p.* Chalmers, L. R. 8 Ch. 289; 42 L. J. Bkr. 2. 37. Bloomer *v.* Bernstein, 43 L. J. C. P. 375; L. R. 9 C. P. 588. Morgan *v.* Bain, L. R. 10 C. P. 15; 44 L. J. C. P. 47. *In re* Phœnix Bessemer Steel Co., 46 L. J. Ch. 115; 4 Ch. D. 108. *Ex p.* Stapleton, 10 Ch. D. 586. *Ex p.* Lambton, L. R. 10 Ch. 105; 44 L. J. Bkr. 81 (building a ship). See also Benjamin on Sales, 679 sq., 756.

101. The usage of trade is an implied condition in sale, as in every mercantile contract (*a*), and as such held to be incorporated in the agreement. So a sale, in simple terms, implies the usual credit given in that line of trade. But it is an exception to this rule, that if the usage be local, and/'or' unknown to one of the parties, it (*b*) has no effect; and that no custom will be admitted in contradiction of the express words of the contract (*c*).

(*a*) See Newman *v.* Cazalet, Park, 900; 1 Ill. 326. Sheriff *v.* Stein's Assignees, 1828; 7 S. 47; 1 Ill. 160; 4 Murr. 454. Stewart *v.* Gordon, 1831; 9 S. 466; 1 Ill. 104. Hodgson *v.* Davies, 2 Camp. 530; 11 R. R. 789. Dickinson *v.* Sitwell, 4 Camp. 279. Smith *v.* Wilson, 3 Barn. & Ald. 728. Woodhouse *v.* Swift, 7 Car. & P. 310. Athya & Co. *v.* Rowell, 1856; 18 D. 1299. Armstrong & Co. *v.* M'Gregor & Co., 1875; 2 R. 339. Towill & Co. *v.* Brit. Agric. Assoc., 1875; 3 R. 117. *Supra*, § 83; *infra*, § 524 (4). Notes to Wigglesworth *v.* Dallison in 2 Smith's L. C. 529, 9th ed.; and 1 *Id.* 528, 10th ed.
(*b*) To be binding it must be known, or taken to be known, to both. Mollett *v.* Robinson, L. R. 7 H. L. 802; 44 L. J. C. P. 362.
(*c*) Yeats, *supra*, § 99 (*c*). Kirchner *v.* Venus, 12 Moo. P. C. 399. Holman *v.* Peruv. Nitrate Co., 1878; 5 R. 657. Fleet *v.* Murton, L. R. 7 Q. B. 126; 41 L. J. Q. B. 49. Abbot *v.* Bates, 43 L. J. C. P. 150.

101A. '(3.) *Warranty implied in Trade Mark.*—By 51 and 52 Vict. c. 28, § 17, repealing 25 and 26 Vict. c. 88, § 19, 20, on the sale or contract for the sale of any goods to which a trade mark or mark or trade description has been applied, the seller is deemed to warrant that the trade mark is a genuine trade mark, and not forged or falsely applied, or that the trade description is not a false description within the meaning of the Act; unless the contrary be expressed in a signed writing delivered at the time of the sale or contract to and accepted by the vendee. Trade description includes any statement of weight, measure, etc., or of the place or country where the goods sold were made or produced, or the material or mode of manufacture, etc. (*a*).'

(*a*) See further in the Act.

102. Express or Special Conditions.—These are employed to introduce some point of agreement not naturally implied in the contract, or to alter what is so implied. They may either regulate the payment of the price; or arrange the delivery; or suspend or dissolve the sale in particular events; or give special warranties.

102A. *Reservation of Right of Disposal.*—'Where there is a contract for the sale of specific goods, or where goods are subsequently appropriated to the contract, the seller may, by the terms of the contract or appropriation, reserve the right of disposal of the goods until certain conditions are fulfilled. In such case, notwithstanding the delivery of the goods to the buyer, or to a carrier or other bailee or custodier for the purpose of transmission to the buyer, the property does not pass until the conditions imposed by the buyer are fulfilled (*a*).

'Where goods are shipped, and by the bill of lading the goods are deliverable to the order of the seller or his agent, the seller is *primâ facie* deemed to reserve the right of disposal (*b*).

'Where the seller draws on the buyer for the price, and transmits the bill of exchange and bill of lading to the buyer together, to secure acceptance or payment of the bill of exchange, the buyer is bound to return the bill of lading if he does not honour the bill of exchange, and if he wrongfully retains the bill of lading the property in the goods does not pass to him (*c*). So a stipulation for payment in cash against bill of lading "is strong evidence of an intention that the property shall not pass; but the question is one of intention to be determined from all the circumstances" (*d*).'

'*Stipulations as to time*, other than those relating to time of payment, are generally of the essence of the contract (*e*); but it depends on the terms of the contract (*f*).

'Where under a contract of sale the price is payable on a day certain, irrespective of delivery, and the buyer wrongfully neglects or refuses to pay such price, the seller may maintain an action for the price, though the property has not passed and the goods have not been appropriated to the contract (*g*).'

(*a*) Sale of Goods Act, 1893, § 19 (1). Mirabita *v.* Ottoman Bank, 3 Ex. D. 164; 47 L. J. Ex. 418.

(*b*) *Ib.* § 19 (2). Mirabita, *cit.* Ogg *v.* Shuter, *infra*, (*d*), and § 104.

(*c*) 1 Bell's Com. 238 (259, M'L.'s ed.). Brandt & Co. *v.* Dickson, 1876; 3 R. 375. Clarke & Co. *v.* Miller & Son's Tr., 1885; 12 R. 1035. Brodie *v.* Todd, *infra*, § 104. Hills *v.* Buchanan, 1786; 3 Pat. 47. Shepherd *v.* Harrison. 38 L. J. Q. B. 105, 177; L. R. 4 Q. B. 196, 493; 5 H. L. 116; 40 L. J. Q. B. 148. See below, § 109, 418, 1302 *fin.*

(*d*) See Blackburn on Sale, p. 148. Benjamin on Sales, 369. Van Casteel *v.* Booker, 3 Ex. 691, and other cases cited in § 1308. Ogg *v.* Shuter, 44 L. J. C. P. 161; L. R. 10 C. P. 159; rev. on facts, 45 L. J. C. P. 44; 1 C. P. D. 47. Compare the state of facts in Brandt *v.* Dickson and Clarke *v.* Miller, *supra* (*c*).

(*e*) Bowes *v.* Shand, 2 App. Ca. 455; 46 L. J. Q. B. 56. Reuter *v.* Sala, 4 C. P. D. 246.

(*f*) Sale of Goods Act, § 10 (1). See below, § 115, 127.

(*g*) The Act, § 49 (2).

103. (1.) *Express Conditions as to Payment* (*a*).—'Unless a different intention appears from the terms of the contract, stipulations as to time of payment are not deemed to be of the essence of the contract of sale (*b*).' The accustomed credit, held to be incorporated in the contract by force of usage, may by special agreement be rejected; if so rejected *tempestivè* (*c*). An agreement to pay at six months, by a bill at two or three months, has been held credit at nine months (*d*). A special condition of "ready money" suspends the passing of the property even in a question with creditors (*e*).

(*a*) See above, § 92, and below, § 127.

(*b*) Sale of Goods Act, § 10 (1).

(*c*) Arnot *v.* Watt, 1825; 4 S. 4; 1 Ill. 105. Hodgson, *sup.* § 101 (*a*). See above, § 100, 101. Athya *v.* Rowell, 1856; 18 D. 1299.

(*d*) Helps *v.* Winterbottom, 9 B. & Ad. 431. See Smith's Merc. Law, 674.

(*e*) See below, § 109. § 1308. Anderson *v.* Ford, 1844; 6 D. 1315.

104. If it be stipulated that "a bill shall be given for the price," it is generally sufficient to send the bill without undue delay, reasonable time being taken to examine the goods; but if stipulated "to be sent in course," that is an absolute condition (*a*).

(*a*) Brodie *v.* Todd & Co., May 20, 1814; F. C.; 1 Ill. 105. Comp. Colvin *v.* Short, 1857; 19 D. 890. Ogg *v.* Shuter, *cit.* § 102A.

105. The stipulation of "a bill" imports the buyer's own bill (*a*). But the seller may object to the credit if the sale be made by a broker for the seller, provided the seller intimate his dissent as soon as he has an opportunity of inquiring into the buyer's credit (*b*); or if there have been undue concealment; or if there be a change on the condition of the buyer between the time of the bargain and the time of tendering the bill (*c*).

(*a*) Somervail & Co. *v.* Stein, 1794; Bell's Cases, 2; 1 Ill. 106. Observe that this case was reversed; 3 Paton, 462.

(*b*) Hodgson *v.* Davies, *sup.* § 101 (*a*); 89 (*l*), 219 (*f*).

(*c*) Brandt & Co., § 102A (*c*). See § 100.

106. The stipulation of "a discountable bill" imports such a bill, in time and in credit, as will produce money at the banks.

107. The stipulation of "an approved bill" seems to import only a bill to which no reasonable objection can be made, and which ought to be approved; otherwise everything would be left to the caprice of the party (*a*).

(*a*) Lord Ellenborough in Hodgson *v.* Davies, *supra*, § 101 (*a*). See Camidge *v.* Allenby, 6 B. & Cr. 373; 5 L. J. K. B. 95. Smith *v* Mercer, 37 L. J. Ex. 24; L. R. 3 Ex. 51.

108. (2.) *Express Conditions as to Delivery.*—Where the goods are sold "on arrival of" (or "by") a certain ship, 'or "*ex* ship" A (*a*),' it is a conditional sale, binding only if there shall be such arrival 'of the ship, and if the goods are on board on her arrival, there being a double condition precedent.' In construing all such stipulations, the object is to find the true and honest meaning of the contract, which is the business of a jury (*b*). 'If the contract asserts that the goods are on board the vessel named, there is only one condition precedent, the arrival of the vessel (*c*).' Where the delivery is to be "on arrival, not beyond" a certain day, it is a condition that the goods shall arrive in time for delivery on that day (*d*). Where there is an entire contract for a quantity to be delivered within a certain time, and part is delivered, the buyer may return that part if the rest be not delivered; and as this privilege endures till expiration of the term, the seller cannot sooner demand payment. But if the term pass without return of the part delivered, the seller has action for the price of what is delivered (*e*).

'*Instalment Deliveries.*—Where there is a

contract for the sale of goods to be delivered by stated instalments, which are to be separately paid for, and the seller makes defective deliveries in respect of one or more instalments, or the buyer neglects or refuses to take delivery of or pay for one or more instalments, it is a question in each case, depending on the terms of the contract and the circumstances of the case, whether the breach of contract is a repudiation of the whole contract, or a severable breach giving rise to a claim for compensation only (*f*).

'Unless otherwise agreed, a buyer is not bound to accept delivery by instalments (*g*), nor to demand it (*h*).'

(*a*) Johnson *v.* Macdonald, 9 M. & W. 600; 12 L. J. Ex. 99.

(*b*) Hawes *v.* Humble, 2 Camp. 327, note; 1 Ill. 106. Boyd *v.* Siffkin, 2 Camp. 326; 11 R. 721. Hayward *v.* Scougal, 2 Camp. 56. Splidt *v.* Hall, 2 Camp. 57, note. Thornton *v.* Simpson, 6 Taunt. 556. See M'Laren's Bell's Com. i. 470. Bell on Sale, 111. Benjamin on Sales, 560 sqq. Johnson *v.* Macdonald, *cit.* Smith *v.* Myers, 39 L. J. Q. B. 210; 41 *ib.* 91; L. R. 5 Q. B. 429; *ib.* 7 Q. B. 139.

(*c*) Hale *v.* Rawson, 4 C. B. N. S. 85; 27 L. J. C. P. 189. Gorrissen *v.* Perrin, 2 C. B. N. S. 681; 27 L. J. C. P. 29.

(*d*) Alewyn *v.* Prior, 1 Ry. & Moo. 406; 1 Ill. 107. Colvin *v.* Short, 1857; 19 D. 890 (cash on 23rd Nov. in exchange for warrants held an essential condition).

(*e*) Oxendale *v.* Wetherell, 9 B. & Cr. 386; 1 Ill. 107; 33 R. R. 207. But see Hall & Sons and Linn, cited § 100.

(*f*) Sale of Goods Act, § 31 (2). **Mersey Steel and Iron Co. *v.* Naylor,** 51 L. J. Q. B. 576; 9 Q. B. D. 648; 9 App. Ca. 434. And see as to contracts for delivery by instalments, Simpson *v.* Crippin, L. R. 8 Q. B. 14; 42 L. J. Q. B. 28. Roper *v.* Johnson, 42 L. J. C. P. 65. Ogle *v.* Vane, 36 L. J. Q. B. 175; 7 B. & S. 855; 37 L. J. Q. B. 77. Tyers *v.* Rosedale, etc., Iron Co., 42 L. J. Ex. 185; 44 *ib.* 130. Honck *v.* Muller, 7 Q. B. D. 92; 50 L. J. Q. B. 529. Turnbull *v.* M'Lean, 1874; 1 R. 730. Higgin *v.* Pumpherston Oil Co., 1893; 20 R. 532. Barr *v.* Waldie, 1893; 21 R. 224. Ireland & Son *v.* Merryton Coal Co., 1894; 21 R. 989. Benjamin on Sales, 54, 582, 584, 888. 2 Smith's L. C. 39, and above, § 33 (*b*), 46, 91 (6).

(*g*) The Act, § 31 (1). Reuter *v.* Sala, 4 C. P. D. 239; 48 L. J. Q. B. 492.

(*h*) Kingdom *v.* Cox, 5 C. B. 522.

109. Suspensive Conditions, if expressly stipulated, may delay the sale, and (even against creditors) bar the passing of the property, though delivered (*a*). 'The condition suspends the contract of sale, and delivery, unless it takes place in such circumstances as to infer waiver of the condition, is not referable to a pure and absolute contract, and therefore does not pass the property (*b*).'

(1.) *Goods 'on Approbation or' on Sale and Return.*—This is a sale either (1) on approval 'of the goods' generally, or within a certain time; in which case the sale is suspended (though the seller may be bound) till the buyer have declared his option (*c*): or (2) 'it is' an arrangement with retail dealers, in which goods are sent to them 'by wholesale dealers' on an agreement that those 'goods' only are to be 'held as' transferred which the former can dispose of. In such contracts this is a legitimate condition suspensive (*d*). But such a case must always be viewed as subject to the law of reputed ownership (*e*).

(2.) *Goods on Hire with Option to buy.*—Goods or furniture or other things may be taken on hire, with an option to keep them as sold at a price (*f*).

'When an owner parts with possession of his moveable property—a pianoforte, a sewing machine, a thrashing mill, or a quantity of furniture—and a question arises with the creditors of the possessor, it is necessary to inquire what is the real nature of the contract. A sale on credit, with a collusive agreement for a hypothec for the price, may be unavailing (*g*). But a *bonâ fide* sale, under the condition that the property shall not pass until a certain sum has been paid, whether expressed as hire payable periodically, or as a price payable by instalments, does not transfer the property until the condition is purified; and the seller is preferred to the property against the buyer or others claiming under him. The doctrine of reputed ownership does not apply if the possession can be ascribed to a known and definite contract (*h*).

'But this state of the law is now subject to the provisions of the 25th section of the Sale of Goods Act, 1893, and the 9th section of the Factors Act, 1889 (applied to Scotland by the Factors (Scotland) Act, 1890), which are nearly in the same terms. It is enacted that where a person, having sold goods, continues or is in possession of the goods or of the documents of title to the goods, the delivery or transfer by him, or by a mercantile agent acting for him, of the goods or documents of title, under any sale, pledge, or other disposition thereof, to any person receiving the same in good faith and without notice of the previous sale, shall have the same effect as if the person making the delivery or transfer were expressly authorised by the owner of the goods to make it (*i*).

'Where a person, having bought or agreed to buy goods, obtains with the consent of the seller possession of them or of the documents of title, the delivery or transfer by him, or by a mercantile agent acting for him, of the goods or documents of title, under any sale, pledge, or other disposition thereof, to any person receiving the same in good faith and without notice of any lien or other right of the original seller in respect of the goods, shall have the same effect as if the person making the transfer or delivery were a mercantile agent in possession of the goods or documents of title with the owner's consent (*k*). This enactment overrides many of the decisions above cited.

(*a*) 1 Stair, 14. § 4. 5. Elch. on Stair, 80. 2 More, p. lxxxviii. 3 Ersk. 3. § 11. Comyn's Dig. *Agreement*, a. 4. Pothier, Oblig. No. 198. Macartney *v.* M'Credie's Crs., 1799; M. *Sale*, Apx. 1; 1 Ill. 107. Cowan *v.* Spence, 1824; 3 S. 28. Wight *v.* Forman, 1828; 7 S. 175. See Brodie *v.* Todd & Co., May 20, 1814; F. C.; 1 Ill. 105. Brandt & Co. *v.* Dickson, 1876; 3 R. 375. Ellis *v.* Mortimer, 1 N. R. 257. Moakes *v.* Nicholson, 19 C. B. N. S. 290; 34 L. J. C. P. 273 (goods being shipped in buyer's ship to be paid for in cash against bill of lading in hands of seller's agent, property does not pass till payment). See Benjamin on Sales, 328 sqq.; and above, § 47, 48, 103 sq.; below, § 116 (*b*).

(*b*) Comp. *per* Lord Young in Clarke & Co. *v.* Miller & Son's Tr., 1885; 12 R. 1035, 1042. See below, § 1315 (*g*), and Pinder & Co. *v.* Fullerton, 1889; 2 Sel. Sh. Ct. Ca. 528.

(*c*) Gibson *v.* Bray, Holt, N. P. Ca. 556; 8 Taunt. 76, note; 19 R. R. 460. Graham & Co. *v.* Pollock, 1760; M. 14,198. Marshall & M'Kell *v.* Kirkwood, 1747; Elch. *Sale*, No. 6. Humphries *v.* Carvalho, 16 East, 45; 14 R. R. 280. Moss *v.* Sweet, 16 Q. B. 493.

(*d*) More's Stair, p. lxxxviii. See 1 Bell's Com. 288 (M'L.'s ed. note). Bell on Sale, 111, and below, § 1315. Brodie's Stair, 901, 909, and the opinions in Brown *v.* Marr, 1880; 7 R. 427 (where the Second Division inclined to hold Sale and Return to be a sale with a *resolutive* condition; but see, *contra*), Macdonald *v.* Westren, 1888; 15 R. 988. Moss *v.* Sweet, *cit.*, and *ex p.* White, *in re* Nevill & Co., L. R. 6 Ch. App. 397; 40 L. J. Bkr. 73; aff. in H. L. *sub nom.* Fowle *v.* White, 20 L. T. 78; 21 W. R. 465, do not determine this point. See § 229 *fin.* and § 1315 (*g*). The risk remains with the owner. Pinder & Co. *v.* Fullerton, *cit.*

(*e*) See below, § 1315.

(*f*) Cowan and Wight, *supra* (*a*).

(*g*) Cropper & Co. *v.* Donaldson, 1880; 7 R. 1108. See below, § 1317.

(*h*) Cowan *v.* Spence, and Wight *v.* Forman, *citt.* (*a*). Marston *v.* Kerr's Tr., 1879; 6 R. 898. Cropper & Co. *v.* Donaldson, 1880; 7 R. 1108. Duncanson *v.* Jefferis' Tr., 1881; 8 R. 563. Hogarth *v.* Smart's Tr., 1882; 9 R. 964. *Ex p.* Powell, *in re* Matthews, 1 Ch. Div. 501; 45 L. J. Bkr. 100. Murdoch & Co. *v.* Greig, 1889; 16 R. 396. *In re* Robertson and *in re* Blanchard, 47 L. J. Bkr. 94, 113; 8 Ch. Div. 601; 9 Ch. Div. 419. Lee *v.* Butler, 1893, 2 Q. B. 318 (where the ordinary terms of a hire-purchase agreement are found—approved in Helby *v.* Matthews, *infra*). In England the validity of such contracts against creditors in bankruptcy depends on the existence of a custom of trade; and in the case of furniture, pianofortes, etc., the Courts now take judicial notice of such a custom. Crawcour *v.* Salter, 51 L. J. Ch. 495; 18 Ch. Div. 30; overruling *ex p.* Powell, *cit.* The later Scotch cases ignore such a distinction. See § 1315, 1317.

(*i*) 56 and 57 Vict. c. 71, § 25 (1).

(*k*) *Ib.* § 25 (2). A hire-purchase agreement, so expressed that the hirer is not obliged to buy, but has only an option to buy, and may terminate the agreement by returning the thing hired, is not a sale or agreement to sell, and so is not affected by the Act, and the owner may recover the article from anyone taking through the hirer. **Helby** *v.* **Matthews**, 1895; A. C. 471.

110. Dissolving Conditions have effect only against the party and his heirs, not against creditors (*a*).

(*a*) Pothier, Oblig. No. 224. Contrast the sounder doctrine of Stair, 1 Stair, 14. § 5, with the more questionable doctrine of Erskine, 3 Ersk. 3. § 11. 1 Bell's Com. 238-39 (259, 260, M'L.'s ed.). *Supra*, § 47-50.

111. Special Warranties (*a*).—These are given where the party, instead of trusting to the implied obligation, requires the condition to be expressly described and warranted. They become absolute qualifications of the contract, whether they relate to the mode of payment, or to the quality of the commodity, or to the time of delivery. So every affirmation of quality made to the buyer as a ground of reliance is a warranty (*b*). 'The rule is, that every affirmation at the time of sale of personal chattels is a warranty, *provided it appears to have been so intended* (*c*).' But the eulogies which dealers are accustomed to make of their goods are not to be received as warranties. They are understood in the ordinary intercourse of trade as boastful recommendations, which the buyer is to take or reject according to his prudence (*d*). If, however, the article be expressly purchased to answer a particular purpose, that is a warranty (*e*). If the article be taken expressly "with all faults," that will not save the seller from a warranty express or necessarily implied (*f*).

(*a*) See above, § 95 and § 97. As to warrandice against Eviction, see below, § 121.

(*b*) *Per* Buller, J., in Pasley *v.* Freeman, 3 T. R. 59; 1 Ill. 208. Button *v.* Corder, 7 Taunt. 405. Shepherd *v.* Kain, 5 B. & Ald. 240; 1 Ill. 100; 24 R. R. 344. There is an important distinction between warranties in the contract of Insurance and warranties in Sale. In the former, no question is admitted as to the *materiality* of any deviation from the warranty (see below, § 475 et seq.); in the latter, materiality seems to be essential to the plea of breach of warranty.

(*c*) Cases in 2 Smith's L. C. 166; 2. 71 (1. 52, 10th ed.); 1 Bell's Com. 466, note, M'L.'s ed. Brodie's Stair, 988. Scott *v.* Steel, 1857; 20 D. 257. Stewart *v.* Jamieson, 1863; 1 Macph. 525. Roberts & Co. *v.* Yule, 1896; 23 R. 855.

(*d*) Benjamin on Sale, 610. 1 Smith's L. C., *cit.*

(*e*) See the above cases, and those under § 95 and 97A.

(*f*) Shepherd, *supra* (*b*). Mellish *v.* Motteux, Peake, 115; 3 Ill. 105. Jones *v.* Bowden, 4 Taunt. 847. "At least fraud vitiates a sale even where the article is sold with all faults." Baglehole *v.* Walters, 3 Camp. 154; 1 Ill. 98; 13 R. R. 778. Pickering *v.* Dowson, 4 Taunt. 779. Fletcher *v.* Bowsher, 2 Stark. 561; 20 R. R. 735.

112. Obligations of the Seller.—The *obligations* of the one party form the *rights* of the other rights and obligations being in all contracts counterparts.

113. (1.) *Delivery.*—The primary duty of the seller is to deliver the thing sold (*a*).

(*a*) See further, § 1299 et seq.

114. He is bound to deliver (*a*) the thing so as to complete the transfer; that being the great object of the contract to the buyer. 'This obligation may be specifically enforced (*b*).' And so there is an implied warranty that the seller has a good title enabling him to sell (*c*), 'unless the circumstances show that the parties only intended to pass such interest as the seller himself had in the thing sold (*d*).' But possession of moveables presumes property; and in the rapid intercourse of trade, the buyer of goods is not allowed to stop the bargain on pretence of want of title, or on mere doubts as to the possibility of a challenge (*e*). But a claim of warrandice arises on eviction (*f*). 'The contract of sale also includes, unless the circumstances show a different intention, an implied warranty that the goods shall be free from any charge or incumbrance in favour of a third party, not declared or known to the buyer when the contract was made (*g*).

Statutory Rules as to Delivery (*h*).—'Whether it is for the buyer to take possession of the goods, or for the seller to send them to the buyer, is a question depending in each case on the contract express or implied. Apart from any such contract, the place of delivery is the seller's place of business if he have one, and, if not, his residence: Provided that specific goods which the parties know to be in some other place when the contract is made are to be delivered there (*i*). Where the goods are in the hands of a third person, there is no delivery unless and until such third person acknowledges to the buyer that he holds the goods on his behalf; but this enactment does not affect the operation of the issue or transfer of documents of title (*k*). Unless otherwise agreed, the expenses of and incidental to putting the goods in a deliverable state must be borne by the seller (*l*).'

(*a*) Sale of Goods Act, § 27.
(*b*) Sutherland *v.* Montrose Shipbuilding Co., 1860; 22 D. 665, 671.
(*c*) Sale of Goods Act, 1893, § 12 (1).
(*d*) Donell. Com. xiii. 2. 19 sqq. This is the correct result of Morley *v.* Attenborough, 3 Ex. 500; 18 L. J. Ex. 148. Bagueley *v.* Hawley, L. R. 2 C. P. 265; 36 L. J. C. P. 328. See Benjamin on Sales, 643 sqq.; below, § 121, 122, 895 *ad fin.*; also, Leith Heritages Co. *v.* Edin. and Leith Glass Co., 1876; 3 R. 879.
(*e*) 1 Stair, 14. § 1. Brown on Sale, 232. Dig. lib. 19. tit. 1, De Act. Empt. 1. 30. § 1. Domat, liv. 1. t. 2. § 2. Pothier, Cont. de Vente, No. 1. The rule is different in sales of land, where sound title alone gives right. See below, § 890, 1313. As to the law of England, see Eichholz *v.* Bannister, 17 C. B. N. S. 708; 34 L. J. C. P. 105. Benjamin on Sales, 606 sqq.
(*f*) See below, § 121.
(*g*) Sale of Goods Act, 1893, § 12 (3).
(*h*) See above, § 91, as to quantity.
(*i*) Sale of Goods Act, § 29 (1).
(*k*) The Act, § 29 (3), altering the law of Scotland, as stated in Black *v.* Incorp. of Bakers, 1867; 6 Macph. 136. 1 Bell's Com. 195. *Infra*, § 1305.
(*l*) The Act, § 29 (5). Bell on Sale, 79.

115. *Time of Delivery.*—The delivery must be made at the time and in the manner stipulated in the contract (*a*); and if there be no stipulation as to time, the delivery must be immediately on the buyer performing all the conditions stipulated, reasonable time being allowed to prepare for the delivery (*b*), 'and notice given of such performance, if it be not a matter within the privity and knowledge of the seller, as, *e.g.*, the arrival of the buyer's ship (*c*).

'If by the contract the seller is bound to send the goods to the buyer, but no time for sending them is fixed, the seller is bound to send them within a reasonable time (*d*). Demand or tender of delivery may be treated as ineffectual unless made at a reasonable hour, what is a reasonable hour being a question of fact (*e*).'

(*a*) See Benjamin on Sales, 690, as to meaning of "forthwith," "reasonable time," "as soon as possible," etc.; also, Startup *v.* Macdonald, 6 M. & G. 593. Cf. Grieve, Son, & Co. *v.* König, 1880; 7 R. 521. Taylor *v.* Maclellans, 1891; 19 R. 10. As to damages for delay in delivery, see Webster & Co. *v.* Cramond Iron Co., 1875; 2 R. 752. Addison on Contr. p. 952, 8th ed. Horn *v.* Midland Ry. Co., 42 L. J. C. P. 59; L. R. 8 C. P. 131. Hydraulic Engineering Co. *v.* M'Haffie, 4 Q. B. D. 670. *Supra*, § 33.
(*b*) Cooper *v.* Green, 1791; M. 10,100. See 1 Ill. 108. See Morton *v.* Lamb, 7 T. R. 125; 1 Ill. 96; 4 R. R. 395. Rawson *v.* Johnston, 1 East, 203; 6 R. R. 252. The Sale of Goods Act, § 29; *infra*, § 117.
(*c*) Armitage *v.* Insole, 14 Q. B. 728. Stanton *v.* Austin, L. R. 7 C. P. 651; 41 L. J. C. P. 218.
(*d*) The Act, § 29 (2). Robb *v.* Cruickshank, 1840; 2 D. 988. Hick *v.* Raymond & Reid, 1893; A. C. 22. Ellis *v.* Thompson, 3 M. & W. 445.
(*e*) *Ib.* § 29 (4). Startup *v.* Macdonald, 6 M. & G. 593.

116. Sometimes the goods are stipulated to remain with the seller till convenient for the buyer to remove them; in which case the seller is truly custodier for the buyer. The perishing of them without fault of the seller will discharge his obligation to deliver (*a*), and the goods to certain effects are held delivered. 'So if a specific thing, or a particular portion of a specific thing, be sold, it is a condition of the contract that the thing (*e.g.* a field of potatoes to be grown) shall be in existence at the intended time of delivery; and if it never come into existence, or perish without fault of the seller, he is not liable (*b*).' But if they are allowed to remain till the term of payment has arrived, and the buyer fail, or his bill for the price be dishonoured, the seller may retain the goods (*c*), 'unless he is barred by having given his assent, express or implied, to a sub-sale previously intimated to him (*d*). This result is effected in virtue of the vendor's lien for the price; and it is held that the lien is not lost, or that it revives on the buyer's insolvency, even when he has relinquished it by the terms of his contract, as by agreeing to hold as bailee for the buyer (*e*). The vendor's lien operates even when the buyer is not insolvent, if the period of credit expires and the goods are still in the vendor's possession (*f*); also when the goods have been sold without any stipulation as to credit. These provisions are all repeated in the Sale of Goods Act (*g*), with this addition that the seller may exercise his lien, even if he is in possession as agent or bailee or custodier for the buyer (*h*), and that whether the buyer is solvent or insolvent.'

(*a*) See above, § 87.
(*b*) Taylor *v.* Caldwell, 3 B. & S. 826; 32 L. J. Q. B. 164. Appleby *v.* Myers, 36 L. J. C. P. 331; L. R. 2 C. P. 651. Howell *v.* Coupland, L. R. 9 Q. B. 462; 43 L. J. Q. B. 201. See above, § 29, 87. Sale of Goods Act, § 7.
(*c*) New *v.* Swain, 1 Dan. & Ll. 193; 1 Ill. 412. See Hurry *v.* Mangles, 1 Camp. 452; 1 Ill. 389; 10 R. R. 727. Harman *v.* Anderson, 2 Camp. 243; 1 Ill. 397; 11 R. R. 706. See Bayley, J., in Bloxam *v.* Sanders, 4 B. & Cr. 948; 1 Ill. 92. 2 Ross' L. C. 48; 28 R. R. 519.
(*d*) 1 Bell's Com. 243 (M'L.'s ed.). M'Ewan & Co. *v.* Smith & Co., 1847; 9 D. 434; rev. 6 Bell's App. 340; 2 H. L. Ca. 309. Fleming *v.* Smith & Co., 1881; 8 R. 548. Hurry, *cit.* Stoveld *v.* Hughes, 14 East, 308. Miles *v.* Gorton, 2 C. & M. 504. Townley *v.* Crump, 4 Ad. & Ell. 58. Pearson *v.* Dawson, E. B. & E. 448; 27 L. J. Q. B. 248. Knights *v.* Whiffen, 40 L. J. Q. B. 51; L. R. 5 Q. B. 660. Woodley *v.* Coventry, 2 H. & C. 164; 32 L. J. Q. B. 185. Gunn *v.* Bolckow & Co., L. R. 10 Ch. 491; 44 L. J. Ch. 732. Farmeloe *v.* Bain, 1 C. P. D. 445; 45 L. J. C. P. 264. Mercht. Bkg. Co. *v.* Phœnix Bessemer Steel Co., 5 Ch. D. 205; 46 L. J. Ch. 418. See below, § 1303; and Benjamin on Sales, 735, 744 sq., 752. Cf. 56 and 57 Vict. c. 71, § 47 (Sale of Goods Act).
(*e*) Townley *v.* Crump, 4 A. & E. 58. Dodsley *v.* Varley, 12 A. & E. 632. Grice *v.* Richardson, 47 L. J. P. C. 48; L. R. 3 App. Ca. 319.
(*f*) New *v.* Swain, *cit.*, and Benjamin on Sales, 812.
(*g*) The Sale of Goods Act, § 41 (1).
(*h*) *Ib.* § 41 (2).

117. *Place of Delivery.*—If a place be fixed at which delivery is to be made, the goods must be delivered at that place; and they are held as still the seller's till brought thither for delivery, the intermediate risk being with the seller (*a*). If no place be fixed, 'the place of delivery is the seller's place of business, and if he have none, his residence. But if specific goods are sold and known to the parties to be at some other place,' the delivery is to be where the goods are at the time of purchase (*b*). If the buyer be at a distance the seller's duty and risk end with delivery to the proper carrier (*c*). It is sometimes a matter of doubt what is the point or port of delivery; and on this it may depend by what rule the measurement or weight is to be adjusted. Thus a cargo of timber sold at so much per English cubic foot is a very different bargain (in consequence of the difference of measurement) if to be measured at Rotterdam or at Aberdeen (*d*). The question will depend on the terms of the order as understood by merchants, and it is for the jury to fix it on proof of mercantile usage and understanding.

(*a*) See above, § 88. But the seller is not answerable for the necessary result of the transit, *e.g.* for iron becoming rusted. Bull *v.* Robinson, 10 Ex. 342; 24 L. J. Ex. 165.
(*b*) Pothier, Cont. de Vente, No. 52. Benjamin on Sales, 673. Sale of Goods Act, § 29 (1).
(*c*) Milne & Co. *v.* Miller, Feb. 1, 1809; F. C.; 1 Ill. 88. Spence *v.* Ormiston, 1687; M. 3153. Dunlop & Co. *v.* Lambert, 1837; 15 S. 884, 1232; rev. 1839, M'L. & R. 663; 6 Cl. & F. 600. Beesley & Co. *v.* M'Ewan, 1884; 12 R. 384. The condition that the buyer pays cost, freight, and insurance does not infer suspension of delivery to the port of arrival. De Laurier *v.* Wyllie, 1889; 17 R. 167. See Ireland *v.* Livingstone, L. R. 5 H. L. 408; 41 L. J. Q. B. 201.
(*d*) Schuurmans *v.* Stephen, 1833; 11 S. 779; 1 Ill. 93. See above, § 91 (3).

118. If the goods are to be sent to a distance, and no directions be given, the rule is, that they are to be delivered in the usual way (*a*). If any directions be given by the buyer as to the carriage, they must be followed as far as possible (*b*); and in that case the buyer must stand to the loss (*c*). At all events, the goods must be despatched with due care (*d*), so as to fix a demand on the carrier (*e*), to secure safe carriage (*f*), and to enable the buyer to insure (*g*).

(*a*) Copeland *v.* Lewis, 2 Starkie, 33; 1 Ill. 108.
(*b*) Harle & Ogilvie, 1749; M. 10,095; Elch. *Presump.* 31; 1 Ill. 109.

(*c*) Vale *v.* Bayle, Cowp. 294.
(*d*) Sword *v.* Milloy, Feb. 17, 1813; F. C.
(*e*) Buckman *v.* Levi, 2 Camp. 414. Fleet Bros. *v.* Morrison, 1854; 16 D. 1122. Hastie *v.* Campbell, 1857; 19 D. 557.
(*f*) Clark *v.* Hutchins, 14 East, 475; 13 R. R. 283. Cothay *v.* Tute, 3 Camp. 129; 13 R. R. 774.
(*g*) Hoog *v.* Kennedy & M'Lean, 1754; M. 10,096. Hesseltines *v.* Arrol & Co., 1802; M. 10,111. Elton, Hammond, & Co. *v.* Porteous, Dec. 13, 1808; F. C. Andrew *v.* Ross, Dec. 6, 1810; F. C. Arnot *v.* Stewart, Nov. 25, 1813; F. C.; aff. 3 Dow, 374; 6 Paton, 289. Johnston & Sharp *v.* Baillie, June 2, 1815; F. C. Cooper *v.* Green, 1791; M. 10,100. Cook *v.* Ludlow, 2 B. & P. 119. Fleet *v.* Morrison, *cit.* Hastie *v.* Campbell, *cit.* (commission agent). 1 Bell's Com. 444 (474, M'L.'s ed.).

118A. *Statutory Rules as to Delivery to a Carrier.*—'When the seller is authorised or required to send the goods to the buyer, delivery to a carrier, whether named by the buyer or not, for the purpose of transmission to the buyer, is *primâ facie* deemed to be delivery to the buyer (*a*). Unless otherwise authorised by the buyer, the seller must make a reasonable contract with the carrier on behalf of the buyer, having regard to the circumstances and the nature of the goods, failing which, loss or damage in transit entitles the buyer to decline to treat the delivery to the carrier as a delivery to himself, or he may hold the seller liable in damages (*b*). Unless otherwise agreed, where goods are sent by the seller to the buyer by a route involving sea-transit, under circumstances in which it is usual to insure, the seller must give such notice to the buyer as may enable him to insure; and if he fails to do so, the goods are at his risk during the sea-transit (*c*). Where the seller agrees to deliver at his own risk at a place other than that where they are when sold, the buyer, unless it is otherwise agreed, takes any risk of deterioration in the goods necessarily incident to the course of transit (*d*).'

(*a*) The Act, § 32 (1). Dunlop & Co. *v.* Lambert, *cit.* § 117 (*c*); and above, § 117, 118, etc.
(*b*) *Ib.* § 32 (2); above, § 118. Bell on Sale, p. 84.
(*c*) Bell on Sale, p. 89. See Smith *v.* Lascelles, 2 T. R. 187; 1 R. R. 457 (agent's duty in forwarding to principal; see Hastie, *cit.*).
(*d*) The Act, § 33. Bull *v.* Robson, 10 Ex. 344; 24 L. J. Ex. 165. Beer *v.* Walker, 46 L. J. C. P. 672. See Dixon *v.* Jones, 1884; 11 R. 739. This is a qualification of the general rule as to risk in § 20 of the Act, and above, § 88 (*d*).

118B. *Acceptance and Examination.*—'Where goods are delivered to the buyer, which he has not previously examined, he is not deemed to have accepted them unless and until he has had a reasonable opportunity of examining them for the purpose of ascertaining whether they are in conformity with the contract (*a*). Unless otherwise agreed, the seller when he tenders delivery is bound, on request, to afford the buyer a reasonable opportunity of examining the goods for the said purpose (*b*).

'The buyer is deemed to have accepted the goods when he has intimated to the seller that he has accepted them, or when the goods have been delivered to him and he does any act in relation to them which is inconsistent with the ownership of the seller, or when after the lapse of a reasonable time he retains the goods without intimating his rejection of them (*c*). In the absence of special agreement, the buyer who refuses to accept delivered goods is not bound to return them to the seller. It is enough if he intimates unconditionally his refusal to accept (*d*).'

Buyer's Neglect or Refusal of Delivery.—'When the seller is ready and willing to deliver, and requests the buyer to take delivery, and the buyer does not within a reasonable time take delivery, he is liable to the seller for any loss so occasioned, and also for a reasonable charge for the care and custody of the goods. But this enactment does not affect the seller's rights where the buyer's neglect or refusal amounts to a repudiation of the contract (*e*).'

(*a*) The Act, § 34 (1). *Supra*, § 99 (*h*), (*i*).
(*b*) The Act, § 34 (2).
(*c*) The Act, § 35. *Supra*, § 99, esp. notes (*a*), (*d*), (*k*), as to rejection; for acceptance is a material question chiefly in regard to rejection. The cases in England as to acceptance under the Statute of Frauds are not necessarily in point in dealing with acceptance in the sense of the text.
(*d*) The Act, § 36. See above, § 99 (*a*).
(*e*) Sale of Goods Act, 1893, § 37. See below, § 128. Bell on Sale, 109.

119. If the goods are to be delivered free on board (*a*) a foreign ship, it is sufficient if the seller put them on board such ship. He is not bound, when he has an adverse interest, to deliver them into the buyer's hand, nor to transfer them in the books of the warehouse where they lie (*b*).

(*a*) See Jack *v.* Roberts, 1865; 3 Macph. 554. Glengarnock Iron Co. *v.* Cooper & Co., 1896; 22 R. 672. Benjamin on Sales, 315.
(*b*) Wackerbarth *v.* Masson, 3 Camp. 270; 1 Ill. 112. Wetherell *v.* Coope, *ib.* 272. This section and the cases cited seem only to show that contracts are to be performed strictly according to their terms.

120. *Buyers' Remedies.*—On the seller failing to deliver, the buyer may, at his choice, annul the bargain, or insist for performance with damages (*a*).

'Where the seller wrongfully neglects or fails to deliver, the buyer may maintain an action for damages for non-delivery. The measure of damages is the estimated loss directly and naturally resulting in the natural course of events from the seller's breach of contract (*b*). Where there is an available market (*c*) for the goods, the measure of damages is to be ascertained *primâ facie* by the difference between the contract price and the market or current price at the time or times when the goods ought to have been delivered, or if no time was fixed, then at the time of the refusal to deliver (*d*).

'In any action for breach of contract to deliver specific or ascertained goods, the Court may, if it thinks fit, on the application of the plaintiff, direct that the contract shall be performed specifically, without giving the seller the option of retaining the goods on payment of damages. The judgment or decree may be conditional, or upon such terms and conditions as to damages, payment of the price, and otherwise as to the Court may seem just; and the application may be made by the plaintiff at any time before judgment or decree. This provision is supplementary to and not in derogation of the right of specific implement in Scotland (*e*).

'Where there is a breach of warranty (*i.e.* in Scotland a failure to perform a material part of the contract (*f*)) by the seller, or where the buyer elects or is compelled to treat any breach of a condition on the part of a seller as a breach of warranty, the buyer is not by reason only of such breach of warranty entitled (in England) to reject the goods, but he may (1) set up against the seller the breach of warranty in diminution or extinction of the price, or (2) maintain an action against the seller for damages for breach of warranty (*g*). The measure of damages is the estimated loss directly and naturally arising in the ordinary course of events from the breach of warranty. In the case of breach of warranty of quality such loss is *primâ facie* the difference between the value of the goods at the time of delivery and the value they would have had if they had answered to the warranty (*h*). The buyer may maintain a second action for the same breach of warranty if he has afterwards suffered further damage (*i*). This enactment does not prejudice or affect the buyer's right of rejection in Scotland as declared by the Act (*k*).'

(*a*) See above, § 33. Notes to Cutter *v.* Powell in 2 Smith's L. C. 1. Benjamin on Sales, 872 sq., 894 sq. See *per* L. P. Inglis in Linn *v.* Shields, 1863; 2 Macph. 88.

(*b*) Sale of Goods Act, § 51 (1), (2). Grebert Borgnis *v.* Nugent, 15 Q. B. D. 85. Duff & Co. *v.* Iron Bdgs. Co., 1891; 19 R. 199.

(*c*) Dunkirk Coll. Co. *v.* Lever, 9 Ch. D. 20.

(*d*) The Act, § 51 (3). This 51st section of the Act is founded on the rules laid down in Hadley *v.* Baxendale, 9 Ex. 341; 2 Smith's L. C. 594 (9th ed.), 523 (10th ed.). See above, § 33.

(*e*) Sale of Goods Act, 1893, § 52.

(*f*) The Act, § 62 (1), § 11 (2).

(*g*) *Ib.* § 53 (1).

(*h*) *Ib.* subs. 2 and 3.

(*i*) *Ib.* § 53 (4).

(*k*) *Ib.* § 53 (5) and § 11 (2).

121. (2.) *Warrandice.* — The secondary obligation of the seller is to warrant against eviction (*a*). This obligation on the seller is implied in sale, and consequent on eviction. Eviction is the loss of a thing, in whole or in part, to the buyer, by the judicial establishment of a right in another preferable to the seller's; or by such right being admitted by the seller; or by the emerging of an unquestionable burden on the subject purchased, which the buyer is compelled to discharge (*b*).

(*a*) See as to warranties, *ante*, § 95, 111; and as to warranty of title, etc., § 114.

(*b*) 3 Ersk. 3. § 9. 1 Domat, t. 2. § 10. Pothier, Vente, Nos. 83, 85.

122. The obligation of warrandice is implied or express. Where a full price is paid, or what the parties consider as such, the warrandice is absolute. It is an engagement that the buyer shall be protected against eviction on any ground existing antecedently to the sale (*a*). To entitle the buyer to redress, there must be eviction; for it is only eviction that grounds an action of warrandice (*b*). The eviction must be *ex defectu juris,* not *ex natura rei,* nor proceeding from accident or violence (*c*). And it must be a loss, strictly speaking, not subsequent to the sale, as by a supervenient law (*d*). Partial loss must be indemnified, and burdens removed (*e*).

(*a*) 2 Ersk. 3. § 25.

(*b*) Inglis *v.* Anstruther, 1771; M. 16,633; 2 Ill. 103. Swan *v.* Martin, 1865; 3 Macph. 853. This statement is qualified in § 895.

(*c*) 2 Ersk. 3. § 29.

(*d*) Plenderleith *v.* E. Tweeddale, 1800; M. 16,639; 2 Ill. 103. Alexander *v.* Dundas, June 9, 1812; F. C. E. Hopetoun's Trs. *v.* Coplands, Dec. 8, 1819; F. C. Hamilton *v.* Calder, 1823; 2 S. 357. See § 895, and above, § 111.

(*e*) Pothier, Vente, No. 99.

123. Warrandice from fact and deed is a more limited obligation, viz. protection against eviction by reason of the seller's own act or omission, past or future.

124. Simple warrandice protects the buyer only against the future act and deed of the seller.

125. Express warrandice is a special bargain altering the implied engagement. The buyer is entitled to redress on eviction, provided he shall have given notice of the challenge. And although he is not bound to defend himself before eviction (*a*), he is *entitled* to defend himself; and if he choose to do so, he will be held to undertake the risk of all omissions in his defence, with the expense of the contest.

(*a*) 2 Stair, 3. § 46. 2 Ersk. 3. § 29, 32. Downie *v.* Campbell, Jan. 31, 1815; F. C.

126. The buyer, on eviction, may claim the whole loss and damage as at the time of eviction, deducting the intermediate profits drawn. But he is entitled only to such law expense as he may have *bonâ fide* laid out in defending himself, either with the assent of the seller, or without any offer on the seller's part to give instant indemnification, or to defend against eviction (*a*).

(*a*) Hill *v.* Yeaman, 1769; M. 16,631; Hailes, 328. These propositions are chiefly applicable to sales of land; as to the warrandice of which, see below, § 894. See also as to warrandice in the sale of debts, § 1469. Eichholz *v.* Bannister, *supra*, § 114; and Benjamin on Sales, 606, 620. A different view, viz. that in eviction of moveables the buyer can claim only the restitution of the sum paid for the right, is expressed by Stair and Bankton, and disapproved by Ersk., 2 Inst. 3. § 30. See § 895; and as to expenses, see Stephen *v.* L. Adv., 1878; 6 R. 282.

127. Obligations of the Buyer.—(1.) *To pay the Price* (*a*).—The chief obligation of the buyer is to pay the price, according to the terms express or implied; *i.e.* on delivery, or at the day appointed, or at the time when, by usage or the expiration of the accustomed credit, the price is due (*b*). The payment must be by a legal tender, if insisted on (*c*); or it may be in such notes as may have been received without objection, or which have been stipulated (*d*); 'and if made in accordance with the seller's request, as by post, it discharges the buyer, even if the money never reaches the seller's hands (*e*).' When instead of cash the buyer's note or a bank-cheque is taken in payment, and dishonoured, this does not discharge the buyer (*f*). 'If a cheque received in payment is not presented within reasonable time, and the drawer is prejudiced by the delay, the seller is held to have made the cheque his own, and the payment is absolute (*g*).' When bank-notes, or a bill or note of a third party, are offered and taken as cash, and without the indorsation of or recourse on the buyer, the seller has no remedy, if they should prove bad by insolvency of the bank or third party, unless the buyer had known of the insolvency, or had omitted some observance necessary for procuring payment (*h*). 'But the buyer is no longer responsible for the price (though he may be responsible on the security) if it can be shown that a bill or note, either his own or that of a third party, was taken with the intention that it should operate as immediate payment. This, however, must be clearly shown; and in the absence of agreement, express or implied, a payment by bill or note is understood to be conditional (*i*).' If the seller, on presenting the buyer's bank-cheque to the banker, agree to receive in payment a bill on a third person, the buyer is discharged, although that bill should be dishonoured (*k*). If the goods are to be paid for in ready money on delivery, delivery of them may be refused unless payment is so made; but if delivered without requiring payment, the buyer will be entitled to set off against a demand for the price a sum due to him by the seller (*l*). It is not, however, a waiver of the condition of ready money, if the buyer has been allowed to take away part of the goods without having paid for them (*m*). If the seller negotiate by discounting the bill of the buyer, it is held to certain effects as payment; so that the seller cannot after that retain the goods. But this circumstance will not deprive him of his right to come against the buyer on the bill being dishonoured (*n*).

(*a*) See above, § 92 and 103.
(*b*) See above, § 100–1.
(*c*) See below, § 1334 et seq.
(*d*) See Warwick *v.* Noakes, Peake, 67; 3 R. R. 653. Polglass *v.* Oliver, 2 C. & J. 15. Caine *v.* Coulton, 1 H. & C. 764; 32 L. J. Ex. 97.
(*e*) Warwick, *cit.* Benjamin on Sales, 699, 700.
(*f*) Everet *v.* Collins, 2 Camp. 515; 1 Ill. 112; 11 R. R. 785.
(*g*) Hopkins *v.* Ware, L. R. 4 Ex. 268; 38 L. J. Ex. 147. See 45 and 46 Vict. c. 61, § 74.
(*h*) Camidge *v.* Allenby, 6 B. & Cr. 373; 1 Ross' L. C. 366; 30 R. R. 358. Read *v.* Hutchinson, 3 Camp. 352. Sard *v.* Rhodes, 1 M. & W. 153. Guardians of Lichfield *v.* Green, 1 H. & N. 884; 26 L. J. Ex. 140. Fenn *v.* Harri-

son, 3 T. R. 757; 1 Ross' L. C. 352. Smith *v.* Mercer, L. R. 3 Ex. 51; 37 L. J. Ex. 24. Hopkins *v.* Ware, L. R. 4 Ex. 208; 38 L. J. Ex. 147. Benjamin on Sales, 717.

(*i*) Sibree *v.* Tripp, 15 M. & W. 23. Guardians of Lichfield, and cases cited note (*h*). M'Laren's Bell's Com. i. 538.

(*k*) Smith *v.* Ferrand, 7 B. & Cr. 19. Anderson *v.* Langdale, 3 B. & Ad. 660.

(*l*) Cornforth *v.* Rivett, 2 M. & Sel. 510. See Bell on Sale, 108; and above, § 100 (*g*).

(*m*) Payne *v.* Shadbolt, 1 Camp. 427.

(*n*) Horncastle *v.* Farran, 3 B. & Ald. 497; 1 Ill. 453; 22 R. R. 461. Bunney *v.* Poyntz, 4 B. & Ad. 568; 1 Ill. 383. It rather seems that the right to retain is lost by merely taking the bill. Hewison *v.* Guthrie, 2 Bing. N. C. 755. See Chambers *v.* Davidson, L. R. 1 P. C. 296; 4 Moore, P. C. N. S. 158; 36 L. J. P. C. 17. And the rule in the text would be more accurately stated thus: If the creditor negotiate the bill or note for value, and without rendering himself liable, it operates as payment though dishonoured; and in all cases the creditor must account for the bill before he can revert to the original contract, and sue for the price. Smith's Merc. Law, 532. Benjamin on Sales, *ll.cc.* Griffith *v.* Owen, 13 M. & W. 64. Caine *v.* Coulton, *cit.* Price *v.* Price, 16 M. & W. 232.

128. (2.) *To take Delivery.*—The next obligation of the buyer is to take delivery of the goods, if they be in the condition stipulated or implied, at the time when the seller is bound to deliver (*a*). And he will be liable in warehouse rent, or damages, if he shall refuse to do so (*b*). 'Where there is an available market, the measure of damages is *primâ facie* the difference between the contract price and the market price at the date of repudiation, the seller being bound, if he resell, to do so at once (*c*). It was laid down that judicial authority for reselling must be obtained (*d*); but this rule was not strictly observed, except in the case of horses, and in many cases it would be inconvenient in practice. It is only when the vendor means to claim damages that he must resell; and on the buyer's default he may in some circumstances retain the article to himself after notice, or he may store it for the vendee, and sue for the price and warehouse rent (*e*).

'Subject to the statutory provisions as to the transfer of bills of lading and similar documents of title (*f*), the unpaid seller of goods has by implication of law, whether the property in the goods has passed to the buyer or not—(1) a lien on the goods, or right to retain them, for the price while he is in possession of them (*g*); (2) in case of the buyer's insolvency, a right of stopping the goods *in transitu* after he has parted with the possession (*h*); (3) a right of resale as limited by the Sale of Goods Act. Where the property has not passed to the buyer, he has besides a right of withholding delivery similar to and coextensive with his rights of lien and stoppage *in transitu* (*i*).

'In Scotland, continuing a provision of the Mercantile Law Amendment Act, 1856, the Sale of Goods Act allows a seller of goods to attach them while in his own hands or possession by arrestment or poinding, just as a third party can (*k*).

'Retention and stoppage *in transitu* are considered, in accordance with the original arrangement of this book, in Part II., Chap. II. (Of Delivery of Moveables), § 1299–1309.

'Here, as in the case of the seller's failure to deliver, when the contract is for future delivery, the date of breach with reference to which damages are assessed is the time of stipulated delivery, and not the time when notice of the intention to break the contract is given (*l*). But in either case action may, it seems, be brought upon repudiation, without waiting for the stipulated time of performance (*m*).'

(*a*) Drew *v.* Ogilvie, Heggie, & Co., 1833; 11 S. 342; 1 Ill. 113. Action has been refused in England on a contract of sale, where the seller had not the goods, or any hope of having them by consignment, but meant to go into the market to supply them. This may be doubted as a general proposition. If on such a bargain the goods were procured and tendered, could they be refused? See Bryan *v.* Lewis, 1 Ryan & Moodie, 386; 1 Ill. 113. See below, as to the effect of sale when completed by delivery, § 1299 et seq. See also as to sales in market, § 665. The doctrine referred to and doubted by Prof. Bell is overruled. Hibblewhite *v.* M'Morine, 5 M. & W. 462. M'Callan *v.* Mortimer, 9 M. & W. 636. Thackoorseydas *v.* Dhondmull, 6 Moo. P. C. 300. Sikes *v.* Wild, 1 B. & S. 587. Sale of Goods Act, 1893, § 5; and above, § 90.

(*b*) Sale of Goods Act, 1893, § 37; and above, § 118B.

(*c*) Warin & Craven *v.* Forrester, 1876; 4 R. 190; aff. *ib.* H. L. 75. Hain *v.* Laing, *infra.* See above, § 100.

(*d*) Bell on Sale, 109. Hain *v.* Laing, 1853; 15 D. 667. See Cal. Ry. Co., *infra*, § 129 (*q*).

(*e*) 1 Bell's Com. 443 (472, M'L.'s ed.), and the author's text, *ante.* Thomson Brs. *v.* Thomson, 1888; 13 R. 88. Wilson, Ronald, & Co. *v.* Curle & Robertson, 1884; 2 Sel. Sh. Ct. Ca. 506. The distinctions which in England have grown out of the English system of pleading have no place in our law, but the rules as to the measure of damages are the same. Maclean *v.* Dunn, 4 Bing. 722. Benjamin on Sales, 744 sqq. 767 sqq.

(*f*) Sale of Goods Act, § 47. Factors Act, 1889 (52 and 53 Vict. c. 45), § 10.

(*g*) See above, § 116; below, § 1300, 1300B.

(*h*) See below, § 1304, 1307 sqq.

(*i*) Sale of Goods Act (56 and 57 Vict. c. 71), § 39. The last provision is introduced because in England a man can have no "lien" over his own property. There seems to be no reason to doubt that, notwithstanding the repeal by § 60 of the Sale Clauses of the Mercantile Law Amendment Act of 1856, vendor's retention in Scotland is exactly equivalent to lien in England, and only secures the price.

(*k*) 19 and 20 Vict. c. 60, § 3. As to which, see Lochhead *v.* Graham, 1883; 11 R. 201. Browne *v.* Ainslie & Co., 1893; 21 R. 173.

(*l*) Howie *v.* Anderson, 1848; 10 D. 355. Boorman *v.* Nash, 9 B. & C. 145. Philpott *v.* Evans, 5 M. & W. 475.

Ripley *v.* M'Clure, 4 Ex. 345. Cort *v.* Ambergate Ry. Co., 17 Q. B. 127; 20 L. J. Q. B. 460.

(*m*) Hochster *v.* La Tour, 2 E. & B. 678; 22 L. J. Q. B. 455. Frost *v.* Knight, L. R. 5 Ex. 322; 7 Ex. 111; 39 L. J. Ex. 227; 41 *ib.* 79. In such cases the ascertainment of damages is necessarily more speculative.

129. Peculiarities in the Sale of Horses.—The common rules apply to the sale of horses; the peculiarities relate to the implied or special warranty.

The general rule that all latent faults are under the implied condition of soundness, while obvious faults only are excepted from it, 'applied' in the sale of horses 'under the former law (*a*). The Mercantile Law Amendment Act and Sale of Goods Act, excluding implied warranties in sales, apply to the sale of horses (*b*).' But where there is any express condition, it rules the question; while general and vague assurances are not to be held as express agreements altering the implied engagements. Warranty generally of soundness (whether implied as 'formerly' in Scotland, or express as in England) is an engagement of difficult construction (*c*). It seems to comprehend all constitutional diseases affecting the life of the horse; all accidental injuries which affect the life; all diseases and accidents attended with lameness; or rendering, or tending certainly to render, the horse prematurely unfit for work (*d*); all defects or bad habits, indicative or symptomatic of disease,—it being the disease, however, which in such case amounts to unsoundness (*e*). Opinions differ extremely as to slighter faults, whether they amount to unsoundness, as temporary lameness (*f*). Bad corns, if concealed, have been held unsoundness (*g*); so running thrush (*h*); roaring, proceeding from organic defect; and crib-biting, when inveterate, have also been held unsoundness (*i*). 'While an ordinary cold or other ailment curable in a few days is not a breach of warranty of soundness (*k*), on the other hand, a purchaser is understood to go to market to buy an article of which he can have immediate use (*l*), and therefore a disease which is curable, but only with great care and protracted surgical treatment, may be unsoundness (*m*). Although, as has been indicated above, a general warranty of soundness does not bind a seller as to defects which are obvious, on the other hand a buyer who, relying upon it, omits to make a minute examination, is protected against defects which, though not apparent, might readily have been detected by such an inspection (*n*).'

Those faults relative to temper, steadiness, timidity, use, etc., which, however important, are not unsoundness, must be guarded against by express warranty; and it is a question of evidence, whether such engagement has been undertaken, and how far it has been complied with (*o*).

A horse in which a defect has been discovered, comprehended under the seller's engagement, must be returned immediately, or as soon as the fault is discovered, 'and after it might have been discovered with ordinary diligence, the right of rejection is determined'; or if there be a time limited 'during which the warranty is to subsist, or' within which the horse, if objected to, is to be returned, that makes the rule between the parties (*p*). 'If the seller denies the alleged unsoundness, and refuses to take back the horse, the buyer was held bound to place it in neutral custody until he should resell it (*q*). This, however, appears to be no longer necessary (though still expedient), the law being declared by the Sale of Goods Act, § 36 and 20 (*r*). But if the seller uses a horse so returned to him as his own (*s*), he is barred from suing for the price of it. So when a buyer refuses to receive or returns a horse sold to him, the seller, if he intends to claim damages for breach of contract, must place it in neutral custody and resell. It was formerly the practice to obtain a judicial warrant (*t*), but the present law only requires the unpaid seller to give notice to the buyer or alleged buyer, as in the case of other goods (*u*).'

(*a*) Ralston *v.* Robertson, 1761; M. 14,238; 1 Ill. 98. Lindsay *v.* Wilson, 1771; 5 B. Sup. 585. Brown *v.* Gilbert, 1791; M. 14,244.

(*b*) See *ante*, § 97A. Oliphant, Law of Horses. Young *v.* Giffen, 1858; 21 D. 87; and see Robeson, Rough, and Rose, cited under § 97A.

(*c*) See Richardson *v.* Brown, 1 Bing. 344. As to authority of agents and servants to warrant, see below, § 225.

(*d*) See Hume's Rep. 667–669, 671, 697, 702. Fulton *v.* Watt, 1850; 32 Jur. 648.

(*e*) Wright *v.* Blackwood, 1833; 11 S. 722. Fielder *v.* Starkin, 1 H. Bl. 17; 2 R. R. 700. Eaves *v.* Dixon, 2 Taunt. 343. See Liddard *v.* Kain, 2 Bing. 183; 1 Ill. 117; 27 R. R. 582. Budd *v.* Fairmaner, 8 Bing. 48; 34 R. R. 619. Brown *v.* Boreland, 1848; 10 D. 1460.

(*f*) Elton *v.* Jordan, 1 Starkie, 127; 18 R. R. 754. Coates *v.* Stephens, 2 M. & R. 157.

(*g*) Hamilton *v.* Hart, 1830 ; 8 S. 596.
(*h*) Ralston *v.* Robb, 1808 ; M. *Sale*, Apx. 6. Fisher *v.* Ure, 1846 ; 9 D. 17.
(*i*) Basset *v.* Collis, 2 Camp. 523. Deuchars *v.* Shaw, 1833 ; 11 S. 612. Broenenburgh *v.* Haycock, Holt, N. P. 630 ; 1 Ill. 116.
(*k*) Dykes *v.* Hill, 1860 ; 22 D. 1523. Newlands *v.* Leggatt, 1885 ; 12 R. 820.
(*l*) Ralston *v.* Robb (*h*). Kiddell *v.* Burnard, 9 M. & W. 668. Holliday *v.* Morgan, 1 E. & E. 1 ; 28 L. J. Q. B. 9.
(*m*) Gardiner *v.* M'Leavy, 1880 ; 7 R. 612. See Benjamin on Sales, 504 sqq.
(*n*) Margetson *v.* Wright, 7 Bing. 603 : 33 R. R. 582. Holliday *v.* Morgan, *cit.*
(*o*) Geddes *v.* Pennington, 1817 ; 5 Dow, 159 ; 6 Pat. 312. Begbie *v.* Robertson, 1828 ; 6 S. 1014. Scott *v.* Steel, 1857 ; 20 D. 253. Thomson *v.* Miller, 1859 ; 21 D. 726. Wilson *v.* Turnbull & Co., 1896 ; 23 R. 714.
(*p*) Brown *v.* Nicolson, 1624 ; M. 14,229. Aiton *v.* Fairie, 1668 ; M. 14,230. Kinnaird *v.* M'Dougal, 1694 ; 4 B. Sup. 184. Russel *v.* Ferrier, 1792 ; Bell's Cases, 479. Bennoch *v.* M'Kail, Jan. 27, 1820 ; F. C. ; 1 Ill. 104. Fielder *v.* Starkin, *cit.* (*e*). Buchanan *v.* Parnshaw, 2 T. R. 745. Caswell *v.* Coare, 1 Taunt. 566 ; 10 R. R. 606. Pollock *v.* Macadam, 1840 ; 2 D. 1026. Robson *v.* Thomson, 1864 ; 2 Macph. 593. Bywater *v.* Richardson, 1 Ad. & E. 508 (warranty to continue till 12 o'clock next day). Chapman *v.* Gwyther, 7 B. & S. 417 ; 35 L. J. Q. B. 142 ; L. R. 1 Q. B. 463 ("I warrant sound for one month"). Head *v.* Tattersall, 41 L. J. Ex. 4 ; L. R. 7 Ex. 7. Hinchcliffe *v.* Barwick, 49 L. J. Q. B. 495 ; 5 Ex. D. 177. Elphick *v.* Barnes, 5 C. P. D. 321.
(*q*) M'Bey *v.* Gardiner, 1857 ; 20 D. 1151. See Robson *v.* Thomson, *cit.* Cal. Ry. Co. *v.* Rankin, 1882 ; 10 R. 63.
(*r*) See above, § 118B.
(*s*) Croan *v.* Vallance, 1881 ; 8 R. 700. Newlands *v.* Leggatt, 1885 ; 12 R. 820 (improper medical treatment at buyer's own hand).
(*t*) The practice was general if not universal ; but though recognised in the opinions of judges (*e.g.* M'Bey *v.* Gardiner, *cit.*) is not supported by direct authority (see Ellershaw *v.* Martin, 1890 ; 6 Sh. C. R. 281.
(*u*) 56 and 57 Vict. c. 71, § 39, 48. *Supra*, § 128.

130. Sales by Auction.—The contract of sale by auction is formed by the offer to buy and acceptance; the offer being by the bidding; the acceptance by the fall of the hammer (*a*), or by the running of a sand-glass, or by the judicial close of the biddings, by the judge (*b*) or auctioneer declaring the last offer to be accepted (*c*). '*Primâ facie* each lot is deemed to be the subject of a separate contract of sale (*d*). Until the acceptance by fall of hammer or otherwise, the bid may be retracted; and so also there is no implied contract by mere advertisement that all the articles advertised for sale will be exposed (*e*).'

(*a*) Payne *v.* Cave, 3 T. R. 148 ; 1 Ill. 117 ; 1 R. R. 679. Warlow *v.* Harrison, 1 E. & E. 295 ; 28 L. J. Q. B. 18 ; 29 L. J. Q. B. 14.
(*b*) The "judge of the roup" is not an arbiter to decide all questions arising out of the sale, but only to see fairplay, and decide matters arising while the sale is going on. Strachan *v.* Auld, 1884 ; 11 R. 756.
(*c*) There is no reason why the vendor should not be his own auctioneer. Flint *v.* Woodin, 9 Hare, 622. See Jeffrey *v.* Aiken, 1826 ; 4 S. 722. Sugden, Vend. & Purch. 44.
(*d*) Chapman *v.* Couston, Thomson, & Co. 1871 ; 9 Macph. 675 ; aff. 1872, 10 Macph. H. L. 74. Sale of Goods Act, 1893, § 58 (1).
(*e*) Harris *v.* Nickerson, 42 L. J. Q. B. 171 ; L. R. 8 Q. B. 286 ; where Warlow *v.* Harrison is questioned. See above, § 74.

131. (1.) *The Exposure* may be at the pleasure of the bidders, or at an upset price; and must in either case be so conducted that the subject may fall to the highest real bidder. Much doubt has arisen as to the lawfulness of biddings for the exposer. He may set a price below which the thing is not to be sold. This is best and most openly done by fixing an upset price; as is done by the judge in judicial sales, or in voluntary sales on the owner's estimate of the worth of the thing. After much doubt, it was at one time held as settled in England, that without fixing an upset price, the exposer might accomplish the same object by the defensive precaution of appointing one to bid for him in order to prevent the thing from being sold below a certain price; but that he could use no unfair means of enhancing the price, as by appointing more than one to bid for him, so as to give the appearance and excitement of a competition; or by allowing his bidder to go on for the purpose generally of taking advantage of the eagerness of competition (*a*). But that doctrine has been thrown into doubt, and all private interference considered as a fraud (*b*). In Scotland we condemn absolutely such interference, and do not adopt the rule of merely limiting the owner's interference to a fair defensive precaution for preventing a sale at an undervalue (*c*). It has been said that if there be no upset price, and no agreement to sell at the pleasure of the company, the owner may bid (*d*); but that is not law, or is at least too broadly laid down. A power may be reserved to the exposer to offer (*e*). But if the sale is declared to be "without reserve," or "at the pleasure of the company," the plain meaning and effect of this, even in England, is held to be, to bar all biddings in behalf of the seller (*f*). 'The remedy, where there has been unfair bidding by or on behalf of the exposer, is to reduce all the offers after the last *bonâ fide* offer, and to hold the person who made it to be the purchaser; not to reduce the sale *in toto*, if justice can be done otherwise (*g*).'

It is implied in fair exposure, that the description shall not be 'misleading or' deceitful (*h*).

Statutory Provisions.—'The Sale of Goods Act, 1893, enacts:—Where a sale by auction is not notified to be subject to a right to bid on behalf of the seller, it shall not be lawful for the seller to bid himself, or to employ any person to bid at such sale, or for the auctioneer knowingly to take any bid from the seller or any such person. Any sale contravening this rule may be treated as fraudulent by the buyer (*i*).

'A sale by auction may be notified to be subject to a reserved or upset price, and a right to bid may also be reserved expressly by or on behalf of the seller, in which case, but not otherwise, the seller, *or* any *one* person on his behalf, may bid at the auction (*k*).'

(*a*) Conolly *v.* Parsons, 3 Ves. jun. 625; 1 Ill. 118. Bexwell *v.* Christie, Cowp. 395; 1 Ill. 119. Howard *v.* Castle, 6 T. R. 642; 3 R. R. 296. Bramley *v.* Alt, 3 Ves. jun. 620. Smith *v.* Clarke, 12 Ves. jun. 477; 8 R. R. 359. Hill *v.* Gray, 1 Starkie, 434; 1 Ill. 16; 18 R. R. 802. Sugden on Vendors, 9 et seq.

(*b*) Crowder *v.* Austin, 3 Bing. 368; 1 Ill. 121; 28 R. R. 646. See also Lord Tenterden in Wheeler *v.* Collier, 1 Mood. & Malk. 126. Thornett *v.* Haynes, 15 M. & W. 367. Green *v.* Baverstock, 32 L. J. C. P. 181; 14 C. B. N. S. 204.

(*c*) Gray *v.* Stewart, 1753; M. 9560. Cree *v.* Durie, Dec. 1810; F. C. Anderson *v.* Stewart, Dec. 16, 1814; F. C. Faulds *v.* Corbet, 1859; 21 D. 587. Rutherfurd *v.* Macgregor & Co., 1891; 18 R. 1061 (law agent of trustee in sequestration). The American law is similar, 2 Kent, Com. 539.

(*d*) More's Notes on Stair, xci.

(*e*) See Thom *v.* Macbeth, 1875; 3 R. 161.

(*f*) Meadows *v.* Tanner, 5 Maddox, 34. Parfitt *v.* Jepson, 46 L. J. C. P. 529.

(*g*) Faulds *v.* Corbet, *cit.* Shiell *v.* Guthrie's Trs., 1874; 1 R. 1083.

(*h*) Hill *v.* Gray, *supra* (*a*). Addison on Contr. 461. Pollock on Contr. 524. Torrance *v.* Bolton, L. R. 8 Ch. 118; 42 L. J. Ch. 177. Caballero *v.* Henty, L. R. 9 Ch. 447; 43 L. J. Ch. 635.

(*i*) Sale of Goods Act, 1893, § 58 (3). Bexwell, Thornett, etc., *citt.* Mainprice *v.* Westley, *cit.* § 132 (*h*).

(*k*) *Ib.* § 58 (4).

132. (2.) *The Biddings* among the real bidders must be fair, and the competition not defeated or restrained by combination or collusion among them (*a*). It is the implied duty of the judge of the roup, or auctioneer, to give to offerers a fair opportunity of bidding (*b*).

Particular conditions as to biddings are frequently introduced in articles of sale: as, that the exposer shall be allowed one or more biddings (*c*); that each bidding shall exceed the preceding in a certain sum; that the time to be allowed for bidding shall be fixed by the expiration of a specified time, as the running of a sand-glass, etc. (*d*); and that other offerers besides the highest shall continue subject to the contract for a certain time, in case of the highest offerer failing. This latter precaution is taken in sales of land; the offers are subscribed; and the rule is, that the stipulation being for the exposer's benefit, the offerers have no *jus quæsitum*, or right to insist on the bargain, if the highest offerer should fail; but if called upon by the exposer, they have the full benefit as well as burden of the contract (*e*). The pasting up of the conditions of sale on the auctioneer's box, or on the door or walls of the auction room, or the publication of them in printed catalogues to be had in the room, is sufficient notice of the conditions (*f*). And these conditions are not to be controlled by any verbal declaration of the auctioneer (*g*).

'The auctioneer is not responsible for a breach of the conditions of sale or for unfair interference, unless he has had knowledge of it (*h*). He is personally responsible for fulfilment of the contract if he does not disclose the vendor's name (*i*), or if from the terms of the contract it appears that he is dealing personally (*k*). If an auctioneer be employed to sell for ready money goods which he has in his possession, and if there be nothing to the contrary in the conditions of sale, it is presumed that he has authority to receive payment of the price (*l*). An auctioneer has no implied authority to warrant the goods entrusted to him for sale (*m*).'

(*a*) Aitchison *v.* ——, 1783; M. 9567; 1 Ill. 120. Murray *v.* M'Whan, 1783; M. 9567. Bramley and Smith, *supra*, § 131 (*a*). Fuller *v.* Abrahams, 3 Brod. & Bing. 116; 6 Moore, 316; 23 R. R. 626.

(*b*) Burns *v.* Monypenny, 1807; M. Apx. *Sale*, 1; 1 Ill. 117.

(*c*) See cases, *supra*, § 131 (*a*).

(*d*) Burns, *supra* (*b*).

(*e*) Walker *v.* Gavin, 1787; M. 14,173; 1 Ill. 120. Hannay *v.* Stothart, 1788; M. 14,194; Hailes, 1046. Currie's Crs. *v.* Hannay, 1791; M. 3162; Bell's Cases, 148. Faulds *v.* Corbet, 1859; 21 D. 587. Shiell *v.* Guthrie's Trs., 1874; 1 R. 1083. It is sometimes a condition that the party preferred shall find caution within a certain time, under pain of forfeiture of his right (Menzies *v.* Barstow, 1840; 2 D. 1317. Kennedy *v.* Ramsay's Trs., 1847; 9 D. 1333); or that the buyer shall satisfy himself before the sale as to the validity of the title. Young *v.* Grierson, 1849; 11 D. 1482.

(*f*) Mesnard *v.* Aldridge (Lord Kenyon), 3 Esp. 271; 1 Ill. 121. Hain *v.* Laing, 1853; 15 D. 667. Macdonald & Fraser *v.* Henderson, 1882; 10 R. 92. See below, § 155 *fin.* White & Co. *v.* Dougherty, 1891; 18 R. 972.

(*g*) Horsfall *v.* Fauntleroy, 10 B. & Cr. 755. See Murray *v.* Selkrig, Jan. 26, 1815; F. C. Higginson *v.* Clowes, 15 Ves. 521; 10 R. R. 112. White & Co. (*f*).

(*h*) Mainprice *v.* Westley, 6 B. & S. 420; 34 L. J. Q. B. 229. See Warlow *v.* Harrison, *cit.* § 130 (*a*).

(*i*) Franklyn *v.* Lamond, 4 C. B. 637; 16 L. J. C. P. 221.

(*k*) Wolfe *v.* Horne, 2 Q. B. D. 355; 46 L. J. Q. B. 534.

(*l*) Benjamin on Sales, 606, 608.

(*m*) Payne *v.* L. Leconfield, 51 L. J. Q. B. 642.

CHAPTER III

OF THE CONTRACT OF HIRING

133. Nature of the Contract (*a*).—By this contract, one party, in consideration of a certain hire, which the other engages to pay, agrees to give, during a certain time, or to a certain effect, the temporary use of a certain subject; or personal service and labour; or both combined (*b*).

(*a*) Consult 3 Ersk. Pr. 3. § 6. 1 Stair, 15. 3 Ersk. 3. § 14. Pothier, Pand. xix. t. 2. § 1. *Ib.* Cont. de Louage. 1 Domat, tit. 4. Jones on Bailments. Story on Bailments, 247. 2 Kent, Com. 582.

(*b*) This contract is in some degree analogous to sale. It is a sale of the use or service; but it is necessarily distinguished from sale, as being temporary instead of permanent, and as the risk does not shift, but remains with the Locator or Letter of the subject or of the labour.

134. The essentials of the contract are: a subject let and hired; the hire or consideration to be given for it; and the time or occasion during which the use or occupation, or benefit, is to be given, or which is to be allowed for the performance of the work.

135. The reciprocal obligations are: to deliver the thing for use, or to perform the service; to pay the hire; to restore or deliver the thing hired, or about which the work is to be performed, after the time is expired or the occasion past.

136. It is a mutual consensual contract, completed by consent, and proved (as in sale) by parole or written evidence (*a*): In land by writing; in moveables by parole; but if reduced to writing, the terms are not alterable by parole evidence (*b*).

(*a*) Pothier, Louage, No. 2.

(*b*) Pollock & Dickson *v.* M'Andrew, 1828; 7 S. 189. See below, § 2257.

I. HIRING OF MOVEABLES.

137. Description of this Contract. — The hiring of moveables is a reciprocal engagement to give and secure the use of the thing during a certain time or occasion, in consideration of a hire which the other engages to pay. It implies a thing to be used and returned. So, things which are consumed by use are not the proper subjects of hiring. These are called "fungibles," "quarum natura est ut aliæ aliarum ejusdem generis rerum vice fungantur: res quæ pondere, numero, et mensura constant." They are to be restored not identically, but in kind, by measure, weight, or number. The consumption of fungibles may be either natural and absolute, as of corn, wine, etc.; or civil, in which the substance is not altered, but the uses of it destroyed, as of paper for writing (*a*).

(*a*) 3 Ersk. 1. § 18. Pothier, Tr. du Prêt de Consumption, No. 23 et seq. 1 Bell's Com. 452 (481, M'L.'s ed.).

138. (1.) *The Subject* may be certain and definite, as the hire of a particular horse or ship; or it may to a certain extent be indeterminate, as in engaging freight with a shipping company, or in jobbing a carriage or horses.

139. (2.) *The Use* may be according to stipulation, or according to the implied use of the subject.

140. (3.) *The Hire* must be either certain, or ascertainable by reference to a standard.

141. Obligations of the Lessor.—These are analogous to those of sale. He is bound (1.) 'in letting an article for immediate use, and where nothing is to be done to it by the hirer to put it into a serviceable state,' to furnish the subject fit and free for use (*a*). 'And if he knows, or in the circumstances ought to know or to suspect, a defect in the thing let, making it unfit for the purpose for which it is let, and omits to inform the lessee of his knowledge or suspicion, or to make inquiry so as to verify or negative the suspicion, he is answerable in damages. But there is not in general an implied warranty against latent defects (*b*).' If it be a definite subject, he is discharged by the accidental perishing of it; this being also a discharge of the hire. A partial destruction by accident will entitle the lessee to abatement of the hire, or to abandon the contract. When the subject is indefinite, the obligation of the lessor is absolute to furnish the article, the destruction of any one not discharging the obligation. Insolvency is no defence to the lessor against an action for implement; but the demand resolves into damages, there being no *jus in re* to the lessee to be a ground of preference.

(*a*) Sutton *v.* Temple, 12 M. & W. 60. Fowler *v.* Locke, *infra*, and cases in § 408. As to gratuitous lenders, see below, § 196.

(*b*) Pothier, Contr. de Louage, P. ii. ch. i. Nos. 118–120. Blakemore *v.* Bristol and Ex. Ry. Co., 8 E. & B. 1051; 27 L. J. Q. B. 167; 1 Smith's L. C. 228. Searle *v.* Laverick, 43 L. J. Q. B. 43; L. R. 9 Q. B. 122. Fowler *v.* Locke, *infra*. See § 196.

142. (2.) The lessor is also bound to warrant the use, and in so doing to protect the lessee in possession; to maintain the thing free from all faults or defects impeding the use, and in a state fit for the purpose stipulated; to indemnify the lessee for any loss occasioned by the want of a subject thus fit, or arising from any supervening incapacity, not from inevitable accident (*a*); and to suffer abatement or loss of hire if the subject by accident become wholly or partially useless (*b*).

(*a*) See Fowler *v.* Locke, 41 L. J. C. P. 99; 43 *ib.* 394; L. R. 7 C. P. 272; 10 *ib.* 90.

(*b*) 3 Ersk. 3. § 15. Wilson *v.* Norris, March 10, 1810; F. C.; 1 Ill. 121. See afterwards, relative to agricultural leases, § 1208, 1253. As to the application of these rules to a bowing contract, see Logan *v.* Hamilton, 1872; 16 Journ. of Jur. 271. A bowing contract does not dispossess owner of cows in a question under Contagious Diseases Act. Robertson *v.* Local Authority of Perthshire, 1883; 10 R. Just. 68.

143. Obligations of the Lessee.—The lessee is bound to pay the hire stipulated or customary, with deduction of an abatement for temporary or partial deprivation of the use by defect or fault of the lessor (*a*).

(*a*) 3 Ersk. 3. § 16. Pothier, Louage, No. 134. Story, p. 274.

144. He is bound to take only the stipulated use, or that which is implied, according to the *bonâ fide* agreement of the parties, and to indemnify the lessor for all excessive use assumed (*a*).

(*a*) Ersk. *ut sup.* Pothier, Louage, No. 159. Story, p. 72. Straton *v.* ——, 1610; M. 3148; 1 Ill. 122. Moffat *v.* Moffat, 1624; M. 10,073. Guthrie's Erskine's Prin. iii. 3. 5, note. See as to taking horses beyond the stipulated distance, Campbell, Shaw, and Gardners, *infra.* In the remarkable case of Seton *v.* Paterson, 1880, 8 R. 236, two judges of the Second Division held that one who hires a horse for an ordinary ride becomes liable for all accidents if he takes it into a grass field and gallops there. This seems to go beyond the cases referred to. See, however, Addison on Contr. 348, 349, as to gratuitous loans; and below, § 197.

145. He is bound to bestow due care on the subject (*a*), 'which implies the application of absolutely necessary repairs and remedies such as a prudent man would use for the preservation of his own property, with recourse against the lessor for the expense so incurred, if the occasion of it was not due to the lessee, and if due notice was given to the owner (*b*).' The hirer of animals is bound to provide them with food, to pay for the shoeing of horses let on time (*c*), and to restore them in proper condition, with the exception of fortuitous loss 'and of ordinary tear and wear (*d*),' when the time shall have expired or the occasion shall be over (*e*). 'A hirer is not liable for faults of ostlers, and persons to whom the horse has been properly entrusted (*f*). But he is liable for negligence of his own servant, even when acting outwith the scope of his employment (*g*).' Where there is loss total or partial, the *onus probandi* is laid on the lessee in whose custody the thing was at the time (*h*).

(*a*) 3 Ersk. 3. § 15. Johnston *v.* Rankin, 1687; M. 10,080; 1 Ill. 122. Trotter *v.* Buchanan, 1688; M. 10,080. Binny *v.* Vean, 1679; M. 10,079. Robertson *v.* Ogle, June 23, 1809; F. C. Marquis *v.* Ritchie, 1823; 2 S. 366. Cooper *v.* Barton, 3 Camp. 5, n.; 13 R. R. 736. Bray *v.* Mayne, 1 Gow, 1; 21 R. R. 786. Dean *v.* Keat, 3 Camp. 4; 13 R. R. 735. Garside *v.* Trent and Mersey Nav. Co., 4 T. R. 462, 581; 2 R. R. 468.

(*b*) 1 Bell's Com. 453 (482, M'L.'s ed.). Addison on Contr. 345.

(*c*) Handford *v.* Palmer, 2 Brod. & Bing. 359.

(*d*) See Shroder *v.* Ward, 13 C. B. N. S. 410; 32 L. J. C. P. 150.

(*e*) See Trotter, *cit.* Campbell *v.* Kennedy, 1828; 6 S. 806. M'Pherson *v.* Sutherland, 1791; Hume, 296. Shaw *v.* Donaldson, 1792; Hume, 297. Gardners *v.* M'Donald, 1792; Hume, 299.

(*f*) Smith *v.* Melvin, 1815; 8 D. 261.

(*g*) Coupé Co. *v.* Maddick, 1891; Q. B. 413; disting. from Storey *v.* Ashton, and cases in § 547 (*c*).

(*h*) Binny, Robertson, and Marquis, *supra* (*a*). Pothier, Louage, No. 199. See Code Civ. Art. 1732 et seq. See Pyper *v.* Thomson, 1843; 5 D. 498. Pullars *v.* Walker, 1858; 20 D. 1238. Moes, Moliere, & Tromp *v.* Leith Shipping Co., 1867; 5 Macph. 988. Wilson *v.* Orr, 1879; 7 R. 266. Seton *v.* Paterson, *supra.* By the English and American law, the *onus* of proving negligence is laid on the lessor.

II. HIRING OF ORDINARY LABOUR.

146. Nature of this Contract.—The contract of hiring of labour is an engagement, on the one part, to perform certain work, or to labour during a certain term, in consideration of a certain hire; on the other part, to pay that hire. It applies to common labour (*a*); to skilled labour; to care and custody; to carriage.

(*a*) See as to hiring of artisans, below, § 190.

147. This strictly is an engagement to do certain work on materials furnished to the workman, the material being "bailed" or delivered to the temporary possession of the workman, to have the labour bestowed on it. Where the thing is to be prepared of materials to be furnished by the workman (as in the general case of manufactures), the contract partakes of sale. It is the executory sale of the English law (*a*).

(*a*) See above, § 90. Pothier, Louage, No. 394. Story on Bailments, 277.

148. Obligations of Workman.—His obligations are to do the work or labour stipulated or implied, and within the time appointed. There is an implied warranty that these duties shall be well performed, otherwise the hire shall not be due, nor damages demandable.

149. Such contracts are frequently made on a specification and estimate, from which in the course of the work there may arise a deviation. In such cases two sets of questions may be raised. Thus, if more be done than is bargained for, the employer is not bound to take it, unless the excess be slight or unavoidable (*a*), 'or it consist of extra work ordered or assented to by him in the knowledge that it involves extra expense (*b*)'; or, if it must necessarily be taken as incorporated with his own materials, he will not be liable for a greater hire of labour than he at first engaged to pay. But if he have acquiesced in the deviation, the *quantum meruit*, ascertained by measure or value, will be the rule, as in contracts for the building or repairing of houses (*c*). If the work have been imperfectly or unskilfully done, 'or not according to contract,' the employer is not bound to take it, and is entitled to damages unless he shall have acquiesced (*d*). If the work be united with his materials, 'it was said in the earlier editions of this book that' it seems not yet to be settled whether the employer shall have right to the subject without paying, or the workman shall be bound to indemnify (*e*). 'In such a case, however, the liability of the employer depends on the utility or inutility of the work. He is bound to pay so far only as he is benefited. But if there is a special contract to complete a certain piece of work, the mere fact that part performance or imperfect performance has been beneficial does not in England render the owner liable to pay the *quantum meruit* (*f*). Where the workman fails to finish work upon the employer's premises, and the employer proceeds to finish it by other workmen or contractors, the employer has a right, at least under the usual clause in contracts for building, etc., to retain the materials and tools brought upon the premises for that purpose, subject to the workman's claim for the value of the materials, and a reasonable hire for the use of the tools (*g*). The employer may retain the contract price in respect of a claim of damages for non-implement of such a mutual contract (*h*); and if damages for delay be fixed at a certain sum for the period during which the work is unfinished, that will be held as pactional damages, and not a penalty subject to modification (*i*), unless the sum stipulated be exorbitant and unconscionable, when it will not be allowed to the full amount (*k*). Claims of damages for imperfect work, or of repayment of sums paid for work not done, discovered after the completion of a building or other executory contract, will be barred by a final settlement proceeding on the reports of inspectors appointed by the employer (*l*).'

(*a*) See § 151.
(*b*) Peacock *v.* M'Kenzie, Scott *v.* Hatton, and Wilson *v.* Wallace, *infra* (*c*). Lovelock *v.* King, 1 Moo. & Ry. 60. Dobson *v.* Hudson, 1 C. B. N. S. 659; 26 L. J. C. P. 153. Sometimes extras are allowed by the contract only upon an order in writing: Myers *v.* Sarl, 30 L. J. Q. B. 9. Russel *v.* Sa da Bandiera, 13 C. B. N. S. 149; 32 L. J. C. P. 68. M'Elroy & Sons *v.* Tharsis Co., 1877; 5 R. 161; rev. 1878, *ib.* H. L. 171.
(*c*) Peacock *v.* M'Kenzie, 1825; 3 S. 306; 1 Ill. 123. Scott & Morris *v.* Hatton, 1827; 6 S. 233. Brown *v.* Perth Road Trs., 1832; 10 S. 667; 1 Ill. 34. Duchess of Buccleugh *v.* Nairn, 1712; M. 4051. Gordon *v.* Millar, 1839; 1 D. 832. Smail *v.* Potts, 1847; 9 D. 1043. Wilson *v.* Wallace & Connell, 1859; 21 D. 507. Weatherstone *v.* Robertson, 1852; 1 Stuart, 333.
(*d*) In England the employer seems to be held at law entitled to take what has been done amiss, without paying for it. This probably arises from the rules of English pleading. Correct this statement of Prof. Bell by Addison on Contr. 395–96, 406.
(*e*) Ellis *v.* Hanlen, 3 Taunt. 52; 1 Ill. 124; 12 R. R. 595. 2 Kent, Com. 590. Story on Bailments, 287.
(*f*) Sinclair *v.* Bowles, 4 M. & R. 3; 9 B. & C. 94. Munro *v.* Butt, 8 E. & B. 752. See cases below, § 152 (*e*), and 2 Smith's L. C. 19 sqq.
(*g*) Kerr *v.* Dundee Gas Co., 1861; 23 D. 343. *In re* Winter (*ex p.* Bolland), 8 Ch. D. 225; 47 L. J. Bkr. 52.
(*h*) Johnston *v.* Robertson, 1861; 23 D. 646.
(*i*) *Ib.*, and see *supra*, § 34.
(*k*) Forrest & Barr *v.* Henderson & Coulborn, 1869; 8 Macph. 187.
(*l*) Ayr Road Trs. *v.* Adams, 1883; 11 R. 326. Muldoon *v.* Pringle, 1882; 9 R. 916. See as to this case, above, § 27A, and Kilmarnock Mags. *v.* Reid, 1897; 24 R. 388.

150. The degree of care requisite on the part of the workman is that implied in ordinary diligence (*a*).

(*a*) See below, § 232.

151. Obligations of Employer.—His obligation is to pay the hire at the time, and in the way, stipulated or implied. If the employment be general to labour, or on time, the hire is due as the work is done and added to the employer's materials. If the work be unskilfully performed, and such as the employer would not have been bound to receive if completed, the hire will not be due (*a*). 'But, unless the terms of the contract strictly exclude any other meaning (*b*), the exact performance of all the particular details of a stipulated work is not a condition precedent of the right to some remuneration. In a building contract, for example, the builder is entitled to recover the price, subject to deduction of such a sum as will make defective work correspond with the specification, and of such loss as the employer may have suffered by non-performance (*c*). In a contract for work to be done according to plans and specifications, there is no implied warranty by the employer that the work can be done in the very way described. Extra work contemplated by the contract is to be paid at the rates provided in the contract; but if additional or varied work, so different as not to be within the contract at all, becomes necessary, it appears that the contractor may refuse to go on with the contract, or go on and claim *quantum meruit*; but in the latter case, he ought perhaps to give notice of the footing on which he is to proceed (*d*).'

(*a*) 1 Bankt. 20. § 26. Pothier, Louage, No. 433.
(*b*) See above, § 149 (*f*).
(*c*) See, *e.g.*, Macbride *v.* Hamilton & Son, 1875; 2 R. 775. Gibson & Stewart *v.* Brown & Co., 1876; 3 R. 328, and cases in § 149 (*g*), (*h*), (*k*). With us such questions are determined according to the principle of mutuality in contracts (§ 71), and we are not troubled with various questions of pleading which occur in the English books. These, however, afford assistance in the construction of contracts upon this subject. See 2 Smith's L. C., notes to Cutter *v.* Powell. Addison on Contr. 391, 396, etc.
(*d*) Thorn *v.* Lord Mayor of London, L. R. 1 App. Ca. 120; 45 L. J. Ex. 487.

152. Risk.—In proper *locatio operis*, where the subject on which the work is to be bestowed belongs to the employer, the risk is with the employer—*res perit domino.* The hire is not forfeited, or repayment demandable, if the thing should, without fault of the workman, perish with the work on it (*a*). Such is the case of repairs to a ship which is burnt before being finished (*b*); 'or of building work performed on the ground of the employer (*c*).' As to printer's work burnt in the printing-office, usage has been held to alter the general rule (*d*). But if the workman be hired to accomplish some particular operation which he undertakes to do 'for a specific sum,' and the whole perishes before he has completed his undertaking, '*i.e.* in the phraseology of the English law, if the contract be *entire*,' the loss of his work would seem to fall on him (*e*); yet in those cases of executory contracts where the price is paid periodically, and the subject appropriated to the employer at the several payments, the whole would perish to the employer. If the workman is to make an article of manufacture of materials to be found by himself, the risk is with the workman, and the unfinished work perishes to him. It is an incomplete executory sale, and he cannot claim the price of his labour.

(*a*) Pothier, Louage, No. 434.
(*b*) Menetone *v.* Athawes, 3 Burr. 1592 ; 1 Ill. 124.
(*c*) M'Intyre *v.* Clow & Co., 1875 ; 2 R. 278. Richardson *v.* Dumfries Rd. Trs., 1890 ; 17 R. 805. See 1 Bell's Com. 456 (486, M'L.'s ed.).
(*d*) Gillet *v.* Mawman, 1 Taunt. 137 ; 2 Taunt. 325, n.
(*e*) See Gillet (*d*). Adlard *v.* Booth, 7 Car. & P. 108. Taylor *v.* Caldwell, 3 B. & S. 826 ; 32 L. J. Q. B. 164. Cutter *v.* Powell, 6 T. R. 220 ; 2 Smith's L. C. 1, and notes there. Appleby *v.* Myers (Ex. Cham.), L. R. 2 C. P. 651 ; 36 L. J. C. P. 331. Anglo-Egypt. Nav. Co. *v.* Rennie, L. R. 10 C. P. 271, 571 ; 44 L. J. C. P. 130. M'Intyre, *cit.* See 1 Bell's Com. *cit.* ; 2 Smith's L. C. *cit.* Addison on Contr. 399 sqq., 929 sqq. See above, § 29, and below, § 570, 1298.

III. HIRING OF SKILLED LABOUR.

153. Nature of the Contract.—The engagement here is to bestow attention, art, and skill on the act to be performed; skill being presumed in all professional persons, according to the rule, "Spondet peritiam artis, et imperitia culpæ annumeratur." The *selection* for superior skill is with the employer (*a*); but he is entitled to rely on ordinary *skill* (*b*). The rate of hire is settled by the contract, or by the ordinary wages of such labour, or by the usage of the parties, or by *quantum meruit* (*c*). The time is regulated in the same way, by agreement or by usage, as in the hiring of clerks and managers (*d*).

(*a*) As to his wilful selection of unqualified persons, see Addison on Contr. 414.
(*b*) Pollock *v.* Wilkie, 1856 ; 18 D. 1311.
(*c*) Stewart *v.* Clyne, 1831 ; 9 S. 382 ; 1833, 11 S. 727 ; aff. 1835, 2 S. & M'L. 45 ; 1 Ill. 125. Sinclair *v.* Erskine, 1831 ; 9 S. 487. Landless *v.* Wilson, 1880 ; 8 R. 299. See below, § 538.
(*d*) Beeston *v.* Collyer, 2 C. & P. 607 ; 4 Bing. 309 ; 29 R. R. 576. Huttman *v.* Boulnois, 4 C. & P. 208 ; 4 Bing. 510. Mabon *v.* Elliot, 1808 ; Hume, 393. Moffat *v.* Shedden, 1839 ; 1 D. 468. Campbell *v.* Fyfe, 1851 ; 13 D. 1041. Hoey *v.* M'Ewan & Auld, 1867 ; 5 Macph. 814. See below, § 174, 570.

154. The Rules of Responsibility derived from the above principle are:

(1.) That one not a professor of the art is liable only for the best exertion of his skill, such as it may be (*a*).

(2.) That, by a professional man, a specific act is to be done according to rule, if a rule be fixed (*b*). When the rule is obscure, professional usage may excuse error (*c*).

(3.) Where express directions are given to such a person, slight deviations, within the fair limits of professional discretion, are justifiable (*d*).

(4.) That if the object be safely attainable by a known method, the professional man takes the risk of deviation from that method. In general, the criterion is reasonable care and skill (*e*).

(5.) That if the act be difficult or complicated, want of success is not an absolute test of responsibility. 'But the onus of showing that injury to goods, sustained in undergoing a delicate process of manufacture, was not the fault of the workman to whom they were entrusted for that purpose, lies on the workman (*f*).'

(6.) The responsibility is only for actual damage: as in killing a lame horse; blundering an objectionable adjudication (*g*). 'It is a good answer to a claim of damages that the pursuer could not have received the expected benefit even if the person employed had performed his duty, in other words, that no damage has resulted from the act or default; though the relevancy of such a defence in the special case of one entrusted with a statutory duty, such as the recording of a writ, was doubted (*h*). The general rule is, that an agent is bound to reinstate his employer in the position in which he would have been if he had duly performed his duty; and so, if the error can be corrected, a law agent may be allowed so to discharge his liability, as by paying off prior encumbrances on property he has been employed to purchase, or even over which he has lent his client's money (*i*). But if by his culpable nondisclosure of material facts, or negligence in making necessary investigations, his employer has been led into a losing transaction, which a reasonable man, knowing the facts, would not have agreed to, an agent may be required to relieve the employer of the contract, *e.g.* by repaying a sum lent out on a bad security, and receiving an assignation to the debt and security (*k*).'

(7.) It is no defence to a messenger-at-arms, that he has not injured or betrayed the interest of his employers; or to an agent bungling an act in which adverse parties are concerned (as a loan), that he was employed by one of them (as by the granter of the bond): he acts for both parties; and the person injured, or who is to receive the security, is he for whose behoof the law will interfere, and by whom the order is held to be given (*l*). 'But while this rule holds good where the terms of the employment, or professional usage, make it a law agent's duty to attend to the interests of both parties to a transaction, one who professes any art is, in general, liable for want of skill or negligence only to his employer, and not to those who may have been intended to benefit by his work, but with whom he has not contracted (*m*). But clear irregularity in using diligence makes a law agent as well as his employer liable for the injury done to the person against whom it is put in force (*n*).'

(8.) When the hiring is on time, with a salary, incapacity or negligence of the person employed will free the employer, but not if acquiesced in without complaint (*o*), 'or known and explained to the employer at the time of engagement (*p*).'

(*a*) Jones on Bailments. 1 Bell's Com. 459 (489, M'L.'s ed.).

(*b*) Atkinson *v.* Macbean, 1756; M. 13,965; 1 Ill. 126. Chatto & Co. *v.* Marshall, Jan. 17, 1811; F. C. Lillie *v.* Macdonald, Dec. 13, 1816; F. C.; aff. 1819, 1 Bligh, 315. See Campbell *v.* Clason, 1838; 1 D. 270, 278. Struthers *v.* Lang, 1826; 4 S. 418; 2 W. & S. 563. Rowand *v.* Stevenson, 1827; 5 S. 903; 6 S. 272; aff. 4 W. & S. 177. Sim *v.* Clark, 1831; 10 S. 85; aff. 6 W. & S. 452; 1 Ill. 128; 3 Ill. 108. Haldane *v.* Donaldson, 1836; 14 S. 610; aff. 1 Rob. 226; 3 Ill. 107. Frame & Co. *v.* Campbell, 1836; 14 S. 914; aff. M'L. & Rob. 595; 3 Ill. 107. Brown *v.* M'Kie, 1852; 14 D. 358. See below, § 219 (7), and other cases, chiefly as to law agents and messengers-at-arms, in 1 Ill. 126 sqq., 222.

(*c*) Graham *v.* Alison, 1830; 9 S. 130; aff. 1833, 6 W. & S. 518; 1 Ill. 129. See also M'Lean *v.* Grant, 1805; M. Apx. *Reparation*, 2. See note in 1 Ill. 130.

(*d*) Burnet *v.* Clark, 1771; M. 8491; 1 Ill. 129 (farrier). Laing *v.* L. Ch. Baron, 1753; Elch. *Mandate*, 4 (carpenter). M'Aulay *v.* Ferguson, 1799; Hume, 324.

(*e*) Lennox *v.* Grant, 1784; M. 14,381. Grant *v.* M'Leay, 1791; Bell's Ca. 319; 1 Ill. 126. Shilcock *v.* Passman, 7 C. & P. 289. Duncan *v.* Blemdell, 3 Starkie, 6. See below, § 219. M'Intyre *v.* Gallagher, 1883; 11 R. 64 (plumber work).

(*f*) Hinshaw *v.* Adam, 1870; 8 Macph. 933.

(*g*) M'Lean, *supra* (*c*). Murray & Son *v.* Taylor, 1828; 6 S. 802; 1 Ill. 131. Campbell *v.* Campbell & Clason, 1838; 1 D. 270; 1839, 2 D. 1113; 1843, 5 D. 1081. See Graham, *supra* (*c*). Haldane, *supra* (*b*).

(*h*) Davidson *v.* Mackenzie, 1856; 19 D. 226. See 1 Bell's Com. 461; and M'Laren's Bell's Com. i. 531, note.

(*i*) Donald's Trs. *v.* Yeats, 1839; 1 D. 1249. Campbell *v.* Clason, *cit.*

(*k*) Graham *v.* Hunter's Trs., 1831; 9 S. 543. Haldane, *supra* (*b*). Stuart *v.* Miller, 1840; 3 D. 255; and cases *infra*, § 219 (*pp*).

(*l*) Grant *v.* Forbes, 1758; M. 2081; aff. 6 Paton, 731; 1 Ill. 221. Struthers, *supra* (*b*). Wilson *v.* Riddel, 1826; 4 S. 732; 1 Ill. 131. Haldane, *supra* (*b*). See below, § 219 (7). Mackintosh *v.* Pitcairn, 1851; 14 D. 187. Fleming *v.* Robertson, 1859; 21 D. 548, 982; H. L. 1861; 4 Macq. 167; 23 D. H. L. 8. See also M'Alister *v.* Gemmill, 1862; 24 D. 956; aff. 1863, 1 Macph. H. L. 1. 1 Bell's Com. 461 (490, M'L.'s ed.).

(*m*) Goldie *v.* Goldie, 1842; 4 D. 1489. Fleming *v.* Robertson, *cit.* (*per* Lord Campbell, C.). See Rae *v.* Meek, 1888; 15 R. 1033. Tully *v.* Ingram, 1891; 19 R. 65.

(*n*) Authorities in Smith & Co. *v.* Taylor, 1882; 10 R. 291. Mackersy *v.* Davis & Sons, 1895; 22 R. 369. See further as to privity of contract and *jus quæsitum tertio*, Blumer & Co. *v.* Scott & Sons, 1874; 1 R. 379.

(*o*) Fraser *v.* Laing, 1831; 9 S. 418; 1 Ill. 131. Harmer *v.* Cornelius, 5 C. B. N. S. 236; 28 L. J. C. P. 85.

(*p*) Gunn *v.* Ramsay, 1801; Hume, 384

IV. HIRING OF CARE AND CUSTODY.

155. Description of this Contract.—This is the contract which regulates the duties of depositaries for hire, wharfingers, warehousemen, livery stablers, and persons who keep depasturing fields for cattle. The engagement is for safe keeping: And this implies a secure place of custody (*a*); a warehouse water-tight, secure from attacks without and fire within, and free from vermin (*b*), or whatever is injurious to that kind of commodity;—a grazing field guarded against the escape of cattle, 'the intrusion of savage and dangerous beasts,' and free from pitfalls and dangers (*c*). It implies the personal care of the lessor and his servants, to prevent injuries incident to property in that situation (*d*). 'The onus is said to be on the warehouseman or depositary to show that injury did not occur through his fault, but it necessarily varies in different contracts and circumstances (*e*).' By express contract, or even by notice (*f*), these liabilities are alterable in extent of responsibility (*g*). 'Where, as in the case of luggage deposited in a cloakroom or carried in a steamship, the ticket given to the passenger or depositor is relied on as giving notice of the terms of the bailment, it must be shown that the conditions were either known to him or that he had reasonable notice of their existence. The rule may be thus expressed: where one of two contracting parties delivers to the other a document (ticket or voucher) in a common form, stating the terms on which he enters into the proposed contract (his "offer"), and the other accepts and acts upon it without objection, the latter, if his attention has been sufficiently drawn to the fact that there are conditions, is held, on the principle of personal bar, to accept the offer as it is made, and is bound by the terms of the document, whether he reads it or not (*h*). He is not so bound if the transaction is such that the receiver of the ticket may suppose that it contains no conditions (*i*), or where it is misleading (*k*), or fraudulent, or perhaps where the conditions are unreasonable or absurd (*l*).'

(*a*) See Searle *v.* Laverick, *supra*, § 141 (*b*).
(*b*) White *v.* Humphreys, 11 Q. B. 44.
(*c*) Smith *v.* Cook, L. R. 1 Q. B. D. 79; 45 L. J. Q. B. 79. Broadwater, *cit. infra.* 1 Bell's Com. 458 (488, M'L.'s ed.). M'Lean *v.* Warnock, 1883; 10 R. 1052. Sutherland *v.* Hutton, 1896; 23 R. 718.
(*d*) Jones on Bailments, 91–2. Davidson *v.* Davidson, 1749; M. 10,081; 1 Ill. 131. Hagart *v.* Inglis, 1832; 10 S. 506. See below, § 210. Laing *v.* Darling, 1850; 12 D. 1279. Robertson *v.* Connolly, 1851; 13 D. 779; 14 D. 315. Allan & Poynter *v.* Williamson, Jan. 5, 1870; 14 J. of J. 119; 7 S. L. R. 214. Snodgrass *v.* Ritchie & Lamberton, 1890; 17 R. 712 (storekeeper, flour in bags).
Leck *v.* Maestaer, 1 Camp. 138; 1 Ill. 132; 10 R. R. 660. Cailiff *v.* Danvers, Peake, 114; 3 R. R. 666. Clarke *v.* Earnshaw, 1 Gow, 30; 21 R. R. 796. Broadwater *v.* Blot, Holt's Cases, 547; 17 R. R. 677. Wood *v.* Curling, 15 M. & W. 626; 16 M. & W. 628.
(*e*) Mackenzie *v.* Cox, 9 C. & P. 632. Reeve *v.* Palmer, 5 C. B. N. S. 84. But see Robertson, *cit.*, and cases in note (*g*), and Sutherland, *cit.* (*c*).
(*f*) See Lightbody's Tr. *v.* Hutchison, 1886; 14 R. 4. *Infra*, § 244 (*a*), (*o*), 435.
(*g*) Whitehead *v.* Straiton, 1667; M. 10,074; 1 Ill. 131. Birnie *v.* Straiton, 1680; M. 10,079. Maxwell *v.* Todridge, 1684; M. 10,079 (early cases as to notice limiting common law liability).
(*h*) Stevenson *v.* Henderson, 1873; 1 R. 215; aff. 1875, 2 R. H. L. 71; L. R. 2 Sc. App. 470. Handon *v.* Cal. Ry. Co., 1880; 7 R. 966. Van Toll *v.* S.-E. Ry. Co., 12 C. B. N. S. 75; 31 L. J. C. P. 241. **Harris** *v.* **G. W. Ry. Co.,** 1 Q. B. D. 515; 45 L. J. Q. B. 729 (*per* Blackburn, J.). Parker *v.* S.-E. Ry. Co., 2 C. P. D. 415; 46 L. J. C. P. 768. **Watkins** *v.* **Rymill,** 10 Q. B. D. 178. **Richardson, Spence, & Co.** *v.* **Rowntree,** 1894; A. C. 217. Burke *v.* S. E. Ry. Co., L. R. 5 C. P. D. 1; 49 L. J. C. P. 107. See Pollock on Contr. 45; and Highland Ry. Co. *v.* Menzies, 1878; 5 R. 887. See cases in § 244, and above, § 132 (*f*).
(*i*) See Parker, Henderson, Harris, *citt.*
(*k*) Henderson, *cit.*
(*l*) See Parker, *cit.* (*per* Bramwell, L. J.).

156. Responsibility.—The commencement of a warehouseman's and of a wharfinger's responsibility is different. The warehouseman, or the wharfinger when employed as such, is a mere custodier, and his responsibility begins with the arrival of the goods at the warehouse, and the act of custody, as by applying the crane of the warehouse (*a*). But a wharfinger has the duty of attending to the landing and receiving of the goods; and his responsibility will commence as soon as the goods are landed on the wharf, or put out of the hands of the carrier or porter for embarkation (*b*).

(*a*) Thomas *v.* Day, 4 Espin. 262; 6 R. R. 857.
(*b*) Cobban *v.* Downe, 5 Espin. 41; 3 Ill. 108; 8 R. R. 825. Leigh *v.* Smith, Ryan & Mood. 224. *Infra*, § 236 (3). Wood *v.* Curling, *cit.* §. 155 (*d*). A wharfinger is also bound to use reasonable care to have the berth to which he invites a vessel and the approaches to it in proper order. The Moorcock, 14 P. D. 64. The Calliope, 1891; A. C. 11. Comp. Buchanan and Renney, *citt. infra*, § 656 (*a*).

V. HIRING OF CARRIAGE.

157. Objects of this Contract.—The carrying trade, now so important a branch of commercial intercourse, is either inland, by land or water; or sea-carriage. The former, together with the general principles of the contract, may here be considered (*a*).

(*a*) The peculiarities of sea-carriage will be discussed below, § 405 et seq.

158. The contract of carriage may be viewed, 1. as relative to goods; 2. as relative to persons.

159. Carriage of Goods.—This contract, which is the *locatio operis mercium vehundarum*, is for safe carriage of commodities, and delivery of them in good condition, in consideration of a hire, stipulated or implied.

The contract of carriage may be Express, depending on the terms of the agreement; or Implied, from the status of a common carrier, with goods fixed on him by receipt, or parole proof, and which by his office he is as much bound to carry as if there were a special contract. He is bound to take the goods offered, and can justifiably refuse them only if dangerous from their nature, or from popular tumult; or if he does not profess to carry such goods (*a*); or has no convenient means of doing so; or if not brought in due time for packing (*b*).

(*a*) A common carrier is bound only to take such goods as he publicly professes to carry (Johnson *v.* Midl. Ry. Co., 18 L. J. Ex. 366; 4 Ex. 397. M'Andrew *v.* Electr. Tel. Co., 17 C. B. 3; 25 L. J. C. P. 26); and is at liberty to refuse them (*e.g.* dogs and live stock) except under special contract regulating the terms and conditions of carriage. M'Manus *v.* L. and Y. Ry. Co., 4 H. & N. 327; 28 L. J. Ex. 353. Oxlade *v.* N.-E. Ry. Co., 15 C. B. N. S. 680. Harrison *v.* L. and B. Ry. Co., 2 B. & S. 122; 29 L. J. Q. B. 218; 31 *ib.* 113. Austin *v.* M. S. and L. Ry. Co., 16 Q. B. 600; 20 L. J. Q. B. 440. Wood *v.* Burns, 1893; 20 R. 602 (pianos carried "only at owners' risk"). But the contract must be conformable to the Act 17 and 18 Vict. c. 31, in the case of railway and canal companies. See § 244A.
(*b*) Edwards *v.* Sherrat, 1 East, 604. Batson *v.* Donovan, 4 B. & Ald. 32; 1 Ill. 139; 22 R. R. 599. Carr *v.* L. and Y. Ry. Co., 7 Ex. 707. Tattan *v.* G. W. Ry. Co., 27 L. J. Q. B. 184. Aldridge *v.* G. W. Ry. Co., 15 C. B. N. S. 582. Addison on Contr. 525 sq. *Infra*, § 244A. By statute no carrier or warehouse owner is bound to carry or receive any goods which are specially dangerous; and nitro-glycerine,

and goods so declared in any order of the Privy Council, are "specially dangerous." See Farrant *v.* Barnes, 11 C. B. N. S. 553; 31 L. J. C. P. 137 (damages due to carrier at common law). Hearne *v.* Garton, 28 L. J. Q. B. 306 (knowledge of consignor necessary to conviction). 38 Vict. c. 17 (Explosives Act), especially § 34, 35, 37, 43, 88. And as to ships, see 57 and 58 Vict. c. 60, § 301, 445 sqq. See also 8 and 9 Vict. c. 33, § 98 (railway); 33 and 34 Vict. c. 78, § 53 (tramway).

160. Responsibility of the Carrier.—The essential peculiarity in the contract with a *common carrier* is, that holding himself out in a public character, he is under certain fixed responsibilities. A common carrier is one who, for hire, undertakes the carriage of goods, 'generally, or of certain classes of goods,' for any of the public indiscriminately, from and to a certain place (*a*). 'One of the termini may be beyond the seas (*b*); and in the case of shipowners and carriers by sea, it has been held in England that they are liable as common carriers, though trading without any fixed terminus, and letting the vessel only to one person for each voyage (*c*).'

(*a*) See Riley *v.* Horne, 5 Bing. 224; 30 R. R. 576. Dickson *v.* G. N. Ry. Co., 18 Q. B. D. 176.
(*b*) Crouch *v.* L. and N.-W. Ry. Co., 14 C. B. 255; 23 L. J. C. P. 73.
(*c*) Liver Alkali Co. *v.* Johnston, L. R. 7 Ex. 267; 41 L. J. Ex. 110; discussed in Scaife *v.* Tarrant, L. R. 10 Ex. 358; 44 L. J. Ex. 235; and **Nugent** *v.* **Smith,** 1 C. P. D. 243; 45 L. J. C. P. 697. See Brind *v.* Dale, 2 M. & R. 80 (carman).

160A. '*Railway Companies* are not common carriers of passengers, and so not liable as insurers (*a*). But they are common carriers of goods, subject to any special limitation or exemption by their Act of Parliament, profession, practice, or special stipulation which they may lawfully make (*b*). Under the equality clauses in their special Acts and the Railway Clauses Consolidation Act, railway companies are bound to charge equally to all persons for the carriage, on the same journey and under the same circumstances, of all goods (*c*); and money paid in excess in contravention of such clauses may be recovered back (*d*). But while they are not common carriers of goods which they do not profess to carry, railway and canal companies are required by the Railway and Canal Traffic Act to make proper arrangements, and afford all reasonable facilities, for the receiving, forwarding, and delivering of traffic (which includes passengers and their luggage, goods, animals, etc.), without unreasonable delay, and without giving any undue or unreasonable preference or advantage to any particular person or company, or any particular kind of traffic, or subjecting any persons or kind of traffic to undue or unreasonable prejudice or disadvantage; and so that no obstruction may be offered to the public desiring to use their railways and canals as a continuous line of communication (*e*).

'The Acts of 1873 (Regulation of Railways Act (*f*) and the Railway and Canal Traffic Act, 1888 (*g*)) followed upon this statute, and have amended it, and established a special tribunal—the Railway and Canal Commission—for administering the law under it and under enactments in special Acts relating to traffic facilities, undue preferences, or other matters mentioned in § 2 of the Act of 1854. This Commission has now power to hear and determine disputes as to the legality, and to enforce payment, of tolls, rates, or charges which have been brought into dispute (*h*); and also, in addition to or substitution for other relief, to award damages (*i*). These Acts make the jurisdiction of the Railway and Canal Commissioners exclusive, an appeal on points of law being allowable (*k*).

'The provisions of these Acts do not extend to facilities for storing goods after delivery to consignees, as by letting surplus land as a coal depôt (*l*), nor to rates charged by a railway company for the use of docks not connected with their railway business (*m*). But they apply to undue and unreasonable disadvantage imposed upon a particular kind of traffic, *e.g.* by charging in excess of the authorised rates to such an extent as to impede or prevent traffic, although there be no preference of a particular person or class (*n*).'

(*a*) Blake *v.* G. W. Ry. Co., 7 H. & N. 987; 31 L. J. Ex. 346. Wright *v.* Mid. Ry. Co., Readhead *v.* Mid. Ry. Co., and other cases below, § 170.
(*b*) Palmer *v.* Gr. Junction Canal Co., 4 M. & W. 749. Pickford *v.* Grand Junc. Ry. Co., 10 M. & W. 399. Parker *v.* G. W. Ry. Co., 7 Scott's N. R. 835. Dickson *v.* G. N. Ry. Co., 18 Q. B. D. 176. 8 and 9 Vict. c. 32, § 82.
(*c*) Pickford, *cit.* Baxendale *v.* L. and S.-W. Ry. Co., L. R. 1 Ex. 137; 35 L. J. Ex. 108. Evershed *v.* L. and N.-W. Ry. Co., L. R. 3 App. Ca. 1029; 48 L. J. Q. B. 22. Murray *v.* Glas. and S.-W. Ry. Co., 1883; 11 R. 205. Hull, Barnsley, etc., Ry. Co. *v.* Yorksh. & Derbysh. Coal, etc., Co., 18 Q. B. D. 761. Denaby Main Coll. Co. *v.* Manch. Sheff., etc., Ry. Co., 11 App. Ca. 97.
(*d*) Sutton *v.* G. W. Ry. Co., 38 L. J. Ex. 177; L. R. 4 H. L. 226. Lanc. Ry. Co. *v.* Gidlow, 45 L. J. Ex. 625;

L. R. 7 H. L. 517. Evershed, *cit.* Yeats's Trs. *v.* G. & S.-W. Ry. Co., 1889; 16 R. 535.

(*e*) 17 and 18 Vict. c. 31, § 2. See 26 and 27 Vict. c. 92, § 30; 31 and 32 Vict. c. 119, § 12 (equal charges when company works steam vessels in connection with railway); 36 and 37 Vict. c. 48, § 11 (forwarding through traffic) and 16 (agreements between railway and canal companies).

(*f*) 36 and 37 Vict. c. 48.

(*g*) 51 and 52 Vict. c. 25.

(*h*) *Ib.* § 10. (*i*) *Ib.* § 12.

(*k*) 36 and 37 Vict. c. 48, § 6; 51 and 52 Vict. c. 25, § 8, 17. N. B. Ry. Co. *v.* N. B. Grain Storage Co., 1897; 24 R. 687. 1 Smith's L. C. 203. Perth Gen. Station Co., 24 R. H. L. 44; 1895, A. C. 479.

(*l*) West *v.* L. and N.-W. Ry. Co., L. R. 5 C. P. 622; 39 L. J. C. P. 282.

(*m*) East and W. India Dock Co. *v.* Savill, 39 Ch. D. 524.

(*n*) Aberdeen Coml. Co. *v.* G. N. of S. Ry. Co., 1878; 6 R. 67. G. W. Ry. Co. *v.* Ry. Comrs., 50 L. J. Q. B. 483. See the following cases decided under the Acts:—Hozier *v.* Cal. Ry. Co., 1855; 17 D. 302. Napier *v.* Glas. and S.-W. Ry. Co., 1865; 4 Macph. 87. Wannan *v.* Sc. Cent. Ry. Co., 1864; 2 Macph. 1373. Pickford *v.* Cal. Ry. Co., 1866; 4 Macph. 755. S.-E. Ry. Co. *v.* Ry. Comrs., 50 L. J. Q. B. 201. Murray *v.* Glas. and S.-W. Ry. Co., 1883; 11 R. 205. Cal. Ry. Co. *v.* Cross, 1889; 16 R. 585. N. B. Ry. Co. *v.* N. B. Grain Stor., etc., Co., 1897; 24 R. 687.

161. To raise the liability, the carrier must be legitimately charged with the goods.

162. A common carrier by land is so charged, by delivery of the goods to him, or to some one empowered to act for him (*a*). But it is not sufficient to lay them down in a common yard of an inn, where other carriers' goods are (*b*); nor to deliver them to the carriers' servants on the road, between the two points of his journey (*c*), unless the servants be sent round or commissioned to receive goods (*d*); nor to deliver a letter to the postman on the street (*e*); nor to deliver them in a state insecure and unfit for carriage (*f*): yet if the defect of security be manifest, and the carrier undertake the carriage notwithstanding, it is enough (*g*).

(*a*) 3 Chitty, Com. Law, 380 (p. 320, ed. 1856). Williams *v.* Cranston, 2 Starkie, 82; 1 Ill. 133; 19 R. R. 681. Bain *v.* Brown & Blackburn, 1824; 3 S. 362. Bain *v.* Sinclair, 1825; 3 S. 533. Syms *v.* Chaplin, 5 Ad. & E. 634; 3 Ill. 109. Tod *v.* Wilson, 1799; Hume, 306. Reid *v.* Mackie, 1830; 8 S. 948. Lovell *v.* L. C. and D. Ry. Co., 45 L. J. Q. B. 476; and as to luggage in the carriage with passengers; see Talley and Bergheim, *infra*, § 235, 244; also, § 240. As to the liability of forwarding agents and carriers' agents, see Wight *v.* Inglis, 1828; 6 S. 572. Bates *v.* Cameron, 1855; 18 D. 186. Hodgman *v.* W. Mid. Ry. Co., 33 L. J. Q. B. 233.

(*b*) Selway *v.* Holloway, 1 Raym. 46; 1 Ill. 135. Buckman *v.* Levi, 3 Camp. 414; 1 Ill. 109. Clarke *v.* Hutchins, 14 East, 475; 13 R. R. 283.

(*c*) Howey & Co. *v.* Lovell, 1826; 4 S. 752. Buckman, *supra* (*b*). Clayton *v.* Hunt, 3 Camp. 27.

(*d*) Clayton, *supra* (*c*)

(*e*) Hawkins *v.* Rutt, Peake, 186. 1 Bell's Com. 464, n. (493, M'L.'s ed.).

(*f*) They must be properly addressed. Cal. Ry. Co. *v.* Hunter & Co., 1858; 20 D. 1097. See Wilson & Co. *v.* Scott, 1797; Hume, 302. Weir *v.* Howie, 1798; Hume, 304.

(*g*) Stuart *v.* Crawley, 2 Starkie, 323; 20 R. R. 691.

163. The obligations incumbent on a carrier are either, 1. under his contract; or 2. under certain rules of public policy.

164. (1.) *Under his Contract.*—These are, that the vehicle shall be sufficient for safely carrying the goods; that they shall be properly packed and placed in the vehicle, 'unless the consignor has undertaken this responsibility himself (*a*)'; that ordinary care, and the regular course of the journey, shall be observed in the transit (*b*); and that the goods shall be delivered according to the undertaking. In all these points the presumption is against the carrier where any damage is sustained; and the *onus probandi* is laid on him (*c*). 'The consignee is not barred from recovering damages by breaking bulk (*d*).'

(*a*) Rain *v.* G. and S.-W. Ry. Co., 1869; 7 Macph. 439; below, § 166.

(*b*) A railway company is bound to forward goods, especially if perishable, with reasonable speed. Macdonald & Co. *v.* Highland Ry. Co., 1873; 11 Macph. 614. Finlay *v.* N. B. Ry. Co., 1870; 8 Macph. 959. Anderson *v.* N. B. Ry. Co., 1875; 2 R. 443. M'Connachie *v.* G. N. of S. Ry. Co., 1875; 3 R. 79. Bates *v.* Cameron, 1855; 18 D. 186. Taylor *v.* G. N. Ry. Co., L. R. 1 C. P. 385; 35 L. J. C. P. 210. Horn *v.* Midland Ry. Co., 41 L. J. C. P. 264; 42 *ib.* 59; L. R. 8 C. P. 131 (measure of damages—special notice). As to damages for delay in carriage by sea, see The Parana, 1 P. D. 452; 45 L. J. Pr. 108; rev. 2 P. D. 118. Comp. § 170 (*n*). The company is bound to give notice, when receiving goods, of any known unusual cause of delay, such as a block. M'Connachie, *cit.* Comp. § 170 (*s*). In a contract to furnish or carry by a ship or other vehicle at a set time, the measure of damage will be the increased freight payable for another means of conveyance (Connal, Cotton, & Co. *v.* Fisher, Renwick, & Co., 1883; 10 R. 824. Featherston *v.* Wilkinson, L. R. 8 Ex. 122; 42 L. J. Ex. 78); or if no other conveyance can be procured, the loss directly caused by the goods being left on the merchant's hand, so far as fairly brought within the contemplation of both parties at the time of the contract. Horn, *cit.* Wilson *v.* Lanc. and Y. Ry. Co., 9 C. B. N. S. 632. See above, § 33; below, § 242.

(*c*) 3 Chitty, Com. Law, 37. Langley *v.* Brown, 1 Moore & Pay. 583; 1 Ill. 135. Lyon *v.* Lamb, 1838; 16 S. 1188. Parry *v.* Roberts, 3 Ad. & E. 120. See Myers *v.* L. and S.-W. Ry. Co., L. R. 5 C. P. 1. Story on Bailments, § 529; below, § 167 (*b*), 170. See, as to the onus where delay occurs from an accident that cannot be accounted for by the carrier, Anderson, *cit.* See § 2031.

(*d*) But his doing so without notice is an element to be considered in weighing the evidence. Johnston & Sons *v.* Dove, 1875; 3 R. 202; and by delay after receipt in giving notice of damage he will be barred from objecting to the condition of the goods. Stewart *v.* N. B. Ry. Co., 1878; 5 R. 426.

165. The vehicle in land-carriage, whether cart, waggon, wain, van, or other carriage or coach used in transporting goods, must not only in itself, but in all accessories, as tackle, horses, drivers, etc., be sufficient (*a*): as in water-carriage, the ship, boat, barge, etc., must be seaworthy; not merely in itself, hull and rigging, tight, staunch, and strong for the voyage, but also properly manned and navigated; with the necessary stores and documents for safety (*b*).

(*a*) Robinson *v.* Dunmore, 2 B. & P. 416; 3 Ill. 108; 5 R. R. 635. Upshare *v.* Aldie, Comyn's Rep. 25; 1 Ill. 167. Low *v.* Booth, 13 Price, 329; 1 Ill. 137. Heughan *v.* Rae, 1776; 5 B. Sup. 577; Hailes, 725. See Curtis *v.* Drinkwater, 2 B. & Ald. 169. Readhead *v.* Midland Ry. Co., *infra*, § 170 (*x*).
(*b*) See of Ships, below, § 408.

166. The goods must be skilfully packed 'by the carrier,' so as to undergo in safety the concussion of the journey (*a*); a question peculiarly fit for a jury (*b*). 'Negligence of the consignor in performing *his* duty,—in packing or securing,—will discharge the carrier, unless it be such as the carrier with ordinary diligence could notice and remedy (*c*).' They must be so placed as to be safe from injury and depredation (*d*); and not in an overloaded vehicle (*e*).

(*a*) Lawrie *v.* Angus, 1677; M. 10,107; 1 Ill. 136. Ctss. of Glasgow *v.* Thermes, 1758; M. 10,099. Sprott *v.* Brown, 1803; M. 10,114. Jones & Co. *v.* Ross, 1830; 8 S. 495. Crofts *v.* Waterhouse, 3 Bing. 319; 1 Ill. 147; 28 R. R. 631. Rain *v.* G. and S.-W. Ry. Co., 1869; 7 Macph. 439. Paxton *v.* N. B. Ry. Co., 1870; 9 Macph. 50. G. W. Ry. Co. *v.* Blower, 41 L. J. C. P. 268; L. R. 7 C. P. 662.
(*b*) See Low *v.* Booth, 13 Price, 329; 1 Ill. 137.
(*c*) Stuart *v.* Crawley, 2 Starkie, 324; 20 R. R. 691. Richardson *v.* N.-E. Ry. Co., L. R. 7 C. P. 75; 41 L. J. C. P. 60 (both cases as to the securing of dogs). See further as to cattle, Rain and Paxton, *citt.*; and below, § 244A, and § 168 (*n*). Comp. Radley *v.* L. and N.-W. Ry. Co., 46 L. J. Ex. 573; L. R. 1 App. Ca. 754.
(*d*) Curtis, *sup.* § 165 (*a*).
(*e*) Israel *v.* Clark, 4 Espin. 259.

167. The carriage must be performed with the care and skill necessary for safety; on land, by having careful and skilful drivers, and by due observance of the rules of carriage; at sea, by sailing according to the rules of good seamanship (*a*). The presumption is against the carrier, where no extraordinary accident has caused the damage (*b*). Care must be taken in the transit to prevent injury from concussion or explosion (*c*); to cover and protect the goods from the weather (*d*); and due vigilance must be exercised to prevent depredation (*e*). 'But while carriers are bound to take all reasonable precautions for the security of goods carried, which do not involve any unusual expenditure, and the providing of which does not require unusual sagacity or foresight, they are not responsible under the contract, and where the edict is excluded by special agreement (see § 235, 244A), for damage arising from wholly unusual and unexpected causes (*f*).'

(*a*) See below, § 235.
(*b*) Langley *v.* Brown, 1 Moore & P. 583; 1 Ill. 135. Sprott, *supra*, § 166 (*a*). Stein *v.* Stenhouse, Feb. 2, 1811; F. C.; 1 Ill. 138. Jones & Co., *supra*, § 166 (*a*). Riley *v.* Horne, 5 Bing. 224; 30 R. R. 576. Lyon *v.* Lamb, 1838; 16 S. 1188. Wood & Co. *v.* Peebles Ry. Co., 1860; 22 D. 1393. See above, § 164 (*c*).
(*c*) Siordet *v.* Hall, 4 Bing. 607; 29 R. R. 651. Buller *v.* Fisher, 3 Esp. 67; 1 Ill. 170; 4 R. R. 902.
(*d*) Robinson, *supra*, § 165 (*a*). Webb *v.* Page, 6 M. & G. 204. Walker *v.* Jackson, 10 M. & W. 168.
(*e*) Batson, *supra*, § 159 (*b*). See Pearcey *v.* Player, 1883; 10 R. 564.
(*f*) Ralston *v.* Cal. Ry. Co., 1878; 5 R. 671. Comp. Nugent *v.* Smith, and the other cases, *infra*, § 168 (*n*), which suggest that the rule is hardly different even when the edict applies. See § 237.

168. The thing carried must be delivered according to the undertaking (*a*); either to the person indicated by the contract, or according to the address, the carrier being liable for porters (*b*); or to one properly authorised to receive them (*c*); or to another carrier, in order to complete the transit, if on that line of road the latter part of the journey is performed by another (*d*); or to the consignor stopping the goods *in transitu*. 'If there be no special direction as to delivery, a carrier is discharged by delivery to a named consignee who demands goods at another place than that to which they are addressed (*e*). In some earlier cases the undertaking of a carrier receiving goods addressed to a place beyond the terminus of his ordinary journey or line of railway was held to be only to deliver to the carrier occupying the next part of the route; but in the absence of special conditions (*f*), a carrier receiving goods to be conveyed to a place beyond his terminus is now held responsible for their safe carriage during the whole of their transit, though during part of the way they should be conveyed by another carrier, the latter being regarded as his agent (*g*). Such also is the liability under the contracts of those who collect goods for transmission by ship or rail to different parts of the world under the name of express companies, forwarding contractors, or general carriers (*h*). The liability of the carrier extends to the safe custody and redelivery of the goods to the sender's order, when they are rejected by the consignee, or cannot for other reasons be delivered to him (*i*).'

A carrier may retain the goods for the

price of their carriage, but not for a general balance or the hire of former carriages (*k*).

The carrier will be discharged of his obligation to deliver under the contract, if the goods have perished by inevitable accident (*l*); by internal defect, or some peculiar peril of the article carried (*m*), 'such as the "inherent vice" of animals causing them injury by their own acts, and without negligence of the carrier (*n*)'; or even by the carrier's own act, if compelled by manifest necessity, as jettison in crossing a ferry, to save life (*o*).

(*a*) Story on Bailments, 345 et seq. Bishop *v.* Mersey and Cl. Nav. Co., 1830; 8 S. 558; 1 Ill. 141. Rae *v.* Hay, 1832; 10 S. 303. Catley *v.* Wintringham, Peake's Ca. 150; 3 R. R. 670. Golden *v.* Manning, 2 Blackst. 916. Syeds *v.* Hay, 4 T. R. 260; 2 R. R. 377. Gibson *v.* Inglis, 4 Camp. 72; 1 Ill. 143; 15 R. R. 727. Sleatt *v.* Fagg, 5 B. & Ald. 342. Griffiths *v.* Lee, 1 Car. & Pay. 638. Geraldes *v.* Donison, Holt's Cases, 346; 17 R. R. 645. Joliffe, 4 T. R. 248. Gilmour *v.* Clark, 1853; 15 D. 478. Bates & Co. *v.* Cameron & Co., 1855; 18 D. 186.

(*b*) Armstrong *v.* Edin. and Leith Shipping Co., 1825; 3 S. 333; 1 Ill. 143. Hyde & Co. *v.* Trent and My. Nav. Co., 5 T. R. 389. See Edinburgh Shipping Co. *v.* Ogilvie, 1819; 2 Mur. 136. Golden, *supra* (*a*). M'Kean *v.* M'Iver, L. R. 6 Ex. 36; 40 L. J. Ex. 30. L. and N.-W. Ry. Co. *v.* Bartlett, 7 H. & N. 400; 31 L. J. Ex. 92. As to porters at railway stations, see Bunch *v.* G. W. Ry., *infra*, § 235. Hodkinson *v.* L. and N.-W. Ry. Co., 14 Q. B. D. 228 (making porter passenger's agent).

(*c*) Denniston *v.* Harkness, 1791; Bell's Cases, 260; 1 Ill. 144. Bain *v.* Bowie & Sons, 1821; 1 S. 14; 1 Ill. 133. Edinburgh Shipping Co., *supra* (*b*). Cal. Ry. Co. *v.* Harrison & Co., 1879; 7 R. 151 (delivery to buyer of goods consigned to seller's order—damages). As to constructive delivery, see Heugh *v.* L. and N.-W. Ry. Co., L. R. 5 Ex. 51; 39 L. J. Ex. 48; Redfield on Carriers, § 127; Angell on Carriers, § 323.

(*d*) See *supra* (*c*). In our practice the subsequent carrier may be sued by the consignee or owner for wrong delivery or damage on his part of the journey, on the footing of contract by agency or by reception of the goods for conveyance. See Campbell *v.* Cal. Ry. Co., 1889; 8 Sh. C. R. 7. It may be questioned whether the later carrier may not be sued by the consignee for damage suffered on the track of the first carrier, on the principle that the two are truly joint adventurers, or mutual agents, the first being the second's agent to make a single contract for through carriage. See Gill in note (*g*); Smith's Merc. Law, 320.

(*e*) Cork Distilleries Co. *v.* G. S. and W. Ry. Co. (Ireland), L. R. 7 H. L. 269. L. and N.-W. Ry. Co. *v.* Bartlett, *cit.*

(*f*) Aldridge *v.* G. W. Ry. Co., 33 L. J. C. P. 161. Zunz *v.* S.-E. Ry. Co., 38 L. J. Q. B. 289; L. R. 4 Q. B. 539. Kent *v.* Midland Ry. Co., 44 L. J. Q. B. 18; L. R. 10 Q. B. 1. Fowles *v.* G. W. Ry. Co., 7 Ex. 699; 22 L. J. Ex. 76.

(*g*) Bates *v.* Cameron, 1855; 18 D. 186. Cal. Ry. Co. *v.* Hunter, 1859; 20 D. 1097. Scottish Central Ry. Co. *v.* Ferguson & Co., 1863; 1 Macph. 750; 1864, 2 Macph. 781. Metzenburg *v.* Highland Ry. Co., 1869; 7 Macph. 919. 1 Bell's Com. 464, 465 (494, M'L.'s ed.). Cf. Mackenzie *v.* Howey, 1802; Hume, 312. Wilson & Co. *v.* Scott, 1797; Hume, 302. Muschamp *v.* Lancaster Ry. Co., 8 M. & W. 421. Bristol and Exeter Ry. Co. *v.* Collins, 7 H. of. L. Ca. 194; 29 L. J. Ex. 165. Gill *v.* Manch. S. and L. Ry. Co., L. R. 8 Q. B. 186; 42 L. J. Q. B. 89. See § 170.

(*h*) Bates *v.* Cameron, 1855; 18 D. 186. Ciceri & Co. *v.* Sutton & Co., 1889; 16 R. 814; aff. 1890, 15 App. Ca. 144; 17 R. H. L. 40.

(*i*) Metzenburg, *cit.* But see below, § 235.

(*k*) Stevenson *v.* Likly, 1821; 3 S. 204; 1 Ill. 138. See below, § 1424.

(*l*) See below, § 237 sqq.

(*m*) Arg. from Lawrence *v.* Aberdeen, 5 B. & Ald. 107; 1 Ill. 304. Gabay *v.* Lloyd, 3 B. & Cr. 793; 27 R. R. 486. Gosling *v.* Higgins, 1 Camp. 451; 10 R. R. 726. Alston *v.* Herring, 11 Ex. 822, and cases in (*n*).

(*n*) Blower *v.* G. W. Ry., L. R. 7 C. P. 655; 41 L. J. C. P. 268. Kendall *v.* L. and N.-W. Ry. Co., L. R. 7 Ex. 373; 41 L. J. Ex. 184. Gill *v.* Manch. S. and L. Ry., L. R. 8 Q. B. 186; 42 L. J. Q. B. 89. Nugent *v.* Smith, 45 L. J. C. P. 697; L. R. 1 C. P. D. 423. Ralston *v.* Cal. Ry. Co., *supra*, § 167 (*f*).

(*o*) 2 Kent, 604. Story on Bailments, 367.

169. (2.) *Responsibilities under Public Policy.*—These are different in principle and effect from those under the contract. As shipmasters, innkeepers, and stablers have facilities for associating themselves or their servants with robbers, thieves, and pilferers of all descriptions, it has been deemed expedient to admit against them a legal presumption of negligence or collusion, and to allow of no excuse or justification for loss or injury to the goods entrusted to their care, without proof of inevitable accident. But as this is a part of the great doctrine of care or diligence prestable, it is better to take the whole in one view (*a*).

(*a*) See below, § 235.

170. Carriage of Persons.—This contract differs from the contract for the carriage of goods, in so far as the protection of human life has required a stricter rule both of sufficiency and of vigilance. (1.) *Passengers and Luggage.*—Carriers of this description are not at liberty to refuse a passenger, if room be left unengaged (*a*); if a place be engaged, it must be made good to the passenger; and the coachman is bound to receive and take charge of the usual luggage allowed to a passenger (*b*).

'*Through Contracts.*—As in the case of goods (§ 168), a railway company is liable to a passenger taking from it a through ticket, even for accidents occurring in the course of the journey on the line of another railway company (*c*). The contract of the company issuing the through ticket is, that the passenger shall be carried to his destination with due and reasonable care; and the company is liable for the negligence of all parties whose care is directly necessary for the passenger's safe conveyance (*d*); and for the sufficiency and safety of all parts of the road of transit (*e*). The same rule applies to the carriage of the passenger's luggage under a through ticket (*f*), It is not liable for an accident occurring to its passenger through the negligence, not of its own servants, but of those of another company using the line, but not under its control, or concerned with his conveyance (*g*). It has also been laid down, and appears to be sound, that apart from contract, the fact that a person is a passenger casts a duty on the railway company or other carrier to carry him safely (*h*). So an action lies against a railway company upon whose line an accident occurs, though it has not issued the ticket to the passenger, or directly contracted with him, either upon the ground that the company issuing the ticket was its agent, or (it would appear) upon the ground of quasi-delict (tort), or at least that by receiving the passenger and taking benefit by carrying him, it assumes a duty towards him (*i*).'

(2.) *Vehicle, etc.*—The coach must be strong and fit for the journey; road-worthy, as far as human foresight can provide (*k*), with steady horses and suitable harness (*l*). There must be provided drivers of competent skill and steadiness; and for any failure in that respect the coachmaster is liable (*m*).

'Passengers are entitled to be conveyed with reasonable speed (*n*). A railway company issuing tickets (*o*) to passengers is liable for any personal inconvenience caused by its negligent delay in breach of the conditions of the contract contained in the ticket, time-tables, or other documents referred to on the ticket; but not for such consequences as could not naturally be contemplated as the result of such breach, *e.g.* catching cold by walking home late at night, or pecuniary loss by missing an appointment (*p*). And a passenger is entitled to recover such expense caused by delay as would be incurred in the circumstances by a reasonable man who had no recourse against a railway company (*q*).'

(3.) *Care.*—The degree of care that is requisite exceeds in vigilance that of the ordinary contract of carriage. The safeguard to which, by the policy of the law, the lives and limbs of passengers are entrusted, is extreme vigilance and caution; enforced by penal statutes (*r*), and by a very strict civil responsibility. So, if the coachman is guilty of furious driving; if he allow an extra number of passengers; if he carry the reins so loose as not to keep the command of his team on any sudden interruption or alarm; if he do not give due notice to outside passengers in passing any obstacle, as under a gateway, 'or in the case of railway companies, of any block or unusual risk on the line (*s*)'; if he permit collision with another carriage, by not observing the rules of the road,—the coach proprietors are liable for the damage thence arising (*t*).

'The passenger injured in a collision is not prevented from recovering damages from the culpable owner of the other ship or train or car, by reason of the contributory fault of the master or driver of the ship or vehicle in which he was travelling (*u*).

'Although in such cases the carrier's liability rests primarily on contract, a claim similar to assythment accrues to a passenger's heirs, wife, children, or parents on his death by the carrier's fault. Indeed, it is now settled in England, after much discussion, that a railway is liable for damage done by its servants to passengers or goods lawfully on their premises or in their carriages, provided it be done by misfeasance, *i.e.* by active wrongdoing, and not merely by non-feasance or omission (*v*). It does not appear that this distinction has been recognised in our law. The carrier of passengers does not, like the carrier of goods (*infra*, § 235 sq.), warrant or insure their safe conveyance. He is bound to take "due care," *i.e.* a very high degree of care, and he contracts that his carriages, bridges, and other means of conveyance are reasonably fit for the purposes to which they are to be applied (*w*). But that does not imply responsibility for the consequences of a latent defect in his carriage which no skill, care, or foresight could have prevented or detected (*x*).

'The onus of proving sufficiency and due care is said to lie on the carrier, and the breaking down of a coach or train is *primâ facie* evidence of negligence (*y*).

'A carrier is not bound to carry merchandise as luggage (*z*). But he may be liable for the loss of what is obviously merchandise, and is taken as luggage without objection (*aa*).

'Railway companies are also bound to keep

their stations and the accesses to them in a safe condition, and to give passengers reasonable facilities for getting into their trains and alighting from them in safety; but this, of course, does not dispense with ordinary care on the part of the passengers (*bb*).'

(4.) *The Rules of the Road* which are thus to be observed are, in *meeting* a carriage or horse, etc., to keep to the left hand; in *passing*, to keep to the right, the foremost bearing to the left; in *crossing*, to bear to the left, and pass behind the other carriage (*cc*). But these rules will not hold invariably in crowded streets, or where the street or road is broad, and there is no fault chargeable on the coachman (*dd*). 'Where there are tramway-cars, passing carriages take the left of car passed (*ee*).'

(*a*) 3 Chitty, Coml. Law, 370, p. 320, ed. 1856. As to railway companies, see G. N. Ry. Co. *v.* Hawcroft, 21 L. J. Q. B. 178.

(*b*) *Per* Chambre, J., 2 B. & P. 419. See Clark *v.* Gray, 4 Esp. 177; 1 Ill. 167. The carrier is not liable for luggage of another taken with passenger; *e.g.* if servant be travelling with master's luggage, master not being in the train. Becher *v.* G. E. Ry. Co., 39 L. J. Q. B. 122; L. R. 5 Q. B. 241. Campbell *v.* Cal. Ry. Co., 1852; 14 D. 806; but there is a tendency to excessive refinement in the cases. See them in 1 Smith's L. C. 202. As to what is personal luggage, see Hudston *v.* Midland Ry. Co., 38 L. J. Q. B. 213; L. R. 4 Q. B. 366. Macrow *v.* G. W. Ry. Co., 40 L. J. Q. B. 300; L. R. 6 Q. B. 612.

(*c*) G. W. Ry. Co. *v.* Blake, 7 H. & N. 997; 31 L. J. Ex. 346. Buxton *v.* N.-E. Ry. Co., 37 L. J. Q. B. 258; L. R. 3 Q. B. 549.

(*d*) Thomas *v.* Rhymney Ry. Co., L. R. 6 Q. B. 266; 40 L. J. Q. B. 89. Eistens, *infra* (*i*). Horn *v.* N. B. Ry. Co., 1878; 5 R. 1055.

(*e*) John *v.* Bacon, 39 L. J. C. P. 365; L. R. 5 C. P. 437. Foulkes, *infra*.

(*f*) Hooper *v.* L. & N.-W. Ry. Co., 50 L. J. C. P. 103.

(*g*) Wright *v.* Midl. Ry. Co., 42 L. J. Ex. 89; L. R. 8 Ex. 137.

(*h*) *Per* Blackburn, J., in Austin, *cit.* (*i*). See Foulkes, *infra*. Hamilton (*i*).

(*i*) Foulkes *v.* Metr. Distr. Ry. Co., 49 L. J. C. P. 361; 5 C. P. D. 157. Marshall *v.* York N. & B. Ry. Co., 11 C. B. 655; 21 L. J. C. P. 34. Austin *v.* G. W. Ry. Co., 36 L. J. Q. B. 201; L. R. 2 Q. B. 442. Martin *v.* G. Indian Pen. Ry. Co., 37 L. J. 27; L. R. 3 Ex. 9. Collett *v.* L. & N.-W. Ry., 16 Q. B. 989. Taylor *v* Manch. and Sheff., etc., Ry. Co., 1895; 1 Q. B. 134. Kelly *v.* Metr. Ry. Co., 1895; 1 Q. B. 944. Meux *v.* G. E. Ry. Co., 1895; 2 Q. B. 387. See as to travelling without ticket, Hamilton *v.* Cal. Ry. Co., 1856; 18 D. 998; 1857, 19 D. 457; and § 168 (*d*). See, however, Eistens *v.* N. B. Ry., 1870; 8 Macph. 980.

(*k*) Anderson *v.* Pyper & Co., 1820; 2 Mur. 261; 1 Ill. 144. Christie *v* Griggs, 2 Camp. 79. Sharp *v.* Gray, 9 Bing. 457. Lyon *v.* Lamb, 1838; 16 S. 1188. See § 408. M'Glashan *v.* Dundee and Perth Ry. Co., 1848; 10 D. 1397. Cargill *v.* Dundee, etc., Ry. Co., 1848; 11 D. 216.

(*l*) Crofts *v.* Waterhouse, 11 Moore, 137; 3 Bing. 319; 1 Ill. 147; 28 R. R. 631. See Readhead, *infra* (*x*).

(*m*) See cases, 1 Ill. 144 et seq. M'Arthur *v.* Croall, 1852; 24 Jur. 170; 1 Stu. 296.

(*n*) G. N. Ry. Co. *v.* Hawcroft, 21 L. J. Q. B. 179. Hamlin *v.* G. N. Ry. Co., 1 H. & N. 408. Briddon *v.* G. N. Ry. Co., 28 L. J. Ex. 51. Buckmaster *v.* G. E. Ry. Co., 23 L. T. N. S. 471. Jarvie, *infra* (*s*). Leblanch, Clark, and Greenfield, *infra* (*p*). Cases as to delay in transit of goods, § 164.

(*o*) As to the right forcibly to extrude passengers travelling without tickets, or with invalid or inapplicable tickets, and refusing to pay the fare, under the usual bye-laws, contrast Highland Ry. *v.* Menzies, 1878, 5 R. 887, and Butler *v.* Manch. Sheff. and Linc. Ry. Co., 21 Q. B. D. 207. A railway company is said to have power to assign certain seats to passengers. Scott *v.* G. N. of Scot. Ry. Co., 1895; 22 R. 287.

(*p*) See cases in (*n*). Denton *v.* G. N. Ry. Co., 5 E. & B. 568; 25 L. J. Q. B. 129. Hurst *v.* G. W. Ry. Co., 19 C. B. N. S. 310; 34 L. J. C. P. 264. Hobbs *v.* L. & S.-W. Ry. Co., L. R. 10 Q. B. 111; 44 L. J. Q. B. 49. As to exclusion of liability by notice, see above, § 74. Hough *v.* R. M. St. Packet Co., 52 L. J. Q. B. 640. M'Cartan *v.* N.-E. Ry. Co., Q. B. D., May 1885. Leblanch (*q*). Clark *v.* N. B. Ry., and Greenfield *v.* N. B. Ry., 1886; 2 Sh. Ct. R. 92, and 300, and *infra* (*bb*).

(*q*) Leblanch *v.* L. & N.-W. Ry. Co., 1 C. P. D. 286; 45 L. J. C. P. 521.

(*r*) 50 Geo. III. c. 48. 3 Geo. IV. c. 85. 7 Geo. IV. c. 33, § 2. 9 Geo. IV. c. 49. 2 and 3 Will. IV. c. 120. 3 and 4 Will. IV. c. 47. As to railways, 3 and 4 Vict. c. 97, which is not repealed as to Scotland. 31 and 32 Vict. c. 119, § 22–24.

(*s*) Jarvie *v.* Cal. Ry. Co., 1875; 2 R. 623. Cf. § 164 (*b*).

(*t*) Allan *v.* M'Leish, 1819; 2 Mur. 158; 1 Ill. 144. Gunn *v.* Gardner, 1820; 2 Mur. 194. Anderson *v.* Pyper & Co., 1820; *ib.* 261. Edin. and Glas. Un. Canal Co. *v.* Johnston, 1832; 10 S. 505. Mayhew *v.* Boyce, 1 Starkie, 423; 18 R. R. 796. Jackson *v.* Tollet, 2 Starkie, 37; 19 R. R. 673. Dudley *v.* Smith, 1 Camp. 167; 10 R. R. 661. Israel *v.* Clark, 4 Esp. 259. Jones *v.* Boyce, 1 Starkie, 493; 18 R. R. 812. Aston *v.* Heaven, 2 Esp. 533; 5 R. R. 750. Curtis *v.* Drinkwater, 2 Barn. & Ad. 169. Morton (Cooley's Factor) *v.* E. and G. Ry. Co., 1845; 8 D. 288.

(*u*) Mills *v.* Armstrong **(The Bernina)**, 12 P. D. 58; aff. 13 App. Ca. 1; overruling Thorogood *v.* Bryan, 8 C. B. 115, and other cases. See Adams *v.* Glas. and S.-W. Ry. Co., 1875; 3 R. 215.

(*v*) See § 544, 2029, 2030, and the cases of Marshall, Martin, Collett, Austin, etc., *supra* (*i*). The practice in assessing damages in case of personal injuries to passengers is explained in Phillips *v.* L. and N.-W. Ry. Co., 5 Q. B. D. 78; 49 L. J. Q. B. 233. Young *v.* Glas. Tram. Co., 1882; 10 R. 242.

(*w*) Grote *v.* Chester, etc., Ry. Co., 2 Ex. 251. Francis *v.* Cockrell, 39 L. J. Q. B. 113, 291; L. R. 5 Q. B. 184, 501.

(*x*) **Readhead** *v.* **Midland Ry. Co.**, 36 L. J. Q. B. 181; 38 L. J. Q. B. 169; L. R. 4 Q. B. 379. As to the duty of examining carriages, etc., see Richardson *v.* G. E. Ry. Co., 1 C. P. D. 342.

(*y*) Lyon *v.* Lamb, *cit.* (*k*). M'Glashan *v.* Dundee and Perth Ry. Co., Cargill *v.* Dundee and Perth Ry. Co., and Sharp, *cit.* (*k*). Crofts, *supra* (*l*). Carpue *v.* L. and B. Ry. Co., 5 Q. B. 747; 13 L. J. Q. B. 133. Ayles *v.* S.-E. Ry. Co., 37 L. J. Ex. 104; L. R. 3 Ex. 146. See § 164 (*c*).

(*z*) Cahill *v.* L. and N.-W. Ry. Co., 10 C. B. N. S. 154; 30 L. J. C. P. 289. G. N. Ry. Co. *v.* Shepherd, 8 Ex. 30; 21 L. J. Ex. 286. Belfast and Ballymena Ry. Co. *v.* Keys, 9 H. L. Ca. 556.

(*aa*) G. N. Ry. Co. and Belfast and Ballymena Ry. Co., *citt.* As to liability for luggage, see § 235, *infra*. In general it is a jury question what is personal luggage in the circumstances of each case. Phelps *v.* L. & N.-W. Ry. Co., 19 C. B. N. S. 321; 34 L. J. C. P. 259.

(*bb*) Potter *v.* N. B. Ry. Co., 1873; 11 Macph. 664 (platform—duty of guard to warn not to alight, etc.; cf. Aitken *v.* N. B. Ry. Co., 1891; 18 R. 836). Stewart *v.* Cal. Ry. Co., 1869; 8 Macph. 486. Thomson *v.* N. B. Ry. Co., 1876; 4 R. 115. Cassidy *v.* N. B. Ry. Co., 1873; 11 Macph. 341. Siner *v.* G. W. Ry. Co., 38 L. J. Ex. 67; L. R. 4 Ex. 117. Cockle *v.* L. and S.-E. Ry. Co., 39 L. J. C. P. 226; L. R. 7 C. P. 321. Bridges *v.* N. L. Ry. Co., 40

L. J. Q. B. 188; L. R. 6 Q. B. 377; 43 L. J. Q. B. 151 (H. L.); L. R. 7 H. L. 213. Lewis *v.* L. C. and D. Ry. Co., 43 L. J. Q. B. 8; L. R. 9 Q. B. 60. Weller *v.* L. B., etc., Ry. Co., 43 L. J. C. P. 137; L. R. 9 C. P. 126. Jackson *v.* Metr. Ry. Co., L. R. 3 App. Ca. 193; 46 L. J. C. P. 376. Robson *v.* N.-E. Ry. Co., 2 Q. B. D. 85; 46 L. J. Q. B. 50. Rose *v.* N.-E. Ry. Co., 2 Ex. D. 248; 46 L. J. Ex. 374. A passenger may exclude a claim for damages for negligence by agreeing to travel at his own risk. Macauley *v.* Furness Ry. Co., 43 L. J. Q. B. 4; L. R. 8 Q. B. 57. Hall *v.* N.-E. Ry. Co., 44 L. J. Q. B. 164; L. R. 10 Q. B. 437. Gallin *v.* L. and N.-W. Ry. Co., L. R. 10 Q. B. 212; 44 L. J. Q. B. 89; *supra* (*p*). See as to carriage doors left unfastened, Gee *v.* Metr. Ry. Co., 42 L. J. Q. B. 105; L. R. 8 Q. B. 161. *Qu.* whether the law is in a satisfactory state as to the responsibility of railway companies for damage by overcrowding, and for loss by robbery or theft during conveyance in trains. See Cobb *v.* G. W. Ry. Co., 1894, A. C. 419.

(*cc*) Wayde *v.* Carr, 2 Dow. & Ry. 255; 25 R. R. 554.

(*dd*) Wordsworth *v.* Willan, 5 Esp. 273.

(*ee*) Ramsay *v.* Thomson & Sons, 1881; 9 R. 140. Jardine *v.* Stonefield Laundry Co., 1887; 14 R. 839. Having regard to the reasons for the new rule, it seems to apply only to a car occupying the rails. An ordinary vehicle on the rails is able to give way and allow a faster carriage to pass on its right according to the general rule.

VI. HIRING OF SERVICES.

171. Different Kinds.—The hiring of services includes, 1. the hiring of domestic servants; and 2. the hiring of workmen in a manufactory (*a*).

(*a*) 3 Ersk. Pr. 3. § 5. 3 Ersk. 3. § 14, 18. See above as to Hiring of Ordinary Labour, § 146; and of Clerks, § 153.

172. Hiring of Domestic Servants.—This is a contract for the hire of services to be performed in the domestic economy of a house, garden, or farm, or in personal attendance.

173. (1.) *Proof of Contract.*—The contract may be either verbal or in writing (*a*).

If the engagement be for a year, or during the term which, by general or local usage, is fixed as the ordinary duration of the particular service, the contract may be proved by parole evidence or oath of party; and if unconditional, will effectually bind the parties (*b*). Commonly "earnest" is given as the test of engagement; but is not indispensable, unless where established by custom, when there is *locus pœnitentiæ* till it has been given. When given, the return of the earnest will not dissolve the engagement (*c*).

For a longer term a probative writing is required, till which there is *locus pœnitentiæ* 'at least' as to the excess beyond the usual term, in absence of *rei interventus*; and oath of party will not supply the want of it (*d*).

(2.) *Tacit Relocation.*—From term to term the engagement is held to be renewed in all its parts by tacit relocation, without writing, where due interruption or warning is not given by either of the parties that the engagement is to terminate (*e*).

(*a*) 3 Ersk. 3. § 14. Tait's Justice of Peace, *voce Servant.*

(*b*) Forbes *v.* Milne, 1827; 6 S. 75; 1 Ill. 147. Mabon *v.* Elliot, 1808; Hume, 393.

(*c*) Wallace *v.* Wishart, 1808; Hume, 353.

(*d*) Caddel *v.* Sinclair, 1749; M. 12,416; Elch. *Writ*, 2. Cf. Hume, 390. Dale *v.* Dumbarton Glass Co., 1829; 7 S. 609; 1 Ill. 150. Paterson *v.* Edington, 1830; 8 S. 431. Dumbarton Glass Co. *v.* Cotesworth, 1847; 9 D. 732. Currie *v.* M'Lean, 1864; 2 Macph. 1076. Dickson on Evid. § 564, 834. Napier *v.* Dick, 1805; Hume, 388. Neill *v.* Vashon, 1807; Hume, 20. Stewart & Macdonald *v.* M'Call, 1869; 7 Macph. 544. See below, § 190, 1188; Fraser, M. & S. 30; and Pickin *v.* Hawkes, 1878; 5 R. 732.

(*e*) See below, § 187, 190. Baird *v.* Don, 1779; 5 B. Sup. 514; Hailes, 889; M. 9182; 1 Ill. 147. E. of Mansfield *v.* Scott, 1831; 9 S. 780; aff. 1833, 6 W. & S. 277. Maclean *v.* Fyfe, Feb. 4, 1813; F. C. Tait *v.* Mackintosh, 1841; 13 Jur. 280; 16 F. C. 658.

174. Duration.—The term of duration is different in different employments and places; and it is held that rural servants, 'including grieves and overseers (*a*), gamekeepers (*b*), and in some cases gardeners (*c*),' are engaged for a year (during the revolution of the seasons), work or no work (*d*). Generally speaking, domestic servants, in town or country, are engaged for six months (*e*); and it is no alteration of this, although the engagement bear to be at the *rate* of so much a year (*f*). It has been said that in one case a governess was held to be engaged for a year (*g*); but this is not now held to be law, 'and the tendency of modern decisions, especially in regard to superior servants in whom trust is reposed, is to hold the engagement (in the absence of express contract) to be during mutual pleasure, and determinable by reasonable notice on either side (*h*).' The engagement may be prolonged to any term, 'even for life, if the terms be not unreasonable or illegal (*i*).' Sometimes the engagement is indefinite; to be closed on the one part by a month's warning, 'or by such warning as is reasonable or usual,' on the other by payment or forfeiture of a month's wages, 'or reasonable compensation (*k*).' The engagement usually terminates only by warning (*l*).

(*a*) Baron Hume, Dec. 393. Finlayson *v.* M'Kenzie, *infra* (*d*).

(*b*) Armstrong *v.* Bainbridge, 1846; 9 D. 29, 1198. Cameron *v.* Fletcher, 1872; 10 Macph. 301. Ross *v.* Pender, 1874; 1 R. 352.

(c) Mabon v. Elliot, 1808; Hume, 393. Groom v. Clark, 1859; 21 D. 831.
(d) Ersk. and Tait, *ut sup.* § 173 (a). Finlayson v. M'Kenzie, 1829; 7 S. 717; 1 Ill. 148. Armstrong, *cit.* (b).
(e) Baird, *supra*, § 173 (e).
(f) See Cameron, *cit.* Fraser, M. & S. 51.
(g) Wood, Nov. 14, 1804. See next note.
(h) Fraser, M. & S. 50. Moffat v. Shedden, 1839; 1 D. 468 (tutor). Campbell v. Fyfe, 1851; 13 D. 1041 (newspaper editor). London Shipping Co. v. Ferguson, 1850; 13 D. 57 (commercial agent — business discontinued). Dowling v. Henderson, 1890; 17 R. 921 (do.). Forsyth v. Heatheryknowe Coal Co., 1880; 7 R. 887 (manager of colliery — colliery discontinued). See as to teachers of schools, Robson v. Overend, 1878; 6 R. 233. Morrison v. Abernethy School Board, 1876; 3 R. 945. *Infra*, § 187 (c).
(i) Fraser, M. & S. 3. 1 Bell's Com. 302 (322 M'L.'s ed.). Wallis v. Day, 2 M. & W. 272. 1 Smith's L. C. 412, 414. Pollock on Contract, 335, 3rd ed.
(k) Silvie v. Stewart, 1830; 8 S. 1010; 1 Ill. 148. Forsyth, *cit.* Morrison, *cit.*
(l) See below, § 179, 187.

175. **Service.**—The essentials of the contract are,—service on the one hand; hire or wages on the other.

176. The service is regulated either by special contract or engagement; as the service of a butler, of a valet, of a groom, of a gardener, etc.; or by custom, general or local.

The rule as to service is, that the master is entitled to require the servant to perform all that fairly belongs to the line of service for which he is engaged; that slight deviations from such line of engagement will not be held to justify a servant's disobedience of his master's orders: But that, if such deviations, though slight, be often repeated, or if what is required be a manifest departure from the line of the servant's engagement, he will not be bound to obey; as when a servant is turned from rural to domestic service, or *vice versâ* (a).

(a) Fairie v. M'Vicar, 1775; 2 Hutchison, J. of P. 166, note 3; 1 Ill. 148. Thomson v. Douglas, 1807; Hume, 392. Stuart v. Richardson, 1806; Hume, 390. Gunn v. Ramsay, 1801; Hume, 384. Peter v. Terrol, 1818; 2 Mur. 28. Wilson v. Simson, 1844; 6 D. 1256. Moffat v. Boothby, 1884; 11 R. 501.

177. The price of the labour to be performed by a domestic servant is given in the hire or wages, accompanied in the ordinary case by board and lodging. Strictly speaking, a sum allowed for board and lodging is not *wages*, though generally called *board-wages* (a).

'*Implied Agreement to Pay Wages.*—When wages are not stipulated, an obligation to pay them may be implied. In the ordinary case there is a presumption from the continuous residence and service that wages are due, but this presumption is readily rebutted by circumstances indicating that the services were rendered gratuitously from good feeling or self-interest, or in return for board and lodging (b). There is less room for the presumption in some cases where service is given by near relatives; but if the servant at the commencement of the service is very young, the presumption that wages are payable after his services have become valuable is stronger (c). It is much more difficult to establish an implied contract for *extra* remuneration (d).'

(a) See below, § 186.
(b) Anderson v. Halley, 1847; 9 D. 1222. Thomson v. Thomson's Tr. 1889; 16 R. 333.
(c) Shepherd v. Meldrum, 1812; Hume, 394. M'Naughton v. M'Naughton, 1813; *ib.* 396. Smellie v. Gillespie, 1833; 12 S. 125; 1835, 13 S. 700. See 13 S. 544; 14 S. 12. Adam v. Peter, 4 D. 599. Alcock v. Easson, 1842; 5 D. 356. Ritchie v. Ferguson, 1849; 12 D. 119. See the cases reviewed in Fraser, M. & S. 39 sqq.
(d) M'Whirter v. Guthrie, 1821; Hume, 760. Money v. Hannan & Kerr, 1867; 5 S. L. R. 32. Latham v. Edin. and Gl. Ry. Co., 1866; 4 Macph. 1084.

178. The servant's express obligation is, to serve in the capacity, at the place, and for the time for which he engages, or to pay damages (a). A collateral and implied obligation is, to be faithful, honest, and observant of all the decencies of domestic life: to avoid insolence in his intercourse with his master and his family; to keep his master's hours; and not absent himself without leave (b).

(a) Campbell v. Price, 1831; 9 S. 264. Anderson v. Moon, 1837; 15 S. 412.
(b) 3 Ersk. 3. § 14. Tait, J. P. *Serv.* Lady Crawford v. Reid, 1822; 1 S. App. 124; 1 Ill. 148. Hamilton v. M'Lean, 1824; 3 S. 379. Silvie v. Stewart, 1830; 8 S. 1010. Matheson v. M'Kinnon, 1832; 10 S. 825. See Callo v. Brouncker, 4 C. & P. 518. Stirling, Gordon, & Co. v. Calderhead's Exrs., 1832; 11 S. 180. Elder v. Bennett, 1802; Hume, 386. Wilson v. Simson, 1844; 6 D. 1256. Edwards v. Mackie, 1848; 11 D. 67. M'Kellar v. Macfarlane, 1852; 15 D. 246. A. v. B., 1853; 16 D. 269. Greig v. Sanderson, 1864; 2 Macph. 1278.

179. The stipulated time of service may be abridged (a) by the death of the servant; in which case his representatives will be entitled to rateable wages for the time during which the service continued (b); or 'it is said by Professor Bell in previous editions' by inability from hurts received *in his master's service* (c), which will excuse the servant's non-performance, without forfeiting his wages. 'But this distinction has not been approved (d). The true principle is, that contracts for personal services are subject to the implied condition that the parties contracting shall be alive to receive or perform them, and not incapacitated by any illness of which they were not cognisant at the time of contracting (*e*). When, therefore, it becomes impossible to perform the contract, as by the lengthened illness or the death of the servant, the death of the master, the dissolution by death (but not by bankruptcy or agreement) of a firm of employers, or (probably) by the insanity of the master or his illness compelling him to retire from the business for which the servant is engaged, the contract is determined (*e*).' Sickness or inevitable accident, though not incurred in his master's service, will excuse non-performance for a short time; but if the inability should continue long, and a substitute should be required, the master will be discharged from his counter-obligation to pay wages (*f*).

(*a*) See above, § 174.
(*b*) M'Lean *v.* Fyfe, Feb. 4, 1813; F. C. See Hoey *v.* M'Ewan & Auld, 1867; 5 Macph. 814.
(*c*) White *v.* Baillie, 1794; M. 10,147; 1 Ill. 148.
(*d*) Fraser, M. & S. 140, 316.
(*e*) Hall *v.* Wright, E. B. & E. 746; 29 L. J. Q. B. 43, *per* Pollock, C. B. Hoey *v.* M'Ewan & Auld, *cit.* (*b*) (death). Puncheon *v.* Haig's Tr., 1790; M. 13,990 (bankruptcy). Tasker *v.* Shepherd, 6 H. & N. 575; 30 L. J. Ex. 207. Boast *v.* Firth, and cases cited above, § 29 (*g*). Farrow *v.* Wilson, L. R. 4 C. P. 744; 38 L. J. C. P. 326. Manson *v.* Downie, 1885; 12 R. 1103. It is a breach if the master disables himself from performing the contract by giving up the business in which the servant is employed. Ross *v.* M'Farlane, 1894; 21 R. 396; and cases cited there. See below, § 570. On the servant's death or inability, wages are due for the period actually served; see Fraser, M. & S. 138; and above (*b*). As to wages on the master's death, etc., see below, § 185-6.
(*f*) Manson *v.* Downie, *cit.* (*e*).

180. Although there should be no stipulation as to change of place, a domestic or personal servant may be removed from town to country, or from country to town, and required to accompany the master's family or person; but not to leave Scotland: nor to go to a distant part of the country without an engagement for his return, and indemnification for time and expense (*a*). A servant engaged for *local* employment cannot be compelled to go to a distant part of the country (*b*).

(*a*) See Baird *v.* Don, 1779; 5 B. Sup. 514; M. 9182; Hailes, 839; 1 Ill. 147. See Fraser, M. & S. 82 sq.
(*b*) Tait, J. of P. 348.

181. Enlisting in the King's service 'was formerly,' by the Mutiny Act, admitted not only to exempt the servant from damages for breach of contract, but to entitle him to wages during the time of his actual service. But this exception 'was' merely statutory, and against the rule of the common law (*a*). 'This was altered in later Mutiny Acts, and now, by the Army Act, 1881, while a soldier has certain privileges in regard to civil procedure, there is nothing to prevent him from being adjudged liable in damages for breach of contract, or at least to forfeiture of wages already earned (*b*).'

No other voluntary engagement will excuse the servant. So marriage during the currency of the engagement is no legitimate excuse for not fulfilling the obligation; and although a husband will be entitled to have the society of his wife, and to require her to leave her service, he will be liable in damages for her breach of contract (*c*). Imprisonment for debt will not excuse a servant's absence; the wages will be forfeited, and damages due (*d*).

(*a*) See Clerk *v.* Murchison, 1799; M. 9186; 1 Ill. 150. M'Donell *v.* Dixon, 1805; M. *Mut. Cont.* Apx. No. 3. Taylor *v.* Guthrie, 1798; Hume, 382.
(*b*) 44 and 45 Vict. c. 58, § 96, 144. Fraser, M. & S. 324, 801. As to the militia, see 38 and 39 Vict. c. 69, § 78; and as to apprentices enlisting, 44 and 45 Vict. c. 58, as cited; and Fraser, M. & S. 348.
(*c*) Fraser, M. & S. 323, 369.
(*d*) *Ib.* 322.

182. Dismissal.—The master must receive a domestic servant, and give bed and board during the time agreed on. And so he is not entitled prematurely to dismiss the servant, paying wages; but will be liable besides for board-wages and for damages. The servant cannot lawfully be dismissed for a slight fault, but only for a serious breach of engagement, or for insolence (*a*). 'A master may justify dismissal by causes not assigned by him at the time, and even by causes not known to him till afterwards (*b*). Damages for wrongful dismissal are to be assessed, as by a jury, with reference to the loss actually suffered; and although some account may be taken of the fault on the one side or the other, the fact that wages have, or might easily have, been earned in other employment of a similar kind, which a reasonable man would have accepted, between the date of dismissal and the natural termination of the engagement, is admitted in modern practice to modify the damages (*c*).'

(*a*) Erskine, Tait, Silvie, and other cases, *supra*, § 178 (*b*). Graham *v.* Thomson, 1822; 1 S. 7; 1 Ill. 149. Batchelor *v.* M'Gilvray, 1831; 9 S. 549. Thomson *v.* Stewart, 1888; 15 R. 806.

(*b*) Smith's Merc. Law, 523. Macpherson *v.* Bentinck, Feb. 25, 1869; 13 J. of J. 209; 6 S. L. R. 376. Watson *v.* Burnett, 1862; 24 D. 479. Spotswood *v.* Barrow, 5 Ex. 110; 19 L. J. Ex. 226. Boston Deep Sea Fishing Co. *v.* Ansell, 39 Ch. D. 39. Fraser, M. & S. 120.

(*c*) Stuart *v.* Richardson, 1806; Hume, 390. Cameron *v.* Fletcher, Ross *v.* Pender, *cit.* § 174 (*b*). Hoey, *cit.* § 179 (*b*). Addison on Contr. 450. 2 Smith's L. C. 50. Mayne on Damages, 158. And below, § 185. Reid *v.* Explosives Co., 19 Q. B. D. 264. Brace *v.* Calder, 1895; 2 Q. B. 253. In earlier cases both in England and Scotland there was a different tendency. Fraser, M. & S. 163, 164; 2 Smith's L. C. 44 sqq.

183. The master has been held entitled to dismiss a servant on paying wages and board-wages (*a*): But he is not entitled capriciously, and without cause shown, to compel the servant to reside out of the family while the service continues; the engagement (especially of a female) being on the faith of the protection of the master's house (*b*).

(*a*) Cooper *v.* Henderson, 1825; 3 S. 435; 1 Ill. 149. See above, § 182; and as to managers, below, § 189.

(*b*) Graham *v.* Thomson, *supra*, § 182 (*a*). *Sed quære?*

184. Wages.—The master must pay the wages stipulated or usual. This payment is (according to the usage) either half-yearly or yearly, the servant's claim prescribing in three years (*a*).

(*a*) 3 Ersk. 3. § 14. Cooper, *supra*, § 183 (*a*). See below, § 629; and above, § 153. Scott *v.* E. Mansfield, 1831; 9 S. 780; aff. 1833, 6 W. & S. 277.

185. If the master should become unable to perform his engagement, the servant has still right to his wages as a creditor, under deduction of what he earns elsewhere during the time engaged for (*a*).

(*a*) Puncheon *v.* Haig, 1790; M. 13,990; 1 Ill. 149. See above, § 179, 182.

186. On the master's death, wages to the next term are due, provided the servant is ready to perform his part; and not only proper wages are due, but board-wages (*a*) also, if the establishment of the deceased be broken up. Upon the master's executry the servant has a preference, by privilege, for the term's wages; but not for board, which is not wages (*b*).

On the master's bankruptcy or insolvency, the servant has a preferable claim over the other creditors to the same extent as against the executry on death (*b*).

(*a*) See above, § 177. (*b*) See below, § 1404.

187. Termination of Service.—(1.) *Warning.*—There must be warning on either part to put an end to the engagement (*a*), 'unless it be dispensed with by the contract (expressly, or by implication from the temporary character of the employment), or by usage (*b*).' This must, 'in yearly or half-yearly engagements,' be forty days before the term, 'or termination of the engagement,' unless by agreement or local usage a shorter time is sufficient (*c*). The proof of warning may raise questions. It is not necessary that the warning shall be judicial, as in the warning of tenants; and, 'while it is enough that either party distinctly shows by his conduct that he does not intend to renew the engagement,' it is not warning that the master has been inquiring after another servant, or the servant after another place (*d*). 'Reasonable notice only, not formal warning forty days before the term, is required in the case of clerks, tutors, and others, not domestic servants (*e*).'

(*a*) See above, § 173 *fin.*

(*b*) Morrison *v.* Allardyce, 1823; 2 S. 434. London Shipping Co. *v.* Ferguson, 1850; 13 S. 51. Fosdick *v.* N. B. Ry. Co., 1850; 13 D. 281.

(*c*) Anderson *v.* Wishart, 1818; 1 Mur. 429. Morrison *v.* Allardyce, 1823, 2 S. 434. Cameron *v.* Scott, 1870; 9 Macph. 233.

(*d*) M'Lean *v.* Fyfe, Feb. 4, 1813; F. C. Anderson, *cit.* Fraser, M & S. 59.

(*e*) Moffat and Campbell, *supra*, § 153 (*d*); so in cases such as a public schoolmaster's, where the tenure is during pleasure. Morrison *v.* Abernethy School Board, 1876; 3 R. 945. The dismissal of public school teachers is now regulated by 45 and 46 Vict. c. 18. See Hinds *v.* Dunbar School Board, 1883; 10 R. 930.

188. (2.) *Character.*—It has been sometimes held that the master must, at the termination of the contract, give to the servant a character; but this is only a *moral*, not a *legal* obligation, and cannot be enforced. Although not bound to comply with the servant's demand for a character, he *may* give one, even unfavourable to the servant, and in so doing is privileged to speak. But if a bad character be given, and not truly, the master will be liable to the servant in damages (*a*). 'So an employer may be made liable in damages for knowingly or recklessly and without belief (*b*) giving a false character in favour of a servant, by relying on which a third party suffers loss (*c*).'

(*a*) Fell *v.* L. Ashburton, Dec. 12, 1809; F. C.; 1 Ill. 149. Carrol *v.* Bird, 3 Esp. 201; 6 R. R. 824. See Christian *v.* Kennedy, 1818; 1 Mur. 427. Anderson *v.* Wishart, 1818; 1 Mur. 429, 439. Matheson *v.* Mackinnon, 1832; 10 S. 825; *infra*, § 2054. A like privilege exists in assigning a reason for dismissal. Watson *v.* Burnett, 1862; 24 D. 494.

(*b*) See Derry *v.* Peck, 14 App. Ca. 337, 365, 374.

(*c*) Anderson, *cit.* Foster *v.* Charles, 6 Bing. 396; 7 *ib.* 105; 31 R. R. 446; and see Fraser, M. & S. 133, as to the application of 32 Geo. III. c. 56.

189. Managers, etc.—The engagement of a manager, cashier, or other servant in a bank, must depend entirely on the contract; but the importance of having the absolute command over such persons and in such establishments, where many objections may occur which cannot be brought to any known or recognised breach of duty, is held to give a bias in the construction of such contracts favourable to the uncontrolled power of dismissal without reason assigned (*a*).

(*a*) Pollock *v.* Comml. Bank, 1829; 3 W. & S. 430. Mitchell *v.* Smith, 1836; 14 S. 358. Fosdick *v.* N. B. Ry. Co., 1850; 13 D. 281. Perhaps this absolute power of dismissal may not always be inconsistent with a claim for damages in lieu of notice. See Morrison, § 187 (*c*). Forsyth *v.* Heatheryknowe Coal Co., 1880; 7 R. 887. Starr-Bowkett Bdg. Socy. *v.* Munro, 1884; 21 S. L. R. 291. Pearce *v.* Foster, 17 Q. B. D. 536 (dismissal of principal clerk for extensive speculation on Stock Exchange).

190. Hiring of Artisans.—The hiring of artisans is a contract on time, or by piecework, for labour to be performed in a manufactory along with other workmen. The contract on time is, like that of domestic service, verbal for a year or a shorter term, but requires writing for a longer period (*a*). 'As tacit relocation is founded on custom, it has no place where warning is excluded by usage or contract, and operates to renew the engagement only for such a period as is usual, not therefore, in an engagement of artisans for a year, for another year (*b*).'

(*a*) Paterson *v.* Edington, 1830; 8 S. 931; 1 Ill. 150. See Dale *v.* Dumbarton Glass Work, 1829; 7 S. 369. Dumbarton Glass Co. *v.* Cotesworth, 1847; 9 D. 732.

(*b*) Lennox *v.* Allan & Son, 1880; 8 R. 38; *supra*, § 173 (2).

191. (1.) *The Obligation of the Artisan* is, to perform his stipulated work with due subordination and regularity, and observance of the rules of the establishment, during the term agreed on. The Legislature interposed to compel fulfilment of workmen's engagements, by empowering one or more justices of the peace, in certain descriptions of manufacture, on complaint upon oath, to apprehend, inquire, and, if necessary, imprison the workman not beyond three months to hard labour; or to abate his wages, if he 'should' refuse to enter to his work, or if he 'should' desert his service before expiration of the term, or if he 'should' be guilty of any misconduct or misdemeanour respecting the service (*a*). 'A later statute on this subject, the Master and Servant Act, 1867 (*b*), modified the severity of these Acts, took away the power of summary apprehension, and while retaining the compulsitor of imprisonment as a penalty for failure to pay a fine or damages, really substituted a civil suit for a criminal complaint. In 1875, however, this Act also was repealed (*c*), and the Employers and Workmen Act passed in its place (*d*). This Act makes the Sheriff a sort of arbiter between masters and workmen, with very wide discretionary powers to adjust disputes, rescind contracts, apportion wages, award damages, require security for performance, etc.; but with no power to enforce any orders (except against apprentices, who may be imprisoned) unless by the ordinary means of enforcing decrees of damages in the Small Debt Court, namely, by poinding or arrestment (*e*).'

(*a*) 20 Geo. II. c. 19. 6 Geo. III. c. 25. 4 Geo. IV. c. 34.

(*b*) 30 and 31 Vict. c. 141.

(*c*) 38 and 39 Vict. c. 86, § 17, repealing also former statutes. See also, for repeal of obsolete statutes, 52 and 53 Vict. c. 24.

(*d*) 38 and 39 Vict. c. 90.

(*e*) Among the cases decided under this Act are Wilson *v.* Glasg. Tramway Co., 1877; 5 R. 981 (Sheriff's jurisdiction to rescind arbitration clause). Clemson *v.* Hubbard, 1 Ex. D. 179; 45 L. J. M. C. 69. Leslie *v.* Fitzpatrick, 3 Q. B. D. 229; 47 L. J. M. C. 22 (infant). Hindley *v.* Haslam, 3 Q. B. D. 481 (counter claims). Grainger *v.* Aynsley; 6 Q. B. D. 182 (contractor is within the Act). Warburton *v.* Heyworth, 6 Q. B. D. 1; 50 L. J. Q. B. 137 (forfeitures in case of women, etc., within Factory Acts). Fraser, M. & S. part iii. ch. 1.

192. (2.) *The Obligation of the Master* is to pay the wages stipulated or implied (*a*); and in this he is placed, 'in many trades,' under certain restraints as to the mode of payment—not by truck, but by money (*b*).

'Wages in the enumerated trades must be paid in the current coin of the realm only; and contracts as to the place where and the manner in which or the persons with whom wages shall be expended, are illegal, null, and void (*c*). Payment in goods is illegal, null, and void, and wages not paid in current coin may still be recovered at law. The master is not entitled to plead against a claim for wages compensation in respect of furnishings from his store, or goods supplied by any person under his order or direction, or by any agent; and such an employer, person, or agent cannot sue the workmen for or in respect of goods so supplied (*d*). Payment may be by bank-notes or drafts, if the artificer consents; but payments by orders or cheques to be cashed in part at the master's store (*e*), or in orders for goods at a store, even if the employer be not interested in the store (*f*), are illegal evasions of the Act. Penalties may be recovered for illegal payments and contracts (*g*). Certain deductions from wages for medical attendance, medicine, rent, materials, etc., are permitted (*h*). And a payment to discharge an obligation of the employee at his desire is to be a payment in cash to the employee (*i*).

'In the hosiery manufacture the Truck Act has been supplemented by a special Act prohibiting deductions (previously permitted) from wages for frame rents or other charges (*k*). Deductions for sharpening tools, and contracts for spending wages at particular shops are prohibited, and the Acts are applied to knitted and other articles made by artificers at their own homes (*l*).'

The master is bound also to give to the workman a full supply of work (if his wages depend on the price) during the term agreed on (*m*). And (as the counterpart of the restraints on the workman) the Legislature 'gave' them certain facilities for recovering payment of wages (*n*), 'now repealed; but the workman as well as the employer may avail himself of the procedure for settling disputes or claims under the Employers and Workmen Act.'

(*a*) Grieve *v.* Gordon, 1821; 1 S. 39; 1 Ill. 150.
(*b*) 12 Geo. I. c. 34. 1 Geo. IV. c. 93. Monteith & Co. *v.* Blackie, 1827; 5 S. 280; 1 Ill. 150.
(*c*) 1 and 2 Will. IV. c. 37, § 2. Hewlett *v.* Allan, 1894; A. C. 383.
(*d*) The existing Truck Acts are 1 and 2 Will. IV. c. 37, and 50 and 51 Vict. c. 46. See Fraser, M. & S. 442. Philips *v.* M'Innes, 1874; 2 R. 224 (foreman an "employer"). M'Farlane *v.* Birrell, 1889; 16 R. Just. 28 (deduction for rent; § 23 of Act).
(*e*) Pillar *v.* Llynvi Coal Co., 38 L. J. C. P. 394; L. R. 4 C. P. 752.
(*f*) Finlayson *v.* Braidbar Quarry Co., 1864; 2 Macph. 1297.
(*g*) The Act, § 9 sqq.
(*h*) The Act, § 23 sqq. Cutts *v.* Ward, L. R. 2 Q. B. 357; 36 L. J. Q. B. 161.
(*i*) Hewlett *v.* Allan, *cit.*
(*k*) 37 and 38 Vict. c. 48. Willis *v.* Thorp, L. R. 10 Q. B. 383; 44 L. J. Q. B. 137. See 38 and 39 Vict. c. 90, § 11.
(*l*) 50 and 51 Vict. c. 46, § 6, 8, 10.
(*m*) But see Fraser, M. & S. 137.
(*n*) 4 Geo. IV. c. 34. As to the Arbitration Act, see Fraser, M. & S. part iii. ch. 2.

193. Combination Laws. — Masters and workmen have reciprocally great power over each other by means of combination. Formerly the combinations of the masters were the more powerful and oppressive, from their unity of counsels, their comparative wealth, and ability to wait for the effect of their plans, and from better information and greater prudence. More recently, workmen have learnt to organise their proceedings, to collect a common fund, and to proceed by union of purpose, and too frequently by force. The great objects of the late statutes on this subject are, to give perfect freedom to voluntary agreement; and to prevent all threats, intimidation, and violence (*a*). 'Combinations either of masters or workmen for the purpose of restricting freedom of contracts for the employment of workmen are illegal at common law, and their rules cannot be enforced (*b*). But it has been enacted that the purposes of a trade union shall not, by reason merely that they are in restraint of trade, be unlawful so as to render void or voidable any agreement or trust (*c*). Further, where the rules of a society operated in illegal restraint of trade (*e.g.* by rules prohibiting its members from taking piece-work), it was held that it could not take the benefits of the Friendly Societies Act (18 and 19 Vict. c. 63, § 44) with regard to the settlement of disputes and the security of property (*d*). And the relaxation of the rule above mentioned is accompanied by such restrictions, that it is still difficult, but not impossible (*e*), to separate the "friendly" from the trade purposes of an ordinary trade union so as to get rid of the taint of illegality (*f*). By registration, however, under the Trade Union Act, 1871, these bodies obtain certain privileges for the protection of their property and rights (*c*).'

(*a*) 53 Geo. III. c. 40. 5 Geo. IV. c. 95. 6 Geo. IV. c. 129. Repealed by 34 and 35 Vict. c. 32. Barclay's Digest, 153. Sir W. Erle, The Law Relating to Trades Unions, 1869. Guthrie's Trade Union Act, 1873. Wright on the Law of Conspiracy. 22 Vict. c. 34, as to the meaning of the words "molestation" or "obstruction." Walsby *v.* Anley, 3 El. & El. 516; 30 L. J. M. C. 131. Wood *v.* Bowron, L. R. 2 Q. B. 21; 36 L. J. M. C. 5. Skinner *v.* Kitch, L. R. 2 Q. B. 393; 36 L. J. M. C. 116. R. *v.* Rowlands, 5 Cox, C. C. 436. R. *v.* Druitt, 10 Cox, C. C. 592.
(*b*) Hilton *v.* Eckersley, 6 E. & B. 47; 25 L. J. Q. B. 199. Hornby *v.* Close, *infra.* Farrar *v.* Close, L. R. 4 Q. B. 602; 38 L. J. M. C. 132; and above, § 40.
(*c*) 34 and 35 Vict. c. 31, § 3.
(*d*) Hornby *v.* Close, 10 Cox, C. C. 393; 8 B. & S. 175; 36 L. J. M. C. 43. The F. S. Act is now 59 and 60 Vict. c. 25.
(*e*) See above, § 40 (*l*).
(*f*) The Trade Union Act, *cit.* § 4 and 5. M'Kernan *v.* United Masons' Assn., 1874; 1 R. 453. Shanks *v.* Do., 1874; *ib.* 823. Manners *v.* Fairholme, 1872; 10 Macph. 520. Rigby *v.* Connel, 14 Ch. D. 482; 49 L. J. Ch. 328. Duke *v.* Littleboy, 49 L. J. Ch. 802. Amalg. Ry. Servants of Scotland *v.* Motherwell Branch, 1880; 7 R. 867. Aitken *v.* Associated Carpenters, etc., 1885; 12 R. 1206. *Supra*, § 40.

CHAPTER IV

OF THE CONTRACT OF LOAN

194. Nature and Kinds of Loan.—Loan is a real contract, by which the owner of a thing gives, for the temporary accommodation of another, the use or services derivable from it (*a*). There are two kinds of loan; one Proper, where a thing is lent for use, under an obligation to restore the same thing to the owner; the other Improper, in which the thing lent is transferred, on an obligation by the borrower to restore as much of the same kind, and of equal goodness. The former is Commodate, or Loan for Use; the latter Mutuum, or Loan for Consumption (*b*).

(*a*) See 1 Stair, 11. 3 Ersk. 1. § 18–25. 1 Bell's Com. 255. Pothier, Tr. de Prêt à l'Usage et de Consomption. Story on Bailments, 156. 2 Kent, Com. 573. Van Leeuwen, 337, 349.

(*b*) The distinction is of importance in bankruptcy, where, under the one contract, the lender, as *creditor dominii*, is entitled to have his property restored; under the other he is a personal creditor, entitled only to a dividend. See § 211, 1315.

195. Commodate. — This (*quasi commodo datum*) is a real contract of loan, for a certain use, without hire, and on an engagement, express or implied, that the identical thing lent shall be restored to the owner. The loan is either on time; or for a special occasion; or at will, which is also called Precarium (*a*).

(*a*) 3 Ersk. 1. § 20. Van Leeuwen, 349.

196. The loan is not complete till the thing has been delivered. But the terms on which the delivery is to be made may be proved by parole evidence. 'The lender, as he lends for beneficial use, is responsible for defects in the article lent, which make it dangerous or unprofitable for the purpose of the loan, and which are known to him (*a*).'

(*a*) Dig. xiii. 6. l. 17. s. 5; l. 18. s. 2 and 3; l. 22 (de pign. act.). Story on Bailments, § 275. Blakemore *v.* Brist. and Ex. Ry. Co., 8 E. & B. 1035; 27 L. J. Q. B. 167. M'Carthy v. Young, 6 H. & N. 329. See above, § 141.

197. The borrower is bound to limit his use of the thing lent to that which is expressed or implied in the loan (*a*), and any excess will make the borrower responsible for any loss or damage (*b*). He must himself only take the use, not communicate it to others (*c*). He is bound to the most vigilant care (*d*), but is not liable for inevitable accidents occurring in the proper course of the use contemplated (*e*); 'or for damage done by the fault of third parties without any negligence of his own (*f*).' He is bound to restore the thing without faulty deterioration; and, according to the several kinds of the contract, either on the occasion being answered, or on the term having expired, or when the restoration is demanded; and if he fail, he will be liable for the damages consequent on his misconduct; or the lender may, in particular circumstances, be entitled to reject the thing, and insist for its value.

(*a*) Pothier, Prêt à l'Us. No. 2021.

(*b*) Coggs *v.* Bernard, 2 Ld. Raym. 909. 1 Smith's L. C. 175, 190.

(*c*) Bringloe *v.* Morrice, 2 Salk. 271; 1 Mod. 210.

(*d*) Pothier, *ut sup.* No. 48. See below, § 234.

(*e*) Jones on Bailments, 67. Story, § 240. 2 Kent, 575. Comp. Addison on Contr. 724–9 with Seton *v.* Paterson, *supra*, § 144.

(*f*) Claridge *v.* S. Staffordsh. Tram. Co., 1892; 1 Q. B. 422.

198. The borrower is entitled to *retain* for the reimbursement of extraordinary expense laid out on the thing, but not for any extraneous cause (*a*).

(*a*) Dig. cited above, § 196.

199. The property remains with the owner. The risk also is with him, unless the borrower shall be in fault; and as the loan is gratuitous, the slightest fault will make him responsible (*a*).

(*a*) Authorities, *ut supra*. Colville *v*. Fleming, 1693; 1 Fount. 544; 1 Ill. 151. Buchanan *v*. Baillie, 1696; 1 Fount. 712. See below, § 232.

200. Mutuum (*quasi de meo tuum*) is a real contract, by which one gives and transfers a fungible to another without hire, for use by consumption, on an engagement to restore as much of the same thing at the stipulated term. The loan of money (*a*) does not fully accord either with *Mutuum*, if interest stipulated or implied be held as profit and not as mere restitution; or with *Locatio Rei*, which is not proper to fungibles. But, setting aside the subtilty of the Roman law, the loan of money seems practically referable to *Mutuum* (*b*).

(*a*) As to proof of loan of money, see *infra*, § 2257, 202A.
(*b*) 1 Stair, 11. § 5. 3 Ersk. 1. § 18; Van Leeuwen, 337.

201. The obligation of the borrower confers only a personal right on the lender to demand the equivalent; *ex. gr.*, if a commodity, to require an equal quantity of the same kind and quality, without regard to the difference of market value at the time. And so action will lie for the thing or its value as at the time and place stipulated for restoration, or otherwise at the time when a legitimate demand for restitution of the thing lent may be made. If money be lent, the current coin or nominal value of the sum lent is to be restored, not the intrinsic value (*a*).

(*a*) 1 Stair, 11. § 5. 3 Ersk. 1. § 18. 33 Vict. c. 10, § 6. 34 Vict. c. 47.

202. There is no counter-obligation on the lender. The property being transferred, he is liable neither for risk nor expense.

202A. '*Acknowledgments of Debt and I O U's* do not require to be stamped (*a*). A holograph writing signed by the granter simply acknowledging receipt of money, and found in the possession of the lender, is enough to raise a presumption of loan, and *in dubio* implies an obligation to repay, requiring no further evidence (*b*), except (it may be) to prove the handwriting, or the fact of delivery, or the authority of the writer to bind the borrower (*c*). While such a document raises a presumption of loan, and an I O U proves it, no such presumption arises from the mere payment of money. Thus the signature of the alleged borrower on the back of a cheque drawn in his favour does not show that the sum in the cheque was a loan, and does not even open the way to a proof *prout de jure* of the intention with which the payment was made, for loan of money can be proved only by writ or oath (*d*). But the granter of an I O U will in general be allowed to prove that the money for which it was given was received not in loan but on some other footing, or that it does not import a loan (*e*). An acknowledgment of debt, forming part of a transaction between third parties, and not delivered to the alleged creditor, is not proof of the debt, the obligation depending more on the creditor's possession of it than on the document itself (*f*).

'It has always been the rule of the law of Scotland that loan cannot be proved by parole, but only by writ of the borrower (*g*); and it has lately been settled by a majority of the whole Court that, like other obligations not needing writing for their *constitution*, loan does not require a solemnly attested deed as evidence of it, but only sufficiently clear writing or writings under the borrower's hand, parole being admissible to identify and set up the writings, but not to prove the obligation to repay (*h*).'

(*a*) See above, § 22 *fin*. Macpherson *v*. Munro, 1854; 16 D. 612. Hamilton's Exrs. *v*. Hope, 1853; 15 D. 594, 599. Welsh's Trs. *v*. Forbes, 1885; 12 R. 851 (agreement—afterstamping—proof). Cases cited in following notes and in Addison on Contr. 1249.

(*b*) Thomson *v*. Geikie, 1861; 23 D. 693. Allan *v*. Murray, 1837; 15 S. 1130. Martin *v*. Crawford, 1850; 12 D. 960. Fraser *v*. Bruce, 1857; 20 D. 115 (borrower's signature in lender's Savings Bank passbook). Christie's Exrs. *v*. Muirhead, 1870; 8 Macph. 461. **Haldane** *v*. **Speirs**, 1872; 10 Macph. 537, 541 (*per* L. P. Inglis). Ross *v*. Fidler, Nov. 24, 1809; F. C. M'Keen *v*. Kevan's Trs., 1864; 2 Macph. 392 (effect of partial production of correspondence). Todd *v*. Wood, 1897; 24 R. 1104.

(*c*) *Per* L. P. Inglis in Haldane, *cit*. Christie's Exrs. *cit*. Woodrow & Son *v*. Wright, 1861; 24 D. 31.

(*d*) Haldane *v*. Speirs, *cit*. See Robb *v*. Robb's Trs. 1884; 11 R. 881.

(*e*) Thomson, *cit*. Addison, Contr. 1048. See Neilson's Trs. *v*. Neilson, 1883; 11 R. 119; and Welsh's Trs. *v*. Forbes, 1885; 12 R. 851 ("received on loan" = agreement, not receipt).

(*f*) Duncan *v*. Shand, 1873; 11 Macph. 254. Dunn's Trs. *v*. Hardy, 23 R. 621.

(*g*) See, *e.g.*, Hamilton's Exrs. *v*. Struthers, 1858; 21 D. 51. Bowe & Christie *v*. Hutchison, 1868; 6 Macph. 642. Haldane, *supra*. M'Adie *v*. M'Adie's Exr., 1883; 10 R. 741. Williamson *v*. Allan, 1882; 9 R. 859.

(*h*) **Paterson** *v*. **Paterson**, 1897; 25 R. 144. Bryan *v*. Butters, 1892; 19 R. 490.

CHAPTER V

OF THE CONTRACTS OF PLEDGE, AND DEPOSIT

I. PLEDGE.

203. Nature and Constitution of Pledge.—Pledge is a real contract, by which one places in the hands of his creditor a moveable subject, to remain with him in security of a debt or engagement, to be re-delivered on payment or satisfaction; and with an implied mandate, on failure to fulfil the engagement 'at the stipulated time or on demand (*a*),' to have the pledge sold by judicial authority (*b*).

(*a*) As to the effect of a stipulation that the debtor's right to the pledge shall *ipso facto* cease if repayment be not made within a certain time (pactum legis commissoriæ), see Stair, Ersk., and Domat, *cit.* (*b*). Addison on Contr. 745.

(*b*) See as to the doctrine of Pledge as a *real* security, and the distinction between Pledge, Hypothec, and Retention, § 1363, 1385, and 1410. As to the title of the pledgor, warranty, and the effect of a limited title in the pledgor, see Addison on Contr. 747, 748. See as to factor's power to pledge, *infra*, § 225 (*e*), 229, etc.
See 3 Ersk. Prin. 1. § 13. 1 Stair, 13. § 11. 3 Ersk. 1. § 33. 1 Bell's Com. 238 (258, M'L.'s ed.); 2. 21 sqq. 3 Domat, 3. tit. 7. § 1. Pothier, Tr. du Cont. de Nantissement. Story on Bailments, § 286. 2 Kent, 577. Van Leeuwen, 353. Royal Bank *v.* Saunders's Trs., 1881; 8 R. 805, 816, 821; aff. 1882, 9 R. H. L. 67, 71, 75; L. R. 7 App. Ca. 366. Bridges *v.* Ewing, 1836; 15 S. 8.

204. Pledge is constituted by the delivery of the subject, on terms or conditions, proved either by writing or by witnesses. The right of the creditor is continued by possession (*a*).

(*a*) Upon the question whether actual or corporeal possession is necessary, or constructive possession by an agent is enough, see below, § 1364.

205. The subject of pledge must be capable of delivery; such as corporeal moveables, goods, wares, and merchandise. Debts also may be pledged, when identified with the document, as in bills and notes. And so may title-deeds, as corporeal moveables, but not as carrying any interest in the land (*a*); 'and except in the case of a law agent's right of retention for his business accounts, such impignoration seems to be unavailing even against the proprietor pledging them, who may reclaim them as accessory to his right of property, much less against singular successors and creditors (*b*).'

(*a*) Hogg *v.* Muir, Wood, & Co., May 18, 1820; 2 Bell's Com. 22 sqq. Innes *v.* Craig, 1821; 1 S. 85; 20 F. C. 406. Menzies *v.* Murdoch, 1841; 4 D. 257. Hamilton *v.* Western Bank, 1856; 19 D. 152. Natl. Bank *v.* Forbes, 1858; 21 D. 79.

(*b*) Christie *v.* Ruxton, 1862; 24 D. 1182. See below, § 1442, 1448.

206. The Creditor's Obligation is, to restore the subject of the pledge on payment of the debt; bestowing ordinary care in the custody of the subject while in his possession (*a*).

The Right of Property remains with the pledger, subject to the burden; and so the risk is with him. The creditor has no right of use during his possession; and the security expires with loss of possession. 'But it is not loss of possession extinguishing the security if the pledgee, having an assignable interest in the pledge, sub-pledges or even sells the pledge. In such a case the pledger, while he may claim damages for a wrongful act of the pledgee, cannot demand back the goods without tendering the full amount of the debt (*b*).'

(*a*) Coggs *v.* Bernard, 1 Smith's L. C. 177, 191. Syred *v.* Carruthers, E. B. & E. 469; 27 L. J. Mag. C. 273 (loss by fire).

(*b*) See Hamilton and Natl. Bank, *citt.* Johnston *v.* Stear, 15 C. B. N. S. 331; 33 L. J. C. P. 130; 1 Smith's L. C. 195, 228. Donald *v.* Suckling, 35 L. J. Q. B. 232; L. R. 1 Q. B. 585. Halliday *v.* Holgate, 37 L. J. Ex. 174; L. R. 3 Ex. 299. Mulliner *v.* Florence, 3 Q. B. D. 484; 47 L. J. Q. B. 700. As to return of the pawn to the pledger for a purpose not inconsistent with the continuance of the pledge, see Reeves *v.* Capper, 5 Bing. N. C. 140. Martin *v.* Read, *infra.* N. W. Bank *v.* Poynter & Co., 1894; A. C. 56; 22 R. H. L. 1.

207. Power to Sell.—By the Roman law, the contract included a mandate to sell. But with us the subject of the pledge cannot be sold without the order of a judge, which is obtained on a summary application to the Sheriff (*a*). In England and America no judicial authority is necessary (*b*).

(*a*) 1 Stair, 13. § 11. 3 Ersk. 1. § 33.

(*b*) Pothonier *v.* Dawson, Holt, 383; 1 Ill. 151. Pigott *v.* Chubley, 33 L. J. C. P. 134; 15 C. B. N. S. 301. Martin *v.* Read, 11 C. B. N. S. 730; 31 L. J. C. P. 126; 1 Smith's L. C. 192, 196. 2 Kent, 582. This is the rule also in France; Code Civil, No. 2078.

208. Montes Pietatis, etc.—On the principles of Pledge are grounded the Montes Pietatis of the Continent; the system of the warehousing of goods for the duties (*a*); and the occasional relief granted to traders by Government in the way of loan on goods deposited.

(*a*) See below, § 1368.

209. Pawnbroking is one species of Pledge, affording a resource to poverty, and a ready means to traders and manufacturers of raising occasional supplies. In order to prevent fraud and oppression, it has been subjected to special regulations by the Legislature. The great lines of this restraining policy are—1. That each pawnbroker shall take out an annual licence, and have his name as pawnbroker over his door; 'and therefore a secret partnership in the business of a pawnbroker is illegal and void (*a*).' 2. That he shall not take pawns before or after certain hours of the day, nor from persons intoxicated, or under twelve years of age. 3. That he shall record a description of each article pawned, with a special note of the name and abode of the pawner, and deliver a 'pawn-ticket in a statutory form' to the pawner, by which the article may be reclaimed. 4. That a certain rate of interest may be claimed; but 'the existing Act does not apply to advances of more than £10 on a single article.' 5. That the pawnbroker shall keep the article, 'if pledged for 10s. or under,' unsold for a year 'and seven days of grace, after which it becomes his property.' 6. That, in order to prevent depredations by workmen and apprentices, the pawnbroker shall be liable to certain penalties for taking in pawn unfinished goods. 7. That the pawns are forfeited at the end of the year, to the effect of entitling the pawnbroker to have them sold, unless notice be given for a further indulgence of three months. 8. That the sale must be public, after advertisement, if the sum advanced be above 10s., while certain goods must be sold by themselves. 9. That an account of the sale shall be entered in a book if 10s. have been advanced on the pawn, and the surplus proceeds of the sale, 'subject to any set-off the pawnbroker may have a right to,' paid over to the pawner, if claimed within three years (*b*). '10. The pawnbroker is bound to insure, and must, subject to certain deductions, make good the value of pledges destroyed or damaged by fire (*c*).'

On this Act it has been held a fraud—1. To advance more than £10 on one article, by dividing the sum into several tickets of £10 each (*d*). 2. That the expiration of the year does not, 'in the case of pledges for more than 10s.,' transfer the pawn; so that after the year, the pawn, if unsold, may be redeemed (*e*). 3. That no provision is made for securing a public sale or accounting for articles pledged for less than 10s. (*f*). 'That the indemnity given by the Act to a pawnbroker delivering the pledge to a person presenting the pawn-ticket does not affect the rights of the true owner of an article pledged without his knowledge or assent (*g*). The pawnbroker may sue for the deficit if the pawn when sold does not realise the amount lent (*h*).'

(*a*) Gordon *v.* Howden, 1843; 5 D. 698; rev. 4 Bell, 254; 12 Cl. & F. 242. See Fraser *v.* Hill, 1852; 14 D. 336; rev. 1 Macq. 392; 1854, 16 D. 789.

(*b*) 30 Geo. II. c. 24. 25 Geo. III. c. 48. 39 and 40 Geo. III. c. 99. 5 and 6 Will. IV. c. 62. 2 and 3 Vict. c. 47–9. 10 Vict. 98. 13 and 14 Vict. c. 33. 19 and 20 Vict. c. 27. 23 Vict. c. 21. 25 and 26 Vict. c. 101, § 311 sq. The Acts relating to pawnbrokers are now consolidated by 35 and 36 Vict. c. 93.

(*c*) 35 and 36 Vict. c. 93, § 27. As to burglary, see Shackell *v.* West, 2 E. & E. 326.

(*d*) Ross *v.* Equitable Loan Co., 1826; 5 S. 192; 1 Ill. 152.

(*e*) Walter *v.* Smith, 5 B. & Ald. 439. See Lundie *v.* Buchanan, 1862; 24 D. 620.

(*f*) Henderson *v.* Wilson, 1834; 12 S. 313. Lundie, *supra* (*e*). See Scoular *v.* M'Loughlin, 1862; 34 Jur. 302; 1864, 2 Macph. 955.

(*g*) Singer Mang. Co. *v.* Clark, 5 Ex. D. 37; 49 L. J. Ex. 224. Comp. as to ownership, Brown *v.* Marr, 1880; 7 R. 427; and above, § 109; below, § 527, 1320.
(*h*) Jones *v.* Marshall, 24 Q. B. D. 269.

II. DEPOSIT.

210. Nature and Kinds of Deposit.—Deposit is a real contract, in which a corporeal moveable is delivered by the owner (or depositor) for custody on his account; the depositary engaging without hire to keep it safely, and restore it on demand (*a*). If hire be stipulated, the contract is *Locatio operis*. See above, § 155.

(*a*) See 1 Stair, 13. § 1. 3 Ersk. 1. § 26. 1 Bell's Com. 257 (277, M'L.'s ed.). Pothier, Tr. de Depôt.

211. Deposit is Proper or Improper. It is Proper, where a specific subject (or a fungible made specific) is placed in deposit, to be specifically returned: Improper, where fungibles not kept distinguishable are deposited for the return of an equal quantity; as money with a banker. In the former the property remains unchanged, the rule being, "Rei depositæ proprietas apud deponentem manet sed et possessio." In the latter the property is not preserved, the depositor being a mere creditor (*a*).

(*a*) Pothier, Tr. de Depôt, No. 18 et seq. and No. 82. S. Austral. Ins. Co. *v.* Randell, L. R. 3 P. C. 101. Marine Bank *v.* Fulton Bank, 2 Wallace, 256. Thompson *v.* Riggs, 5 Wallace, 663.

212. The Obligation of the Depositary is to keep the thing with reasonable care, and not to use it unless with permission express or implied; nor to penetrate into or disclose any secret which may be included in the trust, as by breaking open a packet or box (*a*). But he is not liable for the contents of a packet, casket, etc., if restored precisely as he received it, and uninjured (*b*). 'Reasonable care in a gratuitous depositary is such care as a man of common prudence generally exercises about his own property of like description (*c*). But, while it is generally enough to repel the presumption of negligence in a gratuitous bailee that he has taken the same care of the thing deposited as of his own goods, the loss of his own property at the same time is no defence when it is proved that he has been guilty of negligence (*d*).'

The thing deposited is subject to attachment by creditors of the depositor, and to retention by the depositary for what he may have expended on the subject, but not for any debt otherwise due (*e*).

There is a distinction to be observed between the simple deposit for *custody*, and for *safe keeping*. The latter implies a greater degree of care and vigilance, and may either be expressly enjoined, or implied from the very nature of the deposit, as in the case of jewels or plate sent to a banker's while a family is in the country (*f*). The risk is with the owner when the thing perishes without fault (*g*). But if the thing be not restored in due time, the depositary will be liable for damages or the value, with the benefit to the depositor of his oath *in litem* (*h*).

Joint depositaries are liable *in solidum* (*i*).

(*a*) Story on Bailments, § 61. Rooth *v.* Wilson, 1 B. & Ald. 59; 18 R. R. 431. See Norvel *v.* Ramsay, 1763; M. 12,290. Logan *v.* Logan, 1823; 2 S. 253; 1 Ill. 21. Doorman *v.* Jenkins, 2 A. & E. 256.
(*b*) E. of Cassilis *v.* Simpson, 1826; M. 3452; 1 Ill. 152. 3 Ersk. 1. § 26.
(*c*) Giblin *v.* M'Mullen, L. R. 2 P. C. 317; 38 L. J. P. C. 25. Johnston's Claim, L. R. 6 Ch. 212; 40 L. J. Ch. 286.
(*d*) Doorman *v.* Jenkins, *cit.* (*a*). Giblin, *cit.* Stiven *v.* Watson, 1874; 1 R. 412.
(*e*) See below, § 574, 1414. The depositary cannot refuse re-delivery on the ground that the subject of the deposit is not the property of the depositor; Gelot *v.* Stewart, 1871, 9 Macph. 957; but eviction by the true owner will be a good defence, and legal interpellation by adverse claimants may require him to retain. *Ib.* p. 960. Addison on Contr. 775, 777.
(*f*) Coggs *v.* Bernard, 2 Ld. Raymond, 909; 1 Ill. 166; 1 Smith's L. C. 199, 224; 167, 189, 10th ed. Story on Bailments, 68 sqq. Giblin *v.* M'Mullen, *cit.*
(*g*) Douglas *v.* Bishop of Caithness, 1665; M. 3541; 1 Ill. 152.
(*h*) 1 Stair, 13. § 10. White *v.* Crocket, 1661; M. 9233.
(*i*) 3 Ersk. 1. § 26. Cf. E. Dundonald *v.* Masterman, L. R. 7 Eq. 504; 38 L. J. Ch. 350.

213. The Obligation of the Depositor is to reimburse the depositary of his necessary charges, and to receive back the deposit.

214. Sequestration is classed as a species of deposit, and is either voluntary or judicial, the subject being placed in the hands of a neutral party, to abide the issue of some controversy or reference on which the right depends (*a*).

(*a*) Ersk. 1. § 30. See below, § 2338.

215. Consignation of Money is deposit (*a*). The occasions are: redemption of a wadset or pledge; refusal of the creditor to take his money; a sum *in medio* in a competition by multiplepoinding; a demand for money, suspended; 'deposit of money with a stakeholder to abide the result of a lawful game or race (*b*); or with an auctioneer or bank to abide the fulfilment of the conditions of a sale (*c*).' The risk is with him who is in fault, or who consigns only a part, or in improper hands selected by himself (*d*). The consignatary must keep the sum consigned in safety till called for, and is not entitled to part with it; and, as a counterpart, is not liable for interest. But now consignation is made in banks, and bank interest is due (*e*).

(*a*) 1 Stair, 13. § 6. 3 Ersk. 1. § 31.

(*b*) Calder *v.* Stevens, 1871; 9 Macph. 1074. Applegarth *v.* Colley, 10 M. & W. 733.

(*c*) Addison on Contr. 775.

(*d*) Scott *v.* Somerville, 1665; M. 10,118; 1 Ill. 152. Mowatt *v.* Lockhart, 1673; M. 10,118.

(*e*) See 20 and 21 Vict. c. 18, § 5. 9 Geo. IV. c. 23, § 2.

CHAPTER VI

OF THE CONTRACT OF MANDATE AND FACTORY; OR PRINCIPAL AND AGENT

216. Nature and Proof of Mandate.—Mandate is a consensual contract, completed by acceptance of the mandate (*a*). The mandate and the acceptance may both be proved by parole evidence, or by writing, or by circumstances (*b*), 'and this, even where a contract made by an agent is in writing, to the effect of introducing into the contract, *e.g.* as the purchaser of land, a party not named in the written document (*c*).'

(*a*) 1 Stair, 12. 3 Ersk. 3. § 31. Pothier, Tr. du Cont. de Mandat. 1 Bell's Com. 259, 476. Jones on Bailments, 52. Paley on Principal and Agent. Story on Bailments, § 137. 2 Kent, 568. Van Leeuwen, b. iv. c. 26. Story on Agency.

(*b*) Anderson *v.* Buck, 1841; 3 D. 975 (custom of trade). Humfrey *v.* Dale, 26 L. J. Q. B. 137; 27 *ib.* 395. Duncan *v.* Clyde Trs., 1851; 13 D. 518; aff. 1853, 25 Jur. 331; 15 D. (H. L.) 36 (possession of document of debt). E. Galloway *v.* Grant, 1857; 19 D. 865. Woodrow & Son *v.* Wright, 1861; 24 D. 31. Pickin *v.* Hawkes, 1878; 5 R. 676. Calder *v.* Dobell, L. R. 6 C. P. 486; 40 L. J. C. P. 224. *Infra*, § 219 (7). M'Laren's Bell's Com. i. 510, note.

(*c*) Boswell *v.* Selkrig, 1811; Hume, 350. Horne *v.* Morrison, 1877; 4 R. 977. Cases in Dickson on Ev. § 570, and see below, § 224A, note (*d*).

217. Mandate was in the Roman law, and is still in Scotland, a binding contract, by which one empowers another to manage any business for him without hire. But it has with us been almost superseded by agency or factory, which is the employment of another for hire, to do business as factor for the employer (*a*).

(*a*) 3 Ersk. 3. § 31. M'Donald *v.* Kellie, 1821; 1 S. 101; 1 Ill. 152. Paley, Principal and Agent, 100. Davidson *v.* Robertson, 1815; 3 Dow, 218. 2 Kent, Com. 613.

218. Gratuitous Mandate is constituted by consent, and binds the mandatary who accepts (*a*) to execute the order express or implied, to account for his intromissions, and to restore what is entrusted in him; empowers him to do all that is necessary to fulfil the order; entitles him to reimbursement of his advances or outlays, and relief from his engagements, but gives him no right to remuneration; and, leaving the property and risk of the things entrusted to him with the mandant, it entitles the mandant to revoke the mandate *rebus integris* (*b*). 'A gratuitous agent will not be held bound to the highest degree of diligence if he act fairly and to the best of his ability, or, as it is sometimes said, he will be liable only for gross negligence. But the latter phrase is rather misleading, and his responsibility is properly described in the same terms as that of a depositary (*c*), *supra*, § 212. A skilled workman, when he undertakes, even gratuitously, to perform any act within the scope of his art, *spondet peritiam*, and is responsible for want of skill (*d*).'

(*a*) The law of Scotland does not recognise a distinction, which seems to be admitted in England, between nonfeasance and malfeasance; and which mainly proceeds on the ground that an engagement without consideration is a *pactum nudum*, which will not sustain an action. Smith, Merc. Law, 116. Story, § 164 sqq. Coggs *v.* Bernard, 1 Smith's L. C. 200, 216, 218. The author refers to the rule that no action for non-performance will lie against a gratuitous promiser; but if his undertaking has commenced, he will be liable to his principal for damage by his misconduct, since he has prevented another from being employed, which is held a sufficient consideration to support the contract.

(*b*) 3 Ersk. 3. § 35, 40. See Pothier, Mand. No. 38. Jones on Bailments, 93. 2 Kent, 569. Story on Bailments, 196.

(*c*) Grierson *v.* Muir, 1802; Hume, 329. See Stiven *v.* Watson, 1874; 1 R. 412.

(*d*) Kay *v.* Simpson, 1801; Hume, 328. See Shiells *v.* Blackburn, 1 H. Bl. 158; 2 R. R. 750. Wilson *v.* Brett, 11 M. & W. 113. M'Donald *v.* M'Donald, 1807; Hume, 344. Beal *v.* S. Devon Ry. Co., 3 H. & C. 337. Moffatt *v.* Bateman, L. R. 3 P. C. 115. 1 Smith's L. C. 227 sqq.

219. Mercantile Agency or Factory.—In this more useful relation, where the agent receives an adequate reward for his exertions, it is important to distinguish between General and Special agency, both as in relation to the parties themselves and to the public; the one raising a general credit, the other requiring special powers.

General Agents.—An agent or factor for a merchant residing abroad is held 'by a presumption of fact founded on the improbability that credit should be given to a foreigner' as his general agent, and as such is responsible to the merchants here for the price of goods furnished to his principal on his order (*a*); 'but this is not a rule of law; and in each case it is a question of evidence whether the agent in this country of a disclosed foreign principal guarantees the solvency of his constituent, or binds him as a party to the contract (*b*). But when a foreigner instructs a commission agent or commission merchant in this country to purchase goods for him, there is, in the absence of evidence to the contrary, a general usage that no privity of contract exists between the foreign correspondent and the seller in this country (*c*).' In the same way, one who, acting as factor for a merchant, has been recognised by him in a train of dealings as his general representative, will, by his engagements for his principal within the scope of an agent's authority, bind him, although he may have received special instructions; but still this power will be restrained and qualified by the character of power, as derived from many instances, and within the fair scope of those dealings (*d*).

Special Agents (*e*) are persons employed in a particular line,—as a riding agent, a collecting agent, a law agent. Their powers are similar to those of a factor, but limited to the particular line entrusted to them:—

(1.) *Brokers* are limited agents, employed in the negotiation of contracts relative to property not entrusted to their custody; having power to bind their principals, in relation to the particular transaction, by the entry in their books, and the passing of "Bought and Sold notes" between the parties, reserving to the principal a power of objecting to the credit of the buyer (*f*). And this office of a broker, though sometimes confounded with that of factor, is carefully to be distinguished; as he is in no shape empowered to bind the principal without particular mandate (*g*), or the possession of the goods (*h*). 'In modern practice he frequently performs the further function of passing a delivery order to the seller for his signature, and passing it when signed to the purchaser; but in all this he is merely an intermediary or negotiator, and so long as he acts in this way only as a broker, not assuming to have any use, property, or possession of the goods either for himself or another, he incurs no personal liability (*i*). Neither, as a general rule, can one sue on a contract which he has made, as a broker, for a named principal (*k*). He may, however, make himself liable and entitled to sue on the contract by making it in his own name (*l*), and evidence of custom (as explaining, not contradicting the contract) is admitted to show that in particular trades brokers not disclosing the names of principals at the time of the contract are personally liable (*m*). But a custom which is such as to alter the essential character of a contract (as by converting a broker employed to buy, into a principal to sell to his employer) is not binding on a principal who is ignorant of it (*n*).'

Stockbrokers who buy and sell in the public funds, or in the funds 'shares or stock' of joint-stock companies, are special agents. 'Those who employ them are bound by the rules and usages of the Stock Exchange (*o*), so far as they are not unreasonable or unlawful (*p*). In the practice of the Stock Exchange there are generally intermediate sales between the seller and ultimate purchaser to whom the shares are transferred (see § 400, 403J);

and the contract of the first purchaser (jobber) is held to be that he will either take the shares himself at settling day, in which case he is bound to accept and register a transfer, and to indemnify against calls made between the executory sale and the registration of the transfer, or that he will give the name of a transferee to whom no reasonable objection can be made, and who is willing and able to accept and pay for the shares (*q*). The contract imports no undertaking by the seller that the company will register the transferee (*r*).' Provincial stockbrokers take orders for the purchase or sale of stocks in London or elsewhere; they employ brokers of their own selection as correspondents to execute those orders for buying or selling at a distance, which they transmit: they are directly liable for the correct execution of those orders, and cannot relieve themselves by shifting the responsibility to those whom they employ, and of whom their employers know nothing.

Shipbrokers employed in the buying and selling and freighting of ships are special agents; they adjust the terms of venditions, charter-parties, and bills of lading, and settle with passengers the room and terms of their passage. 'They are entitled by usage, apart from employment, to commission from the shipowner or shipbuilder, provided—1. that the negotiations terminate in a contract, and 2. that they have been effectually originated by them, even although the charty-party or contract be completed by another broker, or by the principal without their intervention (*s*).'

Insurance Brokers are also special agents for effecting insurance, selecting proper underwriters, arranging the premium and terms of the policy, and keeping an account on the one hand with the assured, and on the other with the underwriters, debiting or crediting each with the premium, as middlemen for settling the payment of it. 'The insurance broker is agent for both parties: for the insured to effect the policy; and when, in accordance with usual practice, it is left in his hands, also by implied mandate to collect and adjust in case of loss; for the underwriter as to the premium, but no farther. He is also a principal to receive the premiums from the assured, and pay them to the underwriter, the rule of law being that the broker is the debtor of the underwriter for the premiums, and the underwriter the debtor of the assured for losses (*t*).'

(2.) *Supercargoes* are special agents, but coming very near to the character of general factor; being presumed to be invested with full power over the cargo and its destination, and the investment of the proceeds for a return; being so accredited by the possession of the goods (*u*).

(3.) *A Ship's-husband* is a special agent to act with regard to a particular ship as shipbroker, to manage the outfit and provide necessaries, and to settle the freight and charter-party. But he holds no general authority, even to insure the ship. See below, § 449.

(4.) *A Procurator to draw or accept Bills* is a special agent, whose powers must be examined in order effectually to bind the principal. See below, § 321.

(5.) *Wharfingers*, though with possession of goods, are special agents; having no power beyond their particular business or special mandate (*v*).

(6.) *A Traveller* or *Rider* for a manufacturing or mercantile house is a limited agent. His powers are regulated by his appointment; but he has a tacit mandate by custom to receive payment for his principal, and to take orders for him, to the effect of binding him to performance (*w*).

(7.) *A Law Agent* (*x*) is not a general, but a limited agent. The adverse party is not entitled to rely on him as holding a general authority. As between the agent and client, a mandate must be proved, by writing, correspondence, delivery of papers, signing of papers in an action conducted by the agent, revising or approving of the agent's papers or proceedings, or paying his accounts (*y*), 'or by possession of the service copy of a summons (*z*).' But it is not enough that proceedings have been publicly carried on by the agent in the client's name (*aa*), nor that one has given information to an agent relative to a suit, unless he has authorised him to act for him (*bb*). In relation to third parties, the agent may employ a sub-agent when necessary (*cc*). 'But, while agreements between law agents acting for the same client to share fees or profits are now lawful, "a law agent authorised and acting for a client whom he discloses shall incur no liability to any other law agent employed by him, except such as he shall expressly undertake in writing" (*dd*).' The powers of a law agent are those necessary or usual in that business or employment. A power to recover payment of debt is held to confer a discretionary power in the use of diligence (*ee*); but a messenger has no such power, nor is he entitled to receive payment (*ff*).

Power to refer or compromise—Counsel.—'It is said by Professor Bell that' neither agent nor counsel has with us power to enter into a reference of the cause in which he is employed (*gg*). 'But the case cited applies only to law agents, and there can be no doubt that it is within the province of counsel to bind his client by a reference of the subject-matter of the cause. His authority, unless openly withdrawn and repudiated, is absolute over the whole conduct of the litigation for which he is retained, including the abandonment or compromise of a claim or a defence, or of the whole cause (*hh*); but of course it does not extend to matters collateral or external to those embraced in the action (*ii*).'

Negligence of Law Agent.—A law agent is responsible for professional negligence or want of skill, as in not using the due means for recovering a debt (*kk*); not duly negotiating a bill; using a wrong stamp; not objecting to an insolvent cautioner in a suspension; taking a bad and informal security (*ll*); 'omitting, without express assent of the buyer or lender for whom he acts, to have the records searched for incumbrances (*mm*)'; laying an action on a wrong statute or section of a statute (*ll*); 'ignorance of changes in professional practice, whether occasioned by decisions or statutes (*nn*); executing diligence on an obviously informal and inept decree (*oo*); want of reasonable care and skill and due communication of the facts when employed to lend money and select or advise as to securities (*pp*). But a law agent does not guarantee that his advice shall be correct in law. He is liable only for "want of reasonable skill," or for "gross ignorance," and must show himself acquainted with the ordinary practice of his profession (*qq*). He is not personally liable for what he does *bonâ fide* in obedience to the orders of counsel in the conduct of a cause (*rr*).

'(8.) *Patent Agents.*—There is now a Register of Patent Agents, under rules made by the Board of Trade, and an Institute of Patent Agents formed under Royal Charter (*ss*).'

(*a*) Burgess *v.* Buck, 1829; 7 S. 824; 1 Ill. 153.

(*b*) Hood *v.* Cochrane, Jan. 16, 1818; F. C. Millar *v.* Mitchell, 1860; 22 D. 833. Cf. Athya & Co. *v.* Buchanan, 1872; 45 Sc. Jur. 16. Smith's Merc. Law, 151, 173. M'Laren's Bell's Com. i. 543, note. 2 Smith's L. C. 406. Gadd *v.* Houghton, 1 Ex. D. 357; 46 L. J. Ex. 71. Green *v.* Kopké, 18 C. B. 549. Paice *v.* Walker, L. R. 5 Ex. 173; 39 L. J. Ex. 107.

(*c*) Bennett *v.* Inveresk Paper Co., 1891; 18 R. 975 (explaining in accordance with the text Lord Blackburn's *dicta* in Armstrong *v.* Stokes, L. R. 7 Q. B. 598; 41 L. J. Q. B. 253; Elbinger Actien-Gesellschaft *v.* Claye, 42 L. J. Q. B. 151; L. R. 8 Q. B. 313; and Hutton *v.* Bullock, L. R. 8 Q. B. 331; L. R. 9 Q. B. 572; which appear to have been curiously misunderstood). See Delaurier *v.* Wylie, 1889; 17 R. 167, 171, 191. Girvin, Roper, & Co. *v.* Monteith, 1895; 23 R. 129. Irvine & Co. *v.* Watson, 5 Q. B. D. 414; 49 L. J. Q. B. 531. Ireland *v.* Livingstone, L. R. 5 H. L. 408; 41 L. J. Q. B. 201. *Ex p.* Miles, 15 Q. B. D. 39 (defn. of comn. agent—stoppage *in transitu*).

(*d*) Fenn *v.* Harrison, 3 T. R. 757; 1 Ill. 157. 1 Ross' L. C. 350. Whitehead *v.* Tuckett, 15 East, 400; 3 Ross' L. C. 140; 13 R. R. 509. Baines *v.* Ewing, 35 L. J. Ex. 194; L. R. 1 Ex. 320. Grant *v.* Norway, 10 C. B. 665. Maclean & Hope *v.* Fleming, 1871; 9 Macph. H. L. 38. Smith's Merc. Law, 124. M'Laren's Bell's Com. i. 510.

(*e*) It cannot be said that the distinction of general and special agents is very satisfactory, so far as the terminology is concerned; and it must be noticed that the rule that general agents bind their principals, even although they exceed their instructions, applies to the agents here classified as special, so long as they do not exceed the powers which by his conduct or by the usage of trade the principal holds them out as possessing. See authorities in note (*d*).

(*f*) Hodgson *v.* Davies, 2 Camp. 530; 1 Ill. 104; 11 R. R. 789. Benjamin on Sales, 270. See above, § 89, 105. A broker or agent employed to sell has *primâ facie* no authority to receive payment otherwise than in money. Catterall *v.* Hindle, 35 L. J. C. P. 161; L. R. 2 C. P. 368. Pearson *v.* Scott, 9 Ch. D. 198; 47 L. J. Ch. 705. In England, where much litigation has taken place as to the effect of broker's notes and the entry in his books, with regard to the Statute of Frauds, it seems now to be held that the entry in the books constitutes the contract, and that the notes, being identical, are sufficient evidence of it. As to this and the effect of variance in the terms of the entry and the notes, see the exhaustive exposition in Benjamin on Sales, 251–270.

(*g*) Baring *v.* Corrie, 2 B. & Ald. 137; 1 Ill. 159; 20 R. R. 383. See *ex parte* Dyster, 2 Rose, 351. M'Call & Co. *v.* Black & Co., 1820; 2 S. Ap. 188; 1 Ill. 161. Whitehead, *supra* (*d*). Borries *v.* Imperial Ottoman Bank, L. R. 9 C. P. 38; 43 L. J. C. P. 3; and comp. 2 Smith's L. C. 121.

(*h*) Pickering *v.* Busk, 15 East, 38; 1 Ill. 158; 13 R. R. 364. See cases in note (*g*).

(*i*) Fowler *v.* Hollins, L. R. 7 H. L. 757; 44 L. J. Q. B. 169; affg. 41 L. J. Q. B. 277, and L. R. 7 Q. B. 616. Southwell *v.* Bowditch, 1 C. P. D. 374; 45 L. J. C. P. 374, 630.

(*k*) Fairlie *v.* Fenton, L. R. 5 Ex. 172; 39 L. J. Ex. 107. Addison on Contr. pp. 40, 61, 7th ed.

(*l*) Short *v.* Spackman, 2 B. & Ad. 962. Jones *v.* Littledale, 6 A. & E. 486. 2 Smith's L. C. 400. Mackenzie & Aitken *v.* Robertson, 1886; 13 R. 494.

(*m*) Humfrey *v.* Dale, 7 E. & B. 266; E. B. & E. 1004; 26 L. J. Q. B. 137; 27 *ib.* 390. Fleet *v.* Murton, L. R. 7

Q. B. 126; 41 L. J. Q. B. 49. Hutchison *v.* Tatham, L. R. 8 C. P. 482; 42 L. J. C. P. 260. Imperial Bank *v.* St. Katherine's Dock Co., 5 Ch. D. 195; 46 L. J. Ch. 335. Southwell *v.* Bowditch, *cit.* (*i*). Pike *v.* Ongley, 18 Q. B. D. 708. 1 Smith's L. C. 556; 2. 396.

(*n*) Mollett *v.* Robinson, L. R. 7 H. L. 802; 44 L. J. C. P. 362.

(*o*) Marr *v.* Buchanan, 1852; 14 D. 467. Matthews *v.* Auld & Guild, 1874; 1 R. 1224. Risk *v.* Auld & Guild, 1881; 8 R. 729. Sutton *v.* Tatham, 10 A. & E. 27. Grissell *v.* Bristowe, L. R. 4 C. P. 36; 38 L. J. C. P. 10. Coles *v.* Bristowe, L. R. 4 Ch. Ap. 3; 38 L. J. Ch. 81. Maxted *v.* Paine, L. R. 4 Ex. 81; 40 L. J. Ex. 57. Bowring *v.* Shepherd, L. R. 6 Q. B. 309; 40 L. J. Q. B. 129. Duncan *v.* Hill, 40 L. J. Ex. 137; 42 *ib.* 179; L. R. 8 Ex. 242.

(*p*) Nickalls *v.* Merry, L. R. 7 H. L. 530; 45 L. J. Ch. 575. Pearson *v.* Scott, 9 Ch. D. 198; 47 L. J. Ch. 705. Mollett *v.* Robinson, *supra* (*n*). Sweeting *v.* Pearce, 9 C. B. N. S. 534; 30 L. J. C. P. 109. Neilson *v.* James, 9 Q. B. D. 546; 51 L. J. Q. B. 369. Perry *v.* Barnett, 15 Q. B. D. 389.

(*q*) Coles *v.* Bristowe, *cit.* Nickalls *v.* Merry, *cit.*, and cases in (*o*) and (*p*). Brown *v.* Black, L. R. 15 Eq. 363; 8 Ch. 939.

(*r*) Stray *v.* Russell, 1 E. & E. 888. London Founders' Assn. *v.* Clarke, 20 Q. B. D. 576.

(*s*) Wilkinson *v.* Martin, 8 C. & P. 1. Burnell *v.* Bouch, 9 C. &. P. 620. Hill *v.* Kitching, 3 C. B. 299; 15 L. J. C. P. 251. Gibson *v.* Crick, 1 H. & C. 142; 31 L. J. Ex. 304. Wilkinson *v.* Alston, 48 L. J. Q. B. 37, 733. Mansell *v.* Clements, L. R. 9 C. P. 139. Moss *v.* Cunliffe & Dunlop, 1875; 2 R. 657. White *v.* Munro, 1876; 3 R. 1011. Walker, Donald, & Co. *v.* Birrell, Stenhouse, & Co., 1883; 11 R. 369. Jacobs & Co. *v.* M'Millan & Son, 1894; 21 R. 623. Menzies & Bruce Low *v.* M'Lennan, 1895; 22 R. 299 (construction of agreement to pay commission on sale of brewery).

(*t*) Jenkins *v.* Power, 6 M. & S. 282; 18 R. R. 575. Power *v.* Butcher, 10 B. & C. 329; 34 R. R. 432. Stewart *v.* Aberdeen, 4 M. & W. 211. Baines, *supra* (*d*). **Xenos** *v.* **Wickham**, L. R. 2 H. L. 296; 36 L. J. C. P. 313 (see s.c. 14 C. B. N. S. 460; 33 L. J. C. P. 13, 16, for Lord Blackburn's statement of the general course of business; and comp. 1 Bell's Com. 599 (646, M'L.'s ed.); 1 Arnould, Ins. 157–227). Beckwith *v.* Bullen, 8 E. & B. 683; 27 L. J. Q. B. 162. Sweeting *v.* Pearce, 9 C. B. N. S. 534; 30 L. J. C. P. 109. G. W. Ins. Co. *v.* Cunliffe, L. R. 9 Ch. 525; 43 L. J. Ch. 741. Freebairn *v.* Stevenson, May 25, 1810; F. C. Pitcairn *v.* Adair, Feb. 7, 1809; F. C. Bertram *v.* Richmond, 1802; M. 7122, and Apx. *Insur.* No. 10, note; 16 F. C. 557. Selkrig *v.* Pitcairn, 1808; M. Apx. *Insur.* No. 10. As to the broker's liability for negligence in effecting insurance, etc., see cases in Addison on Contr. 869. Cahil *v.* Dawson, 3 C. B. N. S. 106; 26 L. J. C. P. 252. Elliot *v.* Wilson, 1776; 2 Pat. 411. Gilbert *v.* Galloways, June 12, 1811; F. C. Stone *v.* Aberdeen Ins. Co., 1849; 11 D. 1041. See as to "Lloyd's," 34 Vict. c. 21 (Lloyd's Act); and as to lien, below, § 1452.

(*u*) Davidson *v.* Gwynne, 12 East, 396; 1 Ill. 270; 11 R. R. 420.

(*v*) Monk *v.* Whittenbury, 2 B. & Ad. 484; 1 Ill. 163. See above, § 156; below, § 236, 1434. Benjamin on Sales, 183, 153.

(*w*) Milne *v.* Harris, James, & Co., 1803; M. 8493; 1 Ill. 83. James, Wood, & James *v.* Telford, 1823; 3 S. 167; 2 S. App. 219. See Dickson *v.* Nicholson, 1885; 17 D. 1011 (retention for commission). As to commercial travellers' commission, see Lockwood *v.* Levick, 8 C. B. N. S. 603; 29 L. J. C. P. 340. Laurie *v.* Lloyd & Co., 1873; 11 Macph. 413; aff. 2 R. H. L. 1. Lloyd's Exrs. *v.* Wright, 1870; 7 Sc. Law R. 216. Green *v.* Bartlet, 32 L. J. C. P. 261; 14 C. B. N. S. 681 (auctioneer).

(*x*) As to law agents, see above, § 154; 36 and 37 Vict. c. 63; and for fuller information, Begg on Law Agents, 2nd ed., 1883; Addison on Contr. p. 816.

(*y*) Campbell *v.* Gray, 1821; 1 S. 37. Murdoch *v.* Bryan, 1827; 2 W. & S. 568. Wallace *v.* Miller, 1821; 1 S. 40. Young *v.* M'Gill, 1823; 2 S. 346. Grant *v.* Wilson, 1804; Hume, 336. Grant *v.* Wishart, 1845; 7 D. 274.

(*z*) Dickie *v.* Brash, 1836; 16 S. 353. Muir *v.* Stevenson, 1850; 12 D. 512.

(*aa*) Balfour *v.* Lyle, 1833; 11 S. 906. This case does not apply to the text. See, however, Robertson *v.* Foulds, 1860; 22 D. 714. Stephen *v.* Skinner, 1863; 2 Macph. 287.

(*bb*) Scott *v.* Donaldson, 1831; 10 S. 107. Tod & Wright *v.* Brydone, 1823; 2 S. 157.

(*cc*) Kerr *v.* Marshall, 1816; 1 Mur. 69. Robertson *v.* Winchester, 1823; 2 S. 599. M'Ara *v.* Phillips, 1825; 4 S. 296. Megget *v.* Milne, 1828; 6 S. 981. See Wallace *v.* Murdoch, 1828; 6 S. 1018. See Cameron, *infra.*

(*dd*) 36 and 37 Vict. c. 63, § 21. M'Larens *v.* M'Dougall, 1881; 8 R. 626. Livesey *v.* Purdom & Son, 1894; 21 R. 911 (Scotch law agent employing English solicitor not personally liable).

(*ee*) M'Kenzie *v.* M'Lean, 1830; 8 S. 306. Sanderson *v.* Campbell, 1833; 11 S. 623. Cameron *v.* Mortimer, 1872; 10 Macph. 461, 817.

(*ff*) 3 Ersk. 4. § 3.

(*gg*) Livingston *v.* Johnston, 1830; 8 S. 594. See Comrie *v.* Grigor, 1862; 24 D. 985; 1863, 1 Macph. 357. Orr *v.* Meikle & Smith, 1867; 39 Jur. 557.

(*hh*) Gilfillan *v.* Brown, 1833; 11 S. 548. M'Kenzie *v.* Girvan, 1843; 2 Bell's App. 43, 53 (*per* L. Campbell). Currie *v.* Glen, 1846; 9 D. 308. Forbes *v.* Duffus, 1837; 12 F. C. 321. Duncan *v.* Salmond, 1874; 1 R. 329. Macintosh *v.* Fraser, 1860; 22 D. 421. Batchelor *v.* Pattison, 1876; 3 R. 914. Prestwich *v.* Poley, 34 L. J. C. P. 189; 18 C. B. N. S. 806. Strauss *v.* Francis, L. R. 1 Q. B. 179; 35 L. J. Q. B. 133. Holt *v.* Jesse, 3 Ch. D. 377; 46 L. J. Ch. 254. Cf. King *v.* Pinsoneault, 44 L. J. P. C. 42; L. R. 6 P. C. 245.

(*ii*) Wauchope *v.* N. B. Ry. Co., 1863; 2 Macph. 326. Swinfen *v.* Swinfen, 26 L. J. C. P. 97; 18 C. B. 485; 1 C. B. N. S. 364; 24 Beav. 549; 2 De G. & J. 381. Swinfen *v.* L. Chelmsford, 5 H. & N. 890; 29 L. J. Ex. 382. Chambers *v.* Mason, 5 C. B. N. S. 59; 28 L. J. C. P. 10.

(*kk*) See Hay *v.* Baillie, 1868; 7 Macph. 32.

(*ll*) Highgate *v.* Boyle, 1823; 2 S. 204. Pentland *v.* Wight, 1833; 11 S. 804; 3 Ill. 107. M'Farlane's Exrs. *v.* Ferguson, 1834; 12 S. 284. Morrison *v.* Ure, 1826; 4 S. 656. Brown *v.* Wemyss, 1829; 7 S. 626. Carruthers *v.* Little, 1829; 7 S. 712. Sim *v.* Clark, 1831; 10 S. 85; aff. 6 W. & S. 452; 1 Ill. 129. M'Leod *v.* M'Donald, 1835; 13 S. 287. Haldane *v.* Donaldson, 1836; 13 S. 610; aff. 1 Rob. 226; 3 Ill. 107. Frame & Co. *v.* Leslie, 1836; 14 S. 914; aff. M'L. & Rob. 595. See above, § 154. Anderson *v.* Torrie, 1857; 19 D. 356. Urquhart *v.* Grigor, 1857; 19 D. 853.

(*mm*) Graham *v.* Hunter's Trs., 1831; 9 S. 543. Fearn *v.* Gordon & Craig, 1893; 20 R. 352. Above, § 154 (5).

(*nn*) Lee *v.* Walker, L. R. 7 C. P. 121; 41 L. J. C. P. 91 (patent agent). See Cox *v.* Leech, 1 C. B. N. S. 617; 26 L. J. C. P. 125. Hunter *v.* Caldwell, 10 Q. B. 69, 83.

(*oo*) Smith & Co. *v.* Grant, 1858; 20 D. 1077. The opinions in this case go farther, and make the agent responsible for the omission of the justices and their clerk to have the declaration signed on which a warrant of imprisonment proceeded.

(*pp*) Ronaldson *v.* Drummond & Reid, 1881; 8 R. 767. Sim, Haldane, etc., *citt.* Black *v.* Curror & Cowper, 1885; 12 R. 990. Stewart *v.* M'Clure, Naismith, & Co., 1886; 13 R. 1062; rev. 1888, 15 R. H. L. 1. Ostler *v.* Dill, 1886; 14 R. 12. Stirling *v.* Mackenzie, Gardner, & Alexander, 1886; 14 R. 170. Rae *v.* Meek, 1888; 15 R. 1033; rev. 1889, 14 App. Ca. 558; 16 R. H. L. 31. Apart from special undertaking, law agents seem not to be responsible for the selection of investments. Oastler and Rae, *citt.* Cleland *v.* Brownlie, Watson, & Beckett, 1892; 20 R. 152; and a law agent is not liable for simple omission to advise trustees that a certain investment made by their author is improper. Currors *v.* Walker's Trs., 1889; 16 R. 355. See above, § 154 (6).

(*qq*) Landell *v.* Purves, 1842; 4 D. 1300; rev. 1845, 4 Bell's App. 46; 12 Cl. & F. 98. Cooke *v.* Falconer's

Reprs., 1850; 3 D. 157. Hume *v.* Baillie, 1852; 14 D. 824. Hay *v.* Baillie, *cit.* Hamilton *v.* Emslie, 1868; 7 Macph. 173. Wallace *v.* Fisher & Watt, 1870; 9 Macph. 75. See above, § 154, and cases in (*ll*) and (*nn*). A law agent or messenger-at-arms is not liable to a stranger for a wrong done by his client through him, of which he is ignorant, *e.g.* for doing diligence on a larger sum than is due. Henderson *v.* Rollo, 1871; 10 Macph. 104. Cf. Wilson *v.* Purvis, 1890; 18 R. 72. See § 154 *fin.*

(*rr*) Batchelor *v.* Pattison, 1876; 3 R. 914.

(*ss*) 51 and 52 Vict. c. 50, § 1. Register of Patent Agents' Rules, 1889. Institute of Patent Agents *v.* Lockwood, 1893; 20 R. 315; rev. 1894, A. C. 347; 21 R. H. L. 61.

220. **Obligations of the Agent.**—The agent must perform what he undertakes, or what the mandant or principal is entitled to rely upon as undertaken; otherwise he will be liable in damages (*a*). But there is an *exception* to this, where by illness or inevitable accident the agent is prevented from performing the undertaking.

(*a*) Marr *v.* Buchanan, 1852; 14 D. 467. Gilmour *v.* Clark, 1853; 15 D. 498. Hastie *v.* Campbell, 1857; 19 D. 557. Story on Agency, § 217. Mayne on Damages, 468 sqq. Johnson *v.* Kershaw, L. R. 2 Ex. 82; 36 L. J. Ex. 44. Ireland *v.* Livingstone, L. R. 5 H. L. 395; 41 L. J. Q. B. 201. Cassaboglou *v.* Gibbs, 11 Q. B. D. 797 (measure of damages). It has been held that an agent bound to relieve his principal of a contract made in excess of his powers, is vested with rights of action, *e.g.* of reduction or damages for fraud, which would have been competent to the principal against the other party to the contract. Milne *v.* Ritchie, 1882; 10 R. 365.

221. He must act with the care and diligence of a man of ordinary prudence in the line of the employment (*a*).

(*a*) See below, § 234. Ramsay, Bonnar, & Co. *v.* Mackersy, 1840; 2 Bell's App. 30. Houldsworth *v.* B. L. Co. Bank, 1850; 13 D. 376. See § 153, 154.

222. He must account to the mandant or principal for his administration, and pay over, restore, or give up to him all that he may have received in his name, or as acting for him (*a*). But, acting with due precaution, he is not liable for the buyer's insolvency, unless on a *del credere* commission (*b*). 'An agent is bound to maintain the most entire good faith, and make the fullest disclosure of all facts and circumstances concerning his principal's business. He cannot, therefore, deal on his own account in the business of the agency without the principal's full knowledge and assent; and if he do so (as by secretly buying for himself what he is employed to sell, or secretly selling his own goods to the principal who employs him to buy, or by taking any profit whatever from the other party arising out of the business), the principal is entitled to claim from him, and the agent is bound to account for, any benefit or profit he has obtained (*c*); or in his option, and if the third parties dealing with the agent were cognisant of the agent's employment and position, to repudiate and avoid the transaction (*d*). Any surreptitious or concealed dealing between one principal and the agent of another principal is a fraud (*e*).'

In accounting or in paying money, the rules are, that the agent must, in remitting money, follow any directions given by the principal, or take the risk of the remittance (*f*); that he must, when no directions are given, remit through a chartered bank, or at least a banker reputed at the time to be in good credit, or follow the mercantile custom or local usage (*g*); that if he pay into his own general account, he will be liable to the risk of the banker's failure (*h*); that if he put his own name as drawer or indorser on the bill by which the money is sent, he will be liable as indorser (*i*).

(*a*) Ford *v.* Crichton, 1728; M. 4065; 1 Ill. 153. Wilson & Co. *v.* Old, 1786; M. 4066. Chalmers *v.* Young, 1766; M. 8489; Hailes, 8.

(*b*) Watson *v.* Hood, 1822; 1 S. 492; 1 Ill. 154. See below, § 286. Robinson & Fleming *v.* Middleton, 1859; 21 D. 1089.

(*c*) Pender *v.* Henderson, 1864; 2 Macph. 1428. Robertson *v.* Dennistoun, 1865; 3 Macph. 829. Cunningham *v.* Lee, 1874; 2 R. 83. **Gray's Trs.** *v.* **Drummond & Reid,** 1881; 8 R. 956 (commission paid by auctioneer to law agent). Edin. Nor. Tram. Co. *v.* Mann & Beattie, 1891; 18 R. 1140; aff. 1893, A. C. 69; 20 R. H. L. 7. Morrison *v.* Thomson, L. R. 9 Q. B. 480; 43 L. J. Q. B. 215. **De Busche** *v.* **Alt,** 8 Ch. D. 286; 47 L. J. Ch. 381. Boston Deep Sea Fishing Co. *v.* Ansell, 39 Ch. D. 339. Addison on Contr. 458. Pollock on Contr. 273, 363. Snell's Pr. of Eq. 470. Smith's Merc. Law, 523. *Infra*, § 370, 403H. As to the principal's knowledge, see G. W. Ins. Co. *v.* Cunliffe, 43 L. J. Ch. 741; L. R. 9 Ch. 525.

(*d*) Watt *v.* Macpherson's Trs., 1877; 4 R. 601; rev. 1878, 5 R. H. L. 9; L. R. 3 App. Ca. 254. Cleland *v.* Morrison, 1878; 6 R. 156. Panama & S. Pac. Tel. Co. *v.* India Rubber, etc., Co., L. R. 10 Ch. 515; 45 L. J. Ch. 121. Mollett *v.* Robinson, L. R. 7 H. L. 802; 44 L. J. C. P. 362. New Sombrero Phosph. Co. *v.* Erlanger, L. R. 3 App. Ca. 1218; 48 L. J. Ch. 73. Gillies *v.* M'Lean, 1885; 13 R. 12. Maffett *v.* Stewart, 1887; 14 R. 506.

(*e*) *Per* James, L. J., in Panama, etc., Co., *cit.*

(*f*) Warwick *v.* Nokes, Peakes, 67; 3 R. R. 653.

(*g*) Baines *v.* Turnbull, 1795; M. 1486; Bell's Cases, 322; 1 Ill. 154. M'Kenzie's Trs. *v.* Jones & Co., 1822; 2 S. 75. Knight *v.* L. Plymouth, 3 Atkins, 480. See Ramsay, Bonnar, & Co. *v.* Mackersy, *infra*, § 223. Houldsworth *v.* B. L. Bank, 1850; 13 D. 376.

(*h*) Massey *v.* Banner, 1 Jac. & Wal. 241; 1 Ill. 155; 21 R. R. 150. Baines, *cit.*

(*i*) Le Fevre *v.* Lloyd, 1 Marsh. 318; 5 Taunt. 749; 15 R. R. 644. See Lucas *v.* Groning, 2 Marsh. 460. Scott *v.* M'Kenzie & Lindsay, 1795; M. 10,101; Bell's Cases, 138. Goupy *v.* Harden, 2 Marsh. 454; 7 Taunt. 159; 17 R. R.

478. Webster *v.* M'Calman, 1848; 10 D. 1133. Chiene *v.* Western Bank, 1848; 10 D. 1523. N. B. Bank *v.* Ayrshire Iron Co., 1853; 15 D. 782.

223. *Sub-agents (a).*—He must answer for delegates named by him, whether with or without permission. If named without permission, he must answer absolutely; if with permission, 'whether express or implied from conduct, usage, or the nature of the business,' he will be safe, if in *bonâ fide* he believed the delegate to be competent and solvent (*b*).

(*a*) As to the maxim "delegatus non potest delegare," see Smith's Merc. Law, pp. 115, 116.

(*b*) Thomson & Duncan *v.* Logan, 1754; 5 B. S. 276; 1 Ill. 156. Ramsay, Bonnar, & Co. *v.* Mackersy, 1840; 2 D. 1003; rev. 1843, 2 Bell's App. 30; 9 Cl. & Fin. 845. M'Vicar *v.* Macgregor, 1808; Hume, 347. Western Bank *v.* Bairds, 1862; 24 D. 859. See Macgregor's Tr. *v.* Cox, 1883; 10 R. 1028. De Busche *v.* Alt, *cit.*, and Smith's Merc. Law, *cit.*

224. Obligations of the Principal.—The principal is bound to fulfil the engagements undertaken by the mandatary within the limits of his powers, and so to relieve the mandatary (*a*).

(*a*) Hall & Co. *v.* Stewart, 1813; 2 Dow, 29; 1 Ill. 156. Murray *v.* Campbell, 1827; 6 S. 147. Thomson *v.* M'Taggart, 1823; 2 S. 320. M'Braire *v.* Hamilton, 1826; 2 W. & S. 66. See § 226.

224A. '*Undisclosed Principal—Election.*—In all cases the intention of the parties to a contract determines whether the principal or the agent is liable on the contract, and entitled to enforce it: the question is, to whom was credit given? (*a*). Subject to this general rule, it is held—1. That a contract with a known agent is a contract with his principal, and that if the principal be named or known at the time, there is *primâ facie* no contract with the agent (*b*); unless expressly or by clear implication he assumes liability (*c*). 2. That if the principal is not named, the agent is personally bound (*d*). 3. That in general (*e*) one who is really an agent, even though not known to be so, contracts for his undisclosed principal, and binds him as well as himself (*f*). But in this case the other contracting party, when sued, may avail himself of a set-off or other equity against the agent which has accrued before the disclosure (*g*). 4. That the other contracting party, on discovering the principal (*h*), may elect (both being liable under 2 and 3) to give credit to the agent only, whereby he liberates the principal; and this may be effected by statements or by conduct which cause the principal to alter his position (*i*); and in like manner by taking to the principal he will liberate the agent (*k*). A party contracting with an agent is not deprived of his right to elect the principal as his debtor by reason of the principal's having made payment to the agent, or of the state of accounts between them having been changed, unless by his conduct he has led the principal to believe that he has settled with the agent, or *perhaps* (as when the agency was not known to him) the payment was made when the principal had reason to believe that the other party still relied on the agent's credit alone (*l*).'

(*a*) **Millar *v.* Mitchell**, 1860; 22 D. 833. Calder *v.* Dobell, 40 L. J. C. P. 224; L. R. 6 C. P. 486. Heald *v.* Kenworthy, *infra* (*l*). M'Laren's Bell's Com. i. 541, note. As to the rules of evidence, see Benjamin on Sales, 206 sqq. 2 Smith's L. C. 400 sqq.

(*b*) Brown *v.* Macdougal, 1802; M. Apx. *Factor*, 1. Cowan & Sloan *v.* Davidson, Jan. 14, 1814; F. C. Watson *v.* Bank of Scotland, 1813; 1 Dow, 40; 5 Pat. 555 (rev. M. Apx. *Mandate*, 3). King *v.* Shirra, 1817; 3 Ill. 112. Fleming *v.* Findlay & Co., 1832; 10 S. 739. Craw *v.* Coml. Bank, 1840; 3 D. 193. Williams & Co. *v.* Newlands, 1861; 23 D. 1355. Farrar & Rooth *v.* N. B. Bkg. Co., 1850; 13 D. 1190. **Thomson *v.* Davenport**, 9 B. & C. 78; 2 Smith's L. C. 368; 32 R. R. 578. Owen *v.* Gooch, 2 Esp. 568. Deslandes *v.* Gregory, 2 E. & E. 602; 29 L. J. Q. B. 93; 30 *ib.* 36. See above, § 219 (*i*) to (*m*).

(*c*) Sorley's Trs. *v.* Graham, 1832; 10 S. 319. Woodside *v.* Cuthbertson, 1848; 10 D. 604. Webster *v.* M'Calman, 1848; *ib.* 1133. Millar *v.* Mitchell, *cit.* Tanner *v.* Christian, 4 E. & B. 591. Parker *v.* Winlow, 7 E. & B. 942. Pollock on Contr. 94. 2 Smith's L. C. 397 sqq. Signing "as agent" is generally enough to save the agent from personal liability, but the question is one of construction or of circumstances. Gadd *v.* Houghton, L. R. 1 Ex. D. 357; 46 L. J. Ex. 71. Deslandes *v.* Gregory, *cit.* (*b*); but the refinements of previous English cases will probably not be considered in Scotland. (See Smith's L. C. *cit.* Benj. on Sales, 212.) As to brokers, see Fowler *v.* Hollins, L. R. 7 H. L. 757; 44 L. J. Q. B. 169. Southwell *v.* Bowditch, 1 C. P. D. 174; 45 L. J. C. P. 374, 630; and as to bills of exchange, 45 and 46 Vict. c. 61, § 26; and below, § 313, 321.

(*d*) 1 Bell's Com. 492 (536, M.L.'s ed., and note at p. 540). Addison on Contr. 326. Smith's Merc. Law, 173. An agent cannot discharge himself by parole of liability upon a written contract by showing that it was intended to be a contract with his principal; but parole may be used to charge an undisclosed principal, as that merely adds a new party and does not qualify the written contract. Truman *v.* Loder, 11 A. & E. 595. Higgins *v.* Senior, 8 M. & W. 834; 11 L. J. Ex. 199. 2 Smith's L. C. 404, 407, 412. Benjamin on Sales, 206 sq. *Supra*, § 216.

(*e*) A contract may by its terms exclude the liability or right of any principal. Humble *v.* Hunter, 12 Q. B. 310; 17 L. J. Q. B. 350.

(*f*) Notes to Thomson *v.* Davenport, 2 Smith's L. C. 380. Irvine & Co. *v.* Watson, 5 Q. B. D. 414; 49 L. J. Q. B. 531. Macphail & Son *v.* Maclean's Tr., 1887; 15 R. 47. It has been maintained in an able judgment of Lord Stormonth Darling, that the liability of a latent or unavowed *dominus litis* for the expenses of a litigation depends on the question whether the party behind and the nominal pursuer or defender are truly principal and agent, the degree of interest and control in each being elements in the proof of agency. Fraser *v.* Malloch, 1896,

23 R. 619, where all the authorities as to *dominus litis* are considered.

(*g*) See below, § 573, 1450 ; and Maspons *v.* Mildred & Co., 9 Q. B. D. 530 ; 8 App. Ca. 874.

(*h*) A mere assignee in security does not become a principal, and so liable for the debts of the business, lease, etc., assigned, unless he has held himself out as such principal. Eaglesham & Co. *v.* Grant, 1875 ; 2 R. 960. Miller *v.* Downie, 1876 ; 3 R. 960. Newcastle Chem. Manure Co. *v.* Oliphant & Jamieson, 1881 ; 9 R. 110. Cf. Macphail & Son *v.* Maclean's Tr., *supra* (*f*).

(*i*) Hood *v.* Cochrane, Jan. 16, 1818 ; F. C. Young *v.* Smarts, 1831 ; 10 S. 130. Stevenson *v.* Campbell & M'Lean, 1836 ; 14 S. 562. Carswell *v.* Scott, 1839 ; 1 D. 1215. Williams *v.* Newlands, 1861 ; 23 D. 1355. **Paterson** *v.* **Gandasequi**, 15 East, 62 ; 2 Smith's L. C. 355 ; 13 R. R. 368. Priestley *v.* Fernie, 3 H. & C. 977 ; 34 L. J. Ex. 173. (See Meier *v.* Küchenmeister, 1881 ; 8 R. 642.) Curtis *v.* Williamson, L. R. 10 Q. B. 57 ; 44 L. J. Q. B. 27. Scarf *v.* Jardine, L. R. 7 App. Ca. 345 ; 51 L. J. Q. B. 612. Calder *v.* Dobell, *supra* (*a*).

(*k*) Ferrier *v.* Dods, 1865 ; 3 Macph. 561.

(*l*) Heald *v.* Kenworthy, 10 Ex. 739 ; 24 L. J. Ex. 76. Armstrong *v.* Stokes, L. R. 7 Q. B. 598 ; 41 L. J. Q. B. 252. Irvine & Co. *v.* Watson, 5 Q. B. D. 414 ; 49 L. J. Q. B. 239, 531 ; modifying the qualifications of the general rule in Thomson *v.* Davenport, etc., see 2 Smith's L. C. 389 ; and Davidson *v.* Donaldson, 9 Q. B. D. 623. Cf. Hall & Co., § 224.

224B. '*Misrepresentations* made or *Fraud* committed *by agents*, acting in the course of their employment and for their principals' benefit, have the same effect as if they had been made or committed by the principals ; *i.e.* the person misled or deceived may rescind a contract so induced, or he may claim damages against the principal, founding on the agent's wrong, for there is no sensible distinction between fraud and any other wrong (*a*). But when one is induced by the fraud of the servants or agents of a corporation to become a shareholder in it, and its declared insolvency or liquidation has made it impossible for him to rescind the contract, he can no longer claim damages from the company, because he remains a member of it, and has himself contracted to contribute to the payment of its debts and liabilities (*b*). An agent or servant or director is always personally liable in damages for fraud committed in the business of his principal ; for all persons directly concerned in the commission of a fraud or other wrong are to be treated as principals (*c*). An agent is not liable for a misrepresentation innocently made by him on behalf of his principal (*d*) ; nor in general for the fraud of his co-agent in which he does not participate (*e*).'

(*a*) *Supra*, § 13A, 14, and cases there cited. **Barwick** *v.* **Engl. Jt. St. Bk.**, L. R. 2 Ex. 259 ; 36 L. J. Ex. 147 ; 2 Bell's Com. 618 (509, M'L.'s ed.). M'Laren's Bell's Com. i. 468, 515, notes. **Nat. Exch. Co.** *v.* **Drew,** 1855 ; 2 Macq. 103. New Brunswick Ry. Co. *v.* Conybeare, 9 H. L. Ca. 714. Proudfoot *v.* Montefiore, L. R. 2 Q. B. 511 ; 36 L. J. Q. B. 225. Udell *v.* Atherton, 7 H. & N. 173. Mackay *v.* Coml. Bk. of N. Brunswick, L. R. 5 P. C. 394 ; 43 L. J. P. C. 31. Swire *v.* Francis, L. R. 3 App. Ca. 106 ; 47 L. J. P. C. 18. Jardine's Trs. *v.* Dawson, etc., 1864 ; 2 Macph. 1101. Union Bank *v.* Makin, 1873 ; 11 Macph. 499. Traill *v.* Smith's Trs., 1876 ; 3 R. 770. Clydesdale Bank *v.* Paul, 1877 ; 4 R. 626. Rose *v.* Spavens, 1880 ; 7 R. 925. Beresford's Trs. *v.* Gardner, 1877 ; 4 R. 363. **Houldsworth** *v.* **City of Glasg. Bk.,** 1879 ; 6 R. 1164 ; aff. 1880, 7 R. H. L. 53 ; L. R. 5 App. Ca. 317. N. of Scot. Bkg. Co. *v.* Behn, Möller, & Co., 1881 ; 8 R. 423. Clavering, Son, & Co. *v.* Goodwins, Jardine, & Co., 1891 ; 18 R. 652 (fraud of company officers in issuing share certificates). Brit. Mut. Bkg. Co. *v.* Charnwood Forest Ry. Co., 18 Q. B. D. 714. And as to the law on this point and the controversy arising out of the case of Cornfoot *v.* Fowke, 6 M. & W. 358, see 2 Smith's L. C. 80 sqq. Benjamin on Sales, 416 sqq., 427 sqq.

(*b*) See below, § 403B. **Houldsworth** *v.* **City of Glasgow Bank,** *cit.*, explaining Addie *v.* Western Bank, 1864, 2 Macph. 809 ; 3 Macph. 899 ; rev. 1867, 5 Macph. H. L. 81 ; L. R. 1 Sc. App. 156. Burgess's case, 15 Ch. D. 507 ; 49 L. J. Ch. 541. See further as to fraud or malice by companies or corporations, *infra*, § 2044.

(*c*) Cullen *v.* Thompson & Kerr, 1861 ; 23 D. 574 ; rev. 4 Macq. 424 ; 24 D. H. L. 10. Smith & Co. *v.* Taylor, 1882 ; 10 R. 291. Swift *v.* Winterbotham (Jewsbury), L. R. 8 Q. B. 244 ; 9 Q. B. 301 ; 42 L. J. Q. B. 111 ; 43 *ib.* 56. Weir *v.* Barnett and Weir *v.* Bell, L. R. 3 Ex. D. 32, 238 ; 47 L. J. Ex. 704. Story on Agency, § 308 sqq.

(*d*) Eaglesfield *v.* M. Londonderry, 4 Ch. D. 693 ; aff. in H. L. 38 L. T. 303.

(*e*) Cargill *v.* Bower, 10 Ch. D. 502 ; 47 L. J. Ch. 649.

225. Agent's Powers.—The rules observed as to the agent's powers are : that where the terms are express, the limits are absolute (*a*) ; that his power and his duty must be regulated by the ordinary acts and skill and knowledge of persons in that line (*b*) ; but that where any power is necessary or reasonable to be exercised, in order to the accomplishment of the purpose, it is implied (*c*) ; and that an agent or factor at a distance, and in difficult circumstances, will be discharged if he act with sound discretion (*d*). A factor has power to sell or even to pledge the goods of his principal for advances (*e*) ; 'but apart from this power allowed to persons possessing the character of factor, an agent, however wide his authority in conducting his principal's business, has no implied power to borrow money on his credit (*f*), or to grant obligations out of the ordinary course of business, *e.g.* gratuitous or cautionary obligations (*g*). An agent in possession of securities, and authorised to use them for the purpose of raising money, binds the principal to any extent to which money is truly advanced, although he has fraudulently exceeded a limit fixed by his principal, and applied the difference to his own purposes. *Secus*, if he be lawfully in possession of the securities, but without such authority (*h*).'

Mercantile mandates are extended, restrained, or qualified, and, in general, are aided, by the settled rules and usage of trade (*i*).

In cases of partial execution, it is necessary to distinguish whether the mandate be indivisible, or such as may be executed effectually in parts (*k*).

Under due observance of the distinction between general authority and limited powers, third parties are entitled to deal with a factor or agent as principal (*l*); either in purchasing the goods in his hands, or in taking them in pledge, or in advancing money on a consignment of them. But no one is entitled to trust a limited agent beyond the strict limits of his employment, without calling for and perusing the authority by which his powers are extended. And no sub-factor or third party is entitled to rely on possession of goods given him by the agent, as raising a lien, or resulting right of retention, for a general balance (*m*).

'A person professing to contract as agent, but having no authority or no responsible principal, or exceeding his powers, is liable to third parties, not on the contract, but on his implied undertaking that he had authority, for the loss actually sustained by reason of such third parties not having the valid contract he professed to make with them (*n*). A factor or commissioner whose factory empowers him to sue actions in his principal's affairs may sue in his own name (*o*).'

(*a*) York Buildings Co. *v.* Carnegie, 1764; M. 4054; 1 Ill. 159. Alexander *v.* Calder, 1687; M. 10,085. Young *v.* Finlay, 1716; M. 10,088. Drummond *v.* Ross, 1824; 3 S. 315. Hallilly *v.* Railton, 1830; 5 Mur. 325. Bridges *v.* Willison's Trs., 1831; 10 S. 43. Horsfall *v.* Fauntleroy, 10 B. & Cr. 755; 1 Ill. 120. See below, § 229–31. Forbes *v.* Campbell, 1845; 7 D. 1068. Duncan *v.* Clyde Trs., 1851; 13 D. 518; aff. 1853, 25 Jur. 331. See § 560, 561.

(*b*) Chapman *v.* Walton, 10 Bing. 62; 3 Ill. 106. M'Naughton *v.* Allhusen, 1847; 10 D. 236. Broadhead *v.* Yule, 1871; 9 Macph. 921. So it was held that an architect has power to employ a surveyor or measurer to measure plans and issue schedules to tradesmen. Black *v.* Cornelius, 1879; 6 R. 581.

(*c*) Gordon, 1750; Elch. *Factor*, 9; 1 Ill. 160. Brown *v.* Brown, 1779; M. 5593. Molle *v.* Riddell, Dec. 13, 1811; F. C. Thomson *v.* M'Taggart, 1823; 2 S. 320; 2 Ill. 157. Thomson *v.* Fullerton, 1842; 5 D. 379. Graves *v.* Legge, 2 H. & N. 210; 26 L. J. Ex. 316. Dingle *v.* Hare, 7 C. B. N. S. 145; 29 L. J. C. P. 144. On this principle the servant of a horse-dealer usually employed to sell horses for his master has implied power to warrant; Howard *v.* Sheward, L. R. 2 C. P. 148; 36 L. J. C. P. 42; while the servant of a private person sent on a solitary occasion to sell a horse has no such authority. Brady *v.* Todd, 9 C. B. N. S. 592; 30 L. J. C. P. 223. In such a case, however, if the master repudiate a warranty given by his servant without authority, it seems that the sale is void, and he cannot keep the price. *Per Cur.* in Brady *v.* Todd. Addison on Contr. 52 (8th ed.). An auctioneer has no implied authority to warrant goods (horses) sent to him for sale. Payne *v.* Leconfield, 51 L. J. Q. B. 642.

(*d*) Hay *v.* Gray, 1675; M. 10,083; 1 Ill. 160. O'Reilly, Hill, & Co. *v.* Jaffrey, 1821; 1 S. 60. Pease, etc., *v.* Smith, 1821; 1 S. 23. Auchie & Co. *v* Burns, 1822; 1 S. 538. M'Aulay *v.* J. & D. Fergusson, 1799; Hume, 324. Douglas *v.* Brunton's Trs., 1836; 14 S. 843. Johnston *v.* Kershaw, L. R. 2 Ex. 83; 36 L. J. Ex. 44. Ireland *v.* Livingston, 41 L. J. Q. B. 201; L. R. 5 H. L. 395.

(*e*) See below, § 229, 1314, 1317A, 1364, 1417.

(*f*) Sinclair, Moorhead, & Co. *v.* Wallace & Co., 1880; 7 R. 874. Hawtayne *v.* Bourne, 7 M. & W. 599. Ross, Skolfield, & Co. *v.* State Line Co., 1875; 3 R. 134. Woodrow & Son *v.* Wright, 1861; 24 D. 31.

(*g*) Colvin *v.* Dixon, 1867; 5 Macph. 603. Hamilton *v.* Dixon, 1873; 1 R. 72.

(*h*) Brocklesby *v.* Temperance Bdg. Soc., 1895; A. C. 173.

(*i*) Auchie & Co., *supra* (*d*). Shirreff *v.* Stein's Assignees, 1828; 4 Mur. 454 and 468; 1 Ill. 160. Stein's Assignees *v.* Shirreff, 1828; 7 S. 47. Anderson *v.* Buck, 1841; 3 D. 975. Marr *v.* Buchanan, 1852; 14 D. 467. Swinburne *v.* Western Bank, 1856; 18 D. 1025. Cropper *v.* Cook, L. R. 3 C. P. 192. See § 219 (*o*), (*p*).

(*k*) This sentence appears to refer to the rule, that the performance of an entire contract must be complete as a condition precedent to the exaction of the counterpart. See above, § 152.

(*l*) See Edmunds *v.* Bushell, L. R. 1 Q. B. 97; 35 L. J. Q. B. 20.

(*m*) M'Call & Co. *v.* Black & Co., 1824; 2 S. App. 188; 1 Ill. 161. Johnson & Manly *v.* Findlay, Duff, & Co., 1826; 4 S. 407. See Pultney *v.* Keymer, 3 Esp. 181; and Pochin *v.* Robinows & Marjoribanks, 1869; 7 Macph. 622. 1 Bell's Com. 483 (518, M'L.'s ed.). As to the effect of a mandate "to act and vote" in a sequestration in bankruptcy in making the principal liable for the expenses of litigation, see Barclay *v.* Glendronach Disty. Co., 1868; 7 Macph. 9. Cf. Buchanan *v.* Wallace, 1882; 9 R. 621.

(*n*) See 2 Smith's L. C. 382 sqq. Pollock on Contr. 103 sqq. Benjamin on Sales, 210. M'Laren's Bell's Com. i. 543. Thomson *v.* Dudgeon, 1851; 13 D. 1029. **Collen *v.* Wright**, 7 E. & B. 301; 8 *ib.* 647. Dickson *v.* Reuter's Tel. Co., 3 C. P. D. 1; 47 L. J. C. P. 1. See below, § 403H *fin.*

(*o*) Bow *v.* Cowan's Hosp., 1825; 4 S. 276. Whyte *v.* Maxwell, 1850; 12 D. 955.

226. *Remuneration.*—The mandant is bound to reimburse the mandatary of his advances (*a*); to pay the stipulated or common hire (*b*); or in absence of stipulation or usage, the *quantum meruit* (*c*); and to 'repay advances and' repair any direct damage sustained by the mandatary in the performance of the mandate (*d*).

(*a*) See Robinson *v.* Fleming & Middleton, 1859; 21 D. 1089.

(*b*) Trustees are strictly mandataries according to the principles of the gratuitous contract, and not entitled to recompense without express agreement. See below, § 1991 et seq. As to commission, see above, § 219, note (*s*).

(*c*) See Kennedy *v.* Glass, 1890; 17 R. 1085.

(*d*) 3 Ersk. 3. § 38. Duchess of Buccleugh *v.* Nairne, 1712; M. 4062; 1 Ill. 162. Smith *v.* E. Winton, 1715; *ib.* Campbell *v.* Rose, 1752; 5 B. Sup. 802. Pitcairn *v.* Anderson, 1775; M. 3161; Hailes, 650. Boyes *v.* Scott Waring, 1832; 1 S. App. 122. Stevenson *v.* Duncan, 1842; 5 D. 167. Drummond *v.* Cairns, 1852; 14 D. 611. Mackenzie *v.* Blakeney, 1879; 6 R. 1329. Risk *v.* Auld & Guild, 1881; 8 R. 729. Sutton *v.* Tatham, 10 A. & E. 27, and cases in 2 Smith's L. C. 147. See also *ib.* p. 548 sqq. Smith's Merc. Law, 133. Addison on Contr. 479.

227. Risk.—The risk of goods, etc., is with the mandant or principal, unless fault be established against the factor (*a*).

(*a*) See Hastie *v.* Campbell, 1857; 19 D. 557.

228. Recall of Mandate.—The factory or mandate, as having relation to the public as well as to the parties, may be recalled, by revocation as between the parties, if done *tempestivè*, though that may not be sufficient to affect third parties unless accompanied by notice (*a*): by death, which is revocation (*b*); but transactions begun previous to the death may go on, and those done in ignorance of the death are effectual (*c*): by renunciation, if not made *re infecta* (*d*): by appointment of a new factor or agent to do the same act (*e*): but the mandate seems to subsist notwithstanding supervening insanity (*f*), 'at least until recalled by some public act, or till parties dealing with the agent are put in bad faith by having knowledge of the principal's insanity (*g*). And an authority coupled with an interest cannot be revoked, whether it be conferred originally on a creditor (*procurator in rem suam*), or arise by reason of the agent or factor incurring liabilities to third parties in the business of the agency (*h*).'

(*a*) Borthwick, 1676; 3 B. Sup. 115; 1 Ill. 162. See below (*c*), Patten and Walker. N. of Sc. Bkg. Co. *v.* Behn, Möller, & Co., 1881; 8 R. 432.

(*b*) Ld. Duffus *v.* Forrester, 1628; M. 3166. See Scott *v.* Stewart, 1834; 7 W. & S. 211. Life Assoc. of Scotld. *v.* Douglas, 1886; 13 R. 910.

(*c*) Campbell *v.* Anderson, 1826; 5 S. 86; 3 W. & S. 384. Kennedy *v.* Kennedy, 1843; 6 D. 40. Smout *v.* Ilberry, 10 M. & W. 1. See as to England, Smart *v.* Sandars, 5 C. B. 895, 917; 16 L. J. C. P. 39. Kiddell *v.* Farnell, 26 L. J. Ch. 818. Benjamin on Sales, 75, n.

(*d*) There is in general no implied condition, even in an agency for a fixed period, that the principal shall continue to carry on his business. Rhodes *v.* Forwood, L. R. 1 App. Ca. 256; 47 L. J. Ex. 396. Engl. and Scot. Mar. Ins. Co., M'Clure's Claim, L. R. 5 Ch. 737; 39 L. J. Ch. 685. Patmore & Co. *v.* Cannon & Co., 1892; 19 R. 1004. State of California Co. *v.* Moore, 1895; 22 R. 562. Comp. Emmens *v.* Elderton, 13 C. B. 495; 4 H. L. Ca. 624. Tasker *v.* Shepherd, 6 H. & N. 575; 30 L. J. Ex. 207.

(*e*) Patten *v.* Carruthers, 1770; 2 Pat. 238. Walker *v.* Somerville, 1837; 16 S. 217.

(*f*) Pollock *v.* Paterson, Dec. 10, 1711; F. C. Wink *v.* Mortimer, 1849; 11 D. 995. Ivory's Ersk. Inst. i. note, 244. 2 Kent's Com. 645. See below, § 376. As to the effect of bankruptcy, see M'Laren's Bell's Com. i. 525. Bell on Compl. Title, 89. Broughton *v.* Stewart, Primrose, & Co., Dec. 17, 1814; F. C.

(*g*) 1 Bell's Com. 489 (525, M'L.'s ed.). Drew *v.* Nunn, 4 Q. B. D. 661; 48 L. J. Q. B. 591. Pothier, Obl. 1. 1. 5, 81. Story, Agency, § 481. Smout *v.* Ilberry, *cit.* (*c*). 2 Smith's L. C. 381, 490.

(*h*) Broughton *v.* Stewart, Primrose, & Co., *cit. Infra*, § 229, 1459. Yates *v.* Hoppe, 9 C. B. 541. M'Ewan *v.* Woods, 11 Q. B. 13; 17 L. J. Q. B. 207. Gaussen *v.* Morton, 10 B. & C. 731. Clerk *v.* Lawrie, 2 H. &. N. 200.

229. Institorial Power is an implied mandate raised by acquiescence, or common usage, in several situations.

(1.) *Consignment.*—It is a frequent arrangement in trade to consign goods to a likely market, getting perhaps an advance of money on them, or being allowed to draw bills on the faith of the consignment. A mandate is implied empowering the consignee to sell the goods at the price and time most expedient in his judgment (*a*); and if the consignee have made or got advances on the goods, or accepted bills, his mandate to sell is held to subsist and to be assignable till he is reimbursed or relieved (*b*). This rests on common law in Scotland; but in England a factor has such power only by Act of Parliament (*c*). 'There is a tendency to confuse the relation of agent and principal when it takes this form with that of buyer and seller. When the agent is bound to pay to the principal at a price fixed beforehand without reference to the price at which he sells, being at liberty to sell at any price and take payment in any form or at any time he himself may fix, his real position is that of buyer and not agent, and the principal has no right to the specific proceeds of the agent's sales, but is merely a creditor for the original price (*d*).'

(*a*) O'Reilly, Hill, & Co. *v.* Jaffray, 1821; 1 S. 60; 1 Ill. 160. Ure & Miller *v.* Jaffray, Jan. 31, 1818; F. C.; 1 Bell's Com. 478 (509, M'L.'s ed.); 1 Ill. 163. Smart *v.* Sandars, 3 C. B. 380; 5 C. B. 895.

(*b*) Broughton *v.* Stewart & Co., Dec. 17, 1814; F. C.; 1 Ill. 163. Gillies *v.* M'Kay, 1828; 6 S. 939.

(*c*) 4 Geo. IV. c. 83, as amended by 6 Geo. IV. c. 94. See above, § 225; and 52 and 53 Vict. c. 45, § 7. As to the Factors Acts, see *infra*, § 1317A, 1317B, 1364, 1417, 1450.

(*d*) *Ex p.* White, *in re* Nevill, L. R. 6 Ch. App. 397; 40 L. J. Bkr. 73; aff. in H. L. 21 W. R. 465. See § 109 as to Sale and Return.

230. (2.) *Procuration.*—When acts of management have been recognised by the principal (as in the drawing and indorsing of bills by a clerk, or in receipts by clerks for shop accounts), a mandate authorising the person whose acts are so recognised is implied (*a*).

(*a*) Davidson *v.* Robertson, 1815; 3 Dow, 218; 1 Ill. 163. Bayley on Bills, 316. Thomson on Bills, 220. Murray *v.* Campbell, 1827; 6 S. 147. See below, § 321; and M'Laren's Bell's Com. i. 512.

231. (3.) *Institor.*—When one places another at the head of an establishment, he is held to bind himself by the dealings of such substitute 'within the lawful and ordinary course of business'; and the person who has the management of a shop 'or business' has a presumed general authority to bind his principal by his proper acts of administration as shopkeeper 'or manager' (*a*). 'But the largest powers of a general manager, even when he has power to accept bills and open a bank account, do not *imply* the power of borrowing money on the principal's credit (*b*).'

(4.) *Præpositura.*—A wife is *præposita negotiis domesticis*; or authorised to bind her husband in any trade, etc., which she superintends with his acquiescence (*c*). And a similar authority is held to be given to the person placed at the head or in management of the domestic establishment (*d*).

(5.) *Exercitor.*—One in the command of a ship has an implied power to bind his principal (*e*).

(6.) *Bank Agent.*—Institorial power as applied to banks has raised many questions; with regard to which distinctions seem admissible between the managers and officers at the proper domicile of the bank, and agents or branch establishments at a distance. In the former case, the public is entitled to trust to the full unlimited institorial power in dealing with any officer placed in the apparent trust of receiving money; in the latter, the agent or manager has certain general powers, but which are to be admitted with great caution, and rather to be taken as a limited agency, regulated by the terms of his appointment,—the principal being liable only for acts done by the agent in the proper character of agent (*f*).

(*a*) 1 Stair, 12. § 16. 3 Ersk. 3. § 46. Bruce & Co. *v.* Beat, 1765; M. 4056; 1 Ill. 164. Wilson *v.* Deans, 1675; M. 6021. Anderson *v.* Sanderson, 2 Starkie, 205; 19 R. R. 703. See as to Commercial Travellers, Milne *v.* Harris, James, & Co., 1803; M. 8493. Telford *v.* James, Wood, & James, 1824; 2 S. App. 24; above, § 219 (6). Finlayson *v.* Braidbar Quarry Co., 1864; 2 Macph. 1297. Montgomery *v.* N. B. Ry. Co., 1878; 5 R. 796. Woodrow & Son *v.* Wright, 1861; 24 D. 31. Fraser, M. & S. 252 sq., 258. Morrison *v.* Statter, 1885; 12 R. 1152 (head shepherd on led farm—buying sheep not within general mandate).

(*b*) Hawtayne *v.* Bourne, 7 M. & W. 595. Sinclair, Moorhead, & Co. *v.* Wallace & Co., 1880; 7 R. 874. (As to this case, see note in Smith's Merc. Law, p. 143, 10th ed.) Cf. Ross, Skolfield, & Co. *v.* State Line Co. (*f*). Cf. Woodrow & Son, *cit.*

(*c*) 1 Ersk. Pr. 6. § 15; Inst. § 20. Buchanan *v.* Dickie, 1828; 6 S. 986; 1 Ill. 163. But see Purves *v.* Smith, 1628; M. 4049. See below, § 1566.

(*d*) Hamilton *v.* Forrester, 1825; 3 S. 572. See Mortimer *v.* Hamilton, 1868; 7 Macph. 158.

(*e*) 1 Stair, 12. § 18. 3 Ersk. 3. § 43. Abbott on Shipping, 100. Lindsay & Allan *v.* Campbell, 1800; M. *Mandate*, Apx. 2. See below, § 450.

(*f*) Paisley Bank *v.* Gillon, 1798; 1 Ill. 164. Watson *v.* Bank of Scotland, 1806; M. *Mandate*, Apx. 3; 1 Dow, 40; 5 Pat. 655. Normand *v.* Comml. Bank, 1823; 2 S. 482. Craw *v.* Comml. Bank, 1840; 3 D. 193. Chanter *v.* Borthwick, 1848; 10 D. 1544. Natl. Bank *v.* Martin, 1848; 11 D. 1. Ross, Skolfield, & Co. *v.* State Line Co., 1875; 3 R. 134 (power of manager of shipping co. to draw bills on sub-agent in anticipation of freight). Bank of Upper Canada *v.* Bradshaw, L. R. 1 P. C. 479; 4 Moo. P. C. N. S. 406. Cherry *v.* Colon. Bk. of Austral., L. R. 3 P. C. 24; 38 L. J. P. C. 49. Swift *v.* Jewsbury, L. R. 9 Q. B. 301; 43 L. J. Q. B. 56. Mackay *v.* Comml. Bank of N. Brunswick, L. R. 5 P. C. 394; 43 L. J. P. C. 31. Bank of N. S. Wales *v.* Owston, 4 App. Ca. 270; 48 L. J. P. C. 25 (malicious prosecution).

CHAPTER VII

RESPONSIBILITY FOR NEGLECT

232. Doctrine of Risk in Culpa. — The general rule respecting Risk in the contracts already explained (with the exception of Sale 'according to the common law of Scotland') is, "Res perit domino" (*a*). In Sale, on the principles already explained, the risk is with the buyer; in location, with the lessor; in commodate, with the lender; in pledge, with the debtor; and in mandate, with the employer. But this doctrine of risk applies to the case of *accidental* loss only,—not to that in which there is a *fault*, either actual or presumed. Where there is fault, the great rule is, that he by whose fault or neglect the loss has arisen is liable for the consequences. The proper method of applying this practically is by the verdict of a jury; but lawyers (especially where jury trial has not prevailed) have endeavoured to frame a set of artificial rules for measuring due diligence and care. These attempts have reference to the several degrees of reliance which, in the several contracts, it is necessary or convenient that parties should repose in each other's diligence in the performance of their part. And the principles on which this depends resolve into the two doctrines of—1. Diligence prestable in the ordinary course of contracts; and 2. The peculiar responsibility of common carriers.

(*a*) See 3 Ersk. Pr. 1. § 8. 3 Ersk. 1. § 24. 1 Bell's Com. 435 sqq. Jones on Bailments. Pothier, Apx. to Tr. des Oblig. Story on Bailments, 9 et seq. 2 Kent, 559 et seq. 6 Toullier, 239. Thomasius, de usu practico doctrinæ de culparum prestatione in contractibus, tom. ii. p. 1006. See above, § 87, 153, 198, 204, 227.

233. In order to settle a scale by which to regulate the degree of care or diligence to be observed in the several contracts, and to which lawyers might in their reasonings refer, two extreme points have been fixed, with a middle point or average: the one extreme is the vigilance of a miser, or at least of a very prudent and careful man; the other, the prodigality of a spendthrift, amounting to folly in one's own affairs, and approximating to fraud in the management of another man's concerns; the middle point is the ordinary diligence of a man of ordinary prudence. Neglect of the middle or average care and attention is called "*culpa levis*"; the want of extreme vigilance is called "*culpa levissima*"; the want of that care which even careless and prodigal persons observe in their own affairs, is called "*culpa lata, dolo proxima*" (*a*).

'But the classification of negligence into three degrees is now discredited and disused, and even that of negligence and gross negligence has been questioned. Negligence is in all cases a jury question, to be decided according to the circumstances; for in different cases there are different degrees of responsibility for negligence varying according to the kind and extent of the duty neglected; *e.g.* according as an agent acts gratuitously or not, or in the cases mentioned in the next paragraph (*b*).'

(*a*) Story on Bailments, § 11 to 24.
(*b*) See below, § 234, note (*d*). Mackintosh *v.* Mackintosh, 1864; 2 Macph. 1357. Grill *v.* Gen. Screw Collier Co., 35 L. J. C.P. 321; 37 L.J.C.P. 205; L.R. 3 C.P. 476. Giblin *v.* M'Mullen, 38 L.J.P.C. 25; L.R. 2 P.C. 317. 1 Smith's L.C. 186, 189.

234. Rules of Liability.—The general rules for applying the scale are these:—

(1.) *Culpa Lata.*—In contracts beneficial only to the owner (as deposit and gratuitous mandate), the possessor of the property is bound to good faith, and liable for *culpa lata* only. But this must of course be much regulated by circumstances, since what in some cases and with some persons may be held an innocent omission, and no other than what was to be expected, will in other circumstances and with other persons be gross and faulty neglect (*a*). This obligation to care may be enlarged, by officiousness in undertaking the trust; or, practically, where the public is entitled to rely on the skill of a professional or official person (*b*).

(2.) *Culpa Levis.*—In contracts reciprocally beneficial, the care of a man of ordinary prudence is required: so *culpa levis* will ground responsibility as against the hirer in location; the creditor in pledge; the mandatary or agent in factory; and the partners in society (*c*).

(3.) *Culpa Levissima.*—In contracts beneficial only to him who has the possession (as commodate), vigilance is required; and the possessor is liable for slight neglect, or *culpa levissima* (*d*).

(4.) *Fraud, etc.*—The regular rule of responsibility is altered by fraud, which at all times grounds responsibility; by forcible or faulty withholding of possession; and by public policy, in the cases included under the next section.

(*a*) Story, § 62, 80, 173, 215, etc.

(*b*) Shiells *v.* Blackburn, 1 H. Blackst. 158; 1 Ill. 166; 2 R. R. 750. Wilkinson *v.* Coverdale, 1 Esp. 74. Smith *v.* Lascelles, 2 T. R. 187; 1 R. R. 457. See Story, *supra.* 2 Kent, Com. 539. See above, § 153, 154. Wilson *v.* Brett, 11 M. & W. 113.

(*c*) Story, § 173, 397, 443, etc. 1 Bell's Com. 459, etc. Clydesdale Bank *v.* Beatson, 1882; 10 R. 88 (loss of notes by bank-teller).

(*d*) Story, § 237. These general rules, though long established, are not very precise; and indeed, *à priori*, it is scarcely possible to fix a criterion or rule of care. The general direction in point of law already alluded to (§ 232), with the verdict of a jury on the particular circumstances of each case, will best determine questions of this sort.

235. Responsibility of Carriers, etc. (*a*).—The ordinary rule of responsibility under the obligations of the contract, is enlarged in certain cases supposed to be peculiarly exposed to the dangers of collusion and carelessness. The rule is, that common carriers, innkeepers, and stablers are responsible for the loss of things committed to their charge, although no neglect can be proved, if such loss do not arise from natural and inevitable accident, the act of God or of the king's enemies. This policy was established in Rome by the Prætor's edict. It has been adopted by most of the nations of modern Europe who have recognised the Roman law. In England it has been referred to the custom of the realm. The object is safety to employers on occasions in which the danger of collusion and fraudulent association is imminent: and to this end, a presumption has been introduced, that fraud or negligence has occasioned the loss; to which the only admissible answer is evidence that the loss has proceeded from an act of God or of the king's enemies (*b*).

'But this extraordinary responsibility ceases when the carrier has fulfilled his duty by conveying the goods to the place directed, and offering them, if a carrier by land, to the proper person. If the consignee does not exist, or cannot be found, or refuses or delays to receive the goods, the carrier becomes an ordinary depositary or warehouseman, bound only to exercise due care, and to deliver the goods to the consignor on being paid his ordinary charges (*c*), including his reasonable expenses incurred for preservation of the goods after the termination of the transit (*d*). Neither does it exist to the full extent if the goods carried are not placed in the exclusive custody and control of the carrier, *e.g.* if a railway passenger chooses to have his luggage in the carriage in which he travels, in which case the company is not answerable for loss or injury to which the passenger's own negligence has contributed (*e*). After the transit has ceased, the carrier's liability continues for such time as may be reasonable and usual for allowing the consignee to take possession of the goods (*f*); after which he has only the responsibility of a warehouseman (*g*). In haulage contracts (*e.g.* where a railway company carries a merchant's goods in his own waggons) it seems that the company is a common carrier of the goods (coals), and in returning empty waggons to the pit is liable for the same care as in a contract of location (*h*).'

(*a*) See above, § 157 et seq.

(*b*) Dig. lib. 4. tit. 9; Nautæ, Caupones, Stabularii. 1

Domat, 16. § 1. 1 Stair, 13. § 3. 3 Ersk. 1. § 28. Jones on Bailments, 103 et seq. Forward *v.* Pittard, 1 T. R. 27; 1 Ill. 170; 1 R. R. 142. Story, § 462, 571. 2 Kent, 592, 598. Bourne *v.* Gatliffe, 8 Scott, N. R. 604; 11 C. & F. 45. Bristol, etc., Ry. Co. *v.* Collins, 7 H. of L. Ca. 194; 29 L. J. Ex. 41. Oakley *v.* Portsmouth Ry. Co., 11 Ex. 618; 25 L. J. Ex. 99. Briddon *v.* G. N. Ry. Co., 28 L. J. Ex. 51. Williamson *v.* White, June 21, 1810; F. C. M'Pherson *v.* Christie, 1841; 3 D. 930. Denholm *v.* London & Edinburgh Shipping Co., 1865; 37 Jur. 421. Finlay *v.* N. B. Ry. Co., 1870; 8 Macph. 959.

(*c*) *Supra*, § 155, 168. Heugh *v.* L. & N.-W. Ry. Co., 39 L. J. Ex. 48; L. R. 5 Ex. 51. Metcalfe *v.* L. & B. Ry. Co., 4 C. B. N. S. 318; 38 L. J. C. P. 385. Mitchell *v.* L. & Y. Ry. Co., 44 L. J. Q. B. 107; L. R. 10 Q. B. 256. Chapman *v.* G. W. Ry. Co., 5 Q. B. D. 278; 49 L. J. Q. B. 420 (goods left till called for). M'Kean *v.* M'Ivor, 40 L. J. Ex. 30; L. R. 6 Ex. 36.

(*d*) G. N. Ry. Co. *v.* Swaffield, 43 L. J. Ex. 89; L. R. 9 Ex. 132.

(*e*) Bunch *v.* G. W. Ry. Co., 13 App. Ca. 31; aff'g. 17 Q. B. D. 215, and disapproving Bergheim *v.* G. E. Ry. Co., 3 C. P. D. 318; 40 L. J. Q. B. 318. Talley *v.* G. W. Ry. Co., L. R. 6 C. P. 40; 40 L. J. C. P. 9. Comp. § 236 (*i*). In general, carriers of passengers are liable during the transit as common carriers for their luggage. G. W. Ry. Co. *v.* Goodman, 12 C. B. 313; 21 L. J. C. P. 197. Williams *v.* G. W. Ry. Co., 10 Ex. 15. Campbell *v.* Cal. Ry. Co., 1852; 14 D. 806. Cohen *v.* S.-E. Ry. Co., 2 Ex. D. 253; 46 L. J. Ex. 617.

(*f*) Hyde *v.* Trent Nav. Co., 5 T. R. 389; 2 R. R. 620. Shepherd *v.* Br. & Ex. Ry. Co., 37 L. J. Ex. 113; L. R. 3 Ex. 189. Patscheider *v.* G. W. Ry. Co., 3 Ex. D. 153.

(*g*) Cairns *v.* Robins, 8 M. & W. 258. Heugh, *cit.* (*c*). As to shipowners, see § 408 *fin.*

(*h*) Barr *v.* Cal. Ry. Co., 1890; 18 R. 139. Watson *v.* N. B. Ry. Co., 1876; 3 R. 637. But the latter case does not warrant the distinction.

236. Persons subject to the Rule.—All persons are subject to the rule, who, in the capacity of Carriers, Innkeepers, or Stablers, hold themselves out to the public generally as trustworthy in those employments, and undertake all its responsibilities for hire (*a*).

(1.) *Public Carriers* by water, or masters and owners of merchant ships employed in transporting goods generally for hire; smacks; passage-boats; canal-boats; steam-packets; barges; ferry-boats; lighters; are within this description (*b*). So are

(2.) *Land Carriers.*—Waggoners, carriers, mail and stage coach owners, canal and railway carriers (*c*), taking a price for carriage; carters and porters who offer themselves for hire to carry goods from one part of a city to another (*d*). Hackney coachmen are not within the rule, unless when employed as carriers and paid for carriage (*e*).

(3.) *Wharfingers* have sometimes been said to be under the rule, almost in the character of carriers; but this does not seem to be settled. Wharfingers and warehousemen are on the same footing; and unless where (as sometimes happens) the wharfinger or warehouseman combines the character of carrier or lighterman, his liability seems to be only under the contract (*f*).

(4.) *Innkeepers, Vintners, and Stablers* are also liable for things placed under their charge or that of their servants, or brought by guests or employers (*g*) within the house or premises (*h*). But to this there is an exception, where the guest undertakes specially the care of his own effects (*i*); which will not, however, be inferred from merely locking up the articles for greater security (*k*). 'An innkeeper's liability is limited to £30 for any kind of traveller's property, not being a horse or other live animal, or its gear, or any carriage, except where the injury has arisen from the wilful act or neglect of him or his servants, and except the thing have been deposited expressly for safe custody, provided always he print and display conspicuously in the hall or entry to his inn the terms of the Act introducing this limitation (*l*).'

Where persons are not properly innkeepers, but letters of lodgings, they seem not to be within the rule; though the question is not settled (*m*).

(5.) *Post Office.*—In the great carrying establishment of the post office, instead of the policy of this law, penal statutes have been enacted to enforce and secure vigilance in the officers employed (*n*). But although the Postmaster-General and the establishment are not liable, postmasters who carry on the details of this business are bound by all the liabilities of their contract (*o*).

(*a*) 3 Ersk. 1. § 20, with Ivory's notes. Jones on Bailments, 106. Story, § 495. 2 Kent, Com. 598. Morse *v.* Slue, 1 Vent. Rep. 190, 238. See 17 and 18 Vict. c. 31; 8 and 9 Vict. c. 33, § 82. *Supra*, § 160A, note.

(*b*) Erskine, Jones, and Story, *ut sup.* Bain *v.* Sinclair, 1825; 3 S. 533; 1 Ill. 134. Coggs *v.* Bernard, 2 Ld. Raym. 917; 1 Ill. 166; 1 Smith's L. C. 177. Hyde *v.* Trent and Mersey Nav. Co., 5 T. R. 389; 1 Ill. 143; 2 R. R. 620. As to lightermen, see Liver Alkali Co. *v.* Johnson, L. R. 7 Ex. 267; 41 L. J. Ex. 110, as considered in Scaife *v.* Tarrant, L. R. 10 Ex. 358; 44 L. J. Ex. 235; and **Nugent *v.* Smith,** 1 C. P. D. 423; 45 J. 697; and Maclachlan on Shipping, 115 sq. Shipowners and similar carriers are said to be under this rule or custom, though they may not be "common" carriers as defined above, § 159, 160, in the sense of being obliged to carry for the first comer. Liver Alkali Co., and other cases cited above. See § 436.

(*c*) Campbell *v.* Cal. Ry. Co., 1852; 14 D. 806. See 8 and 9 Vict. c. 33, § 86, 89. 17 and 18 Vict. c. 31. 26 and 27 Vict. c. 92, § 30. 31 and 32 Vict. c. 119, § 14 sqq. See above, § 160A, 170, etc.

(*d*) Jones on Bailments, 104–6. Ewing *v.* Millar, 1687; M. 9235; 1 Ill. 166. Manners *v.* Stewart 1769 · M. 9245.

Middleton *v.* Fowler, 4 Salk. 282. Forward *v.* Pittard, *cit.* § 235. Clarke *v.* Grey, 4 Esp. 117. 1 Selwyn, *Nisi Prius*, 348. Harris *v.* Packwood, 3 Taunt. 264; 15 R. R. 755. Story on Bailments, § 496. 2 Kent, 598.

(*e*) Upshore *v.* Aidee, Comyn's Rep. 25; 1 Ill. 167. 1 Selwyn, N. P. 347. Jeremy, Law of Carriers, 13. Ross *v.* Hill, 2 C. B. 877; 15 L. J. C. P. 182. Powles *v.* Hider, 6 E. & B. 207. Brind *v.* Dale, 2 M. & Rob. 80. See as to furniture removers, Scaife *v.* Tarrant, *infra*, § 244 (*p*). Pearcey *v.* Player, 1883; 10 R. 564.

(*f*) Ross *v.* Johnson, 5 Bur. 2825; 1 Bell's Com. 467. Sideways *v.* Todd, 2 Starkie, 400; 20 R. R. 703. Garside *v.* Trent and Mersey Nav. Co., 4 T. R. 581; 1 Ill. 122; 2 R. R. 468. *In re* Webb, 8 Taunt. 443; 20 R. R. 520.

(*g*) See Bennett *v.* Mellor, and Medawar *v.* Grand Hotel, *cit. infra.* 1 Bell, Com. 469.

(*h*) 3 Ersk. 1 § 29. White *v.* Crockett, 1661; M. 9233; 2 B. Sup. 294; 1 Ill. 167. Forbes *v.* Steel, 1687; M. 9233. Chisholm *v.* Farlane, 1714; M. 9241; 4 B. Sup. 906. Hay *v.* Wordsworth, 1801; M. *Nautæ*, etc., Apx. 1. Williamson *v.* White, June 1, 1810; F. C. Meikle *v.* Skelly, Feb. 16, 1813; F. C. Hagart *v.* Inglis, 1832; 10 S. 506; 1 Ill. 132. Calye's Case, 8 Coke, 32; 1 Smith's L. C. 131; 115, 10th ed. York *v.* Grindstone, 1 Salk. 388. Thomson *v.* Lacy, 3 B. & Ald. 283; 22 R. R. 385. Bennett *v.* Mellor, 5 T. R. 273; 2 R. R. 593. Laing *v.* Darling, 1850; 12 D. 1279.

(*i*) See Gordon *v.* Murray, 1700; M. 9237. Hay *v.* Williamson, 1704; M. 9238. Farnworth *v.* Packwood, 1 Starkie, 249. Burgess *v.* Clements, 4 M. & S. 306; 16 R. R. 473; Kent *v.* Shuckard, 2 B. & Ad. 803. Richmond *v.* Smith, 8 B. & Cr. 9; 32 R. R. 326. Jones *v.* Taylor, 1 Ad. & Ell. 522. Negligence of the guest relieves the innkeeper. M'Pherson *v.* Christie, 1841; 3 D. 930. Armisted *v.* Fuller, 17 Q. B. 261. Cashill *v.* Wright, 6 E. & B. 891. Oppenheim *v.* White Lion Hotel Co., L. R. 5 C. P. 515; 40 L. J. C. P. 231. Morgan *v.* Ravey, 6 H. & N. 265. Medawar (*l*). Comp. § 235 (*e*).

(*k*) 1 Stair, 13. § 3.

(*l*) 26 and 27 Vict. c. 41. Spice *v.* Bacon, 46 L. J. Ex. 713; L. R. 2 Ex. D. 463. Medawar *v.* Grand Hotel Co., 1891; 2 Q. B. 11.

(*m*) May *v.* Wingate, 1694; M. 9236; 1 Ill. 168. Leslie *v.* Richardson, 1700; 4 B. Sup. 494. Watling *v.* M'Dowall, 1825; 4 S. 86. See Scott *v.* Yates, 1800; Hume, 207. Holder *v.* Soulby, 8 C. B. N. S. 254; 29 L. J. C. P. 246. Dansey *v.* Richardson, 3 E. & B. 144; 23 L. J. Q. B. 223.

(*n*) 12 Ch. II. c. 35. 1 Vict. c. 32, 33, 34. Whitefield *v.* Despenser, Cowp. 754. Farries *v.* Elder, 1799; M. 10,103; 1 Ill. 169. Ivory's Erskine, p. 601, note. 31 and 32 Vict. c. 110; 32 and 33 Vict. c. 73; 33 and 34 Vict. c. 38, as to Telegraphs.

(*o*) Story on Bailments, 461. 2 Kent, Com. 610.

237. Extent and Proof of Liability.—The rule is, that persons thus responsible must restore the thing in the same condition in which it was received, barring inevitable accident (*a*); and that they will be liable for damage by total or by temporary loss (*b*).

(*a*) 1 Stair, 13. § 3. 3 Ersk. 1. § 28. 1 Bankt. p. 379, § 1. 1 Selwyn, N. P. 345. Jones on Bailments, 104. The author seems to use the terms "inevitable accident," and "pure accident," 1 Bell's Com. 579, comp. 470, 559 (625, 499, 606, M'L.'s ed.), as equivalent to "act of God." This exception is thus defined by James, L. J.: "A common carrier is not liable for any accident as to which he can show that it was due to natural causes, directly and exclusively, without human intervention, and that it could not have been prevented by any amount of foresight, pains, and care reasonably to be expected from him." **Nugent *v.* Smith,** 45 L. J. C. P. 19, 697; 1 Q. B. D. 423, in which case, and in Nitro-Phosphate Co. *v.* St. Katherine's Dock Co., L. R. 9 Ch. D. 503; 39 L. T. 433, the definition is much discussed. See Nicholls *v.* Marsland, 2 Ex. D. 1; 46 L. J. Ex. 174. The Merchant Prince, 1892; Prob. 9, 179 (collision of ships—onus); above, § 167. The exception covers inherent defect or vice in the thing carried. Cases in § 167, 168.

(*b*) Ogilvie *v.* Taylor, 1828; 6 S. 691; 1 Ill. 169. Millen *v.* Brash, 51 L. J. Q. B. 167.

238. (1.) *Robbery and Theft.* — Neither Robbery nor Theft is in Scotland held to be inevitable accident (*a*). The great object of the policy of the rule is to guard against the collusion to which employers are thus exposed; and the presumption is, that co-operation, not mischance, has led to the loss (*b*). And yet in one case, where there was no room for suspicion, 'theft by housebreaking' was held a good defence (*c*). 'Owners of seagoing ships are not liable for loss or damage, without their actual privity, to gold, silver, diamonds, watches, jewels, or precious stones, by robbery, embezzlement, making away with or secreting thereof, unless the true value is inserted in bills of lading or otherwise declared in writing (*d*).'

(*a*) In England and in America the carrier or innkeeper is regarded as an insurer. See 1 Bell, Com. 469.

(*b*) Forbes *v.* Steel, 1687; M. 9233; 1 Ill. 167. Chisholm *v.* Farlane, 1714; M. 9241; 4 B. Sup. 906. Gordon *v.* Murray, 1700; M. 9237. Brouster *v.* Lees, 1707; M. 9239.

(*c*) Watling *v.* M'Dowall, 1825; 4 S. 83. The text had "robbery."

(*d*) 17 and 18 Vict. c. 104, § 503. Williams *v.* African St. S. Co., 1 H. & N. 300; 26 L. J. Ex. 69. Gibbs *v.* Potter, 10 M. & W. 70. The previous provision in 26 Geo. III. c. 86 was repealed by 17 and 18 Vict. c. 120.

239. (2.) *Fire* 'was,' in Scotland, held an inevitable accident in the sense of the law, so as to free the carrier or innkeeper from responsibility, unless where fraud or collusion 'could' be shown (*a*). 'But by the Mercantile Law Amendment Act carriers for hire of goods within Scotland are liable to make good to the owners all losses arising from accidental fire, while such goods are in their custody or possession (*b*). Owners of seagoing ships are by statute not liable to make good loss arising without their actual fault or privity to goods on board their ships by reason of any fire happening on board such ships (*c*).'

(*a*) M'Donnel *v.* Ettles, Dec. 15, 1809; F. C.; 1 Ill. 170; Ivory's Ersk. p. 600, note; p. 674, Nicolson's ed. It was otherwise in England and in America. Forward *v.* Pittard, 1 T. Rep. 27; 1 Ill. 170; 1 R. R. 142. Hyde *v.* Trent and Mersey Nav. Co., 5 T. Rep. 389; 1 Ill. 143; 2 R. R. 620.

(*b*) 19 and 20 Vict. c. 60, § 17.

(*c*) 57 and 58 Vict. c. 60, § 502. See Hunter *v.* M'Ewan (or M'Gown), May 16, 1811; F. C.; rev. 1819, 1 Bligh, 573; 6 Pat. 460. Moorewood *v.* Pollock, 1 E. & B.

743; 22 L. J. Q. B. 250. This came in lieu of a like enactment in 26 Geo. III. c. 86, repealed by 17 and 18 Vict. c. 120. It applies only to the shipowner's liability as carrier, and does not relieve him from contributing in general average when goods are injured by reason of fire on board. Schmidt *v.* R. M. Steamship Co., 45 L. J. Q. B. 646.

240. (3.) *Servants.*—Fraud and negligence of servants are no excuse. Servants are identified with their master, and the policy of the law is to protect against them, and all possibility of collusion (*a*). But the goods must be delivered to servants regularly, and so as to charge the master (*b*).

(*a*) 1 Stair, 13. § 3. Garnet *v.* Willan, 5 Barn. & Ald. 53; 1 Ill. 140; 24 R. R. 276. See § 244 (*x*); and above, § 162. 1 Will. IV. c. 68, § 5, 8. See as to ships, 57 and 58 Vict. c. 60, § 503; and comp. M'Donnel, *cit.* § 239 (*a*).

(*b*) Howey & Co. *v.* Lovell, 1826; 4 S. 752; 1 Ill. 134.

241. (4.) *Perils of the Sea* excuse only when unavoidable, as rocks, sandbanks, or collision by force of the winds. They furnish no defence if the ship or goods be exposed to danger by unskilfulness 'or negligence (*a*) in navigating or managing the carrying ship (*b*),' or by deviation from the proper course of the voyage (*c*). 'Damage directly done to the cargo by rats is not within the exception of sea perils; and the shipowner is responsible for it under the ordinary terms of the contract, that risk not being peculiar to the sea (*d*). But he will not (it seems) be liable if he has used every effort to extirpate or exclude them (*e*). And if rats gnaw a hole by which sea-water gets in and damages the cargo, that is within the exemption, the sea being the immediate cause of the loss (*f*).'

(*a*) As to the onus shifting where damage is alleged to be due to severe weather, see Williams *v.* Dobbie, 1884; 11 R. 982.

(*b*) In Woodley *v.* Michell, 11 Q. B. D. 47, it was held that a collision caused by fault of *either* of the colliding ships was not within the excepting clause in a bill of lading; but that was corrected by Wilson, Sons, & Co. *v.* Owners of Cargo *per* Xantho, 12 App. Ca. 503. Comp. Sailing Ship Garston Co. *v.* Hickie & Co., 18 Q. B. D. 17.

(*c*) Trent and Mersey Navig. Co. *v.* Wood, 4 Doug. 287; Abbott, 329, 337; 1 Ill. 170. Buller *v.* Fisher, 3 Esp. 67; 4 R. R. 902. Smith *v.* Scott, 4 Taunt. 126; 13 R. R. 568. Lloyd *v.* G. Iron Screw Collier Co., 3 H. & C. 284; 33 L. J. Ex. 269. Grill *v.* G. Iron Screw Collier Co., L. R. 1 C. P. 600; 3 *ib.* 476; 35 L. J. C. P. 321; 37 *ib.* 205; *infra*, § 408, 425, 435. As to rivers, see Angell on Carriers, 168; Parsons on Shipping, i. 253 sq.

(*d*) Dale *v.* Hall, 1 Wils. 281. Laveroni *v.* Drury, 8 Ex. 166; 22 L. J. Ex. 2. Hunter *v.* Potts, 4 Camp. 203; 2 R. R. 353. Kay *v.* Wheeler, L. R. 2 C. P. 302; 37 L. J. C. P. 180.

(*e*) Hamilton, Fraser, & Co. *v.* Pandorf & Co., 12 App. Ca. 518.

(*f*) Hamilton, Fraser, & Co., *cit.*

242. (5.) *Proof.*—The value, which in our old law was ascertained by oath *in litem* alone, is now to be investigated by all fair sources of evidence (*a*).

(*a*) Brouster *v.* Lees, 1707; M. 9239; 1 Ill. 170. M'Ausland *v.* Dick, 1787; M. 9246. Williamson *v.* White, June 21, 1810; F. C.; 1 Ill. 167. But see Scott *v.* Gillespie, 1827; 5 S. 669. Gowans *v.* Thomson, 1844; 6 D. 606. Crawcour *v.* St. George Steampacket Co., 1842; 5 D. 10. Campbell *v.* Cal. Ry. Co., 1852; 24 Jur. 455; 1 Stu. 742.

242A. '(6.) *The Measure of Damages* is the market price of the goods at the port of delivery, apart from any circumstances peculiar to the plaintiff, or accidental as between him and the carrier, *e.g.* a sale by the plaintiff before arrival (*a*).'

(*a*) G. W. Ry. Co. *v.* Redmayne, L. R. 1 C. P. 329. Rodocanachi *v.* Milburn, 18 Q. B. D. 67. The Parana, 1 P. D. 452; 45 L. J. P. D. & A. 108; rev. 2 P. D. 118. See above, § 33, 164 (*b*).

243. Limitation of Responsibility.—The responsibility established on principles of public policy, only formerly limited by contract, is limited now by legislative enactment (*a*).

(*a*) See below, § 436.

244. The responsibility for carriage was formerly limited by special contract, either express; or implied, from notice, and the requiring of an additional payment to compensate greater risk. This had to a certain extent been admitted as effectual, on the principle of implied assent, not of mere notice; in which respect the Scottish rule was more correct than the English (*a*). But the various and difficult questions which arose on the construction of notices, and on the evidence of their being communicated to the parties, led to legislative regulation 'limiting responsibility in certain cases.'

The responsibility of mail-contractors, stage-coach proprietors, or other common carriers by land, is (*b*) limited as to gold or silver coin, or gold or silver manufactured or unmanufactured, watches, clocks, trinkets, jewellery, bank-notes 'of any bank in England, Scotland, or Ireland, bills, cheques,' deeds, 'engravings, china, furs, glass (*c*), lace (*d*), maps, orders, or securities for payment of money, paintings (*e*), pictures (*e*), plate or plated articles, silks (*f*), manufactured or not, and whether or not wrought up with other articles; stamps, precious stones,' etc., 'contained in any parcel or package (*g*),' whether delivered for carriage on hire or accompanying passengers, when beyond the vale of £10; unless the description and value be declared (*h*), and an increased charge paid, 'if demanded (*i*),' at the commencement of the carriage (*k*). In such cases the carrier may charge an additional sum, according to a table to be affixed in his office, which shall be sufficient notice (*l*), 'to all persons sending such goods, without further proof of its having come to their knowledge (*m*)'; but he is bound to give a receipt if required (*n*). They cannot limit their responsibility for other articles by any notice (*o*); but special contracts are not affected by the Act (*p*). 'Special contracts, however, exempting common carriers from all responsibility even for their own misconduct, though formerly held invalid (*q*), were maintained in later cases not within the Railway Traffic Act (*r*). The liability of common carriers for goods extends to passengers' luggage, even when carried with the passenger in the carriage (*s*), and so the Act applies to such luggage, and a declaration must be made, and extra charge paid in order to fix liability for value above £10 (*t*). The Act protects carriers even when goods are negligently carried beyond their destination (*u*). It protects from liability for loss (*v*), even when occasioned by the gross negligence of the carrier's servants (*w*), but not for loss by their felonious acts or delicts (*x*).'

(*a*) Whitehead *v.* Straiton, 1667; M. 10,074; 1 Ill. 131. Bain *v.* Brown, 1824; 3 S. 362; 1 Ill. 134. Chatto & Co. *v.* Pyper, 1827; 4 Mur. 353. Maving *v.* Tod, 1 Starkie, 72; 1 Ill. 172; 16 R. R. 779. Leeson *v.* Holt, 1 Starkie, 187; 18 R. R. 758. Clarke *v.* Gray, 4 Esp. 117; 1 Ill. 167. Cobden *v.* Bolton, 2 Camp. 108. Kerr *v.* Willan, 2 Starkie, 53; 18 R. R. 337. Davis *v.* Willan, 2 Starkie, 279; 19 R. R. 722. Munn *v.* Baker, *ib.* 255. Rowley *v.* Horne, 3 Bing. 2; 28 R. R. 551. Beck *v.* Evans, 16 East, 247; 14 R. R. 340. Wilson *v.* Freeman, 3 Camp. 527. Bodenham *v.* Bennet, 4 Price, 31; 1 Ill. 137; 18 R. R. 686. Clayton *v.* Hunt, 3 Camp. 27; 1 Ill. 135. Harris *v.* Packwood, 3 Taunt. 264; 15 R. R. 755. Marsh *v.* Horne, 4 B. & Cr. 322. See as to Shipowners, § 236 (*b*), 436. See above, § 155.

(*b*) Where the loss occurs on land, the Act applies though the carriage contracted for is partly by water. Baxendale *v.* G. E. Ry. Co., and Leconteur *v.* L. and S.-W. Ry. Co., *infra* (*p*), (*t*).

(*c*) Treadwin *v.* G. E. Ry. Co., L. R. 3 C. P. 308; 37 L. J. C. P. 83.

(*d*) Not machine-made lace, 28 and 29 Vict. c. 94, § 1.

(*e*) Woodward *v.* L. and N.-W. Ry. Co., 3 Ex. D. 121; 47 L. J. Ex. 263 (not commercial designs, as for carpets). Henderson *v.* L. and N.-W. Ry. Co., L. R. 5 Ex. 90 (includes frames).

(*f*) Brunt *v.* Midland Ry. Co., 2 H. & C. 889; 33 L. J. Ex. 187. Bernstein *v.* Baxendale, 6 C. B. N. S. 259; 28 L. J. C. P. 265.

(*g*) Whaite *v.* L. and Y. Ry. Co., L. R. 9 Ex. 67; 43 L. J. Ex. 47 (uncovered waggon).

(*h*) Robinson *v.* S.-W. Ry. Co., 19 C. B. N. S. 51; 34 L. J. C. P. 235. M'Cance *v.* L. and N.-W. Ry. Co., 3 H. & C. 343; 34 L. J. Ex. 39.

(*i*) Behrens *v.* G. N. Ry. Co., 30 L. J. Ex. 153; 31 *ib.* 299; 7 H. & N. 950.

(*k*) "The Carriers Act," 1 Will. IV. c. 68; see 1 Ill. 491. Bradley *v.* Waterhouse, 1 M. & M. 154. 17 and 18 Vict. c. 31. 28 and 29 Vict. c. 94. Smith's Merc. Law, 306. 1 Smith's L. C. 210. Hart *v.* Baxendale, 6 Ex. 788.

(*l*) *I.e.* of the extra charge. Peek *v.* N. Staff. Ry. Co., 1 E. B. & E. 958.

(*m*) Carriers Act, § 2. (*n*) § 3. (*o*) § 4.

(*p*) Baxendale *v.* G. E. Ry. Co., L. R. 4 Q. B. 244; 38 L. J. Q. B. 137. Walker *v.* Y. and N. Midl. Ry. Co., 2 E. & B. 760 (notice of terms and assent). Van Toll *v.* G. E. Ry. Co., 31 L. J. C. P. 241 (ticket with notice). Scaife *v.* Tarrant, 44 L. J. Ex. 36, 234; L. R. 10 Ex. 358 (furniture remover). Shaw *v.* G. W. Ry. Co., 1894; 1 Q. B. 373. See as to railway and canal companies, § 244A.

(*q*) Lyon *v.* Mells, 5 East, 438; 7 R. R. 726. Addison on Contr. 541, 543.

(*r*) Peek *v.* N. Staff. Ry. Co., 32 L. J. Q. B. 241, 246; 10 H. L. Ca. 473. Gallin *v.* L. and N.-W. Ry. Co., L. R. 10 Q. B. 212; 44 L. J. Q. B. 89; and other cases cited in 1 Smith's L. C. 240, 244; and comp. Steel & Craig *v.* State Line Co., 1877; 4 R. H. L. 103; L. R. 3 App. Ca. 72.

(*s*) See above, § 235.

(*t*) Leconteur *v.* L. and S.-W. Ry. Co., L. R. 1 Q. B. 54; 35 L. J. Q. B. 40. Talley *v.* G. W. Ry. Co., L. R. 6 C. P. 44; 40 L. J. C. P. 9. Bergheim, § 235 (*e*). Kent *v.* Midl. Ry. Co., L. R. 10 Q. B. 1; 44 L. J. Q. B. 18. Naish *v.* G. and S.-W. Ry. Co., 1882; 2 Sel. Sh. Ct. Ca. 61.

(*u*) Morritt *v.* N.-E. Ry. Co., 1 Q. B. D. 302; 45 L. J. Q. B. 289.

(*v*) "Loss" includes temporary loss by the carrier. Millen *v.* Brasch, 10 Q. B. D. 142. The carrier is not liable for consequences flowing from the loss. *Ib.* Piancini *v.* L. and S.-W. Ry. Co., 18 C. B. 226.

(*w*) Hinton *v.* Dibbin, 2 Q. B. 646; 11 L. J. Q. B. 113. Morritt, *cit.* (*u*). Naish, *cit.*

(*x*) § 8. Campbell *v.* N. B. Ry. Co., 1875; 2 R. 433. Butt *v.* G. W. Ry. Co., 11 C. B. 140. G. W. Ry. Co. *v.* Rimell, 18 C. B. 575; 27 L. J. C. P. 201. Metcalfe *v.* L. B., etc., Ry. Co., 4 C. B. N. S. 307; 27 L. J. C. P. 205, 333. Vaughton *v.* L. and N.-W. Ry. Co., 43 L. J. Ex. 75; L. R., 9 Ex. 93. Macqueen *v.* G. W. Ry. Co., 44 L. J. Q. B. 131; L. R. 10 Q. B. 569. See § 240. The word "servants" in the Act extends to servants of carriers, receiving-house keepers, etc., employed by railway companies. 1 Will. IV. c. 68, § 5. Machu *v.* L. and S.-W. Ry. Co., 2 Ex. 415. Stephens *v.* L. and S.-W. Ry. Co., 18 Q. B. D. 121.

244A. '*The Railway and Canal Traffic Act.*—The exception of special contracts in this statute having enabled railway companies to create for themselves exemptions from responsibility even for their own misconduct, the Railway and Canal Traffic Act (*a*) was passed to prevent them from imposing on the public unreasonable and improper conditions. Under this Act (which is extended to the steam vessels used by railway companies for their through traffic and the traffic carried on thereby, so far as its provisions are applicable to them (*b*)), railway and canal companies are liable for the loss of or injury done to horses, cattle, or other animals, or to articles, goods, or things, by their fault in receiving (*c*), forwarding, and delivering them, notwithstanding any notice, condition, or declaration by the company contrary to or limiting their liability. But companies may make such conditions with respect to receiving, forwarding, and delivering such things as the Court before which any question relating thereto shall be tried, shall adjudge to be "just and reasonable." The Act limits the amount of damages to be recovered for the loss of or injury to animals, unless a declaration of their value, if higher than the sums limited, shall be made at the time of delivery, and a higher charge paid, as under the Carriers Act. Further, no special contract respecting the receiving, forwarding, or delivering animals, articles, goods, etc., is binding, unless signed by the person with whom it is made, or the person delivering them for carriage. This enactment is held to require conditions limiting the common law liability of carriers both to be just and reasonable, and to be embodied in a *signed* special contract (*d*). The reasonableness of conditions depends on the circumstances of each case; but a condition that the company shall not be liable for any damage or delay, however caused, has been held bad (*e*), except under "owner's risk notes," the consignee having a *bonâ fide* choice to have his goods carried at a higher rate in the ordinary way (*f*). Exemption by contract from damage of a specified kind, as by leakage or breakage, does not relieve from responsibility from such damage, when it is caused by the carrier's negligence (*g*). In the case of fish or such perishable goods, a condition that the company shall not be responsible for loss of market by delay, or for other loss or injury, unless caused by fault or negligence, has been held valid (*h*). The statute does not apply to traffic beyond the company's own lines (*i*).'

(*a*) 17 and 18 Vict. c. 31. See above, § 160A.

(*b*) 31 and 32 Vict. c. 119, § 14, 16. See 34 and 35 Vict. c. 78, § 12. Doolan *v.* Midl. Ry. Co., L. R. 2 App. Ca. 792.

(*c*) Hodgman *v.* W. Midl. Ry. Co., 35 L. J. Q. B. 85; 6 B. & S. 560.

(*d*) Simons *v.* G. N. Ry. Co., 18 C. B. 805; 26 L. J. C. P. 25. Peek *v.* North Staffordshire Ry. Co., E. B. & E. 958, 986; 32 L. J. Q. B. 241; 10 H. L. Ca. 473. M'Manus *v.* Lanc. Ry. Co., 2 H. & N. 693; 4 H. & N. 327; 28 L. J. Ex. 359. Baxendale *v.* G. E. Ry. Co., L. R. 4 Q. B. 244; 38 L. J. Q. B. 137 (contract need not be signed if owner is setting it up). Doolan *cit.* (*b*). M. S. and L. Ry. Co. *v.* Brown, 8 App. Ca. 703. Peebles & Son *v.* Cal. Ry. Co., 1875; 2 R. 346. It applies to passengers' luggage, Zunz *v.* S.-E. Ry. Co., 38 L. J. Q. B. 209; L. R. 4 Q. B. 539. Cohen *v.* S.-E. Ry. Co., 46 L. J. Ex. 417; 2 Ex. D. 253.

(*e*) Peek, Simons, and M'Manus, *citt.* Gregory *v.* W. Midl. Ry. Co., 2 H. & C. 944; 33 L. J. 155. Harrison *v.* L. B. & S. C. Ry. Co., 29 L. J. Q. B. 209; 31 L. J. Q. B. 113; 2 B. & S. 122, 152. Allday *v.* G. W. Ry. Co., 34 L. J. Q. B. 5; 5 B. & S. 903. Rooth *v.* N.-E. Ry. Co., 36 L. J. Ex. 83; L. R. 2 Ex. 173. Lord *v.* Midland Ry. Co., 36 L. J. C. P. 170; L. R. 2 C. P. 239. Garton *v.* Bristol & Exeter Ry. Co., 1 B. & S. 112; 30 L. J. Q. B. 273. Aldridge *v.* G. W. Ry. Co., 15 C. B. N. S. 582; 33 L. J. C. P. 161. Ashendon *v.* L. B. & S. C. Ry. Co., 5 Ex. D. 190. Lewis *v.* G. W. Ry. Co., 3 Q. B. D. 195; 47 L. J. Q. B. 131. Gordon *v.* G. W. Ry. Co., 51 L. J. Q. B. 58. Finlay *v.* N. B. Ry. Co., 1870; 8 Macph. 959.

(*f*) Lewis *v.* G. W. Ry., Peek, and Rooth, *citt.* Manch. S. and L. Ry. Co. *v.* Brown, 8 App. Ca. 703; 52 L. J. Q. B. 132. Forman *v.* G. W. Ry. Co., 38 L. T. R. 851. Dickson *v.* G. N. Ry. Co., 18 Q. B. D. 176 (dog). G. W. Ry. Co. *v.* M'Carthy, 12 App. Ca. 218. As to the meaning of "at owner's risk" in different cases, see Mitchell *v.* L. and Y. Ry. Co., L. R. 10 Q. B. 256; 44 L. J. Q. B. 107; and as to shipowners, above, § 159, note.

(*g*) Phillips *v.* Clark, 26 L. J. C. P. 168; 2 C. B. N. S. 163. M'Manus *v.* Lanc. and Y. Ry. Co., *cit.* See Moes, Moliere, & Tromp *v.* Leith, etc., Shipping Co., 1867; 5 Macph. 988; and Ohrloff *v.* Briscall, L. R. 1 P. C. 231.

(*h*) Beale *v.* S. Devon Ry. Co., 5 H. & N. 875. Finlay, *cit.* (*e*). M'Connachie *v.* G. N. of Scot. Ry. Co. 1875; 3 R. 79. Brown *v.* Manch. S. and L. Ry. Co., 51 L. J. Q. B. 599. As to cattle, see Rain *v.* G. and S.-W. Ry. Co., 1869; 7 Macph. 439. Gill *v.* Manch. S. and L. Ry. Co., L. R. 8 Q. B. 186; 42 L. J. Q. B. 86. M'Manus, Harrison, etc., *citt.*; and above, § 166 (*c*), 168 (*b*).

(*i*) Zunz *v.* S.-E. Ry. Co., *supra* (*d*).

CHAPTER VIII

OF CAUTIONARY OBLIGATIONS

245. Nature and Kinds of Cautionry.—Cautionry is an accessory obligation or engagement, as surety for another, that the principal obligant shall pay the debt or perform the act for which he has engaged, otherwise the cautioner shall pay the debt or fulfil the obligation (*a*). The design of the cautioner's interposition, however, is, 'according to the common law,' not to save the creditor from the necessity of demanding and enforcing payments from his debtor, but to insure him against loss if these measures should fail to procure satisfaction. When the creditor 'wished' to lay on the cautioner the burden of execution against the debtor, he 'took' him bound as joint obligant; the effect of which 'was, before the Mercantile Law Amendment Act,' to deprive the cautioner of the benefit of discussion (*b*).

The cautioner's engagement implies that he is bound for the whole debt (*c*); that 'though' the principal obligant is 'no longer, in the absence of special stipulation, to be' required to perform his engagement before the cautioner shall be compellable to answer (*d*), 'the creditor shall use all proper precautions to secure payment of the debt by him, as by retaining and making available securities, etc. (*e*)'; that satisfaction or extinction of the principal obligation shall discharge the cautioner; and that the cautioner, engaging at the request or for the benefit of the principal debtor, shall, if compelled to fulfil his engagement, have relief or indemnification against the principal (*f*).

(*a*) See 1 Stair, 17. § 3 et seq. 3 Ersk. Pr. 3. § 21. 3 Ersk. 3. § 61. 1 Bell's Com. 347.

(*b*) Discussion is abolished, unless specially stipulated, by 19 and 20 Vict. c. 60, § 8, in obligations for payment of debt, but not in obligations *ad factum præstandum*. See below, § 252.

(*c*) Grant *v.* Strachan, 1721; M. 14,633; 1 Ill. 71. See above, § 52; below, § 255.

(*d*) See below, § 252. See above, (*b*).

(*e*) See § 262 sqq.

(*f*) In the application of terms, "Adpromissor" is a surety in addition to the original obligant; "Expromissor" is a new debtor substituted in place of the original debtor, who is thereby discharged.

246. A cautionary obligation is commonly an engagement of friendship, and gratuitous; and in an old case it was held *pactum illicitum* for the cautioner to stipulate for a valuable consideration (*a*). But this would probably be otherwise determined now, since the principles of insurance have come to be better understood (*b*), and it is a daily practice to engage for the credit of others, on commission.

(*a*) King *v.* Kerr, 1711; M. 9461; 1 Ill. 174. Formerly a consideration was necessary by the law of England; but that law is now assimilated to that of Scotland by 19 and 20 Vict. c. 97, § 3; 1 Smith's L. C. 330 sq. (292, 318, 10th ed.)

(*b*) See More's Stair, lxv. *Ex p.* Adney, Cowper, 460. See below, § 282.

247. Cautionry is Proper or Improper:—Proper, where the engagement is avowedly as cautioner; Improper, where both cautioner and principal are bound as principals; in which case the rights of a cautioner are renounced as to the creditor, but reserved as to the principal debtor (*a*).

(*a*) 3 Ersk 3. § 61 *in fin.* Montgomery *v.* Brown, 1713; M. 3586; 1 Ill. 173.

248. Proof.—Cautionary obligations, correctly speaking, can be proved only by writing, duly executed according to the requisites of the statutes (*a*); or recognised as a privileged writ (*b*).

(*a*) Auchinleck *v.* Gordon, 1580; M. 12,382; 1 Ill. 173. Deuchar *v.* Brown, 1672; M. 12,386. Reid *v.* Proudfoot, 1758; M. 12,344. Crichton *v.* Syme, 1772; 5 B. Sup. 640; Hailes, 483. Wallace *v.* Wallace, 1782; M. 17,056. Walker *v.* Duncan, 1785; M. 17,057. Edmonston *v.* Laing, 1786; M. 17,057; Hailes, 992. Paterson *v.* Wright, Jan. 31, 1810; F. C.; aff. 1814, 6 Pat. 38; 1 Ill. 176. By the law of England, the contract of surety is required to be in writing. See the 4th section of the Statute of Frauds. See § 249A, 282 (*a*). Church of England Assur. Co. *v.* Hodges, 1857; 19 D. 414. Chaplin *v.* Allan, 1842; 4 D. 616.

(*b*) Angus *v.* Coult, 1749; Elch. *Cautioner*, 18; M. 17,040. The case cited has not been regarded as well decided; 1 Ill. 174. Dickson on Evid. § 645. It scarcely bears, however, on the clause in the text, which stands in need of no authority.

249. Exceptions are admitted to the above rule. Thus, a writing of which the subscription is acknowledged is good evidence of cautionry (*a*). And an improbative writing, or an oath on reference, will establish the obligation, where the creditor has, with the knowledge of the cautioner, proceeded in reliance on his engagement, and *rei interventus* has taken place (*b*).

Although parole proof will not, otherwise than as just mentioned, be admitted to establish cautionry for future furnishings (*c*), yet where the cautioner's engagement is an integral part of a contract competent to be proved by parole evidence, the same proof 'was till 1856' admitted of the cautionary obligation (*d*).

(*a*) Brown *v.* Campbell, 1794; Bell's Ca. 115; 1 Ill. 174. Sinclair *v.* Sinclair, 1795; Bell's Ca. 140. But see *contra*, Dickson on Evid. § 600 (3). Church of England Assur. Co. *v.* Hodges, 1857; 19 D. 414. See Fogo *v.* Milligan and other cases, below, § 2232, and 3 Ill. 72.

(*b*) Hunter *v.* Carson, 1824; 2 S. 596; 1 Ill. 176. Grant *v.* M'Donald, 1827; 5 S. 317; 1 Ill. 175. Campbell, 1752; Elch. *Cautioner*, 22. Brebner *v.* Freeland, 1803; M. 17,060. See 1 Ill. 175. Robertson & Co. *v.* Galloway, 1821; 1 S. 191. Taylor *v.* Simson, 1836; 14 S. 935. Hardie *v.* Macdonald, 1844; 6 D. 762. Johnston *v.* Grant, 1844; 6 D. 875; 7 D. 390. Church of England Assur. Co., *supra* (*a*). See Hume's Dec. 92, 94, 103, 105. Ballantyne *v.* Carter, 1842; 4 D. 419. Natl. Bank *v.* Campbell, 1892; 19 R. 885. See the note in 1 Ill. 175.

(*c*) M'Ewan *v.* Crawford, Feb. 13, 1816; F. C. See Hume's Rep. 178–81. Grant *v.* Johnston, 1844; 6 D. 875; 7 D. 390. Simpson *v.* Fleming, 1857; 20 D. 77.

(*d*) Gibb *v.* Walker, 1751; Elch. *Cautioner*, 19. Carruthers *v.* Bell, Nov. 13, 1812; F. C. Rhind *v.* M'Kenzie, Feb. 20, 1816; F. C. See M'Ewan, *supra* (*c*).

249A. 'In 1856 the Mercantile Law Amendment Act assimilated our law to that of England, founded on the Statute of Frauds (§ 4), and Lord Tenderden's Act (9 Geo. IV. c. 14). It enacts that "all guarantees, securities, or cautionary obligations made or granted by any person for any other person, and all representations and assurances as to the character, conduct, credit, ability, trade, or dealings, of any person, made or granted to the effect or for the purpose of enabling such person to obtain credit, money, goods, or postponement of payment of debt, or of any other obligation demandable from him, shall be in writing, and shall be subscribed by the person undertaking such guarantee, security, or cautionary obligation, or making such representations and assurances, or by some person duly authorised by him or them, otherwise the same shall have no effect" (*a*).

'Although the words of this enactment seem to go beyond the terms of the English statute, which have been held to make the memorandum in writing necessary only as evidence of the contract, not to constitute it (*b*), yet as the expressed purpose of the Legislature was to remedy the inconvenience felt by reason of the laws of Scotland being different from those of England and Ireland in some particulars of common occurrence in trade, it is difficult to hold that writing is made indispensable to the *constitution* of the contract of cautionry. This, however, is not a question of practical importance; and there is no room to doubt that in all cases the contract can be proved only by writing, which must in ordinary cases be probative or holograph: improbative guarantees being effectual only *in rei mercatoria* or when followed (as they generally are) by *rei interventus* (*c*). An undertaking to give a guarantee when required is a good "cautionary obligation" in the sense of the Act (*d*).'

(*a*) 19 and 20 Vict. c. 60, § 6. See below, § 281.
(*b*) Laythoarp *v.* Bryant, 2 Bing. N. C. 744. Reuss *v.* Picksley, 35 L. J. Ex. 218; L. R. 1 Ex. 342. Buxton *v.* Rust, L. R. 7 Ex. 1, 279; 41 L. J. Ex. 1, 173. Bailey *v.* Sweeting, 9 C. B. N. S. 843; 30 L. J. C. P. 150, etc.
(*c*) See above, § 248–9. See the notes in M'Laren's Bell's Com. i. 402 sqq., and 1 Smith's L. C. 288 sqq. Clapperton, Paton, & Co. *v.* Anderson, 1881; 8 R. 1004. Walker's Trs. *v.* M'Kinlay, 1880; 7 R. H. L. 85, 88 (Lord Blackburn). Chaplin, § 248. Paterson *v.* Wright, Jan. 31, 1810; F. C.; aff. 1814, 6 Pat. 38. Wylie & Lochhead *v.* Hornsby, 1889; 16 R. 902 (blank paper stamped and signed—proof of mandate).
(*d*) Wallace *v.* Gibson, 1895; A. C. 354; 22 R. H. L. 56.

250. Construction and Extent.—A cautionary obligation offered conditionally is effectual only on compliance with the condition; as an offer to be cautioner for a composition to be paid to creditors, in which the consent of all concerned is an implied condition (*a*). So an obligation to be signed by several is not binding on those who sign first, unless all have signed; but if the signature of the others be not expressly or manifestly a condition, and a bank or creditor has been induced to rely on the names of those who have already subscribed, they will be bound (*b*).

(*a*) Culcreuch Cotton Co. *v.* Mathie, 1823; 2 S. 513.
(*b*) Blair *v.* Taylor, 1836; 14 S. 1069. See Paterson *v.* Bonar, 1844; 6 D. 987. Evans *v.* Bremridge, 2 K. & J. 174; 8 De G. M. & G. 101; 25 L. J. Ch. 334. Rice *v.* Gordon, 11 Beav. 465. Cooper *v.* Evans, L. R. 4 Eq. 45; 36 L. J. Ch. 431. The co-obligants are also free if one of the signatures be forged. Scottish Provincial Assur. Co. *v.* Pringle, 1858; 20 D. 465. Cf. B. L. Co. Bank *v.* Thomson, 1853; 15 D. 314. Craig *v.* Paton, 1865; 4 Macph. 192. The qualification in the latter part of the sentence is perhaps too strongly stated; as in general the creditor ought to see that he gets a valid obligation. See Prov. Assur. Co., *cit.* Hence judicial bonds of caution, where the charger has not such a duty laid upon him, are valid against the other cautioners, although one of the signatures should be forged. Simpson *v.* Fleming, 1860; 22 D. 679.

251. Cautionry as an accessory obligation may be less extensive than the principal obligation, as for a part only; but it cannot be more extensive, though it may be more strict (*a*). There must be a subsisting obligation against the principal, though not necessarily such as lawyers call perfect; a natural obligation, though it will not sustain action against the principal, may be made good against the cautioner (*b*). The cautioner is entitled in all other respects to plead every defence which the principal debtor has against the demand (*c*). The extinction of the principal discharges the accessory engagement (*d*). Cautionary obligations are very strictly interpreted, though not so literally as to evade the true and fair construction of the engagement (*e*). There must, at entering into the engagement, be perfect fairness of representation, so far as the creditor is concerned, otherwise the cautioner will be free (*f*). Where any precautionary stipulations are made or plainly implied, they must be strictly observed, otherwise the cautioner will be free (*g*).

'But fraud of the debtor does not affect the liability of the cautioner to an innocent creditor (*h*). And the universal obligation to make disclosure which holds in contracts of insurance does not apply to guarantees. While the cautioner is entitled to know the real nature of the transaction and the extent of his liability, the creditor is not bound at his peril to volunteer information as to the principal debtor's credit, or anything which is not part of the transaction itself, such even as that the obligation is in substitution for a previous guarantee by another, or that a new cash credit is to be applied (there being no actual agreement to that effect) to pay off an old debt to the bank (*i*). But a creditor may become bound to inquire into and inform his surety of circumstances in the debtor's conduct. such as may reasonably create a suspicion of fraud, for wilful ignorance is equivalent to knowledge (*k*).'

(*a*) 3 Ersk. 3. § 64–5. Pothier, des Oblig., Nos. 368-377. Lady Charteris *v.* L. Belhaven, 1649; 1 B. Sup. 387. Ewing *v.* Malloch, 1681; 3 B. Sup. 398. See Booth *v.* Comml. Bank, 1823; 2 S. 273; 1 Ill. 180. Stevenson *v.* Adair, 1872; 10 Macph. 920 (cautioner for minor apprentice). Jackson *v.* M'Iver, 1875; 2 R. 882. See as to cautionry for interest only, Royal Bank *v.* Rankin, 1844; 6 D. 1418, 1425. Forsyth *v.* Wishart, 1859; 21 D. 449. Molleson *v.* Hutchison, 1892; 19 R. 581. M. Bell's Convg. 250.
(*b*) 3 Ersk. 3. § 64. —— *v.* Crichton, 1612; M. 2074; 1 Ill. 177. Hepburn *v.* Brown, 1700; M. 2076. Shaw *v.* M'Farlan, 1623; M. 2874. Taylor *v.* L. Braco, 1748; M. 16,813. These are cases in which the principal's obligation was invalid, and the decisions varied. Prof. Bell says (1 Ill. 177), that they "may be reconciled on the ground that, wherever the cautioner engages aware of the objection, he is barred *personali exceptione* from the plea; when the bond has been negligently and ineffectually executed to bind the principal, and taken by the creditor, the cautioner will not be liable." The English cases exclude the Statute of Frauds, § 4, where the surety's (?) liability is not accessory at all, but is intentionally undertaken as an independent obligation. See Smith's Mercantile Law, p. 572; 1 Smith's L. C. 288 sqq.; and particularly Mr. J. A. Dixon's learned note in 1 M'Laren's Bell's Com. 407. See also below, § 282; and Stevenson *v.* Adair, *cit.*
(*c*) Johnston *v.* L. Romanno, 1680; M. 2076; 1 Ill. 177. Nimmo *v.* Brown, 1700; M. 2076. Innes *v.* Comrs. of Supply, 1728; M. 2079. Crichton, *supra* (*b*). Halyburton *v.* Graham, 1735; M. 2073. Herdman *v.* Borthwick, 1699; M. 2078.
(*d*) Doull *v.* Hume, 1695; M. 2077; 1 Ill. 185. Low *v.* E. Rosebery, 1812; More's Notes on Stair, p. cxi; 1 Ill. 178. See below, § 260; and cases in 1 Ill. 184 sqq.

(*e*) Dick *v.* Nisbet, 1697; M. 2090; 1 Ill. 178. Hamilton *v.* Calder, 1706; M. 2091; 1 Ill. 179. Forbes *v.* Saltoun's Exrs. 1735; Elch. *Caut.* 4, also 14 and 15. Glasgow University *v.* E. Selkirk, 1790; Bell's Cases, 134. **Houston** *v.* **Spiers,** March 4, 1820; F. C.; aff. 3 W. & S. 392; 1 Ill. 180. Angus *v.* Coult, 1749; M. 17,040; Elch. *Cautioner*, 18. (See above, § 248 (*b*).) Forbes *v.* Welsh, 1829; 7 S. 732; 1 Ill. 179. Cochrane & Co. *v.* Mathie, 1821; 1 S. 82; 1 Ill. 336. Frazer *v.* M'Turk, 1822; 1 S. 483; 1 Ill. 210. Sime *v.* Duncan & Co., 1824; 2 S. 516; 1 Ill. 213. See below, § 285.

(*f*) **Smith** *v.* **Bank of Scotland,** 1813; 1 Dow, 272; 1829, 7 S. 244; 1 Ill. 180; 3 Ross' L. C. 66; 14 R. R. 67. Fishmongers' Co. *v.* Maltby, 1 Dow, 294. Pidcock *v.* Bishop, 3 Barn. & Cr. 605; 27 R. R. 430. Stein's Assignees *v.* Brunton, 1833; 11 S. 373. See below, § 289, 291, 301. Lee *v.* Jones, 14 C. B. N. S. 386; 17 *ib.* 482; 34 L. J. C. P. 131. Wardlaw *v.* Mackenzie, 1859; 21 D. 940. Royal Bank *v.* Rankin, 1844; 6 D. 1418. Falconer *v.* N. of Scot. Bkg. Co., 1863; 1 Macph. 177, 704. M'Dougall & Herbertson *v.* Northern Assur. Co., 1864; 2 Macph. 935. Davies *v.* L. and Prov. Mar. Ins. Co., 8 Ch. D. 469; 47 L. J. Ch. 511.

(*g*) Dick, Hamilton, and Forbes, *supra* (*e*). British Guarantee Assn. *v.* Western Bank, 1853; 15 D. 834. Haworth *v.* Sickness, etc., Ass. Co., 1891; 18 R. 563.

(*h*) French *v.* Cameron, 1893; 20 R. 966. Wallace's Factor *v.* M'Kissock, 1898; 25 R. 642.

(*i*) North Br. Ins. Co. *v.* Lloyd, 10 Ex. 523; 24 L. J. Ex. 14. Hamilton *v.* Watson, 1843; 5 D. 280; aff. 4 Bell's App. 67; 12 Cl. & F. 109. Lee *v.* Jones, *cit.* Falconer, *cit.* *Infra*, § 301. See Wallace's Factor *v.* M'Kissock, *cit.*

(*k*) Owen *v.* Homan, 20 L. J. 323; 4 H. L. Ca. 997.

252. Discussion.—The benefit of discussion ("beneficium ordinis") is a corollary to the accessory nature of the engagement, the cautioner being 'by common law' entitled to insist that the creditor shall first call upon and (in law language) "discuss" the principal debtor, if the cautioner have not expressly or virtually dispensed with this right; and that he shall give the cautioner all the benefit and relief derived from the principal debtor's estate (*a*).

'But by the Mercantile Law Amendment Act, 1856, when one is bound as cautioner for a principal debtor, it is not necessary for the creditor to whom such cautionary obligation is granted, "before calling on the cautioner for payment of the debt to which such cautionary obligation refers, to discuss or do diligence against the principal debtor, as now required by law; but it shall be competent to such creditor to proceed against the principal debtor and the said cautioner, or against either of them, and to use all action or diligence against both or either of them, which is competent according to the law of Scotland" (*b*). But the Act is not to "prevent any cautioner from stipulating in the instrument of caution that the creditor shall be bound, before proceeding against him, to discuss and do diligence against the principal debtor" (*b*).'

(*a*) 1 Stair, 17. § 5. 3 Ersk. 3. § 61. Smith, 1626; 1 B. Sup. 34; 1 Ill. 182. Ritchie *v.* Paterson, 1629; *ib.* 308. Crosbie *v.* Findlay, 1627; 1 B. Sup. 238.

(*b*) 19 and 20 Vict. c. 60, § 8. Morrison *v.* Harkness, 1870; 9 Macph. 35. Ewart *v.* Latta, 1863; 1 Macph. 965; rev. 1865, 3 Macph. H. L. 36; 4 Macq. 983.

253. Discussion has been held to import not merely a *demand* of payment, but enforcement of it, by registered denunciation of the principal, and warrant to imprison, though actual imprisonment is not required (*a*); by poinding, or arrestment and forthcoming, of his moveables; or by adjudication of his heritable estate (*b*). But there is a tendency to relax this rule; and it is a sufficient answer to a demand for discussion, that the principal debtor is out of the kingdom, and has no estate or effects in it (*c*); or that he is bankrupt, and his estate sequestrated (*d*); or that the cautionary obligation is judicial, as in a suspension, or advocation, or for loosing of arrestment (*e*); or that the cautioner is bound in a bill as cautioner (*f*); or that he is bound as co-principal, as in a bank-credit bond (*g*), 'or as in a mercantile guarantee (*h*); or similar primary obligation (*i*).'

(*a*) 1 and 2 Vict. c. 114, § 5.

(*b*) 1 Stair, 17. § 5. 3 Ersk. 3. § 61. See Macfarlan *v.* Anstruther, 1870; 9 Macph. 117.

(*c*) Elams *v.* Fisher, 1757; M. 2110; 1 Ill. 182.

(*d*) Galloway *v.* Robertson & Co., 1825; 4 S. 134. Buchanan *v.* Dennistouns & Co., 1831; 9 S. 557; 3 Ill. 71. The death of the principal debtor does not deprive the cautioner of the benefit of discussion as against his heirs. Wishart *v.* Wishart, 1835; 13 S. 769; rev. 1837, 2 S. & M'L. 564.

(*e*) Dickie *v.* Thomson, 1743; M. 2110.

(*f*) M'Dougal *v.* Foyer, Feb. 13, 1810; F. C.

(*g*) Montgomery *v.* Brown, 1713; M. 3586; 1 Ill. 173.

(*h*) Blackwood *v.* Forbes, 1848; 10 D. 920. See Wilson *v.* Tait, 1837; 15 S. 221; H. L. 1 Rob. 137, and cases therein cited; cf. below, § 282.

(*i*) Morrison *v.* Harkness, 1870; 9 Macph. 35.

254. The right of discussion entitles the cautioner to insist on the application by the creditor of all money of the debtor coming into his hand, and of all securities, direct and indirect, which he holds over the estate of the debtor, and which are not appropriated to other debts (*a*). But it has been held that a landlord having a cautioner bound for rent is not obliged to have recourse to the ruinous diligence of sequestration on his hypothec before coming on the cautioner; it being the chief use of the cautioner's obligation to avoid this necessity (*b*). The exercise of the right, however, may be stipulated by the cautioner, 'in which case the "exercise" of the right of hypothec implies that the sale of the effects must be carried out (*c*)'; and the cautioner may, on payment, demand an assignation to the hypothec (*d*).

(*a*) See below, § 255, note (*a*).
(*b*) M'Queen *v.* Frazer, June 11, 1811; F. C.; 1 Ill. 193. Grant *v.* M'Donald, 1827; 5 S. 194. See Grant *v.* Fenton, 1853; 15 D. 424; and M'Ewan *v.* M'Donald, 1852; 14 D. 809.
(*c*) M'Kenzie *v.* Fraser (M'Tavish *v.* Scott), 1827; 5 S. 559; rev. 4 W. & S. 410. See 2 Hunter, Landl. & Ten. 155.
(*d*) See below, § 270. M. Bell's Convg. 286.

255. Relief is a right on the part of the cautioner to indemnification against the principal debtor. It rests on two grounds: an equitable right to require the creditor to communicate the full benefit of his contract; and an obligation *ex mandato* of the principal debtor, for whose benefit the cautioner has engaged. By the former, the cautioner is entitled to an assignation of the debt and diligence (*a*); and, on satisfying the creditor, comes into his place, and may proceed as principal creditor (*b*). 'The cautioner is also entitled to the benefit of accessory securities held by the creditor, whether the surety knew of them or not (*c*). And any act of the creditor by which he voluntarily does away or even impairs such security, directly or indirectly, *pro tanto* liberates the cautioner (*d*). It is held that this rule applies to securities received by the creditor after the contract of cautionry (*e*).' By the latter, he is entitled in his own person to take legal measures for his relief against threatened distress, or against the possible consequences of the failing condition of the principal debtor (*b*).

(*a*) *I.e.* if he makes payment in full; for payment of a dividend by the trustee of a sequestrated cautioner does not give this right. Ewart, *supra*, § 252 (*b*). But an assignation is not necessary to entitle a cautioner to sue for relief who has paid an overdue debt, against the payment of which the principal debtor has no defence. Craigie *v.* Graham, 1710; M. 14,649.
(*b*) 3 Ersk. 3. § 65. Thomson *v.* Heriot, 1627; M. 2113; 1 Ill. 183. Kinloch *v.* M'Intosh, 1822; 1 S. 457; 1 Ill. 184. Simpson *v.* Gardiner, 1826; 4 S 492. Boswell *v.* Montgomerie, 1836; 14 S. 554. Spence *v.* Brownlee, 1834; 13 S. 199; 3 Ill. 112. Gilmour *v.* Finnie, 1832; 11 S. 193. See Lesly *v.* Gray, 1665; M. 211; 1 Ill. 183. Rigg *v.* Broomhalls, 1676; M. 3353 (assignation to enable cautioner paying in full to proceed against co-cautioners). Wait *v.* Panton, 1697; M. 3356. Wood *v.* Gordon, 1695; M. 3355. See below, § 266. Alston *v.* Denniston, 1828; 7 S. 112. Low *v.* Farquharson, 1831; 9 S. 411. Gray *v.* Thomson, 1847; 10 D. 145. See 1 Bell's Com. 348.
(*c*) See cases below, and Duncan, Fox, & Co. *v.* N. & S. Wales Bk., 6 App. Ca. 1; 50 L. J. Ch. 355.
(*d*) Fleming *v.* Thomson, 1826; 2 W. & S. 277. Storie *v.* Carnie, 1830; 8 S. 853. Sligo *v.* Menzies, 1840; 2 D. 1478. See below, § 263, 557. Mayhew *v.* Crickett, 2 Swans. 185. Wulff *v.* Jay, L. R. 7 Q. B. 756; 41 L. J. Q. B. 322. Bechervaise *v.* Lewis, L. R. 7 C. P. 377; 41 L. J. C. P. 161; 2 Wh. & Tud. L. C. 1002. Story, Eq. Jur. 326. Snell's Pr. of Eq. 490. See below, § 264.
(*e*) See Campbell *v.* Rothwell, 47 L. J. Ex. 144. Forbes *v.* Jackson, 19 Ch. D. 615; 51 L. J. Ch. 690.

256. Discharge of Cautioner.—The cautioner may be discharged directly; or indirectly and consequentially.

257. (1.) *By Direct Discharge*, the cautioner may be freed while the principal debtor continues bound. 'So also by the expiry of seven years in cases to which the Septennial Limitation applies (*infra*, § 600 sqq.).'

258. (2.) *By Satisfaction*, or payment, or expiration, or extinction of the principal obligation, the cautioner is discharged as well as the principal (*a*).

(*a*) Forbes *v.* Lady Saltoun's Exrs., 1735; Elch. *Cautioner*, 4; 1 Ill. 184. Doull, *supra*, § 251 (*d*).

259. (3.) *By Change on Obligation.*—The cautioner is freed by an essential change, consented to by the creditor without the knowledge (*a*) or assent of the cautioner, either on the principal obligation or transaction, or in respect to the person relied on (*b*); 'and that even though the original agreement may, notwithstanding such variance, be substantially carried out' (*c*). 'It is held in England that' when it is not self-evident, without inquiry, that the alteration is immaterial, and cannot prejudice the surety, the Court will not order an inquiry, the surety himself being in such a case the sole judge whether he will remain liable or not (*d*).

'The Mercantile Law Amendment Act, 1856, affirming previous decisions, enacted that a guarantee or cautionary obligation to or for a firm should not be binding as to events occurring after a change in the constitution of the firm, unless a contrary intention appeared by express stipulation or by necessary implication from the nature of the firm or otherwise (*e*). The Partnership Act, 1890, adopts from the Indian Contract Act a shorter provision to a similar effect' (*f*).

(*a*) There is, however, no authority for saying that one who knows that the creditor is going to give time, or to do something which if done without his consent may discharge him, is bound to warn the creditor against it, and that by mere silence he is barred from afterwards pleading that he has been discharged. *Per* L. Blackburn in Polak *v.* Everett, 1 Q. B. D. 669; 45 L. J. Q. B. 369. Allan, B. Allan & Milne *v.* Pattison, 1893; 21 R. 195.

(*b*) **Houston** *v.* **Speirs**, March 4, 1820; F. C.; 1829, 3 W. & S. 392; 4 Bligh, N. S. 515; 33 R. R. 68; 1 Ill. 180. Hammond *v.* Neilson, June 24, 1812; F. C.; 1 Ill. 184. Thomson *v.* Speirs, 1822; 1 S. 478; 1 Ill. 185. Kemp *v.* Allan, 1824; 3 S. 104; 1 Ill. 160. Wallace *v.* Donald, 1824; 3 S. 304. Scott *v.* Campbell, 1834; 12 S. 447. Padon *v.* Bank of Scotland, 1826; 5 S. 175; 1 Ill. 185. See below, § 289 *fin.* Bonar *v.* M'Donald, 1847; 9 D. 1537; aff. 7 Bell, 379; 3 H. L. Ca. 226. Stewart, Moir, & Muir *v.* Brown, 1871; 9 Macph. 763.

(*c*) Bonar *v.* M'Donald, *cit.*, *per* L. Cottenham.

(*d*) Holme *v.* Brunskill, 3 Q. B. D. 495; 47 L. J. Q. B. 610. Comp. L. Wood in Forsyth *v.* Wishart, 1859; 21 D. 449. Croydon Gas Co. *v.* Dickenson, 2 C. B. D. 46; 46 L. J. C. P. 157, and below, § 262 *fin.*

(*e*) 19 and 20 Vict. c. 60, § 6. 19 and 20 Vict. c. 97, § 4. See Bodenham *v.* Purchas, 2 B. & Ald. 39; 3 Ross' L. C. 661; 20 R. R. 342. Christie *v.* Royal Bk., 1839; 1 D. 745; aff. 1841, 2 Rob. 118. Miller *v.* Thorburn, 1861; 23 D. 359. Aytoun *v.* Dundee Banking Co., 1844; 6 D. 1409. Bell's Convg. 257. Montefiore *v.* Lloyd, 33 L. J. C. P. 49; 15 C. B. N. S. 203. Leathley *v.* Spyer, 39 L. J. C. P. 302; L. R. 5 C. P. 595. Backhouse *v.* Hall, 34 L. J. Q. B. 141; 6 B. & S. 507 (necessary implication).

(*f*) 53 and 54 Vict. c. 39, § 18.

260. (4.) *By Discharge of Debtor.*—By the creditor discharging the principal debtor, or compounding the debt, without the cautioner's assent, the cautioner is freed (*a*); unless such discharge shall be so qualified as not to injure the cautioner's claim of relief (*b*). 'In a contract to give time to or release the debtor, a reservation of all the creditor's remedies against the surety has the effect of so qualifying the discharge, because it rebuts the presumption that a total discharge of the debt is intended, and it prevents the surety's rights against the principal debtor from being impaired, the debtor's consent that the creditor shall have recourse against the surety implying his consent that the surety shall in turn have recourse against him (*c*).'

(*a*) Doull *v.* Home, 1695; M. 2077; 1 Ill. 185. Wingate *v.* Martin, 1829; 8 S. 186; 1 Ill. 195. Hall *v.* Wilcox, 2 Mood. & M. 58; 1 Ill. 188. British Lin. Co. Bank *v.* Thomson, 1853; 15 D. 314.

(*b*) Leitch *v.* Haderwick, 1680; M. 2077; 1 Ill. 186. Smith *v.* Ogilvies, 1821; 1 S. 159; aff. 1 W. & S. 315. Lewis *v.* Anstruther, 1852; 15 D. 260. Kearsley *v.* Cole, 16 M. & W. 128; 16 L. J. Ex. 115. Cragoe *v.* Jones, L. R. 8 Ex. 81; 42 L. J. Ex. 68. Nevill's case, 40 L. J. Ch. 1; L. R. 6 Ch. 43; and cases in § 261A (*e*), 262 (*a*). Montgomerie Bell's Convg. 353. Snell's Pr. of Eq. 488.

(*c*) Kearsley *v.* Cole, *cit.* (*per* Parke, B.). See references in last note.

261. To the above rule there is an exception in bankruptcy. When in England a commission of bankruptcy has been issued against the principal debtor, or in Scotland sequestration has been awarded, the creditor may, by acquiescence, allow the debtor to be discharged, or even, as a *debitum justitiæ*, concur in the discharge without freeing the cautioner (*a*): And the creditor 'might' agree to a composition in bankruptcy without discharging the cautioner, provided the cautioner 'had' been previously called on to satisfy the debt,—the creditor being entitled after such notice to take what he 'could' get (*b*). 'Now it is expressly provided by 19 and 20 Vict. c. 79, § 56, that no act of the creditor, in voting or drawing a dividend, or in assenting to a discharge of the bankrupt, or to a composition, discharges a co-obligant of the debtor; but he may obtain an assignation from the creditor, and take his place in the sequestration, if he prefers that course (*c*).'

(*a*) Anderson *v.* Wood, 1821; 1 S. 28; 1 Ill. 186. Brown *v.* Carr, 7 Bing. 508.

(*b*) Whitelaw *v.* Steins, May 20, 1814; F. C. See also Aikman *v.* Fisher, 1835; 14 S. 56; 3 Ill. 114. Brit. Lin. Bank, *supra*, § 260 (*a*).

(*c*) See White *v.* Robertson, 1864; 2 Macph. 553.

261A. '(5.) *By Discharging a Co-Cautioner.*—The Mercantile Law Amendment Act provides that "after the passing of this Act, where two or more parties shall become bound as cautioners for any debtor, any discharge granted by the creditor in such debt or obligation to any one of such cautioners, without the consent of the other cautioners, shall be deemed and taken to be a discharge granted to all the cautioners; but nothing herein contained shall be deemed to extend to the case of a cautioner (*a*) consenting to the discharge of a co-cautioner who may have become bankrupt" (*b*). This rule has been held not to apply to separate cautionary obligations for specific sums, though parts of the same debt (*c*). And in all such cases the distinction is to be observed between a total release or discharge of the cautioner's (or principal's) (*d*) obligation, and one which may be construed as merely an agreement by the creditor not to sue him, as when the creditor's rights and claims against the other obligants are reserved entire (*e*).'

(*a*) *Qu.* Whether this word was not intended to be "creditor"? see Morgan and *ex p.* Jacobs, *infra.*

(*b*) 19 and 20 Vict. c. 60, § 9. See § 269.

(*c*) Morgan *v.* Smart, 1872; 10 Macph. 610. But if it

was the intention of the statute to assimilate our law on this point to that of England, and if it be settled in England (**Dering** *v.* **E. Winchelsea,** 2 B. & P. 270; 1 Wh. & Tud. L. C. 106; 3 Ross' L. C. 28; 1 R. R. 41. Craythorne *v.* Swinburne, 14 Ves. 161; 9 R. R. 264. Whiting *v.* Burke, L. R. 6 Ch. 342. Steel *v.* Dixon, 17 Ch. D. 825; 50 L. J. Ch. 591), and in Scotland (notwithstanding Lawrie *v.* Stewart, June 6, 1823; F. C. and 2 S. 368. See Pollock *v.* Pollock, 1745; M. 2125. Elch. *Caut.* 16. Smiton *v.* Miller, 1792; M. 2138; 1 Bell's Com. 352 (370, M'L.'s ed.). Stirling *v.* Forrester, 1821; 1 S. App. 37; 6 Pat. 818; 3 Bligh, 590. 1 Bell's Com. 349 (367, M'L.'s ed.). Brodie's Stair, 942), that the rights of co-sureties to contribution are bottomed on equity, and do not spring from contract, then it is difficult to support this decision. See, however, Ward *v.* Natl. Bank of New Zealand, 8 App. Ca. 755. See as to the construction of the guarantee in Morgan *v.* Smart,—a guarantee for a limited sum, part of a specific debt,—Ellis *v.* Emmanuel, 1 Ex. D. 157; 46 L. J. Ex. 25.

(*d*) See § 260 (*b*), 262 (*a*).

(*e*) Church of England Assur. Co. *v.* Wink, 1857; 19 D. 1079. Cases in § 262 (*a*). *Ex p.* Jacobs, L. R. 10 Ch. App. 211; 44 L. J. Bkr. 34. *Ex p.* Good, 5 Ch. D. 46; 46 L. J. Ch. 65.

262. (6.) *By giving Time.*—The cautioner is not freed by the creditor merely forbearing or abstaining from enforcing payment, 'nor by a mere agreement not to sue, whereby the cautioner's recourse is not impaired (*a*)'; but he will be freed by the creditor agreeing 'by positive contract' to "give time" to the debtor beyond the limits of the original obligation, so as to tie up the cautioner, by virtue of that agreement, from having the same remedy he might otherwise have had (*b*). 'In a course of mercantile dealing under guarantee the usual or stipulated period of credit is looked to, and the taking of bills in the ordinary course of trade is not *per se* a giving of time such as to liberate a cautioner (*c*). Under a continuing guarantee (§ 284, *infra*) a cautioner may no doubt be discharged by express agreement for "giving time"; but the mere sale of goods at unusual and unreasonable periods of credit affords a defence to the cautioner rather on the ground that the transaction is not within the terms of his obligation, and the question to be determined is whether there has been a material deviation from the contract (*d*).'

(*a*) **Crawford** *v.* **Muir**, 1873; 1 R. 91; aff. 1875, 2 R. H. L. 148; L. R. 2 H. L. 456. Smith *v.* Harding, 1877; 5 R. 147. Green *v.* Wynn, L. R. 4 Ch. 204; 38 L. J. Ch. 204. Bateson *v.* Gosling, L. R. 7 C. P. 9; 41 L. J. C. P. 53. Addison on Contr. 664. See above, § 260, 261, 261A.; and as to such agreements in winding up companies, Webb *v.* Hewitt, 3 Kay & J. 438. Natal Invest. Co. (Nevill's case), 40 L. J. Ch. 1; L. R. 6 Ch. 43. Helbert *v.* Banner, L. R. 5 H. L. 28; 40 L. J. Ch. 410.

(*b*) Fleming *v.* Wilson, 1823; 2 S. 296; 1 Ill. 187. Hume *v.* Youngson, 1830; 8 S. 295. Farquharson *v.* Hutchison, 1826; 4 S. 676. Sheriff's Tr. *v* Giles, 1824; 3 S. 214; 1 Ill. 192. Macartney *v.* M'Kenzie, 1830; 8 S. 862; rev. 5 W. & S. 504. **Rees** *v.* **Berrington,** 2 Ves. jun. 240; 3 R. R. 3. See 2 White & Tudor's L. C. 992. English *v.* Darbey, 2 B. & P. 61; 5 R. R. 543. Goring *v.* Edmonds, 6 Bing. 95; 31 R. R. 358. Philpot *v.* Bryant, 4 Bing. 717. *Ex p.* Glendinning, 1819; Buck's Bkr. Ca. 517; 1 Ill. 189. Samuell *v.* Howarth, 3 Meriv. 272; 1 Ill. 191, and 3 Ill. 115; 17 R. R. 81. Combe *v.* Woolfe, 8 Bing. 156; 3 Ill. 115; 34 R. R. 659. Orme *v.* Young, Holt, N. P. 84; 17 R. R. 611. Creighton *v.* Rankin, 1840; 1 Rob. 99, 132. Stuart *v.* Campbell, 1852; 14 D. 443. Richardson *v.* Harvey, 1853; 15 D. 628. Forsyth *v.* Wishart, 1859; 21 D. 449. Warne & Co. *v.* Lillie, 1867; 5 Macph. 283. Bowe & Christie *v.* Hutchisons, 1868; 6 Macph. 642. Caledonian Bank *v.* Kennedy's Trs., 1870; 8 Macph. 862. Stewart, Moir, & Muir *v.* Brown, 1871; 9 Macph. 763. Nicolsons *v.* Burt, 1882; 10 R. 121. **Oakeley** *v.* **Pasheller,** 4 Cl. & F. 207. Oriental Finance Corpn. *v.* Overend, L. R. 7 H. L. 348; 41 L. J. Ch. 332. Petty *v.* Cook, 40 L. J. Q. B. 281; L. R. 6 Q. B. 90. Rouse *v.* Bradford Banking Co., 1894; A. C. 586 (principal becoming merely a surety by subsequent agreement known to creditor is within these rules).

(*c*) Griffith *v.* Wylie, 1809; Hume 96 (see also p. 97). Warne & Co., *cit.* Stewart, Moir, & Muir, *cit.* Bowe & Christie, *cit.* Swire *v.* Redman, 1 Q. B. D. 369.

(*d*) Calder & Co. *v.* Cruikshanks' Tr., 1889; 17 R. 74. As to the criterion of materiality, see above, § 259.

263. (7.) *By Neglect of Creditor.*—The cautioner is freed by the creditor's extreme neglect of legal proceedings against the principal obligant (*a*), especially if such proceedings have been already begun against the estate of the principal (*b*); or by omission to complete or to take advantage of a security in competition (*c*); or by undue neglect in negotiating a bill (*d*); 'or by breach of a term in the contract of cautionry, as when one had agreed to see a debt paid by instalments, and on the debtor's failure to pay the first instalment, the creditor, without notice to the cautioner, took proceedings on a bill for the full sum, and thus materially changed the debtor's position (*e*).' But mere delay to institute proceedings will not, in the common case, liberate the cautioner; nor the discontinuance of personal diligence commenced against the principal debtor; nor delay or forbearance in enforcing a right of hypothec against a tenant (*f*).

(*a*) Smith *v.* Campbell, 1829; 7 S. 789; 1 Ill. 194. Smith *v.* Wright, 1829; 8 S. 124. Macfarlan *v.* Anstruther, 1870; 9 Macph. 117. Comp. the cases under last §.

(*b*) 3 Ersk. 3. § 66. Boyes *v.* Ogilvie, 1738; Elch. *Caut.* 7; 1 Ill. 191. M'Millan *v.* Hamilton, 1729; M. 3390; 1 Ill. 196. Sinclair *v.* Sinclair, 1744; M. 3524. Anderson *v.* Wood, 1821; 1 S. 28; 1 Ill. 186. Wallace *v.* Donald, 1825; 3 S. 304.

(*c*) Storie *v.* Carnie, 1830; 8 S. 853. Fleming *v.* Thomson, 1825, 4 S. 224; rev. 1826, 2 W. & S. 277; 1 Ill. 192. See above, § 255, note; and Carter *v.* White, 25 Ch. D. 666.

(*d*) National Bank *v.* Robertson, 1836; 14 S. 402; 3 Ill. 114.

(*e*) Murray *v.* Lee, 1882; 9 R. 1040.

(*f*) See above, § 254, and below, § 288. Clapperton, Paton, & Co. *v.* Anderson, 1881; 8 R. 1004.

264. (8.) *By giving up Funds, etc.*—The cautioner is freed by the creditor giving up funds over which he has a right of retention (*a*); or renouncing any security over the debtor's estate without the cautioner's consent (*b*); or neglecting to claim on an estate on which the cautioner was entitled to rely (*c*).

(*a*) Hamilton *v.* L. Kinbrachmont, 1628; M. 2087; 1. B. Sup. 158; 1 Ill. 195. Wallace, *supra*, § 263 (*b*). Stirling *v.* Forrester, 1824; 1 S. App. 37. See above, § 255.

(*b*) Wallace *v.* L. Elibank, 1717; M. 3389; 1 Ill. 192. Boyes, *supra*, § 263 (*b*).

(*c*) Fleming, *supra*, § 263 (*c*). Wingate *v.* Martin, 1829; 8 S. 185; 1 Ill. 195. Hume, *supra*, § 262 (*b*). M'Kenzie's Trs. *v.* Fraser, 1830; 4 W. & S. 410. Drummond *v.* Rannie, 1836; 14 S. 437; 3 Ill. 114.

265. (9.) *By Liberation of Debtor.*—When the creditor has imprisoned or apprehended the debtor, it does not seem to invalidate his claim against the cautioner that he has afterwards liberated the debtor (*a*). The cautioner will still be liable to the creditor, although the debtor shall have escaped from prison; but he will not be liable to the magistrates, on their paying the debt to the creditor; on the contrary, they must indemnify him if he should be called on (*b*).

(*a*) M'Millan *v.* Hamilton, 1729; M. 3390; 1 Ill. 196. Graham *v.* Little, 1730; M. 3364. The words "imprisoned or" appear to have crept in *per incuriam*, as they are not supported by the cases cited, and are contrary both to 3 Ersk. 3. § 66, and 1 Bell's Com. 359. See also above, § 263.

(*b*) Magistrates of Dundee *v.* E. Findlater, 1668; M. 3348. Magistrates are relieved from liability for the escape of prisoners, 2 and 3 Vict. c. 42. Lamb *v.* Mags. of Jedburgh, 1865; 3 Macph. 1105.

266. Recall of Cautionry.—Cautionary obligations may be recalled in certain cases (*a*); as, where one engages for a cash credit, he may, by giving notice to the bank, stop further advances on his responsibility. So, a cautioner for a bank agent, trustee, factor *loco tutoris*, etc., may put an end to his responsibility on reasonable notice, and proper measures taken for recalling the power delegated on his credit (*b*); but a cautioner for an absolute obligation cannot withdraw without taking the debtor in his own hand; nor can a cautioner for a certain term of years (as in a lease) withdraw his security (*c*). 'The cautioner's death generally puts an end to the liability of his estate for the future, if notified to the creditor by his executor, at all events in cases in which the deceased had himself power to recall (*d*).'

(*a*) See cases in § 255 (*b*). M. Bell's Convg. 283.

(*b*) Taylor *v.* Adie, 1818; Hume, 114. Kinloch *v.* Mackintosh, 1822; 1 S. 491. Below, § 287.

(*c*) See Spence *v.* Brownlee, 1834; 13 S. 199.

(*d*) Coulthart *v.* Clementson, 5 Q. B. D. 42. Bradbury *v.* Morgan, 31 L. J. Ex. 462; 1 H. & C. 249. B. L. Bk. *v.* Monteith, 1858; 20 D. 557. 1 Bell's Com. 369 (387), and below, § 288. The terms of the obligation must be looked to. See 1 Smith's L. C. 36.

267. Division.—Although co-cautioners are each ultimately liable to the creditor for the whole debt, they are, in the first instance, entitled to the benefit of Division, provided they have not expressly renounced that benefit. By this each is liable only for his own proportion, while the other cautioners are solvent; and parole evidence, or circumstantial proof, is competent to one co-obligant against another, to prove that he is only a cautioner (*a*).

(*a*) 3 Ersk. 3. § 63. Drummond *v.* Nicolson's Crs., 1697; M. 12,329; 1 Ill. 196. Smollet *v.* Bell, 1793; M. 12,354. See M'Phersons *v.* Haggart, 1881; 9 R. 306. The law of Scotland as to this is made that of England by 19 and 20 Vict. c. 97, § 5.

268. In the Roman law, the obligation of co-cautioners was undertaken by the "stipulatio," in which each answered or engaged for the whole debt. The consequence was, that each was liable, *singuli in solidum*; and that there was not in law any obligation or ground of action to the several cautioners against each other, but on any one of them paying the debt it was extinguished, and all the rest of the cautioners discharged. Two remedies in equity were afterwards introduced: the *Beneficium Divisionis*, by which any one might insist on the others being called on to pay their share; and the *Beneficium Cedendarum Actionum*, by which any one cautioner, on paying the debt, was entitled to require the creditor to assign his right to him (*a*). This is not *necessary* with us; and on that ground it was once held that an assignation could not be demanded (*b*). But it is now settled that an assignation *may* be demanded (*c*).

(*a*) Inst. lib. 3. tit. 21. § 4, *de Fidejussoribus*. Dig. 46. t. 1. l. 39. Cod. lib. 8. tit. 14. l. 11, *de Fidejussoribus*.

(*b*) 3 Ersk. 3. § 68. Home *v.* Crawford, 1666; M. 3347; 1 Ill. 197.

(*c*) Erskine *v.* Manderson, 1780; M. 1386; as corrective of the older cases, M. 3355–56. See 3 Ersk. 5. § 11. Gilmour *v.* Finnie, 1832; 11 S. 193; above, § 255, and below, § 557.

269. Relief among Co-Cautioners.—The relief or remedy arising to co-cautioners *inter se*, cannot be impaired or discharged by the creditor without discharging the co-cautioners (*a*).

(*a*) 3 Ersk. 3. § 68. Skirling *v.* Crichton, 1686; 2 B. Sup. 94; 1 Ill. 197. Dingwall *v.* Murray, 1693; 4 B. Sup. 107. See Nicolson *v.* E. Balcarras, 1708; M. 3357. Wallace *v.* L. Elibank, 1717; M. 3389; 1 Ill. 192. Smith *v.* Ogilvies, 1821; 1 S. 159; aff. 1 W. & S. 315; 1 Ill. 186. See above, § 261A.

270. But where any one of the co-cautioners seeks relief against the others, he must communicate the benefit of any deduction or "ease," which may have been allowed to him in paying the debt; and the benefit of any security which he may hold, 'without the knowledge and acquiescence of the co-cautioner (*a*),' over the estate of the principal (*b*). But this does not hold if the cautioners be bound each for a specific sum (*c*). Where a cautioner who holds a collateral security is creditor in other debts, he is not bound to renounce the benefit of his security (*d*); and a personal guarantee by a third party to any of the cautioners he is not bound to communicate (*e*).

(*a*) Hamilton & Co. *v.* Freeth, 1889; 16 R. 1022. Bell's Com. i. 349.
(*b*) 3 Ersk. 3. § 70. Fisher's Crs. *v.* Campbell, 1778; M. 2134; 1 Ill. 199. Campbell *v.* Campbell, 1775; M. 2132. Milligan *v.* Glen, 1802; M. 2140, and *Cautioner*, Apx. 2. Nicol *v.* Doig & Baxter, June 16, 1807; 1 Ill. 199; 1 Bell's Com. 349 (367, M'L.'s ed.). Humble *v.* Lyon, 1792; Hume, 83. Cowan *v.* Thom, 1802; Hume, 85. See above, § 62. Steel *v.* Dixon, 17 Ch. D. 825; 50 L. J. Ch. 591.
(*c*) Lawrie *v.* Stewart, 1823; 2 S. 327. M. Bell's Conveyancing, 287 sqq. *Sed quære?* See above, § 261A, note (*c*).
(*d*) Campbell, *supra* (*b*).
(*e*) Coventry *v.* Hutchinson, 1830; 8 S. 924. See as to this section, 3 Ersk. Pr. 3. § 27, note in 16th ed.

271. Cautioners may be bound in the same or in several deeds; and at the same time, or at several times. The general rule is, that cautioners are entitled to mutual relief, whether their obligation be in one or in several deeds, being all bound for behoof of the debtor, and at his request (*a*).

(*a*) Walker *v.* Inglis, 1827; 5 S. 726; aff. 1830, 4 W. & S. 40; 1 Ill. 197. Finlayson *v.* Smith, 1827; 6 S. 264. Alston *v.* Dennistoun & Co., 1828; 7 S. 112. See Clark & Highgate *v.* Wilson, 1830; 8 S. 1025. Low *v.* Farquharson, 1831; 9 S. 411. See Smiton, and cases in § 272. Dering *v.* E. Winchelsea, 2 B. & P. 270; 1 White & T. L. C. 106; 3 Ross' L. C. 28; 1 R. R. 41. Whiting *v.* Burke, L. R. 6 Ch. 342. And as to the effect of bankruptcy, see Maxwell's Crs. *v.* Heron, 1792; M. 2136; rev. 3 Paton, 350. Cranston *v.* M'Dowals, 1798; M. 2552.

272. But where cautioners are already bound, and new cautioners are introduced, it is held that if this be only at the desire of the debtor, and not of the former cautioners, the new cautioner is bound as if he had been originally a co-cautioner, and has no other relief than such a cautioner has: And if he be introduced at the request of the former cautioners, or with their assent or acquiescence, to relieve them from a demand, he is cautioner for them, and will have total relief against them (*a*).

(*a*) Murray *v.* Butler, 1722; aff. Robertson's Ap. 465; 1 Ill. 200. Lockhart *v.* L. Semple, 1738; Elchies, *Caut.* 9. Wallace *v.* Fleming, 1685; M. 14,642. Pollock *v.* Pollock, 1745; M. 2125. Loch *v.* L. Nairn, 1701; M. 14,644. Smiton *v.* Miller, 1792; M. 2138; 1 Bell's Com. 352. The view taken in Chancery in England is different —Craythorne *v.* Swinburne, 14 Ves. 160; 1 Ill. 202; 9 R. R. 264; but it was rejected in the Court of Session—Lennox *v.* Campbell, May 18, 1815; F. C. It seems to be a question of intention—Walker *v.* Inglis, *cit.*, § 271 (*a*); but in the absence of circumstances showing the contrary, the presumption is that the new cautioner interposed on behalf of the principal debtor. See Thorburn *v.* Howie, 1863; 1 Macph. 1169. Inglis *v.* Bethune, 1798; Hume, 87. M'Phersons *v.* Haggart, *cit.*, § 267 (*a*).

273. Judicial Cautionry.—Cautionary obligations are employed in judicial proceedings, to secure the efficacy of jurisdiction; to relieve from arrestment or inhibition (*a*); to secure debts brought under suspension in the course of execution or diligence; to secure the person of the debtor for the purpose of personal execution by imprisonment when *in meditatione fugæ*, or when indulged by an incarcerating creditor with temporary liberation.

(*a*) See below, § 2282.

274. (1.) *Caution judicio sisti.*—This is caution to abide judgment within the jurisdiction of the Court. It is exacted from persons *in meditatione fugæ*; and the pursuer of a *cessio bonorum* may, on such caution, procure a personal protection or warrant of liberation (*a*). By the ordinary form of the bond, the cautioner undertakes that the defender shall appear to answer to any action to be brought within six months; and it has sometimes been held that this entitles the creditor to have the person of the defender produced in Court, open to personal diligence (*b*). But this is not the lawful effect of the bond; and it would appear that the cautioner would not be held to forfeit his bond if the debtor were pointed out within Scotland, although he were in prison, or had taken sanctuary, or procured a personal protection (*c*).

The creditor is not bound to call on the cautioner till the decree is about to be extracted (*d*); and he must allow him a reasonable time to present the debtor (*e*).

The obligation *de judicio sisti* is discharged, by death of the debtor (*f*); by notice to the creditor, with presentment of the debtor's person in Court (*g*); by presentment on the creditor's requisition; and by decree extracted, without requisition to present the debtor (*h*).

(*a*) See below, § 2318. Heron *v.* Dickson, 1773; M. 8550; Hailes, 556; 1 Ill. 202. British Linen Co. *v.* Clarkson, 1765; M. 2054. See Scott *v.* Carmichael, 1775; M. 2057; Hailes, 663. 6 and 7 Will. IV. c. 56, § 1, 15. Muir *v.* Collett, 1866; 5 Macph. 47. As to *cessio*, see 39 and 40 Vict. c. 70, § 26, 43 and 44 Vict. c. 34, 44 and 45 Vict. c. 22.

(*b*) Cowan *v.* Aitchison, 1797; M. 2061; and Tasker *v.* Mercer, 1802; M. *Caution jud. sist.* Apx. 2, seem both questionable. See note in 1 Ill. 205.

(*c*) See Watt *v.* Adamson & Shaw, 1828; 7 S. 177. Buston *v.* Fenwick, 1786; Hume, 400. The cautioner is bound to produce the debtor in Court, although he should have taken sanctuary; and it is not enough to present him under the protection of a passed note of suspension. M'Neil *v.* Black, 1804; Hume, 103. Harding *v.* Turnbull, 1797; Hume, 402. Cheyne *v.* Macdonald, 1863; 1 Macph. 960. Douglas *v.* Wallace, 1842; 5 D. 338.

(*d*) Alexander *v.* Ford, 1823; 2 S. 472.

(*e*) Fell *v.* Lyon, 1830; 8 S. 543.

(*f*) Park *v.* Storie, 1680; 3 B. Sup. 318.

(*g*) Lindsay *v.* Fairfoul, 1633; M. 2031. M'Culloch, 1666; M. 369. Stevenson *v.* Chisholm, March 11, 1812; F. C. See Pain *v.* M'Knight, 1803; Hume, 404. Muir *v.* M'Callum, 1810; Hume, 405. Clark *v.* Bremner, 1881; 9 R. 372.

(*h*) Telfer *v.* Muir, 1774; M. 2054; 1 Ill. 203. Brown & Co. *v.* Wilson, 1790; M. 2059. Stewart *v.* Fraser, July 8, 1809; F. C.

275. (2.) *Caution judicatum solvi.*—In proper maritime cases the defender was formerly bound to find caution *de judicio sisti et judicatum solvi* (*a*). But now it is incompetent for the Sheriff, in exercise of his Admiralty jurisdiction, to require such caution from any defender domiciled in Scotland; unless special grounds, stated in the interlocutor, shall make it necessary (*b*). 'And it is also abolished in maritime cases in the Court of Session (*c*).' The effect of this caution, 'which is still given in some cases, *e.g.* in a general loosing of arrestments (*d*),' is, that the cautioner is absolutely liable for all that shall be found due to the pursuer; that where caution is found in the Sheriff Court, he is not discharged by suspension presented to the Court of Session (*e*); that he is not relieved by decree of absolvitor, till such judgment shall be final; and that the death of the party is no liberation to the cautioner (*f*).

(*a*) 1681, c. 16. 1 Will. IV. c. 69, § 23. Rowand *v.* Freeman, 1755; M. 2043; 1 Ill. 205. Herries *v.* Liddesdale, 1755; 5 B. Sup. 295. British Linen Company *v.* Clarkson, 1765; M. 2054; 1 Ill. 202. Cockburn *v.* Inglis, 1776; 5 B. Sup. 407; 1 Ill. 204.

(*b*) 1 and 2 Vict. c. 119, § 22.

(*c*) 13 and 14 Vict. c. 36, § 24.

(*d*) M'Dougall's Tr. *v.* Law, 1864; 3 Macph. 68.

(*e*) Myles *v.* Lyall, 1797; M. 2063; 1 Ill. 205.

(*f*) Dundas *v.* M'Leod, 1774; M. 2040; 1 Ill. 206.

276. (3.) *Caution in Suspension and Advocation.*—This security to the creditor is given, in suspension (which is a stay or sist of diligence already in the course of execution), by caution for the principal sum in the charge, with expenses (*a*); in advocation (which 'was' an appeal from an inferior judge to the Court of Session), the caution 'was' only for the expense in the inferior court, and in the Court of Session (*b*). The cautioner is not bound till his caution is accepted, and may, in the interim, withdraw on the debtor's insolvency (*c*). The cautioner's obligation, both in suspension and in advocation, is not merely personal for the suspender or advocator; but is continued as surety for the heir on the death of the debtor (*d*).

(*a*) See Buchanan *v.* Douglas, 1853; 15 D. 365; 2 Macq. 48. Knox *v.* Patterson, 1861; 23 D. 1263. Logan *v.* Weir, 1870; 8 Macph. 1009 (juratory). As to the effect of a judicial reference, see Stewart *v.* Hickman & Marriot, 1843; 6 D. 151. Potter *v.* Bartholomew, 1847; 10 D. 97.

(*b*) 6 Geo. IV. c. 121, § 41. Act of Sed. June 14, 1799. 1 and 2 Vict. c. 86, § 3 and 4, and Act of Sed. Dec. 24, 1838. The process of advocation is abolished, and no caution is now required in appeals to the Court of Session; 31 and 32 Vict. c. 100, § 65. Mackay's Practice, 179 sqq.

(*c*) Stewart *v.* Mitchell, 1786; M. 2157; 3 Ill. 116.

(*d*) Act of Sed. Jan. 29, 1650. Wilson *v.* Ewing, May, & Co., 1836; 14 S. 262; 3 Ill. 116.

277. (4.) *Caution by Bond of Presentation* is used when a creditor, having personal diligence ready to be executed, or his debtor actually apprehended or in prison, grants an indulgence, on condition of the debtor presenting himself at an appointed time as free as at the time of giving the indulgence; otherwise to pay the debt (*a*). The cautioner undertakes that the debtor shall be personally presented, at a particular place, and on a day and hour specified. The bond is satisfied, and the cautioner freed, by the debtor's death. He is freed for a time by the debtor's sickness, or by inevitable accident; provided the debtor be presented as soon as the impediment is removed. If the debtor be imprisoned by another creditor, it seems to be sufficient to give notice to the holder of the bond of his place of confinement (*b*). But it will not free the cautioner that the debtor is under protection or in sanctuary (*c*).

(*a*) It must be in writing. Chaplin *v.* Allan, 1842 ; 4 D. 616.
(*b*) Polstead *v.* Scott, 1681 ; M. 1807 ; 1 Ill. 206, note.
(*c*) Henderson *v.* Graham, 1710 ; M. 1809.

278. The bond of presentation is strictly but not judaically interpreted, and the most rigid compliance with the condition is required (*a*).

(*a*) M'Gowan *v.* Neilson, 1829 ; 8 S. 142 ; 1 Ill. 206. M'Farlane *v.* Whitson, 1834 ; 12 S. 699. See cases in § 274, note (*c*).

279. Letters of Credit and Recommendation.—(1.) *A Letter of Credit* is a mandate authorising the person addressed to pay money, or furnish goods, to another, on the credit of the writer. When bought at a banker's, it constitutes a debt against the writer; and being a draft on the person addressed, it goes, when answered, into account between him and the writer, but raises no debt to the person paying against the payee. When given for accommodation, and without value paid, it raises, on being answered, a debt not only against the holder of the letter, who receives the money, but also against the writer *ex mandato*, in favour of the person addressed, who has paid the money. A person going abroad gets a power to draw on the writer's correspondent to a certain amount; or a trader, entering into a new line of trade, or settling in a new place, gets a letter of credit or recommendation to dealers in that market; and the chief difficulty is to distinguish between a letter pledging the writer's credit and a mere introduction, under which the person addressed is to follow his own discretion in giving credit (*a*).

(*a*) As to the law of letters of credit and circular notes, see Orr & Barber *v.* Union Bank, 1852 ; 14 D. 395 ; rev. 1854 ; 1 Macq. 513. Cal. Ins. Co. *v.* B. L. Co., 1859 ; 21 D. 1197 ; aff. 4 Macq. 107. *In re* Agra & Masterman's Bank, L. R. 2 Ch. App. 391 ; 36 L. J. Ch. 222. Conflans Quarry Co. *v.* Parker, L. R. 3 C. P. 1 ; 37 L. J. C. P. 51 ; and discussion of these cases in Thorburn, Comm. on Bills of Exch. Act, Intr. 8–22 ; also *ex p.* Coupland, L. R. 5 Ch. 167 ; 39 L. J. Ch. 287 ; *ex p.* Barber, L. R. 9 Eq. 725 ; 39 L. J. Bkr. 39. Union Bank of Canada *v.* Cole, 47 L. J. C. P. 100.

280. (2.) *Letters of Recommendation.* — Generally stated, where a Letter of Recommendation specifies a sum as the limit of credit to be allowed to the bearer; or when it applies specially to a transaction, or dealing, or course of dealing, in which credit is necessary, and is accompanied by an assurance of safety, it will be held as a guarantee. More particularly, the rules seem to be these:—When a representation is made as to character or credit, in consequence of and in answer to inquiries, the expressions used are to be construed largely in favour of the person making such representation, so as not, without great difficulty, to entrap him into a guarantee (*a*). But if the person making the representation states what he knows to be false, to the effect of inducing another to deal with the person recommended, he will be held liable as by a guarantee (*b*). A mere introduction, conceived in general terms of confidence or approbation of the character, conduct, and credit of the person as one with whom it is safe to deal, is held to be only recommendation, not superseding further inquiry or the exercise of a sound discretion; and not amounting to a guarantee (*c*). But when, instead of being thus limited, there is a distinct specific transaction mentioned, with an assurance that it may be safely entered into, it is more easily to be held a guarantee of that particular dealing (*d*).

A letter of recommendation covers only future dealings, unless the contrary be very clearly expressed (*e*).

(*a*) Haycraft *v.* Creasy, 2 East, 92 ; 1 Ill. 210 ; 6 R. R. 380. Rankine *v.* Murray & Muir, May 15, 1812 ; F. C. ; 1 Ill. 207. As to this case, see Prof. George Moir in Ersk. Pr. iii. 3, note E in 16th ed., p. 399. See also 3 Ersk. 26. § 6. Vinn. *ad loc.* Dig. l. 17. t. 1. 2, and l. 4. t. 1. 23. 31, l. 50. t. 14. 2. Bankt. vol. iii. p. 75. Johnston *v.* Owen, 1845 ; 7 D. 1046.
(*b*) Balfour & Co. *v.* Russel, March 8, 1815 ; F. C. Pasley *v.* Freeman, 3 T. R. 51 ; 2 Smith's L. C. 64 ; 1 R. R. 634 ; 1 Ill. 208. Eyre *v.* Dunsford, 1 East, 318 (see 11 R. R. 501 n., 20 R. R. 605 n.). Foster *v.* Charles, 6 Bing. 396 ; 31 R. R. 446. Corbet *v.* Brown, 8 Bing. 33 ; 34 R. R. 615. Ross *v.* Lindsay, 1820 ; Hume, 116. Wilson & Corse *v.* Wood, 1797 ; Hume, 85. Park *v.* Gould, 1851 ; 13 D. 1049.
(*c*) Kembles *v.* Mitchell, 1831 ; 9 S. 648 ; 1 Ill. 208. Rankine, *supra* (*a*). Taylor & Cunningham *v.* Waddell, 1804 ; Hume, 93. Johnston, *cit.*
(*d*) Corbet, *supra* (*b*). Hunter *v.* Carson, 1824 ; 2 S. 596 ; 1 Ill. 208. Fraser *v.* Tait & Kerr, 1822 ; 1 S. 483. See below, § 284, 285.
(*e*) Dykes *v.* Watson, 1825 ; 4 S. 70. Downie *v.* Barr, 1840 ; 3 D. 59.

281. (3.) *Verbal Introductions* 'followed' the same rules in general (*a*). But the greater readiness and confidence with which one speaks in conversation of a friend's situation and circumstances, not only has with us required such assurances to be much more express and specific than when expressed in writing; but this consideration has in England led to a statute, 'Lord Tenterden's Act,' whereby no action is maintainable by reason of any representation or assurance of credit, unless made in writing, and signed by the party to be charged therewith (*b*). 'And, as has been stated above (§ 249A), this rule has been extended to Scotland, so that no verbal introduction or representation can now be held a guarantee. All oral representations as to a third person's ability, etc., are within the Act, if they are made in order to procure money or credit for that third person, whether they are fraudulent or not; and no action will lie, even when they are fraudulently made for the purposes of the person making them, as that the money obtained may be applied to the liquidation of a debt due to the person making them (*c*).'

(*a*) Haycraft, § 280 (*a*). Hunter, § 280 (*d*). M'Ivor *v.* Richardson, 1 M. & S. 557; 1 Ill. 209.

(*b*) 9 Geo. IV. c. 14, § 6.

(*c*) Lyde *v.* Barnard, 1 M. & W. 101; 1 Smith's L. C. 55 sq. Paton *v.* Clydesdale Bank, 1895; 23 R. 38; revd. 1896, A. C. 381; 23 R. H. L. 22.

282. Mercantile Guarantees.—Guarantees, used in mercantile transactions, are either applicable to a special future transaction; or prospectively to a specific course of dealing. If intended to cover previous dealings, it must be clearly expressed. A guarantee 'must now' be in writing; 'although formerly it might' be by parole, provided it 'were' followed by *rei interventus*, without which it 'was' not conclusively binding (*a*). 'It is sometimes a difficult question whether an undertaking is a guarantee requiring to be proved by writing,. or a primary obligation capable of proof by parole. If one says, "Do this, or give these goods to A, and I will see you paid," he himself gives the order and is the principal debtor; *secus*, when he says, "If A does not pay you, I will." It is a question of fact, and if A or the original debtor continues liable, there is a guarantee or cautionary obligation (*b*). There can be no suretyship unless there be a principal debtor (*c*).' It is not unlawful, nor unfrequent in practice, to allow a commission or percentage for engaging in such a guarantee (*d*).

(*a*) 19 and 20 Vict. c. 60, § 6. See above, § 248 sq., 281. As to the terms "guarantee" and "caution," see Wilson *v.* Tait, 1840; 1 Rob. 137, 150.

(*b*) Birkmyr *v.* Darnell, Salk. 27; 1 Smith's L. C. 287. Morrison *v.* Harkness, 1870; 9 Macph. 35. Milne *v.* Kidd, 1869; 8 Macph. 250. Wilson *v.* Tait and Blackwood *v.* Forbes, *supra*, § 253 (*h*). Stevenson's Tr. *v.* Campbell & Sons, 1896; 23 R. 711.

(*c*) See Lakeman *v.* Mountstephen, 43 L. J. Q. B. 188; L. R. 7 H. L. 17; and above, § 251. So, when one induces another to enter into an engagement by a promise to indemnify him, that is not an agreement within the Statute of Frauds in England, and needs not be in writing. Thomas *v.* Cooke, 8 B. & Cr. 728; 7 L. J. (O. S.) K. B. 49; 32 R. R. 520. Wildes *v.* Dudlow, 44 L. J. Ch. 341; 19 Eq. 198. Reader *v.* Kingham, 13 C. B. N. S. 344; 32 L. J. C. P. 108.

(*d*) *Ex p.* Adney, Cowp. Rep. 460. See 17 and 18 Vict. c. 216, incorporating the Guarantee Association. Burnett, petr., 1859; 21 D. 1197. Donaldson *v.* Findlay & Co., 1860; 22 D. 1471. And see § 246, 286.

283. These engagements may be either Permanent and Continuing guarantees; or Limited by stipulation, in respect of the transaction, of the person, or of the time; 'or *del credere* guarantees.'

284. (1.) *Continuing Guarantees.* — One engaging for "any" dealing of another, trusts entirely to his discretion, and will be liable to any amount of his dealings. Even when such a guarantee is limited to a certain sum, it is binding not for one dealing to that amount only, but for successive dealings (*a*). But where such expressions are accompanied by any clear indications that a particular transaction only is in contemplation, it will be held as limited, and not as a continuing guarantee (*b*). A bank-credit bond is of the nature of a continuing guarantee, being for all sums to be advanced or engaged for till the credit be recalled; and a letter guaranteeing an over-draft on the credit was held to be on the same footing (*c*).

(*a*) Merle *v.* Wells, 2 Camp. 414; 1 Ill. 211. Mason *v.* Pritchard, 2 Camp. 436; 11 R. R. 369. Bastow *v.* Bennett, 3 Camp. 220. Allan *v.* Kenning, 9 Bing. 618; 35 R. R. 648. Downie *v.* Barr, 1840; 3 D. 59. Tennant & Co. *v.* Bunten, 1859; 21 D. 631. Veitch *v.* Murray & Co., 1864; 2 Macph. 1098. Caledonian Bank *v.* Kennedy's Trs., 1870; 8 Macph. 862. Stewart, Moir, & Muir *v.* Brown, 1871; 9 Macph. 763. See cases in Smith's Merc. Law, 580. Addison on Contr. 657 sq. Journ. of Jur. xv. 350.

(*b*) Baird *v.* Corbet, 1835; 14 S. 41. Melville *v.* Hayden, 3 B. & Cr. 593. Kay *v.* Groves, 6 Bing. 276; 3 Ill. 115. Wilson & Corse *v.* Wood, 1797; Hume, 85. Slade & Co. *v.* Black & Knox, 1808; Hume, 95. Scott *v.* Mitchell, 1866; 4 Macph. 551. Rennie *v.* Smith's Trs., 1866; 4 Macph. 669.

(*c*) Sir W. Forbes & Co. *v.* Dundas, 1830; 8 S. 865. See also Houston's Exrs. *v.* Speirs, 1834; 12 S. 879. See below, § 299.

285. (2.) *Limited Guarantees.*—The rule of construction of all such engagements, and of their limitation is very rigid. Being *strictissimi juris*, a limitation to future dealings is presumed; and unless the terms are such as to include existing debts, it will not cover them (*a*). A limitation to a particular transaction is conclusive (*b*); a limitation to a person is strictly to be observed (*c*); and a limitation in time is neither to be extended nor abridged (*d*). But the usage of trade will be held as qualifying the construction (*e*). A guarantee for a certain amount of goods has been held not to restrict the dealing, but to cover it to that amount (*f*).

(*a*) Glyn *v.* Hertel, 8 Taunt. 208 ; 1 Ill. 213. **Smith** *v.* **Bank of Scotland,** 1813 ; 1 Dow, 272 ; 1829, 7 S. 244 ; 1 Ill. 180 ; 14 R. R. 67. Paterson *v.* Wright, Jan. 31, 1810 ; aff. 1814, 6 Pat. 38. Napier & Co. *v.* Bruce, 1840 ; 2 D. 556 ; aff. 1842, 1 Bell's App. 78. Downie *v.* Barr, 1840 ; 3 D. 59.

(*b*) Scott *v.* Mitchell, and Rennie *v.* Smith's Trs., *cit.* § 284 (*b*).

(*c*) Stewart *v.* Scott, 1803 ; Hume, 91 ; 1 Bell's Com. 374. Philip *v.* Melville, Feb. 21, 1809 ; F. C. Bowie *v.* Watson, 1840 ; 2 D. 1061. Raimes *v.* Alexander, 1842 ; 4 D. 1167 ; *infra*, § 288 *fin.* As to change in firm, see § 259.

(*d*) M'Lagan & Co. *v.* Macfarlan, Nov. 19, 1813 ; F. C. Douglas & Co. *v.* Gordon & Co., Dec. 24, 1814 ; F.C. Merle, Mason, Bastow, Melville, *supra*, § 284. Bacon *v.* Chesney, 1 Starkie, 192 ; 1 Ill. 214.

(*e*) M'Lagan, *supra* (*d*). Samuel *v.* Howarth, 3 Meriv. 272 ; 3 Ill. 115 ; 17 R. R. 81. Combe *v.* Wolfe, 8 Bing. 156 ; 34 R. R. 659.

(*f*) Kinross *v.* Cleland, 1687 ; 3 B. Sup. 212 ; 1 Ill. 215. Tennant & Co., *cit.* § 284 (*a*). Cf. Morgan *v.* Smart, and Ellis *v.* Emmanuel, cited in § 261A (*c*) ; and § 289 *infra.*

286. (3.) *Del Credere Guarantee.*—This is an engagement by a 'mercantile' factor, bank agent, insurance broker, or other mandatary, for the solvency of persons who purchase from or deal with him in the concerns of his principal (*a*). The consideration for such an engagement is an additional allowance by higher commission on the transaction. This guarantee is constituted by express agreement; or by accepting of, or charging, or acquiescing in *del credere* commission. The factor is entitled to his commission immediately on the sale; the event being collateral (*b*).

(*a*) Grove *v.* Dubois, 1 T. R. 112 ; 1 Ill. 215. Bize *v.* Dickson, 1 T. R. 285 (both overruled. Barber *v.* Pott, 4 H. & N. 759 ; 28 L. J. Ex. 381. Morris, *infra*). Mackenzie *v.* Scott, 1795 ; Bell's Ca. 138 ; 3 Pat. 525 ; 6 Bro. P. C. 291. See Smith's Merc. Law, 127. 1 Bell's Com. 377. The contract does not fall under the Statute of Frauds in England, and therefore need not be in writing. Le Couturier *v.* Hastie, 8 Ex. 40 ; in H. L. 25 L. J. Ex. 253. Wickham *v.* Wickham, 2 Kay & J. 476. And on similar principles, viz. that it is primarily a contract of mandate, and only incidentally one of cautionry, it would seem not to come within the Merc. Law Amt. Act, § 8. The liability of a *del credere* agent is conditional on the vendee's failure to pay. Morris *v.* Cleasby, 4 M. & S. 566.

(*b*) See § 246, 282.

287. Cautionary Obligations for Officers generally.—Cautionary Obligations are most commonly made use of for securing a precise and subsisting debt; but they are also applied most usefully in many situations of trust, where the engagements and transactions are prospective. In such prospective engagement, while the cautioner is not exposed to the danger of any situation or transaction not fairly in contemplation of the parties at entering into the contract, he is not entitled to withdraw suddenly, and without due notice (*a*).

(*a*) As to the right to withdraw, see Burgess *v.* Eve and Phillips *v.* Foxall, cited below, § 288, and above, § 266.

288. From the nature of a prospective engagement, there are some situations in which a duty of care and vigilance is incumbent on the creditor for protection of the cautioner, as in the care to be taken of an apprentice (*a*). 'But as the purpose of a guarantee of this kind is to protect against dishonesty and misconduct, it is no answer to a claim upon the bond that the employer did not see that the employee did his duty. And the obligor (unless where periodical accounting is made the basis of the contract, and its omission a ground of irritancy or forfeiture) is not discharged even by long neglect in the nature of passive inactivity to demand payment or accounting. To liberate the surety from future liability, there must be a positive act by the employer to his prejudice, such as deliberate continuance of the employment, without notice to the surety, after discovery of dishonesty or gross misconduct, failure to disclose previous discreditable conduct, or such negligence as amounts to connivance or fraud (*b*). Sureties are not discharged if the creditor does something to change their position in consequence of a fraudulent act of the person for whom they are bound (*c*).' And when the cautioner happens to die during the time contemplated (*d*), the cautionary obligation is continued on the heir, not only for the debt incurred during the original cautioner's life, but prospectively for the intromissions or advances after the heir's succession (*e*). 'The obligation ceases on a change of firm, and on the death of the creditor (*f*).'

(*a*) Allan *v.* Paterson, 1663 ; M. 2088 ("a very doubtful decision," 1 Ill. 215). And see below, § 291 and 295.

(*b*) M'Taggart *v.* Watson, 1834 ; 12 S. 322 ; rev. 1835, 1 S. & M'L. 553. Rankin *v.* Creighton, 1838 ; 16 S. 447 ; aff. 1840, 1 Rob. 99. Falconer *v.* Lothian, 1843 ; 5 D. 866. Biggar *v.* Wright, 1846 ; 9 D. 78. Smith *v.* Bk. of Scotland, 1 Dow, 272 ; 14 R. R. 67. French *v.* Cameron, 1893 ;

20 R. 966. Bonthrone *v.* Paterson, 1898; 25 R. 391. Black *v.* Ottoman Bank, 15 Moore P. C. 472. Phillips *v.* Foxall, L. R. 7 Q. B. 293. Burgess *v.* Eve, L. R. 13 Eq. 450; 41 L. J. Ch. 515. Sanderson *v.* Aston, 42 L. J. Ex. 64; L. R. 8 Ex. 73. See § 291, 295.

(*c*) Mayor of Hull *v.* Harding, 1892; 2 Q. B. 494.

(*d*) The duration of the liability is a question of intention to be gathered from the terms of the bond, and from the nature of the office or employment. See Addison on Contr. 654; and cases in § 289 (*f*).

(*e*) University of Glasgow *v.* Miller, 1790; M. 2106; Bell's Cases, 140; Hailes, 1091; 1 Ill. 178. Coml. Bank of Aberdeen *v.* Callander, 1801; Hume, 88. Dudgeon *v.* Laing, 1813; Hume, 102. Paterson *v.* Calder, 1808; M. Apx. *Society*, 4. Morrice *v.* Scott. 1831; 9 S. 480. **Kerr** *v.* **Bremner,** 1839; 1 D. 618; H. L. (as Campbell *v.* Bremner) 1842, 1 Bell's App. 380. Brit. Lin. Co. *v.* Monteith, 1858; 20 D. 557. Cal. Bkg. Co. *v.* Kennedy's Trs., 1870; 8 Macph. 862. Lloyd's *v.* Harper, 16 Ch. D. 290; 50 L. J. Ch. 140. In Shaw's Bell's Commentaries, p. 28 (below, § 294), the doctrine is limited to the case where the cautioner "binds himself and his *heirs*"; but this seems to be incorrect, as "it is a general rule of the law of Scotland that all obligations incurred by the ancestor transmit against his representatives." By the whole Court in Kerr *v.* Bremner, *cit.* Bell's Com. i. 367, 369 (385, 387, M'L.'s ed.). Bell's Convg. 256.

(*f*) 19 and 20 Vict. c. 97, § 7. See above, § 259. Barker *v.* Parker, 1 T. R. 287, 295; 1 R. R. 201. *Supra*, § 285 (*c*).

289. An important point in all such prospective obligations by cautioners is, the extent of the obligation. It is an absolute condition implied in the cautioner's engagement, that the creditor shall deal fairly with him, and not mislead him into any engagement for deficiencies undisclosed (*a*). And there must also be perfect fairness in the cautioner's engagement (*b*).

The ordinary obligation is for *future* intromissions, the principal being trusted on the faith of the cautioner: But it may be otherwise stipulated; and it is to be remarked particularly whether the words are so broad as to extend to *past* as well as to future dealings, or acts of administration (*c*).

Where the obligation of the cautioner is general and unlimited, for all loss by the acts of the principal debtor, declaring that the cautioner shall not be liable in more than a certain sum, the cautionary obligation is held to be a *covering* security, entitling the creditor to apply to all his other resources before coming on the cautioner (*d*). It seems to be different where the intromissions themselves are limited in amount (*e*).

The cautionary obligation for intromissions under a particular employment, lease, etc., is confined to the particular extent and character of intromissions under that collateral contract, 'or bargained in the cautionary writing (*f*). Any material change in the nature of the employee's duties and responsibilities, such as to effect the peril of the surety, or vary the conditions of the contract made with the surety, and not communicated to him, liberates him (*g*).'

(*a*) **Smith** *v.* **Bank of Scotland,** 1813; 1 Dow, 272; 1829, 7 S. 244; 1 Ill. 180; 14 R. R. 67; 3 Ross' L. C. 66. Railton *v.* Matthews, 1844; 6 D. 536; rev. 10 Cl. & F. 934; 3 Bell's App. 56. See 7 D. 748; 8 D. 747. Royal Bank *v.* Ranken, 1844; 6 D. 1814. Falconer *v.* Lothian, 1843; 5 D. 866.

(*b*) Smith, *supra* (*a*). See Burnett *v.* Burnett, 1859; 21 D. 813. Wardlaw *v.* Mackenzie, 1859; 21 D. 940.

(*c*) Kinnear *v.* ——, 1776; 3 B. Sup. 102; 1 Ill. 216. Mags. of Edinburgh *v.* Gardiner, 1766; Hailes, 109. Smith, *supra* (*a*). Dykes *v.* Watson, 1825; 4 S. 69. See above, § 285. Wallace *v.* M'Kissock, 1898; 25 R. 642.

(*d*) Maxton *v.* M'Intosh's Crs., 1777; 5 B. Sup. 408; M. Apx. *Cautioner*, 1; 1 Ill. 218. Borthwick *v.* Balfour & Gibson, Jan. 29, 1819; F. C.; aff. 1822, 1 S. App. 131.

(*e*) See Kinross *v.* Cleland, 1677; 3 B. Sup. 212. See § 285 (*f*).

(*f*) University of Glasgow *v.* E. Selkirk, 1790; M. 2104; Bell's Ca. 134. Mags. of Haddington *v.* Howden, 1816; Hume, 109. Napier & Co. *v.* Bruce, 1840; 2 D. 556; aff. 1842, 1 Bell's App. 78; 8 Cl. & F. 470. Montefiore *v.* Lloyd, 15 C. B. N. S. 203; 33 L. J. C. P. 49. Harrison *v.* Seymour, 35 L. J. C. P. 264; L. R. 1 C. P. 518 (contract divisible—see Skillett, *infra*). See § 288 (*c*).

(*g*) **Bonar** *v.* **M'Donald,** 1847; 9 D. 1537; aff. 1850, 7 Bell's App. 379; 3 H. L. 226. Nicholson *v.* Burt, 1882; 10 R. 121. L. Arlington *v.* Meyricke, 2 Wms. Saund. 403. Pybus *v.* Gibb, 6 E. & B. 911. Skillett *v.* Fletcher, L. R. 1 C. P. 217; 2 C. P. 469; 35 L. J. C. P. 154; 36 *ib.* 206. *Supra*, § 259.

290. Particular Officers. — (1.) *Cautioner for a Bank Agent.*—In order to be secured against the fraud, malversation, or negligence of their agents, and generally for their agent's intromissions, banks take one or more sureties, bound either without limitation, or for a particular sum.

291. This being a prospective and continuing guarantee, the bank and the cautioners are reciprocally bound in duties to each other: the cautioners directly, for solvency, fidelity, and care; the bank directly, for perfect fairness in the contract (*a*), and indirectly, for due vigilance in that superintendence which the nature of the trust prevents the cautioner from assuming (*b*).

(*a*) Smith *v.* Bank of Scotland, 1813; 1 Dow, 272; *cit.* § 289 (*a*).

(*b*) British Linen Co. *v.* Nisbet, 1773; 5 B. Sup. 409; 1 Ill. 216. Anonymous Case, 1 Dow, 296. Thomson *v.* Bank of Scotland, 1822; 1 S. 275; 1824, 2 S. App. 316. Leith Bank *v.* Bell, 1830; 8 S. 721; aff. 5 W. & S. 703. British Guarantee Co. *v.* Western Bank, 1853; 15 D. 834. See above, § 251 (*g*), 288, and below, § 295. Forbes *v.* Welsh, 1829; 7 S. 732. Thistle Friendly Society of Aberdeen *v.* Garden, 1834; 12 S. 745. The bond sometimes excludes or limits the bank's duty in superintending, etc.; but a bond of this kind cannot be construed as a security for advances made with the bank's knowledge upon the agent's personal account. North of Sc. Bkg. Co. *v.* Fleming, 1882; 10 R. 217.

292. Where the cautionry is without restriction, the debt of the principal is the debt against the cautioner. Where the sum is restricted, but the obligation not limited, it is a *covering* security, and the creditor may apply all the debtor's resources, in the first place, before making his demand (*a*).

(*a*) Maxton and Borthwick, *supra*, § 289 (*d*).

293. It is commonly covenanted that the amount of the debt against the cautioner shall be fixed by a stated account, signed by the accountant 'of the bank,' and this is sufficient to fix the sum for which summary diligence may proceed (*a*).

(*a*) Fisher *v.* Stewart (Perth Bank), 1824; 2 S. 583, and 3 S. 426; 1 Ill. 219. See *s. c.* 7 S. 97; and below, § 302.

294. If heirs are bound, the obligation transmits *ipso jure*, as a continuing guarantee, against the heir, on the death of the original cautioner (*a*).

(*a*) See above, § 288 (*d*).

295. (2.) *Cautioner for a Trustee or other Official Person.*—This proceeds on the principles already explained: Where the trustee is under the Sequestration Act, there are certain duties prescribed, the palpable breach of which the creditors have it in their power to check; and neglect of fair superintendence in this respect was in one case held to bar the demand against the cautioner (*a*). But this has been disapproved of, and the creditors held entitled both to the protection of the provisions of the statute on the one hand, and to the full benefit of the cautionary obligation on the other, undischarged by any actual or presumed neglect on the part of the creditors, or of the committee of their number (*b*). In one case, in the sequestration of a land estate, where the creditors had not bestowed due vigilance in checking the intromissions of a judicial factor, it was held that the cautioner was freed (*c*). But the more recent case of M'Taggart (*b*) is against that decision; and in cases of extrajudicial trusts, this was not held a good defence to the cautioner (*d*). Where, in a private trust, the cautioner prescribes the rules of vigilance or of accounting, and these are neglected, the cautioner is free (*e*).

(*a*) Duncan *v.* Porterfield, 1826; 5 S. 102; 1 Ill. 219. Houston's Exrs. *v.* Porterfield, 1826; 5 S. 106. Eadie *v.* How, 1829; 7 S. 356. Dalzell *v.* Menzies, 1831; 9 S. 434.

(*b*) M'Taggart *v.* Watson, 1834; 12 S. 332; 1 S. & M'L. 553; 1 Ill. 221; 3 Ill. 116. See Biggar *v.* Wright, 1846; 9 D. 78; and above, § 288.

(*c*) Pringle *v.* Tate, 1834; 12 S. 918; 1 Ill. 221.

(*d*) Rankin *v.* Creighton, 1838; 16 S. 447; aff. 1 Rob. 99; 3 Ill. 116.

(*e*) Forbes *v.* Welsh, 1829; 7 S. 732. See the old cases, Dick *v.* Nisbet, 1697; M. 2090. Hamilton *v.* Calder, 1706; M. 2091. Wallace & Baillie *v.* Saunders, 1707; M. 2096. As to cautioners for judicial factors, see *infra*, § 2116.

296. (3.) *Caution for a Messenger-at-Arms.*—For the due execution of his duty, a messenger finds caution in the Court of the Lord Lyon, "for the damage, interest, and expense which the lieges shall sustain through the negligence, fraudful or informal execution, of the messenger" (*a*).

(*a*) 1587, c. 46. Form of the bond in Lyon Office.

297. This gives action not only to the employer of the messenger, but to any person suffering oppression or damage by his illegal proceedings as a messenger (*a*); not when he acts, or is employed to act as an agent. It gives action also to the Lord Lyon for his fees (*b*). The responsibility of the cautioner is confined to the messenger's acts in that character alone (*c*); and in point of extent, where a special act of diligence is to be done (as to poind a cargo or arrest a debt), the cautioner will be liable only for what is lost by the messenger's failure in duty; but where he is employed generally to do diligence for recovery of debt, the cautioner is not allowed to go into an inquiry as to the probable inefficacy of the diligence, the law holding the debt to be the measure of the damage (*d*). 'The surety is liable for the expenses of proceedings caused by his negligence, although no notice of these proceedings was given to him; but of course may examine into and question the necessity and propriety of these proceedings (*e*).'

(*a*) Grant *v.* Forbes & Henderson, 1758; M. 2081; aff. 1759; 6 Pat. 731; 1 Ill. 221. Kennedy *v.* M'Kinnon, 1821; 1 S. 210. Stewart *v.* Lowrie, 1813; Hume, 100 (cautioners for J. P. constable). Clason *v.* Black, 1841; 4 D. 743. Struthers *v.* Dykes, 1847; 9 D. 1437; aff. 1850, 7 Bell's App. 390. Cullen *v.* Dykes, 1852; 24 Jur. 177. Cullen *v.* Smith & Thomson, 1847; 9 D. 606, 613.

(*b*) M'Intosh *v.* E. Kinnoull, 1824; 3 S. 190.

(*c*) Welsh *v.* M'Veaghs, 1781; M. 8893. Fraser *v.* Andrew, 1831; 9 S. 345. Potter *v.* Muirhead, 1847; 9 D. 519. Wright *v.* O'Henley, 1827; 5 S. 311.

(*d*) Chatto & Co. *v.* Marshall, June 7, 1811; F. C. See also Dean *v.* Mags. of Ayr, 1803; M. 11,765. Glen *v.* Black, 1841; 4 D. 36. Couper *v.* Bain, 1868; 7 Macph. 101. Henderson *v.* Rollo, 1871; 10 Macph. 104. See Davidson *v.* Mackenzie, 1856; 19 D. 226.

(*e*) Clason and Struthers, *citt.* (*a*).

298. (4.) *Caution for a Notary.*—Such cautioner engages for the notary's "honest and faithful administration of his office conform to law" (*a*). Not only fraud, but also want of skill in the proper office of notary, will subject the cautioners (*b*). But the cautioner is not liable for what is not strictly the business of a notary (*c*). 'Since 1873, it is not necessary to find caution on admission as a notary (*d*).'

(*a*) Bond lodged in Court of Session with the Clerk of Notaries.
(*b*) Stevenson *v.* Tweeddale, 1818; 1 Bell's Com. 366; Hume, 111; 1 Ill. 223.
(*c*) Same case.
(*d*) 36 and 37 Vict. c. 63, § 18 (Law Agents Act).

299. Cautionary Obligation for a Cash Account.—A cash account with a bank is a credit allowed to a person named, in virtue of which he may pass cheques on the bank, draw bills, and operate in all the various ways in which he might have operated if he had actually had money deposited in the bank (*a*). The loan is made as the money may be required. The repayment is by the replacing of money as funds come in. The debt is in perpetual fluctuation. The credit and loan are secured by a bond for such amount of debt, not exceeding a certain limited sum (*b*), as shall ultimately arise on a balance of the deposits and drafts.

(*a*) See above, § 284. See as to the effect of a change of partners, *supra*, § 259.
(*b*) As to the effect of this limitation, see 1 Bell's Com. 366–367 (384, M'L.'s ed.); and comp. above, § 289 (*d*), (*e*); § 285 (*f*).

300. This engagement is undertaken by a bond (*a*), in which the account and all the operations on the credit are stipulated to be in the name of the person for whose benefit the credit is provided; but he and his cautioners are all bound jointly and severally as principals (*b*); the cautioners expressly renouncing the benefit of discussion.

(*a*) This may be by heritable bond; 19 and 20 Vict. c. 91, § 7; below, § 913. M. Bell's Convg. 1162. The bank may withdraw the credit, although they have got a heritable security. Johnstone *v.* Coml. Bank, 1858; 20 D. 790.
(*b*) See as to the liability of the cautioner's heirs, *ante*, § 288, 294. Cases of Morrice and B. L. Co. and Cal. Banking Co.

301. A cautioner interposing in a bank credit already granted will be liable for sums advanced before as well as after the date of his bond, provided there be a fair disclosure of the state of the account, or a distinct stipulation as to past advances. 'But the creditor in such a bond is not bound to disclose the particular application to be made of the money to be advanced, even though it should be intended and applied to pay off an existing credit; for the cautioner interposing for his friend is bound to know his condition (*a*). But if there be misrepresentation or active concealment of a state of matters or application of the money different from what might be expected as in the ordinary course of business, the cautioner will be free (*b*).'

(*a*) Hamilton *v.* Watson, 1842; 5 D. 280; aff. 1845, 4 Bell, 67; 12 Cl. & F. 109. See Lee *v.* Jones, 14 C. B. N. S. 386; 17 C. B. N. S. 482; 34 L. J. C. P. 131. Young *v.* Clydesdale Bk., 1889; 17 R. 231.
(*b*) Falconer *v.* N. of Sc. Bkg. Co., 1863; 1 Macph. 177, 704.

302. It is in such bonds stipulated that, to the effect of authorising a valid charge, the amount of the debt shall be ascertained by a signed account extracted from the bank books. 'According to the practice in keeping such accounts, a balance is struck at the end of each year, when interest is added to the principal, just as if a draft had been made upon the bank, to the effect of extinguishing the cautioner's obligation for interest on previous drafts thus converted into principal, and entitling the bank to interest on the accumulated sum, within the limit of the bond, from the date of each balance (*a*).' The amount so ascertained will be sufficient to authorise summary execution (*b*); but the account so referred to is not to be held conclusive between the parties (*c*); the banker will only thereby have the benefit of caution in a suspension, should any objection be stated against the charge.

(*a*) Reddie *v.* Williamson, 1863; 1 Macph. 228. Gilmour *v.* Bk. of Scotland, 1880; 7 R. 734. Coml. Bk. *v.* Pattison's Trs., 1891; 18 R. 476.
(*b*) See Fisher, *supra*, § 293 (*a*).
(*c*) Swan *v.* Bank of Scotland, 1835; 13 S. 403; rev. 2 S. & M'L. 67; 1839, 2 D. 78. Smith *v.* Drummond, 1829; 7 S. 792; 1 Bell's Com. 364 (382, M'L.'s ed.); and above, § 68. Gilmour *v.* Finnie, 1831; 9 S. 907.

303. In balancing the account, all sums due to the bank, or which the bank shall engage for on account of the person in whose name the account is kept, by orders, drafts, receipts, letters of credit, and bills accepted, indorsed, or discounted, or in any other manner of way, will be included. And although, in the account on which the charge is given, some of those engagements should still be depending on bills in the circle, the result as they afterwards fall 'due' may be brought to augment the balance (*a*).

(*a*) Liddell *v.* Sir W. Forbes & Co., 1820; 1 Bell's Com. 369; 1 Ill. 223. See Brit. Lin. Bank *v.* Thomson 1853; 15 D. 314. Alston's Tr. *v.* Royal Bk., 1893; 20 R. 887.

304. The bank cannot discharge, destroy, or forfeit collateral securities, without freeing the co-obligants in the bond (*a*); but, on the other hand, is not bound to do diligence against the person who holds the credit (*b*).

(*a*) See above, § 256 et seq. As to giving time, transacting, etc., see Cal. Bkg. Co., and cases in § 262.

(*b*) For the septennial limitation of cautionary obligations, see below, § 600.

CHAPTER IX

OF BILLS OF EXCHANGE AND PROMISSORY NOTES

305. Nature of Bills. — Bills are to be viewed not only as obligations of simple form and ready execution, but as part of the circulating medium of the country, by means of which manufacturers and merchants turn credit into a negotiable shape, and are enabled to proceed with their dealings as if paid in cash for their goods, while the buyer is indulged with a delay of payment till the returns of trade fill his hands (*a*).

Bills and Notes (*b*) are properly mercantile instruments; but the use of them has not with us, as in some countries, been restricted to mercantile men, and they have been largely introduced into the ordinary intercourse of life. In that use of them the same rules are applied as in the strict mercantile employment of the instruments.

(*a*) The subject is so extensive, and the adjudged cases so numerous, that it may be sufficient here to lay down the general principles which regulate the doctrine: referring to the institutional writers who have fully treated the matter. See Bayley on Bills. Chitty on Bills. Wilson's Thomson on Bills. 1 Bell's Com. 386. Selwyn's Nisi Prius. 3 Kent, Com. on American Law, 71. Pothier, Cont. de Change. Code de Commerce, liv. i. tit. 8. 1 Pardessus, Droit Com. 327. Merlin, Répert. de Jurisp. tom. vii. p. 395. Van Leeuwen, 437. Byles, Chitty, Parsons, and Story on Bills. Story on Promissory Notes.

(*b*) The term Bills will be hereafter used as including Notes, in so far as appropriate.

306. Kinds and Forms of Bills.—(1.) *A Bill of Exchange* is 'an unconditional order in writing, addressed by one person (drawer) to another, signed by the person giving it, requiring the person to whom it is addressed (drawee) to pay on demand, or at a fixed or determinable future time, a sum certain in money to, or to the order of, a specified person, or to bearer. An instrument which does not comply with these conditions, or which orders any act to be done in addition to the payment of money, is not a bill of exchange. A bill is not invalid by reason that it is not dated; that it does not specify the value given, or that any value has been given therefor; or that it does not specify the place where it is drawn, or the place where it is payable (*a*).' The subscription of the drawee to the address of this letter is the "acceptance" of the order, or the undertaking to pay the money as ordered; and such acceptance completes the obligation.

Foreign Bills of Exchange, properly so called, to which there are three parties,—drawer, drawee, and payee, — are used in transmitting money from one country to another. They are generally drawn in sets or duplicates, each being drawn conditionally, "the others not being paid"; and the payee is furnished with two or three duplicates, to provide for the accidental loss of one or more. These the drawee is to answer only alternatively: The first presented is entitled to payment; the discharged document being a good answer to a demand on the others. A banker, consequently, in discounting a draft which is one of a set, proceeds on the discounter's credit alone, unless all the set is given up, or indemnity taken against the use of those which do not appear.

(*a*) 45 and 46 Vict. c. 61, § 3 (1), (2), (4). (Bills of Exchange Act, 1882, referred to in this chapter as The Act.)

307. (2.) *Inland Bills*, in which also there may be three parties, but sometimes only two,—the drawer, requesting the money to be paid to himself, or his order; and the drawee, to whom the request is addressed,—are generally used for settling and constituting a debt in such a form, that the bill may either remain with the original creditor, ready for immediate execution at the time of payment; or be conveyed to another in place of money. 'An inland bill is, or on the face of it purports to be, both drawn and payable within the British Islands, or drawn within the British Islands upon some person resident therein. Unless the contrary appear on the face of the bill, the holder may treat it as an inland bill (*a*).'

(3.) *A Promissory Note* proceeds from the debtor, is signed by him alone, and contains, in form, an 'unconditional' promise or engagement to pay at a 'fixed or determinable future time,' to the creditor, or to his order, 'or to bearer,' a certain sum (*b*) 'in money. A note payable to maker's order is not a promissory note, unless and until it is indorsed by the maker (*c*). A note is not invalid by reason only that it contains also a pledge of collateral security, with authority to sell or dispose thereof (*d*).'

Promissory notes are the nearest in nature and use to inland bills; being a mere acknowledgment of debt, and engagement to pay to the original creditor; and capable, like the others, of being transferred as money to another person.

The obligation, in any of these terms, completed by the acceptance of the drawee of the bill, or by the subscription of the maker of the note, is transmissible by indorsement, '*i.e.* indorsement completed by delivery'; which is either an order on the back of the instrument, signed by the payee, and directing the 'whole' amount to be paid to a person named; or the subscription of the payee's name on the back without any such order, which is called a blank indorsation, and is an authority to the holder of the instrument to demand payment of it when due (*e*).

(*a*) Act, § 4. See *ib.* § 83 (4), § 72 (2). This is nearly the same as 19 and 20 Vict. c. 60, § 12 (Merc. Law Amendment Act, Scotland, which is repealed—see sched.), and § 97 (3) repeats the saving of the existing stamp laws. As to promissory notes, see the Act, § 83 (4).

(*b*) An acknowledgment of the receipt of money, accompanied by a promise to pay it when required, is a note under the Stamp Acts. See below, § 328. Vallance *v.* Forbes, 1879; 6 R. 1099.

(*c*) Act, § 83 (1), (2). See Duncan's Trs. *v.* Shand, 1872; 10 Macph. 984.

(*d*) *Ib.* § 83 (3). Blyth *v.* Forbes, 1879; 6 R. 1102. Macfarlan *v.* Johnston, 1864; 2 Macph. 1210. Wise *v.* Charlton, 4 A. & E. 786. But the insertion of extraneous provisos and conditions will turn a document promising to pay into an agreement, and deprive it of the character of a note. Davies *v.* Wilkinson, 10 A. & E. 98. Kirkwood *v.* Smith, 1896; 1 Q. B. 582.

(*e*) See below, § 329. The Act, § 2, 32, etc.

308. (4.) *Bank Cheques.*—Besides bills and notes, there is another form of order to transfer money, viz. Bank Cheques (*a*). These are orders addressed to a banker to pay a certain sum to the bearer of the cheque. 'It is negotiable, being defined "a bill of exchange drawn on a banker payable on demand," and the provisions of the law as to bills payable on demand, except in regard to summary diligence, apply to cheques (*b*). An indorsee or holder in due course (*c*), therefore (not one who holds merely as an agent for the payee or indorsee) (*d*), has an indefeasible title to it, though it may have been obtained from the drawer by fraud to which he was not a party (*e*). A banker is bound to pay his customer's cheques if he has sufficient funds in his hands, and is answerable to him in damages for loss caused by his wrongful refusal (*f*); and no pretext for refusal will be allowed short of a legal right of retention, or some equally good objection, such as arrestment (*g*), countermand of payment, or notice of the customer's death (*h*), or the customer's sequestration or notour bankruptcy.' There is no day of payment, the order being general; and the presumption of knowledge of dishonour applicable to ordinary bills taken by an indorsee after the day of payment (*i*) is not held to apply to one receiving a cheque after its date; though that may be a circumstance to weigh with the jury in evidence (*k*). 'If the holder of a cheque does not present it for payment within a reasonable time after its issue (which is a question of fact to be determined with regard to the nature of the instrument, usage, and the circumstances of the case), the drawer, if he had funds to meet it at the time when such presentment should have been made, is discharged to the extent to which he suffers damage by the delay, *e.g.* by the failure of the banker; and to the extent of such damage the holder of the cheque is made a creditor of the banker in lieu of him (*l*). If there be no loss, a cheque is, it has been said, valid for six years (*m*).' Such instruments 'were' exempt from the stamp laws, if truly dated and drawn payable to the bearer on demand, and upon a banker within ten miles (*n*); 'but all cheques are now subject to a stamp duty of one penny (*o*). By 16 and 17 Vict. c. 59, § 19, bankers are authorised to pay to the bearer the amount of any cheque drawn on them payable to order purporting to be indorsed by the payee, and it is not incumbent on them (paying in good faith and in the ordinary course of business) to prove that the indorsement, or any subsequent indorsement, was made by or by the direction of the payee. But a third party cashing such a cheque is not protected by the statute (*p*). And this provision is confirmed by the Bills Act of 1882, which adds that a banker so paying is deemed to have paid in due course, though the indorsement has been forged or made without authority (*q*).

'*Crossed Cheques.*—Formerly the crossing of a cheque, whether generally or specially, left the document negotiable, and was merely a direction to the drawee to pay only to a banker, or rather a caution that he must take care not to pay to any but a banker (*r*). Subsequently statutes now repealed were passed to regulate such documents (*s*); and now by the Bills of Exchange Act, a cheque may be crossed by the drawer, or by a holder, or, again, to his agent for collection or to himself by the banker to whom it has been crossed, and either (1) generally, or (2) specially, or (3) with the words "not negotiable." In the first case the drawee is directed to pay only to a banker; in the second only to the banker to whom it is crossed, or to his agent for collection; and in the third only to a banker, or the banker indicated, as the case may be (*t*). The crossing is a material part of the cheque, and may not be obliterated, added to, or altered, except as authorised in the Act (*u*). The drawee must refuse payment of a cheque crossed to more than one banker, except when one is an agent for collection. A drawee paying in contravention or disregard of the crossing, is liable to the true owner for any loss through such payment, unless the cheque at presentment does not appear to be crossed, or to have had a crossing which is obliterated, or added to, or altered, and the drawee pay the cheque in good faith and without negligence (*v*). A banker paying according to the crossing in good faith and without negligence, and—when the cheque comes into the hands of the payee —also the drawer, are in the same position and have the same rights as if the cheque were paid to the true owner (*w*). One who takes a cheque crossed "not negotiable" has not, and cannot transfer, a better title than the person from whom he took it had (*x*). A banker who in good faith and without negligence receives payment for a customer of a crossed cheque, incurs thereby no liability to the true owner, if his customer prove to have no title or a defective title to the cheque (*y*).'

(*a*) As to the nature of a draft (precept), see 1 Stair, 12. § 1; Carter *v.* M'Intosh, 1862; 24 D. 925; and below, § 311, 1459, 1461. And as to the liability of indorsers of bank cheques, see Edinbr. and Glasgow Bank *v.* Samson, 1858; 20 D. 1246. Macdonald *v.* Union Bank, 1864; 2 Macph. 963. As to the effect of cheques in proof of payment, see § 566; of loan, § 2357 (*f*); of donation *mortis causa*, § 1874.

(*b*) Act, § 73 sqq. M'Gilchrist *v.* Arthur, 1794; M. 877. Clydesdale Bank *v.* M'Lean, 1883; 10 R. 719; aff. 1883, 11 R. H. L. 1; 9 App. Ca. 95. B. L. Bank *v.* Carruthers & Ferguson, 1883; 10 R. 923.

(*c*) *Infra*, § 333A.

(*d*) Clydesdale Bank *v.* Royal Bank, 1876; 3 R. 586.

(*e*) Clydesdale Bank *v.* M'Lean, *cit.* (*b*). Keene *v.* Beard, 8 C. B. N. S. 372; 29 L. J. C. P. 287. Currie *v.* Misa, L. R. 10 Ex. 153; 1 App. Ca. 554; 44 L. J. Ex. 94; 45 *ib.* 852.

(*f*) Agra Bank *v.* Hofmann, 34 L. J. Ch. 285. Marzetti *v.* Williams, 1 B. & Ad. 424. Rolin *v.* Steward, 14 C. B. 595; 23 L. J. C. P. 148. Cumming *v.* Shand, 5 H. & N. 95; 29 L. J. Ex. 129.
(*g*) Ireland *v.* N. of Sc. Bkg. Co., 1880; 8 R. 215.
(*h*) Act, § 75. Waterston *v.* City of Glasgow Bank, 1874; 1 R. 470. See Currie *v.* Misa, *cit.* (*c*). Clydesdale Bank *v.* M'Lean, *supra* (*b*).
(*i*) See below, § 332.
(*k*) Rothschild *v.* Corney, 9 B. & Cr. 390; 33 R. R. 209. See the Act, §§ 36 (3) and 73.
(*l*) 45 and 46 Vict. c. 61, § 74. See as to reasonable time, etc., the cases cited in Prideaux *v.* Criddle, L. R. 4 Q. B. 455; 38 L. J. Q. B. 232. Hopkins *v.* Ware, L. R. 4 Ex. 268; 38 L. Ex. 147. London and County Bank *v.* Groome, 51 L. J. Q. B. 224; 8 Q. B. D. 288.
(*m*) Laws *v.* Rand, 3 C. B. N. S. 442; 27 L. J. C. P. 76.
(*n*) 55 Geo. III. c. 184. Swan *v.* Bank of Scotland, 1835; 2 S. & M'L. 67; 3 Ill. 118.
(*o*) 54 and 55 Vict. c. 39, § 32, 34, 38. A post-dated cheque is included in this provision, the Court at the trial having only to deal with the instrument on the face of it. Bull *v.* O'Sullivan, 40 L. J. Q. B. 141; L. R. 6 Q. B. 209. Royal Bk. *v.* Tottenham, 1894; 2 Q. B. 715.
(*p*) Ogden *v.* Benas, 43 L. J. C. P. 259; L. R. 9 C. P. 513. See Clydesdale Bank *v.* Royal Bk., 1876; 3 R. 586. Arnold *v.* Cheque Bank, 45 L. J. C. P. 562; 1 C. P. D. 578; and comp. Cal. Ins. Co. *v.* B. L. Bank, 1859; 21 D. 1197; aff. 1861, 23 D. H. L. 3; 4 Macq. 107; 33 S. J. 692.
(*q*) Act, § 60. See § 90 as to good faith.
(*r*) Bellamy *v.* Marjoribanks, 21 L. J. Ex. 70; 7 Ex. 389. Caslon *v.* Ireland, 5 E. & B. 765; 25 L. J. Q. B. 113. Simmons *v.* Taylor, 2 C. B. N. S. 528; 4 *ib.* 463. Bobbett *v.* Pinckett, 1 Ex. D. 368; 45 L. J. Ex. 555. Smith *v.* Union Bank, 1 Q. B. D. 31; 45 L. J. Q. B. 149.
(*s*) 19 and 20 Vict. c. 25; 21 and 22 Vict. c. 79; 39 and 40 Vict. c. 81.
(*t*) Act, § 76, 77. (*u*) *Ib.* § 78.
(*v*) *Ib.* § 78. See Smith and Bobbett, *citt.*
(*w*) *Ib.* § 80. (*x*) *Ib.* § 81.
(*y*) See Clydesdale Bank, *supra* (*p*). Matthiesen *v.* City and County Bank, 5 C. P. D. 7; 48 L. J. C. P. 529.

309. Essentials of Bills.—The essentials of a bill or note are,—the engagement to pay; the person to whom payment is to be made, called the payee; the sum engaged for; 'but not' the time of payment, 'for if no time of payment is expressed, a bill is payable on demand (*a*)'; and the stamp (*b*). '"When a bill is wanting in any material particular, the person in possession of it has a *primâ facie* authority to fill up the omission in any way he thinks fit." In order that an instrument so completed may be enforceable against any person who became a party thereto before its completion, it must (besides being delivered (*c*)) be filled up within a reasonable time (which is a question of fact), and strictly in accordance with the authority given; but it is valid and effectual to all purposes, and without any such limitation, in the hands of one to whom it is negotiated in due course after such completion (*d*).'

(*a*) 45 and 46 Vict. c. 61, § 10.
(*b*) See below, § 328, and above, § 306.
(*c*) See Baxendale *v.* Bennett, 3 Q. B. D. 525; 47 L. J. Q. B. 624.
(*d*) 45 and 46 Vict. c. 61, § 20. See below, § 313, 321 (*g*), and cases there cited.

310. The engagement is by acceptance of the order or request in a bill to pay; or by the words of promise in a note. Thus the engagement by note is at once perfect: the engagement by acceptance includes drawing and acceptance (*a*). 'A mere acknowledgment of debt is not a note, and a mere authority or request to pay is not a bill (*b*).'

(*a*) See below, § 313.
(*b*) Smith's Merc. Law, 224. As to I O U's, see Woodrow & Son *v.* Wright, 1861; 24 D. 31. Bowe & Christie *v.* Hutchison, 1868; 6 Macph. 643. Purvis *v.* Dowie, 1869; 7 Macph. 764. Haldane *v.* Speirs, 1872; 10 Macph. 537. Morgan *v.* Morgan's Exrs., 1866; 4 Macph. 321. Fesenmayor *v.* Adcock, 16 M. & W. 449. Douglas *v.* Holme, 12 Ad. & E. 641; 10 L. J. Q. B. 43. Smith's M. L., *cit.* Addison on Contr. 1048; and above, § 202A, below, § 328 *fin.*

310A. 'Capacity for Bills.—Capacity to incur liability as a party to a bill is coextensive with capacity to contract (*a*). The power of a corporation to make itself liable on a bill depends on the law in force for the time relating to corporations; so a trading corporation has such power, and other corporations have it only if it is given by their constitution or charter (*b*). If one of the parties has no capacity or power to incur liability on a bill, the holder may yet enforce it against any other party thereto (*c*).'

(*a*) 45 and 46 Vict. c. 61, § 22. M'Lean *v.* Angus, 1887; 14 R. 448 (married women—see below, § 1612).
(*b*) The Act, *ib.* *Infra*, § 403L. And see as to ordinary firms, *infra*, § 321, 354. See Chalmers's Digest, pp. 57, 61 sqq.
(*c*) The Act, *ib.*

311. Drawing.—The drawing of a bill 'where the drawee has in his hands funds available for the payment thereof,' is a transference to the payee of the 'sum for which it is' drawn, 'or of any smaller sum due by the drawee to the drawer,' completed by presentment (*a*).

The bill must be drawn absolutely and unconditionally; but it is not in this sense held a condition if the 'foreign' bill be drawn in sets payable "if the others be not paid" (*b*). It is no bill if drawn with a condition; for that is contrary to the nature of a bill (*c*); but such a draft has been held to operate as an assignation intimated (*d*). 'An order to pay out of a particular fund is not unconditional in the sense of § 3 of the Act; but an unqualified order to pay, coupled with (1) an indication of a particular fund out of which the drawee is to reimburse himself, or of a particular account to be debited with the amount, or (2) a statement of the transaction which gives rise to the bill, is unconditional (*e*).'

The payment must be in money, not in commodities (*f*), 'and the sum must be certain (*g*).'

The drawer must sign before producing the bill in judgment; but it is enough if his name be in the body of the bill, written by himself (*h*). Summary diligence will not, however, be given on such a bill (*i*).

The drawer must sign before any diligence can proceed on the instrument; but he may sign after the death of the acceptor (*k*). The drawer, by signing the bill, engages conditionally to pay it, should the drawee not accept or not pay; provided due notice be given to the drawer of the dishonour. 'See below, § 333E.'

(*a*) Mitchel *v.* Mitchel, 1734; M. 1464; 1 Ill. 479. Stewart *v.* Ewing, 1744; M. 1493. Gavin *v.* Kippen, 1768; M. 1495. Spottiswoode *v.* M'Neill, 1778; M. 1495. Falconar *v.* Campbell, 1824; 2 S. 630. See below, § 315, 339, and 1465. Carter *v.* M'Intosh, 1862; 24 D. 925. Watt's Trs. *v.* Pinkney, 1853; 16 D. 279 (drawee not accepting not liable to summary diligence). See London Jt. St. Bk. *v.* Stewart & Co., 1859; 21 D. 1327. B. L. Co. *v.* Carruthers, 1883; 10 R. 923 (sum in cheque greater than the funds in bank). The additions to the text are from the Act of 1882, which retains for Scotland the former law of Scotland, differing from that of England. See the Act, § 53, and above, § 308 (*a*); below, § 1461.

(*b*) As to such bills, see the Act, § 71.

(*c*) 1 Selwyn, N. P. 269, 328. 3 Kent, 76. Thomson, and cases cited by him, in notes, p. 11. Visc. Garnock *v.* D. Queensberry, 1721; M. 1401. Campbell *v.* Campbell, Bell's Cases, 111. See M'Dowall *v.* D. of Douglas, 1731; M. 1541. Alexander *v.* Thomas, 16 Q. B. 333. Crouch *v.* Credit Foncier of England, L. R. 8 Q. B. 874; 42 L. J. Q. B. 183. 45 and 46 Vict. c. 61, § 3; *supra*, § 306.

(*d*) See *supra* (*a*).

(*e*) Act, § 3 (3). Macfarlan *v.* Johnston, 1864; 2 Macph. 1210. Blyth *v.* Forbes, 1879; 6 R. 1102.

(*f*) Bayley, 178, 196. Leslie *v.* Robertson, 1713; M. 1397. Douglas *v.* Erskine, 1715; M. 1397. Bruce *v.* Wark, 1729; M. 1399. Comp. Bovill *v.* Dixon, 1854; 16 D. 619; 1856, 3 Macq. 1.

(*g*) Pirie's Reprs. *v.* Smith's Exrs., 1833; 11 S. 473. Morgan *v.* Morgan's Exrs., 1866; 4 Macph. 321. Tennent *v.* Crawford, 1878; 5 R. 433. Ritchie *v.* M'Lachlan, 1870; 8 Macph. 814 (order to pay account—but see § 1461 (*g*)). See above, § 306; below, § 325.

(*h*) Ferguson *v.* Blair, 1758; M. 1443.

(*i*) A. *v.* B., 1750; M. 1442; Elchies, *Bill*, 47. See M'Bean *v.* Macpherson, 1806; Hume, 57; Bell's Convg. 435.

(*k*) Erskine says, a bill without the creditor's name is null. In this he goes too far. It will not authorise summary diligence, but it will sufficiently ground an action, even at the instance of the intended creditor. 3 Ersk. 2. § 28, with Ivory's Notes. Fair *v.* Cranston, 1801; M. 1677. Ogilvie *v.* Moss, 1804; M. *Bill*, Apx. 1. See Disher *v.* Kidd, 1810; Hume, 64. Innes *v.* Gordon, 1802; Hume, 47. Below, § 321 (*g*), 324.

312. Signing as Agent, etc.—The bill may be drawn, 'indorsed, or accepted,' for another, so as effectually to bind him, if he have by procuration or otherwise granted authority to that effect. But if the 'person so signing' is not careful to set forth 'that he signs for or on behalf of a principal, or in a' representative character, he will himself be liable (*a*); '"but the mere addition to his signature of words describing him as an agent, or as filling a representative character, does not exempt him from personal liability" (*b*). In determining whether a bill is the bill of an agent signing it or of his principal, the construction most favourable to the validity of the bill is to be adopted (*c*). "A signature by procuration operates as notice that the agent has but a limited authority to sign, and the principal is only bound by such signature if the agent in so signing was acting within the actual limits of his authority" (*d*).' The principal is not liable to the bill-holder, where the agent draws in his own name (*e*).

(*a*) Connel *v.* M'Lelland, 1782; M. 1485; 1 Ill. 224. Douglas *v.* E. of Dunmore, 1800; M. *Bill*, Apx. 15. Clark *v.* Bank of Scotland, 1823; 2 S. 210. 45 and 46 Vict. c. 61, § 26. Webster *v.* M'Callum, 1848; 10 D. 1133. Chiene *v.* Western Bank, 1848; 10 D. 1523. See below, § 321. Jones *v.* Littledale, 6 A. & E. 486.

(*b*) Act, § 26, and cases in note (*a*). Dutton *v.* Marsh, L. R. 6 Q. B. 361; 40 L. J. Q. B. 175. Alexander *v.* Sizer, L. R. 4 Ex. 102; 38 L. J. Ex. 59. Eaton, Hammond, & Sons *v.* M'Gregor's Exrs., 1837; 15 S. 1012. Brown *v.* Sutherland, 1875; 2 R. 615. Comp. Grahame *v.* Macfarlans & Co., 1869; 7 Macph. 640; and above, § 224A.

(*c*) Act, § 26. M'Meekin *v.* Easton, 1889; 16 R. 363.

(*d*) Act, § 25. See below, § 321.

(*e*) Telford *v.* James, Wood, & James, 1822; 2 S. 290; rev. 1 S. App. 220. Leadbitter *v.* Farry, 5 M. & Sel. 345. Ducarry *v.* Gill, 1 Mo. & Mal. 450. Bank of Scotland *v.* Watson, 1813; 1 Dow, 40; 5 Pat. 651; 14 R. R. 11. North Brit. Bank *v.* Ayrshire Iron Co., 1853; 15 D. 782. See the Act, § 23.

313. Acceptance 'is the signification by the drawee of his assent to the order of the drawer, and it' is indicated by the drawee signing his name to the address, or by adding to his subscription the word "ACCEPTS." Acceptance of a blank will entitle the holder to fill it up with any sum to which the stamp is applicable, so that it shall be effectual to any one acquiring right to the bill as an onerous indorsee (*a*). 'And it is now enacted that "where a simple signature on a blank stamped paper is delivered by the signer in order that it may be converted into a bill, it operates as a *primâ facie* authority to fill it up as a complete bill for any amount the stamp will cover, using the signature for that of the drawer, or the acceptor, or an indorser"; but this is subject to the same limitation which applies to the completion of an imperfect bill by the possessor of it (*b*).'

(*a*) Smith *v.* Taylor, 1824; 2 S. 755; 1 Ill. 225. See Fairlie *v.* Brown, 1824; 3 S. 5.

(*b*) 45 and 46 Vict. c. 61, § 20. See above, § 309, and below, § 321 (*g*), and cases there cited. Russell *v.* Banknock Coal Co., 1897; 24 R. 1009.

314. *Proper Acceptance.*—To the proper and efficient purposes of a bill, and for summary execution, no other acceptance is available in Scotland but a written acceptance (*a*); and although a verbal acceptance may reasonably be thought sufficient, as by intimation of the draft, to complete a transfer by draft on the holder of the drawer's fund, this has been decided not to be sufficient in competition (*b*). Formerly it was held in England that a verbal acceptance was sufficient; but the law 'was put,' by statute, on the same footing as in Scotland (*c*). 'Afterwards the Mercantile Law Amendment Act, 1856, required the acceptance to be in writing, and signed by or for the acceptor; and this was, so late as 1878, held to mean that there must be not only a signature of the acceptor, but, contrary to the practice of merchants and others, written words of acceptance (*d*). An Act was immediately passed (41 and 42 Vict. c. 13) providing that an acceptance consisting merely of the signature of the acceptor should be sufficient; and the law is now that the acceptance is invalid unless written on the bill, and that the mere signature of the drawee without additional words is sufficient; but that it must not express that the drawee will perform his promise by any other means than the payment of money (*e*). Except a referee in case of need (*f*), or an acceptor for honour (below, § 322), no one can be a party to a bill as acceptor who is not a proper drawee or addressee (*g*); and a stranger to the bill who signs (for security or other purpose, in the nature of an *aval*) incurs no liability to the drawer or acceptor, but incurs the liabilities of an indorser to a subsequent holder in due course (*h*).

'*Time of Acceptance.*—A bill may be accepted when incomplete; or when overdue, or dishonoured by non-acceptance, or non-payment; and "when a bill payable after sight is dishonoured by non-acceptance, and the drawee subsequently accepts it, the holder, in the absence of any different agreement, is entitled to have the bill accepted as of the date of the first presentment to the drawee for acceptance" (*i*).'

(*a*) Hay *v.* Boyd, 1822; 3 Mur. 9.

(*b*) Cullen *v.* Maclean, 1833; 11 S. 733; 1 Ill. 226. See § 311, 315, 339, etc.

(*c*) 1 and 2 Geo. IV. c. 78, § 2.

(*d*) 19 and 20 Vict. c. 60, § 11; 19 and 20 Vict. c. 97, § 6. Hindhaugh *v.* Blakey, 1 C. P. D. 136; 47 L. J. C. P. 345.

(*e*) 45 and 46 Vict. c. 61, § 17.

(*f*) *Ib.* § 15.

(*g*) **Walker's Trs. (Steele)** *v.* **M'Kinlay,** 1879; 6 R. 1132; aff. 7 R. H. L. 85; 5 App. Ca. 754.

(*h*) **Walker's Trs.,** *cit.* 45 and 46 Vict. c. 61, § 56. See Macdonald *v.* Whitfield, L. R. 8 App. Ca. 733, and Jenkins *v.* Coomber, 1898; 2 Q. B. 168. (Steele *v.* M'Kinlay not affected by Act of 1883.)

(*i*) Act, § 18. *Ex p.* Swan, L. R. 6 Eq. 344. Roberts *v.* Bethell, 12 C. B. 778; 22 L. J. C. P. 69.

315. *Promise to accept.*—To certain effects, however, something less than a written acceptance is admitted to bind the party, 'though not to make a bill.' Where one has made a written *promise* to accept a bill already drawn, on the faith of which money is advanced, this, although it will not make a negotiable instrument, or authorise summary execution as a proper acceptance, will, as an obligation, bind the drawee, and ground an action against him, by one taking the bill on the faith of it (*a*). But a promise to accept a draft not yet drawn has been held not binding, except to one induced to advance money on the promise; and even then this has been doubted (*b*). Where the drawee, having funds of the drawer in his hands, has had the draft presented to him while so indebted for money, he will be bound to answer it; and a protest for non-acceptance or non-payment will, even against competing creditors, be held equal to an assignation intimated (*c*).

(*a*) Shepherd *v.* Campbell, 1823; 2 S. 346; 1 Ill. 225. Pearson *v.* Dunlop, Cowp. 573; 1 Ross' L. C. 434. Miln *v.* Prest, 4 Camp. 393. Johnson *v.* Collings, 1 East, 98; 1 Ross' L. C. 439. Hoare *v.* Dresser, 7 H. L. Ca. 290. Grant *v.* Hunt, 1 C. B. 44. Reynolds *v.* Peto, 11 Ex. 418. See § 311.

(*b*) Bayley, 188. Bank of Ireland *v.* Archer, 11 M. & W. 383. As to letters of credit (undertakings that the granter's agent or correspondent shall honour the grantee's draft), see *supra*, § 279, 280; 1 Bell's Com. 371 (388–9, M'L.'s ed.).

(c) Gordon v. Anderson, 1712; M. 1490. Stewart v. Ewing, 1724; M. 1462; 1 Ill. 480. Mitchel v. Mitchel, 1734; M. 1464. Gavin v. Kippen & Co., 1768; M. 1495. Spottiswoode v. M'Neill, 1778; *ib.* See § 311, § 339, and § 1465, and cases there cited.

316. '*General and Qualified Acceptances.*—By the Bills of Exchange Act, 1882, "an acceptance is either general or qualified. A general acceptance assents without qualification to the order of the drawer. A qualified acceptance in express terms varies the effect of the bill as drawn. In particular, an acceptance is qualified which is" (*a*)'

Conditional.—Acceptance may be conditional, although the drawing may not; for by the unconditional draft there is an absolute obligation saving the bill from that uncertainty which accords not with the nature of the instrument (*b*). Such an acceptance becomes absolute when the condition is fulfilled, 'but cannot be the ground of summary diligence.' The bill-holder (*porteur*) has his option to take a conditional 'or other qualified' acceptance, or to protest for non-acceptance, and take his recourse instantly against the drawer. '"Where a qualified acceptance is taken" (except a partial acceptance of which due notice has been given), "and the drawer or an indorser has not expressly or impliedly authorised the holder to take a qualified acceptance, or does not subsequently assent thereto, such drawer or indorser is discharged from his liability on the bill." And a drawer or indorser receiving notice of a qualified acceptance, and not expressing his dissent to the holder within a reasonable time, is deemed to have assented to it (*c*).' Every condition or variation on the acceptance must be in writing 'on the face of the bill, and in clear and unequivocal terms incorporated in the acceptance (*d*).'

(*a*) 45 and 46 Vict. c. 61, § 19.
(*b*) Bayley, 177–8. 1 Selw. 283. Thomson, 222. See above, § 311.
(*c*) Sproat v. Matthews, 1 T. R. 182; 1 Ross' L. C. 475. 1 Selw. 283. 1 Stair, 11. § 7. Smith v. Vertue, 9 C. B. N. S. 214. Byles on Bills, 186. 45 and 46 Vict. c. 61, § 44.
(*d*) Meyer & Co. v. Decroix & Co., 1891; A. C. 520.

317. The necessity of making the acceptance conditional may arise from the circumstance of the drawee having, at the time the bill is presented to him, no funds of the drawer; and yet, expecting to be in possession of funds by the arrival of a ship with a consignment, or by a sale of goods in his hands, he may be willing to engage if such should be the case. So a condition of arrival or of sale will be good (*a*).

(*a*) 1 Stair, 11. §7. See cases, Bayley, 178, 196. Thomson, 222. 1 Sel. 283.

318. *Qualified Acceptance.*—An acceptance in the character of cautioner is not in effect different from simple acceptance: it imposes no condition on the engagement, and is available only in settling the question of relief as between joint acceptors, or between drawer and acceptor (*a*). 'It has no effect against a third party taking the bill by indorsation (*b*).'

(*a*) Campbell v. Gibson, 1753; Elch. *Bill*, 54; 1 Ill. 226. See M'Kellar v. Campbell, June 7, 1811; F. C.; 1 Ill 72. Sharp, *infra*. Walker's Trs. v. M'Kinlay, 1879; 6 R. 1132 (*per* L. P. Inglis); aff. 1880, 7 R. H. L. 85; 5 App. Ca. 754. 1 Bell's Com. 400 (425, M'L.'s ed.).
(*b*) M'Dougall v. Foyer, Feb. 13, 1810; F. C.; 1 Ill. 182. Sharp v. Hervey, 1808; M. *Bill of Exch.*, Apx. 22; 1 Ill. 239. Fergusson v. Gordon & Co., 1825; 4 S. 165. Drummond v. Campbell, 1813; Hume, 71. Walker's Trs., *cit.*, and cases in § 312 (*b*).

319. *Partial Acceptance.*—The acceptance may vary from the draft in amount, as for a part of the sum drawn for. But the drawer will not be liable in recourse for the balance, if such an acceptance be taken without protest 'as to the balance in the case of a foreign bill' and notice (*a*).

(*a*) Bayley, 199. 45 and 46 Vict. c. 61, § 19 (2) (*b*), § 44 (2).

320. *Local Acceptance and qualified as to Time.*—The acceptance may vary from the draft, in time, or in the mode or place, of payment. The rule is, that the place must be made exclusive by the words "and not elsewhere," in order to form a condition of the acceptance, and to make the bill payable only at that place; and that the change must be acquiesced in by the bill-holder (*a*). 'The acceptance of one or more of the drawees, but not of all, is also a qualified acceptance (*b*).'

(*a*) 1 and 2 Geo. IV. c. 78, § 1; repealed and re-enacted by 45 and 46 Vict. c. 61, § 19 (2) (*c*) (*d*). Rowe v. Young, 1820; 2 Bligh, 391; 1 Ill. 226; 21 R. R. 91. See below, § 337, 1461.
(*b*) The Act, *ib.* (*e*).

320A. '*Effect of Acceptance.*—The acceptor of a bill, by accepting it, (1) Engages that he will pay it according to the tenor of his acceptance; (2) Is precluded from denying to a holder in due course, *a.* the existence of the drawer, the genuineness of his signature, and his capacity and authority to draw the bill (*a*);

b. In the case of a bill payable to drawer's order, the then capacity of the drawer to indorse, but not the genuineness or validity of his indorsement; *c.* In the case of a bill payable to the order of a third person, the existence of the payee and his then capacity to indorse, but not the genuineness or validity of his indorsement (*b*).'

(*a*) London and S.-W. Bank *v.* Wentworth, 5 Ex. D. 96; 49 L. J. Ex. 657. The presumption (which may now, however, be redargued by parole) is that the acceptor is the principal debtor and the proper party to pay the bill. Catto, Thomson, & Co. *v.* Thomson & Son, 1867; 6 Macph. 54. See § 333B.

(*b*) 45 and 46 Vict. c. 61, § 54. Garland *v.* Jacomb, L. R. 8 Ex. 216. Beeman *v.* Duck, 11 M. & W. 251. Robinson *v.* Yarrow, 7 Taunt. 455; 18 R. R. 537. Cooper *v.* Meyer, 10 B. & C. 468; 34 R. R. 493.

321. *Acceptance by Procuration.*—When one becomes a party to a bill or note by the subscription of his agent duly authorised, he is said to act by procuration. Such procuration is most regularly constituted by a written power of attorney, or letter of procuration; and, while unrecalled, or recalled without notice, the writer will be bound by the signature of his representative (*a*). Procuration may be proved by circumstances inferring acquiescence and implied authority; contrary to our former wholesome rule in Scotland, which required writing to confer such a power. This doctrine was established by a decision of the House of Lords, as conformable to the Mercantile Law of England (*b*). Every limitation of a power so extraordinary must be strictly observed. And although, in the case of a bill signed by the party himself, third persons are not bound to inquire into the making of the bill; yet, where the subscription bears to be by procuration, they must use due caution in taking the bill, by insisting for a sight of the procuration: they otherwise run the risk of the powers which it confers (*c*). There is in partnership an implied procuration in every partner, but limited to the trade of the company (*d*). 'In the Act of 1882, the word "person" is defined to include "a body of persons, whether incorporated or not," and "banker" to include "a body of persons, whether incorporated or not, who carry on the business of banking" (*e*). And it is provided that "where a person signs a bill in a trade or assumed name, he is liable thereon as if he had signed it in his own name," and that "the signature of the name of a firm is equivalent to the signature by the person so signing of the names of all persons liable as partners in that firm" (*f*).' The signing of a blank or skeleton bill is a '*primâ facie*' authority to fill up any sum the holder chooses, to the extent which the stamp will cover (*g*).

(*a*) Thomson, 220. Bayley, 82, 316. See above, § 312.

(*b*) Davidson *v.* Robertson, 1815; 3 Dow, 218; 1 Ill. 163. See Lawson *v.* Mathew, 1823; 2 S. 443; 1 Ill. 227. Porthouse *v.* Parker, 1 Camp. 82; 10 R. R. 637. Jones *v.* Turnour, 3 Car. & Pay. 204. Millar *v.* Little, 1831; 9 S. 318. Maiklem *v.* Walker, 1833; 12 S. 53. Anderson *v.* Buck, 1841; 3 D. 975. See Swinburne & Co. *v.* Western Bank, 1856; 18 D. 1025. London Jt. St. Bk. *v.* Stewart, 1859; 21 D. 1327. Miller *v.* Potter, Wilson, & Co., 1875; 3 R. 105.

(*c*) Attwood *v.* Munnings, 7 B. & Cr. 278; 1 Ill. 227; 31 R. R. 194. See above, § 312 (*a*). Stagg *v.* Elliott, 12 C. B. N. S. 373; 31 L. J. C. P. 260. Union Bank *v.* Makin, 1873; 11 Macph. 499. North of Scot. Bk. *v.* Behn, Möller, & Co., 1881; 8 R. 423.

(*d*) Green *v.* Deakin, 2 Starkie, 347; 1 Ill. 243. Blair Miller *v.* Douglas, Jan. 22, 1811; F. C.; 1 Ill. 244. Johnston, Sharp, & Co. *v.* Philips, 1822; 1 S. App. 244; 1 Ill. 245. Turnbull *v.* M'Kie, 1822; 1 S. 331. Johnston *v.* Cliftonhall Coal Co., 1852; 15 D. 84. Blair Iron Co. *v.* Alison, 1855; 18 D. H. L. 49; 27 Jur. 614. Matheson *v.* Fraser, 1820; Hume, 758. Swinburne, *cit.* (*b*). North British Bk. *v.* Ayrshire Iron Co., 1853; 15 D. 782. Ross, Skolfield, & Co. *v.* State Line Co., 1875; 3 R. 134. See further as to Bills by Firms, Chalmers's Digest, 61 sq. Smith, Merc. Law, 38–41. Clark on Partn., 229 sqq.; and *infra*, § 354.

(*e*) 45 and 46 Vict. c. 61, § 2. See as to Bills by Companies, etc., *infra*, § 403L.

(*f*) *Ib.* § 23.

(*g*) Pagan *v.* Wylie, 1703; M. 1660; 1 Ill. 227. Graham *v.* Gillespie & Co., 1795; M. 1453. See Pothier, Cont. de Change, No. 99. 1 Bell's Com. 391 (416, M'L.'s ed.). Ogilvie *v.* Moss, 1804; M. Apx. *Bill*, 17. Thomson & Co. *v.* Gall, 1805; Hume, 53. Cameron *v.* Mortimer, 1869; 7 Macph. 382. Duncan's Trs. *v.* Shand, 1872; 10 Macph. 984. Lyon *v.* Butter, 1841; 4 D. 178. Grassick *v.* Farquharson, 1846; 8 D. 1073. Anderson *v.* Lorimer, 1857; 20 D. 74. Jackson *v.* M'Iver, 1875; 2 R. 882. M'Meekin & Russell *v.* Tudhope, 1881; 8 R. 587. The English cases are collected in **London and S.-W. Bank** *v.* **Wentworth,** 5 Ex. D. 96; 49 L. J. Ex. 657. Garrard *v.* Lewis, 10 Q. B. D. 30. Carter *v.* White, 25 Ch. D. 666 (even after acceptor's death). See 45 and 46 Vict. c. 61, § 20; and above, § 309, 313.

322. *Acceptance for Honour.*—When a bill is presented to the drawee, and not accepted, it is said to be dishonoured; and may be returned on the drawer, or indorser, with a charge of interest, exchange, and costs. But one may be interested for the persons thus exposed to loss, so as to interpose in order to prevent the return of the bill and the accumulation of expense, by accepting for the honour of one or other of those whose names stand on the bill. Such an acceptance, 'which is made after protest for non-payment, before the bill is overdue, and with the holder's consent, was formerly required to' be made under protest before a notary and witnesses, the instrument, 'called an Act of Honour,' stating the fact, and being without delay sent to the person for whose honour it 'was' made. 'But now, in order to be valid, it must be written on the bill, and indicate that it is an acceptance for honour; and be signed by the acceptor for honour. Where it does not state for whose honour it is made, it is deemed to be for honour of the drawer. The maturity of a bill payable after sight is reckoned from the date of noting for non-acceptance (*a*).' It is an acceptance not absolute, but only provisional, that if the bill should not be returned dishonoured, but kept till maturity, and then not paid, the acceptor for honour will pay it. The acceptor for honour is entitled to demand from the bill-holder such proofs, at the maturity of the bill, as shall enable him to recover against the person for whose honour he has accepted; and so there must be 'due presentment, and' a formal protest taken by the bill-holder, 'and also notice to the acceptor for honour of the presentment and protest,' before the bill for the honour of the drawer is paid (*b*). 'The acceptor for honour is liable to the holder and to all parties to the bill subsequent to the party for whose honour he has accepted (*c*).' And in case of the acceptor for honour stipulating in his acceptance not merely a protest, but a *refusal*, 'it was required that' the bill 'should' be presented to the drawee, and refused by him (*d*). 'But now it must, as has just been said, be presented and protested for non-payment before being presented for payment to the acceptor for honour, and it must be presented to him not later than the day following maturity, if his address be in the place of protest for non-payment, or forwarded for presentment not later than that day, if elsewhere. The bill must be protested for non-payment, if dishonoured by the acceptor for honour (*e*).' The person so interposing has recourse against him for whom he has accepted, if already liable, and against all who are responsible to that person; but he has no claim against parties subsequent to him (*f*).

The bill-holder may refuse to take an acceptance for honour; but he does not seem entitled to refuse payment for honour.

'*Payment for Honour*.—The Act states the law as to persons intervening to pay a bill *supra* protest for honour, when it has been protested for non-payment. Payment for honour must be attested by a notarial Act of Honour. It discharges all parties to the bill subsequent to the party for whose honour it is made, and the party paying succeeds to the holder's rights against that party and all liable to him. The holder refusing such payment loses recourse against all who would have been discharged by it (*g*).'

(*a*) 45 and 46 Vict. c. 61, § 65.
(*b*) Carstairs *v.* Paton, 1703; M. 1528; 1 Ill. 228. Hoare *v.* Cazenove, 16 East, 301; 14 R. R. 370. Williams *v.* Germaine, 7 B. & Cr. 468; 31 R. R. 248. Mitchel *v.* Baring, 1 M. & M. 381; 34 R. R. 307; 10 B. & Cr. 4. Vandewall *v.* Tyrrel, 1 M. & M. 87. Phillips *v.* Im Thurn, L. R. 1 Ex. 463; 35 L. J. Ex. 220. 6 and 7 Will. IV. c. 58; repealed by 45 and 46 Vict. c. 61, sched.
(*c*) The Act, § 66.
(*d*) Mitchel, *supra* (*b*). See below, § 336–7. 2 and 3 Will. IV. c. 98.
(*e*) 45 and 46 Vict. c. 61, § 67.
(*f*) Smith *v.* Nissen, 1 T. R. 269. *Ex p.* Lambert, 13 Ves. 179; 9 R. R. 169. See *ex p.* Swan, L. R. 6 Eq. 344.
(*g*) Act, § 68.

323. Subscription.—The subscription must be full. If made by initials or marks, it will not warrant summary execution; but in an action such documents are held admissible, on condition that it shall be proved to be the usual mode of subscribing, and to be genuine. These are points in the action to be made out by the pursuer (*a*). 'Where by the Act any instrument or writing is required to be signed by any person, it is not necessary that he should sign it with his own hand, but it is sufficient if his signature is written thereon by some other person by or under his authority; and in the case of a corporation it is enough if the document be sealed with the corporate seal, though the bill or note of a corporation is not required to be under seal (*b*). "No person is liable as drawer, indorser, or acceptor of a bill who has not signed it as such" (*c*).'

'*Forged or Unauthorised Signatures*.—"Subject to the provisions of the Act, where a signature on a bill is forged or placed thereon without the authority of the person whose signature it purports to be, the forged or unauthorised signature is wholly inoperative, and no right to retain the bill, or to give a discharge therefor, or to enforce payment thereof, against any party thereto can be acquired through or under that signature, unless the party against whom it is sought to retain or enforce payment of the bill is precluded from setting up the forgery or want of authority. Provided that nothing in this section shall affect the ratification of an unauthorised signature not amounting to a forgery" (*d*).

'The provisions of the Act referred to are doubtless the estoppels declared against acceptors and indorsers in clauses 54 (2) and 55 (2) (see above, § 320A, and below, § 333E), and the provisions in favour of bankers in clauses 60, 80, and 82.

'As a forged signature (or a bill fraudulently altered) has no efficacy, one who pays such a bill has no remedy against the person whose signature has been forged (*e*). It was maintained, on the authority of a much discussed case (*f*), that a party to the bill paying it could recover, if that person had facilitated the forgery by his negligence, at least if it could be held that that negligence was the proximate cause of the loss. But it has been pointed out that the case cited, on whatever ground it was decided, was one between a banker and his customer, and depended on the law of mandate and the duties of a principal to his agent, and that there is no similar relation between the drawer or acceptor of a bill and all possible indorsers or holders. They are not under a duty to take precautions against possible forgeries after acceptance by minutely scrutinising the document, and taking care that there are no blank spaces that can be made available for fraudulent alterations. The natural protection against forgery is the criminal law, and not the vigilance of parties to exclude its possibility (*g*). Bankers, however, employed by a customer to pay his bill, are bound to pay to the proper payee, and to make sure of the genuineness of all previous indorsements (*h*), unless they (the bankers) have been misled in a material point by their principal (*i*). One who pays to a holder in *bonâ fide* cannot recover the money back on the ground that a prior indorsement was afterwards found to be forged, if such time has elapsed that the holder's position may have been changed (*k*).'

(*a*) Thomson *v.* Shiel, 1729; M. 16,810; 1 Ill. 229 (subscription by initials). M'Ilwraith *v.* M'Mikin, 1785; M. 16,820. Monro *v.* Monro, Nov. 14, 1820; 1 Ill. 229. Stewart *v.* Russell, July 11, 1815; F. C. Cockburn *v.* Gibson, Dec. 8, 1815; F. C. See M'Intosh *v.* Macdonald, 1828; 7 S. 155. Craigie *v.* Scobie, 1832; 10 S. 510. See Dickson on Evid. § 667, 784.

(*b*) 45 and 46 Vict. c. 61, § 97. See § 98 as to summary diligence, and § 100 as to proof; and below, § 403L, as to companies.

(*c*) *Ib.* § 23. The proviso added to this section will be found at § 321 (*f*), *supra*.

(*d*) *Ib.* § 24. See above, § 320A. Maiklem *v.* Walker, 1833; 12 S. 53; and other cases in Mackenzie *v.* B. L. Co., 1880; 7 R. 836; rev. 1881, 8 R. H. L. 8.

(*e*) Hall *v.* Fuller, 5 B. & C. 750; 29 R. R. 383.

(*f*) Young *v.* Grote, 4 Bing. 453; 29 R. R. 552.

(*g*) Scholfield *v.* Londesborough, 1896; A. C. 514; 65 L. J. Q. B. 593.

(*h*) Robarts *v.* Tucker, 16 Q. B. 560.

(*i*) Bank of England *v.* Vagliano, 1891; A. C. 107; 60 L. J. Q. B. 145.

(*k*) Cocks *v.* Masterman, 9 B. & C. 902; 33 R. R. 365. Lond. & R. Plate Bk. *v.* Bk. of L'pool, 1896; 1 Q. B. 7; 65 L. J. Q. B. 80. But see Chalmers' Notes on the Act, § 59.

324. The Payee is either named in the bill or in the indorsement; or the bearer may be the person entitled to demand payment, as in bank notes. Uncertainty as to the payee 'in a bill not payable to bearer' is fatal to the bill (*a*). 'A bill may be drawn payable to or to the order of the drawer; or payable to or to the order of the drawee, *e.g.* a cheque on a banker in his own favour (*b*). Where a bill is not payable to bearer, the payee must be indicated therein with reasonable certainty (*c*). It may be payable to two or more payees jointly, or, contrary to the former law, alternatively to one of two, or one or some of several payees (*d*), or to the holder of an office for the time being (*e*). Where the payee is a fictitious or non-existing person, the bill may be treated as payable to bearer, and this although the payee really exists, but has never been intended by the (fraudulent) drawer to have any right upon the bill (*f*), or although the drawer, being deceived, believed him to be a real person (*g*).'

(*a*) Blanckenhagen *v.* Blundel, 2 B. & Ald. 417. But if a bill be issued blank in the payee's name, the holder may fill it up with his own name. Thomson & Co. *v.* Gall, 1805; Hume, 53. See Bayley on Bills, 37; Smith's Merc. Law, 237. See § 311, etc.; the Bills of Ex. Act, § 20; and Chamberlain *v.* Young, 1893; 2 Q. B. 206.

(*b*) 45 and 46 Vict. c. 61, § 5 (1). See *ib.* § 61.

(*c*) *Ib.* § 7 (1). Duncan's Trs. *v.* Shand, 1872; 10 Macph. 984. M'Cubbin *v.* Stephen, 1856; 18 D. 1224. Cases in (*a*) and (*e*).

(*d*) Act, s. 7 (1). Thomson *v.* Philp, 1867; 5 Macph. 679. Holmes *v.* Jaques, L. R. 1 Q. B. 376; 35 L. J. Q. B. 130.

(*e*) Act, *ib.* This also alters the former law. Yates *v.* Nash, 8 C. B. N. S. 581; 29 L. J. C. P. 306. M'Call *v.* Taylor, 34 L. J. C. P. 365; 19 C. B. N. S. 301. Holmes *cit.* Summary diligence on a bill so drawn is still incompetent. Act, § 98. Fraser *v.* Bannerman, 1853; 18 D. 756.

(*f*) Act, § 7 (3). Bank of England *v.* Vagliano, 1890; A. C. 107. See Act, § 54, 55.

(*g*) Clutton & Co. *v.* Attenborough, 1895; 2 Q. B. 707; aff. 1897, A. C. 90. Vagliano, *cit.*

325. The Debt in a bill or note must be clear, and unquestionable, and pecuniary (*a*). 'The sum payable by a bill is certain in the meaning of the Act, although it is required to be paid with interest (*b*), by stated instalments (*c*), by stated instalments with a provision that on default in payment of any instalment the whole shall become due, or according to an indicated rate of exchange, or one to be ascertained as directed in the bill (*d*). In the event of discrepancy between the sum expressed in words and that in figures, that in words is the sum payable (*e*). When a bill is expressed to be payable with interest, interest runs, unless the bill otherwise provides, from the date of the bill, or if it be undated, from the issue thereof (*f*).' Bills granted for gaming debts are null in the hands of the original party (*g*), and were formerly held to be so even in the hands of an innocent indorsee as against the *loser* (*h*); but no such defence was held competent to a drawer or indorser discounting the bill and receiving money for it (*i*). By statute, the bill seems to be effectual in the hand of a *bonâ fide* indorsee; the granter or maker being entitled, on paying to him, to recover from the original payee as money paid on an illegal consideration.

(*a*) Bayley, 10. Thomson, 10. Smith *v.* Nightingale, 2 Starkie, 375; 20 R. R. 694. See § 311. 33 Vict. c. 10, § 6 (Coinage Act).

(*b*) See above, § 32. Morgan *v.* Morgan, 1866; 4 Macph. 321. Tennent *v.* Crawford, 1878; 5 R. 433. Vallance *v.* Forbes, 1879; 6 R. 1099.

(*c*) Macfarlan *v.* Johnston, 1864; 2 Macph. 1210.

(*d*) See the Act, § 72 (4).

(*e*) 45 and 46 Vict. c. 61, § 9; and above, § 306. Sanderson *v.* Piper, 7 Sc. 415; 5 Bing. N. C. 425. Gordon *v.* Sloss, 1848; 10 D. 1129.

(*f*) *Ib.* § 9 (3). See § 32, as to interest as damages.

(*g*) See Don *v.* Richardson, 1858; 20 D. 1138. See *ante*, § 36 (4).

(*h*) 9 Anne, c. 14, § 1. Shillito *v.* Theed, 7 Bing. 405; 1 Ill. 230; 33 R. R. 532. Hamilton *v.* Russel, 1832; 10 S. 549, and cases there cited. In England, an injunction or an order to cancel will be granted in Chancery at the suit of the acceptor of a bill for a gaming debt, to prevent it from being indorsed to third parties. Lloyd *v.* Gurden, 2 Swans. 180. Wynne *v.* Callander, 1 Russ. 293; 1 Ill. 58. See Smith's Merc. Law, 285.

(*i*) Edwards *v.* Dick, 4 B. & Ald. 212; 23 R. R. 255.

326. Term of Payment and Days of Grace.—The time of payment is important, as regulating the obligation and the effect of the instrument. It is either "on demand"; or "at sight"; or on a day certain "after sight or presentment"; or a day certain "after the date of the bill"; or at "usance," or "double usance," or "triple or half usance,"—usance being a period, differing according to local custom, for drawing bills from one country on another (*a*). 'Under the Bills of Exchange Act, bills payable on demand, or at sight, or on presentation, or in which no time for payment is expressed, are payable on demand. So bills accepted or indorsed when overdue are, as regards the acceptor or indorser, bills payable on demand (*b*). Bills are payable at a determinable future time in the sense of the Act, if they bear to be payable at a fixed period after date or sight, or at a fixed period after a specified certain event, though the time of its happening be uncertain (*c*). Any holder may insert the true date of issue or acceptance in a bill payable at a fixed period after date or sight (*d*). The date upon a bill, acceptance, or indorsement, is, in the absence of contrary proof, deemed to be its true date. And a bill is not invalid because ante-dated, post-dated, or dated on a Sunday (*e*).'

In reckoning time in bills of exchange, months are calendar, not lunar (*f*); weeks are computed by days, and days are reckoned with the exclusion of that on which the bill is dated (*g*), 'or from which the time of payment is to begin to run, and including the day of payment (*h*). Where a bill is payable at a fixed period after sight, the time begins to run from the date of acceptance, or of noting or protesting for non-acceptance or for non-delivery (*i*).'

(*a*) Thomson, 247 sqq.

(*b*) 45 and 46 Vict. c. 61, § 10.

(*c*) *Ib.* § 12. Colehan *v.* Cooke, Willes, 393. Goss *v.* Nelson, 1 Burr. 226; 1 Ross' L. C. 25. Campbell *v.* Campbell, 1793; Bell's Ca. 111.

(*d*) *Ib.* § 12. The *bonâ fide* insertion of a wrong date makes the bill operate as of the date so inserted; and the date inserted is in all cases the date of the bill, if it afterwards comes into the hands of a holder in due course; *ib.*

(*e*) *Ib.* § 13. Gatty *v.* Fry, 2 Ex. D. 275; 47 L. J. Ex. 605. *Supra*, § 44.

(*f*) Beawes, No. 253.

(*g*) Hague *v.* French, 3 B. & P. 173. Campbell *v.* French, 6 T. R. 212; 4 R. R. 5.

(*h*) *Ib.* § 14.

(*i*) *Ib.* § 14 (3); cf. *ib.* § 42, 43, 51. See further as to computation of time, the Act, § 92.

327. In addition to the term specified, a certain indulgence is granted, called "days of grace." In all cases where the bill is drawn "at usance," or where the term of payment is definite, whether after date or after sight, days of grace are allowed (*a*). When the bill is payable "at sight," it 'was' unsettled whether there 'were' days of grace, though the weight of authority 'seemed' to be for the affirmative (*b*). It 'was' not settled in Scotland (*c*). 'But it is now enacted that bills or notes purporting to be payable at sight or on presentation shall bear the same stamp as, and shall for all purposes be deemed to be, bills or notes payable on demand (*d*).' When the bill is made payable "on demand," no days of grace are allowed. The days differ in different countries, but generally are reckoned exclusive of the day on which the bill becomes due. In Great Britain and Ireland three days of grace are allowed, exclusive of the day on which the bill falls due; and when the last day of grace falls on Sunday, 'Christmas day, or Good Friday,' or on a day 'appointed by royal proclamation as a public fast or thanksgiving day,' payment must be made on the preceding 'business' day (*e*). 'When the last day of grace is a bank holiday (other than Christmas day or Good Friday) under the Bank Holidays Act, 1871, or amending or extending Acts, or is a Sunday, and the second day of grace is a bank holiday, the bill is due and payable on the succeeding business day (*f*). As the bill is due and payable "on the last day of grace" (the Act, § 14 (1)), no action on it lies till the whole of that day has expired, although as soon as payment is refused, a right of recourse warranting protest and notice of dishonour immediately accrues to the holder (*g*).'

(*a*) Colman *v.* Sayer, 1 Barnard, 203. Brown *v.* Harraden, 4 T. R. 148. Janson *v.* Thomas, Bayley, 241. Tassell *v.* Lewis, Lord Raymond, 743.

(*b*) Chitty on Bills, 261 (10th ed.). 1 Sel. N. P. 301. Colman, *supra* (*a*).

(*c*) Thomson, 248. See below, § 336, 349.

(*d*) 34 and 35 Vict. c. 74, repealed by 45 and 46 Vict. c. 61, which restores its provisions. See Act, § 10.

(*e*) In England, the rule by usage included Sunday and Christmas day; and by statute (39 and 40 Geo. III. c. 42) it was extended to Good Friday. To remove doubts, it was provided by 7 and 8 Geo. IV. c. 15 (not extending to Scotland), that Christmas, Good Friday, and all days appointed by proclamation for solemn fasts and thanksgiving, should in all such questions be treated and considered as Sunday. Sel. N. P. 300. Smith & Payne *v.* Laing, 1786; M. 1612.

(*f*) 45 and 46 Vict. c. 61, § 14. The bank holidays in England, under the Acts, are Easter Monday, Monday in Whitsun week, first Monday in August, the 26th December, or if that be a Sunday, the Monday following. In Scotland, New Year's day, Christmas day (or if they fall on Sundays, the following Mondays), Good Friday, the first Mondays of May and August. 34 and 35 Vict. c. 17. 38 and 39 Vict. c. 13.

(*g*) The Act, § 14 (1), 47. Kennedy *v.* Thomas, 1894; 2 Q. B. 759.

328. The Stamp.—This is regulated by Act of Parliament. Without a stamp of the proper, or higher, value and proper denomination, the bill or note is void (*a*); and the 'impressed' stamp cannot be supplied or altered, if not at first correct (*b*), 'except when the bill has been written on an impressed stamp of sufficient value, but improper denomination (*c*).' The sum for which the *pro rata* duty is leviable is that which is due at the date of the bill, not the amount as augmented by stipulated interest (*d*). No document which does not contain a promise to pay 'a certain sum' is a note under the Stamp Acts (*e*). 'An acknowledgment of the receipt of money, accompanied by a promise to pay it when required, is a note under the Stamp Acts (*f*).'

'It is obvious that the Stamp Acts require certain documents which are not negotiable documents to be stamped as bills of exchange or promissory notes. In other words, the definitions of such documents in the Bills of Exchange Act and the Stamp Act are not the same. In construing the latter Act, which makes promissory notes include "any document or writing (except a bank note) containing a promise to pay any sum of money," the Courts put a rational limitation upon the words, holding that they apply to documents which consist substantially of a promise to pay a definite sum of money, and nothing else. An agreement, therefore, which includes a promise to pay a certain sum combined with other stipulations, is not within the clauses of the Stamp Act as to bills and notes (*g*); or a promise to pay which is only the recognition of a legal obligation resulting from the contract contained in the writing (*h*).'

Alterations on Bills.—If a bill or note be altered in a material part after it is issued (unless merely for correcting a clerical error), the bill is null, and a new stamp is necessary (*i*). 'Independently, however, of the objection under the Stamp Acts, "where a bill or acceptance is materially altered after issue (*k*), without the assent of all parties liable on the bill, the bill is avoided, except as against a party who has himself made, authorised, or assented to the alteration, and subsequent indorsees." But if the alteration is not apparent, a holder in due course may avail himself of the bill as if it had not been altered, and may enforce payment of it according to its original tenor (*l*). The Act specifies the following alterations "in particular" as material, viz. any alteration of the date, the sum payable, the time or place of payment, and, where a bill has been accepted generally, the addition of a place of payment without the acceptor's assent (*m*).'

The stamp on foreign bills applies only to bills made in Great Britain, not to those made abroad (*n*); and it is not on mere probabilities that a bill bearing a foreign date will be held to have been drawn in England (*o*); 'and by statute bills purporting to be drawn abroad are for the purposes of the Stamp Act deemed to be so drawn, although in fact made within the United Kingdom (*p*).' If really drawn abroad, bills 'were' not liable to the British Stamp Law; nor do the Courts of this country hold it incumbent on them to enforce foreign stamp laws (*q*). 'By the existing statute, however, every bill drawn or expressed to be payable, or actually paid, or indorsed, or in any manner negotiated in the United Kingdom, must have an *ad valorem* stamp, which, in the case of bills drawn or made, or purporting to be drawn or made, out of the United Kingdom, may be denoted by an adhesive stamp. This must be adhibited, before using the bill, by any holder into whose hands an unstamped bill comes. Penalties are imposed for failure to cancel it (*r*). Only one of a set of foreign bills requires to be stamped; and on proof of the loss or destruction of a duly stamped bill forming one of a set, another of the set, not issued or negotiated apart from the lost bill, may be admitted in evidence to prove its contents (*s*).'

(*a*) The provisions of the Stamp and Revenue Acts are not affected by the Bills of Exchange Act, 1882, § 97.

(*b*) 55 Geo. III. c. 184, § 11–29; 9 Geo. IV. c. 23; 9 Geo. IV. c. 49, § 15. M'Intosh *v.* Stewart, 1830; 8 S. 739; 1 Ill. 224. Robertson *v.* Ettles, 1834; 7 W. & S. 176.

(*c*) The Stamp Act, 54 and 55 Vict. c. 39, § 37.

(*d*) Pruessing *v.* Ing. 4 B. & Ald. 204; 23 R. R. 253; 1 Ill. 230.

(*e*) See definitions in § 306, 307. Tennent *v.* Crawford, 1878; 5 R. 433, and cases in § 311 (*g*), and *infra* (*f*). See as to the competency of an unstamped bill *in modum probationis*, Swan *v.* Bk. of Scot., 1835; 2 S. & M'L. 67; 3 Ill. 118. Pilling *v.* Drake, 1857; 19 D. 938. 54 and 55 Vict. c. 39, § 14 (4).

(*f*) Alexander *v.* Alexander, 1830, 8 S. 602; 1 Ill. 224. M'Intosh, *supra* (*b*). Pirie's Reprs. *v.* Smith, 1833; 11 S. 473; 1 Ill. 224. Miller *v.* Farquharson, 1835; 13 S. 117. Leith Bank *v.* Walker, 1836; 14 S. 332. Isles *v.* Gill, 1836; 14 S. 996; 3 Ill. 118. Haddin *v.* M'Ewan, 1838; 16 S. 331. Scott *v.* Scott, 1847; 9 D. 1347. Sutherland *v.* Munro, 1847; 10 D. 87. M'Cubbin *v.* Stephen, 1856; 18 D. 1224. Bankier *v.* Robertson, 1864; 2 Macph. 1153. Macfarlan *v.* Johnston, 1864; 2 Macph. 1210. Morgan *v.* Morgan, 1866; 4 Macph. 321. Vallance *v.* Forbes, 1879; 6 R. 1099.

(*g*) Mortgage Insur. Corp. *v.* Comrs. of Inl. Rev., 21 Q. B. D. 352. Thomson *v.* Bell, 1894; 22 R. 16.

(*h*) *Per* Lord M'Laren in Thomson *v.* Bell, *cit.* See Buck *v.* Robson, 3 Q. B. D. 686; 48 L. J. Q. B. 250 (assignment of debt in form of order, disting. from order to pay).

(*i*) Bayley, 118, and cases there cited. Murdoch & Co. *v.* Lee, 1800; 3 Ill. 118; 1 Bell's Com. 417; 4 Paton, 261. Johnstone & Co. *v.* Attwell, 1801; M. No. 5, Apx. *Writ.* Henderson *v.* Hay, 1802; M. 17,059; 3 Ill. 118. Fairweather *v.* Alison, Feb. 12, 1817; F. C. Sutherland *v.* Morrison, 1823; 2 S. 394. Robertson *v.* Annan, 1825; 4 S. 40. M'Lean *v.* Morrison, 1834; 12 S. 613. M'Ewan *v.* Graham, 1833; 12 S. 110. Whitehead *v.* Henderson, 1836; 14 S. 544. Homes *v.* Purves, 1836; 14 S. 898. Coml. Bank *v.* Paton, 1837; 15 S. 1202. Armstrong *v.* Wilson, 1842; 4 D. 1347. King *v.* Creighton, 1841; 4 D. 62; 1843, 2 Bell's App. 81. M'Rostie *v.* Halley, 1850; 12 D. 816. M'Cubbin *v.* Turnbull, 1850; 12 D. 1123. Edin. and Glasgow Bank *v.* Samson, 1858; 20 D. 1246. Douglas *v.* Douglas's Trs., 1864; 2 Macph. 1389. Simpson *v.* Taylor, 1875; 2 R. 75. Master *v.* Miller, 4 T. R. 320; 2 H. Bl. 140; 1 Smith's L. C. 747; 2 R. R. 399. Bell's Convg. 473.

(*k*) 45 and 46 Vict. c. 61, § 21. See also § 20.

(*l*) The Act, § 64 (1). Burchfield *v.* Moore, 3 E. & B. 687; 23 L. J. Q. B. 263.

(*m*) The Act, § 64 (2). See the cases in note (*i*), which are not confined to the question under the Stamp Laws, and the English cases in Addison, Contr. 779 sqq., and 1 Smith's L. C. 747 sqq. Vance *v.* Lowther, 1 Ex. D. 176; 45 L. R. Ex. 200 (materiality a question of law).

(*n*) Jordaine *v.* Lashbrook, 7 T. R. 601.

(*o*) Abraham *v.* Dubois, 4 Camp. 269. Robertson & Co. *v.* Routledge, 1822; 1 S. 562.

(*p*) 54 and 55 Vict. c. 39, § 36. See 45 and 46 Vict. c. 61, § 4, 51, 72, 97.

(*q*) James *v.* Catherwood, 3 Dowl. & R. 190. Wynne *v.* Jackson, 2 Russell, 252. If, for want of a stamp, a contract made in a foreign country and falling to be governed by the law of that country is void, it cannot be enforced here. Bristow *v.* Sequeville, 5 Ex. 279. Valery *v.* Scott, 1875; 3 R. 965. Guthrie's Savigny, Pr. Int. Law, 228, 321. Westlake's Pr. Int. Law, § 199.

(*r*) The Stamp Act, 54 and 55 Vict. c. 39, § 34–39. Broddelius *v.* Grischotti, 1887; 14 R. 536.

(*s*) 54 and 55 Vict. c. 39, § 39. Presentment for acceptance is not negotiation. Griffin *v.* Weatherby, L. R. 3 Q. B. 753. Sharples *v.* Rickard, 2 H. & N. 57; 36 L. J. Ex. 302.

329. '**Negotiation.**—"A bill is negotiated when it is transferred from one person to another in such a manner as to constitute the transferee the holder of the bill (*i.e.* the payee or indorsee who is in possession of it, or the bearer thereof)" (*a*). When a bill contains words prohibiting transfer, or indicating an intention that it should not be transferable, it is valid as between the parties thereto, but, if the intention is clearly expressed, is not negotiable (*b*).'

Indorsement.—By means of indorsement, bills circulate as paper money, passing from hand to hand, unaffected, 'till past due,' by any latent exception (*c*), and with increasing credit at each indorsement (*d*). Bills originally payable "to the bearer," or to "a certain person or bearer," 'or on which the only or last indorsement is an indorsement in blank (*e*),' may be transferred 'by delivery' without indorsement, but of course without any increase of credit (*f*). Bills, although not taken payable "to order," may in Scotland be indorsed (*g*); but it 'was' otherwise in England (*h*) 'till the Act of 1882. Now bills payable to a specified person without the words "to order," are payable to order if transfer be not excluded by their terms (*i*).' Indorsement to a person named is said to be "in full," 'or according to the Act "in special"'; if it be in blank, the bill is payable to the holder 'or bearer (*k*). Any holder may convert a blank indorsement into a special one (*l*).' Indorsement made in pencil has been held good within the custom of merchants (*m*).

'An indorsement, in order to operate as a negotiation, must be written on the bill itself, and signed by the indorser, whose mere signature is enough (*n*); it must be of the entire bill, one which purports to transfer only a part of the sum payable, or to transfer to two or more indorsees severally, not operating as a negotiation (*o*); it must be by all of several payees or indorsees, unless they are partners, or the indorser has authority to indorse for the others; a payee or indorsee wrongly designated, or whose name is misspelt, may indorse as described, adding, if he think fit, his proper signature; and in the absence of contrary proof, indorsements are presumed to have been made in the order in which they stand on the bill (*p*).'

(*a*) 45 and 46 Vict. c. 61, § 31 (1), (2).
(*b*) *Ib.* § 8 (1). National Bank *v.* Silke, 1891; 1 Q. B. 435.
(*c*) See *ante*, § 325, as to the effect of a gaming debt.
(*d*) The doctrine of procuration, as applicable to drawing and acceptance, is equally so to indorsement. See *ante*, § 321.
(*e*) The Act, § 8, 31.
(*f*) Bayley, 128. Grant *v.* Vaughan, 3 Burr. 1516. Wokey *v.* Poole, 4 B. & Ald. 1; 22 R. R. 594; 1 Ill. 424 (as to Exchequer Bills). The Act, § 31 (2); and below, § 333F. See as to cheques, Keene *v.* Beard, 8 C. B. N. S. 372; 29 L. J. C. P. 287. See above, § 308.
(*g*) Crichton *v.* Gibson, 1726; M. 1446; 3 Ill. 119. Robertson *v.* Burdekin, 1843; 6 D. 17.
(*h*) Bayley, 128. 2 Kent, 77. 1 Pardessus, 358.
(*i*) The Act, § 8 (4).
(*k*) Collins *v.* Martin, 1 B. & P. 648; 3 Ill. 120; 4 R. R. 752. Peacock *v.* Rhodes, Doug. 636; 1 Ill. 58. The Act, § 8, 34.
(*l*) Act, § 34 (4).
(*m*) Geary *v.* Physic, 5 B. & Cr. 234; 1 Ill. 230; 29 R. R. 225.
(*n*) 45 and 46 Vict. c. 61, § 32 (1). Indorsement is valid if made on an allonge or copy, in a country where "copies" are recognised. *Ib.*
(*o*) *Ib.* (*p*) *Ib.* § 32.

330. The indorsement may be restrictive. Thus, it may be payable "to A. B. only," which will prevent him from indorsing it (*a*). 'But where a restrictive indorsement authorises further transfer, all subsequent indorsees take the bill with the same rights, and subject to the same liabilities, as the first indorsee under the restrictive indorsement (*b*).' Or the indorsement may be "for my use"; in which case it is held that this is not a mere direction to apply the contents to the indorser's use, but a restriction which creates a trust in any one who becomes the indorsee; so that he cannot take it for the payee's debt, but must hold the contents as the money of the person interposing the restriction (*c*); yet the payee of such a bill may discount it, the presumption being that he acts for his constituent (*d*), 'or receive payment, or sue upon it; but he has no power to transfer his rights as indorsee, unless the indorsation expressly authorises him to do so (*e*).' Or, it may be "without recourse," in which case no demand can come back on the indorser, who would otherwise be liable (*f*). Or a condition 'might' be annexed to the indorsation which 'would' be available against the acceptor, if the bill 'should' be accepted with such condition in the indorsement (*g*); 'but now a conditional indorsement may be disregarded by the payer, and payment to the indorsee is valid, whether the condition has been fulfilled or not (*h*).'

(*a*) Anchor *v.* Bank of England, Douglas, 615; 1 Ross' L. C. 279. Sigourney *v.* Lloyd, 8 B. & C. 622; 1 Ross' L. C. 286; 32 R. R. 504.
(*b*) Act, § 34 (3).
(*c*) Treuttell *v.* Barandon, 8 Taunt. 100; 3 Ill. 120; 19 R. R. 472. Sigourney *v.* Lloyd, *cit.*, and cases there cited; confirmed in Exch. Cham., 5 Bing. 525; 1 Ill. 231.
(*d*) See Treuttell, *supra* (*c*). (*e*) The Act, § 35.
(*f*) See 45 and 46 Vict. c. 61, § 16, 58.
(*g*) Robertson *v.* Kensington, 4 Taunt. 30.
(*h*) The Act, § 33.

331. Indorsement carries the bill only, but leaves untransmitted the diligence which may have been raised on it, and has no effect in transferring dividends due on the bill out of a sequestrated estate (*a*), 'or any guarantee, or other collateral obligation or security (*b*).'

(*a*) Wallace, Hamilton, & Co. *v.* Campbell, 1821; 1 S. 53; aff. 1824, 2 S. App. 467; 1 Ill. 231. See M'Kechnie *v.* Macfarlane, 1832; 10 S. 126. M'Lachlan *v.* Thomson, 1831; 9 S. 753; and below, § 1460. 2 Bell's Com. 20; i. 428. 3 Ersk. 2, § 31, note. Anon., 1754; 5 Br. S. 820.

(*b*) See Wilson's Thomson, 178, 418. Forbes & Co. *v.* M'Nab, May 29, 1816; F. C.; and cases in note (*a*).

332. It may be made at any time, even after the bill or note is past due, 'until restrictively indorsed, or paid or discharged by or for the acceptor, or in the case of accommodation bills, by or for the person accommodated (*a*)'; but whether it carries the bill discharged of latent exceptions as between the original debtor and creditor, is a question which 'was' differently viewed in Scotland and in England. In England it has not this effect if made after the day of payment, or when marks of dishonour are on the bill (*b*). In Scotland the decisions greatly varied. It 'was' held that indorsement, even after the bill is due, when it 'bore' no marks of dishonour, 'carried' the bill free of latent claims (*c*); but when it 'had' been retired, and so marked, and again put into circulation (*d*), or dishonoured, and noted on the bill as such (*e*), the indorsee 'was' held liable to latent exceptions. When, again, the bill 'was' indorsed or discounted in circumstances which, in the opinion of a jury, ought to have excited suspicion and called for inquiry, 'or, more correctly, in circumstances which showed *mala fides* on his part,' the indorsee 'was' held subject to those objections to which the indorser was liable (*f*).

'*Negotiation of Overdue Bills.*—By the Mercantile Law Amendment (Scotland) Act the law of Scotland was assimilated to the law of England, and it was enacted that an indorsee of a bill indorsed when overdue should take it subject to all objections or exceptions to which it was subject in the hands of the indorser (*g*). This is repealed, and the Bills of Exchange Act provides that an overdue bill when negotiated is "subject to any defect of title affecting it at its maturity, and thenceforward no person who takes it can acquire or give a better title than that which the person who took it had" (*h*). A bill payable on demand is deemed to be overdue in the meaning of the foregoing enactment when it appears on its face to have been in circulation for an unreasonable length of time, which is a question of fact (*i*). Every negotiation is *primâ facie* presumed to have been made before the bill was overdue, unless the indorsement bears date after the maturity of the bill (*k*). Any one taking a bill not overdue with notice that it has been dishonoured, takes it subject to any defect of title attaching to it at the time of dishonour (*l*). The drawer, or a prior indorser, or the acceptor, to whom a bill is negotiated back, may reissue and further negotiate the bill, subject to the provisions of the Act, but cannot enforce the bill against any intervening party on the bill to whom he was liable (*m*).'

(*a*) Hubbard *v.* Jackson, 4 Bing. 390; 29 R. R. 582. Callow *v.* Lawrence, 3 M. & Sel. 95; 15 R. R. 423. So it is in America; 3 Kent, 91. Jones *v.* Broadhurst, 9 C. B. 173. Williams *v.* James, 15 Q. B. 493. Lazarus *v.* Cowie, 3 Q. B. 459. Cook *v.* Lister, 13 C. B. N. S. 543. 45 and 46 Vict. c. 61, § 36 (1); comp. § 59–64 of Act; and below, § 333G.

(*b*) Bayley, 159. See Crossley *v.* Ham, 13 East, 498; 3 Ill. 121. Taylor *v.* Mather, 3 T. R. 83. Brown *v.* Davies, 3 T. R. 80. Boehm *v.* Sterling, 7 T. R. 423. Tinson *v.* Francis, 1 Camp. 19. Smith's Merc. Law, 227. 1 Ross' L. C. 313 sqq.

(*c*) M'Gowan *v.* M'Kellar, 1826; 4 S. 498; 1 Ill. 232. Wilkie *v.* Wilson, Nov. 30, 1811; F. C. Crauford *v.* Robertson, June 30, 1814; F. C. See Adam *v.* Boyd, 1830; 8 S. 914. Muir & Co. *v.* M'Donald, 1831; 9 S. 535; 1 Ill. 232. See 1 Ross' L. C. 333 sq.

(*d*) Smith *v.* Murdoch, 1829; 7 S. 670.

(*e*) Macdonald *v.* Langton, 1836; 15 S. 303; 3 Ill. 122.

(*f*) Gill *v.* Cubitt, 3 B. & Cr. 466; 1 Ill. 232. Strange *v.* Wigney, 6 Bing. 677. Down *v.* Halling, 4 B. & Cr. 330. Backhouse *v.* Harrison, 5 B. & Ad. 1098. See Macdonald, *supra* (*e*). Goodman *v.* Harvey, 4 Ad. & E. 870. Bank of Bengal *v.* Macleod, 7 Moore, P. C. 35. Raphael *v.* Bk. of Engl., 17 C. B. 161; 25 L. J. C. P. 33. Brandao *v.* Barnett, 1 M. & G. 908, 935; 12 Cl. & F. 105. Crouch *v.* Credit Foncier, L. R. 8 Q. B. 374; 42 L. J. Q. B. 183. See Pollock on Contr. 216 sq. See as to bankers' cheques, Rothschild *v.* Corney, 9 B. & Cr. 388; 33 R. R. 209. *Supra*, § 308.

(*g*) 19 and 20 Vict. 60, § 16. Brown *v.* Bain, 1864; 2 Macph. 1143.

(*h*) 45 and 46 Vict. c. 61, § 36 (2); and see § 29, 38; below, § 333A.

(*i*) *Ib.* § 36 (3). Cases in note (*f*). See Act, § 10 (1); and above, § 326.

(*k*) *Ib.* § 36 (4). See § 13 (1), 100; and 2 Bell's Com. 185 (173, M'L.'s ed.).

(*l*) *Ib.* § 36 (5). This does not affect the rights of a "holder in due course," *ib.*; and see *ib.* § 29, 38; and below, § 333A.

(*m*) *Ib.* § 37. See § 59, 61–64. Morris *v.* Walker, 15 Q. B. 589; 19 L. J. Q. B. 401.

333. The scoring and deleting of an indorsation reinstates the indorser, if truly intended so to do (*a*).

(*a*) Adam *v.* Watson, 1827; 6 S. 244; 1 Ill. 234. See Russell *v.* Mather, 1824; 2 S. 648, f. n. The doctrine of procuration applicable to acceptance (see § 321) holds good in relation to indorsement. See 1 Bell's Com. 404 (428, M'L.'s ed.). The Act, § 24, 60.

333A. '*Holder in Due Course.*—A holder in due course is a holder who has taken a bill, complete and regular on the face of it, under the following conditions, namely, (1) that he became the holder of it (*a*) before it was overdue, and without notice of dishonour; (2) that he took it in good faith and for value, and without notice at the time of negotiation to him of any defect in the title of the person who negotiated it (*b*). The title of one who negotiates a bill is defective, when he obtained the bill, or the acceptance of it, by fraud (*c*), duress, force and fear (*d*), or other unlawful means, or for an illegal consideration (*e*), or when he negotiates it in breach of faith, or under such circumstances as amount to a fraud. A holder (whether for value or not) who derives his title through a holder in due course, and who is not himself a party to any fraud or illegality affecting it, has all the rights of that holder in due course as regards the acceptor and parties prior to that holder (*f*).'

(*a*) A holder is "the payee or indorsee of a bill, or one who is in possession of it, or the bearer thereof." The Act, § 2.

(*b*) Jones *v.* Gordon, L. R. 2 App. Ca. 616; 47 L. J. Bkr. 1.

(*c*) See *supra*, § 13 sq.

(*d*) See *supra*, § 12.

(*e*) See the Act, § 27; and above, § 35 sq.

(*f*) 45 and 46 Vict. c. 61, § 29.

333B. '*Consideration and Value.*—The Bills of Exchange Act does not affect our law, that valuable consideration is not necessary to support an obligation (*a*). But want of value (non-onerosity) may be pleaded as evidence when the bill is challenged on another ground, as for illegality, fraud, or failure of the consideration, or because it was an accommodation bill. As regards the law of England, it is provided that any consideration sufficient to support a simple contract, or an antecedent debt or liability, constitutes valuable consideration (*b*). When value has at any time been given for a bill, the holder is deemed to be a holder for value as regards the acceptor and all who became parties to the bill before that time. And a holder who has a lien on the bill is a holder for value to the extent of the sum for which he has a lien (*c*). An antecedent debt constitutes valuable consideration (*d*); as when a banker credits a customer's account with the amount of a bill or cheque (*e*).

'*Presumption of Value and Good Faith.*—Every one whose signature appears on the bill is *primâ facie* deemed to have become a party thereto for value. Every holder of a bill is *primâ facie* deemed to be a holder in due course (*f*); but if in an action on a bill it is admitted or proved that the acceptance, issue, or subsequent negotiation of the bill is affected with fraud, duress, or force and fear, or illegality, the burden of proof is shifted, unless and until the holder proves that, subsequent to the alleged fraud or illegality, value has in good faith been given for the bill (*g*). A thing is deemed to be done in good faith, where it is in fact done honestly, whether it is done negligently or not (*h*).

'The general rule was, that if it were alleged that the bill was not onerous or not for value, this could be proved only by the writ or oath of the holder, unless fraud were relevantly averred or there were facts, admitted or proved *scripto*, inferring that value had not been given (*i*). It is now, however, enacted that "in any judicial proceeding in Scotland any fact relating to a bill of exchange, bank cheque, or promissory note which is relevant to any question of liability thereon, may be proved by parole evidence"; but this, it is provided, does not affect former rules as to caution and consignation in sists of diligence and suspensions (*k*).

'This provision has given occasion to difference of opinion on the bench, and cannot be said to be happily expressed. It was probably intended to assimilate our practice to that of England in regard to proof of value, and of the discharge of bills and notes. If it be read strictly, it applies only to questions of liability arising on the bill or note ("thereon"), and does not affect the rules of evidence in collateral or extrinsic conditions or agreements. It would seem that in a question with a holder in due course, or any one taking under him, this section will not allow a party to the bill to contradict by parole the legal effect, by the law merchant or under the Act, of his contract upon the face of the bill, such contracts being subject to the ordinary rule that written contracts cannot be contradicted or varied by oral evidence. But while this is law in England, and has been so laid down by high authority in Scotland (*l*), it must be admitted that the words of the section have *primâ facie* a much wider range. It may be useful to remember that in England oral evidence is "admissible (1) to show that what purports to be a complete contract has never come into operative existence," (in other words, to qualify the delivery which is necessary (*m*) to complete the contract); "(2) to impeach the consideration for the contract; or (3) to show that the contract has been discharged by payment, release, or otherwise" (*n*), except by renunciation (*o*). In regard to the first of these points, parole has always been admissible in Scotland. If the operation of the Act were to be restricted to the assimilation of our law to that of England, which may have been the intention, and appears to be the inclination of the judicial mind, the changes effected will be only under heads (2) and (3).'

(*a*) See above, § 8, 64. Law *v*. Humphreys, 1876; 3 R. 1192 (correcting opinions in Clark *v*. Clark, 1869; 7 Macph. 335).
(*b*) 45 and 46 Vict. c. 61, § 27. Currie *v*. Misa, L. R. 10 Ex. 153; 1 App. Ca. 554; 45 L. J. Ex. 854.
(*c*) *Ib*. § 27 (2), (3). Attenborough *v*. Clark, 26 L. J. Ex. 138.
(*d*) The Act, § 27 (1) (*b*).
(*e*) Clydesdale Bank *v*. M'Lean, 1883; 10 R. 719; aff. 11 R. H. L. 1; 9 App. Ca. 95. Currie *v*. Misa, *cit*. *Ex p*. Richdale, 19 Ch. D. 409.
(*f*) Stiell *v*. Holmes, 1868; 6 Macph. 994.
(*g*) The Act, § 30 (1), (2). This is partly substituted for 19 and 20 Vict. c. 60, § 15, repealed. Jones *v*. Gordon, *supra*, § 333A (*b*). Addison, Contr. 757. Force and fear *annul* the contract. See above, § 12.
(*h*) The Act, § 90. Jones *v*. Gordon, *cit*.; authorities in § 332, note (*f*).
(*i*) Wallaces *v*. Barrie, 1793; M. 1484. Brock *v*. Newlands, 1863; 2 Macph. 71. Mercer *v*. Livingston, 1864; 3 Macph. 300. Swanson *v*. Gallie, 1870; 9 Macph. 208 (as between co-acceptors). Wilson *v*. Scott, 1874; 1 R. 1003. **Little** *v*. **Smith**, 1845; 8 D. 265, and cases there cited. Alexander *v*. Stewart, 1877; 4 R. 366. Ferguson, Davidson, & Co. *v*. Jolly's Trs., 1880; 7 R. 500. Blackwood *v*. Hay, 1858; 20 D. 631. Gray *v*. Scott, 1868; 6 Macph. 197, etc. etc.
(*k*) The Act, § 100. Simpson *v*. Brown, 1888; 15 R. 716 (caution).
(*l*) See *per* L. P. Inglis and L. M'Laren in National Bk. of Australasia *v*. Turnbull & Co., 1891; 18 R. 629. Gibson's Trs. *v*. Galloway, 1896; 23 R. 414. See Chalmers's Digest, notes to § 21. Thorburn, p. 218.
(*m*) The Act, § 27.
(*n*) Chalmers, note on § 27.
(*o*) The Act, § 62 (1).

333C. '*Delivery.*—Every contract on a bill, whether it be the drawer's, the acceptor's, or an indorser's, is incomplete, and revocable until delivery of the instrument in order to give effect thereto (*a*), provided that where an acceptance is written on a bill, and the drawee gives notice to, or according to the directions of, the person entitled to the bill that he has accepted it, the acceptance then becomes complete and irrevocable (*b*). As between immediate parties, and as regards a remote party other than a holder in due course, the delivery in order to be effectual must be made either by or under the authority of the party drawing, accepting, or indorsing as the case may be; and it may be shown to have been conditional or for a special purpose only, and not for the purpose of transferring the property in the bill (*c*). But if the bill be in the hands of a holder in due course, a valid delivery of the bill by all parties prior to him so as to make them liable to him is conclusively presumed (*d*). Where a bill is no longer in the possession of one who has signed it as drawer, acceptor, or indorser, a valid and unconditional delivery by him is presumed till the contrary is proved (*e*). A promissory note is inchoate and incomplete until delivery thereof to the payee or bearer (*f*).'

(*a*) Delivery means transfer of possession, actual or constructive, from one person to another. 45 and 46 Vict. c. 61, § 2.
(*b*) *Ib*. § 21 (1). See above, § 23, 24.
(*c*) *Ib*. § 21 (2). Martini *v*. Steel & Craig, 1878; 6 R. 342. Castrique *v*. Buttigieg, 10 Moore, P. C. 94. Denton *v*. Peters, L. R. 5 Q. B. 475. As to proof, see the Act, § 100 (*supra*, § 333B), and Abrey *v*. Crux, L. R. 5 C. P. 42; 39 L. J. C. P. 9.
(*d*) But see § 20 of the Act, *supra*, § 313.
(*e*) 45 and 46 Vict. c. 61, § 21.
(*f*) *Ib*. § 84.

333D. 'The holder of a bill may sue on the bill in his own name. If a holder in due course, he holds the bill free from any defect of title of prior parties, as well as from mere personal defences available to prior parties among themselves, and may enforce payment against all parties liable on the bill. Where the holder's title is defective, a holder in due course to whom he negotiates the bill obtains a good and complete title to the bill; and if he obtains payment of the bill, the person who pays him in due course gets a valid discharge for the bill (*a*).'

(*a*) 45 and 46 Vict. c. 61, § 38.

333E. '*Liability of Drawer and Indorsers.*—The *drawer* of a bill by drawing it engages that on due presentment it shall be accepted (*a*) and paid according to its tenor, and that if it be dishonoured he will compensate the holder or any indorser who is compelled to pay it, provided that the requisite proceedings on dishonour be duly taken. And he is precluded from denying to a holder in due course the existence of the payee and his capacity to indorse (*b*). The indorser of a bill by indorsing it engages that on due presentment it shall be accepted and paid according to its tenor, and that if it be dishonoured he will compensate the holder or a subsequent indorser who is compelled to pay it, provided that the requisite proceedings on dishonour be duly taken. He is precluded from denying to a holder in due course the genuineness and regularity in all respects of the drawer's signature and all previous indorsements; and also from denying to his immediate or a subsequent indorsee that the bill was at the time of his indorsement a valid and subsisting bill, and that he had a good title thereto (*c*). Where a person signs a bill, otherwise than as drawer or acceptor, he thereby incurs the liabilities of an indorser to a holder in due course (*d*).'

(*a*) National Bk. of Australasia *v.* Turnbull & Co., 1891; 18 R. 629.
(*b*) 45 and 46 Vict. c. 61, § 55 (1).
(*c*) *Ib.* § 55 (2).
(*d*) *Ib.* § 56. See above, § 314.

333F. '*A Transferor by Delivery* is the holder of a bill payable to bearer who negotiates it by delivery without indorsing it; and he is not liable on the instrument. He warrants, however, to his immediate transferee, being a holder for value, that the bill is what it purports to be, that he has a right to transfer it, and that at the time of transfer he is not aware of any fact which renders it valueless (*a*). The transferee obtains by the transfer for value such title as the transferor had in the bill; *i.e.* a title equivalent to a duly intimated assignation; and in addition the right to have the indorsement of the transferor (*b*).'

(*a*) 45 and 46 Vict. c. 61, § 58, 8 (3). Gompertz *v.* Bartlett, 2 E. & B. 849; 23 L. J. Q. B. 65. See above, § 329 (*f*).
(*b*) *Ib.* § 31 (4). Whistler *v.* Foster, 14 C. B. N. S. 257; 32 L. J. C. P. 161. Hood *v.* Stewart, 1890; 17 R. 749.

333G. '*Discharge of Bills.*—A bill is discharged by payment in due course by or on behalf of the drawee or acceptor, *i.e.* by payment made at or after its maturity to the holder thereof, in good faith and without notice that his title is defective (*a*). Payment by drawer or indorser does not discharge a bill, but if the bill be payable to or to the order of a third party, the drawer who pays may enforce payment against the acceptor, but may not reissue the bill. When a bill is paid by an indorser, or where a bill payable to drawer's order is paid by the drawer, the party paying is remitted to his former rights as regards the acceptor or antecedent parties, and he may, if he thinks fit, strike out his own and subsequent indorsements, and again negotiate the bill (*b*). Payment of an accommodation bill by the person accommodated discharges it (*c*). A banker who in good faith, and in the ordinary course of business, pays a bill drawn on him, and payable to order on demand, is not bound to show the genuineness of indorsements, or that they were authorised, but is deemed to have paid in due course although they were forged or made without authority (*d*).'

(*a*) 44 and 46 Vict. c. 61, § 59 (1). Bills of course are also discharged in the ways in which other obligations are discharged (*infra*, § 555 sqq.), as by renunciation in writing or with delivery of the bill (the Act, § 62), by confusion (*ib.* 61), cancellation (*ib.* 63, 64,—Dominion Bk. *v.* Anderson & Co., 1888; 15 R. 408; aff. 1891, A. C. 592; 18 R. H. L. 21), prescription (*infra*, § 594), etc. As to giving up the bill and its effect in evidence, see below, § 578 (*a*), (*b*), (*c*).
(*b*) 45 and 46 Vict. c. 91, § 59 (2).
(*c*) *Ib.* § 59 (3).
(*d*) *Ib.* § 60. Comp. 16 and 17 Vict. c. 59, § 19; and above, § 308, 323 *ad fin.*

334. Negotiation of Bills.—The negotiation of bills (*a*) consists of three acts—Presentment, Protest, and Notice.

(*a*) The word negotiation is used in a different sense in the Act; see above, § 329.

335. Presentment is the act of showing or offering at the place of payment a draft to the drawee, or a bill to the acceptor, or note to the maker; that in the one case the bill may be accepted or paid, and 'that' in the other payment 'of the note may be' made.

336. (1.) *Presentment for Acceptance.*—The presentment of a draft for acceptance has a double purpose,—to satisfy the bill-holder whether he is to rely on the payment of the debt; and to preserve "recourse," or a demand for indemnification against the drawer and indorsers, if the drawee should not accept. The presentment must be at the drawee's place of residence, when the bill is made payable there; and if the drawee has absconded, 'or is dead, or bankrupt, or is a fictitious person, or one not having capacity to contract by bill, or' is not there to be found, and cannot be heard of at the banking-houses, the bill is to be held as dishonoured (*a*). If the drawee has changed his place of residence, the holder must endeavour to find it out and present the bill there (*b*). If the drawee cannot himself be found, nor his residence discovered, the bill should be presented to some one authorised to act for him (*c*). If the drawee be dead, the presentment to his heirs may be proper, but 'is' not necessary (*d*); and if the bill be payable at a banker's, a presentment at that banker's is sufficient (*e*). 'When authorised by agreement or usage, presentment may be made through the post office. Presentment is excused if the drawee is dead or bankrupt, a fictitious person, or one incapable of contracting by bill; when after the exercise of reasonable diligence presentment cannot be effected; and where, though the presentment has been irregular, acceptance has been refused on some other ground; but not because the holder has reason to believe that the bill on presentment will be dishonoured (*f*).' If, on the bill being presented, acceptance should be refused, this must be shown by a protest, and notice must be given to the drawer and indorsers (*g*). If the time of payment depend on the presentment (as in bills payable "after sight"), the bill-holder is bound within a reasonable time to present for acceptance (*h*), 'because presentment for acceptance is necessary in order to fix the maturity of the instrument. Where a bill expressly stipulates that it shall be presented for acceptance, or where a bill is drawn payable elsewhere than at the residence or place of business of the drawee, it must be presented for acceptance before it can be presented for payment; but in no other case is presentment for acceptance necessary in order to render liable any party to the bill (*i*). So' the time of presentment is somewhat discretionary, or controlled only by the general rule, that there must be no undue or unnecessary delay, which is properly a question for the jury (*k*). 'Subject to the provisions of the Act, when a bill payable after sight is negotiated, the holder must either present it for acceptance, or negotiate it within a reasonable time, failing which drawers and indorsers are discharged (*l*).'

If the bill be drawn "at sight," it need not be presented for acceptance. If the bill be payable "on demand," or if the day of payment be certain, the holder is not required to present it for acceptance, but may present it at once for acceptance and for payment when due (*m*): but an agent must present a bill for acceptance (*n*). The presentment must be made 'to the drawee, or a person authorised to accept or refuse acceptance on his behalf, before the bill is overdue,' at a seasonable time (*o*), and within the known business hours of a banker's or merchant's attendance (*p*). The bill may be left for acceptance for twenty-four hours (*q*); 'but the time depends on usage at the place (*r*). A bill is dishonoured by non-acceptance when, being duly presented, acceptance is refused or cannot be obtained; or when presentment for acceptance is excused and the bill is not accepted (*s*). Subject to the provisions of the Act, when a bill is dishonoured by non-acceptance, an immediate right of recourse against the drawer and indorsers accrues to the holder, and no presentment for payment is required (*t*). The holder of a bill may refuse to take a qualified acceptance, and if he does not obtain an unqualified acceptance, may treat the bill as dishonoured by non-acceptance (*u*).'

(*a*) Bayley, 125. Anon., Lord Raym. 748, on the evidence of merchants. 45 and 46 Vict. c. 61, § 41.

(*b*) Collins *v.* Butler, Strange, 1087. Bateman *v.* Joseph, 12 East, 433; 11 R. R. 443.

(*c*) Firth *v.* Thrush, 8 B. & Cr. 397; 32 R. R. 431.

(*d*) 45 and 46 Vict. c. 61, § 41.

(*e*) Saunderson *v.* Judge, 2 H. Bl. 509; 3 R. R. 492. Harris *v.* Packer, 3 Tyrwhitt, 370.

(*f*) The Act, § 41.

(*g*) See below, § 340. 45 and 46 Vict. c. 61, § 42.

(*h*) Pothier, No. 143. Bayley, 224. Falls *v.* Porterfield, 1766; M. 1593. Muilman *v.* D'Eguino, 2 H. Bl. 565; 1 Ross' L. C. 414; 1 Ill. 234.

(*i*) 45 and 46 Vict. c. 61, § 39.

(*k*) Fry *v.* Hill, 7 Taunt. 397; 1 Ill. 234; 18 R. R. 512. Falls and Muilman, *supra* (*h*).

(*l*) 45 and 46 Vict. c. 61, § 40. And see as to "reasonable time" and diligence, *ib.* § 39 (4), 40 (3). Gladwell *v.* Turner, L. R. 5 Ex. 59; 39 L. J. Ex. 31.

(*m*) Ferguson *v.* Malcolm, 1727; M. 1558; 1 Ill. 235. Jamieson *v.* Gillespie, 1749; M. 1494. See Philpot, 3 C. & P. 244. The Act, § 39.

(*n*) Dunlop *v.* Hamilton & Co., Jan. 16, 1810; F. C. See Ramsay, Bonars, & Co. *v.* Mackersy, 1840; 2 D. 1003; rev. 2 Bell, 30. Houldsworth *v.* Br. Linen Co., 1850; 13 D. 376, as to the duties of agents in negotiating bills.

(*o*) Barclay *v.* Bailey, 2 Camp. 527; 11 R. R. 787. Morgan *v.* Davidson, 1 Starkie, 114.

(*p*) Parker *v.* Gordon, 7 East, 385; 8 R. R. 746. See Robson *v.* Bennet, 2 Taunt. 388; 11 R. R. 614. See Neilson *v.* Leighton, 1843; 5 D. 513; 6 D. 622. 45 and 46 Vict. c. 61, § 41 (1).

(*q*) Bellasis *v.* Hester, 1 Lord Raym. 281. Hayward *v.* Bank of England, Strange, 550; Bayley, 186. Bank of Van Diemen's Land *v.* Bank of Victoria, L. R. 3 P. C. 526.

(*r*) 45 and 46 Vict. c. 61, § 42. Bank of Van Diemen's Land, *cit.*

(*s*) 45 and 46 Vict. c. 61, § 43 (1). See § 17, 19, 41, 44.

(*t*) *Ib.* § 43 (2).

(*u*) *Ib.* § 44 (1). See above, § 316.

337. (2.) *Presentment for Payment.*—Bills must 'subject to the provisions of the Act (*a*),' in order to preserve recourse against the other parties, be duly presented for payment; 'but not necessarily' where acceptance has been previously refused (*b*). The 'usual' evidence of such presentment is a notarial protest (*c*). If payable "on demand" (in which case no days of grace are allowed), the presentment must be 'within a reasonable time after its issue, and after its indorsement respectively, in order to make drawer and indorser liable,' and the risk of delay will be with the bill-holder (*d*). If put into circulation, it must be presented within a reasonable time after it is received, which rather seems to be considered as a question of fact for the jury than of legal construction for the Court (*e*). In general, it seems to be held that a presentment on the day after receipt by post is enough (*f*). If payable so many days "after sight," the bill or note must be presented on the last day of grace after the expiration of that time, reckoned from the day on which the presentment for acceptance took place. If payable at a day certain, the bill or note must be presented on the last day of grace (*g*). It must be presented 'by the holder or one authorised to receive payment on his behalf, at' a reasonable 'hour on a business' day (*h*) 'at the proper place, either to the person designed in the bill as payer, or one authorised to pay, or refuse payment, on his behalf, if with the exercise of reasonable diligence such person can there be found (*i*).' If regular hours be fixed by usage, they must be observed; if payable at a banker's, bank hours must be observed (*k*).

The place of payment may be indicated either in the drawing of the bill or in its acceptance. In the drawing, it is commonly indicated by the mere address of the drawee (*l*). If any other place be mentioned for payment besides that implied in the address, and the bill have not, when so presented, been accepted, it may be protested in that place for non-payment (*m*). If a particular house be mentioned either in the body of the bill or note, or in a marginal note, or in the acceptance, the presentment for payment must be there (*n*). If the place be mentioned in the acceptance, and without the restrictive words, "there only," or "not elsewhere," the acceptance is held to be general, and the presentment for payment need not necessarily be there, but to the acceptor himself. But if the acceptance specify the place with the above restrictive words, the presentment for payment must be at the particular place or house so indicated. And no difference of construction has been admitted of such restrictive specification, whether proceeding from the drawer or from the acceptor (*o*). Bills drawn payable at any other place than the places therein mentioned as the residence of the drawee, if not accepted, are to be protested for non-payment at the place of payment expressed in the draft, without any further presentment to the drawee (*p*). 'A bill in which no place of payment is specified and no address given is to be presented at the drawee's or acceptor's place of business if known, and if not, at his ordinary residence if known. In any cases not already specified, a bill is duly presented if presented to the drawee or acceptor wherever he can be found, or if presented at his last known place of business or residence (*q*). If with reasonable diligence no person authorised to pay or refuse payment can be found when a bill is presented at the proper place, no further presentment to the drawee or acceptor is required. Bills drawn upon or accepted by two or more persons, not partners, must, if no place of payment be specified, be presented to all. If the drawee or acceptor be dead, presentment is to be made to his personal representative, if any, and if with reasonable diligence he can be found. Presentment through the post office is sufficient if authorised by agreement or usage (*r*).' If a bill, at so many days "after sight," have been presented for acceptance, and refused, but afterwards accepted for honour of the drawer, the presentment for payment is correctly made when the bill is at maturity, 'reckoning not from' the acceptance for honour, 'but from the date of the noting for non-acceptance'; and this both in a question with the drawer, and with the acceptor for honour (*s*). 'Where the holder of a bill presents it for payment, he must exhibit the bill to the person from whom he demands payment, and when it is paid in full, must deliver it up to the party paying it (*t*).'

(*a*) 45 and 46 Vict. c. 61, § 45. See below, § 337A.
(*b*) See the Act, § 46.
(*c*) Bayley, 228. Thomson, 306. Hoare *v.* Cazenove, 16 East, 398; 1 Ill. 228; 14 R. R. 370. Gibb *v.* Mather, 8 Bing. 214; 1 Ill. 235; 34 R. R. 648. See § 338.
(*d*) Bayley, 228. 45 and 46 Vict. c. 61, § 45.
(*e*) Bayley, 229, and cases there cited. See Williams *v.* Smith, 2 B. & Ald. 496; 21 R. R. 373; 1 Ross' L. C. 597. See Leith Bank *v.* Walker, 1836; 14 S. 333; 3 Ill. 118.
(*f*) Rickford *v.* Ridge, 2 Camp. 537.
(*g*) See above, § 326–27. Bills not payable on demand must be presented on the day on which they fall due. 45 and 46 Vict. c. 61, § 45 (1); and above, § 326–27.
(*h*) 45 and 46 Vict. c. 61, § 45 (3).
(*i*) *Ib.* § 45 (4).
(*k*) See Neilson *v.* Leighton, *supra*, § 336 (*p*). Chitty on Bills, 215.
(*l*) See Robertson *v.* Burdekin, 1843; 6 D. 17.
(*m*) 2 and 3 Will. IV. c. 98. See *supra*, § 336 (*t*).
(*n*) Ambrose *v.* Hopwood, 2 Taunt. 61. Sanderson *v.* Bowes, Bayley, 175. Dickinson *v.* Brown, 16 East, 110 and 112. Tracothick *v.* Edwin, 1 Starkie, 468. See Masters *v.* Baretto, 8 C. B. 433.
(*o*) 1 and 2 Geo. IV. c. 78. Rowe *v.* Young, 2 Bligh, 391; 21 R. R. 91. Turner *v.* Hayden, 4 B. & Cr. 1; 1 Ill. 236. Selby *v.* Eden, 3 Bing. 611. Fayle *v.* Bird, 6 B. & Cr. 53. Williams *v.* Waring, 10 B. & Cr. 2. *Supra*, § 320; and comp. the Act, § 19 (2) (*c*), with § 45 (4) (*a*).
(*p*) 2 and 3 Will. IV. c. 98. 45 and 46 Vict. c. 61, § 51 (6).
(*q*) 45 and 46 Vict. c. 61, § 45 (4).
(*r*) *Ib.* § 45 (5), (6), (7), (8).
(*s*) Williams *v.* Germaine, 7 B. & Cr. 468; 1 Ill. 228. The Act, § 65 (5).
(*t*) 45 and 46 Vict. c. 61, § 52 (4).

337A. '(3.) *Delay* in making presentment for payment is excused when it is caused by circumstances beyond the control of the holder, and not imputable to his default, misconduct, or negligence. When the cause of delay ceases to operate, presentment must be made with reasonable diligence.

'It is not necessary to present for payment a bill accepted generally, in order to make the acceptor liable (*a*). Presentment for payment is dispensed with (1) when with reasonable diligence it cannot be effected, but not merely because the holder has reason to believe that the bill will on presentment be dishonoured; (2) where the drawee is a fictitious person; (3) as regards the drawer, where the drawee or acceptor is not bound as between himself and the drawer to accept or pay the bill, and the drawer has no reason to believe that the bill would be paid if presented (as, *e.g.*, where the acceptor is an accommodation party (*b*)); (4) as regards the indorser, where the bill was made or accepted for his accommodation, and he has no reason to believe that it would be paid if presented (*c*). (5) It is also dispensed with by waiver of presentment, express or implied (*d*).'

(*a*) 45 and 46 Vict. c. 61, § 52 (1). See § 19.
(*b*) Bk. of Scotland *v.* Lamont & Co., 1889; 16 R. 769.
(*c*) 45 and 46 Vict. c. 61, § 46 (1), (2). Shepherd, *infra* (*d*).
(*d*) *Ib.* § 46 (2) (*e*). Smith's Merc. Law, 245, 252. 1 Bell's Com. 422 (455, M'L.'s ed.). Allhusen & Sons *v.* Mitchell, 1870; 8 Macph. 600. Shepherd *v.* Reddie, 1870; 8 Macph. 619.

337B. 'Dishonour by Non-Payment.—A bill is dishonoured by non-payment when it is duly presented for payment, and payment is refused or cannot be obtained, or when presentment is excused and the bill is overdue and unpaid. Subject to the provisions of the Act, when a bill is dishonoured by non-payment, an immediate right of recourse against the drawer and indorsers accrues to the holder (*a*).'

(*a*) 45 and 46 Vict. c. 61, § 47.

338. Protest.—The protest is a notarial declaration, before witnesses, on presentment, that the bill has been presented; has not been accepted, or not paid (*a*); and that the bill-holder is to enforce payment not only against the acceptor (if the protest be for non-payment), but also against the drawer and indorsers. 'A protest must contain a copy of the bill, must be signed by the notary making it, and must specify the person at whose request it is made, the place and date, the cause or reason for protesting, the demand made, and the answer given, if any, or the fact that the drawee or acceptor could not be found (*b*).' A note is made 'on the day of dishonour' on the bill at protesting (which is termed noting the bill), and from that note and from the notary's book the notary may make out the instrument at any time (*c*); but the mere note on the bill is insufficient to authorise diligence. The protest, 'which must be conform to the noting which is its warrant (*d*),' must be extended on paper stamped with a rateable duty according to the amount of the bill or note (*e*). It is signed by the notary, but the subscription of the witnesses is not indispensable (*f*); 'and though the protest bears that the notary made the demand for payment, the notarial presentment is by custom generally and sufficiently made by his clerk, or even by a banker's clerk (*g*).' And none but a notary can protest a bill; nor can any notary protest a bill drawn or accepted by himself (*h*).

(*a*) See Elder *v.* Young & Co., 1854; 17 D. 56.
(*b*) 45 and 46 Vict. c. 61, § 51 (7). Bartsch *v.* Poole & Co., 1895; 23 R. 328 (bill payable at drawer's office).
(*c*) Brown & Co. *v.* Dunbar, 1807; M. Apx. *Bill*, 21. Chaters *v.* Bell, 4 Esp. 48. Selwyn, Nisi Pr. 361. 45 and 46 Vict. c. 61, § 51 (4), (9), § 93 (cases in which noting is equivalent to protest).
(*d*) M'Pherson *v.* Wright, 1885; 12 R. 942.
(*e*) 55 Geo. III. c. 184. See Barbour *v.* Newal, 1823; 2 S. 289; 1 Ill. 237. Napier *v.* Carson, 1824; 2 S. 622. The stamp duty, where the duty on the bill is not more than 1s., is the same as on the bill; in other cases, 1s. 54 and 55 Vict. c. 39.
(*f*) Inglis *v.* Clark, 1697; M. 16,971, 7724.
(*g*) Stevenson *v.* Stewart, 1764; M. 1578, 1593. Macartney *v.* Hannah, 1817; Hume, 76. Bell's Convg. 491 states the modern usage correctly. See 1 Bell's Com. 414 (438, M'L.'s ed.), and Smith's Merc. Law, 277. Buller, J., in Leftley *v.* Mills, 4 T. R. 170, 2 R. R. 350, doubts as to the sufficiency of a demand by a banker's clerk, at least in regard to foreign bills.
(*h*) Barbour, *supra* (*e*). See Alexander *v.* Scott, 1827; 6 S. 151 (particularly p. 157); 1 Ill. 237. Russell v. Kirk, 1827; 6 S. 133. Allan *v.* Galli, 1829; 7 S. 706. Reid *v.* Grindlay, 1830; 9 S. 31. M'Kenzie *v.* Smith, 1830; 9 S. 52. Leith Bank *v.* Walker, 1836; 14 S. 333; 3 Ill. 118. See next §, at note (*c*).

339. The protest 'was' indispensably necessary, not only for recording in order to authorise summary diligence even against the acceptor or maker (*a*), but also for recourse against the drawer and indorsers. The want of protest 'could' not be supplied, even by oath of the party that he knew of the dishonour of the bill. The bankruptcy of the drawee, or acceptor, or maker of the note, 'did' not, without a protest, ground a claim of recourse. 'But since 1856, it is not necessary to take a protest merely in order to preserve recourse against the drawer and indorsers, or acceptor, for which purpose presentment and dishonour may be proved by any competent evidence (*b*). When a notary cannot be found at the place where the bill is dishonoured, a certificate, signed by a householder or substantial resident and two witnesses, attesting the dishonour of the bill, operates as if it were a formal protest; though apparently not to warrant summary diligence (*c*).'

A notarial protest of presentment of a draft, where the drawee is possessed of funds of the drawer, is equivalent to an intimated assignation (*d*). 'A foreign bill dishonoured by non-acceptance must be protested; and if accepted and not paid, must be protested for non-payment, otherwise drawer and indorsers are discharged (*e*).'

(*a*) See below, § 344.
(*b*) 19 and 20 Vict. c. 60, § 13; 45 and 46 Vict. c. 61, § 51, 52. There are a few cases in which protest is still necessary; see the Act, § 65 (1), 68 (1), 67 (1), (4), 14 (3).
(*c*) 45 and 46 Vict. c. 61, § 94. See *ib.* § 98. Sommerville *v.* Aaronson, 1898; 25 R. 524 (place of dishonour is where first presented and dishonoured).
(*d*) A protest not being necessary in England (except to certain effects under special statutes), questions as to the ambiguity of notice have arisen in England for which there was scarcely room in Scotland. See § 311, 315, 341, and 1465.
(*e*) The Act, § 51 (2).

340. Notice of Dishonour.—This is the announcement made to those against whom recourse is demandable, that the bill or note has been dishonoured, 'by non-acceptance or non-payment'; and that recourse is to be taken (*a*). The use of it is to enable each in his order to take precautions for his safety and indemnification. But it is now settled that due notice forms an absolute and indispensable condition of the drawer's or indorser's responsibility, whether any loss has arisen from want of notice or not; 'and any drawer or indorser to whom such notice is not given is discharged (*b*).' Notice must be given of non-acceptance, if the bill-holder, though not bound to present for acceptance, does so (*c*); 'but the rights of a subsequent holder in due course are not prejudiced by the omission to give notice of such dishonour. Where due notice of non-acceptance is given, notice of subsequent non-payment is unnecessary, unless in the meantime the bill has been accepted (*d*).' It is unnecessary against the acceptor or maker of a note (*e*). Neglect to give notice is a discharge to all the other parties in the bill, on the ground that it is implied in the obligation of each indorser that he shall have such notice; and it is not necessary to show loss from want of notice, the law presuming it (*f*).

It 'was' questioned whether one who has guaranteed payment of a bill is entitled to notice; 'but the question is now decided in the negative (*g*).'

Notice requires to be given within a

certain time, 'which was' different in foreign and in inland bills. The time in foreign bills is regulated by the usage of merchants (*h*); and the rules seem to be, that to one residing in the same place, notice must be given before the expiration of the day after the dishonour, and so that it may reach the person that day (*i*); that for notice by each successive indorsee to the indorser preceding, a day is allowed after the notice to himself (*k*); but this only on the footing that there has not, in the course of the transmission, been undue delay at any one stage: for if notice to any one indorser has been beyond the day, the drawer and prior indorsers are discharged (*l*). To persons resident elsewhere, notice must be despatched by the next post; or if that should be a day of public rest, by the post following (*m*). In inland bills in Scotland, notice within a fortnight 'was' sufficient (*n*); but this extreme latitude 'was' strictly confined to inland bills and notes, and 'did' not apply to bills drawn on or from England or Ireland (*o*).

'*Statutory Rules.*—This was altered by the Mercantile Law Amendment Act, 1856, which made the preceding rules as to foreign bills substantially applicable to inland bills. That provision was repealed by the Bills of Exchange Act, which provides in regard to notice of dishonour: (1) that it must be given by or for the holder or an indorser liable on the bill; (2) that it may be given by an agent in his own name or in name of any party entitled to give notice, whether his principal or not; (3) that notice by or for the holder enures for the benefit of all subsequent holders and all prior indorsers having a right of recourse against the party to whom it is given; (4) that notice by or for an indorser enures for the benefit of the holder and all indorsers subsequent to the party to whom notice is given; (5) that it may be given in writing or orally in any terms which sufficiently identify the bill, and intimate that it has been dishonoured by non-acceptance or non-payment; (6) that the return of the bill to the drawer or indorser is, in point of form, deemed a sufficient notice of dishonour; (7) that a written notice need not be signed, and may be supplemented and validated by oral communication, and misdescription of the bill vitiates the notice only if it misleads; (8) that notice may be given to an agent of the party; (9) that notice must be given to a personal representative of a party known to be dead, if there be any and he can be found with reasonable diligence; (10) that it may be given either to a bankrupt or his trustee; (11) that it must be given to each of several drawers or indorsers, unless they are partners, or one be authorised to receive it for the others; (12) that it may be given as soon as the bill is dishonoured, and must be given within a reasonable time thereafter. It is not given within a reasonable time (in the absence of special circumstances), unless, if the parties giving and receiving it reside in the same place, it is given or sent off in time to reach the latter on the day after the dishonour; and unless, if they reside in different places, it is sent off on the day after the dishonour, if there be a post at a convenient hour on that day, if not, by the next post thereafter. It is further provided, (13) that when the bill is in the hands of an agent, he may either give notice to the parties or to his principal, and in the latter case, within the same time as if he were the holder; and the principal has the same time for giving notice as if the agent had been an independent holder; (14) that a party receiving notice has the same time after receipt for giving notice to antecedent parties that the holder has after the dishonour (*p*).

'Delay in giving notice of dishonour is excused for the same reasons, and to the same extent, as delay in presenting for payment (*q*). And notice of dishonour is dispensed with when, after the exercise of reasonable diligence, it cannot be given to or does not reach the party to be charged; by waiver, express or implied, whether before or after the proper time for notice. As regards the *drawer*: (1) where drawer and drawee are the same; (2) where the drawee is a fictitious person, or without capacity to contract; (3) where the bill is presented for payment to the drawer; (4) where the drawee or acceptor is under no obligation to accept or pay; (5) where the drawer has countermanded payment. As regards the *indorser*: (1) where the indorser knew at the time of indorsing that the drawee was a fictitious person or incapable of contracting; (2) where the bill is presented for payment to the indorser; (3) or was made for his accommodation (r).' A bill-holder may be ignorant of the residence of those whose mere names are on the bill; and all that the law requires in that case is, that he shall use due diligence to discover the residence of the parties, and give notice as soon as it can reasonably be given (s). It is sufficient notice, if a letter properly addressed be in due time put into the post office (t); but an error in the address will make it requisite to prove the actual delivery of the letter (u). The drawer, by consenting to a delay or indulgence to the acceptor, waives the necessity of notice (v).

(a) See as to accommodation bills, *infra*, § 346.

(b) Littlejohn *v.* Allan, 1746; M. 1569, correcting former cases; 1 Ill. 237. Langley *v.* Hogg, 1748; M. 1574. See also Chitty on Bills, 197–8 (302, 10th ed.), and cases cited, and the cases in 3 Ill. 122–5. 45 and 46 Vict. c. 61, § 48 (1).

(c) Miln *v.* Erskine, 1710; M. 1551. Goodal *v.* Dolley, 1 T. R. 712; 1 R. R. 372. Orr *v.* Maginnis, 7 East, 362; 1 Ross' L. C. 520. Roscoe *v.* Hardy, 12 East, 434; 1 Ross' L. C. 619.

(d) 45 and 46 Vict. c. 61, § 48.

(e) 45 and 46 Vict. c. 61, § 52 (3).

(f) See cases, *supra* (b).

(g) Borthwick *v.* Robertson, 1830; 8 S. 857. See National Bank *v.* Robertson, 1836; 14 S. 402; 1 Ill. 235. Watt *v.* National Bank, 1839; 1 D. 827. Walton *v.* Mascall, 13 M. & W. 72. Hitchcock *v.* Humfries, 5 M. & G. 559. Brown *v.* Kirkland, 1861; 23 D. 363.

(h) 12 Geo. III. c. 72, § 41.

(i) Smith *v.* Mullett, 2 Camp. 208; 1 Ross' L. C. 601; 11 R. R. 694. Jamieson *v.* Swinton, *ib.* 373. See Clarkson *v.* Ball, 1831; 10 S. 17. Williams *v.* Smith, 2 B. & Ald. 496; 1 Ross' L. C. 597; 21 R. R. 373. The rule is that the holder must use due diligence to find the indorser's address if he does not know it, and that he has a day to give notice after ascertaining it. Gladwell *v.* Turner, L. R. 5 Ex. 59; 39 L. J. Ex. 31. Byles on Bills, 283.

(k) Jamieson, *supra* (i).

(l) Marsh *v.* Maxwell, 2 Camp. 210.

(m) See Mackenzie *v.* Dott, 1861; 23 D. 1310.

(n) 12 Geo. III. c. 72, § 41. 33 Geo. III. c. 74. Thomson on Bills, 345. Milligan *v.* Barbour, 1829; 7 S. 489; 1 Ill. 237.

(o) Reynolds *v.* Syme, 1774; M. 1598. Ferguson & Co. *v.* Belch, 1803; M. Apx. *Bill*, 13.

(p) 45 and 46 Vict. c. 61, § 49.

(q) *Ib.* § 50 (1). See *supra*, § 337A.

(r) *Ib.* § 50 (2).

(s) Baldwin *v.* Richardson, 1 B. & Cr. 245; 25 R. R. 883. Firth *v.* Thrush, 8 B. & Cr. 387; 1 Ill. 237; 32 R. R. 421. See above, note (i).

(t) Hawkes *v.* Salter, 4 Bing. 715; 1 Ill. 237; 29 R. R. 708. See Stock *v.* Aitken, 1846; 9 D. 75. 45 and 46 Vict. c. 61, § 49 (15).

(u) Milligan, *supra* (n).

(v) Campbell *v.* Patten, 1839; 12 S. 269. 45 and 46 Vict. c. 61, § 50 (2); *supra* (r).

341. In Scotland, the necessity of a protest 'gave' a clear import to the notice of its having been made. In England several difficulties have occurred as to the import of notice, which 'could' occur with us only where no protest 'had' been made. And the rule there adopted 'was,' that the notice must contain all that a protest imports, viz. that the bill was dishonoured, and that the party looks for payment to the indorser (a). Bankruptcy is not equivalent to protest, neither is it equivalent to notice: but 'although' circumstances necessarily inferring knowledge of the dishonour, and of the intention to demand recourse, 'are not' enough 'to dispense with notice of dishonour,' the right to notice may be waived (b).

(a) Solarte *v.* Palmer, 7 Bing. 530; aff. in H. L., 1 Bing. N. S. 194; 3 Ill. 122. This case was overruled, and the rule is that notice of dishonour, *i.e.* that the bill has been presented to the aceptor and not paid, is sufficient. King *v.* Bickley, 2 Q. B. 421. Paul *v.* Joel, 3 H. & N. 455; 4 H. & N. 355. Bailey *v.* Porter, 14 M. & W. 44. Smith's Merc. Law, 246–8. See above, § 340, where the provisions of the Act are given.

(b) Murray & Son *v.* Morrison, 1824; 3 S. 202; 1 Ill. 238. Allan *v.* Macdonald, 1827; 6 S. 260. See above, § 340.

342. Diligence.—The demand upon a bill is made against the acceptor for the contents of the bill, with interest 'from the time of presentment for payment if the bill is payable on demand, and from the maturity of the bill in any other case,' and charges, '*i.e.* the expenses of noting, or when protest is necessary and the protest has been extended, the expenses of protest'; or against the indorsers, 'or drawer,' for the contents of the bill 'with interest and charges as above (a)'; and in the case of a foreign bill, for exchange, being the difference of money where drawn and where payable; and also for re-exchange, being the damage arising from the dishonour of the bill and the necessity of the bill-holder's having recourse back to the place of drawing (b).

(a) The additions are from the Act, § 57, the third subsection of which leaves the Court to exercise discretion as to awarding interest as damages.

(b) 1681, c. 20. Thomson on Bills, 430. Pothier's Cont. de Change, No. 52 and 64; Code de Commerce, No. 167. 1 Pardessus, 461. In America the rule of damage on returned foreign bills is different, and varies in the several States—in some twenty per cent., in others six, seven and a half, etc. See 3 Kent, Com. 116 et seq. The drawer and indorsers are certainly liable for re-exchange, and so, though conflicting opinions have been given, appears to be the acceptor. M'Laren's Bell's Com. i. 431, note. Wilson's Thomson on Bills, 448. See 45 and 46 Vict. c. 61, § 57. *In re* Gen. S. Amer. Co., 7 Ch. D. 637; 47 L. J. Ch. 67. *Ex p.* Robarts, 18 Q. B. D. 286. See as to re-exchange generally, Suse *v.* Pompe, 8 C. B. N. S. 538. Willans *v.* Ayers, 3 App. Ca. 133.

343. The demand on bills or notes may, 'if the holder's title be clear on the face of the bill (*a*),' be enforced summarily, without the necessity of an action, by a decree of registration, after the analogy of the decree by consent (*b*). But the person making the demand must either have the bill to deliver up on payment, or he must give full indemnity if it should be lost (*c*). 'Nothing in the Bills of Exchange Act, or in any repeal effected thereby, extends, or restricts, or any way alters or affects, the law and practice in Scotland in regard to summary diligence (*d*). Consequently, the repeal of § 10 of the Mercantile Law Amendment Act does not affect the provision, that summary diligence shall not be competent on any bill or note issued without a date (*e*).'

(*a*) Smith *v.* Selby, 1829 ; 7 S. 785. Summers *v.* Marianski, 1843 ; 6 D. 286. Fraser *v.* Bannerman, 1853 ; 15 D. 756. See, however, as to partners, *infra*, § 371.

(*b*) 1681, c. 20. 1696, c. 36. 12 Geo. III. c. 72, § 41, 42. 1 and 2 Vict. c. 114. Yuill *v.* Richardson, 1699 ; M. 14,996 ; 1 Ill. 238. See *ante*, § 67, 68. See as to England, 18 and 19 Vict. c. 67 ; and as to foreign bills, Don *v.* Kealey, 1850 ; 12 D. 1016. Elder *v.* Young & Co., 1854 ; 17 D. 56. Mackenzie *v.* Hall, 1854 ; 17 D. 164.

(*c*) In England it was necessary to go into Chancery in such a case. Hansard *v.* Robinson, 7 B. & Cr. 90 ; 31 R. R. 166. See below, § 349A.

(*d*) 45 and 46 Vict. c. 61, § 98.

(*e*) The Act, *l.c.* ; 19 and 20 Vict. c. 60, § 10. Comp. above, § 326, and the definition of "issued" in § 2 of the Act. Cameron *v.* Morrison, 1869 ; 7 Macph. 382.

344. The protest must be registered in the books of a competent Court (*a*), within six months from the date of the bill in case of non-acceptance, or six months from the date of payment in case of non-payment : and it would seem that in a case where protest has been taken at once for non-acceptance and non-payment, the day of payment will be the *terminus a quo* in reckoning the six months (*b*). The instrument itself and the record must be free from erasure ; but an erasure in the extract was held not fatal to diligence, being in a word unimportant (*c*).

(*a*) Sutherland *v.* Gunn, 1854 ; 16 D. 339 (parties in different counties).

(*b*) Yuill, § 343 (*b*). See Thomson on Bills, 403. N. B. Bk. *v.* Thom, 1848 ; 10 D. 1505. Bon *v.* L. Rollo, 1846 ; 12 D. 1310 (bill may be protested for diligence against acceptor at any time within the six months). M'Rostie *v.* Halley, 1849 ; 12 D. 124. Moffat *v.* Marshall, 1838 ; 16 S. 406.

(*c*) Crichton *v.* Watt, 1830 ; 9 S. 68 ; 1 Ill. 238.

345. A co-acceptor of a bill is entitled, on retiring it, to proceed with the diligence to the effect of operating his relief without any assignation (*a*).

(*a*) Walker *v.* Forbes & Co., 1829 ; 7 S. 684 ; 1 Ill. 238.

346. Accommodation Bills.—Although bills and notes properly spring from real transactions, and so are the representatives of actual debts, the easy form of their constitution and transmission has led to their being used in raising money on credit, for accommodation, without any real debt existing between the drawer and drawee, or with the indorsers. These are called Accommodation Bills, or Wind Bills, from the fictitious nature of the transaction. And this sort of transaction is neither unlawful nor without use. 'The Act defines an "accommodation party to a bill" as "a person who has signed a bill as drawer, acceptor, or indorser without receiving value therefor, and for the purpose of lending his name to some other person" (*a*).'

(*a*) 45 and 46 Vict. c. 61, § 28 (1).

347. There are some points in which real and accommodation bills differ. In a real bill the parties are liable as they stand on the bill : the acceptor is the real debtor ; and the drawer, and each indorser in his order, is surety to the bill-holder. In accommodation bills, the acceptor, 'if he be the party accommodating,' is the mandatary of the drawer, who requests him to pay ; and on payment he becomes his creditor *ex mandato* ; 'but any party, whether drawer or acceptor, or indorser, may be the accommodation party.' The bill-holder, indeed, may have received the bill as a real bill ; 'and it is enacted that "an accommodation party is liable on the bill to a holder for value ; and it is immaterial whether when such holder took the bill he knew such party to be an accommodation party or not"' (*a*) ; but to the original parties it is a mere accommodation, and their rights will be regulated on that footing.

(*a*) The Act, § 28 (2). See Boag *v.* Menzies, 1849 ; 11 D. 362. Stewart *v.* Wyllie, 1849 ; 11 D. 1123. Strathern *v.* Masterman & Co., 1850 ; 12 D. 1087.

348. The neglect of 'presentment for payment or of' notice 'of dishonour,' therefore, to the drawer 'or other party accommodated' will not bar recourse on him, if there be no fund in the drawee's hand, or no reasonable ground to expect the bill to be honoured (*a*). Of this the bill-holder must run the risk if he should neglect to give notice. If the drawer have, *at drawing*, effects with the drawee, it will entitle to notice, as if it were not an accommodation bill. And in the same way, if the drawer have good ground, on any other account, to look for acceptance, this will give him right to notice. Where a bill is drawn for the use of another, the dishonour of it must be intimated (*b*).

(*a*) 45 and 46 Vict. c. 61, § 46, 50.

(*b*) See on the subject of this section, Thomson on Bills, 373. Cory *v.* Scott, 3 B. & Ald. 619; 1 Ill. 239. Norton *v.* Pickering, 8 B. & Cr. 610. Henderson *v.* Kerr, 1829; 8 S. 121. Dirom *v.* Boyd, 1827; 5 S. 773. France *v.* Lucy, 1 Ry. & Mo. 341. Claridge *v.* Dalton, 4 M. & S. 226; 16 R. R. 440. Bickerdike *v.* Bollman, 1 T. R. 405; 2 Smith's L. C. 51 sq.; 1 R. R. 242; 1 Ross' L. C. 508-34. 1 Bell's Com. 427. Smith's Merc. Law, 275.

349. Sexennial Prescription.—Bills and notes are intended for immediate use, not as securities for permanent loans. And the want of the ordinary checks on forgery has led to a limitation, by which a bill or note loses all effect as an obligation on the expiration of six years from the time when payment is demandable: *i.e.* from the last day of grace, if payable on a day certain; if on demand, from the date; if at sight (*a*), from the last day of grace after presentment, or the day before if the last be a holiday (*b*).

(*a*) But cf. § 327, 595.

(*b*) 12 Geo. III. c. 72, § 37 and 39. Moffat *v.* Marshall, 1838; 16 S. 406; 3 Ill. 125. See this subject more fully stated below, § 594 et seq.

349A. 'Lost Bills.—If a bill be lost before it is overdue, the holder may apply to the drawer to give him another bill of the same tenor, giving security to the drawer, if required, to indemnify him against all persons whatever in case the lost bill be found; and the drawer may be compelled to grant such a duplicate bill (*a*). And in any action upon a bill the Court may order that the loss of the instrument shall not be set up, provided a sufficient indemnity be given against the claims of any other person upon the instrument (*b*).'

(*a*) 45 and 46 Vict. c. 61, § 69.

(*b*) *Ib.* § 70. See 17 and 18 Vict. c. 125, § 87; 19 and 20 Vict. c. 102, § 90. Conflans Quarry Co. *v.* Parker, L. R. 3 C. P. 1; 37 L. J. C. P. 51. See also the distinction in the case of loss between a bill in a negotiable state and a bill not negotiable, Grant on Banking, 422; Chitty on Bills, 100; 2 Parsons on Bills, 295.

349B. 'Conflict of Laws.—When a bill drawn in one country is negotiated, accepted, or payable in another, the following rules obtain under the statute: (1) The validity of a bill as regards requisites in form is determined by the law of the place of issue; and the validity in form of the other contracts on the bill by the law of the place where each such contract is made, *i.e.* the place of delivery which completes the contract (*supra*, § 333C). But a bill issued abroad is not invalid for want of being stamped according to the law of the place of issue. And a bill issued abroad may be treated as valid between parties to it in the United Kingdom, if it conform as regards requisites in point of form to the law of the United Kingdom. (2) The interpretation of each contract on the bill is determined by the law of the place where such contract is made; provided that the indorsement abroad of an inland bill is construed, as regards the payer, by the law of the United Kingdom (*a*). (3) The holder's duties with regard to presentment, protest, notice, or otherwise, are determined by the law of the place where the act is done or the bill is dishonoured (*b*). (4) Where a bill is drawn out of, but payable in, the United Kingdom, and the sum payable is not expressed in British currency, the amount shall, in the absence of some express stipulation, be calculated according to the rate of exchange for sight drafts at the place of payment on the day when the bill is payable (*c*). (5) When a bill is drawn in one country and is payable in another, the due date thereof is determined according to the law of the place where it is payable (*d*).'

(*a*) Alcock *v.* Smith, 1892; 1 Ch. 238.

(*b*) Horne *v.* Rouqette, 3 Q. B. D. 514; 2 Smith's L. C. 64. Westlake, Pr. Int. Law, § 217.

(*c*) Hirschfield *v.* Smith, L. R. 1 C. P. 340; 35 L. J. C. P. 177.

(*d*) 45 and 46 Vict. c. 61, § 72. Stewart *v.* Gelot, 1871; 9 Macph. 1057 (stamp; cf. Westlake, § 199). As to this section, comp. Guthrie's Savigny's Pr. Int. Law, pp. 231, 239. Westlake, § 213 sqq.

349C. 'Promissory Notes.—Subject to the provisions in Part IV. of the Bills of Exchange Act, the provisions of that Act relating to bills apply, with the necessary modifications (*a*), to promissory notes, the maker being deemed in applying these provisions to correspond with the acceptor of a bill, and the first indorser of a note with the drawer of an accepted bill payable to drawer's order. But the provisions of the Act as to presentment for acceptance, acceptance, acceptance *supra* protest, and bills in a set, are expressly excluded from applying to notes. Protest of a dishonoured foreign note is unnecessary (*b*).

'Besides the special provisions as to notes already mentioned (*c*), it is enacted that a promissory note may be made by two or more makers, who may be liable thereon jointly, or jointly and severally, according to its tenor (*d*). Where a note payable on demand has been indorsed, it must be presented for payment within a reasonable time after the indorsement, otherwise the indorser is discharged. What is reasonable time is determined with regard to the nature of the instrument (*e.g.* bank note or otherwise), the usage of trade, and the facts of the particular case (*e*). A note payable on demand is not overdue, so as to affect the holder with defects of title of which he had no notice, by reason that it appears that a reasonable time for presenting it for payment has elapsed since its issue (*f*).'

(*a*) See Leeds and County Bank *v.* Walker, 11 Q. B. D. 84 (bank note).

(*b*) 45 and 46 Vict. c. 61, § 89.

(*c*) See above, § 307, 333C *in fin.*, etc.

(*d*) 45 & 46 Vict. c. 61, § 85. When a note runs, "I promise to pay," and is signed by two or more persons, it is deemed to be their joint and several note; *ib.* sub-sec. (2). See above, § 61.

(*e*) The Act, § 86 (1), (2). Chartd. Merc. Bank of India *v.* Dickson, L. R. 3 P. C. 574.

(*f*) The Act, § 86 (3).

349D. 'A note in the body of it made payable at a particular place must be presented for payment there in order to make the maker liable. In other cases presentment for payment is not necessary to make a maker liable, but it is necessary in order to make the indorser of a note liable. Where a note is in the body of it made payable at a particular place, presentment there is necessary in order to render an indorser liable; but when a place of payment is indicated only by way of memorandum, presentment at that place is sufficient to render the indorser liable; but a presentment to the maker elsewhere, if sufficient in other respects, shall also suffice (*a*).'

(*a*) 45 and 46 Vict. c. 61, § 87. Cf. *ib.* § 45. Gordon *v.* Kerr, 1898; 25 R. 570 (instalment note).

349E. 'The maker of a promissory note by making it engages that he will pay it according to its tenor; and he is precluded from denying to a holder in due course the existence of the payee and his then capacity to indorse (*a*).'

(*a*) 45 and 46 Vict. c. 61, § 88. Cf. *ib.* § 54 and 89.

CHAPTER X

OF PARTNERSHIP

350. Nature and Kinds of Partnership.—This contract combines the capacities, industry, skill, funds, and credit of several in the prosecution of a common object of trade, manufacture, or professional employment (*a*). It involves the principles of many separate contracts, as Sale, Location, Pledge, Mandate, Trust. Under Partnership may be considered,—Partnership Proper; Joint Trade or Adventure; Joint-Stock Companies; and Public Chartered Companies.

(*a*) See 1 Stair, t. 16. 3 Ersk. 3. § 18, 30. 2 Bell's Com. 611. Montagu, Gow, Collier, Lindley, and Clark (Edinburgh, 1866) on Partnership. 2 Selw. N. P. 1088. 3 Kent, Com. 23. Pothier, Tr. de Société, tit. 3, p. 533. Merlin, Rép. de Juris. tom. 12, p. 662. Pardessus, tom. 3, pp. 1–98. Van Leeuwen, 409. Voet. lib. 17, t. 2.

I. PARTNERSHIP PROPER.

351. Definition.—Partnership may be described as a mutual contract and voluntary association of two or more (*a*) persons for the acquisition of gain or profit, with a contribution for that end of stipulated shares of goods, money, skill, and industry; the stock of the society being held *pro indiviso* in trust for the creditors. It is distinguished from joint purchase, and also from community arising from common property, which, though held *pro indiviso,* involves no trust for the creditors (*b*). It is in legal construction held, on the one hand, to imply an unlimited mandate or procuration to each partner to bind the company in the line of its trade or employment (*c*); and, on the other, a guarantee by each to third parties of all the engagements legally undertaken in the social name. 'Contrary to the rule formerly supposed to exist, that participation in the profits of a business afforded an absolute presumption of the existence of a partnership, it was established in Cox *v.* Hickman that, although a right to participate in the profits of trade is *primâ facie* evidence and an indispensable element of partnership, and there may be cases where partnership may be inferred from such participation alone, as a presumption not of law but of fact, yet the existence of the relation depends on the real intention and contract of parties (*d*). This section is not altered by the Partnership Act of 1890 (*e*).'

(*a*) See below, § 365.
(*b*) 3 Ersk. 3. § 18. Pothier, Tr. de Société, No. 2. Pardessus, t. 3, p. 4. See London Financial Assn. *v*. Kelk, 26 Ch. D. 107, 143; and as to ships, § 449.
(*c*) Ersk. *ut sup*. § 20; and below, § 354.
(*d*) **Cox** *v*. **Hickman,** 30 L. J. C. P. 125; 8 H. L. Ca. 268; Tudor's L. C. 345. Bullen *v*. Sharp, L. R. 1 C. P. 86; 35 L. J. C. P. 105. Holme *v*. Hammond, 41 L. J. Ex. 157; L. R. 7 Ex. 218. Mollwo, March, & Co. *v*. Court of Wards, L. R. 4 P. C. 419. Pooley *v*. Driver, 4 Ch. D. 458; 46 L. J. Ch. 466. Pawsey *v*. Armstrong, 18 Ch. D. 698. Walker *v*. Hirsch, 27 Ch. D. 460. Badeley *v*. Consold. Bank, 38 Ch. D. 238. Adam *v*. Newbigging, 13 App. Ca. 308. So the profits or a proportion of them may by agreement be appropriated to the payment of a debt, and even a certain control over the business conferred upon a creditor, without his being thereby made a partner. Mollwo, March, & Co., *cit*. *Ex p*. Delhasse, 47 L. J. Bkr. 65; 7 Ch. D. 711. Kelly *v*. Scotto, 49 L. J. Ch. 383. Eaglesham & Co. *v*. Grant, 1875; 2 R. 960. Stott *v*. Fender & Crombie, 1878; 5 R. 1104. See below, § 363, 364.
(*e*) 53 and 54 Vict. c. 39, § 1, 2.

352. Partnership Proper has a double operation: one, as it affects the immediate parties to the contract; another, as it relates to the public dealing with the company.

353. Stock.—The stock of the company, as contributed, and increased or diminished by the dealings of the company, is not only common, and held *pro indiviso* by all the partners; but it is vested in them in trust for the creditors of the company in the first place, and afterwards for division among the partners according to the shares of each (*a*).

'*Partnership Property*.—All property and rights and interests in property originally brought into the partnership stock, or acquired whether by purchase or otherwise on account of the firm, or for the purposes and in the course of the partnership business, are called in the Partnership Act, 1890, partnership property, and must be held and applied by the partners exclusively for the purposes of the partnership, and in accordance with the partnership agreement (*b*): Provided that the title to and interest in heritable estate which belongs to the partnership shall devolve according to the nature and tenure thereof, and the general rules of law applicable, but in trust, so far as necessary, for the persons beneficially interested in the land under this section of the Act (*c*).

'Where co-owners of any heritable estate, not itself partnership property, are partners as to profits made by its use, and purchase other land or estate out of the profits to be used in like manner, the land and estate purchased belong to them, in the absence of agreement to the contrary, not as partners, but as co-owners, for the same respective rights and interests as are held by them in the first-mentioned land or estate at the date of the purchase (*d*).

'Unless the contrary intention appears, property bought with the firm's money is deemed to be bought on account of the firm (*e*).

'*Conversion*.—Where land or any heritable interest therein has become partnership property, it shall, unless the contrary intention appears, be treated between the partners (including the representatives of a deceased partner), and also as between the heirs of a deceased partner and his executors or administrators, as personal or moveable and not real or heritable estate (*f*).'

(*a*) Robertson's Crs., 1744; 2 Bell's Com. 619 (508, M'L.'s ed.). Corrie *v*. Calder's Crs., 1761; M. 14,596; 1 Ill. 240. Crooks *v*. Tawse, 1779; M. 14,596. Sime *v*. Balfour, 1804; M. Apx. *Her. and Mov*. 3; 5 Paton, 525. See the sequel of this case in Minto *v*. Kirkpatrick, 1833; 11 S. 632. Lords of Treasury *v*. M'Nair, Feb. 14, 1809; F. C. Murray *v*. Murray, 1805; M. Apx. *Her. and Mov*. 4. Wilson *v*. Threshie, 1826; 4 S. 366. Fox *v*. Hanbury, Cowp. 445. Skipp *v*. Harwood, 2 Swan. 586. Holderness *v*. Shackels, 8 B. & Cr. 612; 32 R. R. 496. See § 380. Farquhar *v*. Hodden, L. R. 7 Ch. 1; 41 L. J. Ch. 260. As to the question what is partnership property, see Lindley on Partn. i. 643 sqq. Pollock on Partn. 53 sqq.
(*b*) 53 and 54 Vict. c. 39, § 20 (1).
(*c*) *Ib*. § 20 (2).
(*d*) *Ib*. § 20 (3).
(*e*) *Ib*. § 21.
(*f*) *Ib*. § 22.

354. Implied Mandate.—Each partner is by the law held to be "præpositus negotiis societatis"; and whatever he does in the company's name or on its credit, in the line of the company's trade, 'notwithstanding any private agreement to the contrary, or want of authority,' is held to be done for the company (*a*), 'unless the party dealing with him knows of such agreement or want of authority, or "does not know or believe him to be a partner" (*b*).' He is empowered in that line to bind the society by bill or mercantile document, whatever their private contract may be (*c*). Nay, even a fraud 'or other wrongful act or omission,' committed by a partner in the line of the company trade, 'or with the authority of his partners,' binds the company (*d*), 'unless the party seeking to charge the company was himself privy to the fraud.' But 'while a partner in a trading firm has power to borrow money for the business on the firm's credit (*e*),' it has been held in England that he is not empowered to bind by "deed," as in a mortgage (*f*).

(*a*) 3 Ersk. 3. § 20. Dewar *v.* Miller, 1766; M. 14,569. Wallace *v.* Campbell, 1821; 1 S. 56; aff. 1824, 2 S. Ap. 467; 1 Ill. 241. Beveridge *v.* Beveridge, 1869; 7 Macph. 1034; aff. 1872, 10 Macph. H. L. 1. Hawken *v.* Bourne, 8 M. & W. 710. Kinnes *v.* Adam & Sons, 1882; 9 R. 698 (title to sue). Mains & M'Glashan *v.* Black, 1895; 22 R. 329 (meeting of creditors—assent to composition).

(*b*) See below, § 355 (*c*), and Partnership Act, 1890, § 5.

(*c*) Wallace, *supra* (*a*). Bonbonus, 8 Vesey, jr. 540; 3 Ross' L. C. 470. Hope *v.* Cust, 1 East, 53. Ridley *v.* Taylor, 13 East. 175; 3 Ross' L. C. 492. See above, § 321.

(*d*) Willet *v.* Chambers, Cowp. 814; 1 Ill. 241. Bolland, 1 Mont. & Macarthur, Cases in Bankruptcy, 315. See above, § 224B. Miller *v.* Douglas, Jan. 22, 1811; F. C. Sandilands, § 355 (*d*). Swan *v.* Steele, 7 East, 209; 3 Ross' L. C. 459; 8 R. R. 618. Sawyer *v.* Goodwin, 36 L. J. Ch. 578. E. of Dundonald *v.* Masterman, 38 L. J. Ch. 350; L. R. 7 Eq. 504. Thomas *v.* Atherton, 10 Ch. D. 185; 48 L. J. Ch. 370. See Partnership Act, 1890, § 10. The primary test of liability is the ordinary course of the partnership business; and on this ground it has been held that, as it is not part of the ordinary business of solicitors to receive money for general purposes of investment, *i.e.* to be invested at their discretion, a firm is not liable for money so received and misappropriated by a partner, although it is liable for money received to be invested on specified securities. Compare Harman *v.* Johnson, 2 E. & B. 61; 22 L. J. Q. B. 297. Plumer *v.* Gregory, L. R. 18 Eq. 621; 43 L. J. Ch. 616, 803. Blair *v.* Bromley, 2 Ph. 354. Atkinson *v.* Mackreth, L. R. 2 Eq. 570; 36 L. J. Ch. 624. Cleather *v.* Twisden, 28 Ch. D. 340. So in regard to bankers holding securities and selling stock, see *ex p.* Eyre, 1 Ph. 227. Marsh *v.* Keating, 2 Cl. & F. 250. Devaynes *v.* Noble, 1 Mer. 572, 611; 15 R. R. 151. In suing a firm on the ground of fraud, it is necessary to aver personal fraud against one or more of the partners by name. Thomson & Co. *v.* Pattison, Elder, & Co., 1895; 22 R. 432.

(*e*) Bank of Austral. *v.* Breillat, 6 Moore, P. C. 152; Story, 124; Clark, 316. Bryan *v.* Butters Brs. & Co., 1892; 19 R. 490 (a special case). See above, § 225 (*f*).

(*f*) Harrison *v.* Jackson, 7 T. R. 207; 3 Ross' L. C. 557; 4 R. R. 422. Swan *v.* Steele, 7 East, 210; 8 R. R. 618. 3 Kent, Com. 40. See Lindley, i. 278, 284; Smith's Merc. Law, 33.

355. To the above rule there are exceptions. Thus, where the dealing is manifestly not a company matter, 'or is proved to have taken place on the credit of the partner alone' (*a*); and wherever the debt 'or obligation' secured is that of a partner, 'even though he may have afterwards applied the funds so obtained to the benefit of the firm,' the *onus probandi* is laid on the creditor to show the assent of the company (*b*). So, where the party contracting with the partner has notice of a limitation of power, the company is not bound (*c*). And where a guarantee or obligation of surety is entered into, it will not bind the company unless it be 'strictly' in reference to, 'and within the scope of,' the company's course of trade, or proof be given of its having been authorised or adopted by the company (*d*). But the full power is implied where the partners have consented to or acquiesced in the obligation (*e*); or where a party applies to his own use the bill or obligation of the company, of which he is as a creditor fairly possessed or vested with the power of disposal (*f*); or where a bill or note of the company, 'being a trading firm,' has found its way into the hands of an onerous and *bonâ fide* holder (*g*).

'It is enacted in the Partnership Act, 1890, that where one partner pledges the credit of the firm for a purpose apparently not connected with the firm's ordinary course of business, the firm is not bound, unless he is in fact specially authorised by the other partners; but this section does not affect any personal liability incurred by an individual partner (*h*). If it has been agreed between the partners that any restriction shall be placed on the power of any one or more of them to bind the firm, no act done in contravention of the agreement is binding on the firm with respect to persons having notice of the agreement (*i*). It is also enacted that a partner's wrongful act or omission in certain cases binds the firm and the partners jointly and severally (*k*); and that where the money or property of a third party is received by a partner within the scope of his apparent authority, and misapplied by him; or is received by the firm in the course of its business, and is misapplied by one or more partners while it is in the custody of the firm, the firm is liable to make good the loss (*l*).

'*Admissions* and representations by any partner concerning the partnership affairs and in the ordinary course of its business are evidence against the firm (*m*). And except in case of fraud by the partner, notice to any partner who habitually acts in the partnership affairs is notice to the firm (*n*).'

(*a*) Blair *v.* Miller, Jan. 22, 1811; F. C.; 1 Ill. 244. Proudfoot *v.* Lindsay, 1825; 3 S. 310. Johnston, Sharp, & Co. *v.* Phillips, 1822; 1 S. Ap. 244. Blair *v.* Bryson, 1835; 13 S. 901. M'Leod *v.* Tosh, 1836; 14 S. 1058; 3 Ill. 126. Duncan *v.* Lowndes, 3 Camp. 478; 1 Ill. 243;

14 R. R. 814. Hope *v.* Cust, 1 East, 53; 5 R. R. 513. Swan *v.* Steele, *cit.* Wells *v.* Masterman, 2 Esp. 730. Green *v.* Deaken, 2 Starkie, 347. Goulding, 2 Glyn & Jam. 118; aff. see Collyer, 337. Crum & Co. *v.* M'Lean, 1858; 20 D. 751. Tupper & Carr *v.* Rowell, 1858; 20 D. 758. Frankland *v.* M'Gusty, Knapp, P. C. 274; 1 Ill. 244. *Primâ facie*, a contract, transaction, or dealing which is not made in the name of the partnership does not bind the firm, even although it may have derived a profit thereby. Emly *v.* Lye, 15 East, 7; 3 Ross' L. C. 552; 13 R. R. 347; and cases cited in 1 Clark on Partn. 219, 232, 246, and Tudor's L. C. 302. Crum & Co., *cit.* Alliance Bank *v.* Kearsley, L. R. 6 C. P. 433; 40 L. J. C. P. 249 (bank account for firm opened in individual name).

(*b*) Result of the above cases (*a*). Leverson *v.* Lane, 32 L. J. C. P. 10; 13 C. B. N. S. 278. Kendal *v.* Wood, 39 L. J. Ex. 167; L. R. 6 Ex. 243. Heilbut *v.* Nevill, L. R. 5 C. P. 245, 478. Garland *v.* Jacomb, L. R. 8 Ex. 216. *Ex p.* Darlington Bkg. Co., 34 L. J. Bkr. 10; 4 De G. J. & S. 581. Smith's Merc. Law, 36, 41. A reasonable belief that the partner had authority is not enough, unless that belief has been induced by the conduct of the other partners. Kendal, *cit.* See Hogarth *v.* Latham, 3 Q. B. D. 643; 47 L. J. Q. B. 339 (partner cannot issue blank acceptances).

(*c*) Galway *v.* Mathew, 10 East, 264; 10 R. R. 289. Tudor's L. C. 293. Smith's Merc. Law, 32. See above, § 354. Partn. Act, 1890, § 5.

(*d*) Sandilands *v.* Marsh, 2 B. & Ald. 673; Tudor's L. C. 285; 3 Ross' L. C. 463. See 3 Kent, Com. 47. M'Nair & Co. *v.* Gray, Hunter, & Speirs, 1803; Hume, 753. Brettel *v.* Williams, 4 Ex. 623; 19 L. J. Ex. 121. Haslcham *v.* Young, 5 Q. B. 833; 13 L. J. Q. B. 205. *In re* West of England Bk., 14 Ch. D. 317; 49 L. J. Ch. 400.

(*e*) Bonbonus, 8 Ves. jr. 540. Sandilands, *supra* (*d*). Cleather, *cit.* § 354.

(*f*) Ridley *v.* Taylor, 3 East, 175; 1 Ross' L. C. 492. Kirkby, Buck's Cases, 511.

(*g*) Bonbonus, *supra* (*e*). See above, § 321, and cases there cited, note (*d*).

(*h*) Partn. Act, 1890, § 7. (*i*) *Ib.* § 8.

(*k*) *Ib.* § 10, 12. See above, § 354 (*c*).

(*l*) *Ib.* § 11.

(*m*) *Ib.* § 15. See below, § 356, note. (*n*) *Ib.* § 16.

356. Joint Responsibility.—The partners are jointly and severally liable as guarantees to the public of the company's obligations, and so may be called on individually, on the company failing to pay the debt; the company, 'at least if it be a Scotch company,' being first called, and the debt constituted against it. In relation to each other, their responsibility is regulated by their contract (*a*).

(*a*) Johnson *v.* Duncan, 1824; 2 S. 625; 1 Ill. 245. Geddes *v.* Hopkirk, 1827; 5 S. 747. Anon., 1741; Kilk. 518; 1 Bell's Com. 619. See below, § 371. Muir & Co. *v.* Collett, 1862; 24 D. 1119. Where one partner admits a company liability which the others dispute, decree will be pronounced against him, reserving his claims of relief, without constituting the claim against the company. Elliot *v.* Aiken, 1869; 7 Macph. 894. Bills by companies constitute the debt against each partner individually, and warrant diligence against each. Thomson *v.* Liddell, and Wallace *v.* Plock, etc., *infra*, § 357 (*b*). See Bullock *v.* Caird, L. R. 10 Q. B. 276; 44 L. J. Q. B. 124 (partner of Scotch company sued in England). After dissolution all the partners must be called. M'Naught *v.* Milligan, 1885; 13 R. 366.

357. Company a separate Person.—The company forms a separate person, competent to maintain its relations with third parties by its separate name or firm, independently of the partners; capable also of holding a lease, but not of holding feudally as a vassal (*a*). A company having a firm, '*i.e.* a social name, as A. B. & Co., or A. & B.,' may sue or be sued by it (*b*); but a company having only a descriptive name can appear judicially only by or with some, 'three, or two, if there are no more,' or all of the individual names (*c*).

(*a*) Denniston, M'Nair, & Co. *v.* M'Farlane, Feb. 16, 1808; F. C.; 1 Ill. 245. Hunter, L. & T. i. 215. See, however, Clark on Partnership, 170; Murray *v.* Hogarth & Co., 1835; 13 S. 453; and Cooke's Circus Co. *v.* Welding, 1894; 21 R. 337.

(*b*) Douglas, Heron, & Co. *v.* Gordon, 1795; 3 Paton, 428. Thomson *v.* Liddell & Co., July 2, 1812; F. C. Campbell *v.* Baird, 1827; 5 S. 335 (indenture with workman). Forsyth *v.* Hare & Co., 1834; 13 S. 42. Wilson *v.* Ewing, May, & Co., 1836; 14 S. 262. Thomson, Bonar, & Co. *v.* Johnstone, 1836; 15 S. 173. Wallace *v.* Plock & Logan, 1841; 3 D. 1047. As to the firm's right to the social name, see below, § 379. Pollock on Partn. p. 15. In England actions may now (since 1876) be brought by and against partners in the name of their firm. Rules of the Supreme Court, 1883, Order xvi., Rules 14 and 15; Order ix., Rules 6–8, etc. It does not appear that this change of practice alters the old doctrine of English law, which refuses to recognise the firm as a separate person. Partn. Act, 1890, § 4. As to infringements of statutes of a quasi-criminal character by partnership firms and incorporated companies, and liability for penalties, see Pharmaceut. Soc. *v.* Lond. and Prov. Supply Ass., 5 App. Ca. 857; 49 L. J. Q. B. 338, 736. Bremridge *v.* Gray, 1886; 14 R. Just. 60. Fletcher *v.* Eglinton Chem. Co., *ib.* 9. L. Adv. *v.* Thomson, 1897; 24 R. 543. Partn. Act, 1890, § 10.

(*c*) Culcreugh Cotton Co. *v.* Mathie, 1822; 2 S. 41. Scott *v.* Napier, 1827; 5 S. 514. Commercial Bank *v.* Pollok's Trs., 1828; 3 W. & S. 365; 13 S. 94. See below, § 399. London & Edinr. Shipping Co. *v.* M'Corkle, 1841; 3 D. 1045. Natl. Exch. Co. *v.* Drew, 1848; 11 D. 179. Antermony Coal Co. *v.* Wingate, 1866; 4 Macph. 1017. Macdonald *v.* Stenhouse, 1878; 2 Sel. Sh. Ct. Ca. 381 (post office employees issuing annual directory).

358. Delectus Personæ.—It is strongly implied, from the exuberant trust reposed by the partners in each other, and the confidential nature of the connection, that no one shall be a partner without the consent of the rest. Hence heirs, assignees, and creditors are excluded, unless it be otherwise stipulated or necessarily implied, as from the long duration of the company (*a*). In the Roman law, a stipulation to that effect was incompetent (*b*). 'One may assign a part or the whole of his interest in a firm, but only to the effect of creating a sub-partnership (*c*), or other right against himself, which is subject to all rights and equities existing between the assignor and his copartners, whether before or after the assignment (*d*). An assignment of a partner's share, whether absolute or by way of mortgage, does not entitle the assignee as against the other partners to interfere in the management during the continuance of the partnership, or to require accounts, or inspect the books, but only to receive the assignor's share of profits, as shown in the account of profits agreed to by the partners. At dissolution the assignee is entitled to receive the assignor's share of assets, and for the purpose of ascertaining that share to an account as from the date of the dissolution (*e*).'

(*a*) Warner *v.* Cunningham, 1798; M. 14,603; aff. 3 Dow, 76; 1 Ill. 246. See Royal Bank *v.* Fairholm, 1770; M. Apx. *Adjud.* 3. Irvine *v.* Irvine, 1851; 13 D. 1367. Hill *v.* Wylie, 1865; 3 Macph. 541. Beveridge *v.* Beveridge, 1869, 7 Macph. 1034; 1872, 10 Macph. H. L. 1. For questions as to the position of trustees, etc., of a deceased partner under wills directing the business to be continued, see Beveridge, and other cases cited, and Morrison (Paterson's Tr.) *v.* Learmont, 1870; 8 Macph. 500. Comp. Vyse *v.* Foster, L. R. 7 H. L. 318; 44 L. J. Ch. 37 (contract providing for purchase by survivors of deceased partner's share). Ewing *v.* Ewing, 1882; 10 R. H. L. 1; 8 App. Ca. 822. See below, § 380.

(*b*) Dig. lib. 17. tit. 2, Pro Socio (ll. 35, 59). Pothier, Tr. de Société, § 145.

(*c*) Socii mei socius meus socius non est. Dig. 50. 17, 47. § 1. Dig. 17. 7, 19, 20.

(*d*) 3 Ersk. 3. § 22. Cassels *v.* Stewart, 1879; 6 R. 936; aff. 1881, 8 R. H. L. 1; 6 App. Ca. 64. Lindley on Partn. i. 697. *Ex p.* Barrow, 2 Rose, 225. See § 364, *infra*. And see the note in M'Laren's Bell's Com. ii. 544.

(*e*) Partn. Act, 1890, § 31.

359. Avowed or Anonymous Partnership.—The former is commonly carried on and known by a firm or social name; in the latter, the trade is apparently carried on by an individual, there being latent or sleeping partners behind. The rules applicable to both are the same, on the latent partnership, or those concerned in it, being discovered (*a*).

(*a*) See below, § 364A, 386. The dormant partner is in the position of an undisclosed principal (see above, § 224A); Beckham *v.* Drake, 9 M. & W. 97; 11 M. & W. 315; but has in ordinary circumstances no power to bind the firm. See Holme *v.* Hammond, L. R. 7 Ex. 218; 41 L. J. Ex. 157 (*per* Cleasby, B.). Lindley, Partn. 125.

360. Constitution of Partnership.—In the constitution of partnership, a distinction is made between questions among the parties themselves, and questions with third parties. As to the parties themselves, there are two questions: Whether there be a contract so constituted as to raise the rights and responsibilities of partners? and, What share of stock and profit each is bound to contribute or entitled to claim? As to third parties, the only question is, Whether one is bound as a partner? for where he is so, it signifies nothing, in respect to the extent of his liability, what share he holds (*a*).

(*a*) See the Act, § 9.

361. (1.) *Evidence as between the Partners.*—Partnership is a consensual contract; and on such evidence as our law admits in proof of consent, the parties will be entitled to their rights as such, or bound to the public. This may be either a solemn written contract of partnership, duly authenticated; or a less formal writing; letters exchanged; minutes; articles subscribed by initials, and afterwards acted upon; articles written in the ledger, or otherwise identified with the trade; or circumstantial proof; or parole evidence of clerks, agents, or persons dealing with the company (*a*). Even where there is a contract, a question may arise whether the transaction in question be a partnership dealing, which will depend on the construction of the contract, and on the homologation or adoption of it by the company as a part of their trade (*b*). 'In all questions between the partners themselves, and not between strangers and the copartnery or one of the partners, the law regards only the contract they have made and the rights which it gives them *inter se* (*c*).'

(*a*) 3 Ersk. 3. § 18, 21. Voet. ad Pand. lib. 17, tit. 1, 2, § 2. Logie *v.* Durham, 1697; M. 14,566; 1 Ill. 246. Fairholm *v.* Marjoribanks, 1725; M. 14,558; 1 Ill. 252. Livingstone *v.* Gordon, 1775; M. 14,551. Learmonth & Co. *v.* Livingston, 1823; 1 S. App. 481. Bland *v.* Short, 1825; 3 S. 419. Dundee Railway Co. *v.* Miller, 1832; 10 S. 269. Alderson *v.* Clay, 1 Starkie, 405; 18 R. R. 788. See *ex p.* Gellar, 1 Rose, 297. Saville *v.* Robertson, 4 T. R. 720. See Fraser *v.* Hill, 1852; 14 D. 335 (Lord Fullerton); 1854, 16 D. 739. Aitchison *v.* Aitchison, 1877; 4 R. 899. Kinnell *v.* Peebles, 1890; 17 R. 416. Lawrie *v.* Lawrie's Trs., 1892; 19 R. 675. Clark on Partn. 64.

(*b*) Maxton *v.* Brown, 1839; 1 D. 367.

(*c*) Cases cited. Walker *v.* Hirsch; 27 Ch. D. 460.

362. Where, in a question between partners, the contract is established, but the shares left doubtful, and no evidence to clear the doubt, the presumption is for equality of rights and of responsibility. But this is a presumption of fact only, and may be overcome by evidence, or by indications of a different rule having been agreed to (*a*). 'A bare obligation to take one into partnership, not expressing the share or interest to be given, is too vague to be enforced either by specific implement or damages (*b*).'

(*a*) M'Whirter *v.* Guthrie, 1822; 1 S. 295; Hume, 760; 1 Ill. 248. Struthers *v.* Barr, 1826; 2 W. & S. 153. Anderson *v.* Russell, 1828; 6 S. 836. Campbell's Trs. *v.*

Thomson, 1829; 7 S. 650; rev. 1831, 5 W. & S. 16. Peacock *v.* Peacock, 2 Camp. 45, and 16 Ves. 56. See Ferguson *v.* Graham, 1836; 14 S. 871. Buchanan *v.* Lennox, 1838; 16 S. 824. See below, § 380. Aberdeen Bank *v.* Clark, 1859; 22 D. 44. Webster *v.* Bray, 7 Hare, 159. Stewart *v.* Forbes, 1 Macn. & G. 137. The Partn. Act, 1890, § 24 (1).

(*b*) M'Arthur *v.* Lawson, 1877; 4 R. 1134. So also it was held, where an obligation to renew a copartnery did not specify any duration, that it imported an obligation (if there was any capable of receiving effect) only to renew for one year or other reasonable period. Trail *v.* Dewar, 1881; 8 R. 583 (2nd Div.—case of medical practitioners). Young *v.* Dougans, 1887; 14 R. 490 (joint-venture in patent).

363. (2.) *Evidence as to Third Parties.—Holding out.*—Responsibility may be incurred not only by the constitution of a proper partnership, but even where there is no proper constitution of partnership as between the parties themselves, and no right to the stock created in the person called upon. 'It was formerly said that' this may be by receiving, as a partner or principal, a share of the profits (*a*); or by an agreement entitling one to share in the profits (*b*); 'but these are now regarded only as indications, cogent, but not conclusive of the existence of a real partnership; and no person who does not hold himself out to the public, or to creditors and customers, as a partner, is liable to third parties for the acts of persons whose profits he shares, unless he and they are really partners *inter se* (*c*). Liability by *holding out* is incurred' by permitting one's name to be used, or credit relied on, as a partner,—as by the name being over the door, or used or continued in bills of parcels, cheques, etc. (*d*). And in such questions, similarity of name, or the continuance of a name in a firm, peculiarly exposes to this sort of responsibility (*e*). 'The rule is an application of the principle of personal exception (see above, § 27A), for a man who holds himself out as a partner, or allows others to do so, is barred *personali exceptione* from denying the character he has assumed, and upon the faith of which creditors have acted (*f*).'

(*a*) Bloxham *v.* Pell, 2 Blackst. 999. Grace *v.* Smith, *ib.*; 1 Ill. 249. **Waugh** *v.* **Carver,** 2 H. Bl. 235; 3 Ross' L. C. 426; 1 Smith's L. C. 908; 14 R. R. 845. Rowlandson, 1 Rose, 89; 13 R. R. 52. Hesketh *v.* Blanchard, 4 East, 144. Cheap *v.* Gramond, 4 B. & Ald. 663; 3 Ross' L. C. 435. Reid *v.* Hollingshead, 4 B. & Cr. 867; 28 R. R. 488. Chuck, 8 Bing. 469; 34 R. R. 762.

(*b*) **Waugh,** *supra* (*a*). *Ex p.* Hamper, 17 Ves. 412; 1 Ill. 280; 11 R. R. 115. *Ex p.* Chuck, *supra* (*a*). M'Kinlay *v.* Gillon, 1830; 9 S. 90; aff. 5 W. & S. 468; 1 Ill. 249.

(*c*) See the authorities in § 351 (*d*). Lindley on Partnership, pp. 40, 45. Clark on Partn. p. 52, requires to be corrected by these later decisions.

(*d*) Young *v.* Axtell, 2 H. Bl. 242; 1 Ill. 252; 14 R. R. 851. **Waugh,** *supra* (*a*). Williams *v.* Keats, 2 Starkie, 290; 17 R. R. 723. Newsome *v.* Coles, 2 Camp. 617; 12 R. R. 758. **Dickinson** *v.* **Valpy,** 10 B. & Cr. 140; 3 Ross' L. C. 581; 34 R. R. 334. Martyn *v.* Gray, 14 C. B. N. S. 824.

(*e*) Spencer *v.* Billing, 3 Camp. 310. But a deceased partner's executor incurs no liability by the continued use of the old name. Lindley, i. 52, 111, 418. Holme *v.* Hammond, L. R. 7 Ex. 218; 41 L. J. Ex. 157. As to retired partners, see § 382, 386.

(*f*) *Per Cur.* in Mollwo, March, & Co. *v.* Court of Wards, L. R. 4 P. C. 419; and see above, § 351.

364. Such responsibility, however, is not incurred by receiving a mere payment, allowance, or wages, proportioned to the profits. So wages may be paid to clerks, commission to a broker, or hire to a lighterman for working a lighter, proportionally to the gains to be made, without involving the responsibility of a partner (*a*); and, by sub-contract with one of the partners, a third person may divide with him his share without being liable as a partner (*b*).

(*a*) Dixon *v.* Cooper, 3 Wils. 40. Shaw *v.* Galt, 16 Ir. C. L. Rep. 357.

(*b*) Fairholm *v.* Marjoribanks, 1725; M. 14,558; 1 Ill. 252. Wilkinson *v.* Frazer, 4 Esp. 182. Dry *v.* Boswell, 1 Camp. 329; 1 Ill. 250. **Waugh** *v.* **Carver,** *cit.* Mair *v.* Glennie, 4 M. & Sel. 246; 16 R. R. 445. *Ex p.* Norfolk, 17 Ves. 457. Smith *v.* Watson, 2 B. & Cr. 401. Geddes *v.* Wallace, 2 Bligh, 270; 1 Ill. 255; 21 R. R. 66. Rowlandson, 1 Rose, 91; 13 R. R. 52. See Eaglesham & Co. *v.* Grant, etc., *supra*, § 351 (*d*), and 358.

364A. (3.) '*Bovill's Act and Partnership Act.*—The principles of the common law above stated were modified, or at least defined, by a statute of 1865 (Bovill's Act), repealed by the Partnership Act of 1890 (*a*), which repeated or added these provisions, namely, (1) the receipt by a person of a debt or other liquidated amount by instalments or otherwise out of the accruing profits of a business; (2) the advance of money by way of loan to a person engaged, or about to engage, in any trade or undertaking, upon a written and signed contract (*b*) that the lender shall receive a rate of interest varying with the profits, or a share of the profits; or (3) a contract for the receipt of a share of the profits as remuneration by the servant or agent of such person; or (4) the receipt, by way of annuity, by the widow or child of the deceased partner of a trader, of a share of the profits made in the business in which such deceased was a partner; or (5) the receipt of a share of the profits of any business, in consideration of the sale of the goodwill of such business, does not of itself constitute the person so receiving a partner, or liable as such. But, in the event of the bankruptcy or insolvency of the trader, the lender of money on such terms, and the seller of the goodwill, are not entitled to recover the money lent, or the profits or interest due to them, till the claims of the other onerous creditors (c) of the trader have been satisfied (a).'

(a) 28 and 29 Vict. c. 86. 53 and 54 Vict. c. 39, § 2, 3, 48.

(b) The contract must show on its face that the contract is really one of loan. Syers v. Syers, 1 App. Ca. 174. *Ex p.* Tennant, 6 Ch. D. 303. *Ex p.* Delhasse, 7 Ch. D. 511; 47 L. J. Ch. 65. Pooley v. Driver, 5 Ch. D. 458; 46 L. J. Bkr. 466. It does not appear that the law is different where there is no writing. Cox v. Hickman, *cit.* § 351.

(c) *Ex p.* Taylor, 12 Ch. D. 366. *Ex p.* Mills, L. R. 8 Ch. 569. *Ex p.* Sheil, 4 Ch. D. 789; 46 L. J. Bkr. 62. *Ex p.* Schofield, 1897; 2 Q. B. 495.

365. Plurality of Persons.—One person cannot make a partnership (a). But he may, contrary to the English rule (b), be a member of several partnerships without confounding their interests; nay, several persons may, by various combinations of their number, make distinct partnerships for separate objects (c). 'Not more than twenty persons can form a company for the purpose of carrying on any business (other than banking), that has for its object the acquisition of gain by the company or its members, nor more than ten persons for carrying on the business of banking, unless the company be registered under the Companies Act, or formed under some other Act of Parliament, or under Letters Patent (d).'

(a) Nairn v. Forbes & Co., 1798; 1 Ill. 252; 2 Bell's Com. 625. Reid v. Chalmers, 1828; 6 S. 1120. Rose v. Moore & Son, 1833; 11 S. 344. Booth v. Coml. Bank, 1823; 2 S. 311. See Young v. Livingston, 1860; 22 D. 983.

(b) Bosanquet v. Wray, 2 Marsh. 319; 16 R. R. 677; Collyer, 383; 1 Ill. 252. The English rule referred to did not apply in equity, and appears to have been modified by the late Judicature and Bankruptcy Acts.

(c) Bertram & Co.'s Crs. v. Baillie & Co.'s Crs., 1795; 1 Ill. 252; 2 Bell's Com. 625. Royal Bank v. Stein, Smith, & Co., Jan. 20, 1813; F. C.; Buch. Ca. 320; 1 Rose, 462. Williams v. Inglis, Borthwick, & Co., June 13, 1809; F. C.; Forrester's Crs. v. Forbes & Co., 1798; 1 I Ill. 252; 2 Bell's Com. 626. Warner v. Smith, 1 De G. J. & S. 337; 32 L. J. Ch. 573. S. Carolina Bk. v. Case, 8 B. & C. 427; 3 Ross' L. C. 508; 32 R. R. 433. Emly v. Lye, 15 East, 6; 3 Ross' L. C. 552; 13 R. R. 347.

(d) 25 and 26 Vict. c. 89, § 4. See below, § 403c *init.*

366. Term of Duration.—Partnership may be either for a fixed time; or indefinite in time, called a partnership at will.

367. A definite term may be fixed for the partnership, either by express limitation of time; or by reference to some event, or expected course of events, as the duration of a lease of premises. But such limitation must be clearly expressed; it will not be inferred from the mere purchase or existence of leasehold property to be used by the company (a). 'If the partnership is continued after the expiration of the term, without any new agreement, the original contract rights and duties of the partners remain the same as they were at the expiration of the term, so far as is consistent with the incidents of a partnership at will (b). A continuance of the business by the partners, or such of them as habitually acted therein during the term, without any settlement or liquidation of the partnership affairs, is presumed to be a continuance of the partnership (c).'

(a) Marshall v. Marshall, Feb. 23, 1816; F. C.; 1 Ill. 253. **Crawshay v. Maule,** 1 Wils. 191, 196; 18 R. R. 126. Aitken's Trs. v. Shanks & Waddel, 1830; 8 S. 753. Cf. Miller v. Walker, 1875; 3 R. 242.

(b) Partn. Act, 1890, § 27. Lindley on Partn. ii. 823. Cox v. Willoughby, 13 Ch. D. 863; 49 L. J. Ch. 237. Neilson v. Mossend Iron Co., 1885; 12 R. 499; rev. 1886, 11 App. Ca. 298; 13 R. H. L. 50. See § 362, note, and § 373.

(c) Partnership Act, 1890, § 27 (2).

368. Partnership without any limitation of time may be dissolved at the will of the parties, or any of them; provided a fair, honest, and equitable discretion be observed, avoiding injury, or the taking of undue advantage (a).

(a) 3 Ersk. 3. § 26. 3 Pardessus, 158. See below, § 378. Partnership Act, 1890, § 26, 32.

369. Obligations of the Partners.—The partners are bound not only to each other, but to the public.

370. (1.) *In relation to each other, and to the Company.*—Each partner is debtor to the company for his share of stock unpaid, and liable to an action on that account. If the share to be contributed by a partner consist of a specific subject, the contract of partnership is only the *titulus transferendi dominii*; and without delivery the transference to the company is not complete, though, as in the common contract of sale, the risk is with the company. A partner becomes debtor to the company by drawing more of the profit than he is entitled to. He may become a creditor to the company by advancing money beyond his share (a); by allowing the profits to which he is entitled to remain undrawn; or a salary, or wages, or an allowance stipulated beyond his share of profit, to remain unpaid. A partner is bound to give his personal attention and services in the company affairs without recompense, unless it be otherwise stipulated (*b*); and this even in winding up a partnership dissolved by the death of a partner (*c*). He is bound to obey such calls as may be necessary to meet the losses and exigencies of the company (*d*); 'and to communicate to the company all benefit procured to himself in matters that naturally fall within the copartnership business, or from any use by him of the partnership property, name, or business connection (*e*). The recent Act provides further that if a partner, without the consent of the other partners, carries on any business of the same nature as and competing with that of the firm, he must account for and pay over to the firm all profits made by him in that business (*f*).'

(*a*) M'Ghie's Crs. *v.* Tait, 1785; M. 14,668; 1 Ill. 253.

(*b*) Beath *v.* Campbell, Rivers, & Co., 1824; 3 S. 251; rev. 1826, 2 W. & S. 25. Duncan *v.* Union Canal Co., 1831; 9 S. 398. Hunter *v.* Cochrane's Trs., 1831; 9 S. 477. See Berry *v.* Lamb, 1832; 10 S. 792. M'Whirter *v.* Guthrie, 1822; 1 S. 295; Hume, 760. Pender *v.* Henderson & Co., 1864; 2 Macph. 1428. Faulds *v.* Roxburgh, 1867; 5 Macph. 373. Anderson *v.* Anderson, 1869; 8 Macph. 157 (joint-ownership—remuneration allowed on implied contract). M'Naughton *v.* Brunton, 1882; 10 R. 111.

(*c*) Burden *v.* Burden, 1 Ves. & Bea. 170; 12 R. R. 210.

(*d*) Douglas, Heron, & Co. *v.* Hair, 1778; M. 14,605; 1 Ill. 254.

(*e*) 3 Ersk. 3. § 20. M'Niven *v.* Peffers, 1860; 7 Macph. 181. Pender *v.* Henderson & Co., *cit.* **Featherstonhaugh** *v.* **Fenwick,** 17 Ves. 298; 11 R. R. 77. Clegg *v.* Edmondson, 8 De G. M. & G. 787. Davie *v.* Buchanan, 1880; 8 R. 319. Cassels *v.* Stewart, 1879; 6 R. 936; aff. 1881, 8 R. H. L. 1; 6 App. Ca. 64. Dean *v.* M'Dowell, 8 Ch. D. 345; 47 L. J. Ch. 537. Partnership Act, 1890, § 29. Aas *v.* Benham, 1891; 2 Ch. D. 244. See above, § 222; below, § 403B *fin.*, 403H.

(*f*) The Act, § 30.

371. (2.) *In relation to Creditors.*—The partners are liable for all debts established against the company (*a*). 'A partner is liable only for debts incurred after he becomes a member of the firm; and when a change occurs in a firm, the new firm and its incoming partner do not become answerable for debts of the old firm, even if the assets be taken over, unless the intention to do so be established by agreement express or implied. But where a new firm, formed by the assumption of a new partner, takes over the whole stock and business of a going concern, without any arrangement for winding up the old company's affairs, or for accounting, it may more readily be presumed to take over its liabilities also (*b*). The purchase of the business and assets of a firm, with an undertaking to pay present and future liabilities of the vendors, does not give a creditor of the vendors a direct claim against the purchasers, the creditor not being a party to the undertaking (*c*). So, on the principle of novation, the old firm and partners are not discharged until the creditor accepts the new firm as his debtors (*d*). A retiring partner may be discharged from existing liabilities by an agreement between himself and the members of the succeeding firm and the creditors, which agreement may be express or may be inferred from the course of dealing between the creditors and the new firm (*e*).'

'The partners' may be charged individually on decreet or diligence directed against the firm (*f*). If their character as partners be denied, they may be entitled, according to circumstances, to have the charge suspended with or without caution (*g*). Each partner is universally liable to the creditors of the company, and cannot therefore, if he himself be a creditor of the company, enter into competition with the other creditors (*h*). But being liable individually only as guarantee of the company credit, he is entitled to relief against the company funds. And so in bankruptcy, the creditors of the company rank on the estate of the individual partners only for what is not paid from the company estate.

(*a*) See above, § 356.

(*b*) Miller *v.* Thorburn, 1861; 23 D. 359. M'Keand *v.* Laird, 1861; 23 D. 846. Nelmes & Co. *v.* Montgomerie & Loudon, 1883; 10 R. 974. Heddle's Exrx. *v.* Marwick & Hourston's Tr., 1888; 15 R. 698. Stephen's Tr. *v.* Macdougall & Co.'s Tr., 1889; 16 R. 779. See Addison on Contr. 343. Lindley on Partn. 214, 785. Comp. below, cases in § 395 (*b*).

(*c*) Henderson *v.* Stubbs, 1894; 22 R. 51.

(*d*) See Bilborough *v.* Holmes, 5 Ch. D. 255; 44 L. J. Ch. 446; and below, § 383, 387, 578.

(*e*) Partnership Act, § 17 (3).

(*f*) Thomson *v.* Liddell & Co., July 2, 1812; F. C.; 1 Ill. 245. Selkrig *v.* Dunlop & Co., 1804; Hume, 277. Wallace *v.* Plock, 1841; 3 D. 1047. Knox *v.* Martin, 1847; 10 D. 50. Drew *v.* Lumsden, 1865; 3 Macph. 384.

(*g*) Anderson *v.* Bolton, Jan. 26, 1810; F. C. Anderson *v.* Currie, 1836; 14 S. 834.

(*h*) Geddes *v.* Wallace, 1820; 2 Bligh, 270; 1 Ill. 255; 21 R. R. 66.

372. Dissolution of Partnership.—Partnership is dissolved differently in relation to the partners, and in relation to third parties.

373. (1.) *Dissolution in relation to Partners.*—A distinction is to be marked between those events which *eo ipso* dissolve the partnership, and those which only afford a ground of dissolution.

Expiration of the term stipulated entitles the partners to separate without previous warning *inter se*; but it does not *ipso facto* dissolve the company (*a*). It still subsists, 'or rather may still subsist,' by tacit renewal (*b*); and as partnership may at the first be constituted by trading on a particular footing, so the continuance of a trade already begun is effectual to bind the parties on the same presumed terms, 'so far as they are not inconsistent with the implied terms of a partnership at will (*c*),' not for a stated period, as at the first, but as a partnership at will or without time (*d*).

(*a*) The contrary seems to be laid down by English writers (Collyer, 62; Smith, Merc. Law, 25); and also to be the law of France (Pothier, No. 139; 3 Pardessus, 140) and America (3 Kent, Com. 53).

(*b*) See Dalgleish & Fleming *v.* Sorley, 1791; Bell's Ca. 490; 1 Ill. 259. Partnership Act, 1890, §. 27.

(*c*) Neilson *v.* Mossend Iron Co., *supra*, § 367.

(*d*) **Featherstonhaugh** *v.* **Fenwick,** 17 Ves. 298; 1 Ill. 255; 3 Ross' L. C. 615; 11 R. R. 77. See above, § 367; and Traill *v.* Dewar, § 362.

374. *The marriage of a female partner* has in England 'and also in Scotland' been held to dissolve partnership, as otherwise a stranger would be introduced (*a*).

(*a*) Nerot *v.* Burnand, 4 Russ. 247; Collyer, 60; 28 R. R. 65. Russell *v.* Russell, 1874; 3 R. 93. But by the Married Women's Property Act, 1881 (44 and 45 Vict. c. 21), a wife's moveable estate is, by operation of law, vested in her as her separate estate; and it may be thought that marriage has not now the effect of dissolving a partnership of the wife. See Lindley, i. 85.

375. *The death* (*a*) of any of the partners *eo ipso* dissolves the partnership (*b*) (leaving the depending contracts to run their course) (*c*), unless heirs shall be expressly declared to be partners (*d*); or unless the contract shall be so conceived as necessarily to imply a right in heirs, as in a contract exceeding the term of human life (*e*). In such cases the heirs will have a right to be admitted as partners, and they may also be bound by taking up the succession: they cannot, of course, be compelled (if they do not represent) to become partners without their own consent (*f*).

(*a*) See § 379 and § 383, below. Partnership Act, 1890, § 33.

(*b*) Royal Bank *v.* Christie, 1841; 2 Rob. 118; 8 Cl. & Fin. 214.

(*c*) See as to the effect of a partner's death, the business and firm continuing substantially the same, upon contracts and obligations, Alexander *v.* Lowson's Trs., 1890; 17 R. 571.

(*d*) 3 Ersk. 3. § 25. Aiton & Co. *v.* Cheap, 1769; M. 14,573; rev. 1 Ill. 256; 2 Pat. 283. **Crawshay** *v.* **Maule,** 1 Swan. 509; Tudor, L. C. 311; 18 R. R. 126. Vulliamy *v.* Noble, 3 Mer. 614; 17 R. R. 143. See Pothier, Tr. de Soc., No. 144. 3 Kent, 55. Code Civ., art. 1868. See above, § 358. Hill *v.* Wyllie, 1865; 3 Macph. 541. Beveridge *v.* Beveridge, 1869; 7 Macph. 1034; 1872, 10 Macph. H. L. 1.

(*e*) Warner *v.* Cunningham, 1798; M. 14,603; aff. 3 Dow, 76; 1 Ill. 246.

(*f*) See M'Laren on Wills and Succession, ii. 307. Smith's Merc. Law, 28.

376. *Insanity* is only a ground of dissolution, not itself a dissolution of the contract. It may be distinguished as temporary or permanent. The former (as delirium, brain fever, etc.) seems to be no ground of dissolution, but a temporary interruption only of the acting or superintendence of the individual. The latter is a ground of dissolution, for the benefit of all concerned; of the person affected by the disease, as well as of the others. But, 'in the absence of special provisions in the contract,' partnership cannot on this ground be dissolved otherwise than by judicial authority, and the exercise of sound judicial discretion (*a*). 'Although in ordinary circumstances the insanity or incapacity of a partner operates a dissolution of the partnership, that result may be obviated by the terms of the contract, *e.g.* where they are such that the partner in question really performs his duty to the partnership by providing capital (*b*).'

(*a*) Sayer *v.* Bennet, 1 Cox, 107; 1 Montagu, 16; 1 Ill. 257. **Waters** *v.* **Taylor,** 2 Ves. & B. 303; Tudor, L. C. 329; 13 R. R. 91. Wrexham *v.* Huddleston, 1 Swan. 514, note. Jones *v.* Noy, 2 My. & K. 125; 3 L. J. Ch. 14. See **Pollock** *v.* **Paterson,** Dec. 10, 1811; F. C.; 1 Ill. 162. Robertson *v.* Lockie, 15 Sim. 285. Jones *v.* Lloyd, 43 L. J. Ch. 826; L. R. 18 Eq. 265. The Act, § 35 (*a*). When a judicial factor has been appointed to take charge of the lunatic partner's affairs, it would seem that the partnership may be closed by agreement, either by notice in terms of the contract or otherwise, the *curator bonis* applying to the Court of Session for special powers. See Ellis, Petr., 1836; 15 S. 262. Bontine's Cur., 1870; 8 Macph. 976. Acct. of Court *v.* Gilray's Cur. 1872; 10 Macph. 715. Clark on Partn. 661. If the partners and the judicial factor differ, a declaratory action or petition to the Court by either side is necessary.

(*b*) Eadie *v.* MacBean's Curator, 1888; 12 R. 660.

377. *Insolvency* (*a*) of a partner is a ground of dissolution: so is bankruptcy under the Act, 1696, c. 5 (*b*); such dissolution taking place by a distinct act of the other partners, or by judicial sentence. Sequestration of itself operates as a dissolution in Scotland; and so a commission of bankruptcy in England (*c*). In England it seems now to be settled that, on the issuing of the commission, the dissolution is held to have taken place with the act of bankruptcy (*d*). No decision on this point has been pronounced in Scotland.

(*a*) See § 379, below. As to a stipulation that on declared insolvency one should cease to be a partner, see Hannan *v.* Henderson, 1879 ; 7 R. 380.

(*b*) Munro *v.* Cowan & Co., June 8, 1813 ; F. C. ; 1 Ill. 257.

(*c*) See Hunter *v.* Evans, etc., 1830 ; 9 S. 159. Partnership Act, 1890, § 33.

(*d*) Smith, 5 Ves. 295. Dutton *v.* Morrison, 17 Ves. 204 ; 11 R. R. 56. Birket, 2 Rose's Cases, 71.

378. *Dissolution and Renunciation.*—The act of the parties, mutual or individual, may dissolve the partnership in certain circumstances. Thus, by mutual consent, whether the appointed term have expired or not, the partnership may be dissolved. And by renunciation, 'after due notice (*a*),' one or more of the partners may retire, and so dissolve the company at a moment's notice, where there is no term fixed (*b*); or even where there is a term fixed, this may be done on just cause for separating being shown, 'such as fraud (*c*) of one of the copartners; or rash and reckless speculation, or unreasonable and impracticable behaviour of a gross kind in the conduct and business of the copartnery (*d*); or when a partner becomes liable to criminal prosecution (*e*); or is permanently disabled from performing his part of the contract, as by insanity (*f*), or bankruptcy and sequestration, or outlawry (*g*); or assigns his whole interest in the copartnery (see § 358); or because there is no longer a reasonable expectation of the joint adventure being profitable (*h*); or when the state of feeling between the partners has become such, that in the judgment of the Court mutual confidence between them is impossible; or when circumstances render it just and equitable to dissolve (*i*).' The former may be by extra-judicial, the latter will require a judicial act (*k*). But such renunciation must be fair; not for the acquisition of undue advantage; avoiding unnecessary injury; and with due notice, where notice does not increase the peril (*l*).

(*a*) Syers *v.* Syers, 1 App. Ca. 174. *Infra* (*l*).

(*b*) Featherstonhaugh, and Crawshay, *citt.*, *infra*. Neilson *v.* Mossend Iron Co., 1884, 12 R. 499; rev. 11 App. Ca. 298 ; 13 R. H. L. 50.

(*c*) Essell, *infra*. Fraud, or misrepresentation, inducing the partnership contract is a ground of reduction of the contract. Mycock *v.* Beatson, 13 Ch. D. 384 ; 49 L. J. Ch. 127 (lien on surplus assets). Adam *v.* Newbigging, 13 App. Ca. 308.

(*d*) Waters, Wood, *infra*. Partnership Act, § 35 (*c*), (*d*).

(*e*) Essell, *infra*. (*f*) See above, § 376.

(*g*) Partnership Act, 1890, § 35 (*b*).

(*h*) Montgomery, Barr, Warner, Crawshay, Baring, *infra*. Partnership Act, § 35 (*e*).

(*i*) Watney, Lyon, Attwood (not for slight disputes), *infra*. Act, § 35 (*f*).

(*k*) Marshall *v.* Marshall, Jan. 20, 1815, and Feb. 23, 1816 ; F. C. ; 1 Ill. 258. Montgomery *v.* Forrester, etc., 1791 ; M. 14,583 ; Hume, 748. Barr *v.* Speirs, May 18, 1802 ; 1 Ill. 258. Warner *v.* Cunningham, 3 Dow, 85 ; 1 Ill. 246. Peacock *v.* Peacock, 16 Ves. 49 ; 3 Ross' L. C. 607 ; 1 Ill. 258 ; 10 R. R. 138. **Featherstonhaugh** *v.* **Fenwick**, 17 Ves. 293 ; 3 Ross' L. C. 615 ; 1 Ill. 255 ; 11 R. R. 77. **Crawshay** *v.* **Maule**, *ib.* 197 ; 1 Swanst. 495 ; Tudor's L. C. 310 ; 18 R. R. 126. Baring *v.* Dix, 1 Cox, 213 ; 1 R. R. 23. See Inst. Justinian, B. 3. tit. 26, § 4. Vinnius, in Inst. 679. Pothier, Tr. de Soc., No. 149 et seq. See above, § 368. Voet. 17. 2. 24. Waters *v.* Taylor, 2 Ves. & Bea. 299 ; 13 R. R. 91 ; Tud. L. C. 329. Dickie *v.* Mitchell, 1874 ; 1 R. 1030 (farm—judicial factor—joint-tenants incapable). Bain *v.* Black, 1846 ; 11 D. 1286 ; aff. 1849, 6 Bell's Ap. 317 ; 21 S. Jur. 210 (a society, not a partnership—impossibility of object being attained). Millar & Co. *v.* Walker, 1875 ; 3 R. 242 (ditto—mining adventure). Essell *v.* Hayward, 30 Beav. 138. Watney *v.* Wells, 30 Beav. 36. Attwood *v.* Maude, L. R. 3 Ch. 369. Lyon *v.* Tweddell, 17 Ch. D. 729 ; 50 L. J. Ch. 571. Snell's Pr. of Eq. 495 sq. Lindley, Partn. i. 570. Blissett *v.* Daniell, 10 Hare, 493 (power of expulsion to be fairly exercised). Wood *v.* Woad, L. R. 9 Ex. 190 ; 43 L. J. Ex. 153 (do.).

(*l*) 3 Ersk. 3. § 26. Featherstonhaugh, *supra* (*k*). Marshall, *supra* (*k*). Pothier, Société, No. 150. 3 Pardessus, 155. M'Niven *v.* Peffers, 1868 ; 7 Macph. 181. Young *v.* Dougans, 1887 ; 14 R. 490 (joint venture in patent).

379. *The effect of a Dissolution* of partnership is different in various circumstances.

Death, etc.—The death of a partner, while it vests in the survivors the power and title to wind up the concern (*a*) (though without remuneration), gives to the heirs of the deceased partner his share of the stock, property, and goodwill, after the debts of the concern are provided for (*b*). As to the goodwill of a mercantile concern, doubts seem to have been entertained; but the approved doctrine seems to be, that if it be of a nature to go with the premises, it is saleable for the benefit of all concerned (*c*); that if personal (as in professional partnership), each partner is entitled, on dissolution of the partnership, to proceed with his own exertions, and the right of the survivor cannot be affected (*d*). Dissolution by death, or justifiable renunciation, entitles any partner, 'or the executor, but not a mere beneficiary or next of kin of the deceased partner (*e*),' to insist on immediately stopping the trade, and bringing the stock and establishment to a public sale (*f*).

Bankruptcy.—The effect of bankruptcy in dissolving a partnership, when the company itself is bankrupt, is to expose it to sequestration (*g*). When one or more partners as individuals become insolvent, and the partnership is dissolved in consequence, the right of the bankrupt partner vests in his creditors, and they can insist on the same course of proceeding as if the partner were dead.

(*a*) Nicol *v.* Reid, 1877; 5 R. 137. Partnership Act, 1890, § 38.

(*b*) Martin *v.* Crompe, Lord Raym. 340. See Aitken's Trs. *v.* Shanks, 1830; 8 S. 753; 3 Ill. 126. Stewart *v.* Simson, 1835; 14 S. 72. See above, § 375, and below, § 387.

(*c*) Crawshay *v.* Collins, 15 Ves. 227; 2 Russ. 325; 10 R. R. 61. Crutwell *v.* Lye, 17 Ves. 335; 11 R. R. 98. Kennedy *v.* Lee, 3 Meriv. 441; 17 R. R. 110. See M'Kirdy *v.* Paterson, 1854; 16 D. 1013. Bell's Tr. *v.* Bell, 1884; 12 R. 85 (heir and executor). Churton *v.* Douglas, 1 Johns. 174; 28 L. J. Ch. 841. Reynolds *v.* Bullock, 47 L. J. Ch. 773. Stewart *v.* Gladstone, 10 Ch. D. 626 (rev. 47 L. J. Ch. 423). Broughton *v.* Broughton, 44 L. J. Ch. 526. 1 Clark on Partn. 430. 2 Bell's Com. 645 (535, M'L.'s ed.). See below, § 1361c.

(*d*) Farr *v.* Pearce, 3 Madd. 78; 18 R. R. 96. See Spicer *v.* James, Rolls, 1830; in Collyer, 104. Austen *v.* Boys, 24 Beav. 598; 2 De G. & J. 626. As to the name of the firm, see Banks *v.* Gibson, 34 L. J. Ch. 591; 34 Beav. 566. Levy *v.* Walker, 10 Ch. D. 436; 48 L. J. Ch. 273.

(*e*) M'Kersies *v.* Mitchell, 1872; 10 Macph. 861.

(*f*) Marshall and Featherstonhaugh, *supra*, § 378 (*k*). Aitken's Trs. and Stewart, *supra* (*b*).

(*g*) See above, § 377. 19 and 20 Vict. c. 79, § 8.

380. The division of stock and profit on dissolution, after paying the debts, is to be made according to the stipulated shares. If there be no rate fixed, the presumption is for equality (*a*), which, however, may be altered by evidence, or circumstances from which another arrangement may fairly be inferred (*b*). The period of division is at the moment of dissolution, with the benefit or loss on impending transactions; and with liability for debt universally against all the partners, and relief according to their shares (*c*). 'If on the death of a partner, or his ceasing to be a partner, the surviving or remaining partners carry on the business with its capital or assets, and there be no special agreement regulating the rights of parties, and no settlement of accounts between partners and executors, and no option in the contract to surviving or remaining partners to buy the interest of the retiring or deceasing partner, or that option be not duly exercised in all material respects, that partner or his representatives are entitled in their option to the profits referable to his capital, or to payment of the capital and interest at five per cent. (*d*).'

(*a*) See 3 Stair, 4. § 3. Struthers *v.* Barr, 1826; 2 W. & S. 153; 1 Ill. 248. M'Whirter *v.* Guthrie, 1823; 1 S. 319. See *ante*, § 353, 362. Partnership Act, 1890, § 24 (1).

(*b*) See Anderson, Campbell's Trs., and Peacock, *ante*, § 362.

(*c*) See Aytoun *v.* Dundee Bkg. Co., 1844; 6 D. 1409.

(*d*) Crawshay, *supra*, § 379 (*c*). **Vyse** *v.* **Foster**, L. R. 7 H. L. 318; 44 L. J. Ch. 37. Willett *v.* Blandford, 1 Hare, 253 (option to purchase). Yates *v.* Finn, 13 Ch. D. 839; 49 L. J. Ch. 188. Laird *v.* Laird, 1855; 17 D. 984 (where the surviving partner was also executor, a complication which gives rise to difficulties which are treated of in Vyse *v.* Foster, *cit.*, and also in Lindley on Partn. ii. 976 sqq. Pollock on Partn. 94 sqq.). M'Kersies *v.* Mitchell, 1872; 10 Macph. 861 (effect of delay, etc.). Partnership Act, 1890, § 42.

381. (2.) *Dissolution in relation to the Public.* i. *Act of Dissolution.*—The partners cannot be discharged of their responsibility to third parties, unless the partnership be dissolved as between the partners.

382. ii. *Notice.*—Besides the act or sentence of dissolution, there must be Notice, in order to put an end to the contract and responsibility of the partners, in so far as the public is concerned (*a*). And if, after dissolution, one allow his name to remain over the shop or in the firm, he will continue to be liable for the debts of the company, or for bills drawn by the firm, if he have not taken effectual means to bring to a close the credit on which the public has relied (*b*). 'But it is further enacted that, where a person deals with a firm after a change in its constitution, he is entitled to treat all apparent members of the old firm as still being members of the firm (*c*). An advertisement in the *Gazette* is notice to all who had not dealings with the firm before the date of the dissolution or change (*d*). Any partner may publicly notify dissolution, and require the others to concur in all acts necessary for that purpose (*e*). Death, bankruptcy, and the retirement of a partner not known to any one dealing with the firm, dissolve the firm, and need no notice (*f*).'

(*a*) Lindley on Partn. i. 406.

(*b*) Williams *v.* Keats, 2 Starkie, 290; 19 R. R. 723. Dolman *v.* Orchard, 2 Car. & Pay. 104. Brown *v.* Bush, 2 Chitty, Rep. 120.

(*c*) The Act, § 36 (1), and *infra*, § 384.

(*d*) *Ib.* § 36 (2). (*e*) *Ib.* § 37.

(*f*) *Ib.* § 36 (3). See below, § 383 *ad fin.*

383. The dissolution, whether by expiration of time or by mutual or partial act of the parties, must be communicated to the customers and to the public in order to affect third parties (*a*); 'the principle being, as in agency, that when a man has established an agency or a firm, and held himself out to others as liable for its debts, they have a right to assume that that liability continues till they have notice to the contrary (*b*). The effect of this principle, it has been held in England, is that a creditor has merely a right of election, in debts incurred before notice, as between a retired partner and those who continue to carry on the business and incur the debt (*c*). But this judgment rests on the theory of English law, that a partnership debt is due by each of the partners as joint, not as joint and several, contractors, and that a retired partner without notice is liable, not under a joint contract made subsequent to his retirement, but on the distinct and inconsistent principle of estoppel (*d*). That distinction appears to be inapplicable in Scots law, in which, although a personal exception on the ground of holding out might be said to operate against the retired partner, his liability is truly founded on a continuing guarantee, or joint and several liability (*e*) for the obligations of a firm which is a separate legal *persona*, the guarantee or liability not ceasing until he has duly intimated its termination (*f*).' It has been held in England not to be necessary to give notice of dissolution by the death of a partner, in order to free his representatives from future liabilities (*g*). In Scotland a case occurred in which the Court avoided any decision on this general question (*h*); 'but it is now fixed that notice of dissolution by death or bankruptcy, which are public facts, is not required for this purpose in the case either of a firm or a joint-stock company (*i*).'

(*a*) Bolton *v.* Mansfield, Hunter, & Co., 1786; 2 Bell's Com. 640; 1 Ill. 259; aff. 3 Paton, 7; correcting Armour *v.* Gibson, 1774; M. 14,575; Hailes, 600. Dalgleish & Fleming *v.* Sorley, 1791; M. 14,545; Bell's 8vo Cases, 487; Hume, 746.

(*b*) **Scarf** *v.* **Jardine,** 51 L. J. Q. B. 612; L. R. 7 App. Ca. 345. Lindley on Partn. i. 429. *Supra*, § 224A, 371.

(*c*) Scarf *v.* Jardine, *cit.*

(*d*) Comp. Scarf *v.* Jardine with the judgments in Kendall *v.* Hamilton, 48 L. J. C. P. 705, 4 App. Ca. 504, from which it is the natural sequence.

(*e*) See 2 Bell's Com. 619 (507, M'L.'s ed.). *Supra*, § 356.

(*f*) See opinions in Blacks *v.* Girdwood, 1885; 13 R. 243.

(*g*) Lord Eldon in Vulliamy *v.* Noble, 3 Meriv. 614; 1 Ill. 256; 17 R. R. 143.

(*h*) Kemp *v.* Allan, 1824; 3 S. 104; 1 Ill. 266. See Aitken *v.* Charles & Co., 1830; 8 S. 446.

(*i*) Christie *v.* Royal Bk., 1839; 1 D. 743; 2 Rob. 118. Aytoun *v.* Dundee Bkg. Co., 1844; 6 D. 409. Oswald's Trs. *v.* City of Glasgow Bk., 1879; 6 R. 461. See the Act, § 33, 36 (3).

384. In giving notice, there is a difference between that which is requisite for those who have dealt with the company and for the public generally.

To Customers who have dealt with the company, and for the purpose of changing the credit on which the company has actually proceeded, notice must be given,—either by letter; or by personal communication; or by change of the firm, or of the name in the notes and cheques of a banking-house; or by evidence of a newspaper advertisement having been actually read by the party. It is not enough to show an advertisement in the *Gazette* or in the newspapers, with a possibility or even probability of the advertisement having been read by the party (*a*).

(*a*) Jenkins *v.* Blizard, 1 Starkie, 418; 1 Ill. 260; 18 R. R. 792. Dunbar *v.* Remington & Co., March 10, 1810; F. C. M'Iver *v.* Humble, 16 East, 169. Barfoot *v.* Goodall, 3 Camp. 147. Grahame *v.* Hope, Peake's Cases, 154; 3 R. R. 673. See Rowley *v.* Home, 3 Bing. 2. Bertram *v.* M'Intosh, 1822; 1 S. 290. Sawers *v.* Tradestown Victualling Socy., Feb. 24, 1815; F. C. Padon *v.* Bk. of Scotland, 1826; 5 S. 175; 1 Ill. 185. Campbell & Co. *v.* M'Lintock, 1803; Hume, 755. Gardner *v.* Anderson, 1862; 24 D. 315.

385. *To the Public at large*, and for the purpose of counteracting possible credit, 'notice in the' *Gazette* 'is by statute enough'; and newspaper advertisements, accompanied with all reasonable means taken in the particular circumstances to publish the dissolution, 'are no longer required' (*a*).

(*a*) Sawers, *supra*, § 384 (*a*). Godfrey *v.* Turnbull, 1 Esp. 371; 1 Ill. 260. Williams *v.* Keats, 2 Starkie, 290; 19 R. R. 723. Grahame, *supra*, § 384 (*a*). Booth *v.* Quin, 7 Price, 193. Thomson *v.* Spiers, 1822; 1 S. 554; 1 Ill. 185. Newsome *v.* Coles, 2 Camp. 617. Lindley on Partn. i 415. Altered by Partnership Act, 1890, § 36.

386. It has been held in England that notice is not necessary in dormant partnership; but this 'was' not in Scotland to be relied on when the partner's concern in the partnership has been known to any, as there are no means of knowing how far such knowledge and credit may have spread (*a*); 'but now a partner not known to a person dealing with the firm is not liable to him for debts contracted after the date of the retirement (*b*).'

(*a*) Evans *v.* Drummond, 4 Esp. 89; 1 Ill. 261. Carter *v.* Whalley, 1 B. & Ald. 11; 3 Ross' L. C. 635. Hay *v.* Mair (Kay *v.* Pollock), Jan. 27, 1809; F. C. 2 Bell's Com. 643 (533, M'L.'s ed.). Powles *v.* Page, 3 C. B. 16. 1 Lindley, 411 sq. Parsons on Partn. 411, 415. Aitken *v.* Charles & Co., 1830; 8 S. 446.

(*b*) Partnership Act, 1890, § 36 (3).

387. Winding up the Concern.—To one effect the partnership continues to subsist, notwithstanding dissolution, *i.e.* for the winding up of the concern, and terminating all the responsibilities of the company. No new debts can be contracted, but only the funds made effectual for answering the demands (*a*). If special stipulation be made as to winding up, and any special powers given for that purpose, they will be effectual (*b*). If no arrangement have been made for winding up, the surviving or solvent partners are entitled to act (*c*); or if any just cause of objection be stated against them (*d*), 'or if all the partners are dead or incapable (*e*), the partnership estate will be sequestrated, and' a neutral person will be judicially appointed to wind up (*f*). If sequestration be necessary, it is competent on the petition of the surviving partners (*g*). The partners will be liable for the expense of an unsuccessful attempt to enforce a debt alleged to be due to the company; and the surviving partners alone have the title to pursue for debts due to the company (*h*).

(*a*) Kilgour *v.* Finlayson, 1 H. Bl. 155, 158. Abel *v.* Sutton, 3 Esp. 108; 1 Ill. 262; 6 R. R. 618. Snodgrass *v.* Hair, 1848; 8 D. 390 (bill for prior debt granted after dissolution invalid). Gordon *v.* M'Cubbin, 1851; 13 D. 1154 (do.). Muir *v.* Dickson, 1860; 22 D. 1070. Wilson *v.* Bruce, 1853; 16 D. 176 (*per* Hope, J.-C.). Lindley, 226 sq., 805. Pollock on Partn. As to the power to grant securities for old debts, see Butchart *v.* Dresser, 4 De G. M. & G. 542. *In re* Clough, 31 Ch. D. 324.

(*b*) See Jameson *v.* Watson, 1852; 14 D. 1021.

(*c*) Grant *v.* Chalmers, 1771; M. 14,581; 1 Ill. 262. Douglas, Heron, & Co. *v.* Gordon, 1792; M. 11,032, 11,045; aff. 3 Paton, 428. Cheyne *v.* Walker, 1828; 7 S. 60. Thom *v.* North Br. Bank, 1850; 13 D. 134. Young *v.* Collins, 1852; 14 D. 540; rev. 1853; 1 Macq. 385; 25 S. Jur. 329; 15 D. H. L. 35. West of Scotland Mall. Iron Co. *v.* Buchanan, 1855; 17 D. 461. Barclay *v.* Lawrie, 1857; 19 D. 488. Russell *v.* Russell, 1874; 2 R. 93. See § 379.

(*d*) Harding *v.* Glover, 18 Ves. 281; 11 R. R. 185. Wilson *v.* Greenwood, 1 Swan. 481; 18 R. R. 118. Dickie *v.* Mitchell, 1874; 1 R. 1030. Gow *v.* Schulze, 1877; 4 R. 928. Allan *v.* Gronmeyer, 1891; 18 R. 784.

(*e*) Dixon *v.* Dixon, 1831; 10 S. 138; 4 D. & A. 446; aff. 6 W. & S. 229. Dickie *v.* Mitchell, *supra* (*d*).

(*f*) Montagu, 167. Drysdale *v.* Lawson, 1842; 4 D. 1061. Bell *v.* Williamson, 1857; 19 D. 704. Young and Russell, *citt.* (*c*).

(*g*) Campbell, Petr., 1830; 8 S. 625, n.

(*h*) Roger *v.* Jameson, 1838; 16 S. 418. Kinnear *v.* Thomson, 1830; 8 S. 512. See Jameson, *supra* (*b*). M'Glashan, Sh. Ct. Pr. 117. Nicoll *v.* Reid, 1877; 5 R. 177.

388. Special stipulations will alter or modify the ordinary rules or effect of the contract, and regulate the rights and interests of the partners, and of their separate creditors; but such private stipulations will not affect the creditors of the company.

389. Such stipulations may be waived or counteracted by the course of practice and dealing between the parties, provided such practice show plainly an intention to alter or discharge the stipulation (*a*).

(*a*) Geddes *v.* Wallace, 1820; 2 Bligh, 270; 1 Ill. 255; 21 R. R. 66. Jackson *v.* Sedgwick, 1 Swanst. 460; 1 Wilson, 297; 18 R. R. 109. Const *v.* Harris, Turn. & R. 496; 24 R. R. 108.

390. The partners may arrange as they think fit their contributions, the shares of profit or of loss, the time at which a balance is to be struck and accounts settled with partners retiring or with the heirs of partners deceasing. The natural period of accounting and striking a balance in such a situation is the moment of dissolution of the partnership (*a*). But there is sometimes a stipulation that the shares of retiring or deceased partners shall be regulated by the immediately preceding 'periodical' balance; which is to be taken as the rule, provided 'that the system of periodical balances' have been acted on by the parties (*b*). 'Such signed balance-sheets are binding on the partners, and can be corrected only on showing an *error calculi*, or some palpable error that may be detected by examination of the balance-sheets themselves (*c*).'

(*a*) See above, § 380.

(*b*) Dig. lib. 17. tit. 2 (Pro Socio) l. 49, § 2. Hay *v.* Sinclair, July 3, 1800; 2 Bell's Com. 646 (536, M'L.'s ed.); 1 Ill. 263. Blair *v.* Douglas, Heron, & Co., 1776; M. 14,577, and Apx. *Society*, No. 1; aff. 6 Paton, 796. Munro *v.* Cowan & Co., June 8, 1813; F. C.; 1 Ill. 257. Buchanan *v.* Muirhead, 1799; M. 14,593; 2 Bell's Com. 648 (538, M'L.'s ed.). *Ex p.* Barber, L. R. 5 Ch. 687. Jackson, *supra*, § 389 (*a*). Pollock, Gilmour, & Co. *v.* Ritchie, 1851; 13 D. 640. M'Laren *v.* Liddell's Trs., 1862; 24 D. 577. Forster *v.* Paterson, 1802; 4 Pat. 295. Orr Ewing & Co. *v.* Orr Ewing, 8 App. Ca. 822; 10 R. H. L. 1 (clause of interest—instalments—construction); Hunter *v.* Dowling, 1893; 3 Ch. D. 213 (death of partner after end of accountable year, but before signing balance-sheets). After dissolution, one partner may compensate a claim against him by his share of a debt due by his creditor to the company which has been divided among the partners. Oswald's Trs. *v.* Dickson, 1833; 12 S. 156. Heggie *v.* Heggie, 1858; 21 D. 31.

(*c*) M'Laren, *cit.* If any correction of an error by extrinsic proof is at all admissible, that error must be specially and precisely averred. *Ib. per* Lord Neaves.

390A. '*Statutory Rules for Distribution of Assets.*—Subject to any agreement,—1. *Losses,* including losses and deficiencies of capital, shall be paid first out of profits, next out of capital, and lastly, if necessary, by the partners individually in the proportion in which they were entitled to share profits.

'2. *The assets* of the firm, including the sums contributed by the partners to make up losses or deficiencies of capital, shall be applied in the following manner and order:—(1) In paying firm liabilities to persons not partners; (2) in repaying to each partner rateably advances by him to the firm as distinguished from capital; (3) in paying to each partner rateably his capital; (4) the residue shall be divided as profits are divisible (*a*).

'Where a partnership contract has been rescinded for *fraud* or misrepresentation of one of the parties thereto, the party entitled to rescind, without prejudice to any other right, is entitled—(1) to retention of the surplus assets for any sum paid by him for his share in the firm and for any capital contributed by him; (2) to stand in the place of the creditors for any payments made by him in respect of the partnership liabilities; (3) to be indemnified by the person guilty of the fraud or misrepresentation against all the firm's debts or liabilities (*b*).'

(*a*) The Partnership Act, 1890, § 44.
(*b*) *Ib.* § 41.

391. Arbitration.—An obligation to refer 'disputes' to arbitration 'was till 3rd July 1894' effectual only if the arbiter or referee 'were' named. And so an agreement to refer "to neutral persons" 'did' not bar judicial proceedings (*a*); and an agreement to refer to the person who 'should' hold a certain office when a dispute 'should' arise (as the Lord Advocate or Solicitor-General for the time) 'was' not binding (*b*). 'But a clause of arbitration which is necessary for adjusting a condition, or liquidating or extricating a part of the contract—which is, in other words, a condition precedent to the bringing of any action—is and was effectual, although arbiters are not named (*c*); and contrary to the rule which holds in regard to references which are independent contracts (*d*), such executorial or ancillary references do not fall by the death of a party (*e*).

'The Arbitration (Scotland) Act, 1894, enacts that an agreement to refer to an unnamed arbiter, or to a person to be named by another person, or to one described as the holder for the time being of any office or appointment, shall not for that reason only be invalid (*f*). It is also provided that, on the failure to nominate an arbiter or one of two arbiters, the Lord Ordinary or Sheriff having jurisdiction may nominate such arbiter, and may also, on the failure of arbiters to agree upon an oversman, nominate an oversman (*g*). Arbiters have always power to nominate an oversman, unless the agreement to refer provides otherwise (*h*).'

(*a*) Mags. of Edin. *v.* Mylne, 1770; aff. 2 Paton, 209; 1 Ill. 263. Ramsay *v.* Strain, 1884; 11 R. 527. Steel Co. *v.* Tancred, Arrol, & Co., *infra* (*b*).
(*b*) Buchanan, § 390 (*b*). See Elgin Lunacy Board, 1874; 1 R. 1155; rev. 1875, 2 R. H. L. 136. Steel Co. of Scotland *v.* Tancred, Arrol, & Co., 1887; 15 R. 215; aff. 1890, 15 App. Ca. 125; 17 R. H. L. 31.
(*c*) Smith *v.* Duff, 1843; 5 D. 749. Hendry's Trs. *v.* Renton, 13 D. 1001, and cases cited in Bell on Arbitration, B. I. ch. v., and in Howden *v.* Dobie & Co., 1882; 9 R. 758. Gilmour *v.* Cal. Ins. Co., 1892; A. C. 85; 20 R. H. L. 13; revg. 18 R. 1219. See Talisker Disty. Co. *v.* Hamlyn & Co., 1893; 21 R. 204. Distinguish clauses agreeing to refer claims arising during the execution of the contract, and those covering every kind of claim that can arise out of the contract. Kirkwood *v.* Morrison, 1877; 5 R. 79. Mackay *v.* Par. Bd. of Barry, 1883; 10 R. 1046. Beattie *v.* Macgregor, 1883; 10 R. 1095. Levy & Co. *v.* Thomsons, 883; 10 R. 1134. An arbiter cannot assess damages unless expressly empowered. Blaikie *v.* Aberdeen Ry. Co., 1852; 15 D. H. L. 20. M'Alpine *v.* Lan. & Ayrshire Ry. Co., 1889; 17 R. 113. See Hope *v.* Crookston Brs., 1890; 17 R. 868. Mackay *v.* Leven Police Comrs., 1893; 20 R. 1093.
(*d*) Ersk. iv. 3. 29. Robertson *v.* Cheynes, 1847; 9 D. 599. A judicial reference does not so fall. Watmore *v.* Burns, 1839; 1 D. 743.
(*e*) Cal. Ry. Co. *v.* Lockhart, 1857; 19 D. 527; aff. 1860, 3 Macq. 808. Orrell *v.* Orrell, 1859; 21 D. 554. Cf. Alexander's Trs. *v.* Dymock's Trs., 1883; 10 R. 1189.
(*f*) 57 and 58 Vict. c. 13, § 1.
(*g*) *Ib.* § 2, 3, 4. (*h*) *Ib.* § 4.

II. JOINT ADVENTURE OR JOINT TRADE.

392. Description and Constitution.—Joint adventure or joint trade is a limited partnership, confined to a particular adventure, speculation, course of trade, or voyage; and in which the partners, either latent or known, use no firm or social name, and incur no responsibility beyond the limits of the adventure (*a*). It is to be established by the same evidence as partnership (*b*). It is not to be inferred from joint ownership in a ship, unless there has been participation in the mercantile employment of the ship in which the joint adventure is said to have consisted (*c*).

'Although joint adventure has been recognised as something distinct from partnership by very recent authorities (*d*), it is difficult to show in what it differs from proper partnership. The distinction is not recognised in England (*e*), and Mr. Bell himself points out (*f*) that Lord Eldon said (*g*), "A joint adventure is as proper a partnership as any other."'

(*a*) 3 Ersk. 3. § 29, with Ivory's Notes. 2 Bell's Com. 649. See Pothier, Société, No. 54. Collyer, 26, 302. Brown *v.* Gibbon, 5 Br. Parl. Ca. 491. *Ex p.* Gellar, 1 Rose, 297. Salomons *v.* Nissen, 2 T. R. 675; 1 R. R. 592. Reid *v.* Hollingshead, 4 B. & Cr. 867; 28 R. R. 488. See Smith *v.* Craven, 1 Cromp. & Jer. 500; 35 R. R. 764. Whyte *v.* M'Intyre, 1841; 3 D. 334. 1 Clark on Partn. 40.

(*b*) See Logan *v.* Brown, 1824; 3 S. 15; 1 Ill. 264. Ferguson *v.* Graham, 1836; 14 S. 871.

(*c*) Logan, *supra* (*b*); *infra*, § 448.

(*d*) See, *e.g.*, Pyper *v.* Christie, 1878; 6 R. 143.

(*e*) Pollock, Partn. 4, 5.

(*f*) 1 Ill. 264.

(*g*) Davison *v.* Robertson, 1815; 8 Dow, 218. Mr. Bell says (2 Com. 649; 539, M'L.'s ed.): "The great peculiarity in the doctrine of joint trade is, that unless where the joint concern is avowed, and a credit raised on the combined responsibility, the liability being the result of the discovery of a partnership which was not relied on as regulating the credit, the limits of the contract are fixed by the actual agreement between the parties."

393. Joint purchase is also to be distinguished from joint trade, as there is in it no partnership (*a*).

(*a*) Hoare *v.* Dawes, 1780; Doug. 356; 1 Ill. 249. Neilson *v.* M'Dougal, 1682; M. 14,551.

394. A company may be party to a joint adventure; and this to the effect of introducing a preference in favour of the creditors of the adventure over the creditors of the proper company, as to the capital embarked in the joint adventure (*a*).

(*a*) Crooks *v.* Tawse, 1779; M. 14,596; 1 Ill. 240.

395. The Liability of the joint adventurers is governed by these rules:—Where goods are purchased 'or money raised' *for* the joint adventure, 'and the dealing, though ostensibly by an individual, is truly and substantially a dealing of the joint adventure,' the adventurers are liable as partners (*a*). But there is no such responsibility for goods, etc., purchased 'on the credit of an individual adventurer' *previously* to the contract, though afterwards brought into stock 'as his contribution' (*b*). The responsibility is *limited* to the adventure (*c*).

(*a*) Logie *v.* Durham, 1697; M. 14,566. Withers & Co. *v.* Cowan, 1790; 1 Ill. 264; 2 Bell's Com. 650. Wilkie *v.* Greig, 1799, *ib.*; 4 Pat. 265. Cunningham *v.* Kinnear, 1764, *ib.*; aff. 2 Pat. 114. Gouthwaite *v.* Duckworth, 12 East, 421–26; 3 Ross' L. C. 541. See Brit. Lin. Bank *v.* Alexander, 1853; 15 D. 277 (liability upon bills made for raising money for common purpose; comp. with N. Brit. Bank *v.* Ayrshire Iron Co., 1853; 15 D. 782, and *In re* Adansonia Fibre Co., Miles's Claim, L. R. 9 Ch. 635; 43 L. J. Ch. 732). Cameron *v.* Young, 1871; 9 Macph. 786. Lockhart *v.* Moodie & Co., 1877; 4 R. 859. 2 Bell's Com. 649.

(*b*) Donaldson *v.* Paul, 1766; M. 14,609; 1 Ill. 264. Saville *v.* Robertson, 4 T. R. 720; 1 Ill. 247. Gouthwaite and Kinnear, *supra* (*a*). Venables & Co. *v.* Wood, 1839; 1 D. 659; 3 Ross' L. C. 529, 540. White *v.* M'Intyre, 1841; 3 D. 334. Lockhart *v.* Brown, 1888; 15 R. 742. See above, § 371, cases in note (*b*).

(*c*) Barton *v.* Hanson, 2 Camp. 97; 3 Ross' L. C. 573; 11 R. R. 524; Jardine *v.* Macfarlan, 1828; 6 S. 564.

396. The Stock of the concern is common property, and (as in partnership proper) is held in trust for the creditors of the concern (*a*). 'At the close of the adventure each partner has a title to sue the treasurer or intromitter for his share of stock and profits (*b*).'

The shares of the adventurers are presumed, as in partnership, to be equal, but capable of being otherwise arranged (*c*).

Implied Mandate.—In dealings within the limits of the concern, each partner is *præpositus negotiis societatis* (*d*); but he has no implied mandate to bind the partners generally.

(*a*) M'Caul's Crs. *v.* Ramsay, 1740; M. 14,608; 1 Ill. 265. Wilson *v.* Threshie, 1826; 4 S. 366; 1 Ill. 240.

(*b*) Pyper *v.* Christie, 1878; 6 R. 143. As to *mora* in claiming, see Stewart *v.* North, 1893; 20 R. 260.

(*c*) Ferguson *v.* Graham, 1836; 14 S. 871. Buchanan *v.* Lennox, 1838; 16 S. 824. M'Gregor *v.* Bainbrigge, 7 Hare, 164, n.

(*d*) Cameron *v.* Young, 1871; 9 Macph. 786 (latent partner liable for repayment of an advance obtained to pay rent of a farm held as a joint adventure). See cases in § 395 (*a*).

III. JOINT-STOCK COMPANIES.

397. General View of Joint-Stock Companies.—The great public benefit resulting from encouragements and facilities to the investment of capital in joint-stock companies for the prosecution of undertakings requiring capital beyond the means and enterprise of an individual, has given great interest to the law applicable to such arrangements. In English practice, many technical difficulties were found to oppose themselves to the free investment of capital in this way; while in Scotland, under a system of jurisprudence which more readily adapts itself to such emergencies, few obstacles of this kind arose. The difficulties to be overcome were these: that in England the company could not sue or be sued without the names of all the partners; that the partners could not sue each other for a company matter, without necessarily including a dissolution; that the shares were not assignable to the effect of freeing the retiring partner; that creditors could not certainly know against whom to apply; and that the responsibility of each was for the whole debts of the concern. In Scotland none of these objections occurred or were formidable, and the unlimited responsibility of the partners was doubted (*a*), 'though now it has been firmly established as a principle of the common law for more than a century (*b*).' But the doubts occurring as to such associations in England led to the same general understanding as to the precautions to be taken in both parts of the island.

The matter 'was afterwards,' however, regulated by a general statute, applicable to the whole empire, passed on the report to the House of Commons on the state of the law relative to partnership, 14th July 1837 (*c*); 'which has been superseded by other Acts of Parliament to be afterwards noticed (*d*).'

(*a*) Stevenson & Co. (or Arran Fishing Co.) *v.* M'Nair, 1757; M. 14,651, 14,667; 5 B. Sup. 340; 1 Ill. 265; 3 Ross' L. C. 580.

(*b*) See Clark on Partnership, 286. Limited liability, however, may exist not only by charter, Act of Parliament, or registration under the Companies Acts (*infra*, § 403c seq.), but also by contract, as where a person takes a policy of insurance from a company binding the proprietors only to the amount of their shares. 25 and 26 Vict. c. 89, § 38 (6). *In re* Athenæum Ins. Soc., Johnson, 80. Lethbridge *v.* Adams, 41 L. J. Ch. 710; L. R. 13 Eq. 547, and cases there cited.

(*c*) The statute referred to is 1 Vict. c. 73, of which the author gave in a former edition an abstract; but as it is now superseded by more recent enactments, it is unnecessary to give that abstract.

(*d*) See § 403A et seq.

398. At Common Law. (1.) *Nature.*—Under the common law, a joint-stock company is contradistinguished from ordinary partnership (*a*), by the administration being vested in certain officers or directors elected by the company, and made known to the public by advertisement or otherwise (*b*)—the individual partners having no power as *præpositi negotiis societatis* to deal with the public; and by the shares being transferable according to a mode prescribed by the contract.

(*a*) Cf. Dove *v.* Young, 1868; 7 Macph. 304.

(*b*) See as to their power to bind the partners by bills, Dickinson *v.* Valpy, 10 B. & Cr. 128; 1 Ill. 266; 34 R. R. 348. See above, § 321; below, § 403L.

399. (2.) *Title to Sue.*—'Until the Companies Act of 1862' joint-stock companies 'were' in Scotland held lawful, however numerous the parties (*a*). And although a joint-stock company cannot in Scotland sue or be sued by the descriptive name, as a private partnership may by its firm (*b*); and although the partners cannot, by subscribing that name, bind the company; the company have been allowed to sue or be sued by the descriptive name, with the addition of the names of all or some of the partners (*c*). 'A company debt must be sued for in the company name, with joinder of partners (the company being unincorporated or unregistered), even when the company has ceased to carry on business and is being wound up (*d*).'

(*a*) See § 365, 403c.

(*b*) Culcreuch Cotton Co. *v.* Mathie, 1822; 2 S. 47; 1 Ill. 266. Sea Insurance Co. *v.* Gavin, 1827; 5 S. 375. See Scott *v.* Napier, 1827; 5 S. 413. Shotts Iron Co. *v.* Hopkirk, 1828; 6 S. 399. Glasgow Bank *v.* Brock, 3 W. & S. 75. Fisher *v.* Syme, 1827; 6 S. 216. Coml. Bank *v.* Pollock's Trs., 1828; 3 W. & S. 365. Downe, Bell, & Mitchell *v.* Pitcairn, 3 W. & S. 472. See above, § 357. Fleming *v.* Ballantyne, 1842; 5 D. 305. Natl. Exch. Co. *v.* Drew, 1848; 11 D. 179. West of Scot. Mall. Iron Co. *v.* Buchanan, 1855; 17 D. 461. Blair Iron Co. *v.* Alison, 1855; 18 D. H. L. 49. Barclay *v.* Lawrie, 1857; 19 D. 488.

(*c*) Joint-stock banking companies in Scotland were by statute allowed to sue and be sued in the name of their officers, provided they annually entered upon oath the name and firm of the society, and of every partner, with his place of residence, and the name and abode of every manager, etc., at the Stamp Office in Edinburgh. 7 Geo. IV. c. 67 (Bankers (Scotland) Act). This Act is not repealed, except § 12 and 16. See 19 and 20 Vict. c. 3 (charter to banks carrying on business before 1825). Clark on Partnership, 547 sq.

(*d*) West of Scot. Mall. Iron Co. and Barclay, *citt.*

400. (3.) *Transfer of Shares.*—The shares of stock may be transferred, if it be so stipulated in the contract. It is usual to require certain precautions or conditions for completing the transference of the share;—to provide that, before transferring a share, the first offer shall be made to the company, or that the transfer shall be made in presence of so many directors, etc. These are held to be intended for the benefit and security of the company, and must, in order to complete the transference, and change the responsibility, as in a question with the company, 'unless waived by them (*a*),' be observed (*b*); but the completion of the bargain and sale, as between the buyer and seller of the share, will, in a question between them, entitle the seller to relief against the buyer, although the company regulations have not yet been complied with (*c*). In order to discharge the seller of the share from his liability to the creditors of the company for future dealings, he 'is not in general required to' give notice of his retirement; 'but he must have ceased to be a partner, and his name must be removed from the register of shareholders (*d*). By statute, contracts for the sale of shares in joint-stock banking companies are void, unless the numbers by which the shares are distinguished are set forth in the contract; or if there is no register by numbers, then the name of the registered proprietor at the time of the contract (*e*).'

(*a*) Turnbull *v.* Allan & Son, 1833; 11 S. 487; aff. 7 W. & S. 281. Drummond (Fife Bank) *v.* Thomson's Trs., 1834; 12 S. 620. Bargate *v.* Shortridge, 5 H. L. Ca. 397.

(*b*) Gibson Craig *v.* Aitken, 1848; 10 D. 567. Morrison *v.* Harrison, 1876; 3 R. 406. The company has a right of lien or retention of a partner's shares for debts due by him to the company. Hotchkis *v.* Royal Bank, 1797; M. 2673; aff. 3 Pat. 618. Burns *v.* Lawrie's Trs., 1840; 2 D. 1348. Bell's Tr. *v.* Coatbridge Tinplate Co., 1886; 14 R. 246. Clark on Partn. 427.

(*c*) Harvey & Reynolds *v.* Kay, 9 B. & Cr. 356; 1 Ill. 266. Weatherley *v.* Turnbull, 1824; 3 S. 92. East Lothian Bank *v.* Turnbull, *ib.* 95. M'Andrew *v.* Robertson, 1828; 6 S. 950. Turnbull, *supra* (*a*). Thomson *v.* Fullarton, 1842; 5 D. 379. See below, § 403J. As to the transmission of railway shares, see 8 & 9 Vict. c. 17, § 14–19. Morrison *v.* Harrison, *supra* (*b*).

(*d*) See below, § 403K.

(*e*) 30 Vict. c. 29 (Leeman's Act). Mitchell (Nelson) *v.* City of Glasgow Bank, 1878; 6 R. 420; 1879, *ib.* H. L. 66; 4 App. Ca. 624. Neilson *v.* James, 9 Q. B. D. 546; 51 L. J. Q. B. 369.

401. Public Chartered Companies.—These companies are of two kinds,—those which hold the character of a corporation, with a privilege of limited responsibility under a royal charter; and those which enjoy a privilege of monopoly under legislative authority.

402. A royal charter enables a company to hold lands, make bye-laws, enjoy the other privileges of a corporation, and trade under a limited responsibility. The shares of such a company are transferable; the company is undissolved by the death or bankruptcy of a partner; and the management and title to pursue are in the officers appointed according to the charter (*a*).

(*a*) See as to corporations, below, § 2176 sq.

403. To give the privilege of monopoly there must be an Act of Parliament, as in the case of the East India Company.

403A. 'After various attempts had been made to regulate joint-stock companies, to facilitate their formation by enabling the Crown to incorporate by letters patent (*a*), and to produce uniformity in the constitution, government, and powers of companies formed by special Acts of Parliament for the construction of railways, canals, harbours, and other works of public utility (*b*), the Act 7 and 8 Vict. c. 110—the first general Joint-Stock Companies Act—established a general registry for such companies, and a code of rules both for their formation and their government (*c*). It was superseded by the Joint-Stock Companies Act, 1856 (*d*), which continued in force, though amended and varied (*e*), till 1862, when a statute was passed to consolidate and amend "the laws relating to the incorporation, regulation, and winding up of trading companies and other associations" (*f*). This Act extends of necessity to all companies formed and registered under the statutes last mentioned (*g*), and to all banking companies of more than ten persons, and other companies consisting of more than twenty persons, formed after Nov. 2, 1862, for the acquisition of gain. All other companies, except railway companies incorporated by statute, and unregistered companies consisting of fewer than seven persons, *may* register themselves as companies with limited or unlimited liability under its provisions (*h*). Another statute makes similar provisions for the regulation of industrial and provident societies (*i*); while the leading statute has been amended by Acts passed to give additional security to creditors and shareholders, chiefly in conformity with the recommendations of a Committee of the House of Commons appointed after the panic of 1866 (*k*).'

(*a*) *E.g.* 1 Vict. c. 73.

(*b*) See The Companies Clauses Consolidation (Scotland) Act, 8 and 9 Vict. c. 17; The Lands Clauses Consolidation (Scotland) Act, 8 and 9 Vict. c. 19; and The Railways Clauses Consolidation (Scotland) Act, 8 and 9 Vict. c. 33, and subsequent Acts, to analyse which would greatly exceed the limits of this work.

(*c*) As to the regulations applicable to existing companies originally formed under the earlier statutes, see 25 and 26 Vict. c. 89, § 196.

(*d*) 19 and 20 Vict. c. 47.

(*e*) By 20 and 21 Vict. cc. 14, 49, and 21 and 22 Vict. cc. 90, 91.

(*f*) 25 and 26 Vict. c. 89 (Companies Act, 1862).

(*g*) *Ib.* § 176.

(*h*) *Ib.* § 180, 196, etc. See below, § 403C.
(*i*) 56 and 57 Vict. c. 39.
(*k*) 30 and 31 Vict. c. 47 and 131 (Companies Act, 1867); 33 and 34 Vict. 104 (Joint-stock Companies Arrangement Act, 1870); 42 and 43 Vict. c. 76 (Companies Act, 1879); 43 Vict. c. 19 (Companies Act, 1880); 46 and 47 Vict. c. 28 (Companies Act, 1883—wages and salaries preferential); 49 and 50 Vict. c. 23 (Companies Act, 1886—winding up—diligence sixty days before liquidation—procedure); 51 and 52 Vict. c. 62 (winding up); 53 and 54 Vict. c. 62 (mem. of association); 53 and 54 Vict. c. 64 (directors' liability); 54 and 55 Vict. c. 43, and 55 and 56 Vict. c. 36 (forged transfers).

403B. '**The Prospectus** is a statement of the purposes, capital, etc., of a proposed company, issued by the promoters. It is the basis on which the original shareholders agree to take shares; and while some allowance is to be made for sanguine expectations, the law requires that it shall be characterised by the utmost candour and honesty (*a*). And it is required by statute that every prospectus or notice inviting persons to subscribe for shares in any joint-stock company shall specify any contract entered into by the company, promoters, directors, or trustees; and if it fail to do so, it is to be deemed fraudulent on the part of the promoters, directors, or trustees knowingly issuing it, as regards any person taking shares on the faith of such prospectus and not having notice of the contract (*b*).

'An original (*c*) shareholder who has been misled by a material misstatement or concealment in a prospectus, may be relieved from his agreement to take shares. With this view he may either repudiate the shares, if the company seeks to make him liable, provided he do so promptly after notice of the fraud, and before he has taken any benefit from his shares, and have in due time given notice to the company of his repudiation (*d*); or he may claim restoration of moneys paid, if he is in a position to restore the shares, and place all parties in the same position as they were (*e*); or he may, but only in case of fraud, recover damages, not against the company afterwards formed (*f*), but against the promoters, or those who have imposed upon him (*g*). The decision in Peek *v.* Derry led to the passing of the Directors Liability Act, 1890, by which directors and promoters are liable to make compensation to all who are deceived into subscribing for shares by untrue statements in a prospectus or notice or relative document which they have authorised, subject to the conditions in the Act (*h*).

'But as one may not at once approbate and reprobate, he cannot, when induced to take shares by misrepresentations of an existing company itself through its agents, recover damages against the company while remaining a member of it. He must rescind his contract to take shares and withdraw from the company before he can claim damages (*i*). If the memorandum of association, contract, or deed of settlement materially differs from the prospectus, one who has taken shares on the faith of the prospectus may at once repudiate them and claim his deposit, and get the register rectified (*k*).

'But creditors of the company who trust to the register have a right to look to him; and if the company is wound up, whether voluntarily or by or under the supervision of the Court, or if it stop payment and a meeting to resolve on liquidation be called before he has taken steps to have his name removed from the register, he loses his right to avoid the contract, and will be a contributory (*l*). A shareholder is bound to make himself acquainted with the memorandum and articles of association within a reasonable time; and as other parties may be induced to take shares on the faith of his name, he will not be allowed, even in a question with the going company, to get rid of liability on the ground of misrepresentation or fraud, if he fail to take steps to have his name removed (*m*). A "promoter" is accountable to a company for money secretly obtained by him, *e.g.* as commission from a vendor to it, just as if he stood towards it in the relation of agent or trustee at the time when the money was obtained (*n*).'

(*a*) Central Ry. Co. of Venezuela *v.* Kisch, 2 App. Ca. 99; 36 L. J. Ch. 849. City of Edin. Brewery Co. *v.* Gibson's Trs., 1869; 7 Macph. 886. Reese River Ming. Co. *v.* Smith, L. R. 2 Ch. 604; 4 H. L. 64; 39 L. J. Ch. 849.
(*b*) 30 and 31 Vict. c. 131, § 38. Cornell *v.* Hay, 42 L. J. C. P. 136; L. R. 8 C. P. 328. Askew's Case, 43 L. J. Ch. 633; L. R. 9 Ch. 664. *Ex p.* Gover, 44 L. J. Ch. 323; 45 *ib.* 83; L. R. 20 Eq. 114; 1 Ch. D. 182. Twycross *v.* Grant, L. R. 2 C. P. D. 469; 46 L. J. C. P. 636. Sullivan *v.* Mitcalfe, 5 C. P. D. 555; 49 L. J. C. P. 815. New Sombrero Phosph. Co., *infra* (*m*). Macmorland's Trs. *v.* Fraser, 1896; 24 R. 65 (on the faith of, etc.).
(*c*) Peek *v.* Gurney, *infra* (*m*). As to purchasers from allottees, see Andrews *v.* Mockford, 1896; 1 Q. B. 372.
(*d*) Bwlch-y-Plum Lead Co. *v.* Baynes, L. R. 2 Ex. 34; 36 L. J. Ex. 183. Estates Investment Co., *ex p.* Ashley,

39 L. J. Ch. 354; L. R. 9 Eq. 263. M'Niell's Case, 39 L. J. Ch. 822; L. J. 10 Eq. 503. Oakes *v.* Turquand (*k*). Reese River Mining Co. (*a*). Kent *v.* Freehold Land Co., L. R. 3 Ch. 493. *In re* Scottish Petroleum Co., 23 Ch. D. 413.

(*e*) Henderson *v.* Lacon, L. R. 5 Eq. 249. Graham *v.* Western Bank, 1865; 3 Macph. 617. **Addie** *v.* **Western Bank,** 1865; 2 Macph. 809; 3 Macph. 899; rev. 1867, 5 Macph. H. L. 80; L. R. 1 Sc. App. 145. Houldsworth *v.* City of Glas. Bank, 1879; 6 R. 1164; aff. 1880, 7 R. H. L. 53; 5 App. Ca. 317. See cases below, and § 13A.

(*f*) Kelner *v.* Baxter, L. R. 2 C. P. 194; 36 L. J. C. P. 94. *In re* Empress Engineering Co., 16 Ch. D. 125.

(*g*) Addie, *cit.* (*e*). Western Bank *v.* Bairds, 1860; 22 D. 497; 1862, 24 D. 859; 1866, 4 Macph. 1071. Gerhard *v.* Bates, 2 E. & B. 476. Lees *v.* Tod, 1882; 9 R. 807. **Smith** *v.* **Chadwick,** 20 Ch. D. 27; 9 App. Ca. 187. **Peek** *v.* **Derry,** 37 Ch. D. 541 (measure of damages, etc.); rev. 14 App. Ca. 337. See above, § 14.

(*h*) 53 and 54 Vict. c. 64. See the Act itself.

(*i*) See above, § 13A. **Houldsworth** *v.* **City of Glasg. Bk.,** 1879; 6 R. 1164; aff. 1880, 7 R. H. L. 53; 5 App. Ca. 317.

(*k*) Downes *v.* Ship, L. R. 3 H. L. 343. See Oakes *v.* Turquand, L. R. 2 H. L. 325; 36 L. J. Ch. 919. City of Edin. Brewery Co., *supra* (*a*).

(*l*) Oakes *v.* Turquand, *supra*, and cases in note (*e*). Reese River Mining Co. *v.* Smith, *cit.* (*a*). Stone *v.* City and County Bk., 3 C. P. D. 282; 47 L. J. C. P. 681 (voluntary winding up). Tennant *v.* City of Glasgow Bk., 1879; 6 R. 554; aff. *ib.* H. L. 69; 4 App. Ca. 615. Mitchell *v.* City of Glasgow Bk., 1878; 6 R. 439; aff. *ib.* H. L. 60; 4 App. Ca. 528. Burgess's Case, 15 Ch. D. 507; 49 L. J. Ch. 541. One whose shares are forfeited for non-payment of calls, his name being removed from the register, thereby ceases to be a member; and after liquidation, being sued for calls, may plead that he was induced to take shares by fraud in the company's prospectus. He is sued as an ordinary debtor, having ceased by the company's own act to be a member. Mount Morgan Gold Mine *v.* M'Mahon, 1891; 18 R. 772. Aaron's Reefs Lim. *v.* Twiss, 1896; A. C. 273.

(*m*) *In re* Barned's Bank, *ex p.* Peel, L. R. 2 Ch. App. 674, 684; 36 L. J. Ch. 757. Oakes *v.* Turquand, *supra* (*k*). 25 and 26 Vict. c. 89, § 19. **Peek** *v.* **Gurney,** 41 L. J. Ch. 436; 43 L. J. Ch. 19; L. R. 6 H. L. 377. Central Ry. Co. of Venezuela, *cit.* (*a*). New Sombrero Phosphate Co. *v.* Erlanger, 5 Ch. D. 73; 3 App. Ca. 1218; 46 L. J. Ch. 425; 48 *ib.* 73. (Delay has two aspects, as it may bring with it a change of circumstances, or as it may infer acquiescence; *per* Lord Penzance, *l.c.*)

(*n*) Emma Silver Mining Co. *v.* Lewis, 4 C. P. D. 396. Bagnall *v.* Carlton, 6 Ch. D. 371. Sydney, etc., Iron Ore Co. *v.* Bird, 33 Ch. D. 85. Edin. N. Tramways Co. *v.* Mann, 1891; 18 R. 1140; aff. 1893, A. C. 69; 20 R. H. L. 7; 1896, 23 R. 1056.

403C. 'Formation of Companies — Memorandum of Association.—All companies formed since 1862 (*a*) may, if consisting of seven or more persons, and must, if consisting of more than ten members, and being banking companies, or of more than twenty, being formed for the purpose of carrying on any other business (than banking) that has for its object the acquisition of gain (*b*), be formed subject to the provisions of the Act of 1862. Companies which ought to be, and are not registered under the Act (§ 4, 6, 17, etc.), are illegal and cannot sue for their debts (*c*).

'Companies are divided by the Act into three classes: 1. Companies limited by shares; 2. Companies limited by guarantee; and 3. Companies with unlimited liability. The partners of the proposed company sign a memorandum of association, which contains the name of the company, the part of the United Kingdom where the registered office is to be, and the objects of the company. By signing it they agree to become members; and being entered on the register, are deemed members (*d*). Where the liability of the partners is to be limited by shares, the memorandum must also contain a declaration of limited liability, and must state the amount of proposed capital divided into shares of a fixed amount. If the liability is limited by guarantee, there is a declaration that if the company be wound up, each member will contribute to the liquidation of its debts whatever may be required, not exceeding a fixed amount (*e*). The memorandum of association must be signed by at least seven members, each signature being attested by at least one witness. Each member must take at least one share, and write the number he takes opposite his name in the memorandum (*f*). It requires the same stamp as if it were a deed (*g*). The liability of the directors or manager of a company otherwise limited, may be unlimited (*h*). Joint-stock banks of issue registered as limited companies are not entitled to limited liability in respect of their notes (*i*). The liability of persons signing the contract or memorandum can only be limited in the statutory way, not by any private arrangement. Thus, trustees having part of their trust estate invested in shares of a company, and being registered as partners, cannot escape from full personal liability as partners, either in a question with creditors of the company or in the way of relief to their copartners, by reason of their being mere trustees, and described as trustees in the register and books of the company (*k*). The same rule applies to executors accepting the shares of their testator and entered on the register of partners (*l*); but the statute permits a transfer of the interest of a deceased member of a company by his "personal representative," although such personal representative may not himself be a member; *i.e.* he may sell the shares and obtain the transfer directly to the purchaser (*m*). But when one holds shares of a company as a trustee or executor, it has been held that on his death his liability, except as to obligations already incurred, ceases, and his title and interest in the shares does not pass to his personal representatives, but accrues to his surviving co-trustees (*n*). So also the liability of shareholders cannot be restricted by issuing shares at a discount (*o*).'

(*a*) See as to English companies formed before the passing of the Joint-Stock Companies Acts, Womersley *v.* Merritt, L. R. 4 Eq. 695; 37 L. J. Ch. 17. Shaw *v.* Simmons, 12 Q. B. D. 117.

(*b*) Harris *v.* Amery, L. R. 1 C. P. 148; 35 L. J. C. P. 89. Smith *v.* Anderson, 15 Ch. D. 247; 50 L. J. Ch. 39, overruling Sykes *v.* Beadon, 11 Ch. D. 170; 48 L. J. Ch. 522. *In re* Siddall, 29 Ch. D. 1.

(*c*) *In re* Padstow Total Loss Association (*ex p.* Bryant), 20 Ch. D. 137; 51 L. J. Ch. 344. Jennings *v.* Hammond, 9 Q. B. D. 225; 51 L. J. Q. B. 493. Shaw *v.* Benson, 11 Q. B. D. 563.

(*d*) 25 and 26 Vict. c. 89, § 11, 23. There must be an absolute agreement to take shares, and notice of the acceptance by the company; and by rectification of the register (below, § 403F), one may be made liable as a shareholder who has simply agreed to take shares. See Buckley, Companies Act, 46, 52. Curror's Trs. *v.* Cal. Her. Sec. Co., 1880; 7 R. 479. Portal *v.* Emmens, 46 L. J. C. P. 179; 2 C. P. D. 201, 664. Stenhouse *v.* City of Glasg. Bk., 1879; 7 R. 102. Molleson & Grigor *v.* Fraser's Trs., 1881; 8 R. 632. Goldie *v.* Torrance, 1882; 10 R. 174. Miln *v.* N. B. Fresh Fish Supply Co., 1887; 15 R. 21.

(*e*) Lion Mut. Mar. Ins. Ass. *v.* Tucker, 12 Q. B. D. 176.

(*f*) A company in which all the shares, except six taken by persons of his family, are held by one man (a "one man company"), who thus limits his liability and obtains a preference over other creditors as a debenture holder, is not contrary to the intent and meaning of the Act. Salomon *v.* Salomon & Co., 1897; A. C. 22.

(*g*) 25 and 26 Vict. c. 89, § 8, 9, 11, 14, etc. See 51 Vict. c. 8, § 11, as to statements of capital to be lodged with registrar.

(*h*) 30 and 31 Vict. c. 131, § 4, 5.

(*i*) 42 and 43 Vict. c. 76, § 6 (repealing 25 and 26 Vict. c. 89, § 182); and see there and § 188 of the principal Act for further provisions as to banks.

(*k*) **Lumsden** *v.* **Buchanan**, 1864; 2 Macph. 704; rev. 1865, 3 Macph. H. L. 89; 4 Macq. 950. Graham *v.* Western Bank, 1866; 4 Macph. 484. Lumsden *v.* Peddie, 1866; 5 Macph. 34. Muir *v.* City of Glasgow Bk., 1878; 6 R. 392; aff. 1879, *ib.* H. L. 21; 4 App. Ca. 337. Smith *v.* City of Glasgow Bk., 1879; 6 R. 1017. Gordon *v.* City of Glasgow Bk., 1879; 7 R. 55. Stenhouse *v.* Do., 1879; *ib.* 102. Such trustees are joint owners, and liable *in solidum*. Lumsden *v.* Buchanan, *cit.* Oswald's Trs., *infra* (*n*). Cuningham *v.* City of Glasgow Bk., 1879; 6 R. 679; aff. *ib.* H. L. 98; 4 App. Ca. 607. Gillespie & Paterson *v.* City of Glasgow Bk., 1879; 6 R. 714; aff. *ib.* H. L. 104; 4 App. Ca. 632. As to fiar and liferenter of shares, see Wishart *v.* City of Glasgow Bk., 1879; 6 R. 823.

(*l*) Buchan *v.* City of Glasgow Bk., 1879; 6 R. 567; aff. 1879, *ib.* H. L. 44; 4 App. Ca. 549.

(*m*) 25 and 26 Vict. c. 89, § 24, 76, and Table A, art. 12 sqq. See Buchan *v.* City of Glasgow Bk., *cit.* (*l*), where the opinions in the House of Lords restrict the operation of these sections to executors as distinguished from trustees. But qu. whether in Scotland a trustee also, though he is not executor, has not a representative character in the sense of the 24th section of the Act? Buchan, *cit.* Wishart *v.* City of Glasgow Bk., 1879; 6 R. 1341. Gordon *v.* City of Glasgow Bk., 1879; 7 R. 55. Stewart's Trs. *v.* Evans, 1871; 9 Macph. 810. As to a *curator bonis*, see Lindsay's Curator *v.* City of Glasgow Bk., 1879; 6 R. 571. Lumsden *v.* Peddie, *cit.* (*k*); and as to a trustee in a sequestration, see Myles *v.* City of Glasgow Bk., 1879; 6 R. 718.

(*n*) Oswald's Trs. *v.* City of Glasgow Bk., 1879; 6 R. 461. As to the registration of assumed trustees, see Bell *v.* City of Glasgow Bk., 1879; 6 R. 548; aff. *ib.* H. L. 55.

(*o*) *In re* Almada and Tirito Co., 48 Ch. D. 415. Klenck *v.* E. I. Exploration Co., 1889; 16 R. 271. *Infra*, 403E, 403F.

403D. '**Articles of Association—Registration.**—The memorandum of association is registered with the Registrar of Joint-Stock Companies. If the company is limited by shares, printed articles of association, stamped and signed by each member in presence of one attesting witness, containing regulations for the company in numbered paragraphs, may, and in the case of other companies must, be delivered to the registrar along with the memorandum. Companies limited by shares are regulated by the articles given in Table A appended to the Act, so far as they are applicable and are not excluded or modified by the registered articles (*a*). That table may be altered as to future companies by the Board of Trade (*b*).'

(*a*) 25 and 26 Vict. c. 89, § 14–17. See § 403C, note (*g*), *supra*.

(*b*) *Ib.* § 71.

403E. 'The memorandum and articles, if any, bind the subscribers; and on registration and payment of the fees, the registrar certifies that the company is incorporated, and in the case of a limited company that it is limited. The partners thereupon become a corporate body (*a*), with perpetual succession, a common seal, and power to hold lands. But its rights and powers as a corporation are limited by its memorandum of association; and as the Act has regard not merely to the interests of the existing shareholders, but to those of persons who may become shareholders in succession, as well as of the outside public, a company registered under it is disabled from entering into a contract or doing any act foreign to its purposes as defined by the memorandum, even with the assent or homologation of all its members (*b*), or although permitted by the articles of association (*c*). 'An incorporated association's assets are its property, and not the property of the shareholders for the time being; and if the directors misapply the assets to purposes for which the company itself cannot lawfully use them, they are liable as soon as any one properly puts the company in motion (*d*).

'The registrar's certificate is conclusive (*e*) evidence that the requisitions of the Act (not being conditions precedent of registration, such, *e.g.*, as the signature of the memorandum by seven partners) with regard to registration have been complied with (*f*). Changes can be made on the memorandum after registration under certain conditions specified in the statute, for the purpose of increasing capital, conversion of shares into stock, or of shares into shares of larger amount, or of change of name (*g*); and, subject to the provisions of the Act, and the conditions contained in the memorandum of association, the company may, by special resolution, passed by three-fourths of the members present, and subsequently confirmed by a majority, vary the articles of association in regard to the management, but not the constitution of the company, including the fundamental right of members to the share of profits originally provided. The power to issue preference shares, if not at first authorised, is thus excluded (*h*). By a subsequent statute, a company is enabled under an order of the Court to have the capital reduced; but no resolution reducing the capital can come into operation till an order of Court confirming the reduction is registered (*i*). It is now settled that the purchase of its own shares by a company is *ultra vires*, although authorised by its articles of association; and even if such a power, or a power to issue shares at a discount, is found in the memorandum, it is void, as being virtually a reduction of capital, and a violation of a statutory condition of the memorandum (*k*). Somewhat more extensive powers to alter the memorandum are given by the Companies Act of 1890 (*l*).'

(*a*) See Sim, Petr., 1863; 2 Macph. 205. M'Kinnon, Petr., 1884; 11 R. 676 (registered company equivalent to "company incorporated by Act of Parliament").

(*b*) **Ashbury Ry. Carriage Co. *v.* Riche**, L. R. 9 Ex. 224; 7 H. L. 653; 43 L. J. Ex. 177; 44 L. J. Ex. 185. *In re* Geo. Newman & Co., 1895; 1 Ch. D. 674. See below, § 2178; and cf. Att.-Gen. *v.* Great E. Ry. Co., 5 App. Ca. 473; 49 L. J. Ch. 545. 1 Smith's L. C. 378 sqq. The powers of other associations are limited and defined by their constitution, which may be in the form, *e.g.*, of "rules." See, *e.g.*, Scott. Prop. Invt. Soc. *v.* Shiell's Trs., 1883; 10 R. 1198; aff. 1884, 10 App. Ca. 119 (*nom.* Small *v.* Smith); 12 R. H. L. 14. Life Assoc. of Scotland *v.* Cal. Her. Sec. Co., 1886; 13 R. 750.

(*c*) Ashbury Ry. Carr. Co., *cit.* Guinness *v.* Land Corporation of Ireland, 22 Ch. D. 349. Trevor *v.* Whitworth, *infra* (*k*).

(*d*) *Per* Lindley, L. J., in Geo. Newman & Co., *cit.* (presents to directors approved by all existing shareholders), and see note (*h*).

(*e*) Barned's Banking Co., Peel's Case, L. R. 2 Ch. Ap. 674; 36 L. J. Ch. 757. Oakes *v.* Turquand, L. R. 2 H. L. 325; 36 L. J. Ch. 949. Glover *v.* Giles, 18 Ch. D. 173; 51 L. J. Ch. 568. Natl. Debenture and Assets Corporation, 1891; 2 Ch. D. 505. (But see *per* L. MacNaghten in Brit. & Amer. Tr. Assn. *v.* Couper, 1894; A. C. 399.) See Princess of Reuss *v.* Boss, 40 L. J. Ch. 655; L. R. 6 H. L. 176.

(*f*) 25 and 26 Vict. c. 89, § 16, 18; see also § 192.

(*g*) *Ib.* § 12, 13, 50, 51. Hoggan *v.* Tharsis Co., 1882; 9 R. 1191.

(*h*) *Ib.* § 50 sqq. Hutton *v.* Scarborough Cliff Hotel Co., 2 Dr. & Sm. 514, 521; 4 De G. J. & S. 672; 34 L. J. Ch. 643. Walker *v.* Lond. Tram. Co., 12 Ch. D. 705; 49 L. J. Ch. 23. Muirhead *v.* Forth, etc., Mut. Ins. Co., 1893; 20 R. 442; aff. 1894, A. C. 72; 21 R. H. L. 1. Waverley Hydr. Co. *v.* Barrowman, 1895; 23 R. 136 (holders of *ultra vires* preference shares are creditors of company). As to the power of the unanimous shareholders to ratify contracts made by the directors which are *ultra vires* and beyond the scope of the memorandum of association, see **Ashbury Co. Lim. *v.* Riche**, *cit.* (*b*). Bonnington Sugar Co. *v.* Thomson's Trs., *infra* (*k*); and below, § 2178.

(*i*) 30 and 31 Vict. c. 131, § 9–20. 40 and 41 Vict. c. 26. *In re* Sharp, Stewart, & Co., L. R. 5 Eq. 407. *In re* Telegraph Constr. Co., L. R. 10 Eq. 384. British and Burmese St. Nav. Co., Petrs., 1879; 7 R. 379. New Zealand and Austr. Land Co., Petrs., 1880; 8 R. 691. Tharsis Sulphur Co. *v.* Hoggan, 1882; 9 R. 507; 10 R. 103. Hoggan *v.* Tharsis Co., *cit.* (*g*). Avery & Co. Lim., 1890; 17 R. 1001. City Prop. Invt. Trust *v.* Thorburn, 1896; 23 R. 400 (no capital lost—petition refused).

(*k*) **Trevor *v.* Whitworth**, 12 App. Ca. 409. Almada & Tirito Co., and Klenck *v.* E. I. Explor. Co., *supra*, § 403c. Gen. Prop. Invt. Co. *v.* Matheson, 1889; 16 R. 282. Gen. Prop. Invt. Co. *v.* Craig, 1891; 18 R. 389 (exception—surrender by insolvent shareholder). Robertson *v.* B. L. Co., 1891; 18 R. 1225. **British & Amer. Trustee, etc., Ass. *v.* Couper**, 1894; A. C. 399. Compare these previous cases: Bonnington Sugar Co. *v.* Thomson's Trs. (Cree *v.* Somervail), 1878; 6 R. 80; 1879, *ib.* H. L. 90; 4 App. Ca. 648. Zulueta's Case, L. R. 5 Ch. 444; 39 L. J. Ch. 361, 598. Hope *v.* Intl. Finan. Soc., L. R. 4 Ch. D. 327; 46 L. J. Ch. 200. *In re* Dronfield Coal Co., 17 Ch. D. 76; 50 L. J. Ch. 387. Buckley, Companies Act, 75, 483.

(*l*) 53 and 54 Vict. c. 62. Scot. Accident Ins. Co., 1896; 23 R. 586.

403F. '**Register of Company.**—The most important record of the company is the register of members, which must be kept at the registered office (*a*) in one or more books. It must be open to the inspection of the members, and cannot be removed or become subject to any right of lien or hypothec (*b*). It contains the names, addresses, and occupations of the members, the number of shares held by each, distinguished by their numbers, the amount paid up thereon, the date at which each name was entered, and at which any person ceased to be a member (*c*). The statement of the amount paid in the register and share certificates is an absolute protection to a shareholder without notice against calls beyond the amount so appearing to be unpaid (*d*). By § 25 of the Act of 1867 (30 and 31 Vict. c. 131), every share in a company is deemed and taken to have been issued and held subject to payment of the whole amount thereof in cash, unless otherwise determined by a contract in writing, filed with the registrar at or before its issue (*e*).

'If the capital be not divided into shares, the names, addresses, and occupations of the directors are kept in a register, a copy of which, and notification of any change, must be sent to the registrar (*f*). In companies whose capital is divided into shares, an annual list of members, with various particulars required by the statute, must also, under severe penalties, be made up, entered in a separate part of the register, and a copy of it sent to the registrar. Notice of changes in the amount of shares, or conversion of capital, must also be sent to the registrar (*g*). The register is *primâ facie* evidence of all matters directed to be inserted in it (*h*). If (1) any name be entered in or omitted from the register without sufficient cause, or if (2) default or unnecessary delay take place in removing any person's name from the register, he, or any member, or the company itself, may apply to the Court of Session by summary petition for an order to rectify the register. The Court in this proceeding may decide any question of title or question necessary for the rectification of the register (*i*). But where serious or complicated questions apart from the mere rectification of the register are raised between the parties, it will require them to bring an appropriate action in lieu of this summary remedy (*k*). In the case of companies registered in England or Ireland, no notice of any trust, express, implied, or constructive, can be entered on the register or received by the registrar (*l*). In Scotland, there is a practice of noticing trusts in the transfer and registration of stocks, but it does not affect the personal liability of the trustees (*m*). A notice of an equitable assignment of shares in security of a debt is not a notice of a trust within the meaning of this clause (*n*).'

(*a*) Notice of the situation of this office, and of any change, must be given to the registrar. 25 and 26 Vict. c. 89, § 39, 40. 46 and 47 Vict. c. 30 (Companies' Colonial Registers Act, 1883) provides for branch registers of members in colonies where companies transact business.

(*b*) 25 and 26 Vict. c. 89, § 32. Garpel Hæmatite Co., 1866; 4 Macph. 647.

(*c*) *Ib.* § 25. As to the penalty for failure, see § 25, 46.

(*d*) Waterhouse *v.* Jameson, 1868; 6 Macph. 591; rev. 1870, 8 Macph. H. L. 88; L. R. 2 Sc. App. 29. Nicol's Case (Burkinshaw *v.* Nicolls), L. R. 7 Ch. 533; 3 App. Ca. 1004; 47 L. J. Ch. 415; 48 *ib.* 179.

(*e*) Burkinshaw *v.* Nicolls, *cit.* Anderson's Case, 7 Ch. D. 75; 47 L. J. Ch. 273. Spargo's Case, L. R. 8 Ch. 60. White's Case, 12 Ch. D. 511; 48 L. J. Ch. 820. Barrow's Case, 14 Ch. D. 432; 49 L. J. Ch. 498. Coustonholm Paper Mills Liqr. *v.* Law, 1891; 18 R. 1076. Ooregum Gold Mg. Co. *v.* Roper, 1892; A. C. 125. Furness & Co. *v.* Cynthiana Liqrs., 1893; 21 R. 239. *In re* Eddystone Marine Ins. Co., 1893; 3 Ch. D. 9. *Ex p.* Welton, 1895; 1 Ch. D. 255. See Appleyard's Case, 18 Ch. D. 587; 50 L. J. Ch. 554.

(*f*) *Ib.* § 45. (*g*) *Ib.* § 26–29.

(*h*) *Ib.* § 37. As to share certificates, see below, § 403H (*a*).

(*i*) *Ib.* § 35. Ward & Henry's Case, L. R. 2 Ch. App. 431; 36 L. J. Ch. 462. *Ex p.* Parker, L. R. 2 Ch. App. 685. Sichell's Case, L. R. 3 Ch. App. 122; 37 L. J. Ch. 373. Stewart's Case, L. R. 1 Ch. App. 574. Kintrea's Case, 39 L. J. Ch. 193; L. R. 5 Ch. 95. Shaw *v.* City of Glasgow Bk., 1878; 6 R. 332. Prop. Inv. Co. *v.* Duncan, 1886; 14 R. 299. See *infra*, § 403J, 403P, 403R.

(*k*) Ward & Henry, *cit.* Blaikie *v.* Coats, 1893; 21 R. 150.

(*l*) 25 and 26 Vict. c. 89, § 30.

(*m*) See above, § 403C, note (*k*); below, § 403R, note (*f*).

(*n*) Soc. Gen. de Paris *v.* Walker, 14 Q. B. D. 424; aff. 11 App. Ca. 20. Bradford Bkg. Co. *v.* Briggs & Co., 31 Ch. D. 19; rev. 12 App. Ca. 29. As to competitions of assignees of unregistered shares, and the effect of notices, see Bradford Bkg. Co., *cit.* Shaw *v.* Cal. Ry. Co., *cit.*, *infra*, § 403J.

403G. 'Name of Company—Register of Mortgages, etc.—No company may be registered by the same name as an existing company, unless that company be in the course of dissolution and consents (*a*). Every limited company, besides having the word "limited" (and "reduced" for a certain time after a reduction in the capital has taken place) last in its name, must have its name affixed on the outside of every office or place where its business is carried on. Its name must also be engraved on the company's seal, and be mentioned in all notices, advertisements, bills, notes, indorsements, cheques, and orders for money or goods, bills of parcels, receipts, and letters of credit. Not only the company, but also its officers are liable for default in these matters; any officer making such default being personally liable for the amount of any such bill, etc., if not duly paid (*b*). Limited companies are also bound to keep registers, open to the inspection of creditors and members, of all mortgages and charges specifically affecting their property (*c*); and, while a mortgage or debenture is not void by reason that it is not duly registered (*d*), directors and officials are subject to penalties for permitting the omission of such entries. But the rule of construction for some time established in England, that such officials, being bound to see that the law is obeyed, are personally disqualified from enforcing a charge which is not registered, so long as it stands in their persons (*e*), is now negatived, at least in cases where there is no concealment (*f*). Limited banking and insurance companies (*g*), and deposit and benefit societies, must post in a conspicuous place in their registered and branch offices, and places of business, a statement of their liabilities and assets, the amount of capital and shares, etc., and must give a copy to every member and creditor of the company on payment of sixpence (*h*).'

(*a*) 25 and 26 Vict. c. 89, § 20. The name may be changed with consent of the Board of Trade, a new certificate being obtained, § 13. See also below, § 1361c.

(*b*) 25 and 26 Vict. c. 89, § 41, 42. 30 and 31 Vict. c. 131, § 10. Penrose *v.* Martyr, E. B. & E. 499.

(*c*) *Ib.* § 43.

(*d*) *Ex p.* Valpy & Chaplin, L. R. 7 Ch. 289, and cases in next note.

(*e*) *Ex p.* Valpy & Chaplin, *cit.* *In re* Winn Hall Colliery Co., L. R. 10 Eq. 515; 39 L. J. Ch. 695. *In re* Native Iron Co., 2 Ch. D. 345; 45 L. J. Ch. 577. Internat. Pulp Co. (Knowles's Mortgage), 6 Ch. D. 556. Globe Iron & Steel Co., 48 L. J. Ch. 295.

(*f*) Wright *v.* Horton, 12 App. Ca. 371. The Act requires registration of the property charged, so that it is necessary in case of a deposit. Smith's Case, 11 Ch. D. 579. As to debentures and the company's power to mortgage and to borrow, see Buckley, Companies Acts, 149 sqq. Lindley on Company Law, 187 sqq.

(*g*) Special provisions as to a deposit to be made before obtaining incorporation, statements of their accounts, etc., by life assurance companies, are made by 33 and 34 Vict. c. 61, and 35 and 36 Vict. c. 41.

(*h*) 25 and 26 Vict. c. 89, § 44.

403H. '**Directors, etc.**—The number, qualification, and powers of directors are generally defined by the articles of association. Generally speaking, they are the agents of the company, and bind it in all matters within the scope of their authority. Persons dealing with the directors or agents of the company are bound to acquaint themselves with the published constitution of the company, and the limits imposed by the deed of settlement or articles on the authority of the directors, but not with bye-laws or private limitations or instructions; and strangers are entitled to assume that the company business in regard to notices of meetings, resolutions, etc., is duly and regularly performed (*a*).

'The management of the company's affairs is confided to the directors, and they are under stringent obligations to perform their duties with diligence and integrity. Courts of Equity will entertain complaints against them at the instance of shareholders, and will restrain illegal or *ultra vires* acts, and require them to account (*b*), subject to the general rule that the company itself is the proper pursuer to recover its own money or property, and that the shareholder must first exhaust the means of redress provided by the constitution of the company (*c*); and they are liable to make good to shareholders losses incurred by their breach of trust or gross negligence (*d*).

'A director is, strictly speaking, a managing partner and not a trustee (*e*); yet, as in a sense he holds a fiduciary position, no director can take any benefit by dealing on behalf of the company with himself or any firm of which he is a partner (*f*); and he may be compelled to make over to the company any benefits so acquired for himself (*g*). Nor is he entitled to payment for work done for the company, unless there is a special contract for remuneration (*h*). The Court in a winding up has power to compel directors or managers to refund moneys misapplied, and to assess damages for misapplication or retention of the company's moneys, for misfeasance or breach of trust (*i*).

'They may also be made liable to third parties for loss in dealings with their company in consequence of material misrepresentations in fact made by them (*k*). And like other agents professing to bind their principals in matters beyond their powers, they are held to warrant their authority, and may be sued, not on the contract which they have made, but for damages for breach of the implied promise or warranty (*l*).'

(*a*) Heiton *v.* Waverley Hydr. Co., 1877; 4 R. 830. Ernest *v.* Nicholls, 6 H. L. Ca. 401. Fountaine *v.* Carmarthen Ry. Co., L. R. 5 Eq. 316; 37 L. J. Ch. 429. Royal Br. Bk. *v.* Turquand, 5 E. & B. 248; 6 *ib.* 327; 24 L. J. Q. B. 327; 25 *ib.* 317. Balfour *v.* Ernest, 5 C. B. N. S. 601; 28 L. J. C. P. 170. Mahony *v.* East Holyford Mining Co., L. R. 7 H. L. 869. Chapleo *v.* Brunswick Bdg. Soc., 6 Q. B. D. 696; 50 L. J. Q. B. 372. So the company is responsible for its servant's fraud in the issue of share certificates. Clavering, Son, & Co. *v.* Goodwins, Jardine, & Co., 1891; 18 R. 652.

(*b*) Wallworth *v.* Holt, 4 My. & C. 619. Harvey *v.* Bignold, 8 Beav. 343. See Maxtone *v.* Muir, 1845; 7 D. 1006.

(*c*) Foss *v.* Harbottle, 2 Hare, 461. Russell *v.* Wakefield Waterworks Co., L. R. 20 Eq. 474; 44 L. J. Ch. 496. Orr *v.* Glasg. & Airdrie Ry. Co., 1858, 20 D. 327; aff. 1860 3 Macq. 799. Lee *v.* Crawford, 1890; 17 R. 1094.

(*d*) Ferguson *v.* Wilson, L. R. 2 Ch. 90. Turquand *v.*

Marshall, L. R. 6 Eq. 112; 4 Ch. 376, 385; 37 L. J. Ch. 582; 38 L. J. Ch. 645. Leslie's Reprs. *v.* Lumsden, 1851; 14 D. 213; 1856, 18 D. 1046. North of Scotland Banking Co. *v.* Thomson, 1854; 16 D. 1011. Western Bank *v.* Bairds, 1862; 24 D. 859. Western Bank *v.* Baird's Trs., 1866; 4 Macph. 1071; 1872, 11 Macph. 96. Inglis *v.* Douglas, 1860; 22 D. 505. Collins *v.* North Br. Bank, 1850; 13 D. 349; 1 Macq. 369. Tulloch *v.* Davidson, 1858; 20 D. 1045, 1319; aff. 3 Macq. 783. Cullen *v.* Johnston, 1862; 4 Macq. 424; 24 D. H. L. 10; 1864, 3 Macph. 935. Gordon *v.* Davidson, 1864; 2 Macph. 758. Overend & Co. Lim. *v.* Gibb, 39 L. J. Ch. 45; 42 L. J. Ch. 67; L. R. 4 Ch. 701; 5 H. L. 480. Parker *v.* Lewis, L. R. 8 Ch. 1035. City of Glasgow Bk. *v.* Mackinnon, 1882; 9 R. 535. Lees *v.* Tod, 1882; 9 R. 807. Cal. Her. Sec. Co. *v.* Curror's Tr., 1882; 9 R. 1115.

(*e*) Forest of Dean Coal Co., 10 Ch. D. 450. Smith *v.* Anderson, 15 Ch. D. 247; 50 L. J. Ch. 39. Wilson *v.* L. Bury, 5 Q. B. D. 518; 50 L. J. Q. B. 90. Poole's Case, 9 Ch. D. 322; 48 L. J. Ch. 48.

(*f*) Aberdeen Ry. Co. *v.* Blaikie Bros., 1854; 1 Macq. 461; 17 D. H. L. 20; 26 Jur. 622. Benson *v.* Heathorn, 1 You. & C. C. C. 326. Imp. Merc. Credit Assur. *v.* Coleman, L. R. 6 Ch. 558; 6 H. L. 189; 40 L. J. Ch. 262; 42 *ib.* 644. Parker *v.* M'Kenna, L. R. 10 Ch. 96; 44 L. J. Ch. 425. Hay's Case, L. R. 10 Ch. 593; 44 L. J. Ch. 721. See § 1998, 2084, *infra*, and 222, 370, *supra*.

(*g*) Huntington Copper Co. *v.* Henderson, 1877; 4 R. 294; aff. 5 R. H. L. 1. Scot. Pacific Coast Min. Co. *v.* Falkner, Bell, & Co., 1888; 15 R. 290. *In re* Cape Breton Co., 29 Ch. D. 795; aff. (*nom.* Cavendish Bentinck *v.* Fenn) 12 App. Ca. 652. Ladywell Mining Co. *v.* Brooks, 35 Ch. D. 400. Cf. Erlanger *v.* New Sombrero Phosphate Co., 3 App. Ca. 1218; 48 L. J. Ch. 73. See above, § 222, 370, 403B *fin.*

(*h*) M'Naughton *v.* Brunton, 1882; 10 R. 111. Dunston *v.* Impl. Gaslight Co., 3 B. & Ad. 125. Evans *v.* Coventry, 8 De G. M. & G. 835; 25 L. J. Ch. 491. Hutton *v.* West Cork Ry. Co., 23 Ch. D. 654.

(*i*) 25 and 26 Vict. c. 89, § 165. Merc. Tradg. Co., Stringer's Case, 38 L. J. Ch. 698; L. R. 4 Ch. 475. County Marine Ins. Co., Rance's Case, 40 L. J. Ch. 277; L. R. 6 Ch. 104. City of Glasgow Bk. *v.* Mackinnon, 1882; 9 R. 535. Pearson's Case, 5 Ch. D. 336; 46 L. J. Ch. 339. Weston's Case, 10 Ch. D. 579; 48 L. J. Ch. 425. Ambrose Lake Tin Mining Co., 14 Ch. D. 390; 49 L. J. Ch. 457. **Bentinck** *v.* **Fenn,** 12 App. Ca. 652. Archer's Case, 1891; Ch. D. 322. As to their liability under § 165 for paying dividends out of capital, see *in re* National Funds Assur. Co., 10 Ch. D. 118; 48 L. J. Ch. 163. *In re* Exchange Bdg. Co., and *in re* Alexandra Palace Co., 51 L. J. Ch. 525, 655; 23 Ch. D. 297.

(*k*) Richardson *v.* Williamson, L. R. 6 Q. B. 276; 40 L. J. Q. B. 145. Cherry *v.* Col. Bank of Australia, 38 L. J. P. C. 49; L. R. 3 P. C. 24. **Beattie** *v.* **Lord Ebury,** L. R. 7 Ch. 777; 7 H. L. 102; 41 L. J. Ch. 392, 804; L. R. 7 Ch. 777; 44 L. J. Ch. 20. Edgington *v.* Fitzmaurice, 29 Ch. D. 459. See Chapleo *v.* Brunswick Ben. Bdg. Soc., 5 C. P. D. 331; 6 Q. B. D. 696; 50 L. J. Q. B. 372. Lees *v.* Tod, 1882; 9 R. 807 (see above, § 14 (*d*)).

(*l*) Authorities in § 225 (*a*), *supra*. Firbank's Exrs. *v.* Humphreys, 18 Q. B. D. 54.

403I. '**Calls.**—One of the most important powers of the directors is that of making calls, *i.e.* of requiring from shareholders payment of moneys due by them in respect of their shares. The liability of shareholders to calls depends on the deed of settlement, or the memorandum or articles of association (*a*). Under the Companies Act, and in most special Acts, the register is *primâ facie* evidence of membership; and in any action for calls it is enough to allege that the defender is a member of the company, and indebted in respect of a call or other moneys due, whereby right of action has accrued to the company (*b*). If calls be unpaid, the directors are generally empowered to declare the shares forfeited, but only where such power is expressly given by the regulations of the company, and the power given must be exercised with the strictest accuracy in complying with all conditions (*c*). In a judicial or voluntary winding up, the Court of Session may, on production by the liquidators of a signed list of contributories, stating the sums due by each, and the date when they became due, pronounce decree against such contributories without notice, to the same effect as if they had severally consented to registration, for execution on a charge of six days, of a legal obligation for payment of such calls and interest (*d*).'

(*a*) See Morice and Bon-Accord Assur. Co. *v.* Bell, 1850; 12 D. 1205. West of Scot. Malleable Iron Co. *v.* Buchanan, 1855; 17 D. 461. Barclay *v.* Lawrie, 1857; 19 D. 488. Watson *v.* Ayrshire Iron Co., 1859; 22 D. 167. Molleson *v.* Fraser's Trs., 1881; 8 R. 630.

(*b*) 25 and 26 Vict. c. 89, § 70. See Whitehaven and Furness Ry. Co. *v.* Bain, 1850; 12 D. 829; 1 Bell's App. 79. G. N. Ry. Co. *v.* Inglis, 1850; 12 D. 1194; 13 D. 1315; aff. 24 Jur. 434. Cal. Ry. Co. *v.* Crum, 1852; 14 D. 495. Drew *v.* Lumsden, 1865; 3 Macph. 384.

(*c*) 25 and 26 Vict. c. 89; Table A, art. 17-22. Clarke *v.* Hart, 6 H. L. Ca. 633. Johnson *v.* Lyttle's Iron Agency, 5 Ch. D. 687; 46 L. J. Ch. 786. See as to forfeitures, Spackman *v.* Evans, L. R. 3 H. L. 171; 37 L. J. Ch. 752. Houldsworth *v.* Evans, L. R. 3 H. L. 263; 37 L. J. Ch. 800. Evans *v.* Smallcombe, L. R. 3 H. L. 249; 37 L. J. Ch. 793, and the other cases *in re* the Agriculturist Cattle Insur. Co. summarised in Buckley's Companies Acts, 419 sqq.; and comp. Stewart's Trs. *v.* Evans, 1871; 9 Macph. 810. See also Ferguson *v.* Central Halls Co., 1881; 8 R. 997 (notice of call to forfeited shareholder not necessary). Mount Morgan Gold Mine *v.* M'Mahon, 1891; 18 R. 772 (forfeited shareholder may plead fraud in action for calls).

(*d*) *Ib.* § 121. It was held that this provision does not apply to calls made by the directors during the subsistence of the company and remaining unpaid; which are to be enforced by the liquidators under § 101 of the Act. Mitchell, Petr., 1863; 1 Macph. 1116. Benhar Coal Co., 1882; 9 R. 763. See Stone *v.* City and County Bank, 3 C. P. D. 282; 47 L. J. C. P. 681. Lumsden, Petr., 1858; 21 D. 110.

403J. '**Transfer of Shares.**— Companies registered under the earlier Joint-Stock Companies Acts may cause their shares to be transferred in the manner formerly in use, or in such other manner as the company may direct; and the shares of members of companies formed under the Act of 1862 may be transferred in the manner provided by the company's regulations (*a*). Unless express power is reserved to the directors to reject a proposed transfer, they have no discretion in the matter, a member having an absolute right to transfer his shares to any one he pleases, provided only the transfer be real and not merely nominal, and there be no trust or reservation of benefit to the transferor (*b*). In general, it is not till the transferee's name is placed on the register that he becomes a member, and the vendor's liability ceases (*c*). Under the Companies Acts, a company is required to register the transferee on the application of the transferor (*d*). In practice, a transfer should be accompanied by the share certificates; but even if it be, the company may delay registering the transfer for a reasonable time for inquiry (*e*). The company by issuing a share certificate is barred from denying that the person named in it is owner of the shares; and if the company cannot give the shares and register his transferee, it is liable in damages (*f*).'

(*a*) 25 and 26 Vict. c. 39, § 178, 22. See Table A, art. 8–16. See above, § 400. See Murray *v.* Bush, L. R. 6 Ch. 246; 6 H. L. 37; 42 L. J. Ch. 586. As to transfers signed and delivered to the transferee or another, blank, see Soc. Gen. de Paris *v.* Walker, *infra* (*e*). France *v.* Clark, 26 Ch. D. 257. Colonial Bk. *v.* Cordy & Williams, 15 App. Ca. 267 (delivery by executors).

(*b*) Weston's Case, L. R. 4 Ch. App. 20; 38 L. J. Ch. 41. Evans *v.* Wood, L. R. 5 Eq. 9. Moffat *v.* Farquhar, 7 Ch. D. 591; 47 L. J. Ch. 355. Bonnington Sugar Co. *v.* Thomson's Trs. (Cree *v.* Somervail), 1878; 6 R. 80; *ib.* H. L. 90; 4 App. Ca. 648. Shaw *v.* Cal. Ry. Co., 1888; 15 R. 504 (action by alleged transferor); 1890, 17 R. 466, 482. See Buckley's Companies Acts, 22 sqq.

(*c*) 25 and 26 Vict. c. 89, § 23, 25. See Murray *v.* Bush, *cit.* (*a*); and § 403F, 403R.

(*d*) 30 and 31 Vict. c. 131, § 26.

(*e*) Soc. Gen. de Paris *v.* Walker, 14 Q. B. D. 424; aff. 11 App. Ca. 20. Colonial Bank *v.* Whinney, 11 App. Ca. 426. As to damages for not registering, see Skinner *v.* City of London Mar. Ins. Co., 14 Q. B. D. 882.

(*f*) Tomkinson *v.* Balkis Consol. Co., 1893; A. C. 396.

403K. 'Liability of Shareholders.—Partners of joint-stock companies begin to be liable for its contracts and deeds only with the commencement of the company. They are not liable for contracts made before that time by the promoters, while the preliminaries are not completed, unless they become so by express adoption or acquiescence (*a*). When the partnership has begun, which in the case of registered companies takes place at registration (*b*), the partners are liable for all contracts with third parties made by its directors or agents in the usual course of business (*c*); but not, of course, for acts not sanctioned by the constitution of the company (*ultra vires*) (*d*). Members of a registered company are of course not liable as individuals upon the company's obligations beyond the amount of their shares if not paid up, or of their guarantee, except in the event of the company carrying on business for more than six months after the number of members is less than seven (*e*).'

(*a*) Mags. of Helensburgh *v.* Cal. Ry. Co., 1852; 15 D. 148; rev. 1856, 2 Macq. 391. Scott *v.* Money Order Co., 1870; 42 Sc. Jur. 212. Molleson, § 403I. Dickinson *v.* Valpy, 10 B. & C. 142; 3 Ross' L. C. 561; 34 R. R. 348. Hutton *v.* Thompson, 3 H. L. Ca. 161. Clark on Partnership, 292. The liability of promoters is a question of fact for a jury in the case of each individual, the issue of fact being whether he authorised his credit to be pledged for matters connected with the formation of the company. Smith's Merc. Law, 79, 80.

(*b*) 25 and 26 Vict. c. 89, § 18.

(*c*) Hawken *v.* Bourne, 8 M. & W. 703. *In re* County Life Assur. Co., L. R. 5 Ch. 288; 40 L. J. Ch. 471 (*de facto* directors).

(*d*) Mags. of Helensburgh, *cit.* (*a*). Edin. North. Tram. Co. *v.* Mann, 1891; 18 R. 1140; aff. 1893, A. C. 69; 20 R. H. L. 7.

(*e*) 25 and 26 Vict. c. 89, § 48.

403L. 'Bills and Notes granted by Companies.—A company cannot be bound by bills or notes, unless express authority to issue them in its name be given in the articles of association or deed of settlement, or the granting of such obligations be usual and necessary in the business carried on by the company (*a*). A bill or note is validly made, accepted, or indorsed by a company registered under the Act of 1862, if it is made, accepted, or indorsed in the name of the company, or by, on behalf, or on account of the company, by any person acting under its authority (*b*), provided always the company have power by its constitution to issue negotiable instruments (*c*).'

(*a*) Bramah *v.* Roberts, 3 Bing. N. C. 963. Steele *v.* Harmer, 14 M. & W. 831. Bank of Australasia *v.* Breillat, 6 Moo. P. C. 152. Peruvian Ry. Co. *v.* Thames, etc., Co., L. R. 2 Ch. App. 617; 36 L. J. Ch. 864. *In re* Land Credit Co. of Ireland, *ex p.* Overend, Gurney, & Co., L. R. 4 Ch. App. 460; 39 L. J. Ch. 27. Bateman *v.* Mid Wales Ry. Co., L. R. 1 C. P. 499; 35 L. J. C. P. 205.

(*b*) 25 and 26 Vict. c. 89, § 47. Gray *v.* Raper, L. R. 1 C. P. 694. Alexander *v.* Sizer, L. R. 4 Ex. 102; 38 L. J. Ex. 59. Cf. Ross, Skolfield, & Co. *v.* State Line Co., 1875; 3 R. 134.

(*c*) 25 and 26 Vict. c. 89, § 47. Peruvian Ry. Co., *supra* (*a*). See above, § 310, 321, 354. As to debentures in the form of promissory notes, see Imp. Land Co. of Marseilles, 40 L. J. Ch. 93; L. R. 11 Eq. 478; Crouch *v.* Credit Foncier Co., 42 L. J. Q. B. 183; L. R. 8 Q. B. 374.

403M. 'Winding up of Companies.—Many Acts, passed to facilitate the winding up and dissolution of companies, are superseded by the Companies Acts, 1862 and 1886, the latter of which applies to the liquidation of companies certain provisions of the Bankruptcy Act, 1856, as to the ranking of claims and to diligence (*a*). All companies registered under the Act of 1862 may be wound up under it, whether formed under it or not (*b*). Also all companies registered under the former Acts (*c*), and all other partnerships and companies consisting of more than seven members, may be wound up under the Act, but not voluntarily (*d*); except railway companies incorporated by Act of Parliament, and not falling within the operation of the Abandonment of Railways Act, 1850, as revived and amended by the later statutes on that subject (*e*). Provision is made for winding up industrial and provident societies and benefit building societies under the Companies Acts, the jurisdiction being in the Sheriff Court (*f*).'

(*a*) 49 Vict., c. 23.
(*b*) 25 and 26 Vict. c. 89, § 79.
(*c*) 19 and 20 Vict. c. 47; 20 and 21 Vict. c. 14; 20 and 21 Vict. c. 49; and 21 and 22 Vict. c. 91. See 25 and 26 Vict. c. 89, § 177–179.
(*d*) 25 and 26 Vict. c. 87, § 199. Aberdeen Provision Society, 1863; 2 Macph. 385.
(*e*) 13 and 14 Vict. c. 83. 30 and 31 Vict. c. 126. 32 and 33 Vict. c. 114.
(*f*) 56 and 57 Vict. c. 39, § 58. 37 and 38 Vict. c. 42, § 32, 34. 57 & 58 Vict. c. 47, § 8.

403N. 'Winding up of Unregistered Companies.—In the winding up of unregistered companies, every one who is liable to contribute to the liabilities of the company, to the adjustment of the rights of members, or to costs, is a contributory to the extent of such liability; or in the event of the death or bankruptcy of a contributory, or the marriage of a female contributory, the personal representatives, trustee, or husband are liable in terms of the provisions of the Act in regard to them (*a*). After the petition for winding up has been presented, and before an order, the Court may, on the application of any creditor, stay proceedings against any contributory or the company, and diligence against the company is void; and after an order no such proceedings for a company debt can be begun or continued without leave of the Court (*b*). By the order for winding up, or a subsequent order, the property and estates of the company may be vested in the liquidators, who may then, after finding such security as the Court requires, raise and defend all actions necessary for realising the effects of the company (*c*). When the company's affairs have been completely wound up, the Court makes an order that the company be dissolved (*d*). Winding up may be ordered by the Court of Session in the case of an unregistered company when it is dissolved, or has ceased to carry on business, or is carrying it on only for the purpose of winding up; whenever it is unable to pay its debts; or when the Court thinks it just and equitable that it should be wound up (*e*).'

(*a*) 25 and 26 Vict. c. 89, § 200, and § 76–78.
(*b*) *Ib.* § 201, 202, 85, 163.
(*c*) *Ib.* § 203, 92–97.
(*d*) *Ib.* § 111.
(*e*) *Ib.* § 199.

403O. 'Winding up of Registered Companies.—Registered companies are wound up—1*st*, by the Court; 2*nd*, voluntarily by the company; or, 3*rd*, voluntarily under the supervision of the Court. It is incompetent to sequestrate the estates of a registered company under the Bankruptcy Act (*a*). Winding up may be ordered by the Court of Session, when a special resolution has been passed to that effect; when the company does not begin business for a year from its incorporation, or suspends business for a year; when the membership is reduced below seven; when it cannot pay its debts (which in Scotland means when the company neglects for more than three weeks, after service of a formal demand under the creditor's hand, to pay or satisfy a debt of more than £50, whenever the *induciæ* of a charge have expired without payment having been made, or when it is proved to the satisfaction of the Court that it is unable to pay its debts (*b*)); when the Court is of opinion that it is just and equitable that it should be wound up (*c*). Although the last clause can be properly applied only to cases *ejusdem generis* with the cases preceding, it has been liberally interpreted to include a power to wind up where the intended business has become practically impossible, as by the failure of the title to a mine, or the failure to obtain a patent (*d*).'

(*a*) Standard Prop. Invest. Co. *v.* Dunblane Hydrop. Co., 1884; 12 R. 328. But such a company may be made notour bankrupt to the effect of equalising diligence and reducing preferences. Clark *v.* Hinde, Milne, & Co., 1884; 12 R. 347.

(*b*) *Ib.* § 80. *In re* Gold Hill Mines Co., 23 Ch. D. 510. *In re* Milford Dock Co., 23 Ch. D. 292. Macdonell's Trs. *v.* Oregonian Ry. Co., 1884; 11 R. 912. Cuninghame *v.* Walkinshaw Oil Co., 1886; 14 R. 87. Comml. Bk. *v.* Lanark Oil Co., 1886; 14 R. 147. Gardner & Co. *v.* Link, 1894; 21 R. 967.

(*c*) *Ib.* § 79. Suburban Hotel Co., L. R. 2 Ch. 737; 36 L. J. Ch. 710. Anglo-Amer. Brush Electric Co. *v.* Scot. Brush Electric Co., 1882; 9 R. 972.

(*d*) Haven Gold Mining Co., 20 Ch. D. 151; 51 L. J. Ch. 242. German Date Coffee Co., 20 Ch. D. 169; 51 L. J. Ch. 564. Suburban Hotel Co., *cit.*

403P. 'Petition for Winding up, and Effect.—Winding up by the Court proceeds on a petition by the company, or a creditor, or a contributory (subject to certain limitations (*a*)), or by all or any of these (*b*). After the winding up has begun, and indeed from the date of "stopping payment" or of declared and irretrievable insolvency (*c*), all dispositions of the company's property, and alterations in the status of members, and all transfers of shares, are void, unless the Court orders otherwise (*d*); and as all the creditors have then acquired a title and interest to enforce the personal liability of all shareholders on the register, it is too late for any shareholder to rescind his contract to take shares for fraud of the company (*e*). All proceedings may be stayed, and an interm liquidator may be appointed (*f*). Until a liquidator is appointed, the company's property is held to be in the custody of the Court, which may order inspection of the papers by a contributory or creditor (*g*). After an order for winding up, actions and proceedings against the company can only be proceeded with by leave of the Court (*h*). The winding up may be stayed on the motion of a contributory or creditor, and meetings of the creditors and contributories may be held in order to ascertain their wishes, to which, when proved by sufficient evidence, the Court may have regard (*i*). In order to determine the validity of conveyances, mortgages, etc., of the company's property, the date of presentment of the petition for winding up is equivalent to bankruptcy (*k*).'

(*a*) 30 and 31 Vict. c. 131, § 40. Martin *v.* Scot. Savings Inv. Soc., 1879; 7 R. 352. Chapel House Coll. Co., 24 Ch. D. 259. See Gardner & Co. *v.* Link, *cit.*

(*b*) 25 and 26 Vict. c. 89, § 82, 84.

(*c*) Muir *v.* City of Glasgow Bk., 1878; 6 R. 392; aff. 1879, *ib.* H. L. 21; 4 App. Ca. 337, and other City Bank cases in those years.

(*d*) 25 and 26 Vict. c. 89, § 153. Rudge *v.* Bowman, L. R. 3 Q. B. 689. Wiltshire Iron Co., *ex p.* Pearson, L. R. 3 Ch. Ap. 443. Barned's Banking Co., L. R. 3 Ch. Ap. 105. Benhar Coal Co., 1879; 6 R. 707.

(*e*) Oakes *v.* Turquand, Tennent *v.* City of Glasgow Bk., and other cases cited above, § 13A, note (*b*), 403B. Edin. Employers, etc., Co. *v.* Griffiths, 1892; 19 R. 550 (circular proposing to remove names of new shareholders not accepted before winding up).

(*f*) 25 and 26 Vict. c. 89, § 85, 151, 163, 201, 202. Benhar Coal Co. *v.* Sime, 1878; 6 R. 316; 1879, *ib.* 706. As to diligence, New Glenduffhill Coal Co. *v.* Muir & Co., 1882; 10 R. 372. Gardner *v.* Hughes, 1883; 10 R. 1138. *In re* Vron Coll. Co., 20 Ch. D. 442; 51 L. J. Ch. 389.

(*g*) *Ib.* § 92, 158. (*h*) *Ib.* § 87. See above (*f*).

(*i*) *Ib.* § 98, 91. See cases tabulated in Buckley's Companies Acts, p. 232.

(*k*) *Ib.* § 164.

403Q. 'The Official Liquidator or Liquidators are appointed and removed, and their powers, remuneration, and the amount of security to be found by them, are fixed by the Court (*a*); or, with certain limitations, by the Lord Ordinary to whom the liquidation is remitted, or in vacation by the Lord Ordinary on the Bills (*b*). Under the sanction of the Court, or by special order without the sanction or intervention of the Court, they may appoint solicitors or law agents to assist them; compromise all claims by or against the company (*c*); sue and defend in its name; carry on its business so far as necessary for the beneficial winding up of the company (*d*); sell its property; and do all other things, including the making and indorsing of bills, necessary for winding up the company and distributing its assets (*e*). The liquidator differs from the trustee in a sequestration, in being merely administrator for the company, in which its property is still vested, while the trustee has an independent title to the bankrupt estate, which is absolutely vested in him (*f*). The liquidator is bound by the company's constitution and its acts and deeds; and so, for instance, where the shares are said, in the articles and memorandum and certificate of registration granted to *bonâ fide* purchasers of shares, to be entirely or to a great extent paid up, he is not entitled, in settling the list of contributories, to make such a purchaser liable beyond the amount, if any, so stated to be payable (*g*).'

(*a*) 25 and 26 Vict. c. 89, § 92, 93. See Western Bank *v.* Douglas, 1860; 22 D. 447 (appointment of liquidators not joint—powers of liquidators). Brightwen & Co. *v.* City of Glasgow Bk., 1878; 6 R. 244. City of Glas. Bk. Liqrs., 1880; 7 R. 1196 (remuneration). Lysons *v.* Liqr. Miraflores Synd., 1895; 22 R. 605 (removal—personal interest).

(*b*) 49 and 50 Vict. c. 23, § 5, 6.

(*c*) A majority of creditors, or of a class of creditors, may bind a minority in regard to a compromise, statutory provisions being complied with. 25 and 26 Vict. c. 89, § 136, 159, 160. 33 and 34 Vict. c. 104. California Redwood Co.,

1885; 13 R. 335; and cases in Buckley, 291, 345 sqq., 515 sqq. In reporting to the Court, the liquidator is bound to state all material facts affecting the compromise, and if he fails to do so, the compromise may be reduced. D. & W. Henderson & Co. *v.* Stewart, 1894; 22 R. 155.

(*d*) Burntisland Oil Co. Liqr. *v.* Dawson, 1892; 20 R. 180. Wreck Recovery Co., 15 Ch. D. 353.

(*e*) 25 and 26 Vict. c. 89, § 95–97, 157, 159, 160. Collie *v.* Cruickshank, 1865; 3 Macph. 1064. He may be liable in the expenses of litigation, although he should have no funds of the company in his hands. Consold. Copper Co. of Canada *v.* Peddie, 1877; 5 R. 413 (2nd Div.). But see Buckley, Companies Acts, 243, for a statement of the practice.

(*f*) Gray *v.* Benhar Coal Co., 1881; 9 R. 225. Clark *v.* West Calder Oil Co., 1882; 9 R. 1017.

(*g*) Jamieson *v.* Waterhouse, 1868; 6 Macph. 591; rev. 1870, 8 Macph. H. L. 88; L. R. 2 Sc. Ap. 29.

403R. '**Contributories.**—The ascertainment of the contributories, or the persons liable for the debts of the company, is the most important part of the proceedings in a winding up. After the order for winding up has been made, the Court settles a list of contributories, distinguishing those who are so in their own names, and those who are so as representing others (*a*). In doing so, the Court may rectify the register of members (*b*). We have seen that after winding up begins it is too late to rectify the register on the ground of the company's fraud in inducing a person to take shares (*c*). But in a winding up one may have his name removed from the register on the ground that he was incapable of contracting, *e.g.* as a pupil (*d*), that he had never agreed to be a partner or shareholder (*e*), or had agreed under a condition prestable by the company that had not been fulfilled (*f*), or that his shares had been forfeited (*g*), or regularly and validly transferred to another who should, and, but for the company's delay or default, would have been registered in respect of them (*h*). On the other hand, the Court will rectify the register by putting upon it the names of persons who have agreed to take shares, either originally (*i*), or upon a transfer (*k*), or whose names have been improperly removed from it (*l*).

'In the case of a registered company, it is the present and past members, or their representatives, who become contributories. When the company is not limited, or when the full amount of the shares is not paid up, each of these members, or his representatives, becomes liable, by being placed on this list, to contribute to such an amount as may be required for payment of debts, costs of winding up, and adjustment of the rights of the contributories *inter se*; but no past member is bound to contribute if he has ceased to be a member a year before the winding up began, or in respect of any liability incurred after he ceased to be a member, or if the present members are able to make up the contributions required, or in a limited company beyond the amount unpaid on his share (*m*).'

(*a*) 25 and 26 Vict. c. 89, § 98, 99.

(*b*) *Ib.* § 98, 35. See above, § 403F *fin.*

(*c*) See above, § 13A, 403B, 403P.

(*d*) Curtis's Case, L. R. 6 Eq. 455; 37 L. J. Ch. 629. Lumsden's Case, L. R. 4 Ch. 31 (affirmance after majority), and cases in Buckley, Companies Acts, p. 38 sqq. See Hill *v.* City of Glasgow Bk., 1879; 7 R. 68.

(*e*) See the Act, § 23, and cases in Buckley's Notes, p. 53 sqq. Lumsden *v.* Buchanan, 1864; 2 Macph. 695; 1865, 3 Macph. H. L. 89; 37 Sc. Jur. 516; 4 Macq. 950. Ker *v.* City of Glasgow Bk., 1879; 6 R. 575; aff. *ib.* H. L. 52; 4 App. Ca. 598. Lindsay's Curator *v.* City of Glasgow Bk., 1879; 6 R. 671. Gillespie *v.* City of Glasgow Bk., 1879; 6 R. 813, and other City of Glasgow Bank cases in 6 Rettie. Cases in § 403C, note (*d*).

(*f*) Pellatt's Case, L. R. 2 Ch. 527; 36 L. J. Ch. 613. *Ex p.* Elkington, L. R. 2 Ch. 571; 36 L. J. Ch. 593. Simpson's Case, L. R. 4 Ch. App. 184; 39 L. J. Ch. 121. Dougan's Case, L. R. 8 Ch. 540; 42 L. J. Ch. 460, and cases in Buckley, p. 58 sqq. Gardiners *v.* Victoria Estates Co., 1885; 12 R. 1356. See *ex p.* Black, Hawthorn, & Co., L. R. 8 Ch. 254; 42 L. J. Ch. 404. As to the proof and presumptions as to assent in the case of trustees and executors, see the cases in § 403C *fin.*

(*g*) *In re* Financial Corpn. (King's Case), L. R. 2 Ch. 714.

(*h*) See § 403F *in fine*, and Buckley, 117–119. Shepherd's Case, L. R. 2 Ch. 16; 36 L. J. Ch. 32. Shewell's Case, 2 Ch. 387; 36 L. J. Ch. 353. Shaw *v.* City of Glasgow Bk., 1878; 6 R. 332. Mitchell *v.* City of Glasgow Bk., 1878; 6 R. 439; aff. 1879, *ib.* H. L. 60; 4 App. Ca 548. Nelson Mitchell *v.* City of Glasgow Bk., 1878; 6 R. 420; aff. *ib.* H. L. 66; 4 App. Ca. 624. The rule is that a man is not relieved from being a contributory by selling his shares, if owing either to his own neglect or that of his transferee, or to any cause except the delay or default of the company, the transferee's name has not been substituted for his at the time of the winding up. *Per* Giffard, V.-C., in Marshall *v.* Glamorgan Iron Co., L. R. 7 Eq. 129; 38 L. J. Ch. 69. See Buckley, pp. 110, 119. But when a seller has done all that he is bound to do to transfer the property in his shares to the purchaser, the latter or the intermediate jobber is (subject to the usages of the Stock Exchange if the sale is effected there) under an implied contract to indemnify him for loss arising from his name being left on the register. Walker *v.* Bartlett, 18 C. B. 863; 25 L. J. C. P. 263. Wynne *v.* Price, 2 De G. & S. 310. Hawkins *v.* Maltby, L. R. 4 Ch. 200; 38 L. J. Ch. 313. Coles *v.* Bristowe, L. R. 4 Ch. 3; 38 L. J. Ch. 81. Grissell *v.* Bristowe, L. R. 4 C. P. 36; 38 L. J. C. P. 10. Nickalls *v.* Merry, L. R. 7 H. L. 530; 45 L. J. Ch. 575, and other cases cited in Addison, Contr. 871 sqq. Buckley, Companies Acts, 121 sqq. 1 Smith's L. C. 612.

(*i*) See the Act, § 23; above, § 403C.

(*k*) See the Act, § 22; above, § 403J. Allan *v.* Wright, etc., 1853; 15 D. 725. Howe *v.* City of Glasgow Bk., 1879; 6 R. 1194.

(*l*) Curtis's Case, L. R. 6 Eq. 455; 37 L. J. Ch. 629. Spackman *v.* Evans, L. R. 3 H. L. 171; 37 L. J. Ch. 752.

(*m*) 25 and 26 Vict. c. 89, § 196, 200, 38. Blakely Ordnance Co., Brett's Case, 40 L. J. Ch. 497; 43 L. J. Ch. 47; L. R. 6 Ch. 800; 8 Ch. 800. See as to directors, 30 and 31 Vict. c. 131, § 5. Barned's Banking Co., Andrews' Case, 3 Ch.

App. 161; 37 L. J. Ch. 87. The Contract Corpn., Weston's Case, L. R. 6 Eq. 17. Brett's Case, *cit.* Webb *v.* Whiffin, H. L. 42 L. J. Ch. 161; L. R. 5 H. L. 711.

403S. 'No one can be made to contribute to the liabilities of a company limited by shares, or by guarantee, beyond the amount unpaid on the shares, or the shares and guarantee, except that the partners of a limited banking company are liable for the amount of notes issued, over and above their limited liability for the other obligations of the company (*a*). Policies of insurance and other contracts may restrict the liability of partners, or restrict the obligation to the funds of the company (*b*). The debt of a contributory arises when the liability commences, but it is payable only when calls are made. So, in the event of his bankruptcy during the subsistence of the winding up, the liquidator may claim for the estimated value of his liability to future calls, and his trustee becomes a contributory in the winding up (*c*). Various provisions are made with regard to sums due by the company to its members, and the pleading of compensation thereon (*d*), the adjustment of the rights of contributories *inter se* (*e*), the enforcement of orders, and the payment of calls. When the winding up is concluded, the Court orders the dissolution of the company, which is reported by the liquidator to the registrar. When it is minuted by the registrar, the company is dissolved (*f*).'

(*a*) 25 and 26 Vict. c. 89, § 8, 9, 38, 182. Directors of limited companies may, if so provided by the memorandum of association, have unlimited liability; 30 and 31 Vict. c. 131, § 4 and 5. See as to the power to have some shares fully paid up, and some not, 30 and 31 Vict. c. 131, § 24. Observe that shares are not paid up unless paid up in *cash*. See above, § 403F.

(*b*) *Ib.* § 3.

(*c*) *Ib.* § 75, 77. Martin's Pat. Anchor Co. *v.* Morton, L. R. 3 Q. B. 206; 37 L. J. Q. B. 98. Hastie's Case, L. R. 7 Eq. 3; 4 Ch. 274; 38 L. J. Ch. 43, 233. Lindley on Partn., 641, 1117, 1180, 1368. Buckley, Companies Acts, 175 sqq. These clauses apply to *contributories*, and therefore, it is thought, not to shareholders becoming bankrupt before liquidation. As to these, see Buckley and Lindley, *citt.* Taylor *v.* Union Her. Sec. Co., 1889; 16 R. 711.

(*d*) The Act, § 38 (7), 101, etc. Grissell's Case, 35 L. J. Ch. 752; L. R. 1 Ch. 528. *Ex p.* Black, Hawthorn, & Co., 42 L. J. Ch. 404; L. R. 8 Ch. 254. Whitehouse & Co.'s Case, 9 Ch. D. 595; 47 L. J. Ch. 801. Cowan *v.* Gowans, 1878; 5 R. 581. Cowan *v.* Shaw, *ib.* 680.

(*e*) See Pell's Case, L. R. 5 Ch. 11. Anglesea Colliery Co., L. R. 1 Ch. 555. Paterson v. Macfarlane, 1875; 2 R. 490.

(*f*) 25 and 26 Vict. c. 89, § 111, 118.

403T. '**Voluntary Winding up** (*a*) may take place—1*st*, when the period of duration fixed by the articles of association expires, or the event occurs upon which, under such articles, dissolution is to take place, and the company has passed a resolution requiring it to be voluntarily wound up; 2*nd*, when the company has passed a special resolution requiring it to be voluntarily wound up; 3*rd*, when it has passed an extraordinary resolution that it cannot, by reason of its liabilities, continue its business, and that it is advisable to wind it up (*b*). A voluntary winding up commences at the date of the resolution authorising it (*c*). After the resolution, the company can only carry on its business so far as necessary for the purpose of winding up; and transfers of shares are invalid without the sanction of the liquidators; but it retains the status of a corporation till the conclusion of the winding up (*d*). The resolution being intimated in the *Gazette*, liquidators are appointed, and their remuneration fixed, at a general meeting, or by the creditors or a committee of creditors, under an extraordinary resolution to that effect (subject to a power of removal by the Court on motion by a contributory); a list of contributories, which is *primâ facie* evidence of liability, is settled by the liquidators; calls are made by them, debts paid, the assets (if there be a surplus) distributed amongst the members according to their rights and interests in the company (*e*), and the rights of contributories adjusted (*f*). Arrangements sanctioned by extraordinary resolution bind the company, and (if acceded to by three-fourths in number and value) the creditors also, subject to a right of appeal to the Court by any contributory or creditor. On application by a liquidator or contributory, the Court may determine any question or exercise any power competent to it under a winding up by the Court (*g*). Liquidators, with the sanction of an extraordinary resolution, may compromise questions with creditors, contributories, or debtors of the company (*h*). Notwithstanding the existence of a voluntary winding up, a creditor, but not a shareholder, may have the company wound up by the Court, if the Court thinks that his rights will be prejudiced by a voluntary winding up (*i*).'

(*a*) National Savings Bank Assoc., L. R. 1 Ch. App. 553; 35 L. J. Ch. 808.

(*b*) 25 and 26 Vict. c. 89, § 129. Wilson *v.* M'Genn & Co., 1876; 3 R. 474. Sdeuard *v.* Gardner, 1876; 3 R. 577. Lawson Seed, etc., Co. *v.* Lawson & Son, 1886; 14 R. 154. Monkland Iron Co. *v.* Dun, 1886; 14 R. 242.

(c) *Ib.* § 130. (d) *Ib.* § 131.
(e) Birch *v.* Cropper (*in re* Bridgewater Nav. Co.), 39 Ch. D. 1 ; rev. 14 App. Ca. 525.
(*f*) *Ib.* § 132-141.
(*g*) *Ib.* § 136-138. See Sdeuard *v.* Gardner, 1876 ; 3 R. 577. (Section 138 gives no power as under secs. 87 and 163 to stay proceedings by creditors or diligence.) Comp. Gardner *v.* Hughes, 1883 ; 10 R. 1138.
(*h*) *Ib.* § 159, 160. Lama Coal Co., Miller's Case, L. R. 2 Ch. 692 ; 36 L. J. Ch. 837. *In re* Dynevor Duffryn Collieries Co., 11 Ch. D. 605 ; 48 L. J. Ch. 314. See above, § 403Q.
(*i*) *Ib.* § 145, 146. Bank of Gibraltar and Malta, L. R. 1 Ch. 69 ; 35 L. J. Ch. 39. *In re* Gold Co., 11 Ch. D. 707 ; 48 L. J. Ch. 281.

403U. ' Voluntary Winding up under Supervision of the Court. — When a voluntary winding up has begun, it may, upon petition, and at the discretion of the Court, be continued under the supervision of the Court, in which case the date of the winding up is held to be that of the resolution to wind up voluntarily (*a*). The effect of such a winding up is similar to that of an order for winding up by the Court, but the Court cannot do everything it could do under a compulsory winding up (*b*).'

(*a*) 25 and 26 Vict. c. 89, § 130, 147 sqq. Weston's Case, L. R. 4 Ch. App. 20. Bank of Gibraltar and Malta, *cit.* Beaujolais Wine Co., L. R. 3 Ch. 15. Brightwen *v.* City of Glasgow Bk., 1878 ; 6 R. 244. Wilson *v.* Hadley, 1879 ; 7 R. 178. Mollison & Co., 1882 ; 9 R. 509. Gardner *v.* Hughes, 1883 ; 10 R. 1138. Clark *v.* Hinde, Milne, & Co., 1884 ; 12 R. 347.
(*b*) *Ib.* Anglo-Italian Bank, L. R. 2 Q. B. 452. Stringer's Case, 38 L. J. Ch. 698 ; L. R. 4 Ch. 475. Beaujolais Co., *cit.* Sdeuard, *cit.* In England, general orders and rules for the conduct of proceedings under the Companies Act have been made, under the authority of the Acts, by the Lord Chancellor, Master of Rolls, and a Vice-Chancellor. Gen. Orders, Nov. 1862 and March 1867 ; Buckley's Comp. Acts, 562, 613. No Act of Sederunt has been passed by the Court of Session ; but liquidators are held to have the same powers as trustees on bankrupt estates (*ib.* § 171).

CHAPTER XI

OF AFFREIGHTMENT

404. Object of Maritime Contracts. — In those contracts and arrangements which relate to the maritime branch of the carrying trade, the object is not only to provide for the safe carriage of merchandise, but also to preserve to the merchant the full power of disposal in sale or mortgage during the transit; to provide for the necessities and accidents which may fall out during the voyage, or at its termination; and to indemnify the merchant or the shipowner for any loss which may arise from the perils of the sea or enemy. The subject may therefore be considered in relation to the contract of carriage or affreightment; to the partial loss during the voyage by jettison or salvage; to the contracts with the carpenters, seamen, and others, for the repairs and management of the ship; and to the indemnity by insurance of total or partial loss during the voyage. The contract of affreightment will be here explained; the other subjects hereafter.

'*Maritime Law.*—In all Admiralty causes, which are causes having reference to shipping, or to contracts or dealings connected with shipping, such as the Courts of Admiralty in Scotland (*a*) and England had jurisdiction to entertain, the law is the same in Scotland and England (*b*).'

(*a*) See Ersk. i. 3. 33.

(*b*) 1 Bell's Com. 546 sqq. (550, M'L.'s ed.). M'Knight *v.* Currie, 1896; A. C. 97. See also Brodie's Suppl. to Stair, p. 547 sq.; ch. ii. (Of Shipping) *passim.* Smith's Merc. Law, Introd. Blairmore Co. *v.* Macredie, 1897; 25 R. 893.

405. Definition and Constitution of Affreightment.—Affreightment is a contract of hiring or location, by which an entire ship, or part of it, is let on hire for the carriage of goods or of persons (*a*), or for some other lawful use to which it may be applied. It is a consensual contract, which requires writing only so far as a stamp is imposed (*b*), and of course is not confined to any particular form of words. Either a regular charter-party is made out; or an engagement less formal, by letter, or by heads of agreement signed by the parties, is sufficient; and often affreightment, especially when not of the whole ship, is left to depend on the bill of lading alone. The affreightment may be of the whole ship, either on time or for the voyage; or of a part, either by the owners of the ship, or by sub-affreightment (*c*) from one by whom the whole ship is freighted from the owners. 'It is a question of intention to be determined by construing the charter-party as a whole, whether in the phraseology of the English law there is a "demise" or "bailment" of the ship, *i.e.* whether the owner has parted with the possession and control of the ship and placed her entirely in the disposal of the charterer, the master and seamen being his servants; or he has merely contracted to carry by his ship and mariners the charterer's goods, or those of persons dealing with him as sub-freighters (*d*). In the former case the charterer assumes to third parties, whether or not aware of the charter-party (*e*), all the liabilities of an owner (*f*). In the latter case, while the charterer may be entitled to employ the ship as a general ship for his own profit, and the master, in signing bills of lading, does so as the charterer's agent and not the owner's, the owner remains in the legal possession of the ship, and thus, on the one hand, may exercise a lien for freight, even though he has no direct action against the shippers of goods dealing with the charterer (*g*), and, on the other hand, may incur liability for repairs and supplies (*h*), or for the negligence of the master and crew both to passengers and shippers of goods and to strangers injured by collision (*i*).'

(*a*) The hire of a whole ship or passage in a ship, for the conveyance of a family or company of persons or an individual, is regulated by the same principles with freight for carriage of goods. But it has been thought expedient to put this contract under special regulations, for greater safety and accommodation. The statutes on this subject, including the Merchant Shipping Act, 1854 (17 and 18 Vict. c. 104, § 291 sqq.), and amending Acts, have been repealed, and the present special rules as to passenger and emigrant ships are in the Merchant Shipping Act, 1894 (57 and 58 Vict. c. 60, § 267–368). Maclachlan on Merchant Shipping, ch. vii.

(*b*) Lidgett *v.* Williams, 4 Hare, 456; 1 Parsons on Shipping, 274.

(*c*) As to this term, see Youle *v.* Cochrane, 1868; 6 Macph. 427 (*per* L. Pr. Inglis).

(*d*) Christie *v.* Lewis, 2 B. & B. 410; 23 R. R. 483 (overruling Hutton *v.* Bragg, 7 Taunt. 14, and other cases). Belcher *v.* Capper, 4 M. & Gr. 502. Newberry *v.* Colvin, 7 Bing. 107; 1 C. & F. 283; 33 R. R. 437. Meiklereid *v.* West, 1 Q. B. D. 428. Baumwoll Manufactur *v.* Furness, 1893; A. C. 9. Manchester Trust *v.* Furness, 1895; 2 Q. B. 539. See below, § 1423. Tudor's L. C. 695. Maclachlan on Shipping, 347.

(*e*) Baumwoll Manufactur *v.* Furness, *cit.* In Sandeman *v.* Scurr, L. R. 2 Q. B. 86; 36 L. J. Q. B. 38; and other cases where notice has been regarded as important, the demise was not total, and the master, etc., had not become to all effects servants of the charterer. See Manchester Trust *v.* Furness, *cit.*

(*f*) Frazer *v.* Marsh, 13 East, 238; 2 Camp. 517; 12 R. R. 336. Belcher *v.* Capper, and Newberry *v.* Colvin, *citt.* Reeve *v.* Davis, 1 A. & E. 312. Trinity House *v.* Clark, 4 M. & S. 238.

(*g*) See below, § 410.

(*h*) See Maclachlan on Shipping, 111 and 342, and below, § 448.

(*i*) Christie *v.* Lewis, *cit.* Saville *v.* Campion, 2 B. & A. 503; 21 R. R. 376. Preston *v.* Tamplin, 26 L. J. Ex. 346; 2 H. & N. 363. Dean *v.* Hogg, 4 M. & S. 188; 10 Bing. 345. Schuster *v.* M'Kellar, 26 L. J. Q. B. 281; 7 E. & B. 704. Marquand *v.* Banner, 6 E. & B. 232; 25 L. J. Q. B. 313. Fenton *v.* Dublin Stpkt. Co., 8 Ad. & E. 843. Steel *v.* Lester, 3 C. P. D. 121; 47 L. J. C. P. 43. Wagstaffe *v.* Anderson, 4 C. P. D. 283; 5 *ib.* 171; 49 L. J. C. P. 485. Youle *v.* Cochrane, 1868; 6 Macph. 427. (Comp. Tharsis Sulphur Co. *v.* Culliford, 22 W. R. 46.) Mitchell *v.* Burn, 1874; 1 R. 900.

406. Charter-Party.—A charter-party is the written instrument in which the contract of affreightment is formally expressed; specifying the ship in whole or in part; the term during which the ship is let, by time or voyage; the hire or freight; the time of loading and unloading; and the charge to be allowed for detention or demurrage. 'Charter-parties are generally on printed forms, blanks being filled up with particulars as to the voyage contemplated. The written words indicate the main purpose of the voyage, and in construction it is legitimate to limit and control the words used in print by the written words selected by the parties themselves (*a*).' This instrument requires a stamp (*b*).

(*a*) Robertson *v.* French, 4 East, 135; 7 R. R. 535. **Glynn *v.* Margetson**, 1893; A. C. 350.

(*b*) 55 Geo. III. c. 78, Sched. part 1. The stamp is 6d., which may be denoted by an adhesive stamp, to be cancelled by the person last executing the instrument; or in the case of charter-parties executed abroad, adhibited and cancelled by any party thereto within ten days after it is received in the United Kingdom, and before it is executed by any one in the United Kingdom. Afterstamping by impressed stamp is competent only within a month after the first execution of the deed. See 54 and 55 Vict. c. 39, § 49–51 and Sched.; the Belfort, L. R. 9 P. D. 215.

407. The charter-party is executed by the owners or their accredited agent (sometimes also by the master) if hired at the owner's residence; abroad by the master alone, or by an agent duly authorised (*a*). It identifies the ship by its name (*b*), the name of the master, the burden or tonnage register measurement, and the place where the ship is at the time (*c*). But the tonnage stated in description is not conclusive between the parties as to the ship's capacity for carriage (*d*); and if it is intended to confine the engagement on either side to a certain tonnage, it must be specified distinctly, and the owners will be bound to that extent (*e*).

(*a*) As to charter-parties by agents, see above, § 224A. Maclachlan on Shipping, 355–360.

(*b*) As to national character, see Lothian *v.* Henderson, 1803; 4 Pat. 484; 3 B. & P. 499; 7 R. R. 829. A specification in the charter-party of the ship's class (at Lloyd's or otherwise) is only a warranty that she possesses such class at the time of executing the agreement. Hurst *v.* Osborne, 18 C. B. 144; 25 L. J. C. P. 209. Routh *v.* Macmillan, 33 L. J. Ex. 38; 2 H. & C. 750. French *v.* Newgass, 3 C. P. D. 163; 47 L. J. C. P. 361. A sailing vessel with an auxiliary screw is not properly described as a steamship. Fraser *v.* Telegr. Constr. Co., L. R. 7 Q. B. 566; 41 L. J. Q. B. 249.

(*c*) Non-compliance with a descriptive statement in a charter-party, as of the place where the ship is, makes the contract voidable, or entitles to damages, according as it is to be construed as a condition precedent, or a collateral agreement or warranty. Behn *v.* Burness, 3 B. & S. 753; 32 L. J. Q. B. 204. Neill *v.* Whitworth, 34 L. J. C. P. 155; 18 C. B. N. S. 435. Corkling *v.* Massey, L. R. 8 C. P. 395; 42 L. J. C. P. 153. Livingston, Conner, & Co. *v.* Calder & Co., 1891; 2 Sel. Sh. Ct. Ca. 542. Bentsen *v.* Taylor, 1893; 2 Q. B. 274 (waiver—damages). See below, § 408 (*r*), (*s*), (*t*).

(*d*) Hunter *v.* Fry, 2 B. & Ald. 421; 21 R. R. 340. Windle *v.* Barker, 6 E. & B. 675; 25 L. J. Ex. 349. Morris *v.* Levison, 1 C. P. D. 155; 45 L. J. C. P. 409. Addison on Contr. 894; below, § 409.

(*e*) Abbott, 180. 2 Boulay Paty, 345, 351. Pust *v.* Dowie, 32 L. J. Q. B. 179; 34 *ib.* 127; 5 B. & S. 20 (ship to carry 1000 tons of weight and measurement). The Norway, Br. & Lush. Ad. 377; 3 Moore, P. C. N. S. 245. M'Kill & Co. *v.* Wright Brs. & Co., 1887; 14 R. 863; rev. 1888, 14 App. Ca. 106; 16 R. H. L. 1 (ship guaranteed to carry not less than 2000 tons deadweight). As to the measurement of ship's tonnage, see 57 and 58 Vict. c. 60, § 77 sqq.

408. (1.) *Obligations of the Owners and Master.*—The obligations under this contract, whether fully expressed or implied in the general agreement, are, that the ship shall 'at the beginning of the voyage (*a*)' be seaworthy, stout, staunch, and strong for the voyage, and furnished with all tackle and apparel necessary for it; and with a fit and proper master and crew (*b*).

'The *warranty of seaworthiness* is implied whether the contract be by charter-party or by bill of lading (*c*); and although the shipowner does not hold himself out as a common carrier (*d*). It imports fitness for the particular kind of cargo to be carried (*e*); and it is violated, though the ship itself be sound and seaworthy, if unseaworthiness be caused by the manner of stowage (*f*). But failure to make use of a part of equipment with which the ship is furnished is negligence of the master or crew, and not unseaworthiness (*g*).' Ignorance of defect in the ship is no defence; nor the most exact survey before setting out (*h*). In warranting the captain's fitness, his knowledge of the particular ports or perils specified is included (*i*).

Pilotage.—The obligation to employ a pilot rests in Scotland on the principles of mercantile law, 'and was' not regulated by the English Pilotage Acts (*k*), 'the master being bound in dangerous localities to have recourse to the best assistance that can be had in the circumstances (*l*).' Whether the owners shall be liable for the unskilfulness of the pilot employed, is a question not decided; but at least to another ship suffering by faulty collision, it is 'at common law' no answer for the owner to say his ship was under a pilot's care (*m*).

The ship must have the proper *clearances* and *papers* for her protection, according to the law and custom of the country to and from which she sails (*n*).

Convoy.—She must sail with convoy, if stipulated or required at the time; and this may either be made an express warranty in the charter-party or bill of lading, or advertisement of the ship (*o*); or it may be left on the implied undertaking during war, and under the operation of those regulations which in most countries form a part of their war policy (*p*). The convoy must be that regularly appointed for the place of destination; it must be joined at the rendezvous ordered for vessels for that destination; its protection must be continued during the voyage, unless prevented by storm or inevitable accident; and the ship must obtain, as the legitimate proof of the convoy's protection, sailing instructions (*q*).

Beginning of Voyage.—The ship must, at the commencing port, be ready for the cargo at the day appointed; a failure in which may either discharge the contract or entitle to damages, '*i.e.* according as it is a condition precedent, or a collateral agreement or warranty. Whether a covenant in a charter-party as to time or place is of the one character or the other, is a question of intention, to be determined by the language used by the parties (*r*). When time is specified in a charter-party, and the parties so contract with regard to it, that it is of the essence of the contract, it is held to be a condition precedent, and any failure justifies rescission (*s*). In all cases, where there is no express mention of time, the law implies that there shall be no unreasonable delay in commencing the voyage. Such implied agreement, however, is not a condition precedent, but a warranty involving damages; and it justifies repudiation of the charter-party only when its purposes are entirely frustrated by the delay (*t*).' The ship must sail at the day appointed, wind and weather serving; but the master must on no account sail in tempestuous weather (*u*).

Voyage—Deviation.—The voyage must be performed according to the rules of good seamanship; and this comprehends a careful avoidance of all deviation from the correct voyage, unless compelled by storm, or enemies, or pirates, or the want of water, 'or justified by settled usage (*v*), or by the duty of saving life (*w*), or by the contract (*x*)'; such deviation lasting no longer than the necessity (*y*).

Care of Goods and Delivery.—Due preparation must be made, and care taken of the goods in loading and unloading (*z*). The goods must be safely delivered (*aa*) 'at the port of discharge agreed upon, which the master is bound to use all reasonable means to reach, even by lightening the ship at the entrance of the port, if that can be done without risk or substantial inconvenience, and if the consignee be ready to take partial delivery (*bb*).'

(*a*) Cohn *v.* Davidson, 2 Q. B. D. 455 ; 46 L. J. Q. B. 305. Cunningham *v.* Colvils, Lowden, & Co., 1889 ; 16 R. 295. *Infra*, § 477. Comp. Kopitoff *v.* Wilson, *infra* (*d*); and see 2 Arnould, Ins. 540. Maclachlan, 276, note. As to a voyage in stages, see Thin *v.* Richards, 1892 ; 2 Q. B. 141.

(*b*) Abbott, 284 ; Story's edition, 222. 1 Emerigon, 373. Valin, l. 3. t. 3. Pothier, Charte-Partie, No. 30. Lyon *v.* Mells, 5 East, 428 ; 1 Ill. 136 ; 7 R. R. 726. Watson *v.* Clark, 1 Dow, 336 ; 14 R. R. 73. Wilkie *v.* Geddes, 3 Dow, 37 ; 15 R. R. 17. Watt *v.* Morris, 1813 ; 1 Dow, 32. Douglas *v.* Scougal, 4 Dow, 267 ; 6 Pat. 179 ; 16 R. R. 69. Lawrie *v.* Angus, 1677 ; M. 10,107. Lamont *v.* Boswell, 1680 ; M. 10,109. Wedderburn *v.* Bell, 1 Camp. 1 ; 10 R. R. 615. Eden *v.* Parkinson, Doug. 734. Schloss *v.* Heriot, 14 C. B. N. S. 59 ; 32 L. J. C. P. 211. Thomson *v.* Gillespie, 5 E. & B. 209 ; 24 L. J. Q. B. 340. Gibson *v.* Small, 4 H. L. Ca. 353. Worms *v.* Storey, 25 L. J. Ex. 1 ; 11 Ex. 427. Tarrabocchia *v.* Hickie, 1 H. & N. 183 ; 26 L. J. Ex. 26. **Steel & Craig** *v.* **State Line Co.** (*c*). *Infra*, § 477.

(*c*) **Steel & Craig** *v.* **State Line Co.**, 1877 ; 4 R. H. L. 103 ; L. R. 3 App. Ca. 72.

(*d*) Kopitoff *v.* Wilson, 1 Q. B. D. 377 ; 45 L. J. Q. B. 436.

(*e*) Lyon *v.* Mells, *cit.* Stanton *v.* Richardson, L. R. 7 C. P. 421 ; 9 *ib.* 390 ; 41 L. J. C. P. 180 ; 43 *ib.* 230 ; in H. L. 45 *ib.* 78.

(*f*) Kopitoff, *cit.* Comp. Cohn *v.* Davidson, *supra* (*a*).

(*g*) Steel & Craig (*c*). Hedley *v.* Pinkney & Co. S. S. Co., 1894 ; A. C. 217. Gilroy, Sons, & Co. *v.* Price & Co., 1891 ; 18 R. 569 ; rev. 1893, A. C. 56 ; 20 R. H. L. 1. In Steel & Craig (*c*) and Seville Sulphur Co. *v.* Colvils, Lowden, & Co., 1888 ; 15 R. 616, faults not in the equipment of the ship, but in getting her ready for sea (failing to close a port-hole, using muddy water in a boiler, and casing a pipe), were held, being committed at the beginning of the voyage, not to be within the exception of errors or negligence of navigation, but to amount to unseaworthiness.

(*h*) 1 Valin, 620. Pothier, Charte-Partie, No. 30. Lyon, *supra* (*b*).

(*i*) Tait *v.* Levi, 14 East, 481 ; 13 R. R. 289.

(*k*) Pothier, Charte-Partie, No. 31. Abbott, 285 ; Story's edition, 224, note. See 1 Bell's Com. 551 sq. (599, M'L.'s ed.). Brodie's Stair, 985, 989, 1004. Maclachlan on Shipping, ch. vi.; and below, § 436. The law relating to pilotage is now contained in 57 and 58 Vict. c. 60, part x. § 575 sqq. (see also 60 and 61 Vict. c. 61). The licensing and control of pilots are left to district pilotage authorities in various districts. Holman *v.* Irvine Harbour Trs., 1877 ; 4 R. 406 (liability for employing unlicensed pilot). These authorities have also power to give exemptions from compulsory pilotage, in addition to those contained in the Act, but subject to regulations to be made by them. The employment of pilots continues to be compulsory in all districts in which it was so before the Act ; § 603 ; subject, however, to powers conferred on the Board of Trade and pilotage authorities, § 599 and 604, to grant to masters and mates pilotage certificates for certain districts.

(*l*) Thomson *v.* Bisset, 1826 ; 4 S. 670. Rex *v.* Neale, 8 T. R. 241. Phillips *v.* Headlam, 2 B. & Ad. 380. 57 and 58 Vict. c. 60, § 596.

(*m*) Neptune the Second, 1 Dod. Ad. Rep. 466. See the Protector, 1 Rob. 45.

(*n*) Abbott, 287 sqq. See Abbott, 296. Maclachlan, 419. 57 and 58 Vict. c. 60, § 14 sqq., 68, 103, 314, 281, etc.; 39 and 40 Vict. c. 36, § 128, 145, etc. Levy *v.* Costerton, 4 Camp. 389 ; 16 R. R. 808. Dutton *v.* Powles, 31 L. J. Q. B. 191 ; 2 B. & S. 191. Kirk *v.* Gibbs, 1 H. & N. 810 ; 26 L. J. Ex. 209.

(*o*) Abbott, 312 sqq.

(*p*) 1 Valin, 691. Abbott, *l.c.* 38 Geo. III. c. 57. 43 Geo. III. c. 57 (both repealed).

(*q*) Abbott, 298 et seq., and the cases there cited. Maclachlan, 420, 562. See as to a blockaded port, The Shepherdess, 5 Rob. 262 ; 3 Ill. 126. Naylor *v.* Taylor, 5 B. & Cr. 718. Medeiros *v.* Hill, 8 Bing. 231 ; 34 R. R. 696.

(*r*) See **Behn** *v.* **Burness,** 1 B. & S. 877 ; 3 B. & S. 751 ; 32 L. J. Q. B. 204. Seeger *v.* Duthie, 8 C. B. N. S. 45 ; 29 L. J. C. P. 253 ; 30 *ib.* 65. Havelock *v.* Geddes, 10 East, 555 ; 10 R. R. 380. Boone *v.* Eyre, 2 W. Bl. 1312 ; 2 R. R. 768. Davidson *v.* Gwynne, 12 East, 381 ; 11 R. R. 420. Dimech *v.* Corlett, 12 Moo. P. C. 199. Abbott, 200 sqq. Cases in Smith's Merc. Law, 291.

(*s*) Glaholm *v.* Hays, 2 M. & Gr. 268. **Behn** *v.* **Burness,** *cit.* Corkling *v.* Massey, 42 L. J. C. P. 153 ; L. R. 8 C. P. 395. Tully *v.* Howling, 2 Q. B. D. 182 ; 46 L. J. Q. B. 388. Collard *v.* Carswell, 1892 ; 19 R. 987. See Mackenzie *v.* Liddell, 1883 ; 10 R. 705 ("commencing from 8th September").

(*t*) M'Andrew *v.* Chapple, 35 L. J. C. P. 281 ; L. R. 1 C. P. 643. Jackson *v.* Union Mar. Ins. Co., 44 L. J. C. P. 27 ; L. R. 10 C. P. 125. Tarrabocchia *v.* Hickie, *cit.* (*b*). See Jones *v.* Holme, 36 L. J. Ex. 192 ; L. R. 2. Ex. 335. Clipsham *v.* Vertue, 5 Q. B. 265. **Nelson** *v.* **Dahl,** 6 App. Ca. 38 ; 50 L. J. Ch. 411 (*per* Ld. Blackburn).

(*u*) Abbott, 298. Maclachlan, 419.

(*v*) Salvador *v.* Hopkins, 3 Burr. 1707. Vallance *v.* Dewar, 3 Camp. 503 ; 10 R. R. 738. Wilson & Co. *v.* Elliot, 1776 ; M. 7096 ; Apx. *Insur.* 1 ; rev. 2 Pat. 411 ; 7 Bro. P. C. 459 (usage barred by terms of contract).

(*w*) Lawrence *v.* Sydebotham, 5 East, 45 ; 8 R. R. 385. The Beaver, 3 C. Rob. 292. Scaramanga *v.* Stamp, 4 C. P. D. 316 ; 5 *ib.* 295 ; 48 L. J. C. P. 478 ; 49 *ib.* 674. Potter & Co. *v.* Burrell & Son, 1897 ; 1 Q. B. 97. Deviation to save property alone is not justifiable. Scaramanga, *cit.*

(*x*) "Liberty to call at ports in any order" in a bill of lading only justifies calling at ports substantially within the course of the voyage described. Leduc *v.* Ward, 20 Q. B. D. 475. Glynn *v.* Margetson, 1893 ; A. C. 351. See also on deviation and on this clause, Caffin *v.* Aldridge, 1895 ; 2 Q. B. 648.

(*y*) Abbott, 308 ; 2 Pardessus, 49 ; 2 Kent, Com. 209. Freeman *v.* Taylor, 8 Bing. 124 ; 3 Ill. 126 ; 34 R. R. 647. Davis *v.* Garret, 6 Bing. 716 ; 31 R. R. 524. M'Andrew *v.* Adams, 1 Bing. N. S. 29. Stewart *v.* Johnston, Jan. 17, 1810 ; F. C. Cf. Russell *v.* Shannon & Co., 1821 ; 1 S. App. 83.

(*z*) Ogilvie & Co. *v.* Taylor, 1828 ; 6 S. 691 ; 1 Ill. 169. Jones & Co. *v.* Ross, 1830 ; 8 S. 495 ; 1 Ill. 138. (These cases so far as they are authorities rather belong to the next note.) Hutchison *v.* Guion, 5 C. B. N. S. 149 ; 28 L. J. C. P. 63. Sack *v.* Ford, 13 C. B. N. S. 90 ; 32 L. J. C. P. 12. Anglo-Afr. Co. *v.* Lamzed, 35 L. J. C. P. 145 ; L. R. 1 C. P. 226. See as to receipt and stowage by the ship, Maclachlan, 413 sqq. Gall & Co. *v.* Jamieson, 1802 ; Hume, 310. Glengarnock Iron Co. *v.* Cooper & Co., 1896 ; 22 R. 672. As to the liability of the shipowner where a stevedore is appointed by the shipper, see Blaikie *v.* Stembridge, 6 C. B. N. S. 894 ; 28 L. J. C. P. 329 ; 29 *ib.* 212. Sack *v.* Ford, *cit.* Sandeman *v.* Scurr, L. R. 2 Q. B. 86 ; 36 L. J. Q. B. 58. Hayn *v.* Culliford, 3 C. P. D. 410 ; 4 *ib.* 182 ; 47 L. J. C. P. 755 ; 48 *ib.* 372. M'Kill & Co. *v.* Wright Brs. & Co., 1886 ; 14 R. 863 ; rev. 14 App. Ca. 106 ; 16 R. H. L. 1 ; or when the shipper has notice of the kind of stowage to be adopted and has assented. Major *v.* White, 7 C. & P. 41. As to statutory provisions regarding loading, see Maclachlan, 416 ; and below, § 451D.

(*aa*) Abbott, p. 321. Edinburgh and Leith Ship. Co. *v.* Ogilvie, 1829 ; 2 Mur. 136 ; 1 Ill. 143. Armstrong *v.* Edinburgh and Leith Ship. Co., 1825 ; 3 S. 323. Bishop *v.* Mersey & Clyde Nav. Co., 1830 ; 8 S. 558 ; 1 Ill. 141. Rae *v.* Hay, 1832 ; 10 S. 303. Urquhart *v.* Brown, 1833 ; 11 S. 567. Provision is made by statute (57 and 58 Vict. c. 60, Part VII., § 492 sq.) for placing the goods in warehouse where the owner fails to land or take delivery of them, or where there is any difficulty about freight. See as to delivery, Gatliffe *v.* Bourne, 4 Bing. N. C. 314. Bourne *v.* Gatliffe, 4 Sc. 1; 3 M. & Gr. 643; 7 *ib.* 850; H. L. 11 C. & F. 45. Kennedy *v.* Dodge, 17 L. T. N. S. 20. Petrocochino *v.* Bott, L. R. 9 C. P. 355; 43 L. J. C. P. 214. British Shipowners' Co. *v.* Grimond, 1876; 3 R. 968 (point of time of delivery). Avon S. S. Co. *v.* Leask & Co., 1890; 18 R. 289 (do. "alongside"). Thorsen *v.* Macdowall & Neilson, 1892; 19 R. 743.

(*bb*) Hillstrom *v.* Gibson, 1870; 8 Macph. 463. Capper *v.* Wallace, 49 L. J. Q. B. 350; 5 Q. B. D. 163. **Nelson** *v.* **Dahl,** 12 Ch. D. 568; rev. 6 App. Ca. 38; 50 L. J. Ch. 411. These cases show that the usual words, "As near thereto as she can safely get," are to receive a reasonable, not a literal construction. See below, § 429.

409. (2.) *Obligations of the Freighter.*—He must furnish a cargo, which implies that it is lawful; and he will be liable in damages if, by lading prohibited or uncustomed goods, the ship shall be detained or forfeited (*a*). If the ship be freighted rateably, the cargo must be full; not according to the tonnage in the description, but according to the fair capacity of the ship (*b*); and if the freight be in a slump sum, the cargo must be such as at least to cover or secure the freight. The freighter must send the cargo ready for embarkation within a reasonable time, if the day be not specially appointed; or on the day fixed by the charter-party; otherwise the master may either hold the agreement as abandoned, and sail on another voyage, or wait and claim damages for detention (*c*). The freighter must pay a sum or freight for the whole ship, or rateably, according to the ton, etc.; or a sum for the voyage, or time; or rateably per day, week, month, etc., of the ship's employment (*d*). And he must avoid undue delay in taking delivery (*e*).

(*a*) Abbott, 343; Story's edition, 270, note 1. Maclachlan, 445. As to dangerous goods, see § 159. As to illegal voyages, see Waugh *v.* Morris, L. R. 8 Q. B. 202; 42 L. J. Q. B. 57.

(*b*) *Supra*, § 407. As to the express contract to load a full and complete cargo, see Jones *v.* Holme, L. R. 2 Ex. 335; 36 L. J. Ex. 192. Carr *v.* Wallachian Petr. Co., L. R. 1 C. P. 636; 2 *ib.* 468; 35 L. J. C. P. 314; 36 *ib.* 236; and below, § 430.

(*c*) Thompson *v.* Inglis, 3 Camp. 428. See Molloy, 2, 4, 73. Smith's Merc. Law, 330, 367. Maclachlan, 546. Postlethwaite *v.* Freeland, 5 App. Ca. 599, 621; 49 L. J. Ex. 630. Lawrie *v.* Jamieson, 6 Bro. P. C. 474; 3 Pat. 493; 1 Bell's Com. 578 (624, M'L.'s ed.).

(*d*) Wilson *v.* Bennet, March 10, 1809; F. C.; 1 Ill. 268. Christy *v.* Rowe, 1 Taunt. 300; 9 R. R. 776. Shepard *v.* De Bernales, 13 East, 565; 12 R. R. 412. Marsh *v.* Pedder, 4 Camp. 257. See below, § 420.

(*e*) See below as to Lay Days and Demurrage, § 431.

410. A receipt for the goods fixes them on the shipowners and master (*a*). But a bill of lading (*b*) is taken from the shipmaster, 'or other person authorised by the owner to grant it (*c*),' in most cases; even where, by hiring on time, the affreighter takes the ship entirely into his own management. 'When the master signs the bill of lading as agent for the freighter and not for the shipowner, the latter has no direct action against the shippers for the freight (*d*).' It is useful not only to fix the condition of the goods, for which the shipmaster and owners are to be responsible, but to entitle the person who shall hold it to demand delivery of the goods (*e*). It must be given to the shipper or holder of the receipt, in exchange for a previous receipt if granted (*f*).

(*a*) See below, § 413. (*b*) See below, § 414.

(*c*) Jessel *v.* Bath, L. R. 2 Ex. 267; 36 L. J. Ex. 149. Hayn *v.* Culliford, *supra*, § 408 (*z*).

(*d*) Mitchell *v.* Burn, 1874; 1 R. 900. See below, § 421, 1423.

(*e*) 2 Valin, 599. Pothier, Charte-Partie, No. 17. Abbott, 256. Haddow *v.* Parry, 3 Taunt. 303; 1 Ill. 268; 12 R. R. 666.

(*f*) Craven *v.* Ryder, 6 Taunt. 433; 2 Marsh. 127; 16 R. R. 644; 1 Ill. 268. Schuster *v.* M'Kellar, 7 E. & B. 704; 26 L. J. Q. B. 281.

411. Affreightment by General Ship.—The master of a general ship, advertised for the voyage as ready to receive goods, is a common carrier.

412. (1.) *The advertisement* is regarded as an offer to receive and carry the goods. It is completed into a special agreement, by fixing the goods with the master under that advertisement; and it so becomes binding on the owners (*a*). But it is not yet settled whether the special terms of that advertisement are to be taken as a warranty, especially if not repeated in the bill of lading; as when a ship is advertised to sail with convoy (*b*). The description of the voyage, however, as stated in the advertisement, is held by merchants as a special engagement (*c*). The advertisement entitles a merchant to bring his goods to the ship, and to insist on them being taken on board, unless the ship has already been filled up, or has been actually engaged (*d*).

(*a*) Phillips *v.* Edwards, 4 H. & N. 813; 28 L. J. Ex. 32. As to the effect of such an advertisement by charterers, see Peek *v.* Larsen, 40 L. J. Ch. 763; L. R. 12 Eq. 378.

(*b*) Abbott, 255. Maclachlan, 389. Tennent *v.* Carmichael, 1843; 5 D. 639. Cranston *v.* Marshall, 5 Ex. 395; 19 L. J. Ex. 340.

(*c*) Peel *v.* Price, 4 Camp. 243; 16 R. R. 785.

(*d*) Thomson *v.* Clark, June 15, 1809; 1 Ill. 269; 1 Bell's Com. 542. See above, § 74. As to passengers, see Yates *v.* Duff, 5 C. & P. 569. Cranston *v.* Marshall, *cit.* (*b*).

413. (2.) *Receipt.*—To close the contract, there is sometimes an intermediate receipt (*a*), sometimes only a bill of lading (*b*). The receipt is used to fix the goods with the master and owners, and is a mere acknowledgment given by the mate, or the person in command of the ship at the time when the goods are put on board. It charges the master and owners with the goods mentioned in it, and binds the contract within the limits of the advertisement (*c*). It is generally held sufficient under the implied conditions of the contract, in coasting vessels and smacks, or steamboats. In more distant voyages, or for the regulation of the delivery of the goods, a bill of lading is taken from the master, and the receipt delivered up (*d*). If the master should sign a bill of lading for delivery to another than the holder of the receipt, or the person pointed out by him, he would make himself liable to both parties; the receipt preserving to the shipper his full right to stop *in transitu*, or transfer the goods, as he may think proper (*e*).

(*a*) See above, § 410.
(*b*) See below, § 414.
(*c*) See Thomson *v.* Small, 1 C. B. 328. Tindall *v.* Taylor, 4 E. & B. 219. Falk *v.* Fletcher, 18 C. B. N. S. 403; 34 L. J. C. P. 146.
(*d*) As to the master's duty to sign a bill of lading, and disputes as to the terms of proposed bills of lading, see Falk *v.* Fletcher, *cit.* Jones *v.* Hough, 5 Ex. D. 115; 49 L. J. Ex. 211. Arrospe *v.* Barr, 1881; 8 R. 602 ("conditions as per charter-party"—"clean" bill of lading). Although brokers may be entrusted with the function of arranging the terms of the contract of carriage to be inserted in the bill of lading, the master is still bound to state matters of fact correctly, such as the fact and date of shipment of cargo, and liable to his owners for negligence or falsehood. Stumore, Weston, & Co. *v.* Breen, 12 App. Ca. 698.
(*e*) Abbott, 257. Craven *v.* Ryder, *cit.* § 410. Ruck *v.* Hatfield, 5 B. & Ald. 632; 1 Ill. 392. See Schuster *v.* M'Kellar, *cit.* § 410. Hathesing *v.* Laing, 43 L. J. Ch. 233; L. R. 17 Eq. 92. Cowasjee *v.* Thomson, 5 Moore, P. C. 165.

414. Bill of Lading.—This instrument has two objects,—to fix the condition of the goods as received on board, and to give a title to some one to demand delivery. It therefore contains a written acknowledgment of the goods received on board, with an obligation to deliver them, "the act of God (*a*), the king's enemies (*b*), fire, and all other dangers and accidents of the seas, etc., of whatever nature and kind soever, excepted" (*c*). This instrument requires a stamp, whether the goods are to be exported or carried coastwise (*d*). 'As between charterer and shipowner, a bill of lading is in general a mere receipt; but it is the contract on which (the goods being received, § 418 (*d*)) the indorsee must rely as between himself and the shipowner (*e*). Being the contract, it may not be qualified by parole evidence (*f*). A reference in the usual terms to the charter-party in the bill of lading incorporates so much of the charter-party only as relates to payment of freight and other conditions to be performed on delivery of the cargo, but does not give the holders constructive notice of its other contents (*g*).'

(*a*) Nitro-Phosph. Co. *v.* St. Katharine's Dock Co., 9 Ch. D. 503. Nicholls *v.* Marsland, 2 Ex. D. 1; 46 L. J. Ex. 174. **Nugent** *v.* **Smith,** 1 C. P. D. 423; 45 L. J. C. P. 697. River Wear Comrs. *v.* Adamson, 2 App. Ca. 743; 47 L. J. Q. B. 193. Maclachlan, 535. Pollock on Contr. 396.
(*b*) The Teutonia, L. R. 4 P. C. 171. The San Roman, L. R. 5 C. P. 301; 42 L. J. Adm. 46. See Geipel *v.* Smith, L. R. 7 Q. B. 404; 41 L. J. Q. B. 153; and Smith & Service *v.* Rosario Nitrate Co., 1894; 1 Q. B. 194, as to exception of "restraints of princes."
(*c*) Abbott, 258. See above, § 237 sqq.
(*d*) 48 Geo. III. c. 149, Sched. part 1. 55 Geo. III. c. 78, Sched. part 1. Duty, 6d. It cannot be stamped after it is executed; and a penalty of £50 is incurred by making a bill of lading not duly stamped. 54 and 55 Vict. c. 39, § 40 and Sched.
(*e*) Sewell *v.* Burdick, 10 App. Ca. 74, 105 (L. Bramwell). Rodocanachi *v.* Milburn, 18 Q. B. D. 67, 75 (L. Esher).
(*f*) Leduc *v.* Ward, 20 Q. B. D. 475.
(*g*) Fry *v.* Chart. Merc. Bk. of India, L. R. 1 C. P. 689; 35 L. J. C. P. 306. Serraino *v.* Campbell, 1891; 1 Q. B. 283. Manchester Trust *v.* Furness, 1895; 2 Q. B. 539. Diederichsen *v.* Farquharson Brs., 1898; 1 Q. B. 150.

415. The description of the goods in the bill of lading deserves particular care, as the master makes himself and his owners liable for them in the condition mentioned (*a*). The goods, if in sound condition, are in the bill stated to be "received in good order," and the obligation is to deliver them in the like good condition (*b*). But if, as frequently happens, the quality or even the quantity is unknown to the master, he usually and properly adds, "quality or quantity unknown," and then is responsible only for the external and apparent quality (*c*).

(*a*) See Shankland *v.* Athya & Co., 1865; 3 Macph. 810.
(*b*) 1 Bell's Com. 557.
(*c*) **Jessel** *v.* **Bath,** L. R. 2 Ex. 267; 36 L. J. Ex. 149. Coulthurst *v.* Sweet, L. R. 1 C. P. 649. The Helene, L. R. 1 P. C. 231. 1 Parsons on Shipping, 198. Moes, Moliere, & Tromp *v.* Leith and Amst. Shipg. Co., 1867; 5 Macph. 988. Clark *v.* Barnwell, 19 Curtis, 130. Lebeau *v.* Gen. Steam Nav. Co., L. R. 8 C. P. 88; 42 L. J. C. P. 1 (effect of innocent misdescription). Tully *v.* Terry, 42 L. J. C. P. 240; L. R. 8 C. P. 679.

416. The risks to which the owners under their obligation to deliver are liable, exclude, by the express exceptions of the bill of lading, all perils of the sea and enemy, and inevitable accidents; and even for those risks to which, by the policy of the law, they are liable, their responsibility has been greatly limited by statute (*a*). 'As a shipowner is bound to carry with reasonable care, this exception does not save him if the loss by perils of the sea, etc., is caused by previous default on his part (*b*).'

(*a*) See below, § 435; above, § 237, 414. As to the clauses giving further exemptions, see § 435.

(*b*) Grill *v.* Gen. Iron Screw Collier Co., L. R. 1 C. P. 600; 3 *ib.* 476; 35 L. J. C. P. 321; 37 *ib.* 205. Wilson, Sons, & Co. *v.* Owners of Cargo of Xantho, 12 App. Ca. 503. "Perils of the sea" are not to be construed differently in a bill of lading or charter-party and in a policy of insurance; but in the latter, which is a contract of indemnity, the effect of negligence is different (see below, § 472 (1)). Wilson, Sons, & Co., *cit.* Hamilton, Fraser, & Co. *v.* Pandorf & Co., 12 App. Ca. 518.

417. Bills of lading are, by the law and usage of merchants, negotiable instruments, passing to 'onerous *bonâ fide* (*a*)' indorsees and other holders untrammelled by any latent claim or exception; and in order to facilitate the use of them as negotiable instruments, they are made out in sets (commonly of three): one for transmission by post; one to go with the cargo; one for the shipper: And all of them contain a clause, as in foreign bills of exchange, that, one being performed, the rest shall be void (*b*). 'The indorsation and delivery of the bill of lading by custom of merchants passes the property of the goods which it represents (*c*); but it did not pass the contract with the carrier so as to enable the transferee to sue on it or be sued for freight or demurrage (*d*). Now, however, by statute it transfers to the consignee named in it, and to the indorsees to whom the property of the goods passes,—not being mere pledgees who have not taken possession or dealt with the goods (*e*),—all rights of action and all liabilities in respect of the goods, just as if the contract in the bill of lading had been made with them; but without prejudice to any right of stoppage *in transitu* (§ 1307), or to any right to claim freight against the original shipper, or to any liability of the consignee or indorsee as such, or by his receipt of the goods (*f*).

'Assignees of bills of lading may become liable for the freight of goods by receiving them in such circumstances as imply a contract to pay freight (*g*); or for demurrage by receiving goods under a bill of lading making them deliverable on paying demurrage, and clearly imposing the liability, the receipt and other circumstances being in such cases evidence of a contract to pay (*h*).'

(*a*) Leask *v.* Scott, L. R. 2 Q. B. D. 376; 46 L. J. Q. B. 576. See 1 Smith's L. C. 734 sqq. Benjamin on Sales, 889; below, § 419.

(*b*) See § 418 (*e*).

(*c*) Cases in § 419 (*a*); and below, 418A, 1302, 1305, 1308. 18 and 19 Vict. c. 111, preamble.

(*d*) Howard *v.* Shepherd, 9 C. B. 297. Thomson *v.* Dominy, 14 M. & W. 403. Arrospe *v.* Barr, 1881; 8 R. 602 (*per* L. P. Inglis).

(*e*) **Sewell** *v.* **Burdick,** 10 App. Ca. 74. See Tod & Son *v.* Merchant Bkg. Co., 1883; 10 R. 1009.

(*f*) 18 and 19 Vict. c. 111, § 1 and 2. Fox *v.* Nott, 6 H. & N. 630; 30 L. J. Ex. 259. Short *v.* Simpson, 35 L. J. C. P. 147; L. R. 1 C. P. 248. Smurthwaite *v.* Wilkins, 11 C. B. N. S. 842; 31 L. J. C. P. 214 (rights and liabilities of consignee or indorsee pass from him by indorsation). The Freedom, L. R. 3 P. C. 594. Dracachi *v.* Anglo-Egyp. Bk., L. R. 3 C. P. 190; 37 L. J. C. P. 71. The St. Cloud, B. & L. Adm. 4. Lewis *v.* M'Kee, 38 L. J. Ex. 62; L. R. 4 Ex. 58. Fowler *v.* Knoop, 4 Q. B. D. 299; 48 L. J. Q. B. 333. See below, § 421.

(*g*) See below, § 425.

(*h*) Stindt *v.* Roberts, 17 L. J. Q. B. 166. Wegener *v.* Smith, 15 C. B. 729. Smith *v.* Sieveking, 24 L. J. Q. B. 257; 5 E. & B. 589. Chappell *v.* Comfort, 31 L. J. C. P. 58. Gray *v.* Carr, L. R. 5 Q. B. 522; 40 L. J. Q. B. 257. See cases in § 421 (*a*), (*l*).

418. In bills of lading, the obligation to deliver the goods is either general, to the bearer, or in blank; or, filled up to a particular person, as consignee, or to his order, or to his assigns; or, to the consignor and his assigns (*a*). The consignee named in the bill of lading, or the indorsee (*b*) of an assignable bill of lading, or the holder of one blank indorsed, is entitled to demand the goods from the master on payment of freight, 'or from one to whom they have been wrongfully delivered, or one who has wrongfully parted with them (*c*).

'A bill of lading is a living instrument, and may be transferred—even after the goods are landed at a London sufferance wharf, and before a wharfinger's or warehouseman's certificate has been given, the master's engagement not being completely fulfilled; or after an actual, but wrongful, delivery of the goods, to the effect of vesting the indorsee with the right to sue the ship for damages (*d*).

'A bill of lading in the hands of a consignee or indorsee for valuable consideration is by statute conclusive evidence of shipment of goods against the master or other person signing it, although the goods may not have been shipped, unless the holder when he received the bill had actual notice that they were not on board. The master or person signing may, however, exonerate himself by showing that he was not to blame, and that the mistake arose wholly from the fraud of the shipper or holder, or one under whom the holder claims (*e*). So it is not conclusive against the shipowner not signing it, for the master is not his agent to sign for goods which he never received. Neither at common law nor under the statute are shipowners liable for non-delivery of goods mentioned in bills of lading but not actually shipped (*f*). The onus of disproving the bill of lading lies, of course, on the ship (*g*); and mere general evidence that all the goods put on board were delivered does not discharge this burden (*h*).

'The shipowner or master, so long as he has no notice or knowledge of any dealing with the other parts of the bill of lading, is excused if he deliver to the person appearing to be the assign of the part first presented to him (*i*). But in a question of ownership between competing holders of two parts of the bill of lading, the property passes to him who first gets possession of any one of the parts as indorsee (*k*). A purchaser is not justified in refusing to accept and pay, under a contract for payment on presentation of bill of lading, on the ground that only one of the set is tendered, and the others are not accounted for (*l*).'

(*a*) See § 1308.

(*b*) As to pledgees by indorsation and their rights, see Bristol, etc., Bank *v.* Midland Ry. Co., *cit. infra*, and N. W. Bk. *v.* Poynter, Macdonald, & Co., 1894; 21 R. 513; rev. 1895, A. C. 56; 22 R. H. L. 1. *Infra*, § 1364.

(*c*) **Barber** *v.* **Meyerstein,** L. R. 4 H. L. 317; 39 L. J. C. P. 187. Mirabita *v.* Imp. Ottoman Bk., 3 Ex. D. 154; 47 L. J. Ex. 418. Pirie & Sons *v.* Warden, 1871; 9 Macph. 523.

(*d*) Pirie & Sons, *cit.* Short *v.* Simpson, 35 L. J. C. P. 147; L. R. 1 C. P. 248 (*per* Willes, J.). Bristol, etc., Bank *v.* Midland Ry. Co., 1891; 2 Q. B. 653.

(*e*) 18 and 19 Vict. c. 111, § 3. Valieri *v.* Boyland, L. R. 1 C. P. 382; 35 L. J. C. P. 215.

(*f*) **Meyer** *v.* **Dresser**, 16 C. B. N. S. 646; 33 L. J. C. P. 289. **Grant** *v.* **Norway**, 10 C. B. 615; 20 L. J. C. P. 93. Hubbersty *v.* Ward, 8 Ex. 330; 22 L. J. Ex. 113. Jessel *v.* Bath, L. R. 2 Ex. 267; 36 L. J. Ex. 149. Maclean & Hope *v.* Munck, 1867; 5 Macph. 893. **Maclean & Hope** *v.* **Fleming**, 1871; 9 Macph. H. L. 38; L. R. 2 Sc. App. 128. Owners of Immanuel *v.* Denholm, 1887; 15 R. 152. Brown *v.* Powell Duffryn Co., L. R. 10 C. P. 562; 44 L. J. C. P. 289. See Grieve, Son, & Co. *v.* König & Co., 1880; 7 R. 521. Cox *v.* Bruce & Co., 18 Q. B. D. 147. Lishman *v.* Christie & Co., 19 Q. B. D. 333 (by charter-party bill of lading conclusive evidence of quantity shipped).

(*g*) Maclean & Hope, *cit.* Horsley *v.* Grimond, 1894; 21 R. 410.

(*h*) Bedouin S. Nav. Co. *v.* Smith & Co., 1895; 22 R. 350; rev. 1896, A. C. 70; 23 R. H. L. 1.

(*i*) Glyn, Mills, & Co. *v.* E. & W. India Dock Co., 6 Q. B. D. 475; 7 App. Ca. 591; 50 L. J. Q. B. 62; 52 *ib.* 146. Pirie *v.* Warden, *cit.* (as to delivery to one claiming ownership, but not holding any bill of lading). Gabarron *v.* Kreeft, L. R. 10 Ex. 274; 44 L. J. Ex. 238.

(*k*) Barber *v.* Meyerstein, *cit.* (*c*).

(*l*) Sanders *v.* Maclean, 11 Q. B. D. 327.

418A. 'A bill of lading is generally made in favour of some person "or his assigns" (*a*). In general, delivery of goods by a seller to a carrier or shipmaster for conveyance to the buyer passes not only the risk (*supra*, § 87, 88, 117 (*c*)), but the property, the shipmaster being the buyer's agent to receive them (*b*). But (1) when a bill of lading is taken from the master, the delivery of the goods to him is not necessarily delivery to the buyer, but to the master as agent or bailee for the consignee indicated by the bill of lading (*c*). (2) *Primâ facie*, delivery on board under a bill of lading to the consignor himself, "his order or assigns," shows his intention to retain the property (or *jus disponendi*) until it is passed by indorsation and delivery of the bill of lading (*d*). (3) It may, however, be shown by evidence that in taking the bill in his own name the consignor was acting on behalf of the buyer, and did not intend to retain the control over the goods (*e*). (4) Even when the delivery is on board the purchaser's own ship, the consignor may, by the terms of the bill of lading, retain control over the goods and prevent the property from passing (*f*). (5) When a bill of exchange for the price of the goods is sent to the buyer for acceptance, along with a bill of lading to the consignor indorsed by him, the buyer is bound to accept the bill of exchange; and if he refuse to do so, he acquires no right to the bill of lading or the goods (*g*). In all these cases the real question is on whose behalf the master has possession, and of this the terms of the bill of lading are important, but not always conclusive, evidence.

'The transfer of a bill of lading by indorsation and delivery, differing formerly from transfers of documents of title to goods on land in which notice to the custodier and his assent were required (§ 1305, *infra*), itself passes the property (*h*).'

(*a*) Without these words it rather seems that a bill of lading is not negotiable. See Henderson *v.* Comptoir d'Escompte, L. R. 5 P. C. 253; 42 L. J. P. C. 60. 1 Smith's L. C. 460. M'Laren's Bell's Com. i. 220.

(*b*) M'Laren's Bell's Com. i. 216, 217. Dunlop *v.* Lambert, 1839; M'L. & R. 663; 6 Cl. & F. 600 Waite *v.*

Baker, 2 Ex. 1. Cork Distilleries Co. *v.* G. S. Ry., L. R. 7 H. L. 269 ; *infra*, § 1302.

(*c*) **Shepherd** *v.* **Harrison**, L. R. 4 Q. B. 196, 493 ; 5 H. L. 116 ; 38 L. J. Q. B. 105, 177 ; 40 *ib.* 148. *Ex p.* Banner, 2 Ch. D. 78 ; 45 L. J. Ch. 73, and the cases in notes (*d*), (*e*), (*f*). Benjamin on Sales, chap. vi., in whose summary at p. 532, and Smith's Merc. Law, 298, most of these propositions are laid down.

(*d*) M'Laren's Bell's Com. i. 220. Arnots *v.* Boyter, 1803 ; M. 14,204. Waite *v.* Baker, and Shepherd, *citt.* Van Casteel *v.* Booker, 2 Ex. 691. Gabarron *v.* Kreeft, L. R. 10 Ex. 274 ; 44 L. J. Ex. 238. Ogg *v.* Shuter, 1 C. P. D. 47 ; 45 L. J. C. P. 44.

(*e*) Joyce *v.* Swann, 17 C. B. N. S. 84. Brown *v.* Hare, 4 H. & N. 822 ; 29 L. J. Ex. 6. Van Casteel, *cit.* Moakes *v.* Nicholson, 19 C. B. N. S. 290 ; 34 L. J. C. P. 273.

(*f*) Turner *v.* Liv. Dock. Trs., 6 Ex. 543. Ellershaw *v.* Magniac, 6 Ex. 570. Falk *v.* Fletcher, 18 C. B. N. S. 403 ; 34 L. J. C. P. 146. Moakes, *cit.* Gabarron, *cit.* Schotsman *v.* L. & Y. Ry. Co., 36 L. J. Ch. 361 ; L. R. 2 Ch. 332. Benjamin on Sales, 827 sqq.

(*g*) Shepherd *v.* Harrison, *cit.* Ogg *v.* Shuter, *cit.* Mirabita *v.* Impl. Ottoman Bank, 3 Ex. D. 164 ; 47 L. J. Ex. 418. Mitchel *v.* Ede, 11 A. & E. 888. Brown, Shipley, & Co. *v.* Kough, 29 Ch. D. 848. See above, § 102A.

(*h*) Blackburn on Sale, 297. Benjamin on Sales, 801. Barber *v.* Meyerstein, *supra*, § 418 (*c*).

419. The right so conferred will control, not only the right of the creditors of the shipper, but even the shipper's right, to stop the cargo unpaid as *in transitu* (*a*), if the holder of the bill have acquired it 'by transference from one who has authority to assign or transfer it (*b*)' for a valuable consideration, and without notice of no satisfaction been given for the goods (*c*). Goods shipped without an order may, even after the signing of the bill of lading, be countermanded by the shipper; but not if shipped on order, and a bill granted (*d*) 'with the intention that it shall operate as immediate payment (*e*).'

(*a*) Buchanan *v.* Swan, 1764 ; M. 14,208 ; 1 Ill. 269. Hastie & Jamieson *v.* Arthur, 1770 ; M. 14,209 ; H. of L., 2 Paton, 251. Bogle *v.* Dunmore & Co., 1787 ; M. 14,216 ; aff. 1 Ill. 269 ; 1 Bell's Com. 199. Cuming *v.* Brown, 1 Camp. 103 ; 9 R. R. 103 ; 9 East, 506. Vertue *v.* Jewell, 4 Camp. 31. See Benjamin on Sales, 889. Barrow *v.* Coles, 3 Camp. 92. Nathan *v.* Giles, 5 Taunt. 658 ; 15 R. R. 581. See below, § 1308.

(*b*) Gurney *v.* Behrend, 23 L. J. Q. B. 265 ; 3 E. & B. 622. Gilbert *v.* Guignon, L. R. 8 Ch. 16. A bill of lading is not negotiable in the same sense as a bill of exchange, for an indorser (except an agent entrusted with it transferring it under the Factors Acts, see § 229, 1316B, 1364) gives no better right by indorsing it than he himself has. See Benjamin on Sales, 891.

(*c*) Wright *v.* Campbell, 4 Burr. 2046. Caldwell *v.* Ball, 1 T. R. 205 ; 1 R. R. 187. Hibbert *v.* Carter, *ib.* 745 ; 1 R. R. 388. **Lickbarrow** *v.* **Mason**, 1 H. Bl. 357 ; 1 Ill. 404 ; 1 Smith's L. C. 674 ; 2 Ross' L. C. 92 ; 1 R. R. 425. Newson *v.* Thornton, 6 East, 17 ; 1 Ill. 407 ; 8 R. R. 378. Salomons *v.* Nissen, 2 T. R. 674 ; 1 R. R. 592. Haille *v.* Smith, 1 B. & P. 563 ; 1 Ill. 270. Davidson *v.* Gwynne, 12 East, 381 ; 11 R. R. 420. Cuming *v.* Brown, *cit.* See below, § 1305 sqq.

The same law prevails in America. Story's Abbott, 389, notes 1 and 2, and cases there cited.

(*d*) The Constantia, 6 Rob. Adm. 32. Addison on Contr. 539.

(*e*) See above, § 127. Benjamin on Sales, 732, 889. See below, § 1308.

420. Payment of Freight.—Freight is the hire due for the carriage of goods, and is either a gross sum for the voyage; or a rateable payment per ton of the ship's burden, or according to the size, weight, etc., of the goods transported (*a*); or by time, at so much per month (*b*), etc. It includes "primage" or "hat money," a small payment for the master's care (*c*); and "petty average," for towing, beaconage, etc. Sometimes a sum is agreed to be paid 'in advance, or' "on lading the goods"; but that, strictly speaking, is not freight, nor redemandable on the voyage not being completed (*d*).

(*a*) *Primâ facie*, the weight or measurement at the port of delivery is the criterion of freight to be paid ; but this rule is varied by proof that such weight or measurement is fallacious by reason of the thing carried altering in bulk or weight during the voyage, or by special agreement. Gibson *v.* Sturge, 10 Ex. 622 ; 24 L. J. Ex. 21. Buckle *v.* Knoop, 36 L. J. Ex. 49 ; L. R. 2 Ex. 333. Coulthurst *v.* Sweet, L. R. 1 C. P. 653. Tully *v.* Terry, L. R. 8 C. P. 679 ; 42 L. J. C. P. 240.

(*b*) See Hogarth *v.* Miller & Co., 1889 ; 16 R. 599 ; varied 1891, A. C. 48 ; 18 R. H. L. 10 (conditions as to efficiency —payment—average, etc). In this case freight does not depend on carriage of the goods, but on the terms of hiring.

(*c*) Howitt *v.* Paul, Sword, & Co., 1877 ; 5 R. 321.

(*d*) Andrew *v.* Moorhouse, 5 Taunt. 435 ; 1 Ill. 275 ; 15 R. R. 544. 1 Bell's Com. 573. Below, § 427, 459 *fin.* Leitch *v.* Wilson, 1868 ; 7 Macph. 150. Hogg *v.* Inglis' Trs., 1777 ; M. 9181, and App. *Mut. Contr.* 1 ; Hailes, 723 ; 5 B. Sup. 505. How *v.* Kirchner, 11 Moo. P. C. 21 (no lien for money payable in advance, not being freight). Kirchner *v.* Venus, 12 Moo. P. C. 361 ; 5 E. Jur. N. S. 395 (ditto, overruling Gilkson *v.* Middleton, 2 C. B. N. S. 134, and Neish *v.* Graham, 8 E. & B. 505). Lidgett *v.* Perren, 11 C. B. N. S. 362. Abbott, 265, 362 sqq. Byrne *v.* Schiller, L. R. 6 Ex. 20, 319 ; 40 L. J. Ex. 40, 177. The Karnak, L. R. 2 P. C. 505. Best *v.* Saunders, 1 Moo. & M. 208. Allison *v.* Bristol Marine Ins. Co., L. R. 1 App. Ca. 209. Hicks *v.* Shield, 26 L. J. Q. B. 205 ; 7 E. & B. 633. Rodocanachi *v.* Milburn, 18 Q. B. D. 67. See Dig. 19. 2. 1. 15, § 6. In England it is settled by the cases cited above that any prepayment in the nature of freight stipulated in the charter-party, being paid for lading the goods on board, is not recoverable on the failure of the voyage, unless the parties have clearly contracted that it shall be treated as a loan independent of freight. By the law of Scotland and the general maritime law, however, an advance against freight or on account of freight may, if there be nothing in the contract to infer a different intention, be recovered on the loss of the ship and cargo, the consideration on which it was advanced having thus failed. Watson & Co. *v.* Shankland, 1871 ; 10 Macph. 142 ; aff. 1873, 11 Macph. H. L. 51 ; L. R. 2 H. L. 304. The H. of L. affirmed the judgment on a special ground not involving assent to the law on which the C. of S. proceeded. The controversy arises from an artificial construction of the contracts in the earlier English cases.

421. Payment of freight is stipulated in the charter-party, and always made a condition of delivery of the goods in the bill of lading, "he or they paying freight" (*a*). Both on the principles of the contract of carriage, and on this condition, the master has a lien for the freight (*b*); but it has been questioned whether the master, if he give up the goods without insisting on payment of the freight does not waive the shipper's obligation for freight, and limit his demand to the person receiving the goods. In several cases, English and Scottish, it has been held that the condition 'in the bill of lading' is not for the shipper's security, and so the personal obligation of the shipper is not discharged, but remains entire under the charter-party (*c*), 'in addition to the liability for freight of the consignee or indorsee receiving the goods as owner, or in such circumstances as to imply an undertaking to pay freight (*d*)'; that 'even' when there is no charter-party, but a bill of lading only, the shipper is 'not' discharged (*e*); but, in an American case, the equitable distinction was taken, that where the consignor has the real interest in the goods, the same rule holds whether the goods are sent under a charter-party or under a bill of lading (*f*). '

'It has become usual for charterers (especially when they make the charter-party as agents) to stipulate that their liability for freight and other prestations under the contract shall cease when the cargo is loaded, the shipowner then relying on his lien over the cargo. This *cesser clause* is sometimes made still wider, conferring a lien for demurrage and dead freight, and exempting the charterer from liability for all claims of every description (*g*). There has been difficulty in some cases in determining how far the exemption extends; *e.g.* whether to demurrage incurred before the completed loading, or to unliquidated damages for detention in the nature of demurrage. The words may be extensive enough to free the charterer from all liability under the charter-party, they may free him absolutely from liabilities accruing both before and after loading. If, however, they are open to construction, not only may the construction be aided by reference to the extent of the equivalent lien given, but as cesser clauses are generally connected with the creation of a corresponding lien, it is a rule of construction, when clauses are so linked or coupled, that the shipowner is not understood to give up rights stipulated for in another part of the charter without compensation. Unless the cesser clause is so expressed as to exclude such a meaning, it will relieve the charterers from so much only of their liability as is commensurate with the lien given to the ship (*h*). Demurrage will be construed in the popular sense, if the word appears to have been so used (*i*), but in a combined lien and cesser clause it does not cover damages for undue detention at the port of loading (*k*). When the cesser of liability exists, it applies, even when the charterer is also consignee, to exclude action upon the charter-party, and restrict the shipowner to the exercise of his lien, or to the contract arising from the receipt of the goods under the bill of lading (*l*).'

(*a*) As to clauses importing the conditions of the charter-party into the bill of lading, see Gray *v.* Carr, *infra* (*g*). Porteous *v.* Watney, 3 Q. B. D. 534; 47 L. J. Q. B. 643, and cases there cited. Howitt *v.* Paul, Sword, & Co., 1877; 5 R. 321. Arrospe *v.* Barr, 1881; 8 R. 602. By the general reference to charter-party in a bill of lading only those conditions are incorporated which are consistent with the contract in the bill of lading, and so in general only those which affect the rights and liabilities of the consignees. Gullischen *v.* Stewart, *infra* (*l*). Gardiner *v.* Trechmann, 15 Q. B. D. 154. De Laurier *v.* Wyllie, 1889; 17 R. 167.

(*b*) See below, § 1423, 1424.

(*c*) Bennett *v.* M'Naught & Co., Dec. 15, 1820; F. C.; 1 Ill. 270. Kelting *v.* Jay, 1823; 2 S. 121. Pillans & Co. *v.* Pitt, 1825; 4 S. 350. Walley *v.* Montgomery, 3 East, 590; 7 R. R. 526. Ward *v.* Felton, 1 East, 507. The Theresa Bonita, 4 Robinson, 236. Cock *v.* Taylor, 13 East, 399; 12 R. R. 378. Moorsom *v.* Kymer, 2 M. & S. 303; 15 R. R. 261. Dougal *v.* Kemble, 3 Bingham, 383; 28 R. R. 648. Laing *v.* Finlayson, 1805; Hume, 313. Lowther *v.* Belfast Harbour Comrs., 16 Ir. C. L. R. 182; 16 Ir. Ch. 34; 17 Ir. Ch. 54. Faith *v.* E. I. Co., 4 B. & Al. 630.

(*d*) 18 and 19 Vict. c. 111, § 1; and cases cited above, § 417. Smith's Merc. Law, 375. Cf. Tobin *v.* Crawford, 5 M. & W. 235; 9 M. & W. 716. Lewis *v.* M'Kee, 38 L. J. Ex. 62; L. R. 4 Ex. 58. Callendar *v.* Cavan, 1853; 16 D. 146. No obligation to pay freight arises in point of law from the mere receipt of the goods under the bill of lading; but from such receipt and the conduct of the consignee or indorsee in regard to it, a contract will be readily inferred, the consideration for the contract being that the master has given up his lien. Möller *v.* Young, 25 L. J. Q. B. 94; 5 E. & B. 755. Sanders *v.* Vanzeller, 4 Q. B. 260; 11 L. J. Q. B. 497. Zwilchenbart *v.* Henderson, 9 Ex. 722; 23 L. J. Ex. 234. Comp. Furness, Withy, & Co. *v.* White & Co., 1895; A. C. 40 (consignee's acceptance of goods warehoused under § 492 sq. of the Act. *Supra*, § 408 (*aa*)).

(*e*) Drew *v.* Bird, 1 Mood. & Malk. 156. Overruled by Domett *v.* Beckford, 2 N. & M. 376; 5 B. & Ad. 521. Sanders, *cit.* See Smith's Merc. Law, 375. Abbott, 279. Maclachlan, 498.

(*f*) Barker *v.* Haven, 17 Johnson's Rep. 234. And see Story's Abbott, 286, note. Shee's Abbott, 361. Brodie's Stair, 994.

(*g*) Oglesby *v.* Yglesias, E. B. & E. 930; 27 L. J. Q. B. 356. Milvain *v.* Perez, 3 E. & E. 495; 30 L. J. Q. B. 90. Bannister *v.* Breslauer, L. R. 2 C. P. 497; 36 L. J. C. P. 195. Christofferson *v.* Hansen, L. R. 7 Q. B. 509. **Gray *v.* Carr**, L. R. 6 Q. B. 623; 40 L. J. Q. B. 257. Kish *v.* Cory, L. R. 10 Q. B. 553; 44 L. J. Q. B. 205. Lockhart *v.* Falk, L. R. 10 Ex. 132; 44 L. J. Ex. 105. Salvesen & Co. *v.* Guy & Co., 1886; 13 R. 85. Gardiner *v.* Macfarlane, M'Crindell, & Co., 1889; 16 R. 658.

(*h*) French *v.* Gerber, 2 C. P. D. 247; 45 L. J. C. P.

880 ; 46 *ib.* 320. Francesco *v.* Massey, L. R. 8 Ex. 101 ; 42 L. J. Ex. 75. Clink *v.* Radford & Co., 1891 ; 1 Q. B. 625. Hansen *v.* Harrold Bros., 1894 ; 1 Q. B. 612. Gardiner *v.* Macfarlane, M'Crindell, & Co., *cit.*

(*i*) French *v.* Gerber, *cit.* Sanguinetti, *infra*, which do not seem to have been cited in Lamb *v.* Kaselack, Alsen, & Co., 1882 ; 9 R. 482.

(*k*) Clink *v.* Radford & Co., *cit.* Dunlop *v.* Balfour, Williamson, & Co. 1892 ; 1 Q. B. 507. Gardiner *v.* Macfarlane, M'Crindell, & Co., *cit.*

(*l*) Sanguinetti *v.* Pacific S. Nav. Co., 2 Q. B. D. 238 ; 46 L. J. Q. B. 105. Beynon *v.* Kenneth, 1881 ; 8 R. 594. Gullischen *v.* Stewart, 11 Q. B. D. 186 ; 13 Q. B. D. 317.

422. The general rule is, that freight is due only for a voyage completed by delivery of the goods at their destined port ; for such, by their contract, is the engagement of the shipowners, and such the counter-engagement of the merchant. But this rule admits of certain distinctions and exceptions ; a part of the freight being demandable in certain cases, though the whole of what has been undertaken has not been done (*a*).

(*a*) Abbott, 369 ; Story's ed. 276. Luke *v.* Lyde, 2 Bur. 887 ; 1 Ill. 273. Hunter *v.* Prinsen, 10 East, 378 ; 10 R. R. 328. Andrew *v.* Moorhouse, 5 Taunt. 435 ; 15 R. R. 544. The Louisa, 1 Dods. Ad. 317. Metcalfe *v.* Britannia Ironworks Co., 1 Q. B. D. 613 ; 2 *ib.* 423 ; 45 L. J. Q. B. 837 ; 46 *ib.* 443. See above, § 420, note.

423. Where the ship is lost or disabled, but the goods are saved, the master may tranship the goods in order to convey them to their destination, and so earn his full freight ; and he may keep the goods a reasonable time for the purpose of completing the voyage (*a*). 'If he abandons the voyage without the charterer's consent, unless the effect of the excepted perils makes it physically impossible to complete the voyage, or impossible except by such expenditure on the ship as no prudent owner would incur, the shipowners are liable in damages (*b*).'

(*a*) Abbott, 313, 369 et seq., and Maclachlan, 428, 500, and cases there cited and commented on. 1 Valin, 636. Pothier, Charte-Partie, No. 59. Luke, *supra*, § 422 (*a*). Christy *v.* Row, 1 Taunt. 300 ; 1 Ill. 268 ; 9 R. R. 776. The Galam, 33 L. J. Adm. 97 ; B. & L. 167 ; 2 Moo. P. C. N. S. 216. Shipton *v.* Thornton, 9 A. & E. 314. Smith's Merc. Law, 357, 361, 379. Notara *v.* Henderson, 39 L. J. Q. B. 167 ; 41 *ib.* 158 ; L. R. 5 Q. B. 346 ; 7 *ib.* 225. The Soblomsten, *infra*, § 425 (*b*). Brodie's Stair, 983.

(*b*) Assicurazioni Generali *v.* S. S. Bessie Morris Co., 1892 ; 2 Q. B. 652. See below, § 485 (*b*).

424. If the goods have arrived at their destined port damaged, the rules are, that where the merchant takes the goods, freight is due, without abatement for damage or expense, unless occasioned by fault or insufficiency of the ship (*a*): 'that, unless the shipper be barred by taking delivery without objection, his illiquid claim for such damages may, contrary to the rule which till lately obtained in England (*b*), be pleaded by way of exception in answer to an action for the freight (*c*)'; that the merchant will not be allowed to pick and choose, but must take or leave the whole goods (*d*). But where the damage arises from mere accident or irresistible force, it has been doubted whether the merchant may abandon the goods for the freight (*e*). In Scotland, as the master is liable only for fault or breach of warranty (*f*), it would seem that there is no legal ground for throwing the risk on the owners, and allowing the merchant to abandon the goods for the freight; the owners having fulfilled their contract by carrying the goods to their port.

(*a*) Luke, *supra*, 422 (*a*). Lutwedge *v.* Grey, 1732 ; Elchies, *Mut. Cont.* 3 ; 1 Cr. & St. 119 ; 1 Ill. 273 ; Maclachlan, 479. Young *v.* Mann, 1857 ; 19 D. 785. See Williams *v.* Dobbie, 1884 ; 11 R. 982.

(*b*) Dakin *v.* Oxley, 15 C. B. N. S. 646. Since the Judicature Act it is no longer necessary to bring a cross action in England, a defendant being now enabled to plead a set-off or counter claim of damages, to the effect not merely of meeting the claim against himself, but of obtaining judgment for any excess found due to him. Rules of the Supreme Court, 1883, Order xix. 3.

(*c*) Taylor *v.* Forbes, 1830 ; 9 S. 113. M'Donald *v.* Thomson, 1843 ; 5 D. 719. Johnston *v.* Robertson, 1861 ; 23 D. 646. Shankland *v.* Athya & Co., 1865 ; 3 Macph. 810. 1 Bell's Com. 556.

(*d*) See Meyer *v.* Dresser, 16 C. B. N. S. 646 ; 33 L. J. C. P. 289. Luke *v.* Lyde, *supra*, § 422 (*a*).

(*e*) 1 Valin, 636. Pothier, Charte-Partie, No. 59.

(*f*) Lawrie *v.* Angus, 1677 ; M. 10,107 ; 1 Ill. 136. Lamont *v.* Boswell, 1680 ; M. 10,109. See Maclachlan, 469–474. Abbott, 366. Dakin *v.* Oxley, *cit.* Griswold *v.* N. Y. Ins. Co., 3 Johns. 321.

425. If by peril of the sea or hostile power the ship have stopped short in her voyage and cannot proceed, or the goods be carried away, freight *pro rata itineris* is due where the goods are taken by the merchant. This proceeds on an implied new contract, the original contract being left unfulfilled (*a*), 'founded on the voluntary acceptance of the goods by the freighter at the intermediate port, not alone, but if attended with such circumstances as to show that the further carriage was intentionally dispensed with (*b*).'

(*a*) Abbott, 380. *Supra*, § 422. Lutwedge, *supra*, § 424 (*a*). Wilson *v.* Bennet, March 10, 1809 ; F. C. ; 1 Ill. 268. Baillie *v.* Mondigliani, Marsh. Insur. 136 ; 1 Ill. 274.

(*b*) Vlierboom *v.* Chapman, 13 M. & W. 238 ; 13 L. J. Ex. 384. The Soblomsten, 36 L. J. Adm. 5 ; L. R. 1 Adm. & E. 293. Metcalfe *v.* Britannia Ironworks Co., *supra*, § 422 (*a*). Hopper *v.* Burness, 1 C. P. D. 137 ; 45 L. J.

C. P. 377. Hill *v.* Wilson, 4 C. P. D. 329; 48 L. J. C. P. 764. Mitchell *v.* Darthez, 2 Bing. N. C. 555. By the general maritime law it seems that such freight is due whether the goods are accepted by the merchant or not. Roccus, 54, 81. Straccha, P. iii. s. 24. Pothier, Charte-Partie, 68, 69. See Notara, § 423 (*a*).

426. If, in the course of the voyage, an obstruction shall arise, as by blockade, and full advantage shall be derived by the merchant going to another port, as convenient as if the original design were fulfilled, 'or equally within the charter-party (*a*),' freight will be due, or the loss divided (*b*).

(*a*) The Teutonia, L. R. 4 P. C. 171; 41 L. J. Adm. 57.

(*b*) The Friends, 1 Edwards, 246; 1 Ill. 274. As to the effect of a blockade on charter-party, see Geipel *v.* Smith, 41 L. J. Q. B. 153; L. R. 7 Q. B. 404.

427. If the voyage be divisible into parts, and these be made clear and distinct, freight may be demanded for the part performed (*a*).

(*a*) Taylor & Co. *v.* Hogg, 1802; M. 10,113; 1 Ill. 274. Mackrell *v.* Simond, Abbott, 393; Maclachlan, 483. Moorsom *v.* Greaves, 2 Camp. 627; 12 R. R. 763. De Silvale *v.* Kendall, 4 M. & S. 37; 16 R. R. 373. Gibbon *v.* Mendez, 2 B. & Ald. 17. Andrew *v.* Moorhouse, *cit.*, § 420; below, § 459 *fin.*

428. If part of the cargo be lost, 'or properly sold at a port of distress,' freight is due for what is delivered, where rateably stipulated; and even where it is not so stipulated, a rateable charge is allowed if the loss be not such as to authorise an abandonment as for a voyage lost (*a*).

(*a*) Ritchie *v.* Atkinson, 10 East, 295; 10 R. R. 307; Spence *v.* Chadwick, 10 Q. B. 517. The Industrie, 1894; P. 58. See Havelock *v.* Geddes, 10 East, 555; 10 R. R. 380. Bornmann *v.* Tooke, 1 Camp. 377; 10 R. R. 707. See 1 Bankt. p. 398. If a lump freight be stipulated, and the charterer does not load a full cargo, or part of the cargo be lost without fault of the shipowner, the whole sum is due. Robinson *v.* Knights, L. R. 8 C. P. 465; 42 L. J. C. P. 211. The Norway, 3 Moore, P. C. N. S. 245. Merchant Shipping Co. *v.* Armitage, 43 L. J. Q. B. 24; L. R. 9 Q. B. 99. Blanchet *v.* Powell's Llantwit Coll. Co., L. R. 9 Ex. 77; 43 L. J. Ex. 50. See Smith's Merc. Law, 372.

429. When the undertaking is to carry goods to a certain port, the duration of the voyage, 'and the accidents of the sea or river at that port (*a*), are' at the risk of the owners; where it is a contract on time, the duration is at the risk of the merchant. Detention during necessary repairs in course of voyage is regulated by this distinction (*b*). 'A ship bound to carry to a port or dock, "or as near thereto as she can safely get," is entitled to discharge under the second alternative, when the impediment to her entering the port or dock (*e.g.* overcrowding), though not permanent, will cause unreasonable delay and detention, *i.e.* such as the parties could not have contemplated when making the contract (*c*).'

(*a*) *E.g.* the depth of water on a bar, or the closing of navigation by ice. Schilizzi *v.* Derry, 4 E. & B. 873; 24 L. J. Q. B. 193. Metcalfe *v.* Britannia Ironworks Co., 1 Q. B. D. 613; 2 *ib.* 423; 45 L. J. Q. B. 837; 46 *ib.* 443. Hudson *v.* Ede, L. R. 2 Q. B. 566; 3 *ib.* 412; 36 L. J. Q. B. 273; 37 *ib.* 166.

(*b*) Havelock *v.* Geddes, 10 East, 555; 3 Ill. 128; 10 R. R. 380. Ripley *v.* Scaife, 5 B. & Cr. 167; 29 R. R. 205. See also Moorsom, § 427 (*a*); and Notara, § 423 (*a*).

(*c*) **Nelson** *v.* **Dahl**, 12 Ch. D. 568; rev. 6 App. Ca. 38; 50 L. J. Ch. 411. See above, cases in § 408 *ad fin.* and 431 (*f*); and cf. Horsley *v.* Price, 11 Q. B. D. 244. As to the construction of the word "port" in charter-parties and policies of insurance, see below, § 471 (*i*).

430. Dead Freight is the consideration which, as damages, one who engages to furnish a full lading, and fails to fill up the ship, must pay for the loss which the owners would otherwise suffer by part of the space being left unoccupied. It is not properly freight, but indemnity, 'or rather damages,' grounded on the covenant to fill up the ship (*a*). Where the freight is rateable on a uniform cargo, there is no difficulty in ascertaining the amount; but where there are different articles to be paid for at different rates, it becomes necessary to take the average on the voyage (*b*). There is no lien for dead freight without a special bargain (*c*).

(*a*) Phillips *v.* Rodie, 15 East, 547; 1 Ill. 275; 13 R. R. 528. Birley *v.* Gladstone, 3 M. & S. 205; 15 R. R. 465. Gladstone *v.* Birley, 2 Meriv. 401. Hunter *v.* Fry, 2 B. & Ald. 421. See M'Gavin *v.* Cuddy, 1843; 6 D. 297. **M'Lean & Hope** *v.* **Fleming**, 1871; 9 Macph. H. L. 38; L. R. 2 Sc. Ap. 128. Gray *v.* Carr, L. R. 6 Q. B. 522; 40 L. J. Q. B. 257. As to the shipowner's right to take in other goods to complete the lading, see Abbott, 325; 3 Kent, Com. 204.

(*b*) Thomas *v.* Clark, 2 Starkie, 450; 20 R. R. 714. Cockburn *v.* Alexander, 6 C. B. 791; 18 L. J. C. P. 74. Warren *v.* Peabody, 8 C. B. 800; 19 L. J. C. P. 43. Gether *v.* Capper, 15 C. B. 696; 18 C. B. 866; 24 L. J. C. P. 69; 25 *ib.* 260.

(*c*) See **M'Lean & Hope**, *cit.*; and above, § 421; below, § 1423.

431. Lay Days and Demurrage.—Lay days are the days stipulated for loading and unloading; and demurrage is the time during which the freighter may detain the ship still longer on certain terms (*a*). These are regulated by the special agreement, in which the expression "working days" excludes Sundays and holidays at the Custom-house; "running days" includes every day, 'and means calendar days and not periods of twenty-four hours (*b*)'; and the general expression "days" is held to mean running days, unless usage has otherwise settled (*c*). 'A fraction of a day is reckoned as a whole day (*d*); and demurrage or despatch money estimated by hours runs continuously day and night (*e*).' The lay days for 'loading or' unloading commence on the ship's arrival at the usual 'or stipulated' (*f*) place of 'loading or' discharge. In some places the port extends far beyond the place of unloading; and it is not on reaching the port in such cases that the lay days begin, 'nor, on the other hand, at the actual discharging berth,' but on arriving at the 'dock or' place of discharge (*g*).

Where the usual time is to be allowed for unloading, or where there is no stipulation on that point, the lay and demurrage days are regulated by the custom of the port and the principles of common law relative to demurrage; and a delay occasioned by the state of the port will not fall on the merchant (*h*).

'A vessel having a "floating clause" in her charter-party, or whose draught prevents her from reaching the usual place of discharge, is bound to lighten, where such is the custom, to enable her to reach the port of discharge (*i*); and the time spent in lightening is reckoned in her lay days (*k*). In charter-parties, as in other contracts which are silent as to the time of performance, the obligation is to load or discharge within a reasonable time, *i.e.* a reasonable time under the existing circumstances (*l*).

'The shipowner and merchant are bound to use reasonable diligence in loading or discharging (*m*); and if delay or unreadiness occurs without fault on either side, and from a cause over which neither party has any control, such as a strike of labourers, or the crowded state of the port, ice, etc., the loss remains where it falls (*n*). Under a general stipulation for despatch in loading and discharging, it has been held that delay at the port of loading cannot be made up by extra despatch in discharging (*o*).'

(*a*) Abbott, 241. Story's Abbott, 184, note.

(*b*) Cases in note (*d*).

(*c*) Cochran *v.* Retberg, 3 Esp. 121; 1 Ill. 276. Brown *v.* Johnson, 10 M. & W. 331; 11 L. J. Q. B. 373. Nieman *v.* Moss, 29 L. J. Q. B. 206. Parker *v.* Winlo, 7 E. & B. 942. Bastifell *v.* Lloyd, 1 H. & C. 388. Pringle *v.* Mollett, 6 M. & W. 80. Benson *v.* Blunt, 1 G. & D. 449. Holman, *infra*, § 432 (*c*). Nielsen *v.* Wait, 16 Q. B. D. 67. Brodie's Stair, 988.

(*d*) Comml. St. Co. *v.* Boulton, L. R. 10 Q. B. 346. Hough *v.* Athya & Co., 1878; 6 R. 961. The Katy, 1895; P. 56 (even when by agreement the lay days are advanced).

(*e*) Laing *v.* Hollway, 3 Q. B. D. 347; 47 L. J. Q. B. 512.

(*f*) Good & Co. *v.* Isaacs & Son, 1892; 2 Q. B. 555 ("berth"). Tharsis Co. *v.* Morel Bros., 1891; 2 Q. B. 647 (do.).

(*g*) Brereton *v.* Chapman, 7 Bing. 559; 3 Ill. 129; 33 R. R. 573. Lacour & Watson *v.* Donaldson, 1874; 1 R. 912. Tapscott *v.* Balfour, L. R. 8 C. P. 46; 42 L. J. C. P. 16. Brown *v.* Johnson, *cit.* Norden St. Co. *v.* Dempsey, 1 C. P. D. 654; 45 L. J. C. P. 764. M'Veagh *v.* Davies, 4 Ex. D. 265; 48 L. J. Ex. 686. **Nelson** *v.* **Dahl,** and other cases in § 429. Dall'Orso *v.* Mason & Co., 1876; 3 R. 419. Bremner *v.* Burrell & Son, 1877; 4 R. 934.

(*h*) Lannoy *v.* Werry, 2 Br. Par. Ca. 60. Rodgers *v.* Forresters, 2 Camp. 483; 11 R. R. 773. Burmester *v.* Hodgson, 2 Camp. 488; 11 R. R. 776. Hill *v.* Idle, 1 Starkie, 111; 16 R. R. 797. Lawrie *v.* Jamieson, 1796; 6 Br. Par. Ca. 474; 3 Pat. 493. Ashcroft *v.* Crow Orchard Colliery Co., 43 L. J. Q. B. 194; L. R. 9 Q. B. 540. **Postlethwaite** *v.* **Freeland,** 4 Ex. D. 155; 48 L. J. Ex. 353; aff. 49 L. J. Ex. 630; 5 App. Ca. 599. Wyllie *v.* Harrison & Co., 1855; 12 R. 92. Kruuse *v.* Drynan & Co., 1891; 18 R. 1110 (failure of railway company to provide waggons no excuse for merchant). Stephens, Mawson, & Goss *v.* Macleod & Co., 1891; 19 R. 38. Gardiner *v.* Macfarlane, M'Crindell, & Co., 1893; 20 R. 414 ("load as customary," etc.). See above, § 421, as to stipulations excluding freighter's liability for demurrage.

(*i*) Hillstrom *v.* Gibson, 1870; 8 Macph. 463. Nielsen *v.* Wait, 16 Q. B. D. 67.

(*k*) Dickinson *v.* Martini & Co., 1874; 1 R. 1185. Nielsen *v.* Wait, *cit.*

(*l*) Hick *v.* Raymond & Reid, 1893; A. C. 22. Taylor *v.* G. N. Ry. Co., *cit. supra*, § 164 (*b*).

(*m*) Fowler *v.* Knoop, 47 L. J. Q. B. 473; 48 *ib.* 333; 4 Q. B. D. 299. Cases in note (*h*).

(*n*) Ford *v.* Cotesworth, 38 L. J. Q. B. 52; 39 *ib.* 188; L. R. 4 Q. B. 127. Hick *v.* Raymond & Reid, 1893; A. C. 22. Cunningham *v.* Dunn, 3 C. P. D. 443; 48 L. J. C. P. 62. Whites *v.* Steamship Winchester Co., 1886; 13 R. 524 (quarantine).

(*o*) Avon S. S. Co. *v.* Leask & Co., 1890; 18 R. 280 (2nd Div., L. Young *diss.*). Qu. Whether this case was rightly decided on the facts, and whether if extra despatch is given there will in general be any room for applying the rule against lumping the time under such a clause?

432. When lay days and demurrage 'days' are stipulated, the shipper's obligation is absolute not to detain the ship beyond the days; and he will be liable for the demurrage, or for the loss arising from further detention, although occasioned by circumstances over which he has no control (*a*); 'as, *e.g.*, the crowded state of the docks (*b*); the state of the weather (*c*); a strike (*d*); or, in short, any ordinary vicissitudes or causes of detention which are not attributable to the shipowner or his agents or servants (*e*). But it is a good defence to an action for demurrage that the detention was due to the fault or negligence of the shipowner or his master (*f*); or to an impediment expressly excepted by the shipowner in the charter-party (*g*). In a general ship a consignee liable for demurrage is not excused because the delay was caused by consignees of other parts of the cargo (*h*).'

(*a*) Barret *v.* Dutton, 4 Camp. 333; 1 Ill. 277; 16 R. R. 798. Barker *v.* Hodgson, 3 M. & S. 267; 15 R. R. 485.

The Angerona, 1 Dodson, 382. Randall *v.* Lynch, 12 East, 179; 11 R. R. 340. Bessey *v.* Evans, 4 Camp. 131. Leer *v.* Yates, 3 Taunt. 387; Holt, 35; 12 R. R. 671. Struck *v.* Tennant, Abbott, 246. Hudson *v.* Ede, L. R. 3 Q. B. 412; 36 L. J. Q. B. 273; 37 L. J. Q. B. 166. Kay *v.* Field, 10 Q. B. D. 241. Coverdale *v.* Grant, 11 Q. B. D. 543; aff. 9 App. Ca. 470. Ford *v.* Coteswortli, *supra*, § 431 (*a*). Hills *v.* Sughrue, 15 M. & W. 253. Kearon *v.* Pearson, 7 H. & N. 386. New St. Tug Co. *v.* M'Clew, 1869; 7 Macph. 733. Lacour & Watson, *supra*, § 431 (*g*).

(*b*) Randall *v.* Lynch, *cit.* Brown *v.* Johnson, 10 M. & W. 331; 11 L. J. Q. B. 373. See Nelson & Co. *v.* Dahl, *supra*, § 429 (*a*), 431.

(*c*) Kearon *v.* Pearson, *cit.* Thiis *v.* Byers, 1 Q. B. D. 244; 45 L. J. Q. B. 511. Fenwick *v.* Schmalz, L. R. 3 C. P. 313; 37 L. J. C. P. 78 (snowstorm not within exception in loading clause of "accidents beyond his control"). Holman *v.* Peruv. Nitrate Co., 1878; 5 R. 657.

(*d*) Budgett *v.* Binnington, 1891; 1 Q. B. 35.

(*e*) Jones *v.* Adamson, 1 Ex. D. 60; 45 L. J. Ex. 64. Thiis *v.* Byers, *cit.* Randall, *cit.* Barret *v.* Dutton, *cit.* Erichsen *v.* Barkworth, 3 H. & N. 894; 28 L. J. Ex. 95 (neglect of consignee to claim the goods). Lamb *v.* Kaselack & Co., 1882; 9 R. 482. Whites *v.* Winchester S. S. Co., 1886; 13 R. 524 (quarantine).

(*f*) Thorsen *v.* Macdowall & Neilson, 1892; 19 R. 743. Taylor *v.* Clay, 9 Q. B. 713; 16 L. J. Q. B. 44. It has been held that, as the shipowner is bound to deliver the cargo over the ship's side, it is a good defence that the delay was caused by the insufficiency of the crew to do so within the lay days. Hansen *v.* Donaldson, 1874; 1 R. 1067. Comp. Maclachlan, 466, and Petersen *v.* Freebody, 1895; 2 Q. B. 294.

(*g*) Hudson *v.* Ede, *cit.* Ashcroft, *cit.* § 431 (*h*). Kay *v.* Field, and Coverdale *v.* Grant, *citt.* Granite City Steamship Co. *v.* Ireland & Son, 1891; 19 R. 124 (detention by railways). Letricheux & David *v.* Dunlop & Co., 1891; 19 R. 209 (do.). Lilly & Co. *v.* Stevenson & Co., 1895; 22 R. 278 (construction of exemption cause—strike). Little *v.* Stevenson & Co., 1895; 22 R. 796; aff. 1896, A. C. 108; 23 R. H. L. 12.

(*h*) Leer *v.* Yates, *cit.* Porteous *v.* Watney, 3 Q. B. D. 534; 47 L. J. Q. B. 643. See Lamb *v.* Kaselack, *cit.* (*e*).

433. When demurrage is stipulated while the ship is waiting for convoy, it ceases as soon as the convoy is ready to sail (*a*). And demurrage while waiting for a cargo ceases when the ship is fully laden and has her clearances ready to sail (*b*). When the vessel is loaded, all future risk is with the shipowners (*c*).

(*a*) Lawrie and Lannoy, *supra*, § 431 (*h*).
(*b*) Barret, *supra*, § 432 (*a*).
(*c*) Pringle *v.* Mollett, 6 M. & W. 80. Lawrie, *cit.*

434. *Damages for Detention.*—When the ship is detained by the shipper after the demurrage days are expired, the damage is to be fixed according to circumstances. The sum fixed for the demurrage may give a *primâ facie* rule for estimating such damage, but not a measure absolute or conclusive (*a*).

(*a*) Moorsom *v.* Bell, 2 Camp. 616; 1 Ill. 278; 12 R. R. 755. The Angerona, *supra*, § 432 (*a*). Randall *v.* Lynch, *ib.*

435. Responsibility of Owners for Goods (*a*).—The owners are responsible under their contract for the goods shipped, in the condition in which they were delivered, barring the perils of the sea, hostile force, and inevitable accident. Under these exceptions are included such dangers and accidents of the sea, rivers, and navigation as are unavoidable; as of rocks, sandbanks, collision (*b*); capture by the enemy or by pirates (*c*); loss by irresistible force of man; (*d*) actual detention by kings, princes, and rulers (*e*). But where the loss, directly or indirectly, arises from want of skill or faulty navigation (as deviation from the right course), the owners will be liable (*f*). 'Even clauses in charter-parties or bills of lading expressly freeing the shipowners from liability for breakage, leakage, collision, and such like, do not exempt them from liability for the negligence of themselves or the crew; they only shift the *onus probandi* (*g*). But more extensive clauses of exemption are now common, and are valid, *e.g.* exempting from all fault of the master or mariners (*h*); or from liability for any damage that can be covered by insurance (*i*). The master is bound, wherever he is not saved by express exemption, to take all reasonable care of the cargo, and when it is damaged by a cause for which he is not responsible, he ought still at the shipper's expense to use all reasonable means to save it from deterioration or destruction by the consequences of the accident, as by unshipping and drying it, when that is a reasonable and ordinary course, and is not attended with delay of the voyage (*k*). As the Carriers Act does not apply to carriers by water, limitation of liability by notice is still open to shipowners (*l*).' The owners are also liable according to the rules of public policy, grounded on the Edict *Nautæ Caupones*, etc. (*m*).

(*a*) See *ante*, § 160, 236 et seq.

(*b*) Abbott, 327 et seq. Buller *v.* Fisher, 3 Esp. 67; 1 Ill. 170; 4 R. R. 902. Smith *v.* Scott, 4 Taunt. 126; 1 Ill. 278. Fletcher *v.* Inglis, 2 B. & Ald. 315; 1 Ill. 303. See § 241.

(*c*) Pickering *v.* Barclay, Abbott, 329. Barton *v.* Wolliford, *ib.* See Cullen *v.* Butler, 5 M. & S. 461; 17 R. R. 400.

(*d*) Brondrett *v.* Hentigg, Holt's Cases, 149; 1 Ill. 288. Hagedorn *v.* Whitmore, 1 Starkie, 157.

(*e*) Atkinson *v.* Ritchie, 10 East, 534; 10 R. R. 372. See above, § 414 (*c*).

(*f*) Stewart *v.* Johnston, Jan. 17, 1810; F. C. Abbott, 327 et seq. Roccus, § 55, 56. Emerigon, vol. i. p. 532. Trent & Mersey Navig. Co. *v.* Wood, Abbott, 327. Grill *v.* Iron Screw Collier Co., L. R. 1 C. P. 600; 3 C. P. 476; 35 L. J. C. P. 321; 37 L. J. C. P. 205. Turnbull *v.* Black & Rankin, 1799; Hume, 300 (faulty loading).

(*g*) Phillips *v.* Clark, 2 C. B. N. S. 156. Czech *v.* Gen.

Steam Nav. Co., L. R. 3 C. P. 14 ; 37 L. J. C. P. 6. Moes, Moliere, & Tromp *v.* Leith and Amst. St. Nav. Co., 1867 ; 5 Macph. 988. Craig & Rose v. Delargy, 1879 ; 6 R. 1279. Horsley *v.* Baxter Bros. & Co., 1893 ; 20 R. 333. See the Nepoter, L. R. 2 Adm. 375 ; 38 L. J. Adm. 63. The Duero, L. R. 2 Adm. 393 ; 38 L. J. Adm. 69. Thrift *v.* Youle, 46 L. J. C. P. 402 ; 2 C. P. D. 432.

(*h*) Cases in (*g*). Steel & Craig *v.* State Line Co., 1877 ; 4 R. 657 ; *ib.* H. L. 103 ; L. R. 3 App. Ca. 72. Cunningham *v.* Colvils, Lowden, & Co., 1889 ; 16 R. 295. Dobell *v.* S. S. Rossmore Co., 1895 ; 2 Q. B. 408. Gilroy, Sons, & Co. *v.* Price & Co., 1891 ; 18 R. 591 ; revd. 1893, A. C. 56 ; 20 R. H. L. 1. Hayn *v.* Culliford, 3 C. P. D. 410 ; 4 *ib.* 182 ; 47 L. J. C. P. 755 ; 48 L. J. C. P. 372. Chartd. Merc. Bank of India, *v.* Netherlds. Ind. St. Nav. Co., 9 Q. B. D. 118 ; 10 *ib.* 521 ; 51 L. J. Q. B. 393 ; 52 *ib.* 220.

(*i*) Taylor *v.* Liverp. and G. W. Co., L. R. 9 Q. B. 546 ; 43 L. J. Q. B. 205. Moore *v.* Harris, L. R. 1 App. Ca. 318 ; 45 L. J. P. C. 55.

(*k*) Notara *v.* Henderson, L. R. 5 Q. B. 346 ; 7 *ib.* 225 ; 39 L. J. Q. B. 167 ; 41 *ib.* 158. Tronson *v.* Dent, 8 Moore, P. C. 419. Garriock *v.* Walker, 1873 ; 1 R. 100. Adam *v.* Morris, 1890 ; 18 R. 153. Comp. § 450 ; and as to rats, see § 241, note.

(*l*) See above, § 236 (*b*), 244 (*a*) (*n*), 244A. Lightbody's Tr. *v.* Hutchisons, 1886 ; 14 R. 4.

(*m*) See above, § 236 et seq.

436. The responsibility of shipowners is limited by the Legislature in certain cases 'where loss or damage happens without their actual fault or privity' (*a*). Thus, the owners of ships occupied in sea voyages are not liable for loss by fire (*b*). But this exemption has been held not to apply to small craft, lighters, and boats concerned in inland navigation (*c*). 'By 57 and 58 Vict. c. 60, § 502, owners of seagoing ships are not liable for loss or damage—1*st*, to any goods or merchandise by fire on board ship (see above, § 239); or, 2*nd*, to any gold, silver, diamonds, watches, jewels, or precious stones, by robbery, embezzlement, making away with or secreting them, unless the true nature or value has been declared in writing on the bill of lading or otherwise at the time of shipping.' Owners are not liable for loss by the fault of the pilot 'when the employment of such pilot is compulsory by statute (*d*); but they are responsible for a pilot who is appointed by them, when they are not required by law to do so (*e*).' Those exemptions do not extend to masters. Owners 'were by earlier statutes' liable only to the amount of the value of the ship and freight (*f*), which 'was' to be calculated at the time of the loss or damage; and the value as to freight 'was' to be only the amount that the ship would have earned had she completed her voyage (*g*).

'The last of these statutes was repealed, and a somewhat different rule enacted by the Merchant Shipping Act, 17 and 18 Vict. c. 104, § 504. But this also has been repealed; and by 25 and 26 Vict. c. 63, § 54, now included in 57 and 58 Vict. c. 60, § 503, it is enacted that the owners of any ship, British or foreign, shall not—where without their actual fault or privity (*h*) (1) loss of life or personal injury is caused to persons carried in their ships; or (2) damage or loss is caused to goods, merchandise, or other things whatsoever on board their ships; or (3) loss of life or personal injury is, by improper navigation (*i*) of their ship, caused to persons in another ship or boat; or (4) loss or damage is so caused to any other ship, or boat, or goods, merchandise, or things on board any other ship or boat—be answerable in damages in respect of loss of life or personal injury, either alone or together with loss or damage to ships, boats, goods, merchandise, or other things, to an aggregate amount exceeding £15 for each ton of the ship's tonnage; nor in respect of loss or damage to ships, goods, merchandise, or other things, whether there be in addition loss of life or personal injury, or not, to an aggregate amount exceeding £8 for each ton of the ship's tonnage; *i.e.* in case of sailing ships, the registered, and in case of steamers, the gross tonnage, without deduction on account of engine room, but excluding the certified berthage of the crew (*k*). A shipowner, whether admitting or not his liability for loss or damage, may apply to the Court of Chancery or the Court of Session for the purpose of determining the amount of such liability, and distributing it among the claimants, and of staying other proceedings (*l*). The limitation does not save the shipowner from interest from the date of collision, or from costs (*m*); and applies only to injury done to or on board ship, not to a pier, or wharf, or anything ashore (*n*).'

(*a*) See *ante*, § 243. 57 and 58 Vict. c. 60, § 502.

(*b*) 26 Geo. III. c. 86, § 2, 3. 52 Geo. III. c. 39, § 50. 53 Geo. III. c. 159, § 2, 4.

(*c*) Hunter & Co. *v.* M'Gown, 1819 ; 1 Bligh, 573 ; 6 Pat. 460 ; 1 Ill. 171 ; 20 R. R. 198.

(*d*) 6 Geo. IV. c. 125, § 53. By 57 and 58 Vict. c. 60, § 633 (which is declaratory of a general principle of the law of principal and agent—The Halley, *infra.* The Agricola, 2 Rob. Adm. 10), no owner or master is answerable to any person for any loss or damage occasioned by the fault or incapacity of any qualified pilot acting in charge of the ship in any district where the employment of such pilot is compulsory by law. See Abbott, 155. Smith's Merc. Law, 364. Maclachlan, 278 sq. The Calabar, L. R. 2 P. C. 238. The Halley, L. R. 2 P. C. 193. Clyde Nav. Trs. *v.* Barclay,

Curle, & Co., 1875; 2 R. 842; aff. 1876, 3 R. H. L. 44; 1 App. Ca. 790. Owners of Strathspey *v.* Owner of Islay, 1891; 18 R. 1049 (contributory fault of master. See Macbrayne *v.* Patience, 1892, 20 R. 224, as to liability of pilot). The Princeton, 3 Adm. D. 90; 47 L. J. Adm. 33. The Daioz, 47 L. J. Adm. 1. As to steam tugs with pilot, see The Ocean Wave, L. R. 3 P. C. 205. The Energy, L. R. 3 Adm. 48; 39 L. J. Adm. 25. The Mary, 5 P. D. 14; 48 L. J. P. D. & A. 66. Smith *v.* St. Lawrence Towboat Co., L. R. 5 P. C. 308. Spaight *v.* Tedcastle, 6 App. Ca. 217. The onus is on the shipowners to prove that the loss is due to the pilot's fault; and that being proved, the onus of proving contributory fault of the ship lies on the party claiming damages. Clyde Nav. Trs., *cit.* The Velasquez, 4 Moo. P. C. N. S. 426; L. R. 1 P. C. 494; 36 L. J. Adm. 19. The Carrier Dove, 2 Moo. P. C. N. S. 261; Br. & L. 113. The Iona, L. R. 1 P. C. 426; 4 Moo. P. C. N. S. 336. The Meteor, 9 Ir. R. Eq. 567. The Guy Mannering, 51 L. J. P. D. 57; L. R. 7 P. D. 52, 132 (Suez Canal).

(*e*) The Peerless, 30 L. J. Adm. 89; 13 Moo. P. C. 444; Lush. 103. The Lion, 37 L. J. Adm. 39; 38 *ib.* 51; L. R. 2 Adm. 102. The Woburn Abbey, 38 L. J. Adm. 28.

(*f*) 7 Geo. II. c. 15. 26 Geo. III. c. 86, § 1. 53 Geo. III. c. 159.

(*g*) Wilson *v.* Dickson, 2 B. & Ald. 2. Cannan *v.* Meaburn, 1 Bing. 465. Hunter & Co. *supra* (*c*). The Dundee, 1 Hag. Ad. 109. Gale *v.* Lawrie, 5 B. & Cr. 156. The Northumbria, L. R. 3 Ad. & Eccl. 6.

(*h*) Kidston *v.* M'Arthur, 1878; 5 R. 936. The Warkworth, 9 P. D. 145.

(*i*) The Warkworth, 9 P. D. 145.

(*k*) This exclusion clause is added in the Act of 1894, in consequence of the conflicting decisions in Burrell *v.* Simpson & Co., 1876; 4 R. 177; and The Franconia, 3 P. D. 164. Marsden on Collisions, 174. See Clarke *v.* E. Dunraven, 1897; A. C. 59 (exclusion of Act by implied agreement as between yachts in a club race).

(*l*) 57 and 58 Vict. c. 60, § 504. Flensburg Shipping Co. *v.* Seligmann, 1871; 9 Macph. 1011. Miller *v.* Powell, 1875; 2 R. 976. Burrell *v.* Simpson & Co., 1876; 4 R. 177; rev. 1877 (Thompson *v.* Simpson), 5 R. H. L. 40; 3 App. Ca. 279 (collision of two vessels belonging to the same owner—comp. Chartd. Merc. Bk. of India *v.* Nethds. India St. Nav. Co., 9 Q. B. D. 118; 10 Q. B. D. 521; 51 L. J. Q. B. 393; 52 *ib.* 220. Rankine *v.* Raschen, 1877; 4 R. 725. Carron Co. *v.* Cayzer, Irvine, & Co., 1885; 13 R. 114 (expenses of application). Leycester *v.* Logan, 26 L. J. Ch. 306. Hill *v.* Audus, 24 L. J. Ch. 229; 1 K. & J. 263. Cope *v.* Doherty, 4 K. & J. 367; 2 De G. & J. 614; 27 L. J. Ch. 600 (as to foreign ships, comp. Westlake Priv. Int. Law, § 192. Foote, Pr. Int. Law, 404-410. The Wild Ranger, 32 L. J. Adm. 49). The Amelia, 1 Moo. P. C. N. S. 471; 32 L. J. Adm. 191. Glaholm *v.* Barker, L. R. 2 Eq. 598; 1 Ch. 223; 35 L. J. Ch. 259, 657. L. and S.-W. Ry. Co. *v.* James, 42 L. J. Ch. 337; L. R. 8 Ch. 241.

(*m*) The Northumbria, L. R. 3 A. & E. 6; 39 L. J. Adm. 3.

(*n*) River Wear Comrs. *v.* Adamson, 1 Q. B. D. 546; 2 App. Ca. 743; 46 L. J. Q. B. 82.

CHAPTER XII

OF GENERAL AVERAGE, AND SALVAGE

I. GENERAL AVERAGE.

437. Nature of it.—The losses which are suffered at sea, when not total, are commonly called average losses; distinguished by the terms "particular average" and "general or gross average." Particular average is the partial loss or damage, directly occasioned by shipwreck, or other accidental misfortune to the ship, in its hull, rigging, anchors, etc., or to the cargo, or any part of it. General average is a loss accomplished by the hand of man, in the voluntary throwing over of something for the common benefit of all concerned in the voyage. The former misfortune falls where it lights; the latter is a sacrifice, for indemnification of which all are bound to contribute. The principles according to which the contribution in general average is to be settled, are those of a partnership by necessity; as explained in the "Lex Rhodia de Jactu," adopted under certain modifications in the several commercial countries of Europe, '"Si levandæ navis gratia jactus mercium factus est, omnium contributione sarciatur, quod pro omnibus datum est"' (*a*).

(*a*) See Dig. lib. 14. tit. 2 ad Leg. Rhod. 1. 1. Casaregis, Disc. de Commercio, disc. 45. 46. Peckius, ad Leg. Rhod. cum notis Vinnii. 2 Valin, 175. 1 Emerigon, 605. Pothier, Tr. des Avaries, No. 108 et seq. 2 Pardessus, 159. Kuricke, 188. Abbott, 497. Stevens on Average. Benecke on Indemnity, 165. 3 Kent, Com. 232. Story on Bailments, § 583. 1 Bell's Com. 583. Brodie's Stair, 1006. Manley Hopkins on Average. Dixon on Average. Weytsen on Gen. Average in Law Times, vol. xlv. p. 391. Arnould on Marine Insur. 770 sqq. Maclachlan on Shipping, ch. xiv. Strang, Steel, & Co. *v.* Scott & Co., 14 App. Ca. 601.

438. The Requisites to Contribution are: That a sacrifice shall have been purposely and advisedly made, by the hand of man, of part of the cargo, or of ship, rigging, etc., for the common safety (*a*); and that the property of those concerned shall be preserved, or still remain to them. In some of the maritime codes, it is required that there shall be a consultation of those concerned on board; but it is sufficient to raise the right to contribution, if, with such deliberate purpose as time and circumstances permit, the sacrifice shall have been resolved upon as necessary to the common safety, in a case of real danger (*b*). It is not indispensable that the thing shall have been actually thrown overboard or destroyed; but sufficient if it have been exposed to loss for the common benefit, and have suffered from such exposure (*c*). Nor is it necessary that the property shall have been saved by means of the sacrifice, provided it be saved. Although the sacrifice, by all deemed necessary, or such as all, if present, would have consented to at the time, may have proved needless in the event, yet those whose goods remain to them must contribute on the principles of partnership by necessity. This, however, is contrary to the rules of some maritime codes (*d*).

(*a*) Hence, if a ship be accidentally stranded, the expenses incurred in discharging the cargo, but not afterwards, as for discharging ship's stores, or of getting the ship afloat, are general average. Job *v.* Langton, 6 E. & B. 779; 26 L. J. Q. B. 97. If a ship be intentionally run on shore to avoid foundering or striking on dangerous rocks, it is held by Prof. Bell, and has been decided in America and Scotland, that the shipowners are entitled to contribution for loss or damage of the ship from the cargo saved. 1 Bell's Com. 589 (635, M'L.'s ed.). Colombian Insur. Co. *v.* Ashby, 13 Pet. 331; 13 Curtis, 176. Tudor's L. C. 97. Thomson *v.* Landale, 1763; M. 13,428. See Moran *v.* Jones, 7 E. & B. 332. But it is said that the practice of merchants is contrary to the rule, Baily on Gen. Aver. 43, 57, 60; and see Maclachlan on Shipping, 672–675.

(b) Emerigon, 609. Abbott, 503. Benecke, 169. Birkley v. Presgrave, 1 East, 220; 6 R. R. 256. Tudor's L. C. 83.

(c) Benecke, 169 et seq.

(d) Benecke, pp. 172 and 179. Cons. del Mare, c. 194. 2 Valin, 194. 1 Emerigon, 616. Code de Com. art. 423.

439. The goods sacrificed, or thrown overboard, must have been regularly on board as part of the cargo. So there is no contribution for the loss of goods stowed on deck, 'unless such mode of carriage is justified by the usage of trade'; for they are held an encumbrance (a), and the sole remedy to the owner is against the master. 'Even if the goods be carried on deck under an agreement to that effect with the owner of them, there is no right to contribution in a question with the other shippers of cargo (b). One who has by his fault occasioned the peril which gives rise to the claim, cannot claim indemnity or contribution on account of his jettisoned goods or of his ship (c).' Goods on board without a bill of lading are *presumed* supernumerary, and are not to be indemnified by average unless *proved* to be regularly on board (d); but if saved, they must contribute.

If goods be thrown over merely to lighten the ship for the convenience of getting into port, there is no contribution (e); but if thrown over to enable the ship to get over a bar as a refuge from the enemy, or for repair necessary to the safety of all concerned, or to be floated from a bank on which she has struck, or to escape from an enemy, contribution will be due (f). Where goods are sent on shore in lighters for debarkation, their loss is not average; but if placed in lighters to lighten the ship for the general safety, contribution will be due (g). Masts, etc., cut away and sacrificed for the ship's safety are average; but not when cut away on account of injury sustained by perils of the sea (h). The sacrifice or cutting up of sails, ropes, etc., for stopping a leak, is average (i). So is damage done in the course of making the sacrifice (k). 'Money paid for salvage services is general average loss (l); and damage done and expense incurred by an abnormal use of the ship's engines for the common safety in, *e.g.*, a stranded ship (m).' The expense of going into port for the general safety, and for unloading, loading, warehouse rent, 'seamen's wages,' etc., in order to repair 'general' average loss, 'with the expense of the repairs occasioned by the sacrifice, and generally extraordinary expenditure properly incurred for the general interest,' is 'general' average (n), 'but not as a general rule, expense incurred for the ship after the cargo is saved, and the community of interest between it and the ship is over (o).' The result of many contending opinions, and various regulations on the question of going into port for repairing sea damage, not itself 'general' average loss, seems to be that the expense, 'beyond the charges of entering the port (as towage, dues, etc.), and of the unloading of the cargo, if necessary for the safety of both ship and cargo (p),' is not average.

'It was thought, and was formerly laid down in this section (q), that the cost of repairing the ship was general average,' in so far as necessary for safety in prosecuting the voyage, and of no further use to the ship; 'but that doctrine is erroneous, the true principle being that, if the damage was incurred by the mere violence of the wind and weather, without voluntary sacrifice on the part of the shipowner for the benefit of all concerned, it falls, with the expenses consequent upon it, within his contract to keep his ship tight, staunch, and strong, and fit for the service. But if for the safety of both ship and cargo transhipment or unloading is necessary, the expense of such unloading, but not that of reloading, is a general average loss. It seems that on principle (although there has been some variation in practice), nothing ought to be charged to general average which is not itself within the definition of a general average sacrifice, or is the direct result of one (r). So a loss, however extraordinary, that is caused in the mere fulfilment of the shipowner's contract, as in repelling a hostile attack (s), or purchasing coal to prosecute the voyage with an auxiliary screw when the vessel is disabled from carrying sail (t), is not a general average loss.'

(a) 2 Valin, 189. Abbott, 542 et seq. The same rule in America; Story's Abbott, 355, note 1. Milward v. Hibbert, 3 Q. B. 120. Miller v. Titherington, 7 H. & N. 954; 31 L. J. Ex. 363. Tudor's L. C. 92. See below, § 470. 39 and 40 Vict. c. 80, § 24; and Maclachlan, 665–669. Burton v. English, 12 Q. B. D. 218; 49 L. T. R. 768 (carried "at merchant's risk"). Deck cargo if jettisoned is not within a clause in bill of lading exempting the ship from loss by jettison. Royal Ex. Shipping Co. v. Dixon, 12 App. Ca. 11.

(b) Johnson v. Chapman, 35 L. J. C. P. 23; 19 C. B. N. S. 563. Wright v. Marwood, 50 L. J. Q. B. 643; 7 Q. B. D. 62.

(c) Schloss v. Heriot, 14 C. B. N. S. 59; 32 L. J. C. P. 211. Strang, Steel, & Co. v. Scott & Co., *cit.* § 437.

(d) Cons. del Mare, 92 et seq. Jugemens d'Oleron, art. 8, No. 22.

(e) 2 Pothier, Avaries, No. 146.

(f) 2 Valin, 195. 2 Pothier, Avaries, Nos. 145-6. Plummer v. Wildman, 3 M. & S. 482; 1 Ill. 280; 16 R. R. 334. Story's Abbott, 350, note. As to goods injured by water applied for the extinction of fire, see Stewart v. West Ind., etc., St. Ship. Co., 42 L. J. Q. B. 84, 191; L. R. 8 Q. B. 88. Whitecross Wire Co. v. Savill, 51 L. J. Q. B. 426; 8 Q. B. D. 653.

(g) Valin and Pothier, *ut supra*. Benecke, 209. Royal Mail St. Pt. Co. v. Engl. Bk. of Rio Jan., 19 Q. B. 362.

(h) Stevens on Average, 15, 16. Benecke, 182 et seq. Shepherd v. Kottgen, 2 C. P. D. 578; 47 L. J. C. P. 67.

(i) Stevens on Average, 18.

(k) Pothier, No. 115. 2 Valin, 190. Marshall, 429. Abbott, 505. Benecke, 177.

(l) Anderson v. Ocean S. S. Co., 10 App. Ca. 107 (towage contract).

(m) The Bona, 1895; P. 125.

(n) **Attwood** v. **Sellar,** 5 Q. B. D. 286; 49 L. J. Q. B. 515. **Svensden** v. **Wallace,** 13 Q. B. D. 69; aff. 10 App. Ca. 404. Rose v. Bank of Australasia, 1894; A. C. 687.

(o) Walthew v. Mavrojani, L. R. 5 Ex. 116; 39 L. J. Ex. 81. Job v. Langton, 6 E. & B. 779; 26 L. J. Q. B. 97. R. M. St. Pt. Co. v. Engl. Bk. of Rio. Jan., 19 Q. B. D. 362 (cargo landed from stranded ship before jettison). See M'Andrew v. Thatcher, 3 Wallace, 347; and 2 Parsons on Mar. Insur. 263. Parsons on Shipping, 390, 392.

(p) See cases in note (o). Hall v. Janson, 4 E. & B. 500; 24 L. J. Q. B. 97.

(q) Da Costa v. Newnham, 2 T. R. 407. Jackson v. Charnock, 8 T. R. 509; 1 Ill. 279. Plummer, *supra* (f). Power v. Whitmore, 4 M. & S. 141. Benecke, 191-207.

(r) Abbott, 508. Cases reviewed in **Attwood** v. **Sellar**, *cit.* (n); and **Svensden** v. **Wallace** (n). Tudor's L. C. 100. Maclachlan, 676. The Copenhagen, 1 C. Rob. 289. Hall v. Jansen, 4 E. & B. 500. Moran v. Jones, 7 E. & B. 523 (questioned in Svensden v. Wallace, *cit.* See Hallet v. Wigram, 9 C. B. 580. Benson v. Chapman, 8 C. B. 950; 2 H. L. Ca. 696. Wilson v. Bank of Victoria, L. R. 2 Q. B. 263; 36 L. J. Q. B. 89.

(s) Covington v. Roberts, 2 B. & P. 378; 9 R. R. 669. Taylor v. Curtis, 6 Taunt. 608; 16 R. R. 686. Maclachlan, 681 sq.

(t) Wilson v. Bank of Victoria, *cit.* Harrison v. Bank of Australasia, L. R. 7 Ex. 39; 41 L. J. Ex. 36. See Robinson v. Price, 2 Q. B. D. 91.

440. The Subjects of Contribution are—the cargo, ship (a), and freight. *The cargo* includes the goods thrown overboard (b); those loaded on deck (c); luggage in chests and boxes (d). But persons or apparel are not liable to contribution (e). *The ship* contributes, deducting stores and provisions, wear and tear, and partial loss (f). And *freight* contributes, deducting wages (g).

(a) See an exception, Covington v. Roberts, *cit.*, § 439 (s).

(b) 2 Pothier, Avar. No. 123. Price v. Noble, 4 Taunt. 123; 1 Ill. 280; 13 R. R. 566.

(c) 2 Valin, 189. Stevens, 54. Gould v. Oliver, 4 Bing. 134.

(d) 3 Ersk. 3. § 55.

(e) Abbott, 527. Price v. Noble, *cit.* Marshall, 432.

(f) Stevens, 55.

(g) *Ib.* 64. See Scaife v. Tobin, 3 B. & Ad. 523. Williams v. Lond. Ass. Co., 1 M. & S. 318. Frayes v. Wormes, 19 C. P. N. S. 159.

441. Valuation and Apportionment.—In valuing and apportioning the contribution, the guiding principle is, that the owner of the property sacrificed is to be placed in the same condition as if his property had been part of what is saved. The rules observed are these:—If the ship reaches her port without further damage, the property sacrificed is to be valued at the market price of the port of delivery, freight, duties, and charges deducted; and it must bear its share of the contribution (a). The goods which arrive in port undamaged are taken at their actual value in the port of discharge, deducting charges, etc. (b); if put back, they are taken at the invoice price (c); if stopped short of their destination, at their value where stopped. If the goods saved be damaged after the jettison, the deteriorated value must be taken. The owner of goods lost pays no contribution for them.

(a) Benecke, 286. The jettisoned goods are to be estimated at the value they would have had if they had arrived at the port of adjustment; and if they would have arrived in a damaged condition, allowance must be made. Fletcher v. Alexander, 37 L. J. C. P. 193; L. R. 3 C. P. 375.

(b) Marshall, 434, 502. Stevens, 51. See 2 Kent, Com. 242.

(c) Abbott, 529. Stevens, 52, 53.

442. Who liable.—The true owner of the goods saved is the person liable to contribution, 'and he becomes so liable only on the vessel's arrival' (a); and the claim 'upon the cargo' may be secured by lien. If average be made a condition in the bill of lading, a consignee taking the goods will be liable. But if there be no such condition, and the goods are given up to a consignee not the owner, without an express or implied contract by him to pay average, the claim lies only against the consignor (b). 'In the case of a general ship it is the duty of the shipowners or master to have the contribution settled and collect the amount; and with that view to require a bond from each owner on delivery of his goods for payment of his proportion of the loss; and for failure to do so they are liable to an action at the instance of an owner entitled to contribution (c). Each owner of jettisoned goods becomes a creditor of ship and cargo saved; and may recover contribution either by direct action or by enforcing through the shipmaster as his agent a lien on each parcel of goods saved (*d*).'

(*a*) Ranking & Co. *v.* Todd, 1870; 8 Macph. 914. See below, § 456.

(*b*) Scaife *v.* Tobin, 3 B. & Ad. 523; 1 Ill. 280. See below, § 1423, 1426.

(*c*) Crookes *v.* Allan, 5 Q. B. D. 38; 49 L. J. Q. B. 201. Huth *v.* Lamport, 16 Q. B. D. 442, 735 (reasonableness of terms of bond). See below, § 472 (5).

(*d*) Strang, Steel, & Co. *v.* Scott & Co., 1889; 14 App. Ca. 601.

II. SALVAGE.

443. Nature of Salvage.—Salvage is a reward or recompense given to those by means of whose labour, intrepidity, or perseverance, a ship, or goods, 'or the lives of persons from a British ship or boat, or from a foreign ship or boat within British waters, or, when the Government of a foreign country has assented to such exercise of the jurisdiction of British Courts, from ships of that country even when beyond British jurisdiction (*a*),' have been saved from shipwreck, fire, or capture (*b*). 'Salvage for life is payable by the owners of the ship or cargo, and as regards the owners of the ship has priority to other salvage claims. Where the ship is lost, or its value is insufficient, the Board of Trade may award such sum as it deems fit out of the Mercantile Marine Fund (*c*).' It rests on plain principles of equity, and a right of lien; but the rate of salvage to be allowed, and the rules applied, are in all countries regulated by particular laws (*d*). 'It is due by those, whether owners of ship or cargo, who would have borne the loss had there been no rescue (*e*); and consequently salvage calculated upon the value of ship, freight, and cargo may be recovered from the shipowners without suing the owners of cargo, if the freight exceed the value of the cargo, so that the merchant has no benefit by the salvage (*f*), or if the peril have been caused by the fault of the ship, making the shipowners liable to the owners of cargo (*g*).'

(*a*) 57 and 58 Vict. c. 60, § 545. See Abbott, 539. Maclachlan, 620. The Fusilier, 2 Moo. P. C. N. S. 51; 34 L. J. Adm. 25. Cargo *ex* Woosung, 44 L. J. Adm. 45; Cargo *ex* Sarpedon, 3 Adm. D. 28. Cargo *ex* Schiller, 2 Adm. D. 145; 46 L. J. Adm. 9. The Coromandel, 1 Swa. Adm. 205.

(*b*) Abbott, 536 sq.; Story's edition, 397, note, 400, note. 2 Kent, Com. 245. 1 Bell's Com. 592. It is only due where successful services have actually been rendered. The Chetah, 5 Moo. P. C. N. S. 278; 38 L. J. Adm. 1. The Edward Hawkins, 15 Moo. P. C. 486; 31 L. J. Adm. 46; Lush. Adm. 515.

(*c*) 57 and 58 Vict. c. 60, § 544.

(*d*) 12 Anne, c. 18. 26 Geo. II. c. 19. 48 Geo. III. c. 130, 132. 49 Geo. III. c. 122. 53 Geo. III. c. 87. 1 and 2 Geo. IV. c. 75, 76. 6 Geo. IV. c. 117. Kames, Stat. Law, *voce* Wreck, 414. 17 and 18 Vict. c. 104, § 458; 24 Vict. c. 10, § 9; 25 and 26 Vict. c. 63, § 59, now all superseded by the Merchant Shipping Act, 1894, cited above (*a*). Maclachlan, ch. xiii.

(*e*) 1 Bell's Com. 597 (642, M'L.'s ed.).

(*f*) Cox *v.* May, 4 M. & S. 151; 16 R. R. 422.

(*g*) Duncan *v.* Dundee, etc., Shipping Co., 1878, 5 R. 742, where it is suggested that the same principle may be applied to a claim for salving a vessel, which is a common carrier, carrying goods for a number of separate owners.

444. Persons entitled to Salvage.—One who is not otherwise in duty bound to interfere for the safety of the ship or cargo, is at common law entitled to recompense for his services in preserving the ship for the owners (*a*).

The master and crew 'of the ship for which salvage services are rendered' have no right to salvage; for they are bound to exert themselves to the utmost for the service and safety of the ship. There is an exception, however, to this rule, in the case of rescue after capture; for capture puts an end to the contract of the master and crew. The saving or rescue of the ship by the master or seamen, from mutiny, does not come under this exception; for their service is not thereby terminated (*b*).

Passengers, 'though bound to render all assistance in danger without title to salvage,' are entitled to salvage, if they continue with the ship after they might have left it, and exert themselves 'in an extraordinary manner' for its safety (*c*). A pilot 'or tug-boat master' is not in general entitled to salvage; but extraordinary exertions of skill, or courage, or intrepidity may raise his professional charge to salvage (*d*). 'Stipulations by seamen abandoning their rights to salvage are inoperative, except in the case of seamen serving in a ship which by the terms of agreement is to be employed on salvage service (*e*).'

A claim as joint salvor must 'when the object of the salvage is a derelict' be supported by evidence of the necessity for interference (*f*); 'and in other cases the salvors are in general subject to the control of the master or owners of the vessel in danger, and their aid may be refused by him (*g*).' No operation, previous to recapture, will entitle a ship which is not present to claim salvage; neither will a ship merely for being in sight at recapture, have any share, unless it 'were' a King's ship (*h*). 'But the Crown or the Board of Admiralty cannot now claim salvage as owners, and no claim for salvage services rendered by the commander or crew of any ship belonging to Her Majesty shall be made without consent of the Board of Admiralty being first obtained (*i*).' Co-operation will give a joint right; but if merely constructive, it will not (*k*).

'The owners of the salving vessel, in addition to expenses, when they have actually suffered loss or risk of their property, have a right to salvage (*l*); but not charterers, unless the vessel be demised to them, or they have a clause giving them the benefit of salvage (*m*).'

It has been doubted whether a convoy is entitled to salvage for recapture of one of the fleet (*n*).

(*a*) The Sappho, L. R. 3 P. C. 690; 40 L. J. P. C. 348. The Scout, L. R. 3 A. & E. 512; 41 L. J. Adm. 42. The Glengaber, L. R. 3 A. & E. 534; 41 L. J. Adm. 84.

(*b*) The Two Friends, 1 Rob. Adm. 271. The Beaver, 3 Rob. 292; 1 Ill. 281. The Trelawney, 4 Rob. Adm. 223. The Governor Raffles, 1813; 2 Dod. Adm. 14. The Warrior, Lush. 476. Salvage may be due to seamen after *bonâ fide* abandonment in consequence of damage to the ship. The Florence, 16 E. Jur. 572. The Vrede, 30 L. J. Adm. 209. Le Jouet, L. R. 3 Adm. & E. 556; 41 L. J. Adm. 95.

(*c*) The Two Friends, *supra* (*b*). Newman *v.* Walters, 3 B. & P. 611; 7 R. R. 886. See the Vrede, Lush. 322; 30 L. J. Adm. 209.

(*d*) The Joseph Harvey, 1 Rob. Adm. 306. The Sarah, *ib.* 313, note. Robinson *v.* Thoms, 1851; 13 D. 592. The Queen, 37 L. J. Adm. 13. The J. C. Potter, L. R. 3 Adm. 292; 40 L. J. Adm. 9. The Æolus, L. R. 4 Adm. 29; 42 L. J. Adm. 14. The Anders Knabe, 4 P. D. 213; 48 L. J. Pr. 53. Akerblom *v.* Price, Potter, & Co., 50 L. J. Q. B. 629; 7 Q. B. D. 129.

(*e*) 57 and 58 Vict. c. 60, § 156; see also *ib.* § 212. The Pride of Canada, Br. & Lush. 208; 1 Mar. Law Ca. 406. The Ganges, 38 L. J. Adm. 61; L. R. 2 Adm. 370. The Rosario, 2 P. D. 41; 46 L. J. Adm. 52.

(*f*) The Bellona, 1 Edw. 63. The Maria, 1 Edw. 175. The Kathleen, 43 L. J. Adm. 39.

(*g*) The Dantzic Packet, 3 Hag. 383. The Champion, Br. & L. 69.

(*h*) The Sparkler, 1 Dod. Adm. 359; 1 Ill. 282.

(*i*) 57 and 58 Vict. c. 60, § 557 sqq.

(*k*) La Belle Coquette, 1 Dod. Adm. 20. The Wanstead, 1 Edw. 268. The Union, 1 Dod. Adm. 346. See below. The Charlotte, 2 Hag. 361. The Genessee, 12 E. Jur. 401. The Atlas, 15 Moo. P. C. 329; 31 L. J. Adm. 210.

(*l*) The Baltimore, 2 Dod. Adm. 132. The Princess Helena, 30 L. J. Adm. 137; Lush. Adm. 190. The Scout, *cit.* The Glengaber, *cit.*

(*m*) The Scout, *cit.* The Alfen, 1 Swa. 189. The Collier, L. R. 1 Adm. 83. See above, § 405.

(*n*) The Wight, 5 Rob. Adm. 315. See below, § 445 (*m*).

445. When due.—The occasions on which salvage is due are—Shipwreck, Recapture, and Derelict.

(1.) *Shipwreck.*—When goods are saved from shipwreck, they may be retained for payment of the salvage (*a*). 'When the salvage occurs in the United Kingdom, they are to be delivered to and taken charge of by the Receiver appointed by the Board of Trade, who may detain them till satisfaction is made of the salvage, or security given for its payment (*b*).' The 'early' provisions 'of an Act of Queen Anne' for compelling persons in certain public situations on the shores of the island, and ships in the neighbourhood, to give aid, and regulating the mode in which their salvage is to be decided 'extended' to Scotland (*c*). But the 'later' Act for compelling other persons to give aid, and regulating their salvage, 'did' not extend to Scotland; this matter 'was' left to the common law (*d*), 'until the passing of the Merchant Shipping Act of 1854. Under that and the statute of 1894 Receivers of Wreck are appointed throughout the United Kingdom, to whom all wreck found must be brought under a severe penalty; and who are invested with power to search for wreck concealed, and to impress men for aiding vessels in distress (*e*).'

(2.) *Recapture.*—A material change has been made by statute on the former rule with regard to salvage of ships retaken from the enemy. Formerly, if a vessel had on capture been condemned as prize, or was carried by the enemy *infra præsidia*, the original owner was completely divested of his property, and the recaptor entitled to keep the subject retaken (*f*). But by statute the owner is entitled to restitution on payment of salvage, at whatever period the recapture may have taken place (*g*). To this, however, by the policy of the Prize Acts, there is an exception of ships taken by the enemy, and set forth as ships of war while in their hand; when retaken, they are deemed prize, not subject to restitution on salvage (*h*).

Co-operation in recapture will, as already said, give joint right; and so a privateer actually co-operating with a King's ship, if not officiously, will be held a joint salvor (*i*); and a King's ship in sight at the capture 'was' entitled to salvage (*k*); but King's boats sent in pursuit are not entitled; unless they actually assist in the capture (*l*); and where the co-operation or recapture is by the convoy ship, the question will depend on the degree of blame imputable to the convoy in first allowing the capture (*m*).

(3.) *Derelict.* — Property derelict is not under the English Salvage Acts, and there is no restraint as to the rate of salvage. It will therefore be allowed according to the merits of the case (*n*).

(*a*) Hartford *v.* Jones, 1 Ld. Raym. 393 ; 1 Ill. 456. See Maclachlan, 633. But the salvor has also a personal action. Duncan *v.* Dundee, etc., Shipg. Co., 1878 ; 5 R. 742. See above, § 443 *fin.*

(*b*) 57 and 58 Vict. c. 60, § 518, etc. Otis *v.* Kidston, 1862 ; 24 D. 419. See below, § 1292 sqq. When a foreign ship is wrecked on the coast of the kingdom, the Consul-General of the country to which she belongs is deemed the owner as to the custody or disposal of the wreck ; 57 and 58 Vict. c. 60, § 521.

(*c*) 12 Anne, c. 18. Com. of Customs *v.* L. Dundas, May 25, 1810 ; F. C. ; 1 Ill. 283.

(*d*) Baring *v.* Day, 8 East, 57 ; 3 Ill. 129. 48 Geo. III. c. 130.

(*e*) 17 and 18 Vict. c. 104, § 439 sqq. 57 and 58 Vict. c. 60, § 510 sqq. The Zeta, L. R. 4 Adm. 460 ; 44 L. J. Adm. 22.

(*f*) L'Actif, 1 Edw. 185.

(*g*) 13 Geo. II. c. 4, § 18. 17 Geo. II. c. 34, § 20. 29 Geo. II. c. 34, § 24. The Santa Cruz, 1 Rob. 68.

(*h*) 45 Geo. III. c. 73. L'Actif, *supra* (*f*). See 27 and 28 Vict. c. 23, and 27 and 28 Vict. c. 25, the existing Prize Act, extended by Prize Courts Act, 1894, 57 and 58 Vict. c. 39.

(*i*) The Wanstead, 1 Edw. 269 ; 1 Ill. 282. The Union, 1 Dod. 346.

(*k*) The Sparkler, 1 Dod. 359. The Bellona, 1 Edw. 68 ; 1 Ill. 281. See above, § 444.

(*l*) La Belle Coquette, 1 Dod. 18.

(*m*) The Wight, 5 Rob. 315.

(*n*) The Gage, 6 Rob. 173 ; 3 Ill. 129. The Lambton, *ib.* 275, note. The Lord Nelson, 1 Edw. 79 ; 1 Ill. 283. The Zeta, L. R. 4 Adm. 460 ; 44 L. J. Adm. 22. The Hebe, 4 P. D. 217. The Aquila, 1 C. Rob. 37.

446. The Amount of Salvage is left to judicial determination in the case of derelict and shipwreck (*a*) ; in the case of recapture, the rate is regulated by statute (after many changes), at one-eighth for the Royal Navy and King's armed ships ; one-sixth for private ships (*b*). 'The amount may be fixed by agreement at the time, subject to the power of a competent court to reduce or increase it to a reasonable sum (*c*).'

(*a*) Provision is made for summary adjudication on salvage claims by 17 and 18 Vict. c. 104, § 460 sqq. ; 25 and 26 Vict. c. 63, § 49. Lawson *v.* Grangemouth Dockyard Co., 1888 ; 15 R. 753. Summers *v.* Buchan, 1891 ; 18 R. 879. As to the circumstances to be considered in determining the compensation for salvage service, see the Clifton, 3 Hagg. 117. Abbott, 541. See Davidson *v.* Jenkins, 1844 ; 6 D. 765. Lawson, *cit.* Bird *v.* Gibb, L. R. 8 App. Ca. 559 ; and Pritchard's Adm. Digest, *s.v.* Salvage, where a collection of salvage awards will be found. As to the distinction between towage and salvage services, see The Clifton, *cit.* The Glenduror, L. R. 3 P. C. 589. The J. C. Potter, L. R. 3 Adm. 292 ; 40 L. J. Adm. 9. The Strathnaver, 1 App. Ca. 38. Owners of Vulcan *v.* Owners of Berlin, 1882 ; 9 R. 1057.

(*b*) See Tudor's L. C. 946 sqq. ; and above, § 444.

(*c*) Buchanan *v.* Barr & Shearer, 1867 ; 5 Macph. 973. The Phantom, L. R. 1 Adm. 58. The Jonge Andres, Swa. 303 ; 11 Moo. P. C. 313. The Waverley, L. R. 3 Adm. 369 ; 40 L. J. Adm. 42. The Medina, 2 Adm. D. 5 ; 45 L. J. Adm. 81. The Silesia, 50 L. J. Adm. 9. The Renpor, 8 P. D. 115.

CHAPTER XIII

OF CONTRACTS FOR REPAIRS AND FURNISHINGS TO SHIPS; AND OF SHIP'S-HUSBAND, MASTER, AND SEAMEN

I. REPAIRS AND FURNISHINGS.

447. Contracts, how made.—Contracts for repairs and furnishings to ships may be made with the owners, with the ship's-husband, or with the master (*a*).

(*a*) As to the rights of part owners on the bankruptcy of one to retain the profits for advances made for the ship, see Smith *v.* De Silva, Cowp. 469. Holderness *v.* Shackles, 8 B. & C. 612; 32 R. R. 496. Glass *v.* Hutton's Trs., 1794; M. 2587. As to the rights of dissentient part owners in regard to the management of ships, see below, § 1330a, 449 (*a*).

448. Liability.—The owners are liable for stores and repairs *pro rata* when the contract is with themselves 'as a body acting together (*a*)'; *singuli in solidum*, when the order is by the master or ship's-husband (*b*), 'or by one of themselves, whose authority is proved (*c*). Of course one assuming to contract for himself or the ship with a person who is ignorant that there are other owners, is liable to the full extent for his own contract (*d*); but as part owner he has no implied general authority to bind his co-owners (*e*).'

The register does not furnish evidence to charge one as owner for furnishings or repairs, unless it be shown that the registry was made by his authority. The question always is, On whose credit was the work done (*f*)? A purchaser is not liable for orders given by, and furnishings previously made to, the seller of the ship; nor the seller for furnishings made on the order of the purchaser, though still the seller's name is left on the register (*g*). For orders by the master, the actual owners or 'employers (*exercitors*), having the use and control of the ship, not necessarily' those whose names are with their own knowledge or consent left still on the register, are liable (*h*), 'the register being merely evidence from which the jury may infer that the persons there named appointed the master (*i*).' The lessee of a ship for the voyage, or on time, 'if the owner be divested of possession and he has assumed the responsibilities of owner,' is liable for furnishings on the master's order (*k*). Mortgagees 'not' in possession, formerly held liable as owners, are now by statute freed, provided their character as mortgagees is stated in the book of registry, and in the certificate (*l*); 'or, more accurately, a mortgagee is not by reason of his mortgage to be deemed owner of a ship (*m*); but if he take possession and use the ship, he will be responsible on the principle above stated for repairs and necessaries (*n*).'

(*a*) 1 Bell's Com. 519 (568, M'L.'s ed.).

(*b*) Gleadon *v.* Tinkler, Holt, 586; 1 Ill. 283. Baldney *v.* Ritchie, 1 Starkie, 338. 1 Bell's Com. 519. M'Givan *v.* Blackburn, 1725; M. 14,672. Stewart *v.* Hall, 1813; 2 Dow, 29. Roccus, n. 11 sq. See above, § 60.

(*c*) Baldney, *cit.* Brodie *v.* Howard, 17 C. B. 109; 25 L. J. C. P. 57. Briggs *v.* Wilkinson, and Mitcheson *v.* Oliver, *citt. infra* (*f*). The G. Eastern, L. R. 2 Adm. 88.

(*d*) See § 225. Bell's Com. *l.c.* *Infra*, note (*f*).

(*e*) Brodie, *cit.*

(*f*) Frazer *v.* Hopkins, 2 Taunt. 5. Smith *v.* Fuge, 3 Camp. 456. Reusse *v.* Myers, *ib.* 475. Young *v.* Brander, 8 East, 10. Briggs *v.* Wilkinson, 7 B. & Cr. 39. Reeve *v.* Davis, 1 Ad. & Ell. 312. Story's Abbott, 63, note 1. See below, § 2214. Hay *v.* Cockburn's Trs., 1850; 12 D. 1298. Fyfe *v.* Harwood, 1859; 21 D. 845. Hamilton & Co. *v.* Landale, 1860; 22 D. 1059. Mitcheson *v.* Oliver, 5 E. & B. 419; 25 L. J. Q. B. 39. Myers *v.* Willis, 18 C. B. N. S.

886; 25 L. J. C. P. 39. Smith *v.* M'Guire, 3 H. & N. 554; 27 L. J. Ex. 465. See Barker *v.* Highley, 32 L. J. C. P. 270; 15 C. B. N. S. 27. Abbott, 21, 90. (Leslie *v.* Curtis, 1836, 14 S. 996, appears to be erroneously decided.) See also 1 Parsons on Shipping, 42, 117. Brodie's Stair, 952. Pickard *v.* Sears, 6 A. & E. 472. Frost *v.* Oliver, 2 E. & B. 301; 22 L. J. Q. B. 353.

(*g*) Young, *supra* (*f*). Trewhella *v.* Rowe, 11 East, 435. Abbott, 20. Carswell & Son *v.* Finlay, 1887; 14 R. 903.

(*h*) Gleadon, *supra* (*b*). Westerdell *v.* Dale, 7 T. R. 306. Menzies & Goalen *v.* Kerr, 1805; 1 Ill. 284; 1 Bell's Com. 520 (569, M'L.'s ed.). Miller & Co. *v.* Potter, Wilson, & Co., 1875; 3 R. 105. M'Kessack & Co. *v.* Molleson, 1886; 13 R. 448.

(*i*) Hibbs *v.* Ross, L. R. 1 Q. B. 534; 35 L. J. Q. B. 193. See 57 and 58 Vict. c. 60, § 9 sqq., 64 (2).

(*k*) Vallejo *v.* Wheeler, Cowp. 144. Rich *v.* Coe, *ib.* 636. Frazer *v.* Hopkins, 2 Taunt. 5. Tinkler *v.* Walpole, 14 East, 226. Cooper *v.* South, 4 Taunt. 802. Frazer *v.* Marsh, 13 East, 238. Jennings *v.* Griffiths, 1 Ryan & Moody, 42. Baker *v.* Buckle, 7 Moore, 349. Preston *v.* Tamplin, 26 L. J. Ex. 346; 2 H. & N. 643. See Maclachlan, 342; and above, § 405.

(*l*) 4 Geo. IV. c. 41, § 43. 6 Geo. IV. c. 110, § 45.

(*m*) 57 and 58 Vict. c. 60, § 34.

(*n*) See below, § 1382 sq.

II. SHIP'S-HUSBAND, MASTER, AND SEAMEN.

449. Ship's-husband.—He is the agent or commissioner for the owners (*a*). He may be a part owner or a stranger. His powers are by a mandate, or written commission by the owners, or by verbal appointment; the latter chiefly where he is also part owner (*b*). His duties are, to arrange everything for the outfit and repair of the ship, stores, furnishings, etc.; to enter into contracts of affreightment; to superintend the papers of the ship. His powers do not extend to the borrowing of money (*c*); but he may grant bills for 'ordinary and necessary' furnishings, stores, repairs, and the necessary engagements, which will bind the owners although he may have received money wherewith to pay them. He may receive the freight; but is not entitled to take bills instead of it, giving up the lien by which it is secured. He has no power to insure for the owners' interest without special authority (*d*); 'or to order unusual alterations or repairs on the ship, such as lengthening, for he is agent of the owners not as proprietors, but as joint adventurers in the employment of the ship (*e*).' He cannot give authority to a law agent that will bind his owners for the expenses of a lawsuit (*f*); nor can he delegate his authority (*g*). 'The Merchant Shipping Act requires the name and address of the managing owner or ship's-husband to be registered at the Custom-house of the port of registry (*h*).'

(*a*) See as to accounting and settlement by a majority of owners, Manners *v.* Raeburn & Verel, 1884; 11 R. 899; and as to owners dissenting from the management, *infra*, § 1300A.

(*b*) 3 Ersk. 3. § 43. Abbott, 61. 1 Bell's Com. 504. Chappell *v.* Bray, 6 H. & N. 145; 30 L. J. Ex. 24. Hunt *v.* Royal Exch. Ass. Co., 5 M. & S. 47.

(*c*) Beynon *v.* Godden, 3 Ex. D. 263. Guion *v.* Trask, 29 L. J. Ch. 337.

(*d*) French *v.* Backhouse, 5 Burr. 2727; 1 Ill. 284. Bell *v.* Humphries, 2 Starkie, 345. It is otherwise if he and the other owners be in partnership, and the order be given as for the firm. Hooper *v.* Lusby, 4 Camp. 66. Abbott, 62.

(*e*) Chappell *v.* Bray, *cit.* Steele & Co. *v.* Dixon, 1876; 3 R. 1003.

(*f*) Campbell *v.* Stein, 1818; 6 Dow, 134.

(*g*) Forbes *v.* Milne & Co., 1822; 2 S. 78.

(*h*) 57 and 58 Vict. c. 60, § 59. Maclachlan, 186. Frazer *v.* Cuthbertson, 6 Q. B. D. 93; 50 L. J. Q. B. 277.

450. Shipmaster. (1.) *Qualifications.*—By ancient sea laws the shipmaster was required to be a part owner; and by some modern codes he must be examined and passed as sufficiently skilful. But in this country 'till lately' the only requisites 'were' the appointment of the owners, and that he must be a British subject. 'It is now imperative that the master and mate of foreign-going ships and home-trade passenger ships going to sea from the United Kingdom shall hold valid certificates from the Board of Trade (*a*). It is not necessary that a master shall be a British subject (*b*).' The master is employed as under a contract of hiring (*c*), but his office implies an important mandate, — the exercitorial power (*d*).

(2.) *Appointment.*—The master is seldom appointed by written contract, but by verbal agreement with the owners or ship's-husband. His name must be entered in the register and in the certificate at first registration of the ship; and no change is to be made of the master without an alteration in the certificate and on the register (*e*). His duties to the owners are undertaken by the mere act of taking his place as master; and so, in relation to third parties, he is vested with exercitorial power and authority (*f*).

(3.) *Powers.*—The exercitorial power confers on the master the sole direction of the course and conduct of the ship; the power to freight the ship abroad, not at home without express 'or implied' authority (*g*); and power, when the ship is advertised for general freight, to receive goods on board. 'He has no power to sign bills of lading for goods not shipped aboard (*h*); or to carry goods freight free (*i*), or for freight payable to another than the owner (*k*); or to discharge a claim of demurrage without payment (*l*).' As to the outfitting of the ship, his powers are, *at home*, superseded by those of the ship's-husband; but his power is implied, unless the owners take the management, or there be a ship's-husband appointed (*m*). *Abroad*, the master is the accredited agent of the owners in fitting out, victualling, and manning the ship; in ordering necessaries; and even in borrowing money for necessaries, although he may have been provided with money by the owners (*n*).

'The limitations of the master's authority as agent may be more generally expressed thus: (1) He has no implied power to pledge the owner's credit at any port, at home or abroad, where the owner or his agent, able and willing to provide funds, is present or can be communicated with in reasonable time, regard being had to the engagements of the ship, or the usual and proper course of her employment (*o*); (2) This power extends, when it exists, only to the procuring of such things as are necessary and proper to enable the vessel to prosecute the voyage and course of trade in which she is engaged, and such as a prudent owner, if he were on the spot, would himself order (*p*).'

He has power 'in case of necessity and the failure of personal credit,' to hypothecate the ship, 'freight, and in extreme cases the cargo,' for necessaries (*q*); and his fault or neglect in performing his duties binds the owners to the extent of the value of the ship (*r*). He has no authority to *sell* either ship or cargo, unless under the pressure of the most extreme, absolute, and well-proved necessity, 'and inability to obtain the owner's directions'; otherwise the sale is null, and the owner will get back his property on payment of salvage (*s*). 'In ordinary circumstances, the master is a stranger to the cargo except for the purpose of safe conveyance; but in cases of instant and unforeseen necessity, especially in the absence of the owner, he may be bound to take measures, as if he were supercargo or agent, for the safety of cargo, by unshipping and reshipping, or otherwise (*t*). The extent of the master's authority (*e.g.* to make contracts to hypothecate the ship or cargo, etc.) is ruled by the law of the ship's flag, *i.e.* of the country to which she belongs (*u*).' In all these points the master himself is bound, 'unless he takes care to confine the credit or obligation to the owners only (*v*).'

(4.) *Dismissal.*—The owners may dismiss the master at once and absolutely, leaving him to his remedy at law (*w*). 'In the absence of extraordinary cause there must be reasonable notice (*x*).'

(*a*) 57 and 58 Vict. c. 60, § 92 sq. Heslop *v.* Cadenhead, 1886; 14 R. Just. 35 (*ex facie* certificated master—vessel really commanded by "ice-master" on whaling voyage).

(*b*) 17 and 18 Vict. c. 120.

(*c*) See as to his remedies for wages, etc., 57 and 58 Vict. c. 60, § 167.

(*d*) 1 Stair, 12. § 18. 3 Ersk. 3. § 43–45. Abbott, 83; Story's ed. 92, note 1.

(*e*) 57 and 58 Vict. c. 60, § 14, 19.

(*f*) See below, § 488.

(*g*) Abbott, 85. 1 Bell's Com. 506.

(*h*) See above, § 418 (*d*).

(*i*) Dewell *v.* Moxon, 1 Taunt. 391.

(*k*) Reynolds *v.* Jex, 34 L. J. Q. B. 251.

(*l*) Holman *v.* Peruv. Nitrate Co., 1878; 5 R. 657.

(*m*) Lindsay & Allan *v.* Campbell, 1800; M. *Mandate*, Apx. 2; 1 Ill. 164. Stewart *v.* Hall, 1813; 2 Dow, 29; 1 Ill. 284. Webster *v.* Seekamp, 4 B. & Ald. 352; 23 R. R. 307. Grant *v.* Norway, 10 C. B. 687; 20 L. J. C. P. 93.

(*n*) Rocher *v.* Busher, 1 Starkie, 27; 1 Ill. 285; 18 R. R. 742.

(*o*) Cases in (*m*) and (*n*). Lond. Joint-Stock Bank *v.* Stewart & Co., 1859; 21 D. 1327. Drain & Co. *v.* Scott, 1864; 3 Macph. 114. N. W. Bank *v.* Bjornstrom, 1866; 5 Macph. 24 (charterer's agents at port abroad bound to advance on account of freight). Benn & Co. *v.* Porret, 1868; 6 Macph. 577. Strickland *v.* Neilson, 1869; 7 Macph. 400. Miller & Co. *v.* Potter, Wilson, & Co., 1875; 3 R. 105. Arthur *v.* Barton, 6 M. & W. 138; 9 L. J. Ex. 187. Gunn *v.* Roberts, L. R. 9 C. P. 331; 43 L. J. C. P. 233. Johns *v.* Simons, 2 Q. B. 425. Beldon *v.* Campbell, 6 Ex. 886. Edwards *v.* Havill, 14 C. B. 107.

(*p*) Benn & Co. and Strickland, *citt.* Webster *v.* Seekamp, *cit.* The Riga, L. R. 3 Adm. D. 516; 41 L. J. Adm. 39. The Anna, 45 L. J. Adm. 98; 46 *ib.* 15; L. R. 1 Adm. D. 253. The burden of proving that advances of money or supplies were necessary lies on the claimant. Benn & Co. and Gunn *v.* Roberts, *citt.* Cary *v.* White, 1 Bro. P. C. 284.

(*q*) See below, § 452 sqq.

(*r*) Ellis *v.* Turner, 8 T. R. 531; 1 Ill. 285; 5 R. R. 441. Rinquist *v.* Ditchell, Abbott, 88. Cary *v.* White, 1 Bro. P. C. 284; Abbott, 94, 99. See above, § 236, 237, 436. Ewbank *v.* Nutting, 7 C. B. 797.

(*s*) **The Fanny and Elmira,** 1 Edw. 117; 3 Ill. 130. Parmeter *v.* Todhunter, 1 Camp. 541. See **The Gratitudine,** 3 Rob. 240; 1 Ill. 286; Tudor's L. C. 30. Cannan *v.* Meaburn, 1 Bing. 243; 1 Ill. 171. Robertson *v.* Clark, 1 Bing. 445; 35 R. R. 676. Hale *v.* R. Ex. Ass. Co., 8 Taunt. 755. See American Cases, Story's Abbott, 10, note 1. Abbott, 5 sq. Hunter *v.* Parker, 7 M. & W. 322. Vlierboom *v.* Chapman, 13 M. & W. 230. Ireland *v.* Thompson, 4 C. B. 149. Lapraik *v.* Burrows, 13 Moore, P. C. 132. The Australia, Sw. Adm. 480. The Bonita, 1 Lush. 252; 30 L. J. Adm. 145. Ridgway *v.* Roberts, 4 Hare, 106. Acatos *v.* Burns, 3 Ex. D. 282; 47 L. J. Ex. 566. Austral. St. Nav. Co. *v.* Morse, L. R. 4 P. C. 222;

8 Moore, P. C. N. S. 482. Wagstaffe *v.* Anderson, 5 C. P. D. 171; 49 L. J. C. P. 485. The Margaret Mitchell, 4 E. Jur. N. S. 1193. The Eliza Cornish, 17 E. Jur. 738; 1 Ecc. & Ad. 36. Cobequid Mar. Ins. Co. *v.* Barteaux, L. R. 6 P. C. 319. Atlant. Mut. Ins. Co. *v.* Huth, 16 Ch. D. 474. Maclachlan, 159 sqq.

(*t*) The Gratitudine, 3 Rob. 240. Cases in § 435 (*k*).

(*u*) Lloyd *v.* Guibert, 35 L. J. Q. B. 74; L. R. 1 Q. B. 115; 6 B. & S. 100. The Karnak, 38 L. J. Adm. 57; L. R. 2 P. C. 565. The Eliza Cornish, 1 Spinks, 36, *supra* (*s*). Kleinwort *v.* Cassa Maritima of Genoa, L. R. 2 App. Ca. 156. Moore *v.* Harris, 1 App. Ca. 331. The Gaetano e Maria, 51 L. J. Adm. 67; 7 P. D. 1, 137. Guthrie's Savigny on Priv. Int. Law, 236. Westlake, Pr. Int. Law, § 208.

(*v*) 1 Bankton, 398. Brodie's Stair, 970. Hussey *v.* Christie, 9 East, 426; 9 R. R. 585. Rich *v.* Coe, Cowp. 636. See below, § 1436. Meier *v.* Küchenmeister, 1881; 8 R. 642. The doubt expressed in this case, whether the principle of election (§ 224A) applies to contracts made by a shipmaster, though supported by an unsatisfactory passage in 1 Bell's Com. 537–38 (585, M'L.'s ed.), is inconsistent with the English authorities. Priestley *v.* Fernie, 34 L. J. Ex. 172; 3 H. & C. 977. Maclachlan, 132, 139. Addison, Contr. 321, 891. In such cases as Benn & Co. *v.* Porret, and the others cited above (note (*o*)), in which masters and owners were sued together, and held liable jointly and severally, the master had assumed full personal liability by signing a bill or other obligation on which the action was brought.

(*w*) See as to removal by Court, 57 and 58 Vict. c. 60, § 472. M'Lagan *v.* Clunie, 1848; 10 D. 847. M'Kellar *v.* Macfarlane, 1852; 15 D. 246. The Roebuck, 31 L. T. Rep. 274. Maclachlan, 210, 244.

(*x*) Creen *v.* Wright, 1 C. P. D. 591.

451. Seamen.—By a statute of Will. IV., the former statutes relative to merchant seamen 'were' repealed, and the system placed on a new footing (*a*). This statute, 'which was repealed by the Merchant Shipping Act of 1854 (*b*), had' two objects: 1. To secure to seamen, on the one hand, the benefit of a simple and equitable written contract, with exact payment of their wages, and summary and effectual means of recovering them; on the other, strict enforcement of the duties of seamen; and 2. To establish a regular office of registry for merchant seamen, with a system of apprenticeship by which the supply may be kept continually full of skilful seamen, and proper care be taken of the interest and safety of seamen while in foreign parts.

Questions may arise as to seamen's wages, in the decision of which it is necessary to have recourse to general principles of jurisprudence. Thus, according to the common maxim, "Freight is the mother of wages"; so that 'by the general maritime law' total loss during the voyage forfeits wages (*c*). This is a rule founded on policy for the additional security of ship and cargo. But it is subject to several exceptions, as when the voyage is lost by the fault of the owners; if the ship be seized for debt; if forfeited for having smuggled goods; if the ship returns without a cargo: and even when the ship is wrecked, but part of it brought home, the seamen are not to be deprived of all consideration for their services (*d*). 'And now, by statute, the right to wages is not dependent on the earning of freight; but in cases of wreck or loss of the ship, proof that the seaman has not exerted himself to the utmost to save the ship, cargo, and stores, shall bar his claim (*e*).'

The seaman has two remedies for his wages, —a personal action on the contract (*f*), and a lien on the ship to her last plank (*g*). On this right (especially as exemplified in the case of the Neptune), although the seaman 'might' lose his personal action for wages if the owners 'earned' no freight, he 'had' his claim against the ship or its vestiges.

(*a*) 5 and 6 Will. IV. c. 19.

(*b*) 17 and 18 Vict. c. 104, which superseded all the former legislative enactments. See below, § 451A–B. It has been held, in a question as to employers' liability (see below, § 547B), that the Merchant Shipping Act does not apply to firemen or stokers in canal boats, or, indeed, to such vessels themselves. Oakes *v.* Monkland Iron Co., 1884; 11 R. 579.

(*c*) Abbott, 477; Story's ed. 457.

(*d*) The Neptune, 1 Hag. Ad. 227; 1 Ill. 285.

(*e*) 57 and 58 Vict. c. 60, § 157.

(*f*) *Ib.* § 164 sq.

(*g*) The Madonna d'Idra, 1811; 1 Dod. 37. Neptune, *supra* (*d*). See below, § 1400.

451A. 'Under the existing statutes, there are at the principal seaports mercantile marine offices, under superintendents whose duty is to facilitate the engagement of seamen, by keeping registers of their names and characters, superintending their engagement, and securing their presence on board ship at the stipulated time, etc. The master of every ship, except ships of less than 80 tons, exclusively employed in the coasting trade, must, in engaging a seaman, enter into a written agreement, in a form sanctioned by the Board of Trade, specifying the nature of the voyage, amount of wages, and other particulars, and signed by the master before it is signed by the seaman (*a*). In the case of foreign-going ships, every such agreement made in the United Kingdom is to be signed by the seaman in presence of a superintendent or deputy-superintendent of a shipping office (shipping master), who must see that the seaman understands it, and must attest it. When the crew is first engaged, this agreement is in duplicate, one part being retained by the superintendent and the other delivered to the master. Some relaxation of these rules is allowed when the services of engaged seamen are lost within twenty-four hours before putting to sea (*b*). Engagements for home-trade ships may be made in the same way (*c*). Running agreements may be made for two or more voyages, in case of foreign-going ships making voyages averaging less than six months; provided they do not extend beyond the next 30th June or 31st December, or the first arrival at the port of destination in the United Kingdom, or first discharge of cargo after such date (*d*). And the owner of several home-trading ships may engage seamen to serve in two or more of said ships (*e*). Erasures, interlineations, and alterations in agreements are inoperative, unless attested to have been made with the consent of all parties by the shipping master, a justice of peace, officer of customs, or consul, or where there is none, by two respectable British merchants (*f*). No stamp is required (*g*). Stipulations by sailors forfeiting their lien on the ship, or depriving them of any remedy for recovery of wages, or abandoning right to wages on loss of the ship, or any right to salvage, are inoperative (*h*).'

(*a*) 57 and 58 Vict. c. 60, § 133. Notwithstanding the existence of the agreement, a seaman may prove its contents or otherwise support his case without producing it; *ib.* § 123.
(*b*) *Ib.* § 115 (4).
(*c*) *Ib.* § 116.
(*d*) *Ib.* § 115, etc.
(*e*) *Ib.* § 116.
(*f*) *Ib.* § 163.
(*g*) *Ib.* § 721. 54 and 55 Vict. c. 39, Sched. *s.v.* Agreement.
(*h*) *Ib.* § 156. See above, 444 (*e*).

451B. '*Seamen's Right to Wages.*—A seaman's right to wages or provisions begins either when he commences work, or at the time specified in the agreement for his commencing work, or being on board, whichever first happens (*a*) Where his service terminates before the period specified, by wreck or loss of the ship, or by his being left on shore abroad under a certificate of his being unfit or unable to proceed on the voyage, he is entitled only to wages prior to such termination of his service (*b*). Wages are forfeited by desertion both at common law and under the Merchant Shipping Act (*c*). The fact of desertion must be entered in the official log-book of the ship, and that, with proof of the seaman's engagement, and his leaving the ship or absence from it, is *primâ facie* evidence of it in any question of forfeiture of wages, and imposes on the seaman the onus of proving a proper discharge or a sufficient excuse (*d*). Illness, if the sailor remain with the ship, except illness caused by the sailor's own wilful act or default, and death, do not operate a forfeiture of wages; nor quitting the ship to enter the Queen's naval service (*e*). The statute provides for forfeiture of wages, or portions thereof, for certain offences and misconduct; for the discharge and settlement of claims of wages before the shipping master; and for the summary recovery of wages and effects by the seaman or his representatives (*f*). The statutory remedies do not exclude a claim at common law for damages by misconduct (*g*). Seamen's wages take precedence of all other charges (*h*). They cannot be arrested or before accrual assigned, and a power of attorney or authority for receipt thereof is not irrevocable (*i*).'

(*a*) 57 and 58 Vict. c. 60, § 155. As to discharge before the voyage begins, see *ib.* § 162.
(*b*) *Ib.* § 158, and see § 188, 189. Gowans *v.* Thomson, 1844; 6 D. 606. Button *v.* Thompson, L. R. 4 C. P. 330; 38 L. J. C. P. 225.
(*c*) *Ib.* § 221. The Westmoreland, 1 W. Rob. Adm. 216. The Two Sisters, 2 W. Rob. 125. As to desertion, see Maclachlan, 240 sqq. Macnaughton *v.* Allhusen & Co., 1843; 6 D. 194; 1847, 10 D. 236. Gowans, *cit.* O'Neil *v.* Rankin & Sons, 1873; 11 Macph. 539.
(*d*) *Ib.* § 228, 231 sqq. Seward *v.* Ratter, 1884; 12 R. 222.
(*e*) See *ib.* § 157, 160, 195, etc.
(*f*) See Macdonald *v.* Fildes, 1848; 10 D. 860. Ramsay *v.* Bruce, 1849; 12 D. 243. Stephens *v.* Duncan, 1862; 1 Macph. 146.
(*g*) Sharp *v.* Rettie, 1884; 11 R. 745. The Act, § 226. See Great N. Steam Fishing Co. *v.* Edgehill, 11 Q. B. D. 225.
(*h*) The Madonna d'Idra, 1 Dods. 37. See Maclachlan, 249).
(*i*) 57 and 58 Vict. c. 60, § 163.

451C. 'The seaman being bound to exert himself to the utmost in the service of the ship (*a*), any promise of extra pay as an inducement to extraordinary exertion is void. But this rule does not affect a bargain for extra remuneration for extraordinary risk or labour which the seaman is not already bound by his contract to undertake (*b*). The seaman is bound to remain with the ship on arrival in port until she is placed in security, under the penalty of forfeiting a month's wages (*c*); not, as formerly, until delivery of the cargo (*d*).'

(*a*) See *supra*, § 451 (*c*).
(*b*) Abbott, 459. 1 Bell's Com. 511. Hartley *v.* Ponsonby, 7 E. & B. 872; 26 L. J. Q. B. 322.
(*c*) 57 and 58 Vict. c. 60, § 225 (*a*).
(*d*) The Baltic Merchant, 1 Edw. 285. Macdonald *v.* Jopling, 4 M. & W. 285. 1 Bell's Com. 503. Abbott, 485.

451D. 'It is a criminal offence to send or attempt to send a ship to sea in such an unseaworthy state that life is likely to be endangered, unless it be proved that in the circumstances the act was necessary or justifiable (*a*). It is an implied term in every contract for service on board ship that the owner, the master, and every agent concerned in loading, preparing, or sending the ship to sea, shall use all reasonable means to ensure the seaworthiness of the ship for the voyage at its commencement, and to keep her in such condition during the voyage. But it is a defence if it be proved that in special circumstances it was reasonable or justifiable to send the ship to sea in an unseaworthy state (*b*).'

(*a*) 57 and 58 Vict. c. 60, § 457.
(*b*) *Ib.* § 458. Provisions are made in this Act for enforcing these provisions. Hedley *v.* Pinkney & Co. S. S. Co., 1894; A. C. 217.

CHAPTER XIV

OF CONTRACTS OF BOTTOMRY AND RESPONDENTIA

452. Nature.—Bottomry (*a*) and *Respondentia* are contracts for money lent to the owners of ship or cargo at home, or to the master in a foreign country, on the condition that if the subject on which the money is lent be lost by sea-risk or superior force of the enemy, the lender shall lose his money; and that if the voyage shall be successful, the money lent shall be repaid, with a certain profit or consideration for interest and risk called marine interest. For repayment, the person of the borrower is bound (*b*); and also, in bottomry, the ship. 'A bottomry bond by a master possessing only the ordinary powers, being by its nature founded on the maritime risk, is not a competent way of creating a personal obligation against the owners. The lender's security is the ship or cargo only, and the personal obligation of the master, who generally binds himself.'

In *respondentia*, the goods (in certain cases) are hypothecated to the lender. 'In *respondentia,* the obligation must be taken for the benefit of the cargo, and greater strictness will in general be observed (*c*). In particular, the master of a British ship must, if at all possible, communicate to the cargo owner the necessity not only for repairs, but for the proposed hypothecation (*d*).'

The master has 'in general' no power to borrow on such contracts in a home port, *i.e.* within the 'United Kingdom' (*e*), unless where there is a dissension among the owners, and a necessity of borrowing for the minority's share of the outfit. 'If the master can within a reasonable time communicate with the owners, even by electric telegraph, whether they be in the same country or not, it is his duty to do so; and if he fails to do so, a bottomry bond will be invalid (*f*). This being the test, the master may, where it is satisfied, borrow on bottomry, although the owner is in the same country (*g*).'

(*a*) 3 Ersk. 3. § 17. 1 Bell's Com. 530. Abbott, 125. Marshall, 573. Park, 869 (8th ed.). 2 Valin, 1 and 9. Pothier, Cont. à la Grosse Aventure. 2 Emerigon, 377. 3 Boulay-Paty, 1–227. 2 Pardessus, Droit Com. 203. 3 Kent, Com. 353 et seq.

(*b*) See Stainbank *v.* Fenning, 11 C. B. 88; 20 L. J. C. P. 226. Stainbank *v.* Shepherd, 13 C. B. 418; 22 L. J. C. P. 341. Benson *v.* Chapman, 6 M. & G. 792; 5 C. B. 330; 8 C. B. 950. Cochrane *v.* Gilkison, 1854; 16 D. 548. Miller & Co. *v.* Potter, Wilson, & Co., 1875; 3 R. 105. 3 Ersk. 3. § 17 is more correct on this point than 1 Bell's Com. 581. See Abbott, 109, 113; Smith's Merc. Law, 412. But a bottomry bond may be conceived as a collateral security merely, and discharged by acceptance or payment of bills drawn by the master for the same debt. The Nelson, 1 Hagg. 169. Stainbank *v.* Shepherd, *cit.* Cochrane *v.* Gilkison, *cit.* The Emancipation, 1 W. Rob. 124. See The Onward, *infra* (*d*).

(*c*) Jacobsen *v.* Hansen, 1850; 12 D. 762. The Lord Cochrane, 2 W. Rob. 320. Dymond *v.* Scott, 1877; 5 R. 196. Anderston Foundry Co. *v.* Law, 1869; 7 Macph. 836. See above, § 450 (3). The Gratitudine, below (*e*). The Karnak, L. R. 2 Adm. 289; 2 P. C. 505; 37 L. J. Adm. 41; 38 *ib.* 57. Duncan *v.* Benson, 1 Ex. 557; 3 Ex. 644; 18 L. J. Ex. 169. Maclachlan, 155, 52.

(*d*) The Onward, L. R. 4 Adm. 38; 42 L. J. Adm. 61. Kleinwort *v.* Cassa Maritima of Genoa, 2 App. Ca. 156. As to the master of a foreign ship, see The Gaetano e Maria, *supra,* § 450 (*u*).

(*e*) 1 Stair, 12. § 18. 3 Ersk. 3. § 44. Abbott, 107–110. **The Gratitudine,** 3 Rob. Adm. Rep. 255, 278; 1 Ill. 286; Tudor's L. C. 30. The Rhadamanthe, 1 Dod. Adm. 201. See above, § 450. "United Kingdom" in the text seems more correct than "British Empire," which stood in former editions.

(*f*) Wallace *v.* Fielden, 7 Moore, P. C. 398. The Bonaparte, 3 W. Rob. 298; 8 Moore, P. C. 459.

(*g*) La Ysabel, 1 Dod. 273. The Trident, 1 W. Rob. 29. The Olivier, 31 L. J. Adm. 137; 1 Lush. 484. See Tudor's L. C. 60; Smith's Merc. Law, 411. The Karnak, *supra* (*c*). The Lizzie, L. R. 2 Adm. 254. The Panama, L. R. 2 Adm. 390; 3 P. C. 199; 38 L. J. Adm. 67; 39 *ib.* 37.

453. The **Form** of the obligation is that of a bond, or of a bill 'of sale,' expressing the sum borrowed or credit given, with the marine interest; the subject on which the money is taken; and the risk, with its commencement and termination. A verbal agreement to give security on the ship will not do. And a bill of exchange is held as evidence that the ship was not intended to be pledged (*a*).

(*a*) *Ex p.* Halket, 19 Ves. 473. Abbott, 113. See Stainbank *v.* Fenning, Stainbank *v.* Shepherd, and Miller & Co., *citt.* § 452 (*b*). Compliance with the statutes as to registry of ship (see below, § 1381) seems to be necessary in the case of British ships. Abbott, 106. Smith's Merc. Law, 514. But see as to the competency of a bond of bottomry over a British ship lying in a British port, the Royal Arch, 1 Swa. Adm. 269; Maclachlan, 58.

454. Subjects.—There must be something at hazard on the voyage, in order to validate this contract. This may be the ship, with its furniture; the cargo; or the freight 'for the time included in the risk' (*a*). But wages cannot be made the subject of bottomry (*b*).

(*a*) Marshall, 584. The Jacob, 4 Rob. Adm. 245. The Staffordshire, L. R. 4 P. C. 194; 41 L. J. Adm. 49.
(*b*) Marshall, 587.

455. Necessity.—As bottomry loans are, strictly speaking, the creatures of necessity alone in the providing for or extricating the ship, the master cannot make an effectual transaction if there should be circumstances which do not evince such necessity; as for a debt of his own (*a*), or in security of a debt already existing on personal credit (*b*); 'or even for the release of the ship itself from arrest (*c*). But where a master has in a foreign port incurred personal debts for repairs or necessaries, he may borrow money on bottomry from one not his creditor to pay such debts (*d*). Or in exceptional cases of extreme urgency, he may grant a bond of bottomry to his creditor if the repairs have been made or the debt incurred on the credit of the ship, *i.e.* in contemplation of a bottomry security (*e*).'

(*a*) The Gratitudine, *supra*, § 452 (*e*). The Roderick Dhu, 1 Swa. Adm. 177. Heathorn *v.* Darling, 1 Moore, P. C. 5. Soares *v.* Rahn, 3 Moore, P. C. 1. See cases above, § 452 (*e*).
(*b*) The Augusta, 1 Dods, 283. Abbott, 115. Gore *v.* Gardiner, 3 Moore, P. C. 79. The Gauntlet, 3 W. Rob. 82. Sword *v.* Howden, 1826; 4 S. 757. The Empire of Peace, 39 L. J. Adm. 12. Cf. Miller & Co. *v.* Potter, Wilson, & Co., 1875; 3 R. 105.
(*c*) See The Ida, L. R. 3 Adm. 542; 41 L. J. Adm. 85; and cases in Maclachlan, 54.
(*d*) The Hebe, 2 W. Rob. 146; 4 Notes of Ca. 368; 10 E. Jur. 231. The Karnak, 37 L. J. Adm. 41; 38 *ib.* 57; L. R. 2 Adm. 289; 2 P. C. 505.
(*e*) The Alexander, 1 Dods. 279. The Laurel, 33 L. J. Adm. 17; B. & L. Adm. 191.

456. Risk.—This alone gives validity to the stipulation for marine or higher interest (*a*). Where the voyage is not begun, and no risk run, the transaction resolves into a common loan at lawful interest. When the borrower has no interest at stake in ship, goods, or freight, there is no marine interest. After the risk is over, the sum due on the contract bears only lawful interest. But if the risk have once begun, and the ship or goods in the bond have been exposed but for a moment to hazard, the marine interest is due (*b*). The risks are commonly specified in the bond. They are the same with those undertaken in a policy of insurance. It is not necessary that they should be set down in the bond, or even that the bond be expressly conditional, being understood and implied when the nature of the bond clearly appears (*c*). But in a question as to the risk run, the ship is held not to be totally lost, however much injured, if she reach the end of the voyage (*d*). 'There is not in respect to this contract any constructive total loss. Nothing but an utter annihilation of the subject hypothecated discharges the borrower on bottomry. The property saved, whatever it may be, continues subject to the hypothecation (*e*).'

Marine Interest.—The amount depends on the estimate made of the risk; for it is not so properly, or solely, interest, as *pretium periculi*. But that estimate may be exorbitant and oppressive under the pressure of the necessity which justifies the transaction; and courts of justice, though unwillingly, may undoubtedly interfere to reduce any such exorbitant charge (*f*). When the condition of the bond is fulfilled, the sum advanced and the maritime interest stipulated are demandable and become an absolute debt, on which the ordinary legal interest runs (*g*).

Security.—In bottomry, the lender has a privilege or claim on the ship itself, and on the freight. He is entitled to apply in Admiralty to have a sale of the ship for his payment (*h*). And in distributing the proceeds among those who may appear to claim, the last bottomry creditor in point of date is entitled to be preferred, as having furnished the means of preserving the ship for the benefit of all previous lenders,—" salvam fecit totius pignoris causam " (*i*). This preference, however, is given only when the loan has been made to the master abroad on necessity; for a later bond by the owners will not thus be preferred (*k*). 'A bottomry bond is entitled to preference over all other creditors (except seamen, including the master, though part owner (*l*), for their wages), even over a mortgage (*m*).' In *respondentia* on goods which are intended for the market, there can be no hypothecation inconsistent with that object (*n*). 'Where the ship, freight, and cargo are all hypothecated, the cargo is not liable until the proceeds of the ship and freight are exhausted (*o*); and the owner of the cargo has relief against the shipowner (*p*).'

Average.—The risk and security which so intimately enter into the nature of this transaction lead to the question of the effect of average on the lender. He seems liable to general average, so as to be bound to contribute from the money which is saved to him by the sacrifice, to the indemnification of the sufferer 'other than the shipowner' (*q*); and he is, of course, liable to simple average, in so far as it may diminish the subject of his security.

(*a*) Stainbank *v.* Shepherd, 13 C. B. 418; 22 L. J. Ex. 341. The Royal Arch, Swa. Adm. 269. The Emancipation, 1 W. Rob. 130. Miller & Co. *v.* Potter, Wilson, & Co., 1875; 3 R. 105.

(*b*) 2 Emerigon, 491. 3 Boulay-Paty, 74 et seq.

(*c*) Simonds *v.* Hodgson, 3 B. & Ad. 59; revg. decision of C. P. in 6 Bing. 120; 3 Ill. 130. The Emancipation, 1 W. Rob. 124.

(*d*) Thomson *v.* R. E. Ass. Co., 1 M. & S. 31; 3 Ill. 130. The Great Pacific (P. C.), 38 L. J. Adm. 14, 15; L. R. 2 P. C. 516. The Hendrica Gazina, 2 Ir. Jur. N. S. 81.

(*e*) Cases in (*d*). 3 Kent, Com. 359. See The Empusa, 48 L. J. Adm. 36.

(*f*) The Zodiac, 1 Hag. Adm. 320. The Huntley, Lush. Adm. 24. Tudor's L. C. 58. Maclachlan, 57. The Sophia Cook, 49 L. J. Adm. 16; 4 P. D. 30. The Cecilia, 4 P. D. 210.

(*g*) 2 Pardessus, 273. 3 Boulay-Paty, 80. Marshall's dictum on this point seems not to be law, v. 2, p. 751 (591, 5th ed.). Cochrane *v.* Gilkison, 1858; 20 D. 213. Broomfield *v.* Southern Ins. Co., L. R. 5 Ex. 192; 39 L. J. Ex. 186.

(*h*) The ship may be detained by arrestment. Lucovich, Petr., 1885; 12 R. 1090.

(*i*) Casaregis, Disc. 16. 2 Valin, 11. 1 Boulay-Paty, 116, 143, and t. 3. 154. The Rhadamanthe, *supra*, 452 (*e*). The Sydney Cove, 2 Dods. 1. The Fortuna, 5 Ir. Jur. N. S. 375.

(*k*) The Rhadamanthe, *supra*, § 452 (*e*).

(*l*) The Daring, L. R. 2 Adm. 260.

(*m*) The Orelia, 3 Hagg. Adm. 83. The Madonna d'Idra, 1 Dods. 40. The Royal Arch, Swa. Adm. 269. The Heligoland, *ib.* 491. The Hersey, 3 Hagg. Adm. 408. The W. F. Safford, 1 Lush. 69. The Union, *ib.* 128. The Janet Wilson, Swa. Adm. 261.

(*n*) 2 Blackst. 458. Park, 615. Marshall, 743 (574, 578, 5th ed.). Busk *v.* Fearon, 4 East, 319.

(*o*) The Bonaparte, 3 W. Rob. 302. The Priscilla, Lush. Adm. 1.

(*p*) Duncan *v.* Benson, *supra*, § 452 (*c*). Benson *v.* Chapman, *supra*, § 452 (*b*). Anderston Foundry Co. *v.* Law, 1869; 7 Macph. 836. As to foreign law on this point, see above, § 450 (*u*).

(*q*) Pothier, Cont. à la Grosse, No. 91. 3 Boulay-Paty, 220. Marshall, 592. Cochrane, *supra* (*g*). See the Great Pacific, *supra* (*d*). Broomfield, *supra* (*g*). The subject is obscure, and the text is at least subject to the limitation inserted.

CHAPTER XV

OF INSURANCE

I. INSURANCE GENERALLY.

457. Nature of Insurance.—Insurance is a contract to indemnify against possible or probable loss, in consideration of a sum or premium paid, or held to be paid (*a*). 'Contracts of insurance are invariably embodied in "policies." The Stamp Act provides that no contract of sea insurance is valid unless expressed in a policy; and imposes penalties on those receiving premiums except on duly stamped policies (*b*). It also imposes a penalty on any one who receives or takes credit for any premium or consideration for any other insurance than sea, and who does not within one month make out and execute a duly stamped policy (*c*).' The insurer undertakes to be responsible for certain risks or perils of the sea, fire, death, etc., to which the party insured may be exposed; being assured, in doing so, that he is free from such other risks as may either arise from the natural or actual condition of the subject, or out of a deviation from the usual course of peril. It is essential to the contract of insurance that there shall be a subject in which the insured has an interest, a premium given or engaged for, and a risk run.

(*a*) Consult Pothier, Tr. du Cont. d'Assurance. Emerigon, Tr. des Assurances, vol. ii. Valin, Com. sur l'Ordonnance de la Marine, vol. ii. l. 3. tit. 6. 3 Boulay-Paty, 233. Park on Insurance. Marshall on Insurance. 2 Selw. Nisi Pr. 871. 2 Kent, Com. 253. Miller on Insurance. 1 Bell's Com. 598. Phillips (of America), Law of Insurance. Arnould on Marine Insurance. Duer on Marine Insurance. Manley Hopkins's Manual of Marine Insurance. Parsons on Marine Insurance.

(*b*) 54 and 55 Vict. c. 39, § 92, 97. (*c*) *Ib.* § 100.

458. (1.) *Subject.*—The subject insured must be a thing at hazard. And it is held to be so, although it may have already perished, 'or been injured, or have arrived safely,' if this be unknown at entering into the insurance (*a*). And in all 'marine' policies, to avoid such questions, the words "lost or not lost" are inserted. So, when a ship or person abroad, or a house in a distant part of the country, is insured, in the belief of their being still extant, the insurance is effectual, 'even to cover a loss sustained before the insured's interest had been acquired, as in the case of goods sold at sea (*b*).'

(*a*) See Smith *v.* Fleming & Co., 1849; 12 D. 138. Bradford *v.* Symondson, 7 Q. B. D. 456; 50 L. J. Q. B. 582.

(*b*) See Sutherland *v.* Pratt, 11 M. & W. 297. Arnould, 235. And one in whose interest a policy has been made before the loss, though without his authority, may ratify it although he knows of the loss. Williams *v.* North China Ins. Co., 1 C. P. D. 757.

459. It is not necessary that the subject should already belong to the insured: it is enough if it exist *in spe*; as profit to be earned (*a*) 'upon goods in which the insured has already an interest (*b*)'; the produce of a fishing voyage (*c*); 'salvage (*d*)'; or freight, 'even on a time policy which expires before the freight can be earned (*e*),' the interest commencing with the ship breaking ground (*f*). The merchant himself, who sends his goods by sea, has an insurable interest in any advances made to the shipmaster, provided the same be insured as freight, or the repayment made to depend on the earning of freight (*g*).

(*a*) Grant *v.* Parkinson, Marsh. 74; 6 T. R. 483; 3 Ill. 132. Barclay *v.* Cousins, 2 East, 544; 6 R. R. 205. Eyre *v.* Glover, 16 East, 218; 3 Camp. 276; 3 Ill. 132; 13 R. R. 801. M'Swinney *v.* R. E. Ass. Co., 14 Q. B. 634; 19 L. J. Q. B. 222. Chope *v.* Reynolds, 5 C. B. N. S. 642; 28 L. J. C. P. 194.

(*b*) Stockdale *v.* Dunlop, 6 M. & W. 224. M'Swinney, *cit.* Wilson *v.* Jones, 35 L. J. Ex. 94; 36 *ib.* 78; L. R. 1 Ex. 193; 2 Ex. 139. Arnould, 71 sqq.

(*c*) Addison & Son *v.* Duguid, 1797; M. 7077; 1 Ill. 286.

(*d*) Yelton *v.* Smith, 1801; M. Apx. *Ins.* 5; 5 Pat. 139.

(*e*) Michael *v.* Gillespie, 26 L. J. C. P. 306; 2 C. B. N. S. 627.

(*f*) Montgomery *v.* Egginton, 3 T. R. 362; 3 Ill. 133; 1 R. R. 718. Warre *v.* Miller, 4 B. & Cr. 538; 1 Ill. 291; 28 R. R. 382. See § 471. Ellis *v.* Lafone, 8 Ex. 546; 22 L. J. Ex. 124. Foley *v.* United Ins. Co., and Barber *v.* Fleming, *infra*, § 471 (*b*) (*d*).

(*g*) De Silvale *v.* Kendall, 4 M. & S. 37; 1 Ill. 275; 16 R. R. 373. Andrew *v.* Moorhouse, 5 Taunt. 435; 15 R. R. 544. Mansfield *v.* Maitland, 4 B. & Ald. 582. Winter *v.* Holdiman, 2 B. & Ad. 649. Baillie *v.* Modigliani, Park, 116; 1 Ill. 274. Taylor *v.* Wilson, 15 East, 324; 13 R. R. 488. Barclay *v.* Stirling, 5 M. & S. 6; 17 R. R. 245. Flint *v.* Flemyng, 1 B. & Ald. 45. Wilson *v.* Martin, 11 Ex. 684; 25 L. J. Ex. 217. Ralli *v.* Jansen, 4 E. & B. 506; 24 L. J. Q. B. 77. Droege *v.* Stuart, 38 L. J. P. C. 71. Currie *v.* Bombay Native Ins. Co., 39 L. J. P. C. 1; L. R. 3 P. C. 72. Williams *v.* North China Ins. Co., 1 C. P. D. 757. See above, § 420, 427.

460. The insurance must be of a lawful subject of trade. Thus, smuggled goods cannot be insured, nor contraband of war; neither can seamen's wages (*a*), nor what is paid in place of wages (*b*). Enemy's property is not insurable; and so, if war have begun before the policy is effected, it is null (*c*); if war break out afterwards, no action will lie on the policy 'for a loss happening before the war' while the war continues, but its effect 'as to such a loss' will revive on peace (*d*). Although a good policy when made, it will not protect against British capture if war break out (*e*).

(*a*) Park, 11 et seq. Marshall, 62 et seq. Jenkins *v.* Power, 6 M. & S. 282. This was on the principle that freight is the mother of wages; but as that rule is abrogated, it may be that the statement in the text is no longer tenable. See above, § 451. Arnould, 43 sq., 88. The master's wages, effects, and commission are insurable. Duff *v.* Mackenzie, 3 C. B. N. S. 16; 26 L. J. C. P. 313. Hawkins *v.* Twizell, 5 E. & B. 883; 25 L. J. Q. B. 160.

(*b*) Webster *v.* De Tastet, 7 T. R. 157; 3 Ill. 133; 4 R. R. 402.

(*c*) Brandon *v.* Nesbitt, 6 T. R. 23; 3 Ill. 132; 3 R. R. 109. Bristow *v.* Towers, *ib.* 35. Kellner *v.* Le Mesurier, 4 East, 396; 7 R. R. 581. Flindt *v.* Waters, 15 East, 260; 13 R. R. 457. Esposito *v.* Bowden, 7 E. & B. 779; 27 L. J. Q. B. 17. Reid *v.* Hoskyns, 5 E. & B. 729; 6 E. & B. 953. Barrick *v.* Buda, 2 C. B. N. S. 563. Clemontson *v.* Blessig, 11 Ex. 135.

(*d*) Furtado *v.* Rogers, 3 B. & P. 191; 6 R. R. 752. See cases in note (*c*).

(*e*) See Furtado's Case.

461. (2.) *Interest.*—The subject insured must be one in which the insured has an interest (*a*); but that interest need not be specified in the policy (*b*). '"Interest" is not limited to property, but extends to every real and actual (*c*) advantage and benefit arising out of or depending on the thing to which it refers (*d*). But one cannot insure a mere expectancy (*e*).'

And this is enforced by the statutes against wager policies, and against policies for covering illegal and criminal voyages. Those statutes prohibit assurances "by way of wagering or gaming," and assurances "interest or no interest, or without further proof of interest than the policy," 'by way of gaming or wagering, or without benefit of salvage to the assurer' (*f*). The interest must be proved otherwise than by the words of the policy (*g*). But these rules, in marine assurances, apply only to the ships of the Crown or of its subjects, not to foreigners (*h*). The effect of stopping *in transitu* a cargo insured, has in one special case been held to destroy the policy, as annihilating the vendee's interest under it (*i*). But this does not decide the general question, 'whether stoppage effects a rescission of the contract.'

(*a*) See above, § 458–59, etc.; Ebsworth *v.* Alliance M. I. Co., 42 L. J. C. P. 305; L. R. 8 C. P. 596, and cases cited. Anderson *v.* Morice, 44 L. J. C. P. 10, 341; 45 *ib.* 11; L. R. 10 C. P. 58, 609.

(*b*) Brown *v.* Hall, Feb. 2, 1810, F. C.; 1814, 2 Dow, 367. See also Godsall *v.* Boldero, 9 East, 72; 1 Ill. 287;

2 Smith's L. C. 271. Crowley *v.* Cohen, 3 B. & Ad. 478. See below, § 470, 518. Symers *v.* Glasgow M. I. Co., 1846; 9 D. 163. If the insured before the loss has lost his interest by sale of the ship insured or otherwise, he cannot in England sue on the policy even as trustee for the purchaser, unless there has been an express or implied agreement to assign the policy or hold it for the purchaser. Powles *v.* Innes, 11 M. & W. 10. Sparkes *v.* Marshall, 2 Bing. N. C. 761. N. of England Oilcake Co. *v.* Archangel Ins. Co., L. R. 10 Q. B. 249; 44 L. J. Q. B. 121. See Rayner *v.* Preston, 50 L. J. Ch. 472; 14 Ch. D. 297; and below, § 509.

(*c*) Seagrave *v.* Union M. I. Co., 35 L. J. C. P. 172; L. R. 1 C. P. 305.

(*d*) **Lucena** *v.* **Crawford,** 2 B. &. P. 269, 302; 6 R. R. 623. Wilson *v.* Jones, § 459 (*b*). Crowley, *supra* (*b*). See below, § 505.

(*e*) Stockdale *v.* Dunlop, 6 M. & W. 233. Anderson *v.* Morice, *cit.*

(*f*) 19 Geo. II. c. 37. 14 Geo. III. c. 48. Park, 552. Murphy *v.* Bell, 4 Bing. 567; 29 R. R. 630. Paterson *v.* Powell, 9 Bing. 320; 35 R. R. 530. The statute applies to a policy on profits or advances. Smith *v.* Reynolds, 1 H. & N. 221. De Mattos *v.* North, 37 L. J. Ex. 117. L. R. 3 Ex. 125. Allkins *v.* Jupe, 2 C. P. D. 357; 46 L. J. C. P. 824. Berridge *v.* Man. Gen. Ins. Co., 18 Q. B. D. 346. As to reinsurance, see § 505.

(*g*) Murphy, *supra* (*f*). Seagrave *v.* Union Mar. Ins. Co., *cit.* (*c*).

(*h*) Thellusson *v.* Fletcher, 1 Doug. 315; 3 Ill. 133. Nantes *v.* Thompson, 2 East, 385; 6 R. R. 458; and Cousins *v.* Nantes, 3 Taunt. 513; 12 R. R. 696.

(*i*) Clay *v.* Harrison, 10 B. & Cr. 99; 34 R. R. 334. "This seems a very questionable case, especially on the principle of the English law of sale." 1 Ill. 287. See Stoppel *v.* Stoddart, 1850; 13 D. 61; 2 Ross' L. C. 772; below, § 1309A.

462. (3.) *Risk.*—The subject must be actually at risk, or it must be *bonâ fide* believed to be so (*a*). And it must be a risk not occasioned by the fault or crime of the insured. So, in life assurance, death by duelling, suicide, or the hands of justice, are not risks under a policy for the benefit of the person or his family whose life is in question, though by special stipulation some of these risks may be included (*b*). Certain risks are, by special agreement or usage, excepted out of the underwriter's responsibility. In marine insurance, stores and certain perishable articles are by memorandum excepted, unless there be total loss, or stranding, or loss to an amount beyond the average damage to perishable commodities in such a voyage (*c*). So extra risks in ordinary fire policies are excepted, and certain diseases in life insurance. The risk must have arisen within the time specified or event referred to in the express or implied agreement of the parties (*d*).

(*a*) See above, § 458 (*a*). (*b*) See below, § 523.

(*c*) Smith *v.* Allan, 1823; 2 S. 309. See below, §§ 472 (8), 489.

(*d*) Park, 31. Marshall, 191.

463. (4.) *Premium.*—This is the consideration given, at entering into the contract, for the engagement to make future indemnification. It is presumed to be paid; the policy bears the receipt of it; and, as between the contracting parties, it is held as paid, entering as matter of account into their respective relations with the policy broker (*a*).

(*a*) Marshall, 268.

463A. **'Subrogation of Insurer paying, and Contribution.**—In the case of insurances on marine and fire risks, or of moneys lent or deposited, which are contracts of indemnity, the insurer, on making payment to the insured, whether of a partial or a total loss, is subrogated in his place, and has, on grounds of equity (and not because in the case of total loss the property of any remnants vests in him), the same right which the insured possessed to sue for damages a wrong-doer who caused the loss, and a right to recover from the insured any damages paid to him. In short, the insurer is, on payment, entitled to enforce all the remedies which the insured has against third parties, to compel them to make good the loss insured against, and to obtain from the assured, who can never be more than fully indemnified under the insurance contract, whatever advantage he may have received from such remedies (*a*). This includes contribution between different insurers to the same person on the same interest (*b*). But in life and accident insurance, where the contract is an absolute agreement to pay a sum certain on the occurrence of an event, the insurer has no concern with any damages or compensation which the insured may be able to claim *aliunde* (*c*).'

(*a*) **Simpson & Co.** *v.* **Thompson,** 1877; 5 R. H. L. 40; 3 App. Ca. 279 (revg. Burrell *v.* Simpson, 1876; 4 R. 177). Mason *v.* Sainsbury, 3 Doug. 64. Clarke *v.* Blything, 2 B. & Cr. 254; 26 R. R. 334. Yates *v.* White, 4 Bing. N. C. 272. Randal *v.* Cockran, 1 Ves. sen. 97. Dickenson *v.* Jardine, 37 L. J. C. P. 321; L. R. 3 C. P. 639 (average contribution). North Br. & Merc. Ins. Co. *v.* Lond. Liv. & Globe Ins. Co., L. R. 5 Ch. 569; 46 L. J. Ch. 537 (fire insurance). Darrell *v.* Tibbits, L. R. 5 Q. B. D. 560; 50 L. J. Q. B. 33 (fire). **Castellain** *v.* **Preston,** 11 Q. B. D. 381 (do.). Dane *v.* Mortgage Ins. Corp., 1894; 1 Q. B. 54. Laird *v.* Securities Ins. Co., 1895; 22 R. 452. West of Engld. F. I. Co. *v.* Isaacs, 1897; 1 Q. B. 226. See as to the application of the principle to a valued policy, North of Eng. Ins. Ass. *v.* Armstrong, L. R. 5 Q. B. 244; 39 L. J. Q. B. 81, which is doubted by L. Blackburn in Burnand *v.* Rodocanachi, 7 App. Ca. 333; 51 L. J. C. P. 548; below, § 482, 506–7.

(*b*) See below, § 506, 507. North Br. Ins. Co. *v.* Lond. Liv. & Globe Ins. Co., *cit.* Sickness & Acct. Ass. Assn. *v.* Gen. Acct. Ass. Corp., 1892; 19 R. 977.

(c) Bradburn v. G. W. Ry. Co., L. R. 10 Ex. 1; 44 L. J. Ex. 9. Cf. Jebsen v. E. and W. Ind. Dock Co., L. R. 10 C. P. 300; 44 L. J. C. P. 181.

II. MARITIME INSURANCE.

464. Description.—Maritime insurance is a contract of indemnity against loss by perils of the sea, fire, enemies, pirates, arrests by kings or states, barratry.

465. Constitution of the Contract.—Although this ranks as a consensual contract, a written instrument, on stamped paper, is by statute requisite to its constitution (*a*). In practice there is a previous note of the contract, called a "Slip," made out for the purpose of collecting the consents of underwriters to the proposed policy. It is intermediate and temporary, and held only to contain a confidential expression of the intention of the persons who sign by their initials to subscribe the policy. But to each party, while the policy is unsigned, there is *locus pœnitentiæ*. The slip has 'by the Revenue laws' no force as a contract of insurance, 'and under the former statutes on this subject, which prohibited unstamped agreements or contracts for insurance to be given in evidence, was' held ineffectual to show even priority of subscription (*b*).

'These enactments, however, are repealed, and it is now the law that a contract or agreement for sea insurance shall not be valid unless expressed in a policy; and any one attempting to insure or be insured against sea risk, unless by a duly stamped policy, incurs a penalty (*c*). Hence a slip is not valid or enforceable in any court; but it may be given in evidence wherever it is, though not valid, material; *e.g.* to show the time when the risk was really undertaken, after which—on the ground that by usage the contract, though of imperfect obligation, and not enforceable by reason of the positive rule of evidence in the statute, is complete when the slip is initialed—the policy is not avoided by non-disclosure to the insurer of material facts becoming known to the insured (*d*), or to show the intention of the parties (*e*).

'It was stated in former editions that' another preliminary proceeding is frequent, which has a different effect. Great insurance companies (*f*) engage by agents at a distance, empowered to take risks, that policies shall be sent; this intermediate engagement binds the company, and an action is competent for delivery of the policy (*g*). 'But since the Act of 1867 (*h*), which first enacted the rule above referred to, this doctrine appears no longer to be correct; and such agents, unless they have power to issue policies, cannot bind the company (*i*). Yet an agent's knowledge of material facts affecting the risk may affect the insurers (*k*).'

(*a*) 35 Geo. III. c. 63. 55 Geo. III. c. 84. Marshall, 247. Park, 16. Liddel & Brunton v. Kerr & Spence, Dec. 17, 1811; 1 Ill. 289. Mills v. Albion Ins. Co., 1826; 4 S. 575; 3 W. & S. 218; 1 Ill. 289 and 321. See 54 and 55 Vict. c. 39, § 93.

(*b*) Liddel, *supra* (*a*). Rodgers v. M'Carthy, Park, 39. Marsden v. Reid, 3 East, 575; 7 R. R. R. 516. Mackenzie v. Coulson, L. R. 8 Eq. 368. Parry v. Great Ship Co., 4 B. & S. 556; 33 L. J. Q. B. 41. Xenos v. Wickham, *infra* (*i*).

(*c*) 54 and 55 Vict. c. 39, § 97. See below, § 466. Fisher v. Liverpool M. I. Co., 43 L. J. Q. B. 114; 9 Q. B. 418.

(*d*) Cory v. Patton, L. R. 9 Q. B. 577; 41 L. J. Q. B. 195, note; 43 *ib.* 181. Lishman v. Northern M. I. Co., L. R. 10 C. P. 179; 44 L. J. C. P. 185. Morrison v. Univ. M. I. Co., L. R. 8 Ex. 40, 197; 42 L. J. Ex. 17, 115. See Fisher, *cit.* Ionides, *infra.* See Pollock on Contracts, 641.

(*e*) **Ionides v. Pacific F. & M. I. Co.,** L. R. 6 Q. B. 674; 7 Q. B. 517; 41 L. J. Q. B. 33, 190.

(*f*) As to Insurance Companies, see 25 and 26 Vict. c. 89, § 89, 205, 209, etc. Arnould, 149, 156, etc.

(*g*) Mills, *supra* (*a*). Christie v. N. B. Ins. Co., 1825; 3 S. 519; 1 Ill. 320. See Mead v. Davidson, 3 Ad. & E. 303. Fowler v. Scott. Eq. Ass. Co., 28 L. J. Ch. 225. Bhugwandass v. Nethds. India Ins. Co., 14 App. Ca. 83.

(*h*) 30 and 31 Vict. c. 23, § 7, repealed by the Stamp Act of 1891.

(*i*) Fisher, *cit.* As to the *delivery* of the policy and the powers of insurance brokers (*supra*, § 219 (1)), see **Xenos v. Wickham,** 14 C. B. N. S. 435; 33 L. J. C. P. 13; 36 L. J. C. P. 313; L. R. 2 H. L. Ca. 296. Roberts v. Security Co., 1897; 1 Q. B. 111. As to the local law governing contracts of insurance, see Guthrie's Savigny's Priv. Internat. Law, 232, 244, 265.

(*k*) See above, § 13A, 14, 224B. Bowden v. Lond. E. & G. Ins. Co., 1892; 2 Q. B. 534.

466. Policy.—This is an ill-drawn and very loosely expressed instrument, but in all its material points now settled by precedents. It must be subscribed, either by the party himself undertaking the risk, hence called Underwriter; or by one authorised to sign for him by written authority or mandate, or at least sanctioned by acquiescence. The subscription is often made by one acting as agent or broker for many underwriters. 'The policy is not valid unless it specifies the particular risk or adventure, the names of the subscribers or underwriters, and the sum or sums insured; and is made for not more than twelve months (*a*).'

(*a*) 54 and 55 Vict. c. 39, § 93 (Stamp Act, 1891). See Inverkeithing Mar. Assur. Assn. *v.* Mackenzie, 1882; 9 R. 1043; and *In re* Arthur Average Assn., L. R. 10 Ch. 542; 44 L. J. Ch. 569.

(1.) *Stamp.*—The policy must be duly stamped when effected (*a*). 'Formerly' the stamp 'could' not afterwards be supplied, 'but policies of sea insurance may now be afterstamped, for the purpose of production in evidence, on payment of a penalty of £100 (*b*). Policies made out of, but in any way enforceable within, the United Kingdom, are subject to the stamp duty, and may be stamped at any time within ten days of the time when they are first received in the United Kingdom on payment of the duty only (*c*).' Nor can the agreement be materially altered, after it has been fully executed and completed (*d*). But to this rule there is, by the statute itself, an exception, that the policy may be altered before the determination of the risk is known; provided that the thing insured shall have remained the property of the original insurer; that there shall be no prolongation of the term of insurance 'beyond the period of six months, or beyond twelve months in all where the policy is originally for a term of more than six months,' or extension of the voyage; and that no additional 'or further' sum shall be insured by 'reason of' the alteration (*e*). Under this exception, an alteration of the time of sailing has been allowed (*f*); and even of the voyage itself, where the ship was detained beyond the stipulated time of sailing (*g*). But it has not been permitted to alter the insurance from "ship and outfit" to "ship and goods," as being an entire change on "the thing insured" (*h*). A correction of an innocent mistake is held no alteration (*i*); and even a waiver of the warranty of seaworthiness has been held no alteration requiring a new stamp (*k*). 'Contracts by carriers by sea and others undertaking risks attending goods on board ship, or to indemnify the owner for loss, are contracts for sea insurance under the existing Stamp Act (*l*).'

(*a*) Nixon *v.* Albion M. I. Co., 36 L. J. Ex. 180; L. R. 2 Ex. 338. G. B. Steamship Premium Ass. *v.* Whyte, 1891; 19 R. 109 (time policy including a number of ships).

(*b*) 54 and 55 Vict. c. 39, § 95.

(*c*) *Ib.* As to policies of mutual insurance, see *ib.* Lion Ins. Co. *v.* Tucker, 12 Q. B. D. 176. United King. Mut. Steamship Ass. Co. *v.* Nevill, 19 Q. B. D. 110.

(*d*) 35 Geo. III. c. 63. 55 Geo. III. c. 184. Roderick *v.* Hovil, 3 Camp. 103. See Rippiner *v.* Wright, 2 B. & Ald. 478; 1 Ill. 289; 21 R. R. 363. Hubbard *v.* Jackson, 4 Taunt. 169; 13 R. R. 574. At common law alterations can only be made, of course, with consent of all the parties. See Arnould, 264.

(*e*) 54 and 55 Vict. c. 39, § 96.

(*f*) 35 Geo. III. c. 63, § 13. Kensington *v.* Inglis, 8 East, 273; 9 R. R. 438. Ramstrom *v.* Bell, 5 M. & S. 267. Ridsdale *v.* Shedden, 4 Camp. 107.

(*g*) Brockelbank *v.* Sugrue, 1 B. & Ad. 81.

(*h*) Hill *v.* Patten, 8 East, 373. See 9 East, 351.

(*i*) Robinson *v.* Touray, 1 M. & S. 217; 3 Camp. 158; 13 R. R. 781; 16 R. R. 284, n. Sawtell *v.* London, 5 Taunt. 359.

(*k*) Weir *v.* Aberdeen, 2 B. & Ald. 320; 20 R. R. 450.

(*l*) 54 and 55 Vict. c. 39, § 92 (2).

467. (2.) *Construction.*—The policy is to be construed according to its plain sense and meaning, as collected from the terms made use of, taken in their ordinary and popular meaning; unless either by the known usage of trade, or by the force of the context, they are to be understood in a peculiar or technical sense (*a*). Part of it being printed and part written, the definite meaning fixed on the former is to be taken; the latter construed according to the obvious intention of the persons who have selected them; 'and the written words, being selected by the parties, control the printed and formal parts of the policy (*b*).'

(*a*) Robertson *v.* French, 4 East, 120; 3 Ill. 135, 145; 7 R. R. 535. Hunter *v.* Leathly, 10 B. & Cr. 871. Comp. above, § 406, 83. See Smith's Merc. Law, 336; *infra*, § 524. Arnould, 276–296.

(*b*) Dict. Lord Ellenborough, 4 East, 136. Gumm *v.* Tyrie, 33 L. J. Q. B. 97. Joyce *v.* Swann (Realm Ins. Co.), L. R. 7 Q. B. 583; 41 L. J. Q. B. 356. Dudgeon *v.* Pembroke, 2 App. Ca. 284; 46 L. J. Q. B. 409. West Ind. Teleg. Co. *v.* Home & Col. M. I. Co., 6 Q. B. D. 51; 50 L. J. Q. B. 41. Alsager *v.* St. Catherine's Dock Co., 14 M. & W. 798. Halhead *v.* Young, 6 E. & B. 320; 25 L. J. Q. B. 290. See Merc. M. I. Co. *v.* Tetherington, 5 B. & S. 765; 34 L. J. Q. B. 11.

468. (3.) *Name of Insured.*—By statute (*a*), every policy is void in which there does not appear the name of the persons interested; or of the consignor or consignee; or of the person residing in Great Britain who shall receive the order for, and effect such policy; or of him who shall give the order to the agent employed to effect the insurance. It is not enough that the policy bears the name of the master or broker as such; but it is sufficient if there be the name of one employed to represent a true interest, by effecting the policy (*b*). It is not necessary that an agent shall be named as such (*c*). A broker who is not general agent for the insured, is within the statute if described as agent (*d*).

(*a*) 28 Geo. III. c. 56. 1 Bell's Com. 604.
(*b*) Bell *v.* Gilson, 1 B. & P. 345; 4 R. R. 823. Cf. Williams *v.* North China Ins. Co., 1 C. P. D. 757.
(*c*) De Vignier *v.* Swanston, 1 B. & P. 346; 4 R. R. 825, n.
(*d*) Same case. See Symers *v.* Glasgow M. I. Co., 1846; 9 D. 168. G. B. A1 Ins. Ass. *v.* Wyllie, 22 Q. B. D. 710, 719.

469. (4.) *Name of the Ship.*—The ship is described by her name and the name of the master. This is for the purpose of identifying the risk; and so, if the name of ship or captain should be mistaken, without any doubt as to the identity, this would not be fatal; though, to prevent all dispute on that subject, it is commonly added, "or by whatever other name the ship shall be called," and "whoever else shall go as captain." Under such a clause, an innocent mistake, when there is clear proof of the identity of the ship intended by the parties, does not vacate the policy (*a*). Goods may be insured by the policy, generally, as goods on board ship or ships, provided they shall be afterwards identified as those understood by the parties. This has been long settled (*b*).

(*a*) Watt *v.* Ritchie, 1782; M. 7074; 1 Ill. 290. Le Mesurier *v.* Vaughan, 6 East, 382; 8 R. R. 500. Park, 21. Ionides *v.* Pacific M. I. Co., *infra*, § 470.
(*b*) Kewley *v.* Ryan, 2 H. Blackst. 343; 1 Ill. 317; 3 R. R. 408. See below, § 470.

470. (5.) *Specification of Subject.*—Generally speaking, the subject of maritime insurance is the ship, or cargo; but under this is comprehended as fit subjects of insurance the freight to be earned by the ship, and the profits to be effected on the sale of the cargo; and besides these, the bottomry and *respondentia* interests that may exist with regard to either. But although it is indispensable that the insured have an interest in the voyage, it is not necessary to specify the nature of such interest in the policy (*a*), 'if it be immaterial to the risk, *i.e.* unless the peculiar nature of the interest alters the risk insured (*b*).'

Whatever be the subject, it must be so clearly described that there may be no doubt as to identity. Thus the ship must be identified (*c*); and when insured with "the body tackle, boats, and other furniture," this will comprehend the provisions on board at the date of the policy (*d*). The goods are identified by the ship, or by their marks or other description. When the insured does not know by what ship the goods are to be sent, he insures goods by "ship or ships"; and as there are many occasions on which both ship and goods are unknown, in such cases a valid insurance 'called an "open policy"' may be effected "on goods to be afterwards declared and valued by ship or ships," the declaration being made by showing an embarkation of goods for behoof of the insured (*e*). When goods are mentioned generally, it is held to apply only to such as are exposed to the ordinary risks—'not extraordinary risks,' as being loaded on deck, 'unless such goods are' usually so loaded (*f*). Profits may be insured under that general term (*g*); and freight may be insured provided it is done expressly (*h*); and under freight may be covered the benefit one derives from carrying his goods in his own ship (*i*). 'Advances of freight may also be insured (*k*).'

Bottomry and *respondentia* interests may also be insured, but they must be so specified, and will not be covered by an insurance on goods (*l*).

(*a*) Carruthers *v.* Shedden, 6 Taunt. 14; 1 Ill. 291. Crowley *v.* Cohen, 3 B. & Ad. 478; 1 Ill. 287. See above, § 461. Joyce *v.* Kennard, L. R. 7 Q. B. 78; 41 L. J. Q. B. 17.
(*b*) See Mackenzie *v.* Whitworth, 1 Ex. D. 36; 45 L. J. Ex. 233. M'Swinney *v.* R. E. Assur. Co., 14 Q. B. 634; 19 L. J. Q. B. 222.
(*c*) Ionides *v.* Pacific Ins. Co., L. R. 6 Q. B. 674; 7 Q. B. 517; 41 L. J. Q. B. 33, 190. Bates *v.* Hewitt, L. R. 2 Q. B. 595; 36 L. J. Q. B. 282.
(*d*) Brough *v.* Whitmore, 4 T. R. 206; 2 R. R. 361. See § 462, 472.
(*e*) Robinson *v.* Touray, 3 Camp. 158; 13 R. R. 781, and see 16 R. R. 284, n.; 1 M. & S. 217. Harman *v.* Kingston, *ib.* 150; 13 R. R. 775. See Entwistle *v.* Ellis, 2 H. & N. 549; 27 L. J. Ex. 105 (goods to be declared). Gledstanes *v.* R. E. Assur. Co., 34 L. J. Q. B. 30. Ionides, *supra.* Davies *v.* Natl. F. & M. Ins. Co. of N. Zealand, 1891; A. C. 485. Stephens *v.* Austr. Ins. Co., L. R. 8 C. P. 18; 42 L. J. C. P. 12 (policies attach on goods as soon as shipped and in order of shipment, and in case of mistake as to order without fraud, assured may rectify his declaration even after loss known. So also in) Impl. M. I. Co. *v.* Fire Ins. Corpn., 4 C. P. D. 166; 48 L. J. C. P. 424.
(*f*) Blackett *v.* Royal Exch. Assur. Co., 2 Tyrwh. 266. Da Costa *v.* Edmonds, 4 Camp. 142; 16 R. R. 763. Milward *v.* Hibbert, 3 Q. B. 120. Wilson *v.* Rankin, L. R. 1 Q. B. 162; 35 L. J. Q. B. 87. Miller *v.* Tetherington, 6 H. & N. 278; 7 H. & N. 954; 30 L. J. Ex. 217; 31 *ib.* 363. See cases in § 439, and Arnould, 27, 282. The former text was vitiated by a clerical or typographical error.
(*g*) Eyre *v.* Glover, 3 Camp. 276; 16 East, 218; 3 Ill. 132; 13 R. R. 801. Grant *v.* Parkinson, Park, 561; 6 T. R. 483. Barclay *v.* Cousins, 2 East, 544; 6 R. R. 505. Lucena *v.* Crawford, 2 B. & P. 315; 6 R. R. v, 623.

Anderson *v.* Morice, L. R. 10 C. P. 609; 44 L. J. C. P. 341.

(*h*) Baillie *v.* Modigliani, Park, 116; 1 Ill. 274. Taylor *v.* Wilson, 15 East, 324; 13 R. R. 488. Barclay *v.* Stirling, 5 M. & S. 6; 17 R. R. 245. Ellis *v.* Lafone, 8 Ex. 546; 22 L. J. Ex. 224. Michael *v.* Gillespy, 2 C. B. N. S. 627; 26 L. J. C. P. 306. Freight does not include passage money. Denoon *v.* Home & Col. Ins. Co., 41 L. J. C. P. 162; L. R. 7 C. P. 341.

(*i*) Flint *v.* Flemyng, 1 B. & Ad. 45; 35 R. R. 205. Miller *v.* Woodfall, 8 E. & B. 493; 27 L. J. Q. B. 120.

(*k*) See above, § 459 (*g*).

(*l*) Glover *v.* Black, 3 Burr. 1394. Phillips on Ins. § 299, 427. Simonds *v.* Hodgson, 3 B. & Ad. 50. Stainbank *v.* Fenning, 11 C. B. 57. Stainbank *v.* Shepherd, 13 C. B. 418. Broomfield *v.* Southern Ins. Co., L. R. 5 Ex. 192; 39 L. J. Ex. 186.

471. (6.) *Commencement and Termination of Risk.*—There must be no uncertainty as to the commencement and termination of the risk (*a*). These must be clearly set forth in respect both of time and of place.

Commencement.—The expression "at and from" covers all perils while the ship lies at the place mentioned (*b*); the risk beginning on the ship at the time mentioned; or date of the policy, if no time be stated; or if "from a port," with her breaking ground. 'Delay in arriving at the port prevents the policy from attaching, if it be such as materially to alter the risk (*c*).' If the insurance be on freight '"at and from a port,"' it begins with the ship being ready for her cargo, 'which has been bought or contracted for and prevented from being received or carried only by the perils insured against; or with her having begun to do something under a charter-party or contract to take the cargo on board with a view to its fulfilment (*d*)'; with the loading, if the insurance be of goods; not however, covering goods already on board, before the commencement of the risk (*e*), unless either so specified or plainly implied (*f*). At and from an island or district, protects a ship sailing from port to port in that island or district for loading, if the whole be held as one place (*g*).

The course of the voyage must be according to the order of ports and places, and for the purpose mentioned in the policy, or as sanctioned by usage (*h*); 'and the risk does not attach if the ship sails for a port not inlcuded in the policy (*i*).'

Termination.—When the insurance is *to* a district or island, the voyage (as to the ship) determines at the first port (*k*) at which she stops to unload (*l*), unless a stipulation be added insuring her to her port of discharge (*m*). Goods are protected till arrival at the port of delivery. The usual termination for the ship is, "till moored twenty-four hours in good safety," which means, that if no loss or damage happens within the twenty-four hours (or a term of quarantine), for which the underwriters are liable, they are discharged (*n*). On goods the policy usually is, "till safely landed," which covers them till landed in the way which usage sanctions (*o*).

In a policy on time, the period is by statute restricted to twelve months (*p*); and in construing the policy, the Courts have gone as far as possible in favouring the intention of the parties (*q*). 'If a ship insured for time is injured by the perils insured against within the time, but the extent of the damage is not ascertained till the time has expired, the ship being kept afloat till then, the insured may, it appears, recover under the policy (*r*).'

(*a*) Park, 31. Phillips, § 918 sqq. 2 Selw. N. P. 877. See 54 and 55 Vict. c. 39, *supra*, § 466.

(*b*) Rotch *v.* Edie, 6 T. R. 413; 13 Ill. 134; 3 R. R. 222. Palmer *v.* Marshall, 8 Bing. 79; 34 R. R. 628. Haughton *v.* Emp. M. I. Ins. Co., L. R. 1 Ex. 206; 35 L. J. Ex. 117. Foley *v.* United F. & Mar. Ins. Co. of Sydney, L. R. 5 C. P. 155; 39 L. J. C. P. 206. See below, § 476.

(*c*) De Wolf *v.* Archangel Ins. Co., L. R. 9 Q. B. 451; 43 L. J. Q. B. 147.

(*d*) Williamson *v.* Innes, 8 Bing. 81; 34 R. R. 629. See cases in § 459 (*f*). Thompson *v.* Taylor, 6 T. R. 478; 3 R. R. 233. Devaux *v.* I'Anson, 5 Bing. N. C. 519. Forbes *v.* Aspinall, 13 East, 331; Tudor's L. C. 204, 170; 12 R. R. 352. Flint *v.* Flemyng, *cit.* Horncastle *v.* Stuart, 7 East, 400; 8 R. R. 649. Mackenzie *v.* Shedden, 2 Camp. 431; 11 R. R. 759. Sellar *v.* M'Vicar, 1 N. R. 23. Barber *v.* Fleming, 39 L. J. Q. B. 25; L. R. 5 Q. B. 59. Smith's Merc. Law, 418. Foley, *cit.* (*b*). See also Jones *v.* Neptune M. Ins. Co., L. R. 7 Q. B. 720; 41 L. J. Q. B. 370 (beginning from the loading—complete loading). Joyce *v.* Realm M. I. Co., L. R. 7 Q. B. 580; 41 L. J. Q. B. 356.

(*e*) Langhorn *v.* Hardy, 4 Taunt. 628; 13 R. R. 708. Spitta *v.* Woodman, 2 Taunt. 416; 3 Ill. 136; 11 R. R. 628. Horneyer *v.* Lushington, 15 East, 46; 13 R. R. 759. Mellish *v.* Alnut, 2 M. & S. 106; 14 R. R. 599. The tendency is to relax this strict rule of construction. See cases in next note.

(*f*) Bell *v.* Hobson, 16 East, 240; 3 Ill. 136; 14 R. R. 337. Gladstone *v.* Clay, 1 M. & S. 118; 14 R. R. 479. Carr *v.* Montefiore, 5 B. & S. 408; 33 L. J. Q. B. 57, 256. Joyce *v.* Realm Ins. Co., L. R. 7 Q. B. 580; 41 L. J. Q. B. 356. Arnould, 378–387.

(*g*) Camden *v.* Cowley, 1 W. Blackst. 417. Cruickshanks *v.* Janson, 2 Taunt. 301; 11 R. R. 584. Warre *v.* Miller, 4 B. & Cr. 538; 1 Ill. 291; 28 R. R. 382.

(*h*) Robertson *v.* Laird, 1790; M. 7099; aff. 3 Pat. 443. Beatson *v.* Haworth, 6 T. R. 530; 3 Ill. 137; 3 R. R. 258. Bottomly *v.* Bovill, 5 B. & Cr. 210. Solly *v.* Whitmore, 5 B. & Ald. 45; 24 R. R. 474. Hammond *v.* Reid, *ib.* 72; 22 R. R. 679. Clason *v.* Simmonds, 6 T. R. 533, n.; 3 R. R. 260. Ashley *v.* Pratt, 16 M. & W. 471; 1 Ex. 257; 17 L. J. Ex. 135. See below, § 492.

(*i*) See below, § 492 (*b*).

(*k*) It is sometimes a question what is "a port" within the policy. See Sea Ins. Co. of Scotland *v.* Gavin, 1827; 5 S. 525; aff. 4 W. & S. 17; 2 Dow & Cl. 124. Harrower *v.* Hutchison, L. R. 4 Q. B. 523; 38 L. J. Q. B. 185; 39 L. J. Q. B. 229. Owners of Afton *v.* Northern Ins. Co., 1887; 14 R. 544; aff. (*nom.* Hunter *v.* North. Ass. Co.) 1888, 13 App. Ca. 717; 15 R. H. L. 72 ("while in port thirty days after arrival"—port of Greenock). Sailing Ship Garston Co. *v.* Hickie & Co., 15 Q. B. D. 580 (charter-party).

(*l*) Camden *v.* Cowley, 1 W. Blackst. 417.

(*m*) Arnould, 421.

(*n*) Waples *v.* Eames, 2 Strange, 1243. Angerstein *v.* Bell, Park, 54. Merc. M. I. Co. *v.* Tetherington, 5 B. & S. 765; 34 L. J. Q. B. 11. Lidgett *v.* Secretan, L. R. 5 C. P. 190; 39 L. J. C. P. 196. Whitwell *v.* Harrison, 2 Ex. 127; 18 L. J. Ex. 465. Stone *v.* Ocean M. I. Co., 1 Ex. D. 81; 45 L. J. Ex. 361 (to a place, generally).

(*o*) Tierney *v.* Etherington; approved of by Lord Mansfield, 3 Burr. 348. Hurry *v.* R. Ex. Assur. Co., 2 B. & P. 430; 5 R. R. 639. Stewart *v.* Bell, 5 B. & Ald. 238; 3 Ill. 138; 24 R. R. 342. Harrison *v.* Ellis, 26 L. J. Q. B. 239; 7 E. & B. 465. As to landing by lighters, see Hurry, *cit.*; Stewart, *cit.*; and Lane *v.* Nixon, L. R. 1 C. P. 412; 35 L. J. C. P. 243. Houlder *v.* Merchts. M. I. Co., 17 Q. B. D. 354.

(*p*) 35 Geo. III. c. 63, § 2. 30 and 31 Vict. c. 23, § 8; now 54 and 55 Vict. c. 39, § 93. Lishman *v.* North. M. I. Co., L. R. 8 C. P. 216; 42 L. J. C. P. 108.

(*q*) Park, 40.

(*r*) Knight *v.* Faith, 15 Q. B. 649; 19 L. J. Q. B. 517.

472. Risks insured against.—These are:—

(1.) *Perils of the Sea*; by winds and waves, lightning, rocks, sands, collision of ships, etc. (*a*); but damage by indirect consequence is not included (*b*): a species of worm infesting the rivers of Africa was held not a loss by sea peril; 'apparently on the principle that in the circumstances the damage fell within the category of wear and tear in the ordinary service of the ship (*c*). Insurance is for protection against casualties, and so underwriters are not liable for loss by inherent defects of the subject insured, or by the natural and regular action of the tide, or even by the chemical action on it of the sea water, etc. (*d*).' Damage to living animals by agitation of the waves has been held loss by peril of the sea (*e*); 'but not their death or deterioration without fault from want of food, nor injury to goods caused by delay arising from bad weather on the voyage (*f*). The policy includes losses of the kinds above indicated, although they were partly due to the negligence of the ship's crew, if not barratrous (*g*). The expression "perils of the sea" means the same whether it occurs in a charter-party, bill of lading, or policy of insurance (*h*).'

(2.) *Fire.*—It is not every loss that happens at sea which is covered by insurance; but fire is expressly included in the policy, and is covered by the insurance (*i*), provided, as to goods, it do not arise from the unfit condition of the goods at embarkation (*k*).

(3.) *Enemies* (*l*).—This applies to capture by public enemies in war; and in a question of insurance it is not necessary that there should be condemnation, or even carrying *intra præsidia* (*m*); for the insurer is liable whether the property be changed by the capture or not. The cases may be either of total or partial loss, as the ship or goods are recaptured and restored or not (*n*); but the insurer is liable to the loss in both cases.

(4.) *Detention of Princes, etc.*—By kings, princes, and people, is meant not enemies merely, but those in amity, 'and of the nation of the assured (*o*)' also; and not a riotous assembly of people, but a national act (*p*).

(4*a*.) '*Pirates, Rovers, and Thieves.*—Acts of piracy are all hostile depredations done at sea without the commission of any state, or beyond the limits of a commission. The English law of piracy includes all such acts committed at sea as would be felony if done on land (*q*).'

(5.) *Jettison.*—The damage or loss suffered in this way is covered by the usual words of the policy, and indeed is strictly a loss by dangers of the sea (*r*); and the claim for indemnity is not limited to the strict case of average contribution, but extends to all jettison *ex justa causa* (*s*). 'The insured may claim indemnity for a loss of this kind without having sought contribution from the parties liable, leaving the insurer to stand in his place in the general average adjustment (*t*).'

(6.) *Barratry.*—This is a peril brought into the policy by special stipulation; for it may be said to be inconsistent with the true relations of the parties, that insurers should answer for the fraud of those appointed by the insured (*u*).

(7.) *Other Perils.*—Difficulties having arisen as to many cases not included under the words of the policy, a sweeping clause of "all other perils" was introduced (*v*). This comprehends such a case as a ship fired on by mistake from a British cruiser (*w*), a ship in dock blown over by a land breeze (*x*), 'but not the explosion of a steam boiler, or the bursting of a pump, or apparently any casualty which is not fairly described as a marine loss, and is not *ejusdem generis* with those enumerated (*y*).'

(7*a*.) '*Running-down Clause*.—Under the ordinary form of policy, insurers are not liable for losses arising from the liabilities imposed on a shipowner by modern rules of law requiring an equal division of the damage in cases of collision (*z*), for loss of life, personal injuries, loss or injury of goods on board, and for similar losses and injuries occasioned on board another vessel by that insured. But since De Vaux *v.* Salvador the policy contains a clause by which the underwriter undertakes the risk of three-fourths of all damages which the shipowner may have to pay in case "the vessel shall by accident or negligence of the master or crew, run down or damage any other ship or vessel," etc. A question arose, and was differently decided in England and Scotland, whether this clause in its original form covered damages paid for loss of life or personal injury to individuals on board either ship (*aa*); but stipulations excluding such liability, and dealing with the expenses of contested claims, are now added (*bb*). It has been held to apply where the collision was with the tug towing the insured ship, the latter having had to pay damages (*cc*).'

(8.) *Exceptions—The Memorandum*.—The difficulty of distinguishing between loss by tear and wear, or by the natural quality and inscrutable decay of certain commodities, has led to the exception by a memorandum, saving the underwriter from all partial losses, '"average, unless general,"' on corn, fish, salt, fruit, flour, and seed, except by jettison or stranding of the ship; and from partial loss under a certain rate on sugar, tobacco, hemp, flax, hides, and skins, unless by general average or stranding (*dd*). 'This memorandum exempts the underwriter from making good any partial loss whatever within its terms, even including expenses and freight incurred in forwarding the subject-matter of the insurance when it is not in danger of total loss (*ee*). But as there can be no partial loss of freight, this does not exclude the insured on freight, who earns his freight by forwarding the goods in another ship, from recovering the freight in such ship from the underwriters, under the suing and labouring clause (*ff*).' The chief doubt relates to stranding (*gg*), 'but it is held under the clause "unless the ship be stranded," that if the ship be stranded the underwriter pays for the articles in the memorandum, whether the loss on them is occasioned by the stranding or not (*hh*)'; and in regard to this, the ship must be rendered immoveable on the strand; and the stranding must be occasioned by some extraordinary or accidental occurrence, and not merely by the ship taking the ground in the usual course 'of navigation' in a tide river or harbour, though in doing so she should be injured by some hard substance (*ii*). Such an accident, however, may give indemnification for loss on goods not within the memorandum. In questions under the memorandum, 'in a policy on goods or a time policy on a ship (*kk*),' two distinct occasions of loss are not to be combined to bring up the average with the percentage; nor is the total loss of some part of the goods under the memorandum to be reckoned as a partial loss on the whole (*ll*), 'unless the goods be made up in packages separately insured, or be of different species (*mm*).'

(*a*) Emerig. 12. Marshall, 166. Park, 34, 136. 2 Selw. N. P. 880, 894. Smith *v.* Scott, 4 Taunt. 126; 1 Ill. 278; 13 R. R. 568. Buller *v.* Fisher, 3 Esp. 67; 1 Ill. 170; 4 R. R. 902. Fletcher *v.* Inglis, 2 B. & Ald. 315; 1 Ill. 303; 20 R. R. 448. Hahn *v.* Corbet, 2 Bing. 205; 27 R. R. 590.

(*b*) Powel *v.* Gudgeon, 5 M. & S. 437; 17 R. R. 385. **De Vaux** *v.* **Salvador,** 4 A. & E. 420. See Montoya *v.* Lond. Ass. Co., 6 Ex. 451. Bondrett *v.* Hentigg, Holt's N. P. 149; 17 R. R. 625. Dent *v.* Smith, L. R. 4 Q. B. 414; 38 L. J. Q. B. 144. Cater *v.* Great W. Ins. Co., L. R. 8 C. P. 552; 42 L. J. C. P. 266. Inman *v.* Bischoff, 6 Q. B. D. 648; 50 L. J. Q. B. 440. Pink *v.* Fleming, 25 Q. B. D. 396. Reischer *v.* Borwick, 1894; 2 Q. B. 548.

(*c*) Rohl *v.* Parr, Park, 142; 1 Esp. 444; 3 Ill. 141; 5 R. R. 742. See Lovell *v.* M'Millan, June 21, 1809; F. C. As to rats, see above, § 241 (*b*).

(*d*) Paterson *v.* Harris, 1 B. & S. 336; 30 L. J. Q. B. 354. Magnus *v.* Buttemer, 11 C. B. 876; 21 L. J. C. P. 119. Corcoran *v.* Gurney, 22 L. J. Q. B. 133; 1 E. & B. 456. See Koebel *v.* Saunders, 17 C. B. N. S. 79; 33 L. J. C. P. 312.

(*e*) Lawrence *v.* Aberdein, 5 B. & Ald. 107; 24 R. R. 299. Gabay *v.* Lloyd, 3 B. & Cr. 793; 27 R. R. 486.

(*f*) Tatham *v.* Hodgson, 6 T. R. 656. Taylor *v.* Dunbar, L. R. 4 C. P. 206; 38 L. J. C. P. 178; Arnould, 713.

(*g*) See below, § 479. Dixon *v.* Sadler, 5 M. & W. 405; 8 M. & W. 895. Redman *v.* Wilson, 14 M. & W. 476; 14 L. J. Ex. 333. Davidson *v.* Burnand, L. R. 4 C. P. 117; 38 L. J. C. P. 73. See Coey *v.* Smith, 1860; 22 D. 955. Trinder & Co. *v.* Thames and Mersey M. I. Co., 1898; 2 Q. B. 114.

(*h*) **Wilson & Sons** *v.* **Owners of Cargo per Xantho,** and **Hamilton** *v.* **Pandorf,** 12 App. Ca. 503, 518.

(*i*) Gordon *v.* Rimmington, 1 Camp. 123; 10 R. R. 656. Busk *v.* R. E. Ass. Co., 2 B. & Ald. 73; 20 R. R. 350.

(*k*) Boyd *v.* Dubois, 3 Camp. 133.

(*l*) As to insurance of war risks as between seller and buyer, see Birkett, Sperling, & Co. *v.* Engholm & Co., 1871; 10 Macph. 170.

(*m*) Goss *v.* Withers, 2 Burr. 683; 1 Ill. 306. Marshall, 493.

(*n*) Hamilton *v.* Mendez, 2 Burr. 1198. Bainbridge *v.* Neilson, 10 East, 328; 1 Ill. 312; 10 R. R. 316. Patterson *v.* Ritchie, 4 M. & S. 393; 16 R. R. 498. Dean *v.* Hornby, 3 E. & B. 180. Powell *v.* Hyde, 5 E. & B. 607; 25 L. J. Q. B. 65. Fowler *v.* E. & I. M. I. Co., 18 C. B. N. S. 919; 34 L. J. C. P. 253.

(*o*) Aubert *v.* Gray, 3 B. & S. 163; 32 L. J. Q. B. 50.

(*p*) Marshall, 408. Touteng *v.* Hubbard, 3 B. & P. 301; 6 R. R. 791. Nesbit *v.* Lushington, 4 T. R. 783; 2 R. R. 519. Lozano *v.* Janson, 2 E. & E. 160: 28 L. J. Q. B. 337. Rodocanachi *v.* Elliott, L. R. 8 C. P. 649; 9 C. P. 518; 42 L. J. C. P. 247; 43 *ib.* 255 (siege and blockade). Stringer *v.* Engl. & Sc. M. I. Co., L. R. 5 Q. B. 599; 39 L. J. Q. B. 214.

(*q*) Hume's Com. i. 480. 1 Stephen's Com. 299 sqq. Palmer *v.* Naylor, 8 Ex. 739; 10 Ex. 382; 23 L. J. Ex. 323. Dean *v.* Hornby, 3 E. & B. 180; 22 L. J. Q. B. 129. Kleinwort *v.* Shepherd, 1 E. & E. 447; 28 L. J. Q. B. 147.

(*r*) Marshall, 434. Arnould, 877.

(*s*) Butler *v.* Wildman, 3 B. & Ald. 398; 22 R. R. vi, 435.

(*t*) Dickinson *v.* Jardine, L. R. 3 C. P. 639; 37 L. J. Q. B. 321.

(*u*) See this more fully stated below, § 479.

(*v*) See Fletcher *v.* Inglis, 2 B. & Ald. 315; 1 Ill. 303; 20 R. R. 448. Walker *v.* Maitland, 5 B. & Ald. 171; 24 R. R. 320. Lawrence *v.* Aberdein, *cit.* (*e*). Gabay *v.* Lloyd, *cit.* (*e*). Lovell *v.* M'Millan, June 21, 1809; F. C. Thompson *v.* Whitmore, 3 Taunt. 227; 1 Ill. 314; 12 R. R. 642. Boyd *v.* Dubois, 3 Camp. 133. Naylor *v.* Palmer, 8 Ex. 739. Davidson *v.* Burnand, L. R. 4 C. P. 117; 38 L. J. C. P. 73.

(*w*) Cullen *v.* Butler, 5 M. & S. 461; 1 Ill. 278; 17 R. R. 400.

(*x*) Phillips *v.* Barber, 5 B. & Ald. 161; 24 R. R. 317. Napier *v.* Wood, 1825; 4 S. 19. Cf. Magnus *v.* Buttemer, 11 C. B. 876; 21 L. J. C. P. 119. Davidson *v.* Burnand, *cit.*

(*y*) **Thames and Mersey M. I. Co. *v.* Hamilton & Co. (Hamilton *v.* Pandorf)**, 12 App. Ca. 484, overruling West India Telegr. Co. *v.* Home & Col. M. I. Co., 6 Q. B. D. 51; 50 L. J. Q. B. 41.

(*z*) See above, § 436. De Vaux *v.* Salvador, 4 A. & E. 420.

(*aa*) Taylor *v.* Dewar, 5 B. & S. 58; 33 L. J. Q. B. 141. Coey *v.* Smith, 1860; 22 D. 955. Xenos *v.* Fox, 38 L. J. C. P. 351; L. R. 4 C. P. 665 (expenses of contested claim). Thompson *v.* Reynolds, 7 E. & B. 172; 26 L. J. Q. B. 93.

(*bb*) Baine & Johnston, *infra.*

(*cc*) Baine & Johnston *v.* M'Cowan (The Niobe), 1890; 17 R. 1016; aff. 1891, A. C. 401; 18 R. H. L. 57 (L. Bramwell *diss.*).

(*dd*) See Bishop *v.* Pentland, 7 B. & Cr. 219; 37 R. R. 177. Mitchell *v.* Calder, 1822; 1 S. 298. See § 462. Navone *v.* Haddon, 9 C. B. 30. Reimer *v.* Ringrose, 6 Ex. 263; 20 L. J. Ex. 175. Gr. Ind. Pen. Ry. Co. *v.* Saunders, 2 B. & S. 266; 31 L. J. Q. B. 206. Under the suing and labouring clause, the underwriter may be liable for what is really particular average. Kidston *v.* Empire M. I. Co., L. R. 1 C. P. 535; 2 C. P. 357; 36 L. J. C. P. 156; but not for general average and salvage. Lohre *v.* Aitchison, 3 Q. B. D. 558; 4 App. Ca. 755; 47 L. J. Q. B. 534; 49 *ib.* 123. See Meyer *v.* Ralli, 1 C. P. D. 358; 45 L. J. C. P. 741.

(*ee*) Gr. Ind. Penins. Ry. Co. *v.* Saunders, *cit.* Booth *v.* Gair, 15 C. B. N. S. 291; 33 L. J. C. P. 99.

(*ff*) Kidston *v.* Empire Mar. I. Co., *cit.* Meyer *v.* Ralli, *cit.*

(*gg*) See Roux *v.* Salvador, 1 Bing. N. S. 526; 1 Ill. 314. Burnett *v.* Kensington, 7 T. R. 210; 4 R. R. 424. Carruthers *v.* Sydebotham, 4 M. & S. 77; 16 R. R. 392. Hearne *v.* Edmunds, 1 Brod. & Bing. 338; 21 R. R. 660. Rayner *v.* Godmond, 5 B. & Ald. 225; 24 R. R. 335. Barrow *v.* Bell, 4 B. & Cr. 736. Wells *v.* Hopwood, 3 B. & Ad. 20. Kingsford *v.* Marshall, 8 Bing. 458; 34 R. R. 756. Craig *v.* Spence, 1794; M. 7109. Hoffman *v.* Marshall, 2 Bing. N. S. 383; 3 Ill. 142. Corcoran *v.* Gurney 1 E. & B. 456; 22 L. J. Q. B. 113. Magnus *v.* Buttemer, *supra* (*x*).

(*hh*) Burnett *v.* Kensington, *cit.*

(*ii*) Wells *v.* Hopwood, and Kingsford *v.* Marshall, *cit.* De Mattos *v.* Saunders, L. R. 7 C. P. 571. Letchford *v.* Oldham, 5 Q. B. D. 538; 49 L. J. Q. B. 458. Thomson *v.* Murison, 1844; 6 D. 1120.

(*kk*) So decided in Stewart *v.* Merchants Marine Ins. Co., 15 Q. B. D. 619. But in Blackett *v.* Royal Exch. Ass. Co., 2 C. & J. 244, the case of a voyage policy on a ship, it was held that different losses during the voyage must be added together to ascertain the percentage under the exempting clause.

(*ll*) See Benecke, 464; and Davy *v.* Milford, 15 East, 559; 1 Ill. 287; see 15 R. R. 279, n. Thompson *v.* R. E. Ass. Co., 16 East, 214; 14 R. R. 388. Allan *v.* Smith, 1823; 2 S. 271. Bondrett *v.* Hentigg, Holt, 149; 17 R. R. 725. See below, § 489.

(*mm*) Hills *v.* Lond. Ass. Co., 5 M. & W. 576. Ralli *v.* Janson, 6 E. & B. 422; 25 L. J. Q. B. 300. Entwisle *v.* Ellis, 2 H. & N. 549; 27 L. J. Ex. 105. Duff *v.* Mackenzie, 3 C. B. N. S. 16; 26 L. J. C. P. 313. Wilkinson *v.* Hyde, 3 C. B. N. S. 30; 27 L. J. C. P. 116.

473. Obligations of the Insured.—The insured proposes to the insurer a seaworthy ship, engaged in a lawful voyage, and safe previous to the time at which the insurance is to commence. The insurer, taking all this for granted, estimates the dangers of the sea and enemy, takes into view all circumstances affecting the risk,—all floating rumours and political speculations,—and fixes, as in a wager, the sum at which he will take the risk of indemnifying the insured for loss. The former of these being conditions precedent, are incumbent on the insured; and if not true, or not observed, the insurance is null. The latter are points of information for calculating the perils of the voyage, and, so far as the knowledge of them depends on the insured, affect the contract only if misstated or concealed, being material to the risk. Thus (besides an obligation to pay the premium, as already mentioned) the insured is under obligations in respect to representation, and to warranty (*a*).

(*a*) Behn *v.* Burness, 3 B. & S. 751; 32 L. J. Q. B. 204.

474. Representation (*a*).—Insurance is a contract of good faith, in which the insurer, in calculating the risks to be run, greatly relies on the statement of the insured. The statement is called a Representation, which, whether fraudulent or innocent (*b*), if material to the risk, must be 'substantially (*c*)' true, or complied with, otherwise there is 'in the option of the insurer' no insurance (*d*). 'The contract, however, continues valid till the party misled has elected to avoid it (*e*).' The information given must not be conjectural where the knowledge is certain; nor given as certain when it is conjectural (*f*). In respect to materiality (which is a question for the jury on the evidence of persons conversant with the subject), it is of chief importance to ascertain whether the statement was an inducement to undertake the risk (*g*). 'The rule is that all should be disclosed which would affect the judgment of a rational underwriter governing himself by the ordinary principles and calculations of his business (*h*); and although the concealment or misstatement be of a fact not directly material to the risk, but yet material to guide the underwriter's judgment (*e.g.* of misconduct or fraud of the insured in regard to former policies), it suffices to avoid the policy (*i*).' There must be no misrepresentation; no false insinuation; no concealment of circumstances material to the risk 'which the underwriter is not presumed to know, or of which he has not waived further information' (*k*); no false ground of speculation suggested by the representation of the insured, however innocently made (*l*). So an error or misleading of the underwriter as to the day of sailing will be fatal (*m*); or as to sailing with convoy, or making a running voyage (*n*); or as to the arrival of the ship (*o*). All intelligence, in the sense of mercantile men on such points, must, if material, be disclosed (*p*). The doctrine that a misrepresentation to the first underwriter in a material point is a misrepresentation to all, though held in one case in England, is to be received with much hesitation, and with strict regard to time and circumstances (*q*). 'An innocent insured is affected by the fraud or neglect of such agents as his shipmaster or ship agents, leading to his ignorance of a fact (*e.g.* the loss of the ship) of which he ought to be aware, and of which it is their function to inform him (*r*). The non-disclosure of material facts known to the agent or broker employed to effect the particular insurance, though not known to the principal, will also entitle the insurer to avoid the contract (*s*). What is expressed as a statement of opinion or expectation, not of actual facts, will not avoid the policy, unless it be fraudulent (*t*). The insured need not mention what the insurer knows—*scientia utrinque par pares contrahentes facit*—or ought to know; what he takes upon himself the knowledge of or what he waives being informed of (*u*). And here the insurer is affected by the knowledge of his agent effecting the insurance (*v*).'

There are some points, however, which it is not necessary to describe or mention—as the draught of water of the ship; or depth of a harbour; or common reports, and matter of general notoriety; or public and political speculations and events (*w*). Neither is the insured bound to state particulars relating to the ship,—her age, build, construction, repairs, etc. (*x*).

(*a*) See below, § 491; above, § 14. Duer, Marine Insurance, vol. ii. ch. xiv. Arnould, p. 507 sqq.

(*b*) Ionides *v.* Pender, 43 L. J. Q. B. 227; L. R. 9 Q. B. 531. Anderson *v.* Pacific M. I. Co., L. R. 7 C. P. 65. Arnould, 514. Dennistoun & Co. *v.* Lillie, below (*m*).

(*c*) See Arnould, 530. But if there be fraud, a trivial discrepancy will avoid the policy; and greater strictness is required in regard to some statements, *e.g.* as to time of sailing. See below, note (*m*), etc. Alexander *v.* Campbell, 41 L. J. Ch. 478.

(*d*) Marshall, 347. 2 Selw. 932. **Carter** *v.* **Boehm**, 3 Burr. 1905; 3 Ill. 139; 1 Smith's L. C. 474. 3 Boulay-Paty, 507. 3 Kent, Com. 282. Observe that any statement of a fact bearing upon the risk introduced into the written policy is in marine insurance to be construed as a warranty; and, *primâ facie* at least, compliance with that warranty is a condition precedent to the attaching of the risk. *Per* L. Blackburn in Standard Life Ass. Co. *v.* Weems, 1884; 11 R. H. L. 51; 9 App. Ca. 671, 684 (Thomson *v.* Weems). See below, § 475.

(*e*) Morrison *v.* Univ. M. I. Co., L. R. 8 Ex. 40, 197; 42 L. J. Ex. 17, 115. See above, § 13A.

(*f*) Stewart, *infra* (*m*). Kinloch, *infra* (*k*).

(*g*) Flinn *v.* Headlam, 9 B. & Cr. 693; 1 Ill. 293; 33 R. R. 291. Baker & Adams *v.* Scot. Sea. Ins. Co., 1856; 18 D. 691. Carr *v.* Montefiore, 5 B. & S. 408. The question of materiality may be differently answered in time policies and voyage policies. **Gibson** *v.* **Small**, 4 H. L. Ca. 353. **Dudgeon** *v.* **Pembroke**, L. R. 9 Q. B. 581; 1 Q. B. D. 96; 2 App. Ca. 284; 43 L. J. Q. B. 220; 46 *ib.* 409. Harvey & Co. *v.* Seligmann, 1883; 10 R. 680.

(*h*) Ionides *v.* Pender, 43 L. J. Q. B. 227; L. R. 9 Q. B. 531. Parsons on Insur. i. 495. Hutchison & Co. *v.* Aberdeen Ins. Co., 1876; 3 R. 682. Stribley *v.* Impl. M. I. Co., 1 Q. B. D. 507; 45 L. J. Q. B. 396. Tate *v.* Hyslop, 15 Q. B. D. 368.

(*i*) Hill *v.* Sibbald, *infra* (*m*). Ionides *v.* Pender, *cit.* Rivaz *v.* Gerussi, 6 Q. B. D. 222; 50 L. J. Q. B. 176. It is a question of fact whether the matter in question falls within the rule above stated, as to which it seems now to be held that the evidence of insurance brokers is admissible. See 1 Smith's L. C. 487 sqq. Arnould, 579. Baker & Adams, *cit.* (*g*). Stribley *v.* Impl. M. I. Co. *cit.* (*h*).

(*k*) Grieve *v.* Young, 1782; M. 7086; 1 Ill. 293. Bain *v.* Kippen, 1783; M. 7087. Keay *v.* Young, 1783; M. 7088. Scougall *v.* Young, 1798; M. 7091. Gillespie & Co. *v.* Douglas, 1803; M. 7095. Allan *v.* Young & Co., 1803; M. 7092. Adam & Mathie *v.* Murray, 1804; M. App. *Ins.* 6. Bogle *v.* Smith, 1804, *ib.* 7; rev. 1809, 5 Pat. 248. Correct Bell's Com. i. 620 accordingly. Bowker & Co. *v.*

Smith, Feb. 9, 1810; F. C. Morrison *v.* Gibbon, Jan. 18, 1811; F. C. Henderson *v.* Tenant, 1812; 1 Dow, 324; 5 Pat. 736. Lambe *v.* Smith, Feb. 15, 1815; F. C. Kinloch *v.* Campbell, June 14, 1815; F. C. Rickards *v.* Murdoch, 10 B. & Cr. 527; 34 R. R. 511. Elton *v.* Larkins, 8 Bing. 198; 34 R. R. 676. Campbell *v.* Russell & Co., 1792; 3 Pat. 340. Mackintosh *v.* Martin, 11 M. & W. 116. **Harrower** *v.* **Hutchinson**, L. R. 4 Q. B. 523; 5 Q. B. 584; 38 L. J. Q. B. 185; 39 L. J. Q. B. 229. Gandy *v.* Adelaide M. Ins. Co., 40 L. J. Q. B. 239; L. R. 6 Q. B. 746. It is not enough to excuse the insured that a material fact was once known to the underwriter, though forgotten, or that the means of knowing it were easily within his reach. Bates *v.* Hewitt, 36 L. J. Q. B. 282; L. R. 2 Q. B. 592; Morrison *v.* Univ. M. I. Co. (*e*).

(*l*) Marshall, 347. Park, 404. 1 Bell's Com. 619. Lindenau *v.* Desborough, 8 B. & Cr. 586, in Life Insurance; 1 Ill. 324. M'Dowall *v.* Frazer, 1 Doug. 259. Rickards, *supra* (*k*).

(*m*) Stirling & Robertson *v.* Goddard, 1822; 1 S. App. 238; 1 Ill. 296. Dennistoun & Co. *v.* Lillie, 1821; 1 S. App. 22; 3 Bligh, 202; 22 R. R. 13. Stewart *v.* Morrison, 1779; M. 7080; 5 B. Sup. 488; Hailes, 818; 1 Ill. 293. Kinloch *v.* Duguid, Jan. 22, 1813; F. C. Hill *v.* Sibbald, June 10, 1809; F. C.; rev. 2 Dow, 263. Smith *v.* Bisset, March 9, 1810; F. C. Colby *v.* Hunter, 1 Mood. & Mal. 81. Nelson *v.* Salvador, *ib.* 309; 31 R. R. 733. Mackintosh *v.* Marshall, 11 M. & W. 116.

(*n*) Reid & Co. *v.* M'Millan, June 25, 1813; F. C.; aff. 1816, 4 Dow, 97; 6 Pat. 197. Bain, Scougall, Kinloch, Morrison, etc., *supra* (*k*). Shoolbred *v.* Nutt, Park, 493; 1 Ill. 303. Haywood *v.* Rodgers, 4 East, 590; 7 R. R. 638.

(*o*) Kirby *v.* Smith, 1 B. & Ald. 672; 19 R. R. 412. Lynch *v.* Hamilton, 3 Taunt. 37; 12 R. R. 591. Smith *v.* Allan, 1808; 5 Pat. 229.

(*p*) Durrel *v.* Bederley, Holt, 283; 3 Ill. 139; 17 R. R. 639.

(*q*) Pawson *v.* Watson, Cowp. 785. Brine *v.* Featherstone, 4 Taunt. 869; 14 R. R. 689. Hill *v.* Sibbald (*m*). Arnould, 541.

(*r*) Proudfoot *v.* Montefiore, L. R. 2 Q. B. 511; 36 L. J. Q. B. 225. Anderson, *cit.* (*b*). Stone *v.* Aberdeen M. I. Co., 1849; 11 D. 1041. It has lately been laid down as a general proposition (though much doubted by the learned editor of Arnould, see pp. 525, 548, 5th ed., and by Lord Watson in **Blackburn** *v.* **Vigors**, *infra*), that concealment by an agent without moral fraud is not a ground for avoiding the policy, but only affects the recovery of a loss connected with the concealment. Stribley *v.* Impl. M. I. Co., *cit.* (*h*). Gladstone *v.* King, 1 M. & S. 35.

(*s*) **Blackburn, Low, & Co.** *v.* **Vigors**, 17 Q. B. D. 553; rev. 12 App. Ca. 531. Blackburn, Low, & Co. *v.* Haslam, 21 Q. B. D. 144.

(*t*) M'Dowall, *cit.* Barber *v.* Fletcher, 1 Doug. 306. Anderson, *supra* (*b*). Dennistoun & Co. *v.* Lillie, *cit.* (*m*). Harvey & Co. *v.* Seligmann, 1883; 10 R. 680.

(*u*) *Per* Lord Mansfield in **Carter** *v.* **Boehm**, *cit.* (*d*), and cases in (*k*).

(*v*) Story on Agency, § 140 sq. Cruikshank *v.* Northern Acct. Ins. Co., 1895; 23 R. 147.

(*w*) Paterson & Co. *v.* Duguid, June 15, 1792; Bell's Ca. 281. Thomson *v.* Buchanan, 1781; M. 7085; Hailes, 886; rev. 2 Pat. 592; 1 Ill. 298. **Carter** *v.* **Boehm** (*d*). Harrower *v.* Hutchinson, *supra* (*k*).

(*x*) Haywood, *supra* (*n*). Freeland *v.* Glover, 7 East, 464; 9 R. R. 803.

475. Warranty.—This is an absolute condition, express or implied, relative to the state or circumstance of the subject insured; which, if not 'strictly and literally' true, or not 'strictly' complied with, defeats the insurance, whether material to the risk or not (*a*). The insured is not bound to disclose what is the subject of 'and covered by' a warranty (*b*).

A warranty may be affirmative, as that a ship was safe on a particular day; or promissory, that the ship shall proceed with the convoy, or sail on a day certain, etc.; and whether of the one nature or of the other, they are either express or implied.

(*a*) M'Dowall *v.* Frazer, 1 Doug. 259. M'Morran & Co. *v.* Newcastle F. I. Co., 1815; 3 Dow, 255; 1 Ill. 298. See above, § 111 (*b*); and below, § 514. Driscoll *v.* Passmore, 1 B. & P. 200, 311; 1 Ill. 302; 4 R. R. 782.

(*b*) Shoolbred *v.* Nutt, Park, 493. Haywood *v.* Rodgers, *cit.* Smith *v.* Bisset, March 9, 1810; F. C.

476. Express Warranties.—These are in the body, or on the face, or margin, or bottom of the policy, or in some print or writing incorporated with it (*a*). Warranty being an absolute condition, it follows that express warranties must be literally fulfilled; and it is not a good answer to say that the state of things was represented truly, according to the belief of the insured: for no ignorance or *bona fides* is an answer to the fact that the condition has not been observed on which alone the insurance was made (*b*). So a warranty to *sail* on a day certain imports that the ship shall be ready to sail, unmoored, and on her actual voyage (*c*); and it must be literally complied with (*d*). A warranty to *depart* on a certain day, means that she shall be out of port on that day (*e*). A warranty that the ship is safe on the day of signing the policy, warrants her safe, not at the moment of signing, but some time during that day (*f*). A policy on a ship "at and from" is a warranty that the ship is at the place mentioned, or will be there shortly, 'or at least within such a time that the risk shall not be materially varied (*g*)'; and a delay of arrival, 'or her arrival in so disabled a state as to be a wreck (*h*),' will be fatal (*i*). To sail with convoy, imports that she shall sail from the rendezvous with a convoy for the voyage of the regular naval force appointed by Government for that purpose (*k*), and that she will keep with the convoy during the voyage (*l*). 'The breach of warranty and the loss do not need to be connected: so, the loss being by shipwreck, breach of warranty to sail with convoy is a good defence (*m*).'

(*a*) Bean *v.* Stupart, 1 Doug. 11. Worsley *v.* Wood, 6 T. R. 710. Routledge *v.* Burrel, 1 H. Bl. 254; 3 R. R. 323. As to construction and evidence of usage, see Prov. Ins. Co. of Canada *v.* Leduc, L. R. 6 P. C. 224; 43 L. J.

P. C. 49 (St. Lawrence). Dryer *v.* Birrell, 1883; 10 R. 585; rev. 1884, 11 R. H. L. 41; 9 App. Ca. 345 (no St. Lawrence). Colledge *v.* Harty, 6 Ex. 205; 20 L. J. Ex. 146.

(*b*) De Hahn *v.* Hartley, 1 T. R. 343; 1 R. R. 221. M'Morran *v.* Newcastle F. I. Co., § 475 (*a*).

(*c*) Nelson *v.* Salvador, *cit.* § 474 (*n*). Wright *v.* Shiffner, 11 East, 515; 3 Ill. 140; 11 R. R. 263. Lang *v.* Anderdon, 3 B. & Cr. 495; 27 R. R. 412. Pettigrew *v.* Pringle, 3 B. & Ad. 514. Graham *v.* Barras, 5 B. & Ad. 1011.

(*d*) Dennistoun & Co. *v.* Lillie, 1 S. App. 22; 3 Bligh, 202; 1 Ill. 297; 22 R. R. 13. Dunmore & Co. *v.* Allan, 1786; M. 7101; Hailes, 996. Monteith *v.* Crosse, 1788; M. 7105. Stirling & Robertson *v.* Goddard, 1822; 1 S. App. 238. Pettigrew, and cases there cited, *supra* (*c*). See Bouillon *v.* Lupton, 15 C. B. N. S. 113; 33 L. J. C. P. 37. Colledge (*a*). Baines *v.* Holland, 10 Ex. 802; 24 L. J. Ex. 204.

(*e*) Moir *v.* R. E. Ass. Co., 3 M. & S. 461; 3 Ill. 140; 16 R. R. 330.

(*f*) Blackhurst *v.* Cockell, 3 T. R. 360; 1 R. R. 717.

(*g*) Mount *v.* Larkins, 1 L. J. C. P. 20; 8 Bing. 108. De Wolff *v.* Archangel Ins. Co., 43 L. J. Q. B. 147; L. R. 9 Q. B. 451.

(*h*) Parmeter *v.* Cousins, 2 Camp. 235; 11 R. R. 702. See Barker *v.* Janson, L. R. 3 C. P. 303; 37 L. J. C. P. 105.

(*i*) Hull *v.* Cooper, 14 East, 479; 13 R. R. 287. See Freeman *v.* Taylor, 8 Bing. 124; 3 Ill. 126; 34 R. R. 647. See above, § 471.

(*k*) Hibbert *v.* Pigou, Park, 694. Audley *v.* Duff, 2 B. & P. 111; 5 R. R. 549. Lilly *v.* Ewer, 1 Doug. 72. D'Eguino *v.* Bewicke, 2 H. Blackst. 551; 3 R. R. 503. Anderson *v.* Pitcher, 2 B. & P. 169; 5 R. R. 565.

(*l*) Jeffrey *v.* Legendre, 4 Mod. 58. See as to Express Warranties by the American law (agreeing in most points with the above), Phillips's Ins. § 754 et seq.

(*m*) Hibbert *v.* Pigou, 1 Marsh. Ins. 375. De Hahn (*b*). *Infra*, § 477 (*b*).

477. Implied Warranties.—The chief implied warranty, and the most important, is—

(1.) *Seaworthiness.*—This 'warranty—which is a condition of the contract, and the breach of which affords a good defence to the insurer, whether of ship, freight, or cargo (*a*), whether the loss can be traced to the breach or not (*b*), and irrespective of the shipowner's honesty or negligence in the transaction (*c*)—' implies that the ship, 'not lighters for landing the cargo (*d*),' shall be stout, staunch, and strong for the voyage 'at the commencement of the risk' (*e*); well and sufficiently rigged 'and equipped,' and with a proper master and crew (*f*). Seaworthiness is presumed, so as to lay the *onus probandi* on the underwriters (*g*); 'and it may be admitted by them, so as to exclude them from disputing it in an action on the policy (*h*).' In order to make out this defence, it will not refute the presumption should the underwriter prove that the ship became unseaworthy after the risk began (*i*). But if the ship spring a leak, or go down without adequate cause, it will, 'in the absence of other evidence, and especially if it occur soon after sailing,' overcome the presumption, and infer 'as a matter of fact' want of seaworthiness (*k*). It is not enough under the warranty of seaworthiness that the insured has had the ship carefully inspected, or fully and expensively repaired. If the ship in point of fact be not seaworthy, no previous care or *bona fides* is an answer to the failure of the condition. 'Seaworthiness is a relative term, depending for its meaning and effect on the nature of the ship and cargo, as well as of the voyage, insured; and it may even be of different degrees in regard to different parts of the same voyage (*l*). It is settled that there is no implied warranty of seaworthiness in a time policy (*m*); but underwriters may have a remedy in respect of unseaworthiness under such a policy, on the ground of wilful concealment or the like (*n*).'

(*a*) Arnould, 638.

(*b*) Forshaw *v.* Chabert, 3 B. & B. 158; 23 R. R. 596; 1 Ill. 290. Quebec M. I. Co. *v.* Comml. Bk. of Canada, L. R. 3 P. C. 234; 39 L. J. P. C. 53 (defect remedied before loss). Daniels *v.* Harris, L. R. 10 C. P. 1; 44 L. J. C. P. 1 (overloading remedied by jettison). Lothian *v.* Henderson, 3 B. & P. 515; 7 R. R. 829. *Supra*, § 476 *fin.*

(*c*) Scougal & Co., and cases in note (*e*).

(*d*) Lane *v.* Nixon, L. R. 1 C. P. 412; 35 L. J. C. P. 243.

(*e*) M'Kellar *v.* Henderson, Nov. 15, 1810; F. C.; 1 Ill. 300. Watt *v.* Morris, 1813; 1 Dow, 32; 5 Pat. 697. Scougal & Co. *v.* Douglas, 4 Dow, 269; 6 Pat. 179. Harvey *v.* Smith, 1818, 1 Mur. 302, 313. **Dixon** *v.* **Sadler,** 5 M. & W. 405; 8 M. & W. 895; Tudor's L. C. 105. **Gibson** *v.* **Small,** 16 Q. B. 152; 4 H. L. Ca. 353. Biccard *v.* Shepherd, 14 Moo. P. C. 471. Hollingsworth *v.* Brodrick, 7 Ad. & E. 40. Busk *v.* R. E. Ass. Co., 2 B. & Ald. 73; 20 R. R. 350. Knill *v.* Hooper, 2 H. & N. 277; 26 L. J. Ex. 377. See above, § 408. The shipowner does not warrant that the vessel shall continue seaworthy during the voyage, or that the master and crew shall continue to do their duty. Dixon *v.* Sadler, Busk, and cases cited. Arnould, 640, 663. Overloading is unseaworthiness. Daniels *v.* Harris (*b*).

(*f*) Wilkie *v.* Geddes, 1815; 3 Dow, 57; 15 R. R. 17. Thomson *v.* Bisset, 1826; 4 S. 670 (pilot). Clifford *v.* Hunter, 1 Mood. & Mal. 103. Wedderburn *v.* Bell, 1 Camp. 1; 10 R. R. 615. Law *v.* Hollingsworth, 7 T. R. 160. This case was supposed to establish the rule that a pilot was required under this warranty, wherever such aid could be got, and was required by the nature of the navigation; but as it is now conclusively settled that the warranty is only that the ship, etc., shall be originally sufficient, the rule must be limited apparently to the case where the ship sails from a port where there is an establishment of pilots, and the navigation requires one. Smith's Merc. Law, 456. Dixon *v.* Sadler, *supra* (*e*). Tudor's L. C. 129. Hollingsworth *v.* Brodrick, *supra* (*e*). Shore *v.* Bentall, 7 B. & Cr. 798; 31 R. R. 302. Forshaw *v.* Chabert, *cit.* Harvey *v.* Smith, 1818; 1 Mur. 302, 313. See Cook *v.* Greenock M. I. Co., 1843; 5 D. 1379 (effect of usage). Stone *v.* Aberdeen M. I. Co., 1849; 11 D. 1041 (towing ropes). Baker & Adams *v.* Scot. Sea Ins. Co., 1855; 17 D. 417; 1856, 18 D. 691.

(*g*) Smith *v.* Bisset, March 9, 1810; F. C. Cairns *v.* Kippen, 1820; 2 Mur. 256. Hutchinson & Co. *v.* Aberdeen Ins. Co., 1876; 3 R. 682. Cases in note (*k*), *infra*.

(*h*) Parfitt *v.* Thomson, 13 M. & W. 392; 14 L. J. Ex. 73. Phillips *v.* Nairne, 4 C. B. 343.

(*i*) Potts *v.* Allan, June 5, 1810; F. C.; rev. 1815, 3 Dow, 23; 1 Ill. 302.

(*k*) Potts *v.* Allan, *cit.* Scougal & Co. *v.* Douglas, *cit.* (*e*). See Watson *v.* Clark, 1813; 1 Dow, 336; 5 Pat. 698; 14 R. R. 73. Anderson *v.* Morice, 44 L. J. C. P. 10, 341; L. R. 10 C. P. 58, 609. Davidson *v.* Burnand, 38 L. J. C. P. 73; L. R. 4 C. P. 117. Pickup *v.* Thames and Mersey I. Co., 3 Q. B. D. 594; 47 L. J. Q. B. 749.

(*l*) Biccard *v.* Shepherd, *supra* (*e*). Forbes *v.* Wilson, 1 Camp. 538. Annen *v.* Woodman, 3 Taunt. 299; 12 R. R. 663. Burgess *v.* Wickham, 3 B. & S. 669; 33 L. J. Q. B. 17. Clapham *v.* Langton, 5 B. &. S. 729; 34 L. J. Q. B. 46. Bouillon *v.* Lupton, 15 C. B. N. S. 113; 33 L. J. C. P. 37. Daniels *v.* Harris, *cit.* (*b*). Quebec M. I. Co. *v.* Com. Bk. of Canada (*b*). So, when a river steamer is sent to her destination oversea, the owner does enough if he disclose to the underwriter the nature of the adventure, and do what can be done to make such a vessel fit for a sea voyage. Burgess *v.* Wickham, 3 B. & S. 669; 33 L. J. Q. B. 17. Clapham *v.* Langton, 34 L. J. Q. B. 46. Turnbull *v.* Janson, 36 L. T. Rep. 635.

(*m*) Gibson *v.* Small, *supra* (*e*). Michael *v.* Tredwin, 17 C. B. 551; 25 L. J. C. P. 83. Jenkins *v.* Haycock, 8 Moo. P. C. 351. Thompson *v.* Hopper, E. B. & E. 1049; 27 L. J. Q. B. 441. Dudgeon *v.* Pembroke, L. R. 9 Q. B. 581; 1 Q. B. D. 96; 2 App. Ca. 284; 43 L. J. Q. B. 220; 46 *ib.* 409. West Ind. Telegr. Co. *v.* Home and Col. M. I. Co., 9 Q. B. D. 51; 50 L. J. Q. B. 41. Kenneth & Co. *v.* Moore, 1883; 10 R. 547. *Supra*, § 474 (*g*).

(*n*) Gibson *v.* Small, *cit.* (*per* Parke, B.). Dudgeon *v.* Pembroke, *cit.*

478. (2.) *Non-deviation* (*a*).—A warranty against deviation is not, like seaworthiness, a condition precedent, but a promissory warranty; and it resolves into a defence grounded on a departure from the engagement not to deviate.

It is no defence against breach of warranty against deviation, that the insurer (*b*) guarded with his utmost vigilance against it.

(*a*) See this more fully stated below, § 492.

(*b*) It is printed thus, not "insured," in all the editions; but the sentence appears to be inconsistent with § 494, etc. It is probably a hasty jotting, and it is not easy to say what is meant.

479. Barratry.—Although it appears inconsistent that underwriters on a ship should be liable for the wrongs done to the owner by a master and crew selected by himself, the importance of full indemnity has led to an express stipulation in all policies, that the underwriters "are contented to bear" losses from "barratry of the master and mariners," *i.e.* those which proceed from any fraudful and illegal act by which the interest of the owners shall suffer (*a*). To constitute barratry, the act must be fraudulent. Thus, when the master runs off with the ship, or enters into any smuggling concern, or evades duties to the loss of the ship, or sinks or deserts the ship, or criminally delays or defeats the voyage; all such acts done with a criminal intention are barratry (*b*). 'But an act is not barratrous if done merely negligently, though it may be in contravention of statutory rules for navigation; nor unless it is done without the owner's consent; but an act done for his benefit without his consent may be; for a master has no right to commit an illegal act even for his owner's advantage, and he must be presumed to have forbidden it (*c*).' The master or crew alone can commit barratry (*d*), and against none but the owners or general freighters (*e*). If the master be owner, he cannot commit barratry against himself; neither can it be the ground of claim against the underwriters, if consented to by the owner (*f*). Barratry may be committed by the owners or master against the general freighter; or with consent of the freighters against the owner, if unknown to the party injured (*g*). A difficulty has been raised as to barratry by a master, himself a *part*-owner only. But it would seem that no exception could be taken against the claim of the other part-owners, not participant in or consenting to the act, more than to the claim of a freighter on the barratry of the owner, or of the owner on barratry with consent of the freighter (*h*).

The loss must take place on barratry during the voyage or time limited by the policy, though not necessarily in the very act of barratry (*i*). In a policy on goods, it is a total loss from the moment that the goods are taken out of the possession of the assured. It is not necessarily so as to the ship (*k*).

(*a*) Emerigon, 336. 2 Valin, 80. Pothier, Assur. No. 64. Abbott, 137; Story's ed. 138. Marshall, 409. Park, 188. 2 Selw. N. P. 901. Phillips, Ins. § 1062. 3 Kent, Com. 305. Vallejo *v.* Wheeler, Cowp. 143; 1 Ill. 304. Lockyer *v.* Offley, 1 T. R. 252; 1 R. R. 194. Earle *v.* Rowcroft, 8 East, 125; 1 Ill. 141; 9 R. R. 385. Hucks *v.* Thornton, Holt, 30; 17 R. R. 594. In insurance against barratry, it has been said that, contrary to the ordinary rule in insurance contracts, it is enough if it be the effective though not the proximate cause of the loss, as when it causes the seizure of the ship or cargo. Vallejo, *cit.*, and cases in Arnould, 773–74. See Cory *v.* Burr, 8 Q. B. D. 313; 9 *ib.* 463; 51 L. J. Q. B. 95, 468; in which Lord Blackburn holds that there is no such exception, 8 App. Ca. 393, 397–98.

(*b*) See cases (*a*). Knight *v.* Cambridge, 8 East, 135; 9 R. R. 392. Ross *v.* Hunter, 4 T. R. 38; 2 R. R. 319. Phyn *v.* R. Ex. Assur. Co., 7 T. R. 505; 4 R. R. 508. Cairns *v.* Kippen, 1820; 2 Mur. 258.

(*c*) Earle *v.* Rowcroft, *supra* (*a*). Phyn *v.* R. Ex. Assur. Co., *cit.* Wilson *v.* Rankin, 6 B. & S. 208; 34 L. J. Q. B. 63; 35 L. J. Q. B. 87; Moss *v.* Byron, 6 T. R. 379. Grill *v.* Gen. Iron Screw Collier Co., L. R. 1 C. P. 600 ; 35 L. J. C. P. 321 (*per* Willes, J.).

(*d*) Nutt *v.* Bourdieu, 1 T. R. 330 ; 1 R. R. 211. Everth *v.* Hannan, 6 Taunt. 375.

(*e*) Vallejo, *supra* (*a*). Soares *v.* Thornton, 6 Taunt. 640 ; 18 R. R. 615.

(*f*) Ross, *supra* (*b*). Stamma *v.* Brown, 2 Strange, 1173. Nutt, *supra* (*d*).

(*g*) Vallejo, *supra* (*a*). Boutflower *v.* Wilmer (Lee, Ch. Jus.), 2 Selw. N. P. 969.

(*h*) See cases in preceding note. So decided, Jones *v.* Nicholson, 10 Ex. 28. Strong *v.* Martin, 1839 ; 1 D. 1245. See Small *v.* U. K. Mut. Mar. Ins. Co., 1897 ; 2 Q. B. 311 (mortgagee).

(*i*) Lockyer, *supra* (*a*). See above, note (*a*). Brown *v.* Smith, 1813 ; 1 Dow, 349 ; 5 Pat. 718 ; 14 R. R. 78.

(*k*) Dixon *v.* Reid, 5 B. & Ald. 597 ; 24 R. R. 481. Falkner *v.* Ritchie, 2 M. & S. 293 ; 15 R. R. 253.

480. **Total Loss** is an expression not to be taken strictly ; as if it were requisite to a claim of indemnity under the contract, that the ship should go to the bottom, or the goods be entirely lost. Insurance is a contract for commercial indemnity ; and a ship is constructively held to be totally lost where it cannot be repaired, so as to proceed on her voyage, at a reasonable expense (*a*) ; or goods totally lost where the object of the voyage is defeated.

This effect of the contract necessarily implies (in cases where the loss is total only constructively) that the wreck of the ship or the vestiges of the goods shall be given up or abandoned to the underwriter (*b*). But where the loss is manifestly and absolutely total (as where a ship is sunk, and never heard of again), there is no other question than whether it be a loss within the policy ; there is no room or necessity for abandonment (*c*). '"Though it has been said that a loss by perils of the sea cannot be total if the thing exists *in specie*, yet that must be taken only to mean if it exist for any useful purpose ; for if a ship be so battered as to be rather a congeries of planks than a ship, or if the cargo be so damaged as to exist only in the shape of a nuisance, in such cases the loss is total without abandonment" (*d*).' Where the insurance is on freight, 'and the voyage is lost by a peril insured against, so that the insured cannot earn the freight, the loss is total, and' no abandonment is necessary, 'for there is nothing to abandon (*e*).' Where the loss is only constructively total (as where portions of the wreck are left, but useless to the insured), the claim for indemnification must be accompanied by abandonment (*f*).

(*a*) Allen *v.* Sugrue, 8 B. & Cr. 561 ; 1 Ill. 305 ; 32 R. R. 483. Thomson *v.* Bisset, 1823 ; 3 Mur. 294. See Dixon and Falkner, *supra*, § 479 (*k*). M'Iver *v.* Henderson, 4 M. & S. 576 ; 3 Ill. 142 ; 16 R. R. 550. **Cologan** *v.* **London Assur. Co.,** 5 M. & S. 447 ; 17 R. R. v, 390. Ionides *v.* Univ. M. I. Co., 14 C. B. N. S. 292 ; 32 L. J. C. P. 176.

(*b*) See below, § 484. **Fleming** *v.* **Smith,** 1846 ; 8 D. 627 ; aff. 1 H. L. Ca. 573 ; 6 Bell's App. 278. Lozano *v.* Janson, 2 E. & E. 160 ; 28 L. J. Q. B. 337. Knight *v.* Faith, 15 Q. B. 649 ; 19 L. J. Q. B. 509. N. of Engl. Iron S. S. Ins. Ass. *v.* Armstrong, L. R. 5 Q. B. 244 ; 39 L. J. Q. B. 81.

(*c*) Mullett *v.* Shedden, 13 East, 304 ; 12 R. R. 347. Mellish *v.* Andrews, 15 East, 13 ; 13 R. R. 352. Bondrett *v.* Hentigg, Holt, 149 ; 1 Ill. 288 ; 17 R. R. 625. Cambridge *v.* Anderton, 2 B. & Cr. 691 ; 1 Ill. 305 ; 26 R. R. 517. Stringer *v.* E. & S. M. I. Co., L. R. 4 Q. B. 676 ; 5 Q. B. 599 ; 38 L. J. Q. B. 321 ; 39 L. J. Q. B. 214. Cossman *v.* West, 13 App. Ca. 160.

(*d*) Smith's Merc. Law, 376, quoting Cambridge, *supra* (*c*). Dyson *v.* Rowcroft, 3 B. & P. 75. Cologan, *supra* (*a*). The leading case on this subject is **Roux** *v.* **Salvador,** the final decision in which by Lord Abinger appears not to have been known to the author when he last revised this work. 3 Bing. N. C. 266 ; Tudor's L. C. 139. Potter *v.* Rankin, *infra*, § 486 (*a*).

(*e*) Idle *v.* R. E. Assur. Co., 8 Taunt. 755 ; 21 R. R. 358. Green *v.* R. E. Assur. Co., 6 Taunt. 68 ; 16 R. R. 571. Mount *v.* Harrison, 4 Bing. 388 ; 29 R. R. 580. Benson *v.* Chapman, 6 M. & G. 792 ; 8 C. B. 950 ; 2 H. L. Ca. 696. Philpott *v.* Swann, 11 C. B. 250. Moss *v.* Smith, 9 C. B. 94. Turner *v.* Scot. M. I. Co., 1851 ; 13 D. 652, 989 ; 1 Macq. 334. **Potter** *v.* **Rankin,** *infra*, § 486 (*a*). Jackson *v.* Union M. I. Co., 44 L. J. C. P. 27 ; L. R. 10 C. P. 125 (what is total loss of freight). Allison *v.* Bristol M. I. Co., 1 App. Ca. 209.

(*f*) See below, § 485.

481. Total loss may be Valued or Not Valued. In the one case the policy is called a valued policy ; in the other, an open policy. In the one, the amount is fixed which the parties agree to be the value on a loss ; in the other, proof must be given of the amount. But there is no difference between them as to the question whether the loss be total or partial (*a*).

(*a*) Lewis *v.* Rucker, 2 Burr. 1170 ; Tudor's L. C. 225. Thellusson *v.* Fletcher, Doug. 315. Allen, § 480 (*a*).

482. (1.) In a *Valued* policy, the sum specified, 'or the proportion of it corresponding to the whole intended cargo, if only a part of the cargo is on board at the time of the loss (*a*),' is demandable on a total loss occurring, 'however the value of the ship may have been diminished before the loss (*b*), provided that' there is no fraud, and where the policy does not exclude proof of interest ; investigation being open to the insurer, to ascertain whether there be fraud (*c*). 'For all the purposes of the contract the valuation in a policy is conclusive between the parties ; and it results from this, and from the principle that marine insurance is a contract of indemnity, that the insured can recover in an action on a valued policy only the balance of the sum in the policy, after deducting what he may have received under other policies (*d*).' At first, it was conceived that the provisions of the statute of 19 Geo. II. c. 37 comprehended all valued policies; but it was afterwards settled that it includes only those in which all proof of interest was dispensed with (*e*).

(*a*) Tobin *v.* Harford, 13 C. B. N. S. 791; 17 *ib.* 528; 34 L. J. C. P. 37. Denoon *v.* Home & Col. M. I. Co., L. R. 7 C. P. 341; 41 L. J. C. P. 161.
(*b*) Lidgett *v.* Secretan, L. R. 6 C. P. 616; 40 L. J. C. P. 257. Barker *v.* Janson, and cases below (*c*).
(*c*) See below, § 498-9. Smith *v.* Fleming, 1849; 12 D. 138. Irving *v.* Manning, 1 H. L. Ca. 287. Barker *v.* Janson, 37 L. J. C. P. 105; L. R. 3 C. P. 303. Tobin *v.* Harford, *cit.* Lidgett *v.* Secretan, *cit.* Williams *v.* North China M. I. Co., 1 C. P. D. 757. Burnand *v.* Rodocanachi, 7 App. Ca. 333; 51 L. J. C. P. 548. As to a partial loss occurring under a valued policy, see Tudor's L. C. 212. Tobin *v.* Harford, *cit.*
(*d*) Irving *v.* Richardson, 1 M. & R. 153. Morgan *v.* Price, 4 Ex. 615. Bruce *v.* Jones, 1 H. & C. 769; 32 L. J. Ex. 132. See below, § 506. North of Eng. Iron S. S. Ins. Co. *v.* Armstrong, 39 L. J. Q. B. 81; L. R. 5 Q. B. 244 (as to which *v. per* Lord Blackburn in Burnand, *cit.*). 2 Smith's L. C. 285. *Supra*, § 463A.
(*e*) Lewis, *supra*, § 481 (*a*). Da Costa *v.* Firth, 4 Burr. 1966. Murphy *v.* Bell, 4 Bing. 567; 1 Ill. 287; 29 R. R. 630. Barker, *supra* (*c*).

483. (2.) In an *Open* policy, proof must be given by the assured of the extent of the loss; the rules as to the adjustment of which will be found below (*a*).

(*a*) See § 500-7. Tobin *v.* Harford, *cit.* § 482 (*a*).

484. Abandonment is a relinquishment to the underwriter, in a case of loss constructively total, of all right, title, and claim to what may be saved; leaving it to him to make the most of it for his own benefit (*a*). 'It operates as an assignation (*b*).'

(*a*) In some countries the right to abandon is limited to certain definite cases. In Hamburgh, only when the ship is missing; in France, on capture, total shipwreck, or stranding and wreck, or arrest of princes. In Great Britain and America, it is admitted in all cases where perils within the policy occasion loss of the ship; or of the voyage, in an insurance of goods.
(*b*) See below, § 487.

485. (1.) *Cases for abandonment*, generally stated, are: where the voyage is lost, or not worth pursuing; where the thing is so damaged, that it is of little or no value to the owner; where the salvage to be paid is very high; where the articles saved are not worth the freight; where, 'even although the ship may have reached her destination and earned her freight (*a*),' further expense is necessary, to a greater amount than the insured will defray, or the insurer undertake, 'or, rather, than an owner of prudence and discretion, if on the spot and uninsured, would incur' (*b*). But more particularly—

Capture is *primâ fronte* a total loss, for abandonment; provided the cause of capture or detention be a risk within the policy (*c*).

Where the loss is by sea risk, the insured is entitled to abandon for total loss, not only where there is certainty, but where there is great probability, of total loss. But a distinction is to be observed between ship and cargo. Insurance of the ship is for indemnity by loss of the ship *on* the voyage (*d*): Insurance of the cargo is for indemnity of loss of the goods or of the intended market; it is insurance of the cargo *and* of the voyage. Defeat of the voyage is total loss to the merchant; but it is not a total loss to the owner of the ship (*e*). But as to goods, it cannot be said in absolute terms, where there is an exception freeing the underwriters from particular average, that loss or retardation of the voyage is a total loss for abandonment; unless some such great injury or damage be sustained by the subject of insurance as to render it of no value, or such as to entitle the insured to abandon (*f*).

(*a*) **Stewart** *v.* **Greenock M. I. Co.,** 1846; 8 D. 323; aff. 1848, 2 H. L. Ca. 159; 1 Macq. 328; 3 Ross' L. C. 344. Cases in next note.
(*b*) Marshall, 443. Park, 332. Brown *v.* Smith, 1813; 1 Dow, 349; 5 Pat. 718; 14 R. R. 78. Lord Mansfield in Goss *v.* Withers, 2 Burr. 683, 697; 1 Ill. 306. Milles *v.* Fletcher, 1 Doug. 231. Hamilton *v.* Mendez, 2 Burr. 1198. See **Roux** *v.* **Salvador,** 3 Bing. N. C. 266; Tudor's L. C. 139. Knight *v.* Faith, 15 Q. B. 649; 19 L. J. Q. B. 509. **Moss** *v.* **Smith,** 9 C. B. 94; 19 L. J. C. P. 225. Phillips *v.* Nairne, 4 C. B. 343. Irving *v.* Manning, 2 C. B. 784; 1 H. L. Ca. 287. Young *v.* Turing, 2 M. & Gr. 593. Grainger *v.* Martin, 2 B. & S. 456; 4 B. & S. 9; 31 L. J. Q. B. 186. Kemp *v.* Halliday, 6 B. & S. 723; L. R. 1 Q. B. 520; 35 L. J. Q. B. 156. M'Corkle *v.* Murison, 1847; 9 D. 1491. Fleming *v.* Smith, 1846; 8 D. 627; aff. 6 Bell's Ap. 278; 1 H. L. Ca. 513. **Shepherd** *v.* **Henderson,** 1881; 8 R. 518; aff. 9 R. H. L. 1.
(*c*) See below, § 487.
(*d*) M'Corkle, *cit.*
(*e*) Fitzgerald *v.* Pole, 5 Bro. P. C. 131; Willes, 641; 15 R. R. 256. Falkner *v.* Ritchie, 2 M. & S. 290; 15 R. R. 253. Gernon *v.* R. E. Assur. Co., Holt, 49; 1 Ill. 309; 16 R. R. 630. Doyle *v.* Dallas, 2 M. & Mal. 48; 1 Ill. 310. See Stewart *v.* Greenock M. I. Co., *cit.* (*a*). Turner *v.* Scot. M. I. Co., *infra* § 487 (*d*).
(*f*) Anderson *v.* Wallis, 2 M. & S. 240; 1 Ill. 308; 14 R. R. 642. Thompson *v.* R. E. Assur. Co., 16 East, 214; 1 Ill. 288. Wilson *v.* R. E. Assur. Co., 2 Camp. 623; 1 Ill. 308. Naylor *v.* Taylor, 9 B. & Cr. 718; 33 R. R. 305. Hudson *v.* Harrison, 3 B. & B. 97; 23 R. R. 575. Reimer *v.* Ringrose, 6 Ex. 263; 20 L. J. Ex. 175. Rosetto *v.* Gurney, 11 C. B. 176; 20 L. J. C. P. 257.

486. (2.) *Abandonment not Compulsory.*—The insured cannot be compelled to abandon. But when entitled to do so, he must, 'unless perhaps where there is nothing to abandon, and the notice can be of no use to the underwriter,' give notice within a reasonable time; that is, the earliest opportunity. 'He may not lie by, waiting to see the state of the markets, or the chances of recovery; and if he unduly delay to abandon, although he may have communicated with the underwriters, he may be held to have elected to treat the loss as partial' (*a*). Although not compelled to abandon, however, he cannot claim for a constructively total loss without abandoning (*b*). He is not bound to do so till he has an opportunity of having correct information (*c*); but the underwriters are entitled in the meanwhile to take precautions against further damage. 'Notice of abandonment is not necessary, when by capture or seizure abroad the subject of insurance is entirely taken out of the power and possession of the insured (*d*).'

(*a*) Mitchell *v.* Edie, 1 T. R. 608; 1 R. R. 318. Hunt *v.* R. E. Ass. Co., 5 M. & S. 47; 1 Ill. 310; 17 R. R. 264. Mellish *v.* Andrews, 15 East, 13; 13 R. R. 351. Barker *v.* Blakes, 9 East, 283; 9 R. R. 558. Davy *v.* Milford, *cit.* § 472 (*ll*). Fleming *v.* Smith, § 485 (*b*). Farnworth *v.* Hyde, 18 C. B. N. S. 835; 34 L. J. C. P. 207; 36 L. J. C. P. 33; L. R. 2 C. P. 204. **Potter** *v.* **Rankin,** 37 L. J. C. P. 257; 39 L. J. C. P. 147; L. R. 5 C. P. 341; L. R. 6 H. L. 83; 42 L. J. C. P. 169. Currie *v.* Bombay Native Ins. Co., L. R. 3 P. C. 72. Kaltenbach *v.* Mackenzie, 3 C. P. D. 467; 48 L. J. C. P. 9. It is not necessary to notify to underwriters on a policy of reinsurance, Uzielli *v.* Boston M. I. Co., 15 Q. B. D. 11.

(*b*) **Roux** *v.* **Salvador,** 1 Bing. N. S. 526; 3 Bing. N. C. 266; Tudor's L. C. 139. See above, § 480.

(*c*) Read *v.* Bonham, 3 B. & B. 147; 23 R. R. 587. Gernon, § 485 (*e*). King *v.* Walker, 3 H. & C. 209; 33 L. J. Ex. 167. 325. Browning *v.* Prov. Ins. Co. of Canada, L. R. 5 P. C. 263.

(*d*) Farnworth, *cit.* Stringer *v.* Engl. and S. M. I. Co., and Cossman *v.* West, § 480 (*c*). See cases in § 480 (*e*).

487. (3.) *Notice.*—It is sometimes a question whether the abandonment is conclusive;—as where a ship has been captured, but is restored; or has been reported as lost. There are two points of importance: 1. Notice of abandonment; 2. Acceptance.

Notice of abandonment is a mere offer, which becomes a contract, transferring the property and settling the interest of the parties, when it is accepted; 'and no particular form is required (*a*).' But before acceptance, if what appeared a total loss becomes not so, as by recapture, recovery, or partial preservation, the policy then is for indemnity only of a partial loss (*b*). 'The question whether there has been a total or a partial loss is determined by the condition of the ship when action is raised (*c*).' When the notice is accepted, the contract is irrevocable, the property, 'with all its incidents, including in the case of a ship the right to freight due or to be earned for carrying the goods of others, although insured with other insurers and to the exclusion of their claim (*d*), but not prepaid freight (*e*),' is transferred, and the underwriters must stand by the abandonment (*f*). 'If after abandonment the insured recovers any part of the insured property, *e.g.* earns freight after recapture, he is accountable to the underwriters for it or its value (*g*).'

(*a*) Currie and Potter, *supra*, § 486 (*a*). As to evidence of acceptance, and acts of the underwriters in salving, etc., which do or do not infer acceptance or personal exception, see Prov. Ins. Co. of Canada *v.* Leduc, L. R. 6 P. C. 224; 43 L. J. P. C. 49. **Shepherd** *v.* **Henderson**, 1881; 8 R. 518; aff. 9 R. H. L. 1.

(*b*) See cases, 1 Ill. 312, 313. Randal *v.* Cochran, 1 Ves. sen. 98. **Case** *v.* **Davidson**, 5 M. & S. 79; 17 R. R. 280. Kerswill *v.* Bishop, 2 Tyr. 602. Sharp *v.* Gladstone, 7 East, 30; 8 R. R. 583. See below, § 489. Benson *v.* Chapman, 5 C. B. 330; 2 H. L. Ca. 720. Rosetto *v.* Gurney, 11 C. B. 176; 20 L. J. C. P. 257.

(*c*) Cases in notes (*b*), (*f*). Blairmore Co. *v.* Macredie, 1897; 25 R. 893.

(*d*) **Stewart** *v.* **Greenock M. I. Co.**, *cit.* § 485 (*a*). Turner *v.* Scot. M. I. Co., 1851; 13 D. 652, 989; 1 Macq. 334. Simpson *v.* Thomson, 1876; 4 R. 177; rev. 1877, 5 R. H. L. 40; 3 App. Ca. 279. Yates *v.* Whyte, 4 Bing. N. C. 272. Miller *v.* Woodfall, 8 E. & B. 493; 27 L. J. Q. B. 120 (A. gives no right to freight when shipowner is carrying his own goods). N. of Eng. Iron S. S. Ins. Co. *v.* Armstrong, 39 L. J. Q. B. 81; L. R. 5 Q. B. 244 (see above, § 463A, 482). Potter *v.* Rankin, § 486 (*a*). Dickinson *v.* Jardine, 37 L. J. C. P. 321; L. R. 3 C. P. 639. But freight earned by transhipping the goods and forwarding them by another ship does not so pass to the underwriters on the ship. Hickie *v.* Rodocanachi, 4 H. & N. 455; 28 L. J. Ex. 273.

(*e*) See The Red Sea, 1895; Pr. D. 20.

(*f*) Bainbridge *v.* Neilson, 1 Camp. 237; 10 East, 329; 1 Ill. 312; 10 R. R. 316. Robertson & Co. *v.* Smith, Stewart, etc., Feb. 10, 1809; F. C.; Buch. Rep. 73; 2 Dow, 474. Patterson *v.* Ritchie, 4 M. & S. 593; 16 R. R. 498. Brotherston *v.* Barber, 5 M. & S. 418; 17 R. R. 378. Parry *v.* Aberdeen, 9 B. & Cr. 411; 1 Ill. 309; 32 R. R. 221. King *v.* Walker, 3 H. & C. 209; 33 L. J. Ex. 325. Cammell *v.* Sewell, 3 H. & N. 617. Prov. Ins. Co. of Canada *v.* Leduc, *cit.* (*a*).

(*g*) Leatham *v.* Terry, 2 B. & P. 479. Whitworth *v.* Shepherd, 1884; 12 R. 204. **Case** *v.* **Davidson**, *cit.* (*b*).

488. (4.) *Duties of Masters.*—The state of things on occasion of a loss constructively total, accompanied by abandonment, exposes the underwriters to abuses. The ship or goods injured, but still worth something, are in the power of a master and crew selected by the insured, while the underwriters are at a distance. But the master, though he continues accountable to the owners, is liable to the underwriters as their agent in case of abandonment (*a*): And the rule of his conduct is, that he can sell ship or cargo only in a case of absolute necessity, and in the exercise of a prudent discretion, as if there were no insurance; or when the ship cannot be repaired at the place where she lies, or the necessary supply of money obtained; or where goods cannot find freight to their market, or are so damaged that they cannot be sent on, or from their nature and condition cannot be kept for an opportunity (*b*).

(*a*) Idle *v.* R. E. Ass. Co., 8 Taunt. 755; 1 Ill. 305; 21 R. R. 538. Somes *v.* Sugrue, 4 C. & P. 276; 1 Ill. 314. See Read *v.* Bonham, *cit.* § 486. Currie, *supra*, § 486 (*a*).

(*b*) See cases, § 487 (*f*). Roux *v.* Salvador, *cit.* § 480 (*d*). Cambridge *v.* Anderton, § 480 (*c*). Robertson *v.* Clarke, 1 Bing. 445; 25 R. R. 676. Doyle *v.* Dallas, 2 Mo. & Mal. 48. Gardner *v.* Salvador, *ib.* 116. Freeman *v.* E. India Co., 5 B. & Ald. 617; 24 R. R. 497. Morris *v.* Robinson, 3 B. & Cr. 196; 27 R. R. 322. Cobequid M. I. Co. *v.* Bartoaux, L. R. 6 P. C. 319. Hall *v.* Jupe, 49 L. J. Q. B. 721.

489. Partial Loss (also called Average Loss) includes damage by stranding; striking on a rock; collision by inevitable accident; loss of boats, masts, yards, etc., by force of the wind and waves; loss while the vessel is before the wind, or lying to the sea; capture, though recaptured; loss and defence, etc., against enemy. Among these, stranding has given occasion to frequent questions, from the mention of it in the memorandum clause, where certain perishable articles are excepted from the insurance, unless on general average, or the "stranding of the ship" (*a*). 'If, after a partial loss has been incurred, the vessel is totally lost during the period of the risk, for which the insurer pays, he cannot be called on also to pay for the partial loss, for he has fulfilled his obligation by paying for the total loss. So, if after a partial loss the vessel is totally lost by a peril not within the policy, the insurer pays for the partial loss only so much as the insured has actually lost, as by expenditure in repairing the damage (*b*). But in the event of a total loss after the period covered by the policy, the underwriters must pay for a previous partial loss, because their liability is fixed as at the expiration of the risk insured (*c*).'

(*a*) Park, 218. See above, § 462, 472 (8), and below as to the rules of Adjustment, § 498.

(*b*) Livie *v.* Janson, 12 East, 648; 11 R. R. 513. Le Cheminant *v.* Pearson, 4 Taunt. 367; 13 R. R. 636. Stewart *v.* Steele, 5 Scott, N. R. 927.

(*c*) Lidgett *v.* Secretan, L. R. 6 C. P. 616; 40 L. J. C. P. 257.

490. Return of Premium (*a*).—Where no risk is run, the premium must be returned: But where the risk is once begun, it is not returnable; and where the assured have been guilty of fraud, they are barred *personali exceptione* from asking back the premium; while fraud by the underwriter will entitle the insured to restitution of the premium. So, where any warranty relative to the state or condition of the ships has not been observed, and there is no fraud, the premium is returnable (*b*): Or where the voyage has never been begun (*c*), there is a return of premium.

For short interest there is a return of premium; as for goods stated in the policy, not sent; or short profits: but there can be no return 'under a valued policy' for the goods being of less value (*d*).

When the policy is void without fault, as by war, before signing, but unknown at the time, 'return is due (*e*). But a policy on an illegal voyage is invalid, and there can be no return of premium after the risk has commenced (*f*).'

When the policy is on an entire voyage, and it has begun, there can be no return of any part of the premium (*g*). But if two or more distinct voyages are included, and any of them not begun, there will be a partial return (*h*). Fraud on either part will affect the right to premium; so fraudulent misrepresentation by the insured will bar the claim for a return after the commencement of the voyage, on account of the absence of risk; and so also fraud of the underwriter will ground an action for recovery of what has been paid (*i*). Sometimes the parties stipulate in the policy for a return of the premium, or part of it, in certain cases. This, of course, forms the rule between them (*k*).

(*a*) See above, § 463; and below, § 491.

(*b*) Feise *v.* Parkinson, 4 Taunt. 640; 13 R. R. 710. Colby *v.* Hunter, 1 Mood. & Mal. 81; 1 Ill. 297. Penson *v.* Lee, 2 B. & P. 330; 5 R. R. 614.

(*c*) See below, § 495.

(*d*) Park, 766. Eyre *v.* Glover, *cit.* § 470 (*g*). Horneyer *v.* Lushington, 15 East, 46; 13 R. R. 759. M'Nair *v.* Coulter, 4 Bro. P. C. 450. See Fisk *v.* Masterman, 8 M. & W. 165.

(*e*) Oom *v.* Bruce, 12 East, 225 ; 3 Ill. 143 ; 11 R. R. 367. Hentig *v.* Staniforth, 5 M. & S. 122 ; 17 R. R. 293.
(*f*) Arnould, Pt. II. ch. v., Pt. III. ch. ix. pp. 676, 1061. 1 Smith's L. C. 384, 2 *ib.* 278. *Supra*, § 35, 460. Wilson *v.* Rankin, L. R. 1 Q. B. 163 ; 35 L. J. Q. B. 87. Dudgeon *v.* Pembroke, *supra*, § 477 (*m*).
(*g*) Tyrie *v.* Fletcher, Cowp. 666 ; Tudor's L. C. 220. Bermon *v.* Woodbridge, 2 Doug. 781. Langhorn *v.* Cologan, 4 Taunt. 330 ; 13 R. R. 613. Tait *v.* Levi, 14 East, 481 ; 13 R. R. 289. Moses *v.* Pratt, 4 Camp. 297 ; 16 R. R. 794.
(*h*) Stevenson *v.* Snow, 3 Burr. 1237. See Long *v.* Allen, Marsh. 370 ; 20 R. R. 89, n.
(*i*) Wilson *v.* Dunkel, 3 Burr. 1361. Tyler *v.* Horne, Park, 455. **Carter** *v.* **Boehm**, 3 Burr. 1905 ; 3 Ill. 139 ; 1 Smith's L. C. 474.
(*k*) Aguilar *v.* Rodgers, 7 T. R. 421 ; 4 R. R. 478. Audley *v.* Duff, 2 B. & P. 111 ; 5 R. R. 549. Kellner *v.* Le Mesurier, 4 East, 396 ; 7 R. R. 581. Dalgleish *v.* Brook, 15 East, 295 ; 13 R. R. 476.

491. Defences of the Underwriter.—The underwriters are discharged of the contract—1. By misrepresentation or concealment on the part of the insured; 2. By breach of warranty; or 3. By deviation.

(1. and 2.) *Misrepresentation* (*a*) of material facts, and *Breach of all such warranties* as are conditions precedent (*b*), annul the contract *ab initio*. Breach of promissory warranties and deviation do not thus annul the contract, but discharge all further operation of the policy. In the former cases the risk never has begun, and there is a right to demand return of the premium, unless the insured has been guilty of gross fraud; in the latter, the risk having been once begun, there is no return of premium (*c*).

(*a*) See above, § 474. (*b*) See above, § 475.
(*c*) See above, § 490.

492. (3.) *Deviation.*—The risk is calculated on the regular course of the voyage; and it is an implied warranty that this course shall be observed. From the moment of deviation, the rest of the risk under the policy is discharged, while the underwriter is liable for loss previously incurred (*a*).

As a breach of warranty, deviation must *actually* have taken place, in order to ground the defence of the underwriter. Instruction or intention to deviate is therefore not enough, if the vessel has not reached the diverging point. If a voyage to a given place be insured, and when the ship sails it is not intended actually to go to that place, she is held not to have sailed on the voyage insured, though lost in the fair way of that voyage (*b*). But when the ultimate *termini* of the voyage on which the ship sails are the same as those described in the policy, it is held that the voyage is the same up to the point of divergence; and that if the voyage terminate before reaching that point, there has been only an *intention* to deviate. Total loss, therefore, before the dividing point is covered; while in case of partial loss, evidence must be shown of the proportion of damage occurring before that point (*c*).

If a deviation have once been made, for however short a time or space, the return of the ship in safety to her course will not revive the policy, so as to subject the underwriter for subsequent loss (*d*).

(*a*) Green *v.* Young, 2 L. Raym. 840.
(*b*) See below, § 495.
(*c*) Kewley *v.* Ryan, *cit.* § 469. Foster *v.* Wilmer, 2 Str. 1249. Marsden *v.* Reid, 3 East, 572 ; 7 R. R. 516. Hare *v.* Travis, 7 B. & Cr. 14 ; 31 R. R. 139. Young *v.* Allan, 1805 ; M. Apx. *Ins.* 9. Simon Israel & Co. *v.* Sedgwick, 1893 ; 1 Q. B. 303.
(*d*) Wilson & Co. *v.* Elliot, 7 Brown's Parl. Ca. 459 ; 4 *ib.* 470 (Tomlin's ed.) ; 2 Pat. App. 481 ; rev. M. Apx. *Ins.* 1 and 7096 ; 5 B. Sup. 485 ; 1 Ill. 317. Hammond *v.* Reid, 4 B. & Ald. 72 ; 22 R. R. 629. Solly *v.* Whitmore, 5 B. & Ald. 45 ; 24 R. R. 274. Middlewood *v.* Blakes, 7 T. R. 162 ; 3 Ill. 140 ; 4 R. R. 405. See Wooldridge v. Boydell, 1 Doug. 16. Tudor's L. C. 169.

493. According to the fair construction of the policy, it is a deviation to depart from the shortest and safest course of the voyage, or (where it is a known and ordinary voyage) from the usual course (*a*). 'The insurers are discharged if the risk be varied, although it may not be increased (*b*): nor is it material that the subsequent loss should be connected with the deviation (*c*).' Inverting the order in which the policy allows the ship to call, or touch, or enter port (*d*), is deviation, unless altered according to any known, regular, and settled course (*e*). Where there is no order of successive ports fixed by the policy, to invert the geographical order, unless sanctioned by usage, is deviation (*f*). So it is also to go to a port mentioned in the policy, but out of the order of the voyage, or for a purpose different from that specified, and not subordinate to the voyage described (*g*). To stay at any port an unusual time is a deviation; but leave to touch at a port is leave also to trade there, if there be no delay thereby occasioned (*h*). To linger unreasonably, and for purposes not in the policy, is a deviation (*i*). These questions of delay are for the jury (*k*).

(a) Pelly v. R. E. Ass. Co., 1 Burr. 348. Bond v. Nutt, Cowp. 601; 3 Ill. 135. Hibbert v. Phyn, 4 Camp. 150. Davies v. Garret, 6 Bing. 716; 3 Ill. 127; 31 R. R. 524. R. E. Shipping Co. v. Dixon, 12 App. Ca. 11.

(b) Company of African Merchants v. Brit. and For. Ins. Co., L. R. 8 Ex. 154; 42 L. J. Ex. 60. Phillips on Ins. 983. Arnould, 474 sq.

(c) Cases above, § 492 (d). Thomson v. Hopper, 26 L. J. Q. B. 18.

(d) Clason v. Simmons, 6 T. R. 533, note; 3 R. R. 260. Ashley v. Pratt, 16 M. & W. 471. Pratt v. Ashley, 1 Ex. 257; 17 L. J. Ex. 135.

(e) Beatson v. Haworth, 6 T. R. 530; 3 R. R. 258.

(f) Gairdner v. Senhouse, 3 Taunt. 16; 12 R. R. 573. See Smith's Merc. Law, 419, 452. Leathly v. Hunter, 7 Bing. 517; 33 R. R. 556.

(g) Solly v. Whitmore, *cit.* § 492. Bottomly v. Bovill, 5 B. & Cr. 210; 29 R. R. 221. Hammond v. Reid, 4 B. & Ald. 72; 22 R. R. 629. Hamilton v. Sheddon, 3 M. & W. 49. African Merchts. v. Brit. and For. M. I. Co., *cit.* Robertson & Co. v. Laird, 1791–96; 3 Pat. 232, 443.

(h) Williams v. Shee, 3 Camp. 469; 14 R. R. 811. Rainer v. Bell, 9 East, 195; 9 R. R. 533. Laroche v. Oswin, 12 East, 131; 11 R. R. 337. Langhorn v. Allnutt, 4 Taunt. 511; 13 R. R. 708. See Smith's Merc. Law, 452. Phillips v. Irving, 7 M. & G. 325. Campbell v. Russell & Co., 1792; 3 Pat. 340.

(i) Inglis v. Vaux, 3 Camp. 447; 14 R. R. 778. See Solly v. Whitmore, *supra* (g). Mount v. Larkins, 8 Bing. 122; 34 R. R. 631.

(k) Langhorn, *supra* (h).

494. Departure from the course may be justified by necessity, provided the new direction into which the ship is forced is pursued in the direct course (a). Such necessity is pleadable from stress of weather, or approach of an enemy, or inevitable accident, or compulsion by a King's ship (b). To go into port for a supply of water or necessary provisions is not a deviation; even though goods should be taken in, provided this does not, directly or indirectly, increase the risk (c). To join convoy is a necessity justifying deviation from the usual course (d). To avoid a port which has become hostile, or has been laid under embargo, will justify a deviation, provided the voyage is not relinquished, and another destination taken; but if the voyage be relinquished, the underwriters are freed (e). In such a case it may seem most prudent to go into the next port, and there do the best possible for all concerned; but this, if not provided for (which it generally is), will not be a voyage under the policy (f). Whether the interruption be a risk within the policy, entitling the insured to abandon, is a different question (g). Letters of marque will entitle a merchant ship to chase an enemy, but not to cruise (h); nor to lie to for bringing the prize into harbour; all deviations of this kind requiring special licence (i). A delay of the voyage, or deviation from the course, to save or aid a ship in distress, or to save life, 'seemed to Professor Bell' to be justifiable (k), but not for the purpose of saving goods wrecked; 'and there was till recently no clear decision on the subject in any British Court. It has recently, however, been held that a deviation to save property merely is not justifiable as between ship and charterer (or insurer); and it seems, though not so decided, that a deviation to save life is justifiable (l).'

(a) Lavabre v. Wilson, 1 Doug. 284.

(b) Smith v. M'Neil, 2 Dow, 538; 3 Ill. 141. Delany v. Stoddart, 1 T. R. 22; 1 R. R. 139. O'Reilly v. Gonne, 4 Camp. 249; 16 R. R. 788. Scott v. Thompson, 1 B. & P. N. R. 181; 8 R. R. 780. Driscol, *cit.* § 475. Forster v. Christie, 11 East, 205; 10 R. R. 470. See Phelps v. Auldjo, 2 Camp. 350; 11 R. R. 725. The Teutonia (Duncan v. Köster), L. R. 4 P. C. 171; 41 L. J. Adm. 4, 57.

(c) Raine v. Bell, 9 East, 195; 9 R. R. 533.

(d) D'Aguilar v. Tobin, Holt, 185; 11 East, 22.

(e) Parkin v. Tunno, 2 Camp. 59; 11 East, 22; 10 R. R. 422. See Oliverson v. Brightman, 8 Q. B. 781; 15 L. J. Q. B. 274. The Teutonia, *supra* (b).

(f) Blackenhagen v. London Ass. Co., 1 Camp. 454, and note; 10 R. R. 729.

(g) See the cases on this subject, collected and commented on in Phillips, § 1023 sqq.

(h) Jolly v. Walker, Park, 636; 8 R. R. 464.

(i) Parr v. Anderson, 6 East, 202; 8 R. R. 461. Lawrence v. Sydebotham, 6 East, 45; 8 R. R. 385.

(k) See Lawrence, *supra* (i). Mason v. Ship Blaireau, 2 Cran. 268; Phillips, § 1023. See Smith's Merc. Law, 454; Tudor's L. C. 126; 25 and 26 Vict. c. 63, § 33 (as to collisions). Gourock Rope Wk. Co. v. Fleming, 1867; 5 Macph. 501. Kirby v. Owners of Scindia, L. R. 1 P. C. 241.

(l) Scaramanga v. Stamp, L. R. 5 C. P. D. 295; 48 L. J. C. P. 478; 49 *ib.* 674. Comp. Crocker v. Jackson, Sprague's Rep. 141. 2 Parson's Mar. Ins. 135.

495. If the voyage insured have never been entered upon, but the vessel have sailed on a different voyage entirely, the risk is not run, the policy is annulled, and the premium must be returned (a). And although, where a vessel is insured *at* a port, and preparations have been begun for the voyage insured, the risk is begun, and a subsequent deviation will discharge the policy without giving a right to a return of premium; yet if preparations for a *different* voyage have been begun, and the ship is afterwards lost at the port before sailing, the policy will be discharged without any return of premium (b).

(a) See above, § 490 and § 492. See Wilson & Co. v. Elliot, *supra*, § 492 (d).

(b) Cunningham v. Tasker, 1819; 1 Bligh, 87; 1 Ill. 317; 1 Bell's Com. 623.

496. Loss.—The claim of the insured involves two points: 1. That the loss has happened within the policy; and 2. That it is either total loss; or, if the policy is not valued, a partial loss to the amount claimed. The burden of proving these points lies on the insured.

(1.) *Proof.*—The great rule is, that the best proof is to be given which can in the circumstances be had (*a*).

The log-book and protests must be shown to the underwriters; but they, if extant, are not properly evidence, unless by the loss of better evidence they become necessary. They may be used to contradict the master or mate; and the log-book, on the whole, is a check rather than proof (*b*). The same holds as to protests: they are not proofs, but may be used as checks to contradict other proofs, and may occasionally supply the loss of the log-book, if they bear that book to have been shown to the magistrate (*c*). Surveys may be made evidence by being sworn to. And parole evidence is competent; as of the master, etc. (*d*).

(*a*) Ferrier *v.* Sandeman, June 29, 1809; F. C.; 1 Ill. 318. Taylor on Ev. § 204, 271.

(*b*) Carleton *v.* Strong, 1 Mur. 25, 32. Cairns *v.* Kippen, 2 Mur. 248. See below, § 2214.

(*c*) Senat *v.* Porter, 7 T. R. 158; 4 R. R. 403.

(*d*) Thomson *v.* Bisset, 3 Mur. 297.

497. Proof afforded in these modes,—that the ship sailed with the cargo insured; that she never arrived at her port; and that she was reported to be lost and the crew saved,—is held sufficient proof of loss, without the necessity of calling, or proving the absence of the crew (*a*).

(*a*) Koster *v.* Reed, 6 B. & Cr. 19; 1 Ill. 318; 30 R. R. 239. See also Ferrier, § 496 (*a*).

498. (2.) *Adjustment of Loss* (*a*).—In adjusting losses, it is necessary to distinguish between valued and open policies.

(*a*) See Losh, Wilson, & Bell *v.* Martin, 1856; 19 D. 101. As to a foreign adjustment, see Power *v.* Whitmore, 4 M. & S. 141. Harris *v.* Scaramanga, 41 L. J. C. P. 170; L. R. 7 C. P. 481. Hendricks *v.* Austral. Ins. Co., L. R. 9 C. P. 460; 43 L. J. C. P. 198. Mavro *v.* Ocean M. I. Co., L. R. 9 C. P. 595; 10 C. P. 414; 43 L. J. C. P. 339; 44 *ib.* 229. Hill *v.* Wilson, 4 C. P. D. 329; 48 L. J. C. P. 764. Robinows & Marjoribanks *v.* Ewing's Trs., 1876; 3 R. 1134. Arnould on Ins. 946. Phillips on Ins. § 1414.

499. The adjustment on a valued policy is at the sum expressed, if there be proof of interest, or such proof at least not excluded, and no fraud (*a*).

(*a*) M'Nair *v.* Graham, etc., 1772; M. 7106; 5 B. Sup. 486; Hailes, 465; rev. 1 Ill. 318; 2 Pat. 224, 297. Wilson *v.* Wordie, 1783; M. 7107. Young *v.* Deas, 1798; M. 7115. Rhand *v.* Robb, 1804; M. Apx. *Insur.* 27. Smith *v.* Fleming, 1849; 12 D. 138. See above, § 482.

500. In adjusting losses on an open policy, the general rules are:—

501. That in a total loss the ship is taken as at the commencing port; stores, wages advanced, and premium of insurance, included. The loss on freight is the amount of the manifest, or freight list, covered with the premiums, etc.

502. The loss on the cargo is estimated by the invoice price, with charges, premium, broker's commission, and charges of moving (*a*).

(*a*) Stevens on Average. Benecke on Indemnity. **Lewis** *v.* **Rucker**, 2 Burr. 1167; Tudor's L. C. 225.

503. In a partial loss, 'the depreciation in' the value of the ship is to be taken, deducting one-third from new materials and labour (*a*). 'That is to say, the insured has made good to him the depreciation in the value of his vessel at the end of the risk, so far as that is caused by the perils insured against. In general the sum properly expended in repairs, or the estimated amount of expenditure, is the measure of this depreciation, under deduction (by settled custom of trade), in the case of wooden ships, of one-third of such cost of repairs in respect of the benefit received by the shipowner in getting new materials instead of old (*b*). But if the insured sells his ship unrepaired, he cannot recover under his contract of indemnity a larger sum than the depreciation in value as ascertained by the sale (*c*).'

(*a*) Stevens on Average, 158. Benecke, 48, 449. Palmer *v.* Blackburn, 1 Bing. 61; 1 Ill. 319; 25 R. R. 599. Poingdestre *v.* R. Ex. Ass. Co., 1 Ry. & Moo. 378. Bousfield *v.* Barnes, 4 Camp. 228; 16 R. R. 780, and pref. vii, viii.

(*b*) Cases in Arnould, 902 sq. Lohre *v.* Aitchison, 2 Q. B. D. 501; 3 *ib.* 558; 4 App. Ca. 755; 46 L. J. Q. B. 715; 47 *ib.* 534; 49 *ib.* 123. The deduction is not made if the ship is on her first voyage. Pirie *v.* Steele, 2 M. & R. 49.

(*c*) Pitman *v.* Univ. Ins. Co., 9 Q. B. D. 192; 51 L. J. Q. B. 561.

504. In valuing the cargo, two methods are followed: Either the invoice is taken, with premium, etc., and the nett proceeds of the sale of the damaged goods are deducted; or the amount of the sales is compared with a *pro forma* account of the same goods taken as if sound. The former is called a salvage loss, on the analogy of salvage; what is paid being as a redemption from total loss. The latter method avoids involving the underwriter in a falling or rising market; the market price of the sound and of the damaged commodity being said to be the scales in which to weigh the depreciation (*a*). 'The rule is thus stated by Lord Mansfield: that, the insurer being bound "to indemnify the merchant to the amount of the prime cost or value in the policy, if the goods arrive, but lessened in value through damages received at sea," he puts "the merchant in the same condition which he would have been in if the goods had arrived free from damage, that is, by paying such proportion or aliquot part of the prime cost or value in the policy, as corresponds with the proportion or aliquot part of the diminution in value occasioned by the damage" (*b*). Thus, if the value in the policy was £100, and the goods at the end of the voyage would have realised £200, but sold as damaged for £150, then the diminution in value (£50) is one-fourth, and the loss to be made good is one-fourth of the value in the policy, or £25.'

(*a*) Stevens on Average. Benecke, 424 et seq.
(*b*) Lewis *v.* Rucker, *cit.* § 502 (*a*). Smith's Merc. Law, 474.

505. Reinsurance.—Although there can be no insurance without an interest, it is not necessary that the insured shall be owner of the thing insured. An underwriter who has insured a ship or goods has an unquestionable interest in the voyage, which, on the common principles of indemnity, he is entitled to protect by insurance. Accordingly, in most of the countries of Europe, and in America, underwriters are allowed to secure themselves against the loss which they may dread under a policy which they have entered into, by opening a policy with other insurers to reassure them against loss (*a*). But the dread of the insane speculations of the time of George II. led to a statute by which this remedy was forbid, except on occasions of the insolvency or bankruptcy of the insurer, or in case of his death; confining it, in short, as a remedy only to creditors or executors (*b*). 'That statute, however, has been repealed, and there is now no statutory prohibition of reinsurance (*c*). It is not a concealment voiding the policy to omit to state that it is a reinsurance (*d*).'

There are two sorts of reinsurance,—that sort which was contemplated in the above-mentioned statute; and as a reinsurance to the *underwriter*, or a policy against any loss that may arise under a subsisting policy. Such a policy, unless in the excepted cases, 'was' unlawful, not only when effected by a native, but when entered into with a foreigner (*e*).

Another form of reinsurance is by the insured against the possible insolvency of the underwriters on his policy. This, although not falling under the prohibition of the statute, seems never to have come into practice in this country (*f*), and indeed is better effected by double insurance.

(*a*) 1 Emerigon, No. 8. 1 Valin, 65. Pothier, Assur. No. 96. Phillips, § 374. Marshall, 101. *Supra*, § 461.
(*b*) 18 Geo. II. c. 37, § 4.
(*c*) 27 and 28 Vict. c. 56, § 1; 30 and 31 Vict. c. 23, § 3.
(*d*) Mackenzie *v.* Whitworth, 44 L. J. Ch. 81; 45 *ib.* 233; L. R. 10 Ex. 142; 1 Ex. D. 36.
(*e*) Andrée *v.* Fletcher, 2 T. R. 161; 1 R. R. 701.
(*f*) Marshall, 102.

506. Double Insurance.—This is a remedy to the insured, who effects insurance of the same risk with more than one set of underwriters. He may sue on both policies to the effect of complete indemnity (*a*). But he cannot draw full indemnity under both policies; for that would amount to a wager policy in the one or the other.

(*a*) Davis *v.* Gildart, Marsh. 104.

507. The policies are all considered as making only one policy, and there is contribution and relief among the several underwriters; the underwriters who pay being entitled to come into the place of the insured to receive rateable contribution from the others (*a*).

(*a*) Davis, § 506 (*a*). Godin *v.* London Assur. Co., 2 Burr. 489; 1 Ill. 319. Irving *v.* Richardson, 2 Mood. & Rob. 153; 2 B. & Ad. 193; 1 Ill. 320. See § 463A, 482. Arnould, 328 sq.

III. INSURANCE AGAINST FIRE.

508. Policy and Premium.—A policy of insurance against fire is a contract for indemnity against losses by fire, occurring within the time limited in the policy, in consideration of a sum paid, or of an annual payment. The contract must be by policy on stamped paper (*a*). But the agreement may be so conclusively fixed before delivery of the policy, as to ground an action for implementing it by the furnishing of a regular policy (*b*); 'for there is not, as in the case of sea insurances, a statute requiring the contract to be embodied in a policy, though those engaging in such a contract without executing a policy are subject to a penalty (*c*).'

(*a*) 37 Geo. III. c. 90. 55 Geo. III. c. 184. 3 and 4 Will. IV. c. 23. The stamp duty is 1d. 54 and 55 Vict. c. 39, Sched., and § 99, 100 ; see *ib.* § 91.

(*b*) Christie *v.* N. B. Ins. Co., 1825 ; 3 S. 519 ; 1 Ill. 320. Mills *v.* Albion F. & L. Ins. Co., 1828 ; 3 W. & S. 218. See below, § 513. See M'Elroy *v.* Lond. Ass. Corp., 1896 ; 24 R. 287.

(*c*) See above, § 465. 54 and 55 Vict. c. 39, § 100. See Rossiter *v.* Trafalgar Ins. Co., 27 Beav. 377.

509. Interest.—There can be no lawful policy of insurance against fire without an interest: it would be a wager policy of the most dangerous description. The interest may be as proprietor (*a*) ; as creditor (*b*) ; as pledgee of goods ; as holder of a lien ; as factor with a balance due ; as a consignee having made advances (*c*): 'and even a custodier, *e.g.* a wharfinger, not responsible to the owner of goods for accidental fire, may, in the absence of an express limitation in the policy to goods for which he is responsible, insure and recover the full value, being trustee for the owner so far as the sum insured exceeds his interest in respect of his own charges (*d*).'

(*a*) As to the effect of change of property, see Forbes and Poole, *infra*, § 513 (*d*). Collingridge *v.* Royal Ex. Assur. Co., 3 Q. B. D. 173 ; 47 L. J. Q. B. 32. Rayner *v.* Preston, 50 L. J. Ch. 472 ; 18 Ch. D. 1. Castellain *v.* Preston, 11 Q. B. D. 380.

(*b*) 31 and 32 Vict. c. 101, § 119, 122 (heritable creditor —altering Pollock *v.* Marnoch, 1859 ; 21 D. 1210). See Glasgow Prov. Invt. Soc. *v.* Westmr. Fire Office, 1887 ; 14 R. 947 ; aff. 1888, 13 App. Ca. 699 ; 15 R. H. L. 89.

(*c*) 14 Geo. III. c. 48. Marshall, 790. Park, 953. 1 Bell's Com. 625. Marks *v.* Hamilton, 7 Ex. 323 ; 21 L. J. Ex. 109 (bankrupt).

(*d*) Waters *v.* Monarch F. & L. A. Co., 5 E. & B. 870 ; 25 L. J. Q. B. 102. L. & N.-W. Ry. Co. *v.* Glyn, 1 E. & E. 652 ; 28 L. J. Q. B. 188. Donaldson *v.* Manchester Ins. Co., 1836 ; 14 S. 601. Dalgleish *v.* Buchanan, 1854 ; 16 D. 332. N. B. Ins. Co. *v.* Moffatt, 41 L. J. C. P. 1 ; L. R. 7 C. P. 25. Martineau *v.* Kitching, 41 L. J. Q. B. 227 ; L. R. 7 Q. B. 436, 457. Gillespie *v.* Miller, Son, & Co., 1874 ; 1 R. 423. A mere agent without possession or a lien has no insurable interest, and an insurance effected by him is void. Bunyon on Fire Ins. 15.

510. Risk.—The risk is, of fire, or of loss by means of fire, within the stipulated period, and not excepted in the policy (*a*). So all damage produced by fire consuming or damaging the property is to be indemnified under the policy. But it is not held a loss by fire if there be no ignition, as in heat by effervescence, or injury by the overheating of a flue (*b*); 'or injury from concussion caused by the explosion of a neighbouring gunpowder magazine (*c*).'

There is in the policy an exception of fire occasioned by the invasion of a foreign army, or by usurped power, or civil commotion (*d*).

(*a*) As to the construction of policies in regard to place, see Pearson *v.* Com. Union Ins. Co., 1 App. Ca. 498 ; 45 L. J. C. P. 761. Wingate *v.* Foster, 3 Q. B. D. 382 ; 47 L. J. Q. B. 525. Gorman *v.* Hand in Hand Ins. Co., 11 Ir. C. L. R. 224.

(*b*) Austin *v.* Drewe, 4 Camp. 360 ; 2 Marsh. 130 ; 1 Ill. 321 ; 16 R. R. 647. Tarleton *v.* Staniforth, 5 T. R. 695 ; 1 B. & P. 470 ; 4 R. R. v. 845. See below, § 513.

(*c*) Everett *v.* Lond. Assur. Co., 19 C. B. N. S. 126 ; 34 L. J. C. P. 299. As to insurance covering "explosion by gas," see Stanley *v.* Western Ins. Co., L. R. 3 Ex. 71 ; 37 L. J. Ex. 73.

(*d*) Drinkwater *v.* Lond. Assur. Co., 2 Wilson, 363. Langdale *v.* Mason, Park, 965.

511. Incidental loss or damage is within the policy; as damage in the removal of furniture, or by the falling of a wall injured by the fire, or by water used to extinguish a fire (*a*). 'Professor Bell held it' doubtful whether one insuring his house possessed by a tenant can claim for rent as part of his loss (*b*); 'but it is now settled that, unless they are expressly insured, a fire policy does not cover remote losses, such as those arising from want of occupancy, loss of profits, or payment of wages to servants thrown out of work by the destruction of the property (*c*).'

(*a*) Johnston *v.* West. of Scot. Ins. Co., 1828 ; 7 S. 53 ; 4 Mur. 189 ; 1 Ill. 322.

(*b*) 3 Kent, Com. 372.

(*c*) Menzies *v.* North Brit. Ins. Co., 1847 ; 9 D. 694. Buchanan *v.* Liverp. and Lond. and Globe Ins. Co., 1884 ; 11 R. 1032. Wright *v.* Pole, 1 A. & E. 621.

512. Duration of the Policy.—The efficacy of the policy is limited to a certain day. 'A policy from a certain day to another day specified covers the whole of the latter day (*a*), and none of the former day (*b*).' Sometimes by the policy fifteen days beyond the proper day of expiration are added, during which it is provisionally declared that the policy shall subsist on payment of the premium. And it has been held that this only gives an option to the insured to continue the insurance, by paying the premium within the fifteen days, notwithstanding any intervening loss; provided the office had not already given notice that they would not renew the contract (*c*).

(*a*) Isaacs *v.* Royal Ins. Co., 39 L. J. Ex. 189 ; L. R. 5 Ex. 296.

(*b*) Sickness and Acct. Ass. Assn. *v.* Gen. Acct. Ass. Corp., 1892 ; 19 R. 977.

(*c*) Salvin *v.* James, 6 East, 571. Acey *v.* Ferme, 7 M. & W. 151. Tarleton, § 510 (*b*).

513. Conditions of Payment of Loss.—Insurance offices against fire generally issue printed proposals, which are by reference incorporated with the policy. It 'was' a stipulation common in such proposals, 'now in disuse,' that the insured 'should,' before claiming for loss, produce a certificate of good character from the ministers, etc., of the parish. The wrongful refusal of such certificate has sometimes given rise to a question whether it be indispensable; and it has been held an absolute condition (*a*). 'The insured is generally bound as a condition of his claim to give notice of loss within a certain time, and deliver full particulars (*b*).'

Another condition commonly stipulated is, that the insured shall give notice of any other insurance effected on the subject, so as to afford the means of contribution, otherwise the policy shall be void. This condition also is effectual (*c*).

'Conditions against the introduction of steam-engines, or changes in the nature of the business carried on in the premises, are to be literally construed and enforced (*d*).'

Another stipulation is against loss by invasion, foreign enemy, or military or usurped power; and in more recent proposals, loss from "riot, tumult, and civil commotion" is added as an exception from the undertaking. This condition saves the underwriters from losses by invasion or by riot (*e*). But there is a remedy under the Riot Act, and underwriters paying such a loss may sue in the name and with the consent of the insured (*f*).

(*a*) Oldman *v.* Bewicke, 2 H. Blackst. 572. Worsley *v.* Wood, 6 T. R. 710; 3 R. R. 323. Tarleton *v.* Staniforth, *cit.* § 510 (*b*).

(*b*) Roper *v.* Lendon, 1 E. & E. 825; 25 L. J. Q. B. 260. Mason *v.* Harvey, 8 Ex. 819; 22 L. J. Ex. 336. Worsley, *cit.* See Shiells *v.* Scot. Ass. Corp., 1889; 16 R. 1014.

(*c*) Marshall, 788. Hort on Apportionment of Losses, 1870. Such stipulation does not apply to a marine policy accidentally overlapping. Australian Agric. Co. *v.* Saunders, 44 L. J. C. P. 391; L. R. 10 C. P. 668. Where a clause provided that if there be "other insurances, whether effected by the insured or any other person covering the same property," the company should be liable to pay only its rateable proportion, it was held that the contribution could be extended only to those who insured the same interest in the same property, and so that there was not contribution between the insurers of a first and a second heritable creditor. Scot. Amic. Her. Sec. Assn. *v.* Northern Assur. Co., 1883; 11 R. 287. See N. B. and Merc. Ins. Co. *v.* Liv. Lon. and Globe Ins. Co., 45 L. J. Ch. 548; 46 *ib.* 537; L. R. 5 Ch. D. 569 (a case of wharfingers and merchants insuring separately the same subject with this clause). As to distinct insurances by different heritable creditors, see Glasgow Prov. Invt. Soc. *v.* Westmr. Fire Office, 1887; 14 R. 947.

(*d*) Glen *v.* Lewis, 8 Ex. 607; 22 L. J. Ex. 228. Stokes *v.* Cox, 1 H. & N. 320, 533; 26 L. J. Ex. 113. A condition against an alteration of the subject insured will readily be implied from the description. Sillem *v.* Thornton, 3 E. & B. 868; 23 L. J. Q. B. 368. See Pim *v.* Reid, 6 M. & G. 1. Mayall *v.* Mitford, 6 A. & E. 670. As to a condition that the policy shall be void if the property pass to any other person, see Forbes *v.* Border Counties Fire Office, 1873; 11 Macph. 278; and cf. Poole *v.* Adams, 33 L. J. Ch. 639. Collingridge, *supra*, § 509 (*a*).

(*e*) Drinkwater *v.* London Assur. Co., Marsh. 790; 1 Ill. 322; 2 Wils. 363. Langdale *v.* Mason, Marsh. 971.

(*f*) Mason *v.* Sainsbury, Marsh. 794. Clark *v.* Inhabit. of Blything, 2 B. & Cr. 254; 26 R. R. 334.

514. Representation and Warranty.—The doctrine of representation and warranty applies to the case of fire insurance as well as maritime (*a*) 'and life insurance' (*b*).

(*a*) M'Morran *v.* Newcastle F. I. Co., 1815; 3 Dow, 257; 1 Ill. 298. Bufe *v.* Turner, 6 Taunt. 338; 1 Ill. 322; 16 R. R. 626. Worsley *v.* Wood, *cit.* § 513. Dobson *v.* Sotheby, 1 Mood. & Malk. 90; 31 R. R. 718. See above, § 474–75. *In re* Univ. Non-Tariff F. I. Co., 44 L. J. Ch. 761; L. R. 19 Eq. 485.

(*b*) See below, § 522.

515. Extent of Loss.—Fire policies are not properly valued policies. They limit, but do not measure, the liability for loss. The loss must be proved, and every possible means of detecting fraud exposed (*a*). The settlement is on the principle of an average loss, not on the principle of abandonment. The underwriters pay not for what has been expended, but only for what is lost to the amount of the sum insured (*b*); which may be ascertained judicially, or by arbitration, or amicably. 'An option may be reserved to the insurer to pay the loss or reinstate (*c*). The impossibility of fulfilling the obligation to reinstate emerging after election made, is no defence to the company (*d*), nor the fact that sums sufficient for reinstatement have been paid to other insured interests (creditors) by other insurers, but not used for reinstatement, the value of the subject having been sufficient at the date of the fire to cover the claimants' loss (*e*).'

(*a*) Bisset *v.* Royal Ex. Assur. Co., 1821; 1 S. 107; 1 Ill. 323. As to fraudulent over-valuation, see Hercules Ins. Co. *v.* Hunter, 1835; 14 S. 147, 1137; 15 S. 800. Campbell *v.* Aberdeen F. I. Co., 1841; 3 D. 1010. M'Kirdy *v.* North Brit. Ins. Co., 1858; 20 D. 463.

(*b*) Hercules Ins. Co. *v.* Hunter, 1836; 14 S. 1137. The Act of 14 Geo. III. c. 78, in the 83rd section, provides that insurance offices may, on the requisition of any one interested, insist on seeing the money of such insurance laid out on rebuilding. Although this be a public Act, it is an English, or more properly a *London* Act, and does not extend to Scotland. See Bisset, *supra* (*a*); and opp. in Westminster Fire Office *v.* Glasgow Prov. Invt. Soc., 1888;

13 App. Ca. 699 ; 15 R. H. L. 89, where *ex parte* Goreley, 4 De G. & S. 477 ; 34 L. J. Bankr. 1, is doubted.

(*c*) Sutherland *v.* Sun Fire Office, 1852 ; 14 D. 775.

(*d*) Brown *v.* Royal Ins. Co., 1 E. & E. 853 ; 28 L. J. Q. B. 275.

(*e*) Glasgow Prov. Invt. Co. *v.* Westminster Fire Office, 1887 ; 14 R. 947 ; 13 App. Ca. 699 ; 15 R. H. L. 89.

516. Assignment of Policy.—Fire policies are in England not assignable at law, but they are in equity: they are assignable in Scotland, provided the interest goes with them (*a*).

(*a*) 1 Bell's Com. 629. 2 Marshall, 800. Lynch *v.* Dalzell, 2 Br. Parl. Ca. 497 ; 1 Ill. 324. Saddlers' Co. *v.* Badcock, 2 Atk. 554.

517. Floating Policies against Fire.—Factors, warehousemen, printers, and others, who have great stores of goods entrusted to them, find it of great advantage to have their warehouses protected against loss by fire, as affording safety to those who employ them. For that purpose they effect a general or floating insurance, applicable to all goods that may be in their warehouse. And although the owner of the goods cannot, under such a policy, be said to be a party to the contract, the insured is allowed to sue on the policy, if he can show that, by contract, or usage, or the course of dealing, he is liable to the owner for the goods. There are other policies effected on similar views, but still more extensive, upon goods belonging to the insured or with him in trust, in all or any of the warehouses, cellars, or granaries in a certain city. To these the same general doctrine applies (*a*).

(*a*) Donaldson *v.* Manchester Fire Office, 1836 ; 14 S. 601 ; 3 Ill. 143. Dalgleish *v.* Buchanan, 1854 ; 16 D. 332. See above, § 509 (*d*). Austral. Ins. Co. *v.* Randell, L. R. 3 P. C. 101 ; 6 Moore, P. C. N. S. 341. Bunyon on Fire Insur. p. 10 sqq. 2nd ed.

IV. INSURANCE UPON LIVES.

518. Nature of it.—Insurance of lives is a contract, not of indemnity, like sea and fire insurance, but of mutual risk (*a*); where one engages to pay a certain sum in the event of the death, or an annuity during the life, of a particular person, in consideration of a premium paid at once or periodically.

(*a*) **Dalby *v.* Ind. & Col. L. A. Co.**, 15 C. B. 365 ; 24 L. J. C. P. 2 ; 3 Ross' L. C. 718 ; 2 Smith's L. C. 282. Law *v.* Lond. Indisp. L. P. Co., 1 K. & J. 223 ; 24 L. J. Ch. 196. Angell on Fire and Life Insurance. Bunyon on Life Insurance.

519. Stamp.—The policy must be stamped (*a*).

(*a*) 55 Geo. III. c. 184. 54 and 55 Vict. c. 39, Sched., and § 91, 98, 99 sq. See above, § 457.

520. Interest.—There can be no valid insurance on life without a pecuniary interest, the policy being limited to the interest 'at the time of effecting the insurance'; and the insured is not entitled to recover more than the amount of it (*a*). A father has no insurable interest in the life of his son (*b*). In a policy opened by one on his own life, his family has an interest sufficient; and as it is assignable, it is useful as a fund of credit. After the creditor is satisfied from another source, such a policy is available to the debtor, or to his creditors generally. It is sometimes made absolute during the whole life of the person insured; sometimes only for a certain number of years.

(*a*) 14 Geo. III. c. 48, § 1, 2, 3. Hebdon *v.* West, 3 B. & S. 579. Seagrave *v.* Union M. I. Co., 35 L. J. C. P. 172 ; L. R. 1 C. P. 305. The Act also requires (§ 2) the insertion in the policy of the name of the person interested. Hodson *v.* Observer L. A. Co., 8 E. & B. 40. Evans *v.* Bignold, 38 L. J. Q. B. 293 ; L. R. 4 Q. B. 622. See Wainwright *v.* Bland, 1 M. & W. 32 ; 1 M. & R. 481. Shilling *v.* Accid. D. I. Co., 2 H. & N. 42 ; 26 L. J. Ex. 266.

(*b*) Halford *v.* Kymer, 10 B. & Cr. 724 ; 1 Ill. 324 ; 3 Ross' L. C. 725 ; 34 R. R. 553. Innes *v.* Equit. Ass. Co., 10 B. & Cr. 727. Shilling, *supra* (*a*). But if the insurers pay, the money belongs to the father. Worthington *v.* Curtis, 1 Ch. D. 419 ; 45 L. J. Ch. 259. See as to insurances on lives of children in Friendly Societies, 59 and 60 Vict. c. 25, § 62 sqq.; as to claims by third parties paying contributions to Friendly Societies, Cruickshank *v.* Munro, 1875 ; 19 J. of J. 502, 2 Sel. Sh. Ct. Ca. 185 (Dove Wilson, S.S.).

521. A creditor has an interest in his debtor's life, in so far as the payment or security of the debt may depend on the continuance of his life. And he may either himself open a policy on his debtor's life, paying the premium, or he may get assigned to him a policy opened by the debtor on his own life (*a*). A policy of the former kind has been held to fall on the debt being paid from another source (*b*); but there 'seemed' to be much reason to question the principle of this decision 'which was afterwards overruled' (*c*); and in cases where the creditor 'had' drawn a dividend from his debtor's estate, insurance offices 'were in use, even before the decision in Dalby *v.* The Indian and Colonial Co., to' settle with the insured for the whole sum, and not merely for the balance, as in an indemnity. 'It is now settled that the only effect of the statute is to make the assured value his interest at its true amount when he makes the contract; and that a subsequent cesser of the interest does not avoid the policy (*d*). But as under the statute the insured can recover no more than the amount of his interest, payment to a creditor of the amount of his debt is a bar to his recovering the sum insured for the same interest in other policies (*e*). It is a question of intention, to be proved by the circumstances of each case (in whatever form the policy may be taken), whether a policy taken or assigned in a loan transaction has been so taken or kept up for the benefit of the creditor, and to the extent of his loan only, or for the benefit and at the expense of the debtor, so that, *quoad* the surplus, it falls within his estate (*f*). So, an agreement that a creditor shall effect a policy and the debtor pay the premiums, *primâ facie*, means that the equitable property in the policy is in the debtor, subject to the security; for what the debtor pays or agrees to pay for is presumably his (*g*).'

The interest is not to be reckoned by the actual value of the life, or diminished to the creditor by collateral securities. While the debt subsists, the policy is good, leaving the collateral securities to be otherwise available (*h*). 'Assignees of life policies may sue upon them in their own names (*i*).'

(*a*) Lindenau *v.* Desborough, 8 B. & Cr. 586; 3 Ross' L. C. 731. See Natl. Bank *v.* Forbes, 1858; 21 D. 79.
(*b*) **Godsal** *v.* **Boldero**, 9 East, 71; 1 Ill. 287; 2 Smith's L. C. 271. De Morgan on Probabilities, 244.
(*c*) **Dalby** *v.* **Ind. & Col. Life Ass. Co.**, *supra*, § 518. Law *v.* London Indisp. L. P. Co., *ib.*
(*d*) Dalby, Law, *cit.*
(*e*) Hebdon *v.* West, § 520 (*a*).
(*f*) M. of Queensberry *v.* Scot. Union Ins. Co., 1839; 1 D. 1203; aff. 1 Bell's App. 183. Lindsay *v.* Barmcotte, 1851; 13 D. 718. White *v.* Cotton, 1846; 8 D. 872. Shand *v.* Blaikie, 1859; 21 D. 878. Forrester *v.* Robson's Trs., 1875; 2 R. 755 (mode of proof—see below, § 1995). See as to such transactions, known in England as borrowing upon annuity, Holland *v.* Smith, 6 Esp. 11; 9 R. R. 801. Drysdale *v.* Pigott, 8 De G. M. & G. 546; 25 L. J. Ch. 878. Gottlieb *v.* Cranch, 4 De G. M. & G. 440; 22 L. J. Ch. 912. Freme *v.* Brade, 2 De G. & J. 582; 27 L. J. Ch. 697. Knox *v.* Turner, L. R. 9 Eq. 155; 5 Ch. 515; 39 L. J. Ch. 206, 750. Bruce *v.* Garden, L. R. 5 Ch. 32; 39 L. J. Ch. 334. Lewis *v.* King, 44 L. J. Ch. 259. Preston *v.* Neele, 12 Ch. D. 760. Bunyon on Life Insur. Ch. 6.
(*g*) Holland, Drysdale, and Bruce, *citt.* (*f*). Salt *v.* M. of Northampton, 1892; A. C. 1.
(*h*) Dwyer *v.* Edie, Park, 639; Marshall, 778; 1 Ill. 324. Anderson *v.* Edie, Park, 915; Marsh. 776. Godsal, *supra* (*b*).
(*i*) See 30 and 31 Vict. c. 145, which gives the same power in England.

522. Representation and Warranty. — The same rule prevails with respect to representation and warranty as in other insurance (*a*). Every material fact 'known to the insured' must be disclosed. It will not relieve from the effect of failure to disclose 'all facts within his knowledge which can reasonably be supposed to influence the judgment of the insurers,' that the omission was innocent, '*i.e.* not fraudulent'; and it is a question for the jury whether it be material (*b*). 'The representations made must be true not only at the time when they are made, but when the risk begins; and if a material change of circumstances occurs before the insurance is made,—if, *e.g.*, that be understood to be at the issuing of the policy or the date of payment of the premium,—it must be disclosed, and, as the risk is not the same, the insurer may refuse the insurance, even if he have accepted a previous proposal (*c*). Innocent misstatements by the assured, *i.e.* misstatements which involve no negligence or want of fair consideration for the interest of the insurers, are not fatal to the policy, unless the truth of the statement be made a warranty or condition of the contract (*d*). Policies often contain a provision that the declaration of the insured shall be the basis of the contract, or a condition precedent of the contract, or the like; and in that case (such declaration not being limited to the knowledge and belief of the assured) the contract is avoided if any of the statements contained in it be untrue, whether known to the assured to be untrue or not (*e*). Such a warranty or condition is a ground of reduction even against onerous assignees of the policy (*f*). But in the case of an insurance on the life of another party, that party is not, in the absence of express conditions or adoption of his statements, agent for the insured, so as to make the latter responsible for his fraud or concealment, or that of the referees (*g*).'

(*a*) See above, § 474, 475. Newcastle F. I. Co. *v.* Macmorran & Co., 3 Dow, 255; 15 R. R. 67. Standard L. A. Co. *v.* Weems, *infra* (*e*) (*per* Lord Blackburn). The knowledge of the insurer's agent of such a fact as that the insured is a one-eyed man affects the principal. Bawden *v.* Lond. E. & G. Ins. Co., 1892; 2 Q. B. 534.
(*b*) Ross *v.* Bradshaw, 1 W. Blackst. 312; 1 Ill. 325. Lindenau, *supra*, § 521 (*a*). Everett *v.* Desborough, 5 Bing. 503; 3 Ross' L. C. 732. Forbes & Co. *v.* Edin. L. A. Co., 1832; 10 S. 451. Borthwick *v.* Ralston's Trs., 1837; 15 S. 1306. Sprott *v.* Ross, 1838; 16 S. 1145. London Ass. Co. *v.* Mansel, 11 Ch. D. 363; 48 L. J. Ch. 331. Rose *v.* Medical L. A. Soc., 1848; 11 D. 151, 158.

(*c*) Canning *v.* Farquhar, 16 Q. B. D. 727. Sickness and Acct. Ass. Assn. *v.* Gen. Acct. Ass. Corp., 1892; 19 R. 977.

(*d*) Foster *v.* Life Ass. of Scot., 1873; 11 Macph. 351. Wheelton *v.* Hardisty, 8 E. & B. 232; 27 L. J. Q. B. 241. Cruikshank *v.* Northern Acct. Ins. Co., 1895; 23 R. 147.

(*e*) Duckett *v.* Williams, 2 C. & M. 348. Anderson *v.* Fitzgerald, 4 H. L. Ca. 484. Cazenove *v.* Brit. L. A. Ass. Co., 6 C. B. N. S. 437; 28 L. J. C. P. 259; 29 *ib.* 160. Geach *v.* Ingall, 14 M. & W. 95. Perrins *v.* M. & G. T. Ins. Soc., 2 E. & E. 317; 29 L. J. Q. B. 242. Fowkes *v.* Manchester & London Ass. Co., 32 L. J. Q. B. 153; 3 B. & S. 917. Macdonald *v.* Law Union Ins. Co., 43 L. J. Q. B. 131; L. R. 9 Q. B. 328. Adamson *v.* Scott. Prov. Ass. Co., 1868; 6 Macph. 442. Foster, Forbes & Co., Wheelton, *citt.* Hutcheson, *infra.* Weems *v.* Standard L. A. Co., 1884; 11 R. 658; aff. 1884, 11 R. H. L. 48; 9 App. Ca. 671 (Thomson *v.* Weems—overruling Hutcheson *v.* Nat. Loan Ass. Co., 1845; 7 D. 467).

(*f*) Scottish Widows Fund *v.* Buist, 1876; 3 R. 1078. Scot. Eq. L. A. Soc. *v.* Buist, 1877; 4 R. 1076; aff. 1878, 5 R. H. L. 64.

(*g*) Wheelton *v.* Hardisty, *cit.*

523. Suicide, Duelling, etc. — There is usually a clause declaring that death at sea, or by suicide, duelling, or the hand of justice, shall not be held as a risk under the policy. Such events have been held, even without express stipulation, fatal to an insurance effected by the guilty person, and not available even to his creditors (*a*). But the objection will not annul a policy effected by a third party interested. 'The condition that the policy shall become void if the assured shall "commit suicide" or "die by his own hands," receives effect whether the insured be sane or not at the time of death; for if it were effectual only where the assured is of sound mind and the act is therefore felonious or a crime (*b*), the condition would be obviously superfluous (*c*). If there be no such express condition, suicide of the insured while insane does not void the policy (*d*); and the exception sometimes added to the condition, that the policy shall be good to the extent of any *bonâ fide* interest vested in a third person at the time of the insured's death, is valid, even though that interest should be merely a lien without any assignation (*e*).' Death in a foreign country, unless excepted, 'or even when excepted, if the exception be waived, as by receipt of premiums after notice (*f*),' is a risk under the policy.

(*a*) Bolland *v.* Disney, 3 Russ. 351; as rev. in H. L. July 9, 1836; 4 Bligh, N. S. 194; 2 Dow & Cl. 1. See above, § 462.

(*b*) 4 Stephen's Com. 143 sqq. 1 Hume's Crim. Law, 300.

(*c*) Borradaile *v.* Hunter, 5 M. & Gr. 639. Dormay *v.* Borradaile, 5 C. B. 380; 16 L. J. C. P. 337. Clift *v.* Schwabe, 3 C. B. 437; 17 L. J. C. P. 2; 3 Ross' L. C. 755. Dufaur *v.* Prof. L. I. Co., 25 Beav. 599; 27 L. J. Ch. 817, and cases cited in following notes.

(*d*) Horn *v.* Anglo-Austr., etc., L. I. Co., 30 L. J. Ch. 511.

(*e*) Moore *v.* Woolsey, 4 E. & B. 243; 24 L. J. Q. B. 40. Jackson *v.* Foster, 1 E. & E. 463; 29 L. J. Q. B. 8. White *v.* Br. Emp. M. L. A. Co., L. R. 7 Eq. 394; 38 L. J. Ch. 53. See U. K. L. A. Co. *v.* Allan, 1838; 16 S. 1277.

(*f*) Wing *v.* Harvey, 2 De G. M. & G. 265. Reis *v.* Sc. Eq. L. I. Co., 2 H. & N. 19.

CHAPTER XVI

OF THE CONSTRUCTION OF CONTRACTS

524. With all the care which can be taken, disputes will arise as to the meaning of contracts; and construction is the art of collecting from proper indications what the parties held out to each other as their meaning and intention in the contract, and what, in concluding their contract, they mutually agreed to, understood, and relied on.

'A Court cannot construe a contract which is so vague as to be no contract. No agreement is a contract unless its terms are certain, or capable of being made certain by reference to some standard which the parties had in their minds (*a*).'

The General Rule is, that the words, according to their plain meaning and obvious intent, are to be taken as conclusive of the mutual intention of the parties; and that constructive or explanatory evidence is to be admitted only where the words are ambiguous and the agreement uncertain (*b*). Words expressive of engagement, when proved by a writing executed at the time, furnish the clearest of all indications of intention. Wherever this precaution of writing has not been followed, and witnesses are to be relied on, the object of the inquiry at the trial must be to get from them as nearly as possible the words made use of.

Ambiguities.—There are two kinds, which are to be dealt with differently: An ambiguity patent or apparent on the face of the contract, which, unless it can be solved by the context and nature of the contract, may be fatal: And a latent ambiguity, arising not from the words, but in their application; and in this case, extraneous evidence is admissible to clear up the difficulty (*c*).

But in bargains there is so much taken for granted, so loose a confidence, so vague an adoption of usage, so great uncertainty as to the ordinary understanding in such cases, and so much ambiguity and imperfection of language, even where the identity of the words is not disputed, that courts of justice are frequently compelled to make an election between different meanings, and sometimes to admit the evidence of usage to qualify the whole. 'It is a golden rule of construction, that the grammatical and ordinary sense of the words used is to be adhered to, unless that would lead to some absurdity, or some repugnancy or inconsistency with the rest of the instrument, in which case the grammatical and ordinary sense of the words may be modified, so as to avoid that absurdity or inconsistency, but no further (*d*). In other words, the more literal or natural construction does not prevail, if it is opposed to the intention as manifest and apparent by the rest of the instrument (or statute), and if the words either are sufficiently flexible to admit of another construction consistent with that intention, or clearly appear to have been used by mistake. The construction must be made upon consideration of the entire instrument, and greater regard is to be had to the clear intent of the parties than to any particular words (*e*).'

Special Rules.—The rules seem to be,—

(1.) That the 'natural and' popular sense of the words, as known and used at the place (*f*) and time, is to be followed, unless the words be technical, 'or have a special meaning affixed to them by usage of trade (*g*).'

(2.) That technical words are to be taken technically, if no doubt can be entertained of the meaning and application: And for their meaning, usage may be resorted to (*h*).

(3.) That the sense which gives validity and effect to the agreement is to be preferred to that which invalidates or defeats it (*i*).

(4.) That usage enters into, extends, limits, and qualifies contracts, especially in matters of trade. But the usage must be consistent with law (*k*) 'and with the terms of the contract (*l*), and reasonable (*m*)'; and either general, universal usage; or usage of the particular trade or line of dealing: or, if local, known and relied on by both parties; and when it is so, it tacitly enters into the contract (*n*). 'Usage, or a course of dealing between the parties, may enter into and qualify a contract (*o*); and subsequent usage operates (by way of personal bar) to put a meaning on what is ambiguous, or even to add to the contract (*p*).'

(5.) That words, however general, are to be confined to the subject and matter of the agreement contemplated by the parties (*q*). 'So, when a particular enumeration is followed by such words as "or other," the latter expression ought, if not enlarged by the context, to be limited to matters *ejusdem generis* with those specially enumerated. The application of this rule, and whether it applies at all, in every case depends on the precise terms, subject-matter, and context of the clause under consideration (*r*).'

(6.) That in the several contracts, sale, location, etc., the *naturalia* of the particular contract are tacitly part of the agreement (*s*); 'but in unusual and innominate contracts conditions are not implied (*t*).'

(7.) That if the meaning and import of the agreement is to be collected from what has passed in correspondence, the meaning is to be taken according to the import of the whole (*u*). And if a series of conversations and communings, or of letters, has resulted in a distinct written agreement, all previous correspondence and communings are discharged 'and excluded from consideration' (*v*).

(8.) That the true point of inquiry in all doubtful cases is not (as in a will) the intention of one party, but that meaning of the terms made use of which the adverse party understood, and on which he was entitled to rely (*w*).

(9.) 'But while "communings," *i.e.* what parties said and did while a contract reduced to a distinct agreement was in negotiation, are to be disregarded in construing it, it is sometimes necessary and proper to look at the surrounding facts and circumstances, and therefore to have evidence of them, in order to judge of the meaning of the words, and their application to the subject-matter of the agreement (*x*). It may even be necessary to consider the whole correspondence and facts to ascertain whether what seems to be an agreement was really such according to the true intent of the parties (*y*).'

(*a*) See M'Arthur *v.* Lawson, Traill *v.* Dewar, and Young *v.* Dougans, *cit.* in § 362. Comp. above, § 92 (1), 174. Pollock on Contracts, p. 42, 3rd ed. Benjamin on Sale, pp. 83–86, 3rd ed. In Davies *v.* Davies, 36 Ch. D. 359, it was held that a covenant by a retiring partner to retire from the business so far as the law allows was too vague to be enforced.

(*b*) Pelly *v.* R. E. Ass. Co., 1 Burr. 341; 1 Ill. 326. Newman *v.* Cazalet, Park, 630. Palmer *v.* Blackburn, 1 Bing. 61; 25 R. R. 599. Inglis *v.* Cunningham, 4 Mur. 73. Yeatts *v.* Pim, 2 Marsh. 141; 16 R. R. 653. Pollock *v.* M'Andrew, 1828; 7 S. 189; 1 Ill. 89. Robertson *v.* French, 4 East, 135; 3 Ill. 145; 7 R. R. 535. Smith *v.* Cooke, 1891; A. C. 297. As to contracts partly printed, see above, § 406, 467.

(*c*) See Best's Pr. of Evid. 311. Morton *v.* Hunter & Co., 1830; 4 W. & S. 379, 386. Logans *v.* Wright, 1831; 5 W. & S. 242.

(*d*) *Per* L. Wensleydale, in Gray *v.* Pearson, 6 H. L. Ca. 61, 106; 26 L. J. Ch. 473; and L. Blackburn, in Cal. Ry. Co. *v.* N. B. Ry. Co., 1881; 8 R. H. L. 23, 30; 6 App. Ca. 114.

(*e*) See 3 Ersk. Inst. 3. 87. 2 Smith's L. Ca. 500. Greenwood *v.* Greenwood, 5 Ch. D. 954; 47 L. J. Ch. 298. Ford *v.* Beech, 11 Q. B. 852; 17 L. J. Q. B. 114. See above, § 11, *init.*; below, § 760. N. B. Oil and Candle Co. *v.* Swann, 1868; 6 Macph. 835. Johnston *v.* Robertson, and cases as to penalties in § 34, *supra.* Mags. of Dundee *v.* Duncan, 1883; 11 R. 145 (omitted words supplied).

(*f*) See Addison on Contracts, 54 sq. Guthrie's Savigny on Priv. Int. Law, 243 sqq. *Supra*, § 91 (3), 117, etc. Crosse *v.* Bankes, 1884; 11 R. 988; rev. 1886, 13 R. H. L. 40.

(*g*) See below (4). Bowes *v.* Shand, L. R. 2 App. Ca. 455; 46 L. J. Q. B. 561.

(*h*) Bowman *v.* Horsey, 2 Mood. & Rob. 85; 3 Ill. 145. See above, § 83. Addison on Contracts, 65. 1 Smith's L. C. 546, etc. Dickson on Evid. § 199 et seq. Mackenzie *v.* Dunlop, 1853; 16 D. 129; aff. 1856, 3 Macq. 22. Hunter *v.* Miller, 1862; 24 D. 1011 (fallow-break not technical). Thomson *v.* Garioch, 1841; 3 D. 625. Jack *v.* Roberts, 1865; 3 Macph. 554. M'Intosh *v.* Ogilvie, 1806; Hume, 822 (see *ib.* 827, 842). Clayton *v.* Greyson, 5 A. & E. 302. Evans *v.* Pratt, 3 M. & G. 759. Fleming *v.* Airdrie Iron Co., 1882; 9 R. 473.

(*i*) Notes to Tranmarr *v.* Scott, 2 Smith's L. C. 492, 498.

(*k*) See below, § 1303, 2235. 1 Smith's L. C. 553. Steel Co. *v.* Tancred, Arrol, & Co., 1887; 15 R. 215.

(*l*) 1 Smith's L. C. 554 sq. Mollett *v.* Robinson, *infra.* Calder *v.* Aitchison & Co., 1831 ; 5 W. & S. 410. Sinclair *v.* M'Beath, 1868 ; 7 Macph. 273.

(*m*) 1 Smith's L. C. 559.

(*n*) See above, § 83. See Mollett *v.* Robinson, 39 L. J. C. P. 290 ; 41 L. J. C. P. 65 ; 44 *ib.* 802 ; L. R. 5 C. P. 646 ; 7 *ib.* 84 ; 7 H. L. 802 ; and cases as to stockbrokers in § 219. Kirchner *v.* Venus, 12 Moore, P. C. 399. Sweeting *v.* Pearce, 30 L. J. C. P. 109 ; 9 C. B. N. S. 534. Holman *v.* Peruv. Nitrate Co., 1878 ; 5 R. 657. Buckle *v.* Knoop, 36 L. J. Ex. 49, 223 ; L. R. 2 Ex. 125. Norden Steamship Co. *v.* Dempsey, 1 C. P. D. 662 ; 45 L. J. C. P. 764. Cf. 1 Smith's L. C. 535 sqq. Dickson on Evid. § 229 sqq.

(*o*) Bourne *v.* Gatliffe, 11 Cl. & F. 45. Cumming *v.* Shand, 5 H. & N. 95 ; 29 L. J. Ex. 129.

(*p*) Mags. of Dunbar *v.* Hers. of Dunbar, 1833 ; 11 S. 879 ; rev. 1835, 1 S. & M'L. 134, 195 ; 3 Cl. & F. 335 (*contemporanea expositio* of a statute). See also Laird & Sons *v.* Clyde Nav. Trs., 1882 ; 9 R. 711 ; aff. 1883, 10 R. H. L. 77 (and as to the different construction of ancient and modern statutes, Thomas *v.* Thomson, 1865 ; 5 Macph. 1160, 1165 (*per* Inglis, J.-C.)). Heriot's Hosp. *v.* Macdonald, 1830 ; 4 W. & S. 98. Masters and Seamen of Dundee *v.* Wedderburn, 1830 ; 8 S. 547. Girdwood & Co. *v.* Campbell, 1830 ; 9 S. 170. Russell *v.* Cowpar, 1882 ; 9 R. 660. Jopp's Trs. *v.* Edmond, 1888 ; 15 R. 271, as to which see 1 Jur. Rev. 103.

(*q*) See 4 Stair, 42. § 21. 3 Ersk. 4 § 9. 2 Smith's L. C. 540. Pollock on Contracts, 483–485. Burnett *v.* G. N. of Scot. Ry. Co., 1883 ; 11 R. 375 ; rev. 1884, 12 R. H. L. 25 ; 10 App. Ca. 147 (where the inferior Court's misapplication of this rule was corrected).

(*r*) *Per Cur.* in Sun Fire Office *v.* Hart (P. C.), 1889 ; 14 App. Ca. 98.

(*s*) Pelly, *supra* (*b*).

(*t*) *Per* L. P. Inglis, in Landless *v.* Wilson, 1880 ; 8 R. 289.

(*u*) Hussey *v.* Horne Payne, 4 App. Ca. 311 ; 48 L. J. Ch. 846.

(*v*) Kain *v.* Old, 2 B. & Cr. 634 ; 3 Ill. 105 ; 26 R. R. 497. Inglis *v.* Buttery, 1877 ; 5 R. 58 ; rev. *ib.* H. L. 87. Even deleted words in the concluded agreement are excluded from consideration. Inglis, *cit.* Comp. Forlong *v.* Taylor's Exrs., *infra.* Gordon *v.* Hughes, June 15, 1815 ; F. C. ; rev. 1819, 1 Bligh, 287 ; 20 R. R. 52 ; and below, § 2257, 2258, 760.

(*w*) Life Ass. of Scot. *v.* Foster, 1873 ; 11 Macph. 351.

(*x*) Inglis *v.* Buttery, *cit.* Shore *v.* Wilson, 9 Cl. & F. 355, 369. Wigram on Extrinsic Evid., 57 sq. (3rd ed.). Addison, Contr. 44. Forlong *v.* Taylor's Exrs., 1838 ; 3 S. & M'L. 177, 210. Philip *v.* Edin. P. & D. Ry. Co., 1857 ; 2 Macq. 514, 525-6. Stewart *v.* S. N.-E. Ry. Co., 1859 ; 3 Macq. 382. Mackenzie *v.* Liddell, 1883 ; 10 R. 705.

(*y*) Hussey *v.* Horne Payne, *supra* (*u*).

BOOK FIRST

PART II

OF RIGHTS ARISING FROM IMPLIED OBLIGATIONS INDEPENDENT OF CONVENTION

INTRODUCTION

525. Amid the accidents of human life many invasions of right occur, and many grounds of action for redress are required which are not derived from convention or express contract. The Roman lawyers, instead of contemplating the rights encroached upon or violated, were accustomed to refer all personal actions to obligations express, or implied, or presumed; and they made three classes of constructive obligations, corresponding to the rights invaded. Those included—1. Obligations arising *quasi ex contractu*; 2. Obligations arising *ex delicto*; 3. Obligations arising *quasi ex delicto*. Without following the subtleties connected with this arrangement, it seems to be simpler to consider all such grounds of action, on account of rights invaded, under the heads of Restitution, Recompense, and Reparation of Injuries.

CHAPTER XVII

OF RESTITUTION, REPETITION, RECOMPENSE, AND NEGOTIORUM GESTIO

I. RESTITUTION.

526. General Rule. — The law gives an action of restitution against one in possession of the property or goods of another without his consent (*a*); or who has, in consequence of error, received payment of money not legally due to him (*b*).

(*a*) 1 Stair, 7. 3 Ersk. Pr. 1. § 5. 3 Ersk. 1. § 10.
(*b*) See § 531. Kinniburgh *v.* Dickson, 1830; 9 S. 153.

527. Stolen Goods.—For things stolen, the owner who has been unlawfully deprived of them has an action not only against the thief, but against third parties, who may even have purchased them *in bonâ fide*, or received them in pledge. In such cases an obligation arising from the natural duty of restitution is presumed (*a*). The only doubt which disturbs the simplicity of this rule arises from the sanction due to a sale in public market. In England, this overcomes the right of the true owner (*b*): but it is not so in Scotland (*c*). With us the privilege of public market 'was under the former law' of force only to overcome the landlord's hypothec, in regard to corn sold there in bulk, and not by sample (*d*).

But if a purchaser in public market (*e*) have fairly disposed of the thing to another before any claim made by the owner, he will not be bound to restore to the owner the price which he has received, unless in so far as it shall exceed what he himself paid; to which extent he is a gainer by the loss of the original owner (*f*).

(*a*) 3 Ersk. 1. § 10, with Ivory's Notes. 1 Bell's Com. 281 (299, M'L.'s ed.).

(*b*) 2 Blackst. 449. 2 Steph. Com. 72. Wilkinson *v.* King, 2 Camp. 335; 1 Ill. 326. See Cole *v.* N.-W. Bk., L. R. 10 C. P. 354. Benj., Sales, 7 sqq. Sale of Goods Act, § 22.

(*c*) Bishop of Caithness *v.* Fleshers of Edinburgh, 1629; M. 9112, 4145; 1 Ill. 417. Ferguson *v.* Forrest, 1639; *ib.* Wright *v.* Butchart, 1662; M. 9112. Forsyth *v.* Kilpatrick, 1680; M. 9120. Henderson *v.* Gibson, 1806; M. *Moveables*, Apx. 1; 1 Ill. 327. See Ramsay *v.* Wilson, 1666; M. 9113. Pringle *v.* Gribton, 1710: M. 9123. Todd *v.* Armour, 1882; 9 R. 901. Sale of Goods Act, § 22 (3).

(*d*) See below, § 665, 1242, 1318–21.

(*e*) The judgment in Faulds *v.* Townsend, 1861, 23 D. 437, seems to extend the doctrine of this paragraph to any purchaser in good faith and without negligence.

(*f*) 3 Ersk. 1. § 10. Scott *v.* Low, 1704; M. 9123. Walker *v.* Spence, 1765; M. 12,802. Faulds *v.* Townsend, *cit.* Todd *v.* Armour, *cit.*

528. It is an exception to the above rule of restitution, that money, bank-notes, and bills payable to the bearer, or blank indorsed, cannot be vindicated against one who acquires them *in bonâ fide*, 'i.e. without notice, or means of knowing wilfully disregarded, that the previous holder was not a *bonâ fide* holder (*a*),' in the course of trade. In such case, the property passes with the possession (*b*).

(*a*) In the sense of the Bills of Exchange Act, a thing is deemed to be done in good faith if it is in fact done honestly, whether it is done negligently or not. 45 and 46 Vict. c. 61, § 90. See 1 Smith's L. C. 472, 734.

(*b*) Crawford *v.* Royal Bank, 1749; M. 875; 1 Ill. 327; 1 Ross' L. C. 229. Swinton *v.* Beveridge, 1799; M. 10,105. Lambton & Co. *v.* Marshall, 1799; M. *Bill*, Apx. 6; 1 Ill. 231. Scott & Co. *v.* Kilmarnock Bank, Feb. 27, 1812; F. C. See 1 Smith's L. C. 455 sqq; and above, § 333A et seq.; and below, § 1333. The Act 19 and 20 Vict. c. 60, § 15, is repealed by the Bills of Exchange Act.

529. But if one in lawful possession of a thing sell it to another without notice, the sale is good (*a*).

(*a*) See below, § 537.

530. Goods got by Mistake, etc.—One who by mistake has received anything (as from a carrier) is liable in restitution; and so one to whom a thing has been transferred, or an obligation undertaken and fulfilled, on a consideration which has failed, is also liable to restitution under the condition, *causa data causa non secuta* (*a*).

(*a*) 3 Ersk. 1. § 10. Webster *v.* Thomson, 1830; 8 S. 528. Pride *v.* St. Anne's Bleaching Co., 1838; 16 S. 1376.

II. REPETITION.

531. General Rule.—Whatever has been delivered or paid on an erroneous conception of duty or obligation may be recovered on the ground of equity; provided the person receiving it has no reason, on natural right, implied donation, or compromise, to rely on the acquisition as his own (*a*). The action by which in the Roman law this was effected was called *Condictio Indebiti*, and the term has been adopted by us. It was an action founded, not on convention, but *quasi ex contractu*; a sort of *pro-mutuum* or *quasi mutuum* (*b*).

(*a*) 1 Stair, 7. § 9. 3 Ersk. 3. § 54. Pothier, Tr. de Cond. Indeb. § 160. Voet. lib. 12. tit. 6. § 7.

(*b*) 1 Stair, 11. § 5.

532. Special Rules.—The special rules on this subject are:—

(1.) *Natural Obligation.*—As restitution is grounded on equity, it has no place if the transference or payment have proceeded on a natural obligation; for that is binding in equity, as a bar, although it would not have grounded a demand at law (*a*).

(*a*) 3 Ersk. 3. § 54.

533. (2.) *Knowledge of no Debt.*—If the payment have been made with full knowledge of the person who makes it that he is under no debt or obligation to pay, it is held a donation, and irrevocable (*a*). 'So "aliment or entertainment given to any person without paction is presumed to be a donation, if the person is major and capable to make an agreement. But entertainment to minors (*b*) or weak persons doth ever infer recompense according to the true value of the benefit received" (*c*); unless they have estate of their own, or a father or guardians be accessible with whom a bargain might be made, or it appear from relationship or otherwise that the advances or aliment were gifted (*d*). In modern practice the tendency is to rely more on the evidence of facts and circumstances showing whether the aliment or advances were intended to be a donation (*e*).'

(*a*) 3 Ersk. 3. § 54. See as to Donations between Husband and Wife, below, § 1616.

(*b*) Rather, "pupils." See Elchies, Notes, 48. Drummond *v.* Swayne, 1834; 12 S. 342.

(*c*) 1 Stair, 8. § 2. 4 *ib.* 45. § 17 (15) and (17). See below, § 2192, as to relief to paupers.

(*d*) See 3 Ersk. 3 § 92. Drummond *v.* Swayne, *cit.*

(*e*) See, *e.g.*, Forbes *v.* Forbes, 1869; 8 Macph. 85. M'Gaws *v.* Galloway, 1882; 10 R. 157. The distinction in regard to repetition between gratuitous charity deliberately bestowed and mistaken fulfilment of an onerous obligation, is illustrated in Masters and Seamen of Dundee *v.* Cockerill, 1869; 8 Macph. 278, and cases there cited.

534. (3.) *Error in Fact or Law.*—If the payment have been made under an unavoidable error in *fact* 'affecting the payee's right to receive the money (*a*),' restitution may be demanded (*b*). 'It was formerly held that' if the person in error have in his own hands the means of correct knowledge, he cannot plead his error arising from gross negligence (*c*). 'But it is now settled that, however careless a person paying in error may have been, he may recover back what he has paid from one who had no right to receive it, provided only he has not intended to waive all inquiry and meant the payee to have the money at all events (*d*). The means of knowledge are material only as affording evidence of actual knowledge (*e*). Money paid under compulsion of legal process cannot be recovered back on the ground of error, because *interest reipublicæ ut sit finis litium* (*f*).'

If the error be in *law*, although sufficient to relieve from an obligation, it 'was' more doubtful whether it affords a good ground of restitution (*g*). In several cases the Court of Session held error in law to ground restitution (*h*); but this doctrine 'was, when the author wrote,' much shaken by a case in the House of Lords (*i*); 'and it rather seems that where there is *bona fides*, and money is paid with full knowledge of the facts, though there be no debt, it cannot be recovered back merely because paid in ignorance of law (*k*). But this rule is subject to the large exception that a party will be relieved against such a payment, if in the circumstances it be inequitable for the party receiving the money to profit by the mistake of the other (*l*).'

(*a*) Chambers *v.* Miller, 13 C. B. N. S. 125; 32 L. J. C. P. 30 (banker's error as to customer's balance as against payee of cheque). Youle *v.* Cochrane, 1868; 6 Macph. 427. See below, § 536.

(*b*) 3 Ersk. 3 § 54. Parole evidence is allowed, even although the payment be by bill. Balfour *v.* Smith, 1877; 4 R. 454. See § 528.

(*c*) Wilson & M'Lellan *v.* Sinclair, 1830; 4 W. & S. 398; 1 Ill. 328.

(*d*) **Kelly** *v.* **Solari**, 9 M. & W. 54; 11 L. J. Ex. 10. Townsend *v.* Crowdy, 8 C. B. N. S. 477; 29 L. J. C. P. 300. Balfour *v.* Smith, *cit.* Dalmellington Iron Co. *v.* G. & S.-W. Ry. Co., 1889; 16 R. 523. See Brownlie *v.* Campbell (Miller), 5 App. Ca. 925, 952; 7 R. H. L. 66. 2 Smith's L. C. 427-432. See above, § 14.

(*e*) Cases cited (*d*). Bell *v.* Gardiner, 4 M. & G. 11.

(*f*) Marriott *v.* Hampton, 7 T. R. 269; 2 Smith's L. C. 409-432; 4 R. R. 439. Moore *v.* Vestry of Fulham, 1895; 1 Q. B. D. 399.

(*g*) See the controversy among the civilians on the distinction between error in law and fact. Voet. lib. 12. tit. 6. § 7. Pothier, Tr. de Cond. Indeb. No. 160. Vinnius, Quest. Sel. lib. 1. c. 47. Huber, lib. 2. tit. 6. § 1. It is settled in France by the rule which they have adopted. Code Civil, § 1377. In England the controversy came to a solemn discussion in Brisbane *v.* Dacres (1813), 5 Taunt. 143; 14 R. R. vi. 718; 1 Ill. 337, and was settled against the right to restitution on mistake in law.

(*h*) 3 Ersk. 3. § 54. Stirling *v.* E. Lauderdale, 1775; M. 2930. Carrick *v.* Carse, 1778; M. 2931; Hailes, 783. Keith *v.* Grant, 1792; M. 2933.

(*i*) Wilson, *supra* (*c*). See Dixon *v.* Monkland Canal Co., *infra*.

(*k*) Dixon *v.* Monkland Canal Co., 1830; 8 S. 826; aff. 1831, 5 W. & S. 445. Bilbie *v.* Lumley, 2 East, 469; 6 R. R. 479. Rogers *v.* Ingham, 3 Ch. D. 351, and cases in 2 Smith's L. C. 421, 430 sq. Pollock on Contr. 439.

(*l*) Stone *v.* Godfrey, 5 De G. M. & G. 76. *Ex p.* James, L. R. 9 Ch. 609. Rogers *v.* Ingham, *cit.* Addison on Contracts, 429 sqq. Dickson *v.* Halbert, 1854; 16 D. 586. It is doubtful whether the rule, as stated above, is that which accords best with the natural development of our law; but the rule of the English common law was thrust upon us by Lord Brougham; and our judges have not yet had occasion to apply to it the modifications to which it is subject in England, in equity and even at common law. See Smith's L. C., and Addison, *ll.cc.*

535. (4.) *Compromise.*—If the payment have been made in the way of transaction or compromise, 'fairly entered into with full disclosure and good faith,' it is not revocable (*a*) 'on the ground of error, because the transaction is an independent obligation, and the Court will be slow to disturb the quiet which is the result of the agreement. To invalidate such a settlement or recover back a payment so made, mere mistake of law is not enough: it must be shown not merely that the payment was not originally due, but that the compromise was procured by unfair means (*b*).

'(5.) *Judgments.*—On a like ground, the impossibility of carrying on the business of courts of law without some kind of finality, error in fact or law is no ground for restitution against a judgment. Error in fact, though produced by perjury, will not avail. In order to found a reduction, there must be error caused by fraud, as by subornation of perjury, or by deceit or corruption practised on judge or jury (*c*).'

(*a*) Ersk. *ut supra.* Oliver, 1798; noted in Ivory's Erskine, p. 673†; 1 Ill. 328. Simpson *v.* White, 1710; 4 B. Sup. 791.

(*b*) Stewart *v.* Stewart, 1836; 15 S. 112; aff. 1839, Macl. & Rob. 401; 6 Cl. & F. 911 (error of law). De Cordova *v.* De Cordova, 4 App. Ca. 692. Calisher *v.* Bischoffsheim, L. R. 5 Q. B. 449; 39 L. J. Q. B. 181. Kippen *v.* Kippen's Trs., 1874; 1 R. 1171. Brown *v.* Graham, 1848; 10 D. 867; 1849, 11 D. 1330 (*error calculi*). Dickson *v.* Halbert, *cit.* See as to discharges of claims of damages obtained by employers from workpeople, M'Donagh *v.* P. & W. M'Lellan, 1886; 13 R. 1000. Lally *v.* Glasgow Iron Co., 1888; 4 Sh. Ct. R. 67. Park *v.* Dove, 5 *ib.* 19; and by a railway company from a traveller injured, N. B. Ry. Co. *v.* Wood, 1891; 18 R. H. L. 27.

(*c*) See Begg *v.* Begg, 1889; 16 R. 550. See 1 Smith's L. C. 669; 2 *ib.* 754, 770, 788, etc.

536. (6.) *Payment to True Creditor by Wrong Debtor.*—In the Roman law there was no *condictio*, if the person who received the payment was really the creditor, and entitled to receive it, although the payment had been made by one erroneously supposing himself the debtor. This is not law with us; though perhaps in equity—where, in consequence of such negligent proceeding by him who pays, the creditor has been led into some expenditure which may bear hard upon him if obliged to refund; or where, in consideration of the payment, he has foregone some advantage, or given up a security, or liberated his debtor—he ought to be entitled to retain what he has got (*a*).

(*a*) 3 Ersk. 3. § 54. Kerr *v.* Rutherford, 1684; M. 2928; 1 Ill. 328. D. of Argyle *v.* Halcraig's Reprs., 1723; M. 2929. See Chambers *v.* Miller, and Youle *v.* Cochrane, *supra*, § 534. Cathcart *v.* Moodie, 1804; M. Apx. *Heir & Exr.* 2. M'Laren on Wills and Succ. § 2406 Aiken *v.* Short, 1 H. & N. 215; 25 L. J. Ex. 321. Addison on Contr. 430. 2 Smith's L. C. 429 sq.

537. Periculum and Sale.—If restitution be demandable, not of money, but of a thing delivered and received unduly, the thing must be restored in the same condition in which it was received, barring accidents. If it have perished by the receiver's fault, or even without his fault if he have received it *in mala fide*, the value must be restored. If it have been sold *in bonâ fide*, the price must be paid over (*a*).

(*a*) See above, § 529.

III. RECOMPENSE.

538. Where one has gained by the lawful act of another, done without any intention of donation, he is bound to recompense or indemnify that other to the extent of the gain (*a*). '"The obligation of recompense is founded on the consideration that the party making the demand has been put to some expense or some disadvantage, and by reason of that expense or disadvantage there has been a benefit created to the party from whom he makes the demand, of such a kind that it cannot be undone. . . . In every case there must be, in order to ground the claim, the loss to one party resulting in a benefit to the other" (*b*).'

A prominent example of the doctrine occurs where one *in bonâ fide* builds on another's ground 'believing it to be his own.' Although the property of the building passes as an accessory to the owner of the ground, he is liable in recompense to the extent of what he has thus acquired (*c*). 'The recompense due in such cases is measured by the enhanced permanent value of the subjects at the time when the true owner resumes possession, arising (apart from any natural increment of value (*d*)) from improvements executed during the subsistence of *bonâ fide* possession (*e*); but it cannot exceed the sum originally expended (*f*).' But in this matter the doctrine of Lord Stair seems to be carried too far, in giving the benefit of this law of recompense to one who *in mala fide* builds on another's ground (*g*). The case between a liferenter and fiar is peculiar when the rebuilding of a ruined or burnt tenement is in question (*h*).

Meliorations.—Those whose right is merely temporary are presumed to make improvements or additions only for their own conveniency, and so, 'except as the rule is modified on equitable grounds by custom or the peculiar character of the possession (*i*), or by the provisions of the Agricultural Holdings Act (*k*),' have no claim of recompense (*l*). So it is when a tenant builds for his own accommodation (*m*). 'It was laid down in previous editions, that' when a right is prematurely terminated, there seems to be room for a claim of recompense; as when a tenant becomes bankrupt after having erected valuable buildings on his farm (*n*). 'But this must depend on the nature of the right and the circumstances attending it; and it has been formally decided that the doctrine does not apply when a lease is prematurely determined by the tenant's death or other cause, as the possibility of such a termination must have been contemplated by the parties (*o*).' So, on the reduction of conveyances, under which the purchasers have *in bonâ fide* made meliorations, the principle of recompense applies; though there seems to be a distinction between simple fiars and heirs of entail as to right to resort to the land in security (*p*). But one who is only a creditor holding a security over the subject meliorated, is not liable for recompense, or for the cost of meliorations made by order of the proprietor (*q*).

Recompense has been held, under the *Lex*

Rhodia de Jactu, due *quasi ex contractu* to those who suffer by loss of goods, etc., sacrificed at sea for the common safety (*r*).

(*a*) Fernie *v.* Robertson, 1871 ; 9 Macph. 437. Landless *v.* Wilson, 1880 ; 8 R. 289 ; and Rankin *v.* Wither, 1886 ; 13 R. 903. These cases afford authority for the wide rule stated ; and show that the right to recompense has place in various relations not specifically noticed in this paragraph. But cases of so-called recompense are often very like claims on quasi-contracts, *e.g. actio contraria negotiorum gestorum* ; and subject to the general principles laid down here there is a tendency to decide each case on its own circumstances. See Kames's Equity, B. i. ch. iii. § 2. Rankine, Landown. p. 78. See also Reedie *v.* Yeaman, 1875 ; 12 S. L. R. 625 (meliorations by husband on wife's property). Paterson *v.* Greig, 1862 ; 24 D. 1370 (by mother as *pro-tutor* or *negotiorum gestor* on son's property). Fernie *v.* Robertson, *cit.* Buchanan *v.* Stewart, 1874 ; 2 R. 78 (trustee in bankruptcy). Nelson *v.* Gordon, 1874 ; 1 R. 1093 (heritable creditor in possession).

(*b*) *Per* L. Pres. Inglis, Stewart *v.* Steuart, 1878 ; 6 R. 145. See *per* Brett, M. R., in Leigh *v.* Dickson, 15 Q. B. D. 60, 64. Falcke *v.* Scot. Imp. Ins. Co., 34 Ch. D. 234 (payment of premiums to save policy of insurance—lien).

(*c*) 3 Ersk. 1. § 11. Jack *v.* Pollock, 1665 ; M. 13,412 ; 1 Ill. 328. Halket *v.* Watt, 1672 ; M. 13,412. Dchss. of Lauderdale *v.* Steill, 1687 ; 2 B. Sup. 105. Rutherford *v.* Rankine, 1782 ; M. 13,422. See below, § 937. Donell. Com. iv. 33, § 18 sqq. Kames's Pr. of Eq. i. 1. ch. iii. § 2, and iii. ch. i. Rankine, Law of Land Ownership, 78 sqq. Yellowlees *v.* Alexander, 1882 ; 9 R. 765. Mags. of Selkirk *v.* Clapperton, 1830 ; 9 S. 9.

(*d*) Douglas *v.* Douglas's Trs., 1864 ; 2 Macph. 1379, *per* Inglis, J.-C.

(*e*) Authorities in note (*c*). And see York Buildings Co. *v.* Mackenzie, 1793 ; M. 13,367 ; rev. 1795–97, 3 Pat. 378, 579 ; cf. 1 Macq. 481, note.

(*f*) L. 38 D. *de rei vind.* (6. 1). Rankine, p. 84.

(*g*) 1 Stair, 8. § 6. See Rutherford, *supra* (*c*). The text is affirmed in Barbour *v.* Halliday, 1840, 2 D. 1279, where a question, however, was raised as to the right of a *mala fide* possessor, not receiving compensation, to remove the erections he had made. The *mala fide* possessor's right to *impensæ necessariæ*, outlays for the necessary maintenance of the subject, accorded by the Roman law, is not affected by this decision.

(*h*) See below, § 1063.

(*i*) M'Tavish *v.* Fraser, 1790 ; Clarke *v.* Brodie, 1801 ; M'Kay *v.* Brodie, 1801, Hume, 546 sq. 2 Hunter, L. & T. 218, 240.

(*k*) 46 and 47 Vict. c. 62. See below, § 1255 sqq.

(*l*) 2 Stair, 1. § 40. 3 Ersk. 1. § 11. Hodge *v.* Brown, 1664 ; M. 13,400. Hunter, L. & T., *l.c.* See below, § 1052, as to liferenters.

(*m*) See Grant *v.* Macleod, 1857 ; 19 D. 127.

(*n*) See Morton *v.* Montgomerie, 1822 ; 1 S. 322 ; 2 Ill. 203. See Pendreigh's Tr. *v.* Dewar, 1871 ; 9 Macph. 1037.

(*o*) Scott's Exrs. *v.* Hepburn, 1876 ; 3 R. 816. The point was not decided in Morton, *cit.*

(*p*) Binning *v.* Brotherstones, 1676 ; M. 13,401. D. of Gordon *v.* Innes, 1824 ; 3 S. 10. Vans Agnew *v.* E. Stair, 1824 ; *ib.* 229, 531. See, however, Steuart's Trs. *v.* Hart, 1875, 3 R. 192, where there was not *bona fides*, and yet, a conveyance having been reduced by the purchaser, on the ground of essential error known to the seller, there was total restitution on both sides, the purchaser being fully indemnified for his expenditure in building. As to retention, which seems to have been the sole remedy of the *bonâ fide* possessor by Roman law, see Donell. Com. iv. 33, § 22, 23. Beattie *v.* L. Napier, 1831 ; 9 S. 639. York Bdgs. Co. *v.* Mackenzie, *cit.* (*e*).

(*q*) Burns *v.* M'Lellan's Crs., 1735 ; M. 13,402 ; Elch. *Hyp.* 2. Selby's Heirs *v.* Jolly, 1795 ; M. 13,438. See Buchanan *v.* Stewart, 1874 ; 2 R. 78.

(*r*) See this doctrine already considered, § 437 et seq.

539. Remuneration for Services.—Where one has been lawfully employed in services relative to a common subject, he has a right to recompense, in respect of the benefit derived from those services by any one taking advantage of them (*a*). So employment in an office requiring skill and attendance is to be recompensed, although at entering on the employment nothing was said as to salary (*b*). But this does not hold as to a political agent (*c*); nor as to a partner employed in extraordinary labour for the company (*d*).

(*a*) Forbes *v.* Ross & Paterson, 1676 ; M. 13,414. Anderson *v.* Anderson, 1869 ; 8 Macph. 157.

(*b*) M'Evers *v.* Rose, 1761 ; M. 13,435. Smellie *v.* Gillespie, 1833 ; 12 S. 125 ; 1835, 13 S. 700. But see Carmichael *v.* Millar, 1830 ; 8 S. 783. See Hardinge *v.* Clark, 1856 ; 18 D. 612. Pinkerton *v.* Addie, 1864 ; 2 Macph. 1271.

(*c*) Bulman *v.* L. Galloway, 1766 ; M. 13,435.

(*d*) See above, § 370.

IV. NEGOTIORUM GESTIO.

540. Nature of it.—*Negotiorum Gestio* is the management of the affairs of one who is absent, 'or incapacitated from attending to his affairs (*a*),' spontaneously undertaken without his knowledge, and on the presumption that he would, if aware of the circumstances, have given a mandate for such interference. An obligation is hence raised by legal construction, to the effect of indemnifying the *negotiorum gestor* (*b*).

(*a*) Maule or Ker *v.* Graham, *infra* ; Fernie *v.* Robertson, § 538 (*a*).

(*b*) 1 Stair, 8. § 3, 4. 3 Ersk. 3. § 52. 2 Pothier, 819. See Johnston *v.* M. Annandale, 1726 ; M. 9281 ; 1 Ill. 329. See below, § 559.

541. Rules.—The rules of this obligation are, that the *negotiorum gestor* is bound to complete the performance of the act which he has begun, as if he held a proper mandate, unless the principal shall relieve him; to account for his intromissions, and restore all that he has received; and to bestow a degree of care and diligence, altering with circumstances,—subjecting him for *culpa levissima*, if his interference be officious, exclusive, and interested; for *culpa levis* only, if he have interfered in the fair course of friendly intercourse, without very strong necessity; and for no more than *culpa lata*, in cases of necessary interference or sudden emergency (*a*). On the other hand, the person for whom the *negotiorum gestor* interferes is bound to indemnify him for expenditure, necessarily, or usefully, or even reasonably and *in bonâ fide*, laid out (*b*); and to relieve him from all engagements undertaken for his benefit in the course of his interference.

(*a*) 3 Ersk. 3. § 53. Maule or Ker *v.* Graham, 1757; M. 3529; aff. 2 Pat. 13; 1 Ill. 329. See above, § 233, note. Cf. Fulton *v.* Fulton, 1864; 2 Macph. 893. Bannatyne's Trs. *v.* Cunninghame, 1872; 10 Macph. 319.

(*b*) Smith's Heirs *v.* E. Winton, 1714; M. 9275. Campbell *v.* Crs. on the Equivalent, 1725; M. 9276. Fernie *v.* Robertson, 1871; 9 Macph. 437.

CHAPTER XVIII

OF REPARATION OF INJURIES

543. General Rule.—The rights of individuals, either to property or to personal liberty, safety, or reputation, are not only protected by penal law, but in civil law they furnish, when invaded, ground of action for reparation. This class of civil remedies has by lawyers been divided into actions grounded on delict, and actions grounded on something short of delict, but which, to the purposes of civil reparation, is so considered—*quasi* delict. The remedies for injury to the person will be discussed hereafter (*a*). Here it is sufficient to state the general principles of the obligation to repair damage.

(*a*) See § 2028 et seq.

544. Delict.—(1.) *Nature of it.*—A delict is an offence committed with an injurious, fraudulent, or criminal purpose. Criminal law looks to the prevention of delict by punishment, example, and terror, without any view to indemnification; while civil jurisprudence, looking only to indemnification, without regard to punishment or example, raises for this purpose, by construction of law, an obligation to repair the damage occasioned by the delict (*a*).

(*a*) 3 Ersk. 1. § 13. Duff *v.* Bradberry, 1825; 4 S. 23; 1 Ill. 329. Clark *v.* Thomson, 1816; 1 Mur. 161. Gordon *v.* Royal Bank, 1826; 5 S. 164.

545. (2.) *Distinction between Damages for Breach of Contract and Delict.*—There is this difference between the responsibility for damage arising from breach of contract, and the liability for damage occasioned by delict, that the former gives reparation of *direct* damage only (*a*); the latter, the highest advantage which, but for the delict, would have been enjoyed. 'But in the latter case, also, the wrong-doer is properly liable only for such loss as is the natural and probable consequence of his own acts; and although all damages which, under ordinary circumstances, might be expected to result from the wrongful act are recoverable, those which are too remote will be excluded (*b*). It has not been unusual to take the wrong-doer's motives (*e.g.* malice) into account in assessing damages for delicts and *quasi* delicts (*c*); but it may perhaps be held that this is done in England mainly because the law of that country does not, as ours does, admit of a pecuniary payment as *solatium* for wounded feelings. It is clear that damages for injuries to property may generally be ascertained as precisely as damages for breach of contract, and are so dealt with in both countries; while in other cases of delict (and even actions for breach of contract which partake of the character of delict, *e.g.* some cases of personal injury), the estimation of *solatium*, or of compensation for bodily suffering, cannot be readily limited by rules, or made a mere matter of calculation. All that can be said in such cases is, that, subject to the general rules above indicated, and to the caution or reservation that it is frequently if not always impossible and unfair to attempt to give an absolutely perfect pecuniary compensation (*d*), damages are to be such compensation as, under all the circumstances, is fair and reasonable (*e*). Damages are given although it may be impossible to say that the person claiming is out of pocket in any definite sum, as where a harbour authority is deprived by a collision of the use of a dredging machine (*f*).

'(3.) *Motive—Malice.*—It seems a truism to say that reparation can be recovered only for the commission of a wrongful, *i.e.* of an illegal, act. Yet it is only lately decided, after some difference of opinion, that an action in itself lawful does not become unlawful, so as to make the doer liable to an action for damages, because it is done with an evil or malicious motive. Thus a man may exercise his right of diverting subterranean water within his own ground so as to deprive his neighbour of it, although he does so from malicious motives and not in the pursuit of his own interests alone (*g*). And one may "procure" the dismissal of a servant or workman, if he employs no unlawful means, and if the dismissal does not involve the breach of an existing contract (*h*). The rule is, in short, that malice in legal questions depends, not on the motive of the actor, but on the illegal nature of the act which he contemplates and commits (*i*).'

(*a*) See *ante*, § 30 et seq.
(*b*) See above, § 31. Pollock on Torts, 30 sqq. Houldsworth *v.* B. L. Bank, 1850; 13 D. 376. Robertson *v.* Connolly, 1851; 13 D. 779. The Argentino, 13 Pr. D. 191; aff. 14 App. Ca. 519 (damages in collision of ships—loss of future charter-party). Scott's Trs. *v.* Moss, 1889; 17 R. 32 (descent of balloon in field after advertisement).
(*c*) See above, § 32. Mayne on Dam. 23. Cases in § 546 (*a*). It has been held that as the degree of a defender's fault is an element in assessing the damages, evidence of the manner in which an accident has happened, or an injury been inflicted, is not to be excluded by an admission of liability. Morton (Cooley's Factor) *v.* E. & G. Ry. Co., 1845; 8 D. 288. Dobie *v.* Aberdeen Ry. Co., 1856; 18 D. 862. Cunningham *v.* Duncan & Jamieson, 1889; 16 R. 383.
(*d*) Phillips *v.* L. and S.-W. Ry. Co., 5 Q. B. D. 78; 49 L. J. Q. B. 233.
(*e*) Phillips, *cit.* Mayne, *cit.* H. Smith on Negl. 13 sq., 175 sq. Below, § 552. Damages for death or personal injury are not reduced by sums paid under a policy of insurance. Hicks *v.* Newport, etc., Ry. Co., 4 B. & S. 403. Bradburn *v.* G. W. Ry. Co., 44 L. J. C. P. 9; L. R. 10 Ex. 1. Yates *v.* Whyte, 4 Bing. N. C. 272. But this is subject to the insurer's claim to a portion of the damages recovered.
(*f*) Owners of Sand Pump Dredger *v.* S.S. Greta Holme, 1897; A. C. 596.
(*g*) Mayor of Bradford *v.* Pickles, 1895; 1 Ch. 145; aff. 1895, A. C. 587. See below, § 966, 969.
(*h*) **Allen** *v.* **Flood**, 1898; A. C. 1; revg. 1895, 2 Q. B. 91.
(*i*) *Per* Lord Watson, in Allen *v.* Flood, p. 94.

546. (4.) *Action and Title.*—The civil action for reparation grounded on delict is not, like the penal action in criminal law, confined to the delinquent. The wrong-doer's representative is liable for reparation 'so far as he has assets (*in quantum lucratus est*)'; in which we follow the rule of the canon rather than of the civil law (*a*). 'It has sometimes been thought that, when a claim for damages and *solatium* on account of personal injury arises, it vests *ipso facto* and *ipso jure* by the commission of the injury, and being a debt passes to the legal representatives of the sufferer. It has now been decided that, unless there has been patrimonial loss, *i.e.* direct injury to the estate passing to the executor, no action is competent to him (*b*). On the other hand, if the injured person has raised action against the delinquent, the usual effect of litiscontestation follows, and on the pursuer's death his executor may insist in the action (*c*). The law on this point has been of late development, because of the practice of our Courts to allow action by certain relatives of deceased persons against those who wrongfully or negligently caused the death, not in a representative capacity, but in their own right. This right is limited to the lawful (*d*) children or parents, husband or wife, of the deceased (*e*).

'When one has received reparation, or has brought an action to judgment, for a delict, he cannot again sue on the ground of a subsequent increase or development of the damages. The prospective damages ought to be assessed once for all, for "*nemo debet bis vexari pro unâ et eâdem causâ*" (*f*). On the same principle, the executor or relatives of one who has raised an action of damages for personal injury, and afterwards dies in consequence of the injury, cannot raise a separate action for his own loss by the pursuer's death (*g*). Different relatives cannot raise simultaneous or concurrent actions, and a married woman cannot sue for the death of a child, her husband being the proper pursuer (*h*).

'When two persons have been injured by the same wrong, they may insist for damages in the same action, the summons applying the claim to the pursuers separately, and asking separate sums of damages (*i*).'

(*a*) 3 Ersk. 1. § 15 *in fin.* M'Naughton *v.* Robertson, Feb. 17, 1809; F. C.; 1 Ill. 330. Morrison *v.* Cameron, May 25, 1809; F. C. Tulloch *v.* Davidson, 1858; 20 D. 1045; aff. 1860, 3 Macq. 783. Evans *v.* Stool, 1885; 12 R. 1295. 4 Inst. 12. 1. Dig. 47. 10. 13. As to the maxim *Actio personalis moritur cum personâ*, see the cases cited in this and following notes. Broom's Legal Maxims. Pollock on Torts, p. 52 sqq. Peek *v.* Gurney, L. R. 6 H. L. 377; 43 L. J. Ch. 19; and Hatchard *v.* Mège, 18 Q. B. D. 771.

(*b*) Bern's Exr. *v.* Montrose Asylum, 1893; 20 R. 859. Auld *v.* Shairp, 1874; 2 R. 191.

(*c*) Hagart's Tr. *v.* Hope, June 1, 1821; F. C.; 2 Sh. App. 125. Neilson *v.* Rodger, 1853; 16 D. 325. Green *v.* Borthwick, 1896; 24 R. 211 (br. of promise—decl. of marriage).

(*d*) Weir *v.* Coltness Iron Co., 1889; 16 R. 614 (mother cannot sue for death of bastard). Clarke *v.* Carfin Coal Co., 1891; A. C. 412; 18 R. H. L. 63.

(*e*) Eistens *v.* N. B. Ry. Co., 1870; 8 M. 980. Greenhorns *v.* Addie & Miller, 1855; 17 D. 860. Horn *v.* N. B. Ry. Co., 1878; 5 R. 1055.

In England there is no claim of damages for the death of a relative by fault or negligence, except under statute. 9 and 10 Vict. c. 93 (Lord Campbell's Act); 27 and 28 Vict. c. 95. See Addison, Torts, 608.

(*f*) Guthrie Smith on Damages, 41. Addison on Torts, 767 sqq. Authorities in Brunsden *v.* Humphrey, 14 Q. B. D. 141, which seems to introduce a questionable exception. The right to sue a second action for a continuing nuisance, and to sue on a subsequent subsidence of land due to the same mining operation, are hardly exceptions to the rule. See below, § 965.

(*g*) Darling *v.* Gray & Sons, 1891; 18 R. 1164; aff. 1892, A. C. 576; 119 R. H. L. 31.

(*h*) Whitehead *v.* Blaik, 1893; 20 R. 1045. Darling *v.* Gray, *cit.* As to claims for slander, etc., of undischarged bankrupt, and trustee's right, see Thom *v.* Bridges, 1857; 19 D. 721. Jackson *v.* M'Kechnie, 1875; 3 R. 130; of wife, *infra*, § 1610. As to the measure of damages where party injured has died after raising an action, see M'Master *v.* Cal. Ry. Co., 1885; 13 R. 252.

(*i*) Harkes *v.* Mowat, 1864; 24 D. 701. Mitchell *v.* Grierson, 1894; 21 R. 367.

547. (5.) *Responsibility of Master for Delict 'or Quasi Delict' of Servant.*—Distinctions are necessary as to the responsibility of a master, or of one having authority, for the delicts of servants. If a master give express directions, in obeying which damage is done, he is liable for it. Where something is directed to be done, or is in the common line of the servant's duty, but no special directions are given, the servant's act, and even his exercise of discretion, is the act and discretion of the master, and he is liable (*a*). Where the master has not ordered or authorised the thing to be done, and especially where he has forbidden it, he is not liable; 'but so long as the servant is acting within the general scope of his employment, a prohibition as to the manner or place of doing an act within that employment does not relieve the master from liability for the servant's negligence (*b*).' And if the servant wilfully or maliciously do an injurious act, 'for his own private ends, and so as in doing it to divest himself of the character of servant,' his master will not be liable (*c*). 'And as no master is presumed to authorise his servant to do an illegal act, he will not be liable for a crime or fraud committed by his servant, though in the course of his business, unless with his knowledge his business be benefited by it (*d*). A person is not liable for the negligent acts of a tradesman or independent contractor employed by him, committed during the course of the work (*e*).'

(*a*) Baird *v.* Graham, 1852; 14 D. 615. Hill *v.* Merricks, 1813; Hume, 397. Mackintosh *v.* Mackintosh, 1864; 2 Macph. 1357. Baldwin *v.* Casella, 41 L. J. Ex. 167; L. R. 7 Ex. 325. Below, § 2031. Martin *v.* Wards, 1887; 14 R. 814 (servant assuming work beyond line of his ordinary duty).

(*b*) Fraser *v.* Younger & Son, 1867; 5 Macph. 861. L. Keith *v.* Keir, *infra* (*c*). Limpus *v.* London Omn. Co., 1 H. & C. 526; 32 L. J. Ex. 34. Ward *v.* Gen. Omn. Co., 42 L. J. C. P. 265. Stevens *v.* Woodward, 6 Q. B. D. 318; 50 L. J. Q. B. 231. Betts *v.* De Vitre, L. R. 3 Ch. 423; 37 L. J. Ch. 325. Black and Percival, *infra* (*e*).

(*c*) 3 Ersk. 1. § 15. Ld. Keith *v.* Keir, June 10, 1812; F. C.; 1 Ill. 330. See as to the report of this case, Baird *v.* Hamilton, 1826; 4 S. 790. **Linwood** *v.* **Hathorn**, May 14, 1817; F. C.; 1821, 1 Sh. Ap. 20; 3 Bligh, 193; 22 R. R. 8. Thornburn *v.* Ellis, May 24, 1811; F. C. M'Kenzie *v.* M'Leod, 10 Bing. 385. M'Manus *v.* Cricket, 1 East, 106. Campbell *v.* Barry, 1748; M. 10,071; 1 Ill. 87. See below, § 554, 2031. Dalrymple *v.* M'Gill, 1804; Hume, 387. Mitchell *v.* Crasweller, 13 C. B. 237; 22 L. J. C. P. 100. Storey *v.* Ashton, 38 L. J. Q. B. 223; L. R. 4 Q. B. 476. Baird, *cit.* Hunter *v.* E. & G. Canal Co., 1836; 14 S. 717. **Reid** *v.* **Bartonshill Coal Co.**, 1855; 17 D. 1017; H. of L. 20 D. 13; 3 Macq. 266. Fraser, M. & S. Ch. xiii., and 1 Smith's L. C. 383.

(*d*) Waldie *v.* D. Roxburghe, 1822; 1 S. 322; aff. 1825, 1 W. & S. 1. Wardrope *v.* D. Hamilton, 1876; 3 R. 876. Limpus and Ward, *citt.* Lyons *v.* Martin, 8 A. & E. 512. Clydesdale Bank *v.* Paul, 1877; 4 R. 626. Cf. Poulton *v.* L. & N.-W. Ry. Co., L. R. 2 Q. B. 534; 36 L. J. Q. B. 294. Young *v.* Colt's Trs., 1832; 10 S. 666. Lundie *v.* MacBrayne, 1894; 21 R. 1085.

(*e*) **M'Lean** *v.* **Russel**, 1849; 11 D. 1035; 12 D. 887; 3 Ross' L. C. 181. N. B. Ry. Co. *v.* Leadburn Ry. Co., 1865; 3 Macph. 343. Nisbett *v.* Dixon, 1852; 14 D. 973. Stephen *v.* Thurso Comrs., 1876; 3 R. 535. Quarman *v.* Burnett, 6 M. & W. 499 (jobmaster). Anderson *v.* Glas. Tramway Co., 1893; 21 R. 318. Rapson *v.* Cubitt, 9 M. & W. 710. Butler *v.* Hunter, 7 H. & N. 826; 31 L. J. Ex. 214. Reedie *v.* L. & N.-W. Ry. Co., 4 Ex. 244. Ellis *v.* Sheffield Gas Co., 2 E. & B. 767. Taylor *v.* Greenhalgh, L. R. 9 Q. B. 487; 43 L. J. Q. B. 168. But notwithstanding the employment of a contractor, the employer remains liable himself where he has a personal duty resting upon him, as by statute, by the possession of property upon which he causes hazardous operations to be performed (see Percival *v.* Hughes, 51 L. J. Q. B. 388; 52 L. J. Q. B. 719; 9 Q. B. D. 441; 8 App. Ca. 443. Black *v.* Christchurch Fin. Co., 1894; A. C. 48), or by contract express or implied (Francis *v.* Cockerell, L. R. 5 Q. B. 501; 39 L. J. Q. B. 291. Rourke *v.* White Moss Coll. Co., 2 C. P. D. 205).

547A. (6.) '*Fault of Master or of Fellow-Servants.*—It is a rule of law that the master who employs a servant (not an agent) is responsible to persons outside his business for the fault or negligence of that servant in matters in which he is employed, and this rule is expressed in the maxim *Qui facit per alium facit per se.* But a series of decisions has settled this exception, that a master or employer is not so liable to a fellow-servant, because the fellow-servant in entering the employment contemplates and undertakes the natural and ordinary risks of the employment, and one of these risks is the possible negligence of a fellow-servant who has been selected with due care by the employer (*a*). A foreman, or manager (*b*), or the master of a ship, appointed by the employer (*c*), is a fellow-servant with the workmen or seamen under him, in the sense of the rule; although the Scotch Courts, until overruled, distinguished where the fault was that of such a superior servant, or "deputy master" "representing" the master (*d*).

'The defence of common employment is available only when the defender (*i.e.* the person sought to be made liable for the fault of his servant) can show that the pursuer was in his service. The exemption depends on the relations between the three parties, and there is no room for it where there is no legal relation of which the workman's undertaking can be an implied term. Hence certain cases have been overruled in which the servants of independent contractors working towards the same end, such as the building of a house, were held to be fellow-servants with each other and with the servants of the employer, in a common employment (*e*).

'On the other hand, as the exemption rests on an implied contract to take the risk of negligence of those employed by the same employer in the same work or undertaking, it is not limited to the case where the injured party is able to see and calculate the hazards to which he is exposed. All persons employed under the same employer for the purposes of the same business, however different their duties and although the departments in which they are engaged are quite distinct, are within the meaning of the rule, so that, *e.g.*, porters at a railway station are fellow-workmen with the company's platelayers making repairs on the line, or carpenters working on the roof of an engine-shed (*f*). But it follows from the terms in which the principle is stated that an employer who carries on businesses quite distinct in character or in locality or in both, may not be exempt from liability for the fault of a servant in one concern, by which one of his servants in another has been injured; for example, if a man is both a banker and a brewer, and his bank clerk is run over by his drayman. In such a case there is not a common employment for the same general purpose. It has been held that the seamen in two ships belonging to the same owner, which come into collision at sea or in a river, are not in a common employment in the sense of the rule (*g*).

'A master is still liable in reparation to a servant if he has personally failed to use reasonable care in carrying on the work, in furnishing the machinery or material used, in keeping the machinery in proper repair, in selecting his managers and other servants or in organising the work (defective system) (*h*).

'A master is not answerable, except under the Workmen's Compensation Act, 1897, for injuries to which the servant has contributed by his own fault (see § 2031), or which the servant was equally able with his employer to foresee and guard against, or which occur without fault in a necessarily dangerous employment which the servant has undertaken with full knowledge of all the risks (*i*). But when an accident occurs by breakdown of plant or machinery, a defect may often be inferred from the circumstances; and when this is so, and when it is proved that the defect could have been discovered by proper inspection (*k*), the employer has to discharge the onus of showing that it occurred without his fault (*l*).

'*Volenti non fit injuria.*—The doctrine of common employment may almost be regarded as a development of the principle expressed by the maxim *Volenti non fit injuria,* which has a wider application and is not confined to questions between masters and servants. The maxim would require distinct and separate notice, if space permitted. But here, as in the whole subject of reparation of injuries, it is impossible to deal with details, and it is undesirable to classify the multitude of cases reported with no apparent utility. In questions between employer and employed, the maxim imports that the latter expressly or by implication agreed to take upon himself the risks attending the particular work which he was engaged to do, and in doing which he has been injured. The mere fact of his knowing the danger and continuing at his work does not always infer his acceptance of the risk; and the question whether he has done so is one of fact and not of law (*m*).'

(*a*) **Reid** *v.* **Bartonshill Coal Co.**, 1855; 17 D. 1017; revd. 1858, 3 Macq. 268.

(*b*) **Wilson** *v.* **Merry & Cunningham**, 1867; 5 Macph. 807; aff. 1867, 6 Macph. H. L. 85; L. R. 1 Sc. App. 326.

(*c*) Hedley *v.* Pinkney & Sons, 1893; A. C. 222. Leddy *v.* Gibson, 1873; 11 Macph. 304.

(*d*) See, *e.g.*, Brownlie *v.* Macaulay, 1860; 22 D. 975. Sommerville *v.* Gray, 1863; 1 Macph. 768.

(*e*) **Johnson** *v.* **Lindsay & Co.**, 1891; A. C. 371, overruling Woodhead *v.* Gartness Mineral Co., 1877; 4 R. 469. Maguire *v.* Russel, 1885; 12 R. 1071. Congleton *v.* Angus, 1887; 14 R. 309. Wingate *v.* Monkland Iron Co., 1884; 12 R. 91; and restoring Gregory *v.* Hill, 1869; 8 Macph. 282. See M'Callum *v.* N. B. Ry., 1893; 20 R. 385. Cameron *v.* Nystrom, 1893; A. C. 308 (stevedore and shipowner—see also Union S.S. Co. *v.* Claridge, *infra*). It seems still to be possible that the servant of A. may, on a particular occasion and for a particular purpose, become the servant of B., notwithstanding that he continues in A.'s service, and is paid by him. See Union S.S. Co. *v.* Claridge (P. C.), 1894; A. C. 185. Cairns *v.* Clyde Trs. 1898; 25 R. 1021. At least Rourke *v.* White Moss Coll. Co., 2 C. P. D. 205; 46 L. J. Q. B. 283, and Murray *v.* Currie, L. R. 6 C. P. 24; 40 L. J. C. P. 27, have not been overruled.

(*f*) Morgan *v.* Vale of Neath Ry. Co., L. R. 1 Q. B. 149; 35 L. J. Q. B. 23. *Secus*, if a railway accident be caused by a train belonging to a different company from that in whose employment the person injured is. Warburton *v.* G. W. Ry. Co., 36 L. J. Ex. 9; L. R. 2 Ex. 30. Swanson *v.* N.-E. Ry. Co., 3 Ex. D. 341; 47 L. J. Ex. 372. Adams *v.* G. & S.-W. Ry. Co., 1875; 3 R. 215. A pilot in a compulsory pilotage district is not excluded by this rule from recovering damages from the shipowner for the negligence of his servants. Smith *v.* Steele, 44 L. J. Q. B. 60; L. R. 10 Q. B. 125.

(*g*) The Petrel, 1893; P. D. 321.

(*h*) See below, note (*i*), and § 2031. Macaulay *v.* Buist, 1846; 9 D. 245. Stark *v.* M'Laren, 1871; 10 Macph. 31. Wilson, *supra* (*b*). Sneddon *v.* Mossend Iron Co., 1876; 3 R. 868. M'Killop *v.* N. B. Ry., 1895; 23 R. 768. Grant *v.* Drysdale, 1883; 10 R. 1159. Fraser *v.* Fraser, 1882; 9 R. 896. Walker *v.* Olsen, 1882; 9 R. 946. Welsh *v.* Moir, 1884; 12 R. 590 (machine put to improper use—latent defect). Gibson *v.* Nimmo, 1895; 22 R. 491 (defective system). Macdougall *v.* Udston Co., 1896; 23 R. 505 (do.). Sword *v.* Cameron, 1839; 1 D. 493 (do.). Reid *v.* Bartonshill Co., *sup.* (*a*) (do.).

(*i*) Robertson *v.* Adamson, 1862; 24 D. 1231. Cook *v.* Bell, 1857; 20 D. 137. Crichton *v.* Keir, 1863; 1 Macph. 407. Pollock *v.* Cassidy, 1870; 8 Macph. 615. Senior *v.* Ward, 1 E. & E. 385. Woodley *v.* Metr. Ry. Co., 2 Ex. D. 384; 46 L. J. Ex. 521. M'Gee *v.* Eglinton Iron Co., 1883; 10 R. 955. Wilson *v.* Wishaw Coal Co., 1833; 10 R. 1021. Grant *v.* Drysdale, 1883; 10 R. 1159. Rooney *v.* Allans, 1883; 10 R. 1224. Fraser and Walker, *citt.* (*h*). Macfarlan *v.* Thompson & Co., 1884; 12 R. 232. Fraser *v.* Hood, 1887; 15 R. 178 (vicious horse). M'Ternan *v.* White & Bee, 1890; 17 R. 368 (continuing to work with drunken fellow-workman). There are cases in which the servant's knowledge of the circumstances leads rather to the inference that there was no danger and no fault. *E.g.* Watt *v.* Neilson & Co., 1888; 15 R. 772. Mulligan *v.* M'Alpine, 1888; 15 R. 789. Fraser, M. & S. Ch. x. part 1. Robb *v.* Bulloch, Lade, & Co., 1892; 19 R. 971.

(*k*) Gavin *v.* Rogers, 1889; 17 R. 206.

(*l*) Comp. § 164, 170, 553 (*a*). Fraser *v.* Fraser, and Walker *v.* Olsen, *citt.* (*h*).

(*m*) **Smith** *v.* **Baker**, 1891; A. C. 325. Wallace *v.* Culter Paper Co., 1892; 19 R. 925. Smith *v.* W. Forbes & Co., 1897; 24 R. 699. Wilkinson *v.* Kinneil Coal Co., 1897; 24 R. 1001 (attempt to save life). Thomas *v.* Quatermaine, § 547B (*h*). Yarmouth *v.* France, § 547B (*f*).

547B. (7.) '*Employers' Liability Act*, 1880.—The House of Lords having carried the doctrine stated in the previous section beyond reason, the rule which the Scotch Courts had previously adopted (*a*) was, subject to several limitations, restored by statute from 1st January 1881 (*b*); viz. that an employer is answerable to his servants for the negligence of those to whom he delegates his authority.

'By this Act a workman (*i.e.* any railway servant, and any one to whom the Employers and Workmen Act, 1875, applies (*c*)), "or in case the injury results in death, his legal personal representatives and any persons entitled in case of death" (*d*), have, in the enumerated cases, the same right of compensation and remedies against the employer as if the workman had not been in the service of the employer or engaged in his work (*e*), unless he knew of the defect or negligence which caused the injury and failed to give information of it to his employer or some one in authority, or was aware that the employer or such person already knew of such defect or negligence (*f*); or unless he have contracted not to claim under the Act (*g*). The defence of contributory negligence, and also that founded on the maxim *Volenti non fit injuria* (known danger), are not taken away by the Act (*h*). But the latter cannot be pleaded where the injury arises from the employer's breach of a statutory regulation (*i*). The cases in which this right is given are: Where personal injury is caused to a workman

'(1.) "By reason of any defect in the condition of the ways, works, machinery, or plant connected with or used in the business of the employer" (*k*), provided always that "the defect arose from, or had not been discovered or remedied owing to the negligence of the employer, or of some person in the service of the employer, and entrusted by him with the duty of seeing that the ways, works, machinery, or plant were in proper condition" (*l*).

'(2.) "By reason of the negligence of any person in the service of the employer who has any superintendence entrusted to him, whilst in the exercise of such superintendence"; such person being defined as "a person whose sole or principal duty is that of superintendence, and who is not ordinarily engaged in manual labour" (*m*).

'(3.) "By reason of the negligence of any person in the service of the employer to whose orders or directions the workman at the time of the injury was bound to conform, and did conform, where such injury resulted from his having so conformed" (*n*).

'(4.) "By reason of the act or omission of any person in the service of the employer, done or made in obedience to the rules or bye-laws of the employer, or in obedience to particular instructions given by any person delegated with the authority of the employer in that behalf" (*o*), provided always that the injury resulted from some impropriety or defect in such rules, bye-laws, or instructions, not being a rule or bye-law approved or accepted by a department of Government under or by virtue of any Act of Parliament (*p*).

'(5.) "By reason of the negligence of any person in the service of the employer who has the charge or control of any signal, points, locomotive engine, or train upon a railway" (*q*).

'In order to give a right of action under the Act, notice of the injury, stating the name and address of the person injured, and the cause and date of the injury, must be given in the way specified within six weeks, and the action must be commenced within six months, or in case of death within twelve months, from the occurrence of the accident (*r*). The amount recoverable is limited to the estimated earnings, for three years preceding the injury, of a person in like employment in the district (*s*); and the action must be brought in the Sheriff Court, though it may be removed to the Court of Session for jury trial (*t*).'

(*a*) Macaulay *v.* Brownlie, 1860; 22 D. 975. Sommerville *v.* Gray & Co., 1863; 1 Macph. 768. Wilson *v.* Merry & Cunningham, *cit.*

(*b*) 43 and 44 Vict. c. 42.

(*c*) This definition excludes domestic or menial servants, and all persons, such as clerks, shopmen, time-keepers, watchmen, who are not engaged in manual labour; 38 and 39 Vict. c. 90, § 10; also, it would seem, such persons as omnibus or tramway conductors and drivers (Morgan *v.* Gen. Omn. Co., 13 Q. B. D. 832. Cook *v.* Metr. Tram. Co., 18 Q. B. D. 683; the contrary opinions of two judges in Wilson *v.* Glas. Tram. Co., 1898; 5 R. 981, being unnecessary to the judgment); and seamen, see *ib.* § 13; 43 and 44 Vict. c. 16, § 11. Fraser, M. & S. 237-8; but not firemen or stokers in canal boats exclusively employed in canal navigation. Oakes *v.* Monkland Iron Co., 1884; 10 R. 579.

(*d*) See above, § 546; below, § 2030. Fraser, M. & S. 218.

(*e*) 43 and 44 Vict. c. 42, § 1. It is a necessary condition that the relation of employer and employee subsists between the person injured and the defender. So one employed by a contractor cannot sue the principal. Nicolson *v.* Macandrew & Co., 1888; 15 R. 854. Robertson *v.* Russell, 1885; 12 R. 634. Sweeney *v.* Duncan & Co., 1892; 19 R. 870. Compare Morrison *v.* Baird & Co., 1882; 10 R. 271.

(*f*) *Ib.* § 2, subs. 3. See above, § 547A *fin.* M'Monagle *v.* Baird & Co., 1881; 9 R. 364. Haston *v.* Edinburgh Tramways Co., 1887; 14 R. 624 (horses are plant—sufferer's knowledge of defect). Fraser *v.* Hood, 1887; 15 R. 178 (do.). Wilson *v.* Boyle, 1889; 17 R. 62. Yarmouth *v.* France, 19 Q. B. D. 647 (do.). Weblin *v.* Ballard, 17 Q. B. D. 122.

(*g*) Griffiths *v.* E. of Dudley, 51 L. J. Q. B. 543; 9 Q. B. D. 357. Wright *v.* Howard, Baker, & Co., 1893; 21 R. 25 (contract by notices).

(*h*) Thomas *v.* Quartermaine, 17 Q. B. D. 414; 18 Q. B. D. 685. See above, § 547A *fin.*

(*i*) Baddeley *v.* E. Granville, 19 Q. B. D. 423.

(*k*) Act, § 1, subs. 1. M'Giffin *v.* Palmer's Shipbdg. Co., 10 Q. B. D. 5 (condition of the ways—accidental obstruction). M'Quade *v.* Dixon, 1887; 14 R. 1039. Howe *v.* Mark, Finch, & Co., 17 Q. B. D. 187 (not works in course of construction). Robinson *v.* Watson, 1892; 20 R. 144 (railway co.'s waggons at colliery). Simpson *v.* Burrell & Paton, 1896; 23 R. 590 (stevedore not responsible for defect in ship—not being bound to inspect). Maclachlan *v.* Peveril Co., 1896; *ib.* 753. M'Multy *v.* Primrose, 1897; 24 R. 442 (stair in unfinished house—injury to bricklayer). Ferris *v.* Cowdenbeath Coal Co., 1897; 24 R. 615 (manhole in coal-pit part of way).

(*l*) Act, § 2, subs. 1. Fraser *v.* Fraser, 1882; 9 R. 896. Walsh *v.* Whiteley, 21 Q. B. D. 371 (mere fact that machine is dangerous to workman employed to work it not a "defect" unless it implies negligence of master; L. Esher, M. R., *diss.* See Bruce *v.* Barclay, 1890; 17 R. 811. Robb *v.* Bulloch, Lade, & Co., 1892; 19 R. 971).

(*m*) Act, § 1, subs. 2, and § 8. Shaffers *v.* Gen. St. Nav. Co., 10 Q. B. D. 356. Osborne *v.* Jackson, 11 Q. B. D. 619 (foreman assisting in manual labour; comp. M'Manus, *infra*, and Kellard *v.* Rooke, 21 Q. B. D. 367). Macleod *v.* Pirie, 1893; 20 R. 381 ("estate manager").

(*n*) Sec. 1, subs. 3. M'Manus *v.* Hay, 1882; 9 R. 425. Dolan *v.* Anderson & Lyell, 1885; 12 R. 804. Sweeney *v.* M'Gilvray, 1886; 14 R. 105.

(*o*) Sec. 1, subs. 4.

(*p*) Sec. 2, subs. 2.

(*q*) Sec. 1, subs. 5. As to the question whether "railway" includes tramway, see Fraser, M. & S. 235. Doughty *v.* Firbank, 10 Q. B. D. 358. Gibbs *v.* G. W. Ry. Co., 11 Q. B. D. 22 (charge or control of points).

(*r*) Act, § 4 and 7. Moyle *v.* Jenkins, 51 L. J. Q. B. 113; 8 Q. B. D. 116. Keen *v.* Millwall Dock Co., 51 L. J. Q. B. 277; 8 Q. B. D. 482. Stone *v.* Hyde, 51 L. J. Q. B. 452; 9 Q. B. D. 76. Thomson *v.* Robertson & Co., 1884; 12 R. 121 (notice). Clark *v.* Adams, 1885; 12 R. 1092. M'Govan *v.* Tancred, Arrol, & Co., 1886; 13 R. 1033 (notice, how proved). Trail *v.* Kelman, 1887; 15 R. 4.

(*s*) Act, § 3.

(*t*) Act, § 6. M'Avoy *v.* Young's Paraffin Co., 1881; 9 R. 100. Morrison *v.* Baird & Co., *cit.* (*e*).

547C. (8.) '*Workmen's Compensation Act*, 1897.—From 1st July 1898 employers of workmen on railways, in factories, mines, quarries, and engineering works, whether they or their representatives are guilty of negligence or wrong-doing or not, are made liable, under the conditions stated in the Act, to pay compensation to their workmen for accidental injuries arising out of or in the course of the employment. If the injury is attributable to the serious and wilful misconduct (which is not mere "contributory fault") of the workman, any compensation claimed is disallowed. Special machinery is provided for working the provisions of this remarkable statute, which is only saved from being revolutionary and tyrannical by the possibility under the conditions of modern life of insuring (*a*).'

(*a*) 61 and 62 Vict. c. 37. A. of S., June 3, 1898.

548. (9.) *Effect of a Penalty.*—The imposition of a penalty by statute is no discharge of the civil claim for reparation, 'at least if it exist independently of the statute, or if the statute imposes a duty which has not been fulfilled' (*a*).

(*a*) 3 Ersk. 1. § 14. See above, § 36; and cases there in note (*c*) *in fine*.

549. (10.) *Effect of Impracticability of Restoration.*—Where exact restoration is impracticable, damages are due, to be ascertained by the verdict of a jury.

550. (11.) *Joint and Several Liability.*—Although in criminal law each party is liable only to his own punishment, in civil reparation, the partners or associates in a crime perpetrated by united counsels and means, are liable *singuli in solidum*, unless the acts are distinct (*a*). 'The rule is extended to claims arising from *quasi* delicts; although it is thought to be contrary to principle and inconvenient in its application to acts or omissions which are not tainted with fraud or moral delinquency (*b*). Under this rule it has been held that a discharge granted to one wrong-doer for a partial payment or satisfaction, not being a renunciation of the whole claim, does not liberate the others (*c*); and in England that judgment against one of several joint delinquents, though unsatisfied, is a bar, for reasons of public policy, to an action against the others (*d*).

'*Relief among Wrong-doers.*—There is no contribution or relief among wrong-doers (*e*). It has, however, been decided that in Scotland one who has paid damages to the person injured under a joint and several decree is not precluded from obtaining relief against his co-debtors, for in doing so he founds only on the decree, and does not need to go behind it or found on the joint wrong (*f*). The rule applies alike whether the wrong is a delict or a *quasi* delict, a crime or merely a negligent omission. But weighty opinions distinguish in favour of the case of those whose liability has not arisen from conscious and therefore moral wrong, and who are not to be disabled from recovering against co-delinquents; and that whether it has been brought to judgment or not (*g*).'

(*a*) 1 Stair, 9. § 5. Hay *v.* Elphinstone, 1763; M. 14,658; 1 Ill. 330. D. of Athole *v.* Dalgleish, 1822; 1 S. 511. 3 Ersk. 1. 15. Smith *v.* O'Reilly, 1800; Hume, 605. M'Donnell *v.* Macdonald, 1813; 2 Dow, 66. Bannerman *v.* Fenwicks, 1817; 1 Mur. 252. **E. Kinnoull** *v.* **Ferguson,** 1841; 3 D. 778; aff. 1 Bell's App. 652; 9 Cl. & F. 251. North British Ry. Co. *v.* Leadburn Ry. Co., 1865; 3 Macph. 340. Leslie *v.* Lumsden, 1848; 14 D. 213. **Western Bank** *v.* **Douglas, etc.,** 1860; 22 D. 448, 475. Croskery *v.* Gilmour's Trs., 1890; 17 R. 697. If different defenders are called in one action for different delicts, they cannot be sued conjunctly and severally for a slump sum of damages; but separate sums must be concluded for. Barr *v.* Neilsons, 1868; 6 Macph. 651. Taylor *v.* M'Dougall, 1885; 12 R. 1304.

(*b*) See Palmer *v.* Wick, etc., S.S. Co., *infra* (*f*), *per* L. Watson.

(*c*) Western Bank *v.* Bairds, 1862; 24 D. 859. See Delaney *v.* Stirling, 1893; 20 R. 506.

(*d*) King *v.* Hoare, 13 M. & W. 494; 14 L. J. Ex. 29. Brinsmead *v.* Harrison, L. R. 7 C. P. 547; 40 L. J. C. P. 190.

(*e*) Dig. xxvii. 3. 1. § 13, 14 (de tutelæ, etc.). "Nec enim ulla societas maleficiorum, vel communicatio justa damni ex maleficio est."

(*f*) **Palmer** *v.* **Wick & Pulteneytown S.S. Co.,** 1893; 20 R. 275; aff. 1894, A. C. 318; 21 R. H. L. 39.

(*g*) Opp. in Palmer, *cit.* See Croskery *v.* Gilmour's Trs. and Western Bank *v.* Douglas, *citt.* Gardiner *v.* Main, 1894; 22 R. 100. See Pollock on Torts, 170. 1 Smith's L. C. 168; 2 *ib.* 546. Savigny, Obligationen-Recht, i. 256 sqq.

551. (12.) *Effect of Punishment on Civil Remedy.*—The punishment of the crime does not extinguish the civil claim of damage, except where the punishment is capital (*a*).

(*a*) 1 Hume, 279. Foster's Criminal Law, 287. Kames's Law Tracts, Tr. 1.

552. (13.) *Solatium.*—Reparation includes not merely the pecuniary loss, but also a *solatium* for injury (*a*).

(*a*) Black *v.* Cadell, 1804; M. 13,905; aff. 5 Paton, 567; 1 Ill. 331. Brown *v.* M'Gregor, Feb. 26, 1813; F. C. See Greenhorn *v.* Addie, 1855; 17 D. 860. Evans *v.* Stool, *supra*, § 546.

553. Quasi Delict.—(1.) *Nature of it.*—Gross negligence or imprudence, though it should bear no such character of fraud, malice, or criminal purpose as to subject the person to criminal cognisance, is, as a ground for an action for damages, held as a delict, to the effect of making the person guilty of the imprudence or negligence liable to indemnify the person who suffers by the fault. These are by lawyers called *quasi* delicts (*a*).

Injury 'by which the author here means "harm" or damage' to the property of another (even where it appears that extraordinary vigilance and skill might have prevented loss) will not ground an action of damages: 'that is to say, there is often *damnum sine injuria*, and damages will be given only when there is a legal wrong, an invasion of another's right; in other words, a breach of duty (*b*). The duties which have to be considered in questions of this kind are infinitely various, and the most general statement of those which do not arise out of contract, have not the sanction of the criminal law, and breaches of which are described as *quasi* delicts or negligence, is that they arise from the possession of property or from the relations of life (§ 2026 sqq.), or are imposed by statute. It is a *quasi* delict or negligence when a man unintentionally, *i.e.* without malice or fraud, but from want of care, interferes with the rights of another so as to cause him to suffer loss. So (*c*)'—

(2.) '*Collision of Ships.*'—If negligence or want of competent skill be shown, as in cases of collision of ships (*d*); as to which the rules are 'now contained in "Regulations for preventing Collisions at Sea," enacted under the Act of 1894 by the Queen's Order in Council of 27th November 1896 (*e*). The rules of maritime law in regard to damages in cases of collision were thus stated by Lord Stowell': (1) that where no blame is imputable to either party, but the damage is by storm 'or other *vis major* or inevitable accident (*f*),' the loss falls where it lights, and neither is liable to the other; (2) that where both are to blame for want of the requisite vigilance or skill, the loss is apportioned between them (*g*); (3) that if the suffering party alone has been to blame, he must bear the burden; and (4) that if the fault is with the vessel which has run down and injured the other, the latter will be entitled to an entire compensation (*h*). 'If it is proved in case of collision that any of the regulations for preventing collisions contained in or made under any of the Merchant Shipping Acts from 1854 to 1894 has been infringed, the ship infringing (*i*) it is to be deemed in fault, unless the circumstances have made a departure from the regulations necessary (*k*).'

(3.) *Keeping dangerous Dogs, etc.*—Carelessness in the keeping of a dangerous dog 'or other animal,' or in the management of firearms, subjects to damages in reparation (*l*). 'It was formerly held that the owner's knowledge of the dangerous or mischievous character of a domesticated animal must in all cases be proved in order to render him liable (*m*); but now, in any action for injury to sheep or cattle, it is not necessary to prove a previous propensity in a dog to injure sheep or cattle; and the occupier of the place where the dog is kept or allowed to stay is liable, unless he proves that he is not the owner, and that it was kept or allowed to remain on the premises without his sanction or knowledge (*n*). Cattle includes horses (*o*). There is little doubt that carelessness, as above stated, is still the ground of liability; and will be readily inferred if a dog is allowed to stray from home and worries sheep or cattle (*p*). The "*scienter*," *i.e.* the owner's or custodier's knowledge of the animal's vicious propensity, must still be proved in the case of other domesticated animals, and in the case of injuries done by dogs to persons or other animals than sheep or cattle (*q*). And one who keeps a dog or bull, or the like, which he knows to be of a ferocious disposition, or a wild beast, is not merely bound to take all proper precautions for its control, but, at all events in a question with one who is lawfully on the ground and is not himself in fault, is absolutely bound to prevent mischief, and must at his peril keep the animal from doing hurt. In other words, in such a case it is unnecessary for the injured person to adduce evidence of substantive negligence (*r*). A distinction has been taken between the effect of *scientia* in a question between the owner and one of the public, and in one between the owner and a servant employed in attending to the animal alleged to be vicious, the latter having possibly equal knowledge of its propensities with the master (*s*). Apart from the vice or ferocity of the animal, its owner is liable, according to the ordinary rules of law, for negligence in using or guarding it, as for careless or reckless driving of horses or cattle in public places (*t*), or failure in maintaining fences. Indeed the *scientia*, so much discussed in the cases cited, is just an element in the proof of negligence, having the effect when established of shifting the *onus probandi*.'

(4.) *The use of diligence* (as arrestment, etc., in security) is always *periculo petentis*; and where injury arises, will entitle to reparation, if nimious or groundless (*u*). 'This distinction is to be observed: (*a*) A person using any legal right or remedy to which he is absolutely entitled, and which he can use without applying to a Court for a special warrant, is not liable in damages for doing so; unless either (1) there be an inherent vice in the form or regularity of the writ itself, or in the manner in which it is used; or (2) it be averred and proved that he obtained his diligence or put it in force maliciously and without probable cause. This applies to arrestments of all kinds, poindings, and inhibitions, in which it may be said that the creditor merely *utitur jure suo* (*v*). But (*b*) in the case of warrants to apprehend as *in meditatione fugæ*, or to imprison under a decree for aliment under the Act of 1882, petitions for *cessio bonorum*, process captions, applications for interdict, and sequestrations for rent, the warrant or order of Court is not obtained purely as a matter of course, but upon a precise statement, often *ex parte*, in order to induce the Court to grant the requisite authority. In such cases the applicant is answerable for the correctness of his statements, and is liable in damages if it be simply proved that his application was wrongful or illegal (*w*). There can be no action of damages for merely raising or insisting in an action at law (*x*).'

(5.) *Carelessness of Public Officers.*—Carelessness on the part of public officers, magistrates, or road trustees, or their managers or workmen, has in Scotland been held to render them liable as trustees for reparation, with relief against the trust fund, though not in their private capacities. It 'was' otherwise in England (*y*).

(*a*) 3 Ersk. 1. § 15. Black and Brown, *supra*, § 552 (*a*). Smith *v.* Milne, March 8, 1810; F. C.; rev. 2 Dow, 390. Innes *v.* Mags. of Edin., 1798; M. 13,189. Chapman *v.* Parlan, 1825; 3 S. 401; 1 Ill. 331. Brown & Co. *v.* Stewart, 1824; 3 S. 127. Mack *v.* Allan & Simson, 1832; 10 S. 349. It is impossible to indicate within the space at command the various heads of *Negligence*. The following notes are retained from former editions. As to negligent or injurious use or management of property, see Guthrie Smith on Damages. **Black** *v.* **Cadell**, 1804; M. 13,905; aff. 5 Pat. 567. Hislop *v.* Durham, 1842; 4 D. 1168. (See **Prentice** *v.* **Assets Co.**, *infra.*) Thomson *v.* Gray, 1842; 5 D. 377. Samuel *v.* E. & G. Ry. Co., 1850; 13 D. 312. Davidson *v.* Monklands Ry. Co., 1855; 17 D. 1038. **Kerr** *v.* **Earl of Orkney**, 1857; 20 D. 298. Mackintosh *v.* Scott & Co., 1859; 21 D. 363. Tennent *v.* E. of Glasgow, 1862; 1 Macph. 133; aff. 1864, 2 Macph. H. L. 22. Mackintosh *v.* Mackintosh, 1864; 2 Macph. 1357 (muir-burning). **Campbell** *v.* **Kennedy**, 1864; 3 Macph. 121 (water-pipe in upper flat, as to which see also Weston *v.* Tailors of Potterrow, 1839; 1 D. 1218. Carstairs *v.* Taylor, 40 L. J. Ex. 129; L. R. 6 Ex. 217, where the injury was caused by rats gnawing the pipe). Robertson *v.* Adamson, 1862; 24 D. 1231. Macmartin *v.* Hannay, 1872; 10 Macph. 411. Cleghorn *v.* Taylor, 1856; 18 D. 664. Chalmers *v.* Dixon, 1876; 3 R. 461 (vapours from burning heap of ironstone refuse). Macfeat *v.* Rankin, 1879; 6 R. 1043 (unfenced quarry—cf. Ross *v.* Keith, 1888; 16 R. 86; Royan *v.* M'Lennans, 1889; 17 R. 103; and **Prentice** *v.* **Assets Co.**, 1890; 17 R. 484, where the cases are reviewed, and the general rule fixed as to pits, etc., adjoining public roads). Laurent *v.* L. Advocate, 1869; 7 Macph. 607 (alterations injuring neighbour). Cameron *v.* Fraser, 1881; 9 R. 26 (ditto—contractors). Sinnerton *v.* Merry & Cunningham, 1886; 13 R. 1012. Findlay *v.* Angus, 1886; 14 R. 312 (sufficiency of door fastening in place frequented by children). Brady *v.* Parker, 1887; 14 R. 783 (unfenced pit or well of hoist in warehouse). It seems, notwithstanding some dicta in Cleghorn, *cit.*, that the elements of damage and property are not sufficient to create liability, but that there must be fault either of commission or omission. Campbell, *cit.* Pirie & Sons *v.* Mags. of Aberdeen, 1871; 9 Macph. 412.

See as to the brocard *res ipsa loquitur*, Scott *v.* London Dock Co., 34 L. J. Ex. 220; 3 H. & C. 596. Briggs *v.* Oliver, 4 H. & C. 403; 35 L. J. Ex. 163. Kearney *v.* London, Brighton, etc., Ry. Co., 39 L. J. Q. B. 200; 40 L. J. Q. B. 285. Anderson *v.* N. B. Ry. Co., 1875; 2 R. 443. Lyon *v.* Lamb, 1838; 16 S. 1188. Macaulay *v.* Buist, 1846; 8 D. 245, 248. Milne *v.* Townsend, 1892; 19 R. 830. Welfare *v.* L. B. & S. C. Ry., L. R. 4 Q. B. 693; 38 L. J. Q. B. 241. *Supra*, § 170 (*x*), *infra*, § 970. Railway companies are not liable for fire communicated by sparks from locomotives, unless they are proved to have been negligent, *e.g.* in the construction or management of the engine. Vaughan *v.* Taff Vale Ry. Co., 29 L. J. Ex. 247; 5 H. & N. 679. Smith *v.* L. and S.-W. Ry. Co., 39 L. J. C. P. 68; 40 L. J. C. P. 21. Jones *v.* Festiniog Ry. Co., L. R. 3 Q. B. 733; 37 L. J. Q. B. 214. Powell *v.* Fall, 49 L. J. Q. B. 428 (locomotive on road). Murdoch *v.* G. and S.-W. Ry. Co., 1870; 8 Macph. 768. Port-Glasgow and Newark Sailcloth Co. *v.* Cal. Ry. Co., 1892; 19 R. 608. City of Peking, 1888; 14 App. Ca. 40 (collision of ships). See below, § 964–970. There is a class of cases which perhaps ought to be referred to the head of *quasi* delicts rather than either to that of recompense or damages for breach of contract: viz. those in which one who has by representations or conduct induced another to incur expense or loss in reliance upon an informal or incomplete agreement, and has fraudulently or in bad faith refused to bind himself so as to be liable in specific implement, has been held liable to make good specific expenditure so caused. See **Walker** *v.* **Milne**, 1823; 2 S. 379; 3 S. 82, 333. Bell *v.* Bell, 1841; 3 D. 1201. Heddle *v.* Baikie, 1846; 8 D. 376.

Allan *v.* **Gilchrist**, 1875 ; 2 R. 587. M'Arthur *v.* Lawson, 1877 ; 4 R. 1134. But see Alderson *v.* Maddison, 5 Ex. D. 293 ; 49 L. J. Ex. 801 (rev. on another point). Pollock on Contracts, 495 sqq.

(*b*) **Mogul S.S. Co.** *v.* **M'Gregor, Gow, & Co.**, 1892 ; A. C. 25 ; affg. 23 Q. B. D. 598, and esp. *per* Bowen, L. J. ; citing authorities. **Allen** *v.* **Flood**, 1898 ; A. C. 1.

(*c*) In previous editions, "yet."

(*d*) Vanderplank *v.* Miller, Mood. & Mal. 169. See 57 and 58 Vict. c. 60, § 418-423.

(*e*) The Regulations are to be found in Marsden, Collns., 296, 314, 471 ; Guthrie Smith on Dams., 166, 411 ; and 9 P. D. 247 sqq. See as to steam pilot vessels, O. in C., Aug. 19, 1892, in Stat. R. & O., 1892, p. 633. There are also local rules in the Clyde, Mersey, and other rivers. The text originally stood thus, in lieu of the passage in single inverted commas : "That the ship going to windward is to keep to windward, and the ship which has the wind free is to bear away." Handyside *v.* Wilson, 3 Carr. & P. 528 ; 33 R. R. 695.

(*f*) As to "inevitable accident," see above, § 237.

(*g*) Le Neve *v.* Hay, 1824 ; 2 S. App. 395. Clyde Shipping Co. *v.* Glasgow & Londonderry S. P. Co., 1859 ; 21 D. 898 and 1131. Boettcher *v.* Carron Co., 1861 ; 23 D. 322. Little *v.* Burns (*k*). See above, § 436.

(*h*) Le Neve *v.* Hay, *cit.*, and the cases there quoted by Lord Gifford. The Woodrop Sims, 2 Dod. Ad. 83. Montgomerie *v.* D. & J. Craig, 1826 ; 4 S. 769 ; 4 Mur. 167.

(*i*) There is not infringement if, in the circumstances, a competent seaman could not, exercising reasonable care, know that the regulation is applicable. Baker *v.* Theodore H. Rand, 12 App. Ca. 247.

(*k*) 57 and 58 Vict. c. 60, § 419 (4). The Fanny M. Carville (P. C.), 44 L. J. Adm. 34. Maclachlan, ch. vi. Marsden on Collisions at Sea (4th ed.), ch. 2. Little *v.* Burns, 1881 ; 9 R. 118. Stoomvahrt Maatschappy Nederlander *v.* P. & O. Co. (The Khedive), 5 App. Ca. 876. The Benares, 9 P. D. 16. Hine Brs. *v.* Clyde Trs., 1888 ; 15 R. 498. The Glamorganshire, 13 App. Ca. 454. So, where a collision has occurred, there is an onus on the vessel which, by the regulations, is required to "keep out of the way" of the other. Hilda *v.* Australia, 1884 ; 12 R. 76.

(*l*) Brown & Co., *supra* (*a*). Sarch *v.* Blackburn, 4 Carr. & P. 294 ; 34 R. R. 805. Dixon *v.* Bell, 5 M. & S. 198 ; 17 R. R. 308. As to firearms and explosives, see Galloway *v.* King, 1872 ; 10 Macph. 788. King *v.* Pollock, 1874 ; 2 R. 42. As to dangerous articles generally, especially in places to which the public have access, see Clark *v.* Chambers, L. R. 3 Q. B. D. 327 ; 47 L. J. Q. B. 429, where many English cases are referred to ; and comp. Campbell *v.* Ord & Maddison, 1873, 1 R. 149, with Mangan *v.* Atherton, 4 H. & C. 388 ; 35 L. J. Ex. 161 ; and M'Gregor *v.* Ross & Marshall, 1883 ; 10 R. 725.

(*m*) **Orr** *v.* **Fleeming**, 1853 ; 11 D. 486 ; rev. 1885, 2 Macq. 14.

(*n*) 26 and 27 Vict. c. 100. M'Intyre *v.* Carmichael, 1870 ; 8 Macph. 570. Murray *v.* Brown & Porteous, 1881 ; 19 S. L. R. 253. See 28 and 29 Vict. c. 60, applicable to England.

(*o*) Wright *v.* Pearson, 38 L. J. Q. B. 312 ; L. R. 4 Q. B. 582.

(*p*) Cases in note (*n*), and many Sheriff-Court cases, *e.g.* Barr *v.* M'Isaac, 1864 ; 1 Sel. Sh. C. C. 498. Howison *v.* White, 1892 ; 8 Sh. Ct. R. 318, where others are cited.

(*q*) **Clark** *v.* **Armstrong**, 1862 ; 24 D. 1315. Renwick *v.* Von Rotberg, 1875 ; 2 R. 855. Smith, *infra* (*t*). Cowan *v.* Dalziels, 1877 ; 5 R. 241. Gladman *v.* Johnson, 36 L. J. C. P. 153. Stiles *v.* Cardiff St. Nav. Co., 33 L. J. Q. B. 310. Baldwin *v.* Casella, 41 L. J. Ex. 167 ; L. R. 7 Ex. 325. Applebee *v.* Percy, 43 L. J. C. P. 365 ; L. R. 9 C. P. 647.

(*r*) **Burton** *v.* **Moorhead**, 1881 ; 8 R. 892. 1 Stair, 9. § 5. Inst. iv. 9. Ll. 40-42 D. de aed. ed. (21, 1). May *v.* Burdett, 9 Q. B. 101 ; 16 L. J. Q. B. 64. Cox *v.* Burbidge, 17 C. B. N. S. 245 ; 32 L. J. C. P. 89. Smillies *v.* Boyd, 1886 ; 14 R. 150. Daly *v.* Arrol, *ib.* 154. Fraser *v.* Bell, 1887 ; 14 R. 811. See Hennigan *v.* M'Vey, 1882 ; 9 R. 411 (boar) ; *infra* (*t*). Read *v.* Edwards, 17 C. B. N. S. 245 ; 34 L. J. C. P. 31 (dog addicted to hunting game). It is said that the general rule requiring proof of *scienter* will not be extended. Smith, *infra* (*t*). And the recent cases go far in increasing the responsibility of owners of dogs, etc. There is a penalty for keeping dangerous dogs. See the Dogs Act, 34 and 35 Vict. c. 56. Henderson *v.* M'Kenzie, 1876 ; 3 R. 623.

(*s*) Clark *v.* Armstrong, *cit.* (*q*), *per* Lord Benholme.

(*t*) Brown *v.* Fulton, 1881 ; 9 R. 36 (horse entrusted to boy). Phillips *v.* Nicoll, 1884 ; 11 R. 592 (cow led through street from slaughter-house). Harpers *v.* G. N. of S. Ry. Co., 1886 ; 13 R. 1139. Illidge *v.* Goodwin, 5 C. & P. 190. Cox *v.* Burbidge, *cit.* (*r*). Ellis *v.* Loftus Iron Co., L. R. 10 C. P. 10 ; 44 L. J. C. P. 24 (horse). Smith *v.* Cook, 1 Q. B. D. 79 ; 45 L. J. Q. B. 122. **Clark** *v.* **Armstrong**, 1862 ; 24 D. 1315 (bulls). Hudson *v.* Roberts, 6 Ex. 699 ; 20 L. J. Ex. 299 (do.). Jackson *v.* Smithson, 15 M. & W. 561 (rams). Tillett *v.* Ward, 10 Q. B. D. 17.

(*u*) Clark *v.* Thomson, 1816 ; 1 Mur. 161. See below, § 2031 sqq.

(*v*) Neilson *v.* Smith, 1821 ; 1 S. 8 ; Hume, 31. Duff *v.* Bradberry, § 544. L. Duffus *v.* Davidson, 1828 ; 4 Mur. 558. Brodie *v.* Young, 1851 ; 13 D. 737. Henning *v.* Hewatson, 1852 ; 14 D. 487. Baillie *v.* Hume, 1853 ; 16 D. 151. Macfarlan *v.* Macfarlan, 1842 ; 5 D. 1. Inglis *v.* M'Intyre, 1861 ; 23 D. 1240. Meikle *v.* Sneddon, 1862 ; 24 D. 720. Wolthekker *v.* Northern Agricult. Assn., 1862 ; 1 Macph. 211. Petersen *v.* M'Lean & Hope, 1868 ; 6 Macph. 218. Other cases in Birnie on Issues, 35, 36. Mackinnon *v.* Hamilton, 1866 ; 4 Macph. 852. Leconte *v.* Douglas, 1880 ; 8 R. 175 (excess). Kinnes *v.* Adam, 1882 ; 10 R. 693 (sequestration). Nelmes & Co. *v.* Gillies, 1883 ; 10 R. 890 (poinding including third party's goods). Taylor *v.* Rutherford, 1888 ; 15 R. 608 (intermediary—debt collector).

(*w*) Wolthekker, *cit.* **Kennedy** *v.* **Fortwilliam Comrs.**, 1877 ; 5 R. 302.

Medit. Fugæ.—Swayne *v.* Fife Bkg. Co., 1835 ; 13 S. 1003. Carne *v.* Manuel, 1851 ; 13 D. 1253. Ford *v.* Muirhead, 1858 ; 20 D. 949. Maclean *v.* Colthart, 1865 ; 3 Macph. 719. Macmeekin *v.* Russel, 1881 ; 8 R. 587.

Cessio Petitions under Act of 1880.—Smith & Co. *v.* Taylor, etc., 1882 ; 10 R. 290.

Interdicts.—Reid *v.* Bruce, 1855 ; 17 D. 1100. Abel's Exrs. *v.* Edmunds, 1863 ; 1 Macph. 1061. Arnot *v.* Dowie, 1863 ; 2 Macph. 119. Robinson *v.* N. B. Ry., 1864 ; *ib.* 841. Miller *v.* Hunter, 1865 ; 3 Macph. 740. Kennedy *v.* Fortw. Comrs., *cit.* Glasgow City and District Ry. Co. *v.* Glas. Coal Exch. Co., 1885 ; 12 R. 1287. Fife *v.* Orr, 1895 ; 23 R. 8. Gibson *v.* Clark, 1895 ; 23 R. 294. In some cases damages have been refused for obtaining an interdict, which was ultimately found to be wrongful or illegal, *e.g.* Moir *v.* Hunter, 1832 ; 11 S. 32. Mudie *v.* Miln, 1828 ; 6 S. 967. **Jack** *v.* **Begg**, 1875 ; 3 R. 35 ; the reason being either that the interdict was of the nature of a possessory judgment and therefore right at the time (see *per* Lord Gifford in Kennedy *v.* Fortwilliam Comrs., *cit.*), or because the person claiming damages was himself a wrong-doer, and the interdict recalled only for reasons not affecting the merits.

Sequestrations for Rent.—Urquhart *v.* M'Kenzie, 1834 ; 3 S. 84. Oswald *v.* Graeme, 1851 ; 13 D. 1229. Robertson *v.* Galbraith, 1857 ; 19 D. 1016. Duffy *v.* Gray, 1858 ; 20 D. 580. Watson *v.* M'Culloch, 1878 ; 5 R. 843.

Process Caption.—Hunter *v.* Kerr, 1842 ; 4 D. 1175.

The recording of a protest on a bill is a judicial proceeding, and falls under class (*a*). Gardiner *v.* Martin, 1864 ; 2 Macph. 1183. But it is unnecessary to aver malice and want of probable cause in claiming damages for recording a protest and charging thereon when the bill had been paid before it was protested, for a charge is diligence falling under class (*b*). Gibb *v.* Edin. Brewery Co., 1873 ; 11 Macph. 705. This appears to rest on the principle, which applies to every case of diligence, that when the debt is paid there is no longer any valid warrant. See also Wilson *v.* Mackie, 1875 ; 3 R. 18. As to decrees taken after payment, see Davies & Co. *v.* Brown & Lyell, 1867 ; 5 Macph.

842. Ormiston *v.* Redpath & Co., 1866; 4 Macph. 488. Pollock *v.* Goodwin's Trs., 1898; 25 R. 1051 As to carriers of passengers ejecting or causing the apprehension of persons refusing to comply with their lawful regulations, see Highland Ry. Co. *v.* Menzies, 1878; 5 R. 887. Apthorpe *v.* Edin. Tramways Co., 1882; 10 R. 344. Lundie *v.* MacBrayne, 1894; 21 R. 1085.

(*x*) Addison on Torts, 621, 5th ed. Cree *v.* Collier, 1821; 1 S. 170. Gordon *v.* Royal Bank, 1826; 5 S. 164. Aitken *v.* Finlay, 1837; 15 S. 683. Mudie *v.* Miln, 1828; 6 S. 967. Lyon *v.* Reid's Trs., 1835; 13 S. 984. Cleland *v.* Laurie, 1848; 10 D. 1372. Kinnes *v.* Adam, *cit.* (*v*).

(*y*) M'Lachlan *v.* Road Trs., 1827; 4 Mur. 216. Millar *v.* Road Trs., 1828; 4 Mur. 568. Aiken *v.* Douglas, 1836; 14 S. 204. Murray *v.* Douglas, 1837; 15 S. 890. Findlater *v.* Duncan, 1838; 16 S. 1150. Harris *v.* Baker, 4 M. & Sel. 27; 16 R. R. 370. Hall *v.* Smith, 2 Bing. 156. As to Findlater, see below, § 2031.

554. (6.) *Responsibility of Master for Servant.*—One is liable for the faults or gross negligence of those in his employment or under his command, according to the rules already laid down (*a*).

(*a*) See above, § 547. Fraser *v.* Dunlop, 1822; 1 S. 243; 1 Ill. 332. Baird *v.* Hamilton, 1826; 4 S. 790. Waldie *v.* D. of Roxburghe, 1822; 1 S. 344; aff. 1 W. & S. 1. Ld. Keith and Linwood, *supra*, § 547 (*c*). Sword *v.* Cameron, 1839; 1 D. 493. Fraser on M. & S. 261 sqq.

BOOK FIRST

PART III

OF EXTINCTION OF OBLIGATIONS

INTRODUCTION

555. Obligations are extinguished, either—1. By actual fulfilment of the engagement, payment, performance, or satisfaction made to the creditor; or, 2. By virtual fulfilment, compensation, novation, or confusion; or, 3. By discharge on the part of the creditor; or, 4. By presumed abandonment or satisfaction.

CHAPTER XIX

OF PAYMENT AND PERFORMANCE

I. PAYMENT.

556. General Rule.—Payment or prestation by the true debtor in the obligation to the true creditor, satisfies and extinguishes the engagement (*a*). But the creditor is not bound to accept of a partial payment, or of anything but proper payment according to the obligation (*b*).

(*a*) 1 Stair, 18. § 3. 3 Ersk. 4. § 1–6. Kilkerran, 284.
(*b*) 3 Ersk. 4. § 1.

557. By whom Payment may be made.—Payment, to the effect of extinguishing the obligation, may be made not only by the debtor himself, but by any one acting for the debtor: or even by a stranger, where the debt is pecuniary, and due, and demanded (*a*); or where any penal effect may arise from delay; or where the creditor has no interest in demanding performance by the proper debtor. The debtor cannot prevent any stranger from paying and demanding an assignation if the creditor chooses to grant it. But the creditor cannot be compelled to grant an assignation, unless the debtor shall consent, and the granting of the assignation shall not interfere with any other interest of the creditor himself (*b*). 'If he be pressing his debtor by diligence, he is bound at his request to assign the debt to any friend who interposes to pay the debt for him, provided he have no good reason for refusing. But the right to an assignation is founded in equity, and the right to demand or to refuse must alike be supported by a reasonable interest (*c*).'

(*a*) 3 Inst. 30, *pr.* See 1 Smith's L. C. 338. Benjamin on Sales, 752. Walter *v.* James, L. R. 6 Ex. 124; 40 L. J. Ex. 104.
(*b*) M'Gilvray *v.* M'Arthur, 1826; 4 S. 697; 1 Ill. 332. Austin *v.* Grant, 1827; 5 S. 701. But see Rainnie *v.* Milne, 1822; 1 S. 355. Smith *v.* Gentle, 1844; 6 D. 1164. Cuningham's Trs. *v.* Hutton, 1847; 10 D. 307. Russell *v.* Mudie, 1858; 20 D. 125. Fleming *v.* Burgess, 1867; 5 Macph. 856 (trustee in sequestration paying). Will *v.* Elder's Trs., 1867; 6 Macph. 9. Guthrie *v.* Smith & M'Connachy, 1880; 8 R. 106. See above, § 255, 268; and below, § 1238.
(*c*) Fleming and Will, *citt.* 3 Ersk. 5. § 11. Sligo *v.* Menzies, 1840; 2 D. 1478.

558. Payment made by one interested in the debt (as co-obligant or surety) will take away the right of the creditor, but will not extinguish the debt of the principal obligant. The person so paying is entitled to an assignation, to the effect of operating his relief (*a*).

(*a*) See Guthrie *v.* Smith & M'Connachy, *cit.*; and below, § 910A.

559. Payment is presumed to have been made by the proper debtor where the evidence is ambiguous, even in the case of bills and promissory notes (*a*).

Payment made by one administering for the debtor in any representative capacity, as tutor, trustee, factor, etc., is presumed to be made from the funds of the principal, and so to extinguish the debt; otherwise it is *negotiorum gestio* (*b*).

(*a*) Webster *v.* Thomas, Jan. 15, 1819, F. C., and cases there cited; 1 Ill. 333. Jackson *v.* Williamson, 1825; 4 S. 296. Ewing *v.* E. Strathmore, 1825; 4 S. 313; aff. 1832, 6 W. & S. 56. Soutar's Reps. *v.* Soutar, 1827; 5 S. 876. See 3 Ersk. 4. § 6; Dickson, Evid. § 396. Brown *v.* Kerr, 1809; Hume, 62. M'Kenzie *v.* Orr, 1838; 16 S. 311; aff. M'L. & R. 117. Tod *v.* Dunlop, 1838; 1 D. 231. Wood *v.* Northern Revn. Co., 1848; 11 D. 254. Fairbairn *v.* Fairbairn, 1868; 6 Macph. 640. Welsh *v.* Welsh's Trs., 1877; 5 R. 542. Below, § 566.

(*b*) 3 Ersk. 4. § 6. Trotter *v.* Robertson, 1672; M. 11,526. Donaldson *v.* Walker, 1711; M. 11,511. Jackson, *supra* (*a*). See M'Lachlan *v.* Henderson, 1831; 9 S. 753. Above, § 540.

560. To whom Payment may be made.—Payment will extinguish the debt in the following cases:—If made to the true creditor, or to his heir with his title completed, provided they shall be in full capacity to discharge the debt (*a*); or if made to one duly authorised by the creditor to receive it, as assignee, trustee, factor, etc. (*b*). But a wife has no such power (*c*); neither has a messenger or officer of the law employed to do diligence for the debt; so that payment to him is no extinction of the debt, unless, as is sometimes the case, such messenger is employed as agent (*d*). 'In general, payment to an agent who has authority to take payment must be in cash, and not by a mere settlement of accounts.'

(*a*) 3 Ersk. 4. § 3. See Halkerton *v.* Drummond, 1729; M. 1799; 1 Ill. 333. Howes *v.* Campbell, 1758; *ib.* Somerville *v.* Smith, 1823; 2 S. 509.

(*b*) Haggart *v.* Miller, 1838; 16 S. 1038; 3 Ill. 145. Duncan *v.* Clyde Trs., 1851; 13 D. 518; aff. 1853, 25 Jur. 331. Falconer *v.* Dalrymple, 1870; 9 Macph. 212. See above, § 219 (*f*), (*m*), etc.; below, § 564.

(*c*) Except as to her own earnings, property, or income, within the Acts of 1877 and 1881. 40 and 41 Vict. c. 29, § 3; 44 and 45 Vict. c. 21, § 1 (2).

(*d*) Pierson *v.* Scott, 47 L. J. Ch. 705. Addison on Contracts, 136, 332.

561. Bonâ fide Payment.—Payment is good if made *in bonâ fide* to one to whom the debtor has been led or allowed by the creditor to believe in point of fact (*a*) that he has given authority to receive it (*b*); as to the original creditor after assignation or diligence not duly intimated (*c*); or after 'sequestration in' bankruptcy unknown to the debtor (*d*); or by tenants to a landlord after a sale of the estate; or by tenants after the landlord has granted an heritable bond, if either it has not been intimated (*e*), or, though intimated, if the creditor has not taken posession or demanded the rents; or, though he has taken decree of maills and duties, if he has allowed it to remain for a long time without a charge or claim against the tenant (*f*). Payment made *in bonâ fide* to the creditor after arrestment of the funds of one abroad is good, if there has not been personal notice given to the debtor (*g*); and it has been held that even a payment made by a debtor at a distance from home, after arrestment used at his dwelling-house, was good (*h*). Payment to one who had been factor, without notice of recall of the factory, is good (*i*): so also, if made to one possessed of the documents of debt, with apparently a good title to receive payment (*k*); or to one by acquiescence allowed to receive rents for an apparent heir (*l*).

(*a*) *Ignorantia juris neminem excusat.* See § 11, 534.

(*b*) 1 Stair, 18. § 3. 3 Ersk. 4. § 3.

(*c*) 3 Ersk. 4. § 3, and cases there cited. Lyon *v.* Law, 1610; M. 1786; 1 Ill. 334. Hume *v.* Hume, 1632; M. 848. Hamilton *v.* E. Rothes, 1759; M. 1802. Blackwood *v.* E. Sutherland, 1703; M. 1793 (overruled by Laidlaw, *infra*). Comp. E. of Strathmore *v.* Hers. of Rescobie, 1888; 15 R. 364.

(*d*) 54 Geo. III. c. 137, § 38 *in fin.* 19 and 20 Vict. c. 79, § 111.

(*e*) York Buildings Co. *v.* Gardner, 1736; M. 1784; Elch. *Bona and Mala fides*, 2; 1 Ill. 334. Home *v.* Kello Tenants, 1666; 1 B. Sup. 522. M'Gill *v.* Crawford, 1716; M. 1783. See Robertson *v.* Orme, 1755; 5 B. Sup. 838. Garden *v.* Lindsay, 1757; *ib.* 855.

(*f*) Garden, *supra* (*e*).

(*g*) 54 Geo. III. c. 137, § 3. 19 and 20 Vict. c. 91, § 1.

(*h*) Laidlaw *v.* Smith, 1838; 16 S. 367; aff. 2 Rob. 490. See Scott *v.* Fludyer, 1770; Hailes, 348.

(*i*) 3 Ersk. 4. § 3. A mercantile factor in possession of goods has power to receive payment of the price, not a broker. See above, § 219, 225, 229. Benjamin on Sales, 740.

(*k*) But mere possession of the document of debt by a factor for trustees for the purpose of uplifting interest was held not to presume authority to uplift principal. Duncan *v.* Clyde Trs., *supra*, § 560 (*b*). See Addison on Contracts, 143.

(*l*) Somerville *v.* Smith, 1823; 2 S. 509.

562. But to prevent collusion between tenants and landlords to the prejudice of singular successors, a tenant's payment of rent before the legal term is not a *bonâ fide* payment to save him from the demand of a creditor or purchaser (*a*). This, however, does not prevent a payment after the legal and before the conventional term (*b*). Nor does it apply to the payment of a debt before the time of payment (*c*). It holds respecting the payment of feu-duties, and it would seem also to hold as to the interest of heritable debts. 'The presumption of collusion does not operate in favour of the trustee on the landlord's sequestrated estate, who takes the estate *tantum et tale* (*d*), and it seems reasonable to hold that the rule may be set aside by evidence of good faith on the part of the tenant (*e*).'

(*a*) 3 Ersk. 4. § 5. Gray *v.* Campbell, 1629 ; M. 10,023. E. of Lauderdale *v.* Tenants of Swinton, 1662 ; *ib.* Lady Traquair *v.* Houatson, 1667 ; *ib.* 10,024.

(*b*) York Buildings Co., *supra*, § 561 (*e*).

(*c*) Ersk. *ut supra*.

(*d*) Davidson *v.* Boyd, 1868 ; 7 Macph. 77. See Hunter, L. & T. ii. 437. Haggart *v.* Miller, 1838 ; 16 S. 1058.

(*e*) So held in Cooper's Trs. *v.* Smillie, 1880, and Glas. & W. of Scot. Savings Invt. Co. *v.* Mills, 1882 ; 2 Sel. Sh. Ct. Ca. 261, 258. See Laidlaw *v.* Smith, *cit.* § 561 (*h*).

563. Indefinite Payments.—Where several debts are due, the debtor may, in making the payment (*a*), appropriate it to a particular debt, under this limitation, that the creditor cannot be compelled to take a partial payment. If there be no distinct appropriation by the debtor, the creditor may by his receipt appropriate it (*b*). If there be no appropriation by either of the parties, the creditor may, 'at the time or afterwards, before action (*c*),' ascribe it to which debt he pleases: to interest, for example, and not to the principal debt (*d*); or to the worst secured debt; or to a debt bearing no interest instead of one on which interest runs; or to a debt in danger of prescribing, leaving a more recent one unpaid (*e*). It has even been held that he was not bound to apply it to a debt which he was employed to recover (*f*). But this is to be received under the equitable limitation, that the debtor shall not, by such appropriation of the creditor, be left exposed to penal consequences; nor have the payment ascribed to a disputed debt, 'or one for which the debtor is liable only in a representative character (*g*), or to a part of the debt which is illegal (*h*)'; nor a cautioner 'wholly (*i*)' deprived of the benefit of the payment where the debtor is insolvent; nor a payment, as understood at the time of payment, ascribed differently on emerging circumstances (*k*); nor a dividend from a sequestrated estate applied otherways than to the whole debt (*l*). 'When no appropriation has been made by either party, and especially, *e.g.*, in the case of an account current between the parties, such as a banking account, the law appropriates payments to the various debts in their order: it presumes, for instance, where there is a running account, that the parties intended to apply the first item on the credit side to discharge the first item on the debit side, and so on (*m*). But this rule suffers exception, when a particular mode of dealing, or express arrangement, shows a different intention of the parties (*n*).'

(*a*) Specific appropriation of money or debts receives effect in several cases, as here, in compensation (§ 574), and retention (§ 1414); but a mere obligation to appropriate a fund in a particular way cannot create a security or *jus in re*. An obligation to pay a debt out of certain profits has no more effect than an obligation to pay. Graham & Co. *v.* Raeburn & Verel, 1895 ; 23 R. 84. *Infra*, § 1333.

(*b*) 3 Ersk. 4. § 2. Forbes *v.* Innes, *infra* (*e*). Campbell *v.* Falconer, 1828 ; 6 S. 830 ; 1 Ill. 337.

(*c*) Simson *v.* Ingham, 2 B. & C. 65 ; 3 Ross' L. C. 689 ; 26 R. R. 273. Cox *v.* Troy, 5 B. & Ald. 474 ; 24 R. R. 460. Phillpott *v.* Jones, 2 A. & E. 42. Campbell *v.* Dent, 2 Moore, P. C. 292. Scott's Trs. *v.* Alexander's Tr., *infra* (*m*).

(*d*) See Watt *v.* Burnett's Trs., 1839 ; 2 D. 132. Wauchope *v.* N. B. Ry. Co., 1863 ; 2 Macph. 326. Sandeman *v.* Scott, 1849 ; 11 D. 405 ; 1 Macq. 293. Tudor's L. C. 27, 28.

(*e*) Ersk. *ut supra*. Duck *v.* Maxwell, 1717 ; M. 6804 ; 1 Ill. 335. Paterson *v.* ——, 1744 ; cited by Ersk. *ut supra* ; 5 B. Sup. 726. Forbes *v.* Innes, 1739 ; M. 6813 ; Elchies, *Ind. Pay.* 1 ; 5 B. Sup. 690. Harwood, 1742 ; *ib.* 726. Strettel *v.* Potts, 1779 ; M. 6815. Good *v.* Smith, 1779 ; M. 6816 ; Hailes, 837. Reid *v.* Maxwell, 1782 ; M. 6818. M'Leod *v.* M'Kenzie, 1821 ; 1 S. 89. Cochran & Co. *v.* Mathie, 1821 ; *ib.* 82. Houston's Exrs. *v.* Speirs, 1824 ; 3 S. 180 ; 4 S. 566 ; 3 W. & S. 392. Maitland *v.* Cockerell, 1827 ; 6 S. 109. Clyne *v.* Swanson, 1830 ; 8 S. 391. Hotchkis *v.* Kirk, 1832 ; 10 S. 289. Bremner *v.* Mabon, 1837 ; 16 S. 213. See below, § 616. Williams *v.* Griffith, 5 M. & W. 300. Mackenzie *v.* Orr, 1838 ; 16 S. 311 ; aff. M'L. & R. 117. Couper *v.* Young, 1849 ; 12 D. 190. Cullen *v.* Mitchell, 1850 ; 22 Jur. 646 ; 1852, 1 Macq. 190.

(*f*) M'Leod, *supra* (*e*). Dickson *v.* Moncrieff, 1853 ; 16 D. 24.

(*g*) Semple *v.* Comistoun, 1705 ; M. 6803. Goddard *v.* Cox, 2 Str. 1194 ; Tudor's L. C. 4, 23, etc. Dig. de solut. (46, 3).

(*h*) *Supra*, § 36 (6). See, however, Smith's Merc. Law, 679. Addison on Contracts, 150 (may be applied to a debt on which, though not illegal, action is prohibited).

(*i*) Ersk. *l.c.* See Smith's Merc. Law, 680.

(*k*) See Christie and Jackson, *infra* (*m*). Addison on Contracts, 150. Simson *v.* Ingham, *supra* (*c*). Hooper *v.* Keay, 1 Q. B. D. 178. Thompson *v.* Hudson, L. R. 6 Ch. 320 ; 40 L. J. Ch. 28.

(*l*) Ersk. *ut supra*. M'Raith *v.* Campbell, 1680 ; M. 6801. Duchess of Buccleuch *v.* Douall, 1725 ; M. 6807. M'Nee *v.* Balmanno, 1825 ; 3 S. 39 ; 2 W. & S. 7. Bannatyne's Reps. *v.* Brown's Trs., 1825 ; 3 S. 407. Allan *v.* Allan & Co., 1831 ; 9 S. 519. **Devaynes** *v.* **Noble (Clayton's Case)**, 1 Mer. 585 ; 3 Ross' L. C. 643 ; Tudor's L. C. 1 ; 15 R. R. 151. Dickson *v.* Moncrieff, 1853 ; 16 D. 24.

(*m*) **Devaynes** *v.* **Noble**, *supra* (*l*). **Bodenham** *v.* **Purchas**, 2 B. & Ald. 39 ; 3 Ross' L. C. 661 ; 20 R. R. 342. Mills *v.* Fowkes, 5 Bing. N. C. 455. Simson *v.*

Ingham, *supra* (*c*). Houston's Exrs. *v.* Speirs, 1829; 3 W. & S. 392. **Christie** *v.* **Royal Bank**, 1839; 1 D. 745; aff. 1841, 2 Rob. 118; 3 Ross' L. C. 668. Lang *v.* Brown, 1859; 22 D. 113. Campbell *v.* Montgomerie, 1839; 1 D. 1147. Jackson *v.* Nicoll, 1870; 8 Macph. 408. M'Laren *v.* Bradley, 1874; 2 R. 185. Scott's Trs. *v.* Alexander's Tr., 1884; 11 R. 407. Cuthill *v.* Strachan, 1894; 21 R. 549. Where a copy of such an account kept by the creditor was sent to the debtor, the creditor was held to have lost his right to change the entries in the account. Hooper *v.* Keay, *supra* (*k*).

(*n*) Copland *v.* Toulmin, 7 C. & F. 349. Henniker *v.* Wigg, 4 Q. B. 795. Wickham *v.* Wickham, 2 K. & J. 478. Merriman *v.* Ward, 1 J. & H. 371. City Disc. Co. *v.* M'Lean, L. R. 9 C. P. 692; 43 L. J. C. P. 344. *In re* Hallett's Estate, 13 Ch. D. 696; 49 L. J. Ch. 415. Pollock & Co. *v.* Murray & Spence, 1863; 2 Macph. 14. As to indefinite payments to beneficiaries by trustees holding two distinct funds, see Beith *v.* Mackenzie, 1875; 3 R. 185.

564. Evidence of Payment. — (1.) *The General Rule* is: "unumquodque eodem modo solvitur quo colligatur."

565. So payment of an obligation constituted by writing must be proved by written evidence, as in a money debt. But parole evidence is sufficient where the contract is parole, and payment an integral part of it, as in sale for ready money (*a*). 'So, when payment forms part of a series of intromissions or agency transactions, where payment is made by third parties on behalf of the debtor, parole has sometimes been admitted (*b*). A receipt neither holograph nor tested, the signature being proved, is generally, and always in payment of rents and *in re mercatoriâ*, sufficient evidence of payment (*c*). Payment of bills and notes may, it appears, be proved by parole (*d*.)'

(*a*) Crawford *v.* Munro, 1823; 2 S. 213; 1 Ill. 338. Macdonald *v.* Callender, 1786; M. 12,366. Parole evidence of payment is not allowed when the sale is upon credit, even for a few days. Tod *v.* Flockhart, 1799; Hume, 498. Shaw *v.* Wright, 1877; 5 R. 245.

(*b*) Birnie's Assignees *v.* Darroch, 1842; 4 D. 366. Glasgow Infirmary *v.* Caldwell, 1857; 20 D. 1. Tosh *v.* Ogilvie, 1873; 1 R. 255. See 4 Ersk. 2. § 21. Dickson, Ev. § 590. Mackenzie *v.* Brodie, 1859; 21 D. 1048. As to payment of wages, see Brown *v.* Mason, 1856; 19 D. 137.

(*c*) M'Laren *v.* Howie, 1869; 8 Macph. 106; *supra*, § 20. As to the effect of receipts, see Gordon *v.* Trotter, 1833; 11 S. 696. Swan *v.* Baird, 1836; 15 S. 251. Macfarlan *v.* Watt, 1828; 6 S. 556 (markings on a bill). Smith's Merc. Law, 681; and Lee *v.* Lanc. and Y. Ry. Co., L. R. 6 Ch. 527. Fleming *v.* Brown, 1861; 23 D. 443 (legacy).

(*d*) 45 and 46 Vict. c. 61, § 100. See above, § 333B *ad fin.*

566. (2.) *Presumed Payment.*—Payment is not in general to be presumed, unless the circumstances are irreconcilable with the subsistence of the debt (*a*). But it is presumed from the document 'of debt' being found in possession of the debtor 'or cautioner,' according to the maxim, *Chirographum apud debitorem repertum præsumitur solutum* (*b*). This presumption, however, yields to proof, 'which may be by parole (*c*)'; as in a bill sent for acceptance, and kept by the drawee; or a receipt or document lost, and falling into the debtor's hands; or a bill stolen from a messenger (*d*). 'When a cheque is proved or admitted to have been granted by a debtor to his creditor and paid, the presumption is, in the absence of contrary evidence, that it was a payment to account of the debt (*e*).'

(*a*) Graham *v.* Veitch, 1823; 2 S. 594; 1 Ill. 338. See M'Kie *v.* Watson, 1837; 16 S. 73; 3 Ill. 145. Irvine *v.* Lang, 1840; 2 D. 804. Gordon *v.* Glendonwyn, 1838; 16 S. 645. Johnstone *v.* Watson, 1848; 6 Bell's Ap. 245. Melrose *v.* Bruce, 1855; 17 D. 965. Patrick *v.* Watt, 1859; 21 D. 637. Tosh *v.* Ogilvie, *supra.*

(*b*) 3 Ersk. 4. § 5. Gordon *v.* Johnston's Heirs, 1703; M. 11,408. Rollo *v.* Simpson, 1710; M. 11,411. Stewart *v.* Central Bank, 1859; 21 D. 1180.

(*c*) Ersk. *l.c.* Henry *v.* Miller, 1884; 11 R. 713. Cf. Cameron *v.* Panton's Trs., 1891; 18 R. 728 (*per* L. O.).

(*d*) Ersk. *ut supra.* Fithie *v.* E. Northesk, 1693; 4 B. Sup. 70. Ross *v.* Drummond, 1699; *ib.* 464. Edward *v.* Fyfe, 1823; 2 S. 431. See above, § 559. As to the mode of proof, see Dickson on Evid. § 952.

(*e*) Nicoll *v.* Reid, 1878; 6 R. 216. Haldane *v.* Speirs, 1872; 10 Macph. 537. Robb *v.* Robb's Trs., 1884; 11 R. 881. *Infra*, § 2257 (*g*).

567. From three consecutive discharges of periodical payments (as rents, interests, feu-duties, or salaries), payment of all preceding is presumed '(*apocha trium annorum*) (*a*); and it appears that the presumption may be redargued by parole (*b*).' But it is not enough that there have been three consecutive payments without a discharge (*c*). 'Nor does the presumption arise where arrears are constituted by bill or bond, although there are consecutive discharges for the following terms (*d*).' It was doubted whether the presumption holds where the discharges are by a factor (*e*); but such discharge has been held sufficient. One discharge for three consecutive years does not raise the presumption: nor is it enough to show irregular payments amounting in all to three years' rent or interest (*f*).

'*Silence — Mora.* — Payment is presumed from taciturnity, *i.e.* where the relation of the parties and the whole circumstances, coupled with long silence (but not silence or failure to make a demand alone), lead to the reasonable inference of payment or abandonment (*g*). In claims which require constitution, mere delay (*mora*) is enough to found a plea of abandonment or waiver, at least when it is such that it may have caused the party against whom the claim is made to have altered his position or lost evidence (*h*).'

(*a*) 3 Ersk. 4. § 10, and cases cited. Errol *v.* Cruickshanks, 1605; M. 11,392; 1 Ill. 339. Williamson *v.* Balgillo, 1631; M. 11,393. D. of Buccleuch *v.* M'Turk, 1845; 7 D. 927. Hunter, L. & T. ii. 416 (443). See below, § 585.
(*b*) Buccleuch, *cit.* Hunter *v.* Kinnaird, *infra* (*f*). Cameron *v.* Panton's Trs., 1891; 18 R. 729 (*per* L. Kincairney).
(*c*) Morrison *v.* East Nisbet Tenants, 1631; M. 11,394; 1 Ill. 339.
(*d*) Ersk. *l.c.* Patrick *v.* Watt, 1859; 21 D. 637.
(*e*) Ld. Wedderburn *v.* Nisbet, 1612; M. 6322; 1 Ill. 339, note. Preston *v.* Scott, 1667; M. 11,397. Earl Marischal *v.* Fraser, 1682; M. 11,399, 3551. Blackadder *v.* Cockburn, 1687; M. 3552; 3 B. S. 648.
(*f*) Hunter *v.* L. Kinnaird's Trs., 1829; 7 S. 548. Here receipts for balance of year's rent for five successive years were held to raise the presumption. A presumption of waiver was held to apply to penal rent for miscropping, where the landlord had given receipts for the ordinary rents for a series of years without reservation. Baird *v.* Mount, 1874; 2 R. 104.
(*g*) Cullen *v.* Wemyss, 1838; 1 D. 32. Ryrie *v.* Ryrie, 1840; 2 D. 1210. Seath *v.* Taylor, 1848; 10 D. 377. Thomson *v.* Smith, 1849; 12 D. 276. Moncrieff *v.* Waugh, 1859; 21 D. 216. Thomson's Trs. *v.* Monteith's Tr., 1834; 12 S. 842. M'Kie *v.* Watson, *supra*, 566 (*a*). Spence *v.* Paterson's Trs., 1873; 1 R. 46.
(*h*) See above, § 27A. Cook *v.* N. B. Ry. Co., 1872; 10 Macph. 513. Stewart *v.* North, 1893; 20 R. 260.

568. Physicians' and lawyers', '*i.e.* counsel's' fees are presumed to have been paid (*a*). But in the case of the former, this presumption does not hold during the deathbed sickness (*b*). And if a promise or contract shall be established, the presumption will not hold (*c*). Nor will it hold if local custom be different, 'as it now generally is, unless in the case of those who are merely consulting physicians or surgeons (*d*). Tavern bills are presumed to be paid, unless the tavern-keeper prove the subsistence as well as the constitution of the debt, which he may do *prout de jure* (*e*).'

(*a*) Johnston *v.* Bell, 1716; M. 11,418; 1 Ill. 339. Russell *v.* Dunbar, 1717; M. 11,419. Malcolm *v.* Balfour, 1744; Elch. *Presump.* 15. Park *v.* Langlands, 1755; M. 11,421. Hamilton *v.* Gibson, 1781; M. 11,422. Sanders *v.* Hewat, 1822; 1 S. 310. See below, § 1403.
(*b*) Cases *supra* (*a*).
(*c*) Johnston, *supra* (*a*). M'Kenzie *v.* Town of Burntisland, 1728; M. 11,421.
(*d*) Flint *v.* Alexander, 1795; M. 11,422. Sanders, *supra* (*a*).
(*e*) Barnett *v.* Colvill, 1840; 2 D. 337.

II. PERFORMANCE.

569. Rules.—Obligations *ad factum præstandum* may be implemented by any one representing the debtor, or by his authority, or by one interposing for his relief from the obligation; provided in those several cases the creditor have no interest to insist on the debtor himself fulfilling his obligation.

570. Where the engagement is peculiarly personal, it is discharged by the death or incapacity of the debtor (*a*).

(*a*) See above, § 179. Fraser, M. & S. 102. Hall *v.* Wright, 29 L. J. Q. B. 43. Robinson *v.* Davidson, L. R. 7 Ex. 469. Stubbs *v.* Holywell Ry. Co., L. R. 2 Ex. 211; 36 L. J. Ex. 166. Hoey *v.* M'Ewan & Auld, 1867; 5 Macph. 814. Smith *v.* Riddell, 1886; 14 R. 95. As to partial performance and supervening incapacity, see Sims Reeves *v.* Edin. Choral Union, 1871; 2 Sel. Sh. Ct. Ca. 121 and note.

571. When the obligation relates to a specific subject, the destruction of the subject, without fault, extinguishes the obligation; if the subject be destroyed by fault of the obligor, the obligation resolves into a claim of damage (*a*).

(*a*) See above, § 29.

CHAPTER XX

OF COMPENSATION

572. Nature of Compensation.—The concurrence of two liquid debts reciprocally due may be made to operate as payment from the moment of concourse (*a*). This is called in England "Set-off"; with us, "Compensation." It rests on two principles—the expediency of abating lawsuits, and the avoiding of injustice; and this doctrine is in Scotland established and regulated by statute.

(*a*) 1592, c. 141. 1 Stair, 18. § 6. Moore's Notes, p. cxxxviii. 3 Ersk. Prin. 4. § 2. 3 Ersk. 4. § 11–19. 2 Bell's Com. 124. In England the provisions of the Common Law Procedure Act, 23 and 24 Vict. c. 126, which gave an extended right of set-off to defendants, have been still further enlarged by the "Supreme Court Judicature Acts, 1873–1894," and the rules made under them. In particular, counter-claims for damages may be set up; and a defendant pleading a set-off may obtain all such relief as he has properly claimed by his pleading, and as the Court might have granted in an action instituted for the same purpose. In Scotland the reform of procedure has not extended so far in this direction.

573. The General Rules of compensation are—

(1.) The debts must be of the same nature. So, an obligation to deliver grain or goods cannot be set off against a pecuniary obligation (*a*); but a claim for damage sustained in the carriage of goods has been allowed to be set off against freight (*b*). 'This, however, is not properly compensation under the statute 1592, c. 141; but rests on the ground that a party who has failed to fulfil his part of a mutual contract is not entitled to insist on performance of the counterpart (*c*).'

(2.) The debts must both be due: So there is no compensation between a present debt, and one that is future or contingent (*d*).

(3.) The debts must both be liquid, "certum an et quantum debeatur" (*e*); it being, however, sufficient that the debt shall be instantly verified by writ or oath (*f*). But the bankruptcy of one of the parties seems to entitle the other in equity to *retain* (*g*) till the illiquid debt be constituted, or in security of a future 'or contingent' debt. 'So an indorser of a bill cannot plead compensation against a claim by the acceptor while his indorsee holds the bill; but he is entitled to retain what he owes to the acceptor, the debtor in the bill, until he is relieved of his contingent liability, and when he pays and again becomes holder of the bill he has a proper right of compensation (*h*).'

(4.) The parties must be debtor and creditor, each in his own right, and at the same time (*i*). A factor will, to this effect, be held as principal where he has sold goods consigned to him without notice to the buyer of his being only a factor (*k*); but if, before the goods are delivered, the purchaser has notice that they belong to a third party, there will be no compensation on a debt of the factor (*l*). And when the sale is by a broker without disclosing the name of his principal, the buyer cannot plead compensation on a debt due by him to the broker (*m*). 'The rule is, that if a principal by his conduct induces a buyer to believe that his agent is contracting on his own account, he is subject to all the equities pleadable by a party contracting with the agent which have arisen before the principal is disclosed; *e.g.* to compensation upon a debt existing before such disclosure, though it may not have existed at the time of the contract (*n*). Compensation cannot be pleaded if the party contracting knows that the other party is an agent, though he may not know who the principal is (*o*). A factor entrusted with the possession of goods is presumed to have authority to sell in his own name, and a purchaser's right to a set-off against him is not defeated by a private prohibition by his principal to sell in his own name (*p*). It would seem that when an agent sues for the price of goods sold by him as his own, or for a debt due to his principal, having himself no beneficial interest in the claim, the buyer or debtor may plead compensation on a debt due to him by the principal (*q*). On this principle an executor or trustee, dealing as such with a bank, is not exposed to a plea of compensation or retention upon a debt due to the bank by the testator (*r*).'

(5.) Difficult questions have arisen as to compensation between company debts and debts of the partners. The rules seem to be these: In the common case there is no concourse of debt and credit between the debt of the company and the debt of any individual partner; the company forming an entirely separate person in law (*s*). But it 'is now settled that' a company, called upon to pay a debt to one who is debtor of a partner, may arrange with that partner to enable them to satisfy the debt by assigning his debt to the company, so as to make a concourse (*t*). Such arrangement, however, cannot be made after bankruptcy (*u*). Where the company debt is demanded from a partner, or where the company is bankrupt or dissolved, the partner may set off the debt due to him against the company debt (*v*). 'After the dissolution of a solvent company, each partner has a right to a share of the debts due to the firm; and hence there is then a proper *concursus debiti et crediti* between a debt due by a partner and a debt due to the company by his creditor in that debt, to the extent of his share (*w*).'

(6.) If any one has an interest in extinguishing the debt claimed, he may plead compensation (*x*).

(*a*) 3 Ersk. 4. § 15. Elliot *v.* Ellis, 1631; M. 2649; 1 Ill. 340. Tullialan *v.* Condie, 1664; M. 2559.

(*b*) Taylor *v.* Forbes, 1830; 9 S. 113.

(*c*) M'Donald *v.* Thomson, 1843; 5 D. 719. Scottish N.-E. Ry. Co. *v.* Napier, 1859; 21 D. 700. Johnston *v.* Robertson, 1861; 23 D. 646. Burt *v.* Bell, 1861; 24 D. 13. See Pillans & Co. *v.* Pitt, 1825; 4 S. 350. Stewart & Co. *v.* Dennistoun, 1854; 16 D. 1062. See above, § 71.

(*d*) 3 Ersk. 4. § 15.

(*e*) Dun *v.* Craig, 1824; 3 S. 274. Mowat *v.* Denham, 1828; 7 S. 88. Cargill *v.* Baxter, 1829; 7 S. 662. Finlayson *v.* Russell, 1829; 7 S. 698. Ewing *v.* E. Strathmore, 1825; 4 S. 310; 6 W. & S. 56. Dunbar *v.* Davidson, 1826; 4 S. 124 (a pursuer *in forma pauperis*). Downe, Bell, & Mitchell *v.* Pitcairn, 1829; 3 W. & S. 472. M'Intyre *v.* M'Donald, 1854; 16 D. 485. Drew *v.* Drew, 1855; 17 D. 559. Scot. N.-E. Ry. Co. *cit.* (*c*). Urie *v.* Lumsden, 1859; 22 D. 38. Kerr *v.* Fife, etc., Ry. Co., 1860; 22 D. 564. Mackie *v.* Riddell, 1874; 2 R. 115.

(*f*) 3 Ersk. 4. § 16, and cases there cited. Sligo *v.* Fotheringham, 1777; 5 B. Sup. 420. Seaton *v.* ——, 1683; M. 2566; 1 Ill. 340. M'Dowal *v.* Agnew, 1707; M. 2568. Ross *v.* Mags. of Tain, 1711; M. 2568. Munro *v.* Macdonald's Exrs., 1866; 4 Macph. 687 (action sisted till counter-action ready for hearing).

(*g*) See below, of Retention, § 1410; and wherein it differs from Compensation. Sim *v.* Lundy, 1868; 41 Jur. 136.

(*h*) Hannay & Son's Tr. *v.* Armstrong & Co., 1875; 2 R. 399; aff. 1877, 4 R. H. L. 43. Thomson on Bills, 583.

(*i*) 3 Ersk. 4. § 13. Ferguson *v.* Muir, 1711; M. 2659; 1 Ill. 341. Auld *v.* Riddel, July 6, 1810; F. C. Pearson *v.* Bushby, March 10, 1814; F. C. Lumsden *v.* Allan & M'Kie, 1823; 2 S. 585. Campbell *v.* Little, 1823; 2 S. 429. Hay *v.* Brown, 1825; 4 S. 348 (trustee). Anderson & Co. *v.* Collier, 1829; 7 S. 462; 1 Ill. 342. Fleming *v.* Findlay & Co., 1832; 10 S. 739. M'Intyre, *supra* (*e*). Stuart *v.* Stuart, 1869; 7 Macph. 366. Lavaggi *v.* Pirie & Co., 1872; 10 Macph. 312. Johnston *v.* Johnston, 1875; 2 R. 986 (intervention of trust—party pleading compensation must have a right to sue for the debt pleaded on). Semenza *v.* Brinsley and Dresser *v.* Norwood, *citt. infra* (*o*).

(*k*) Belches *v.* Johnston, 1770; M. *Compens.* Apx. 2; 1 Ill. 342. Baxter *v.* Bell & Maxwell, 1800; *ib.* No. 4. Gall *v.* Murdoch, 1821; 1 S. 75. Hitchiner & Co. *v.* Steuart & Ninian, 1803; M. 14,206. Johnson *v.* Scott & Son, Nov. 14, 1818; F. C. See **George** *v.* **Clagett**, 7 T. R. 359; 2 Smith's L. C. 135; 4 R. R. 462. See Alexander *v.* Monteath, 1846; 8 D. 810. Miller & Paterson *v.* M'Nair, 1852; 14 D. 955. Maspons *v.* Mildred & Co., 51 L. J. Q. B. 605; 9 Q. B. D. 531. Montagu *v.* Forwood, 1893; 2 Q. B. 352.

(*l*) Moor *v.* Clementson, 2 Camp. 22; 11 R. R. 653.

(*m*) **Baring** *v.* **Corrie**, 2 B. & Ald. 137; 1 Ill. 159; 2 Smith's L. C. 123; 20 R. R. 383. Liddell *v.* Young & Son, 1852; 14 D. 647. Matthews *v.* Auld & Guild, 1874; 1 R. 1224. This rule applies even if the buyer knows that the broker is also a merchant, if he does not know in the particular case that he is selling his own goods. Cooke & Son *v.* Eshelby, 12 App. Ca. 271.

(*n*) Lavaggi *v.* Pirie & Co., *supra* (*i*). George *v.* Clagett, *supra* (*k*). Sims *v.* Bond, 5 B. & Ad. 393. Salter *v.* Purchell, 1 Q. B. 213. 2 Smith's L. C. 137 sq. Smith's Merc. Law, 165 sq. M'Laren's Bell's Com. i. 527.

(*o*) Semenza *v.* Brinsley, 18 C. B. N. S. 467; 34 L. J. C. P. 161. Dresser *v.* Norwood, 14 C. B. N. S. 574; 32 L. J. C. P. 201; 17 C. B. N. S. 466; 34 L. J. C. P. 38.

(*p*) **Baring** *v.* **Corrie**, *supra* (*m*), and cases in previous notes. *Ex parte* Dixon, 4 Ch. D. 133; 46 L. J. Bkr. 20. Means of knowledge is not here equivalent to actual knowledge, but may be evidence of it. Borries *v.* Imp. Ottoman Bank, L. R. 9 C. P. 38; 43 L. J. C. P. 3.

(*q*) Thornton *v.* Maynard, L. R. 10 C. P. 695; 44 L. J. C. P. 382. Middleton *v.* Pollock (*ex parte* Nugee), L. R. 20 Eq. 29; 44 L. J. Ch. 584; 2 Smith's L. C. 141.

(*r*) Gray's Trs. *v.* Royal Bank, 1895; 23 R. 199.

(*s*) M'Kie *v.* M'Dowall, 1774; M. 2575.

(*t*) Galdie *v.* Gray, 1774; M. 14,598. Thomson *v.* Stephenson, 1855; 17 D. 739. See cases in note (*v*).

(*u*) Cauvin *v.* Robertson, 1783; M. 2581. See Doe *v.* Dainton, 3 East, 149.

(*v*) Bogle *v.* Ballantyne, 1793; M. 2581. **Scott** *v.* **Hall & Bisset**, June 13, 1809; F. C. Salmon *v.* Padon & Vannan, 1824; 3 S. 405. Russell *v.* M'Nab, 1824; 3 S. 63. Low *v.* Lizars, 1839; 16 S. 1092. Oswald's Trs. *v.* Dickson, 1833; 12 S. 156. Hill *v.* Lindsay, 1847; 10 D. 78. Thomson *v.* Stephenson, *cit.* Heggie *v.* Heggie, 1858; 21 D. 31. Raleigh *v.* Hughson & Dobson, 1861; 23 D. 352.

(*w*) Mitchell *v.* Canal Basin Co., 1869; 7 Macph. 480.

(*x*) M'Bride *v.* Melvill, 1680; M. 2570. Town of Aberdeen *v.* Strachan, 1709; M. 2570. Rae *v.* Clerk, 1738; M. 2571. Middleton *v.* E. Strathmore, 1743; M. 2573. But see Lord Kilkerran's doubt, *ib.*

574. The Exceptions to these Rules are—that there is no compensation in deposit (*a*). Specific appropriation bars compensation; as in the case of an obligation by the debtor to pay certain debts; or where money is given for the purpose of retiring a bill; or when a bill is given to the banker for discount, or sent for payment (*b*); 'or where the debtor's obligation is expressly alimentary or for the maintenance of the creditor (*c*).' A debt prescribed cannot compensate a debt not prescribed, unless upon a reference to oath in the short prescriptions (*d*); and a debt acquired after bankruptcy, or after diligence to attach the debt claimed, is not a sufficient ground of compensation (*e*). 'The fact that a party has a cautioner or collateral security for his debt is not destructive of a right of compensation (*f*).'

(*a*) 1 Stair, 13. § 8. 3 Ersk. 4. § 17, 18. Campbell *v.* Campbell, 1781; M. 2665; 1 Ill. 343. *Supra*, § 212.

(*b*) Douglas *v.* Buchtrig's Crs., 1699; M. 2624. Stewart *v.* Bisset, 1770; M. *Comp.* Apx. 2; Hailes, 342. Farrar & Rooth *v.* North Br. Bank, 1850; 12 D. 1190. Gray's Trs. *v.* Royal Bank, 1895; 23 R. 199.

(*c*) Reid *v.* Bell, 1884; 12 R. 178.

(*d*) Carmichael *v.* Carmichael, 1719; M. 2677; 1 Ill. 343. Baillie *v.* M'Intosh, 1753; M. 2680. Clark *v.* Buchanan, 1773; M. 2665. Miller *v.* Baird, Dec. 7, 1819; Hume, 480. See below, § 575, 620.

(*e*) Crawford *v.* E. Moray, 1662; M. 2613. Mousewell's Crs. *v.* Lawrie, 1662; M. 2614. Cauvin *v.* Robertson, 1783; M. 2581. Mill *v.* Paul, 1825; 4 S. 22. M'Lure *v.* Brown, 1678; M. 2617.

(*f*) Hannay & Son's Tr. *v.* Armstrong & Co., 1875; 2 R. 399; aff. 1877, 4 R. H. L. 43.

575. Operation.—Compensation operates according to these rules:—It must be pleaded 'and sustained' (*a*), not having with us (as it had by the Roman law) any effect *ipso jure*; so it does not stop prescription (*b*) 'till pleaded (*c*).' And it must be pleaded before decree; not being competent by suspension after judgment pronounced (*d*). Even where the decree is in absence, the general rule holds (*e*); but it has been sometimes relaxed (*f*). It is, however, competent to be stated by suspension against a decree of registration in cases of insolvency (*g*), or where the party is *vergens ad inopiam* (*h*). When pleaded, it operates retrospectively to the period of concourse, and so stops interest (*i*).

'The right to compensate passes against assignees, if once vested against the cedent by concourse before assignation. But there can be no compensation if concourse is prevented by intimated assignation before the counter debt arises (*k*).'

(*a*) Grahame *v.* Auchterlony, 1693; 4 B. Sup. 86. Cowan *v.* Gowans, 1878; 5 R. 581.

(*b*) 1 Stair, 18. § 6; corrected by 3 Ersk. 4. § 12. Lord Kilk. in **Maxwell** *v.* **M'Culloch**, 1738; M. 2550; 1 Ill. 343. Baillie, *supra*, § 574 (*d*). Cleland *v.* Stevenson, 1669; M. 2682.

(*c*) See above, § 574; and below, § 620 (*b*).

(*d*) Martin *v.* Livingston, 1632; 1 B. Sup. 78. Nicoll *v.* Blair, 1664; 2 B. Sup. 340. Logan *v.* Coutts, 1678; M. 2641; 1 Ill. 343. Brown's Executors *v.* Davidson, 1694; 4 B. Sup. 142. Gordon *v.* Melvil, 1697; M. 2642. Anderson *v.* Schaw, 1669; M. 2646. Downie *v.* Rae, 1832; 11 S. 51. See Shiells, *infra* (*k*).

(*e*) Paterson's Crs. *v.* Macaulay, 1742; M. 2646. Cunningham & Co. *v.* Wilson & Co., Jan. 17, 1809; F. C.

(*f*) Baillie *v.* Dawson, 1733; Elch. *Comp.* 1. A. *v.* B., 1747; M. 2648. Corbet *v.* Hamilton, 1707; M. 2642; 5 B. Sup. 747.

(*g*) Hill *v.* Kippen, 1822; 2 S. 35.

(*h*) Barclay *v.* Clark, 1683; M. 2641. M'Laren *v.* Bisset, 1736; M. 2646.

(*i*) Cleland, *supra* (*b*). Campbell *v.* Carruthers, 1756; M. *Tack*, Apx. 1.

(*k*) 2 Bell's Com. 138 (131, M'L.'s ed.). Shiells *v.* Ferguson, Davidson, & Co., 1876; 4 R. 250. MacGregor's Tr. *v.* Cox, 1883; 10 R. 1028 (trustee in bankruptcy). Elmslie *v.* Grant, 1830; 9 S. 200 (tenant—maills and duties). Chambers' Factor *v.* Vertue, 1892; 20 R. 257.

CHAPTER XXI

OF NOVATION, DELEGATION, CONFUSION, AND DISCHARGE

I. NOVATION.

576. A debt is extinguished by novation in two several ways: Novation properly so called, and Delegation.

Nature of it.—Novation is the substitution of a new engagement or obligation by the same debtor to the same creditor, to the effect of extinguishing the original debt (*a*).

(*a*) 1 Stair, 18. § 8. 3 Ersk. Pr. 4. § 9. 3 Ersk. 4. § 22. Pallet *v.* Rodgers, 1675; 1 B. Sup. 733. Douglas, Heron, & Co. *v.* Brown, 1785; M. 7070; Hailes, 979; 1 Ill. 344.

577. Delegation is the substitution of a new debtor for the old, with consent of the creditor. The person thus substituted was in the Roman law called Expromissor (*a*). 'There is no novation without the assent of three parties,—the original debtor, the new debtor, and the creditor accepting the new debtor and discharging the former obligation (*b*).'

(*a*) 1 Stair, 18. § 8. 3 Ersk. Pr. 4. § 9. 3 Ersk. 4. § 22. Hay *v.* Hall, 1697; M. 11,520; 1 Ill. 344. Clerk *v.* Broadlees' Crs., 1712; 1 B. Sup. 88. Davidson *v.* Ranken, 1733; M. 7061; Elch. *Society*, 1. Buchanan & Co. *v.* Somerville, 1799; M. 3402. Dudgeon *v.* Reid, 1829; 7 S. 729. Hunter *v.* Falconer, 1835; 13 S. 252. Dunlop's Tr. *v.* M'Kechnie, 1845; 7 D. 494. Campbell *v.* Cruickshank, 1845; 7 D. 548. Fox & Sons *v.* Anderson, 1849; 11 D. 1194. Pearston *v.* Wilson, 1856; 19 D. 197. Dundas *v.* Morison, 1857; 20 D. 225 (taking of bills not a discharge of rents). Muir *v.* Dickson, 1860; 22 D. 1070. M'Intosh & Son *v.* Ainslie, 1874; 10 Macph. 304.

(*b*) Authorities in last note. Cf. Addison on Contracts, 162 sqq.; *supra*, § 371.

578. Novation not presumed.—Novation 'or delegation' is not to be presumed where the circumstances are consistent with the subsistence of the original debt (*a*), unless the old security be given up (*b*), or the new one expressly taken in satisfaction, or a new debtor taken in place of the old. Any other alteration on the security is held to be for the convenience and intermediate security or use of the creditor, and in corroboration of the original engagement; as where the creditor in a book-debt takes a bond or bill for the amount (*c*).

'In all cases it is a question of fact whether the tripartite agreement to innovate has been entered into (*d*). In the case of a company or firm subject to change by the retirement of old and the introduction of new partners, comparatively slight evidence is sufficient to show that a customer who continues his dealings with the new firm accepts it as his debtor in place of the old (*e*). But the amalgamation of one joint-stock company with another is not to be assimilated in this respect to a mere change of partners (*f*). And on a Life Assurance Company transferring its business to another company, or amalgamating with it, a policy-holder is not deemed to have abandoned his claim against the former company by paying premiums to the latter, or by any other act, or to have accepted in lieu thereof the liability of the transferee company, unless such abandonment and acceptance have been signified by some writing signed by him or his authorised agent (*g*).'

(*a*) King *v.* Taylor, 1629; M. 11,518; 1 Ill. 344. Binny *v.* Scot, 1675; M. 7057. Callender *v.* Colzier, 1677; 1 B. Sup. 781, and 3 *ib.* 138. Kincaid *v.* Deas, 1696; M. 7060. Thomson *v.* Kerr, 1736; Elch. *Presump.* 6. Ross's Crs., 1713; 5 B. Sup. 96. Grant *v.* Donaldson, 1715; M. 7060. Bank of Scotland *v.* Bank of England, 1781; M. 14,121;

Hailes, 870. Rutherford *v.* Anderson, 1785; M. 7069; Hailes, 968. Skinner *v.* Paterson, 1823; 2 S. 312. Buchanan & Co. *v.* Adam, 1833; 11 S. 762. Cox *v.* Tait, 1843; 5 D. 1283. Pattie *v.* Thomson, 1843; 6 D. 350.

(*b*) Stevenson *v.* Duncan, 1806; Hume, 245. Journeymen Dyers *v.* Thomson, 1802; Hume, 244. Fraser and other cases in note (*c*), *infra.* The case of Hope Johnston *v.* Cornwall, 1895, 22 R. 314, ignores the importance of giving up the bill, and in any view is so special that it cannot be regarded as involving any principle.

(*c*) Gordon *v.* Gordon, 1678; M. 7059. D. of Norfolk *v.* Annuitants of York Bdgs. Co., 1752; M. 7062; 1 Ill. 345. Davidson *v.* Ranken, 1733; M. 7061; 1 Elch. *Soc.* 1. Dougal *v.* Gordon, 1795; M. 851. Moubray *v.* White, 1824; 3 S. 100, 323. Edgar & Lyon *v.* Robinson, 1825; 3 S. 513. Linning *v.* Douglas, 1821; 1 S. 89. Skinner, *supra* (*a*). Wilson & Corse *v.* Gardner, 1807; Hume, 247. Pearson *v.* Donald, 1839; 1 D. 615. Fraser *v.* Maclennan, 1849; 12 D. 208. Roy's Trs. *v.* Stalker, 1850; 12 D. 722. Cullen *v.* Wright, 1863; 1 Macph. 734. Pollock & Co. *v.* Murray & Spence, 1863; 2 Macph. 14. Anderson *v.* M'Dowal, 1865; 3 Macph. 727. Scott *v.* Sinclair, 1865; 3 Macph. 918. M'Intosh & Son *v.* Ainslie, 1872; 10 Macph. 304.

When the personal obligation under a bond and disposition in security is transmitted by agreement in virtue of the Conveyancing Act, 1874, to a disponee of the security subject, the creditor, though no party to the transmission, gets an additional obligant in the disponee, and delegation does not take place. 37 and 38 Vict. c. 94, § 47. Univ. of Glas. *v.* Yuill's Tr., 1882; 9 R. 643.

(*d*) See cases in Addison on Contr. 162; and under § 577.

(*e*) Buchanan *v.* Somerville, Buchanan & Co. *v.* Adam, Dunlop's Tr. *v.* M'Kechnie, Campbell *v.* Cruickshank, Pearston *v.* Wilson, Muir *v.* Dickson, *cit.* § 577, 578 (*a*). *In re* Family Endowment Soc., L. R. 5 Ch. 518; 39 L. J. Ch. 306. Smith's Merc. Law, 52 sqq. See above, § 383, 384.

(*f*) Family Endowment Soc., *cit.* *In re* Medical L. A. Soc. (Spencer's Case), L. R. 6 Ch. 362; 40 L. J. Ch. 455. Lindley on Company Law, 258–61. Buckley on the Companies Acts, 403 sqq.

(*g*) 35 and 36 Vict. c. 41, § 7.

579. Effect of Novation.—Novation of either kind extinguishes the debt, with its accessories. But a special stipulation may preserve them; or the old debtor may guarantee the credit of the new. If the old debtor knew, while the creditor was ignorant, that the substituted debtor was insolvent, the original debt will subsist.

II. CONFUSION.

580. Nature of Confusion.—When the same person becomes both creditor and debtor in an obligation, without any right of relief against another, the *jus crediti* is suspended (*a*); and if no interest of the creditor interferes to make it desirable to keep up the debt, it is held to be satisfied and extinguished '*confusione*' (*b*).

Where the creditor has an interest to keep up the debt, it is only suspended, not extinguished (*c*). So the debt may be assigned and money borrowed on it; or it may be kept up for the benefit of children, as by an heir of entail; or, in contemplation of a divergence of the lines of succession, it may be made available to a particular heir; or where the creditor succeeds to the debtor in a character entitled to relief, the debt will not be entirely extinguished, but the right of relief will remain (*d*). 'It rather seems that where one becomes full and absolute creditor and debtor in the same debt without relief, confusion operates at once and irrevocably, unless by taking an assignation of the debt or security he keeps it up as a separate right (*e*).'

(*a*) 1 Stair, 18. § 9. Cf. below, § 997.

(*b*) 3 Ersk. Pr. 4. § 10. 3 Ersk. 4. § 23. Hart *v.* Hart, 1630; M. 3035 and 5566; 1 Ill. 346. Hogg *v.* Brack, 1832; 11 S. 198. See Lord Blantyre *v.* Dunn, *infra*, § 1266. Elder *v.* Watson, 1859; 21 D. 1122. Murray *v.* Parlane's Tr., 1890; 18 R. 287.

(*c*) Cunningham *v.* Lady Cardross, 1680; M. 3038. Cuming *v.* Irvine, 1726; M. 3042; 1 Cr. & St. 103. Murray *v.* Neilson, 1728; M. 3043. Codrington *v.* Johnstone, 1824; 2 S. Ap. 118. Lawrie *v.* Donald, 1830; 9 S. 147. Welsh *v.* Barstow, 1837; 15 S. 537. Mackenzie *v.* Orr, 1838; 16 S. 311; aff. M'L. & Rob. 117. Fleming *v.* Imrie, 1868; 6 Macph. 363.

(*d*) Gordon *v.* Maitland, 1757; M. 11,161. Crawford *v.* Hotchkis, March 11, 1809; F. C. Macalister *v.* Macalister, 1865; 4 Macph. 245; below, § 914.

(*e*) See Forbes & Co. *v.* Duncan, 1802; M. App. *Tailzie*, 2. Codrington, *cit.* Hogg, *cit.* D. Roxburghe *v.* Wauchope, 1825; 1 W. & S. 41. V. Strathallan *v.* Drummond, 1828; 6 S. 881. There is some difficulty in extracting a more precise formula from the cases. See Bell's Conveyancing, p. 348–9. Nicolson's Ersk. Inst. iii. 4. 23–27. Murray *v.* Parlane, *cit.* (*b*). It is clear that while one who advances money to pay prior charges upon an estate is entitled to have an assignation to these securities, which will be preferable to subsequent securities existing at the date of the assignation; an absolute owner paying up prior securities cannot keep them up for his own benefit against subsequent incumbrances. Mackenzie *v.* Orr, *cit.* Love *v.* Storie, 1863; 2 Macph. 22. See 1 Stair, 18. § 9. Ersk. *l.c.* Guthrie's Erskine's Principles, iii. 4. 10 (16th ed. p. 432).

581. Operation.—Confusion takes place where the debtor succeeds to the creditor; where the creditor succeeds to the debtor, and to the extent of the right thus arising; where a stranger succeeds to both; where the creditor and debtor intermarry 'previous to July 18, 1881,' and the debt is moveable (*a*).

(*a*) 3 Ersk. 4. § 23, 24. Codrington, *supra*, § 580 (*c*). See Hogg, *supra*, § 580 (*b*). See 44 and 45 Vict. c. 21.

III. DISCHARGE.

582. Nature of Discharge.—A discharge is properly the acknowledgment of payment or performance actually made; but it may be granted independently of performance or payment, which is called Acceptilation.

Proof.—Express discharge must be established by evidence equally available with that which constitutes the obligation (*a*). 'An agreement to discharge mutual debts by setting one against the other must be proved by writ or oath (*b*).'

Effect.—A discharge extinguishes the debt; but it is frequently combined with an assignation; as, where a cautioner is called upon to pay a debt, he gets from the creditor a discharge of his own obligation, and an assignation of the debt, for the purpose of operating his relief without the necessity of raising an action (*c*).

(*a*) Although donation may be proved by parole evidence (*supra*, § 64), it has not yet been held that a donation which consists in the renunciation or discharge of a debt vouched by writing may be so proved. But when the discharge is effected by delivery and destruction of such a document, parole is competent. Anderson's Trs. *v.* Webster, 1883; 11 R. 35; where the decision, though put on narrower grounds, might perhaps have been referred to the larger principle now admitted in regard to donation.

(*b*) See Hannay & Son's Tr. *v.* Armstrong Bros., 1875; 2 R. 399; aff. 4 R. H. L. 43. Cowan *v.* Shaw, 1878; 5 R. 680. Mackenzie *v.* Brodie, 1859; 21 D. 1058. M'Laren *v.* Howie, 1869; 8 Macph. 106.

(*c*) 3 Ersk. 4. § 8; also § 7. See above, § 557. As to reduction of discharge on ground of mistake, see M'Farlane *v.* M'Farlane's Trs., 1897; 24 R. 574.

583. **Construction.**—A special discharge, with a general clause superadded, is limited to debts of the same kind with that specially discharged (*a*).

(*a*) 3 Ersk. 4. § 9. 1 Stair, 18. § 2. Talbot *v.* Guydet, 1705; M. 5027; 1 Ill. 347. Logan *v.* Mitchell, 1797; M. 11,379. Ewen (or Graham) *v.* Mags. of Montrose, 1824; 2 S. 612; rev. 1825, 1 W. & S. 595; 4 W. & S. 346.

584. The words of a general voluntary discharge include all debts of which, at the date, the granter could demand payment, except those of an extraordinary description; as cautionry, feu-duties, heritable burdens, etc. (*a*); 'except also claims of which the granter was ignorant, or which he must be presumed not to have contemplated (*b*). A wider construction is given to a discharge which from its conception is plainly intended to be universal; and so' a general discharge in bankruptcy comprehends all debts of every description, present, future, and contingent, contracted previous to the date of the first deliverance on the petition for sequestration; 'or, in an extrajudicial arrangement, previous to the date of the discharge, or other date specified (*c*).'

(*a*) 3 Ersk. 4. § 9. Campbell *v.* Napier, 1678; M. 5035; 1 Ill. 347. Oliphant *v.* Newton, 1682; M. 5035. M'Taggart *v.* Jeffrey, 1828; 6 S. 641; 4 W. & S. 361. Ewen, *cit.* Adam *v.* M'Dougal, 1831; 9 S. 570. See Neilson's Trs. *v.* Neilson's Trs., 1883; 11 R. 119 (construction).

(*b*) Greenock Banking Co. *v.* Smith, 1844; 6 D. 1340. Purdon *v.* Rowat's Tr., 1856; 19 D. 206. Dickson *v.* Halbert, and cases in § 11 *ad fin.*, and § 534. Lyall *v.* Edward, 6 H. & N. 337; 30 L. J. Ex. 193. Moon's Trs. *v.* Carmichael, 1836; 14 S. 1026. M. of Tweeddale *v.* Hume, 1848; 10 D. 1053. Rennie *v.* Walker, 1800; M. Apx. *Presumption*, 4. Haselgrove *v.* House, 6 B. & S. 975; 35 L. J. Q. B. 1; L. R. 1 Q. B. 101.

(*c*) 54 Geo. III. c. 137, § 59 and 61. 19 and 20 Vict. c. 79, § 140, 147. Harris *v.* Churchill, 1822; 1 S. 370. Adam, *cit.* Brit. L. Co. *v.* Esplin, 1849; 11 D. 1104. Whyte *v.* Knox, 1858; 20 D. 970.

585. **Presumed Discharge.**—Discharge is presumed, from three consecutive receipts for rents or other periodical payments (*a*), and from the settlement of a factor's 'or other' periodical accounts (*b*). 'There is also in many circumstances a presumption of discharge or of payment from *mora*, or even apart from delay from the relations and actings of parties (*c*).'

(*a*) See *ante*, § 567.

(*b*) 3 Ersk. 4. § 10. M'Arthur *v.* M'Arthur, 1821; 1 S. 41, 87. Walker *v.* Drummond, 1836; 14 S. 780; 3 Ill. 146. Glasgow Infirmary *v.* Caldwell, 1858; 20 D. 1. Laing *v.* Laing, 1862; 24 D. 1362. Fell *v.* Rattray, 1869; 41 S. Jur. 236. See M'Adie *v.* M'Adie's Exr., 1883; 10 R. 741.

(*c*) Wilson *v.* Wilson, 1783; M. 11,646. Stuart *v.* M'Conochie's Exrs., 1836; 14 S. 412. Russell's Trs. *v.* Russell, 1885; 13 R. 331; and see Dickson on Evid. § 618 sqq.

CHAPTER XXII

EXTINCTION OF OBLIGATIONS BY LIMITATION AND PRESCRIPTION

586. Distinction between Limitation and Prescription.—The mere lapse of time in some cases bars action on an obligation; in others, it extinguishes the obligation entirely. But in order correctly to mark the principle on which this doctrine proceeds, it is necessary to distinguish between Limitation properly speaking, and what more correctly is called Prescription. Limitation is a denial of action on an instrument or document of debt, after the lapse of a certain time, without regard to the actual subsistence of the debt; as in holograph writings, bonds of caution, bills and notes. Prescription is a legal presumption of abandonment or of satisfaction, and so extinguishes the debt; as in the long negative prescription, the decennial, quinquennial, and triennial prescriptions. This distinction is grounded on a real difference in principle; and although it may seem unimportant, it enters into all arguments on the more nice and difficult questions in this department.

I. LIMITATION.

587. Limitation of action is either by convention or by statute; the former being a condition in the obligation, the latter established on grounds of public expediency.

588. Conventional Limitation depends entirely on the will of the parties. Thus—

An obligation stipulated to be binding for a certain time, is extinguished by the lapse of that time; as an obligation to guarantee a loan during six months; or an obligation to pay a sum of money, provided a demand shall be made within a year; or to pay an annuity during a certain term of years. In such stipulations it is important to observe the distinction between engagements to *endure* for a certain time, and engagements for collateral matters to *take effect* provisionally within a time certain. The expiration of the limited time extinguishes the one; it only points the application of the other.

An obligation may be limited to a particular event (as the provision of a sum on A.'s attaining a certain age); in which case by predecease the obligation is extinguished, the condition becoming impossible. Obligations are also sometimes specially limited to the person of the debtor or of the creditor; in which case the death of the party, or incapacity to perform the thing undertaken, will extinguish the right and discharge the obligation. So an obligation by an artist to paint a picture, or an agreement to give the use of a thing to one during life, or an obligation to pay an annuity during life, expires with the life of the person.

589. Statutory Limitation.—The laws by which the effect of written obligations is limited to a certain term, proceed on the obvious expediency of protecting persons against demands after the ordinary checks against forgery may have been removed; or against the consequences of too easily putting their hand to cautionary engagements after so transitory an act may have been forgotten. There are statutes of this description establishing the vicennial, the quinquennial, the sexennial, and the septennial limitations.

590. Vicennial Limitation.—By statute, "holograph missive letters, and holograph bonds, and subscriptions in compt-books without witnesses, not being pursued for within twenty years, shall prescrive in all time thereafter, except the pursuer offer to prove by the defender's oath the verity of the said holograph bonds, and letters, and subscriptions in compt-books" (*a*). The statute seems to contemplate only contracts or obligations; and it 'was' doubted whether it is to be held as quite settled by the case below (*b*), that a writing not itself an obligation, but a collateral proof merely, falls under the Act. 'It is now settled that it extends to all holograph writs on which an obligation can be founded, *e.g.* a receipt for money (*c*). Its operation is excluded by action raised within the twenty years (*d*); or probably by pleading compensation (*e*); or by such recognition after the twenty years as may be held to raise a personal exception against the defender pleading the statute (*f*).'

(*a*) 1669, c. 9. 3 Ersk. 7. § 26.
(*b*) Bank of Scotland *v.* ——, 1747; 5 B. Sup. 748; 1 Ill. 348.
(*c*) Mouat *v.* Banks, 1856; 18 D. 1093.
(*d*) Simpson *v.* Brown, 1792; Bell's 8vo Ca. 380.
(*e*) Dickson on Evid. § 435.
(*f*) Dickson on Evid. § 417. Wyse *v.* Wyse, 1847; 9 D. 1405.

591. The time runs from the date of the writing, not from the day of payment, or purifying of a condition (*a*).

(*a*) Home *v.* Donaldson, 1773; M. 10,992; Hailes, 511; 1 Ill. 348. See Wyse *v.* Wyse, *cit.*

592. After the lapse of the statutory period, the authenticity of the writing, not that of the subscription merely, 'but not, in order to exclude the prescription, the subsistence of the obligation (*a*),' must be established by the debtor's oath, or that of his heir (*b*); and in that case it is not necessary to prove the debt (*c*).

The vicennial prescription does not run against a minor (*d*).

(*a*) Ersk. *l.c.*
(*b*) 3 Ersk. 7. § 26. Correct Sir G. M'Kenzie's Obs. on the Act, 2 Parl. Ch. II. sess. 1, c. 9. E. of Leven *v.* Arnot, 1715; M. 10,991; 1 Ill. 348. Graham *v.* Cochran, 1725; M. 10,992. Brown *v.* Crawford, 1441; M. 9417. Dalzell *v.* L. Lindores, 1784; M. 10,994; Hailes, 984.
(*c*) Muir *v.* Cunningham, 1675; 4 B. Sup. 269. E. of Leven, *supra* (*b*). Wyse, § 590 (*f*).
(*d*) 1669, c. 9 *in fin.* See Gray *v.* Fothringham, 1700; M. 10,987.

593. Quinquennial Limitation.—By statute, "all bargains concerning moveables, or sums of money provable by witnesses, shall only be provable by writ or oath of party, if the same be not pursued for within five years after the making of the bargain" (*a*). Under this limitation are comprehended sales of moveables, and the contracts of hiring, loan, deposit, pledge (*b*), 'if not constituted by writ (*c*).' But it has been held not to apply to a consignment of goods not being a sale, or account of furnishings, 'or any accounting between agent and principal' (*d*). It has sometimes been held that *actions* raised on holograph writings fall under the quinquennial prescription of the Act, 1685, c. 14, and on this Erskine (*e*) speaks ambiguously. There does not appear to be any ground for such an opinion in either of the statutes. 'After the five years, both the subsistence and the constitution of the debt must be proved by the debtor's writ or oath (*f*).'

(*a*) 1669, c. 9. 3 Ersk. Pr. 7. § 8. 3 Ersk. 7. § 20.
(*b*) White *v.* Spence, 1683; M. 11,065; 1 Ill. 349. Ewart *v.* Murray, 1730; M. 11,067. Nobles *v.* Armstrong, June 1, 1813; F. C. As to sales of farm stocking by valuation, see Lawson *v.* Milne, 1839; 1 D. 603, and Mackintosh *v.* Taylor, 1849; 11 D. 1244.
(*c*) E. Southesk *v.* Reddie, 1682; M. 11,066, 12,326. Hunter *v.* Thomson, 1843; 5 D. 1285.
(*d*) M'Farlane *v.* Brown, 1827; 5 S. 205. M'Kinlay *v.* M'Kinlay & Co., 1851; 14 D. 162.
(*e*) 3 Inst. 7. § 27, 43.
(*f*) Campbell *v.* Grierson, 1848; 10 D. 361. White and Nobles, *supra.* Kennard & Sons *v.* Wright, 1865; 3 Macph. 946.

594. Sexennial Limitation.—This is, strictly speaking, a statutory limitation of action (*a*), by which no bill of exchange, or inland bill, or promissory-note, "shall be of force or effectual to produce any diligence or action in Scotland, unless such diligence shall be raised and executed, or action commenced thereon, within the space of six years from and after the term at which the sums in the said bills and notes become exigible." But it is provided "that it shall be lawful and competent at any time after the expiration of the said six years, in either of the cases mentioned, to prove the debt contained in the bill or note, and that the same is resting owing, by the oath or writ of the debtor." "The years of minority of the creditor are not to be reckoned" (*b*).

(*a*) See above, § 349.
(*b*) 12 Geo. III. c. 72; made perpetual by 23 Geo. III. c. 18, § 55. 1 Bell's Com. 393. Dickson on Evid. § 424 sqq. See Patrick *v.* Watt, 1859; 21 D. 637 (minority—subsequent payments and lapse of time).

595. (1.) *The terminus a quo* is the time at which the debt is exigible (*a*). This is the last day of grace in bills and notes at a fixed term (*b*); the date of the bill itself, if payable on demand (*c*).

In bills and notes at sight, the point 'was' left unsettled: it 'could' not be till presentment, and the safe course 'was' to hold the presentment of the bill to be the *terminus a quo* (*d*). 'But now a bill payable at sight or on presentation is a bill payable on demand (*e*); and so the *terminus a quo* is the date of the bill, at least if that be the date of issue (*f*). But in bills payable at a certain period after demand or notice, time runs from expiry of that period (*g*).'

(*a*) See above, § 326–7.
(*b*) Douglas, Heron, & Co. *v.* Grant, 1793; M. 4602; aff. 6 Bro. Parl. Cases, 276; 3 Pat. 503; 1 Ill. 349.
(*c*) Stephenson *v.* Stephenson's Trs., 1807; M. *Bill*, Apx. 20.
(*d*) Thomson on Bills, 674. Moffat *v.* Marshall, 1838; 16 S. 406.
(*e*) See § 327. 45 and 46 Vict. c. 61, § 10.
(*f*) See English cases in Chalmers's Digest, p. 271.
(*g*) Broddelius *v.* Grischotti, 1887; 14 R. 536.

596. (2.) *The Effect of the Limitation* is, that by mere elapse of time the instrument, as a ground of action or diligence, is extinct, but the debt left unaffected. Therefore diligence cannot proceed on the registered protest (*a*); and in order to establish the debt, the action must not be laid on the *bill*, but on the *debt*, to be established by other proofs than the bill. A certain degree of looseness, however, has crept into practice, which has confounded in some degree the principles on which this matter should be regulated. Actions laid on the bill have been sustained as sufficient to justify a reference to oath, 'a mention of the bill by way of description being almost unavoidable (*b*),' and to entitle the pursuer to judgment on an affirmative oath, or even on a defence admitting the debt (*c*). But the 'strictly' correct decision was pronounced in a case where a summons laid on the bill was held incompetent, reserving action in the proper form (*d*). A decree in absence on such incompetent libel, with all diligence by adjudication or otherwise following on it, would be ineffectual in competition.

(*a*) Douglas, Heron, & Co. *v.* Richardson, 1784; M. 11,127. Armstrong *v.* Johnstone, 1804; M. 11,140.
(*b*) *Per* L. Fullerton in Darnley, *infra.*
(*c*) Campbell *v.* Stuart, 1797; M. 1648; 1 Ill. 349. Philip *v.* Milne, 1800; M. *Bill.* Apx. 9. See Clarkson's Trs. *v.* Gibson, June 8, 1820; F. C. Sinclair *v.* Sinclair, 1823; 2 S. 513. V. Strathallan *v.* Drummond, 1828; 6 S. 881. Darnley *v.* Kirkwood, 1845; 7 D. 595. Galloway *v.* Moffatt, 1845; 7 D. 1088.
(*d*) Stirling *v.* Lang, 1830; 8 S. 638.

597. Another important consequence has been argued as necessarily following from the extinction of the bill as an obligation or ground of action; namely, that one who is bound only by signing the bill as a cautioner, with notice to that effect, but no otherways than by the *verborum obligatio* of the bill, is discharged by the lapse of the six years which terminates its existence (*a*). But a different construction of the Act has been adopted, and the cautioner held liable, if, on reference to oath, the debt is admitted not to have been paid (*b*).

(*a*) Arg. ex Russell *v.* M'Nab, 1822; 2 S. 88; 1 Ill. 350.
(*b*) Philip *v.* Milne, 1800; M. *Bill*, Apx. 13. M'Neil *v.* Blair, 1825; 3 S. 459. Laidlaw *v.* Hamilton, 1826; 4 S. 636. Baird *v.* Little's Tr., 1827; 5 S. 820. Wilson *v.* Strang, 1830; 8 S. 625. Christie *v.* Henderson & Murdoch, 1833; 11 S. 744. Black *v.* Black, 1838; 16 S. 1220. Paul *v.* Allison, 1841; 3 D. 874. Drummond *v.* Crichton, 1848; 10 D. 340. Boyd *v.* Fraser, 1853; 15 D. 342. It is quite settled that in proving the debt it is enough that value has been received by one obligant on the bill, although the deponent may have been merely a cautioner and may have received nothing. Christie, Boyd, etc., *citt.* But it appears to be erroneous to regard Christie *v.* Henderson, Black *v.* Black, etc., as settling the principle that, when one of joint acceptors (or any "accommodation party") depones on reference to his oath that he never paid the bill, but says nothing about payment by the principal debtor or co-

obligants, or depones that he does not know if they paid it, "resting owing" is established. It may be settled that it is not necessary to refer to the oaths of all of several co-acceptors before resting owing can be proved. But in construing the oath, the question in this, as in all cases, is *quid juratum est*, and the onus is on the creditor. See § 599 (*c*); and Campbell's Trs. *v.* Hudson's Exr., 1895; 22 R. 943. Christie *v.* Henderson was decided before Darnley *v.* Kirkwood, *ibi cit.*, and the cases of Alcock and Cullen, § 632; and it really depended on the terms of the oath.

598. (3.) *Interruption.*—The bill or note may be preserved in force 'against all of the obligants' by diligence or a judicial demand 'against one of them' (*a*). In order to be effectual to preserve the bill by judicial demand, the action must be called in court, or at least there must be citation. But protest, with decree of registration, is not diligence to this effect; the diligence must be executed (*b*). Nor is it available to preserve the bill in force, that the creditor has made affidavit and claimed under a private trust (*c*): but where, in the course of such trust, the debt has been *recognised*, it will be a bar to the plea on the statute (*d*). It is sufficient to lodge a claim in a sequestration; but this must be correctly done in terms of the Act (*e*). So, a claim made in a multiplepoinding or any process of competition, 'or pleading compensation on the bill in a suspension,' is held equivalent to an action (*f*). But an action of cognition and sale of a minor's land is not an action of that description (*g*).

(*a*) Gordon *v.* Bogle, 1784; M. 7532; 1 Ill. 352. Roy *v.* Campbell, 1850; 12 D. 1028. Paxton *v.* Forster, 1842; 4 D. 1515. But see the doubts of Lords Young and R. Clark in Milne's Trs. *v.* Ormiston's Trs., 1893; 20 R. 523. See below, § 620, 623.

(*b*) 12 Geo. III. c. 72. Douglas, Heron, & Co. *v.* Richardson, 1784; M. 11,127; 1 Ill. 349. Scott *v.* Brown, 1828; 7 S. 192; 1 Ill. 350. Henderson *v.* Stewart, 1830; 9 S. 180. Fraser *v.* Urquhart, 1831; 9 S. 723. M'Lachlan *v.* Henderson, 1831; 9 S. 753. Walker *v.* Easton, 1831; 9 S. 759. Boag *v.* Fisher, 1849; 11 D. 362 (*med. fugæ* warrant insufficient). Cochrane *v.* Prentice, 1841; 4 D. 76 (action dismissed as incompetent does not interrupt).

(*c*) Watson *v.* Auchincloss, 1822; 1 S. 395; 1 Ill. 352. Blair *v.* Horn, 1858; 21 D. 45; 1859, 21 D. 1004.

(*d*) Ettles *v.* Robertson, 1833; 11 S. 397; 1 Ill. 352. See Watson *v.* Hunter & Co., 1841; 3 D. 583. Dickson on Evid. § 432 sq. Blair *v.* Horn, *cit.* (at p. 49, *per* L. J.-C. Inglis).

(*e*) 54 Geo. III. c. 137, § 52. 19 and 20 Vict. c. 79, § 109. Crawford's Trs. *v.* Haig, 1827; 5 S. 705. M'Callum & Dalgleish *v.* Christie, 1833; 11 S. 321.

(*f*) National Bank *v.* Hope, 1837; 16 S. 177; 3 Ill. 146. Lindsay *v.* E. Buchan, 1854; 16 D. 600. Ross *v.* Robertson, 1855; 17 D. 1144.

(*g*) Ferrier *v.* E. Erroll, June 9, 1812; F. C.; 1 Ill. 362. See below, § 620. See as to a judicial reference, Dunn *v.* Lamb, 1854; 16 D. 944.

599. (4.) *Proof after Six Years.*—When the six years have expired before the action has been raised, the only sufficient proof of the debt is by writing or oath of the debtor (*a*). 'The statute does not introduce a mere presumption of payment, but enacts specific and imperative rules as to probation, which are not affected by the Bills of Exchange Act, 1882 (*b*). It not only limits the mode of proof to the alleged debtor's writ or oath; but it shifts the *onus probandi* from the debtor in the bill to the creditor. After the lapse of six years the holder of the bill has to prove in the statutory way: (1) that the debt was originally due; and (2) that it is resting owing (*c*).'

Such proof, if within the six years, must amount to an acknowledgment of the debt, superseding the bill (*d*), 'or if antecedent to or contemporary with the bill, such as to be independent of it and not innovated and extinguished by the bill (*e*)'; and so payment of interest within the six years, or of part of the sum in the bill, is not enough (*f*). If the acknowledgment refer only to the bill as the document on which the debt depends, it seems not sufficient to sustain action after the six years (*g*).

If the proof offered be subsequent to the six years, it seems sufficient that the acknowledgment shall refer to the bill, and recognise the debt as subsisting (*h*). 'While both constitution and resting owing must be proved by the oath on reference, the creditor is entitled to have from the debtor more than a mere oath of credulity; *i.e.* it is not always enough to say that he believed or understood that the debt was paid by some one, without assigning satisfactory, or at least probable, grounds for the belief (*i*).' The debt is restored, not as if the bill were re-established to run a new course of six years, but as a debt subject to the prescription of forty years (*k*), only as against him who recognises the obligation (*l*). But the privilege of summary execution does not revive in consequence of the acknowledgment of the debt (*m*).

The limitation does not affect the claim of recourse of one who signs an accommodation bill for another (*n*).

(*a*) Wood *v.* Howden, 1843; 5 D. 507.

(*b*) 45 and 46 Vict. c. 61, § 100.

(*c*) **Darnley** *v.* **Kirkwood**, 1845; 7 D. 595 (*per* Ld. Fullerton). M'Gregor *v.* M'Gregor, 1860; 22 D. 1264.

The waiver of the plea of prescription by concurring in a proof *prout de jure* does not alter the rule as to the *onus probandi*, which remains upon the party founding on the bill. Simpson *v.* Stewart, 1875; 2 R. 673. Kerr's Trs. *v.* Ker, 1883; 11 R. 108.

(*d*) Russell *v.* Fairie, 1792; M. 11,130; Bell's Ca. 125; 1 Ill. 353. Lindsay *v.* Moffat, 1797; M. 11,137. M'Tavish *v.* Lady Saltoun, 1825; 3 S. 328. Hunter *v.* Duff, 1831; 9 S. 702. Blair *v.* Horn, 1858-9; 21 D. 45, 1004. Easton *v.* Hinshaw, 1873; 1 R. 23. Nisbet *v.* Neil's Trs., 1869; 7 Macph. 1097.

(*e*) See above, § 576 sqq. Campbell *v.* Campbell, 1779; M. 1648. Blake *v.* Turner, 1860; 23 D. 15. Nisbet, *cit.* (*d*).

(*f*) Horsburgh *v.* Bethune, Feb. 13, 1811; F. C. Ferguson *v.* Bethune, March 7, 1811; F. C. Darnley, *cit.*

(*g*) See Stirling *v.* Lang, 1830; 8 S. 638; 1 Ill. 350. See Nisbet *v.* Neil's Trs., 1869; 7 Macph. 1097.

(*h*) Russell, *supra* (*d*). Scott *v.* Gray, 1784; M. 11,126; Hailes, 939. Black *v.* Shand's Crs., 1823; 2 S. 110 (payment of interest marked in debtor's books by his clerk sufficient). M'Indoe *v.* Frame, 1824; 3 S. 207. M'Kenzie *v.* Noble, 1827; 5 S. 367. Elder *v.* Marshall, 1830; 9 S. 133. See Blair, *supra* (*d*). Watson *v.* Hunter & Co., 1841; 3 D. 583. Wood (or Hislop) *v.* Howden, 1843; 5 D. 507 (which has been questioned). M'Gregor *v.* M'Gregor, 1860; 22 D. 1264 (writ of agent). Rennie *v.* Urquhart, 1880; 7 R. 1030. Storeys *v.* Paxton, 1878; 6 R. 293. Campbell's Trs. *v.* Hudson's Exr. 1895; 22 R. 943. As to admissions on record, see **Darnley** *v.* **Kirkwood**, 1845; 7 D. 595. Noble *v.* Scott, 1843; 5 D. 723. Campbell's Trs., *cit.*

(*i*) Paul *v.* Allison, 1841; 3 D. 874. Fyfe *v.* Carfrae, 1841; 4 D. 152. Black *v.* Black, 1838; 16 S. 1220 (as to which *qu.* ?). Mackay *v.* Ure, 1849; 11 D. 982. **Darnley** *v.* **Kirkwood**, 1846; 8 D. 441. Drummond *v.* Crichton, 1848; 10 D. 340.

(*k*) Ferguson, *supra* (*f*). M'Indoe, *supra* (*h*). Drummond *v.* Lees, 1880; 7 R. 452.

(*l*) Houston *v.* Yuill, 1822; 1 S. 417; Hume, 479. M'Neil *v.* Blair, 1823; 2 S. 155. M'Indoe, *supra* (*h*). Allan *v.* Ormiston, 1817; Hume, 477. Boyd *v.* Fraser, 15 D. 342.

(*m*) Armstrong *v.* Johnston, 1804; M. 11,140; 1 Ill. 349.

(*n*) Ralston *v.* Lamont, 1792; M. 11,130; 1 Ill. 355. Jolly *v.* N'Neil, 1829; 7 S. 666. Hall *v.* Arnot, 1837; 16 S. 263. Comp. Roy *v.* Campbell, 1850; 12 D. 1028; and Buchanan *v.* Macdonald, 1840; 2 D. 1444.

600. Septennial Limitation of Cautionary Obligations.—It has been provided, as a protection against "facility to engage as cautioners for others, who, afterwards failing, have left a growing burden on their cautioners without relief," that "no man binding or engaging for hereafter, for and with another conjunctly and severally, in any bond or contract for sums of money, shall be bound for the said sums for longer than seven years after the date of the bond; but that from and after the said seven years the said cautioner shall be *eo ipso* free of his caution." This, however, is subject to certain conditions (*a*).

(*a*) 1695, c. 5. 3 Ersk. 7. § 22, 24. 1 Bell's Com. 356. See Opinion of the Court in Stewart *v.* Douglas, 1712; M. 11,151; 1 Ill. 355.

601. (1.) *To what Cases applicable or not.*—The Act provides that "whoever is bound for another, either as express cautioner or as principal or co-principal, shall be understood to be a cautioner or have the benefit of this Act, provided that he have either a clause of relief in the bond, or a bond of relief apart, intimated personally to the creditor at his receiving of the bond." He only is held a cautioner who has total relief. So, co-obligants stipulating for mutual relief are not cautioners within the meaning of the Act (*a*), although it should be known that one was only a cautioner (*b*). Nor is total relief (as to a cautioner) sufficient to raise the plea under the Act, unless the cautioner be "bound with and for another," or as "express cautioner." If he be so, it is sufficient (*c*), 'except where one signs a bill "as security" (*d*).' But if he "be bound as principal or co-principal," the bond must contain a "clause of relief," 'or must show by its express language that he is a cautioner and so entitled to relief (*e*),' or there must be a bond of relief "apart" (*f*), intimated personally to the creditor at his receiving of the "bond" (*g*). Although it is not indispensable to give notarial intimation, yet mere private knowledge is not enough (*h*). It must be either notice judicial, if not notarial (*h*); or at least notice established by clear written evidence (*i*).

(*a*) Ballantyne *v.* Muir, 1708; M. 11,010; 1 Ill. 355. Park's Crs. *v.* Maxwell, 1785; M. 11,031. See Muir *v.* Ferguson, 1728; M. 11,014 ("questionable," see 1 Ill. 355). Smith *v.* Ogilvie, 1821; 1 S. 159; aff. 1825; 1 W. & S. 315.

(*b*) Smith, *supra* (*a*).

(*c*) Ross *v.* Craigie, 1729; M. 11,014. Scott *v.* Rutherford, 1715; M. 11,012. Douglas, Heron, & Co. *v.* Riddick, 1792; M. 11,032, 11,048; see 4 Paton, 133. Yuille *v.* Scott, 1827; 6 S. 137; aff. 1831, 5 W. & S. 436; 8 S. 485; 1 Ill. 456.

(*d*) Sharp *v.* Hervey, 1808; M. Apx. *Bill of Exch.* 22.

(*e*) Stocks *v.* M'Lagan, 1890; 17 R. 1122.

(*f*) Ross, *supra* (*c*). Smith *v.* Bell, 1829; 7 S. 771; 1 Ill. 356. Douglas, Heron, & Co., *supra* (*c*). Burnet *v.* Middleton, 1742; M. 11,018; Elch. *Caut.* 13.

(*g*) Bell *v.* Herdman, 1727; M. 11,039.

(*h*) Same case. Burnet, *supra* (*f*).

(*i*) M'Rankin *v.* Schaw, 1714; M. 11,034. Drysdale *v.* Johnston, 1839; 1 D. 409.

602. To give the benefit of the statute, the obligation must be for a sum of money, to be paid within the seven years (*a*). 'So when one is bound as cautioner not for the principal sum of a debt, but only for interest during the not payment of the principal, or it would seem for an annuity, he cannot plead the limitation against a demand for payments becoming due seven years after the date of the bond (*b*).' It is not available to cautioners *ad facta præstanda* (*c*); or to judicial cautioners (*d*); or cautioners in marriage contracts (*e*); or cautioners for the discharge of an office (*f*), or cautioners for relief (*g*), or for a composition in bankruptcy (*h*), or in 'separate bonds *ex post facto*, or' bonds of corroboration (*i*). One engaging by a missive letter to procure security to the creditor, or binding himself as guarantee for debts due, or for mercantile credit, is not within the protection of the Act (*k*). One guaranteeing a bond by missive letter not referred to in the bond is not entitled to the protection of the Act (*l*). Action of relief by one cautioner against another is not cut off by the statute (*m*). 'And as it qualifies the terms of the contract, and does not merely cut off the remedy by action, the statute does not apply to a bond which is governed by a foreign law (*n*).'

(*a*) Balvaird *v.* Watson, 1709; M. 11,005; 1 Ill. 356. Borthwick *v.* Crawford, 1715; M. 11,008. Millers *v.* Short, 1762; M. 11,027. Anderson *v.* Wood, 1821; 1 S. 31.

(*b*) Molleson *v.* Hutchison, 1892; 19 R. 581.

(*c*) Stewart *v.* Campbell, 1726; M. 11,010. Robertson *v.* Mackinlay, 1736; M. 11,010; Elchies, *Caut.* 5, 6. Sir R. Monro *v.* Bain, 1741; M. 11,017; Elchies, *Caut.* 10. Marshall *v.* Thom, 1736; *ib.* 5.

(*d*) Hope *v.* Foulis, 1715; M. 11,009. M'Kinlay *v.* Ewing, 1781; Hailes, 881. Hog *v.* Low, 1826; 4 S. 708. Gallie *v.* Ross, 1836; 14 S. 647.

(*e*) Stewart, *supra* (*c*). Kerr *v.* Bremner, 1839; 1 D. 618: 1842, 1 Bell's App. 280.

(*f*) Strang *v.* Fleet, 1709; M. 11,005.

(*g*) Forbes *v.* Dunbar, 1726; M. 11,014. Bruce *v.* Stein, 1793; M. 11,033.

(*h*) Cuthbertson *v.* Lyon, 1823; 2 S. 291. See the limitation in 19 and 20 Vict. c. 79, § 144.

(*i*) Caves *v.* Spence, 1743; M. 11,020; Elchies, *Caut.* 12. Scott *v.* Rutherford, 1715; M. 11,012. Lady Gordon *v.* Tyrie, 1748; M. 11,025; see Elch. *Caut.* 10. Monteith *v.* Pattison, 1841; 4 D. 161. Tait *v.* Wilson, 1836; 15 S. 221; aff. 1840, 1 Rob. 137.

(*k*) More *v.* Forbes, 1710; M. 11,011. Caves, *supra* (*i*). Hog & Co. *v.* Holden, 1765; M. 11,029. Howison *v.* Howison, 1784; M. 11,030; 3 Ill. 146.

(*l*) Howison, *supra* (*k*). Tait *v.* Wilson (*i*).

(*m*) Forbes, *supra* (*g*).

(*n*) Alexander *v.* Badenach, 1843; 6 D. 323.

603. (2.) *How the Obligation may be prolonged.*—In order to continue the obligation beyond the seven years, in cases to which the Act applies, it is necessary that the bond shall be renewed or corroborated; or such negotiations at least for that purpose commenced by the cautioner as to bar the plea on the statute 'by showing his intention to continue the obligation' (*a*); or that the creditor shall have "done diligence within the seven years" (*b*); or that the creditor shall at least have obtained decree against the cautioner within the seven years, it being doubtful whether a mere citation, or even a summons called and in dependence, is sufficient (*c*). But the effect of interruption by diligence or decree is only to preserve to the creditor his claim against the cautioner for the debt, with such interest as shall have fallen due within the seven years (*d*). 'Payment of interest beyond the seven years does not perpetuate the obligation, and interest so paid in error may be recovered by the cautioner (*e*).'

(*a*) 3 Ersk. 7. § 24, to be noted for correction. Douglas, Heron, & Co. *v.* Riddick, 1793; M. 11,048; 4 Pat. 133; 1 Ill. 357. Gordon *v.* Campbell, 1715; M. 11,037. Yuille *v.* Scott, 1830; 8 S. 485. Wallace *v.* Campbell, 1749; M. 11,026. Stocks *v.* M'Lagan, 1890; 17 R. 1122. M'Gregor's Exrs. *v.* Anderson's Trs., 1893; 21 R. 7.

(*b*) 1695, c. 5. Irvine *v.* Copland, 1752; M. 11,043; Elchies, *Caut.* 21. Reid *v.* Maxwell, 1780; M. 11,043; Hailes, 850.

(*c*) Douglas, Heron, & Co., *supra* (*a*). Clark *v.* Stuart, 1779; M. 11,043. "A very doubtful note of this case, which is nowhere more fully reported." 1 Ill. 358. Ewing *v.* Semple, 1739; 5 B. Sup. 211. Stewart *v.* Douglas, 1712; M. 11,039.

(*d*) 3 Ersk. 7. § 24. Correct the first annotator by the text, and Ivory's note. Semple *v.* Ewing, Nov. 1741; 5 B. Sup. 713. Reid (*b*). Stewart (*c*).

(*e*) Carrick *v.* Carse, 1778; M. 2931. Yuille *v.* Scott, 1830; 8 S. 485; aff. 1831, 5 W. & S. 436.

604. (3.) *Minority.*—There is no interruption to the running of the term of limitation on account of minority (*a*).

(*a*) Ramsay *v.* Miller, 1706; 4 B. Sup. 644; 1 Ill. 358. Stewart *v.* Douglas, 1712; *ib.* 913; M. 11,151.

II. PRESCRIPTION.

605. Principle.—The doctrine of prescription is distinguished from that of limitation. It infers, by operation of the law itself, from the mere lapse of time, a presumption of abandonment or of payment. Payment or satisfaction or abandonment is the inference from the lapse of the long term of forty years; payment is the inference from the lapse of certain shorter terms which have been appropriated to debts of different kinds.

606. Negative and Positive distinguished.—The Long Prescription is Negative or Positive. The abstinence of a creditor from demanding fulfilment of a right or obligation during forty years has been held a fair ground to presume satisfaction and abandonment or payment: in consideration of the danger of demands upon false evidence; of the probability of payment and loss of documents; of the equity of discouraging forgotten debts; and of the disfavour to one guilty of such negligence. This is "Negative Prescription." The "Positive" is the application of the same principle to the fortification of a title to land. Where one has had a long continuance of uninterrupted possession as owner, on a title apparently good, the law, on grounds of policy, for the settling of men's minds and the encouragement of improvement, holds the title so fortified as unexceptionable (*a*).

(*a*) 3 Ersk. 7. § 8–15. Gordon *v.* Glendonwyn, 1838; 16 S. 645; 3 Ill. 147. See below, § 2002.

607. Negative Prescription.—(1.) *Nature and Requisites.*—By the lapse of forty years from the day of payment, and neglect during that time to take document upon the debt, without excuse from incapacity or nonage, a debt or right is held to be discharged or abandoned. Three statutes have been passed on this subject. The words of the first (1469, c. 29) are: "That the party to whom the obligation is made, that has interest therein, sall follow the said obligation within the space of forty years, and take document thereupon: And gif he dois not, it sall be prescrived and be of nane avail, the said forty years being runnin and unpersewed by the partie." By a subsequent Act (1474, c. 55), it is provided that, "in time to cum, all obligations made or to be made, that beis not followed within forty years, sall prescrive and be of nane avail" (*a*). By a still later statute (1617, c. 12), it is declared, "that all actions competent of the law on heritable bonds, reversions, contracts, or utherris whatsoever, sall be persued within the space of forty years after the date of the same, except the said reversions be incorporated in the body of an infeftment; and that in the course of the said forty years' prescription, the years of minority and lesse age sall noways be counted, but only the years during which the parties against whom the prescription is used were majors, and past twenty-one years of age."

(*a*) As to the effect of these earlier statutes, see L. Deas in Chisholm *v.* Chisholm Batten, 1864; 3 Macph. 202, 225. Kermack *v.* Kermack, 1874; 2 R. 156.

608. (2.) *To what Cases applicable or not.*—The statutes were at first held to apply only to simple and unilateral obligations; but now abandonment is presumed in respect to all absolute rights and obligations whatever, mutual or unilateral, heritable or moveable, if not insisted on within the term (*a*).

(*a*) 1617, c. 12. 3 Ersk. 7. § 8. Lauder *v.* Colinslie, 1630; M. 10,655; 1 Ill. 359. Paul *v.* Reid, Feb. 8, 1814; F. C. Ogilvie *v.* Ogilvie, 1630; M. 6541 (marriage contract). Kirk-Session of Aberscherder *v.* Gemrie, 1633; M. 10,972 (loan of church bell). Mags. of Linlithgow *v.* Mitchell, 1822; 1 S. 553 (toll duties). See Barr *v.* Hamilton, 1823; 2 S. 556. Barns *v.* Barns's Trs., 1857; 19 D. 626 (right to challenge illegal act of trustees). Paterson *v.* Wilson, 1859; 21 D. 322 (right to exhibition of unfeudalised disposition). Trinity Hospital *v.* Loc. of S. Leith, 1848; 11 D. 266 (inhibition of teinds). Pearson *v.* Malachi, 1892, 20 R. 167 (obl. to create real burden). Baird *v.* Mags. of Dundee, 1862; 24 D. 447; 1 Macph. H. L. 6. Chisholm, *supra*, § 607. It applies to a claim against an executor for payment of a legacy (Jamieson *v.* Clark, 1872; 10 Macph. 399); and to a claim by a co-obligant, who has paid more than his share, against his co-debtors for reimbursement, *e.g.* against an underpaying heritor in an interim locality (Sinclair *v.* Campbell's Trs., 1877; 4 R. 1126; rev. 1878, 5 R. H. L. 119); to a right to levy harbour dues at a part of a port (Dundee Comrs. *v.* Dougall, 1848; 11 D. 6; aff. 1 Macq. 317). It does not apply to *res meræ facultatis*; *infra*, § 999, 2017.

609. Where the obligation is incorporated in the body of an infeftment used as a title, the action on it does not prescribe (*a*). And where it is prestable periodically, the several terms' payments may be severally extinguished by prescription, while the general obligation subsists (*b*); as in the case of feu-duties (*c*), rents, and annuities (*d*). Interests are extinguished by prescription periodically, term after term; or by extinction of the principal debt by negative prescription, the whole interests fall as accessories.

(*a*) 1617, c. 12. 3 Ersk. 7. § 12. Stuart *v.* Cuming, 1711; M. 10,722; 1 Ill. 359. The statute speaks only of "*reversions* incorporated in the body of an infeftment," and the authorities cited do not support the proposition in the text. But even a reversion will be worked off by the positive prescription. See Scott *v.* Bruce Stewart, 1776; Hailes, 811; 5 B. S. 542; *infra*, § 2008. 3 Ross' L. C. 464 sqq. Nicolson *v.* Keith, 1810; Hume, 470. See below, § 2016.

(*b*) 3 Ersk. 7. § 13. Kames's Elucid. art. 33. Henderson *v.* Burt, 1858; 20 D. 402.

(*c*) L. Gairntully *v.* Commissary of St. Andrews, 1638; M. 10,750.

(*d*) Lockhart *v.* D. of Gordon, 1730; M. 10,736. Anstruthers *v.* C. of Rothes, 1779; M. 10,713. It is different in the case of a liferent right. Stuart *v.* Cuming (*a*).

610. The right to set aside a deed, settlement, or instrument on *extrinsic* objections, falls by the negative prescription; a challenge on *intrinsic* objections appearing *ex facie* does not prescribe (*a*).

(*a*) 3 Ersk. 7. § 9. Ainslie *v.* Watson, 1738; M. 10,736; 1 Ross' L. C. 196. See below, § 871 et seq.; 2015 et seq. Paton *v.* Drysdale, 1725; M. 10,709; 1 Ross' L. C. 194.

611. In order to ground the plea of prescription, the right must have been neglected or abandoned during the whole term of forty years, without any document taken on it, or payment of interest or of principal made. See the several statutes cited above, § 607.

612. It is not necessary to the plea of negative prescription, that the debtor shall *bonâ fide* believe the debt to be paid; nor is reference of non-payment to his oath a good answer to the plea of the long prescription (*a*).

(*a*) 3 Ersk. 7. § 15. Napier *v.* Campbell, 1703; M. 10,656; 1 Ill. 360. See as to *mala fides* proceeding from the title, Kinloch *v.* Rocheid, 1800; M. *Prescription*, Apx. 4; and 1808, *ib.* 7. See below, § 2004. Kermack *v.* Kermack, 1874; 2 R. 156.

613. (3.) *Terminus a quo.*—The term of prescription, by the construction, though not by the express words of the Act, runs from the day of payment (*a*), not from the date of the bond, as in the vicennial limitation. The day of payment is the day specified in a pure or future obligation; or the event stipulated, if the obligation be conditional; or the eviction, if the obligation be of warrandice, the statute excepting from the ordinary rule "all actions of warrandice, which shall not prescrive from the date of the bond or infeftment whereupon the warrandice is sought, but only from the date of the distress, which shall prescrive, it not being pursued within forty years, as said is" (*b*).

(*a*) Butter *v.* Gray, 1665; M. 11,183; 1 Ill. 360. Kames's Elucid. art. 33. 3 Ersk. 7. § 36.

(*b*) 1617, c. 12. See Elliot *v.* M. Lothian, 1808; Hume, 465. Horne *v.* M. Breadalbane, 1835; 13 S. 296; 1838, 16 S. 815 (revd. on another point, 1842, 1 Bell's App. 1; see) Lennox *v.* Hamilton, 1843; 5 D. 1357. Sinclair *v.* M. Breadalbane, 1844; 6 D. 378; rev. 1846, 5 Bell, 353. Hope *v.* Hope, 1864; 2 Macph. 670. So, when an agent commits an error in legal proceedings, prescription runs against the client's claim of damages, not from the date of the error, but from the date when it is detected, and the client damnified by it. Cooke *v.* Falconer's Reprs., 1850; 13 D. 157.

614. (4.) *The effect* of the prescription is extinction of the debt; or, more properly, a perpetual exception to the action of debt (*a*). And the pleas in answer to the exception are—1. Interruption; 2. Minority; 3. *Non valens agere.*

(*a*) Kermack *v.* Kermack, 1874; 2 R. 156.

615. Interruption.—The term of prescription may be interrupted by taking document on the debt, either judicially or extrajudicially. And the effect of that is not to suspend the running of the term of prescription, but to break it off and to render it necessary to begin a new course of prescription.

616. (1.) *Extrajudicial interruption* may be express or implied. Express interruption is by a new voucher, document, or acknowledgment of the debt, as showing it not merely to be subsisting, but insisted on (*a*): such is a bond of corroboration (*b*); an engagement to pay interest (*c*); a special submission of the debt (*d*); 'or a state by executors acknowledging the debt (*e*).' But it has been said (though it would seem not entirely free of doubt) that an assignation intimated is insufficient to interrupt (*f*).

Implied interruption is by partial payment, or by payment of interest, evincing that the debt is neither paid nor abandoned, 'which must be proved by writ (*g*).' But indefinite payment secretly ascribed by the creditor to the debt will not interrupt (*h*).

(*a*) Pitmedden *v.* Monro, 1705; M. 11,261; 1 Ill. 360. Haliburton *v.* Graham, 1736; M. 11,015; Elch. *Presc.* 8. Aitken *v.* Malcolms, 1776; Hailes, 148. See M'Tavish *v.* L. Saltoun, 1825; 3 S. 472.

(*b*) Haliburton, *supra* (*a*).

(*c*) Skene *v.* Campbell, 1686; M. 11,256.

(*d*) Vans *v.* Murray, June 14, 1816; F. C. See Buchanan *v.* Buchanan, 1765; M. 11,676. Hay *v.* King's Adv., 1756; M. 11,276; 2 Pat. 266, 272. Garden *v.* Rigg, 1743; M. 11,274; Elch. *Presc.* 25; 1 Pat. 409.

(*e*) Briggs *v.* Swan's Exrs., 1854; 16 D. 385.

(*f*) 3 Ersk. 7. § 38.

(*g*) Kermack *v.* Kermack, 1874; 2 R. 156.

(*h*) 3 Ersk. 7. § 39. Garden, *supra* (*d*).

617. (2.) *Judicial interruption* is by 'citation,' action, or diligence; in either case notice being given to the true debtor of a demand for the particular debt in question.

618. Interruption by *citation* is not competently made unless the debtor be lawfully (*a*) cited specially to pay the debt in question (*b*); and then it is only a temporary interruption, requiring to be renewed every seven years (*c*).

(*a*) Campbell *v.* M'Neil, 1799; M. 11,120; 1 Ill. 361. Baillie *v.* Doig, 1790; M. 11,286.

(*b*) See Vans and Garden, *supra*, § 616 (*d*). 3 Ersk. 7. § 38. M'Dowal *v.* M'Dowal, 1739; Elch. *Presc.* 19. Menzies *v.* Forbes, 1779; M. 11,258.

(*c*) 1669, c. 10. Camerons *v.* M'Donald, 1761; M. 11,331.

619. In order to interrupt by *action*, the summons must be called in court, and must be libelled upon a legal title to the debt; or at least there must be in the pursuer a radical title completed, and capable of operating *retro* (*a*).

(*a*) Blair *v.* Sutherland, 1736; M. 11,270; Elch. *Presc.* 7; 1 Ill. 361. E. of Home *v.* Steel, 1765; M. 5555. Robertson *v.* Robertson, 1776; M. *Presc.* Apx. 2; Hailes, 707. See § 2018. Cooke *v.* Falconer's Reprs., 1850; 13 D. 157 (action).

620. It is not strictly necessary that a special action should be raised for the debt: it is sufficient to enter a claim in a proper process of competition; as ranking and sale, multiplepoinding, or sequestration (*a*). Even a claim lodged in a process as a counter demand, and in defence, has been held an interruption (*b*). But a claim lodged with a trustee under a private trust is not sufficient; nor the production of a claim in a process of cognition and sale by tutors (*c*); nor a claim of retention made judicially by a law agent without producing his account (*d*). And it has also been held that where, in an action of relief against a co-obligant, the creditor was examined, and produced his ground of debt in the action, this was no interruption (*e*).

(*a*) See above, § 598. Crawford *v.* Simpson, 1732; M. 11,049; 1 Ill. 362. Thomson *v.* Simson, 1774; *ib.*; Hailes, 591. Douglas, Heron, & Co. *v.* Richardson, 1784; M. 11,127; 1 Ill. 349. Graham *v.* Macfarlane, May 30, 1811; F. C. See Menzies *v.* Forbes, 1699; M. 11,258. 54 Geo. III. c. 137, § 52. 19 and 20 Vict. c. 79, § 109. Crawford's Trs. *v.* Haig, 1827; 5 S. 705; 1 Ill. 352.

(*b*) Sloan *v.* Birtwhistle, 1827; 5 S. 742. See above, § 575.

(*c*) Ferrier *v.* E. Errol, July 9, 1812; F. C. See above, § 598.

(*d*) Couper's Executors *v.* Ogilvie, 1753; M. 11,107.

(*e*) V. Arbuthnot *v.* Douglas, 1795; M. 11,133; Bell's Ca. 83. See Kames's Eluc. 254, and comp. above, § 598.

621. In interruption by *diligence*, it is not enough to extract a decree of registration; or even to raise horning, without giving a charge; or poinding, without following it up by execution (*a*). Informal diligence will not interrupt (*b*).

(*a*) Johnston *v.* L. Belhaven, 1672; M. 11,237; 1 Ill. 363. Thomson *v.* E. Linlithgow, 1708; M. 11,264. Wright *v.* Wright, 1717; M. 11,268. M'Nicol *v.* M'Neill, 1821; 1 S. 166. See Lauder *v.* Colinslie, 1630; M. 10,655; 1 Ill. 359. Douglas, Heron, & Co., *supra*, § 620 (*a*).

(*b*) Cameron *v.* M'Donald, 1761; M. 11,331. E. of Hopetoun *v.* York Bdgs. Co., 1784; M. 11,285; 1 Ill. 364. Grant *v.* York Bdgs. Co., 1784; M. 11,283; H. L. 1785; 3 Pat. 17.

622. (3.) *When interruption may be made.*—Prescription runs *de momento in momentum*, and the interruption may be on the last moment of the fortieth year (*a*).

(*a*) 3 Ersk. 7. § 30.

623. (4.) *By whom.*—Interruption by a co-creditor having a *pro indiviso* right is available to all the creditors in the obligation; and interruption to one of several persons bound *in solidum* is an interruption against all (*a*).

(*a*) Clerk *v.* E. of Home, 1747; M. 10,662. Gordon *v.* Bogle, 1784; M. 7532; Hailes, 947; 1 Ill. 364. See cases in § 625. Cooke *v.* Falconer's Reprs., § 619 (*a*).

624. Minority.—Besides interruption, there are two answers to the plea of prescription: 1. Minority; or, 2. *Non valens agere.*

625. The years of minority of the immediate creditor must be deducted from the term of negative prescription (*a*); so also must the time during which a child is *in utero* (*b*). By the words of the statute, the rule applies only to incapacity from infancy, or "less age."

(*a*) 1617, c. 12. 3 Ersk. 7. § 35. E. of Marchmont *v.* Home, 1714; M. 11,154; 1 Ill. 364. Dalrymple *v.* Duncan, 1737; Elch. *Presc.* 14. Blair *v.* Sutherland, 1741; *ib.* 8; 1 Ill. 361. Ruddiman *v.* Trades Maiden Hosp., 1746; *ib.* 28; M. 11,155. Inveraw *v.* E. Breadalbane, 1747; M. 11,156. Cuming *v.* York Bdgs. Co., 1790; M. 11,170. See below, § 2022.

(*b*) Campbell *v.* Wilson, 1765; 5 B. Sup. 917; rev. 2 Pat. 198. It is said in 1 Ill. 365—"I should say that they (*i.e.* the months *in utero*) were to be deducted if the child died; but I can see no reasoning for lengthening out so long a term as the forty years' prescription by this addition." This criticism appears, however, to be sufficiently answered both by the words of the statutes (see Napier on Prescr. 526 sqq., 628), and by the principle that the *nasciturus habetur pro nato* wherever *his own* interests require it. L. 7, *Dig. de statu hom.* (i. 7). Savigny, System, vol. ii. 12 sq. (§ 62).

626. The rule is absolute, that minority must be discounted, whether the minor have guardians or not. 'But where there is a body of creditors having a right to pursue a common claim, the minority of one or more does not exclude the operation of the statutes, there being some capable of asserting their right (*a*).'

(*a*) Allan (or Dickson) *v.* Brander, 1839; 1 D. 678; aff. 1842; 1 Bell's Ap. 167. M'Innes *v.* Brander, 1844; 6 D. 512. Cf. below, § 627 (*a*).

627. Non valens agere cum effectu.—This is an answer in equity to the plea of prescription, and proceeds on the principle, not on the words of the law; for no man can be held to abandon a right by abstaining from an act which he has no capacity to perform, or which is of no avail if performed. Under this principle, prescription does not run where the creditor is in a state of personal disability: as by imprisonment abroad; by a wife's disability while under *cura maritalis*; by furiosity (*a*). But forfeiture or outlawry does not bar the running of prescription (*b*); 'nor a disability which is due to the *laches* of the creditor himself (*c*).' Claims which cannot at the time be made effectual do not prescribe; so a fiar, while excluded by a liferenter, is under no necessity to bring forward his claim (*d*).

(*a*) D. of Lauderdale *v.* E. Tweeddale, 1678; M. 11,193; 1 Ill. 365. Whiteford *v.* E. Kilmarnock, 1682; M. 11,196–7. O'Neill *v.* Mags. of Dumfries, 1803; M. 11,201. M'Kie *v.* Stewart, 1665; M. 11,204. Gaw *v.* E. Wemyss, 1675; M. 11,183, compared with Taylor *v.* Gibson, 1675; M. 6055. See Dirlet. and Stewart, 374. See below, § 2023. Graham *v.* Watt, 1843; 5 D. 1368; aff. 1846, 5 Bell's Ap. 172. The plea does not apply where the right was in a person of full age and *valens agere* during the period of minority founded on. Buchanan *v.* Bogle, 1847; 9 D. 686. Cf. Allan *v.* Brander, § 626.

(*b*) Robertson *v.* King's Advocate, 1758; 5 B. Sup. 357. Campbell *v.* Wilson, 1765; *ib.* 915, 926. Brodie *v.* Shedden, Feb. 20, 1821; F. C. See Wemyss *v.* King's Adv., 1766; 5 B. Sup. 933.

(*c*) E. of Fife *v.* Duff, 1887; 15 R. 238.

(*d*) Elliot *v.* Aitchison, 1724; M. 11,209. Brown *v.* Hepburn, 1680; M. 11,028. Scot *v.* ——, 1756; 5 B. Sup. 854. M'Ghie *v.* Tinkler, 1776; M. 11,112; 1 Ill. 372. Lawrie *v.* Donald, 1830; 9 S. 147. See M'Neill *v.* M'Neal, 1858; 20 D. 735, and below, § 2023.

628. Triennial Prescription.—The shorter prescriptions were introduced chiefly in order to establish a presumption of payment in particular cases, where injustice might be suffered by forgetfulness or the loss of vouchers. And the rule is, that the defender in such cases, defending himself on the ground of payment having been made, requires no proof of this beyond the legal presumption.

In debts arising out of a course of service, or of dealing, and not founded on written obligation, the law has raised, on the expiration of three years, a double presumption: 1*st*, That no such debt ever existed; and 2*nd*, That if it ever did exist, it has been paid. The words of the Act are: "That all actions of debt for house-maills, men's ordinaries, servants' fees, merchants' accounts, and others the like debts that are not founded upon written obligations (*a*), be pursued within three years, otherways the creditor shall have no action, except he either prove by writ or by oath of his party" (*b*).

(*a*) See Dickson on Evid. § 493–6; and below, § 630 *fin.*

(*b*) 1579, c. 83. 3 Ersk. Pr. 7. § 6. 3 Ersk. Inst. 7. § 17.

629. (1.) *Description of Debts.*—The Act applies to the following debts, namely:—1. To traders' accounts 'of the nature of shopkeepers' accounts,' whether in retail or in wholesale (*a*); but not 'to' the price of goods consigned between foreign merchants (*b*), 'or to the larger "mercantile" dealings, such as the sale of goods sold by manufacturers in Scotland to foreigners (*c*)'; nor bargains of moveables (*d*); nor contracts for repairs (*e*); nor accounts between masters and owners of a ship (*f*). 2. To workmen's wages, 'whether paid by time or measurement (piece-work)' (*g*). 3. To writers' accounts, 'including disbursements by the agent in the ordinary course of professional duty' (*h*); 'a stockbroker's account for promoting a railway (*i*)'; salaries to factors (*k*); claims of the clerk to a submission (*l*); 'of an advocate's clerk for his fees (*m*); engineers' and surveyors' accounts for plans or work (*n*); but not to an engineer's or other party's charges for going to London to give evidence before a committee of Parliament, that being out of the ordinary course of his employment (*o*).' It does not apply to cash advances, though it does to commission on advances (*p*); nor to the agent's travelling 'and other' expenses 'in a special employment out of his ordinary business' (*q*); nor to advances for articles purchased and sent abroad by a factor to his constituent (*r*); 'nor to general accountings between agent and principal (*s*), or an agent's claim for commission on wholesale purchases (*t*), or a mandatary's claim for reimbursement of his outlays (*u*).' 4. To furnishings to a family or domestic establishment (*v*). 5. To servants' wages; each term running a separate course (*w*). 6. To house-rents, where the lease is verbal; each term running also a separate course (*x*). 7. To aliment furnished 'on contract express or implied' (*y*); 'but not to a claim of relief for alimentary advances against the father of a bastard (*z*)'; and each term's aliment, like rents and wages, runs a separate course. Even where the aliment was payable weekly, it was held that this rule applied, and that it was not a continuous account (*aa*).

This prescription is no defence against an action for money recovered *ex mandato* (*bb*), or for money advanced (*cc*), 'or where there are mutual accounts properly stated, as an account current (*dd*).'

(a) Ord v. Duffs, 1630 ; M. 11,083 ; 1 Ill. 366. Bruce v. Jack, 1760 ; 1 B. Sup. 609. See as to these cases, Laing & Irvine v. Anderson, *infra*, *per* L. Pr. Inglis. As to a single purchase, see Gobbi v. Lazzaroni, 1859 ; 21 D. 801. See *contra*, M'Gregor v. Stewart, 1811 ; Hume, 472 (which, however, falls rather within the same class of cases as those in note (d)) ; and cases in Dickson on Evid. § 485.

(b) Hamilton & Co. v. Martin, 1795 ; M. 11,120. M'Farlan v. Brown, 1827 ; 5 S. 189 ; 1 Ill. 349. Anderson & Child v. Wood, 1809 ; Hume, 467. M'Kinlay v. M'Kinlay, 1851 ; 14 D. 162. See (c), (bb), *infra*.

(c) Laing & Irvine v. Anderson, 1872 ; 10 Macph. 74. Cf. Sandys v. Lowden, 1874 ; 2 R., Just. 7.

(d) Baird v. Montgomerie, 1688 ; M. 11,092. Smith v. Miller, 1827 ; 5 S. 314. See Gobbi, *supra* (a).

(e) Bell v. ——, 1755 ; 5 B. Sup. 840.

(f) Butchart v. Mudie, etc., 1781 ; M. 11,113 ; Hailes, 885.

(g) Bayne v. ——, 1692 ; M. 11,092. Tweedie v. Williamson, 1694 ; M. 11,092. Mackay v. Carmichael & Christie, 1851 ; 14 D. 207.

(h) Dallas v. M'Kenzie, 1695 ; 4 B. Sup. 271. Mason v. E. Aberdeen, 1709 ; M. 11,094. M'Adam v. Fogo, 1786 ; Hailes, 875. Campbell v. Stein, 1813 ; 6 Dow, 116. Wallace v. M'Kissock, 1829 ; 7 S. 542. Smith v. Bell, 1829 ; 7 S. 771. See Deans v. Steele, 1853 ; 16 D. 317. M'Andrew v. Hunter, 1851 ; 13 D. 1111. Cullen v. Smeal, 1853 ; 15 D. 868. Richardson v. Merry, 1863 ; 1 Macph. 940.

(i) White v. Cal. Ry. Co., 1868 ; 6 Macph. 415.

(k) Smith v. E. of Winton, 1714 ; M. 11,096. Grubb v. Porteous, 1835 ; 13 S. 603.

(l) Farquharson v. L. Advocate, 1755 ; M. 11,108.

(m) Fortune's Exrs. v. Smith, 1864 ; 2 Macph. 1005.

(n) Stevenson v. Kyle, 1850 ; 12 D. 673. Johnston v. Scott, 1860 ; 22 D. 393.

(o) Blackadder v. Milne, 1851 ; 13 D. 820. Barr v. E. & G. Ry. Co., 1864 ; 2 Macph. 1250.

(p) Scott v. Gregory's Trs., 1832 ; 10 S. 375. Ker v. Mags. of Kirkwall, 1827 ; 5 S. 812. See Drummond v. Stewart, 1740 ; M. 5858. Tod's Trs. v. Melville, 1836 ; 14 S. 432. Maclaren v. Bradley, 1874 ; 2 R. 185.

(q) Moncreiff v. Durham, 1836 ; 14 S. 830 ; 3 Ill. 147. Richardson v. Merry, 1863 ; 1 Macph. 940.

(r) Grubb, *supra* (k).

(s) M'Kinlay v. M'Kinlay, 1851 ; 14 D. 162.

(t) Brown v. Brown, 1891 ; 18 R. 889.

(u) Sadler v. M'Lean, 1794 ; M. 11,119 ; Bell's Ca. 104. Grant v. Fleming, 1881 ; 9 R. 257.

(v) Russell v. E. Argyle, 1613 ; M. 11,082 ; 1 Ill. 368. Guthrie v. M. of Annandale, 1724 ; M. 11,101.

(w) 1579, c. 83. Robertson v. M. of Annandale, 1740 ; 1 Cr. & St. 293. M'Dougal v. Campbell, 1830 ; 8 S. 959. Smellie v. Cochrane, 13 S. 544 ; 14 S. 12. Alcock v. Easson, 1842 ; 5 D. 356.

(x) Ferguson v. Muir, 1737 ; M. 11,103. Cuming's Trs. v. Simpson, 1825 ; 3 S. 377.

(y) Hamilton v. Lady Ormiston, 1716 ; M. 11,100. Cuming v. Andrew, 1722 ; M. 11,101. Forsyth v. Simson, 1791 ; M. 11,081 ; Bell's Ca. 361. Finlayson v. Gown, July 7, 1809 ; F. C. M'Dowal v. M'Lurg, 1807 ; M. *Presc.* Apx. 6. Taylor v. Allardyce, 1858 ; 20 D. 401. Ligertwood v. Brown, 1872 ; 10 Macph. 832. The prescription does not apply to poor-rates. Munro v. Graham, 1857 ; 20 D. 72.

(z) Thomson v. Westwood, 1842 ; 4 D. 833. Thom v. Jardine, 1836 ; 14 S. 1004. Butchart v. Scott, 1839 ; 1 D. 1128. Moncrieff v. Waugh, 1859 ; 21 D. 216. Finlayson and M'Dowal, *citt.*

(aa) Fraser v. M'Keich, 1838 ; 16 S. 1045. A *general* obligation to pay advances for aliment may result in a continuous account, prescription running from the date of the latest advance. Bracken v. Blasquez, 1891, 18 R. 819, where the last paragraph of Lord M'Laren's opinion referring to this section must be misreported.

(bb) Frier v. Paterson, 1826 ; 4 S. 396. Anderson & Child, *cit.* (b). Fortune's Exrs., *cit.* (m).

(cc) Paterson v. Mackenzie, 1825 ; 3 S. 620. Smith v. Bell, *supra* (h). See Ormistoun v. Hamilton, 1712 ; 5 B. S. 90 ; Robertson's Ap. 61.

(dd) Boyes v. Gray, 1829 ; 7 S. 815. Murray v. Wright, 1870 ; 8 Macph. 722. M'Kinlay v. M'Kinlay, *cit.* (b), (s). M'Kinlay v. Wilson, 1885 ; 13 R. 210. See Batchelor's Trs. v. Honeyman, 1892 ; 19 R. 903.

630. (2.) *How elided.*—It is sufficient to elide the prescription if a 'competent' action 'or proceeding (including submission) in which the claim might have been enforced' have been raised in a competent court (a) ; or if, in defence, an account as a counter claim have been produced judicially (b). But it has not been held enough that the creditor has a lien (c) ; though in England, perhaps more correctly, the matter has been viewed differently, the remedy only being held discharged by the statute of limitations, but not the debt (d).

It will also be sufficient to show by written mandate 'or contract' the constitution of the debt (e), so as to bring it within a different class of debt from that provided for in the Act. But it is not for this purpose sufficient to show a written order for goods with a carrier's receipt (f), or a letter from a country writer employing a town agent (g). 'A mere written order, followed by furnishings or work done, is not enough to take the debt out of the statute, as being founded upon written obligation (h). But the statute does not apply where the pursuer refers to a written contract, or to letters containing the substance of the agreement under which the debt was incurred (i), provided always the writings be such as to create an obligation against the debtor sued (k); nor where the pursuer's failure to sue timeously is due to the conduct of the defender, *e.g.* concealment, whether fraudulent or not (l).'

(a) See M'Laren v. Buik, 1829 ; 7 S. 483 ; 1 Ill. 372. Cochrane v. Prentice, 1841 ; 4 D. 76. Dunn v. Lamb, 1854 ; 16 D. 944. Eddie v. Monkland Ry. Co., 1855 ; 17 D. 1041. Cf. Gobbi v. Lazzaroni, 1859 ; 21 D. 801. Thomas v. Stiven, 1868 ; 6 Macph. 777.

(b) Sloan v. Birtwhistle, 1827 ; 5 S. 742 ; 1 Ill. 362. See above, § 598. Eddie, *cit.*

(c) Mason v. E. of Aberdeen, 1709 ; M. 11,094 ; 1 Ill. 367. M'Adam v. Fogo, 1780 ; M. 6252 ; Hailes, 875. See M'Callum v. Christie, 1833 ; 11 S. 321.

(d) Spiers v. Hartley, 3 Esp. 81. Higgins v. Scott, 2 B. & Ad. 419 ; 3 Ill. 151.

(e) Sadler v. M'Lean, 1794 ; M. 11,119 ; Bell's Ca. 104.

(f) Bell v. ——, 1755 ; 5 B. Sup. 840. Douglas v. Grierson, 1794 ; M. 11,116 ; Bell's Cases, 97, and cases cited.

(g) Wallace v. M'Kissock, 1829 ; 7 S. 542.

(h) Ross v. Shaw, 1784 ; M. 11,115. Douglas (f).

(i) Watson v. L. Prestonhall, 1711 ; M. 11,095. See

Blackadder *v.* Milne, 1851, 13 D. 821, as explained in Barr *v.* E. & G. Ry. Co., 1864, 2 Macph. 1250; and White *v.* Cal. Ry. Co., 1868; 6 Macph. 418.

(*k*) North Br. Ry. Co. *v.* Smith Sligo, 1873; 1 R. 309. Chalmers *v.* Walker, 1878; 6 R. 199. Chisholm *v.* Robertson, 1883; 10 R. 760. See 1 Bell's Com. 332; and Brown *v.* Brown, 1891; 18 R. 889.

(*l*) Cal. Ry. Co. *v.* Chisholm, 1886; 13 R. 773.

631. (3.) *The terminus a quo* is the day of payment of termly debts, as servants' wages, house-rents, aliment: the close of the account, which is the date either of the last unpaid article (*a*), or of the last article preceding an interruption of three years, or of the last article preceding the day of the death of the debtor, 'for an account ceases with the death of the debtor, and furnishings to his widow or successor form a new account (*b*).' But it is a continuous account if it proceed without interruption, although each year's account should be summed up, and interest charged on it (*c*). And where a town agent has been employed by a country agent for several clients, as the country agent is himself the debtor, all the accounts form one continuous account in a question of triennial prescription: the whole is saved from prescription if the last article is within the three years; and a payment of one of the intermediate accounts by one of the clients will not avail the country agent as an interruption or breach of the continuity (*d*).

(*a*) Beck *v.* Learmonth & Co., 1831; 10 S. 81; 1 Ill. 369. See Fisher *v.* Ure, 1836; 14 S. 660; 3 Ill. 147.

(*b*) Graham *v.* Stonebyres, 1670; M. 11,086. Ross *v.* Saltoun, 1680; M. 11,089. Wilson *v.* Tours, 1680; M. 11,089. Lady Ormiston *v.* Hamilton, 1709; M. 11,093. Wright's Exrs. *v.* Dickson, 1753; M. 11,106. Lesly *v.* Mollison, Nov. 15, 1808; F. C. Wilson *v.* Rutherford, 1826; 4 S. 433. Lyon *v.* Mitchell, 1819; Hume, 481. Kennedy *v.* M'Dougal, 1741; M. 11,104; 5 B. Sup. 710. Stewart *v.* Scott, 1844; 6 D. 889 (account contrived to evade prescription, as to which see also Aytoun *v.* Stoddart, 1882; 9 R. 631).

(*c*) Whyte *v.* Currie, 1829; 8 S. 153. As to changes of firm, see Torrance *v.* Bryson, 1840; 3 D. 186. Stewart *v.* Scott, *cit.* Barker *v.* Kippen, 1841; 3 D. 965. Wotherspoon *v.* Henderson's Trs., 1868; 6 Macph. 1052.

(*d*) Fisher, *supra* (*a*). Elder *v.* Hamilton, 1833; 11 S. 591.

632. (4.) *Proof after Three Years.*—In debts falling under the Act, it is necessary after the term to prove both the constitution and the subsistence of the debt by the writing or the oath of the debtor, or of his representatives; 'but even' in a concern under the sole superintendence of a manager, 'it is not competent to prove' by his writing or oath, 'for the statute requires proof by the writ or oath of party' (*a*). 'The Act has received a very liberal interpretation in regard to the proof of resting owing by writ (*b*); and it has even been held that, the constitution and resting owing of a debt being established by the debtor's writ, the amount may be proved by extrinsic evidence (*c*).' And on a reference to the defender's oath, it seems to be sufficient that he shall swear that payment has been made in his usual way, by money having been given to his steward, son, wife, etc., for that purpose, where they have had the superintendence (*d*). '"In such a case the presumption of payment is with the defender; and unless the contrary is made out by the oath, he ought to have the benefit of it" (*e*). The constitution of the debt may be proved by the writ, and the resting owing by the oath of the party (*f*).'

If the original debtor have died, a distinction has been taken as to the demand against the heir. If he have died within the three years, and so there has not yet arisen any presumption of payment, proof of the constitution of the debt, with the heir's oath negative of payment, 'was said to' be sufficient to support the action. If the three years expired before the original debtor's death, the presumption of law 'was' held to attach, and 'that' the heir's oath negative of payment 'did' not overturn it (*g*.) 'But this doctrine is authoritatively negatived, and it is fixed that the creditor must prove both the constitution and subsistence of the debt by the oath of the heir, whether the debtor died during or after the currency of the three years. This proceeds on the ground that the application of the statute does not rest on any presumption of payment, but excludes all considerations except the simple element of dates (*h*). Thus it was held that a defender pleading the statute needs not aver payment or extinction of the debt (*i*).'

(*a*) Donaldson *v.* Murray, 1766; M. 11,110; 1 Ill. 370. Bryson *v.* Aytoun, 1825; 4 S. 182. See 3 Ersk. 7. § 18; and 4. § 11–13. Wilson and Lesly, *supra*, § 631 (*b*). Nisbet's Trs. *v.* Morrison's Trs., 1829; 7 S. 307. Smith *v.* Falconer, 1831; 9 S. 474. See Duncan *v.* Forbes, 1829; 7 S. 821. Buchanan *v.* Mags. of Dunfermline, 1828; 7 S. 35. Bertram & Co. *v.* Stewart's Trs., 1874; 2 R. 255; and Duncan, *cit.* As to a wife where she is *præposita*, see below, § 1566.

(*b*) M'Andrew *v.* Hunter, 1851; 13 D. 1111. Stevenson *v.* Kyle, 1850; 12 D. 673. Smith *v.* Falconer, 1831; 9 S. 474. Fiske *v.* Walpole, 1860; 22 D. 1488. Mitchell *v.* Moultry, 1882; 10 R. 378. Judicial admissions supersede the necessity of proving by writ or oath. Ritchie *v.* Little, 1836; 14 S. 216.

(*c*) Smith, Stevenson, and Bertram, *citt.* Fife *v.* Innes, 1860; 23 D. 30.

(*d*) Goodall *v.* Hay Newton, 1825; 8 S. 387 f. n. Mette *v.* Dalyell, 1830; *ib.* 387. Smith, *supra* (*a*). Mackay *v.* Ure, 1849; 11 D. 982. Stirling *v.* Stewart, 1697; 4 B. Sup. 383; 1 Ill. 371.

(*e*) 1 Ill. 371; see below, § 2268.

(*f*) Deans *v.* Steel, 1853; 16 D. 317.

(*g*) Lesly, *supra*, § 631 (*b*). Granger's Exrs. *v.* Hamilton, 1833; 11 S. 591. See Ritchie *v.* Little, 1836; 14 S. 216. Auld *v.* Aikman, 1842; 4 D. 1487.

(*h*) **Cullen** *v.* **Smeal,** 1853; 15 D. 868. See Cowbrough & Co. *v.* Robertson, 1879; 6 R. 1301.

(*i*) **Alcock** *v.* **Easson,** 1842; 5 D. 357.

633. (5.) *Minority* is not pleadable as an exception to the triennial prescription (*a*); nor interruption, as in the long prescription (*b*); nor is there any deduction of the time of absence from the kingdom (*c*), nor of the *annus deliberandi* (*d*).

(*a*) Brown *v.* Brodie, Jan. 26, 1709; M. 11,150; 5 B. Sup. 915; 1 Ill. 372.

(*b*) M'Laren *v.* Buik, 1829; 7 S. 483. See Dunn *v.* Lamb, Eddie *v.* Monkland Ry. Co., *supra*, § 630 (*a*).

(*c*) M'Ghie *v.* Tinkler, 1776; M. 11,112.

(*d*) D. of Argyll *v.* Campbell, 1736; Elch. *Prescrip.* 10.

634. Quinquennial Prescription.—Ministers' stipends and multures are presumed to be paid after five years from the term of payment (*a*). And the like presumption holds as to rents, or maills and duties, after five years from the tenant's removing from the lands (*b*); and the dependence of a sequestration for rents '*currente termino*' does not bar the prescription (*c*).

(*a*) 1669, c. 9. 3 Ersk. 7. § 20, with Ivory's note, pp. 766–7. Nisbet *v.* Baillie, 1729; M. 11,059; 1 Ill. 372. Fairholm *v.* Livingston, 1725; M. 11,058. Hunter, L. & T. ii. 163, 464. Comp. § 593, above.

(*b*) Murray *v.* Trotter, 1709; M. 11,054. Johnston's Ex. *v.* Johnston, 1897; 24 R. 611.

(*c*) Cochrane *v.* Ferguson, 1830; 8 S. 324. A sequestration for past-due rent seems to bar the prescription. Hogg *v.* Low, 1826; 4 S. 702. Or pleading compensation in respect of rents against a claim by the tenant. M'Donald *v.* Jackson, 1826; 5 S. 28. Cf. Nicolson *v.* M'Allister's Trs., 1832; 11 S. 759. See also Heddle *v.* Baikie, 1847; 9 D. 1254. The statute extends to urban tenements. Boyes *v.* Henderson, 1823; 2 S. 190.

635. Decennial Prescription of Tutorial Accounts.—The reciprocal obligation on tutors and curators, and on their wards, to account and reimburse, is extinguished, or presumed to be satisfied, if ten years have expired from the termination of the guardianship (*a*).

(*a*) 1696, c. 9. 3 Ersk. 7. § 25. See below, § 2086 and 2097.

BOOK SECOND

OF REAL RIGHTS IN PROPERTY HERITABLE AND MOVEABLE

PART I

REAL RIGHTS IN HERITABLE PROPERTY

INTRODUCTION

636. Rights in which there is an immediate connection with the subject itself, may relate either to Territorial possessions, or to Moveables — goods, sums of money, debts, and effects of all kinds. They admit, as territorial, or as unconnected with land, of very remarkable differences in respect of the forms of transference; the extent and nature of the use: and the duties implied in ownership.

Territorial property is naturally connected more intimately with the military and political arrangements necessary for public safety, and more liable to peculiarities in national jurisprudence; while Moveable property is left to the undisturbed guidance of rules and principles of more universal application.

A double system of jurisprudence, in relation to the subjects of property, has thus arisen in Scotland, as in most European nations;—the one regulating Land and its accessories according to the spirit and arrangements of the feudal system; the other regulating the rights to Moveables according to the principles of Roman jurisprudence which prevailed before the establishment of feus.

These different systems it may be proper to consider separately; taking first into view the jurisprudence of Land rights, and proceeding afterwards to the doctrines of property in Moveables.

637. Without entering in detail into the history of the feudal law of territorial property in Scotland, it may be sufficient to observe that it was originally arranged on principles of military duty and subordination, fitted more for defence than for conquest. Before the Union with England, considerable advances had been made towards the converting of the ancient military tenure and law of feus into a system more suited to agriculture; and although the spirit of agricultural and general improvement spread rapidly in Scotland after the Union, the progress of improvement received a check in the rebellions of 1715 and 1745, which after a time led to still further emancipation from the trammels of the feudal law. The restraints of feudal subordination are now abolished in all that relates to the possession and use of land; while the conveyancing of land continues to be regulated by the strict principles of the feudal system (*a*).

(*a*) The labours of a Royal Commission, appointed to review this department of the law, may be expected soon to lead to legislative remedies for the more complex and expensive operations in feudal conveyancing, and the establishment of a simple, more certain, and more economical system. The author was chairman of this Commission, and the improvements which he anticipated from their labours have to a large extent been realised.

CHAPTER I

OF PROPERTY IN THE SOVEREIGN

I. PROPERTY HELD IN TRUST FOR THE PUBLIC.

638. Res Publicæ.—Many things by law excepted from the ordinary rules of appropriation are reserved for the use of the public (*a*). These are called *Res Publicæ* in the books of the Roman law. Under this class are—Seas and Shores; Rivers and Harbours; Roads; Bridges; Fairs and Markets. These are all necessary for public use and intercourse, and as such are vested in the Crown in trust for the subject.

(*a*) 1 Craig, 16. 2 Stair, 1. § 5. 2 Ersk. Pr. 1. § 2, and 6. § 5. 2 Ersk. 1. § 5, 6.

639. Seas.—The main ocean is common to all nations, in which they meet on a footing of equal right. No nation has pre-eminent jurisdiction there, except over its own subjects within its own ships (*a*). But the sovereign, as a guardian of the people, and for their defence, and the purposes of their trade and intercourse, is proprietor of the narrow seas within cannon-shot of the land, and the firths, gulfs, and bays around the kingdom (*b*).

(*a*) Forbes *v.* Cochrane, 2 B. & C. 448; 26 R. R. 402. See American case of The Mariana Flora, 11 Wheaton's Reports, 38. See The Franconia, *infra*, § 640 (*a*).

(*b*) 2 Stair, 1. § 5. 2 Ersk. 1. § 6. The Twee Gebroeders, 3 C. Rob. Ad. 336. 2 Grotius, 3. § 10. Bynkershoek, Qu. Juris Pub. lib. 1. c. 8. Vattel, liv. i. c. 23, § 289. See 9 Geo. II. c. 35, § 23. 4 and 9; and the American statute, March 2, 1799. 6 and 7 Vict. c. 79. Mayor of Colchester *v.* Brooke, 7 Q. B. 339; 15 L. J. Q. B. 59. Gann *v.* Free Fishers of Whitstable Co., 11 H. L. Ca. 192; 35 L. J. C. P. 29. Foreman *v.* Do., L. R. 4 H. L. 266; 38 L. J. C. P. 345. *Infra*, § 645.

640. This right to the narrow seas comprehends, That of free and uninterrupted navigation: The right of fishing, and of taking all wreck and goods found at sea, except such as are claimed and identified: The right to forbid passage to enemies: The right to levy tolls or duties: The jurisdiction over those seas (*a*), and right of search, that the subjects may be safe and the revenue protected (*b*): The right of flag, as the emblem of British sovereignty in those seas.

The first two are the great public uses, to which the other rights are subservient.

(*a*) In the case of The Franconia (Queen *v.* Keyn), L. R. 2 Ex. D. 63, 46 L. J. Mag. Ca. 17, it was held that the jurisdiction of the English Courts as established by law did not extend to the trial of offences by foreigners in foreign vessels within the territorial waters of Great Britain. But this judgment is corrected by the Territorial Waters Jurisdiction Act, 1878 (41 and 42 Vict. c. 73), which provides for the arrest and trial of foreigners for offences on the open sea within the territorial waters of Her Majesty's dominions, although committed on board or by means of a foreign ship. But no proceedings are to be taken under the Act except with the consent and on the certificate of one of H. M. Secretaries of State. And the definition of these "territorial waters" is (sec. 7) "such part of the sea adjacent to the coast of" Her Majesty's dominions "as is deemed by international law to be within the territorial sovereignty of H. M."; and "for the purpose of an offence" within the Act, "any part of the open sea within one marine league of the coast, measured from low-water mark."

As to the Crown's right to the *solum* below these territorial waters—below low water—including the right to submarine minerals, see L. Adv. *v.* Clyde Nav. Trs., 1891; 19 R. 174; Rankine, Landownership, 215–217.

(*b*) The St. Louis, 2 Dodson Ad. 245. 9 Geo. II. c. 35, § 23. 4. 9.

641. Sea-Shores.—The shore 'or foreshore' comprehends all that is covered by the sea in ordinary tides—the land which lies between high and low water-mark. This holds true both in Scotland (*a*) and in England (*b*).

(*a*) 2 Stair, 1. § 5. 2 Ersk. 6. § 17. The definition here given is not consistent with some dicta in Scots cases (*e.g. per* L. Moncreiff in Officers of State *v.* Smith, *infra,* and the interlocutor in Agnew *v.* L. Adv., 1873; 11 Macph. 309. See Dalrymple *v.* Chalmers, 1886; 13 R. Just. 34); but it is in harmony with the express decision in Att.-Gen. *v.* Chambers, 4 De G. M. & G. 206, 23 L. J. Ch. 662, that in the absence of contrary usage, the Crown's right to the sea-shore landwards is limited by the average of the medium high tide between the spring and the neap tides in each quarter of the moon throughout the year. Rankine, Landownership, 217.

(*b*) Sir H. Constable's case in 5 Reports, 107 B. See also the cases cited next note.

642. In England the shore covered by the sea belongs to the Crown; and all that is gained by sudden recess of the sea is held as the *incrementa* of that original property. The exception to this is, that what is gained to the land by gradual and imperceptible addition goes to the neighbouring proprietor (*a*), while that which is gained to the shore by similar imperceptible change is added to the right of the Crown (*b*).

The shore, according to the law of Scotland, shifts with the shifting of the tide; always corresponding to the above description of whatever is covered by the sea in ordinary tides. It is not, as in England, held to be the property reserved to the sovereign; but 'while it is not (*c*)' presumed to be granted, 'it may be, and in most places has been, acquired by prescriptive possession' as part and pertinent of the adjacent land, under the burden of the Crown's right as trustee for the public uses. 'Doubt has been entertained as to the nature and extent of the Crown's right in the foreshores of Scotland (*d*); but the law seems to be now fixed substantially in harmony with the statements of Professor Bell in this and the following sections. The result of recent decisions is, that while the foreshore, like other land in Scotland, is originally vested in the Crown, it may be alienated by express grant, subject always to the rights of navigation, and other rights which the public may have in it; and that a Crown title, more especially a barony title, to lands adjoining the sea-shore, without any express grant or boundary indicating an intention to convey the foreshore, but explained by possession, or an *ex facie* valid title followed by prescriptive possession, is sufficient to constitute a right of property in the foreshore (*e*).'

(*a*) **The King** *v.* **Lord Yarborough,** 1824; 3 B. & Cr. 91; aff. in H. L., 5 Bing. 163; 2 Bligh, N. S. 147; 2 Ill. 1; 27 R. R. 292. Att.-Gen. *v.* Chambers, 4 De G. & J. 55.

(*b*) Scratton *v.* Brown, 4 B. & Cr. 485; 28 R. R. 344. *In re* Hull & Selby Ry. Co., 5 M. & W. 327.

(*c*) See *per* L. Benholme in Agnew *v.* L. Adv. (*e*).

(*d*) See, *e.g.*, Scrabster Harb. Trs. *v.* Sinclair, 1864; 2 Macph. 884. Baillie *v.* Hay, 1866; 4 Macph. 625; also the cases cited below, § 643, 644, and L. Adv. *v.* Maclean, 1866; 38 Jur. 584. **Officers of State** *v.* **Smith,** 1846; 8 D. 711; aff. 6 Bell's App. 487. Gammel *v.* Comrs. of Woods, etc., 1854; 13 D. 854; aff. 3 Macq. 419. Dss. Sutherland *v.* Watson, 1868; 6 Macph. 199.

(*e*) Agnew *v.* L. Adv., 1873; 11 Macph. 309. L. Adv. *v.* L. Blantyre, 1879; 6 R. H. L. 72. Buchanan *v.* L. Adv., and Geils *v.* L. Adv., 1882; 9 R. 1218. Young *v.* N. B. Ry. Co. (L. Adv. *v.* Young), 1885; 13 R. 314; aff. 1887, 12 App. Ca. 554; 14 R. H. L. 53. Mags. of Montrose *v.* Comml. Bk., 1886; 13 R. 947 (burgh charter).

643. The shore, so far as capable of appropriation, may in England be part of the manor of a subject, 'but always subject to the public right of passage (*a*).' In Scotland it may be conveyed by the Royal grant, subject to the public use; and grants of the adjacent land are under that implied burden.

If the sea or sea-shore be the boundary of any man's property, the grant is construed to include the shore to the ebb-mark, and to extend or recede with the waters (*b*); the shore, or what is covered at ordinary high water, being still subject to the use of the public. It has also been permitted to such owner to prevent by artificial operations the encroachment of the sea, and even by such means to gain by encroachment on the sea. Whether those decisions are to be entirely approved of, or whether the strict construction to which Royal grants are subject (*c*) should not lead to a different conclusion, may be doubted. But at all events, the grantee who gains by embankment in such cases must hold the shore as still subject to the public uses (*d*).

It has been held that there is no substantial distinction between a grant of land as bounded by the *sea*, and as bounded by the *sea-shore*; and that the shore is given in both cases subject to public use (*e*). But after a grant so bounded, nothing remains in the

Crown but the public trust; and no one can, by subsequent grant or otherwise, be allowed to interpose between the grantee and the shore (*f*).

(*a*) **Mayor of Colchester** *v.* **Brooke**, 7 Q. B. 339; 15 L. J. Q. B. 59, and cases in § 639, 645.

(*b*) **Campbell** *v.* **Brown**, Nov. 18, 1813; F. C.; 2 Ill. 2. Boucher *v.* Crawford, Nov. 30, 1814; F. C. As to which case see *per* L. Wood, 8 D. 760. Blyth's Trs. *v.* Shaw Stewart, 1883; 11 R. 99. See § 738, 935.

(*c*) See The Elsebe, 5 Rob. Adm. 182.

(*d*) Hagart *v.* Fyfe, 1870; 9 Macph. 127. **Hunter** *v.* **L. Adv.**, 1869; 7 Macph. 899.

(*e*) Mags. of Culross *v.* E. Dundonald, 1769; M. 12,810; Hailes, 291; 5 B. Sup. 556. Mags. of Culross *v.* Geddes, Dec. 7, 1809; F. C.; Hume, 554. Campbell, *supra* (*b*). Leven *v.* Mags. of Burntisland, 1812; Hume, 554. Cameron *v.* Ainslie, 1848; 10 D. 446. It has been held in some cases, that a charter granting land as bounded by the "sea-flood" or the "full sea" excludes the sea-shore, and as a bounding charter prevents the grantee from acquiring the sea-shore by prescription. **Berry** *v.* **Holden**, 1840; 3 D. 205. Mags. of St. Monance *v.* Mackie, 1845; 7 D. 852. See Kerr *v.* Dickson, 1840; 3 D. 154; aff. 1 Bell's App. 499. Suttie *v.* Gordon, 1837; 15 S. 1037. Smart *v.* Mags. of Dundee, 1797; 3 Pat. 606; 8 Bro. Par. Ca. 119. Todd *v.* Clyde Trs., 1840; 2 D. 357; aff. 1841, 2 Rob. 333. But, on the other hand, a superior granting a feu so bounded cannot, at least where his own boundary is the same, interject himself by acquiring land from the sea between the feuar and the actual sea-flood. **Hunter** *v.* **L. Adv.**, 1869; 7 Macph. 899. Mags. of Montrose *v.* Comml. Bk., 1886; 13 R. 947.

(*f*) Campbell and Boucher, *supra* (*b*). L. Reay *v.* Falconer, 1781; M. 5151; Hailes, 890. See Macalister *v.* Campbell, 1837; 15 S. 490.

644. A right to the shore includes, by implication, sea-greens, which are occasionally covered by the water; rocky islands also occasionally covered, with their sea-weed, etc.; 'minerals, which may be acquired under a barony title by prescription even below low water-mark (*a*); and also a right to prevent strangers, or neighbours having no right of servitude, from taking any use of the foreshore except the uses reserved to the public' (*b*). In England the original right of the Crown comprehends everything but imperceptible additions (*c*).

(*a*) Wemyss' Trs. *v.* L. Adv., 1896; 24 R. 216.

(*b*) 2 Ersk. 6. § 17. Bruce *v.* Rashiehill, 1714; M. 9342; 2 Ill. 3. E. Morton *v.* Covingtree, 1760; M. 13,528. Macalister, *supra*, § 643 (*f*). Innes *v.* Downie, 1807; Hume, 552. Paterson *v.* M. Ailsa, 1846; 8 D. 752. **L. Saltoun** *v.* **Park**, 1857; 20 D. 89. Nicol *v.* Blaikie, 1859; 22 D. 335. **Colquhoun** *v.* **Paton**, 1859; 21 D. 996. **Baird** *v.* **Fortune**, 1859; 21 D. 1848; rev. 1861, 4 Macq. 127. Pirie *v.* Rose, 1884; 11 R. 490. See Lindsay *v.* Robertson, 1868; 7 Macph. 239, and L. Adv. *v.* Sharp, 1878; 6 R. 108. Below, § 647.

(*c*) The Elsebe, *supra*, § 643 (*c*). Benest *v.* Pipon, 1829; 1 Knapp, P. C. 60.

645. Uses for which the Seas and Shores are held.—Of these uses, navigation and fishing are the chief: the former being the primary, and inalienable.

(1.) *Navigation* is a use for the public, not to be interrupted or encroached on by grant of ferry, or by exercise of any ancient right of ferry. And those sailing in the course of the ferry cannot be stopped or impeded of their right of free navigation, unless it be shown that they are encroaching on the proper right of passage from shore to shore (*a*).

(*a*) 2 Ersk. 1. § 6. Campbell *v.* Campbell, and Ferguson *v.* Dowall, Jan. 18, 1815; F. C.; aff. 6 Pat. 417; 2 Ill. 4. See also Grant *v.* Goodson, 1781; M. 12,820; 2 Pat. 582; 3 Pat. 679. Colquhoun *v.* D. Montrose, 1793 and 1804; M. 12,827 and 14,283; 4 Pat. 221. See § 652–3; **Agnew** *v.* **L. Adv.**, 1873; 11 Macph. 309, 330. Cases in § 639.

646. (2.) *Fishing* is a secondary use for which the Crown holds the seas and shores (*a*) for the public benefit; but it is not 'in all cases' inalienable, like that of navigation. So the right of sea-fishing for salmon may be granted, either expressly by a grant of the fishing of salmon, or by a clause *cum piscationibus*, followed by possession of salmon-fishing (*b*).

The grant of salmon-fishing in the sea is the only monopoly of sea-fishing which has always been admitted. A grant of white sea-fishing has occasionally been made, but the effect of it has been questioned (*c*), and has never been fully tried. It 'seemed to Professor Bell' to be sufficient to control the public right as to floating fish; but, 'he added,' a monopoly of this kind of fishing, in any particular spot, is not granted by a general clause *cum piscationibus* with possession (*d*). 'According to the latest authorities, however, every subject has a title to use the shore for taking floating white fish in a proper mode, and the Crown's right to white fishings in the sea appears to be only a trust for the public, and therefore inalienable (*e*). An exclusive' right to take oysters, mussels, etc., which are fixed to the spot, is effectual 'within the three-mile limit,' where expressly granted (*f*). 'Such a right may also be acquired by prescription on a general title including "fishings" (*g*).' Lobster-fishing seems to stand in the middle between floating fish and oysters and mussels; 'and while the validity of an exclusive right has not been determined,' it is 'at all events' not conferred without express grant, or exclusive possession on a general grant (*h*). The fishing of small shell-fish, bait, etc., is open to the public, and at least is not barred by the general grant of salmon-fishing and other fishings without exclusive possession (*i*).

(*a*) See as to **Blundell** *v.* **Catterall** (*infra*, § 647), Rankine on Landownership, 229; and as to the use of the sea-shore by fishermen under 29 Geo. II. c. 23, repealed, except § 1, 17, by 31 and 32 Vict. c. 45, § 71, 11 Geo. III. c. 31, § 11 (white herring fishing), and otherwise,—Hoyle *v.* M'Cann, 1858; 21 D. 96. M'Callum *v.* Patrick, 1868; 7 Macph. 163. Mackinnon *v.* Ellis, 1878; 5 R. 832. Nicol, Lindsay, and L. Adv. *v.* Sharp, *supra*, § 644 (*b*). **L. Adv.** *v.* **M'Douall**, 1873; 11 Macph. 688; rev. 1875, 2 R. H. L. 49, 55 (*per* L. Cairns, C.). Scott *v.* Gray, 1887; 15 R. 27. As to a servitude or privilege of beaching boats, Stephen *v.* Aiton, 1875; 2 R. 470; aff. 1876, 3 R. H. L. 4. And a proprietor cannot by building a pier at his own hand exclude fishermen from the use of any part of the foreshore. E. Stair *v.* Austin, 1880; 8 R. 183. Cf. Baillie *v.* Hay, 1866; 4 Macph. 625. As to white fishing in tidal part of river, see Bowie *v.* M. of Ailsa, 1887; 14 R. 649.

(*b*) 1 Craig, 16. § 38. 2 Stair, 3. § 69. 2 Ersk. 6. § 15. Ramsay *v.* Kellies, 1776; 5 B. Sup. 445; Hailes, 722; 2 Ill. 4. See § 671, 754, 1112. It remains with the Crown where not alienated. **Comrs. of Woods, etc.** *v.* **Gammell**, 1851; 13 D. 854; 3 Macq. 419. D. Sutherland *v.* Ross, 1836; 14 S. 960. Anderson *v.* Anderson, 1867; 6 Macph. 117; 5 Irv. 499.

(*c*) See Ramsay, *supra* (*b*). 2 Stair, 1. § 5. 2 Ersk. 6. § 17.

(*d*) Same case. See 29 Geo. II. c. 23, § 1.

(*e*) See **Dss. Sutherland** *v.* **Watson**, 1868; 6 Macph. 199. L. Adv. *v.* M'Douall, *cit.* (*a*). Gilbertson *v.* Mackenzie, 1878; 6 R. 610 (Solway—comp. Coulthard *v.* Mackenzie, 1879; 6 R. 1322. Mackenzie *v.* Murray, 1881; 9 R. 186). Comp. Bowie *v.* M. of Ailsa, *cit.* (*a*).

(*f*) Grant *v.* Rose, 1764; M. 12,801; aff. 1769, 6 Pat. 779. Ramsay, *supra* (*b*). Maitland *v.* M'Clelland, 1860; 23 D. 216. Mags. of St. Andrews *v.* Wilson, 1869; 7 Macph. 1105.

(*g*) Dss. Sutherland, *supra*. See D. Buccleuch *v.* Mags. of Edinr., 1843; 5 D. 846. D. Argyll *v.* Robertson, 1859; 22 D. 261. Lindsay *v.* Robertson, 1868; 7 Macph. 239. Agnew *v.* Mags. of Stranraer, 1822; 2 S. 42. Erskine *v.* Mags. of Montrose, 1819; Hume, 558. The Board of Trade has power to authorise the establishment of oyster and mussel fishings by private individuals. 31 and 32 Vict. c. 45; 46 and 47 Vict. c. 22, § 8, 27, 30. See 3 and 4 Vict. c. 74 (crim. law); 10 and 11 Vict. c. 92 (do.); 47 and 48 Vict. c. 27 (cockles); 49 and 50 Vict. c. 53; 57 and 58 Vict. c. 60, § 745.

(*h*) 5 B. Sup. 556–7. D. Portland *v.* Gray, 1832; 11 S. 14. Stewart on Fishing, 69.

(*i*) Hall *v.* Whillis, 1852; 14 D. 324.

647. (3.) *Other Uses*, as the taking of kelp on the shore, the convenience of bathing, etc., are not understood to be uses necessary for the public, and inalienable; but seem to go with the express or implied grant, provided the primary and secondary public uses are left uninjured (*a*). 'But the right of the public to use the sea-shore for recreation may be vindicated by the Crown against a seaboard owner having a bounding title (*b*); and perhaps by members of the public also (*c*).'

(*a*) E. Morton *v.* Covingtree, 1760; M. 13,528; 2 Ill. 3. See, in England, **Blundell** *v.* **Catterall**, 5 B. & Ald. 268; 2 Ill. 5; 24 R. R. 353. See, as to fishing, above, § 646 (*a*); as to seaware, Paterson, Saltoun, and Pirie, *citt.* § 644 (*b*); and below, § 990 *fin.*

(*b*) **Officers of State** *v.* **Smith**, 1846; 8 D. 711; aff. 1849, 6 Bell's App. 487.

(*c*) Hagart *v.* Fyfe, 1870; 9 Macph. 127. Keiller *v.* Mags. of Dundee, 1886; 14 R. 191 (mags. of burgh). Rankine on Landownership, 230. *Contra*, Cameron *v.* Ainslie, 1848; 10 D. 446.

648. Navigable Rivers.—Navigable rivers are, like the sea, public; and are, for similar purposes, vested in the Crown. They are held as highways, or common passages. It is not tide rivers only which are held public; but rivers above tide-water, where fit for the transportation of the country products, though that should only be *down* the stream, are public rivers (*a*). 'As far as the tide reaches, the *solum* of the river belongs to the Crown, just as it is proprietor of the narrow seas within the three-mile line (§ 639); above the highest reach of the tide the channel belongs to the adjoining owners, as in the case of a private river (below, § 1101). Hence, while the interest of an owner in a stream is such as to entitle him to prevent any erection in the *alveus* which perceptibly affects the flow of water upon his land, whether there be actual damage or not (*infra*, § 1102), the interest of the public in a navigable stream extends only to prevent such erections by the proprietors of the *alveus* as interfere with the navigation (*b*).'

(*a*) Grant *v.* D. Gordon, 1776; 3 Pat. 679; 1778–82; M. 12,820, 14,297; aff. 2 Pat. 582. Colquhoun *v.* D. Montrose, 1793; M. 12,827; 14,281; 1804, 4 Pat. 221; M. 14,283; 2 Ill. 6. See § 968, 645. Bowie *v.* M. of Ailsa, 1887; 14 R. 649 (white fishing in tidal river).

(*b*) Colquhoun's Trs. *v.* Orr Ewing, 1877; 4 R. 344; rev. *ib.*, H. L. 116; 2 App. Ca. 839. Comp. cases below, § 650; and above, § 647 (*b*), (*c*).

649. (1.) *The Stream* of a navigable river is a highway for the people, of which the use is in the public without grant, and which no grant or exercise of secondary use can impede or hinder.

650. (2.) *The Banks* of public rivers are either the *alveus* or proper shore ('foreshore') left dry by the tide at ebb, or the proper banks above the reach of the water. The former is free for the public use, but subject to any grants not detrimental to the navigation (*a*). The latter are not vested in the Crown, but belong to the owners of the land bordering on the river (*b*), 'who, just like riparian proprietors on non-navigable rivers, have an exclusive right of access, on which neither the public nor adjoining owners may encroach (*c*)'; and in England it has been held that they can be appropriated for the purposes of navigation, 'as for a towing path,' only by the force of custom (*d*).

(*a*) See L. Advocate *v.* Hamilton, etc., 1849; 11 D. 391; 1 Macq. 46; 24 Jur. 379. **L. Blantyre** *v.* **Clyde Trs.,** 1867; 5 Macph. 508; aff. 9 Macph. H. L. 6; 1880, 7 R. 659. See 6 R. H. L. 72.
(*b*) 2 Stair, 1. § 5. See M'Intyre's Trs. *v.* Mags. of Cupar, 1867; 5 Macph. 780, 786. Gibson *v.* Bonnington Sugar Co., 1869; 7 Macph. 394.
(*c*) Lyon *v.* Fishmongers Co., L. R. 1 App. Ca. 622; 46 L. J. Ch. 68. North Shore Ry. Co. *v.* Pion, 1889; 14 App. Ca. 612.
(*d*) Ball *v.* Herbert, 3 T. Rep. 253; 2 Ill. 6; 1 R. R. 695. It seems to be so in Scotland also. Carron Co. *v.* Ogilvie, 1806; 5 Pat. 61.

651. Navigable Lakes do not, generally speaking, appear to be *inter regalia*, as rivers are (*a*). If wholly within the land of one proprietor, the lake goes as a pertinent of the land. If not so, but touching the estates of various proprietors, the lake and its *solum* rateably belongs to them all (*b*); 'the *solum* belonging to them separately for such uses as digging marl, or taking minerals below it, and the water being enjoyed in common for boating, fishing, and fowling. The *solum* can be divided, or the use of the water regulated, only by consent or judicial authority (*c*).' But if such lakes form great channels of communication in a district of country, there seems to be some reason to regard them as *res publicæ*; not to be held as implied in a grant of the adjacent land, but to be regulated in the conveyance, and in the exercise of the use, by the same rules which prevail with regard to a public river (*d*).

(*a*) See Bristow *v.* Cormican, 3 App. Ca. 641 (Lough Neagh).
(*b*) 2 Stair, 3. § 73. See below, § 1110. 2 Bankt. 3. § 12.
(*c*) Cochrane *v.* E. Minto, 1815; 6 Pat. 159. Macdonald *v.* Farquharson, 1836; 15 S. 259. Baird *v.* Robertson, 1836; 14 S. 396; 1839, 1 D. 1051. Menzies *v.* Macdonald, 1854; 16 D. 827; aff. 2 Macq. 463; 19 D. H. L. 1. Scott *v.* Napier, 1869; 7 Macph. H. L. 35. Mackenzie *v.* Bankes, 1877; 5 R. 278; aff. 1878, *ib.* H. L. 192. Stewart's Trs. *v.* Robertson, 1874; 1 R. 334.
(*d*) M'Donell *v.* Cal. Canal Comrs., 1830; 8 S. 881. See Swan's Trs. *v.* Muirkirk Iron Co., 1850; 12 D. 622. Colquhoun's Trs. *v.* Orr Ewing, 1877; 4 R. 344, 350.

652. Ferries.—The right of ferry, in public rivers and arms of the sea, is vested in the Crown for the use of the public (*a*). Ferries are public or private.

(1.) *Public Ferries* are under the management of the trustees of the roads connected with them, or under the regulation of the justices of peace, or ruled by special Acts of Parliament (*b*). The right of ferry, 'which, whether public or private, imports the exclusive right of conveying passengers and their luggage (and, it may be, carriages) across a narrow sea, loch, or river (*c*),' is not permitted to interfere with the general navigation; or to supersede the right of any subject of the Crown to navigate in the course of the passage, as a part of the sea (*d*), provided it be not done for avoiding the regular ferry; nor, on the other hand, is any one entitled, under the pretence of the general right of navigation, to interfere with or encroach on the right of passage. As the ferryman is not bound to carry a passenger to any point but his own landing-place, he cannot prevent others from navigating to other points (*e*).

(*a*) 1 Craig, 15. § 15. 2 Ersk. 6. § 17.
(*b*) See 4 Geo. IV. c. 56. 3 and 4 Will. IV. c. 33. Edinr., etc., Ry. Co. *v.* Arthur, 1854; 17 D. 252.
(*c*) Ferguson *v.* Dowall, and Campbell *v.* Campbell, *infra* (*e*). Walker *v.* Jackson, 10 M. & W. 161; 12 L. J. Ex. 165. As to the nature of the right, see Baillie *v.* Hay, 1866; 4 Macph. 625 (incorporeal right—piers as adjuncts not assessable under local Act; comp. Edinr., etc., Ry. Co., *cit.* (*b*)). Stirling Crawford *v.* Clyde Trs., 1881; 8 R. 826 (terminus in private ground). Cases in note (*e*), and § 653 (*c*). Tripp *v.* Frank (*e*). Newton *v.* Cubitt, 5 C. B. N. S. 627; 12 *ib.* 32; 13 *ib.* 864; 28 L. J. C. P. 176; 31 *ib.* 246; 9 Jur. N. S. 544. Hopkins *v.* G. N. Ry. Co., 2 Q. B. D. 224; 46 L. J. Q. B. 265.
(*d*) See § 645. Hunter *v.* Moir, 1830; 9 S. 86. Moir *v.* Hunter, 1832; 11 S. 32. North Br. Ry. Co. *v.* Mackintosh, 1890; 17 R. 1065 (Queensferry Acts).
(*e*) Tarbet *v.* Bogle, 1731; M. 4167; 2 Ill. 7. Campbell *v.* Campbell and Ferguson *v.* Dowall, Jan. 18, 1815; F. C.; aff. 6 Pat. 417. Trs. of Kinghorn Ferry *v.* Crichton, 1821; 1 S. 209. Tripp *v.* Frank, 4 T. Rep. 666; 2 R. R. 495. Greig *v.* Mags. of Kirkcaldy, 1846; 8 D. 1247, and 13 D. 975.

653. (2.) *Private Ferries* are such as the sovereign has granted to individuals, with the benefit of a certain monopoly, for the public benefit (*a*). The monopoly empowers the grantee to levy fair and reasonable rates (*b*). It does not exclude neighbouring heritors from having a boat to transport themselves and their family, and servants, and workmen. But as the condition of enjoyment of the right is that the grantee shall provide safe and convenient boats and boatmen for the passage, no rival ferry is allowed to interfere with the right (*c*). 'Ferries are subject to regulation, in regard to rates, etc., by the justices of peace and commissioners of supply, and it seems they may authorise the owner of the ferry to substitute a bridge and levy pontages on it (*d*). But there seems to be reason for holding that the right of ferry is properly an exclusive privilege of conveying by boats only, so that an action for disturbance or infringement does not lie against one who interferes with the right otherwise than by means of boats, *e.g.* by building a bridge. And it has been decided in England that there is no action for diverting the traffic against a railway company building a railway bridge beside the ferry (*e*).'

(*a*) It may be acquired by prescription. D. Montrose *v.* MacIntyre, 1848 ; 10 D. 896. Greig *v.* Mags. of Kirkcaldy, 1851; 13 D. 975.

(*b*) Mags. of Montrose *v.* Scott, 1755 ; M. 4167 ; 2 Ill. 7. See Cumming *v.* Smollett, 1852 ; 14 D. 855.

(*c*) Martin *v.* Thomson, June 16, 1818 ; F. C. Campbell, *supra*, § 652 (*e*). Hunter *v.* Moir, 1830 ; 9 S. 86. Moir, *supra*, § 652 (*d*). Weir *v.* Aiton, 1858 ; 20 D. 968.

(*d*) *Supra*, § 652. Martin *v.* Easton, 1830 ; 8 S. 952. Cumming *v.* Smollett, 1852 ; 14 D. 885, and cases therein cited.

(*e*) Hopkins *v.* Great N. Ry. Co., 2 Q. B. D. 224 ; 46 L. J. Q. B. 265, overruling R. *v.* Cambrian Ry. Co., L. R. 6 Q. B. 422 ; 40 L. J. Q. B. 169.

654. Ports and Harbours.—The sovereign has the sole right of erecting (*a*) or of holding public ports and harbours ; limited occasionally by the effect of royal or parliamentary grants to communities or to subjects. 'A right to a free port may be constituted by express grant (*b*), or by prescription upon a charter of royal burgh (*c*), or even, though that is not determined, on a barony title (*d*).' The duty of providing for the public safety in navigation is naturally accompanied by the power of exacting shore and harbour dues, to prevent the burden of the artificial operations or civil establishments necessary for the safety of navigation from becoming a load upon the subjects generally. A port or harbour has accordingly been described as comprehending —1. The natural access which makes a safe landing-place ; 2. The artificial operations by which it is improved for the convenience or safety of navigation ; and, 3. The civil power and privilege of monopoly within a certain district or precinct, and of levying 'anchorage and quayage' dues. 'The limits of the port are fixed either by the terms of the grant or prescriptive possession ; and the Board of Trade has statutory powers to define and extend the limits of public ports (*e*).' The right to levy dues, and the duty of keeping up the harbour in a state fit for navigation, are counterparts. And the right and duty, as vested in a grantee, depend on the original right of the Crown, and the limits of it (*f*).

(*a*) As to the rights of parties who erect private piers on the sea-shore of their own lands, with or without the permission of the Admiralty, or now of the Board of Trade (46 Geo. III. c. 153 ; 10 and 11 Vict. c. 27, § 12 ; 25 and 26 Vict. c. 69, § 15), see Colquhoun *v.* Paton, 1853 ; 16 D. 206 ; 1855, 18 D. 108 ; 1859, 21 D. 996. E. of Stair *v.* Austin, 1880 ; 8 R. 183. And comp. Officers of State *v.* Smith, *cit.* § 642 (*d*), and Crawford *v.* Clyde Trs., 1881 ; 8 R. 826.

(*b*) 2 Stair, 3. § 61. 2 Ersk. 6. § 17. See Dundee Harb. Trs. *v.* Dougall, 1848 ; 11 D. 6 (see pp. 20, 22), 1464 ; 1852, 1 Macq. 317 ; 15 D. H. L. 3 (charter from subject superior).

(*c*) Macpherson *v.* Mackenzie, 1881 ; 8 R. 706.

(*d*) *Infra*, § 755. See Gann *v.* Whitstable F. Fishers, Foreman *v.* Do., above, § 639.

(*e*) 54 Geo. III. c. 159, § 14 ; 9 and 10 Vict. c. 102 ; 16 and 17 Vict. c. 107, § 9 ; 25 and 26 Vict. c. 69, § 17 ; 37 and 38 Vict. c. 30. Nicholson *v.* Williams, L. R. 6 Q. B. 632 ; 40 L. J. Mag. Ca. 159.

(*f*) 1 Craig, 15. § 15. 2 Ersk. 6. § 17. M'Farlane *v.* Mags. of Edinr., 1827 ; 5 S. 665 ; aff. 4 W. & S. 76. Bruce *v.* Sandeman, *ib.* 668 ; 2 Ill. 7. Mags. of Campbelton *v.* Galbreath, 1844-45 ; 7 D. 220, 255, 482.

655. In regard to the power of levying dues, the rules seem to be—

(1.) That such dues are leviable as are sanctioned by immemorial usage (*a*).

(2.) That the fair construction of the grant, as affected by usage, is to be applied to new modes of navigation — to steamboats for example (*b*).

(3.) That such dues form a fund for the maintenance, 'including leading lights (*c*),' and repairs of the harbour, and not for the emolument of the grantee (*d*).

(4.) That the improvement as well as repairs of the harbour, 'though not the extension of it,' form a necessary burden on the grantee 'to the extent of the dues and revenues ; the grantee being bound to that extent to keep the port and harbour and its appurtenances in a proper state of repair, and to furnish such improved accommodation and conveniences to the parties resorting to it as are proper and suitable to the nature and extent of the port. When this duty is fulfilled, any surplus revenue belongs to himself (*e*).' But in one case, where the parliamentary grant of the harbour appropriated "the haill benefit" to the maintenance of the clergy, it seemed to be held that this controlled the application of the dues so far as mere improvements were concerned (*f*).

(5.) 'It was thought' that, in so far as applied to the harbour, the dues levied do not subject the grantee of the harbour to poor-rates (*g*); 'but the contrary rule is now settled in regard both to Crown grantees and public trustees (*h*).'

(6.) That the grantee is not bound to repair or improve the harbour out of his own means, and is not entitled to levy additional dues, without authority of Parliament, in order to indemnify himself for any extraordinary expenditure, or improvement, or repair (*i*). The proper course on such occasions is to apply to Parliament for a special Act (*k*).

(7.) That a third party is not entitled to insist on having the dues assigned to him by the grantee, in order that he may repair the harbour (*l*).

(*a*) Cowan *v.* Mags of Edin., 1828; 6 S. 586; 2 Ill. 12. See the principle exemplified and applied in the construction of statutes relative to Leith Harbour—Mags. of Edinburgh *v.* Shipowners of Leith, 1838; 16 S. 1171. Christie, *infra* (*d*). Girdwood (*b*). Mags. of Campbelton, *supra*, § 654 (*f*). Mags. of Renfrew *v.* Hoby, 1854; 16 D. 348; aff. 2 Macq. 478; 19 D. H. L. 2.

(*b*) M'Farlane, *supra*, § 654 (*f*). Girdwood & Co. *v.* Campbell, 1827; 6 S. 124; 1830, 9 S. 170.

(*c*) Bruce *v.* Aiton, 1885; 13 R. 358.

(*d*) Christie *v.* Landale, 1828; 6 S. 813. See also Stein (*l*).

(*e*) Officers of State *v.* Christie, 1854; 16 D. 454; 18 D. 727. See Home *v.* Allan, 1868; 6 Macph. 189.

(*f*) Ministers of Edinburgh *v.* Mags. of Edinburgh, 1838; 16 S. 400.

(*g*) Heritors of South Leith *v.* Mags. of Edinburgh, 1833; 15 S. 204. Inspr. of N. Leith *v.* Leith Dk. Comrs., 1852; 15 D. 95; rem. 1855, 2 Macq. 28; 18 D. H. L. 1.

(*h*) Adamson *v.* Clyde Navn. Trs., 1863; 1 Macph. 974; aff. 1865; 3 Macph. H. L. 100; 4 Macq. 931. Gardiner (Miles) *v.* Leith Dock Comrs., 1864; 2 Macph. 1234; aff. 1866, 4 Macph. H. L. 14; L. R. 1 Sc. Ap. 17. **Mersey Dock and Harb. Bd. *v.* Jones**; *Ib.* *v.* **Cameron,** 11 H. L. Ca. 443; 35 L. J. Mag. Ca. 1; 3 Macph. H. L. 102. See below, § 1138.

(*i*) Christie's Case, *supra* (*d*). Cases in (*e*).

(*k*) See Home *v.* Allan (*e*), and cases cited by Mr. Rankine, Landownership, 251, note 57. As to borrowing on security of dues, the cases and statutes will be found in Mags. of Renfrew *v.* Murdoch, 1892; 19 R. 823.

(*l*) Stein *v.* Stirling, 1825; 4 S. 180. See Hume, 557. Exercise of the right to levy dues at any one spot within the limits of the grant preserves it over the whole extent. Mags. of Edinr., *infra*, § 658 (*a*). Mags. of Campbelton, *supra*, § 654 (*f*). But a contrary open and uninterrupted practice to land goods at a particular place without paying dues infers dereliction at that point. Dundee Harbour Trs. *v.* Dougall, 1848; 11 D. 6 and 1464; aff. 1 Macq. 317; 1 Stu. 660; 15 D. H. L. 3; 24 Jur. 385. Mags. of Renfrew *v.* Hoby, *supra* (*a*).

656. The public is entitled to insist that the harbour shall be maintained, as far as the means afforded by the dues lawfully leviable extend; but beyond this the only remedy is by an application to Parliament.

'*Harbour Trustees.*—Many private and local Harbour Acts have been passed since the growth of commerce required facilities which the common law could no longer give; and the usual clauses in such Acts, having been collected in the Harbours, Docks, and Piers Clauses Act, 1847 (*a*), are, with the compulsory powers given by the Lands Clauses Act, 1845, incorporated in whole or in part in subsequent special Acts. Additional powers for improving and maintaining the harbours of royal burghs are given by the Burgh Harbours Act of 1853 (*b*); and the General Pier and Harbour Act of 1861 (*c*) enables the Board of Trade to make provisional orders for the construction and maintenance of harbours, of which the estimated cost does not exceed £100,000.'

(*a*) 10 and 11 Vict. c. 27. 25 and 26 Vict. c. 69, § 5 (Harbours Transfer Act). See as to harbour trustees as parliamentary commissioners for the public in contrast to Crown grantees, L. P. Inglis in Oswald *v.* Ayr Harbour Trs., 1883; 10 R. 472, 481; and generally as to the powers of such trustees, the same case, *l.c.*, and as aff'd., 1883, 10 R. H. L. 85; 8 App. Ca. 623, and cases in § 655. They are liable for negligence in performing their duties, *e.g.* in buoying the approach to their harbour. Buchanan *v.* Clyde Trs., 1884; 11 R. 531. Renney *v.* Mags. of Kirkcudbright, 1890; 18 R. 294; revd. 1892, A. C. 264; 19 R. H. L. 11 (duty of harbour-master in berthing, etc.). See above, § 156 (*b*).

(*b*) 16 and 17 Vict. c. 93. Mags. of Renfrew *v.* Murdoch, 1892; 19 R. 822.

(*c*) 24 and 25 Vict. c. 45; 25 Vict. c. 19; 25 and 26 Vict. c. 69, § 11. As to loans from the Public Works Commissioners, see 24 and 25 Vict. c. 47; 26 and 27 Vict. c. 81; 29 and 30 Vict. cc. 30, 72; 38 and 39 Vict. c. 89 (Public Works Loan Act); 39 and 40 Vict. c. 31; 41 Vict. c. 18; 42 and 43 Vict. c. 77; 44 and 45 Vict. c. 38; 45 and 46 Vict. c. 62, § 7; 48 and 49 Vict. c. 61; 50 and 51 Vict. c. 37, § 4.

657. Although the sovereign has right to open harbours, he has no power to order the shutting or opening of the ports, so as to regulate the exports and imports. This power, however, may be exercised during war, by Orders in Council, as a part of the war policy. The use of the port is free to the public on payment of the legal dues, when the harbour is once opened.

658. Grants of ports and harbours are in all respects held under the conditions which qualify the Crown's right as trustee for the public. But they confer a monopoly within the precincts prescribed, so that no one can erect a harbour on his own ground within those precincts, to the effect of exempting ships and goods from the harbour dues exigible under the grant (*a*). 'He may, however, erect a quay on his own ground within the bounds of the grant, paying always to the grantee the dues leviable (*b*).'

(*a*) Mags. of Edinburgh *v.* Scott, 1836; 14 S. 922; 2 Ill. 8. Mags. of Campbelton, § 654 (*f*). See above, § 655, note (*l*).

(*b*) Cases in note (*a*). M'Farlane, § 654 (*f*). Leith Dock Comrs. *v.* Colon. Life Ass. Co., 1861; 24 D. 64. In such a case, quayage dues, not being earned, are not exigible. Mags. of Campbelton, *cit.*

659. Highways.—'A right of highway confers on the public a right to use the surface of the ground for the ordinary purposes of locomotion; and is vested in the Crown, and subject to the management of statutory trustees for the use of the public. Unless there be an express right by purchase or otherwise, it implies no right of property in the soil (*a*), which, with the minerals underneath (*b*), and the trees and herbage that grow on its sides (*c*), is presumed to belong to the owners of the adjoining lands (*d*).' Highways are vested in the Crown, on the principle already stated; but they are placed under regulations for the public benefit by special statute, or by the General Road Acts. Whether streets in cities and towns, or roads in the country, they are public passages. They are not to be encroached upon by private proprietors or communities on the one hand (*e*); nor can the pretence or reality of public advantage authorise encroachment on private property on the other, except by Act of the Legislature, and on full indemnification. One difference there is, however, between a public road and a road acquired in the way of servitude. The former is held to be capable of extension with a change in the mode of travelling or conveyance, 'provided it is capable, without having its existing character altered by engineering, of being used by the changed mode of conveyance'; the latter is strictly limited to the extent of the possession (*f*).

(*a*) **Galbreath** *v.* **Armour**, 1845; 4 Bell's App. 374. Waddell *v.* E. Buchan, 1868; 6 Macph. 690 (see Aitken's Trs. *v.* Rawyards Coll. Co., 1894; 22 R. 201). Thomson *v.* Murdoch, 1862; 24 D. 975. Campbell *v.* Walker, 1863; 1 Macph. 825. Kelvinside Estate Co. *v.* Donaldson's Trs., 1879; 6 R. 995. See 12 App. Ca. 149, 159.

(*b*) Cases cited, and *per* L. Campbell in M. of Breadalbane *v.* M'Gregor, 1848; 7 Bell's App. 43, 60.

(*c*) Cases cited, and Dawson *v.* Ritchie, 1888; 32 J. of J. 159; 4 Sh. Ct. Rep. 104 (Sh. Ct. of Fife).

(*d*) Cases in (*a*). Wishart *v.* Wyllie, 1853; 1 Macq. 389.

(*e*) But the owner of lands intersected by a public footpath, or even a cart road, may put stiles or gates across it for grazing purposes or the protection of his crops, provided they are not obstructive, *i.e.* are capable of being easily opened or crossed by ordinary passengers. Sutherland *v.* Thomson, 1876; 3 R. 485. Hay *v.* E. Morton's Trs., 1861; 24 D. 116. Kirkpatrick *v.* Murray, 1856; 19 D. 91. Rodgers *v.* Harvie, 1829; 7 S. 287. Wood *v.* Robertson, March 9, 1809; F. C.

(*f*) Forbes *v.* Forbes, 1829; 7 S. 441; 2 Ill. 10. See *infra*, § 1010. Thomson *v.* Murdoch, 1862, 24 D. 975, where public and servitude roads are further distinguished. Mackenzie *v.* Bankes, 1868; 6 Macph. 936. As to the constitution of public rights of way by prescription, see the cases in § 1010, *infra*. Scot. Rights of Way Soc. *v.* Macpherson, 1887; 14 R. 875; aff. 1888, 15 R. H. L. 68; 13 App. Ca. 744.

660. (1.) *Streets of Burghs* (*a*) are, on the above footing, held by the magistrates under the Crown for the public benefit, and under the burden of the public use. They cannot be appropriated by the magistrates, either for public building (*b*), or by feuing (*c*): nor can they be encroached on by individuals (*d*). No encroachment can be made on private property for the convenience of the public, without the authority of Parliament (*e*); and even when power is given under Police Acts to regulate the line of houses about to be rebuilt, it is under the implied condition of full indemnification (*f*).

(*a*) See Muirhead, Police Government in Burghs (1893), pp. 145 sqq. As to a street which forms part of a public highway, see Threshie *v.* Mags. of Annan, 1845; 8 D. 276. As to public and private streets under the General Police Acts (13 and 14 Vict. c. 33; 25 and 26 Vict. c. 101; and now 55 and 56 Vict. c. 55), see Cargill *v.* Mags. of Portobello, 1863; 2 Macph. 244. Campbell *v.* Leith Police Comrs., 1866; 4 Macph. 853; rev. 1870, 8 Macph. H. L. 31. Millar's Trs. *v.* Leith Police Comrs., 1873; 11 Macph. 932. Dundee Police Comrs. *v.* Mitchell, 1876; 3 R. 762. Kinning Park Comrs. *v.* Thomson & Co., 1877; 4 R. 528. Mags. of Edinburgh *v.* Paterson, 1880; 8 R. 197. Harris *v.* Mags. of Leith, 1881; 8 R. 613. Johnstone Police Comrs. *v.* Donald, 1882; 9 R. 613. Mags. of Leith *v.* Gibb, 1882; 9 R. 627 (old walk intervening prevents property from "abutting"). Old Aberdeen Police Comrs. *v.* Leslie, 1884; 11 R. 733 (footways continue to be maintained by proprietors). Phillips *v.* Dunoon Police Comrs., 1884; 12 R. 159 (levelling—appeals).

(*b*) Miller *v.* Swinton, 1740; M. 13,527; 2 Ill. 10. Mags. of Montrose *v.* Scott, 1762; M. 13,175.

(*c*) Young *v.* Dobson, Feb. 2, 1816; F. C.

(*d*) Sir W. Forbes *v.* Ronaldson, 1783; M. 13,185. Gordon *v.* Royal Bank, 1819; 1 S. App. 452; see also 5 S. 164.

(*e*) Smellie *v.* Struthers, 1803; M. 7588. Newall *v.* Dumfries Comrs., 1828; 6 S. 884; rev. 4 W. & S. 137.

(*f*) Dougall *v.* Hutchison, 1827; 5 S. 224. See Strachan *v.* Edin. Impt. Comrs., 1837; 15 S. 637. Burnet *v.* Bush, 1849; 12 D. 44. Michie's Trs. *v.* Grant, 1872; 11 Macph. 51. Schulze *v.* Mags. of Galashiels, 1894; 23 R. 682.

661. (2.) *Roads* or *Highways Proper* are under the regulation of the General Road Act, 'now of the Roads and Bridges Act of

1878'; of Special Acts; and of the same general principles with other public rights.

At first the public highways were under the direction of the commissioners of supply and justices of peace of the county. Afterwards, in almost every county, Acts of Parliament were passed for regulating the roads; and giving power to trustees to arrange the statute labour, and to levy tolls, and borrow money on the produce of them. The abuses which prevailed in the obtaining and administering of those local Acts led to a general system of administration of roads and highways, by 4 Geo. IV. c. 49, amended and consolidated by 1 and 2 Will. IV. c. 43. The object of these laws 'was' to reform the old and imperfect arrangements, and reduce to a uniform system the management of all the highways, with a reservation of whatever 'might' be peculiarly necessary in certain situations. For that purpose (while local Acts 'were' continued as necessary for each county) it 'was' by the general Act for Scotland provided,—that the old Acts of the seventeenth century, and such recent Acts as 'were' of the nature of general laws, 'should' be repealed; and the rules newly established 'were' declared to extend to all local Acts 'then' in force, or to be enacted, for making (etc.) roads in Scotland. The qualifications of trustees, and their powers and proceedings, 'were' regulated; with the officers to be elected, the books and accounts to be kept, etc. Their powers to borrow money 'were' defined, and the nature of the security to be given over the tolls prescribed (*a*). Rules 'were' established for levying of tolls, with certain exemptions. Powers 'were' conferred for widening all turnpike roads to twenty feet of clear passable road (*b*), and for taking ground for that purpose without paying for it, but reserving the owner's claim of damages for fences removed or injured; and also for widening roads to forty feet, on giving compensation for the ground taken above twenty feet. Powers 'were' also given to purchase lands necessary for improving the roads. Some very just and useful rules 'were' laid down for the taking of materials (*c*). Rules 'were' also laid down for the prevention of nuisances and obstructions, regulating buildings on the sides of roads, and providing for the safety of passengers (*d*). And certain limitations in point of time 'and of jurisdiction (*e*) were' established for actions and complaints and appeals in matters relating to the roads (*f*).

On the interpretation and effect of this general Act it 'was' held, under the 4 Geo. IV. c. 49,—That each local Act 'was' to be read as if the general Act were incorporated in it (*g*); but this 'did' not apply to pontage Acts (*h*): That all 'specific' regulations in local Acts, not inconsistent with the rules of the general Act, 'were' effectual, notwithstanding the extension of the general Act (*i*): And, That the provisions of the Act for limitation of actions 'superseded' the rules of local Acts (*k*).

On the general policy of the law relating to highways, where any unwarranted obstruction has been occasioned *de recenti* by trustees or others, it may be removed *brevi manu* (*l*).

In the general Act there 'was' an exemption from toll of persons passing along their own lands, or being proprietors or occupiers of land through which private roads run. This 'did' not authorise an evasion by means of the purchase of small patches (*m*).

The trustees 'were' not entitled to compel the public to use the road, by shutting up a parish road, so as to bring travellers within the toll (*n*).

(*a*) Farquharson *v.* Burnett, 1851; 13 D. 586. Breadalbane Trs. *v.* M. Breadalbane, 1846; 8 D. 1062.

(*b*) Mackintosh *v.* West of Stirlingshire Trs., 1849; 12 D. 85. Walkinshaw *v.* Orr, 1860; 22 D. 627; 23 D. 80.

(*c*) Yeats *v.* Taylor, 1863; 1 Macph. 221. Graham *v.* Renfrewshire Road Trs., 1849; 11 D. 682; 1851, 13 D. 1012. Lyell's Trs. *v.* Forfarshire Road Trs., 1882; 9 R. 792 (2nd Div., doubted by Professor Rankine, Landownership, p. 801). Whitson *v.* Perth Co. Council, 1897; 24 R. 519.

(*d*) M'Leish *v.* Crightons, 1883; 10 R. Just. 47 (steam thrashing-machine near road). Elgin Rd. Trs. *v.* Innes, 1886; 14 R. 48 (removal of barbed wire fence—see 56 & 57 Vict.). Fraser *v.* Mags. of Rothesay, 1892; 19 R. 817 (duty of fencing where drop on side of road).

(*e*) Beckett *v.* Hutcheson, 1864; 2 Macph. 482; aff. 1866, 4 Macph. H. L. 6. Mitchell *v.* Morrison, 1832; 10 S. 230. Simson and Wilson, *infra* (*f*).

(*f*) 4 Geo. IV. c. 49. 1 and 2 Will. IV. c. 43. Simson *v.* Harley, 1830; 8 S. 977; 2 Ill. 8. Wilson *v.* Leith Walk Trs., 1831; 9 S. 725. Dudgeon *v.* Roberton, 1859; 21 D. 351. Orr *v.* Hill, 1841; 3 D. 1235. Sommerville *v.* Gordon, 1842; 5 D. 383. Swan *v.* Mackintosh, 1867; 5 Macph. 599. Comp. below, § 1136 (*f*).

(*g*) Menzies *v.* Duff, 1827; 5 S. 884. Mitchell *v.* Frew, 1827; 5 S. 909.

(*h*) Armstrong *v.* Stobbs, 1830; 8 S. 980. See Spottiswoode *v.* Laing, 1855; 18 D. 302.

(*i*) Sir W. Baillie *v.* M'Kenzie, 1826; 4 S. 834. MacCallum *v.* Spiers, 1827; 5 S. 541.

(*k*) Selkirk *v.* Laidlaw, 1826; 4 S. 695.
(*l*) Glasgow Road Trs. *v.* White, 1825; 4 S. 303.
(*m*) Merry *v.* Dallas, 1828; 7 L. 90. See Renfrewshire Road Trs. *v.* Reid, 1861; 23 D. 539.
(*n*) Glasgow Road Trs. *v.* White, 1828; 7 S. 115. As to the powers of road trustees in shutting up roads, see Walker *v.* Weir, 1817; 6 Pat. 281. Murray *v.* Stewart, 1839; 2 D. 12. Forbes *v.* Morison, 1851; 14 D. 134. Hart *v.* Carruthers, 1830; 8 S. 356. Campbell *v.* Walker, 1863; 1 Macph. 825. Love *v.* Lang, 1872; 10 Macph. 782. Murray *v.* Arbuthnot, 1870; 9 Macph. 198. Shearer *v.* Hamilton, 1871; 9 Macph. 456 (closing as cart road, closes also as footpath). M'Gavin *v.* M'Intyre, 1874; 1 R. 1016. M'Kerron *v.* Gordon, 1876; 3 R. 429. Pollok *v.* Thomson, 1858; 21 D. 173 (R. Trs. can't shut up a public footpath). L. Blantyre *v.* Dickson, 1885; 13 R. 116 (do.). Hope Vere *v.* Young, 1887; 14 R. 425 (cart road—footpath—public right of way, prior to use as statute labour road). Lanarkshire Rd. Trs. *v.* L. Belhaven's Trs., 1891; 18 R. 949 (level crossing—power to remove).

662. There are other statutes relative to roads which demand attention: as, An Act relative to Highland Roads (*a*); and, An Act to provide for the conveyance of the mails by railroads, and granting certain powers to the Postmaster-General (*b*); 'the Acts regulating the use of locomotives on public roads (*c*), etc.'

(*a*) 3 and 4 Will. IV. c. 33. 25 and 26 Vict. c. 105 (transferring to county trustees). 41 and 42 Vict. c. 51, § 3, 4.
(*b*) 1 and 2 Vict. c. 98. 7 and 8 Vict. c. 85, § 11. 10 and 11 Vict. c. 85, § 16. 31 and 32 Vict. c. 119, § 36-7. 36 and 37 Vict. c. 48, § 18–20.
(*c*) 24 and 25 Vict. c. 70. 28 and 29 Vict. c. 83. 41 and 42 Vict. c. 58. Smith *v.* Wood, 1882; 10 R. Just. 31. English cases in Rankine, 808.

663. (3.) *Parish Roads.*—These 'were till 1845' maintained still on the old system of statute labour, under the management of justices of peace and commissioners of supply. The labour and a contribution of road and bridge money 'were' supplied by tenants, cottars, and labourers, and the inhabitants of royal burghs. The legal breadth of such roads 'was' twenty feet, with a discretion, in certain circumstances, to widen the road or change the direction. The proportions of labour and the penalties or conversions 'were' settled by the statutes (*a*). 'The Act 8 and 9 Vict. c. 41 abolished in the option of the road trustees the personal performance of service and the conversion thereof as a poll-tax, and substituted an assessment on lands according to the real rental.'

(*a*) 1617, c. 8. 1661, c. 38. 1686, c. 8. 5 Geo. I. c. 33. 11 Geo. III. c. 53. 1 and 2 Will. IV. c. 43, § 70. Tait, Blair, and Hutchison on Justices of Peace. See Kilmalcolm Rd. Trs. *v.* Cal. Ry. Co., 1863; 2 Macph. 355; aff. 1865, 4 Macq. 937; 3 Macph. H. L. 84.

663A. 'Roads and Bridges Act, 1878.—In all counties in which tolls and statute labour were not abolished by local Acts before 1878, the Roads and Bridges Act of that year has superseded and repealed as from 1st June 1883 all local Acts. In counties where tolls and statute labour were so abolished, the Act may be adopted. It vests the management of roads in county road trustees and burgh local authorities. The county road trustees consisted of the commissioners of supply, and a certain number of trustees elected by the ratepayers, but by the Local Government Act 1889 they were superseded by the Councils (*a*). It abolishes all tolls (including pontages), statute labour, and statute labour conversion money, bridge money, and road assessments hitherto existing, and causewaymail; and substitutes rates and assessments for the repair and maintenance of highways. Most of the provisions of the General Turnpike Act are repeated or incorporated in this statute (*b*).'

(*a*) 52 and 53 Vict. c. 50, § 11.
(*b*) 41 and 42 Vict. c. 51. See also 43 Vict. c. 7; 46 and 47 Vict. c. 62, § 24; 48 and 49 Vict. c. 61, § 5; 52 and 53 Vict. c. 50, § 16, 37, etc. Under this statute the following cases have occurred:—Kelvinside Estate Trs. *v.* Lanarkshire Road Trs., 1884; 11 R. 1097; rev. 1886, 14 R. H. L. 18 (lighting—transference of obligation under local statute). Russell *v.* Lanarkshire Road Trs., 1884; 12 R. 298 (assessment—unlet property). Johnstone *v.* Mags. of Glasgow, 1885; 12 R. 596 (fencing—transference of obligation from county road trustees to burgh local authority). Sutherlandshire Road Trs. *v.* Lawson, 1885; 12 R. 818 (transference of obligations—road partly in adjacent county). Mags. of Glasgow *v.* Hillhead Comrs., 1885; 12 R. 864; aff. 1886, 13 R. H. L. 110; 11 App. Ca. 699 (bridges situated in more than one county or burgh). D. of Hamilton *v.* Lanarkshire, etc., Road Trs., 1885; 12 R. 1249 (debt, commissioners' duties). Lanarkshire, etc., Road Trs. *v.* Lady Torphichen's Trs., 1885; 12 R. 1252. Dumbartonshire Road Trs. *v.* Orr Ewing & Co., 1886; 13 R. 472 (bridges and ferries on Leven). Govan Comrs. *v.* Armour, 1887; 14 R. 461 (assessment—owners and occupiers—exemptions). Lanarkshire Road Trs. *v.* Mags. of Glasgow, 1887; 14 R. 890 (bridge partly in county, partly in burgh—Secretary of State—management). Lang *v.* Morton, 1893; 20 R. 345 (road vested in R. Trs. though they cease to maintain it and omit from list under § 41). Graham *v.* Mags. of Perth, 1896; 23 R. 602 (causewaymail).

664. Fairs and Markets.—Fairs and markets are intended for the encouragement of manufactures and trade; affording a place of resort for demand and supply; relaxing occasionally the monopolies of cities, and protecting the fair dealer by the regulation and control of public officers. The right of fairs and markets is vested in the Crown for the use of the subject (*a*); and the right to hold a particular fair or market is commonly granted to a burgh or an individual, for the benefit of the inhabitants of the community or district (*b*). No market or fair can be held without a grant from the Crown, 'or Parliament (*c*),' or prescription implying a grant. Such grant has also been held as implied in a charter of regality or barony. But all grants of fair or market are made subject to any rights which have already been conferred, and are not to be interfered with (*d*).

(*a*) See Blackie *v.* Mags. of Edinr., 1884; 11 R. 783 (*per* L. Fraser, p. 789).
(*b*) As to the powers of magistrates in regard to a market-house, see Blackie *v.* Mags. of Edinr., 1884; 11 R. 783; aff. 1886, 11 App. Ca. 665; 13 R. H. L. 78.
(*c*) Authorities in Blackie, *cit.* p. 789.
(*d*) Falconar *v.* L. Glenbervie, 1642; M. 4146. Farquharson *v.* E. Aboyne, 1619; M. 4147. Mags. of Stirling *v.* Murray, 1706; M. 4148; 2 Ill. 11.

665. The privileges of market are directed to the safety and freedom of dealings there. One great privilege of a market, by the usage of Scotland, in early times, was the freedom from arrestment of person or goods for previous debts (*a*). In England it is a privilege of open market to bar the reclaiming of stolen goods, *bonâ fide* purchased there. But this is not law in Scotland; the true owner may recover his property notwithstanding such sale. The only exception to this 'was,' that corn subject to the landlord's hypothec, when sold in open market in bulk, and not by sample, 'could' not 'under the law existing before 1867' be reclaimed by the landlord (*b*).

(*a*) Gibson *v.* Ker, 1552; M. 4145.
(*b*) See above, § 527–8, also § 1320, 1242.

666. The power of levying market customs is regulated by Act of Parliament, or by usage, and the reasonable occasions of the market; and except on those grounds no market dues can be levied (*a*). 'Burgh customs cannot be adjudged or arrested (*b*).'

(*a*) Mags. of Edinburgh *v.* Fleshers, 1790; M. *Bur. Roy.* Apx. 6; rev. 4 Paton, 375; 2 Ill. 11. Boog *v.* Mags. of Burntisland, 1775; M. 1991. Tod *v.* Mags. of St. Andrews, 1781; M. 1997. Fergusson *v.* Mags. of Glasgow, 1786; M. 1999; Hailes, 922. Skene *v.* Ross, 1794; Bell's Ca. 46, 116. Fleshers of Kirkcaldy, 1822; 2 S. 96. Mags. of Edinburgh, 1826; aff. 2 W. & S. 588. Cowan *v.* Mags. of Edinr., 1828; 6 S. 586. See Fleshers of Glasgow *v.* Mags., 1802; M. *Bur. Roy.* Apx. 11. Mags. of Dunbar *v.* Kelly, 1829; 8 S. 128. Hill *v.* Mags. of Edinr., 1830; 8 S. 449. Mags. of Wigton *v.* M'Clymont, 1834; 12 S. 289. Mags. of Lochmaben *v.* Beck, 1841; 4 D. 16. Boyd & Latta *v.* Haig, 1848; 10 D. 1433 (causewaymail in Edinburgh). See Mags. of Linlithgow *v.* Edin. and Glas. Ry. Co., 1859; 21 D. 1215; 3 Macq. 691 (transit customs or toll—railway). Kerr *v.* Mags. of Linlithgow, 1865; 3 Macph. 370. Maxwell *v.* Mags. of Dumfries, 1866; 4 Macph. 764 (effect of usage and desuetude on tables of bridge customs). Mags. of Kilmarnock *v.* Mather, 1869; 7 Macph. 548 (effect of decree of declarator). Graham *v.* Mags. of Perth, 1896; 23 R. 602 (petty customs within extended boundary under G. P. Act, 1862, § 13, 2nd Div.).
(*b*) Mags. of Lochmaben, *cit.* Kerr, *cit.* Phin *v.* Mags. of Auchtermuchty, 1827; 5 S. 690.

II. ROYAL PATRIMONY.

667. Reserved Property.—The Crown's right in land consists either of Reserved Rights, or of the Annexed Property or Patrimony of the Crown (*a*).

(*a*) 1 Craig, 16. 2 Stair, 3. § 35–6 and 60. 2 Ersk. 6. § 13 et seq.

668. The rights of subjects to land being derived from the Crown by grant, certain rights are by implication reserved from all such grants. These are—

669. (1.) *Mines.*—Mines of gold, and all mines yielding a certain proportion of silver, are *inter regalia* (*a*). Such mines were formerly held inalienable by the Crown; but they were dissolved from the Crown in the end of the sixteenth century, and allowed to be feued to the proprietor of the ground, or to strangers on the owner's refusal. The permission to feu to the proprietor is held to give him a *jus quæsitum* to demand such feu; not in his character as vassal of the Crown, but as owner of the soil (*b*), 'though holding of a subject (*b*). When such a grant is made to the proprietor of lands, it has the effect, unless at least the grantee does something to show his intention to keep the estates separate, of uniting the mines and the lands, so that the former are carried by an adjudication of the lands in preference to a later adjudication of the mines (*c*), or by a general conveyance of the lands (*d*).'

(*a*) 1424, c. 12. 1592, c. 12. See below, § 740.
(*b*) E. Hopetoun *v.* Officers of State, 1750; M. 13,527; 2 Ill. 12. D. Argyle *v.* Murray, 1739; M. 13,526; 5 B. Sup. 680.
(*c*) Oughterlony *v.* E. Selkirk, 1755; M. 164; 5 B. Sup. 836.
(*d*) E. Breadalbane *v.* Jamieson, 1875; 2 R. 826.

670. (2.) *Forests* are tracts of land for the keeping of deer. By the old laws of Scotland, the King had the privilege of killing deer not appropriated and within enclosures; and ground kept as chases for deer belonged to the King. The forest laws were oppressive chiefly in two ways:—1. The forests being unenclosed, continual encroachments were made on the property of neighbouring proprietors. 2. Cattle trespassing or found at any time in the King's forests, though unenclosed, were forfeited. Till the end of the seventeenth century no man was bound to herd his cattle, so as to prevent their trespassing on the property of others, except in haining time while the corn was on the ground; and when the trespass was committed on enclosed grounds, the proprietor against whom the trespass was committed could do no more than drive the cattle off his land. But it was different with the King's forests; and hence arose great oppression. The grant of a right of forestry conferred on the grantee the same privilege as if the ground included had been originally a King's forest, and greatly extended the oppression of the forest laws. On occasion of a grant of this kind made to a subject, a judicial inquiry and report were ordered as to the nature and effect of those grants, and a representation was made to the King against the granting of new forests. A grant of land in which a royal forest lies does not carry the forest without express words (*a*).

(*a*) 2 Ersk. 6. § 14. M. Athole *v.* L. Faskalie, 1680; M. 4653; 2 Ill. 12. See below, § 753. Robertson *v.* D. Athole, May 22, 1810; F. C. D. Athole *v.* MacInroy, 1862; 24 D. 673.

671. (3.) *Salmon-Fishing.*—The right to fish salmon 'universally, and not merely, as the original text bears,' otherways than by angling, within sea-mark or where the sea ebbs and flows, or in rivers, is *inter regalia.* This right is communicable by grant (*a*).

(*a*) See above, § 646; and below, § 754, 1112 et seq.

672. Annexed Property.—The royal patrimonial estate consisted of lands, castles, strongholds, and palaces throughout the country. These were often dissipated and transferred from the Crown; and a series of statutes with regard to them extends from the beginning of the fifteenth century down to modern times, in which two great objects may be distinguished: one to counteract the grants which, from necessity, or in a spirit of profusion, the Crown had been induced to make; another to encourage the operations of feuing or leasing of the royal property for a fair exchangeable value in annual payments and in furtherance of the agricultural improvement of the country (*a*). In modern times, the hereditary possessions and revenues of the Crown have been given up to the disposal of Parliament, and a settled sum appropriated for maintaining the royal household and dignity. In the beginning of William IV.'s reign, a more unreserved renunciation than formerly was made of all the King's patrimony and heritable revenues to the consolidated fund (*b*), and a civil list of £510,000 settled on the King. The whole of the King's patrimony and revenues in Scotland were on that occasion placed under the care of the Commissioners of Woods and Forests (*c*); and by commission from them, the levying and management was entrusted to certain officers who had formerly acted in the Court of Exchequer. On the accession of the reigning Queen, a similar renunciation was made of her Scottish revenues, lands, castles, and feu-duties, to be administered by the proper officers as Parliament should appoint; a certain sum being appropriated for supporting the royal dignity and household, freed from the burden of many pensions and salaries formerly paid out of the civil list (*d*).

(*a*) 1455, c. 41. 1457, c. 71. 1587, c. 29. 25 Geo. II. c. 41. History of the Exchequer. 3 Will. IV. c. 13.
(*b*) 1 Will. IV. c. 25.
(*c*) 2 and 3 Will. IV. c. 112. 3 and 4 Will. IV. c. 69. 14 and 15 Vict. c. 42. By 29 and 30 Vict. c. 62, § 7, the management of the Crown's interests in the bed of the sea and foreshore is transferred to the Board of Trade. See Officers of State *v.* L. Dunglas, 1838; 1 D. 300. As to the management of the royal parks of Holyrood and Linlithgow, see 35 and 36 Vict. c. 15 (Parks Regulation Act, 1872).
(*d*) 1 Vict. c. 2. As to the Crown private estates, see 25 and 26 Vict. c. 37. 36 and 37 Vict. c. 61. 37 and 38 Vict. c. 94, § 60.

673. The hereditary keepers of the royal palaces and parks have no right, without express grant, to exhaust or sell the soil or minerals, but merely to preserve from waste (*a*).

(*a*) Officers of State *v.* E. Haddington, 1826; 2 W. & S. 468; and 5 W. & S. 479; 2 Ill. 12.

674. Principality of Scotland.—The lands held to belong to the King's eldest son, as Prince and Steward of Scotland, were in the fifteenth century erected by Parliament, to remain with the Crown till the birth of a son, and to vest in the eldest son as a perpetual appanage and personal provision, settled and limited for ever. The principality reverts to the Crown when there is no Prince: And

The charters, while there is no Prince, must bear to be granted by the sovereign, in place and right of the Prince and Steward of Scotland (*a*). When there is a Prince who is minor, the charter must be granted by the sovereign, as his administrator (*b*).

(*a*) Johnston *v.* Riccarton, 1608; M. 11,685; 2 Ill. 15.
(*b*) Purves *v.* L. Luss, 1680; M. 11,686. Hamilton *v.* Bargany Vassals, 1626; M. 11,686. See below, § 933, as to Orkney and Shetland.

CHAPTER II

OF THE SUBJECT SUPERIOR

675. Superiority and Vassalage distinguished.—The property of land in Scotland is held either directly and immediately under the Crown as paramount superior of all feudal subjects; or indirectly, either as vassal to some one who holds his land immediately from the Crown, or as a sub-vassal in a still more subordinate degree (*a*). The two separate estates of Superiority and Vassalage are held reciprocally either by the Sovereign and his immediate vassal; or by the Crown's immediate vassal, and his vassal under him; or successively by vassals still lower, down to the last step of the ownership of land (*b*).

(*a*) Craig, Jus Feudale. Hope's Minor Practics. Dirleton's Doubts, and Stewart's Answers. Stair's Inst. b. 2 and 3; with notes of Lord Elchies and of More and Brodie. Ersk. b. 2 and 3. Ross' Lectures. Duff, Menzies, and Montgomerie Bell on Conveyancing.

(*b*) In England, this long protracted chain, from the King to his vassals and their sub-vassals indefinitely, is unknown. By a statute passed in the reign of Edward I. (called the statute *Quia emptores*, 18 Ed. I. c. 1), the direct effect of a conveyance by a landholder to a purchaser is to place the purchaser in the seller's stead as a vassal of the Crown, and to banish from the system subordinate vassalage. With us this is left to be accomplished in each individual case by a particular operation of conveyancing, to be afterwards described in treating of Confirmation. A freehold or allodial title is not unknown in Scotland, but its occurrence is exceptional; see below, § 697 (*a*), 932 sqq., 1165, 1172; Ersk. Pr. 2, 3, 4.

676. The estates of superiority and of vassalage are separate estates, not burdens on each other. The proprietor who immediately holds possession of the land, cultivating it by himself or his tenants, and reaping the immediate fruits of the soil, is said to have the "*dominium utile*," or "property." The right which the superior holds is called the "*dominium directum*," or "superiority."

677. The superior's estate, or *dominium directum*, is held immediately over the vassal. From the first the superior could dispose of the superiority without the vassal's consent; and clearly he may now do so, to the effect of changing the superior on the vassal (*a*). But he cannot create a mid-superiority between the vassal and himself; and he cannot split his right of superiority, to the effect of multiplying superiors on the vassal (*b*).

(*a*) See below, § 688, 703, 855 sqq.

(*b*) See below, § 857 and 859.

678. The vassal's estate, or *dominium utile*, is held under the superior as over-lord. The superior by whose grant he directly holds is called his *immediate* superior; the superior of whom that superior holds is called the vassal's *mediate* superior. The vassal was originally not permitted to alienate the land, so as to change the vassal on the superior.

But now the vassal's power of disposal is unrestrained, and the superior 'was' bound to receive either a creditor or a purchaser as his vassal, unless there 'were' some restraint by special condition (*a*); of which hereafter (*b*). 'By the present law the new vassal is received by force of law (implied entry) without any act on the part of the superior (*c*).'

(*a*) 1469, c. 36. 20 Geo. II. c. 50, § 12, 13.
(*b*) See § 861 sq.
(*c*) 37 and 38 Vict. c. 94, § 4. See below, § 775A.

679. Of these two estates, and the relation which they bear to each other, it may be observed that the superior is entitled at all times to have a vassal; the vassal (at all times when necessary to him) to have a superior; the duties being reciprocal (*a*).

(*a*) See below, § 705, 735.

680. Feudal Holdings.—The kinds of holding enumerated in the older books are: 1. The Military, or Ward-holding; 2. Blench; 3. Feu; 4. Burgage; and 5. Mortification. Of these, Feu, Blench, and Burgage alone remain. 'Blench is, in practice, in all points but the prestation, and Burgage has been, by Act of Parliament (*a*), in all points except the register of sasines, assimilated to Feu.'

(*a*) 37 and 38 Vict. c. 94, § 25.

681. (1.) *Ward-holding*, the ancient military holding, once the prevailing tenure of the feudal law, was abolished by 20 Geo. II. c. 50, and has become mere matter of history. The clause of *tenendas* was: "Per servitium wardam et relevum in feudo et hæreditate in perpetuum." The service was military, "ut cum armis et equis ad domini imperium quoties mandaverit paratus sit"; but there was seldom any specific obligation to this effect. The words of the *reddendo* were: "Reddendo inde mihi et successoribus meis debita et servitia tali tenend. generi assueta, omnium aliorum onerum aut præstationum loco."

The fixed return or duty consisted of military and personal service. The occasional or incidental rights '(casualties)' were—Ward, Marriage, Recognition, Non-entry, Relief or Fine, and Escheat (*a*).

(*a*) 2 Stair, 3, § 31. 2 Ersk. 4. § 2. See below, § 704.

682. (2.) *Blench-holding* was of old a sort of honorary holding, "ob præclara in rempublicam merita, et partam bello gloriam." It was without service or prestation, except as a mere badge or acknowledgment of superiority. The *tenendas* was "in libera alba firma feodo et hæreditate pro perpetuo"; the *reddendo*, a pair of gilt spurs, or a rose noble, or a penny, etc., *si petatur tantum*. And this, with a merely nominal return, continues to be the holding into which the ward-holding of all lands held originally ward of the Crown was converted by the 20th of Geo. II., and those of the Principality by 25 Geo. II. c. 20 (*a*).

(*a*) 2 Ersk. Prin. 4. § 3; 2 Inst. 4. § 7. 20 Geo. II. c. 50, § 2. 25 Geo. II. c. 20.

683. (3.) *Feu-holding* was deemed an ignoble holding, in which, instead of military service, agricultural labour or services were exacted. But it now forms the great and important holding of land in Scotland. The *tenendas* is "in feudifirma feodo et hæreditate." The *reddendo*, 'whether fixed or incidental (casualties) (*a*),' is a feu-farm or rent in cattle, grain, money, or services, generally agricultural. It is the holding into which all ward-holdings of subjects were converted by the Legislature in abolishing the military holding (*b*); and it is now the prevailing tenure (*c*).

(*a*) See below, § 704. (*b*) 20 Geo. II. c. 50, § 4.
(*c*) 2 Ersk. Prin. 4. § 2; Inst. § 5.

684. It may be observed of these several holdings, that during the military age of feus, wherever the expression of the *tenendas* was ambiguous, the presumption was for ward-holding; and that, ward-holding having been abolished, the presumption is now for feu-holding.

685. (4.) *Burgage-holding* is a peculiar sort of military holding appropriate to royal burghs. The sovereign is superior; each individual holding directly of the Crown (the magistrates being commissioners) for the service of watching and warding. This holding will afterwards be considered as a separate system (*a*).

(*a*) 2 Ersk. 4. § 8. See below, § 838 et seq.

686. (5.) *Mortification* was a species of religious holding for the service of prayers and masses for the dead. It was chiefly used in the bestowing of lands on the Church, or in the endowing of hospitals, colleges, etc.

The holding was abolished on the Reformation, and mortified lands declared to belong to the Crown; lands mortified to the use of hospitals and corporations being now held, like others, in feu or blench by trustees (*a*).

(*a*) 1587, c. 29. 2 Ersk. 4. § 10, 11.

687. Superior's Title.—The original *dominium directum*, or superiority, in the Crown as over-lord, is not a right of use of the lands, but only a right to the civil fruits of feu-duty, etc., and to the casualties. So the right or *dominium utile* conferred on the Crown vassal may be converted into an intermediate superiority by the granting of a sub-feu, which, transferring the *dominium utile* to a sub-vassal, leaves a mere superiority or *dominium directum* in the vassal of the Crown.

688. The right which, relatively to the feudal vassal, the Crown has thus in all lands, or which, under the King or other superior, is held by a subject relatively to his own vassal, is an estate—constituted in the Crown *jure coronæ*; in a subject, by a conveyance to the lands themselves. But although, in the proper and pure language of feudal conveyancing, the superiority is transferred by conveying the lands themselves, so great a relaxation has been introduced in consequence of the recognised existence of the separate estates of superiority and vassalage, that a conveyance of the "*superiority* of the lands" specified has occasionally been used by conveyancers as a legitimate mode of conveying the superiority, where that alone was intended. It is a practice condemned by Lord Stair (*a*); and though it has in one case been sanctioned so far as to sustain a vote under the former law of elective franchise (*b*), in the other cases on this subject either the sasine proceeded on a precept, duly assigned, authorising infeftment in the lands (*c*); or the lands were conveyed "so far as may be extended to the right of superiority" (*d*): or the conveyance was founded on to some limited extent only, as for a title in a removing of tenants, or a conveyance merely of feu-duties (*e*). The feu-duties may be assigned without conveying the lands (*f*).

(*a*) 2 Stair, 4. §. 1. See Pringle *v.* Pringle, 1890; 17 R. 1229. Orr *v.* Moir's Trs. (Mitchell), 1892; 19 R. 700; revd. 1893, A. C. 238; 20 R. H. L. 27.

(*b*) Hamilton *v.* Bogle, Feb. 23, 1819; F. C.; 2 Ill. 16; 1 Ross' L. C. 22.

(*c*) M'Kenzie *v.* M'Kenzie, 1822; 2 S. 90.

(*d*) Hill *v.* D. Montrose, 1828; 6 S. 1133.

(*e*) Lagg *v.* Tenants, 1624; M. 13,757. Park *v.* Robertson, May 16, 1816; F. C. In Gardner *v.* Trinity House of Leith, 1841, 3 D. 534, a title to the superiority was held a good title to pursue a declarator of non-entry; and while the point has not been expressly decided, it is now thought, on the authority of the cases of Hamilton and Gardner, *citt.*, that, except perhaps in a question of prescriptive consolidation (Bell's Convg. 780, 781, and *infra*, § 689, 2009, 2017; note in 2 Ill. 17), a title to the "superiority" is equivalent to a title to the lands. See Norton *v.* Anderson, July 6, 1813, F. C.; and comp. 20 Geo. II. c. 51. Fleeming *v.* Howden, 1868; 6 Macph. 782. Graham *v.* D. Hamilton, 1869; 7 Macph. 976; rev. 1871, 9 Macph. H. L. 98; L. R. 2 Sc. App. 66.

(*f*) Douglas of Kelhead *v.* Vassals, 1671; M. 9306. See 4 Stair, 8. § 2; and below, § 703, 857.

689. The superior's sasine in the "lands" may, with possession, be a good title of prescription to carry the property (*a*). *

(*a*) Bruce *v.* Bruce Carstairs, 1770; M. 10,805: Hailes, 378; aff. 1772, 2 Pat. 258; 2 Ill. 17. Middleton, 1774; M. 10,944; 5 B. Sup. 614. Walker *v.* Grieve, 1827; 5 S. 469. Waddell *v.* Pollock, 1828; 6 S. 999. L. Elibank *v.* Campbell, 1833; 12 S. 74. See Bald *v.* Buchanan, 1786; M. 15,084; 2 Ill. 54. See below, § 821, 2009, 2017.

690. Rights or Estate of the Superior.—The superior's estate or *dominium directum* consists of—1. Permanent rents, viz. feu or blench duties and services; 2. Occasional rights or casualties, viz. the payments to be made on the entry of an heir or singular successor, 'or periodically (*a*).'

(*a*) See below, § 704B.

691. Military and Civil Services.—Military services 'to subject superiors' are abolished by the statutes passed on occasion of the Rebellion of 1715 (*a*). Civil services may still be continued, but are demandable only within the year (*b*); 'and provision is made for their commutation by agreement or by the sheriff, and the conversion of their money value into feu-duty (*c*).'

(*a*) 2 Ersk. 5. § 2. 1 Geo. I. c. 54. See also Act of Sederunt, March 10, 1756.

(*b*) D. Argyle *v.* Tarbert's Crs., 1762; M. 14,495; 2 Ill. 18. Kinross Feuars *v.* Bruce, 1693; M. 13,071. Edinburgh Treasurer *v.* Sheins, 1696; M. 4188. D. Hamilton *v.* Mather, 1835; 14 S. 162; aff. 2 S. & M'L. 586. Hope *v.* Aitken, 1872; 10 Macph. 347.

(*c*) 37 and 38 Vict. c. 94, § 20, 21.

692. Blench-duties.—Considering feu and blench holding as now the only surviving feudal tenures, it is only in the former that the rent or duty is of consequence enough to raise a question. Blench-duty, payable *si petatur tantum*, must be demanded within the year, otherwise it is not actionable (*a*).

(*a*) Archbishop of St. Andrews *v.* L. Torsonce, 1610; M. 15,011; 2 Ill. 18. L. Sempill *v.* Blair, 1627, *ib.*; 1 B. Sup. 232.

693. Feu-duties vary exceedingly, 'being' sometimes almost a quit-rent; sometimes an ample rent, as in a lease, constituting as a real burden of annuity a valuable estate; sometimes accompanied by a certain stipulation of kain poultry, etc.

The feu-duty may be made payable in kind, as in grain, or in money, or alternatively in either; 'and, in feus granted since 1874, it must be of fixed amount or quantity (*a*).'

(*a*) 37 and 38 Vict. c. 94, § 23; *infra*, § 704B.

694. (1.) *Kind.*—If payable in kind, as corn, it may be demanded in kind, whether the land produce it or not, unless otherwise stipulated in the grant (*a*); and the vassal is bound to bring it to the superior if within the barony (*b*). The superior cannot restrain the feuar from growing other grain than that stipulated for the feu-duty; but he is entitled, under a general stipulation of grain or victual feu-duty, to demand *in kind* such grain as the vassal grows on the land, although more valuable than the sort of grain cultivated at the date of the charter (*c*). If the feu-duty be payable in produce no longer to be found on the land (as peats, or coal, or lime, which have been exhausted), the obligation is not by such exhaustion extinguished (*d*), unless there shall be an express specification of "such as are produced in the land."

(*a*) M'Leod *v.* Ross, 5 B. Sup. 615; 2 Ill. 19; aff. 2 Paton, 430. D. Hamilton *v.* Mather, *supra*, § 691.
(*b*) Treasurer of Edinburgh, *supra*, § 691 (*b*).
(*c*) Same case. M. Tweeddale *v.* Aytoun, 1841; 4 D. 213. Ferguson's Trs. *v.* Kinghorn Mags., 1876; 3 R. 401.
(*d*) Monro *v.* M'Kenzie, 1763; M. 14,497; 2 Ill. 19.

695. (2.) *Money.*—If the feu-duty be payable in money, no interest is due on arrears 'without express stipulation' (*a*); the superior must demand his feu-duties, 'when interest runs from the date of the action (*b*).' And this rule of their payment is so far different from that of a common debt.

(*a*) 2 Craig, 3. § 37. Kerr *v.* Simpson, 1790; Bell's Ca. 290; 2 Ill. 19. Napier *v.* M'Gavin, 1831; 9 S. 655. Wallace *v.* E. Eglinton, 1835; 13 S. 564. Edin. Mags. *v.* Horsburgh, 1735; 13 S. 571. Wallace *v.* Crawford's Trs., 1838; 1 D. 162. M. Tweeddale's Trs. *v.* E. Haddington, 1880; 7 R. 620, 642.
(*b*) M. Tweeddale *v.* Aytoun, 1842; 4 D. 862.

696. (3.) *Alternatively.*—If the obligation be alternative, as so much grain, or so much money in lieu thereof, or the value as converted by the fiars, the option will be with the vassal, unless it is otherwise indicated by the conception of the *reddendo*; or unless the delivery become imprestable, or be so long delayed that the superior shall not be bound to take it (*a*).

Where, in the *reddendo*, there is a stipulation of kain poultry, convertible at certain prices, it was held that, even although the option seemed by the words to be with the superior, he could not claim the *ipsa corpora* (*b*).

(*a*) See Anstruther *v.* Mags. of Pittenweem, 1742; Elch. *Alternative*, 1; Notes, p. 23. M'Leod, *supra*, § 694 (*a*).
(*b*) Hope *v.* Speares, 1838; 16 S. 1007. Hope *v.* Aytoun, 1872; 10 Macph. 347.

697. Means of compelling Payment of Feu-duties. — The superior may compel payment (*a*) of his feu-duties either by means of his real right and preference as superior, or by hypothec, or by poinding of the ground, 'or by adjudication,' or by personal action against the vassal; or he may have forfeiture of the feu (*b*).

(1.) *Real Security.*—The superior has, by means of his real right in the lands, a preference over purchasers and creditors, in voluntary or judicial sales, and in rankings of creditors. It extends over the whole lands feued, though divided in sub-feuing or on sale; each owner or sub-feuar having relief against the others for excessive payment (*c*). 'When the charter of the lands provides for the allocation of the feu-duty upon sale in lots or subinfeudation (*d*), or the superior agrees to an allocation, it is effected, without prejudice to the rights of heritable creditors not parties thereto, by indorsing on the deed of conveyance, before or after it is recorded in the register of sasines, a memorandum of allocation in a statutory form signed by the superior (*e*).'

(*a*) When lands are taken under compulsory powers, a title is completed under § 80 of the Lands Clauses Consolidation Act by registration of the conveyance; and the company so taking the lands does not become vassal of the original owner's superior, but only bound to pay him compensation for his interest in the lands, in terms of that Act, which provides separately for the cases in which the whole or only a part of the estate under one title is taken; 8 and 9 Vict. c. 19, § 80, 107, 108, 126. Elgin Mags. *v.*

Highland Ry. Co., 1884; 11 R. 950. Inverness Mags. *v.* Highland Ry. Co., 1893; 20 R. 551. See Monkland Ry. Co. *v.* Macfarlane, 1864; 2 Macph. 519.

(*b*) Sandeman, below (*e*), *per* L. Watson, 12 R. H. L. 70–72. Duff's Feudal Convg. p. 85.

(*c*) V. Stormont *v.* Blair, 1682; 2 B. Sup. 13; 2 Ill. 19. Ors. of Eyemouth, 1757; 5 B. Sup. 556. Wemyss *v.* Thomson, 1836; 14 S. 233. See Little Gilmour *v.* Balfour, 1839; 1 D. 403. Knight *v.* Cargill, 1846; 8 D. 991. Nisbet *v.* Smith, 1876; 3 R. 781. Sandeman *v.* Scot. Prop. Invt. Co., 1883; 10 R. 614; rev. 10 App. Ca. 553; 12 R. H. L. 67.

(*d*) Duff's Feudal Convg. p. 80 (§ 54, end). See below, § 888. See as to the construction of a clause providing for allocation, Campbell *v.* Deans, 1890; 17 R. 661 (heritable creditors infeft under bond and d. in s. not "singular successors").

(*e*) 37 and 38 Vict. c. 94, § 8.

698. (2.) *Hypothec.*—The superior has a hypothec, for security and satisfaction of the last or current feu-duty, over the crop and *invecta et illata*, similar but preferable to the hypothec of a landlord (*a*).

(*a*) 2 Stair, 4. § 7. 2 Mackenzie, 6. § 12. 2 Ersk. 6. § 63. Ross, vol. ii. p. 392. Hamilton *v.* Borland, 1756; M. 15,109; 2 Ill. 20. Yuille *v.* Lawrie, 1823; 2 S. 155. See below, § 1234. 2 Bell's Com. 27.

699. (3.) *Poinding of the Ground* is a peculiar action and diligence for attaching and securing (in order to payment of the superior's duties as *debita fundi*) not only the effects brought upon the land by the vassal, 'singular successors (*a*), and sub-vassals (*b*),' but those also brought on the land by tenants, to the extent of their year's duty (*c*). Questions may arise as to the degree of control which a superior may exercise for security of his feu-duties (*d*). Where a tenant, for example, pays only a small rent with a grassum, it would seem that the superior would be entitled to use his diligence to the extent of a fair rent; and either to hold the grassum as anticipated rent, or to demand legal interest on the grassum (*e*). The superior has no preference *ipso jure* (except in his real right over the lands themselves), his right over the moveables being no more than a privilege to poind, which must be made real by poinding of the ground,—a declaratory action, the calling of which in court (*f*), 'followed by the due and timeous completion of the diligence (*g*),' operates by litigiosity to secure the preference against all diligence not completed into a real right (*h*). 'The superior's privilege appears to be unaffected by the restrictions placed by the bankruptcy statutes on poindings of the ground by heritable creditors (*i*).'

(*a*) Rollo *v.* Murray, 1629; M. 4185.

(*b*) Duff's Feudal Convg. p. 85. Moncrieff *v.* Balnagown, 1630; M. 4185.

(*c*) 4 Stair, 23. § 5, 10; 2 *ib.* 4. § 8. 4 Ersk. 1. § 11. 1469, c. 37. Below, § 2285.

(*d*) See Hamilton, *supra*, § 698 (*a*).

(*e*) See below, § 721.

(*f*) *Qu.* service of which? See below, § 2285 (*g*).

(*g*) Henderson *v.* Grant, 1896; 23 R. 659. See below, § 2285, and § 914 (*k*).

(*h*) Tullis *v.* White, June 18, 1817; F. C.; 2 Ill. 20. Hay *v.* Marshall, 1824; 3 S. 223; and 2 W. & S. 71. Bell *v.* Cadell, 1831; 10 S. 100; see the note of L. O. Kinnear *v.* Watson, 1832; 11 S. 46. Campbell's Trs. *v.* Paul, 1835; 13 S. 237. It has been held that a superior cannot poind the ground for arrears of feu-duties after he has parted with his right to the land, poinding of the ground being available only to one who has a real right in the land. Scot. Her. Co. *v.* N. B. Prop. Inv. Co., 1885; 12 R. 550, doubted in Maxwell's Trs. *v.* Bothwell Sch. Bd., 1893; 20 R. 958.

(*i*) See below, § 2285. *Per* L. Deas in Royal Bank *v.* Bain, 1877; 4 R. 985, 990; and the reasoning of Lord Kinnear in Millar's Trs. *v.* Miller & Son's Tr., 1886; 13 R. 543, 547, upon an analogous point.

699A. (4.) '*Adjudication* is competent, as upon other *debita fundi* (*a*).'

(*a*) Duff's Feudal Convg. p. 85. 1 Bell's Com. 716. **Sandeman *v.* Scot. Prop. Invt. Co.**, 1885; 12 R. H. L. p. 71, *per* L. Watson.

700. (5.) *Personal Action* is competent at the superior's instance against the original vassal himself *ex contractu*, the vassal by acceptance of the feu becoming personally liable for the feu-duties (*a*) 'and whole obligations of the feu (*b*), and continuing so liable even after he has sold the lands,—until the purchaser was received by the superior under the former law (*c*), but, since 1874, until the purchaser is infeft and notice of change of ownership has been given to the superior in terms of the Conveyancing (Scotland) Act, 1874 (*d*)'; or against singular successors entering as vassals, for the feu-duties of their own time (*e*); or against sub-vassals 'to the extent of their sub-feu-duties (*f*)'; or against tenants in the lands while in possession (*g*), or intromitters with the fruits during their intromission (*h*); 'or against the original vassal (and his representatives) who has undertaken an express personal obligation for the feu-duties, even after transference to a purchaser and his entry with the superior (*i*).' The vassal's personal obligation is co-ordinate, and not alternative with the real right; and so the vassal cannot renounce his feu '("refute")' to the effect of discharging the personal obligation, whether his right is by charter or by contract. This is now settled law (*k*). 'It is only the *vassal* who is personally bound; and so, in the absence of a permanent personal obligation on his representatives, his heir may renounce the feu, and the representatives of the deceased vassal are liable only for prestations due at his death (*l*).'

(*a*) Moncrieff *v.* Balnagown, 1630; M. 4185; 2 Ill. 22. Bp. of Galloway *v.* Vassals, 1632; M. 4186. Wallace *v.* Ferguson, 1739; M. 9195. Scottish Drainage, etc., Co. *v.* Campbell, 1887; 15 R. 108; aff. 1889, 14 App. Ca. 139; 16 R. H. L. 16.

(*b*) M. Tweeddale's Trs. *v.* E. Haddington, 1880; 7 R. 620. 37 and 38 Vict. c. 94, § 4 (2), (3).

(*c*) **Hyslop** *v.* **Shaw**, 1863; 1 Macph. 535. Wallace, *supra* (*a*). M. Tweeddale's Trs., *supra*.

(*d*) 37 and 38 Vict. c. 94, § 4 (2). Dundee Pol. Comrs., *infra* (*i*). Aiton, below (*l*).

(*e*) Rollo *v.* Murray, 1629; M. 4185.

(*f*) Duff's Feudal Convg. p. 85. Moncrieff (*a*). Sandeman *v.* Scot. Prop. Invt. Co., 1881; 8 R. 790. M. Tweeddale and Hyslop, *citt.*

(*g*) It has been decided that the superior cannot sue an action of maills and duties for recovery of his feu-duties, on the ground that that gives a right of constant possession, and the superior has no right of possession, being excluded by his own grant. Prudential Ass. Co. *v.* Cheyne, 1884; 11 R. 871; where it is said that the statement in the text is inaccurate, and that tenants can be made liable only as intromitters, and only to the extent of their rent (*per* L. Rutherfurd Clark, p. 880). In Nelson's Trs. *v.* Tod, 1896, 23 R. 1000, this decision was extended to an action of maills and duties by the heritable creditor of a superior against the vassal. *Sed quære?*

(*h*) Biggar *v.* Scott, 1738; M. 4191; Elch. *Sup. & Vas.* 4. Rollo, *cit.* Hamilton *v.* L. Burleigh, 1712; M. 4189. Crs. of Eyemouth, *supra*, § 697. Duff's Feud. Convg. § 56 (5).

(*i*) King's Coll. of Aberdeen *v.* Hay, 1852; 14 D. 675; rev. 1854, 1 Macq. 526. Brown's Trs. *v.* Webster, 1852; 14 D. 680; rev. 1855, 2 Macq. 40. Small *v.* Millar, 1849; 11 D. 495; rev. 1853, 1 Macq. 345. **Royal Bank** *v.* **Gardyne**, 1851; 13 D. 912; rev. 1853, 1 Macq. 358. Dundee Pol. Comrs. *v.* Straton, 1884; 11 R. 586. Burns *v.* Martin, 1886; 12 R. 1343; rev. 1887, 14 R. H. L. 20; 12 App. Ca. 184. See *per* Lords Curriehill and Deas in Henderson *v.* Norrie, 1866; 4 Macph. 690.

(*k*) 3 Craig, 1. § 9. 2 Stair, 4. § 48, and 11. § 6. See Moncrieff, *supra* (*a*). Biggar, *supra* (*h*). Wallace, *supra* (*a*). Redfern *v.* Maxwell, March 7, 1816; F. C. M. Abercorn *v.* Marnoch's Trs., June 26, 1817; F. C. Napier *v.* M'Gavin, 1831; 9 S. 655. Hunter *v.* Boog, 1834; 13 S. 203; 2 Ross' L. C. 205. Mitchell's Trs. *v.* Pearson, 1834; 12 S. 322. M. Abercorn *v.* Grieve, 1835; 14 S. 168. Balfour *v.* Cook, 1817; Hume, 771.

(*l*) Aiton *v.* Russell's Exrs., 1889; 16 R. 625. Macrae (Buchanan's Factor) *v.* Mackenzie's Tr., 1891; 19 R. 139. Marshall *v.* Callander Hydro. Co., 1895; 22 R. 954; aff. 1896, A. C. 223; 23 R. H. L. 55.

701. (6). *Tinsel of the Feu.*—The last remedy against non-payment of the feu-duties is Tinsel of the Feu, or Irritancy *ob non solutum canonem*, which is a forfeiture of the vassal's right for breach of the feudal contract 'by the neglect of payment of the feu-duty for two full years, and is expressly reserved from the effect of implied entry (*a*).' This irritancy is provided by statute, '1597, c. 246,' and sometimes enforced by conventional stipulation. But in all cases it requires a declarator (*b*), the forfeiture being purgeable at the bar (*c*) before decree of declarator is extracted (*d*). 'The decree is not final till the extract is recorded in the appropriate register of sasines (*e*).' As this remedy proceeds on the principle of *forfeiture*, the superior cannot both insist on the forfeiture and demand arrears (*f*). The annulling of the vassal's right is not necessarily attended with nullity of securities granted by the vassal; but unless the holders of such securities come forward to purge the irritancy, the superior will be entitled to the lands free of the burden (*g*). 'The irritancy of a feu *ob non sol. can.* annuls sub-feus granted by the vassal, and not confirmed or recognised by the superior, whose security and remedies for his feu-duties cannot be impaired by any act of the vassal (*h*).'

(*a*) 37 and 38 Vict. c. 94, § 4 (3).

(*b*) Proceedings before the Sheriff to enforce this irritancy were made competent where the subjects do not exceed £25 in value. 16 and 17 Vict. c. 80, § 32. Hope *v.* Aitken, 1872; 10 Macph. 347. Maxwell's Trs. *v.* Bothwell Sch. Bd., 1893; 20 R. 958. See 40 and 41 Vict. c. 50.

(*c*) Prior of Pluscardin *v.* Sheriff of Moray, 1583; M. 7225; 2 Ill. 25. Wardlaw *v.* Hepburn, 1605; M. 7227. Carruthers *v.* Johnston, 1737; M. 7235. Lockhart *v.* Shiells, 1770; M. 7244. Baillie *v.* Town of Lanark, 1693; M. 7254. Rait *v.* Spence, 1848; 11 D. 126. Hope, *cit.*

(*d*) Ballenden *v.* D. Argyle, 1792; M. 7252; Bell's Ca. 157. Maxwell's Trs. (*b*) (purged by payment of arrears due by vassal himself, apart from predecessors, and without interest). The distinction between legal and conventional irritancies stated by 2 Ersk. 5. § 27, is said no longer to obtain. **Tailors of Aberdeen** *v.* **Coutts**, 1840; 1 Rob. 296, 316. But in regard to leases and other contracts the distinction is still recognised; and it is laid down that conventional irritancies are not purgeable, but are enforced according to their terms; although where they are of a highly penal nature, the Court may possibly interfere to mitigate the hardship. Stewart *v.* Watson, 1864; 2 Macph. 1414. Lyon *v.* Irvine, 1874; 1 R. 512. Hannan *v.* Henderson, 1879; 7 R. 380. Glasgow Mags. *v.* Hay, 1883; 10 R. 635. Conditions fenced by irritancies are construed, like other conditions in feu-contracts, according to the true intention of parties. See Napier *v.* M'Gavin, 1831; 9 S. 655. Glasgow Mags. *v.* Hay, *cit.* See below, § 868 (*b*), (*m*).

(*e*) 50 and 51 Vict. c. 69, § 4.

(*f*) M'Vicar *v.* Cochrane, 1748; M. 15,095. Napier, *cit.* Edinburgh Mags. *v.* Horsburgh, 1834; 12 S. 593.

(*g*) Drummond *v.* Hamilton's Crs., 1686; M. 7235. 2 Ersk. 5. § 79. Cf. *infra*, § 789, and 2 Ersk. 7. § 21.

(*h*) **Sandeman** *v.* **Scot. Prop. Invt. Co.**, 1883; 10 R. 614; rev. 1885, 12 R. H. L. 67; 10 App. Ca. 553. Cassels *v.* Lamb, 1885; 12 R. 722.

702. Retention by Vassal of Feu-duties.—The vassal has right to retain the feu-duties wherever any essential condition of the feu-contract is unperformed on the part of the superior. But the failure must be on the part of the superior in the proper character of superior (*a*).

(a) Kerr v. Simpson, 1790; M. 2692; Hailes, 1092; aff. 1792, 3 Pat. 238; 2 Ill. 26. Cockburn v. Heriot's Hospital, 1825; 4 S. 128; 2 W. & S. 293. See Heriot's Hospital v. Gibson, 1809; 2 Dow, 301. Gibson v. Heriot's Hospital, 1811; Hume, 15. Ainslie v. Edin. Mags., 1839; 2 D. 64; 1842, 4 D. 639. Arnott's Trs. v. Forbes, 1881; 9 R. 89. Thom v. Chalmers, 1886; 13 R. 1026 (no retention for mere dispute). Shaw's Bell's Com. 735. *Supra*, § 71; *infra*, § 861 sqq.

703. Sale of Feu-duties.—A superior may dispose of his feu-duties without selling his superiority. There was of old a form of conveyance by which, under the title of *alienatio feudifirmæ feudifirmarum*, the prohibition of alienation of the Crown lands was evaded; to prevent which, so far as the Crown was concerned, a statute was made after the Act of Annexation, '1587, c. 29' (a). But a similar conveyance, assigning the feu-duties payable to the superior, with power to uplift and discharge the same, and to use all modes of recovery competent to the superior, to be held blench of the superior, is an effectual constitution of a real right to the feu-duties (b).

(a) 1597, c. 239. See M'Kenzie's Obs. 15 Par. James VI. c. 239. Dundas v. Officers of State, 1779; M. 15,103; aff. 1780, 2 Pat. 516.
(b) Douglas of Kelhead v. Vassals, 1671; M. 9306; 2 Ill. 27. And see below, § 855 et seq. *Supra*, § 688. Duff's Feud. Convg. § 56.

704. Casualties of Superiority.—The subsisting casualties are—Non-entry; Relief, or Composition; and Escheat. The casualties of ward, marriage, and recognition are abolished (a).

'The Conveyancing (Scotland) Act, 1874, contains the following provisions for the abolition of all casualties, (b), except those constituted by special stipulation and payable at fixed intervals (c), in feus created after its commencement, and, by the redemption or commutation of casualties under previously existing feu-rights, for their gradual extinction.'

(a) See above, § 681 sqq. 20 Geo. II. c. 43.
(b) See the definition in § 3 of the Act.
(c) 37 and 38 Vict. c. 94, § 23.

704A. '*Redemption of Casualties.*—In feus created before October 1, 1874, the casualties may be redeemed on terms agreed on between the superior and feuar (a). Failing such agreement, casualties not consisting of a fixed amount payable in money or fungibles at fixed periods or intervals, may be redeemed by the proprietor of the feu on payment of the highest casualty, estimated as at the date of redemption, with fifty per cent. additional, in cases where the casualties are exigible only on the death of the vassal; and where they are exigible on each sale or transfer as well as on the vassal's death, on payment of two and a half times the amount of the casualty, estimated as aforesaid (b). Where the casualty consists of a sum calculated on the footing of an annual sum being paid for each year from the date of the last entry, the price of redemption is to be eighteen times such sum. No redemption can take place but by agreement till all casualties already due or accrued are paid, and redemption applies only to future and prospective casualties (c). In the superior's option, the redemption money may be converted into additional feu-duty equal to four per cent. on the capital, the amount of which is fixed by a signed and recorded memorandum in a statutory form, whereupon the superior's right to all casualties is held to be discharged (d). The vassal, except in the case last cited, is entitled on payment or tender of the redemption money to have, and cause to be recorded, a discharge of the redeemed casualties, to which the consent of any creditor in a heritable security affecting the superiority is necessary (e). Casualties subject to the fetters of an entail may be redeemed, the money being consigned or applied in the way directed by the Act (f). A mid-superior may in the same way redeem the casualties payable to his over-superior (g).'

(a) Edin. Mags. v. Edin. Roperie Co., 1877; 4 R. 1032; aff. 1878, 6 R. H. L. 1 (divided feu). Morris v. Brisbane, 1877; 4 R. 514 (feuar's title).
(b) Morris v. Brisbane, *cit.* M'Laren v. Burns, 1886; 13 R. 580.
(c) 37 and 38 Vict. c. 94, § 15.
(d) *Ib.* § 17, and Sch. G. (e) *Ib.* § 16, and Sch. F.
(f) *Ib.* § 18. (g) *Ib.* § 19.

704B. 'In feus granted after 1st October 1874, the annual feu-duty must be of fixed amount or quantity, and no casualties or duties are payable by law irrespective of express agreement. Casualties stipulated for must be payable not on the succession of an heir or the acquisition of a singular successor, but at fixed intervals. A permanent increase or reduction of the feu-duty of certain amount and at a certain time or times, or payment of a casualty in the form of a periodical fixed sum or quantity, may also be stipulated (*a*).'

(*a*) 37 and 38 Vict. c. 94, § 23. Browne, Petr., 1875; 2 R. 488.

705. Non-Entry.—This is not so properly a casualty as the enforcement of the vassal's obligation to enter as such. 'It is not within the definition of casualties in the Act of 1874 (*a*).' The superior is entitled to have a vassal, feudally vested; or to take possession of the lands himself, or to draw the rents, if there be no vassal. Non-entry gives occasion to the exercise of this right; and it may proceed either from the heir's neglect to enter in the room of his predecessor, or from the neglect of a disponee to complete his feudal title.

'The recent legislation, which dispenses with the intervention of the superior in completing titles, by making infeftment an implied entry, and provides for the gradual abolition of casualties as uncertain and contingent burdens on land, preserves and protects the pecuniary rights of the superior. Non-entry could hardly co-exist with the implied entry by infeftment; and yet the declarator of non-entry, by giving the superior actual possession of the lands, was his most efficient means of enforcing some of these rights. The policy of the Act has therefore led to the apparent abolition of non-entry, and the remedy connected with it; while the old law has with some changes been substantially retained, so far as it serves for the protection of these money claims. It is enacted that since 1st October 1874, no lands shall be deemed to be in non-entry; but a superior entitled according to the former law to sue a declarator of non-entry may raise, against the successor of any vassal, whether infeft or not, an action, in a statutory form, of declarator and for payment of any casualty exigible at the date of action, and the implied entry created by the Act of 1874 cannot be pleaded in defence against such action. A decree for payment in such an action has the same effect as a decree of declarator of non-entry until payment of the casualty and expenses. Till such payment, but not afterwards, the superior under the decree has right to the rents due for the period while he is in possession of the lands under the decree, over and above any arrears of feu-duties and the other rights due and competent under the former law prior to the date of payment of the casualty, by which the decree ceases to have the effect of a decree of non-entry (*b*).

'So much of the old law still survives under this clumsy and anomalous enactment, that it seems proper in the following paragraphs to retain the present tense wherever that can be done without actually misleading.'

(1.) *When Lands are in Non-Entry.*—Lands 'were' in non-entry in the following cases: where the heir 'neglected' to renew his investiture with the superior on his ancestor's death (*c*); where the vassal himself, or (after his death) his heir, 'delayed' to take sasine on an unexecuted precept; where the service of an heir 'was' reduced; where the lands 'had' been sold and resigned *in favorem* of the purchaser, but the new vassal 'did' not come to the superior for his charter, or 'did' not take sasine on that charter; for although there 'was,' in consequence of this, no forfeiture, the lands or rents 'fell' as a *surrogatum* to the superior for the want of a vassal (*d*). 'Apart from the enactment above cited, the last-mentioned case cannot now occur, resignation *in favorem* being virtually abolished (*e*).'

(*a*) 37 and 38 Vict. c. 94, § 3. L. Adv. *v.* Moray, 1890; 17 R. 945.
(*b*) 37 and 38 Vict. c. 94, § 4, subs. 4, and Sch. B.
(*c*) See Darroch *v.* Ranken, 1855; 17 D. 935.
(*d*) 2 Ersk. 5. § 30, 42.
(*e*) 37 and 38 Vict. c. 94, § 4 (1), § 26, etc.

706. (2.) *Declarator of Non-Entry.*—Of old, the superior entered at once into possession of the lands by sentence of his own Baron Court; but 'in modern times' a process of Declarator of Non-Entry 'was' requisite. This is called the General Declarator of Non-Entry. Before citation in it, the vassal 'was' not in contumacy, and the superior 'could' demand only his feu-duties or (in blench-holding) his retour-duties. Citation unobeyed infers contumacy; and from that moment the superior has right to demand the full rents, unless there be a reasonable excuse for not entering; and he 'was' entitled on decree to enter into possession, and to have action of maills and duties, or poinding of the ground. The decree for thus accomplishing the purpose of making the feu-duties effectual is called, though improperly, the Special Declarator of Non-Entry (*a*).

(*a*) 2 Ersk. 5. § 29, 36, 42. 2 Stair, 4. § 22. Byres *v.* Law, 1626; M. 13,791; 2 Ill. 27. Douglas of Kellhead *v.* Vassals, 1671; M. 9306. Faa *v.* L. Powrie, 1673; M. 9307. Copland *v.* Fraser, 1771; 5 B. Sup. 610. Coltart *v.* Tait, 1782; M. 9313. Robin *v.* Drummond, 1823; 2 S. 404. Donaldson's Trs. *v.* Chalmers, 1833; 11 S. 367. Marshal *v.* Mather, 1835; 14 S. 30. Wallace *v.* E. Eglinton, 1836; 14 S. 599. See below, § 713. Hill *v.* Mackay, 1824; 2 S. 681. Preston *v.* Dundonald's Crs., 1799; Hume, 770. Hill *v.* Kyd, 1812; *ib.* 771. Tod's Trs. *v.* Graham, 1869; 8 Macph. 264.

707. The object of the action of general declarator 'was' to have it declared that the tenement is void; that the bygone feu-duties, or in blench-holding the retour-duties, belong to the superior from the vassal's death to the date of citation; that he has right to poind the ground for the full rent or duties, bygone from citation, and future till the heir's entry; and that he has right to a year's rent for the heir's entry. 'By the statutory entry the superior is deprived of his non-entry duties, without any substitute being given him, and he has not now an action for bygone feu-duties or retour-duties accruing before 1st October 1874 (*a*).'

(*a*) L. Adv. *v.* Moray, 1890; 17 R. 945.

708. The superior's title to pursue is his sasine in the lands themselves (*a*), 'or in the superiority (*b*).'

(*a*) Park *v.* Robertson, May 16, 1816; F. C.; 2 Ill. 16. See below, § 710.
(*b*) See above, § 688 (*c*).

709. The nature of the action, and the parties to be called, vary with circumstances. Where the vassal 'had' died, the action 'was' a simple declarator of non-entry, and the heir 'was' a proper party (*a*). Where the vassal 'had' alienated his fee, and on the procuratory there 'had been' resignation, the superior's action 'was' reduction-improbation of such conveyance, with declarator of non-entry; and there seems to be no necessity to call the heir, but only the disponee. If a vassal infeft disponed with procuratory, and died, his heir 'could' not be compelled to enter (either by the superior or by the disponee); and it seems not to be necessary to call the heir (*b*). But if the heir 'chose' in such circumstances to enter, the superior 'was bound to' receive him on the proper evidence of his right being produced (*c*). 'But there was no room for such an entry of the heir if the purchaser had already obtained a charter from the superior: and it is now settled, upon the construction of the statute of 1874, that the implied entry effected by the purchaser's infeftment extinguishes the mid-superiority, and makes the purchaser liable for composition, subject (it would seem) only to the proviso that the superior cannot exact it as long as the vassal lives on whose entry the last payment was made (*d*); and that the payment of relief or composition is due on the entry of the vassal last infeft, and not (if the superior should have delayed making a demand for it) on the entry of any intermediate disponee, for the statute does not increase the superior's right to demand casualties (*e*). So long, however, as the purchaser's or disponee's title is unrecorded, the heir is still entitled to demand an entry upon payment of relief duty only (*f*).' If a disposition have been granted to the heir, with a procuratory, and he sell, the disponee is not bound to take an assignation to the procuratory, but may compel the heir to complete his title (*g*). 'The case referred to establishes the rule, that if on a sale there be no obligation expressed to accept the seller's title as it stands, an unentered seller is bound to enter with the superior (*h*); or under the new system, at least where there is in the disposition the usual clause of relief (see § 892, 895), to relieve a purchaser, who by infeftment obtains an implied entry, of the casualty exigible by the superior (*i*).'

The tenants and sub-vassals must be called in all cases 'under the law prior to 1874 (*k*).'

(*a*) Napier *v.* Kincaid, 1743; Elch. *Non-entry*, 2; 2 Ill. 28; 2 Ross' L. C. 315.
(*b*) Dundas *v.* Drummond, 1769; M. 15,035; Hailes, 275. Haig *v.* Forbes, 1821; 1 S. 8. Dundee Mags. *v.* Kidd, 1829; 7 S. 801. Mackenzie *v.* Mackenzie, 1838; 16 S. 1326. See Hamilton Mags. *v.* Swin, 1854; 15 D. 437. Cauvin's Hosp. *v.* Falconer, 1863; 1 Macph. 1164. Mackenzie *v.* Mackenzie, 1842; 5 D. 246. Tod's Trs. *v.* Graham, 1869; 8 Macph. 264. D. Argyll *v.* Dalgleish's Trs., 1873; 11 Macph. 616.
(*c*) Piggot *v.* Colvil, 1829; 8 S. 213. Cf. Fullarton *v.* Hamilton, 1833; 12 S. 117.
(*d*) 37 and 38 Vict. c. 94, § 4 (2), (4). Ferrier's Trs. *v.* Bayley, 1877; 4 R. 738. Rossmore's Trs. *v.* Brownlie, 1877; 5 R. 201. Sivwright *v.* Straiton Estate Co., 1878; 5 R. 922. Lamont *v.* Rankin's Trs., 1879; 6 R. 739; aff. 1880, 7 R. H. L. 10. Jurid. Rev. i. 81.
(*e*) See Mounsey *v.* Palmer, 1884; 12 R. 236. Stuart *v.* Hamilton, 1889; 16 R. 1030.

(*f*) D. Hamilton *v.* Guild, 1883; 10 R. 1117. Hope *v.* D. Hamilton, 1883; 10 R. 1122. See below, § 712.
(*g*) Gardiner *v.* Anderson, 1799; M. 15,037. See § 723. Mackenzie, *supra* (*b*).
(*h*) See below, § 723.
(*i*) Straiton Estate Co. *v.* Stephens, 1880; 8 R. 299.
(*k*) See 37 and 38 Vict. c. 94, Sch. B.

710. The grounds of defence relevant to exclude the superior in a declarator of non-entry 'were': the heir's sasine, '*i.e.* the existence of an entered vassal' (*a*); 'the delivery to the vassal of a charter by progress, containing no reservation of bypast duties and casualties (*b*)'; the terce, to the extent of a third; or, courtesy as to the whole; the superior's refusal of a charter, or not being himself entered, and so not able to give an entry; or the title so perplexed that the true superior cannot be discovered,—the vassal having a right to call on the superior to show his title, that he may be satisfied of his safety to enter with him (*c*); the superior's tinsel of superiority (*d*). 'These points are still important, as the action of declarator and for payment substituted for the declarator of non-entry can be sued only by a superior who would, but for the Act, be entitled to sue a declarator of non-entry, and the decree in the action has the effect of and operates as a decree of non-entry according to the former law (*e*).'

The superior, though entitled to compel a vassal to enter, has no right to infeft him without his consent (*f*). 'But the vassal is not entitled to refuse to enter, or pay the duties, where the superior is in the substantial right, has an *ex facie* title, and there is no competition on the ground of alleged defects in the superior's title (*g*).'

(*a*) Hay *v.* Auchenames, 1630; M. 9291; 2 Ill. 29. Fullarton *v.* Denholm, 1678; M. 9293. Stuart *v.* Jackson, 1889; 17 R. 85 (not a mere liferenter). See § 709 (*c*), 723. Morris *v.* Brisbane, 1877; 4 R. 515. This defence may be excluded by an obligation in the charter to enter and be infeft within a certain period. Dick Lauder *v.* Thornton, 1890; 17 R. 320.
(*b*) Glasgow Tailors *v.* Blackie, 1851; 13 D. 1073. L. Adv. *v.* Rollo, 1872; 10 Macph. 1024.
(*c*) Chalmers *v.* Vassals, 1745; M. 9330, 15,091; Elch. *Non-entry*, 3; 1 Pat. 404. See below, § 736A.
(*d*) Dickson *v.* Elphinston, 1802; M. 15,024. See below, § 735.
(*e*) 37 and 38 Vict. c. 94, § 4 (4).
(*f*) E. Eglinton *v.* Caldwell, 1581; M. 15,026. Laing *v.* Scrymgeour, 1582; M. 15,026. Stewart *v.* Burnside, 1794; Bell's Ca. 75. See below, § 878.
(*g*) Gibson-Craig *v.* Cochrane, 1841; 16 S. 1332; aff. 1841, 2 Rob. 446; 2 Ross' L. C. 329. Innes *v.* Gordon, 1844; 7 D. 141. E. Breadalbane *v.* Macdougall, 1880; 8 R. 42; aff. 1881, *ib.* H. L. 92. Mackenzie *v.* Munro, 1869; 7 Macph. 676. See M. Bell's Convg. 1130. Mackenzie, *supra*, § 709 (*b*).

711. In order to procure an entry, and avoid the penal consequences of non-entry, the heir must offer proof by retour of his right (for calling him as a defender does not imply an acknowledgment of his title); the relief and non-entry duties, viz. a year's rent; the full rents after decree, unless there shall be a good or colourable excuse; and such a charter for signature as the superior is bound to grant (*a*). And in this, though the vassal is entitled to prescribe such destination as he pleases within the limits of the legal succession, the superior does not seem bound to comply when the destination goes beyond it (*b*).

(*a*) Hill *v.* Mackay, *supra*, § 706 (*a*). Piggot *v.* Colvil, 1829; 8 S. 213; 2 Ill. 29. Fullarton, *supra*, § 710 (*a*). Douglas *v.* Carlyle, 1671; M. 9292; 2 Ill. 30. Powrie *v.* Smith, 1687; M. 9296. Rolland *v.* Vassal, 1554; M. 9314. L. Melvil *v.* Bruce, 1677; M. 9321. Robin *v.* Drummond, 1823; 2 S. 404. Spottiswoode *v.* Fraser, 1771; M. 8004. See above, § 706.
(*b*) See below, § 718, 725. D. Hamilton *v.* E. Hopetoun, 1839; 1 D. 689.

712. If the proper heir offer to enter, the superior must, 'if there be no contrary provision in the title (*a*),' comply, and has no title to inquire into any conveyances which may have been granted (*b*), to insist on the entry of a disponee, or to select among the disponees a vassal for himself. He may be compelled to give an entry to any one legally entitled to an entry. This 'was' done by an order of Court in the process of non-entry, requiring the superior to lodge a charter, and by the Court refusing to give decree in the declarator of non-entry till this be complied with (*c*).

(*a*) Dick Lauder *v.* Thornton, 1890; 17 R. 320.
(*b*) See Monteith *v.* Ingels, 1869; 7 Macph. 523. Rossmore's Trs. *v.* Brownlie, D. Hamilton, and Hope, *citt. supra*, § 709 (*d*), (*f*).
(*c*) Piggot, *supra*, § 711 (*a*). Hill *v.* Mackay, 1824; 2 S. 681; 2 Ill. 28. Observe Gordon *v.* Grant & Lumsden, June 29, 1814; F. C., to be denied, as not law; 2 Ill. 31.

713. The superior is entitled to feu-duties or retour-duties before, and (unless there be some justification) to full rents after citation; and to possession from decree. So he has poinding of the ground for the duties before, and for rents after citation. And he may assume possession on decree, and remove a tenant by force of his decree, but not till after the next Whitsunday (*a*).

(*a*) 2 Ersk. 6. § 26. Coltart *v*. Tait, 1782 ; M. 9313 ; 2 Ill. 27. See above, § 706. Mackintosh *v*. Tytler, 1870 ; 8 Macph. 772.

714. No effectual declarator of non-entry 'could' take place during the *annus deliberandi* (*a*).

(*a*) Lockhart *v*. Chiesly, 1708 ; M. 6878 ; 2 Ill. 31. Baillie *v*. Brown, 1710 ; M. 6879. See below, § 1685. The period is not limited to six months by 31 and 32 Vict. c. 101, § 61.

715. Relief, or **Composition,** is the acknowledgment or consideration given by one who enters as vassal to the superior for receiving him (*a*). Of old, every vassal paid this fine. It seems originally to have been the purchase-money for an entry, while yet the fee was personal ; and by consuetude was continued, so that, even when the grant became hereditary, the renewal was still held to be under the implied burden of such payment. The fine was lighter for an heir ; heavier for one demanding an entry under a conveyance, voluntary or judicial. The heir's fine is called Relief ; the singular successor's (purchaser's or creditor's), Composition for an entry. An heir is the proper successor to the fee, and entitled, by the express or implied nature of the grant, to an entry as subsidiary grantee or universal successor to all the rights of the deceased. A singular successor has no such right as in relation to the superior, and is entitled to compel an entry only by statute, and on payment of a fine.

(*a*) It is doubted whether the composition payable for the entry of singular successors is properly a casualty, 1 Bell's Com. 24 ; but it is commonly understood and spoken of as such, and has been held to be included in an obligation to relieve of "casualties." Edinr. Gas Light Co. *v*. Taylor, 1843 ; 5 D. 1325. See Stirling *v*. Ewart, 1842 ; 4 D. 684 ; aff. 1844, 3 Bell's App. 128 (*per* Hope, J.-C., and L. Brougham). Stuart *v*. Jackson, 1889 ; 17 R. 85. It remains a question whether it is *suâ naturâ* a *debitum fundi* recoverable by poinding the ground. It is so if stipulated and taxed in the feu-contract. Morrison's Trs. *v*. Webster, 1878 ; 5 R. 800. Stewart *v*. Gibson's Trs., 1880 ; 8 R. 270. It is included in the definition of "casualties" in the Conveyancing Act, 1874 (37 and 38 Vict. c. 94), § 3 (7). Straiton Estate Co. *v*. Stephens, 1880 ; 8 R. 299. See the Act, § 5.

716. (1.) *Amount of Relief*.—The relief payable by an heir is a year's feu or blench duty, in addition to the duty payable for the year. This doubling of the feu-duty, or of the blench-duty, is the implied fine between the superior and the heir ; and the superior never can, but by special agreement, demand a year's rent of the land for the fine of an heir, but only the duplicand (*a*). Singular successors, on the contrary, require a special stipulation to bar the superior's claim for the year's rent as his fine.

(*a*) It has been twice decided that, without a special stipulation, no relief is due in feu-holding for the entry of an heir. Kincaid *v*. L. Hatton, 1610 ; M. 13,579 ; 2 Ill. 31. E. Dundonald *v*. Barr, Nov. 24, 1736 ; Elch. *Sup. & Vass.* 2. 2 Stair, 4. § 27. But this has been much doubted by Erskine ; 2 Ersk. 5. § 48. And a disponee who is also the heir of the last entered vassal is bound to pay relief duty only, irrespective of the form of his title. Mackenzie *v*. Mackenzie, and M. Hastings *v*. Oswald, *infra*, § 718. Mackintosh *v*. Mackintosh, 1886 ; 13 R. 692. As to trustees under a *mortis causa* deed who hold for the heir of the testator, see § 724, below.

717. (2.) *Who are Heirs*.—The superior 'was' bound to enter as an heir the heir of investiture, or person entitled by the destination of the existing charter to succeed ; failing the heir of investiture, the heir at law. The heir entitled to an entry as such 'might' demand it, although he 'had' bought the estate, and 'held' a disposition as purchaser, not being compellable to use that disposition. An heir 'might' even demand to be entered on the footing of an heir under a 'deed of' settlement, provided it 'were' not hurtful to the superior. But one who 'was' not heir *alioquin successurus* 'was' not entitled to an entry as heir merely because he 'was' heir by a deed of settlement: he 'was' a singular successor. The Crown taking by forfeiture, or the Crown's donatary, 'was' entitled to enter without paying as a singular successor (*a*).

(*a*) Blair *v*. Montgomery, 1680 ; M. 15,045 ; 2 Ill. 32. D. Gordon *v*. Commissioners on Forfeited Estates, 1772 ; M. 15,050 ; Hailes, 472. See below, § 730, and cases under next section.

718. The superior 'was' not bound to enter the heir otherwise than by precept of *clare constat*, or by a charter not assignable ; nor 'could' he be required to grant such a charter as the heir 'could' assign, to the effect of entering a stranger as vassal (*a*). Nor 'was' he bound, under a destination to heirs and assignees, to enter a disponee from one infeft, without payment of a composition as singular successor ; a grant to heirs and assignees being intended only to include assignees before sasine (*b*). Nor 'was' the superior bound to give entry on an entail conceived in such terms as to exclude all chance of compositions for singular successors, confining the fee to substitutes in destination as heirs of investiture; but 'he was' entitled to make a reservation in his charter of all rights and casualties, as if the destination had never been made or the charter granted (*c*), 'to the effect apparently of obtaining a year's rent or other composition on the succession of an heir of the new tailzied investiture, who should not be also an heir of the old investiture (*d*). If, however, he had recognised the destination under an entail by entering the first heir, and had received, or waived, composition for a singular successor, he thus "enfranchised" all the heirs of the new investiture, and could not afterwards demand a composition from subsequent substitutes who were not heirs of line of the predecessor. This could only be secured, if at all, by express stipulation, reservation being insufficient (*e*). On the other hand, if a new investiture is introduced (by virtue of an implied entry under the statute) by a disponee's infeftment, the superior, whose rights in regard to casualties are not to be prejudiced by such entry, may claim composition, not merely from such disponee, but, if he has not paid it, from his heirs (*f*).'

(*a*) Musselburgh Mags. *v.* Brown, 1804; M. 15,038; 2 Ill. 37.

(*b*) 2 Stair, 4. § 32. Boyd *v.* Linlithgow Vassals, 1751; Elch. *Sup. & Vass.* 13; 2 Ill. 34. Inverness Mags. *v.* Duff, 1769; M. 15,059. Brisbane *v.* L. Semple, 1794; M. 15,061. Thomson, Petr., May 22, 1810; F. C. See § 727.

(*c*) Aberdeen Mags. *v.* Burnet, 1808; M. Apx. *Sup. & Vass.* 10; 2 Ill. 32. Lockhart *v.* Denham, 1760; M. 15,047; 2 Ross' L. C. 329, 388. Mackenzie *v.* M'Kenzie, 1777; M. 15,053; Hailes, 760; 5 B. Sup. 613; 2 Ross' L. C. 407. D. Argyle *v.* E. Dunmore, Nov. 19, 1795; M. 15,068; 2 Ross' L. C. 335. D. Hamilton *v.* Baillie, 1827; 6 S. 94. Wallace *v.* E. Eglinton, 1836; 14 S. 599. See above, § 711, and below, § 725. D. Hamilton *v.* E. Hopetoun, 1839; 1 D. 689.

(*d*) Mackenzie (*c*). M. Hastings, *infra* (*e*).

(*e*) Stirling *v.* Ewart, 1842; 4 D. 684; aff. 1844, 3 Bell's App. 128; 2 Ross' L. C. 340. Adv.-Gen. *v.* Swinton, 1854; 17 D. 21 (a very special case—Johnstone *v.* D. Buccleuch, 1892; 19 R. H. L. 39; A. C. 625). M. Hastings *v.* Oswald, 1859; 21 D. 871. Heriot's Hosp. *v.* Carnegys, 1884; 12 R. 30. L. Adv. *v.* Moray, 1894; 21 R. 553.

(*f*) Stuart *v.* Hamilton, 1889; 16 R. 1030. See above, § 709, and Ferrier *v.* Bayley, *ibi cit.* (*d*), and below, § 775A *fin.*

719. (3.) *Amount of Composition.* — A singular successor, whether purchaser or creditor (*a*), pays a year's rent of the land, without regard to the amount of the feu or blench duty, and the superior is not to be deprived of this payment without express consent (*b*). Creditors were first privileged to enter on tender of a year's maill, as the lands were set for the time (*c*), unless the superior were himself the debtor, in which case he is bound to enter the creditor gratis (*d*). Purchasers used at first to force an entry in the character of creditors; but on the relaxation of the rigid maxims of feudal law, they were empowered in their own right to demand an entry on resignation on the same terms with creditors (*e*). 'By the more recent law, any one infeft on a conveyance by a person publicly infeft, or whose title could be made public by confirmation, or infeft on a decree of special service, adjudication, or sale, might compel an entry by confirmation (*f*). Subject superiors are bound also to give precepts of *clare constat* to heirs entitled to ask them (*g*).'

(*a*) See, for the meaning of the words "singular successors," Campbell *v.* Deans, 1890; 17 R. 661.

(*b*) Boyd, Inverness Mags., Brisbane, and Thomson, cited above, § 718 (*b*). Edinburgh Mags. *v.* Horsburgh, 1834; 12 S. 593. See L. Blantyre *v.* Dunn, 1858; 20 D. 1188.

(*c*) 1469, c. 36. 1669, c. 18. 1681, c. 7.

(*d*) Seton's Crs. *v.* Seton, 1702; M. 15,046. Couper *v.* Stewart, 1742; M. 15,058.

(*e*) 20 Geo. II. c. 50, § 12, 13.

(*f*) 10 and 11 Vict. c. 48, § 6, re-enacted by 31 and 32 Vict. c. 101, § 97, 100; which are amended by 32 and 33 Vict. c. 116, § 5, and mostly repealed by 56 Vict. c. 14.

(*g*) 31 and 32 Vict. c. 101, § 101. 37 and 38 Vict. c. 94, § 4 (1).

720. The year's rent to be paid by a singular successor is the actual rent of the lands at the time when the new charter is to be granted,—the rise or fall in rent affecting the superior's claim (*a*); 'or the sum for which they might be let if they are then in the possession of the vassal himself (*b*)'; but under deduction of feu-duties and annual burdens imposed with the superior's consent, and a reasonable allowance for annual repairs on perishable subjects (*c*), of public burdens, and 'if the vassal be not titular' of one-fifth for teind (*d*).

(*a*) Heriot's Hospital *v.* Hepburn, 1715; M. 7998; 2 Ill. 35. Anderson *v.* Marshall, 1824; 3 S. 334. Hence in an implied entry under the Conveyancing Act, 1874 (*infra*, § 736A, 775A), the measure of the casualty is not the rent of the year, being prior to the Act, when the infeftment was registered, but that of the statute, that being the actual date of entry. Houstoun *v.* Buchanan, 1892; 19 R. 524.

(*b*) L. Blantyre *v.* Dunn, 1858; 20 D. 1188.

(*c*) Aitchison *v.* Hopkirk, 1775; M. 15,060; Hailes, 612; 5 B. Sup. 613.

(*d*) Reid *v.* Fullarton, 1819; 4 S. 227, note, and 1 Bell's Com. 25; 2 Ill. 36. Thomson *v.* Simson, 1825; 4 S. 224.

721. In estimating the rent these rules are observed:—The composition to be paid by the vassal for land on which he has built houses is the rent augmented by that of the houses (*a*). If the land be sub-feued for building, the superior is entitled only to the feu-duty paid to his vassal, not to the rent of the houses built on the ground (*b*). The effect of a sub-feu for a large price, with elusory feu-duties, is to give to the superior a right to the feu-duty with the interest of the grassum (*c*). It is not yet settled whether the superior is to have any casualty falling to his vassal from a sub-vassal in the year of the vassal's entry (*d*). 'The composition also includes the average annual value of minerals in course of being worked (*e*); and of shootings let or capable of being let (*f*).'

(*a*) Anderson, *supra*, § 720 (*a*). Aitchison, *supra*, § 720 (*c*). 1 Bell's Com. 24. As to composition for part of a line of railway, see Hill *v*. Cal. Ry. Co., 1877; 5 R. 386. In ascertaining what is rent, the rule for determining what are fixtures is the same as between landlord and tenant. Marshall *v*. Tannoch Chemical Co., 1886; 13 R. 1042. *Infra*, § 1473.

(*b*) Bell on Conveyance of Land, 316, note. Elchies' Annot. on Stair, 177. Hay *v*. L. Yester, 1634; 1 B. Sup. 201. L. Almond *v*. Hope, 1639; M. 15,056. Monkton *v*. L. Yester, 1639; M. 15,020. Cowan *v*. Elphinston, 1639; M. 15,055. Ross *v*. Heriot's Hospital, June 6, 1815; aff. 2 Bligh, 707; 6 Pat. 640; 2 Ross' L. C. 193.

(*c*) Campbell *v*. Hamilton, 1832; 10 S. 734.

(*d*) Campbell, *supra* (*c*).

(*e*) Allan's Trs. *v*. D. Hamilton, 1878; 5 R. 510. Sivwright *v*. Straiton Estate Co., 1879; 6 R. 1208. Comp. *infra*, § 1042, 1598, 1772. When a fixed rent and not a lordship was paid for them, it was held the true average value. Sturrock *v*. Carruthers' Trs., 1880; 7 R. 709.

(*f*) Stewart *v*. Bulloch, 1881; 8 R. 381. See Leith *v*. Leith, 1862; 24 D. 1059.

722. (4.) *Who are Singular Successors* (*a*).—A superior 'was' not bound to enter a *corporation*, which never dies, for he would so lose the heir's relief (*b*). This must be matter of special stipulation or of compromise (*c*). 'An entry of managers of a corporation and their successors in office for its behoof is an entry of the corporation (*d*). But as, under the Conveyancing Act of 1874, express entry with the superior is abolished, his rights to casualties being saved, corporations may now hold lands and have their title complete under the provisions of that Act. In feus granted before 1874 (see above, § 704B), they are bound—in the absence of stipulations to a different effect, as are also trustees—to pay composition at fixed periods appointed in the Act, differing according to the terms of the original investiture (*e*).'

(*a*) See below, § 783. Campbell *v*. Deans, 1890; 17 R. 661 (heritable creditor).

(*b*) 2 Stair, 3. § 41. 2 Ersk. 7. § 7; and 2. 12. 27. Hamilton *v*. Glasgow Univ., 1713; rev. Robertson's Ap. 172; 2 Ill. 36. Hill *v*. Edinr. Merchant Co., Jan. 17, 1815; F. C. See Campbell *v*. Orphan Hospital, 1843; 5 D. 1273. Gardner *v*. Trinity House of Leith, 1845; 7 D. 286. Learmonth *v*. Trinity Hospital, 1854; 16 D. 580.

(*c*) E. Mansfield *v*. Gray, May 22, 1829; 7 S. 642. E. Zetland *v*. Carron Co., 1841; 3 D. 1124.

(*d*) Campbell (*b*). E. Lauderdale *v*. Hogg, 1897; 24 R. 914.

(*e*) 37 and 38 Vict. c. 94, § 5; superseding 32 and 33 Vict. c. 116, § 113, which re-enacted 13 Vict. c. 13, § 2, as to casualties of lands conveyed for religious purposes. See Crawford *v*. Dempster, 1879; 6 R. 708. E. Home *v*. Lyell, 1887; 15 R. 193. See also § 724, below.

723. In conveyances to a *purchaser*, it may be observed that 'as the law stood before the Conveyancing Act of 1874, and as it remains in theory,' the disponee is not bound to enter, although he shall have been infeft base, or shall have assumed possession of the lands, if the fee be full by the disponer continuing infeft and alive; and that when the fee does fall into non-entry, and there are successive disponees, the superior cannot insist for more than one entry, and that from the last disponee (*a*). If the disponer be not yet infeft, the purchaser may insist (if not otherwise stipulated) on his completing his title so as to render the fee full, that the purchaser may not be compelled during the disponer's life to enter (*b*). But if the disponer should die, and so the fee fall into non-entry, the disponee cannot insist on the disponer's heir entering (*c*). If, however, so inclined, the heir may by entering delay the necessity of the purchaser's entering, and the superior is not entitled to object (*d*).

(*a*) Gordon *v*. Grant, June 29, 1814; F. C.; 2 Ill. 31; not law, though relied on in 3 Ersk. 396, note 158. See above, § 710, 712, note; and Mounsey *v*. Palmer, 1884; 12 R. 236.

(*b*) Gardiner *v*. Anderson, 1799; M. 15,037; 2 Ill. 29. See above, § 709.

(*c*) Dundas *v*. Drummond, 1769; M. 15,035; Hailes, 275; 2 Ill. 36. Confirmed, Hamilton *v*. E. Lauderdale, 1778; 5 B. Sup. 615.

(*d*) As to this section, see **Hyslop** *v*. **Shaw**, 1863; 1 Macph. 535, 550; and above, § 709.

724. *Trust-disponees* of the vassal (especially where other interests than those of the heir at law are introduced) must enter as singular successors. But having once entered, it would appear that the superior 'was' not 'before 1874' entitled, while a trustee 'survived,' to insist on a disponee from him entering, or to take advantage of any peculiarity in the state of the *personal* right, to declare non-entry; as, for example, to proceed on the ground of the purposes of the trust being exhausted (*a*). 'And now trustees for the heir are liable only for such casualties as would have been payable by him if he had taken by succession (*b*).'

(*a*) Grindlay *v.* Hill, Jan. 18, 1810; F. C.; 2 Ill. 37. Hill *v.* Mackay, 1824; 2 S. 574; 2 Ill. 28. D. Buccleuch *v.* Johnston, 1891; 18 R. 587; aff. 1892, 19 R. H. L. 39; A. C. 625. See as to their liability for composition under the Conveyancing Act, above, § 722. M. Huntly *v.* E. Fife, 1885; 14 R. 1091. As to the completion of the title of the heir of the last surviving trustee, see 37 and 38 Vict. c. 94, § 43; *infra*, § 2001.

(*b*) 50 and 51 Vict. c. 69, § 1; which is not retrospective. Stuart *v.* Jackson, 1889; 17 R. 85.

725. Although a substitute 'might' not be entitled to insist on an entry as heir under a deed of entail (*a*), or a vassal to require the superior to grant an unqualified charter of resignation on the procuratory in an entail, a *purchaser* demanding his entry on payment of a composition 'was' entitled to make what alteration he 'pleased' on the destination in the original charter; to change it, for example, from a male fee by a general destination to heirs female, or heirs whatsoever: but not to go beyond the line of succession by introducing an utter stranger (*b*).

(*a*) See above, § 718.

(*b*) See above, § 711. Aberdeen Mags. *v.* Burnet, 1808; M. *Sup. & Vass.* Apx. 10; 2 Ill. 32.

726. (5.) *Taxing of Composition.*—It is a frequent practice to fix at a certain sum (or, in technical phrase, to tax) the composition payable on entering with the superior. The presumption is against taxing, and the taxing clause is strictly interpreted (*a*). 'The benefit of a clause of taxation in the charter is not lost by its omission in charters by progress (*b*); and the superior may be bound by a clause in his own titles to enter the vassal on payment of a taxed composition (*c*).'

(*a*) E. Zetland *v.* Carron Co., 1841; 3 D. 1124 (duplicand of feu-duty over and above feu-duty). E. Mansfield *v.* Gray, 1829; 7 S. 642. Cases under § 727. Dundee Mags. *v.* Duncan, 1883; 11 R. 145 (2nd Div.), is an example of liberal interpretation of a taxing (?) clause.

(*b*) Stewart *v.* Russell, June 3, 1813; F. C.

(*c*) Learmonth *v.* Trinity Hosp., 1854; 16 D. 580.

727. Unless 'the taxing clause is' clearly made to comprehend singular successors, the superior is not thereby excluded from demanding his full composition from them. Where the charter with such a clause is conceived in favour of the grantee "and his heirs and assignees," that is held to mean only assignees of the personal right before investiture, but not to give the benefit of the taxed composition to purchasers from the grantee infeft (*a*), 'unless the terms of the deed distinctly express an intention to do so (*b*).' But where the superior is bound to enter "singular successors" on their tendering a double of the feu-duty, it is effectual (*c*).

(*a*) Inverness Mags., Boyd, and Thomson, *supra*, § 718 (*b*). Salmon *v.* L. Boyd, 1751; M. 4181; 2 Ill. 37. L. Carnegy *v.* Cranburn, 1663; M. 10,375. M'Lachlan *v.* Tait, 1823; 2 S. 303. 2 Stair, 3. § 5; 2 *ib.* 4. § 32. 2 Ersk. 7. § 5.

(*b*) Hamilton *v.* Dunn, 1853; 15 D. 925. Harvie *v.* Stewart, 1870; 9 Macph. 129. Inverkeithing Mags. *v.* Ross, 1874; 2 R. 48. D. Montrose *v.* Provan's Tr., 1887; 14 R. 378.

(*c*) Innes *v.* Reid's Trs., 1822; 1 S. 479; 2 Ill. 37.

728. (6.) *Retention of Charter for Composition.*—The superior 'might' secure himself in payment of his composition by retaining the charter till the composition 'was' paid (*a*): but if he 'delivered' it, the entry 'might' be completed by sasine, and then the claim for the composition 'became' merely personal,—there is no poinding of the ground for it as for a *debitum fundi*.

(*a*) See 1 Bell's Com. 26; 2 Ross' L. C. 165; and above, § 715, note.

729. A composition once incurred has been held not to be discharged by the superior obtaining a decree of declarator *ob non solutum canonem* (*a*).

(*a*) Edinburgh Mags. *v.* Horsburgh, 1835; 12 S. 593; 13 S. 571. See Mitchel's Trs. *v.* Pearson, 1834; 12 S. 322.

730. Escheat.—Escheat is the forfeiture to the superior of the annual profits of the land while the vassal remains in a state of rebellion against his superior or the Crown. Formerly, the death of a vassal, where no heir could be traced, or in technical words, the failure of the vassal's blood, reinstated the superior in the fee. But the Sovereign is now *ultimus hæres*, taking (by the donatary) the fee, with all its burdens and all real debts created by the vassal, to the extent of the fee (*a*). The superior is bound to enter the donatary on declarator, without exacting the composition of a singular successor (*b*). Where the Crown is superior, there is consolidation *ipso jure*.

Rebellion against the superior by disclamation, now obsolete, or by purpresture, now superseded, or by alienation, forfeited the fee. Rebellion, civil or criminal, formerly excluded the vassal; now, only the rebellion consequent on crime in penal law has that effect (*c*).

The escheat falls on the heir's rebellion, although not yet entered, as if he were entered; on the rebellion of liferenters, tercers, husbands by courtesy, holders of real burdens; on the rebellion of a tenant, the liferent going to the landlord.

Relaxation restores the vassal *de futuro*, but does not affect the superior's right for the past (*d*).

(*a*) 2 Ersk. 5. § 53. Balnagoun *v.* Dingwall, 1662; M. 3409; 2 Ill. 37.
(*b*) Boyd *v.* Linlithgow Vassals, 1751; Elch. *Sup. & Vass.* 13; 2 Ill. 34. See above, § 717.
(*c*) 20 Geo. II. c. 50, § 11. (*d*) 2 Ersk. 5. § 65.

731. Escheat was of two kinds: one not properly feudal, called Single Escheat; the other, 'called Liferent Escheat,' directly affecting the feudal estate.

732. (1.) By *Single Escheat* the rebel's moveables fell to the Crown as *bona vacantia*. The Crown or the donatary had a year in which to levy them, which of course burdened the superior's right of liferent escheat; and the waste thus occasioned was compounded for by giving a year's rent.

733. (2.) *Liferent Escheat* gives to the superior, while his vassal lives and continues in rebellion, right to possession of the fee. But it is merely the usufruct which falls; the fee is in the rebel, with every power of disposal which does not interfere with the usufruct. It falls by sentence of death and escape—the sentence terminating the vassal's capacity to hold the fee, the existence of the vassal excluding the heir; or by denunciation of the vassal for a criminal cause, unrelaxed for a year (*a*).

(*a*) M'Rae *v.* Hyndman, 1836; 15 S. 54; 2 Ill. 38; aff. 1839, M'L. & R. 645.

734. The liferent escheat is burdened with the vassal's debts made real on the lands (*a*). But not with personal debts; nor with debts in virtue of voluntary deeds after denunciation; nor with subsequent debts or deeds; nor with obligations to convey, if not followed by infeftment within year and day of denunciation (*b*).

(*a*) Css. Sutherland *v.* Crs. of Skelbo, 1771; M. *Sup. & Vass.* 1; 2 Ill. 38.
(*b*) 2 Ersk. Pr. 5. § 33.

735. Tinsel of Superiority.—The superior 'was' bound when required to enter his vassal (*a*). If the superior's titles 'were' not complete, he 'was' bound to complete them; and to this effect the vassal 'might' charge him to enter within forty days, under certification that he 'would' "tyne his superiority." The vassal 'might' then bring a process of declarator of tinsel of superiority during the 'vassal's' life (*b*), and, on obtaining decree of declarator, take his entry with the next superior, whether Crown or subject (*c*). The remedy under this Act, however, was formerly held competent only to adjudgers and heirs, not to purchasers; and against the superior's heirs unentered, not singular successors holding the personal right. But the remedy 'was' not thus confined in modern practice (*d*).

(*a*) See § 710, 736A. 1469, c. 36. 1669, c. 18. 2 Stair, 4. § 6. 20 Geo. II. c. 50, § 12, 13. 3 Ersk. 8. § 79. The law in this and the following sections appears to be superseded by the provisions of the Act 37 and 38 Vict. c. 94, by which the formal renewal of investiture ceases to be necessary or competent.
(*b*) The text had "superior's life" here; and the correction suggested in the seventh edition from 3 Ersk. 8. § 80, and Dickson *v.* Elphinston (*c*), has been confirmed by the Court in Rossmore's Trs. *v.* Brownlie, 1877; 5 R. 201.
(*c*) 1474, c. 57. Dickson *v.* Elphinston, 1802; M. 15,024; 2 Ill. 30. Rossmore's Trs., *cit.*
(*d*) Spalding *v.* Napier, 1709; M. 15,033; 2 Ill. 38. Christie *v.* The Crown, 1776; 5 B. Sup. 608.

736. The importance to the vassal of obtaining a complete title to enable him to remove tenants, to grant heritable securities, to make effectual provisions for his children, has led to a strict construction of the Act (*a*), in which the words "fraud and guile" are held to indicate any delay to the prejudice of the vassal. The Court accordingly 'admitted' of no delay, but instantly 'gave' decree of declarator (*b*).

The superior, in losing his tenant for life, 'did' not forfeit his feu-duty, but only the casualties of superiority. The effect 'was' not to punish the immediate superior, but only, by giving the vassal an entry with his mediate superior, to save him from the inconvenience of the want of a feudal title, and to meet any proof of non-entry on the part of his immediate superior (*c*).

(*a*) 1474, c. 57.
(*b*) Dickson, *supra*, § 735 (*c*).
(*c*) Hay *v.* Auchenames, 1632; 2 Ill. 38. 3 Stair, 5. § 47. Wallace *v.* Crawford's Exrs., 1838; 1 D. 162.

736A. 'Additional facilities were given by the Titles to Land Consolidation (Scotland) Act of 1868 (*a*), for enabling the vassal to obtain an entry; but these provisions seem to be repealed, or at least superseded, by the Act of 1874, abolishing formal entry with the superior; and giving the vassal by infeftment an implied entry, "whether the superior's own title or that of any over-superior has been completed or not" (*b*).'

(*a*) 31 and 32 Vict. c. 101, § 104–110, amending the Lands Transference Act of 1847 (10 and 11 Vict. c. 48, § 8–14), and the Titles to Land (Scotland) Act, 1858 (21 and 22 Vict. c. 76, § 23–26, etc.).
(*b*) 37 and 38 Vict. c. 97, § 4. See below, § 775A.

CHAPTER III

OF THE VASSAL

737. Vassal's Estate.—The vassal acquires, by the charter of the superior, the right of property and exclusive use of the lands and teinds, and also of the pendicles, parts, and pertinents of the land—whether above the surface, as houses, woods, and enclosures, or below it, as coal, limestone, and minerals—with all the legal privileges belonging to the lands (*a*). But this right is under exception of all *regalia* (*b*), unless expressly granted to him; and also of teinds, unless plainly meant to be included or (if already feudalised) expressly conveyed. When the identity of the land is unquestionable, the grant includes all that forms a proper part of the land from the sky to the centre (*c*). It is otherwise in a lease, which is superficial only.

(*a*) 2 Stair, 3. § 75. 2 Ersk. Pr. 6. 2 Ersk. 6.

(*b*) See above, § 669 et seq.

(*c*) Bruce *v.* Erskine, 1716; M. 9642; 2 Ill. 39. Dick *v.* E. Abercorn, 1769; M. 12,813 (grant of lake includes the soil). Menzies *v.* E. Breadalbane, June 10, 1818; F. C.; aff. 1822, 1 S. App. 225 (reservation of mines and minerals does not extend to peculiarly fine freestone—but see Jamieson *v.* N. B. Ry. Co., 1868; 6 S. L. R. 188. Nisbet Hamilton *v.* N. B. Ry. Co., 1885; 13 R. 454). Cf. D. Hamilton *v.* Bentley, 1841; 3 D. 1121. Forth and Clyde Nav. Co. *v.* Wilsons & Co., 1848; 11 D. 122 (reservation of quarries, stone, and coal does not extend to ironstone). Livingstone *v.* Clark, 1821; 1 S. 48. Logan *v.* Wright, 1831; 5 W. & S. 242. Baird *v.* Robertson, 1836; 14 S. 396 (solum of lake). See below, § 740, 940.

738. Charter (*a*).—In the charter may be distinguished—1. The grant of the lands; and 2. The grant of the pertinents.

(1.) *Grant of the Lands.*—Lands are conveyed by the general name where an estate has been erected into a barony (*b*); or by the names, or situation, or boundaries (*c*) of the particular lands in the common case.

If the lands be described by *boundaries*, the effect is different as against the grantee and against third parties. And if the boundary be the sea, or the sea-shore, the right is extended or limited as the sea recedes or advances (*d*). If the boundary be a stream or river, the property may be subject to alteration; extended by *alluvio* or imperceptible addition to the bank, or by gradual and imperceptible variation of the channel; or the stream may cease to be the boundary in consequence of some violent and manifest change or *avulsio* (*e*). If the boundary (as in urban or suburban property) be by walls, the expression may exclude, or include, or divide the wall (*f*). 'If it be by a roadway, the *solum* of the roadway is *primâ facie* excluded from the grant (*g*); whereas if it be by a river, *primâ facie* half the *alveus* is included in the grant (*h*).' The grantee cannot acquire by prescription what is beyond his express boundaries (*i*), 'though he may so acquire a servitude (*k*), and apparently an incorporeal right such as salmon-fishings (*l*).'

If described by *measurement*, it may be either taxative or demonstrative. When the subject is by name or otherwise, 'as by physical boundaries, or even by possession,' clearly pointed out, 'unless the words are distinctly taxative, or the extent is an inherent quality of the grant or conveyance,' a superadded measurement is 'not' generally to be held as taxative. When the measurement is used descriptively only, it is considered as demonstrative (*m*). 'Words importing extent or measurement may be distinctly taxative, as by adding the word "only" (*n*), by being combined with a plan (*o*), or when the extent is made an inherent quality of the bargain, as when the price or feu-duty is rateably according to the measurement (*p*).'

(*a*) See the charter more fully explained below, § 757 et seq.
(*b*) E. Argyle *v.* Campbell, 1668; M. 9631; 2 Ill. 38.
(*c*) As to parole evidence to explain the meaning of a description of boundaries, see Dalhousie's Tutors *v.* Minr. of Lochlee, 1890; 17 R. 1060; aff. 1891, 18 R. H. L. 72.
(*d*) See above, § 643. As to the mode of ascertaining the boundary line of shore ground *ex adverso* of conterminous properties on rivers or bays of the sea, see **Campbell** *v.* **Brown**, Nov. 18, 1813; F. C. M'Taggart *v.* Macdouall, 1867; 5 Macph. 534. Laird *v.* Reid, 1871; 9 Macph. 669, 1009. Keith *v.* Smyth, 1884; 12 R. 66 (salmon-fishings). Gray *v.* Fleming & Richardson, 1885; 12 R. 530. Tain Mags. *v.* Murray, 1887; 15 R. 83. Crook *v.* Seaford Corpn., L. R. 6 Ch. 551.
(*e*) See below, § 935 et seq.
(*f*) See below, § 1078.
(*g*) Louttit's Trs. *v.* Highland Ry. Co., 1892; 19 R. 791. See below, § 992 (*d*).
(*h*) **Morris** *v.* **Bicket**, 1864; 2 Macph. 1082; aff. 1866, 4 Macph. H. L. 44. Gibson, below (*m*). Micklethwait *v.* Newlay Bridge Co., 1886; L. R. 33 Ch. D. 133. See M'Intyre's Trs. *v.* Cupar Mags., 1867; 5 Macph. 780.
(*i*) Young *v.* Carmichael, 1671; M. 9636; 2 Ill. 40. Thomson *v.* Grieve, 1688; 2 B. Sup. 118. Wilson *v.* Dundas, 1695; 4 B. Sup. 236. Suttie *v.* Gordons, 1837; 15 S. 1037. *Infra*, § 739, 993, 2002 sqq. Kerr *v.* Dickson, 1840; 3 D. 154; aff. 1 Bell's App. 499. Hepburn *v.* D. Gordon, 1823; 2 S. 525 (within a parish). **Gordon** *v.* **Grant**, 1850; 13 D. 1 (do.). Berry *v.* Holden, 1840; 3 D. 205. St. Monance Mags. *v.* Mackie, 1845; 7 D. 582. Fleming *v.* Baird, 1841; 3 D. 1015. Reid *v.* M'Coll, 1879; 7 R. 84. N. B. Ry. *v.* Hutton, 1896; 23 R. 522.
(*k*) **Beaumont** *v.* **L. Glenlyon**, 1843; 5 D. 1337.
(*l*) E. Zetland *v.* Tennent, 1873; 11 Macph. 469. See E. Dalhousie *v.* M'Inroy, 1865; 3 Macph. 1168.
(*m*) Douglas *v.* Lyne, 1630; M. 2262. Rochead *v.* Borthwick (lease), 1679; M. 2264; 3 Ill. 151. Ure *v.* Anderson, 1834; 12 S. 494. Yeaman *v.* Gilruth, 1792; Hume, 783 (lease). Fleming, *supra* (*i*). Gibson *v.* Bonnington Sugar Co., 1869; 7 Macph. 394 (river boundary and measurements). Menmuir *v.* Airth, 1863; 1 Macph. 929 (lease). Stewart *v.* Greenock Harb. Trs., 1866; 4 Macph. 282 (effect of measurement and boundaries together in making a bounding title). Blyth's Trs. *v.* Shaw Stewart, 1883; 11 R. 99 (boundary by low-water mark, and measurements). The authorities cited by Prof. Bell, as well as the shape and turn of the sentences, suggest that the "not" now inserted was omitted by accident, and not deliberately. The general rule, as it is now stated, is recognised in all the cases cited. A reference to previous possession in describing lands conveyed by a general name may be taxative, Murray *v.* Oliphant, 1634; M. 2262; and it will in general control measurements, Deas *v.* Kyle, 1664; M. 10,604. Oliver *v.* Suttie, 1840; 2 D. 514. Hardie *v.* Kinloch, 1842; 5 D. 64. Gregson *v.* Alsop, 1897; 24 R. 1080 (cases on leases). But, on the other hand, such a reference must yield to subsequent possession clearly indicative of a different construction of the title-deed, Gardner *v.* Scott, 1839; 2 D. 185; rev. 1843, 2 Bell's App. 129; or may be shown by the context to be merely demonstrative, Critchley *v.* Campbell, 1884; 11 R. 475.
(*n*) Duff, Feud. Convg. 47. M. Bell's Convg. 592.
(*o*) N. B. Ry. *v.* Moon's Trs., 1879; 6 R. 640. N. B. Ry. *v.* Hawick Mags., 1862; 1 Macph. 200. See Currie *v.* Campbell's Trs., 1888; 16 R. 237. Plans affect any question between parties only if incorporated in the titles, and only for the purpose for which they are therein referred to. Keith *v.* Smyth, 1884; 12 R. 66. See Dickson on Evid. § 1044, 1047. *Infra*, § 2233 (*a*).
(*p*) Hepburn *v.* Campbell, 1781; M. 14,168. See also Rochead, *cit.* (*m*). Gray *v.* Hamilton, 1801; M. Apx. *Sale*, 2. Brown *v.* Kyd, 1813; Hume, 700.

738A. '*Description by Reference.*—If lands have been particularly described in a prior deed or instrument, recorded in the appropriate Register of Sasines, it is sufficient in any subsequent conveyance to specify the county, or in burgage lands the burgh and county, and to refer in a statutory form to the particular description in the prior recorded deed (*a*). And where several lands are conveyed by the same deed to the same person by particular description, a clause may be inserted, declaring that in future conveyances, the lands, or certain portions of them, shall be designed by a general name or by general names respectively; and on the deed, or an instrument upon it, being recorded in the Register of Sasines, such general name or names may be used in all subsequent conveyances, deeds, and discharges, provided that reference in a statutory form be made in the conveyances, deeds, and discharges to the prior deed so recorded (*b*).'

(*a*) 37 and 38 Vict. c. 94, § 61, repealing 31 and 32 Vict. c. 101, § 11, which consolidated 21 and 22 Vict. c. 76, § 15, and 23 and 24 Vict. c. 143, §. 34. Murray's Trs. *v.* Wood, 1887; 14 R. 856. See also Cattanach's Tr. *v.* Jamieson, 1884; 11 R. 972.
(*b*) 31 and 32 Vict c. 101, § 13.

739. (2.) *Parts and Pertinents* are such accessory parts, and fixtures, and appendages to land, or houses, or such separate possessions, or privileges, as accompany the occupation and use of the land, or have for forty years been so enjoyed along with it. They are, 'if consistent with the title (*a*),' carried without being named or described in the charter (*b*). Even tenements lying separate and discontiguous from the main subject, 'or expressly included in the titles of another,' may be thus carried, unless excluded by a bounding charter which does not specify them (*c*). 'Possession for the prescriptive period is the proper mode of explaining what are the parts and pertinents of lands (*d*); and in the case of promiscuous possession may result in establishing common property, or commonty, or servitude (*e*). The possession must be as part and pertinent in virtue of the titles (*f*). Every proprietor is entitled to claim such accessories and incidents as are necessary to the reasonable enjoyment of his property, *e.g.* necessary ways and passages (*g*). *Quando aliquid conceditur*,

conceditur etiam id sine quo res ipsa esse non potest. So a right to minerals implies the power to dig mines (*h*); a right to fishings, access over the adjoining lands when they belong to another (*i*); and the right to a canal, the use of the bank as a towing-path (*k*).'

(*a*) See § 738, 2004 *fin.* Officers of State *v.* E. Haddington, 1831; 5 W. & S. 570. So a right of hunting over another man's ground, though of course it may be the subject of contract, cannot be acquired as a part and pertinent. **E. Aboyne** *v.* **Farquharson**, Nov. 16, 1814; F. C. Comp. Patrick *v.* Napier, 1867; 5 Macph. 683 (angling). As to title-deeds as accessories of lands, see below, § 890A.

(*b*) 2 Stair, 3. § 73. 2 Ersk. 6. § 4. Bruce *v.* Erskine, 1709; M. 9638; 2 Ill. 40. Bruce and Menzies, *supra*, § 737 (*c*). Nisbet *v.* King, 1624; M. 9628. L. Burley *v.* Syme, 1662; M. 9630. See below, § 750. **Gordon** *v.* **Grant**, 1850; 13 D. 1, 7. **L. Adv.** *v.* **Hunt**, 1865; 3 Macph. 426; rev. 1867; 5 Macph. H. L. 1; L. R. 1 Sc. App. 85.

(*c*) Forsyth *v.* Durie, 1632; M. 9628; 2 Ill. 40. Young *v.* Wright, 1649; 1 B. Sup. 390. Young, Thomson, and Wilson, *supra*, § 738 (*i*). Css. Moray *v.* Wemyss, 1675; M. 9636. Crawford *v.* Crawford, 1714; M. 9641. Perth Mags. *v.* E. Wemyss, 1829; 8 S. 82. E. Fife's Trs. *v.* Cumming, 1830; 8 S. 326. **Baird** *v.* **Fortune**, 1859; 21 D. 848; rev. 1861, 4 Macq. 127. L. Adv. *v.* Hunt, *cit.* N. B. Ry. *v.* Hutton, 1896; 23 R. 522. See below, § 746.

(*d*) Cases in notes (*b*) and (*c*); below, § 2002 sqq.

(*e*) **Carnegie** *v.* **M'Tier**, 1844; 6 D. 1381, and authorities there cited.

(*f*) *Infra*, 2004.

(*g*) 2 Stair, 7. § 10. 2 Ersk. 6. § 4, 9. See below, § 992, 1010.

(*h*) **Rowbottom** *v.* **Wilson**, 8 H. L. Ca. 348, 360; 30 L. J. Q. B. 49. Blair *v.* Ramsay, 1875; 3 R. 25; aff. *ib.* H. L. 41. Turner *v.* Ballendene, 1832; 10 S. 415; aff. 1834, 7 W. & S. 163. Cf. Cal. Ry. Co. *v.* Sprot, 1854; 16 D. 559, 955; rev. 1856, 2 Macq. 449.

(*i*) Matthew *v.* Blair, 1612; M. 14,623. Miller *v.* Blair, 1825; 4 S. 217. L. Adv. *v.* Sharp, 1878; 6 R. 108. *Infra*, § 1120.

(*k*) Swan *v.* Muirkirk Iron Co., 1850; 12 D. 622. See Yuille *v.* Rushbury, 1888; 15 R. 828 (patent of a Theatre Royal).

740. Among pertinents, mines of minerals and coal, and quarries of limestone, marble, freestone, etc., are included (*a*). These occasionally are separate tenements. 'They may, for instance, be reserved by a superior or disponer, who may retain either a mere right to work, of the nature of a servitude or real burden or condition, or an absolute property in the strata (*b*).' Under pertinents, *regalia* cannot be included (*c*).

(*a*) 2 Ersk. 6. § 5. Bruce *v.* Erskine, 1716; M. 9642; 2 Ill. 39. L. Burley, *supra*, § 739 (*b*). Oughterlony *v.* E. Selkirk, 1755; M. 164; 5 B. Sup. 837. See Anstruther *v.* Anstruther, 1792; 3 Pat. 483. Anderson *v.* Cadells, 1803; 4 Pat. 532. Addie *v.* Gillies, 1848; 10 D. 826. Harvie *v.* Stewart, 1870; 9 Macph. 129. E. Breadalbane *v.* Jamieson, 1875; 2 R. 826. G. & S. W. Ry. *v.* Bain, 1893; 21 R. 134.

(*b*) 2 Ersk. 6. § 5. **Graham** *v.* **D. Hamilton**, 1869; 7 Macph. 976; rev. 1871, 9 Macph. H. L. 98. Blair *v.* Ramsay, 1875; 3 R. 25; aff. *ib.* H. L. 41. Bain *v.* D. Hamilton, 1865; 3 Macph. 821; 1867, 6 Macph. 1. Harvie *v.* Stewart, 1870; 9 Macph. 129. Dunlop *v.* D. Hamilton, 1884; 11 R. 963; aff. 1885, 10 App. Ca. 813; 12 R. H. L. 65 (reservation by one infeft in lands of liberty to work the minerals is at least *primâ facie* a reservation of the estate in the minerals, and not of a mere privilege). Davidson *v.* D. Hamilton, 1822; 1 S. 411. Ker *v.* Simson, 1790; M. 2692; 1792, 3 Pat. 238. Dunlop *v.* Corbet, June 20, 1809; F. C. Dixons *v.* Buchanan, 1825; 4 S. 355; 1829, 7 S. 324. Fleeming *v.* Howden, 1868; 6 Macph. 782, 790. Orr *v.* Moir's Trs. (Mitchell), 1892; 19 R. 700; revd. 1893, 20 R. H. L. 27; A. C. 238. As to what are minerals, see Bell *v.* Wilson, 35 L. J. Ch. 337; L. R. 1 Ch. 303. Hext *v.* Gill, 41 L. J. Ch. 293, 761; L. R. 7 Ch. 699. Midland Ry. Co. *v.* Haunchwood Brick, etc., Co., 20 Ch. D. 552; 51 L. J. Ch. 778; and cases cited above, § 737 (*c*). **Gillespie** *v.* **Russel**, 1854; 17 D. 1 (cf. 18 D. 677; 19 D. 897). **Glasgow Mags.** *v.* **Farie**, 1887; 14 R. 346; rev. 1888, 13 App. Ca. 657; 15 R. H. L. 94 (clay in surface and subsoil not a mineral in sense of Railways and Waterworks Clauses Acts—cf. Midland Ry. Co. *v.* Robinson, 1889; 15 App. Ca. 19). Rights of hunting and fishing may be reserved if apt terms be used. Hemming *v.* D. Athole, 1883; 11 R. 93. D. Richmond *v.* Duff, 1867; 5 Macph. 310.

(*c*) See § 669 *supra*, and 748 and 750 *infra*.

741. Woods and trees are pertinents, or rather parts, of the lands on which they grow (*a*).

(*a*) 2 Ersk. 6. § 14. See Paul *v.* Cuthbertson, 1840; 2 D. 1286; and below, § 1226, 1303, 1473, 1754, etc.

742. Orchards, though lying discontiguous from the principal subject, are held to be pertinents (*a*).

(*a*) Bruce *v.* Dalrymple, 1709; M. 9638; 2 Ill. 40.

743. Houses and buildings (including mills (*a*), though sometimes a separate tenement), enclosures, and fixtures (*b*), are pertinents. Fortalices in the old law were not so held (*c*).

(*a*) 2 Stair, 3. § 71. 2 Ersk. 6. § 4, 5. Rose *v.* Ramsay, 1777; M. 9645, and Apx. No. 1, *Part and Pert.*; Hailes, 756; 2 Ill. 40. Downie *v.* Alexander, 1777; M. Apx. *Implied Assig.* 1.

(*b*) Arkwright *v.* Billing, Dec. 3, 1819; F. C. Niven *v.* Pitcairn, 1823; 2 S. 239. Graham *v.* Lamont, 1875; 2 R. 438 (fences). See below, § 1473.

(*c*) 2 Stair, 3. § 65-6. Home *v.* Home, 1612; M. 9627. See below, § 752.

744. Seats in the parish church are held to be pertinents of the lands whose owners have possessed them as such (*a*); 'and when allocated in respect of a property, cannot be disjoined from it (*b*).'

(*a*) Lithgow *v.* Wilkinson, 1697; M. 9637; 2 Ill. 42. Duff *v.* Brodie, 1769; M. 9644; Hailes, 297. Peden *v.* Paisley Mags., 1770; M. 9644. 2 Ersk. 6. § 11. D. Roxburghe *v.* Millar, 1876; 3 R. 728, 745 (*per* L. Deas); rev. 1877, 4 R. H. L. 76.

(*b*) Stephen *v.* Anderson, 1887; 15 R. 72.

745. Servitudes which are concomitant privileges, intended for giving the full exercise and enjoyment of the right of property, are pertinents (*a*).

(*a*) Borthwick *v.* Borthwick, 1638; M. 9632; 2 Ill. 127. See below, § 979 et seq.

746. Separate tenements and patches of land, houses, etc., may become pertinents of an estate in land by possession as such during the term of prescription (*a*).

(*a*) 2 Ersk. 6. § 3. Young *v.* Carmichael, 1671; M. 9636; 2 Ill. 40. Css. Moray *v.* Wemyss, 1675; M. 9636 Dalrymple *v.* E. Stair, 1841; 3 D. 837. King *v.* E. Stair, 1844; 6 D. 821; aff. 1846, 5 Bell's App. 82, 100.

747. The right of trout-fishing 'and of angling generally' in a river passing through the lands goes as a pertinent; but not the right of salmon-fishing (*a*). The rules seem to be these:—Trout-fishing in a private river 'or loch' is a pertinent of the lands, but may be reserved, or even transferred to a stranger (*b*). In a public river, access to the banks or to the water by a boat gives to any one a right to fish; 'but this is negatived as regards the non-tidal part of a river by the case of Grant *v.* Henry (*c*); and it is not so in the case of a private stream or loch (*d*).' Long possession and use of fishing will 'not (*e*)' confer on the public a right to fish. Salmon-fishing granted by the Crown to a stranger gives him, by access (*f*), a right also to fish trout; but not in close-time, when he has no privilege of access. In fishing trout the proprietor of a private river is to do nothing hurtful to the salmon-fishing (*g*). A right in another to salmon and other fishing may be effectual to exclude the proprietor of the ground from trouting, provided it be exercised by excluding, not by mere abstinence on the proprietor's part. The proprietors of the shores of a loch have *presumptione* common right of sailing and fishing 'over the whole loch, and may communicate the right by conveyance of part of their estate,' unless excluded by express grant, or exclusive possession on a general title (*h*). 'A right claimed by a seaboard proprietor as a pertinent, to share in a capture of whales stranded below his floodmark, has been negatived (*i*).'

(*a*) See above, § 671; below, § 1100 et seq. M'Donald *v.* Farquharson, 1836; 15 S. 259.

(*b*) **Scott** *v.* **Napier**, 1869; 7 Macph. H. L. 35, and cases in § 651, *supra*; and notes (*d*) and (*g*) *infra*. It may be questioned whether trout-fishing can be constituted into a separate feudal estate unconnected with land. It is decided that it cannot be acquired as a servitude. Patrick *v.* Napier, 1867; 5 Macph. 683.

(*c*) Grant *v.* Henry, 1894; 21 R. 358.

(*d*) Fergusson *v.* Shirreff, 1844; 6 D. 1363. Montgomery *v.* Watsons, 1861; 23 D. 635.

(*e*) Fergusson, Montgomery, and Grant, *supra*.

(*f*) Rather by implication, on the principle that the greater includes the less; at least it can only be on this principle in the case of a private river. Fergusson, *supra* (*d*). Hence the statement which follows, that the right ceases in close-time, may be doubted.

(*g*) Carmichael *v.* Colquhoun, 1787; M. 9645; Hailes, 1033; 2 Ill. 42 Mackenzie *v.* Rose, 1830; 8 S. 816; aff. 6 W. & S. 31. See 8 and 9 Vict. c. 26, and 23 and 24 Vict. c. 45, against trout-poaching. Stewart on Rights of Fishing, chap. xv. See below, § 1121. As to an agricultural tenant, see D. Richmond *v.* Dempster, 4 Irv. 10. Maxwell *v.* Copland, 1868; 7 Macph. 142; aff. 1871, 9 Macph. H. L. 1. As to eel-cruives, see Braid *v.* Douglas, 1800; M. Apx. *Property*, 2.

(*h*) See above, § 651; below, § 1111.

(*i*) Bruce *v.* Smith, 1890; 17 R. 1000.

748. *Regalia* are excepted from the ordinary rule of pertinents; and even when granted by the Crown to a vassal, they are not held to be transferred from that vassal by a conveyance of the land, unless expresssly mentioned (*a*).

(*a*) 2 Stair, 3. § 60. 2 Ersk. 6. § 13. L. Adv. *v.* Sinclair, 1865; 3 Macph. 981; aff. 5 Macph. H. L. 97; L. R. 1 Sc. App. 174. L. Adv. *v.* M'Culloch, 1874; 2 R. 27. E. Breadalbane *v.* Jamieson, 1875; 2 R. 826 (gold and silver mines). Cases in § 750 (*c*).

749. Regality and Barony.—There are two species of royal grants of land which deserve to be particularly distinguished, though in modern times one of them has been abolished, and the other has much fallen from its ancient splendour. These are grants of Regality and grants of Barony.

(1.) *Regality* was an erection and feudal grant of land *in liberam regalitatem*, with a high and almost royal jurisdiction. Scotland was in former times divided into the Royalty, where the King's jurisdiction was exercised by his ordinary judges; and Regality, where, under such grants as these, jurisdiction civil and criminal was exercised by the Lord of Regality. Regalities were abolished by statute on occasion of the Rebellion of 1745 (*a*).

(*a*) 20 Geo. II. c. 43. 2 Stair, 3. § 45. 2 Ersk. 3. § 46.

750. (2.) *Barony* was the erection of land *in liberam baroniam*, as one feudal tenement, accompanied also by extensive jurisdiction within appointed limits. The barony, though consisting of many separate lands and portions, is designated by a general name. And it is accompanied by pertinents and privileges not attendant on the property of ordinary estates. Barony is truly the only feudal dignity conferred on territorial proprietors; lordship, earldom, etc., being only nobler titles for a barony, as connected with personal dignities (*a*).

As the name of the barony is *nomen universitatis*, a charter or disposition of the barony not only conveys all the lands and separate portions included in the barony, 'or prescriptively possessed,' but all the pertinents belonging to it (*b*). And among those pertinents held to be conveyed, if not excepted, are such *regalia* as have been granted to or conferred on the baron (*c*). 'But a barony title, though a good title for prescription even of *regalia*, is not (it seems) enough to carry them of itself unless they are expressly granted (*d*).'

(*a*) 2 Stair, 3. § 45. 2 Ersk. 3. § 46, and 2. 6. § 18.
(*b*) Compare § 874, below.
(*c*) 2 Stair, 3. § 60. 2 Ersk. 6. § 18. E. Argyle *v.* Campbell, 1668; M. 9631. Wemyss' Trs. *v.* L. Adv., 1896; 24 R. 216.
(*d*) L. Adv. *v.* Cathcart, 1871; 9 Macph. 744 (*per* L. P. Inglis). D. Montrose *v.* M'Intyre, 1848; 10 D. 896. Cases in § 748, 754.

751. Jurisdiction, originally very extensive, but abolished, or at least restricted to the necessary enforcement of duties, rents, etc., within the barony, was a privilege conferred by the erection of a barony (*a*).

(*a*) 1 Ersk. 4. § 25–29. 20 Geo. II. c. 43; c. 50, § 18. See 5 B. Sup. 750–763.

752. Fortalices were the King's castles and forts for public defence, which were in the custody of Constables, but are now ranked only as country-seats, and held as implied in grants of barony (*a*).

(*a*) 2 Stair, 3. § 65–6.

753. The right of forestry is not conferred by erection into a barony, but may be conveyed by a conveyance of the barony (*a*).

(*a*) 2 Ersk. 6. § 18. See *supra*, § 670.

754. A right to salmon-fishing is not conferred by mere erection of lands into a barony, unless specially granted; but the charter of a barony is a good title by prescription to carry salmon-fishing 'though without mention of fishings' (*a*), 'whether the possession proved be possession by the Crown vassal, or by one deriving right from him, *e.g.* where the barony has been subdivided (*b*). But the extent of the salmon-fishing so acquired is measured by the possession (*c*). An express grant of salmon-fishings carries the fishing in rivers in or bounding the barony, even when there has been adverse possession by one not having a title to which his possession can be ascribed (*d*).'

(*a*) 2 Ersk. 6. § 18. See above, § 646, 671, and below, § 1112. See Nicol (Milne's Trs.) *v.* L. Adv., 1868; 6 Macph. 972. D. Richmond *v.* E. Seafield, 1870; 8 Macph. 530. L. Adv. *v.* Cathcart, 1871; 9 Macph. 744. L. Adv. *v.* M'Douall, 1873; 11 Macph. 688; rev. 1875, 2 R. H. L. 49.
(*b*) L. Adv. *v.* M'Culloch, 1874; 2 R. 26.
(*c*) L. Adv. *v.* Cathcart, 1871; 9 Macph. 744. L. Adv. *v.* L. Lovat, 1880; 5 App. Ca. 273; 7 R. H. L. 122 (where prescriptive possession of salmon-fishings in part of a river, where alone they were at the time of any commercial value, with certain exercise of rights in the rest of the river, sufficed under a barony title to establish a right to the fishings in the whole river opposite the barony lands).
(*d*) D. Argyll *v.* Campbell (Lochnell), 1891; 18 R. 1094.

755. A right to ports and harbours is not created, but may be carried, by a charter of barony (*a*).

(*a*) 2 Ersk. 6. § 18. See above, § 654 sqq.; and Rankine, Landownership, 244.

CHAPTER IV

OF THE FEUDAL TITLE TO LAND

756. General View.—The leading principles of feudal conveyancing are:—That the superior is over-lord of the fee, while the vassal holds directly of him, as if his proprietary rights were derived from the superior's grant. The grant of land is by a charter from the superior, 'registered in the Register of Sasines, formerly' with an instrument of sasine (*a*), recorded in the public register. On any termination of the vassal's right (*i.e.* on transmission of it by death to his heir, or on voluntary transference to a purchaser, or on a compulsory judicial conveyance to a creditor), recourse must be had, 'by the law previous to 1874,' to the superior in order to have a renewal of the grant, which he 'was' bound to give (on service, resignation, or adjudication), and which, like the original grant, 'was' completed by sasine 'or charter' recorded (*b*). And if the vassal choose to give only the *dominium utile* to another, without transferring his whole right, or to burden it with debt, he may do so by a grant, in subinfeudation, of the land, to be held of himself as an intermediate superior; he himself continuing vassal to his own superior, and the sub-feu being completed by sasine duly recorded.

Thus, no real right to the property, and no real burden on land, can be created without a feudal grant completed by sasine, and published in the public record, 'or by its modern equivalent, viz. registration of the writ by which it is created.'

Feudal grants are either—1. Original; or 2. by Progress, on the occasion of the transmission of the land from the original vassal.

(*a*) See below, § 770A.

(*b*) It is now unnecessary to obtain from the superior a renewal of the investiture. See § 775.

I. ORIGINAL GRANTS.

757. *Nature of the Vassal's Title.*—Originally, a feudal vassal swore fealty on receiving a grant from his superior, and was thereupon invested in the land, by the hand of the superior himself, before the *Pares Curiæ.* The written title was rather a record of what had already passed, than itself the grant; it was called *Breve Testatum.* The charter afterwards introduced expressed, in terms of conveyance, the superior's grant. And if the superior was not himself to give the investiture, the charter was accompanied by a precept commanding his bailie to give sasine. This precept afterwards became part of the charter.

An instrument of sasine under the hand of a notary was the proof of the investiture, and was ordered to be registered for public inspection within a certain time (*a*). Thus there are three points to be marked: The charter containing the precept of sasine; the sasine and instrument; and the registration of the sasine (*b*).

(*a*) 2 Ersk. Pr. 3. 2 Stair, 3. 2 Ersk. 3. 2 Ross, 117, etc.

(*b*) Professor Bell wrote in 1839 at the end of this title, "The complicated requisites of this part of the feudal title (the charter and sasine), as in a long course of practice they have grown up and been accumulated, have suggested the obvious improvement of simplifying the proceedings, and abolishing forms which have now become useless. And in the report of the Law Commissioners will be found suggestions for very extensive alterations. How far those suggestions may appear to the wisdom of Parliament fit to be adopted, it is not easy to anticipate; but to whatever length improvement shall be carried, it will still be necessary to keep in mind the rules and principles which regulate the present practice." See the alterations which have been stated in the additions to this chapter, § 763A, 770A, 771A, 774A, 778A, 805A, 809A, 820A, 825A, 828A, etc.

758. Charter and Precept.—The charter is properly a grant of land, forming the *titulus transferendi dominii*; and so far is complete without a precept of sasine. The precept of sasine belongs 'by the older law' to the *modus transferendi*, being the mandate to give tradition. And such precept 'might' be unnecessary, if the superior himself 'chose' to give sasine *propriis manibus*; or it 'might' be supplied by a separate precept. But by the 'modern' practice 'until 1868,' the charter is a compound deed, containing a grant of the feudal subject, and a precept authorising a person to represent the superior, and to give sasine in the land to the vassal. 'The precept of sasine is not now necessary (*a*); although the practically obsolete instrument of sasine would probably not be effectual if the charter or disposition contained no precept (*b*). The difference in essentials between a feu-charter, a feu-contract, and a feu-disposition is, in effect, immaterial (*c*).'

(*a*) 31 and 32 Vict. c. 101, § 5.

(*b*) *Infra*, § 771, 771A.

(*c*) 1 Jur. Styles, 32 (3rd ed.). Duff's Feudal Convg. 133. Aiton *v.* Russell's Exrs., 16 R. 625 (*per* L. P. Inglis). Macrae *v.* Mackenzie's Trs., 1891; 19 R. 138 (*per* L. Kinnear).

759. The parts of the charter, properly so called, are the dispositive clause, the *tenendas*, and the *reddendo*; these expressing the grant and its conditions. The precept of sasine is not, as a part of the charter, indispensable, but has been superadded to the proper charter (*a*).

(*a*) As to the clause of warrandice, see § 894, below; clause of relief from burdens, § 895A, below.

760. (1.) *The Dispositive Clause.*—This contains (besides the name and description of the granter and grantee, and the cause of granting) the grant *de præsenti* of the superior to the vassal, the description of the subject, and the destination or line of succession to which the superior gives his consent. The words of conveyance must import a grant *de præsenti*. Words of preterite or of future grant will not do, unaccompanied by words *de præsenti*. 'The word "dispone" appears to have been indispensable, at least in gratuitous deeds (*a*). But since 31st December 1868 it has been competent for the owner of lands to settle the succession to them by *mortis causa* deed, which is not invalid (if granted by a person then alive, or granted after that date) because "the grantor has not used the word 'dispone' or other word or words importing a conveyance *de præsenti*" (*b*); and it is not now "competent to object to the validity of any deed or writing as a conveyance of heritage coming into operation after" 7th August 1874, "on the ground that it does not contain the word 'dispone,' provided it contains any other word or words importing conveyance or transference, or present intention to convey or transfer" (*c*).'

The subject of the grant must be described (*d*); both its extent and local situation; and its nature, as of fee or liferent, etc. (*e*): and in all questions on such points, this clause contains the proper evidence. Where the dispositive clause is clear and without ambiguity, the grant is not to be enlarged or limited by the words of any subsequent 'or other' clause (*f*). If ambiguous, 'or susceptible of more than one meaning,' other clauses may be referred to in aid of the construction (*g*). The destination is here set forth, forming the contract between the superior and vassal as to the heirs whom the superior shall be bound to receive as such, on payment of a double feu-duty (*h*), or the persons to be regarded as purchasers, and so held liable for a full composition (*i*). This clause contains the essence of the charter, which is the grant (*k*). And if the deed were to stop here, sasine might be obtained by means of a separate precept, or by the judicial process of adjudication in implement (*l*).

(*a*) Hamilton *v.* Macdowal, March 3, 1815 ; F. C. Glassford's Tr. *v.* Glassford, 1864 ; 2 Macph. 1317. See M. Bell's Convg. 583. Kirkpatrick *v.* Kirkpatrick's Trs., 1873 ; 11 Macph. 551 ; 1874, 1 R. H. L. 37.

(*b*) 31 and 32 Vict. c. 101, § 20. See below, § 1691.

(*c*) 37 and 38 Vict. c. 94, § 27. See below, § 1691, 1692.

(*d*) See above, § 738 sq.

(*e*) See N. B. Ry. *v.* Edin. Mags., 1893 ; 20 R. 725.

(*f*) **Shanks** *v.* **Ceres Kirk-session,** 1797 ; M. 4295 ; 1 Ross' L. C. 42. Forrester *v.* Hutchison, 1826 ; 4 S. 824. **E. Aboyne** *v.* **Farquharson,** Nov. 16, 1814 ; F. C. ; aff. 1818, 6 Pat. 380. Allan *v.* Cameron's Crs., 1780 ; M. 10,265 ; aff. 1781, 2 Pat. 572 (real burden not expressed in dispositive clause). Chancellor *v.* Mosman, 1872 ; 10 Macph. 995. Lee *v.* Alexander, 1882 ; 10 R. 230 ; aff. 1883, 8 App. Ca. 853 ; 10 R. H. L. 91. So, although a simple assignation of an unexecuted procuratory of resignation and precept of sasine is sufficient (*infra*, § 853) to transmit a personal right to land, an assignation to titles when made in corroboration of a precise grant can neither enlarge nor control that grant as specifically set forth in the dispositive clause. Graham *v.* Don, Dec. 15, 1814 ; F. C. ; 1 Ross' L. C. 50. Hamilton *v.* Montgomery, 1834 ; 12 S. 349. Renton *v.* Anstruther, *infra*, § 852-3. Brownlie *v.* Miller (Campbell), 1878 ; 5 R. 1076 ; aff. 1880, 7 R. H. L. 66 ; 5 App. Ca. 925. **Strachan** *v.* **Whiteford,** 1776 ; M. Apx. *Adjud.* 7 ; 2 Ross' L. C. 480 ; as explained in Watson *v.* Wilson, 1868 ; 6 Macph. 258.

(*g*) Menzies' Lectures, 551. L. Adv. *v.* Sinclair, 1865 ; 3 Macph. 981 ; aff. 1867 ; 5 Macph. H. L. 97 ; 1 App. Ca. 174. L. Adv. *v.* M'Culloch, 1874 ; 2 R. 27. Sutherland *v.* Sinclair, 1801 ; M. Apx. *Tailzie*, 8. Orr *v.* Moir's Trs., 1892 ; 19 R. 700 ; revd. (Orr *v.* Mitchell) 1893, A. C. 238 ; 20 R. H. L. 23.

(*h*) See *supra*, § 717. (*i*) See *supra*, § 722 sqq.

(*k*) 2 Stair, 3. § 14. 2 Ersk. 3. § 21-23 ; and 6. § 1-17. 2 Ross, 164. 1 Jurid. Styles, 15. 1 Bell's Forms of Deeds, 12. Henderson *v.* Henderson, 1667 ; M. 11,339 ; 2 Ill. 326. Simson *v.* Barclay & Gemmel, 1752 ; Elch. *Testament*, 12 ; and Notes, 486 ; 5 B. Sup. 794 ; 1 Ross' L. C. 1 ; 2 Ill. 43 and 326. Ogilvie *v.* Mercer, 1793 ; M. 3340 ; aff. 1796, 3 Pat. 434 ; 1 Ross' L. C. 13. Montgomery *v.* Innes & Foulis, 1795 ; Bell's Fo. Ca. 203 ; 1 Ross' L. C. 7. Stewart *v.* Stewart, 1803 ; Hume, 880 ; 1 Sandford's Her. Succ. 62.

(*l*) But see M. Bell's Convg. 583.

761. (2.) *The Tenendas* clause sets forth the holding thus:—"To be holden and to hold, all and sundry the said lands, etc., by B., etc., of and under me, etc., as their immediate lawful superiors of the same, in feu-farm (or in blench-farm), fee and heritage, for ever, by all the righteous meaths and marches," etc. Where such a clause was omitted in a charter, formerly the presumption was for ward-holding; now the tenure would be presumed to be feu, or blench if held of the Crown (*a*).

(*a*) 2 Stair, 3. § 15. 2 Ersk. 3. § 24. 2 Ross, 164. See cases in § 760 (*f*). See also § 820A.

762. (3.) *The Reddendo* clause expresses the regular return to be made by the vassal of services, or of feu or blench duty; and also the occasional or casual return on the entry of an heir or singular successor, 'or periodically.'

763. These clauses express all the parts of the proper charter, and, with the authenticating or testing clause, make a perfect grant, transferring the *jus ad rem*, and forming the *titulus transferendi dominii* to be completed by sasine, the *modus transferendi dominii*.

763A. 'It was competent and sufficient, in granting writs or charters of renewal by subject superiors, to refer to the *tenendas* and *reddendo* as set forth at length either in the recorded writ or charter produced to the superior, or in any charter or other writ recorded in any public register (*a*).'

(*a*) 31 and 32 Vict. c. 101, § 100. This provision since 1874 applies only to charters of novodamus, precepts or writs of *clare constat*, and writs of acknowledgment. 37 and 38 Vict. c. 94, § 4 (1). See below, § 755A.

764. (4.) *The Precept of Sasine* 'which under the new system of titles is unnecessary (*a*), and since 1845 has been used only in a short statutory form (*b*), was' an order or mandate addressed by the superior to his bailie, by means of which the conveyance 'was' to be completed by sasine. The precept commands the bailie to give "actual, real, and corporal possession" to the vassal or his attorney, by delivery of "earth and stone," or such other symbols as law has prescribed for tradition of the subject of the grant (*c*). This precept plainly bears the marks of having been once a separate deed, and is awkwardly incorporated with the charter, by being added at the end of it. It was first made part of the charter by a statute for regulating the tenor of Crown charters; and the practice was imitated by subject superiors in their grants or dispositions (*d*).

(*a*) 31 and 32 Vict. c. 101, § 5 ; repeating 21 and 22 Vict. c. 76, § 5.

(*b*) 8 and 9 Vict. c. 35, § 5 and Sch. A, in 31 and 32 Vict. c. 101, Sch. A.

(*c*) It was not necessary that the precept should specify the symbols. Barstow *v.* Stewart, 1858 ; 20 D. 612.

(*d*) 2 Stair, 3. § 16, 19. 2 Ersk. 3. § 33. 2 Ross, 65, 161. 1672, c. 7.

765. Where sasine is to be given *propriis manibus*, no precept is necessary. A charter or even an instrument bearing the fact of sasine being so given, signed by the superior 'along with the notary,' and containing words of *de præsenti* alienation, is enough. But in practice, sasine *propriis manibus* is almost obsolete, and never used but in sasines to wives and children under family settlements (*a*). 'A short statutory form has been provided, by which a husband may give his wife infeftment *propriis manibus*, by recording any conveyance, granted in his favour, with a warrant of registration on behalf of himself and his wife, signed by himself (*b*).'

(*a*) 2 Stair, 3. § 19. 2 Ersk. 3. § 38. Menzies, 593. M. Bell's Convg. 661, 671.
(*b*) 31 and 32 Vict. c. 101, § 15, and Sch. H, No. 3.

766. The precept, being a mandate, expired formerly by the death of either party. This was remedied by Act of Parliament (*a*); and the *jus quæsitum* which a purchaser has in the warrant for completing his title (as being a procuratory *in rem suam*) was made effectual by declaring "that procuratories of resignation and precepts of sasine shall in all time coming continue in full force, and be sufficient warrants not only for making of resignations and taking sasine in favour of the parties to whom they are or shall be granted, but likewise in favour of their heirs, assignees, and successors, having right to the said procuratories and precepts, either by a general service, or by disposition and assignation, or by adjudication, as well after as before the death of the granters, or parties to whom they are granted, or both; providing always that the instruments of resignation and sasines taken after the death of either party express the titles of those to whom the sasine is granted, and that the same be deduced therein, otherways to be void and null." 'If the granter be divested, the precept does not necessarily fall; though it may become useless by reason of the prior infeftment of a disponee under another disposition by the same author (*b*).'

(*a*) 1693, c. 35; 9 Act. Parl. p. 461, c. 73. 3 Ersk. 3. § 42. An exception is made from the statute of the precept of *clare constat* for entering an heir, which is necessarily personal, and not assignable.
(*b*) Pringle *v.* Pringle, 1890; 17 R. 1229. See below, § 790 *fin.*, 929.

767. The precept of sasine, according to the above Act, is a warrant to give sasine to the person named as grantee (*a*), or to his heir proved by service, or to the assignee of the grantee. But in these two last cases the connecting evidence (or *mid-couple*) must be shown to the person who gives sasine, and published to the witnesses, and expressed in the instrument. While a precept of sasine is still unexecuted, the charter containing it is called an open charter; and the precept may be assigned either in whole or in part 'by the grantee, but not by the granter (*b*).'

(*a*) See Fogo *v.* Fogo, 1840; 2 D. 651; 4 D. 1063; aff. 1843, 2 Bell's App. 195; 2 Ross' L. C. 36; and below, § 1693.
(*b*) Gammel *v.* Cathcart, 1849; 12 D. 19; aff. 1852, 1 Macq. 362; 15 D. H. L. 31.

768. The mandate is to give heritable state and sasine, real, actual, and corporal possession. The party to whom sasine is to be given (or whose heir or assignee under the Act of 1693 is entitled to take sasine under the precept) must be named (*a*). The lands must be described so as to be known, or capable of identification by written evidence (*b*). The possession to be delivered is *corporal*, not *actual*, possession of the lands or subjects themselves. The possession 'was' delivered symbolically, by delivery of some token or badge (*c*).

(*a*) See Blackwood *v.* Colvil's Reprs., 1740; M. 14,657; 2 Ross' L. C. 18. M. Bell's Convg. 646. See below, § 876.
(*b*) See below, § 876.
(*c*) See below for the present law.

769. Sasine. — Sasine 'according to the old law was' the delivery of possession by certain symbols, as earth and stone for lands, clap and happer for mills, etc.; and this symbolical delivery 'was' indispensable, while without it, 'or its modern equivalent, registration,' real and actual possession of the land is of no avail in completing the title, and not necessary to its completion. Of this symbolical possession the only evidence admissible 'was' a notarial instrument duly recorded.

770. (1.) *Ceremony.* — Sasine 'was, till 1st October 1845,' given by delivery, on the ground of the lands, of the proper symbol, by the bailie of the superior to the attorney of the vassal; the warrant to that effect being read and published by the notary to the witnesses present; and instruments being taken, by placing a piece of money in the hands of the notary, for the purpose of calling the attention of him and of the witnesses to the ceremony. The ceremony 'was' this:—The bailie, attorney, notary, and two witnesses, being on the ground, the attorney of the vassal 'or disponee' delivers the deed containing the precept, with the proper connecting title, 'if any,' to the bailie, requiring him to perform the duties according to the mandate. The bailie delivers the warrant and its accompaniments to the notary, to be read and published to all present. The notary reads the warrant and the connecting evidence. The bailie delivers the symbols to the attorney. The attorney receives the symbols (*a*), and takes instruments in the hands of the notary, by giving him a piece of money. And the notary and witnesses see, and must by their subscription attest, the truth of the ceremony as stated in the instrument (*b*).

(*a*) See above, § 769. Barstow *v.* Stewart, 1858; 20 D. 612.

(*b*) 2 Ersk. 3. § 35. Primrose *v.* Dury, 1612; M. 14,326; 2 Ill. 44. Lady Lamertoun *v.* Polwarth, 1680–2; M. 14,309, 14,321. Urquhart *v.* Officers of State, 1752; M. 9921; aff. 1755, Cr. St. & Pat. 586. Livingstone *v.* L. Napier, 1762; 5 B. Sup. 587. Henderson *v.* Dalrymple, 1776; M. *Memb. of Parl.* Apx. 2; 5 B. Sup. 586; Hailes, 695. Douglas *v.* Chalmers, 5 B. Sup. 587. Don *v.* Waldie, Feb. 4, 1813; F. C. Davidson *v.* M'Leod, 1827; 6 S. 8; 2 Ross' L. C. 65; 2 Ill. 45. See below, § 869 et seq.

770A. 'In 1845 important changes were made as to sasine. The statutory form of precept (when used) is a mandate to "any notary-public to whom these presents may be presented to give to the said A. B., or his foresaids, sasine of the lands and others above disponed" (*a*). It is not necessary to proceed to the lands in which sasine is to be given, or to perform any act of infeftment thereon; but sasine is effectually given by producing to the notary the precept of sasine and relative writs, and by expeding and recording in the appropriate register of sasines an instrument setting forth that sasine had been given in the lands according to a form annexed to the statute (*b*). But in 1858 this mode of taking sasine was dispensed with (*c*). It is no longer necessary for infeftment to expede and record an instrument of sasine; and it is sufficient for the person in whose favour a conveyance (*d*) is granted, to record the conveyance itself in the appropriate register of sasines. On the conveyance, bearing a warrant of registration in a statutory form (*e*) specifying the person on whose behalf it is presented, and signed by that person or his agent, being recorded along with the warrant, it has the same effect as if the conveyance had been followed by an instrument of sasine recorded at the date of recording the conveyance, in favour of the person on whose behalf the conveyance is presented for registration.'

(*a*) 8 and 9 Vict. c. 35, Sch. A.

(*b*) 8 and 9 Vict. c. 35, § 1 and Sch. B, in 31 and 32 Vict. c. 101, Sch. A, No. 2.

(*c*) By the Titles to Land Act, 21 and 22 Vict. c. 76, now consolidated with other Acts in 31 and 32 Vict. c. 101.

(*d*) The word "conveyance" includes every writ by which lands are transmitted. See § 36 of the Act, and 31 and 32 Vict. c. 101, § 3.

(*e*) 31 and 32 Vict. c. 101, § 15 and Sch. H. Johnston *v.* Pettigrew, 1865; 3 Macph. 954.

771. (2.) *The Instrument of Sasine* (which 'was until 1858' the only admissible evidence of the sasine) is an attestation by the notary and witnesses, subscribed by them, that symbolical possession was duly given to the vassal (*a*). It 'consisted until 1845' of an invocation, "in the name of God"; the date, by the day and year, and also by the year of the sovereign's reign; and the date 'was' important as regulating the recording. There is then set forth the compearance and name of the attorney, and the name of the person whom he represents; the compearance and name of the bailie as representing the superior; the description of the charter as in the attorney's possession, with such a narrative as may connect it with the precept; the exhibition of the charter by the attorney to the bailie, with a request to execute his office as bailie; the bailie's compliance, by delivering the charter and precept to the notary for publication; the reading of the precept, which must be *verbatim* engrossed in the instrument, so far as it relates to the lands in which sasine is given (*b*); the giving of sasine and real and corporal possession by delivery of the 'appropriate' symbols by the bailie to the attorney (*c*); the taking of instruments by the attorney in the notary's hand; and the attestation that those things were done on the ground of the land, at a certain hour of the day of the date of the instrument, in presence of the witnesses duly named and described. The conclusion is the notary's Latin docquet, authenticating the instrument, and again attesting the truth of the ceremony as seen, known, and heard by the notary and witnesses personally present (*d*).

(*a*) 2 Stair, 3. § 16. 2 Ersk. 3. § 34–8.
(*b*) Don *v.* Waldie, Feb. 4, 1813; F. C.; 2 Ill. 45. Lamertoun *v.* Polwarth, 1680; M. 14,309; 2 Ill. 44.
(*c*) Brechin Town Council *v.* Arbuthnot, 1840; 3 D. 216. *Infra*, § 871.
(*d*) The detail of questions which may arise on this instrument will be given below, § 869 et seq.

771A. 'Under the form introduced by the Infeftment Act of 1845, there is no invocation, nor is any date necessary, nor is the appearance of an attorney or bailie mentioned; the instrument beginning thus: "At there was by (or on behalf of) A. B., presented to me, notary-public subscribing, a disposition (or other deed) granted by C. D., and bearing date as in the precept of sasine hereinafter inserted." Then there is stated the import of the deed, and that it contains an obligation to infeft (the nature of which is specified); and the precept of sasine must be inserted. Whereupon the notary says: "In virtue of which precept, I hereby give sasine to the said A. B. of the lands and others above described." This is followed by a reference to burdens, if any, a testing clause without date, and the subscriptions of the notary and witnesses; but there is no docquet (*a*). The date of presentment at the register of sasines is the date of the instrument and of the infeftment (*b*).'

(*a*) 8 and 9 Vict. c. 35, Sch. B, in 31 and 31 Vict. c. 101, Sch. A.
(*b*) 8 and 9 Vict. c. 35, § 3.

772. (3.) *Registration of the Sasine.*—The laws establishing the record of sasines had two objects in view: the first was to guard against forgery, by making conveyances known; the next (suggested as an improvement on the system) was to give information to all persons interested in knowing the state of the property (*a*). Hence the rule in the statutes 'was' twofold: that the sasine shall be recorded within sixty days; and that priority of registration shall give preference (*b*). 'Under the more modern system, instruments of sasine in the new form may be recorded at any time during the life of the person in whose favour they are expede (*c*); and all conveyances and instruments registrable with warrants in the register of sasines, may be recorded at any time in the life of the person on whose behalf they are presented for registration, and are preferable according to the date of registration (*d*).'

The words of the Act 1617 as applicable to sasines are: "That there shall be a public register in which all instruments of sasine shall be registered within threescore days after the date of the same"; "the extract of the which register shall make faith in all cases, except where the writs so registered are offered to be improven; and if it shall happen any of the said writs which are appointed to be registered as said is, not to be duly registered within the said space of threescore days," "the same to make no faith in judgment, by way of action or exception, in prejudice of a third party who hath acquired a perfect and lawful right to the said lands and heritages; but (*i.e.* without) prejudice always to them to use the said writs against the party maker thereof, his heirs and successors" (*e*).

(*a*) As to the effect of registration on the title of one holding under a latent trust, see Her. Revers. Co. *v.* Millar, 1892; 19 R. H. L. 43.
(*b*) 1503, c. 89. 1540, c. 77. 1555, c. 46. 1587, c. 64. See Convention of Holyrood in 1598, 4 Act. Parl. c. 184. 1600, c. 36, 4 Act. Parl. 237. Act of Sederunt, Jan. 6, 1604. 1617, c. 16. The sasines of burgage subjects were excepted from these Acts, and regulated by another statute. See below, § 843. 2 Ersk. 3. § 39 sqq. Lindsay *v.* Giles, 1844; 6 D. 771 (computation of sixty days).
(*c*) 8 and 9 Vict. c. 35, § 3.
(*d*) 31 and 32 Vict. c. 101, § 142.
(*e*) 1617, c. 16; 4 Act. Parl. 545. Simpson *v.* Blackie, 1678; M. 13,553; 2 Ill. 45. Grey *v.* Tenants, 1626; M. 13,540. Compare Keith *v.* Sinclair, 1703; 4 B. Sup. 542; M. 13,562, with **Paterson** *v.* **Douglas**, 1705; M. 13,564; aff. 1714, Robertson's Ap. 99; 2 Ross' L. C. 78. See below, § 774, 880.

773. The requisites of registration under this Act, and subsequent Acts and regulations, 'were': The instrument must be recorded within threescore days from the date of the sasine. On being presented to the keeper of the record, it must be entered in a minute-book, with a general description of the lands, and a reference to the pages of the record where the transcript is to be found (*a*); while the instrument, with the notary's docquet, must be transcribed *verbatim et literatim*, either in the General Record at Edinburgh or, 'till 1869–71,' in the Particular Record of the county where the lands lie (*b*); all records being, after a certain time, deposited in the Register House at Edinburgh (*c*). In deciding in what Particular Register (*c*) the sasine 'should' be recorded, it is to be observed that although in baronies, and under clauses of union, sasine 'might' be taken at a particular part of the lands, the instrument must be registered either in the record of each county within which any of the lands lie, or in the General Register (*d*). After being recorded, there must be a certificate (*e*) written on the back of the instrument, stating the fact of recording, with an exact reference to the page of the record where the instrument is to be found recorded. The preference of the sasine depends on the priority of its being duly booked and inserted in the register (*f*).

(*a*) 1617, c. 16. 1693, c. 14. 1696, c. 18.

(*b*) The Particular Registers are abolished by the Land Registers (Scotland) Act, 1868, and the General Register in Edinburgh is now the only competent register for all writs relating to lands not held burgage (31 and 32 Vict. c. 64, § 8, 27); and it is divided according to the counties of Scotland (*ib.* § 3; 54 Vict. c. 9). But the abolition of the distinction between burgage and feu holding leaves the writs of all lands held burgage at 1st October 1874 to be recorded in the Burgh Registers. 37 and 38 Vict. c. 94, § 25. See Begg's Conveyancing Code, p. 362.

(*c*) Act of Sederunt, Jan. 17, 1756. Stair, Apx. § 3. 2 Ersk. 3. § 40 sqq.

(*d*) Dalrymple *v.* E. Carnwath, 1711; 4 B. Sup. 862; 2 Ill. 83. See below, § 874.

(*e*) Gibson Craig *v.* Cochran, 1838; 16 S. 1332 (error in certificate).

(*f*) 1693, c. 13.

774. The rules of recording 'were' these: The sasine is held as recorded within the sixty days, if the date of presentment as proved by the minute-book is within that time, and the instrument has been actually recorded, or is still in the keeper's hand (*a*). The instrument, as appearing in the record, must be correctly transcribed, in order to have effect in competition against third parties having acquired a perfect and lawful right to the lands (*b*). And so, if incorrectly recorded, or imperfectly, the error or omission of an essential part is fatal (*c*); and after expiration of the sixty days an error cannot be corrected (*d*) unless by a new sasine (*e*). Between sasines, both entered in the minute-book, but reversed in order in the transcription, the preference rather seems to be 'not' with the sasine first actually recorded, though last presented (*f*), 'but with that first entered in the minute-book (*g*); and that is the rule with regard to writs authorised to be registered under the Conveyancing Acts since 1858 (*h*).

'The looseness of the words of the Act 1617, above quoted, caused much controversy as to the effect of an instrument of sasine unrecorded or imperfectly recorded. It is now settled that such a sasine is an absolute nullity. It does not exhaust the precept or create a real right of any kind. The exception in the statute ("but prejudice," etc.) was introduced chiefly or solely with regard to reversions and other writs therein appointed to be registered, the effect of which as creating a personal right it was proper to save. This does not prevent the statute from making a sasine unrecorded null for the purpose which a sasine is intended to serve, viz. the creation of a real right; and the words of the clause referred to have no meaning in regard to a sasine beyond this, that there may be persons who are barred *personali exceptione* from objecting to the apparent title (*i*).'

(*a*) Stair, Apx. § 3. M'Kenzie *v.* M'Leod, 1768; M. 8800. E. Fife *v.* Gordon, 1774; M. 8850; 2 Ill. 46. Skelly *v.* Duff, 1774; 5 B. Sup. 589. Dunbar *v.* Sutherland, 1790; M. 8799. Maclaine *v.* Maclaine, 1852; 14 D. 870; aff. 1855, 27 S. Jur. 550; 18 D. H. L. 44.

(*b*) Grey *v.* Hope, 1790; M. 8796.

(*c*) M'Queen *v.* Nairne, 1823; 2 S. 539. Dennistoun *v.* Spiers, 1824; 3 S. 200.

(*d*) Dundas *v.* Dennistoun, 1824; 3 S. 281; correcting Tait, Petr., 1822; 1 S. 229. See § 770A, 774A.

(*e*) See below, § 774A, 879. M. Bell's Convg. 670.

(*f*) L. Cardross *v.* Foulis, 1678; M. 13,554; 2 Ill. 47. E. Mar *v.* Lady Kincardine, 1684; M. 13,557. Drummond *v.* Ramsay, June 24, 1809; F. C. Adam *v.* Duthie, June 19, 1810; F. C. Douglas *v.* Dunlop, 1835; 13 S. 505; 3 Ill. 152.

(*g*) Maclaine, *cit.* (*a*). 8 and 9 Vict. c. 35, § 3. 21 and 22 Vict. c. 76, § 19. Writs transmitted by post and received at the same time are deemed to be presented and registered contemporaneously; 31 and 32 Vict. c. 64, § 6; 31 and 32 Vict. c. 101, § 142.

(*h*) 31 and 32 Vict. c. 101, § 142.

(*i*) **Young** *v.* **Leith**, 1847; 9 D. 932; aff. 1848, 2 Ross' L. C. 81, 103; in which the cases are reviewed. See especially, Paterson, *supra*, § 772 (*e*), and the cases cited in § 879, *infra*. Ceres Sch. Bd. *v.* M'Farlane, 1895; 23 R. 279 (singular successor of superior). See also Crawford *v.* M'Michen, 1729; 2 Ross' L. C. 112 (unregistered sasine not a title for prescription). Professor Bell has not, as was pointed out in Young *v.* Leith, been quite consistent or correct in his statements as to the effect of an unregistered sasine. See Com. i. 697; and below, § 879, 880.

774A. 'By the Infeftment Act of 1845, instruments of sasine were ordered to be recorded in manner theretofore in use (*a*); and it was declared that the date of presentment and entry set forth on the instrument by the keeper of the record should be taken to be the date of the instrument and infeftment, and that the instrument might be recorded at any time during the life of the party in whose favour it was expede (*b*). It was also provided that, in case of error or defect in the instrument or in the recording, it should be competent of new to make and record an instrument, to have effect from the date of recording it, as if no previous instrument had been made or recorded (*c*). Similar provisions are made with regard to the recording in the Registers of Sasines of deeds generally, by the Consolidation Act of 1868 (*d*).'

(*a*) 8 and 9 Vict. c. 35, § 2. (*b*) *Ib.* § 3.
(*c*) *Ib.* § 4. See as to correcting errors in recording, Innes, Petr., Dec. 20, 1816; F. C. Dundas *v.* Dennistoun, 1824; 3 S. 400. D. Montrose, Petr., 1846; 8 D. 822. Maclaine, *supra*, § 774 (*a*). Menzies, Convg. 585. M. Bell, Convg. 671.
(*d*) 31 and 32 Vict. c. 101, § 142, 143.

774B. 'Under the present law, by which the "conveyance" may be recorded instead of expeding and recording an instrument of sasine, provision is made in the case of conveyances which affect separate lands or interests, or which contain clauses of a private nature (such as the purposes of a trust), or matter unnecessary for the completion of the disponee's title or the protection of the public, for expeding a notarial instrument in favour of the grantee, setting forth generally the nature of the conveyance, and containing those parts of it by which the lands are affected; and on this instrument being recorded, it is equivalent to a recorded sasine (*a*). The granter of the deed is also authorised to insert a clause of direction, limiting the recording where the conveyance itself is recorded, to particular parts of the conveyance (*b*). Provisions are likewise made for the case where the conveyance, before being recorded, is acquired by a third party. Where this is by an assignation, it may be recorded along with the conveyance itself, and a warrant of registration (*c*); or, either in that case, or where the party has right by general assignation (*d*), service (*e*), adjudication (*f*), or otherwise, he may expede and record a notarial instrument to the above effect and setting forth the mid-couple, with a warrant of registration (*g*). The date of entry in the minute-book is now the date of registration (*h*). The provisions of an Act by which instruments of sasine and of resignation *ad remanentiam* bearing erasures were declared to be not challengeable except on fraud, are now extended to all instruments (*i*).'

(*a*) 31 and 32 Vict. c. 101, § 17, 23, and Sch. J.
(*b*) *Ib.* § 12.
(*c*) 32 and 33 Vict. c. 116, § 2. 37 and 38 Vict. c. 94, § 33.
(*d*) 31 and 32 Vict. c. 101, § 19.
(*e*) *Ib.* § 46. 37 and 38 Vict. c. 94, § 31.
(*f*) 37 and 38 Vict. c. 94, § 62.
(*g*) 31 and 32 Vict. c. 101, § 23. See as to the nature of a notarial instrument as a title to heritage, Kerr's Tr. *v.* Ritchie's Tr., 1888; 15 R. 520; and as to its application, § 780 *fin.*, 782, 805A, 825A, 828 sqq., 852, 910A, 1692, 1692A.
(*h*) *Ib.* § 142.
(*i*) 6 and 7 Will. IV. c. 33. 31 and 32 Vict. c. 101, § 144. 37 and 38 Vict. c. 94, § 54.

II. GRANTS BY PROGRESS.

775. Transmission to Successors.—The original charter and sasine present the simple view of the feudal title, and the constitution of the relation of superior and vassal. The right of the vassal, so completed, was originally personal to the grantee himself; it now descends to heirs or to assignees (*a*). And the renewal of the fee to a successor of either of these descriptions 'was' effected, 'as stated in the following paragraphs,' by a new grant, with a precept and sasine duly recorded. 'But in reading these sections, it must be remembered that it is now unnecessary, even where there is a provision to the contrary in any statute in force in 1874, or in any deed, for a person having right by succession, bequest, gift, or conveyance to any lands, to obtain from the superior any charter, precept, or other writ by progress in order to the completion of his title; and it is incompetent for superiors to grant such writs, except charters of *novodamus*, precepts or writs from Chancery or of *clare constat*, or writs of acknowledgment (*b*).'

(*a*) "Assignees," in the technical sense, are assignees of an unexecuted warrant for sasine, or now of a conveyance unrecorded—assignees before infeftment (§ 727, above); but a wider signification is here attached to the term.
(*b*) 37 and 38 Vict. c. 94, § 4, subs. 1.

775A. '*Implied Entry under the Conveyancing Act*, 1874.—It will be convenient to state here the rules which have been substituted for the formal renewal of investiture by the superior, which is now abolished.

'A proprietor duly infeft (*a*) is now held to be entered with the nearest superior (*b*) (whether his title be completed or not (*c*)) as at the date of recording his infeftment, to the same effect as if that superior had granted a writ of confirmation (see below, § 806 sqq.).

Such an implied entry confers no more extensive rights than those contained in the original feu-charter or the last writ of entry (*d*): nor does it validate a subfeu where subinfeudation is prohibited; or release the last entered proprietor and his heirs and representatives from personal liability for feudal obligations (*e*) till notice of the change of ownership has been given to the superior. A form of notice of change of ownership is provided by the statute, as well as means for preserving evidence that such notice has been given (*f*). This implied entry is not to prejudice or affect the superior's rights and remedies under the previously existing law or the feu-right, so far as they have not ceased to be operative in consequence of the Act or otherwise, in regard to feu-duties, casualties, and arrears due at or prior to the date of such entry; but it does not entitle a superior to claim any casualty sooner than he otherwise could do by law or the conditions of the feu-right (*g*).'

(*a*) As to the effect of the infeftment of a heritable creditor, see Campbell *v.* Deans, 1890; 17 R. 661; and of a liferenter, see Stuart *v.* Jackson, 1889; 17 R. 85.

(*b*) The statute bears, "the nearest superior whose estate" would, according to the previous law, "have been not defeasible at the will of the proprietor so infeft," in order to exclude the granter of a disposition with an *a me vel de me* precept upon which the grantee has taken infeftment. The alternative holding is, however, made ineffective by this clause. See cases in § 709 (*d*), (*f*).

(*c*) See M. Bell's Convg. 1140. *Infra*, § 778, 793, 881.

(*d*) This is in conformity with the principle that a mere alteration in a charter by progress, *e.g.* the omission or insertion of a reservation in favour of the superior, could not change the conditions or extent of the feu-right, which is always measured by the original charter. 2 Craig, 12. 9. 2 Ersk. 3. § 20. Graham *v.* D. Hamilton, 1842; 4 D. 482. Threipland *v.* Rutherford, 1848; 10 D. 1079. Hutton *v.* Macfarlan, 1863; 2 Macph. 79. Boyd *v.* Bruce, 1872; 11 Macph. 243. Heriot's Hosp. *v.* Carnegys, 1884; 12 R. 30. See below, § 805.

(*e*) See Marshall (*g*).

(*f*) 37 and 38 Vict. c. 94, § 4 (2) and Sch. A. See above, § 700.

(*g*) *Ib.* subs. 3. By the former law an entry by the superior operated as a discharge of all arrears of feu-duties and casualties. Duff's Feudal Convg. 225. M. Bell's Convg. 739. Tailors of Glasgow *v.* Blackie, 1851; 13 D. 1073. L. Adv. *v.* L. Rollo, 1872; 10 Macph. 1024. **Marshall** *v.* **Callander & Trossachs Hydr. Co.**, 1895; 22 R. 954; 1896, A. C. 223; 23 R. H. L. 55. As to this clause of the Act, see above, § 709, 710, 715, etc. Comp. Mags. of Edinr. *v.* Whitehead, 1876; 3 R. 663 (recording in superior's chartulary).

776. (I.) **Transmission to Heirs.**—The rules of succession under which the heir has right will be afterwards explained (*a*). But assuming those rules at present, the title of the person who has right as heir under the destination is completed by grant or charter from the superior, with sasine recorded. And this renewed grant proceeds either on the superior's knowledge of the heir's right, or on the verdict of an inquest.

In studying the history of the heir's title, the points to be marked are: The acknowledgment of the heir originally by the over-lord, with the swearing of fealty and investiture before the *Pares Curiæ*; the inquiry before them as an inquest into the heir's title; the introduction of a more regular judicature for ascertaining the heir's title, by a verdict under the superintendence of the King's judge, the sheriff of the county.

Of the method of completing the heir's title, a very general idea will here suffice; the proper place for the explanation of it in detail will be found under the doctrines of Succession (*b*).

(*a*) See below, § 1637 et sqq.

(*b*) See below, § 1817 et sqq.

777. (A) *Entry by Precept of Clare Constat.*—The precept of *clare constat* is a mandate by the superior to his bailie, stating the death of the vassal last vest and seized in the lands; declaring the superior's knowledge and conviction that the person named in the instrument is nearest and lawful heir to the deceased in the said lands, and therefore commanding his bailie to infeft him as heir (*a*).

(*a*) 3 Stair, 5. § 26. 2 Stair, 3. § 14. 3 Ersk. Pr. 8. § 34. 8 Ersk. 8. § 71. 1 Juridical Styles, 384. 6 Bell's Forms of Deeds, 564.

778. This species of entry, 'which is excepted from the general abolition of charters and writs by progress by the Conveyancing Act of 1874 (*a*),' can be given only by a superior who is feudally invested; or by one who, although not yet invested, is truly the superior, and whose precept is held to become effectual, *jure accretionis*, on his subsequent investiture (*b*). The superior can thus enter only the heir at law or of investiture. The fee not being by the vassal's death reinvested in the superior, so as to enable him to make a *new* grant, he can only recognise the fact of the fee opening in terms of the destination of succession, as expressed or implied in the grant. In proof of the character of the heir entitled to an entry, the superior may proceed upon other documents than the investiture itself, and enter an heir of provision who falls within the destination. It is not essential that, in the precept, the precise description and character under which the heir takes should be set forth, provided the meaning of the precept be clear (*c*). A precept of *clare constat* has been found an incompetent mode of entering one who is not the heir immediately next in succession (*d*). The precept is strictly personal, falls by death 'of the grantee,' and cannot be assigned. 'Formerly it fell by the death either of granter or grantee, but since the Lands Transference Act of 1847, it remains valid during the life of the grantee notwithstanding the granter's death. It falls if the grantee die without taking infeftment (*e*).' But if sasine has been taken on such a precept granted before the superior was infeft, it subsists to the effect of being capable of confirmation after the death of the parties (*f*). And the superior may grant a precept of *clare constat* to himself where he is the heir. The sasine on the precept of *clare constat*, duly recorded, completes the feudal right of the heir.

(*a*) 37 and 38 Vict. c. 94, § 4 (1).
(*b*) See below, § 881.
(*c*) Crichton's Crs. *v.* Christian Knowl. Socy., 1798; M. 15,115. Ogilvy *v.* Ogilvy, Dec. 16, 1817; F. C.; Hume, 724. See below, § 779C, 1820.
(*d*) See below, § 1819.
(*e*) 1693, c. 35. 10 and 11 Vict. c. 48, § 15. 31 and 32 Vict. c. 101, § 103.
(*f*) Lockhart *v.* Ferrier, 1837; 16 S. 76. See below, § 811, 813.

778A. 'Since 1st October 1858, instead of precepts (which are not abolished), the Crown and subject superiors may grant a shorter document called a Writ of *Clare Constat*, in the form of a statutory schedule, which may be recorded with a warrant of registration in the appropriate register of sasines. On being so recorded, the writ of *clare constat* has the same effect as if a precept from Chancery or of *clare constat* had been granted, and an instrument of sasine thereon had been expede and recorded at the date of recording the writ, in favour of the person on whose behalf such writ is presented for registration. Subject superiors are bound to grant such writs if required by the heir; but the heir must, if required, produce a charter or other writ showing the *tenendas* and *reddendo*, and pay or tender to the superior his duties or casualties. Where the lands are held of the Crown or of the Prince, or where the heir is required by the superior, he must also produce a decree of general or of special service establishing his right to succeed to the lands (*a*); and in the former case the application for the writ must be made in the same manner as when a precept from Chancery is applied for. All writs and precepts from Chancery must be recorded in the appropriate register of sasines before the first term of Whitsunday or Martinmas after their dates, and in the Register of Crown Writs (*b*). Further, under the Act of 1868 every charter or writ from the Crown or from a subject superior operates as a confirmation of the whole prior deeds necessary to be confirmed in order to complete the investiture of the person obtaining such charter or writ (*c*).'

(*a*) 31 and 32 Vict. c. 101, § 84, 85, 101, and Sch. W; re-enacting 21 and 22 Vict. c. 76, § 11; and 10 and 11 Vict. c. 51, § 18, 19.
(*b*) *Ib.* § 86, 87. (*c*) *Ib.* § 115.

779. (B) *Entry by Service.*—The use of the Service (properly so called) is to prove by the verdict of an inquest the heir's right (either at law or by provision) to succeed to the person who was last feudally vested in the special estate in question, and so entitle him to demand an entry or renewal of the feudal grant of that estate from the superior feudally vested in the estate (*a*). But another form of service has been introduced, which merely establishes the general character of heir to the person, without relation to any particular lands. The former is called "Special Service," the latter "General Service"; and the details of the nature and doctrine of each will be afterwards given (*b*).

(*a*) See the proper office of service more accurately stated below, § 1824.
(*b*) See below, § 1824 to 1853. The forms of services have been altered, and the details of these alterations will be stated below, § 1828, etc.

779A. '*Vesting of Estates in Heirs without Service.*—The use and importance of service is materially affected by the provision in the Conveyancing Act of 1874, that "a personal right to every estate in land descendible to heirs shall, without service or other procedure, vest or be held to have vested in the heir entitled to succeed thereto, by his survivance of the person to whom he is entitled to succeed, whether such person shall have died before or after the commencement of this Act, provided the heir shall be alive at the date of the commencement of this Act, if such person shall have died before that date (*a*) (1st October 1874); and such personal right shall, subject to the provisions of this Act, be of the like nature and be attended with the like consequences, and be transmissible in the same manner, as a personal right to land under an unfeudalised conveyance, according to the existing law and practice" (*b*). It is a result of this enactment that whenever it is applicable (that is, in all successions opening after 1st October 1874, and in all cases where one possessing as apparent heir survives that date), possession as apparent heir no longer exists in the law of Scotland, for the heir becomes at once owner of the lands under a complete personal right (*c*).'

(*a*) Main *v.* Lamb, 1880; 7 R. 688.
(*b*) 37 and 38 Vict. c. 94, § 9.
(*c*) M'Adam *v.* M'Adam, 1879; 6 R. 1256.

779B. '*Completion of Title to Deceased Heir not Served or Infeft.*—The title of an heir or disponee of a proprietor vested under the provision above recited with a personal right to lands, or of a person acquiring right from such heir or disponee, may be made up in like manner as if the person making up a title holds a disposition from the proprietor last infeft, and a disposition and assignation from each intervening heir or disponee, in favour of their respective immediate successors. A petition in a statutory form is presented to the Sheriff of Chancery or of the county, which is carried through as if it were a petition for special service; and when decree is obtained, which is equivalent to decree of special service, the extract of it may be recorded in the appropriate register of sasines to the effect of infeftment (*a*).'

(*a*) *Ib.* § 10. See Mowbray's Hendry's Styles, 158 (ed. 1878). 1 Jur. Styles, 321.

779C. 'It is provided that an erroneous statement of the character in which an heir is entitled to succeed shall be no objection to any precept or writ from Chancery or of *clare constat*, or to any decree of service, general or special, or to any writ of acknowledgment (whether obtained before or after the commencement of the Act), or to any other decree or petition; provided such heir was in truth entitled to succeed as heir to the lands specified (*a*).'

(*a*) 37 and 38 Vict. c. 94, § 11. See below, § 1830. 2 Ross' L. C. 522. M. Bell's Convg. 1099. Mowbray, Convg. Act, p. 80 (ed. 1874).

780. (1.) *Special Service.* — Under the Special Service, the verdict of the jury, confirmed by the sheriff's signature, and returned into Chancery, entitles the heir to demand his entry and have his title completed by sasine. If he hold of the Crown, he obtains at once a precept from Chancery, directing the sheriff, as the King's bailie, 'since 1845 any notary-public (*a*),' to give infeftment. If he hold of a subject, he is in the same way entitled to demand a precept from his superior for the same purpose. By the infeftment thus authorised, when duly recorded, the feudal grant is renewed, and the title to the lands again complete (*b*). 'Since 1847, however, every decree of special service, being recorded in Chancery and extracted, has the effect of a disposition from the ancestor infeft to the heir served, vesting him with a personal right to the lands. He may complete his feudal title to the lands by recording the extracted decree in the Register of Sasines, with a warrant of registration thereon, in the same way as a conveyance. If the person served shall not have been infeft, his heirs or assignees may complete their title as if the extracted decree were an unrecorded conveyance, in the manner provided by the Titles to Land Act, 1868, for that case (*c*).'

(*a*) See 8 and 9 Vict. c. 35, § 6, superseded by 10 and 11 Vict. c. 51, § 18, both repealed by 31 and 32 Vict. c. 101, § 4.
(*b*) 3 Ersk. Pr. 8. § 28. 3 Stair, 5. § 28 et seq. 3 Ersk. 8. § 59, 79, 80. 1 Juridical Styles, 303. 5 Bell's Forms, 514. 1 and 2 Geo. IV. c. 38, § 11.
(*c*) 31 and 32 Vict. c. 101, § 46, 23, amending 10 and 11 Vict. c. 47, § 21 and 22. See Moreton's Trs. *v.* Moreton, 1854; 16 D. 1108, the evil of which is remedied by the Act cited.

781. (2.) *General Service.*—A General Service, proving the heir's right to the general character of heir at law, or heir of provision according to the destination of the charter or disposition, when returned to Chancery, entitles the heir to take the benefit of all unexecuted precepts or procuratories of his ancestor, and thereon to obtain infeftment, and to take all rights belonging to the heir which do not require infeftment (*a*).

(*a*) 3 Stair, 4. § 33, and 5. § 25. 3 Ersk. Pr. 8. § 29. 3 Ersk. 8. § 63–66. 31 and 32 Vict. c. 101, § 37.

782. (3.) *Effect of Service* (*a*).—It is of importance, in considering the transmission of the fee to heirs, to observe with regard to these forms of service, that a special service, 'which formerly included' a general service in the same character, 'does not since 1847 imply or operate as a general service to the deceased in the same character, except as to the lands embraced in it' (*b*); and that neither the precept from the Crown nor the precept from a subject superior, following on such a service, is assignable (*c*). If sasine 'did' not follow on a special service where the ancestor was infeft, the inchoated right of the heir 'expired,' and 'till 1868' the next heir 'had to' serve heir, not to the person thus served heir and not infeft, but to the *vassal last infeft* (*d*). But where the ancestor has not been infeft, the title of the heir is so far completed by the retour of the general service, or of the special service including a general, as to enable him to take sasine on the unexecuted precept; or to dispose of the succession and assign the unexecuted precept or procuratory. And his heir may, on his death, take up the right by general service to him. The infeftment on a precept or procuratory thus transmitted will be complete and valid, provided the retours, one or more, or assignations, be produced and read at the giving of sasine, and "deduced" in the instrument (*e*). 'A decree of general service to a proprietor infeft is now equivalent to a general disposition by such proprietor, to the effect of enabling the heir, or those deriving right from him, provided he has survived 1st October 1874, to expede and record all notarial instruments competent to a general disponee, in terms of the Titles to Land Act, 1868, or the Conveyancing Act, 1874 (*f*). A general service by the heir of one so served, or of a general disponee, has the like effect as a transmission of the right to the lands; and such services are sufficient links, like general dispositions, for connecting the person expeding a notarial instrument with the person last infeft (*g*).'

(*a*) See above, § 779A sqq.
(*b*) 10 and 11 Vict. c. 47, § 23; re-enacted by 31 and 32 Vict. c. 101, § 47. See below, § 1927A.
(*c*) See above, § 778.
(*d*) See above, § 780 *in fin.*
(*e*) In relation to this distinction, the register of retours of general services, or of special as including general services, is very important. See below, another anomalous mode of entry as heir, § 835.
(*f*) 37 and 38 Vict. c. 94, § 31. See below, § 1692, 1692A.
(*g*) *Ib.*

783. (II.) **Transmission to Singular Successors.**—Singular successors are distinguished from successors by the law of descent, as taking the land by a special or singular title, 'in any other character than that of heir of the last investiture,' either as purchasers, 'or gratuitous disponees,' or as creditors attaching the heritable estate of their debtor by adjudication, judicial sale, or sequestration (*a*).

(*a*) 2 Ersk. 7. § 1. 3 Ersk. 8. § 1. Duff's Feud. Convg. p. 216. Campbell *v.* Deans, 1890; 17 R. 661 (bondholder).

784. (A) **Transmission to Purchasers.**—The disposal of land to a purchaser is in general regulated by the principles of the contract of sale already explained (*a*), taken along with some peculiarities in the application of these principles to land, which will be afterwards stated (*b*).

(*a*) See above, § 85–132. (*b*) See below, § 889 sqq.

785. As every feudal proprietor holds as vassal either of the Crown or of some subject superior, and at the same time has a power of granting base fees to be held of himself, it may be the object of the parties in a sale of land either to convey it to the purchaser as it stands in the seller (the purchaser becoming vassal to the seller's superior, and the seller being dropped out of the feudal chain); or to leave in the seller a superiority intermediate between his own superior and the purchaser, the purchaser in this last case becoming vassal of the seller. Sometimes a superiority is thus reserved because it is valuable, on account of the stipulated feu-duty; and formerly, lands held of the Crown by the seller gave him, as Crown vassal, the elective franchise, which belonged to Crown vassals only, though 'this' occasion for the creation of intermediate superiority has passed away.

Sometimes, 'under the system of titles

existing until 1874,' the purchaser 'might' prefer to have his title completed as vassal to the seller, because he 'was' thus vested instantly with the *dominium utile*, which is the valuable estate, and secured against competitors; while some time 'was' necessary to complete the title in entering with the superior, during which there 'was' danger of being cut out by purchasers or creditors of the seller.

It may be proper, in order to explain this matter clearly, to consider — 1. The transmission of the seller's whole estate; 2. The transmission of the base right or *dominium utile* alone; and 3. The combination of both in the 'more' modern disposition, empowering the purchaser immediately to complete his title to a base fee, convertible by confirmation into a public holding under the seller's superior. 'The disposition contains many clauses which are common to it and to the charter (*a*).'

(*a*) *Supra*, § 758 sqq.

786. *Modes of Completing the Title.*—The vassal's estate continues unextinguished in his person, till with his consent, and 'formerly' with the sanction and authority of his superior (*a*), a new sasine shall supplant the first, and transmit the estate. The regular way of accomplishing this 'was' by means of resignation in the superior's hands, either for the purpose of conveying the vassal's whole estate to the superior himself, or for the purpose of obtaining from him a new grant in favour of another. The former is called "Resignation *ad remanentiam*"; the latter, "Resignation *in favorem*." Another irregular mode of conveyance was introduced, by which the vassal disponed his estate with a precept of sasine to be held of his superior; a subsequent confirmation of this imperfect deed by the superior being held sufficient to ratify it. This is called a title by "Confirmation."

(*a*) See § 775 sqq.

787. *Resignation ad Remanentiam.*—The superior is reinvested in the *dominium utile*, and the vassal's estate merged in the superiority, or in other words, the two estates are consolidated, by a simple disposition containing words of conveyance *de præsenti*, which the vassal completes by resigning *propriis manibus* in his superior's hands. The same effect is produced by the vassal granting a disposition containing a procuratory of resignation or mandate to persons whose names are left blank, to compear before the superior, or his commissioners in his name, wherever they may be (it not being necessary, as in sasine, to perform this ceremony on the ground of the lands), and there to resign and surrender, upgive, overgive, and deliver the lands described, in the superior's hands "*ad perpetuam remanentiam*, to the effect that my right of property of the said lands shall be consolidated with the said B.'s right of superiority thereof." But if the resignation be made *propriis manibus*, there is no procuratory or mandate; the vassal merely signs the instrument of resignation (*a*). When resignation is not *propriis manibus*, a procuratory of resignation is executed in presence of a notary (*b*), and an instrument of resignation *ad remanentiam* is extended and recorded. 'In 1858, the instrument of resignation *ad remanentiam* was made unnecessary, the procuratory, or the conveyance containing the clause of resignation *ad remanentiam*, being itself registered with a warrant of registration. The instrument, however, remained competent, and a new form was given, which might be registered at any time during the life of the person in whose favour it was expede (*c*). By the Conveyancing Act of 1874, however, it is provided that consolidation of superiority and mid-superiority or superiority and property may be effected by the proprietor of the two estates executing a minute in a specified form, which is recorded in the Register of Sasines, to the same effect as resignation *ad perpetuam remanentiam* (*d*). But no consolidation effected under the Act or otherwise can affect or extend the rights or interests of any over-superior (*e*).' The symbol is not, as in sasine, earth and stone, but staff and baton (*f*).

(*a*) 1555, c. 38. 1563, c. 81. 2 Stair, 11. § 3. 2 Ersk. 7. § 19 and 20. 2 Ross, 225. *Infra*, § 791.

(*b*) 2 Ersk. 7. § 19.

(*c*) 31 and 32 Vict. c. 101, § 18, re-enacting 21 and 22 Vict. c. 76, § 4.

(*d*) 37 and 38 Vict. c. 94, § 6. See above, § 775 sqq. *Infra*, § 821.

(*e*) *Ib.* § 7. It is thought that procuratories and instruments of resignation *ad remanentiam* are not "writs by progress" of a kind falling under the prohibition in § 4 (1) of the statute, and that they are therefore still competent.

(*f*) Act of Sed., Feb. 11, 1708. Carnegy *v.* Cruikshank's Crs., 1729; M. 14,316; 2 Ill. 48. E. Aberdeen *v.* Duncan,

1742; M. 14,316; Elch. *Sup. & Vass.* 7. Redfearn *v.* Maxwell, March 7, 1816; F. C.

788. Resignation *ad remanentiam* is to be distinguished from a renunciation. The vassal's estate is not a burden to be thrown off, but an estate of which the conveyance is completed by a ceremony strictly feudal, and equivalent to sasine (*a*).

(*a*) 3 Craig, 1. § 21. 2 Stair, 11. § 1–6. Kames' Eluc. art. 11. Landale *v.* Landale, 1752; M. 14,469; Elch. *Service*, No. 6; Elch. Notes, 424; 5 B. Sup. 794; 2 Ill. 48; 2 Ross' L. C. 253. Finlay *v.* Morgan, 1770; M. 14,480, 6904; 2 Ross' L. C. 265. See **E. Zetland** *v.* **Glover Incorp. of Perth**, 1870; 8 Macph. H. L. 144. **Sandeman** *v.* **Sc. Prop. Invt. Soc.**, 1883; 10 R. 614; revd. 12 R. H. L. 67; 10 App. Ca. 553.

789. In order to render the resignation effectual, it is necessary that, where the feudal grant by which the vassal's estate was created has been completed by infeftment, any one coming into the place of the vassal so infeft must himself be infeft before he can effectually resign for the purpose of reinvesting the superior. On the other hand, the superior must be infeft, in order to be capable of receiving an effectual resignation in his own favour (*a*). If there be an intermediate superiority, there can be no resignation *ad remanentiam* from the sub-vassal to the first or higher superior. Where the land is effectually resigned, and the vassal's estate consolidated with the superior's, it goes to the superior with all its burdens (*b*).

(*a*) See below, § 793.
(*b*) 2 Stair, 11. § 5, 6. 2 Ersk. 7. § 21. A real burden may be created by reservation in a disposition with resignation *ad remanentiam*. Wilson *v.* Fraser, 1822; 1 S. 316; aff. 1824, 2 S. App. 162. It is held that by resignation *ad remanentiam* the subaltern estate is extinguished and the lands held in future on the superiority titles, *e.g.* Barstow (Park's Cur.) *v.* Black, 1870, 8 Macph. 671, where a destination in the titles of the *dominium utile* was evacuated by the consolidation. Nevertheless, it was held that a right of fishing acquired by prescription by the vassal upon a feu-right "with fishings," the superior having no right to salmon-fishings, was not destroyed by consolidation, although, as the case is stated, the superior had no title to which it could be referred. E. Zetland *v.* Glover Incorp. of Perth, 1870; 8 Macph. H. L. 144. See Walker's Reps. and Trinity Hosp., *infra*, § 821 (*a*).

790. Formerly a procuratory of resignation, like a precept of sasine, was held, on the principle of mandate, to expire on the death of either party; but by the same statute which perpetuated the precept of sasine, procuratories of resignation also are declared to subsist after the death of the parties, and to the benefit of heirs or assignees, provided "that the instruments of resignation express the titles of those in whose favour the resignation is made, and that the same be deduced therein." (See above, § 766.)

'A procuratory of resignation does not fall by the divestiture of the granter, unless the disposition itself be extinguished by the prior infeftment of another disponee (*a*).'

(*a*) Cheyne *v.* Smith, 1832; 10 S. 622. See above, § 766 *fin.*

791. The ceremony of resignation 'in the ancient form' takes place before a notary and witnesses, in presence of the superior, or of his commissioners for receiving resignation; and an instrument of resignation is extended and signed by the notary and witnesses, and also by the vassal if the resignation be made *propriis manibus* (*a*). This instrument (which operates as a sasine consolidating the property and superiority) is recorded, and so the title is complete (*b*).

(*a*) 1555, c. 38. 1563, c. 81.
(*b*) 1669, c. 3. 2 Ersk. 7. § 20. See as to consolidation, below, § 821.

792. *Resignation in Favorem.*—This 'was' a provisional resignation by the vassal in the hands of the superior, on the condition and requisition that the superior 'should' grant a new charter to the person named. Such resignation, which the vassal might at all times have made with the consent of the superior, the superior 'was latterly (*a*)' bound to receive; and a singular successor in whose favour such resignation 'should' be made, 'might' demand an entry from the superior. The deed of conveyance in this case, as in a sale to the superior, 'was originally' accompanied by or 'contained' a procuratory for resigning in the hands of the superior; 'and since 1847 it contained in lieu of this a clause of resignation declared to be equivalent to it (*b*).' And the holder of such a deed 'was,' on the superior's refusal to give him an entry, entitled either to charge the superior within fifteen days to accept resignation and enter him as vassal, on the tender of a year's rent and arrears, and so to proceed as on an obligation *ad factum præstandum*; or, after 'the expiry of' such charge, he 'might' resort to the next superior, and so up to the Crown, which refuses no vassal (*c*).

(*a*) 20 Geo. II. c. 50, § 12.
(*b*) 10 and 11 Vict. c. 48, § 3. 21 and 22 Vict. c. 76,

§ 5. 31 and 32 Vict. c. 101, § 8; repealed by S. L. Rev. Act, 1893 (No. 1).

(*c*) 2 Ross, 240. 2 Ersk. 7. § 22, also 7.

793. Resignation, in order to be effectual, requires the concurrence of a vassal infeft, and so having the feudal right to be resigned, and of a superior also infeft, and so capable of receiving provisionally the feu. Without resignation, the feu continues with the vassal last infeft (*a*).

(*a*) 3 Craig, 1. § 14. 3 Stair, 2. § 8. 2 Ersk. 7. §. 18. Grieve *v.* Williamson, 1760; M. 3022; 2 Ross' L. C. 152; 2 Ill. 49. Landale, *supra*, § 788. See above, § 789; and cf. 1 Bell's Com. 719 (756, M'L.'s ed.). But if the superior at any time of his life completes a valid title to the superiority, it will by accretion validate a resignation and charter granted while he had not that title. Innes *v.* Gordon, 1844; 7 D. 141. Norton *v.* Anderson, July 6, 1813; F. C. Martin *v.* Wight, 1841; 3 D. 485. Mackenzie *v.* Mackenzie, 1838; 16 S. 1326. *Infra*, § 882.

794. The ceremony, 'before its abolition as regards Crown charters in 1847 (*a*), proceeded,' like that of resignation *ad remanentiam*, before a notary and witnesses. If the resignation 'was' to be made to the Sovereign as superior, one of the macers of Exchequer 'appeared' as procurator in presence of the Judge of Exchequer, and by the symbol of a pen 'resigned' the lands in his hands as commissioner of the Crown. If the resignation 'was' to be made in the hands of a subject superior, the procurator for the disponer 'made' the resignation by the symbol of staff and baton; then, changing hands and acting for the disponee, he 'received' back the symbol as attorney for the disponee, in token of the superior having accepted the condition and acceded to the new grant (*b*). On this ceremony an instrument 'was' sometimes extended in the case of a Crown holding, but not usually where the lands 'held' of a subject (*c*).

(*a*) 10 and 11 Vict. c. 51, § 17; repealed by 31 and 32 Vict. c. 101, § 4, Sch. A (1).

(*b*) 3 Craig, 1. § 17. 2 Ersk. 7. § 17 and 22. Act of Sed., Feb. 11, 1708. E. Aberdeen *v.* Duncan, 1742; M. 14,316; Elch. *Sup. & Vass.* 7; 2 Ill. 48.

(*c*) 1 Bell's Forms of Deeds, 215. Instruments of resignation *in favorem* were long disused, and were abolished by 8 and 9 Vict. c. 35, § 9. Renton *v.* Anstruther, 1848; 11 D. 37; 2 Ross' L. C. 146. Duff's Feudal Convg. 226.

795. There is a marked distinction between this form of resignation and resignation *ad remanentiam*. In resignation *ad remanentiam* the resignation is in itself the infeftment of the superior, and the instrument is full evidence of it, completing the investiture when duly recorded. In resignation *in favorem* the resignation 'was' only the surrender, empowering the superior to make a new grant; and this grant he 'made' by his charter, in which he 'recited' the surrender, the instrument of resignation not being extended except where the lands 'held' of the Crown.

796. The transmission by resignation *in favorem* 'was' completed by a charter from the superior (called, from the preceding ceremony, charter of resignation), bearing a precept for infeftment; by sasine taken on the precept; and by the recording of the sasine. The feudal estate 'was' thus vested in the new vassal, and thereby, 'but not sooner (*a*),' the sasine of the former vassal 'was' superseded, and he denuded of the fee.

(*a*) Purves *v.* Strachan, *infra*, § 802.

797. While the disposition and procuratory were separate deeds, the procuratory was necessary as the connecting link of the title. The inconvenience of this (formerly very important) was, to a certain extent, corrected by a statute which dispensed with the production of the procuratory after possession for forty years. This Act is of little consequence now, for the procuratory, 'long before the abolition of such deeds, was' invariably incorporated with the conveyance (*a*).

(*a*) 1594, c. 218. 2 Ersk. 7. § 25. 2 Stair, 3. § 19.

798. The procuratory 'might,' under the provisions of the statute, be executed, and the title completed, in favour of an heir or assignee of the purchaser, provided the title 'were' deduced in the 'instrument' (*a*). It 'was' necessary in the instrument of resignation to express the title of the heir or assignee, and deduce the same where a procuratory 'was' executed in favour of another than the person to whom it 'was' granted. This, in the case of a Crown holding, 'was' generally (though gradually falling into neglect) complied with by extending an instrument of resignation (*b*). In the case of a resignation in the hands of a subject superior, the Act 'was' held to be sufficiently complied with by expressing and deducing the title in a clause called the "quæquidem" of the charter. 'But it was decided that the omission of this deduction of titles in a charter of resignation did not involve its nullity, although no instrument of resignation was expede (*c*). The Infeftments Act, abolishing instruments of resignation, made it necessary to deduce the titles in the charter (*d*).'

(*a*) 1693, c. 35. *Supra*, § 766, 790.
(*b*) See above, § 794.
(*c*) Renton *v.* Anstruther, § 794.
(*d*) 8 and 9 Vict. c. 35, § 9.

799. The charter of resignation 'differed' from the original charter, as being the echo of the resignation (*a*); as proceeding on the consideration of the composition paid for an entry; and in having a clause of *quæquidem*, deducing the title as flowing by resignation from the person last infeft.

(*a*) See below, § 805.

800. Till resignation 'had' been made, the superior 'had' no power to grant a new charter otherwise than by confirmation of an infeftment (*a*) proceeding from the vassal infeft (*b*); 'but a charter of novodamus need not be preceded by resignation (*c*).'

(*a*) See below, § 806.
(*b*) Grieve *v.* Williamson, 1760; M. 3022; 2 Ill. 49; 2 Ross' L. C. 152.
(*c*) 50 and 51 Vict. c. 69, § 3.

801. If a superior 'had' accepted of a resignation *in favorem*, he 'was' personally bound to the disponee to grant him a charter when demanded; and this *jus quæsitum* 'bound' the superior to refuse a new resignee (*a*).

(*a*) 2 Ersk. 7. § 23.

802. The resigner 'was' not divested of the feudal estate till sasine 'was' taken on the charter of resignation. And yet the lands 'were' held as if in non-entry, the superior not being entitled to demand his feu-duties from a vassal from whom he 'had' accepted a resignation; nor from the disponee, who 'was' not yet entered (*a*).

(*a*) Dirleton, *voce* De Resignationibus, 6 and 7; Duobus investitis, etc., p. 170. Hope's Min. Pract. tit. 5. § 14, to be corrected by 3 Craig, 1. § 17, 18. Stewart's Answer to Dirleton. 3 Stair, 2. § 12. 2 Ersk. 7. § 23, 24. Bell, Conveyance of Land, 262. Arbuthnot *v.* Barclay, 1677; 3 B. Sup. 209; 2 Ill. 49. Purves *v.* Strachan, 1677; M. 6890; 3 B. Sup. 194; 2 Ross' L. C. 140. Cf. § 786, 788, 793, *supra*.

803. The resignee 'was' not invested till infeftment 'had' been taken, and so a simple renunciation before infeftment 'discharged' his right (*a*).

(*a*) 3 Stair, 2. § 12.

804. Resignation 'was till 1847' the only regular form of transmission recognised by statute, and the superior 'was' not bound to enter the heir in any other way (*a*).

(*a*) 20 Geo. II. c. 50, § 12. See above, § 775, 786, 792; below, § 806 (*a*).

805. As the superior, in entering a singular successor, 'acted' by compulsion of the statute, it 'was' *salvo jure* (*a*). 'And a charter by progress, whether by the Crown or a subject superior, being merely "the echo of the resignation" (*supra*, § 799), carried in general no higher or other right than it was competent to the resigner to convey (*b*), of which his original right was the measure.'

(*a*) See Heriot's Hosp. *v.* Carnegys, 1884; 12 R. 30.
(*b*) E. Perth *v.* d'Eresby Trs., 1875; 2 R. 538; aff. 1877, 5 R. H. L. 26; 3 App. Ca. 297; and cases in § 775A, note (*c*).

805A. 'New forms and new rules as to resignation *in favorem* were latterly established, and though now superseded by the Act of 1874 (*a*), require still to be kept in mind.

'(1.) *Where lands are held of the Crown or Prince.*—The party in right of the deed which was the warrant for resignation, might apply to the Presenter of Signatures either for a charter of resignation, or, instead of a charter, for a writ of resignation to be engrossed on the deed, both in statutory forms. Such writ of resignation being recorded with the deed and a warrant of registration, had the same effect as a charter of resignation followed by sasine duly recorded. To prevent the creation of a mid-superiority, it is provided that such recording is not to have the effect of an instrument of sasine following on the deed (*b*).

'(2.) *Where lands are held of a Subject Superior*, and a new investiture by resignation was required, the superior granted, in favour of the party in right of the deed which was the warrant for resignation, either a charter of resignation, or a writ of resignation engrossed on such deed, in statutory forms. The deed with writ of resignation written thereon is as effectual as if a charter of resignation had been granted: and the superior was bound if required to grant a charter or writ in the statutory form instead of a charter in the old form. The party requiring such writ or charter must be entitled to demand an entry by resignation, and, if required, produce to the superior a charter or other writ showing the *tenendas* and *reddendo* of the lands resigned; and he must also pay or tender such duties or casualties as the superior was entitled to demand. It was competent to record in the appropriate register of sasines, with a warrant of registration, either the deed bearing the writ of resignation, or the charter of resignation, or a notarial instrument expede on the charter; and the recording of any of these had the same effect in all respects as if a charter of resignation had been granted, and had been followed by an instrument of sasine, duly recorded according to the former practice, in favour of the party on whose behalf the deed and writ, or charter, or instrument was presented for registration. But the recording of the deed along with such writ has not the effect of an instrument of sasine following on the deed (*c*). Every charter or writ, whether from the Crown or a subject superior, operates as a confirmation of the whole prior deeds necessary to be confirmed in order to complete the investiture of the party obtaining such writ or charter (*d*).'

(*a*) See § 775.
(*b*) 31 and 32 Vict. c. 101, § 81, repealed by S. L. Rev. Act, 1893 (No. 1); 21 and 22 Vict. c. 76, § 8. See 10 and 11 Vict. c. 51, § 24.
(*c*) *Ib.* § 99; amending 21 and 22 Vict. c. 76, § 9, and 23 and 24 Vict. c. 143, § 33, and repealed by S. L. Rev. Act, 1893 (No. 1).
(*d*) *Ib.* § 115; amending various prior enactments.

806. *Confirmation.*—Resignation (as already explained) 'was' the regular way of placing the purchaser in the room of the seller, and vesting him with the full estate which the seller holds under the superior. There 'was' another mode of accomplishing the same end, but it 'required till 1847' the spontaneous act of the superior to confirm and make it effectual (*a*). It 'consisted' of two parts,—a conveyance, containing a precept of sasine proceeding from the seller himself, and requiring infeftment to be given to the disponee, to be held of the disponer's superior. But as the disponer 'had' no power to authorise such a sasine, it 'was' necessary that it be confirmed by the charter of the superior, reciting the conveyance or disposition by the vassal, with the sasine following on it, and ratifying, approving, and confirming them (*b*). This is called entry by confirmation (*c*).

(*a*) Power was given to compel him to do so. 31 and 32 Vict. c. 101, § 97; repeating 10 and 11 Vict. c. 48, § 6, as altered by 21 and 22 Vict. c. 76, § 7; now repealed by S. L. Rev. Act, 1875. But such charters cannot now be given at all. See above, § 775.
(*b*) In England, as explained already (§ 675 (*b*)), the conveyance by the vassal is in itself sufficient, without express confirmation, to invest the grantee as vassal of the Crown; 18 Edw. I. c. 1, Quia Emptores, etc. Whether such a rule may not now be safely introduced in Scotland, deserves to be considered; but it is a mistake to imagine that such a law ever was enacted in Scotland,—an express confirmation having always been required to complete the disponee's title as a fee held of the granter's superior. See Kames's Statute Law, note 18. 2 Ross, 258. Bell, Conveyance of Land, 281. Lord Stair's proposal, 2 Stair, 4. § 6.
(*c*) See below, the alternative mode of entry, § 818.

807. The vassal's conveyance of his feu, with a precept of sasine to be held from him of his superior (*a me de superiore meo*), 'was' effectual to confer a good title of possession in regard to tenants, so as to entitle the purchaser to draw the rents; but it 'was' null and ineffectual, in so far as respects the superior and the feudal right, until confirmed by the superior's charter. Till then the disponer 'was' still undivested; his death before confirmation 'opened' the casualty of non-entry; his creditors 'might' attach the estate; and the disponee 'had' no more than a right transmissible by general service, although the superior 'might' confirm after the disponee's death (*a*).

(*a*) The Queen *v.* Cranston, 1566; M. 3007; 2 Ill. 50. L. Balmernoch *v.* Coutfield, 1620; M. 3007. Douglas *v.* Somerville, 1713; M. 3008. Rowand *v.* Campbell, 1824; 3 S. 196; see 5 S. 903; 1830, 4 W. & S. 177; 1 Ill. 128. Struthers *v.* Lang, 1826; 4 S. 418; aff. 1827, 2 W. & S. 563.

808. No effective base infeftment 'could' follow upon a precept authorising sasine, to be held of the superior. The superior's sanction and confirmation 'was' essentially necessary to give such a sasine any feudal effect. And the complete title 'required' the vassal's conveyance; sasine proceeding on it, duly recorded; and the superior's charter of confirmation (*a*).

(*a*) See below, cases in § 810 (*a*).

809. The charter of confirmation refers by name and description to the deed and sasine confirmed; expressly ratifies, approves, and perpetually confirms them; and decerns and ordains that this confirmation shall be as valid and effectual as if they were *verbatim* recited, or as if the confirmation had been made and granted before the taking of the infeftment (*a*). The sasine confirmed is identified by the date, but not by this exclusively; other features in the description may serve the purpose as well (*b*). And confirmation generally of all deeds granted by such a person, of lands described or enumerated, is good (*c*).

(*a*) 1 Jurid. Styles, 69 (4th ed. 412). 1 Bell's Forms of Deeds, 193 et seq. In practice the sasine always precedes the confirmation; and notwithstanding the above words of confirmation, it has been doubted whether it would be a good title if the confirmation were prior to the date of the sasine. Adam, *infra* (*b*). See M. Bell's Convg. 731 sqq.
(*b*) Adam *v.* Drummond, June 12, 1810; F. C.; 2 Ill. 50.
(*c*) Drummond *v.* Drummond, 1793; M. 6936.

809A. 'It has been already stated that by the Titles to Land Consolidation Act, a writ of *clare constat* or a writ of resignation operates as a confirmation (*a*). The Act further provided that, in place of a charter, a writ of confirmation might be written on the deed to be confirmed, in a prescribed form, both as to Crown and other holdings. The superior was bound to grant an entry by confirmation under the usual condition (*b*).'

(*a*) See *ante*, § 778A, and § 805A (1).
(*b*) 10 and 11 Vict. c. 48, § 6, 7; 21 and 22 Vict. c. 76, § 7; substantially re-enacted and improved by 31 and 32 Vict. c. 101, § 82, 97 to 100, 114, 115, 116: see S. L. Rev. Act, 1893 (No. 1). 32 and 33 Vict. c. 116, § 5; but see S. L. Rev. Act, 1893 (No. 2), and § 775.

810. The first confirmed infeftment is the first effectual, though the sasine should be last in date or last recorded (*a*). And the confirmation is held, in the case of a Crown charter, to be of the date of passing the seals (*b*): in the case of a subject superior's charter, it has been held to be of the date of delivery, not of subscribing (*c*). The date which the charter bears will, however, be held the true date, unless in particular circumstances of the withholding of delivery.

(*a*) 1578, c. 66. 2 Ersk. 7. § 14. Hope's Min. Pract. tit. 5. § 1 and 3. Polmaise *v.* Tenant, 1580; M. 3026; 2 Ill. 51. Henderson *v.* Campbell, 1821; 1 S. 103. See cases in § 820, *infra*, and Gardner, *infra*, § 813.
(*b*) Miln *v.* Powfowlis, 1678; M. 3028. Clackmannan *v.* E. Wigtown, 1680; M. 3029. Cardross *v.* Dalzell, 1682; M. 3030. Cockburn's Crs. *v.* Sinclair, 1691; 2 B. Sup. 128. The date of signing or sealing (which last was in 1858 dispensed with, unless required by the receiver) is the date of a Crown charter. 31 and 32 Vict. c. 101, § 78; amending and repeating 10 and 11 Vict. c. 51, § 15, and 21 and 22 Vict. c. 76, § 32.
(*c*) Dalziel *v.* E. Mar, 1685; 2 B. Sup. 81. "This," says Harcarse, "seems not very well founded"; 2 Ill. 52.

811. The confirmation of a sasine to be held *a se* operates *retro*, giving the same effect to the sasine as if confirmed of its date, or as if it had proceeded on the superior's own precept (*a*).

(*a*) 2 Stair, 3. § 28. 2 Ersk. 7. § 15. Bp. of Aberdeen *v.* V. Kenmure, 1680; M. 3011; 2 Ill. 52. Lockhart *v.* Ferrier, 1837; 16 S. 76; 3 Ill. 153; 2 Ross' L. C. 129; *supra*, § 778.

812. But the operation of the confirmation *retro* is stopped or barred by the existence of any real right adverse to the grantee's. So a base right or feu granted by the vassal, and completed by sasine, will bar the confirmation as a completion of the conveyance of the *dominium utile*, leaving to it the effect of carrying the superiority (*a*).

(*a*) M'Kenzie *v.* Ross & Ogilvie, 1791; M. 275; 2 Ill. 52. Hope's Min. Pract. *ut supra*, § 810 (*a*). 1 Bell's Com. 682 (722, M'L.'s ed.). D. Argyll *v.* Dalgleish's Trs., 1873; 11 Macph. 616. Gardner, *infra*, § 813.

813. Confirmation 'might' take place at any time, if there 'were' no impediment; and it is important to observe that it 'was' as valid after the death of the disponer, or of the disponee, as during their lives (*a*); and that this applies to a sasine on a precept of *clare constat* 'granted by a mid-superior unentered,' if taken during the life of the parties (*b*). 'The sasine of the disponer's heir upon a precept of *clare constat* is not an impediment to the confirmation of the disponee's infeftment (*c*). But if the disponer grant a second conveyance to a stranger who is first entered with the superior, that entry is an impediment to the original disponee's confirmation, a mid-superiority being constituted in the *bonâ fide* third party, which at least becomes indefeasible by prescriptive possession (*d*).'

(*a*) Johnston *v.* E. Queensberry, 1634; M. 3020; 2 Ill. 52. M'Dowall *v.* Hamilton, 1793; M. 8807; 2 Ross' L. C. 127.
(*b*) Lockhart, *supra*, § 811. The precept is now effectual during the life of the grantee. See above, § 778.
(*c*) Fullarton *v.* Hamilton, 1833; 12 S. 117. See above, § 709.
(*d*) **Gardner** *v.* **Scott**, 1839; 2 D. 185; rev. 1843, 2 Bell's App. 129; *supra*, § 810.

814. The confirmation adopts the title such as it is (*a*).

(*a*) Adam *v.* Drummond, June 12, 1810; F. C.; 2 Ill. 50. Bell, Election Law, 242. Bell's Conveyance of Land, 288, note. Kibble *v.* Stewart, June 16, 1814; F. C.; 2 Ill. 52.

815. Confirmation 'was' not the regular form of transmission to singular successors, but it has been found both effectual as such, and a legitimate mode of altering the destination of the investiture, without any resignation (*a*). The charter of confirmation 'was' sometimes (though not by good conveyancers) combined with the charter of resignation, for the purpose of being used alternatively. If sasine be taken on the precept, and resignation made on the procuratory in the same disposition, and one title be completed by charter of resignation and sasine, another by a clause of confirmation of the sasine already taken, it has been held that they are not inconsistent; that the disponee may use either as his title; and that the existence of the one does not annul the other (*b*).

(*a*) Gibson-Craig *v.* Cochran, 1838; 16 S. 1332; aff. 1841, 2 Rob. 446. See below, § 822.

(*b*) Campbell *v.* Haldane, 1754; 5 B. Sup. 809; Elchies, *Memb. of Parl.* 61, and Notes, 282; 2 Ill. 52. Stewart *v.* E. Fife, 1827; 5 S. 383. See 2 Ross' L. C. 157 sqq. Menzies' Convg. 811. M. Bell's Convg. 743. Below, § 822.

816. *Subinfeudation.*—When the feudal proprietor of land disposes only of the *dominium utile* of the whole or of part of his estate (as in feuing it out for building, or in selling the estate, with reservation of the mid-superiority), he creates a sub-vassalage, or base fee, to be held of himself; the principles of which operation have already been explained in treating of the original charter (*a*).

(*a*) See above, § 756 et seq.

817. As, under a conveyance of the whole estate with a restricted precept of sasine to hold *a me de superiore meo*, no effectual base sasine can be taken; so, under a conveyance of the *dominium utile* with a precept *de me*, no sasine can be taken which can either constitute a public right holding of the seller's superior, or even become the subject of confirmation to that effect (*a*).

(*a*) See § 808, 820.

818. *Alternative Holding.*—The old contract of alienation of land was accompanied by, or contained, three mandates for completing the right: a procuratory for resigning *in favorem*; a precept of sasine, to be held of the superior, *a me de superiore meo*; and a precept of sasine, *de me*, to be held of the disponer himself (*a*). The modern disposition, 'prior to the alterations introduced in 1858 and 1868, combined' these. It 'contained,' besides the dispositive clause, an obligation to infeft the disponee, either to be held of the disponer's superior, or to be held of the disponer himself; and for that purpose there 'were' a procuratory of resignation, and a precept of sasine, which, to serve the purpose of the two precepts of sasine formerly used, 'was' conceived in terms *indefinite*, and equally applicable to a public and to a base right (*b*). 'These clauses are now abolished or in disuse, and the implied entry under the Conveyancing Act of 1874 has made the "double manner of holding" impossible and unnecessary (*c*).'

(*a*) 1540, c. 105. 1693, c. 13 and 35. Hope's Min. Pract. Spottiswood's Notes, 217.

(*b*) 2 Ersk. 7. § 16. Bp. of Aberdeen *v.* V. Kenmure, 1680; M. 3011; 2 Ill. 52; 2 Ross' L. C. 1. Bell's Conveyance of Land, 250 et seq. M. Bell's Convg. 683.

(*c*) 31 and 32 Vict. c. 101, § 5, etc., repeating previous enactments. 37 and 38 Vict. c. 94, § 4.

819. The effect of sasine taken on this indefinite precept 'was' to complete at once a base right, or perfect feudal estate of *dominium utile*; and to be convertible by the superior's confirmation into a sasine for a public holding, so as to place the disponee exactly in the place of the disponer, provided there 'were' no mid-impediment (*a*).

(*a*) 2 Ross' L. C. 1 sqq. See above, § 812, 813.

820. The true criterion by which to determine whether a precept conceived in terms indefinite or ambiguous is public or base, is found in the obligation to infeft. If it be an obligation to infeft by two manners of holding, one to be held *de me*, the other *a me de superiore meo*, the precept is alternative. If it be only to be held *a me de superiore meo*, it is a *public* precept, and no sasine can proceed upon it that will be effectual without confirmation. If it be to hold *de me*, the precept is *base*, and cannot be confirmed to the effect of creating a public holding. Sasine under a definite precept can give no tenure but of the specific kind expressed (*a*).

(*a*) Bellenden *v.* Ker's Trs., 1823; 2 S. 329; aff. 1825, 1 W. & S. 381; 2 Ill. 53; 2 Ross' L. C. 2. Rowand *v.* Campbell 1824; 3 S. 196; 1 Ill. 128. Peebles *v.* Watson, 1825; 4 S. 290. M'Nair *v.* M'Nair, 1827; 5 S. 372. Struthers *v.* Lang, 1826; 4 S. 418; aff. 1827, 2 W. & S. 563. Rowand *v.* Stevenson, 1827; 5 S. 903; aff. 4 W. & S. 177. See § 877.

820A. 'It is not necessary or usual to insert in any conveyance a clause of obligation to infeft or a precept of sasine (*a*). A clause expressing the manner of holding was introduced into modern dispositions in a form provided by statute, viz.: "To be holden the said lands and others *a me*," or "*a me vel de me*," as the case may be. The meaning of this clause, which is now ineffectual, was declared to be:—1. If the lands are to be holden *a me*, that they are to be holden from the grantor of and under his immediate lawful superiors, as the grantor or his predecessors held or might have holden, and that the title of the disponee may be completed either by resignation or confirmation, or both, the one without prejudice of the other. 2. If the lands be disponed to be holden *a me vel de me*, that they are either to be holden of the grantor in free blench, for payment of a penny Scots yearly if asked only, and freeing and relieving the grantor of all feu-duties and other duties and services exigible out of the lands by his immediate superiors; or to be holden from the grantor of and under his immediate superiors in the same manner as the grantor or his predecessors held, or might have holden, and that the title of the disponee may be completed either by resignation or confirmation, or both, the one without prejudice of the other. 3. Where no manner of holding is expressed, the conveyance implies that the lands are to be holden in the same manner as if there were a clause expressing the holding to be *a me vel de me*, where the titles contain no prohibition of subinfeudation or against an alternative holding, and *a me* where the titles contain such prohibition (*b*).'

(*a*) 31 and 32 Vict. c. 101, § 5; re-enacting 21 and 22 Vict. c. 76, § 5.

(*b*) *Ib.* § 6. See *ib.* § 147; re-enacting 21 and 22 Vict. c. 76, § 28. See 10 and 11 Vict. c. 48, § 1, 2, Sch. A, and 23 and 24 Vict. c. 143, § 36. Colquhoun *v.* Walker, 1867; 5 Macph. 773 (an alternative holding does not contravene a prohibition against sub-feuing). As to sub-feuing, see below, § 866.

821. *Consolidation.*—The two estates of superiority and vassalage are sometimes vested separately in the same person. It was long contended that the absurdity of a man being his own vassal necessarily inferred *ipso jure* a consolidation of estates thus circumstanced. But this subtilty has been fully refuted, and there is an end to all those doubts and questions. Consolidation of the two estates separately vested can be directly accomplished only by resignation *ad remanentiam* in the proprietor's hands, as his own superior (*a*), 'or by the statutory equivalent of resignation (*b*).' But if, on a title to the superiority (which correctly is constituted by sasine in the lands), there has been possession for forty years, it has been held to work off the base infeftment in the property, and so to consolidate the two estates; a most important qualification of the general doctrine (*c*). 'The extinction of the base right by prescriptive possession unequivocally referable to the superiority title, has the effect of overcoming the general presumption in favour of the more beneficial title, and bringing the property by consolidation under the fetters of an entail affecting the superiority (*d*).'

(*a*) See above, § 787. 2 Ersk. 7. § 19, and 3. 8. § 81. Bell, Conveyance of Land, 319, 335. B. Supplicant, 1634; M. 6917; 2 Ill. 54. Elies, Supplicant, 1687; M. 3086. Morton's Daughters, 1668; M. 6917. Porteous *v.* Bell, 1757; 5 B. Sup. 855. Campbell *v.* Wilson, 1765; 5 B. Sup. 915. L. Elibank *v.* Purves, 1833; 12 S. 74; 2 Ill. 17; 3 Ross' L. C. 534. **Bald** *v.* **Buchanan**, 1786; M. 15,084; 2 Ill. 54; 2 Ross' L. C. 210. See as to the effect of the consolidation, Walker's Reps. *v.* Heriot's Hosp., 1839, 1 D. 1132, compared with Trinity Hospital *v.* Nisbett's Trs., 1851; 13 D. 1161. **Barstow (Park's Curator)** *v.* **Black**, 1870; 8 Macph. 671. **E. Zetland** *v.* **Glover Incorpn. of Perth**, 1870; 8 Macph. H. L. 144.

(*b*) Consolidation is now effected by merely recording a minute. 37 and 38 Vict. c. 94, § 6.

(*c*) Bruce *v.* Bruce Carstairs, 1770; M. 10,805; Hailes, 378; aff. 1772, 2 Pat. 258; 2 Ill. 17. Walker *v.* Grieve, 1827; 5 S. 469. See above, § 689; and below, § 2009, 2017, 2019.

(*d*) L. Elibank, *supra* (*a*). See E. Glasgow *v.* Boyle, 1887; 14 R. 419. Bontine *v.* Graham, 1837; 15 S. 711; aff. 1840, 1 Rob. App. 347. Wilson *v.* Pollok, 1839; 2 D. 159. See below, § 2020.

822. *Combination of Resignation and Confirmation.*—In the making up of the titles to land, either where sasine 'was' taken on the indefinite precept, and it 'was' desirable to have an entry by resignation, and at the same time to avoid the circuitous operation of consolidating the property and superiority by resignation *ad remanentiam*, or where one 'wished' to have alternatively a title both by confirmation and by resignation, it 'was' the practice to take a charter of resignation with a clause of confirmation. The intention of this 'was' to make the disponer (hitherto base infeft) hold public by the confirmation, and so to render his procuratory valid and the charter of resignation following on it effectual to carry the whole estate, property, and mid-superiority; or to give the benefit, such as it is, of a double title,—one by confirmation, and another by resignation; which being constituted, the one without prejudice of the other, have been found not inconsistent with each other (*a*).

(*a*) See above, § 815, and the cases there cited. § 820A.

823. (B) **Transmission to Creditors** (*a*).—The estate of the debtor may be transferred to creditors,—1. By adjudication for debt; 2. By judicial sale; 3. By adjudication on a trust bond; 4. By adjudication in implement; 'and 5. By forfeiture of the reserved right of redemption (*b*).'

Adjudication for Debt.—By statute, a creditor is empowered to proceed to adjudge his debtor's estate in satisfaction of his debt; and in virtue of the decree of adjudication to demand, 'under the law as it existed before 1874,' a charter of adjudication from the superior, on which he 'might' be infeft (*c*). At first the superior had his choice to take the land to himself, paying the debt; or to enter the creditor as vassal, provided he should tender a year's rent of the land. But 'afterwards' the superior must enter the adjudger, *periculo petentis* and *salvo jure*, on payment of a year's rent; and if he himself 'were' the debtor, he 'was' bound to enter the adjudger without a composition (*d*).

(*a*) The view here to be given of adjudication is intended merely to explain the nature of a feudal title by charter of adjudication and sasine, in the person of an individual creditor. The particular forms and varieties of adjudication, with the regulations relative to *pari passu* preference, will demand attention hereafter. See below, § 2299 et seq. M. Bell's Convg. 1190.
(*b*) *Infra*, § 914 (8).
(*c*) 2 Ersk. Pr. 12. § 1, 2, 6, 7, 13–19. 2 Ersk. 12. § 39–46. 1 Bell's Com. 701 et seq.
(*d*) 1469, c. 37. 1669, c. 18. 1672, c. 19. 1681, c. 17. 1690, c. 20.

824. (1.) *Decree* (*a*).—The creditor's right is constituted by an action and decree called Adjudication. It is either "Special," 'now obsolete,' in which the debtor appears and consents to the adjudication of a certain portion in value equal to the debt, and a fifth part more (*b*); or "General," of the whole estate, in which last case the decree pronounced by the Court adjudges from the defender, and decerns and adjudges to belong and pertain to the creditor, for payment and satisfaction to him of the debt, annual-rents, etc., accumulated into one principal sum, the specific lands described, with "all right, title, and interest whatever of and concerning the same competent to the said debtor, with all charters, dispositions," etc. This is intended to comprehend all possible rights belonging to the debtor. The decree concludes with a decerniture against the superior to enter the creditor as vassal (*c*). 'The confirmation of the trustee on a sequestrated estate operates as a decree of adjudication from the date of the sequestration (*d*).'

(*a*) See below, § 2300. And for the recent alterations on adjudications, see below, § 825A and 828A.
(*b*) The special adjudication was virtually abolished by 10 and 11 Vict. c. 48, § 18; and by c. 49, § 10, as to burgage subjects, and is now in disuse. 31 and 32 Vict. c. 101, § 59.
(*c*) Norvall *v.* Blair, 1782; M. 94; 2 Ill. 55. Lesly *v.* Irvine, 1692; 1 Fount. 538, 543. Peadie, Petr., 1776; M. *Process*, Apx. 2. Graham *v.* Hunter, 1828; 7 S. 13. 1 Bell's Com. 719.
(*d*) 19 and 20 Vict. c. 79, § 102 (2).

825. Adjudication may proceed against a debtor, proprietor of heritage, 'or of any right in its nature heritable (*a*),' for his own 'liquid (*b*)' debt (*c*): or against the heir of a deceased heritable proprietor, held to represent him on taking benefit of his estate; or required, 'formerly' by charges to enter heir, 'afterwards by the service of an action of constitution (*d*),' to make his election whether to enter under the condition of so far representing his ancestor, or to abandon the estate to the adjudger; in which last case adjudication is competent against the estate itself so abandoned (*e*): or against the debtor succeeding to an estate, and required by a charge to make up his titles to it, so as to open it to the diligence of the charger (*f*).

(*a*) Smith *v.* Frier, 1857; 19 D. 384. Royal Bank *v.* Fairholm, 1770; M. Apx. *Adjud.* 3. Learmonts *v.* Shearer, 1866; 4 Macph. 540. Glover's Trs. *v.* City of Glas. Union Ry. Co., 1869; 7 Macph. 338 (railway—superfluous lands).
(*b*) 2 Ersk. 12. § 9. 1 Bell's Com. 739 (775, M'L.'s ed.).
(*c*) 2 Ersk. Pr. 12. § 1, 4, and 15. 2 Ersk. 12. § 6, 39, 40.
(*d*) See below, § 1854–8A. 31 and 32 Vict. c. 101, § 60.
(*e*) 1540, c. 106. 1621, c. 27. 2 Ersk. Pr. 12. § 5. 2 Ersk. 12. § 47 et seq. 1 Bell's Com. 711.
(*f*) Ersk. *loc. cit.* 1621, c. 27.

825A. 'Formerly the proceedings against an heir were complicated and tedious, particularly as to charges. These were simplified by the Lands Transference Act of 1847 (10 and 11 Vict. c. 48, § 16, 17). And since the Titles Acts of 1858 and 1860 (*a*) it is provided that, in actions of constitution and adjudication against an unentered heir on account of his ancestor's debt or obligation, for the purpose of attaching the ancestor's heritable estate, it is unnecessary to raise a separate summons of constitution and a separate summons of adjudication. Both actions may be combined in one summons, whether the heir renounce the succession or not. Such actions, and actions of adjudication against him for his own debt or obligation, in order to attach his ancestor's estate, may be insisted in after the lapse of six months from the date of his becoming apparent heir (*b*). In all cases of adjudication, except where the subjects are heritable securities, a decree is equivalent to a conveyance from the ancestor, owner, or seller of the lands, though *incapax*, in favour of the adjudger, who was before 1874 entitled to charge the superior to grant an entry by confirmation, and may now complete his title by registration of the decree, or of a notarial instrument thereon (*c*).'

(*a*) Re-enacted by 31 and 32 Vict. c. 101, § 60.
(*b*) *Ib.* § 61. See 37 and 38 Vict. c. 94, § 9.
(*c*) 37 and 38 Vict. c. 94, § 62 ; partly repealed by S. L. Rev. Act, 1892 (No. 2). 31 and 32 Vict. c. 101, § 15.

826. (2.) *Abbreviate.*—After the decree is pronounced, an abridgment or "abbreviate" is made out and signed by the extractor, and recorded in a register called the Register of Abbreviates of Adjudication, 'which is now united with the Register of Inhibitions (*a*),' within sixty days of the date of the decree. If the time of recording have expired, a new term is granted, reserving all objections (*b*).

(*a*) 31 and 32 Vict. c. 64, § 17.
(*b*) 2 Ersk. 12. § 43. 1661, c. 31. Reg. 1695, art. 24. 1 and 2 Geo. IV. c. 38, § 18. Seton *v.* Glass, 1750 ; 5 B. Sup. 239 ; 2 Ill. 56. Sibbald, Petr., 1764 ; *ib.* 373. Smellome, 1774 ; M. 206 ; 5 B. Sup. 273. See below, § 2300 (4). Bruce, Petr., 1828 ; 6 S. 620. Cathcart *v.* Maclaine, 1846 ; 9 D. 305. Key, Petr., 1855 ; 17 D. 681. Martin, Petr., 1857 ; 20 D. 55.

827. (3.) *Charter and Sasine.*—To the completion of the decree of adjudication as a feudal right, there 'were' required, a charter of adjudication from the superior (which is granted in obedience to and in terms of the decree), and a sasine thereon duly recorded. The decree of adjudication is also a judicial assignation, by virtue of which sasine or resignation 'might' proceed on a precept or procuratory unexecuted (*a*).

(*a*) Pierce *v.* Limond, 1791 ; M. 244 ; 2 Ill. 56 ; 2 Ross' L. C. 464.

828. The charter of adjudication, and sasine thereon duly recorded, complete the feudal right of the creditor. But it must be observed, that although in the decree of adjudication general words are used to carry "all right and interest," and these may be effectual in vesting a personal right to rents, etc., and in carrying a right to an unexecuted precept of sasine, the description of the subject must in the charter of adjudication and sasine, 'or in the recorded decree or notarial instrument,' be precise, in order to complete the feudal right (*a*).

(*a*) Graham *v.* Hunter, 1828 ; 7 S. 13 ; 2 Ill. 56.

828A. 'In 1847, it was made competent, where the debtor was infeft in the lands adjudged, to grant a warrant in the decree to infeft the pursuer (*a*). Under the later law, the decree or a charter of adjudication, or a notarial instrument on the decree or charter, may be recorded in the register of sasines, to the effect of operating infeftment (*b*). Where the subjects adjudged are heritable securities, the adjudger, on recording the abbreviate of adjudication or an extract decree in the appropriate register of sasines, is in the same position as if an assignation of such securities had been granted to him by the ancestor or person or creditor, in trust or otherwise, whose estate is adjudged, and as if such assignation had been recorded in the register of sasines at the date of recording the abbreviate or extract decree (*c*).'

(*a*) 10 and 11 Vict. c. 48, § 19.
(*b*) 37 and 38 Vict. c. 94, § 62. 31 and 32 Vict. c. 101, § 15.
(*c*) 37 and 38 Vict. c. 94, § 65.

829. (4.) *Redemption and Legal.* — The transmission accomplished by adjudication, and charter and sasine 'or infeftment in the modern form,' has not at once the effect of a sale of the vassal's estate to the creditor: It is a right redeemable at first ; a mere security, or *pignus prætorium.* It may be extinguished by payment or intromission with the rents (*a*). It has not the effect of an absolute conveyance either to give the adjudging creditor of the superior a right to enter vassals, or to bar a charter of confirmation of an existing base right (*b*). It is to be held as transferring the land in satisfaction of the debt only after the lapse of a certain period allowed to the debtor for redeeming his estate, and with a declarator. This period for redemption is 'ten years, and is' called the "Legal"; and at any time during the legal, the debtor, 'but the debtor only, and therefore not one who is merely a debtor to him (*c*),' on paying the debt, or showing it to be paid by intromission with the rents, is entitled to have his estate restored (*d*).

(*a*) E. Dalhousie *v.* L. Hawley, 1713; M. 9992; 2 Ill. 56.

(*b*) M'Kenzie *v.* Ross & Ogilvie, 1791; M. 275. See below, § 2302. Grindlay *v.* Drysdale, 1833; 11 S. 896; and see the cases in next section, and authorities in 1 Ross' L. C. 133, 146 sqq.

(*c*) Macleod's Trs. *v.* Murray, 1891; 18 R. 830 (debtor in bond of annuity—*jus tertii*).

(*d*) See on this section, the cases in § 830–1. **Cochrane** *v.* **Bogle**, 1849; 11 D. 908; aff. 1850, 7 Bell's App. 65. It seems that the right of redemption may be exercised by an heir when served, although he has previously renounced. **Stewart** *v.* **Lindsay**, Dec. 7, 1809; F. C.; 1 Ross' L. C. 304; and authorities, *ib.* p. 306 sqq.

830. On the expiration of the term of redemption, the right to redeem may be foreclosed, either by an action brought for declaring the power expired, or by prescription. The former is the "Declarator of Expiry of the Legal"; on the pronouncing and extracting of which, the creditor's right under his charter of adjudication and sasine 'or other infeftment' becomes absolute (*a*).

(*a*) **Campbell** *v.* **Scotland**, 1794; M. 321; Bell's Cases, 8vo, p. 15; fol. p. 109; 2 Ill. 57; 1 Ross' L. C. 155. Ormiston *v.* Hill, Feb. 7, 1809; F. C. **Stewart** *v.* **Lindsay**, Nov. 26, 1811; 1 Bell's Com. 705 (744, M'L.'s ed.); 1 Ross' L. C. 164. As to the grounds on which a decree of declarator of expiry of the legal obtained in absence may be opened up, see Landale *v.* Carmichael, 1794; M. 305; Bell's Ca. 109; 1 Ross' L. C. 174; 1 Bell's Com. 705, 737 (743, 773, M'L.'s ed.). Paul, *infra*, § 2016, 2017 *init.* Grieve (or Dingwall) *v.* Burns, 1871; 9 Macph. 582.

831. (5.) *Prescription.* — The same absolute right is produced 'by possession (*a*)' if forty years (*b*) have been allowed to elapse, 'not' after sasine has been taken on the adjudication, without redemption, 'but, as the decisions show, and as Professor Bell has said in other passages (*c*), after the expiry of the legal.' It thus operates *retro,* so as even to make effectual an entail executed by the adjudger before declarator or prescription (*d*).

(*a*) Anderson *v.* Nasmyth, 1758; M. 10,676; 1 Ross' L. C. 152. Home *v.* Crs. of Eyemouth, 1740; Elch. *Adjud.* 23.

(*b*) The shortening of the period of prescription by the Conveyancing Act of 1874 does not extend to this case. *Infra*, § 2012.

(*c*) See 1 Bell's Com. 705 sqq. (744, M'L.'s ed.); *infra*, § 2012, 2302.

(*d*) Johnston *v.* Balfour, 1745; M. 10,789; Elch. *Prescr.* 26; 2 Ill. 58. Spence *v.* Bruce, Jan. 21, 1807; 1 Bell's Com. 706 n. (745, M'L.'s ed.); 1 Ross' L. C. 206. Dalyell *v.* Dalyell, Jan. 17, 1810; F. C. Robertson *v.* D. Athol, 1808; Hume, 463; 1815, 3 Dow, 108; 1 Ross' L. C. 208; 1 Bell's Com. 706, 707. Cochrane *v.* Bogle, *cit.* § 829 (*d*). Ged *v.* Baker, 1740; M. 10,789; Elch. *Adjud.* 28; *Prescr.* 22; 1 Ross' L. C. 200. M'Lellan *v.* Cutler, 1762; 5 B. S. 893. **Caitcheon** *v.* **Ramsay**, 1791; M. 10,810; 3 Ross' L. C. 434. Ormiston, *cit.* § 830.

832. *Adjudication in Security.*—An adjudication is competent not only for satisfaction of debts actually due, but 'also, when the debtor is *vergens ad inopiam*,' on debts not yet due, or even on contingent debts in certain circumstances; '*e.g.* if the debtor's estate is likely to be attached by the diligence of other creditors before the arrival of the term, or the bond be payable on the granter's death, or for relief of a cautioner.' But such adjudication is in security only. It never can, by declarator or otherwise, be converted (like the ordinary adjudication for debt) into an absolute right of property: but it confers the right of ranking on the estate, and entitles the creditor to payment of a dividend on bankruptcy, or to consignment of the dividend if the debt be contingent (*a*).

(*a*) 2 Ersk. 12. § 42. Nisbet *v.* Stirling, 1759; M. 59. Dunlop's Crs. *v.* Brown & Collinson, 1781; M. 62. M'Neil's Crs. *v.* Saddler, 1794; M. 122. D. Queensberry's Exrs. *v.* Tait, July 11, 1817; F. C. See below, § 2305. 1 Bell's Com. 315, 714, 741 (332, 752, 777, M'L.'s ed.); 1 Ross' L. C. 287.

833. *Adjudication under Judicial Sale* (*a*). —Decree of Judicial Sale is truly an adjudication, proceeding at the instance of a creditor holding a real security over the estate where the debtor is insolvent; or, without insolvency, at the instance of an apparent heir of the debtor as trustee for the creditors and for his own eventual interest. The object of the action is to have the debtor's estate brought to public sale, and the price divided among the creditors. It differs from adjudication so far that there is no legal—no power or time left for redemption; it is an absolute adjudication to the purchaser. The decree adjudges the estate as in a common adjudication, but irredeemably, to pertain and belong to the purchaser, and 'formerly ordained' the superior to infeft and seise the purchaser as vassal in the lands. 'During its dependence all separate adjudications are suspended (*b*).'

The decree of sale 'was' followed by a charter of sale and adjudication, containing a precept for infeftment. And sasine being taken and duly recorded, the feudal title 'was' complete (*c*). 'Now, however, a decree of sale is equivalent to a conveyance by the ancestor or owner of the lands in favour of the purchaser, who may complete his title by infeftment on it in the same way as on a decree of adjudication (*d*) This is esteemed a title of a very eligible kind. 'It does not, however, protect against the claims of third parties not deriving their right from the bankrupt, and not called as parties to the action of sale (*e*).'

(*a*) See below, § 2333. M. Bell's Convg. 823.
(*b*) 19 and 20 Vict. c. 91, § 4. Cf. § 835 (*g*), below.
(*c*) 2 Ersk. 12. § 59 et seq. 1681, c. 17. 1690, c. 20. 1695, c. 24. 54 Geo. III. c. 137, § 10. 3 Jur. Styles, 435 et seq.
(*d*) 37 and 38 Vict. c. 94, § 62; *supra*, § 828A.
(*e*) Rollo *v.* Dundas, 1739; Elch. *Ranking and Sale*, 5; 1 Ross' L. C. 335. Urquhart *v.* Officers of State, 1753; M. 9919; aff. Cr. St. & P. 586. Middlemore *v.* Macfarlan's Reps., March 5, 1811; F. C. (see 1803, M. *Heir Appar.* Apx. 2). 2 Bell's Com. 278 (258, M'L.'s ed.).

834. *Adjudication on Trust Bond.*—Taking advantage of the facilities provided for creditors, two indirect methods of proceeding were devised: the one for compelling the superior to enter a purchaser before the law had provided means for that purpose; the other for entering heirs tentatively, without the necessity of their assuming that character and responsibility. (1) If a purchaser was in danger of being refused by the superior, he took a bond from the seller for the price, and so adjudged the estate as a creditor. (2) Sir Thomas Hope invented the mode of proceeding on the part of an heir desirous of challenging adverse deeds, and yet unwilling to incur responsibility as representative. By this device the heir grants a bond to a confidential person for a sum above the value of the estate; on such bond, the holder, as a creditor, charges the heir to enter, and on his refusal adjudges the estate or *spes successionis* of the heir. The holder of the bond then proceeds to challenge the adverse deed; and finally, in case of success, the bondholder, being a trustee, conveys the bond and adjudication to the heir, in whose person, *confusione*, the debt is extinguished. It was first doubted whether this formed a good title to carry land, but afterwards it was recognised as a good and valid title (*a*).

(*a*) 3 Ersk. 8. § 72. See below, § 1859. M'Laren on Wills, § 208. M. Bell's Convg. 1106. Duff's Feud. Convg. 489.

835. *Adjudication in Implement.*—Adjudication in Implement is a judicial method of completing a conveyance to the vassal's estate; 'and it is available whether the title which it is used to establish be absolute or qualified, the adjudication being itself irredeemable as regards the persons from whom the right is adjudged (*a*).' It is in the form of an adjudication, and is founded upon an obligation by the vassal (*b*) to convey, or upon a conveyance without precept or procuratory (*c*). The decree decerns and adjudges the lands heritably and irredeemably to the pursuer, in implement and satisfaction to him of the obligation; and 'formerly ordained' the superior to enter the pursuer as vassal absolutely. 'The decree itself is now equivalent to a conveyance for the purpose of infeftment (*d*). It has precisely the effect, and no more, of a deed voluntarily granted in implement of an imperfect conveyance (*e*).' Sasine duly recorded, proceeding on a charter of adjudication in implement, in terms of the decree, 'now, infeftment on the decree, without charter,' completes the right of the adjudger, and is as absolute a transference as if the right were completed on the vassal's disposition (*f*). It is irredeemable, and is not superseded, like an adjudication for debt, by a ranking and sale (*g*).

Adjudication in implement has been attempted to be used for facilitating the entry of heirs; but this attempt has been discountenanced and abandoned (*h*).

(*a*) 3 Stair, 2. § 45; 4 Stair, 51. § 9. 2 Ersk. 12. § 47. M. Bell's Convg. 816. Macgregor *v.* Macdonald, 1843; 5 D. 888; 2 Ross' L. C. 489. Watson *v.* Wilson, 1868; 6 Macph. 258; both explaining Strachan *v.* Whiteford, 1776; M. Apx. *Adjud.* 7.
(*b*) When directed against an heir for implement of an ancestor's obligation, it had to be preceded by charges and action of constitution, as in ordinary adjudication. 1 Bell's Com. 749 (783, M'L.'s ed.) Laurie *v.* Laurie, 1854; 16 D. 860.
(*c*) In many cases the necessity for adjudication in implement is removed by the provision in the new statutes that disponees under general dispositions without the executive clauses, may complete their titles by notarial instruments in statutory form. 31 and 32 Vict. c. 101, § 19; and 37

and 38 Vict. c. 94, § 29. Smith *v.* Wallace, 1869; 8 Macph. 204.

(*d*) See 37 and 38 Vict. c. 94, § 62, referred to above, § 828A (*b*).

(*e*) Paton *v.* Renny, 1835; 13 S. 509. See Monteith *v.* Ingels, 1869; 7 Macph. 523. *Infra*, § 1692, 1692A.

(*f*) 2 Ersk. 12. § 50. 3 Jur. Styles, 333. 1 Bell's Com. 748 (782, M'L.'s ed.).

(*g*) Hutchinson *v.* Wood, 1830; 8 S. 982; 2 Ill. 58. Campbell *v.* Macvicar, 1752; M. 277; 1 Ross' L. C. 121. Wood *v.* Scott, 1833; 11 S. 355. Bontine *v.* Graham, 1839; 1 D. 631. Somerville *v.* Bontine, 1839; 1 D. 906. Watson and Macgregor, *citt.* The act and warrant of the trustee in a sequestration is equivalent to a decree of adjudication in implement as well as in payment. Laurie, *supra* (*b*).

(*h*) Dunlop *v.* Cochrane, July 4, 1820; F. C.; aff. 1824, 2 S. App. 115. See Murray *v.* Ramsay & Co., Jan. 17, 1811; F. C. As to declarator and adjudication, see 1 Bell's Com. 751 (785, M'L.'s ed.); 1 Ross' L. C. 320 sqq. M. Bell's Convg. 1004, 1010. 37 and 38 Vict. c. 94, § 62, 65. Miles *v.* N. B. Ry. Co., 1867; 5 Macph. 402. *Infra*, § 1993 *fin.*

CHAPTER V

OF THE FEUDAL TITLE TO PATRONAGE AND TEINDS

I. PATRONAGE.

836. Nature and History.—Patronage is the right of presenting to the vacant office of the ministry in a parish church a person duly qualified to officiate as a clergyman. On the abolition of Popery, the right of presentation in patrons was reserved (*a*). It was afterwards abolished (*b*), and restored by a statute, 'till 1875' in observance (*c*). The right originally belonged to the founder of a church; or, if not claimed by him, was held to be vested in the Pope. Patronages which were appendant to a lordship or barony held by the Church before the Reformation, were as accessories annexed to the Crown (*d*): Those which belonged to archbishops, bishops, and chapters, 'were till 1875' in the Crown; and those which belonged to subjects, either appendant or separate from land, 'were till that date' still with them.

'Church Patronage Act, 1874.—By the Act 37 and 38 Vict. c. 82, the right of electing and appointing ministers to vacant churches and parishes is vested in the congregations, subject to regulations as to the mode of procedure to be made from time to time by the General Assembly. The Church courts have right to decide finally upon the appointment, admission, and settlement of ministers (*e*). The Act took effect at 1st Jan. 1875, from which date the Acts 10 Anne, c. 12, and 6 and 7 Vict. c. 61 (Lord Aberdeen's Act), were repealed. Compensation was made payable to private patrons presenting a petition to the sheriff to determine the amount within six months after the passing of the Act (6th Aug. 1874). It is payable by the heritors out of the first four years' stipend after the occurrence of a vacancy, and must be applied for when the vacancy occurs (*f*). If no appointment be made by the congregation within six months after the occurrence of a vacancy, the appointment devolves on the presbytery (*g*). Certain provisions are made by the Act for the case of small congregations, *i.e.* where the communicants do not exceed twenty-five. The Act does not affect or interfere with the patron's or titular's right to teind existing at its date, or the right of ann, or the laws as to the disposal of vacant stipend.'

Title to Patronage.—The right of patronage 'might' be in a subject as an accessory of his land; or as vested in him by infeftment; or as a right never feudalised, and vested or transferred by disposition without infeftment (*h*). And if once vested by infeftment, patronage must ever after, like land, be transferred by sasine (*i*). Patronage 'was' held to be in the Crown where no other right appears, to the effect of operating as a good title of prescription (*k*). A grant of patronage by the Crown to a subject 'was' not objectionable on the annexing Acts, and 'did' not require a dissolution, as these Acts do not specify patronage as a right to be annexed to the Crown (*l*); and when lands annexed to the

Crown have been dissolved, the dissolution 'extended' to the patronage (*m*).

Rights of Patronage.—The rights of the patron are the following:—

(1.) *Presentation.*—The principal right 'was' that of presentation; and this right as to a second minister 'belonged' as accessory to that of the first charge (*n*). But this right of presentation may be excepted from the grant; and where it is so, the grant 'was' not a prescriptive title (*o*). The right of presentation 'might' be exercised by a woman (*p*); by a liferenter (*q*); by a commissioner (*r*); by the tutors of a pupil; by a minor with his curators; but whether a minor having curators 'could' present without their concurrence 'was' doubtful (*s*). If the patron, 'now the congregation,' shall neglect to present, or the presentee within six months to declare his acceptance in writing, the right devolves on the presbytery (*t*). When parishes of which the patronages are separate 'were' united, the presentation 'was' alternate (*u*). A substitution in presenting will not exclude the patron then in possession from presenting (*v*).

This right of presentation, 'Professor Bell added in his last edition (1839),' has lately given occasion to questions agitated with great heat, as connected with a question of conflicting jurisdiction between the Church and the Supreme Civil Court. Those questions arose from the right of rejection claimed by congregations, as fortified by an Act of the General Assembly of the Church in 1835, providing that no one should be admitted on the patron's presentation, if a major part of the male heads of families, communicants, should dissent from his call. But this Act has been held in the Civil Courts to be *ultra vires* of the General Assembly; and a person who had been rejected under the provisions of that Act was ordered to be restored (*w*). 'These unfortunate decisions and the controversy arising out of them ended in the schism of 1843, and the formation of the "Free Church."'

(2.) *Teinds.*—The patron has right to all the teinds not heritably disponed (*x*).

(3.) *Vacant Stipends.*—The patron has right to the vacant stipends, to be applied to pious uses within the parish; and now, by statute, in aid of the fund for clergymen's widows (*y*).

(4.) *Seat in Church, etc.*—The patron has right to a seat in the church, and a burial-place in the churchyard (*z*).

(*a*) 1567, c. 7. 1592, c. 115. 1612, c. 1.

(*b*) 1649, c. 23. 1690, c. 23. Cullen *v.* Sprot, 1841; 3 D. 561; aff. 1842, 1 Bell's App. 595.

(*c*) 10 Anne, c. 12. (*d*) 1587, c. 29.

(*e*) Cassie *v.* Gen. Assembly, 1878; 6 R. 221.

(*f*) See E. Strathmore *v.* Rescobie Hers., 1888; 15 R. 364.

(*g*) Craig *v.* Anderson, 1893; 20 R. 942. The Court of Session has still jurisdiction to decide whether, in each particular case, the right of appointment has devolved on the presbytery. Stewart *v.* Paisley Presby., 1878; 6 R. 178. The cases below in note (*t*) are still authoritative. Cassie, *supra* (*e*).

(*h*) 2 Craig, 8. § 37. 2 Stair, 8. § 35. 1 Ersk. 5. § 15. Parson of Morham *v.* L. Bearford, 1666; M. 9897; 2 Ill. 59. See L. Adv. *v.* Graham, 1844; 7 D. 183.

(*i*) Urquhart *v.* Officers of State, 1752; M. 9915; aff. M. 9923; Elch. *Patronage*, 5 and 7; 5 B. Sup. 257. See E. Hopetoun, *infra* (*u*).

(*k*) E. Home *v.* L. Adv., 1758; 5 B. Sup. 867; M. 10,777; aff. 2 Pat. 25. Brodie *v.* E. Moray, 1777; M. 9937; Apx. *Patr.* 1; 2 Hailes, 767. See below, § 2003.

(*l*) Donaldson *v.* Officers of State, 1755; M. 9926; 5 B. Sup. 279. Lockhart *v.* Officers of State, 5 B. Sup. 279. Murdoch *v.* Gordon, 1783; M. 9942; 2 Hailes, 917. See L. Adv. *v.* L. Dundas, 1830; 8 S. 755; aff. 1831, 5 W. & S. 723. The doctrine of the text is correct so far as regards rights of patronage belonging to bishops and dignified clergy as such; but feudalised rights of patronage appended to lordships and baronies belonging to popish prelates were carried to the Crown by the Act of Annexation, and could not be given out without a dissolution. 1 Ersk. 5. § 10. Peebles Mags. *v.* Officers of State, 1800; Hume, 457. Duncan, Par. Law, 96. See Connell on Par. 456 sqq.

(*m*) Graham *v.* Officers of State, 1758; M. 9927; 2 Ill. 60.

(*n*) Town of Haddington *v.* E. Haddington, 1680; M. 9901. Town of Dundee *v.* E. Lauderdale, 1683; M. 9904. Cochran *v.* Officers of State, 1749; M. 9909. Cunningham *v.* Wardrop, 1762; M. 9933; rev. 6 Pat. 734.

(*o*) L. Adv. *v.* E. Mansfield, 1830; 8 S. 765. The grant of patronage might be subject to the condition that the presentation be made only with the approbation of the disponer. L. Adv. *v.* Stirling Mags., 1846; 8 D. 450. See further as to construction of such grants—Brown, *infra* (*p*). Graham *v.* Smith, 1859; 22 D. 185.

(*p*) See Brown *v.* Johnstone, 1830; 8 S. 899; 2 Ill. 60.

(*q*) D. Roxburghe *v.* Duchess, June 25, 1818; F. C. See Forbes *v.* M'William, 1762; M. 9931; 2 Pat. 36.

(*r*) Tait *v.* Keith, 1778; M. 9938; aff. 2 Pat. 447. Bailie *v.* Morrison, 1822; 1 S. 363, and Presby. of Inverness *v.* Fraser, 1823; 2 S. 384; 2 Ill. 61. Presby. of Strathbogie, below (*t*).

(*s*) 2 Bank. 8. § 100. Connell on Parishes, 521. More's Sup. to Stair, p. xliii.

(*t*) 1 Ersk. 5. § 16. 10 Anne, c. 12. 5 Geo. I. c. 29, § 8. Connell on Parishes, 496. Applegirth *v.* Thomson, 1682; M. 9959; 2 Ill. 62. Proc. for the Church *v.* E. Dundonald, 1762; M. 9961. Paisley Presby. *v.* Erskine, 1770; M. 9966. Strathbogie Presby. *v.* Forbes, 1776; 5 B. Sup. 534; M. 9972; Apx. *Patr.* 2; 2 Hailes, 712. L. Dundas *v.* Zetland Presby., 1795; M. 9972; Bell's Ca. 169. The period of six months ran from the date of the deliverance of the presbytery sustaining objections by parishioners to a presentee under the Aberdeen Act, 6 and 7 Vict. c. 61. By 7 and 8 Vict. c. 44, the presbytery's *jus devolutum* was made applicable in parishes *quoad sacra*. See Duff *v.* Officers of State, 1864; 2 Macph. 469; and above, notes (*e*), (*g*).

(*u*) Officers of State *v.* Gordon, 1821; 1 S. 129. E. Hopetoun *v.* E. Rosebery, 1835; 13 S. 685. See 7 and 8 Vict. c. 44, § 5.

(*v*) Invernytie *v.* Nairn, 1677; M. 9899. As to the presentation of an assistant and successor during the life of the incumbent, see Campbell *v.* Stirling, March 4. 1813; F. C.; aff. 1816, 6 Pat 238. Luke *v.* Brown, 1832; 10 S. 307; aff. 6 W. & S. 241. Clark *v.* Stirling, 1841; 3 D. 722.

(*w*) E. Kinnoull *v.* Auchterarder Presby., 1838; Report by Mr. Charles Robertson; 16 S. 661; aff. 1839, M'L. & R. 220. Strathbogie Presby. *v.* The Minority, 1839, 1840, 2 D. 258, 585, 1047, 1380; 1842, 4 D. 1298. Edwards *v.* Cruickshank, 1840; 3 D. 282. **E. Kinnoull** *v.* **Ferguson**, 1841; 3 D. 778; aff. 1842, 1 Bell, 662. Middleton *v.* Anderson, 1842; 4 D. 957. E. Kinnoull *v.* Ferguson, 1843; 5 D. 1010. Cruickshank *v.* Gordon, 1843; 5 D. 909, etc. By 6 and 7 Vict. c. 61 (Lord Aberdeen's Act), the parishioners might state and establish by proof before the presbytery relevant objections to the presentee's gifts and qualities, either generally or with reference to the particular parish.

(*x*) 2 Ersk. 10. § 49. See below, § 837.

(*y*) 1 Ersk. 5. § 13. 54 Geo. III. c. 169. Dundee Mags. *v.* Nicol, 1829; 8 S. 66. Stirling Mags. *v.* Gordon, 1837; 15 S. 657. E. Kinnoull *v.* Gordon, 1842; 5 D. 12; rev. 1845, 4 Bell, 126. Livingstone *v.* Grant, 1850; 13 D. 394; aff. 1860, 32 Jur. 514. Cheyne *v.* Dundee Mags., 1866; 4 Macph. 1002. The provisions of the Act of Geo. III. apply to *quoad sacra* churches under 7 and 8 Vict. c. 44, but not to parliamentary churches under 5 Geo. IV. c. 90, unless these have been erected into *quoad sacra* churches prior to the collation of the minister. Irvine *v.* Ministers' Widows' Fund, 1838; 16 S. 1024. Grant *v.* Macintyre, 1849; 11 D. 1370. Cheyne *v.* Cook, 1863; 1 Macph. 963.

(*z*) Ersk. *ut supra*. L. Torphichen *v.* Gillon, 1765; M. 9936; 2 Ill. 63. Acts of Assembly, Aug. 9, 1649. Connell on Parishes, 546. This has been doubted. Duncan, Par. Law, 218.

II. TEINDS (*a*).

837. Nature and History.—A tenth part of the produce of lands was early claimed by the clergy as their right, and gradually came to be by law appropriated to their maintenance. How teinds came to be held by laymen as a separate estate, or a yearly payment out of land, can be understood only by attending to the several situations in which they originally stood. Teinds of lands which had belonged to the Church were, previous to the Reformation, either feued out by churchmen separately from the land for an annual duty, as ground-rent, or they were feued out along with the lands (*cum decimis inclusis et nunquam antea separatis*), so that the grantee enjoyed land and teind together; and although such grants by churchmen were annulled by 1564, c. 88, unless confirmed by the Crown, confirmation was easily obtained. Those which were not feued out, but still in the hands of the Church, at the Reformation, fell on that event to the Crown; and those which were feued out, but not confirmed, also fell to the Crown. The right to teinds which had been constituted as a separate estate was completed by infeftment, the Crown having right to the duties payable for land; and this right sometimes remained with the Crown, sometimes was bestowed on a subject.

After the Reformation, teinds of land belonging to the Church at that time were conferred on Lords of Erection, and were vested in them by sasine; while certain teinds which continued after the Reformation to be payable to the bishops of the Reformed Church, were left in the hands of the Crown on the abolition of Episcopacy, and were granted out in many instances to subjects.

Title.—The original right to teinds was vested in the clergy without sasine, but now the right can be completed only by sasine. Teinds feued out by the churchmen were vested by sasine. Teinds granted by the Crown to laymen, after the Reformation, were vested by sasine. To teinds originally granted along with the lands as *decimæ inclusæ*, when constituted as a separate estate on the alienation of the land, the title was by sasine. Teinds to which in none of these ways an heritable right could be shown, belonged to the patron of the parish, subject to stipend, by 1649, c. 39; 1690, c. 23; '1693, c. 41' (*b*); and these are either held by the title which gives the patronage, or where granted to others than the patron, the right is completed by sasine. Such being generally the state of this peculiar sort of estate, the titles to it are a charter and sasine of a barony carrying the teinds as an integral part of it (*c*); a charter and infeftment in land *cum decimis inclusis*, with pertinents, the intention being clear to include teinds, carries the titularity (*d*); a conveyance of teinds completed by infeftment (*e*); a grant of patronage *cum decimis* carries the titularity of the teinds, not the mere patron's right (*f*); a personal right by adjudication without sasine has been held a good title to prescribe a right to teinds (*g*). 'A decree of valuation of teinds is not a title upon which a proprietor of lands can acquire by prescription a right to the teinds of other lands not included in the valuation (*h*).'

(*a*) See below, § 1146 et seq., of teinds as a burden on land and provision for the clergy.

(*b*) See Lochore & Capledrae Coal Co. *v.* Common Agent of Ballingry, 1878 ; 5 R. 763.

(*c*) Trotter *v.* Hog, 1736 ; Elch. *Teinds*, 2 ; 2 Ill. 63. L. Adv. *v.* Balfour, 1860 ; 23 D. 147. A charter erecting lands into a burgh does not carry teinds. Learmonth *v.* Edinburgh Mags., 1859 ; 21 D. 890 ; and see pp. 894, 897 as to the text.

(*d*) Dunning *v.* Crs. of Tillibole, 1748 ; Elch. *Teinds*, 26 ; M. 15,659. Scott *v.* Muirhead, 1672 ; M. 15,638. Callander *v.* Carruthers, 1698 ; M. 15,649. See Blair *v.* Dunbar Mags., 1836 ; 14 S. 945 ; 2 Ill. 101 ; and as to titles conveying teinds by implication, Mackintosh *v.* L. Abinger, 1877 ; 4 R. 1069 ; and the cases cited in the report.

(*e*) Minister of Morbattle *v.* Moir, 1745 ; M. 15,657 ; Elch. *Teinds*, No. 23.

(*f*) Spalding *v.* Small, 1753 ; M. 15,670. Stewart *v.* Scott, 1797 ; M. 15,703. See Sands *v.* E. Wemyss, 1842 ; 5 D. 74. Coll. of Glasgow *v.* E. Eglinton's Trs., 1845 ; 7 D. 965.

(*g*) Gordon *v.* Kennedy, 1758 ; 5 B. Sup. 358. Irvine *v.* Burnet, 1764 ; M. 10,830. See Watt's Trs. *v.* Kings, 1869 ; 8 Macph. 132 (teinds named only in warrandice clause of feu-charter.

(*h*) Macleod *v.* Paterson (Smith), 1869 ; 7 Macph. 614 : aff. 1873 ; 11 Macph. H. L. 62.

CHAPTER VI

OF THE FEUDAL TITLE TO BURGAGE PROPERTY

838. Kinds of Burghs.—Burghs are of two kinds: Royal Burghs, connected with the Royalty of Scotland; and Burghs of Regality and Barony, connected with the Regality. In the former there 'was, till recently,' a peculiar system of feudal holding and conveyancing; the latter is regulated by the ordinary rules and principles. Royal burghs were immediately under the protection of the Crown, the feudal service or *reddendo* being a species of military duty for the safety of the community, namely, watching and warding. Burghs of Regality and Barony had a constitution analogous to these, but were held under the lord of regality or baron to whom they belonged, according to the charter of erection.

I. ROYAL BURGHS (*a*).

839. Constitution.—The Royal Burgh is a corporation or legal person created by a charter from the Crown, and holding its lands and privileges from the Crown by the tenure of watching and warding. The charter in favour of the burgh does not require or perhaps admit of sasine, and the fee is always full (*b*).

(*a*) See below, § 2162.
(*b*) 2 Stair, 3. § 38. 2 Ersk. 3. § 34, 38; 2. 4. § 8 and 9. M. Tweeddale *v.* Town of Musselburgh, 1740; M. 6896; 2 Ill. 64. Ayton *v.* Kirkcaldy Mags., 1833; 11 S. 676. Brodie's Stair, p. 245, note.

840. Burgage Holding.—Each burgage proprietor holds immediately of the Crown "for services of burgh used and wont." The magistrates 'gave' him entry and sasine: but it is as Commissioners of the Crown empowered to enter vassals, and receive resignations, and give sasine. If the burgh is annihilated, the burgage holders continue as Crown vassals (*a*). Where there 'was' no provost, one of the magistrates (with the town-clerk as notary) 'entered' vassals; and where there 'was' no magistrate or clerk, the sheriff and sheriff-clerk 'were' held competent to give sasine (*b*).

(*a*) 2 Stair, 3. § 38. 2 Ersk. 4. § 8, 9. Urquhart *v.* Clunes, 1758; M. 15,079; 2 Ill. 64. Lockhart *v.* Kennedy, 1662; 1 B. Sup. 482.
(*b*) Thomson *v.* M'Kitrick, 1662, 1666; M. 6892. Duff *v.* Elgin Mags., 1823; 2 S. 117.

840A. 'Abolition of Burgage Tenure.—Proprietors, and all others having any estate in land held burgage, have now the same right and interest in such estate as would have belonged to them under the Conveyancing Act of 1874, had the tenure been feu; and since October 1, 1874, there is no distinction between feu and burgage estates in land so far as regards the conveyances relating thereto, or the completion of titles, or subinfeudation, or anything to which that Act relates. Similar provisions are made as to lands held by the tenure of booking in Paisley (*a*).'

(*a*) 37 and 38 Vict. c. 94, § 25, 26. M'Cutcheon *v.* M'William, 1876; 3 R. 565 (*per* L. Currichill, Ordy.). *Infra*, § 843 *fin.*

841. Title.—Each burgess holds immediately of the Crown; but he can receive his entry only from the magistrates, insomuch that in competition a charter and sasine from the Crown 'did' not avail against a subsequent entry by the magistrates (*a*).

(*a*) 1567, c. 27. Css. Kincardine *v.* E. Mar, 1686; M. 6894; 2 Ill. 65. See below, § 846, as to feuing.

842. The title of each burgage holder 'was' completed by sasine given by one of the magistrates and the town-clerk as notary (*a*). 'Under the existing system, the deed constituting the title of a burgage holder may itself be registered in the proper register of sasines; the town-clerk, if appointed before 8th March 1860, writing the warrant of registration if required, and receiving certain fees. Town-clerks appointed after that date have no exclusive right of preparing or expeding any deed relating to lands (*b*).'

(*a*) 1567, c. 27.
(*b*) 31 and 32 Vict. c. 101, § 136, 151, 153. See 37 and 38 Vict. c. 94, § 25.

843. The sasine must be recorded in the books of the burgh. 'The burgh registers of sasines are not affected by the Land Registers Act of 1868; and in them must still be recorded all writs affecting lands which immediately prior to 1st October 1874 were held burgage (*a*).'

By statute after the model of the Act 1617, c. 16, all "instruments of sasine of tenements within burghs royal, or liberties, or freedoms thereof, holding in burgage, shall be insert in the town-clerk's books of the several burghs *respective*, within threescore days after the date of the same," the extract to make faith in all cases where the writ is not to be improven; and "if it shall happen any of the said writs which are appointed to be insert as said is, not to be duly insert within the said space of sixty days, then the same to make no faith in judgment, by way of action or exception, in prejudice of a third party who hath acquired a perfect and lawful right to the said tenements, without prejudice always to them to use the writs against the parties makers thereof and their heirs and successors" (*b*). By statute, the practice of omitting the docquet in the registration 'was' corrected, and its registration required in future, but dispensed with as to sasines before the statute (*c*). 'But the Infeftment Act of 1845 dispensed with the notary's docquet (*d*), and the subsequent Acts of 1847 and 1860 assimilated the forms of burgage conveyancing to those in use in feu holdings (*e*).'

(*a*) 31 and 32 Vict. c. 64, § 27. 37 and 38 Vict. c. 94, § 25.
(*b*) 1681, c. 11; 8 Act. Parl. 248, c. 13. Compare § 772, 773, above; and see below, § 847.
(*c*) 10 Geo. IV. c. 19. (*d*) 8 and 9 Vict. c. 35, § 7.
(*e*) 10 and 11 Vict. c. 49, § 5, 7. 23 and 24 Vict. c. 143. 31 and 32 Vict. c. 101, § 7, 8. 37 and 38 Vict. c. 94, § 26.

844. Transmission to Singular Successors.—(1.) *Purchasers.* The conveyance of burgage property to a purchaser 'was' made by disposition, containing words of transference *de præsenti* (*a*), with a procuratory for resigning in the hands of the magistrates in favour of the disponee. It 'was' strictly regulated by the feudal principle; and so a precept 'was' in such a case invalid and incapable of confirmation, and there 'could' be no base right granted by a burgage holder so as to constitute a sub-vassalage in the tenement. The receiving of resignation by the symbol of staff and baton, and giving of sasine by earth and stone, 'was' one act and proceeding; and one instrument 'was' evidence of both, the town-clerk being notary (*b*).

(2.) *An Adjudger* 'was' entered and infeft at once by the magistracy, in obedience to the decree of adjudication, if the debtor himself 'were' infeft; if his right 'were' still personal, the entry 'was' by an instrument of adjudication, resignation, and sasine.

(3.) *An Heritable Creditor* strictly ought to be entered by means of a procuratory of resignation in the bond. But the constitution of a burden by annualrent right held of the granter has been found valid (*c*); and under the sanction of this decision, the practice 'was' introduced, of granting heritable bonds, with precepts to hold of the granter, over burgage subjects.

(*a*) See above, § 760.
(*b*) Act of Sed., Feb. 11, 1708. See Thomson *v.* M'Kitrick, 1662; M. 6892; 2 Ill. 65. The disposition of burgage subjects has not since 1860 required a clause of obligation to infeft, or a procuratory or clause of resignation; but it implies, and may express, that the lands are "to be holden of Her Majesty in free burgage." See 31 and 32 Vict. c. 101, § 7 (re-enacting 10 and 11 Vict. c. 49, § 1, and 23 and 24 Vict. c. 143, § 6), and 37 and 38 Vict. c. 94, § 26. See above, § 775A, etc.
(*c*) Bennet *v.* Sclanders, 1711; M. 6895.

845. Transmission to Heirs.—If an heir at law of one infeft 'was' to be entered, the magistrates, on a cognition by two or more witnesses of the claimant's character as heir in the fee, 'gave' sasine forthwith by earth and stone of the land, and hasp and staple of the house; and an instrument of cognition and sasine 'was' extended and recorded (*a*). (In Edinburgh, however, there 'was' in practice no cognition (*b*).) If the claim 'were' under the destination of a deed, the magistrates 'required' proof by a service as heir of provision, and thereupon 'gave' sasine (*c*). If the ancestor 'had' not been infeft on his disposition, the magistrates 'required' a general service as heir of provision to prove the right under the disposition; and on production of such service, they 'gave' sasine on the original procuratory (*d*). If the title 'was' to be completed in favour of one purchasing from the heir, they 'required' a general service of the heir. In some burghs a form of special service 'was' introduced, in which the proceedings in the ordinary special service 'were' followed in the Burgh Court, but without any brieve from Chancery. A claim 'was' made with a prayer for service and cognition. It 'was' remitted to a jury, and the Court 'interposed' a decree to the verdict (*e*). The sasine duly recorded 'completed' the title in all those cases. 'Since 1860, the service of heirs in burgage subjects is by petition to the sheriff, as in other cases (*f*). It is also competent for the heir of a person who dies infeft in burgage subjects to obtain a writ of *clare constat* signed by the chief magistrate and town-clerk, which, being recorded in the appropriate register of sasines, has the full effect of cognition and sasine (*g*). This remains in force, and may be recorded at any time during the life of the grantee (*h*).'

(*a*) 3 Ersk. 8. § 72. 1 Jur. Styles, 4th ed. 562.
(*b*) 1 Jur. Styles, 4th ed. 565.
(*c*) 1 Jur. Styles, 4th ed. 572.
(*d*) 1 Jur. Styles, 4th ed. 569. Cumming's Crs. *v.* Maconochie, 1783; M. 14,446; 2 Ill. 65. Edgar *v.* Maxwell, 1743; 5 B. Sup. 730.
(*e*) Duff, Feudal Convg. 516. See Menzies, Convg. 838.
(*f*) 31 and 32 Vict. c. 101, § 27–46; 37 and 38 Vict. c. 94, § 9–14. See 10 and 11 Vict. c. 47, and 23 and 24 Vict. c. 143.
(*g*) 31 and 32 Vict. c. 101, § 102; improving 23 and 24 Vict. c. 143, § 7.
(*h*) *Ib.* § 103.

846. Power to Feu Burgage Subjects.—Although it has been doubted whether magistrates can convey the burgh lands to be held burgage, it is not doubted that, under certain conditions, they may, 'by a public sale and by an act of council,' feu, for a feu-duty adequate to the rent, where the act is unequivocally beneficial to the burgh; but they cannot part with a superiority (*a*).

Sometimes there is a confounding of holdings; and it is doubtful whether the subject is to be held in burgage or in feu; or whether the titles are to be made up in the usual way or *more burgagio.* The rule seems to be, that *in dubio* the tenure is to be held burgage, with a ground-annual; the holdings of burgage and feu not being inconsistent to this extent (*b*). 'The better opinion seemed to be that the private owners of burgage lands could not convey them to be held in feu (*c*); but that the magistrates might competently grant feu-rights of land belonging to the burgh for an adequate feu-duty (*d*). A feu-duty, however, could not be validly stipulated in a burgage holding (*e*), until the recent statute abolishing the distinction of feu and burgage estates expressly provided that proprietors of lands previously held burgage may grant feus, and that the titles of all such feus granted before the Act shall be unchallengeable on the ground that such feus are of land held by burgage tenure, or that the titles have been recorded in the burgh register of sasines (*f*).'

(*a*) 2 Stair, 3. § 38. 2 Ersk. 4. § 9. See 3 Geo. IV. c. 91, § 5–8. Dean *v.* Irvine Mags., 1752; M. 2522; 2 Ill. 66. Dawson *v.* Glasgow Mags., 1824; 3 S. 136; 1826, 2 W. & S. 230; 1827, 6 S. 19; affirmed with findings, 1830, 4 W. & S. 81. Kilmarnock Mags. *v.* Inhabitants, 1776; 5 B. Sup. 406. Stewart *v.* Paisley Mags., 1822; 1 S. 246. Selkirk Mags. *v.* Clapperton, 1828; 6 S. 955.
(*b*) Edgar, *supra*, § 845 (*d*). Dawson, *supra* (*a*). See Perth Mags. *v.* Stewart, 1830; 9 S. 225; 1835, 13 S. 1100. E. Fife's Trs. *v.* Aberdeen Mags., 1842; 4 D. 1245. Donald's Trs. *v.* Yeats, 1839; 1 D. 1249.
(*c*) 2 Bankt. 3. 68. Duff, Feud. Convg. 51, 509. See, however, Dr. Mowbray's note in Hendry's Man. of Convg. quest. 793.
(*d*) Cases in previous notes and next section. 2 Ersk. 4. § 9. See Brodie's Stair, pp. 245–6, note.
(*e*) Arbroath Mags. *v.* Dickson, 1872; 10 Macph. 630.
(*f*) 37 and 38 Vict. c. 94, § 25. M'Cutcheon, above, § 840A.

847. The community may have held lands in feu before its erection into a burgh, or may purchase and hold lands in feu. These are to be held according to the common rules; and whatever effect may be given to the privileges of the burgh over the lands so held, their tenure is not burgage (*a*). Sasine in such lands, which, though lying within the territory of the burgh, are not held in burgage, must be recorded in the county register (*b*). And where lands or tenements are granted out in feu by the magistrates, the sasine must also (though the subject be within the territory of the burgh) be recorded in the county register (*c*). Where the matter is doubtful, it is advisable to record the sasine in both registers.

(*a*) 2 Ersk. 4. § 9.
(*b*) 1681, c. 11. 49 Geo. III. c. 42.
(*c*) Davie *v*. Denny, June 2, 1814; F. C.; 2 Ill. 67. Dixon *v*. Lawther, 1823, 2 S. 176, is not to be relied on. See Brechin Town Council *v*. Arbuthnot, 1840; 3 D. 216, and cases in § 846.

II. BURGHS OF REGALITY AND BARONY.

848. Constitution.—Burghs of Regality and Barony are erected by the Crown to be held of lords of regality or barons. They are sometimes erected with a constitution and jurisdiction in the magistrates and community, independently of the superior. Sometimes, of old, they were made dependent on the superior for their set. But this sort of dependence was abolished by 20 Geo. II. c. 50.

849. Holding and Title.—The feudal holding of such a community is regulated by the ordinary principles (*a*); but burghs under the old constitution so far still proceed on the analogy of royal burghs, that the magistrates act as commissioners having power to receive resignations.

(*a*) As to the rights of feuars and inhabitants within burghs of barony, see Henderson *v*. Malcolm, June 29, 1815; F. C. Peterhead Mags. *v*. Mercht. Maiden Hosp., 1840; 3 D. 99. Hamilton Mags. *v*. D. Hamilton, 1846; 8 D. 844; aff. 1850, 7 Bell's App. 1. Home *v*. Young, 1846; 9 D. 286. Muir *v*. Glasgow Mags., 1859; 21 D. 603.

850. The record for the sasines in such burgh is the County 'Division of the' General Register.

CHAPTER VII

OF THE TRANSMISSION OF INCOMPLETE OR PERSONAL RIGHTS TO LAND

851. Nature of a Personal Right to Land.—The feudal title, 'as has been explained,' is completed by sasine duly recorded. But the right of the grantee or disponee 'or adjudger,' before sasine, or of an heir before entry and infeftment, or of one named in a destination, is imperfect, and called "Personal," in opposition to the "Real" right. Two questions of importance occur respecting personal rights to land:—1. The effect of the conveyance of a personal right in divesting the granter; and 2. The discharge, or sopiting, of a personal fee remaining under a destination or marriage-contract.

852. Conveyance of a Personal Right.—The personal right to land may be conveyed, and a feudal title completed, in one of two ways: By voluntary disposition, containing an assignation to the unexecuted precept or procuratory in the disposition by which the seller himself holds his right, 'or even by a simple assignation of an unexecuted procuratory (or precept) without a direct disposition, provided the intention be clear to transmit the personal fee (*a*),' when, in virtue of the assignation, the buyer may, under the Act 1693, c. 35 (*b*), be infeft; or by a disposition, containing a precept of sasine, which, although proceeding *a non habente potestatem* (*i.e.* from one who is not himself infeft), and therefore in the first instance ineffectual, will yet authorise a sasine to be taken provisionally;—so as to become effectual *jure accretionis*, if the disponer's feudal title shall be afterwards completed by a sasine in his person without any mid-impediment intervening (*c*). 'Now, any person having right to an unrecorded conveyance of land may assign the conveyance by an assignation in a statutory form, either written upon the deed or separate; and when the conveyance and the assignation, or a notarial instrument setting forth the assignee's right, are recorded in the Register of Sasines, they give him the same right as if the lands had been conveyed to him by the original disposition, and infeftment had been taken thereon (*d*).'

(*a*) Livingstone *v.* Napier, 1762; M. 15,418, 15,461; aff. 1765, 2 Pat. 108; 2 Ross' L. C. 425, 521. **Renton** *v.* **Anstruther,** 1837; 16 S. 184; aff. 1843, 2 Bell's App. 214; 2 Ross' L. C. 435. M. Bell's Convg. 761.

(*b*) See § 766 and 790.

(*c*) 3 Stair, 2. § 2. 2 Ersk. 7. § 26. Henderson *v.* Campbell, 1821; 1 S. 103; 2 Ill. 51. See below, § 881. E. Fife *v.* Duff, 1862; 24 D. 936; aff. 1863, 1 Macph. H. L. 19; 4 Macq. 469.

(*d*) 31 and 32 Vict. c. 101, § 22, 23—§ 22 being repealed and re-enacted by 32 and 33 Vict. c. 116, § 2. See as to personal rights descending to heirs, 37 and 38 Vict. c. 94, § 9, 10. *Supra*, § 779A, 779B.

853. Although the disponer holds in such a case nothing but the personal right, his conveyance will not so fully exhaust that right as to preclude a subsequent disponee from acquiring, by means of the first sasine, a preference. This was at one time doubted, and the judgments of the Court varied on the question. But it was at last fully settled, that a conveyance by one holding a personal right is completed only with the completion of the disponee's title by sasine; and that, if double conveyances be granted, the first sasine will carry the land (*a*).

(*a*) 2 Ersk. 7. § 26 *in fin.* Rule *v.* Purdie, 1710; M. 2844; 2 Ill. 67; Erskine *v.* Hamilton, 1710; M. 2846; and Sinclair *v.* Sinclair, 1733; M. 2848, were overruled by **Bell** *v.* **Gartshore,** 1737; M. 2848; 5 B. Sup. 198; 2 Ross' L. C. 410. Henderson, *supra*, § 852 (*c*). See Renton, *cit.* § 852, and observe the distinction between a personal fee, which may be made real without the intervention of any third party, and a *jus crediti* or obligation to convey; as to which see Laurie *v.* Laurie, 1854; 16 D. 860. Edmond *v.* Aberdeen Mags., 1855; 18 D. 47; aff. 1858, 20 D. H. L. 5; 3 Macq. 116. Smith *v.* Wallace, 1869; 8 Macph. 204. M. Bell's Convg. 771.

854. Discharge or Sopiting of Personal Fees.—Under the destinations of settlements, and in consequence of securities, voluntary or by adjudication, by one who afterwards acquires right to the estate, there sometimes remain personal rights to lands, or affecting them, which in completing the feudal title are neglected or not taken up. On a divergence of the lines of succession, such personal fee may fall to an heir different from him who holds the feudal right; and by making up titles on the personal right, a part of the estate, or valuable interest in it, may be carried off. Rights of this kind, therefore, arising from destinations, ought never to be neglected, but ought either to be taken up and completed along with the other feudal titles, or merged and sopited. This is accomplished either by a new disposition or settlement granted by one who is in the substantial right of the personal fee (*a*), or by a new charter and investiture (*b*). But it is not enough to extinguish the personal fee that a title shall be made up in a character which includes the right to the fee, unless a new destination be given to it. As to incumbrances, it would seem that they are held as extinguished *confusione* (*c*).

(*a*) **Edgar** *v.* **Maxwell,** 1736; M. 3089; 2 Ill. 68; aff. 1742, 1 Pat. 334; 2 Ross' L. C. 522, 596 (case of Elshieshiells). Harvie *v.* Craig Buchanan, Dec. 12, 1811; F. C.; Buchanan's Cases. "Upon the case of Elshieshiells, Lord Kilkerran adds: 'Where one has it in his power to make up his right to an estate by either of two titles, *e.g.* upon the destination in his contract of marriage, or upon the ancient investitures of the estate, and is under no restraint which of the two he shall choose; if he choose to make up his titles on the one, *e.g.* upon the ancient investiture, and conveys away the estate, as in this case, no subsequent heir can take up the estate upon the provision in the contract of marriage, and thereupon quarrel that conveyance.' In other words, where one has a perfectly formal feudal title to an estate, and likewise a substantial interest in a separate personal right to that estate, although on the investiture coming to a close the personal right will survive and rule the descent of the land if unaltered, yet the person so in right of both is in capacity to alienate the estate gratuitously, and so to defeat the personal right (provided he is under no limitation), although he has not made up his titles to the personal right." 2 Ill. 69. See Pattison *v.* Dunn's Trs., 1866; 4 Macph. 1104; aff. 1868, 6 Macph. H. L. 147. M'Laren on Wills, § 860. *Supra*, § 821; *infra*, § 2019, 2020.

(*b*) **Molle** *v.* **Riddell,** Dec. 13, 1811; F. C.; 2 Ill. 69; 2 Ross' L. C. 619; aff. 1816, 6 Pat. 168. Zuille *v.* Morrison, March 4, 1813; F. C. See L. Reay *v.* M'Kay, 1823; 2 S. 520; aff. 1825, 1 W. & S. 306; 2 Ill. 579. E. Glasgow *v.* Boyle, 1887; 14 R. 419.

(*c*) D. Gordon *v.* The Crown, 1750; M. 9597; 2 Ill. 71. Robertson *v.* Davidson, 1751; M. 3044; 5 B. Sup. 792. As to prescription, see below, § 2019, 2020. "Upon the case of Robertson, Lord Monboddo states the difficulty in feudal form as resolvable on the general principle, that one having several rights in his person, and choosing to make up a title to any one of them, is thereby presumed to renounce and repudiate the rest, to the effect that it should not be used by any creditor, or taken up by any heir, but not be so extinguished as not to be competently used to defend the right on which the title is made up against any prior or preferable right. He observes also, that the Court had no occasion to determine the question of the succession dividing, the principal right going to one heir and the incumbrance to another. But if the case were happening, the Lords would, it is believed, find that the heir to the principal right, on which the titles were made up, would carry all." 2 Ill. 71. See as to a burden on land acquired by purchase, in regard to the succession of the purchaser, Dennison *v.* Fea's Trs., 1873; 11 Macph. 392.

CHAPTER VIII

OF THE SALE OF SUPERIORITY—CONDITIONS IN FEUDAL GRANTS—OBJECTIONS TO SASINES—ACCRETION—PROVING OF THE TENOR—AND GROUND-ANNUALS (*a*)

(*a*) This chapter was in the former edition entituled, "Review of some important Questions relative to the Transmission of Feudal Estates," and embodied the above subjects. It seems to have been intended as an appendix to the preceding chapters of this book.—*Note by Mr. Shaw.*

I. SALE OF THE SUPERIORITY.

855. Superior's Power.—Of old the vassal was not entitled to dispose of the feu without his superior's consent; but at no time does the superior appear to have been under restraint in transmitting his superiority to another. The rules as to such transmission are these:—

856. (1.) The superior may, without the vassal's consent, sell his right or estate of superiority; so that when the conveyance is completed by sasine, the vassal holds of the new as he did formerly of the old superior (*a*).

(*a*) 2 Ersk. 5. § 4. Dreghorn *v.* Hamilton, 1774; M. 15,015; 5 B. Sup. 607; 2 Ill. 71.

857. (2.) The superior cannot, without his vassal's consent, create a superiority intermediate between them; his powers of alienation being so far restrained by force of his grant to the vassal as to give the vassal a right to object. Such a conveyance is not, however, a nullity; nor has any one a right to oppose it but the vassal. Even without the vassal's consent, the superior may sell a part of his feu-duties, and assign his right to demand them and enforce their payment. But the disponee is only his assignee to the feu-duties, unless the vassal consent or acquiesce (*a*).

(*a*) 2 Stair, 4. § 5. 2 Ersk. 5. § 4. Douglas *v.* Torthorell, 1671; M. 9306, 9292, 15,012; 2 Ill. 72. Monimusk *v.* M. Huntly, 1682; M. 15,015. Hotchkis *v.* Walker's Trs., 1822; 2 S. 70. See above, § 703, 677, 688. See as to the effect of heritable securities and other temporary rights to be holden *a me vel de me*, granted by the superior, Home *v.* Smith, 1794; M. 15,077. Williams & James *v.* Maclaine's Trs., 1872; 10 Macph. 362. Arnott's Trs. *v.* Forbes, 1881; 9 R. 89. Duff's Feud. Convg. 68, 275. M. Bell's Convg. 763, 1177.

858. (3.) The superior succeeding by forfeiture to his vassal, and so becoming superior of the sub-vassal, may revive the intermediate superiority, if he have not barred himself by accepting the sub-vassal (*a*). But where the Crown has become superior in place of the Church, the vassal is a proper Crown vassal under the Act of Annexation, and no intermediate superiority can in such circumstances be now raised (*b*).

(*a*) E. Argyle *v.* M'Leod, 1672; M. 15,013; 2 Ill. 72. See also D. Gordon *v.* M'Intosh, 1714; M. 10,975.
(*b*) Stewart *v.* L. Abbotshall, 1610; M. 15,012.

859. (4.) The superior cannot split the superiority into parts, where there is one feu and one *reddendo*, so as to compel the vassal to seek his entry from more than one superior (*a*). So, when heirs-portioners succeed to land, the entry must be by the whole or by the eldest; and, strictly, it is only the eldest who is superior. And in the same way joint superiors must concur; but it is no splitting of superiority to vest it in two or more jointly and *pro indiviso* (*b*). The mere circumstance, however, of separate subjects, holding of the same superior, coming into the person of the same vassal, will neither entitle him to demand one charter and a single entry, nor to object to the superior selling his right to different parties; for this is not to multiply superiorities, but to continue them (*c*). And although the superior should have included the separate subjects in one charter, they still may be disjoined by a sale of the superiorities separately, provided the charter shall contain distinct *quæquidem* and *reddendo* (*d*).

(*a*) See above, § 677. 2 Craig, De Feud. § 35. 2 Stair, 4. § 5. Maxwell *v.* M'Millan, 1741; M. 8817; 5 B. Sup. 696; 2 Ill. 72. Sinclair *v.* Sinclair, 1754; Elch. *Sup. & Vass.* 16; 5 B. Sup. 812. D. Montrose *v.* Colquhoun, 1781; M. 8822; Hailes, 877; aff. 6 Paton, 805. Graham *v.* Westenra, 1826; 4 S. 615.
(*b*) 2 Stair, 4. § 17. Baillie *v.* Lady Idington, 1678; 3 B. Sup. 234. Lady Luss *v.* Inglis, 1678; M. 15,028. Cargills *v.* Muir, 1837; 15 S. 408. See below, § 1053, 1659.
(*c*) Dreghorn *v.* Hamilton, 1774; M. 15,015; 5 B. Sup. 607. See Lee *v.* Alexander, 1883; 10 R. H. L. 91.
(*d*) Lamont *v.* D. Argyle, June 23, 1813; F. C.; rev. 1819, 6 Paton, 410; 2 Ill. 74. Dreghorn, *supra* (*c*).

860. The effects of this in the operations formerly so frequent for election purposes, were, that the vassal himself had right to object to the splitting of the superiority, or the interjection of a mid-superior; but that no such right was conferred on the freeholders; to them it was *jus tertii* (*a*).

(*a*) Campbell *v.* Laurie, 1781; M. 7786; 2 Ill. 74. Hotchkis *v.* Walker's Trs., 1822; 2 S. 70. Colquhoun *v.* Dickson, 1824; 3 S. 59. See Stewart *v.* Houston, 1823; 2 S. 300. Mure *v.* Westenra, 1824; 3 S. 17.

II. CONDITIONS IN FEUDAL GRANTS.

861. General View.—In order to understand the effect of conditions in feudal rights, and their effect against heirs and purchasers, it is necessary to premise the general doctrine of real burdens. By the law of Scotland, the right to lands sold may be limited or burdened by reservation of certain parts of the land, as coal, lime, mines, etc. (*a*); or by reservation of certain uses, as servitudes; or by reservation, in a well-known form, of a certain burden or faculty to burden to a limited extent. All of these depend on the principle that the seller excepts from the transference, and reserves, as under his original right, some part of the subject, or some of the rights or powers of a proprietor. And all that the law requires in order to give effect to such reservation is, that it shall be clear and certain, and duly published to all concerned (*b*).

The efficacy of conditions introduced into the title by which the property is transferred, depends on another principle, and much doubt has been entertained as to their effect.

In the sale of moveables, no condition is effectual to limit the right of the buyer, unless in so far as it *suspends* the sale, or reserves the property untransferred. If once transferred by delivery, the property passes unqualifiedly; and the strongest *resolutive* condition that the property shall *revert* to the seller in a particular event, has no effect on creditors or purchasers from the buyer (*c*). So it is in a question between seller and purchaser in a sale of land, where the above established mode of qualifying the transference by reservation is not followed. The seller who claims performance of a condition of pre-emption, or the performance of any act, or the observance of any stipulation, against the creditors of the purchaser, can be ranked only as a personal creditor for fulfilment of the condition as an engagement of the purchaser; but can have no preference, as by real right, on the land (*d*). It was attempted to provide for this imperfection, and produce the effect of a real qualification of the right to land when sold or conveyed in a deed of settlement, by means of irritant and resolutive clauses. But this device, applied first to fortify provisions of entail, was found ineffectual: and a statute was necessary to overcome the right of an owner to the uncontrolled disposal of property, and render the resolutive clauses effectual (*e*).

We have seen the inefficacy of such resolutive clauses in qualifying the owner's right in moveables. But the peculiarity of the feudal contract allows the introduction of another principle, viz. the force of a condition as entitling the superior to refuse a renewal of the feu, if the conditions stipulated in his contract with the vassal have not been observed, and to insist on such condition against singular successors as well as against heirs. In considering the subject, it is to be observed: That some conditions are *inter naturalia* of feus—as annual payments or services to the superior; and these, if not contrary to the Act of 20 Geo. II. c. 50, § 10, are held effectual both against heirs and purchasers. Other conditions, however, are not *inter naturalia*, but properly engagements *ad facta præstanda*, stipulated in the shape of conditions. Such is a clause of pre-emption, by which the vassal is bound to offer the feu back to the superior before disposing of it to a stranger (*f*); and after some doubts whether it was under the prohibition of the Act of Geo. II., this has been held legitimate and effectual to entitle the superior to refuse an entry to heirs or singular successors. Such also is a clause prohibiting sub-feu, 'now inept.' These, however, if not *inter naturalia*, partake so much of a legitimate stipulation for preserving the rights of the superior, that there has been little difficulty in giving effect to them. Other conditions of a more personal description have occasioned much difficulty: such are conditions, 'now inept by statute,' that the superior's agent shall be employed to draw out the charters, which occasioned great doubt here and in the House of Lords, and 'the question was' left undetermined (*g*). Others, again, have been introduced for preserving the plan of a town, preventing nuisances and encroachments, completing streets and pavements, etc.; as to which also much doubt 'was' entertained whether they are real burdens, or if not properly so, whether they are not engagements so interwoven with the feudal title, that the superior may refuse an entry to singular successors contravening the prohibition or not complying with the condition. The doctrine which hitherto has regulated such cases is, that the condition is effectual to the superior, so as to entitle him not only passively to refuse an entry, but judicially to insist on compliance with the condition (*h*).

The rules, therefore, seem to be:—1. That lawful conditions for maintaining valuable interests (*i*) on the part of the superior, when inserted in the vassal's investiture and published in the record of sasines (*k*), 'might' be enforced by the superior refusing an entry to an heir or a singular successor if the condition be not complied with (*l*); 2. That if such lawful conditions be enforced by irritant and resolutive clauses, the superior not only 'had' the passive right of refusing an entry, but 'has' an active title to challenge and reduce 'the act or deed done in contravention,' as to which the judges seem now to think that irritant and resolutive clauses are not necessary (*m*); 3. That when such a condition does not enter into the sasine and appear in the register, though it will affect the personal right before sasine, it will be ineffectual against a purchaser from the vassal infeft (*n*).

'The conditions which are here treated of are to be distinguished from real burdens in the more limited sense afterwards (§ 915-924) explained. These are, generally, reserved rights to payment of a definite sum of money, constituted against the lands, giving the creditor an absolute preference, but not in their own nature enforceable. On the other hand, an inherent condition of the feudal right running with the land may be enforced by personal action against the vassal (*o*) for the time being, by the party or parties for whose benefit it is imposed: and its pecuniary value may be indefinite. It must not be of a purely personal nature (*p*), and generally relates to the use or employment of the land, and payments for or in respect thereof (*q*). The following passage has been accepted as an authoritative statement of the law on this subject (*r*):—

'"To constitute a real burden or condition, either in feudal or burgage rights, which is effectual against singular successors, words must be used in the conveyance which clearly express or plainly imply that the subject itself is to be affected, and not the grantee and his heirs alone; and those words must be inserted in the sasine which follows on the conveyance, and of consequence appear upon the record. In the next place, the burden or condition must not be contrary to law or inconsistent with the nature of this species of property; it must not be useless or vexatious; it must not be contrary to public policy, for example, by tending to impede the commerce of land, or create a monopoly. The superior, or the party in whose favour it is conceived, must have an interest to enforce it (*i*). Lastly, if it consists in the payment of a sum of money, the amount of the sum must be distinctly specified (*s*). If these requisites concur, it is not essential that any *voces signatæ*, or technical form of words, should be employed. There is no need of a declaration that the obligation is real, that it is a *debitum fundi*, that it shall be inserted in all the future infeftments, or that it shall attach to singular successors (*t*). It is sufficient if the intention of the parties be clear, reference being had to the nature of the grant, which is often of great importance in ascertaining its import. Neither is it necessary that the obligation should be fenced with an irritant clause, and far less with irritant and resolutive clauses. The construction of the words employed will be affected by the nature of the grant (*u*). If the condition is one usually attaching to the lands in a feudal or burgage holding, in particular if it has a *tractus futuri temporis*, or is of a continuous nature, which cannot be performed, and so extinguished, by one act of the disponee or his heir, words less clear and specific will suffice to create it than when the burden appears to be of a personal nature; for example, the payment of a sum of money once for all in terms of a family settlement."'

(*a*) See above, § 740.

(*b*) See below, § 919; and as to the distinction between real burdens and such inherent conditions of the feudal grant, see M. Tweeddale's Trs. *v.* E. Haddington, 1880; 7 R. 620; and below, p. 359.

(*c*) See above, § 102 sqq., 109, 110.

(*d*) 1 Stair, 14. § 5. As to the effect of a condition in a minute of sale, and the right to have it made a real burden in the disposition to follow thereon, see Corbett *v.* Robertson, 1872; 10 Macph. 329.

(*e*) 1685, c. 22.

(*f*) See below, § 865, and cases there cited.

(*g*) See below, § 867.

(*h*) See below, § 868. **Tailors of Aberdeen** *v.* **Coutts,** 1840; 2 S. & M'L. 609; 1 Rob. 296; 3 Ross' L. C. 269.

(*i*) Tailors of Aberdeen, *cit.* The onus of showing that the superior has no interest lies upon the vassal who seeks to be released from the condition. Campbell *v.* Clydesdale Bank, 1868; 6 Macph. 943 (*per* L. Neaves). **E. Zetland** *v.* **Hislop,** 1882; 9 R. H. L. 40; 7 App. Ca. 427 (*per* L. Watson). See Edinr. Mags. *v.* Macfarlan, 1858; 20 D. 156. Naismith *v.* Cairnduff, 1876; 3 R. 863. Below, § 862.

(*k*) In any conveyance or deed affecting the lands, it is sufficient to refer to real burdens or conditions as set forth in a deed already recorded in the Register of Sasines. 31 and 32 Vict. c. 101, § 10. See also § 146, *ib.*; and below, § 861A.

(*l*) **Preston** *v.* **E. Dundonald's Crs.,** March 6, 1805; M. 6569; Apx. *Pers. and Real,* 2; 1 Bell's Com. 28, note; 2 Ill. 74; 3 Ross' L. C. 289; 4 Pat. 331. Campbell *v.* Harley & Dunn, 1823; 2 S. 299; 1 W. & S. 690; 6 S. 679. Brown *v.* Burns, 1823; 2 S. 261.

(*m*) Stirling *v.* Johnstone, 1757; M. 2343; 5 B. Sup. 323. They are not necessary. Tailors of Aberdeen, *cit.* 1 Bell's Com. 26, n. Colquhoun *v.* Walker, 1867; 5 Macph. 773.

(*n*) See Preston, *supra* (*l*). Below, § 864. Croall *v.* Edinr. Mags., 1870; 9 Macph. 323.

(*o*) For examples of such conditions of tenure in favour of the vassal, see below, § 895A.

(*p*) See, *e.g.*, Campbell *v.* Harley, *infra*, § 867.

(*q*) M. Tweeddale's Trs. *v.* E. Haddington, *cit.* (*b*). **E. Zetland** *v.* **Hislop,** 1882, *cit.* (*i*). Arbroath Mags. *v.* Dickson, 1872; 10 Macph. 630, 635 (*per* L. Pres. Inglis). Tennant *v.* Napier Smith's Trs., 1888; 15 R. 671.

(*r*) Opinion of Lord Corehouse in **Tailors of Aberdeen,** *cit.* (*h*), adopted by H. L., and referred to in all subsequent cases.

(*s*) Edinr. Mags. *v.* Begg, 1883; 11 R. 352. Smith Sligo *v.* Dunlop & Co., 1885; 12 R. 907.

(*t*) See, *e.g.*, Boswall *v.* Inglis, 1849; 6 Bell's App. 427.

(*u*) Hemming *v.* D. Athole, 1883; 11 R. 93.

861A. 'The Conveyancing Act of 1874 makes the following provisions with regard to real burdens on land:—

'It is lawful to record in the appropriate register of sasines any writing by which any real burden on land is assigned, conveyed, or transferred, or is extinguished or restricted.

'Unless so recorded, no deed dated after 1st October 1874, assigning, conveying, or transferring a real burden on land, is effectual in competition with third parties. It is only from the date of registration that such deeds have effect in competition; and registration makes intimation unnecessary. Real burdens may be assigned, conveyed, or transferred, and extinguished or restricted, and titles may be completed to them, as nearly as may be in the same manner as in the case of heritable securities requiring infeftment, as defined by the titles to Land Consolidation Act of 1868, the provisions and forms of which, and of the Conveyancing Act, 1874, as to the transference, extinction of, and completion of title to, such heritable securities, apply as nearly as may be to real burdens upon land. Such real burdens, except ground-annuals, are made moveable as to succession, to the same extent and effect as heritable securities (*a*).

'Reservations, conditions, and real burdens affecting land may be effectually imported into any deed relating to it by reference to a recorded deed, instrument, or writing applicable to the land, or to the estate of which it forms a part, in which they are set forth at full length. And feuing conditions applicable to a whole estate or part of it may be embodied in a deed and recorded, so as to be imported by reference into subsequent deeds or conveyances (*b*).'

(*a*) 37 and 38 Vict. c. 94, § 30. 31 and 32 Vict. c. 101, § 117, 124. See Mowbray's Hendry's Styles, 305. *Infra*, § 910, 1485A.

(*b*) 37 and 38 Vict. c. 94. § 32. N. B. Ry. *v.* Edinr. Mags., 1893; 20 R. 725 (reference to Act). *Infra*, § 917 sqq.

862. Requisites.—Conditions in the grant intended to protect the casualties of the superior require, to their efficacy, besides an interest (*a*) existing in the superior, that the condition shall be lawful, and that it shall be incorporated in the title.

(*a*) See above, § 861 (*c*). Waddell *v.* Campbell, 1898; 25 R. 456 (a case of direct contract, where interest is irrelevant).

863. (1.) *The condition must be lawful*; that is to say, neither at common law exceptionable as *pactum illicitum* (*a*), nor falling under the prohibitions in the statute of George II. After the abolition or decay of the military system of feus, conditions were frequently introduced into feu-holdings similar in import to the casualties of marriage and recognition, and called clauses *de maritagio* and *de non alienando sine consensu superiorum*. These it was the object of the Act to abolish, an additional feu-duty being substituted in their stead. The words of the Act are—"That the casualty of marriage consequent upon such holding, and all such prohibitory clauses restraining the power of alienation, be taken away and discharged"; and it is declared lawful for the subjects-superior or vassals in lands so held to apply to the Court of Session to modify such additional feu-duty by the vassal as they shall judge a reasonable recompense (*b*). Conditions of pre-emption and prohibitions to sub-feu are not held to be forbidden by this enactment (*c*).

(*a*) See E. Zetland *v.* Hislop, 1881; 8 R. 675; rev. 1882, 9 R. H. L. 40, 7 App. Ca. 427. See § 35 sqq. above.

(*b*) 20 Geo. II. c. 50, § 10.

(*c*) See § 865-866.

864. (2.) *Must be incorporated in the Title.*—The condition, in order to be effectual against singular successors, must be incorporated in the title. A condition lawfully bargained for by the superior will qualify the vassal's right, and that of his heirs or assignees, while the right remains personal; but unless it appear in the sasine duly recorded, it will not affect the feudal right or singular successors (*a*).

(*a*) See above, § 861 (*n*).

865. The Clause of Pre-emption is an obligation by the vassal to give the first offer to the superior if he mean to sell his land. It is intended, not for preserving the feudal influence of the superior (the abolition of which was the object of the Act), but for conferring on him a valuable right to the re-purchase of the estate; and 'although there are some judicial opinions indicating that the question, whether it is within the Act 20 Geo. II., is still undecided (*a*), it' is legitimate and effectual (*b*).

(*a*) Preston and Farquharson, *infra*. E. Mar *v.* Ramsay, 1838; 1 D. 116. Lumsden *v.* Lorimer, 1841; 3 D. 1199. Lumsden *v.* Stewart, 1843; 5 D. 501. Strathallan *v.* L. Grantley, 1843; 5 D. 1318. M. Bell's Convg. 579. Shaw's Bell's Com. 750. The opinion of all the judges in Tailors of Aberdeen (§ 861 (*h*)) was "that the validity of a clause of pre-emption still remains matter of doubt."

(*b*) Preston *v.* E. Dundonald, 1781; 2 Bell's Com. 28, n.; 2 Ill. 76. See above, § 861 (*l*). Irving *v.* M. Annandale, 1767; M. 2343. Farquharson *v.* Keay, 1800; M. *Clause*, Apx. 3. Preston, 1805; *supra*, § 861 (*l*).

866. The Prohibition to Sub-Feu is a condition intended to preserve the superior's casualty of composition for an entry. It prohibits alienation to be held base (*de me*). The effect of such a clause 'was,' that although a sub-feu will not be null, the superior 'could' not be compelled to enter his vassal the mid-superior when the lands 'fell' into non-entry, and so the sub-feuar 'suffered' the inconvenience of non-entry; and that an heritable security, as being a mere burden and no alienation, is not thus defeasible (*a*). 'A disposition with an alternative precept is not a contravention of this condition (*b*). Prohibitions to sub-feu or to grant conveyances with an alternative holding, made after 1st October 1874, are null and void, and not capable of being enforced; and all (private) Acts of Parliament to the contrary are repealed (*c*).'

(*a*) See cases, *supra*, § 861 (*b*). 31 and 32 Vict. c. 101, § 147. Darroch *v.* Ranken, 1855; 17 D. 935.
(*b*) Colquhoun *v.* Walker, 1867; 5 Macph. 773.
(*c*) 37 and 38 Vict. c. 94, § 22. Browne, Petr., 1875; 2 R. 488.

867. Special Stipulations for preserving the superior's right are good as personal engagements. They seem not to be effectual as real burdens; and it has been much doubted whether the superior is bound to give an entry to the vassal on any other condition than compliance with the stipulation (*a*). 'Monopolies of superiors' agents in preparing and recording sasines or conveyances or other deeds relating to any estate in land, and similar restrictions, whether contained in charters or in previous Acts of Parliament, are annulled and incapable of being enforced (*b*).'

(*a*) Stewart *v.* Burnside, 1794; M. 15,027; Bell's Cases. 75; 2 Ill. 76; 2 Ross' L. C. 161. M'Ritchie *v.* M'Donald & M'Neill, 1801; 2 Ill. 77; 1 Bell's Com. 26; 2 Ross' L. C. 165. Campbell *v.* Harley, 1823; 2 S. 299; 1 W. & S. 690; 6 S. 679; 2 Ill. 75. Napier *v.* M'Gavin, 1831; 9 S. 655.
This section is hardly intelligible, and seems to have been left incomplete by Prof. Bell. The cases scarcely bear upon the text; and one at least appears to have been misunderstood by him. See M'Laren's Bell's Com. i. 25, and 2 Ross' L. C. 165.
(*b*) 37 and 38 Vict. c. 94, § 22. Edin. Mags. *v.* Whitehead, above, § 775A.

868. 'Building Restrictions have become, by reason of the great increase of cities, the most important class of conditions inherent in the grant. Although several leading cases had occurred during Professor Bell's life, it is evident that he had not matured his opinions on this subject when he printed his last edition of this work in 1839. The two sentences which he wrote are therefore followed by a somewhat fuller summary of the points which are now settled.'

A condition may be inserted for the purpose of preventing encroachments or abuses, or for enforcing a particular plan of building which it may be of consequence to the value of the property to preserve; and 'when Professor Bell wrote,' it still 'remained' a doubt whether, when clearly made a condition, it 'would' not have effect against the vassal by contract, and against purchasers by force of the condition (*a*). The construction of such clauses is according to the fair understanding of the parties (*b*). 'It is now quite understood that conditions of this kind, when applied to the lands themselves in accordance with the rules already explained, may be enforced by and against singular successors (*c*). It is rightly said above (though with reference to a case which gives no light on the point) that the construction of such clauses is according to the fair understanding of the parties; and it has often become a question whether it was intended to impose a real burden by means of a *feuing plan.* The mere exhibition of a plan to intending feuars does not of course impose on them any obligation to adhere to it; nor even a reference to it in the titles, if it be made only for the purpose of identifying the subjects or ascertaining their extent (*d*). It must appear from the charter itself that the plan was intended to form part of the contract; as when it is incorporated by being signed and referred to in the charter in such terms as to make the intention clear (*e*). It is imported into the contract only for such purposes as are mentioned or necessarily implied in the titles (*f*).

'*Primâ facie* such restrictions are enforceable only by, or against (*g*), the superior, who alone is a party to the contract of feu. But neighbouring feuars holding from the same superior may also have a right to enforce them on the principle of *jus quæsitum tertio.* In order to this, however, it is not enough that similar conditions are found in feu-charters from a common superior, and that the proprietor seeking to enforce them against his neighbour has an interest in their observance: it must be expressed or be clearly implied in the feuar's title, that in accepting his feu he contemplated and agreed that the burden should be imposed upon him (*h*). For example, this will be inferred, as generally happens, from clauses establishing or implying a mutuality of rights and obligations between the feuars, as where a feuar stipulates that a condition laid upon himself shall also be inserted in his neighbours' titles; or from a sufficient reference to a common building plan (*i*). The feuar vindicating such a right must aver and prove his interest and his title (*k*). Either superior or co-feuars may be barred by acquiescence from objecting to infringements of the condition, and held to have abandoned their right to enforce it (*l*);

but such abandonment is not inferred from the permission of slight or isolated deviations, or such as the particular feuar has no interest to forbid; and it extends only to such restrictions as are in fact waived or abandoned (*m*). There is a presumption in favour of the free use of property; and restrictions of this kind are to be interpreted, if ambiguous, in favour of freedom, and in all cases strictly (*n*).'

(*a*) Dirom *v.* Butterworth, June 5, 1812; F. C.; 2 Ill. 77. **Gordon** *v.* **Marjoribanks** (New Club case), March 10, 1814; 18 F. C. p. 25, note; 6 Dow, 87; 6 Pat. 351. Schultze *v.* Campbell, Nov. 29, 1815; F. C. Young & Co. *v.* Dewar, Nov. 17, 1814; F. C. Stewart *v.* Burke, Dec. 9, 1820; F. C. Walker *v.* Renton, March 11, 1825; F. C.; 3 S. 455. Pollock *v.* Turnbull, 1827; 5 S. 195. See also Heriot's Hospital *v.* Gibson, 1809; 18 F. C. 25, note; 2 Dow, 301; 2 Ill. 26. Deas *v.* Edinburgh Mags., 1772; 2 Pat. 259.

(*b*) Scott *v.* Cairns, 1830; 9 S. 246. Carson & Co. *v.* Miller, 1863; 1 Macph. 604. Free St. Mark's Trs. *v.* Taylor's Trs., 1869; 7 Macph. 415. Stewart *v.* Meikle, 1874; 1 R. 408. Campbell *v.* Clydesdale Bank, 1868; 6 Macph. 943. M'Ewan *v.* Shaw Stewart, 1880; 7 R. 682 ("three square storeys"; comp. Campbell *v.* Allan, 1855; 18 D. 267. Cochrane *v.* Paterson, 1882; 9 R. 634). Welsh *v.* Jack, 1882; 10 R. 113. And see below (*n*); and above, § 701 (*c*).

(*c*) See above, § 861, and Tailors of Aberdeen, there cited. Johnston, below (*l*).

(*d*) Heriot's Hospital *v.* Gibson, *supra* (*a*). Walker *v.* Renton, and Gordon *v.* Marjoribanks, *ib.* Barr *v.* Robertson, 1854; 16 D. 1049. Carson & Co., and Free St. Mark's Trs., *supra* (*b*). Croall *v.* Edinr. Mags., 1870; 9 Macph. 323 (restriction by plan in articles of roup but not in charter). See N. B. Ry. *v.* Todd, 1846; 5 Bell's App. 184, 200.

(*e*) Dirom (*a*). Gordon and other cases in (*d*). Henderson *v.* Nimmo, 1846; 2 D. 869. Skinner *v.* Diey, 1855; 18 D. 158. Edinr. Mags. *v.* Macfarlane, 1858; 20 D. 156. In Glasgow Feuing Co. *v.* Watson's Trs., 1887; 14 R. 610, a feu-contract was partially reduced (rectified) on the ground of error in an incidental obligation so constituted, even against an onerous purchaser on the faith of the records.

(*f*) Barr *v.* Robertson, *supra* (*d*).

(*g*) See below, § 992, 994.

(*h*) **Macritchie's Trs.** *v.* **Hislop**, 1879; 7 R. 384; rev. 1881; 8 R. H. L. 95; 6 App. Ca. 560. N. B. Ry. Co. *v.* Moore, 1891; 18 R. 1021. Johnston *v.* Macritchie, *infra* (*l*). And see Skinner, Dirom, Carson, Free St. Mark's, Edinr. Mags., *citt.*, and cases in (*i*) below.

(*i*) M'Gibbon's Trs. *v.* Rankin, 1871; 9 Macph. 423. Alexander *v.* Stobo, 1871; *ib.* 599. Allan's Trs. *v.* Dixon's Trs., 1868; 7 Macph. 193; aff. 1870, 8 Macph. H. L. 182. Beattie *v.* Ures, 1876; 3 R. 634. Dalrymple *v.* Herdman, 1878; 5 R. 847 (superior has no power to discharge without consent of co-feuars). Walker & Dick *v.* Park, 1888; 15 R. 477 (no *jus quæsitum*—jurisdiction of dean of guild). Guthrie *v.* Young, 1871; 9 Macph. 544. Robertson *v.* North Br. Ry. Co., 1874; 1 R. 1213. (See L. Watson's doubt as to this case, 8 R. H. L. 104.) As to a lost building plan, see Sutherland *v.* Barbour, 1887; 15 R. 62. Power reserved to a superior to dispense with the condition or obligation excludes mutuality. Turner *v.* Hamilton, 1890; 17 R. 494. Thomson *v.* Alley & M'Lellan, 1882; 10 R. 433.

(*k*) Macritchie's Trs., *cit.* (*per* Lord Watson). See Gould *v.* M'Corquodale, 1869; 8 Macph. 185. Dennistoun *v.* Thomson, 1872; 11 Macph. 121. Stewart *v.* Bunten, 1878; 5 R. 1108. Charlton *v.* Scott, 1894; 22 R. 109. Stevenson *v.* Steel Co. of Scotland, 1896; 23 R. 1079 (no *jus quæsitum*). See above, § 861 (*i*).

(*l*) Campbell's Trs. *v.* Clydesdale Bank, 1868; 6 Macph. 943. Fraser *v.* Downie, 1877; 4 R. 942. Brown *v.* Burns, 1823; 2 S. 298. E. Moray *v.* Pearson, 1842; 4 D. 1411. Muirhead *v.* Glasgow Highland Society, 1864; 2 Macph. 420. Johnston *v.* Macritchie, 1893; 20 R. 539.

(*m*) Ewing *v.* Campbell, 1877; 5 R. 230. Gould *v.* M'Corquodale, and Stewart *v.* Bunten, *citt.* (*k*). Macritchie's Trs., *cit.* (*h*). E. Zetland *v.* Hislop, 1882; 9 R. H. L. 40; 7 App. Ca. 427. Johnston *v.* Walker's Trs., 1897; 24 R. 1061.

(*n*) Heriot's Hosp. *v.* Ferguson, 1773; M. 12,817; aff. 3 Pat. 674. Russell *v.* Cowpar, 1882; 9 R. 660. Hood *v.* Traill, 1884; 12 R. 362. Assets Co. *v.* Lamb & Gibson, 1896; 23 R. 569 (too strict). See, besides the cases cited in note (*b*), many cases of construction in Rankine on Landownership, pp. 398–402; and on the whole of this subject the decisions are so numerous that reference must be made to Professor Rankine's book, chap. xxvii., for fuller details and references.

III. OBJECTIONS TO SASINE (*a*).

869. Different Kinds of Objections.—The objections to sasine are Intrinsic or Extrinsic.

(*a*) See *supra*, § 771, as to the instrument of sasine.

870. (1.) *Intrinsic Objections, i.e.* objections appearing *ex facie* of the instrument, are fatal, if *in essentialibus*. Sasine is regarded as an *actus legitimus*, requiring a regular instrument in proof of it, which must be perfect as to all necessary particulars of the act (*a*).

(*a*) D. Monmouth *v.* Scott, 1667; M. 12,266; 2 Ill. 78. 2 Stair, 3. § 16. 2 Ersk. 3. § 34 sqq. 1 Bell's Com. 674. Bell's Conveyance of Land, 186 sqq. The notary's instrument is the only admissible evidence of sasine, and it is much to be regretted that from the time when the records were introduced, the instrument of sasine should not have been held conclusive proof of the ceremony. It may be expected (said Professor Bell) that, in consequence of the report of the Law Commissioners, the law in this respect will be altered. See above, § 770A, 771A, 774A.

871. As to the essential points, in reciting the ceremony, there are no *verba solemnia* absolutely indispensable; and so it is enough if the ceremony in all its essentials be stated in plain and intelligible words (*a*). The reading of the charter and precept must be stated, and in the instrument the precept transcribed, or as much of it as relates to the land (*b*). The testing clause and subscriptions are also transcribed, though perhaps not indispensable (*c*). The omission of the Christian name of the bailie has been held not fatal (*d*); nor a confounding of the names of the bailie and attorney, if capable of being extricated and understood (*e*); nor the omission of a date, if it can be consistently presumed, or if not essential (*f*); but when it is important, the omission is fatal (*g*); 'and the year of the King's reign and year of God must correspond, at least if both be mentioned (*h*).' The omission to state in the instrument the delivery of "heritable state and sasine, real, actual, and corporal possession," is fatal (*i*). Although the instrument commonly and correctly bears that sasine was given on the grounds of the several parcels "respectively and successively," yet, where the expression is not exclusive of this fact (as that sasine was taken "on the ground ofthe said lands"), and the words are such as accord with the supposition of the correct delivery of sasine (*k*), it seems to be sufficient. Where the words are exclusive of the supposition of successive acts (as if the instrument should bear that sasine was taken on a particular spot), it will be bad as to all the separate portions, 'except that of which it was correctly taken.' The statement in the instrument that a wrong symbol has been used is fatal (*l*). And although it has been held a sufficient sasine where the symbol was not specified, but the instrument bore only that the usual symbols were used (*m*), this was a very old sasine, and the judgment is not to be relied on absolutely. The instrument is null if the notary's docquet do not bear that he was personally present, and the words *vidi, scivi, et audivi* (*n*). An error in the docquet as to the number of pages is not held fatal, if demonstrably a clerical error (*o*).

(*a*) Douglas *v.* Chalmers, Gordon *v.* Brodie, Livingston *v.* L. Napier, 1762–1773; 5 B. Sup. 587; 2 Ill. 44, 78. Davidson *v.* M'Leod, 1827; 6 S. 8; 2 Ill. 45; 2 Ross' L. C. 65.

(*b*) Don *v.* Waldie, Feb. 4, 1813; F. C. Gordon *v.* E. Fife, 1827; 5 S. 550.

(*c*) Bell's Conveyance of Land to a Purchaser, 203.

(*d*) Morton *v.* Hunters & Co., 1828; 7 S. 172; aff. 1830, 4 W. & S. 379.

(*e*) Hilton *v.* Cheynes, 1676; M. 14,331. Douglas, *supra* (*a*). Henderson *v.* Dalrymple, 1776; 5 B. Sup. 586; Hailes, 695; 2 Ill. 44.

(*f*) Hamilton *v.* Hamilton, 1824; 2 S. 640. Gordon's Trs. *v.* Eglinton, 1851; 13 D. 1381. D. Argyle *v.* Dalgleish's Trs., 1873; 11 Macph. 616.

(*g*) M'Millan *v.* Campbell, 1831; 9 S. 551. Dickson's Trs. *v.* Goodall, 1820; Hume, 925.

(*h*) Brechin Town Council *v.* Arbuthnot, 1840; 3 D. 216. Lindsay *v.* Giles, 1844; 6 D. 771. M'Farlan, Petr., 1853; 15 D. 708. Haig *v.* Haig, 1857; 19 D. 449. Smith, *cit. infra*, § 872 (*a*).

(*i*) Davidson, *supra* (*a*).

(*k*) 2 Ersk. 3. § 45. Maxwell *v.* L. Portrack, 1628; M. 14,318. L. Hermiston *v.* Butler, 1630; M. 14,326. Gordon *v.* Brodie, 1773; 5 B. Sup. 587; Hailes, 535; Bell, Election Law, 254. See M'Intosh *v.* Inglis, 1825; 4 S. 190. M. Bell's Convg. 652.

(*l*) Carnegy *v.* Cruickshanks, 1729; M. 14,316; 2 Ill. 48. E. Aberdeen *v.* Duncan, 1742; M. 14,316; Elch. *Sup. & Vass.* 7. Brechin Town Council, *supra* (*h*). M. Bell's Convg. 648.

(*m*) Urquhart *v.* Officers of State, 1753; M. 9921; Elch. *Sasine*, 8; 5 B. Sup. 257; aff. 1755, 1 Cr. St. & P. 586; 2 Ill. 44.

(*n*) Primrose *v.* Dury, 1612; M. 14,326. M'Intosh, *supra* (*k*).

(*o*) D. Roxburghe *v.* Hall, 1731; M. 14,332. Clark *v.* Waddel, 1752; M. 14,333. M'Lean *v.* D. Argyle, 1777; 5 B. Sup. 590. Morrison *v.* Ramsay, 1826; 5 S. 150. M'Ghie *v.* Leishman, 1827; 5 S. 758. Dickson *v.* Cuninghame, 1829; 7 S. 503. But see A. of S., Jan. 17, 1756, and M. Bell's Convg. 650.

872. At common law, if any essential part of the instrument was written on an erasure not duly authenticated, it was held fatal; as the date, the king's reign, the name of the lands (*a*). But, by statute, the law as to erasures is placed on a new footing, and no erasure is fatal unless proved to have been made fraudulently, or where the record is not conformable to the instrument as presented for registration (*b*).

(*a*) Innes *v.* E. Fife, 1827; 5 S. 559; aff. 2 W. & S. 637; 2 Ill. 80. M'Millan *v.* Campbell, 1831; 9 S. 551. E. Cassillis *v.* Kennedy, 1831; 9 S. 663. Hoggan (Smith) *v.* Ranken, 1835; 13 S. 461; aff. 1840, 1 Rob. 173. Howden *v.* Ferrier, 1835; 13 S. 1097.

(*b*) 6 and 7 Will. IV. c. 33. See below, § 875.

873. (2.) *Extrinsic Objections.*—Although much to be regretted (as tending to shake the stability of land rights by parole evidence), extrinsic objections, *i.e.* objections to the truth of the statement in the instrument, are still competent as grounds of reduction, if supported by sufficient proof.

874. Sasine in Separate Tenements.—As sasine must be taken on the ground of the lands, the ceremony 'had to be' separately performed on each tenement, either where the lands lie discontiguous, or where they hold of different superiors, or where they are held by different tenures, or where they have been acquired by different titles; and defects in those points may, as grounds of reduction of the sasine, be established either by reference to the instrument or by extraneous evidence (*a*).

If the land shall have been erected into a barony, sasine on any part, or on a part appointed, and by the symbol of earth and stone, is sufficient for the whole (*b*). The Crown has also power, by a clause of union in a charter, to unite subjects lying locally discontiguous, or requiring different symbols: so as to make sasine at any point of the lands, or at a place specified, good for the whole; or to make one symbol serve (*c*). But it is indispensable that sasine shall be duly recorded, either in the General Register of Sasines, or in the Particular Register of each shire in which any of the united parcels lie (*d*). The rules for sasine under such charters are:—If in the charter of a barony, or in a clause of union, a place is appointed for taking sasine, it must be taken at that place; otherwise only the contiguous portions derived from the same superior will be carried (*e*). If no place be named, but sasine is authorised *super aliquam partem fundi*, etc., it may be taken on any part of the barony or united lands (*f*). Separation of a part does not dissolve the union, but each part is held to be joined to each; and neither the part alienated nor the part retained is deprived of the benefit (*g*). A clause of union has no effect in dispensing with separate sasine, where the subjects are derived from different sources or held of different superiors, but only when they are locally discontiguous, or require different symbols. The Crown alone can give such dispensation; a subject superior can only communicate the privilege when conferred. But the objection on this ground being extrinsic, if the years of prescription have run, the presumption is *omnia rite et solemniter acta esse* (*h*). 'An instrument of sasine in the more modern form is effectual whether the lands contained in it be contiguous or discontiguous, or are held by the same or different titles, or of one or more superiors (*i*). The recording of a conveyance under the existing law has the same effect (*k*).'

(*a*) 2 Ersk. Pr. 3. § 21. 2 Ersk. 3. § 36, 44–5. Bk. of Scot. *v.* Ramsay, 1729; M. 16,404; 2 Ill. 82. Grant *v.* Rowand, 1837; 15 S. 563. Campbell *v.* Campbell, 1819; Hume, 723. Questions of the nature stated in the text cannot arise under the new forms of infeftment.

(*b*) 2 Ersk. 3. § 46.

(*c*) 2 Craig, 7. § 17, 19. 2 Stair, 3. § 44–5. 2 Ersk. 3. § 45. Montgomerie *v.* Dalrymple, March 2, 1813; F. C.; 2 Ill. 82.

(*d*) See Dalrymple *v.* E. Carnwath, 1711; 4 B. Sup. 862. See 31 and 32 Vict. c. 64, § 3 (Land Registers Act).

(*e*) Lauriston *v.* Dunnipace, 1636; M. 14,330. Bk. of Scot., *cit.* (*a*).

(*f*) Skene *v.* Ogilvie, 1768; M. 8792; Hailes, 210; rev. 2 Pat. 141.

(*g*) 2 Craig, 7. § 19, to be corrected by 2 Stair, 3. § 45, and 2 Ersk. 3. § 45. Skene and Montgomerie, *supra*. Dundas *v.* Freeholders of Linlithgow, 1767; M. 8793; Hailes, 210; rev. 2 Pat. 141; 2 Ill. 83. Lyall *v.* Skene, 1768; 2 Pat. 138. Brown *v.* Kyd, 1813; Hume, 717.

(*h*) Heron *v.* Syme, 1771; M. 8684, *bis*; Hailes, 401. Scott *v.* Bruce Stewart, 1779; M. 13,519; 5 B. Sup. 588; Hailes, 730, 811. Wood's Trs. *v.* Ferrier, 1832; 10 S. 773; aff. 7 W. & S. 147. Montgomerie, *supra* (*c*).

(*i*) 8 and 9 Vict. c. 35, § 1.

(*k*) 31 and 32 Vict. c. 101, § 15.

875. Erasures in Sasines.—There is this important distinction between deeds, and instruments of sasine or of resignation, that the former are of the essence of the conveyance, the latter only the notice of it; and that, in the latter, an entry on the record consistent with the deed of conveyance is all that is truly useful. In a deed, words erased are presumed to have been different when the deed was signed, unless the alteration be authenticated by the tenor of the testing clause. In an instrument the same presumption holds, unless the alteration is authenticated by the docquet of the notary. In practice, it happened that vitiations were more frequent in sasines than in deeds, and that they were less accurately authenticated, from the less familiar use of Latin in the docquet. But some cases occurred which gave great alarm, where vitiations in sasines were found fatal to the titles of an estate, while every sasine coming into improper hands was exposed to such fatal operations (*a*). These obvious dangers led to a statute (*b*), whereby no challenge of an instrument of sasine or instrument of resignation shall receive effect by reduction or exception, on the ground that any part of it is written on an erasure, unless it be proved that it has been done for the purpose of fraud, or unless the record is not conformable to the instrument as presented for registration. The law is to apply only to cases in which the objection has been judicially made after the 12th May 1835, and it does not apply to sasines *propriis manibus*, for those are conveyances rather than mere instruments of sasine. 'It was enacted that, in case of any error or defect in a sasine in the modern form, or in the recording of it, a new instrument may be made and recorded, taking effect from the date of recording it (*c*); and again, that in case of any error or defect in any instrument, or any warrant of registration, or in the recording of any deed or instrument, or warrant of registration, in the Sasine Registers, it shall be competent of new to make and record the instrument, or to record the deed or instrument with the old or a new warrant, as the case may require (*d*). And the Act 6 and 7 Will. IV. c. 33 is made applicable to all instruments (*e*). With regard to deeds, instruments, and writings recorded in the Sasine Registers, it is further provided that they cannot be challenged on the ground that any part of the record is written on erasure, unless such erasure is proved to have been made for the purpose of fraud, or the record is not conformable to the writ as presented for registration (*f*).'

(*a*) Hoggan *v.* Ranken, and Howden *v.* Ferrier, *citt.* § 872; 2 Ill. 81.
(*b*) 6 and 7 Will. IV. c. 33. See above, § 872.
(*c*) 8 and 9 Vict. c. 35, § 4.
(*d*) 31 and 32 Vict. c. 101, § 143; see definition clause, § 3 (9).
(*e*) *Ib.* § 144.
(*f*) 37 and 38 Vict. c. 94, § 54.

876. **Precept of Sasine.** (1.) *General Precept.*—The precept must contain a warrant to give infeftment to a certain person, and in certain lands. But it seems not to be necessary that either the person or the lands should be *named*, provided they shall be sufficiently distinguished and identified (*a*). Hence, if the lands be described in such a way as to be capable of identification by written evidence, the sasine will be good, provided written evidence to identify the lands be produced to the notary, and read and published and stated in the instrument (*b*); and in such a case the extract of a sasine from the record is sufficient where the sasine is lost (*c*). A precept to infeft A. *nominatim*, and his heirs and assignees, is a good warrant of sasine in favour of a person, though not named, who shall produce to the notary proof of his character of heir or assignee (*d*). A precept to infeft "the heirs of A." is not good to sustain a sasine, if taken in the same terms (*e*); but if sasine be taken to B., and a general service be produced and "deduced" in the instrument, proving B. to be the heir, it seems to be sufficient (*f*). 'Exact specification in the precept of the symbols to be used in giving sasine in the old forms was not necessary (*g*).'

(*a*) See M. Bell's Convg. 646. *Supra*, § 768.
(*b*) York Buildings Co. *v.* D. Norfolk, 1739; Elch. *Serv. & Conf.* 8; 2 Ill. 83; 2 Ross' L. C. 28. Wallace *v.* Dalrymple, 1742; M. 6919; Elch. *Sasine*, 3. Graham's Crs. *v.* Hyslop, 1753; M. 49. Belches *v.* Stewart, Jan. 21, 1815; F. C. Hill *v.* D. Montrose, 1833; 11 S. 958; 2 Ross' L. C. 34.
(*c*) 1617, c. 16. (*d*) 1693, c. 35.
(*e*) 2 Ersk. 3. § 33. Blackwood *v.* E. Sutherland, 1740; M. 14,327; 2 Ross' L. C. 18. Melville *v.* Smiton's Crs., 1794; M. 14,237. Peacock *v.* Glen, 1826; 4 S. 742.
(*f*) See Barstow *v.* Stewart, 1858; 20 D. 612. Menzies, Convg. 561.
(*g*) Barstow, *supra*. Brechin Town Council *v.* Arbuthnot, 1840; 3 D. 216.

877. (2.) *Special Precept.*—If the precept be special in its nature, it is not a warrant under which sasine of a different description can be given; as a precept for "sasine in security," or "in liferent," will not authorise a sasine in fee or in property. It has been thought, however, that a precept to infeft one in trust may, when such trustee has power to sell, be assigned to a purchaser so as to authorise a sasine in his person; and at least where the precept is to infeft the trustee and his assignees, a purchaser may be infeft on the assigned precept. A precept for sasine generally, or in fee, will authorise a sasine in security or in trust. The greater being held to include the less, it is good if the sasine be of the same nature, and by the same symbols (*a*).

(*a*) Mitchell *v.* Adam, 1767; M. 14,335; L. Pitfour in Hailes, 185; 2 Ill. 85; 2 Ross' L. C. 418. See 1 Bell's Com. 697, notes. More *v.* Bonthrone, 1805; Hume, 238. Cockburn *v.* Cameron, 1836; 14 S. 889. Melvin *v.* Dakers, 1843; 5 D. 1217. Houlditch *v.* Spalding, 1847; 9 D. 1204. See above, § 820, and Barstow, § 876 (*f*).

878. (3.) *Mandate presumed from Possession of Precept.*—The possession of the precept presumes a mandate to take sasine. But this may be redargued by him in whose name it is taken: as where sasine would infer representation; or where it is taken differently from the warrant, in leaving out conditions protected by irritancies (*a*); 'or where the charter or disposition has not been delivered (*b*).'

(*a*) 2 Stair, 3. § 17. 2 Ersk. 3. § 33 *in fin.* 2 Craig, 7. § 6. See above, § 710 (*f*). Paul *v.* Boyd, 1833; 11 S. 292.
(*b*) Menzies, Convg. 563. Gray *v.* Dinning, 1838; 1 D. 227.

879. (4.) *Exhausting of the Precept.*—The precept is exhausted when duly executed. By such execution only does the fee become full in the person of the disponee, so as to extinguish the feudal right which enables the granter to issue a precept. But when not duly executed, or so as not to complete the feudal right in another, and entirely to divest the granter, the precept is still in force. And so a fatal error in the *taking* of sasine may be remedied by a new sasine; the precept in that case is not exhausted. A fatal error in the *instrument*, as it annuls the sasine, leaves the feudal right undivested, and the precept still in force. Even a fatal error in the *recording* (as to a certain extent it destroys the sasine) has also the effect of permitting a new sasine to be taken, as on an unexhausted precept. This has been doubted on the words of the Act of 1617. But, according both to legal principle and the practice of conveyancers, the precept is in such a case good authority for a new sasine (*a*).

(*a*) 1599, Act of Sed. pp. 29, 30. 1600, c. 36. 1617, c. 16. 1669, c. 3. Stewart's Ans. to Dirl. 275 (*b*). Kibble *v.* Stewart, June 16, 1814; F. C.; 2 Ill. 86. Baxter *v.* Watson, May 15, 1818; 1 Bell's Com. 697; Hume, 718. Kibble *v.* Stevenson, 1830; 9 S. 233; aff. 5 W. & S. 553. Fulton *v.* M'Allister, 1831; 9 S. 442. Young *v.* Leith, 1847; 9 D. 932; aff. 2 Ross' L. C. 103. Haig *v.* Haig, 1857; 19 D. 449. See the effect of these cases more fully stated in § 774.

880. Registration of Sasine.—The record of the sasine must be complete. And so, if lands are omitted in an essential part of the record of the instrument, the sasine is held not recorded as to them (*a*). An erroneous transcription of the date of the instrument in the record annuls the registration (*b*). An error in the record as to the year of the King's reign in transcribing the date of the precept is fatal (*c*). The effect of omitting to record, or of not recording in due time, or of omitting any subject, or of any error which annuls the registration, is not to destroy the sasine to all intents. Against the granter, and his heirs and representatives, it is effectual (*d*): But it is null against a third party who has completed his real right; nor will it be a good answer to him in competition, or a bar to his completing his right, that he was aware of the existence of a prior right of which the sasine was not duly recorded, unless he be participant in the fraud. So, an adjudger, or creditor obtaining a security, etc., with sasine duly recorded, will prevail in a competition notwithstanding private knowledge of the error (*e*).

(*a*) Grey *v.* Hope, 1790; M. 8796; 2 Ill. 46. Stewart *v.* E. Fife, 1827; 5 S. 383; 2 Ill. 85.
(*b*) M'Queen *v.* Nairne, 1824; 2 S. 637.
(*c*) Denniston *v.* Speirs, 1824; 3 S. 285 and 400. See above, § 871 (*h*).
(*d*) 1617, c. 16. See above, § 772, 774. Simpson *v.* Blackie, 1678; M. 13,553.
(*e*) Leslie *v.* M'Indoe's Trs., 1824; 3 S. 48; 2 Ill. 85. See also Lang *v.* Dixon, June 29, 1813; F. C.; decided on the ground of acquiescence and homologation. Young *v.* Leith, 1847; 9 D. 932; 2 Ross' L. C. 81.

IV. ACCRETION.

881. Principle.—A sasine taken on the precept of one who has the right but is not infeft, is ineffectual. It, however, may become effectual on the subsequent completion of his title. This is the doctrine comprised in the maxim, *Jus superveniens auctori accrescit successori.* It is held to depend on the principle of warrandice express or implied; the law doing what the granter is bound to do (*a*).

(*a*) 3 Stair, 2. § 1, etc. 2 Ersk. 7. § 3. 1 Bell's Com. 698. Wilson *v.* Webster, 1836; 14 S. 1117; 3 Ill. 153. *Supra*, § 778, 793, 852. Martin *v.* Wight, 1840; 3 D. 485 (trustees).

882. The Rules of this doctrine are—

(1.) A conveyance of land with sasine proceeding from one in the substantial right, but whose title is not complete, is made perfect by the subsequent completion of the granter's title (*a*). So, if an heir or disponee convey the land to which his right as yet is only personal, and the disponee is infeft, the subsequent sasine of the granter makes valid the imperfect conveyance. So, also, if one infeft on an indefinite precept, unconfirmed, dispone with a precept to be held *a me*, a subsequent confirmation of his sasine will validate the public sasine proceeding from him (*b*). So, in the same way, if one, infeft public without confirmation (and so having no complete feudal right), dispone with a precept, the subsequent completion of his title by confirmation will render valid, *accretione*, the otherwise inefficacious infeftment of the grantee.

(2.) If the granter of the precept have at the time no right to the subject, but acquire a right by subsequent title, it may be doubted whether accretion will take place (*c*). The ground of this doubt is, that there can be no proper conveyance where there is no right existing; that law may *fictione* supply solemnities, but not substantial right; and that in such cases there is nothing but an implied obligation to convey, which requires a different mode of completion (*d*). 'But it has now been decided that in such a case accretion does take place (*e*).'

(3.) If one not yet infeft grant a conveyance or an heritable bond, and on the precept sasine be taken, and the granter die without his title being completed, and his heir make up titles to the land, this will not avail the grantee; nor will the heir's title accresce to his sasine (*f*).

(4.) Accretion is available to infeftments according to their priority in date; and even when the title is completed on the application of one of the competitors, and with the intention of validating his right alone, it nevertheless will accresce to the other if his sasine be prior in date (*g*). But where the title is completed on the *diligence* of any creditor, it has been said by Lord Stair to accresce only to that creditor (*h*).

(5.) The effect of accretion is important in bankruptcy; and, on the principle stated by Lord Stair, it would appear that after bankruptcy no accretion to render valid the securities of particular creditors to the prejudice of the general body, should take place in consequence of an act of the trustee intended for the general benefit. But the point is not settled (*i*).

(*a*) 3 Stair, 2. § 1. 2 Ersk. 7. § 2, 3; 1 Bell's Com. 698 (737, M'L.'s ed.); 2 Ross' L. C. 306. Innes *v.* Gordon, 1844; 7 D. 141. M'Gibbon *v.* M'Gibbon, 1852; 14 D. 605. E. Fife *v.* Duff, 1862; 24 D. 936; aff. 1 Macph. H. L. 19; 4 Macq. 469.

(*b*) Henderson *v.* Campbell, July 5, 1821; F. C.; 1 S. 104; 2 Ill. 51. Macdonald Lockhart *v.* Ferrier, 1837; 16 S. 76.

(*c*) Dirleton & Stewart, *v.* *Jus Superveniens*. 2 Ersk. 7. § 2. See 2 Stair, 3. § 14. Buchan *v.* Cockburn, 1739; M. 6528; 2 Ill. 86. Town of Musselburgh *v.* Scot, 1675; M. 7759. Forbes *v.* Innes, 1668; M. 7759. Stewart *v.* Hutchison, 1681; M. 7762 (cases of consenters).

(*d*) In consultation with the late Mr. Jamieson, Professor Bell and he differed in opinion; that sound lawyer inclining to hold the maxim applicable.

(*e*) Swan *v.* Western Bank, 1866; 4 Macph. 663. Cf. Munro *v.* Brodie, 1844; 6 D. 1249. Glassford's Exrs. *v.* Scott, 1850; 12 D. 893. Smith *v.* Wallace, 1869; 8 Macph. 204. See below, § 890 (*h*).

(*f*) Keith *v.* Grant, 1792; M. 2933; 2 Ill. 87; 3 Ross' L. C. 308. This was delivered by L. J.-C. Macqueen, and assented to by all the Court, except L. Henderland, who doubted (as Stewart does—Dirleton & Stewart, *ut supra*) whether, being bound in warrandice, the completion of his title does not accresce.

(*g*) 3 Stair, 2. § 2. Neilson *v.* Murray, 1738; M. 7773; Elch. *Jus Superv.* 1. Paterson *v.* Kelly, 1742; M. 7775; Elchies' Notes, 236. Alison *v.* Chalmers, 1708; M. 7773. See Henderson, *supra* (*b*).

(*h*) Stair, *supra* (*a*).

(*i*) 1 Bell's Com. 699 (737–8, M'L.'s ed.). See Tatnal *v.* Reid, 1827; 5 S. 277. Baron Norton *v.* Anderson, July 6, 1813; F. C. Redfearn *v.* Maxwell, March 7, 1816; F. C. See Wilson *v.* Webster, 1836; 14 S. 1117.

V. PROVING OF THE TENOR.

883. Loss of Titles.—The loss of titles, 'or their accidental or inadvertent destruction, or obliteration, or cancellation (*a*),' may be supplied 'or cured,' by an action called Proving of the Tenor; and when the deed is of the nature of a title, or ground of a permanent right, this process is necessary in order to supply the defect (*b*). It can proceed only before the Court of Session, 'and there only in the Inner House (*c*); or it may be before the Court of Teinds, as well as the Court of Session, in the case of lost valuations and sub-valuations of teinds (*d*).' Two points are necessary to the effect of completing the title:—1. The tenor of the deed; and 2. The *casus amissionis*. Being a dangerous though a useful remedy, great strictness of proof is required in making out these points (*e*). 'In certain cases, as where a deed is founded on by way of exception, and is not the foundation of the original suit constituting the pursuer's title to sue, and where the fact in question might be proved otherwise without any such deed; or where it is shown that the party prejudiced by the deed has destroyed it, a formal action of proving the tenor is not required, and the import of the writ may be proved incidentally in the course of a process (*f*).'

(1.) *Proof of the Tenor.*—When the deed is of a nature not to be extinguished by mere delivery to the debtor, attention is chiefly or entirely to be directed to the proving of the tenor; the fact of the loss of the deed being enough in the ordinary case. The proof of the tenor will vary with circumstances. In some cases, that proof will consist of scrolls and copies, aided by parole evidence; in other cases, more suspicious, or more special in terms, conditions, provisions, etc., adminicles will be required, *i.e.* authentic writings which of themselves make faith without the aid of parole evidence, as sasines, instruments of resignation, retours of service, precepts of *clare constat* (*g*). Where the deed is not of a permanent nature, but such as may be extinguished by mere delivery, as a bond 'or a bill (*h*),' it is not to be expected that there shall be found adminicles; and then the proof of the tenor by scrolls, parole, copies, etc., must be supported by clear evidence of *casus amissionis* (*i*). 'The proof of *casus amissionis* is of equal delicacy and importance in the case of testamentary writings, in regard to which the party founding on them must exclude the supposition that the testator intentionally destroyed them (*k*).' In proving the tenor of a deed, if it should be established by the defender that it was informal, not duly authenticated, or not written on a stamp as required by law, the action would fail. But the presumption in those points would be in favour of the deed on proof of the *casus amissionis* (*l*). Great difficulty has been found in sustaining a proving of the tenor of judicial proceedings; and so of titles by adjudication (*m*).

(2.) *Proof of Casus Amissionis.*—The point here is to prove that a deed once existing has accidentally perished, and has not been intentionally destroyed by one having power to cancel it (*n*). The same strict evidence, however, of a *casus amissionis* is not required in such cases as in the restoring of obligations (*o*).

(*a*) Cunningham *v.* Mouat's Trs., 1851; 13 D. 1376. Winchester *v.* Smith, 1863; 1 Macph. 685. Cousin *v.* Gemmell, 1862; 24 D. 758. Graham *v.* Graham, 1847; 10 D. 45.

(*b*) 4 Stair, 32. § 1 et seq. 4 Ersk. 1. § 54. Maxwell *v.* Maxwell, 1742; M. 15,820; Elch. *Tenor*, 4, and Notes, 483; 2 Ill. 88. See Seton, 1766; 5 B. Sup. 924. See Browne *v.* Orr, 1872; 10 Macph. 397 (interest, where deed recorded).

(*c*) Balnagoun *v.* M'Kenzie, 1663; M. 15,790. Smart *v.* Ewing, 1673; 3 B. Sup. 149. Fraser *v.* Fraser Davies, 1784; M. 15,830. Robertson *v.* Blair Hyndman, 1833; 11 S. 775. Lillie *v.* Lillie, 1832; 11 S. 160. Inch's Trs. *v.* Inch, 1855; 17 D. 1138.

(*d*) 1707, c. 9. Alexander *v.* Oswald, 1840; 3 D. 40. L. Lynedoch *v.* Liston, 1841; 3 D. 1078. See Richmond *v.* Offrs. of State, 1869; 7 Macph. 956.

(*e*) Fraser, *supra* (*c*). Rannie *v.* Ogg, 1891; 18 R. 903 (exclusively parole evidence ?). Skinners and Furriers of Edin. *v.* Baxter, 1897; 24 R. 744.

(*f*) Maxwell, *cit.* (*b*). Drummond *v.* Thomson's Trs., 1832; 12 S. 620; aff. 7 W. & S. 564; and cases in Dickson on Evid. § 1291–1297. Shaw *v.* Shaw's Trs., 1876; 3 R. 813. Selkirk Presb. *v.* D. Buccleuch, 1869; 8 Macph. 121 (churchmen). Clark *v.* Clark's Trs., 1860; 23 D. 80 (title resting on contract proveable by parole). Gilchrist *v.* Morrison, 1891; 18 R. 599.

(*g*) Gordon *v.* Gray, 1749; 5 B. Sup. 766; M. 15,823. D. Roxburghe's Trs. *v.* Young, 1835; 13 S. 476. Walker *v.* Brock, 1852; 14 D. 362. Watson *v.* Erskine, 1847; 19 Jur. 523. Falconar *v.* Stephen, 1848; 11 D. 220, 1338. Jenkinson *v.* Campbell, 1850; 12 D. 854. Cunningham *v.* Mouat's Trs., 1851; 13 D. 1376. Winton & Co. *v.* Thomson & Co., 1862; 24 D. 1094. Sanquhar Mags. *v.* Officers of State, 1864; 2 Macph. 499. M'Leod *v.* Leslie, 1865; 3 Macph. 840. Richmond *v.* Officers of State, 1869; 7 Macph. 956. Ritchie *v.* Ritchie, 1871; 9 Macph. 820. In these cases and in modern practice (see, *e.g.*, 2 Mackay's Practice, 321), the distinction in these two sentences as to the use of the word adminicles is not observed; and the word is loosely used to include writings of all kinds tending to prove the tenor.

(*h*) Campbell *v.* York Buildings Co., 1780; M. 15,828. Carson *v.* M'Micken, May 14, 1811; F. C. Macfarlane *v.* M'Nee, 1826; 4 S. 509.

(*i*) Gordon, *supra* (*g*), and cases in 2 Ill. 89, 90. M'Kean *v.* ——, 1857; 19 D. 448. Russell's Trs. *v.* Russell, 1862; 24 D. 1141. A testament wilfully destroyed by one of the parties interested in it was proved without adminicles, in Leckie *v.* Leckie, 1884; 11 R. 1088.

(*k*) Kerr *v.* Kerr, 1830; 9 S. 204. Dow *v.* Dow, 1848; 10 D. 1465. Forrester *v.* Forrester, 1835; 15 S. 690; 1836, 16 S. 1064. Boyter *v.* Rintoul, 1832; 5 D. & A. 215; aff. 6 W. & S. 394. Lang *v.* Bruce, 1838; 1 D. 59. Cunningham, *supra* (*g*). Winchester *v.* Smith, 1863; 1 Macph. 685. Ritchie *v.* Ritchie, *cit.* (deed destroyed by adverse party). Bonthrone *v.* Ireland, 1883; 10 R. 779. See below, note (*n*).

(*l*) Blackwood *v.* Hamilton, 1713; M. 15,819; rev. Robertson's App. 211.

(*m*) Lady Airth *v.* Blackwood, 1707; M. 15,813, 11,359. Duncan *v.* Arnott, 1827; 5 S. 840. L. Lynedoch *v.* Liston, 1841; 3 D. 1078. Shaw Stewart *v.* Macfarlane, 1835; 13 S. 765. Clyne *v.* Johnstone, 1833; 11 S. 131. D. Argyle *v.* Maclean, 1781; M. 15,828. As to hornings, executions, etc., see 1579, c. 94. 4 Ersk. 1. § 58. By statute, copies of lost or destroyed pleadings (not interlocutor sheets, Cofton *v.* Cofton, 1875; 2 R. 599) may be proved in the process and authenticated to the satisfaction of the Court, both in the Court of Session (31 and 32 Vict. c. 100, § 15) and Sheriff Court (39 and 40 Vict. c. 70, § 11).

(*n*) 4 Stair, 32. § 4–7. 4 Ersk. 1. § 54. Muir *v.* Niddrie, 1663; M. 15,789. Moffat *v.* Moffat, Jan. 31, 1809; F. C. Paterson *v.* Houston, 1837; 16 S. 225. See above (*k*). Graham *v.* Graham, 1847; 10 D. 45. Donald *v.* Kirkaldy, 1787; M. 15,831; aff. 1788, 3 Pat. 105; see 9 R. 872. Smith *v.* Ferguson, 1882; 9 R. 866.

(*o*) Ersk. *ut supra.* Gordon *v.* Gray, 1749; M. 15,823; 5 B. Sup. 776. Carson *v.* M'Miken, May 14, 1811; F. C. Murray *v.* Dun, 1834; 12 S. 764. D. Roxburghe, *supra* (*g*). M'Leod *v.* M'Lean, 1835; 13 S. 581. Brechin Mags. *v.* Guthrie, Martin, & Co., 1835; 14 S. 154. Forbes *v.* Welsh, 1827; 5 S. 497. Kerr *v.* Kay, 1830; 8 S. 1008.

VI. GROUND-ANNUALS.

884. Nature of them.—Out of the peculiar state of Church lands as affected by the Reformation, and from the great demand in more recent times for building ground in towns, a description of estate called "Ground-Annuals" has arisen, intermediate between that of the superior and that of the vassal, of the nature of a perpetual annuity. "Annual" is technically used to mean a yearly duty or revenue; and when payable from land, it seems formerly to have been distinguished by the different names of ground-annual, top-annual, and feu-annual, the distinctions of which are not very accurately ascertained (*a*).

(*a*) Skene, De Verb. Sig. *Annual*. 1 Craig, 10. § 38. 2 Stair, 5. § 7. 1551, c. 10; 2 Act. Parl. 489.

885. Ground-Annuals out of Church Property.—One-fourth part of the territory of Scotland is reckoned to have been the property of the Church at the time of the Reformation; in the administration and cultivation of which, by means of feus, rental-rights, and kindly tenantry, the early agriculture of Scotland was chiefly promoted. At the Reformation, this property, which all merged in the Crown, was parcelled out in various lordships erected by the Crown, the grantees being called Lords of Erection, not as being of the order of nobility, but merely feudal lords. In 1587, this profusion, by which the Crown greatly suffered, was checked by a general annexation of the Church lands, with the exception of the lordships of erection. Other grants were subsequently made, however, and were stopped only by another Act of Annexation, 1592, with the exception only of those lands which had been granted to Lords of Parliament (*a*). The lands which belonged to the Knights Templars were excepted from the Annexation Acts, and hence the successors of the Knights Templars are the proper superiors of those lands. In the beginning of the seventeenth century, the Lords of Erection resigned their superiorities to the Crown, with the exception of the feu-duties; and for those feu-duties a redemption-price was to be given, such as King Charles I. should award. The king's decree-arbitral settled the rate of this redemption at 1000 merks for each chalder of victual, or £100 of money of feu-duty; and the feu-duties were to be retained till that price should be paid, no power being given of interposing superiors between the King and the former Church vassals (*b*). But no benefit accrued to the Crown from this reserved power of redemption; and it was on the eve of the Union renounced, that the feu-duties might remain irredeemably and for ever with the Lords of Erection, and those having right from them (*c*).

(*a*) 1587, c. 29. 1592, c. 121. 1633, c. 10, § 4. 1690, c. 13 and 29. 1707, c. 11. 2 Ersk. 10. § 18.
(*b*) 1653, c. 10 and 14. 1690, c. 23, 29.
(*c*) 1707, c. 11.

886. In virtue of that series of statutes, property of this sort came to stand thus:—The Crown was superior of Church lands, the vassals holding formerly of the Church being entitled to an entry with the Crown wherever they had not recognised the lord of erection as an intermediate superior. A feu-duty was payable as a "ground-annual" to the successor of the lord of erection, the holding of the Crown being blench, under the real burden of the feu-duties. This real burden has by practice been usually conveyed by resignation and infeftment only (*a*).

(*a*) E. of Aberdeen *v.* Forbes, 1699; M. 7974; 2 Ill. 91. Blair *v.* Murray, 1790; 2 Bell's Com. 283; 2 Ill. 91. Heriot's Hospital *v.* Hepburn, 1714; M. 8986–9; Robertson's App. 118. Inverness Mags. *v.* Bell's Trs., 1827; 6 S. 160. Coll. of St. Andrews *v.* Newark's Crs., 1762; M. 10,171. Duff's Feudal Conveyancing, 200.

887. Ground-Annuals in Building Feus.—The usual course with those who speculate in building ground is to grant sub-feus to builders, from whom they stipulate for a high feu-duty. But if sub-feus be prohibited, and there is great demand for building ground (as formerly in Edinburgh, where the grants from the town and from the Governors of Heriot's Hospital contain such exclusions), those who take the land in feu with the intention of again disposing of small portions to builders, find their advantage in stipulating for an annual rent from the builder rather than in demanding a price payable at once. This is accomplished by the creation of a "ground-annual." The disposition is granted to be held public (*a me de superiore meo*), in compliance with the condition of the feu-charter; but the subject is charged with an annual payment to the granter, and his heirs and assignees. Either a burden or annuity is reserved which is declared a real burden, or a bond and disposition in security of the annuity is granted by the purchaser, on which infeftment is taken; and in either way the payment appears in the Register of Sasines as a real burden. When the payment is by proper ground-annual, it is postponed to the feu-duty. It gives no active title to enter into possession, though, as a *debitum fundi*, it may be made the foundation of poinding the ground (*a*). No interest is due on ground-annuals (*b*). Like a burden by reservation, the ground-annual is transmissible by assignation to third parties, and by general service to heirs (*c*).

(*a*) See § 887A, 914, and Bell's Trs., below.
(*b*) Scott Moncrieff *v.* L. Dundas, 1835 ; 14 S. 61. See above, § 695.
(*c*) See below, § 923. As to an obligation to build in a contract of ground-annual, see Marshall's Tr. *v.* Macneill & Co., 1888 ; 15 R. 762. As to extinction *confusione*, see Murray *v.* Parlane's Tr., 1890 ; 18 R. 287.

887A. 'But when a bond and disposition in security of the annuity forms part of the contract, as in the existing practice it usually does, the person in right of the ground-annual has an active title, and has all the remedies of a heritable creditor in a bond and disposition in security (*a*). In this form the burden not only attaches to the lands ; but in the event of a sale, the personal liability of the purchaser or grantee in the original contract of ground-annual and of his heirs continues, unless there be an express provision to the contrary ; and his singular successors in the land, if they have become personally bound, are relieved by parting with the lands (*b*).'

(*a*) Bell's Trs. *v.* Copeland & Co., 1896 ; 23 R. 651 (poinding of ground in competition with trustee in seqn.).
(*b*) **Small** *v.* **Millar**, 1849 ; 11 D. 495 ; rev. 1853, 1 Macq. 345 ; 21 S. Jur. 143. **Gardyne** *v.* **Royal Bank**, 1851 ; 13 D. 912 ; rev. 1853 ; 1 Macq. 358 ; 28 S. Jur. 410. Brown's Trs. *v.* Elmsley, 1852 ; 14 D. 675 ; rev. 1855 ; 2 Macq. 40 ; 18 D. H. L. 16 ; 27 S. Jur. 346 ; overruling Peddie *v.* Soot's Trs., 1846 ; 8 D. 560. See Dundee Police Comrs. *v.* Straton, 1884 ; 11 R. 586.

888. Care is usually taken by builders, in feuing out ground from which a ground-annual is payable, to have the payment so divided and apportioned, that, in disposing of the several lots when built upon, each purchaser may be liable only for his own share of the ground-annual. But even if such precaution be not taken at the first, purchasers who receive and complete their right with a burden of only a portion of the ground-annual are liable for no more,—at least have been held no further liable to poinding of the ground, which is a process of execution (*a*).

(*a*) Thomson *v.* Scott, 1828 ; 6 S. 526 ; 2 Ill. 92. See above, § 697.

CHAPTER IX

OF THE SALE OF LAND

889. Evidence of Contract.—Written evidence is indispensable to the contract of sale of lands (*a*), 'even when the contract is only founded on to the effect of sustaining a claim of damages (*b*).' There is generally a previous agreement in writing, to fix the bargain while the necessary examination of titles and preparation of the formal conveyances are in progress. This is in the form of 'holograph or probative' missives or minutes of sale (*c*), to which the doctrines already explained as to 'consent,' authentication, *locus pœnitentiæ*, *rei interventus*, and homologation are applicable (*d*). A promise in writing to dispone land, if delivered, 'and forming a complete unilateral obligation in itself (*e*),' is good without acceptance (*f*); and a virtual obligation to dispone lands has been inferred from an assignation to the perpetual rents of the subject (*g*).

'With regard to the effect of a concluded contract of sale, it is to be observed that, while a purchaser in general takes the subject free from all personal obligations of his predecessor and from all burdens not appearing on the title or records, his knowledge of any prior right, such as an onerous contract of sale made by his author, or even such notice of it as ought to have put him on his inquiry, will be sufficient ground for setting aside even a completed feudal right in his favour (*h*).'

(*a*) 1 Stair, 10. § 9. 3 Ersk. 2. § 2. 1 Bell's Com. 328 (345, M'L.'s ed.). Cases in following notes. See Aberdein *v.* Stratton's Trs., 1867; 5 Macph. 726, and Shiell *v.* Guthrie's Trs., 1874; 1 R. 1083 (*supra*, § 132), where it is held that no exception exists even in the case of sales by auction. As to purchases or sales by agents, see above, § 216.

(*b*) Allan *v.* Gilchrist, 1875; 2 R. 587.

(*c*) 1 Bell's Forms of Deeds, 144. Cockburn *v.* Trotters, 1639; M. 4187; 2 Ill. 92. Stewart *v.* Bissett, 1765; 5 B. Sup. 902. As to the effect of conditions in minutes of sale, see Corbett *v.* Robertson, 1872; 10 Macph. 329.

(*d*) See *ante*, §§ 18–27. Bell on Title to Land, 141. E. Aberdeen *v.* Laird, 1823; 2 S. 461. Rait *v.* Galloway, 1833; 12 S. 131. As to consent and concluded bargain, offer and acceptance, etc., see above, § 72, etc., 524 (7), and Johnston *v.* Clark, 1855; 18 D. 70. Milne *v.* Robertson, 1836; 14 S. 533; aff. 2 S. & M'L. 494. Dickson *v.* Blair, 1871; 10 Macph. 41. Colquhoun *v.* Wilson's Trs., 1860; 22 D. 1035. Heiton *v.* Waverley Hydr. Co., 1877; 4 R. 830. Westren *v.* Millar, 1879; 7 R. 173. Whyte *v.* Lee, 1879; 6 R. 699 (authorised agent). As to authentication (holograph, probative, etc.), Goldston *v.* Young, 1868; 7 Macph. 188. Weir *v.* Robertson, 1872; 10 Macph. 438 (writer's name in the body of unsigned holograph missive). Mitchell *v.* Scott's Trs., 1874; 2 R. 162. Scottish Lands, etc., Co. *v.* Shaw, 1880; 7 R. 756 (dictation to amanuensis). Caithness Flagstone Co. *v.* Sinclair, 1880; 7 R. 1117; aff. 1881, 8 R. H. L. 78 (do.). Gavine's Tr. *v.* Lee, 1883; 10 R. 448. M'Laren *v.* Law, 1871; 44 S. Jur. 17. Stewart *v.* Burns, 1877; 4 R. 427.

(*e*) See above, § 8. Ersk. Pr. 16th ed. 310, note (*e*).

(*f*) Fergusson *v.* Paterson, 1748; M. 8440. Muirhead *v.* Chalmers, 1759; M. 8444. Barron *v.* Rose, 1794; M. 8463. Malcolm *v.* Campbell, 1891; 19 R. 278 ("agree to sell" for so much, delivered, not valid without written acceptance). Goldston *v.* Young, *cit.* (*d*).

(*g*) Sinclair *v.* Couper, 1667; M. 16,464. Fullarton *v.* Muir, 1699; M. 16,465. But see note in 2 Ill. 93.

(*h*) See above, § 880. Leslie *v.* M'Indoe's Trs., and Lang *v.* Dixon, there cited. Marshall *v.* Hynd, 1828; 6 S. 384. Airdrie Mags. *v.* Smith, 1850; 12 D. 1222. Morrison *v.* Somerville, 1860; 23 D. 232. Petrie *v.* Forsyth, 1874; 2 R. 214. Stodart *v.* Dalzell, 1876; 4 R. 236. See Snell's Princ. of Equity, 30 sqq. As to partial reduction (rectification) on the ground of error in incidental obligations, see Glasgow Feuing Co. *v.* Watson's Trs., 1887; 14 R. 610.

890. Seller's Title.—There are two obligations implied in a sale of lands,—one, to give an unexceptionable title; the other, to warrant or indemnify the seller in case of eviction. As to the title, it is implied in a sale of lands (although commonly expressed in the previous minutes or agreement) that the seller shall give one that is unexceptionable, in which respect it differs from a sale of moveables. The rules on this subject are: That in a sale of land the buyer has an absolute right to a good title, '*i.e.* such a title as will secure him not merely from eviction, but from risk of trouble and expense (*a*)'; and unless he shall have unequivocally discharged this right, he is not bound to take a defective title with warrandice, or to wait till his right is challenged (*b*). It is a sufficient ground of exception to the title if it be liable to challenge (*c*); and although at one time it seems to have been held sufficient to offer a progress against which no challenge had been made, with warrandice in case of challenge (*d*), this is not law, and has been uniformly rejected in subsequent cases (*e*). But the buyer must either take the title offered or give up the bargain, and he is not entitled to insist on a deduction from the price (*f*). A reasonable time, however, must be allowed to the seller, on such an objection being started, to furnish an unexceptionable title; and the necessary discretion for that purpose can be excluded only by fixing a day against which the title must be completed by the seller (*g*). If it be specially and clearly agreed that the title shall be taken as it stands, or that the buyer shall be held to have examined the titles and satisfied himself, all that is demandable in absence of an actual challenge is warrandice (*h*). 'The bargain is binding if there be merely feudal defects in the title, resolving into a question of expense, but it is not binding if the title be radically bad, *i.e.* if the seller have no right at all to the lands which he professes to sell, or be absolutely unable to give a "marketable" title' (*i*). While formidable objections exist, the buyer is not bound to pay the price; and accordingly, a known method of trying the validity of objections to titles is by suspension of a threatened charge for payment of the price (*k*). 'A purchaser who enters into possession must pay interest if he fails to pay the price or consign it in his own name and that of the seller; and that although the delay in payment should be due to the seller's failure to furnish a sufficient progress of title-deeds (*l*). The purchaser who states a reasonable objection to the title offered him, which is repelled by the Court, is generally found entitled to the expenses of the process in which the doubt is removed; but there is no absolute rule, that one who states a plausible objection shall get the expenses of clearing his title (*m*).'

(*a*) Dunlop *v.* Crawford, 1849; 11 D. 1062; 1850, 12 D. 518. Hope *v.* Hamilton, 1851; 13 D. 1268. Kerr *v.* M. of Ailsa, 1852; 14 D. 864; aff. 1 Macq. 736. D. Devonshire *v.* Fletcher, 1874; 1 R. 1056. Dick, *infra*. See also § 912, below. M. Bell, Convg. 702 (3rd ed.).

(*b*) Nairne *v.* Scrymgeour, 1676; M. 14,169; 2 Ill. 94. Lockhart *v.* Johnston, 1742; M. 14,170. L. Maxwell *v.* Tait, 1743; Elchies, *Tailzie*, 21. Smith *v.* Aitken, 1827; 5 S. 340. Dick *v.* Donald (Cuthbertson), 1826; 2 W. & S. 522, and 9 S. 93; 1831, 5 W. & S. 712. Robertson *v.* Rutherford, 1841; 4 D. 121. Dunlop and Kerr, *supra*. Brown *v.* Cheyne, 1833; 12 S. 176. Traill *v.* Connon, 1877; 5 R. 25.

(*c*) Cases, *supra* (*b*). Little, *infra* (*e*).

(*d*) Paton *v.* Gordon, 1682; M. 14,170.

(*e*) Little *v.* Dickson, 1749; M. 14,177.

(*f*) E. Morton *v.* Cuninghan, 1738; M. 14,175; 2 Ill. 99. Aikman *v.* Hepburn & Cheap, 1772; M. 14,179; Hailes, 509; 5 B. Sup. 586; aff. 1773, 2 Paton, 326. See § 893.

(*g*) Smith *v.* Aitken, 1829; 8 S. 84. Dick, *supra* (*b*). Raeburn *v.* Baird, 1832; 10 S. 762. Nairne, *supra* (*b*). Hutchinson & Son *v.* Scott, 1830; 8 S. 377. As to the case where the purchaser is unable to give entry at the date stipulated, see Kelman *v.* Barr's Tr., 1878; 5 R. 816. Hunter *v.* Carsewell, 1822; 1 S. 248. Heys *v.* Kimball & Morton, 1890; 18 R. 381.

(*h*) See below, § 892.

(*i*) Rowand *v.* Cochrane, 1769; M. 14,178; Hailes, 312. Hay *v.* Panton, 1783; M. 14,183. Anderson *v.* Matheson, Dec. 4, 1818; F. C. Carruthers *v.* Stott, 1826; 4 S. 35. Smith, *supra* (*b*). Sorley's Trs. *v.* Graham, 1832; 10 S. 319. Young *v.* Grierson, 1849; 11 D. 1482. Waddell *v.* Pollock, 1828; 6 S. 999. Rodger *v.* Brown, 1859; 21 D. 1022. Hamilton *v.* Western Bank, 1861; 23 D. 1033. See above, § 882 (2); below, § 893, 894, and Brownlie *v.* Miller, § 893 (*h*). Davidson *v.* Dalziel, 1881; 8 R. 990. Carter *v.* Lornie, 1890; 18 R. 353 (tender of valid title pending action). Gilfillan *v.* Cadell & Grant, 1893; 21 R. 269 (do.).

(*k*) Waddell *v.* Pollock, 1828; 6 S. 999.

(*l*) Grandison's Trs. *v.* Jardine, 1895; 22 R. 925. Ersk. iii. 3. 79.

(*m*) Kerr and Dunlop, *supra* (*a*). Dundee Calendering Co. *v.* Duff, 1869; 8 Macph. 298. Howard & Wyndham *v.* Richmond's Trs., 1890; 17 R. 990.

890A. '*Delivery of Title-Deeds.*—The clause of assignation of writs and evidents in use for conveyances and deeds under the conveyancing statutes is: "and I assign the writs, and have delivered the same according to inventory"; and it is adaptable according to circumstances (*a*). The clause, when unqualified, imports an absolute and unconditional assignation to such writs and evidents, and to all open procuratories, clauses, and precepts, if any, and as the case may be, therein contained, and to all unrecorded conveyances to which the disponer has right (*b*). The writs are accessories of the estate, so far as they are required to instruct the owner's title, but *quoad ultra* they have been held severable if not separate property (*c*).'

(*a*) 31 and 32 Vict. c. 101, Sch. B (1), (2).
(*b*) *Ib.* § 5, 8. As to this clause in bonds and dispositions in security, see § 914 (1), below.
(*c*) Christie *v.* Ruxton, 1862; 24 D. 1182. Porteous *v.* Henderson, 1898; 25 R. 563. M. Bell's Convg. 690 (3rd ed). See as to pledge of titles, § 1384, below.

891. Sale under a Power of Sale.—In securities over land for debt, it has become the uniform practice to give to the creditor a power, under certain precautions, to sell the subject of the security for satisfaction of the debt; and questions often arise out of the exercise of such powers. The doctrine on this subject is, that although such power is a mandate, it is as procurator *in rem suam* that the creditor is authorised to act; and it is held not revocable by the granter's death or bankruptcy (*a*). A creditor proceeding regularly, under such a power, to sell the lands, is not to be interrupted by a process of ranking and sale raised by other creditors (*b*); and sequestration under the Bankrupt Act has no effect in interrupting the creditor in the exercise of those powers (*c*). The precautions enjoined or made conditions of the power must be carefully observed; and if there be no express stipulation, the Court of Session will in equity interpose to order all reasonable precautions to be observed. A publication in a newspaper containing advertisements only, is sufficient compliance with the condition of advertising in a newspaper (*d*). If the burdens exceed the price, the purchaser has not the same protection as under the Bankrupt Acts (*e*), but must, 'under the former law,' trust to his right as assignee of the preferable securities paid off and conveyed to him (*f*). 'Now sales carried through under a heritable security and the Titles to Land Consolidation Act, 1868, are as valid as if made by the granter of the heritable security: the creditor selling is bound to count and reckon for the price, and consign the surplus, if any, after paying all previous incumbrances; upon which the disposition by him to the purchaser has the effect of completely disencumbering the lands sold of all securities and diligences posterior to that of the selling creditor, as well as of his security and diligence (*g*). If there be no surplus, the lands are disencumbered by registration of a certificate by a notary, along with the disposition by the creditor to the purchaser (*h*).' The creditor exposer of the lands to sale cannot bid at the auction (*i*), as he is to a certain extent trustee for the debtor, and bound to act with due regard to the debtor's reversionary interest; and is liable to restraint judicially, on the undue exercise of his power (*k*). 'He will also be restrained if he proceed to sell with a reckless disregard of the interests of postponed heritable creditors (*k*); but such a creditor cannot insist on obtaining an assignation of the first heritable debt upon payment, unless he can show it to be necessary in order to enable him to recover his debt (*l*).

'A creditor under a bond and disposition in security, who has exposed the security subjects at a price not exceeding the amount due under his own and any prior and *pari passu* securities, may now obtain, after intimation and inquiry, a decree of the sheriff declaring the debtor's right extinguished, and that he (the creditor) is vested in the lands as absolute proprietor as at the date of the decree, and the lands are disencumbered as in the case of a sale under the previous Acts, saving the personal obligation of the debtor for any surplus of the debt above the sum at which the subjects were exposed. The extract decree is recorded in the register of sasines, and the title of any purchaser from this creditor is indefeasible, without prejudice to any competent claim of damages against the petitioning creditor (*m*).'

(*a*) Steven, Glen, & Currie *v.* Fleming, Feb. 19, 1811; F. C.; 2 Bell's Com. 295 (275, M'L.'s ed.); 2 Ill. 96. Robertson *v.* Paton, May 23, 1815; F. C.; Hume, 58. Marshall *v.* Dunlop, Jan. 19, 1821; F. C.; Hume, 666. See Beveridge *v.* Wilson, 1829; 7 S. 279.
(*b*) Simson *v.* Graham, 1831; 10 S. 66. Bell *v.* Gordon, 1838; 16 S. 657; 3 Ill. 154. Marshall *v.* Dunlop, *cit.*
(*c*) Beveridge, *supra* (*a*).
(*d*) Dickson *v.* Dumfries Mags., 1831; 9 S. 282. Ogilvie *v.* Crombie, 1804; Hume, 657. Morrison *v.* Millar, 1818; Hume, 720. Hagart *v.* Robertson, 1834; 13 S. 234. Nisbet *v.* Cairns, 1864; 2 Macph. 863. Fleming *v.* Imrie, 1868; 6 Macph. 363. The forms to be observed in carrying out such a power, as well as the effect of the clause itself, are now governed by 31 and 32 Vict. c. 101, § 119, as repealed and re-enacted by 32 and 33 Vict. c. 116, § 7; and amending 10 and 11 Vict. c. 50, § 3; and must be strictly observed. Stewart *v.* Brown, 1882; 10 R. 192. Howard & Wyndham *v.* Richmond's Trs., 1891; 17 R. 990 (period of advertising). Ferguson *v.* Rodger, 1895; 22 R. 643 (do.).
(*e*) 1695, c. 6. 54 Geo. III. c. 137, § 42. See L. Alloway in Beveridge (*a*). 19 and 20 Vict. c. 91.
(*f*) See *contra*, Wilson *v.* Stirling, 1843; 8 D. 1261. See § 892.
(*g*) 31 and 32 Vict. c. 101, § 119, 121–123. Stewart *v.* Brown, and cases in note (*d*). Nicholson's Trs. *v.* M'Laughlin, 1891; 19 R. 49 (sale by one of two *pari passu* creditors);

corrected by 57 and 58 Vict. c. 44, § 11. Adair's Tr. *v.* Rankin, 1895 ; 22 R. 975 (sale by postponed bondholder).

(*h*) 37 and 38 Vict. c. 94, § 48, and Sch. L, No. 1.

(*i*) Maxwell *v.* Drummond's Trs., 1823 ; 2 S. 122. Jeffrey *v.* Aiken, 1826 ; 4 S. 722. Taylor *v.* Watson, 1846 ; 8 D. 400. Stirling's Trs., Petrs., 1865 ; 3 Macph. 851. But a heritable creditor, concurring with the trustee in his debtor's sequestration in selling, may purchase the subjects ; 19 and 20 Vict. c. 79, § 120. Cruickshank *v.* Williams, 1849 ; 11 D. 614. The trustee in the sequestration cannot purchase ; *ib.* § 120. Howard (*d*). Brown *v.* Burt, 1848 ; 11 D. 338. See Abercrombie (Whyte's Tr.) *v.* Burt, 1851 ; 13 D. 679. Frazer *v.* Hankey & Co., 1847 ; 9 D. 415 (sale to trustee not void but voidable). See 1 Bell's Com. 38.

(*k*) Dicta in Beveridge, *supra* (*a*). Stewart *v.* Brown, *cit.* (*per* L. P. Inglis).

(*l*) Kerr *v.* M'Arthur's Trs., 1848 ; 11 D. 301. Cuninghame's Trs. *v.* Hutton, 1847 ; 10 D. 307. Boswell *v.* Ayrshire Bkg. Co., 1841 ; 3 D. 352. Govan *v.* Simpson or Govan, 1758 ; 2 Pat. 27. See 19 and 20 Vict. c. 79, § 113–117.

(*m*) 57 and 58 Vict. c. 44 (Her. Securities Act, 1894), § 8–13. As to *pari passu* bondholders, see § 11.

892. Clearing of Burdens.—The seller is bound to discharge all incumbrances (*a*), 'including casualties (*b*).' Burdens by real security (*c*) remain, 'except in sales under bonds in virtue of the Titles Consolidation and Conveyancing Acts (*d*), and in the cases to be mentioned below,' as incumbrances on the land, although extending beyond the price which the purchaser has agreed to pay. A receipt from the creditors whose debts are paid off, with a discharge of the price by the seller, will not free the land. The purchaser must trust for the fortification of his title to the due vesting by assignation in his own person of the preferable debts when paid off (*e*). But in judicial sales, and in sales under the Sequestration Act, the burden is limited to the amount of the price. Payment of the price to creditors, as ranked in judicial sale, disburdens the land (*f*); and in sequestration, payment of real securities to the amount of the price, with a discharge by the trustee, completely disencumbers the land (*g*). In judicial sales, the holders of heritable securities, when they receive payment, grant not a discharge and renunciation, but a discharge and assignation of their debts to the purchaser, by which the extinction of the debts *confusione* is prevented, and they are kept up in fortification of the purchaser's right. But they are not held to form a separate estate in the purchaser, so that they can be transferred by him separately from the land, to the effect of being excluded from a ranking and sale of the land if the purchaser should become bankrupt (*h*). The purchaser is entitled to retain the price till incumbrances shall be purged (*i*); but this right is subject to equitable limitation (*k*). It may be restrained conventionally, by limiting the right of retention to a certain number of years (*l*); or if the years of prescription have expired, and warrandice be given with security for relief, the Court will in equity interpose to order payment of the price (*m*). 'Or the right to have the burdens purged may be excluded by the terms of the missives of sale or articles of roup, stipulating that the seller is not to clear them off, or imposing them on the purchaser himself (*n*).'

(*a*) Paton *v.* Stuart, 1825 ; 3 S. 653. Ralston *v.* Farquharson, 1830 ; 8 S. 927, and cases in following notes. As to allocation of feu-duties, see Nisbet *v.* Smith, 1876 ; 3 R. 781. Robertson *v.* Douglas, 1886 ; 13 R. 1133.

(*b*) Gardiner *v.* Anderson, 1799 ; M. 15,037. Straiton Estate Co. *v.* Stephens, 1880 ; 8 R. 299.

(*c*) See below, § 897 et seq.

(*d*) Last section, notes (*f*), (*g*).

(*e*) See above, § 891.

(*f*) 1695, c. 6. Seton's Crs. *v.* Scott, 1788 ; M. 13,371 ; Hailes, 1054 ; aff. 3 Pat. 682 ; 2 Ill. 98.

(*g*) 54 Geo. III. c. 137, § 42. 19 and 20 Vict. c. 91. Ferrier *v.* Pennicuik, July 8, 1812 ; F. C. ; 2 Ill. 98. M'Lane *v.* Robertson, Nov. 29, 1825 ; 4 S. 232. Kirkland & Sharp *v.* Russel, 1824 ; 2 S. 630.

(*h*) Seton's Crs., *supra* (*f*).

(*i*) Cargill *v.* Craigie, 1822 ; 1 S. Ap. 134. Robertson *v.* M'Gregor, 1840 ; 3 D. 213. And is not liable in interest—Rodger *v.* Brown, 1859 ; 21 D. 1022.

(*k*) Calderwood (Durham's Tr.) *v.* Graham, 1800 ; M. 16,641.

(*l*) Smith *v.* Somervill, 1706 ; M. 14,184. Young *v.* Grierson, 1849 ; 11 D. 1482. Comp. § 890 (*g*) ; and Stewart *v.* M'Callum, 1868 ; 6 Macph. 382 ; aff. 1870, 8 Macph. H. L. 1.

(*m*) Marjoribanks *v.* Nisbet, 1715 ; M. 14,187. See Mitchell *v.* Thomson's Trs., 1827 ; 6 S. 135.

(*n*) Davidson *v.* Dalziel, 1881 ; 8 R. 990. Below, § 910A.

893. Extent of Subject Sold.—The seller is bound to convey and deliver the whole subject sold (*a*). And so the purchaser is entitled to everything included in the description, but not to demand anything which it excludes (*b*). Thus, when in a judicial sale lands were sold on which a ground-annual was constituted, the purchaser was held not entitled to the benefit of that separate estate (*c*). 'And a purchaser may resile or claim damages under the clause of warrandice, if not apprised, at the time of the agreement, that the property is held under any material reservation in favour of the superior, as of the minerals (*d*).'

A description by measurement entitles the purchaser to insist for the quantity described, and no more ; any valid objection on account of error entitling him to the option of giving up the purchase, if it amount to error *in substantialibus* (*e*).

If the description include a subject not intended to be sold (as formerly a freehold qualification relied on by the buyer), the question will depend either on warranty or on the effect of error. When there is any room for doubt, the purchaser must secure himself by a distinct warranty, under which he will have action for the subject of that warranty. If there be no warranty, he can have remedy against the deficiency only on one of two grounds: either he must make out a case of misrepresentation and fraud; or he must prove an error *in substantialibus* sufficient to annul the whole contract (*f*). He can have no remedy on the principle of the *actio quanti minoris* of the civil law,—a doctrine not recognised in Scotland (*g*). But it was held not enough to raise this plea, '*i.e.* for repayment of part of the price under the warrandice,' that the subject sold was 'described as' a superiority of forty shillings of old extent, 'the old electoral qualification,' if there was no warrandice of a vote (*h*).

(*a*) As to time of entry ("immediate" possession), see Heys *v.* Kimball & Morton, 1890; 17 R. 381.

(*b*) E. Morton *v.* Cuningham, 1738; M. 14,175; 2 Ill. 99. Wilson *v.* Campbell's Crs., 1764; M. 13,330. Lloyds *v.* Paterson, 1782; M. 13,334; Hailes, 897. York Buildings Co. *v.* Ferguson, 1780; 2 Pat. 541. Ross *v.* Martin, 1888; 15 R. 282.

(*c*) Blair *v.* Murray, 1790; 2 Bell's Com. 283; 2 Ill. 91 and 99. As to representations or warrandice of extent and value in judicial sales, see 2 Bell's Com. 284. Traill *v.* Dangerfield, 1870; 8 Macph. 579.

(*d*) Robertson *v.* Rutherford, 1841; 4 D. 121. This was extended by two judges of the Second Div. (revg. L. Young, Ord.; *diss.* L. Gifford) to a reservation of minerals in a villa feu. White *v.* Lee, 1879; 6 R. 699. See above, § 14 (*h*). Louttit's Trs. *v.* Highland Ry. Co., 1892; 19 R. 791 (*per* L. M'Laren).

(*e*) Hannay *v.* Bargaly's Crs., 1785; M. 13,334. Gray *v.* Hamilton, 1801; M. *Sale*, Apx. 2. Hepburn *v.* Campbell, 1781; M. 14,168. E. Morton, *supra* (*a*). See above, § 890.

(*f*) See Mackenzie *v.* Girvan, 1840; 3 D. 318 (L. Cuninghame's judgment acquiesced in); aff. 1843, 2 Bell's App. 43. Robertson *v.* Rutherford, 1841; 4 D. 121. E. Moray *v.* Pearson, 1842; 4 D. 1411. Hamilton *v.* Western Bank, 1861; 23 D. 1033. Dobbie *v.* Duncanson, 1872; 10 Macph. 810. Ferguson *v.* Mossman, 1797; 3 Pat. 531. Davidson *v.* Anstruther Mags., 1845; 7 D. 342. Wood *v.* Edinburgh Mags., 1886; 13 R. 1006. Woods *v.* Tulloch, 1893; 20 R. 477; and see above, § 11, 13 sqq.

(*g*) But see Louttit's Trs. (*d*), especially L. M'Laren's opinion; and see in § 99A, above, this principle applied by statute to the sale of goods.

(*h*) M'Lean *v.* M'Neill, 1757; M. 14,164. **Gordon** *v.* **Hughes**, June 15, 1815; F. C.; rev. 1 Bligh, 287 (overruling so far M'Lean's case). Balmer *v.* Hogarth, 1830; 8 S. 718 (compromised on appeal); 10 S. Apx. 862; 4 S. Jur. 390. See *supra*, § 99, 890. **Brownlie** *v.* **Miller**, 1878; 5 R. 1076; aff. 1880, 7 R. H. L. 66, 71; 5 App. Ca. 925. M'Kirdy *v.* Anstruther, 1839; 1 D. 855. Oliver *v.* Suttie, 1840; 2 D. 514.

894. Warrandice.—Keeping in view the double obligation incumbent on a seller of land, and the buyer's right to insist for a complete title, if a sale of land has been completed by the execution of those deeds by which the property is transferred, there is still implied, and commonly expressed in the conveyance (*a*), an obligation of warrandice to indemnify the purchaser in case of eviction. This is absolute in sale where a full price is paid, unless a limitation has been stipulated (*b*); 'and an express clause of absolute warrandice will receive full effect even in a gratuitous conveyance (*c*). In a disposition of land the dispositive clause is the measure of the warrandice, which therefore does not cover representations as to incidental matters made before the conveyance. These are ruled by the general law of fraud and error (*d*). So a clause of absolute warrandice cannot enlarge the disponee's right if the dispositive clause show that it was merely intended to put him in the granter's place. The real bargain between the parties is to be considered (*e*).'

The obligation may be personal or real.

(1.) *Personal warrandice* is an obligation expressed or implied, to indemnify the purchaser in case of eviction. 'It does not become heritable, *i.e.* prestable by the granter's heir, merely because it relates to heritage or heritable debt (*f*).'

(2.) *Real warrandice* is also either express or implied. It is express, where one heritable subject is conveyed to the purchaser of another, in security and real warrandice against eviction of that other, "so that in case of eviction (*g*) the said A. shall have immediate access to the said lands." In this case the security is completed by sasine in the warrandice lands bearing the above qualification, and the right so created is merely provisional (*h*). Effect is given to this provisional right by a declaratory action proceeding on the conveyance and the eviction, and concluding for immediate entry to possession, and payment of the maills and duties. Warrandice is implied where landowners make exchange or excambion of their lands with each other; in which case the person who shall by eviction lose the subject conveyed to him may have recourse upon his original property by a declaratory action similar to that on express warrandice (*i*); but it is doubtful whether, without being specified in the sasine, this right is effectual against third parties (*k*).

(*a*) By 31 and 32 Vict. c. 101, § 8, in a deed of conveyance the obligation is expressed thus: "I grant warrandice." This, unless specially qualified, implies absolute warrandice as regards the lands, and the writs and evidents; and warrandice from fact and deed, as regards the rents.

(*b*) Ramsay *v.* Cunningham, 1830; 8 S. 399; 2 Ill. 100. Blair *v.* Dunbar Mags., 1833; 14 S. 445. Galloway *v.* Gardner, 1838; 1 D. 74.

(*c*) 2 Ersk. 3. § 27. Coventry *v.* Coventry, 1834; 12 S. 895. Strong *v.* Strong, 1851; 13 D. 548. Macalister *v.* Macalister, 1866; 4 Macph. 495.

(*d*) Gordon *v.* Hughes, and Brownlie *v.* Miller, § 893 (*h*). N. B. Ry. *v.* Edin. Mags., 1893; 20 R. 725.

(*e*) Leith Heritages Co. *v.* Edin. and Leith Glass Co., 1876; 3 R. 789. See above, § 114.

(*f*) Stirling Crawford's Trs. *v.* Stirling Stuart, etc. (Dss. Montrose *v.* Stuart), 1886; 14 R. 131; aff. 1887, 13 App. Ca. 81; 15 R. H. L. 19.

(*g*) Smith Sligo *v.* Dunlop & Co., 1885; 12 R. 907.

(*h*) 2 Ersk. 3. § 28. Blair *v.* Blair, 1741; Elchies, *Warr.* No. 5. See Kilkerran, 592.

(*i*) E. Melrose *v.* Ker, 1623; M. 3677. Wards *v.* Balcomie, 1629; M. 3678.

(*k*) Balfour *v.* Moncrieff, 1788; M. 10,267.

895. (3.) *Effect of Warrandice.*—Warrandice is not an obligation to *protect*, but only to *indemnify* in case of eviction (*a*); and out of this peculiarity (too often overlooked) arise several important consequences. Thus there is no action of warrandice till judicial eviction, unless the ground of demand be unquestionable, and proceeding from the fault of the seller; 'or the obligation to relieve be disputed, in which case the action may be brought when eviction is threatened' (*b*). Indemnification must be made for a partial eviction. A burden must be removed; but if transacted by the buyer, he can demand only indemnification (*c*), 'which in every case extends to all the consequences of a contravention of the warrandice. The remedy of a breach is not restitution, which is appropriate to a contract annulled on fraud or error, but indemnification only (*d*).' A servitude, 'unless of a very burdensome description, so as to amount to essential error as to the subject,' does not, however, seem to be a burden in this sense (*e*); neither will the purchaser have any claim of warrandice if the purpose of his purchase is defeated as a nuisance (*f*). The purchaser is entitled, 'if there be no limitation in the terms of the obligation,' to demand the whole worth of the 'lost' subject at the time of eviction, and not merely the sum which he has paid (*g*). The person bound in warrandice is entitled to have notice of the claim or attempt to evict (*h*). But the buyer is not bound to enter into a litigation in defence of the right, provided he give due notice (*i*). If he undertake the defence without notice, and omit the proper plea, the seller will be free. The seller is not bound to defend against the claim; and if the buyer choose to do so while the seller declines it, and fails, he is not entitled to the expense of litigation (*k*). Warrandice indemnifies only against loss from defective right, and from losses properly anterior to the sale; but not from burdens natural to the right (*l*), nor from losses caused by supervenient laws (*m*), or arising from the nature or legal effects of ownership (*n*). To protect the purchaser against these, a special stipulation is required (*o*).

(*a*) 2 Stair, 3. § 46. 3 Ersk. 3. § 9. Inglis *v.* Anstruther, 1771; M. 16,633; Hailes, 412; 2 Ill. 102. Below (*c*).

(*b*) Stair and Ersk. *supra*, and 2 Ersk. 3. § 32. E. Home *v.* E. Lothian, 1663; M. 16,584. Grieve *v.* Hepburn, 1635; M. 16,579. Smith *v.* Ross, 1672; M. 16,596; 2 B. Sup. 624. Hepburn *v.* D. Buccleuch, 1710; M. 16,617. Sutherland's Crs. *v.* Ross, 1749; M. 16,629. L. Melville *v.* Erskine's Trs., 1842; 4 D. 385. Downie *v.* Campbell, Jan. 31, 1815; F. C. See Leith Heritages Co. *v.* Edinr. and Leith Glass Co., 1876; 3 R. 789, 796 (*per* L. Ormidale).

(*c*) Logan *v.* L. Luss, 1632; M. 9224. Grieve *v.* Hepburn, 1735; M. 16,579. Dewar *v.* Aitken, 1780; M. 16,637.

(*d*) 2 Ersk. 3. § 30. Welsh *v.* Russell, 1894; 21 R. 769. Comp. § 126, above.

(*e*) More's Stair, p. 92. 2 Ersk. 3. § 31. Urquhart *v.* Halden, 1835; 13 S. 844. *Supra*, § 893.

(*f*) Murray *v.* Buchanan, 1776; M. 16,636; Hailes, 66. A lease—the purpose of the purchase (lace-working) had not been made known to the landlord.

(*g*) Houston *v.* Corbet, 1717; M. 16,619; Hill *v.* Yeaman, 1769; M. 16,631; Hailes, 328. Lord Napier's Trs. *v.* Drummond, 1777; Hailes, 750; 5 B. Sup. 636. 2 Ersk. 3. § 30. Galloway *v.* Gardner, 1838; 1 D. 74. In Cairns *v.* Howden, 1870, 9 Macph. 284, the question was raised, but not decided, whether, when the subject sold has fallen in value, the buyer is entitled to recover the full price, or only the value at the time of eviction. In addition to the authorities there referred to, see Gluck, Com. vol. xx. pp. 297–330. Donell. *Tract. de Evictionibus* (*Recit.* i. 597, and t. ix. p. 1447 sqq., ed. Lucens.); also Com. xiii. 2. 18. Kames' Pr. of Eq., B. i. c. 4. § 5. The case of Cairns suggests the larger question whether the rule in the text is consistent with justice, and whether every case should not be determined on its own merits.

(*h*) Lyon *v.* Dunlop, 1620; M. 16,572. Brown *v.* Logan, 1630; M. 16,579. Clark *v.* Gordon, 1681; M. 16,605.

(*i*) 2 Stair, 3. § 46. 2 Ersk. 3. § 32. Downie *v.* Campbell, Jan. 31, 1815; F. C.; 2 Ill. 103.

(*k*) Inglis, *supra* (*a*). Stephen *v.* L. Adv., 1878; 6 R. 282.

(*l*) Drummond *v.* Stewart, 1549; M. 16,565. Cuninghame *v.* Cuthbertson, 1829; Sh. Teind Cases, 175. M'Ritchie's Trs. *v.* Hope, 1836; 14 S. 578. Brownlie, *supra*, § 893 (*h*).

(*m*) 2 Stair, 3. § 46. 2 Ersk. 3. § 29. Watson *v.* Law, 1667; M. 16,588; 2 Ill. 103. Muirhead *v.* L. Colvil,

1715; 5 B. Sup. 125. Sprot *v.* Heriot's Hosp., 1829; 7 S. 682. See Holiday *v.* Scot, 1830; 8 S. 831. See next section.

(*n*) Lumsden *v.* Gordon, 1682; M. 16,606. Plenderleith *v.* E. Tweeddale, 1800; M. 16,639.

(*o*) See E. Hopetoun *v.* Jardine, July 3, 1811; F. C. Alexander *v.* Dundas, June 9, 1812; F. C. D. Roxburghe *v.* M. Lothian, 1838; 16 S. 341.

895A. 'Obligations to Relieve from Public Burdens.—In conveyances and deeds under the conveyancing statutes, the clause of relief runs thus: "I bind myself to free and relieve the said disponee and his foresaids of" (in the case of feus) "all feu-duties, casualties, and public burdens," or (in the case of burgage) "all ground-annual, cess, annuity, and other public burdens." The clause may be adapted to circumstances; and it imports, unless qualified, an obligation to relieve of all feu-duties or other duties and services or casualties, payable or prestable to the superior, and of all public, parochial, and local burdens, due from or on account of the lands conveyed, prior to the term of entry (*a*).

'Special clauses of relief from public burdens have occasioned many questions. When an obligation of this kind is granted by a superior to a vassal, and is made an inherent part of the feudal (*b*) contract, it passes to the vassal's heirs and disponees with the lands ("runs with the lands") without special assignation (*c*). When, however, the relation of superior and vassal does not exist between the obligor and obligee, or, as it is said in England, there is no "privity of estate" between them, although an ordinary obligation of warrandice passes to a purchaser by a conveyance of the lands with the writs, an obligation to relieve from public burdens, or from future augmentations of stipend, will not pass without an express assignation (*d*). In general obligations of this kind (*e.g.* to relieve from public burdens imposed, or to be imposed, or from burdens due and exigible, or that may become due and payable from the lands in all time coming), the parties are held to have in view burdens exigible at the time or that may thereafter become exigible by virtue of any law or practice existing at the time; but no burdens imposed for the first time by supervenient laws, *i.e.* by laws enacted after the date of the obligation (*e*). The reason of this rule is, obviously, that burdens of the latter kind are not in the contemplation of the persons who enter into the obligation. And in construing clauses of relief, as in other questions of construction, the meaning of the parties as expressed in the contract is the rule and limit of liability (*f*). Hence a burden similar in name to one existing at the date of the obligation may be so altered in its incidence or in its objects as to be excluded from the obligation to relieve (*g*). It has been decided, however, that poor-rates levied in respect of ownership under the Poor Law Amendment Act of 1845 are not a new kind of burden, but fall under a clause of relief from public burdens granted before that date, the object and incidence of the rate being the same as under the former law, and the changes in the law being natural and necessary improvements in administration (*h*).

'After the question had been raised and reserved in a number of cases, in which superiors endeavoured to obtain some restriction of their liabilities under such clauses, it has now been settled that obligations of relief in such terms are not limited to the amount of feu-duty payable (*i*). The growth of towns and other causes sometimes make the liability of a superior exceed the whole value of the feu-duty. "This," said Lord Westbury, "may show that the contract of the superior was originally improvident, but does not affect the legal construction or validity of the obligation" (*k*).'

'Warrandice against payment of teinds and stipends does not necessarily, or even usually, protect against future augmentations of stipend. In order to have this effect the obligation must contain that term, or words admitting of no other construction (*l*).'

(*a*) 31 and 32 Vict. c. 101, § 5, 8, and Sch. B (1), (2).

(*b*) See Durie's Trs. *v.* E. Elgin, 1889; 16 R. 1104 (a case of mere personal obligation to grant a feu-right with such a clause).

(*c*) Lennox *v.* Hamilton, 1843; 3 D. 435. **Stewart** *v.* **D. Montrose**, 1860; 22 D. 755; aff. 1863, 4 Macq. 499; 1 Macph. H. L. 25. Hope *v.* Hope, 1864; 2 Macph. 670. See Stewart *v.* M'Callum, 1868; 6 Macph. 382; aff. 1870, 8 Macph. H. L. 1. Murray *v.* Css. Rothes, 1874; 2 R. 106; and as to the *ipso facto* transference of such liability to the singular successors of superiors, Pagan *v.* Rae, 1860; 22 D. 806. As to such an obligation in a conveyance with resignation *ad rem.* to the Crown, see Orr Ewing *v.* E. Cawdor, 1884; 11 R. 471; aff. 1884, 12 R. H. L. 12.

(*d*) Horne *v.* Breadalbane's Trs., 1841; 3 D. 435; rev. 1842; 1 Bell's App. 1. Sinclair *v.* Breadalbane, 1844; 6 D. 378; rev. 1846, 5 Bell's App. 353. Spottiswoode *v.* Seymer, 1853; 15 D. 458.

(*e*) Scott *v.* Edmond, 1850; 12 D. 1077. Campbell's

Trs. *v.* Scot. Union Ins. Co., 1893; 21 R. 167. Sprot *v.* Heriot's Hospital, 1829; 7 S. 682. 2 Stair, 3. § 46.

(*f*) See, *e.g.*, Duff *v.* E. Seafield, 1883; 11 R. 126 (obligation by tacksman of teinds in excambion to relieve of augmentation "in all time coming" held to expire at termination of granter's tack). Jopp's Trs. *v.* Edmond, 1888; 15 R. 271 (construction by actings of parties). Lanark Mags. *v.* Honyman, 1890; 17 R. 1226.

(*g*) Dunbar's Trs. *v.* British Fisheries Soc., 1877; 5 R. 350; aff. 1878, 5 R. H. L. 221; 3 App. Ca. 1298 (road money). Stewart *v.* E. Seafield, 1876; 3 R. 518 (road money, schoolmaster's salary, school rate). Scott, Sprot, and Campbell's Trs., *citt.* (*e*).

(*h*) Lees *v.* Mackinlay, 1857; 20 D. 6. Hunter *v.* Chalmers, 1858; 20 D. 1311. Paterson's Trs. *v.* Hunter, 1863; 2 Macph. 234. Nisbet *v.* Lees, 1869; 7 Macph. 881. Preston *v.* Edinr. Mags., 1870; 8 Macph. 502. Wilson *v.* Musselburgh Mags., 1868; 6 Macph. 483.

(*i*) Dunbar's Trs. *cit.* (*g*). Cf. Preston *v.* Edinr. Mags., and Hunter *v.* Chalmers, *supra*. Reid's Trs. *v.* Dss. Sutherland, 1881; 8 R. 509.

(*k*) D. Montrose *v.* Stewart, *cit.* (*c*).

(*l*) Alexander *v.* Dundas, June 9, 1812; F. C. Cuningham *v.* Cuthbertson, Jan. 27, 1829; F. C.; Sh. Teind Ca. 175. M'Ritchie's Trs. *v.* Hope, 1836; 14 S. 578. Pedie *v.* Heriot's Hosp., 1839; 1 D. 871. Paterson *v.* D. Hamilton, 1843; 5 D. 1313. Stevenson *v.* Spens' Trs., 1858; 20 D. 651. Campbell *v.* Dingwall's Trs., 1865; 4 Macph. 50. E. Rosslyn *v.* N. B. Ry., 1865; *ib.* 140. Cases in note (*c*) *supra*. It must be admitted that the cases on the subject are not always consistent. See also 2 Connel on Teinds, 103 sqq. Duff, Feud. Convg. p. 89, § 57.

CHAPTER X

OF HERITABLE SECURITIES

896. General View.—Land is a source of credit, directly and indirectly:—Indirectly, in so far as the credit of the owner of the land is augmented, either by the rents of his lands, which may be attached for his debt, or by the value of the estate, which also may be attached and brought to sale for debt. And even after his death, the value of his land may be appropriated by his creditors, not only in preference to the right of succession of his heir, but in preference also to the claims of the creditors of the heir; provided advantage shall be taken of this privilege, by completing the proper diligence within three years after the debtor's death (*a*). The diligence or execution by which land is made available for debt is either Adjudication or Judicial Sale (*b*), or Sequestration in Bankruptcy (*c*). And the land may be secured exclusively for the benefit of a particular creditor by Inhibition, which is a prohibition against the voluntary alienation of the land, or further contraction of debt, to the prejudice of the inhibitor's claim (*d*). Land is made directly the means of security to creditors, by the creation of a burden entitling the creditor to appropriate the rents and uses of the land until the debts shall be paid. The right conferred on the creditor may 'sometimes' be considered as a separate estate, distinct from the property (*e*).

(*a*) See below, § 1931. (*b*) See above, § 824, 833, 891.
(*c*) See below, § 2341. (*d*) See below, § 2306.
(*e*) 2 Stair, 10. 2 Ersk. 8. 2 Ross, 320. As to heritable securities in the succession of the creditor, see below, § 1485.

897. Real securities on heritable estates are constituted in various forms, and either by base or public holding. In the latter, the superior is entitled to his composition; but if he be himself the debtor, he must enter the creditor gratis. The chain of feudal titles to the land continues unbroken and unaffected by these rights in security; which are held as excrescences on the property, and may be created or dissolved without affecting the radical right to the estate, or touching the progress of titles. As mere accessories of the debt, they are discharged by its extinction, or annihilated by renunciation, without any feudal form of reconveyance (*a*). 'The rights of the debtor and creditor are in all material respects the same as those of pledgor and pledgee (see § 206, 207); and so the creditor can only demand payment of his debt under the personal obligation of the debtor on condition of restoring the whole of the impignorated lands (*b*).'

(*a*) 2 Stair, 10. § 13. Hope's Min. Pract. 6. § 2. 2 Ersk. 8. § 18. 2 Ross, 368. Conf. § 904, 909, 910A. N. Albion Prop. Invt. Co. *v.* M'Bean's Cur., 1893; 21 R. 107. See authorities in 2 Ross' L. C. 706–720.
(*b*) N. Albion Prop. Co. *cit.* (*a*). M'Kirdy *v.* Webster's Trs., 1895; 22 R. 340.

898. Whatever be the form in which a heritable security is created, it requires, in order to its effect as a real right, the constitution of a *jus in re.*

899. Such securities are reducible to two classes: one in which the real right is constituted by infeftment in favour of the creditor; the other in which the real right depends on the force of a condition qualifying the right of property.

900. The securities which depend for their effect on sasine to the creditor are: Wadset; Infeftment of Annualrent; Heritable Bond; Disposition in Security; and Absolute Disposition with Back-Bond. And these are distinguishable into two classes,—the one including Wadset, Annualrent right, and absolute Disposition with Back-Bond, as being *dispositions* under reversion: the other comprehending Heritable Bond and Disposition in Security, as infeftments in *security* merely, in which the land is pledged or burdened, but not transferred; the right not being convertible into property by a discharge of the reversion; and the efficacy of the infeftment depending on the subsistence of the debt, to which it is a mere accessory (*a*). 'No real security over land can be created for an indefinite sum, or to unspecified creditors (*b*).'

(*a*) 2 Ersk. 8. § 2–36. 1 Bell's Com. 670 et seq.
(*b*) 2 Ersk. 3. § 50. Tailors of Aberdeen *v.* Coutts, *supra*, § 861 and § 861 (*r*). See below, § 916, 919. As to the question whether failure to specify the rate of interest makes the burden indefinite, see Forbes & Welsh *v.* Forbes, 1894; 21 R. 630.

901. Wadset.—This is a security created by disponing the land to the creditor, but redeemably, on payment of a specified sum; the security being completed by sasine duly recorded. The creditor is called the Wadsetter; the debtor the Reverser. This form is now little used.

902. The right of reversion is either incorporated in the conveyance, as a condition of the disposition; or expressed in the form of a contract (*a*); or the power of redemption may be in a separate deed, called a Reversion, which, in order to limit and qualify the real right, must be recorded in the Register of Sasines (*b*). The right of reversion remains unextinguished till declarator of expiry of the right, and may competently be claimed by one having a title to the lands (*c*).

(*a*) The form of a contract was introduced about 1661; and when this security is used in present practice, this is the form made use of. Mackintosh, *infra*, § 904.
(*b*) 2 Ersk. Pr. 8. § 1. 2 Stair, 10. § 1 et seq. 2 Ersk. 8. § 3 et seq. 1469, c. 28. 1617, c. 16. 2 Ross, 329. Dallas, Styles, 709 et seq. 2 Bell's Forms of Deeds, 27 et seq.
(*c*) L. Dundas *v.* Anderson, 1836; 14 S. 951; 2 Ill. 104. See Wright *v.* Turner, 1855; 17 D. 629; and comp. with it M'Andrew *v.* Reid, 1868; 6 Macph. 1063.

903. The estate created in the creditor or wadsetter, when this form of security was in use, might have been held public or base.

904. When the entry was public as vassal of the superior, the reinvestment of the debtor or reverser was necessary on redemption. This was formerly secured by letters of regress, binding the superior to enter his old vassal on redemption; but under 20 Geo. II. c. 50, the necessity of such an express obligation was superseded, and the wadsetter's conveyance on redemption entitled the reverser to enter on paying a year's rent. Letters of regress came to be used only for the purpose of forcing the superior to enter the reverser as vassal without composition; and even singular successors in the superiority must so enter the reverser, if letters of regress have been granted and recorded in the Register of Sasines. Where the wadset is held base, a resignation *ad remanentiam* restores the fee to the vassal. Erskine's doctrine is doubtful, that a mere renunciation is sufficient (*a*).

(*a*) 2 Ersk. Pr. 8. § 6. 2 Ersk. 8. § 16–18. Correct by 2 Stair, 10. § 13. Wauchope *v.* D. Roxburghe, Dec. 14, 1815; F. C.; aff. 1825, 1 W. & S. 41. See Chisholm *v.* Chisholm-Batten, 1864; 3 Macph. 202, 221. Mackintosh *v.* Tytler, 1870; 8 Macph. 772. See also 31 and 32 Vict. c. 101, § 132, 134, and 3 (interpretation clause).

905. Where the reverser wishes to have back his land, and the security discharged, he must either use the order of redemption prescribed in the wadset; or, without the formality of a premonition and order of redemption, as in the old practice, he must call the creditor in an action of declarator of redemption, concluding that the lands shall be declared to have reverted to the debtor; and the decree in this action extinguishes the feudal right of wadset, and restores the debtor to his full right (*a*). If the debtor shall, on the other hand, be unable to redeem his land, the wadsetter may have his right made absolute, and the security converted into a right of property, by an action of declarator of expiry of the redemption (*b*).

(*a*) 2 Ersk. 8. § 17 et seq., and § 23. 2 Stair, 10. § 14 sqq. 2 Bell's Deeds, 52. Campbell *v.* Campbell, 1786; M. 16,552; Hailes, 993; 2 Ill. 104. L. Alva *v.* Erskine, 1791; M. 16,555.
(*b*) 2 Ersk. 8. § 14, 16.

906. Wadsets are either Proper, in which the wadsetter takes the land in pledge, the rents and profits going in extinction of the interest; or Improper, in which the wadsetter takes the rents generally to account of principal and interest. In the former, the wadsetter holds as a proprietor; in the latter, he holds as a steward of the wadset subject (*a*).

(*a*) 2 Ersk. 8. § 26–7.

907. The loan may be enlarged by an extension of the security, called an "Eik to the Reversion"; which, like the principal security, requires to be recorded in order to have effect against third parties (*a*).

(*a*) 2 Ersk. 8. § 30. 2 Bell's Deeds, 46. See Turner *v.* M'Intyre, 1816; Hume, 660.

908. Infeftment of Annualrent (*a*).—This was at first a perpetual annuity from land, not redeemable; a feudal estate secured and completed by sasine. But a little before the Reformation, a redemption clause came gradually to be added to the security, by which it approached to the nature of a wadset. In this state it was an impignoration of a rent out of the land, as the wadset was of the land itself, for the debt. On the Reformation, it underwent another change, by the addition of a power of requisition on the part of the lender. It is seldom used, but is still a legitimate form of real security (*b*).

(*a*) See *ante*, § 884, as to ground-annuals.
(*b*) 2 Ross, 372. 2 Stair, 10. § 1 et seq. 2 Ersk. 8. § 31; and as to extinction and discharge, 2 Ersk. 8. § 34, and notes. Macdonald *v.* Macdonald's Trs., 1829; 7 S. 826. As to bonds of annualrent and rent charges for improvements under the Montgomerie and Rutherfurd Acts, and the Improvement of Land Acts, see 38 and 39 Vict. c. 24; 41 and 42 Vict. c. 28; 45 and 46 Vict. c. 53, § 6. Rankine on Land Ownership, 961, etc.

909. Heritable Bond.—This is the first of that class of securities which are mere accessory burdens, annihilated by the extinction of the debt, or discharged by renunciation. The heritable bond first brought into use was an obligation to infeft the lender in an annualrent for security of the principal sum under reversion, and with a power of requisition of the principal, and a corresponding obligation to repay the principal sum (*a*). This security was imperfect, as giving a right only to levy the interest from the lands; and it was converted into a combination of the common personal bond, with a real right of annualrent payable out of the land, accompanied by a conveyance of the lands themselves in security (*b*). The sasine in an annualrent payable out of the lands, and in the lands themselves in security, when duly recorded in the Register of Sasines, vests a feudal estate; but still it is of the nature of a mere burden, which payment of the debt, or *confusio*, or mere renunciation of the security, will extinguish (*c*).

(*a*) Dallas, 694. 8, and 701.
(*b*) 2 Ross, 376. 1 Jur. Styles, 394. 2 Bell's Deeds, 93. 2 Ersk. 8. § 35. Hogg *v.* Brack, 1832; 11 S. 198; 2 Ill. 104. See E. Dalhousie *v.* L. Hawley, 1713; M. 9992; 2 Ill. 56. Railton *v.* Muirhead, 1834; 12 S. 757. Brown *v.* Rae, 1835; 13 S. 256; 2 Ill. 104.
(*c*) See above, § 904.

910. Bond and Disposition in Security.—This consists of a bond (*a*) accompanied by a disposition of the lands themselves, redeemably and under reversion, for real security of the principal, interest, and penalties, accompanied by a power of sale to the creditor under certain conditions and precautions (*b*). The right is completed by infeftment duly recorded. The exercise of the power of sale has given rise to many questions (*c*).

(*a*) See above, § 67–8.
(*b*) 1 Jur. Styles, 401 et seq.
(*c*) See above, § 891.

910A. 'A statutory form has since 1847 been provided for this form of security, the effect of the various clauses in which is explained, and provision is made for the transmission of the creditor's right, for the discharge and restriction of the security, etc. (*a*). Infeftment by means of sasine and recording of the instrument is no longer necessary. The registration of heritable securities of all kinds in the Register of Sasines is as effectual as if they had contained an obligation to infeft, procuratory of registration, and precept of sasine; and as if sasine had been given in favour of the creditor, and an instrument of sasine had been duly recorded of the date of the registration of the deed (*b*). A warrant of registration must be written on such deeds (*c*). The date of registration is the date of the deed in competitions, and in all questions under the Bankruptcy Statutes, from the Act 1696, c. 5, downwards (*d*). Heritable securities may be registered at any time during the lifetime of the grantee; and if they have not been so registered, they are as full and sufficient warrants for completing the title of the party having right to them as if they had been bonds and dispositions in security in the form in use prior to 1847; and the title may be completed in a manner provided by the Act, or by service (*e*) or notarial instrument, as the circumstances of the case may require (*f*). The bond and disposition in security is now the usual form of security for money instantly advanced.

'*Transmission against Successors.*—By statute a heritable security for money over a landed estate, and the personal obligations for payment in it, are transmitted (1) against a person taking the estate by succession, gift, or bequest (*g*), and they burden his title as they burdened his ancestor's or author's; and (2) against a person taking the estate by conveyance, when an agreement to that effect appears in the conveyance, and they then form a like burden (*h*). A conveyance in consideration of a price composed of such a transmission and a sum of money must be stamped according to the whole price (*i*).

'The security and obligations are not extinguished, as against a person once bound, by the mere passing on of the estate to another person, whether the person bound be the granter of the security or one taking under this provision of the Act (*k*); but the inability of the creditor to reinstate in the security a divested obligant, on payment by him, will release him (*l*). A person taking an estate in the circumstances first contemplated by the Act (*i.e.* by "lucrative title") is not, however, liable for the debts of his ancestor or author beyond the value of that ancestor's or author's estate to which he has succeeded (*m*).'

(*a*) See 31 and 32 Vict. c. 101, § 120, 126, 128, 131–5; 32 and 33 Vict. c. 116, § 6, 7, 8; 10 and 11 Vict. c. 50. Love *v.* Storie, 1863; 2 Macph. 22. 37 and 38 Vict. c. 94, § 47, 48, 49, 63, 64, 65.

(*b*) 32 and 33 Vict. c. 116, § 6. 31 and 32 Vict. c. 101, § 3, 134, 135.

(*c*) 32 and 33 Vict. c. 116, § 9. 37 and 38 Vict. c. 94, § 33.

(*d*) 31 and 32 Vict. c. 101, § 148, 142, 120.

(*e*) Hare, Petr., 1889; 17 R. 105. See § 1485A, below.

(*f*) 31 and 32 Vict. c. 101, § 120. 32 and 33 Vict. c. 116, § 8.

(*g*) Welch's Exrs., below.

(*h*) 37 and 38 Vict. c. 94, § 47, and Sch. K. Ritchie & Sturrock *v.* Dullatur Feuing Co., 1881; 9 R. 358. **Wright's Exrs.** *v.* **M'Laren**, 1891; 18 R. 841, and cases cited there. See Kippen *v.* Stewart, 1852; 14 D. 533. Reid *v.* Lamond, 1857; 19 D. 265.

(*i*) Inl. Rev. *v.* City of Glasgow Bk., 1881; 8 R. 389.

(*k*) Glas. Univ. *v.* Yuill's Trs., 1882; 9 R. 643. See Johnston *v.* M'Kinnon, 1888; 5 Sh. Ct. Rep. 123.

(*l*) N. Albion Prop. Invt. Co. *v.* M'Bean's Cur., 1893; 21 R. 90 (partial discharge). M'Kirdy *v.* Webster's Trs., 1895; 22 R. 340 (feu of security subject). Above, § 558, 897.

(*m*) 37 and 38 Vict. c. 94, § 12. Welch's Exrs. *v.* Edin. Ass. Co., 1896; 23 R. 772.

911. Securities for Future Debts.—In practice, the commerce of money required facilities in the mode of security beyond those afforded by the forms now enumerated. Hence such expedients as an eik to the reversion in wadsets; a clause declaring that the wadset should stand effectual for all debts, engagements, and sums to be advanced; or a clause in annualrent rights, that all other debts and engagements should be discharged before the power of redemption should be exercised. All those expedients were liable to abuse, as covers to fraud on the eve of insolvency; and by 1696, c. 5, it was enacted, "That all dispositions or other rights that shall be granted for hereafter for relief or security of debts to be contracted for the future, shall be of no force as to any such debts as shall be found to be contracted after the sasine or infeftment following on the said disposition or right" (*a*). Under this Act, a security for money of which part only is advanced at completing the security, is bad as to the part which is not advanced at that time (*b*), but not if the obligation for the balance is absolute (*c*). So also, under this Act, heritable security for a cash account is ineffectual (*d*). But in construing this Act against fraud, the *delivery* of the sasine duly recorded is held the date of the sasine (*e*); and the difficulties at common law and under this Act are overcome by disposition and back-bond, or by a form authorised by statute (*f*).

(*a*) See 19 and 20 Vict. c. 91, § 7.

(*b*) Dempster *v.* Kinloch, 1750; M. 10,290; 2 Ill. 105; 2 Ross' L. C. 632. Johnston *v.* Warden, 1777; 5 B. Sup. 386. Turner *v.* M'Intyre, 1816; Hume, 660. Black *v.* Curror & Couper, 1885; 12 R. 990 (*per* L. Ordinary).

(*c*) Fulton *v.* Lead, 1826; 4 S. 740. 2 Ross' L. C. 636.

(*d*) Pickering *v.* Smith, Wright, & Gray, 1788; M. 1155; 2 Ill. 105; 2 Ross' L. C. 645. Stein's Crs. *v.* Newnham & Co., 1789; M. 1158 and 1236; 1793, M. 14,127; 2 Ross' L. C. 648; Hailes, 1071; 3 Pat. 345. But see below, § 913; Bell's Tr. *v.* Bell, 1884; 12 R. 85.

(*e*) Dunbar's Crs. *v.* Abercromby, 1789; M. 1156; Bell's 8vo Ca. 57, note; 2 Bell's Com. 236 (220, M'L.'s ed.); 2 Ross' L. C. 638. Drummond *v.* Campbell, 1791; Bell's Cases, 54; 2 Ross' L. C. 734.

(*f*) See below, § 913.

912. Absolute Disposition with Back-Bond is a form of security which confers, by the disposition and sasine, a right of property, 'which is absolute as regards third parties who deal with the disponee on the faith of the public records; and, in questions with the disponer himself, or persons acquiring an interest in the estate or the personal contract through him, is' qualified only by a personal obligation or back-bond to denude on payment of the debt (*a*). 'The disponee is a *quasi* trustee, though his trust is not pure, being partly *in rem suam* (*b*). Such a disposition with back-bond is not a "heritable security" in the sense of the conveyancing statutes (*c*), and therefore it does not carry the remedies conferred by these statutes, and in the creditor's succession it passes to his heir in heritage (*d*).' This obligation to denude comes to have the force of a real limitation of the right, by registration of the back-bond in the record of sasines and reversions. While it remains unrecorded, the borrower is exposed to the risk of the lender's bankruptcy (*e*). It covers all advances and debts, whether before or after the date of the sasine, 'or recorded disposition; but if the back-bond be recorded or produced judicially, the security is restricted to sums advanced at that date (*f*). The *ex facie* absolute disponee is so affected by the terms of the back-letter, though unrecorded, that he cannot hold the estate conveyed in security of advances made after intimation of an onerous and *bonâ fide* assignation of the reversionary right to a third party (*g*). The disponee is vested with all the rights of a proprietor, so that he is entitled to possess and administer the estate, —his appropriate remedy, if the granter has been allowed to retain possession, being an action, not of maills and duties, or of poinding the ground, but of declarator and removing (*h*). The remedy of simple ejection is not competent (*i*). On the other hand, the terms of the borrower's right of redemption and reconveyance may be proved as between him and the disponee by the same kind of evidence which would be competent and sufficient to prove a trust against an *ex facie* absolute disponee (*k*); and that right subsists against the disponee and his representatives until it is extinguished by declarator (*l*), or by a fair sale to a *bonâ fide* purchaser. The disponee has power to sell by public roup, or even, it is thought, by private bargain, before or after the back-bond is recorded (*m*); and if he do so unfairly and without due regard to the interest of his debtor, the remedy of the latter is not a rescission of the sale (the buyer being in good faith), but an action of damages (*n*), or an interdict of a proposed sale (*o*). In a sale by prior creditors holding bonds and dispositions in security, the disponee has merely the rights of a creditor holding a security (*p*). If the granter is allowed to remain in ostensible possession, the creditor or his trustee in bankruptcy cannot challenge a lease granted by him (*q*); while, if the disponee possess, he is liable as a proprietor for the prestations of the feu and the local burdens imposed on owners, and his tenure is subject to the real burdens of the feu (*r*), with relief against prior creditors, in a question with whom he also is a creditor (*s*).'

(*a*) See Clark *v.* City of Glas. Ass. Co., 1850; 12 D. 1047; revd. 1854, 1 Macq. 668. Gardyne *v.* Royal Bank, 1851; 13 D. 912; revd. 1853, 1 Macq. 358. Campbell *v.* Bertram, 1865; 4 Macph. 23. Rankin, *infra* (*h*). This statement appears to be too general in view of M'Bride *v.* Cal. Ry. Co., 1894; 21 R. 620; and Forbes's Tr. *v.* Macleod, 1898; 25 R. 1012, following on Her. Rev. Co., below (*e*).

(*b*) Wight *v.* Duggan, 1797; M. 12,761; 3 Pat. 610. Leckie, below (*f*). Forbes, above (*a*). Below, § 1995.

(*c*) 31 and 32 Vict. c. 101, § 3. 37 and 38 Vict. c. 94, § 3. 57 and 58 Vict. c. 44, § 18. *Quære* whether a disposition without back-bond comes under the definition, where truly in security? and see Forbes, above (*a*).

(*d*) 31 and 32 Vict. c. 101, § 3 and § 117.

(*e*) 1696, c. 25. 1 Bell's Com. 672 (714, M'L.'s ed.); and 2 *ib.* 236, 272. 2 Bell's Deeds, 291. See Tierney *v.* Court, 1832; 10 S. 664; 2 Ill. 107. See, however, Her. Reversionary Co. *v.* Millar, 1892; 19 R. H. L. 43, and Forbes, above (*a*); and comp. § 1468, 1994, below.

(*f*) Drummond, § 911 (*c*). Riddel *v.* Niblie's Crs., 1782; M. 1154; 2 Ross' L. C. 721. Keith *v.* Maxwell, 1795; M. 1163; Bell's Ca. 234; 2 Ross' L. C. 723. Maitland *v.* Cockerell, 1827; 6 S. 109. James *v.* Downie, 1836; 15 S. 12. Russell *v.* E. Breadalbane, 1829; 7 S. 767; aff. 1831. 5 W. & S. 256. Leckie *v.* Leckie, 1854; 17 D. 77. Robertson *v.* Duff, 1840; 2 D. 279. Hay's Tr. *v.* Davidson, 1853; 15 D. 583. 1 Bell's Com. 684 (725, M'L.'s ed.). *Infra*, § 1367.

(*g*) Natl. Bk. *v.* Union Bank, 1885; 13 R. 380; rev. 1886, 12 App. Ca. 53; 14 R. H. L. 1.

(*h*) Rankin *v.* Russell, 1868; 7 Macph. 126. Scottish Her. Sec. Co. *v.* Allan, Campbell, & Co., 1876; 3 R. 333. See Scot. Pr. Invt. Co. *v.* Horne, *infra* (*l*). Her. Sec. Inv. Ass. *v.* Wingate's Tr., § 1317.

(*i*) 57 and 58 Vict. c. 44, § 5, and above note (*c*).

(*k*) Robertson *v.* Duff (*f*), esp. *per* L. Fullerton. Natl. Bk. *v.* Union Bank, *cit.* (*g*). The transaction is not, however, a proper trust. *Per* L. Pres. Inglis and L. Watson in Natl. Bk. *v.* Union Bank, *cit.*

(*l*) Thomson *v.* Threshie, 1844; 6 D. 1106. Smith *v.* Smith, 1879; 6 R. 794. Scottish Pr. Invt. Co. *v.* Horne, 1881; 8 R. 737.

(*m*) Duncan *v.* Mitchell & Co., 1893; 21 R. 37 (construction of registered back-letter giving power to sell by private bargain).

(*n*) Simson *v.* M'Millan, 1770; 2 Pat. 227. Parks *v.*

Alliance Her. Sec. Co., 1880 ; 7 R. 546. Baillie *v.* Drew, 1884 ; 12 R. 199.
(*o*) Lucas *v.* Gardner, 1876 ; 4 R. 194.
(*p*) Stewart *v.* Brown, 1882 ; 10 R. 192. See City of Glasg. Bk. *v.* Nicolson's Trs., 1882 ; 9 R. 689.
(*q*) Abbott *v.* Mitchell, 1870 ; 8 Macph. 791.
(*r*) Clark, Gardyne, and Campbell, *citt.* (*a*). Marshall's Tr. *v.* Macneill & Co., 1888 ; 15 R. 762.
(*s*) City of Glasgow Bank, *cit.* (*p*).

913. Securities in Relief and for Cash Accounts.—To avoid the inconvenience of the absolute disposition and back-bond, and chiefly to facilitate cash accounts with bankers and securities in relief to cautioners, it was provided that heritable securities may be given for cash accounts, or for relief of cautioners in cash accounts, on condition that the principal sum and interest to become due under the bond should be limited to a certain definite sum, 'to be specified in the security,' not exceeding the amount of the principal sum and three years' interest (*a*). In construing this Act, it is fixed that a security for 'a credit not exceeding' a certain sum "and three years' interest thereon" is a sufficient compliance with the Act (*b*); 'and that an inhibition does not affect a cash-credit bond as a security for advances subsequent to its date (*c*).'

(*a*) 33 Geo. III. c. 74, § 12 ; continued by 54 Geo. III. c. 137, and 19 and 20 Vict. c. 91, § 7. See 31 and 32 Vict. c. 101, § 3, 134 ; and above, § 299 sqq.
(*b*) Morton *v.* Hunters & Co., 1828 ; 7 S. 172 ; aff. 1830, 4 W. & S. 379 ; 2 Ill. 107.
(*c*) Campbell's Tr. *v.* De Lisle's Exrs., 1870 ; 9 Macph. 252.

914. Effect of Heritable Securities. (1.) *Title - Deeds.*—A heritable creditor is not entitled to demand possession of the title-deeds of the land; though sometimes it may be necessary for him to have exhibition of them, in order to satisfy an assignee; or even to have them so deposited as to avoid the danger of a law-agent's right of retention (*a*). *After* the term of payment, there seems to be no room to doubt the creditor's right to have such exhibition of the title-deeds as may be necessary in negotiating a loan by assignation. But it has been held that he has no such right *before* the term of payment (*b*). It is sometimes stipulated that the title-deeds shall remain in neutral custody, 'or be delivered to the creditor (*c*). The clause of assignation of writs under the modern conveyancing statutes is in effect the same as that formerly in use (*d*).'

(*a*) See below, § 1438.
(*b*) Hamilton *v.* Brown, 1839 ; 1 D. 725. See Bain *v.* Duncan, 1892 ; 29 S. L. R. 335 (exhibition only, not loan, of writs).
(*c*) M'Neill *v.* Blair, 1835 ; 14 S. 14 ; 2 Ill. 105. Malcolm *v.* Carmichael, 1854 ; 16 D. 825.
(*d*) 31 and 32 Vict. c. 101, § 118, 119, and Sch. FF. M. Bell's Convg. 1161 (3rd ed.).

(2.) *Expense of Transfers.*—The expense of any transfers of the security made necessary by the debtor's failure to pay at the stipulated term, falls on the creditor who makes such transfer for his own convenience, not on the debtor. 'The clause in the statutory form of a bond and disposition in security obliging the granter for the expenses of assigning and discharging the security, means that any discharge, assignation, or other deed necessary to be granted by the creditor on the debtor's making payment shall be at the debtor's expense' (*a*).

(*a*) Bell *v.* Eliot, 1835 ; 14 S. 3 ; 2 Ill. 105. 32 and 33 Vict. c. 116, § 7.

(3.) *Possession.*—The creditor is entitled to enter into possession, or by decree of maills and duties to take the rents, and sequestrate the tenant's 'effects' (*a*). When a creditor takes possession, his intromissions with the rents go to payment of his interest, and to diminution or extinction of the principal, and discharge of his security. But although he has taken possession, he is not bound to intromit beyond the interest; and may safely pay over the balance to the debtor, without being responsible to postponed creditors. If, however, he has taken possession in opposition to the diligence of such creditors, and to their exclusion, he will be bound to account strictly, and either to pay to such creditors the balance after taking his interest, or to hold such balance in diminution of his debt (*b*). 'The assignation to rents in a bond and disposition in security in the statutory form entitles the creditor *inter alia*, "on default in payment, to enter into possession of the lands disponed in security, and uplift the rents thereof . . . and to make all necessary repairs on the buildings, subject to accounting to the debtor for any balance of rents actually recovered beyond what is necessary for payment" of the principal, interest, and penalty, and of all expenses incurred in reference to such possession, including the expenses of management, insurance, and repairs (*c*). It has been doubted whether under this statutory clause the creditor is entitled to take possession without some judicial proceedings (*d*). In many cases, however, under this or stronger clauses, or by arrangement, possession has been taken *de plano*; and it has been held that, without any diligence, a heritable creditor, by virtue of the assignation to rents intimated by registration, has a completed real right to the rents, preferable in competition to the arrestment of a personal creditor (*e*). Any creditor in possession of lands disponed in security may let them for not more than seven years (*f*), and may obtain a sheriff's warrant to let lands for not more than twenty-one years, and minerals for not more than thirty-one years (*g*). It has long been settled law that a heritable creditor has no lien over the moveables on the security lands, but must proceed to affect them by diligence. By a decree of maills and duties he will obtain the benefit of the landlord's hypothec over the crop, stock, and moveables of the tenants, to be made effectual by a sequestration; by a poinding of the ground he may attach the effects of the landlord, and those of the tenants to the extent of the rents due by them (*h*). By taking possession, a heritable creditor incurs the ordinary liabilities of a proprietor arising from the condition of the property, whether to the public or to neighbouring owners (*i*).'

(*a*) Railton *v.* Muirhead, 1834; 12 S. 757. Robertson's Trs. *v.* Gardner, 1889; 16 R. 705. Obviously, a process of maills and duties is not competent where a debtor is in the natural possession of the bonded property. Rowat *v.* Chalmers, 1890; 17 R. 1088. See below (*h*) *fin.* As to creditor of superior, see § 700 (*g*), above.

(*b*) Brown *v.* Rae, 1835; 13 S. 256. City of Glasg. Bk. *v.* Nicolson's Trs., 1882; 9 R. 689. For the creditor's duty of accounting after a sale, see above, § 891.

(*c*) 31 and 32 Vict. c. 101, § 119, repeating and amending 10 and 11 Vict. c. 50, § 2. See above (*b*).

(*d*) Neils *v.* Lyle, 1863; 2 Macph. 168. M'Rosty *v.* Phillips, 1897; 13 Sh. Ct. Rep. 274; 14 *ib.* 69. And see 57 and 58 Vict. c. 44, § 3 *fin.*

(*e*) Webster *v.* Donaldson, 1780; M. 2902. 1 Bell's Com. 757 (793, M'L.'s ed.). Budge *v.* Brown's Trs., 1872; 10 Macph. 958. See Wylie, *infra* (*h*); and compare Chambers's Factor *v.* Vertue, 1893; 20 R. 257 (maills and duties—preference to tenant's set-off), with Stevenson & Lauder *v.* Dawson, 1896; 23 R. 469 (no maills and duties —preference of house factor's retention).

(*f*) 57 and 58 Vict. c. 44, § 6. (*g*) *Ib.* § 7.

(*h*) *Per* L. Corehouse in Railton *v.* Muirhead, *supra* (*a*), Comp. Budge, *cit.*; Royal Bank *v.* Bain, 1877; 4 R. 985, etc. A creditor, although in possession under a decree of maills and duties, may poind the ground. Henderson *v.* Wallace, 1875; 2 R. 272; or the holder of a ground-annual—Bell's Trs. *v.* Copeland & Co., 1896; 23 R. 650; but not an adjudger, or *ex facie* absolute disponee; *infra*, § 2285 (*d*); or the holder of a bond over a registered lease—Luke *v.* Wallace, 1896; 23 R. 634.

After remarkable fickleness in legislation, it is now enacted that no poinding of the ground which has not been carried into execution by sale of the effects sixty days before the date of a sequestration or liquidation is available in competition with the trustee or liquidator; except for the interest on the current half-yearly term, and arrears of interest for one year previous to such term. 42 and 43 Vict. c. 40, § 3, repeating (except a like restriction as to actions of maills and duties, which remains repealed) 19 and 20 Vict. c. 79, § 118, which had been repealed by 37 and 38 Vict. c. 94, § 55 (Conveyancing Act, 1874). 50 and 51 Vict. c. 69, § 2. 49 Vict. c. 23, § 3 (4) (liquidations). See 46 and 47 Vict. c. 39 (Statute Law Revision Act); above, § 699 (superior), and below, § 2285. The restriction applies to a poinding by the holder of a ground-annual. Bell's Trs., *cit.*

As to the creditor's remedies when the proprietor is in the natural possession of the subjects, see Blair *v.* Galloway, 1853; 16 D. 291. M'Farlane *v.* Campbell, 1857; 19 D. 623. Rowat, *cit.* 57 and 58 Vict. c. 44, § 5. And as to the effect of extraordinary stipulations as to removal for failure to pay interest or principal, see Wylie *v.* Her. Sec. Invt. Assn., 1871; 10 Macph. 253. Scot. Prop. Invt. Co. *v.* Horne, *supra*, § 912 (*l*).

(*i*) Baillie *v.* Shearer's Factor, 1894; 21 R. 499. See § 553 (*a*), 964, 970.

(4.) *Payment.*—Although in such securities a term is fixed for payment (generally the next term 'of Whitsunday or Martinmas'), it is not understood that payment is then to be exacted, but the money is to lie on a permanent loan for at least some reasonable time; the term being appointed only in order to make the debt absolute instead of future. But payment may be required at that term, and enforced by personal diligence; or the money may be offered by the debtor, 'or by a postponed creditor on sale by him (*a*).' To guard against the inconveniences thus arising, certain terms of premonition are commonly stipulated, which the parties are bound to observe, and not easily presumed to discharge, 'or they are inferred' (*b*).

(*a*) Adair's Trs. *v.* Rankin, 1895; 22 R. 975. 31 and 32 Vict. c. 101, § 122.

(*b*) Munro *v.* Dunlop, 1838; 16 S. 335. See as to 32 and 33 Vict. c. 116, § 7, above, § 891 (*d*). The creditor calling up the debt may charge on the personal obligation and also sell. M'Whirter *v.* M'Culloch's Trs., 1887; 14 R. 918. M'Nab *v.* Clarke, 1889; 16 R. 610.

(5.) *Debt on an Entailed Estate.*—Where a debt is made a burden on an entailed estate, the heir in possession may (unless prohibited by the entail) pay the debt, and take an assignation to it, so as to keep it up against the estate. It has been held that a proprietor in fee simple may pay up a debt heritably secured on his estate, by means of a trustee, to the effect of keeping up the security (*a*).

(*a*) M'Kenzie *v.* Gordon, 1838; 16 S. 311; aff. 1839, M'L. & R. 117. *Supra*, § 580.

(6.) *Catholic Securities.* — When a real security extends over several estates, on one of which there are other securities, the debt of the catholic security falls to be paid rateably from all; and the purchaser of the estate on which there are no other securities is not entitled on an assignation to the catholic security to discharge the estate over which it alone extends, keeping up the debt against the others, to the prejudice of the creditors holding the securities over them; 'the equitable rule being, that while the catholic creditor is entitled to operate payment as he best can out of the subjects of his security, he may not arbitrarily or nimiously take his payment out of subjects over which there is a secondary security. He must take payment, in the first instance, out of the subject which has no other security over it, or assign his right to the second creditor. As the rules on this subject are equitable, the circumstances of each case must be considered' (*a*).

(*a*) E. Moray *v.* Mansfield, 1836; 14 S. 886; 2 Ill. 112. See 2 Ersk. 12. § 66. 2 Bell's Com. 523 (417, M'L.'s ed.). Boswell *v.* Ayrshire Bkg. Co., 1841; 3 D. 352. Littlejohn *v.* Black, 1855; 18 D. 207. Morton (Liddell's Cur.) *v.* Liddell, 1871; 10 Macph. 292. Nicol's Tr. *v.* Hill, 1889; 16 R. 416. Ferrier *v.* Cowan, 1896; 23 R. 703. Rose, and Moncrieff *v.* Skene, *citt.* § 1935, below.

(7.) '*Power of Sale.*—The power of sale in a bond and disposition in security may be exercised whether the creditor is or is not in possession of the security subjects. It has already been commented on (*a*).'

(*a*) *Supra*, § 891. 32 and 33 Vict. c. 116, § 119.

(8.) '*Foreclosure.*—Any creditor under a bond and disposition in security, who has exposed the security subjects for sale at a price not exceeding what is due under his security and any prior and *pari passu* security, and has failed to find a purchaser, may petition the sheriff to find that the debtor has forfeited his right of redemption, and that the petitioner has right to the security subjects as absolute proprietor, subject to the burdens mentioned in the bond, at the latest upset price; and, on an extract decree being recorded in the appropriate register of sasines, the creditor has right to the subjects as under an irredeemable disposition of the date of the decree, the subjects being disburdened of all securities and diligences posterior to his security. The sheriff may, instead, order a re-exposure at a price fixed by him, and if the creditor then buy in, a similar result may be obtained (*a*). The extract decree must be stamped as a conveyance on sale (*b*). The personal obligation of the debtor is reserved, so far as not extinguished by the price at which the subjects have been acquired (*c*).'

(*a*) 57 and 58 Vict. c. 44, § 8–13, and Sch. D.
(*b*) Tod *v.* Inland Revenue, 1897; 24 R. 934; rev. 1898, 25 R. H. L. 29. See 61 and 62 Vict. c. 10, § 6.
(*c*) 57 and 58 Vict. c. 44, § 9.

915. Securities Qualifying the Right of Property.—When land is disponed under the burden of a sum to be paid, or under burden of a power reserved, or under the burden of a power granted to another to burden the right with payment of a specific sum, the real securities thus created are incorporated as qualifications of the right of property which the conveyance bestows, and which the sasine on that conveyance renders complete.

916. The force and effect of such securities may be considered either in relation to the grantee, or in relation to third parties. Against the disponee and his heirs, the obligation implied in the condition is effectual, provided it be clear (*a*); and it may be made effectual by inhibition or adjudication. Against third parties it is effectual only in so far as a real right is created, accompanied with these three requisites: that the burden shall affect the land itself, not the disponee merely; that it shall be of specific extent; and that it shall be published in the record of sasines (*b*).

(*a*) See below, § 1781 sqq.
(*b*) See above, § 861 sqq.; 37 and 38 Vict. c. 94, § 30; and as to ranking of debts by real burden, 1 Bell's Com. 692.

917. (1.) *Reserved Burden.*—A burden reserved is effectually constituted where, in a conveyance of land, a specific sum is declared (in terms appropriate) a burden on the land, and on the right of the disponee; and where this condition enters the infeftment, and is recorded (*a*). 'Should the disponee, in a case of pure burden, part with the land to a singular successor, any implied personal obligation on the disponee and his heirs to pay the burden is at an end, and the singular successor is under no personal obligation (*b*).'

(*a*) 2 Stair, 3. § 55. 2 Ersk. 3. § 49–51. 3 Bell's Deeds, 35 et seq. 1 Bell's Com. 685 (726, M'L.'s ed.). See § 861A.

(*b*) Scot. Drainage Co. *v.* Campbell, 1887; 15 R. 108.

918. The condition may be imposed either in the disposition and sasine, so as to affect the base fee and *dominium utile*; or by confirmation, to affect the public right; or where the title is completed by resignation, the burden must appear in the sasine (*a*); or where the conveyance is to the superior of the lands, if the burden appear in the disposition and instrument of resignation *ad remanentiam* to the superior, it is enough, although this was said to be rather an extinction of a right than a new constitution (*b*).

(*a*) 2 Ersk. 3. § 49.

(*b*) Wilson *v.* Fraser, Feb. 13, 1822; F. C.; 1 S. 316; aff. 1824, 2 S. App. 162; 2 Ill. 107.

919. In point of expression, it is necessary, 'although there are no indispensable *voces signatæ*,' that the burden shall be specifically and pointedly stated as a real debt and burden on the lands disponed (*a*); the strongest expression of mere personal obligation, though conditional, '*i.e.* although the conveyance be "granted and accepted under that condition," or the deed be "granted under the conditions following, appointed to be engrossed in the infeftments" (*b*),' being insufficient (*c*). It must be precise and clear in amount, and in the name of the creditor, either in the recorded sasine, or in a list recorded in the Register of Sasines as relative to it (*d*). 'See above, § 861 *fin.*'

(*a*) Where a real burden is duly imposed (see *infra*, § 920) by a general disposition, the lands are fixed and ascertained, in the old conveyancing, by the infeftment following on the charter of adjudication in implement, in the new, by the notarial instrument. Cowie *v.* Cowie's Tr. (Muirden), 1893; A. C. 674; 20 R. H. L. 81; revg. 18 R. 706, and explaining Williamson *v.* Begg, 1887; 14 R. 720. Comp. *supra*, § 835; *infra*, § 1692, 1692A.

(*b*) 1 Bell's Com. 686 (727, M'L.'s ed.). Stewart, *infra*, etc.

(*c*) 2 Ersk. 3. § 49. 1 Bankt. 579. Stewart *v.* Hoome, 1792; M. 4649; 2 Ill. 107; 1 Bell's Com. 686; 3 Ross' L. C. 13. Martin *v.* Paterson, 1808; M. *Pers. and Real*, Apx. No. 5; 3 Ross' L. C. 16. M'Intyre *v.* Masterton, 1824; 2 S. 664. Forbes's Trs. *v.* Gordon's Assignees, 1833; 12 S. 219. Tailors of Aberdeen *v.* Coutts, *supra*, § 861 (*h*). Baird's Trs. *v.* Mitchell, 1846; 8 D. 464; 3 Ross' L. C. 293. Mackenzie *v.* L. Lovat, 1727; Robertson's App. 607; 3 Ross' L. C. 1. Mags. of Arbroath *v.* Dickson, 1872; 10 Macph. 630. Davidson *v.* Dalziel, 1881; 8 R. 990.

(*d*) 2 Ersk. 3. § 50. Innes *v.* Duff, 1719; M. 10,244; Mackenzie *v.* L. Lovat, 1719; both rev. 1721, Robertson's App. 372, 355; 3 Ross' L. C. 1. Calderwood's Crs., 1730; M. 10,245. M'Lellan's Crs., 1734; 1 Bell's Com. 690; 2 Ill. 108. Smith's Crs. *v.* Smiths, 1738; M. 10,246; Elchies' Notes, 329. Broughton's Crs. *v.* Gordon, 1739; M. 10,247; Elch. Notes, 329; 5 B. Sup. 665; 3 Ross' L. C. 6. Allan *v.* Cameron's Crs., 1780; M. 10,265; aff. 2 Pat. 572; 2 Ill. 109; 3 Ross' L. C. 10. Place *v.* M'Nab's Trs., Feb. 24, 1821; 1 Bell's Com. 689; Hume, 544. Chalmers, § 921 (*a*). Stein's Crs. *v.* Newnham & Co., 1789; M. 1158, 14,127; aff. 3 Pat. 345. Erskine *v.* Wright, 1843; 8 D. 863 (real burden sustained in favour of children of persons pointed out). Tod *v.* Dunlop, 1838; 1 D. 231.

920. The burden, 'although effective as a qualification of the personal right against the disponee and his creditors (*a*), in order to become real' must be declared in the dispositive clause (*b*).

(*a*) Lamont *v.* Lamont's Crs., 1789; M. 5494; 1 Bell's Com. 685, 692 (726, 732, M'L.'s ed.).

(*b*) Ersk. *ut supra*. Allan, *supra*, § 919 (*d*). Williamson *v.* Begg, *cit.* Cowie's Tr. (Muirden) *v.* Cowie (H. L.), *cit.* § 919.

921. The burden must be incorporated in the recorded sasine by which the burdened estate is conveyed (*a*); 'and, once on record, it may be dealt with in deeds by reference to the recorded writ (*b*).'

(*a*) 2 Ersk. 3. § 51. Stenhouse *v.* Innes, 1765; M. 10,264; 2 Ill. 109. Broughton's Crs., *supra*, § 919 (*d*). L. Elibank *v.* Dornock's Crs., 1765; 5 B. Sup. 906. Chalmers *v.* Redcastle's Crs., 1791; 2 Ill. 110; 1 Bell's Com. 687, 689. Place, *supra*, § 919 (*d*). See § 910A, 861A.

(*b*) 31 and 32 Vict. c. 101, § 10. 37 and 38 Vict. c. 94, § 32, and Sch. H.

922. A reserved burden, though real (and so giving the remedy of poinding of the ground (*a*)), gives no active title to raise an action of maills and duties so as to affect the rents (*b*); nor power to assume possession, 'unless there be an express power of sale (*c*).' In order to accomplish that, adjudication must be led; and a personal bond is commonly granted by the disponee, collateral with the burden, and referred to in the reservation (*d*).

(*a*) See 1 Bell's Com. 692 (732, M'L.'s ed.). Duff's Feud. Convg. 136 (4). A. *v.* B., M. 10,550 (Kilkerran); below, § 2285, *init*.

(*b*) 4 Stair, 35. § 24, and 4. 23. § 5.

(*c*) Wilson, *supra*, § 918 (*b*).

(*d*) 2 Stair, 10. § 1. Baillie *v.* Laidlaw, 1821; 1 S. 108; 2 Ill. 110.

923. A burden by reservation is not in the creditor's person a feudal estate; requires no sasine in the creditor's person; is carried by general service (*a*); and is transferable by assignation (*b*). 'Real burdens are, by the Conveyancing Act, 1874, declared to be moveable as regards succession; and as they may be assigned or discharged as nearly as may be in the form applicable to heritable securities, the registration of the assignation in the proper register supersedes the necessity of intimation (*c*).'

(*a*) Cuthbertson *v.* Barr, 1806; M. *Serv. & Conf.*, Apx. No. 2; 2 Ill. 110. See Andrews *v.* Laurie, 1849; 12 D. 344; and *supra*, § 861A.

(*b*) Miller *v.* Brown, 1820; 1 Bell's Com. 691; Hume, 540; 3 Ross' L. C. 29. Baillie, § 922 (*d*).

(*c*) 37 and 38 Vict. c. 94, § 30. 31 and 32 Vict. c. 101, § 117, etc. See above, § 910A; below, § 1485A.

924. (2.) *Faculty to Burden.*—This is a power reserved by the granter of a conveyance (or conferred on another as the condition of it), to burden the lands disponed with a specific sum. It may be viewed either as a mere power, or as exercised in conformity with the condition (*a*).

(*a*) 2 Ersk. 3. § 50. 1 Bell's Com. 40 sqq. 3 Ross' L. C. 38–68.

925. While the right exists as a mere power, it has been thought that there is room for a distinction between a right reserved to the granter, and the right conferred on a stranger. The granter reserving the right has been held to have more ample power, and his creditors a right to adjudge for his debts, even after his death, without distinction between anterior and subsequent creditors (*a*). A stranger, it has been suggested, will not confer on his creditors any right but that of adjudging during his life, on the principle that he is bound to exercise the power in their favour (*b*). The faculty forms a burden on the disponee, whose creditors can take his estate only under the condition.

(*a*) Elliot *v.* Elliot, 1698; M. 4130; 2 Ill. 111; 3 Ross' L. C. 63. Rusco's Crs. *v.* Blair, 1723; M. 4117; 3 Ross' L. C. 65.

(*b*) More's Sup. to Stair, cxcii. M'Lean's Children *v.* M'Lean, 5 B. Sup. 444. But see Morris *v.* Tennant, 1855; 27 Jur. 546; H. L. 1858, 30 Jur. 493. M'Laren on Wills, § 2035 (3rd ed.). Colville *v.* James, 1862; 1 Macph. 41.

926. When the faculty has been exercised in due form, a real burden is constituted on the estate.

927. In the creation of such a power it must be made specific, both as to the extent of the power to be exercised, and as to the person by whom it is to be exercised.

928. The power remains with the disponer before sasine is taken on the conveyance in which it is declared. After sasine, it is vested as a real right in the person to whom it is reserved or given. It may be exercised by testamentary deed or on deathbed; and is regarded so much as a mere power, that it expires with that person if he should die without exercising it (*a*).

(*a*) Pringle *v.* Pringles, 1765; M. 3287; 5 B. Sup. 444; rev. 1767, 2 Pat. 130; 2 Ill. 111. M'Lean, *supra*, § 925 (*b*).

929. In order to confer a real right and preference on the person in whose favour the power is to be exercised (*a*), the deed of exercise must be completed by sasine recorded, or adjudication with sasine. It may seem anomalous that a warrant for sasine should be given by one not the proprietor of the land; but it is correctly given in virtue of the power reserved or granted (*b*).

(*a*) "A faculty to burden is a real right; but it is an important question what rights granted in consequence of such faculty are real"; Kilkerran, 186; 2 Ill. 111. Cunningham, *infra* (*b*). "The difference is to be marked between the exercise of the faculty to the effect of creating a real burden, as in a question with the disponee and his heirs, and considered merely as an effectual destination or bequest to regulate succession. See Hyslop *v.* Maxwell, 1834; 12 S. 413." 2 Ill. 112. The latter kind of faculty may be exercised by a personal deed. Bannatine's Trs. *v.* Cunninghame, 1869; 7 Macph. 993.

(*b*) 2 Ersk. 3. § 50. Rome *v.* Graham's Crs., 1719; M. 4113; 2 Ill. 111; 3 Ross' L. C. 38. Sinclair *v.* Sinclair, 1724; M. 4123. Ogilvie *v.* Ogilvies, 1735, 1737; M. 4125; Elchies, *Faculty*, 1; 3 Ross' L. C. 43. Douglas's Crs. *v.* Stewart, 1737; Elch. *ib.* 3. Cunningham *v.* Cunningham's Crs., 1739; M. 4133; Elch. *ib.* 5; 5 B. Sup. 681; 3 Ross' L. C. 51. Henderson *v.* Henderson's Crs., 1760; M. 4141; 3 Ross' L. C. 59. Montier *v.* Baillie, 1773; M. 15,859; Hailes, 530. Anderson *v.* Young & Trotter, 1784; M. 4128; 3 Ross' L. C. 66. See also Cheyne *v.* Smith, 1832; 10 S. 622 (procuratory), and Pringle *v.* Pringle, 1890; 17 R. 1229 (precept) as to infeftment after granter's divestiture; and comp. § 766, above.

930. The exercise of the faculty by personal deed raises to him in whose favour it is exercised a personal debt against the disponee; and the person so favoured, or the creditors of him who holds the power, may proceed to attach the faculty, but there is no preference to either till the burden be made real (*a*).

(*a*) Learmonth *v.* E. Lauderdale, 1671; M. 4099. Davidson *v.* Town of Aberdeen, 1708; M. 4109. Rome, Ogilvie, and Cunningham, *supra*, § 929 (*b*). Bannatine's Trs., *supra*, § 929 (*a*).

931. Powers in Road and Canal Acts.—In those cases where power is given to sell, or borrow money, there are sometimes special provisions introduced respecting the form of conveyance. In such cases, the particular Act prescribes the form in which the conveyance is to be given; and the terms of the statute must be strictly adhered to (*a*).

(*a*) See 8 and 9 Vict. c. 17, § 40 seq.; 26 and 27 Vict. c. 118, § 12 sqq. (Companies Clauses Consol. Acts). Dundee Union Bank *v.* Dundee and Newtyle Ry. Co., 1844; 6 D. 521.

CHAPTER XI

OF UDAL RIGHTS IN ORKNEY AND ZETLAND

932. Nature.—In Orkney and Zetland the land appears, while under the Kings of Norway, to have been held free from all burdens analogous to feudal duties or services, and liable only to a Government tax called SKAT. The lands so held were called SKATLAND; and an exemption from Skat was given to such lands as were enclosed for cultivation, called UDAL or free lands. There was nothing analogous to feus (*a*). The title to lands was judicial, by an entry of the heir in presence of the Foude or Governor's Court, a decree of that Court being the title (*b*). The law of succession was different from the feudal. The children had equal shares (as is still the law of Norway), leading to a minute division of land (*c*). No alienations could be made without the judicial consent of the heirs; and the term of prescription was thirty years (*d*).

(*a*) E. of Galloway *v.* E. of Morton, 1752; M. 16,393.
(*b*) 2 Stair, 3. § 11. 2 Ersk. 3. § 18. 2 Bankt. 3. § 10, 17 et seq. Peterkin's Notes on Orkney. Sinclair *v.* Hawick, 1624; M. 16,393.
(*c*) See Charter, Dec. 3, 1498; Peterkin's Notes, 97; also Apx. p. 95. Sinclair *v.* Hawick, 1624; M. 16,393; Peterkin's Notes, Apx. 94.
(*d*) See Dundas *v.* Orkney Heritors, 1777; 5 B. Sup. 609. See Rankine, Landownership, 46, note.

933. History.—Those islands, held at one time of the Crown of Denmark by the Earls of Orkney, came, on failure of those earls, into the family of Sinclair by investiture. They were annexed to the Crown of Scotland in the fifteenth century; and, after much confusion, and a partial adoption of feudal titles in many parts of those islands, there was a new annexation to the Crown a little after the middle of the seventeenth century. A grant was made to the Earl of Morton in 1707, the reversionary right of which in the Crown was discharged in 1742. The right was afterwards purchased by the family of Dundas. The lands of Orkney and Zetland stand now in one of two situations. Some lands are held feudally of the Crown; and others, and a considerable part, still continue to depend on the judicial title of udal property, convertible into feu at the option of the proprietors, to be held either of the Crown or of Lord Dundas (*a*). And it is provided that vassals whose valuation does not exceed £20 Scots may possess by their udal right without renewal of infeftment (*b*).

(*a*) Rendall *v.* Robertson, Dec. 15, 1836; 15 S. 265. Beatton *v.* Goudie, 1832; 10 S. 286; 1 Ill. 113.
(*b*) 1690, c. 32 *in fin.*

CHAPTER XII

OF OWNERSHIP OF LAND

934. Accession.—There are several modes in which a landowner's property may be enlarged by the accession of other land to that which formerly belonged to him.

935. (1.) *Alluvion* is a process of gradual and imperceptible addition to land, by the slow retiring of a river or of the sea, or by the successive accumulation of soil brought down by a stream, or floated in by the sea. Such addition becomes a part of the property (*a*).

(*a*) 2 Stair, 1. § 35. 2 Ersk. 1. § 14. See above, § 642, 738.

936. (2.) *Alvei Mutatio and Avulsio.*—This gradual addition is to be distinguished on the one hand from "alvei mutatio," and on the other from "avulsio." The former of these is the change frequently occasioned by a river which bounds the property of conterminous heritors deviating from its course; the latter is the violent tearing away of a part of the ground of one proprietor, and depositing it in a shape capable of identification along the bank of another's land. In neither of these cases is there an acquisition by accession; unless, by acquiescence on the part of the proprietor whose land is diminished, a right shall be conferred on the other (*a*).

(*a*) Instit. de Rerum Div. lib. 2, t. 1. § 21. M. of Tweeddale *v.* Ker, 1822; 1 S. 397; 2 Ill. 113. See below, § 947. Mags. of Edin. *v.* Scot, 1836; 14 S. 922, 933 (minerals below). Rankine on Landownership, 100.

937. (3.) *Planting or Building on Another's Land.*—The property of the ground carries that of buildings, fixtures, or trees united to the soil. Buildings by a tenant remain to the landlord. Even buildings by the owner of ground, with materials of another, follow the property of the soil, leaving it (as a question of recompense) to be determined how the owner of the materials is to be indemnified (*a*). The claim for recompense gives no ground for retaining the property in security of the amount (*b*).

(*a*) 2 Ersk. 1. § 15, and 3. 1. § 11. See Stenhouse *v.* Young, 1741; 5 B. Sup. 711; 2 Ill. 114. M'Nair *v.* L. Cathcart, 1802; M. 12,832. Laird *v.* Fenwick, 1807; M. *Liferenter*, Apx. 3; 2 Ill. 145. But only a *bonâ fide* possessor upon a supposed good title of property is entitled to recompense. Barbour *v.* Halliday, 1840; 2 D. 1279. Thomson *v.* Fowler, 1859; 21 D. 453. *Supra*, § 538.

(*b*) Sinclair *v.* Sinclair, 1829; 7 S. 343; 2 Ill. 114. Unless where the owner has seen and acquiesced. Beattie *v.* L. Napier, 1831; 9 S. 639.

938. Exclusive and Absolute Right.—The right of ownership may be exercised either directly by the proprietor himself, or by his tenants.

939. The chief attribute of property is the right of deriving from land and its accessories all the uses or services of which they are capable. This right may be considered, in relation to others, as "exclusive"; or in relation merely to the subject, as "absolute." The exclusive right may suffer limitation wherever the public interest requires it; the absolute use also may be restrained on similar principles, where it tends to the injury or discomfort of the public. Both the exclusive and the absolute use may be extended or restrained by agreements, expressed or implied, which constitute servitudes (*a*); 'they are limited by the public necessities (*b*); and by the law of neighbourhood (*c*), and the law of nuisance (*d*)'; and they are under the burden of public taxes (*e*).

(*a*) *Infra*, § 979 sqq.
(*b*) *Infra*, § 956 sqq. 2 Ersk. 1. 2.
(*c*) *Infra*, § 964 sqq. 2 Ersk. 1. 2.
(*d*) *Infra*, § 973 sqq. (*e*) *Infra*, § 1122 sqq.

I. EXCLUSIVE USE.

940. Nature and Effect of Exclusive Use.—The right to the exclusive occupation and use of land leads, in its exercise, to many difficult cases of interference between conterminous proprietors, and between landowners and the public. The proprietor of land has the exclusive right to the use and occupation, not merely of the surface, but of what is below, and what is above the surface, "a cœlo usque ad centrum." 'In other words, where there is no division of the underground estate and surface between different proprietors, as where mineral strata are "reserved" or separately owned (*supra*, § 737, 740), the vertical measurement of a landowner's property, whether it be landed property or house property, is unlimited (*a*).'

(*a*) Cf. Glas. City and Distr. Ry. Co. *v.* M'Brayne, 1883; 10 R. 894. Glasg. Coal Exch. Co. *v.* Glasg. City and Distr. Ry. Co., 1883; 10 R. 1283. Cf. as to flats, § 1086.

941. So he has a right to have his neighbour prevented from projecting a building over his land (*a*); or resting it on his wall (*b*); or the rain-drop from his neighbour's roof from falling on his ground (*c*); or trees from overshadowing it (*d*); or even a cornice or ornament from extending beyond the line of the boundary, however innocuously (*e*). When any of these rights to exclude are found to exist, they are held presumptive, though not conclusive of a right of property, and do not necessarily imply servitude merely (*f*).

(*a*) Miln *v.* Mudie, 1828; 6 S. 967. Hazle *v.* Turner, 1840; 2 D. 886. Urquhart *v.* Melville, 1853; 16 D. 307. M'Intosh *v.* Scott & Co., 1859; 21 D. 363. Cf. Arrol *v.* Inches, 1887; 14 R. 394.
(*b*) See Leonard *v.* Lindsay & Benzie, 1886; 13 R. 958.
(*c*) Garriochs *v.* Kennedy, 1769; M. 13,178; 2 Ill. 114. See Stirling *v.* Finlayson, 1752; M. 14,526; 2 Ill. 130. *Infra*, § 1004.
(*d*) Halkerston *v.* Wedderburn, 1781; M. 10,495. See Rankine on Landownership, 524. Lemmon *v.* Webb, 1895; A. C. 1.
(*e*) Miln *v.* Mudie, *cit.* (*a*).
(*f*) Scouller *v.* Pollock, 1832; 10 S. 241. Comp. Jack *v.* Lyall, 1833; 11 S. 711; aff. 1 S. & M'L. 77.

942. He may insist on the removal of conduit pipes which have been laid below the surface of his land, or roots of trees which shoot into his ground (*a*). 'Generally, he has not merely the remedies more usual in practice of interdict and damages, but that of restitution or restoration by an action *ad factum præstandum*, for "where the party injured can be restored precisely to his former state, the method ought to be followed, both as the most natural and as the completest reparation" (*b*).'

(*a*) See below, § 967. Galbreath *v.* Armour, 1845; 4 Bell's App. 374. See Halkerston, *cit.*, and Rankine, *l.c.*
(*b*) Ersk. iii. 1–14. Stair, i. 9. 4. Miln *v.* Mudie, *supra* § 941. Hazle *v.* Turner, *ib.* Jack *v.* Begg, 1875; 3 R. 35. Sommers *v.* Mags. of St. Monance, 1882; 26 J. of J. 615; 2 Sel. Sh. Ct. Cases, 439 (Sheriff Crichton — rebuilding boundary wall). Leonard *v.* Lindsay & Benzie, 1886; 13 R. 958.

943. He may prevent others from coming on his land for taking fuel, however necessary to them, and however inexhaustible the supply; or from hunting on his land, or setting foot upon it, or encroaching, however inoffensively (*a*).

(*a*) Baird *v.* Thomson, 1825; 3 S. 448. E. Breadalbane *v.* Livingstone, 1790; M. 4999; aff. 1791, 3 Pat. 221. See below, § 956 et seq., for limitations of these rights.

944. Individual benefit or convenience will not justify the invasion of this exclusive right of property (*a*); 'nor does the absence of actual damage prevent the person whose property is invaded from vindicating his right to exclusive use (*b*).' The right must be purchased if the party be desirous of using it. Such questions are most apt to occur relative to the placing of sign-posts in towns. And the rules seem to be: That in the common case no conveniency of one proprietor or inhabitant can entitle him to place his sign-board on the more conspicuous wall of his neighbour (*c*); that the mere circumstance of a wall being the front wall of a common close, lane, or *cul de sac*, does not render it common, so as to entitle tradesmen in that close to place their sign-boards there (*d*); and although acquiescence is said to confer such a right, it does not seem that anything short of a written consent or prescription will be sufficient for that purpose (*e*).

(*a*) Farquharson *v.* Farquharson, 1740 ; M. 12,779 ; Elchies, *Property*, 5 ; 5 B. Sup. 668 ; 2 Ill. 161. See below, § 1102.

(*b*) Miln and Hazle, *supra*, § 941 (*a*) ; and authorities as to water, § 648, 650, 1102. But see Leonard *v.* Lindsay & Benzie, 1886 ; 13 R. 958.

(*c*) Murray *v.* Mackenzie, 1812 ; Hume, 520. Dickson *v.* Morton, 1824 ; 3 S. 310 ; 2 Ill. 114. Alexander *v.* Butchart, 1875 ; 3 R. 156.

(*d*) Murdoch *v.* Dunbar, 1783 ; M. 13,184. Munro *v.* Davidson, 1808 ; Hume, 518. Lowrie *v.* Drysdale, May 13, 1812 ; F. C.

(*e*) Buchanan *v.* Carmichael, 1823 ; 2 S. 526. See next section. M'Arly *v.* French's Trs., 1883 ; 10 R. 574.

945. Effect of Acquiescence.—The exercise of the exclusive right may be barred by acquiescence. This doctrine has of late acquired considerable importance from the effects ascribed to it ; and it is necessary to distinguish clearly the principle on which it depends.

946. The principle seems to be, that mere acquiescence may, as *rei interventus*, make an agreement to grant a servitude, or to transfer property, binding, or may bar one from challenging a judicial sentence ; but that where there is neither previous contract nor judicial proceeding, there must be something more than mere acquiescence, something capable of being construed as an implied contract or permission, followed by *rei interventus*. Where great cost is incurred by operations carried on under the eye of one having a right to stop them, or where, under the eye and with the knowledge of him who has the adverse right, something is allowed to be done which manifestly cannot be undone, the law will presume an agreement or conventional permission as a fair ground of right (*a*). 'There may be acquiescence or personal bar where a violation of a man's exclusive right, or a nuisance, is only prospective, provided expense is incurred in operations which will manifestly and certainly result in an invasion of the rights of the person seeking to prevent them. But in most cases there can be no acquiescence until injury arises, and silence, or *non-repugnantia*, for a period does not bar from objecting when a nuisance is distinctly increased or an encroachment extended (*b*). In pleading, the circumstances from which acquiescence is to be inferred ought to be specified (*c*).'

(*a*) M. of Abercorn *v.* Langmuir, May 20, 1820 ; F. C. ; 2 Ill. 115. Aytoun *v.* Melville, 1801 ; M. *Property*, Apx. 6. Stirling *v.* Haldane, 1829 ; 8 S. 131. M'Nair *v.* Cathcart, 1802 ; M. 12,832 ; 2 Ill. 113. Moir *v.* Alloa Coal Co., 1849 ; 12 D. 77. Ewen v. Turnbull's Trs., 1857 ; 19 D. 513. Cairncross *v.* Lorimer, 1858 ; 20 D. 995 ; aff. 1860, 3 Macq. 827 (see above, § 27A). **Wark** *v.* **Bargaddie Coal Co.**, 1856 ; 18 D. 772 ; rev. 1859, 3 Macq. 467. Scott *v.* Fothringham, 1859 ; 21 D. 737. Muirhead *v.* Glasg. Highland Socy., 1864 ; 2 Macph. 420. Cowan *v.* Kinnaird, 1865 ; 4 Macph. 236. Bank of Scotland *v.* Stewart, 1891 ; 18 R. 957.

(*b*) Johnston *v.* Scott, 1834 ; 12 S. 492. **D. Buccleuch** *v.* **Cowan**, 1866 ; 5 Macph. 211. Stirling and Ewen, *citt.* Robertson *v.* Stewart, 1872 ; 11 Macph. 189. Houldsworth *v.* Burgh of Wishaw, 1887 ; 14 R. 920. And as to prospective nuisances, see Trotter *v.* Farnie, and Arnott *v.* Brown, and cases in § 976 sq. *infra*.

(*c*) Scott *v.* Fothringham, 1859 ; 21 D. 737. D. Buccleuch *v.* Cowan, 1866 ; 4 Macph. 475.

947. Although it is rightly said that mere acquiescence cannot confer a right of property, it may confer a right of use of property or servitude (*a*).

(*a*) L. Melville *v.* Douglas, 1828 ; 7 S. 186 ; and 1830, 8 S. 841 ; 2 Ill. 115. Monro *v.* Jervey, 1821 ; 1 S. 154. See Johnston *v.* Scott, 1834 ; 12 S. 492. Comp. § 936, 944, 994, 1103. 2 Ersk. 9. § 3 *fin.* And see Sanderson *v.* Geddes, 1874, 1 R. 1198, as explained in Grahame *v.* Mags. of Kirkcaldy, 1882 ; 9 R. H. L. 91, an explanation which is authoritative in regard to the effect of the case as a precedent, but is hardly consistent with the terms of the judgment of the 2nd Div. See also D. Buccleuch *v.* Mags. of Edinr., 1865 ; 3 Macph. 528.

948. Right to Game.—The exclusive possession of land is the foundation on which the Scottish game laws rest, the right of hunting and killing game being an incident of property in land. Game is not property in Scotland ; nor does it belong to the sovereign ; nor was there originally any restraint on the killing of game within one's own land. But in the seventeenth century the right of killing game was, from favour to landowners, restricted to proprietors of a certain measure of property (viz. a ploughgate), or those having authority from such proprietor (*a*). To the qualification thus established has been added the necessity of a licence, for the increase of the revenue (*b*). This right has been made the subject of many penal regulations for the preservation and the protection of the privilege (*c*). A severe law has been passed against midnight destroyers of game (*d*), and for guarding against trespasses in the day-time (*e*).

(*a*) 2 Craig, 8. § 13. 1555, c. 51. 1621, c. 31. 1685, c. 20. 1707, c. 13. Pollock, Gilmour, & Co. *v.* Harvey, 1828 ; 6 S. 913 ; 2 Ill. 116. As to the ploughgate, see Innes, Legal Antiq. 241. Irvine, Game Laws, 241.

(*b*) 48 Geo. III. c. 55. 52 Geo. III. c. 93. 3 Vict. c. 17. 11 and 12 Vict. c. 30. 23 and 24 Vict. c. 90. 33 and 34 Vict. c. 57 (Gun Licence Act).

(*c*) 13 Geo. III. c. 54. 57 Geo. III. c. 90. See E. of Cassillis *v.* Sloan, 1826 ; Sh. Justiciary Cases, 146.

(*d*) 9 Geo. IV. c. 69 (Night Poaching Act). See below, § 961.

(*e*) 2 and 3 Will. IV. c. 68. See also an Act for the Prevention of Poaching, 25 and 26 Vict. c. 114. 38 and 39 Vict. c. 47. 40 and 41 Vict. c. 28. And the Ground Game Act, 43 and 44 Vict. c. 47.

949. (1.) *Right to Kill Game.*—Property in land in Scotland gives the qualification to kill game. It is not enough to have property in England (*a*). But such qualification gives no right to hunt on another's ground without permission from the proprietor (*b*).

(*a*) E. of Mansfield *v.* Henderson, Jan. 18, 1810; F. C.; 2 Ill. 116.
(*b*) Baird *v.* Thomson, 1825; 3 S. 448; 2 Ill. 114. E. of Breadalbane *v.* Livingstone, 1790; 2 Ill. 117; M. 4999; 3 Pat. 221. Kelly *v.* Smith, 1780; M. 4995.

950. Leave from a qualified person gives the right to hunt (*a*) on that person's ground, or to have possession of game without challenge (*b*).

(*a*) The generic term for pursuing game in whatever mode. Trotter, *infra* (*b*).
(*b*) Trotter *v.* M'Ewan, July 8, 1809; F. C. But the Acts do not forfeit the game found in the possession of an unqualified person. Scott *v.* Everett, 1853; 15 D. 288.

951. The right of hunting in a forest may, as a delegation from the owner, be conveyed to another, to the effect of giving to the assignee a qualification to kill game.

952. The right to kill game does not exist as a real right separate from the land, by sasine or lease; it is only a personal privilege in respect of the right of property (*a*). 'In accordance with this strict principle, it was held that a lease of shootings was not protected against singular successors of the lessor by the Act 1449, c. 17 (*b*). But as such leases have become ordinary sources of profit to landowners, shootings are now regarded rather as property than mere personal privileges (*c*); and, while it has not yet been held that, like fishings, they may be held as a separate estate independent of the land, the rents which they yield or might yield are treated as part of the ordinary return of the ground,—as rents received substantially for the use and occupation of the land. Hence such rents, or the value of unlet shootings, are computed in ascertaining the amount of the free rents of an estate due under an entail to a widow for her jointure or locality (*d*), and to children for their provisions (*e*), or in computing the year's rental payable as composition on the entry of a vassal (*f*); and they are now, whether let or unlet, included in the valuation roll, and are subject to all assessments, rates, or taxes imposed according to the annual value of lands and heritages (*g*). So a lessee of a shooting-lodge and shootings is liable to assessment as a tenant and occupant of "lands and heritages" in the sense of the Poor Law Act (*h*). And, whether or not it includes the occupancy of a house or lodge, a lease of shootings affords a qualification for the electoral franchise (*i*).'

(*a*) E. of Aboyne *v.* Innes, June 22, 1813; F. C.; aff. 1819, 6 Pat. 444. See the sequel in M. Huntly *v.* Nicol, 1858; 20 D. 374; and Id. *v.* Eund. 1896; 23 R. 610; also Hemming *v.* D. of Athole, 1883; 11 R. 93. As to joint-owners, see Campbell *v.* Campbell, Jan. 24, 1809; F. C.
(*b*) Pollock, Gilmour, & Co. *v.* Harvey, 1828; 6 S. 913. Birkbeck *v.* Ross, 1865; 4 Macph. 272. E. of Fife *v.* Wilson, 1859; 22 D. 191. Cf. Campbell *v.* M'Kinnon, 1867; 5 Macph. 636, 651; aff. 8 Macph. 40. See *infra*, § 1207.
(*c*) See Farquharson, Petr., 1870; 9 Macph. 66.
(*d*) Macpherson *v.* Macpherson, 1839; 1 D. 794; aff. 5 Bell's App. 280. Menzies *v.* Menzies, 1852; 14 D. 451.
(*e*) Sinclair *v.* Duffus, 1842; 5 D. 174.
(*f*) Stewart *v.* Bullock, 1881; 8 R. 381.
(*g*) 49 and 50 Vict. c. 15, amending 17 and 18 Vict. c. 91, § 42.
(*h*) Crawford *v.* Stewart, 1861; 23 D. 965.
(*i*) Dawson *v.* Watson, 1869; 8 Macph. 10. Richardson *v.* Stewart, 1878; 6 R. 17. Girvan *v.* Campbell, 1875; 3 R. 1. Paterson *v.* Johnston, 1879; 7 R. 17.

953. A tenant has no qualification, or leave to kill game, merely by having the possession of land (*a*), 'even under an agricultural lease for 999 years (*b*)'; and a lease with leave to shoot, though as a lease of the land it is good against singular successors, under the Act of 1449, c. 17 (*c*), will not be effectual to confer the privilege of shooting to the prejudice of a purchaser of the lands (*d*), 'unless it be a lease conferring the right to exclusive occupation of the land, as may happen when the land cannot be profitably used for any other purpose (*e*).' But the landlord may hunt on his tenant's ground, paying surface damage (*f*). 'When the game on a farm is increased by the landlord beyond a fair average stock, the tenant has a claim for damages for the extraordinary damage (*g*).'

(*a*) M. of Tweeddale *v.* Somner, June 18, 1808; F. C. E. of Hopetoun *v.* Wight, Jan. 17, 1810; F. C. As to rabbits, etc., see below, § 1224.
(*b*) Welwood *v.* Husband, 1874; 1 R. 507. See Wemyss *v.* Wilson, 1847; 10 D. 194; 6 Bell's App. 394. Wemyss *v.* Gulland, 1847; 10 D. 204. Smellie *v.* Lockhart, 1844; 2 Broun, 194. E. Kinnoull, *v.* Tod 1859; 3 Irv. 501; 32 Jur. 154.
(*c*) See below, § 1224.
(*d*) Pollock, Gilmour, & Co. *v.* Harvey, 1828; 6 S. 913.
(*e*) Farquharson, Petr., 1870; 9 Macph. 66. See Birkbeck *v.* Ross, Crawford *v.* Stewart, E. of Fife *v.* Wilson, etc., *supra*, § 952.

(*f*) Ronaldson *v.* Ballantyne, 1804; M. 15,270; 2 Ill. 117. See below, § 961.

(*g*) Wemyss *v.* Wilson, 1847; 10 D. 194; 6 Bell's App. 394. See Morton *v.* Graham, 1867; 6 Macph. 71. Syme *v.* E. of Moray, 1867; 6 Macph. 217. Broadwood *v.* Hunter, 1856; 18 D. 574. Inglis *v.* Moir's Tutors, 1871; 10 Macph. 204. Cadzow *v.* Lockhart, 1875; 2 R. 928; 1876, 3 R. 666. Kidd *v.* Byrne, 1875; 3 R. 255 (liability of game tenant; comp. Eliott's Trs. *v.* Eliott, 1894; 21 R. 858). Cameron *v.* Drummond, 1888; 15 R. 489 (damage by removal of wire-netting on fence round plantation). See now 40 and 41 Vict. c. 28.

954. (2.) *Possession and Sale of Game.*—The old laws relative to the possession and sale of game are repealed (*a*), and the rules seem now to be: That penalties are imposed on those having in their possession muirfowl or ptarmigan from 10th December to 12th August, or partridges from 1st February to 1st September, or pheasants from 1st February to 1st October (*b*). A qualified person may possess or buy and sell game; and an unqualified person may buy from, or sell to, a qualified person. Authority given by a qualified person to buy *his* game will be a good defence in a prosecution, throwing the *onus probandi* on the prosecutor, to show the game not to be that of the licenser. An unqualified person not having leave is subject to penalties for having game in his possession; but under this law the sale of game is now open and avowed.

(*a*) 13 Geo. III. c. 54. Possession of a licence to shoot does not exempt an unqualified person from the penalties. Stevenson *v.* Melville, 1863; 35 Jur. 610.

(*b*) 1 and 2 Will. IV. c. 68. See for England, 1 and 2 Will. IV. c. 32. 23 and 24 Vict. c. 90 extends to the United Kingdom the provisions of the English Act. See also 43 and 44 Vict. c. 47, § 4 (Ground Game Act). Barclay's Digest, 486.

955. Prosecutions for offences against the game laws must be *in 'foro' delicti*, and may be maintained by the agent of a game association, in the character of informer, for the penalties (*a*).

(*a*) Buchanan *v.* Weir, May 22, 1818; F. C.; 2 Ill. 117. Gray *v.* Bonnar, Jan. 23, 1816; 19 F. C. Apx.

956. Limitation of Exclusive Use.—The exclusive right of a landowner yields wherever public interest or necessity requires that it should yield.

957. Access must on this principle be allowed for extinguishing a fire, for pursuing a criminal, for destroying dangerous or noxious animals (*a*).

(*a*) Colquhoun *v.* Buchanan, 1785; M. 4997 (farmer's right to destroy foxes). See § 939, 944.

958. On the same principle with the above, rest the laws for the enclosing of lands and straightening of marches, which to a certain extent interfere with the proprietor's exclusive right, for the public benefit (*a*).

(*a*) 1661, c. 41. 1669, c. 17. 1685, c. 39. 1 Ersk. 4. § 3, and 2. 6. § 4. 2 Hutchison's J. P. 498. Tait's J. P. 253. See Strang *v.* Steuart, 1864; 2 Macph. 1015; aff. 1866, 4 Macph. H. L. 5 (as to property in march fences, and their origin in agreement apart from statute).

959. In the construction of those laws, it is held that they apply not to every proprietor of a patch of land, but have in view the improvement of large estates (*a*); that the conterminous proprietor must be called as a party (*b*); that the line of fence is to be fixed by the Sheriff, 'who is required to visit the marches personally, and who, under the later statute (1669), but not under the earlier one, has jurisdiction exclusive of the Court of Session (*c*)'; and where a stream is the boundary, the fence is to be on the one side, or the stream divided for watering (*d*); that considerable portions of ground may be exchanged, provided they bear a reasonable relation in value to the whole march (*e*); and that entailed lands are comprehended under these laws, provided the exchanged or purchased portion be duly brought under the entail (*f*). 'In construing the former Act as to "repairing" existing fences, it is held that that word includes the rebuilding of a ruinous march fence with alterations in its style, if recommended by experience (*g*).'

(*a*) Penman *v.* Douglas, 1739; M. 10,481; Elchies, *Planting*, 3; 2 Ill. 117. 2 Ersk. 6. § 4. E. of Peterborough *v.* Garioch, 1784; M. 10,497. E. of Cassillis *v.* Paterson, Feb. 28, 1809; F. C. L. Adv. *v.* Sinclair, 1872; 11 Macph. 137.

(*b*) Ord *v.* Wright, 1738; M. 10,479; Elchies' Notes, 331.

(*c*) Ld. Adv. *v.* Sinclair, *cit.*

(*d*) E. of Crawford *v.* Rig, July 21, 1769; M. 10,475. Pollock *v.* Ewing, 1869; 7 Macph. 815.

(*e*) 1 Ersk. 4. § 3. Chalmers *v.* Pew, 1756; M. 10,485. Pew *v.* Miller, 1754; M. 10,484. E. of Kintore *v.* E. Kintore's Trs., 1886; 13 R. 997.

(*f*) Ramsay *v.* Primrose, 1702; M. 10,477.

(*g*) Paterson *v.* MacDonald, 1880; 7 R. 958.

960. On the same principle also depends that power of taking the property of individuals, which the Legislature occasionally exercises in the course of public improvements, by roads, bridges, canals, etc.,—a power which implies as a condition, that the value of what is taken shall be paid to the proprietor. 'The value must be assessed with reference to the interest and loss of the proprietor, and not to the value after the board or company has acquired it (*a*). And as compulsory powers are given for public purposes, a contract not to exercise them is void; and thus the value assessed is not to be diminished by reason of a contract by the company or trustees not to use their powers to the full extent (*b*). The provisions in favour of persons whose property is taken are regarded almost as terms of a contract sanctioned by Parliament. So any one of these has a right to require the company to comply literally with the Act, so far as it makes provision for his interest; and such provisions or conditions may not be relaxed or modified by any Court (*c*).' In order to preserve the property, and protect the landholder's interest against encroachment beyond the strict limit of necessity, it is provided by the standing orders of both Houses of Parliament, that no Act of Parliament which touches private property shall be passed without certain notices being given, affording full opportunity of being heard (*d*).

'Such Acts are strictly construed as to the extent and mode of the interference with property (*e*). Reference to plans exhibited or notices given prior to the passing of a statute interfering with private property is excluded, except in so far as they are incorporated in the statute (*f*). Failure to give due notice of the Act, even to a party whose rights under a previous statute are affected, does not touch the validity of an Act (*g*).

'Acts conferring power to interfere with private property now generally incorporate the Lands Clauses Consolidation Act, 8 Vict. c. 19; and Lands Clauses Consolidation Amendment Act, 23 and 24 Vict. 106; the Railways Clauses Consolidation Act, 8 and 9 Vict. c. 33; and Railways Clauses Consolidation Amendment Act, 26 and 27 Vict. c. 92; and other Consolidation Acts, or parts of these (*h*).'

(*a*) Stebbing *v.* Metr. Bd. of Works, L. R. 6 Q. B. 37; 40 L. J. Q. B. 1. Cf. Hillcoat *v.* Archb. of Canterbury, 19 L. J. C. P. 376; 10 C. B. 327.

(*b*) Oswald *v.* Ayr Harbour Trs., 1882; 10 R. 472; aff. 8 App. Ca. 623; 10 R. H. L. 85.

(*c*) Herron *v.* Rathmines, etc., Impt. Comrs., 1892; A. C. 499.

(*d*) In Railroad and other Acts, provisions are made for invasions of amenity, for severing of fields, etc.; and the question in those cases will turn, not as on nuisance at common law, but on the construction of the condition under which power is given to make the railway. See Bell's Dict. *s.v.* Private Bills.

(*e*) Moncreiffe *v.* Perth Harbour Trs., 1843; 5 D. 879; aff. 1846, 5 Bell's App. 333. Baxter *v.* N. B. Ry. Co., 1846; 8 D. 1212. Dundee Gas Co. *v.* Mags. of Dundee, 1847; 9 D. 1084. Dalgleish *v.* Stirling, etc., Ry. Co., 1847; 9 D. 505. E. P. and D. Ry. Co. *v.* Leven, 1848; 10 D. 1013; aff. 1 Macq. 284. Galloway *v.* Mayor of London, L. R. 1 H. L. 34; 35 L. J. Ch. 477.

(*f*) North British Ry. Co. *v.* Tod, 1846; 8 D. 726; rev. 5 Bell's App. 184.

(*g*) Edinburgh and Dalkeith Ry. Co. *v.* Wauchope, 1839; 1 D. 1151; aff. 1842, 1 Bell's App. 252.

(*h*) See below, § 978 *fin.* The enormous mass of case law upon this subject makes it impossible even to summarise the principles which have now been settled in regard to compulsory expropriation by public companies and corporations. The law may be found in such works as Deas on Railways, Hodges on Railways, Lloyd on Compensation, Ingram on Compensation, Godefroi and Shortt's Law of Railway Companies, or Mr. Rankine's Notes on the Lands Clauses Act in the Apx. to the Law of Landownership, pp. 812–865. See the Waterworks Clauses Acts, 10 and 11 Vict. c. 17; 26 and 27 Vict. c. 93; 33 and 34 Vict. c. 70; 36 and 37 Vict. c. 89.

961. Enforcement of Exclusive Right.—In order to enforce the right of exclusive possession, and protect property exposed to depredators, contrivances have been employed to detain, or hurt, or even to destroy the trespasser. The principles applicable to this matter seem to be, that to *detain* a trespasser is lawful, and such engines as have lately been contrived for that sole purpose seem to be unexceptionable. To repel by force a midnight robber who breaks into a house is lawful; and as the life and safety of the owner are in such cases put in peril in the attack and defence, safeguards and means of protection to prevent the necessity of such conflicts, and produce the same end, seem unexceptionable,—as a watch-dog, or even a spring-gun, or a man-trap. But those blind and indiscriminating means of defence, which are so often applied to the protection of gardens, and orchards, and enclosed grounds, are very questionable even where notice of the danger is given. Such engines are illegal, even with notice, for preventing a mere trespass on grounds unenclosed (*a*), although most frequently employed in this way for the preservation of game. By statute, these engines are now prohibited in England; but it was thought there was no occasion that the Act should extend to Scotland, as this evil was already provided for by the common law (*b*). The statute, however, for protection against persons going at night into enclosures armed for the purpose of taking or destroying game, does extend to this country (*c*); and to this has been added an Act against trespassers in the day-time.

'In ordinary cases of trespass, where there is no offence against these or any other statutes, the only way of enforcing exclusive right of possession and excluding intruders is a civil process of interdict (*d*); but this remedy will not be granted where no right is asserted and no appreciable injury is done, at least in regard to unenclosed ground open to the public (*e*). The use of force to eject a trespasser is unlawful (*f*). The Trespass (Scotland) Act, 1865, makes it an offence to lodge in premises, or light a fire, or encamp on land without the owner's permission (*g*).'

(*a*) Craw, Syme's Just. Ca. pp. 188, 202. Shaw's Just. R. 194; 2 Ill. 118. See Vere *v.* Lord Cawdor, 11 East, 568. Dean *v.* Clayton, 2 Marsh. 577. Elliott *v.* Wilkes, 3 Barn. & Ald. 304.

(*b*) 7 and 8 Geo. IV. c. 18. Repealed by 24 and 25 Vict. c. 95. The Act 24 and 25 Vict. c. 100, § 31, makes it a misdemeanour to set such engines, punishable with penal servitude or imprisonment; but the enactment does not extend to spring-guns or other engines set in a dwelling-house for protection thereof from sunset to sunrise. This appears to be the law of Scotland also, according to the text. See Hume, Crim. Law, i. 219. L. Adv. *v.* Kennedy, 1838; 2 Swin. 213.

(*c*) 9 Geo. IV. c. 69. 2 and 3 Will. IV. c. 68. 7 and 8 Vict. c. 29. 40 and 41 Vict. c. 28.

(*d*) Watson *v.* E. Errol, 1763; M. 4991. Hay's Trs. *v.* Young, 1877; 4 R. 398. Steuart *v.* Stephen, 1877; 4 R. 873.

(*e*) Winans *v.* Macrae, 1885; 12 R. 1051. Robertson *v.* Wright, 1885; 13 R. 174.

(*f*) E. Eglinton *v.* Campbell, 1770; M'Laur. 505. L. Adv. *v.* Kennedy, 1838; 2 Swin. 213.

(*g*) 28 and 29 Vict. c. 56.

II. ABSOLUTE USE OF LAND.

962. General Rule.—The landowner has (under the exceptions to be immediately stated) a right to do what he pleases with his property within its limits, and to derive from it all the uses and services of which it is capable.

963. Limitations.—This right is subject to limitations, by Neighbourhood, by the law of Nuisance, and by Servitude (*a*).

(*a*) See next chapter.

964. (1.) *By Neighbourhood.*—The principles on which this limitation is regulated are:—One is not, by the faulty or careless use of his property, to occasion any real or actual damage to the property of another: and the remedies are either preventive, by interdict; or reparative, by action of damages (*a*). And a neighbouring proprietor is not bound to wait till a threatened or impending mischief shall be done, but is entitled to protection where there is reasonable fear of injury. But mere inconvenience to a neighbour from a beneficial or blameless exercise of a proprietor's right within his own limits will not entitle him to damages, or to an interdict, anticipating evil, and restraining such proprietor in his operations (*b*). No one, however, is entitled, even within his own limits, to act wantonly, with the mere purpose of producing inconvenience and loss to his neighbour — *in æmulationem vicini.* This, however, is never to be presumed, but must be proved (*c*). Under the guidance and restraint of these principles, a proprietor may exhaust, convert, or destroy the substance of his ground, whether surface or internal materials (*d*).

(*a*) As to the application of these remedies, see *infra*, § 976, 977. Bank of Scotland *v.* Stewart, 1891; 18 R. 957. Jack *v.* Begg, 1875; 3 R. 35, 43, etc.

(*b*) See above, § 946; and below, § 976–7.

(*c*) See Rankine on Landownership, 319.

(*d*) 2 Ersk. 1. § 2 et seq., and tit. 9. § 1 et seq.

965. A proprietor may dig or build on any part of his ground, even to the very verge, though the consequence should be to stop all his neighbour's lights, but not to the danger of property or life (*a*). 'A proprietor's absolute use of his land is limited by neighbourhood, so far as he is obliged to afford to his neighbour's property such support as its natural situation in relation to his requires. So far at least as the natural soil is concerned, the reciprocal right of support exists as a common law right incident to the ownership of land both in England and Scotland; the rules of law in both countries being the same (*b*), whether the support required is lateral, as in the ordinary case of adjoining superficial estates, or vertical, when the mineral strata are separated from the estate in the surface (*c*). It has been solemnly decided in England that the right of support which exists "of common right" in regard to the soil, may be acquired for buildings by prescription after the analogy of the English law of "ancient lights" (*d*). It has not been held that the identity of the two systems of law extends so far; or rather, that the Scots law of prescription can be applied in the same way. On the contrary, there is authority for saying that with us the owner of land is entitled in the ordinary course of management to erect buildings on his land, and to have the natural and ordinary support for them from his neighbour's adjacent soil or mineral strata; but not to lay any extraordinary or unnatural weight upon his soil materially increasing the burden of his neighbour (*e*).'

(*a*) 2 Ersk. 1. § 2, and t. 9. § 10. Somerville *v.* Somerville, 1613; M. 12,769; 2 Ill. 118. See Wilson *v.* Richardson, 1688; M. 12,777. Dunlop *v.* Robertson, 1803; Hume, 515. Glassford *v.* Astley, 1808; *ib.* 506; M. *Property*, Apx. 7. Blackwood *v.* Bell, 1825; 4 S. 26. Murray *v.* Johnston, 1834; 13 S. 119. Callender *v.* Eddington, 1826; 4 Mur. 108; 2 Ill. 119. Douglas *v.* Monteith, 1826; *ib.* 130. Robertson *v.* Strang, 1825; 4 S. 6. See § 970. Thomson *v.* Gray, 1842; 5 D. 377. M'Intosh *v.* Scott & Co., 1859; 21 D. 363.

(*b*) Cal. Ry. Co. *v.* Sprot, 1854; 16 D. 559; revd. 1856, 2 Macq. 449. **Andrew** *v.* **Buchanan,** 1871; 9 Macph. 554; rev. 1873, 11 Macph. H. L. 13; L. R. 2 Sc. App. 286.

(*c*) *Infra*, § 970. Dunlop's Trs. *v.* Corbet, June 20, 1809; F. C. Cal. Ry. *v.* Sprot, *cit.* Id. *v.* L. Belhaven, 1856; 2 Macq. 56. Bonomi *v.* Backhouse, E. B. & E. 622; aff. in H. L., 34 L. J. Q. B. 181; 9 H. L. Ca. 503. **Rowbotham** *v.* **Wilson,** 8 H. L. Ca. 347; 30 L. J. Q. B. 49. Dalton *v.* Angus, 6 App. Ca. 740; 50 L. J. Q. B. 689. **White** *v.* **Dixon,** 1881; 9 R. 375; aff. 1883, 10 R. H. L. 45; 8 App. Ca. 833. Aitken's Trs. *v.* Rawyards Coll. Co., 1894; 22 R. 201. A feuar may agree to bear any risk arising from the proper working of the minerals. Andrew *v.* Buchanan, *cit.* See Rowbotham *v.* Wilson, *cit.* Bank of Scotland *v.* Stewart, 1891; 18 R. 957 (construction of alleged agreement in reservation of minerals—acquiescence). D. Buccleuch *v.* Wakefield, 39 L. J. Ch. 441; L. R. E. & I. App. 377. Hext *v.* Gill, 41 L. J. Ch. 293, 761; L. R. 7 Ch. 699. Smith *v.* Darby, 42 L. J. Q. B. 140; L. R. 7 Q. B. 716. Aspden *v.* Seddon, 44 L. J. Ch. 359; L. R. 10 Ch. App. 394. A distinct subsequent subsidence, though arising from the same excavation, is a new cause of action. Mitchell *v.* Darley Main Coll. Co., 14 Q. B. D. 121; aff. 11 App. Ca. 127. Bonomi *v.* Backhouse, *cit.* See above, § 546 *fin.* A clause in an agricultural lease providing for damage done to the surface by mining includes damage by subsidence. Govrs. of Stewart's Hosp. *v.* Waddell, 1890; 17 R. 1077. As to gaspipes and the company's right to support, see Mid and E. Calder Gaslight Co. *v.* Oakbank Oil Co., 1891; 18 R. 788, and cases there cited. As to the relative liability of lessor and lessee to a person injured, see cases at end of § 2031.

(*d*) Dalton *v.* Angus, *cit.*

(*e*) Hamilton *v.* Turner, 1867; 5 Macph. 1086. Bain *v.* D. Hamilton, 1867; 6 Macph. 1. Cf. Neill's Trs. *v.* Dixon, 1880; 7 R. 741. The difficulties of the English judges in Dalton *v.* Angus, *cit.*, and the absence of Mr. Rankine's usual clearness of exposition (Landownership, p. 409 sqq.), show the uncertainty of the law on this point. See M'Intosh *v.* Scott, *cit.* (*a*); and Percival *v.* Hughes, 9 Q. B. D. 441; 8 App. Ca. 443, as to newly built houses. Campbell's Trs. *v.* Henderson, 1884, 11 R. 520, only decides that if one by digging *in suo* without specific fault causes the fall of his neighbour's wall, which is itself insufficient and unsuitable for its place and purpose, he is not answerable.

966. A proprietor may establish, on the very verge of his ground, manufactories; erect chimneys, furnaces, steam-engines, or lime-kilns; open quarries of stone or mines of coal; however disagreeable or inconvenient in direct or consequential effect, provided he avoid nuisance, and act not in mere spite or malice —*in æmulationem vicini* (*a*).

The restraint which is grounded on the principle of *æmulatio vicini* may affect acts positive or negative (*b*). And so, to entitle one to redress against any operation of a proprietor on this ground, a case must be made out of mere malice, or at least useless caprice or annoyance (*c*). But it will not on this ground be lawful to interfere with the site of a useful erection, on merely showing that it might have been placed elsewhere with equal convenience to the owner, and less offence to his neighbour (*d*). 'On the other hand,' where one objects to the proceeding with any innocuous operation on a subject of common interest, he may be opposed by showing that his opposition is merely *in æmulationem vicini* (*e*).

(*a*) Dewar *v.* Fraser, 1767; M. 12,803; Hailes, 177; 2 Ill. 119. Ralston *v.* Pettigrew, 1768; M. 12,808; Hailes, 234. See Ross *v.* Baird, 1829; 7 S. 361; and below, § 972.

(*b*) See Rankine, L. O. 320.

(*c*) But see the qualification by Lord Watson in Mayor of Bradford *v.* Pickles, 1895; A. C. 587; and above, § 545 (3).

(*d*) Dewar, *supra* (*a*).

(*e*) Ritchie *v.* Purdie, 1833; 11 S. 771. See Graham *v.* Greig, 1838, 1 D. 171, where Lord Jeffrey says that the plea of emulation can apply only "to active uses on the part of the proprietor to whom it is objected, and has nothing to do with his resistance of usurped uses by one who is not a proprietor. The law allows no inquiry into the motives of such resistance. It is enough that the party is sole owner, and does not choose to submit or consent."

967. A proprietor cannot project his walls or roof beyond the boundary line, or so construct his roof as to throw the eavesdrop on his neighbour's ground (*a*).

(*a*) 2 Ersk. 9. § 9. See above, § 942.

968. The inferior ground must receive the natural drainage of the upper ground; but is not bound to submit to what is produced by artificial changes on the condition of the water. So the inferior must receive the superfluous water, even under the operations of draining, in all the variations of agricultural improvement, 'subject to equitable regulation by the Court, if the superior owner should unduly press his right, to the injury of the lower' (*a*).

This rule extends to levels for draining coal (*b*); 'and the proprietor of lower workings is bound to receive the water which naturally, and in the ordinary course of mining operations, flows to him from the workings of his neighbour to the rise. Hence, as a mineral proprietor is entitled to work out the whole of his minerals without reference to his neighbour's interests (*c*), the lower proprietor must protect himself against the invasion of water from above by leaving a barrier of his own minerals upon the march (*d*). The higher proprietor is not liable for injury by mere gravitation and percolation, even when his proper and ordinary workings have caused subsidence of the surface, and consequent sits and dislocation of drains (*e*). But the superior heritor or lessee is not entitled to resort to unusual means, as by pumping, for getting rid of the water in his workings, and throwing it on the lower (*f*).'

It applies also to natural streams and rivers as the legitimate channels for the drainage consequent on habitation, as a natural use of the ground (*g*). But such drainage will not be allowed into a mill-course, which is artificial and private property (*h*). This absolute right must, however, yield to public necessity; but whether this be at the disposal of the common law has not been cleared (*i*). An *opus manufactum* for gain will not be permitted, to the effect of throwing an unnatural quantity of water on the inferior tenement (*k*). And the draining of a lake seems a questionable operation, 'in this respect, that the Court will probably, if called upon, restrain or regulate the operations,' so far as hurtful to the inferior ground (*l*).

(*a*) 2 Ersk. 9. § 2. Campbell *v.* Bryson, 1864; 3 Macph. 254. As to outfalls, see 10 and 11 Vict. c. 113 (Drainage of Lands Act). Rankine on Landownership, 426.

(*b*) Aitken *v.* Dewar, 1734; Elch. *Property*, 3; 2 Ill. 119.

(*c*) **Irving** *v.* **Leadhills Co.**, 1856; 18 D. 833; aff. 1859, 21 D. H. L. 10; 34 L. T. 34. Smith *v.* Kenrick, 7 C. B. 515; 18 L. J. C. P. 172. See § 965 as to support.

(*d*) Durham *v.* Hood. 1871; 9 Macph. 474. Baird *v.* Monkland Iron Co., 1862; 24 D. 1418.

(*e*) Wilsons *v.* Waddell, 1876; 3 R. 288; aff. 4 R. H. L. 29; 2 App. Ca. 95. Smith *v.* Fletcher (Smith *v.* Musgrave), 43 L. J. Ex. 70; 47 *ib.* 4; L. R. 9 Ex. 64; 2 App. Ca. 781.

(*f*) Durham *v.* Hood, 1871; 9 Macph. 474. See below, note (*k*), and § 1109. Baird *v.* Williamson, 15 C. B. N. S. 376; 33 L. J. C. P. 101. Lomax *v.* Stott, 39 L. J. Ch. 834. Bankier Distillery Co. *v.* Young & Co., 1892; 19 R. 1083; aff. 1893, A. C. 691; 20 R. H. L. 76. Cf. Fletcher *v.* Rylands, § 969.

(*g*) Downie *v.* E. of Moray, 1825; 4 S. 167; 2 Ill. 120. Correct this by Montgomerie & Fleming *v.* Buchanan's Trs., 1853; 15 D. 853. Campbell *v.* Bryson, *cit.*; and below, § 1106.

(*h*) Eyre *v.* E. of Moray, 1827; 5 S. 912.

(*i*) Town of Edinburgh *v.* Cathcart, 1736; Elch. *Property*, 3.

(*k*) Miller *v.* Stein, 1792; Bell's Ca. 334. Russel *v.* Haig, 1791; M. 12,823; Bell's Ca. 344; 3 Pat. 403. Hope *v.* Wauchope, 1779; M. 14,538; 2 Pat. 286, 338, 520. See below, § 1108, 1102, 1106, 971.

(*l*) Mayor of Berwick *v.* Haining, 1661; 2 B. Sup. 292; M. 12,772 (Mackenzie's Works, vol. i. p. 24. Pleadings). See § 651, 1110. Campbell *v.* Bryson, 1864; 3 Macph. 254. Montgomerie & Fleming *v.* Buchanan's Trs., 1853; 15 D. 853.

969. The inferior heritor is not entitled to cause the water to be thrown back on the land of the superior heritor, either by damming up a stream, or by impeding the natural drainage. But the superior heritor may clear his land of superfluous water, without regard to consequential effects on the inferior tenement (*a*). 'And on the same principle, neither a mine-owner nor any other is responsible for injury to the well or stream of another (in the absence of some specific right to such stream or well), by digging or other operation within his own ground, whereby its hidden and undefined sources of supply are diverted (*b*). But one may not foul his well so as by hidden percolation to pollute his neighbour's (*c*).'

(*a*) See Hope, *supra*, § 968 (*k*). See above, § 968; below, § 1108.

(*b*) Blair *v.* Hunter, Finlay, & Co., 1870; 9 Macph. 204. Acton *v.* Blundell, 12 M. & W. 324; 13 L. J. Ex. 289. **Chasemore** *v.* **Richards**, 7 H. L. C. 349; 29 L. J. Ex. 81. Mayor of Bradford *v.* Pickles, 1895; A. C. 587. See **Fletcher** *v.* **Rylands**, 35 L. J. Ex. 154; 37 *ib.* 161; L. R. 1 Ex. 265; 3 H. L. 330; 1 Smith's L. C. 789; and below, § 1109.

(*c*) Ballard *v.* Tomlinson, 29 Ch. D. 115. See Snow *v.* Whitehead, 27 Ch. D. 588.

970. Although a proprietor may, to the very verge of his property, dig his ground and remove the earth, he is not entitled to do any direct injury to his neighbour; or to take away the support of his property; or to occasion reasonable apprehensions of danger; or within burgh to infringe the rules of the Dean of Guild, who has jurisdiction over buildings (*a*). 'When a proprietor, in exercising his legal right within his own property, causes damage to another, he is responsible only if he carries on his operations negligently, and fails to use all proper precautions; *e.g.* in muir-burning, to prevent the fire from extending beyond his boundary (*b*); or, in building or altering buildings on the verge of his property, to avoid structural injury to his neighbour's house (*c*), or unnecessary injury by dust, steam, or otherwise, to his trade or goods (*d*). In such cases, as well as in damage from water in worn or defective pipes which overflows from an upper floor or adjacent property (*e*), the liability of the proprietor clearly rests upon negligence, which has to be proved. In the class of cases which falls under what English lawyers call the principle of **Fletcher** *v.* **Rylands** (*f*), negligence is still the ground of liability. The only difference is that in such cases the proprietor is doing something or keeping something upon his property which is in its nature dangerous and not necessary (or usual?) in the ordinary management of the particular kind of property, and he is therefore bound to observe a higher degree of diligence to prevent injury to his neighbour. Hence in such cases the mere occurrence of damage (as by the overflow of an artificial reservoir (*g*), the escape of a wild animal (*h*), or the ignition of a heap of combustible materials (*i*)), is proof of negligence, and makes him *primâ facie* answerable. He can excuse himself by showing that the occurrence was the consequence of *vis major* or the act of God (*k*), or, it would seem, of the wrongful act of a third party; but not on the ground that a road or footway within his bounds has been placed under the jurisdiction of a police board, unless it has been entirely taken over by that board (*l*).'

(*a*) 2 Ersk. 1. § 2. Ralston *v.* Pettigrew, 1768; M. 12,808; Hailes, 234; 2 Ill. 119 (brick kiln injuring shrubs). Ferguson *v.* Marjoribanks, Nov. 12, 1816; F. C.; 2 Ill. 120. Pirnie *v.* M'Ritchie, June 5, 1819; F. C. Murray *v.* Gullan, 1825; 3 S. 639. Robertson *v.* Strang, 1825; 4 S. 6; 2 Ill. 118. Gray *v.* Greig, 1825; 4 S. 104. Dunlop, Glassford, and Murray, *supra*, § 965 (*a*). *Supra*, § 941, and cases in § 553.

(*b*) Mackintosh *v.* Mackintosh, 1864; 2 Macph. 1357.

(*c*) M'Intosh *v.* Scott, 1859; 21 D. 363. Laurent *v.* L. Adv., *infra.*

(*d*) Cameron *v.* Fraser, 1881; 9 R. 26. Laurent *v.* L. Adv., 1869; 7 Macph. 607.

(*e*) **Weston** *v.* **Tailors of Potterrow**, 1839; 1 D. 1218. **Campbell** *v.* **Kennedy**, 1864; 3 Macph. 121. Moffat & Co. *v.* Park, 1877; 5 R. 13. *Supra*, § 553.

(*f*) 35 L. J. Ex. 154; 37 *ib.* 161; L. R. 1 Ex. 265; 3 H. L. 330, and cases cited below, note (*k*), and § 1108; 1 Smith's L. C. 789.

(*g*) **Kerr** *v.* **E. Orkney**, 1857; 20 D. 298, 303; and cases in § 1108, *infra.*

(*h*) See above, § 553 (3). Cowan *v.* Dalziel, and Burton *v.* Moorhead, *ibi citt.*

(*i*) Chalmers *v.* Dickson, 1876; 3 R. 461.

(*k*) See above, § 237, note (*a*). Tennant *v.* E. Glasgow, Pirie *v.* Mags. of Aberdeen, cited in § 1108, *infra.* Potter *v.* Hamilton and Strathaven Ry. Co., 1864; 3 Macph. 83.

(*l*) Baillie *v.* Shearer's Factor, 1894; 21 R. 498.

971. One may erect a bulwark for the defence of his land against the encroachments of a river, to the effect of preserving the ground such as nature placed it. He may fortify, but not raise the bank. And it has been settled by the House of Lords, that he may not "erect any bulwark or other *opus manufactum* upon the banks of the river, which may have the effect of diverting the stream of the river in time of flood from its accustomed course, and throwing the same upon the lands of a neighbouring proprietor" (*a*).

(*a*) **Menzies** *v.* **E. Breadalbane**, 1828; 3 W. & S. 235; 2 Ill. 161. See below, § 1102, 1108. Burgess *v.* Brown, 1790; Hume, 504. See below, § 1102. Murdoch *v.* Wallace, 1881; 8 R. 855.

972. The inconveniences or restraints imposed by neighbourhood on the use and enjoyment of property,—the interruption of light, of prospect, or of air, the want of a proper access to property, the inconvenience of irregular marches,—all these must be endured, unless either the person who suffers shall buy the privilege; or the dominant proprietor shall consent or acquiesce; or the Legislature, for purposes of public policy, shall interfere, as in the laws regulating marches (*a*).

(*a*) *Supra*, § 958.

973. (2.) *Limitation by the Law of Nuisance.*—The landowner's right to the absolute use of his property is qualified by the law of nuisance, which in some degree may be considered as part of the law of neighbourhood (*a*).

'Since Professor Bell wrote, various statutes have been passed to provide for the removal or suppression of nuisances injurious to public health. The Nuisance Removal Acts, 11 and 12 Vict. c. 123, and 12 and 13 Vict. c. 111, were superseded by 19 and 20 Vict. c. 103 (1856); which in its turn was repealed by the Public Health (Scotland) Act, 1867 (*b*). This Act was repealed in 1897 by a new Public Health (Scotland) Act, which defines (§ 16) statutory nuisances, and gives the local authorities powers of inspection, and for removal of nuisances; enacts regulations for watercourses, factories, sewers, etc., and subjects certain trades to regulation by the local authority and Local Government Board, which is the central sanitary authority for Scotland (c). This, and the like enactments, do not affect the rights of neighbouring proprietors at common law (d).'

(a) Between public and private nuisance there is no useful distinction in the law of Scotland. In England, public nuisance is punishable, and the nuisance removable by indictment; private nuisance is remedied by civil action at the suit of an individual. See for some important information on this subject, Report of the French Institute, with Remarks, 2 Edin. Med. and Surg. Journal, p. 290.

(b) 30 and 31 Vict. c. 101; amended by various statutes. See also the Factory and Workshop Acts, 41 Vict. c. 16, § 3, 4, 33–37; 54 and 55 Vict. c. 75, etc. The Smoke Acts, 20 and 21 Vict. c. 73; 28 and 29 Vict. c. 102. Dumfries Local Authority *v.* Murphy, 1884; 11 R. 694. The Alkali Act, 44 and 45 Vict. c. 37, amended by 48 and 49 Vict. c. 61, § 5, and 55 and 56 Vict. c. 30. The Burgh Police Act, 1892, 55 and 56 Vict. c. 55. The Explosives Act, 38 and 39 Vict. c. 17.

(c) 60 and 61 Vict. c. 38. See also the Local Government (Scotland) Act, 1889, 52 and 53 Vict. c. 50.

(d) Pentland *v.* Henderson, 1855; 17 D. 542.

974. *Definition.*—The description of nuisance in Scotland is the same whether the public or the individual be regarded. Whatever obstructs the public means of commerce and intercourse, whether in highways or navigable rivers; whatever is noxious or unsafe, or renders life uncomfortable to the public generally, or to the neighbourhood (a); whatever is intolerably offensive to individuals in their dwelling-houses, or inconsistent with the comfort (b) of life, whether by stench (as the boiling of whale blubber (c)), by noise (as a smithy in an upper floor (d)), or by indecency (as a brothel next door), is a nuisance (e).

Conventional Nuisance.—But what is not at common law a nuisance, may conventionally be declared so, in respect to some particular piece of ground or area; and so, in feuing ground, it is frequently stipulated that the vassal shall not be allowed to establish a brewery, tanwork, soapwork, distillery, etc. The chief difficulty in such cases arises where the enumeration is qualified by the words, "whereby a nuisance can be created." The rule seems to be, that the operations or works prohibited are not to be put to the test of what strictly is a nuisance at common law, but to be measured by the fair meaning of the parties as amounting to what is offensive in the circumstances and situation, 'or affecting the value or amenity of houses or property which the condition is intended to protect, or the comfort of the persons living in them' (f). It has been held that even the indirect effects (if necessary or probable) consequent on any particular use or employment of ground may be a nuisance; as in England in the case of a person keeping premises for pigeon-shooting, causing idle persons to assemble on the highway with fire-arms, noise, and alarm (g).

(a) 1698, c. 8. Leith *v.* Mags. of Aberdeen, 1748; Elch. *Pub. Pol.* 9; 2 Ill. 121 (soapwork). Dewar *v.* Fraser, 1767; M. 12,803; Hailes, 177; 2 Ill. 119 (limekiln). Ralston *v.* Pettigrew, 1768; M. 12,808; Hailes, 234 (brick-kiln). Palmer *v.* M'Millan, 1794; M. 13,188; Bell's Ca. 11. Jameson *v.* Hillcoats, 1800; M. *Property*, Apx. 4. Scott *v.* Cox, July 5, 1810; F. C. Farquhar *v.* Watson, Jan. 19, 1813; F. C. Vary *v.* Thomson, 1805; M. *Pub. Pol.* Apx. 4. Stewart *v.* Thomson, 1807; M. *Pub. Pol.* Apx. 5. Kelt *v.* Lindsay, July 8, 1814; F. C. Eyre *v.* E. of Moray, 1827; 5 S. 912. Downie *v.* E. of Moray, 1825; 4 S. 109. Harrold *v.* Watney, 1898; 2 Q. B. 20 (defective fence along highway). Ogston *v.* Aberdeen Tram. Co., 1895; 23 R. 340; rev. 1896, A. C. 111; 24 R. H. L. 8 (putting salt on snow in street). Att.-Gen. *v.* Tod-Heatley, 1897; 1 Ch. 560.

(b) Although not injurious to health, Farquhar *v.* Watson, *cit.* Walter *v.* Selfe, 4 De G. & Sm. 315. Hislop *v.* Fleming, *infra* (e).

(c) Dowie, *infra*, § 976. Trotter, *ib.* Or chemical works, Jameson *v.* Hillcoats, *cit.* Anderson *v.* Burnett, 1849; 12 D. 131. Fraser's Trs. *v.* Cran, 1877; 4 R. 794; 5 R. 290; 1879, 6 R. 451.

(d) Kinloch (e). Johnston *v.* Constable, 1841; 3 D. 1263. Frame *v.* Cameron, 1864; 3 Macph. 290.

(e) Clark *v.* Gordon, 1760; M. 13,172; 2 Ill. 122. Kinloch *v.* Robertson, 1756; M. 13,163. Fleming *v.* Ure, 1750; M. 13,159. Robertson *v.* Campbell, 1802; M. *Pub. Pol.* Apx. 3. In Paterson *v.* Beattie, 1845, 7 D. 561, it was held that a monument erected in a churchyard to the memory of persons convicted of sedition was not a nuisance. See as to a slaughter-house, Palmer, *cit.*, Kelt, *cit.*, Porteous, *cit.* (f). Swinton *v.* Peddie, *infra*, § 976. Pentland *v.* Henderson, 1857; 17 D. 542; a hospital for infectious diseases. Mutter *v.* Fyfe, 1848; 11 D. 211, 303. Metrop. Asylum District *v.* Hill, 6 App. Ca. 193; 50 L. J. Q. B. 353. As to byres and stables within burghs, Manson *v.* Forrest, 1887; 14 R. 802. Robertson *v.* Thomas, *ib.* 822. As to smoke, Cooper & Wood *v.* N. B. Ry. Co., 1863; 1 Macph. 499; 2 *ib.* 116; and above, § 973 (b). As to calcining ironstone and charring coals and the like, Heriott *v.* Faulds, 1804; M. 15,255. M'Callum *v.* Forth Iron Co., 1861; 23 D. 729. Galbraith's Tr. *v.* Eglinton Iron Co., 1868; 7 Macph. 167. **Hislop *v.* Fleming** (Kelvinside Estate Co.), 1882; 10 R. 426; aff. 1886, 13 R. H. L. 43; 11 App. Ca. 686. **Inglis *v.* Shotts Iron Co.**, 1881; 8 R. 1006; aff. 1882, 9 R. H. L. 78; 7 App. Ca. 518.

(f) Newington Feuars *v.* Lauder, June 16, 1815; F. C. Porteous *v.* Grieve, 1839; 1 D. 561. **E. Zetland *v.* Hislop,** 1881; 8 R. 675; rev. 1882, 9 R. H. L. 40; 7 App. Ca. 427 (where earlier cases are referred to). And as to the construction of such stipulations, see Anderson *v.* Aberdeen Agric. Hall Co., 1879; 6 R. 901. Mutter *v.* Fyfe, *cit.* (e). Ewing *v.* Hastie, 1879; 5 R. 439 ("to be used only as dwelling-houses"—cf. with regard to use as school under such clause, Colville *v.* Carrick, 1883; 10 R. 1241. German *v.* Chapman, 47 L. J. Ch. 250; 7 Ch. D. 271). On such conditions see also § 868, as to building restrictions in feu-contracts, the legal rules applicable to which are precisely similar. Frame *v.* Cameron, 1864; 3 Macph. 290. There is a general presumption in favour of freedom in the use of property, so that in the ordinary run of such cases, the onus of showing that a particular use or operation is a nuisance lies on the pursuer. Frame, *cit.*; and cf. E. Zetland *v.* Hislop, *cit.*

(*g*) The King *v.* Moore, 3 B. & Ad. 184; 2 Ill. 122; 1 L. J. M. C. 30. Dowie, § 976 (*a*). Walker *v.* Brewster, 37 L. J. Ch. 33; L. R. 5 Eq. 25. See as to schools, Harrison *v.* Good, 40 L. J. Ch. 294; L. R. 11 Eq. 338, and cases *supra* (*f*). And as to the principle in the text as affecting landlords and lessors, Henderson *v.* Stewart, 1818; Hume, 522. Dunn *v.* Hamilton, 1837; 15 S. 853; aff. 3 S. & M'L. 356. Pirie *v.* Mags. of Aberdeen, 1871; 9 Macph. 412. Anderson *v.* Aberdeeen Agric. Hall Co., 1879; 6 R. 901. As to annoyance caused by the ordinary use of a highway, see Anderson, *cit.* Hammersmith Ry. Co. *v.* Brand, L. R. 4 H. L. 171, 192, 198. Truman *v.* L. B. and S. C. Ry. Co., 25 Ch. D. 423.

975. In England, dovecots are a nuisance. In Scotland, the right to erect 'or rebuild' them, 'though not the right to retain them when lawfully erected,' is, on the same principle, restrained to persons having land yielding ten chalders of victual yearly (*a*).

(*a*) 1617, c. 19. Brodie *v.* Gordon, 1752; M. 3602; Apx. *Dovecot.* Kinloch *v.* Wilson, 1731; M. 3601. Murray *v.* Turnbull, 1797; M. 7628. Easton *v.* Longlands, 1832; 10 S. 542; 5 D. & A. 285.

976. Under the above general description, questions may arise which lead to distinctions. Thus there are some operations which are destructive of health, and unquestionably nuisances; while there are others innoxious to health, but intolerable in a populous neighbourhood, or dangerous in the neighbourhood of a public seminary; as to which, the verdict of a jury is the proper test by which to settle the question (*a*).

It has been questioned whether, by removal of what is offensive to a greater distance from human habitation, it may not be rendered legal (*b*). The intended establishment may be such as to admit of doubt whether the apprehensions of those who complain are reasonable (*c*), and whether proposed means of curing the offence may not render it unobjectionable (*d*). The proper course is to interdict what is at the time unquestionably a nuisance, leaving the party to proceed with experiments to prove that it is now abated (*e*). 'But it is not unusual, as an indulgence, not as a right, to allow the party complained of, while the operations causing the nuisance are going on, and without at once granting interdict, to make experiments at the sight or with the advice of a man of skill nominated by the Court, or to introduce improvements with the view of carrying on the works without nuisance (*f*).'

(*a*) Dowie *v.* Oliphant, Dec. 11, 1813; F. C. Swinton *v.* Peddie, 1837; 15 S. 775; H. L. 1839; M'L. & R. 1018; 2 Ill. 122. See below, § 978.

(*b*) Same case as stated in Trotter *v.* Farnie, 1830; 9 S. 144.

(*c*) See Cowper Essex *v.* Acton Local Board, 1889; 14 App. Ca. 153, 160 (apprehensions must be reasonable).

(*d*) Trotter, *supra* (*b*), and 10 S. 423; 5 W. & S. 649.

(*e*) See Fraser's Trs. *v.* Cran, *supra*, § 974 (*c*). M'Neill *v.* Scott, 1866; 4 Macph. 608.

(*f*) Johnston *v.* Constable, 1841; 3 D. 1263. Swinton and Fraser's Trs., *citt.* Cases below in § 977. D. of Buccleuch *v.* Cowan, 1873; 11 Macph. 675 (and previous reports there cited as to agreement after verdict for experiments and remit). Cal. Ry. Co. *v.* Baird, 1876; 3 R. 839. Att.-Gen. *v.* Colney Hatch Asylum, L. R. 4 Ch. 146; 38 L. J. Ch. 265.

977. One is not bound to submit to the erection of what is avowedly a nuisance, or manifestly threatens to be so; but may by interdict stop the operations. Nor will it be a sufficient answer, that it is intended to apply remedies in order to remove what is offensive, unless it can be demonstrated that the proposed remedies will be successful (*a*). But interdict will not be granted in doubtful cases; or against what is admitted not yet to be a nuisance, but only such as may become a nuisance by abuse (*b*); 'or when abatement has been effected under a remit from the Court after verdict against the defender (*c*).

(*a*) Trotter, *supra*, § 976 (*b*).

(*b*) Scott *v.* Leith Police Comrs., 1832; 8 S. 845; and 1835, 13 S. 646. Arnott *v.* Brown, 1847; 9 D. 497; 10 D. 95; aff. 1852, 24 Jur. 421; 1 Stu. 694; 1 Macq. 229. Lady Willoughby D'Eresby's Trs. *v.* Strathearn Hydr. Estab. Co., 1873; 1 R. 35. Manson *v.* Forrest, 1887; 14 R. 802.

(*c*) Home *v.* Duns Police Comrs., 1882; 9 R. 924.

978. The doctrine of nuisance must, 'it was said by Professor Bell,' be taken under two qualifications:—

(1) 'It is said' that one is not to complain of a nuisance, if he *come to the nuisance* (*a*). This proceeds on the ground of personal exception; 'but it can hardly be said to be established by the cases cited, or any later cases in which the plea has been raised (*b*). In England it seems to be settled that one who comes to a nuisance, or any other neighbour, can be prevented from challenging it only by the acquisition of a prescriptive right by the offending party (*c*); and even that, as no such prescriptive right can be

acquired except against one who is entitled to challenge the user, one may acquire a right to object to operations of his neighbour by changing the use of his own property so as to make those operations nuisances which were previously innoxious, *e.g.* by building in his garden beside an engine which his neighbour has had for more than the prescriptive period (*d*). It would seem that there is no sufficient authority in our law for this plea, in any correct or intelligible sense, except where it rests either upon acquiescence or prescription (*e*).'

And (2) that a place in which already offensive works exist may be rendered still more offensive, without entitling the complainers to an interdict; provided the increase be not carried so far as to render the *accumulated nuisance* intolerable or dangerous (*f*). 'But this "qualification" (if it be not too strongly stated to be at all admissible) is to be carefully guarded. It does not mean that a place may be *appropriated* to manufactures and works of an offensive nature so as to exclude all complaint of nuisance; that a place may be a proper and convenient place for carrying on a disagreeable and offensive work, or one in which such a work may be a reasonable use of his property by the person complained of (*g*). It should not be pressed further than this, that, apart from rights acquired by acquiescence and prescription, the question what is a nuisance must receive a different answer according to the circumstances of different localities; for one does not expect to find the same quality of air, the same freedom from noise, smoke, filth, and other like annoyances and discomforts in a town or city as in the country, or even in one part of a town or one suburb, as in another (*h*). And while the right to object to an existing nuisance may be excluded by acquiescence (*i*) or by prescription (*k*), the extent to which it is so excluded is limited by the actual user or possession, and those injured are entitled to challenge and interdict any material increase of the pollution or annoyance (*l*). It is no answer to the complaint that others besides the defender are polluting a river or the air (*m*). And what might not be held a nuisance in a town or populous neighbourhood by reason of its causing a certain amount of discomfort, will yet be actionable if it cause a sensible injury to the value of property (*n*).

'In regard to injuries to property by companies or public bodies under statutory powers for the construction of works or buildings, it is settled that no action lies for using such works or buildings in the way which the Legislature has authorised, although such use would be a nuisance at common law, unless it be done negligently; and it is negligence if the company fail to make such reasonable exercise of all statutory or common law powers which they possess as may prevent, so far as possible, damage to others (*o*). Statutory authority to do a certain thing does not sanction the commission of a nuisance to one's neighbours, unless what is authorised cannot be done without causing a nuisance; but in the absence of negligence, what amounts to a nuisance will be justified not only if the terms of the statute are imperative, but even when they are merely permissive (*p*). The compensation given to adjoining owners for injuriously affecting their property is due only for injury done by reason of the execution of the works, not by the statutory use of them when executed (*q*).'

(*a*) Colvil *v.* Middleton, May 27, 1817; F. C.; 2 Ill. 122. Duncan *v.* E. Moray, June 9, 1809; F. C.; 2 Ill. 123. Lawrence *v.* Obee, 3 Camp. 514.

(*b*) Ewen *v.* Turnbull's Trs., 1857; 19 D. 573. Cooper & Wood *v.* N. B. Ry. Co., 1863; 1 Macph. 499. **Hislop *v.* Fleming (Kelvinside Estate Co.)**, 1882; 10 R. 426; aff. 1886, 13 R. H. L. 43; 11 App. Ca. 686.

(*c*) Elliotson *v.* Feetham, 2 Bing. N. C. 134. Bliss *v.* Hall, 5 Sc. 504. Hole *v.* Barlow, 4 C. B. N. S. 336; 27 L. J. C. P. 208 (*per* Byles, J.). Tipping *v.* St. Helens Smelting Co., L. R. 1 Ch. App. 66, see below (*h*). See 1 Smith's L. C. 268.

(*d*) Sturges *v.* Bridgman, 11 Ch. D. 852; 48 L. J. Ch. 785.

(*e*) See above, § 27A. Hislop, *cit.* Rankine on Landownership, 325.

(*f*) Glasgow Water Co. *v.* Aird, Dec. 20, 1814; F. C.; 2 Ill. 123. Balleny *v.* Comb, Feb. 3, 1813; F. C. Charity *v.* Riddel, 1808; M. Apx. *Pub. Pol.* 6. Dowie, § 976 (*a*). Colvil, *supra* (*a*).

(*g*) Cases in note (*f*). Trotter *v.* Farnie, *supra*, § 976 (*b*), (*d*). Cavey *v.* Leadbitter, 13 C. B. N. S. 470; 32 L. J. C. P. 104. Bamford *v.* Turnley, 3 B. & S. 62; 31 L. J. Q. B. 286.

(*h*) See above, § 976; and cases in note (*g*). **St. Helens Smelting Co. *v.* Tipping**, 11 H. L. Ca. 642; 35 L. J. Q. B. 66. Hislop *v.* Fleming (Kelvinside Estate Co.), *supra* (*b*).

(*i*) *Supra*, § 946.

(*k*) Duncan *v.* E. Moray, *supra* (*a*). D. of Buccleuch *v* Cowan, 1866; 5 Macph. 214, 227, 234.

(*l*) Balleny, *cit.* (*f*). Russel *v.* Haig, 1790–92; M. 12,823; Bell's 8vo Ca. 338; 3 Pat. 403. Ewen *v.* Turnbull's Trs., 1857; 19 D. 513. D. of Buccleuch *v.* Cowan, *cit.*

(*m*) D. of Buccleuch *v.* Cowan, *cit.* Ewen, *cit.* Crossley *v.* Lightowler, L. R. 3 Eq. 279; 2 Ch. 478; 36 L. J. Ch. 584. St. Helens Smelting Co., *cit.* Mackay *v.* Greenhill, 1858; 20 D. 1251.

(*n*) St. Helens Smelting Co., *cit.* (*h*). Dewar *v.* Fraser, and Ralston *v.* Pettigrew, etc., *citt.*, § 974 (*a*). See and compare Salvin *v.* Brancepeth Coll. Co., 44 L. J. Ch. 149; L. R. 9 Ch. 705, and Inglis *v.* Shotts Iron Co., 1881; 8 R. 1006; aff. 1882, 9 R. H. L. 78; 7 App. Ca. 518; also Bamford and Crossley, *citt.* (*g*), (*m*).

(*o*) Geddis *v.* Proprs. of Bann Reservoir, 3 App. Ca. 430.

(*p*) Metrop. District Asylum *v.* Hill, 6 App. Ca. 193; 50 L. J. Q. B. 353. L. B. & S. C. Ry. Co. *v.* Truman, 11 App. Ca. 45.

(*q*) **Hammersmith Ry. Co. *v.* Brand,** L. R. 4 H. L. 171; 38 L. J. Q. B. 265. Glasg. Union Ry. Co. *v.* Hunter, 1869; 7 Macph. 408; rev. 1870, 8 Macph. H. L. 156. Cal. Ry. Co. *v.* Walker's Trs., 1881; 8 R. 401; aff. 1882, 9 R. H. L. 19; 7 App. Ca. 259. Att.-Gen. *v.* Metr. Ry. Co., 1894; 1 Q. B. 384.

CHAPTER XIII

OF SERVITUDES

979. Description of Servitude. — Servitude (*a*) is a burden on land or houses, imposed by agreement—express or implied—in favour of the owners of other tenements; whereby the owner of the burdened or "servient" tenement, and his heirs and singular successors in the subject, must submit to certain uses to be exercised by the owner of the other or "dominant" tenement; or must suffer restraint in his own use and occupation of the property. Presupposing those extensions or restraints of the exclusive or absolute right of use which naturally proceed from the situation of conterminous properties, a servitude is a further limitation of that right in favour of the owner of another subject.

Servitudes may be viewed either as real rights and privileges to the one proprietor, or as real burdens on the ground of the other; according as they are taken in relation to the subject benefited, or to that which is burdened. Servitude differs from property; it is an accident of property, "non pars substantiæ sive fundi, sed accidens."

The law does not recognise as servitudes affecting singular successors many burdens or privileges or uses of property which may be made the subject of personal contract (*b*). Servitudes properly constituted are effectual against singular successors in the servient tenement, and available to singular successors in the dominant, though not followed by infeftment; and it has therefore been held essential that this burden should be limited to such uses or restraints as are well established and defined, leaving others as mere personal agreements (*c*). What shall be deemed a servitude of a regular and definite kind is a secondary question, as to which the only description that can be given generally seems to be, that it shall be such a use or restraint as by law or custom is known to be likely and incident to the property in question, and to which the attention of a prudent purchaser will, in the circumstances, naturally be called (*d*).

(*a*) See 2 Stair, 7, and 4, 45. § 17. More on Stair, ccxx. Brodie's Stair, p. 332. 2 Ersk. 9.

(*b*) Nicholson *v.* Melvill, 1708; M. 14,516; 2 Ill. 123. See below, § 1000. Patrick *v.* Napier, 1867; 5 Macph. 683. Scott *v.* Howard, 1880; 7 R. 997; aff. 1881, 8 R.H.L. 59; 6 App. Ca. 295.

(c) Cochran v. Fairholm, 1759; M. 14,518. Cleghorn v. Dempster, 1805; M. 16,141; rem. 1813, 2 Dow, 40. Town of Falkland v. Carmichael, 1708; M. 10,916. Jaffray v. D. Roxburghe, 1775; M. 14,517, 2340; 1 Pat. 632. Sinclair v. Town of Dysart, 1779; M. 14,519; aff. 2 Pat. 554. Dyce v. Hay, 1849; 11 D. 1266; aff. 1852, 1 Macq. 305; 24 Jur. 465; 1 Stu. 783. Harvey v. Lindsay, 1853; 15 D. 768. Mags. of Earlsferry v. Malcolm, 1829; 7 S. 755; 1832, 11 S. 74. Aikman v. D. Hamilton, 1830; 8 S. 943; rev. 6 W. & S. 64. Patrick, *cit.* Murray v. Peddie, 1880; 7 R. 804.

(d) N. B. Ry. v. Park Yard Co., 1897; 24 R. 1148; revd. 1898, A. C. 643, 653.

980. Classification of Servitudes.—Lawyers class servitudes as Natural, Legal, or Conventional. But what are called *natural* servitudes are not properly servitudes; such as the burden of receiving the water of the superior tenement. The *legal* are more properly police regulations for public safety in cities; though in this class liferents by terce and courtesy have also incorrectly been ranked. The *conventional* alone are properly servitudes, by which those rights of use, which belong to proprietors by nature and law, are altered or modified.

Another distinction has been made between servitudes of *Continuous* and *Interrupted* use; and again between servitudes *Manifest* and *Not manifest.* And both those distinguishing features may be of importance in the question of the constitution or extinction of servitude (*a*).

(a) 2 Stair, 7. § 5. 2 Ersk. 9. § 6.

981. Servitudes have been classed as Prædial and Personal. Those have been called *prædial,* of which the benefit is conferred on another subject, or *prædium*; those have been called *personal* which are conferred on a person independently of property (*a*). But, practically, the only servitudes in Scotland are prædial. Usufruct, or liferent, ranked by lawyers as the principal personal servitude, is more correctly to be considered as limited property; and the servitudes which are enjoyed by individuals, independently of any property of their own, have still reference to some *prædium* (royal burgh, etc.), the inhabitants of which hold the right (*b*). Prædial or proper servitudes are Positive or Negative.

(a) 2 Ersk. 9. § 5.

(b) Cleghorn and Sinclair, *supra,* § 979 (*c*). Feuars of Dunse v. Hay, 1732; M. 1824; 2 Ill. 124. Servitudes of bleaching, golfing, etc., have been sustained in the person of the magistrates of a royal burgh for the use of the inhabitants over the lands of a neighbouring proprietor. Sinclair, *cit.* Murray v. Mags. of Peebles, Dec. 8, 1808; F. C. Cleghorn v. Dempster, *cit.* § 979. Home v. Young, 1846; 9 D. 286. Mags. of Dundee v. Hunter, 1843; 6 D. 12; 1868, 20 D. 1067. See below, § 993 (*h*). That privilege has been denied to a burgh of barony (Feuars of Dunse, *cit.*); but some doubt may be entertained as to the precise effect of this case. See Dyce v. Hay, *cit.* § 979; and Smith v. Comrs. of Police of Denny, 1879; 6 R. 858; aff. 1880, 7 R. H. L. 28; 5 App. Ca. 489. A public right of way may be established by prescriptive use; but it seems no other public servitude or burden can be imposed upon private property in that way; see, *e.g.*, M. Breadalbane v. M'Gregor, 1846; 9 D. 210; 1848, 7 Bell's App. 43. Harvey v. Lindsay, Dyce v. Hay, etc., *citt.* § 979. As to the right of the inhabitants of small unincorporated communities to wells, greens, etc., see Henderson v. E. Minto, 1860; 22 D. 1126. Dyce v. Hay, Harvey v. Lindsay, Smith v. Police Comrs. of Denny, *citt.* L. Melville v. Denniston, 1842; 4 D. 1231. In the other cases of this kind, the right sustained in favour of the inhabitants or burgesses has always been a right over subjects belonging in property to the burgh as a quality of the right vested in the magistrates. Jaffray v. D. Roxburghe, Cochran v. Fairholm, Sinclair v. Mags. of Dysart, Mags. of Earlsferry v. Malcolm, *citt.* § 979. Dyce and Cleghorn, *citt.* Home v. Young, 1846; 9 D. 286. Sanderson v. Lees, 1859; 22 D. 24. Paterson v. Mags. of St. Andrews, 1879; 7 R. 712; aff. 1881, 8 R. H. L. 117; 6 App. Ca. 833. Grahame v. Mags. of Kirkcaldy, 1879; 6 R. 1066; 1881, 8 R. 395; 1882, 9 R. H. L. 91; 7 App. Ca. 547. Aikman v. D. Hamilton, 1830; 8 S. 943; H. L. 6 W. & S. 64. Sharp v. D. Hamilton, 1829; 7 S. 679. Murray v. Mags. of Forfar, 1893; 20 R. 908. A practice by the magistrates of alienating or dilapidating the common property does not derogate from the right of the inhabitants to what remains. Cases in Murray, *cit.* at pp. 915, 918.

982. The right conferred in *positive* servitude controls that of exclusive use and occupation, which is a part of the right of property (*a*), and enables the dominant proprietor to exercise some act of absolute use over the servient subject which otherwise might have been prevented; as to rest a beam on the servient wall, to take water from a fountain, to use a road, to pasture cattle, to take fuel (*b*).

In *negative* servitude the dominant owner holds a restraint over the servient, by which the servient is limited in that absolute use (*c*) of his tenement which entitled him to derive from it every benefit of which it is capable. So he may be restrained from any building which may interrupt light or prospect, or perhaps from building at all on the servient tenement (*d*).

(a) *Supra,* § 940.

(b) 2 Stair, 7. § 5. 2 Ersk. 9. § 1.

(c) *Supra,* § 962.

(d) Stair, *ut supra.* 2 Ersk. 9. § 35.

983. But the most frequent servitudes known in our practice are: 1. Those relating to lands and other rural subjects,—as a servitude of road or passage, of aqueduct, of watering of cattle, of pasturage, of fuel or feal and divot; or 2. Those relating to houses or buildings in town or country,—as the servitude of support, of stillicide, of light, of prospect.

Urban servitudes relate to houses for habitation, although in the country; *Rural* relate to fields, enclosures, gardens, etc., although in a city.

984. Exercise of Servitude.—As servitudes are thus limitations on the absolute or on the exclusive right of the servient tenement, they are passive merely, not active. The owner of the servient tenement is not bound to do anything (*a*). Where one has a servitude of drain, he must himself be at the expense of cleaning and repairing it (*b*). So the dominant of a road must keep it in order for his own use. The dominant of a servitude of support must repair the wall for his own security, though an opposite doctrine is sometimes laid down (*c*). And any stipulation to the contrary imposes a personal obligation superadded to the servitude (*d*).

(*a*) 2 Ersk. 9. § 1.
(*b*) Parson of Dundee *v.* Inglish, 1687; M. 14,521. Gray *v.* Maxwell, 1762; M. 12,800. Carlile *v.* Douglas, 1731; M. 14,524. See below, § 1012.
(*c*) 2 Stair, 7. § 6. 2 Ersk. 9. § 8. Murray *v.* Brownhill, 1715; M. 14,521. Nicolson *v.* Melvill, 1708; M. 14,516. See below, § 1003.
(*d*) Same cases. See Cooper & M'Leod *v.* Edinr. Impt. Trs., 1876; 3 R. 1106.

985. It is a part of the servitude that the owner of the dominant tenement has right to access for performing, at his own expense, all the operations necessary for preserving and making use of the servitude (*a*). But it is only where such access becomes necessary by derangement, or immediately impending damage, that such intrusion on the proprietary right is justifiable. It were otherwise a right of way over another's ground (*b*).

(*a*) See Waddell *v.* Russell, 1781; 2 Pat. 579.
(*b*) Weir *v.* Glenny, 1832, as revd. 7 W. & S. 244; 2 Ill. 132. See below, § 1012.

986. The benefit of servitude is limited to the dominant tenement; and is confined to the necessary use of that tenement as fairly in contemplation of the parties in creating the servitude (*a*). So a servitude of fuel does not entitle the proprietor of the dominant subject to supply fuel to a limework opened on his land, nor to communicate the right to his feuars (*b*). Nor does a servitude of taking slates entitle the owner of the dominant subject to take slates for sale (*c*); nor a servitude of passage, or of pasturage, entitle the dominant to extend it to another tenement (*d*).

(*a*) Brown *v.* Kinloch, 1775; M. 14,542; 2 Ill. 125. 2 Ersk. 9. § 5. See Gibb *v.* Bruce, 1837; 16 S. 169; and Graham *v.* D. Hamilton, as revd. 1871, 9 Macph. H. L. 98, 103 (*per* L. Hatherley, C.). Mags. of Dunbar, *infra*, § 988.
(*b*) Leslie *v.* Cumming, 1793; M. 14,542. Carstairs *v.* Brown, 1829; 7 S. 607. See below, § 1014.
(*c*) Murray *v.* Mags. of Peebles, Dec. 8, 1808; F. C.
(*d*) Scott *v.* Bogle, July 6, 1809; F. C. E. Aboyne *v.* Innes, June 22, 1813; F. C.; 2 Ill. 116. E. Breadalbane *v.* Menzies, 1743; Elchies, *Servitude*, 3; 5 B. S. 710, 724. See below, § 1010. Stewart *v.* Caithness, 1788; Hume, 731. Anstruther *v.* Caird, 1861; 24 D. 149.

987. The owner of the servient tenement is no further limited than the servitude requires. So he is not restrained from watering his own cattle along with those of the dominant owner, if there be enough for both. So also he may restrict the dominant owner to a part, if not detrimental to the servitude; or substitute one road for another, if equally convenient; or enclose a road, placing stiles or gates of easy access (*a*).

(*a*) 2 Ersk. 9. § 36. Watson *v.* Dunkennar Feuars, 1667; M. 14,529; 2 Ill. 125. Dunikier Vassals *v.* The Laird, 1670; 2 B. Sup. 466. E. Southesk *v.* L. Melgum, 1680; M. 14,531. Beveridge *v.* Marshall, Nov. 18, 1808; F. C. Bruce *v.* Wardlaw, 1745; M. 14,525. See Urie *v.* Stewart, and other cases in § 1010 (*c*). Mags. of Renfrew *v.* Speirs, 1823; 2 S. 458. See below, § 1010, 1011. Borthwick *v.* Strang, 1799; Hume, 513.

988. But the owner of the servient tenement can do nothing to diminish the use or convenience of the servitude to the owner of the dominant (*a*). Nor can the owner of the dominant enlarge his use so as to increase the burden on the servient, unless in so far as such change of use may have become necessary in order to make the servitude effectual to the extent originally granted (*b*).

(*a*) M'Grigor *v.* Maclean, 1896; 24 R. 86.
(*b*) 2 Ersk. 9. § 4. L. Garleton *v.* Stevenson, 1677; M. 14,536; 2 Ill. 126. See Bruce *v.* Dalrymple, 1741; Elch. *Servitude*, 2. Mags. of Dunbar *v.* Sawers, 1829; 7 S. 672. Greenhill *v.* Allan, 1825; 4 S. 160. Scouller *v.* Robertson, 1829; 7 S. 344. Allans *v.* Mags. of Rutherglen, 1801; 4 Pat. 269.

989. A negative servitude is not to be evaded, or the prohibited act justified, on pretence that, if the servitude be insisted on, the 'servient owner' (*a*) may do acts still more offensive 'to the dominant tenement' (*b*).

(*a*) The original text had "dominant."
(*b*) Greenhill, *supra*, § 988 (*b*).

990. Effect of Servitudes on Singular Successors.—The constitution of servitudes may be considered as between the original parties, or as against singular successors.

In relation to singular successors, there are important differences between positive and negative servitudes. In all servitudes the *titulus transferendi* is a grant express or implied; the *modus* is the exercise of the right conferred by the grant. But this exercise is manifested by possession in positive servitudes; while negative servitudes, which are mere prohibitions, are not thus made manifest. Hence, positive servitudes not constituted by disposition and sasine must, in order to be effectual against singular successors, be followed by possession (either continuous or otherwise, according to circumstances), unless both the dominant and servient proprietors' rights remain still personal (*a*): negative are effectual by mere force of the grant. Positive servitudes may be constituted by prescription; negative cannot. The rule which denies effect to servitudes not already known and recognised (*b*) is strictly observed with regard to negative servitudes. Singular successors are left to their own vigilance, aware of what is naturally suggested by the peculiarity of the situation, and safe enough if the effectual servitudes be of a known description; a servitude of light, for example, or of prospect. As to positive servitudes of an anomalous nature, they are less likely to escape detection, as the possession betrays them; and long usage has been more easily admitted to rank them among proper servitudes,—as bleaching, walking, or golfing (*c*), cutting wood (*d*), taking of slates or stones for the use of the dominant tenement (*e*); 'taking drift sea-ware (not growing sea-tangle) for manure (*f*).'

(*a*) 2 Ersk. 9. § 3. Gun *v.* Brown, 1829; 7 S. 274; 2 Ill. 127.

(*b*) See above, § 979.

(*c*) Cochran *v.* Fairholm, 1759; M. 14,518; 2 Ill. 123. Jaffray *v.* D. Roxburghe, 1775; M. 14,517. Sinclair *v.* Town of Dysart, 1779; M. 14,519; aff. 2 Pat. 254. Cleghorn *v.* Dempster, 1813; 2 Dow, 40. Home *v.* Young, 1846; 9 D. 286. Dyce *v.* Hay, 1849; 11 D. 1266; 1 Macq. 305. Harvey *v.* Lindsay, 1853; 15 D. 768. See Sanderson *v.* Lees, 1859; 21 D. 1011; 1859, 22 D. 24. St. Andrews Ladies' Golf Club *v.* Denham, 1887; 14 R. 686 (possessory judgment).

(*d*) Garden *v.* E. Aboyne; Elch. *Servitude*, 1; 2 Ill. 127; 1734, M. 14,517.

(*e*) Murray *v.* Mags. of Peebles, Dec. 3, 1808; F. C.; 2 Ill. 125. See § 981, note.

(*f*) Fullerton *v.* Baillie, 1697; M. 13,524. E. Morton *v.* Covingtree, 1760; M. 13,528 (see 11 Macph. 332). Baird *v.* Fortune, 1859; 21 D. 848; rev. 1861, 4 Macq. 127; 23 D. H. L. 5. Macalister *v.* Campbell, 1837; 15 S. 490. See above, § 644, 647.

991. Constitution of Positive Servitudes.—Positive servitudes are constituted either by Grant or by Prescription.

992. (1.) *By Grant* such a servitude may be constituted, in the charter either of the dominant or of the servient tenement; or in a separate deed, contract, missive, or other authentic writing 'holograph or tested' (*a*). And it will be effectual against singular successors, either if it qualify the recorded sasine, or if the grant be followed by such possession or use as it admits of; possession being in this case the badge, but not the measure of the right (*b*).

'*Implied Grant and Implied Reservation.*—A servitude cannot be constituted *rebus ipsis et factis* (*c*). But (1) continuous and manifest (apparent) servitudes may be created by implied grant upon the severance of two tenements previously possessed together. When an owner conveys a part of his tenement as it has been possessed by himself, all such uses or easements over the portion retained, which are necessary to the reasonable and comfortable enjoyment of the part granted, and have been and are at the time of the grant used by the owner of the whole for the benefit of the part granted, pass to the grantee, although not mentioned (*d*). (2) If, on the other hand, the granter intends to reserve any right over the tenement conveyed, he must expressly reserve it by the terms of his grant; for a granter "cannot derogate from his grant." The only exception to this is in the case of servitudes (at least ways) of necessity, *i.e.* without which the property not granted would be inaccessible or useless (*e*). When the severance occurs by simultaneous conveyances to different parties, the presumption is in favour of the constitution into a servitude of a benefit enjoyed in the manner above stated during the unity of possession, at least where the two grantees have notice of the two transactions (*f*).'

(*a*) 2 Ersk. 9. § 3. Turnbull *v.* Blanerne, 1622; M. 14,499; 2 Ill. 127. Pennimuir *v.* ——, 1632; M. 14,502.

Kincaid *v.* Stirling, 1750 ; M. 8404 ; Elch. *Servitude*, 4. Garden, *supra*, § 990 (*d*). Dinwiddie *v.* Corrie, 1821 ; 1 S. 164. Davidson *v.* D. Hamilton, 1822 ; 1 S. 385. Sievwright *v.* Wilson & Borthwick, 1828 ; 7 S. 210. Argyllshire Comrs. of Supply *v.* Campbell, 1885 ; 12 R. 1255. Servitudes may be constituted by statute. Cal. Ry. Co. *v.* Sprot, 1854 ; 16 D. 559, 955 ; rev. 1856, 2 Macq. 449. Cal. Ry. Co. *v.* L. Belhaven, 1857 ; 3 Macq. 56. M'Culloch *v.* Dumfries Waterworks Comrs., 1863 ; 1 Macph. 334. They may be established against a superior and other feuars by a feuing plan. Henderson *v.* Nimmo & Colquhoun, 1846 ; 2 D. 869. Crawford *v.* Field, 1874 ; 2 R. 20. Newport Ry. Co. *v.* Fleming, 1879 ; 7 R. 179 ; aff. 1883, 8 App. Ca. 265 ; 10 R. H. L. 30. See above, § 868.

(*b*) Pittaro *v.* Stewart, 1673 ; M. 14,503 ; 2 Ill. 128. See next section, *in fin.*

(*c*) **Cochrane** *v.* **Ewart**, 1860 ; 22 D. 358 ; aff. 1861, 4 Macq. 117, overruling Preston's Trs. *v.* Preston, 1844 ; 22 D. 366. Comp. above, § 739 ; below, § 994.

(*d*) **Baird** *v.* **Fortune**, 1859 ; 21 D. 848 ; rev. 1861, 4 Macq. 127. Cochrane *v.* Ewart, *cit.* M'Gavin *v.* M'Intyre, 1874 ; 1 R. 1016. Gow's Trs. *v.* Mealls, 1875 ; 2 R. 729. Alexander *v.* Butchart, 1875 ; 3 R. 156. Walton *v.* Mags. of Glasgow, 1876 ; 3 R. 1130. M'Laren *v.* Glasgow Union Ry. Co., 1878 ; 5 R. 1042. Heron *v.* Gray, 1880 ; 8 R. 155. See Carnegie *v.* M'Tier, 1844 ; 6 D. 1381, 1399, etc. Argyllshire Comrs., *cit.* (boundary by lane and possession). Louttit's Trs. *v.* Highland Ry. Co., 1892 ; 19 R. 791 (boundary by private roadway does not imply unlimited access thereby). Cullens *v.* Cambusbarron Co-op. Soc., 1895 ; 23 R. 209. Polden *v.* Bastard, 36 L. J. Q. B. 92 ; L. R. 1 Q. B. 156. Watts *v.* Kelson, 40 L. J. Ch. 126 ; L. R. 6 Ch. 166. Barkshire *v.* Grubb, 18 Ch. D. 616 ; 50 L. J. Ch. 731. Bayley *v.* G. W. Ry. Co., 26 Ch. D. 434. Birmingham Bkg. Co. *v.* Ross, 28 Ch. D. 295.

(*e*) **Suffield** *v.* **Brown**, 33 L. J. Ch. 249 ; 4 De G. J. & S. 185. Crossley *v.* Lightowler, 36 L. J. Ch. 584 ; L. R. 2 Ch. 478. Wheeldon *v.* Burrows, 48 L. J. Ch. 853 ; L. R. 12 Ch. D. 31. Union Her. Sec. Co. *v.* Mathie, 1886 ; 13 R. 670. Anderson *v.* Handley, 1881 ; 2 Sel. Sh. Ct. Ca. 532. Russell *v.* Watts, 1885 ; 10 App. Ca. 660 ; 55 L. J. Ch. 158. Broomfield *v.* Williams, 1897 ; 1 Ch. 602. See below, § 997. Dig. 8. 4. 10 ; 8. 2. 3 ; 8. 3. 29 sqq., etc. Donell. Com. xi. 9. 27, xi. 17. 7, etc.

(*f*) Swansborough *v.* Coventry, 9 Bing. 305 ; 2 L. J. C. P. 11 ; 35 R. R. 660. Allen *v.* Taylor, 16 Ch. D. 355 ; 50 L. J. Ch. 178. Russell *v.* Watts, *cit.*

993. (2.) *By Prescription* alone, with possession, a positive servitude may be established, without any grant or other title in writing, except charter and sasine in the dominant subject; law presuming a title (*a*). But the possession must be clear and unequivocal (*b*). 'Mere non-user for the prescriptive period of an inherent right of property will not enlarge a servitude in favour of a neighbour clearly defined by the titles (*c*).' And it must continue during forty years (*d*), uninterrupted by minorities or otherwise; and no presumption from acquiescence short of that term will be sufficient (*e*). The servitude must be possessed 'by any *de facto* possessor on a probable title (*f*)' as accessory to a dominant tenement, and 'will' not be excluded by a bounding charter (*g*). Royal burghs may, as the Crown's vassal, possess for individuals, but not burghs of barony (*h*). The possession is in this case not merely the badge, but also the measure of the right: *tantum præscriptum quantum possessum* (*i*). 'Yet changes and substitutions, *e.g.* in the line of a public or private way (*infra*, § 1010), being apparently consented to or acquiesced in on each side, do not hinder the acquisition of a right, the use and possession of which as a definite subject is otherwise sufficient for prescription (*k*).'

(*a*) 2 Ersk. 9. § 3. Grant *v.* Grant, 1677 ; M. 10,876 ; 2 Ill. 128. E. Breadalbane *v.* Menzies, 1743 ; Elchies, *Serv.* 3. Ross *v.* Ross, 1757 ; Elchies, *Serv.* No. 5. Porteous *v.* Allan, 1773 ; M. 14,512 ; Hailes, 280 ; 5 B. Sup. 595. See D. Roxburghe *v.* Town of Dunbar, 1713 ; M. 10,883. Rodgers *v.* Harvie, 1827 ; 5 S. 917 ; 3 W. & S. 251. Hilson *v.* Scott, 1895 ; 23 R. 241 (title *a non domino* founding property not servitude). A servitude acquired by prescription is binding on the vassal's superior, who has a title to interrupt. M. Breadalbane *v.* Campbell, 1851 ; 13 D. 647. 2 Stair, 7. § 3. 2 Ersk. 9. § 4.

(*b*) Purdie *v.* Steel, 1749 ; M. 14,511 ; 2 Ill. 129. M'Nab *v.* Munro Ferguson, 1890 ; 17 R. 397. D. Athole *v.* M'Inroy, 1889 ; 17 R. 456 ; aff. 1891, A. C. 629 ; 18 R. H. L. 46. See, as to the effect of prescription where a servitude of way was said to have begun as a personal privilege, Rome *v.* Hope Johnstone, 1884 ; 11 R. 653.

(*c*) See Blair *v.* Strachan, 1894 ; 21 R. 661.

(*d*) The period of prescription for servitudes is not altered by the Conveyancing Act of 1874, 37 and 38 Vict. c. 94, § 34.

(*e*) Campbell *v.* D. Argyle, 1836 ; 14 S. 799. Craufurd *v.* Menzies, 1849 ; 11 D. 1127. Black *v.* Mason, 1881 ; 8 R. 497. Brodie *v.* Mann, 1884 ; 11 R. 925 ; rev. 1885, 12 R. H. L. 52 ; 10 App. Ca. 378. As to interruption, see § 999. A right established by uninterrupted possession for the necessary period is lost only by evidence of acquiescence in interruption and stoppage of its exercise for forty years. Mags. of Elgin *v.* Robertson, 1862 ; 24 D. 301. See Davidson *v.* E. Fife, 1863 ; 1 Macph. 874 ; and Hill *v.* Ramsay, 1805 ; 5 Pat. 299.

(*f*) Drummond *v.* Milligan, 1890 ; 17 R. 316.

(*g*) Saunders *v.* Hunter, 1830 ; 8 S. 605. Liston *v.* Galloway, 1835 ; 14 S. 97. Beaumont *v.* L. Glenlyon, 1843 ; 5 D. 1337. See above, § 738. The word "must," which stood here in former editions, appears to have been a typographical error.

(*h*) Feuars of Dunse *v.* Hay, 1732 ; M. 1824 ; 2 Ill. 124. See § 981 (*b*).

(*i*) Ersk. *ut supra* (*a*).

(*k*) Hozier *v.* Hawthorne, 1884 ; 11 R. 766.

994. Constitution of Negative Servitudes.—Negative servitudes can be constituted only by grant; being incapable of possession, and so of prescription (*a*). The deed must be authentic and binding, but does not require sasine, or publication in the record (*b*). It must also be in such terms as unequivocally to create a 'permanent' burden or restraint on the proprietor of the servient tenement, 'not a mere personal or temporary obligation on the granter (*c*).' So, the mere circumstance of having made no objection to a neighbouring proprietor opening a window in his gable, will not infer a grant of servitude of light or prospect (*d*), though an express permission to open such windows may imply a servitude.

A negative servitude may be established by a building plan (*e*) (see above, § 868); or by articles of roup; 'or by necessary implication from the terms of restrictions in the titles of neighbouring feuars (*f*); or even by implied grant (*g*).'

(*a*) 2 Ersk. 9. § 35.

(*b*) Town of Edinburgh *v.* Town of Leith, 1630; M. 14,500; 2 Ill. 129. Clelland *v.* M'Kenzie, 1739; M. 14,506. Gray *v.* Ferguson, 1792; M. 14,513; aff.; see note in 7 S. 212, for opinion of judges. Mutrie *v.* King, June 26, 1810; F. C. Mearns *v.* Massie, 1800; Hume, 736. M'Gown *v.* Kidd, *ib.* 740. Boswall *v.* Inglis, 1848; 10 D. 888; aff. 1849, 6 Bell's App. 427. Cowan *v.* Stewart, 1872; 10 Macph. 735. N. B. Ry. Co. *v.* Park Yard Co., 1897; 24 R. 1148; rev. 1898, A. C. 643.

(*c*) Cowan *v.* Stewart, *cit.* Sievwright *v.* Wilson & Borthwick, 1828; 7 S. 210. Banks & Co. *v.* Walker, 1874; 1 R. 981. Comp. Ross *v.* Cuthbertson, 1854; 16 D. 732. Trs. of Free St. Mark's *v.* Taylor's Trs., 1869; 7 Macph. 415.

(*d*) Morris *v.* M'Kean, 1830; 8 S. 304; 2 Ill. 130. Forbes *v.* Wilson, 1724; M. 14,505. Dundas *v.* Blair, 1886; 13 R. 759. See Craig *v.* Gould, 1861; 24 D. 20. Cowan (*b*). A superior's approval of his vassals' buildings does not bind him to protect their lights. King *v.* Barnetson, 1896; 24 R. 81.

(*e*) Young & Co. *v.* Dewar, Nov. 17, 1814; F. C.; 2 Ill. 77. Gordon *v.* Marjoribanks, March 16, 1814; 18 F. C. p. 25, note; aff. 6 Paton, 351. Walker *v.* Renton, 1825; 3 S. 455. Pollock *v.* Turnbull, 1827; 5 S. 195. See above, § 868.

(*f*) See above, § 868.

(*g*) Heron *v.* Gray, 1880; 8 R. 155, doubted by Mr. Rankine, Landownership, 365; but if the doctrine of implied grant is to be received, there appears to be no sufficient reason for the doubt. See cases cited in § 992.

995. Extinction of Servitudes.—Servitudes are extinguished in several ways.

(1.) *By Change of Circumstances.*—Where, by a change of circumstances, the servitude is no longer available, it is either extinguished absolutely, or suspended till matters are restored to their former condition; as a servitude of prospect destroyed by the building of a house on intermediate property over which there is no servitude; or a servitude of way for the watering of cattle, where the spring is destroyed. While the impossibility of exercising the servitude remains, it may be held as extinguished, but will revive when the obstruction is removed. 'Land acquired under compulsory powers is taken free of servitudes' (*a*).

(*a*) Oban Town Council *v.* Callander Ry. Co., 1892; 19 R. 912. Cf. § 697 (*a*). 53 and 54 Vict. c. 70, § 22 (Housing of Working Classes Act).

996. The extinction either of the servient or of the dominant tenement destroys the servitude. But the extinction must be total; otherwise, with revival, the servitude will revive (*a*).

(*a*) 2 Stair, 7. § 4. 2 Ersk. 9. § 37.

997. (2.) *By Confusion.*—Servitudes are extinguished by confusion, when the dominant and servient tenements come both into one person (*a*). But the doctrine of Erskine, that the servitude can revive only by a constitution *de novo*, must be taken with some limitation. Wherever a separation or disunion may be anticipated (*b*), the effect seems to be to produce rather a combination of the two rights, as if the proprietor had divided himself into two persons, with a *suspension* rather than an extinction of the servitude. Nor would it in such a case seem to be necessary, on a subsequent separation of the tenements, to constitute the servitude *de novo*. During the union of the rights, the owner's use may indeed be said to be exercised *jure proprietatis*; but it seems that if, in the exercise of the right or otherwise, the owner has indicated no intention of extinguishing the servitude, it would, on separation of the tenements, revive (*c*).

(*a*) 2 Ersk. 9. § 37. See above, § 580.

(*b*) As in the case of estates held by different titles, see, *e.g.*, Preston *v.* Preston's Trs., 1844; 22 D. 366.

(*c*) Donaldson's Trs. *v.* Forbes, 1839; 1 D. 449. Cochrane *v.* Ewart, 1860; 22 D. 358; aff. 1861, 4 Macq. 117. Gow's Trs. *v.* Mealls, 1875; 2 R. 729. Carnegie *v.* M'Tier, 1844; 6 D. 1381, 1390, 1399, 1407–8. See above, § 992.

998. (3.) *By Renunciation.*— Servitudes, not being estates or property, but burdens or accidents of property, may be extinguished by the renunciation or discharge of the dominant proprietor (*a*).

(*a*) 2 Ersk. 9. § 37.

999. (4.) *By Prescription or Abandonment.*—Positive servitudes may be extinguished *non utendo*, by prescription (*a*); a new term of negative prescription commencing after every interruption. But abstinence from the exercise of the full extent of the right will not extinguish or limit a servitude where it is *res meræ facultatis* (*b*). Negative servitudes, 'it is said in former editions,' may be extinguished by abandonment in the titles (*c*); 'or rather it is more correct to say that the case cited (*d*) shows that if a grant of servitude in a minute of sale be not inserted in a subsequent disposition of the dominant property, its abandonment is to be inferred, or it is to be held a merely personal arrangement. But if a servitude be once validly constituted, it is not lost by its mere omission for forty years from the titles of the servient tenement, for with these the dominant owner has no concern (*e*). Abandonment of the servitude in whole or in part may, however, be inferred from non-user for a period less than forty years, if there be also conduct on the part of the dominant owner clearly showing an intention to relinquish it, or from such conduct as infers acquiescence, or raises a personal bar apart from lapse of time (*f*). The prescription of a negative servitude runs from the first act of the servient owner inconsistent with it; of a positive servitude from the last act of user or possession (*g*).'

(*a*) See § 993 (*d*).
(*b*) Bethune *v.* Ogilvie, 1670; M. 10,912; 2 Ill. 138. Nicholson *v.* L. Bightie, 1662; M. 11,291. Monro *v.* M'Kenzie, 1760; M. 14,533. Rodgers *v.* Harvie, 1827; 5 S. 917; 3 W. & S. 251. See Leck *v.* Chalmers, 1859; 21 D. 408. Gellatly *v.* Arrol, 1863; 1 Macph. 592. Smith *v.* Stewart, 1884; 11 R. 92; and below, § 2017.
(*c*) Sievwright *v.* Borthwick & Wilson, 1828; 7 S. 210.
(*d*) See other cases above, § 994 (*c*).
(*e*) Boswall *v.* Inglis, 1848; 10 D. 888; aff. 1849, 6 Bell's App. 427.
(*f*) Hill *v.* Ramsay, 1810; 5 Pat. 299 (non-user of road and its being ploughed over by the owner of the ground). Muirhead *v.* Glasg. Highland Soc., 1864; 2 Macph. 420 (buildings erected in partial contravention of serv. of lights, etc.). Campbell *v.* M'Kinnon, 1867; 5 Macph. 636. Mags. of Rutherglen *v.* Bainbridge, 1886; 13 R. 745. See above, § 868.
(*g*) 2 Ersk. 9. § 37. Wilkie *v.* Scott, 1688; M. 11,189.

1000. Particular Servitudes.—Many servitudes are enumerated at great length in the books of the Civilians, which are nothing more than agreements, express or implied, on the part of the owners of land or houses to renounce the exercise of certain points of their right, absolute or exclusive: In other words, to abstain from certain uses of their property, which the dominant proprietor may desire to prevent; or to grant to the dominant the privilege of certain uses of their tenement, from which they might otherwise exclude him. Our servitudes are few and well known; and there are not many individual servitudes on which a particular commentary seems to be necessary (*a*).

(*a*) 2 Stair, 7. § 4. 2 Ersk. 9. § 37. As to "hunting," etc., on another's land, see § 739, 952.

1001. Urban Servitudes.—Recurring to the distinction of Urban and Rural Servitudes (*a*), the chief difference between them in nature and effect is, that the rural are all positive servitudes; the urban chiefly negative, but some also positive.

(*a*) See above, § 983.

1002. Urban servitudes relate to buildings, whether in town or country.

1003. (1.) *Support.*—This servitude (*oneris ferendi*, and *tigni immittendi* of the Civilians) gives a right to rest the whole, or part, of a beam of a building on the house, wall, or property of another; controlling and limiting the otherwise exclusive right belonging to the servient proprietor (*a*). In regard to this servitude, an exception to the ordinary rule of servitudes is said to exist; viz. that the servient is bound not merely to suffer the burden, but to maintain in sufficiency the wall, etc., on which the support is rested. But with us this requires a special contract.

(*a*) 2 Stair, 7. § 6. 2 Ersk. 9. § 8. Murray *v.* Brownhill, 1715; M. 14,521; 2 Ill. 124. Young *v.* Cuddie, 1831; 9 S. 500; 2 Ill. 130. See above, § 984; below, § 1086.

1004. (2.) *Stillicide.*—A proprietor has a right to insist that the rain from his neighbour's house shall not fall on his property, either in drops from the eaves or collected in a spout. This servitude restrains that right, and imposes on him the burden of receiving the rain from the dominant tenement. If only the eaves-drop, it is properly *stillicide*; if the collected water (*flumen*), the servitude is distinguished by the addition of *fluminis* (*a*).

(*a*) 2 Ersk. 9. § 9. Clark *v.* Gordon, 1760; M. 13,172; 2 Ill. 125. Stirling *v.* Finlayson, 1752; M. 14,526; 2 Ill. 130. See above, § 941, and cases there cited. Buchanan *v.* Bell, 1774; M. 13,178. Steele *v.* Oliver & Boyd, 1832; 10 S. 857. As to alteration of height of eaves, see Harvey *v.* Walters, L. R. 8 C. P. 162; 42 L. J. C. P. 105.

1005. (3.) *Light or Prospect.*—The servitude of light or of prospect is a restraint on the absolute use, to the effect of preventing the servient proprietor from building, or raising any obstruction by which the light in the one case, or the prospect in the other, of the dominant tenement shall be obstructed (*a*). For light, an ell's distance has been held sufficient (*b*). A servitude of this kind may indirectly arise from a stipulated tolerance of windows looking into the servient tenement (*c*).

(*a*) 2 Ersk. 9. § 10. Simson *v.* Hill, 1649; 1 B. Sup. 396; 2 Ill. 131. Ogilvie *v.* Donaldson, 1678; M. 14,534. Blackwood *v.* Bell, 1825; 4 S. 26; 2 Ill. 118. Greenhill *v.* Allan, 1825; 4 S. 160; 2 Ill. 127. See above, § 965.

Baird *v.* Ross, 1829; 7 S. 766; rev. 1832, 6 W. & S. 127; 1836, 14 S. 528. Boswall *v.* Inglis, *supra*, § 994 (*b*). Cases in § 868. Russell *v.* Cowpar, 1882; 9 R. 660.

(*b*) Ogilvie *v.* Donaldson, 1678; M. 14,534; 2 Ill. 131.

(*c*) Forbes *v.* Wilson, 1724; M. 14,505. See above, § 994.

1006. A servitude may be created for protecting a house or garden from being looked in upon by a neighbour. Such a servitude is a limitation of that natural right of absolute use which entitles the owner of a tenement to open a window in his wall (*a*). Independently of this servitude, the only protection against such invasion of privacy is the power of erecting an obstruction over against the window (*b*).

(*a*) Forbes, *supra*, § 1005 (*c*).

(*b*) See Glassford *v.* Astley, 1808; M. *Property*, Apx. 1.

1007. (4.) *Altius non Tollendi; or Not to Build.*—These are restraints on the servient owner's legal power of building on his own ground, one of the absolute uses of property (*a*). And it has been held, that under such a servitude the servient proprietor is not entitled to erect a shed supported on iron pillars with a flat leaden roof (*b*); 'or even to build a cellar (*c*).'

(*a*) Walker *v.* Wishart, 1825; 4 S. 148; 2 Ill. 131. Mutrie *v.* King, June 26, 1810; F. C.; 2 Ill. 129. See cases cited under § 868. Cowan *v.* Stewart, 1872; 10 Macph. 735.

(*b*) Mags. of Edinburgh *v.* Brown, 1833; 11 S. 255. It was held that a proprietor might build a chimney as high as four storeys, notwithstanding a servitude restricting him from building a house above one storey high. Banks & Co. *v.* Walker, 1874; 1 R. 980.

(*c*) Mags. of Edinr. *v.* Paton & Ritchie, 1858; 20 D. 731. Comp. Malloch *v.* Gray, 1872; 10 Macph. 774. Cases above, § 868.

1008. It is also said that there is a servitude *altius tollendi.* This, however, is, properly speaking, no servitude, but a restoration of the natural power of the proprietor,—an exception in favour of an individual from the operation of some general servitude *altius non tollendi*; and it may be doubted how far such an exemption will be effectual against third parties.

1009. Rural Servitudes.—There are several well-known servitudes of this class.

1010. (1.) *Passage.* — This is of three degrees: Foot-road, Horse-road, and Cart or Coach road; to which may be added, Loaning for cattle (*a*). This kind of servitude infers no obligation on the servient proprietor to maintain the road; nor does it prevent him, 'when the servitude road is not fixed by contract in a definite line (*b*),' from changing the direction, provided the new course shall be equally convenient; or even from placing gates or stiles of easy access (*c*).

The distinctions between a public road and a servitude road (*d*) are, that the former is open to all the Queen's subjects, the latter only to the dominant proprietor (*e*); that the former varies in extent with changes in the mode of conveyance, the latter is limited to the actual extent of use (*f*); that the trustees on a highway, whatever power they may have to shut up other roads, cannot at common law interrupt a servitude road (*g*); 'that a public right of way must be between two public places as its termini (*h*); that in the one case the title to sue is in every member of the public; in the other, only in the owner of the dominant tenement (*i*); that an action at the instance of any individual for vindication of a public road seems to be *res judicata* against the whole public, if fairly tried; while an action in regard to a servitude road is *res judicata* only between the parties and their successors (*k*).'

'The local authority must vindicate public rights of way, and may erect guide-posts upon, and maintain these ways (*l*).'

(*a*) 2 Ersk. 9. § 12. Malcolm *v.* Lloyd, 1886; 13 R. 512. As to loaning, see Chatto *v.* Lockhart, 1790; Hume, 734. Questions about drove-roads have generally been questions of public right. Porteous *v.* Allan, 1769; M. 14,512; 5 B. S. 598. Campbells *v.* Campbells, 1777; 5 B. S. 599. M. Breadalbane *v.* M'Gregor, 1846; 9 D. 210; rev. 1848, 7 Bell's App. 43. As to kirk-roads, see Neilson *v.* Sheriff of Galloway, 1623; M. 10,880. Fardell *v.* Wemyss, 1673; *ib.* These also have generally arisen as public rights of road; see Bruce *v.* Wardlaw, 1748; M. 14,525. Urie, *infra* (*c*). Smith *v.* Knowles, 1825; 3 S. 652 (see *per* L. Neaves in M'Gavin *v.* M'Intyre, 1874; 1 R. 1024). As to peat-roads, see Ross *v.* Ross, *infra.* Dingwall *v.* Farquharson, 1797; 3 Pat. 564. As to shooting access, see M'Inroy *v.* D. Athole, 1891; 18 R. H. L. 46; A. C. 629. The use of a road may be limited by express condition to certain purposes. Gibb *v.* Bruce, 1837; 16 S. 169. But if a road be fit for all purposes, an exclusion of a particular use, such as driving loose cattle, will not be readily established. Swan *v.* Buist, 1834; 12 S. 316 (comp. Forbes and Mackenzie, *infra* (*f*).

(*b*) Hill *v.* M'Laren, 1879; 6 R. 1363. Grigor *v.* M'Lean, 1896; 24 R. 86 (width). Thomson's Trs. *v.* Findlay, 1898; 25 R. 407 (as to which, see Jur. Rev., Oct. 1898).

(*c*) Urie *v.* Stewart, 1747; M. 14,524; 2 Ill. 126. Ross *v.* Ross, 1751; M. 14,531; Elch. *Serv.* 5. Wood *v.* Robertson, March 9, 1809; F. C. See cases in § 987. Kirkpatrick *v.* Murray Stewart, 1856; 19 D. 91. Oliver *v.* Robertson, 1869; 8 Macph. 137 (servient owner not in general entitled to lock gates, though giving the dominant a key. Mags. of Glasgow *v.* Bell, 1776; 5 B. S. 598). L. Donington *v.* Mair, 1894; 21 R. 829. Blair *v.* Strachan, 1894; 21 R. 66 (substitution). As to gates on a public road or footpath, see Wood, *cit.*; and above, § 659. Where a right of way is found to exist in a particular direction, the Court if necessary will define the precise line. Mackintosh *v.* Moir, 1872; 10 Macph. 517.

(*d*) See Galbraith *v.* Armour, 1845; 4 Bell's App. 374. Thomson *v.* Murdoch, 1862; 24 D. 975.

(*e*) See Torrie *v.* D. Athole, 1849; 12 D. 328; aff. 1 Macq. 55.

(*f*) Forbes *v.* Forbes, 1829; 7 S. 441; 2 Ill. 8. This is subject to the qualification that the road is capable, without engineering operations, of being used for any novel mode of conveyance, *e.g.* for carts on their introduction. Mackenzie *v.* Bankes, 1868; 6 Macph. 936. Malcolm *v.* Lloyd. *cit* (*a*).

(*g*) Calder *v.* Learmonth, 1831; 9 S. 343; 2 Ill. 131. M'Gavin *v.* Macintyre, 1874; 1 R. 1016. Conversely, if a road managed by road trustees be abandoned by them, it does not remain as a public right of way unless there be evidence of prescriptive use from one public place to another. Winans *v.* L. Tweedmouth, 1888; 15 R. 540.

(*h*) Rodgers *v.* Harvie, 1826; 4 Murr. 25; 5 S. 917; aff. 3 W. & S. 251; 7 S. 287; 8 S. 611. Cuthbertson *v.* Young, 1851; 13 D. 1308; 14 D. 300; aff. 1854, 1 Macq. 455. Burt *v.* Barclay, 1861; 24 D. 218. Campbell *v.* Lang, 1851; 13 D. 1179; aff. 1853, 1 Macq. 451; 15 D. H. L. 41. Darrie *v.* Drummond, 1865; 3 Macph. 496. Scott *v.* Drummond, 1866; 4 Macph. 819; 1867, 5 Macph. 771. Jenkins *v.* Murray, 1866; 4 Macph. 1046. Duncan *v.* Lees, 1870; 9 Macph. 274, 855.

(*i*) Torrie, *cit.* (*e*). As to caution for expenses, see Jenkins *v.* Robertson, 1869; 7 Macph. 739. Potter *v.* Hamilton, 1870; 8 Macph. 1064.

(*k*) White *v.* E. Morton, 1866; 4 Macph. H. L. 53; L. R. 1 Sc. App. 70. Jenkins *v.* Robertson, 1867; 5 Macph. H. L. 27; L. R. 1 Sc. App. 117. Torrie *v.* D. of Athole, *cit.* (*e*).

(*l*) 57 and 58 Vict. c. 58, § 42, 29. Alston *v.* Ross, 1895; 23 R. 273.

1011. (2.) *Watering.—Aquæ haustus* is a servitude of leave to water cattle, 'or take water for domestic or other purposes,' at a stream or well in the servient tenement. It may be acquired by long use (*a*); and does not bar the servient proprietor from the same use of the stream, or prevent him from covering over the stream, provided he leave sufficient for the servitude, and free access to the water at a fit watering-place (*b*).

(*a*) Macnab *v.* Ferguson, 1890; 17 R. 397.

(*b*) 2 Ersk. 9. § 13. Beveridge *v.* Marshall, Nov. 18, 1808; F. C.; 2 Ill. 126. *Supra*, § 987, 995. Waddell *v.* Russel, 1781; 2 Pat. 579 (mineral well). Brand (Thorburn) *v.* Charters, 1842; 4 D. 345. Mackenzie *v.* Learmonth, 1849; 12 D. 132. Smith *v.* Denny Police Comrs., 1879; 6 R. 858; aff. 1880, 7 R. H. L. 28; 5 App. Ca. 489. L. Melville *v.* Denniston, 1842; 4 D. 1231.

1012. (3.) *Aqueduct* is a right to conduct water by conduits, canals, pipes, etc., in the servient tenement. The dominant tenement is bound, by the implied nature of the servitude, to maintain the aqueduct in a fit condition to prevent injury to the servient by his operations, or by the insufficiency of the conduits; and the servient proprietor is bound (when it becomes necessary, and within the limits of due discretion) to allow access for repairs. The dominant proprietor is not bound to repair injury by restagnation from floods (*a*).

(*a*) 2 Ersk. 9. § 13. Parson of Dundee *v.* Inglish, 1768; M. 14,521; 1 Ill. 124. Carlile *v.* Douglas, 1731; M. 14,524. Wallace *v.* Morrison, 1761; M. 14,511; 2 Ill. 131. Weir *v.* Glenny, 1832; 10 S. 290; 7 W. & S. 244. Preston *v.* Erskine, 1714; M. 10,919; 10 D. 526, note. Christie *v.* Wemyss, 1842; 5 D. 242. L. Blantyre *v.* Dunn, 1848; 10 D. 509. Kincaid *v.* Stirling, 1752; M. 8403; Elch. *Serv.* 6. Stirling *v.* Haldane, 1829; 8 S. 131. Preston's Trs. *v.* Preston, *supra*, § 992 (*c*). Pringle *v.* D. Roxburghe, 1767; 2 Pat. 134. Dicksons & Laings *v.* Burgh of Hawick, 1885; 13 R. 133 (conveyance of ground occupied by mill-lade). See above, § 984, 985; and below, § 1108.

1013. (4.) *Pasturage* is the right to feed cattle or sheep on another's ground, or on a common. It is constituted by charter of the dominant tenement, *cum pastura*, etc., either specific or interpreted by use; or by obligation or contract, with possession; or by prescription, grounded on words in the title sufficient to sustain it (*a*). The number of cattle or sheep to be admitted to pasture is either specified in the grant; or (in the ordinary case of several servitudes of pasturage on a common) the right of each is proportioned to the number of cattle or sheep which the several dominant tenements can fodder in winter (*b*). The servitude is not to be extended by communication to others; the servient tenement being entitled to all the use left unoccupied by the dominant (*c*). The right is settled rateably among the commoners in an action of *sowming and rouming*, in which there are two issues of fact,—the whole extent of pasturage, and the several proportions. But this action is not competent against the proprietor 'as sole defender' (*d*). The servitude of pasturage on the sides of a loch does not include a right to cut the herbage (*e*), 'or kill the game (*f*),' and is limited to the stock of cattle on the dominant tenement (*g*).

(*a*) 2 Ersk. 9. § 14. D. Athole *v.* Stewart, 1825; 4 S. 197; 2 Ill. 132. Haining, *infra*, § 1014. See below, § 1087 sq., as to commonty, and cases there in note.

(*b*) 2 Ersk. 9. § 15. E. Breadalbane *v.* Menzies, 1741; 5 B. Sup. 710.

(*c*) E. Breadalbane *v.* Menzies, 1743; Elchies, *Servitude*, 3; 5 B. Sup. 724. 2 Ersk. 9. § 5. See above, § 986.

(*d*) Ersk. *ut supra*, § 15. Dunlop *v.* Drumelzier, 1679; M. 14,531. See below, § 1088. Culross *v.* Erskine, 1704; 4 B. S. 589.

(*e*) Cuninghame *v.* Dunlop, 1836; 15 S. 295.

(*f*) Forbes *v.* Anderson, Feb. 1, 1809; F. C. E. Aboyne *v.* Farquharson, Nov. 16, 1814; F. C.; aff. 1818, 6 Pat. 380.

(*g*) Cuninghame *v.* Dunlop, 1837; 16 S. 1080. E. Breadalbane, *cit.* (*b*).

1014. (5.) *Fuel, Feal, and Divot* is a right by servitude to cut and remove peat and turf for fuel, or for fences, etc. It commonly accompanies pasturage, but is also a separate servitude, and may be separated or lost by non-use or consent (*a*).

(*a*) 2 Ersk. 9. § 17. Brown *v.* Kinloch, 1775 ; M. 14,542 ; 2 Ill. 125. Carstairs *v.* Brown, 1829 ; 7 S. 607. Haining *v.* Town of Selkirk, 1668 ; M. 2459 ; 2 Ill. 132. See above, § 986. Dinwiddie *v.* Corrie, 1821 ; 1 S. 164. Grierson *v.* Sandsting School Board, 1882 ; 9 R. 437.

1015. (6.) *Materials for Building.*—Among rural servitudes has been ranked a power to take materials for building—wood, stone, slates (*a*).

(*a*) See Garden *v.* E. Aboyne, 1734 ; M. 14,517 ; 2 Ill. 127 ; Murray *v.* Mags. of Peebles, Dec. 8, 1808 ; F. C. Sharp *v.* D. Hamilton, 1829 ; 7 S. 679 ; 2 Ill. 132. Aikman *v.* D. Hamilton, 1830 ; 10 S. 943 ; 6 W. & S. 64. Keith *v.* Stonehaven Har. Trs., 1829 ; 7 S. 405 ; 5 W. & S. 234.

1016. Thirlage.—There are several rights which lawyers frequently class with servitudes, although, properly speaking, they are not servitudes, and depend in a great degree on other principles. One of these is Thirlage (*a*).

(*a*) Among these are also classed Usufruct or Liferent, and Commonty. See below, § 1037 and 1071 et seq.

1017. Nature of Thirlage.—Thirlage is a restriction of lands, and their inhabitants, to a particular mill, for the grinding of grain; with the burden of paying such duties and services as are expressed or implied in the constitution of the right. It is not a servitude (which consists *in patiendo* merely), nor a restraint on the absolute or exclusive use of property (*a*). But being devised originally as an expedient for indemnifying the builder of a mill for extraordinary outlay in a rude age, it has degenerated in times of more improved manufacture into a burdensome and inexpedient tax on the produce of land, and is now in a state of gradual extinction.

(*a*) See Macdowall *v.* Milliken's Trs., 1798 ; Hume, 737 (obs. of reporter). Harris *v.* Mags. of Dundee, 1863 ; 1 Macph. 833. Stobbs *v.* Caven, 1873 ; 10 Macph. 530.

1018. Thirl, Multures, etc.—The territory subject to the monopoly is called the Thirl or Sucken. Multures (*Moliturœ*) are a proportion of grain paid to the miller for the grinding of the rest. Insucken Multures may be called the monopoly price of grinding; Outsucken Multures, the price paid by those not astricted. Dry Multures are duties in grain, or money, paid whether grain be ground or not; and Knaveship or Sequels are a perquisite or allowance paid to the miller's servant (*a*).

(*a*) 2 Ersk. 9. § 18, 19, 20.

1019. Constitution of Thirlage.—Thirlage is constituted differently in different circumstances. It may be Implied, or created by Grant, or raised by Prescription.

1020. (1.) *Implied.*—A title to ground prescription of Thirlage is implied from the existence of King's Mills, and mills in Kirk lands (*a*). It was also held once that no title to ground prescription of thirlage was required in a Barony Mill (*b*); but the favour for freedom has relaxed this rule, and it is only when a Baron is infeft in the barony mill and multures thereof that he can claim thirlage, or the use of resorting to the mill (*c*): and even in that case, an exception of particular lands is given, either by a clause "cum multuris" in a feu right; or where the mill is still in the hands of the Baron, or before it has been conveyed by a feu "cum multuris" in the *tenendas*, with a special duty *pro omni alio onere* in the *reddendo* (*d*).

(*a*) 2 Stair, 7. § 16. 2 Ersk. 9. § 28. Stuart *v.* Abstractors, 1662 ; M. 10,854 ; 2 Ill. 133. Maxwell *v.* Stot, 1740 ; M. 16,017 ; Elch. *Multures*, 184. Miller *v.* Montgomery, 1809 ; Hume, 742. M'Alister *v.* D. Argyll, 1831 ; 9 S. 763 ; aff. 1832, 6 W. & S. 98.

(*b*) 2 Ersk. 9. § 22.

(*c*) Nicolson *v.* Tillicoultry Feuars, 1662 ; M. 10,856. E. Hopetoun *v.* Bathgate Brewers, 1753 ; M. 16,029. Bruce *v.* Stein, 1769 ; M. 16,061. Robertson *v.* Shaw, 1744 ; 5 B. Sup. 627.

(*d*) M'Pherson *v.* M'Intosh, 1681 ; M. 15,985. Buntin *v.* Boyd, 1682 ; M. 15,986.

1021. (2.) *Grant.*—In the constitution of thirlage by *grant*, it is held that an express agreement in writing is good against the party and his heirs, by force of the contract; against third parties, only if followed by possession. A reservation of the thirlage to a certain mill in a sale of lands is a good constitution of thirlage. A sale of the mill, with the multures of the granter's lands, will also constitute thirlage. And a clause in a lease may constitute thirlage against the tenants, but not to the effect of binding singular successors; it expires with the lease (*a*).

(*a*) 2 Ersk. 9. § 21. Scott, 1776 ; 5 B. Sup. 627. But such a clause constitutes a permanent right or servitude of thirlage if the lands are sold separately from the mill during the currency of the leases, the disposition being silent as to the multures. M'Dowall *v.* Milliken's Trs., 1798 ; Hume, 737.

1022. (3.) *Prescription.* — To establish thirlage by Prescription, there is required (contrary to the rule in servitudes) a written title, unless in Royal mills, or Church mills, or in Barony mills conveyed with multures (*a*). Clear use of the servitude is also necessary to constitute the right against third parties. In evidence of such use, payment of dry multures will be enough; but payment of insucken multures will not, unless accompanied by services (*b*). Payment of dry multures will even imply a title, being exclusive of any other supposition than astriction (*c*).

(*a*) 2 Ersk. 9. § 28. Stuart and Maxwell, *supra*, § 1020 (*a*). Hopetoun, Bruce, Robertson, *supra*, § 1020 (*c*). Harris *v.* Mags. of Dundee, 1863; 1 Macph. 833.
(*b*) Ersk. *ut supra*. M'Alister *v.* D. Argyll, 1831; 9 S. 763; aff. 1832, 6 W. & S. 98.
(*c*) Kinnaird *v.* Drummond, 1675; M. 10,862.

1023. (4.) *Lightest Presumed.*—Where the words of the constitution of thirlage are indefinite, the degree and nature of the servitude are determined by usage; with a presumption, or bias of construction, for the lightest (*a*): And the sufficiency of the mill is an implied condition (*b*).

(*a*) See below, § 1029. Hence wheat is not included where none grew on the lands at the constitution of the thirlage, and there was no flour mill on the lands. Dalgleish *v.* L. Dundas, 1812; Hume, 743, and cases in next note.
(*b*) 2 Ersk. 9. § 27. Couston *v.* Pitreavie, 1760; M. 16,047; 2 Ill. 134. Wright *v.* Rannie, 1768; M. 16,057. Maxwell *v.* Vassals, 1766; M. 16,057.

1024. Kinds of Thirlage.—The several kinds of thirlage are attended with different effects.

1025. (1.) *Grana Crescentia; Growing Corns.*—This includes all the grain raised upon the lands, whether carried to the mill, or sold in the shape of corn to dealers, or even malted as barley (*a*). But it does not include seed corn; horse corn; rent corn to the proprietor of the mill as landlord, where stipulated to be delivered unground; nor feu-duty corn deliverable to the proprietor of the mill as superior, though afterwards converted into money; nor teind-sheaves; nor grain purchased (*b*); nor ground meal or malt imported into the thirl (*c*).

(*a*) 2 Ersk. 9. § 23. E. Wigton *v.* Town of Kirkintilloch, 1736; Elch. *Mult.* 3; 2 Ill. 134. Forbes *v.* Walker, 1744; M. 16,022.
(*b*) L. Innerwick *v.* Hamilton, 1635; M. 15,972. Stewart *v.* Abstractors, 1662; M. 15,974. Garden *v.* Watson, 1697; M. 15,990. Haxton *v.* Melvil, 1709; M. 16,003. L. M'Leod *v.* Ross, 1778; M. 16,070. See note 202 in Ivory's Ersk. p. 441, and various cases, Brown's Syn. *Thirlage*, 2535.
(*c*) E. Wigton, *supra* (*a*).

1026. A clause astricting lands in general terms has been held to import thirlage of *omnia grana crescentia* (*a*).

(*a*) L. Kilkerran *v.* Blair, 1755; 5 B. Sup. 830. Yeaman *v.* Dunbar, 1759; M. 16,044. E. Wigton, *supra*, § 1025 (*a*).

1027. (2.) *Grindable Corn.*—This does not include all grain capable of being ground; but only such as is required to be so (even that which is necessary for the tenant's family), the mill being fitted to grind it. What is not so required to be ground may, notwithstanding this servitude, be sold without paying multure (*a*). By usage, however, this has been held as extensive as thirlage of *grana crescentia* (*b*).

(*a*) 2 Ersk. 9. § 24. Lockhart *v.* Paterson, 1731; M. 16,015. Lockhart *v.* Durham, 1736; M. 16,016; Elch. *Mult.* 2. Low *v.* Beatson, 1742; Elch. *Mult.* 9; M. 16,021. Town of Musselburgh *v.* Wauchope, 1743; M. 16,021; Elch. *Mult.* 11.
(*b*) Greig *v.* Reid, 1781; M. 16,068. By "usage" is here meant the practice of the parties beyond the years of prescription. See Beattie *v.* Low, 1787; Hume, 729. Milne *v.* Kyd, 1787; Hume, 728. Stobbs *v.* Caven, 1873; 10 Macph. 530.

1028. (3.) *Invecta et Illata.*—This thirlage comprehends all grain brought into the thirl, whether of the growth of the lands or not, and ground within the thirl; or that "tholes fire and water," *i.e.* suffers an operation which the mill, or its appurtenances of kiln, etc., are fitted to perform; not baking or brewing (*a*). It does not thus include meal or flour bought out of the thirl, and brought in and baked within it, if there be no fraud (*b*); nor malt imported and brewed there, under the same qualification (*c*); nor grain imported at a harbour within the thirl, to be carried beyond the thirl for grinding and baking, even where the bread is afterwards brought for retail into the thirl (*d*); nor ale imported from a brewery, nor bread from a bakehouse, in the vicinity (*e*).

(*a*) 2 Stair, 7. § 19, 20. 2 Ersk. 9. § 25.
(*b*) M'Kenzie *v.* Town of Elgin, 1624; M. 15,965; 2 Ill. 135. Gray & Clark *v.* Reid, 1749; M. 16,024. Bakers of Perth *v.* The Millers, 1749; M. 16,025. Mags. of Haddington *v.* The Bakers, 1788; M. 16,071. E. Fife *v.* King, 1807; M. *Thirlage*, Apx. 2. See Miller *v.* Stocks, 1814; Hume, 744.
(*c*) Haddington, *supra* (*b*). M. Abercorn *v.* Town of Paisley, 1798; M. 16,074.
(*d*) Bakers of Dundee *v.* Just, Feb. 23, 1813; F. C.
(*e*) Arnot *v.* Kirkcaldy, 1757; M. 16,035.

1029. (4.) *Effect of Possession and Use.*—It may be observed respecting the several kinds of thirlage, that the above terms by which they have been distinguished are not, strictly speaking, *voces signatæ*; but the nature and extent of the burden may be modified by possession and use (*a*). Thirlage does not operate as a restraint on the mode of culture; the tenant, for example, may lay down his land in grass, provided there be no fraud in the operation (*b*). Grain may be liable to a second multure; grain, for example, growing where it is liable to a thirlage of *grana crescentia*, and carried into a thirl where it is liable to a thirlage of *invecta et illata*, will be liable to both, unless the mills belong to the same proprietor (*c*). The lightest thirlage is to be presumed (*d*); and no combination of different sorts of thirlage is to be inferred, but must be imposed in words perfectly clear and free from doubt (*e*).

(*a*) Greig, *supra*, § 1027 (*b*).
(*b*) 2 Ersk. 9. § 24. Grant *v.* Milne, 1755; M. 16,034; 2 Ill. 136. Slowan *v.* Hathorn, 1765; M. 16,052. Chalmers *v.* Wilson, 1769; M. 16,060. Ayton *v.* Bruce, 1785; M. 16,069.
(*c*) Elphinston *v.* Leith, 1749; M. 16,026.
(*d*) 2 Ersk. 9. § 27. M'Alister *v.* D. Argyll, 1831; 9 S. 763; rev. 1832, 6 W. & S. 98. See above, § 1023.
(*e*) Mags. of Glasgow *v.* Dawson, 1827; 6 S. 19; rev. 4 W. & S. 81.

1030. Exercise of Thirlage.—In the exercise of the right of monopoly conferred by thirlage, the monopolist is exposed to evasions. In repressing these, the grain seems of old to have been liable to seizure (*a*); but the remedy afterwards established was by summons of abstracted multures before the Judge Ordinary. The evasion is of difficult detection, and recourse must be had to data such as the case affords, as the quantity of grain known to have been growing on the lands, or used in baking, etc. But it has been held that, under the operation of this right, the natural use of property is so far restrained, that mills for carrying on the same operation within the thirl, or capable of performing the same operation, are not to be permitted. A distinction, however, has been taken in these cases. So, where the new mill is unfit, without alteration, to grind the astricted grain, it has been held enough to find caution that no such alteration shall be made (*b*). But where a corn mill is erected within the thirl, or the machinery of the new mill is fit, without alteration, to do the work of the thirl, it has been ordered to be demolished or altered, so as to be incapable of encroachment (*c*); a judgment not now likely to be repeated.

(*a*) 2 Craig, 8. § 9.
(*b*) M'Leod *v.* Roberts, 1757; M. 16,037; 2 Ill. 137. Lockhart *v.* Denholm, 1757; M. 16,039.
(*c*) 2 Ersk. 6. § 5. Urquhart *v.* Tulloch, 1752; M. 16,028. Miller *v.* Corse, 1760; M. 16,048. Mags. of Glasgow *v.* Rae Crawford, Feb. 11, 1813; F. C.

1031. Extinction of Thirlage.—Thirlage is extinguished, either by express deed; by prescription; by extinction or insufficiency of the mill; or by commutation, under a statute.

(1.) *By Discharge Express and Implied.*—This may be accomplished by a discharge and renunciation on the part of the owner of the mill (*a*); or by a clause *cum molendinis et multuris* in a charter from a person who is proprietor both of the land and of the mill. It is sufficient if these words shall be inserted in the *tenendas* of a subject's charter; not so if the charter be from the Crown (*b*). But the doctrine of Erskine, that payment of insucken multures and other circumstances will bar the effect of such a clause, though supported by one decision (*c*), is to be received with some qualification (*d*). It is not sufficient to have a clause in the *reddendo, pro omni alio onere*, for this cannot be construed as the discharge of an existing burden (*e*).

(*a*) 2 Ersk. 9. § 37, 38.
(*b*) Ersk. *ut supra.* Veitch *v.* Duncan, 1665; M. 15,975; 2 Ill. 138. Stuarts *v.* Abstractors, 1662; M. 10,854. Wedderburn *v.* Durie, 1641; M. 16,020.
(*c*) M'Nab *v.* E. Breadalbane, 1758; M. 16,041.
(*d*) Coltart *v.* Fraser, 1768; M. 16,058; aff. 1774, 2 Pat. 332. D. Roxburghe *v.* Muir, 1785; M. 16,070.
(*e*) Monteith *v.* Abbotscarse Feuars, 1716; M. 16,009.

1032. (2.) *By Prescription.*—Thirlage is extinguished by prescription, provided the abandonment has been complete. It may be restricted by a prescriptive use of abstraction inconsistent with the thirlage (*a*).

(*a*) Bruce Stuart *v.* Erskine, 1741; M. 16,020.

1033. By extinction of the mill for forty years, the right to thirlage may be lost. The exemption 'or suspension' arising from destruction of the mill may be put an end to by rebuilding the mill within the forty years, provided the new mill be not beyond the limits of the thirl (*a*).

(*a*) Ballardie *v.* Bisset, 1781; M. 16,063. Webster *v.* Millar's Trs., 1828; 6 S. 573. Kinloch *v.* Morrison, 1830; 9 S. 244. See Harris *v.* Mags. of Dundee, 1863; 1 Macph. 833. Forbes's Trs. *v.* Davidson, 1892; 19 R. 1022.

1034. (3.) *By Excambion.*—Thirlage may be extinguished by the transference consequent on judicial excambion, under the Act 1695, c. 23 (*a*).

(*a*) Jardine *v.* Douglas, 1793; M. 14,152; 2 Ill. 138.

1035. (4.) *By Commutation.* — Thirlage may be extinguished by commutation. In order to further the improvement of lands under thirlage, it has been enacted that it shall be competent to proprietors of lands thirled, or of mills holding this monopoly, to apply to the Sheriff to have the burden commuted into an annual payment. The parties immediately concerned must be cited, and all interested called edictally. The nature and extent of the right must be ascertained by a decree of declarator, which is subject to advocation. The commutation is then struck by a jury of heritors, or tenants of £30 of yearly rent, whose verdict is directed to be recorded in the Register of Sasines, converting the thirlage into a payment in grain or money. This verdict is made irreversible after having been recorded for three years. The payment comes in place of the thirlage, payable in grain or by fiars prices, as the person paying may choose; and landlords paying the commutation where the lands are let, are entitled to recover it from their tenants as rent. A set of similar provisions is enacted for the thirlage of *invecta et illata* in towns and villages (*a*).

(*a*) 39 Geo. III. c. 55. Orr *v.* Adam, 1822; 2 S. 16; 2 Ill. 139. Bakers of Dundee *v.* Mags. of Dundee, 1804; M. 16,076. Dss. Sutherland *v.* Reid's Trs., 1881; 8 R. 514. Forbes's Trs. *v.* Davidson, *cit.* § 1033 (commutation by voluntary agreement—construction—effect of discontinuance of mill).

1036. (5.) *Effect of Insufficiency of the Mill.*—Where the mill is insufficient for the work of the thirl, those who are under the servitude are not bound as of old to pay multure, but are entitled to carry for manufacture elsewhere what is necessary for their families, after giving notice, and waiting forty-eight hours without having their work done (*a*), and even to require what for other purposes may be necessary to be manufactured within a reasonable time, otherwise to be free to go elsewhere (*b*).

(*a*) Lockhart *v.* Vassals, 1736; Elch. *Mult.* 2; 2 Ill. 139. E. Wigton *v.* Town of Kirkintilloch, 1736; *ib.* 3. Landale *v.* Meldrum, 1745; M. 16,023. Forbes's Trs. *v.* Davidson, *cit.* § 1033.

(*b*) Clark's Tr. *v.* Hill, 1828; 6 S. 659.

CHAPTER XIV

OF LIFERENT

1037. Definition.—The Romans classed three several rights under Servitude:—Usus, or the right to such of the fruits of a subject as the *usuarius* or his family could consume; Habitation, the right to possess a house in one's own person or in the person of another; Usufruct, a right to use and enjoy a subject during life, without wasting its substance. This last corresponds with *Liferent* in the law of Scotland, which is more of the nature of limited property than of servitude. It is the right to use and enjoy a subject during life, without destroying the substance. The person entitled to such enjoyment for life is called the Liferenter; the person whose property is burdened with the liferent is called the Fiar; and the reversionary right of use and enjoyment, after the liferent has expired, is called the Fee (*a*).

(*a*) 2 Stair, 6. 2 Ersk. 9. § 39 et seq.

1038. Kinds of Liferent.—Liferent is either Legal or Conventional. Legal liferents are two in number, connected with the conjugal relation of marriage, viz. Terce and Courtesy, which will more fitly be considered hereafter in treating of Marriage (*a*).

(*a*) See § 1596 et seq., and § 1605 et seq.

1039. Conventional liferent is either reserved out of a grant or conveyance, or newly created by direct conveyance of a liferent right of use (*a*).

(*a*) For the constitution of liferent by deed of settlement, marriage-contract, etc., see § 1708 et seq., and § 1953 et seq.

1040. Liferent by Reservation.—This form of liferent is constituted by a conveyance of land or other heritable subject in fee, reserving to the granter the liferent use. This may be either by one who is infeft in the land, or by one who holds only a personal right. In the former case, the liferent reserved depends on the granter's sasine in fee, the new conveyance being truly a limitation or restriction of it from a fee to a liferent. In the latter case, the liferenter can have no real right without an infeftment in his own person. The liferenter by reservation 'had' by force of his original sasine a right to enter vassals; the liferenter by constitution 'had' no such power (*a*).

(*a*) 2 Craig, 22. § 5. 2 Stair, 6. § 11. 2 Ersk. 9. § 42. See § 1055 et seq.; 1048.

1041. Liferent by Constitution is created in a marriage-contract, settlement, or other conveyance, by disponing an estate to one in liferent, and another in fee; or to two or more in conjunct fee and liferent; or by an annuity of a certain sum payable out of the estate. The right of the liferenter is not (like a servitude) constituted without sasine. It requires a sasine in the liferenter to confer a real right effectual against singular successors (*a*).

(*a*) 2 Ersk. 9. § 41.

1042. Subjects of Liferent.—The proper subjects of liferent are such only as are not consumed by use. And so coal, stone, lime, minerals, etc., as accessories of land, are excluded, though they may be expressly given in liferent; and if let for rent, the rent may be carried by a general settlement (*a*). But liferenters of lands are to a certain extent, or in particular circumstances, allowed a limited use of things consumable; and this either expressly or by tacit assent and usage, as the lime, coal, etc., necessary for the liferenter's beneficial possession of the land (*b*).

'In liferents by constitution the extent of the liferenter's right depends on the granter's intention; and it has been held that, as it is in itself a partial estate, it may be terminated by a resolutive condition, which could not so affect a fee (*c*). When a proprietor creates a liferent, *eo nomine*, of a particular subject, the legal definition of liferent as applied to the circumstances determines the rights of liferenter and fiar *inter se*; and so, when *going* mines form part of the subject, it is because the proprietor treated the minerals as subjects bearing fruit, that the returns from the mines are presumed to pass with the other fruits of the subject to the liferenter (*d*). There is no such presumption as to the proceeds of *unopened* mineral fields or quarries, let or wrought, without the granter's express or implied direction, by trustees after the commencement of the trust (*e*). When a truster directs a mixed estate to be converted, and gives a liferent of the *universitas*, or directs the income of the residue, or of a proportion of the estate, to be paid to his widow or child, then the intention is held to be that the natural produce of the *capital* of the estate is to be paid to the liferenter, like the interest accruing on a sum of money (*f*). So, where a trust estate includes mineral leases held by the truster, and nothing irresistibly indicates the intention to give the income in its existing state of investment, a liferent of the free annual income of the residue does not include the whole profits realised from the leases, but only the interest on these profits regarded as part of the residue; or rather it implies a right to receive the income of the estate when put in a proper state of investment (*g*). On the other hand, trustees authorised to carry on a work or manufactory as part of a trust estate are entitled to deduct from the income before paying it to the liferenter what is actually required for the maintenance and renewal of buildings and plant, but not to set aside a sum for depreciation (*h*).'

(*a*) Swinton *v.* Dss. of Roxburghe, Feb. 1, 1814; F. C.; 2 Ill. 140. Belscheir *v.* Moffat, 1779; M. 15,863. Waddell *v.* Waddell, Jan. 21, 1812; F. C.

(*b*) 2 Ersk. 9. § 57. See Eiston *v.* Eiston, 1831; 9 S. 716. D. of Roxburghe *v.* Dss. of Roxburghe, Jan. 19, 1816; F. C.

(*c*) Chaplin's Trs. *v.* Hoile, 1890; 18 R. 27; 1891, 19 R. 237.

(*d*) Guild's Trs. *v.* Guild, 1872; 10 Macph. 911. Wardlaw *v.* Wardlaw's Trs., 1875; 2 R. 368; and cases in notes (*a*) and (*b*). Ferguson, *infra*.

(*e*) Campbell's Trs. *v.* Campbell, 1882; 9 R. 725; aff. 1883, 10 R. H. L. 651; 8 App. Ca. 641. Baillie's Trs. *v.* Baillie, 1891; 19 R. 220 (opened but not going). Nugent's Trs. *v.* Nugent, 1898; 25 R. 475 (liferent by reservation).

(*f*) Wood *v.* Menzies, 1871; 9 Macph. 775. Ferguson *v.* Ferguson's Trs., 1877; 4 R. 532. Freer's Trs. *v.* Freer, 1897; 24 R. 437 (terminable instalments under contract).

(*g*) Ferguson, *cit.*; which is explained by Lord M'Laren in Strain's Trs. *v.* Strain, 1893; 20 R. 1025; and compare § 721, 1598, 1772.

(*h*) Ellis *v.* Ellis's Trs., 1895; 22 R. 764.

1043. The Roman law admitted of a *quasi* or improper usufruct in fungibles, of which the liferenter was, on expiration of the usufruct, to deliver to the fiar as much of the same kind, and as good in quality, as he had received for use. To this we have nothing analogous but the liferent of money (*a*), or steel-bow in a lease, 'or the liferent of a stocked farm, under which the liferenter is bound to keep up the stock, substantially to the same extent, description, and value (*b*).' In the liferent of money, the fruits, *i.e.* the interest of the money, may be regarded as the liferenter's proper right; but it has been held that the liferenter of a sum is entitled to the actual use of the capital, on due security being given to the fiar, or on the money being reinvested, with due protection to the fiar (*c*); and the debtor in a sum so secured will pay at his own risk, if the fiar be not called (*d*).

Furniture, not being consumable by use, though liable to deterioration by tear and wear, may be liferented; and in marriage contracts, it is a frequent provision that the wife shall have the furniture in liferent. The rule of the Roman law of usufruct in fungibles will not apply here; the liferenter will not be bound to replace or renew the articles. Difficulties arise sometimes with creditors of the husband in regard to such liferents. In such cases, the real right is not complete without possession, and the wife is not held as in possession during the marriage, so that her claim is only personal, not real or preferable (*e*).

(*a*) 2 Ersk. 9. § 40.
(*b*) Rogers' Trs. *v.* Scott, 1867; 5 Macph. 1078. Comp. Groves *v.* Wright, 2 Kay & J. 347. Phillips *v.* Beale, 32 Beav. 25. Cockayne *v.* Harrison, 41 L. J. Ch. 509; L. R. 13 Eq. 432.
(*c*) Kinross *v.* Hunthill, 1661; M. 8262; 2 Ill. 141. Salton *v.* Crawford, 1697; 4 B. Sup. 377. Fleming *v.* Fleming, 1661; M. 8256. Jordan *v.* Harris, 1680; M. 8264. Malcolm *v.* Neilson, 1731; M. 8266.
(*d*) Wilkie *v.* Hamilton, 1692; 4 B. Sup. 2. Malcolm, *supra* (*c*).
(*e*) See below, § 1946. In a note to the case of Cochran *v.* Cochran (Culross case), 1775, M. 8280; 2 Ill. 141, the author says: "It would seem—1. That a liferent of furniture gives the full use of it everywhere, *salva substantia*. 2. That giving the liferent of the furniture of a house is only demonstrative, and the furniture may be carried thence. 3. That where, as in the Culross case, it is combined with a mansion-house, it is to be held only as an accessory to the possession of the house."

1044. Rights of Liferenter.—The liferenter has, during life, right to all the uses and services derivable from the land, but under the qualification that the substance of the property shall not be consumed (*a*). So he has rights to all fruits, natural and civil.

(*a*) See Rogers' Trs. *v.* Scott, 1867; 5 Macph. 1078. As to his powers of suing and being sued, and protecting the property, see Hardie *v.* Mags. of Port-Glasgow, 1864; 2 Macph. 746. Denovan *v.* Johnston, 1832; 10 S. 206. M'Christie *v.* Fisher, 1825; 4 S. 11 (removing).

1045. (1.) *Natural Fruits.*—All the natural or spontaneous, and all the industrial fruits, belong to the liferenter; the right to the spontaneous fruits 'not actually severed from the soil, as cut trees (*a*),' ceasing with his death; the right to the industrial crop in the ground at his death going to his executors without rent (*b*).

(*a*) Lang, § 1046 (*b*).
(*b*) 2 Ersk. 9. § 65. Guthrie *v.* L. Mackerston, 1671; M. 15,891; 2 Ill. 142. Cockburn *v.* Brown's Exrs., 1748; M. 15,911; Elch. *Liferenter*, 5. See M. of Tweeddale *v.* Somner, Nov. 19, 1816; F. C. (hay sown with white crop goes to heir; overruling Gordon *v.* Gordon, 1806; Hume, 188).

1046. A liferenter's right to cut growing timber depends on the kind of timber. The general rule is, that the liferenter has no right to cut timber, even though planted by himself (*a*). The exceptions are—(1) *silvæ cæduæ*, where the wood is laid out in portions (haggs) or lots for annual cutting, and regarded as part of the crop of the land (*b*). (2) A conjunct fiar, or a liferenter by reservation, is entitled to cut the timber which has come to maturity, though not laid out in haggs, but which according to local usage is cut at maturity (*c*). (3) To the extent of maintaining the houses, etc., in tenantable condition, liferenters are entitled to have wood of mature growth, notice being given to the fiar before cutting (*d*); even under a discretionary power to cut what shall not be injurious to the estate, the fiar is entitled to notice (*e*). (4) The liferenter is entitled to windfalls and underwood (*f*).

(*a*) 2 Stair, 3. § 74. 2 Ersk. 9. § 58. Mousewell's Crs. *v.* Children, 1683; M. 8253; 4 B. Sup. 138; 2 Ill. 142. Gray *v.* Seton, 1789; M. 8250; Hailes, 1067. See below, § 1058 and 1070.
(*b*) Stair, *supra* (*a*). Lang *v.* D. Douglas, 1752; Elch. Notes, *Liferent*, 6. See Mousewell, *supra* (*a*). Dss. Hamilton *v.* D. Hamilton, 1722; Robertson's Ap. 443. M'Alister's Trs. *v.* M'Alister, 1851; 13 D. 1239. Dashwood *v.* Magniac, 1891; 3 Ch. 306.
(*c*) Ferguson *v.* Ferguson, 1737; M. 8254; Elch. *Liferent*, 1. A liferenter by constitution is entitled to cut coppicewood which is in use to be cut at intervals of years, if he is in possession when the usual period arrives, but not to anticipate the period. M'Alister, *cit.*
(*d*) Stanfield *v.* Wilson, 1680; M. 8244. E. Dunfermline *v.* E. Callander, 1683; M. 8244. Dickson, *infra* (*f*). M'Alister, *cit.*
(*e*) Dingwall *v.* Duff, 1833, 1834; 12 S. 216 and 541. See below as to Heirs of Entail, § 1754.
(*f*) Dickson *v.* Dickson, 1823; 2 S. 154. He is not entitled to sell trees blown down by an extraordinary storm. M'Alister, *supra*. As to what are windfalls, see Swinburne *v.* Ainslie, 30 Ch. D. 485.

1047. (2.) *Civil Fruits* (*a*).—The right of the liferenter of land to the civil fruits of the land, the rents, whether of corn, or grass farms (*b*), or houses (*c*), or mills (*d*), is regulated by the legal terms of payment; so that if he survive the term of Whitsunday, his executors have right 'at common law' to the first half of the year's rent; if he survive the term of Martinmas, to the whole year's rent from the Whitsunday preceding to the Whitsunday following. And it is sufficient, in either of those cases, that he live until the morning of the term day (*e*). This rule, according to the legal terms, is not subject to alteration by any conventional *postponement* (*f*); but conventional *anticipation* (*f*) of the term of payment will vest the right at the stipulated term (*g*).

'*Apportionment Acts.*—In 1834 these rules of the common law were modified by the first Apportionment Act referred to in Professor Bell's note, which was held in 1844 to extend to Scotland, although its phraseology is entirely that of the law of England (*h*). This Act altered the rule of the common law, and made rents reserved or rent charges granted apportionable between heir and executor, the latter having right to the rent due up to the day of the predecessor's death. But it applied only to the executors of persons having limited or determinable interests, *i.e.* liferenters, heirs of entail, etc., not fee-simple proprietors, and to payments due under a written instrument executed, or if testamentary, coming into operation since the date of the Act (*i*). The rule of the common law stated in the text appears to be entirely altered by the Apportionment Act, 1870, by which all rents, annuities, dividends, and other periodical payments in the nature of income, whether reserved or made payable under an instrument in writing or otherwise, are, like interest on money lent, considered as accruing from day to day, and are apportionable in respect of time accordingly (*k*). The apportioned part is payable or recoverable at the date when the entire portion of which it is part becomes due and payable, or in the case of a rent, annuity, or other such payment determined by death, re-entry, or otherwise, when the next entire portion would have been payable if not so determined (*l*). The persons entitled to such apportioned parts have the same remedies for recovering the same when payable (allowing proportionate parts of all just allowances) as they would have had for the entire portions if entitled thereto; but these remedies are to be directed, not against the person primarily liable to pay the entire portion of rent reserved out of or charged on lands or heritage, but against the heir or other person who, but for the apportionment, would be entitled to the entire or continuing rent, he being still alone entitled to receive the entire or continuing rent in the first instance (*m*). Annual sums made payable in policies of insurance are not apportionable (*n*); nor sums as to which it is expressly stipulated that no apportionment shall take place (*o*). Under the interpretation clause the word "dividend" does not apply to profits in a private trading partnership (*p*). The Act applies to all instruments, even if dated or coming into operation before its passing (*q*).'

(*a*) Kames' Elucid, art. 9. 2 Ersk. 9. § 64.

(*b*) Carnegie *v.* Carnegie's Exrs., 1668; M. 15,887; 2 Ill. 143. Trotter *v.* Rochead, 1681; M. 15,899. Johnston *v.* M. Annandale, 1727; M. 15,913. Pringle *v.* Pringle, 1741; M. 15,907; Elch. *Heir and Executor*, 1. Campbell *v.* Campbell, 1745; M. 15,908; Elch. *Heir and Executor*, 3. Kerr *v.* Turnbull, 1760; 5 B. Sup. 876. M. of Queensberry *v.* Montgomerie, Feb. 18, 1814; F. C. Elliot's Trs. *v.* Elliot, 1792; M. 15,917. Swinton *v.* Gawler, June 20, 1809; F. C. Innes *v.* D. Gordon, 1822; 2 S. 3. Trotter *v.* Cunningham, 1837, 2 D. 140. Blaikie *v.* Farquharson, 1849; 11 D. 1456. Campbell *v.* Campbell, 1849; 11 D. 1426.

(*c*) Binny *v.* Binny, Jan. 28, 1820; F. C. King *v.* Jaffray, 1828; 6 S. 420.

(*d*) Guthrie *v.* L. Mackerston, 1671; M. 15,891.

(*e*) Brunton *v.* ——, 1642; M. 15,885. Paterson *v.* Smith, 1704; M. 15,902. Tolquhoun's Exrs. *v.* Credrs., 1740; M. 15,607; Elch. *Liferenter*, 2.

(*f*) Campbell *v.* Campbell, M. Queensberry *v.* Montgomerie, Swinton *v.* Gawler, etc., *citt.* (*b*). Petley *v.* Mackenzie, 1805; Hume, 186. Lockhart *v.* Lockhart, 1839; 1 D. 443. Kynynmond, *infra*, § 1049 (*a*). L. Herries *v.* Maxwell's Cur., 1873; 11 Macph. 396. Campbell *v.* Campbell, 1849; 11 D. 1426.

(*g*) There is an English statute of 4 and 5 Will. IV. c. 22, the second section of which deserves attention. See below, as to this statute. It does not alter the rule as to the executor's rights to forehand or postponed rents here laid down; but gives him a proportion of the forehand rent growing due in the term in which the ancestor died. L. Herries, *cit.*

(*h*) **Brydges** *v.* **Fordyce**, 1844; 6 D. 968; aff. 6 Bell, 1; 1 H. L. Ca. 1; and see as to its interpretation, Campbell *v.* Campbell, 1849; 11 D. 1426. Blaikie *v.* Farquharson, 1849; 11 D. 1456. Baillie *v.* Lockhart, 1855; 2 Macq. 258. Paul (Hard) *v.* Anstruther, 1862; 1 Macph. 14; aff. 1864, 2 Macph. H. L. 1. Duff's Trs. *v.* Shand's Trs., 1864; 2 Macph. 1342. L. Adv. *v.* Stevenson, 1866; 4 Macph. 322. E. Dalhousie *v.* Crokat, 1868; 6 Macph. 659. Bannatine's Trs. *v.* Cunningham, 1872; 10 Macph. 319. Riddell's Trs. *v.* Riddell, 1857; 21 D. 800.

(*i*) Cases cited, and Brown *v.* Amyot, 3 Hare, 173; 13 L. J. Ch. 232. Knight *v.* Boughton, 12 Beav. 312; 19 L. J. Ch. 16. Wardroper *v.* Cutfield, 33 L. J. Ch. 605. Plummer *v.* Whitley, Johns. 585. Lock *v.* de Burgh, 20 L. J. Ch. 384. 1 M'Laren on Wills and Succ. 210 sqq.

(*k*) 33 and 34 Vict c. 35, § 2.

(*l*) *Ib.* § 3.

(*m*) *Ib.* § 4. Hasluck *v.* Pedley, L. R. 19 Eq. 371; 44 L. J. Ch. 143.

(*n*) *Ib.* § 6.

(*o*) *Ib.* § 7. Cunningham's Trs. *v.* Duke, 1873; 11 Macph. 543 (annuity). Maxwell's Trs. *v.* Scott, 1873; 1 R. 122 (assignation of rent on sale of land). As the Act is intended to remedy the common law, and to apply to cases not regulated by express stipulation, it does not affect the minister's ann, which is ruled by the Act 1672, c. 13. Latta *v.* Edin. Eccl. Comrs., 1877; 5. R. 266.

(*p*) *Ib.* § 5. Jones *v.* Ogle, L. R. 8 Ch. 192; 42 L. J. Ch. 334. See *In re* Griffith (Carr *v.* Griffith), 12 Ch. D. 655. See also as to dividends, Cameron's Factor *v.* Cameron, 1873; 1 R. 21. Pollock *v.* Pollock, L. R. 18 Eq. 329; 44 L. J. Ch. 168.

(*q*) Capron *v.* Capron, L. R. 17 Eq. 288; 43 L. J. Ch. 677. Hasluck *v.* Pedley (*m*). *In re* Cline, L. R. 18 Eq. 213. Constable *v.* Constable, 11 Ch. D. 681; 48 L. J. Ch. 621. See further the following cases under this Act, Learmonth *v.* Sinclair's Trs., 1878; 5 R. 548. Straker *v.* Wilson, L. R. 6 Ch. 503; 40 L. J. Ch. 630. Clive *v.* Clive, L. R. 7 Ch. 433; 41 L. J. Ch. 386. Swansea Bank *v.* Thomas, 4 Ex. D. 94; 48 L. J. Ex. 344. *In re* Wearmouth Crown Glass Co., 19 Ch. D. 640.

1048. A liferenter infeft in the liferent of a superiority has a right to the feu-duties, as the ordinary fruits or profits of the land; but he has no right to the casualties, unless the liferent be by reservation, in which case he 'had' power to enter heirs or singular successors (*a*).

(*a*) 2 Ersk. 9. § 42. 20 Geo. II. c. 50. See above, § 1040; and below, § 1055. Ewing *v.* Ewing, 1872; 10 Macph. 678. As to terce, see below, § 1598.

1049. A liferent interest in a heritable bond, or an annuity secured on land, if payment be stipulated termly at Whitsunday and Martinmas, or Candlemas and Lammas, falls 'at common law' under the rule above laid down (*a*); but if stipulated to be paid termly and continually during all the days of the liferenter's or creditor's life, he will have the fractional payments corresponding to the survivance (*b*).

(*a*) See § 1047. 2 Ersk. 9. § 66. Murray Kynynmond *v.* Cathcart, 1739; M. 15,906; 2 Ill. 234. Henderson *v.* Murray, 1624; M. 15,878; 2 Ill. 145. Lindsay *v.* Heriot, 1630; M. 15,881. Colebrooke *v.* Gibson-Craig, 1835; 13 S. 756.

(*b*) E. of Dalhousie *v.* Gilmour, 1787; M. 15,915; 2 Ill. 232. See below, § 1498. See last section; Cunningham's Trs. *v.* Duke, *cit.* § 1047 (*o*).

1050. The liferenter has the dividends or interest of bank stock. But 'it has been held in certain cases that' he has no right to the bonus on accumulations,—only to the interest of it. The difficulty here rests on the consideration that the bonus in such cases arises from a stoppage and accumulation of dividends, retained by order of the bank directors, and so is truly an extra dividend. But, 'where the company has no power to increase its capital, and has used accumulated profits as "floating" capital and afterwards distributed them among shareholders,' it has been held rather as an additional capital, and the liferenter entitled only to the interest on it (*a*). 'When, however, a company has power either to divide or to capitalise its profits, and validly exercises that power, the liferenter's and fiar's rights are regulated by such exercise of the power; and, according to the real nature of the transaction, what is paid as dividend goes to the liferenter, and what is paid by the company to its shareholders as capital, or appropriated as an increase of its capital stock, enures to the benefit of all who are interested in the capital, and so to the fiar and liferenter according to their respective rights (*b*).'

(*a*) Rollo *v.* Irving, 1801; M. 8282; rev. (*nom.* Irving *v.* Houston) 4 Paton, 521; 1 Ill. 425, commented on in Bouch *v.* Sproule, 12 App. Ca. 385. Cuming *v.* Cuming's Trs., 1824; 2 S. 620. Thomson *v.* Lyell, 1836; 15 S. 32 (liferenter's right to dividend declared before, but payable after his death). Brander *v.* Brander, 4 Vesey, 800. See below, § 1344.

(*b*) Bouch *v.* Sproule, 12 App. Ca. 385; revg. 29 Ch. App. 635. Armitage *v.* Garnett, 1893; 3 Ch. 337.

1051. As a liferenter has no right to those things of which the substance is consumed by use, so he is not entitled to draw the rents of subjects which he would not be allowed to take into his natural possession; *ex gr.* the rent of coal; for such rents are truly the price of the substance (*a*).

(*a*) D. Roxburghe *v.* Dss. Roxburghe, Feb. 11, 1814; F. C.; 2 Ill. 145. See Waddell *v.* Waddell, Jan. 21, 1812; F. C. See above, § 1042.

1052. (3.) *Meliorations.*—Liferent expands with the extension of the subject;—as the liferent of land on which houses come to be built (*a*); or of which the value or rents are improved by the opening of a road, bridge, canal, railway, or other communication. But if the liferenter's right be enlarged by means of meliorations *bonâ fide* made by the fiar, he must, in taking benefit by the melioration, pay the interest of such expenditure (*b*). 'A liferenter's improvements are presumed to be made for the purpose of enhancing his own benefit and enjoyment of the estate, and so give no claim of recompense (*c*).'

(*a*) Mitchell's Crs. *v.* Warden, 1742; M. 8275; Elch. *Liferenter*, 3; 2 Ill. 145.

(*b*) Laird *v.* Fenwick, 1807; M. *Liferenter*, Apx. 3. See 2 Ill. 145, and Hacket *v.* Watt, 1672; M. 13,412. On the subject of this section, see 1 M'Laren, Wills and Succ. 410, 411; 2 *ib.* 285; 2 Fraser, H. & W. 1426.

(*c*) *Supra*, § 538. Morrisons *v.* Allan, 1886; 13 R. 1156 (liferenter believing that he had a larger right).

1053. (4.) *Voting.*—The liferenter of an estate, or even of a superiority, whether by reservation or new constitution, was formerly entitled to vote for a member of Parliament; provided the lands which he held in liferent were of a sufficient extent, and held of the Crown. The fiar exercised the right in the liferenter's absence (*a*). Under the existing law, a liferenter so entitled formerly to a vote is still entitled to a vote (*b*); and where a liferenter and fiar have right to any subject to which a right of voting is now annexed, the right of voting is in the liferenter, not in the fiar (*c*).

(*a*) 1681, c. 21. Wight on Elections, 238. Bell on Elections, 91.

(*b*) 2 and 3 Will. IV. c. 65, § 7.

(*c*) *Ib.* § 8. 6 Will. IV. c. 78, § 10. 31 and 32 Vict. c. 48, § 14.

1054. Powers of the Liferenter.—These correspond with the rights already stated.

1055. (1.) *Entry of Vassals and Custody of Titles.*—A liferenter by reservation 'had' power, in virtue of his original infeftment, to enter heirs and singular successors. At one time it was conceded that he might so enter *heirs*, for the fiar himself being compellable to enter an heir, suffered nothing by the liferenter doing so. But the liferenter could not enter a *singular successor* without an encroachment on the fee, the fiar not being bound to enter a stranger. As heirs and singular successors now stand on the same footing, a liferenter by reservation 'might' enter either an heir or a singular successor; and as an accompanying right, he is entitled to the composition (*a*). A liferenter by constitution has no right to enter heirs or singular successors (*b*). Neither 'had' a proprietor who, being himself uninfeft, dispones the land, reserving his own liferent, any right to enter heirs or singular successors. He never had a feudal right, and so cannot give a feudal title. A liferenter by reservation is entitled to the custody of the title-deeds (*c*).

(*a*) 2 Craig, 22. § 5. 2 Ersk. 9. § 42. Clark *v.* Wemyss, 1596; M. 8251; 2 Ill. 146. Crawfordjohn *v.* Glaspen, 1611; M. 8352.

(*b*) Henderson *v.* M'Kenzie, 1836; 14 S. 540. Unless such power is expressly conferred in the constitution of his right. Gibson-Craig *v.* Cochrane, 1838; 16 S. 1332; aff. 2 Rob. 446.

(*c*) Wallace *v.* Deas, 1831; 10 S. 164.

1056. (2.) *Granting of Feu Rights.*—Although a liferenter by reservation may enter vassals, he is not entitled to grant a feu effectual beyond the liferent; and even although the fiar consent to the feu, if he be not infeft in the fee at the time, the feu will not be effectual beyond the liferent, unless in so far as the fiar or his heirs are barred *personali exceptione* (*a*).

(*a*) Redfearn *v.* Maxwell, March 7, 1816; F. C.; 2 Ill. 146.

1057. (3.) *Granting of Leases.*—A liferenter has no power to grant a lease, the term of which shall last beyond his own life (*a*). Sometimes, however, power is reserved, or conferred, in constituting the liferent, to grant leases for a definite term; and sometimes the liferenter and the fiar concur in granting a lease of certain duration beneficial for both.

(*a*) 2 Ersk. 9. § 57; and 6. § 21. Fraser *v.* Middleton, 1794; M. 8256 and 7849; 2 Ill. 146. Fraser *v.* Croft, 1898; 25 R. 496. See below, § 1183.

1058. (4.) *Sale of Trees.*—The liferenter, as he is not in general entitled to cut timber, so he cannot sell trees; and although coppice-wood and woods laid out in haggs may be sold as well as cut, the liferenter's right ceases with his life, and so also does the right of the purchaser, the fiar being entitled to stop the cutting (*a*).

(*a*) 2 Stair, 3. § 74. 2 Ersk. 9. § 58. See above, § 1046, and cases there.

1059. (5.) *Patronage.*—In the reservation or constitution of a liferent, the exercise of the right of patronage 'might' be vested in the liferenter (*a*).

(*a*) Lady Forbes *v.* L. Forbes, 1760; M. 9932; rev. 2 Paton, 36; 2 Ill. 147. D. of Roxburghe *v.* Dss. of Roxburghe, June 25, 1818; F. C. More's Notes on Stair, p. ccxiii. See above, § 836.

1060. Liabilities of Liferenter.—He is not liable for the debts of the disponer if the fee be sufficient to discharge them; for the fiar is the proper representative and debtor (*a*).

(*a*) Stewart *v.* Stewart, 1792; Bell's Ca. 220; 2 Ill. 140. Nixon *v.* Borthwick, 1806; M. *Liferenter*, Apx. 2. See Forbes *v.* Forbes, 1763; 2 Pat. 84. 3 Ersk. 9. § 61, note. Waddell *v.* Waddell, 1818; 6 Dow, 279; 6 Pat. 374.

1061. (1.) *Taxes, Feu-Duties, etc.* — The right of the liferenter, 'unless exempted by the terms of the grant (*a*),' is subject to the burden of the public taxes, feu-duties, minister's stipend, etc., during the liferent (*b*). But those which are only occasional, and are by law laid upon heritors, are not burdens on the liferenter 'by constitution'; as the building of kirks and manses (*c*), and also the repairing of them (*d*).

(*a*) Clark *v.* Clark, 1871; 9 Macph. 435. Rodger's Trs. *v.* Rodger, 1875; 2 R. 294. Kinloch's Trs. *v.* Kinloch, 1880; 7 R. 596.

(*b*) 2 Ersk. 9. § 61. Stamford *v.* Tenants, 1636; M. 13,070; 2 Ill. 148. L. Elshiesheils *v.* Lady Elshiesheils, 1688; M. 13,070. Lumsden *v.* Robertson, 1704; M. 13,072.

(*c*) 1663, c. 21. 2 Ersk. 10. § 57. Minister of Morcham *v.* Binston, 1679; M. 8499. See below, § 1164, 1171.

(*d*) Ersk. *ut supra*. Lady Anstruther *v.* Anstruther, May 14, 1823; 2 S. 306; and F. C. See 2 Stair, 6. § 19.

1062. (2.) *Repairs, etc.*—A liferenter must keep up the liferented tenement by necessary and proper repairs (*a*). He may be called on by the fiar to make such ordinary repairs as are necessary to preserve the tenement in a habitable and tenantable condition (*b*). And if the fiar shall repair the tenement, the liferenter must pay the interest of the expenditure on necessary repairs (*c*).

(*a*) 2 Ersk. 9. § 60. See Borthwick *v.* Borthwick, 1696; M. 8245; 2 Ill. 148. Cunningham *v.* Cunningham, 1733; M. 8275. Scott *v.* Haliburton, 1823; 2 S. 435. See above, § 1046 (*d*). The liferenter of a stocked farm is bound to keep up the stock, and leave it substantially of the same kind and value as when he received it. Rogers' Trs. *v.* Scott, 1867; 5 Macph. 1078.

(*b*) Scott, *supra* (*a*).

(*c*) Ersk. *ubi cit.* Laird *v.* Fenwick, 1807; M. *Liferenter*, Apx. 4; 2 Ill. 145. See below, § 1063.

1063. The natural and irreparable decay of a subject liferented, or its accidental destruction by fire or other calamity, will affect the right of the liferenter and of the fiar according to the following rules: Neither the liferenter nor the fiar will be bound to rebuild. If the fiar do rebuild or repair the subject, the liferenter must, in order to enjoy the subject, pay proportionally to his interest in its restoration. The liferenter may continue to draw the rent of the subject, such as it remains, without repairing the damage. If the liferenter repair the subject, he will have right to indemnification from the fiar taking the benefit of it, to the extent of the *lucrum* accruing to him, or the fee will be burdened with the principal sum expended, but not with the interest during the liferent. If the area of a house burnt or destroyed should be sold, the liferenter will be entitled to the interest of the price, the fiar to the reversion (*a*).

(*a*) 2 Ersk. 9. § 60. Scott *v.* Forbes, 1755; M. 8278; 2 Ill. 148. Halliday *v.* Gardine, 1706; M. 13,419. See above, § 1062. See also § 538, 1253. Nelson *v.* Gordon, 1874; 1 R. 1097.

1064. The liferenter in certain circumstances must find caution (*cautio usufructuaria*) to maintain the buildings, woods, etc., without waste. The old laws on this subject were directed chiefly to the prevention of waste, while lands were in ward; and in modern times such caution will not be required, unless where there is shown some reasonable cause to fear waste or neglect on the part of the liferenter (*a*).

(*a*) 1491, c. 25; 2 Act Parl. 324, § 6. 1535, c. 15; *ib.* 344, § 14. 2 Ersk. 9. § 59. 1594, c. 226. Ralston *v.* Leitch, 1803; Hume, 293. Scott, *cit.* Bell *v.* Bell, 1827; 6 S. 221.

1065. (3.) *Aliment of Fiar.*—The liferenter of lands is, 'or was, according to ancient decisions,' bound to aliment the fiar as heir of investiture, when he has no other means of subsistence (*a*); but the burden has been held personal to the liferenter, and not effectual against his creditors (*b*). There is no claim to aliment where the fiar has renounced the succession, and takes the estate by a singular title (*c*), or after he has sold the land (*d*). This aliment is not due from an annuitant on the estate (*e*), nor from the liferenter of a sum of money (*f*); 'and the whole doctrine has been discredited by Sir Geo. Mackenzie and by opinions in the House of Lords (*g*).'

(*a*) 2 Ersk. 9. § 62–3. 1491, c. 25. More's Notes on Stair, 216.

(*b*) Blair *v.* Scott, 1737; Elch. *Aliment*, 5. In 2 Ill. 149 the author mentions that this judgment was on the ground that this aliment was not founded on the statute 1491, but introduced by custom, *ad exemplum* of a ward superior and vassals. And he adds in a note: "Mr. Erskine puts the case on another footing (ii. 9. § 63), viz., 'That the heir would have had no claim of alimony from his own creditors, if the estate had been carried off by them after the liferenter's death, and ought to be still less entitled to it from the creditors of the liferenter.' This reasoning is not conclusive; for if the liferent be affected by this burden, the creditors of the liferenter can take it only under the burden."

(*c*) Lyon *v.* Gray, 1712; M. 383. Blair, *supra* (*b*).

(*d*) Sandilands *v.* Sandilands, 1700; M. 385.

(*e*) Stewart *v.* Campbell, 1780; M. 398; 5 B. Sup. 377; Hailes, 861.

(*f*) Mirrie *v.* Pollock, 1731; M. 397.

(*g*) Mackenzie, Obs. 101. Maule *v.* Maule, 1825; 1 W. & S. 266.

1066. Extinction of Liferent.—Liferent is extinguished (1) by the death of the liferenter; (2) by renunciation of the liferent, even without recording; the liferent being a burden of which, by renunciation, the fee is relieved (*a*).

(*a*) 2 Ersk. 9. § 68. 1 Bank. 668. § 33. See also next section. See as to discharge of liferents, Pretty *v.* Newbigging, 1854; 16 D. 667. Foulis *v.* Foulis, 1857; 19 D. 362; M'Laren on Wills and Succ. ii. 435; as to consolidation of fee and liferent, Martin *v.* Bannatyne, 1861; 23 D. 705.

1067. Joint Liferent.—Where two or more have conferred upon them a liferent right, and a question arises as to the way in which the right is to be enjoyed, it is held that the exercise of the right is to be regulated on the principles which rule the administration of common property (*a*). The expiration of the right, in whole or in part, by the death of one or more of the joint liferenters, may raise a question of some nicety. So, if a subject be given to A. and B. in liferent, without any indication of survivance, the subject (if in contemplation of parties a divisible one) will divide, and part fall to the fiar, while the liferent subsists as to the others; if the subject be indivisible, or such as would suffer by division, the fiar would seem to have right to the *pro indiviso* possession, while the surviving liferenter would retain his liferent. If the joint liferent arise by operation of law (as by the succession of heirs portioners), the same rule has been applied, though that decision has been objected to (*b*).

(*a*) See below, § 1072.
(*b*) M. Tweeddale *v.* Dods, June 14, 1821; 1 Sandford on Succession, 28; and note in 2 Ill. 150. See below, § 1219, and 1882. Tulloch *v.* Welsh, 1838; 1 D. 94. Barber *v.* Turner, 1835; 13 S. 422. Tennant *v.* Morris, 1856; 18 D. 382; aff. 1858, 20 D. H. L. 7; 30 Jur. 493. Fergus *v.* Conroy, 1872; 10 Macph. 968.

1068. Rights of Fiar.—The fiar's right to the use and possession of the land is under burden of the liferenter's right.

1069. The fiar therefore cannot interfere with the liferenter's possession, unless for the necessary preservation of his own right: as to prevent waste on cause shown (*a*).

(*a*) See above, § 1063.

1070. He may work coal, lime, minerals, etc., which are excepted from the liferent; but he must leave enough for the liferenter's use, and he is liable for surface damage. He must not hurt the amenity of the liferenter's possession; yet if there be a going coal, however disagreeable the effects may be, the liferenter is not entitled to stop it. The fiar may not cut the ornamental timber, though he may make the necessary thinnings, not hurting the amenity (*a*).

(*a*) Dss. Hamilton *v.* D. Hamilton, 1723; Robertson's Ap. 443; 2 Ill. 150. D. Roxburghe *v.* Dss. Roxburghe, Jan. 19, 1816; F. C.; 2 Ill. 140. Dickson *v.* Dickson, 1823; 2 S. 153. Tait *v.* Maitland, 1825; 4 S. 253.

CHAPTER XV

OF COMMON PROPERTY, COMMON INTEREST, COMMONTY, RUNRIDGE LANDS, COMMON RIGHT IN WATER AND IN FISHING

1071. General Nature of Rights in Common.—Although undivided right and possession of land is the best arrangement both for the public and for the individual, there being in that situation no opposition or interruption to the free use and enjoyment of property; yet it frequently happens that land is held in common, either by design and by joint purchase, or by accident in the course of succession, or by the settlement of a former proprietor, or by the concurrence of separate rights in one subject of common use.

Of rights thus in common, three kinds may be distinguished:—1. Common Property, in which the several parties have, *pro indiviso*, the same equal but undivided right, each being entitled to the joint use and enjoyment of the subject, and mutual consent being necessary in all acts of management or disposal; 2. Common Interest, in which there is a mixture of property in one, restrained or qualified by an interest in another for the maintenance and preservation of the subject; and 3. Commonty, in which a right, not of common property, but only of common use, is conferred on several persons by the proprietor of the subject. These distinctions are not sufficiently marked by our institutional writers, but they are very important.

I. COMMON PROPERTY.

1072. Description.—Common property is a right of ownership vested *pro indiviso* in two or more persons, all being equally entitled to enjoy the uses and services derivable from the subject, and the consent of all being requisite in the management, alteration, or disposal of the subject. This common and undivided right is continued either by necessity, if a subject belonging to several be indivisible, or voluntarily, if the subject be divisible, until it shall be divided.

1073. Although the whole subject cannot be disposed of otherwise than by mutual consent, each joint owner may sell his own *pro indiviso* right, the purchaser coming into his place. The right may also be 'disponed in security (*a*), and' adjudged to the same effect.

(*a*) Schaw *v.* Black, 1889; 16 R. 336.

1074. Management.—In relation to a common subject, difficulties may arise in the course of administration, or respecting operations on the subject. The following rules seem to be established:—

1075. (1.) *In re communi melior est conditio prohibentis* (*a*).—So one co-proprietor may prevent another from removing tenants, unless better rents or better security shall be offered (*b*); 'or from sequestrating tenants for rent (*c*); and the principle is extended so as to entitle third parties (neighbours or tenants) to object to acts in which all the co-owners do not concur (*d*).' He may prevent any extraordinary use of the subject that may be attempted without his consent; as the letting of a lease with privilege of shooting (*e*). He may also prevent any operations on the common subject by which its condition is to be altered; as, in a common stair or passage, he whose property lies next adjoining, is not, without the consent of the rest, entitled to break the wall, and strike out a door (*f*). In this respect the different effects of Common Property and Common Interest are to be marked, and it is necessary to discriminate carefully whether the right be of the one class or of the other (*g*).

The exception to this rule is, that necessary operations in rebuilding, repairing, etc., are not to be stopped by the opposition of any of the joint owners.

(*a*) Dig. 10. 3. § 28 (*communi div.*); 8. 2. 27, § 1 (*de serv. pr. rust.*); 8. 5. 11 (*si serv. vind.*).

(*b*) Bruce *v.* Hunter, Nov. 16, 1808; F. C.; 2 Ill. 150. Murdoch *v.* Inglis, 1679; 3 B. Sup. 297. Grozier *v.* Downie, 1871; 9 Macph. 826.

(*c*) Stewart & Gibb *v.* Waud, 1842; 4 D. 622.

(*d*) Miller *v.* Cathcart, 1861; 23 D. 743 (declarator of marches). See, as to the right of each of several co-owners to prevent encroachments or injury to the property and maintain claims of damages, Lade *v.* Largs Baking Co., 1863; 2 Macph. 17. Johnston *v.* Craufurd, 1855; 17 D. 1023. Laird *v.* Reid, 1871; 9 Macph. 699. Schaw *v.* Black, *cit.* § 1073. 1 Mackay's Practice of Ct. of Sess. 288.

(*e*) Campbell & Stewart *v.* Campbell, Jan. 24, 1809; F. C. Wilson *v.* Buchanan, 1860; Hume, 120.

(*f*) A. *v.* B., 1680; M. 2448. Halliday *v.* Bruce, 1681; M. 2449. Anderson *v.* Dalrymple, 1799; M. 12,831. Reid *v.* Nicol, 1799; M. *Property*, Apx. 1. Sandy *v.* Innes, 1823; 2 S. 195; 2 Ill. 152. Anderson *v.* Saunders, 1831; 9 S. 564. Alexander *v.* Couper, 1840; 3 D. 249. Gellatly *v.* Arrol, 1863; 1 Macph. 592. Dow & Gordon *v.* Harvey, 1869; 8 Macph. 118. Taylor *v.* Dunlop, 1872; 11 Macph. 25.

(*g*) Ritchie *v.* Purdie, 1833; 11 S. 771. See below, § 1086.

1076. Where anything is built or planted on the common subject, it accresces to the common right (*a*).

(*a*) See above, § 937. See Leck *v.* Chalmers, 1859; 21 D. 408.

1077. Where parties cannot agree, either the will of the majority rules, or the ordinary state must be continued.

1078. Where a wall is common between conterminous proprietors, the expense of erection or of necessary repairs is common, in the proportions of the value of the share which each has in the subject. But operations on a common wall which are not necessary are to be done only by common consent (*a*). A division wall in urban subjects has been held common, though built by one of the proprietors 'partly on his own and partly on his neighbour's land (*b*). The right of adjoining feuars in a mutual gable is often regulated by their titles; but at common law a proprietor of ground which, by its situation in a town or village, by a feuing plan, or by other circumstances, is dedicated to building purposes, is entitled to build half the thickness of his gable wall beyond his own boundary; and when this "common" or "mutual gable" is afterwards used by the adjacent feuar, there emerges to the builder a real and preferable right, arising from the nature of the subject, and founded on the doctrine of recompense, to recover from his neighbour half of the expense of building it. This payment is exigible, if there be no special provision in the titles (*c*), and if not in fact previously paid by the superior (*d*), only when the gable is so used; and the right transmits against singular successors without special mention in the conveyance (*e*).'

(*a*) Warren *v.* Marwick, 1835; 13 S. 944. Graham *v.* Greig, 1838; 1 D. 171. Begg *v.* Jack. 1874; 1 R. 366. Dow & Gordon *v.* Harvey, 1869; 8 Macph. 118. See below, note (*e*) *fin.*

(*b*) Wallace *v.* Brown, 1808; M. Apx. *Pers. & Real*, 4; 2 Ill. 152. Ness *v.* Ferries, 1825; 4 S. 7. M'Kenzie *v.* M'Kenzie, 1829; 8 S. 74. Thorburn *v.* Pringle, 1832; 10 S. 822. Skinner *v.* Bell, 1833; 11 S. 353.

(*c*) Sinclair *v.* Brown Bros., 1882; 10 R. 45.

(*d*) Robertson *v.* Scott, 1886; 13 R. 1127.

(*e*) Wallace and cases *supra* (*b*). **Hunter** *v.* **Luke**, 1846; 8 D. 787. **Law** *v.* **Monteith**, 1855; 18 D. 125. See E. Moray *v.* Aytoun, 1858; 21 D. 33. Walker *v.* Shearer, 1870; 8 Macph. 494 (customary right in Aberdeen to "take band"). Guthrie *v.* Young, 1871; 9 Macph. 544. Sanderson *v.* Geddes, 1874; 1 R. 1198. Jack *v.* Begg, 1875; 3 R. 35. Glasg. Royal Infy. *v.* Wyllie, 1877; 4 R. 894 (gable built by common author). Berkeley *v.* Baird, 1895; 22 R. 372 (do.). The feuar using a gable already built, may insert fireplaces and vents, and heighten it, if he inflict no injury on the adjoining property. Lamont *v.* Cumming, 1875; 2 R. 784. Rodger *v.* Russell, 1873; 11 Macph. 671. See Rankine on Landownership, ch. xxxii.

1079. (2.) *Division.*—Where property in land or houses is held in common, and a division is possible, it is a rule that no one is bound to remain in community, but may insist for a division. To this, however, there is an exception in the special case of Conjunct

Rights to husband and wife, where the common right is, by its very constitution and the connection of the parties, indivisible (*a*). 'It is said to be a general rule, applying to joint estates other than land, as, *e.g.*, under trusts, that they may be divided when they cannot be specifically enjoyed by the joint owners (*b*).'

(*a*) See Milligan *v.* Barnhill, 1782; M. 2486; Hailes, 897. See Brock *v.* Hamilton, 1852; repd. 19 D. 701, note; below, § 1082.

(*b*) Bruce's Trs. *v.* Bruce's Tr., 1894; 21 R. 593 (joint estate in husband and wife living separately).

1080. If the parties cannot agree, the subject must be divided, where that is possible. Of old, co-adjudgers were entitled to have the property adjudged by them divided by brieve of division; but this clumsy expedient has, in the progress of improvement, been superseded by the process of judicial sale.

1081. Joint proprietors may 'still competently (*a*)' insist by brieve of division to have the subject divided. A brieve is directed from Chancery to the Sheriff. All parties having interest are called. The rights of parties are fixed by decree. A remit is made to a jury to measure, value, and divide the subject. The verdict settles the shares; and lots being cast, the division is fixed by decree of the Court. Extract and possession complete the separate rights of the parties in their shares of what formerly was common.

The same effect may be produced by an action of declarator and division, 'a remedy which has entirely superseded the brieve of division in practice,' concluding that proper persons shall be appointed to survey, examine, and divide the subject; that the division shall be ratified; that the several portions shall be declared to belong to the several parties; that they shall be ordained to execute the necessary deeds; and finally, in cases where a division may prove inexpedient or impracticable, that the subject shall be sold and the price divided (*b*).

In the ordinary case, this purpose is now accomplished by private arrangement and reference.

'It is provided, under the present system of land rights, that the title of the parties to their shares of the subject divided, whether it be commonty or common property or runrig lands, may be completed by recording an extract of the decree of division, whether pronounced by a Court or arbiters (*c*).'

(*a*) M'Neight *v.* Lockhart, 1843; 6 D. 128. Brock *v.* Hamilton, *cit.*

(*b*) Anderson *v.* Anderson, 1857; 19 D. 700. M'Bride *v.* Paul, 1862; 24 D. 546. Frizell *v.* Thomson, 1860; 22 D. 1176. Such actions may be in the Sheriff Court, if the value of the subject do not exceed £50 a year, or £1000 value. 40 and 41 Vict. c. 50, § 8 (3).

(*c*) 37 and 38 Vict. c. 94, § 35.

1082. If the subject be indivisible (*a*), it may be sold at the instance (*b*) of any of the parties, and the price divided, unless where it is a thing of common and indispensable use, as a staircase or vestibule (*c*).

(*a*) This is ascertained by a remit to a man of skill to report on the divisibility, and make up a scheme of division. And the question of divisibility is to be answered in a reasonable way, with due regard to the rights and interests of all the parties. Thom *v.* Macbeth, 1875; 3 R. 161. Bryden *v.* Gibson, and Milligan *v.* Barnhill, *infra* (*c*). Brock and Anderson, *citt.* A trustee who, as such, is a co-owner, may sue an action of division and sale, although he has no power of sale. Craig *v.* Fleming, 1863; 1 Macph. 612.

(*b*) This action cannot be maintained by joint beneficiaries under a trust. Kennedy & Tullis *v.* Maltmen of Glasgow, 1885; 12 R. 1086.

(*c*) Milligan *v.* Barnhill, 1782; M. 2486; Hailes, 897; 2 Ill. 153. See Bryden *v.* Gibson, 1837; 15 S. 486.

1083. Joint property arising in the course of succession to females admits of some distinctions necessary to be observed. If daughters or sisters succeed *ab intestato* to heritage, they are heirs-portioners and joint-owners. They are entitled to equal shares, with this difference, that where there is a right in its nature, exercise, or use not capable of division, it goes as a *præcipuum* to the eldest,—as a peerage, an office, the mansion-house, with its garden, orchard, and offices (*a*). But superiorities, though going to the eldest on account of the vassal's right to hold of one superior, yet are not indivisible in succession, since the feu-duties may be divided. And so, if there be one superiority, the eldest takes it, under the burden of paying a compensation to her younger sisters (*b*); if there be more than one, the eldest has the choice, the second the next, and so on, compensation, 'except in the case of a blench superiority (*c*),' being made to the younger (*d*). If the subject of the succession be such as not to be divisible without injury, as a brewery, it will be ordered to be sold and the price divided (*e*). 'Each heir-portioner has a separate title or estate, and may sue in questions relating to the property without concurrence of the others, contrary to the rule which generally obtains in the case of joint proprietors, whose right is *pro indiviso* in regard to the title as well as the possession (*f*).'

(*a*) 3 Ersk. 8. § 5–13. Cowie *v.* Cowies, 1707; M. 2453, 5362; 2 Ill. 153. Peadie *v.* Peadies, 1743; M. 5367; 5 B. Sup. 728. Ireland *v.* Govan, 1765; M. 5373. Forbes *v.* Forbes, 1774; M. 5378. M'Lauchlan *v.* M'Lauchlan, 1807; M. *Heir Port.* Apx. 3. Dinniston *v.* Welsh, 1830; 8 S. 935. See Halbert *v.* Bogie, 1857; 19 D. 762. M'Laren on Wills and Succession, i. 78–81; and below, § 1659.

(*b*) Houston *v.* Dunbar, 1744; M. 5369. Rae *v.* Rae, 1809; Hume, 764.

(*c*) M'Neight *v.* Lockhart, 1843; 6 D. 128.

(*d*) Houston, *supra* (*b*).

(*e*) Bryden *v.* Gibson, 1837; 15 S. 486.

(*f*) Cargill *v.* Muir, 1837; 15 S. 408. M'Neight *v.* Lockhart, 1843; 6 D. 128, 136. See above, cases in § 1075 (*d*).

1084. If daughters take a succession not *ab intestato*, but by a conveyance or settlement to them *nominatim*, or by description, equally among them, though the eldest may be entitled to indivisible subjects, it is not as a *præcipuum*; but she must give compensation to the rest (*a*).

(*a*) Cathcart *v.* Rocheid, 1773; M. 5375; 2 Ill. 154. Wight *v.* Inglis, 1798; M. Apx. *Heir Port.* 1; and see M'Lauchlan, *supra*, § 1083 (*a*). See Dinniston, *supra*.

1085. (3.) *Custody of Title-Deeds.*—In cases of common property, disputes arise to whom the right of custody of the title-deeds belongs. The general rules are: That the person who has the chief interest in the common property has the custody, subject to an obligation to make the titles forthcoming to any of the rest having occasion for them; that where no one has pre-eminence over the rest, the title-deeds (if the parties should not agree) ought to be deposited in neutral custody; that the eldest heir-portioner has custody of the title-deeds (*a*); that although all the other shares should come to be vested in one, this right in the eldest heir-portioner remains unimpaired; and that transumpts, where necessary, are to be made at the common expense (*b*).

(*a*) Denholms *v.* Denholms, 1638; M. 2447. 3 Ersk. 8. § 13.

(*b*) Stevenson *v.* Pitcairn, 1711; M. 2456; 2 Ill. 154. Cowie, *supra*, § 1083 (*a*). Cunningham *v.* Lady Cardross, 1680; M. 2449.

II. COMMON INTEREST.

1086. Nature.—A species of right differing from common property takes place among the owners of subjects possessed in separate portions, but still united by their common interest. It is recognised in law as "Common Interest." It accompanies and is incorporated with the several rights of individual property. In such cases a sale or division cannot resolve the difficulties which may arise in management; but the exercise and effect of the common interest must, when dissensions arise, be regulated by law or equity. Thus, in the common wall of one of the large tenements of Edinburgh, consisting of many floors belonging to different proprietors, there is no common property among the owners of the several floors, but a combination of individual property with common interest (*a*).

'In such tenements the original titles and the possession following on them show the intention of the builder and form "the law of the tenement" (*b*), any special burden or restriction being valid against singular successors only if transmitted in their titles (*c*). Where it is not modified by the titles, the general rule is that the ground on which the tenement is built, with the area, courts, or greens attached, *primâ facie* belongs in property to the lowest heritor (*d*); that the uppermost heritor appears to be owner of the roof, and so entitled to alter, but not to raise it, subject to the limitations arising from the common interest of the lower proprietors (*e*); that the boundary between the flats is an ideal line drawn through the centre of the joists (*f*); that the close, stair, and staircase (with walls enclosing it) are the common property of all the owners of the tenement (*g*); and that' each is proprietor of the wall of his own floor and can prevent all encroachments upon it; but he is bound to the rest (having a common interest in it) to support it, and is (*h*) entitled to alter it, 'as by opening a door in it, but not' to such an extent as to encroach on or endanger the common interest (*i*).

And so this common interest is distinguishable from *Servitude*, in so far as each person concerned is bound by the common interest to maintain his own wall, which in mere servitude he would not be obliged to do. It is also distinguishable from *Property*, in so far as no one having merely a common interest is entitled to break or touch the wall or space which belongs to another; he has only the right to prevent injury and insist on support. But each party may make alterations and changes on his own wall, notwithstanding the common interest which is vested in others, provided he does not endanger that common interest, or expose those who hold it to reasonable alarm (*j*). It is different in common *property*, no one common proprietor being entitled, without the consent of all the rest, to alter the state of the common subject (*k*); 'and, while an owner of a flat is entitled to make innocuous operations and alterations on his own walls, he is not allowed, without his neighbour's consent, to make any change on what belongs in property to the latter, or even on what is common, as a gable or staircase (*l*).' This rule, however, is qualified, as already explained, by the exception of acts done *in æmulationem vicini* (*m*). 'To warrant an objection to operations by a proprietor *in suo* by neighbouring owners on the ground of common interest, there must be injury to the security, light, or air of the objectors; mere injury to amenity is not enough (*n*).

'Where neighbouring owners or tenants have a common interest in anything, as in a road giving a common access, or an area or green for light and common use, their rights are ruled on similar principles—that is to say, by the titles constituting their rights, as interpreted "by law or equity." Any one of the community is entitled to maintain the existing state of possession against the others (*o*). So in regulating the use of a garden or square in a city, when the titles gave a right and interest, but not a right of property in the area, and did not define the system of management, the Court had recourse to the past possession and administration to fix the measure of the proprietors' rights (*p*).'

(*a*) 2 Stair, 7. § 6. 2 Ersk. 9. § 11. 2 Bankt. 7. § 9.

(*b*) Gellatly *v.* Arrol, 1863; 1 Macph. 592. Walker *v.* Braidwood, 1797; Hume, 512.

(*c*) Deans *v.* Abercromby, 1681; M. 10,122, 12,774. Alexander *v.* Couper, 1840; 3 D. 249. Blanc *v.* Greig, 1856; 18 D. 1315.

(*d*) Johnston *v.* White, 1877; 4 R. 721. Barclay *v.* M'Ewen, 1880; 7 R. 792. Boswell *v.* Mags. of Edinr., 1881; 8 R. 986. Sutherland *v.* Barbour, 1887; 15 R. 62. The lower heritor's ownership generally depends on the terms of the titles, and is subject to limitation by the common interest of the other proprietors; see cases cited, and Stewart *v.* Blackwood, *infra* (*k*). For example, the right of ownership *a cœlo usque ad centrum* cannot be freely exercised as to the open ground, before or behind, so held by the owner of a ground floor. Urquhart *v.* Melville, 1853; 16 D. 307. Arrol *v.* Inches, 1887; 14 R. 394.

(*e*) Taylor *v.* Dunlop, 1872; 11 Macph. 25. Watt *v.* Burgess's Trs., 1891; 18 R. 766. Sanderson's Trs. *v.* Yule, 1897; 25 R. 211 (several property where top flat divided—right of one owner to put out storm window). Sharp *v.* Robertson, 1800; M. Apx. *Property*, 3. Cuddie *v.* M'Kechnie, 1804; Hume, 516.

(*f*) Alexander *v.* Butchart, 1875; 3 R. 156. Dickson *v.* Morton, 1824; 3 S. 310. M'Arly *v.* French's Tr., 1883; 10 R. 574 (prescriptive encroachment by signboard). Murray *v.* M'Kenzie, 1812; Hume, 520. Walker (*b*). Gray *v.* Greig (*k*).

(*g*) Anderson *v.* Dalrymple, 1799; M. 12,831. Reid *v.* Nicol, 1799; M. Apx. *Property*, 1. Graham *v.* Greig (*l*). Ritchie *v.* Purdie, 1833; 11 S. 771. Anderson *v.* Saunders, 1831; 9 S. 564. Gellatly (*b*). Taylor *v.* Dunlop (*l*).

(*h*) The original text was "is not."

(*i*) Todd *v.* Wilson, 1894; 22 R. 172.

(*j*) Johnston *v.* White (*d*). Gellatly *v.* Arrol (*b*). Todd Wilson, *cit.* (*i*). Cochran's Trs. *v.* Cal. Ry., 1898; 25 R. 572.

(*k*) Ferguson *v.* Marjoribanks, Nov. 12, 1816; F. C.; 2 Ill. 120. Pirnie *v.* Macritchie, June 5, 1819; F. C. Murray *v.* Gullan, 1825; 3 S. 639. Gray *v.* Greig, 1825; 4 S. 104. M'Nair *v.* M'Lauchlan, 1826; 4 S. 546; 2 Ill. 155. See a good illustration of the distinction in Stewart *v.* Blackwood, 1829; 7 S. 362. Hall *v.* Corbet, 1698; M. 12,775. Robertson *v.* Rankin, 1784; M. 14,534. M'Kean *v.* Davidson, 1823; 2 S. 480. Brown *v.* Boyd, 1841; 3 D. 1205. Walker, Gellatly, Graham *v.* Greig, Taylor *v.* Dunlop, and other cases cited.

(*l*) Walker, Gellatly, etc., *citt.* Graham *v.* Greig, 1838; 1 D. 171. Taylor *v.* Dunlop, 1872; 11 Macph. 25. Munro *v.* Jervey, 1821; 1 S. 161 (prescription).

(*m*) See above, § 1075, 966.

(*n*) Barclay *v.* M'Ewen, *cit.* Calder *v.* Merchant Co. of Edinr., 1886; 13 R. 623.

(*o*) Bennet *v.* Playfair, 1877; 4 R. 321. Taylor's Trs. *v.* M'Gavigan, 1896; 23 R. 945. Mackenzie *v.* Carrick, 1869; 7 Macph. 419.

(*p*) Governors of George Watson's Hospital *v.* Cormack, 1883; 11 R. 320.

III. COMMONTY.

1087. Nature and Origin.—This is a right neither of common property nor of common interest, but of joint perpetual use, conferred, or presumed to be conferred, by the proprietor of land for the common use of many. The right to have common property divided does not therefore extend to this species of right; but the Legislature interposed in the end of the seventeenth century, and, with a view to the agricultural improvement of the country, empowered each person having a right to commonty to apply for having the common divided judicially (*a*). In England there is no such process. A private Act of Parliament 'was' required for the division of an English Common (*b*).

(*a*) 1695, c. 23.

(*b*) A number of General Inclosure Acts have been passed in modern times, beginning with 41 Geo. III. c. 109. See 6 and 7 Will. IV. c. 115, which first rendered a special private Act unnecessary; 8 and 9 Vict. c. 118, and a number of amending Acts. Stephen's Com. i. 664 sqq.

1088. This peculiar right of usufruct in a Common arose at first from the grants made by feudal lords and proprietors to their feuars and tenants, of rights to pasture their cattle on the grazing ground or wastes of the barony. Sometimes, also, by vicinage and custom, cottagers were suffered to establish a right of common over those wastes and pasture lands. Neighbouring towns, too, and hamlets, permitted reciprocal encroachments on their pasture ground, and so established commonty of pasture by mutual agreement or forbearance (*a*). The right is distinguishable from usufruct as being not personal, but an accessory (*b*) of the real property of the commoner; from liferent, as being perpetual, and without any reversionary right of fee in another; and from servitude, as being not a burden, but of the nature of limited property. There is a servitude of pasturage; but it is distinguishable from commonty, being a burden which in the division of the common gives to the person entitled to the servitude no right to demand a share, while the holder of it cannot be compelled to abandon his right to pasture, and take a share of the common instead of it (*c*). 'Commonty is also distinguished from the servitude in this respect, that it cannot be acquired by prescription beyond the limits of a bounding charter (*d*).'

(*a*) Mr. Rankine (Landownership, 496–8) points out how these sentences give a view of the origin of Commonty, which is entirely at variance with the results of modern inquiries into primitive land rights.

(*b*) L. Blantyre *v.* Jaffray, 1856; 19 D. 167.

(*c*) E. Fife's Trs. *v.* Cumming, 1831; 9 S. 336; 2 Ill. 155. **Gordon** *v.* **Grant,** 1849; 13 D. 1. See above, § 1013.

(*d*) Hepburn *v.* D. Gordon, 1823; 2 S. 525. Gordon *v.* Grant, *cit.* Beaumont *v.* L. Glenlyon, 1843; 5 D. 1337. See above, § 738–9.

1089. Constitution.—Commonty is constituted by a grant *cum communiâ*; or *cum communiis*; or "with commonty": Or by a grant of "parts and pertinents," accompanied by the explanatory possession of common pasturage (*a*). Servitude is created by a grant *cum communi pastura in commune de B.*; or *cum privilegio communitatis*; or "with parts, pertinents, and pendicles, with common pasturage"; or "with pasturage of cattle, and privilege of commonty."

(*a*) Rattray *v.* Graham, 1724; M. 2463; 2 Ill. 156. **E. Wigton** *v.* **Feuars of Biggar,** 1739; 5 B. Sup. 209, 602; Elchies, *Commonty*, 2; 2 Ill. 155. Johnston *v.* D. Hamilton, 1768; M. 2481. **Laurie** *v.* **D. Hamilton,** 1771; M. Apx. *Commonty*, 2; Hailes, 460. D. Buccleugh *v.* Erskine, June 16, 1812; F. C. See 16 S. 422. Watt *v.* Paterson, 1813; 2 Dow, 25. Bain *v.* Mags. of Wick, 1834; 12 S. 522. E. Airlie *v.* Rattray, 1835; 13 S. 691. Carnegie *v.* M'Tier, 1844; 6 D. 1381. Gordon *v.* Grant, *cit.* E. Fife's Trs. *v.* Cumming, 1830; 8 S. 326; 1831, 9 S. 336.

1090. Rights of the Over-lord.—As the right of commonty is derived from the paramount proprietor of the whole barony or estate, it may seem that there is an *ipso jure* reservation to himself of a right of commonty in his whole lands. But although there *may* be such reservation and continuance of the over-lord's right, yet, if the reservation be *not* made, he will lose the privilege, unless the right be preserved by possession; or there be persons holding servitudes under him, and possessing on them; or the possession shall be continued by the lord's tenants (*a*). If the over-lord's right be continued by possession, it will not be measured by the precise extent of that possession, but will extend according to the proportion of land still in his hands, unfeued, rated along with those of the feuars (*b*). Servitudes form burdens on the proprietor's right of common (*c*). The over-lord had at one time right to a *præcipuum*, an allowance for his right of property over the servitudes; now he takes only what is not allotted to parties having commonty (*d*). The superior has no *præcipuum* nor right of commonty on account of his *dominium directum*, and the feu-duties payable to him must be deducted from his valuations (*e*). And the holder of the *dominium utile* has the share of commonty corresponding to the land in his possession according to its valued rent, including feu-duties and other prestations payable to the Crown or other superiors (*f*).

(*a*) Trotter *v.* E. Marchmont, 1736; 1 Cr. S. & P. 186; 2 Ill. 157. D. Buccleugh *v.* Erskine, *supra*, § 1089 (*a*).

(*b*) Balfour *v.* Douglas, 1757; M. 2480. See below, § 1096.

(*c*) Stewart *v.* Mackenzie, 1748; M. 14,541; Elch. *Commonty*, 7. Lawrie *v.* D. Hamilton, *cit.*

(*d*) Hog *v.* E. Home, 1724; M. 2462. E. Wigton *v.* Feuars of Biggar, *supra*, § 1089 (*a*). Henderson *v.* M'Gill, 1782; M. 2487.

(*e*) L. Adv. *v.* Balfour, 1838; 16 S. 420; 3 Ill. 154.

(*f*) L. Adv. *cit.* See L. Blantyre *v.* Jaffray, 1856; 19 D. 167.

1091. The Exercise of the Right, according to the proportion of the property of the commoners, may be either by themselves or their tenants (*a*). 'Any one commoner may prohibit and prevent another from taking or giving an extraordinary use of the common property, as by letting a right to shoot over it (*b*), or granting to a stranger a right to cut peats (*c*), or even by altering its condition by agricultural or other improvements (*d*). The ordinary use is for pasturage, the amount of stock permissible being fixed, as in the servitude, by a process of souming and rouming (*e*); but the right of commonty includes the minerals (*f*), and may include the privilege of fuel, feal, and divot (*g*).'

(*a*) Barrowman *v.* Murray, 1668; 1 B. Sup. 572; 2 Ill. 158. See Scott *v.* M'Dowall, 1857; 19 D. 769.
(*b*) Campbell *v.* Campbell, Jan. 24, 1809; F. C. See above, § 1075.
(*c*) Wilson *v.* Buchanan, 1800; Hume, 120.
(*d*) Innes *v.* Hepburn, 1859; 21 D. 832. *Infra*, § 1096 (*f*).
(*e*) See above, § 1013.
(*f*) Johnston *v.* D. Hamilton, 1768; M. 2481; 16 F. C. 688. Baird & Co. *v.* Feuars of Kilsyth, 1878; 6 R. 116. But see Henderson *v.* Makgill, 1782; M. 2487. Spence *v.* E. Zetland, 1839; 1 D. 415. Bonshaw's Trs. *v.* D. Queensberry, 1764; M. 2481.
(*g*) See above, § 1014.

1092. **The Division** of a Common is accomplished by a process before the Court of Session, the object of which is to ascertain the rights and interests of the several claimants, and to estimate and to divide the common according to the value and interest of the several parties concerned. 'An action of division of commonty may proceed in the Sheriff Court, if the value of the divisible subject do not exceed £1000 (*a*). The decree of division has the effect of a conveyance to the parties, and may be recorded in the Register of Sasines (*b*).'

(*a*) 40 and 41 Vict. c. 50, § 8 (3).
(*b*) 37 and 38 Vict. c. 94, § 35.

1093. (1.) *The Title* required in the pursuer of this action is an interest as a commoner. Servitude is not enough (*a*).

(*a*) 1695, c. 23. Lawson *v.* D. Buccleuch, 1737; M. 2472; 2 Ill. 158. **Stewart** *v.* **Feuars of Tillicoultry**, 1739; M. 2409; Elchies, *Com.* 4. Lawrie, *supra*, § 1089 (*a*). Gall *v.* Greenhill, May 31, 1810; F. C. Stewart *v.* Mackenzie, 1748; M. 2476, 14,541. Maitland *v.* Lambert, 1769; M. 2483. **Gordon** *v.* **Grant**, 1849; 13 D. 1. See Graham's Tr. *v.* Boswell, 1830; 9 S. 121. Spence *v.* E. Zetland, 1839; 1 D. 415. Craig *v.* Fleming, 1863; 1 Macph. 612 (trustee).

1094. The proprietor has no right to insist in a division, if there be only servitudes, and no right of commonty; although the servitudes should exhaust the whole use of the surface (*a*).

(*a*) Stewart, *supra*, § 1093 (*a*), and other cases there cited. See Maitland *v.* Lambert, 1769; M. 2483.

1095. (2.) *The Proceedings* comprehend the production of the titles of the commoners, and proofs of possession; the perambulation of the common; the valuation of the right of each; the ascertainment and valuation of servitudes; the ascertaining of the mines and minerals; and the casting or allocating of the whole (*a*).

(*a*) As to the effect of the decree and completion of title, see § 1081. See also A. of S., June 18, 1852. Bruce *v.* Bain, 1883; 11 R. 192.

1096. (3.) *The Rules of Division* are:—1. To divide among the commoners according to their several rights and interests, taking the valuation of their respective lands according to the valued rent in the cess books (*a*); 'exceptions being allowed only of mosses, which are divided according to frontage (*b*), and commons in Shetland, which are divided according to merk's lands (*c*).' 2. To give to the commoners the share nearest to their own property. 3. To preserve the servitudes over the divided portions; or to commute them, if those holding the right will consent, and to give a portion of land in their stead (*d*). 4. To allow to the baron or proprietor a share of commonty corresponding only to the lands for which possession has taken place, not to the whole barony, under the burden of servitudes (*e*). 5. To lay on each commoner the burden of any improvement which he may have made prematurely while under a usurped possession (*f*). And 6. To continue as common such mosses as are indivisible (*g*).

(*a*) 1695, c. 23. E. Wigton *v.* Feuars of Biggar, 1739; M. 2467; 5 B. Sup. 206; 2 Ill. 155. D. Douglas *v.* Baillie, 1740; M. 2574; Elch. *Com.* 5; 2 Ill. 158. Sharp *v.* Carlile, 1748; M. 2478. Small *v.* Ferguson, 1804; M. Apx. *Commonty*, 3.
(*b*) Campbell *v.* L. Douglas, 1804; M. Apx. *Commonty*, 4.
(*c*) Bruce *v.* Grierson, 1823; 2 S. 573. Spence *v.* E. Zetland, 1839; 1 D. 415.
(*d*) E. Wigton, *supra* (*a*). Lawrie, Gall, Gordon, *citt.* § 1093 (*a*).
(*e*) Balfour *v.* Douglas, 1757; M. 2479; Elch. *Com.* 8. D. Buccleugh *v.* Erskine, June 16, 1812; F. C.; 2 Ill. 158. § 1090 *supra*. As to feu-duty due to superior, see L. Adv. *v.* Balfour, 1838; 16 S. 420.
(*f*) Kinloch, Petr., Jan. 14, 1814; F. C. See Innes *v.* Hepburn, 1859; 21 D. 832.
(*g*) See Campbell *v.* L. Douglas, 1804; M. *Commonty*, Apx. 4. Johnston *v.* Johnston, 1831; 10 S. 70. L. Blantyre *v.* Jaffray, 1856; 19 D. 167.

1097. The exceptions from the operations of this Act are—the King's commons, and the commons of royal burghs (*a*).

(*a*) Sandilands *v.* Mags. of Falkland, Jan. 19, 1809; F. C.; 2 Ill. 159. Hunter *v.* Mailler, 1854; 16 D. 641.

Henderson *v.* Mags. of Abernethy, June 29, 1815; F. C. (in notes). Rattray *v.* Graham, 1724; M. 2463. 10 Geo. IV. c. 132.

IV. RUNRIDGE LANDS.

1098. Nature and Origin.—This is a species of right and possession which seems to have arisen from out of the practice of the common defence and watching, and the common ploughing and labouring, necessary or natural in the occupation of burgh acres and lands in the neighbourhood of towns. It is different from common property. The right of the several parties to the alternate ridges is absolute. But in the end of the seventeenth century, the Legislature, with a view to the improvement of agriculture, introduced a power of dividing (or rather of allotting into consolidated portions) the scattered ridges, according to the rights of the parties (*a*).

(*a*) 1695, c. 23. 3 Ersk. 3. § 59. Davidson *v.* Kerr, 1748; Elch. *Com.* No. 6, and *Runridge*, No. 1; 2 Ill. 159. Davidson *v.* Heddell, 1829; 8 S. 219. **Lady Gray** *v.* **Richardson**, 1876; 3 R. 1031; aff. 1877, 4 R. H. L. 76; 3 App. Ca. 1.

1099. Division.—According to the statute, and the construction put on it, the rules are:—That the division is to be made with due regard to mansion-houses, however poor and mean (*a*); that no regard is to be had to former possession, but due attention paid to the general interest (*b*); that not burgh acres only should be excluded, but patches of four acres (*c*); that small detached parcels of land, surrounded by great estates, are not within the remedy of the Act (*d*).

(*a*) Taylor *v.* E. Callander, 1698; M. 14,141; 2 Ill. 159. Gray *v.* Wardrop, 1777; M. *Runridge*, Apx. 1; 5 B. Sup. 580; Hailes, 741.

(*b*) Russell *v.* York Buildings Co., 1774; M. 14,144; 5 B. Sup. 580; Hailes, 554.

(*c*) Chalmers *v.* Pew, 1756; M. 10,485; 2 Ill. 117. Heritors of Inveresk *v.* Milne, 1755; M. 14,142; overruled by Lady Gray *v.* Blairs, 1782; M. 14,151; Hailes, 846; 2 Ill. 160. Buchanan *v.* Clark, 1766; M. 14,142; Hailes, 158. Jardine *v.* L. Douglas, 1793; M. 14,152; 2 Ill. 138. Burns *v.* Bogle, 1829; 7 S. 415.

(*d*) Hall *v.* Callander, 1744; M. 14,141; 2 Ill. 160. Morrison *v.* Drysdale, 1780; M. 14,151; 5 B. Sup. 582. As to the completion of title after division, see § 1081.

V. COMMON RIGHT IN WATER.

1100. Nature.—This is a common right and interest in the several proprietors, opposite or successive, by or through whose lands water flows. Each has right to the water as it passes or runs through his land, for all family purposes and uses to which, without deterioration, destruction, or waste, it can be applied; for trout-fishing by rod or even by net, where there is no right of salmon-fishing thereby injured; and for taking salmon by rod or spear (*a*).

(*a*) M'Kenzie *v.* Rose, 1830; 8 S. 816; aff. 6 W. & S. 31; 2 Ill. 43. Cases below, § 1104, etc.

1101. Opposite Proprietors on the banks have half the land (*a*) covered by the stream, but no property in the water. They are on an equal footing in respect to the use of the water which flows between them, and which is held to be equally divided. But they have no right to alter the channel, or to take an aqueduct from the river so as to diminish the stream. A watercourse for a mill may be prevented, if the objector can show that any use or expectation is thereby destroyed, or any amenity injured (*b*). But a pipe to supply the family with water may be taken (*c*).

(*a*) See the curious case of Jameson *v.* Dundee Police Comrs., 1884, 12 R. 300, as to the effect of prescriptive use as a sewer within burgh, and of the General Police Act.

(*b*) 2 Stair, 7. § 12. 2 Ersk. 9. § 13. Bannatyne *v.* Cranston, 1624; M. 12,769. Kelso *v.* Boyds, 1768; M. 12,807; Hailes, 224; 2 Ill. 160. Mags. of Linlithgow *v.* Elphinston, 1767; 5 B. Sup. 935. Hamilton *v.* Edington & Co., 1793; M. 12,824. Braid *v.* Douglas, 1800; M. *Prop.* Apx. 2. Johnson *v.* Ritchie, 1822; 1 S. 304. D. Roxburghe *v.* Waldie, 1821; Hume, 524. Colquhoun's Trs. *v.* Orr-Ewing, 1877; 4 R. H. L. 116. Mason *v.* Hill, 5 B. & Ad. 1. Embrey *v.* Owen, 6 Ex. 367. Miner *v.* Gilmour, 12 Moore P. C. 156.

(*c*) Ogilvie *v.* Kincaid, 1791; M. 12,824; Hume, 508.

1102. An opposite heritor is not entitled to change the direction or level (*a*) of the stream; or to augment its force; or to build in the bed of the river a bulwark for his own protection, which shall have any of these effects, or which shall make the water in its natural channel overflow, or leave its old course (*b*). 'The interest of each heritor in the stream is such as to entitle him to prevent the opposite proprietor from performing without his consent any operation within the *alveus*, even on his own side of the *medium filum*, which may cause a sensible alteration in the flow of the water such as may possibly tend to damage opposite or lower riparian owners, although they cannot qualify any present damage (*c*). But a proprietor may strengthen the banks and even raise bulwarks and embankments on his own ground, for the purpose of protecting his land against the stream or the tide, provided he can show that there is no possibility of material damage to the other side in ordinary floods, the *onus probandi* being on him (*d*).'

(*a*) D. Roxburghe *v.* Waldie, 1821 ; Hume, 524.

(*b*) D. Gordon *v.* Duff, 1735 ; M. 12,778 ; Elchies, *Prop.* 2 ; 2 Ill. 161. Town of Nairn *v.* Brodie, 1738 ; M. 12,779 ; Elch. *Prop.* 4. Fairly *v.* E. Eglinton, 1744 ; M. 12,780 ; Elch. *Prop.* 7. Menzies *v.* Mags. of Aberdeen, 1748 ; M. 12,787 ; Elch. *ib.* 8. Farquharson *v.* Farquharson, 1741 ; M. 12,779 ; 5 B. Sup. 688 ; Elch. *ib.* 5. **Menzies** *v.* **E. Breadalbane,** 1826 ; 4 S. 783 ; rev. 3 W. & S. 235. See above, § 971.

(*c*) **Morris** *v.* **Bicket,** 1864 ; 2 Macph. 1082 ; aff. 1866, 4 Macph. H. L. 44 ; L. R. 1 Sc. App. 47. **Colquhoun's Trs.** *v.* **Orr-Ewing & Co.,** 1877 ; 4 R. 344 ; rev. *ib.* H. L. 116 ; 2 App. Ca. 839. See M'Intyre's Trs. *v.* Mags. of Cupar, 1867 ; 5 Macph. 780. D. Roxburghe *v.* Waldie's Trs., 1879 ; 6 R. 663. Robertson *v.* Foote & Co., 1879 ; 6 R. 1291. M'Gavin *v.* M'Intyre Brs., 1890 ; 17 R. 818 ; aff. 1893, A. C. 268 ; 20 R. H. L. 49. Kensit *v.* G. E. Ry. Co., 27 Ch. D. 122.

(*d*) Farquharson and Menzies, *citt.* Morris, *cit.* Jackson *v.* Marshall, 1872 ; 10 Macph. 913. See Nield *v.* L. and N.-W. Ry. Co., 44 L. J. Ex. 15 ; L. R. 10 Ex. 4. Lindsay *v.* Thomson, 1866 ; 5 Macph. 29.

1103. The privilege of doing any of those things is to be purchased, or may be acquired by sufferance, or by acquiescence implied from the permission of expensive operations (*a*).

(*a*) Aytoun *v.* Douglas, 1800 ; M. *Prop.* Apx. 5. See above, § 946–7.

1104. Successive Proprietors have the use of the stream as it passes their lands. But in ascertaining the nature and extent of the use, regard must be paid to the size of the stream, and to its condition of purity or pollution. There is a certain order of uses, primary and secondary, according to which, when they come into collision (especially in less considerable streams), the parties are bound to exercise their rights. The primary uses are for the support of animal life in man and beast, and for other domestic purposes of cooking, washing, etc. ; the secondary uses comprehend other purposes, of manufacture, etc. (*a*).

(*a*) See Miller and Russel, below, § 1106. **Dunn** *v.* **Hamilton,** 1837 ; 15 S. 853 ; aff. 1838, 3 S. & M'L. 356. Hood *v.* Williamson, 1861 ; 23 D. 496. **D. Buccleuch** *v.* **Cowan, etc.,** 1866 ; 5 Macph. 214 ; 11 Macph. 675 ; aff. 1876, 4 R. H. L. 14.

1105. The superior heritor has the full use of the water, in passing, for the primary use of drink for man or beast, and for the family purposes of cooking, washing, bleaching, brewing for domestic use. He may even for those uses take off an aqueduct, provided he return what is unused unpolluted to its channel before leaving his property (*a*). This use is not forfeited, but may be resumed by the superior heritor, even although, while he has not used it, works may have been erected by the inferior heritors which will require for secondary purposes the whole water. But this will be under qualification of the law of prescription (*b*).

(*a*) See M'Lean *v.* Hamilton, 1857 ; 19 D. 1006. Ogilvie, and other cases in § 1101. Hood *v.* Williamson, 1861; 23 D. 496. Bonthron *v.* Downie, 1878 ; 6 R. 324.

(*b*) Hunter & Aitkenhead *v.* Aitken, 1880 ; 7 R. 510.

1106. In its course, therefore, the stream is not to be polluted by any manufactory ' or sewage (*a*),' so as to be made unfit for the use of man or beast ; but this under the qualification, that larger rivers are, ' or, perhaps, by use and prescription more readily become (*b*),' the natural conduits to the sea, for all the usual, and natural, and necessary uses of the subject, or for ' the pollutions arising from ' habitation (*c*). 'It is a good defence to a complaint by an inferior heritor that the stream has been from time immemorial devoted to secondary purposes, such as manufactories, so as to supersede the primary purposes (*d*) ; but it is not a sufficient defence apart from prescription,—if it be proved that the party complained of materially contributes to the pollution,—that others are also polluting it to the effect of creating a nuisance (*e*). Even forty years' pollution does not prevent an inferior heritor from objecting to a material increase of the pollution (*f*).'

(*a*) Montgomerie & Fleming, *infra* (*c*). Cal. Ry. Co. *v.* Baird, 1876 ; 3 R. 839. Scott *v.* Scott, 1881 ; 8 R. 851.

(*b*) See Rankine, Landownership, 434.

(*c*) Miller *v.* Stein, 1791 ; M. 12,823 ; Bell's Ca. 334 ; 2 Ill. 119. Russel *v.* Haig, 1791 ; M. 12,823 ; Bell's Ca. 338 ; 3 Pat. 403. Downie *v.* E. Moray, 4 S. 167. Dunn, *supra*, § 1104 (*a*). See *supra*, § 968. Montgomerie & Fleming *v.* Buchanan's Trs., 1853 ; 15 D. 853. Ewen *v.* Turnbull's Trs., 1857 ; 19 D. 513. D. Buccleuch, *supra*, § 1104 (*a*). Rigby & Beardmore *v.* Downie, 1872 ; 10 Macph. 568. Dumfries Waterworks Comrs. *v.* M'Culloch, 1874 ; 1 R. 975 (sheepwashing in a lake supplying town with water). Cal. Ry. Co., *cit.* Moncreiffe *v.* Perth Pol. Comrs., 1886 ; 13 R. 921 (public river—sewage—salmon-fishings). See the Rivers Pollution Prevention Act, 1876, 39 and 40 Vict. c. 75 ; 48 and 49 Vict. c. 61, § 5 ; 56 and 57 Vict. c. 31. Mags. of Portobello *v.* Mags. of Edin., 1882 ; 10 R. 130. Guthrie, Craig, & Co. *v.* Mags. of Brechin, 1885 ; 12 R. 469 (appeal).

(*d*) Russel *v.* Haig, *cit.* Downie *v.* E. Moray, *cit.* Rigby & Beardmore, *cit.* Robertson *v.* Stewarts, 1872 ; 11 Macph. 189.

(*e*) D. Buccleuch, *cit.* § 1104 (*a*). Mackay *v.* Greenhill, 1857 ; 20 D. 1251.

(*f*) D. Buccleuch, *cit.* § 1104 (*a*). Ewen, *cit.* (*c*). Milne Home *v.* Comrs. of Duns, 1882 ; 9 R. 924. M'Gavin *v.* M'Intyre Brs., *cit.* § 1102.

1107. The superior heritor is not entitled to change the course of the stream, 'or alter its natural flow, in regard either to its force, volume, or direction (*a*); or even to alter its natural quality, as, *e.g.*, by adding hard water from mineral workings, so as to make it unfit for special uses to which it has been or might be put by a lower heritor, though not unfitting it for the primary purposes (*b*)'; or to waste it in any course of deviation for manufacturing or agricultural purposes, even though he should return the water into the old channel. He cannot, therefore, take it off for irrigation (*c*), or for a distillery, or for a salt-work, or for a mill (*d*). If, in the exercise of his secondary use, the superior heritor has erected a manufactory, the improvement of which may require more water than was used at first, he cannot be deprived of the right to take it by the erection in the meantime of works by inferior heritors, which may require the water not to be diminished (*e*). A proprietor cannot object to the erection of works which do not interfere with the primary uses of the stream, on the ground of possible detriment to some work that he may afterwards think of erecting (*f*); 'nor to the performance of ordinary rural operations (such as dragging timber) which injuriously affect secondary uses by a lower heritor (*g*).'

(*a*) The storing or impounding of water for power, etc., is only allowed subject to regulations, each case depending on circumstances, such as the size of the stream, prescriptive possession, etc. See L. Glenlee and M. Abercorn, *infra* (*d*). L. Blantyre *v.* Dunn, 1848; 10 D. 509, 521. Hunter & Aitkenhead *v.* Aitken, 1880; 7 R. 510. See § 1108; and as to the straightening and embanking of a natural streamlet, Murdoch *v.* Wallace, 1881; 8 R. 855.

(*b*) So held, though not decided, by the H. of L. in Bankier Disty. Co. *v.* Young & Co., 1893; A. C. 691; 20 R. H. L. 76; affg. 19 R. 1083.

(*c*) See Rankine, Landownership, 424.

(*d*) 2 Stair, 7. § 12. Bannatyne *v.* Cranston, 1624; M. 12,769. Kelso *v.* Boyds, 1768; M. 12,807; 2 Ill. 160. L. Glenlee *v.* Gordon, 1804; M. 12,834; 2 Ill. 162. See above, § 1101, and § 971. Cruickshanks *v.* Henderson, 1791; Hume, 506. M. Abercorn *v.* Jamieson, 1791; Hume, 510. Lanark Twist Co. *v.* Edmonstone, 1810; Hume, 520. M'Lean *v.* Hamilton, 1857; 19 D. 1006. Hood, *cit.* § 1104. Cowan *v.* L. Kinnaird, 1863; 1 Macph. 972; 1865, 4 Macph. 236. Morris and Colquhoun's Trs., *citt.* § 1102 (*c*). As to the right of inferior proprietors to compensation for the diversion, under the Public Health Act, of springs feeding a stream, see Peterhead Granite Co. *v.* Peterhead Par. Bd., 1880; 7 R. 536.

(*e*) Lyon & Gray *v.* Bakers of Glasgow, 1749; M. 12,789 (a special case).

(*f*) Dunn, *supra*, § 1104 (*a*).

(*g*) Armistead *v.* Bowerman, 1888; 15 R. 814.

1108. The superior heritor is not entitled, by any *opus manufactum*, to increase the force of the stream upon his inferior neighbour; nor is the inferior heritor entitled to throw back the water on his superior neighbour (*a*). 'When a stream, whose origin is of a permanent character, flows in an artificial or partly artificial channel, inferior proprietors upon that channel, who do not *primâ facie* possess in such a case any right to the unimpeded flow of the water, may by grant or prescriptive possession acquire rights similar to owners along a natural watercourse (*b*). But the water in an artificial conduit for draining mines, or other purpose of a temporary character, may, it seems, be discontinued or diminished by the upper proprietor, although the lower heritor should lose an accidental or resulting benefit which he has enjoyed for forty years (*c*).'

(*a*) Fairlie *v.* E. Eglinton, 1744; M. 12,780; Elch. *Prop.* 7; 2 Ill. 162. See above, § 969. Burgess *v.* Brown, 1796; Hume, 504. Baillie *v.* L. Saltoun, 1821; Hume, 523. As to injuries caused by superior heritors having dammed back the water of a stream, see Henderson & Thomson *v.* Shaw Stewart, 1837; 15 S. 868. **Kerr** *v.* **E. Orkney,** 1857; 20 D. 298. Tennant *v.* E. Glasgow, 1862; 1 Macph. 133; aff. 1864, 2 Macph. H. L. 22. Pirie *v.* Mags. of Aberdeen, 1871; 9 Macph. 412. Css. of Rothes *v.* Kirkcaldy Comrs., 1879; 6 R. 974. Filshill *v.* Campbell, 1887; 14 R. 592. **Fletcher** *v.* **Rylands,** 35 L. J. Ex. 154; L. R. 1 Ex. 265; aff. L. R. 3 H. L. 330; 37 L. J. Ex. 161. Nichols *v.* Marsland, L. R. 10 Ex. 255; 2 Ex. D. 1; 46 L. J. Ex. 174. Smith *v.* Fletcher, *supra*, § 968. Box *v.* Jubb, 4 Ex. D. 76; 48 L. J. Ex. 417. Hurdman *v.* N.-E. Ry. Co., 3 C. P. D. 168; 47 L. J. C. P. 368.

(*b*) **L. Blantyre** *v.* **Dunn,** 1848; 10 D. 509. Mackenzie *v.* Woddrop, 1854; 16 D. 381. Sutcliffe *v.* Booth, 32 L. J. Q. B. 136. Nuttall *v.* Bracewell, L. R. 2 Ex. 1; 36 L. J. Ex. 1. Holker *v.* Porritt, L. R. 8 Ex. 107; 10 Ex. 59; 42 L. J. Ex. 85; 44 *ib.* 52. Rameshur Pershad *v.* Koonj Behari, L. R. 4 App. Ca. 121. Roberts *v.* Richards, 50 L. J. Ch. 297.

(*c*) Munro *v.* Ross, 1846; 1 D. 1029. Irving *v.* Leadhills Mining Co., 1856; 18 D. 833. Heggie *v.* Nairn, 1882; 9 R. 704. Comp. Arkwright *v.* Gell, 5 M. & W. 283. Wood *v.* Waud, 3 Ex. 748. Bridges *v.* L. Saltoun, 1873; 11 Macph. 588.

1109. Springs rising in the superior ground could not, by the Roman law, be stopped, if perennial, tributary, or feeders to the stream below. Those which only occasionally overflowed might, for useful purposes, be stopped. With us *aqua pluvia* or drainage may be stopped by the superior heritor; but a rivulet passing the various lands may not so be stopped; and springs rising in one man's lands, and flowing down to those of others, may not be stopped (*a*). 'A person who works minerals is not responsible for pumping dry the springs in a neighbouring property;

and he may dispose as he pleases of the water which is collected in his mines (*b*).'

(*a*) Kelso *v.* Boyds, 1768; M. 12,807; Hailes, 224; 2 Ill. 160. Mags. of Linlithgow *v.* Elphinston, 1767; M. 12,805; Hailes, 203; 5 B. Sup. 935. MacNab *v.* Robertson, 1896; 23 R. 1098; aff. 1897, A. C. 109; 24 R. H. L. 34.

(*b*) Blair *v.* Hunter, Finlay, & Co., 1870; 9 Macph. 204. Cf. Irving *v.* Leadhills Co., 1856; 18 D. 833. See above, § 968, 969. As to the percolation of sewage, see Ballard *v.* Tomlinson, and Snow *v.* Whitehead, *supra*, § 969.

1110. Lakes which give a permanent source to rivers are not to be drained by the owner of the ground in which they are situated. But if the lake do not supply a stream, it is entirely within the power of the owner of the ground, provided there be no servitude over it (*a*).

(*a*) Mags. of Linlithgow, *supra*, § 1109 (*a*). See above, § 651. Cunninghame *v.* Dunlop, 1836; 15 S. 295; 1838, 16 S. 1080. Rankine, Landownership, 167 sqq.

1111. Lakes surrounded by the ground of various proprietors are common property; but they are not under the Act 1695, nor divisible otherwise than by consent or Act of Parliament (*a*).

(*a*) See above, § 651, 747.

1112. **Salmon-Fishing** (*a*). (1.) *Title.*—The right of fishing salmon (otherwise than by the rod in rivers, or within sea-mark, where the sea ebbs and flows) belongs to the Crown, and is communicable to subjects only by grant (*b*). The right may be given either with the land or separately. The royal grant is *cum piscatione salmonum*, which vests the right directly (*c*), the extent depending on the limits expressed, and the construction of the grant (*d*): Or *cum piscariis*, or *cum piscationibus*, which grounds a title for prescribing a right of salmon-fishing, provided the possession is by the exercise of fishing salmon by net and coble, not merely by rod and spear (*e*). 'Such a clause occurring even in a charter by a subject superior, is a sufficient title for prescription, at least where the earlier titles show that the fishings have been given out by the Crown (*f*). A grant of barony is also a sufficient title for prescription without mention of fishings (*g*).' A right to fish salmon with the rod is not 'in general' conferred by a grant of fishing, though followed by rod fishing (*h*). 'The possession must be by net and coble fishing, or some equally clear and unequivocal exercise of the right (*i*). Rod fishing seems to be sufficient possession in streams where fishing by net and coble is impracticable or unprofitable or less profitable (*k*).'

Among the several grants which may subsist on the same river, the peculiar migratory habits of the fish confer on the successive grantees a common interest, like that in running water. On this principle a sort of corporation of the heritors interested in a river is established by a statute, of which the object is to regulate this as a branch of national wealth (*l*). But this common interest does not confer on proprietors of salmon-fishing in a river any interest to object to one fishing (in a lawful manner) opposite to his own lands, beyond their limits, although the person fishing has himself no right of salmon-fishing (*m*).

(*a*) See above, § 646, 671, and 754. By 7 and 8 Vict. c. 95, no one can fish in the sea within a mile of low-water mark, without permission of the owner of the salmon-fishing. The offence of salmon-poaching is punishable under that statute; 9 Geo. IV. c. 39; and 25 and 26 Vict. c. 97, § 27, etc. See Stewart on Rights of Fishing.

(*b*) Leslie *v.* Ayton, 1593; M. 14,249; 2 Ill. 12. L. Garlies *v.* Torhouse, 1605; M. *ib.* See above, § 646, 671. The proposition of the text (and of § 671) is not subject to the limitations under which it is stated by the author: the right of salmon-fishing being a *jus regale*, and the Crown's rights being universal both geographically (within the realm), and it seems also with respect to the method of fishing. **Comrs. of Woods, etc.** *v.* **Gammell**, 1851; 13 D. 854; aff. 1859, 3 Macq. 419. D. Sutherland *v.* Ross, 1836; 14 S. 960. Anderson *v.* Anderson, 1867; 6 Macph. 117; 5 Irv. 499. Ogston *v.* Stewart's Trs., 1893; 21 R. 282; 1896, A. C. 120; 23 R. H. L. 16.

(*c*) Without any necessity for possession or exercise of the right, which is *meræ facultatis.* Mackenzie *v.* Davidson, 1841; 3 D. 646. **Lady Gray** *v.* **Richardson**, 1876; 3 R. 1031; aff. 4 R. H. L. 76; 3 App. Ca. 1. See Higgins *v.* E. Moray, 1884; 12 R. Just. 1.

(*d*) 2 Ersk. 6. § 6, 15. Grant *v.* D. Gordon, 1778, 1781; M. 14,297, 12,820; Hailes, 654; 5 B. Sup. 547; aff. 2 Pat. 582; 3 Pat. 679. Brodie *v.* Mags. of Nairn, 1796; M. 12,830. Warrand's Trs. *v.* Mackintosh, 1888; 15 R. 833; revd. 1890, 15 App. Ca. 52; 17 R. H. L. 13. The grant must, it seems, be express, unless followed by usage. L. Adv. *v.* Northern Lights Comrs., 1874; 1 R. 950.

(*e*) Ersk. *ut sup.* Maxwell *v.* Portrack, 1628; M. 14,250; 2 Ill. 13. Forbes *v.* Udney, 1701; M. 7812. D. Queensberry *v.* V. Stormont, 1773; M. 14,257; Hailes, 543. Smollett *v.* Colquhoun, 1779; see 14 S. 963, note. Mags. of Inverness *v.* Duff, 1775; M. 14,257. Chisholm *v.* Fraser, 1801; M. *Salm. Fish.* Apx. 1. Forbes *v.* Leys, Masson, & Co., 1824; 2 S. 515. D. Sutherland *v.* Ross, 1836; 14 S. 960. See below, § 1119 et seq. Warrand's Trs., *cit.*

(*f*) L. Adv. *v.* Sinclair, 1865; 3 Macph. 981; aff. 1867, 5 Macph. H. L. 97; L. R. 1 Sc. Ap. 174. Stuart *v.* M'Barnet, 1867; 5 Macph. 753; aff. 6 Macph. H. L. 123. E. Zetland *v.* Glovers of Perth, 1868; 6 Macph. 292; aff. 1870, 8 Macph. H. L. 144.

(*g*) See above, § 754.

(*h*) D. Sutherland, *supra* (*e*).

(*i*) Anderson, *cit.* (*b*). Milne *v.* Smith, 1850; 13 D. 112. Ramsay *v.* D. Roxburghe, 1848; 10 D. 661. L. Abercromby *v.* M. Breadalbane, 1843; 5 D. 1389. D. Richmond *v.* E. Seafield, 1870; 8 Macph. 530.

(*k*) See Stuart, *cit.* (*f*). E. Dalhousie *v.* M'Inroy, 1865; 3 Macph. 1168. L. Abercromby, *cit.* L. Adv. *v.* L. Lovat, 1880; 7 R. H. L. 122, 135; 5 App. Ca. 273. D. Roxburghe *v.* Waldie's Trs., 1879; 6 R. 663. Sinclair *v.* Threipland, 1890; 17 R. 507. Ogston, *cit.* (*b*). Warrand *v.* Mackintosh, 1890; 15 App. Ca. 52, 70 (*per* Lord Watson). Twenty years seems to be now the period of prescription. Ogston, *cit.* 37 and 38 Vict. c. 94, § 34.

(*l*) 9 Geo. IV. c. 39, § 10. See 25 and 26 Vict. c. 97, which provides for the formation of District Boards for the management of matters under the Salmon Fishery Acts. See also 26 and 27 Vict. c. 50; 27 and 28 Vict. c. 118; 31 and 32 Vict. c. 123; and 45 and 46 Vict. c. 78. Campbells, Petrs., 1883; 10 R. 819.

(*m*) Mackenzie *v.* Gilchrist, and Mackenzie *v.* Houston, 1829, 1830; 7 S. 297; 8 S. 117, 796; aff. 5 W. & S. 422; 2 Ill. 162. See L. Somerville *v.* Smith, 1859; 22 D. 279. Stuart, *supra* (*f*). Forbes *v.* Leys, Masson, & Co., 1831; 9 S. 933; aff. 5 W. & S. 384.

1113. (2.) *Protection.*—The public interest is combined with that of the private proprietors of fishings, in all those regulations which are directed to prevent the destruction of spawning fish, and also in those which are directed to prevent the obstructing of fish in their migration into rivers (*a*). The regulations relate to the time during which fish may be taken; to the machinery by which they may be taken; to the limits within which certain engines are prohibited.

(*a*) Hay *v.* Mags. of Perth, 1863; 1 Macph. H. L. 41; 4 Macq. 535.

1114. (3.) *Close Time.*—A time is fixed by statute within which no person shall take any salmon, or fish of the salmon kind, from any river, stream, estuary, or sea-coast in Scotland. This time 'always continues for 168 days, and under the Act of 1862 (25 and 26 Vict. c. 97) the close time for each district of Scotland is fixed by bye-laws of the Commissioners appointed under the Act, and in the greater number of cases extends from August 27 to February 10, with an extension of the time for rod fishing generally to October 31. The powers of the Commissioners under this Act are now transferred to the Fishery Board for Scotland (*a*). There is a weekly close time of not less than thirty-six hours, extending from 6 P.M. on Saturday to 6 A.M. on Monday, subject to variation by the Commissioners (*b*).'

(*a*) 45 and 46 Vict. c. 78.

(*b*) 25 and 26 Vict. c. 97, § 7; 31 and 32 Vict. c. 123, § 15. Custar *v.* Chalmers, 1878; 5 R. Just. 36. Osborne *v.* Anderson, 1887; 14 R. Just. 12.

1115. (4.) *Machinery.*—As to the method pursued in the taking of salmon, there is an absolute prohibition of all fixed machinery within certain limits; and regulations for diminishing the evils of such machinery in the situations where it is permitted.

1116. There is a prohibition of all fixed machinery for fishing of salmon in the rivers and waters of Scotland, where the sea ebbs and flows. This prohibition comprehends cruives or zairs (*a*); stent-nets; bulwarks across the river with nets; hang-nets and stake-nets; sights (artificial shallows to disclose the passing of the salmon); towing-paths; nets having one end fastened to the shore, and the other floating; all modes, in short (*primâ fronte* at least), except net and coble; 'a phrase which is symbolical of the proper legal mode of fishing, viz. by a net which is not to be fixed, or stented, or in any manner settled or made permanent in the river; but it is to be used by the hand, and is not to quit the hand, and is to be kept in motion during the operation of fishing (*b*). But erections or operations on the banks or in the *alveus,* such as a bulwark or bridge, if otherwise lawful, are not prohibited, unless they impede the passage of the fish up or down the river (*c*).' There is an absolute prohibition also of the use of light or fire in the taking of salmon, grilse, sea-trout, or other fish of the salmon kind (*d*).

(*a*) See Mags. of Dumbarton, *infra* (*d*). Fraser *v.* Duff, 1829; 8 S. 14; aff. 5 W. & S. 57. Mackenzie *v.* Renton, 1840; 2 D. 1078. L. Adv. *v.* L. Lovat, 1880; 7 R. H. L. 122.

(*b*) *Per* L. Westbury in Hay *v.* Mags. of Perth, 1863; 1 Macph. H. L. 41; 4 Macq. 535. See, however, Allan's Mortification *v.* Thomson, 1879; 7 R. 221 (drift or hang nets). E. Wemyss *v.* E. Zetland, 1890; 18 R. 126 (do.).

(*c*) See above, § 971, 1102. Trotter *v.* Hume, 1757; M. 12,798. Forbes *v.* Smyth, *infra* (*d*). Macbraire *v.* Mather, 1871; 9 Macph. 913. West *v.* Aberdeen Harb. Comrs., 1876; 4 R. 207. D. Sutherland *v.* Ross, 1877; 4 R. 765; aff. 1878, 5 R. H. L. 137; 3 App. Ca. 736.

(*d*) 1424, c. 11. 1503, c. 72. 1535, c. 16. 1581, c. 111. 9 Geo. IV. c. 39, § 6. Fishers of Don, 1693; M. 14,287; 2 Ill. 163. D. Queensberry *v.* M. Annandale, 1771; M. 14,279; Hailes, 442. Colquhoun *v.* D. Montrose, 1793 and 1807; M. 12,827, 14,281–3; 4 Pat. 221. Dirom *v.* Littles, 1797; M. 14,282. E. Fife *v.* Gordon, 1807; M. *Salmon-Fishing*, Apx. 2. E. Kinnoul *v.* Hunter, 1802; M. 14,301; aff. 4 Pat. 561, 671. D. Athole *v.* Dalgleish (Maule), March 7, 1812; F. C.; Buchanan's Cases, 254; aff. 1816, 5 Dow, 282; Feb. 4, 1817; F. C.; 1823, 2 S. 442; rev. 1 W. & S. 590; 2 Ill. 163, 164. Mags. of Dumbarton *v.* Graham, Jan. 16, 1813; aff. 6 Pat. 163. Scott *v.* Kerse, Dec. 11, 1812; F. C. D. Athole *v.* Wedderburn, 1826; 5 S. 153. Forbes *v.* Smyth, 1824; 2 S. 721; aff. 1 W. & S. 583. See Fraser *v.* Duff, 1829; 8 S. 14; aff. 5 W. & S. 57. L. Gray *v.* Syme, 1835; 13 S. 1089. Cunninghame *v.* Taylor, 1804; Hume, 715. Mackenzie *v.* Renton, 1840; 2 D. 1078. Cases in Stewart's Rights of Fishing, pp. 158, 164, etc., and the bye-laws of the Commissioners of Salmon Fisheries, 31 and 32 Vict. c. 123, Sched. Hay *v.* Mags. of Perth, 1861; 24 D. 230; rev. 1863, 1 Macph. H. L. 41; 4 Macq. 535. See 22 and 23 Vict. c. 70 (Tweed Act). 20 and 21 Vict.

c. 148, § 58 (cairn nets). Mackenzie *v.* Murray, 1881; 9 R. 186 (paidle net). D. Roxburghe *v.* Waldie's Trs., 1879; 6 R. 663.

1117. In construing the statutes as to the limits within which machinery is thus prohibited, viz. "the rivers and waters of Scotland, where the sea ebbs and flows" (*a*), it has been held, That the prohibition extends to all rivers and estuaries to the fullest extent to which the sea ebbs and flows, and down to the *fauces terræ* at the mouth of the firth, and the sands dry at low water, as well as in the channel (*b*): That it does not comprehend the proper shores of the sea (*c*): That stake nets are prohibited in the landlocked estuary of a river, being the intermediate space between what is strictly the river and strictly the sea, but where the river and fresh water still exists with predominating influence; and that they cannot lawfully be placed either in the channel of such river or estuary, or on the sands which are left dry by the ebbing of the sea (*d*). 'Now, however, under the powers conferred by the Act of 1862, the Commissioners of Salmon Fisheries have by bye-laws fixed and defined the limits which divide each river or estuary in Scotland from the sea, so far as they were not already fixed by statute or judicial decision.' There is an exception in the statute of 1563 (prohibiting machinery where the sea ebbs and flows), "that it shall not be extended to the cruives and yairs being upon the water of Solway" (*e*); this exception not being touched by the 'more' recent statute (*f*).

(*a*) Stat. Alex. II. c. 16. Rob. I. c. 12. 1424, c. 11. 1427, c. 6. 1429, c. 131. 1457, c. 86. 1469, c. 38. 1477, c. 74. 1488, c. 16. 1535, c. 17. 1563, c. 68. 1579, c. 89. 1581, c. 111. 1685, c. 20. The statute of 1862 provides for the determination by the Commissioners of the limits of the different estuaries within which the prohibitions of the earlier statutes are to apply.

(*b*) D. Athole, *supra*, § 1116 (*d*). Little *v.* Grierson, 1824; 3 S. 370. Carnegie *v.* Brand, 1826; 4 S. 809. Carnegie *v.* Ross's Trs., 1829; 7 S. 284.

(*c*) E. Kintore *v.* Forbes, 1826; 4 S. 648; aff. 1828; 3 W. & S. 261; 2 Ill. 165. M'Kenzie *v.* Syme, 1830; 8 S. 1013. Dss. Sutherland *v.* Gilchrist, 1836; 14 S. 959.

(*d*) M'Kenzie *v.* Horne, 1838; 16 S. 1286; aff. 4 M'L. & R. 977. See D. Sutherland *v.* Ross, 1844; 6 D. 425; aff. 3 Bell's App. 315. As to the right to use stake nets for white fishing, see Gilbertson, Coulthard, and Mackenzie, *infra* (*f*).

(*e*) 1563, c. 68. Murray *v.* E. Selkirk, 1821; 1 S. 111; rev. 2 S. Ap. 299; 2 Ill. 165. M'Whir *v.* Oswald, 1833; 11 S. 552; 1 S. & M'L. 393.

(*f*) 9 Geo. IV. c. 39, § ult. See Solway Act, 44 Geo. III. c. 45; 25 and 26 Vict. c. 97, of which § 33 applies to the Solway the provisions of the English Salmon Fisheries Act, 24 and 25 Vict. c. 109. By that Act and the Amendment Act, 28 and 29 Vict. c. 121, § 9, fixed engines are made illegal in the Solway, unless lawfully exercised at the time of the passing of the Act by virtue of a grant, charter, or immemorial usage. See Stewart on Rights of Fishing, chap. xvii. Report of the Special Commissioners appointed to inquire into recent Legislation on Salmon Fisheries in Scotland (July 1871), p. xxxvi sqq. 40 and 41 Vict. c. 241. Johnstone *v.* Mackenzie & Beattie, 1869; 6 S. L. R. 727. Gilbertson *v.* Mackenzie, 1878; 5 R. 610. Coulthard *v.* Mackenzie, 1879; 6 R. 1322. Mackenzie *v.* Murray, 1881; 9 R. 186. D. of Buccleuch *v.* Kean, 1890; 17 R. 829.

1118. The machinery permitted in rivers and streams is regulated on this principle, that there shall be a sufficient passage left to the young fry, and, to a certain extent, for the full-grown fish. The cruives, zairs, etc., 'where permitted by grant or prescription, were, by the old rules,' not to be kept up during close time; and all boats, oars, nets, etc., 'were' to be removed. The hecks and obstructions 'were' to be of the width asunder of three inches, for the passage of the fry. The hecks of all cruives 'were to' be pulled up every Saturday night at six o'clock, and 'to' remain open till Monday morning at sunrise, and during the whole of close time (*a*). 'These erections are now regulated by a bye-law of the Commissioners, ratified by Act of Parliament in 1868. They may also be acquired and demolished by district boards (*b*).'

(*a*) 1424, c. 11. 1477, c. 73. 1489, c. 15. 9 Geo. IV. c. 39, § 7 and 9. See the Tweed Act, *supra*, § 1116 (*d*) *fin.*

(*b*) 25 and 26 Vict. c. 97, § 6 (6). 31 and 32 Vict. c. 123, § 13. D. of Fife *v.* George, 1897; 24 R. 549.

1119. Rights of Heritors.—The common interest which results from the migratory habits of the fish gives to each heritor on a river, having a grant of salmon-fishing, a title to challenge all unlawful modes of fishing (*a*).

(*a*) 9 Geo. IV. c. 39, § 10. Colquhoun *v.* D. Montrose, 1807; M. 14,283; 4 Pat. 221; 2 Ill. 163. Chisholm *v.* Fraser, 1801; M. *Salmon-Fishing*, Apx. 1; 2 Ill. 13. D. Athole, *supra*, § 1116 (*d*). E. Kintore, *supra*, § 1117 (*c*). Fraser *v.* Duff, 1829; 8 S. 14; 4 W. & S. 57. Forbes *v.* Leys, Masson, & Co., 1831; 9 S. 933; 5 W. & S. 384. Johnstone *v.* Mackenzie & Beattie, *supra*, § 1117 (*f*). Munro *v.* Munro, 1845; 7 D. 358; 8 D. 1029.

1120. A grant of fishing separate from the property of the bank implies, as a pertinent, the right of 'access and of' drawing the nets on the bank, 'foreshore, or beach'; but where the grantee has but one bank, and his opposite neighbour has a right of fishing, neither has an implied right to use the bank *ex adverso*. The grantee, although he has the privilege of using the bank, has it only so far as necessary for his fishing; and he can give no leave to another to angle, to the effect of using the bank (*a*). 'In large rivers, the owner of fishings on one bank has no right for any purpose to pass across the *medium filum* (*b*), or, in the absence of contrary possession, above or below perpendiculars dropped upon the *medium filum* from his land boundaries (*c*); in smaller streams it is usual to adjust the mode or hours of fishing by agreement (*d*). A right of fishing in a navigable river from certain lands may be defined by possession or the nature of the stream; and its extent is not affected by the formation of a bank in the channel, from which fishing can be carried on (*e*). By possession the right to fish for salmon in a river may be extended beyond the lands named in the grant, so as to entitle the grantee to fish even *ex adverso* of the lands of another proprietor, whether on the same or the other side of the river (*f*). The marches of salmon-fishings as between adjoining owners on the coast are fixed, in the absence of definition in the titles, in the same way as boundaries on the foreshore (*g*).

'An early statute provided that in all weirs or mill-dams there should be a slope or pass in mid-channel, as big as could be conveniently allowed without prejudicing the going of the mills (*h*). The matter is now regulated by a bye-law of the Commissioners (*i*).'

(*a*) 2 Ersk. 6. § 15. Matthew *v.* Blair, 1612; M. 14,263; 2 Ill. 165. L. Monimusk *v.* Forbes, 1623; M. 10,840, 14,264. Miller *v.* Blair, 1825; 4 S. 217. Forbes *v.* E. Kintore, 1826; 4 S. 656. See above, § 739. Forbes *v.* Smyth, 1824; 2 S. 721; 1 W. & S. 583. Berry *v.* Wilson, 1841; 4 D. 139. Mackenzie *v.* Davidson, 1841; 3 D. 646. Richardson *v.* Hay, 1862; 24 D. 775. E. Dalhousie *v.* M'Inroy, 1865; 3 Macph. 1168. L. Adv. *v.* Sharp, 1878; 6 R. 108 (foreshore and beach).

(*b*) Macbraire *v.* Mather, 1871; 9 Macph. 913. Mather *v.* Macbraire, 1873; 11 Macph. 522. D. Roxburghe *v.* Waldie's Trs., 1879; 6 R. 663. Robertson *v.* Foote & Co., 1879; 6 R. 1290.

(*c*) Keith *v.* Smyth, and Gray *v.* Fleming & Richardson, *citt.* § 738 (*c*).

(*d*) Milne *v.* Smith, 1850; 13 D. 112. Brown *v.* Kirkcudbright, 1678; M. 10,844. See Stuart *v.* M'Barnet, *supra*, § 1112 (*f*).

(*e*) Wedderburn *v.* Paterson, 1864; 2 Macph. 902. E. Zetland *v.* Glovers of Perth, 1868; 6 Macph. 292; aff. 1870, 8 Macph. H. L. 144. Milne *v.* Smith, *cit.* (*d*). Macbraire, *cit.* (*b*). E. Zetland *v.* Tennent's Trs., 1873; 11 Macph. 469.

(*f*) Ramsay *v.* D. Roxburghe, 1848; 10 D. 661. D. Richmond *v.* E. Seafield, 1870; 8 Macph. 530. D. Roxburghe *v.* Waldie's Trs., 1879; 6 R. 663.

(*g*) Keith *v.* Smyth, 1884; 12 R. 66. See above, § 738.

(*h*) 1696, c. 33. Forbes *v.* Leys, Masson, & Co., 1831; 9 S. 933; aff. 5 W. & S. 384. M. Ailsa *v.* Paterson, 1867; 5 S. L. R. 5.

(*i*) 25 and 26 Vict. c. 97, § 6 (6); 31 and 32 Vict. c. 123, § 11, 12. Kennedy *v.* Murray, 1869; 7 Macph. 1001.

1121. Whether a proprietor may be prevented from angling on his own bank, seems to depend on the question whether this operation be detrimental to the salmon-fishing of the grantee. In the general case he cannot be prevented (*a*).

(*a*) Forbes, *supra*, § 1120 (*a*). M'Kenzie *v.* Rose, 1830; 8 S. 816; aff. 6 W. & S. 31; 2 Ill. 43. See above, § 747. Guthrie *v.* Dunbar, 1855; 17 D. 1002. L. Somerville *v.* Smith, 1859; 22 D. 279. D. Sutherland *v.* Ross, 1836; 14 S. 906. Anderson *v.* Anderson, 1867; 6 Macph. 117. Stuart *v.* M'Barnet, 1867; 5 Macph. 753; 6 Macph. H. L. 123.

CHAPTER XVI

OF PUBLIC BURDENS ON LAND.

1122. Public Burdens generally.—The proprietor's right to his land is charged with the burden of paying such public taxes as are necessary for the great objects of protection, government, and religious instruction. These are either such as are directly payable to Government; or such as are appropriated for the maintenance of the clergy; or such as are levied for support of the poor; and other parochial burdens (*a*).

(*a*) A public burden must have a public object, and have its origin in public authority. Traill *v.* Dangerfield, 1870; 8 Macph. 579. For a more ample account of the public burdens upon land, including the property and income tax, inhabited house duty, police, and many other rates imposed by modern statutes, reference must be made to Mr. Rankine's Treatise on the Rights and Burdens incident to Ownership of Lands, Part IV. pp. 628–714.

I. LAND-TAX.

1123. Nature and History.—The cess or land-tax is a tax, not on the land itself, but on the rent of land; assessed upon each district according to a certain invariable canon, and subdivided among the several proprietors by the Commissioners of Supply. It 'was' placed under the superintendence of the Commissioners for the affairs of Taxes (*a*); 'and after various changes, its collection is now committed to the Treasury, with the aid of local Commissioners, and is regulated by the Taxes Management Act, 1880 (*b*).'

(*a*) 3 Will. IV. c. 13, § 4.
(*b*) 43 and 44 Vict. c. 19. As to land-tax, valued rent, and Commissioners of Supply, see Rankine, pp. 190 sqq., 688 sqq. The Local Government Scotland Act, 1889 (52 and 53 Vict. c. 50, § 102), preserves the administration of the Commissioners of Supply in regard to the land-tax.

1124. This tax became a permanent source of revenue in the end of the seventeenth century, superseding the occasional subsidies of the feudal government; and the old methods of valuing lands 'according to the old and new "extent"' for the levying of subsidies, were altered in 1643, and finally superseded in 1670. A new valuation was then established, which (like the valuation in England in 1692) has ever since furnished the rule of assessment (*a*). The land-tax, formerly a tax annually imposed, was, during Mr. Pitt's administration, made perpetual at the rate of four shillings in the pound. The proportion payable by Scotland is settled at £47,974. The tax has been made redeemable, so that each landowner may purchase exemption from his share of the burden (*b*).

(*a*) 1597, c. 277. 1640, c. 34. 1645, c. 6. 1656, c. 14 and 25. 1670, c. 3. 1672, c. 4. 1690, c. 6 and 9.
(*b*) 38 Geo. III. c. 5, and c. 60. See below, § 1131.

1125. Mode of Assessment.—The land-tax is levied by charging a particular sum on each county, according to the valuation settled in the seventeenth century, leaving it to be assessed on the estates of individuals by Commissioners named in the Act (*a*). It is a personal burden on the landholder in respect of his land, not a burden on the land itself, or *debitum fundi.* And the arrears of land-tax 'were' recoverable 'formerly' by process ordered by the Commissioners to be issued as for Crown debt (*b*); 'now by poinding and sale under a sheriff's warrant (*c*).' But the claim for arrears does not affect singular successors (*d*).

(*a*) See 17 and 18 Vict. c. 91, for the new mode of settling valuations. Below, § 1136. As to the Cess Rolls, and the functions still performed in this matter by the Commissioners of Supply, see the authorities summarised in Rankine on Landownership, 192. Renfrew & Brown *v.* Mags. of Glasgow, 1861; 23 D. 505. L. Adv. *v.* Commrs. of Supply of Edinr., 1861; 23 D. 933; aff. 4 Macq. 387; 24 D. H. L. 7. Trades House of Glasgow *v.* Hers. of Govan, 1887; 14 R. 910.
(*b*) 3 Will. IV. c. 13, § 5.
(*c*) 43 and 44 Vict. c. 19, § 97.
(*d*) Graham *v.* Hers. of Clackmannan, 1664; M. 10,164; 2 Ill. 166.

1126. The burden is proportioned between counties and burghs in the ratio of one-sixth to be paid by the burghs.

1127. (1.) *Counties.*—The land-tax payable by counties is levied on the proprietors of the land, and of subjects connected with it yielding a yearly revenue, under the direction, 'or rather according to the allocation,' of the Commissioners of Supply, named in the Act by which the land-tax is imposed; and the rent, as ascertained by them, is called the valued rent (*a*).

(*a*) 38 Geo. III. c. 5, § 131. 6 and 7 Will. IV. c. 65, § 12, altered and re-enacted by 43 and 44 Vict. c. 19, § 81.

1128. The qualification to be a Commissioner of Supply 'was,' that he shall possess, in property, superiority, or liferent, land valued at £100 Scots of valued rent yearly; the same land affording a qualification both to the superior and to every successive vassal whose infeftment to that extent still subsists (*a*); or that he 'should' be the eldest son of one qualified, as holder of £100 Scots of valuation, to be himself a Commissioner (*b*). He must be of lawful age; and he must, before acting, take and subscribe the oath of allegiance and abjuration, and the assurance (*c*). 'The qualification is now fixed by 17 and 18 Vict. c. 91, § 19, and 19 and 20 Vict. c. 93; 20 Vict. c. 11; 28 Vict. c. 38; 42 and 43 Vict. c. 42, § 10. The persons qualified are those named as *ex officio* Commissioners in any Act of Supply; proprietors (*d*) of heritable property worth £100 a year, or the husbands of such proprietors; eldest sons of proprietors of heritable property appearing in the valuation roll as worth £400; the factor (*e*) of the proprietor of property worth £800, in the proprietor's absence. Buildings not agricultural are estimated in regard to this qualification at half their rent appearing on the valuation roll (*f*).'

(*a*) Gordon *v.* Anderson, 1766; M. 2444; 2 Ill. 166. Hay *v.* Hepburn, 1735; M. 2436; Elch. *Com. of Supply*, 1. See also M. 8929; Elchies, *Jurisdiction*, 7. The provisions of the Acts, as applicable to England, do not extend to Scotland.
(*b*) Hay *v.* Hepburn, *cit.*
(*c*) Sutherland *v.* Sutherland, 1751; M. 2436. The oath of allegiance alone is now taken in the terms prescribed by 30 and 31 Vict. c. 75, § 5; see 21 and 22 Vict. c. 48; 22 Vict. c. 10.
(*d*) Boyd *v.* Lanark Comrs., 1876; 14 S. L. R. 489. Leslie *v.* Orkney Comrs., 1883; 20 S. L. R. 362.
(*e*) Walker *v.* Zetland Comrs., 1870; 8 Macph. 443. Craigie *v.* Aberdeenshire Comrs., 1879; 7 R. 52.
(*f*) See Journal of Jurisprudence, vol. xi. p. 554.

1129. The Commissioners of Supply proportion and allot the tax as it affects the county. They also 'divided' valuations at the desire of those having interest, subject to the review of the Court of Session (*a*); 'but this duty is now laid upon the sheriff (*b*). The Commissioners of Supply conducted the general business of the county, in regard to police rating, valuation, court-houses, and other matters, most of which have now been transferred to the County Council (*c*).'

(*a*) See the cases in Rankine on Landownership, 192.
(*b*) 52 and 53 Vict. c. 50, § 102 (Local Govt. (Scotland) Act, 1889).
(*c*) *Ib.* § 11. This Act is amended and extended to parishes by the Local Govt. (Scotland) Act, 1894 (57 and 58 Vict. c. 58).

1130. (2.) *Burghs.*—The proportion of land-tax laid on burghs is allocated among the several burghs by the Convention of Royal Burghs; and the share laid on each is again, by stentmasters chosen by the magistrates, allocated on the inhabitants, according to their 'rents and living, goods and gear, which they have within the burgh':

by which are understood the rent of houses, the profit of trade or calling, and personal estate; 'the rent being now fixed according to the value in the annual valuation roll (*a*).'

(*a*) See 17 and 18 Vict. c. 91, § 33. Renfrew & Brown *v.* Mags. of Glasgow, 1861; 23 D. 505.

1131. Redemption of Land-Tax.—By the first Act authorising the redemption of the land-tax, and by subsequent Acts amending and consolidating the system, it is provided that application may be made to two Commissioners of Supply to have the proportion of land-tax adjusted to the lands of which the exemption is to be purchased, and a certificate granted to that effect. The Commissioners appointed by the Redemption Acts may then bargain for the sale of it. When the sale is completed, and the land-tax of the lands redeemed, that land, or rather the owner of it, is thenceforward exempt from land-tax; subject, of course, to any future imposition on land, of which the share is to be ascertained correctly by schedule. The Commissioners must still, after such exemption of particular lands, state in the certificate of assessment the land-tax charged on the parish, till all be redeemed; and they are to receive from the Commissioners of Taxes a certificate of the redeemed portion. Powers are given by the Act to sell lands under entail, for redeeming the land-tax of the entailed estate, under certain precautions (*a*). Sales under these Acts must be fair in all respects; and any unfairness, as a collusive lease with a view to affect the price, will be relevant to reduce the sale (*b*). But an error of judgment in the Court, in executing the Act, will not annul the sale (*c*).

(*a*) 38 Geo. III. c. 60; 39 Geo. III. c. 6 and 21; 41 Geo. III. c. 72: consolidated by 42 Geo. III. c. 116, and amended by 53 Geo. III. c. 142; 57 Geo. III. c. 100; and 1 and 2 Geo. IV. c. 123. 4 and 5 Will. IV. c. 11 and 60. Harrison's Analysis of these Acts. Eliott *v.* Wilson, 1826; 4 S. 425: aff. 1828, 3 W. & S. 69; 2 Ill. 400. Wilson *v.* Elliot, 1826; *ib.* 732; 2 Ill. 403. Lawrie *v.* Lawrie, 1806; M. *Publ. Bur.* Apx. 2; and 2 Dow, 556.
(*b*) Hamilton *v.* Millar, 1830; 9 S. 165.
(*c*) E. of Wemyss *v.* Montgomery, 1824; 2 S. Ap. 1.

II. SCHOOLS.

Parochial burdens are directed to three objects: 1. Education; 2. The maintenance of the poor; 3. The maintenance of the clergy.

1132. Parochial Schools (*a*). (1.) *Tax.*—Provision 'was' made for the maintenance of schools by means of a tax upon landholders or heritors and tenants; 'which is now levied half on owners and half on occupiers, along with the assessment for relief of the poor (*b*).'

(2.) *Schoolmaster.*—The parochial schoolmaster 'had to' be qualified in morals, literature, and religion, and such branches of education as the minister and heritors 'should' require, and to the satisfaction of the presbytery of the bounds (whose decision on the qualifications required 'was' not subject to any appeal); and he 'had till 1861 to' sign the Formula and Confession of Faith of the Church of Scotland (*c*). The appointment 'prior to 1872 was' for life, or during good behaviour, and the schoolmaster 'continued' under the superintendence of the presbytery (*d*); 'but is now during the pleasure of the school board, reasonable notice of removal or dismissal being given, as required by the common law (*e*), and the dismissal being valid only if made after the notices and in conformity with the regulations of the Public School Teachers Act, 1882 (*f*).'

'In 1861 the 14th section of 43 Geo. III. c. 54 was partly repealed, and the jurisdiction in complaints against schoolmasters on the ground of immoral conduct and cruel and improper treatment of pupils, but not on the ground of neglect of duty or disqualification, was transferred from the presbytery to the final judgment of the sheriff (*g*).

'The power of applying to the sheriff for removal of a teacher appointed previous to 1872, on the ground of immoral conduct, or improper or cruel treatment of his scholars, is now vested in the school board (*h*). The school board has also power, when they consider any such teacher incompetent, unfit, or inefficient, to require a special report regarding the school and teacher, from Her Majesty's inspector, on which, if they see cause, they may remove him. Such removal must, however, be confirmed by the Education Department; and the teacher's right to a retiring allowance under the Act of 1861 is saved. The acts of the school board in this matter are not subject to review by any Court; but may be set aside, at least so far as regards a refusal of the retiring allowance, on the ground of material deviation from the statutory regulations, oppression, or bad faith (*i*). The teachers of burgh schools, not having held office under the old law *ad vitum aut culpam*, may be dismissed or removed as formerly upon any reasonable ground by the school board, to which the powers of the magistrates were transferred by the Act (*k*). Parochial schools and burgh schools are now regulated by the Education (Scotland) Act, 1872; which places all under the government of school boards elected by the ratepayers of the several school districts, which generally, though not always, correspond with the area of parishes and burghs.'

(*a*) M'Culloch *v.* Allan, 1793; M. 7471; rev. 4 Pat. 119. 35 and 36 Vict. c. 62. See § 1, 11, 24, 46; see also Amending Acts, 41 and 42 Vict. c. 78; 46 and 47 Vict. c. 56. School Board of Peebles *v.* Mags. of Peebles, 1874; 1 R. 686. Selkirk Parish School Board *v.* Burgh School Board, 1875; 2 R. 761. Lochgilphead School Board *v.* S. Knapdale School Board, 1877; 4 R. 389.

(*b*) 35 and 36 Vict. c. 62, § 44. *Infra*, § 1136A. See Steuart *v.* E. Seafield, 1876; 3 R. 518 (obligation to relieve of schoolmaster's salary not applicable to this rate). Hogg *v.* Auchtermuchty Par. Board, 1880; 7 R. 986 (minister's manse and glebe not exempt, 2nd Div.). Gillanders *v.* Campbell, 1884; 12 R. 309 (do. 1st Div.).

(*c*) Act of Privy Council, Dec. 10, 1616, in Kames' Statute Law, 457. 1633, c. 5. 1693, c. 22. 1696, c. 26. 43 Geo. III. c. 54. Murray *v.* Donaldson, 1834; 13 S. 128. Simpson *v.* D. Buccleuch, 1835; *ib.* 1066. See Macalpine *v.* Campbell, 1840; 2 D. 481. Mathieson *v.* Dunsmure, 1829; 8 S. 252. Ross *v.* Findlater, 1826; 4 S. 514. The qualification of schoolmasters is now fixed by certificate of competency obtained by examination under regulations made by the Scottish Education Department, 35 and 36 Vict. c. 62, § 56 sqq., or by university degrees, *ib.* § 59.

(*d*) Murray and Simpson, *supra* (*c*). Gordon *v.* Bell's Trs., 1843; 6 D. 222. Presby. of Elgin *v.* Mags. of Elgin, 1861; 23 D. 287, 311 (Burgh School).

(*e*) 35 and 36 Vict. c. 62, § 55. Morrison *v.* Abernethy School Board, 1876; 3 R. 945. Fraser, M. & S. 51, 60, etc. *Supra*, § 174, 187, 189.

(*f*) 45 and 46 Vict. c. 18. Hinds *v.* Dunbar School Board, 1883; 10 R. 930. Barvas School Board *v.* Macgregor, 1891; 18 R. 647.

(*g*) Fleming *v.* Dickson, 1862; 1 Macph. 188. Naysmith *v.* Dalhousie, 1865; 3 Macph. 565. Macpherson *v.* Hers. of Kilmallie, 1873; 11 Macph. 309.

(*h*) 35 and 36 Vict. c. 62, § 60, subs. 1.

(*i*) *Ib.* subs. 2. Robb *v.* Logiealmond School Board, 1875; 2 R. 417, 698. Morison *v.* Glenshiel School Board, 1875; 2 R. 715. Macfarlane *v.* Mochrum School Board, 1875; 3 R. 88. Marshall *v.* Ardrossan School Board, 1879; 7 R. 359.

(*k*) 35 and 36 Vict. c. 62, § 24. Mitchell *v.* Elgin School Board, 1883; 10 R. 982. See Presby. of Elgin, *supra* (*d*), and Whyte *v.* Haddington School Board, 1874; 1 R. 1124. *Infra*, § 2189.

1133. (3.) *Education.*—'Formerly' the heritors and minister, 'now the school board elected by the ratepayers,' determine what branches of education are to be taught in the school (*a*). The schools 'were' also under presbyterial visitation at least once a year (*b*); 'a power which is abolished, but is not transferred to the school board (*c*)'; and 'while' it 'was' prescribed that the Bible 'should' be read as a regular exercise, and the Shorter Catechism taught, 'the Act of 1872 does not enjoin, though it may be said to recognise or sanction, the giving of religious instruction, declaring it expedient that school boards should be at liberty to continue the existing custom (*d*). And while every public school is open at all times to the inspection of any of Her Majesty's inspectors, it is no part of such inspector's duties to inquire into religious instruction, or examine any scholar in religious knowledge (*e*).'

(*a*) 43 Geo. III. c. 54, § 16. 35 and 36 Vict. c. 62, § 23, 24, etc. Hunter *v.* Kelso School Board, 1875; 2 R. 520.

(*b*) Acts of Assembly, 1766, c. 13. 1800, c. 11.

(*c*) 35 and 36 Vict. c. 62, § 23. Kelso School Board *v.* Hunter, 1874; 2 R. 228.

(*d*) 35 and 36 Vict. c. 62, preamble.

(*e*) *Ib.* § 66. 53 and 54 Vict. c. 43, § 8. There is a "conscience clause" allowing children to be withdrawn from any religious instruction or observance, § 68. 53 and 54 Vict. c. 43, § 6; and no Parliamentary grant can be made for religious instruction, *ib.* § 67.

1134. (4.) *Schoolhouse, etc.*—By 'a former' Act (*a*) it 'was' provided, that in every parish there 'should' be a schoolmaster (*b*), or in certain parishes two, at the discretion of the heritors and minister, subject to the review of the quarter-sessions. A schoolhouse, a house for the master, and a garden, 'had to' be provided by the heritors, with the advice of the presbytery, to be defrayed by assessment and relief according to the valued rents; a majority of the heritors, with consent of the schoolmaster, being empowered to remove the site of the school when they 'should' think it necessary, the jurisdiction in this matter being in the quarter-sessions without appeal (*c*). 'The school boards of burghs must now provide necessary schools and schoolmasters' houses (*d*); and the town council of every burgh has to pay to the school board each year "such sum as has been the custom" of the burgh prior to 1872 to pay to the burgh school (*e*).

'The duty of ascertaining the amount of school accommodation required in any parish or burgh, and of making provision for the education of all persons in a parish or burgh, is now laid on school boards, subject to the approval of the Education Department. The various provisions of the present statute are too extensive to be detailed here (*f*).'

(*a*) 43 Geo. III. c. 54.
(*b*) See Lord Belhaven *v.* Presby. of Hamilton, 1845 ; 7 D. 1061.
(*c*) Anderson *v.* Hers. of Bourtie, Nov. 26, 1808 ; F. C.; 2 Ill. 166. Dawson *v.* Allardice, Feb. 18, 1809 ; F. C. Gartshore *v.* Adams, 1858 ; 20 D. 712. Ainslies *v.* Tainsh, 1872 ; 10 Macph. 336. See as to the former law on this subject, Duncan on Parochial Law, pp. 761, 806, 819.
(*d*) 35 and 36 Vict. c. 62, § 37, 54, etc.
(*e*) *Ib.* § 46. Dunbar School Board *v.* Mags. of Dunbar, 1876 ; 3 R. 631. Perth School Board *v.* Mags. of Perth, 1878 ; 6 R. 45. Hunter *v.* School Board of Lochgilphead, 1886 ; 14 R. 135 (illegal uses of school buildings). School Board of Greenock *v.* Mags., 1890 ; 17 R. 967.
(*f*) 35 and 36 Vict. c. 62, § 25 sqq. L. Adv. *v.* Stow School Board, 1876 ; 3 R. 469.

III. POOR-RATES.

1135. Means for Support of the Poor (*a*).—During the reigns of the five Jameses and of Mary—that is, during the fifteenth and the greater part of the sixteenth century—various statutes were passed of extreme severity for repressing vagabonds and masterful beggars. Those laws, on the Reformation, were combined with provisions for the aged and impotent poor; not resulting, as in England, in the establishment of a permanent *fund* for the poor, but at all times restricted to the *actual* necessity, as it arises, of the disabled and impotent poor. The funds for the support of the poor are two-fold (*b*): 1. Those arising from voluntary contributions at the church doors, mortifications, etc.; and 2. A sum levied by assessment, in supplement of those funds. Here the latter only is to be considered, in so far as a burden is thereby imposed on landholders and residenters in parishes.

(*a*) See below, of the Condition and Provision for the Poor, and of the Law of Parish Settlements, § 2190 et seq.
(*b*) 1 Ersk. 7. § 63, with Ivory's notes. Dunlop, Burn, and Monypenny on the Poor Law. Dunlop, Parochial Law, p. 161. Guthrie Smith's Digest of the Poor Law, 3rd ed., 1878.

1136. The Assessment for levying the funds necessary for the poor 'was before 1846' regulated by the heritors and kirk-session in landward parishes, and by magistrates in burghs (*a*); all proprietors of land and houses liable in payment of poor-rates being entitled to vote by themselves or by proxy at meetings of heritors and kirk-session, in relation to the administration of the poor laws, though not entered in the cess-rolls, nor in the books of the collector of cess (*b*).

'**Poor Law Amendment Act, 1845.**—In parishes partly burghal and partly landward, the administration of the funds provided for the poor was vested in the heritors, kirk-session, and burgh magistrates, acting as one body (*c*). In the few parishes in which the funds requisite for the relief of the poor continued to be provided without assessment, the administration remained unchanged (*d*); but where an assessment is levied, a parochial board was formed under the Act of 1845. It consisted in rural parishes of owners and occupants of lands and heritages of more than £20 a year of annual value, and of members elected by the kirk-session and the ratepayers; and in burghal parishes of members elected by owners and occupants, with four persons named by the magistrates and four by the kirk-session. In mixed parishes, the provost and magistrates of any burgh in the parish were members of the board, along with the heritors and elected members (*e*). To these boards were committed the functions of the heritors and kirk-session in distributing the funds for relief of the poor, and other duties, *e.g.* the administration in rural parishes of the sanitary laws (*f*).'

(*a*) 1579, c. 74. 1594, c. 147. 1597, c. 268. 1600, c. 19. Proclamation, Aug. 11, 1693. 1672, c. 18. 1698, c. 21.
(*b*) Robertson *v.* Murdoch, 1830 ; 8 S. 587. See as to mandates (which must be signed, but need not be probative or stamped) in meetings of heritors and kirk-session under old system, and in elections of parochial board under the recent system, Robertson, *cit.* 8 and 9 Vict. c. 83, § 22. Thompson *v.* Muir, 1871 ; 10 Macph. 178 ; aff. 1876, 3 R. H. L. 1. Laurie *v.* Thomson, 1874 ; 1 R. 402.
(*c*) Mags. of Dunbar *v.* Heritors of Dunbar, 1833 ; 11 S. 879 ; as rev. 1835, 1 S. & M'L. 134. Currie *v.* Lockhart, 1841 ; 3 D. 799. See also Minr. of Dalry *v.* Newall, 1791 ; M. 14,557. E. Galloway *v.* Dalry, Feb. 22, 1810 ; F. C.
(*d*) 8 and 9 Vict. c. 83, § 17, 22.
(*e*) *Ib.*
(*f*) See below, § 2190 sqq. 8 and 9 Vict. c. 83. 30 and 31 Vict. c. 101 (Public Health Act, repd. 1897). All actions for anything done in execution of the Poor Law Act (not including actions upon contracts made by boards, etc. (Mackay *v.* Beattie, 1860 ; 22 D. 1486), or actions, such as declarators or reductions, proper to the Supreme Court (Thompson *v.* Muir, 1871 ; 10 Macph. 178. Ferguson *v.* Malcolm, 1850 ; 12 D. 732)), must be brought in the Sheriff Court and within three calendar months after the fact committed, and a month's notice of the action must be given. 8 and 9 Vict. c. 83, § 86. Knox *v.* Montgomery, 1865 ; 3 Macph. 890. Knox *v.* M'Arthur, *ib.* M'Laren *v.* Steele, 1857 ; 20 D. 48. Mackay *v.* Chalmers, 1858 ; 21 D. 443. M'Coll *v.* Babtie and Beattie, 1882 ; 9 R. 470. See Guthrie Smith's Poor Law, p. 96 sqq., and comp. above, § 661 (*c*), (*f*).

1136A. 'Local Government Board and Parish Councils.—By 8 and 9 Vict. c. 83, § 91, all former statutes were repealed, in so far as they are at variance or inconsistent with the provisions of that Act; but they continue in force in all other respects. By this Act a Board of Supervision was appointed to inquire into the management of the poor, and control the proceedings of parochial boards (*a*); and provisions made for the election of these parochial boards, on which was conferred the power of assessment. The powers of the Board of Supervision are now vested in the Local Government Board for Scotland (*b*); and popularly elected Parish Councils are created (*c*), which take the place and are deemed to be a continuance of the respective parochial boards, and subject to their liabilities and to the provisions of Acts of Parliament relating to or dealing with the powers and duties of parochial boards (*d*). Various modes of assessment were allowed by the Act; but subsequently they were abolished, excepting that by which one-half of the assessment is imposed on the owners as a class, and the other half upon the tenants or occupants as a class, of all lands and heritages, including shootings and deer forests (*e*), within the parish or combination, rateably according to the annual value (*f*). The 35th section of the 8 and 9 Vict. c. 83 also permits a parochial board to continue to assess according to any mode established by local Act of Parliament, or by usage prior to 1845 (*g*). The parochial board, now parish council, is authorised by § 36, and in some cases required (24 and 25 Vict. c. 37), to classify lands and heritages equitably, and fix different rates of assessment for them (*h*). Power to borrow money on the security of the assessments is given to Parochial Boards by statute (*i*).'

(*a*) As to the powers of this board, see Clark *v.* Board of Supervision, 1873; 1 R. 261.
(*b*) 57 and 58 Vict. c. 58, § 3 (Local Government (Scotland) Act, 1894).
(*c*) *Ib.* § 8, sqq.
(*d*) *Ib.* § 22, 23. Par. Coun. of Kilmarnock *v.* Ossington's Trs., 1896; 23 R. 833.
(*e*) 49 Vict. c. 15.
(*f*) 24 and 25 Vict. c. 37. Galloway *v.* Nicolson, 1875; 2 R. 650.
(*g*) Croll *v.* Scot. Central Ry. Co., 1861; 23 D. 747.
(*h*) N. B. Ry. Co. *v.* Paterson, 1887; 14 R. 478 (classification must be exhaustive—railways). Bruce *v.* Fordoun Ratepayers, 1889; 16 R. 568 (classn. may be abandoned without consent of B. of S.).
(*i*) 49 and 50 Vict. c. 51.

1136B. 'Valuation of Lands.—By the Valuation of Lands Act of 1854, 17 and 18 Vict. c. 91, a valuation roll is now prepared annually by officers (assessors) appointed for the purpose, according to which the poor-rates and all other public local assessments leviable upon the real rent (*a*) are assessed and collected. This roll contains the name or description of the subjects,—*i.e.* of all lands and heritages capable of yielding rent, even although exempt from taxation or not actually yielding profit (*b*),—the names of the proprietor, tenant, and occupier, and the yearly rent or value. An appeal against the assessor's valuation is allowed to the magistrates of burghs, or, in counties, to the Commissioners of Supply, from whose determination there is an appeal, upon a case stated at the instance either of the party complaining or of the assessor, to two judges of the Court of Session, named for the purpose by Act of Sederunt (*c*). When the roll is completed, copies are furnished to the clerks of the several parish councils, etc., and it is in force as the valuation roll of the county or burgh for the year from Whitsunday preceding to Whitsunday following. The "lands and heritages" valued in the roll include lands and houses; shootings and deer forests, whether actually let or not (*d*); fishings (*e*); water power (*f*); woods (*g*), copse, and underwood yielding revenue; ferries (*h*); piers, harbours, docks (*i*), etc.; canals, railways (*k*), including tramways in the streets of towns (*l*); mines and quarries actually worked (*m*); coalworks, waterworks (*n*); limeworks, brickworks, ironworks, gasworks (*o*), factories; all buildings and pertinents thereof, and all machinery fixed or attached (*p*) to any lands or heritages (*q*). The term also includes prisons (*r*), the right of gathering seaware for manufacturing kelp, and using the seashore for its manufacture (*s*), gas-pipes and water-pipes laid along highways (*t*); but not commuted multures (*u*).'

(*a*) The Act is applicable only to local, not to imperial taxation; but the same valuation roll may be made available for both purposes, when the surveyor of public taxes is appointed assessor under the Valuation Act, as provided by 20 and 21 Vict. c. 58. See Menzies *v.* Solr. of Inland Rev., 1878; 5 R. 531. So the valuation roll is not conclusive in questions as to the amount of provisions between an heir of entail and younger children—Leith *v.* Leith, 1862; 24 D. 1059, 1082; nor in estimating the composition due to a superior. Hill *v.* Cal. Ry. Co., 1877; 5 R. 386. It is provided that nothing in the Act shall "exempt from or render liable to assessment any person or property not previously exempt from or liable to assessment." 17 and 18 Vict. c. 91, § 41. 30 and 31 Vict. c. 80, § 9 (railways, etc.). 58 and 59 Vict. 41. M'Laren *v.* Clyde Nav. Trs., 1865; 4 Macph. 58; aff. 1868, 6 Macph. H. L. 81. E. Traquair's Trs. *v.* Hers. of Innerleithen, 1870; 9 Macph. 234.

(*b*) Menzies, 1873; 11 Macph. 989. Renfrew Prison Bd., 1865; 4 Macph. 1137. Barony Parish, 1877; 4 R. 1149. Univ. of Glasgow, 1870; 11 Macph. 982. Univ. of Edin. *v.* Greig, 1865; 3 Macph. 1151; rev. 6 Macph. H. L. 97; etc.

(*c*) 17 and 18 Vict. c. 91, § 8. 20 and 21 Vict. c. 58. 30 and 31 Vict. c. 80, § 8. 42 and 43 Vict. c. 42, § 4. See 11 Macph. 991, 992. M'Gregor *v.* Menzies, 1874; 1 R. 1144. Rule *v.* L. Abinger, 1883; 10 R. 502.

(*d*) Crawford *v.* Stewart, 1861; 33 Jur. 498; 23 D. 965. Middleton *v.* L. Adv., 1876; 3 R. 599. 49 Vict. c. 15.

(*e*) L. Herries, 1883; 11 R. 397 (white fishings in Solway).

(*f*) Shaws Water Co. *v.* Greenock Police Comrs., 1862; 24 D. 1302; rev. 1863, 1 Macph. H. L. 59. Fleming, Reid, & Co. *v.* Greenock Assr., 1884; 11 R. 857.

(*g*) Allan *v.* Dunlop, 1858; 20 D. 1354. L. Forbes, 1861; 24 D. 1458. Innes, 1875; 4 R. 1147.

(*h*) Anderson *v.* Gillanders, 1853; 15 D. 577. Baillie *v.* Hay, 1866; 4 Macph. 625. E. P. & D. Ry. Co. *v.* Arthur, 1854; 17 D. 252 (see 17 and 18 Vict. c. 91, § 22). Scottish Central Ry. Co., 1863; 1 Macph. 1198. L. Blantyre, 1877; 4 R. 1150.

(*i*) Stonehaven Harbour Trs., 1865; 4 Macph. 1139. Adamson *v.* Clyde Nav. Trs., 1863; 1 Macph. 974; 1865, 3 Macph. H. L. 101; 4 Macq. 931. Clyde Trs., 1866; 4 Macph. 1143. Kirkwall Harbour Trs., 1881; 9 R. 1243. Clyde Trs., 1873; 11 Macph. 979.

(*k*) Anderson *v.* Union Canal Co., 1839; 1 D. 648; 1847; 9 D. 402. Edin. and Glasgow Ry. Co. *v.* Adamson, 1853; 15 D. 537; 2 Macq. 331. Duncan *v.* Scot. N.-E. Ry. Co., 1867; 6 Macph. 152; rev. 1870, 8 Macph. H. L. 53; 2 Sc. Ap. 20. See below, § 1136D.

(*l*) Craig *v.* Edin. Tramways Co., 1874; 1 R. 947.

(*m*) See 8 and 9 Vict. c. 83, § 37. 17 and 18 Vict. c. 91, § 42. Heritors of Kirkmabreck, 1861; 24 D. 1456. Carron Co., 1864; 4 Macph. 1133. Summerlee Iron Co., 1875; 4 R. 1146. Blantyre Par. Bd. *v.* Lanarksh. Assessor, 1883; 10 R. 773. L. Elphinstone *v.* Do., 1888; 15 R. 637.

(*n*) Dundee Waterworks Comrs. *v.* Dundee Road Trs., etc., 1883; 11 R. 390. Mags. of Glasgow *v.* City Par., etc., 1884; 12 R. 3.

(*o*) These are valued in the same manner as railways under § 23 of the Act. See 50 and 51 Vict. c. 51, and below, § 1136D. Falkirk Gas Co., *infra* (*t*). Phœnix Gas Light Co., L. R. 1 Q. B. 241. Edin. Gas Co., 1887; 14 R. 583.

(*p*) Pollok, 1862; 24 D. 1457. Graham Bros., 1873; 11 Macph. 982–3. As to telegraph and telephone wires and posts, see Elect. Tel. Co. *v.* Salford, 11 Ex. 181. Lanc. Telephone Co. *v.* Overseers of Manchester, 14 Q. B. D. 267. Guthrie Smith's Poor Law, p. 109.

(*q*) 17 and 18 Vict. c. 91, § 42.

(*r*) Renfrewshire Prison Board, 1865; 4 Macph. 1137.

(*s*) British Seaweed Co., 1866; 4 Macph. 1139. Gordon, 1866; 4 Macph. 1141.

(*t*) Hay *v.* Edin. Water Co., 1850; 12 D. 1240; aff. 1854, 1 Macq. 682; 17 D. H. L. 1; 26 Jur. 246. Falkirk Gas Co., 1864; 4 Macph. 1133.

(*u*) Campbell, 1864; 4 Macph. 1132. D. Sutherland, 1869; 11 Macph. 980. M'Leod, *ib.*

1136C. 'The yearly value of lands and heritages is taken to be "the rent at which, one year with another, such lands and heritages might, in their actual state (*a*), be reasonably expected to let from year to year"; and if they are "*bonâ fide* let for a yearly rent, conditioned as the fair annual value thereof, without grassum or consideration other than the rent," it is taken as the yearly rent or value under the Act (*b*). In assessments for the support of the poor, the gross value is fixed by the valuation roll, in making up which this rule is followed. But the parochial board is still bound to make deduction of the probable annual cost (which may be ascertained by striking an average) of repairs, insurance, and other expenses necessary to maintain the lands and heritages in their actual state, as well as of all rates, taxes, and public charges (*c*).'

(*a*) See Paterson *v.* Comrs., 1878; 9 R. 1237, and Lanarksh. Co. Coun. *v.* Wishart, 1891; 7 Sh. Ct. R. 295, as to unfinished property. Cal. Ry. Co. *v.* Lanarksh. Assessor, 1896; 23 R. 691 (houses of railway co.'s employees).

(*b*) 17 and 18 Vict. c. 91, § 6. N. B. Ry. Co. *v.* Leith Assessor, 1884; 11 R. 558. Gosnell *v.* Edin. Assessor, 1883; 10 R. 665. Marr Typefdg. Co. *v.* Edin. Assr., 1884; 11 R. 563; 12 R. 571. Dundee Harbour Trs. *v.* Assessor, 1886; 13 R. 829; cases in 14 R. 579–582, 589; 18 R. 939, 941, 945. Craigton Cemy. Co. *v.* Lanarksh. Assessor, 1889; 16 R. 802 (cemetery). Aberdeen Cemy. Co., 1891; 18 R. 936 (do.). Crawford *v.* Haddington Assessor, 1896; 23 R. 685 (goodwill of public-house). As to subjects in the occupation of the owner, or not *bonâ fide* let at their fair value, see Guthrie Smith on the Poor Law, p. 129. Rankine on Landownership, 205.

(*c*) 8 and 9 Vict. c. 83, § 37. Anderson *v.* Union Canal Co., 1839; 1 D. 648; 1847, 9 D. 402. E. & G. Ry. *v.* Adamson, 1853; 15 D. 537; 1855, 17 D. 1007. Edinr. and Glasgow Ry. Co. *v.* Meek, 1864; 3 Macph. 229. Edinr. and Glasgow Ry. Co. *v.* Hall, 1864; 4 Macph. 301. Glasgow Gas Light Co. *v.* Adamson, 1863; 1 Macph. 727. Croll, *supra*, § 1136A. Steuart *v.* Par. Bd. of Keith, 1869; 8 Macph. 26. Mags. of Glasgow *v.* Hall, 1887; 14 R. 319.

1136D. 'The ordinary mode of rating being inapplicable to railways and canals passing through many parishes, the proportion of their annual value on which assessment is made for each parish is according to the distance for which the line or canal passes through or is situated in such parish, in proportion to its whole length (*a*). The computation is to be made of the whole railway or canal as a *unum quid*, including stations, which are not to be separately assessed, and everything necessary for the convenient use of the railway (*b*). A special valuation roll is made up for the railways and canals of Scotland by the assessor of railways and canals, setting forth the yearly value of the whole lands and heritages belonging to each railway or canal company (or commissioners acting under statute (*c*)), the names of the parishes in which the undertaking is situated, its total length, and its length in each parish and county, the cost of the several stations, wharfs, docks, and places of business, etc. (*d*). From the *cumulo* yearly rent or value of the undertaking, the following deductions are made: a sum equal to five per cent. of the whole cost of the stations, wharfs, docks, depôts, counting-houses, and other places of business, and one-half of the annual expense of maintaining or repairing the permanent way of railways (repairs of stations, wharfs, etc., not being allowed by the assessor (*e*)). The total mileage of the canal or railway (including ferries) bears the same proportion to the mileage in the parish as the *cumulo* value, after these deductions have been made, bears to the amount assessable in each parish, with the addition of five per cent. of the cost of any station, wharf, etc., situated within such parish (*f*). Statutory provision is made for making good any deficiency in parochial assessments, during the progress of the works, caused by the compulsory taking of assessable lands by promoters under the Lands Clauses Act (*g*).'

(*a*) 8 and 9 Vict. c. 83, § 45. See above, § 1136B (*o*).
(*b*) Edinr. and Glasg. Ry. Co. *v.* Adamson, 1853; 15 D. 537; aff. 2 Macq. 331. Dundee, etc., Joint Line *v.* Arbroath Assr., 1883; 11 R. 396.
(*c*) Caln. Canal Comrs. *v.* County Council of Inverness, 1894; 21 R. 1045 (see 22 R. 149).
(*d*) 17 and 18 Vict. c. 91, § 20. Comrs. of Supply of Argyll *v.* Caln. Canal Comrs., 1872; 10 Macph. 639. N. B. Ry. Co. *v.* Wallace, 1884; 12 R. 6 (revenue derived from working lines of other companies).
(*e*) 17 and 18 Vict. c. 91, § 22; amended by 30 and 31 Vict. c. 80, § 3, 4.
(*f*) *Ib.* See Edinr. and Glasgow Ry. Co. *v.* Adamson, *cit.* E. P. and D. Ry. Co. *v.* Arthur, 1855; 17 D. 252; 20 D. 677. N. B. Ry. Co. *v.* Greig, 1866; 4 Macph. 645. Edinr. and Glasgow Ry. Co. *v.* Hall, 1866; 4 Macph. 301. Edinr. and Glasg. Ry. Co. *v.* Meek, *cit.* § 1136C (*c*). Glasgow, Barrhead, and Neilston Ry. Co. *v.* Caln. Ry. Co., 1855; 17 D. 1148; rev. 1860, 22 D. H. L. 1. Guthrie Smith's Poor Law, 150 sqq. Deas on Railways.
(*g*) 8 and 9 Vict. c. 19, § 127. Hall *v.* Glasg. Union Ry. Co., 1881; 8 R. 687. Stratton *v.* Metr. Board of Works, L. R. 10 C. P. 76; 44 L. J. M. C. 33.

Parishes are in three situations: 1. Landward; 2. Burghal; and 3. Mixed.

1137. (1.) *Landward Parishes.*—In these parishes (including burghs of barony and regality) (*a*), every inhabitant 'was' liable to a proportion of the tax, there being a double assessment—one in respect of land as heritors, and one in respect of personal property as inhabitants (*b*).

(*a*) Gammell, 1822; Dunlop, Par. Law, 410, and Apx. No. 10.
(*b*) 1579, c. 74. 1663, c. 16. Proclamation, Aug. 11, 1692. See § 1136A.

1138. Heritors are liable in their parish to an assessment in respect of all their landed property within the parish; not for landed property in other parishes, unless by convention or Act of Parliament it has been otherwise settled (*a*). Wadsetters and liferenters are liable to assessments as heritors (*b*). Saltworks, coalworks, and mills are assessed as real property (*c*). Harbour dues 'were' not subject to taxation in so far as applied to the keeping up or improving of the port (*d*). It would seem that superiors are not liable for their feu-duties, the land being already fully assessed (*e*). A canal company is assessable for poor-rates in a landward parish through which the canal runs, in proportion to the annual value of the portion of the canal in that parish (*f*). The exemptions are, the royal property (*g*), and the manses and glebes of 'parish—not of *quoad sacra* parish (*h*)'—clergymen, churches, churchyards, and schoolhouses (*i*). 'Parish councils have power to exempt individuals on the ground of poverty (*k*).'

(*a*) See below, § 1144; above, 1136A.
(*b*) 1663, c. 16. Dunlop, Par. Law, 230. Tutors, curators, commissioners, trustees, adjudgers, wadsetters, or other persons in actual receipt of the rents and profits of lands and heritages, including corporations, are liable to assessment as owners. 8 and 9 Vict. c. 83, § 1. See Hay *v.* Edinr. Water Co., 1854; 1 Macq. 682.
(*c*) Collector of Inveresk *v.* Mags. of Musselburgh, 1794; M. 10,585; 2 Ill. 167. Bakers of Paisley *v.* Mags. of Paisley, 1836; 15 S. 200. See above, § 1136B.
(*d*) Heritors of South Leith *v.* Mags. of Edinr., 1833; 15 S. 204. See as to deductions under the present law, § 1136B, 1136C, 1136D. This statement is not now law. Trustees occupying property yielding or capable of yielding a net annual value above the cost of repairs, insurance, and the expenses of maintaining the property in its actual condition, are liable to be assessed for the surplus, although bound to apply it for public purposes, such as the extension and improvement of the harbour. Adamson *v.* Clyde Trs., 1860; 22 D. 606; 1863, 1 Macph. 974; aff. 1865, 3 Macph. H. L. 100; 4 Macq. 931. **Mersey Dock Trs.** *v.* **Cameron**, 1865; 3 Macph. H. L. 102, note; 11 H. L. Ca. 443. **Gardiner** *v.* **Leith Dock Comrs.**, 1864; 2 Macph. 1234; aff. 1866, 4 Macph. H. L. 14; L. R. 1 Sc. Ap. 17. Univ. of Edinr. *v.* Greig, 1865; 3 Macph. 1151; rev. 1868, 6 Macph. H. L. 97; L. R. 1 Sc. Ap. 349. Greig *v.* Heriot's Hospital, 1866; 4 Macph. 675. Comrs. of Supply of Argyll *v.* Caln. Canal Comrs., 1872; 10 Macph. 639. Reg. *v.* Metr. Board of Works, L. R. 4 Q. B. 15; 38 L. J. Mag. Ca. 24 (sewers, etc.). Reg. *v.* St. Martin's, Leicester, L. R. 2 Q. B. 403; 36 L. J. Mag. Ca. 99 (constabulary).
(*e*) Dunlop, Par. Law, 410. Heritors of South Leith, *supra* (*d*). See below, § 1164 (*b*).
(*f*) Anderson, *supra*, § 1136C (*c*). See above, § 1136D.
(*g*) L. Adv. *v.* Edinr. Police Comrs, 1850; 12 D. 456. L. Adv. *v.* Oliver, 1852; 14 D. 356. Adamson, Univ. of Edinr., and cases cited, note (*d*); and below, § 1145.
(*h*) Tevendale *v.* Taylor, 1871; 15 J. of J. 274.

(*i*) Heritors of Cargill *v.* Tasker, Feb. 29, 1816; F. C. Dunlop, 412 (manses). Forbes *v.* Gibson, 1850; 13 D. 341; aff. 1 Macq. 106 (do.). No poor-rates can be imposed in respect of any church, chapel, or premises exclusively appropriated to religious worship; 28 and 29 Vict. c. 36. Steel *v.* Bain, 1870; 14 J. of J. 526; 2 Sel. Sh. Ct. Ca. 337 (Dove Wilson, S.S.—not on landlord drawing rent); and Sunday and ragged schools may be exempted by the board. 32 and 33 Vict. c. 40. Scientific and literary societies are also exempt. 6 and 7 Vict. c. 36. See Guthrie Smith on the Poor Law, p. 182. See for further exemptions, 31 and 32 Vict. 110 (Post Office Telegraphs). 23 and 24 Vict. c. 112 (Defence Acts). 17 and 18 Vict. c. 104, § 430 (lighthouses managed by Northern Lights Comrs.). 17 and 18 Vict. c. 106 (places for militia stores). M'Isaac *v.* Mackenzie, 1869; 7 Macph. 598.

(*k*) 8 and 9 Vict. c. 83, § 42.

1139. The rule for assessing the property of a heritor is the real rent 'or "annual value" (*a*), of which the valuation roll now affords an authoritative estimate (*b*)'; but 'by the old law' a discretion 'was' given to the heritors and kirk-session to take either that or the valued rent, provided they 'applied' the same rule throughout. Where the real rent 'was' taken, a deduction of one-fourth 'was' given for repairs; 'but deductions are now made on the principle above stated, except where a custom has prevailed to the contrary (*c*).' The valued rent 'was' taken as in the assessment for the county taxes (*d*). 'It was held under the old law that' wherever the heritors 'took' the valued rent, and that 'was' found to be unequal and unjust, the Court of Session 'might' interfere to direct the real rent to be taken; as, in a landward parish containing a large town population, where the valued rent of the town was very small compared with the country district, 'to direct assessment upon' the real rent with a proper deduction for repairs, etc., from the rent of houses (*e*).

(*a*) 8 and 9 Vict. c. 89, § 34.
(*b*) See above, § 1136B.
(*c*) See above, § 1136C. Croll, *ib. cit.*
(*d*) See above, § 1127. Scott *v.* Fraser, 1773; M. 10,577; Hailes, 522; 2 Ill. 167. Hers. of Cargill, *supra*, 1138 (*i*).
(*e*) Crawford *v.* Harkness, 1838; 16 S. 1072. See above, § 1136A.

1140. The inhabitants of a parish (though they should not be heritors, nor, strictly speaking, householders, but only residents in the parish) 'were' liable to half of the assessment laid on the parish, in respect of their personal property, wherever situate; and individually they 'were' liable, both as heritors in the parish of domicile, to their share of the heritors' assessment, and as inhabitants according to their whole substance, unless so far as already assessed (*a*). They 'were' held so liable in every parish where they 'could' be considered as residents, in so far as not assessed elsewhere (*b*). But clergymen 'were' not liable as inhabitants on the amount of their stipend (*c*); nor, it would seem, 'were' parochial schoolmasters (*d*).

(*a*) 1579, c. 74. Procl. Aug. 11, 1692. See Lawrie *v.* Dreghorn, 1797; M. 10,587; 2 Ill. 167. Gammell *v.* Weir, 1822; Dunlop, Apx. 10. Cochran *v.* Manson, 1823; 2 S. 201.
(*b*) Buchanan *v.* Parker, 1827; 5 S. 391. Also Cochran, *supra* (*a*).
(*c*) See 8 and 9 Vict. c. 89, § 47, 49. Gillon *v.* Meek, 1851; 14 D. 248.
(*d*) Cargill, *supra*, § 1138 (*i*).

1141. Landed property in another parish 'was' to be taxed there, not included in the personal charge for the parish of residence (*a*).

(*a*) Cochran, *supra*, § 1140 (*a*).

1142. The rule of assessment 'was' partly judicial, partly discretionary; and the Court cannot, in the way of suspension, interfere with it (*a*).

(*a*) Gammell, *supra*, § 1140 (*a*); settled by compromise. Ross *v.* Carrick, Dec. 16, 1800; M. *Poor*, Apx. 3. Crawford *v.* Harkness, *supra*, § 1139.

1143. (2.) *Burghal Parishes.*—In these all indwellers 'were' liable who 'might' spend £100 Scots yearly, or 'were' stented to be worth 2000 merks in free goods. And one who 'was' a burgess, having a place of business within the burgh, although residing with his family in a neighbouring parish, 'was' held an indweller liable to assessment (*a*). The assessment in the parish of residence is in respect of the whole personal estate—money lent, stock in the funds, bank stock, money on security—but not including the produce of land in another parish (*b*).

(*a*) 1579, c. 74. Procl. Aug. 29, 1693. Buchanan, *supra*, § 1140 (*b*). Dunlop, 428 seq.
(*b*) Lawrie and Cochran, *supra*, § 1140 (*a*). See § 1136A.

1144. (3.) *Mixed Parishes* are partly landward, partly burghal. It was held in the Court of Session that each part of the parish was liable to the support of its own poor; but this was reversed in the House of Lords, and the poor of both districts held as the poor of one parish (*a*). Where lands 'had' been disjoined by Act of Parliament from a landward parish and annexed to the royalty of a royal burgh and different parish, but with a provision "still to remain liable for parochial burdens as if the Act never had been passed," it was held that they were liable to both assessments, according to the value of the whole property (*b*). But where the lands in question were disjoined from the parish to which they originally belonged, but were included within the royalty of a burgh, they were by the House of Lords (reversing the judgment of the Court of Session) held assessable only in the royalty, but not in the original parish, nor even any compensation due to that parish (*c*). 'Owners of lands are not now liable to be assessed in more than one parish or combination (*d*).'

(*a*) Mags. of Dunbar *v*. Heritors of Dunbar, 1835; 1 S. & M'L. 134. Currie *v*. Lockhart, 1841; 3 D. 799.
(*b*) M'Craw *v*. Allan, 1839; 1 D. 513; aff. 2 Rob. 507. M'Craw *v*. Cunningham, 1837; 2 S. & M'L. 773. Burns *v*. Ewing, 1837; 15 S. 936; rev. M'L. & R. 435.
(*c*) M'Craw, *supra* (*b*). See below, § 2171.
(*d*) 8 and 9 Vict. c. 83, § 46. Allan *v*. Insprs. of Edinr. and S. Leith, 1849; 11 D. 1391; aff. 1 Macq. 293.

1145. (4.) *Crown Property.*—The property of the Crown may be distinguished—1. As the original annexed property of the Crown; or 2. As property of the Church annexed in 1587; or 3. As property purchased or otherwise acquired by the Crown for the public service. The first description of Crown property is exempt from public taxes, unless when held as a beneficiary possession by a subject (*a*). The second is liable to such taxes as the clergy were liable to pay. And the third is liable as if it still remained in the hands of a subject, but exempt in so far as it has been increased in value by meliorations for the public service (*b*). 'But this statement is erroneous, and the views formerly entertained have been corrected by judgments of the House of Lords. The exemption of the Crown is found to rest upon the principle that it is not bound by a statute unless expressly named; and as it is not named in any statute imposing assessments, it is exempt. And the exemption does not extend to property held for public or even national purposes (as a university or national gallery), but is confined to such as belongs to the Crown, and is occupied by its servants for the purposes of the administration of the government (*c*). But this exemption, having proved unjust and invidious, has now been practically abandoned by the Treasury, which makes contributions in respect of Government property in aid of local rates according to a valuation made, and from time to time revised, by its own officers (*d*).'

(*a*) Canongate *v*. E. Haddington, 1816; Dunlop, 77, note; 2 Ill. 168. Ross *v*. E. Haddington, 1824; 3 S. 115. See The King *v*. Hurdis, 3 T. R. 497.
(*b*) Bruce *v*. Veitch, Nov. 28, 1810; F. C. Barrack Comrs. *v*. Milroy, Nov. 21, 1815; F. C. Officers of Ordnance *v*. Hers. of North Leith, 1825; 4 S. 89. See above, § 1138 (*d*).
(*c*) Mersey Dock Trs. *v*. Cameron; Gardiner *v*. Leith Dock Comrs.; Univ. of Edinr. *v*. Greig, and other cases cited in § 1138 (*d*).
(*d*) See Guthrie Smith, Poor Law, 122.

IV. TEINDS.

1146. Provisions for the Clergy.—The clergy of Scotland are maintained by an annual payment or stipend out of the produce of the land, and in country parishes are entitled to a manse and glebe. The annual payment is supplied from the teinds of the parish; the manse or dwelling-house is supplied by the contribution of the heritors, according to the extent of their property; and the glebe is a portion of land designed for the minister out of church lands, or temporal lands nearest to the church (*a*).

(*a*) 2 Stair, 8. 2 Stair, 3. § 40. 2 Ersk. 10. Connell on Teinds and Parishes.

1147. History of Teinds as a Burden on Land.—Teinds, which were at one time entirely appropriated to the maintenance of the clergy, came afterwards to be held by laymen, either separate from or along with their lands. In the progress of this somewhat curious revolution, an Act of annexation was passed in 1587, by which the lands of the church which had been held of the Crown before the Reformation were restored to the Crown. But although that Act does not seem to have comprehended teinds, or the spirituality of benefices, a design appears to have been formed, on the accession of Charles I., to supply the wants of the Crown by a resumption of teinds as well as of lands. The threats of this proceeding excited great alarm; and in justification of the measure, two objects were professed as in view, in themselves fair and reasonable: 1. To make a competent provision for the clergy, and for education; and 2. To free owners of land from the great oppression suffered in the drawing and levying of teinds in kind. In the settling of these disputes, it was arranged that teinds to whomsoever payable, should be liable to be valued, so as to be levied by a *modus* instead of being drawn in kind; and that the landowner should further be entitled to purchase the teind at a certain rate. This arrangement was ratified by the Acts of 1633, c. 17, and 1690, c. 23.

Thus teinds, which in Scotland were formerly levied in kind, came to be regarded as a fixed burden on land, subject to be redeemed or purchased by the proprietor of the ground; and even while unredeemed, to be payable according to a fixed *modus* or valuation, like the land-tax.

1148. Teinds may therefore be taken—1. As an estate in relation to the title of improprietor or titular; in which view they have already been considered (*a*). 2. As a charge on land, affording a fund for the clergy entitled to a stipend; in which view they are now to be considered.

(*a*) See above, § 837.

1149. All lands are liable to the burden of teind, with the exception of lands granted *cum decimis inclusis*; and of lands of which the teinds are redeemed, though still liable to a share of any augmentation of stipend. 'Ministers' glebes, even when feued to laymen, are exempt (*a*).'

(*a*) 1578, c. 62. 1621, c. 10. 2 Ersk. 10. § 16. Cranstoun *v.* Elliot, 1800; M. Apx. *Stipend*, 3. Wilson *v.* Agnew, 1831; 9 S. 357.

1150. To whom Payable.—Teinds are payable either to the titular; or to a tenant; or to the clergyman, so far as his stipend has been allocated on the landowner.

1151. Kinds of Teinds.—Teinds are in one of three situations—Drawn in kind, or Valued, or Redeemed.

1152. (1.) *Drawn Teinds—Parsonage and Vicarage.*—Teinds drawn in kind may be generally described as one-tenth of the annual produce of the land; and not a personal tax, but a prædial burden. While teinds are subject to be drawn in kind, they are distinguished as Parsonage or Vicarage (*a*).

(*a*) 2 Ersk. 10. § 24.

1153. Parsonage teinds are payable out of grain raised by culture, and the terms are Whitsunday and Michaelmas. They are properly due to the parson, and are technically called *Decimæ Rectoriæ* (*a*).

(*a*) 1672, c. 13. 2 Ersk. 10. § 13.

1154. Vicarage teinds were properly payable to the vicar; and where there was no vicar, to the parson. They are payable out of minor and accidental products—cattle, fowl, eggs, etc.; and are regulated chiefly by usage (*a*).

(*a*) As to fish teinds, see Johnstone *v.* Chalmers, 1780; 2 Pat. 559. Scott *v.* Methuen, 1851; 13 D. 991.

1155. Between these two kinds of teinds there is a remarkable difference. The right to parsonage teinds cannot be lost by prescription; vicarage may be lost *non utendo* (*a*).

(*a*) 3 Ersk. 7. § 13. Hunter *v.* D. Roxburghe, 1796; M. 15,728.

1156. Teinds are *debita fructuum*, not *debita fundi*; arrears do not affect singular successors. But all intromitters with the rent are liable to a personal action for arrears (*a*).

(*a*) 2 Ersk. 10. § 42. As to the defence of *bonâ fide* perception, see Macrae *v.* Assets Co., 1894; 21 R. 1080.

1157. The right of the titular or patron to his tenth of teinds to be drawn in kind is as good as that of the proprietor of the land to his nine-tenths. But in the actual *drawing* of the teind, the right was formerly more oppressive than a *pro indiviso* right of the ordinary description. Remedies were provided against this evil by several statutes, but they were imperfect; and before the establishment of a better system, relief was chiefly obtained by means of private agreements: either by tacks to the proprietor of his own teinds, by which he was saved from the drawing in kind, paying a fixed rent; or by usage of rental bolls, which was a tacit agreement to pay so many bolls for teind, according to a valuation, subject to interruption by notice, and offer of the actual produce on the part of the landowner, or by inhibition of teinds on the part of the titular. But at last the general plan already alluded to was adopted, for giving to each heritor the drawing of his own teind, and the option of purchasing exemption (*a*).

(*a*) 1633, c. 17, 19. 1690, c. 23, 30. 1693, c. 21, 25. 1707, c. 11. 2 Ersk. 10. § 24-5.

1158. (2.) *Valued Teinds.*—The two parts of this improved system are, valuation, and sale of the teinds (*a*). The benefits derived from this improved system were, that the rent was fixed instead of being variable; so that valuations of an early date became favourable to the heritor, even when in grain, much more when in money, insomuch that valuations in the seventeenth and beginning of the eighteenth century are not above one-thirtieth of the teindable produce of the present day.

(*a*) The jurisdiction in the valuation and sale of teinds is in the Court of Session as a Commission of Teinds. 6 Geo. IV. c. 120, § 54, etc. When lands are sold in parcels, the titular is entitled to recover his valued teinds from each purchaser as an intromitter, to the amount of the fruits intromitted with, unless and until the teinds are properly divided and allocated. Univ. of Glasgow *v.* Pollok, 1868; 6 Macph. 878.

1159. Valuation was appointed to be settled judicially, by commissioners and sub-commissioners named in the statute. The rule of valuation was by a proof of the teind where drawn or separated from the stock, a deduction of a fifth being allowed; and by taking one-fifth of the whole, 'whether the lands were grass lands or corn lands, or even unfit for tillage and not producing teindable fruits,' when stock and teind were possessed jointly by the heritor (*a*). 'The rent under a current lease is taken in general to be the true value (*b*). Valuations by the sub-commission are subject to review by the Court of Teinds as coming in place of the High Commission, and the Court must be satisfied that the heritors and patron and minister were parties to the proceedings; but in old valuations, if the titular was represented, the presence of a stipendiary minister was not necessary (*c*).'

As to the particulars included in a valuation: The rents of quarries, minerals, mosses, etc. (*d*), and of supernumerary houses not necessary for agriculture, are deducted (*e*). Uncommon expenditure in improvement is a ground of reasonable deduction (*f*). Orchards are deducted, as not giving such fruits as are the subject either of parsonage or of vicarage (*g*).

(*a*) 2 Stair, 8. § 14. 2 Ersk. 10. § 30, 33. 1 Connell, 260, 297, 312. Hay *v.* D. Roxburghe, 1757; M. 15,750; 2 Ill. 168. Doul, 1708, and Hume, 1711; *ib.* and 2 Ersk. 10. § 29. See L. Glenlyon *v.* Clark, 1842; 5 D. 69. Houston *v.* Common Agent of Haddington, 1868; 6 Macph. 235. Burt *v.* Home, 1878; 5 R. 445 (lands covered with houses valued at estimated agricultural rent). L. Adv. *v.* D. of Athole, 1885; 12 R. 881.

(*b*) 1 Connell, 185 sqq. Fothringham *v.* Elder, 1870; 9 Macph. 172.

(*c*) Ferguson *v.* Gillespie, 1795; M. 15,768; aff. 3 Pat. 534. M'Neil *v.* Minrs. of Campbeltown, 1809; 5 Pat. 244. D. Gordon *v.* Gillan, 1825; 1 W. & S. 295; Sh. T. C. 64. Kirkwood *v.* Grant, 1865; 4 Macph. 4. Jamieson *v.* Little, 1867; 5 Macph. 14. Ministers of Old Machar *v.* The Heritors, 1868; 6 Macph. 504; rev. 8 Macph. H. L. 168. See also Ministers of Islay *v.* The Heritors, 1868; 6 Macph. 1074. Elder *v.* Fothringham, 1869; 7 Macph. 341. Deans of Chapel Royal *v.* Johnstone, 1869; 7 Macph. H. L. 19; L. R. 1 Sc. App. 426. M'Neil's Trs. *v.* Campbell, 1872; 11 Macph. 211. Ainslie *v.* Officers of State, 1869; 11 Macph. 260. Hay *v.* Minr. of Peebles, 1886; 13 R. 585.

(*d*) Heritors of Calder *v.* Univ. of Glasgow, 1834; M. 15,739. Paul *v.* Nicol, 1869; 7 Macph. 967; rev. 1871, 9 Macph. H. L. 121. Richmond *v.* Common Agent of Orwell, 1867; 5 Macph. 557. Plummer *v.* Common Agent of Selkirk, 1867; 6 Macph. 124. Houston, *cit.* Stevenson *v.* Mags. of Rutherglen, 1874; 2 R. 174.

(*e*) Hers. of Calder, *cit.*

(*f*) Same case. Smith *v.* Officers of State, Dec. 17, 1817; F. C. See Buchanan on Teinds, 200.

(*g*) Hay, *supra* (*a*). As to the surrender of teinds, see Mitchell *v.* L. Douglas, Jan. 24, 1798; F. C.; and M. 14,827. E. Minto *v.* Pennell, 1873; 1 R. 156. Colquhoun *v.* Fogo, 1873; 11 Macph. 919. Fogo *v.* Colquhoun, 1867; 6 Macph. 105.

1160. (3.) *Redeemed Teinds—Sale.*—Teinds in the hands of titulars were made redeemable at nine years' purchase of the valued teind, the *modus* being made so low on account of the liability of such teinds to stipend; and the value in victual is convertible in this process of sale at a medium, according to the fiars of the last seven years. Teinds in the hands of patrons are redeemable at six years' purchase. The privilege of a sale confined by 1633, c. 17 and 19, to two years from the valuation, is not now so limited (*a*).

(*a*) Ramsay Irvine *v.* Maule, 1794; M. 15,698; 2 Ill. 169.

1161. In completing the sale of teinds, the purchaser receives a disposition with precept of sasine. The sentence is not an adjudication of teinds to the heritor, but a mutual personal decree *ad factum præstandum*, decerning the pursuer to pay to the titular a certain sum, as nine years' purchase (or six years' purchase) of the teinds, parsonage and vicarage, of the pursuer's lands of A., with interest till the titular shall give a valid heritable right to the teinds, and declaring the pursuer to have right to the teinds, specifying the crop and year. All teinds may be the subject of this action, except teinds allocated to the minister for stipend; teinds reserved in the sale of the land; bishop's teinds vested in the Crown; teinds belonging to colleges and hospitals. All the excepted teinds may be *valued*, but not *sold*.

1162. Stipend, Augmentation, and Locality.—The teinds forming a charge on land, while unexhausted, afford a fund for the augmentation of ministers' stipends. The stipend is not a burden on the *dominium directum*, but only on the *dominium utile*; on property, not superiority (*a*). The localling or apportioning of the burden on the unexhausted teind is under the jurisdiction of the Court of Session as Commissioners of Teinds (*b*). No new augmentation is to be allowed till the expiration of fifteen years from any former augmentation previous to the Act 48 Geo. III.; nor till after the expiration of twenty years from any augmentation after the Act (*c*).

In awarding a stipend, it has been held by the whole Court that any extraordinary size of glebe is to be taken into account (*d*); 'but not the increased income derived from feuing the ground (*e*).'

(*a*) Pedie *v.* Heriot's Hospital, 1839; 1 D. 871. See also M'Donald *v.* Heriot's Hospital, 1830; 4 W. & S. 98. Jackson *v.* Cochrane, 1873; 11 Macph. 475. As to the question whether Crown property is exempt from teind-duties, see E. of Moray *v.* M'Diarmid, 1869; 8 Macph. 142; and cases cited by L. O. and L. Neaves.

(*b*) 48 Geo. III. c. 133; 6 Geo. IV. c. 120, § 54, etc. See Act of Sed., Nov. 12, 1825.

(*c*) Dow *v.* Coll. of Glasgow, 1825; Sh. T. C. 77. Gardner *v.* Hers. of Rathven, 1838; 1 D. 158. A fund is provided for small stipends by 50 Geo. III. c. 84.

(*d*) Stewart *v.* L. Glenlyon, 1835; 13 S. 787.

(*e*) Leck *v.* Hers. of Kilmalcolm, 1875; 3 R. 32. See below, § 1176.

1163. Augmented stipends, not localled on any particular heritor, may be demanded from *any* heritor to the extent of his teinds, with relief against the other heritors. But, 'in practice, the necessity for such a step is obviated by making up interim schemes of locality (A. of S. July 5, 1809; A. of S. June 20, 1838), which regulate the payments of heritors, subject to their right to relief when the final scheme is approved (*a*).' If the stipend shall have been localled, such locality gives the limits of the heritor's responsibility to the minister. It is an appropriation of the burden fixed judicially, under the superintendence of the common agent of all the heritors. 'A judgment *in foro contentioso* in one locality, in which the issue is distinctly raised, is *res judicata* in another subsequent locality in the same parish (*b*).' The stipend is to be allocated in this order: first, on teinds never erected (*c*): secondly, on teinds vested in titulars, and by them demandable from heritors (*d*): the whole, if not valued, or at least the valued teind: thirdly, on teinds let by the titular to tacksmen: fourthly, on teinds purchased by the heritor, and on the teinds of the titular's (*e*) own land: fifthly, on the teinds of bishops in the hands of the Crown (*f*): and lastly, on the teinds of colleges and pious foundations.

(*a*) Weatherstone *v.* M. Tweeddale, 1833; 12 S. 1. M'Cartney *v.* Campbell, March 4, 1817; F. C. Oswald *v.* Martin, 1835; 14 S. 32. Haldane *v.* Ogilvy, 1871; 10 Macph. 62. M'Neill's Trs. *v.* Campbell, 1872; 10 Macph. 783. Sinclair's Trs. *v.* Campbell's Trs., 1877; 4 R. 1126; rev. 1878, 5 R. H. L. 119. Mackenzie *v.* L. Advocate, 1878; 5 R. 589. Duncan *v.* Brown, 1882; 10 R. 332. E. of Fife *v.* Duff, 1887; 15 R. 238. As to obligations to relieve from stipend, see § 895.

(*b*) Bonar *v.* Lord Advocate, 1870; 9 Macph. 58. Thomson *v.* Lord Advocate, 1872; 10 Macph. 849, and cases there cited. Cheape *v.* Lord Advocate, 1871; 9 Macph. 377. Dundas *v.* Waddell, 1878; 6 R. 345; rev. 1880, 7 R. H. L. 19. Maclachlan *v.* Stuart, 1885; 12 R. 1107.

(*c*) See Learmonth *v.* Mags. of Edinr., 1859; 21 D. 890.

(*d*) Lord Advocate *v.* Landale, 1867; 40 S. Jur. 363.

(*e*) Patrons of parsonages within the Acts 1690, c. 23, and 1693, c. 41, have the same privilege. Lochore and Capledrae Coal Co. *v.* Common Agent of Ballingry, 1878; 5 R. 763.

(*f*) Common Agent of Prestonkirk *v.* Ferguson, 1846; 9 D. 61. L. Adv. *v.* Gordon's Trs., 1868; 6 Macph. 250; aff. 1871, 9 Macph. H. L. 73. L. Adv. *v.* E. Galloway, 1873; 11 Macph. 896. Cheape, *cit.* (*b*).

V. CHURCH.

1164. Building and Repairing.—It is now settled that the expense of building and of repairing the parish church lies on the heritors; so the term "parishioners" has been construed by inveterate usage (*a*). In the description of heritors, neither titulars of teinds, nor superiors, nor liferenters, 'nor owners of coal-mines, nor long-lease holders (*b*),' are included (*c*). The heritors are entitled, without the intervention of the presbytery, to determine on repairing or rebuilding (*d*); and in a landward parish the assessment is according to the valued rent, but the heritors may take the real rent. When the parish is mixed (both landward and burghal), the building or repairing of a church is a parochial charge to be defrayed by all the owners of lands and houses in proportion to their real rents (*e*). 'It seems that disjunction and erection of lands into a *quoad sacra* parish, under the Act of 1844, does not affect the liability of heritors to the ecclesiastical burdens of the old parish (*f*).'

In the question of repairing or rebuilding the church, the heritors may, without concurrence of the presbytery, resolve to rebuild, the majority binding the minority; but any one is entitled to bring the resolution under review by suspension (*g*). The presbytery may, where necessary, decern for a new church, after appointing a visitation, and report by tradesmen, with public notice from the pulpit (*h*); but this under review of the 'Sheriff and Lord Ordinary on Teind Causes, whose decision is final (*i*).' The heritors, however, are not bound to rebuild, if the church be repairable, *i.e.* wherever the repairs will make it safe as originally built (*k*). The heritors are not bound, where the church is in good repair, or repairable, to enlarge it for an augmented population (*l*). The presbytery have nothing to say as to the style of architecture, provided the church afford due accommodation (*m*). In rebuilding a church (though not in the repairing), accommodation must be provided for the parishioners; and the rule is, to provide for two-thirds of all examinable persons in the parish (*n*).

The additional churches which by statute are provided for the Highlands and Islands of Scotland, are originally to be built, and the stipend paid, from the Government fund. The church is to be repaired from the produce of the seat-rents, guaranteed by the heritor or heritors who apply for the church, and who are, "with their heirs and successors in their land," bound for what may further be necessary for repairs, to the extent of one per cent. on the original cost (*o*). The minister's house and offices are to be repaired from a certain proportion of the seat-rents; what more is necessary being defrayed by the minister (*p*).

'The heritors are also bound to provide and maintain churchyards (*q*). And by a modern statute, power is given to local authorities to provide burying-grounds (*r*).'

(*a*) 1563, c. 76. 1572, c. 54. Act of Privy Council, Sept. 13, 1563. 2 Ersk. 10. § 63. Kirk-session of Lauder *v.* Gallowshiels, 1630; M. 7913. Boswell *v.* D. Portland, 1834; 13 S. 148; 3 Ill. 156. Williamson *v.* Kirkcaldy, 1685; M. 7914.

(*b*) Bell *v.* Wemyss, 1805; M. Apx. *Kirk*, 4. M'Laren *v.* Clyde Trs., 1865; 4 Macph. 58; aff. 1868, 6 Macph. H. L. 81.

(*c*) Bruce Carstairs *v.* Greig, 1773; M. 2333; 2 Ill. 170; 1 Hailes, 524; aff. 3 Pat. 675. Murray *v.* Scott, 1794; M. 15,092. Minr. of Moreham *v.* Binston, 1679; M. 8499; 2 Ill. 148. Anstruther *v.* Anstruther's Trs., 1823; 2 S. 306. See § 1171.

(*d*) Boswell, *supra* (*a*).

(*e*) Harlow *v.* Hers. of Peterhead, 1802; rev. 4 Pat. 356; Connell's Sup. to Law of Parishes, p. 25; Dunlop's Par. Law, 10. Boswell, *supra* (*a*). The Valuation Act, 17 and 18 Vict. c. 91, does not alter the rule of liability. Macfarlane *v.* Monklands Ry. Co., 1864; 2 Macph. 518. Scot. N.-E. Ry. Co. *v.* Gardiner, 1864; 2 Macph. 537. M'Laren *v.* Clyde Trs., *cit.* D. of Abercorn *v.* Presby. of Edinburgh, 1869; 7 Macph. 875; 1870, 8 Macph. 733. E. of Traquair's Trs. *v.* Heritors of Innerleithen, 1870; 9 Macph. 234 (lands let on long leases rated according to rent in Valuation Roll). Bruce *v.* Bruce, 1873; 11 Macph. 755. Her. of Kinghorn *v.* Mags. of K., 1897; 24 R. 704 (repairs—custom of parish—old decree). See the proviso in § 33 of that Act, that where the area of a church has been divided according to the valued rent, assessments for its repair shall continue to be imposed according to this rule; a proviso which does not exclude other cases in which valued rent continues to be the rule, at least in regard to repairs. D. of Abercorn, *supra*. And as to assessments for parochial buildings, see 25 and 26 Vict. c. 58; 29 and 30 Vict. c. 75. Downie *v.* M'Lean, 1883; 11 R. 47. As to church bells and their use, see M'Naughton *v.* Mags. of Paisley, 1835; 13 S. 432. Kirk-session of Peebles *v.* Mags., 1874; 1 R. 1139; aff. 1875; 2 R. H. L. 117.

(*f*) Mags. of Fortrose *v.* Maclennan, 1880; 8 R. 124. D. Abercorn *v.* Presby. of Edinr., 1870; 8 Macph. 733. Cf. D. Roxburghe *v.* Millar, 1876; 3 R. 728; rev. 1877, 4 R. H. L. 76.

(*g*) Boswell, *supra* (*a*).

(*h*) M'Neill *v.* Nicolson, 1828; 6 S. 422; 3 Ill. 155.

(*i*) 31 and 32 Vict. c. 96. Walker *v.* Presby. of Arbroath, *infra* (*q*). Presby. of Deer *v.* Heritors of Pitsligo, 1876; 3 R. 975. Heritors of Pitsligo *v.* Gregor, 1879; 6 R. 1862. Mags. of Arbroath *v.* Presby. of Arbroath, 1883; 10 R. 767.

(*k*) Murray *v.* Presby. of Glasgow, 1833; 12 S. 191; 3 Ill. 156. A church seems to be repairable when moderate and judicious repairs will put it in a "sufficient and serviceable" condition for a considerable time. Cunninghame *v.* Deans, Dec. 12, 1811; F. C. Gordon *v.* Gordon, 1846; 18 S. Jur. 595. M'Leod, *infra* (*l*). E. of Glasgow *v.* Miller, 1831; 9 S. 370; aff. 1834, 7 W. & S. 185. Bertram *v.* Presby. of Lanark, 1864; 2 Macph. 1413. Hamilton *v.* Presby. of Hamilton (Campbell *v.* Jack), 1827; 6 S. 47; 8 S. 196; 9 S. 167, 796.

(*l*) L. Lynedoch *v.* Smythe, 1828; 6 S. 791. E. of Glasgow *v.* Miller, 1834; 7 W. & S. 185. See also M'Leod *v.* Carment, 1830; 8 S. 475.

(*m*) Same cases.

(*n*) Same cases. Minr. of Tingwall *v.* Heritors, 1787; M. 7928. Connell, Sup. 34, 44, 125. Hamilton, *supra* (*k*). M'Neill, *supra* (*h*). As to the allocation of seats, see D. of Roxburghe, *supra* (*f*). D. of Abercorn, *supra* (*f*). Stiven *v.* Heritors of Kirriemuir, 1878; 6 R. 174. Stephen *v.* Anderson, 1887; 15 R. 72. Mackay *v.* Wood, 1889; 17 R. 38 (Brechin corporation sittings). Rankine on Landownership, 157.

(*o*) 4 Geo. IV. c. 79. 5 Geo. IV. c. 90, § 18. It may be doubted whether this is personal, or a real burden on the lands. The reason of the thing should favour the latter opinion. See 7 and 8 Vict. c. 44, § 14, 15.

(*p*) 5 Geo. IV. c. 90, § 18. Macdougall *v.* D. Portland, 1892; 20 R. 105 (minister—heritors—control as to repairs).

(*q*) Mags. of Greenock *v.* Stewart, 1777; M. 8019; 5 B. S. 414; rev. 1779, 2 Pat. 486. Ure *v.* Ramsay, 1828; 6 S. 916. Kirk-session of S. Leith *v.* Scott, 1832; 11 S. 75. Walker *v.* Presby. of Arbroath, 1876; 3 R. 498; aff. 4 *ib.* H. L. 1. 1563, c. 76. 1597, c. 232. Duncan, Par. Law, 231 sqq. Rankine on Landownership, 634. As to the rights of private parties to burying-places, see Hill *v.* Wood, 1863; 1 Macph. 360. Turner *v.* Committee of Greenock West Church, 1869; 7 Macph. 538. Wright *v.* Lady Elphinstone, 1881; 8 R. 1825 (heritors hold churchyards in trust for purposes for which churchyards were instituted, and cannot divert them from those uses). Wright *v.* Wright, 1881; 9 R. 15 (right to remove tombstones *inter familiam*). Russell *v.* M. of Bute, 1882; 10 R. 302. Steel *v.* St. Cuthbert's Kirk-session, 1891; 18 R. 911 (rights of kirk-session—extension of church over burying-ground). Mitchell, Petr., 1893; 20 R. 902 (disinterment and removal). Fraser *v.* Turner, 1893; 21 R. 278 (right to compromise question as to extent of churchyard). See Cunningham *v.* Edmiston, 1871; 9 Macph. 869 (lair-holders in proprietary cemetery).

(r) 18 and 19 Vict. c. 68 (Bain v. C. of Seafield, 1884; 12 R. 62; 1887, 14 R. 939); 20 and 21 Vict. c. 42; 44 and 45 Vict. c. 27; 49 and 50 Vict. c. 21. See also 30 and 31 Vict. c. 101, § 16, 43, 96. Fulton v. Dunlop, 1862; 24 D. 1027.

VI. MANSE.

1165. Provision for Manse.—The Legislature endeavoured by various statutes to afford a remedy to the Reformed clergy against the alienation of manses on the eve of the Reformation. Where a parish church was not provided with a manse, the heritors were directed to build one at their own charge, and to repair those already built (*a*).

(*a*) 1563, c. 72. 1572, c. 48. 1592, c. 116. 1649, c. 45; renewed by 1663, c. 21.

1166. Title to a Manse.—The minister of a parish is entitled to a manse, whether it be a landward parish; or a parish partly town, partly landward; or a parish partly landward, partly burgh royal: landward being held to apply to a territory properly termed rural in opposition to urban (*a*). The minister of a parish in a royal burgh is not entitled to a manse on the Act of 1663 (*b*). If, in a parish where the clergyman is entitled to a manse, he cannot be provided with one, a compensation is given by statute (*c*).

(*a*) 1649, c. 45. 1663, c. 21. King's College of Aberdeen v. Heritors, 1748; Elch. *Manse*, 2; 2 Ill. 169. Minrs. of Dunfermline v. Heritors, 1805; M. *Manse*, Apx. 1; aff. 1812; see note in 2 W. & S. 604; 5 Pat. 593. Adamson v. Paston, Feb. 14, 1816; F. C. Auld v. Mags. of Ayr, 1825; 4 S. 99; rev. 1827; 2 W. & S. 600; and 1828, 6 S. 1087. Baikie v. Logie, 1827; 5 S. 546. The second minister of a parish is not entitled to a manse and glebe. Heritors of Elgin v. Troop, 1769; M. 8508; 1 Hailes, 283. Adamson, *supra*. Carnegie v. Speid, 1849; 11 D. 1250. See L. Panmure v. Presby. of Brechin, 1855; 18 D. 197.

(*b*) Thomson v. Heritors of Dunfermline, 1750; M. 8504; Elch. *Manse*, 4. Duncan's Par. Law, 415.

(*c*) 5 Geo. IV. c. 72, § 2.

1167. The minister is also entitled to house-rent till his manse shall be built, or the question of right settled (*a*).

(*a*) Steel v. Lochmaben Heritors, 1712; M. 8502, 5131; 2 Ill. 169. Potter v. Heritors of Kippen, 1708; 4 B. Sup. 691. Gardiner v. Dingwall, 1823; 2 S. 409; 1825, 4 S. 246. See Auld, *cit.*

1168. What a Manse includes.—A manse is held to include a stable, byre, barn, and other offices, with a garden (*a*); and the expense is not now limited to the maximum of £1000 Scots, appointed in the Act of 1663, but is extended to the expense of a competent manse (*b*).

(*a*) 2 Ersk. 10. § 57. Connell on Parishes, 291. Anderson, Petr., 1791; M. 5152; 2 Ill. 169. Carmichael v. M'Lean, 1837; 15 S. 1020. Heritors of Balfron v. Niven, 1863; 1 Macph. 324. E. Glasgow v. Murray, 1868; 7 Macph. 6. Maxwell v. Presby. of Langholm, 1867; 40 S. Jur. 13 (garden wall).

(*b*) Dingwall v. Gardiner, Nov. 27, 1816; F. C.; aff. 3 Bligh, 72; 1 S. App. 10; 2 Ill. 170. Mags. of Elgin v. Gatherer, 1841; 4 D. 25.

1169. Building and Repairing.—The presbytery may order whatever is necessary to make the manse habitable and capable of lodging the clergyman and his family (*a*); and where the defects or disrepair cannot otherwise be remedied, they may order a new manse (*b*). A manse, if in repair or repairable, is not to be enlarged to suit the accommodation or family of the minister; but where a new manse is to be built, due regard must be paid to the change of times, and proper accommodation of the minister's family (*c*). But the power of the presbytery in questions of manse is limited to that conferred by the Act of 1663 (*d*).

(*a*) Contrast Robertson v. E. Rosebery, 1788; M. 8515, with Heritors of Strathblane v. Hamilton, 1827; 5 S. 913; 2 Ill. 171.

(*b*) Hamilton v. Clason, 1826; 4 S. 551. Hers. of Olrig v. Phin, 1851; 13 D. 1332. Hers. of Kingoldrum v. Haldane, 1863; 1 Macph. 325. Hers. of Insch v. Storie, 1869; 8 Macph. 363. Elliott v. Hunter, *infra*.

(*c*) Shiells v. Hers. of Channelkirk, June 15, 1818; 3 Ill. 157. Mackenzie v. Mackenzie, 1835; 13 S. 1014. Carmichael v. M'Lean, 1837; 15 S. 1020. Elliott v. Hunter, 1867; 5 Macph. 1028. Hers. of Balfron v. Niven, 1858 (repd. 1863); 1 Macph. 324. E. Glasgow v. Murray, 1868; 7 Macph. 6. E. Cawdor v. Ross, 1867; 39 S. Jur. 553.

(*d*) Auld v. Mags. of Ayr, 1827; 2 W. & S. 600; 1828, 6 S. 1087; 2 Ill. 169.

1170. The minister is by statute entitled to have the manse in good and sufficient repair; and, on the other hand, if it be so, he is chargeable with the burden of maintaining it in tenantable condition. On application of the heritors to the presbytery, the manse will be surveyed and declared sufficient, or what is called a *free manse*. The effect of this declaration is to impose the burden of repairs on the minister during his incumbency (*a*).

(*a*) 1612, c. 8. 1663, c. 21. 2 Ersk. 10. § 58. D. Hamilton v. Scott, 1813; 1 Dow, 393; 5 Pat. 745; 3 Bligh, 88; 2 Ill. 171. Minr. v. Hers. of Botriphney, 1805; 2 Ill. 171; Connell on Par. 309; 1 Dow, 399. Shiells and Elliott, *supra*, § 1169 (*c*). Duncan, Par. Law, 437. By 31 and 32 Vict. c. 96, § 12, the heritors may apply to the Sheriff for a decree of free manse, which is operative for fifteen years or till the prior death of the incumbent. Hers. of Pitsligo v. Gregor, 1879; 6 R. 1062. In the case of Parliamentary churches, the manse is to be repaired by the minister himself, in so far as the proportion of the seat-rents is not sufficient. 5 Geo. IV. c. 90, § 18.

1171. The persons liable to the expense are the heritors (*a*); but under this description of "heritor" is included neither a superior (*b*) nor a liferenter (*c*). Tenants are not liable for part of the expense of building a manse (*d*). Owners or holders of seats in the parish church, not being heritors, are not liable for the repair of the manse (*e*). The proprietors in a burgh parish, where the minister is entitled to a manse, seem to be liable along with the heritors of the landward part; the magistrates, 'where the assessment was on the valued rent,' being primarily liable, along with the heritors, reserving to them relief against proprietors or inhabitants of the burgh (*f*). 'But this rule does not apply to assessments on the real rent, individual owners being then liable, in the burghal as in the landward parish, according to their real rents appearing in the Valuation Roll (*g*). The obligation is not a *debitum fundi*, and does not transmit against singular successors (*h*).'

(*a*) Minr. of Morham *v.* Binston, 1679; M. 8499; 2 Ill. 148. Miller *v.* Craig, 1769; Hailes, 329; 2 Ill. 170. As to heritors' right to prevent a minister from letting his manse, see Hers. of Aberdour *v.* Roddick, 1872; 10 Macph. 221 (cf. Inland Rev. *v.* Fry, 1895; 22 R. 422); or to compel him to live in it, Hers. of Pitsligo, *cit.*

(*b*) Bruce Carstairs *v.* Greig, 1773; M. 2333; 1 Hailes, 522; aff. 3 Pat. 675. Dundas *v.* Nicholson, 1778; M. 8511; Hailes, 802. Murray *v.* Scott, 1794; M. 15,092.

(*c*) Anstruther *v.* Anstruther, 1823; 2 S. 306.

(*d*) Miller, *supra* (*a*). See cases in § 1164 (*e*).

(*e*) Fairie *v.* Leitch, Feb. 2, 1813; F. C.

(*f*) See cases, § 1166. Lockhart *v.* Mags. of Lanark, 1832; 10 S. 243. See § 1164. Mags. of Elgin *v.* Gatherer, 1841; 4 D. 25. Harlow *v.* Peterhead Hers., 1802; 4 Pat. 356.

(*g*) Downie *v.* M'Lean, 1883; 11 R. 47.

(*h*) 2 Stair, 3. § 40 *ad fin.* Guthrie *v.* Mackerstoun, 1672; M. 10,137. Blair *v.* Fowler, 1676; M. 10,168. See Webster *v.* Hendrie & Graham, 1885; 2 Sel. Sh. Ct. Ca. 81 (Lanarkshire).

VII. GLEBE.

1172. Arable Glebe.—Every minister of a parish, of which any part lies in the country, or is properly a landward or country parish, is entitled to a glebe of four acres of arable land, or sixteen soums of pasture ground (*a*).

(*a*) 1593, c. 161. 1606, c. 7. 1644, c. 31. 1663, c. 21. 2 Stair, 3. § 40. 1 Ersk. Pr. 5. § 16. 3 Inst. 10. § 59. Anderson *v.* Parishioners, 1664; M. 5121; 2 B. Sup. 136; 2 Ill. 172. Fullarton *v.* Richmond, 1779; M. 5123. But where there are two ministers of the same parish, only the first minister is entitled to a glebe. Adamson *v.* Paston, Feb. 14, 1816. See L. Panmure *v.* Presby. of Brechin, 1855; 18 D. 197, and 22 D. 1357. Procurator for Church *v.* Offirs. of State, 1828; S. Teind C. 148. As to a minister's proof of his title to land claimed as a glebe, see Presby. of Selkirk *v.* D. Buccleuch, 1869; 8 Macph. 121. As to united parishes, see 39 Vict. c. 11. Minr. of Brydekirk *v.* Minr. of Hoddam, 1877; 4 R. 798.

1173. The glebe is to be designed from kirk lands (*a*) in a particular order (*b*), which order must still be observed (*c*). The land nearest to the kirk and manse, or most commodious for the minister, though not nearest to the kirk, is to be taken (*d*). The provision of the Act to this effect is construed to be for the benefit of the heritors as well as the minister; and he is not to choose land remoter and better, if there be kirk lands nearer his manse (*e*). Temple lands are held not to be kirk lands (*f*). It is only where there are no church lands that the glebe is to be designed out of temporal lands (*g*), the power to design temporal lands depending entirely on there being no kirk lands; and although doubts have been entertained on the subject, there has been no judgment to the contrary (*h*).

(*a*) As to what are church lands, see Cochrane *v.* Smith, 1859; 22 D. 260 (*per* L. Benholme). Mags. of Montrose, *infra* (*h*). Kingsbarns, *infra* (*e*). Wilson *v.* Forbes' Trs., June 10, 1818; F. C.; rev. 1822, 1 S. App. 249.

(*b*) 1593, c. 161. 1606, c. 7. 1644, c. 31. 2 Stair, 3. § 40. 2 Ersk. 10. § 59. See Belshes *v.* Moore, 1827; 4 S. 347; 2 W. & S. 550; 2 Ill. 173.

(*c*) E. Galloway *v.* Nicholson, 1823; 2 S. 398.

(*d*) Anderson *v.* Thomas, May 22, 1810; F. C.; aff. 2 Dow, 433.

(*e*) Minr. of Fraserburgh *v.* Heritors, 1680; M. 5140; 2 Ill. 173. Minr. of Kingsbarns *v.* Erskine, 1794; M. 5140; Bell's Ca. 27.

(*f*) Duncan *v.* Parishioners of Kilpatrick, 1698; M. 5140. Ross *v.* Vassals, 1700; M. 7985. L. Torphichen, 5 B. S. 753.

(*g*) 1644, c. 31. 1663, c. 21. 2 Stair, 3. § 40. 2 Ersk. 10. § 59. Kingsbarns, *supra* (*e*).

(*h*) Minr. of Kingsbarns *v.* Balfour Hay, 1799; M. *Glebe*, Apx. 2. The note in Connell on Parishes, 370, relative to Balfour Hay's case, is not to be relied on. See Dunlop's Parochial Law, 120. See Belshes, *supra* (*b*). Mags. of Montrose *v.* Scott, 1832; 10 S. 212.

1174. The glebe is to contain at least four acres of arable land, *i.e.* of land in use to be cultivated as such (*a*); and if there be no arable lands near the church, the minister is to have sixteen soums of grass (each soum being pasture for one cow or ten sheep) designed in like manner out of pasture church lands next adjoining to the church (*b*). If there be no manse or glebe ground, the minister is to receive a compensation out of the public funds (*c*).

(*a*) 1663, c. 21. Steele *v.* Dalrymple, 1748; M. 5161; 2 Ill. 173. Minr. of Dunfermline *v.* Black, 1751; Elch. *Glebe*, 5. Grierson *v.* Ewart, 1778; M. 5162. Hailes, 799, 888. See Minr. of Panbride *v.* Maule, May 18, 1809. F. C.

(*b*) 1606, c. 7. 2 Ersk. 10. §. 59.

(*c*) 5 Geo. IV. c. 72, § 2.

1175. Grass Glebe.—The minister is entitled, over and above his proper glebe, to grass for a horse and two cows (*a*), to be designed out of kirk grass lands, not out of arable lands, *i.e.* lands *de facto* in a course of cultivation (*b*); or if there be no such lands near the manse, to £20 Scots yearly (*c*). Lands rich, and occasionally ploughed, are not properly grass lands by merely being for a long time kept as pasture lands (*d*). The minister may insist on having his grass glebe out of kirk lands, although 'such a glebe' equally good and convenient can be given out of other lands (*e*).

(*a*) 1663, c. 21. Beaton *v.* Dallas, 1734; Elch. *Glebe*, 1; 2 Ill. 172. Forbes *v.* Miller, 1755; M. 5127; 5 B. Sup. 304. Pringle *v.* His Minister, 1765; 5 B. Sup. 903. Dundas *v.* Somerville, 1805; M. *Glebe*, Apx. 5; 2 W. & S. 357, n. Carfrae *v.* Heritors of Dunbar, May 13, 1814; F. C. Belshes, *supra*, § 1173 (*b*). E. Moray *v.* Nicol, 1863; 3 Macph. 39.

(*b*) Hodges *v.* Bryce, 1756; M. 5162; 2 Ill. 174. Minr. of Panbride *v.* Heritors, May, 18, 1809; F. C. Stewart M'Kenzie *v.* M'Crae, 1825; 4 S. 146; 1828, 6 S. 422. See Wilkie *v.* Simpson, 1769; 2 Pat. 222. Grierson *v.* Ewart, *cit.* § 1174 (*a*). M'Millan *v.* Presby. of Kintyre, 1867; 6 Macph. 39.

(*c*) Sometimes this has been extrajudicially arranged; but it is only where the statutory equivalent has been judicially settled and acquiesced in, that the minister is held to be excluded from his right to a grass glebe. Minr. of Dollar *v.* D. Argyll, 1807; M. *Glebe*, Apx. 7; 2 Ill. 172. Panbride, *supra* (*b*). Anderson *v.* Thomas, May 22, 1810; F. C.; aff. 1814; 2 Dow, 433.

(*d*) Bruce *v.* Carstairs, 1826; 4 S. 626.

(*e*) Belshes *v.* Moore, as reversed, 1827; 2 W. & S. 558.

1176. Relief to Heritors.—The heritor whose land is taken for manse or glebe is entitled to relief from the other heritors, though their lands should be temporal lands (*a*); and in the same way, where a sum in lieu of grass is appointed to be paid to the minister, it is to be allocated at once on all the heritors (*b*). 'The obligation is not a *debitum fundi*, but personal (*c*). Not only at common law, but by statute, 1572, c. 48, the minister is disabled from selling, feuing, or putting any person in possession of his glebe after his relation with the cure ceases (*d*), except to the extent of reaping a crop previously sown by the incumbent or his tenant (*e*). By 29 and 30 Vict. c. 71, the minister may, with the consent of the presbytery, let on lease for eleven years the glebe, or part of it, reserving five acres; or under the authority of the Teind Court, obtained in a petition presented with consent of the heritors and presbytery, may feu the glebe or part of it for building or other uses (*f*).'

(*a*) 2 Ersk. 10. § 60. This is incorrectly stated by Professor Bell. When church lands are designed, the claim of relief is only against the owners of other church lands, not against the owners of temporal lands. Mags. of Montrose *v.* Scott, 1832; 10 S. 211; and so also where the money allowance is given in lieu of grass. Ferguson and Durie, *infra*.

(*b*) Ferguson *v.* Glasgow, 1745; M. 5157; Elch. *Glebe*, 3; 2 Ill. 174. Durie *v.* Thomson, 1755; M. 5161. The glebe and churchyard are designed by the presbytery, subject to review by the Court of Session—Campbell *v.* Morgan, 1850; 12 D. 1262. Walker *v.* Presby. of Arbroath, *infra*; and now by the Sheriff, with an appeal to the Lord Ordinary in Teind Causes—31 and 32 Vict. c. 96 (Ecclesiastical Buildings Act). See as to procedure by the heritors and presbytery, and their liability, and as to this Act, Campbell *v.* Stirling, March 4, 1813; F. C.; aff. 6 Pat. 238. Maxwell *v.* Gordon, 1816; 4 Dow, 279. Robertson *v.* Murdoch, 1830; 8 S. 587. Boswell *v.* D. Portland, 1834; 13 S. 148. M'Neel *v.* Robertson, 1836; 14 S. 849. E. Glasgow *v.* Miller, 1831; 9 S. 370; aff. 1833, 7 W. & S. 185. Sanderson & Muirhead *v.* Macfarlan, 1868; 6 Macph. 701. Walker *v.* Presby. of Arbroath, 1876; 3 R. 498; aff. 4 R. H. L. 1. Presby. of Deer *v.* Hers. of Pitsligo, 1876; 3 R. 975. Heritors of Pitsligo *v.* Gregor, 1879; 6 R. 1062. Mags. of Arbroath *v.* Presby. of Arbroath, 1883; 10 R. 767. Cook's Forms of Procedure in Church Courts (ed. 1882), pp. 173–218. Duncan's Par. Law, ch. x.

(*c*) 2 Stair, 3. § 40 *ad fin.* Snow *v.* Hamilton, 1675; M. 10,167. Cf. *supra*, § 1171 *fin.*

(*d*) Mackie *v.* Neill, 1736; Elch. *Glebe*, 2. Minr. of Little Dunkeld *v.* D. Atholl, 1791; M. 5153; Bell's 8vo Ca. 235. Minr. of Falkland *v.* Johnston, 1793; M. 5155. Learmonth *v.* Paterson, 1858; 20 D. 420.

(*e*) Anstruther *v.* Carstairs, 1807 (Carnbee case); Duncan's Par. Law, 520. M'Callum *v.* Grant, 1826; 4 S. 527. Taylor *v.* Stewart, 1853; 2 Stu. 538.

(*f*) M'Leod *v.* Macinroy, 1870; 8 Macph. 955. Gloag *v.* Hers. of Galashiels, 1873; 1 R. 187; 37 and 38 Vict. c. 94, § 36. As to an excambion, see Bain *v.* Css. of Seafield, 1884; 12 R. 62; 1887, 14 R. 939.

CHAPTER XVII

OF LEASES

1177. Leases Generally (*a*).—Property in the hands of tenants may consist either of lands or other subjects let out for cultivation or pasture, or the deriving of some other product from the possession; or of houses, manufactories, etc., for the habitation or use of the tenant. These may be taken separately.

'A lease, otherwise called a tack, is a contract of location—personal in its essence, but in some circumstances possessing by statute a real quality—whereby certain uses of land, or other subjects of certain kinds, are let on hire (set) for a return in money, produce, or services (*b*). The granter of the uses is called the landlord or lessor, and the grantee is called the tenant, lessee, or tacksman. The returns or prestations are in the general case called rent, if in money or produce and periodical, and when rent is paid for minerals it is often called royalty or lordship (*c*).

'The principles of the contract are here dealt with under the heading of the Agricultural Lease, at one time the more prevalent form of the contract, but the peculiarities of other leases are noticed from time to time, and in the case of Urban Leases have separate treatment later on (*d*).

'A new and anomalous tenure has been created in certain parishes called "Crofting Parishes," in the counties of Argyll, Inverness, Ross and Cromarty, Sutherland, Caithness, Orkney, and Shetland, by the Crofters' Holdings (Scotland) Act, 1886. It is not expedient to encumber this book with its details (*e*). It does not give crofters a right of property (*f*).

'*Allotments.*—Other forms of lease which have been subjected to special conditions by statute are the Small Holding and the Allotment; but the Acts have not been much used (*g*).'

(*a*) 2 Stair, 9. 2 Ersk. 6. § 20, 64. Bell on Leases. Hunter on Landlord and Tenant. Rankine on Leases, 2nd ed. 1893.

(*b*) *Infra*, § 1186.

(*c*) 2 Bankt. 9. § 1. 2 Mackenzie, 6. § 5. 2 Stair, 9. § 1. 2 Ersk. 6. § 20. 2 Ross, 456. 1 Bell's Com. 65. 1 Hunter, L. & T. 79. Rankine, Leases, 1.

(*d*) *Infra*, § 1272 sqq.

(*e*) 49 and 50 Vict. c. 29. 50 and 51 Vict. c. 24. 51 and 52 Vict. c. 23. 54 and 55 Vict. c. 41. Rankine on Leases, ch. 23. Fraser *v.* Macdonald, 1888; 15 R. 181. M'Nab *v.* Campbell, 1888; 15 R. 472. L. Abinger *v.* Cameron, 1888; 15 R. 598 (subdivision before Act passed). Traill's Trs. *v.* Grieve, 1890; 17 R. 1115 (enlargement—farm let under a lease). D. Sutherland *v.* Reed, 1890; 18 R. 252 (jurisdiction of ordinary Civil Courts). Swanson *v.* Grieve, 1890; 18 R. 371. Livingstone *v.* Beattie, 1891; 18 R. 735 (sub-tenant not "crofter" within the Act). M'Lean *v.* M'Lean, 1891; 18 R. 885 (power of bequest—"member of family"). Stuart & Stuart *v.* Macleod, 1891; 19 R. 223 (jurisdiction—sequestration). Mackenzie *v.* Cameron, 1894; 21 R. 427 (bequest of croft—jurisdiction). Colquhoun *v.* Cameron, 1894; 22 R. 23 (do.). Mackenzie *v.* Munro, 1894; 22 R. 45 (cessio—removing). Macdonald *v.* Macdougall, 1896; 23 R. 941 (division of estate—crofter's right to seaware). Dalgleish *v.* Livingston, 1895; 22 R. 646.

(*f*) MacDonald *v.* Dalgleish, 1894; 21 R. 900.

(*g*) 55 and 56 Vict. c. 31, 54. 57 and 58 Vict. c. 58, § 26. See also below, § 1282 (*a*).

I. AGRICULTURAL LEASES.

1178. Nature and Principles.—An agricultural lease is an agreement entered into for the raising of a gross produce to be divided (after defraying necessary charges) between the landlord furnishing the land, and the tenant supplying capital, industry, and agricultural skill. In the connection between landlord and tenant in agricultural leases, the matter which chiefly demands the attention of lawyers and of legislators is the union or opposition of their interests. While this contract confers on the tenant a permanent interest or estate, it fully reserves to the landlord on his part rights of great value, combining in one common concern their most important interests without the dangers or consequences of partnership.

1179. The division of profits ought to be made in the largest proportions to each that their respective means and situations afford, giving the highest rent to the landlord, and the largest profit to the farmer, with due assurance to each for the preservation of his peculiar estate or interest in the land. To the attainment of these objects, it is requisite that the landlord's right to the land as owner shall be preserved, and, at the close of the lease, his estate restored to him unimpaired or improved; that the tenant shall have absolute security for the continuance of his right during a term sufficient to indemnify him fairly for the employment of his industry and capital, and for the value of his improvements; and that the rent payable to the landlord out of each year's produce shall maintain an average proportion to that produce, varying with the changes to which it is naturally subject (*a*).

(*a*) See below, § 1213–15.

1180. Title to Grant a Lease.—In considering the constitution of a lease, the first question regards the title to grant it.

1181. The granter of a lease must be either the proprietor of the subject let (*a*), or one entitled to the full use and possession of the subject, or one in the administration of it. The proper title, therefore, of the granter of a lease as heritable proprietor is an infeftment. Where the granter is not infeft, the lease does not confer an effectual or permanent right (*b*), though it may be made perfect by the granter's subsequent infeftment, provided no mid-impediment has intervened. A sasine previous to that of the granter will defeat the lease. The granter's death uninfeft will defeat it, if a stranger shall come into the feudal right who is not bound to represent him,—as a purchaser, or a stranger substitute in a tailzied succession, or a creditor adjudging the land. The heir of the granter of the lease, however, taking the land as his representative, will be bound by the contract (*c*). A lease by an apparent heir is not secure to the tenant. Even if the granter have been three years in possession, it is not good on the statute of 1695 against an adjudger (*d*); and its effect against a subsequent heir passing by the granter was at one time doubted (*e*), though afterwards it was found effectual (*f*). A liferenter may effectually grant a lease, his title being complete either on his original infeftment, if it be a reserved liferent; or by sasine, if a liferent by new constitution; or by marriage, as in a lease granted by a husband of his wife's land (*g*).

(*a*) Cuninghame *v.* Ayrshire Assessor, 1895; 22 R. 596 (Crown lease of submarine minerals).

(*b*) See a curious application of this by the Second Division in Reid's Tr. *v.* Watson's Trs., 1896; 23 R. 636; and see Weir *v.* Dunlop & Co., 1861; 23 D. 1293.

(*c*) 2 Ersk. 6. § 21. Lowdon *v.* Murray, 1752; M. 5270; 2 Ill. 174. Gordon *v.* Milne, 1780; M. 7008, 10,309.
(*d*) Lowdon, *supra* (*c*).
(*e*) Same case. See below, § 1930.
(*f*) Knox *v.* Irvine, 1760; M. 5276.
(*g*) Grieve *v.* Pringle, 1797; M. 5951; 2 Ill. 286. See above, § 1057; and below, § 1183, 1269. As to a lease by one who has granted an absolute disposition with unrecorded back letter, see Abbott *v.* Mitchell, 1870; 8 Macph. 791.

1182. The power of granting leases may be under restraint by limitations on the granter's right as proprietor, by the temporary nature of his right, by the diligence of creditors, by the administrative character in which he acts. The reduction of the granter's right will be fatal to the lease (*a*). Long leases granted, 'by persons dying before 16th August 1871,' to the heir's prejudice on death-bed will, as acts of extraordinary administration, be challengeable (*b*). But ordinary leases for a fair rent are not on this ground exceptionable (*c*).

(*a*) Macniven *v.* Murray, 1847; 9 D. 1138. Eliott *v.* Eliott's Trs., 1894; 21 R. 858.
(*b*) 3 Ersk. 8. § 97. Christison *v.* Ker, 1735; M. 3226; 2 Ill. 175. Bogle *v.* Bogle, 1759; M. 3235. No deed made by a person dying after that date can be challenged *ex capite lecti*. 34 and 35 Vict. c. 81. This is not affected by 46 and 47 Vict c. 39, Sched. (Stat. Law Rev. Act, 1883).
(*c*) Semple *v.* Semple, June 1, 1813; F. C. Gordon, *supra*, § 1181 (*c*). See below, § 1786 et seq.

1183. Although a liferenter may grant a lease effectually, it is limited to the duration of the liferent (*a*). And an heir of entail, though not properly a liferenter, is often, by the prohibitions of the entail, prevented from granting long leases (*b*). 'But his tenant is entitled to possess until the next Whitsunday after the end of the liferent, or rather until the first Whitsunday which occurs at least forty days after the end of the liferent, as warning must be given. (See below, § 1269.)'

(*a*) Above, § 1057; below, § 1269.
(*b*) See below, § 1196, 1752, and 1764.

1184. Leases granted by temporary administrators endure only during the office (*a*). So of a lease by tutors, and curators 'for lunatics' (*b*). So also a lease by a husband of his wife's estate will last only during his administration (*c*). 'But a lease by a wife, with her husband's concurrence, or by her alone, where the *jus mariti* and husband's right of administration are renounced or excluded, is valid for the duration expressed (*d*).' But the Court in one case gave power to a testamentary tutor to let leases for nineteen years (*e*). 'The inexpediency of this rule led to the practice of applying to the Court for authority to grant leases, and in many cases the Court of Session authorised tutors nominate and factors *loco tutoris* to grant leases of ordinary administration (*f*). Subsequently the renewing or granting a lease for a period of years was included among the acts, for doing which judicial factors, tutors at law, and curators of insane persons were enabled by the Pupils' Protection Act of 1849 to obtain special powers from the Court (*g*). And now any tutor, curator, or judicial factor has the same powers as trustees with regard to leasing, viz. as ordinary powers, of leasing agricultural lands for not more than twenty-one years, and minerals for not more than thirty-one years, of removing tenants, and, with regard to agricultural or pastoral subjects, of granting abatements of rent and accepting renunciations (*h*); and of applying to the Court of Session for power to grant long leases, or of granting them with certain consents (*i*).'

(*a*) 2 Craig, 10. § 1. 2 Stair, 9. § 3. "The doctrine seems too broadly laid down in general, that the lease cannot exceed the duration of the office. If the tutor should die, his fair act of administration will last during the pupillarity. In Lothian (*c*) the title of the tutor was itself imperfect." Author's note in 2 Ill. 175.
(*b*) See below, § 2084. A. *v.* M. Huntly, 1672; M. 16,285; 2 Ill. 175. L. Reay *v.* Anderson, 1800; M. 16,385. Ross *v.* Ross, March 9, 1820; F. C. 1 Ersk. 7. § 16. Former editions had merely the words "and curators" here. But a minor and his curators may grant leases enduring beyond minority. The correct doctrine is stated below, § 2096.
(*c*) Grieve, *supra*, § 1181 (*g*). Lothian *v.* Somerville, 1724; M. 16,337. See Gibson *v.* Aitken, 1798; Hume, 205. Keggie *v.* Christie, May 25, 1815; F. C. Below, § 1594.
(*d*) Keggie, *cit.* Gowan *v.* Pursell, 1822; 1 S. 418. 1 Hunter, L. & T. 164. Rankine, Leases, 24. There is nothing in the Married Women's Property Act, 1881 (44 and 45 Vict. c. 21), which affects the law here stated, that Act, § 2, excluding the *jus mariti* and right of administration only from rents and income. See the provision in § 5 of this Act, for dispensing with the husband's consent to deeds in cases of desertion and separation.
(*e*) Forbes, petr., 1838; 1 D. 355. See also Colt *v.* Colt, 1800; M. 16,387. Slade, petr., 1831; 10 S. 167. Russell, petr., 1840; 2 D. 721. M'Kenzie, petr., 1842; 4 D. 456. Halkett, petr., 1847; 10 D. 146. Spiers' Tutors, petrs., 1848; 10 D. 1474. Morison, petr., 1857; 19 D. 493; 1861, 23 D. 1313. Morison, petr., 1857; 20 D. 276. Pearson, petr., 1865; 3 Macph. 883. Douglas, petr., 1867; 6 Macph. 178 (father as administrator). Brown's Tutors, petrs., 1867; 5 Macph. 1046.
(*f*) See cases in note (*e*).
(*g*) 12 and 13 Vict. c. 51, § 7, 25, 28. Kincaid, petr., 1856; 18 D. 1208. Fraser, petr., 1857; 19 D. 801. See 1 Hunter, L. & T. 170–187. Pattison's Cur., 1890; 17 R. 303. As to trustees, see below, § 1998A, B.
(*h*) 30 and 31 Vict. c. 97, § 2; and 50 and 51 Vict. c. 18, as extended by 47 and 48 Vict. c. 63, § 2.
(*i*) 30 and 31 Vict. c. 97, § 3. Rankine, Leases, 9.

1185. The power of the proprietor to let leases is under restraint by the diligence of creditors. So by inhibition a lease of extraordinary duration, or for an inconsiderable rent, will be objectionable; but if according to the course of ordinary administration, it will be good (*a*). By adjudication, or ranking and sale, the debtor's powers are so far limited that he can grant no lease beyond ordinary administration; but by mercantile or common sequestration, 'the bankrupt' being deprived of the possession, leases even of ordinary duration are bad (*b*). 'As any creditor in possession of lands disponed in security may let them for not more than seven years (*c*), it is thought that the proprietor's power to lease is ousted to the same effect.'

(*a*) Gordon *v.* Milne, 1780; M. 7008. E. Breadalbane *v.* M'Lachlan, 1802; 2 Bell's Com. 150 n.; Hume, 242. Wedgewood *v.* Catto, Nov. 13, 1817; F. C. 2 Hunter, L. & T. 571.

(*b*) Carlyle *v.* Lowther, 1766; M. 8380. York Buildings Co. *v.* Fordyce, 1778; M. 8380; aff. 2 Pat. 500. *Id. v.* Threipland, 1778; M. 8383; aff. 2 Pat. 496. As to heirs of entail, see E. Wemyss *v.* Murray, Nov. 17, 1815; F. C.; aff. 1 Bligh, 339; 6 Pat. 465, 561. Comp. Stewart *v.* Campbell, 1834; 13 S. 7. Lindsay *v.* Webster, 1841; 4 D. 231. King *v.* Wieland, 1858; 20 D. 960. As to the effect of a heritable creditor entering into possession under a clause in his bond giving him "power to output and input tenants," see Forsyth *v.* Aird, 1853; 16 D. 197. Blair *v.* Galloway, 1853; 16 D. 291. Macfarlane *v.* Campbell, 1857; 19 D. 623.

(*c*) 57 and 58 Vict. c. 44, § 6.

1186. Constitution of Lease.—The contract of location is consensual, and in its own nature merely personal (*a*); 'and its nature is not so altered by the statute aftermentioned that its constitution and validity are questions of heritable right, which cannot be competently entertained by the Sheriff Court (*b*)'; but by statute it is made real against singular successors in land, provided certain requisites shall be complied with (*c*). 'A lease, when constituted, may be altered by consent of parties, shown by probative writ, or by oath, or even (except where the change affects the rent (*d*)) by oral or informal written evidence followed by *rei interventus* (*e*).'

(*a*) Stewart *v.* Watson, 1864; 2 Macph. 1414, 1422, *per* L. Neaves. Campbell *v.* M'Kinnon, 1867; 5 Macph. 636; aff. 1870, 8 Macph. H. L. 40. Dirl. and Stewart, *Tack*, p. 296. 1 Stair, 15. § 4; 2 *ib.* 9. § 1. 2 Ersk. 6. § 23.

(*b*) Robertson *v.* Cockburn, 1875; 3 R. 21.

(*c*) 1449, c. 17.

(*d*) Law *v.* Gibsone, 1835; 13 S. 396. Turnbull *v.* Oliver, 1891; 19 R. 154. Rattray *v.* Leslie's Tr., 1892; 19 R. 853. Cf. Baillie *v.* Fraser, 1853; 15 D. 747.

(*e*) **Wark** *v.* **Bargaddie Coal Co.**, 1856; 18 D. 772; rev. 21 D. H. L. 41; 3 Macq. 467. Kirkpatrick *v.* Allanshaw Coal Co., 1880; 8 R. 327.

1187. (1.) *Verbal Lease.*—A lease of land (*a*) is not to be proved by parole evidence, if for more than for a single year; but only by writ or oath as against the granter and his heirs (*b*).

(*a*) See 1 Hunter, L. & T. 365; Rankine, Leases, 113, as to the non-application of this rule to leases of subjects which are not heritage, *e.g.* rents, feu-duties, customs, steam-power.

(*b*) Baillie *v.* Somerville, 1611; M. 8398; 2 Ill. 175. Low *v.* Lyell, 1611; M. 8398. Johnston *v.* Logan, 1621; M. 8399. Stewart *v.* Leith, 1766; M. 15,178; Hailes, 174. A. *v.* B., 1791; M. 15,181. Jackson *v.* Graham, 1705; M. 12,413. Neill *v.* E. Cassillis, Nov. 22, 1810; F. C.; see 2 Ill. 176. Maxwell *v.* Grierson, 1812; Hume, 849. Paterson *v.* E. Fife, 1865; 3 Macph. 423 (admission of lease for years must be taken as it stands, and does not open the way for proof of alleged conditions). Fowlie *v.* M'Lean, 1868; 6 Macph. 254. Gowans' Trs. *v.* Carstairs, 1862; 24 D. 1382. As to evidence by writ, see Gibson *v.* Adams, 1875; 3 R. 144. Sellar *v.* Aiton, 1875; 2 R. 381. Wilson *v.* Mann, 1876; 3 R. 527. A separate condition or agreement made before the date of a written lease can of course be proved only by writ or oath. Philip *v.* Cumming's Exrs., 1869; 7 Macph. 859. Stewart *v.* Clark, 1871; 9 Macph. 616. See also Garden *v.* E. Aberdeen, 1893; 20 R. 896 (innominate contract relative to lease). For cases as to proof of alleged rights, interests, or liabilities under leases between the tenant and third parties, see Seth *v.* Hain, and M'Vean *v.* M'Vean, *infra*, § 1995 (*c*). Stewart & Craig *v.* Phillips, *infra*, § 2257 (*k*).

1188. Although all authorities agree that a verbal lease for a year is good, such a lease for more than one year is not effectual even for a year (*a*), 'except where the lessee has taken possession (*b*).'

(*a*) 2 Stair, 9. § 4. 2 Ersk. 6. § 30.

(*b*) 1 Hunter, L. & T. 365. Rankine, Leases, 112. Fowlie *v.* M'Lean, *cit.* Cf. Forbes *v.* Wilson, 1873; 11 Macph. 454, 465. Clark *v.* Lamont, Jan. 27, 1816; F. C. *Infra*, § 1194 (*b*).

1189. A lease for more than one year, though the writing be imperfect, 'or a verbal lease,' may by *rei interventus* be fixed on the granter and his heirs as an effectual contract, provided such *rei interventus* shall distinctly apply to a right of longer duration than a single year. But a lease established *rei interventu* has no effect against singular successors without possession (*a*). 'Where *rei interventus* is founded on as validating a verbal or informal lease for a term of years, there must be a concluded agreement (*consensus in idem placitum*) (*b*), and proof of the concluded agreement by writ or oath of party, or judicial admission (*c*).'

(*a*) Stewart *v.* Leith, 1776; M. 15,178; Hailes, 174. Skene *v.* ——, 1637; M. 8401; 2 Ill. 23. M'Kenzie *v.* Trotter, 1729; M. 8437; 2 Ill. 175. M'Rory *v.* M'Whirter, Dec. 18, 1810; F. C. See *ante*, § 26. Pratt *v.* Abercromby, 1858; 21 D. 19. Bathie *v.* L. Wharncliffe, 1873; 11 Macph. 490. Campbell *v.* Dougal, 1813; Hume, 861. Mackenzie *v.* Mackenzie, 1799; Hume, 801. Css. Moray *v.* Stewart, 1772; M. 4392; rev. 2 Pat. 317. Ballantine *v.* Stevenson, 1881; 8 R. 959. Bell *v.* Goodall, 1883; 10 R. 905 (*rei int.* by granting sub-lease).

(*b*) *Supra*, § 25. Fraser *v.* Brebner, 1857; 19 D. 401. D. Hamilton *v.* Buchanan, 1877; 4 R. 328, 854; aff. 1878, 5 R. H. L. 69. Erskine *v.* Glendinning, 1871; 9 Macph. 656.

(*c*) Gowans' Trs. *v.* Carstairs, 1862; 24 D. 1382. Walker *v.* Flint, 1863; 1 Macph. 417. Emslie *v.* Duff, 1865; 3 Macph. 854. Fowlie *v.* M'Lean, 1868; 6 Macph. 254. Philip *v.* Cumming's Exrs., 1869; 7 Macph. 859. Sinclair *v.* M'Beath, 1869; 7 Macph. 273. Campbell *v.* M'Kinnon, 1867; 5 Macph. 636; aff. 1870, 8 Macph. H. L. 40. Sellar *v.* Aiton, 1875; 2 R. 381. Forbes *v.* Wilson, 1873; 11 Macph. 454. See Ivory's Ersk. B. ii. note 96.

1190. (2.) *Written Lease.*—In a question with the granter and his representatives, it is necessary to the validity of a written lease for years that it shall be authenticated in terms of the statutes, and delivered; or fortified by *rei interventus* (*a*); or sanctioned by homologation; or if in the shape of a mere offer, it must be followed by real evidence of acceptance (*b*); or it may be in the shape of written articles and conditions for the general regulation of the plan of leasing the estate, if proved by written (*c*) evidence to have been adopted by the parties (*d*); or, finally, a written obligation to grant a lease has been held equivalent to a lease (*e*). These are all effectual modes of binding the granter and his representatives, in whatever terms conceived, if legitimate; and this independently of possession, in so far as not necessary in *proof* of the agreement.

Against singular successors, whatever is effectual and binding on the granter and his representatives, as above, will bind them (*f*), under two qualifications,—that the lease is special and definite in subject, in rent, and in the term of duration; and that possession shall have followed as the requisite badge of real right under the statute (*g*).

(*a*) Ross *v.* Ross, 1790; Hume, 774. Graham *v.* Gowans, 1792; *ib.* 784. Campbell *v.* Macpherson, 1793; *ib.* 786. See Hamilton *v.* D. Queensberry's Exrs., 1833; 12 S. 206. *Ante*, § 26. See Spencer, Sutherland, & Co. *v.* Hay, 1845; 8 D. 283. Pratt *v.* Abercromby, 1858; 21 D. 19. Gray *v.* Low, 1859; 21 D. 293. M'Leod *v.* Urquhart, 1808; Hume, 840. Barbour *v.* Chalmers, 1891; 18 R. 610. Below, § 1194.

(*b*) Css. Moray *v.* Stewart, 1772; M. 4392, 4396; Hailes, 485; rev. 1773; 2 Pat. 317; 2 Ill. 176. M'Pherson *v.* M'Pherson, May 15, 1815; F. C. M'Arthur *v.* Simpson, 1804; M. 15,181. Clark *v.* Lamont, Jan. 27, 1816; F. C. Murdoch *v.* Moir, June 18, 1812; F. C. Cairns *v.* Gerrard, 1833; 11 S. 737. Russel *v.* Fraser, 1835; 13 S. 752. L. Elibank's Trs. *v.* Pentland, 1828; 7 S. 502; aff. 1831, 5 W. & S. 28. Burnet *v.* M'Kimming, 1835; 14 S. 74. D. Hamilton *v.* Buchanan, *supra*, § 1189 (*b*) (proof allowed to show to which of two offers possession was to be ascribed, or whether to both).

(*c*) See E. Mansfield *v.* Henderson, 1856; 18 D. 989. See § 1187.

(*d*) Macra *v.* Mackenzie, 1828; 6 S. 935; 2 Ill. 177. See Pratt, *supra* (*a*). E. Aboyne *v.* Ogg, 1810; Hume, 847.

(*e*) Garioch *v.* Forbes, 1750; M. 15,177. Grant *v.* Richardson, 1788; M. 15,180. Arbuthnot *v.* Campbell, 1793; Hume, 785. As to the fulfilment of an obligation to execute "a lease containing all usual and necessary clauses," see Wilson *v.* Douglas, 1868; 7 Macph. 112.

(*f*) See cases (*a*), (*b*). Skene *v.* Spankie, 1790; 1 Bell on Leases, 313, note. Burnet, *supra* (*b*). Carruthers *v.* Thomson, 1836; 14 S. 464; 2 Ill. 176. Singular successors are bound by a clause of reference, forming an essential part of the lease. Montgomerie *v.* Carrick, 1848; 10 D. 1387.

(*g*) 1449, c. 17. 2 Stair, 9. § 4. 2 Ersk. 6. § 25. 1 Bell on Leases, 30. See below, § 1194. Wilson *v.* Mann, 1876; 3 R. 527. As to leases for 99 years constituted by (prescriptive) possession following upon advertisement, see Campbell *v.* M'Kinnon, § 1189 (*c*); upon an informal tack, Carlyle *v.* Baxter, 1869; 41 S. Jur. 342.

1191. Thus a binding written contract of lease, followed by possession, is the sole title of that real estate of lease effectual against purchasers and creditors which is so important in agriculture. The statute '(1449)' protects absolutely one who holds such a lease, with possession conformable; and without possession no lease has effect against singular successors.

1192. A written lease must, in order to be effectual to ground an action, be on stamped paper (*a*). The stamp may be supplied 'without penalty within thirty days after first execution (*b*), or' at any time on payment of certain penalties, though the practice of sisting process till the stamp be obtained 'was' at least of doubtful propriety (*c*); and no consent of the parties can waive the objection (*d*).

(*a*) 55 Geo. III. c. 184; repealed by 33 and 34 Vict. c. 99. An agreement for a lease is subject to the same duty, 54 and 55 Vict. c. 39, § 75–78. Rollo *v.* Reid, 1787; M. 16,944; 2 Ill. 177. M'Niven *v.* Hunter, 1836; 14 S. 685. Church *v.* Sharpe, 1843; 5 D. 876. Hutchison *v.* Ferrier, 1851; 13 D. 837; aff. 1 Macq. 196; 15 D. H. L. 7. Forsyth *v.* Aird, 1853; 16 D. 197.

(*b*) 54 and 55 Vict. c. 39, § 15 (2) (*a*), (*d*).

(*c*) See 31 and 32 Vict. c. 100, § 41 (repealed, except as to the deliverance of the judge, by 33 and 34 Vict. c. 99), and 54 and 55 Vict. c. 39, § 14; above, § 22.

(*d*) Robb *v.* Forrest, 1831; 5 W. & S. 740.

1193. Duration of the Lease (*a*).—The written lease, according to the requisites of the contract of location (*b*), must fix the Term 'of Duration,' the Rent, and the Subject.

(*a*) See below, § 1215. (*b*) See above, § 134.

1194. The statute '(1449)' is in favour of such tenants as have "terms and zeires," they being entitled to "remain with their tacks unto the isshew of their termes." There is a marked distinction, however, between the parties to the lease and strangers in this respect.

(1.) *Granter and Heirs.*—A lease of any duration will be effectual against the granter and his heirs: as to possess "without ish"; or "as long as the grass groweth up, and the water runneth down" (*a*). If the term be not mentioned, it is construed to be for one year only, or for the most limited term which the words admit of (*b*).

(2.) *Singular Successors.*—In order to make a lease effectual against singular successors, it must have a definite term of duration (*c*). But exceptions are admitted to this rule:—Where the purchaser is made aware specially of the nature of the lease, and taken bound to warrant it, the lease will be effectual against him (*d*); and it will also be effectual where the purchaser homologates the agreement (*e*). Where the duration depends on the payment of debt, the lease is held, in a question with singular successors, to be without a definite ish in the sense of the Act (*f*).

(*a*) 1449, c. 17. 2 Stair, 9. § 16, 27. *Arg. ex.* 2 Ersk. 6. § 24. Stewart *v.* V. Ayr, 1631; M. 11,182, 15,191; 2 Ill. 178. Carruthers *v.* Irvine, 1717; M. 15,195. Kerr *v.* Waugh, 1752; M. 10,307. Ridpath *v.* White, 1737; M. 15,196. Fraser *v.* King's Advocate, 1758; M. 15,196; 1 Hailes, 406; rev. 2 Pat. 66; 1 Bell on Leases, 44; 2 Ill. 178. Irvine *v.* Knox, 1760; M. 5276, 15,199. E. Hopetoun *v.* Hunter's Trs., 1863; 1 Macph. 1074; rev. 1865, 3 Macph. H. L. 50; 4 Macq. 972. E. Hopetoun *v.* Wight, 1863; 1 Macph. 1097; aff. 2 Macph. H. L. 35; 4 Macq. 729.

(*b*) 2 Stair, 9. § 16. Ridpath, *supra* (*a*). Clark *v.* Lamont, Jan. 27, 1816; F. C. Russell *v.* Freen, 1835; 13 S. 752 (term fixed by reference to advertisement). M'Leod *v.* Urquhart, 1808; Hume, 840 (parole). Dunlop *v.* Steel Co. of Scotland, 1879; 7 R. 283. Thomson *v.* Thomson, 1896; 24 R. 269 (for life). See above, § 1188. Agreements for the use of property generally, if no term is stated, may be terminated by either party on reasonable notice. Fifeshire Road Trs. *v.* Cowdenbeath Coal Co., 1883; 11 R. 18; see Lanarkshire Road Trs. *v.* L. Belhaven's Trs., 1891; 18 R. 949 (level-crossing).

(*c*) See the cases in (*a*). Hamilton *v.* Tenants, 1626; M. 15,188. Oswald *v.* Robb, 1688; M. 15,194. But see E. Hopetoun, *supra* (*a*). Campbell *v.* M'Kinnon, 1867; 5 Macph. 636; aff. 1870, 8 Macph. H. L. 40.

(*d*) Wight *v.* E. Hopetoun, 1763; M. 15,199; M. 10,461.

(*e*) Scott *v.* Straiton, 1771; M. 15,200; Hailes, 404; aff. 3 Paton, 666. See below, § 1200.

(*f*) Bennet *v.* Turnbull, 1628; M. 15,237; 2 Ill. 178. Geichen *v.* Walkinshaw, 1628; M. 15,238. Pringle *v.* Fleming, 1629; M. 15,238. Stewart, *supra* (*a*). Thomson *v.* Reid, 1664; M. 15,239. Cockburn *v.* Sampson, 1698; M. 15,247. Auchinbreck's Crs. *v.* M'Lauchlan, 1748; M. 15,248. Robertson *v.* Spalding, 1754; Elch. *Tack*, 20. Lesly *v.* Orme, 1779; M. 15,530; aff. 2 Dow, 112; 1 Bligh, 510; 2 Pat. 533; 1 Bell's Com. 68; 2 Ill. 391. See Jordanhill's Crs. *v.* E. Crawford, 1752; M. 10,307; Elch. No. 18, *Tack*; 5 B. Sup. 797; 2 Ill. 179. Wight, *supra* (*d*). See 2 Stair, 9. § 11, 28. See as to long leases, below, § 1196A.

1195. A question of some difficulty, however, arises on the construction of the statute 1449, in so far as a lease may have a definite term, and yet be equal to a perpetuity. It was manifestly not the design of that Act to create a species of leasehold estate equal to property (*a*), but only to protect proper tenants against singular successors. And not only by the words of the Act, but by the spirit and design of it, the term ought to be limited to the proper temporary character of a lease, while any attempt to create estates of perpetuity by way of lease must depend on other safeguards than the Act of Parliament (*b*). To what length of lease, then, the protection of the Act should be extended, is a question on which much doubt has been entertained (*c*). The common term is of nineteen years, which, whether it corresponds to any physical revolution of the seasons or not, seems to give no recognised rotation of crops. A double term of nineteen, or thirty-eight years, has been usually recognised as fit for improving leases; while in mineral or coal leases a longer term still has been common, having regard to the extraordinary expense and slow returns. Long terms have also been sanctioned as suitable to building leases, where a large expenditure is necessary at the first, and the houses built remain long habitable. Amidst these varieties it may perhaps be held that leases for the usual period, either of agricultural or even of improving leases, will be good against singular successors; that liferent leases, or leases terminating with a liferent, will be effectual; that building leases for such reasonable term as to indemnify the expense will be protected; and that mining leases may be greatly prolonged. But there are no cases which settle on any satisfactory footing the doubts which may be raised on this subject, and all that can be safely laid down is, that a lease in which a definite term is named, but with a renewal from term to term, is not effectual against singular successors (*d*); that though a lease for 2000 years, or even for 400 years, has been held not protected by the statute (*e*), those were cases not turning entirely on the point of duration: and that the criterion adopted in questions under entail prohibitions, annulling long leases as *alienations*, is not correct to be adopted in ordinary cases, where the singular successor has notice of the term of duration from the written lease followed by possession.

(*a*) 2 Stair, 9. § 24 et seq.
(*b*) Alison *v.* Ritchie, 1730; M. 15,196; 2 Ill. 179. Jordanhill's Crs., *supra*, § 1194 (*f*). Campbell *v.* Siller, 1785; M. 15,223; Hailes, 978. See below, § 1196A, 1214–5.
(*c*) Jordanhill's Crs., *supra*, § 1194 (*f*). 1 Bell on Leases, 49 et seq.
(*d*) Crichton (Stewart) *v.* V. Ayr, 1631; M. 11,182, 15,191. Oswald *v.* Robb, 1688; M. 15,194. *Arg. ex.* Wight and Scott, *supra*, § 1194 (*d*) and (*e*). But see Campbell *v.* M'Kinnon, 1867; 5 Macph. 636; aff. 1870; 8 Macph. H. L. 40. It seems to be effectual at least for the term expressed. Scott *v.* Straiton, 1771; M. 15,200; aff. 3 Pat. 666. Lumsden *v.* Stewart, 1843; 5 D. 501; See § 1196A.
(*e*) Alison, *supra* (*b*). Jordanhill's Crs., *supra*, § 1194 (*f*). See *contra*, E. Elgin *v.* Wellwood, 1821; 1 S. App. 44. Fraser *v.* L. Adv., 1758; M. 15,196; rev. 2 Pat. 66.

1196. (3.) *Heirs of Entail.*—Where the lease is granted by one who holds the land under restraint against alienation (as by an heir of entail under prohibitions against alienating or disponing, or by a tutor or other temporary administrator), it must, in order to be effectual, not only be of definite duration, but of a duration not equivalent to alienation (*a*), nor beyond the duration of the administrative authority (*b*).

(*a*) 1 Bell's Com. 69. Lesly, *supra*, § 1194 (*f*). 1 Bell, Leases, 126, note. See below, § 1752. *Supra*, § 1183–4.
(*b*) See below, § 2084.

1196A. '*Registration of Long Leases.*—Probative leases of heritable subjects, for a specific rent, of thirty-one or more years' duration, and leases containing an obligation upon the granter to renew the same from time to time at fixed periods, or upon the termination of a life or lives, or otherwise, provided they be renewable so as to endure for thirty-one years or upwards, may now be recorded in the General Register of Sasines (*a*); in which case, if valid and binding as in a question with the granters, they are to be effectual in competition according to the date of recording, and, as against any singular successor whose infeftment is posterior in date to such registration, in the same manner as if the grantee had entered into actual possession of the subjects leased at the date of registration (*b*). But no lease, except of burgage subjects, executed after the passing of the Act (unless where the same shall have been executed in terms of an obligation to renew as above mentioned, and of date prior to the Act) is to be registrable where the name of the lands of which the subject consists or forms a part, and (if it be not mineral) the extent thereof,—not to exceed fifty acres,—shall not be set forth (*c*).'

(*a*) 20 and 21 Vict. c. 26, § 1, 17.
(*b*) *Ib.* § 2, 12, 16. Rodger *v.* Crawfords, 1867; 6 Macph. 24. See below, § 1212A.
(*c*) 20 and 21 Vict. c. 26, § 18.

1197. Rent.—This is an essential part of the contract of location (*a*); but there is a distinction in this (as in regard to the term of duration) between questions with the granter and his heirs, and questions with singular successors.

(*a*) See further, below, § 1227.

1198. (1.) *Granter and Heirs.*—In questions with the granter of the lease and his heirs, the rent may be merely nominal, or it may be effectually discharged, or stipulated to be retained for debt. This is taken for granted in all the cases which have occurred with singular successors (*a*).

(*a*) Ross *v.* Blair, 1627; M. 15,167; 2 Ill. 180. Sinclair *v.* M'Beath, 1788; Hume, 773. Campbell *v.* Welsh, 1785, 3 Pat. 32.

1199. (2.) *Singular Successors.*—In questions with singular successors, there must under the statute be a rent payable to the proprietor of the land (*a*). And that rent must stand undischarged, as some equivalent for the possession of which the purchaser of the land is deprived (*b*). Nor can there be any stipulation available against singular successors by which the tenant shall be empowered to apply the rent in extinction of debt (*c*).

(*a*) 1449, c. 17. Below, § 1201.
(*b*) 2 Stair, 9. § 29. 2 Ersk. 6. § 29. Ross, *supra*, § 1198. Auchinbreck *v.* M'Laughlan, 1748; M. 15,248; Elch. *Tack*, 14; 2 Ill. 180. L. Cranstoun's Crs. *v.* Scott, 1757; M. 15,218; 5 B. Sup. 830. Ross *v.* Dss. Sutherland, 1838; 16 S. 1179.
(*c*) Stair, *ut supra*. Cranstoun, *supra* (*b*). Douglas's Crs. *v.* Carlyle, 1757; M. 15,219. See below, § 1212.

1200. There may, however, be, in consequence of the purchaser's agreement or acquiescence, a personal exception which shall bar him from challenging such application of the rents; as where the purchaser, with full knowledge of the leases, is taken bound to warrant them (*a*).

(*a*) See above, § 1194.

1201. The doctrine as to rent, delivered by Craig, is that there must be a rent, or something in its stead (*a*). And in so far as singular successors are concerned, the doctrine, as Erskine lays it down, is that the rent in money, or grain, or service, must be expressed in the lease, and that, although below the true value, it will afford to the tenant an absolute security against removing (*b*). It is at the same time said that the rent must not be elusory (*c*). But as there is no criterion according to which this can be ascertained, or the requisite rent fixed, the result on the whole seems to be, that a rent or annual return of some kind is essential to the character of a lease (*d*); that where rental-rights now exist, they are effectual against heirs, and even against singular successors with or without a grassum, provided the tenant has a written rental-right with possession (*e*); and that, in consideration of a grassum, the rent may be reduced to the lowest rate (a common resource for raising money to provide for younger children by heirs of entail) (*f*)—the effect of which leases against singular successors has never been doubted. A discharge of the rent, however, in satisfaction of debt, or a right to retain it for interest, or in extinction of the principal, is not good against singular successors; but it would seem that on the principle under which grassums and low rents have been sanctioned, the debt of the granter of a lease may so far be provided for by taking the debt as a grassum, and reducing the rent to a low rate.

(*a*) 2 Craig, 10. § 2. (*b*) 2 Ersk. 6. § 24.
(*c*) This does not apply to leases registered under the Act of 1857; § 1196A (*b*) above.
(*d*) 2 Ersk. 6. § 20, 24. 1449, c. 17. 2 Stair, 9. § 20. 1 Hunter, L. & T. 474. Rankine, Leases, 137.
(*e*) 2 Ersk. 6. § 37. See below, § 1279.
(*f*) See below, § 1229, 1752.

1202. Where the right of retention stipulated is not on account of a debt unconnected with the lease, but intended to render effectual some undertaking or counter obligation on the part of the 'landlord'—as the completing of fences, the building of farm offices, or for specified meliorations—it will be effectual against singular successors (*a*). In such case neither creditors nor purchasers have reason to complain, since, by the lease and possession, they have full means of learning how the stipulations and the rent stand, and so may regulate the price or their credit accordingly. Where the obligation is not in the lease, but separate, the same does not hold (*b*). Even where the retention for meliorations depends on local custom, it has been held effectual against singular successors (*c*). But it has been held that a stipulation of retention of part of the rent for personal services as ground officer, was not binding on a singular successor (*d*).

(*a*) Arbuthnot *v.* Colquhoun, 1772; M. 10,424. Stewart *v.* M'Ra, 1834; 13 S. 4. See below, § 1256.
(*b*) Turner *v.* Nicolson, 1835; 13 S. 633. See § 1210.
(*c*) Bell *v.* Lamont, June 14, 1814; F. C. See Gordon *v.* Robertson, 1826; 2 W. & S. 115. Gordon *v.* Thomson, 1831; 9 S. 735. Shirreff *v.* L. Lovat, 1854; 17 D. 177; 2 Hunter, L. & T. 239. Dickson on Evid. § 237.
(*d*) Ross *v.* Dss. Sutherland, 1838; 16 S. 1179. 1 Bell's Com. 74. See for specific stipulations of the lease, improvements, particular outlays, etc., below, § 1256. As to retention of rent generally, see below, § 1231.

1203. (3.) *Money Rent.*—Rent may be in money, grain, or other produce of the subject.

1204. Where the rent is in money, it is generally made payable at two terms in the year, Whitsunday and Martinmas (*a*), held to be the "legal terms." Sometimes the term of payment is *before* the crop is reaped, sometimes *after*, and the terms thus stipulated are called the "conventional terms"; the rent payable by anticipation being called "forehand rent," that which is payable after the crop is reaped being called "back rent." The terms of payment of rent are important in questions with purchasers, between fiar and liferenter (*b*), and between heirs and executors (*c*). 'But questions of vesting and apportionment do not affect the title of the landlord in possession to levy the rents payable after his succession, for leases are real contracts, and the obligations of landlord and tenant transmit to and against their heirs, whatever questions of accounting or division may exist in regard to the succession of the one or the other (*d*).'

(*a*) See below, § 1230. (*b*) See § 1047.
(*c*) Kames' Elucid. art. 9. 2 Ersk. § 64. 1 Bell on Leases, 220. 1 Hunter on L. & T. 387, ii. 326. Rankine, Leases, 319. Carnegie *v.* Carnegie's Exrs., 1688; M. 15,887; 2 Ill. 143. Pringle *v.* Pringle, 1741; M. 15,907; 2 Ill. 180. M. Queensberry *v.* Montgomerie, Feb. 18, 1814; F. C.; 2 Ill. 144, 233. Elliot's Trs. *v.* Elliot, 1792; M. 15,917; 2 Ill. 235. Swinton *v.* Gawler, June 20, 1809; F. C.; 2 Ill. 234. See also Murray Kynynmound *v.* Cath-

cart & Rocheail, 1739; M. 5415, 15,906. And below, § 1230 and 1499. Innes *v.* D. Gordon, 1822; 2 S. 3. Trotter *v.* Cunninghame, 1839; 2 D. 140.

(*d*) Lennox *v.* Reid, 1893; 21 R. 77.

1205. (4.) *Grain Rent.*—Where the rent is in grain or otherwise payable in produce, it is to be satisfied from the produce of the farm, if there be any. If there be none, the tenant is bound and entitled to deliver fair marketable grain of the same kind (*a*). If agreed to be converted into money, or if the grain be tendered and refused, it will be converted according to the fiars (*b*). If the fault of not delivering the grain be with the tenant, he will be liable to pay a conversion according to the market price (*c*). The tenant failing to deliver grain when stipulated will be liable for damage, where the landlord has engaged to deliver grain to a merchant and is disappointed (*d*). In order to reconcile with the imperial standard the measures of capacity according to which rents payable in grain are exigible under Scottish leases, it is ordered that an inquisition shall be taken (in like manner as in fixing the fiars prices) of the value, according to the standard established by the Act, of all rents in grain payable according to the measures formerly used in the county, to be transmitted to and enrolled at Edinburgh; the conversion to be the rule of future payment, according to tables to be made out and published (*e*). But it has been held that the fifteenth section of that Act annulling agreements in which any other than the standard weights and measures are specified, without stating the ratio or proportion, does not apply to leases (*f*).

(*a*) E. Elgin *v.* Wellwood, 1825; 3 S. 422; 2 Ill. 181. See Baillie *v.* Fraser, 1853; 15 D. 747 (conversion into fixed money rent).

(*b*) 2 Ersk. 6. § 40. Barclay *v.* Simpson, 1682; M. 4413. As to fiars prices, see 1 Ersk. 4. § 6. 2 Hunter, L. & T. 290. 2 Connell on Tithes, 431. 2 Hutchison, J. of P. 98. Geo. Paterson, Histor. Acct. of Fiars Prices. W. Hector, Fiars Prices, a Memorandum, Paisley, 1878. N. Elliot, The Position of the Fiars Prices, Edinr. 1879. Knox *v.* Law, 1771; M. 4420. Mylne *v.* Horne, 1850; 12 D. 883. Howden *v.* E. Haddington, 1851; 13 D. 522. 31 and 32 Vict. c. 82, § 5 (County General Assessment Act).

(*c*) Ersk. *supra* (*b*). E. Elgin, *supra* (*a*).

(*d*) Ersk. *supra* (*b*).

(*e*) 5 Geo. IV. c. 74, § 18 and 19. 5 and 6 Will. IV. c. 63, § 15, 16. 41 and 42 Vict. c. 49. 52 and 53 Vict. c. 21.

(*f*) Henry *v.* M'Ewan, 1832; 10 S. 572; aff. 7 W. & S. 411. See Miller *v.* Mair, 1860; 22 D. 660. 2 Hunter, L. & T. 298. *Supra*, § 91 (4).

1205A. '(5.) *Lordship or royalty* is a return commonly stipulated in leases of minerals, at the rate of so much in money for each ton of the output of mineral. It is usual to agree for rent or lordship alternatively, in the option of the lessor, who is given a power of inspecting the lessee's books for the purpose of checking the output. The clauses of such leases are generally so fully detailed as to make the documents codes exclusive of the common law on most points (*a*).'

(*a*) 2 Hunter, L. & T. 299. Rankine, Leases, 291. *Infra*, § 1208 (*c*).

1206. Subject of the Lease.—The subject of the lease must be described so as to be fully identified. Where measure enters into the description, the statute (*a*) is to be attended to, by which a standard yard is fixed, and the rood of land is to contain 1210, the acre 4840 square yards, according to that standard yard.

(*a*) 5 Geo. IV. c. 74, § 2; and see 5 and 6 Will. IV. c. 63; 41 and 42 Vict. c. 49; and above, § 91, 1205. Thomson *v.* Garioch, 1841; 3 D. 625. Miller *v.* Mair, *cit.* As to descriptions which refer to the extent of the subject, see above, § 738, 893; and Oliver *v.* Suttie, 1840; 2 D. 514. Menmuir *v.* Airth, 1863; 1 Macph. 929. Hardie *v.* Kinloch, 1842; 5 D. 64. Gregson *v.* Alsop, 1897; 24 R. 1080 ("as occupied by A."). 2 Hunter, L. & T. 180-186. Rankine, Leases, 195. *Qu.* whether there can be a lease, giving a real right, of a going business with stock? Walker (Paterson's Tr.) *v.* Paterson's Trs., 1891; 19 R. 91.

1207. The proper subject of lease is land, and the Act of 1449 speaks of "the ground." But mills, fishings, collieries, etc., fall under the same rules with leases of lands (*a*).

(*a*) 2 Stair, 9. § 2. 2 Ersk. 6. § 27. 1 Bell on Leases, 31-33. Glas. Tram. Co. *v.* Glas. Corpn., 1897; 24 R. 628; 1898, A. C. 631; 35 S. L. R. 967 (tramways in burgh). M'Nab *v.* Robertson, 1896; 23 R. 1098; 24 R. H. L. 34 (water rights). Cunninghame *v.* Ayrshire Assessor, 1895; 22 R. 596 (submarine minerals). Compare § 1187 (*a*), above. As to leases of land for sporting purposes, see Farquharson, petr., 1870; 9 Macph. 66; and above, § 952.

1208. The contract of lease implies a subject let: so, if it turn out that no such thing exists as the parties intended to be the object of agreement, the tenant cannot be bound to pay rent (*a*). Where the subject fails (as where a house is burnt (*b*); where a farm is by a flood or a hurricane reduced to sterility; where a coal is exhausted suddenly and unexpectedly), the tenant's obligation to pay rent will be discharged (*c*). Where the destruction is partial, the point is more doubtful; and the distinction seems to be, that if it be permanent, though partial, the failure of the subject let will give relief by entitling the tenant to renounce the lease, unless a deduction shall be allowed (*d*); but that if it be not permanent but temporary or occasional, it will not entitle the tenant to relief (*e*). The ground of this distinction is, that while the contract implies the existence and warrandice of the subject, it is, in so far as belongs to the produce of that subject, a contract of risk (*f*). In the decisions, however, relief has been given to a greater extent than that distinction would authorise; thus, devastation of the crop by storm, etc., if *plus quam tolerabile*, has been admitted as a ground of abatement (*g*); but as the tenant takes the risk of the seasons, it must at least be some extraordinary event that will justify such a decision (*h*). 'And the rule has now been laid down, that if a tenant, through no fault of his own, loses part of the subject let to him, he is entitled to an abatement of rent, *i.e.* he ceases to be debtor for the rent to the extent to which he has been deprived of the subject let (*i*).' Devastation by public calamity rests on another footing, as of this the tenant undertakes no risk, and it ought to fall on both alike (*k*). If the failure is by a supervenient law, it is held that the risk of such law is with the tenant; as in a lease of fishings in the North Esk, in which the close time was lengthened by 9 Geo. IV. c. 38 (*l*). 'The tenant is entitled to damages under the contract for the undue exercise by the landlord of his reserved powers, *e.g.* in regard to game (*m*), his wrongful use of his neighbouring lands, as by discharging by drainage an undue quantity of water upon the farm (*n*), or for failure to perform his obligations under the lease, as in contracts generally (*o*). In all claims of the nature here spoken of, the tenant may be deprived of his remedy by failure to give timeous notice (*p*).'

(*a*) 1 Stair, 15. § 2, 3. 2 Ersk. 6. § 41. 2 Hunter, L. & T. 188, 451. See above, § 29, 141. E. Wemyss *v.* Campbell, 1858; 20 D. 1423. Webster *v.* Lyell, 1860; 22 D. 1423. Menmuir *v.* Airth, 1863; 1 Macph. 929.

(*b*) See below, § 1253, 1274A. The tenant may abandon his lease, although the repair of the subject may occupy only a few weeks, the rule being that the lease is terminated, in his option, by the destruction of the subject so that it is no longer fit for the purpose for which it is let, but not by partial destruction or injury causing only considerable inconvenience. Drummond *v.* Hunter, 1869; 7 D. 347. Duff *v.* Fleming, 1870; 8 Macph. 769. Allan *v.* Markland, 1882; 10 R. 383.

(*c*) Lindsay *v.* Home, 1612; M. 10,120. Wilson *v.* Mader, 1699; M. 10,125. Gray *v.* Hog, 1706; 4 B. Sup. 635; 2 Ill. 181. Murdoch *v.* Fullarton, 1829; 7 S. 404. White *v.* Moncrieff, 1849; 11 D. 1031 (abatement allowed). Thomson *v.* Gordon, 1869; 7 Macph. 687. Sinclair *v.* Mossend Iron Co., 1854; 17 D. 258. Gowans *v.* Christie, 1871; 9 M. 485; aff. 1873, 11 Macph. H. L. 1. Fleeming *v.* Baird, 1871; 9 Macph. 730. Shotts Iron Co. *v.* Deas, 1881; 8 R. 530. The cases last cited show that a tenant's right to abandon his lease on this ground, or to claim abatement, may be excluded by implied intention, where there are breaks at specified periods, as is usual in leases of minerals; and that he must observe stipulations in the lease intended to meet the case of supervening failure of the subject. *E.g.* a report by an engineer or an award by arbiters as to the exhaustion of coal, or unworkability, may be a condition precedent of the right to abandon. Waddell's Trs. *v.* Monkland Iron Co., 1885; 13 R. 237. Cf. Merry & Cunningham *v.* Brown, 1859; 21 D. 1337; aff. 1863, 1 Macph. H. L. 14. Shotts Iron Co. *v.* Deas, *cit.* In mineral leases, indeed, it is generally difficult to apply the common law principle, owing to the nature of the subject and the fulness of the stipulations. Fleeming *v.* Baird, *cit.* Where, however, a general clause provides for the termination of the lease if the minerals become, without the lessee's fault, not worth the expense of working, it may be operative if, the condition and quality of the minerals being unaltered, there be a great and permanent depreciation of their market value. Dixon *v.* Campbell, 1824; 2 S. App. 175. Shotts Iron Co. *v.* Deas, *cit.*

(*d*) Edmistone *v.* Preston, 1675; M. 15,172. Hamilton *v.* ——, 1667; M. 10,121. Futt *v.* L. Ruthven, 1671; 2 B. Sup. 504. Foster *v.* Adamson, 1762; M. 10,131. Heriot's Hospital *v.* Angus, 1709; M. 10,126. Sharp's Factor *v.* Monboddo, 1778; M. 10,134. Walker *v.* Bayne, May 30, 1811; F. C.; 3 Dow, 233; 6 Pat. 217. L. Kinnaird *v.* Matthewson, 1802; 4 Pat. 429.

(*e*) Steedman *v.* Kennedy, 1741; Elch. *Tack*, No. 9. Gowans and Fleeming, *cit.*

(*f*) Stair, *cit.* (*a*) Gowans, *cit.* (*c*).

(*g*) 2 Ersk. § 41.

(*h*) E. Eglinton *v.* Tenants, 1742; M. 10,128; Elch. *Tack*, 8. Lindsay, *supra* (*c*).

(*i*) Muir *v.* M'Intyre, 1887; 14 R. 470. Duncan *v.* Brooks, 1894; 21 R. 760. Anderson *v.* Calder, 1895; 11 Sh. Ct. Rep. 303 (public-house licence).

(*k*) Wilkie *v.* Kerr, 1762; M. 10,120; Ersk. *supra* (*g*). See below, § 1253. Tacksman of Customs *v.* Greenhead, 1667; M. 10,121.

(*l*) Holiday *v.* Scott, 1830; 8 S. 831; 2 Ill. 103. Goldie *v.* Williamson, 1796; Hume, 793. See Donald *v.* Leitch, 1886; 13 R. 790 (loss of hotel licence).

(*m*) See cases above, § 953 (*g*).

(*n*) Macdonald *v.* Johnstone, 1883; 10 R. 959.

(*o*) Above, § 30. Below, § 1223.

(*p*) Lowndes *v.* Buchanan, 1854; 17 D. 63. Sinclair *v.* Mossend Co., 1854; 17 D. 258. Bargaddie Coal Co. *v.* Wark, 1860; 23 D. 44. Thomson *v.* Gordon, 1869; 7 Macph. 687. Below, § 1274A.

1209. Possession on the Lease.—This is the proper completion of the real right of the tenant. Formerly it was questioned whether registration in the record of reversions would supply the want of possession; and the answer was in the negative (*a*). In order to secure leases against singular successors, they were at one time completed by sasine; but since 1449, possession is the sole badge of real right, 'except in the case of leases registered under the Act of 1857 (*b*).' Without possession commenced and continued, the tenant is a personal creditor on his contract (*c*); but possession continued gives full effect in competition, or against singular successors (*d*). Assignation of the lease with intimation to the landlord is not sufficient (*e*). 'The tenant is entitled to sue for specific implement of the obligation to give possession (*f*), as well as damages for breach of it (*g*).'

(*a*) Dirleton and Stewart, *Tack*.
(*b*) Above, § 1196A. (*c*) *Supra*, § 1186.
(*d*) 2 Craig, 10. § 7, 11. 2 Ersk. 6. § 25. 3 Stair, 2. § 6. Bell on Leases, 52 et seq. Johnston *v.* Cullen, 1676; M. 15,231; 2 Ill. 182. 2 Stair, 9. § 7. 1 Bell's Com. 66. Above, § 1191. Hutchison *v.* Ferrier, 1852; 1 Macq. 196. Wallace *v.* Campbell, 1750; M. 2805, 2811; Elch. *Tack*, 17.
(*e*) Grant *v.* Adamson, 1802; Hume, 810. See below, § 1212.
(*f*) Millat *v.* Marshall, 1878; 2 Sel. Sh. Ct. Ca. 226, and authorities cited there.
(*g*) 2 Hunter, L. & T. 178, 534, 541. See Goskirk *v.* Edin. Ry. Access Co., 1863; 2 Macph. 383. Seaforth's Trs. *v.* Macaulay, 1844; 7 D. 180.

1210. (1.) *Under the Lease.*—The possession must be under the lease (*a*). So, if the possession have begun on a verbal lease, and the term of entry by the written lease is not yet arrived, a singular successor will not be affected by such written lease. So, also, if an unexpired lease is at its close to be followed by a new one, written out and executed between the parties, possession under the old lease will not make valid the new (*b*). But if the right under the new lease is to begin from its date, although the old lease be not expired, and not renounced, the possession will be held to proceed upon the new lease, provided there be such difference of rent, etc., as fairly to show the possession to be on the new lease (*c*). It has been held (but may be doubted) that by a separate and subsequent missive a prolonged term of possession was good against a purchaser (*d*).

(*a*) In Eliott's Trs. *v.* Eliott, 1894, 21 R. 858, some effect was given to a lease on which possession followed, although it was reduced. Comp. E. Fife *v.* Wilson, 1864; 3 Macph. 323.
(*b*) L. Drum *v.* Jamieson, 1602; M. 15,209; 2 Ill. 182. Johnston *v.* Monzie, 1760; 5 B. Sup. 877. L. Cranstoun's Crs. *v.* Scott, 1757; M. 15,218; 5 B. Sup. 830. Douglas's Crs. *v.* Carlyle, 1757; M. 15,219. Scott *v.* Graham, 1769; M. 15,220. Redhead *v.* Kerr, 1792; Bell's 8vo Ca. 202; rev. 3 Pat. 309; 1 Bell's Com. 68. Pratt *v.* Abercromby, 1858; 21 D. 19.
(*c*) Neilson *v.* Menzies, 1671; M. 15,231. "This is a very doubtful decision, and the case is reported differently by Gosford": M. 7770; 2 Ill. 183. E. Cassillis *v.* Montgomery, 1686; 3 B. Sup. 600. See 1 Bell on Leases, p. 63 et seq. Montgomerie *v.* Vernon, 1895; 22 R. 465.
(*d*) Thomson *v.* Terney, 1791; Hume, 780. See Turner *v.* Nicolson, 1835; 13 S. 633; 2 Ill. 205. Birkbeck *v.* Ross, 1865; 4 Macph. 272.

1211. (2.) *Actual Possession.*—Possession must be actual. But it may be either natural or civil; a tenant possessing by his sub-tenant as effectually as if himself resident and sole cultivator of the farm (*a*).

(*a*) 2 Ersk. 1. § 22, 25, and Ivory's note, 102. See below, § 1212.

1212. Leases as Securities for Money.—It was of old frequently attempted to render leases available securities for debt; and in more recent times the great expenditure necessary in particular branches of industry has made it desirable that a tenant (especially of ground for the erection of manufactories) should have the means of borrowing money on the security of an assignation to his lease. The former attempts, we have seen, proved abortive (*a*). The more modern proposal, to secure the loan by sub-lease or assignation, has hitherto proved unsuccessful. So far as the matter can be stated as settled, the rules seem to be: Actual possession as sub-tenant or assignee will make the right effectual to the lender, even although there should be a clause excluding assignees and sub-tenants; unless the landlord should object to it (*b*). And if the security be by assignation of the principal lease, when a sub-lease has been already granted, possession by levying the surplus rent, or intimation of the conveyance to the sub-tenant, will complete the right; which truly resolves into an assignation of the surplus rent (*c*). But it is not enough to intimate the assignation of a lease to the landlord (*d*). Nor is it enough to intimate the assignation of a sub-lease to the principal tenant; possession, natural or civil, must follow in order to complete the right effectually against singular successors (*e*). An assignation to the lease, with delivery of it to the assignee, followed by a written sub-lease from the assignee to the principal tenant, under which alone (without any power of ascribing his possession to the principal lease) his possession proceeds, seems to be the most effectual completion of the conveyance which can be adopted in the present state of the law (*f*). It has been attempted, under leases of very long duration, to create securities by heritable bond, but this has been found ineffectual (*g*).

(*a*) See above, § 1194 and 1201.
(*b*) Wallace *v.* Harvey, 1627; M. 67; 2 Ill. 183. Wallace *v.* Campbell, 1750; M. 2805, 2811; Elch. *Tack*, 17. See below, § 1218.
(*c*) Sime's Trs. *v.* Fidler, 1806; M. *Tack*, Apx. 13.
(*d*) Grant *v.* Adamson, 1802; Hume, 811. Yeoman *v.* Elliot, Feb. 2, 1813; F. C. Russel *v.* E. Breadalbane, 1822; 2 S. 62; 1 W. & S. 620; 5 S. 891; 1831, 5 W. & S. 257. See Kennedy *v.* Forsyth, 1829; 7 S. 435. Brock *v.*

Cabbell, 1822; 2 S. 52; 3 W. & S. 75; 8 S. 647; aff. 5 W. & S. 476. Hamilton *v.* Stewart, 1830; 8 S. 799. Clark *v.* West Calder Oil Co., 1882; 9 R. 1017.

(*e*) Hardie Douglas *v.* Hay's Tr., 1794; M. 2802; Bell's fo. Ca. 50; as corrected in Yeoman's case, *supra* (*d*). Inglis & Co. *v.* Paul, 1829; 7 S. 469. Benton *v.* Craig's Tr., 1864; 2 Macph. 1365.

(*f*) Cases, *supra* (*d*). M'Phail *v.* Sutherland, 1833; 11 S. 396. M'Dougall & Herbertson *v.* Northern Ass. Co., 1864; 2 Macph. 935. The assignee becomes tenant, and his liability for the rent continues after the discharge of his debt and retrocession of the tenant by the assignee, unless the landlord release him. Ramsay *v.* Comm. Bank, 1842; 4 D. 405. See, as to the responsibility of creditors taking possession of a farm on the bankruptcy of the tenant, Kirkland & Sharpe *v.* Gibson, 1831; 9 S. 596; aff. 6 W. & S. 340. Dundas (E. Strathmore's Tr.) *v.* Morrison, 1853; 15 D. 752; 1855, 20 D. 225. Moncrieff *v.* Ferguson, 1896; 24 R. 47. 2 Hunter, L. & T. 596 sqq. Rankine, Leases, 557. Goudy on Bankruptcy, 280. *Infra*, § 2000 (*i*).

(*g*) Grieve *v.* Grieve's Crs., 1790; Hume, 778. But see next section.

1212A. 'Securities over Registered Leases.—The party in right of a recorded lease may assign it, in accordance with the conditions and stipulations of the lease, in security of payment of borrowed money, or annuities, or provisions to wives or children; and the recording of the bond and assignation in security, in the register in which the lease is recorded, has the effect of completing the right under it, and constituting a real security over the lease to the extent assigned (*a*). But it has been held that the debt does not become *debitum fundi*, so as to warrant a poinding of the ground (*b*). The creditor is entitled, in default of payment of the capital sum for which it has been granted, or of a term's interest, or of a term's annuity, for six months after the same shall have fallen due, to obtain from the Sheriff, after intimation to the lessee and the landlord, a warrant to enter on possession of the subjects, to uplift the rents from the sub-tenants, and to sub-let the subjects; but he is not personally liable to the landlord in any of the obligations and prestations of the lease, unless and until he enter into possession (*c*). A power is also conferred on the creditor to sell the lease in terms of the Heritable Securities Act of 1847 (*d*).'

(*a*) 20 and 21 Vict. c. 26, § 1, 4. See above, § 1196A. Rodger *v.* Crawfords, 1867; 6 Macph. 24. It has been held that such a security is moveable *quoad* the succession of the creditor. Stroyan *v.* Murray, 1890; 17 R. 1170.

(*b*) Luke *v.* Wallace, 1896; 23 R. 634. Above, § 914 (3).

(*c*) 20 and 21 Vict. c. 26, § 6.

(*d*) *Ib.* § 20. 10 and 11 Vict. c. 50.

1213. Permanency of the Lease.—The greater part of Scotland is in the hands of tenants, who contribute to the cultivation of it by their capital or credit, skill and industry, in reliance on certainty of possession, and on such returns from the land during the stipulated period, as one year with another may replace their outlay, and afford a fair profit (*a*).

(*a*) See above, § 1178–9.

1214. Transmissibility of the Lease—and Delectus Personæ.—Leases at will, and for services which were deemed base by military vassals, were the first stage of tenancy in Scotland; and it was at that time a great object to keep the ground so let in the hands of the selected tenants, and to prevent it from coming into hostile possession. With the permanency of the right arose the science of agriculture, properly so called; and such permanency came naturally to be regulated on an estimate of the rotation necessary for the indemnification of the tenant. To complete the security of the tenant, however, it is not only necessary to protect him against creditors of the landlord and purchasers of the land; but also, in order to give him full confidence to engage with energy in his labour and improvements, that his right should be available to his heirs and family, and even to those to whom, amidst the misfortunes and accidents of life, he may find it necessary to make it over, on his own or his family's incapacity to reap advantage from it. But the *delectus personæ* begun in an early age, and recommended by the nearness of the connection of landlord and tenant, and the discomfort to the landlord from the introduction of a disagreeable or troublesome tenant, have contributed to give great force to the landlord's right of choice of his tenant's successor.

1215. Farms are either already improved, and ready for successful cultivation; or such as require improvement: and for these a difference of duration of lease is suitable, in order to enable the tenant to perform his part, proportioned to the great difference of outlay, expense, and industry (*a*). Where the farm is fully improved, and the houses and fences in good condition, nothing more is requisite on the part of the tenant than good cultivation, in order to do justice to himself and to the landlord, by producing good crops without exhaustion of the soil, affording a fair rent and reasonable profit, and enabling him to restore the land uninjured on quitting possession. Short leases are sufficient for this purpose; and so grass farms may be 'let' from year to year; but corn farms require one, or two, or three rotations or courses of crops. In the richer soil of England, leases are commonly very short. In Scotland, the ordinary length of leases is nineteen or twenty-one years; which, however, do not seem to correspond with any particular course of rotation. Where the farm is in a state of dilapidation, the soil exhausted, the farm out of order, and much labour and outlay necessary to prepare it for successful cultivation, either the landlord must be at the charge of restoring the farm, or the tenant, if he undertake the burden, must be allowed a longer lease than would in ordinary circumstances be required, or the rent must be made lower; so that in the one way or the other the tenant may be indemnified. An improving lease, if the rent is kept up at an average rate, is generally of double the length of the ordinary lease—thirty-eight or forty-two years.

(*a*) See above, § 1193–5.

1216. (1.) *Assignees and Sub-Tenants.*—Between the two cases above stated a practical distinction is observable. In a lease of ordinary length, by the law of Scotland, the *delectus personæ* has full operation; and assignees and sub-tenants are excluded, unless by stipulation admitted; while in England the leasehold estate is absolute, and implies a power to assign. In longer leases, by the law of Scotland, the tenant may, without leave of the landlord, assign or sub-set; and unless there is a stipulated exclusion, the tenant's assignees, or heirs, or creditors, may enjoy the land, or be entitled to demand a compensation if deprived of it.

The general rule, then, as to assignees and sub-tenants, is, that where there is no stipulated exclusion of them, the law presumes and gives effect to the landlord's selection of a tenant, and exclusion of all of whom he does not approve (*a*). This at first was held to exclude even heirs-at-law; now it excludes only assignees and sub-tenants (*b*). To the above rule, 'which extends to sporting leases (*c*),' these exceptions are admitted:—Creditors adjudging their debtor's lease are not excluded, without an express clause of exclusion (*d*). In improving leases of long duration (*e*), and in liferent leases (*f*), the possession may be effectually assigned or sublet, if there be no clause of exclusion. If 'in a lease of such endurance' there be a clause of exclusion of assignees, it is 'not' held also to exclude sub-tenants (*g*).

(*a*) See below, § 1274, as to Urban Tenements, where a different rule prevails.

(*b*) 2 Ersk. 6. § 31, 32. 1 Bell, Leases, 145, 175 et seq., 187. Thomson *v.* Watson, 1750; M. 10,337; 2 Ill. 185. Rattray *v.* Graham, 1623; M. 10,366. Lady Binny *v.* Sinclair, 1672; M. 10,382. Hume *v.* Lyal, 1680; M. 10,391. Alison *v.* Proudfoot, 1788; M. 15,290. E. Peterborough *v.* Milne, 1791; M. 15,293. See E. Glasgow *v.* Hamilton, 1851; 13 D. 1290. Gray *v.* Low, 1859; 21 D. 293.

(*c*) Mackintosh *v.* May, 1895; 22 R. 345.

(*d*) 2 Stair, 9. § 26. 2 Ersk. 6. § 32. Elliot *v.* D. Buccleuch, 1747; M. 10,333; Elchies, *Tack*, 12, and Notes, p. 444. Kinloch *v.* Fullerton's Crs., July 6, 1791; n. r.; 1 Bell's Com. 77; (73, M'L.'s ed.); see M. 15,309, note. See above, § 1212 (*f*); below, § 1218.

(*e*) Simson *v.* Gray, 1794; M. 15,294. E. Cassillis *v.* M'Adam, 1806; M. 15,301, note. See D. Portland *v.* Baird & Co., 1865; 4 Macph. 10. Pringle *v.* Maclagan, 1802; Hume, 808. It does not appear that the implied power is confined to improving leases. 1 Hunter, L. & T. 239.

(*f*) 2 Ersk. 6. § 32. Duff *v.* Fowler, 1672; M. 10,282.

(*g*) Trotter *v.* Dennis, 1770; M. 15,282. 1 Bell's Com. 77 (73, M'L.'s ed.). Ivory's Ersk. B. ii. note 111. 1 Hunter, L. & T. 249.

1217. Where the lease contains express power to assign or sub-set, the whole stipulations are available to any assignee or subtenant who shall acquire right (*a*).

(*a*) M'Guffog *v.* Agnew, 1822; 1 S. 342; 2 Ill. 186.

1218. Where the lease contains a clause of exclusion, the construction and effect are regulated thus:—Express exclusion of assignees excludes creditors adjudging (*a*); and although on bankruptcy (where bankruptcy is not made a stipulated forfeiture of the lease) the tenant may himself continue in possession (*b*), and communicate to his creditors the benefit of the lease, no manager or trustee is admitted; that being regarded as a virtual assignation (*c*). At one time such exclusion was held fatal to the lease on the marriage of a female tenant, as being a legal assignation to the husband; but the rule is now settled the other way, the husband not taking the lease as assignee, but as administrator for the wife (*d*). A lease excluding assignees, "unless approved of by the landlord," has the same force with an unqualified exclusion; the tenant has no right under such a clause to require the landlord to justify his refusal (*e*). 'Neither, if he does assign a reason, is that subject to the review of the Court (*f*).' A clause of exclusion, fortified by a declaration of irritancy on bankruptcy, will effectually prevent any arrangement for continuing the lease to the benefit of creditors on bankruptcy. A stipulation of residence on the farm, with exclusion of assignees and sub-tenants, will bring the lease to an end if the tenant shall have absconded; and without such condition of residence, his leaving the country is considered an abandonment (*g*). 'So, if a clause requiring residence be guarded by an irritancy, and the tenant refuse to reside (*h*). In a lease granted for manufacturing or commercial purposes, an ordinary clause of exclusion would probably not prevent the tenant from assuming partners, and conveying to them an interest under it (*i*).' Clauses of exclusion are personal to the landlord, and confer no right of challenge upon any one not coming in his right (*k*). Neither are creditors entitled to take advantage of such a 'clause' to get rid of the tenant's obligation to continue the lease, or to avoid a claim of damages (*l*).

(*a*) Elliot *v.* D. Buccleuch, 1747; M. 10,333; Elch. *Tack*, 12, and p. 444; 2 Ill. 186. Cunningham *v.* Hamilton, 1770; M. 10,410. See below, § 1260.

(*b*) Bankruptcy does not of itself determine a lease. See 1 Bell's Com. 76. Fraser *v.* Robertson, 1881; 8 R. 347. See below, § 1249 sq.

(*c*) 1 Bell's Com. 80 (76, M'L.'s ed.). 1 Bell on Leases, 181. Durham *v.* Henderson, 1773; M. 15,283; Hailes, 515. Laird *v.* Grindlay, 1791; M. 15,294; Bell's 8vo Cases, 296. E. Dalhousie *v.* Wilson, 1802; M. 15,311. Munro *v.* Miller, Dec. 11, 1811; F. C. Watson *v.* Douglas, Dec. 13, 1811; F. C. Sydserf *v.* Todd, March 8, 1814; F. C. Comp. Dobie, *infra* (*k*). Young's Trs. *v.* Anderson, 1809; Hume, 843.

(*d*) 2 Craig, 10. § 6. 2 Ersk. 6. § 31. 1 Bell's Com. 76. Hume *v.* Taylor, 1734; M. 5700. Elliot, *supra* (*a*). Gillon *v.* Muirhead, 1775; M. 15,286; Hailes, 631. Forrester *v.* Milligan, 1830; 8 S. 992.

(*e*) 1 Bell's Com. 78 (73, M'L.'s ed.). 1 Bell, Leases, 181. D. of Roxburgh *v.* Archibald, 1785; M. 10,412, n. Elliot, *supra* (*a*). Irvine *v.* Valentine, 1791; 1 Bell's Com. 78, note; Hume's Sess. Pap.; aff. 3 Pat. 287. Muir *v.* Wilson, Jan. 20, 1820; F. C. M. Breadalbane *v.* Whitehead, 1893; 21 R. 138.

(*f*) D. Portland *v.* Baird & Co., 1865; 4 Macph. 10. See Wight *v.* E. Hopetoun, 1855; 17 D. 364.

(*g*) 1 Bell's Com. 81. Copland *v.* Gordon, 1805; M. *Tack*, Apx. 20. Forbes *v.* Duncan, June 2, 1812; F. C. Hog *v.* Morton, 1825; 3 S. 617. Scott *v.* Wotherspoon, 1829; 7 S. 481. Tennant *v.* M'Donald, 1836; 14 S. 976. Richardson *v.* Scott, 1835; 13 S. 972. See below, § 1260. Hamilton *v.* Somerville, 1855; 17 D. 344. Lyon *v.* Irvine, 1874; 1 R. 512. Moncrieff *v.* Hay, 1842; 5 D. 253. Fraser *v.* M. Abercorn, 1835; 14 S. 77. Williamson *v.* Johnston, 1848; 11 D. 332. Lindsay & Hogg *v.* Nisbet, 1855; 17 D. 788. Anstruther *v.* Greenshields, 1855; 18 D. 59.

(*h*) Edmond *v.* Reid, 1871; 9 Macph. 782; and cases in § 1249, *infra*.

(*i*) Dick *v.* Skaills, 1706; 4 B. Sup. 642. Borrows *v.* Colquhoun, 1852; 24 Jur. 443; 1 Stu. 733; rev. 1854, 1 Macq. 691; 26 Jur. 641; 1 Hunter, L. & T. 236.

(*k*) 2 Ersk. 6. § 31, as corrected by Hay *v.* Wood, 1801; M. 15,297. Deuchar *v.* L. Minto, 1798; M. 15,295. M'Coag *v.* M'Sporan, 1803; Hume, 813. Murdoch *v.* Murdoch's Trs., 1863; 1 Macph. 330. Dobie *v.* M. Lothian, 1864; 2 Macph. 788. As to implied waiver of objection by landlord, see L. Elphinston *v.* Monkland Iron Co., 1886; 11 App. Ca. 332; 13 R. H. L. 98.

(*l*) Kinloch *v.* Mansfield, 1836; 14 S. 905. See Bidoulac *v.* Sinclair's Tr., 1889; 17 R. 144.

1219. (2.) *Heir of the Tenant.*—The death of the tenant may raise questions of much importance both to the landlord and the tenant's family (*a*). The tenant's heir-at-law succeeds to the lease, although there be no express destination to heirs. Where a lease is granted to two tenants, and their heirs and successors, the heir of the tenant who dies first is entitled to continue the joint possession with the survivor (*b*). Where the tenant is succeeded by daughters, they, as heirs-portioners, take the lease *pro indiviso*. The *pro indiviso* share of each descends to her heirs; but if such heirs-portioners succeed as liferenters in a lease provided to a man "during his lifetime and that of his heirs," this seems to be limited to the life of his immediate heirs; and so the death of one of the heirs-portioners will put an end to her *pro indiviso* share, instead of giving the succession to the survivor, who can take only as *her* heir (*c*). A lease, terminating with a liferent to any "person to be condescended on by the tenant by a writing under his hand," was held to be effectually destinated to his "eldest daughter then in life" (*d*). Although it is of importance to the tenant, in many situations, to have the power of regulating the succession to the lease, a destination of the lease to heirs, with a clause excluding assignees and sub-tenants, is held to prevent the tenant from naming an heir; *hæredes nati*, not *hæredes facti*, being intended (*e*); 'or, in other words, the successor takes by contract with the lessor, and not by inheritance from the lessee (*f*).' A conveyance *inter vivos* to the heir-at-law will indeed be effectual (*g*); but the tenant has been held to have no power to name an heir different from the heir-at-law, without the landlord's assent (*h*).

'*Bequest of Lease.*—It is provided by the Agricultural Holdings (Scotland) Act, 1883, that a tenant may by will or other testamentary writing bequeath his lease, subject to certain provisions, viz. that the legatee shall within a limited time (twenty-one days after the tenant's death, unless unavoidably prevented) intimate the bequest to the landlord or his known agent, which implies acceptance of the bequest; that the landlord within a month thereafter may intimate to the legatee that he objects to receive him as tenant, failing which the lease is binding on both parties as from the death of the late tenant; that if the landlord objects, the legatee may apply to the Sheriff to adjudicate on the reasonableness of the landlord's objections to him, the Sheriff's judgment being final; that pending such proceedings the legatee has possession, unless the Sheriff otherwise direct; and that if the legatee does not accept, or the bequest is declared null, the lease shall descend to the tenant's heir, as if there had been no bequest (*i*).'

(*a*) As to the liability of a deceased tenant's estate for damages, where the heir and executor both decline to take up the lease, see Bethune *v.* Morgan, 1874 ; 2 R. 186.

(*b*) Dickson *v.* Dickson, 1825 ; 2 S. 462 ; 2 Ill. 190. See Macalister *v.* Macalister, 1859 ; 21 D. 560 ; Burns *v.* Martin, 1885 ; 12 R. 1343 ; rev. 1887, 12 App. Ca. 84 ; 14 R. H. L. 20 ; and Bain *v.* Mackenzie, 1896 ; 23 R. 528 (passive representation) ; Marquis *v.* Prentice, 1896 ; 23 R. 595 (vesting—cond. *si sine liberis*), as to destinations in contracts of lease.

(*c*) M. Tweeddale *v.* Dods, 1821 ; 2 Ill. 150. *Sed quære?* Sandford on Heritable Succ. i. 26–28. 1 Hunter, L. & T. 212. See note in 2 Ill. *cit.*, and above, § 1067 ; and see Pratt *v.* Abercromby, 1858, 21 D. 19, for an opinion, that where a lease is to heirs of the body, but heirs-portioners are excluded, the lease goes to the eldest daughter. Crighton (Duff) *v.* Lady Keith, 1857 ; 19 D. 713.

(*d*) Irvine *v.* Thom, 1827 ; 5 S. 534.

(*e*) See also § 1922 (4), below.

(*f*) *Per* L. Kinnear in Bain, *cit.* (*b*). Macalister, and other cases *citt.* (*b*). Rankine, Leases, 81.

(*g*) Hepburn *v.* Burn, 1759 ; M. 10,409.

(*h*) 1 Bell Leases, 157. Deuchar *v.* L. Minto, 1798 ; M. 15,295. Cuninghame *v.* Grieve, 1803 ; M. 15,298 ; *Tack*, Apx. 9 ; 4 Pat. 571 ; 6 Pat. 16 ; 1 Bell, Leases, 162, note. Lowden *v.* Adam, 1805 ; M. *Tack*, Apx. 10. Gray *v.* Low, 1859 ; 21 D. 293. Murdoch *v.* Murdoch's Trs., 1863 ; 1 Macph. 330.

(*i*) 46 and 47 Vict. c. 62, § 29.

1220. Management and Cultivation (*a*).—The interests of the landlord and of the tenant are nearly the same during the early part of the lease, and diverge only as the lease draws towards its close. It is at first for the benefit of the tenant as well as of the landlord to keep the land in good heart and cultivation. But gradually, as the lease advances, the interest of the tenant, in contemplation of his removal, prompts him to seek the largest possible profits while his possession continues. To avoid litigation on questions so doubtful as the settling of the rules of good husbandry suggests, the parties commonly fix certain points by the lease. The general principle of such conventional arrangement is, that injury to the landlord is to be prevented, without unduly restraining the spirit of improvement and fair profit on the part of the tenant. And the most approved practice seems to be to leave the tenant less fettered towards the commencement of the lease, and even at the close to introduce only negative regulations for preventing the breaking up of old pasture land, or the exhausting of the land by a bad course of cropping ; as the taking, for example, of two white crops in succession. Positive regulations are chiefly directed to the rotation of crops, and to secure the consumption of the straw made on the farm, and, as far as possible, the application to the land of the manure made from its produce. Such views have directed Lord Kames and others to certain proposals for arranging the adverse interests of landlord and tenant, and have of late years dictated many extensive systems of leasehold management in Scotland (*b*).

(*a*) See this subject resumed below, § 1257 et seq.

(*b*) Kames' Gentleman Farmer, Supplement, 6th edition. 1 Bell, Leases, 246, 258, and in Apx. No. 2, p. 161, will be found a very valuable collection of the practical arrangements throughout Scotland on this matter. See also 2 Hunter, L. & T. 474 et seq.

1221. (1.) *Positive Regulations.*—Where positive regulations of the course of cultivation are introduced, the rules are, 'that if 'they are' clear, 'and their violation has not been acquiesced in (*a*),' they will be enforced ; where they are fortified by a penalty, it is subject to modification according to the damage actually sustained (*b*) ; and where an additional rent is stipulated, such rent is held the conventional value of the different use and possession which the tenant may derive from the farm, and as such not subject to modification (*c*). 'A purchaser is not readily bound by the acquiescence of the seller of an estate in violation of the terms of a written lease (*d*).'

(*a*) Murray's Trs. *v.* Gordon, 1806; Hume, 823; M. Apx. *Tack*, 12. Hunter *v.* Broadwood, *infra* (*c*). Taylor *v.* Duff's Trs., 1869; 6 Macph. 351. Lamb *v.* Mitchell's Trs., 1883; 10 R. 640. See § 1222.

(*b*) M'Kenzie *v.* Craigie, June 18, 1811; F. C.; 1 Ill. 43; aff. 6 Pat. 117. M'Kenzie *v.* Gilchrist, Dec. 13, 1811; F. C. Pollock *v.* Paton, 1777; M. *Tack*, Apx. 4; Hailes, 766. Don *v.* Brew, 1879; 2 Sel. Sh. Ct. Ca. 117.

(*c*) Fraser *v.* Ewart, Feb. 25, 1813; F. C. Graham *v.* Straiton, 1789; 16 F. C. 423, note; 3 Pat. 119, 367. See Morrison *v.* Blair, 1823; 2 S. 241. Miller *v.* L. Gwydir, 1824; 3 S. 65; aff. 2 W. & S. 52. Lawson *v.* Ogilvie, 1832; 10 S. 531; aff. 1834, 7 W. & S. 397; 2 Ill. 191. Little *v.* Mutter, 1797; Hume, 797. Hunter *v.* Clark, 1810; Hume, 852. Hunter *v.* Broadwood, 1854; 16 D. 441. Threipland *v.* Munro, 1861; 23 D. 1252. Baird *v.* Mount, 1874; 2 R. 101 (landlord barred from claiming additional rent for miscropping payable at usual terms by granting receipts for ordinary rents without reservation). See above, § 34.

(*d*) Hall *v.* M'Gill, 1847; 9 D. 1557. Carnegie *v.* Guthrie, 1866; 5 Macph. 253.

1222. (2.) *Implied Regulations.* — There are certain implied obligations of the tenant relative to the cultivation and management of his farm, which may be judicially enforced. Thus, he is bound, according to the nature of location, to enter to the farm; in which it is implied that he shall properly stock it, both from the necessary obligation to cultivate it properly, and from the implied engagement to afford security for the rent (*a*). He is also bound to labour it honestly and *tanquam bonus vir* during the whole stipulated term (*b*); but this implied obligation will yield to express rules laid down and observed (*c*). Where no rules have been prescribed, and the landlord has not objected to the tenant's operations during the lease, he has no right to claim damages at the close (*d*).

(*a*) Randiford *v.* Crombie, 1623; M. 15,256; 2 Ill. 191. Scott *v.* Wotherspoon, 1829; 7 S. 481; 2 Ill. 189. Horn *v.* M'Lean, 1830; 8 S. 329. See below, § 1258.

(*b*) 2 Ersk. 6. § 39, with Ivory's Notes, and cases there cited. Murray *v.* Balcanqual, 1665; M. 15,257. L. Haddo *v.* Johnston, 1633; M. 7539. Maxwell *v.* M'Kiming, 1776; 5 B. Sup. 515. Thomson *v.* Oliphants, 1824; 3 S. 275. E. Wemyss *v.* Hope, Feb. 7, 1809; F. C. (lease of coal). Fleming *v.* Macdonald, 1860; 22 D. 1025. Carron Co. *v.* Donaldson, 1858; 20 D. 681. Bairds *v.* Harper, 1865; 3 Macph. 543.

(*c*) Stark *v.* Edmonston, 1826; 5 S. 45. Mackenzie *v.* Munro, 1860; 23 D. 144. Below, § 1261.

(*d*) Fraser *v.* Maitland, 1824; 2 S. Ap. 37. Eliott's Trs. *v.* Eliott, 1894; 21 R. 858 (excessive stock of game). See § 1221.

1223. (3.) *Remedies.*—A Court may interfere for the prevention of any inequitable departure from the implied, or any breach of the express (*a*), obligations of the lease, 'and may award damages for a transgression, as in other contracts (*b*).' But it is not the office of a judge to prescribe positive regulations of cropping or cultivation to be followed (*c*). 'The judge ordinary (*i.e.* the Sheriff) may appoint inspectors of fields alleged to have been miscropped, or of fences and buildings not maintained according to the requirements of the lease, and may assess the damages upon such inspection (*d*). The judge ordinary has also power to authorise the landlord, or on the landlord's application to appoint a manager, to cultivate the farm where the tenant deserts the farm, or fails to make such preparations as are necessary for carrying out the stipulated rotation (*e*); also to compel the tenant to implement the lease by taking possession and paying the rent (*f*). But the remedy for a breach of an express regulation is, after the expiry of the lease, damages, not specific implement (*g*).'

(*a*) As to prohibitions of particular trades, see L. Macdonald *v.* Campbell, 1889; 16 R. 540 (selling spirits—recall of permission); cf. E. of Zetland *v.* Hislop, 1881; 8 R. 675; rev. 9 *ib.* H. L. 40; 7 App. Ca. 427 (sup. and vassal).

(*b*) Above, § 30 sqq. 2 Hunter, L. & T. 529. Rankine, Leases, 410.

(*c*) Meldrum *v.* Gibb, 1737; Elch. *Tack*, 4; 2 Ill. 192. M'Kenzie *v.* Craigie, June 18, 1811; F. C.; 1 Ill. 43. M'Kenzie *v.* Gilchrist, Dec. 13, 1811; F. C. See 1 Bell on Leases, 256, note. Cathcart *v.* Sloss, 1864; 3 Macph. 76.

(*d*) Hall *v.* M'Gill, 1847; 9 D. 1557. Irvine *v.* Scott, 1856; 18 D. 1090. Gordon's Trs. *v.* Melrose, 1870; 8 Macph. 906. Baird *v.* Mount, 1874; 1 R. 1119. Dickson *v.* Graham, 1877; 4 R. 717. Lees *v.* Marr Typefounding Co., 1877; 4 R. 1088.

(*e*) Brock *v.* Buchanan, 1851; 13 D. 1069. Affleck *v.* Affleck, 1862; 24 D. 291. Gibson *v.* Clark, 1895; 23 R. 294.

(*f*) Robertson *v.* Cockburn, 1875; 3 R. 21. As to the competency of charging upon an extract registered lease, see Hendry *v.* Marshall, 1878; 5 R. 687.

(*g*) Sinclair *v.* Caithness Flagstone Co., 1898; 25 R. 703.

1224. Tenant's Use of the Land. — The tenant's right of possession of the land comprehends—

(1.) *The Exclusive Possession*, with all the rights to prohibit encroachment which the landlord would himself have enjoyed if the lands had been in his natural possession (*a*). The tenant is 'at common law' entitled, for preservation of his crop, to kill rabbits 'unless reserved (*b*), and foxes (*c*),' but not to destroy pigeons (*d*), 'or to fish with rod or net in streams or lochs within the lands (*e*).' The tenant's right to exclude others is under the exception of the landlord's right to come upon the farm in exercise of his reserved interest in mines, etc.; of his right to preserve or cut timber; and even of his privilege of hunting and shooting — responsible, of course, in all those cases for any surface damages which he may occasion (*f*).

(2.) *Absolute Use.*—The tenant has also the absolute use, in so far as necessary for habitation, and for the cultivation and reaping of the fruits of the land. 'But he is not entitled to convert the buildings or premises let to a use not contemplated in the contract, as to use them for a posting station (*g*).' He has the benefit of any servitude belonging to the subject (*h*), and a right to suitable accommodation in the parish church out of the area belonging to the landlord (*i*). The tenant of a grass field has been held entitled to enter it at Candlemas, and dress it for the ensuing season, without leave of the tenant in possession, who is not entitled to graze it at that season (*k*). It 'was' not settled whether the tenant (if otherwise qualified to kill game) 'had' the right of hunting or shooting on the farm; but it 'is now decided' that, without the landlord's express permission, he has no such right (*l*). 'By the Ground Game Act, 1880, every occupier of land has, as incident to and inseparable from his occupation of the land, a concurrent right with the landlord or a game tenant to kill and take ground game (*i.e.* hares and rabbits) on the land; but, if with fire-arms, only by himself and one other person authorised in writing to kill such game; and under other restrictions (*m*).'

(*a*) See above, § 940 et seq. As to the tenant's right to give strangers access or passage over the land let, see Stewart *v.* Stephen, 1877; 4 R. 873. The tenant cannot recover damages from the landlord for dispossession by another, unless the latter, being called upon, has wrongfully failed to protect him. Menzies *v.* Whyte, 1888; 15 R. 470.

(*b*) Moncrieff *v.* Arnot, 1828; 6 S. 530; 2 Ill. 192. See Porter *v.* Stewart, 1858; 3 Irv. 57; 30 Jur. 518. North *v.* Cumming, 1864; 3 Macph. 173. Inglis *v.* Moir's Tutors, 1871; 10 Macph. 204. Wood *v.* Paton, 1874; 1 R. 868. 2 Hunter, L. & T. 192, 210 sqq. See cases in § 953 *ad fin.*

(*c*) Colquhoun *v.* Buchanan, 1785; M. 4997.

(*d*) Easton *v.* Longlands, 1832; 10 S. 542.

(*e*) D. Richmond *v.* Dempster, 1861; 4 Irv. 10; 33 Jur. 133. Maxwell *v.* Copland, 1868; 7 Macph. 142; aff. 1871, 9 Macph. H. L. 1.

(*f*) 1 Bell on Leases, 433. Ronaldson *v.* Ballantyne, 1804; M. 15,270; 2 Ill. 117. Lanlon *v.* Watt, 1874; 1 Sel. Sh. Ct. Ca. 280 (game tenant's watcher). Robertson *v.* Ross & Co., 1892; 19 R. 967 (stipulated damages—severance). Below, § 1226. As to game, above, § 953.

(*g*) Baillie *v.* M'Kie, 1842; 4 D. 1520. D. Argyle *v.* M'Arthur, 1861; 23 D. 1236. See below, § 1274.

(*h*) Wood *v.* Robertson, March 9, 1809; F. C. As to a road, see Duncan *v.* Scott, 1876; 3 R. H. L. 69. Galloway *v.* Cowden, 1885; 12 R. 578.

(*i*) Skirving *v.* Vernor, 1796; M. 7930.

(*k*) Hamilton *v.* Cunningham, 1830; 8 S. 955. See Addie *v.* Young, 1862; 24 D. 799.

(*l*) M. Tweeddale *v.* Somner, June 18, 1808; F. C.; 2 Ill. 116. E. Hopetoun *v.* Wight, Jan. 17, 1810; F. C. See above, § 953.

(*m*) 43 and 44 Vict. c. 47. See Brown *v.* Thomson, 1882; 9 R. 1183. Fraser *v.* Lawson, 1882; 10 R. 396. Stuart *v.* Murray, 1884; 12 R. Just. 9. Niven *v.* Renton, 1888; 15 R. Just. 42. Richardson *v.* Maitland, 1897; 24 R. Just. 32.

1225. Reserved Rights of the Landlord.—The landlord's rights are either reserved, as not included in the lease; or stipulated, as rent.

1226. The reserved rights comprehend the following particulars:—

(1.) *Mines and Minerals, Clay, Lime, and Shell-marl.* — The landlord has an implied right to work these, and even to open the ground, so far as may be necessary for that purpose, on paying surface damage; but he is not entitled, without stipulation, to manufacture the rude materials on the land (*a*).

(2.) *Woods* are also reserved to the landlord, the tenant being entitled to the yearly fruits, thinnings for repairs, willow twigs while young for basketwork, etc. (*b*). The planting on farms is specially protected by statute (*c*). 'The tenant under a building lease is entitled to cut trees, at least so far as may be necessary for his reasonable enjoyment (*d*).'

(3.) *Kelp* on the shores of a farm does not belong to the tenant (*e*).

(4.) *Hunting.*—The landlord has by implication the right to hunt or shoot over his tenant's farm (*f*).

'(5.) *Resumption* of parts of the subject by the landlord may be stipulated for, and compensation for the tenant's loss by resumption is implied (*g*). Compensation generally takes the form of a proportionate deduction from the full rent (*h*). The power of resumption may be general, or may relate to special parts of the subject, or to special purposes—such as feuing, planting, or mining (*i*).'

(*a*) 2 Stair, 9. § 31. 2 Ersk. 6. § 22. Colquhoun *v.* Watson, 1668; M. 15,253; 2 Ill. 193. Smith *v.* M'Gill, 1768; M. 15,266; Hailes, 223. Bethune *v.* Jervice, 1778; M. 15,267; 5 B. Sup. 517; Hailes, 786. 1 Bell on Leases, 205. M'Callum *v.* Forth Iron Co., 1861; 23 D. 729.

(*b*) 2 Ersk. 6. § 22. Touch *v.* Ferguson, 1664; M. 15,252. Bogue *v.* Wight, 1806; M. *Planting*, Apx. 2.

(*c*) 1685, c. 39. 1698, c. 16. Ferguson *v.* M'Nidder, 1734; M. 10,479. Robertson *v.* Robertson, 1744; M. 10,484; Elchies' Notes, 331. Stirling *v.* Christie, 1762; M. 9403; 5 B. Sup. 536, 888. Logan *v.* Howatson, 1775; M. 10,492; Hailes, 644. Cooper *v.* Campbell, 1805; M. *Planting*, Apx. 1. Gillies *v.* M'Donald, 1824; 3 S. 254.

(*d*) Gordon *v.* Rae, 1883; 11 R. 67.

(*e*) Campbell *v.* Campbell, 1795; M. 9646.

(*f*) Ronaldson, M. Tweeddale, and E. Hopetoun, *supra*, § 1224 (*f*) and (*l*).
(*g*) Menmuir *v*. Airth, 1863 ; 1 Macph. 1071. 2 Hunter, L. & T. 215.
(*h*) Trotter *v*. Torrance, 1891 ; 18 R. 848 (whether buildings included). Robertson, above, § 1224 (*f*).
(*i*) As to breaks, see below, § 1271A, 1278 *fin*.

1227. Landlord's Right to Rent (*a*).—Rent, according to its legal definition, is the stipulated annual return or consideration paid by the tenant to the landlord for the use and possession of the farm, and for the produce derived from it. The great object in all stipulations respecting rent is to reconcile the interest of the landlord and the tenant in the varying results of the operation of the skill, industry, and capital of the tenant upon the natural and inherent powers of the soil, which is the property of the landlord. To do justice to both parties, and prevent loss on either side by sudden changes on the value of money and of farm produce, the yearly rent, or a considerable portion of it, should be regulated by the fiars of such grain or other produce as the farm is likely to yield, and in such proportions of the several kinds as are likely to be raised; and a maximum and minimum should be fixed, above or below which the augmentation of the money conversion, or its diminution, ought not to go. The same rules may be applied to dairy farms or sheep farms, the conversion of the cheese or wool being made by arbitration. 'If no rent be agreed upon, the true annual value is payable, the occupant being presumed to be a tenant upon that footing (*b*).

'Rents prescribe which are not pursued within five years after the tenant's removal from the lands (*c*).'

(*a*) See above, § 1197, 1201.
(*b*) Young *v*. Cockburn, 1674 ; M. 11,624. Glen *v*. Roy, 1882 ; 10 R. 239. See above, § 92 (*c*) ; and comp. Thomson *v*. Thomson, 1896 ; 24 R. 269.
(*c*) 1669, c. 9. Above, § 634.

1228. (1.) *Grassum*.—Rent is naturally periodical; but sometimes part is paid by anticipation in grassum. And so grassum (which is a fine paid for a lease during a term of years) is, when analysed, a proportion taken from each year's rent, and paid at once by anticipation; either to supply some necessity for ready money, or to disappoint some future possessor of the estate. At one time, grassums were much used as a fund of provision for the families of the proprietors of entailed estates: more recently, for defeating indirectly the interest of subsequent heirs of entail.

1229. Purchasers and creditors have, generally speaking, no right to challenge leases let on grassums (*a*). Neither have heirs of entail any such right, where there is no prohibition to alienate or let leases with diminution of the rental; but such prohibitions strike against grassums (*b*).

(*a*) 2 Ersk. Pr. 6. § 10. 2 Ersk. 6. § 37. See above, § 1201.
(*b*) Queensberry Leases, 1 Bligh, 339, 534 ; 5 Dow, 297 ; 2 Ill. 392. D. Hamilton *v*. Esten, 1816 ; 2 Bligh, 196. Wellwood *v*. Wellwood, 1823 ; 2 S. 475. E. Elgin *v*. Wellwood, 1821 ; 1 S. Ap. 44. See below, § 1752.

1230. (2.) *The Legal Terms* for payment of rent are Whitsunday and Martinmas, subject to alteration according to the agreement of the parties (*a*). The entry to the houses and grass is generally at Whitsunday; to the arable land at the separation of the crop, or at Martinmas. The first half-year's rent is regularly payable at the Whitsunday after entry; the second half-year's rent is payable at the second Martinmas. The rent may be stipulated "forehand," *i.e.* payable at the Martinmas after entry to the houses and grass; and at Whitsunday, while the first crop is still on the arable land; or at Lammas and Candlemas of the first year. "Back-rent" is payable, one half at the Martinmas after the separation of the first crop, and the other at the following Whitsunday; or at Candlemas and Lammas, after the first crop is reaped (*b*). 'The term Whitsunday has been held to be subject to construction by the conduct of parties, showing that they intended the 26th of May, or Whitsunday Old Style (*c*).'

(*a*) See above, § 1204.
(*b*) The effect of these arrangements on hypothec, and on the succession of the landlord and of the tenant, will deserve attention. See § 1204 and 1499. As to the rights of a purchaser, see Penman *v*. Ker, 1828 ; 6 S. 940. Lady Murray's Trs. *v*. Jardine, 1865 ; 3 Macph. 845. E. Glasgow's Trs. *v*. Clark, 1889 ; 16 R. 545. Rankine, Leases, 313.
(*c*) Hunter *v*. Barron's Trs., 1886 ; 13 R. 883.

1231. Enforcing Payment of Rent.—The payment of rent may be enforced by personal diligence; or by diligence against the crop and stocking; or by force of irritancy, or forfeiture of the lease; 'and the landlord in possession at the conventional term for payment is the person entitled to enforce payment (*a*).' There is no retention of rent admitted on the ground of illiquid claims of damage (*b*). 'But the tenant may refuse to pay, or even rescind the bargain, if he does not get possession of the subject let, or of any essential part or requisite of it (*c*), or if the landlord insist on violating a material condition of the lease (*d*). Wider views on this subject are held by the Courts than formerly were accepted; and it has been well said that the general rules regulating retention under other contracts (*infra*, § 1410 sqq.) should be applied; and it thus becomes a question of intention whether non-performance of some duty by the landlord is "conditional with respect to" the tenant's obligation to pay rent (*e*). In order to fix on the landlord a claim of damage there must be a distinct effective complaint (*f*).' It is competent to insist in personal 'diligence' and in sequestration for rent—'where the latter may yet be pursued'—at one and the same time (*g*).

(*a*) Lennox *v.* Reid, 1893; 21 R. 77.
(*b*) Dun *v.* Craig, 1824; 3 S. 274; 2 Ill. 194. Heriot *v.* Halket, 1825; 3 S. 479. Fraser *v.* Kinloch, 1828; 6 S. 1117. Mouat *v.* Denham, 1828; 7 S. 88. Johnston *v.* Inglis, 1832; 10 S. 260. See Bowie *v.* Duncan, 1807; Hume, 839. Dods *v.* Fortune, 1854; 16 D. 478. Dickson *v.* Porteous, 1852; 15 D. 1. M'Rae *v.* M'Pherson, 1843; 6 D. 302. Humphrey *v.* Mackay, 1883; 10 R. 647. Sutherland *v.* Urquhart, 1895; 23 R. 284. Comp. Macdonald *v.* Johnstone, 1883; 10 R. 959. Below, § 1256.
(*c*) Gray *v.* Renton, 1840; 3 D. 203. Kilmarnock Gaslight Co. *v.* Smith, 1872; 11 Macph. 58. Guthrie *v.* Shearer, 1873; 1 R. 181; cf. Sawers *v.* M'Connell, 1874; 1 R. 392. Muir *v.* M'Intyres, 1887; 14 R. 470. Munro *v.* M'Geoch, 1888; 16 R. 93, explained in Stewart *v.* Campbell, 1889; 16 R. 346. Sivwright *v.* Lightbourne, 1890; 17 R. 917 (no formal lease—proof b. a. allowed). Johnstone *v.* Hughan, 1894; 21 R. 777. Duncan *v.* Brooks, 1894; 21 R. 760 (peat allotment). See below, § 1253 (*a*), (*e*), 1256 (*h*); and above, § 71.
(*d*) Davie *v.* Stark, 1876; 3 R. 1114.
(*e*) Cases in (*c*), (*d*). *Per* L. M'Laren in Sivwright, *cit.*
(*f*) Broadwood *v.* Hunter, 1855; 17 D. 340. Emslie *v.* Young's Trs., 1894; 21 R. 710. Johnstone *v.* Hughan, *cit.* Eliott's Trs. *v.* Eliott, 1894; 21 R. 858.
(*g*) Booth *v.* Pentland, 1831; 5 W. & S. 228.

1232. (1.) *Personal Diligence.*—The tenant is, under his contract (*a*), liable in his person and funds to summary diligence for the rent. On registration of the lease under a clause to that effect, personal diligence may be issued for the rent as summarily as if the debt were constituted by bond. And diligence may thus be raised at the first for the whole periodical payments of the rent, to the effect of authorising a charge for each term's rent as it falls due, "the term of payment being first come and bygone" (*b*). The charge on personal diligence must be definite (*c*). Although a creditor is entitled to a warrant *de meditatione fugæ*, if the tenant be about to leave the country, 'and if imprisonment is competent for his debt (*d*),' it is very doubtful whether he can insist for caution to the full amount of all future rents, without giving a reasonable allowance for the value of the abandoned lease (*e*).

(*a*) Distinguish the case of a sub-tenant, not under contract with the landlord. Maxwell *v.* D. Queensberry's Exrs., 1827; 5 S. 935; rev. 1831, 5 W. & S. 771. M'Lachlan *v.* Sinclair & Co., 1897; 13 Sh. Ct. Rep. 362. Rankine, Leases, 190. Below, § 1252.
(*b*) 3 Jurid. Styles, 634. 2 Bell on Leases, 4.
(*c*) M'Martin *v.* Forbes, 1824; 3 S. 275; 2 Ill. 194.
(*d*) Below, § 2318.
(*e*) M'Gill *v.* Ferrier, 1838; 16 S. 934. With great deference, I cannot hold this case to settle the law in favour of so unjust a right. This case is also impugned in 2 Hunter, L. & T. 349. Rankine, Leases, 333. See Hart *v.* Anderson's Trs., 1890; 18 R. 169.

1233. (2.) *Hypothec* (*a*).—The landlord 'of agricultural subjects held under leases, writings, or bargains current at the 11th of November 1881' has security for his rent by hypothec; with the power of having the hypothecated subjects converted into a specific pledge, and finally applied to his payment, by the process of sequestration and sale (*b*). 'But at the date mentioned, the landlord's right of hypothec for the rent of all other land (including the rent of any buildings thereon), exceeding two acres in extent, let for agriculture or pasture, ceased and determined (*c*). Nor can a conventional security over the tenant's crop, valid against creditors, be created by the lease (*d*).'

(*a*) See below, § 1276, for Urban Hypothec.
(*b*) 2 Ersk. 6. § 56. 2 Ross, 392. Kames's Law Tracts, No. 4; Elucid. art. 10. 1 Bell, Leases, 362. 2 Hunter, L. & T. 360.
(*c*) 43 Vict. c. 12 (Hypothec Abolition (Scotland) Act, 1880). This clause was held not to apply to buildings separately let for a distinct rent, though in the same lease and for the same purpose (a dairy), the buildings being on separate but adjoining lands. Clark *v.* Keirs, 1888; 15 R. 458. See Jackson *v.* Rodger, 1891; 7 Sh. Ct. Rep. 202 (lands and more valuable mill).
(*d*) M'Gavin *v.* Sturrock's Tr., 1891; 18 R. 576.

1234. Hypothec is a real right of security similar to pledge, but not requiring possession (*a*); 'and it is extended so far as to give the landlord a right to obtain an interdict against the sale and removal of the crop and stock, unless the tenant shall find caution for the current rent (*b*). This rule applies still to urban subjects. Further, the landlord may obtain from the Judge Ordinary a warrant to "carry back," so as to subject to sequestration what has been removed from the premises. This warrant is not to be granted without notice to the tenant, except on special causes stated, such as that the removal was clandestine or under the cloud of night (*c*). The tenant is bound to occupy and stock the farm or house with his own stock, so as to give the landlord security for his rent (*d*).'

(*a*) See below, § 1385.

(*b*) Preston *v.* Gregor, 1845; 7 D. 942. Cathcart *v.* Sloss, 1864; 3 Macph. 76, 521. 2 Hunter, L. & T. 414.

(*c*) See below, § 1239 (*b*). Donald *v.* Leitch, 1886; 13 R. 790. Gray *v.* Weir, 1891; 19 R. 25. Johnston *v.* Young, 1890; 18 R. Just. 6. M'Laughlan *v.* Reilly, 1892; 20 R. 41.

(*d*) L. Stonefield *v.* M'Arthur, 1800; M. *Removing*, Apx. 3; *supra*, § 1222; *infra*, § 1258.

1235. *Subjects.*—The subjects of hypothec are various, according to the nature of the lease. In arable farms, 'held under bargains current at Martinmas 1881,' the hypothec extends over the produce of the land, and the cattle and sheep fed on it (*a*); and over the stocking and horses used in husbandry (*b*); but it 'was' doubted whether it extends over the tenant's furniture (*c*). 'The Hypothec Amendment Act of 1867 enacted that it should not be competent to include in a sequestration for the rent of any farm or lands, any household furniture, or agricultural implements, or manure, lime, drain tiles, feeding stuff, or other material not the produce of or made upon the farm, and not at the time incorporated with the soil, or consumed, or applied to the purpose for which it may have been procured. But if manure or any of the enumerated materials have been brought upon the lands in fulfilment of a specific obligation in the lease, they may be included in the sequestration (*d*).' In grass farms, it extends over the grass-mail, if the fields are let out in pasture; but not over the 'sheep and' cattle of others taken in to pasture (*e*), 'except to the extent of grass-mail for sheep, cattle, or other live stock, so long as that or any part of it is unpaid, even after the removal of the stock from the lands (*f*).' In dairy farms, the cheeses made and stored are subject to the hypothec (*g*).

(*a*) 1 Stair, 13. § 15; 4 Stair, 25. 2 Ersk. 6. § 56-61. M'Dowal *v.* Jamieson, 1781; M. 6215; 2 Ill. 194. Crichton *v.* E. Queensberry, 1672; M. 6203.

(*b*) Hepburn *v.* Richardson, 1726; M. 6205. Napier *v.* Kissock, 1825; 4 S. 307. See Henderson *v.* Warden, 1847; 17 S. Jur. 271 (implements of husbandry).

(*c*) Alison *v.* Campbell's Crs., 1748; M. 6246. See M'Clymonts *v.* Cathcart, 1848; 10 D. 1489.

(*d*) 30 and 31 Vict. c. 42, § 6.

(*e*) Correct 1 Bank. 17. § 10, by 2 Ersk. 6. § 63. Brown *v.* Sinclair, 1724; M. 6204. M'Kye *v.* Nabony, 1780; M. 6214.

(*f*) 30 and 31 Vict. c. 42, § 5. Steuart *v.* Stables, 1878; 5 R. 1024.

(*g*) Goldie *v.* Oswald, 1839; 1 D. 426.

1236. *Sub-Tenant.*—The right operates differently where there is no other person concerned in the possession than the original tenant, and where there is a sub-tenant. It also operates differently against the crop, and against the cattle and stocking.

1237. Where there is a sub-tenant, there is not only a hypothec to his immediate landlord, the tenant (*a*); but if the landlord have not authorised or assented to the sub-lease, the sub-tenant is liable to hypothec for the principal tenant's rent also.

If the landlord have sanctioned the sub-lease, the sub-tenant is saved from responsibility to any greater amount than his own rent. And he is also safe from the landlord's hypothec to any extent, if he have paid his rent regularly and in *bonâ fide* to the tenant (*b*). The principal tenant is primarily liable to the landlord, not a mere cautioner for the sub-tenant. If the landlord have proceeded to sequestrate the effects of the sub-tenant, he may abandon that proceeding without discharging the principal tenant, who has it in his power to sequestrate, or, on paying the rent, to take up the landlord's sequestration. But if the landlord should not only abandon his diligence, but give time to the sub-tenant, the principal tenant will be freed (*c*).

(*a*) Christie *v.* M'Pherson, Dec. 14, 1814; F. C. Stevenson *v.* Cooper, 1822; 1 S. 312. See below, § 1239 (*d*).

(*b*) 2 Ersk. 6. § 63. L. Saltoun *v.* Club, 1700; M. 1821; 2 Ill. 195. Blane *v.* Morrison, 1785; M. 6232.

(*c*) Williamson *v.* Forbes, 1830; 8 S. 405.

1238. A cautioner for rent, 'but not a stranger,' may, on paying the rent to the landlord, insist for an assignation to the hypothec (*a*). But the landlord will not lose his recourse on the cautioner by neglecting to enforce his hypothec (*b*), provided he does not give time to the tenant (*c*).

(*a*) Stewart *v.* Bell, May 31, 1814; F. C.; 2 Ill. 195. Christie *v.* M'Pherson, Dec. 14, 1814; F. C. M'Arthur *v.* Forbes, 1822; 2 S. 91. Stevenson *v.* M'Culloch, 1821; 1 S. 30. Bannatyne *v.* Finlayson, 1824; 2 S. 751. Graham *v.* Gordon, 1841; 3 D. 479; rev. 2 Rob. 251; 1842, 4 D. 903. See above, § 254, 557, and Steuart *v.* Stables, 1878; 5 R. 1024.

(*b*) M'Queen *v.* Fraser, June 11, 1811; F. C.; 1 Ill. 193. See above, § 254.

(*c*) See Williamson, *supra*, § 1237 (*c*). M'Dougall & Herbertson *v.* Northern Assur. Co., 1864; 2 Macph. 935 (as to liberation by change in the terms of the lease).

1239. *Effect.*—The hypothec over the crop entitles the landlord to retain the entire crop at the tenant's risk, if the rent is not yet due, or at least to the full amount of the rent; 'and even, it has been held, although the rent is not in arrear, and the tenant is not *vergens ad inopiam* (*a*)'; but if *bonâ fide* sold, or given in payment of debt, while enough is left for the rent, the landlord cannot attach, by poinding for debt, what remains, and seek restitution of what has been so disposed of, as under hypothec. 'Intromission with the effects subject to hypothec may infer liability for the whole rent; or at least for the value of what has been withdrawn from the landlord's security, as by a sale under a poinding (*b*).' The hypothec covers the rent of the year of which that crop is the produce; remaining effectual, 'under leases or bargains subsequent to 15th July 1867, only for three months after the conventional or legal term of payment of the last portion of each year's rent (*c*),' while the crop is in the tenant's possession (*d*). The crop cannot be sequestrated for the rent of a former year; and if such sequestration be taken, the landlord will be liable in damages (*e*).

(*a*) Preston *v.* Gregor, 1845; 7 D. 942.

(*b*) Steuart *v.* Peddie, 1874; 2 R. 94. Jack *v.* M'Caig, 1880; 7 R. 465. See Jackson *v.* Lind, 1745; M. 6245. A. *v.* B., 1744; M. 6228. 1 Stair, 13. § 5. 2 Ersk. 6. § 60. 2 Bell's Com. 32. Small *v.* Boyd, 1877; 1 Sel. Sh. Ct. Ca. 307. The landlord's right to retain on the premises for current rent is unlimited till caution is found, and so it appears that the liability of an intromitter, whether poinding creditor or purchaser, is for the whole rent growing due; but after the term intromitters are held liable only for the past due rent. Authorities cited. Cf. Rankine, Leases, 358–364, 372. Miller *v.* Rankin, 1881; 2 Sel. Sh. Ct. Ca. 276. Miller *v.* Ballingall, 1887; 4 Sh. Ct. Rep. 87. Chalmers *v.* Brown, 1890; 6 *ib.* 197.

(*c*) 30 and 31 Vict. c. 42, § 4.

(*d*) Correct 2 Ersk. 6. § 58, by 2 Ersk. Pr. 6. § 26. Pringle *v.* Scott, 1736; M. 6216; 2 Ill. 196. Rutherford *v.* Scott, 1736; M. 6226. Hay *v.* Keith, 1623; M. 6188. Crawfurd *v.* Stewart, 1737; M. 6193. Taylor *v.* Davidson, 1750; M. 6197. Brims *v.* Ferrier, May 31, 1815; F. C.; 2 Ill. 197; printed Bruce. M'Clymonts *v.* Cathcart, 1848; 10 D. 1489. E. Cassillis *v.* Ramsay's Crs., 1816; Hume, 230. It is not settled whether the hypothec covers an additional pactional rent for miscropping. Witham *v.* White & Young, 1866; 38 S. Jur. 586. Robertson *v.* Clark, 1842; 4 D. 1317. 2 Hunter, L. & T. 362. As to the questions whether this hypothec extends to interest on improvement money, and to the surplus rent payable by a sub-tenant to the principal lessee, see Scott *v.* Anderson, 1865; 1 Sel. Sh. Ct. Ca. 305. Ross *v.* M'Laren's Tr., 1869; *ib.* 309.

(*e*) Horn *v.* M'Lean, 1830; 8 S. 454; 2 D. & A. 238.

1240. The hypothec over the cattle and stocking is effectual for each year's rent successively as it falls due; the hypothec expiring as to each year's rent, if no sequestration follow within three months after the last term's payment of the rent (*a*).

(*a*) Hepburn *v.* Richardson, 1726; M. 6205. 2 Hunter, L. & T. 367. Hunter *v.* North of Engl. Bkg. Co., 1849; 12 D. 65. Henderson *v.* Warden, 1847; 17 S. Jur. 271 (work horses).

1241. *Competition.*—The landlord is not entitled to a preference as against the superior for his feu-duties (*a*); nor to farm-servants claiming wages (*b*); nor to funeral expenses (*c*); nor to the Crown (*d*); 'nor to poor-rates and school-rates; and if he sell under his sequestration, he must, it seems, pay out of the proceeds the current poor-rates and school-rates, and land and assessed taxes (*e*).' But the landlord is entitled to retain the crop on the farm; to stop poinding; 'but not, after it has been actually removed,' to recover and bring back under the operation of his hypothec, and subject to sequestration, the crop for the rent of the year of which it is the produce; 'nor, as formerly, to bring back' at any time within three months the stocking for the rent of the current year (*f*).

'The Bankruptcy Act does not affect this hypothec (*g*), and the landlord's preference over all unprivileged creditors (*h*) is thus preserved even in the insolvency of the tenant.'

(*a*) 2 Ersk. 6. § 63. Yuille *v.* Lawrie, 1823; 2 S. 155; 2 Ill. 20.

(*b*) See below, § 1404.

(*c*) Rowan *v.* Barr, 1742; M. 11,852; 2 Ill. 197. See below, § 1403, 1406.

(*d*) See below, § 1247.

(*e*) As to the preference of poor-rates, see 8 and 9 Vict. c. 83, § 88. 43 Geo. III. c. 150, § 33. 52 Geo. III. c. 95, § 13, 14. Below, § 1409. Adamson *v.* Ambrose, 1858; 1 Sel. Sh. Ct. Ca. 315. 1 Bell's Com. 739. N. B. Prop. Invt. Co. *v.* Paterson, 1888; 15 R. 885. As to school-rates, see 35 and 36 Vict. c. 78, §. 44. See also 43 and 44 Vict. c. 19 (Taxes Management Act), § 88, 97, etc. 20 and 21 Vict. c. 72, § 32 (county police). 52 and 53 Vict. c. 50, § 62 (7) (county rates).

(*f*) Crichton *v.* E. Queensberry, 1672; M. 6203. Rorison *v.* Shaw, 1766; M. 6211; Hailes, 42. Smart *v.* Ogilvie, 1796; 3 Pat. 490. See § 1239. 30 and 31 Vict. c. 42, § 4.

(*g*) 19 and 20 Vict. c. 79, § 119.

(*h*) See below, § 1402 sqq.

1242. The landlord 'was at common law' entitled to vindicate the corn grown on the farm, even against *bonâ fide* purchasers, unless sold in bulk in public market (*a*). There 'was' no such right of vindication against the purchasers of stocking (*b*). 'But the case (Barns *v.* Allan) above cited, by showing the injustice of the law, led to an inquiry by a Royal Commission, in consequence of whose report it was enacted that the landlord's hypothec should cease and determine — 1. When any agricultural produce has been *bonâ fide* purchased for its fair marketable value from the tenant, and has been actually delivered to the purchaser, and removed from the lands, and the price has been paid; 2. When such produce has been *bonâ fide* purchased at public auction from the tenant, or one acting by his authority, after seven days' written notice by the tenant or such party given to the landlord or his factor or known agent, without sequestration having been obtained and registered previous to or during the currency of such notice. But this enactment, which is still applicable to leases current at Martinmas 1881, does not apply to any produce which the tenant is not entitled legally or by the terms of his lease to carry off the lands, or which is subject to a subsisting registered sequestration (*c*).

'The landlord's hypothec is saved by the Sale of Goods Act, 1893 (*d*).'

(*a*) Smart, *supra*, § 1241 (*f*). 1 Bell on Leases, 375. 2 Hunter, L. & T. 400. **E. Dalhousie** *v.* **Dunlop & Co.**, 1828; 6 S. 626; aff. 1830, 4 W. & S. 420; 2 Ill. 198. **Barns** *v.* **Allan & Co.**, 1864; 2 Macph. 1119.

(*b*) Hay *v.* Elliot, 1639; M. 6219; 2 Ill. 197. Scott *v.* ——, 1678; M. 6223. Tennant *v.* M'Brayne, 1833; 11 S. 471. See below, as to Urban Tenements, § 1277.

(*c*) 30 and 31 Vict. c. 42, § 3.

(*d*) 56 and 57 Vict. c. 71, § 61 (5).

1243. The hypothec is communicated to an assignee to rents (*a*); to a creditor infeft in security, 'if he has taken possession (*b*)'; but not to adjudgers uninfeft.

(*a*) Wedderburn *v.* Mann, 1707; M. 10,399. 2 Hunter, L. & T. 364. Comp. § 1238, above.

(*b*) See Railton *v.* Muirhead, 1834; 12 S. 757. Hood *v.* Martin's Crs., 1835; 13 S. 923.

1244. (3.) *Sequestration.*—By this process the real security of hypothec is converted into a special pledge, and the subject of it brought to sale for payment of the rent. While the effects sequestrated remain after sequestration in special pledge, no one is entitled to intromit with them without judicial authority; and his doing so is a breach of sequestration, punishable as a contempt of court (*a*). But where horses and corn have been sequestrated, and part of the sequestrated corn thrashed out by the tenant and given for the subsistence of the horses, it has been held justifiable (*b*).

(*a*) Love *v.* Foster, 1832; 11 S. 280; 2 Ill. 198.

(*b*) Millar *v.* Paterson, 1831; 9 S. 792. Gordon *v.* Fiddler, 1823; 2 S. 486. Gordon *v.* Suttie, 1836; 14 S. 954. See opinions in M'Glashan *v.* D. Atholl, June 29, 1819; F. C. (corn used for farm servants).

1245. The process of sequestration is competent, 'in leases of farms or land for agricultural purposes current at Martinmas 1881,' either during the currency of the term, or after the rent is due; 'but in the case of urban leases (*a*), and leases granted after July 15, 1867, only for three months after the year's rent or last portion thereof is payable (*b*).' It commences by a summary application to the Judge Ordinary, but with a different prayer in the two cases now mentioned. When the rent is already payable, the prayer is to sequestrate, take inventory, and grant warrant to sell. When the application is made before the term (*c*), the prayer is only to sequestrate in security, and take inventory. But 'there is some authority for saying that' this latter process is not, after the term, convertible into a proceeding in which the effects may be sold (*d*). 'In practice the two forms are commonly combined for the rent of successive terms, and in either case there may be a prayer for decree of payment, and on the arrival of the term of payment it may be granted (*e*).' The usual procedure in a sequestration for sale 'was,' that the Sheriff granted a warrant to take inventories; and on a report made to him of the effects inventoried, he sequestrated them. By Act of Sederunt, however, he may, on the application, pronounce an interlocutor sequestrating the crop, stocking, and effects, and grant warrant to take inventories, and serve the application on the tenant (*f*). This inventory is the criterion and measure of what is sequestrated (*g*).

After sequestration, a warrant is, on application of the landlord, granted by the Sheriff, authorising the sale of the articles sequestrated. But such warrant must be carried into execution at the sight of the Clerk of Court, or some one authorised by the Sheriff (*h*).

(*a*) *Infra*, § 1277.
(*b*) 30 and 31 Vict. c. 42, § 4. See below, § 1277 (*a*).
(*c*) See as to the necessity of showing cause for sequestration in security, Donald *v*. Leitch, 1886; 13 R. 790.
(*d*) Miller *v*. Paterson, 1831; 9 S. 792; 2 Ill. 198.
(*e*) 16 and 17 Vict. c. 80, § 27. Duffy *v*. Gray, 1858; 20 D. 581.
(*f*) Act of Sederunt, Nov. 12, 1825, and July 11, 1839.
(*g*) Horsburgh *v*. Morton, 1825; 3 S. 596. The owner of effects wrongly sequestrated, *e.g.* not affected by the landlord's hypothec, may appear in the sequestration, and claim to have them withdrawn from it. Lindsay *v*. E. Wemyss, 1872; 10 Macph. 708. Macdonald *v*. Westren, 1888; 15 R. 988; or he may seek to interdict a sale. Pulsometer Enging. Co. *v*. Gracie, 1887; 14 R. 316.
(*h*) Act of Sederunt, *ut supra*.

1246. A report of the sale must be made within fourteen days after the warrant shall have been issued, and the roup rolls lodged in process, with an account of expenses, and a state of the debt, showing the exact difference between the debt and the proceeds of the sale (*a*). 'The Clerk of each Sheriff Court keeps a register of all sequestrations granted for rent, whether in rural or urban subjects (*b*).'

(*a*) Cargill *v*. Baxter, 1829; 7 S. 662. Act of Sederunt, *supra*, § 1245 (*f*).
(*b*) 30 and 31 Vict. c. 42, § 7.

1247. As by virtue of his hypothec the landlord has no preference over the Crown, so even by sequestration and a warrant to sell he does not acquire such preference (*a*). But after sale of the effects, an order on the Sheriff-Clerk to pay the price to the landlord seems to prevail over the Crown (*b*).

(*a*) Ogilvie *v*. Wingate, 1791; M. 6884 and 7889; 2 Ill. 199; 3 Paton, 273; 2 Bell's Com. 54. Robertson *v*. Jardine, 1802; M. 7891. Adam *v*. Sutherland, 1863; 2 Macph. 6. See above, § 1241.
(*b*) See Tait's Justice of Peace, 256. 2 Bell's Com. 56; 1 Ersk. 3. § 31.

1248. (4.) *Irritancy of the Lease.*—This is another, though an indirect, mode of enforcing the payment of the rent; and it is either by force of stipulation, or by law.

1249. At common law, the tenant's breach of engagement grounded an action of declarator and removing; and the conventional penalty was at one time held to strengthen it into an absolute forfeiture not purgeable. But it is not so held now. A conventional forfeiture of the lease on failure to pay rent is independent of the claim of damage for the breach of the contract. It is an agreement that the tenant shall forfeit his lease if he shall fall two years' rent in arrear; 'or, sometimes, in the event of sequestration for rent being awarded in consequence of the rent being in arrear; or, in the event of the bankruptcy of the tenant, or his failing to implement the conditions of the lease (*a*).' When a lease is to be forfeited *extra ordinem*, and without any forfeiting clause, it must be done by declarator before the Court of Session (*b*). But if there be a conventional forfeiture, the Sheriff (*c*) may decern the tenant to remove on account of the breach of condition (*d*). 'A conventional irritancy cannot be purged (*e*). The exercise of the landlord of his option to irritate bars his claim to damages, if it be not reserved (*f*).

'The bankruptcy of a company which is a tenant, at all events if sub-tenants and assignees are excluded, puts an end to the lease, there being no *persona* to be tenant after the company is dissolved (*g*). But the bankruptcy of one of two joint tenants has not this effect (*h*).'

(*a*) *E.g.* as to residence and management, Drummond *v*. M'Pherson, 1799; M. *Tack*, Apx. 6. Cameron *v*. Cameron, Dec. 18, 1810; F. C. Stirling *v*. Millar, June 29, 1813; F. C. Edmond *v*. Reid, 1871; 9 Macph. 782.
(*b*) As to this, however, see Hamilton *v*. Hamilton, 1845; 8 D. 308.
(*c*) See below, § 1250. Wylie *v*. Her. Sec. Invt. Assn., 1871; 10 Macph. 253. Scottish Prop. Invt. Soc. *v*. Horne, 1881, 8 R. 737, as to jurisdiction in conventional irritancies.
(*d*) Scott *v*. Wotherspoon, 1829; 7 S. 481; 2 Ill. 189. Horn *v*. M'Lean, 1830; 8 S. 329; 2 Ill. 191. Aberdeen College *v*. L. Northesk, 1675; M. 7230; 2 Ill. 199. Ogilvie *v*. Duff, 1834; 12 S. 857. Hall *v*. Grant, 1831; 9 S. 612. Hogg *v*. Gordon, 1780; 2 Pat. 516. Hamilton, (*b*). Lindsay *v*. Hogg, 1855; 17 D. 788. Anstruther *v*. Greenshields, 1855; 18 D. 59. Forbes *v*. Ure, 1856; 18 D. 577. Stewart *v*. Watson, 1864; 2 Macph. 1414. Rankin *v*. M'Lauchlan, 1864; 3 Macph. 128. Lyon *v*. Irvine, 1874; 1 R. 512. Houldsworth *v*. Brand's Trs., 1875; 2 R. 683. Stewart *v*. Rutherfurd, 1863; 1 Macph. 511. Guild *v*. Maclean, 1897; 25 R. 106, where the lessor was not held bound to give reasons for his opinion that there was a breach. D. Hamilton *v*. Warnocks, 1872; 1 Sel. Sh. Ct. Ca. 294. For instances of conditions fenced by irritancies, see § 1218.
(*e*) Stewart, Rankin, Lyon, *citt.*
(*f*) Walker's Trs. *v*. Manson, 1886; 13 R. 1198. Buttercase, (*h*). Comp. Bidoulac *v*. Sinclair's Tr., 1889; 17 R. 144; and § 1271, below.
(*g*) Campbell *v*. Calder Iron Co., 1805; 1 Bell's Com. 82. Walker *v*. M'Knights, 1886; 13 R. 599.
(*h*) Young *v*. Gerrard, 1843; 6 D. 347. Buttercase's Tr. *v*. Geddie, 1897; 24 R. 1128.

1250. After the example of feus, there appears to have been formerly a stipulation in leases (*a*) of irritancy *ob non solutum canonem*; under which it was held competent to require from tenants, who had fallen into arrear, caution for the rent of the remaining years of the lease. In several cases where no such irritancy had been incurred, it appears formerly to have been the practice to require caution from tenants *vergentes ad inopiam* (*b*). But the only competent ground for judicially requiring caution for future rents was the irritancy (*c*). And this has been taken as the groundwork of an Act of Sederunt, by which it is declared that when a full year's rent shall fall in arrear, 'or the tenant shall desert his possession and leave it unlaboured,' instead of a declarator of irritancy, an action shall be competent before the Judge Ordinary to compel payment of arrears, with caution for five years' rent, otherwise to remove (*d*).

(*a*) In the earlier editions misprinted "cases."

(*b*) L. Kinnaber *v.* Rough, 1594; M. 15,301; 2 Ill. 199. Lawson *v.* Scott, 1627; M. 15,302. Stevenson *v.* Job, 1629; M. 15,303.

(*c*) Binning *v.* Sinclair, 1672; M. 15,304. Cunningham *v.* Halyburton, 1677: M. 15,305. See above, § 1218.

(*d*) Act of Sederunt, Dec. 14, 1756, § 5. Oliver *v.* Weir's Trs., 1870; 8 Macph. 876. Mackenzie *v.* Mackenzie, 1848; 10 D. 1009. 2 Hunter, L. & T. 124 sqq. The fourth section also provides that where a tenant has irritated his lease by suffering two full years' rent to fall in arrear, the lessor may declare the irritancy, and obtain a decree of removing before the Sheriff. This A. of S. seems to apply only to agricultural tenancies. See as to urban leases, Wright *v.* Wightman, 1875; 3 R. 68. 2 Hunter, L. & T. 127–8.

1251. In construing this Act of Sederunt, it has been held that a full year's rent means the *amount* of a full year's rent (*a*). The amount must be due not only at raising the action, but at the date of decree; the landlord, however, not being bound to accept of a partial payment, so as to defeat his remedy (*b*); and payment of a part in the course of legal diligence will not discharge the proceeding (*c*). By consignation of the rent before decree the irritancy is purged, so that the judge shall not be warranted in requiring caution for five crops (*d*). The Act of Sederunt applies to tenants possessing on verbal tacks (*e*).

'A statutory irritancy enforceable before the Judge Ordinary has been introduced in regard to leases for more than twenty-one years (*f*).

'And by the Agricultural Holdings Act, 1883, it is provided that where the landlord has no right of hypothec, *i.e.* in leases dated subsequent to Martinmas 1881, he may raise an action before the Sheriff, when six months' rent of the holding is due and unpaid, to have the tenant removed at the next term of Whitsunday or Martinmas as if the lease were then determined, and that the Sheriff shall decern for removing unless the arrears of rent are paid, or caution found for the same and one year's further rent. In this case the provisions of the Act of S., 1756, § 5, are declared not to apply (*g*).'

(*a*) Urquhart *v.* M'Kenzie, 1824; 3 S. 56; 2 Ill. 200. See as to calculating the year's rent and credits to be allowed to the tenant, Hamilton *v.* Cuthill, 1831; 9 S. 926; 4 D. & A. 297.

(*b*) Campbell *v.* Robertson, 1763; M. 13,867.

(*c*) Marshall *v.* Read, 1803; Hume, 569. Sutherland *v.* M'Kenzie, 1854; 26 S. Jur. 466.

(*d*) M'Donald *v.* Jardine, 1825; 4 S. 230. See M'Christie *v.* Fisher, 1825; 4 S. 11. Kennedy *v.* Alison, 1807; Hume, 578.

(*e*) Monro *v.* Brown, 1827; 5 S. 807.

(*f*) 16 and 17 Vict. c. 80, § 32, *in fine*. 55 and 56 Vict. c. 17, sch. form 11.

(*g*) 46 and 47 Vict. c. 62, § 27; repealing 43 Vict. c. 12, § 2 and 3.

1252. Obligations of a Sub-Tenant.—The tenant's obligations may be either incumbent on himself, or on his sub-tenant, as in the natural possession. By convention the sub-tenant may be directly liable to the landlord for the prestations in the lease. If there be no such convention, there seems to be no direct obligation by the sub-tenant to the landlord (*a*).

(*a*) Purves *v.* Gentle, 1797; Hume, 794. 2 Hunter, L. & T. 174. Rankine, Leases, 190. Comp. § 1232 (*a*), above.

1253. Repairs and Meliorations.—From the nature of the contract, warrandice is implied on the landlord's part to make the subject effectual to the tenant, or fit for its purpose, and so to put the houses and fences in due repair (*a*). On the other hand, the tenant is liable for the effect of negligence (*b*). It is not, however, to be reckoned a fault for which he is responsible if the loss has been occasioned by the officious act of his servant, not within the scope of the servant's employment (*c*). The implied obligation on the landlord does not make it incumbent on him to restore the houses on their destruction by extraordinary and inevitable accident (*d*). The rule has been settled in the House of Lords, that neither the landlord nor the tenant is bound to restore; and that the loss accrues to each according to his interest, reserving to the tenant any right of relief he may have by abandonment, or by abatement of rent (*e*);

and that any hardship arising from the rule is to be avoided by special agreement.

(*a*) 2 Ersk. 6. § 39. Buchanan *v.* Stark, 1776; 5 B. Sup. 515. Belshes *v.* Caddels, 1776; *ib.* 516; Hailes, 688; 2 Ill. 200. Middleton *v.* Meggat, 1828; 7 S. 76. Kinloch *v.* Fraser, 1829; 7 S. 819. Gordon *v.* Ruxton, 1797; Hume, 798. Haining & Douglas *v.* Grierson, 1807; Hume, 829. Anderson *v.* Abel, 1854: 16 D. 796. Downie *v.* Campbell, Jan. 31, 1815; F. C. Napier *v.* Ferrier, 1847; 9 D. 1354. Lowndes *v.* Buchanan, 1854; 17 D. 63. Goskirk *v.* Edinr. Ry. Access Co., 1863; 2 Macph. 383. Kippen *v.* Oppenheim, 1847; 10 D. 242. Duncan *v.* M'Dougal, 1796; Hume, 792. Sprot *v.* Morrison, 1853; 15 D. 376. Harrold *v.* Pollexfen, 1844; 6 D. 1103. Baird *v.* Graham, 1852; 14 D. 615. Burnet *v.* Stewart, 1863; 1 Macph. 524. Barclay *v.* Neilson, 1878; 5 R. 909. Reid *v.* Baird, 1876; 4 R. 234 (landlord bound to give urban tenant a wind- and water-tight house, or pay damages for flooding, etc.); and other cases in § 1274A. As to express stipulations by the lessor for meliorations and repairs, see Paterson *v.* E. Fife, 1865; 3 Macph. 423 (mode of proving). M'Master *v.* Cameron, 1812; Hume, 858. 2 Hunter, L. & T. 245 sq., etc. Barclay *v.* Neilson, *cit.*

(*b*) 1426, c. 75. Sutherland *v.* Robertson, 1737; M. 13,979; Elch. *Reparation*, 2. Hardie *v.* Black, 1768; M. 10,133. M'Lellan *v.* Kerr, 1797; M. 10,134.

(*c*) M'Kenzie *v.* M'Leod, 10 Bing. 385.

(*d*) Walker *v.* Bayne, May 30, 1811; F. C.; rev. 1815, 3 Dow, 233; 6 Pat. 217. See above, § 1063, 1208.

(*e*) *Ib.* York Buildings Co. *v.* Adams, 1741; M. 10,127. Clark *v.* Baird, 1741; M. 10,128. Swinton *v.* M'Dougall, Jan. 16, 1810; F. C. Walker, in H. L., *supra* (*d*). See Devon Iron Co. *v.* E. Mansfield, 1839; 2 D. 268. Drummond *v.* Hunter, 1869; 7 Macph. 347. D. Hamilton's Trs. *v.* Fleming, 1870; 9 Macph. 329.

1254. There are two kinds of disrepair: one allied to injury or dilapidation, and arising from negligence or hard usage; the other from the inevitable and imperceptible tendency of all the works of man to decay and destruction by use. With the exception of the latter (tear and wear) the tenant is bound 'at common law and generally by express bargain' to maintain and restore the houses and fences as he received them (*a*). But an exception has been admitted to this rule, in relation to fences erected by the landlord after the tenant's entry. Where such fences are not stipulated to be erected, and are not of a kind which the landlord may be compelled to erect (as march fences with contiguous heritors), the landlord is not entitled by erection of them to enlarge the tenant's obligation to uphold (*b*). It has also been held, 'said Professor Bell in the previous editions,' though at one time otherwise decided, that a tenant is not bound to repair fences spontaneously erected by himself, which he is not entitled to remove (*c*). 'But the cases cited by the author do not conflict with one another, and do not support his statement. It seems that while a tenant is not entitled to remove *houses* erected by him during his lease, he is not bound to repair them; and that he may remove *fences* erected by him for his own accommodation, and not as a permanent improvement of the farm; but if he leaves them, he must put them in good repair. Something may depend on the nature and position of the fence and the conditions of the lease (*d*).'

(*a*) 2 Ersk. 6. § 39. Whites *v.* Houston, 1707; M. 15,258; 2 Ill. 202. Campbell *v.* Browne, 1776; 5 B. Sup. 518. See Taylor *v.* Brown, 1800; Hume, 308. Mossman *v.* Brocket, 1810; Hume, 850. Johnstone *v.* Hughans, 1894; 21 R. 777.

(*b*) Dudgeon *v.* Howden, Nov. 22, 1813; F. C.

(*c*) Oliphant *v.* Thomson, 1822; 1 S. 307; as contrasted with Andrew *v.* Morison, Jan. 19, 1811; F. C. Hamilton *v.* Hamilton, 1845; 8 D. 308; 1846, 9 D. 53.

(*d*) See D. Buccleuch *v.* Tod's Trs., 1871; 9 Macph. 1014. 1 Hunter, L. & T. 312.

1255. It is implied in the contract of lease, that any buildings, fences, or improvements which the tenant may spontaneously make, are made in contemplation of his own interest, and for his own use only. And so 'at common law' he has no claim for such meliorations at the end of his lease, without special stipulation (*a*). But he has been held entitled to remove trevisses, mangers, etc., with which he had fitted up a barn as a temporary stable (*b*); 'also wire fencing put up for his own convenience in the management of the farm (*c*); and, being a nurseryman, to take away greenhouses, hotbed frames, and such like erections (*d*)'; and if the tenant's possession be terminated abruptly and prematurely, he ought in equity to be entitled to recompense. The most distinct example of this emergent claim for recompense occurs where houses or fences have been built by a tenant whose lease excludes assignees and sub-tenants, and the tenant is prematurely deprived of the use of them. In such a case, it is equitable that, the landlord getting the benefit while the tenant has not derived the expected advantage, the creditors of the tenant or his family should be allowed a proportion of the value of the meliorations (*e*). 'But in the case referred to, a certain sum was expended by the tenant under a special stipulation in the lease, which bound the landlord to repay it at the issue of the lease; and it has been decided that it does not support the equitable exception which Professor Bell and other writers have founded upon it. There is no rule, at common law, that money expended by a tenant not under agreement can be claimed by him or his representatives, either at the ish of the lease or at its premature termination (*f*).'

(*a*) 2 Ersk. 6. § 39. Whites, *supra*, § 1254 (*a*). Ducat *v*. Css. Aboyne, 1803; M. 15,264; 2 Ill. 202. Ivory's Note, Ersk. p. 372, No. 119. Jollie, *infra*, § 1256 (*c*). M'Kay *v*. Brodie, 1801; Hume, 549. Murray *v*. Bisset, 1805; Hume, 818. Hamilton, *cit*. Thomson *v*. Fowler, 1859; 21 D. 453. Officer *v*. Nicolson, 1807; Hume, 827 (custom of barony).

(*b*) Scott *v*. Ewart, 1824; 3 S. 344. See M. Tweeddale *v*. Hume, 1848; 10 D. 1053.

(*c*) D. Buccleuch *v*. Tod's Trs., 1871; 9 Macph. 1014. See above, § 1254.

(*d*) Syme *v*. Harvey, 1861; 24 D. 202. The same was held upon evidence of acquiescence or agreement, where an urban tenant built greenhouses greatly in excess of the requirements of his house, in Ferguson *v*. Paul, 1885; 12 R. 1222.

(*e*) Morton *v*. Lady Montgomerie, 1822; 1 S. 344.

(*f*) Scott's Exrs. *v*. Hepburn, 1876; 3 R. 816. See Thomson *v*. Fowler, *cit*. Pendreigh's Exrs. *v*. Dewar, 1871; 9 Macph. 1037. Above, § 538.

1256. The repairing or building of houses and fences is generally made the subject of express stipulation. The tenant usually agrees to accept them as in good and sufficient repair; or he takes an assignation to the obligation on the outgoing tenant under the expiring lease, in which case it is incumbent on the incoming tenant to see the repairs complete; and commonly this is settled by survey of skilled or neutral persons. Sometimes the stipulation is directed to secure that the houses, etc., shall be of equal value at the termination of the lease; and in that case it is held that if, on the whole, the tenant leaves what is of equal value, though the whole is not in complete repair, it is sufficient compliance with the covenant (*a*). The tenant sometimes undertakes to make the necessary repairs and meliorations on being allowed their value at the end of the lease, and questions arise on the construction of such stipulations (*b*). In such cases an obligation to uphold, with a right to indemnification of any excess of value in additions, restrains the tenant to mere renewal or rebuilding of what becomes ruinous, and to make necessary or suitable improvements, but gives no right to pull down old houses, or erect new ones not necessary or suitable to the farm (*c*). Express clauses as to buildings supersede local customs, as to indemnification for meliorations (*d*). A claim for meliorations under an express clause in a lease, 'but not under a separate missive (*e*),' is good against singular successors (*f*); but retention of the farm at the end of the lease for meliorations is not allowed, unless assented to by the purchaser or supported by local custom (*g*). 'Neither is it competent to retain the rent, at least during the currency of the lease, in respect of the landlord's non-implement of an engagement to expend money in meliorations (*h*), such retention being in general competent only if there be really defective possession (*i*). Compensation will operate where the circumstances are appropriate (*k*).' The burden of meliorations may be made effectual against succeeding heirs of entail to the extent of three-fourths, provided care be taken to follow out the directions of the Act of 10 Geo. III. c. 59, § 9 (*l*).

(*a*) M'Donald *v*. Robertson, 1830; 8 S. 974; 2 Ill. 203.

(*b*) See Purves *v*. Gentle, 1797; Hume, 794. Taylor *v*. Brown, 1808; Hume, 308. Grant *v*. Baird, 1810; Hume, 855. See *ib*. 858. M'Donald *v*. Brown, 1839; 2 D. 184. Napier *v*. Ferrier, 1847; 9 D. 1354. Dods *v*. Fortune, 1857; 19 D. 275. D. Hamilton's Trs. *v*. Fleming, 1870; 9 Macph. 329 (effect of such stipulation where there is *damnum fatale*). Frier *v*. E. Haddington, 1871; 10 Macph. 118. Barclay *v*. Neilson, 1878; 5 R. 909. L. Adv. *v*. E. Home, 1891; 18 R. 397. The landlord's remedy under the lease need not exclude his claim for damages. Allan's Trs. *v*. Allan & Son, 1891; 19 R. 215.

(*c*) Sinclair *v*. Manson, 1821; 1 S. Ap. 1. Jollie *v*. Graham, 1827; 6 S. 236; rev. 1831, 5 W. & S. 280; 1834, 12 S. 789; aff. 1835, 2 S. & M'L. 24.

(*d*) Gordon *v*. Thomson, 1831; 9 S. 736. See Gordon *v*. Robertson, 1825; 3 S. 656; rev. 1826, 2 W. & S. 115. Sheriff *v*. L. Lovat, 1854; 17 D. 177. See 2 Hunter, L. & T. 239 sq. As to local custom, see also Learmonth *v*. Sinclair's Trs., 1878; 5 R. 548. And for the provision under the recent statute for removal of tenant's fixtures and buildings, see below, § 1256A (8); and as to such fixtures generally, § 1473, 1475, below.

(*e*) Bruce, *infra* (*f*). Turner, *infra* (*g*).

(*f*) 2 Bankt. 9. § 25. Ray *v*. Finlayson, 1680; M. 15,216. M'Dowal *v*. M'Dowal, 1760; M. 15,259; contrasted with Arbuthnot *v*. Colquhoun, 1772; M. 10,424; Hailes, 464. Morrison *v*. Patullo, 1787; M. 10,425. Bruce *v*. M'Leod, 1822; 1 S. Ap. 213. Fraser *v*. Maitland, 1824; 2 S. Ap. 37. See Stewart *v*. E. Dunmore's Trs., 1837; 15 S. 1059. Barr *v*. Cochrane, 1878; 5 R. 1877. Dunn's Trs. *v*. E. Zetland, 1862; 24 D. 801. *Supra*, § 1202. As to the purchaser's claims against tenants for fulfilment of stipulations of this kind in the lease, see Hall *v*. M'Gill, 1847; 9 D. 1557. Hamilton *v*. Fleming, 1793; Hume, 787. See as to heirs of entail, Ross *v*. Hawkins, 1848; 10 D. 1288. Mackenzie *v*. Mackenzie, 1849; 11 D. 596. E. Fife's Trs. *v*. E. Fife, 1852; 1 Stu. 271. Runcie *v*. Lumsden, 1857; 19 D. 965. Macdonald *v*. Johnston, 1883; 10 R. 959; and cases in note (*l*) *infra*. And as to the right of a landlord to retain money of the tenant on his bankruptcy for a claim by the former in respect of dilapidation, Munro *v*. Fraser, 1858; 21 D. 103. Such a stipulation may be effectual against the lessor's personal representatives, as well as his heir. M'Gillivray's Exrs. *v*. Masson, 1857; 19 D. 1099. See Waterson *v*. Stewart, 1881; 9 R. 155.

(*g*) Campbell *v*. Gemmel, 1790; Hume, 779. Bell *v*. Lamont, June 14, 1814; F. C. Stewart *v*. M'Ra, 1834;

13 S. 4. Turner *v.* Nicholson, 1835 ; 13 S. 633. M'Neil *v.* Sinclair, 1807 ; Hume, 834 ; and see *ib.* 854.

(*h*) Dods *v.* Fortune, 1854 ; 16 D. 478. Cf. Guthrie *v.* Shearer, 1873 ; 1 R. 181. Drybrough *v.* Drybrough, 1874 ; 1 R. 909. The decisions in regard to retention of rent for non-fulfilment of obligations incumbent on the landlord are (as Mr. Hunter justly remarks) far from uniform ; and in various cases (*e.g.* Dickson *v.* Porteous, 1852 ; 15 D. 1) have confined the tenant's right beyond what is reasonable or just. See 2 Hunter, L. & T. 255 sq., 280–286. Rankine, Leases, 303.

(*i*) Cases in § 1231 (*b*), (*c*).

(*k*) Above, § 572. Davidson's Trs. *v.* Urquhart, 1892 ; 19 R. 808. Smith *v.* Harrison & Co.'s Tr., 1893 ; 21 R. 330. Lovie *v.* Baird's Tr., 1895 ; 23 R. 1. Jaffray's Tr. *v.* Milne, 1897 ; 24 R. 602.

(*l*) Dillon *v.* Campbell, 1780 ; M. 15,432 ; 2 Ill. 205. Webster *v.* Farquhar, 1791 ; Bell's Ca. 207 ; M. 15,439. Taylor *v.* Bethune, 1791 ; Bell's Ca. 214. Tod *v.* Moncrieff, 1823 ; 2 S. 113 ; aff. 1825, 1 W. & S. 217. Fraser *v.* Fraser, 1827 ; 5 S. 722 ; 8 S. 409 ; aff. 5 W. & S. 69. Innes *v.* D. Gordon's Exrs., 1827 ; 6 S. 279 ; aff. 4 W. & S. 305. Barclay *v.* E. Fife, 1829 ; 7 S. 708. See below, § 1766–1771. See above, (*f*).

1256A. 'The Agricultural Holdings Act applies only to holdings either wholly agricultural or wholly pastoral, or in part agricultural and as to the residue pastoral, or in whole or in part cultivated as a market garden. It does not apply to a holding let to a tenant during his continuance in an office, appointment, or employment of the landlord (*a*). Nor does it apply to a hotel and land let together as one subject (*b*) ; or to land which is of such value or extent that it is merely an adjunct of a house, the principal subject let (*c*). A tenant who has made improvements specified in the schedule to this Act, is entitled on quitting his holding at the determination of a tenancy (*d*) to obtain from his landlord, by certain procedure, such a sum as fairly represents the value of the improvement to an incoming tenant, the valuation being exclusive of what is justly due to the inherent capabilities of the soil (*e*). The general right thus conferred is qualified by the conditions noted in the following paragraphs. The subject of compensation for improvements which must be left by the tenant on the holding is contiguous to that of fixtures which may be removed by him, and the latter is also treated in the Act.

(1.) '*Improvements made before the commencement of the Act* (1st January 1884) do not entitle to compensation, except boning with undissolved bones, claying or spreading blaes, liming, marling, application of purchased manure, consumption on the holding of cake or other feeding stuff not produced on the holding (being the improvements set forth in the third part of the schedule), if made within ten years before said date under no express obligation (*f*). Additions are made to the schedule, with regard to market gardens, by a later statute (*g*).

(2.) '*Improvements in the first part of the schedule,* viz. erection or enlargement of building, formation of silos, laying down of permanent pasture, making water meadows or works of irrigation, making gardens, making roads or bridges, making or improving water-courses, ponds, wells, or reservoirs, or water supply works for domestic or agricultural purposes, making permanent fences, reclaiming waste land, weiring or embanking land and sluices against floods, entitle to compensation if the landlord or his agent has previously consented in writing to the execution of the improvement, whether unconditionally or upon conditions as to compensation or otherwise (*h*).

(3.) '*Drainage,* the improvement specified in the second part of the schedule, entitles to compensation only if, between two and three months before beginning it, the tenant has given notice in writing of his intention, and the proposed manner of doing the work. In this case, failing an agreement, the landlord may elect to do the drainage himself, charging interest ; and the right to compensation under the Act is excluded by stipulations limiting the outlay in any lease current at the passing of the Act or relative writing made prior to the passing of the Act (*i*).

(4.) '*Reservations.*—Specific compensation provided by any agreement or custom for improvements executed at any time under a lease current at 1st January 1884, is substituted for compensation under the Act. In a tenancy under a lease beginning after the said date, a written agreement (*k*) made after the date of the Act, securing to the tenant fair and reasonable compensation, having regard to the circumstances existing at the time of making the agreement, for an improvement specified in the third part of the schedule, is valid, and excludes the compensation under the Act. This provision applies to those improvements under leases current at 1st January 1884, contained in the third part of the schedule, and enumerated above (1), for which specific compensation is not provided by any written agreement or custom (*l*). But an agreement depriving the tenant of his right to claim compensation is void (*m*).

(5.) '*Deductions from the compensation* payable are to be allowed in respect of any benefit the landlord has given the tenant in consideration of executing the improvement; in the case of compensation for manures, in respect of the value of manure that would have been produced by consuming on the holding, according to the rules of good husbandry or the terms of any written contract, any crops sold or removed off the holding in the last two years of the tenancy, unless a return of manure has been made in respect of such produce. The landlord is further entitled to deduction from the compensation payable to the tenant of any rent payable for the holding; of rates, taxes, etc., interest, insurance premiums, for which the tenant is liable as between them; of sums payable for breach of any stipulation of the lease or contract relative thereto; or for any deterioration committed or permitted by the tenant; but such breach, if connected with cultivation and management, and such deterioration, must have taken place within four years. The tenant, on the other hand, may have added to the compensation any sum due to him for breach of any stipulation or contract (*n*).

(6.) '*Procedure.*—Written notice must be given four months before the determination of the tenancy (*o*) of the tenant's intention to claim compensation under the Act, without which he is not entitled to compensation. Counter notice of any claim by the *landlord* may be given within fourteen days thereafter (*p*). Such notices shall state, so far as reasonably may be, the particulars and amount of the claim (*q*). Failing agreement as to the amount and time of payment of compensation, the difference shall be settled by arbitration. Copious details of the procedure in the arbitration are given in the Act (*r*). When the sum claimed as compensation exceeds £100, there is a right of appeal, on certain specified grounds, to the Sheriff, whose decision is final (*s*). The Sheriff, on the landlord's application, has power to charge the holding or estate with the compensation money payable by him, subject to certain limitations and conditions (*t*).

(7.) '*An incoming tenant* may buy (with the landlord's consent, except in the case of market gardens) the outgoing tenant's improvements or part of them, to the effect of recovering compensation at the end of his tenancy, such as his predecessor could have claimed if he had remained in the tenancy (*u*).

'*A change of tenancy*—which appears to mean a new lease or letting—does not of itself deprive a tenant, "who has remained in his holding during a change or changes of tenancy," of his right to claim compensation when he does quit his holding (*v*). And the compensation given by the Act, when it is available, but not otherwise, is exclusive of compensation that might be claimed by any agreement or custom (*w*).

(8.) '*Tenants' Fixtures.* — It is further enacted that any engine, machinery, fencing, or other fixture affixed to his holding, or any building erected by a tenant, for which he is not under the Act or otherwise entitled to compensation, and which is not so affixed or erected in pursuance of an obligation to, or instead of a building or fixture belonging to the landlord, shall be the property of the tenant, and removable by him before, or within a reasonable time after, the termination of the tenancy. But this is subject to these provisions: full payment of rent, and performance or satisfaction of all other obligations to the landlord, before removal of such fixture or building; making good of all damage occasioned by the removal; giving the landlord a month's notice of the intention to remove; the landlord's right to elect, before the expiration of such notice, to purchase the fixture or building, the value in such event being fixed by the statutory procedure (*x*). This enactment extends to market gardens (*y*), from which also the tenant may remove the fruit trees and bushes which he has planted, but not permanently set out (*z*).'

(*a*) The principal Act, 46 and 47 Vict. c. 62, § 35, 42. 60 and 61 Vict. c. 22, amending as to market gardens. Rankine, Leases, 250 sqq.

(*b*) Mackintosh *v.* L. Lovat, 1886 ; 14 R. 282.

(*c*) Taylor *v.* E. of Moray, 1892 ; 19 R. 399.

(*d*) See the definition in § 42 of the Act, which includes a determination by renunciation. Strang *v.* Stuart, 1887; 14 R. 637.
(*e*) The Act, § 1.
(*f*) The Act, § 2. A provision with regard to other kinds of improvements made before the Act has ceased by lapse of time to be operative.
(*g*) 60 and 61 Vict. c. 22, § 3 (3).
(*h*) The Act, § 3. (*i*) The Act, § 4.
(*k*) See Gardiner *v.* L. Abercromby, 1892; 9 Sh. Ct. Rep. 33.
(*l*) The Act, § 5. (*m*) The Act, § 36.
(*n*) The Act, § 6. Soot *v.* L. Wharncliffe's Trs., 1885; 1 Sh. Ct. Rep. 189. Hunter *v.* Barron's Trs., 1886; 3 *ib.* 33. Birrell *v.* Baird, 1887; 3 *ib.* 462.
(*o*) Hunter *v.* Barron's Trs., 1886; 13 R. 883. Strang *v.* Stuart, (*d*). Sinclair *v.* Clyne's Tr., 1887; 15 R. 185. Black *v.* Clay, 1893; 21 R. 41; aff. 1893, A. C. 368; 21 R. H. L. 72. The qualified right of the tenant to enter the lands for the reaping and removal of his crops, after the ish of the lease, does not affect the date of its determination. Black *v.* Clay, *cit.* Waldie *v.* Mungall, 1896; 23 R. 792.
(*p*) The Act, § 7.
(*q*) Sinclair *v.* Brown, 1892; 19 R. 780.
(*r*) The Act, § 8, 11, 19, and amending Act, 52 and 53 Vict. c. 20.
(*s*) The Act, § 20. See Sinclair *v.* Clyne's Tr., *cit.* Gardiner, *cit.*
(*t*) The Act, § 24–26.
(*u*) The Act, § 37. 60 and 61 Vict. c. 22, § 3 (4).
(*v*) The Act, § 39. (*w*) The Act, § 38.
(*x*) The Act, § 30. Rankine, Leases, 280. As to the general law of fixtures, see § 1473, 1475, below; also § 1255, above. Brand's Trs. *v.* Brand's Tr., 1876; 3 R. H. L. 16.
(*y*) 60 and 61 Vict. c. 22, § 3 (1). (*z*) *Ib.* § 3 (5).

1257. Stocking, Cropping, etc.—It is implied in the contract that the tenant shall possess and labour the farm *tanquam bonus vir.* Under this obligation the following points seem fixed:—

1258. (1.) *Stocking.*—The tenant is bound to enter into possession with a sufficient stock (*a*); and he may be removed on summary application to the Sheriff, if he shall fail to stock the farm (*b*). But failure of any essential stipulation on the part of the landlord will free the tenant (*c*).

(*a*) Randifuird *v.* Crombie, 1623; M. 15,256; 2 Ill. 191. Scott *v.* Wotherspoon, 1829; 7 S. 481; 2 Ill. 189. Horn *v.* M'Lean, 1830; 3 S. 329; 2 Ill. 191. Thomson *v.* Handyside, 1833; 12 S. 557. Edmond *v.* Abel's Exrs., 1862; 24 D. 559. Cathcart *v.* Sloss, 1864; 3 Macph. 76, 521. M'Dougall *v.* Buchanan, 1867; 6 Macph. 120. Robertson *v.* Cockburn, 1875; 3 R. 21. *Supra,* § 1222.
(*b*) Tait *v.* Gordon, 1828; 6 S. 1055; 2 Ill. 206. This case has not been accepted as an authority for the general statement in the text; and it is still left uncertain whether the Sheriff can summarily remove on the ground of failure to stock a farm. See Horn *v.* M'Lean, 1830; 8 S. 329. 2 Hunter, L. & T. 132, and M'Dougall *v.* Buchanan (*a*). **Macdonald** *v.* **Mackessack,** 1888; 16 R. 168. Dove Wilson, Sh. Ct. Prac. 486, 487. It would appear that the Sheriff Court must have jurisdiction to remove, at least within the limit of £1000 or £50 a year. 40 and 41 Vict. c. 50, § 8.
(*c*) Duncan *v.* M'Dougall, 1796; Hume, 792. See Guthrie, *supra,* § 1256 (*h*).

1259. (2.) *Cropping.*—He is not entitled unduly to exhaust the soil; and it is on this general principle that questions as to rotation of crops, or regulations on that subject, are to be settled (*a*).

(*a*) See above, § 1220. 2 Ersk. 6. § 39, and cases cited by Mr. Ivory, pp. 372, 373. Murray *v.* Balcanqual, 1665; M. 15,257; 2 Ill. 191. Maxwell *v.* M'Kiming, 1776; 5 B. Sup. 515. E. Wemyss *v.* Hope, Feb. 7, 1809; F. C. Fraser *v.* M'Donald, 1834; 12 S. 684; 2 Ill. 206. Carron Co. *v.* Donaldson, 1858; 20 D. 681.

1260. The tenant cannot, where assignees and sub-tenants are excluded, abandon the possession and cultivation to others (*a*).

(*a*) E. Dalhousie *v.* Wilson, 1802; M. 15,311. See above, § 1218. Graham *v.* Stevenson, 1792; Hume, 781. As to applications for interim management where the tenant is absent, or fails to cultivate, see above, § 1223.

1261. (3.) *Dung and Straw.*—The tenant is bound to use the dung made on the farm in its cultivation during his possession, and on the same principle to consume by his cattle the fodder from which dung is produced (*a*). But there is room for distinctions in the application of this implied obligation during the last year's possession. These arise from the impossibility of the tenant using the straw or applying the dung in the cultivation of the farm after his possession is at an end. The general usage in Scotland is, for the tenant leaving the houses and grass at Whitsunday to have access to cut down his corn after the new tenant is in possession, and along with his crop to be allowed to carry off the straw, and take away or sell the dung (*b*); though in some counties a usage prevails of giving the straw to the new tenant. In leases this is commonly regulated by stipulation: as, that the fodder shall be consumed on the farm; that none shall be sold or carried off at any time, hay excepted; and that dung shall be laid on the farm the last year of the lease. These clauses truly make steelbow of the straw and dung left by each tenant to his successor. Doubts, however, have arisen on the construction of these clauses as affected by usage. The Court of Session have held that the words are to be interpreted by the usage. The House of Lords have viewed the matter differently; and leaving, on the one hand, the ordinary rule and usage untouched where no stipulation is made, they have, on the other, given full effect to the plain words of the stipulation as exclusive of any usage (*c*). The custom of a particular estate has not the force of an express stipulation to prevail against the general rule, 'or a clause in a lease' (*d*).

(*a*) D. Roxburghe *v.* Archibald, 1785; 5 B. Sup. 519; 2 Ill. 206. Finnie *v.* Trotter, 1767; M. 15,260–1; 2 Ill. 206–7, see note there. Pringle *v.* M'Murdo, 1796; M. 6575. E. Northesk *v.* Rolland, 1797; M. 15,254. See note in 2 Ill. 207 as to sub-leases. Scott *v.* Durham, May 27, 1813; F. C. See Gordon, below (*c*). Carnegie *v.* Scott, 1852; 14 D. 528. Hence in a question between a tenant's heir and executor the dung is heritable. Reid's Exr. *v.* Reid, 1890; 17 R. 519.

(*b*) Jamieson *v.* ——, 1792; M. 15,263. D. Roxburghe, *supra* (*a*). Drysdale *v.* Wemyss, 1848; 10 D. 467; aff. 6 Bell's App. 455. M'Ewan *v.* Paterson, 1803; Hume, 571. Philp *v.* Morton, 1816; Hume, 865.

(*c*) D. Roxburghe *v.* Roberton, 1816; Hume, 867; rev. 2 Bligh, 156; 6 Pat. 610; 2 Ill. 207. Gordon *v.* Robertson, 1825; 3 S. 656; 4 S. 13; rev. 1826, 2 W. & S. 115. Gordon *v.* Anderson, 1833; 11 S. 647; aff. 7 W. & S. 545. Stirling *v.* Yuille, 1827; 6 S. 251. See below, § 1264. Wilson *v.* Swan, 1804; Hume, 817. See above, cases in § 1256 (*b*); below, § 1264 (*d*). Greig & Tosh *v.* Mackay, 1869; 7 Macph. 1109. L. Elibank *v.* Scott, 1884; 11 R. 494. M'Duff *v.* Balfour, 1892; 19 R. 440.

(*d*) Allan *v.* Thomson, 1829; 7 S. 784. See in England, Smith's Leading Cases, 305 et seq. vol. i. p. 594, 8th ed. Officer *v.* Nicolson, 1807; Hume, 827. Anderson *v.* Tod, 1809; Hume, 842.

1262. (4.) *Grass.*—When the lease terminates at Whitsunday and Martinmas, it may be doubted what the tenant's right is in relation to sown grass. The entry to the natural grass is at Whitsunday, and so the removal is at Whitsunday; the entry to the arable land is at Martinmas, and so is the removal. Formerly the hay was only from natural grass; but in the modern system, grass sown down with grain is a crop, for which the preparation is laborious and expensive. The rule has altered with the practice, and seems now to be, that the tenant in such a case has the away-going crop of grass (*a*).

(*a*) Sinclair *v.* Dalrymple, 1744; M. 5421; 2 Ill. 209. M. Tweeddale *v.* Somner, Nov. 19, 1816; F. C. Wight *v.* Inglis, 1796; M. 5446. Keith *v.* Logie's Heirs, 1825; 4 S. 267. Lyall *v.* Cooper, 1832; 11 S. 96. See 2 Ill. 210. 2 Hunter, L. & T. 486. Rankine, Leases, 388. Harvey *v.* King's College, 1845; 8 D. 151. M. Tweeddale *v.* Murray, 1846; 8 D. 411; as rev. 6 Bell's App. 125.

1263. (5.) *Fallow, etc.* — In respect to fallow 'or green crop' left by the outgoing tenant, 'or other expenses incurred by him under his lease, in order to keep up the continuity of good husbandry,' it has been held that, independently of express stipulation, he, 'or even the landlord, if the landlord prepare the ground (*a*),' has right to claim its value; and this has proceeded on the principle, that as the tenant might have taken a crop from the land instead of leaving it fallow, and as the incoming tenant reaps the advantage which the other has abstained from taking, he is in equity entitled to the value (*b*).

(*a*) Marshall *v.* Walker, 1869; 7 Macph. 833. Simson's Tr. *v.* Carnegie, 1870; 8 Macph. 811.

(*b*) Purves *v.* Rutherford, 1822; 2 S. 59; 2 Ill. 210. Alexander *v.* Gillon, 1847; 9 D. 524. Brown *v.* Coll. of St. Andrews, 1851; 13 D. 1355. Sheriff *v.* L. Lovat, 1854; 17 D. 177. Erskine's Trs. *v.* Crombie, 1870; 9 Macph. 54 (turnips to be taken at market value). Thomson *v.* Jamieson, 1874; 1 R. 895.

1264. (6.) *Steelbow.*—It was a frequent practice formerly for the landlord to stock the farm, on an agreement by the tenant to restore the articles, or their equivalents, at the end of the lease. This was called "steelbow," and is a species of *mutuum*. In questions relative to the landlord's right in steelbow in competition with creditors, although in the earlier cases steelbow stock did not fall under the escheat of the tenant, but under that of the landlord (*a*), yet it was in one case held to belong to the tenant, and to be liable for his debts (*b*). In a more recent case, preference on the steelbow stocking of a farm was given to the landlord over the tenant's creditors; but this seems to have proceeded chiefly on the principle of hypothec (*c*). Those covenants relative to straw and dung in the last year of the lease, which now so commonly occur, rest on the principle of steelbow. The tenant sometimes gets the straw and dung of the last year of his predecessor's possession at his entry, and leaves the straw and dung of the last year of his own possession to the succeeding tenant. If he do not get this at his entry, he is entitled to the value of what he leaves (*d*). When he gets it from his predecessor, he is held bound to leave the dung and fodder unconsumed, without any claim for the value (*e*). 'The qualities of steelbow are denied to contracts relating to other subjects than farms (*f*).'

(*a*) 2 Stair, 3. § 81; 1 *ib.* 11. § 4. 2 Ersk. Pr. 6. § 2. 2 Ersk. 6. § 12; and 3 Ersk. 1. § 18. 1 Hunter, L. & T. 325.

(*b*) Turnbull *v.* Ker, 1624; M. 14,777; 2 Ill. 210.

(*c*) Butter *v.* M'Vicar, 1764; M. 6208; 5 B. Sup. 899. See *contra*, note in 2 Ill. 211; and Stewart *v.* Rose, 1816; Hume, 229. See also Torrance *v.* Traill's Trs., 1897; 24 R. 837. Macneal *v.* Smith, 1886; 2 Sh. Ct. Rep. 331.

(*d*) Heriot *v.* Halket, 1826; 4 S. 446; 2 Ill. 210. Berry *v.* Allen, 1827; 5 S. 212; aff. 1829, 3 W. & S. 417; 2 Ill. 208. See above, § 1261.

(*e*) Stirling *v.* Yuille, 1827; 6 S. 251.

(*f*) Paterson's Tr. *v.* Paterson's Trs., 1891; 19 R. 91.

1265. Tacit Relocation.—In order to put an end to the lease, notice must be given forty days before Whitsunday preceding its stipulated termination 'or a stipulated break,' that advantage is to be taken of its close. This must be regular and binding notice (*a*). The parties are otherwise held, 'if there be nothing in the lease or in their conduct inconsistent with the presumption,' to renew their agreement 'in all its terms (*b*) till the next break, or, at the termination,' for another year; and so from year to year, till notice shall be duly given (*c*). But this general rule and presumption admit of some qualifications. So there is no tacit relocation in judicial leases (*d*), nor in the lease of pasture fields (*e*). And it is doubtful whether it has place in a lease of an arable farm for a year (*f*). Tacit relocation is not a renewal of the lease for the original term, but only for a year (*g*); and the original lease expires, so as to liberate the cautioners (*h*).

(*a*) M'Intyre *v.* M'Nab's Trs., 1829; 8 S. 237; aff. 5 W. & S. 299; 2 Ill. 211. See below, § 1268A, 1271, 1278. 16 and 17 Vict. c. 80, § 29.

(*b*) Cases in (*c*). Wemyss *v.* Drysdale, 1848; 10 D. 467; aff. 1849, 6 Bell's App. 455, 461.

(*c*) 2 Stair, 9. § 23. 2 Ersk. 6. § 35. 2 Bell on Leases, 132. Forsyth *v.* Bruce, 1827; 6 S. 101. M'Intyre, *supra* (*a*). Hume *v.* M'Leod's Reprs., 1808; Hume, 583 (available to heir of lessee). Trotter *v.* Lanceman, 1804; Hume, 814. Robertson & Co. *v.* Drysdale, 1834; 12 S. 477. Blain *v.* Ferguson, 1840; 2 D. 546. Bett *v.* Murray, 1845; 7 D. 447. Wilson *v.* Stewart, 1853; 16 D. 106.

(*d*) 2 Ersk. 6. § 36.

(*e*) M'Harg, petr., 1805; M. *Removing*, Apx. No. 4.

(*f*) 2 Stair, 9. § 23. 2 Ersk. 6. § 36. Forsyth, *supra* (*c*).

(*g*) 2 Stair, 9. § 23. 2 Ersk. 6. § 35. But if the term is less than a year, it appears to be a renewal only for that shorter term. Stair and Ersk., *citt.* Rankine, Leases, 534. Hunter *v.* Peebles, 1894; 10 Sh. Ct. Rep. 269.

(*h*) Forbes *v.* Lady Saltoun's Exrs., 1735; Elch. *Cautioner*, 4.

1265A. '*Notice required by the Agricultural Holdings Act.*—"Notwithstanding the expiration of the stipulated endurance of any lease, the tenancy shall not come to an end unless written notice has been given by either party to the other of his intention to bring the tenancy to an end—(A) in the case of leases for three years and upwards, not less than one year, nor more than two years, before the termination of the lease (*a*); (B) in the case of leases from year to year, or for any other period less than three years, not less than six months before the termination of the lease." Failing such notice by either party, the lease is renewed by tacit relocation for another year, and thereafter from year to year. The form of this notice is that prescribed by the Sheriff Courts Act, 1853, and comes in place of the notice required by that Act. This section does not affect the landlord's right to remove a tenant sequestrated in bankruptcy, or who has incurred an irritancy or other liability to be removed; and it does not apply to stipulations for resuming land for building, planting, feuing, or other purposes, or to subjects let for less than a year (*b*).'

(*a*) Compare authorities in § 1256A (*a*); and see Gould *v.* Paterson, 1895; 12 Sh. Ct. Rep. 284.

(*b*) 46 and 47 Vict. 62, § 28.

1266. Removing (*a*).—Leases terminate by Removing or by Renunciation.

(*a*) 2 Craig, 9. § 2. 1546, c. 3. 1555, c. 39. 2 Ross, 509. Act of Sederunt, Dec. 14, 1756. 2 Ersk. 6. § 45. 2 Bell, Leases, 51. In L. Blantyre *v.* Dunn, 1858, 20 D. 1188, it was not formally determined that, when a tenant under a long lease acquires the subject let in property, the lease is utterly extinguished *confusione*, and does not continue to subsist as a separate estate; but it was held that the lease was at least sopited, and that the owner could not be his own tenant, owing rent to himself; that each term's rent was extinguished *confusione* during the union of rights; and that the superior was entitled to the actual value of the subjects at the date of entry as his composition, not merely to the rent in the long lease.

1267. (1.) *Proceedings.*—Under the old law, removing proceeded on a precept in the landlord's name, as granter of the lease, or as purchaser, heir, joint-proprietor, etc., infeft in the lands (*a*). This precept was executed against the tenant personally or at his dwelling-house, and also on the ground of the lands and at the parish church, forty days before the 15th day of May of the year in which the lease was to expire (*b*). This was followed by action of removing before the Sheriff, or before the Court of Session; decree in the former being carried into immediate execution by precept of ejection; decree in the latter requiring a charge, as the Court of Session never executed its own decrees (*c*).

'In a removing or ejection, the question of the pursuer's title is antecedent to all others (*d*), subject to the general principle in questions between the original lessor and his lessee (or that lessee's representatives) that the latter cannot impugn his author's title, unless by clear *primâ facie* evidence of divestiture (*e*), or even demand production of it.'

(*a*) 1555, c. 39. 2 Stair, 9. § 41, 43. 2 Ersk. 6. § 51, 53. 2 Bell, Leases, 51 et seq., and Apx. 333. Paxton *v.* Hunter, 1749; M. 16,121; 2 Ill. 211. See also as to heirs, Ersk. *ut supra*, and cases. Elphinston *v.* Guthrie, 1625; M. 13,270. Bruce *v.* Hunter, Nov. 16, 1808; F. C. (common proprietors); comp. also Stewart *v.* Wand, 1842; 4 D. 622; and above, § 1075, 1083; and 2 Hunter, L. & T. 12. As to tercer, Lady Maxwell *v.* Tenants, 1630; M. 15,842.

(*b*) 1690, c. 39. 24 Geo. II. c. 23. 2 Craig, 9. § 2. 2 Stair, 9. § 39. 2 Ersk. 6. § 46. Kames' Elucid. art. 34. Dss. Buccleugh *v.* Davidson, 1715; M. 13,836. E. March *v.* Dowie, 1754; M. 13,843. Campbell *v.* Johnstone, 1793; M. 13,849.

(*c*) Stainhill *v.* Burd, 1675; M. 13,894. Pringle *v.* E. Home, 1739; M. 13,894; Elchies, *Ejection*, 1; Notes, 119.

(*d*) Sinclair *v.* Leslie, 1887; 14 R. 792. See below, § 1268.

(*e*) 2 Stair, 1. § 27. 2 Stair, 9. § 41. 4 Stair, 26. § 8. 2 Ersk. 6. § 51. King *v.* Wieland, 1858; 20 D. 960. Dunlop & Co. *v.* Meiklem, 1876; 4 R. 11. Dennistoun, M'Nair, & Co. *v.* M'Farlane, 1808; M. Apx. *Tack*, 15. Traill *v.* Traill, 1873; 1 R. 61.

1268. A better form was introduced by Act of Sederunt, 14th December 1756. Where the tenant is bound by the lease to remove without warning, a charge of horning on the registered tack, given forty days before the Whitsunday of the expiration of the lease, is a good warrant for a precept of ejection by the Sheriff within six days after the term of removal (*a*). Alternatively with the process under the Act of 1555, an action of removing before the Judge Ordinary of the county where the lands lie, is by the Act of Sederunt made competent (*b*). This proceeding may be by summons or by summary application (*c*); and on due citation, the calling in court (*d*) forty days before Whitsunday is equivalent to a warning in terms of the Act 1555. The Sheriff proceeds thereupon to decern in the removing (*e*), following up his decree with a precept of ejection within forty-eight hours. In these proceedings there has been some relaxation from the strictness of the rule under the Act of 1555. But 'in proceedings by a landlord against tenants who derive their rights from others than himself,' infeftment is still necessary as a title to pursue (*f*); 'it was enough, however, in the case of an apparent heir, if he were infeft before decree, or at all events before calling in court (*g*).' Where there is a sub-lease, and the tenant has quitted the natural possession after the landlord has recognised the sub-tenant, warning to the sub-tenant is enough; but if the sub-tenant be not recognised, the tenant must be warned (*h*). If assignees and sub-tenants are allowed, and the lease have been assigned or the farm sub-let, and intimation made to the landlord, the assignee or sub-tenant must be called; if there be no intimation, this is not necessary (*i*). Advocation 'or appeal' is not competent against a decree of removing (*k*); 'the competent mode of review being by suspension before execution of the Sheriff's decree (*l*).'

(*a*) See 2 Craig, 9. § 11. 4 Stair, 26. § 14. 2 Ersk. 6. § 50. 2 Bell, Leases, 69. Brown *v.* Peacock, 1822; 1 S. 337; 2 Ill. 212. Heron *v.* Rollo, 1825; 4 S. 118, and cases there cited. A. S. § 1. 2 Hunter, L. & T. 25 sq. *Infra*, § 1271. Maclaren *v.* M. Breadalbane, 1831; 10 S. 163. Blain *v.* Ferguson, 1840; 2 D. 546. Jamieson *v.* Thomson, 1802; Hume, 807. Heddle *v.* Baikie, 1841; 3 D. 370.

(*b*) Cameron *v.* M'Donald, 1804; M. 13,875. Nisbet *v.* Aikman, 1866; 4 Macph. 284.

(*c*) Tait *v.* Gordon, 1828; 6 S. 1055. See Nicolson's Ersk. i. 436, note; Wilson's Sheriff Court Pr. 482.

(*d*) Comp. § 1268A.

(*e*) A. S. § 2. Carruthers *v.* V. Stormont, 1764; M. 13,868. Hay, petr., June 2, 1810; F. C. Stevenson *v.* Baird, 1821; 1 S. 88.

(*f*) 2 Ersk. 6. § 52. Paton *v.* MacIntosh, 1757; M. 5273. Ferguson *v.* Morrison, 1802; M. 13,806. Brown *v.* Lang, 1802; Hume, 565. Stewart *v.* Burns, 1802; *ib.* 568. Campbell *v.* Mackellar, 1808; M. *Removing*, Apx. No. 5. Milne *v.* Petrie, 1807; Hume, 581. Johnston *v.* Martin, March 3, 1810; F. C. Scott *v.* Fisher, 1832; 10 S. 284. Penman *v.* Martin, 1822; 1 S. 485. Wilson *v.* Wilson, 1859; 21 D. 309. See above, § 1267 *fin.*

(*g*) Johnston, *cit.* Mackintosh *v.* Munro, 1854; 17 D. 99. See Mackenzie *v.* Gillanders, 1853; 16 D. 158. Traill *v.* Traill, 1873; 1 R. 61. See above, § 779A. A heritable creditor infeft on a bond, with power to output and input tenants, may pursue a removing even without a decree of maills and duties. Forsyth *v.* Aird, 1853; 16 D. 197. Blair *v.* Galloway, 1853; 16 D. 291. As to tacksmen, see 2 Ersk. 6. § 51, notes. M'Ilreavie *v.* Smith, 1810; Hume, 851. Johnston *v.* Dickson, 1831; 9 S. 452. Logie *v.* Corsie, 1847; 9 D. 1164. Ritchie *v.* Dickson, 1857; 19 D. 949. Wilson *v.* Wilson, 1859; 21 D. 309. Cameron *v.* Robertson, 1867; 39 S. Jur. 256. As to joint-proprietors, see § 1075, 1083, 1267 (*a*).

(*h*) D. Queensberry *v.* Barker, July 7, 1810; F. C. Thomson *v.* Harvie, 1823; 2 S. 408. 2 Ersk. 6. § 36. 2 Hunter, L. & T. 52.

(*i*) A. S. § 3.

(*k*) 6 Geo. IV. c. 120, § 44. Gibson *v.* Scott, 1826; 4 S. 407. M'Nair *v.* L. Blantyre's Trs., 1833; 11 S. 935. Roy *v.* E. Wemyss, 1840; 2 D. 1345. Fletcher *v.* Davidson, 1874; 2 R. 71. Contrast § 1268B, below.

(*l*) 1 and 2 Vict. c. 86. Graham *v.* Gordon, 1843; 5 D. 1207. M'Dougall *v.* Galt, 1863; 1 Macph. 1012. 2 Mackay's Practice, 491. 2 Hunter, L. & T. 92–98. This does not apply to a summary decree of ejection. Robb *v.* Brearton, 1895; 22 R. 885.

1268A. 'By the Sheriff Court Act, 1853, it is "competent to raise a summons of removing at any time," *i.e.* not only forty days before Whitsunday (*a*), "provided there be an interval of at least forty days between the date of the execution of the summons and the term of removal; or, where there is a separate ish as regards land and houses or otherwise, between the date of the execution of the summons and the ish which is first in date" (*b*). A probative lease specifying the term of endurance is equivalent to an extract decree of removing, provided (1) notice in the statutory form be given within the prescribed period (*c*) before the expiration of the term, or where there are separate terms, before the term which comes first; and (2) that a certificate by the sheriff-officer or messenger, or acknowledgment by the tenant or his known agents of such notice, be indorsed on the lease. The officer ejecting must have as his warrant the lease, and a written authority from the landlord or his factor or agent; and the removal must take place within six weeks from the expiration of the term of endurance (*d*). The same effect is given to a letter of removal granted by the tenant (*e*).'

(*a*) Grainger *v.* Geils, 1857; 19 D. 1010.
(*b*) 16 and 17 Vict. c. 80, § 29. Lyon *v.* Irvine, 1874; 1 R. 512. Leslie *v.* Jessiman, 1893; 10 Sh. Ct. Rep. 130. Leny *v.* Cameron, 1894; *ib.* 133 (summons only notice).
(*c*) This was forty days in the Act of 1853, but has been altered; see above, § 1265A.
(*d*) 16 and 17 Vict. c. 80, § 30. See Taylor *v.* E. Moray, 1892; 19 R. 399. 55 & 56 Vict. c. 17, sch. form 10 (extract).
(*e*) *Ib.* § 31.

1268B. '*Ejection of Possessors without Title.*—Summary petitions of removing or ejection are competent before the Judge Ordinary, without any warning, against persons who have no legal title, or who have merely precarious possession (*a*); and indeed one who has no title of possession at all may, it seems, be ejected by a proprietor without any judicial warrant; though it is generally inexpedient to do so (*b*). In such petitions appeal is a competent mode of review (*c*). Such a possessor has no right of action for illegal ejection, though he may have for assault or violence.'

(*a*) 2 Ersk. 6. § 49. E. Elgin's Trs. *v.* Walls, 1833; 11 S. 585. Nisbet *v.* Aikman, 1866; 4 Macph. 284. Hally *v.* Lang, 1867; 5 Macph. 951. Comp. Gordon and Stewart, *infra*, § 1269. Whyte *v.* Haddington Sch. Bd., 1874; 1 R. 1124. Robb *v.* Brearton, *supra*, § 1268 (*l*). Chisholm *v.* Chisholm, 1898; 14 Sh. Ct. Rep. 146 (squatter ejected by squatter). 2 Hunter, L. & T. 101 sq.
(*b*) Macdonald *v.* Dss. Leeds, 1860; 22 D. 1075. Macdonald *v.* Watson, 1883; 10 R. 1079. Edmonstone *v.* Jeffray, 1886; 13 R. 1038.
(*c*) Clarke *v.* Clarkes, 1890; 17 R. 1064. Barbour *v.* Chalmers & Co., 1891; 18 R. 610.

1268C.—'*Violent Profits* are penal damages incurred by one who takes or keeps possession without a legal title; and in actions of removing or summary ejection a defender must find caution for them at giving in his defences (*a*), unless he instantly verify a defence excluding the action (*b*). It is a good answer to a claim for violent profits that the defender was possessing in good faith, and the question when good faith comes to an end is determined according to the circumstances (*c*). The amount of violent profits, which may be demanded in an action upon the bond or in an action *eo nomine* (*d*), is by custom double the rent of houses in burghs (*e*), and in other subjects the greatest profit which the pursuer can prove that he would have made (*f*).'

(*a*) 2 Ersk. 6. § 54. A. of S., July 10, 1839, § 34. Robb *v.* Menzies, 1859; 21 D. 277. Cases, *infra.* Rankine, Leases, 508 sqq.
(*b*) Wilson *v.* Henderson, 1823; 2 S. 428, as in new edn. Johnstone *v.* Maxwell's Trs., 1845; 7 D. 1066. Oliver *v.* Weir's Trs., 1870; 8 Macph. 786.
(*c*) Barbour *v.* Bell, 1831; 9 S. 334. Houldsworth *v.* Brand's Trs., 1876; 3 R. 304. Rankine, Landownership, 72; Leases, 508.
(*d*) D. Buccleuch *v.* Hyslop, 1822; 2 S. 6; aff. 2 S. App. 43. E. Wemyss *v.* D. Queensberry's Exr., 1823; 2 S. 107; aff. 2 S. App. 70. Houldsworth *v.* Brand's Trs., 1877; 4 R. 369.
(*e*) 1 Stair, 9. § 27; 2. 9. § 44. Ersk. *l.c.* 2 Bell on Leases, 83.
(*f*) Stair, *l.c.* Gardner *v.* Beresford, 1877; 4 R. 1091. Houldsworth *v.* Brand's Trs., *cit.* D. Gordon *v.* Innes, 1828; 6 S. 996; aff. 4 W. & S. 305; 1832, 10 S. 16. See an action for simple damages, Tod *v.* Fraser, 1889; 17 R. 226; and cf. Houldsworth *v.* Brand's Trs., *cit.* Baird *v.* Kerr, 1894; 10 Sh. Ct. Rep. 153.

1269. In liferent leases and leases from liferenters there is a peculiarity as to the termination of the possession. Where the liferent tenant, or the liferenter of lands, has held the natural possession, no new possession is to be taken by his heir or representative; but the removing may be summary between terms, the heir or representative being entitled to reap the crop on paying a proportion of the rent, and having right to recompense for labour in preparing the ground (*a*). If subtenants have held under the person having such right, they are not to be summarily ejected, but may remain till the next Whitsunday (*b*).

(*a*) 2 Craig, 9. § 13. 2 Stair, 9. § 9, 23, 38. 2 Ersk. 6. § 49. Gordon *v.* Michie, 1794; M. 13,851; 2 Ill. 214. Stewart *v.* Grimmond, 1796; M. 13,853; Hume, 561. Thomson *v.* Marston, 1628; M. 8252. Johnstone's Trs., 1803; M. 15,207; and Udney *v.* Brown, *ib. cit.* 1 Hunter, L. & T. 126. See M. Tweeddale *v.* Sommer and M. Tweeddale *v.* Murray, *supra*, § 1262. This doctrine is said to apply only to leases for the life of the tenant, warning being necessary in leases for the life of the granter. 2 Hunter, L. & T. 60, 80. Ersk. *ubi cit.*, and Ivory's note, 133. The liferenter of lands is, of course, not within the category of tenants.
(*b*) 1491, c. 26. 2 Ersk. 6. § 49. 2 Stair, 9. § 23, 38.

1270. (2.) *Way-going Crop.*—Much difficulty has arisen about way-going crops in leases with Whitsunday entries. The general rule as to arable farms is, that the tenant is entitled to reap the crop which has been sown before the term of removal, 'whether or not that be the natural termination of the lease (*a*)'; the right of exclusive possession being his during seed-time (*b*). But he is not entitled to the use of the barns in thrashing, etc., the corn (*c*).

(*a*) Wemyss *v.* Drysdale, 1848; 10 D. 467; aff. 1849, 6 Bell's App. 455.

(*b*) Brodie *v.* Murdoch, 1777; M. *Tack*, Apx. 3; 2 Ill. 213. Scott *v.* Brodie, 1802; M. *Tack*, Apx. 8; 4 Pat. 311. See above, § 1261-4, as to dung and straw, grass, fallow, and steelbow. Fullarton *v.* Crawford, March 4, 1814; F. C. Harvey *v.* King's Coll. of Aberdeen, 1845; 8 D. 151. M. Tweeddale *v.* Murray, 1846; 8 D. 411; rev. 6 Bell, 125. M. Tweeddale *v.* Hume, 1848; 10 D. 1053. Hunter *v.* Miller, 1862; 24 D. 1011; aff. 1 Macph. 49; 4 Macq. 560. Bairds *v.* Harper, 1865; 3 Macph. 543. Wood *v.* Paton, 1874; 1 R. 868 (right to protect way-going crop from rabbits).

(*c*) M'Ewan *v.* Paterson, 1803; M. 13,891; Hume, 571. See M'Leod *v.* Bruce, 1809; Hume, 842. Anderson *v.* Tod, *ib.* Gordon *v.* Robertson, 1826; 2 W. & S. 115. Finlayson *v.* Pedie, 1829; 7 S. 329. Gatherer *v.* Cumming's Exrs., 1870; 8 Macph. 379.

1271. Renunciation.—A renunciation during the currency of the lease requires writing, formal and binding. But if the lease itself be informal, it is said that the renunciation may also be informal. In such case, however, it will require corroborative circumstances to the renunciation to balance *rei interventus* on the lease (*a*). No particular form of renunciation is required, further than that it must contain a clear and explicit notice to the right party forty days before Whitsunday (*b*). If the term be expired, renunciation may be proved by oath of party, but not by parole evidence (*c*). When the renunciation of the lease is in the shape of an obligation to remove without warning, it will not save from the necessity of giving a regular warning, unless it be dated at the regular time for giving warning (*d*). 'An accepted renunciation imports a discharge by both parties of all claims under the lease, *hinc inde*, so far as not reserved (*e*); but a renunciation effectual without acceptance does not discharge the landlord's claims (*f*).'

(*a*) 2 Craig, 9. § 2. 2 Stair, 9. § 35. 2 Ersk. 6. § 44. As to implied renunciation, see 2 Stair, 9. § 36. Milne *v.* Forbes, 1830; 8 S. 990. Hopkirk *v.* Kelly, 1834; 13 S. 223. Kennedy *v.* Carlyle, 1836; 15 S. 102.

(*b*) M'Intyre *v.* M'Nab's Trs., 1829; 8 S. 237; aff. 1831, 5 W. & S. 299; 2 Ill. 211.

(*c*) Schaw *v.* Palmer, 1605; M. 12,301; 1 Bell, Leases, p. 524, note. Carlisle *v.* Lawson, 1734; Elch. *Tack*, 1; cited by Kilk. in Edmonston *v.* Bryson, 1744; M. 12,415, 13,884.

(*d*) Perth Mags. *v.* Andrew, 1798; Hume, 562. Lockhart *v.* Twaddle, 1800; *ib.* 564. Paxton *v.* Slack, 1803; *ib.* 568. M'Laren *v.* M. Breadalbane, 1831; 10 S. 163. See Stevenson *v.* Baird, 1821; 1 S. 84. See above, § 1268A, and 16 and 17 Vict. c. 80, § 31.

(*e*) Jenkin *v.* Younger, 1825; 3 S. 639. Waterson *v.* Stewart, 1881; 9 R. 155. Lyons *v.* Anderson, 1886; 13 R. 1020. Walker's Trs. *v.* Manson, 1886; 13 R. 1198. Comp. § 1249 (*f*), above.

(*f*) Bidoulac *v.* Sinclair's Tr., 1889; 17 R. 144. Cf. Buttercase's Tr., § 1249, above. Scott & Chisholme *v.* Brown, 1893; 20 R. 575.

1271A. '*Breaks.*—In leases for a considerable time of subjects of any kind (*a*) it is common to stipulate for breaks, but these will be of more frequent occurrence in leases of subjects as to which the contract is at the outset of doubtful advantage, such as minerals. Breaks may be stipulated for by either party or by both, and it is of moment to make clear as well which party is intended to hold the option (*b*) as what intimation is required for its valid exercise. A break in the landlord's option is a reserved power of total resumption of the subject let; and a break in the tenant's option is a renunciation, the acceptance of which has been prearranged. Where a break is simply stipulated for, no reasons need be given for exercising the right to break (*c*). It is a question of construction whether the right is transmissible and to whom it transmits (*d*).'

(*a*) See also, as to urban subjects, § 1278 *fin.*, *infra.*

(*b*) Johnston *v.* Gordon, 1805; Hume, 822. Grant *v.* Sinclair, 1861; 23 D. 796.

(*c*) E. Rosebery *v.* Brown, March 7, 1811; F. C. Stewart *v.* Rutherfurd, 1863; 35 S. Jur. 307. Houldsworth *v.* Brand's Trs., 1875; 2 R. 683.

(*d*) Murray *v.* Brodie, 1806; Hume, 825. Ross *v.* M'Finlay, 1807. See 2 Hunter, L. & T. 118. Rankine, Leases, 476.

II. URBAN LEASES.

1272. 'The accepted division of leases into Rural and Urban leases, according to the subject of location, is neither essential nor exhaustive (*a*). The nominal distinction of the letting of an agricultural holding or rural tenement, and the letting of an urban tenement, is merely that, in the former, the principal subject of location is the surface of the soil—it may be with accessory buildings or other non-rural subjects;

while in the latter the *prædium* is a building—it may be with accessory ground or other non-urban subjects; but there are subjects of proper lease which fall under neither head, such as minerals, game, water-power. The general rules as to all three classes have been noticed in the foregoing sections.' In considering the doctrine of leases as applied to other than agricultural subjects—'at least to urban subjects'—there are some points on which a real or supposed difference exists.

'The chief distinctions as regards urban subjects are—(1) in the implied power to assign or sub-let (*b*); (2) in the obligation to maintain being the landlord's (*c*); (3) in the survival of the landlord's hypothec (*d*); (4) in the notice and mode of removing (*e*); (5) in the prescription of rents due under a verbal lease (*f*); and (6) in the removal of fixtures (*g*).'

(*a*) 1 Hunter, L. & T. 241. 2 Stair, 9. § 43; Brodie's note 6. Rankine, Leases, 167. Compare § 983, *supra* (servitudes).
(*b*) *Infra*, § 1274. (*c*) *Infra*, § 1274A.
(*d*) *Infra*, § 1275 sqq. (*e*) *Infra*, § 1278.
(*f*) *Supra*, § 628 sqq.
(*g*) *Supra*, § 1256; *infra*, § 1276 *fin*., 1473, 1475.

1273. Constitution and Effect.—Here the same rules apply as in agricultural subjects. Verbal leases are good only for a year; while *rei interventus* may, if clearly applicable, establish a right for a longer term. Possession is the completion of the lease; and it is equally effectual, under the Act 1449, against singular successors in other subjects as in agricultural leases (*a*). As a tenant in land is bound to enter and stock the farm, so is the tenant of a house bound to furnish it (*b*). 'It was said that' the landlord of an inn is not to set up a rival inn without abating rent (*c*). 'But the case quoted for this proposition, if it is well decided, is to be supported only on the ground of sterility (a road having been diverted); and it has been settled that from the mere granting of a lease no contract can be implied by which the granter is restricted in the use of his other property (*d*). Actions for house rents, not founded on written obligations, prescribe if not pursued within three years (*e*).'

(*a*) 2 Ersk. 6. § 27. 1 Bell, Leases, 34. Rae *v.* Finlayson, 1680; M. 10,211; 2 Ill. 214. Waddel *v.* Brown, 1794; M. 10,309. See above, § 1190-1. Macarthur *v.* Simpson, 1804; M. 15,181; 1 Bell's Com. 65 (63, M'L.'s ed.).
(*b*) Thomson *v.* Handyside, 1833; 12 S. 557. See Whitelaw *v.* Fulton, 1871; 10 Macph. 27. Wright *v.* Wightman, 1875; 3 R. 68. Gardner *v.* Anderson Bros., 1889; 6 Sh. Ct. Rep. 57 (auctioneer's rooms).
(*c*) Campbell *v.* Watt, 1795; Hume, 788.
(*d*) Craig *v.* Millar, 1888; 15 R. 1005. To that effect an express condition seems to be required. See, *e.g.*, Davie *v.* Stark, 1876; 3 R. 1114.
(*e*) 1579, c. 83. Above, § 628 sqq.

1274. Power to Assign or Sub-set.—The rule (differently from agricultural leases) is, that the tenant, even for a single year, has power to assign or sub-set, when not expressly prohibited (*a*). But it is implied that the appropriate use of the subject shall not be altered or encroached upon '(inverted)' (*b*), or an inn or shop shut up (*c*); and when the use of the subject is combined with the arrangements of a manufactory, the *delectus personæ* prevails to prevent sub-lease or assignation (*d*).

(*a*) 2 Bankt. 9. § 12. 1 Bell, Com. 76; 2 *ib*. 32. 1 Bell, Leases, 184. 2 Ersk. 6. § 32, note. 1 Hunter, L. & T. 242. Rankine, Leases, 167. Aitchison *v.* Binny, 1748; M. 10,405; Elchies, *Tack*, 13; Notes, 444; 2 Ill. 214. Anderson *v.* Alexander, July 10, 1811; F. C. See above, § 1216. Hatton *v.* Clay & M'Luckie, 1865; 4 Macph. 263. As to leases for a year or less, see 1 Hunter, L. & T. 246. Rankine, Leases, 168. Murray *v.* M'Robbie, 1874; 1 Sel. Sh. Ct. Ca. 278. And as to furnished houses, Hunter and Rankine, *ubi citt.*
(*b*) Gordon *v.* Crawford, 1825; 4 S. 95. See above, § 1224. Leechman *v.* Sievewright, 1826; 4 S. 683. Reid *v.* Keith, 1868; 6 Macph. 768; rev. 1870, 8 Macph. H. L. 110; L. R. 2 Sc. App. 39 (sales by auction in shop). D. Argyll *v.* M'Arthur, 1861; 23 D. 1236. Baillie *v.* M'Kie, 1842; 4 D. 1520. Leck *v.* Fulton & Thomson, 1854; 17 D. 408. Hood *v.* Miller, 1855; 17 D. 411.
(*c*) Graham *v.* Stevenson, 1792; Hume, 781. In this case damages were given for shutting up an inn, contrary to the fair meaning of the lease; but while the tenant of a shop may be ordained to plenish and keep it in fair condition by fires, etc., he will not be ordered to keep it open and carry on business in it. Whitelaw *v.* Fulton, 1871; 10 Macph. 27.
(*d*) E. Elgin's Trs. *v.* Walls, 1833; 12 S. 585. See above, § 1218. This doctrine has been questioned; see 1 Hunter, L. & T. 242; 1 Bell, Com. 76; but see also Rankine, Leases, 167.

1274A. *Repairs.*—'The landlord of an urban tenement is bound, like the landlord of a rural subject (*a*), to put the subject of lease into a tenantable condition at entry (*b*). But he is further bound to maintain it during the lease in the like condition (*c*), excepting deterioration arising out of the tenant's fault or negligence (*d*), or those of a third party (*e*). A breach of this obligation may infer any of four remedies on the tenant's part—(1) a right to execute the necessary repairs on the landlord's failure, deducting the expense from the rent (*f*); (2) a claim for damages (*g*); (3) a right of refusing to enter, or of abandoning the possession (*h*); and (4) a right to retain the rent (*i*).

'The exercise of the remedy of repairing may be safeguarded by application to the Sheriff, or, in burgh, to the Dean of Guild, whose warrant will settle the necessity and expense of the repairs (*k*). Refusal to possess is not justified unless, owing to the extent and duration of the deprivation of accommodation, occupation of the premises is a thing out of reason (*l*). All remedy may be lost by acceptance of the premises in disrepair, or by continuing to occupy without objection (*m*).

(*a*) *Supra*, § 1253 sqq.

(*b*) 2 Ersk. 6. § 43. Compare § 141–2 and § 1208, *supra*.

(*c*) Ersk. *ut supra*. 2 Ersk. Pr. 6. § 17. 1 Bankt. 20. § 15; 2 *ib.* 9. § 20. 1 Hunter, L. & T. 222. Rankine, Leases, 230. *Supra*, § 33. Allan *v.* Robertson's Trs., 1891; 18 R. 932. M'Dougall *v.* Gray, 1894; 11 Sh. Ct. Rep. 69 (not to light stair).

(*d*) 1 Bankt. 20. § 20. Ersk. *ut supra*. Sutherland *v.* Robertson, 1736; M. 13,979. Hardie *v.* Black, 1768; M. 10,133. M'Lellan *v.* Ker, 1797; M. 10,134.

(*e*) Allan, *cit.* (*c*). See Stewart *v.* Smith, 1895; 12 Sh. Ct. Rep. 336 (house wrecked by railway). Lusk *v.* Todd, 1897; 13 Sh. Ct. Rep. 265.

(*f*) Ersk. *ut supra*. Baird *v.* Inglis, 1671; 2 B. S. 562. Hamilton *v.* ——, 1667; M. 10,121. Deans *v.* Abercromby, 1681; M. 10,122.

(*g*) Reid *v.* Baird, 1876; 4 R. 234. Wilson, Guthrie, & Co. *v.* Wright, 1891; 8 Sh. Ct. Rep. 51. Dickie *v.* Colville, 1894; 10 Sh. Ct. Rep. 282.

(*h*) Kippen *v.* Oppenheim, 1847; 10 D. 242 (vermin). Compare § 1208, *supra*.

(*i*) *Supra*, § 71, 1231. Rankine, Leases, 304.

(*k*) Ersk. *ubi cit.*

(*l*) Allan *v.* Markland, 1882; 10 R. 383 (fire). Compare § 1208, *supra*. Drummond *v.* Hunter, 1869; 7 M. 347 (fire). Duff *v.* Fleming, 1870; 8 M. 769 (fire). Scot. Her. Sec. Co. *v.* Granger, 1881; 8 R. 459 (defective drainage). Reid *v.* Baird, *supra* (*g*).

(*m*) Henderson *v.* Munn, 1888; 15 R. 859. Drummond, *cit.* *Supra*, § 27. Contrast, as to known danger, Webster *v.* Brown, 1892; 19 R. 765, with Shields *v.* Dalziel, 1897; 24 R. 849; Hill *v.* Hubner, 1897; *ib.* 875; and Smith *v.* Baker & Sons, 1891; A. C. 325. Rice *v.* Muirhead, 1896; 12 Sh. Ct. Rep. 177.

1275. Hypothec.—In urban subjects, comprehending dwelling-houses, shops, warehouses, cellars, manufactories, breweries, etc., the hypothec is over the *invecta et illata*. And the same rule applies to dwelling-houses in the country which are let merely as such.

1276. *Invecta et illata* comprehend household furniture, plate, paintings, books, and all moveables belonging to the tenant, 'but not necessarily those belonging to (*a*)' his family (*b*). It does not seem to comprehend cash, bonds, bills, or other documents of debt. Neither does it seem to comprehend wearing apparel (*c*). Shop goods, raw materials of manufacture, implements of trade, etc., are subjects of hypothec; but the goods are vendible till sequestrated (*d*); 'and in questions with *bonâ fide* purchasers without notice of the sequestration even afterwards — to make the hypothec effectual against them, the shop must be closed, or the sequestrated goods removed (*e*).' The shop-books are not subject to hypothec, to the effect of entitling the landlord to levy the debts. Goods of third parties in a warehouse, or cellar, or inn, are not subject to hypothec, whether they be there on pledge or deposit, for manufacture, for sale, or *in transitu* (*f*). But where the tenant has furniture on hire, a different rule has been introduced, in consideration of the landlord's right to have the house furnished, and the presumed consent of the hirer that the furniture let shall supply the requisite security. So, where the tenant has the furniture on hire from a broker, the articles are liable to the hypothec of his landlord (*g*). Where furniture is with the tenant on gratuitous loan, it seems now to be held that it is to be classed with hired furniture and liable to hypothec (*h*). But when taken possession of, or detained in a house against the will of the owner, furniture is not subject to the landlord's hypothec (*i*); or when deposited in the house, it is not so liable (*k*). 'An exception to the general rule has been allowed in the practice of some inferior courts, where specific articles, not being ordinary and necessary parts of the furniture ("plenishing") of a house or shop, are lent gratuitously or let on hire—at least where there is a known custom of hiring out such articles, as in the case of pianofortes and sewing-machines. In such cases the landlord cannot be presumed to rely on the security of the particular thing, or the owner of it "to take the hazard of the rent" (*l*). This exception, however, is not recognised but negatived, in regard to articles let for hire, by the latest decision of the Supreme Court (*m*); and the general principle seems to apply to all furniture taken on hire by the tenant or his family (*n*). Trade fixtures, attached by the tenant to the subject, thus become the landlord's, subject to the tenant's right of removing them (*o*).'

(*a*) Bell *v.* Andrews, 1885; 12 R. 961 (pianoforte presented to tenant's daughter residing with him). In editions previous to the 9th, the words here were "the tenant *and* his family."

(*b*) 2 Ersk. 6. § 64. Bell, Leases, 387, note. 2 Pothier, 277, § 241–3. Anon., 1672 ; 2 B. Sup. 670 ; 2 Ill. 215. Css. of Callander *v.* Campbell, 1703 ; M. 6244. Christie *v.* M'Pherson, Dec. 14, 1814 ; F. C. ; 2 Ill. 196. As to the right of hypothec in relation to cautioners for the rent, see above, § 1238.

(*c*) Css. of Callander, *supra* (*b*). 2 Bell's Com. 30. 2 Hunter, L. & T. 375.

(*d*) 2 Ersk. 6. § 64. As to plants in a nursery, see Begbie *v.* Boyd, 1837 ; 16 S. 233. 2 Hunter, L. & T. 373.

(*e*) More's Notes on Stair, lxxxiii. 2 Hunter, L. & T. 380. Below, § 1277.

(*f*) Cowan *v.* Perry, 1804 ; 2 Bell's Com. 30, 31 ; 2 Ill. 215. Girdwood & Co. *v.* Wilson, 1834 ; 12 S. 576. Pulsometer Co. *v.* Gracie, 1886 ; 14 R. 316 (samples in commission agent's office). Compare § 1245 (*g*), above.

(*g*) Wauchope *v.* Gall & Ross, 1805 ; Hume, 227. Stewart *v.* Bell, May 31, 1814 ; F. C. and Apx. Penson & Robertson, petrs., June 6, 1820 ; F. C. Nelmes & Co. *v.* Ewing, 1883 ; 11 R. 193 (billiard-table, etc.).

(*h*) Wilson *v.* Spankie, Dec. 17, 1813 ; F. C. ; 2 Ill. 215. See Fountainhall's note, 2 B. Sup. 670. 2 Bell's Com. 31, where a different view is suggested. Cowan (*f*). Graham's Trs. *v.* Currie, 1896 ; 12 Sh. Ct. Rep. 129. In Adam *v.* Sutherland, 1863, 2 Macph. 6, the question is left open ; and see Macdonald *v.* Westren, 1888 ; 15 R. 988 (goods on sale or return). Rankine, Leases, 346.

(*i*) Jaffray *v.* Carrick, 1836 ; 15 S. 43.

(*k*) Cowan, *supra* (*f*). Adam, *supra* (*h*).

(*l*) See the following Sheriff Court cases :—Milne *v.* Singer Manufg. Co., 1881 ; 25 J. of J. 499. Singer Manufg. Co. *v.* Docherty, 1882 ; 26 J. of J. 445. Stevenson *v.* Donaldson, 1884 ; 28 J. of J. 277. Wheeler & Wilson Co. *v.* M'Ritchie & Bruce, 1884 ; *ib.* 498. Watson *v.* Singer Manufg. Co., 1884 ; *ib.* 658 ; 1 Sh. Ct. Rep. 20. See 4 Stair, 25. § 3. 2 Bell's Com. 30 (29, M'L.'s ed.). L. Deas in Adam *v.* Sutherland, and Nelmes & Co. *v.* Ewing, *citt.* ; and as to custom, the English cases cited in § 109 (*f*), *supra* ; and Marston *v.* Kerr's Tr., 1879 ; 6 R. 898. Comp. below, § 1314–1317.

(*m*) Bell *v.* Andrews, *supra* (*a*).

(*n*) See Dickson *v.* Singer Manufg. Co., 1886 ; 30 J. of J. 658 ; 2 Sel. Sh. Ct. Ca. 269 (Fifeshire). M'Dougall's Trs. *v.* Maver & Son, 1889 ; 5 Sh. Ct. R. 325. Duncanson & Henderson *v.* Maver & Son, 1894 ; 11 Sh. Ct. Rep. 232. Middleton *v.* Macbeth, 1894 ; *ib.* 9. Park *v.* Storrey, 1897 ; 14 *ib.* 44.

(*o*) Brand's Trs. *v.* Brand's Tr., 1876 ; L. R. 1 App. Ca. 762 ; 3 R. H. L. 16. Miller *v.* Muirhead, 1894 ; 21 R. 658. Smith *v.* Harrison & Co.'s Tr., 1894 ; 21 R. 330. Compare § 1473, 1475, below.

1277. The hypothec gives security for each year's rent successively over the *invecta* ; the same space of three months after the term, which is allowed in following the hypothec on cattle in agricultural farms, being given to make it effectual in urban tenements (*a*). In the rent so secured will be included whatever is so combined with the rent as a consideration for the use of the particular subject, that it fairly makes a slump consideration for the whole (*b*). In competition with other rights, it will not prevail over the Crown, or the superior, or servants, or undertakers for funeral expenses (*c*). It will not bar the tenant from selling his goods in his shop or warehouse. But a buyer, though he has paid the price, if he have not got delivery, will not prevail against the landlord (*d*) ; yet it has been doubted in particular cases whether the buyer will not prevail. And as to one who has got delivery by the key of the repository (that repository being the landlord's), it would seem that the warehouse of a trader would, in a sale of this kind, in the ordinary course of trade, be held to be open market, and the purchaser safe. By statute (*e*) it has been provided, that goods imported into the owner's cellar may be effectually sold by him on observing certain requisites ; and such a sale would seem to protect the buyer against the landlord. By another statute (*f*), distillers are allowed to warehouse spirits somewhat on the same footing with goods under the statute last referred to, but there is no such provision for sale, and the landlord was preferred to a purchaser who had received an order of delivery (*g*) ; the purchaser being declared entitled to an assignation to the hypothec as extending over other effects.

(*a*) Dick *v.* Lands, 1630 ; M. 6243 ; 2 Ill. 216. See above, § 1240, 1245. M'Leod *v.* Thomson's Crs., 1805 ; Hume 226 (hypothec effectual by sequestration within, though sale not till after, three months). As to retaining and "carrying back" the subjects hypothecated, see above, § 1234, 1239.

(*b*) Catterns *v.* Tennant, 1834 ; 12 S. 686 ; rev. 1 S. & M'L. 695. See Auld *v.* Baird, 1827 ; 5 S. 264. Kilmarnock Gas Co. *v.* Smith, 1872 ; 11 Macph. 58 ; and Herit. Sec. Invt. Assoc. *v.* Wingate & Co.'s Tr., 1880 ; 7 R. 1094 (where there was an attempt to create a security over moveables, giving the lender the benefit of the landlord's hypothec). Sandeman *v.* Thomson, 1866 ; 1 Sel. Sh. Ct. Ca. 75 (steam power—separable let).

(*c*) See above, § 1241, 1247 ; below, § 1404. Adam *v.* Sutherland, 1863 ; 2 Macph. 6.

(*d*) Kinniel *v.* Menzies, 1790 ; M. 4973. 19 and 20 Vict. c. 60, § 4 ; re-enacted by 56 and 57 Vict. c. 71, § 61 (5). See Herit. Sec. Invt. Assoc., *supra* (*b*). Above, § 1276.

(*e*) 6 Geo. IV. c. 112, § 9. See below, § 1306.

(*f*) 4 Geo. IV. c. 94.

(*g*) Wyld & Co. *v.* Richardson, 1832 ; 10 S. 538.

1278. Removing.—The regular possession in urban subjects is from Whitsunday to Whitsunday ; 'and, as in agricultural leases, tacit relocation takes place where the steps towards removing are not duly taken (*a*).' Where a garden in which vegetables are cultivated is let along with a house, the rule in practice sanctioned by the Court is that possession of the garden is given at Candlemas ; but the small gardens and greens of houses in town are entered to along with the house (*b*). 'The custom of many places postponed the date of actual removal and entry to a date later than the legal term, and in order to remove the inconvenience which arose from this customary term being different in different places, it is enacted by the Removal Terms Scotland Act, 1886 (which followed the earlier Act of 1881 relating to burghs only), that in leases, subsequent to the Act, of dwelling-houses, shops, and other buildings and their appurtenances, including a dwelling-house or building let along with land for agricultural or other purposes, a Whitsunday or Martinmas entry or removal shall, in the absence of express stipulation, be held to be at noon of the 28th of May and the 28th of November respectively; or of the day following, if any of these days fall upon a Sunday (*c*). There is nothing in this Act to affect the obligation to pay rent at the term of Whitsunday or Martinmas; but it has been held that furniture is not before the 28th of May hypothecated for the rent falling due at Martinmas, that being due for a period which did not begin till 28th May (*d*).'

The mode of warning and removing from urban subjects (including houses in the country without land) is generally regulated by local custom; the forms of the statute 1555, or even of the Act of Sederunt 14th December 1756, not being necessary (*e*). But there must be warning or verbal notice, or chalking of the door by a burgh officer, forty days before the term of removal (*f*). In Edinburgh, the custom is to give warning at Candlemas; but that is not an absolute rule (*g*). The same term of warning must be given by the tenant to the landlord, in order to put an end to the lease on his part. 'By the Act of 1886, above referred to, it is provided that when a house (other than a dwelling-house or building let along with land for agricultural purposes) is let for a period not exceeding four calendar months, notice of removal must be given "as many days before the date of ish as shall be equivalent to at least one-third of the full period of duration of the lease" (*h*). All notices of removal from houses not let along with land for agricultural purposes may be given by posting registered letters (*i*).' A summary process of removing has been provided for subjects let for less than a year, at a rent not exceeding £30 (*k*).

The parties may stipulate for a break in the term; which, according to its fair construction, will entitle the tenant to remove, or the landlord to resume possession. But a break in favour of the landlord 'for his own personal benefit or occupation' will not entitle a trustee or agent for him to take the benefit of it (*l*).

(*a*) Above, § 1265.
(*b*) Renton *v.* Younger, 1823; 2 S. 214; 2 Ill. 217.
(*c*) 49 and 50 Vict. c. 50, which repeals 44 and 45 Vict. c. 39.
(*d*) Thomson *v.* Barclay, 1883; 10 R. 694. Donald *v.* Leitch, 1886; 13 R. 790. Sawers *v.* Kinnair, 1897; 25 R. 45. See M'Intyre *v.* M'Nab's Trs., 1831; 5 W. & S. 299.
(*e*) 2 Ersk. 6. § 47. Riddel *v.* Zinzan, 1671; M. 13,828. Lundin *v.* Hamilton, 1758; M. 13,845. Robb *v.* Menzies, 1859; 21 D. 277. Scott *v.* Boyd & Latta, 1829; 7 S. 592. Chirnside *v.* Park, 1843; 5 D. 864. Lambert *v.* Smith, 1864; 3 Macph. 43 (notice to tenant's wife). Slowey *v.* Moir, 1865; 4 Macph. 1 (do.). Dunlop & Co. *v.* Meiklem, 1876; 4 R. 11. Gilchrist *v.* Westren, 1890; 17 R. 363. Robb *v.* Brearton, 1895; 22 R. 885. 2 Hunter, L. & T. 82.
(*f*) Tait *v.* Sligo, 1766; M. 13,864; 2 Ill. 218. Jollie *v.* Stevenson, 1781; M. 13,865. See Robb *v.* Menzies (*e*). Robertson *v.* Draffan, 1885; 1 Sh. Ct. Rep. 81.
(*g*) Jack *v.* E. Kellie, 1795; M. 13,866. Tenants of houses there have now, in general, till 15th March to retake them.
(*h*) 49 and 50 Vict. c. 50, § 5. (*i*) *Ib.* § 6.
(*k*) 1 and 2 Vict. c. 119, § 8. Lees, Small Debt Handbook, 129. And see 16 and 17 Vict. c. 80, § 29, 30. Shotts Iron Co. *v.* Paton, 1857; 19 D. 755.
(*l*) Davidson *v.* Girvan, 1838; 16 S. 1125. And see § 1271A, above.

III. RENTALLERS AND KINDLY TENANTS.

1279. Nature of the Right.—That sort of right which, originating in villenage in England, became copyhold, and is now of so much importance in the territorial law of that part of the island, arose in a manner nearly similar in Scotland; but it is now to be found existing only in particular districts, under the name of Rental-right and Kindly Tenancy. The villains of the ancient law grew into kindly tenants (*a*), under the Crown, the Church, and the Barons. They held their land at first by sufferance, or at will; for the performance, probably, of agricultural services in the mains of the manor or barony. They were enrolled in the rental book of the King's stewart, or in that of their lord; and this, or a copy of the entry, was their sole title. They came to be admitted to a sort of hereditary right; their widows being permitted to continue their possession, and their sons to succeed. Rental-rights had no ish, or term of expiration; and so the alternative was, either to regard them, the rentallers, as perpetual tenants (which they could not effectually be against singular successors, without sasine), or as liferenters.

(*a*) See 2 Ross's Lect. 478 sqq. Craig, 275. 2 Stair, 9. § 15. 2 Ersk. 6. § 37, 38. D. Montrose *v*. Provan's Trs., 1887; 14 R. 378.

1280. The Crown Rentallers were by statute declared to be mere liferenters (*a*). But the King's kindly tenants of the four towns of Lochmaben were, by successive warrants and protections of the King, in 1592, 1602, 1664, declared to have right to continue their possession undisturbed, and at the old rent, as long as they should pay the same; and the Act of 1587 was not held to operate after a barony was vested in a subject. Accordingly, in an action of declarator, it was held "that the pursuers had such a right of property to the lands that they could not be removed, and might dispone these rights to extraneous persons" (*b*). It has been further held, that the *dominium utile* of those lands has been fully dissolved from the Crown, and so is liable in teind-duty for the minister's stipend (*c*). The right of those kindly tenants may also serve as the ground of real securities for debt by feudal form (*d*).

(*a*) 1587, c. 68.
(*b*) Kindly Tenants of Lochmaben *v*. V. Stormont, 1726; M. 15,195, 15,185; aff. 1 Cr. & St. 77; 2 Ill. 218.
(*c*) M. Queensberry *v*. Wright, 1838; 16 S. 439.
(*d*) Irvine & Jop *v*. Collins, 1795; M. 10,316; Bell's Cases, 145. Mounsey *v*. Kennedy, Nov. 30, 1808; F. C.

1281. Church Rentallers.—On the eve of the Reformation, the possessions of the kindly tenants of the Church seem to have been much disturbed, by the anxiety of the clerical lords and monasteries to feu out their lands. But the number and influence of those tenants induced the Legislature to give them protection to a certain extent (*a*); and when questions arose with singular successors in kirk lands, those rights were viewed as ordinary leases, and, being without ish, they were held good only for a year. Afterwards they were construed to be liferents (*b*), renewable at will to the heir, but not alienable; the *delectus personæ* being strict.

(*a*) 1563, c. 77.
(*b*) 2 Craig, 9. § 24. 2 Stair, 9. § 15, 20. 2 Ersk. 6. § 37. 2 Ross, 480.

1282. Ordinary Rentallers, holding of subjects, were considered as mere liferenters; or if heirs were mentioned, the first heir only was held to have right (*a*).

(*a*) 2 Ersk. 6. § 38. E. Galloway *v*. Tailzifer, 1631; M. 7194; 2 Ill. 218. Ahannay *v*. Aiton, 1632; M. 15,191. Wilson *v*. Wilson, 1859; 21 D. 309. 1 Hunter, L. & T. 423, 483, ii. 123. A kind of rental right held in perpetuity under Building Associations was introduced by 18 and 19 Vict. c. 88 (Dwelling-Houses (Scotland) Act, 1855); repealed by 53 and 54 Vict. c. 70, Sch. 7.

BOOK SECOND

PART II

REAL RIGHTS OF PROPERTY AND POSSESSION IN MOVEABLES

INTRODUCTION

1283. The law of property in moveables is less peculiar than that of territorial property. Moveables were of little consideration under our early law. Possession was the badge of property in them while a man lived; and by equal division among his family on his death, those of his moveables were disposed of which were not requisite for the heir's equipment for his feudal duties (*a*). Moveables unaffected by any of the rules of the feudal law, remained under the rules of a jurisprudence immediately derived from the Civilians; in many of its doctrines modified, and in some respects improved, by the Canonists. In modern times, moveable property is frequently of much greater value than property in land. It is the part of the wealth of the people most generally diffused, and the most frequent subject of transaction and of transference. And although it makes not so great a figure in our law books, the modes of its transference being simple, and less exposed to those blunders and mistakes out of which so much litigation and so many doubts arise, a correct knowledge of the rules by which it is regulated, and of their combinations, is of great consequence in the daily transactions of life. Besides money, jewels, and goods in immediate possession, one may have shares in Government or bank stock; ships; commodities and money in distant countries; or in the hands of manufacturers, factors, bankers, debtors. And those funds, so various and so widely scattered, may be subject to the laws of various countries, so as, on marriage, on death, or on bankruptcy, to give rise to many questions of conveyance and succession, in the decision of which the principles of international law mingle with those of the law of Scotland.

Referring to future discussions for the nicer discriminations between heritable and moveable property (*b*), the moveable estate may here be described as comprehending whatever moves, or is capable of being put in motion and transferred from place to place, without change of nature and structure, or destruction of anything to which it may be attached. And in the same class are comprehended all personal debts.

(*a*) See below, § 1903 sqq. (*b*) See below, § 1470–1504.

1284. Ownership in moveables is a right of exclusive and absolute use and enjoyment, with uncontrolled powers of disposal, provided no use be made of the subject, and no alienation attempted, which, for purposes of public policy, convenience, or justice, are, by the general disposition of the common law, or by special enactments of the Legislature, forbidden; or from which, by obligation or contract, the owner has bound himself to abstain. Of restraints on grounds of policy in agriculture and in commerce, there are examples in the laws regulating exports and imports, which directly by prohibition, or indirectly by high duties, impose embargoes on commodities; in the corn and distillery laws; in the laws relating to forestalling and regrating; in the navigation laws for the encouragement of British shipping (*a*). Restraints by contract are chiefly indirect—by the operation of pledge, retention, and hypothec, as qualified rights of property.

The subjects composing the moveable estate may be distinguished into two classes—Corporeal and Incorporeal.

(*a*) Many of these restraints have been either abolished or modified.

CHAPTER I

MODES OF ACQUIRING PROPERTY IN CORPOREAL MOVEABLES

1285. Nature of Corporeal Moveables.—Moveables corporeal in Scottish law correspond with chattels in England. They include all things which, being themselves capable of motion or of being moved, may be perceived by the senses—seen, touched, taken possession of: as ships; household furniture; goods and effects of all kinds; farm stock and implements; horses, cattle, and other animals; corn, money, jewels, wearing apparel.

1286. Modes of Acquisition.—The property or ownership of moveables corporeal is acquired by modes which have been distinguished into original and derivative; the former having reference to the first act of appropriation, or subsequent change of the thing appropriated; the latter being by transference from one who has already acquired the ownership. The latter is in the present day the more frequent and important mode of acquiring property; yet the original modes of acquisition sometimes occur in argument, or for decision. The original modes of acquisition depend either on the first effectual apprehension of a subject having no owner; or on a natural, accidental, or intentional change, by which a new subject of property is produced. The former is called "Occupancy," the latter "Accession." The derivative mode of acquisition is by sale or other "Transference."

I. OCCUPANCY.

1287. Definition.—Occupancy is the act of apprehending, with a purpose of appropriation, things which have no owner. It is distinguished as applicable to two classes of cases; one comprehending things never before appropriated; the other, things which have at one time been appropriated, but have ceased to belong to anyone. The same rule was followed in both cases in the Roman law; but in Scotland, property is acquired by occupancy only in the former case. In the latter, the right goes to the Crown, and is generally given as a donation either to the finder or to another.

1288. As to things not hitherto appropriated, the general rule is, that they belong to the occupant: "quod nullius est, fit occupantis." Shells, pearls, pebbles, or precious stones on the seashore; animals *feræ naturæ*, beasts, birds, fish,—fall under this rule (*a*): so that game, salmon, etc., taken by a trespasser belong to the taker, unless when forfeited by statute (*b*); and the only proper exception is of royal fish, which belong to the Crown (*c*).

(*a*) As to theft of such things, see Wilson *v.* Dykes, 1872; 10 Macph. 444.

(*b*) Scott *v.* Everitt, 1853; 15 D. 288. It appears that in England the property of animals *feræ naturæ* is in the owner of the land in which they are started and captured, and not in the captor. Blades *v.* Higgs, 12 C. B. N. S. 501; 32 L. J. C. P. 182; 34 L. J. C. P. 286.

(*c*) 2 Stair, 1. § 33. 2 Ersk. 1. § 10.

1289. Property, how Vested.—The act of appropriation is effectual to vest the property only when complete. But it is held complete while fairly proceeding towards full accomplishment. So, if one wound an animal to death, or so that it cannot escape, or if one, without wounding it, have an animal in pursuit, and not beyond reach, another coming in and taking the animal does not deprive the first of his right—the first being deemed the lawful occupant (*a*).

(1.) *In Whale-fishing*, an important branch of national industry, this general principle is not found to answer all the exigencies of the situation, and particular rules are established. Where a fish is harpooned with the line attached, it is a fast fish, and belongs to the striker; and this is also the rule where the harpoon has come out of the fish, or has been detached from the line, but the fish is so entangled in the line as to continue in the power and management of the striker. Another striking the fish is held a friendly harpoon. Where one has struck a fish, and another comes unsolicited and does an act which occasions the unfixing of the first striker's harpoon, and then kills it himself, he kills it for the first striker. Where, without any such interference, the line breaks, or is not in management, it is a loose fish (*b*). There appear to be in some fishing stations peculiar rules; as in the south whale fishery, a rule that where a fish is harpooned with a droug (which is a harpoon with a short line and buoy attached to it), a share is given (*c*). 'The conventional rule observed in one locality cannot be applied in another where a different mode of fishing is used; and if no conventional rules have been established applicable to such place and mode of fishing, the general law of occupancy will solve the question, viz. that the person first engaged, so long as he continues the pursuit with a reasonable prospect of success, excludes the interference of another. In the northern seas the common law of occupancy has been entirely set aside by the rule of "fast and loose" (*d*).'

(*a*) 2 Stair, 1. § 33. Sutter, *infra* (*d*).
(*b*) Stair, *ut supra*. Row *v*. Addison & Sons, 1792; Ivory's Ersk. p. 224, Nicolson's ed. 258; aff. 3 Pat. 334; 1 Ill. 374, printed Rose. Littledale *v*. Scaith, 1 Taunt. 243, note. Hogarth *v*. Jackson, 1 M. & M. 58. Skinner *v*. Chapman, 1 M. & M. 59, note; 1 Ill. 374. Hutcheson *v*. Dundee Whale-fishing Co., 1830; 5 Mur. 164.
(*c*) Fennings *v*. L. Grenville, 1 Taunt. 241; 9 R. R. 760 and pref.
(*d*) Sutter *v*. Aberdeen Arctic Co., 1861; 23 D. 465; rev. 1862, 4 Macq. 355.

1290. (2.) *Wild and Domesticated Animals.*—Things which may be appropriated by occupancy are not capable of being so acquired while the possession of the first holder continues; as in the case of wild animals confined (deer in a forest, rabbits in a warren, pigeons in a dovecot, bees in a hive), or tame and domesticated animals, though not confined (*a*). When wild animals confined and appropriated have regained their natural liberty, they are again free to be acquired by occupancy. But a different rule prevails in respect to such animals as have *animum revertendi*; as pigeons, hawks in pursuit of prey, bees hiving while pursued by the owner (*b*); and also as to such as are marked for private property, as deer and swans with collars.

(*a*) 2 Ersk. 1. § 10. See 1 Hume, 82; and above, § 646. As to cats, see Whittingham *v*. Ideson, 8 Upper Can. L. J. 14.
(*b*) 2 Stair, 1. § 33. 2 Ersk. 1. § 10.

1291. (3.) *Things Lost.* — Things already appropriated, but lost, forgotten, or abandoned, fall under a different rule from that which regulates things that have never been appropriated. The rule is, "Quod nullius est fit domini regis." The principle on which this rests is public expediency—to avoid fraud, contests, and litigation, together with some slight purpose of adding to the public revenue (*a*). 'The rule operates only when the article lost can be held as abandoned by the owner. Till then, subject to police regulations under certain Acts of Parliament, the finder is entitled to possession against all but the true owner.'

(*a*) Stair and Ersk. *ut supra*. See Sands *v*. Bell & Balfour, May 22, 1810; F. C.; 1 Ill. 375. See below, § 1293, 1294. The finder of a bank note is entitled to retain it as against everyone but the true owner, therefore against the owner of the shop or premises in which he has found it. Bridges *v*. Hawksworth, 21 L. J. Q. B. 75. Hogg *v*. Armstrong & Mowat, 1874; 1 Sel. Sh. Ct. Ca. 438. The finder is answerable for the same degree of diligence as a depositary. 1 Smith's L. C. 190.

1292. Wrecks. — These belong to the Crown, on the principle (in modern times) of restraint on piracy and peculation. Even by our early law, wreck was given up to the owner if any living thing escaped; or, although there should not be any living creature on board, if there were any marks to identify the property, and if within year and day (or while the thing was extant) satisfactory proof was made to that effect (*a*). It appears to have been found necessary by statute in the fifteenth century, to introduce a rule of reciprocal dealing with other nations in respect to wreck, which was acted on so late as the close of the seventeenth century (*b*). But the old law of wreck, which held the existence of some living creature necessary to the claim of restitution, was rejected by the Court of Session in the beginning of last century (*c*), and half a century afterwards was, on an admirable argument of Lord Mansfield, banished from English jurisprudence (*d*). It may be considered as completely superseded by the modern statutes passed for the preservation of property in this condition (*e*). By those statutes, the officers of the customs and excise 'were' bound to keep all wrecks and goods for the owners; and although the right of the Crown, and those having right from the Crown, is secured by those Acts, the grantee of the Crown 'was,' in like manner with the officers of customs, bound to preserve the property for the owners (*f*). Salvage is claimable against the Crown, or the Crown's grantee, taking the wreck. In particular circumstances, there is so far a departure from the common rule of wreck and of first occupancy, that the person who succeeds in saving the property is entitled, 'though not in the case of wrecks within the United Kingdom (*g*),' not merely to retain it for payment of salvage, but to the entire property. This, with a view to the saving of human life, prevails as the rule of usage in the North Seas (*h*).

(*a*) 3 Stair, 3. § 27. 2 Ersk. 1. § 13. 1 Hume, Crim. Law, 485. 1429, c. 124. Hamilton *v.* Cochrane, 1622; M. 16,791; 1 Ill. 374.

(*b*) 1429, c. 124. Jacobson *v.* E. Crawford, 1674; M. 16,792.

(*c*) Montier *v.* Agnew, 1725; M. 16,796.

(*d*) Hamilton *v.* Davis, 5 Burr. 2732.

(*e*) 12 Anne, c. 18. 5 Geo. I. c. 11. Comrs. of Customs, May 25, 1810; F. C. See below, § 1292A.

(*f*) Comrs. of Customs *v.* L. Dundas, Dec. 2, 1812; F. C. See M. Breadalbane *v.* Smith, 1850; 12 D. 602. A right to wreck may be acquired by prescription. L. Adv. *v.* Hebden, 1868; 6 Macph. 489.

(*g*) See next §.

(*h*) Garrioch, July 7, 1818, n. r.

1292A. 'The Board of Trade has now the superintendence of wrecks, and may, with the consent of the Treasury, appoint any officer of coastguard, customs, or inland revenue, or other person, to be a receiver of wreck for any district (*a*). And no admiral, or other person exercising admiralty jurisdiction, except as after mentioned, is to interfere with wreck (*b*). Whenever any ship is stranded or in distress, the receiver is to proceed to the place; and he may require such persons as he thinks necessary to assist him; require the master or person having the charge of any vessel near at hand to give aid with his men or vessel; and demand the use of any waggon, cart, or horses that may be near at hand. He is to take the command of all persons present, who are required to obey under penalty of a fine, and who, while assisting, may, if necessary, pass or repass over private property; he is to assign such duties to each, and issue such directions, as he thinks fit, for the preservation of the ship, persons, and cargo; to repress plundering and misconduct; but he is not to interfere between the master and his crew as to the management of the ship, unless he is requested to do so by the master (*c*). All cargo and articles washed on shore, or lost or taken from the ship, must be delivered to him; and any person, whether the owner or not, who secretes or keeps possession of, or refuses to deliver them to the receiver, incurs a penalty not exceeding £100; and the receiver may take them by force (*d*). He, or a commissioner appointed by the Board of Trade, or in their absence any justice of the peace, must examine upon oath any person belonging to the ship, or other person, as to the names of the ship, the master, and owners; of the owners of the cargo; the ports or places from and to which the ship was bound; the occasion of the distress; the services rendered; and such other matters as he thinks necessary. This examination is to be taken down in writing, and a copy sent to the Board of Trade, and another to the secretary of Lloyds (*e*). He must also, within forty-eight hours after taking possession of the wreck, cause a description of it to be posted up in the custom-house of the port nearest to the place where the wreck was found or seized; and if the value exceed £20, is to transmit a similar description to the secretary of Lloyds, who is there to post it up (*f*). In the event of no owner establishing a claim to wreck before the expiration of a year from the date at which the same has come into the possession of the receiver, then, if any admiral, etc., has proved to the satisfaction of the receiver that he is entitled to wreck at such place, he must, upon payment of all expenses, fees, and salvage, deliver up possession to such admiral, etc. But if no owner establish his claim within the above period, and if no admiral, etc., other than Her Majesty, is proved to be entitled to it, the receiver is forthwith to sell it; and after payment of all expenses, and such amount of salvage as the Board of Trade may in each case or by any general rule determine, pay the proceeds into the Exchequer (*g*).

'Wrecks and other obstructions in harbours and the approaches to them may be removed by harbour-masters, and sold, and the expense, if it exceed the proceeds of the sale, may be recovered from the owner at the time when the expense is incurred, who, on the other hand, is entitled to receive any surplus of the proceeds of sale (*h*). Further provision is made for the removal and buoying of wrecks in harbours and tidal waters by the Removal of Wrecks Act, 1877 (40 and 41 Vict. c. 16).'

(*a*) 57 and 58 Vict. c. 601, § 566. (*b*) *Ib.* § 539. (*c*) *Ib.* § 511 sqq. (*d*) *Ib.* § 518, etc. (*e*) *Ib.* § 517. (*f*) *Ib.* § 520. (*g*) *Ib.* § 520, etc.

(*h*) 10 and 11 Vict. c. 27, § 56 (Harbour, Docks, and Piers Act, 1847). Arrow Shipping Co. *v.* Tyne Improvement Comrs., 1894; A. C. 508.

1293. Treasure-Trove.—This goes to the Crown or grantee, unless proof of property can be shown, or a reasonable presumption of former ownership (*a*).

(*a*) 1 Craig, 16. § 40. 2 Stair, 1. § 5, and 3. § 60. 2 Ersk. 1. § 12. Cleghorn *v.* Baird, 1696; M. 13,523; 1 Ill. 375. Gentle *v.* Smith, 1788; Baron Hume; 1 Ill. 374. More's Notes, 146. See Sands, and other cases above, § 1291.

1294. Waif and Stray Goods.—These are generally considered as the same in Scotland. Waifs, strictly speaking, are goods stolen and thrown away by the thief; and in England they are forfeited to the Crown, in punishment of the owner's want of due vigilance in following them. Strays belong to the Crown or the grantee; and the property was forfeited by the old law after a year's silence, if the stray was an animal requiring to be fed; but the stray might be vindicated at any time, if inanimate. The grantee must not use or injure the stray; and the property is lost to the owner, if duly advertised and sold for the keep (*a*). The Crown has no claim to goods which have been lodged in a public warehouse and forgot for many years, and where the owner is unknown, unless there shall be evidence of total abandonment (*b*).

(*a*) 2 Ersk. 1. § 12. See Napier *v.* M'Farlane, 1749; 3 Pat. 649.

(*b*) Sands *v.* Bell & Balfour, May 22, 1810; F. C.

1295. Prizes.—What is taken in war belongs to the Crown ('*bello parta cedunt reipublicæ*'), and is now adjudicated in the Court of Admiralty of England (*a*). Prizes are either by way of reprisal, or in open war after a declaration of hostilities. Sea-prize, regularly, is and ought to be by the Royal Navy alone. But prizes 'might' legitimately, 'until the partial abolition of privateeering by the Declaration of Paris (April 16, 1856), made by Great Britain, Austria, France, Russia, Sardinia, and Turkey,' be made during war by private ships under Royal Warrants, as privateers authorised to carry on war against the public enemy and to make captures. It 'might' also be made under Letters of Marque and Reprisal, during peace, where injustice or oppression having been committed on individuals, indemnification has been refused, and Government chooses thus to compel indemnification without necessarily incurring the evils of general warfare. In both cases, privateers 'found' caution for good behaviour to the amount of £1500; or £3000, if more than fifty men. But no precautions 'were' sufficient to prevent abuse (*b*); and the whole privateering system is greatly to be condemned, as contrary to the true spirit of a national contest, and disgraced by a selfish desire for plunder, very nearly allied to piracy (*c*). Commissions to private ships are deemed indispensable on two grounds: that war may be conducted with some regard to a regular system; and that precautions may be taken against the enemy strengthening their hands by the capture of inadequate force opposed to them. But the *enemy* has no right to complain of capture by an uncommissioned ship or to treat the captor as a pirate. The only effect is, that the prize becomes a *droit* of the Admiralty; not prize for the captor. In self-defence, every private ship is entitled to make prize, though uncommissioned. By the law of nations, and the Prize Acts passed in the commencement of each war, prizes, when taken, must be judicially condemned; which forms a great and wholesome restraint on the conduct of captors (*d*). The general rules of condemnation seem to be: That the ships, goods, and effects of either of the belligerents may lawfully be captured: That the goods of an enemy, 'except contraband of war,' on board the ships of a friendly State may 'not' be taken (*e*): That contraband of war, though the property of a neutral, may be taken: That neutral property not contraband cannot be taken, and if on board an enemy's ship, must be restored: That the evidence to acquit or condemn must in the first instance come from the ship taken, the papers on board, and the examination of the master and officers (*f*): That every ship must be provided with genuine papers; and that if there be false or colourable papers, no proper papers on board, papers destroyed, prevarication, and fair ground of suspicion, the costs will be adjudicated, or not, to the claimant, in case of acquittal or restitution: That if capture be made without probable cause, costs and damages will be given; to which effect privateers are bound to find security for good behaviour (*g*).

The point of time at which the property of the prize passes, may be questioned by the original owner with a purchaser or with a recaptor; and when a ship escapes from the captor, or is retaken and ransomed by the owner, he is immediately reinvested. In other circumstances the sentence of condemnation alone passes the property; and in the interim (*h*) the ship is under sequestration, in possession of the Government of the captor, in trust for those to whom the property shall be finally adjudicated. This is now the universal rule.

(*a*) 1681, c. 16. 2 Stair, 2. § 1 et seq. Hendricks *v.* Cunningham, Jan. 30, 1781; rev. May 20, 1782; M. 11,959; 2 Pat. 609. 6 Geo. IV. c. 120, § 57. 27 and 28 Vict. c. 23, 24, 25. 29 and 30 Vict. c. 109, § 38–42 (offences). 53 and 54 Vict. c. 57 (Colonial Prize Courts). 57 and 58 Vict. c. 39.

(*b*) See instructions by Orders in Council, May 16, 1803.

(*c*) Kent, Com. vol. i. p. 96.

(*d*) Wake *v.* Hillary, Bauerman, & Son, 1801; M. *Prize*, Apx. 1. The Flad Oyen, 1 C. Rob. Adm. 135.

(*e*) The alteration was made by the Treaty of Paris, 1856. This, and the abolition of privateering, were the only real modifications made by that Treaty on the rules of prize courts, drawn up in the celebrated statement of 1753, quoted in Maclachlan on Shipping, 548. The whole document and relative papers are to be found in Clark's Cabinet Library of Scarce and Celebrated Tracts, vol. i., International Law (Edin.: T. & T. Clark, 1838).

(*f*) Hendricks *v.* Cunningham, 1782; 2 Pat. 609. Statement of 1753, *cit.* (*e*).

(*g*) See paper by Lord Stowell and Sir John Nichol, published by Wheaton, Dig. of Law of Mar. Captures; and also by More, Notes to Stair, p. clii. Lord Stowell's Judgments from 1798 to 1822 in Robinson's, Edwards', and Dodson's Reports in Admiralty. 1 Ill. 376. Tudor's L. C. *passim*.

(*h*) See The Somerset, 2 Dods. Adm. 56. The Harmony, 2 *ib.* 78. The Gauntlet (R. *v.* Elliot), L. R. 4 P. C. 184; 41 L. J. Adm. 65. Prior to condemnation, there is an inchoate right of property, capable of assignment and giving an insurable interest.

II. ACCESSION.

1296. Nature and Kinds of Accession.—This mode of acquiring property depends on natural increase, by the production of the fruits of vegetables, or the young of animals; or on the accidental or intentional application of skill or art in manufacture; or by commixtion or confusion of substances, whereby an augmentation of value or a new article is produced. Hence natural and industrial accession.

1297. Natural Accession consists of that increase or augmentation which proceeds from the production of fruits, natural or industrial; or from the propagation of animals. It confers the property on the owner of the principal.

1298. Industrial Accession is produced by the art or industry of man, and is either Adjunction, Specification, Confusion, or Commixtion. In all these the rule is, "accessorium sequitur principale"; *i.e.* of two things having intimate connection, the property of the principal draws after it that of the accessory; and the only difficulty is to fix which is the principal. The rules by which this is to be ascertained are: That of two substances, one of which can exist separately, the other not, the former is the principal: That where both can exist separately, the principal is that which the other is taken to adorn or complete: That in the absence of these indications, bulk prevails; next value. And in all such cases where there can be no separation, the property is with the owner of the principal, leaving to the other a claim for indemnification (*a*).

(1.) *Specification* is the forming of a new species from materials belonging to another; a change being produced on the substance: as flour out of corn, wine out of grapes. The questions which occasioned the controversy of the Sabinians and Proculeians (*b*) are resolved with us according to the *media sententia* (*c*), on the plain principles of good sense and natural equity. The rules are:—That if the materials, as a separate existence, be destroyed *in bonâ fide*, the property is with the workman; the owner of the materials having a personal claim for a like quantity and quality, or for the price of the materials: That if still capable of restoration to their original shape, the property is held to be with the owner of the materials; a claim against him for work and indemnity, *in quantum lucratus*, being competent to the workman (*d*).

(2.) *Confusion of Liquids and Commixtion of Solids* have the following effects:—They raise a common property, if the commodities be of the same kind; and of such property *pro indiviso* the shares are in proportion to quantity and value; where either the union is by common consent, or where, having been made by accident or without fault, the commodities are inseparable (*e*). The property is unchanged if the articles be capable of separation. If the union be of substances different, so as to create a *tertium quid*, the property is (according to the rule in specification) with the owner of the materials, or with the manufacturer, according to the possibility or impossibility of restoring the original substances (*f*).

(*a*) 2 Ersk. 1. § 14.
(*b*) 2 Inst. 1. De Rer. Div. § 25. Vinnius, Com. in Inst. 148. Pothier, Tr. de Droit de Propriété, § 188.
(*c*) 2 Stair, 1. § 41. 2 Ersk. 1. § 16.
(*d*) If the parties agree to contribute their materials for a certain purpose the rules of accession do not apply, but the contract forms the rule, and they become joint-owners in shares corresponding to the value of their contributions. Wylie & Lochhead *v.* Mitchell, 1870; 8 Macph. 552. Mr. Guthrie Smith in Journ. Jurispr. (Sept. 1870), xiv. 481.
(*e*) Comp. Wylie & Lochhead, *supra*.
(*f*) 2 Stair, 1. § 34, 36, 41. 2 Ersk. 1. § 14–17. 1 Bell's Com. 276 (295, M'L.'s ed). See 2 Stephen's Com. 22, 24.

CHAPTER II

OF DELIVERY OF MOVEABLES

1299. Modus et Titulus Transferendi.—The derivative mode of acquiring property is Tradition, or Delivery, as the "modus" following on a legal "titulus transferendi" (*a*). Lawyers distinguish, in transference, the *titulus transferendi dominii* and the *modus transferendi dominii*; the former being the conventional will to convey; the latter, the overt act by which the real right is transferred. The *titulus transferendi* is either Voluntary, and that either *inter vivos* or *mortis causa*; or Judicial. The voluntary *titulus transferendi* has already been considered under the Contract of Sale (*b*). Transference of moveables *mortis causa* will be discussed under Succession (*c*); while the judicial will be considered under Diligence (*d*). The *modus transferendi* is tradition or delivery (*e*).

(*a*) Voet. ad Pand. lib. 41. tit. 1. § 35.
(*b*) See above, § 85 et seq.
(*c*) See below, § 1637 et seq.
(*d*) See below, § 2270 et seq.
(*e*) 2 Ersk. 1. § 18 seq.

1300. Nature and Effect of Delivery.—Delivery, as the *modus transferendi* in moveables, is applicable to all the conventional titles of transference known in law. It is the delivery of possession by the owner, with the design of transferring the property to the receiver (*a*). By the laws of England, America, and France, the property of moveables is passed by the completed contract of sale, but the right of possession still remains with the seller (*b*). By the 'common' law of Scotland, neither the right of possession nor the right of property is passed without delivery; the rule being peremptory, "Traditionibus, non nudis pactis, dominia rerum transferuntur" (*c*). And it is not enough, in transferring moveables, by the Scottish law, to give symbolical delivery, or delivery by an instrument of possession. If the things themselves remain in possession of the person transferring, the instrument will avail nothing (*d*).

The material distinction between the Scottish and the other laws alluded to is, that by those laws the property being passed, and the *possession* alone wanting, the seller has only the power of retaining the thing sold till the price be paid; and if bankruptcy should occur, the tender of the price will entitle the buyer to demand the thing. But in Scotland, the *property* being still untransferred, if the seller become a bankrupt, his creditors 'took' the thing sold even should the price be paid or tendered by the buyer. No one can doubt that this rule of the law of Scotland is inconsistent with equity; but it is clearly settled, and is not to be altered except by the Legislature (*e*).

(*a*) 2 Stair, 1. § 11. 2 Ersk. 1. § 19. Brown on Sale, 390.
(*b*) 2 Blackst. Com. 498. 2 Kent, Com. 492. 4 Pothier, Droit de Propriété, p. 419. 2 Stephen's Com. 68. Brodie's Stair, 906. See above, § 87, 88.
(*c*) See Mathison *v.* Alison, 1854; 17 D. 274. M'Arthur *v.* Brown, 1858; 20 D. 1232. Moore *v.* Gledden, 1869; 7 Macph. 1016 (nature and effect of possession). Orr's Tr. *v.* Tullis, 1870; 8 Macph. 936; below, § 1317.
(*d*) 2 Ersk. 1. § 19, 20. Corbet *v.* Stirling, 1666; M.

10,602; 1 Ill. 376. Ker *v.* Scott & Elliot, 1695; M. 9122. Carse *v.* Halliburton, 1714; M. 9125. Henry *v.* Robertson, 1822; 1 S. 375. Borthwick *v.* Grant, 1829; 7 S. 420. Fraser *v.* Frisby, 1830; 8 S. 982. See above, § 86; and below, § 1317.

(*e*) See below as to actual and constructive delivery, § 1302–3. See § 1303, 1300A.

1300A. 'Mercantile Law Amendment Act.—Between 1856 and 1892, the Mercantile Law Amendment (Scotland) Act, now repealed in this respect (*a*), effected an important qualification of the doctrine of delivery. It enacted, that "where goods have been sold, but the same have not been delivered to the purchaser, and have been allowed to remain in the custody (*b*) of the seller, it shall not be competent for any creditor of such seller, after the date of such sale, to attach such goods as belonging to the seller by any diligence or process of law (including sequestration), to the effect of preventing the purchaser or others in his right from enforcing delivery of the same; and the right of the purchaser to demand delivery of such goods shall, from and after the date of such sale, be attachable by or transferable to the creditors of the purchaser." This rule does not affect the landlord's hypothec for rent (*c*). It also enabled the seller to secure a preference by arresting or poinding in his own hands, previous to intimation of a sub-sale (*d*).

'The rule of the common law, that the undelivered goods remain the property of the seller, was not altered by this section. Its only effect was to exclude the diligence of the seller's creditors in competition with the buyer enforcing his contract (*e*); and, being intended to assimilate the law to that of England, it applied only to the sale of a definite existing article or quantity of goods (bargain and sale), and not to an executory agreement for a sale (*f*).'

(*a*) Sale of Goods Act, 1893, § 60 and sched.

(*b*) Where not merely the custody but the beneficial use and uncontrolled possession and power of disposal of the article sold, *e.g.* a horse, remained by the terms of the contract or by sufferance with the seller, in such a way as to show that there was not a true sale, this clause of the Act did not apply. Sim *v.* Grant, 1862; 24 D. 1062. Edmond *v.* Mowat, 1868; 7 Macph. 59. See obs. in Orr's Tr. *v.* Tullis, 1870; 8 Macph. 936; and Robertsons *v.* M'Intyre, 1882; 9 R. 772. But its operation was not excluded by the addition to a true contract of sale of a stipulation by the seller for a right of pre-emption, or a collateral agreement for a share of the surplus price on a resale; such conditions not being inconsistent with a *bonâ fide* sale. Allan & Co.'s Tr. *v.* Gunn & Co., 1883; 10 R. 997. M'Bain *v.* Wallace & Co., 1881; 8 R. 360; aff. *ib.* H. L. 106; 6 App. Ca. 588; or by the seller's continued possession and use upon a contract of loan or hiring. Scott *v.* Scott's Trs., 1889; 16 R. 504.

(*c*) 19 and 20 Vict. c. 60, § 1, 4.

(*d*) Browne & Co. *v.* Ainslie & Co., 1893; 21 R. 173.

(*e*) Wyper *v.* Harvey, 1861; 23 D. 606. Black *v.* Incorp. of Bakers, 1867; 6 Macph. 136 (*per* L. P. Inglis). M'Bain *v.* Wallace & Co., *cit.* (*per* L. Blackburn and L. Watson).

(*f*) M'Meekin *v.* Ross, 1876; 4 R. 154. Comp. § 87, 97A, *supra*.

1300B. '"It was further enacted (*a*), that where a purchaser of goods, *i.e.* of a definite existing article or quantity of goods (*b*), who has not obtained delivery thereof," sells the same, the purchaser from him, or any other subsequent purchaser, is "entitled to demand that delivery of the said goods shall be made to him, and not to the original purchaser; and the seller, on intimation being made to him of such subsequent sale, shall be bound to make such delivery on payment of the price of such goods, or performance of the obligations or conditions of the contract of sale, and shall not be entitled, in any question with a subsequent purchaser, or others in his right, to retain the goods for any separate debt or obligation alleged to be due to the seller by the original purchaser" (*c*). But the seller's right of retention for payment of the price of the goods, or such portion of it as might remain unpaid, or for performance of the obligations or conditions of the contract of sale, or any right of retention competent to the seller, except as between him and the sub-purchaser, or as arising from express contract with the original purchaser, was not affected by this enactment (*d*).'

(*a*) The Act, § 4, also repealed as above.

(*b*) See M'Meekin *v.* Ross, *cit.* Stewart *v.* Fraser & Co., 1878; 2 Sel. Sh. Ct. Ca. 512.

(*c*) 19 and 20 Vict. c. 60, § 2.

(*d*) 19 and 20 Vict. c. 60, § 2. See as to buyer's retention (which is not noticed under Retention, *infra*, chap. viii. § 1410 sqq.), above, § 116.

1300C. 'Sale of Goods Act.—*Transfer of Possession by Completed Contract of Sale.*—This enactment was repealed by the Sale of Goods Act, 1893, being made superfluous and unnecessary by the assimilation of our law to that of England effected by that statute. As already indicated (see above, § 86, 87, etc.), property in moveables is now transferred by the completed contract of sale, and the rule *traditionibus non nudis pactis*, etc., has so far ceased to exist.

'The distinction of the *titulus* and the *modus transferendi dominii* as regards moveables has thus become much less important, the contract of sale effecting the transference *ipso facto*. Delivery remains, however, the *modus* in regard to other legal relations, *e.g.* in donation, and, as will immediately be seen, may be a material fact in some of the conventional and statutory modifications of the new rule.

'In order that a contract of sale may pass the property, the goods must be "ascertained" (*a*)—identified and agreed upon by the parties (*b*).

'In a sale of such goods, the property passes at such time as the parties intend it to be transferred; and to ascertain such intention, regard is had to the terms of the contract, the conduct of the parties, and the circumstances of the case (*c*).

'"Unless a different intention appears," *i.e.* probably, where the intention is not expressly stated in the contract, the Act (*d*) gives rules for ascertaining the intention of parties:—1. Where there is an unconditional contract for the sale of specific goods in a deliverable state, the property passes when the contract is made, and postponement of time of payment or of delivery or of both is immaterial. 2. Where in a contract for sale of specific goods the seller is bound to do something to them for the purpose of putting them in a deliverable state, the property does not pass till such thing is done and the buyer has notice thereof. 3. Where there is a contract for the sale of specific goods in a deliverable state, but the seller is bound to weigh, measure, test, or do some other act or thing with reference to the goods, for the purpose of ascertaining the price, the property does not pass until such act or thing be done, and the buyer has notice thereof (*e*). 4. When goods are delivered to the buyer on approval or "on sale or return," or other similar terms, the property therein passes to the buyer—(1) when he signifies his approval or acceptance to the seller, or does any other act adopting the transaction; (2) if he does not signify his approval or acceptance to the seller, but retains the goods without giving notice of rejection, then on the expiration of any time that may have been fixed, or if none has been fixed, on the expiration of a reasonable time, which is a question of fact (*f*). 5. Where there is a contract for the sale of unascertained or future goods by description, and goods of that description and in a deliverable state are unconditionally appropriated to the contract, either by the seller with the assent of the buyer, or by the buyer with the assent of the seller, the property thereupon passes to the buyer. The assent may be express or implied, and may be given either before or after the appropriation is made. Where the seller delivers the goods to the buyer, or to a carrier or other bailee or custodier, whether named by the buyer or not, for the purpose of transmission to the buyer, and does not reserve the right of disposal, he unconditionally appropriates the goods to the contract.'

(*a*) The Act, § 15. See above, § 86, 90.

(*b*) "Specific goods." The Act, § 62.

(*c*) The Act, § 17. **Seath** *v.* **Moore**, 1886; 11 App. Ca. 350, 370, 380; 13 R. H. L. 57.

(*d*) *Ib.* § 18.

(*e*) Anderson *v.* Morice, L. R. 10 C. P. 58, 609; aff. 1 App. Ca. 713; 46 L. J. Q. B. 11. **Seath** *v.* **Moore**, 11 App. Ca. 350, 370. Mr. R. Brown, Sale of Goods Act, p. 90, points out that the Scots cases on passing of risk illustrate rules 2 and 3, *e.g.* Hansen *v.* Craig & Rose, 1859; 21 D. 432; Anderson & Crompton *v.* Walls & Co., 1870; 9 Macph. 122; Walker *v.* Langdales Chem. Co., 1873; 11 Macph. 906; and that Black *v.* Incorp. of Bakers, 1867, 6 Macph. 136, is overruled by these rules.

(*f*) See above, § 109; below, § 1315.

1301. The simple act of delivery by the hands of the seller to a buyer can seldom take place amidst the wholesale dealings of traders; and it is necessary to note many situations in which distinctions may be taken and questions raised. The situations chiefly deserving of notice are: where the goods to be transferred are in the seller's possession; and where they are in the custody or under the care of another. 'In the following sections the present tense is generally retained, although the law may be modified by the effects of the Sale of Goods Act, 1893. It is still desirable to retain the exposition of the common law of Scotland, and references to the decisions bearing on it.'

1302. Delivery of Goods in the Seller's Possession (*a*).—In the delivery of goods which are in the seller's own hands, or in what law deems to be his custody, these cases may be distinguished:—

(1.) *Actual Delivery.*—The simple act is exemplified in purchasing a book in a shop, and bringing it away; delivery into the buyer's cart, or warehouse, or shop (*b*); delivery into the buyer's ship, or into a ship hired on time, and entirely at his command (*c*); delivery into a bonded warehouse for the buyer, and at his own risk (*d*); delivery into the warehouse of a public warehouseman, used by the buyer as his own (*e*), or to a carrier's warehouse to be there at the buyer's order (*f*); delivery of the key of a warehouse or cellar in which the goods are placed (*g*). In all these examples the delivery 'was' held to be actual and complete, effectually to transfer the property beyond recall or stoppage (*h*). 'But when the sale is by express or implied agreement for cash on delivery, the inadvertent transference of the goods into the buyer's custody, there being no consent to delay of payment, is not delivery, and does not pass the property; and the seller, if he do so without delay, may demand restoration of the goods (*i*).'

(*a*) 2 Ersk. 1. § 18, 19. 1 Bell's Com. 172 (183, M'L.'s ed.). Brown on Sale, 390.

(*b*) Collins *v.* Marquis's Crs., 1804; M. 14,223; 1 Ill. 377. Blakey *v.* Dinsdale, Cowp. 661.

(*c*) Fowler *v.* M'Taggart, 7 T. R. 442; 1 East, 522; 3 East, 396; 4 R. R. 485. Inglis *v.* Usherwood, 1 East, 515. Bohtlingk *v.* Inglis, 3 East, 381; 7 R. R. 490. See Robertsons & Aitken *v.* More, 1801; M. *Sale*, Apx. 3; 1 Ill. 383. Baxter *v.* Pearson, July 8, 1807; F. C.; 1 Ill. 393; Hume, 688; 1 Bell's Com. 175 (186, M'L.'s ed.). The statement in the text has been regarded as too limited; many cases, especially in England, showing that delivery is in general effected when the goods are placed without special restriction in the hands of a shipmaster as a common carrier for conveyance to the buyer. See **Dunlop** *v.* **Lambert,** 1839; M'L. & R. 663; revg. 15 S. 884, 1232. M'Laren's Bell's Com. i. 218. 1 Bell's Com. 203 (where this seems to be correctly stated), and above, § 418A.

(*d*) Strachan *v.* Knox & Co., Jan. 21, 1817; F. C.; 1 Ill. 380.

(*e*) Richardson *v.* Goss, 3 B. & P. 127; 6 R. R. 727. Leeds *v.* Wright, *ib.* 320; 7 R. R. 779. Scott *v.* Pettit, *ib.* 469; 7 R. R. 804. Dixon *v.* Baldwen, 5 East, 175, 188; 7 R. R. 681. These cases, and those in the next note, relate to the termination of the *transitus* in questions of stoppage, and not to this subject. See below, § 1308 (*v*). But the text does not here stand in need of authorities.

(*f*) Foster *v.* Frampton, 6 B. & Cr. 107; 1 Ill. 411; 30 R. R. 255. Black *v.* Cassels, 1828; 6 S. 894. See last note.

(*g*) 2 Ersk. 1. § 19. See 2 Inst. 1. § 44. Dig. l. 41. tit. 1. 9. § 6. Maxwell & Co. *v.* Stevenson & Co., 1831; 5 W. & S. 269. More *v.* Dudgeon, and Somervail & Co. *v.* Stein, in 1 Bell's Com. 175 (186–7, M'L.'s ed.).

(*h*) See as to goods rejected as not conform to sample, Jowitt *v.* Stead, 1860; 22 D. 1400.

(*i*) 1 Bell's Com. 237 (258, M'L.'s ed.); *supra*, § 100, 103, 109; *infra*, § 1308 (*c*). Richmond *v.* Railton, *ibi cit.* Benjamin on Sales, 287. Fraud in obtaining delivery raises another question. See Watt *v.* Findlay, and Richmond, *infra*, *l.c.*

1303. (2.) *Constructive Delivery.*—When goods sold are in the seller's custody, but some impediment prevents the completion of the act of delivery, the rule is, 'in some peculiar cases,' that wherever the delivery is as far perfected, and the commodity as much separated from the seller's stock as in the circumstances is possible for the completing of the transfer, the property is passed; with this sole qualification, that if the price be unpaid, the seller may retain the goods in security. The effect produced is analogous, in short, to that which takes place in England by completion of the contract. So that the bankruptcy of the seller will not entitle his creditors to take the goods if the price be paid or secured, but only to retain possession if the price should not be paid. Such are 'some of' the following cases:—Where the delivery of goods sold by entire contract is necessarily protracted (of a cargo of corn, for example), and an interruption takes place in the course of the delivery, the unloading and delivery of part is 'not' held delivery of the whole, 'and' (*a*) the part undelivered may be retained for the price if unpaid (*b*). 'Professor Bell wrote, in the earlier editions, that' where the thing sold is not yet separated from the soil, and cannot instantly be separated and delivered, it is held as delivered, and the property passed, subject to retention for the price, when the commodity is marked for the buyer (*c*). 'But the case cited refers only to growing corns publicly sold, as to which there is a custom, and which are poindable after Whitsunday or Midsummer; and the contrary has been determined with regard to trees, which are *partes soli*, and can be transferred only by actual removal and delivery (*d*).' Where cattle are sold while grazing, and are marked for the buyer; or sold by public roup, and put into the seller's field till they can be removed; or wine is sold and placed in a bin for the buyer; the delivery seems, 'according to two decisions,' to be complete if the price is paid (*e*). 'These were cases in which it was natural and usual for the subject of sale to remain in the seller's possession; doubt was cast upon them as laying down any general rule by subsequent authorities; and the points involved were afterwards solved in most cases by the Mercantile Law Amendment Act (*f*), and now by the Sale of Goods Act, 1893.'

'*Contract for building a Ship or making a specific Article.*'—When a manufacture in the workman's hand unfinished is purchased, and the price paid; or when, by periodical payments, it is appropriated as it advances, the law holds it as delivered (*g*). But in this class of cases some doubts remain where the delivery is left imperfect, not from *necessity*, but in mere *convenience* to the buyer. There seems, however, upon the whole, now to be a prevailing opinion that the distinction is to be disregarded when no question arises respecting the payment of the price (*h*). 'Perhaps the true principle in Scots law is, that when a *specific* thing in the hands of a manufacturer or artificer is purchased, the manufacturer becomes custodier or bailee for the purchaser so long as he holds it for the completion of his work, and what he adds, *i.e.* actually affixes (*i*) to it, becomes the property of the purchaser by accession; the qualification of the hard rule, "traditionibus," etc., being here allowed from favour to trade, and partly because some of the manufacturers and artificers to whom the exception applies do not derive credit from the possession of goods which they are known to be making for others. In the case of a ship paid for by instalments, the case which is most commonly referred to, the law of England reaches the same result more easily than ours, because the passing of property is there the effect of *contract*, and no more is required than clear evidence that the contract is complete. The last Scots case upon the subject was decided upon the Mercantile Law Amendment Act (*k*); but, notwithstanding the difficulties which undoubtedly surround the question, and which were felt in that case by the judges both in Scotland and the House of Lords, the rule of Simpson *v.* Duncanson's Creditors may be held to be settled (*l*).

'Constructive delivery also takes place where the seller, after the contract of sale, continues to hold the article on a different or inferior title, such as location or deposit, subject to the buyer's right of property. Delivery is important as the means of obtaining possession, and in cases of this kind the buyer has civil possession through the seller, who holds for him (*m*).'

In English practice, whenever the custom of trade has sanctioned sales of goods in which the custody is left with the seller, and the goods are distinguished or marked for the buyer, or there is an agreement to pay warehouse rent, and the rent is received from the buyer, the property is held to be completely transferred (*n*), provided nothing remains to be done in ascertaining or preparing the goods (*o*).

'In the law of Scotland, there could, as a general rule, be no delivery to a purchaser, such as to pass the property, of goods which remain in the actual possession of the seller, except probably in one or two of the cases above mentioned (*p*). Constructive delivery by means of a delivery order can only take place where there are three independent persons — the vendor, the vendee, and the custodier of the goods; and if the custodier of the goods is identified with the vendor, *e.g.* if he is the keeper of a warehouse belonging to the vendor, in which goods are stored belonging to the vendor and to others, there is no independent third person who can become, on intimation of the delivery order, custodier for the vendee (*q*).'

(*a*) Originally "though." Professor Bell attempted to apply English authorities on stoppage and delivery to Scots law, sometimes with the effect of producing confusion.

(*b*) 1 Bell's Com. 172 (183, M'L.'s ed.). Collins *v.* Marquis, 1804; M. 14,223; 1 Ill. 377. Slubey *v.* Hayward, 2 H. Bl. 504; 2 Ross' L. C. 212; 1 Ill. 384; 3 R. R. 486. Hammond *v.* Anderson, 1 N. R. 71; 8 R. R. 763. See Hanson *v.* Meyer, 6 East, 614; 1 Ill. 90; 8 R. R. 572. Tudor's L. C. 600; 2 Ross' L. C. 20. Jones *v.* Jones, 8 M. & W. 431. Tanner *v.* Scovell, 14 M. & W. 28. The cases cited refer to stoppage *in transitu*, and to the effect of part delivery in divesting the vendor's lien for the unpaid price; and there is no authority for laying down the general proposition that a partial delivery operates to transfer the property of the whole of a specific quantity of goods sold. Even in question of stoppage and lien a partial delivery has such an effect only when it occurs in such circumstances as to be evidence that the buyer's taking possession of part is constructive possession of the whole—the carrier or warehouseman becoming his bailee. Bolton *v.* L. & Y. Ry. Co., 35 L. J. C. P. 137; L. R. 1 C. P. 431; *ex p.* Cooper, 48 L. J. Bkr. 49; 11 Ch. D. 68; *ex p.* Falk, 14 Ch. D. 496; and 1 Smith's L. C. 730; Smith's Merc. Law, 642; Benjamin on Sales, 788 sqq., and above, § 108.

(*c*) Grant *v.* Smith, 1758; M. 9561; 1 Bell's Com. 176 (187, M'L.'s ed.); 1 Ill. 383.

(*d*) Brodie's Stair, 897. Paul *v.* Cuthbertson, 1840; 2 D. 128. Elder *v.* Allen, 1833; 11 S. 902. Anderson *v.* Ford, 1844; 6 D. 1315.

(*e*) Lang *v.* Bruce, 1832; 10 S. 777; 1 Ill. 386. Gibson *v.* Forbes, 1833; 11 S. 916. See below, § 1315 *fin.*

(*f*) *Supra*, § 1300A. Boak *v.* Meggat, 1844; 6 D. 662. Mathison and Anderson (*q*). Black *v.* Incorp. of Bakers, 1867; 6 Macph. 136. 1 Bell's Com. 180 (191, M'L.'s ed.); 2 Ross' L. C. 567.

(*g*) Mucklow *v.* Mangles, 1 Taunt. 318; 9 R. R. 784. **Simpson *v.* Duncanson's Crs.**, 1786; M. 14,204; 1 Bell's Com. 177, notes (189, M'L.'s ed.). Woods *v.* Russell, 5 B. & Ald. 942; 24 R. R. 621. See Atkinson *v.* Bell, 8 B.

& Cr. 277 ; 32 R. R. 382. Clark *v.* Spence, 4 A. & E. 448 ; 3 Ill. 148. Wood *v.* Bell, 6 E. & B. 355 ; 25 L. J. Q. B. 321. Anglo-Egypt. S. Nav. Co. *v.* Rennie, L. R. 10 C. P. 281 ; 44 L. J. C. P. 130, 292. Boak, *cit.* Orr's Tr. *v.* Tullis, 1870 ; 8 Macph. 936. Wylie & Lochhead *v.* Mitchell, 1870 ; 8 Macph. 552. Spencer & Co. *v.* Dobie & Co., 1879 ; 7 R. 396. Sutherland *v.* Montrose Shipbuilding Co., 1860 ; 22 D. 665. See Tudor's L. C. 621. Benjamin on Sales, 277 sqq., 325 sq. Boak *v.* Meggat, *cit.*, shows that purchase and payment of an unfinished article left in the seller's hands to have an operation completed does necessarily pass the property.

(*h*) Broughton *v.* Aitchison, Nov. 15, 1809 ; F. C. 1 Bell's Com. 180 (191, M'L.'s ed.). Lang and Gibson, *supra* (*e*). See § 1316. See Dryden & Co., 1853, n. r., stated in Shaw's Bell's Com. 124, notes.

(*i*) Seath *v.* Moore, *infra*, esp. 11 App. Ca. 381.

(*k*) **M'Bain** *v.* **Wallace & Co.**, 1881 ; 8 R. 360 ; aff. *ib.* H. L. 106 ; 6 App. Ca. 588. See Brodie's Stair, 900 sqq., and **Seath** *v.* **Moore** (Campbell's Tr.), 1884 ; 12 R. 260 ; aff. 1886, 11 App. Ca. 350 ; 13 R. H. L. 57.

(*l*) See *per* Lord Watson in Seath *v.* Moore, 11 App. Ca. 377, where the remarks on the case itself do not impeach the rule of law as explained in the series of subsequent cases in (*g*).

(*m*) Orr's Tr. *v.* Tullis, 1870 ; 8 Macph. 936 (esp. *per* L. J.-C. Moncreiff), and other cases in § 1315, 1317, in which the main question is whether the transaction has been genuine and *in bonâ fide*. This seems to explain the cases under notes (*e*) and (*g*). *Per* L. Cowan in Mathison, *infra* (*q*). Professor Bell sometimes falls into confusion by attempting to treat stoppage as a branch of the doctrine of lien, or retention, which necessitates the anomalous conception of a right of retention existing after delivery. He has thus been led, as in this paragraph, to speak of the payment of the price as a possible criterion of delivery, with which in truth it has no connection (1 Stair, 14. § 2 ; 1 Bell's Com. 237). Non-payment of the price is the basis of the right of stoppage, but the question of delivery is entirely independent of the fact of payment or non-payment of the price (*per* L. P. Blair in Broughton *v.* Aitchison, *supra* (*h*). Melrose *v.* Hastie, 1851 ; 13 D. 880, etc. etc.). In other passages, as in § 1304, 1 Com. 209, etc., a more accurate statement occurs. Further, the idea of incomplete or imperfect delivery is erroneous ; for goods are either delivered or not delivered. Stoppage is competent, not when the *delivery* of them is incomplete or unfinished, but only when their *transitus* from the seller to the buyer is not at an end. In reading the author's text and the corresponding passages of the Commentaries, the passages which depend on English authorities must often be regarded with suspicion ; delivery being in England important for other purposes than the passing of the property. See M'Laren's Bell's Com. 183, 211, 216, etc. Smith's Merc. Law, 642, 705, etc.

(*n*) Flynn & Field, 1 Atk. 185. Goodall *v.* Skelton, 2 H. Bl. 316 ; 3 R. R. 379. Thackthwaite *v.* Cock, 3 Taunt. 487 ; 12 R. R. 689. Hammond *v.* Anderson, *supra* (*b*). Hurry *v.* Mangles, 1 Camp. 452 ; 10 R. R. 727. Stoveld *v.* Hughes, 14 East, 308 ; 1 Bell's Com. 176, 179 (187, 191, M'L.'s ed.) ; 12 R. R. 523.

(*o*) White *v.* Wilks, 1 Marsh. 2 ; 1 Ill. 92 ; 14 R. R. 735. Bloxham *v.* Saunders, 4 B. & Cr. 941. Busk *v.* Davies, 5 Taunt. 622 ; 15 R. R. 288. Hurry, *supra* (*n*). New *v.* Swain, 1 Dan. & L. 193 ; 1 Ill. 412. Townley *v.* Crump, 4 A. & E. 58 ; 3 Ill. 148. See Tansly *v.* Turner, 2 Bing. N. S. 151. See below, § 1315. But see Benjamin on Sales, book ii. ch. iv. and v. p. 295 sqq., and above, § 1300*c* (2), (3).

(*p*) See below, § 1306, 1317.

(*q*) Anderson *v.* M'Call, 1866 ; 4 Macph. 765. Mathison *v.* Alison, 1854 ; 17 D. 274. Connal & Co. *v.* Loder, 1868 ; 6 Macph. 1095, 1110. Distillers' Co. *v.* Russel's Trs., 1889 ; 16 R. 479. Rhind's Tr. *v.* Robertson & Baxter, 18 R. 623. See below, § 1305, 1306, 1378.

1304. (3.) *Transitus.*—There is another class of cases, in which, though the thing is at the time of the sale in the seller's hands, the delivery to the buyer is not direct and immediate, but circuitous and transitory, through a middle hand (*a*): as where the goods are delivered to a wharfinger to be sent to the buyer, or where they are delivered to a carrier or shipmaster to be transported to him, even though the ship should be freighted by the buyer, if not on time (*b*); or where materials bought are sent to a manufacturer by the buyer's order. In these cases the delivery is complete to pass the property, with reservation of a privilege to reclaim them before they have reached the actual custody of the buyer, if the price be still unpaid (*c*).

(*a*) Dunlop *v.* Scott & Co., Feb. 22, 1814 ; F. C. ; 1 Ill. 390. Dixon *v.* Baldwen, 7 R. R. 681 ; 5 East, 175 ; 1 Ill. 381. Ellis *v.* Hunt, 3 T. R. 464 ; 1 R. R. 743. Fragano *v.* Long, 4 B. & Cr. 219 ; 28 R. R. 226. Noble *v.* Adams, 2 Marsh. 366 ; 17 R. R. 445. Craven *v.* Ryder, 6 Taunt. 433 ; 16 R. R. 644. Ruck *v.* Hatfield, 5 B. & Ald. 632 ; 24 R. R. 507. Litt *v.* Cowler, 7 Taunt. 169 ; 17 R. R. 784. Sale of Goods Act, 1893, § 32. *Supra*, § 118A.

(*b*) Robertsons & Aitken *v.* More, 1801 ; M. *Sale*, Apx. 3. Baxter *v.* Pearson, July 8, 1807 ; F. C. ; Hume, 688 ; 1 Bell's Com. 175 (186, M'L.'s ed.) ; 1 Ill. 393. See § 1302 (*c*), 1308 (*g*).

(*c*) See below, of stopping *in transitu*, § 1307 ; and above, § 1303 (*m*).

1305. Delivery of Goods in the Custody of Another.—The principle which rules delivery in such a case is, that there shall be a complete transfer of the custodier's duty, so as henceforward he shall hold for the buyer instead of the seller. This comprehends all the cases of sale of goods placed in bond warehouses for the duties; or in dock warehouses, provided delivery is given by transfer of the dock warrant 'and the warehousekeeper's acceptance of notice thereof' (*a*); all goods in the hands of wharfingers, 'factors,' or brokers (*b*), to whom notice is given to change the custody, '"whatever may be the precise condition of the goods, even though the quantity be unascertained, provided the mass be sold; even though the price be unascertained, provided it be at a rate which afterwards can be certainly fixed by ascertainment of the quantity; even though the goods be lying in such a state that some preliminary operation is necessary to put them in a state for delivery" (*c*)'; goods sold while in the hands of carriers by sea or land, by transfer of the bill of lading (*d*); goods deposited or left in the carrier's warehouse, 'at the disposal of the seller, when such a change in the carrier's position is made that he comes to hold them' subject to the buyer's order (*e*); 'goods sold when in the hands of a workman employed to perform some operation on them (*f*).

'In all these cases, the assent, express or implied, of the custodier, purchaser, and seller is required according to the decisions in England, and not merely notice to the custodier (*g*). Notice to the custodier is generally given by means of a "delivery order," or by an indorsation on a warrant for delivery, which is according to these authorities merely an authority to the custodier to give delivery, changing upon its presentation and acceptance the constructive possession, and is not a document of title transferring the property (*h*). In Scotland, however, there has been a tendency (contrary to the English cases) to consider the delivery order as giving a title to the property (*i*). The Factors' Acts, contrary to the view adopted by the English judges, dealt with documents of this kind as documents of title (*k*); and the Act of 1877 made an important change in their legal effect, rendering them negotiable in the sense in which a bill of lading is negotiable. It was followed and repeated by the Factors' Act, 1889, and Sale of Goods Act, 1893. It is enacted, that "where any document of title to goods (*l*) has been lawfully endorsed or otherwise transferred to any person as a vendee or owner of the goods, and such person transfers such document by endorsement (or by delivery where the document is by custom, or by its express terms, transferable by delivery, or makes the goods deliverable to the bearer) to a person who takes the same *bonâ fide*, and for valuable consideration, the last-mentioned transfer shall have the same effect for defeating any vendor's lien or right of stoppage *in transitu*, as the transfer of a bill of lading has for defeating the right of stoppage *in transitu*"; and if the last-mentioned transfer was by way of pledge or other disposition for value, the unpaid seller's right of lien or retention or stoppage *in transitu* can only be exercised subject to the rights of the transferee (*m*).'

(*a*) 4 Geo. IV. c. 24, § 82. 6 Geo. IV. c. 105, § 9, as to goods imported. 4 Geo. IV. c. 94, § 66, as to spirits, etc. See also below, § 1363 et seq. Tod & Co. *v.* Rattray, Feb. 1, 1809; F. C.; 1 Ill. 397; 1 Bell's Com. 194 (208, M'L.'s ed.). M'Eachern *v.* Ewing & Co., 1824; 2 S. 724; 1 Ill. 399. See Campbell, Ruthven, & Co. *v.* Brown; Robertson, Harvie, & Co. *v.* Adam's Crs.; and Auchie, Ure, & Co. *v.* Spence, 1 Ill. 395–6; 1 Bell's Com. 195 (209, M'L.'s ed.). Lucas *v.* Dorrien, 7 Taunt. 278. Zwinger *v.* Samuda, *ib.* 265; 18 R. R. 476, 480. See **M'Ewan & Co.** *v.* **Smith,** 1847; 9 D. 434; aff. 6 Bell's App. 340. Melrose & Co. *v.* Hastie & Co., 1850; 12 D. 655; 1851, 13 D. 880, 14 D. 268; 1 Macq. 698. Mathison *v.* Alison, and Anderson *v.* M'Call, § 1303 (*g*). **Hamilton** *v.* **Western Bank,** 1856; 19 D. 152.

(*b*) Brokers in the strict sense of the word are not in general entrusted with the possession of goods. The word "factors," which has been added, ought perhaps to have been substituted for it.

(*c*) *Per* L. P. Inglis, in Black *v.* Incorp. of Bakers, 1867; 6 Macph. 136, 141, 142. In previous editions the following words stood in the place of those now inserted: "(provided nothing remain to be done to ascertain the price or the quantity), or who acknowledge that they hold for the buyer." Professor Bell's misconception of the import of the English cases—not to be wondered at in a wilderness not yet cleared and put in order by Blackburn and Benjamin—has been pointed out by the last editor of the Commentaries (vol. i. p. 200). The authorities quoted by Prof. Bell under the passage deleted are—Main *v.* Maxwell, 1710; M. 9124; 1 Ill. 393. Harman *v.* Anderson, 2 Camp. 243; 1 Ill. 397; 11 R. R. 706. Stonard *v.* Dunkin, 2 Camp. 344; 11 R. R. 704. Hawes *v.* Watson, 2 B. & Cr. 540; 26 R. R. 448. Bloxham *v.* Morley, 4 B. & Cr. 952; 28 R. R. 527. Hanson *v.* Meyer, *supra*, § 1303 (*b*). Wallace *v.* Breeds, 13 East, 522; 1 Ill. 91; 12 R. R. 433. Whitehouse *v.* Frost, 12 East, 614; 11 R. R. vi. 491; "a case scarcely ever mentioned without suggestion of doubt or disapproval." Benjamin on Sales, 297. Busk *v.* Davis, 2 M. & S. 397; 15 R. R. 288. 1 Bell's Com. 183 (194, M'L.'s ed.).

(*d*) Buchanan & Cochrane *v.* Swan, 1764; M. 14,208; 1 Ill. 394. Arthur *v.* Hastie & Jamieson, 1770; M. 14,209; Hailes, 258; rev. 2 Pat. 251. Bogle *v.* Dunmore & Co., 1787; M. 14,216; Hailes, 1018. Young *v.* Stein's Trs., 1789; M. 14,218. See above, § 417–419; below, § 1308.

(*e*) See Foster *v.* Frampton, 6 B. & Cr. 107; 1 Ill. 411; 30 R. R. 255. Black *v.* Cassels, 1828; 6 S. 894. As already (§ 1302 (*f*)) mentioned, these cases relate to stoppage *in transitu*; but the addition to the text makes a true instance of "delivery of goods in the custody of another," although not perhaps of frequent occurrence. See M'Laren's Bell's Com. vol. i. pp. 218, 240–1.

(*f*) Black *v.* Incorpn. of Bakers of Glasgow, 1867, 6 Macph. 136, where it was held that, in a sale of the flour to be made from a certain quantity of grain in the hands of a miller for the purpose of being ground, the property passed only with the conversion of the grain into flour, the sale having been previously intimated to the miller.

(*g*) M'Laren's Bell's Com. i. 194, note. Benjamin on Sales, 151 sq., 765, 787. Connal & Co. *v.* Loder, 1868; 6 Macph. 1095.

(*h*) M'Ewan & Co., *supra* (*a*). Brodie's Stair, 874. Griffiths *v.* Perry, 28 L. J. Q. B. 208. The warehouseman or custodier is not in safety to part with the goods without a delivery order. Smith *v.* Allan & Poynter, 1859; 22 D. 208. See the distinction between a delivery order and a warrant for goods in the Stamp Act, 54 and 55 Vict. c. 39, § 69, 111, repeating previous Stamp Acts. A delivery order requires a penny stamp; a warrant for goods, which is "evidence of the title of any person therein named, or his assigns," a threepenny stamp; *ib.* and sched. See below, § 1378.

(*i*) Hamilton *v.* Western Bank, 1856; 19 D. 152. Pochin *v.* Robinows & Majoribanks, 1869; 7 Macph. 622. Vickers *v.* Hertz, 1871; 9 Macph. H. L. 65. Young *v.* Lambert, 39 L. J. P. C. 21. Kingsford *v.* Merry, 1 H. & N. 503. Tudor's L. C. 724.

(*k*) See Benjamin on Sales, 803.

(*l*) The definition of this term is now to be found in the Sale of Goods Act, § 62. See below, § 1317A.

(*m*) 40 and 41 Vict. c. 39, § 5, *infra*, 1317B. See above, § 417–419; and below, § 1308, note (*r*); 52 and 53 Vict. c. 45, § 10; 56 and 57 Vict. c. 71, § 47. This enactment brings the law into accordance with the understanding of merchants, who have always been disposed to regard the transfer of a paper of this kind as an actual transfer of the property or right to possession of the goods which it represents. The warehousekeeper, instead of remaining the bailee or agent of the owner, must now be taken to assent *in advance*, as Mr. Benjamin (on Sales, 804) suggested, to hold not merely for him, but for anyone to whom his certificate may be indorsed, or to whom the owner grants a delivery order.

1306. 'This section and § 1378 set forth a distinction which appears to have existed between the mode of transference of goods bonded in a warehouse belonging to a third party, and goods bonded in the warehouse of the seller. The Acts, however, upon which the statement was founded are repealed by 16 and 17 Vict. c. 107, which contains no similar provision; and that Act is itself repealed, with a few exceptions, by the Customs Consolidation Act, 1876 (*a*). The officer of excise appears now to have no concern with the custody of the goods so far as the transferee or buyer is concerned, the warehousekeeper being alone answerable for their safe keeping and their proper delivery (*b*).'

(*a*) 39 and 40 Vict. c. 36.
(*b*) Rhind's Tr. *v.* Robertson & Baxter, 1891 ; 18 R. 623. See Smith *v.* Allan & Poynter, 1858 ; 22 D. 208 ; and the general rule in Anderson *v.* M'Call, *supra*, § 1303, *fin.*

1307. Stopping in Transitu.—The doctrine of stopping *in transitu* is, as Lord Stowell has observed, a proprietary right recognised by the general mercantile law of Europe; or rather an equitable extension of the right to retain possession of the goods sold till the price shall be paid, proceeding on the principle and effect of mutual contract (*a*). It is a doctrine of English law adopted in America, and not unknown in Scottish jurisprudence. It was first applied to Scottish bargains of moveables by a decision of the House of Lords in 1790, in place of a rule of presumed fraud *intra triduum*, which had formerly been held to entitle a seller to restitution of his goods, even after delivery (*b*). It proceeds on the ground of a right to retain the goods sold, or to recover them, if they have not yet got into the buyer's hand, in security of the price unpaid (*c*). 'It may be exercised only where the buyer has become bankrupt or insolvent (*d*); but if that condition exist, it is competent even where the goods have been sold on credit (*e*).'

(*a*) Brown on Sale, 433. 6 Rob. Ad. 498. 2 Kent, Com. 540, 552. Code de Commerce, No. 576, 580, 2.
(*b*) Allan, Stewart, & Co. *v.* Stein's Crs., 1790 ; M. 4949 ; 1 Ill. 15, 402 ; 3 Pat. 191.
(*c*) Tucker *v.* Humphrey, 4 Bing. 516 ; 1 Ill. 402. See below, 1309A.
(*d*) The Constantia, 6 Rob. Adm. 321. Wilmshurst *v.* Bowker, 2 M. & Gr. 792. 1 Bell's Com. 223. Sale of Goods Act, § 44.
(*e*) M'Laren's Bell's Com. i. 243. Inglis *v.* Usherwood, 1 East, 515. Edwards *v.* Brewer, 2 M. & W. 375. Dryden & Co. *v.* Hamelin, July 1853 ; Shaw's Bell's Com. 124 ; M'Laren's Bell's Com. i. 243.

1308. (1.) *When Competent or not* (*a*).—'By the Sale of Goods Act, 1893 (§ 45 (1)), the general principle is stated. Goods are deemed to be in course of transit from the time when they are delivered to a carrier by land or water, or other bailee, for the purpose of transmission to the buyer, until the buyer or his agent in that behalf takes delivery of them from such carrier or other bailee.' The rules of this doctrine of stopping *in transitu* are:—

Actual delivery by the seller to the buyer *de manu in manum* puts an end to the transit (*b*); with the exception of goods sold for ready money, and delivered before the price is paid, or where the reciprocal obligations are contemporary, the delivery then being conditional (*c*); and of goods taken into the buyer's custody for safety after insolvency (*d*). Goods delivered into a bond warehouse, or any public warehouse, for the buyer, there to abide the market at his orders, are no longer *in transitu*, or subject to stoppage (*e*).

Goods delivered into the buyer's ship, or into a ship hired by him on time, 'so as to be entirely in his possession and control (*f*),' are no longer *in transitu*; but if the ship is hired only for the voyage, they may be stopped, 'the master being the servant of the shipowners, and not by the terms of the charter-party the agent of the purchaser to receive the goods (*g*). Even where the goods are delivered on board the buyer's ship, the seller may secure his right to stop by taking the bill of lading to himself or his assigns (*h*). But this right ceases when he assigns the bill of lading (*i*). If the contract with the purchaser be fulfilled, and the goods be put on board a vessel not to be conveyed to him, but to be taken elsewhere as to a sub-vendee, by him or one who holds for him on a commercial speculation, the *transitus* between the seller and purchaser is over, the latter having obtained all the possession contemplated, and having sent them on a new voyage (*k*).

'The rule laid down by the Sale of Goods Act is that, where goods are delivered to a ship chartered by the buyer, it is a question depending on the circumstances of the particular case whether they are in the possession of the master as a carrier, or as an agent of the buyer (*l*).' Goods which are still with a workman to be finished, or with a warehouseman or broker for sale, and transferred by notice, or by an entry in the books, or by payment of warehouse rent, or by marking, are no longer *in transitu* (*m*). Goods in dock warehouses are conclusively transferred by indorsation of the dock warrant; the indorsee being *in bonâ fide*, and giving a valuable consideration for the transfer (*n*).

Where goods are still on their passage from the seller to the buyer in the hands of a middleman, they may be stopped (*o*). The description of middleman includes all those who are employed in the transit of goods,—as common carriers by land or water; shipping companies; masters of ships on general freight; packers, wharfingers, and warehousemen aiding in the transit 'or delivery; and the *transitus* continues in such cases until the goods are in the actual or constructive possession of the consignee (*p*).'

But this general rule admits of several exceptions. Thus, if, with the seller's permission, goods be taken by a shipmaster on a special receipt, "as goods shipped by the *buyer*," they are no longer *in transitu* (*q*). So, where a bill of lading transferable is indorsed for value, and without notice and collusion, there can be no stopping as *in transitu* against the indorsee (*r*); but this does not hold where the 'vendee's (*s*)' factor is indorsee, although he be under advance or acceptance on general account (*t*). 'When the transfer of the bill of lading is only in security, the right to stop *in transitu* is not absolutely defeated; but the seller resumes his right subject to the rights of the pledgee, who, however, must in the first instance apply the proceeds of other goods of the insolvent consignee which he may hold to the discharge of his claim (*u*).'

Where the middleman is, by agreement of the parties, '*i.e.* of himself and the buyer,' converted into a special agent of the buyer, there is no stoppage, 'and it is immaterial that a further destination for the goods may have been intimated by the buyer (*v*).' And acts of ownership exercised at the close of a voyage, 'or before arrival at the appointed destination' (if not conditional), will finish the *transitus*, although the goods be still with a middleman (*w*). 'Wrongful refusal of the carrier or custodier to deliver ends the transit; but not the buyer's rejection, while the middleman's possession continues, even if the seller has refused to receive them back (*x*).'

Part payment of the price of goods does not divest the seller of his right to stop 'the goods, or, if the contract be apportionable, such part of them as has not been paid for (*y*),' for the part unpaid (*z*). 'Part delivery, when it does not infer an agreement to give up possession of the whole, does not prevent stoppage of the remainder (*aa*).' Nor is it defeated by any claim made on the goods by a creditor of the buyer; as by an arrestment (*bb*); 'or by a sub-vendee, unless under a *bonâ fide* indorsement of a bill of lading, or transference of a document of title under the Factors Act (*cc*).'

The privilege of stopping *in transitu* is given only to sellers ('including an agent of the seller to whom the bill of lading has been indorsed, and a consignor who buys with his own money or credit') against buyers (*dd*); 'and it implies not only a countermand of the order to deliver to the purchaser, but an order to deliver to the seller, which the carrier is bound to obey (*ee*).'

(*a*) See 1 Bell's Com. 205 (223, M'L.'s ed.). 19 and 20 Vict. c. 60, § 2. *Supra*, § 1307 (*e*).

(*b*) See authorities under § 1302.

(*c*) Bishop *v.* Shillito, 2 B. & Ald. 329, note; 20 R. R. 457; 1 Ill. 410. Cowan *v.* Spence, 1824; 3 S. 42; 1 Ill. 108. M'Cartney *v.* M'Credie, 1799; M. Apx. *Sale*, No. 1; 1 Ill. 406. Brodie *v.* Todd & Co., May 20, 1814; F. C.; 1 Ill. 105. Anderson *v.* Ford, 1844; 6 D. 1315. See Watt *v.* Findlay, 1846; 8 D. 529. Richmond *v.* Railton, 1854; 16 D. 403. Hall & Sons *v.* Scott, 1860; 22 D. 413. Linn *v.* Shield, 1863; 2 Macph. 88. See above, § 100, 103, 1302 *fin.*

(*d*) Steins *v.* Hutchinson, Nov. 16, 1810; F. C.; 1 Ill. 408. See below, § 1310.

(*e*) Strachan *v.* Knox & Co., Jan. 21, 1817; F. C.; 1 Ill. 408. See cases, § 1302 (*e*). Allan *v.* Gripper, 2 Tyr. 217; 37 R. R. 682. Rowe *v.* Pickford, 8 Taunt. 89; 1 Ill. 409; 19 R. R. 466. See § 1303 (*q*). James *v.* Griffin, 1 M. & W.

20 ; 2 M. & W. 623. Edwards v. Brewer, 2 M. & W. 375. Nicholson v. Bower, 1 E. & E. 172. Nichols v. Lefevre, 2 Bing. N. C. 83. M'Laren's Bell's Com. i. 231.

(*f*) See above, § 405, and below, § 1423, as to "demise" of a ship.

(*g*) Fowler v. M'Taggart, 7 T. R. 442 ; 3 East, 396 ; 1 Ill. 379 ; 4 R. R. 485. Bohtlingk v. Inglis, 3 East, 395 ; 7 R. R. 490. Robertsons & Aitken v. More, July 3, 1801 ; M. Apx. *Sale*, No. 3. Baxter v. Pearson, *supra*, § 1304 (*b*). Drake v. M'Millan, 1807 ; Hume, 691. Neish v. Trompousky & Co., 1807 ; *ib.* 693. Schotsmans v. Lanc. and Yorksh. Ry. Co., L. R. 2 Ch. Ap. 332 ; 36 L. J. Ch. 361.

(*h*) Turner v. Trs. of Liverpool Docks, 6 Ex. 543 ; 20 L. J. Ex. 393. Berndtson v. Strang, 36 L. J. Ch. 879 ; 37 *ib.* 665 ; L. R. 4 Eq. 481 ; 3 Ch. Ap. 588. See above, § 103.

(*i*) Van Casteel v. Booker, 2 Ex. 691 ; 18 L. J. Ex. 9. Smith's Merc. Law, 344, 612. M'Laren's Bell's Com. i. 220, *infra* (*q*), and 1 Bell's Com. 214. See Shepherd v. Harrison, L. R. 4 Q. B. 196, 493. Moakes v. Nicholson, 19 C. B. N. S. 290 ; 34 L. J. C. P. 273.

(*k*) Fowler, *supra*. Cowasjee v. Thomson, 5 Moore, P. C. 165. Jones v. Jones, 8 M. & W. 481. Van Casteel v. Booker, *supra*. Kendal v. Marshall, Stevens, & Co., 11 Q. B. D. 356. Morton & Co. v. Abercromby, 1858 ; 20 D. 362. Cowdenbeath Coll. Co. v. Clydesdale Bk., 1895 ; 22 R. 682. *Ex p.* Miles, 15 Q. B. D. 30 (purchase by commission agent). See § 1309A.

(*l*) Sale of Goods Act, 1893, § 45 (5). See cases in (*p*) *infra*.

(*m*) Main v. Maxwell, 1710 ; M. 9124. Lawrie v. Black, 1831 ; 10 S. 1. Harman v. Anderson, 2 Comp. 243 ; 11 R. R. 706. Withers v. Lyss, 4 Camp. 237 ; 1 Ill. 409 ; 16 R. R. 781. Stonard v. Dunkin, 2 Camp. 344 ; 11 R. R. 704. Hawes v. Watson, 2 B. & Cr. 540 ; 26 R. R. 408. *Supra*, § 1303 (*g*).

(*n*) Keyser v. Suse, 3 Gow's Cases, 58. Zwinger v. Samuda, 7 Taunt. 265. Lucas v. Dorrien, *ib.* 278 ; 18 R. R. 476, 480. This is a case of delivery, not of stoppage. See § 1305.

(*o*) Snee v. Prescot, 1 Atk. 243. Wiseman v. Vandeput, 2 Vern. 303. Stokes v. La Riviere, 3 East, 397 ; 7 R. R. 499. Hunter v. Beale, *ib.* 466. See Dixon v. Baldwin, 5 East, 184 ; 1 Ill. 381 ; 7 R. R. 681. Hodgson v. Loy, 7 T. R. 440 ; 4 R. R. 483. Coates v. Railton, 6 B. & Cr. 422 ; 1 Ill. 411. Tucker v. Humphrey, 4 Bing. 516.

(*p*) Smith v. Goss, 1 Camp. 282 ; 1 Ill. 408 ; 10 R. R. 684. Hodgson, *supra* (*o*). Feise v. Wray, 3 East, 93 ; 6 R. R. 651. Tucker, *supra* (*o*). Nicholls v. Hart, 5 Car. & P. 179. Black v. Cassels, 1828 ; 6 S. 894 (goods which lay three months with carrier. See 1 Ill. 411, 412). Rodger v. Comptoir d'Escompte de Paris, L. R. 2 P. C. 393 ; 38 L. J. P. C. 30. Turner v. Liverpool Dock Trs., 6 Ex. 593. James v. Griffin, 1 M. & W. 20 ; 2 M. & W. 622. **Bolton v. L. and Y. Ry. Co.**, L. R. 1 C. P. 431 ; 35 L. J. C. P. 137. Edwards v. Brewer, 2 M. & W. 375. Whitehead v. Anderson, 9 M. & W. 518. **Wentworth v. Outhwaite**, 10 M. & W. 436 ; 2 Ross' L. C. 239. Coventry v. Gladstone, L. R. 6 Eq. 44 ; 37 L. J. Ch. 492. Valpy v. Gibson, 4 C. B. 837. **Barber v. Meyerstein**, L. R. 4 H. L. 317 ; 39 L. J. C. P. 187. *Ex p.* Gibbes, 1 Ch. D. 101 ; 45 L. J. Bkr. 10. *Ex p.* Watson, 5 Ch. D. 35 ; 46 L. J. Bkr. 97. *Ex p.* Rosevear China Clay Co., 11 Ch. D. 560 ; 48 L. J. Bkr. 100. M'Leod & Co. v. Harrison, 1880 ; 8 R. 227. Bethell v. Clark, 20 Q. B. D. 615.

(*q*) 1 Bell's Com. 203, 204 (221, M'L.'s ed.). Fragano v. Long, 4 B. & Cr. 219 ; 28 R. R. 226 ; 1 Ill. 391. Noble v. Adams, 2 Marsh. 366. Craven v. Ryder, *ib.* 129 ; 6 Taunt. 433 ; 16 R. R. 644. Morton & Co. v. Abercromby, 1858 ; 20 D. 362. See above (*g*).

(*r*) 1 Valin, 572. 1 Emerigon, 320. **Lickbarrow v. Mason**, 1 H. Bl. 357 ; 5 T. R. 683 ; 4 B. Parl. Cases, 57 ; 1 Ill. 404 ; 2 Ross' L. C. 92 ; 1 R. R. 425. Wright v. Campbell, 4 Burr. 2046. *In re* Westzinthus, 5 B. & Ad. 817 ; 1 Ill. 413. Bogle v. Dunmore & Co., 1787 ; M. 14,216 ; Hailes, 1018. Tod & Co. v. Rattray, Feb. 1, 1809 ; F. C. ; 1 Ill. 397. Salomons v. Nissen, 2 T. R. 674 ; 1 R. R. 592. Cuming v. Brown ; 9 R. R. 603 ; 9 East, 506. Coxe v. Harden, 4 East, 211 ; 7 R. R. 570. Stoppel & Son v. Stoddart, 1849 ; 11 D. 676 ; 1850, 13 D. 61. Morton & Co. v. Abercromby, 1858 ; 20 D. 362. Rodger v. Comptoir d'Escompte de Paris, *cit.* (*p*). Gurney v. Behrend, 3 E. & B. 622. The Marie Joseph (Pease v. Gloahec), L. R. 1 P. C. 219 ; 35 L. J. P. C. 66.

(*s*) In previous editions, "seller's." But see 52 and 53 Vict. c. 45 (Factors Act, 1889) ; and above, § 229.

(*t*) Patten v. Thomson, 5 M. & S. 350 ; 1 Ill. 409 ; 17 R. R. 350.

(*u*) *In re* Westzinthus, *cit.* Spalding v. Ruding, 6 Beav. 376 ; 15 L. J. Ch. 374. 1 Smith's L. C. 737 sqq. Kemp v. Falk, 7 App. Ca. 573. See Burdick v. Sewell, 10 App. Ca. 74. And see the Sale of Goods Act and Factors Acts as cited above, § 1305 *ad fin.*

(*v*) Richardson v. Goss, 3 B. & P. 126 ; 1 Ill. 380 ; 6 R. R. 727. Scott v. Pettit, *ib.* 469 ; 7 R. R. 804. Dixon v. Baldwin, *supra* (*o*). Leeds v. Wright, 3 B. & P. 320 ; 7 R. R. 709. See doctrine in Tucker, *supra* (*o*). Sale of Goods Act, § 45 (3). See above, § 1305 (*e*). Dodson v. Wentworth, 4 M. & Gr. 1080. Wentworth v. Outhwaite, Bolton v. L. and Y. Ry. Co., Valpy v. Gibson, Whitehead v. Anderson, and other cases, *supra* (*p*). Cowasjee v. Thompson, 5 Moore, P. C. 165. *Ex p.* Barrow, 6 Ch. D. 783 ; 46 L. J. Bkr. 71. *Ex p.* Cooper, *in re* M'Laren, 11 Ch. D. 68 ; 48 L. J. Bkr. 49. The retention by the carrier of his lien for the freight is not inconsistent with his becoming agent for the buyer, though it is strong evidence of the contrary. Whitehead v. Anderson, *supra* (*p*). Allan v. Gripper, *supra* (*c*). *Ex p.* Falk (Kemp v. Falk), 14 Ch. D. 446 ; 7 App. Ca. 753. See Moakes v. Nicholson, 19 C. B. N. S. 290 ; 34 L. J. C. P. 273 ; and 1 Smith's L. C. 818. Benjamin on Sales, 839 sq.

(*w*) Ellis v. Hunt, 3 T. R. 464 ; 1 Ill. 390 ; 1 R. R. 743. Foster, *infra*. Mills v. Ball, 2 B. & P. 457 ; 4 R. R. 653. Nicholas v. Lefevre, 2 B. & Ald. 81 ; 1 Ill. 414. Morley v. Hay, 3 Man. & Ry. 396. The Act, § 45 (2). In general the transit will be at an end if the carrier in fact deliver the goods into the hands of the consignee before their arrival. On the other hand, the carrier cannot extend the vendor's right to stop by unlawfully withholding the goods. See Whitehead, *supra* (*p*). Jackson v. Nichol, 5 Bing. N. C. 508. Coventry, *supra* (*p*). L. and N.-W. Ry. Co. v. Bartlett, 7 H. & N. 400. Foster v. Frampton, 6 B. & Cr. 107 ; 30 R. R. 255. Bird v. Brown, 4 Ex. 786. 1 Bell's Com. 224 (244, M'L.'s ed.). Benjamin on Sales, 845. 1 Smith's L. C. 732.

(*x*) Sale of Goods Act, § 45 (6) (4).

(*y*) Merchant Banking Co. v. Phœnix Bessemer Steel Co., 5 Ch. D. 205 ; 46 L. J. Ch. 418.

(*z*) Hodgson, *supra* (*o*). Van Casteel, *supra* (*i*). Edwards v. Brewer, 2 M. & W. 375. Melrose & Co. v. Hastie, 1851 ; 13 D. 880 ; 14 D. 268. Sale of Goods Act, § 38.

(*aa*) The Sale of Goods Act, § 45 (7). See above, § 1303 (*b*).

(*bb*) Feise, *supra* (*p*). Kinloch v. Craig, 3 T. R. 119 and 783 ; 1 Ill. 395 ; 1 R. R. 664. Brodie's Stair, 884. Dunlop v. Scott & Co., Feb. 22, 1814 ; F. C. Louson v. Craik, 1842 ; 4 D. 1452 (surety for the price. It is thought that a surety who has paid the price would be entitled to stop. Impl. Bank v. London and St. Katherine Dock Co., 5 Ch. D. 195 ; 46 L. J. Ch. 335. Benjamin on Sales, 819. 19 and 20 Vict. c. 97, § 5).

(*cc*) Cases above (*r*). Dixon v. Yates, 5 B. & A. 313. Jenkins v. Usborne, 7 M. & G. 678. 1 Smith's L. C. 733. *Infra*, § 1317B (2).

(*dd*) Butler v. Woolcot, 2 N. R. 64. See Sale of Goods Act, § 38 (2) ; below, § 1416. Louson v. Craik, *cit.* (*bb*). Falk v. Fletcher, 18 C. B. N. S. 403 ; 34 L. J. C. P. 146. Pennell v. Alexander, 3 E. & B. 243. Whitehead v. Anderson, 9 M. & W. 518. Adamson, Howie, & Co. v. Guild, 1868 ; 6 Macph. 347.

(*ee*) The Tigress, B. & L. 38 ; 32 L. J. Adm. 97.

1309. (2.) *Modes of Stopping.*—The most correct and effectual mode of stopping is by warrant of the Judge Ordinary or a magistrate (*a*); 'but this is not usual in practice, and in ordinary cases is made unnecessary by the duty now expressly imposed by statute on the carrier or custodier to obey the directions of the seller (*b*).' In England, bankruptcy alone is not sufficient or equivalent to stoppage (*c*); but in Scotland there is at least a bias toward an opposite rule (*d*). Notice, even verbal, is enough (*e*); but notice to the buyer's creditor is not enough (*f*). 'It must either be given to the person who has the immediate custody of the goods, or so that the middleman (*e.g.* the shipowner) may be able with reasonable care to communicate the stoppage to his servants in charge of the goods (*g*).' It would seem that a seller is not entitled to intercept the voyage of a general ship in order to stop his goods *in transitu* (*h*).

(*a*) Morton & Co. *v.* Abercromby, 1858; 20 D. 362. Stoppel & Co. *v.* Stoddart, 1850; 13 D. 61. Schotsmans, *supra*, § 1308 (*g*).
(*b*) Sale of Goods Act, § 46 (2).
(*c*) Haswell *v.* Hunt, 5 T. R. 231, and 226, 230; 1 Ill. 414; see 2 R. R. 573. Scott *v.* Pettit, *sup.* (*r*). As to the effect of the buyer's insolvency on a contract of sale, see above, § 100.
(*d*) 1 Bell's Com. 227 (248, M'L.'s ed.) sqq., and cases there cited. See Brown *v.* Watson, 1816; Hume, 709; below, § 1310.
(*e*) Robertsons & Aitken *v.* More, 1801; M. *Sale*, Apx. 3; 1 Ill. 393. See Benjamin on Sales, 850.
(*f*) Same case.
(*g*) Whitehead *v.* Anderson, 9 M. & W. 518. See The Tigress, *supra*, § 1308 (*ee*). *Ex p.* Watson, 5 Ch. D. 35; 46 L. J. Bkr. 97. *Ex p.* Falk (**Kemp** *v.* **Falk**), 14 Ch. D. 446; 7 App. Ca. 573. Sale of Goods Act, 1893, § 46.
(*h*) Goodhart *v.* Lowe, 2 Jac. & W. 349; 1 Ill. 410; 22 R. R. 161.

1309A. 'It is a mistake, and one productive of much confusion, to regard the question whether goods have been delivered to the buyer, and the question whether they can be stopped *in transitu*, as identical. The latter question can only arise when delivery has taken place; before delivery, the seller's remedy is his right to *retain*, of which the right to stop *in transitu*, speaking loosely, is an equitable extension. The right to retain ceases upon delivery; the right to stop ceases upon the termination of the *transitus* (*a*). And the *transitus* continues so long as the goods are still in the carrier's hands as such and for the purpose of the original transit, although the carrier was the purchaser's agent to accept delivery so as to pass the property. There has been difficulty in determining whether a fresh transit has not begun; but it is clearly settled that the right of stoppage exists so long as the transit has been caused, either by the terms of the contract or by the directions of the purchaser to the vendor. When the goods are in transit in consequence of fresh directions given by the purchaser, or have reached a particular place, there to be kept till the purchaser gives fresh orders as to their destination, the right to stop has ceased (*b*).

'It has been a subject of controversy whether stoppage *in transitu* rescinds the contract of sale, so as to throw the risk back on the seller, and deprive him of the right to recover the price and charges, if those should exceed the market value of the goods stopped. In Scotland, the opinion that the contract is not rescinded, but that stoppage merely restores to him the right of possession and revests him with the rights of an unpaid vendor, appears to prevail, contrary to the opinion of Professor Bell (*c*); and, though it is said not to be decided, the same view is supported by the greatest weight of authority in England (*d*).

'It is now enacted that—1. A contract of sale is not rescinded by the mere exercise by an unpaid seller of his right of lien, or retention, or stoppage *in transitu*. 2. Where an unpaid seller after exercising such right resells the goods, the buyer acquires a good title thereto as against the first buyer. 3. Where the goods are perishable, or the unpaid seller gives notice to the buyer of his intention to resell, and the buyer does not within a reasonable time pay or tender the price, he may resell and recover from the original buyer damages for any loss occasioned by his breach of contract. 4. Where the seller expressly reserves a right of resale in case of the buyer's default, on or such default resells, the contract of sale is thereby rescinded, but without prejudice to any claim of the seller for damages (*e*).'

(*a*) See 1 M'Laren's Bell's Com. 183, 211, 217, etc. *Supra*, § 1302, 1303, etc. Schotsmans and Berndtson, *supra*, § 1308 (*g*) (*h*).
(*b*) Bethell *v.* Clark, 20 Q. B. D. 215. Lyons *v.* Hoffnung (P. C.), 1890; 15 App. Ca. 391. See above, § 1308 *init.*
(*c*) 1 Bell's Com. 230. Stoppel & Co. *v.* Stoddart, 1850; 13 D. 61. Adamson, Howie, & Co. *v.* Guild, 1868; 6 Macph. 347 (*per* L. Barcaple).
(*d*) Gibson *v.* Carruthers, 8 M. & W. 321; 2 Ross' L. C.

255. **Bloxam** *v.* **Saunders**, 4 B. & Cr. 941; 2 Ross' L. C. 48; 28 R. R. 579. Clay *v.* Harrison, 10 B. & C. 99; 34 R. R. 334. **Wentworth** *v.* **Outhwaite**, 10 M. & W. 450; 2 Ross' L. C. 239. Martindale *v.* Smith, 1 Q. B. 397. Schotsmans *v.* Lanc. and Y. Ry. Co., *supra*, § 1308 (*g*). *Ex p.* Falk (**Kemp** *v.* **Falk**), 7 App. Ca. 573. Smith's Merc. Law, 545–547. 1 Smith's L. C. 811 sqq. Benjamin on Sales, 864 sqq.

(*e*) Sale of Goods Act, 1893, § 48.

1310. (3.) *Rejection on Insolvency.*—The buyer may and ought (*a*) to reject the goods when offered to be delivered, if he be unable to perform his engagement. And (although it has been doubted whether bankruptcy alone would not be sufficient to operate as stoppage (*b*)) it seems to be law, that if the goods be taken by the buyer (*c*), they cannot afterwards be rejected; that if taken only by a clerk, without authority, they may still be rejected by the buyer (*d*); and that if taken *custodiæ causa*, with the intention only of preserving them for the seller, the seller's right to them is preserved (*e*). 'Intimation of the rejection to the seller is necessary, to enable him by acceptance to rescind the contract. But the property is prevented from passing to the insolvent buyer even by ambiguous acts, such as depositation in neutral custody for the benefit of all concerned, provided it appear that the buyer does not take possession in the usual course of trade (*f*).'

(*a*) As to the duty, see Watt and Booker, *infra*. Carnegie & Co. *v.* Hutchison, 1815; Hume, 704. Brown *v.* Watson, 1816; Hume, 709.

(*b*) See above, § 1309.

(*c*) Mitchell *v.* Wright, 1871; 9 Macph. 576 (delivery complete).

(*d*) Wallace & Co. *v.* Miller, 1766; M. 8475; Hailes, 27; 1 Ill. 415. See Heinekey *v.* Earle, 8 E. & B. 410; 28 L. J. Q. B. 79. Brandt & Co. *v.* Dickson, *infra* (*e*).

(*e*) Steins *v.* Hutchinson, Nov. 16, 1810; F. C.; 1 Ill. 408. James *v.* Griffin, 2 M. & W. 623. See Carnegie & Co. *v.* Hutchison, 1815; Hume, 704. Mitchell & Gowans *v.* Phin, Jan. 12, 1813; F. C. Inglis *v.* Port Eglinton Spinning Co., 1842; 4 D. 478. Watt *v.* Findlay, 1846; 8 D. 529, 532. Drake *v.* M'Millan, 1807; Hume, 691. **Booker & Co.** *v.* **Milne**, 1870; 9 Macph. 314. Brandt & Co. *v.* Dickson, 1876; 3 R. 375. Atkin *v.* Barwick, 1 Str. 165; 1 Ill. 415. Bartram *v.* Farebrother, 4 Bing. 579; 1 Ill. 415; 29 R. R. 639. Heinekey *v.* Earle, *cit.* (*d*). Benjamin on Sales, 492. See also Birrell's Tr. *v.* Clark & Rowe, 1874; 18 Journ. of Jur. 495; 1 Guthrie's Sel. Sh. Ct. Ca. 86.

(*f*) Drake, and Booker & Co., *supra* (*e*).

CHAPTER III

OF POSSESSION OF MOVEABLES

1311. Nature of Possession.—Possession is detention, with the design or *animus* of holding the subject as the property of the holder. It differs from custody, which is conditional and limited possession, held not for the custodier, but for another. It is acquired originally by mere occupancy of things not formerly appropriated, and derivatively by tradition (*a*).

(*a*) 2 Stair, 1. § 42. 2 Ersk. 1. § 28 et seq. See above § 1287 and 1299 et seq.

1312. Kinds.—Possession is "Natural," *i.e.* held by the owner himself ostensibly and manifestly; or "Civil," held by others for him, as his servants, clerks, factors, consignees, or persons having the custody or use of the thing (*a*).

(*a*) 2 Ersk. 1. § 22. Union Bank *v.* Mackenzie, 1865; 3 Macph. 765.

1313. Presumption of Property.—Possession (provided it be actual) presumes property in moveables,—*in pari casu potior est conditio possidentis.* It is on this principle that in Scotland a factor in possession of goods has at common law power to pledge, which in England is given by statute (*a*).

(*a*) 2 Stair, 1. § 42. 2 Ersk. 1. § 20. See above, § 229, 114; below, § 1364.

1314. The legal presumption of property from possession may be overcome by other presumptions, or by proof (*a*). In proof of property to counteract the presumption, there must be evidence of right, and also of the loss of possession,—as, that the thing was stolen; that it was given in pledge, in loan, etc. (*b*).

(*a*) Warrender *v.* Thomson, 1715; M. 10,609; 1 Ill. 416. See § 1320. Sharpe *v.* Smyth, 1832; 11 S. 38. Macdougall *v.* Whitelaw, 1840; 2 D. 500. Anderson *v.* Buchanan, 1848; 11 D. 270. Orr's Tr. *v.* Tullis, 1870; 8 Macph. 936. Cases under § 1315.

(*b*) Scott *v.* Fletcher, 1665; M. 11,616. Ramsay *v.* Wilson, 1666; M. 9113 et seq. Pringle *v.* Gribton, 1710; M. 9123.

1314A. 'Sale of Goods by Persons having no Title or a Voidable Title.—Subject to the provisions of the Sale of Goods Act, 1893, a sale of moveables by a person who is not the owner and has not the authority or consent of the owner to the sale, gives the buyer no better title than the seller had, unless the owner is by his conduct precluded from denying the seller's authority to sell (*a*). But the Sale of Goods Act does not affect the provisions of the Factors Acts (*b*) or other Acts (such as the Bills of Lading Act) enabling an apparent owner to dispose of goods as if he were the true owner; or the validity of any contract of sale under any special common law or statutory power of sale, or under judicial authority (*c*).

'When goods are sold by one who has a voidable (reducible) title, not avoided at the time of the sale, a buyer in good faith and without notice acquires a good title to the goods (*d*).'

(*a*) 56 and 57 Vict. c. 71, § 21. Colonial Bk. *v.* Whinney, 11 App. Ca. 426, 435. Hollins *v.* Fowler, L. R. 7 H. L. 757; 44 L. J. Q. B. 169. Cundy *v.* Lindsay, 3 App. Ca. 459; 47 L. J. Q. B. 481. See above, § 27A, and Pickard *v.* Sears, Seton *v.* Lafone, etc., *ibi citt.*

(*b*) See below, § 1317 sqq.

(*c*) The Sale of Goods Act, § 21 (2).

(*d*) The Act, § 23. Cundy *v.* Lindsay, *cit.*, etc.

1315. Reputed Ownership.—Considering the force of the above presumption, and its effect in raising credit in a commercial country, collusive possession of anything is a natural ground on which the creditors of the person allowed so to possess may attach it for debt; creditors trusting to the apparent ownership in their debtor, and giving credit accordingly. It is necessary, however, carefully to distinguish between such possession as is required in the course of legitimate contracts, and such as may be needlessly, carelessly, or fraudulently given to, or left with, one who is not the owner. Possession alone is not a ground on which moveables shall be made to answer for the debt of the possessor, or on which creditors are entitled to rely: for the goods in their debtor's possession may be with him, not as owner, but under some contract requiring temporary possession. Hence, every legitimate cause of possession makes an exception to the credit of apparent ownership (*a*): 'and creditors are bound to know that many honest occasions of possession may arise in the daily complication of human affairs, without any radical title of property in the mere possessor on which they would be entitled to rely as a ground of credit (*b*).' So, in commodate, the possession of the borrower is no lawful ground of credit to him. In hiring, neither the subject let (*c*), nor materials in the hands of a workman under *locatio operis* (*d*), can afford a fair ground of enlarged credit to the possessor. In deposit, though the thing deposited may appear as part of the custodier's stock, it remains separate on his bankruptcy as the property of the depositors. So furniture deposited is not liable to the landlord's hypothec; so also fungibles deposited, if separate and distinguishable, and even money if specifically distinguished (*e*), are not to be held the custodier's. In pledge, the goods remain distinct from the creditor's stock. In factory, goods of the principal are often mingled with the factor's, and difficult cases arise where the identity is lost; but where the distinction is traceable, the rule applies (*f*). Goods on sale and return are not attachable by the consignee's creditors (*g*); nor goods consigned for advances and sale. And goods left with the seller, if properly separated (as wine in a bin, or corn in a warehouse, of which the key is delivered), and marked and distinguished as the buyer's, are not to be taken by the seller's creditors (*h*).

(*a*) 1 Bell's Com. 254 (274, M'L.'s ed.). 1 Selwyn, N.P. 217 et seq., and cases cited. See as to liferent, Scott *v.* Price, 1837; 15 S. 916, 919; as to questions between a husband's creditors and his wife as to furniture, **Shearer** *v.* **Christie,** 1842; 5 D. 132. Campbell *v.* Stewart, 1848; 10 D. 1280. Brown *v.* Fleming, 1850; 13 D. 373. Young *v.* Loudoun, 1855; 17 D. 998. Fraser, Husband and Wife, 691, 1344; and below, § 1549.

(*b*) *Per* L. Ivory in Shearer *v.* Christie, 1842, 5 D. 132, quoted in many recent decisions; in which also the doctrine of this and the two succeeding paragraphs, which are abridged from the Commentaries, *l.c.*, is recognised as correct.

(*c*) See **Orr's Tr.** *v.* **Tullis,** 1870; 8 Macph. 936. Marston *v.* Kerr's Tr., 1879; 6 R. 898 (hire with option to purchase). Robertsons *v.* M'Intyre, 1882; 9 R. 772. Duncanson *v.* Jefferis' Tr., 1881; 8 R. 563. *Supra*, § 1303, *fin.*

(*d*) See above, § 1303 (*g*).

(*e*) See below, § 1333; above, § 1276, *fin.*

(*f*) See 1 Bell's Com. 259–269 (278 sqq., M'L.'s ed.).

(*g*) Gibson *v.* Bray, 8 Taunt. 76; 19 R. R. 640. Macdonald *v.* Westren, 1888; 15 R. 988. Sadler *v.* Whitmore, 5 E. Jur. 315. In regard to the proper contract of sale and return, Prof. Bell says: "In this transaction of sale and return, the property is in suspense till sold, or the election determined; and in the meantime, the creditors of the persons so sending the goods will take them. But any of them sold are sold to the benefit of the person having them on sale or return, and his creditors will be entitled to the price, not the sender of the goods. Bailey *v.* Gouldsmith, Peake, N. P. 56." Bell on Sale, p. 111. See above, § 109.

(*h*) See § 1303, and cases there cited. *Ex p.* Marrable, 1 Glyn & Jam. 402.

1316. Collusive Possession is when the appearance of ownership is carried beyond the purpose or occasion of a legitimate contract, and powers of disposal are ostensibly given or allowed to be assumed. Such neglect, by misleading creditors to trust the possessor on his apparent ownership, justly exposes the owner to the loss of his goods, when attached for the debt of the possessor (*a*). In England, ownership was held originally to give right to the creditors of the owner to take the goods; but a statute of James I. introduced an exception in cases of reputed ownership and collusive possession, giving to the creditors of persons holding such possession a right to attach the subjects of it (*b*). In Scotland, credit raised on apparent ownership has been long favoured, and is the ground of a statutory privilege given to the creditors of an apparent heir in land (*c*). Both proceed on the same principle (*d*).

(*a*) Borthwick *v.* Grant, 1829; 7 S. 420; 1 Ill. 417. Fraser *v.* Frisby, 1830; 8 S. 982.

(*b*) 21 James I. c. 19. 6 Geo. IV. c. 19, § 72. 46 and 47 Vict. c. 52, § 44 (iii.). Smith's Merc. Law, p. 772 sq. 2 Smith's L. C. 223 sqq.

(*c*) 1695, c. 24. See below, § 1929.

(*d*) Knowles *v.* Horsfall, *cit.* § 1306. See Lingard *v.* Messiter, 1 B. & Cr. 308.

1317. Collusive possession proceeds on the appearance of uncontrolled possession and power of disposal; on acquiescence 'by the true owner' in something beyond the possession requisite to a fair contract, the proof of collusion varying, of course, with circumstances. Thus, where possession is continued by a former owner, creditors are more easily misled into a belief of ownership. The same takes place where a disposition or assignation of moveables is made, *retenta possessione*; and in such a case neither an instrument of possession, nor even actual delivery if the thing be immediately restored, has any effect in passing the property so as to counteract the presumption of property arising from possession (*a*).

'*Securities over Moveables without Possession.*—A large number of cases have occurred in late years in which attempts have been made to create securities over moveables without possession, in many cases successfully. Thus such continued possession as is mentioned above is not suffered to prevail in favour of the possessor's creditors, if it be clearly shown that it was had upon a new title, such as location, loan, etc., after a *boná fide* sale (*b*). The Court professes to inquire in all cases into the truth of transactions, and even where there has been a sale, and a transfer of the property, will not allow the seller to retain a security over the article sold, by means of a simulate contract of hiring, or where the transaction is truly a security (*c*). So it has been held that a person may acquire moveables by purchase (*e.g.* the machinery in a mill or the furniture of an inn), taking delivery of them through a tenant or other bailee, and leave them in his possession on a contract of hire or of "hire and purchase," without exposing them to the diligence of the tenant's creditors (*d*); or may sell under a clause of pre-emption articles which he retains in his possession (*e*).

'Many of these cases can hardly be reconciled; but while the principle of reputed ownership has become less important in practice than it was when Prof. Bell wrote, and while Lord Young has frequently dissented and held, where the form of sale has been honestly adopted and where the lender has received a proprietary title, that a conveyance of moveables with the intention of making a security is to be sustained as such, the true rule seems to be best stated in the words of Lord Kincairney: "I am disposed to think that a conveyance of moveables has been sustained, to the effect of constituting a security for an advance, where the transaction has been in reality a pure sale, although the whole object of it has been to effect a security, and although there may be an understanding that the ownership shall revert to the borrower when that purpose has been served; and it seems to me that the rule of law, that an assignation of moveables without delivery is totally ineffectual, has not yet been relaxed by decisions to any greater extent" (*f*).

'Several of the cases (*e.g.* M'Bain *v.* Wallace and Liddell's Tr. *v.* Warr & Co., *citt.*) were decided on the ground that they fell under sec. 1 of the Mercantile Law Amendment Act, 1856 (*g*); and it may perhaps be asked whether, if that Act had not existed, any question would have been raised. That section, however, has been repealed by the Sale of Goods Act, 1893, § 60; and sec. 17 of the same Act makes delivery no longer essential to pass the property in a sale of specific or ascertained goods. But sec. 61, subsec. 4 declares that "the provisions of the Act relating to contracts of sale do not apply to any transaction in the form of a contract of sale which is intended to operate by way of mortgage, pledge, charge, or other security" (*h*). Although the cases on the subject are discussed or noted here, it is thought that this clause of the Sale of Goods Acts really makes most of them superfluous.'

(*a*) See above, § 1300, and cases there referred to. Breichan *v.* Muirhead, 1810; Hume, 215 (conveyance of tavern furniture to wife). Johnstone *v.* Sprott, 1814; Hume, 448 (pledge of horses, etc., to servant). Cargill *v.* Millar, 1820; Hume, 223 (goods in shop kept by wife). Brock *v.* Cabbell, 1831; 5 W. & S. 476 (security over lease). Macdougal *v.* Whitelaw, 1840; 2 D. 500. Anderson *v.* Buchanan, 1848; 11 D. 270. Sim *v.* Grant, 1862; 24 D. 1033. Benton *v.* Craig, 1864; 2 Macph. 1365. Edmond *v.* Mowat, 1868; 7 Macph. 59. See cases in § 1303, 1314, and in note (*b*). Hewat's Tr. *v.* Smith, 1891; 19 R. 403 (pictures conveyed by marriage contract).

(*b*) Orr's Tr. *v.* Tullis, 1870; 8 Macph. 936. Robertsons *v.* M'Intyre, 1882; 9 Macph. 772. Liqr. of W. Lothian Oil Co. *v.* Mair, 1892; 20 R. 64. Liddell's Tr. *v.* Warr & Co., 1893; *ib.* 989. Mitchell's Trs. *v.* Gladstone, 1894; 21 R. 586; Brechin Auction Co. *v.* Reid, 1895; 22 R. 711; and other cases, *supra*, § 1315 (*c*). **M'Bain *v.* Wallace & Co.**, 1881; 8 R. 360; aff. *ib.* H. L. 106; 6 App. Ca. 588 (decided on the Merc. Law Amend. Act, sec. 1; see § 1300A, 1303); and comp. M'Caul's Tr. *v.* Thomson, 1883, 10 R. 1064, with Anderson *v.* Buchanan, 1848, 11 D. 270,—a case which has been much doubted, and in which the opinion of Lord Moncreiff, who dissented, has since been repeatedly cited as giving a clear and correct view of the law. Stiven *v.* Scott & Simson, 1871; 9 Macph. 923. Pattison's Tr. *v.* Liston, 1893; 20 R. 806.

(*c*) Cropper *v.* Donaldson, 1880; 7 R. 1108. Heritable Sec. Invt. Assoc. *v.* Wingate's Tr., 1880; *ib.* 1094.

(*d*) See Union Bank *v.* Mackenzie, 1865; 3 Macph. 765. Duncanson *v.* Jefferis' Tr., 1881; 8 R. 563. Hogarth *v.* Smart's Tr., 1882; 9 R. 964. Thomson *v.* Scoular, 1882; 9 R. 430.

(*e*) Allan & Co.'s Tr. *v.* Gunn & Co., 1883; 10 R. 997. Cases cited above in these notes, and above in § 109.

(*f*) Robertson *v.* Hall's Tr., 1896; 24 R. 120, 127.

(*g*) See above, § 1300A.

(*h*) Robertson *v.* Hall's Tr., *cit.* 56 and 57 Vict. c. 71, § 17, 61 (4).

1317A. 'The Effect given to Possession by the Factors Acts.—As a general rule, a person in possession of goods can confer on another by sale or pledge no better title than he himself has; and therefore it must be shown that the seller or pledger of goods not his own has authority from the owner to sell or pledge. In the case of a factor for selling goods, it was held in England, contrary to the decisions in Scotland (*a*), that his possession of goods in that character, or of a bill of lading or other symbol of possession, did not imply power to pledge them for advances (*b*). This was found to be inconvenient; and by the influence of the banking interest the earlier Factors Acts were passed; and a series of Acts followed—known by the same name—which, founded on the principle of personal exception or estoppel, established, at least for the cases to which they extend, the general rule that, when the owner of goods has clothed anyone with apparent authority to act as his agent in dealing with them, he is bound by the agent's acts in selling or pledging the goods just as if he had given express authority. In other words, the ostensible possession of the goods, or of the documents which are their symbols, is the badge and criterion, not indeed of property, but of the *jus disponendi*, so far as the public is concerned; so that third parties dealing in good faith with the holder are *not* to be prejudiced by latent claims against the goods by the person from whom he has derived possession. The earlier Acts applied to agents entrusted with possession of goods or documents of title to goods. An Act of 1877 extended the principle to the case of buyers or sellers left in possession of the documents of title to goods.

'It was held that this complicated and ill-digested series of enactments, "The Factors Acts, 1823 to 1877" (*c*), applied to Scotland (*d*). They were repealed by the "Factors Act, 1889," which consolidated and amended their provisions (*e*). The brief summary of these Acts given in previous editions is here retained for the sake of historical connection, and particularly of the decisions as to their effect.

'By the Act 6 Geo. IV. c. 94, it was provided as follows (*f*):—

'(1.) *Consignor of Goods deemed the true Owner.*—The person in whose name goods are shipped is to be deemed the true owner thereof, so far as to entitle the consignee to a lien thereon in respect of any money or negotiable security advanced by him to such person, or received by such person to his use, if he has not notice by the bill of lading or otherwise, at or before the advance or receipt, that such person is not the actual and *bonâ fide* owner of the goods; and such person shall be taken for the purposes of the Act to have been entrusted with the goods for the purpose of consignment or sale, unless the contrary be made to appear (*g*).

'(2.) *Agent entrusted with Goods or Documents of Title to Goods to be deemed the true Owner of the Goods.*—So also a person entrusted with, and in possession of, a bill of lading or any of the warrants, certificates, or orders mentioned in the Act, is to be deemed the true owner of the goods described therein, so far as to give validity to any contract or agreement made by him for the sale or disposition of the goods, or the deposit or pledge thereof, if the buyer, disponer, or pawnee has not notice, by the document or otherwise, that such person is not the actual and *bonâ fide* owner of the goods (*h*). Various decisions having shown that this Act was insufficient for its purpose, it was provided by the statute of 1842, that any agent entrusted with the possession of goods, or of the documents of title to goods (which are defined (sec. 4) to be "any bill of lading, India warrant, dock warrant, warehousekeeper's certificate, warrant or order for the delivery of goods, or any other document used in the ordinary course of business as proof of the possession or control of goods, or authorising or purporting to authorise, either by indorsement or by delivery, the possessor of such document, to transfer or receive goods thereby represented"), shall be deemed the owner of the goods so far as to give validity, against the owner and all other persons interested in the goods, to any agreement by way of pledge, lien, or security *bonâ fide* made with him, as well for any original loan, advance, or payment made on the security of such goods or documents, as also for any further or continuing advance in respect thereof, notwithstanding that the person claiming the pledge or lien has notice that the possessor of the goods is only an agent (*i*).

'In construing these enactments it was held, and is still law (*k*), that they apply (as does the remainder of the Acts) only to dealings in mercantile transactions and by agents for sale (*l*), not to clerks, servants, and the like (*m*), or to a wharfinger (*n*) or warehouseman entrusted with the goods as such, even though he also carries on business as a factor or agent to sell (*o*). It was also held that a vendor allowed by the buyer to retain possession of the documents of title (*p*), and a vendee obtaining possession of them (*q*), were not agents entrusted with them in the sense of these Acts.

'(3.) *Vendor retaining Documents of Title and Vendee obtaining them to be within the Acts.*—This led to the passing of the Factors Act of 1877, by which it was enacted, *inter alia*, that on a sale of goods, if the vendor or any person on his behalf continues or is in possession of the documents of title, a pledge, sale, or other disposition of the goods or documents by the vendor, or any person or agent entrusted by the vendor with the goods or documents within the meaning of the Acts, so continuing or being in possession, should be as valid as if such vendor or person were an agent or person entrusted within the meaning of the Acts, provided that the person to whom the pledge, sale, or other disposition is made had not notice that the goods were previously sold (*r*). It was further enacted that on a sale, or contract for the sale of goods, the vendee or a person on his behalf having obtained possession of the documents of title from the vendor or his agents, a sale, pledge, or other disposition of such goods or documents by such vendee or person should be as valid as if the vendee or person were an agent entrusted by the vendor with the documents within the meaning of the Acts, provided the person to whom the sale, pledge, or disposition was made had not notice of any lien or other right of the vendor in respect of the goods (*s*).

'(4.) *Revocation of Agency without Notice.*—As it was decided under the previous statutes that an agent whose power of sale had been revoked was not within the operation of the Acts (*t*), the same statute provided further, that a revocation of the entrustment or agency of an agent who continues in possession of goods or documents of title should not prejudice or affect the title or rights of any purchaser or lender without notice of such revocation (*u*).

'(5.) *Notice to Third Parties, Antecedent Debts, etc.*—The 3rd section of the Act of 1825 provided that if a factor entrusted as aforesaid deposited or pledged goods as security for a pre-existing debt or demand, he who so took the deposit or pledge without notice should acquire such right, title, or interest as, and no further or other than, was possessed by the person making the deposit or pledge (*v*). And further (sec. 4), any person might contract for the purchase of goods with any agent entrusted with the goods, or to whom they might be consigned, and receive and pay for the same to the agent, notwithstanding he should have notice that the party with whom he contracts was an agent, if such contract and payment were made in the ordinary and usual course of business, and he had not at the time of the contract or payment notice that the agent was not authorised to sell or to receive the price. Also (sec. 5) any person might accept any goods or any such document as aforesaid, or deposit or pledge from any factor or agent, notwithstanding he should have notice that the party was a factor or agent; but, in such case, he should acquire such right, title, or interest, and no further or other than was possessed by the factor or agent at the time of the deposit or pledge. These provisions, as well as the other provisions of the Act, were partly a confirmation or declaration of the common law (*w*), and were to be read along with the amendment in the Act of 1842, which was to this effect: that the Act protects such loans, advances, and exchanges (*x*) only as shall be made *boná fide* and without notice that the agent has not authority to make the contract or agreement, or is acting *mala fide* against the owner; and "nothing herein shall be construed to extend to or protect any lien or pledge for, or in respect of, any antecedent debt" (*v*) of the agent to the pledgee, nor to authorise an agent in deviating from any express orders or authority received from the owner; but that, to the effect of protecting such *boná fide* loans, etc. (though made with notice of the agent not being owner, but without notice of the agent's acting without authority), and to no further or other intent or purpose, the contract or agreement shall be binding on the owner and all other persons interested in the goods (*y*).

'(6.) *An agent entrusted*, in the sense of the Acts, is defined to be an agent possessed of a document of title, whether derived immediately from the owner of the goods or obtained by reason of his being entrusted with the possession of the goods or of any other document or title thereto (*z*). Contracts pledging or giving a lien upon a document of title as defined above are taken to be respectively pledges of and liens upon the goods to which it relates. And where any loan or advance shall be *boná fide* made to any agent entrusted with, and in possession of, goods or documents of title, on the faith of a written agreement to consign, deposit, transfer, or deliver them, and they shall actually be received by the person making the loan or advance without notice that the agent was not authorised to make the pledge or security, the loan or advance is deemed to be a loan or advance on the security of such goods or documents of title, though the goods or documents are not actually received by the lender till the period subsequent thereto (*aa*).

'The same section contained definitions or explanations in regard to advances: and provided that the agent in possession of goods or documents of title should be taken to have been entrusted with them by the owner, unless the contrary can be shown in evidence (*bb*).

'(7.) *Saving of true Owner's Rights.*—It was provided that the Act (of 1825) should not prevent the true owner of the goods from recovering them from his factor or agent before a sale, deposit, or pledge, or from the assignees of the factor or agent in the event of his bankruptcy; nor from the buyer the price of the goods, subject to any right of set-off on the part of the buyer against the factor or agent; nor from recovering the goods deposited or pledged upon repayment of the money or restoration of the negotiable instrument advanced on the security thereof to the factor or agent, and upon payment of such further money, etc., as may have been advanced by the agent to the owner; nor from recovering from any person any balance remaining in his hands as the produce of a sale of the goods after deducting the money or negotiable instrument advanced on the security thereof, etc. (*cc*).'

(*a*) Colquhoun *v.* Findlay, Duff, & Co., Nov. 15, 1816; F. C. Ede & Bond *v.* Findlay, Duff, & Co., May 15, 1818; F. C. Johnston *v.* Scott & Son, Nov. 14, 1818; F. C. Johnson & Manley *v.* Findlay, Duff, & Co., 1826; 4 S. 407. 1 Bell's Com. 483 (517, M'L.'s ed.).

(*b*) See Smith's Merc. Law, 128.

(*c*) 4 Geo. IV. c. 83. 6 Geo. IV. c. 94. 5 and 6 Vict. c. 39. 40 and 41 Vict. c. 39, § 1. All repealed by 52 and 53 Vict. c. 45 (1889); applied to Scotland by 53 and 54 Vict. c. 40 (1890).

(*d*) See above, § 229 (*c*).

(*e*) See note (*c*).

(*f*) The summary of this Act is taken from the fifth edition of Abbott on Shipping, 381, as quoted in **Cole** *v.* **North-Western Bank**, L. R. 10 C. P. 360; 44 L. J. C. P. 233, and there adopted by Blackburn, J., and the other judges.

(*g*) 6 Geo. IV. c. 94, § 1. See Cole (*f*), Johnson (*p*). *Infra*, § 1517B (4). **Maspons** *v.* **Mildred & Co.**, 9 Q. B. D. 530; 8 App. Ca. 874.

(*h*) 6 Geo. IV. c. 94, § 2.

(*i*) 5 and 6 Vict. c. 39, § 1. Kaltenbach *v.* Lewis, 24 Ch. D. 54; 10 App. Ca. 617. The preamble of this Act is of some importance.

(*k*) See definition of mercantile agent in 52 and 53 Vict. c. 45, § 1.

(*l*) See Cole, *cit. infra* (*o*). M'Ewan *v.* Smith, and Jenkins, *infra* (*q*).

(*m*) Wood *v.* Rowcliffe, 6 Hare, 183. Lamb *v.* Attenborough, 1 B. & S. 831; 31 L. J. Q. B. 41. See Heyman *v.* Flewker, 13 C. B. N. S. 519; 32 L. J. C. P. 132.

(*n*) Monk *v.* Whittenbury, 2 B. & Ad. 484; 36 R. R. 637.

(*o*) Fuentes *v.* Montis, L. R. 3 C. P. 268; 4 *ib.* 93; 37 L. J. C. P. 97; 38 *ib.* 95. Cole *v.* N.-W. Bank, L. R. 9 C. P. 470; 10 C. P. 354; 43 L. J. C. P. 194; 44 *ib.* 233. Comp. Baines *v.* Swainson, 4 B. & S. 270; 32 L. J. Q. B. 281, and Vickers *v.* Hertz, 1871; 9 R. H. L. 65; L. R. 2 Sc. App. 113.

(*p*) Johnson *v.* Credit Lyonnais Co., 2 C. P. D. 224; 3 C. P. D. 32; 47 L. J. C. P. 232.

(*q*) Jenkins *v.* Usborne, 8 Scott N. R. 505; 7 M. & G. 78. Van Casteel *v.* Booker, 2 Ex. 691; 18 L. J. Ex. 9.

M'Ewan v. Smith, 1849; 6 Bell's App. 340; 2 H. L. Ca. 310.

(r) 40 and 41 Vict. c. 39, § 3.

(s) Ib. § 4.

(t) Fuentes v. Montis, cit. (o).

(u) 40 and 41 Vict. c. 39, § 2.

(v) Jewan v. Whitworth, L. R. 2 Eq. 692; 36 L. J. Ch. 127. M'Nee v. Gorst, L. R. 4 Eq. 315. Kaltenbach v. Lewis, cit. (i). Martinez & Gomez v. Allison, 1890; 17 R. 332.

(w) Per L. Tenterden in the fifth edition; see above (f).

(x) See 5 and 6 Vict. c. 39, § 2 (as to substitution of goods under security).

(y) 5 and 6 Vict. c. 39, § 3.

(z) 5 and 6 Vict. c. 39, § 4 (occasioned by Phillips v. Huth, 6 M. & W. 572; and Hatfield v. Phillips, 14 M. & W. 665; 12 Cl. & F. 343. See definition in § 1317A (1). The provision in the text is repeated by the Act of 1889, § 2 (3).

(aa) 5 and 6 Vict. c. 39, § 4. See Bonzi v. Stewart, 4 M. & G. 295. Portalis v. Tetley, L. R. 5 Eq. 140. Cole v. N.-W. Bank, cit. (o). Supra, § 1317A (2).

(bb) 5 and 6 Vict. c. 39, § 4. Baines v. Swainson, 4 B. & S. 270; 32 L. J. Q. B. 281.

(cc) 6 Geo. IV. c. 94, § 6.

1317B. **'The Factors Act, 1889.**—(1.) In this Act a "Mercantile Agent" is one having in the customary course of his business as such agent authority either to sell goods or to consign goods for the purpose of sale, or to buy goods, or to raise money on the security of goods (a). A person is deemed to be in possession of goods or of the documents of title to goods, where the goods or documents are in his actual custody, or are held by any other person subject to his control or for him or on his behalf (b). "Document of Title" includes any bill of lading, dock warrant, warehousekeeper's certificate, and warrant or order for the delivery of goods, and any other document used in the ordinary course of business as proof of the possession or control of goods, or authorising or purporting to authorise, either by endorsement or delivery, the possessor of the document to transfer or receive goods thereby represented (c). "Pledge" includes any contract pledging, or giving a lien or security on goods, whether in consideration of an original advance, or of any further or continuing advance, or of any pecuniary liability (d). A pledge of documents of title is deemed to be a pledge of the goods (e).

'(2.) Where a mercantile agent is, with the owner's consent—which for the purposes of the Act is presumed, in the absence of evidence to the contrary (f)—in possession of goods or of the documents of title, any sale, pledge, or other disposition of the goods made by him (personally or through a clerk or other person authorised in the ordinary course of business so to contract on his behalf (g)) in the ordinary course of business of a mercantile agent, shall, subject to the provisions of the Act, be as valid as if he were expressly authorised by the owner; provided that the person taking under the disposition acts in good faith, and has not at the time of the disposition notice of the mercantile agent's want of authority (h). Such disposition is valid even after the owner's consent has been recalled, if the person taking has not at the time thereof notice that the consent has been determined (i).

'(3.) Where a mercantile agent pledges goods as security for a debt or liability due from the pledgor to the pledgee before the time of the pledge, the pledgee acquires no further right to the goods than could have been enforced by the pledgor at the time of the pledge (k). The consideration necessary for the validity of a sale, pledge, or other disposition of goods may be either a cash payment, or the delivery or transfer of other goods, or of a document of title, or of a negotiable security, or any other valuable consideration; but where the consideration is not a cash payment, the pledgee acquires no right or interest in the goods in excess of the value of the goods, documents, or security, when so delivered or transferred in exchange (l).

'(4.) *Consignors and Consignees.*—Where the owner of goods has given possession to another person for the purpose of consignment or sale, or has shipped the goods in the name of another person, and the consignee has not had notice that such person is not the owner of the goods, the consignee has the same lien for advances made to or for the use of such person as if that person were owner of the goods, and may transfer the lien to another person. But this enactment does not limit or affect the validity of any sale, pledge, or disposition by a mercantile agent (m).

'(5.) *Sellers and Buyers.*—The 8th and 9th sections of the Factors Act, 1889, are now repeated in the 25th section of the Sale of Goods Act. They may hereafter be repealed in a Statute Law Revision Act. The latter section (Sale of Goods Act, § 25 (1)) is in lieu of the third section of the Factors Act, 1877, which applied only to documents of title (*n*). It is provided that where a person, having sold goods, continues or is in possession of the goods or documents of title, the delivery or transfer by him or a mercantile agent acting for him of the goods or documents under any sale, pledge, or other disposition to any person receiving the same in good faith and without notice of the previous sale, has the same effect as if the person making the transfer or delivery were expressly authorised by the owner of the goods to do so (*o*).

'Where a buyer or one who has agreed to buy obtains with consent of the seller possession of the goods or documents of title, the delivery or transfer by him or by a mercantile agent acting for him of the goods or documents of title under any sale, pledge, or disposition thereof, to a person receiving the same in good faith and without notice of any lien or other right of the original seller in respect of the goods, has the same effect as if the person making the transfer or delivery were a mercantile agent possessing the goods or documents with the owner's consent (*p*).

'Subject to the provisions of the Sale of Goods Act, 1893 (*q*), the unpaid seller's right of lien or retention or stoppage *in transitu* is not affected by any sale or other disposition which the buyer may have made, unless the seller has assented thereto; provided that where a document of title has been lawfully transferred to any person as buyer or owner of the goods, and that person transfers the document to a person who takes it in good faith and for valuable consideration, then if such second transfer was by way of sale, the unpaid seller's right of lien or retention or stoppage *in transitu* is defeated; if it was by way of pledge or other disposition for value, the said lien, retention, or stoppage *in transitu* can only be exercised subject to the rights of the transferee (*r*).

'As between buyer and seller this section puts all documents of title, which words have the same meaning in the Sale of Goods Act and in the Factors Act, 1889 (*s*), on the same footing as bills of lading.

'By the custom of merchants, bills of lading when transferred carry the property of the goods represented (*supra*, § 417); but the other documents of title with which they are classed in the Acts under consideration merely give, when transferred, a contract right effectual against the granter and any principal whom he may represent, intimation to the warehousekeeper or custodier being necessary to the constitution of a real right. So a pledge or security created by indorsation and delivery of a document of title not being intimated to the holder of the goods, though good against an unpaid seller to the pledgor, is ineffectual against a subsequent arrestment by another creditor of the buyer (pledgor) (*t*).'

(*a*) 52 and 53 Vict. c. 45, § 1 (1). Hastings *v.* Pearson, 1893; 1 Q. B. 62.
(*b*) *Ib.* § 1 (2), repeating 5 and 6 Vict. c. 39, § 4.
(*c*) *Ib.* § 1 (4), repeating the same Act, adding warehouse-keeper's certificates therein omitted. As to wharfinger's certificates, see Gunn *v.* Bolckow, Vaughan, & Co., L. R. 10 Ch. 491; 44 L. J. Ch. 732. As to iron warrants, Merchant Bank *v.* Phœnix Co., 5 Ch. D. 205; 36 L. J. Ch. 418.
(*d*) *Ib.* § 1 (5).
(*e*) *Ib.* § 3.
(*f*) *Ib.* § 2 (4). *Supra*, § 1317A, at (*bb*).
(*g*) *Ib.* § 6.
(*h*) *Ib.* § 2 (1). This reproduces and alters secs. 2 and 4 of 6 Geo. IV. c. 94, and sec. 4 of 5 and 6 Vict. c. 39. See § 1317A (6). It is thought that it does not alter the rule stated at § 1317A (2), as founded on Monk *v.* Whittenbury, and Cole *v.* N.-W. Bank.
(*i*) *Ib.* § 2 (2). See above, § 1317A (4).
(*k*) *Ib.* § 4. Substituted for Factors Act, 1825, § 3, as qualified by Factors Act, 1842, § 3. See § 1317A (5). Probably this applies to pledges of documents of title; see § 3 of this Act.
(*l*) *Ib.* § 5; altering 5 and 6 Vict. c. 39, § 4; and in lieu of § 2 of same Act.
(*m*) *Ib.* § 7. Above, § 1317A (1).
(*n*) See § 1317A at notes (*p*), (*q*), (*r*).
(*o*) Sale of Goods Act, § 25 (1).
(*p*) Sale of Goods Act, § 25 (2). Sec. 4 of the Factors Act, 1877, applied only to documents of title. See § 1317A (3).
(*q*) 56 and 57 Vict. c. 71, § 25 (2).
(*r*) Sale of Goods Act, § 47, reproducing in the proviso § 10 of the Factors Act, 1889.
(*s*) Sale of Goods Act, § 62, and above, subs. (1).
(*t*) **Robertson & Baxter** *v.* **Inglis**, 1897; 25 R. 758; aff. 1898; *ib.* H. L. 70.

1318. Recovery of Possession when Lost.—Besides the provisions of the criminal law operating indirectly for the protection of property, the owner is by civil process entitled to follow and recover his property; or to demand restitution; or to insist for damages for the loss of it.

1319. The owner is entitled to follow after and recover his property without the aid of a judge, provided he *ex incontinenti* follow it; but not *ex intervallo* (*a*).

(*a*) 2 Ersk. 1, § 23.

1320. The owner may proceed judicially against anyone who shall illegally possess himself of his property. The action is summary, grounded on the *jus in re*. It comes in place of the *rei vindicatio* of the Roman law; has for its object the recovery of the subject to the use of the owner; and requires, as a title to pursue, the right of ownership, with proof of the loss of possession (*quomodo desiit possidere*), as by fraud, theft, deposit, loan, etc., in order to counteract the presumption of property which arises from possession (*a*). Goods, therefore, bought but not delivered, cannot be so vindicated by the buyer in a summary process; the action in such cases is personal, grounded on the contract or *jus ad rem*; the demand is as a creditor, not as proprietor. The action of restitution can be directed only against the possessor, or one who has fraudulently put away the thing in order to evade the action. It will not lie against a purchaser in *bonâ fide* from one acquiring the goods by fraud; but one who has bought goods that have been stolen will be liable to such demand of restitution, even where they have been bought in public market (*b*).

(*a*) Russel *v.* Campbell, 1699; 4 B. Sup. 468; 1 Ill. 417. See § 1313.

(*b*) Bishop of Caithness *v.* Fleshers of Edinburgh, 1629; M. 4145. Forsyth *v.* Kilpatrick, 1680; M. 9120. Mackay *v.* Forsyth, 1758; M. 4944. Alexander *v.* Black, Jan. 17, 1816; 1 Bell's Com. 287 (307, M'L.'s ed.). Henderson *v.* Gibson, 1806; M. *Moveables*, Apx. 1. See above, § 120, 527. E. Fife's Trs. *v.* Snare, 1849; 11 D. 1119; 1 Bell's Com. 287 (307, M'L.'s ed.).

1321. The owner who cannot recover his property is entitled to maintain, against the party by whose fault or delict he has lost it, an action of damages; and the establishment of his right to the thing itself will entitle him to indemnification on account of the want of it.

CHAPTER IV

OF PROPERTY IN SHIPS

1322. Navigation Laws.—The right of property in a ship is conveyed by written title, registered in a particular way. The rules respecting the titles and ownership of this species of property have arisen with the growth of a system of national policy for the encouragement of British shipping and navigation. The series of statutes enacted for this purpose had for their object to breed up a race of skilful and able seamen, to augment the shipping of Great Britain, and to encourage ship-carpenters. They began with the Long Parliament, and have been continued down to the present 'reign' (*a*).

(*a*) 12 Chas. II. c. 18. 1661, c. 45. 26 Geo. III. c. 60. 4 Geo. IV. c. 41; repealed, 6 Geo. IV. c. 105; re-enacted, 6 Geo. IV. c. 104-110. 3 and 4 Will. IV. c. 54, 55. See also c. 56 and 57, and 5 and 6 Will. IV. c. 19. Abbott on Shipping, 12th ed. 38 seq.; Story's ed. 25 et seq. 1 Bell's Com. 151 et seq. 8 and 9 Vict. c. 88, 89. See § 1323A.

1323. Under these laws there are two descriptions of ships privileged:—

(1.) *British Ships* 'enjoyed' a monopoly of the British trade with her colonies and settlements; of the coasting trade; of the importation, not only from the place of growth, but from any port in Asia, Africa, or America in which they 'might' happen to be, of goods known by the name of enumerated articles—this right being shared, however, with the ships of the country in which those articles 'were' produced, or from which they 'were' accustomed to be brought; and of fisheries for importation. These privileges 'were' confirmed and protected by forfeitures and alien duties (*a*).

(2.) *Foreign Ships* 'were' also privileged to share with British ships in the importation into this country of commodities produced abroad, in respect of being vessels of the country of produce, or of manufacture, or from which the goods 'were' imported (*b*). In order to enjoy this privilege, it 'was' requisite that the ship 'should' be of the build of such country; or prize of war to such country, and as such condemned and adjudged; or forfeited to such country under the Slave Trade Laws, and as such condemned; or British built, not being a prize of war from British subjects. The ship must in those several cases be owned by subjects of that country, and three-fourths of the crew must be subjects of that country (*c*).

(*a*) 3 and 4 Will. IV. c. 54, § 2. (*b*) *Ib.* § 3 et seq. (*c*) *Ib.* § 15.

1323A. 'The Navigation Laws, in so far as they impeded free intercourse in trade among all nations, have been repealed (*a*); and thus practically the distinction between British and foreign ships, so far as relates to trade, is abolished. But in regard to the property of British ships, the system of registration introduced by them is substantially maintained. Subsequently to the repeal of the Navigation Acts, a statute was passed (*b*), in which, and in amending Acts (*c*), were embodied not only the rules as to registration, but also all matters relating to ships; and by another statute, all statutes affecting shipping from the 8 Eliz. are repealed (*d*). The Merchant Shipping Act, 1854, and Acts amending, have been consolidated by the Merchant Shipping Act, 1894 (*e*).'

(*a*) See 12 and 13 Vict. c. 29, and 17 and 18 Vict. c. 5.
(*b*) 17 and 18 Vict. c. 104 (Merchant Shipping Act, 1854).

(c) 18 and 19 Vict. c. 91. 25 and 26 Vict. c. 63; etc.
(d) See 17 and 18 Vict. c. 120. 1 Bell's Com. 151 seq.; M'L.'s ed. 159 seq.
(e) 57 and 58 Vict. c. 60.

1324. Registration of Ships.—Registration is the test of the right to enjoy the privilege of a British ship (a). Ships not duly registered 'may be detained till the master produces the certificate (b), and ships' are liable to forfeiture (c) 'if they unduly assume the character of British ships; they have no protection as such; and cannot claim the privilege of limited liability (d).' The registry is to be made by the 'principal officer' of the customs in any port in 'the United Kingdom' or the Isle of Man, 'and by him together with the governor in Guernsey and Jersey, by the governor in Malta and Gibraltar,' and by certain other officers in 'other British possessions (e),' on proof of ownership, by 'declaration of ownership, builder's certificate, and other statutory evidence (f)': and the name given to the ship at first, and in which she is registered, is not to be changed 'without permission of the Board of Trade (g).'

(a) 3 and 4 Will. IV. c. 55, § 2. 57 and 58 Vict. c. 60, § 2, 3.
(b) *Ib.* § 2 (3), 692.
(c) *Ib.* § 69, 76.
(d) 57 and 58 Vict. c. 60, § 72, 502. The Andalusian, 3 P. D. 182; 47 L. J. Adm. 65. *Supra*, § 436. When a share in a ship passes by succession to an unqualified person, he must apply for an order of the Court of Session to have the share sold. *Ib.* § 28. Roy *v.* Hamilton & Co., 1867; 5 Macph. 573. See § 1326.
(e) *Ib.* § 4.
(f) *Ib.* § 9, etc.
(g) *Ib.* § 47. Bell *v.* Bank of London, 28 L. J. Ex. 116.

1325. Description of British Ships entitled to Privilege.—'In order to be registered as a British ship, a vessel must be owned either (1) by a natural born British subject, who, if he has at any time sworn allegiance to a foreign sovereign or state, or has otherwise become a citizen or subject of a foreign state, must subsequently have taken the oath of allegiance to the Queen, and who must, while owner of the ship, reside within the Queen's dominions, or be a partner of a firm carrying on business within the Queen's dominions; (2) by a person made a denizen by letters of denization, or naturalised, provided he reside or be a partner as aforesaid, and have taken the oath of allegiance, after being made a denizen, or naturalised; or (3) by a body corporate, under and subject to the laws of, and having its principal place of business in, the United Kingdom or a British possession (a).

'Registry is not required in the case (1) of ships not above fifteen tons in burden, employed only on the rivers or coasts of the United Kingdom, or of some British possession within which their managing owners reside; (2) of vessels not above thirty tons in burden, and not having a whole or fixed deck, employed entirely in fishing or the coasting trade in Newfoundland or parts adjacent, or the Gulf of St. Lawrence (b).

'When a ship has been altered so as not to correspond with the particulars stated in the register book and certificate (*infra*, § 1326), either a new registration must be made, or the particulars of the alteration must be endorsed on the former certificate (c).'

(a) 57 and 58 Vict. c. 60, § 1. R. *v.* Bjornsen, 34 L. J. M. C. 180; 10 Cox, Cr. Ca. 74. R. *v.* Arnaud, 9 Q. B. 806. See 33 and 34 Vict. c. 14, nothing in which is to qualify an alien to be owner of a British ship, § 14.
(b) 57 and 58 Vict. c. 60, § 3. Benyon *v.* Cresswell, 12 Q. B. 899.
(c) *Ib.* § 48 sqq.

1326. Certificate of Registry.—The certificate bears testimony to the ownership: the name and port of the ship; 'the details as to build and description given in the surveyor's certificate; the particulars as to the history of the ship stated in the statutory declaration of ownership; the name of' the master: and is proof of the ship being entitled to the privileges of a British ship (a). The shares held by different persons are specified, the owners not exceeding 'sixty-four' in number (b). Corresponding with the registry is a book to be kept by the 'registrar' at the port (c). Penalties are imposed on the master if he have not the certificate when called for; and a summary remedy is provided against any person wilfully detaining a registry certificate for any purpose but lawful navigation of the ship (d). On every change of the master 'or owners,' the certificate must be delivered up to the 'registrar, etc.,' at the port where the ship happens to be, that 'he' may indorse on it the change of master, and send notice to the ship's port, and take new security for the penalties (e). The loss of the certificate may, under certain precautions, be repaired by 'granting a new certificate; and it may also be replaced, when worn out or obliterated (f).

A ship ceases to be British, and her certificate must be delivered up, if she be actually or constructively lost, taken by an enemy, burnt, or broken up, or become the property of unqualified persons. In the latter case, she may be registered again on her property being re-transferred to qualified owners (*g*).'

(*a*) 57 and 58 Vict. c. 60, § 14, etc.
(*b*) *Ib.* § 5. Hibbs *v.* Ross, L. R. 1 Q. B. 534.
(*c*) 57 and 58 Vict. c. 60, § 5, 11.
(*d*) See § 15, 16, etc. It cannot be pledged, or made the subject of a lien. Wiley *v.* Crawford, 1 B. & S. 253 ; 30 L. J. Q. B. 319. Gibson *v.* Ingo, 6 Hare, 112. Harkle *v.* Henzell, 8 E. & B. 828. Bowen *v.* Fox (*f*). Scott *v.* Robertson, 1862 ; 24 D. 572.
(*e*) The Act, § 19, 20.
(*f*) *Ib.* § 18. See Bowen *v.* Fox, 10 B. & Cr. 41 ; 1 Ill. 418.
(*g*) The Act, § 21, 22, etc.

1327.—The certificate 'and other documents' provided by the statute 'are evidence of the matters stated therein pursuant to the statute, or by any officer in pursuance of his duties, subject to all just exceptions (*a*).'

(*a*) 57 and 58 Vict. c. 60, § 64, 695. The use of certified copies is also provided for. The certificate has been held sufficient to justify the recall without caution of arrestments used on a debt due by a former owner of the ship alleged to have fraudulently transferred it. Duffus & Lawson *v.* Mackay, 1857 ; 19 D. 430. Cf. Schultz *v.* Robinson & Niven, 1861 ; 24 D. 120. See, however, as to its effects in establishing the liability of the registered owner for the acts of the master, Myers *v.* Willis, 17 C. B. 77 ; 18 C. B. 886 ; 25 L. J. C. P. 255. Hibbs *v.* Ross, L. R. 1 Q. B. 534 ; 35 L. J. Q. B. 193. Hay *v.* Cockburn's Trs., 1850 ; 12 D. 1298. Miller & Co. *v.* Potter, Wilson, & Co., 1875 ; 3 R. 105. Maclachlan, 111. Dickson on Evid. § 1121, 1122 (2nd ed., omitted in 3rd ed.). See below, § 2214.

1328.—Property in Ships, how acquired.—Property in ships is acquired either by building, or causing to be built; or by purchase; or by capture and condemnation.

(1.) *Building.*—One who builds a ship, or causes her to be built, is owner, and entitled and bound to have the proper certificate of ownership and registry issued (*a*). And the general rule in England is, that delivery by the builder of the survey, ' or "builder's certificate,"' for the purpose of registration, passes the property (*b*). 'Application for registry is made by the person or corporation requiring to be registered as owner, or by his or their agent. He must produce a declaration of ownership, and in the case of the first registry of a ship a builder's certificate (*c*).'

(*a*) Mucklow *v.* Mangles, 1 Taunt. 318 ; 1 Ill. 384 ; 9 R. R. 784. Simpson *v.* Duncanson's Crs., 1786 ; M. 14,204 ; 1 Bell's Com. 177, note ; 1 Ill. 386. Woods *v.* Russell, 5 B. & Ald. 942 ; 24 R. R. 621. Clarke *v.* Spence, 4 A. & E. 448 ; 3 Ill. 148. 17 and 18 Vict. c. 104, § 40. Wood *v.* Bell, 5 E. & B. 772 ; 6 E. & B. 355 ; 25 L. J. Q. B. 158. Baker *v.* Gray, 17 C. B. 462 ; 25 L. J. C. P. 161. *Ante*, § 1303.
(*b*) Wood, *supra* (*a*). Abbott, 1 seq.
(*c*) 57 and 58 Vict. c. 60, § 9, 10.

1329. (2.) *Sale.*—Ships may now be purchased and owned by one or more persons, free from many of the embarrassments of the former law.

Under the former Acts, there was much difficulty in vesting the property of ships in companies consisting of many partners; and some danger in placing the property in trust, lest it might, on the bankruptcy of the trustee, be held to belong to his creditors (*a*). By 'subsequent' Acts, the property of every ship of which there is more than one owner is divided into sixty-four shares, and the proportion held by each owner is to be described in the certificate as consisting of a certain number of those shares. Not more than 'sixty-four' persons may be owners of a ship, excepting minors, legatees, etc., or 'incorporated' joint-stock companies (*b*); 'but any number of persons not exceeding five may be registered as joint-owners of a ship, or any shares in her, and are considered as one person in reckoning the number of persons to be registered. Private firms cannot be registered in the company name. The person appearing on the register as owner has the proper title to transfer the property of his shares, and give valid receipts for the price (*c*), and his title can be disputed only for fraud (*d*); or the invalidity of the bill of sale to him (*e*); or an equitable title derived from himself. The register cannot take notice of any trust; but notwithstanding the statutory rules as to registration, though without prejudice to them, any beneficial or equitable interest of any persons or company may be enforced against registered owners and mortgagees in respect of their interest in the ship, in the same manner as equities may be enforced against them in respect of any other personal property (*f*).'

(*a*) Abbott, 32, 35, 45 (12th ed. 53). 1 Bell's Com. 159. Cambden *v.* Anderson, 5 T. R. 709 ; 1 Ill. 419 ; see 4 R. R. 755. Curtis *v.* Perry, 6 Ves. Jr. 739 ; 6 R. R. 28. *Ex p.* Yallop, 15 Ves. 60 ; 10 R. R. 24. *Ex p.* Houghton, 17 Ves. 251 ; 11 R. R. 73. *Ex p.* Burn, 1 Jac. & W. 378 ; 21 R. R. 186.
(*b*) 6 Geo. IV. c. 110, § 32, 33 ; and 3 and 4 Will. IV. c. 55, § 32, 33. The number was restricted to thirty-two : see § 37 and 44 of 17 and 18 Vict. c. 104 ; but this was

altered by 43 and 44 Vict. c. 18. See 57 and 58 Vict. c. 60, § 5.

(c) The Eastern Belle, 33 L. T. 214.

(d) The Horlock, 2 P. D. 243; 47 L. J. Adm. 5. Bell v. Gow, 1862; 1 Macph. 183.

(e) Orr v. Dickinson, 28 L. J. Ch. 516. Read v. Fairbanks, 13 C. B. 692; 22 L. J. C. P. 206.

(f) 57 and 58 Vict. c. 60, § 5, 24 sq. 56, 57. Ward v. Beck, 13 C. B. N. S. 668; 32 L. J. C. P. 113. Gardner v. Cazenove, 1 H. & N. 423. Liverpool Mar. Cr. Co. v. Wilson, L. R. 7 Ch. 507; 41 L. J. Ch. 498. The Horlock, cit. (d). Watson v. Duncan, 1879; 6. R. 1247. Duthie v. Aiken, 1892; 20 R. 241 (invalid bill of sale—remedy). Chateauneuf v. Capeyron, 7 App. Ca. 127; 51 L. J. P. C. 57. Proof of such equitable interest may fall within the rule of the statute 1696 as to trusts. Carlyle v. Macalpin's Trs., 1864; 2 Macph. 882. This was different under the registry Acts prior to 1854; see Liverpool Borough Bank v. Turner, 1 J. & H. 159; 2 De G. F. & J. 502; 30 L. J. Ch. 379. Morton v. Black, 1843; 5 D. 411. M'Arthurs v. M'Brair, 1844; 6 D. 1174. Boyd's Exrs. v. Martin's Exrs., 1847; 9 D. 1234. Ord v. Barton, 1846; 8 D. 1011. Hay v. Cockburn's Trs., 1850; 12 D. 1298.

1330. '*Bill of Sale.*—The property of a ship, or of shares of a ship, can be transferred only by writing (*a*); and a bill of sale is the universal instrument of transfer of ships in the usage of all maritime countries (*b*). And by statute the transfer of registered ships or shares therein to persons qualified to be owners of British ships must be by bill of sale in a prescribed form, or as near thereto as circumstances will permit (*c*).' Formerly it was required that in the bill of sale the certificate should be recited in words at length, truly and accurately; otherwise to be utterly void and null to all purposes. Under this rule very trivial errors were fatal. But now it is enough if the certificate or the principal contents thereof shall be recited 'in the prescribed form,' and the identity of the ship thereby effectually proved. 'The bill of sale is to be executed before, and attested by, one witness (*d*); and until it is executed and delivered, there is no transfer of the ship (*e*).' Whether the sale be of the whole ship or of shares, there must be a bill of sale; the embarrassments and nullities of the old Acts being now removed (*f*). The sale must be entered in the book of registry, and indorsement made on the certificate by the 'registrar,' or a new registry obtained (*g*).

(a) See 1 Bell's Com. 152 (147, M'L.'s ed.). Maclachlan on Shipping, 33. Schultz v. Robinson & Niven, 1861; 24 D. 120.

(b) The Sisters, 5 C. Rob. Ad. 155. The Eliza Cornish, 1 Ecc. & Ad. 36; 17 E. Jur. 738. Schultz v. Robinson & Niven, *cit.*

(c) 57 and 58 Vict. c. 60, § 24 Sch. 1, A. Union Bank v. Lenanton, 3 C. P. D. 243; 47 L. J. C. P. 409 (unregistered ship built for alien).

(d) *Ib.* It does not require a stamp.

(e) Granfelt v. L. Adv., 1874; 1 R. 782. Chapman v. Callis, 9 C. B. N. S. 769; 30 L. J. C. P. 241.

(f) Abbott, 47 (12th ed.). 1 Bell's Com. 160. See on the subject of this section, 57 and 58 Vict. c. 60, § 24 sqq.

(g) A certificate of sale may be granted by the registrar to enable the owner to dispose out of the country of a whole ship. See 57 and 58 Vict. c. 60, § 39, 51, etc.

1330A. '*Action of Sett and Sale.*—The law of Scotland recognises the right of the owners of half or the major part of a ship to sue for an order on the other owners to buy their shares at a certain rate, or alternatively to sell their own shares to the pursuers at the same rate, or otherwise that the ship be sold by auction (*a*). The pursuer's offer does not oblige him to buy less than the whole of the other shares of the ship (*b*).'

(a) 1 Stair, 16. § 4. 3 Ersk. 3. § 56. Bankton, i. 8. 40; i. 22. 21. 1 Bell's Com. 502. Hutton v. Hay, 1880; 2 Guthrie's Sel. Sh. Ct. Ca. 537, where other authorities are given.

(b) Anderson v. Sillars, 1894; 22 R. 105. As to the remedy of a dissentient part-owner seeking to save himself from responsibility, see Hunter v. Kerr, 1880; 2 Guthrie's Sel. Sh. Ct. Ca. 539.

1331. (3.) *Capture.*—Ships captured and condemned in any Court of Admiralty as prize of war, or ships condemned for breach of the laws for prevention of the slave trade, may be registered, and the property secured to the captor or owner (*a*).

(a) 3 and 4 Will. IV. c. 55, § 5, 9, 29. *Supra*, § 1325.

1332. Mortgage of Ships.—This is now made very simple and effectual, without involving the mortgagee in the responsibilities of ownership, and without requiring possession (*a*).

(a) 3 and 4 Will. IV. c. 55, § 42. Abbott, 49 (12th ed.). And 57 and 58 Vict. c. 60, § 31. See below, § 1379.

CHAPTER V

OF MONEY DEBTS, GOVERNMENT AND BANK STOCK

1333. Money. — Money, the circulating medium of this country, consists of coin and bank-notes. Money is peculiar in this respect, that it cannot, like other moveables, be recognised as identified while in the possession of another than the owner, unless separated and marked for the purpose. Possession in this, as in the case of ordinary moveables, presumes property. Money in possession of an insolvent is a general fund for division among his creditors; and 'it has been said that' no sum or part of it is claimable by anyone unless it be distinguished and ear-marked as specific (*a*). '"When money or notes," said Lord Mansfield, "are paid (? received) *bonâ fide*, and upon a valuable consideration, they never shall be brought back by the true owner; but where they come *mala fide* into a person's hands, they are in the nature of specific property; and if their identity can be traced and ascertained, the party has a right to recover." Hence, in such cases, the question is whether the circumstances afford evidence of *mala fides*; *i.e.* whether the party taking the money or negotiable instrument must have suspected that it was lost, stolen, or fraudulently obtained (*b*). The quaint phrase that "money has no ear-mark" has led to some confusion, and is not now law in the sense that money cannot be specifically claimed. On the contrary, when money, securities, or goods are placed in the hands of another in a fiduciary relation, as agent, depositary, or trustee, so that there is a particular duty with regard to them or their proceeds, and not merely the relation of debtor and creditor, then the goods, securities, or money may be followed and claimed by the true owner in the hands of the agent or trustee (or his trustee in bankruptcy, who takes *tantum et tale*), into whatever form they may have been changed, and although mixed and confounded with other money of his, or with a mass of the like material; and this right ceases only when the means of ascertainment fail (*c*). But it must be distinguished and set aside by an appropriation which is more than a mere designation of a fund belonging or coming to the debtor out of which payment shall be made (*d*).'

(*a*) Hotchkis *v.* Dundee Bank, 1797; 1 Bell's Com. 261; 1 Ill. 423. See M. 2673.

(*b*) Clark *v.* Shee, Cowp. 197. Gill *v.* Cubitt, 3 B. & Cr. 466. Miller *v.* Race, 1 Burr. 452; 1 Smith's L. C. 469; 1 Ross' L. C. 205. Solomons *v.* Bank of England, 13 East 135; 12 R. R. 341. Raphael *v.* Bank of England, 17 C. B. 161. Goodman *v.* Harvey, 4 A. & E. 870. Bank of Bengal *v.* Fagan, 7 Moo. P. C. 72. De Waal *v.* Bank of England, July 1871. London and County Bk. *v.* London and R. Plate Bk., 21 Q. B. D. 535 (stolen securities restored to possession of owner may be held by him, if in *bonâ fide*, against third parties, who had acquired a title from the thief). Dunlop's Trs. *v.* Clydesdale Bank, 1891; 18 R. 751; aff. 1893, A. C. 282; 20 R. H. L. 59 (client's money fraudulently paid into overdrawn bank account by stockbroker). E. of Sheffield *v.* London Jt. St. Bk., 13 App. Ca. 333. London Jt. St. Bk. *v.* Simmons, 1892; A. C. 201. 2 Stephen's Com. 123. See *ante*, § 308, 333A, 528, and 13A, and 45 and 46 Vict. c. 61, § 29, etc.

(*c*) Knatchbull *v.* Hallett, 49 L. J. Ch. 415; L. R. 13 Ch. D. 696. 1 Bell's Com. 264, 267 (283, 286, M'L.'s ed.). Taylor *v.* Plumer, 3 M. & S. 562; 16 R. R. 361. *Ex p.* Cooke, 46 L. J. Bkr. 52; L. R. 4 Ch. D. 123. Harris *v.* Truman & Co., L. R. 9 Q. B. D. 264; 51 L. J. Q. B. 338. Macadam *v.* Martin's Tr., 1872; 11 Macph. 33. Blyth *v.* Maberley's Assignees, 1832; 10 S. 796.

(*d*) Graham & Co. *v.* Raeburn & Verel, 1895; 23 R. 84. See § 563 (*a*).

1334. (1.) *Coin.*—The Gold coin is regulated by statute, and is the only legal tender by the Bank of England. But by others, while the Bank of England continues to pay its notes in legal coin, those notes payable to the bearer on demand are declared a legal tender above £5 (*a*), 'except by the Bank of England or a branch thereof. But Bank of England notes are not a legal tender in Scotland or Ireland (*b*).'

(*a*) 3 and 4 Will. IV. c. 98, § 6. This is an English Act, contd. by 7 and 8 Vict. c. 32.
(*b*) 8 and 9 Vict. c. 38, § 15. 8 and 9 Vict. c. 37, § 6.

1335. 'By the Coinage Act, 1870, a tender of payment is declared to be legal if made in coins issued by the Mint in accordance with the Act, and not called in by proclamation, and not become diminished in weight by wear or otherwise, so as to be of less than the minimum statutory weight. Such tender is legal tender, in the case of gold coins, for a payment of any amount; in the case of' silver coin 'such tender' is a legal tender for forty shillings, 'but for no greater amount (*a*).'

(*a*) 33 Vict. c. 10, § 4. Coins below the current weight or called in are to be cut, broken, or defaced by the receiver; and all disputes as to such coins are to be determined by a summary proceeding under the Summary Jurisdiction Acts. *Ib.* § 18.

1336. 'Bronze' coin is a legal tender only 'for a payment of one shilling, but for no greater amount (*a*).' Tokens to workmen, formerly in use as money, are not now permitted 'under a penalty of £20 (*b*). Her Majesty may, by proclamation, direct that other coins, for payments not above 5s., foreign coins, and gold coined at a branch of the Mint in any British possession, are to be current and a legal tender (*c*).'

(*a*) 33 Vict. c. 10, § 4. 22 and 23 Vict. c. 30, now repealed, introduced bronze coinage.
(*b*) See 57 Geo. III. c. 46; and 57 Geo. III. c. 113. 33 Vict. c. 10, § 5.
(*c*) 33 Vict. c. 10, § 11.

1337. (2.) *Bank-notes* are promissory notes payable to the bearer on demand; passing current as money from hand to hand; transferred by delivery (*a*); and in all questions of identity considered as money, having no earmark (*b*). In England no bank-note can be issued for less than £5 (*c*). In Scotland there 'was' no restriction, 'but now Scotch and Irish bankers' notes cannot be issued except for sums of one pound and multiples thereof (*d*); nor practically for more than £100 (*e*); and such notes, if under £5, cannot be negotiated in England (*f*). The issue of bank-notes is subjected to remarkable and anomalous restrictions by the Bank Acts of 1844 and 1845. Only banks in existence on the 6th May 1844 are now permitted to issue promissory notes payable to bearer on demand, and in England only beyond sixty-five miles from London, the Bank of England having the privilege of "exclusive banking" within that radius. In England the issue is limited to the amount of the average circulation which the banker had during a certain period; in Scotland, to an amount fixed in like manner, *plus* notes against which the banker holds gold and silver (*g*). Bank-notes are exempted from the sexennial prescription, but not from the negative (*h*). And unless the banker pay a composition (*i*), they are liable to stamp duty (*k*).'

(*a*) See as to the liability of the transferor of a bank-note, above, § 333F.
(*b*) See above, § 1333.
(*c*) 7 Geo. IV. c. 6, § 3.
(*d*) 8 and 9 Vict. c. 38, § 5, 16. 8 and 9 Vict. c. 37, § 24.
(*e*) The Stamp Act, 1891, limits "bank-note" (not issued by the Bank of England) for the purposes of the Act to £100. 54 and 55 Vict. c. 39, § 29. There is another definition of bank-notes for the purposes of the Banking Acts, in 17 and 18 Vict. c. 83, § 11.
(*f*) 9 Geo. IV. c. 65.
(*g*) 7 and 8 Vict. c. 32. 8 and 9 Vict. c. 39. 3 and 4 Will. IV. cc. 83, 98. 7 and 8 Vict. c. 32, § 26. The public has been very slow in finding out that the monopoly created by these Acts is a tax upon itself for the benefit of the banks, and that the artificial system of banking greatly aggravates the mischief of the periodical crises which visit the commercial world. See Guthrie on Bank Monopoly (Blackwood, Edin. 1864).
(*h*) 12 Geo. III. c. 72, § 39.
(*i*) 9 Geo. IV. c. 23. 16 and 17 Vict. c. 63, § 7.
(*k*) 54 and 55 Vict. c. 39, § 29 sqq. and sched.

1338. Incorporeal Rights. — Incorporeal rights comprehend all *jura ad res*, the *jus exigendi* in all obligations; and although incapable, in one sense, of possession, they are vested by the completion of the *jus exigendi*, and form, when so vested, a part of the moveable or personal estate. Such are, debts, Government funds, bank stock, patents, and copyright.

1339. Jura Crediti.—In estimating a man's estate and effects, his solvency or insolvency, all obligations and contracts in which he is the creditor may be regarded as property: the *jus exigendi* giving him the right to the subject of the obligation, whether moveables or money. Frequent occasions arise in which it is necessary thus to contemplate *jura crediti* as property; as in bankruptcy, on marriage, or on the death of the owner.

1340. (1.) *Paper Money, etc.*—Paper money, bank-notes, negotiable bills, bank cheques, are moveable; some of them, as bank-notes and cheques 'to bearer (*a*),' are transferable by delivery, others by indorsation only. They are personal estate; are held to be wherever the owner is domiciled; and are regulated in bankruptcy and in succession by the law of the domicile.

(*a*) See above, § 308, 1333, 1337.

1341. (2.) *Debts* (*a*).—Ordinary debts are also part of the personal estate of the creditor, but are not transferable otherwise than by assignation. They are regulated, as the others are, by the law of the domicile.

(*a*) In England, debts are called property or choses in action; moveables, property in possession. In Scotland, according to the language of the Roman law, the former are characterised as incorporeal rights; the latter as corporeal.

1342. Government Stock.—The public debt is either funded or unfunded.

(1.) *The Funded Debt* yields to the creditor a certain interest or annuity, paid regularly at the Bank of England out of the aggregate produce of the taxes. The capital can be obtained only by a sale of the annuity in the Stock Exchange, 'the ownership of stock being nothing more than a right to a perpetual annuity, subject to redemption (*a*).' The statutes (*b*) declare that the annuitants shall be possessed thereof as of personal estate; and so it is held in questions of succession in Scotland (*c*). The transfer of the stock is made by an entry 'in the books kept in the offices of the Accountants-General of the Banks of England and Ireland (*d*),' signed by the person holding the stock, or his attorney; or, in the absence of a trustee in bankruptcy, and in cases of lunacy, it may be made by the secretary of the Bank of England, under an order from the Court of Chancery. 'Ownership of stock may be proved by a copy of the entry in the transfer book of the bank (*e*); production of the books themselves being required only when there is a question about the handwriting of the transfer (*f*). The statute also provides for the issue of stock certificates (with coupons) to stockholders; which are either to bearer and transferable by delivery, or nominal (*i.e.* bearing the owner's name), and not transferable except by devolution of law. When a stock certificate is outstanding, the stock ceases to be transferable at the bank (*g*).'

(*a*) Wildman *v.* Wildman, 9 Ves. 174; 7 R. R. 153.
(*b*) 25 Geo. III. c. 32, § 7, and other statutes. 33 and 34 Vict. c. 71, § 9; by which Act the statutes as to the national debt are consolidated. See 51 and 52 Vict. c. 2 (National Debt Conversion Act, 1888).
(*c*) 36 Geo. III. c. 90. Hog *v.* Lashley, 1791; M. 5479; aff. 3 Paton, 247; 1 Ill. 220. Wildman *v.* Wildman, *cit.*
(*d*) 33 and 34 Vict. c. 71, § 22.
(*e*) Marsh *v.* Collnet, 2 Esp. 665; 5 R. R. 763.
(*f*) Auriol *v.* Smith, 18 Ves. 198. Mortimer *v.* M'Callan, 6 M. & W. 58. See Foster *v.* Bank of England, 8 Q. B. 689; 15 L. J. Q. B. 212.
(*g*) 33 and 34 Vict. c. 71, § 26 sqq.

1343. (2.) *The Unfunded Debt* is constituted either by Exchequer and Navy bills, 'Treasury bills (*a*), or by Exchequer bonds (*b*),' on which money is lent to Government by the Bank of England for the service of the year. They bear interest from their dates, or from six months after they are issued. They are issued according to the regulations of an Act passed in 1808, and by authority of particular statutes are made either with the creditor's name or in blank; passing in the former case by indorsation; in the latter, like bank-notes, from hand to hand. They are personal or moveable estate (*c*). There is another species of transaction (arising from loans by Government), in which Exchequer bills are made use of. For the carrying on of certain public works, fisheries, and the employment of the poor, money is advanced by Government, on securities to be granted to the commissioners of Government under the authority of particular statutes, extending from the 57 Geo. III. down to the present time. 'The statutory provisions on this subject are consolidated, and the previous Acts of Parliament repealed, by the Public Works Loans Act, 1875, and the administration of these loans is committed to the Public Works Loan Commissioners (*d*).' The debts, principal and interest, on the advances so made are declared to be privileged, in so far as to entitle the commissioners to preference over private creditors (*e*); 'except prior *bonâ fide* creditors secured by mortgages, who have not assented to the priority of the Government loan; and if there be more than one such creditor, the assent in writing of three-fourths of them in value effects the postponement to such charge, even of those who do not assent (*f*).'

(*a*) 40 and 41 Vict. c. 2.
(*b*) 17 and 18 Vict. c. 23. 29 and 30 Vict. c. 35.
(*c*) 48 Geo. III. c. 1, referred to in subsequent Acts, down to the last, 1 and 2 Vict. c. 93, but repealed by 29 and 30 Vict. c. 25, § 1. Wookey *v.* Poole, 1820, 4 B. & Ald. 1; 1 Ill. 424; 1 Ross' L. C. 251; 22 R. R. 594. Brandao *v.* Barnett, 12 Cl. & F. 787. *Ex p.* South-E. Ry. Co., 9 E. Jur. 650. 29 and 30 Vict. c. 25.
(*d*) 38 and 39 Vict. c. 89. For amending Acts, see the Index of Statutes.
(*e*) 57 Geo. III. c. 34, § 44. 1 and 2 Vict. c. 88, repealed.
(*f*) 38 and 39 Vict. c. 89, § 18.

1344. Bank Stock.—The shares of the stock of chartered banks are of the nature of property, and may be sold (*a*).

(*a*) See as to liferenter's rights, above, § 1050.

(1.) *Bank of England Stock* is declared by statute to be of the nature of personal estate; it is transferable by contract, registered in the books of the bank within seven days of the date of the contract; and the transfer must be made within fourteen days. The dividends are payable half-yearly at the bank.

1345. (2.) *Bank of Scotland Stock* is assignable by an entry in the books of the bank, signed by the cedent and assignee. It is disposable by will; is attachable by adjudication, but so as not to divide the share; and on the bankruptcy of a stockholder, the bank may order his shares to be sold, after certain public notices (*a*). 'Scotch bank stocks are now transferred in the same way as the shares of other limited liability companies (*b*), the banks reserving the right of preparing the deed of transfer.'

(*a*) 1695, Act. Parl. vol. ix. p. 494. 14 Geo. III. c. 32. 44 Geo. III. c. 23.
(*b*) See above, § 403J.

1346. (3.) *Royal Bank Stock* is declared moveable, descendible to executors, but not attachable. It can be transferred only in presence of the court of directors, who may stop the transfer till the stockholder's debt to the bank shall be paid (*a*).

(*a*) 5 Geo. I. c. 20. Royal Bank *v.* Fairholm, 1770; M. *Adjud.* Apx. No. 3; 1 Ill. 425.

1347. (4.) *British Linen Company Stock* is personal, and saleable by a signed transfer in presence of the directors, with a power of retention for the debts of the stockholder to the bank (*a*).

(*a*) Burns *v.* Lawrie's Trs., 1840; 2 D. 1348.

CHAPTER VI

OF PATENTS, COPYRIGHT, AND TRADE MARKS

1348. General View.—The right of a person to enjoy the profits of his useful invention, or literary composition, seems to rest securely on the same foundation on which property depends; namely, occupancy, with skill, labour, expense, and intellectual exertion employed in the acquisition or production. But a more narrow view has been taken of this matter; and instead of considering the invention or the composition as itself the subject of property, it has been held that, as the purchase of the individual machine or book gives the power of imitating or of copying it, either such copy or the original may be sold, and so copies multiplied to make gain. With this view, in the case of discoveries in the useful arts, concurs the interest which the public has to prevent the undue raising of prices, and restraining of industry and improvement according to the caprice or self-interest of monopolists. The Legislature has therefore interposed, on the one hand, to secure for a certain but limited time to the authors of useful inventions, or of literary compositions, a monopoly of sale and profit; and, on the other, to protect the interests of the public.

I. PATENTS.

1349. Principle.—The power which the Crown assumed of granting monopolies, at one time grossly abused, was taken away in England in the reign of James I.; in Scotland, in Charles I.'s time. There was, however, a reservation of power to the Crown to give letters patent "for the sole working and making of any manner of manufacture within the realm to the first and true inventor; so they be not contrary to the law, nor mischievous to the State, by raising prices of commodities at home, or hurt of trade, or generally inconvenient" (*a*). The law of England and of Scotland has been the same since the Union (*b*). The right to a patent monopoly of a useful invention is granted on the principle of a compromise or bargain between the inventor and the public. If left to the common law, the inventor would be deprived of the benefit of his invention. If he held a monopoly of it for ever, the public interest would suffer by high prices imposed by him wherever the use of his invention was valuable, and so would be deprived of the advantage of the discovery by other persons. On these grounds the bargain proceeds, by which there is given to the public the full benefit of the discovery, on a fair disclosure of it in its most beneficial shape, and in terms so plain and intelligible that it may be used without danger of useless expense, and without the necessity of further experiment; and the public, on the other hand, is restrained for a time from interfering with the gains. But although this be now the settled principle of the arrangement, it was not till Queen Anne's time that, by a provision introduced into the patent, a specification of the invention was made the condition of the right. The condition is, that the patentee shall, by an instrument in writing, 'either along with his application or within nine months afterwards (*c*),' particularly describe and ascertain the nature of his invention, and in what manner the same is to be performed.

'The grant of a patent is an exercise of the Crown's prerogative, upon the conditions above mentioned, with others specified in the Letters Patent. Before 1883, Letters Patent in the usual form did not exclude the Crown from the use of the patented invention, the principle being that the Crown in granting an exclusive privilege is not itself bound by the exclusion, unless it be expressly declared to that effect (*d*). It is now enacted, however, that a patent shall have to all intents the like effect against the Crown as against subjects; but that the officers of any department may use the invention for the services of the Crown on terms to be agreed on, or in default of agreement to be settled by the Treasury after hearing parties (*e*).'

(*a*) See 21 James I. c. 3. 1641, c. 76. 5 and 6 Will. IV. c. 83. Godson on Patents, 1823; Supplement, 1832. Davies' Cases on Patents. Report of the Committee of the House of Commons, June 12, 1829. 2 Kent, Com. on American Law, 366. Merlin Répert. de Jurispr. *voce* Brevet d'Invention. Renouard, Tr. de Bre. d'Inv. 15 and 16 Vict. c. 83. 16 and 17 Vict. c. 5 and 115. 22 Vict. c. 13; all repealed by 46 and 47 Vict. c. 57. 48 and 49 Vict. c. 63. 49 and 50 Vict. c. 37. 51 and 52 Vict c. 50 (amending Acts), etc. (Patents, Designs, and Trade Marks Acts, 1883 to 1888). Caldwell *v.* Vanvlissingen, 9 Hare, 415; 21 L. J. Ch. 97. Coryton on Patents. Hindmarch on Patents. Webster's Cases on Patents. Curtis on Patents. Agnew on Patents.

(*b*) See Godson on Patents, 42 et seq. 1 Bell's Com. 108.

(*c*) 46 and 47 Vict. c. 57, § 8.

(*d*) Feather *v.* The Queen, 35 L. J. Q. B. 200; 6 B. & S. 257. Dixon *v.* London Small Arms Co., 46 L. J. Q. B. 617; 1 App. Ca. 632.

(*e*) 46 and 47 Vict. c. 57, § 27, and Sched. I. Form D.

1350. Persons entitled to Patent.—The persons (*a*) entitled to apply for a patent are the inventor or discoverer of a new manufacture, 'or his personal representative applying within six months of his decease (*b*),' provided he is the first publisher of the invention (*c*); or the introducer of a foreign invention into this country. As to the former, a person is not the inventor who has learned the thing from another (*d*); 'or has taken it from, or has been anticipated by, a book published or circulated in this country, or from the specification of a prior patent (*e*).' But 'to invalidate a patent, the previous publication must give what is essential to the patent; *i.e.* must convey such knowledge as to enable the public, *i.e.* not necessarily ordinary workmen, but educated men conversant with the subject (*f*), to see the discovery and carry the invention into practical operation (*g*).' It will not deprive one of the title that he has employed another in the investigation (*h*), provided the invention is not distinctly the separate and independent invention of such assistant (*i*). 'The first importer, whether a British subject or an alien friend (*k*), of' a foreign invention, by the introduction of which the country is benefited, has, by the uniform construction of the statute from its passing to the present day, been held entitled to the privilege (*l*).

(*a*) Any person may apply for a patent, whether a British subject or not. 46 and 47 Vict. c. 57, § 4 (Patents, etc., Marks Act, 1883); and "person" in the Act includes a body corporate. The Act, § 117.

(*b*) The Act, § 34.

(*c*) Godson, Sup. 4. See next section, (*f*), (*x*), (*y*).

(*d*) The King *v.* Arkwright, Dav. Cases, 129; 1 Ill. 431. Tennant, *ib.* 429. Hill *v.* Thompson, 8 Taunt. 895; 20 R. R. 488. Roebuck, Garbet, & Co. *v.* Stirling, 1774; 5 B. Sup. 522; Hailes, 566; aff. 2 Paton, 346; 1 Ill. 426. Murdoch & Co. *v.* Chivers, 5 B. Sup. 524. **Neilson *v.* Househill Coal Co.**, 1842; 4 D. 1187; 5 D. 86; 2 Bell's Ap. 1; 9 Cl. & F. 788. Neilson *v.* Baird, 1843; 6 D. 51. Pickard & Curry *v.* Prescott, 1890; 17 R. 1102; aff. 1892, 19 R. H. L. 56; A. C. 263. As to contemporaneous inventors, see the Act, § 7, 13; and Smith *v.* Davidson, 1857; 19 D. 691. Forsyth *v.* Riviere, 1 Webster Pat. Rep. 97. Cornish *v.* Keene, *ib.* 508.

(*e*) Neilson *v.* Househill Co., *cit.* Stead *v.* Williams, 8 Scott, N. R. 872; 2 Webs. P. R. 142. Booth *v.* Kennard, 2 H. & N. 84. Hills *v.* Evans, 2 De G. F. & J. 300; 31 L. J. Ch. 457. Lang *v.* Gisborne, 31 Beav. 133; 31 L. J. Ch. 769. Neilson *v.* Betts, L. R. 5 H. L. 1; 40 L. J. Ch. 317. Pickard *v.* Prescott, 1892; A. C. 263; 19 R. H. L. 56.

(*f*) King, Brown, & Co. *v.* Brush Elect. Light Corp., 1890; 17 R. 1266; aff. 1892, A. C. 376; 19 R. H. L. 20. Comp. § 1352 (*g*).

(*g*) Hills *v.* Evans, *cit.* Betts *v.* Menzies, 10 H. L. Ca. 117; 31 L. J. Q. B. 233. Plimpton *v.* Malcolmson, 3 Ch. D. 531; 45 L. J. Ch. 505. Plimpton *v.* Spiller, 6 Ch. D. 412; 47 L. J. Ch. 211. Stonor *v.* Tod, 4 Ch. D. 58; 46 L. J. Ch. 32. Patterson *v.* Gaslight and Coke Co., 3 App. Ca. 239; 47 L. J. Ch. 402. United Telephone Co. *v.* Harrison, 21 Ch. D. 720; 51 L. J. Ch. 705. If it be shown that, though described in a book sent to this country, that book was never used or placed in a position where it could be known to persons concerned in matters of the kind, there is not prior publication. Plimpton's cases, cited; and see United Telephone Co., *cit.* Harris *v.* Rothwell, 35 Ch. D. 416 (foreign specification in Patent Office Library).

(*h*) Bloxam *v.* Elsee, 1 Car. & P. 558; 6 B. & Cr. 169; 30 R. R. 275. Minter *v.* Wells, 1 Webs. P. R. 132. Allan *v.* Rawson, 1 C. B. 551.

(*i*) Godson, Sup. 4. R. *v.* Arkwright, *cit.* (*d*). Barker *v.* Shaw, 1 Webs. P. R. 126.

(*k*) See above, note (*a*). Chappell *v.* Purday, 11 M. & W. 318. Beard *v.* Egerton, 3 C. B. 97; 15 L. J. C. P. 270. See Milligan *v.* Marsh, 2 E. Jur. 1083.

(*l*) Edgeberry *v.* Stephens, 2 Salk. 477. Wood *v.* Zimmer, Holt, 58; 17 R. R. 605. Nickels *v.* Ross, 8 C. B. 679. Crane *v.* Price, 5 Scott, N. R. 338; 4 M. & G. 580; 1 Webs. P. R. 411.

1351. Subject of Patent.—The description of the subject as contained in the statute 'of James I., which is still authoritative (*a*),' is "any manner of new manufacture within this realm, to the true and first inventor and inventors of such manufacture, which others, at the time of making such letters patent, shall not use, so as they be not contrary to law, nor mischievous to the State, by raising prices of commodities at home, or hurt of trade, or generally inconvenient." As "Manufacture" is the word used by the Legislature in describing the subject of such patents, it must be a subject vendible, the law being made for the encouragement of trade. A mere principle or method, therefore, is no proper subject of patent, though, if embodied in a manufacture, it may, '*i.e.* embodied in a practical mode of carrying the principle or idea into effect, described in the specification' (*b*). But although *described* in the specification as a method, it will be good if truly a patent for a process or thing produced (*c*). 'The statement that' anything made by the hand of man may be the subject of a patent (*d*) 'appears to be too vague and general, and to require too many limitations to be practically useful.' It must be something material and useful (*e*).

It must not have been publicly used 'or published in any part of the United Kingdom (*f*). Public user means use in public so as to come to the knowledge of others than the inventor, not necessarily use by the public (*g*). And experiments by the inventor, if kept private so far as possible (*h*), or even manufacture of the patented articles by the inventor shortly before the date of the patent, if they are kept secret and not offered for sale (*i*), will not invalidate a patent (*k*). Prior use in the colonies, not being "within the realm," does not invalidate (*l*). Exhibition of an invention at an industrial or international exhibition, certified as such by the Board of Trade, or publication of a description of it, or use there, does not, subject to certain conditions, prejudice the inventor's right to obtain letters patent within six months from the opening of the exhibition. 46 and 47 Vict. c. 57, § 39 (*m*).'

Even a new process of manufacture has been held a lawful subject of patent, though to be carried on by known implements or elements acting upon known substances so as to produce some other known substance, provided it be in a manner cheaper, better, or more expeditious (*n*); 'but not a mere working direction improving an old or known process (*o*). So a new combination or arrangement of things formerly in use, but so as to produce either a new effect or a better effect than before, may be the subject of a patent (*p*); or even, it has been held, a new application of any means or contrivance, provided, in either case, the new combination or application be so much out of the track of the former use as not naturally to suggest itself, but to require some thought and study (*q*). But the cases show that this rule must be applied with great discrimination, and very rarely in mechanical inventions. In chemical inventions it has been held that there is more room for allowing patents for new applications of known processes (*r*).' The improvement of an old commodity, or engine, provided the old part be not described as new, and that the old (if protected) be not invaded, is a fair subject of patent (*s*).

A discovery or invention imported may also be the subject of a patent (*t*). It must be an invention, discovery, or first disclosure, as at the obtaining of the patent; insomuch that the improver of a machine under an existing patent, 'though he may obtain a patent for his improvement,' cannot, without consent of the patentee, use his invention till the expiration of the first patent, 'if the old invention have to be used in the combination, or with the addition of the new invention (*u*). But the Board of Trade, on the application of the second patentee, may order the patentee of the earlier invention to grant licences to subsequent inventors on reasonable terms (*v*).' A patent cannot be had for the *idea* of a machine not reduced into practice at the date of the specification, though the inventor afterwards discovers a method of accomplishing it; but if he have discovered improved methods before enrolling the 'complete' specification, the patent will, 'or rather may,' cover them (*w*).

If the invention or discovery 'and disclosure' have truly been made by the patentee, it will not invalidate his patent that a model of a similar machine imported from abroad had been seen before the date of the patent, no such machine having been made and introduced into this country previously (*x*); 'or that another party had simultaneously made the invention, but did not use it for his own trade till after the filing of the specification (*y*).' If a patent be granted for a complex invention, there must be novelty in all the 'essential' parts 'as stated in the specification,' else the whole patent will be bad (*z*).

(*a*) See 46 and 47 Vict. c. 57, § 46.

(*b*) Boulton & Watt *v.* Bull, 2 H. Bl. 463; 1 Ill. 426; 3 R. R. 439. Hornblower *v.* Boulton & Watt, 8 T. R. 98; Davies P. Ca. 221. The King *v.* Wheeler, 2 B. & Ald. 350; 20 R. R. 465. Hadden *v.* Pirie & Co., 1823; 2 S. 423. Minter *v.* Wells, 1 C. M. & R. 505. Neilson *v.* Baird, 1843; 6 D. 51. Neilson *v.* Househill Co., § 1350 (*d*). Neilson *v.* Harford, 1 Webs. P. R. 331. Betts *v.* Menzies, 10 H. L. Ca. 117; 31 L. J. Q. B. 233. Electric Tel. Co. *v.* Brett, *cit.* (*s*). Jupe *v.* Pratt, 1 Webs. P. R. 145. *Infra* (*w*).

(*c*) Hornblower, *supra* (*b*).

(*d*) The King *v.* Wheeler, *supra* (*b*).

(*e*) Hill *v.* Thompson, 8 Taunt. 375; 3 Mer. 629; 2 B. Moo. 424; 17 R. R. 156; 20 R. R. 488. Huddart *v.* Grimshaw, Dav. Cases, 297. Manton *v.* Manton, *ib.* 333, 348. Walker *v.* Congreve, Godson, 68. Brunton *v.* Hawkes, 4 B. & Ald. 541; 23 R. R. 382; 1 Ill. 430. See cases cited, § 1350 (*d*). Burch *v.* Glen, 1857; 20 D. 648, note. Morgan *v.* Seaward, 1 Webs. P. R. 187; 2 M. & W. 544. Lewis *v.* Marling, *infra* (*f*). Tetley *v.* Easton, 2 C. B. N. S. 706; 26 L. J. C. P. 209.

(*f*) Lewis *v.* Marling, 10 B. & Cr. 22; 34 R. R. 313. Jones *v.* Pearce, Godson, Sup. 10. See Brown *v.* Annandale & Co., 1841; 3 D. 1180; aff. 1842, 1 Bell's App. 70. Brown *v.* Kidston, 1852; 14 D. 826; and other cases on prior publication; above, § 1350.

(*g*) Carpenter *v.* Smith, 9 M. & W. 300; 1 Webs. P. R. 543. Stead *v.* Williams, and Stead *v.* Anderson, 8 Scott, N. R. 872; 2 Webs. P. R. 130, 149; 7 M. & G. 818. Hutchison, Main, & Co. *v.* Pattullo, 1888; 15 R. 644. Gill *v.* Cutler, 1895; 23 R. 371.

(*h*) Templeton *v.* Macfarlane, 1847; 10 D. 4. *Re* Newall & Elliott, 4 C. B. N. S. 294. *Re* Adamson's Patent, 6 De G. M. & G. 420; 25 L. J. Ch. 456 (dedication to public by inventor's public use).

(*i*) Bramah *v.* Hardcastle, Holt, 81; 1 Webs. P. R. 44. Betts *v.* Menzies, *cit.* (*b*). Morgan *v.* Seaward, *cit.* (*e*). Smith *v.* Dickinson, 3 B. & P. 630.

(*k*) As to unsuccessful experiments by others, see Hills *v.* London Gaslight Co., *infra* (*r*). Galloway *v.* Bleaden, 1 Webs. P. R. 525. Stead *v.* Williams, *cit.* Daw *v.* Ely, L. R. 3 Eq. 496.

(*l*) Rolls *v.* Isaacs, 19 Ch. D. 268; 51 L. J. Ch. 170.

(*m*) On the subject of prior user, see Heath *v.* Smith, 2 Webs. P. R. 268. Neilson *v.* Betts. L. R. 5 H. L. 1; 40 L. J. Ch. 317. To invalidate a patent, it is not necessary that the prior use should be continued to the date of the patent. Neilson *v.* Househill Co., § 1350 (*d*).

(*n*) See this doctrine laid down by Lord Tenterden as the opinion of the Court in Wheeler's case, *supra* (*b*). See also Lewis, *supra* (*f*). Hullett *v.* Hague, 2 B. & Ad. 370; 36 R. R. 687. Saunders *v.* Aston, 3 B. & Ad. 881; 37 R. R. 574. Approved in Murray *v.* Clayton, L. R. 7 Ch. 570. Cannington *v.* Nuttall, *infra* (*p*). See Harwood *v.* G. N. Ry. Co., 35 L. J. Q. B. 27; 11 H. L. Ca. 654. Ormson *v.* Clark, 32 L. J. C. P. 8, 291; 13 C. B. N. S. 337; 14 *ib.* 475. Betts, *cit.* (*b*).

(*o*) Patterson *v.* Gaslight & Coke Co., § 1350 (*g*). **Badische Anilin Fabrik** *v.* **Levinstein**, 29 Ch. D. 366; rev. 12 App. Ca. 710.

(*p*) Morton *v.* Middleton, 1863; 1 Macph. 718. Templeton *v.* Macfarlane, 1848; 10 D. 796; aff. 1 H. L. Ca. 595. Crane *v.* Price, 4 M. & G. 486; 5 Scott, N. R. 388; 1 Webs. P. R. 409; 12 L. J. C. P. 81. Sellers *v.* Dickinson, 5 Ex. 312. Lister *v.* Leather, 8 E. & B. 1004; 27 L. J. Q. B. 295. Curtis *v.* Platt, 35 L. J. Ch. 852. Cannington *v.* Nuttall, 40 L. J. Ch. 739; L. R. 5 H. L. 205. Saxby *v.* Clunes, 43 L. J. Ex. 228 (H. L). Murray *v.* Clayton (*n*). Badische Anilin Fabrik, *cit.* Saxby *v.* Gloucester Waggon Co., 7 Q. B. D. 305; 50 L. J. Q. B. 577.

(*q*) Penn *v.* Bibby, L. R. 2 Ch. Ap. 127; 36 L. J. Ch. 455. See, however, Harwood *v.* G. N. Ry. Co., *cit.* (*n*). Brook *v.* Aston, 8 E. & B. 478; 28 L. J. Q. B. 175. Steiner *v.* Heald, 6 Ex. 607; 20 L. J. Ex. 410. Horton *v.* Mabon, 31 L. J. C. P. 255; aff. 16 C. B. N. S. 141. Dudgeon *v.* Thomson, 1876; 4 R. 256; aff. 1877, *ib.* H. L. 88; 3 App. Ca. 34. Jordan *v.* Moore, L. R. 1 C. P. 624; 35 L. J. C. P. 268. Saxby *v.* Gloucester Waggon Co., *cit.* (*p*).

(*r*) Young *v.* Fernie, 4 Giff. 577; 10 E. Jur. N. S. 926. See Unwin *v.* Heath, 5 H. L. Ca. 505; 25 L. J. C. P. 8. Hills *v.* London Gaslight Co., 5 H. & N. 312; 29 L. J. Ex. 409. See Badische Anilin Fabrik, *cit.* (*o*).

(*s*) Hill, *supra* (*e*). Lewis *v.* Davis, 3 C. & P. 502; 33 R. R. 690. Morton, *cit.* (*p*). Electric Telegraph Co. *v.* Brett, 10 C. B. 838; 20 L. J. C. P. 123. See below, § 1352 (*n*).

(*t*) Prale *v.* Millar & Son, 1863; 1 Macph. 450. *Supra*, § 1350 *fin.*

(*u*) M'Farlane *v.* Price, 1 Starkie, 109; 18 R. R. 760. *Ex p.* Fox, 1 V. & B. 67; 1 Webs. P. R. 431. Lister *v.* Leather, 8 E. & B. 1004, 1017; 27 L. J. Q. B. 295.

(*v*) 46 and 47 Vict. c. 57, § 22.

(*w*) Bloxam *v.* Elsee, *cit.* § 1350. Crossley *v.* Beverley, 9 B. & Cr. 63. See above (*b*); below, § 1353A. Badische Anilin Fabrik, *cit.* (*o*).

(*x*) Lewis, *supra* (*f*).

(*y*) Smith *v.* Davidson, 1857; 19 D. 691. See § 1350 (*d*).

(*z*) Brunton *v.* Hawkes, *cit.* (*e*). See above (*p*); below, § 1352 (*m*). Kerr *v.* Clark & Co., 1868; 7 Macph. 51. Kay *v.* Marshall, 8 Cl. & F. 245; 2 Webs. P. R. 51. Morgan *v.* Seaward, *cit.* (*e*). Templeton, *cit.* (*p*). Hill, *cit.* (*e*).

1352. Specification.—The specification is intended at once to give to the public the full benefit of the invention, and to limit the patentee's power of restraining the invention and industry of others. It must therefore be precise, unambiguous, and clear. Until of late years, the course of judicial decisions has gone on too critical a construction of the words of specifications (*a*); but now the rule is, that a fair and not too astute construction shall be put on them (*b*).

'With regard to specifications, it is enacted that "a provisional specification must describe the nature of the invention, and be accompanied by drawings, if required (*c*). A complete specification, whether left on application or subsequently, must particularly describe and ascertain the nature of the invention, and in what manner it is to be performed, and must be accompanied by drawings, if required. A specification, whether provisional or complete, must commence with the title, and, in the case of a complete specification, must end with a distinct statement of the invention claimed" (*d*). By the decisions' these points seem to be fixed:—The invention must be fully and fairly described, and the specification 'accepted at the Patent Office.' The title and general designation, 'and the provisional specification, which is to be read along with the title,' under which the patent has been obtained must exactly accord with the 'final' specification (*e*); and the description must detail the invention intelligibly and unambiguously (*f*), particularly the method and effect; omitting nothing useful or necessary to understand the description, 'and to enable a workman of ordinary skill to construct the machine or perform the process protected (*g*)'; containing nothing to mislead (*h*); and specifying the most advantageous mode, so as to require no further research or experience to verify or perfect the disclosure, and to occasion no useless expense (*i*), 'and so as to show what cannot be used without infringing the patent (*k*).' The terms made use of are to be understood according to the acceptation of practical men at the time of the enrolment (*l*). And nothing shall be included in the patent which is not original (*m*).

'So, in a patent for an improvement or addition to an old invention, what is new must be described and distinguished from the parts that are old (*n*). And if any one of the parts of an invention consisting of distinct parts is old, the whole patent is void (*o*); and the same holds if one patent is taken out for several distinct inventions, one of which is not new, or is not an improvement (*p*). But a patent for a combination is not, if properly expressed as such, a claim that each part of the combination is new, and it is not therefore necessary to distinguish in the specification the new parts from the old (*q*); unless the patentee intends also to claim one or more of the parts as being themselves novel and useful inventions (*r*).'

In order to give time for preparing a proper specification, the application for a patent 'might' be preceded by a caveat to prevent surprise. But that will not prevent disclosure, nor debar other inventors; and the preference of the pretensions of rival candidates must be decided on evidence (*s*). 'Although caveats are still used in various proceedings in regard to patents, and have merely the effect of entitling to notice (*t*), they are superseded in this use by the provisional specification.'

(*a*) Hill *v.* Thompson, *cit.* § 1351 (*e*); 1 Ill. 428.

(*b*) Russel *v.* Crichton, 1839; 1 D. 893. Russel *v.* Cowley, 1 C. M. & R. 864. See below, § 1353. Sellers *v.* Dickinson, 5 Ex. 312; 20 L. J. Ex. 417. Harrison *v.* Anderston Foundry Co., 1875; 2 R. 357; rev. 3 R. H. L. 55; 1 App. Ca. 574. Hinks *v.* Pat. Safety Lighting Co., 46 L. J. Ch. 185; 4 Ch. D. 607. Hutchison, Main, & Co. *v.* Pattullo, 1888; 15 R. 644.

(*c*) As to the office of the provisional specification, see Stonor *v.* Todd, 4 Ch. D. 58; 46 L. J. Ch. 32; and the cases in (*e*) *infra*.

(*d*) 46 and 47 Vict. c. 57, § 5. The last two requirements are directory, and non-compliance with them does not invalidate the patent. Vickers, Sons, & Co. *v.* Siddell, 1890; 15 App. Ca. 495. 49 & 50 Vict. c. 38, § 2.

(*e*) Bloxam, *supra*, § 1351 (*w*). See below, § 1353A. Dudgeon *v.* Thomson, 1873; 11 Macph. 863. **Penn** *v.* **Bibby**, L. R. 2 Ch. Ap. 127; 36 L. J. Ch. 455. Wright *v.* Hitchcock, 39 L. J. Ex. 97. Bailey *v.* Roberton, 1877; 4 R. 545; aff. 1878, 5 R. H. L. 179; 3 App. Ca. 1055. United Telephone Co. *v.* Harrison, 21 Ch. D. 743; 51 L. J. Ch. 705. Gillies *v.* Dunbar, 1877; 5 R. 337. Vickers, Sons, & Co. *v.* Siddell, *cit.* Nuttall *v.* Hargreaves, 1892; 1 Ch. D. 23.

(*f*) Campion *v.* Benyon, 3 B. & B. 5; 23 R. R. 549. Turner *v.* Winter, 1 T. R. 602; 1 R. R. 311. Hastings *v.* Brown, 1 E. & B. 450.

(*g*) Burch *v.* Glen, 1857; 20 D. 648. Knox *v.* Paterson, *ib.* Sykes *v.* Wilson, 1866; 4 Macph. 349. Prale *v.* Millar & Co., 1863; 1 Macph. 450. Morton, *infra* (*k*). Beard *v.* Egerton, 8 C. B. 165; 19 L. J. C. P. 39. Bailey, *cit.* (*e*). Plimpton *v.* Malcomson, 3 Ch. D. 531; 45 L. J. Ch. 505. Wegmann *v.* Corcoran, 13 Ch. D. 65. **Badische Anilin Fabrik** *v.* **Levinstein**, 29 Ch. D. 366; rev. 12 App. Ca. 710.

(*h*) Turner, *supra* (*f*). Felton *v.* Greaves, 3 C. & P. 611; 33 R. R. 706. Savory *v.* Price, Ry. & Moo. 1; 27 R. R. 723. Wegmann and Plimpton, *cit.* (*g*). Simpson and Stevens, *infra* (*i*). Sturtz *v.* De la Rue, 5 Russ. 322; 1 Webs. P. R. 83; 29 R. R. 24. Hills *v.* London Gaslight Co., 5 H. & N. 572; 29 L. J. Ex. 409. Badische Anilin Fabrik, *cit.*

(*i*) The King *v.* Elsee, 11 East, 109. The King *v.* Wheeler, 2 B. & Ald. 350; 20 R. R. 465. Ld. Cochran *v.* Smethurst, 1 Stark. 208; 18 R. R. 761. Arkwright *v.* Nightingale, Dav. on Patents, 56. Boville *v.* Moore, *ib.* 401. Turner *v.* Winter, *cit.* (*f*). Wood *v.* Zimmer, Holt's Ca. 58; 17 R. R. 605. The King *v.* Metcalf, 2 Stark. 249; 19 R. R. 713. Astley *v.* Taylor, 1821; 1 S. Ap. 54. Crossley *v.* Beverly, M. & M. 283; 9 B. & Cr. 63. Campion *v.* Benyon, *cit.* (*f*). Simpson *v.* Holliday, L. R. 1 H. L. 315; 35 L. J. Ch. 811. Stevens *v.* Keating, 2 Ex. 772. Morgan *v.* Seward, 2 M. & W. 544; 1 Webs. P. R. 179. Neilson *v.* Harford, 1 Webs. P. R. 318. Hills, *cit.* (*h*).

(*k*) Morton *v.* Middleton, 1863; 1 Macph. 718.

(*l*) Turner, *supra* (*f*). Elliott *v.* Turner, 2 C. B. 446. Hills *v.* Evans, 31 L. J. Ch. 457. Bickford *v.* Skewes, 1 Q. B. 938. Morton *v.* Middleton, 1863; 1 Macph. 718. Kerr *v.* Clark & Co., 1868; 7 Macph. 51. Simpson, and Crossley *v.* Beverly, *supra* (*i*).

(*m*) Huddart *v.* Grimshaw, Dav. Cases, 295. Brunton *v.* Hawkes, *cit.* § 1351 (*e*). Campion, *supra* (*f*). Wood, *supra* (*i*).

(*n*) Crane *v.* Price, 4 M. & G. 580; 5 Scott, N. R. 338; 1 Webs. P. R. 413. Nickels *v.* Ross, 8 C. B. 723. Dangerfield *v.* Jones, 13 L. T. N. S. 144. Ormson *v.* Clark, § 1351 (*n*). See above, § 1351 (*s*). In a combination patent for improvements on part of a machine, it is not enough to describe the whole machine as improved, but the specification must show wherein the improvement consists, — "it must assign the *differentia* of the new combination." Foxwell *v.* Bostock, 4 De G. J. & S. 298. Parkes *v.* Stevens, 38 L. J. Ch. 626 ; L. R. 8 Eq. 358 ; 5 Ch. 36.

(*o*) Cases *supra*, § 1351 (*z*).

(*p*) Morgan *v.* Seaward, *supra* (*i*). Cornish *v.* Keene, 1 Webs. P. R. 505.

(*q*) **Harrison** *v.* **Anderston Foundry Co.**, 1875 ; 2 R. 857 ; rev. 3 R. H. L. 55 ; L. R. 1 App. Ca. 574. Comp. Holmes *v.* L. and N.-W. Ry. Co., 12 C. B. 831. Lister *v.* Leather, 27 L. J. Q. B. 295 ; 8 E. & B. 1004 and 1017. Morton *v.* Middleton, *cit.* (*k*). Henderson *v.* Clippens Oil Co., 1881 ; 9 R. 232 ; aff. 10 R. H. L. 38 ; 8 App. Ca. 873.

(*r*) **Clark** *v.* **Adie**, L. R. 10 Ch. 667 ; aff. L. R. 2 App. Ca. 215 ; 46 L. J. Ch. 585. This requirement of a specific claim for subordinate parts of a combination limits or overrules the doctrine laid down in Sellers *v.* Dickinson, Lister *v.* Leather, Parkes *v.* Stevens, *citt.*, and other cases, to the effect that a combination patent may be infringed by taking a *material* part of the combination, if new, though not separately claimed. Comp. as to combinations, Pennycook Patent Glazing Co. *v.* Mackenzie & Co., 1882 ; 9 R. 414. As to infringement of combination patents, see Gwynne *v.* Drysdale & Co., 1886 ; 13 R. 684. Proctor *v.* Bennis, 36 Ch. D. 740.

(*s*) See below, § 1353A, as to provisional specifications.

(*t*) *E.g.* in applications for extension, the Act, § 25. Agnew on Patents, 161, 162. R. *v.* Cutler, 3 C. & K. 215. *In re* Somerset's Patent, 13 Ch. D. 399, note.

1353. Amidst the evils arising from the rigid construction to which specifications and patents were exposed, new powers were bestowed on 'the law officers of the Crown, the Judicial' Committee of the Privy Council, 'and on the Comptroller-General of Patents, subject to appeal to the law officers,' which greatly tend to correct the evils of the former law (*a*). These, generally stated, are: A power 'to the Comptroller and law officers (*b*)' to allow the specification to be corrected, 'by disclaimer, correction, or explanation,' if by mistake or ignorance entered erroneously, 'but not, under the law prior to 1883, so as to convert a bad specification, containing no sufficient description of any useful invention, into a specific, definite, practical description; and no amendment shall be allowed that would make the specification as amended claim an invention substantially larger than, or substantially different from, the invention claimed by "the specification as it stood before the amendment" (*c*)': A power 'to the Judicial Committee of the Privy Council, now expiring by the repeal of the statute conferring it (*d*),' so far to control a verdict at law opening a patent on account of others being said to have known the thing before, and 'in that case, or when the patentee had discovered prior use or invention by persons unknown to him,' to confirm the patent as effectual (*e*): A power 'to the Court in an action for infringement,' when a patent has been held good, to grant a certificate 'that the validity of the patent came in question,' that shall meet any future trial, and give the patentee the benefit, 'formerly' of triple costs, 'now of full costs, charges, and expenses as between solicitor and client (*f*)': And, finally, a power 'to the Judicial Committee on the application of the patentee or his assignees, six months before the expiration of the original term (*g*), to advise the Queen' to renew 'or extend' the patent, for a limited term, on being satisfied that there are sufficient grounds to justify the indulgence (*h*), 'having regard to the nature and merit of the invention in relation to the public, to the profits made by the patentee as such, and to all the circumstances of the case.'

(*a*) 5 and 6 Will. IV. c. 83, and later Acts, now repealed.

(*b*) The law officers are the Attorney-General and Solicitor-General of England. 46 and 47 Vict. c. 57, § 117. Knox *v.* Paterson, 1857 ; 20 D. 40.

(*c*) 46 and 47 Vict. c. 57, § 18 (8). 51 and 52 Vict. c. 50, § 5. Ralston *v.* Smith, 11 H. L. Ca. 223 ; 35 L. J. C. P. 49. R. *v.* Mill, 10 C. B. 379. Seed *v.* Higgins, 8 H. L. Ca. 550 ; 30 L. J. Q. B. 314. Perry *v.* Skinner, 2 M. & W. 471. Wallington *v.* Dale, 7 Ex. 88 ; 23 L. J. Ex. 29. Tetley *v.* Easton, 2 C. B. N. S. 706. Thomas *v.* Welch, L. R. 1 C. P. 192 ; 35 L. J. C. P. 200. Cannington *v.* Nuttall, *cit.* § 1351 (*p*). When a patent has been amended (unless when the patentee has been allowed by the judge to apply for the amendment during the dependence of an action for infringement under sec. 19 of the Act), the patentee must bring fresh proceedings for infringement, and is not allowed to enforce an interdict obtained before the amendment. Dudgeon *v.* Thomson, 1877 ; 4 R. H. L. 88 ; 3 App. Ca. 34.

(*d*) 5 and 6 Will. IV. c. 83, § 2, not repealed *quoad hoc* by 46 and 47 Vict. c. 57, § 113, and sched., as to patents existing at 1883. Jablochkoff's Patent, 1891; A. C. 293.

(*e*) Agnew on Patents, p. 220.

(*f*) 46 and 47 Vict. c. 57, § 31.

(*g*) Marshall's Patent, 1891; A. C. 104.

(*h*) The Act, § 25. *In re* Bett's Patent, 1 Moo. P. C. N. S. 49. Ledsam *v.* Russell, 14 M. & W. 574 ; 16 *ib.* 633 ; 1 H. L. Ca. 687. Hardy's Patent, 6 Moo. P. C. 441. Napier's Patent, 13 *ib.* 370. Norton's Patent, 1 Moo. P. C. N. S. 339. Poole's Patent, L. R. 1 P. C. 514. Claridge's Patent, 7 Moo. P. C. 394. Hill's Patent, 1 Moo. P. C. N. S. 258. Newton's Patent, 14 Moo. P. C. 156. Trotman's Patent, L. R. 1 P. C. 118. Saxby's Patent, L. R. 3 P. C. 294 ; 7 Moo. P. C. N. S. 82. Normand's Patent, L. R. 3 P. C. 193. Blake's Patent, 4 Moo. P. C. N. S. 535. Bovill *v.* Finch, 39 L. J. C. P. 277 ; L. R. 5 C. P. 523. Lake's Patent, 1891; A. C. 240 (insufficient accounts). Bower-Barff Patent, 1895; A. C. 675.

1353A. 'Under the existing law, an *application* for a patent is made to the Patent Office, and is supported by a declaration in a statutory or prescribed form; and must be accompanied by either a provisional or complete specification. These documents are referred to an examiner, who ascertains whether the nature of the invention is fairly described, the application, specification, and drawings, if any, prepared in the prescribed manner, and the invention sufficiently indicated in the title. Upon his report the Comptroller accepts or refuses the application, or requires an amendment; subject to an appeal to the law officers (*a*). A complete specification may be lodged at any time within nine months after the application (*b*); and will be sent to an examiner for comparison with the provisional specification, the Comptroller's refusal to accept it being subject to appeal (*c*). For two months after the acceptance of a complete specification has been advertised, any person may give notice of opposition to the granting of a patent on certain specified grounds (*d*). The patentee has provisional protection between the date of acceptance of his application and the sealing of the patent (*e*); and from the date of the acceptance of a complete specification he has the same privileges and rights as if a patent for the invention were sealed, except that he cannot before the sealing institute an action for infringement (*f*). A Register of Patents is kept at the Patent Office, which is *primâ facie* evidence of the matters directed to be inserted therein (*g*).'

(*a*) 46 and 47 Vict. c. 57, § 5-7. 51 and 52 Vict. c. 50, § 2.
(*b*) *Ib.* § 8. (*c*) *Ib.* § 9.
(*d*) *Ib.* § 10, 11. 51 and 52 Vict. c. 50, § 4.
(*e*) *Ib.* § 14. (*f*) *Ib.* § 15.
(*g*) *Ib.* § 23.

1353B. **'Infringement—Revocation.**—If a patent right be infringed, the patentee may raise his action for the damages sustained (*a*); and he may also obtain an interdict restraining the offender from the further use of the invention (*b*).

'But it is an offence summarily punishable for a seller to represent falsely that an article is patented when no patent has been granted for it (*c*); nor may a person represent a patent as still existing when it has expired (*d*), or assert an exclusive right to the trade name, being the only name of his patented article, after his term has expired (*e*). And it is enacted, in confirmation of the common law, that where any person claiming to be a patentee threatens any other person with legal proceedings or liability in respect of any alleged manufacture, use, sale, or purchase of his invention, the person aggrieved may obtain an interdict against such threats, and recover any damage sustained, if the alleged manufacture, etc., was not in fact an infringement of the inventor's legal rights; but this provision does not apply if the inventor with due diligence commences and prosecutes an action for infringement of his patent (*f*).

'An action for infringement of a patent may be successfully defended, on the ground, either (1) that there has been no infringement, or (2) that the patent is void.

'A patent right is infringed by one who makes for sale (*g*), sells, or imports for sale (*h*), or uses, or applies in any way for his own profit or benefit (*i*), the patented art or invention, without the licence or assent of the patentee. Intention is of no moment in this question (*k*), and ignorance of the patent seems in strict law to be no defence (*l*). In determining the question of infringement, the substance and not the mere form of the invention is considered,—whether the mode of working is essentially or substantially different (*m*),—so that a difference introduced merely to disguise or conceal the imitation (*n*), or the use of a known mechanical or even chemical equivalent, will be no protection (*o*).

'The invalidity of the patent may be established by objections to the form of the letters patent, or of the specification, which are properly objections to the title to sue; or by showing that the article was not a fit subject for a patent, that the patentee was not truly the inventor, that there had been "prior use" or publication, that the invention is not generally useful, or that the specification is insufficient, etc.; the objection that the patent is void in law being always open at the trial as an answer to the patentee's issue of infringement (*p*).

'Moreover, apart from all allegations as to infringement, the patent may be repealed in England, formerly by means of a *scire facias*, but now by a petition to the High Court of Justice, or in Scotland by an action of reduction at the instance of the Lord Advocate, or of anyone having an interest with concurrence of the Lord Advocate,—

which may be given only upon just cause shown (*q*).'

(*a*) As to the measure of damages, see United Horse Shoe and Nail Co. *v.* Stewart & Co., 1886 ; 14 R. 266 ; rev. 1888 ; 13 App. Ca. 401 ; 15 R. H. L. 45.

(*b*) As to procedure, see 46 and 47 Vict. c. 57, § 28 sqq. An interdict against one may be enforced against another who is assumed by him as a partner for the purpose of infringing. Harvie *v.* Ross, 1886 ; 14 R. 71. As to the competency and effect of interdict against one residing beyond the territory, see Gill *v.* Cutler, 1895 ; 23 R. 371.

(*c*) 46 and 47 Vict. c. 57, § 105.

(*d*) Cheavin *v.* Walker, 5 Ch. D. 862 ; 46 L. J. Ch. 265, 686.

(*e*) Linoleum Manufg. Co. *v.* Nairn, 7 Ch. D. 834 ; 47 L. J. Ch. 430.

(*f*) 46 and 47 Vict. c. 57, § 32. Wren *v.* Weild, L. R. 4 Q. B. 736 ; 38 L. J. Q. B. 88, 327. Halsey *v.* Brotherhood, 16 Ch. D. 518 ; 19 Ch. D. 389 ; 49 L. J. Ch. 786 ; 51 *ib.* 233. Johnson *v.* Edge, 1892 ; 2 Ch. 1. Skinner *v.* Shaw & Co., 1893 ; 1 Ch. 413.

(*g*) Jones *v.* Pearce, 1 Webs. P. R. 122. Muntz *v.* Foster, 2 *ib.* 101. It is not infringement to make an article for amusement, or for a *bonâ fide* experiment, or as a model and not for profit, etc. Jones, *cit.* Higgs *v.* Goodwin, E. B. & E. 529 ; 27 L. J. Q. B. 421. Frearson *v.* Loe, L. R. 9 Ch. D. 48.

(*h*) Gibson *v.* Brand, 4 M. & G. 179 ; 4 Scott, N. R. 844. Walton *v.* Lavater, 8 C. B. N. S. 181 ; 29 L. J. C. P. 275. Elmslie *v.* Boursier, L. R. 9 Eq. 222 ; 39 L. J. Ch. 328. Wright *v.* Hitchcock, L. R. 5 Ex. 37 ; 39 L. J. Ex. 97. Betts *v.* Willmott, L. R. 6 Ch. App. 239. Von Heyden *v.* Neustadt, 14 Ch. D. 233 ; 50 L. J. Ch. 126. As to mere exposure for sale, comp. Minter *v.* Williams, 1 Webs. P. R. 137, with Oxley *v.* Holden, 5 C. B. N. S. 667. There is no infringement by a foreigner who makes and delivers abroad to a buyer in this country an article protected by a British patent. Badische Anilin Fabrik *v.* Basle Chem. Wks., 1898 ; A. C. 200.

(*i*) Betts *v.* Neilson, 40 L. J. Ch. 317 ; L. R. 5 E. & I. App. 1 ; 3 Ch. App. 429 (mere transmission through England for shipment there). Nobel's Explosives Co. *v.* Jones, 50 L. J. Ch. 582 ; L. R. 17 Ch. D. 721 ; 8 App. Ca. 5 (do.). And anyone taking part in the wrong may be restrained and is answerable. Nobel's Co., *cit.* Betts *v.* De Vitre, *infra* (*k*).

(*k*) Stead *v.* Anderson, 2 Webs. P. R. 156. Stevens *v.* Keating, 2 *ib.* 175 ; 2 Ex. 772 ; 19 L. J. Ex. 57. Heath *v.* Unwin, 15 Sim. 552 ; 5 H. L. Ca. 505 ; 25 L. J. C. P. 8. Wright *v.* Hitchcock, *cit.* (*h*). Cf. Betts *v.* Willmott, *cit.* (*h*). Betts *v.* De Vitre, L. R. 3 Ch. 441 ; 37 L. J. Ch. 325.

(*l*) Wright *v.* Hitchcock, *cit.* (*h*). Curtis *v.* Platt, 11 L. T. N. S. 245. Honiball's Patent, 9 Moo. P. C. 378. See Betts *v.* Willmott, 18 W. R. 946.

(*m*) Morgan *v.* Seaward, § 1351 (*e*). Hill *v.* Thompson, *ib.* Stead *v.* Anderson, *cit.* Thorn *v.* Worthing Skating Rink Co., 6 Ch. D. 415.

(*n*) Dudgeon *v.* Thomson, 1876 ; 4 R. 256 ; aff. 1877, *ib.* H. L. 88 ; L. R. 3 App. Ca. 34. Barrett *v.* Vernon, 35 L. T. 755. Henderson *v.* Clippens Oil Co., *supra*, § 1352 (*q*). Murchland *v.* Nicholson, 1893 ; 20 R. 1006.

(*o*) Morgan, *cit.* Sellers *v.* Dickinson, § 1351 (*p*). Curtis *v.* Platt, 35 L. J. Ch. 852 ; L. R. 1 H. L. 337. Harwood *v.* G. N. Ry. Co., 11 H. L. Ca. 654. Stevens *v.* Keating, *cit.* (*k*). Muntz *v.* Foster, *cit.* (*g*). Electric Teleg. Co. *v.* Brett, 10 C. B. 838 ; 20 L. J. C. P. 123. **Unwin** *v.* **Heath**, 5 H. L. Ca. 505 ; 25 L. J. C. P. 8. **Badische Anilin Fabrik** *v.* **Levinstein**, 24 Ch. D. 156 ; 29 *ib.* 366 ; rev. 12 App. Ca. 710. Proctor *v.* Bennis, 36 Ch. D. 740.

(*p*) See above, § 1350–1352. Sykes *v.* Wilson, 1866 ; 4 Macph. 349. Dudgeon *v.* Thomson, 1873 ; 11 Macph. 863. **Harrison** *v.* **Anderston Foundry Co.**, 1874 ; 2 R. 122, 857 ; rev. 1876, 3 R. H. L. 33 ; 1 App. Ca. 574.

(*q*) 46 and 47 Vict. c. 57, § 26, 109. **Gillespie** *v.* **Young**, 1861 ; 23 D. 1357.

1354. Period.—This is, in ordinary cases, fourteen years from the date of the patent, '*i.e.* from the date of application'; but sometimes the term is enlarged by the Legislature in particular cases, or now by the Committee of Privy Council (*a*).

(*a*) 46 and 47 Vict. c. 57, § 13, 17. See above, § 1353 *fin.*

1355. Assignment.—The patent, 'or a separate and distinct part of it (*a*),' may be assigned under certain limitations. It may also be communicated by licence. It may be entirely assigned to another. But 'under the terms of old patents' the benefit 'was' not transferable to more than five (*b*); the patent becoming void if at any time vested in more, or if books 'were' opened for the subscription of more than five, or if the benefit 'were' divided into more than five shares, or if the patentees 'acted' as a body corporate. 'The Patent Act of 1852, however, enacted that, notwithstanding any proviso in former letters patent, it should be lawful for more than twelve persons to have an interest in them: and in the present form of patent there is no limitation of the number of assignees (*c*).' The benefit may be exercised on a licence under the hand of the patentee, and such licence, 'if an exclusive licence,' will be a ground of action for damages on account of invasion (*d*). The patent is held as part of the patentee's estate on bankruptcy, and so passes to his assignees in England, and to his trustee in sequestration in Scotland (*e*). 'During the period of the licence a licensee is barred from disputing the validity of the patent; though he is entitled to plead that the true construction of the patent does not include what he has done so as to subject him to payment of royalties (*f*). In an assignment or licence there is no implied warranty of the validity of the patent (*g*); and in the absence of fraud, royalties paid under a licence cannot be recovered back if the patent be afterwards found void (*h*). It is therefore important to make special agreements as to such matters.

'Assignments and licences must, and will on proof of title, be entered on the Register of Patents; and the person for the time being entered on the register as proprietor of a patent shall, subject to any rights appearing by the register to be vested in any other person, have power absolutely to assign, grant licences as to, or otherwise deal with the same: provided that any equities in respect of the patent may be enforced in like manner as in respect of any other personal property (*i*).'

(*a*) Dunnicliff *v.* Mallet, 7 C. B. N. S. 209; 29 L. J. C. P. 70. Walton *v.* Lavater, 8 C. B. N. S. 184; 29 L. J. C. P. 275. The patentee may assign his patent for any place in or part of the United Kingdom or Isle of Man. 46 and 47 Vict. c. 57, § 36.

(*b*) Bloxam *v.* Elsee, 6 B. & Cr. 169; 1 C. & P. 568; 1 Ill. 429.

(*c*) 15 and 16 Vict. c. 83, § 36. 46 and 47 Vict. c. 57, sched.

(*d*) Renard *v.* Levinstein, 2 H. & M. 633. Derosne *v.* Fairie, 1 Webs. P. R. 154.

(*e*) See below, § 1480.

(*f*) Clarke *v.* Adie, 46 L. J. Ch. 598; 2 App. Ca. 423 (2nd appeal). Crossley *v.* Dixon, 10 H. L. Ca. 293. Trotman *v.* Wood, 16 C. B. N. S. 479. Noton *v.* Brooks, 7 H. & N. 499. Baird & Co. *v.* Neilson, 1842; 1 Bell's App. 219; 8 Cl. & Fin. 726. Walton *v.* Lavater, *cit.* (*a*). Axmann *v.* Lund, 18 Eq. 330; 43 L. J. Ch. 655.

(*g*) Hall *v.* Condor, 2 C. B. N. S. 22; 26 L. J. C. P. 138. Smith *v.* Scott, 28 L. J. C. P. 325; 6 C. B. N. S. 771. Smith *v.* Neale, 2 C. B. N. S. 67; 26 L. J. C. P. 143.

(*h*) Taylor *v.* Hare, 1 B. & P. N. R. 260; 1 Webs. P. R. 292. Lawes *v.* Purser, 6 E. & B. 930; 26 L. J. Q. B. 25. Lovell *v.* Hicks, 2 Y. & Coll. 46. Henderson *v.* Mostyn Copper Co., 3 C. P. 202.

(*i*) 46 and 47 Vict. c. 57, § 23. See Chollet *v.* Hoffmann, 7 E. & B. 686; 25 L. J. C. P. 249. Hassall *v.* Wright, L. R. 10 Eq. 509.

II. COPYRIGHT.

1356. Principle.—Although the foundation on which a right of exclusive privilege may be argued at common law is the same in the case of a mechanical invention and of a literary composition, there is a remarkable difference in the considerations on which the limited monopoly of each ought to stand. In the arts, the public is concerned in the invention being opened to them at no very distant period: for no use being derivable from the invention without the absolute possession of the individual machine or manufacture, the public is entirely in the power of the monopolist; and yet the invention would probably have been made by others, if not restrained. But in the case of a book, not only is it impossible that any other person could have composed the same book, but it is a kind of production of which the public has the benefit, by the knowledge diffused; and the value of which, and consequently the power of keeping up extravagant prices, is restrained by the interest of the author himself. There are not, therefore, the same reasons for limiting the monopoly of an author, as in setting bounds to that of the inventor.

1357. Unpublished and Published Works.—(1.) *Unpublished Works* are property at common law, and the publication of them is an invasion of the right of the owner: 'nor is the circulation of a few copies of etchings, poems, or other works, among private friends, such publication as to deprive the author of his right to protection (*a*).' Under this rule are comprehended,—works fit or intended for publication, though a gift or sale (*b*) of the manuscript may have been made (*c*); works prepared for publication of a special sort; dramatic works (*d*); private letters, which, although written and sent beyond recall, are communicated with no intention of publication (*e*); 'lectures delivered not to the general public, but to a class limited or selected by contract or otherwise, so as to imply a restriction on the use to be made of the lecture (*f*).' The law of England and that of Scotland proceed on different grounds in denying the right 'of the receiver' to publish letters. In England, it is on the ground of property alone; in Scotland, on the ground chiefly of a just and expedient interference for the protection of reputation. 'Practically, however, the rule is the same in both countries, viz. that the copyright of letters belongs exclusively to the writer and his representatives, subject only to the receiver's right to use and publish them on a legitimate and necessary occasion, *e.g.* in order to maintain a lawsuit, or vindicate his character if it be aspersed by the writer (*g*).'

(*a*) P. Albert *v.* Strange, 2 De G. & S. 696; 1 Macn. & G. 25; 18 L. J. Ch. 120; and the cases in following notes, esp. Jefferys *v.* Boosey, § 1358, and Caird *v.* Sime (*f*). As to private exhibition or circulation, see also Turner *v.* Robinson, 10 Ir. Ch. R. 121, 516.

(*b*) *Sed qu.* as to sale; Cox *v.* Cox, 11 Hare, 118. And see below, § 1417 *fin.*

(*c*) D. of Queensberry *v.* Shebbeare, 4 Burr. 2330; 1 Ill. 433. White *v.* Gerock, 2 B. & Ald. 298; 22 R. R. 786.

(*d*) Machlin *v.* Richardson, Ambler, 694. Colman *v.* Walker, 5 T. R. 245. Levy *v.* Rutley, 40 L. J. C. P. 244; L. R. 6 C. P. 523. *Infra*, § 1359 (2).

(*e*) Dodsley *v.* M'Farquhar, 1775; M. *Lit. Prop.* Apx. 1; 5 B. Sup. 509; 1 Ill. 434. Cadell & Davies *v.* Stewart, 1804; M. *Lit. Prop.* Apx. 4; 5 Pat. 493. Pope *v.* Curle, 2 Atk. 342. Thomson *v.* Stanhope, Amb. 737. Gee *v.* Pritchard, 2 Swan. 402; 19 R. R. 87. Granard *v.* Dunkin, 1 Ball & B. (Ir. Ch. R.) 209. Perceval *v.* Phipps, 2 Ves. & B. 28; 13 R. R. 1. See Davis *v.* Miller, 1855; 17 D. 1166, as to a letter to a newspaper countermanded. Oliver *v.* Oliver, 11 C. B. N. S. 139 (receiver of letter has property in the *corpus* of the letter). See Folsom *v.* Marsh, 2 Story's R. 111 (quoted in Shortt, Law of Works of Lit. and Art, p. 38).

(*f*) Abernethy *v.* Hutchinson, 3 L. J. Ch. 202; 1 H. &

T. 28. Caird *v.* Sime, 1885; 13 R. 23; rev. 1887, 12 App. Ca. 326; 14 R. H. L. 37.

(*g*) Cases in note (*c*). See further, 1 Bell's Com. 116 (111, M'L.'s ed.); and White *v.* Dickson, 1881, 8 R. 896, which does not state any very clear rule.

1358. (2.) *Published Works* are now protected by statute alone. By the first statute on this subject, a monopoly was given for fourteen years (or in certain circumstances for twenty-eight); secured not only by the common law remedies, but also by penalties and forfeitures, provided the work was entered in Stationers' Hall. By a later Act, the author's monopoly 'was' declared to extend to twenty-eight years, or (if the author be alive at the end of that time) during his natural life, and to be independent of an entry in Stationers' Hall; but the entry 'was' enforced by penalties. And by a still later Act, the author is relieved from the furnishing of some of the copies (*a*). 'It was at first held in England, contrary to the Scots decisions cited, that there was a common law copyright, which entitled the author and his representatives to protection even after the lapse of the statutory term (*b*). But it was afterwards settled that, whether or not there was a common law copyright before the Act of Queen Anne, since that Act copyright in *published* works of literature (and now of art) exists only under the statutes (*c*).'

(*a*) 8 Anne, 19, extended to the United Kingdom by 41 Geo. III. c. 107. 54 Geo. III. c. 156. 6 and 7 Will. IV. c. 110. Midwinter *v.* Hamilton, 1748; M. 8295; 1 Ill. 436. Hinton *v.* Donaldson, 1773; M. 8307; 5 B. Sup. 508. Millar *v.* Taylor, 4 Burr. 2303. Donaldson *v.* Beckett, 4 Burr. 2408; 2 Br. Par. Ca. 145. Cadell & Davies *v.* Stewart, 1804; M. *Lit. Prop.* 13; 5 Pat. 493. Jefferys *v.* Boosey, 4 H. L. Ca. 815; 24 L. J. Ex. 81. Reade *v.* Conquest, 9 C. B. N. S. 755; 30 L. J. C. P. 269.

(*b*) Millar *v.* Taylor, *cit.*

(*c*) Donaldson *v.* Beckett, *cit.* Jefferys *v.* Boosey, and Reade *v.* Conquest, *citt.*

1358A. '**Existing Statutory Rules.**—Since July 1842, the law of copyright has been on a new footing (*a*). The copyright (*b*) in a book first (*c*) published in this country after that date, and in the lifetime of the author (*d*), is to endure over the whole British dominions for his life (*e*), and for the further term of seven years commencing at his death; but if the seven years expire before the end of forty-two years from the first publication, the copyright is to endure for forty-two years. If a book be published after the death of its author, the copyright is to endure for forty-two years from the first publication, and be the property of the proprietor of the author's manuscript, from which the book has been first published (*f*). If a book has been published before 1st July 1842, the copyright is to endure for the full term provided as to books published after the above date; but if such copyright belong to a publisher, or other person who has acquired it for other consideration than love and affection, it is to endure only for the term which subsisted therein at the above date; unless the author if he be living, or his representatives if he be dead, and the proprietor of such copyright, before the expiration of such term, agree to accept of the benefits of the Act in respect of that book, and cause a minute thereof to be entered in the Book of Registry; in which case the copyright is to endure for the full term provided for books to be published after the above date (*g*). Copyright in periodical works is secured to the publisher where the author has been employed and actually (*h*) paid by a publisher, but only under the condition of not republishing the article in a separate form without the consent of the author for twenty-eight years; the property of the article reverting to the author for the remainder of the term given by the Act to authors (*i*).

'The Judicial Committee of the Privy Council may license the republication of any work which the proprietor refuses to publish after the death of the author (*k*). Copies of all books are to be delivered to the British Museum, and, on demand within twelve months of publication, to the Bodleian Library, the Public Library at Cambridge, the Advocates' Library at Edinburgh, and the Trinity College Library, Dublin (*l*).'

(*a*) 5 and 6 Vict. c. 45.

(*b*) Copyright is "the sole and exclusive right of printing or otherwise multiplying copies of any subject to which the word is applied." *Ib.* § 2. Hence unauthorised gratuitous distribution of a book is an infringement of copyright. Novello *v.* Sudlow, 12 C. B. 177. Ager *v.* P. and O. S. Nav. Co., 26 Ch. D. 637. Copyright is personal property. *Ib.* § 25.

(*c*) See Hedderwick *v.* Griffin, 1841; 3 D. 383. Guichard *v.* Mori, 9 L. J. Ch. 227. Clementi *v.* Walker, 2 B. & Cr. 861.

(*d*) The privileges conferred on authors by the statutes on this subject extend to alien friends, at least if residing at the time of publication in this country, or in the colonies, even although by the laws of the colony in which they reside they are not entitled to copyright there. Jefferys *v.*

Boosey, 4 H. L. Ca. 815; 24 L. J. Ex. 81. Low v. Routledge, 35 L. J. Ch. 114; L. R. 1 Ch. App. 42; 37 L. J. Ch. 454; L. R. 3 H. L. 100. But the qualification as to residence is contrary to the opinions of Lords Cairns and Westbury in Low v. Routledge, and is probably inconsistent with the 2nd sec. of the Naturalisation Act, 1870 (33 Vict. c. 14).

(e) Low v. Routledge, *cit.* (*d*).

(*f*) *Ib.* § 3. See Maclean v. Moody, 1858; 20 D. 1154.

(*g*) *Ib.* § 4. Marzials v. Gibbins, L. R. 9 Ch. 518; 43 L. J. Ch. 774. *Ex p.* Hutchins & Romer, 4 Q. B. D. 90, 483; 48 L. J. Q. B. 29, 505.

(*h*) Richardson v. Gilbert, 1 Sim. N. S. 336; 20 L. J. Ch. 553.

(*i*) *Ib.* § 18, 19. Smith v. Johnson, 4 Giff. 632; 33 L. J. Ch. 137. Murray (Mayhew) v. Maxwell, 1 J. & H. 312. Sweet v. Benning, 16 C. B. 459; 24 L. J. Ch. 175. Low v. Ward, 37 L. J. Ch. 841; L. R. 6 Eq. 415. Henderson v. Maxwell, 4 Ch. D. 163; 5 Ch. D. 892; 46 L. J. Ch. 59. Articles in newspapers registered at Stationers' Hall are within § 18. Cox v. Land and Water Journal Co., 39 L. J. Ch. 152; L. R. 9 Eq. 324; overruled by Walter v. Howe, 17 Ch. D. 708; 50 L. J. Ch. 621. See Mayhew v. Maxwell, 1 J. & H. 312; and Platt v. Walter, 17 L. T. N. S. 157. M'Cormick v. M'Cubbin, 1822; 1 S. 541; 20 F. C. 664. Orr's Tr. v. Tullis, 1870; 8 Macph. 936, 941. The name of a newspaper is not copyright under the Acts, but the proprietor may prevent its use by another, and assign his right in it and the goodwill. Kelly v. Hutton, L. R. 3 Ch. App. 703; 37 L. J. Ch. 917. See § 1360 (*d*). The Newspaper Libel and Registration Act, 1881 (44 and 45 Vict. c. 60), does not extend to Scotland.

(*k*) *Ib.* § 5. (*l*) *Ib.* § 6–10.

1358B. 'The proprietorship of all copyrights of books and all assignments thereof, and of dramatic and musical pieces, whether in manuscript or otherwise, and licences affecting such copyright, are registered in a Book of Registry at Stationers' Hall; and the certificates of such registry given by the officers of the Stationers' Company are evidence in all Courts, and are *primâ facie* proof of the proprietorship or assignment or licence, but subject to be rebutted by other evidence; and in the case of dramatic or musical pieces are *primâ facie* proof of the right of representation or performance (*a*). By entering the first part of encyclopædias and other periodical works, protection is secured for the whole (*b*). No copyright is acquired by registration until the actual publication of the work (*c*). A form of assignment is also provided in the case of books entered in a specified way, which may be made by a mere entry in the Book of Registry, without being subject to stamp or any duty, and is as effectual as if made by deed (*d*). Remedies are provided for entries in the Book of Registry by which any person is aggrieved (*e*), and for piracy (*f*). Books pirated become the property of the proprietor of the copyright (*g*). The omission to register does not affect the copyright of a book; but registration pursuant to the Act is a condition precedent to the right to sue for the infringement thereof (*h*). Proceedings for any "offence" against the Act are subject to a limitation of twelve months after the offence is committed (*i*).'

(*a*) 5 & 6 Vict c. 45, § 11. Jefferys v. Kyle, 1856; 18 D. 906; aff. 1859, 3 Macq. 611.

(*b*) *Ib.* § 19.

(*c*) Maxwell v. Hogg, 36 L. J. Ch. 433; L. R. 2 Ch. 307. Correspondent Newspaper Co. v. Saunders, 11 E. Jur. N. S. 540. Henderson v. Maxwell, 46 L. J. Ch. 891; 5 Ch. D. 892.

(*d*) *Ib.* § 13. See below, § 1361.

(*e*) *Ib.* § 14. *Ex p.* Davidson. 2 E. & B. 577; 18 C. B. 297; 25 L. J. C. P. 237. *In re* Graves, L. R. 4 Q. B. 715. *Ex p.* Hutchins & Romer, 4 Q. B. D. 90, 483; 48 L. J. Q. B. 29, 505.

(*f*) *Ib.* § 15, 16.

(*g*) *Ib.* § 23. Hole v. Bradbury, 12 Ch. D. 886; 48 L. J. Ch. 673.

(*h*) *Ib.* § 24. Murray v. Bogue, 1 Drew. 353; 22 L. J. Ch. 457. Stannard v. Lee, 40 L. J. Ch. 489; L. R. 6 Ch. 346. Goubaud v. Wallace, 36 L. T. Rep. 704. Thomas v. Turner, 33 Ch. D. 292 (date of first publication—first edition).

(*i*) *Ib.* § 26. Stewart v. Black, 1846; 9 D. 1026. Hogg v. Scott, 43 L. J. Ch. 705; L. R. 18 Eq. 444. Clark v. Bell, 1804; M. Apx. *Lit. Prop.* 4.

1359. Subject of Copyright—Piracy.—(1.) *General Rule.*—There is no exclusive privilege in any subject of inquiry. No one, by writing on any subject, can preoccupy it to the exclusion of another; and a prior cannot obstruct a subsequent publication without proof of identity (*a*).

(2.) *Dramatic Composition* is protected against *publication* by persons admitted to the representation (*b*); and further, protected against *representation* though printed (*c*).

(3.) *Lectures* are protected against publication in certain cases (*d*); 'namely, by the statute, when the lecturer has given two days' notice to two justices living within five miles of the place where they are delivered; but it is provided that the statute, which enacts penalties and forfeiture, shall not extend to lectures delivered in any university or public school or college, or on any public foundation, or by anyone in virtue of, or according to, a gift, endowment, or foundation; and that the law relating thereto shall remain the same as if the Act had not been passed. When the statute does not apply, it is now settled that the lecturer's common law right in his work is not lost by his communicating it to a limited or selected audience, not the general public without restriction, there being an implied contract with such an audience that, while they may take full notes for their own use, they shall not afterwards publish the lectures for profit (*e*).'

(4.) *Quotations.*—The most difficult questions which have arisen on the subject of these statutes regard the evidence of identity of the publication complained of with the original publication; or, in other words, in what cases an author is entitled to vindicate as his own exclusive right what has been published by another. The difficulty exists only when the publication is of the nature of a review, or when it is derived from sources of information open to all. As to quotations in encylopædias, reviews, etc., it is for a jury to say whether an unfair advantage has been taken to pilfer part of the work, so as, under pretence of reviewing, to give the substance, and so to reduce the value of the work itself (*f*). In works professing to give accurate information of facts accessible to all, it is often difficult to prove the piracy; as in almanacs, road-books, directories, 'time-tables, digests of legal decisions, dictionaries, encyclopædias, catalogues, and such-like': and here also the matter is fit to go to the jury (*g*), 'evidence of the manner in which the pirated work was actually done being competent, when comparison of results fails to establish the infringement (*h*).'

(5.) *Abridgments, Translations, etc.*—Abridgments, translations, and notes are allowable and protected (*i*). An abridgment must be fair; not a colourable shortening of the work, but the expression of its substance in the abridger's own language (*k*).

(6.) *Indecent 'or Immoral' Publications.*—In England, a composition, whether published or unpublished, if so objectionable as not to be fit for publication, will not be protected at the suit of the author against publication by another (*l*); 'nor one which involves in its publication a fraud on the public, as by professing falsely to be a translation from a well-known foreign writer (*m*).'

(*a*) Matthewson *v.* Stockdale, 12 Ves. Jr. 274; 1 Ill. 437. Wilkins *v.* Aikin, *infra* (*f*). Longman *v.* Winchester, 16 Ves. Jr. 269. Pike *v.* Nicholas, L. R. 5 Ch. 251; 39 L. J. Ch. 435.

(*b*) Macklin *v.* Richardson, Ambler, 694; 1 Ill. 433. Coleman *v.* Walthen, 5 T. R. 245. Boucicault *v.* Chatterton, 5 Ch. D. 267; 46 L. J. Ch. 305.

(*c*) Morris *v.* Harris, 1 Jac. & W. 481; 1 Ill. 439. Murray *v.* Elliston, 5 B. & Ald. 657. 3 and 4 Will. IV. c. 15. By 5 and 6 Vict. c. 45, the words "dramatic piece" comprehend "every tragedy, comedy, play, opera, farce, or other scenic, musical, or dramatic entertainment"; and the property of them and of musical compositions is preserved to the authors or proprietors in respect of printing and publishing for the same period provided in the Act for the duration of the copyright of books; and they are also protected against the representation of dramatic or musical pieces after having been published. The first representation or performance of such pieces as have not been printed is the date of the first publication, and the exclusive right is extended to the term of copyright given by the Act, counting from the first publication. Reade *v.* Lacy, 1 J. & H. 524; 30 L. J. Ch. 655. Reade *v.* Conquest, 9 C. B. N. S. 755; 30 L. J. C. P. 209. Novello *v.* Sudlow, 12 C. B. 177; 21 L. J. C. P. 169 (gratuitous distribution to society). Marsh *v.* Conquest, 17 C. B. N. S. 418; 33 L. J. C. P. 319. Lyon *v.* Knowles, 5 B. & S. 751; 32 L. J. Q. B. 71. Wood *v.* Boosey, L. R. 3 Q. B. 223; 37 L. J. Q. B. 84. Chatterton *v.* Cave, 44 L. J. C. P. 386; 46 *ib.* 97; 47 *ib.* 545; 2 C. P. D. 42; 3 App. Ca. 483. Fairley *v.* Boosey, 4 App. Ca. 711; 48 L. J. Ch. 697. *Ex p.* Hutchins & Romer, *supra*, § 1358B (*c*). Chappell *v.* Boosey, 21 Ch. D. 232; 51 L. J. Ch. 625. Wall *v.* Taylor, 9 Q. B. D. 727; 11 *ib.* 102. Dick *v.* Bates, 12 Q. B. D. 79; 13 *ib.* 843 (private representation). Eaton *v.* Lake, 20 Q. B. D. 378 (assignment or consent to representation must be in writing). It is not piracy to turn a novel into a drama, which is acted. Reade *v.* Conquest, *cit.* Toole *v.* Young, 43 L. J. C. P. 170; L. R. 9 C. P. 523; unless (it seems) the drama be also printed and published. Tinsley *v.* Lacy, 1 H. & M. 747; 32 L. J. Ch. 535. As to songs, see Lover *v.* Davidson, 1 C. B. N. S. 182. Chappell *v.* Sheard, 2 K. & J. 117. Chappell *v.* Davidson, 18 C. B. 192; 25 L. J. C. P. 225. Clark *v.* Bishop, 25 L. T. Rep. 908. Leader *v.* Purday, 7 C. B. 4; 18 L. J. C. P. 197. See further, as to musical compositions, 45 and 46 Vict. c. 40.

(*d*) Abernethy *v.* Hutchinson, 1 H. & T. 28; 3 L. J. Ch. 209; 1 Ill. 433. Lawrence *v.* Smith, 3 Jacob, 471; 23 R. R. 123; 1 Ill. 435. 5 and 6 Will. IV. c. 65. Nicols *v.* Pitman, 26 Ch D. 374.

(*e*) Abernethy, *cit.* Nicols *v.* Pitman, *cit.* Caird *v.* Sime, 1885; 13 R. 23; rev. 12 App. Ca. 326; 14 R. H. L. 37.

(*f*) Roworth *v.* Wilkes, 1 Camp. 97. Wilkins *v.* Aikin, 17 Ves. Jr. 422; 11 R. R. 118. Campbell *v.* Scott, 11 Sim. 31. Bohn *v.* Bogue, 10 E. Jur. 420. Pike *v.* Nicholas, L. R. 5 Ch. 251; 39 L. J. Ch. 435. Lennie *v.* Pillans, 1843; 5 D. 416.

(*g*) Murray *v.* M'Farquhar, 1765; M. 8309; 1 Ill. 437. Taylor & Skinner *v.* Bayne, 1776; M. 8308 (road-book). Annan *v.* Boule, 2 Br. Ch. Ca. 80. Cary *v.* Kearsley, 4 Esp. 168; 6 R. R. 646. Templer *v.* Murray, 1 East, 362. Matthewson *v.* Stockdale, 13 Ves. Jr. 273. Cary *v.* Longman, 1 East, 358; 6 R. R. 285. Hogg *v.* Kirby, 8 Ves. 215; 7 R. R. 30. Kelly *v.* Morris, 35 L. J. Ch. 423; L. R. 1 Eq. 697 (directory). Morris *v.* Ashbee, L. R. 7 Eq. 34. Morris *v.* Wright, L. R. 5 Ch. App. 279 (directory). Walford *v.* Johnston, 1846; 18 S. Jur. 423; 20 D. 1160 (Clyde Bill of Entry and Shipping List—comp. Maclean *v.* Moody, 1858; 20 D. 1154). Alexander *v.* Mackenzie, *infra* (*i*). Hotten *v.* Arthur, 1 H. & M. 603; 32 L. J. Ch. 771 (advertising catalogues). Macfarlane & Co. *v.* Oak Foundry Co., *infra* (*m*) (do.). White *v.* Briggs, 1890; 18 R. 222 (do.). Harpers *v.* Barry, Henry, & Co., 1892; 20 R. 133 (do.). Leslie *v.* Young & Sons, 1893; 20 R. 1077; alt. 1894, A. C. 335; 21 R. H. L. 57 (time-tables). Sweet *v.* Benning, 16 C. B. 459; 24 L. J. C. P. 175 (law digest). Jarrold *v.* Houlston, 3 K. & J. 708. Pike *v.* Nicholas, *supra* (*f*). Scott *v.* Stanford, 36 L. J. Ch. 729; L. R. 3 Eq. 718. Hogg *v.* Scott, L. R. 18 Eq. 444; 43 L. J. Ch. 705.

(*h*) Harpers *v.* Barry, Henry, & Co., *cit.* (*g*).

(*i*) Wyatt *v.* Barnard, 3 Ves. & B. 77; 13 R. R. 141. Cary, *supra* (*g*). Alexander *v.* Mackenzie, 1847; 9 D. 748

(book of styles). Blacks *v.* Murray, 1870; 9 Macph. 341 (notes and illustrations of standard work taken from other books). Murray *v.* Bogue, 1 Drew. 353; 22 L. J. Ch. 457. Saunders *v.* Smith, 3 M. & Cr. 711 (notes on leading cases). Campbell *v.* Scott, 11 Sim. 31. Translations of foreign books protected by the International Copyright Acts (*infra*, § 1360A) may be prevented by the foreign author for ten years. 49 and 50 Vict. c. 33, § 35.

(*k*) Newbery, Lloft's R. 775. Gyles *v.* Wilcox, 2 Atk. 143; 1 Ill. 437. Bell *v.* Walker, 1 Br. Ch. Ca. 451. Dickens *v.* Lee, 8 E. Jur. 183. Folsom *v.* Marsh, 2 Story's R. 100. Story's Exrs. *v.* Holcombe, 4 M'Clean, 308. Tinsley *v.* Lacy, 1 H. & M. 747; 32 L. J. Ch. 535.

(*l*) Walcot *v.* Walker, 7 Ves. Jr. 1. Lawrence *v.* Smith, *cit.* (*d*). Stockdale *v.* Onwhyn, 5 B. & C. 173; 29 R. R. 207.

(*m*) Wright *v.* Tallis, 1 C. B. 893; 14 L. J. C. P. 283. See Macfarlane & Co. *v.* Oak Foundry Co., 1883; 10 R. 801.

1360. (7.) *Book.* — This word in the 'earlier' Act has been held to comprehend and protect a work consisting of a single sheet printed separately; a part of a book, as a tale or song in a book; and notes on a book (*a*). 'The existing statute defines a book "to mean and include every volume, part or division of a volume, pamphlet, sheet of letter-press, sheet of music, map (*b*), chart, or plan, separately published" (*c*).'

(8.) *The Title of a Book* or other publication is protected, 'though rather as a sort of trade-mark than as copyright'; as the title of a periodical work, review, magazine, or newspaper. A title is held to be property, as well as the work itself, and is often very valuable (*d*).

(9.) *Engravings, Music, etc.*—The Legislature has extended the same protection to property in engravings, busts, music, patterns of linens, etc. (*e*); 'also to pictures, drawings, and photographs, when registered (*f*).' But in regard to engravings, it is no piracy to make a second engraving from the same picture (*g*).

(*a*) Hime *v.* Dale, 11 East, 224; 1 Ill. 438. Clementi *v.* Golding, 11 East, 244. White *v.* Gerock, § 1357 (*c*). Blacks *v.* Murray, 1870, 9 Macph. 341, as to notes on a standard author. Cary *v.* Longman, *sup.* (*g*) (additions and corrections on existing book). See also Hedderwick *v.* Griffin, 1841; 3 D. 383.

(*b*) Altering the previous statutes, which dealt with maps as artistic works. Stannard *v.* Lee, L. R. 6 Ch. 346; 40 L. J. Ch. 489.

(*c*) 5 & 6 Vict. c. 45, § 2. As to newspapers, see above, § 1358A (*i*). As to advertising catalogues of tradesman, see Cobbett *v.* Woodward, L. R. 14 Eq. 407; 41 L. J. Ch. 656. Grace *v.* Newman, L. R. 19 Eq. 623; 44 L. J. Ch. 298. Maple & Co. *v.* Junior Army and Navy Stores, 21 Ch. D. 369. Macfarlane & Co. *v.* Oak Foundry Co., etc., *sup.* (*g*).

(*d*) Hogg *v.* Kirby, *cit.* § 1359 (*g*). Constable & Co. *v.* Brewster, 1824; 3 S. 215. Edinburgh Correspondent, 1822; 1 S. (N. E.) 407, note; 1 Ill. 439. Bradbury *v.* Dickens, 28 L. J. Ch. 667; 27 Beav. 53. Metzler *v.* Wood, 8 Ch. D. 606; 47 L. J. Ch. 625. Weldon *v.* Dicks, 10 Ch. D. 247; 48 L. J. Ch. 201. Kelly *v.* Byles, 13 Ch. D. 682; 49 L. J. Ch. 181 (title "post office" directory). Dicks *v.* Yates, 18 Ch. D. 706; 50 L. J. Ch. 809. Chappell *v.* Davidson, 2 K. & J. 123. Chappell *v.* Sheard, *ib.* 117.

(*e*) 8 Geo. II. c. 13. 7 Geo. III. c. 38. 17 Geo. III. c. 57. 54 Geo. III. c. 56. 54 Geo. III. c. 23; *ib.* c. 156. See also as to engravings, 6 and 7 Will. IV. c. 59; 15 and 16 Vict. c. 12. Colnaghi *v.* Ward, 12 L. J. Q. B. 1. Bogue *v.* Houlston, 5 De G. & S. 267; 21 L. J. Ch. 470. Gambart *v.* Sumner, 5 H. & N. 5; 29 L. J. Ex. 98. Gambart *v.* Ball, 14 C. B. N. S. 306; 32 L. J. C. P. 96. Graves *v.* Ashford, L. R. 2 C. P. 410; 36 L. J. C. P. 139. Graves *v.* Logan, 1868; 7 Macph. 204. Dicks *v.* Brooks, 15 Ch. D. 36; 49 L. J. Ch. 812. As to music, *supra*, § 1359 (*c*).

(*f*) 25 and 26 Vict. c. 68. Turner *v.* Robinson, 10 Ir. Ch. R. 121, 510. Graves's Case, L. R. 4 Q. B. 715. *Ex p.* Graves, L. R. 3 Ch. App. 642. *Ex p.* Beal, L. R. 3 Q. B. 387; 37 L. J. Q. B. 161. Graves *v.* Walker, 39 L. J. Q. B. 31. Nottage *v.* Jackson, 11 Q. B. D. 627. Tuck *v.* Priester, 19 Q. B. D. 48, 629.

(*g*) De Berenger *v.* Wheble, 2 Starkie, 548; 1 Ill. 440. Bach *v.* Longman, Cowp. 628. Clementi *v.* Golding, *supra* (*a*).

1360A. 'Extension to Foreign Authors.— Her Majesty in Council may, on compliance with certain conditions, extend the privilege of copyright to authors of books, prints (*a*), dramatic pieces, articles of sculpture, and other works of art first published in foreign countries which give the same privilege to British authors and artists, for any period not exceeding the term to which such productions would be protected if published in the United Kingdom (*b*). In the same way, foreign authors of dramatic pieces and musical compositions may for such period have the sole liberty of representing and performing them; and the authorised translations of foreign books are allowed an exclusive privilege for five years on certain conditions.'

(*a*) Avanzo *v.* Mudie, 10 Ex. 203.

(*b*) 7 and 8 Vict. c. 12. 15 and 16 Vict. c. 12. 49 and 50 Vict. c. 33. Cassell *v.* Stiff, 2 K. & J. 279. Boucicault *v.* Delifield, 33 L. J. Ch. 38. Wood *v.* Boosey, L. R. 2 Q. B. 340; 3 *ib.* 223; 37 L. J. Q. B. 84. Wood *v.* Chart, L. R. 10 Eq. 204; 39 L. J. Ch. 641. Boucicault *v.* Chatterton, 5 Ch. D. 267. Boosey *v.* Fairley, 7 Ch. D. 301; 4 App. Ca. 711; 47 L. J. Ch. 186; 48 *ib.* 697. See 5 and 6 Vict. c. 45, § 17; 9 and 10 Vict. c. 58 (duties on importation of books and engravings); 16 and 17 Vict. c. 107, § 44, 46, 160; and 18 and 19 Vict. c. 96, § 39, 40; 39 and 40 Vict. c. 36, § 102; and Cooper *v.* Whittingham, 15 Ch. D. 501 (as to prohibition of importation of foreign reprints of books where the copyright is subsisting); and 38 and 39 Vict. c. 53, as to copyright in Canada.

1361. Assignment. — Literary property 'correctly registered at Stationers' Hall (*a*)' may be assigned either before or after publication, provided it be done in writing. In all actions in which another than the author is prosecutor, a written title is necessary under the statute (*b*); 'but a formal assignment attested by two witnessess is not now required (*c*). The intention to assign the copyright must be clear; an assignment of copyright being distinguished from a mere agreement for publication or licence to publish (*d*).'

(*a*) Low *v.* Routledge, 33 L. J. Ch. 717.
(*b*) 54 Geo. III. c. 156. Power *v.* Walker, 4 Camp. 8; 3 M. & S. 7; 1 Ill. 436; 15 R. R. 378. Morris *v.* Kelly, 1 Jac. & W. 481; 21 R. R. 216. Stewart *v.* Black, 1846; 9 D. 1046. Fullarton *v.* M'Phun, 1850; 13 D. 219. March *v.* Conquest, 17 C. B. N. S. 418; 33 L. J. C. P. 319 (dramatic representation). Jefferys *v.* Boosey, 24 L. J. Ex. 81; 4 H. L. Ca. 815 (assignment by foreigner). Low *v.* Routledge, L. R. 1 Ch. 42; 35 L. J. Ch. 114 (do.). Layland *v.* Stewart, 4 Ch. D. 419; 46 L. J. Ch. 103. The form of assignment by entry on the register, which is exempt from stamp-duty, is regulated by 5 and 6 Vict. c. 45, § 13. Registration of an assignment of the right of representation of a dramatic piece is not required. Lacy *v.* Rhys, 4 B. & S. 873; 33 L. J. Q. B. 157.
(*c*) Jefferys *v.* Boosey, *cit.* Jefferys *v.* Kyle, 1856; 18 D. 906; aff. 1859, 3 Macq. 611 (receipt for price in writing sufficient). Cumberland *v.* Copeland, 1 H. & C. 194; 31 L. J. Ex. 353.
(*d*) Reade *v.* Bentley, 3 K. & J. 271; 27 L. J. Ch. 254; 4 K. & J. 656 (joint adventure—half-profits). Hole *v.* Bradbury, 12 Ch. D. 886; 48 L. J. Ch. 673.

1361A. '**Infringement** is the reproduction of the copyright work or a material part of it so as to interfere with the proprietor's profit and enjoyment. Recitation from memory is not piracy (*a*); nor dramatising a novel (*b*); nor (apart from the International Copyright Acts) a translation (*c*); nor the fair use of common materials or a common subject (*d*); nor a *bonâ fide* abridgment (*e*). Copyright may be infringed by one who does not know of the owner's right, and without any *animus furandi* (*f*).'

(*a*) Coleman *v.* Wathen, 5 T. R. 245. Murray *v.* Elliston, 5 B. & Ald. 657; 24 R. R. 519. Cases on dramatising novels in § 1359 (*c*), *supra*.
(*b*) Cases above, § 1359 (*c*).
(*c*) Cases above, § 1359 (*i*), 1360A.
(*d*) *Supra*, § 1359 (*a*).
(*e*) *Supra*, § 1359 (5).
(*f*) Lee *v.* Simpson, 3 C. B. 883; 16 L. J. C. P. 105. See Shortt, Law of Literature and Art, 199, 200.

1361B. '**Copyright of Designs.**—Previous statutes (*a*) are repealed by the Patents, Designs, and Trade Marks Act, 1883 (*b*), which contains the existing law on the subject. The owner of a registered design has copyright in it within the United Kingdom (*c*) for five years, *i.e.* the exclusive right to apply it to any article of manufacture, or to any substance to which it is applicable according to the definition of design in the class in which it is registered (*d*). A design is "any design applicable to any article of manufacture, or to any substance artificial or natural, whether the design is applicable for the pattern, or for the shape or configuration, or for the ornament thereof, or for any two or more of such purposes, and by whatever means it is applicable, whether by printing, painting, embroidering, weaving, sewing, modelling, casting, embossing, engraving, staining, or any other means whatever, manual, mechanical, or chemical, separate or combined, not being a design for sculpture" protected by the Sculpture Copyright Act of 1814 (*e*). The design in which copyright is claimed must be new (*f*); and not previously exhibited, except at an industrial or international exhibition certified by the Board of Trade. Before delivery on sale of any articles to which the design has been applied, a prescribed number of specimens of the design must be furnished to the Comptroller of Patents, etc., and each article sold and delivered must be marked with the prescribed mark, words, or figures, denoting that the design is registered, failing which the copyright ceases (*g*). It is not an objection to the registration of a design for shape or configuration that it incidentally secures a mechanical advantage which might have been protected by a patent, but that is merely an incident. The question whether a design is useful is irrelevant, and the only test of infringement is similarity of shape or figure as judged by the eye (*h*).'

(*a*) 5 and 6 Vict. c. 100. 6 and 7 Vict. c. 65. 13 and 14 Vict. c. 104. 21 and 22 Vict. c. 70. 24 and 25 Vict. c. 73. 38 and 39 Vict. c. 93.
(*b*) 46 and 47 Vict. c. 57, § 113, and schedule. 51 and 52 Vict. c. 50, § 6, 7.
(*c*) Potter & Co. *v.* Braco de Plata Co., 1891; 18 R. 511.
(*d*) 46 and 47 Vict. c. 57, § 50, 60.
(*e*) The Act cited, § 60.
(*f*) Adams *v.* Clementson, 12 Ch. D. 712. Lazarus *v.* Charles, 42 L. J. Ch. 507; L. R. 16 Eq. 117. Lemay *v.* Welch, 28 Ch. D. 24. Hunter, Walker, & Co. *v.* Falkirk Iron Co., 1887; 14 R. 1072; 1888, 15 R. 665; aff. (*nom.* Hecla Foundry Co. *v.* Walker, Hunter, & Co.), 1889; 14 App. Ca. 551; 16 R. H. L. 27.
(*g*) The Act, § 50, 51. See under the former Acts, Holdsworth *v.* M'Crae, L. R. 2 H. L. 380; 36 L. J. Q. B. 297. Jewitt *v.* Eckhart, 8 Ch. D. 404; and cases noted in Shortt, Lit. and Art, 281 sqq. Carron Co. *v.* Ritchie, Watson, & Co., 1857; 19 D. 281.
(*h*) Hunter, Walker, & Co. *v.* Falkirk Iron Co., *cit.* (*f*).

III. TRADE NAMES, TRADE MARKS, AND GOODWILL (*a*).

1361C. '(1.) *Trade Names and Trade Marks.*—In general, a man may call himself by, or trade under, any name he likes (*b*), and he may also take advantage to himself by stating to the public that he has been in the employment of a well-known trader or manufacturer (*c*). But when a name has become known as appropriated to the business of a particular person or company, no other person may carry on business under that name, or use it or one only colourably different, in a way calculated (*d*) to deceive the public, and induce them to deal with him in the belief that they are dealing with that person or company, or getting his goods (*e*).

'By the common law, a trader who puts upon the goods which he manufactures, selects, or has exclusive means of procuring and selling (as a seam of ore or a mineral water), a distinctive (*f*) mark or name, indicating that they are produced or selected or made by him (*g*), may acquire by exclusive use, even for the shortest time, a right to have the trade mark or trade name, if used so as to deceive the public and so injure his business, protected by interdict, and by damages for its infringement or violation; and the right may be transmitted to a purchaser or legatee (*h*). One may be protected in the exclusive use of a merely descriptive name (as distinguished from a "fancy" or arbitrary name) where it has become known as indicating his goods only, or (at least?) where it is appropriated with the purpose of passing off as his the goods of another (*i*). The common law as here stated is qualified, so far as regards trade marks, by the Act referred to below, par. 3.

'(2.) *Goodwill* has been called, by Lord Eldon, the probability that the old customers of a trader will continue, on his retirement, to buy their goods from his successor in business, whether in the former place of business or another (*k*). But this, if it was intended to be a definition, is much too narrow. Goodwill includes all the advantage of the reputation and connection of the firm or business, which may be the result of years of work and the expenditure of much money. It has been firmly settled, though the rule has been not unreasonably regretted by the highest recent authorities (*l*), that one who sells a goodwill, or a partner who was at the dissolution of a firm not entitled to any share of the goodwill of the firm's business, may not be restrained from setting up in the same or a similar trade, even next door to the old concern (*m*). Parties must protect themselves by special covenants against this. But the seller of goodwill, or such a partner, may not canvass his former customers or the customers of the old firm, use a trade name of the old firm, or represent himself as continuing the former business (*n*).

'It has been said that when the profits of a business result almost entirely from confidence in the personal skill of the party employed, as in the case of a surgeon or lawyer, the goodwill is too insignificant to be taken notice of; at least to be recognised as a subject of commerce after the death of the practitioner (*o*). But this is a statement of fact rather than of law, and if the business connection of a solicitor, a dentist, a chiropodist, or a professional musician, finds a purchaser before or after his death, there is surely no reason why a Court of law should not give effect to the bargain (*p*).

'Goodwill is intimately connected in its nature and character with trade marks, and under the statute by which these are now regulated and protected, they can when registered be assigned and transmitted only in connection with the goodwill of the business concerned in the particular class of goods for which they have been registered, and are determinable with that goodwill (*q*).

'(3.) *Registration of Trade Marks.*—Since 1875 there has been a Register of Trade Marks, as defined by the Acts, registration in which is, after the lapse of five years without challenge, conclusive evidence of right to the mark (*r*), but is not a bar to rectification of the register by the Court (*s*). Without such registration no one is entitled to institute proceedings to prevent or recover damages for the infringement of a trade mark capable of being registered under the Act. In the case of a trade mark in use before 13th August 1875, such proceedings are allowed upon a certificate by the Comptroller that registration has been refused (*t*).

'For the purposes of the Acts a trade mark must contain at least one of these particulars: (1) a name of an individual or firm, printed, impressed, or woven in some particular and distinctive manner; or (2) a written signature or copy of a signature of the individual or firm applying for registration thereof; or (3) a distinctive device, mark, brand, heading, label, ticket, or fancy word or words not in common use. Other particulars regarding registration and its effects must be sought for in the Acts (*u*).

'By the Merchandise Marks Act, 1887 (*v*), the vendor of goods to which a trade mark or trade description has been applied is deemed to warrant that the mark is a genuine trade mark, and not forged or falsely applied, and that the trade description is not a false trade description within the meaning of the Act, unless the contrary is expressed in a signed and delivered writing.

'That Act, which repeals the earlier Act of 1862, makes certain specified acts in violation of the rights to trade marks and trade descriptions (as defined in § 3) criminal offences, and provides for their prosecution, which may be at the instance of the procurator-fiscal, or of the party injured, with his concurrence (*w*). Such offences may be prosecuted by the Board of Trade (*x*), and in England and Scotland by the Board of Agriculture (*y*).'

(*a*) Reference must be made for the law of trade marks to Tudor's Leading Cases, notes on Croft *v.* Day. Sebastian on Trade Marks. Application for registration in the Register of Trade Marks, kept by the Comptroller of Patents, Designs, and Trade Marks, is equivalent to public user. 51 and 52 Vict. c. 50, § 17, amending 46 and 47 Vict. c. 57, § 75.

(*b*) Merchant Bkg. Co. *v.* Merchants Jt. St. Bk., 9 Ch. D. 560; 47 L. J. Ch. 828. Levy *v.* Walker, 10 Ch. D. 436; 48 L. J. Ch. 273. Still less is a man to be prevented from trading in his own name because it happens to be like another's, if he does not use it in a manner calculated to deceive. **Croft** *v.* **Day**, 7 Beav. 232; Tudor's L. C. 563. Burgess *v.* Burgess, 3 De G. M. & G. 896. Massam *v.* Thorley's Cattle Food Co., 14 Ch. D. 748. As to partnership names, see above, § 379 (*d*).

(*c*) Boswell *v.* Mathie, 1884; 11 R. 1072.

(*d*) Intention to deceive is not required to give a right to interdict in regard to a trade name or trade mark. Singer Co. *v.* Kimball & Morton, 1873; 11 Macph. 267 (*per* L. Pr. Inglis). Millington *v.* Fox, 3 My. & Cr. 338. Singer Manufg. Co. *v.* Loog, 8 App. Ca. 15.

(*e*) Cases in preceding notes. Singer Co. *v.* Wilson, 2 Ch. D. 434; 45 L. J. Ch. 490; 47 L. J. Ch. 481; 3 App. Ca. 376. Lee *v.* Haley, L. R. 5 Ch. 155; 39 L. J. Ch. 284. Hendriks *v.* Montagu, 17 Ch. D. 638; 50 L. J. Ch. 456 (registration of company name). G. N. of Scot. Ry. Co. *v.* Mann, 1892; 19 R. 1035 (hotel name fixed to heritable subject). Cowan *v.* Millar, 1895; 22 R. 833. Crawford's Tr. *v.* Lennox, 1896; 23 R. 747 (hotel sign—pleading). But see, as to "innocent mistake" and the evidence of infringement, Bass, Ratcliffe, & Gretton *v.* Laidlaw, 1886; 13 R. 898; and Thomson & Co. *v.* Robertson, 1888; 15 R. 880.

(*f*) A new name invented for a new article, and coming to be used as the sole name of that article, cannot be appropriated even by the inventor. Leonard & Ellis *v.* Wells, 26 Ch. D. 288; but its exclusive use by the original inventor may be an important element in showing that the defender's use of the words is calculated to deceive. Eno *v.* Dunn, 1890; 15 App. Ca. 252. See below, note (*t*).

(*g*) Wood *v.* Lambert & Butler, 32 Ch. D. 247.

(*h*) **Leather Cloth Co.** *v.* **Amer. Leather Cloth Co.**, 11 H. L. C. 538; 35 L. J. Ch. 53. Wotherspoon *v.* Currie, L. R. 5 H. L. 508; 42 L. J. Ch. 130. Johnston & Co. *v.* Orr Ewing, 7 App. Ca. 219. Somerville *v.* Schembri, 12 App. Ca. 453. Montgomerie *v.* Thompson, 1891; A. C. 217 (name of town where ale brewed—"Stone ale").

(*i*) Reddaway *v.* Bayham, 1896; A. C. 199. Cellular Clothing Co. *v.* Maxton & Murray, 1898; 25 R. 1098. See Bayer *v.* Baird, 1898; 25 R. 1142.

(*k*) Cruttwell *v.* Lye, 17 Ves. Jr. 335; 11 R.R. 98. Churton *v.* Douglas, Johns. 174; Sebastian, 268 sqq. See above, § 91, 379.

(*l*) Trego *v.* Hunt, *infra*.

(*m*) Cruttwell *v.* Lye, 17 Ves. 335; 11 R. R. 98.

(*n*) **Trego** *v.* **Hunt**, 1895, A. C. 7, disapproving of opinions in Pearson *v.* Pearson, 27 Ch. D. 145; upholding Labouchere *v.* Dawson, 41 L. J. Ch. 427; L. R. 13 Eq. 322; and reviewing the cases. See above, § 379.

(*o*) See Smith's Merc. Law, 212. Bain *v.* Munro, 1878; 5 R. 416.

(*p*) See Donald *v.* Hodgart's Trs., 1893; 21 R. 246. As to the value of the goodwill of a public-house, see Llewellyn *v.* Rutherford, L. R. 10 C. P. 456; 44 L. J. C. P. 281. Philp's Exr. *v.* Philp's Exr., 1894; 21 R. 482.

(*q*) 46 and 47 Vict. c. 57, § 70.

(*r*) 46 and 47 Vict. c. 57, § 64, 76; amended by 51 and 52 Vict. c. 50, § 10, etc.

(*s*) Herbert *v.* Cowie Brs., 1897; 24 R. 361.

(*t*) The Act, § 77. Orr Ewing *v.* Registrar of Trade Marks, 4 App. Ca. 498. The following trade mark cases in Scotland may be referred to:—Wilkie *v.* M'Culloch & Co., 1823; 2 S. 423. Singer Manufg. Co. *v.* Kimball & Morton, 1873; 11 Macph. 267. Charleson *v.* Campbell, 1876; 4 R. 149 (name of hotel). Lochgelly Iron and Coal Co. *v.* Lumphinnans Iron Co., 1879; 6 R. 482. Dunnachie *v.* Young & Sons, 1883; 10 R. 874 (generic or descriptive name—"Glenboig" clay). Montgomerie *v.* Donald, 1884; 11 R. 506 (ditto—"Water of Ayr" hones). Stuart *v.* Scot. Val de Travers Co., 1885; 13 R. 1 ("granolithic"—descriptive name—distinctive word—registration). Bulloch, Lade, & Co. *v.* D. & C. Gray, 1875; 1 Guthrie's Sel. Sh. Ct. Ca. 554; 19 J. of J. 518. Cowie Brs. *v.* Herbert, 1897; 24 R. 353 (different views of same building—deception of foreign (Burmese) buyers—absence of evidence of actual deception).

(*u*) 46 and 47 Vict. c. 57, § 64.

(*v*) 50 and 51 Vict. c. 28, § 17.

(*w*) Burns *v.* Turner, 1897; 25 R. Just. 38.

(*x*) 54 and 55 Vict. c. 15.

(*y*) 57 and 58 Vict. c. 19.

CHAPTER VII

OF THE REAL RIGHT OF PLEDGE AND OF HYPOTHEC

1362. General View. — There are rights inferior to property in moveables, which are of great importance in the intercourse of a commercial country, — namely, Pledge, Hypothec, and Retention (*a*). They are useful to the owner of the thing, as enabling him to supply himself with money or credit, without parting with the ownership. They are useful to creditors, as affording the means of security for debt.

(*a*) See next chapter.

I. PLEDGE.

1363. Nature of Pledge. — Pledge has already been viewed as a contract imposing reciprocal obligations on the parties (*a*). The real right, or *jus in re*, thereby conferred, vests in the holder a power over the subject, to retain it in security of the debt for which it is pledged; and, if necessary, to have it sold judicially for payment. And this real right in the pledgee qualifies so far, and restrains the right of property in the pledger or owner (*b*).

(*a*) See above, § 203–208.
(*b*) 1 Stair, 13. § 11. 3 Ersk. 1. § 33.

1364. Effect. — Pledge is different from property. It gives no power to sell without the warrant of a judge, 'or a special agreement'; nor to make use of the subject; and the fruits, if reaped, go to the extinction of the debt. The right conferred is merely to retain in security, and to resist all attempts by the owner, or those in his right, to recover the possession till the debt be satisfied. But it is a real right completed by delivery and possession (*a*), which delivery can be given effectually only by one having the ownership or disposal. This, with continued possession of the thing impledged, is necessary to the creation and continuance of the real right in the pledgee (*b*). A factor who has the goods of his principal in his hand can effectually pledge them, or take advances on their consignment. A different rule prevailed in England till a statute 'was passed' for regulating the powers of factors (*c*). But the pledge or mortgage of ships is effectual in the mode pointed out in the statute 'as to this,' without any possession on the part of the mortgagee (*d*).

The *property* in pledge is still with the owner; continued in him by the civil possession of the pledgee. But the real right of pledge cannot be held by the pledgee by mere civil possession through the owner (*e*); 'nor even, it has been said, by constructive possession through a warehouseman or third party (*f*). This has been questioned (*g*).

But the law seems practically to stand thus. In England, where the pledgee has a "special property" in the thing pledged, the delivery may be either actual or constructive, *e.g.* by delivery order or bill of lading (*h*). In Scotland, while it is denied that a delivery order intimated, the meaning and effect of which is to transfer the property, can constitute a valid pledge of goods,—pledge being a contract in which the property does not pass,—it is not doubted that an *ex facie* absolute transfer by a delivery order, subject to an obligation to re-transfer on repayment of an advance, is effectual as a security, not only for a present advance, but for subsequent advances made in reliance upon it (*i*). A delivery order bearing on its face to be qualified is not valid either to transfer property, to which it gives no immediate right, or as a security (*k*). And it is now clear that in Scotland, as in England, a pledgee whose right has been duly completed may re-deliver the goods for a limited purpose to the pledger as well as to a third party, *e.g.* he may hand a bill of lading to the pledger that the latter may sell the goods for him as his agent (*l*).'

(*a*) Stair and Ersk. *supra*, § 1363 (*b*). Johnston *v.* Sprott, Dec. 8, 1814; Hume, 448. See above, § 204. Moore *v.* Gledden, 1869; 7 Macph. 1016.
(*b*) Tod & Son *v.* Mercht. Bkg. Co., 1883; 10 R. 1009.
(*c*) 6 Geo. IV. c. 94. See above, § 225, 1317A seq.; and below, § 1417.
(*d*) See below, § 1379.
(*e*) Dig. lib. 13. tit. 7. De Pign. Act. 1. 37. Voet. ad Pandect. lib. 20. tit. 1. § 12. Clark *v.* W. Calder Oil Co., 1882; 9 R. 1017. See above, § 1212.
(*f*) Cases cited below, (*i*).
(*g*) 2 M'Laren's Bell's Com. 21, note.
(*h*) Young *v.* Lambert, 39 L. J. P. C. 21; L. R. 3 P. C. 142. Barber *v.* Meyerstein, 39 L. J. C. P. 187; L. R. 4 H. L. 317.
(*i*) Hamilton *v.* Western Bk., 1856; 19 D. 152 (see 21 D. 86). Mackinnon *v.* Nanson & Co., 1868; 6 Macph. 974. See 1 Bell's Com. 684, and § 912, 1367.
(*k*) Mackinnon, *cit.*
(*l*) North-Western Bk. *v.* Poynter, Macdonald, & Co., 1894; 21 R. 513; revd. 1895, A. C. 56; 22 R. H. L. 1. It is otherwise if there be no agency, but a direct sale by the pledgee. Tod & Son, *supra* (*b*). See above, § 418.

1365. Pledge operates as a security for the whole debt, and is not weakened by payment of a part of the debt, but remains as complete for the last shilling as for the whole (*a*).

(*a*) 2 Ersk. 12. § 67 *in fin.*

1366. The right of ownership presumed from the possession of moveables is qualified or limited by the condition of the contract under which, or in reference to which, that possession is held; but the limitation goes no further. Thus a moveable in possession of a workman is his only to the effect of a lien for the price of his labour; or if pledged, it is the pledgee's only to the extent of the debt for which it is pledged. So, if one claims right to goods in the possession of another, he must prove the conditions and purpose of the possession, in order to make out his right to the recovery of the thing. If there be no proof but the admission of the possessor, that admission must be taken with the condition annexed to it, and this will sufficiently prove a right of pledge (*a*).

(*a*) Murray *v.* Cunningham, 1668; 1 Br. Sup. 575; 1 Ill. 440. Harriot *v.* Cunningham, 1791; M. 12,405. See Johnston, *supra*, § 1364 (*a*). See above, § 1315; below, § 2218.

1367. Tacit Extension of Pledge.—It is an important question, whether a pledge is maintainable against third parties for more than the original advance, where additional advances have been made to the 'debtor (*a*). The rules seem to be these': When an absolute conveyance is made, though only intended as a security, and a new loan takes place during its subsistence, 'before intimation of a subsequent conveyance of the reversion (*b*),' the restitution is not demandable without payment of the whole debt. This is peculiarly applicable to heritable securities by absolute disposition with an unrecorded backbond (*c*) So also in the case of a ship mortgaged under the old law, where the conveyance was strictly analogous to absolute disposition and backbond (*d*). So, in creating a security for a loan by assignation of a debt, it has been held tacitly extended to subsequent advances (*e*). All these cases proceed on the ground of a right ostensibly universal and absolute requiring to be resolved—not being mere securities *ex facie*. Where a jewel or other moveable has been given in pledge without limitation of the security, it may seem that, on the principle which regulated the above cases, the universal right presumed from possession will effectually cover further advances, which cannot be supposed to be made but on that footing (*f*). But if there be proof to limit the pledge to the specific advance made at the time of its consitution, there does not appear to be any ground on which, as against purchasers or creditors, the original security by pledge can be held as extended (*g*). The security may be expressly extended to cover a further advance, but not after diligence by third parties to attach the subject, or after sequestration.

(*a*) In previous editions, "made to the creditor."
(*b*) National Bank *v.* Union Bank, 1885; 13 R. 380; revd. 1886, 12 App. Ca. 53; 14 R. H. L. 1.
(*c*) See above, § 912. Brough's Crs. *v.* Jollie, 1793; M. 2585; 1 Ill. 440.
(*d*) Balleny *v.* Raeburn & Co., June 7, 1808; F. C.
(*e*) Dougal's Crs., 1794; Bell's Ca. 41. See above, § 912; and below, § 1453. Robertson *v.* Duff, *ibi cit.* 1 Bell's Com. 684 (724–5, M'L.'s ed.).
(*f*) See Hamilton *v.* Western Bank, 1856; 19 D. 152. Natl. Bank *v.* Forbes, 1858; 21 D. 79.
(*g*) Demaimbry, Preced. in Chanc. 412. See the author's notes, 1 Ill. 441. Rintoul & Co. *v.* Bannatyne, 1861; 1 Macph. 137.

1368. Bonding of Goods for Duties.—On the principle of pledge, the 'bonding or' warehousing system has been introduced. Originally suggested by Sir Robert Walpole, proposed as a general measure of revenue by Dean Tucker, and revised and reduced to practice during Mr. Pitt's administration, it has been improved by successive statutes (*a*). It is connected immediately with the system of the navigation laws and shipping, and is intended to promote two great objects of national policy: the encouragement of importation for the home market, by the storing of goods without advancing the duties; and the promotion of the carrying trade of the country, by the storing of goods for foreign markets on the same terms. A collateral effect is produced on the doctrines of common law, in the peculiarity introduced in certain operations of transference and security over moveables.

(*a*) These were consolidated by an Act in 1823, afterwards in 1825, and finally in 1833. See 43 Geo. III. c. 132. 4 Geo. IV. c. 24. 4 Geo. IV. c. 94, § 66 et seq. 6 Geo. IV. c. 105 and c. 112. 3 and 4 Will. IV. c. 57. 1 Bell's Com. 186 et seq. 8 and 9 Vict. c. 91; repealed by 16 and 17 Vict. c. 107 (Customs Consolidation Act), which with subsequent Acts is again repealed by 39 and 40 Vict. c. 36 (Customs Laws Consolidation Act, 1876). See also various amending Acts. Index of Statutes.

1369. The Commissioners of the Treasury are from time to time to appoint what ports are be warehousing ports 'or places,' and, 'subject to their directions, the Commissioners of Customs are to appoint' in what warehouses of special or of ordinary security in those ports goods may be secured (*a*).

(*a*) 3 and 4 Will. IV. c. 57, § 2. 39 and 40 Vict. c. 36, § 12–16.

1370. Warehouses are accommodated to the two several occasions of goods prohibited to be used or sold in this country, and of goods which may be so used or sold. For the former, warehouses of special security are provided to prevent evasion of the prohibitory laws; and these are either to be specially appointed, or warehouses connected with wharfs and within walls, and published in the London and Dublin Gazettes. For the other case, warehouses of ordinary security are held sufficient; the goods being bonded only for duties, but allowed to be sold in the country (*a*).

(*a*) 3 and 4 Will. IV. c. 57, § 3, 7. 39 and 40 Vict. c. 36, § 12, etc. The distinction here pointed out appears not to be specifically repealed in the existing Act.

1371. Duties, how Secured.—The duties are secured by bond and pledge.

1372. The bond is either a *general* bond by the proprietor of the warehouse, with two sureties "for the payment of the full duties of importation on all such goods as shall at any time be warehoused therein, or for the due exportation thereof"; or 'formerly' a *special* bond "by the importers of the separate quantities of goods upon each importation, in respect of the particular goods imported by them respectively." Such special bond 'might,' on a sale of the goods without being removed, be superseded by the bond of the buyer of those goods (*a*). 'But special bonds by the owners of goods appear to be recognised by the present Act only on the removal of goods to another warehousing place, on taking them out for special purposes with leave, or on clearance for exportation (*b*).'

(*a*) 3 and 4 Will IV. c. 57, § 8.
(*b*) 39 and 40 Vict c. 36, § 13, 89, 96, 104, 165 sq.

1373. The pledge of the goods subsists while they remain in the warehouse. They may be sold by the owner while in the warehouse, and a fresh security given by the buyer, and the former released. The goods must be removed from the warehouse, 'either for home use or exportation,' within 'five' years. After that time, 'unless the goods are examined, duty paid for any deficiency or difference in quantity, and the goods rewarehoused,' the commissioners are entitled to sell them for the duties, 'after one month's notice to the warehousekeeper' (*a*).

(*a*) 3 and 4 Will. IV. c. 57, § 29, 30. 39 and 40 Vict. c. 36, § 92, 93.

1374. For recovering payment of the duties, the Crown may proceed upon the personal bond of the warehousekeeper or importer; or the sureties may be called upon, and on payment they get assignment to the lien over the goods; or the goods may, at the appointed time, be sold by order of the Commissioners of the Customs.

1375. In clearing goods from the warehouse, if lawful to be sold, payment of the duties is the sole condition on which they can be removed; if prohibited, it is necessary to give security for exportation (*a*).

(*a*) 3 and 4 Will. IV. c. 57, § 16. 39 and 40 Vict. c. 36, § 97, 98, etc.

1376. In the case of goods imported and warehoused, facilities are provided for examining them, sorting, separating, repacking, and selling them in whole or in part, without removal or payment of the duties (*a*).

Spirits warehoused under the 4 Geo. IV. may be viewed, shown, and examined for sale under certain precautions (*b*).

(*a*) 3 and 4 Will. IV. c. 57, § 9, 10, 31. 39 and 40 Vict. c. 36, § 95, etc.
(*b*) 4 Geo. IV. c. 94, § 77. See 39 and 40 Vict. c. 36, § 42, 95, 96, 103; 43 Vict. c. 14, § 3; 43 and 44 Vict. c. 24, etc.

1377. Provision is made for preserving the rights of parties, both owners of imported goods, and shipmasters having lien for freight on all goods and merchandise landed in docks, and lodged in the custody of the proprietor of the said docks (*a*).

(*a*) 3 and 4 Will. IV. c. 57, § 14. 25 and 26 Vict. c. 63, § 66 sqq. See below, § 1415.

1378. '**Transfer of Bonded Goods.** — See above, § 1306.'

1379. Mortgages of Ships.—By the Act which regulates the sale of ships (*a*), the mortgaging or granting of securities over that valuable species of property is also regulated. There are two methods of giving security over such property,—by mortgage, and by assignment.

(*a*) 3 and 4 Will. IV. c. 55, § 42. See above, § 1330. 57 and 58 Vict. c. 60, § 66 sq.

1380. Mortgage is a transfer of the whole ship, or of a share, for security of debt, 'in a specified form, stating the number and date of the ship's registry, and other particulars (*a*).' The transfer is entered 'by the registrar of the ship's port, in the order in which it is received,' in the Book of Registry (*b*), and 'formerly was' indorsed on the certificate 'of registry'; and the 'date of' entry 'on the Book of Registry fixes the priority of mortgages *inter se* (*c*). There is no such indorsement on the certificate of registry under the existing law. When, however, the ship is mortgaged out of the country in which its port of registry is situated, a certificate of mortgage is furnished by the registrar, upon which a record of all mortgages made thereunder is to be indorsed by a registrar or British consular officer. Mortgages indorsed on this certificate have priority over all mortgages entered on the register after the date of the entry of the certificate there, and *inter se* according to the date of indorsement (*d*). An unregistered mortgage is not void; its effect as against other liens and charges not registered depends on its date and notice of them to the mortgagee (*e*).'

(*a*) 57 and 58 Vict. c. 60, § 31, Sched. 1.
(*b*) *Ib.* § 32.
(*c*) See 57 and 58 Vict. c. 60, § 33.
(*d*) *Ib.* § 39 sqq.
(*e*) Liverpool Mar. Cr. Co. *v.* Wilson, L. R. 7 Ch. 507; 41 L. J. Ch. 798. Bell *v.* Blyth, L. R. 4 Ch. 136; 38 L. J. Ch. 178. Keith *v.* Burrows, 1 C. P. D. 722; 45 L. J. C. P. 876 (decided in H. L. on another point).

1381. Another method of giving security over a ship is by assignment to a trustee for selling the ship or share in satisfaction of debt. To be effectual, it must be entered in the same way (*a*).

(*a*) See as to bills of sale, *supra*, § 1329: and as to their use for creating securities, 25 and 26 Vict. c. 63, § 3. Myers *v.* Willis, 17 C. B. 77; 18 C. B. 886; 25 L. J. C. P. 39, 255. Gardner *v.* Cazenove, 1 H. & N. 423; 26 L. J. Ex. 17. Ward *v.* Beck, 13 C. B. N. S. 668; 32 L. J. C. P. 113. The Innisfallen, L. R. 1 A. & E. 72; 35 L. J. Adm. 110.

1382. It is provided that the creditor is to be held no further as an owner of the ship than may be necessary for 'making the ship or share available as a security for' the debt; that the owner shall not thereby cease to be owner, except in the same respect (*a*); and that a subsequent act of bankruptcy 'by the mortgagor,' or assignment under a commission, shall not affect the interest of the creditor under his mortgage, 'but the mortgage shall be preferred to the interest or right of his assignees (*b*). But the mortgagee's statutory title does not exclude the operation of the Acts against preferences by bankrupts (*c*).'

(*a*) Hence his contracts with third parties made providently while in possession are binding upon the mortgagee. Collins *v.* Lamport, 4 De G. J. & S. 500; 34 L. J. Ch. 196. The Innisfallen, *supra*. Johnson *v.* R. M. Steam Packet Co., L. R. 3 C. P. 38; 37 L. J. C. P. 33. But the mortgagee may prevent a ship from sailing uninsured or in an unseaworthy state, and that without incurring liability to a charterer. Laming & Co. *v.* Seater, 1889; 16 R. 828.
(*b*) 57 and 58 Vict. c. 60, § 34 sqq. Gardner, *supra*, § 1381.
(*c*) Anderson *v.* Western Bank, 1859; 21 D. 230.

1382A. 'Every registered mortgagee has power absolutely to dispose of the ship or share mortgaged; but if there are several persons registered as mortgagees, a subsequent mortgagee cannot, except under the order of a competent Court, do so without the concurrence of every prior mortgagee (*a*). Subject to any equities existing between him and the mortgagor, and subject also to the legal liens and equities of third parties (*b*), the mortgagee is entitled to take possession of the ship, and to draw her earnings (*c*). He is therefore entitled to freight, if he take possession before it becomes payable (*d*). He may employ the ship, if he do so prudently, and he then becomes liable for the necessary disbursements of the ship (*e*). The mortgagor's equitable interests remain until the mortgagee has recouped himself out of the ship's earnings, or until repayment, when the mortgagor is entitled to a re-transfer; or until a sale (*f*). The transmission of a mortgage by death, bankruptcy, or otherwise, must be registered; and a transfer must be indorsed on the mortgage (*g*); and the discharge thereof is likewise to be entered upon the register (*h*).'

(*a*) 57 and 58 Vict. c. 60, § 35. As to priorities between mortgagees and other incumbrancers, see cases in § 1380 (*c*).
(*b*) 57 and 58 Vict. c. 60, § 57. The Cathcart, L. R. 1 A. & E. 314.
(*c*) Williams *v.* Alsup, 30 L. J. C. P. 353; 10 C. B. N. S. 417.
(*d*) Rusden *v.* Pope, L. R. 3 Ex. 269; 37 L. J. Ex. 139. Brown *v.* Tanner, L. R. 3 Ch. 597; 37 L. J. Ch. 923. Wilson *v.* Wilson, 41 L. J. Ch. 423; L. R. 14 Eq. 32. Tanner *v.* Phillips, 42 L. J. Ch. 125. Beynon *v.* Godden, 3 Ex. D. 263. Keith *v.* Burrows, 2 App. Ca. 636; 46 L. J. C. P. 801.
(*e*) Havilland, Routh, & Co. *v.* Thomson, 1864; 3 Macph. 313. Russell *v.* Baird, 1839; 1 D. 931.
(*f*) Marriott *v.* Anchor Rev. Soc., 3 De G. F. & J. 177; 30 L. J. Ch. 571. De Mattos *v.* Gibson, 30 L. J. Ch. 145.
(*g*) 57 and 58 Vict. c. 60, § 31, etc., and Sched. 1.
(*h*) *Ib.* § 32. See as to this section, Maclachlan, 42 sq., 112, 504.

1383. Pledge of Debts.—The pledge of debts cannot be fully accomplished except in those cases in which the debt or *jus exigendi* goes with the document (*a*).

(*a*) See above, § 205; and below, § 1459.

1384. Pledge of Title-Deeds.—The pledge of title-deeds has not, according to the law of Scotland, the effect of burdening the estate or subject, but, 'it was said,' confers merely a right of retention of the *ipsa corpora* of the title-deeds (*a*). 'Title-deeds of a land estate cannot, however, be pledged (*b*).' In England the original rule was the same with the Scottish. But gradually there came to be admitted, as a consequence of the pledge, an equitable right to a conveyance of the estate itself. This has been admitted, much to the regret of the highest authorities in English jurisprudence (*c*).

(*a*) 2 Bell's Com. 24.
(*b*) Christie *v.* Ruxton, 1862; 24 D. 1182. *Supra*, § 205, 890A. Disting. titles necessary to make a prescriptive progress, and ancient writs of the lands. Porteous *v.* Henderson, 1898; 25 R. 563.
(*c*) *Ex p.* Hooper, 1 Mer. 7. See 1 Wh. & Tud. L. C. 726. Snell's Pr. of Eq. 319.

II. HYPOTHEC.

1385. Distinction between Hypothec and Pledge.—Hypothec differs from pledge in giving security to the creditor without possession, and is admitted in cases in which it is expedient to raise such security without impeding the ordinary use of the thing. Hypothecs were numerous in the Roman law, and are still largely admitted on the Continent; but it is against the principle and spirit of the law of Scotland to admit a real right or security which is not attended with some badge manifest and palpable. Hypothecs, therefore, on account of the false credit which may be induced by the owner's possession, are limited to a very few cases (*a*).

(*a*) 1 Stair, 13, 14. 3 Ersk. 1. § 34. 2 Bell's Com. 26. 2 Pothier, 945. Chev. dal Pozzo, Obs. sur le Régime Hypothécaire.

1386. Conventional Hypothecs.—Conventional hypothecs in the law of Scotland are bottomry and *respondentia* (*a*).

(*a*) These have been already explained. See above, § 452 et seq.

1387. Tacit Hypothecs.—The only tacit hypothecs admitted in the law of Scotland are those introduced by consuetude, of which everyone is aware, and in which it is held to be for the common advantage of the parties to give a security thus extensive, so far as it can be done without interrupting the ordinary use or employment of the subject of security; and those introduced by statute for the protection of the public revenue.

The hypothecs introduced by consuetude are those in favour of landlords and of law agents, in a few maritime cases, and in privileged debts. Of these the landlord's hypothec, favourable to tenants, as saving them from personal and sudden diligence for their rent, has been already considered (*a*).

(*a*) See above, § 1234 et seq., § 1275 et seq.

1388. Law Agent's Hypothec.—This hypothec has been encouraged, as tending to keep open the courts of justice to poor men. Under it the agent is entitled to have decree in his own name for the expense found due to his client by the adverse party. There is an implied agreement that the agent shall, in security of his professional remuneration, have this right (*a*). In England the right goes much further, extending over the subject of the lawsuit itself (*b*). 'It is now lawful for the Court in which an action or proceeding depends to charge the law agent's taxed expenses of or in reference to such action upon property of any kind therein recovered or preserved on behalf of the client (*c*).'

(*a*) 2 Bell's Com. 35 et seq. 2 Pothier, 703 et seq. Mill *v.* Wright, Jan. 12, 1802; 2 Bell's Com. 37; 1 Ill. 442. Alison's Trs. *v.* Johnston Wylie, Nov. 29, 1808; F. C.; 1 Ill. 442; Hume, 454. M'Kenzie *v.* Ross, 1823; 2 S. 401. M'Tavish *v.* Pedie, 1826; 4 S. 704; 1828, 6 S. 593. Clapperton *v.* M'Lauchlan, June 8, 1802; 2 Bell's Com. 37; 1 Ill. 442. Ellis *v.* Mackenzie, 1831; 9 S. 585. See below, of Retention, § 1437. A. of S., July 10, 1839; s. 106. Cullen *v.* Smith, 1845; 8 D. 771. Peddie *v.* Davidson, 1856; 18 D. 1306.

(*b*) 2 Bell's Com. 35. 23 and 24 Vict. c. 127, § 28, as to orders charging property with costs. Pulling on Attorneys, 380.

(*c*) 54 and 55 Vict. c. 30, § 6. Carruthers *v.* Finlay & Wilson, 1897; 24 R. 363.

1389. Against the right of the agent to a decree in his own name for the expense of the action which he conducts, it will not avail as a defence that his own client is solvent, and able to pay his full demand (*a*). Even where he has allowed decree to go out in the name of the client, he is entitled, if the decree should be suspended, to appear in the suspension, and still have the decree for the original expenses in his own name (*b*).

(*a*) Russell *v.* Greig & Peddie, 1826; 4 S. 403; 1 Ill. 442.

(*b*) M'Tavish, *supra*, § 1388 (*a*). Until decree for expenses, an agent has not, except in the cases mentioned below (§ 1391–2), even a contingent claim against the opposite party, and therefore if he hold a sum of money belonging to that party, his subsequently emerging claim cannot compete with an arrestment in his hands previous to the decree. Crawford *v.* Gemmells, 1864; 3 Macph. 306.

1390. Compensation on a debt due by the client is not pleadable by the party against whom the agent requires decree, so as to defeat the agent's claim for expenses (*a*). But if decree has been pronounced in the client's name, and on a demand or charge for payment the adversary has pleaded compensation, the agent cannot afterwards come forward to defeat that plea by a demand for the expenses in his own name; for to that effect compensation is payment. If expenses have been found against the client in another part of the litigation, 'whether in the same judgment or at an earlier period of the cause,' the amount may be set off in compensation (*b*).

(*a*) Smith *v.* Gemmell, 1802; M. 6257; 1 Ill. 443. Miller *v.* Geils, 1848; 10 D. 1384. Munro *v.* Bothwell, 1846; Arkley, 118.

(*b*) Warburton *v.* Hamilton, 1826; 4 S. 631. Graham *v.* M'Arthur, 1826; 5 S. 49. Gordon *v.* Davidson, 1865; 3 Macph. 938. Stothart *v.* Johnston's Trs., 1823; 2 Mur. 549. Halliday *v.* Halliday, 1828; 6 S. 406. Compensation has been admitted where there were decrees for expenses in different contemporaneous actions relating to the same subject-matter. Portobello Pier Co. *v.* Clift, 1877; 4 R. 685. See Paterson *v.* Wilson, 1883; 11 R. 358, and Strain *v.* Strain, 1890; 17 R. 566.

1391. The parties cannot, by a collusive settlement, fraudulently deprive the agent of his right to a decree for costs. In England it is deemed indispensable to an attorney, in challenging a compromise, to show a clear case of collusion (*a*). In Scotland this distinction has not yet been clearly established; but it is countenanced in two cases (*b*), and rests upon plain principles of equity and expediency. Wherever expenses have been found due, or damages have been awarded, or where otherwise expenses must necessarily follow on the decree, it has not been permitted to the client, without consent or acquiescence of the agent, to settle extrajudicially, or by compromise, so as to defeat the agent's claim (*c*). Where the success of the client and his title to expenses are not thus demonstrated, or where the compromise is made previous to the calling of the cause in court, the agent cannot prevent or challenge it, or insist on proceeding for his costs, 'and as far as the client's own interests are concerned there is no limitation of his right to compromise' (*d*).

(*a*) Chapman *v.* Haw, 1 Taunt. 341 ; 1 Ill. 443 ; 9 R. R. 786. Nelson *v.* Wilson, 6 Bing. 568. Hart *v.* Payne, 1 B. & Ad. 660.

(*b*) Sloss & Gemmell *v.* Kennedy, 1823 ; 2 S. 302. M'Lean & M'Dowall *v.* Auchinvole, 1824 ; 3 S. 190. Macqueen *v.* Hay, 1854 ; 17 D. 107. Barr *v.* Wotherspoon, 1850 ; 13 D. 305. Cheyne *v.* Cheyne, 1832 ; 10 S. 202. Murray *v.* Kidd, 1852 ; 14 D. 501. Smith *v.* Smith, 1871 ; 9 Macph. 538. Clark *v.* Henderson, 1875 ; 2 R. 428.

(*c*) Hamilton *v.* Bryson, June 17, 1813 ; F. C. Rox *v.* Stewart, July 3, 1818 ; F. C. Sloss, *supra* (*b*). Tod & Wright *v.* Wilson & M'Lennan, 1822 ; 1 S. 358. M'Kenzie *v.* Ross, 1823 ; 2 S. 401. Hamilton *v.* Dixon, 1824 ; 3 S. 242. Barr *v.* Wotherspoon, 1850 ; 13 D. 305. Macgregor & Barclay *v.* Martin, 1867 ; 5 Macph. 583.

(*d*) Anderson *v.* Walker, 1830 ; 8 S. 299.

1392. The agent may even proceed with the action when his client has withdrawn, to the effect of having expenses awarded or modified, that he may have decree for them (*a*).

(*a*) Hamilton and Rox, *supra*, § 1391 (*c*). M'Tavish *v.* Pedie, 1826 ; 4 S. 704 ; 1 Ill. 442. Cases in § 1391. When the client dies, after being found entitled to expenses, his representatives must be sisted before the agent can get decree. Baillie *v.* Campbell, 1872 ; 10 Macph. 414.

1393. Even without decree in his own name, the agent may by formal notice (but for which there does not seem to be any prescribed form) stop the party from paying the expenses awarded to his adversary ; and such notice will have the effect of making the party hold the fund for the agent (*a*). An arrestment, if previous to such notice, will prevail against the agent ; if subsequent, it will not avail (*b*).

(*a*) M'Kenzie, *supra*, § 1391 (*c*). 2 Bell's Com. 37. Unless after the agent's omission to exercise his privilege of taking decree in his own name, the position of parties has changed, as by a third party acquiring a *jus quæsitum* in the expenses decerned for. See Fleming *v.* Love, 1839 ; 1 D. 1097.

(*b*) Stephen *v.* Smith, 1830 ; 8 S. 847 ; 1 Ill. 444.

1394. An agent superseding another, and paying his account, is entitled to the benefit of his hypothec (*a*) ; 'and the agent superseded, when expenses are awarded, may obtain decree in his own name for his unpaid proportion (*b*).'

(*a*) See Beveridge's Forms of Process, 620.

(*b*) M'Tavish, *cit.* § 1392. Hunter *v.* Pearson, 1835 ; 13 S. 495.

1395. It has been doubted whether a friend of the client, advancing money to the agent, has the benefit of the hypothec. In England this is discountenanced as "maintenance." It was denied in the Court of Session in one case, but collusion was suspected (*a*). It was admitted in an earlier case (*b*), and in a later case allowed to a cautioner in a suspension (*c*).

(*a*) Rennie & Playfair *v.* Aitken, June 8, 1811 ; F. C. ; 1 Ill. 444.

(*b*) Campbell *v.* Montgomery, 1790 ; M. 6259.

(*c*) Henderson *v.* Young, 1828 ; 7 S. 142.

1396. The same rule appears to be held applicable to expenses in a submission as to those in an action (*a*).

(*a*) See Stephen, *supra*, § 1393 (*b*). Pollock *v.* Scott, 1831 ; 9 S. 432. Mackenzie *v.* Robertson, 1831 ; 9 S. 798. See Bell on Arbitration, 230.

1397. Maritime Hypothecs.—These are admitted for the purpose of giving security in certain cases, without compelling the workman or furnisher to stop and impede the use of the ship. They are recognised only in certain definite and known cases of necessity, namely, for foreign repairs ; for damage done to the goods of freighters by delay, etc. ; 'for damage to another vessel by collision (*a*) ; for salvage' ; and for the wages of the 'master and' seamen employed in navigating the ship. The effect of the hypothec is to give preference over the price of the ship when sold (*b*).

(*a*) M'Knight *v.* Currie, 1895 ; 22 R. 607 ; aff. 1897, A. C. 97 ; 24 R. H. L. 1. The damage for which the lien is claimed must be done by the ship, or in the course of the ship's navigation. See Macknight, *cit.*

(*b*) See The Bold Buccleuch (Harmer *v.* Bell), 7 Moore P. C. 267. The City of Mecca, 6 P. D. 106 ; 50 L. J. Adm. 17, 53. Macknight, *cit.* Maclachlan, 65, etc., 632. 57 and 58 Vict. c. 60, § 167.

1398. (1.) *Hypothec on Ship for Repairs* is strictly confined to repairs made 'and necessaries supplied' abroad, and does not cover such repairs 'and necessaries' as are made 'or supplied' in this country (*a*). 'In relation to the rights and remedies of persons having claims for repairs done or supplies furnished to or for ships, all ports in Great Britain and Ireland, the Islands of Man, Guernsey, Jersey, Alderney, and Sark, and the islands adjacent to any of them, are deemed home ports (*b*).'

(*a*) 3 Ersk. 1. § 34. 1 Bell's Com. 525 (573, M'L.'s ed.). Hamilton *v.* Wood, 1788 ; M. 6269 ; Hailes, 1039 and 1052 ; aff. 3 Paton, 148 ; 1 Ill. 445. Wood & Co. *v.* Weir's Crs., Jan. 31, 1810 ; 1 Bell's Com. 527 (575, M'L.'s ed.) ; 2 Bell's Com. 98 (93, M'L.'s ed.). See Stewart *v.* Hall, 1813 ; 2 Dow, 29 ; 1 Bell's Com. *l.c.* See below, as to lien, § 1420, 1436. Abbott, 99. In England a lien was supposed to be created by statute ; 3 and 4 Vict. c. 65, § 6 ; and see 24 Vict. c. 10, § 4–6. Maclachlan, 66–68, 108. But it is determined that there is no such lien. The Henrich Bjorn, 11 App. Ca. 270. The Rio Tinto, 9 App. Ca. 356.

(*b*) 19 and 20 Vict. c. 60, § 18 ; and for England, 19 and 20 Vict. c. 97, § 8.

1399. (2.) *Hypothec to Freighters.*—This gives security over the ship to the owners of the goods, for loss by improper interruption of the voyage, or for damage done by improper stowage, etc. (*a*); 'but the remedy does not seem ever to have been applied.'

(*a*) 2 Bell's Com. 39.

1400. (3.) *Hypothec for Seamen's Wages.*—Strictly speaking, this is properly no hypothec, but a *jus retinendi et insistendi.* But it is effectual against the ship to her last plank (*a*); 'and cannot be renounced (*b*). It also affects the freight (*c*). The master has now the same lien and remedies as seamen, so far as the case permits (*d*). He was held in England to have a maritime lien on the ship, not only for his wages under this statute, but also for expenditure necessary for the prosecution of the voyage made in his capacity of master (*e*); and the House of Lords having overruled the decisions to this effect (*f*), it is enacted that the master or anyone properly acting in his place has the same remedies and lien for disbursements made and liabilities duly incurred on account of the ship as the master has for his wages (*g*). When he makes a contract beyond his ordinary powers, the owner, if he takes the benefit of it, is bound to indemnify him for any expense necessarily incurred for its fulfilment; and so the master, having made a charter-party abroad and incurred expense for its performance, was allowed repayment of his disbursements out of the freight (*h*).'

(*a*) 3 Ersk. 2. § 34. 1 Bell's Com. 513 (562, M'L.'s ed.); 2 *ib.* 103 (99 M'L.'s ed.). 17 and 18 Vict. c. 104, § 181 et seq. Seamen of the Golden Star *v.* Miln, 1682; M. 6259; 1 Ill. 445. Sands *v.* Scott, 1708; M. 6261. The Madonna d'Idra, 1 Dod. 37; 1 Ill. 285. The Neptune, 1 Hag. 227. See above, § 451. And as to priorities, see The Elin, 8 P. D. 39, 129.
(*b*) 57 and 58 Vict. c. 60, § 156. The Ganges, L. R. 2 Adm. 370.
(*c*) See cases in Maclachlan, 249.
(*d*) 57 and 58 Vict. c. 60, § 167. The Tecumseh, 3 W. Rob. 109. See as to the master's possessory liens, § 1436.
(*e*) The Feronia, L. R. 2 Adm. 65; 37 L. J. Adm. 60; and other cases.
(*f*) Hamilton *v.* Baker (The Sara), 1889; 14 App. Ca. 209.
(*g*) 57 and 58 Vict. c. 60, § 167. Morgan *v.* Castlegate S.S. Co., 1893; A. C. 38. The Orienta, 1895; P. 49.
(*h*) Bristowe *v.* Whitmore, 31 L. J. Ch. 467; 9 H. L. Ca. 391.

1401. (4.) *Hypothec for Average Loss.*—This, although established in the early maritime codes, and recognised on the Continent, seems scarcely to exist in the law of Scotland (*a*).

(*a*) 1 Bell's Com. 40.

1402. Hypothec for Privileged Debts.—Certain debts are privileged; and although not strictly referable to the principle of hypothec, they produce as to moveables the same effect as a universal hypothec over the whole property of the debtor. They are called "privileged debts"; and this privilege rests on various grounds, sometimes of humanity and charity, and sometimes of expediency in encouraging useful institutions.

1403. (1.) *Medical Attendance on Death-bed, and Funeral Expenses.*—This privilege is grounded on considerations of humanity and decency (*a*). It includes the medical expense of the last sickness (without any absolute connection with the sixty days of death-bed) (*b*), and the expense of interment. These are held equal in privilege, and come in *pari passu* (*c*). The expense of moderate and suitable mournings for the family is also included (*d*). The funeral expense of a tenant is preferable to the landlord's hypothec (*e*); 'and may be claimed in the sequestration for rent (*f*).' There is no preference, however, over the husband's estate for his wife's funeral expense, but only a preference on her own funds (*g*).

(*a*) 3 Ersk. 9. § 43.
(*b*) Douglas *v.* Queensberry's Crs., 1674; M. 11,826; 1 Ill. 445. Kirkland *v.* Burklae, 1682; 2 B. Sup. 25, and 3. 440. Auchinleck *v.* Dinmuir, 1697; M. 11,834. Russel *v.* Dunbars, 1717; M. 11,419. Peter *v.* Monro, 1749; M. 11,852; Elch. *Fun. Charges*, 3. Rowan *v.* Barr, 1742; M. 11,852; Elch. *Fun. Charges*, 2. Park *v.* Langlands, 1755; M. 11,421. Lawson *v.* Maxwell, 1784; M. 4473; Hailes, 493, 509. Sanders *v.* Hewitt, 1822; 1 S. 310.
(*c*) Peter, *supra* (*b*).
(*d*) 1 Bell's Com. 157. Kirkland, *supra* (*b*). Dunipace *v.* Watson, 1750; M. 11,452. Hall *v.* M'Auley, 1753; M. 4855; Elch. *Fun. Charges*, 5. Rowan, *supra* (*b*). Sheddan *v.* Gibson, 1802; M. 11,855.
(*e*) Rowan, *supra* (*b*). *Supra*, § 1241.
(*f*) Drysdale *v.* Kennedy, 1835; 14 S. 159.
(*g*) Auchinleck, *supra* (*b*). See below, § 1572.

1404. (2.) *Servants' Wages.*—This is only for the term current at the death or bankruptcy, whether a year, half-year, or month (*a*). The servants privileged are, domestic servants, farm-servants, reapers, and other occasional servants for agricultural labour (*b*). It has been doubted whether a gardener is within the privilege; but certain combinations of outdoor labour and domestic service have been admitted as sufficient (*c*). In Scotland, neither artificers, clerks, nor overseers are 'at common law' entitled to the privilege (*d*). 'But since June 29, 1875, the wages of clerks, shopmen, and servants employed by a bankrupt are entitled to the same privileges as those of domestic servants, to an extent not exceeding four months' wages prior to the date of sequestration, or of the concourse of diligence for the distribution of the estates of a notour bankrupt, and not exceeding £50. The wages of workmen employed by the bankrupt are similarly entitled to a privilege to an extent not exceeding two months' wages prior to the same date (*e*).' The privilege to farm-servants has been found to prevail over the landlord's hypothec (*f*); 'and it seems the better opinion, and has been held in the local Courts, that the same rule applies to domestic servants, though not to the classes of persons embraced in the statute of 1875 (*g*).'

(*a*) 3 Ersk. 9. § 43. Crawford *v.* Hutton, 1680; M. 11,832; 1 Ill. 446.
(*b*) M'Lean *v.* Shirreffs, 1832; 10 S. 217.
(*c*) 3 Ersk. 9. § 43. Melvil *v.* Barclay, 1779; M. 11,853. Act of Sed., Jan. 23, 1779. Lockhart *v.* Paterson, 1804; M. *Priv. Debt*, 2. See White, *infra* (*d*).
(*d*) White *v.* Christie, 1781; M. 11,853; 1 Ill. 447. Ridley *v.* Haig's Crs., 1789; M. 11,854; Hailes, 1061. Marshall *v.* Philp, 1828; 6 S. 515. Maben *v.* Perkins, 1837; 15 S. 1087.
(*e*) 38 and 39 Vict. c. 26, repealing 19 and 20 Vict. c. 79, § 122. 46 & 47 Vict. c. 28 (lign.). 51 & 52 Vict. c. 62, § 1 (6) (deceased insolvent).
(*f*) M'Glashan *v.* D. of Atholl, June 29, 1819; F. C.; 1 Bell on Leases, 414.
(*g*) Fraser, M. & S. 147–150. Boag *v.* M'Laine, 1880; 2 Sel. Sh. Ct. Ca. 360 (Sheriff Fraser). *Contra* Grant *v.* Chalk, 1880; 2 *ib.* 364. Tait *v.* Neilson, 1881; 2 *ib.* 366. Dobbie *v.* Thomson, 1880; 7 R. 983.

1405. (3.) *Current Rent of the Dwelling-House.*—A privilege is given to the landlord for a year's, 'or rather perhaps a term's,' rent of the house in which the tenant dies (*a*).

(*a*) 3 Ersk. 9. § 43. Lady Dunipace *v.* Watson, 1750; M. 11,852; 1 Ill. 447. 3 Stair, 8. § 72. More's Notes, ccclxxii. Burton on Bankr. p. 4. The landlord can enforce his claims by sequestration, and so this privilege is rarely asserted. But it appears to stand on the same basis as the previous classes of privileged debts, and to be subject to the same limitation to what is "reasonable." Peter *v.* Monro, *cit.*, § 1403 (*b*). And see 51 & 52 Vict. c. 62, § 1 (6).

1406. (4.) *Ministers' Widows' Fund.*—This fund enjoys a privilege or universal hypothec, preferable even to funeral expenses (*a*).

(*a*) 19 Geo. III. c. 20.

1407. (5.) *Friendly Societies.*—The debts due to the society by office-bearers dying or becoming bankrupt, from sums coming into their hands in the course of their office, are directed to be paid before any of the other debts are paid or satisfied (*a*).

(*a*) 59 and 60 Vict. c. 25, § 35.

1408. (6.) *Exchequer Bills.*—There is a universal hypothec for Exchequer bills granted in loans by Government (*a*).

(*a*) See above, § 1343. 38 and 39 Vict. c. 89, § 18. 39 and 40 Vict. c. 31, § 7. Holden *v.* M'Farlane, June 9, 1821; 1 S. 62.

1409. (7.) *Taxes.*—Besides the privilege by writ of extent for the recovery and preservation of the public revenue (*a*), special hypothecs have been established by the Legislature for the securing of particular taxes, the arrears being made a charge on the manufactures and materials (*b*); and there is a General Post Office hypothec, which operates as a privilege for all debts and arrears of postage (*c*); 'a preference to all debts of a private nature for poor rates (*d*); and for assessments under the Roads and Bridges Act (*e*); and the like.'

(*a*) See below, § 2291. 51 & 52 Vict. c. 62, § 1.
(*b*) 28 Geo. III. c. 37, § 21. 43 Geo. III. c. 150. See also 6 Geo. IV. c. 107. 43 and 44 Vict. c. 19, § 88, etc. (Taxes Management Act, 1880).
(*c*) 9 Anne, c. 10, § 30. See 3 and 4 Vict. c. 96; 10 and 11 Vict. c. 85.
(*d*) 8 and 9 Vict. c. 83, § 88. Adamson *v.* Ambrose, 1858; 1 Guthrie's Sh. Ct. Ca. 315.
(*e*) 41 and 42 Vict. c. 51, § 85.

CHAPTER VIII

OF RETENTION OR LIEN

1410. General View and Definition of Retention.—This right results from possession, and so far is different from hypothec, and analogous to pledge. Strictly speaking, it is applicable to corporeal subjects only, but is extended to debts. In this shape it is carefully to be distinguished from compensation. Compensation is payment and extinction of mutual debts; whereas retention of a debt is nothing more than an implied security for performance (*a*); a power of suspension, or right to withhold payment or performance till satisfied of some counter demand. Compensation, therefore, can be pleaded only where the debt in extinction of which it is meant to be applied is due and liquid; whereas retention may be pleaded in security of debts, future, contingent, or illiquid (*b*). Retention depends on possession, and expires with the loss of it. But it is not in every case that the mere circumstance of possession confers a right of retention. It is a right which arises only as the counterpart of a mutual contract (*c*); or by usage and common understanding in certain known cases, in which, for the convenience of commerce, it is held to be acquiesced in and implied between the parties. Within these limits, retention may be described as a right to retain a subject legitimately in one's possession until a debt shall be paid, or an engagement performed, the *jus exigendi* of which is in the possessor. 'In special circumstances equity requires an extension of the principle, irrespective of usage or mutual contract, as where one who founds on a liquid debt is shown on probable grounds to be under an obligation to account to the debtor for larger sums (*d*). The security does not cover the expense of keeping or taking care of the thing retained during the detention, *e.g.* the shipwright's charges for the occupation of his slip by a ship detained under his lien for repairs (*e*).'

(*a*) See Borthwick *v.* Scot. Widows' Fund, 1864; 2 Macph. 395.
(*b*) 3 Ersk. 4. § 20 et seq. Sibbald *v.* Gibson, 1852; 15 D. 217. Hamilton *v.* Western Bk., 1857; 19 D. 152.
(*c*) Meikle & Watson *v.* Pollard, 1880; 8 R. 69. See above, § 71; below, § 1419.
(*d*) Ross *v.* Ross, 1895; 22 R. 461.
(*e*) Somes *v.* Brit. Emp. Shipping Co., E. B. & E. 353; 28 L. J. Q. B. 220; 8 H. L. Ca. 338; 30 L. J. Q. B. 229. See Stephen *v.* Swayne, 1861; 24 D. 158; and above, § 128. *Qu.* as to Lord M'Laren's distinction between lien and retention in Gladstone *v.* M'Callum, 1896; 23 R. 783.

1411. Kinds of Retention.—Retention is Special or General.

(1.) *Special Retention* arises in the course of a particular contract, and operates as a security for fulfilment of the counterpart (*a*).

(2.) *General Retention* extends in certain cases beyond the immediate transactions out of which the possession has arisen, and operates as a security for the general balance of account between the parties (*b*).

(*a*) 1 Stair, 18. § 7. 3 Ersk. 4. § 20 et seq. 2 Bell's Com. 91. See § 1419 et seq.
(*b*) See below, § 1431 et seq.

1412. Requisite Possession.—In order to confer the right of retention of corporeal moveables, there must be possession. But, 1. It is not such possession as a workman has who is employed to build a house, or repair a ship in a roadstead, or to cut down timber (*a*); 'or a clerk, secretary, or servant to write up books (*b*).' 2. It must be actual possession; not merely civil, and by fiction or construction of the law. So goods in a carrier's hand, though constructively delivered so as to pass the property if the price be paid, are not, in respect to a question of retention, in the possession of the consignee (*c*). But, 3. It will be enough if the goods are in the hands of clerks or servants, or anyone entrusted (as manufacturer, wharfinger, or warehousekeeper) to prepare, or carry, or keep the goods subject to the employer's order. So, again, it will not be sufficient to constitute retention, that there has been an intention of delivering possession, nor even that this intention has been partially executed, if legitimate possession has not been actually completed (*d*).

(*a*) Callum *v.* Ferrier, 1822; 2 S. 102; aff. 1 W. & S. 399; 1 Ill. 447. Haywood *v.* Waring, 4 Camp. 291. See Cooper *v.* Barr & Shearer, *infra*, § 1420.
(*b*) Gladstone *v.* M'Callum, *cit.* § 1410. See § 1414 (*a*).
(*c*) Kinloch *v.* Craig, 3 T. R. 119; aff. 1 W. & S. 783; 1 Ill. 395; 1 R. R. 664. Young *v.* Stein's Trs., 1789; M. 14,218. Sweet *v.* Pym, 1 East, 5; 1 Ill. 448; 5 R. R. 497. Harvey *v.* Lydiard, 1 Starkie, 123. Nichols *v.* Clent, 3 Price, 547. 2 Bell's Com. 91. *Supra*, § 1304. Correct the text by § 1303, note (*m*).
(*d*) Wilson *v.* Balfour, 2 Camp. 579; 1 Ill. 449.

1413. The possession must be lawful; not acquired by fraud; nor by a void contract, nor by informal diligence (*a*); nor by mere accident 'or mistake' (*b*).

(*a*) Glendinning's Crs. *v.* Montgomery, 1745; Elch. *Arrest.* 24, and notes, 40; 1 Ill. 449; M. 2573, 1449; disapproved in subsequent cases; see 2 Bell's Com. 93 (89 M'L.'s ed.), and Harper *v.* Faulds, 1791; M. 2666; Bell's Ca. 440, 474. Dickson *v.* Nicholson, 1855; 17 D. 1011 (monies collected by traveller). See Addison on Contracts, 424; and Brown *v.* Marr, 1880; 7 R. 427.
(*b*) Mackenzie *v.* Newall, 1824; 3 S. 206; 1 Ill. 458. Louson (Craik's Tr.) *v.* Craik, 1842; 4 D. 1452.

1414. Possession of a confidential nature, as in deposit (*a*), or with a specific appropriation inconsistent with the retention claimed (*b*), will not ground retention.

(*a*) 1 Stair, 13. § 9. Appin's Crs. *v.* Fraser, 1760; M. 749; 1 Ill. 450. See § 212, 574. As to claim by servants to retain their master's goods or money in their possession for wages, see Burns *v.* Bruce, 1799; Hume, 29. Dickson *v.* Nicholson, *supra*, § 1413. Cf. § 1412 (1).
(*b*) Stewart *v.* Bisset, 1778; M. *Compen.* Apx. 2; Hailes, 342. Harper and Mackenzie, *supra*, § 1413. Lucas *v.* Dorrien, 7 Taunt. 278; 1 Moore, 29; 1 Ill. 398; 18 R. R. 480. See Burn *v.* Brown, 2 Starkie, 272; 19 R. R. 719. Chisholm *v.* Fraser, 1825; 3 S. 630; 1 Ill. 463. M'Kie *v.* M'Kinnell, 1822; 1 S. 465. Borthwick *v.* Bremner, 1833; 12 S. 121. See below, § 1451. Frith *v.* Forbes, 32 L. J. Ch. 10 (consignee's lien excluded in consignment expressly subject to claim of a third party—see Phelps, Stokes, & Co. *v.* Comber, 29 Ch. D. 813; and Brown, Shipley, & Co. *v.* Kough, 29 Ch. D. 848). Hewitt *v.* Elliot (Stephenson's Trs.), 1775; 2 Pat. 381 (see Bell's 8vo Ca. 458, 474). Brown *v.* Sommerville, 1844; 6 D. 1267. Lawrie *v.* Denny's Tr. 1853; 15 D. 404. Natl. Bank *v.* Forbes, 1858; 21 D. 79. Gray's Trs. *v.* Royal Bank, 1895; 23 R. 199 (monies lodged in a bank by executors of deceased debtor).

1415. The right of retention terminates with the loss of possession (*a*), unless the possession is taken 'away' by undue means (*b*). But, 1. The possession of goods by a factor who sells and delivers them is transferred to the price unpaid, so as to extend his lien over it (*c*). 2. If a shipmaster 'were' compelled to place goods in the King's warehouse, or in dock warehouses, under the Dock Acts, the possession 'was' not lost, nor the lien discharged (*d*); but if he voluntarily 'placed' them in a private bond warehouse, he 'lost' his lien (*e*). 'This distinction does not seem to be retained under the Merchant Shipping Act, 1894. A shipowner may, subject to the responsibilities which he thereby undertakes as a warehouseman, retain goods for freight on board his ship on demurrage for a reasonable time, and, after landing them, he retains his right over them so long as they are in his own possession (*f*). In ports in the United Kingdom, if there be not a person ready to take delivery and pay freight, the shipowner may avail himself of the provisions of the Merchant Shipping Act, landing the goods with certain notices, and lodging them with a warehouseman under a stop order for freight, which preserves his lien. The goods may be sold by the warehouseman if the lien be not discharged within ninety days, or sooner if they be perishable (*g*).' 3. If he has quitted possession by error or mistake, the lien will subsist (*h*). 4. The lien may be reserved by agreement. '5. Possession legally obtained under contract for a continuing purpose is not to be displaced by inference from equivocal acts (*i*).'

(*a*) Kruger *v.* Wilcox, Amb. 252; 1 Burr. 494; I Ill. 451; Tudor's L. C. 353. Sweet *v.* Pym, *supra*, § 1412 (*c*).

(*b*) Wallace *v.* Woodgate, 1 C. & P. 575. *Infra*, § 1447.
(*c*) Drinkwater *v.* Goodwin, Cowp. 251; 1 Ill. 469. Houghton *v.* Matthews, 3 B. & P. 485; 7 R. R. 815.
(*d*) 4 Geo. IV. c. 24, § 83; re-enacted, 6 Geo. IV. c. 112, § 45. Ward *v.* Felton, 1 East, 507; 1 Ill. 271. Wilson *v.* Kymer, 1 M. & S. 157. See Johnston *v.* Duncan, 1827; 5 S. 660; 1 Ill. 451. 3 and 4 Will. IV. c. 57, § 47. See below, § 1424.
(*e*) Johnston, *supra* (*d*).
(*f*) See Meyerstein *v.* Barber, 36 L. J. C. P. 48; L. R. 2 C. P. 36 (*per* Willes, J.). Mors le Blanch *v.* Wilson, 42 L. J. C. P. 70; L. R. 2 C. P. 227. The difficulty does not seem to be insuperable. See § 1412. Reeves *v.* Capper, 5 Bing. N. C. 136.
(*g*) 57 and 58 Vict. c. 60, § 494 sqq. Mierbrodt *v.* Fitzsimon, 44 L. J. Adm. 45; L. R. 6 P. C. 306. Wilson *v.* London, etc., Stm. Nav. Co., L. R. 1 C. P. 61; 35 L. J. C. P. 9. Glyn & Co. *v.* E. and W. India Dock Co., 6 Q. B. D. 475; 7 App. Ca. 591; 50 L. J. Q. B. 62; 52 *ib.* 146.
(*h*) *Ex p.* Morgan, 12 Ves. 6; 1 Ill. 451; 8 R. R. 272. *Ex p.* Doughty, Montagu on Lien, 11. See above, § 1413.
(*i*) Cooper *v.* Barr & Shearer, 1873; 11 Macph. 651; rev. 1875, 2 R. H. L. 14.

1416. The right does not revive on recovering possession, if it have once effectually ceased (*a*); and there is no stopping *in transitu* to preserve a lien, that being a right only as between vendor and vendee (*b*).

(*a*) 2 Bell's Com. 95. Whithead *v.* Vaughan, Cook's B. L. 579; 1 Ill. 452. Jones *v.* Pearl, 1 Strange, 556. Hartley *v.* Hitchcock, 1 Starkie, 408; 18 R. R. 790. See below, § 1449.
(*b*) Kinloch *v.* Craig, 3 T. R. 783; 1 Ill. 395; 1 R. R. 664. See above, § 1308–10. See Edwards *v.* Southgate, 10 W. R. (Ex.) 528 (lien of shipping agent on bill of lading).

1417. Effect of Retention.—The effect of retention of corporeal subjects is to deprive the owner of the use and benefit of the thing retained till the counterpart be performed or the debt satisfied. The effect of retention of a debt is to deprive the creditor of his money retained till satisfaction be given (*a*). Whether it entitles the creditor who claims retention to take active steps for making effectual his debt, as in pledge, by sale of the thing retained, admits of distinctions. And, 1. A factor having power to sell, may, by means of sale, make effectual the sums which he has advanced on the goods in his hand (*b*). 2. He may transfer the lien, and on such transference raise money; the assignee having the same right to retain which his cedent had. And although, when a factor sends goods to a consignee or sub-factor, without giving notice of his representative character, such consignee or sub-factor will have an effectual right of retention against the principal for money advanced on the goods (*c*), he can have no lien for his general balance against the primary factor, beyond the amount of the primary factor's right to retain against his principal. 3. In the common case of goods prepared for the market, 'not in the possession of a factor,' and useful only as commodities in trade, a court of law will authorise a sale, as in pledge; but it seems very doubtful whether such authority can be granted for disposing of a thing not of that description, to the effect of conferring on the purchaser the full property (*d*). In lien over an author's unpublished compositions, for example, it does not seem competent for a Court to order publication and sale without the author's consent. 'In the general case, and apart from the specialties that belong to the character of factors, a right of retention is a mere personal right, which is inseparable from the contract out of which it springs, and which the person entitled to it cannot realise by sale or transference (*e*). But a right of retention once vested in a carrier or other legitimate possessor remains, notwithstanding the sale of the goods by the owner and indorsation and delivery of a bill of lading or other document representing them (*f*).'

(*a*) 3 Ersk. 4. § 20.
(*b*) Broughton *v.* Stewart, Primrose, & Co., Dec. 17, 1814; F. C; 1 Ill. 452.
(*c*) See above, § 1364.
(*d*) See Thames Iron Co. *v.* Patent Derrick Crane Co., 1 J. & H. 93; 29 L. J. Ch. 714. Parker *v.* Brown & Co., 1878; 5 R. 979 (sale of grain in damaged and deteriorating condition, with consignation of proceeds subject to pleas of parties).
(*e*) Donald *v.* Suckling, L. R. 1 Q. B. 585; 35 L. J. Q. B. 232 (*per* Blackburn, J.). Legg *v.* Evans, 6 M. & W. 36; 9 L. J. Ex. 132. See Mulliner *v.* Florence, 3 Q. B. D. 484; 47 L. J. Q. B. 700; and below, § 1428 (*c*).
(*f*) Small *v.* Moats, 9 Bing. 592. Gledstanes *v.* Allan, 12 C. B. 202. See below, § 1424.

1418. Discharge and Waiving of Retention.—This may be either, 1. 'By agreement' before possession begins (*a*); or, 2. By 'agreement implied from the' custom of trade 'or dealing between the parties' (*b*); or, 3. By contract 'after it has been constituted'; or, 4. By document restrictive of the claim to personal credit, 'or bill making the principal direct creditor for the price' (*c*); '5. By the unauthorised sale and delivery of the article retained, which puts an end to possession (*d*). It is enough to exclude any alleged lien if any of the terms of the contract between the parties (as where credit is allowed, or a security taken payable at a distant day) be inconsistent with the subsistence of a lien (*e*). A limitation which merely takes away the right of action, but leaves the debt subsisting, does not destroy a lien which has once been established (*f*). A claim to hold against the owner tendering satisfaction of the debt on a different ground, is held as a waiver of the lien (*g*).'

(*a*) Davis *v.* Bowsher, 5 T. R. 488 ; 1 Ill. 470 ; 2 R. R. 650 ; Walker *v.* Birch, 6 T. R. 258 ; 1 Ill. 452. Robertson's Tr. *v.* Royal Bank, 1890 ; 18 R. 12.

(*b*) Green *v.* Farmer, 1 Blackst. 651 ; 1 Ill. 457. Crawshay *v.* Homfray, 4 B. & Ald. 50. Fisher *v.* Smith, L. R. 4 App. Ca. 1 ; 48 L. J. Ex. 411.

(*c*) Johnston *v.* Duncan, 1827 ; 5 S. 660 ; Ayton *v.* Colvil, 1705 ; M. 6710 ; 1 Ill. 465. Horncastle *v.* Farren, 3 B. & Ald. 497 ; 22 R. R. 461. Miller & Paterson *v.* M'Nair, 1852 ; 14 D. 955. Chambers *v.* Davidson, L. R. 1 P. C. 296 ; 36 L. J. P. C. 17. See as to this section, 2 M'Laren's Bell's Com. 91, 92 ; and below, § 1444.

(*d*) See above, § 1417 ; and Mulliner *v.* Florence, *ibi cit.* (*e*). Cf. White *v.* Spettigue, 13 M. & W. 603 ; 14 L. J. Ex. 99.

(*e*) Chambers *v.* Davidson, *cit.* Chase *v.* Westmore, 5 M. & S. 180 ; 17 R. R. 301 ; Tudor's L. C. 679. Pinnock *v.* Harrison, 3 M. & W. 532. Smith's Merc. Law, 704. Walker *v.* Kirchner, 11 Moore, P. C. 21. Alsager *v.* St. Katharine's Dock Co., 14 M. & W. 794 ; 15 L. J. Ex. 54. Tamvaco *v.* Sampson, L. R. 1 C. P. 363 ; 35 L. J. C. P. 196. Kirchner *v.* Venus, 12 Moore, P. C. 360. Hewison *v.* Guthrie, 2 Bing. N. C. 759. Cowell *v.* Simpson, 16 Ves. Jr. 275. Bock *v.* Gorrissen, 2 De G. F. & J. 434 ; 36 L. J. Ch. 42. Angus *v.* M'Lachlan, 23 Ch. D. 330. Bank of Africa *v.* Salisbury Gold Mining Co., 1892 ; A. C. 281 (subsequent agreement not implying waiver or limitation of lien).

(*f*) Spears *v.* Hartley, 3 Esp. 81 ; 6 R. R. 814. *In re* Broomhead, 16 L. J. Q. B. 355.

(*g*) Chilton *v.* Carrington, 15 C. B. 95.

1419. Special Retention.—This, 'as already stated,' is part of the law of mutual contract, entitling one to withhold performance, or retain possession of that which forms the subject of the contract, till the counter obligation be performed (*a*).

(*a*) See *supra*, § 1411. **Harper** *v.* **Faulds,** 1791 ; M. 2666 ; Bell's Ca. 432 ; 1 Ill. 453 ; 2 Ross' L. C. 708.

1420. (1.) *Retention of Ship.*—Retention of a ship is competent for repairs, but not for furnishings of necessaries and outfit. This right of retention depends on possession, and is not, like hypothec (*a*), confined to the case of repairs made abroad. It is effectual for repairs made on the vessel in a home port. But ship-carpenters repairing a ship in an open harbour or roadstead, have not, 'the ship not being placed in their exclusive charge,' the possession necessary to sustain the right (*b*).

(*a*) See above, § 1398.

(*b*) *Ex p.* Bland, 2 Rose, 91 ; 1 Ill. 454. Watkinson *v.* Bernardiston, 2 P. Williams, 367. Franklin *v.* Hosier, 4 B. & Ald. 341 ; 23 R. R. 305 ; and cases there cited. Hamilton *v.* Wood, 1788 ; M. 6269 ; 3 Pat. 148. See above, § 1410, 1412, 1415 *fin.* Thames Ironworks Co. *v.* Derrick Co., 1 J. & H. 93 ; 29 L. J. Ch. 714. Cooper *v.* Barr & Shearer, 1873 ; 11 Macph. 651 ; rev. 1875, 2 R. H. L. 14. Ross & Duncan *v.* Baxter & Co., 1885 ; 13 R. 185. Williams *v.* Alsup, above, § 1382A (*c*). *Ex p.* Willoughby, 16 Ch. D. 604 (engineer furnishing engines—price partly paid).

1421. The right may be excluded by a special contract to make the repairs on credit; and even an implied contract by the usage of trade will discharge the lien, unless where the debtor is *vergens ad inopiam* (*a*).

(*a*) Raitt *v.* Mitchell, 4 Camp. 146 ; 1 Ill. 454 ; 16 R. R. 765. 2 Bell's Com. 98.

1422. (2.) *Retention for Carriage.*—This is admitted both in water and in land carriage.

1423. Retention is admitted wherever the possession is clearly with the shipowners (*a*). In water carriage, difficulties have occurred from the nature of the contract, as having the effect of placing the freighter in possession, or leaving the possession with the owners. The distinction seems to rest on the question whether it be a contract of *locatio operis* for carriage, or a contract of *locatio rei*. In the former case there is lien for freight (*b*), for average, and for passage money (*c*); but not 'in any case' for dead freight without a special bargain (*d*), nor for wharfage dues (*e*), 'nor for money paid in advance in the nature of freight (*f*).' Retention would seem not competent where a ship is hired on time, and at the disposal of the freighter. This case does not appear to have been decided; but the principles recognised in the cases already referred to may sanction that opinion (*g*).

(*a*) Hutton *v.* Bragg, 2 Marsh. 339 ; 7 Taunt. 14 ; 1 Ill. 454 ; 17 R. R. 431. Trinity House *v.* Clerk, 4 M. & S. 288. See above, § 405.

(*b*) *Supra*, § 405, 421. Saville *v.* Campion, 2 B. & Ald. 503 ; 21 R. R. 376. Tait *v.* Meek, 8 Taunt. 280. Yates *v.* Railston, 8 Taunt. 280 and 302 ; 19 R. R. 524. Christie *v.* Lewis, 2 B. & B. 410 ; 23 R. R. 483. Campion *v.* Colvin, 3 Bing. N. C. 17 ; 3 Ill. 127. Gledstanes *v.* Allen, 12 C. B. 202. How *v.* Kirchner, 11 Moore, P. C. 34, and cases cited above, § 1418 (*e*).

(*c*) *Supra*, § 437 ; *infra*, § 1426. Wolfe *v.* Summers, 2 Esp. 631 ; 2 Camp. 201.

(*d*) **Maclean & Hope** *v.* **Fleming**, 1871 ; 9 Macph. H. L. 38 ; L. R. 2 H. L. 128. Phillips *v.* Rodie, 15 East, 547 ; 13 R. R. 528. **Gray** *v.* **Carr**, L. R. 6 Q. B. 522 ; 40 L. J. Q. B. 257. Pearson *v.* Goschen, 17 C. B. N. S. 352 ; 33 L. J. C. P. 265.

(*e*) Bishop *v.* Ware, 3 Camp. 360 ; 14 R. R. 755. *Supra*, § 430. Faith *v.* E. I. Co., 4 B. & Ald. 630 ; 23 R. R. 423.

(*f*) How *v.* Kirchner, *cit.* Kirchner *v.* Venus, 12 Moore, P. C. 361, and other cases referred to at § 420, note (*c*). See Maclachlan, 509.

(*g*) See cases, *supra* (*b*), and § 410, 1300.

1424. The right extends over every part of the goods consigned to the same person, for the freight of the whole goods consigned to him 'under one contract' (*a*), entitling the shipmaster to payment before delivering the goods. 'The freight named in the bill of lading is *primâ facie* the amount for which lien may be enforced, and, even though nominal, precludes the shipowner from claiming a larger sum from a *bonâ fide* indorsee (*b*); but if the bill of lading bear "on payment of freight as per charter-party," it gives a lien for freight against the indorsee at the rate named in the charter-party (*c*).' The shipmaster is not entitled to detain 'the goods' on board; but he may place them with a wharfinger, or in bond, reserving the lien (*d*). But there is no lien for a general balance (*e*). 'It is sometimes said, on the authority of English cases, that a right to retain for a general balance may be established in favour of a carrier by usage or special agreement, though not so as to affect third parties (*f*). But such an agreement seems to be inconsistent with the character of a common carrier bound to take for conveyance all the goods brought to him by the public (*g*).'

(*a*) Malcolm *v.* Bannatyne, Nov. 15, 1814; F. C.; 1 Ill. 455. Soldergreen *v.* Flight, cited in Hanson *v.* Meyer, 6 East, 622; 8 R. R. 572. Abbott, 234, 323. Maclachlan, 434, 513. Möller *v.* Young, 5 E. & B. 71, 755; 25 L. J. Q. B. 94.

(*b*) Gilkison *v.* Middleton, 2 C. B. N. S. 134. Foster *v.* Colby, 3 H. & N. 705; 28 L. J. Ex. 81. Merc. & Exch. Bk. *v.* Gladstone, L. R. 3 Ex. 233; 37 L. J. Ex. 130. Brown *v.* North, 8 Ex. 1; 22 L. J. Ex. 49. Weguelin *v.* Collier, L. R. 6 H. L. 286; 42 L. J. Ch. 758. See also Keith *v.* Burrows, 2 C. P. D. 163; 2 App. Ca. 636; 46 L. J. C. P. 452, 801; and Gumm *v.* Tyrie, 6 B. & S. 298; 34 L. J. Q. B. 124.

(*c*) Cases in § 421. Smith *v.* Sieveking, 24 L. J. Q. B. 257; 5 E. & B. 589. As to claims against sub-freighters generally, see Maclachlan, 434, 514. Youle *v.* Cochrane, 1868; 6 Macph. 427. Mitchell *v.* Burn, 1874; 1 R. 900.

(*d*) Tait, *supra*, § 1423 (*b*). See, however, above, § 1415, 1302.

(*e*) Stevenson *v.* Likly, 1824; 3 S. 204. See above, § 168.

(*f*) Rushforth *v.* Hadfield, 6 East, 518; 7 East, 227; 8 R. R. 520. Wright *v.* Snell, 5 B. & Ald. 550; 24 R. R. 413. Butler *v.* Woolcott, 2 B. & P. 64; 9 R. R. 615. Oppenheim *v.* Russell, 3 B. & P. 42; 6 R. R. 604. Brandao *v.* Barnett, 2 Scott, N. C. 113.

(*g*) See the cases cited; esp. *per* Best, J., in Rushforth *v.* Hadfield. *Per* L. Moncreiff in Ridley *v.* Sloan, 1837; 15 S. 469. Also *per* L. Young in Peebles & Son *v.* Cal. Ry. Co., 1875; 2 R. 346. Addison, Contr. 568.

1425. There is a lien for land carriage (*a*), similar to that for freight; but not for booking (*b*). 'This lien covers the charges on luggage left at a cloakroom by one who is only a hirer or bailee (*c*). A stipulation or notice that a railway company shall be entitled to retain goods for a general balance due by the consignee or owners was held not to be "reasonable" in the sense of the Railway and Canal Traffic Act (*d*). The Railways Clauses Act creates a right in railway companies to detain and sell carriages and goods for a general balance of tolls. But it is now settled that this provision applies only to tolls for the use of the line, and not to charges for goods conveyed by the company as carriers (*e*).'

(*a*) Skinner *v.* Upshaw, 2 Raym. 752; 1 Ill. 456. Higgins *v.* Bretherton, 5 C. & P. 2.

(*b*) Lambert *v.* Robinson, 1 Esp. Ca. 119.

(*c*) Singer Mftg. Co. *v.* L. & S.-W. Ry. 1894; 1 Q. B. 833.

(*d*) 17 and 18 Vict. c. 31, § 7. Scottish Central Ry. Co. *v.* Ferguson, Rennie, & Co., 1861; 2 Macph. 781. Peebles & Son *v.* Cal. Ry. Co., 1875; 2 R. 346. But in these cases the question whether that Act is at all applicable to such agreements does not appear to have been raised.

(*e*) 8 and 9 Vict. c. 33, § 90. Wallis *v.* L. & S.-W. Ry. Co., L. R. 5 Ex. 62; 39 L. J. Ex. 57. Highland Ry. Co. *v.* Jackson, 1876, 3 R. 850, overruling an elaborate judgment of Lord Shand in Cal. Ry. Co. *v.* Guild, 1873; 1 R. 198; and certain opinions in Peebles & Son *v.* Cal. Ry. Co., *cit.* See further on this clause of the Act, North Br. Ry. Co. *v.* Caxton, 1870; 8 Macph. 998.

1426. (3.) *Retention for Average Loss* is accomplished by the interference of the shipmaster, who is entitled to detain the cargo for the respective shares (*a*); 'but the owners of cargo have no lien upon the ship (*b*).'

(*a*) See The Galam, 2 Moore, P. C. N. S. 216. The Söblomsten, 32 L. J. Adm. 41. Dickinson *v.* Jardine, L. R. 3 C. P. 639; 37 L. J. C. P. 321. Crookes *v.* Allan, 5 Q. B. D. 38; 49 L. J. Ex. 201. *Supra*, § 442.

(*b*) Crookes *v.* Allan, *cit.* The North Star, 29 L. J. Adm. 73; 1 Lush. 45.

1427. (4.) *Retention for Salvage* is a most natural and equitable right to those who, having saved the ship, cannot be compelled to deliver it up till salvage be paid (*a*). 'Under the Merchant Shipping Act the receiver of wreck detains the ship, cargo, or apparel saved till payment of salvage, or security found, or arrestment or detention by competent court (*b*).'

(*a*) Hartford *v.* Jones, 1 Raym. 393; 1 Ill. 456. The Two Friends, 1 Rob. Adm. 277. See 12 Anne, st. 2, c. 18, § 2. 4 Geo. I. c. 12. 1 and 2 Geo. IV. c. 76, § 19. Hingston *v.* Wendt, 1 Q. B. D. 367; 45 L. J. Q. B. 440.

(*b*) 57 and 58 Vict. c. 60, § 552. Otis *v.* Kidd, 1862; 24 D. 419. There is also a maritime lien for salvage giving priority independent of possession. See Maclachlan, 633, 702, 704; and above, § 1397.

1428. (5.) *Retention of Innkeepers and Stablers.*—This extends over the goods, horses, and carriages of travellers 'brought to the inn in the ordinary way, as the property of the guest, even though they are not really his, and even although the goods be not of the kind ordinarily brought by travellers for their use on a journey, such as a piano hired for the temporary use of the guest, but not over the known property of a third person,' for the expense of keep, or of entertainment, while in his stable or inn upon that journey (*a*). But it has been held that a livery stablekeeper, who is not bound to take in horses, 'and who has the custody of them only as the owner's servant and for his use,' has not in England a lien for the keep of them without an express agreement, 'such a lien being inconsistent with the nature of the contract' (*b*). 'The innkeeper's lien is not lost by occasional and temporary absences *animo revertendi* (*c*); nor by his allowing the guest to go away without paying his bill, his luggage remaining in the inn (*d*); but not being a general lien, it does not revive upon the return of the guest, if the innkeeper has suffered him to go away permanently with his luggage without paying his bill (*e*). In another sense this lien is general, extending over all the guest's property received by the innkeeper in his premises, and so over horses and carriages for the personal expenses under the same contract (*f*).'

(*a*) Johnson *v.* Hill, 3 Starkie, 172; 23 R. R. 764. Thompson *v.* Lacy, 3 B. & Ald. 283; 1 Ill. 456; 22 R. R. 385. Nayler *v.* Mangles, 1 Esp. 109; 5 R. R. 752. York *v.* Greenaugh, 2 Raym. 866. Turrill *v.* Crawley, 13 Q. B. 197; 18 L. J. Q. B. 153. Broadwood *v.* Granara, 10 Ex. 417; 24 L. J. Ex. 21. Threlfall *v.* Borwick, 41 L. J. Q. B. 266; L. R. 7 Q. B. 711; 44 L. J. Q. B. 87; L. R. 10 Q. B. 210. M'Kichen *v.* Muir, 1849; 1 J. Shaw, Justy. R. 233. Robins & Co. *v.* Gray, 1895; 2 Q. B. 591 (commercial traveller's baggage).

(*b*) Wallace *v.* Woodgate, Ryan & Mood. 193. Judson *v.* Etheridge, 1 C. & M. 743. See 2 Bell's Com. 104. Smith *v.* Dearlove, 6 C. B. 132. Orchard *v.* Rackstraw, 9 C. B. 698; 19 L. J. C. P. 303. In England this distinction is also and mainly rested on the ground that the livery stablekeeper does not, like a trainer of race-horses, confer an additional value on the horses by bestowing his skill and labour, but it may be doubted if such a distinction exists in Scottish practice.

(*c*) Allen *v.* Smith, 12 C. B. N. S. 638; 31 L. J. C. P. 306; aff. in Ex. Ch. 9 E. Jur. N. S. 1284. By 41 and 42 Vict. c. 38, an innkeeper has power after six weeks to sell goods left at his inn, subject to certain provisions as to notices, etc. The Act probably applies to Scotland.

(*d*) Snead *v.* Watkins, 1 C. B. N. S. 267; 26 L. J. C. P. 27.

(*e*) Jones *v.* Thurloe, 8 Mod. 172. Jones *v.* Pearl, 1 Str. 557.

(*f*) Mulliner *v.* Florence, 3 Q. B. D. 484; 47 L. J. Q. B. 700. See Smith *v.* Dearlove, *cit.* (*b*).

1429. (6.) *Retention of Cattle for Grass-Maill.*—This arises as the counterpart of the contract for depasturing cattle. 'There is an absence of decisions in support of such a right of retention; and it may sometimes be difficult to establish such possession by the lessor as is required for retention. In the case of milch cows the owner has possession for the purpose of milking (*a*).'

(*a*) See Jackson *v.* Cummins, 5 M. & W. 342; and above, § 1235. And comp. the case of livery stablekeepers, above.

1430. (7.) *Retention by Persons bestowing Labour and Skill.*—Retention is given to workmen on the contract of *locatio operarum* (*a*), for the price of their labour on goods in their possession, where there is no special agreement for payment at a future time (*b*). And a trainer of race-horses has been held to have a lien, though 'in England' a livery stabler has not (*c*). 'An accountant, factor, or man of business, has, on the principle of mutual contract, a right to retain books and papers put into his hands for recovery of debts, or for other purposes under the contract, until he is paid for his trouble and outlay under the contract of employment (*d*). It has been said that this is "a new departure"; but though it may not be consistent with the peculiar principle of English law (*e*), it naturally results from the principles recognised by the law of Scotland (*f*).'

(*a*) Castellain *v.* Thompson, 13 C. B. N. S. 105; 32 L. J. C. P. 79.

(*b*) *Ex p.* Ockenden, 1 Atk. 233; 1 Ill. 456. Green *v.* Farmer, 4 Bur. 2214. Chase *v.* Westmore, 5 M. & S. 180; Tudor's L. C. 679. Blake *v.* Nicholson, 3 M. & S. 167 (printer). Brook *v.* Wentworth, 3 Anst. 881. See Harper *v.* Faulds, 1791; Bell's Ca. 440; M. 2666.

(*c*) Bevan *v.* Waters, 1 M. & M. 285. See above, § 1428. Power to the owner by usage or contract to run the horses at races, the owner selecting the jockey, is inconsistent with the continuance of this lien. Forth *v.* Simpson, 13 Q. B. 680; 18 L. J. Q. B. 263. The owner of a stallion has in England a lien on a mare received into his stable to be covered. Scarfe *v.* Morgan, 4 M. & W. 270.

(*d*) Meikle & Wilson *v.* Pollard, 1880; 8 R. 69. Robertson *v.* Ross, 1887; 15 R. 67. Cf. York Bdgs. Co. *v.* Robertson, 1805; M. *Hypothec*, Apx. 2. These cases overrule Brown *v.* Sommerville, 1844; 6 D. 1267, a case previously doubted. Ferguson *v.* Cameron, July 1891 (Sh. C. of Lanarkshire). Robertson *v.* B. L. Co., 1891; 18 R. 1225, 1232. See Gladstone *v.* M'Callum, 1896; 23 R. 783.

(*e*) See § 1428.

(*f*) See, *e.g.*, above, § 71, 1411. 2 Bell's Com. 91, 97 (87, 91 M'L.'s ed.). Bell's 8vo Cases, 471 sq. Opinions of Lords Cuninghame and Moncreiff in Brown *v.* Sommerville, *cit.* Begg on Law Agents, pp. 205, 206.

1431. General Retention.—This proceeds not on the reciprocal rights of the particular contract out of which the possession arises, but on the footing of an agreement, express or implied, in certain cases, for the continuing of possession already begun, in security of debts unconnected with the original contract (*a*). It has sometimes been contended that in Scotland the right of retention goes further than the English lien, so as to comprehend all cases where there is legitimate possession and a debt due to the possessor; and that retention is in such case a necessary substitute for the diligence of arrestment, which a creditor possessed of his debtor's effects cannot use in his own hand. But there is no ground for this distinction (*b*).

(*a*) See Hamilton *v.* Western Bank, 1857; 19 D. 152.

(*b*) 2 Bell's Com. 105 (101 sqq., M'L.'s ed.). More's Notes on Stair, Note Q. p. 131. Harper *v.* Faulds, 1791; M. 2666; Bell's Ca. 440; 1 Ill. 453; 2 Ross' L. C. 708. M'Kenzie *v.* Newal, 1824; 3 S. 206; 1 Ill. 458. Stuarts & Fletcher *v.* M'Gregor & Co., 1829; 7 S. 622. See L. Ivory in Hamilton, *cit.* Hope, J.-C., in Sibbald *v.* Gibson 1852; 15 D. 217. Paul & Thain *v.* Royal Bank, 1869; 7 Macph. 361. Borthwick *v.* Scot. Widows' Fund, 1864; 2 Macph. 595.

1432. (1.) *By Contract.*—A right of general retention is sometimes raised by express contract. Where the agreement is clear and explicit, it is effectual; and it is the only way of establishing a general lien, where there is no such lien recognised at common law, or established by usage (*a*). 'But there can be no retention either by usage or contract, if the existence of such a right is inconsistent with the terms or meaning of the contract (*b*).'

(*a*) See the doctrine delivered by Sir W. Grant in Gladstone *v.* Birley, 2 Mer. 401; 1 Ill. 459, and Lord Chief Justice Tindal's remarks in Bleadon *v.* Hancock, M. & Malk. 467. See Bock *v.* Gorrissen, 2 De G. F. & J. 434; 30 L. J. Ch. 39; and cases cited in § 1423 (*d*). Wiltshire Iron Co. *v.* G. W. Ry. Co., L. R. 6 Q. B. 101, 776; 40 L. J. Q. B. 43, 308 (effect of debtor's bankruptcy).

(*b*) Cases in § 1418 (*e*). Forth *v.* Simpson, § 1430 (*c*). Cases in § 1423 (*f*), and § 1428 (*b*). Jackson *v.* Cummins, § 1429 (*a*).

1433. Lien has in England 'and Scotland' been allowed to be raised by implied contract, inferred from advertisement, in the case of manufacturers not bound to work otherwise than on their own conditions (*a*). But it is requisite that the advertisement shall be clear and specific, and known to the party, so as to be equal to a contract, and that the goods proceed from the owner as under such implied agreement (*b*). Such contract by advertisement, however, is with great difficulty admitted in the case of common carriers to raise a lien (*c*). There 'was' no example of retention in Scotland by advertisement; but the principle on which it may be justified as implying a contract is clear; 'and in the case of a bleacher, the principle has been expressly recognised, to the effect of giving a lien for bills granted for work done, as well as for the open account, the lien being limited to the account for work done within a year (*d*).'

(*a*) Kirkman *v.* Shawcross, 6 T. R. 14; 1 Ill. 459; 3 R. R. 103. But see Bowman *v.* Malcolm, 11 M. & W. 833.

(*b*) Wright *v.* Snell, 5 B. & Ald. 350; 24 R. R. 413.

(*c*) Oppenheim *v.* Russell, 3 B. & P. 42; 6 R. R. 604. Rushforth *v.* Hadfield, 6 East, 519; 8 R. R. 520. See above, § 1425. Tudor's L. C. 689–691.

(*d*) Anderson's Trs. *v.* Fleming, 1871; 9 Macph. 718. See below, § 1435.

1434. (2.) *Retention by Usage of Trade.*—Usage of trade, when general and known, has been admitted as a good ground of general retention in several branches of manufacture in England; as calico-printers, dyers, wharfingers, and packers (*a*). But this requires a long course of dealing in old-established trades, 'may be varied by local usage (*b*),' and is not easily admitted in new branches of manufacture (*c*). 'It was found that there is no such lien in the case of storekeepers (*d*) or scourers (*e*); but it is now decided that by usage, both in England and Scotland, calenderers and packers have a right to retain for a general balance (*f*).'

(*a*) 2 Bell's Com. 105. Addison on Contracts, 425–6, 475. See Harper *v.* Faulds, 1791; M. 2666; Bell's 8vo Ca. 432; 2 Ross' L. C. 708. Cases of Smith *v.* Aikman, Strong *v.* Phillips, etc., *infra.* *In re* Witt & Co., 2 Ch. D. 489; 45 L. J. Bkr. 118 (packers—alleged cesser of usage). Hired rollers delivered to calico-printers by customers, who represent them to be their own, cannot be retained against the hirer under this usage. Mitchell *v.* Heys & Sons, 1894; 21 R. 600.

As to wharfingers, see Addison on Contracts, 427. Tudor's L. C. 706. Dresser *v.* Bosanquet, 4 B. & S. 460; 32 L. J. Q. B. 57. Moet *v.* Pickering, L. R. 8 Ch. D. 172; 47 L. J. Ch. 527. 10 and 11 Vict. c. 47 (Harbours Clauses Act). 14 and 15 Vict. c. 43 (do.).

As to dyers, *qu.* ?—the decision in Kirkman *v.* Shawcross, *cit.*, resting upon notices; see Tudor's L. C. 706.

(*b*) Holderness *v.* Collinson, 7 B. & C. 212.

(*c*) Bleadon, *supra*, § 1432 (*a*). See Rushforth, *supra*, § 1433 (*c*). Smith's Merc. Law, 701.

(*d*) Laurie & Co. *v.* Anderson, 1853; 15 D. 404. Laurie *v.* Black, 1831; 10 S. 1. Reid *v.* Watson, 1836; 14 S. 223.

(*e*) Smith *v.* Aikman, 1859; 22 D. 344. See Rose *v.* Hart, 8 Taunt. 499; 20 R. R. 533.

(*f*) *In re* Witt, 2 Ch. D. 489; 45 L. J. Bkr. 118. Strong *v.* Phillips & Co., 1878; 5 R. 770.

1435. The course of dealing between the parties has also been held a good ground of lien; as in bleaching 'there is a lien for the whole account for work done within the year,' where one piece of goods is sent in after another, and the parties settle periodically, delivering the several pieces as they are ready (*a*).

(*a*) Hunter *v.* Austin & Co., 1794; 1 Ill. 460. M'Culloch *v.* Pattison & Co., 1794; 1 Ill. 461. Aberdeen & Smith *v.* Paterson, 1812; 2 Bell's Com. 109; Hume, 127. Handyside v. M'Intosh, 1805; Hume, 651. Brown v. Sommerville, 1844; 6 D. 1267. Laurie & Co. v. Anderson, 1853; 15 D. 404. Bovill v. Dixon, 1854; 16 D. 619. Anderson's Trs. v. Fleming, 1871; 9 Macph. 718. Miller v. Hutchison & Dixon, 1881; 8 R. 489.

1436. Shipmaster's Lien.—There is no lien to a shipmaster for the price of repairs for which he has bound himself personally; for though he may hypothecate the ship for repairs abroad, he cannot convert the hypothec into a right to retain possession (*a*). 'The master seems to have a possessory lien over cargo for freight and general average (*b*). He has also been allowed a lien over particular cargo saved by him for the expenses incurred in saving it (*c*).'

(*a*) Hussey v. Christie, 9 East, 432; 1 Ill. 462; 9 R. R. 585.
(*b*) Cleary v. M'Andrew, 2 Moore, P. C. N. S. 216.
(*c*) Hingston v. Wendt, 1 Q. B. D. 367; 45 L. J. Q. B. 440.

1437. Recognised Classes of General Retention.—There are certain well-established and known rights of retention, introduced from considerations of expediency or of justice in particular departments, of which the details are important.

1438. Retention by Law Agent.—(1.) *General Rule.*—This entitles a law agent, 'his personal representatives after his death (*a*), or his trustee in bankruptcy (*b*),' to retain his client's title-deeds, securities, documents of debt, and other papers, which come lawfully into his possession in the course of his employment (*c*), until he shall receive satisfaction for the amount of his business or professional account (*d*), 'even although partly incurred before the deeds were put into the agent's hands (*e*).' It does not cover the balance on the cash-account between the parties; nor advances of money, even in situations where the law agent is the natural channel of communication in the transaction, 'or even where there is an express agreement to that effect, for title-deeds are not capable of being impignorated'; nor a yearly salary as agent (*f*); 'nor commission on money transactions (*g*); nor cautionary obligations (*h*).' But an agent employed to borrow money has been found entitled to retain his client's title-deeds till the account of expenses paid by him to the lender's agent shall be repaid (*i*).

(*a*) Wilson v. Lumsdaine, 1837; 15 S. 1211. Paul v. Meikle, 1868; 7 Macph. 235.
(*b*) Inglis v. Moncrieff, 1851; 13 D. 622. The trustee's right is subject, of course, to all equities affecting the bankrupt. As to other assignees, see *per* L. Fullerton in Renny & Webster v. Myles, *cit. infra* (*c*). *Infra*, § 1442.
(*c*) Renny & Webster v. Myles, 1847; 9 D. 619. Richardson v. Merry, 1863; 1 Macph. 940.
(*d*) 3 Ersk. 4. § 21. 2 Bell's Com. 111. See above, as to hypothec, § 1388. Renny & Webster, *cit.* As to the expense of constituting the agent's claim against the client, see Gray v. Graham, 1851; 13 D. 693; aff. 1855, 2 Macq. 435. Palmer v. Lee, 1880; 7 R. 651.
(*e*) Menzies v. Murdoch, 1841; 4 D. 257. Comp. Kerr v. Beck, 1849; 11 D. 510. Renny & Webster, *cit.*
(*f*) Cuthbert v. Ross, 1697; 4 B. Sup. 374; 1 Ill. 462. York Buildings Co. v. Dalrymple, 1738; Elch. *Hyp.* 9. Lidderdale's Crs. v. Naismith, 1749; M. 6428. Moncrieff v. Colvil's Crs., 1799; 2 Bell's Com. 112. Grant's Reprs. v. Robertson, 1801; M. *Hyp.* Apx. 1. Skinner v. Paterson, 1823; 2 S. 354. Christie v. Ruxton, 1862; 24 D. 1182. Largue v. Urquhart, 1883; 10 R. 1229 (law agent also factor).
(*g*) Paul v. Dickson, 1839; 1 D. 867.
(*h*) Grant's Reprs. v. Robertson, and Lidderdale's Crs. v. Naismith, *supra* (*f*). See Kemp v. Youngs, *infra* (*i*).
(*i*) Inglis & Weir v. Renny, 1825; 4 S. 113. See Kemp v. Youngs, etc., 1838; 16 S. 500. Paul *cit.* (*g*).

1439. (2.) *Exceptions.*—Comprehensive as the right of retention of title-deeds, securities, and documents of debt is, there is a clear exception of all papers which have been put into the agent's hands for a special purpose, 'or at least under a special agreement,' inconsistent with the claim of retention (*a*). And the agent has no right to retain the proceedings in a process which he has been employed to conduct (*b*), 'or the funds recovered in such process (*c*).'

(*a*) Chisholm v. Fraser, 1825; 3 S. 442; 1 Ill. 463.
(*b*) Callman v. Bell, 1793; M. 6255. Forsyth v. Syme, Feb. 18, 1791, referred to in Callman's case. See Finlay v. Syme, 1773; M. 6250.
(*c*) Cullen v. Smith, 1845; 8 D. 77. See above, § 1388.

1440. (3.) *Expiration.*—This expires, like all other liens, with the loss of possession; but it is not loss of possession if the title-deeds, etc., are lodged by the agent in process (*a*); nor where the country agent sends papers to town (*b*); nor where the town agent has sent the papers to the country. And when the country agent has papers to retain, he may retain both for his own and for the Edinburgh agent's 'or the parliamentary solicitor's' account (*c*).

(*a*) Callman and Forsyth, *supra*, § 1439 (*b*).
(*b*) 2 Bell's Com. 112.
(*c*) Walker v. Phin, 1831; 9 S. 691; 1 Ill. 463. Kemp v. Youngs, etc., 1838; 16 S. 500. Renny v. Rutherfurd, 1840; 2 D. 676; 1841, 3 D. 1134.

1441. (4.) *Effect.*—It confers no active right, 'and so does not bar the triennial prescription (*a*),' but merely entitles the agent to retain the papers, until either his account shall be paid; or a preference admitted in bankruptcy, if his account be unexceptionable; or security found, 'or consignation made,' if his accounts be disputed 'and the circumstances urgent' (*b*). 'The exercise of the right is subject to the equitable control of the Court (*c*). A law agent is bound to deliver up his client's papers to the trustee in the client's sequestration; but he may reserve his right over them to the effect of obtaining a preference over the funds in the sequestration (*d*).'

(*a*) Mason *v.* E. of Aberdeen, 1709; M. 11,094. Foggo *v.* M'Adam, 1780; M. 6252; Hailes, 875.

(*b*) Johnstone *v.* Bell, 1823; 2 S. 144; 1 Ill. 463. Paul *v.* Mathie, 1826; 4 S. 420. Gilfillan *v.* Henderson, 1828; 6 S. 880. Dobie *v.* Scales, 1831; 9 S. 609. Ferguson & Stuart, *infra* (*c*). Skinner, *infra* (*d*).

(*c*) Ferguson & Stuart *v.* Grant, 1856; 18 D. 536.

(*d*) Johnstone and Paul, *citt.* Skinner *v.* Henderson, 1865; 3 Macph. 867. See Renny *v.* Rutherfurd & Kemp, 1841; 3 D. 1134. Renny & Webster *v.* Myles, 1847; 9 D. 619. Adam & Winchester *v.* White's Tr., 1884; 11 R. 863. 2 Bell's Com. 113 (108, M'L.'s ed.). In a ranking and sale or judicial sale it is for the Court to judge whether it is proper in the interest of the creditors to order production of the titles. Findlay *v.* M'Intosh, 1842; 4 D. 1550; aff. 1845; 4 Bell's App. 361. Clason *v.* Jones, 1847; 9 D. 1512. See also 25 and 26 Vict. c. 89, § 115 (Companies Act). Observe that when an agent lends titles to another upon a borrowing receipt obliging the borrower to return them on demand, he is entitled to have them restored without discussing the validity of his claim to retention, the borrower holding them only for inspection. Crawford *v.* Hodge, 1831; 10 S. 11. Duncan *v.* Fea, 1824; 2 S. 636. Murray *v.* Sinclair, 1847; 2 D. 594, 1194.

1442. The effect of this right against third parties (*a*) is the most extraordinary of the consequences of the principle once admitted. 1. Against personal creditors in bankruptcy, this right is equally effectual as against the client himself (*b*). 2. Against singular successors and heritable creditors an agent may retain the title-deeds of his client, to the effect frequently of defeating their real security (*c*); and in this respect it may be doubted whether the right, admitted at first with great reluctance, has not been carried too far (*d*). 'The law on this point is quite settled, though it will be confined in practice strictly within the limits of former decisions (*e*). It will also be restricted by applying, where the circumstances admit, the principle of personal bar against agents who have been employed in obtaining the security (*f*).' 3. It has even been held effectual to an agent employed by an apparent heir three years in possession of the estate, but who afterwards renounced, against the heritable and personal creditors of the defunct (*g*). 4. It is not effectual by an agent of an heir of entail against 'anyone not representing that heir; as' a creditor of the entailer adjudging (*h*); 'or a substitute heir of entail (*i*). 5. It appears not to be effectual to the agent of one of several joint-owners, or persons having different estates in the same subject (as of fee and liferent), against the others (*k*).'

(*a*) As to a law agent's right to retain a *mortis causa* deed against the beneficiaries and persons claiming under them, see Paul *v.* Meikle, 1868; 7 Macph. 235.

(*b*) Newlands' Crs. *v.* Mackenzie, 1793; M. 6254; 1 Ill. 464. Hotchkis *v.* Thomson, 1794; M. 6256; Bell's Ca. 1. See Menzies *v.* Murdoch, 1841; 4 D. 257.

(*c*) M'Vicar *v.* Lady Kirmin, 1736; Elch. *Hyp.* 3. Lidderdale's Crs. *v.* Naismith, 1749; M. 6248; 1 Ill. 462. Newlands and Hotchkis, *supra* (*b*). Finlay *v.* Syme, 1773; M. 6250; Hailes, 516. Hamilton of Provanhall's Crs., 1781; M. 6253; Hailes, 876. Campbell *v.* Smith, Feb. 1, 1817; F. C. Campbell & Clason *v.* Goldie, 1822; 2 S. 16. Cameron *v.* Burns, 1824; 3 S. 176. Dobie *v.* Scales, 1831; 9 S. 609. See Grant *v.* Bain, 1840; 2 D. 618. Menzies *v.* Murdoch, 1841; 4 D. 257. As to ranking and sale, see Findlay and Clason, *citt.*, above, § 1441.

(*d*) See Rattray *v.* Cruttenden & Co., 1828; 6 S. 568. Campbell, Cameron, etc., *supra* (*c*).

(*e*) Kemp, Renny & Webster, and other cases, *citt.* Callander and Scott, *infra* (*h*), (*i*). Gray *v.* Graham, *supra*, § 1438 (*d*). Smith *v.* Lamont, 1858; 20 D. 912. Malcolm *v.* Carmichael, 1854; 16 D. 825. Cases in (*d*).

(*f*) Wilson *v.* Lumsdaine, 1837; 15 S. 1211. Allan *v.* Sawers, 1842; 4 D. 1356. Paterson *v.* Currie, 1846; 8 D. 1005. Gray *v.* Graham, *supra*, § 1438 (*d*). Inglis *v.* Moncrieff, 1851; 13 D. 622.

(*g*) Cameron, *supra* (*c*).

(*h*) Callander *v.* Laidlaw, 1834; 12 S. 417.

(*i*) Scott & Gillespie *v.* Thomson, 1854; 17 D. 124. Murray *v.* Elibank, 1829; 8 S. 161.

(*k*) Smith *v.* Lamont, 1858; 20 D. 912. Campbell & Clason, and Scott & Gillespie, *citt.*

1443. It has been much questioned whether the agent is bound to allow inspection of the deeds, or entitled absolutely to withhold them. The rules seem to be these: 1. A third party is entitled to have the retained deeds exhibited in evidence of a fact, or in support of a right adverse to the client; but not to have them produced to be used as a title in any right derived from the client (*a*). 2. That the client himself is not entitled to have them produced even in *modum probationis* (*b*). 3. That although creditors and others deriving right through the client cannot insist on having possession of title-deeds which the client himself cannot insist for, a substitute heir of entail is not precluded from inspection of the title-deeds by the right of retention pleadable against the heir in possession (*c*).

(*a*) Dalrymple *v.* E. of Selkirk, 1751; Elch. *Hyp.* 17; 1 Ill. 465. See Montgomerie *v.* A. B., 1845; 7 D. 53. Paul *v.* Meikle, 1868; 7 Macph. 235. M'Intosh *v.* Chalmers, 1883; 11 R. 8.

(*b*) Finlay, *supra*, § 1442 (*c*). See Ferguson & Stuart *v.* Grant, 1856; 18 D. 536.

(*c*) Murray *v.* Scott, 1829; 8 S. 161.

1444. (5.) *Waiver.*—The agent's right of retention may be waived, but this must be done expressly. It is not to be presumed that it is the intention of the parties to waive it; nor inferred from the agent taking a bond, bill, or other security for the amount of his account (*a*), unless a long term of payment has been fixed, in which case it is not to be supposed that the parties intended the titles to be confined during so long a time (*b*).

(*a*) Ayton *v.* Colville, 1705; M. 6247, 6710; 1 Ill. 465. Linning *v.* Douglas, 1821; 1 S. 90. Skinner *v.* Paterson, May 21, 1823; 2 S. 354, and F. C.; 1 Ill. 462. See Renny *v.* Rutherfurd, 1841; 3 D. 1134. Gray *v.* Graham, 1855; 2 Macq. 435. M'Creadie *v.* Reid, 1822; 1 S. 367; 1 Ill. 466. Gairdner *v.* Milne & Co., 1858; 20 D. 565. Hewison *v.* Guthrie, 2 Bing. N. C. 755. Palmer *v.* Lee, 1880; 7 R. 651.

(*b*) See Cowell *v.* Simpson, 16 Ves. Jr. 283; 10 R. R. 181; 1 Ill. 466. Hewison, *cit.* Cases in § 1418 (*e*), and 2 Bell's Com. 114 (109, M'L.'s ed.).

1445. Factor's Retention.—Much of the foreign trade of the country is carried on by means of factors (*a*), and is greatly promoted by the factor having a general lien, entitling him, without insisting on payment or retention for each transaction, to rely on a right of retention in the end for the general balance that may be due to him. This right might almost be ranked among the special liens, from the peculiar nature of the contract of factory, as a right resulting out of the *actio contraria* of the contract by which the principal engages to indemnify the factor. Both in England and in Scotland an implied agreement is held to subsist, that for the balance which shall arise on his general account (whether consisting of advances on the particular goods, or of money paid for the principal, or of duties on other goods, or in whatever way arising), the factor shall have security by retention or lien over all the goods and effects of the principal which, coming into his possession as factor (*b*), may be in his actual or civil possession at the time the demand for the balance is made (*c*).

(*a*) As to non-mercantile factors, see 3 Ersk. 4. § 21. Wright's Trs. *v.* Allan, 1840; 3 D. 243. Largue *v.* Urquhart, 1883; 10 R. 1229.

(*b*) See § 1448 (*b*).

(*c*) 1 Stair, 18. § 7. 3 Ersk. 4. § 21. 2 Bell's Com. 114 (109, M'L.'s ed.). Chalmers *v.* Bassily, 1666; M. 9137; 1 Ill. 467. Stephens *v.* Crs. of York Buildings Co., 1735; M. 9140. Kruger *v.* Wilcox, cited in Godin, 1 Burr. 494; Ambler, 252; 1 Dick. 269; Tudor's L. C. 353. Sibbald *v.* Gibson & Clark, 1852; 15 D. 217.

1446. (1.) *To whom given.*—This general lien is given only to factors—not to a wharfinger (*a*), 'nor to a storekeeper (*b*),' nor to a broker (*c*), nor even to a broker who also acts as factor (*d*); the combination of the two characters in the same person not entitling him to extend the lien from dealings in the one character to dealings in the other. And although a factor may assign over his lien to another, or may, by consigning to a sub-factor, without notice of his being himself a factor, and taking advances from such sub-factor on the credit of the goods, raise a lien for those advances, which will be effectual against his principal, there is no resulting lien to such sub-factor for the general balance due to him by the primary factor (*e*).

(*a*) Monk *v.* Whittenbury, 2 B. & Ad. 484; 1 Ill. 467; 36 R. R. 637. Richardson *v.* Goss, 3 B. & P. 119; 1 Ill. 380; 6 R. R. 727. See above, § 1434.

(*b*) Lawrie *v.* Anderson (Denny's Tr.), 1853; 15 D. 404. *Supra*, § 1434.

(*c*) M'Call & Co. *v.* Black & Co., 1824; 2 S. App. 188.

(*d*) Same case. Dixon *v.* Stansfeld, 10 C. B. 398.

(*e*) Colquhoun *v.* Findlay, Duff, & Co., Nov. 15, 1816; F. C. Ede & Bond *v.* Findlay, Duff, & Co., May 15, 1818; F. C. Johnston *v.* Scott & Co., Nov. 14, 1818; F. C. Johnson & Manly, 1819. M'Call & Co., *supra* (*c*), as decided in the Court of Session, and not invalidated by the decision in the House of Lords; 1 Bell's Com. 485 (519, M'L.'s ed.).

1447. (2.) *Subjects.*—The factor's lien extends over goods and property sent to him by the principal; goods bought for the principal; bills, policies of insurance, etc., of the principal, which have come into the factor's hands as factor, and are still in his actual possession, or in the hands of others under his orders; and the price of goods sold and demandable by him as factor (*a*). But things under special appropriation are excepted (*b*). So are goods which the factor has sold, and which he cannot be allowed to retain against the purchaser for any balance due by the principal (*c*). If, indeed, he have sold them while under a *del credere* commission, he may be entitled to retain or to stop *in transitu* against the purchaser, the price being unpaid. But if the bill for the price has been paid, or has been indorsed to the principal, and settled by him with the purchaser, by composition or otherwise, the factor cannot retain against the purchaser on pretence of the guarantee to cover his general balance (*d*).

(*a*) Stephens *v.* Crs. of York Buildings Co., 1735; M. 9140; 1 Ill. 469. Drinkwater *v.* Goodwin, Cowp. 251. Jourdain *v.* Lefevre, 1 Esp. 66. See 1 Burr. 493, 494. Hudson *v.* Grainger, 5 B. & Ald. 27; 3 Ill. 151; 24 R. R. 268. See above, § 1417; Miller & Paterson *v.* M'Nair,

1852; 14 D. 955. Gairdner *v.* Milne & Co., 1858; 20 D. 565 (proceeds of policy of insurance). Scott & Neill *v.* Smith & Co., 1883; 11 R. 317 (goods rejected by purchaser, and held by seller's agent).

(*b*) See above, § 1414. 1 Bell's Com. 262. Davis *v.* Bowsher, 5 T. R. 588; 2 R. R. 650. 2 Bell's Com. 119.

(*c*) Stirling & Sons *v.* Duncan, 1823; 1 S. App. 389.

(*d*) Stirling, *supra* (*c*).

1448. (3.) *Extent of the Lien.*—It covers all salary; commission; expenses; advances of cash; engagements and guarantees which the principal is aware of, or has authorised. But it will not cover debts due previous to the factory; nor debts afterwards assigned to the factor by creditors of the principal, unless where he has, at the principal's desire, interposed to pay the debts (*a*); 'nor debts incurred in transactions extrinsic to the factorial relation (*b*).'

(*a*) Pearson *v.* Crichton, 1672; M. 2625; 1 Ill. 471. Marsh *v.* Chambers, 2 Strange, 1234. Houghton *v.* Matthews, 3 B. & P. 485; 7 R. R. 815. Sibbald *v.* Gibson & Clark, 1852; 15 D. 217.

(*b*) Miller & Paterson *v.* M'Nair, 1852; 14 D. 955. Dixon *v.* Stansfeld, 10 C. B. 398. Addison on Contracts, 474.

1449. (4.) *Possession Requisite.*—The lien depends on possession, 'which may be by others under the factor's orders (*a*)'; but the regaining of possession by fair means, in the course of the factory, will restore the lien; differently from the rule in the common case of retention. This is a consequence of the broader right on which a factor's lien rests (*b*).

(*a*) Wilmot *v.* Wilson, 1841; 3 D. 815.

(*b*) Whitehead *v.* Vaughan, Cook's B. L. 547; 1 Ill. 452; 8 R. R. 524 n. This decision may be questionable, in so far as the possession was not recovered fairly. See above, § 1416, and 2 Bell's Com. 95, 117 (90, 112, M'L.'s ed.).

1450. (5.) *Factor's Powers.*—The power which a factor has now by statute in England, he has always had at common law in Scotland. He may pledge as well as sell (*a*). A factor sells either as factor (as when his invoice bears, "A., debtor to B. as factor for C. D.," or "C. D., debtor to A. by D."), or in his own name without mention of the factory. In both cases he has lien over the price not to be defeated by the principal. Where no balance is due to the factor for which a lien can be claimed, the principal has action for the price in preference to the factor's creditors. When the factor has sold in his own name, concealing the principal, the buyer may set off a debt due to him by the factor, against the principal's demand for the price (*b*).

(*a*) See above, § 1364. 6 Geo. IV. c. 94.

(*b*) Warner *v.* M'Kay, 2 Gale, 86; 1 M. & W. 591. See above, § 224A, 573 (4), 1317A.

1451. Banker's Retention.—A banker is a money factor, and in all cases where he acts as agent he has a right of retention, extending over all unappropriated paper in his hands belonging (*a*) to customers, for security of his balance on the general account (*b*): but not including bills discounted (*c*), or bills appropriated, 'such as bills indorsed to him for the special purpose of negotiation' (*d*), 'or securities known to belong truly to the customer's principals (*e*).' The practice in Scotland is to indorse bills sent to a banker; and if taken to account, or credit be given, it is held a discount, and the bill belongs to the banker, and on his bankruptcy goes to his creditors; but if not taken to account or credit, but intended to lie for recovery as agent, the banker has a lien for his balance, and on his bankruptcy his creditors have no right to take the bills as his (*f*). 'Banking companies generally and other companies may have (*g*) by their constitution a lien over their own stock, in security of advances made to shareholders (*h*). The banker's lien does not cover debts not yet due, if the debtor be neither bankrupt nor *vergens ad inopiam* (*i*).'

(*a*) See **Brandao** *v.* **Barnett**, 12 Cl. & F. 787; 3 C. B. 519. Farrar & Rooth *v.* N. B. Bkg. Co., 1850; 12 D. 1190. Attwood *v.* Kinnear & Co., 1832; 10 S. 817. It does not extend over boxes containing securities belonging to their customer, of which he retains the key. Leese *v.* Martin, L. R. 17 Eq. 224; 43 L. J. Ch. 193.

(*b*) 2 Bell's Com. 118. Jourdain *v.* Lefevre, 1 Esp. 66; 1 Ill. 469. Davis *v.* Bowsher, 5 T. R. 588. Robertson's Tr. *v.* Royal Bank, 1890; 18 R. 12.

(*c*) Carstairs *v.* Bates, 3 Camp. 301. Giles *v.* Perkins, 9 East, 12. Thompson *v.* Giles, 2 B. & C. 422; 26 R. R. 392, 400. Patten, *infra* (*f*).

(*d*) Haig *v.* Buchanan, 1823; 2 S. 412. Matheson *v.* Anderson, 1822; 1 S. 486. Borthwick *v.* Bremner, 1833; 12 S. 121. See above, § 1414. Brandao *v.* Barnett, *supra* (*a*). Vanderzee *v.* Willis, 3 Br. Ch. Ca. 21. It is not enough to exclude the general lien that a security appears to have been deposited to cover a special advance. Jones *v.* Peppercorn, Johns. 430; 28 L. J. Ch. 153. *In re* European Bank, L. R. 8 Ch. 41. London Chart Bk. of Australia *v.* White, 4 App. Ca. 413; 48 L. J. P. C. 75.

(*e*) Natl. Bk. *v.* Dickie's Tr., 1895; 22 R. 740. See Misa *v.* Currie, 1 App. Ca. 544; 45 L. J. Ex. 414. Cf. Gray's Trs. *v.* Royal Bank, 1895; 23 R. 199.

(*f*) *Ex p.* Sargeant, 1 Rose, 153. Carstairs, *supra* (*c*). Glen *v.* Natl. Bank, 1849; 12 D. 353. Farrar & Rooth, *cit.* (*a*). Patten *v.* Royal Bank, 1853; 15 D. 617.

(*g*) Bank of Africa *v.* Salisbury Gold Mining Co., 1892; A. C. 281. Bell's Tr. *v.* Coatbridge Tinplate Co., 1886; 14 R. 246.

(*h*) Burns *v.* Laurie's Trs., 1840; 2 D. 1348. Hague *v.* Dandesan, 2 Ex. 741; 17 L. J. Ex. 769. *In re* London & Birm. Bank, 34 L. J. Ch. 418; 34 Beav. 332. Murray *v.* Pinkett, 12 Cl. & F. 764. *In re* Stockton Malleable Iron

Co., 2 Ch. D. 101; 45 L. J. Ch. 168. *In re* Gen. Exch. Bank (*re* Lewis), L. R. 6 Ch. 818; 40 L. J. Ch. 429. New London & Brazil Bank *v.* Brocklebank, 51 L. J. Ch. 404, 711. *In re* Hoylake Ry. Co. (*ex p.* Littledale), L. R. 9 Ch. 257; 43 L. J. Ch. 529; *ex p.* Stringer, 9 Q. B. D. 436. 8 and 9 Vict. c. 17, § 16 (Comp. Clauses Act); 25 and 26 Vict. c. 10, Sched. I. cl. 10.

(*i*) Paul & Thain *v.* Royal Bank, 1869; 7 Macph. 361. See Ireland *v.* North of Sc. Bkg. Co., 1880; 8 R. 215 (refusal to pay cheque from money lodged on current account).

1452. Policy Broker's Retention.—This also is a factor's lien. It entitles the broker, on the principles of bankruptcy, 'even though the principal himself be an agent, if the broker have not notice that he is so (*a*),' to retain the policy, and also to retain sums paid to him for a loss; but not to recover under the policy, unless he hold a special power so to do (*b*); nor to retain the premium 'on the bankruptcy of the underwriter,' or apply it in double insurances to indemnify the assured (*c*).

(*a*) Westwood *v.* Bell, 4 Camp. 349; 16 R. R. 800; 2 Bell's Com. 121 (116, M'L.'s ed.). Addison, Contr. 475. If the broker know that he is dealing with an agent, he has still a particular lien for premium and charges on each policy. Fisher *v.* Smith, 4 App. Ca. 1; 48 L. J. Ex. 411. Losh, Wilson, & Bell *v.* Douglas & Co., 1857; 20 D. 58. 2 Bell's Com. 122 (116, M'L.'s ed.).

(*b*) 2 Bell's Com. 120 (115, M'L's ed.). Whitehead *v.* Vaughan, *cit.*, § 1449. Levy *v.* Barnard, 8 Taunt. 149; 1 Ill. 437; 19 R. R. 484. Leslie & Thomson *v.* Linn, 1783; M. 2627. Wilmot *v.* Wilson, 1841; 3 D. 815.

(*c*) Selkrig *v.* Pitcairn & Scott, 1805; M. *Insur.* Apx. 10; 2 Bell's Com. 121 (116, M'L.'s ed.).

1453. Trustee's Retention.—This rests on the presumed agreement to make advances or undertake responsibilities on the security of the trust estate (*a*).

(*a*) E. Bedford *v.* L. Balmerino, 1662; M. 9135; 1 Ill. 474. Dougall's Crs., 1794; Bell's Ca. 41; 1 Ill. 440. Wight *v.* Kidd, 1828; 7 S. 70. See below, § 1996, 1998 (10); and above, § 912, 1367. Brodie *v.* Wilson, 1837; 15 S. 1195. Robertson *v.* Duff, 1840; 2 D. 279. Henderson *v.* Norrie, 1866; 4 Macph. 691.

1454. Cautioner's Retention.—This is a general lien, which originally was admitted on the footing of a presumed agreement, to one who, having goods in his hand belonging to another, or being due money to him, engaged as cautioner for him. Afterwards it was extended even to goods or money coming into the cautioner's hand after having engaged as cautioner (*a*).

(*a*) Town of Aberdeen *v.* Strachan, 1709; M. 2570; 1 Ill. 474. Innes *v.* Leslie, 1635; M. 2620. M. Clydesdale *v.* Cochrane, 1729; M. 2689. Balfour *v.* Lazini, 1746; M. 2575. Murray's Crs. *v.* Chalmers, 1744; M. 2626. Brough's Crs. *v.* Jollie, 1793 and 1795; M. 2585; Bell's Ca. 191; 1 Ill. 440. 2 Bell's Com. 123 (118, M'L.'s ed.). D. Queensberry's Exrs. *v.* Tait, 1822; 1 S. 428. Brodie *v.* Wilson, and Robertson *v.* Duff, *citt.* Christie *v.* Keith, 1838; 16 S. 1224 (cautioner's lien subsists after debt ranked on principal debtor's estate). M'Pherson *v.* Wright, 1885; 12 R. 942.

CHAPTER IX

OF WRITTEN TRANSFERENCE OF MOVEABLES; AND OF ASSIGNATION OF DEBTS

I. WRITTEN TRANSFERENCE OF MOVEABLES.

1455. When Writing required.—It is sometimes necessary from circumstances to employ writing in the transference of moveables. On some occasions it is requisite in law; and in others it is usual, but not essential.

1456. (1.) *Consignment of Goods.*—Writing is necessary in consignment 'of goods' from a distance. By means of correspondence, bill of lading, written mandate to a factor, etc., goods consigned to a distant place are appropriated to certain persons. The property is thus effectually vested in those who are declared to have the beneficial interest, and who have notice of it (*a*). On the bankruptcy of the consignor after notice, his creditors cannot take the consigned goods, nor can the consignee claim lien over them to the prejudice of the person receiving the notice. The consignee becomes, on notice, the custodier of the person for whom the goods are sent (*b*).

(*a*) As to notice, see Arnott *v.* Drysdale, 1863 ; 1 Macph. 796.

(*b*) 2 Bell's Com. 12. Stonehewer *v.* Inglis, 1697 ; M. 7724 ; 1 Ill. 475. Gray *v.* L. Ross, 1706 ; M. 7724. Arthur *v.* Hastie & Jamieson, 1770 ; Hailes, 258, 381 ; M. 14,209 ; 2 Pat. 251 ; 2 Bell's Com. 12. Hunter & Co.'s Tr. *v.* Hamilton's Tr., 1791 ; Bell's Ca. 385. Auchterlony's Crs., 1732 ; M. 7737. Fisher *v.* Miller, 1 Bing. 150 ; 25 R. R. 607. Hodgson *v.* Anderson, 3 B. & Cr. 842. Pearson, Wilson, & Co. *v.* Brock, 1842 ; 4 D. 1509. See below, § 1465 (*h*), (*i*) ; and above, § 1305 *fin.* Brown, Shipley, & Co. *v.* Kough, 29 Ch. D. 848.

1457. (2.) *Writing required by Statute.*—Writing is by statute requisite, in order to pass the property completely of goods in a bond warehouse in the actual possession of the owner of the goods (*a*). It is also required in conveying a patent, or the property of a book or copyright (*b*); and in transferring ships, writing is requisite in the vendition or mortgage (*c*).

(*a*) See above, § 1306, 1378. (*b*) See above, § 1361. (*c*) See above, § 1330.

1458. (3.) *Usage.*—Writing is commonly used in complicating transactions, involving a transfer of moveables; or where the conveyance is of a *universitas*; or where the intention is to create a security. But such conveyance is not held effectual, without delivery, to exclude purchasers or creditors poinding. And momentary delivery of possession, together with an instrument of possession, will not be sufficient if the actual possession be returned to, and left with the owner (*a*).

(*a*) Thomson *v.* Chirnside, 1558 ; M. 827 ; 1 Ill. 476. Corbet *v.* Stirling, 1666 ; M. 10,602. See above, § 1314 sqq.

II. ASSIGNATION OF DEBTS.

1459. Principle.—The *jus crediti* in debts being such as cannot be transferred by delivery, the principle on which this transference is accomplished is that of the conversion of the engagement to pay to the original creditor, into an obligation to pay to the assignee. It most resembles the change of custody in the transferring of corporeal moveables (*a*). There was at first no power implied in debts, to substitute another creditor for the original one. To evade which, in practice, it was usual to take bonds in blank; but this was afterwards prohibited (*b*): or to take a mandate from the original creditor, empowering the assignee to demand and discharge the debt; such mandate (as "in rem suam") being held, contrary to the ordinary case of mandates, to be irrevocable (*c*). The latter is the form of assignation at present,—a mandate with cession and surrogation into the cedent's place. The assignee's right is completed by notice or intimation to the debtor (*d*).

Debts which are extinguished cannot be assigned (*e*); 'nor perhaps those which have not begun to exist (*f*).'

'The institutional writers and judges have not limited the creditor's power of assigning debts and contracts, except in cases where it is barred by the nature of the subject, by immemorial custom, or by the principle of *delectus personæ* (*g*), the most obvious examples of which occur in the law of leases and partnership. Assignation of contracts is excluded wherever the contract involves personal confidence, or where personal considerations are of the essence of the agreement, or its terms or nature and circumstances show that it was to be fulfilled on one or both sides only by the parties themselves (*h*).'

(*a*) 3 Stair, 1. § 2, 3, etc. 3 Ersk. 5. § 2. 2 Bell's Com. 16.
(*b*) 1696, c. 25. As to writs blank in the creditor's name, see 3 Ersk. 2. § 6. Duncan's Trs. *v.* Shand, 1872; 10 Macph. 984. Clapperton, Paton, & Co. *v.* Anderson, 1881; 8 R. 1004.
(*c*) Stair and Ersk. *ut supra*. 3 Ersk. 3. § 40. Struthers *v.* Commercial Bank, 1842; 4 D. 460 (*per* L. Fullerton). Ritchie *v.* M'Lachlan, 1870; 8 Macph. 815. See above, § 228.
(*d*) 3 Ersk. 5. § 3. Buchan *v.* Farquharson, 1797; M. 2905; 1 Bell's Com. 289 (308, M'L.'s ed.); 1 Ill. 476.
(*e*) See above, § 555 et seq. Jackson *v.* Nicoll, 1870; 8 Macph. 408.
(*f*) Bedwells & Yates *v.* Tod, Dec. 2, 1819; F. C. (assignation of legacy intimated to executor during testator's life). See, however, Percy *v.* Clements, 43 L. J. C. P. 155. Brice *v.* Bannister, 3 Q. B. D. 569; 47 L. J. Q. B. 722. Holroyd *v.* Marshall, 10 H. L. Ca. 191; 33 L. J. Ch. 193. *Ex p.* Nichols, *in re* Jones & Barber, 22 Ch. D. 782. Campbell's Trs. *v.* Whyte, 1884; 11 R. 1078. See also § 1461 (*h*).
(*g*) 3 Ersk. 5. § 2. 3 Stair, 1. § 2; 1. 10. § 16, etc.
(*h*) See § 358, 1214; and as to contracts of service and apprenticeship, § 179, etc., Fraser, M. & S. 122, 361 sqq. In the recent case of Grierson, Oldham, & Co. *v.* Forbes, Maxwell, & Co., 1895; 22 R. 812, the discussion of certain subtleties of English law appears to be out of place, unless the judges intended to construe an English contract. The English decision which is said to have been followed has been questioned in England, and ought not to be regarded as laying down for Scotland the very wide rule for which it is quoted. See Benjamin on Sale, pp. 61, 371. Pollock on Contracts, 436.

1460. Kinds of Debts.—Debts are either such as are incorporated (*a*) with the document, as in the case of bills and notes; or such as are independent of the document by which they may be proved. The former pass by indorsation (*b*); the latter require a written assignation and notice. Assignation is necessary to convey diligence (*c*), and also dividends (*d*). Indorsation of a bill on which diligence has been done or dividends declared, will not give right to them.

(*a*) See Savigny, Obligationenrecht, § 62. Pollock on Contracts, 234 sqq.
(*b*) See Bovill *v.* Dixon, 1854; 16 D. 519; rev. 1856, 3 Macq. 1. Commercial Bank *v.* Kennard, 1859; 21 D. 864. Connal & Co. *v.* Loder, 1868; 6 Macph. 1095.
(*c*) Gordon *v.* Richardson & Co., 1806; 2 Bell's Com. 19; 1 Ill. 482. Frier *v.* Richardson & Co., 1806; M. Apx. *Bill*, 19. See above, § 331; below, § 1467.
(*d*) Wallace, Hamilton, & Co. *v.* Campbell, 1821; 1 S. 53; aff. 1824, 2 S. App. 467.

1461. Deed of Assignation.—The deed of assignation contains words of transference and cession of the bond or other document, and of the debt therein contained (*a*); with a surrogation of the assignee into the creditor's place, and power to uplift and discharge (*b*). 'Words directly importing assignation or conveyance are not indispensable; any words giving authority or directions which, if fairly carried out, will operate a transference are sufficient to make an assignation (*c*). So a bill operates, when presented, as an assignation of funds of the drawer in the hands of the drawee (*d*), and if accepted "payable at" a banker's, operates on presentment as an intimated assignation of the acceptor's monies in the bank (*e*). An order to pay, written upon or referring to an open account or other debt due by a third party to the writer, has always been accounted within this principle (*f*). Unless the sum be certain, such an order is not a bill (see § 311); and it has been thought that it requires an assignation stamp (10s.) (*g*).

'One who assigns a thing or an obligation which is not his, assigns all the rights which he has to make it his; and the law implies that a cedent confers on his assignee everything that is necessary to make his assignation effectual (*h*).'

(*a*) See M'Cutcheon *v.* M'William, 1876; 3 R. 565.
(*b*) 3 Stair, 1. § 4. Farquhar *v.* Hunters, 1715; M. 16,467; 1 Ill. 477.
(*c*) Carter *v.* M'Intosh, 1862; 24 D. 925.

(*d*) Watt's Trs. *v.* Pinkney, 1853; 16 D. 279; and other authorities in § 311 (*a*), *supra*.

(*e*) Brit. Lin. Co. *v.* Rainey's Tr., 1885; 12 R. 825. See Chalmers on Bills, 235.

(*f*) See **Carter** *v.* **M'Intosh** and other cases in § 1465, *infra*, especially those in note (*h*). See also 1 Stair, 12. § 1; Brodie's Stair, p. 416 note; 2 Bell's Com. 20 (19, M'L.'s ed.). Dicta in Ritchie *v.* M'Lachlan, 1870; 8 Macph. 815, which appear to require recognition by the debtor in the case of such a procuratory or mandate *in rem suam*, can refer to recognition only as evidence of intimation. To require recognition by the debtor as a condition of the transference of the right is altogether erroneous, for the transference is by assignation or procuratory *in rem suam*, which in the civil law and ours are identical in operation, and require no consent of the debtor. L. 3 Cod. *de her. vel. act. vend.* (4. 39). L. 1 Cod. *de Novat.* (8. 42). Donell. Com. xv. 64. 12. In all our books there is no other passage which even suggests that the debtor's concurrence has anything to do with the matter. See in the Sheriff Courts, A. B. *v.* Inglis, 1892; 9 Sh. Ct. R. 165 (erroneously reading Ritchie *v.* M'Lachlan), and Smith *v.* Paterson, 1894; 10 Sh. Ct. Ca. 171, where Sheriff Balfour explains the correct principle.

(*g*) See Lawrie *v.* Ogilvy, 6 Feb. 1810; F. C.

(*h*) Miller *v.* Muirhead, 1894; 21 R. 658 (*per* Lord R. Clark).

1461A. '*Transmission of Moveables Act.*—An Act of Parliament was passed in 1862 for the purpose of abbreviating and simplifying the forms of transmission of moveable estate in Scotland. It provides forms of assignation which may be used in the transmission of personal bonds or conveyances of moveable estate, but not of moveable estate to which the owner has not already a conveyance or assignation. It is applicable to bonds and assignations of every kind, decrees, policies of assurance, protests of bills, etc.; and the moveable estate affected by it includes "all personal debts and obligations, and moveable or personal property or effects of any kind." The form of assignation provided simply states the consideration, and assigns the bond or other deed described; any connecting title or other circumstances regarding the nature and extent of the right assigned being a necessary part of the description of the deed. The assignation may be either a separate writ, or written upon the bond or conveyance itself. It is registrable in the books of any Court, in terms of any clause of registration contained in the bond or conveyance assigned; and upon intimation has the same effect as an intimated assignation under the old form (*a*).'

(*a*) 25 and 26 Vict. c. 75, § 1, 4. See M. Bell's Convg. 296 sqq. Craigie, Law of Convg. 236 sqq.

1462. Intimation.—There are two points in the doctrine of intimation; the interruption of *bona fides* on the part of the debtor, and the completion of the transference. Intimation is necessary for both purposes, not merely to give preference in competition, but as a step of diligence to complete the assignee's right (*a*). Assignation is completed by intimation, even though the deed of assignation should not itself be delivered (*b*). 'Even an unintimated assignation, if delivered, is valid against the granter, who cannot dispute his own deed, and against his personal representatives (*c*). But a special provision in the Bankruptcy Act, giving the trustee's confirmation the effect of an intimated assignation, prevents such an assignation from receiving effect against the creditors in a sequestration (*d*).'

(*a*) Drummond *v.* Muschet, 1492; M. 843; 1 Ill. 477. Meldrum *v.* L. Anstruther, 1622; M. 844. Wallace *v.* Edgar, 1663; M. 837. Fraser *v.* Fraser, 1678; M. 844. Thom *v.* Thom, 1683; 2 B. Sup. 49. M'Dowal *v.* Fullarton, 1714; M. 840. Campbell's Trs. *v.* Whyte, 1884; 11 R. 1078.

(*b*) M'Lurg *v.* Blackwood, 1680; M. 845; 1 Ill. 477. See 3 Ersk. Pr. 5. § 2.

(*c*) 3 Ersk. 5. § 3. Grant *v.* Gray (Lillie's Trs. *v.* Suter's Tr.), 1828; 6 S. 489.

(*d*) 19 and 20 Vict. c. 79, § 102, 111. But for this provision there might be room for contending, notwithstanding some authorities (Sinclair *v.* Sinclair, 1726; M. 2793. Montgomerie Bell's Convg. 307, etc.), that the trustee takes the bankrupt estate subject to the bankrupt's obligation. See below, § 1468. On the other hand, it seems that an unintimated assignation may be defeated by diligence at the instance of individual creditors of the assignor. 3 Ersk. 5. § 3. As to this, however, see below, § 1468, and the English cases (Pickering *v.* Ilfracombe Ry. Co., L. R. 3 C. P. 235; 37 L. J. C. P. 118, etc.), as stated in Pollock on Contracts, 229. Addison on Contracts, 1271. *Inf.* § 2278A.

1463. Regular intimation is made by the assignee giving notice, in presence of a notary and witnesses, to the debtor personally, or at his dwelling-house (or to the treasurer of an incorporation); the procurator of the assignee reading the deed of assignment of the special debt, or leaving a written schedule or copy of it; the date of such intimation being the criterion of preference in all competitions and questions on bankruptcy (*a*). If the debtor be out of Scotland, the intimation must be at the Record Office of Citations (*b*).

(*a*) 3 Ersk. 5. § 3, 5. Scott *v.* L. Drumlanrig, 1628; M. 846; 1 Ill. 477. Lawrie *v.* Hay, 1696; M. 849. Keir *v.* Menzies' Crs., 1739; M. 738, 850; 5 B. Sup. 656; Elch. *Arrest.* 10 (intimation to treasurer of corporation). Watson *v.* Murdoch, 1755; M. 850.

(*b*) 6 Geo. IV. c. 120, § 51. 1 and 2 Vict. c. 118. A. of S., July 11, 1828; December 24, 1838. An opinion is expressed by Professor Montgomerie Bell (Conveyancing, 312), that the forms of intimation provided by the Act of 1862 (*infra*, § 1464A) are applicable even where the debtor is abroad.

1464. The legitimate and regular proof of intimation is by a notarial instrument, duly authenticated, bearing the fact of notice to the debtor. It is an *actus legitimus*, and must be correct in form and authentication.

1464A. 'While the old forms of intimation are not abolished, the Act of 1862 already mentioned provides that an assignation shall be validly intimated, (1) by a notary-public delivering to the debtor a certified copy before two witnesses, the evidence of which is a certificate by the notary in a statutory form, either apart or written on the assignation; or (2) by the holder of the assignation, or anyone authorised by him, transmitting a certified copy by post to the debtor; in which case the debtor's written acknowledgment of the receipt of the copy is sufficient evidence of intimation. If the deed containing the assignation contain other conveyances or trust purposes, a copy of the part respecting "the subject-matter of the assignation" is enough (*a*). When a corporation is the debtor, intimation ought to be made to the treasurer (*b*): or in the case of an incorporated bank, both to the manager at the head office, and to the agent at the branch where the money is lying or payable (*c*). In the case of companies registered under the Companies Act, 1862, it may be left or sent by post addressed to the company at their registered office (*d*). To railway companies it may be made in the same way, at the principal office, or to the secretary, or if there be no secretary, to one of the directors (*e*). Intimation, in the case of ordinary partnerships, ought to be made to all partners, unless a manager be formally appointed: intimation to one who is *de facto* managing partner is not sufficient (*f*).'

(*a*) 25 and 26 Vict. c. 85, § 2.
(*b*) Keir *v.* Menzies' Crs., *cit.* § 1463.
(*c*) M. Bell's Convg. 313.
(*d*) 25 and 26 Vict. c. 89, § 62.
(*e*) 8 and 9 Vict. c. 17, § 137. 8 and 9 Vict. c. 33, § 130.
(*f*) Hill *v.* Lindsay, 1846; 8 D. 472. See Watson *v.* Murdoch, *cit.* § 1463. Hill *v.* Lindsay, 1847; 10 D. 78. But see 53 & 54 Vict. c. 39, § 16. As to trustees, see Watt's Trs., § 1465 (*h*). Miller *v.* Learmonth, 1870; 42 S. Jur. 418 (H. L.). Jameson *v.* Sharp, 1887; 14 R. 643. As to building societies, see Grigor Allan *v.* Urquhart, 1887; 15 R. 56.

1465. But, 'apart from the Act of 1862,' notarial interposition is not in all cases necessary: so judicial notice is sufficient, 'as by execution of a summons by the assignee, or lodging a claim in a multiplepoinding in which the debtor is a party (*a*). The assignation to rents in a heritable security is intimated to the debtor's tenants by service of an action of maills and duties (*b*), but not by service of a poinding of the ground (*c*).' And if the debtor be a party to the assignation, it is enough (*d*). Acknowledgment of notice in writing on the back of the assignation, or by letter, 'which proves its own date, contrary to the usual rule in holograph writings,' is sufficient (*e*); but a letter written to the debtor is not sufficient (*f*). A promise to pay, if proved by writing, is sufficient (*g*). So a draft accepted, or presented and protested, 'or presented and a demand made,' is equivalent to an assignation duly intimated when the drawee is debtor in a money debt (*h*); not so when he has only effects in his hand; though it would seem that such draft would, as an assignment, affect the proceeds, when realised, of goods in the drawee's hands at the presentment, if there be no mid-impediment (*i*). Partial payment, or payment of interest 'to the assignee,' is 'proof of' notice (*k*); but mere private knowledge is not 'pleadable as equivalent to notice in a competition (*l*),' though such knowledge legitimately proved is a sufficient bar to the debtor's paying to the cedent (*m*). 'Registration in the books of Council and Session is not equivalent to intimation (*n*); but registration in the Register of Sasines, etc., is sufficient (*o*).''

(*a*) White *v.* Neish, 1622; M. 854; 1 Ill. 478. Elphinston *v.* Ord, 1624; M. 858. Ogilvie *v.* Ogilvie, 1681; M. 863. Dougal *v.* Gordon, 1795; M. 851. Campbell *v.* Campbell, 1861; 23 D. 159. **Carter** *v.* **M'Intosh,** 1862; 24 D. 925.
(*b*) Chambers' Factor *v.* Vertue, 1892; 20 R. 257.
(*c*) Royal Bank *v.* Dixon, 1868; 6 Macph. 995. Lang *v.* Hislop, 1854; 16 D. 908.
(*d*) Turnbull *v.* Stewart & Inglis, 1751; M. 868.
(*e*) M'Gill *v.* Hutcheson, 1630; M. 860. See Gray *v.* D. of Hamilton, 1708; Robertson's Ap. 1; 2 Bell's Com. 19. E. of Aberdeen *v.* E. of March, 1730; Cr. & St. Ap. 44. Newton & Co. *v.* Collogan, 1785; M. 850. Wallace *v.* Davies, 1853; 15 D. 688.
(*f*) Bayne *v.* Cunningham, 1679; M. 863.
(*g*) Home *v.* Murray, 1674; M. 863. 3 Ersk. 5. § 4. 2 Bell's Com. 18.
(*h*) Mitchel *v.* Mitchel, 1734; M. 1464. Gavin *v.* Kippen, 1768; M. 1495. Spottiswood *v.* M'Neill, 1778; M. 1495. Falconer *v.* Campbell, 1824; 2 S. 534. Brierly *v.* Mackintosh, 1843; 5 D. 1100; aff. 5 Bell's App. 1. Watt's Trs. *v.* Pinkney, 1853; 16 D. 279 (intimation to body of trustees—bill or draft). B. L. Bank *v.* Carruthers & Fergusson, 1883; 10 R. 923 (cheque refused for want of "sufficient funds" passes the right to the smaller sum at the drawer's credit). See above, § 308 (*a*), 311 (*a*), 1461. Brodie's Stair, p. 419.

(*i*) Stewart *v.* Ewing, 1744 ; M. 1493. See above, § 311, 315, 339, and 1456.
(*k*) Livingstone *v.* Lindsay, 1626 ; M. 860.
(*l*) L. Rollo *v.* L. Niddrie, 1665 ; 1 B. Sup. 510. Dickson *v.* Trotter. 1778 ; M. 873 ; Hailes, 675.
(*m*) Leith *v.* Garden, 1703 ; M. 865. See Dickson, *supra* (*l*).
(*n*) Tod's Trs. *v.* Wilson, 1867 ; 7 Macph. 1100.
(*o*) Paul *v.* Boyd's Trs., 1835 ; 13 S. 818. Edmond *v.* Mags. of Aberdeen, 1855 ; 18 D. 47 ; aff. 1858, 3 Macq. 118. 3 Ersk. 5. § 6.

1466. Some assignations require no intimation: as—1. The conveyance to a trustee in sequestration (*a*); or assignment under an English commission of bankruptcy (*b*). 2. Judicial assignations (*c*). 3. Marriage, 'previous to July 18, 1881,' as an assignation to the husband of rights falling under the *jus mariti*; but the husband being liable to a personal exception, as bound by his wife's warrandice, this can be effectual only to his creditors (*d*). 4. 'It seems to have been a misapprehension to say that' an assignation in England of a debt due in England 'requires no intimation'; but 'that' it seems to be different where the assignation, though in England, is of a Scottish debt (*e*). 'In fact, ordinary assignments of things in action in England, though valid without notice against the original creditor and his representatives, including assignees in bankruptcy (*f*), do not give a right *in rem* perfecting the assignee's right in competition with subsequent assignees, until intimated to the debtor (*g*). But it appears to be settled that the necessity and the validity in essentials of notice of an assignation of a fund locally situated in Scotland is to be judged, like diligence, by the rules of Scots law (*e*). 5. Where the assignee is himself the debtor or person to whom intimation should be made (*h*).'

(*a*) 54 Geo. III. c. 137, § 30. 19 and 20 Vict. c. 79, § 102 ; but by § 111 of the Bankruptcy Act, if a debtor in ignorance of the sequestration pay his debt in *bonâ fide* to the bankrupt, he is not obliged to pay it a second time to the trustee.
(*b*) 3 Ersk. 5. § 7. Selkrig *v.* Davies, 1814 ; 2 Dow, 230 ; 1 Ill. 481.
(*c*) 3 Stair, 1. § 13. 3 Ersk. 5. § 7.
(*d*) See Robertson *v.* Halkerston, 1673 ; M. 5776 ; 1 Ill. 481. Stracey Till *v.* Jamiesons, 1763 ; M. 2858, 5946. 2 Bell's Com. 18, 19. See below, § 1561.
(*e*) Gray, *supra*, § 1465 (*e*). See Wallace *v.* Davies, 1853 ; 15 D. 688. Donaldson *v.* Ord, 1855 ; 17 D. 1053. Carrick *v.* Dickie's Assignee, 1822 ; 1 S. 447. Connal & Co. *v.* Loder, etc., 1868 ; 6 Macph. 1095. See Bar, Internat. Law, § 76 ; p. 301 of Gillespie's Transl. Story, § 395.
(*f*) Burn *v.* Carvalho, 4 My. & Cr. 690. See Snell's Pr. of Eq. 89. Pollock on Contracts, 226. Addison on Contracts, 1271.
(*g*) 36 and 37 Vict. c. 66, § 25 (6) (Judicature Act) ; and the authorities in last note.

(*h*) Russell *v.* E. of Breadalbane, 1827 ; 5 S. 891 ; aff. 1831, 5 W. & S. 256. Montgomery *v.* Montgomery, 1673 ; M. 841. E. of Argyle *v.* Macdonald, 1676 ; M. 842. Paul *v.* Boyd's Trs., 1835 ; 13 S. 818.

1467. Effect of Assignation.—The assignation substitutes the assignee in the cedent's place; and he may proceed 'to sue or to do diligence either' in the cedent's name, 'while he is alive, or in his own' (*a*). If he is to proceed in his own name 'to execute diligence begun in the cedent's name,' he must have judicial authority so to do. The messenger employed to execute diligence is not judge of the validity of conveyances; and he is not entitled, where diligence has been issued in the cedent's name, to execute it in the name of the assignee. The Court has held, on a report of the Writers to the Signet on the practice, that no diligence, either by arrestment, horning, or poinding, issued in the name of the cedent, can be executed in the name of the assignee (*b*). 'The assignee may proceed in his own name without confirmation after the cedent's death (*c*).'

(*a*) Grier *v.* Maxwell, 1621 ; M. 828 ; 1 Ill. 481.
(*b*) 2 Stair, 1. § 17. 3 Ersk. 5. § 8. Stewart *v.* Hay, 1745 ; M. 834 ; Elch. *Assig.* No. 6 ; Notes 43. Fogo *v.* Scott, 1769 ; M. 3693 ; Hailes, 319. Young *v.* Buchanan, 1799 ; M. 8137. Menzies, Conveyancing, 252 (3rd ed. 261).
(*c*) 1690, c. 26. 1693, c. 15. See 1 and 2 Vict. c. 114, § 7. See Mags. of Wick *v.* Forbes, 1849 ; 12 D. 299.

1468. Right of the Assignee.—The general rule is, *Assignatus utitur jure auctoris* (*a*). And so all defences competent to the debtor against the original creditor, existing at the date when the assignation is completed, and constituted otherwise than by the debtor's oath, will be effectual against the assignee; as a claim on a back-bond (*b*), a claim of compensation (*c*), etc. It is otherwise as to an indorsee (*d*). But 'the debtor may be precluded, or barred, from setting up against assignees defences which he may have against the original creditor, either by the nature or terms of the original contract (*e*), or by his subsequent actings (*f*); and' exceptions grounded on latent trusts 'or equities in favour of third parties,' though pleadable 'on the principle of personal bar (*g*)' against the cedent and against his creditors, 'who in sequestration take the subject, whether heritable (*h*) or moveable, *tantum et tale*, as it stood in the bankrupt' (*i*), will not be effectual against onerous 'and *boná fide*' assignees, 'who found on an independent title, the true owner being barred *personali exceptione* from challenging rights so acquired from his trustee' (*k*).

(*a*) 3 Ersk. 5. § 8, 9. Scottish Widows' Fund *v.* Buist, 1876; 3 R. 1078.

(*b*) Scott *v.* Montgomery, 1663; M. 10,187; 1 Ill. 482. See below, § 2263. Mangles *v.* Dixon, 3 H. L. Ca. 702. Phipps *v.* Lovegrove, L. R. 16 Eq. 80. Cavendish *v.* Geaves, 24 Beav. 163. Snell's Princ. of Eq. 92. The assignee's right is subject to conditions affecting the assignor's title, so that *resoluto jure dantis resolvitur jus accipientis.* Johnstone-Beattie *v.* Dalzell, 1868; 6 Macph. 333. Ker's Trs. *v.* Weller, 1863; 2 Macph. 371; aff. 1866; 4 Macph. H. L. 8.

(*c*) 2 Bell's Com. 138 sq. (131, M'L.'s ed.). Shiells *v.* Fergusson, Davidson, & Co., 1876; 4 R. 250. Cavendish (*b*). Graeme's Tr. *v.* Giersberg, 1888; 15 R. 691 (personal bar against cedent).

(*d*) See above, § 1460.

(*e*) *In re* Agra and Masterman's Bk., *ex p.* Asiatic Bkg. Corpn., L. R. 2 Ch. 391; 36 L. J. Ch. 222. *In re* Blakeley Ordnance Co., L. R. 3 Ch. 154; 37 L. J. Ch. 418. Webb *v.* Herne Bay Comrs., L. R. 5 Q. B. 642; 39 L. J. Q. B. 220. Merchant Bkg. Co. *v.* Phœnix Bessemer Steel Co., 5 Ch. D. 205; 49 L. J. Ch. 418. And see as to the limits of this principle, Crouch *v.* Credit Foncier, L. R. 8 Q. B. 374; 42 L. J. Q. B. 183.

(*f*) Higgs *v.* Northern Assam Tea Co., L. R. 4 Ex. 387; 38 L. J. Ex. 233 (see L. R. 10 Eq. 458). *In re* Bahia and San Francisco Ry. Co., L. R. 3 Q. B. 584; 37 L. J. Q. B. 376. Mangles *v.* Dixon (*b*). Adam & Forsyth *v.* Forsyth's Trs., 1867; 6 Macph. 31.

(*g*) Her. Revy. Co. *v.* Millar, *infra* (*k*), *per* L. Watson.

(*h*) Her. Revy. Co. *v.* Millar, *infra* (*k*).

(*i*) Dingwall *v.* M'Combie, 1822; 1 S. 501. Gordon *v.* Cheyne, 1824; 2 S. 675. See Edmond *v.* Mags. of Aberdeen, 1855; 18 D. 47; aff. 1858, 3 Macq. 116. Littlejohn *v.* Black, 1855; 18 D. 207. Howden *v.* Fleeming, 1867; 5 Macph. 568; rev. 1868, 6 Macph. H. L. 113; L. R. 1 Sc. App. 368. Davidson *v.* Boyd, 1868; 7 Macph. 77 (prepayment of rent to bankrupt). Watson *v.* Duncan, 1879; 6 R. 1247 (unregistered bill of sale of ship followed by possession—doubting Tod's Trs. *v.* Wilson, 1869; 7 Macph. 1100). North Br. Ry. Co. *v.* Lindsay, 1875; 3 R. 168. Graeme's Tr. *v.* Giersberg (*c*).

(*k*) **Redfearn** *v.* **Somervail**, 1813; M. Apx. *Pers. and Real*, 3; 1 Dow, 50; 5 Pat. 707. Attwood *v.* Kinnear & Son, 1832; 10 S. 817. Burns *v.* Lawrie's Trs., 1840; 2 D. 1348. Scot. Wid. Fund *v.* Buist, *supra* (*a*). **Her. Revy. Co.** *v.* **Millar,** 1891; 18 R. 1166; rev. 1892, A. C. 598; 19 R. H. L. 43.

1469. Warrandice.—Assignation, as a sale of the debt, implies warrandice. The *implied* warrandice is, that the debt is due, and the title to assign good. The cedent is not, without special stipulation, held to warrant the solvency of the debtor (*a*); differently from indorsation, which, being a new bill, is of course a warrandice of solvency. *Express* warrandice is either absolute, or from fact and deed, or a special warrandice of solvency. Warrandice from fact and deed is that commonly stipulated, and secures only against such acts or deeds of the cedent as may hurt the right of the assignee. Warrandice absolute is *debitum subesse.* Warrandice specially of solvency will protect the assignee both against the insolvency of the debtor, and in case of the debt being questionable, against the loss of the money in that way (*b*). In practice and in style-books, it is usual to express only warrandice from fact and deed; and in the common case, warrandice is required only to this extent, there being in assignations no implied warrandice of solvency; but in an onerous transaction, the warrandice truly ought to extend at least to warrandice of the truth of the debt. 'Although not expressed, warrandice *debitum subesse, i.e.* that the debt is truly due, is implied in all assignations, and is not excluded by the ordinary clauses of warrandice from fact and deed, etc. (*c*).'

(*a*) 2 Ersk. 3. § 25. See Anon., 1671; 2 B. Sup. 519; 1 Ill. 483.

(*b*) Riddel *v.* Whyte, 1707; M. 16,616; 1 Ill. 484. Barclay *v.* Liddel, 1671; M. 16,593–4; 1 Ill. 483.

(*c*) Ferrier *v.* Graham's Trs., 1828; 6 S. 818. Sinclair *v.* Wilson & M'Lellan, 1829; 7 S. 401. Reid *v.* Barclay, 1879; 6 R. 1807 (bond with cautioners—warrandice that cautioners bound).

CHAPTER X

OF THE DISTINCTION BETWEEN HERITABLE AND MOVEABLE PROPERTY

1470. General View.—In many general arrangements of one's affairs,—on the occasion of marriage, of death, of bankruptcy; in questions also relating to diligence for the recovery of debt,—it is necessary to distinguish precisely the lines which separate property into heritable and moveable. "Moveables" are 'or, rather, were' assigned by marriage, and 'became' common between the spouses; they fall to the executor in succession; they remain with the seller of land or of houses; they are removeable by a tenant on leaving his farm; they are attached by arrestment, and carried by poinding; and in bankruptcy and succession they are regulated by the law of the owner's domicile. Things which are deemed "Heritable" go by succession to the heir; they are not assigned by marriage; they go with land to the buyer; they remain for the landlord at the end of a lease; they are affected by inhibition, and attached and carried by adjudication; and they are regulated by the territorial law, not by that of the owner's domicile.

The character of any subject or fund, as, in these important respects, heritable or moveable, may be either—1. By its Nature, as being immoveable, like lands or houses; or as moveable, like furniture or cattle: or, 2. By Connection or Accession to some subject which has by nature the character of moveable or immoveable: or, 3. By Destination of the owner, either as in connection with something else, or in regard to succession. But in some respects a distinction is to be observed between the character of heritable or moveable, considered as in a question of succession, or as in a question of the competency of diligence (*a*).

(*a*) 2 Stair, 1. § 2. 2 Ersk. 2. 2 Bell's Com. 1 et seq. 1 M'Laren on Wills and Succession, 183 sqq. Fraser, Husband and Wife, 688 sqq.

I. CORPOREAL SUBJECTS.

1471. Natural Character.—Corporeal subjects are distinguished as heritable or moveable, according to their nature; their 'accession to or' connection with others; or the destination impressed on them.

1472. They are heritable or moveable by nature, as they are capable or incapable of being moved. Land, and parts of land, as minerals, lime, coal, or stone, in mines and quarries, and generally things which are naturally immoveable, are in law heritable 'till separated from the land.' Whatever moves, or is capable of being moved from place to place without injury or change of nature in itself, or in the subject with which it is connected, is moveable (*a*).

(*a*) 2 Stair, 1. § 2. 2 Ersk. 2. § 4, 7. Bruce *v.* Erskine, 1707; M. 14,092. Stewart *v.* Stewart, 1761; M. 5436. Paul *v.* Cuthbertson, *infra*, § 1473 (*c*). M. Breadalbane's Trs. *v.* Pringle, 1854; 16 D. 359 (thinnings of woods).

1473. Accession or Connection.—Things, though in themselves by nature moveable, may become heritable by accession. So, what has been by art so annexed 'or adapted' to land (although not built in or fixed to it) that it cannot be removed without destruction, or change of nature or of use, in the one or in the other subject, is heritable by accession, as buildings, fixtures in houses, mills, machines, 'including such parts of machinery as, though not physically fixed to the greater machines, form part of the general apparatus (*a*),' or vessels erected on a spot to which by their own weight they are, while entire, immoveably fixed (*b*). So, what is by growth connected with the soil is heritable, as trees and natural fruits not requiring seed and cultivation (*c*). There is, however, a general exception of industrial fruits. These go with the property of the seed and labour (*d*), as manufactures in which the productive powers of the soil are employed. Hay of the second crop from grass seed sown with white crops has been held heritable in a question of succession, but considered as an industrial crop in a question between landlord and tenant (*e*).

(*a*) **Fisher** *v.* **Dixon,** *infra* (*b*).

(*b*) 2 Stair, 2. § 4. 2 Ersk. 2. § 4 and 5, with Ivory's Note, p. 241. 1 Bell's Com. 752. Hyslop's Tr. *v.* Hyslop, Jan. 18, 1811; F. C., "not entitled to any weight as a precedent," 2 Ill. 219—see next case. Arkwright *v.* Billinge, Dec. 3, 1819; F. C.; see 2 Ill. 41. Niven *v.* Pitcairn, 1823; F. C.; 2 S. 239. See **Fisher** *v.* **Dixon,** 1843; 5 D. 775; aff. 1845, 4 Bell's App. 286; 12 Cl. & F. 312. M'Knight *v.* Irving, 1805; Hume, 412; 2 Hunter, Landl. and Ten. 284 sq. Syme *v.* Harvey, 1861; 24 D. 202. Dowall *v.* Miln, 1874; 1 R. 1180 (heir and executor—requires consideration; Hellawell *v.* Eastwood, *infra*, cited as authoritative, and Longbottom *v.* Berry not cited and ignored). Moore (Bell's Tr.) *v.* Bell, 1884; 22 S. L. R. 59; 12 R. 85. N. B. Ry. *v.* Ass. of Rys. and Canals, 1887; 25 S. L. R. 4 (rating). M'Gregor *v.* Tolmie, 1860; 22 D. 1183 (heritable creditor; see also Arkwright and Niven, *citt.* Cox *v.* Stead, 1833; 11 S. 672; aff. 7 W. & S. 497). **Brand's Trs.** *v.* **Brand's Trs.** (Bain *v.* Brand), 1874; 2 R. 258; rev. 1876, 3 R. H. L. 16; 1 App. Ca. 762; 1878, 5 R. 607. Nisbet *v.* Mitchell Innes, 1880; 7 R. 575 (seller and purchaser). Cochrane *v.* Stevenson, 1891; 18 R. 1208 (do.—pictures attached to wall). See also Tod's Trs. *v.* Finlay, 1872; 10 Macph. 422. Marshall *v.* Tannoch Chem. Co., 1886; 13 R. 1042 (superior and vassal). Walmesley *v.* Milne, 29 L. J. C. P. 361. Longbottom *v.* Berry, L. R. 5 Q. B. 123; 39 L. J. Q. B. 37. Holland *v.* Hodgson, L. R. 7 C. P. 328; 41 L. J. C. P. 146. Sheffield, etc., Bdg. Soc. *v.* Harrison, 15 Q. B. D. 358. D'Eyncourt *v.* Gregory, L. R. 3 Eq. 382; 36 L. J. Ch. 107. Hellawell *v.* Eastwood, 6 Ex. 295; 20 L. J. Ex. 154 (not followed in later cases, though quoted for its statement of principles). Turner *v.* Cameron, 39 L. J. Q. B. 125. Observe that the relaxation in favour of trade fixtures of the general rule "inædificatum solo solo cedit" (as to which, see the opinions in Wake *v.* Hall, 8 App. Ca. 195) applies in questions between landlord and tenant, or superior and vassal, but not as between heir and executor, or heritable and general creditors. Mather *v.* Fraser, 2 Kay & J. 536. Brand's Trs. *v.* Brand's Trs., Fisher *v.* Dixon, Marshall *v.* Tannoch Co., Longbottom *v.* Berry, etc., *citt.* 2 Smith's L. C. 192–206, and 207, 208. As to agricultural fixtures, see above, § 1256A. And upon fixtures generally, see the notes to **Elwes** *v.* **Mawe,** in 2 Smith's L. C. 183–222. Amos and Ferard on Fixtures, 3rd ed., 1883. Rankine's Landownership, 104 sqq. 1 Hunter, Landlord and Tenant, 294 sqq.

(*c*) Stewart *v.* Stewart's Exrs., 1761; M. 5436. See Paul *v.* Cuthbertson, 1840; 2 D. 286. Burns *v.* Fleming, 1880; 8 R. 226 (shrubs in villa garden).

(*d*) Stair and Ersk., *ut supra*. As to plants in a nursery, see Begbie *v.* Boyd, 1837; 16 S. 232. Gordon *v.* Gordon, 1806; Hume, 188.

(*e*) Sinclair *v.* Dalrymple, 1744; M. 5422; 2 Ill. 209. Wight *v.* Inglis, 1196; M. 5446. M. of Tweeddale *v.* Somner, Nov. 19, 1816; F. C. Keith *v.* Logie's Heirs, 1825; 4 S. 272. Lyal *v.* Cooper, 1832; 11 S. 96; 2 Hunter, Landl. and Ten. 456, and above, § 1262.

1474. Things in their nature heritable may become moveable, as part of an *universitas* or mass which is regarded as moveable. So, a share of heritable subjects forming part of the stock of a trading company is a trust estate in the partners, and moveable, the subjects themselves becoming part of the *universitas*, and merging in the general fund of the company for the benefit of the creditors, and ultimately of the partners (*a*).

(*a*) Corse, petr., Dec. 16, 1802; M. *Her. & Mov.* Apx. 2; 2 Ill. 219. Sime *v.* Balfour, 1804; *ib.* 3; 5 Paton, 525; 1 Ill. 240. Minto *v.* Kirkpatrick, 1833; 11 S. 632. Murrays *v.* Murray, 1805; M. *Her. & Mov.* Apx. 4. See below, § 1996. Irvine *v.* Irvine, 1851; 13 D. 1367; 2 Bell's Com. 3.

1475. Destination.—This may operate either where there is a manifest purpose of such an annexation or connection as would by accession characterise the thing as heritable, or where there is a destination in point of succession to the heir or the executor. So materials prepared for completing the wainscoting or windows of a house are held heritable (*a*). It 'was' doubtful whether the same principle applies to dunghills, or manure prepared to be spread upon the land in agriculture (*b*); but it seemed to be the opinion of the Court, that in distinguishing between plants in a nursery for sale, and those in a nursery for the use of an estate, this principle operates (*c*). 'As a tenant is bound to apply all dung produced on a farm for its cultivation, it is heritable in a question between his heir and executor (*d*). Fixed machinery erected by a tenant for working minerals, or for farming purposes, being annexed to the subject of the lease, which is heritable, is likewise heritable *destinatione* in a question between his heir and executor. But in a question with the landlord, the tenant or his heir has a right of severance (*e*).' Heirship moveables 'were' by destination heritable (*f*). Books, 'jewels,' and furniture may by destination be made heritable in succession (*g*). But the character thus accidentally impressed on subjects by destination, although it has ruled questions of succession, is not admitted to change them in respect to diligence (*h*).

(*a*) Johnston *v.* Dobie, 1783; M. 5443; Hailes, 919; 2 Ill. 219. See Gordon *v.* Gordon, 1806; Hume, 188. See as to money so devoted, below, § 1492.

(*b*) Lees *v.* Wilson, 1808; Hume, 191. See below, Reid's Exr. *v.* Reid.

(*c*) Gordon, *supra* (*a*). Begbie *v.* Boyd, 1837; 16 S. 232.

(*d*) Reid's Exr. *v.* Reid, 1890; 17 R. 519.

(*e*) **Brand's Trs.** *v.* **Brand's Trs.**, 1874; 2 R. 258; rev. 1876, 3 R. H. L. 16; 1 App. Ca. 762; see 5 R. 607. Reid's Exr. *v.* Reid, *cit.* Miller *v.* Muirhead, 1894; 21 R. 658 (assignation in security to landlord of fixtures). Cf. Turner *v.* Cameron, § 1473 (*b*).

(*f*) 3 Stair, 5. § 9. 3 Ersk. 8. § 17. 1474, c. 53. The right to heirship moveables is abolished. 31 and 32 Vict. c. 101, § 160.

(*g*) Veitch *v.* Young, 1808; M. *Serv. & Conf.* Apx. 4. Baillie *v.* Grant, 1859; 21 D. 838. As to questions with third parties, not heirs, see Kinnear *v.* Kinnear's Trs., 1875; 4 R. 705. M. of Bute *v.* Mss. of Bute's Trs., 1880; 8 R. 191.

(*h*) Forbes *v.* Drummond, 1772; 5 B. Sup. 583. Turner *v.* Cameron, § 1473 (*b*).

II. INCORPOREAL SUBJECTS.

1476. Natural Character.—Incorporeal subjects follow the same order and analogy with corporeal subjects.

1477. Incorporeal rights are heritable or moveable, according to the subject-matter.

1478. Rights to land, whether of property or of liferent, made real by infeftment, and debts secured upon land, are heritable (*a*).

(*a*) 2 Ersk. 2. § 5. Drysdale *v.* Drysdale, 1627; 1 B. Sup. 236; 1 Ill. 220. See below, § 1485, 1485A.

1479. Simple personal debts and engagements, whether presently due or payable at a future term, with interest from that term, are moveable (*a*); also shares of companies, public or private (*b*), bank stock (*c*), and Government stock (*d*); 'bill debts, legacies, and provisions, though bearing interest (*e*); and claims of damages, though arising in respect of heritable property (*f*).' Arrears of the annual returns of debts and funds, themselves heritable, are held to be moveable, though secured on land. So arrears of rents and of feu-duties, and arrears and savings of interest of heritable bonds, or of reversions of the price of lands sold judicially, are moveable. These are all considered as cash *in bonis* of the person in right of them (*g*). The price of lands sold is moveable, where the sale is by the owner; not where the sale 'before 1874 (*h*) was' by an apparent heir,—the price in this last case coming in place of the lands as a *surrogatum* (*i*), 'the apparent heir not being an owner. It is now fixed that, independently of all presumptions or questions of intention, a completed contract of sale, even though compulsory, makes the price of lands moveable in the succession of the owner, if he die before executing a conveyance (*k*). The same rule applies in regard to the succession of the creditor, when the subject of a heritable security is extrajudicially sold with his consent; but in judicial sales the creditor's interest remains heritable until payment of his debt (*l*). Sale of a pupil's heritage by his tutor or factor *loco tutoris* under judicial authority does not convert the proceeds into moveable estate: but after the owner attains minority it is carried by his will (*m*).'

(*a*) 2 Ersk. 2. § 7. Tuffie *v.* Campbell, 1808; and Hogg *v.* Grieve, 1807; Hume, 189. Fraser *v.* Bowie, 1804; Hume, 210. Haining *v.* Young, 1808; Hume, 214. Gray *v.* Walker, 1859; 21 D. 709. Muirhead *v.* Muirhead's Factor, 1867; 6 Macph. 95.

(*b*) Corse, Murrays, and Sime, *supra*, § 1474 (*a*). Irvine *v.* Irvine, 1851; 13 D. 1367. 8 Vict. c. 17, § 7. 25 and 26 Vict. c. 89, § 22.

(*c*) Bruce *v.* E. Kincardine, 1683; 3 B. Sup. 478; 2 Ill. 220. Murray *v.* Blackwood, 1710; M. 5478. Sir G. Dalrymple *v.* Halket, 1735; M. 5478. See above, § 1344.

(*d*) Hog *v.* Hog, 1791; M. 5479; 3 Pat. 247; 2 Ill. 420.

(*e*) 2 Ersk. 2. § 9, 10. Tuffie, Hogg, Fraser, *citt.* (*a*). Fraser, Husband and Wife, 721, 722.

(*f*) Cal. Ry. Co. *v.* Watt, 1875; 2 R. 917. Kelvinside Estate Co. *v.* Donaldson's Trs., 1879; 6 R. 995. But see, for the distinction between continuing breaches of real contracts, and those in which the covenant is broken once for all, and the ultimate damage has accrued, Addison on Contracts, 1287.

(*g*) 2 Ersk. 9. § 64. Martin *v.* Agnew, 1755; M. 5457; 5 B. Sup. 830. Spalding *v.* Spalding, 1792; M. 5257; Bell's Ca. 244. Innes *v.* D. Gordon, 1822; 2 S. 3. See below, § 1484, 1496, 1499, 1505. 2 Ersk. 2. § 7. Shaw's Bell's Com. 718. Johnston *v.* Cochran, 1829; 7 S. 226.

(*h*) See above, § 779A.

(*i*) Emslie *v.* Groat, 1817; Hume, 197. See below, § 1493.

(*k*) **Heron** *v.* **Espie**, 1856; 18 D. 917 (where the price of lands taken by a railway company under statutory powers, fixed by arbitration and deposited, was held to be moveable as to succession). See Deas on Railways, 149. Moncreiff *v.* Miln, 1856; 18 D. 1286. Cal. Ry. Co. *v.* Watt, and Kelvinside Estate Co. *v.* Donaldson's Trs., *supra* (*f*). See below as to the converse case of a purchase of land, § 1492. And comp. Garland *v.* Stewart, 1841; 4 D. 1; below, § 1600.

(*l*) 2 Bell's Com. 6. 1 M'Laren on Wills and Succession, 195. *Infra*, § 1486, 1488. 19 and 20 Vict. c. 79, § 102.

(*m*) Brown's Tr. *v.* Brown, 1897; 24 R. 962. See below, § 1486.

1480. Rights having a tract of future time are heritable. Such are liferents; also debts giving a periodical right without having relation to a capital sum or principal, as an annuity (*a*). It 'was' suggested that patent rights and copyright, as having a tract of future time, seem to be heritable (*b*). But this 'had' never been decided 'when Mr. Bell wrote; and it is now settled that patents are moveable, being destined to executors, and subject to legacy duty (*c*). And copyright is personal property by statute (*d*).'

(*a*) 2 Stair, 1. § 4. 2 Ersk. 2. § 6. Ewing *v.* Drummond, 1752; M. 5476; Elch. *Her. & Mov.* 16; 2 Ill. 221. See below, § 1498. See above, § 1479 (*a*); below, § 1495. Crawford's Trs. *v.* Crawford, 1867; 5 Macph. 275. Hill *v.* Hill, 1872; 11 Macph. 247. Gordon *v.* Scott, 1873; 11 Macph. 334.
(*b*) More's Notes on Stair, cxli. 1 Bell's Com. 115 (121, M'L.'s ed.).
(*c*) Lord Adv. *v.* Oswald, 1848; 10 D. 969. 46 and 47 Vict. c. 37, Sched. I., Form D. See Hill *v.* Hill, 1872; 11 Macph. 247 (*per* L. Pres. Inglis).
(*d*) 5 and 6 Vict. c. 45, § 25.

1481. Titles of honour, and offices to continue after the patentee's or officer's life, are heritable (*a*).

(*a*) 2 Ersk. 2. § 6. 1 Bell's Com. 124 (120, M'L.'s ed.).

1482. The *jus crediti* under a trust admits of distinctions, not according to the subjects vested in the trustees, but according to the nature of the subject demandable. If the trust be for vesting heritable subjects in the trustees, with a right in others to demand delivery or conveyance of the specific subjects, 'or a share of them,' the *jus crediti* is heritable, descending to the heirs of the persons favoured (*a*). If the *jus crediti* under the trust be merely to demand a sum of money, or share of the general trust fund (which is the ordinary case), it is moveable, descending to executors (*b*), 'and being arrestable in the hands of the trustees (*c*).'

(*a*) Durie *v.* Coutts, 1791; M. 4624; 2 Ill. 221.
(*b*) Grierson *v.* Ramsay, 1780; M. 759; Hailes, 855. See Wilson *v.* Smart, May 31, 1809; F. C. Angus *v.* Angus, 1825; 4 S. 279. Burrell *v.* Burrell, 1825; 4 S. 314. See below, § 1996, 1493, 1488, 1672. Somerville's Trs. *v.* Gillespie, 1859; 21 D. 1148. Scott *v.* Scott, 1846; 8 D. 892. Meiklam's Trs. *v.* Meiklam's Trs., 1852; 15 D. 159. Johnston *v.* Johnston, 1857; 19 D. 706; aff. 3 Macq. 619. Smith's Trs. *v.* Grant, 1862; 24 D. 1142. Auld *v.* Anderson, 1876; 4 R. 211. Kippen's Trs. *v.* Kippen's Exrs., 1889; 16 R. 668. See cases in § 1493 (*d*), etc.
(*c*) Learmonts *v.* Shearer, 1866; 4 Macph. 540. Grierson and Wilson, *citt.* (*b*).

1483. Accession or Connection.—Incorporeal are, like corporeal subjects, characterised as heritable by accession or connection with immoveable subjects.

1484. On this principle, feu-duties and casualties of superiority, rents of land, interest of heritable bonds and annuities, are heritable, though the arrears be moveable (*a*).

(*a*) Poldean's Crs. *v.* Sharp, 1738; Elch. *Her. & Mov.* 8; and Notes, p. 134; 2 Ill. 222. See above, § 1479.

1485. Rights connected with or affecting lands, though not feudalised, are heritable; as servitudes, teinds, patronage, reversions, faculties and rights to challenge deeds relating to heritage (*a*).

Heritable securities, whether by heritable bond or disposition in security, or by real burden, or by adjudication, are 'by the common law' heritable; even although in these cases infeftment shall not yet have been taken (*b*). Bonds also having a clause of infeftment, though not completed by sasine, are heritable. But if, by the conception of the bond, the infeftment is suspended till a subsequent day, or till a condition shall be fulfilled, the debt will be moveable (*c*).

'Since 31st December 1868, all heritable securities (*d*), of whatever date granted or obtained, and in whatever terms they may be conceived, are moveable as regards the succession of the creditor opening after that date (*e*), unless executors are expressly excluded by the bond or a subsequent minute in a statutory form, in which case the rules of the former law still prevail (*f*). But all heritable securities continue to be heritable *quoad fiscum,* and as regards all rights of courtesy and terce competent to the creditor's husband or wife, and in computing legitim; and no heritable security, whether granted before or after marriage, pertains to the husband *jure mariti,* or to the wife *jure relictæ,* unless the husband or relict has right or interest therein otherwise (*g*). It has been held that this enactment extends only to intestate succession, and that persons taking the right to heritable bonds by destination may still make up their title by service (*h*). But, of course, one who deals by will with his "heritable" or "moveable estate" is held to use these terms in the sense impressed on them by the statute (*i*).'

(*a*) 2 Ersk. 2. § 5. See above, § 1478. Milne *v.* Wills, 1869; 7 Macph. 406; and Telfer *v.* Fulton, 1810; Hume, 192 (seats in church). 2 Stair, 1. § 3. 2 Ersk. 2. § 14.
(*b*) Drysdale *v.* Drysdale, 1627; 1 B. Sup. 236; 2 Ill. 222. Reid *v.* Campbell, 1728; M. 5538. Cleland *v.* M'Aulay, 1734; M. 5554. Monro *v.* Alexander, 1795; M. 5548. M'Nicol *v.* M'Calman, Jan. 31, 1816; F. C. Mead *v.* Anderson, 1828; 6 S. 1034; aff. 4 W. & S. 328. Bailie's Trs. *v.* Crosse, 1832; 10 S. 617. See Marshall *v.* Lyell, 1859; 21 D. 514. Napier *v.* Orr, 1864; 3 Macph. 57. Hughson *v.* Hughson, Nov. 22, 1822; F. C.
(*c*) 2 Ersk. 2. § 5. Nasmith *v.* L. Hay, 1615; M. 5513. Anderson *v.* Anderson, 1623; M. 5513. Gordon *v.* Kerr,

1683; M. 5514. Stewart *v.* Stewart, 1705; M. 2767. Fisher *v.* Pringle, 1718; M. 5516. Menzies's Crs. *v.* Exrs., 1738; M. 5519. Gray *v.* Cairncross, 1711; M. 5462. Hadaway *v.* Barker, 1830; 8 S. 800.

(*d*) 31 and 32 Vict. c. 101, § 3. "Heritable securities" do not include ground annuals or absolute dispositions with back-bonds. As to securities over registered leases, see Stroyan *v.* Murray, 1890; 17 R. 1170.

(*e*) Brown *v.* Macdonald, 1870; 8 Macph. 439.

(*f*) *Ib.* § 117. See below, § 1491. Guthrie *v.* Guthrie, 1880; 8 R. 34.

(*g*) *Ib.* Hodge *v.* Hodge, 1879; 7 R. 259.

(*h*) Hare, petr., 1889; 17 R. 105.

(*i*) Hughes' Trs. *v.* Corsan, 1890; 18 R. 299.

1486. The above 'common law' rule does not hold as to the constructive security of a ranking and sale; or a disposition in a cessio; or in sequestration (*a*); nor as to securities taken by a tutor, or by a factor *loco tutoris*, '*curator bonis*, or father as administrator-in-law' (*b*). 'Such acts have not the effect of altering the pupil's succession (*c*); but changes made during tutorial administration by operation of public law have the ordinary effect upon the character of the pupil's estate as to succession (*d*).' And if a tutor be compelled, or in the fair course of administration called on, to pay a heritable debt, his application of moveable funds to that purpose cannot be challenged by the executors (*e*).

(*a*) Henderson *v.* Stewart, 1796; M. 5534; 2 Ill. 224. Ross *v.* Ross, 1806; Hume, 187.

(*b*) Ross *v.* Ross' Trs., 1793; M. 5545. **Lady C. Graham** *v.* **E. of Hopetoun**, 1798; M. 5599. Moncreiff *v.* Milne, 1856; 18 D. 1286. Nisbet *v.* Rennie, 1818; Hume, 221. **Heron** *v.* **Espie**, 1856; 18 D. 917. Morton *v.* Young, Feb. 11, 1813; F. C. (father). V. Strathallan *v.* Glenlyon's Trs., 1837; 15 S. 971. Kennedy *v.* Kennedy, 1843; 6 D. 40. Ld. Adv. *v.* Anstruther, 1842; rep. 13 D. 450. See Campbell *v.* Grant, 1869; 8 Macph. 227. Macfarlane *v.* Greig, 1895; 22 R. 405 (division and sale—factor *loco absentis*). Cases in § 1482 (*b*), 1479 *fin.* See also as to a wife's estate,—Gow *v.* Lang, 1807; Hume, 220. Berford *v.* Brown, 1832; 10 S. 609. Spence *v.* Paterson's Trs., 1873; 1 R. 46. Fraser, Husband and Wife, 703 sqq.

(*c*) Kennedy and Graham, *citt.* (*b*). 1 Bell's Com. 133 (129, M'L.'s ed.). Cases in 1 M'Laren on Wills and Succession, 221–2.

(*d*) Fraser, Guardian and Ward, 261–265. Graham, *cit.* L. James Stuart, petr., 1855; 17 D. 378.

(*e*) Lady C. Graham, *supra* (*b*).

1487. Where one abroad has empowered a person at home to act for him in investing money remitted, the accessory character of a heritable bond or other real security 'by common law' will be impressed upon the fund so as to regulate his succession, although the principal may be ignorant of what has been done (*a*). But any will which he may make is construed according to the law of his domicile (*b*). If the investment have been made known to him, and approved of, the succession will be regulated accordingly (*c*).

(*a*) Davidson *v.* Kyde, 1797; M. 5597; aff. 4 Pat. 63; 2 Ill. 225. M'Millan *v.* M'Millan's Trs., 1824; 3 S. 217. See Marshall *v.* Lyell, 1859; 21 D. 514.

(*b*) Trotter *v.* Trotter, 1826; 5 S. 78; aff. 3 W. & S. 407.

(*c*) Lady Ramsay *v.* Cowan, 1835; 11 S. 967. Comp. Nicholson's Assignee *v.* Macalister's Trs., 1841; 3 D. 675. Williamson *v.* Paul, 1849; 12 D. 372. 2 M'Laren on Wills and Succession, 96. Pringle's Trs. *v.* Hamilton, 1872; 10 Macph. 621.

1488. The effect of accessory heritable security superadded to debts, 'admitted' of distinctions 'under the old law.' Thus, where lands, or voluntary securities on land, or adjudications, are conveyed to creditors in security of personal debts, those debts are made heritable, and so continue while the security is in force (*a*). The same effect follows where a trust is granted for the security of creditors, and the trustee is infeft, and the creditors have acceded; it is the same as if granted to themselves (*b*). But where a trust has been granted for the sole and immediate purpose of paying the debts by a sale, the succession of the creditors is not changed. The *jus crediti* against the trustee rather than the heritable security 'was' regarded in this question (*c*). Formerly, it seems to have been held that the effect of the trust (especially where the creditors adjudged in corroboration of it) was to make the debt heritable, and that it became moveable only when the subject was sold (*d*).

(*a*) Trents *v.* E. Lauderdale, 1740; 5 B. Sup. 217; 2 Ill. 226. Fraser's Trs. *v.* Fraser, 1749; M. 5491. Watson *v.* M'Donald, 1794; M. 5497. Massie's Trs. *v.* Massie, 1816; Hume, 193. Duncan *v.* Rae, Feb. 15, 1810; F. C. Meiklam's Trs. *v.* Meiklam's Trs., 1852; 15 D. 159. Napier *v.* Orr, 1864; 3 Macph. 57. This effect does not now follow in regard to the creditor's succession. 31 and 32 Vict. c. 101, § 107.

(*b*) 2 Ersk. 2. § 15.

(*c*) Cave *v.* Murray, 1736; Elch. *Her. & Mov.* 4. Grierson *v.* Ramsay, 1780; M. 759; Hailes, 855; 2 Ill. 221. M'Ewan *v.* Thomson, 1793; M. 5596. Kyle's Trs. *v.* Whyte, 1827; 6 S. 40. See below, § 1493. Hawkins *v.* Hawkins, 1843; 5 D. 1035. Johnston *v.* Johnston, 1860; 3 Macq. 619, 633, 637.

(*d*) Smith's Exrs. *v.* His Heir, 1737; Elch. *Her. & Mov.* 6. Murray Kynynmond *v.* Cathcart, 1739; M. 5590, 5415, 15,906; Elch. *ib.* 10. Dunbar *v.* Brodie's Exrs., 1748; M. 5591; Elch. *ib.* 14.

1489. Accessory moveable security, 'such as a bond of corroboration, or a bill,' does not change the succession of a heritable debt (*a*).

(*a*) 2 Ersk. 2. § 16. Craw *v.* E. of Kellie, 1628; M. 5550; 2 Ill. 227. E. of Mar *v.* Hamilton, 1664; M. 5550. Wishart *v.* E. of Northesk, 1683; M. 5552. D. of Hamilton *v.* E. of Selkirk, 1740; M. 5554 and 5615; aff. 1 Cr. & Stew. 271.

1490. Destination.—An incorporeal right may be altered from its natural character of heritable or moveable by destination express or implied, 'the question turning upon the intention of the creditor or proprietor (*a*).'

(*a*) 2 Ersk. 2. § 14. Waugh *v.* Jamieson, 1676; M. 5526; 2 Ill. 228. Yates's Trs. *v.* Yeats, 1832; 10 S. 565.

1491. Express destination, by the exclusion of executors in a personal bond, makes the bond heritable (*a*). The assignation of a bond containing such an exclusion will, 'it was thought, according to the former law,' without repeating the exclusion or being conceived to heirs or assignees, continue the original condition of the debt (*b*). 'Bonds secluding executors are still heritable (*c*), but they may be bequeathed by will (*d*). And any security made real by registration of the deed or of an instrument in the Register of Sasines, may be made heritable by recording in that register a minute excluding executors in a statutory form. A similar minute may be endorsed upon an unrecorded conveyance, and recorded along with it. The exclusion of executors may now be removed by recording a minute to that effect, or by assigning, conveying, or bequeathing the security without expressing or repeating the exclusion (*e*).'

(*a*) 2 Ersk. 2. § 11, 12. 1661, c. 32. Ross *v.* Ross, July 4, 1809; F. C.; 2 Ill. 228. Muir *v.* Muir, 1687; M. 5524. Crawford *v.* E. Traquair, 1692; M. 5525. See below, § 1562.

(*b*) Sandilands *v.* Sandilands, 1680; M. 5498. Lockhart *v.* Muirhead, 1708; M. 5498. Kennedy *v.* Kennedy, 1747; M. 5499; Elch. *Her. & Mov.* 13; Notes, 182; 5 B. Sup. 749. See Ross (*a*). Bell's Conveyancing, 252; 2 Bell's Com. 6. 2 Ersk. 2. § 12. See below (*e*).

(*c*) 31 and 32 Vict. c. 101, § 117.

(*d*) *Ib.* § 20.

(*e*) *Ib.* § 117. Marshall's Analysis, 153, and App. 145, where forms of such minutes are given.

1492. Sums directed to be laid out by trustees on 'land, and, though perhaps not necessarily, sums directed, before 1868, to be laid out on' heritable securities, 'and also, it seems, in a question with children claiming legitim, money required to complete, after a testator's death, buildings which he had begun to build and contracted for (*a*),' are heritable (*b*). 'The principle is, that what ought to have been done according to a testator's direction, shall be held to have been done; and when he has not specified a time for doing it, he is held to mean within a reasonable time, *i.e.* within a year after his death. This rule applies to questions of conversion and vesting (*c*).'

(*a*) Robson *v.* Macnish, 1861; 23 D. 420. Malloch *v.* M'Lean, 1867; 5 Macph. 335. Cooper *v.* Jarman, L. R. 3 Eq. 98; 36 L. J. Ch. 85.

(*b*) Dick *v.* Gillies, 1828; 6 S. 1065; 2 Ill. 230. Burrell *v.* Burrell, 1825; 4 S. 314; 2 Ill. 222. See cases in § 1493 (*d*), (*i*). E. Stair *v.* Stair's Trs., 1825; 1 W. & S. 72; 2 W. & S. 414, 614. Fergusson *v.* Fergusson, 1834; 12 S. 456. Howat's Trs. *v.* Howat, 1838; 16 S. 622. Campbell's Trs. *v.* Campbell, 1838; 16 S. 1251. Carfrae *v.* Carfrae, 1842; 4 D. 605. Macpherson *v.* Macpherson, 1852; 1 Macq. 243. Dickson's Tutors *v.* Scott, 1853; 16 D. 1. Moncrieff *v.* Menzies, 1857; 20 D. 94. Whyte *v.* Whyte, 1860; 22 D. 1335. Romanes *v.* Riddell, 1865; 3 Macph. 248 (heritable security). See 1 M'Laren, Wills, etc., 215–216.

(*c*) E. Stair and Dickson's Tutors, *citt.* (*b*). Love's Trs. *v.* Love, 1879; 7 R. 410. Fulton's Trs. *v.* Fulton, 1880; 7 R. 566. As to contracts for purchase of land uncompleted at intestate's death, see Hudson *v.* Cook, L. R. 13 Eq. 417; 41 L. J. Ch. 306; and comp. above, § 1479 *fin.*, 1487.

1493. Destination to the effect of altering a heritable debt 'or other heritable subject' to moveable, is inferred from a direct trust and instruction to sell heritable subjects and convert them into money (*a*): *Multo magis*, when the land is actually sold (*b*). It is not implied from a mere power to sell, or a process having been raised for payment, for this is not conclusive of intention as to succession (*c*). 'The general rule is, that where the exercise of a power to sell is indispensable to the execution of a trust, or the intention that there should be a sale is clearly indicated, the beneficiary has not a right to claim a specific heritable subject or a share of heritage, but only to call on the trustees for payment of a share of the estate or residue. The interest of the beneficiary is therefore moveable, the power being construed as an *implied direction* (*d*). In trusts and instructions containing a power to sell, such phrases as "pay over" or "divide," applied to heritable or mixed subjects, have been held capable of construction with regard to the nature of the subject and of the trust purposes, and so not to necessitate a sale, but to admit of specific or *pro indiviso* conveyances to the beneficiaries (*e*). In other cases, where conversion by destination has taken place, the actings or the election of the beneficiaries, *e.g.* in taking specific conveyances instead of money, may operate reconversion (*f*). If there is not an absolute direction to sell, but the right to sell is made to depend on the will or discretion of the trustees, or is limited to cases of necessity or particular purposes, then until the necessity arises or the discretion is acted upon, or after the particular purposes are answered, there is no change in the quality of the property, and the heritable property remains heritable (*g*). But postponement of the sale, if there be no contingency in the direction, does not prevent conversion (*h*). In questions between the heirs and executors of the testator himself with regard to subjects falling under a direction to sell, it is settled that in order to change the character of the succession, so as to disinherit the heir, or to defeat the executor, it is necessary to deal with the estate so as to give it to some other person (*i*); and the undisposed of balance of a mixed estate directed to be realised, will be divided between heir and executor, according to the proportionate value of the heritable and moveable estates (*k*).' Even a process of adjudication was held not to alter the character of the debt, the creditor having died before decree (*l*). 'Mere investment by trustees for the preservation of the estate does not effect conversion into heritage or *vice versâ* (*m*).'

(*a*) Dick, *supra*, § 1492 (*b*). Angus *v.* Angus, 1825; 4 S. 279; 2 Ill. 222. Blair *v.* Blair, 1849; 12 D. 97, 113. L. Adv. *v.* Smith, 1852; 12 D. 585; 1 Macq. 760. Smith's Trs. *v.* Grant, 1862; 24 D. 1142.

(*b*) See above, § 1479, 1488; below, § 1600.

(*c*) 2 Ersk. 2. § 16. Reid *v.* Campbell, 1728; M. 5584; 2 Ill. 230. Munro *v.* Munro, 1735; M. 11,357; Elch. *Her. & Mov.* 2. M'Kenzie *v.* Dewar, 1772; M. 5778; Hailes, 505. Cathcart, *cit. infra* (*d*). Strachan *v.* Mowbray, 1843; 5 D. 687. Grindlay *v.* Grindlay's Trs., 1853; 16 D. 27. Speirs and Buchanan, *infra* (*d*). Duncan's Trs. *v.* Thomas, 1882; 9 R. 731. *Contra*, Boag *v.* Walkinshaw, 1872; 10 Macph. 872.

(*d*) **Buchanan** *v.* **Angus**, 1860; 22 D. 979; 1862, 4 Macq. 374. L. Adv. *v.* Blackburn's Trs., 1847; 10 D. 166. L. Adv. *v.* Williamson; 13 D. 436; aff. 1843, 2 Bell's App. 89. Cathcart *v.* Cathcart, 1830; 8 S. 803. Speirs *v.* Speirs, 1850; 13 D. 81. Somerville's Trs. *v.* Gillespie, 1859; 21 D. 1148 (intention inferred from physical impossibility of dividing the subjects. See also Boag, Weir, and Fotheringham's Trs., *infra*). Weir *v.* L. Adv., 1865; 3 Macph. 1006. Sheppard's Trs. *v.* Sheppard, 1885; 12 R. 1193. See Mackenzie *v.* Mackenzie, 1868; 6 Macph. 375. Melrose *v.* Melrose, 1869; 7 Macph. 1050. Boag *v.* Walkinshaw, 1872; 10 Macph. 872. Fotheringham's Trs. *v.* Paterson, 1873; 11 Macph. 848. Nairn's Trs. *v.* Melville, 1877; 5 R. 128. Brown's Trs. *v.* Brown, 1890; 18 R. 185. Playfair's Trs. *v.* Playfair, 1894; 21 R. 836. See above, § 1482.

(*e*) Buchanan *v.* Angus, and cases above (*d*). Auld *v.* Anderson, 1876; 4 R. 211. Hogg *v.* Hamilton, 1877; 4 R. 845. See Wardlaw's Trs. *v.* Wardlaw, 1880; 7 R. 1070. Baird *v.* Watson, 1880; 8 R. 233. Resulting inconvenience, not amounting to absolute necessity in order to the execution of the trust—as where in a trust of long endurance the beneficiaries entitled to a conveyance of heritage become very numerous—does not affect the question of conversion, unless the truster has indicated his intention in regard to such an event. Duncan's Trs. *v.* Thomas (*c*). Aitken *v.* Munro, 1883; 10 R. 1097. Sheppard's Trs. *v.* Sheppard, 1885; 12 R. 1193. Anderson's Exrx. *v.* Anderson's Trs., 1895; 22 R. 254. Comp. Weir *v.* L. Adv., 1865; 3 Macph. 1007; and 1 M'Laren, Wills and Succn. 217.

(*f*) Grindlay *v.* Grindlay's Trs., 1853; 16 D. 27. Nicolson's Assignee *v.* Macalister's Trs., 1841; 3 D. 675. Williamson *v.* Paul, 1849; 12 D. 372. Hogg (*e*).

(*g*) Buchanan *v.* Angus, *cit.* (*d*). Aitken *v.* Munro, 1883; 10 R. 1097. 1 M'Laren on Wills, etc., 216, 218–219. L. Adv. *v.* Hamilton, 1856; 18 D. 636. See Fraser, H. & W. 737–739. Mackenzie *v.* Mackenzie, 1868; 6 Macph. 375. Wardlaw's Trs. *v.* Wardlaw, 1880; 7 R. 1070. Seton's Tr. *v.* Seton, 1868; 13 R. 1047.

(*h*) M'Gilchrist's Trs. *v.* M'Gilchrist, 1870; 8 Macph. 689.

(*i*) See Cathcart, *cit.* (*d*). Patrick *v.* Nichol, 1838; 1 D. 207. Gardner (Pearson) *v.* Ogilvie, 1857; 20 D. 105 (*per* Lords Curriehill and Deas). White *v.* White, 1860; 22 D. 1335. Neilson *v.* Stewart, 1860; 22 D. 646. Thomson *v.* Tennant's Trs., 1868; 7 Macph. 114 (esp. *per* L. Cowan). See the earlier cases in 1 M'Laren, Wills and Succn. 208 sqq.; and the principle stated by L. P. Campbell in **Kers** *v.* **Wauchope**, 1812; 5 Pat. 559; 1 Ross' L. C. 432. Comp. also Finnie *v.* Lords of Treasury, 1836; 15 S. 165. Grindlay *v.* Grindlay's Trs., 1853; 16 D. 27.

(*k*) Cowan *v.* Cowan, 1887; 14 R. 670.

(*l*) Carnegie *v.* Carnegie, 1700; M. 5537.

(*m*) Cases in note (*g*), and § 1486 (*b*). Melrose *v.* Melrose, *cit.* (*d*). Carfrae *v.* Carfrae, 1842; 4 D. 605. White *v.* White, 1860; 22 D. 1335.

1494. A charge of horning on a heritable debt makes it moveable (*a*); but the registration of a bond in order to a charge has not that effect (*b*); 'and bonds secluding executors remain heritable *destinatione*, notwithstanding the use of personal diligence (*c*).'

(*a*) Donaldson *v.* Donaldson, 1624; M. 5571; 2 Ill. 230. Montgomery *v.* Stewart, 1666; M. 5584. Seaton's Exrs. *v.* E. Nithsdale, 1672; M. 5572. Bannatyne *v.* Bonar, 1683; M. 5581. Gray *v.* Panton, 1705; M. 5581. Douglas *v.* Dickson, 1751; M. 5576; 5 B. Sup. 793.

(*b*) Yeaman *v.* Yeaman, 1687; M. 5484.

(*c*) Bannatyne and Gray, *citt.* (*a*).

1495. Formerly, bonds bearing interest were held to be *quasi feuda*, as having by the fixed yearly profit some resemblance to permanent rights (*a*). But still the natural character of the obligation prevailed wherever the presumption could fairly be entertained against permanency. And so the debt was held moveable, either before the term of payment (*b*), or where interest was stipulated from the date, but not payable till the arrival of the term of payment of the bond, and no stipulation of interest afterwards (*c*). But wherever interest was stipulated to be paid before the term of payment, or where the term of payment was very distant, or already past, and the bond stipulated for interest, the debt was held heritable (*d*). By statute, an alteration was made in order to enlarge the fund for younger children, by declaring bonds of this description moveable as to succession, though still heritable as to the fisk and *jus relictæ* (*e*).

(*a*) 2 Ersk. 4. § 9, 10. See 1 Ross' Lect. 44. Fraser, Husband and Wife, 718.

(*b*) Smith *v.* Anderson, 1624; M. 5503; 2 Ill. 231. Douglas *v.* M'Michael, 1629; M. 5504. Carnousie *v.* Meldrum, 1630; M. 5505. Meuse *v.* Craig's Exrs., 1748; M. 5506. See Gray *v.* Walker, 1859; 21 D. 709.

(*c*) Porteous *v.* Veitch, 1627; M. 5463.

(*d*) 2 Ersk. 2. § 9. Ross *v.* Graham, Nov. 14, 1816; F. C. Hughson *v.* Hughson, Nov. 22, 1822; F. C. Gray, *cit.* (*b*). Downie *v.* Downie's Trs., 1866; 4 Macph. 1067. Crawford's Trs. *v.* Crawford, 1867; 5 Macph. 275. Dawson's Trs. *v.* Dawson, 1896; 23 R. 1006.

(*e*) 1641, c. 57. 1661, c. 32. 2 Ersk. 2. § 9, 10. Hughson, Ross, and Downie, *citt.* (*d*). 2 Bell's Com. 7. 3 Stair, 4. § 24. Below, § 1583.

1496. Although, by connection with heritage, the *jus crediti* both of rents, and of principal and annual payments in heritable bonds, is heritable (*a*), yet the accruing payments, as they arise, become moveable as soon as they vest *in bonis* of the creditors. As to which the following rules are observed:—

(*a*) See above, § 1484.

1497. (1.) Where the payment is not connected with the produce of land, the right vests *de die in diem*; as the interest of bonds, though the bonds themselves be heritable *destinatione*.

1497A. Apportionment.—'The rules of the common law stated in the following sections have been altered by the Apportionment Acts. All periodical payments are now considered as accruing from day to day, and are apportionable in respect of time between heir and executor (*a*).'

(*a*) See above, § 1047.

1498. (2.) Under a right having *tractum futuri temporis*, as in the case of annuities, if the periodical payment 'were' termly, the right to the payments 'did' not vest *de die in diem*, but at the specified term; a special stipulation to pay daily and continually having the effect, however, of changing it into a right vesting *de die in diem* (*a*).

(*a*) E. Dalhousie *v.* Gilmour, 1789; M. 15,915; 2 Ill. 332. See above, § 1049, 1480. See § 1497A.

1499. (3.) Rents of lands vest and become moveable at the legal terms of Whitsunday and Martinmas. Postponing the term does not alter this (*a*), but anticipation does; for at the actual term "dies et cedit et venit," and the rent due is *in bonis* of the landlord (*b*). 'So even forehand rents are held as accruing and apportionable, if the landlord dies during the term, for the occupation during which they are payable (*c*).'

(*a*) Carnegie *v.* Carnegie, 1668; M. 15,887; 2 Ill. 143. Innes *v.* D. Gordon, 1822; 2 S. 3; 2 Ill. 221.

(*b*) M. Queensberry *v.* Montgomery, Feb. 18, 1814; F. C.; 2 Ill. 233. See Swinton *v.* Gawler, June 20, 1809; F. C., and cases in next note. Trotter *v.* Cunninghame, 1839; 2 D. 140. Blaikie *v.* Farquharson, 1849; 11 D. 1456. Baillie *v.* Lockhart, 1855; 2 Macq. 258.

(*c*) L. Herries *v.* Maxwell's Curator, 1873; 11 Macph. 396. See § 1497A.

1500. (4.) Payments connected with the rents of lands, or payable in victual (land's produce), fall under the same rule (*a*).

(*a*) 2 Ersk. 9. § 66. Carruthers *v.* Barclay, 1738; M. 5413; 2 Ill. 233. Baillie *v.* Cuthbert, 1684; M. 15,900. Murray Kynynmond *v.* Rochead, 1739; M. 5415; Elch. *Her. & Mov.* 10 and 11. L. Daer *v.* D. Hamilton, 1740; Elch. *Her. & Mov.* 11; 5 B. Sup. 695. See § 1497A.

1501. (5.) The rents of grass farms follow the same rule as those of corn farms: The rent is for the crop, not for the possession. And whether the rent be made payable at Martinmas after entry, and the following Whitsunday, or as a slump rent at the Martinmas after entry, if the landlord survives Martinmas, the whole goes 'at common law' to his executor; if he dies before Martinmas, his executor gets only the half (*a*).

(*a*) Pringle *v.* Pringle, 1741; M. 5419; Elch. *Heir & Ex.* 1; 2 Ill. 143. Sinclair *v.* Dalrymple, M. 5421; 2 Ill. 234. Kerr *v.* Turnbull, 1760; M. 5430; 5 B. Sup. 876. Swinton *v.* Gawler, June 20, 1809; F. C. Johnston *v.* M. Annandale, 1727; M. 15,913. Elliot's Trs. *v.* Elliot, 1792; M. 15,917. Campbell *v.* Campbell, 1745; M. 15,908; Elch. *H. & Ex.* 3. Petley *v.* M'Kenzie, 1805; Hume, 186. Campbell *v.* Campbell, 1849; 11 D. 1426. See § 1497A.

1502. (6.) The rents of houses are regulated by the legal terms of Whitsunday and Martinmas; the rent of the first half-year vesting the moment the possession begins (*a*).

(*a*) Binny *v.* Binny, Jan. 28, 1820; F. C.; 2 Ill. 235. See L. Monboddo's note on L. Daer's case, *supra*, § 1500 (*a*). King *v.* Jaffray, 1828; 6 S. 422. See § 1497A; 2 Bell's Com. 8.

1503. (7.) Interest stipulated at the legal terms is as rent at those terms. But if conventional terms be stipulated, the question is ruled by the stipulations (*a*).

(*a*) Murray Kynynmond and L. Daer, *supra*, § 1500 (*a*). See § 1497A.

1504. (8.) In all cases in which payments are regulated by terms, an adjudication before the legal term will carry the right which vests at the term; an arrestment after the term will carry the rent due at that term; and an adjudger after arrestment will be postponed on the rent due at the term previous. But a distinction has been introduced between interests due on a heritable bond and interest falling due under an adjudication. In the former case, an adjudication of the bond and debt is held to carry the bond and future interests, but not the arrears; in the latter, the adjudication of the debt and diligence carries the adjudication, with the whole accumulated sum and interest, including arrears. And although the ground on which this distinction was first established may seem now to be subverted by the opposite view more recently taken of an adjudication as being a mere *pignus prætorium*, it seems to be settled as above, by the latest cases on the subject (*a*).

(*a*) Ramsay *v.* Brownlee, 1738; M. 5538; Elch. *Adjud.* 20; 2 Ill. 235. Baikie *v.* Sinclair, 1786; M. 5545; Hailes, 988; aff. 1787, 3 Pat. 64. Ryder *v.* Ross's Crs., 1794; M. 5549; Bell's Ca. 52. See 2 Bell's Com. 10. Cochrane *v.* Bogle, 1849; 11 D. 909; aff. 7 Bell's App. 65. Fraser, Husband and Wife, 696.

1505. (9.) Arrears of feu-duty, rent, and interest are moveable (*a*).

(*a*) Keirie *v.* Nicolson, 1671; M. 5448; 2 Ill. 236. L. Elibank *v.* M'Kenzie, 1711; M. 5462. Campbell *v.* Campbell, 1743; M. 5247. Martin *v.* Agnew, 1755; M. 5457; 5 B. Sup. 830; 2 Ill. 220. Johnston *v.* Cochran, 1829; 7 S. 226. See above, § 1479. Willock *v.* Ouchterlony, 1769; M. 5539; aff. 1772, 3 Pat. 659.

BOOK THIRD

OF RIGHTS ARISING FROM MARRIAGE AND CONSTITUTION OF A FAMILY; AND OF THE LAWS OF SUCCESSION

PART I

OF MARRIAGE; AND PARENT AND CHILD

CHAPTER I

OF MARRIAGE

1506. Constitution of Marriage (*a*).—The contract of marriage is the most important known in law. It is constituted by consent of the parties, but its effects both upon them and upon others are beyond their control, established and regulated by the public law. It binds the parties beyond recall; confers on their children the status and the right of legitimacy; establishes the relations of consanguinity and affinity; and is the direct fountain of the laws of succession. It produces its effects and is accompanied by the duties and rights which attach to married persons in whatever part of the world it may have been entered into, or whithersoever the parties may have wandered from their original domicile; those rights and duties depending not so much on the *lex loci contractus*, as on the laws and regulations of the country in which the married pair are domiciled.

By the law of Scotland, marriage is a consensual contract, requiring no particular solemnity, nor even written evidence, but deliberate and unconditional consent alone. There is no restraint on account of nonage, but that which proceeds from incapacity of consent in persons under puberty (*b*). There is no absolute necessity for publication, or solemnity, or celebration, or particular place or time of celebration. There is no necessity for the consent of parents or of guardians (*c*).

(*a*) See 1 Stair, 4. 1 Ersk. 6. 1 Blackst. Com. 15. Pothier, Tr. de Mariage, v. iii. p. 129. 2 Kent, Com. 75. Story, Conflict of Laws, § 107. Fraser on Husband and Wife, 2nd ed., 1876. Report of the Royal Commission on the Laws of Marriage, 1868. 2 Stephen's Com. 253 seq. Bishop on the Law of Marriage and Divorce. Friedberg, Das Recht der Eheschliessung in seiner geschichtlichen Entwicklung, Leipzig, 1865. Murray, Property of Married Persons, 1891. See below, § 1941 et seq., for Marriage Contracts and Family Settlements.

(*b*) Below, § 1523.

(*c*) 2 Craig, 18. § 18 et seq. 1 Stair, 4. § 6. 1 Mackenzie, 6. 1 Ersk. 6. § 2 et seq. 1 Ersk. Pr. 6. § 2 et seq. Report of Royal Comm. xvi.

1507. In England, till 1757, the contract of marriage seems to have been as little encumbered with forms as in Scotland (*a*). But by the Marriage Act of that year it was required that the consent of parents or guardians should be given where the parties were under twenty-one years of age; and that there should be publication by banns in a lawful chapel for three Sundays, and by celebration openly in the parish church, or in a chapel wherein marriage had usually been celebrated. And these requisites were imposed under the pain of nullity of the marriage (*b*). By later statutes, some relaxation is made in these regulations; and in marriage accomplished by fraud, the guilty party is deprived of the benefit of the other's property (*c*).

(*a*) **Dalrymple** *v.* **Dalrymple**, 1811; Dodson's Report; 2 Hagg. Cons. Rep. See, however, **The Queen** *v.* **Millis**, 1842; 10 Cl. & F. 534; Dix's Rep. Fraser, H. & W. 273, 205 sqq.

(*b*) 26 Geo. II. c. 33.

(*c*) 4 Geo. IV. c. 76, and 5 Geo. IV. c. 32. 6 and 7 Will. IV. c. 85 and 86. 1 Vict. c. 22. 3 and 4 Vict. c. 72. 19 and 20 Vict. c. 119. 23 Vict. c. 24. See 19 and 20 Vict. c. 119, § 7 and 8, for the case where one of the parties is resident in Scotland. As to Quakers, 23 and 24 Vict. c. 18, and 35 and 36 Vict. c. 10. As to British subjects abroad, 4 Geo. IV. c. 91; 12 and 13 Vict. c. 38; 31 and 32 Vict. c. 61: all repealed by the Foreign Marriage Act, 1892; 55 and 56 Vict. c. 23. As to marriages at sea, 57 and 58 Vict. c. 60, § 253 (merchant ships). 42 and 43 Vict. c. 29 (navy). 55 and 56 Vict. c. 23, § 12, etc. (do.).

1508. Modes of Marriage.—Marriage is regular or irregular. In both kinds the essential requisite of the contract is unconditional consent *de præsenti* to marriage (*a*). The party must be of the age of puberty; and neither under the influence of force, nor of fraud, nor of essential error, in consenting to the marriage. So, if the consent be invalidated by error, or force and fear, or incapacity from extreme intoxication, there is no marriage (*b*). A promise of marriage, not being *de præsenti*, is not of itself marriage (*c*); nor is it even a ground of action for declaring marriage, or compelling implement of the engagement (*d*). But it may be a good ground of action for damages and solatium (*e*), such actions being now declared proper jury cases (*f*); and if followed by consummation, it will make marriage (*g*).

(*a*) 1 Ersk. 6. § 11. See below, § 1515. Lowrie *v.* Mercer, 1840; 2 D. 953 (*per* L. Moncreiff, p. 960). Fraser, H. & W. 294 sqq.

(*b*) 1 Stair, 4. § 6. 1 Ersk. 6. § 23. Thomson *v.* Wright, 1767; M. 13,915; 2 Ill. 237. Johnston *v.* Brown, 1823; 2 S. 495; Ferg. Cons. Rep. 229. See below, § 1520.

(*c*) See below, § 1515, 1519.

(*d*) Stair and Ersk. *ut supra*.

(*e*) Graham *v.* Burn, 1685; M. 8472. Hog *v.* Gow, May 27, 1812; F. C. See § 25.

(*f*) 6 Geo. IV. c. 120, § 28. 1 Will. IV. c. 69, § 2. But see 13 and 14 Vict. 36; 29 and 30 Vict. c. 112. Mackay, C. of S. Practice Manual, 324 sqq. In such actions the promise may be proved *prout de jure*, the parties being competent witnesses (16 Vict. c. 20, § 3); and it may be inferred from conduct and correspondence. Murray *v.* Napier, 1861; 23 D. 1243. Nor is a direct refusal necessary to constitute a breach. Stoole *v.* M'Leish, 1870; 8 Macph. 613. Cattanach *v.* Robertson, 1864; 2 Macph. 839. See Frost *v.* Knight, 39 L. J. Ex. 227; L. R. 5 Ex. 322; 7 Ex. 111. As to justification of the breach, see Thomson *v.* Wright, *supra* (*b*). Fletcher *v.* Grant, 1878; 6 R. 59. Fraser, H. & W. 490–494. As to the defence of *mora*, see Colvin *v.* Johnstone, 1890; 18 R. 115.

(*g*) See below for questions of Foreign Relations, § 1537.

1509. Regular Marriage.—A regular marriage in Scotland requires 'either' the publication of banns 'or notice to the Registrar of Births, Marriages, and Deaths for the parish or district'; and that the ceremony shall be performed by a clergyman, before at least two credible witnesses.

1510. (1.) *Banns* are proclaimed 'on two, or in the minister's discretion, on one (*a*), formerly' on three several Sundays in the parish church (*b*) of the parties, while the people are met for divine service. They announce a purpose of marriage between the parties, proclaimed by their names and designations or descriptions; requiring all concerned to state any objection which they may know to the union. The only express regulations relating to banns are ecclesiastical, and have been recognised by the Legislature no further than by general statutory prohibitions against "clandestine and unorderly" marriages, under pecuniary penalties (*c*). A certificate of the session-clerk is received as evidence of proclamation of banns (*d*). 'The certificate must now be accompanied by a copy of a statutory schedule, which, upon the solemnisation of the marriage, is produced to the minister and signed by the spouses, by two witnesses, male or female, present at the ceremony, and by the minister. It must then be transmitted within three days to the registrar of the parish, who forthwith enters it in the duplicate register (*e*). The registrar is bound upon requisition to attend the solemnisation of a marriage, for which he is entitled to a fee and his expenses (*f*).'

(*a*) Act viii. Ass., May 28, 1880. Cook's Forms of Procedure and Practice, 41, 5th ed. 1882. Fraser, H. & W. 282.

(b) As the proclamation of banns is properly an ecclesiastical regulation, it falls to be made in the church of a district erected into a parish *quoad sacra*, under 7 and 8 Vict. c. 44, for persons residing in its district or parish. Hutton *v.* Harper, 1875; 2 R. 893; aff. 1876, 3 R. H. L. 9. See L. Adv. *v.* Ballantyne, 1859; 3 Irv. 352.

(c) 1 Ersk. 6. § 10. Fergusson's Consist. Law, 108. Ch. 51 of the 4th Lateran Council in 1215, Sac. Sanct. Concilia, tom. 9, p. 202. Statutes of Honorius in 1217, c. 56; *ib.* tom. 11, p. 262. Gregory IX. in 1237, *ib.* 550, 578, c. 13. Council of Trent, 1563, *ib.* tom. 14, p. 876. Scottish Prov. Councils at Perth, 1269, c. 65. 1 Book of Discipline, General Assembly, 1638, art. 21. Directory for Worship, 1644. Acts of Assembly, 1690, c. 5; 1711, c. 5; 1784, c. 8. Statute 1661, c. 34; 7 Acta Parl. 231. 1698, c. 6; 10 Acta Parl. 149. 10 Anne, c. 7. 4 and 5 Will. IV. c. 28. 17 and 18 Vict. c. 80, § 46, 68. 18 and 19 Vict. c. 29. In practice, proclamation on three successive Sundays was not generally observed. Bell's Law Dict., *Banns*; and Cook's Proced. in Ch. Courts, 5th ed., 40 sq. Report of Royal Comm. xvii.

(d) 1 Ersk. 6. § 10. See above, § 1507 (b).

(e) 17 and 18 Vict. c. 80, § 46. See 23 and 24 Vict. c. 85.

(f) 17 and 17 Vict. c. 80, § 47.

1510A. '(2.) *Marriage Notice Act.*—On the preamble that it is expedient to encourage the celebration of regular marriages in Scotland, the Marriage Notice (Scotland) Act, 1878, provides that regular marriages may be celebrated by clergymen upon production to them of a certificate, by the Registrar or Registrars of Births, Marriages, and Deaths for the parishes or districts in which the parties have resided for not less than fifteen days, to the effect that notice of the intended marriage has been given, that all the requirements of the law have been complied with, and no objections stated. This certificate has the same effect as a certificate of proclamation of banns. On notice of the intended marriage being given to the registrar, the particulars are entered in the Marriage Notice-Book which he keeps, and a public notice of the intended marriage in a statutory form is posted for seven consecutive days in a conspicuous place on the door or outer wall of his office. Objections must be stated in writing, subscribed by the person taking the same, and lodged by him personally; and the objector must also subscribe a declaration of their truth, which exposes him, if false, to the penalties of perjury. Objections as to residence, or of a formal character, not involving a legal impediment to the marriage, are disposed of by the Sheriff on a report by the registrar. Such objections as involve a legal impediment to the marriage (a) prevent the issuing of a certificate of notice until production of a certified judgment of a competent Court (b) to the effect that the parties are not disqualified by the objection from contracting marriage. Provision is made for parties unable to write signing by marks in a statutory form any notice, declaration, or other writ under the Act. The registrar's certificate of notice is valid only for three months (c).'

(a) Even though withdrawn by the objector, as the statute has been construed in the Sheriff Court of Aberdeen. 27 J. of J. 214; 2 Sel. Sh. Ca. 238.

(b) *I.e.* the Court of Session; see case cited in note (a).

(c) 41 and 42 Vict. c. 43. See as to the responsibility incurred by a person objecting to the issuing of a certificate of proclamation of banns, Henderson *v.* Henderson, 1855; 17 D. 348.

1511. (3.) *Ceremony.*—It is not required to a regular marriage *in facie ecclesiæ*, that the ceremony shall be performed in church; but it must be performed by a clergyman (a). The want of his presence does not, indeed, affect the validity of the marriage (b); but it exposes the parties and celebrator to penalties (c). The clergyman must be either of the Kirk of Scotland (d); or of the Episcopal communion, duly qualified by the taking of the oaths of allegiance and abjuration (e); 'or, now, after due proclamation of banns in the parish church (f), or notice under the Act, of any other religious body (g). A clergyman of the Church of Scotland is not obliged to celebrate a marriage not preceded by due proclamation of banns (h); but may be compelled by the Court of Session to proclaim the banns and celebrate the marriage (i).'

(a) Fraser, H. & W. 287, 293.

(b) 1 Ersk. 6. § 11. Ferg. Consist. Law, 111. Canons of Perth, art. 65. See Carruthers *v.* Johnston, 1705; M. 2252; 1 Ill. 237. Crawford's Trs. *v.* Hart, 1802; M. 12,698 (parties to clandestine marriage entitled to legal provisions *jure relictæ* and *jure mariti*; cf. Fraser, H. & W. 255, 256).

(c) 1661, c. 34. 1672, c. 9. 1690, c. 27. 1698, c. 6.

(d) 1661, c. 34. 1695, c. 12. See 2 Hume's Crim. Law, 327. Ivory's Ersk. p. 125, n. 143.

(e) 10 Anne, 7.

(f) 4 and 5 Will. IV. c. 28. See L. Adv. *v.* Ballantyne, 1859; 3 Irv. 352.

(g) See last section. (h) 41 and 42 Vict. c. 43, § 11.

(i) Fraser, H. & W. 290.

1512. Two witnesses legally capable of giving testimony must be present, who know the parties.

1513. No special form of words is necessary. But there is generally a solemn admonition by the clergyman to the parties. The question of mutual acceptance is solemnly put, and an answer required, as in the Roman *stipulatio*. And a declaration 'is' made by the clergyman that the parties are married.

1514. Clandestine and Irregular Marriages. —*Clandestine* marriage (*a*) is as effectual in law as the most regular; but the parties, celebrator, and witnesses are liable to penalties. Those penalties are seldom exacted; though occasionally they are enforced against trafficking priests (*b*), 'or persons who unwarrantably assume the character of a minister of religion (*c*).' Marriages are deemed clandestine which 'were, before the statutes above referred to (*d*),' celebrated by a clergyman not of the Established Church, or 'now are celebrated' by a layman assuming the character of a clergyman, or without banns or 'notice at the registrar's office (*e*). There is no penalty under the Acts here cited, except for the celebration of a marriage with a religious ceremony without proclamation of banns or notice to the registrar (*f*). And it is erroneous to include in this category (*i.e.* under the Acts against clandestine marriages) *irregular* marriages contracted by declaration or consent,' before a magistrate, or before witnesses only, or by written acknowledgment or confession of the parties (*g*). Present unconditional consent in any of those circumstances is marriage; *ipsum matrimonium* (*h*); but the expression of present consent in a written 'antenuptial' contract of marriage 'in the common style,' being accompanied by an obligation to solemnise the marriage, is not marriage; it is only *sponsalia de futuro* (*i*). 'The parties do not in this case *intend* to be bound till the nuptial ceremony is performed. But where an irregular marriage is in question, a promise or undertaking to solemnise the marriage at a future time does not suspend the contract, if it be otherwise clear that there is a deliberate acknowledgment of a present marriage (*k*).'

(*a*) Fraser, H. & W. 229 sqq.

(*b*) 1661, c. 34. 1695, c. 12. 1698, c. 6. 1 Hume's Crim. Law, 463 et seq. Carruthers and Crawford, *supra*, § 1511 (*b*). L. Adv. *v.* Wylie, 1 Hume, 466, note 2; 2 Ill. 238. L. Adv. *v.* Robertson, March 18, 1818; *ib.* note 4. L. Adv. *v.* Rutherford & Cogan, April 15, 1812; *ib.* note 3.

(*c*) L. Adv. *v.* Dickson, 1844; 2 Broun, 278. L. Adv. *v.* Ballantyne, 1859; 3 Irv. 352. As to exchange of consent before magistrates and collusive convictions, see 1 Hume's Crim. Law, 465. Fraser, H. & W. 257, 303. 1 Nicolson's Ersk. 144, notes. Report of Royal Comm. xviii. and App. 155. See § 1514A.

(*d*) See § 1511 (*e*), (*f*).

(*e*) A person celebrating a marriage with a religious ceremony, without having exhibited or produced to him a certificate or certificates of proclamation of banns, or of notice under the Marriage Notice Act, is liable to a penalty of fifty pounds. 41 and 42 Vict. c. 43, § 12. See above, § 1510A.

(*f*) See Fraser, H. & W. 229, 250 sqq. L. Adv. *v.* Ballantyne, *cit.* (*c*). 41 and 42 Vict. c. 43, § 12.

(*g*) Fraser, H. & W. 294 sqq.

(*h*) 1 Ersk. 6. § 11. **Dalrymple** *v.* **Dalrymple,** Dodson's Report, and 2 Hagg. Cons. Cases, 129; 2 Ill. 238; Clark's Cabinet Lib. of Scarce and Celd. Tracts, Edin. 1838. See M'Kie *v.* Ferguson, 1781; Hume, 355; Fergusson's Cons. R. 155. Currie *v.* Turnbull, 1806; *ib.* 373. **Walker** *v.* **M'Adam,** 1807; M. *Proof*, Apx. 4; aff. 1813, 1 Dow, 148; 5 Pat. 675. Anderson *v.* Fullarton, 1795; M. 12,690; Hume, 365. Stewart *v.* Menzies, *cit.* § 1519 (*b*) (condition). Lowrie *v.* Mercer, 1840; 2 D. 953. Leslie *v.* Leslie, 1860; 22 D. 993. Lockyer *v.* Sinclair, 1846; 8 D. 582 (intention of parties). Imrie *v.* Imrie, 1891; 19 R. 185 (do.). Op. in M'Kenzie *v.* Stewart, 1848; 10 D. 611. Fleming *v.* Corbet, 1859; 21 D. 1034. Roxburgh *v.* Watson, 1868; 7 Macph. 19 (evidence of relations). Forster *v.* Forster, 1869; 7 Macph. 797; aff. 1872, 10 Macph. H. L. 68. Robertson *v.* Stewart, 1874; 1 R. 532; rev. 2 R. H. L. 80.

(*i*) 1 Ersk. 6. § 3. See Lockyer *v.* Sinclair, *cit.*

(*k*) See above, § 25. Edmeston *v.* Cochrane, 1804; M. *Proof*, Apx. 2. Currie, *cit.* (*h*). Ritchie *v.* Wallace, 1792; Hume, 363.

1514A. '*Registration of Irregular Marriages.* —When a person is convicted before a magistrate or justice of the peace of an irregular marriage, either party to the marriage is authorised and required to register the marriage in the parish where the conviction is obtained; and the magistrate or justice is bound under a penalty to give notice of the conviction to the registrar. When an irregular marriage is established by declarator in a competent Court, either party is authorised to register the marriage in the parish of the domicile, or of the usual residence of the parties; and the clerk of Court is bound under a penalty to give notice to the registrar (*a*). No irregular marriage is valid, unless one of the parties has lived in Scotland twenty-one days preceding it, or has at the time usually resided there. Within three months after an irregular marriage has been contracted, the parties may jointly apply to the Sheriff for a warrant to register the marriage; and this being granted upon proof of the marriage and of residence in Scotland for the requisite time, and the marriage registered, a certificate of registration by the registrar is evidence of a valid marriage (*b*). Parties may establish the validity of marriages and their legitimacy, and that they are natural-born subjects, in the Court for Matrimonial Causes in England (*c*); and a declarator that the party is a natural-born subject is made competent in the Court of Session (*d*).'

(*a*) 17 and 18 Vict. c. 80, § 48, 49.
(*b*) 19 and 20 Vict. c. 96 (L. Brougham's Act).
(*c*) 21 and 22 Vict. c. 93.
(*d*) *Ib.* § 9.

1515. Promise of Marriage.—The most explicit promise or declaration of marriage to take effect in a certain future event, will not be purified into a legitimate proof of marriage by the event (*a*); nor will a written declaration of marriage found in one's repositories after death, or so framed as to be effectual only after death, be a legal constitution of marriage. A man may *de præsenti* declare a woman to be his *wife*, but he cannot otherwise effectually give her the rights of his *widow* (*b*).

But a 'mutual' promise of marriage in writing, 'or proved by writing,' or admitted on reference to oath (*c*), although not of itself marriage, nor a binding engagement to ground an action for implement, is, when followed by sexual intercourse, a legal ground of declarator of marriage; and when so declared, unites the parties as husband and wife as effectually as a regular marriage *in facie ecclesiæ*. In proper marriage (*sponsalia de præsenti*) the law presumes or takes no account of sexual intercourse; *consensus, non concubitus, facit matrimonium*. In marriage by promise *subsequente copula*, the sexual intercourse is not presumed; but, being proved, the consent to marriage is inferred (*d*).

(*a*) See above, § 1508; and below, § 1519.
(*b*) Anderson *v.* Fullarton, 1795; M. 12,690; Hume, 365. See also **Walker** *v.* **M'Adam,** 1807; M. Apx. *Proof*, 4; 1813, 1 Dow, 148; 5 Pat. 675; Fergusson's Cons. Rep, 189.
(*c*) Below, § 1518, 1519. See as to oath on reference, Longworth *v.* Yelverton, *infra*, § 1517 (*f*).
(*d*) 1 Stair, 4. § 6. 4 Stair, 3. § 42. 4 Stair, 45. § 19. Pennycook *v.* Grinton, 1752; M. 12,677; Elchies, *Proof*, 10; 2 Ill. 239. Reid *v.* Laing, 1823; 1 S. App. 440. **Dalrymple**, *supra*, § 1514 (*h*). Walker, *supra* (*b*). Innes *v.* Innes, 1835; 13 S. 1050; 2 S. & M'L. 417. 1 Bankt. 5. § 2. 4 Bankt. 45, 46 sqq. Op. in Browne *v.* Burns, 1843; 5 D. 1288, 1294. It has been doubted whether promise and *copula* do not constitute very marriage without any judicial sentence. See Lowrie *v.* Mercer, 1840; 2 D. 953, 960. Browne, *cit.* **Longworth** *v.* **Yelverton,** 1862; 1 Macph. 161; rev. 1864, 2 Macph. H. L. 49; 4 Macq. 745; and separate report. Maloy *v.* Macadam, 1885; 12 R. 431. Report of Royal Comm. p. xix. *Infra*, § 1520 *fin.* But the statement of the text, that a promise with subsequent *copula* does not constitute marriage unless declared by a decree of a competent Court, is supported by the learned and elaborate exposition of L. Fraser, H. & W. 323 sqq.; and by **The Queen** *v.* **Millis**, 10 Cl. & F. 534; Dix's Rept. (1842). It has been held that, in order to constitute marriage, both the promise must be given and the *copula* must commence in Scotland. Longworth, *cit.* Macdonald *v.* Macdonald, 1863; 1 Macph. 854.

1516. Marriage by Habit and Repute.—Cohabitation, 'which means constant living together in one house as husband and wife (*a*),' and habit and repute of marriage, 'in almost all countries creates a presumption of marriage (*b*); and,' if it be in Scotland, makes a marriage (*c*); 'or, more accurately, the two circumstances combined always afford strong evidence of marriage, and in Scotland, where marriage may be effected by *de præsenti* consent without proof of the precise time and place when such consent was interchanged, evidence which must be generally conclusive (*d*).' If the habit and repute of marriage have begun in avowed concubinage 'or adultery,' a very palpable and recognised change of purpose, 'or at least a very clear and undivided reputation of marriage after the parties have become at liberty to marry,' must be shown in aid of the proof by public opinion (*e*). It must be a general repute of the neighbourhood, not the report of one or two persons; and it must, as a very questionable kind of evidence, be supported by conduct or acquiescence uniform and consistent (*f*).

(*a*) **Lowrie** *v.* **Mercer**, 1840; 2 D. 953. Hamilton *v.* Hamilton, 1839; 2 D. 89; aff. 1842, 1 Bell's App. 736.
(*b*) Goodman *v.* Goodman, 28 L. J. Ch. 745. Piers *v.* Piers, 2 H. L. Ca. 331. Lyle *v.* Illwood, 44 L. J. Ch. 164; L. R. 19 Eq. 98. Collins *v.* Bishop, 48 L. J. Ch. 31. Hill *v.* Hibbit, 25 L. T. Rep. 183. Sastry Velaider Aronegary *v.* Sembecutty Vaigalie, 6 App. Ca. 364; 50 L. J. P. C. 28. Dysart Peerage Ca., 6 App. Ca. 489.
(*c*) M'Culloch *v.* M'Culloch, 1759; M. 4591; rev. 2 Pat. 33; 2 Ill. 241. See **Sassen** *v.* **Campbell**, 1824; 3 S. 159; rev. 2 W. & S. 309. Lowrie *v.* Mercer, *cit.* (*a*).
(*d*) See L. Redesdale in Cuninghame, *infra* (*f*); L. Moncreiff in Lapsley (*e*), and Lowrie (*a*); and L. Cranworth in Campbell (*e*).
(*e*) Farrell *v.* Barrie, 1828; 6 S. 472. Elder *v.* M'Lean, 1829; 8 S. 56. See Lowrie, *cit.* **Lapsley** *v.* **Grierson,** 1845; 8 D. 34; aff. 1 Cl. & F. 498; 20 S. Jur. 362. Cuninghame, *infra* (*f*). **Campbell** *v.* **Campbell** (Breadalbane case), 1866; 4 Macph. 867; aff. 5 Macph. H. L. 115. Thomas *v.* Gordon, *infra* (*f*). Wall *v.* De Thoren, 1874; 1 R. 1036. De Thoren *v.* Att.-Gen., 1 App. Ca. 686; 3 R. H. L. 28.
(*f*) **Cuninghame** *v.* **Cuninghame** (Balbougie), 1810; 15 F. C. 616, note; Hume, 376; revd. 1814, 2 Dow, 482; Fergusson, Cons. Rep. 122, 212. Thomas *v.* Gordon, 1829; 7 S. 872. See Farrell, *supra* (*e*). Adair *v.* Adair, 1829; 7 S. 597; 2 Ill. 248. Hamilton *v.* Hamilton (*a*). Lowrie (*a*). Sceales *v.* Sceales, 1867; 37 Jur. 191. Campbell, *cit.* (*e*). Napier *v.* Napier, 1801; Hume, 367. Longworth *v.* Yelverton, 1862; 24 D. 696. Forbes *v.* Css. Strathmore, Elch. *Proof*, 9; Ferg. Cons. R. 113; 6 Pat. 684.

1517. Proof of Marriage.—Marriage is judicially established by action of declarator in the Court of Session, now the great Consistory (*a*); or the question may arise incidentally in the course of another cause (*b*). In such judicial inquiries, a regular marriage is not, 'it is said,' to be set aside on pretence of a purpose different from marriage, or on probabilities arising out of subsequent acts and circumstances. An irregular marriage suggests doubts, and justifies an investigation into the deliberate purpose of the parties (*c*). 'But while it must be extremely difficult to prove that there was no real intention to marry when there has been a regular and public celebration, there is no decision which fixes the distinction here alleged; and there seems to be no sufficient reason for supporting a simulate marriage against the truth more than another simulate contract (*d*).'

In this and other consistorial causes, either the whole cause or any issue or issues of fact connected with it, may, at the discretion of the Court, be tried by jury; 'but it has never been done'; and the old consistorial oath is changed for the oath usual in other courts of justice (*e*). The decree 'is never pronounced in absence without evidence (*f*); and' once pronounced, 'could' not be challenged or reduced after a year (*g*). 'A decree of declarator in a consistorial action is *res judicata* or conclusive against all the world, as a judgment *in rem* (*h*). And in such actions the parties are now competent witnesses (*i*). A marriage *per verba de præsenti* may be declared after the death of one of the parties (*k*); but it is still undecided whether this is competent where the marriage is alleged to have been constituted by promise and subsequent *copula* (*l*).'

(*a*) 1 Will. IV. c. 69, § 33.

(*b*) See Farrell *v.* Barrie, 1828; 6 S. 472; 2 Ill. 241 (action against executors for money). Adair *v.* Adair, 1829; 7 S. 597; 2 Ill. 248 (declarator of legitimacy by son after death of parties). Pirie *v.* Ochterlony, 1787; Hume, 248 (multiplepoinding for distributing a succession). Downie *v.* Douglas, 1792; Hume, 251 (do.). Lenaghan *v.* Monkland Co., 1857; 19 D. 976 (assythment by widow). Beattie *v.* Baird, 1863; 1 Macph. 273. Rudland *v.* Gilbert, 1844; 16 S. Jur. 97 (action for debt of alleged wife). L. Fraser (H. & W. 1241–42) questioned Farrell *v.* Barrie; but there is no doubt as to the competency of deciding *incidenter* whether there has been a marriage, in cases where that is necessary for the decision of a question of pecuniary liability or patrimonial right. Wright *v.* Sharp, 1880; 7 R. 460. M'Donald *v.* Mackenzie, 1891; 18 R. 502. Sharp *v.* Sharp, 1898; 25 R. 1132 (nullity proved by way of exception). Incidental judgments are conclusive only between the parties to them.

(*c*) Dow *v.* Eadie, Dec. 9, 1811; Ferg. Cons. Rep. 43. See below, § 1520, and cases there. Browne *v.* Burns, 1843; 5 D. 1288. A. *v.* B., 1843; 6 D. 342, 932. Sassen *v.* Campbell, *cit.* § 1516. Lockyer *v.* Sinclair, 1846; 8 D. 582.

(*d*) In one case effect was refused to a regular marriage on the ground that it was without real consent on both sides. **M'Gregor** *v.* **Jolly,** 1824; 4 S. 254; rev. 3 W. & S. 85. Comp. Dow, *cit.* (*c*). See the opinions on both sides in Fraser, H. & W. 428–436. It is not doubted that fraud vitiates even a regular marriage *in facie ecclesiæ*. Allan *v.* Young and Cameron *v.* Malcolm, *infra*, § 1520 (*d*). Fraser, H. & W. 456 sqq.

(*e*) 11 Geo. IV. and 1 Will. IV. c. 69, § 36. Consistorial actions are now tried before the Lord Ordinary, without any jury, the evidence being recorded by a shorthand writer. 24 and 25 Vict. c. 86, § 13. 31 and 32 Vict. c. 100, § 100.

(*f*) 11 Geo. IV. and 1 Will. IV. c. 69, § 36. As to the effect of this clause in excluding an oath on reference, see Longworth *v.* Yelverton, 1865; 3 Macph. 654; aff. 1866, 5 *ib.* H. L. 144.

(*g*) See below, § 1536.

(*h*) Longworth *v.* Yelverton, *cit.* (*f*). See Lockyer *v.* Ferryman, 1876; 3 R. 882; aff. 1877, 4 R. H. L. 32; 2 App. Ca. 519.

(*i*) 16 and 17 Vict. c. 20, § 3 and 4; and 37 and 38 Vict. c. 64, § 1.

(*k*) Walker *v.* M'Adam, § 1514 (*h*). See Green, *infra*.

(*l*) Maloy *v.* M'Adam, 1885; 12 R. 431. Green *v.* Borthwick, 1896; 24 R. 211. See § 1515, 1520 *ad fin.*, 1534.

1518. In proving marriage, there must be *primâ facie* evidence either of regular celebration, or of unconditional consent to marriage *de præsenti*; or of a promise and engagement, followed by sexual intercourse. The promise can be proved only by writing or oath of the promiser (*a*). In the other cases the evidence may be parole; or written (*b*); or, 'perhaps, where the interests of third parties, as of the wife by a regular marriage, are not affected (*c*),' by confession on reference; or by a train of facts and circumstances (*d*); habit and repute and cohabitation inferring acknowledgment (*e*). But wherever by evidence of any of those descriptions present (*f*) matrimonial consent is proved, it makes perfect marriage (*g*).

(*a*) Above, § 1515. Campbell *v.* Honeyman, and Ross *v.* M'Leod, *infra*, § 1519 (*a*). Stewart, *ib.* (*c*). Harvie *v.* Crawford, *ib.* (*d*). Monteith and Mackenzie, *ib.* (*f*). Little *v.* Halliday, 1855; 17 D. 578. 37 and 38 Vict. c. 64, § 3. L. Fraser suggests (H. & W. 388) that third parties (*e.g.* a parochial board) having interest may be entitled to prove marriage by a promise *cum copula* entirely by parole. Compare § 1995 (2), below.

(*b*) See Forster *v.* Forster, 1869; 7 Macph. 797; aff. 1872, 10 Macph. H. L. 69.

(*c*) Gray *v.* Leny, 1801; Hume, 414. Pattinson *v.* Robertson, 1846; 9 D. 226. **Longworth** *v.* **Yelverton,** 1865; 3 Macph. 654; aff. 1866, 5 *ib.* H. L. 144.

(*d*) Aitchison, *cit. infra* (*g*). Craigie, *cit. infra* (*e*).

(*e*) 1 Stair, 4. § 6. 4 Stair, 45. § 19. 1 Ersk. 6. § 2 et seq. Above, § 1516. Dalrymple and Walker, *supra*, § 1514 (*h*). Craigie *v.* Hoggan, 1837; 15 S. 379, and 16 S. 584; aff. M'L. & Rob. 942; 2 Ill. 250.

(*f*) Anderson *v.* Fullerton, 1795; M. 12,690; Hume, 365. Hamilton *v.* Hamilton, 1839; 2 D. 89; aff. 1842, 1 Bell's App. 736. See Aitchison, *infra*, Craigie, *cit.*, and above, § 1514 *fin.*

(*g*) Aitchison *v.* Incorp. of Solicitors, 1838; 1 D. 42. Craigie and Walker, *supra* (*e*). Campbell *v.* Campbell, 1867; 5 Macph. H. L. 115, 134. Ivory's Ersk. 1, note 139. Leslie *v.* Leslie, 1860; 22 D. 993. Macdonald *v.* Macdonald, 1863; 1 Macph. 854. Wall *v.* De Thoren, 1874; 1 R. 1036. Robertson *v.* Stewart, 1874; 1 R. 532; rev. 1875, 2 R. H. L. 80.

1519. To establish marriage by promise and *copula*, the promise of marriage must precede the *copula*; or if the promise be after connection, it must be followed by intercourse in such circumstances as to connect the intercourse with the promise (*a*). The promise must be unconditional; and a declaration or promise of marriage conditionally, if there shall be a child born of the connection, is not marriage (*b*). It must not be an inference from mere courtship, or intention to marry; but the *copula* must follow either on positive engagement and promise accepted (*c*), 'clearly' established by writing, or oath, or circumstantial evidence; or on courtship and conduct amounting to an engagement (*d*). 'The antecedent promise must be proved by writ or oath (*e*); and the fact of courtship having gone on for some time, and other circumstances, are only available to aid in the construction of the writing which proves the promise. The promise itself need not be contained, though it must be distinctly proved, in the writings founded on (*f*).'

(*a*) White *v.* Hepburn, 1785; M. 12,686; 2 Ill. 243. Kennedy *v.* M'Dowall, 1800; Ferg. Cons. Rep. 163. Sim *v.* Miles, Nov. 20, 1829; F. C.; 8 S. 89. See also **Campbell** *v.* **Honeyman,** 1830; 8 S. 1039; 5 W. & S. 92; 2 Dow & Clark, 265. Craigie, *supra*, § 1518 (*e*). Bankton, *ut supra*, § 1515. Fraser, H. & W. 379 sqq. Ross *v.* M'Leod, 1861; 23 D. 972. Surtees *v.* Wotherspoon, 1873; 11 Macph. 384.

(*b*) Kennedy, *supra* (*a*). Stewart *v.* Menzies, 1833; 12 S. 179; 1836, 14 S. 427; aff. 1841, 2 Rob. 547. *Supra*, § 1514 (*h*). Surtees (*a*). M'Intosh *v.* Shillinglaw, 1829; 1 S. Jur. 135.

(*c*) Stewart *v.* Lindsay, 1818; Hume, 380; see 5 W. & S. 151, note. See as to this case, Fraser, H. & W. 375 sq.

(*d*) White, *supra* (*a*). Smith *v.* Grierson, 1755; M. 12,391; Ferg. Cons. Rep. 134. Stewart, *supra* (*c*). Campbell, *supra* (*a*). Harvie *v.* Inglis, 1837; 15 S. 964; 1839, 1 D. 536. See Cockburn *v.* Logan, 1676; M. 12,386. Harvie *v.* Crawford, 1732; M. 12,388. Cameron *v.* Cameron, 1814; Ferg. Cons. Rep. 139.

(*e*) See above, § 1515, 1518.

(*f*) Campbell, Ross, and other cases, *supra citt.* Monteith *v.* Robb, 1844; 6 D. 934. Mackenzie *v.* Stewart, 1848; 10 D. 611. **Longworth** *v.* **Yelverton,** 1862; 1 Macph. 161; rev. 2 Macph. H. L. 49; 4 Macq. 745. Morrison *v.* Dobson, 1869; 8 Macph. 347.

1520. Marriage Irrevocable.— Marriage, once established by clear, deliberate, and conclusive consent, cannot be annihilated or recalled by retractation, subsequent writing, disclamation, or conduct of the parties (*a*). But the evidence may be invalidated, when, the marriage not being regular, 'and probably even if it be regular (*b*),' the circumstances are ambiguous or inconclusive, and such as are fairly to be ascribed to deception, fraud, or an intention 'on both sides (*c*)' short of full and deliberate consent and purpose of marriage (*d*). Marriage being once lawfully contracted, no second marriage can have the effect of annulling it; or entitling the party in a second ceremony or attempt to marry, to bar, *personali exceptione*, the party in the first from vindicating their conjugal rights (*e*). But a question of great difficulty remains: whether promise with *copula* so constitutes marriage *ipso jure*, that it may be insisted on in prejudice of a second marriage solemnly celebrated. This is a question as yet undecided (*f*).

(*a*) Mackenzie *v.* Mackenzie, March 8, 1810; F. C.; 2 Ill. 245. See M'Gregor *v.* Jolly, § 1517 (*d*). Craigie, *supra*, § 1518 (*e*). Lowrie *v.* Mercer, 1840; 2 D. 953, 961 (*per* L. Moncreiff).

(*b*) See above, § 1517 (*d*).

(*c*) A mental reservation on one side only, the other party truly intending to contract marriage, does not prevent marriage; at all events, if the parties have in any measure acted upon the ostensible contract. See above, § 27A. Stewart *v.* Menzies, *cit.* § 1519 (*b*) Fleming *v.* Corbet, 1859; 21 D. 1045; and other authorities in Fraser, H. & W. 436 sqq. Bell *v.* Graham, 13 Moore, P. C. 242.

(*d*) Allan *v.* Young, 1773; Ferg. Cons. Rep. 37 (fraud). Cameron *v.* Malcolm 1756; M. 12,668; Ferg. Cons. Law, 156 (do.). M'Gregor *v.* Jolly, § 1517 (*d*). Macinnes *v.* More, 1781, 1782; M. 12,683; 2 Pat. 598; 3 Pat. 40; 2 Ill. 247. Taylor *v.* Kello, 1786; M. 12,687; rev. 3 Pat. 56. See opinion of Court in Ritchie *v.* Wallace, 1792; Hume, 363. Richardson *v.* Irving, 1785; Hume, 361. M'Gregor *v.* Campbell, 1801; M. 12,697. Farrell, *supra*, § 1517 (*b*). Cuninghame, Adair, and Thomas, *supra*, § 1516 (*f*). See above, § 1508 (*b*), § 1517 (*c*). Anderson *v.* Fullarton, 1795; Hume, 365 (writing not delivered). **Sassen** *v.* **Campbell,** 1824; 3 S. 159; alt. 2 W. & S. 309. Stewart (*c*). Robertson *v.* Stewart, 1874; 1 R. 532; rev. 1875, 2 R. H. L. 80. Imrie *v.* Imrie, 1891; 19 R. 185 (written declaration torn up). Morrison *v.* Dobson, and cases in § 1519 (*d*). As to force and fear, see above, § 12, and Fraser, H. & W. 444; as to error, see above, § 11; 1 Stair, 4. § 6; 4 Stair, 40. § 24. Fraser, H. & W. 448. Above, § 1508.

(*e*) Cochrane *v.* Campbell, 1746, 1753; M. 10,456; 5 B. Sup. 789; Elch. *Proof*, 7; 1 Cr. & St. 519; 3 W. & S. 135, note; Ferg. Cons. Rep. 84. Napier *v.* Napier, 1801; Hume, 367. Reid *v.* Robb, 1813; Hume, 378. See also M'Gregor, *supra* (*a*). Bell's Report of a Putative Marriage, *infra*, § 1525. Wright *v.* Wright's Trs., 1837; 15 S. 767.

(*f*) See Pennycook *v.* Grinton, 1752; M. 12,677; Elch. *Proof*, 10; 2 Ill. 239. Stewart, *supra*, § 1519 (*b*). See above, § 1515 (*d*).

1521. In declarators of marriage where a second marriage has been attempted, and of course the interests of the party to that marriage, or perhaps of children, are deeply interested, the question was raised in the House of Lords, whether it was not necessary to call those parties, and on a search of precedents it was found that no such necessity exists; it being competent for the party, however, to appear or interpose in the suit (*a*).

(*a*) Wright *v.* Wright's Trs., 1837 ; 15 S. 767. See precedents quoted in **M'Gregor** *v.* **Jolly,** 3 W. & S. 202, n. See also **Dalrymple** *v.* **Dalrymple,** Dod. Rep. ; 2 Hag. 129 ; 2 Ill. 238. Compare Longworth, *supra*, § 1518 (*c*).

1522. Impediments to Marriage.—All persons may, by the law of Scotland, effectually enter into marriage who are legally capable of consent, not already married, not divorced on account of adultery with the person with whom it is proposed to intermarry, and not within the forbidden degrees.

1523. (1.) *Incapacity.*—This may either be incapacity of consent or incapacity of conjugal duties. Incapacity of consent is from nonage or from mental infirmity. Males under fourteen, females under twelve, are incapable of consent, and therefore of marriage. But minors after puberty may marry, or by solemn consent ratify a previous marriage ; and this without consent of parents or guardians (*a*). Idiots are incapable of marriage ; and madmen unless during a lucid interval (*b*).

(*a*) 1 Stair, 4. § 6. 4 Stair, 45. § 19. 1 Ersk. 6. § 2. Dig. l. 23. t. 2. l. 4. De Rit. Nup. 1 Fraser, H. & W. 51. Johnston *v.* Ferrier, 1770 ; M. 8931 ; Hailes, 368 ; 2 Ill. 249. This case rejects for the law of Scotland the rule *malitia supplet ætatem* ; which, however, our criminal law applies in cases of rape. L. Adv. *v.* Fulton, 1841 ; 2 Swin. 564.

(*b*) Blair *v.* Blair, 1748 ; M. 6293. **Walker** *v.* **M'Adam,** 1807 ; M. *Proof*, Apx. 4 ; 1 Dow, 176 ; 5. Pat. 675. See below, § 2105, 2108 ; and as to proof of lucid interval, Fraser, H. & W. 75 sqq. As to intoxication, see Johnston *v.* Brown, Nov. 15, 1823 ; F. C. ; 2 S. 495, and Ferg. Cons. Rep. 229 ; and above, § 14 ; and as to outlawry, Macrae *v.* Macrae, 1836 ; 15 S. 54. Kynnaird *v.* Leslie, 35 L. J. C. P. 233.

1524. Incapacity of conjugal duties is a *ground* on which marriage may be declared void, at the instance of either of the parties, but is not in itself a nullity pleadable by others (*a*).

(*a*) 1 Stair, 4. § 6. 1 Ersk. 6. § 7. See Thomson *v.* Wright, 1767 ; M. 13,915 ; 2 Ill. 237. L. Adv. *v.* Masterton, 1837 ; 1 Swin. 427. A. *v.* B., 1863 ; 1 Macph. 1163. C. *v.* M., 1876 ; 3 R. 693. A. *v.* B., 1884 ; 11 R. 1060 ; aff. 1885, 12 R. H. L. 36. The case last cited, and the practice in the English Court, show a tendency to infer incapacity on evidence which falls short of showing the absolute impossibility of *copula*. See Fraser, H. & W. 80–104. The text here appears to recognise the competency of a challenge of the marriage by the impotent spouse himself. L. Fraser in some passages restricts the remedy to "the aggrieved spouse" (*e.g.* pp. 81, 98) ; but there seems to be neither reason nor authority for laying down such an absolute rule. Fraser, H. & W. 99, 100. It is proper that a challenge on this ground should be made promptly ; for a party may be barred from doing so by delay, inferring acquiescence. 2 Craig, 18. 18. Fraser, H. & W. 94. Reynolds *v.* Reynolds, 45 L. J. Pr. 89 ; L. R. 1 P. D. 405. Cuno *v.* Cuno, 41 L. J. P. & Matr. 37 ; L. R. 2 H. L. 300.

1525. (2.) *Impediment from previous Marriage.*—There can be no second marriage where the parties to the first are alive, and undivorced (*a*) ; and neither *bona fides* nor personal exception will protect the second marriage against challenge (*b*).

(*a*) 1 Stair, 4. § 6. 1 Ersk. 6. § 7. See Dalrymple, *supra*, § 1521 (*a*). Campbell, § 1519 (*a*). M'Gregor, § 1520 (*a*). Cases in § 1516 (*e*). Fraser, H. & W. 135.

(*b*) See Bell's Report of a Putative Marriage ; and below, of legitimacy of the children, § 1627. Fraser, H. & W. 151.

1526. (3.) *Impediment from Adultery.*—Although adultery was declared by the Legislature in 1600 to annul a marriage between the guilty parties, it does not seem ever, except in one case, to have been practically admitted to bar the succession of the issue (*a*). 'But it seems to be the law that such a marriage is invalid wherever one of the parties has been divorced for adultery committed with the other, at least if the paramour be named in the decree of divorce (*b*).'

(*a*) 1600, c. 20. 1 Stair, 4. § 7. 3 Stair, 3. § 42. 1 Ersk. 6. § 43. See Dig. l. 34. t. 9. l. 13. Decretal, l. iv. t. 7. c. 6. Lyle *v.* Douglas, 1670 ; M. 329 ; 2 Ill. 250 ; 2 B. Sup. 147, 468. Fraser, H. & W. 140.

(*b*) Campbell *v.* Campbell, 1866 ; 4 Macph. 867 ; aff. 5 Macph. H. L. 115. Beattie (Bell) *v.* Beattie, 1866 ; 5 Macph. 181.

1527. (4.) *Impediment from Relationship.*—Relationship is either of consanguinity or affinity. In *consanguinity*, or relationship by blood, the forbidden degrees comprehend ascendants and descendants to the most remote degree ; collaterals *in loco parentis*, '*i.e.* where the collateral is brother or sister to the direct ascendant of the other party,' also *in infinitum* ; and those of the whole or half blood, who are within the second degree ; cousins-german and all of more remote degree being free to intermarry (*a*). In *affinity* or relationship by marriage, the husband and wife being *one* (*b*), the blood-relations of each are held as related by affinity in the same degree to the one spouse as by consanguinity to the other. But it is no legal impediment to marriage that one of the parties has had illicit connection with a near relation of the other,—as where a man married a woman who (unknown to him) had lived in concubinage with his brother (*c*). The view on which, in England, it had been considered as lawful for a husband to marry his sister-in-law after the death of his wife, has never been admitted in Scotland (*d*), 'and such a marriage is invalid (*e*) ; as well as a marriage between an uncle and niece by affinity, or aunt and nephew by affinity (*f*).' And by a recent 'English' statute, all marriages subsequent to August 1835, within the prohibited degrees of affinity, are null, and not merely voidable (*g*).

(*a*) 1567, c. 15. 1 Stair, 4. § 4. 1 Ersk. 6. § 8, 9. 1 Hume's Crim. Law, 447.
(*b*) It is laid down that in order to constitute affinity the marriage must be consummated by *copula*. 1 Stair, 4. § 6; and authorities in Fraser, Husband and Wife, 106, 120.
(*c*) Hamilton *v.* Wylie, 1827; 5 S. 716; 2 Ill. 250.
(*d*) 1567, c. 15. 1690, c. 5, art. 24. 1 Stair, 4. § 6. 1 Ersk. 6. § 9. 1 Bankt. 5. § 47. 1 Mack. 6. § 5. Ferg. Cons. Law, 171. 1 Hume's Crim. Law, 449, 450. 2 Phillimore, Eccles. Cases, 16.
(*e*) **Fenton** *v.* **Livingstone,** 1856; 16 D. 104; 18 D. 865; opinions in H. L. 1859, 3 Macq. 497; 1861, 23 D. 366.
(*f*) Purves' Trs. *v.* Purves, 1895; 22 R. 513.
(*g*) 5 and 6 Will. IV. c. 54.

1528. Dissolution of Marriage.—Marriage is dissolved only by death or by divorce (*a*).

(*a*) Nicolson, de Nuptiis, as quoted by Stair, 1 Stair, 4. § 6, and 4 Stair, 45. § 19. 1 Ersk. 6. § 37.

1529. (1.) *Death.*—Although the death of either party dissolves marriage, this effect is not produced by civil death (*a*).

(*a*) Ersk. *ut supra.*

1530. (2.) *Divorce for Adultery.*—Divorce, either for adultery or for desertion, dissolves marriage (*a*).

Divorce for adultery formerly proceeded by an action before the Commissaries of Edinburgh, in which great care was taken to prevent collusion (*b*). It now proceeds by an action before the Court of Session (*c*); the success of which depends on proof of criminal intercourse with the defender (*d*). This must in each case depend on the circumstances of the case, but at least it is not indispensable to prove the identity of the paramour (*e*). The Lord Ordinary is required to administer the oath of calumny; and when the pursuer is abroad, a commission may be granted to take the oath (*f*).

'*Collusion* is regarded as an offence against public order, and is a bar to divorce (*g*). The Lord Advocate may enter appearance in an action of divorce or declarator of nullity of marriage, lead proof, and maintain such pleas as he considers warranted by the circumstances; and the Court may order the proceedings in any case to be laid before the Lord Advocate, that he may determine whether to enter appearance (*h*).'

Evidence and Procedure.—Sufficient evidence of the ground of action, 'including the marriage (*i*),' is required, even where appearance shall not be made for the defender (*k*). 'This rule excludes judicial, but not extrajudicial admissions by the defender (*l*).' It is also provided that the cause, or any issue connected with it, may be tried by jury (*m*). It may be important, in the proof of adultery, to have the *date* of the marriage fixed; and it was held competent to conjoin a declarator to this effect with the divorce (*n*). 'In consistorial actions the summons must be served personally, when the defender is not in Scotland; and this may be done by any person authorised by the pursuer, although not an officer of the law. If the defender's residence is unknown, edictal citation must be made; but in that case service is required on the children of the marriage, if any, and also on one or more of the next of kin, exclusive of the children, if known and resident within the United Kingdom (*o*). In an action of divorce at the instance of a husband, the alleged paramour may be called as a co-defender, without prejudice to the competency of adducing him as a witness; and if the adultery is proved, he may be found liable in expenses (*p*), including those which the husband may have been ordained to pay to the wife during the cause (*q*). The parties are now competent witnesses (*r*).'

(*a*) 1 Stair, 4. § 7. See as to the wife's expenses of suit, below, (*q*), and § 1620.
(*b*) St. Aubin *v.* O'Brien, 1814; Ferg. Con. Ca. 276; 2 Ill. 250. **Ford** (Greenhill) *v.* **Ford,** 1822; 1 S. 275; 1824, 2 S. App. 435. Shaw *v.* Gould, L. R. 3 H. L. 55; 37 L. J. Ch. 433. Graham *v.* Graham, 1881; 9 R. 327.
(*c*) 1 Will. IV. c. 69, § 33.
(*d*) See King *v.* King, 1842; 4 D. 567. M'Iver *v.* M'Iver, 1859; 21 D. 655. Murray *v.* Murray, 1847; 9 D. 1556. Campbell *v.* Campbell, 1860; 23 D. 99. Tulloh *v.* Tulloh, 1861; 23 D. 639 (pregnancy and non-access of husband; see also Pegg *v.* Pegg, 1859; 21 D. 820. Fullerton *v.* Fullerton, 1873; 11 Macph. 720). Walker *v.* Walker, 1871; 9 Macph. 1092 (latitude of time). Soeder *v.* Soeder, 1897; 24 R. 278 (do.). Collins *v.* Collins, 1882; 9 R. 785; 10 R. 250; aff. 1884, 11 R. H. L. 19; 9 App. Ca. 205. Whyte *v.* Whyte, 1884; 11 R. 710 (evidence of indecent conduct with other persons than the alleged paramour admitted in corroboration). Robertson *v.* Robertson, 1888; 15 R. 1001. Wilson *v.* Wilson, 1898; 25 R. 788 (single witness to each of separate acts).
(*e*) Smith *v.* Smith, 1838; 16 S. 499; 3 Ill. 158. Pegg and Tulloh, *citt.* Gray *v.* Gray, 1865; 37 Jur. 566.
(*f*) A. B. *v.* C. D., 1838; 16 S. 1143. Orde *v.* Murray, 1846; 8 D. 535. Hook *v.* Hook, 1862; 2 Macph. 488.
(*g*) Cases in (*b*). Fraser, H. & W. 1194.

(*h*) 24 and 25 Vict. c. 86, § 8. Ralston *v.* Ralston, 1881 ; 8 R. 371.
(*i*) See Lacy *v.* Lacy, 1869 ; 7 Macph. 369. Fraser, H. & W. 1148.
(*k*) 1 Will. iv. c. 69, § 36. See cases in note (*d*) as to sufficiency of proof.
(*l*) Campbell (*d*). A. *v.* B., 1858 ; 20 D. 407. Fullerton (*d*).
(*m*) 1 Will. iv. c. 69, § 37. See above, § 1517 (*c*).
(*n*) Sim *v.* Sim, 1834 ; 12 S. 633.
(*o*) 24 and 25 Vict. c. 86, § 10. 31 and 32 Vict. c. 100, § 100.
(*p*) 24 and 25 Vict. c. 86, § 7. Kydd *v.* Kydd, 1864 ; 2 Macph. 1074. Miller *v.* Simpson, 1863 ; 2 Macph. 225. Fraser *v.* Fraser & Hibbert, 1870 ; 8 Macph. 400 (jurisdiction against co-defender—lease).
(*q*) Andrews *v.* Andrews, 1873 ; 11 Macph. 401. Munro *v.* Munro, 1877 ; 4 R. 332, 344.
(*r*) 16 and 17 Vict. c. 20, § 3, 4 ; and 37 and 38 Vict. c. 64, § 1. See below, § 2244.

1531. Adultery might, by our old law, be tried criminally. But the civil action of divorce is a private remedy, and may be discharged by the party, or met by personal exception (*a*). The discharge of the private remedy, or *remissio injuriæ* '(condonation),' bars the action. It is inferred from cohabitation after knowledge of the offence (*b*) ; involving of course many nice points of evidence, in distinguishing between knowledge and mere suspicion (*c*) ; and from long delay of the action, importing acquiescence (*d*). 'Condonation completely extinguishes the condoned offence as a ground of divorce ; so that it cannot be revived to that effect by any subsequent fault ; and a condition attached to the forgiveness is void. But in an action of divorce for subsequent adultery with the same person, the forgiven adultery may be used in evidence (*e*).'

(*a*) 1563, c. 64. 1581, c. 105. 1592, c. 19. 1701, c. 11. It is not barred by decree of separation *a mensa et thoro* previously obtained by the pursuer. **Geils** *v.* **Geils,** 1850 ; 13 D. 333 ; 1852, 1 Macq. 255. Ritchie *v.* Ritchie, 1861 ; 4 Macq. 162.
(*b*) Aitken *v.* Macree, Feb. 6, 1810 ; F. C. ; 2 Ill. 251. Watson's Crs. *v.* Cruikshanks, 1681 ; M. 330 ; 3 B. Sup. 407. Anon., 1758 ; 5 B. Sup. 863. Greenhill, *supra*, § 1530 (*b*). See below, § 2033. Fraser, H. & W. 1176, sqq.
(*c*) Fairlie *v.* Fairlie, in H. L. 1815 ; 6 Pat. 121 ; see below, § 1533 (*b*). Stedman *v.* Stedman, 1742 ; 6 Pat. 675. Legrand *v.* Legrand, 1782 ; 2 Pat. 596. **Wemyss** *v.* **Wemyss,** 1866 ; 4 Macph. 660. Ralston *v.* Ralston, 1881 ; 8 R. 371. **Collins** *v.* **Collins,** *infra* (*e*).
(*d*) Duncan *v.* Maitland, March 9, 1809 ; F. C. Lockhart *v.* Henderson, 1799 ; M. *Adultery*, Apx. 1. See Best *v.* Best, 2 Phillim. Eccles. Cases, 161. Anon., *supra* (*b*). A. *v.* B., 1853 ; 15 D. 976. Wemyss, *cit.* Hellon *v.* Hellon, 1873 ; 11 Macph. 290.
(*e*) Lockhart, *cit.* (*d*). **Collins** *v.* **Collins,** 1882 ; 9 R. 785 ; 10 R. 250 ; aff. 1884 ; 11 R. H. L. 19 ; 9 Ap. Ca. 205.

1532. *Lenocinium* is a bar to divorce at the instance of the husband. It comprehends all that misconduct on the part of a husband by which he becomes the pander to his wife's guilt, exposes her to pollution, or encourages and promotes licentious conduct (*a*). 'There is no reason why the plea of connivance should not be sustained, if pleaded, against a wife seeking a divorce (*b*).'

(*a*) Sir G. M'Kenzie's Crim. Law, *voce* Adultery, § 6. Mackenzie *v.* His Wife, 1745 ; M. 333 ; 2 Ill. 251. Donald *v.* Donald, 1863 ; 1 Macph. 741. **Wemyss** *v.* **Wemyss,** 1866 ; 4 Macph. 660. Munro *v.* Munro, 1877 ; 4 R. 332. Marshall *v.* Marshall, 1881 ; 8 R. 702. Hunter *v.* Hunter, 1883 ; 11 R. 359.
(*b*) See Fraser, H. & W. 1185, 1189, 1192.

1533. Recrimination is no bar to divorce (though admitted as such in the Roman, Canon, and English law) (*a*) ; but it may entitle the party first injured to have divorce preferably to the other, with all the benefit thence accruing (*b*). When there are mutual actions of divorce, the Court will, on demand of the party, pronounce decree, without abiding the discussion of the pecuniary effect (*c*). 'Mutual guilt in modern practice entitles the parties to mutual divorces, the effect of which seems to be that neither can claim any interest in the estate of the other (*d*).'

(*a*) Logan *v.* Wood, 1561 ; M. 339 ; 2 Ill. 252. Correct 1 Bank. 5. § 128, by Lockhart *v.* Henderson, 1799 ; M. *Adult.* Apx. No. 1. Fraser, H. & W. 1196 sqq.
(*b*) Fairlie *v.* Fairlie, *supra*, § 1531 (*c*).
(*c*) M'Intyre *v.* M'Intyre, 1821 ; 1 S. 199. Walker *v.* Walker, 1871 ; 9 Macph. 460, 1091. Fraser *v.* Walker, 1872 ; 10 Macph. 837. See *infra*, § 1622.
(*d*) M'Intyre, *supra* (*c*). Warrender *v.* Warrender, 1836 ; 14 S. 1099. Donald *v.* Donald, 1863 ; 1 Macph. 741. Brodie *v.* Brodie, 1870 ; 8 Macph. 854. Thomson (Donald) *v.* Donald's Exr., 1871 ; 9 Macph. 1869. Cases in (*c*), *supra*. The Sess. Pa. in the later cases of Fairlie, June 15, 1819, F. C., show that the text correctly states the principle of that case, only one stage of which is reported in 6 Pat. 121.

1534. The action for divorce being entirely personal to the offended party, is barred, or after being commenced the action falls, by death ; and cannot competently be commenced or continued (*a*) by the heir or representative of the injured party (*b*). 'But defences to an action of divorce may be maintained by the defender's creditors (*c*) ; and, by statute, by the children and next of kin of the defender (*d*).'

(*a*) See Ritchie *v.* Ritchie, 1874 ; 1 R. 826. Fraser, H. & W. 1144, 1145. Compare § 1517 *fin.*, above.
(*b*) Clement *v.* Sinclair, 1762 ; M. 337 ; 2 Ill. 252. See Menzies *v.* Stevenson, Nov. 21, 1835 ; 14 S. 47 ; and F. C. An action of divorce or separation in the name of an insane wife is incompetent. Thomson *v.* Thomson, 1887 ; 14 R.

634 (Qu. As to tutor-dative after cognition ?). See below, § 1622, as to the effect of divorce on the estates.

(*c*) Ford *v.* Ford (Greenhill *v.* Ford), 1822 ; 1 S. 296 ; aff. 1824, 2 S. App. 435.

(*d*) 24 and 25 Vict. c. 86, § 10.

1535. (3.) *Divorce for Desertion.*—Wilful desertion by either spouse, if obstinately persisted in for four years, is a ground of divorce by the law of Scotland (*a*). The action may be raised after a year's desertion, provided four years of desertion shall have elapsed before decree. The party complained against must be within Scotland ; or if absence abroad be part of the offence, 'it was held that' personal notice must be given, unless by concealment and ignorance of the place of residence that is rendered impossible (*b*). 'But where jurisdiction exists, the matter of notices is now regulated by the Conjugal Rights Act of 1861 (*c*).' To prevent collusion an oath of calumny is required. The proceedings prescribed by the statute 'were' in practice supplanted by others. There was formerly a sentence of excommunication, on pronouncing of which "the malicious and obstinate defection of the party offender" was declared "ane sufficient cause of divorce." The proceeding 'until 1861 was,' first, a decree of adherence ; secondly, a charge to adhere, and denunciation ; thirdly, an application to the presbytery, which 'declined' to interfere, when a protest 'closed' the proceeding, and 'was' in practice held equivalent to the excommunication of the old law ; after which an offer to adhere 'came' too late to bar the divorce (*d*). 'But since the Conjugal Rights Act of 1861 these preliminaries are unnecessary, the lapse of four years giving a right to sue for divorce (*e*). This provision, however, does not seem to alter the principle of the law as to non-adherence or wilful defection, but only the form of process (*f*). And so the rule remains, that the defender must be proved to have been and continued in malicious and obstinate "defection" without a reasonable cause (*g*).' A sufficient ground of separation, 'such as cruelty (*h*), or adultery, whether committed before or after the commencement of the separation (*i*),' is a good defence : 'but as the action is founded on the pursuer's willingness to adhere, a wife suing a divorce for desertion cannot always successfully plead as her ground of action a desertion which consists in her having left his house by reason of his cruelty without having been actually driven from it (*k*).'

(*a*) 1573, c. 55. 1 Stair, 4. § 8. 1 Ersk. 6. § 44. Fraser, H. & W. 1207. Gregor *v.* M'Gregor, 1836 ; 14 S. 707 ; 2 Ill. 252. See as to the protection from the husband and his creditors of property acquired by deserted wives, *infra*, § 1540A, 1560B.

(*b*) Blake *v.* Blake, 1826 ; 4 S. 803 ; 2 Ill. 256. Downie (Buchanan) *v.* Downie, 1837 ; 16 S. 82 ; 3 Ill. 158. See A. B. *v.* C. D. (Duke *v.* Duke), 1845 ; 7 D. 556. O'Rourke *v.* O'Rourke, 1849 ; 11 D. 976. Smith *v.* Smith, 1854 ; 16 D. 544. Carswell *v.* Carswell, 1881 ; 8 R. 901.

(*c*) 24 and 25 Vict. c. 86, § 10 ; as to which, see above, § 1530 *fin.*, and M'Callum, *infra* (*e*). The remedy is not available against a foreigner by domicile who has married a Scotch woman in Scotland. Gordon *v.* Gordon, 1847 ; 9 D. 1293. A. B. *v.* C. D., *cit.* (*b*). See Redding *v.* Redding, 1888 ; 15 R. 1102.

(*d*) Murray *v.* M'Lauchlan, 1838 ; 1 D. 294. It is an undecided question, as to which conflicting opinions have been given, whether an honest offer to adhere may not receive effect after the action of divorce has been raised, on the ground that no previous action of adherence is now required. Muir *v.* Muir, Winchcombe *v.* Winchcombe, Auld *v.* Auld, *citt. infra* (*g*) (*f*). Lilley *v.* Lilley, 1881 ; 12 R. 145. See Fraser, H. & W. 1214. If the 11th sec. of the Conjugal Rights Act affects procedure only, it seems to be the better opinion that the substantial right of offering still to adhere is not *in all circumstances* taken away from the deserting spouse.

(*e*) 24 and 25 Vict. c. 86, § 11. M'Callum *v.* M'Callum, 1865 ; 3 Macph. 550.

(*f*) Bowman *v.* Bowman, 1866 ; 4 Macph. 384 (*per* L. Pr. Colonsay). Auld *v.* Auld, 1884 ; 12 R. 36 (*per* L. Pr. Inglis). See A. B. *v.* C. D., 1853 ; 16 D. 111. Mackenzie *v.* Mackenzie, 1893 ; 20 R. 636 ; aff. 1895, 22 R. H. L. 32 ; A. C. 384.

(*g*) A. *v.* B., 1868 ; 40 Jur. 497. See Chalmers *v.* Chalmers, 1868 ; 6 Macph. 547. Muir *v.* Muir, 1879 ; 6 R. 1353. Winchcombe *v.* Winchcombe, 1881 ; 8 R. 726. Young *v.* Young, 1882 ; 10 R. 184 (defender's penal servitude). Barrie *v.* Barrie, 1882 ; 10 R. 208. Willey *v.* Willey, 1884 ; 11 R. 815. **Watson *v.* Watson**, 1890 ; 17 R. 736 (remonstrance a question of circumstances). Gibson *v.* Gibson, 1894 ; 21 R. 470 (seven judges—do.). The difference of opinion between the First Div. (Bowman, Auld, Barrie, Lilley, Chalmers, M'Callum, *citt.*) holding the affirmative, and the Second Div. (Gould, Winchcombe, Muir, Willey, *citt.*) holding the negative, as to the need of remonstrance to ground a divorce, came up, in Watson, *cit.*, before the whole Court, a majority of which expressed the opinion stated above in this note. See also Mackenzie, *cit.* (*f*), and cases in (*k*). As to *mora*, see Mackenzie *v.* Mackenzie, 1883 ; 11 R. 105. Willey, *cit.* Contrast § 1560B, below.

(*h*) Letham (*i*). Auld (*f*). Other causes than these are pleadable. Chalmers, *cit.* Gould *v.* Gould, 1887 ; 15 R. 229.

(*i*) Letham *v.* Letham, 1823 ; 2 S. 284. A. B. *v.* C. D., *cit.* (*b*). Bowman *v.* Bowman, *cit.* (*f*). A. *v.* B., 1896 ; 23 R. 588.

(*k*) Bowman *v.* Bowman, *cit.* Contrast Gibson *v.* Gibson, *cit.*, with Murray *v.* Murray, 1894 ; 21 R. 723 (wife extruded from house). And see Mackenzie, *cit.* (*f*). In Gow *v.* Gow, 1887, 14 R. 443, the Second Division almost seems to have taken a different view. But Bowman *v.* Bowman does not appear to have been considered, and the report is very brief, and does not necessarily imply that the wife was unwilling to adhere.

1536. The rule that decrees of the Commissary Court in consistorial causes cannot be reduced after year and day from the sentence (*a*), 'was' in observance (*b*). 'But while no such rule can apply to the consistorial jurisdiction now vested in the Court of Session, it appears that it extended at any time only to exclude reductions of their own decrees by the Commissaries (*c*). A decree in a consistorial cause will not be reduced on the mere allegation of perjury; there must be an averment of subornation or knowledge of the perjury of witnesses, amounting to fraud of the party obtaining the decree (*d*).'

(*a*) Instructions to Commissaries, 1563; confirmed by 1592, c. 25, and 1606, c. 6.
(*b*) Gardiner *v.* M'Arthur, May 16, 1823; F. C.; 2 S. 276, note; 2 Ill. 252. Donald *v.* Thom, May 16, 1823; F. C.; 2 S. 275. Menzies *v.* Menzies, 1835; 14 S. 47. Stewart *v.* Stewart, 1863; 1 Macph. 449.
(*c*) Lockyer *v.* Ferryman, 1876; 3 R. 882. Fraser, H. & W. 1236.
(*d*) Forster *v.* Grigor, 1871; 9 Macph. 445. Lockyer *v.* Ferryman, *cit.*

1537. Foreign Marriages.—The questions arising as to foreign marriages chiefly relate to the constitution of the marriage (*a*) or its dissolution.

As marriage is a contract *juris gentium*, it is effectual wherever constituted according to the forms of the country in which it is contracted (*b*). 'Difficult questions arise with regard to personal capacity. In general, a person must have capacity according to the law of his domicile. But, at least if one party be domiciled in this country, his marriage here is valid, notwithstanding a personal incapacity of the other in her domicile which is of a kind not recognised by our law (*c*).'

It has been held in Scotland, that wherever the marriage may have been contracted or the adultery committed, an action for dissolving the marriage is competent in the Consistory Court of Scotland, provided the parties are domiciled in Scotland; the husband's domicile, '—which, if it does not necessarily mean his permanent domicile, governing his succession and other legal relations, at least means in questions of *status* one constituted by residence of a much more permanent and continuous character than the forty days' residence formerly held in Scotland to be sufficient to found jurisdiction in such cases (*d*),—' being that of the wife, 'even where there is a formal deed of separation (*e*), but not necessarily after judicial separation (*f*)'; and that there is no collusion for evading the law of other countries (*g*). 'There is not, as was once thought, jurisdiction on the ground of personal citation in the *locus delicti* (*h*).'

(*a*) As to the marriage of British subjects abroad, see above, § 1507 (*c*).
(*b*) Pertreis *v.* Tondear, 1 Hagg. Cons. 136; 2 Hagg. Cons. 417. Story, Conf. of Laws, 100 et seq., and the authorities cited. Fraser, H. & W. 1297 sqq. Forbes *v.* L. Strathmore, 1756; Elch. 365; 5 B. Sup. 853; 2 Ill. 253. MacCulloch *v.* MacCulloch, 1759; M. 4591; 2 Ill. 241. Scruton *v.* Gray, 1772; M. 4822; Hailes, 499 (no jurisdiction by arrestment in action as to personal status). Brook *v.* Brook, 9 H. L. 193. Scrimshire *v.* Scrimshire, 2 Hagg. 408. *In re* Wright, 25 L. J. Ch. 621.
(*c*) Sotomayor *v.* De Barros, L. R. 5 P. D. 94; 49 L. J. P. D. & A. 1; see Fraser, H. & W. 1533. Beattie *v.* Beattie, 1866; 5 Macph. 181. Westlake, Priv. Int. Law, 52 sqq. Fraser, H. & W. 1297 and 1538. Guthrie's Savigny's Priv. Int. Law, pp. 153, 164, 171, 300, where the authorities will be found; and discussions on the doctrine of the Lords Justices in the earlier stage of the case of Sotomayor *v.* De Barros (3 P. D. 1; 47 L. J. P. D. & A. 23). Of course no country recognises the validity of marriages which are forbidden by an absolute and prohibitory law of its own. Brook *v.* Brook, *cit.* Fenton *v.* Livingstone, 1859; 3 Macq. 497. The Sussex Peerage, 11 Cl. & F. 85.
(*d*) **Pitt** *v.* **Pitt**, 1862; 24 D. 1444; rev. 2 Macph. H. L. 28; 4 Macq. 627. Jack *v.* Jack, 1862; 24 D. 467. Hook *v.* Hook, 1862; 24 D. 488. Wilson *v.* Wilson, 1872; 10 Macph. 573. Carsewell *v.* Carsewell, 1881; 8 R. 901. Stavert *v.* Stavert, 1882; 9 R. 519. See Niboyet *v.* Niboyet, 4 P. D. 1; 48 L. J. P. D. & A. 1. Harvey *v.* Farnie, 8 App. Ca. 43. Low *v.* Low, 1891, 19 R. 115, shows how the rule that jurisdiction depends on the complete or absolute domicile may lead to great hardship and inconvenience. Dombrowitzki *v.* Dombrowitzki, 1895; 22 R. 906.
(*e*) Warrender, *infra* (*g*).
(*f*) *Arg. ex* 24 and 25 Vict. c. 86, § 6.
(*g*) Gordon *v.* Eaglesgraaf, 1699; 2 Ill. 253. Brunsdon *v.* Wallace, 1789; M. 4784; Hailes, 1063. Pirie *v.* Lunan, 1797; M. 4594. French *v.* Pilcher, 1800; M. *Forum Comp.* Apx. 1. Wyche *v.* Blount, 1801; *ib.* 2. Morecombe *v.* M'Lelland, 1801; *ib.* 3; Ferg. Cons. Rep. 29. Murray *v.* Lindley, 1805; *ib.* 11 (prorogation—contradicted in Ringer, *infra*). Lindsay *v.* Tovey, 1807; *ib.* 12; 1 Dow, 118. Utterton *v.* Tewsh, 1812; Ferg. Cons. Law, 42. Sugden *v.* Lolly, 1812; *ib.* 13. R. *v.* Lolly, R. & R. C. C. 237; 2 Cl. & F. 567, n. Edmonstone *v.* Edmonstone, and Forbes *v.* Forbes, June 1, 1816; F. C. Levett *v.* Levett, and Kibblewhite *v.* Rowland, Dec. 21, 1811; F. C. Blake *v.* Blake, 1826; 4 S. 803. Sharp *v.* Orde, 1829; 8 S. 49. Warrender *v.* Warrender, 1834; 12 S. 847; 2 S. & M'L. 154. Ringer *v.* Churchill, 1840; 2 D. 307. Duke *v.* Duke (A. B. *v.* C. D.), 1845; 7 D. 556. Bennie *v.* Bennie, 1819; 11 D. 1211 (domicile of origin). Geils *v.* Geils, 1850; 13 D. 321; aff. 1852, 1 Macq. 255. Shields *v.* Shields, 1852; 15 D. 142. Tulloh *v.* Tulloh, 1861; 23 D. 639. Pitt and cases *supra* (*b*) and (*d*). Dolphin *v.* Robins, 7 H. L. Ca. 390; 3 Macq. 563. Shaw *v.* Gould (*in re* Wilson's Trusts), 35 L. J. Ch. 243; 37 L. J. Ch. 433; L. R. 3 H. L. 55. Beattie (*c*). Report of Royal Comm. xxvi. Fraser on the Conflict of Laws in Cases of Divorce, Edinr., 1860. Fraser, H. & W. 1251–1316.
(*h*) Jack *v.* Jack, Pitt *v.* Pitt, and Stavert *v.* Stavert, *citt.*

1538. Adherence.—In marriage, the parties bind themselves to live together till death part them; and the mutual obligation may be enforced by an action called an action of adherence (*a*). To this (on the part of the wife) is added a separate action for aliment (*b*);

in which she is allowed sufficient for her subsistence, and for carrying on her action, with a due aliment on decree of adherence being pronounced. The decree of adherence may be followed by a charge on letters of horning. But there is no further means of enforcing the duty than either by decree and diligence for a suitable aliment, or by an action of divorce after four years' desertion. 'Desertion is no defence to an action for implement of an antenuptial contract (*c*); but the pursuer's cruelty or adultery is a good defence to an action of adherence (*d*); or a decree of protection under the Conjugal Rights Act (*e*). But not desertion which may be put an end to by a *bonâ fide* offer to adhere; nor in general a voluntary contract of separation (*f*).'

(*a*) Fraser, H. & W. 867 sqq. Lang *v.* Lang, 1851; 13 D. 1108. A. B. *v.* C. D., 1853; 16 D. 111.

(*b*) See below, § 1545. As to the obligation of a wife, having separate estate, to aliment her husband, see Fingzies *v.* Fingzies, 1890; 28 S. L. R. 6 (O. H.).

(*c*) Smith *v.* Smith, 1866; 4 Macph. 279.

(*d*) Lang *v.* Lang, and A. B. *v.* C. D., *citt.*

(*e*) 24 and 25 Vict. c. 86, § 3.

(*f*) See above, § 1535; below, § 1544.

1539. **Separation.**—What in England is called a divorce *a mensâ et thoro*, is in Scotland distinguished as a mere separation. It is competent, notwithstanding the engagement to adhere, either judicially or by voluntary agreement.

1540. (1.) *Judicial Separation* proceeds on satisfactory evidence of life being endangered; or of a fair and reasonable ground of apprehension of personal violence; or of continued annoyance, wearing out and exhausting the party; or of adulterous practices (*a*). 'Maltreatment as a ground of separation is in its nature "continuous and cumulative"; and therefore continued cohabitation is no defence to a suit for separation. So also, a return to cohabitation, while it imports forgiveness or condonation of past injuries, does not, like condonation of adultery, bar the injured party from founding on the forgiven injuries if the maltreatment be renewed, the true issue being whether the injured spouse can live with the other with safety to person and health. In this case, therefore, the reconciliation or condonation is in its nature conditional (*b*).'

(*a*) Fraser, H. & W. 877. Baillie *v.* Murray, 1714; Ferg. Cons. Law, 184; 2 Ill. 257. M'Lelland *v.* Fulton, 1813; *ib.* 185. Dss. Gordon *v.* D. Gordon, 1697; *ib.* 190. Letham *v.* Provan, 1823; 2 S. 284. Sinton (Irvine) *v.* Irvine, 1833; 11 S. 402. Muirhead *v.* Muirhead, 1846; 8 D. 786. Macfarlane *v.* Macfarlane, 1847; 9 D. 500; 1849, 11 D. 533. Borthwick *v.* Borthwick, 1848; 10 D. 1312. **Paterson** *v.* **Russell,** 1849; 11 D. 21; rev. 7 Bell's App. 337. Fulton *v.* Fulton, 1850; 12 D. 1104 (violence under influence of drink only). Steuart *v.* Steuart, 1870; 8 Macph. 821 (excitable temper verging on insanity no defence). Montgomery Moir *v.* Moir, 1751; Elch. *Husband and Wife,* 35; 6 Pat. 687. M'Gaan *v.* M'Gaan, 1880; 8 R. 279. Paterson *v.* Paterson, 1861; 24 D. 215 (refusal of sexual intercourse not a ground of separation). Strain *v.* Strain, 1885; 13 R. 132 (wilfully or with reckless indifference to the wife's health communicating venereal disease). As to adultery as a ground for judicial separation, see Wilson *v.* Wilson, 1866; 4 Macph. 732. Symington *v.* Symington, 1874; 1 R. 871. As to insane spouse, see above, § 1534 (*b*). As to title to sue when former husband not proved dead, see Sharp *v.* Sharp, 1898; 25 R. 1132.

(*b*) Shand *v.* Shand, 1832; 10 S. 384. Irvine and Macfarlane, *citt.* (*a*). Graham *v.* Graham, 1878; 5 R. 1093. Collins *v.* Collins, *cit.* § 1531 (*e*). Authorities in Fraser, H. & W. 901. See above, § 1531.

1540A. '*Decree of Separation and Custody of Children.*—The effect of the decree of separation, which may be obtained at the instance of either spouse (*a*), is to suspend the rights of the spouses over each other's persons (*b*). After decree obtained at the instance of a wife, it is provided by statute that all property which would otherwise fall under the *jus mariti*, acquired by her or coming to or devolving upon her, shall be regarded as property belonging to her from which the *jus mariti* and right of administration are excluded, may be disposed of by her as if she were unmarried, and on her death passes to her heirs and representatives as if her husband had been dead. If she again cohabits with her husband, her property (*c*), subject to any written agreement between her and her husband, is held to her separate use, exclusive of the *jus mariti* and right of administration. The wife, when so separate, is capable of suing and being sued, and liable for wrongs and injuries as if unmarried; and the husband is not liable for her obligations or contracts, wrongful acts or omissions, or for costs incurred in any action she may sue or defend. If the husband fail to pay any aliment awarded to the wife, he is liable for necessaries supplied to her use (*d*). In actions of separation and divorce, the Court has the widest and most general discretion to make interim and final orders as to the custody, maintenance, and education of pupil children of the marriage, during pupillarity (*e*), but only before decree of divorce or separation has been pronounced (*f*). It has common law powers as to the custody of children, which may be exercised in the action of divorce or separation, or under a separate application. There is no general rule that the guilty father shall be deprived of his common law right to the custody of the children; but the Court is to exercise its discretion according to the whole circumstances (*g*). A judicial separation, which in the ordinary and now invariable form bears to be for all time coming, cannot be recalled by the Court (*h*), but it may be waived by mutual consent of the spouses, upon which all their respective rights revive (*i*), with the statutory exception above noticed (*k*).'

(*a*) See Pickard *v.* Pickard, 33 L. J. Pr. & D. 158; 3 Sw. & T. 523. Forth *v.* Forth, 36 L. J. Pr. & D. 122. Calder, petr., 1841; 3 D. 615. As to jurisdiction, see Le Mesurier, 1895, A. C. 517 (*per* L. Watson). Hood *v.* Hood, 1897; 24 R. 973. Above §, 1537.
(*b*) Fraser, H. & W. 906.
(*c*) 24 and 25 Vict. c. 86, § 19. (*d*) *Ib.* § 6.
(*e*) Watson *v.* Watson, 1895; 23 R. 219.
(*f*) *Ib.* § 9. M'Farlane *v.* M'Farlane, 1847; 9 D. 904. Lang *v.* Lang, 1869; 7 Macph. 445. Ketchen *v.* Ketchen, 1870; 8 Macph. 952. Steuart *v.* Steuart, 1870; 8 Macph. 831. Symington *v.* Symington, 1874; 1 R. 871; altered 1875, 2 R. H. L. 41; 1875, 2 R. 974. Shirer *v.* Dixon, 1885; 12 R. 1013 (inquiry before proof—procedure—expenses). M'Callum *v.* M'Callum, 1893; 20 R. 293 (procedure).
(*g*) Lang, *cit.* Lilley *v.* Lilley, 1877; 4 R. 397. Bloe *v.* Bloe, 1882; 9 R. 894. Bowman *v.* Graham, 1883; 10 R. 1234. Fraser, P. & C. 70. See below, § 2068; and as to the Guardianship of Infants Act, 1886, § 2083.
(*h*) Strain *v.* Strain, 1890; 17 R. 297, correcting Fraser, H. & W. 907.
(*i*) Winton *v.* Grieve, 1830; 2 S. Jur. 370. Palmer *v.* Bonnar, Jan. 25, 1810; F. C. Fraser, *l.c.*
(*k*) *Supra* (*c*).

1541. (2.) *Voluntary Separation.*—Although it was at first doubted (*a*), it is now settled, that a separation may be effected by mutual consent. But courts of law, though they wink at the practice, will not interfere to aid or complete such contracts by awarding aliment, if not settled by the parties (*b*); 'or in any way authorising a separation of consent, except upon evidence of one or more of the legal grounds for separation above stated (*c*). But under statute they may settle the custody of the children (*d*).'

(*a*) 1 Ersk. 6. § 20. Drummond *v.* Rollock, 1624; M. 6152; 2 Ill. 258; see 1 B. Sup. 349. Fraser, H. & W. 911.
(*b*) Bell *v.* Bell, Feb. 22, 1812; F. C. See Macdonald *v.* Macdonald's Trs., 1863; 1 Macph. 1065. Scott *v.* Scott, 1894; 21 R. 853 (child born three months after separation). Contrast with Hay, below, § 1545 (*g*).
(*c*) Macfarlane *v.* Macfarlane, 1847; 9 D. 400.
(*d*) 49 and 50 Vict. c. 27, § 5. Mackellar *v.* Mackellar, 1898; 25 R. 883. See below, § 2083.

1542. The husband has been held entitled to assign a separate residence to his wife; but this is not a settled point, and the power is very questionable (*a*).

(*a*) Colquhoun *v.* Colquhoun, 1804; M. *Husband and Wife*, Apx. 5; 2 Ill. 258.

1543. The wife is not entitled to separate herself from her husband and family, unless for protection and safety against such danger or insult as will justify judicial separation (*a*); and she cannot exclude him from any separate house to which she may have removed (*b*). Her remedy is judicial separation.

(*a*) Letham, *supra*, § 1540 (*a*).
(*b*) Russell *v.* Russell, 1820; Hume, 224.

1544. Separation by mutual consent is revocable by either party; 'but the revocation does not affect arrears or accumulations of aliment under the separation deed' (*a*). If, however, the grounds stated in the contract be sufficient for a judicial separation, the agreement will receive effect as irrevocable (*b*) 'until final decree in an action of adherence (*c*).' But a voluntary contract is no defence against an action for judicial separation (*d*). A contract of separation is occasionally combined with post-nuptial provisions, and those may be irrevocable, though the separation may not (*e*). 'It is revoked by service of a summons of divorce (*f*). It is not revocable after the dissolution of the marriage (*g*), or by creditors (*h*). The Court must be satisfied that the revocation is *bonâ fide* with the intention of adherence, and not a device for defeating claims of aliment, etc. (*i*).'

(*a*) Livingstone *v.* Begg, Feb. 6, 1666; M. 6153; 2 Ill. 258. E. Argyle *v.* Css. Argyle, 1695; M. 6054. Palmer *v.* Bonnar, Jan. 25, 1810; F. C. Dickson *v.* Hunter, 1827; 5 S. 266; aff. 1831, 5 W. & S. 455. Malcolm *v.* Mack, 1805; Hume, 2. See Lawson *v.* Bain, 1830; 9 S. 923. M'Millan *v.* M'Millan, 1871; 9 Macph. 1067.
(*b*) Shand *v.* Shand, 1832; 10 S. 384.
(*c*) A. B. *v.* C. D. (Richmond *v.* Richmond), 1853; 15 D. 372; 16 D. 111; 25 S. Jur. 257.
(*d*) Lawson *v.* M'Culloch, 1797; M. 6157.
(*e*) Miller *v.* Brown, *cit.* (*g*). Sutherland *v.* Syme, 1772; Hailes, 479. Macgregor's Tr. *v.* Macgregor, Jan. 22, 1820; F. C. Davidson *v.* Davidson, 1867; 5 Macph. 710. See Palmer and Dickson, *citt.* (*a*).
(*f*) Warrender *v.* Warrender, 1835; 2 S. & M'L. 154. Shand, *supra* (*b*).
(*g*) Palmer and Dickson, *citt.* Miller *v.* Brown, 1776; M. 6456; 5 B. Sup. 473; Hailes, 678.
(*h*) Macgregor, *supra* (*e*).
(*i*) Palmer and Dickson, *citt.* Hood *v.* Hood, 1871; 9 Macph. 449.

1545. Aliment.—A wife is entitled to separate aliment in all cases of her husband's desertion; or in judicial separation; during an action of 'separation or' divorce, 'in the discretion of the Court if she be pursuer (*a*), but not after decree of divorce has been pronounced (*b*)'; the question formerly being proper in such cases to the Commissary Court, but now being competent to the Court of Session, or, 'to a very limited extent,' to the Sheriff Court (*c*). But she is not *de jure* entitled to aliment without proof; the Court being vested with a discretionary power to give or to withhold aliment according to circumstances (*d*); 'or to alter its amount (*e*). And, unless the husband, by failing to appear, or expressly, admits his desertion, a claim for aliment can be maintained by a wife only in an action which concludes for a decree of adherence or of separation as well as for aliment (*f*). Hence it appears that these being proper consistorial actions, the Sheriff's jurisdiction to award aliment to a deserted or maltreated wife, where there is no contract of separation, extends only to the granting of interim aliment in case of absolute necessity, if the marriage is not denied, for a definite period, that the rights of parties may be determined by the competent Court (*g*). A *bonâ fide* offer to entertain the pursuing wife at bed and board extinguishes the ground of action (*h*).'

(*a*) Fraser, H. & W. 837 sqq. Fraser *v.* Abernethy, 1774; Hailes, 572; 2 Ill. 260. De la Motte *v.* Jardine, 1789; M. 447; Hailes, 1060. Gray (Croall) *v.* Croall, 1832; 11 S. 185. Kennedy (Currie) *v.* Currie, 1833; 12 S. 171. Scott *v.* Selbie, 1835; 13 S. 278. Craigie *v.* Craigie, 1837; 15 S. 836. See M'Farlane *v.* M'Farlane, 1844; 6 D. 1220; 1848, 10 D. 962 (wife having separate estate). Alexander *v.* Alexander, 1849; 12 D. 117. As to alimony of widow, see below, § 1572; and aliment of wife voluntarily separate, above, § 1541.

(*b*) Stewart *v.* Stewart, 1872; 10 Macph. 472. Ritchie *v.* Ritchie, 1874; 1 R. 826. Shirrefs *v.* Shirrefs, 1896; 23 R. 807.

(*c*) 1 Will. IV. c. 69, § 32–3. 24 and 25 Vict. c. 86, § 15. 37 and 38 Vict. c. 31.

(*d*) Kennedy, *supra* (*a*). Maxwell *v.* Wallace, 1808; M. Apx. *Husb. and Wife*, No. 7. M'Naughton *v.* M'Naughton, 1850; 12 D. 703. Baxter *v.* Baxter, 1845; 7 D. 639 (husband insolvent). Williamson *v.* Williamson, 1860; 22 D. 599. Donald *v.* Donald, 1860; 22 D. 1118; 1862, 24 D. 499. Lang *v.* Lang, 1868; 7 Macph. 24. Thomson *v.* Thomson, 1890; 17 R. 1091 (rate). See as to aliment pending a declarator of marriage, Sassen *v.* Campbell, Jan. 20, 1819; F. C.; rev. 1826, 2 W. & S. 309. Browne *v.* Burns, 1843; 5 D. 1288. And in a declarator of nullity of marriage, Ballantyne *v.* Ballantyne, 1866; 4 Macph. 494. As to bygone aliment for years in which wife has kept herself, see Donald, *cit.* M'Millan *v.* M'Millan, 1871; 9 Macph. 1067. See below, § 1620.

(*e*) Stewart *v.* Stewart, 1887; 15 R. 113.

(*f*) Coutts *v.* Coutts, 1866; 4 Macph. 802. Crombie *v.* Crombie, 1868; 6 Macph. 776.

(*g*) Benson *v.* Benson, 1854; 16 D. 555. Rennie *v.* Rennie, 1863; 1 Macph. 389. Hood *v.* Hood, 1871; 9 Macph. 449 (action before Sheriff upon agreement); 13 J. of J. 350, 351 (June 1869). Smith *v.* Smith, 1874; 1 R. 1010. M'Donald *v.* M'Donald, 1875; 2 R. 705. Hay *v.* Hay, 1882; 9 R. 667 (birth of child after decree of separation).

(*h*) Paterson *v.* Paterson, 1861; 24 D. 215. Hood (*g*). Crombie, *cit.* (*f*). Arthur *v.* Gourlay, 1769; 2 Pat. 184.

1546. Communio Bonorum, or Common Stock.—Marriage, considered as the origin and establishment of a family, has in contemplation not merely the contracting parties, but the interest of their children, as members of the domestic society, for intermediate subsistence, education, and future provision (*a*).

(*a*) 1 Stair, 4. § 9, 17. 1 Ersk. 6. § 12.

1547. The moveable property of the parties 'at common law' is, *ipso jure*, assigned to the husband as a fund, to be under his uncontrolled power ('*jus mariti*') during the marriage (*a*). It is the fund of maintenance of the parties and of their children during the marriage, and is divisible in certain shares after the marriage is dissolved. 'But by the Married Women's Property (Scotland) Act, 1881, this assignation of the wife's moveable property is excluded in the case of marriages contracted after its passing (July 18, 1881); and it remains vested in her as her separate estate (*b*).'

(*a*) See as to the *jus mariti*, below, § 1561; and charges on the common stock, § 1568 et seq.; and as to the phrase *communio bonorum*, Shearer *v.* Christie, 1842; 5 D. 132. Muirhead *v.* Muirhead's Factor, 1867; 6 Macph. 95. Fraser *v.* Walker, 1872; 10 Macph. 837. Fraser, H. & W. 648 sqq. Ersk. Pr., 16th ed. p. 65. Murray's Property of Married Persons, 10.

(*b*) See below, § 1560D.

1548. What Communio Bonorum comprehends, or Not.—(1.) *Moveables.*—'In marriages contracted before July 18, 1881 (*a*), and where the wife has not obtained a protection order, or been judicially separated, or been reasonably provided for by the husband, in the event of her surviving him, by irrevocable deed made before that date (*b*), or her estate has not been brought under the Act by mutual deed (*c*),' the moveable or personal estate of either party forms the common stock 'or fund subject to the *jus mariti*,' including personal debts, or sums due; goods belonging to either at the time of the marriage; and effects or debts acquired or falling to either during the marriage 'and prior to the said date (*d*),' by their own industry (*e*), by gift, by succession, or otherwise; with all rents, fruits, and profits (*f*). 'Claims of damage arising to the wife during the marriage and before July 18, 1881, are thought to fall under the *jus mariti*, although a wife is entitled to sue without her husband's concurrence for reparation of wrongs of a strictly personal character, such as slander (*g*). And legitim, vesting *ipso jure* on her father's death, may under such marriages be sued for by the husband, unless discharged before the marriage, or the wife be entitled to elect between it and a conventional provision (*h*).'

(*a*) 44 and 45 Vict. c. 21, Married Women's Property (Scotland) Act, 1881.
(*b*) 44 and 45 Vict. c. 21, § 3 (1).
(*c*) 24 and 25 Vict. c. 86, § 1, 6, 19 ; and 37 and 38 Vict. c. 31 ; 44 and 45 Vict. c. 21, § 4 ; see above, § 1540A ; below, § 1560B.
(*d*) 44 and 45 Vict. c. 21, § 3 (2).
(*e*) Observe that a wife's earnings by her own industry were protected since January 1, 1878. 40 and 41 Vict. c. 29, § 3. See below, § 1560C.
(*f*) 1 Ersk. Pr. 6, § 6, and 1 Inst. 6, § 12.
(*g*) Milne *v.* Gauld's Trs., 1841 ; 3 D. 345. See Gale *v.* Bennet, 1857 ; 19 D. 665. Smith *v.* Stoddart, 1850 ; 12 D. 1185. Horn *v.* Sanderson, 1872 ; 10 Macph. 295. Bern's Exr. *v.* Montrose Asylum, 1893; 20 R. 859 (*per* L. Young—husband's title to sue after wife's death). Fraser, H. & W. 574, 701 ; and below, § 1561, 1610.
(*h*) Macdougal *v.* Wilson, 1858 ; 20 D. 658. See Stevenson *v.* Hamilton, 1838 ; 1 D. 181. Lowson *v.* Young, 1854 ; 16 D. 1098. Miller *v.* Learmonth, 1871 ; 10 Macph. 107 ; aff. 1875, 2 R. H. L. 62. See below, § 1587 (*o*).

1549. All moveables, money, bonds, bills, etc., in the wife's possession, are presumed to be the husband's (*a*). Money lent or deposited by the wife is presumed to be part of the *communio bonorum* (*b*). So is money applied by a wife in payment of her own debt (*c*). This presumption, however, yields to proof (*d*); 'and in dealing with it the recent statutes referred to must be kept in view.'

(*a*) M'Donald *v.* Doig, 1793 ; M. 5848 ; 2 Ill. 264. Thomas *v.* City of Glasgow Bk., 1879 ; 6 R. 607. Fraser, H. & W. 689. Mortgages of companies under the companies Clauses Act (8 and 9 Vict. c. 17, § 46) and shares of companies under the Companies Acts (25 and 26 Vict. c. 89, § 22) are moveable estate.
(*b*) Fenton *v.* Carnegie, 1635 ; M. 5801.
(*c*) Rigg *v.* Cunningham, 1727 ; M. 5801.
(*d*) Lauder *v.* Hog, 1677 ; 3 B. Sup. 130. Cockburn *v.* Burn, 1679 ; M. 5794. Dods *v.* Wood, 1766 ; Hailes, 12. Boaz *v.* London, 1829 ; 7 S. 555. See above, § 1315.

1550. The fund must not only accrue, but vest (*a*), during the marriage, in order to characterise it as moveable, and so falling under the *communio bonorum*; the Scottish law, 'when the husband's domicile is in Scotland,' regulating what shall fall under it, the foreign 'law, when the wife's property is situated abroad, determining' whether the thing is personal or real (*b*), 'and also the effect of the marriage on the wife's heritable estate (*c*). So money lent on real security in England, being moveable, falls under the *communio bonorum* (*d*).' Legacies fall under the *communio*, although liferented by a third party, who happens to survive the dissolution of the marriage (*e*). But conditional bonds do not vest before the purifying of the condition (*f*). 'It is on this ground that policies of insurance on a married woman's life in favour of herself or her executors, etc., have been held not to fall under the *jus mariti*, but to pass to her own representatives, because payment of the sum insured is (it is said) contingent on the continued payment of the premiums, and is not due till after the dissolution of the marriage (*g*). In like manner such a policy on the wife's life, payable to the husband, was held to belong to him as not having vested during the marriage, and not to be subject to a claim under the old law by the representatives of the predeceasing wife (*h*). On the other hand, a policy in the husband's favour, whether on his own or his wife's life, has been held to be part of his estate at his death, and so subject to claims of legitim and *jus relictæ*, and that although the wife whose life is insured is still living (*i*). By statute, policies of insurance effected by a married woman on her own or her husband's life for her separate use, vest in her exclusive of the *jus mariti* and right of administration. And policies effected by a married man on his own life and expressed to be for the benefit of his wife or children, or both, are a trust in him, or other trustees named, for their benefit, exclusive of creditors and not revocable or reducible, unless there be fraud against creditors or he become bankrupt within two years (*k*).'

(*a*) See below, notes (*g*), (*h*), (*i*). Fraser, H. & W. 744 sqq.
(*b*) Scott *v.* Dickson, 1663 ; M. 5799 ; 2 Ill. 262. Wallace *v.* Lister, 1821 ; 1 S. 17. Lawson *v.* Bannatyne, 1614 ; M. 5798. Egerton *v.* Forbes, Nov. 27, 1812 ; F. C. Newlands *v.* Chalmers, 1832 ; 11 S. 65. Clarke *v.* Newmarch, 1836 ; 14 S. 488. See Craigie *v.* Gairdner, June 12, 1817 ; F. C. Milligan *v.* Milligan, 1826 ; 4 S. 438 ; 2 Ill. 459. Robertson *v.* Gilchrist, 1828 ; 4 S. 446. And 4 Geo. IV. c. 98, § 1. Ivory's notes on Ersk. p. 894, note 611. Guthrie's Savigny's Priv. Intl. Law, 181, notes.
(*c*) Tennent *v.* Welch, 1889 ; 16 R. 876 ; revd. 1891, A. C. 639 ; 18 R. H. L. 72.
(*d*) M. Breadalbane's Trs. *v.* Breadalbane, 1843 ; 15 S. Jur. 389. Downie *v.* Christie, 1866 ; 4 Macph. 1067. See Hall's Trs. *v.* Hall, 1854 ; 16 D. 1057. Monteith *v.* Monteith's Trs., 1882 ; 9 R. 982.

(e) Frazer v. Bowie, 1804; Hume. 210. Haining v. Young, 1808; ib. 214.

(f) Fotheringham v. E. Home, 1694; M. 5764. Philp v. Corrie, *infra*, § 1552 (f).

(g) Smith v. Kerr, 1869; 7 Macph. 863 (2nd Div.). Thomson's Trs. v. Thomson, 1879; 6 R. 1227 (2nd Div.).

(h) Wight v. Brown, 1849; 11 D. 459 (2nd Div.).

(i) Muirhead v. Muirhead's Factor, 1867; 6 Macph. 95 (1st Div.). Pringle's Trs. v. Hamilton, 1872; 10 Macph. 621. Chalmers' Trs. v. Chalmers, 1882; 9 R. 743. Under the altered law it may be of less importance to reconcile the apparent conflict between these two classes of cases, or to determine which view, if they really differ in principle, is the right one. But it seems that the opinions in Wight v. Brown were given with reference to a theory (*communio bonorum*) which was really useful only in regard to the claim of the predeceasing wife's representatives to a share of the matrimonial estate, which has now been taken away (*infra*, § 1580); and that the cases in notes (g) and (h), as well as in this note, really turn upon the terms of the policy indicating the intention with which it has been made. See Ersk. Pr. (16th ed.), p. 65. Fraser, H. & W. 698, 981. Galloway v. Craig, 1861; 4 Macq. 267. Inglis v. Inglis, 1869; 7 Macph. 435.

(k) 43 and 44 Vict. c. 26 (Married Women's Policies of Assurance (Scotland) Act, 1880). Kennedy's Trs. v. Sharpe, 1895; 23 R. 146 (widower's policy). Such policies may be surrendered by the trustee with the wife's concurrence. Schumann v. Scot. Widows' Fund, 1886; 13 R. 678.

1551. '*Fraud on Marital Rights.*'—The wife cannot, after betrothment or proclamation of banns, gratuitously alienate any fund or right, or discharge any debt which falls under the *communio bonorum* (a). If there have been no banns proclaimed, or not regularly, the validity of such a conveyance will depend on grounds of reduction or preference at common law (b). 'But since the Married Women's Property Act, 1881, it is difficult to see how any conveyance by a woman about to marry can be a fraud on her husband, who has no prospective right in her property.'

(a) 1 Ersk. 6. § 22. Swyne v. Swyne, 1605; M. 6029; 2 Ill. 265. Fletcher v. ——, 1611; M. 6029. Scott v. Brown, 1633; M. 6030. Lady Bute v. Sheriff of Bute, 1665; M. 6030; 1 B. Sup. 520; 2 B. Sup. 423. Auchinleck v. Williamson, 1667; M. 6033. Ogilvie v. Ogilvie, 1679; 2 B. Sup. 240. Gilchrist & Grant v. Pringle, 1682; M. 6032. M'Lellan v. M'Lellan, 1722; M. 6028.

(b) M'Dougal v. Aitken, 1623; M. 6027. See Fraser, H. & W. 679. 1 Wh. & Tud. L. C. 446.

1552. (2.) *Heritable subjects*, lands, houses, things attached to land, servitudes, teinds, patronage, do not fall under the *communio*. The price also of lands 'sold during the marriage' (a), and real securities and heritable bonds, are excluded; nor does the uplifting of heritable debts 'during the marriage' make them fall into communion, 'if the money can be traced; the presumption being, even after a long lapse of time, that the parties had no intention of altering the character of the property in the husband's favour (b). And the husband is personally liable in repayment if he has appropriated the money, and the wife may rank on his estate for it (c). The presumption, however, may be redargued: and if the annual proceeds of separate estate have been expended with the wife's consent for the benefit of the family, she cannot insist on repetition (d).' Bonds with a clause of infeftment are excluded from the *communio bonorum* (e). Rights having a tract of future time (f), and bonds after the term of payment, if they bear interest, are excluded (g). But it seems doubtful what shall be the effect of excluding executors in a bond (h).

Although heritable subjects and debts are excluded, their fruits, rents, and interests, 'except arrears of interest under an adjudication (i),' are not (k) 'excluded, when the marriage has been contracted before 18th July 1881; but in marriages contracted after that date, the rents and produce of heritable property in Scotland belonging to the wife are not subject to the *jus mariti* and right of administration of the husband; and under all marriages, whether contracted before or after the Act, the *jus mariti* and right of administration are excluded from the income of heritable subjects to which the wife may acquire right after the 18th July 1881, except where, before that date, the husband has by irrevocable deed or deeds made a reasonable provision for his wife in the event of her surviving him (l).'

Industrial crops, of which the seed is sown before the dissolution of the marriage, are reckoned as part of the common fund; but not if the seed is not actually sown (m).

(a) Hill v. King, 1719; M. 5697; 2 Ill. 260. Boaz v. Loudon, 1829; 7 S. 555. See below, § 1615.

(b) Cockburn v. Burn, 1679; M. 5794. Stewart v. Gillies, 1687; M. 5793. Rollo v. Forest, 1685; M. 5795. Scott v. Parks, 1693; M. 5777. Ogilvies v. E. Eglinton, 1609; M. 5794. Anderson v. Laidlaw, 1816; Hume, 218. Nisbet v. Rennie, 1818; Hume, 221. Baird v. Haddow, 1842; 4 D. 564. **Heron** v. **Espie**, 1856; 18 D. 917, 920, 927. Smith v. Frier, 1857; 19 D. 384. Cuthill v. Burns, 1862; 24 D. 849. Spence v. Patterson, 1873; 1 R. 46. **Welch** v. **Tennent**, 1889; 16 R. 876; rev. 1891, A. C. 639; 18 R. H. L. 72. Although heritable securities are now made moveable as regards the succession of the creditor (31 and 32 Vict. c. 101, § 117; *supra*, § 1485A), the Act provides that "no heritable security, whether granted before or after marriage, shall to any extent pertain to the husband *jure mariti*, where the same is or shall be conceived in favour of the wife, or to the wife *jure relictæ*, where the same is or shall be conceived in favour of the husband, unless the husband or relict has or shall have right and interest therein otherwise; declaring, nevertheless, that this provision shall in no way prejudice the rights and interests of wife or husband, or of the creditors of either, in or to the bygone interest and annualrents due under any such heritable security, and *in bonis* of the husband or wife respectively prior to his or her death; and further providing that where legitim is claimed on the death of the creditor, no heritable security shall to any extent be held to be part of the creditor's moveable estate in computing the amount of the legitim."

(*c*) Sutherland *v.* Syme, 1772; Hailes, 479. M'Lellan *v.* Hathorn, 1758; M. 6098. Meldrum *v.* Wilson, 1842; 15 S. Jur. 90. See Laidlaw *v.* Laidlaw's Tr., 1882; 10 R. 374.

(*d*) Lees *v.* Wilson, 1808; Hume, 191. Hutchison *v.* Hutchison, 1843; 5 D. 469. Baxter's Exr. *v.* Baxter's Trs., 1886; 13 R. 1209; aff. 1888, 13 App. Ca. 385; 15 R. H. L. 37 (*nom.* Edward *v.* Cheyne). Cf. Tennent *v.* Tennent's Exr., 1889; 16 R. 876; revd. 1891, A. C. 639; 18 R. H. L. 72. Below, § 1616 (*h*). 2 Ersk. 2. § 16.

(*e*) Gordon *v.* Ogilvie, 1684; M. 5777. Ramsay *v.* Goldie, 1825; 4 S. 108.

(*f*) Pennicuick *v.* Cockburn, 1582; M. 5764. See Philp *v.* Corrie, 1765; 5 B. Sup. 469, 903, 908. Downie *v.* Christie, 1866; 4 Macph. 1067. Above, § 1480.

(*g*) Meuse *v.* Craig's Exrs., 1748; M. 5506, 5778; Elch. *Her. & Mov.* 15; 2 Ill. 232. Pitcairn *v.* Edgar, 1665; M. 5775; 2 Ill. 261. Philp, *supra* (*f*). Gray *v.* Dunlop, 1739; M. 5770; Elchies, *Her. & Mov.* 9, and notes, p. 181. Gray *v.* Walker, 1859; 21 D. 709. Hogg *v.* Grieve, 1807; Hume, 189. Tuffie *v.* Campbell, 1808; Hume, 190. See above, § 1495. Fraser, H. & W. 718.

(*h*) Barclay *v.* Pearson, 1682; M. 5777. See above, § 1491.

(*i*) Ramsay *v.* Brownlie, 1738; M. 5538; Elch. *Adjud.* 20. Baikie *v.* Sinclair, 1786; M. 5545; Hailes, 988; aff. 3 Pat. 64. Ryder *v.* Ross, 1794; M. 5549; Bell's Ca. 52.

(*k*) Donaldson *v.* Hay, 1783; M. 5949; Hailes, 921. Storrar *v.* Lidster's Crs., 1773; 5 B. Sup. 469. Philp, *supra* (*f*). See Ferguson *v.* Cowan, 1819; Hume, 222; 20 D. 662, note. Smith *v.* Frier, 1857; 19 D. 384. Below, § 1594.

(*l*) 44 and 45 Vict. c. 21, § 2, 3. See Poe *v.* Paterson, 1882; 10 R. 356; aff. 1883, *ib.* H. L. 73; 8 App. Ca. 678.

(*m*) Ballingal *v.* Robertson, 1808; Hume, 214. See above, § 1473, and Fraser, H. & W. 694.

1553. In things falling to either of the parties by succession, the character of heritable or moveable in this question depends on the state of the funds at the time when the succession opens; uninfluenced by any change under the executor's management (*a*).

(*a*) Tansh's Crs. *v.* Dunbar, 1744; M. 5842; Elchies, *Husband and Wife*, 22; 2 Ill. 264. Gray *v.* Walker, § 1552 (*g*). Anderson *v.* Laidlaw and other cases in § 1552 (*b*); and above, § 1486. Fraser, H. & W. 725.

1554. (3.) *Paraphernalia.*—The general rule, which assigns to the *communio bonorum* all moveables belonging to the spouses, suffers two exceptions; the one of *Paraphernalia*, the other of *Peculium* (*a*).

(*a*) 1 Ersk. 6. § 15, 41 *in fin.*

1555. The term Paraphernalia, which, strictly speaking, expresses what is over and above the dower, and peculiarly the wife's own, is in the law of Scotland applied to the wife's dress, and the ornaments proper to her person, 'whatever their source' (*a*). These articles the law regards as peculiarly the property of the wife, and not attachable by the creditors of the husband (*b*).

(*a*) Black, § 1557 (*c*). Young, § 1559 (*b*).

(*b*) 2 Craig, 17. § 7. 1 Ersk. Pr. 6. § 8. Fraser, H. & W. 770, 775. Gray *v.* Gray, 1582; M. 5802; 2 Ill. 266. Davidson *v.* M'Cubbin, 1610; M. 5802. E. Leven *v.* Montgomerie, 1683; M. 5803. See Montgomerie *v.* Hart, 1845; 7 D. 1081.

1556. Articles proper to a woman's dress are presumed to be paraphernal (*a*). But this yields to proof by writing; by the character of family jewels (*b*); but where the husband is a jeweller, it has been doubted whether the presumption holds (*c*).

(*a*) Dicks *v.* Massie, 1696, 1697; M. 5821; 2 Ill. 266.

(*b*) E. Leven, *supra*, § 1555 (*b*). Boyd *v.* Dundas, 1781; Fraser, H. & W. 773.

(*c*) Craig *v.* Monteith, 1684; M. 5819, 5820.

1557. Dressing-plate and tea-plate are not paraphernal (*a*). A chest of drawers, or clothes-press, appropriated to a wife's clothes, is paraphernal (*b*). But articles of household furniture, though presented to the wife by her relations on her marriage, are not paraphernal; as bed and table linen, mirror, lady's work-table, etc. (*c*).

(*a*) Css. Wigton *v.* Elphinstone, 1748; M. 5771; Elchies, *Husband and Wife*, 30; 2 Ill. 267. Dicks, *supra*, § 1556 (*a*). Gemmil *v.* Yule, 1735; Elch. *Husband and Wife*, 4.

(*b*) Pitcairn *v.* Pentherer, 1716; M. 5825. Cameron *v.* M'Lean, 1876; 13 S. L. R. 278.

(*c*) Hewat (Black) *v.* Wood, 1803; Hume, 210. Consider the effect of the M. W. P. Act, 1881, *supra*, § 1548.

1558. Articles not peculiar to woman's dress must be *proved* to be paraphernal (*a*).

(*a*) Lady Rankeilor *v.* Ayton, 1709; M. 5824; 2 Ill. 267. Css. Bute *v.* E. Bute, 1711; M. 5824.

1559. Although paraphernalia are the property of the wife, they are not at her disposal *inter vivos*; but she may bequeath them by will. And they admit of a distinction in relation to creditors, proper paraphernalia not being attachable (*a*); but things not properly paraphernal, though specially gifted, being attachable by creditors, with relief to the wife against the husband's estate (*b*).

(*a*) Above, § 1555.

(*b*) Craig, *supra*, § 1556 (*c*), and E. Leven, *supra*, § 1555 (*b*). See Gemmil *v.* Yule, *cit.* Clerk *v.* Sharp, 1717; M. 5996. Shearer *v.* Christie, 1842; 5 D. 132. Young *v.* Johnston & Wright, 1880; 7 R. 760. Consider the effect of the M. W. P. Act, *supra*, § 1548.

1560. (4.) *Peculium.*—A fund may be appropriated to the wife by custom or by special gift. By custom, certain presents are made to a wife (on the sale of lands with her consent), called the lady's gown. This and other analogous gifts are held to be *peculium* (*a*). A sum or provision may be secured to a wife as a *peculium* (*b*), either by herself before marriage (*c*); or by the husband by antenuptial contract, or while solvent, renouncing his *jus mariti* (*d*); 'or purchasing a policy of insurance the sum in which is payable to her heirs after her death (*e*)'; or by a stranger (*f*). 'A provision made for the support and aliment of the wife by a stranger, or by herself or her husband before the marriage, does not fall under the *jus mariti*, at least if declared to be *alimentary* and not assignable (*g*). But such an "alimentary" provision if exorbitant for the grantee's station in life will, in the discretion of the Court (if the *jus mariti* be not excluded), be open to the diligence of creditors *quoad excessum* (*h*). And a post-nuptial provision of a fund falling under the *jus mariti* purchased by an onerous arrangement with a relative of the wife was sustained (*i*). The effect of the Married Women's Property Act of 1881 is to make the whole moveable estate of the wife *peculium* (*k*).'

(*a*) Lady Pitfirran *v.* Wood, 1709; M. 5799; 2 Ill. 267. Mungel *v.* Calder, 1750; M. 5771. Douglas *v.* Kennedy, 1751; M. 6019. Fraser, H. & W. 775. This custom seems to be obsolete.

(*b*) Dirleton and Stewart, *voce* Aliment. See below, § 1614. **Biggart *v.* City of Glasgow Bk.**, 1879; 6 R. 470.

(*c*) Sandilands *v.* Mercer, 1833; 11 S. 665; 2 Ill. 268. See below, § 1944, 1562.

(*d*) Such a post-nuptial provision, so far as payable during the marriage, and in any case if it exceed a reasonable provision, is revocable as a donation *inter virum et uxorem*, and may be attached by creditors. See Kemp *v.* Napier, 1842; 5 D. 558. Dunlop *v.* Johnston, 1865; 3 Macph. 758; aff. 5 Macph. H. L. 22. See below, § 1616, 1944.

(*e*) Wight and Smith, *supra*, § 1550 (*h*) (*g*).

(*f*) 1 Stair, 4. § 9. 1 Ersk. 6. § 14. Annand & Colquhoun *v.* Chessels, 1774; M. 5844; aff. 1775, 2 Pat. 369. Robertson *v.* Gilchrist, 1828; 6 S. 446; 2 Ill. 459. Gordon *v.* Gordon, 1832; 11 S. 36. Young *v.* Loudoun, 1855; 17 D. 998. Hogg's Trs. *v.* Wilson's Trs., 1868; 41 S. Jur. 70. Biggart, *cit.* (*b*).

(*g*) 1 Stair, 4. § 9, 17. 1 Ersk. 6. § 14. 1 Bell's Com. 129 (124, M'L.'s ed.). Fraser, H. & W. 764. See as to the effect of alimentary provisions in marriage contracts, Martin *v.* Bannatyne, 1861; 23 D. 705.

(*h*) Harvey *v.* Calder, 1840; 2 D. 1095. Rennie *v.* Ritchie, 1845; 4 Bell's App. 221. Lewis *v.* Anstruther, 1852; 15 D. 260. See below, § 2276 (*o*) (*p*).

(*i*) Forbes *v.* City of Glas. Bk., 1879; 6 R. 1122.

(*k*) *Infra*, § 1560D. Fraser, H. & W. 791.

1560A. '*Provision for Wife under Conjugal Rights Act.*—After the analogy of the English law of a wife's "equity to a settlement," it was provided by the Conjugal Rights Act of 1861 (*a*), that "when a married woman succeeds to property, or acquires right to it by donation, bequest, or any other means than by the exercise of her own industry, the husband or his creditors, or any other person claiming under or through him, shall not be entitled to claim the same as falling within the *communio bonorum*, or under the *jus mariti*, or husband's right of administration, except on the condition of making therefrom a reasonable provision for the support and maintenance of the wife, if a claim therefor be made on her behalf; and in the event of dispute as to the amount of the provision to be made, the matter shall, in an ordinary action, be determined by the Court of Session according to the circumstances of each case, and with reference to any provisions previously secured in favour of the wife, and any other property belonging to her exempt from the *jus mariti* (*b*). Provided always that no claim for such provision shall be competent to the wife, if, before it be made by her, the husband or his assignee or disponee shall have obtained complete and lawful possession of the property (*c*), or in the case of a creditor of the husband, where he has, before such claim is made by the wife, attached the property by decree of adjudication or arrestment, and followed up the said arrestment by obtaining thereon decree of furthcoming, or has poinded and carried through and reported a sale thereof" (*d*). As it is only in case of dispute that the Court settles the amount, the spouses themselves may apportion the wife's property so that she may hold it free of *jus mariti*; and it may be either an annuity (or annual payment) or a capital sum subject to the wife's power of testing and passing to her heirs (*e*). The statute applies to heritable successions opening to a wife before the date of its passing, to the effect of giving her a right to a provision out of the future rents or termly payments (*f*).'

(*a*) 24 and 25 Vict. c. 86, § 16.

(*b*) Sommer, *infra*. Taylor *v.* Taylor, 1871; 10 Macph. 23 (aliment of children living with wife). Kinnear *v.* Ferguson, 1871; 10 Macph. 54. Jack *v.* Ferguson, 1878; 5 R. 624. Clark, *infra* (*c*). Murray, Property of Married Persons, 50, n.

(*c*) This means more than merely acquiring a title or vested right or even control, though that right should have been assigned away by the husband, and the assignation intimated. There must be actual possession and enjoyment. Sommer *v.* Sommer's Tr., 1871; 9 Macph. 594. Clark *v.* Clark, 1881; 8 R. 723.

(*d*) As to the effect of the vesting clauses of the Bankruptcy Act, 1856, in connection with this provision, see Miller *v.* Learmonth, 1871, 10 Macph. 107, and Fraser, H. & W. 832. Jack *v.* Ferguson, *cit.* (*b*). Reid *v.* M'Walter, 1878; 5 R. 630.

(*e*) Mudie *v.* Clough, 1896; 23 R. 1074.

(*f*) Taylor *v.* Taylor (*b*). Reid *v.* M'Walter (*d*).

1560B. '*Protection Order for Deserted Wife.*—A wife deserted by her husband may obtain from the Court of Session, or from the Sheriff, an order protecting against the husband and his creditors, and any person claiming in or through his right, the property which she has acquired or may acquire by her industry after the desertion, or to which she has after the desertion succeeded, or may succeed or acquire right (*a*). The husband or his creditors may apply for recall of this order, provided they have not lodged answers to the wife's application for it; but the recall, if granted, affects no right or interest onerously and *bonâ fide* acquired from the wife during the subsistence of the order (*b*). The order of protection continues operative until cohabitation is resumed; or until recall, upon the husband's proving that he has ceased from his desertion, and, if required, finding caution. And in this case, rights acquired by the wife as well as those of third parties are not affected; the wife's rights and interests continuing vested in her, exclusive of the husband's *jus mariti* and right of administration. The husband cannot institute an action of adherence against the wife, until the order has been recalled (*c*). After intimation of the order of protection in newspapers, as appointed by the Court, the wife's property belongs to her as if she were unmarried, unless the husband or his assignee or disponee have acquired full and complete lawful possession of it (*d*), or unless it has been attached by arrestment and furthcoming, or a poinding and sale reported, before the date of presenting the petition (*e*). The order has the effect of a decree of separation *a mensa et thoro* in regard to the property of both spouses, and in regard to the wife's capacity to sue and to be sued (*f*).'

(*a*) 24 and 25 Vict. c. 86, § 1. 37 and 38 Vict. c. 31 (extending jurisdiction to Sheriff Court). "Desertion" in the sense of these statutes differs from the "malicious and obstinate defection" of the Act of 1573, c. 55 (*supra*, § 1535). Turnbull, petr., 1864; 2 Macph. 402. Chalmers *v.* Chalmers, 1868; 6 Macph. 547.

(*b*) *Ib.* § 2.

(*c*) *Ib.* § 3.

(*d*) Above, § 1560A (*c*).

(*e*) *Ib.* § 4.

(*f*) *Ib.* § 5. See § 1540A.

1560C. '**The Married Women's Property Act,** 1877, excludes the *jus mariti* and right of administration "from the wages and earnings of any married woman acquired or gained by her" after January 1, 1878, "in any employment, occupation, or trade in which she is engaged" (*i.e.* as a servant or manager, whether paid by salary or a share of profits) (*a*), "or in any business which she carries on under her own name," apart from her husband and not jointly with him or as his agent or assistant (*b*); and "from any money or property acquired by her after the commencement of the Act through the exercise of any literary, artistic, or scientific skill. Such wages, earnings, money, or property, and all investments thereof, shall be deemed to be settled to her sole and separate use, and her receipts shall be a good discharge" for them (*c*).'

(*a*) Ferguson's Tr. *v.* Willis & Co., *infra*, *per* L. Pr. Inglis.

(*b*) M'Ginty *v.* M'Alpine, 1892; 19 R. 935.

(*c*) 40 and 41 Vict. c. 29, § 3. Taken, with some differences, from the English Married Women's Property Act of 1870, 33 and 34 Vict. c. 93, § 1. This enactment does not by implication protect the stock-in-trade or plant by which a married woman's earnings are made, if that be her husband's *jure mariti* or otherwise. Ferguson's Tr. *v.* Willis, Nelson, & Co., 1883; 11 R. 261. Comp. § 1562, below. See, *contra*, Ashworth *v.* Outram, 5 Ch. D. 923; 46 L. J. Ch. 687. In a special case the Act was applied by the majority of the Second Division to a wife's earnings as a washerwoman made in her husband's house, and mixed by her with his estate. Morrison *v.* Tawse's Exx., 1888; 16 R. 247.

1560D. '*Married Women's Property Act,* 1881.—It is proper to state here the provisions of the latest of the series of statutes in favour of women, as to the moveable property of the spouses, and especially as to the *jus mariti*, although these provisions may also have to be mentioned in other parts of the book.

'When a marriage is contracted after the passing of the Act (18th July 1881), and the husband at the time of the marriage has his domicile in Scotland (*a*), the whole moveable or personal estate of the wife, whether acquired before or during the marriage, is, by operation of law, vested in the wife as her separate estate, and is not subject to the *jus mariti* (*b*): in short, it is *peculium*. Any income of such estate is payable to the wife on her individual receipt, or to her order, and to this extent the husband's right of administration is excluded; but the wife is not entitled to assign the prospective income thereof, or unless with the husband's consent, to dispose of such estate (*c*). Except as provided in the Act in the case to be immediately stated, the wife's moveable estate is not subject to arrestment, or other diligence of the law, for the husband's debts, provided that the said estate (except such corporeal moveables as are usually possessed without a written or documentary title) is invested, placed, or secured in the name of the wife herself, or in such terms as clearly distinguish the same from the estate of the husband (*d*). Any money or other estate of the wife, lent or intrusted (*e*) to the husband, or immixed with his funds (*f*), is to be treated as assets of the husband's estate in bankruptcy, under reservation of the wife's, or her assignee's (*g*), claim to a dividend as a creditor for the value of such money or other estate, after the claims of the other creditors of the husband for valuable consideration in money or money's worth have been satisfied (*h*). Nothing in these provisions excludes or abridges the power of settlement by antenuptial contract of marriage (*i*).

'Where a marriage has taken place before the passing of the Act, the provisions just recited apply only to estate and the income thereof, to which the wife may acquire right after the passing of the Act, and not even to such after-acquired property, where the husband has, before the passing of the Act, by irrevocable deed or deeds, made a reasonable provision for his wife in the event of her surviving him (*k*). Parties married before the commencement of the Act may bring themselves within its provisions by mutual deed, in the manner provided by the fourth section of the Act.'

(*a*) This limitation does not appear in the Acts of 1877 (§ 1560*c*) and 1880 (§ 1550).

(*b*) 44 and 45 Vict. c. 21, § 1, subs. 1.

(*c*) *Ib.* subs. 2. See below, § 1614, 1616 as to disposal of income. So a wife can validly discharge or transact as to her legitim without her husband's concurrence. Miller *v.* Galbraith's Trs., 1886 ; 13 R. 764.

(*d*) *Ib.* subs. 3. See Allan *v.* Wishart, 1890 ; 6 Sh. C. R. 185 (furniture in husband's house). Adam *v.* Adam's Tr., 1894 ; 21 R. 676 (do.). Fraser, H. & W. 1517.

(*e*) Anderson *v.* Anderson's Tr., 1892 ; 19 R. 684 (husband's furniture sold to wife and not removed). Adam *v.* Adam's Tr., *cit.*

(*f*) National Bank *v.* Cowan, 1893 ; 21 R. 4.

(*g*) Cochrane *v.* Lamont's Tr., 1891 ; 18 R. 451.

(*h*) *Ib.* subs. 4. Cochrane, *cit.* (*g*). Cf. § 1552, 1617. 53 and 54 Vict. c. 39, § 3 ; above, § 364.

(*i*) *Ib.* subs. 5 ; see *ib.* § 8.

(*k*) *Ib.* § 3. See Poe *v.* Paterson, 1882 ; 10 R. 356 ; aff. 1883, *ib.* H. L. 73 ; 8 App. Ca. 678. Scott's Tr. *v.* Scott, 1889 ; 16 R. 507 ("income thereof" does not make each year's rent a separate subject). Comp. § 1562 (*b*).

1561. Jus Mariti.—'At common law, and in the cases to which the Married Women's Property Act of 1881 does not apply, *i.e.* (1) under marriages contracted before 18th July 1881, where the husband has before that date made a reasonable provision for his wife on her survivance, by an irrevocable deed or deeds; and (2) under all such marriages, whether such provision has been made or not, in regard to the estate and income to which the wife has acquired right before the passing of the Act,' the husband's administration as the head of the family is absolute; and his *jus mariti* comprehends every subject which forms part of the common stock (*a*). It operates *ipso jure* like an assignation, without the necessity of intimation (*b*); and is available to his creditors either on the arrestment of particular funds, 'as interest or rents become due,' or by adjudging the right so as to make it available against the rents of the wife's estate (*c*). A distinction is to be marked relative to an alimentary provision settled on a wife; that it is not attachable for her husband's debt, but the administration of it for behoof of the family may be in the husband (*d*). So a provision to children under the Ministers' Widows' Act is not arrestable, but it falls under the *jus mariti* of the husband of the child (*e*). Although the marriage is an assignation requiring no intimation to complete it, the doctrine of Lord Stair requires some modification, that an assignation before marriage, not intimated, falls by the marriage: for another principle operates in that case, the husband being bound to fulfil his wife's obligation to complete the assignation (*f*). 'The husband sues in his own name for debts due to the wife, and falling under the *jus mariti* (*g*).'

(*a*) See above, § 1548 sqq.

(*b*) Comp. above, § 1466, 1547. *Per* L. Meadowbank in Royal Bank *v.* Stein's Assignees, Jan. 20, 1813 ; F. C. Fraser, H. & W. 679. Auth. in next note.

(*c*) 1 Stair 4. § 9 and 17. Dirl. and Stewart, *Jus Mar. and Jus Relictæ*. 1 Ersk. Pr. 6. § 7 ; 1 Inst. 6. § 13. Sinclair *v.* Clunie's Crs., 1739 ; M. 713, 772 ; 5 B. Sup.

658; Elchies, *Husb. and Wife*, 10; 2 Ill. 269. Menzies *v.* Gillespie's Crs., 1761; M. 5974. Calder *v.* Steel, Nov. 19, 1818; F. C. M'Donell *v.* Clark, Nov. 25, 1819; F. C. See below, § 1594; above, § 1552. Borthwick *v.* M'Farlane, 1844; 6 D. 1290. Smith *v.* Frier, 1857; 19 D. 385; as to which see Fraser, H. & W., 763.

(*d*) Dick *v.* Lady Penkill, 1709; M. 5999. See above, § 1560; below, § 1563.

(*e*) Donaldson *v.* Hay, 1783; M. 5949; Hailes, 921; 2 Ill. 262. 17 Geo. II. c. 11 (Ministers' Widows' Fund).

(*f*). Till *v.* Jamieson, 1763; M. 5946. See above, § 1466.

(*g*) Tait *v.* Wilson, 1831; 9 S. 680. *Supra*, § 1547, 1548 (*h*); *infra*, § 1610. As to a submission by the husband, see Robertson *v.* Cheynes, 1847; 9 D. 599. As to a husband's title to sue for damages for injuries to his deceased wife, see *per* L. Young in Bern's Exr. *v.* Montrose Asylum, 1893; 20 R. 859. Bills due to the wife must be recovered by him by action, not by summary diligence. Smith *v.* Selby, 1829; 7 S. 885.

1562. The *jus mariti* may, 'in the cases in which it still exists (*a*),' be renounced 'by the husband' as to any particular subject or fund (*b*), or as to the administration generally, provided it extend not to the entire renunciation of the husband's right to act as the head of the family. 'It may also be excluded by a third party, conveying or bequeathing a subject or fund to the wife (*c*). It is to be noticed, however, that in marriages to which the common law applies, no exclusion of the *jus mariti*, or declaration that the fund shall be alimentary and inalienable, suffices to secure against a wife's voluntary deeds an estate or fund which is directed to be paid to herself, or in which she receives an absolute fee. In order to effect that purpose, the donor must vest the fee in trustees; for the effect of such a simple gift or destination is that the wife may spend, use, or dilapidate the fund as any other absolute owner (*d*). There may, however, be "a protected succession"; *i.e.* a fee given to a wife (or another) with full power of disposal and administration, but with a right of succession to children, which, it is said, cannot be disappointed by a gratuitous deed, either *inter vivos* or *mortis causa* (*e*). But it does not clearly appear how the person in possession of a fund or estate so "protected" can be prevented from spending or putting it away at pleasure.

'The *jus mariti* may be renounced or excluded in regard to all or any part of the wife's estate, with or without specification, and therefore in regard to *acquirenda* as well as vested rights (*f*).'

The renunciation, to be effectual, must be made unequivocally, and in direct and explicit terms (*g*), 'or at least by clear implication. Such an implication arises from an antenuptial conveyance to trustees, under which the husband can have no right other than that given to him by the agreement of parties (*h*).' But the husband cannot renounce it 'after the marriage,' to the effect of withdrawing his effects from his creditors (*i*); 'though he may effectually do so by an antenuptial contract (*k*), except as regards corporeal moveables to which the principle of reputed ownership may apply (*l*).' A separation, whether voluntary or judicial, is not 'at common law' a renunciation of the *jus mariti* —'even over property which was once the wife's and has been left in her possession during the separation (*m*), and although the husband may be held to have renounced this right with regard to the earnings and profits made by her when separate and without aliment from him (*n*);' but while the husband is bound to furnish the wife with the aliment stipulated or awarded, whatever moveable funds she acquires or succeeds to, strictly speaking, belong to him (*o*). 'A different effect, however, is given to a decree of separation by the Conjugal Rights Act (*p*).'

(*a*) See above, § 1560D *fin.*

(*b*) Exclusion of the *jus mariti* from any particular fund applies to the interest as well as the capital. Robertson *v.* Robertson, 1835; 13 S. 442. Hutchison *v.* Hutchison, 1842; 4 D. 1399; 1843, 5 D. 469. Smith *v.* Frier, 1857; 19 D. 384. Such a renunciation may as a donation be proved by parole. Wright's Exrs. *v.* City of Glasgow Bank, 1880; 7 R. 527.

(*c*) 1 Stair, 4. § 9. 1 Ersk. 6. § 14. Fraser, H. & W 783. Foulis and Collington *v.* Lady Collington, 1667; M. 5828; 2 Ill. 269. Murray's Trs. *v.* Dalrymple, 1745; M. 5842, 2273. Greig *v.* Wemyss, 1670; M. 5832. Walker *v.* Walker's Crs., 1730; M. 5841. M'Pherson *v.* Graham, 1750; M. 6113. Keggie *v.* Christie, May 25, 1815; F. C. Annand, *supra*, § 1560 (*f*). See § 1944. Hutchison *v.* Hutchison, *cit.* Young *v.* Loudon, 1855; 17 D. 998. Balderston *v.* Fulton, 1857; 19 D. 293. Biggart *v.* City of Glasgow Bank, 1879; 6 R. 470.

(*d*) Allan's Trs. *v.* Allan, 1872; 11 Macph. 216. White's Trs. *v.* White, 1877; 4 R. 786. Gibson's Trs. *v.* Ross, *ib.* 1038. Douglas's Trs. *v.* Kay's Trs., 1879; 7 R. 295. Clouston's Trs. *v.* Bulloch, 1889; 16 R. 937. Simson's Trs. *v.* Brown, 1890; 17 R. 581. See 2 M'Laren, Wills and Succn. 62. Fraser, H. & W. 1486. Duthie's Trs. *v.* Kinloch, 1878; 5 R. 858; and below, § 1944, 1956.

(*e*) Arthur & Seymour *v.* Lamb, 1870; 8 Macph. 928. Massy *v.* Scott's Trs., 1872; 11 Macph. 173. Comp. Gibson's Trs. *v.* Ross, *cit.* Lindsay's Trs. *v.* Lindsay, 1880; 8 R. 281 (trust). Dalglish's Trs. *v.* Bannerman's Exrs., 1889; 16 R. 559. See Logan's Trs. *v.* Ellis, 1890; 17 R. 425. Gillon's Trs. *v.* Gillon, 1890; 17 R. 435. Macdonald *v.* Hall, 1893; 20 R. H. L. 88. Muir's Trs. *v.* Muir's Trs., 1895; 22 R. 553. See § 1971, below.

(*f*) Ersk. *cit.* M'Dougall *v.* City of Glasgow Bank,

1879 ; 6 R. 1089 (correcting 1 Bell's Com. 638). Greenhill *v.* Ford, 1824 ; 3 S. 169. Hutchison, *supra* (*b*).

(*g*) Cuthbertson *v.* Pollock, 1799 ; Hume, 206.

(*h*) Rollo *v.* Ramsay, 1832 ; 11 S. 132. Dauney *v.* Pearson, 1841 ; 3 D. 504. Wilson's Trs. *v.* Wilson's Factor, 1868 ; 7 Macph. 136. Morrison *v.* Marshall, 1871 ; 9 Macph. 736. Irvine *v.* Connon's Trs., 1883 ; 10 R. 731. Bruce's Trs. *v.* Bruce's Tr., 1894 ; 21 R. 593. Comp. § 1580A, below.

(*i*) Breichan *v.* Muirhead, 1810 ; Hume, 215. Shearer *v.* Christie, 1842 ; 5 D. 132. See below, § 1619, 1944.

(*k*) See below, § 1944 ; above, § 1315. Sandilands *v.* Mercer, 1833 ; 11 S. 665. Rollo *v.* Ramsay, *supra* (*h*).

(*l*) See above, § 1043, 1315, 1549. Fraser, H. & W. 1344.

(*m*) Henderson *v.* Henderson, 1889 ; 17 R. 18. See Buchanan *v.* Buchanan, 1890 ; 6 Sh. Ct. Rep. 319 (acquiescence).

(*n*) Jameson *v.* Houston, 1770 ; M. 5898. Davidson *v.* Davidson, 1867 ; 5 Macph. 710. Henderson, *cit.* Fraser, H. & W. 699. Comp. § 1560C, above.

(*o*) Henderson *v.* M'Callum, 1794 ; Hume, 202. Ferguson *v.* Thomson, 1877 ; 4 R. 393 (husband divorced).

(*p*) See above, § 1540A, 1560B.

1563. Husband's Administration. — The husband's power of administration and disposal *inter vivos* 'of moveable estate' (*a*) is unlimited (*b*), 'while the *jus mariti* is not excluded or renounced; and the right of administration subsists notwithstanding the exclusion of the *jus mariti*, unless it be itself also renounced or excluded (*c*)'; but he cannot defeat the rights of his wife or children by deeds *mortis causa*; nor by deeds on deathbed, though *ex figura verborum inter vivos*; nor fraudulently (*d*). His power is not suspended till it shall be seen whether the marriage shall continue for a year or produce living offspring (*e*). 'It must be noticed that the right of administration is only partially excluded from recent and future marriages by the Act of 1881, viz. as to the current income of the wife's estate (*f*). Hence, although the wife's furniture in the spouses' house cannot be taken by the husband's creditors (above, § 1560D (*d*)), she cannot claim delivery of it as against him if she separates from him without sufficient cause (*g*).'

(*a*) As to his administration of heritable estate, see below, § 1594.

(*b*) 1 Stair, 4. § 17. 1 Ersk. 6. § 13 sqq. Fraser, H. & W. 796 sqq. Campbell *v.* Campbell, 1769 ; M. 5944 ; 2 Ill. 271. Tailors of Canongate *v.* Daikers, 1697 ; M. 5944.

(*c*) Dick *v.* Lady Pinkhill, 1709 ; M. 5999. Waddel *v.* Waddel, 1837 ; 10 S. Jur. 84, and cases in § 1562 (*f*), (*g*), (*h*), *supra*. Fraser, H. & W. 676, 797 sq. *Supra*, § 1561 (*d*).

(*d*) 3 Ersk. 9. § 16. Agnew *v.* Agnew, 1775 ; M. 8210. Hog *v.* Hog, 1800 ; M. *Legitim*, Apx. 2 ; 4 Pat. 581. Thomson *v.* Thin's Crs., 1675 ; M. 5941. Grant *v.* Grant, 1679 ; M. 5943. Henderson *v.* Henderson, 1728 ; M. 8199. Edgar *v.* Edgars, 1672 ; M. 15,837. Campbell, *supra* (*b*). Sorlies *v.* Robertson, 1761 ; M. 5947 ; Hailes, 459. Millie *v.* Millie, 1803 ; M. 8215 ; aff. 1805, 5 Pat. 160. See below, § 1584 ; and Fraser, H. & W. 1000–1010.

(*e*) Tailors of Canongate, *supra* (*b*). See below, § 1575 et seq.

(*f*) *Supra*, § 1560D.

(*g*) Dempsey *v.* Dempsey, 1885 ; 30 J. J. 106 ; 2 Sh. Ct. Rep. 19 (Sheriffs Crichton and Henderson). Andrew *v.* Andrew, 1884 ; 1 Sh. Ct. Rep. 54.

1564. The husband is bound so to administer the funds as to implement his obligations, express or implied, in the marriage contract; and he cannot defend himself against action on such obligation, on pretence of not payment of tocher, which he ought himself to have recovered (*a*).

(*a*) Erlie *v.* Gordon, 1625 ; M. 6064 ; 2 Ill. 272. Campbell *v.* Campbell, 1665 ; M. 6065. Menzies *v.* Corbet, 1671 ; M. 6066. Stewart *v.* Stewart, 1678 ; M. 6066. Hamilton *v.* Bonar's Heirs, 1682 ; 2 B. Sup. 28. Gowans *v.* Forrest, 1685 ; *ib.* 83. Fraser, H. & W. 1396.

1565. Wife's Præpositura.—Certain departments of domestic economy naturally fall under the wife's management. This is by tacit or express delegation from the husband (*a*).

(*a*) See More's Notes on Stair, xxii. Brodie's Stair, 31, f. n. 1 Ersk. Pr. 6. § 15, 16 ; and Inst. § 20. The rule was in one case extended to the case of a daughter's managing her father's house. Hamilton *v.* Forrester, 1825 ; 3 S. 572. See above, § 231 ; below, § 1613.

1566. The wife is empowered, as by *presumed* mandate, to bind the husband for 'suitable' furnishings to the family 'or herself,' although she may have had money given to her for that purpose; and although he may be insolvent, and she enjoy a pension, furnishings to the family are the husband's debts, not hers (*a*). The creditor will be entitled to the benefit of her oath on reference, for proof of the debt (*b*). But this does not extend to transactions unconnected with the ordinary management of the family, 'in which the husband's credit is not relied on' (*c*). The presumption of *præpositura* is removed 'by private notice to individual tradesmen (*d*), or more properly' by inhibition at the husband's instance; in the use of which he cannot be controlled, although the wife may have redress against any false or calumnious statement on which the inhibition may proceed (*e*), 'and which, being recorded in the General Register of Inhibitions (*f*), is deemed to be notice to all the world, and is effectual even against foreign tradesmen (*g*). Neither inhibition nor private notice is effectual against a creditor who proves that the furnishings he has sold were applied to the use of the husband's wife or family, and that the husband had not provided sufficient aliment for them (*h*), or that by his acts he had passed from the prohibition (*i*).' Mere separation is not a recall of the *præpositura* (*k*); 'but when the parties are living apart, there is not a presumption of *præpositura*, and the husband's liability depends on the circumstances; such as the conduct of the parties, the terms of the separation, the wife's possessing separate estate, the tradesman's knowledge, etc. (*l*).'

(*a*) Robertson *v.* Haldane, 1801; Hume, 208. 1 Stair, 4. § 17. 1 Ersk. 6. § 26. 1 Bell's Com. 479. Fraser, H. & W. 604. Buie *v.* Gordon, 1827; 5 S. 464; 1831, 9 S. 923; 3 S. Jur. 603. L. Fraser (H. & W. 608) doubts the husband's liability where he has supplied the wife with money for necessaries, but the text is supported by Dalling and Alston, below (*b*). See Mortimer *v.* Hamilton, 1868; 7 Macph. 158. As to the wife's own liability, see Walker, Scott, and Sandilands, *citt.* below, § 1611. Robertson *v.* Haldane, *cit.*, and comp. Fraser, H. &. W. 612, 622, 837, 1517.

(*b*) Dalling *v.* M'Kenzie, 1675; M. 6005; 2 Ill. 272. Kincaid *v.* Sanderson, 1621; M. 6021. Alston *v.* Stamfilds, 1682; M. 6007. Cochran *v.* Lyle, 1740; M. 6018. Paterson *v.* Taylor, 1771; M. 12,485; Hailes, 391; 5 B. Sup. 474. Young & Co. *v.* Playfair, 1802; M. 12,486. See Fraser, H. & W. 628. Duncan *v.* Forbes, 1831; 9 S. 540. The opinion in Mitchells *v.* Moultrys, 1882, 10 R. 378 (2nd Div.), that the wife's oath as *præposita* is competent to prove the constitution only, but not the resting owing of the debt, is contrary to Young & Co. *v.* Playfair, *cit.*, which does not seem to have been referred to in argument.

(*c*) Arnot *v.* Stevenson, 1698; M. 6017. See Nairn *v.* Buchanan, 1680; M. 6016. Binny *v.* Smith, 1836; 14 S. 355. Fraser, H. &. W. 612.

(*d*) Buie *v.* Gordon, *cit.* See More's Stair, xxiii.

(*e*) 1 Ersk. 6. § 26. Campbell *v.* L. Ebden, 1675; M. 5879. Auchinlech *v.* E. Monteith, 1675, *ib.* Burton *v.* Corse, 1747; M. 6024; Elch. *Husb. and Wife*, 26. E. Caithness *v.* Css. Caithness, 1747; M. 6025; Elchies, *ib.* 27.

(*f*) See note in Fraser, H. & W. 631. Mann, Byars, & Co. *v.* Millar, 1871; 15 J. J. 383 (whether registration equivalent to publication). Cf. Mackintosh's Trs. *v.* Davidson & Garden, 1898; 25 R. 554 (ditto).

(*g*) Topham *v.* Marshall, 1808; M. Apx. *Inhib.* 2.

(*h*) 1 Stair, 4. § 17; and Brodie's note, p. 31. Gordon *v.* Sempill, 1776; M. 446; and Apx. *Husband and Wife*, 4.

(*i*) Ker *v.* Gibson, 1709; M. 6023.

(*k*) Harman *v.* Macalister, 1826; 4 S. 806.

(*l*) See Fraser, H. &. W. 635–647; and see above, § 1540A, 1560B, etc.

1567. *Express præpositura* may be verbal or by sufferance; as where the wife is employed or allowed to proceed in managing a particular department; as a shop, tavern, lodging-house, etc. (*a*). The goods, furniture, etc., are 'the husband's' *præsumptione juris* (*b*), and he is liable for the debts incurred for furnishings made to her in the course of the trade so permitted. But he will not be liable for money lent to her without proof of its application either to the family or to the permitted trade (*c*). The husband has been held liable on an obligation, by his wife keeping lodgings by his permission, for the value of articles stolen from the lodgings (*d*). The wife may be authorised by writing; and this is *necessary* to entitle her to uplift money, and to make effectual her receipt for money, rents, interests, etc. (*e*). 'These rules and presumptions arise from the law of agency or mandate, applied to the relation of husband and wife, and where the wife is truly *præposita*, seem not to be affected by the legislation of 1877 and 1881 (*f*). There is no decision as to the husband's liability for the debts of a wife who carries on a trade or business in her own name; but the Act of 1877 makes her independent of him in respect of such a business; and it is reasonable to hold that, as he is no longer the principal for whom it is carried on, he shall not be subjected to the responsibilities of a principal. It will be a question of fact in each such case whether the wife has incurred liability as her husband's agent or not (*g*).'

(*a*) Wilson *v.* Deans, 1675; M. 6021; 2 Ill. 273. Muirhead *v.* Douglas, 1609; M. 6020. Brown *v.* Dickson, 1711; M. 6018. Buchanan *v.* Dickie, 1828; 6 S. 986; 1 Ill. 163. James, Wood, & James *v.* Downie, 1837; 15 S. 1151. Lambert *v.* Smith, 1864; 3 Macph. 43 (hiring house and removing). Slowey *v.* Moir, 1865; 4 Macph. 1 (ditto). 1 Ersk. 6. § 26. Fraser, H. & W. 622.

(*b*) Cargil *v.* Miller, 1820; Hume, 223. See above, § 1549.

(*c*) M'Intyre *v.* Graham, 1795; Hume, 203. Mitchelson *v.* Cranston, 1780; M. 5886. Robertson *v.* Haldane, 1801; Hume, 208. Grant *v.* Baillie, 1830; 8 S. 606 (homologation). Gemmil *v.* Yule, 1735; Elch. *Husb. and Wife*, 4 (pledging goods). Tweddell *v.* Duncan, 1840; 2 D. 808; 3 D. 998 (ditto).

(*d*) Scott *v.* Yates, 1800; Hume, 207.

(*e*) Pitarrow *v.* Tenant, 1587; M. 6614. Arnot, *supra*, § 1566 (*c*). Calderwood *v.* Steel, 1693; 4 B. Sup. 50. Nairn *v.* Buchanan, 1680; M. 6016, 1669. Binny *v.* Smith, 1836; 14 S. 355. M'Intyre, *supra* (*c*). But it is at least doubtful whether this old rule or the general law as to proof of mandate would be followed in modern practice. Dickson on Evid. § 567. Fraser, H. & W. 628. Lambert and Slowey, *citt.* (*a*).

(*f*) See above, § 1560C, 1560D.

(*g*) The English Act of 1882 makes a presumption that a married woman contracts with respect to and so as to bind her separate property. 45 and 46 Vict. c. 75, § 1 (3). See Broomfield (Griffith), M. W. P. Act, p. 31. And see below, § 1572, 1612.

1568. Charges on the Common Stock (*a*).—Debts of the husband, debts of the wife before marriage 'if the marriage were contracted before 1st January 1878 (*b*),' debts arising during marriage, and the burdens which accompany the temporary enjoyment of the heritable estate, are all charges on the common fund, 'by the common law; but the rules as to this matter are modified as below by recent legislation.'

(*a*) See above, § 1546. (*b*) Below, § 1571A.

1569. (1.) *Debts of the Husband.*—The personal debts of the husband, at whatever time contracted, are burdens on the common stock, and preferable to the wife's claim for subsistence (*a*). But heritable debts, or such as, if due to the husband, would not have belonged to the common stock, or have augmented the fund to the wife or children, are not chargeable against the stock in a question with wife or children (*b*).

(*a*) 3 Ersk. 9. § 22 *in fin.* Robb *v.* Robb's Crs., 1794; M. 5900; Bell's fol. Ca. 13; 2 Ill. 274. Lisk *v.* Lisk's Crs., 1785; M. 5887; see 2 Ill. 274. Ogilvie's Crs. *v.* Scott, 1687; M. 5892. Turnbull *v.* Turnbull's Crs., 1709; M. 5895. Lee *v.* Watson, 1795; M. 5889. Comp. above, § 1538, 1562 (*i*); below, § 1619, 1944. Fraser, H. & W. 863–4.

(*b*) 1661, c. 32. 3 Ersk. Pr. 9. § 7; more correct than 3 Ersk. Inst. 9. § 22.

1570. (2.) *Debts of the Wife before Marriage.*—'In marriages contracted before the 1st January 1878 (*a*),' such debts of the wife before marriage as would, if due to her, have fallen under the *communio bonorum*, 'including obligations existing or contracted before the marriage, although they may not have become prestable or operative till after it (*b*),' are during the marriage demandable from the husband as administrator (*c*). Even the aliment of her natural children before marriage, if not recovered from the father, is a debt on the common stock (*d*). 'So also is her obligation to support her indigent parents (*e*).' And her heritable debts will also be demandable from him if he have had the *universitas* of his wife's property conveyed to him (*f*); 'or so far as he is *lucratus* by the marriage (*g*).' He will not, however, be liable for any furnishings to her before marriage for which action would not have been competent against her; as while she lived as a child in her father's house (*h*). If the wife's debts be still unpaid at dissolution of the marriage, they become again debts of the wife, and are not demandable from the husband, unless they shall have been fixed during the marriage as debts on his estate (*i*), or unless he shall be *lucratus* by the marriage beyond a reasonable tocher (*k*).

(*a*) Below, § 1571A.

(*b*) Wishart *v.* City of Glasgow Bk., 1879; 6 R. 823. Reid *v.* Moir, *infra* (*e*).

(*c*) 1 Stair, 4. § 17. 1 Ersk. 6. § 16. Fraser, H. & W. 586 sqq. Osborn *v.* Young, 1696; M. 5785; 2 Ill. 275. Gordon *v.* Campbell, 1704; M. 5787. Inglis *v.* Harvey, 1715; M. 5855.

(*d*) Aitken *v.* Anderson, 1815; Hume, 247.

(*e*) Reid *v.* Moir, 1866; 4 Macph. 1060. Foulis *v.* Fairbairn, 1887; 14 R. 1088.

(*f*) Dick *v.* Cassie, 1738; M. 5857; Elch. *Husband and Wife*, 9. Weir *v.* Parkhill, 1738; M. 5857.

(*g*) 1 Ersk. 6. § 18. Leslie *v.* Wallace, 1708; M. 5853.

(*h*) Bannatyne *v.* Clerk, 1768; M. 5860. Css. Caithness *v.* E. Fife, 1774; 5 B. Sup. 473.

(*i*) Wilkie *v.* Stewart, 1678; M. 5868; 3 B. Sup. 222. See next section.

(*k*) 1 Ersk. 6. § 17. Burnet *v.* Lepers, 1665; M. 5863–4. Drummond *v.* Stewart, 1740; M. 5858.

1571. Debts of the wife are fixed on the husband's estate by such diligence as is sufficient to create a security on his estate or effects, which he must relieve (*a*); but personal diligence against the husband for his wife's debt falls on the dissolution of the marriage (*b*). It seems formerly to have been held that such diligence might proceed summarily against the husband (*c*); but this does not seem to be law. The wife's debts do not become proper debts of the husband, though fixed as burdens on his estate; and so he has relief against the wife's estate for what he may be compelled to pay (*d*).

(*a*) 1 Stair, 4. § 17. 1 Ersk. 6. § 17. Wilkie, *supra*, § 1570 (*i*). Bryson *v.* Menzies, 1698; M. 5869; 2 Ill. 275.

(*b*) Douglas *v.* Stirling, 1623; M. 5861. More's Stair, i. 4. 17. f. n., and Notes, xxiii. Elchies' Annot. 21. Fraser, H. & W. 594, 596.

(*c*) A. *v.* B., Elch. *Husb. and Wife*, 15; 5 B. Sup. 743.

(*d*) E. Leven *v.* Montgomery, 1683; M. 5876, 5803, 3217. Gordon *v.* Inglis, 1681; M. 5924. Smith *v.* Drummond, 1829; 1 S. Jur. 334. Robertson *v.* Lyon, 1821; 1 S. 48. Wilkie, *cit.*

1571A. 'In any marriage which takes place after 1st January 1878, the liability of the husband for the antenuptial debts of his wife, including her liability to aliment her indigent parents (*a*), is limited to the value of any property which he shall have received from, through, or in right of his wife, at, or before, or subsequent to the marriage; and any Court in which a husband is sued for such debt has power to direct any inquiry or proceedings which it may think proper for the purpose of ascertaining the nature, amount, and value of such property (*b*).'

(*a*) M'Allan *v.* Alexander, 1888; 15 R. 863.

(*b*) 40 and 41 Vict. c. 29, § 4. See the fuller provisions of the English Act, 45 and 46 Vict. c. 75, § 13, 14.

1572. (3.) *Debts contracted during the Marriage.*—Such debts are burdens on the common fund, if for furnishings to the family, aliment, education, medical attendance, etc.; if for aliment of the family, from the husband's death to the first term, with aliment of a posthumous child (*a*); if for aliment of a wife living in separation, either judicial or agreed to, or necessary and justifiable (*b*); and the funeral expense of the husband (*c*). But the funeral expense of the wife is not a common burden (*d*), and gives no preference as a privileged debt, except on the *jus relictæ*.

'The widow's alimony until the first term of payment of her legal or conventional provisions, measured according to the husband's circumstances, is a debt due by the husband's executry, payable after privileged debts (*e*), but before any division of the free executry is made, and so is preferable to *jus relictæ*, legitim, and legacies (*f*). The widow may obtain from the Court a further or extraordinary aliment, if her provisions, legal or conventional, are found insufficient for her maintenance (*g*); and as this allowance is made on the ground of debt, questions of capital and income do not affect it (*h*).

'A husband is not liable in damages for his wife's delict or quasi delict committed during the marriage (*i*), nor for debts incurred by her in carrying on a separate business or managing her separate estate (*k*).'

(*a*) 1 Stair, 4. § 22. 2 Bank. 6. §. 11. 1 Ersk. 6. § 41, and 3. 9. § 22. Fraser, H. & W. 965, 990. Palmer *v.* Sinclair, June 27, 1811; F. C.; 2 Ill. 276. Moncreiff *v.* Monypenny, 1713; M. 3945. Lord Justice-Clerk *v.* Hamilton, 1709; M. 5909 and 5912. Boswell *v.* Boswell, 1737; M. 5916; Elch. *Aliment*, 6, and notes. Thomson *v.* Douglas, 1856; 18 D. 1240. M'Intyre *v.* M'Intyre's Trs., 1865; 3 Macph. 1074. M'Pherson *v.* Walker, 1869; 8 Macph. 246.

(*b*) 1 Ersk. 6. § 19. Lady Kinfauns *v.* Kinfauns, 1711; M. 5882. See § 1545, above.

(*c*) Dirleton, *Funeral Charges*. Anon., 1708; M. 5927. Moncreiff, *supra* (*a*).

(*d*) 3 Ersk. 9. § 22. Marshall *v.* Finlays, 1747; M. 3948. Gordon *v.* Inglis, 1681; M. 5924. Dicks *v.* Massie, 1695; M. 5828. As to this unsatisfactory distinction, see note in 2 Ill. 277; and Fraser, H. & W. 621, 989.

(*e*) See above, § 1403.

(*f*) Auth. in (*a*), *supra*. Baroness de Blonay *v.* Oswald's Reps., 1863; 1 Macph. 1147. See Ivory's Ersk. pp. 146, 149, 150, 161, notes; and cf. § 1600, below.

(*g*) 1 Stair, 5. § 10. Thomson *v.* M'Culloch, 1778; M. 934. Blake *v.* Bates, 1840; 3 D. 317. Comp. § 1600 *fin.*, below.

(*h*) Thomson *v.* Anderson's Trs., Jan. 27, 1899.

(*i*) Murray *v.* Graham, 1724; M. 6079. Chalmers *v.* Baillie, 1790; M. 6083; Hailes, 1072, 1075, 1791; 3 Pat. 213. Friend *v.* Skelton, 1854; 17 D. 548, 551. **Barr *v.* Neilsons,** 1868; 6 Macph. 651. Milne *v.* Smiths, 1892; 20 R. 95. *Infra*, § 1613 (*c*). See Ritchie *v.* Barclay, 1845; 7 D. 819.

(*k*) **Wright's Exrs. *v.* City of Glasgow Bank,** 1880; 7 R. 527; and cases below, § 1612.

1573. (4.) *Burdens accompanying the Possession of the Heritable Estate*, 'in marriages to which the former law still applies,' as interests, repairs, and expense of cultivation, affect the accruing right of possession.

1574. Division of the Common Stock.—The common fund 'was' restored to the parties as before marriage, or divided in certain proportions according to circumstances:—

1575. (1.) '*Until* 1855,' *if the marriage* '*were*' *dissolved within year and day, and without a living child*, parties 'were' restored as nearly as possible to their former state (*a*); 'but a rule which in practice was excluded by almost every marriage contract (*b*), was entirely abolished by the enactment that "where a marriage shall be dissolved before the lapse of a year and day from its date by the death of one of the spouses, the whole rights of the survivor and of the representatives of the predeceaser shall be the same as if the marriage had subsisted for the period aforesaid" (*c*).'

The tocher 'was' paid back, and the moveable funds still extant restored to the party to whom they originally belonged; and this whether the parties or either of them had been married before or not (*d*). All the reciprocal engagements 'were' discharged if no stipulation 'had been' made to the contrary. There 'was' no claim for terce or courtesy (*e*). Estates conveyed or provisions made to either party in contemplation of the marriage, 'were' restored (*f*). And presents made by relations, etc., 'were' divided equally (*g*).

(*a*) 1 Ersk. 6. § 38 et seq. Dirleton and Stewart, *Jus Mariti*. 1 Stair, 4. § 19. See Note from Fountainhall, M. 12,699, footnote. Fraser, H. & W. 963.

(*b*) Below, § 1943.

(*c*) 18 Vict. c. 23, § 7.

(*d*) Maxwell *v.* Harestanes, 1634; M. 6160; 2 Ill. 277.

(*e*) Lady Maxwell *v.* Garlies, 1600; M. 6159. Maxwell, *supra* (*d*). Somerville *v.* Bell, 1751; M. 6161.

(*f*) Guthrie *v.* Guthrie, 1672; M. 6171. Calder *v.* M'Intosh, 1610; M. 6167. L. Burleigh *v.* Arnot, 1678; M. 6172. See Hunters *v.* Brown, 1766; M. 6164; Hailes, 120. Hood *v.* Jack, 1739; M. 6175. Cuming *v.* Gordon, 1781; M. 6165.

(*g*) Waugh *v.* Jamieson, 1679; M. 6179.

1576. The restitution of tocher must be without deduction (*a*), except of debts of the wife, or her funeral expenses, which the husband 'might' have paid (*b*).

(*a*) 1 Ersk. 6. § 38–9. Covington *v.* Veitch, 1606; M. 6166; 2 Ill. 278. Cases, *supra*, § 1575 (*f*). Neilson, 1776; M. 6165. Gordon *v.* Stewart, 1743; M. 6161.

(*b*) Gordon *v.* Inglis, 1681; M. 6180 and 5924.

1577. Moveables, or money not given in tocher, 'were' to be accounted for under deduction of what 'had' been *boná fide* consumed (*a*).

(*a*) 1 Ersk. 6. § 39, with Ivory's note.

1578. (2.) *If the marriage 'had' subsisted for a year and part of the next day* (*a*), *or if a child 'had' been born* of it which 'had' been heard to cry (*b*), the common fund 'suffered' a division bipartite or tripartite, according as there 'were' children surviving at its dissolution or otherwise. And in this question a child legitimated by the intermarriage of the parents 'was' held to be a living child of the marriage, to the effect of regulating the division of the common fund (*c*).

'This rule of division now applies in all cases, in conformity with the statute above cited (§ 1575).'

(*a*) Waddell *v.* Salmon, 1680; M. 3465; 2 Ill. 277.
(*b*) Irvine *v.* Robertson, 1632; M. 6181. Dobie *v.* Richardson, 1765; M. 6183. See below, § 1943.
(*c*) Crawford's Trs. *v.* Hart, 1802; M. 12,698; 2 Ill. 237.

Independently of convention, the division proceeds thus:—

1579. On the husband's death, if there be children of the marriage, or children existing by any former marriage of the husband, the division is tripartite: the surviving widow has a third, called "Jus Relictæ" (*a*): a third, called "Dead's Part" (*b*), goes according to the husband's will, or to his children as his next of kin; a third, called "Legitim" (*c*) (*Legitima pars liberorum*), goes to the husband's children, whether of that or of a former marriage, in their own right; but of this the wife's children of a former marriage have no part. If there be no surviving children of the father by this or a former marriage, the division is bipartite between the widow, and the next of kin or legatees of the husband.

(*a*) See below, § 1591. (*b*) See below, § 1592.
(*c*) See below, § 1582.

1580. On the wife's death, 'previous to the year 1855':—If there 'were' no surviving children of the husband (of this or a former marriage), the division 'was' bipartite; one-half 'going' to the wife's children of a former marriage, or if she 'had' no children, to her other next of kin, or to her legatees; the other to the surviving husband. If there 'were' children of the husband by this or a former marriage, the tripartite division 'had' the effect of ascertaining the wife's third, that it 'might' go according to her will, or to her children, or her other next of kin, as her representatives; but the other two-thirds 'remained' with the husband as his own, subject only to his children's claim of legitim on his death (*a*). If the children of the marriage 'were' minors, the father 'retained' the whole; but in that case he 'held' the mother's third as administrator-in-law for the children, and their debtor accountable to them or their representatives for it; and the father 'was' liable for interest while he 'held' this part of the fund—subject, however, to an equitable compensation for aliment (*b*). Where there 'were' specific subjects (as furniture), to a third of which the wife was entitled, the father would seem to hold these as trustee for his children; so that on his subsequent bankruptcy, so far as the identical things 'remained' to which the wife had right, the children should be preferable to his creditors.

'By 18 Vict. c. 23, § 6, it is enacted, that "where a wife shall predecease her husband, the next of kin, executors, or other representatives of such wife, whether testate or intestate, shall have no right to any share of the goods in communion; nor shall any legacy or bequest or testamentary disposition thereof by such wife affect or attach to the said goods, or any portion thereof."'

(*a*) 3 Ersk. 9. § 21. Fraser, H. & W. 1528, 977. Home *v.* Christie, 1606; M. 8161; 2 Ill. 279. See Menzies *v.* Livingstone, 1839; 1 D. 601. **Kennedy** *v.* **Bell,** 1859; 22 D. 269; 1864, 2 Macph. 583. Smith *v.* Barlas, 1857; 19 D. 267.
(*b*) Steele's Trs. *v.* Cooper, 1830; 8 S. 926. Menzies, *supra* (*a*).

1580A. '*Husband's Right in Wife's Separate Estate on her predecease.*—After the 18th July 1881, the husband of any woman who shall die domiciled in Scotland shall take by operation of law the same share and interest in her moveable estate which is taken by a widow in her deceased husband's moveable estate according to the law and practice of Scotland, and subject always to the same rules of law in relation to the nature and amount of such share and interest, and the exclusion, discharge, or satisfaction thereof, as the case may be (*a*). But the Act (Married Women's Property Act, 1881) does not affect contracts made between married persons before or during marriage (sec. 8), and so when a wife's whole estate is disposed of by antenuptial contract, the husband cannot claim this *jus relicti* in contravention of the contract (*b*). Nor does this statute entitle him to claim on his wife's divorce as if she were dead (*c*).'

(*a*) 44 and 45 Vict. c. 21, § 6. See below, § 1894, as to the husband's right to administer the executry. This and the 5th and 7th sections of the Act apply to marriages contracted before the passing of the Act. Poë *v.* Paterson, 1882; 10 R. 356; aff. 1883, *ib.* H. L. 73; 8 App. Ca. 678. Of course in such marriages the *jus mariti* must have been excluded. Fotheringham's Tr. *v.* Fotheringham, 1889; 16 R. 873 (estate in wife constituted by convention). Simons' Tr. *v.* Neilson, 1890; 18 R. 135 (do.). Observe the separate enactment of the Conjugal Rights Act as to wives separated or protected under it, above, § 1540A.

(*b*) Buntine *v.* Buntine's Trs., 1894; 21 R. 714.

(*c*) Eddington *v.* Robertson, 1895; 22 R. 430. *Infra*, § 1622.

1581. (3.) *Effect of Convention.*—By convention the legal rights may be altered thus:—

Renunciation by the wife of her *jus relictæ* 'before the opening of the succession' will, on the husband's death without children, make the whole dead's part (*a*). Or if there be children, the division on the husband's death will be bipartite between the dead's part and legitim; the children taking the legitim as their own; while, as dead's part, the other will go according to the will, or fall to them as their father's next of kin (*b*). On the wife's death (*c*), after renunciation of her third, the whole remains with the husband, subject only to a claim of legitim by the children on his death. If the children have all renounced, or been forisfamiliated, the division is bipartite between the husband and wife. If only some of the children have renounced, or been forisfamiliated, the rest take the whole legitim. If both wife and children have renounced, the whole becomes dead's part. 'As *jus relictæ* vests *ipso jure* at the moment of the husband's death, a subsequent discharge by the widow, *e.g.* by accepting a testamentary provision, leaves the division tripartite if there be children, the executor drawing the widow's third in lieu of the conventional provision (*d*).' The renunciation must in all such cases be express, or at least clearly implied, not inferred from ambiguous circumstances (*e*).

(*a*) Jervey *v.* Watt, 1762; M. 8170; 2 Ill. 279. Nisbet *v.* Nisbet, 1726; M. 8181; aff. Robertson's Ap. 594; 2 Ill. 279, 281.

(*b*) Johnston *v.* Johnston, 1814; Hume, 290.

(*c*) See above, § 1580 *fin.*, 1580A.

(*d*) **Fisher** *v.* **Dixon,** 1840; 2 D. 1121; aff. 1843, 2 Bell's Ap. 63. Campbell's Trs. *v.* Campbell, 1862; 24 D. 1321. See *infra*, § 1591.

(*e*) M'Auley *v.* Bell, 1712; M. 3848. Riddel *v.* Dalton, 1781; M. 6457. M'Kinnon *v.* M'Donald, 1763; M. 6451. Tod *v.* Wemyss, 1770; M. 6451; Hailes, 385. Miller *v.* Brown, 1776; M. 6456; 5 B. Sup. 473; Hailes, 678. Sutherland *v.* Syme, 1772; Hailes, 479. See Milne *v.* Innes, 1822; 2 S. 59. Stewart *v.* Stewart's Trs., 1891; 18 R. 1114. See below, § 1590, 1591.

1582. Legitim or Bairn's Part (*a*).—Legitim, which is generally stated as a share of the goods in communion belonging to the children on dissolution of the marriage, is more correctly a right of succession to a share of the father's moveable estate, vesting in the children *ipso jure* on their father's death, but expiring with the predecease of the children, and not transmissible in that event to their heirs (*b*).

'*Legitim in Mother's Separate Estate.*—Since 18th July 1881, the children of any woman who may die domiciled in Scotland shall have the same right of legitim in regard to her moveable estate which they have according to the law and practice of Scotland in regard to the moveable estate of their deceased father, subject always to the same rules of law in relation to the character and extent of the said right, and to the exclusion, discharge, or satisfaction thereof, as the case may be (*c*).'

(*a*) See above, § 1579.

(*b*) 3 Ersk. 9. § 15 et seq. Fraser, H. & W. 973. Kilkerran in Robertson *v.* Kerr, 1742; M. 8202-5; 2 Ill. 281. Jervey, *supra*, § 1581 (*a*). **Shearer** *v.* **Christie,** 1842; 5 D. 132. **Fisher** *v.* **Dixon,** 1840, 2 D. 1121; 1841, 3 D. 1181; 1843 (H. L.), 2 Bell's Ap. 63. See below, § 1949.

(*c*) 44 and 45 Vict. c. 21, § 7. See § 1580A.

1583. The rules according to which the right of children to their legitim is regulated are:—1. Legitim is due, 'at common law (*a*),' on the father's death only (*b*). 2. If the wife survive the husband, the legitim is a third; if she has predeceased, or renounced her share, the legitim is a half (*c*). 'So also when the estate consists of moveable bonds bearing a clause of interest (*d*), the widow's right being excluded by statute, the division is bipartite (*e*).' 3. All the father's existing children, of whatever marriage, including both legitimated and posthumous children, are entitled to a share of the legitim, unless they have renounced or been forisfamiliated (*f*). 4. In legitim there is no representation or substitution of the children of a deceased child to the parent (*g*). 5. If the father have left only one child, legitim is due, although that child is heir (*h*). 6. The eldest son has a share with the rest, but is excluded from it if there be a heritable estate which he refuses to collate, or share with the other children (*i*). 7. By renunciation or forisfamiliation, the legitim accrues to the other children, and even to the heir, if he be the only other child, 'or if the right of the other children has been discharged or satisfied (*k*). 8. Heritable securities are not reckoned in ascertaining legitim (*l*).'

(*a*) See last section, *ad fin.*
(*b*) 3 Ersk. 9. § 15 et seq. Nisbet, *supra*, § 1581 (*a*).
(*c*) 3 Ersk. 9. § 17. Nisbet and Jervey, *supra*, § 1581 (*a*). Johnston, *supra*, § 1581 (*b*).
(*d*) Above, § 1495.
(*e*) 1661, c. 32. 2 Ersk. 2. § 9. Dawson's Tr. *v.* Dawson, 1896; 23 R. 1006.
(*f*) See below, § 1587. 3 Stair, 8. § 45. 3 Ersk. 9. § 23.
(*g*) 3 Stair, 8. § 44 and 52. 3 Ersk. Pr. 9. § 6–9. 3 Ersk. Inst. 9. § 17. 18 Vict. c. 23, being limited to property on which the father could test, does not introduce representation in legitim.
(*h*) Howden *v.* Crichton, 1821; 1 S. 14; 2 Ill. 281. See Collier *v.* Collier, July 6, 1833; F. C.; and Justice, *infra.*
(*i*) Kennedy *v.* Kennedy, 1622; M. 8163; 2 Ill. 281. Justice *v.* Murray, 1737; M. 8166; Elchies, *Legitim*, 2. Marshall *v.* Finlays, 1747; M. 8166, 3948, 5929. Johnston *v.* Johnston, 1814; Hume, 290. See Little Gilmour and other cases below, § 1912. **M. Breadalbane** *v.* **M. Chandos,** 1836; 14 S. 309; aff. 2 S. & M'L. 377.
(*k*) Sinclair *v.* Sinclair, 1768; M. 8188; Hailes, 247. Hog *v.* Hog, 1791; M. 8193; Bell's Ca. 491; aff. 3 Pat. 247. **L. Panmure** *v.* **Crokat,** 1856; 18 D. 703. *Infra*, § 1590.
(*l*) 31 and 32 Vict. c. 101, § 117. Above, § 1485A, 1552 (*b*).

1584. Legitim is diminished by every deed of the father *inter vivos* and *in liege poustie* disposing of his moveable funds (*a*); provided it be not fraudulently contrived, in order to disappoint the children without touching the father's own right during his life (*b*). 'And all moveable debts are to be deducted before division (*c*), including provisions by antenuptial contract to the wife and children (*d*) and executry expenses (*e*).'

(*a*) Agnew *v.* Agnew, 1775; M. 8210; 2 Ill. 271. **Hog (Lashley)** *v.* **Hog,** 1800; M. Apx. *Legit.* 2; as revd. 4 Pat. 581. Hay *v.* Angus, 1795; Hume, 281. Black *v.* Black, 1795; *ib.* 290. Millie *v.* Millie, 1803; M. 8215; aff. 1807, 5 Pat. 160; 2 Ill. 282. Craigie *v.* Craigie, 1811; Hume, 288.
(*b*) Hog, Millie, etc., *supra* (*a*). See below, § 1585 (*c*), (*e*).
(*c*) Cases in next section. 1 Stair, 5. § 6. 3 Ersk. 9. § 22. 1 Bell's Com. 635.
(*d*) 3 Ersk. 9. § 16. Wilson's Trs. *v.* Pagan, 1856; 18 D. 1096. **Keith's Trs.** *v.* **Keith,** 1857; 19 D. 1040. Even a reasonable post-nuptial provision to a wife is said to be preferable to the children's claim for legitim. See Lawrie, *infra*, § 1585 (*a*), (*d*). Fraser, H. & W. 988, 1011. As to contract provisions for children of second marriage, see Bishop's Trs. *v.* Bishop, 1894; 21 R. 728.
(*e*) M. Breadalbane's Trs. *v.* Dss. Buckingham, 1842; 4 D. 1259.

1585. Legitim may be defeated by an 'irrevocable' deed *inter vivos*, though the term of payment is after the husband's death, 'and although a liferent or any annuity is reserved (*a*)'; but not by a deed *mortis causa* (*b*), 'or by one which does not absolutely divest the father (*c*),' though it may be diminished by rational provisions for his wife made by a husband having no other means of providing (*d*); nor *per ambages* (*e*); nor on deathbed 'by delivering cash or securities transmissible by delivery, or lending money on heritable security' (*f*). And no deed or settlement of the father regulating the succession to the legitim is effectual, even where the child is a bankrupt, a pupil, or an idiot (*g*).

(*a*) 3 Ersk. 9. § 16. Johnston *v.* Johnston, 1697; M. 8198. Balmain *v.* Graham, 1721; M. 8199; 2 Ill. 526. Lawrie *v.* Edmond's Trs., 1816; Hume, 291. See 3 J. of J. 410–11. Collie *v.* Pirie's Trs., 1851; 13 D. 506; Boustead *v.* Gardner, 1879; 7 R. 139 (annuity out of business). 1 M'Laren on Wills, etc., 122. Fraser, H. & W. 1004, 1011.
(*b*) Millie, *supra*, § 1584 (*a*). Justice, *supra*, § 1583 (*i*). Allan *v.* Allan, 1763; 5 B. Sup. 897; 2 Ill. 282. M'Donald *v.* M'Donald, 1801; Hume, 288. Johnston *v.* Johnston, 1814; Hume, 290. Wilson's Trs., *supra*, § 1584 (*d*). Grant *v.* Gunn's Trs., 1833; 11 S. 484. See below, § 1589 (*b*).
(*c*) Nicolson's Assignee *v.* Hunter, 1841; 3 D. 675; 16 F. C. 728. Milroy *v.* Milroy, 1803; Hume, 285. Hog, § 1584 (*a*). Buchanan *v.* Buchanan, 1876; 3 R. 556. The disponee must obtain possession. Craigie, *cit.* § 1584 (*a*). Buchanan, *cit.* Fraser, H. & W. 1003.
(*d*) Balmain and Lawrie, *supra* (*a*). The limitation to a husband having no other means of providing is hardly warranted. See above, § 1584.
(*e*) Dirleton, *Legitim Lib.* 3 Stair, 4. § 24. 3 Ersk. 9. § 16. Hog, *supra*, § 1584 (*a*). Anderson *v.* Miller, 1799; Hume, 282. As to *pleading* that a gift or alienation was made in fraud of legitim, see Boustead *v.* Gardner, *cit.* (*a*).
(*f*) **Hog (Lashley)** *v.* **Hog,** 1791; M. 4619 and 8492; Bell's Ca. 491. Milroy, *cit.* Allan, *supra* (*b*). The Act 34 and 35 Vict. c. 81 (the inclusion of which in the Statute Law Revision Act of 1883 does not revive the law previous to its passing) abolishes reductions *ex capite lecti* of deeds, instruments, and writings; but does not affect other transactions. See Fraser, H. & W. 1005–1007.
(*g*) Allan *v.* Callender, 1762; M. 8209. Christie *v.* Christie, 1681; M. 8197. Robertson *v.* Kerr, 1742; M. 8202; Elchies, *Legitim*, 6. Morton *v.* Young, Feb. 11, 1813; F. C. Anderson, *supra* (*c*).

1586. The right to legitim vests *ipso jure* 'in each child as a creditor' on the child's survivance (*a*); 'and it extends to a third (or half) of the whole moveable estate which the father or mother possessed at the time of death, the share of each child being fixed and ascertained as at that time, and not at the period of realisation (*b*). It seems that when the child has an option of taking legitim, or a testamentary provision in lieu of it, the vesting of the legitim carries the right of election also to his representatives (*c*). An election made under substantial error is invalid, and may be retracted, subject to the rules as to homologation (*d*).'

(*a*) Yeaman *v.* Yeaman, 1680; M. 8176, 5484; 2 Ill. 283. Russell *v.* Brown, 1687; M. 8177. Sibbald *v.* Procr.-Fiscal, 1623; M. 8176. Jervey *v.* Watt, 1762; M. 8170; 2 Ill. 279. Stevenson *v.* Hamilton, 1838; 1 D. 181. Macdougal *v.* Wilson, 1858; 20 D. 658. Fisher *v.* Dixon, *infra* (*b*).

(*b*) Lees *v.* Wilson, 1808; Hume, 191. Haining *v.* Young, 1808; Hume, 214. M. Breadalbane's Trs. *v.* Dss. Buckingham, 1842; 4 D. 1259; 1843, 15 S. Jur. 389. M'Murray *v.* Govan, 1852; 14 D. 1048. **Fisher** *v.* **Dixon,** 1840; 2 D. 1121; 1841, 3 D. 1181; 1843, 2 Bell's App. 63. E. Dalhousie *v.* Crokat, 1868; 6 Macph. 659. Gilchrist *v.* Gilchrist's Trs., 1889; 16 R. 1118. As to questions whether policies of insurance form part of the estate subject to legitim or *jus relictæ*, see above, § 1550; and as to cases in which the division is postponed, Ross *v.* Masson, 1843; 5 D. 483. As to interest on legitim, which is generally at 5 p. c., see Sime *v.* Balfour, 1804; M. *Her. and Mov.* Apx. 4 (see 11 S. 632). Menzies *v.* Livingston, 1838; 16 S. 1268. Minto *v.* Kirkpatrick, 1833; 11 S. 632. Ballingall *v.* Robertson, 1808; Hume, 214. Ross *v.* Ross, 1896; 23 R. 802 (exceptions—delay in election owing to minority, etc.). Grant *v.* Grant's Trs., 1898; 25 R. 948; and cases above cited.

(*c*) M'Murray *v.* Govan, *cit.* (*b*). Lowson *v.* Young, 1854; 16 D. 1103. See *contra*, Stewart's Trs. *v.* Stewart, 1851; 14 D. 298.

(*d*) See § 11, 13 sqq., *supra*; and § 1587 (*b*), 1591, 1940, *infra*. Inglis' Trs. *v.* Inglis, 1887; 14 R. 740; 1890, 17 R. H. L. 76. Comp. § 1591 (*l*). Dawson's Trs. *v.* Dawson, 1896; 23 R. 1006 (election by widow—*per* L. Kinnear).

1587. *Discharge.*—The right to legitim is discharged or satisfied in one or other of the following modes:—By express discharge (*a*); by a provision accepted 'with full knowledge of the facts,' having a condition annexed that acceptance shall discharge the legitim (*b*); 'or by a special provision accepted under a general settlement of the father's whole moveable estate, whether it be contained in one or several deeds (*c*): but acceptance of a special provision under a partial settlement of the father's moveable estate, or a settlement which does not plainly disclose an intention to dispose of the legitim, does not exclude the legatee from legitim (*d*)'; by a reasonable (*e*) provision being made for the child in an antenuptial marriage contract of the parents, accompanied by an express exclusion of the right to legitim. But the words, "for all he can ask or claim by the father's death," 'or any words which merely raise an implication or presumption,' are not sufficient to discharge the legitim. The proper words are, "to discharge the legitim or bairn's part of gear" (*f*). But such a condition in a post-nuptial contract is not effectual, unless acceded to by the child (*g*).

It is no sufficient forisfamiliation or bar to legitim, that a child has been married and has left the father's house, without a discharge of the legitim (*h*). And a child being married in England, and in the English marriage contract a large sum given "as her portion," it was held no bar to her claim of legitim, 'and the general rule settled that a gift by a father in the marriage contract of his child does not exclude legitim, unless it be distinctly stated that the sum given is to be accepted in full of all legal claims' (*i*). Legitim is not held to be excluded by a larger provision being given to the child (*k*); nor by a marriage contract in which the whole stock and conquest of the marriage is settled (even if so settled on the child), unless it expressly bear to be in satisfaction of the legitim (*l*). 'But if, by antenuptial contract, the whole moveable estate is settled upon the children, or upon the wife, whether in liferent or even in fee, no fund is left out of which legitim can be claimed (*m*), at least while the liferent subsists (*n*).'

And it may be for the interest of a husband's creditors that a more ample provision made to his wife by her father shall be rejected, and recourse had to her legitim, if the conventional provision exclude the husband. 'But in such a case the wife's right of election, being personal to herself, cannot be controlled by the husband or his creditors; though it is said that the Court would not allow an unfair election by her of a small protected interest in place of a greatly larger interest which would benefit creditors (*o*). Cases of this kind are now provided for by the Conjugal Rights Act (*p*). A lunatic cannot of course elect; but he does not lose his right to do so even if he take temporary benefit out of the estate. The right may be exercised by him after his recovery, or by his representatives on his death. In cases of urgent necessity, if for instance third parties have a pressing interest in the division of a trust estate, the Court will authorise an election to be made by a *curator bonis* (*q*). But such an election will not be allowed to affect the character of his succession (*r*).'

(*a*) 3 Ersk. 9. § 23. Lawson *v.* Lawson, 1777; M. 8190, and *Legitim*, Apx. 1; 2 Ill. 283. Anderson *v.* Anderson, 1743; M. 5054; Elch. *Execr.* 12. Hepburn *v.* Hepburn, 1785; M. 5056. Fisher *v.* Dixon, *supra*, § 1586 (*b*). Clark *v.* Burns & Stewart, 1835; 13 S. 326. **M. Breadalbane's Trs.** *v.* **Mss. Chandos,** *infra* (*i*). Trevelyan *v.* Trevelyan, 1873; 11 Macph. 516.

(*b*) M'Gill *v.* Lady Oxenford, 1671; M. 8179. Begg *v.* Lapraik, 1737; M. 12,851; Elch. *Legitim*, 3. Campbell *v.* Campbells, 1738; M. 8187, 9265; Elch. *ib.* 4. Nisbet, *infra*, § 1588 (*a*). Hog, *infra* (*h*). Johnston, *infra* (*g*). Sime, *supra*, § 1586 (*b*). Paterson *v.* Moncrieff, 1866; 4 Macph. 708. Ross *v.* Mackenzie, 1842; 5 D. 151. Davidson's Trs. *v.* Davidson, 1871; 8 Macph. 995. Macfarlane's Trs. *v.* Oliver, 1882; 9 R. 1138. See below, § 1940, 1949.

(*c*) Henderson *v.* Henderson, 1782; M. 8191. **Collier** *v.* **Collier**, July 6, 1833; F. C., and 11 S. 912. **M. Breadalbane's Trs.** *v.* **Dss. Buckingham**, 1840; 2 D. 731. Nicolson's Assignee, § 1585 (*c*). Minto *v.* Kirkpatrick, 1842; 4 D. 1224. L. Panmure, *supra*, § 1583 (*k*). Keith's Trs. *v.* Keith, 1857; 19 D. 1040. See Crellin *v.* Muirhead's Tr., 1892; 20 R. 51.

(*d*) Collier *v.* Collier, *cit.* See **White** *v.* **Finlay,** *infra*, § 1592 (*c*).

(*e*) Where there is an express exclusion in an antenuptial contract, it is not necessary that an *equivalent* provision should be given in lieu of it. Maitland *v.* Maitland, 1843; 6 D. 244. See E. Kintore, *infra* (*f*).

(*f*) 3 Ersk. 9. § 23. Stirling *v.* Luke, 1732; Elch. *Legitim*, 1; Cr. & St. 215; 11 R. 1019, f. n. Burden *v.* Smith, 1738; Elch. *Mut. Cont.* 7; rev. Cr. & St. 214. Home *v.* Watson, 1757; 5 B. Sup. 330. Stephen *v.* Straiton, 1803; Hume, 286. See below, § 1590, 1592. Cases in note (*a*). Keith's Trs. (*c*). E. Kintore *v.* Css. Kintore, 1884; 11 R. 1013; aff. 1886, 11 App. Ca. 394; 13 R. H. L. 93. The proposition of Professor Bell in the text is perhaps too widely expressed, and is hardly necessitated by the authorities. It is enough that no mere implication, however strong, suffices to discharge legitim. See Meldrum *v.* Anderson, 1885; 2 Sh. Ct. R. 28 (*per* Sheriff Dove Wilson).

(*g*) Johnston *v.* Paterson, 1825; 4 S. 234; 1829, 7 S. 229.

(*h*) **Hog** *v.* **Lashley**, 1791; M. 4619, 8193; Bell's Ca. 491; 3 Pat. 247. Dirl. and St., *Bairn's Part.* Clark and Breadalbane, *citt.* (*a*).

(*i*) **M. Breadalbane** *v.* **Mss. Chandos,** 1836; 14 S. 309; aff. 2 S. & M'L. 377. Keith's Trs., *cit.* (*c*). Trevelyan, *cit.* (*a*). Somerville's Trs. *v.* Dickson's Trs., 1887; 14 R. 770. Rait *v.* Arbuthnott, 1892; 19 R. 687.

(*k*) Howden *v.* Crichton, 1821; 1 S. 18.

(*l*) See cases above (*a*); and below, § 1949.

(*m*) Fisher's Trs. *v.* Fisher, 1844; 7 D. 129. Home *v.* Watson (*f*). See above, cases in (*c*), (*d*), (*f*).

(*n*) Bell *v.* Bell, 1897; 25 R. 310 (liferent to husband—legitim from mother's estate).

(*o*) Lowson *v.* Young, 1854; 16 D. 1098. Stevenson *v.* Hamilton, 1838; 1 D. 181. Macdougall *v.* Wilson, 1858; 20 D. 656. See Millar *v.* Birrell, 1876; 4 R. 87; also *supra*, § 1560D, note (*b*). The effect of the election of legitim is not necessarily an entire "forfeiture" of the conventional provision; but only a diminution of it so far as to provide compensation to the legatees who suffer by the withdrawal of the legitim. Macfarlane's Trs. *v.* Oliver, 1882; 9 R. 1138. See the cases on equitable compensation, *infra*, § 1590 (*e*), 1940 (*c*).

(*p*) See above, § 1560A. See Fraser, H. & W. 830 sqq.

(*q*) Morton *v.* Young, Feb. 11, 1813; F. C. Cowan *v.* Turnbull's Trs., 1845; 7 D. 872; 1848, 6 Bell's App. 222. Morrison's Curator *v.* Morrison's Trs., 1880; 8 R. 205.

(*r*) Kennedy *v.* Kennedy, 1843; 6 D. 40. Hope, petr., 1858; 20 D. 390. Cowan, *cit.*

1588. '*Collatio bonorum inter liberos.*'—Advances will be imputed to the legitim in the following circumstances:—If made for the purpose of setting the child up in trade, or for a settlement in the world, or for a marriage portion (*a*). This equalising of the right is called *collatio bonorum inter liberos.* If the advances be not made from the common stock, there is no such collation; as when a father makes an advance from his heritage (*b*). Advances for aliment, education, or apprenticeship, 'or on loan, these being due to the executry,' will not be imputed to the legitim (*c*); 'nor payments of an onerous or remuneratory nature (*d*).'

(*a*) 3 Stair, 8. § 45. 3 Ersk. 9. § 24. Fraser, H. & W. 1033 sqq. Russell *v.* Brown, 1687; M. 8177; 2 Ill. 283. Skinner *v.* Skinner, 1755; M. 8172; Hailes, 674. Nisbet *v.* Nisbet, 1726; M. 8181; aff. Robertson's Ap. 594. Macdougall's Crs. *v.* Macdougall, 1804; M. *Bankrupt*, Apx. 21. Webster *v.* Rettie, 1859; 21 D. 915. Johnston *v.* Cochran, 1829; 7 S. 226. Nicolson's Assignee *v.* Hunter, 1841; 3 D. 675. Kay *v.* Kay, 1844; 16 Jur. 550. Nisbet's Trs. *v.* Nisbet, 1868; 6 Macph. 567. Douglas *v.* Douglas, 1876; 4 R. 105. Welsh *v.* Welsh's Trs., 1878; 5 R. 542. Malcolm *v.* Campbell, 1889; 17 R. 255.

(*b*) 3 Stair, 8. § 46. 3 Ersk. 9. § 25. D. Buccleuch *v.* Tweeddale, 1677; M. 2369. Marshall *v.* Marshall's Trs., 1829; 8 S. 110. Nicolson's Assignee *v.* Hunter, March 3, 1841; F. C. As to the question whether interest is to be added to the sum to be collated, see Johnston, and Nisbet's Trs. *v.* Nisbet, *citt.*; and Monteith *v.* Monteith's Trs., 1882; 9 R. 982, 985.

(*c*) Irving *v.* Irving, 1694; 4 B. Sup. 144. Skinner, *supra* (*a*). Webster, *supra* (*a*) (loans).

(*d*) Minto *v.* Kirkpatrick, 1833; 11 S. 632.

1589. A father may, during his life, give to a child what sums he pleases, reserving the child's right to legitim (*a*), either in express words, or by declaring that the child shall continue a bairn in the house (*b*). 'Collation takes place only *inter liberos, i.e.* among children claiming legitim; and therefore not in a question with the widow (*c*), or with a residuary legatee (*d*), even though he should be a child himself claiming legitim (*e*).'

(*a*) 3 Stair, 8. § 45. 3 Ersk. 9. § 25. Corsan *v.* Corsan, 1631; M. 2367, 12,849; 2 Ill. 285. Skinner, *supra*, § 1588 (*a*).

(*b*) Begg *v.* Lapraik, 1737; M. 2379 and 12,851; Elch. *Forisfam.* 1. Spence *v.* Stevenson, 1766; M. 8178. Douglas, and other cases above, § 1588 (*a*). It is said that the father, who has made advances during his life, may in a *mortis causa* deed effectually declare his intention that they shall not diminish the share of legitim falling to the child receiving them. Monteith *v.* Monteith's Trs., 1882; 9 R. 982 (*per* L. J.-C. Moncreiff and L. Young).

(*c*) 3 Stair, 8. § 46. 1 Bell's Com. 101. Trevelyan *v.* Trevelyan, 1873; 11 Macph. 516.

(*d*) Clark *v.* Burns & Stewart, Breadalbane *v.* Chandos, and Keith's Trs. *v.* Keith, *supra*, § 1587 (*a*) and (*c*).
(*e*) Fisher *v.* Dixon, *supra*, § 1586 (*b*). Monteith (*b*).

1590. The effects of a discharge of legitim are:—A discharge (*a*) by all the children makes the division bipartite between husband and wife; or if the wife be already dead, and her share paid, it converts the whole into dead's part (*b*). A discharge by one child, 'in the father's lifetime,' operates like the death of that child (*c*); and the virtual discharge by the heir of the right to legitim by refusing to collate, will produce the same effect (*d*). A discharge of legitim after the father's death accrues, 'on the principle of equitable compensation, to the fund burdened with the conventional provision elected in lieu of it, *i.e.* generally' to the person entitled to the residuary right of succession (*e*). 'A discharge of legitim does not prevent the children who have granted it from taking as next of kin upon intestacy, or under an ultimate destination as "nearest heirs" (*f*).'

(*a*) See above, § 1587 and 1581.
(*b*) Instruction to Commissaries, Feb. 28, 1688, in Act of Sed. p. 99; and see as to the rule of succession in that case, Chisholm *v.* Chisholm, 1672; M. 8180; 2 Ill. 285. Foubister *v.* ——, 1604; M. 8181. See below as to the power over, and modification of, legitim by the father, § 1949. See above, § 1581, 1583.
(*c*) M'Gill *v.* Oxenford, 1671; M. 8179. Henderson *v.* Henderson, 1728; M. 8187. Hog *v.* Lashley, *supra*, § 1587 (*h*). Fisher *v.* Dixon, below (*e*). Buchanan *v.* Buchanan's Trs., 1876; 3 R. 566. Douglas *v.* Douglas, 1876; 4 R. 105. Jack's Trs. *v.* Marshall, 1879; 6 R. 543. *Supra*, § 1583 (*i*).
(*d*) M. Breadalbane, *supra*, § 1587 (*i*); and 1841, 3 D. 357. Peat *v.* Peat, 1839; 1 D. 508. See 1 M'Laren on Wills, 482.
(*e*) Henderson, *supra* (*c*). **Fisher** *v.* **Dixon,** 1840; 2 D. 1121; 1841, 3 D. 1181; aff. 1843, 2 Bell's App. 63. Campbell's Trs. *v.* Campbell, 1862; 24 D. 1321. L. Panmure *v.* Crokat, 1856; 18 D. 703. Nisbet's Trs. *v.* Nisbet, 1868; 6 Macph. 567. Davidson's Trs. *v.* Davidson, 1871; 9 Macph. 995. As to the effect of electing between two conventional provisions, see Peat, *cit.* Nisbet's Trs. *v.* Nisbet, 1851; 14 D. 145. Harvey (Macdowall) *v.* Harvey, 1862; 1 Macph. 345. See above, § 1587 (*o*); below, § 1940 (*c*).
(*f*) Wilson *v.* Gibson, 1840; 2 D. 1236. Maitland *v.* Maitland, 1843; 6 D. 244. Balderston *v.* Fulton, 1857; 19 D. 293.

1591. Jus Relictæ or Widow's Share.—The share to which the relict is entitled, or which 'devolved' on her executors on her predecease (*a*), has already been explained (*b*). It is a share of the moveables of the husband domiciled in Scotland (*c*), a half or a third, according to the rules already laid down. 'It does not extend to a heritable security (*d*), or to a bond with a clause of interest (*e*). It is to be remembered that a surviving husband has now precisely the same right in the separate estate of his wife (*f*).' The wife takes this right *ipso jure* (*g*), 'and is entitled to interest on it from the husband's death (*h*).' She may dispose of it by testament; and without a will it descends to her children or next of kin. The husband cannot encroach upon it more than upon the legitim, by *mortis causa* or by fraudulent deeds (*i*). It may be renounced, provided it be clearly expressed; and this may be effectually done in a postnuptial contract of separation, provided it be onerous, and so irrevocable (*k*). 'An election and renunciation may be recalled on sufficient grounds (*l*). Like legitim, *jus relictæ* may be constructively discharged by acceptance of a provision under a settlement disposing of the total moveable estate (*m*), and it will be satisfied by taking, or assenting with full knowledge of the facts (*n*) to, a testamentary or marriage contract provision, either expressed to be in lieu of *jus relictæ*, or forming part of a total settlement of the moveable estate (*o*). In a case of partial intestacy acceptance of provisions declared to satisfy the legal rights need not exclude the *jus relictæ* from the moveables fallen into intestacy (*p*). The *jus relictæ*, like legitim, is said to be taken by the widow as a creditor, not as an heir (*q*).'

(*a*) See above, § 1580 *fin.*
(*b*) See above, § 1579 et seq.
(*c*) Nisbett *v.* Nisbett's Trs., 1835; 13 S. 517; 2 Ill. 286. See Fraser, H. & W. 991.
(*d*) Above, § 1485A. (*e*) Above, § 1495.
(*f*) See above, § 1580A.
(*g*) 3 Ersk. 9. § 30. M'Aulay *v.* Bell, 1712; M. 3848; 2 Ill. 279.
(*h*) M'Intyre *v.* M'Intyre's Trs., 1865; 3 Macph. 1074.
(*i*) 3 Ersk. 9. § 15. Milroy *v.* Milroy, 1803; Hume, 285. See above, § 1585.
(*k*) See Miller *v.* Brown, 1776; M. 6456; 5 B. Sup. 473; Hailes, 678. Sutherland *v.* Syme, 1772; Hailes, 479. See below, § 1946. Keith's Trs. (*o*); see above, § 1581 (*e*). Johnston *v.* Coldstream, 1843; 5 D. 1297. Howden *v.* Crichton, 1821; 1 S. 16.
(*l*) Stewart *v.* Bruce's Trs., 1898; 25 R. 965 (hurry—inadequate information—no independent advice). Comp. § 1586, above.
(*m*) See above, § 1587. Stewart *v.* Stephen, 1832; 11 S. 139. Ross *v.* Masson, 1843; 5 D. 483. Dunlop *v.* Greenlees' Trs., 1865; 3 Macph. H. L. 46. Cross *v.* Boyes, 1801; Hume, 484. See Thomson *v.* Smith, 1849; 12 D. 276; Caithness' Trs. *v.* Caithness, 1877; 4 R. 937; Ersk. Pr. p. 536, note (16th ed.); and Fraser, H. & W. 1069, as to the effect of accepting a liferent of the husband's whole moveable estate.
(*n*) See cases in § 1940, note (*c*) *fin.* Dawson's Trs. *v.* Dawson, 1896; 23 R. 1006.
(*o*) **Keith's Trs.** *v.* **Keith,** 1857; 19 D. 1040. Steuart's Trs. *v.* Steuart, 1891; 18 R. 1114 (foreign marriage contract—construction). See Campbell's Trs. *v.*

Campbell, 1862; 24 D. 1321. Baxter's Trs. *v.* Baxter's Exr., 1884; 11 R. 996; aff. 1887, 13 App. Ca. 373; 15 R. H. L. 33, 37; below, § 1940 (*c*); above, § 1586 (*d*).

(*p*) Hamilton's Trs. *v.* Boyes, 1898; 25 R. 899.

(*q*) Inglis *v.* Inglis, 1869; 7 Macph. 435. M'Intyre (*h*). Tait's Trs. *v.* Lees, 1886; 13 R. 1104. Buntine *v.* Buntine's Trs., 1894; 21 R. 714 (*jus relicti*).

1592. Dead's Part (*a*).—The husband, 'or a wife having separate estate,' may dispose by testament of the share belonging to him, called the dead's part; and if he do not exercise this power, the dead's part descends to his children or other next of kin (*b*). 'When one is appointed executor and universal legatory, there being wife and children claiming their thirds, this is a bequest of dead's part only, with right of administering the estate as executor (*c*). It must be remembered that bonds bearing interest and heritable securities, though they remain heritable in regard to the *jus relictæ* and legitim, are now moveable and form part of the dead's part (*d*).' In marriage contracts there is no necessity for stipulating a discharge of the dead's part, as of the legitim, since it is at all times within the husband's power. And the general words "all that the child can ask or take through the father's death," though usually held to apply to the dead's part only, will, where the word legitim is used in the clause, be held as construed by that word to mean only the bairn's part (*e*). 'Where the words are "ask or demand," they do not apply to dead's part, to which a child has no legal claim (*f*). A discharge of "executry," if unqualified by the other language of the instrument, is a discharge of the right of succession to dead's part (*g*).'

(*a*) See above, § 1579. (*b*) See below, § 1861.

(*c*) **White** *v.* **Finlay,** 1861; 24 D. 38.

(*d*) See above, § 1485A, 1495, 1552 (*b*). The terms of the 6th and 7th sections of the Married Women's Property Act of 1881 seem to make them heritable also as to the rights now given to a husband and children in the separate estate of a wife and mother. See § 1580A, 1582.

(*e*) See cases, *supra*, 1587 (*a*), (*f*). Sinclair *v.* Sinclair, 1770; M. 8188; aff. 2 Pat. 199. Pringle *v.* Pringle, 1741; Elch. *Legitim*, 5. See Wilson *v.* Gibson, 1840; 2 D. 1236. Johnston *v.* Miller, 1847; 9 D. 1389.

(*f*) Sinclair and Pringle, *citt.* (*e*). Fraser, H. & W. 1076.

(*g*) Clark *v.* Burns & Stewart, 1835; 13 S. 326.

1593. Heritable Estates.—The rights of the spouses as to the heritable estates are either such as arise during the marriage, or such as arise after its dissolution (*a*). 'The quality of being heritable or real is attached to property by the *lex rei sitæ*, and by that law the nature and extent of the spouses' rights to it are determined (*b*).'

(*a*) See above, § 1552.

(*b*) Welch *v.* Tennant, 1889; 16 R. 876; rev. 1891, A. C. 639; 18 R. H. L. 72. Above, § 1550.

1594. During the marriage, 'if it have been contracted before the 18th July 1881,' the husband has the sole administration and possession of the wife's heritable estate 'to which she has acquired right before the said date,' as well as of his own. He draws the rents, interests, and profits (*a*). But it has been held that the husband cannot compel his wife to bring an action against her mother to deprive her of heritable property, and have it vested in herself (*b*). The husband, in the administration of the wife's estate, is under restraint so far that he can grant no lease to endure beyond his own life without his wife's concurrence (*c*). This right of administration to the effect of taking the rents, etc., his creditors may adjudge 'if the *jus mariti* be not excluded; but they cannot attach the mere right of administration (*d*).

'In the case of marriages contracted after 18th July 1881, the rents and produce of heritable property in Scotland belonging to the wife are, by the Married Women's Property Act, 1881, no longer subject to the *jus mariti* and right of administration of the husband (*e*).

'In the case of marriages contracted before the Act, the old law applies to all the wife's heritage (and moveables, *supra*, § 1560D) if the husband have before the date of the Act made a reasonable provision by irrevocable deed for her in the event of her surviving him (*f*). But if no such provision have been made, the old law applies in such marriages only to *acquisita* before the date of the Act, and the *jus mariti* and right of administration are excluded from the rents and produce or income of heritable property in Scotland to which the wife may acquire right after the passing of the Act (*f*).'

(*a*) 1 Stair, 4. § 17. 1 Ersk. 6. § 27.

(*b*) Ferguson *v.* Cowan, 1819; Hume, 222.

(*c*) Above, § 1184. Grieve *v.* Pringle, 1797; M. 5951; 2 Ill. 286. Gibson *v.* Aitken, 1798; Hume, 205. See as to a lease falling to the wife as tenant, Gillon *v.* Muirhead, 1775; M. 15,286; 2 Ill. 188. Hume *v.* Taylor, 1734; M. 15,700.

(*d*) See above, § 1552, 1561. Crawcour *v.* Graham, 1847; 6 D. 589, 597. Cases in Fraser, H. & W. 813, note (*c*). Loudon *v.* Young, 1856; 18 D. 856; 19 D. 140. The language of the text is inaccurate—the distinction between *jus mariti* and right of administration not being drawn clearly enough.

(*e*) 44 and 45 Vict. c. 21, § 2. It is not said, as it is in regard to income of moveable estate, that a wife may not assign prospective rents and produce. This enactment gives her absolute power of dealing with the rents and produce of her heritable estate without the consent, and even against the will, of her husband. See Fraser, H. & W. 813.

(*f*) 44 and 45 Vict. c. 21, § 3. See above, § 1560D.

1595. **Terce.**—After dissolution of the marriage, there arises a liferent of the land, total or partial, to the survivor. The wife's liferent is called Terce; the husband's Courtesy (*a*).

(*a*) See below, § 1605.

1596. Terce is a liferent of a third part of the heritable estate in which the husband dies infeft as of fee, provided by law to a widow who has not accepted of a conventional provision (*a*).

(*a*) 2 Craig, 22. § 26. 2 Stair, 6. § 12, 13. 2 Ersk. Pr. 9. § 26. 2 Ersk. Inst. 9. § 45. 1 Bell's Com. 57. See as to Liferent, above, § 1037 et seq.

1597. (1.) *Who Entitled.*—The terce may be claimed by 'one who is held and reputed' (*a*) the widow (*b*) of a deceased proprietor infeft as of fee, 'even' if the marriage has 'not' subsisted for year and day, or produced a living child (*c*); and provided 'by statute' she has not, 'in the full and fair knowledge of her rights,' accepted a conventional provision, or has done so with reservation of her right to terce (*d*); 'provided also the right to terce be not excluded by the entail or other deed, not made by the husband himself, regulating the succession to the estate (*e*).' It may be questioned whether a conventional provision, which, if effectual, would have been fatal to the terce, will exclude it if that provision be defeated (*f*).

(*a*) 1503, c. 77. Craik *v.* Penny, 1891 ; 19 R. 339.

(*b*) An alien could not formerly take terce. Stewart *v.* Hoome, 1792 ; M. 4649. **Nisbett** *v.* **Nisbett's Trs.**, 1834; 12 S. 293; 1835, 13 S. 517. But this is changed by the Naturalisation Act, 1870 ; 33 and 34 Vict. c. 10, § 2, 10.

(*c*) 1 Jurid. Styles, 342. 1503, c. 77. 2 Stair, 6. § 17. 2 Ersk. Pr. 9. § 26, and Inst. § 51. Crawford's Trs. *v.* Hart, 1802 ; M. 12,698 ; 2 Ill. 237 (legitimation *per subsequens matrimonium*). Paxton *v.* Paxton, 1840 ; 2 D. 1102. The title of the Act of 1855 applies to intestate moveable succession only ; but the enactments are not confined to that subject, and the terms of the 7th section are wide enough to apply to terce. 18 Vict. c. 23, § 7 ; *supra*, § 1575 (1). Fraser, H. & W. 1083.

(*d*) M'Kenzie's Observ. 3; Parl. Cha. II. c. 10. 2 Stair, 6. § 17. 2 Ersk. Pr. 9. § 26 ; Inst. § 44, 45. 1681, c. 10. Lady Craigleith *v.* Prestongrange, 1681 ; M. 6450, 15,845; 2 Ill. 286. Jankouska *v.* Anderson, 1791 ; M. 6457, 15,868. Lowthian *v.* Ross, 1797 ; M. 4631 ; and *Foreigner*, Apx. 9 ; rev. 3 Pat. 621. See Lowthian *v.* Aglionby, *infra*, § 1598 (*l*). Css. Findlater *v.* E. Seafield, Feb. 8, 1814 ; F. C. Douglas, Heron, & Co. *v.* Cant, 1783 ; M. 11,461, 15,866. Cowan *v.* Kerr, 1830 ; 9 S. 188. **Nisbett** (*b*). Borthwick *v.* Pringle, 1870 : 8 Macph. 622 (acquiescence and abandonment). Hamilton's Trs. *v.* Boyes, 1898 ; 25 R. 899 (partial intestacy —widow getting terce and conventional provision). The cases of Jankouska, Lowthian, and Nisbett relate to conventional provisions subject to foreign laws. See as to ignorance of legal rights, Hope *v.* Dickson, 1833 ; 12 S. 222 ; Cooper *v.* Cooper's Trs., 1885 ; 12 R. 473 ; rev. 1888, L. R. 13 App. Ca. 88 ; 15 R. H. L. 21 (foreign minor) ; 1 Bell's Com. 58 ; and above, § 11 *fin.*, 27 ; below, § 1619, 1946.

(*e*) Gibson *v.* Reid, 1794 ; M. 15,869. Kerr *v.* Reid, 1795 ; Bell's Ca. 195. Newton *v.* Newton, 1866 ; 5 Macph. 1056 ; aff. 1870, 8 Macph. H. L. 66 ; L. R. 2 Sc. App. 13.

(*f*) Mowat's Crs. *v.* Lauder, 1697 ; M. 6395. See *contra*, § 1947. Fraser, H. & W. 1116.

1598. (2.) *The Subjects* out of which terce is demandable are, in general, all heritable subjects and rights in which the husband was infeft (*a*). And in a question with the husband's representatives, 'though not with creditors,' it will not bar the widow of her terce that the husband's infeftment has been reduced on informalities in making up his titles (*b*). In particular, terce is due from corporeal heritage, as lands, houses, barns, etc. It may be doubted whether from the mansion-house and garden (*c*); though, if the mansion-house be let, or if there be more than one, the widow may claim her terce (*d*). 'It may also be claimed' from incorporeal subjects, as securities on land by infeftment (*e*); but burdens by reservation do not seem to be comprehended within the description of subjects liable to terce (*f*). Terce is not due from superiorities; and it has been held (but with strong expression of doubt) that no terce is due from the large feu-duties which are now sometimes levied from lands in the neighbourhood of towns (*g*). Reversions (*h*); patronage (*i*); leases, as not feudal; coal, etc., as not proper for liferent—give no terce (*k*). Nor 'formerly' subjects held burgage (*l*); within which exception, however, subjects in burghs of regality and barony 'were' not included, nor tenements within the royalty not held burgage (*m*). 'But even before the abolition of burgage tenure, the widows of persons dying infeft in burgage property were entitled to terce, with service and kenning as in other property from which terce could be claimed (*n*). It is due from teinds, if vested by special infeftment, not when united with the stock or held on a personal title (*o*).'

(*a*) 2 Stair, 6. § 16. 2 Ersk. Pr. 9. § 27, and Inst. § 48, 49. See also 2 Craig, 22. § 26–29. Css. Dunfermline *v.* Her Son, 1627 ; M. 14,707, 15,837 ; 2 Ill. 287. 1 Bell's Com. 59.

(*b*) Rose *v.* Fraser, 1790; M. *Terce*, Apx. 1. Hamilton *v.* Boswell, 1716; M. 3117; aff. 1720, Robertson's Ap. 346 (courtesy). See Campbell *v.* Brown, 1829; 1 S. Jur. 83. Smith *v.* Ranken, 1835; 13 S. 461; aff. 1840; 1 Rob. 173.

(*c*) Montier *v.* Baillie, 1773; M. 15,859; Hailes, 530. *Sed quære?* See below, § 1603, and Fraser, H. & W. 1097.

(*d*) Mead *v.* Swinton, 1796; M. 15,873. See Logan *v.* Galbraith, 1665; M. 15,842; 1 B. Sup. 507.

(*e*) 1 Bell's Com. 59, is too absolutely expressed as to real burdens by reservation. See Shaw's Bell's Com. 607. 31 and 32 Vict. c. 101, § 117.

(*f*) See below, § 1600 (*d*).

(*g*) 2 Ersk. 9. § 49. 2 Craig, 22. § 34. L. Glenbervie *v.* Luss, 1541; M. 15,835. L. Lamington *v.* His Mother, 1628; M. 15,840, 8240; 1 B. Sup. 246. Lady Dunfermline, *supra* (*a*). **Nisbett** *v.* **Nisbett's Trs.**, 1835; 13 S. 517. See 1 Bell's Com. 58, and L. Moncreiff in 13 S. 532, 533.

(*h*) M'Dougall *v.* M'Dougall, 1801; M. *Terce*, Apx. 3.

(*i*) D. Roxburghe *v.* Dss. Dowager, June 25, 1818; F. C.; 2 Ill. 61.

(*k*) Lamington, *supra* (*g*). Belschier *v.* Moffat, 1779; M. 15,863; 2 Ill. 140. Waddel *v.* Waddel, Jan. 21, 1812; F. C. See above, § 721, 1042; below, § 1772.

(*l*) 2 Craig, 22. § 34. 2 Stair, 6. § 16, and 1. 4. § 21. 2 Bank. 6. § 11. 2 M'Kenzie, 9. § 43. Lowthian (Ross) *v.* Aglionby, 1801; M. *Annualrent*, Apx. 2; aff. 4 Pat. 464.

(*m*) Rose *v.* Fraser, 1790; M. 15,867; *Terce*, Apx. 1. Wallace *v.* ——, 1649; 1 B. Sup. 395. Park *v.* Gib, 1769; M. 15,855; Hailes, 306.

(*n*) 24 and 25 Vict. c. 86, § 12 (Conjugal Rights Act).

(*o*) Arbuthnot *v.* Arbuthnot's Trs., 1805; Hume, 294; 1 Bell's Com. 57. Moncrieff *v.* Tenants of Newton, 1667; M. 15,733, 15,844. Lady Dunfermline, *cit.* (*a*).

1599. The infeftment of the husband must be "of fee" as at the time of his death (*a*); and real, not merely nominal, or in trust (*b*).

(*a*) 2 Craig, 22. § 27. 2 Stair, 6. § 12. 2 Ersk. 9. § 45.

(*b*) Cumming *v.* L. Adv., 1756; M. 15,854, 4268; 5 B. Sup. 843; 2 Ill. 290.

1600. The terce is diminished by all transferences and real burdens completed by infeftment before the husband's death (*a*). But to exclude the terce, sasine must be actually and duly taken and recorded (*b*). Resignation *in favorem* will not have this effect; but resignation *ad remanentiam* will (*c*). Real burdens by reservation affect the terce, although it is doubted whether the terce includes rights of this description (*d*). A trust conveyance or absolute disposition and sasine, with a back-bond, will not deprive the widow of her terce; though debt so secured will diminish her right (*e*). An adjudication not completed by infeftment, though with a charge to the superior, does not bar the terce (*f*). 'There must be a charter, or its modern equivalent, a recorded decree or abbreviate of adjudication (*g*).' Conveyances in defraud of the terce, or undue delay in taking infeftment, will defeat the terce in a question with third parties, creditors or purchasers; but the wife will, as a personal right, be entitled to redress or relief (*h*). And if lands liable to terce have been sold after the husband's death, the widow may claim indemnification against the seller (*i*); and even against the purchaser she would seem to have a real right of restitution. The Court will interfere to give reasonable aliment, if the terce should be inadequate or accidentally defeated, or if the husband's means consist of funds not yielding terce (*k*); 'but this will be done only on the ground that in the circumstances of the estate the widow's provisions are not suitable to its free income, and not because merely of her needs and to the effect of extinguishing or unfairly encroaching on the rights of other heirs or beneficiaries (*l*).'

(*a*) Campbell *v.* Campbell, 1776; 5 B. Sup. 627. Belschier *v.* Moffat, 1779; M. 15,863; Hailes, 838. Arbuthnot *v.* Arbuthnot, 1805; Hume, 294. Bartlet, *infra* (*e*).

(*b*) M'Culloch *v.* Maitland, 1788; M. 15,866; 5 B. Sup. 843; 2 Ill. 290. Boyd *v.* Hamilton, 1805; M. 15,874. Cases in note (*f*). Robson *v.* Macnish, 1861; 23 D. 429. Rossborough's Tr. *v.* Rossborough, 1888; 16 R. 157 (sale by bondholder—terce due till disposition recorded).

(*c*) See above, § 787–792.

(*d*) Stewart *v.* Hoome, 1792; M. 4649. 1 Bell's Com. 58, 686, n. See § 1598.

(*e*) Bartlet *v.* Buchanan, Feb. 21, 1811, and Nov. 27, 1812; F. C. It is doubted whether terce is due from estate held by trustees in which the husband has never himself been infeft. Fraser, H. & W. 1092. More's Notes on Stair, 219. 1 M'Laren on Wills, etc., § 162.

(*f*) Hunter's Crs. *v.* Douglas, 1715; M. 15,850; overruled by Carlyle *v.* Lyon's Crs., 1725; M. 15,851, 147. Hamilton *v.* Wood, 1770; M. 15,858; Hailes, 332.

(*g*) 31 and 32 Vict. c. 101, § 62, 129.

(*h*) M. Annandale *v.* Scott, 1711; M. 15,848. Carruthers *v.* Johnston, 1706; M. 15,846, 2252. Thomson *v.* M'Culloch, 1778; M. 434; Hailes, 797; 5 B. Sup. 376. 2 Ersk. 9. § 46.

(*i*) Bell *v.* Halliday, 1825; 4 S. 286. See Boyd (*b*), Bartlet (*e*).

(*k*) Thomson, *supra* (*h*); see Lord Braxfield's Opinion; Hailes, 797. Blake *v.* Bates, 1840; 3 D. 317. 1 Bell's Com. 60. Fraser, H. & W. 969 sq., where the authorities are referred to. Comp. § 1572, above.

(*l*) Howard's Exr. *v.* Howard's Cur., 1894; 21 R. 787.

1601. (3.) *Service.*—The process for making the terce effectual consists of two parts: one called Serving to the terce, for vesting the right; the other called Kenning to the terce, for giving actual possession. 'In practice, however, "kenning" is nearly obsolete; and the widow's rights as to terce are generally settled by submission, in which the arbiter assigns to her either a certain portion of the estate, or a fixed sum out of the rents, either being secured to her against the creditors of the heir in possession (*a*).'

(*a*) Boyd *v.* Hamilton, *infra*, § 1604 (*b*).

1602. Service to the terce is a judicial process proceeding on a brieve from Chancery, and directed to the Sheriff of the shire in which the lands lie (*a*). 'The process is not to be stopped except by objections that are readily, if not instantly, verifiable (*b*).' A jury is impannelled to return an answer as to the lands out of which the claimant has a right to terce. To this verdict the Sheriff interpones his authority, and decerns. The effect is to vest in the widow a right of possession *pro indiviso*, with the benefit of the landlord's hypothec; and to vest her with a right to demand a third of the interest of heritable debts, or a third of the rents 'as at the husband's death' (*c*). It has been held that, without such service, the widow does not transmit to her executors the rents of the terce lands not drawn by her (*d*). But it has been well observed, that this decision would require to be reconsidered (*e*).

(*a*) In one case, where the lands lay in different shires, a commission was granted to an advocate as Sheriff in that part. But L. Elchies doubts of this. Lawson *v.* ——, 1742; Elchies, *Terce*, 1; Notes, 484. M'Laren, Wills and Succn. i. § 213; Fraser, H. & W. 1101 n.; and Nicolson, Ersk. Inst. ii. 9. § 50, note, say that in this case the brieve is addressed to the Sheriff of Edinburgh, referring to 1 and 2 Geo. IV. c. 38, § 11, the statute abolishing the jurisdiction of the macers of the Court of Session.

(*b*) Auth. in § 1597, note (*a*). As to procedure and appeals, see Craik *v.* Penny, *ibi cit.*

(*c*) 2 Ersk. 9. § 50. Veitch *v.* ——, 1632; M. 16,087; 2 Ill. 291. Robson *v.* Macnish, 1861; 23 D. 429. Fea *v.* Traill, *infra.*

(*d*) M'Leish *v.* Rennie, Feb. 21, 1826; 4 S. 485; and F. C. See Borthwick *v.* Pringle, 1870; 8 Macph. 622.

(*e*) More's Notes on Stair, p. ccxviii. 1 M'Laren on Wills, etc., § 211. See 2 Stair, 6. § 15. 2 Ersk. 9. § 55. As to the rights of a widow unserved, see 2 Craig, 22. § 33. M'Leish (*d*). Fea *v.* Traill, 1731; M. 16,115. Fraser, H. & W. 1095, 1107.

1603. (4.) *Kenning* to the terce is a secondary process, dividing the subject between the heir and the widow, and giving liferent infeftment to the widow in her third. In the division the widow has a third of the lands, and of the barn and barnyard. Where there are more houses than one, the heir has the best. The widow gets possession of the mansion-house, if not to be inhabited by the heir (*a*). Sasine 'was' given on this process by delivery of earth and stone, and an instrument of possession follows.

(*a*) 2 Stair, 6. § 14. Montier *v.* Baillie, 1773; M. 15,859; 2 Ill. 288. Logan *v.* Galbraith, 1665; M. 15,842; 1 B. Sup. 507. Mead *v.* Swinton, 1796; M. 15,873. See above, § 1598. Fraser, H. & W. 1097.

1604. (5.) *Extent and Effect.*—Terce is a liferent conferring a *pro indiviso* right of possession before kenning; a proper liferent possession after kenning (*a*). It is effectual against third parties, according to the measure of the husband's infeftment, which in this respect is also the wife's (*b*), and so it draws back to the husband's death (*c*). Against the heir 'it operates' as an assignment of all rents and profits 'uplifted' from the term subsequent to the husband's death (*d*); against tenants for their 'unpaid' rents (*e*); 'against creditors, however, uplifting rents in *bonâ fide*, a subsequent service to the terce gives no claim of repetition (*f*).' But as a title to remove, the instrument of possession on the kenning is necessary (*g*).

'*Lesser terce* occurs where the widow of a former owner is enjoying a terce, and the widow of a later fiar must, till it cease, be content with a terce of the remaining two-thirds (*h*).'

(*a*) As to the rights of a tercer in possession, see above, § 1044 sqq. Bell *v.* Bell, 1827; 6 S. 221. Ralston *v.* Leitch, 1803; Hume, 293.

(*b*) Boyd *v.* Hamilton, 1805; M. 15,874; 2 Ill. 291. Yeoman *v.* Oliphant, 1666; M. 15,843.

(*c*) Carlyle *v.* Lyon's Crs., 1725; M. 15,851.

(*d*) Lady Dunfermline *v.* Her Son, 1628; M. 15,839. Crichton *v.* Hamilton, 1532; M. 15,835. Semple *v.* Crawford, 1624; M. 15,837. Tenants of Easthouses *v.* Hepburn, 1627; M. 15,838. Wamphray *v.* ——, 1669; 2 B. Sup. 440. See Bell *v.* Halliday, *cit.*, § 1600 (*i*).

(*e*) A. *v.* B., 1632; M. 15,842.

(*f*) Milne *v.* Wood, 1770; M. 15,858; Wamphray, *cit.* M'Leish, *cit.*, § 1602.

(*g*) Lady Maxwell *v.* Tenants, 1630; M. 15,842. Fraser, H. & W. 1108; 2 Hunter, L. & T. 14. See further as to the rights of a widow who has been served and kenned, cases in § 1600 *fin.*

(*h*) Alex. II. c. 9. 2 Craig, 22. § 30. 2 Stair, 6. § 16. 2 Ersk. 9. § 47. Fraser, H. & W. 1100.

1605. Courtesy.—This is a right in the surviving husband of an heiress (where the marriage has produced a living heir to her estate), to continue during the husband's life the possession of the heritable estate in which his wife died infeft as heiress to her predecessor (*a*).

(*a*) 2 Craig, 22. § 40. 2 Stair, 6. § 19. 2 Ersk. 9. § 52. 1 Bell's Com. 61. Fraser, H. & W. 1118 sqq. See above, § 1037 et seq.; below, § 1948.

1606. The requisites are:—That there shall have been a child born of the marriage which shall have been heard to cry (*a*); that there shall be no heir of the wife by a former marriage, 'who survives his mother and is served' (*b*); that the land shall have come to the wife, 'not by singular title, but' by succession, as heir of line, tailzie, or provision (*c*); and that the wife shall have died infeft, and even if her infeftment be irregular it is held sufficient (*d*). There is no exception, as 'there was' in terce, of lands held burgage 'or of feu-duties' (*e*).

(*a*) See above, § 1575. Roberton *v.* Moderator of Gen. Assembly, 1833; 11 S. 297. A child legitimated by subsequent marriage appears to satisfy the condition. Crawford's Trs. *v.* Hart, 1802; M. 12,698.

(*b*) Darleith *v.* Campbell, 1702; M. 3113; 2 Ill. 292. Fraser, H. & W. 1122. More's Notes on Stair, 219. See, however, 37 and 38 Vict. c. 94, § 9; *supra*, § 775A, 779A.

(*c*) Lawson *v.* Gilmour, 1709; M. 3114. Hodge *v.* Fraser, 1740; M. 3119; Elchies, *Husband and Wife*, 13. Primrose *v.* Crawford, 1771; M. *Courtesy*, Apx. 1; Hailes, 458. Paterson *v.* Ord, 1781; M. 3121; Hailes, 879. Knight *v.* Robinson, 1786; M. 8815. Watt *v.* Wilkin, 1885; 13 R. 218.

(*d*) 2 Ersk. 9. § 52. Hamilton *v.* Boswell, 1716; M. 3117; Robertson's Ap. 192. Porteous *v.* Bell, 1757; 5 B. Sup. 855. L. Clinton *v.* Trefusis, 1869; 8 Macph. 370.

(*e*) See above, § 1598. 2 Craig, 22. § 43. 2 Stair, 6. § 19. Skene, *voce* Curialitas. 2 Ersk. 9. § 54. Gordon *v.* Clark, 1715; M. 3116. See 2 Ill. 293. L. Clinton (*d*).

1607. The 'current interests of the' wife's personal debts are effectual against the courtesy, with relief to the husband against the wife's other property (*a*).

(*a*) 2 Ersk. 2. § 55. Fraser, H. & W. 1126 n. Monteith *v.* Next of Kin, 1717; M. 3117; 2 Ill. 293.

1608. No service or title is necessary, as in terce, to enable the husband to continue his possession; and as his right is merely a right of possession, 'or rather on the ground of *bonâ fide* perception, or waiver,' rents not levied or fruits not reaped do not vest, and are not demandable by the husband's heir (*a*).

(*a*) 2 Ersk. 9. § 52, 55. M'Aulay *v.* Watson, 1636; M. 3112, 1740; 1 B. Sup. 358; 2 Ill. 294.

1609. Husband Wife's Curator.—Marriage affects chiefly the status of the wife. The husband is curator of his wife (*a*). Her person is sunk, but not so completely as by the English law (*b*).

(*a*) 1 Ersk. 6. § 19–21. Scott *v.* Paton, 1703; M. 6050; 2 Ill. 294. Ross, petr., 1704, *ib.* M'Pherson *v.* M'Intosh, 1773; M. 6052; Hailes, 510. Finlay *v.* Hamilton, 1748; M. 6051. M'Lachlan *v.* Campbell, May 25, 1809; F. C. Jeffrey *v.* Matheson, 1826; 4 S. 773. Wight *v.* Dewar, 1827; 5 S. 549. Borthwick, § 1610 (*a*) (subsequent concurrence). M'Kenzie *v.* Ewing, Nov. 19, 1830; 9 S. 31, and F. C.; aff. 6 W. & S. 462. Paul *v.* Gibson, 1834; 12 S. 431; aff. 7 W. & S. 462. Laird *v.* Milne, 1833; 12 S. 54. Willox *v.* Farrell, 1849; 11 D. 1206. Borthwick *v.* M'Farlane, 1844; 6 D. 1295. Horn *v.* Sanderson, 1872; 10 Macph. 295. Fraser, H. & W. 516, 566, 804, etc.

(*b*) 1 Blackst. 442. 2 Stephen, 275.

1610. Her *deeds* require his concurrence, unless they be in his own favour (*a*), 'or of the nature of a testament or will (*b*), or relate to her separate estate from which his right of administration is excluded (*c*).' Even when in favour of his relations, 'or in security of his debts,' a deed is null without his concurrence (*d*). In all *actions* at the instance of the wife '—at least in those not relating to her separate estate, from which both *jus mariti* and right of administration are excluded by statute or otherwise (*e*)—' his name is requisite as a party (*f*), 'and he may be liable for expenses (*g*)'; or in his room a *curator ad litem* is named by the Court of Session on summary application, or incidentally by the judge before whom the suit depends (*h*); and it has been held that a wife separated from her husband may bring an action for damages on account of slander against her (*i*). Her written authority must be shown to sanction proceedings as to her 'separate or heritable' property (*k*). She must be a party to any submission in which she has interest (*l*). The husband must be called as a party in all actions against her (*m*). 'It has been stated above that a wife judicially separated, and one who has obtained a protection order, have power to grant deeds and to sue (*n*). And by the Married Women's Property Act, 1881, when a wife is deserted by her husband or living separate from him with his consent, a judge of the Court of Session, or Sheriff Court, may, on petition, dispense with the husband's consent to any deed relating to her estate (*o*).'

(*a*) **Rennie** *v.* **Ritchie**, 1845; 4 Bell's App. 221. Dickson *v.* Blair, 1871; 10 Macph. 41. As to subsequent concurrence, see Bullions *v.* Bayne, 1793; M. 6149 (not sufficient after wife's death). Cochran *v.* Hamilton, 1698; M. 6001. Borthwick *v.* Grant, 1829; 7 S. 420.

(*b*) 1 Ersk. 6. § 28. **Miller** *v.* **Milne's Trs.**, 1859; 21 D. 377. Fraser, H. & W. 564. Cf. § 1580, above.

(*c*) See Fraser, H. & W. 813 sqq. Miller *v.* Galbraith's Trs., 1886; 13 R. 764.

(*d*) Boyle *v.* Crawford, 1822; 1 S. 350; 2 Ill. 294. Brownlee *v.* Waddell, 1831; 10 S. 39. Rennie, *cit.*

(*e*) Fraser, H. & W. 572, 815, etc. Macgown, below, *per* L. M'Laren.

(*f*) See below, § 1620; above, § 1540A, 1548. Horn *v.* Sanderson, 1872; 10 Macph. 295; and as to subsequent concurrence, Lyle *v.* Mackay, 1849; 11 D. 404. Slowey *v.* Robertson, 1865; 4 Macph. 1. Whitehead *v.* Blaik, 1893; 20 R. 1045 (wife's action on death of child ousted by husband's).

(*g*) Macgown *v.* Cramb, 1898; 25 R. 634 (husband active in suit).

(*h*) Davidson, petr., 19 D. 862. And cases in Fraser, H. & W. 568. It is necessary to attend to the true nature of the office of a *curator ad litem*, who represents and binds the absent husband in litigations against third parties, and ought not to be appointed in actions between the husband and wife, in which the husband is a party and is bound by the proceedings. See Fraser, H. & W. 569–572, and authorities there cited.

(*i*) M'Kenzie, *supra*, § 1609 (*a*). See above, § 1548, 1572 *fin.*

(*k*) Aitken *v.* Orr, 1802; M. 16,140. See Stevenson *v.* Hamilton, 1838; 1 D. 181.

(*l*) M'Cally *v.* Inglis, 1821; 1 S. 69. See Wallace *v.* D. Hamilton, 1830; 8 S. 572. Ferguson *v.* Cowan, 1819; Hume, 222.

(*m*) Spence *v.* Thomson, 1739; M. 6080. Freebairn *v.* Grant, 1709; *ib.*

(*n*) See above, § 1540A, 1560B.

(*o*) 44 and 45 Vict. c. 21, § 5. This provision appears to be intended for the benefit of wives not enfranchised by the other clauses of the Act. It applies to marriages contracted before the Act. Poë *v.* Paterson, 1882; 10 R. 356; aff. 1883, 10 R. H. L. 73; 8 App. Ca. 678.

1611. Wife's Personal Obligation. — The general rule is established, that she is incapable of legal obligation; and it has been exemplified in many cases, according to almost every test (*a*).

(*a*) 1 Craig, 15. § 20. 1 Bankt. 5. § 73. 1 Mack. 6. § 12. 1 Stair, 4. § 16. 1 Ersk. Pr. 6. § 15; Inst. § 22 and 25. Fraser, H. & W. 519. Kerr *v.* Shearers, 1715; M. 5991; 2 Ill. 295. Menzies *v.* Gillespie's Crs., 1761; M. 5974. Watson *v.* Robertson, 1772; M. 5976; Hailes, 508. Harvey *v.* Chessels, 1791; M. 5980; Bell's Ca. 255. Scott *v.* Scheniman, 1818; Hume, 221. Lennox & Co. *v.* Auchincloss, 1821; 1 S. 22. Walker *v.* Home, 1827; 6 S. 204. Dollar *v.* Murdoch, 1827; 5 S. 333. Balfour *v.* Lady Strathmore, 1831; 9 S. 558. E. Strathmore *v.* Ewing, 1831; 4 S. 310; 1832, 5 S. Jur. 7; 6 W. & S. 56. **Miller *v.* Milne's Trs.**, 1859; 21 D. 377. Sandilands *v.* Mercer, 1833; 11 S. 665. Jackson *v.* MacDiarmid, 1892; 19 R. 528 (cash credit bond).

1612. Exceptions have been admitted in the following cases: — Diligence has been authorised against her estate for money *in rem versum* (*a*), either as furnishings to her, or debts of hers before marriage (*b*); but not for furnishings to the family, the husband being alive (*c*). This has been allowed more especially 'for necessaries' when she is living separate from her husband (*d*). 'A wife judicially separated has, since 1861, had full power of contracting; and one who has obtained a protection order in a *de facto* separation has the same privilege (*e*).' And above all, such remedies have been given when the wife, living separate, is engaged in trade for herself (*f*). She may grant mandates and other deeds, 'and incur obligations,' relative to her separate property; but not to the effect of binding her person 'or her husband' (*g*). Even personal obligations to sell or dispone her heritable estate, or to infeft a creditor, may be considered as imperfect dispositions, competent to sustain an adjudication in implement, though not to authorise a demand or diligence against the person; and her procuratories or precepts are effectual to validate infeftments (*h*). She may act as a trustee (*i*) 'or executor (*k*)' independently of her husband; but she cannot act as tutor or curator (*l*), 'except in the case of her own children, of whom since 1886 she is tutor after the father's death (*m*). It is said that a husband consenting to his wife undertaking an office becomes liable for the obligations she thereby incurs, if she has no separate estate (*n*).'

(*a*) Zibbis *v.* Orkney, 1609; M. 5982; 2 Ill. 296. Sinclair *v.* Richardson, 1677; M. 5648, 5984. Primrose *v.* Watson, 1610; M. 5982. Douglas *v.* Robertson, 1623; M. 5983. 1 Bell, Com. 663. Fraser, H. & W. 535 sqq. See Macara, below (*g*); and above, § 1572.

(*b*) *Qu.* whether Jackson *v.* MacDiarmid, *cit.* § 1611, ought not to have been brought within this exception. See *per* L. Young, diss. Fraser, H. & W. 536.

(*c*) Walker *v.* Home, 1827; 6 S. 204. See also Rutherford *v.* Halcro, 1630; M. 6071; 1 B. Sup. 315. Nairn *v.* Mercer, 1785; M. 5860; Hailes, 983. Buie *v.* Gordon, 1831; 9 S. 923.

(*d*) 1 Ersk. 6. § 25. Neilson *v.* Arthur, 1672; M. 5984. Robins *v.* Southesk, 1688; M. 5955. See Anderson *v.* Shand, 1833; 11 S. 688. Paul *v.* Gibson, 1834; 12 S. 431; aff. 1834, 7 W. & S. 462 (in both husband banished or imprisoned). Cf. § 1566, 1572, above.

(*e*) See above, § 1540A, 1560B.

(*f*) Russell *v.* Paterson, 1629; M. 5955. Hay *v.* Corstorphin, 1663; M. 5956. Churnside *v.* Currie, 1789; M. 6082. Orme *v.* Diffors, 1833; 12 S. 149. M'Quillan *v.* Smith, 1892; 19 R. 375 (suing for her bastard's aliment). See Ritchie *v.* Barclay, 1845; 7 D. 819. **Biggart *v.* City of Glasgow Bank**, 1879; 6 R. 470.

(*g*) Consider 1 Ersk. Pr. 6. § 15, along with the cases of Ellis *v.* Keith, 1665, as reported by Dirleton, M. 5988. Bruce *v.* Paterson, 1678; M. 5965-6. Pringle *v.* Irvine, 1711; M. 5970. Clark *v.* Gibson, 1826; 4 S. 391. Brown *v.* Bedwell, 1830; 9 S. 136. Buchan *v.* Risk, 1834; 12 S. 511. Gray *v.* Wylie, 1840; 2 D. 1205. Macara *v.* Wilson, 1848; 10 D. 707. Gifford *v.* Rennie, 1853; 15 D. 451. Biggart *v.* City of Glasgow Bank, *cit.* Henderson *v.* Dawson, 1895; 22 R. 895. See above, § 1560, 1560A,B,C,D, 1562, 1567, 1572, and Wright's Exrs. *v.* City of Glasgow Bank, 1880; 7 R. 527. The extended powers conferred on married women by the Act of 1881 (see § 1560C, 1560D, etc.) do not enable them to grant bills or notes. 45 and 46 Vict. c. 61, § 22. M'Lean *v.* Angus, 1887; 14 R. 448.

(*h*) Watson *v.* Henderson, 1802; Hume, 208. As to enforcing by personal diligence a wife's obligations *ad facta præstanda*, see Anderson *v.* Buchanan, 1775; M. 6081; Hailes, 650. Tait *v.* Wilson, 1831; 9 S. 680. Kennedy *v.* Watson, 1848; 11 D. 171. 1 Stair, 4. § 14. 1 Ersk. 6. § 19. Fraser, H. & W. 555. As to her bankruptcy, 19 and 20 Vict. c. 79, § 13. Davidson *v.* Rae, 1885; 1 Sh. Ct. Rep. 147 (cessio).

(*i*) Stoddart *v.* Rutherford, June 30, 1812; F. C. Darling *v.* Watson, 1824; 2 S. 607; aff. 1825, 1 W. & S. 188. Laird *v.* Milne, 1833; 12 S. 54.

(*k*) Spreul *v.* Spreul, 1674; M. 5873.

(*l*) 1 Stair, 6. § 24. 1 Ersk. 7. § 12. Kerbechill, 1586; M. 9585. Stuart *v.* Henderson. 1636; M. 9585. Chalmers's Trs. *v.* Sinclair, 1897; 24 R. 1047. Fraser, Guar. & Ward, 171, 346.

(*m*) See 49 and 50 Vict. c. 27, and below, § 2069A, etc.

(*n*) 1 Stair, 4. § 17. Pattisson *v.* M'Vicar, 1886; 13 R. 550.

1613. The wife's obligation as *præposita* is effectual; but it is so only against the husband (*a*). A bond to take effect after the wife's death is 'said by Professor Bell to be' good; 'but the point, which was discussed in a modern case, has been much doubted' (*b*). And she is bound to indemnify for damage proceeding from her delict (*c*). But, 'while she may be punished corporally for a crime,' she cannot, during her marriage, be imprisoned for 'failure to pay' a fine imposed on her for delinquency (*d*). These are not proper exceptions to the nullity of the wife's obligations, though sometimes so laid down. 'Obligations of the wife may be homologated or adopted by her if she survive the dissolution of the marriage (*e*).'

(*a*) See § 1565 seq. Mitchelson *v.* Lady Cranston, 1780 ; M. 5886 ; 2 Ill. 298. Robertson *v.* Haldane, 1801 ; Hume, 208. Cockett *v.* Beattie, 24 R. Justy. 62 (not *præposita* to refuse vaccination of his child).

(*b*) 1 Ersk. 6. § 28. 1 Ersk. Pr. 6. § 17. Colquhoun *v.* Roseburn, 1720 ; M. 5973. Bruce *v.* Paterson, 1678 ; M. 5965–6. See Miller *v.* Milne's Trs., 1859 ; 21 D. 377.

(*c*) Murray *v.* Graham, 1724 ; M. 6079. Chalmers *v.* Baillie, 1790 ; M. 6083 ; M. 6086 ; 1791, 3 Pat. 213. Crowder *v.* Watson, 1831 ; 10 S. 29 ; aff. 6 W. & S. 271. See above, § 1572 *fin.* Fraser, H. & W. 557.

(*d*) Chalmers, *supra* (*c*). Procr.-Fiscal *v.* M'Luckie, 1796 ; Hume, 204.

(*e*) 3 Ersk. 3. § 47. Gordon *v.* Farquhar, 1766 ; 5 B. Sup. 932. Thomson *v.* Stewart, 1840 ; 2 D. 564.

1614. Wife's Power to Alienate.—The wife may, with her husband's consent, dispose of her own estate, or of her *peculium* (*a*). 'But, whilst the husband in virtue of his right of administration may grant leases of his wife's heritage which are valid during his life (*b*), he has, of course, no power to sell her heritage except with her concurrence (*c*).'

(*a*) 1 Ersk. Pr. 6. § 17. Cunningham *v.* Cunningham, 1686 ; 3 B. Sup. 593 ; 2 Ill. 299. Clerk *v.* Sharp, 1717 ; M. 5996. Pringle *v.* Irvine, 1711 ; M. 5970. Brown *v.* Bedwell, and Buchan *v.* Risk, *citt.* § 1612 (*g*). Reliance Ass. Soc. *v.* Halkett's Fr., 1891 ; 18 R. 617 (income). See above, § 1610, and Dickson *v.* Blair, *ibi cit.* (consent in writing to sale of heritage).

(*b*) Grieve *v.* Pringle, *supra*, § 1181, 1594.

(*c*) Kennedy *v.* Watson, 1848 ; 11 D. 171. *Supra*, § 1594.

1615. Deeds of alienation by the wife of her own property, or in which she consents to concur in conveyance by the husband, are presumed to proceed from the husband's undue influence, the presumption being counteracted by her judicial ratification (*a*); 'which is an effectual protection against challenge on the ground of force, fear, or undue influence applied by the husband, though not against challenge on other grounds (*b*).' Deeds done by the wife with her husband's concurrence, which have the effect of altering her property and bringing it within the *jus mariti*, are objectionable (*c*); and the proceeds of her heritable estate, or money in a heritable bond to her, though allowed to go into a bank, are held to be hers as *surrogatum*, and not to fall under the *jus mariti* (*d*).

(*a*) 1481, c. 84. 1 Ersk. Pr. 6. § 17, and Inst. § 34, 36. See Brisbane, petr., 1850 ; 12 D. 917.

(*b*) Buchan *v.* Risk, 1834 ; 11 S. 511. Ersk. *l.c.* Priestnell *v.* Hutchison, 1857 ; 19 D. 475. Fraser, H. & W. 819.

(*c*) Gow *v.* Lang, 1807 ; Hume, 220. M'Connochie *v.* Patterson, 1816 ; *ib.* Anderson *v.* Laidlaw, 1816 ; Hume, 218.

(*d*) Nisbet *v.* Rennie, 1818 ; Hume, 220. See above, § 1552.

1616. Contracts and Donations between the Spouses.—Although the spouses may enter into contracts with each other, yet, in so far as gratuitous or without equivalent consideration, all that they do is revocable (*a*), and the law presumes donation ; but the contrary may be proved (*b*). There is not, however, required an absolute and scrupulous equality of opposite considerations to bar revocation ; but even where the form of a transaction has been adopted, substantial inequality, 'as at the time when the question is raised by revocation (*c*),' will authorise revocation (*d*). Contracts and mutual settlements, truly onerous, are as effectual as between strangers (*e*), 'except so far as a power of separate revocation has been stipulated (*f*).' And gratuitous deeds or donations, 'which may be established by writ, though not delivered by the husband, who is said to be the proper custodier of his wife's papers (*g*), or by parole proof of facts and circumstances (*h*),' are effectual if not revoked (*i*). A provision by a wife in favour of a husband's children of a former marriage is not revocable after the husband's death (*k*). And an interest in a stranger as one of the contracting parties, provided it be real and not nominal or collusive, 'or a mere substitution or *spes successionis* (*l*),' bars the revocation (*m*) 'so far as the third party is concerned ; but the donor may revoke as against the other spouse and claim repetition, or rank on his estate for the amount of the gift (*n*).'

(*a*) 1 Stair, 4. § 18, and cases there. 1 Ersk. 6. § 29, and cases. Fraser, H. & W. 916 sqq. **Palmer *v.* Bonnar,** Jan. 25, 1810 ; F. C. ; 2 Ill. 258. **M'Diarmid (Marshall) *v.* M'Diarmid,** 1826 ; 4 S. 589 ; aff. 1828, 3 W. & S. 37. M'Neill *v.* Steel's Trs., 1829 ; 8 S. 210. "This case was held in the House of Lords (see the next case, 5 W. & S. 499) as much more decisive of a very important point than it seems to have been ; namely, that a mutual deed between husband and wife is in its nature revocable and ambulatory, like a last will or a deed of separation. It may be correctly held so to be when the contract is combined with a deed of separation (as in Palmer's case, and in Hunter's), but there seems to be no authority for saying that a simple deed or contract of provision is so revocable, except on the ground of *donatio* ; and that again brings back the question of the point of time undetermined." 2 Ill. 300. Dickson *v.* Hunter, 1827 ; 5 S. 266 ; 5 W. & S. 455. Henderson's Trs. *v.* Tulloch, 1833 ; 12 S. 133. See below, § 1617 (*b*) ; as to loans by the wife to the husband, above, § 1560D. Stevenson *v.* Hamilton, 1838 ; 1 D. 181.

(*b*) Brownlee's Crs. *v.* Stevenson, 1735 ; Elchies, *Presum.* 3

Jardine *v.* Currie, 1830; 8 S. 937. **Loudoun *v.* Young,** 1856; 19 D. 140. For instances of remuneratory contracts where revocation was disallowed, see Hepburn (*d*), and cases in note (*e*).

(*c*) *E.g.* if a conventional provision is revoked and the legal rights preferred by reason of an increase of the husband's fortune, the question of inequality will be judged as at the husband's death. See M'Neill *v.* Steel's Trs., and Dickson *v.* Hunter, *supra* (*a*). Thomson *v.* Thomson, and Blaikie *v.* Milne, *infra*, § 1617. Mitchell *v.* Mitchell's Trs., 1877; 4 R. 800.

(*d*) Stewart *v.* Mitchell, 1769; M. 6100; Hailes, 310. Hepburn *v.* Brown, 1814; 2 Dow, 342. See Palmer *v.* Bonnar, and Dickson *v.* Hunter, etc., *supra*. Deeds have been set aside on other grounds than *pecuniary* inequality, as when they have contained a condition of forfeiture upon second marriage, see M'Neill and M'Diarmid, *citt.* (*a*). Thomson *v.* Thomson, 1838; 16 S. 641. Maclachlan *v.* Jaffrey, 1839; 1 D. 1177. As to revocation as donations of deeds altering antenuptial marriage contracts, see Jardine *v.* Currie, Cousin *v.* Caldwell, *infra*, § 1617; and Thomson and Maclachlan, *citt.* Rae *v.* Nielson, 1875; 2 R. 675. Beattie's Trs. *v.* Beattie, 1884; 11 R. 846.

(*e*) Stair and Ersk. *supra* (*a*). Stirling *v.* Crawford, 1716; M. 6111. Shearer *v.* Somerville, 1733; M. 4892. Hepburn, *supra* (*d*). Anderson *v.* Garroway, 1837; 15 S. 435; 2 Ill. 301, and 3 Ill. 159. Wright *v.* Harley, 1847; 9 D. 1151. Cuthill *v.* Burns, 1862; 24 D. 849. Macdonald *v.* Macdonald's Trs., 1863; 1 Macph. 1064. Kidd *v.* Kidds, 1863; 2 Macph. 227. Shaw's Trs. *v.* Shaw, 1870; 8 Macph. 419. Welsh's Trs. *v.* Welsh, 1871; 10 Macph. 16. Mitchell *v.* Mitchell's Trs. (*c*). Croll's Trs. *v.* Alexander, 1896; 22 R. 677. Mudie *v.* Clough, 1896; 23 R. 1074 (mutual settlement of reasonable provision on wife's heirs). See below, § 1866. As to postnuptial settlements, see below, § 1944.

(*f*) Nimmo's Trs. *v.* Hogg's Trs., 1840; 2 D. 458. Wilson's Trs. *v.* Stirling, 1861; 24 D. 163. Barclay *v.* Fairly, 1849; 11 D. 1133. Main *v.* Lamb, 1880; 7 R. 688. Watson *v.* Giffen, 1884; 11 R. 444. As to the effect of a mutual settlement duly executed by one of the spouses, but not by the other, see M'Millan *v.* M'Millan, 1850; 13 D. 187. Millar *v.* Birrell, 1876; 4 R. 87. Morris *v.* Anderson, 1882; 9 R. 952 (surviving liferenter's right to test on savings).

(*g*) Smith *v.* Smith's Trs., 1884; 12 R. 186. See Gibson *v.* Hutchison, 1872; 10 Macph. 923.

(*h*) **Wright's Exrs. *v.* City of Glasgow Bank,** 1880; 7 R. 527. Hutchinson *v.* Hutchinson's Trs., 1842; 4 D. 1399; 5 D. 469 (presumption that wife agrees that her moneys received by husband shall be applied to family expenses). Baxter's Exr. *v.* Baxter's Trs. (Edward *v.* Cheyne), 1886; 13 R. 1209; aff. 1888, 13 App. Ca. 385; 15 R. H. L. 33, 37.

(*i*) As to provisions under the statute of 1881, see above, § 1560D.

(*k*) Gentles *v.* Aitken, 1826; 4 S. 757; 2 Ill. 301. This case does not affirm the general proposition stated in the text, though it is clear that so far as such a deed vests an absolute and unconditional right in a third party it is irrevocable. Ersk. *l.c.* Fraser, H. & W. 918 sqq., 1503 sqq. *Infra*, § 1619. See Thomson *v.* Thomson (*d*). Fernie *v.* Colquhoun's Trs., 1854; 17 D. 232. Kidd *v.* Kidds (*e*). Lang *v.* Brown, 1867; 5 Macph. 789. Somerville's Trs. *v.* Dickson, 1865; 3 Macph. 602; aff. 1867, 5 Macph. H. L. 69. Cases in note (*m*).

(*l*) Davidson *v.* Mossman, 1870; 8 Macph. 807. Thomson (*d*) and Fernie (*k*).

(*m*) 1 Ersk. 6. § 29. Hisleid *v.* Lindsay, 1591; M. 6106. Sanders *v.* Dunlop, 1728; M. 6108. Scott *v.* Cranstoun, 1776; M. 6108; Hailes, 713; rev. 2 Pat. 425. Muir *v.* Stirling, 1663; M. 6107. Hamilton *v.* Bain, 1669; M. 6107. Somerville *v.* Paton, 1680; M. 5990, 6108. Fernie, *supra* (*k*). Mitchell *v.* Mitchell's Trs., *supra* (*c*). Brown *v.* Bedwell, 1830; 9 S. 136; and Standard Prop. Invt. Co., *infra*, 1619 (*i*).

(*n*) *Supra*, § 1571 *fin.* Fraser, H. & W. 919. Williams *v.* Williams, 1844; 7 D. 110.

1617. Donations between husband and wife, 'even when they form part of a contract of separation which becomes irrevocable after the dissolution of the marriage (*a*),' may be revoked after dissolution of the marriage; and they continue pendent, with all their effects, during the giver's life (*b*). When revoked, all that has followed is annulled (*c*). 'The donee holds under a resolutive condition, which is effectual against onerous disponees and creditors, except so far as they may be protected by a personal exception against the donor revoking, or by the presumption of property in moveables arising from possession (*d*).'

(*a*) Palmer *v.* Bonnar, § 1616 (*a*). Dickson *v.* Hunter (*b*). Nisbett *v.* Nisbett's Trs., 1835; 13 S. 517.

(*b*) 1 Ersk. 6. § 32. Maclellan *v.* Hathorns, 1758; M. 6098; 2 Ill. 302. Watson *v.* Gordon's Exrs., 1774; M. 6103. Hepburn, *supra*, § 1616 (*d*). Moffat's Trs. *v.* Gray, 1821; 1 S. 184. M'Diarmid, *supra*, § 1616 (*a*). Dickson *v.* Hunter, 1827; 5 S. 266; aff. 5 W. & S. 455; 2 Ill. 259. Gaywood *v.* Gaywood's Trs., 1828; 6 S. 909. Jardine *v.* Currie, 1830; 8 S. 937. Thomson *v.* Thomson, 1838; 16 S. 641; 3 Ill. 159. Cousin *v.* Caldwell, 1838; 16 S. 1109. Blaikie *v.* Milne, 1838; 1 D. 18 (revocation by insane husband's *curator bonis*). Fernie and Kidd, *supra*, § 1616 (*k*). Rae *v.* Nielson, *cit.* § 1616 (*d*). Melville *v.* Melville's Trs., 1879; 6 R. 1286. Below, § 1619, as to creditors. It is said that an heir or executor cannot revoke, the right to revoke being personal to the donor. 1 Ersk. 6. § 32. Fraser, H. & W. 950. Dunlop *v.* Boyd, 1863; 2 Macph. 1.

(*c*) Sinclair *v.* Shaw, 1739; 5 B. Sup. 658; Elch. *Husband and Wife*, 11. See Kemp *v.* Napier, 1842; 4 D. 558 (arrears of annuity). Fraser, H. & W. 960 sqq.

(*d*) Sinclair, *cit.* Paterson *v.* M'Lean, 1677; M. 10,284. Williams *v.* Williams (Erskine *v.* Erskine's Trs.), 1844; 7 D. 110. Laidlaw *v.* Laidlaw's Tr., 1882; 10 R. 374. *Supra*, § 1313 sqq.

1618. Revocation is either express or implied (*a*). Express is by a deed directly recalling the donation, or disposing of the *universitas* of the estate 'expressly' including the subject of the donation (*b*); 'or by a plea to an action upon the deed of gift (*c*); and it may be private and unknown at the time to the donee (*d*).' Revocation may be implied from deeds inconsistent with the donation (*e*), and has been inferred from the mere contraction of debt when the husband has no other fund of payment (*f*). But that is correctly ascribed by Erskine to another principle, viz. that creditors may exercise the faculty when necessary for their payment (*g*). The mere contraction of debt does not imply an intention to revoke, 'but the burdening of heritage, the subject of a prior donation, is *pro tanto* a revocation (*h*).'

(*a*) 1 Ersk. 6. § 31.

(*b*) Scott *v.* Scott, 1770; M. 11,367; Hailes, 357; 2 Ill. 303. The original text seems too broad, for in general a special bequest or gift must be specially revoked (1 M'Laren, Wills & Succn. 266. 1 Ersk. 6. § 31), and the case cited hardly supports the text. See Fraser, H. & W. 953, 954. It is a question of intention how far a general conveyance to another infers a revocation of a donation *inter conjuges*.

(*c*) Auth. in Fraser, H. & W. 950.

(*d*) Steven *v.* Dunlop, Feb. 1, 1809; F. C. 1 Ersk. 6. § 31.

(*e*) Henderson's Trs. *v.* Tulloch, 1833; 12 S. 133. E. Fife *v.* Mackenzie, 1795; M. 2325; aff. 1797, 3 Pat. 549. 1 Ersk. 6. § 31.

(*f*) Henderson *v.* Saughtonhall, 1683; M. 6095. M'Adam *v.* Trophen, 1684; M. 6096. See Tolmie *v.* Cruickshank, 1859; 21 D. 840. Maclachlan *v.* Jaffrey, 1839; 1 D. 1177 (legacy where funds insufficient).

(*g*) Ersk. *supra* (*a*). See below, § 1619 (*e*).

(*h*) Johnstone's Trs. *v.* Johnstone, 1896; 23 R. 538. 1 Stair, 4. § 18. 1 Ersk. 6. § 31. Fraser, H. & W. 954. Comp. Honeyman, § 1619 (*e*).

1619. The power of revocation is barred by the acceptance, 'after dissolution of the marriage,' of provisions made under that condition (*a*); but if this have proceeded from ignorance or error, it will not operate as a bar (*b*). Revocation is barred by divorce for adultery (*c*). The right to revoke is not renounced by the wife's judicial ratification (*d*). And this right may be exercised by creditors in case of insolvency (*e*); 'to the effect, *e.g.*, of cutting down post-nuptial provisions in favour of a wife to take effect during the husband's life, and those taking effect after his death so far as they are excessive (*f*); but not a reasonable jointure or provision made by him when solvent to take effect at the dissolution of the marriage (*g*). Sequestration in bankruptcy *eo ipso* revokes donations *inter virum et uxorem* (*h*). There is no revocation by a wife of deeds making over her separate property directly to her husband's creditors or other third parties for his purposes, or of her consent to his deeds so dealing with her property; although she may have a claim against the husband on the ground of donation and revocation (*i*).'

(*a*) Dixon *v.* Fisher, 1839; 1 D. 474; aff. 2 Rob. 345. See above, § 1591; below, § 1946. Mitchell *v.* Mitchell's Trs., *supra*, § 1616 (*c*).

(*b*) Hope *v.* Dickson, 1833; 12 S. 222. See above, § 11 *fin.*, 27.

(*c*) Murray *v.* Livingston, 1575; M. 328; 2 Ill. 304. See as to the effect of adultery and divorce, Fraser, H. & W. 952; and below, § 1622.

(*d*) 1 Ersk. 6. § 35. Gordon *v.* Maxwell, 1678; M. 6144. Borthwick *v.* Scott, 1724; M. 6149; correcting 1 M'Kenzie, 6. § 14, and Richardson *v.* Michie, 1685; M. 6147; 2 B. Sup. 85.

(*e*) 1 Ersk. 6. § 31. Honeyman & Wilson *v.* Robertson, 1886; 14 R. 163 (adjudication).

(*f*) Kemp *v.* Napier, 1842; 4 D. 558. **Shearer** *v.* **Christie**, 1842; 5 D. 132. Tolmie, *supra*, § 1618 (*f*). Dunlop *v.* Johnston, 1865; 3 Macph. 758; aff. 1867, 5 Macph. H. L. 22. Miller *v.* Learmonth, and other cases in § 1944, *infra.*

(*g*) Craig *v.* Galloway, 1860; 22 D. 1211; rev. 1861, 4 Macq. 267. *Infra*, § 1944. Fraser, H. & W. 943 sqq.

(*h*) Kemp *v.* Napier, *cit.*

(*i*) See **Standard Prop. Invt. Co.** *v.* **Cowe,** 1877; 4 R. 695; and the authorities there cited. See above, § 1571, 1616 (*k*), (*m*), 1617, etc.

1620. Action and Diligence by Spouses against each other are competent for alimony (*a*), for separation (*b*), and for divorce (*c*). In such cases the husband pays both sides, 'even where the wife is the party at fault (*d*), unless she has separate estate (*e*)'; and it would seem that, in taxing the account of the wife's agent, it is to be taxed as between agent and client, not as between party and party (*f*).

(*a*) Above, § 1545. (*b*) Above, § 1540.

(*c*) Above, § 1530, 1535. Glenbervie *v.* Glenbervie, 1638; M. 6053; 2 Ill. 304 (inhibition *stante matrimonio*). M'Lachlan *v.* Campbell, May 25, 1809; F. C.; 2 Ill. 294 (imprisonment on decree). Thomson, petr., March 7, 1815; F. C. (law burrows against wife). Smith *v.* Smith, 1866; 4 Macph. 279. Fraser, H. & W. 577 sqq. Mackay's Practice of the Court of Session, vol. ii. pp. 554, 578.

(*d*) Gray *v.* Mickle, 1813; Hume, 217. See Donald *v.* Donald, 1863; 1 Macph. 741. Stewart *v.* Stewart, 1863; 1 Macph. 449 (reduction of decree of divorce). Gow *v.* Gow, 1855; 17 D. 477. Milne *v.* Milne, 1885; 13 R. 304 (effect of Married Women's Property Act). Begg *v.* Begg, 1890; 15 App. Ca. 170; 17 R. H. L. 60 (not in general expenses in the H. of L.). Kirk *v.* Kirk, 1876; 3 R. 128.

(*e*) M'Farlane *v.* M'Farlane, 1844; 6 D. 1220; 1848, 10 D. 962. Pitt *v.* Pitt, 1862; 24 D. 1444. Henderson *v.* Henderson, 1888; 16 R. 84. As to this matter, however, the Married Women's Property Act requires now to be considered.

(*f*) Taylor *v.* Binnie, 1831; 10 S. 18 (successful declarator of marriage). Fraser, H. & W. 1233. Lang *v.* Lang, 1849; 11 D. 1217 (unsuccessful wife not liable to husband—cf. Begg, *supra*). It appears that a medium scale is now adopted. King *v.* Patrick, 1845; 7 D. 536. See Mackellar *v.* Mackellar, 1898; 25 R. 883 (petition for custody of children — wife gets costs as party, unless otherwise ordered).

1621. Effect of Dissolution of Marriage (*a*).—The effect of the dissolution of marriage by death has already been stated—where the marriage is prematurely dissolved; and where it has subsisted for a year, or with living progeny (*b*).

(*a*) See above, § 1528 et seq.

(*b*) See above, § 1575, 1579 1605.

1622. Of divorce as a mode of dissolving marriage, the effects are, that the innocent party has the benefit of all legal and conventional provisions 'granted *intuitu matrimonii*, as if the other were dead, and whether these conventional provisions come from the guilty party or his father (*a*),' and the guilty is barred from revoking donations; that the guilty party forfeits the tocher and donations *propter nuptias*; and that the guilty party seems, by personal exception, barred from claiming any benefit from the dissolution (*b*). But death before decree of divorce bars these consequences (*c*).

(*a*) Johnstone Beattie *v.* Dalzell (*b*).

(*b*) 1573, c. 55. 1 Stair, 4. § 20. 1 Ersk. 6. § 46-48. Auchinleck *v.* Stewart, 1540; M. 339; 2 Ill. 304. Anderson *v.* Welsh, 1734; M. 333; Elchies, *Husb. and Wife*, 3. Justice *v.* Murray, 1761; M. 334. In Justice the husband divorced for adultery was allowed to retain the tocher; but the authority of the case is questioned. 1 Ersk. 6. § 48, and Ivory's note. See **Johnstone Beattie** *v.* **Dalzell,** 1868; 6 Macph. 333, 340. As to divorce for desertion, see 1573, c. 55; and Fraser, H. & W. 1220. This forfeiture affects the guilty party's creditors. Johnstone Beattie *v.* Dalzell, *cit.* Greenhill, *infra*, § 1623. See also Johnstone Beattie *v.* Johnstone, Feb. 5, 1867; 5 Macph. 340. **Harvey** *v.* **Farquhar,** 1870; 8 Macph. 971; aff. 1872, 10 Macph. H. L. 26. Ritchie *v.* Ritchie, 1874; 1 R. 826, 987. Ferguson *v.* Jack's Exrs., 1877; 4 R. 393. Stewart *v.* Stewart, 1872; 10 Macph. 474. Thom *v.* Thom, June 11, 1852; 14 D. 861. M'Alister *v.* M'Alister, June 18, 1854; 26 S. Jur. 597. Harvey's Factor *v.* Spittal's Cur., 1893; 20 R. 1016. Eddington *v.* Robertson, 1895; 22 R. 431 (wife divorced—*jus relicti* not due). Taylor's Trs. *v.* Barnett, 1893; 20 R. 1032 (divorce not equivalent to death in propelling a fee); and above, § 1533, 1534, as to mutual divorces.

(*c*) A. *v.* B., 1734; Elchies, *Husb. and Wife*, 2. Clement *v.* Sinclair, 1762; M. 337; 2 Ill. 252. Smith *v.* Smith, 1866; 4 Macph. 279.

1623. The rights of the parties are fixed as at the date of the decree of divorce; and the innocent party can claim no right or interest in any estate afterwards acquired by succession or otherwise (*a*); 'and the right to aliment ceases (*b*).'

(*a*) E. Elgin *v.* Fergusson, 1827; 5 S. 243; 2 Ill. 305. See Greenhill *v.* Ford, 1824; 3 S. 169; 4 S. 473. See 2 S. App. 435. Ferguson *v.* Jack's Exrs., 1877; 4 R. 393. It seems on this principle that the husband, if the innocent party, is entitled to courtesy if the conditions stated above in § 1606 are fulfilled; but that he cannot *jure mariti* continue to take the rents of heritage falling due after the decree of divorce, or demand a share of a succession vested in his wife, but not already in his possession. R. F. *v.* J. J.'s Exrs., 1876; 20 J. J. 270.

(*b*) Stewart *v.* Stewart, 1872; 10 Macph. 472.

CHAPTER II

OF PARENT AND CHILD

1624. Lawful Child. — A lawful child, according to the law of Scotland, is one born in wedlock, or within a certain time after the dissolution of the marriage; or born of parents who, at the conception, were under no impediment to marry, and have since intermarried (*a*).

(*a*) 1 Ersk. Pr. 7. § 36, 37; and Inst. 1. 6. § 49, 52. See below, § 1626–7; and as to illegitimate children, § 2059 et seq. Fraser on the Law of Parent and Child, 2nd ed., Edinr. 1866, ch. i.

1625. (1.) *Bona fides* in both or one of the parents, though it will not validate marriage ('putative marriage') where one of the parties is already married, seems to legitimate the offspring (*a*).

(*a*) 4 Decret. 7. § 14. 2 Reg. Maj. 16. § 73, 74, with Skene's Note. 2 Craig, 18. § 18, 19. 3 Stair, 3. § 42. 1 Ersk. 6. § 51. Bell's Report of a Case of Putative Marriage; 2 Ill. 305. Fraser, P. & C. 22 sqq. **M'Gregor** *v.* **Jolly,** 1825; 4 S. 254; 3 W. & S. 85; 2 Ill. 246. See also Purves's Trs. *v.* Purves, 1895; 22 R. 513 (marriage invalid through affinity.

1626. (2.) *The Presumption of Legitimacy* from the birth of a child during marriage (*a*) is of great value in protecting every man's legitimacy; as expressed in the maxim, "Pater est quem nuptiæ demonstrant." It may indeed be overcome by opposite proofs; but the mere circumstance of birth occurring soon after marriage, 'or more than nine months after the husband's death,' will not be sufficient for that purpose (*b*). 'In the first case indeed there is still a presumption of fact, in accordance with universal feeling, that a man who marries a woman whom he knows to be pregnant is the father of her child (*c*).' Impossibility of access within the period of gestation will overturn the presumption (*d*). Proof of non-access within that period is now admitted, 'even where there has been possibility of access (*e*)'; the English rule, by which such proof was excluded unless the parties were separated by seas, having been abandoned in both countries (*f*). But moral proofs will not be admitted to counteract the presumption of legitimacy—far less moral probabilities (*g*). In England, divorce *a mensâ et thoro* seems to overturn the presumption. But a decree of separation in Scotland has not that effect. 'The presumption may be overcome, and the child proved to be illegitimate, by any competent and sufficient evidence (*h*). A married woman is entitled to sue for the aliment of her adulterine bastard, at least when her husband has left her and has not been heard of for years (*i*).'

(*a*) Where there is only an allegation of a marriage by habit and repute, or of an irregular marriage, neither this presumption nor the general presumption arising from the possession of the status of legitimacy exists. Swinton *v.* Swinton, 1862; 24 D. 833.

(*b*) See Sande, Dec. Fris. 1. 4. tit. 8. dig. 10. 1 Ersk. 6. § 56. Fraser, P. & C. 5 sqq. Sandy *v.* Sandy, 1823; 2 S. 406; 2 Ill. 306 (mother more than nine months a widow). Gardner Peerage case, 1824; Le Marchant's Report. Innes *v.* Innes, 1835; 13 S. 1050; 1837, 2 S. & M'L. 417. Brown & Gourlay *v.* Gourlay, 1796; Hume, 483. Smith *v.* Dick, 1869; 8 Macph. 31. Gardner *v.* Gardner, 1876; 3 R. 696; aff. 1877, 4 R. H. L. 56. Reid *v.* Mill, 1879; 6 R. 659. Kerrs *v.* Lindsay, 1890; 18 R. 365. When a marriage takes place between a man and a woman who has a child, there is no presumption of the legitimacy of the child; if the paternity be disputed, it must be proved. Innes *v.* Innes, and Smith *v.* Dick, *citt.*

(*c*) Gardner *v.* Gardner, Reid, and Kerrs, *citt.*

(*d*) 3 Stair, 3. § 42. The King *v.* Luffe, 8 East, 207; 2 Ill. 307. See Jobson *v.* Reid, 1830; 8 S. 343; 10 S. 594.

(*e*) **Brodie** *v.* **Dyce,** 1872; 11 Macph. 142. Montgomery *v.* Montgomery, 1881; 8 R. 403; and cases in note (*f*).

(*f*) 4 Decret. 17. § 3. 2 Craig, 18. § 20. 3 Stair, 3. § 42. 1 Ersk. 6. § 49. Pendrell *v.* Pendrell, 2 Strange, 924. The King, *supra* (*d*). **Routledge** *v.* **Carruthers,** Jan. 20. 1810; May 19, 1812; F. C.; Buchanan's Cases, 121; 1816, 4 Dow, 391; 2 Bligh, 692. Douglas Cause (2 Paton, 243; 6 Paton, 763).

(*g*) Cases, *supra* (*f*). Banbury Peerage, 1813 ; 2 Ill. 308 ; Le Marchant's Report, and 1 Sim. & S. 154. See, *contra*, Fraser, P. & C. 6 sqq. Sandy, *cit.*, and Mackay, *infra*.

(*h*) Mackay *v.* Mackay, 1855 ; 17 D. 494. Lepper *v.* Brown, 1802; Hume, 488. Aitken *v.* Mitchell, 1806; Hume, 489. Walker *v.* Walker, 1857; 19 D. 290. Tulloh *v.* Tulloh, 1861 ; 23 D. 641. Brodie *v.* Dyce (*e*). Steedman *v.* Steedman, 1887 ; 14 R. 1066 (presumption rebutted—parties living in same village). Tennent *v.* Tennent, 1890 ; 17 R. 1205. Coles *v.* Homer, 1895; 22 R. 716 (sequel to Tulloh, *cit.*). Gurney *v.* Gurney, 32 L. J. Ch. 456 ; 1 H. & M. 413. Atchley *v.* Sprigg, 33 L. J. Ch. 345. Plowes *v.* Bossey, 31 L. J. Ch. 681 ; 2 Dr. & Sm. 145. Morries *v.* Davies, 1837 ; 5 Cl. & F. 163. Heathcote's Divorce, 1 Macq. 535. Hargrave *v.* Hargrave, 9 Beav. 552 ; 2 Stephen's Com. 298. Aylesford Peerage, 11 App. Ca. 1. Sir H. Nicolas on Adulterine Bastardy. The husband is a competent witness to prove non-access. Brodie (*e*). And while the wife cannot be compelled to answer questions inferring her adultery, evidence of her own conduct and statements regarding the child are admissible. Gardner Peerage, Morries *v.* Davies, Walker *v.* Walker, and Tennent *v.* Tennent, *citt.* As to a married woman's claim against her bastard's real father, see Wilkinson *v.* Bain, 1880 ; 8 R. 72. M'Quillan, *infra*.

(*i*) Stewart *v.* Sheedy, 1893 ; 2 Sel. Sh. Ct. Ca. 11. M'Quillan *v.* Smith, 1892 ; 19 R. 375. Robertson *v.* Leitch, 1895; Glasgow Sh. Ct. See Wilkinson *v.* Bain, 1880 ; 8 R. 72.

1627. (3.) *Legitimation of children, by the subsequent marriage of their parents* (*a*), has been referred to various fictions invented to explain its several effects; one, that the parents were married at the time of gestation; another, that the child was not born till the marriage. None of the suppositions entirely accords with the effect. But the general rule is fixed, and not to be shaken on the inadequacy of any fiction to account for it. 'To make it available,' the parties must have been under no legal impediment to marry at the procreation of the child; and so children born of an adulterous intercourse will not be legitimated by the subsequent marriage of their parents. Children legitimated by subsequent marriage will, as lawful children, take precedence of those born afterwards in marriage. And this effect of legitimation would seem to follow although the children should have died before the marriage, so as to confer on their descendants all the rights which belong to the children of one lawfully born. It has been questioned whether the intermediate marriage of either of the parties with another than the parent of the child bars the legitimacy which would otherwise arise from their intermarriage, 'and the question has been determined in the negative' (*b*). But the children of the intermediate marriage cannot be prejudiced by the legitimation.

(*a*) 1 Ersk. 6. § 52. 1 Bankt. 5. 57–8. Fraser, P. & C. 32 sqq.

(*b*) **Kerr** *v.* **Martin,** 1836 ; 14 S. 1104 ; 1840, 2 D. 752. This case leaves the rights of the children of the intervening marriage undetermined.

1628. Difficulties on this subject naturally arise from difference in the laws of different countries, relative to the effect of subsequent marriage in legitimating offspring (*a*); and the following points have been held as law:—Subsequent marriage has no effect to legitimate the previous issue, if the child be born and the marriage take place in a country by the law of which subsequent marriage does not legitimate previous issue (*b*). A person having illegitimate children born in England, will not, by going into Scotland 'without' acquiring a domicile there, and marrying there the mother of those children, legitimate them (*c*). When the domicile of the parents at the birth and at the marriage is actually or constructively in Scotland, the child is legitimate; 'and by later cases the simple rule is established that the question of legitimation *per subsequens matrimonium* is ruled by the law of the domicile of the parents (*i.e.* of the father) at the time of the marriage' (*d*). It has been said that a child born where the law of legitimation is recognised, may be legitimated by the marriage of the parents in a country where it is denied (*e*). The judges of England have held that a child legitimated by subsequent marriage in Scotland, though in point of status legitimate in England, cannot, contrary to the territorial law of England, succeed to lands there (*f*). 'The register of births is corrected on production of an extract of the marriage entry, if the paternity has been acknowledged in terms of the registration statute, or, if no such acknowledgment has been made, it may be corrected by warrant of the Sheriff (*g*).'

(*a*) Fraser, P. & C. 45 sqq.

(*b*) **Shedden** *v.* **Patrick,** 1803 ; M. *Foreign*, Apx. 6 ; aff. 5 Pat. 194 ; 2 Ill. 309 ; 1849, 11 D. 1333 ; 1854, 1 Macq. 535. Strathmore Peerage, 1821 ; 4 W. & S. Apx. No. 5. **Munro** *v.* **Munro,** 1837 ; 16 S. 18 ; rev. 1840, 1 Rob. 492.

(*c*) Ross *v.* Munro, 1827 ; 5 S. 605 ; as revd. 4 W. & S. 589, and Appendix.

(*d*) **Css. Dalhousie** *v.* **M'Douall,** 1838 ; 16 S. 6 ; aff. 1840, 1 Rob. 475. Munro *v.* Munro, *cit.* M'Dowall *v.* Adair, 1852 ; 14 D. 525. Aikman *v.* Aikman, 1859 ; 21 D. 757 ; aff. 1861, 3 Macq. 854. Udny *v.* Udny, 1866 ; 5 Macph. 164 ; aff. 1868, 7 Macph. H. L. 89. *In re* Wright, 2 K. & J. 595 ; 25 L. J. Ch. 621. See Guthrie's Savigny, Priv. Internatl. Law, § 377, 380, pp. 284, 302, 308.

(*e*) See Huber, Prælect. De Conflictu Legum, l. 3. § 10, 12. Voet, de Statutis. Hertius, de Collisione Legum, § 4, 10, 16. 3 Pothier, Tr. 320. Story, Conf. of Laws, 85 et seq.

(*f*) **Birtwhistle** *v.* **Vardill,** 5 B. & Cr. 438 ; aff. 7 C. & F. 935 ; 9 Bligh, 48 ; 1 Rob. 627. See 4 W. & S. Apx. No. 6 ; 6 W. & S. Apx. See **Fenton** *v.* **Livingston,** 1856 ; 18 D. 865 ; rev. 1859 ; 3 Macq. 497 ; 23 D. 366. Shaw *v.* Gould, L. R. 3 H. L. 55 ; 37 L. J. Ch. 433.

(*g*) 17 and 18 Vict. c. 80, § 36. As to letters of legitimation, see below, § 2064.

1629. Maintenance or Aliment.—Besides legitim as a provision for lawful children after the father's death, the children have right during his life to maintenance (*a*), education, and protection. 'Posthumous children have a claim against their father's estate as creditors for aliment (*b*).'

(*a*) See below, § 1978, 1985, as to provisions to children. Fraser, P. & C. 85. As to liability for wages where maintenance, etc., is afforded, see Miller *v.* Miller, 1898 ; 25 R. 995. Gray *v.* Gray, 1892 ; 8 Sh. Ct. Rep. 124.

(*b*) See Hastie and Kerr *v.* Hastie, 1671 ; M. 416, 5922. Muirhead (Fincham) *v.* Muirhead, 1706 ; M. 5927, 16,322. Spalding *v.* Spalding's Trs., 1874 ; 2 R. 237. *Infra*, § 1632 ; *supra*, § 1572.

1630. A child is entitled to maintenance,—1. In the father's house; and for necessary furnishings the father is liable (*a*); or, 2. Elsewhere, if the father's conduct endanger the child's 'moral or physical health or' safety, or if the father choose to give him separate maintenance (*b*). 3. The amount above bare subsistence according to his condition in life, is at the father's discretion (*c*). The mere name of a profession is not enough to satisfy the obligation (*d*); but an occupation in the lower ranks, by which a livelihood may be gained, is sufficient (*e*); 'and one who has been fairly educated to a profession and fairly started in the world must make his own way without further claim on his father, if he be sound in body and mind, and of such age as to be fit for his work (*f*).' The obligation ceases with forisfamiliation (*g*), unless the child shall fall into indigence and want (*h*). It extends to the son's wife in the higher ranks during the son's life; or after, if she be the mother of an heir of entail (*i*).

(*a*) 1 Ersk. 6. § 56. Dick *v.* Dick, 1666 ; M. 409 ; 2 Ill. 311. Buchan *v.* Buchan, 1666 ; M. 411. Barclay *v.* Douglas, 1758 ; M. 9624. Ferne *v.* Wilson, 1680 ; 3 B. Sup. 384. Jameson *v.* Jameson, 1845 ; 8 D. 86. Wallace *v.* Goldie, 1848 ; 10 D. 1510. M'Culloch *v.* Smellie, 1799 ; Hume, 423. Fergusson & Lillie *v.* Stephen, 1864 ; 2 Macph. 804. Couper *v.* Riddell, 1872 ; 44 S. Jur. 484. Fraser, P. & C. 95. 1 Stair, 5. § 7, with Brodie's note, p. 45.

(*b*) Morrison *v.* Morrison, 1716 ; M. 410. Hepburn *v.* Hepburn, 1734 ; *ib.* Bain, *infra* (*c*). **Ketchen** *v.* **Ketchen,** 1870 ; 8 Macph. 952 ; 1871, 9 Macph. 691. Harvey *v.* Harvey, 1860 ; 22 D. 1198. Baillie *v.* Agnew, 1775 ; 5 B. Sup. 526. Cameron, petr., 1847 ; 9 D. 1401.

(*c*) **Maule** *v.* **Maule,** 1823 ; 2 S. 464 ; rev. 1 W. & S. 266. See Bain *v.* Bain, 1860 ; 22 D. 1021 ; and as to amount, Thom *v.* Mackenzie, 1864 ; 3 Macph. 177 : and Smith *v.* Smith, *infra.* The interference of the Court may be prevented by misconduct on the part of the child. A. *v.* B., 1848 ; 10 D. 895. Bain, *cit.*

(*d*) Maule, *supra* (*c*). See Maidment *v.* Landers, May 25, 1815 ; F. C. ; rev. 6 Dow, 257. A. *v.* B., 1858 ; 20 D. 778. Dick, *supra* (*a*) ; and Ayton, *infra*, § 1631.

(*e*) Dick, *supra* (*a*). The limitation to the lower ranks is not now observed in the case of sons. Hunter's Trs. *v.* Macan, 1839 ; 1 D. 817. See Maule, *cit.*

(*f*) Maule and Bain, *citt.* Smith *v.* Smith, 1885 ; 13 R. 126.

(*g*) Campbell *v.* Campbell, 1741 ; M. 448. See Thomson *v.* Gibson & Borthwick, 1851 ; 13 D. 683. Also as to forisfamiliation in the sense of the poor law, Lees *v.* Kemp, 1891 ; 19 R. 6. Mackay *v.* Munro, 1892 ; 19 R. 396. Elgin Par. Bd. *v.* Kinloss Par. Bd. 1893 ; 20 R. 763. Brechin Par. Council *v.* Glasgow Par. Co., 1897 ; 24 R. 587.

(*h*) 8 and 9 Vict. c. 83, § 80.

(*i*) Duncan *v.* Hill, Feb. 17, 1810 ; F. C. Yuill *v.* Marshall, Dec. 21, 1815 ; F. C. Adam *v.* Lauder, 1762–4 ; M. 398 and 400. Chrystie *v.* M'Millan, 1802 ; M. *Aliment*, Apx. 2. Brown *v.* Brown, 1824 ; 3 S. 247. Lauder *v.* Lauder, 1765 ; M. 398, 15,419. De Courcy *v.* Agnew, 1806 ; M. *Aliment*, Apx. 8. Tait *v.* White, 1802 ; *ib.* 3. See Hoseason *v.* Hoseason, cited below, § 1633. Fraser, P. & C. 87, 105. Wallace, *supra* (*a*).

1631. The father is bound to give aliment in the lower ranks till the child is able to earn a livelihood; in the higher, still longer, if the child be destitute, especially in the case of daughters (*a*).

(*a*) 1 Ersk. 6. § 56. Fraser, P. & C. 101 sqq. Cairns *v.* Bellamore, 1687 ; M. 410 ; 2 Ill. 313. Ayton *v.* Colvil, 1705 ; M. 451. Dalziel *v.* Dalziel, 1788 ; M. 450. Maidment, *supra*, § 1630 (*d*). When children had funds of their own, a mother having the means of educating and alimenting them, was, on accounting, held entitled to impute the interest accruing on the child's estate, but not the capital, against her expenditure. Fairgrieve *v.* Henderson, 1885 ; 13 R. 98. A somewhat different rule is said to apply to a father. Galt *v.* Black, 1830 ; 8 S. 332. But decisions may be expected to vary according to the circumstances.

1632. The duty of maintenance devolves on the father's representatives, 'whether in heritage or moveables' if *lucrati* by his succession (*a*); not on the son 'or collateral relations' merely as such (*b*).

(*a*) 1 Ersk. 6. § 58. Lowther *v.* M'Laine, 1786 ; M. 435 ; see note in 2 Ill. 314. Buchanan *v.* Morrison, Jan. 21, 1813 ; F. C. Scott *v.* Sharp, 1759 ; M. 440, and Apx. *Par. & Ch.* 1, and cases in Fraser, P. & C. 108. *Supra*, § 1629, note.

(*b*) 1 Stair, 5. § 10. Anderson *v.* Gibson, 1754 ; M. 427. Malcolm *v.* Malcolm, 1756 ; M. 439. Stuart *v.* Court, 1848 ; 10 D. 1275. Marshall *v.* Gourlay, 1836 ; 15 S. 313. Mackintosh *v.* Taylor, 1868 ; 7 Macph. 67.

1633. The duty devolves on the mother if she be rich, and the father indigent or dead (*a*); and 'after her' the grandfather (*b*) is bound to aliment his destitute grandchildren in his own house, or to allow a reasonable aliment according to his means—'whichever way is less burdensome to him (*c*).' But he is not bound to aliment the wife 'or widow' of his son (*d*). 'Failing the paternal grandfather and ascendants, the ascendants on the mother's side are liable (*c*). A stepmother is not liable (*f*).'

(*a*) 1 Bankt. 6. § 15. 1 Stair. 5. § 7. 3 Ersk. Pr. 1. § 4. (*contra*, 1 Ersk. Inst. 6. § 56). Fraser, P. & C. 86. Buchan, § 1630 (*a*). Macdonald, *infra*. See Barry's Trs. *v.* Barry, 1888; 15 R. 496 (widow's annuity burdened with maintenance).

(*b*) Chrystie, Brown, and Tait, § 1630 (*i*). Belch *v.* Belch, 1798; Hume 1. Hamilton *v.* Hamilton, 1807; *ib.* 3. Jameson *v.* Jameson, 1845; 8 D. 86.

(*c*) Fraser, P. & C. 87, 92. Muirhead, § 1629 (*b*). M'Kissock *v.* M'Kissock, 1817; Hume, 6. Jameson, *cit.* Bell *v.* Bell. 1890; 17 R. 549.

(*d*) Chrystie, Tait, Belch, *citt.* (wife). Duncan, Yuill, Adam, § 1630 (*i*) (widow). Pagan *v.* Pagan, 1838; 16 S. 399 (do.). Hoseason *v.* Hoseason, 1870; 9 Macph. 37 (do.). Fraser, H. & W. 972; P. & C. 87.

(*e*) 1 Ersk. 6. § 56. Fraser, P. & C. 87.

(*f*) Macdonald *v.* Macdonald, 1846; 8 D. 830. See Barry, *cit.*

1634. Indigent parents have a reciprocal right to maintenance from their children, who are in circumstances to afford it (*a*)—'a right preferable to that against their own parents (*b*). A husband, if married before 1st January 1878, is liable for the aliment of his wife's indigent parents during the marriage (*c*): but if married after that date he is liable only *quantum lucratus* by the marriage (*d*).'

(*a*) 1 Ersk. 6. § 57, and cases there quoted by Ivory. 1 Stair, 5. § 6. Fraser, P. & C. 114. White *v.* White, 1829; 7 S. 567; 2 Ill. 314. Muirhead *v.* Muirhead, 1849; 12 D. 356. Landers *v.* Landers, 1859; 21 D. 706. Buie *v.* Stiven, 1863; 2 Macph. 208. Mackenzie *v.* Mackenzie, 1864; 3 Macph. 177. Macdonald *v.* Macdonald, 1846; 8 D. 830. Hamilton *v.* Hamilton, 1877; 4 R. 688.

(*b*) Fraser, P. & C. 85.

(*c*) Reid *v.* Moir, 1866; 4 Macph. 1060. See above, § 1570.

(*d*) Above, § 1571A.

1635. Education.—Education of children seems to be at the father's discretion (*a*), 'subject to the general law in the Education Act of 1872 (*b*).'

(*a*) See 1 Kames' Prin. of Equity, 109. Maule *v.* Maule, 1823; 2 S. 464; rev. 1 W. & S. 266; 2 Ill. 311. See below, § 2068. Fraser, P. & C. 222.

(*b*) 35 and 36 Vict. c. 62, § 69.

1636. Guardianship. — The father, 'and after his death the surviving mother under the provisions of the Guardianship of Infants Act, 1886,' is administrator-in-law for his children (*a*).

(*a*) See below, of Tutors and Curators, § 2067 et seq. Fraser, P. & C. 164. 49 and 50 Vict. c. 27. 54 and 55 Vict. c. 3. See § 2069, 2078A, 2083.

BOOK THIRD

PART II

OF THE LAWS OF SUCCESSION

CHAPTER I

OF SUCCESSION IN GENERAL

1637. General View.—No department of municipal law is more intimately connected with the state of society than that which relates to the rights of heirs and the rules of descent; and in none, perhaps, are differences so essential to be found in comparing the laws and institutions of various countries. While in most European countries, and particularly in England and Scotland, the equal division of the Roman law prevails in relation to the succession in moveables; the law of primogeniture and the preference of males, is the distinguishing character of the descent of land. But in France, in Holland, in Spain, in Normandy, and partly in Denmark, and almost universally in America, the rule of equal partition has been adopted in the descent of land (*a*).

(*a*) 3 Stair, tit. 4. 3 Ersk. tit. 8. 2 Blackst. Com. c. 16. Pothier, Tr. des Successions, Œuv. Posth. tom. 3. Code Civil, Nos. 718–892. Chabot, Com. sur la Loi des Successions. Toullier, Dr. Civ. tom. 4. Van Leeuwin, 63. Kent, Com. on American Law, v. iv. p. 373. Story, Conf. of Laws, § 464. M'Laren on Wills and Succession.

1638. Hæreditas Jacens.—In the law of Scotland the *universitas* of the estates and property of one deceased is called his *Hæreditas*, and comprehends both lands and moveables; the one descending to the heir, the other to the executor; or both to one person, if these characters be united. While it still remains untaken up by the heir, it is called "Hæreditas jacens." The person who takes the benefit of the *hæreditas* is burdened with the debts of the deceased; he is called the representative of the deceased, and considered as *eadem persona cum defuncto.* The act or mode of taking up the succession is either a judicial or an extra-judicial proceeding, by which the heir's right in heritage or in moveables is recognised, and the active title, as well as the passive representation, either universally or to a limited extent conferred and fixed on the successor.

1639. Opening of the Succession.—The natural opening of the succession is by death; natural, not civil death. But the death of a proprietor is not necessarily accompanied by succession: for, 1. In particular crimes (as treason) there is no succession; the criminal's estate being forfeited from the traitor and his heirs, and his blood being corrupted (*a*). 2. Succession may open before death, under the provisions of a strict entail declaring certain acts to infer forfeiture of the estate and devolution of the succession (*b*).

(*a*) 1 Hume, Criminal Law, 546, 550–1, 548.
(*b*) See below, of Entails, § 1761.

1640. In the proof of death, as opening the succession to a particular person, difficulties may arise. Thus, 1. It may be necessary to determine which of two persons dying on the same day, or perishing by the same accident, survived (*a*); or, 2. It may be necessary to ascertain whether a person absent from the country, or missing, is still alive, or was alive at any particular time (*b*); or, 3. In order to ascertain whether a succession has devolved or a bequest accrued to a particular person, his survivance on a particular day must be established (*c*). All such cases are for a jury; and presumptions, proofs, and inferences from the particular circumstances rule the decision. 'In England there is a presumption that a person who has gone abroad and has not been heard of for seven years, is dead; but there is no presumption as to the particular time of death within the seven years (*d*).'

'*Presumption of Life Limitation Acts* (*e*).—Whereas great hardships have arisen from the want of any limitation to the presumption of life as regards persons who have been absent from Scotland (*f*), or have disappeared for long periods of years, it was enacted in 1881 that, for the purposes of the Act, in all cases where a person had left Scotland (*f*), or had disappeared, and where no presumption arose from the facts that he died at any definite date (*g*), he should be presumed to have died on the day which would complete a period of seven years from the time of his being last heard of, at or after such leaving or disappearance (*h*). This statute made provision for the Court, (1) granting authority to persons entitled to succeed, to uplift and enjoy the yearly income of the heritable and moveable estate of the absent person, or for its sequestrating such estate and appointing a judicial factor (*i*); (2) for its granting authority to such persons, after seven years from the date of the former deliverance, to make up a title to and enjoy the fee of the moveable estate; (3) for its granting the same authority in regard to the heritable estate on the lapse of thirteen years from the said former deliverance (*k*); and it also made provision for sales, etc., by *pro indiviso* proprietors where one of them had disappeared (*l*).

'On 3rd July 1891, the first statute was repealed by another of wider scope (*m*), the leading enactment of which provides that the Court of Session, or in certain cases the Sheriff, may, on the application of a person entitled to estate by succession or transmission on the death of a person who has disappeared for seven years, find (1) that the absentee has disappeared, (2) that he was last known to be alive on such a date, and (3) either that he died on a date specified within seven years after the date so found, or, in the absence of proof, that he is presumed to have died at the end of seven years after the date so found; leaving the petitioner, and others entitled to estate on the death, to make up titles and take possession in any competent way, as in the case of an actual death at the date fixed (*n*). The statute does not entitle any person to intestate moveable succession of an absentee who was not a domiciled Scot at the date of the proven or presumed death (*o*). The absent person, or any person deriving right from him preferably to the person who has obtained a title under the Acts, is entitled, within thirteen years after possession (or a registered title, where such is admissible) is obtained under the Acts, to demand and receive the fee or capital, if extant in the hands of the statutory possessor or anyone holding by gratuitous title from him (subject to all claims for meliorations, but free of burdens imposed after the finding of the Court), or to demand and receive the price if the property be sold; but after thirteen years, all claim by the absent person, or those deriving right from him as aforesaid, is barred. In no case is a person who has obtained possession and uplifted income under any of the provisions of the Acts prior to the absent person, or those in his right, appearing and intimating their claim, liable to account for or pay the income received previous to such intimation (*p*). Nothing in the Acts is to prejudice or affect the right of third parties having rights preferable to that of the absent person or to the right of his representatives derived from him (*q*). The Acts do not apply to policies of insurance upon the life of any person absent from Scotland, whose death must be proved under the former law (*r*).

'The case of absentee heirs of entail is provided for to certain effects by yet another statute (*s*).'

(*a*) Case of General Stanwix, Fearne's Posth. Works. R. *v.* Dr. Hay, 1 W. Bl. 640. See Code Civ. de France, § 761–2. Chabot, Tr. de Successions, § 722. 4 Toullier, Droit Civ. 44. Fettes (Ritchie's Trs.) *v.* Gordon, 1825; 4 S. 149. Underwood *v.* Wing, 19 Beav. 459; 2 De G. M. & G. 633; aff. in H. of L. as Wing *v.* Angrave, 8 H. L. Ca. 183; 30 L. J. Ch. 65. Best on Evid. § 1410. Dickson on Evid. § 311.

(*b*) Sommerville *v.* Thomson & Rutherford, May 19, 1815; F. C.; rev. 6 Pat. 393; 2 Ill. 316. L. Ashburton *v.* Baillie, Feb. 7, 1811; F. C. Carstairs *v.* Stewart, 1734; M. 11,633. Lawrie *v.* Drummond, 1670; M. 12,643. See Ruthven *v.* Clark, 1628; M. 11,629. Erskine *v.* Steven, 1622; M. 11,656. French *v.* E. Wemyss, 1667; M. 12,644; and 1694, 4 B. Sup. 163. Hog *v.* Home, 1706; M. 12,645. Henderson *v.* Morton, 1710; M. 12,646. Forrester *v.* Boutcher, 1760; M. 11,674. Reid *v.* Brown, 1834; 12 S. 278. Campbell *v.* Campbell, 1834; *ib.* 382. Bruce *v.* Robson, 1834; *ib.* 486. Garland *v.* Stewart, 1841; 4 D. 1. Stirling *v.* Mackenzie, 1847; 9 D. 923. Chambers *v.* Carruthers, 1849; 11 D. 1359. Fife *v.* Fife, 1855; 17 D. 951 Kennedy *v.* M'Lean, 1851;

13 D. 705. Fairholme *v.* Fairholme's Trs., 1858; 20 D. 813. Barstow *v.* Cook, 1862; 24 D. 790. Tait *v.* Wood, 1866; 4 Macph. 443. Murray *v.* Wright, 1870; 8 Macph. 722. Bruce *v.* Smith, 1871; 10 Macph. 430. Stewart's Trs. *v.* Stewart, 1875; 2 R. 488. Rhind's Trs. *v.* Bell, 1878; 5 R. 527.

(*c*) Hamilton, 1791. See Craig, *infra* (*h*).

(*d*) Knight *v.* Nepean, 5 B. & Ad. 86; 2 M. & W. 894. Watson *v.* England, 14 Sim. 28. *In re* Phené, L. R. 5 Ch. 139; 39 L. J. Ch. 316. *In re* Lewes, 40 L. J. Ch. 602; L. R. 6 Ch. 356. Prudential Ass. Co. *v.* Edmonds, 2 App. Ca. 487. Best, Pr. of Ev. § 409.

(*e*) Stevenson on Presumption of Life, Edin. 1893.

(*f*) 44 and 45 Vict. c. 47, preamble. The Act did not apply to absent persons who had never been in Scotland. Rainham *v.* Laing, 1881; 9 R. 207. Nor to one whose death opened a right of succession not to him—the deceaser—but under the will of another person. Minty *v.* Ellis' Trs., 1887; 15 R. 262.

(*g*) Williamson *v.* Williamson, 1886; 14 R. 226.

(*h*) 44 and 45 Vict. c. 47, § 8. As this Act created a presumption that the absent person died seven years after he was last heard of, a succession which would have opened to him after that date, if he had lived, was not within the provisions of the Act. Craig, etc., petrs., 1882; 9 R. 434.

(*i*) 44 and 45 Vict. c. 47, § 1. It was held that if a liferenter disappeared, the provisions of the Act could not be made available by the fiar, who does not "succeed" to him. Peterhead School Board *v.* Yule's Trs., 1883; 10 R. 763.

(*k*) 44 and 45 Vict. c. 47, § 2–5.

(*l*) *Ib.* § 6. 54 and 55 Vict. c. 29, § 4.

(*m*) 54 and 55 Vict. c. 29.

(*n*) *Ib.* § 1. (*o*) *Ib.* § 3 *fin.*

(*p*) *Ib.* § 6–7. (*q*) *Ib.* § 10. (*r*) *Ib.* § 11.

(*s*) 45 and 46 Vict. c. 53, § 14–16, as amended by 54 and 55 Vict. c. 29, § 8.

1641. Persons capable of Succeeding.—It is indispensable to the vesting of a succession in a particular person, that such person shall be conceived at the opening of the succession, and shall be born alive (*a*); that the person to succeed shall be legitimate; that he shall be a subject of the Queen (*b*); and that he shall be of uncorrupted blood.

(*a*) See above, § 1629; below, § 1642, 1779.
(*b*) See § 1644, 2134.

1642. In intestate succession, the person who is in the right to succeed at the time of the opening of the succession is the heir. But the right of a child already conceived, though not yet born, is admitted in this question, provided there is life after birth; and, on birth, he will exclude one who may have entered as heir, and may compel him to denude. Many difficult questions in evidence respecting conception, birth, parentage, identity, and legitimation by subsequent marriage of parents, occur on such occasions. In succession by deed, the person entitled to succeed according to a particular destination will not be deprived of it, though not born or conceived at the opening of the succession (*a*). 'But in intestate succession, the nearest heir in existence at the opening of the succession acquires an indefeasible right by service, or since 1874 by mere survivance, before the conception of a nearer heir, and is not obliged to denude in his favour. In this case the brocard, *Semel hæres semper hæres*, applies (*b*).'

(*a*) 3 Stair, 5. § 50. 3 Ersk. 8. § 6, 9, 76. Bruce *v.* Melville, 1677; M. 14,880; 2 Ill. 317. L. Mountstewart *v.* M'Kenzie, 1707, 1709, 1710; M. 14,903–6 and 14,914. M'Kinnon *v.* M'Kinnon, 1756; M. 14,938, 6566; 5 B. Sup. 848; 1765, M. 5290; 5 B. Sup. 904; aff. 2 Pat. 252. Douglas Cause; see arguments and speeches, and as decided in the House of Lords, 2 Pat. 243; 6 Pat. 673. Middlemore *v.* M'Farlane, March 5, 1811; F. C. E. Eglinton *v.* Montgomerie (Bourtriehill Case), 1844; 7 D. 425; 9 D. 1167; 1847, 6 Bell's Ap. 136. Home *v.* Logan, 1880; 7 R. 1137. See Stewart *v.* Nicholson (Carnock Case), 1859; 22 D. 72. Campbell *v.* Campbell (Boquhan Case), 1868; 6 Macph. 1035.

(*b*) Grant *v.* Grant's Trs., 1859; 22 D. 53. 37 and 38 Vict. c. 94, § 9.

1643. Legitimacy of birth is indispensable (*a*).

(*a*) See above, § 1624 et seq.

1644. Aliens 'were' excluded from succession in lands, but 'might' be naturalised (*a*). 'Since 1870 aliens may take, hold, and dispose of real and personal property, as if they were natural born subjects (*b*).'

(*a*) See below, § 2134 et seq.
(*b*) 33 and 34 Vict. c. 14, § 2. See below, § 2135.

1645. Corruption of blood bars succession (*a*).

(*a*) See above, § 1639.

1646. Laws of Consanguinity.—The law of succession to land is arranged on the principle of primogeniture and the preference of males; while moveables are disposed of nearly on the principles of the Roman jurisprudence, in equal shares to all the nearest of kin.

1647. In both courses of succession there is perpetual reference to the lines of consanguinity; of which there are three: Descending, Collateral, and Ascending. The first and the last are called "Lineal," in contradistinction to the second; and in them there is *vinculum personarum ab eodem stipite descendentium*,—as all descending in a direct line from one common ancestor.

1648. (1.) *Lineal Descent* includes all issue immediate and remote; each generation forming a degree of descent.

1649. (2.) *Lineal Ascent* comprehends immediate parents and ancestry in the direct line, as high as evidence can reach.

1650. (3.) *Collateral Kindred* also descend from one common ancestor with the deceased, but not, as in lineal succession, from each other. And here it is necessary to distinguish the full from the half blood; and in half blood, the consanguinean from the uterine (*a*).

(*a*) The word "collateral" is here used in a wider sense than in § 1861, *infra*. In the Intestate Moveable Succession Act it seems to be used as here. See *per cur.* in Ormiston *v.* Broad, 1862; 1 Macph. 10. See below, § 1861A.

1651. Persons are connected by full blood (or german), who are born, or descended, of the same father and mother.

1652. Relationship of full blood or of half blood, according to the Books of the Feus, stopped at the seventh degree (*a*); but it is reckoned in Scotland to extend as far as the evidence of propinquity will reach (*b*).

(*a*) Lib. Feud. l. 1. tit. 1. § 4.
(*b*) 2 Craig, 17. § 11. 3 Ersk. 10. § 2.

1653. Half blood is either consanguinean or uterine.

1654. Consanguinean relations are persons born or descended of the same father, but not of the same mother. Uterine relations are persons born or descended of the same mother, but not of the same father. Law recognises no relationship between the consanguinean and the uterine; and there is no succession *ab intestato* of the one to the other.

CHAPTER II

OF SUCCESSION IN LAND

I. INTESTATE SUCCESSION.

1655. Succession in Heritage.—In heritable succession the radical points are:—Primogeniture, and the succession of males and of their issue according to seniority: Representation of parents, by their children taking their place in the succession: Failing males, equal partition among females; their issue taking their portions according to the same rule of representation: and, 'until October 1, 1874,' a deviation in collateral succession where land 'had' been acquired by the owner (called Conquest) (*a*), from the rule of descent observed in the succession to lands coming from an ancestor, called Heritage.

(*a*) See § 1670A.

1656. Lineal Descent.—The several lines already mentioned are observed in succession to heritage.

1657. Referring to the explanation of consanguinity already given (*a*), the following are the rules of the lineal descent of heritage:—

(*a*) See above, § 1647 et seq.

1658. (1.) *Primogeniture and Preference of Males.*—The heritable estate descends *ab intestato* to the lawful issue of the person who died last vest and seised in the land: first, males in their order; and next, females as heirs-portioners. The eldest son, and his issue, male and female in their order, take first; next the second son, with his issue, male and female in their order; and so on through all the sons (with their issue) in their order (*a*).

(*a*) 2 Craig, 13. § 19; 14. § 3 and 7. 3 Stair, 4. § 33. 3 Ersk. 8. § 5.

1659. (2.) *Heirs-Portioners* (*a*).—Failing the male issue and their issue, the female issue inherit *pro indiviso* as heirs-portioners, the issue of those who have died taking their mother's portion (*b*). The father's daughters, of whatever marriage, succeed equally to subjects divisible (*c*). The issue of each daughter take their mother's place; first, sons in their order, then daughters equally. The eldest heir-portioner by legal succession, not by provision (*d*), has a preferable right or *præcipuum*, without compensation to her sisters, to the mansion-house of an estate in the country (*e*). But she has no such right to a house in town, or to a country villa (*f*). She is also entitled as a *præcipuum* to such peerages, dignities, and titles of honour as are not limited otherwise. She has also a preferable right to subjects indivisible, and amongst others to a superiority (*g*); but this on another footing from the right to the *præcipuum*, as she must give compensation for such subjects (*h*). When there are more superiorities or rights to feu-duties than one, they must be divided like other subjects (*i*). The eldest heir-portioner has the custody of the title-deeds (*k*). The subjects to which the heirs-portioners succeed *pro indiviso*, they may insist on having divided; and in such division the eldest has the portion next to the mansion-house; but the others cast lots for their choice (*l*).

(*a*) See above, § 1083.
(*b*) 1 Feud. 8. § ult. 2 Feud. 11 and 36. 2 Craig, 14. § 3. 1 Reg. Maj. 25. § 23; and 2. 28. § 1, 3; 29. § 1, 2, etc. Quon. Att. c. 20. Balf. 221. § 1 and 4. Skene, de Verb. Sig. *voce* Varda. See Hailes, Sutherland Case.
(*c*) 3 Stair, 5. § 11. 3 Ersk. 8. § 13. Wallace *v.* Wallace, 1758; M. 5371; 2 Ill. 319. Smith *v.* Wilson, 1792; M. 5381.
(*d*) Cathcart *v.* Rocheid, 1773; M. 5375; 5 B. Sup. 465. Wight *v.* Inglis, 1798; M. *Heir Por.* Apx. 1. M'Lauchlan *v.* M'Lauchlan, 1807; *ib.* 3. Dinniston *v.* Welsh, 1830; 8 S. 935.
(*e*) 2 Craig, 14. § 7. 3 Stair, 8. § 11. 3 Ersk. 8. § 13. Hawthorn *v.* Gordon, 1696; M. 5361; 2 Ill. 319. Cowie *v.* Cowie, 1707; M. 2453, 5362; 2 Ill. 153. Peadie *v.* Peadies, 1743; M. 5367; 5 B. Sup. 728. Forbes *v.* Forbes, 1774; M. 5378. Ireland *v.* Govan, 1765; M. 5373. See above, § 1083.
(*f*) Wallace, *supra* (*c*). Smith, *supra* (*c*). Thomson *v.* Angus, 1786; Hume, 765. Rae *v.* Rae, Jan. 1810; F. C.; see Hume, 764.
(*g*) Lady Luss *v.* Inglis, 1678; M. 15,028. See above, § 859.
(*h*) See Peadie, Ireland, Forbes, *supra* (*e*). Wight and M'Lauchlan, *supra* (*d*).
(*i*) Rae, *supra* (*f*). (*k*) Same case.
(*l*) Houston *v.* Dunbar, 1742; M. 5367. Inglis *v.* Inglis, 1781; Hume, 762. Chalmers *v.* Chalmers, 1750; M. 5369; Elchies, *Heirs Por.* 4; see 6 D. 138, 143.

1660. (3.) *Representation.*—Where, before the opening of the succession, a descendant has died, who if alive would have succeeded as heir, his place is supplied, and the succession taken, by his lineal descendant. This is called Representation (*a*).

(*a*) 2 Craig, 13. § 39. 3 Stair, 4. § 4. 3 Ersk. 8. § 11.

1661. Collateral Succession.—On the exhaustion of the line of descent (children, grandchildren, and their descendants), the succession, instead of ascending to the grandfather, deviates to the collateral line. The rules are these:—

1662. Heritage, after descending as far as possible, ascends gradually. So, on the death of a middle brother, his younger brothers (and their issue), in their order from elder to younger, succeed before the elder. And elder brothers succeeding to younger are preferred in an inverse order, viz. from younger to elder upwards; each as he succeeds transmitting to his issue (*a*).

(*a*) 3 Ersk. 8. § 8. Johnston *v.* Watson, 1681; M. 14,871; 2 Ill. 319. Grant *v.* Grant, 1757; M. 14,874. See as to Conquest, below, § 1670.

1663. Where a woman dies leaving heritage, her brothers and their issue succeed before her sisters, according to the order now stated. Her sisters, when the succession opens to them, are heirs-portioners (*a*).

(*a*) 3 Stair, 4. § 33.

1664. The full blood, male and female, with their issue, succeed in the first place, according to the above order (*a*).

(*a*) Hope, Min. Pract. tit. 2. 3 Ersk. 8. § 8. Stenhouse *v.* Dewar, 1686; M. 14,872; 2 Ill. 319.

1665. The half-blood consanguinean succeeds after the full blood; brothers first, in the above order. If they are issue of a former marriage, the youngest brother consanguinean first, and gradually upwards; if of a subsequent marriage, the eldest first, and gradually downwards (*a*). Sisters consanguinean succeed to brothers consanguinean as heirs-portioners. The half-blood uterine is excluded (*b*); 'so that even when an intestate inherits from his mother, his father or brothers consanguinean succeed him, to the exclusion of his brother uterine (*c*).'

(*a*) Lady Clarkington *v.* Stewart, 1664; M. 14,867; 2 Ill. 319. 2 Craig, 15. § 19.
(*b*) Gilbert's Case, in 2 Craig, 17. § 9. 8 Stair, 4. § 4. Lennox *v.* Linton, 1663; M. 14,867.
(*c*) Lennox *v.* Linton, *cit.* (*b*).

1666. Ascending Line.—Failing collaterals, the heritage goes to the father.

1667. Heritage ascends to the father and his relations, to the exclusion of the maternal line (*a*).

(*a*) 2 Lib. Feud. 50, and 4. 84. 1 Coke on Littleton, tit. 1. § 3. Harg. and But. Notes, n. 56, 57. See also 1 Howard, Anciennes Loix des François, 13. 2 Blackst. 210. 2 Craig, 13. § 46. 3 Stair, 4. § 35. 3 Ersk. 8. § 9. See Hope, Maj. Pract. Lennox, *supra*, § 1665 (*b*).

1668. The succession never ascends to the mother and her relations. Even the mother's own estate, after vesting in her son or daughter, never ascends to the maternal line again (*a*).

(*a*) 2 Craig, 17. § 9. 3 Ersk. 8. § 9, 10. Lennox, *cit.* § 1665.

1669. Crown Ultimus Hæres.—The Crown, as *ultimus hæres*, takes the *hæreditas* on failure of the three lines of succession now stated. This is a caduciary right, not a right of succession (*a*). 'So the Crown cannot succeed as conditional institute, under a destination to "heirs" (*b*). But the Crown's donatary might pursue a reduction on the ground of deathbed (*c*). Formal procedure for establishing the right is seldom taken; and when the circumstances are precisely ascertained, a royal warrant narrating that the estate has fallen to the Crown is deemed a sufficient title to the donatary (*d*).'

(*a*) 1 Lib. Feud. 1. § 4. 2 Craig, 17. § 11. 3 Ersk. 10. § 2. 3 Stair, 3. § 47. Halcro *v.* Sommerville, 1526; M. 1348; 2 Ill. 496. Tenant *v.* Tenant, 1638; M. 14,897; 2 Ill. 320.

(*b*) Torrie *v.* King's Remembrancer, 1832; 10 S. 597. As to a lease, see Falconar *v.* Hay, 1789; M. 1355. 1 Hunter, L. & T. 187.

(*c*) Goldie *v.* Murray, 1753; M. 3183. Brock *v.* Cochrane, Feb. 2, 1809; F. C. See 1 M'Laren on Wills, etc., § 137. 34 and 35 Vict. c. 81. See below, § 1786, 1815.

(*d*) See Bell's Dict., *Last Heir.*

1670. Succession in Conquest.—The difference between conquest and heritage is this: Conquest is what has come into the person of the deceased by purchase, gift, or other singular title from a stranger, or from one to whom he would not by law have succeeded. Heritage is that to which one has succeeded as heir-at-law to his father or other relation (*a*).

'*Distinction between Heritage and Conquest abolished.*—In successions opening after 1st Oct. 1874, the distinction between fees of conquest and fees of heritage is abolished; and fees of conquest descend to the same persons, in the same manner, and subject to the same rules, as fees of heritage (*b*).'

(*a*) 2 Lib. Feud. 50. 1 Craig, 10. § 26. 3 Stair, 5. § 10. 3 Ersk. 8. § 14.

(*b*) 37 and 38 Vict. c. 94, § 37.

1671. In the succession in land acquired by conquest, the law of Scotland 'did' not accord either with the law of the Feus or with the law of England, but 'was' peculiar (*a*). The rules 'were' these:—

(1.) Succession to conquest, as contradistinguished from succession to heritage, 'took' place *only* where a middle brother or sister (or their issue) 'died,' leaving younger and elder brothers or uncles. The younger brother (or uncle) and his issue 'took' the heritage; the elder and his issue the conquest (*b*). So the conquest of a middle brother dying without issue, or of the son of a middle brother failing issue, 'went' to his immediate elder brother or uncle alive; or if there 'were' no elder, to the next younger alive, failing issue of intermediate brothers or uncles who 'had' died (*c*).

(2.) The conquest of a sister dying without issue 'went' also to her next elder brother; or, failing elder and their issue, to the next younger brother alive, preferably to her sisters (*d*).

(3.) Where there 'were' only sisters, there 'was' equal partition in conquest as in heritage (*e*).

(4.) In conquest, as in heritage, the whole blood 'excluded' the half (*f*): but if there 'were' no brothers or sisters german, or issue of them, the rule 'held' as to brothers consanguinean (*g*).

(5.) There 'was' representation as in heritage.

(6.) If the succession 'came' from the youngest brother dying without issue, the immediate elder brother 'took' both the heritage and the conquest (*h*).

(*a*) 1 Lib. Feud. 1. § 2; also tit. 20. 2 Craig, 15. § 10; *ib.* 77.

(*b*) 3 Stair, 5. § 10. 3 Ersk. 8. § 14. Hope's Min. Pract. p. 170, § 4, note.

(*c*) 3 Ersk. 8. § 14.

(*d*) 3 Stair, 4. § 33. Robertson *v.* Halkerston, 1675; M. 5605; 2 Ill. 310. A. *v.* B., 1670; M. 5608. Cunningham *v.* Cunningham, 1770; M. 14,875.

(*e*) 3 Ersk. 8. § 15. Carse *v.* Russel, 1717; M. 14,873.

(*f*) See Sir G. Lockhart's opinion in Fount. vol. i. p. 6; 3 B. Sup. 241.

(*g*) 2 Craig, 15. § 19. 3 Stair, 5. § 10. Lady Clarkington *v.* Stewart, 1664; M. 14,867.

(*h*) Robertson, *supra* (*d*).

1672. The rules by which it 'was' ascertained what subjects 'were' comprehended in conquest 'were' the following:—The subject must be a heritable subject or debt vested by sasine, or requiring sasine to complete the right (*a*); and this 'comprehended' adjudications (*b*); bonds bearing a clause of infeftment (*c*); subjects purchased and vested in a trustee (*d*); and it would seem, also subjects disponed in trust to be conveyed over to the deceased. Subjects to be sold by trustees, and the produce divided, 'were' not conquest, but moveable estate (*e*). Heritable subjects which do not require sasine 'were' not conquest, but 'went' to the heir in heritage; as leases (*f*), personal bonds excluding executors (*g*). Teinds 'were' not conquest, as they affect the fruit, not the land (*h*).

(*a*) 3 Stair, 5. § 10. 3 Ersk. 8. § 14, etc. D. Hamilton *v.* E. Selkirk, 1740; M. 5554, 5615; 5 B. Sup. 684; 1 Cr. & St. 271; 2 Ill. 320. Robertson, *supra*, § 1671 (*d*). Pitcairn *v.* Pitcairn, as there quoted, M. 5607.

(*b*) A. *v.* B., 1675; M. 5608. Anderson *v.* Anderson, 1677; M. 5609.

(*c*) A. *v.* B., 1676; M. 2448. Menzies' Crs. *v.* Menzies, 1738; M. 5614; Elch. *Her. and Conq.* 2.

(*d*) D. Hamilton, *supra* (*a*). Miller *v.* Miller's Trs., 1831; 9 S. 295, and 7 W. & S. 1. Brown *v.* Campbell, 1855; 17 D. 759.

(*e*) See above, § 1482.
(*f*) E. Dunbar *v.* Heirs, 1625; M. 5605. Fergusson *v.* Fergusson, 1663; *ib.*
(*g*) Begbie *v.* Begbie, 1706; M. 5609. D. Hamilton, *supra* (*a*).
(*h*) Greenock *v.* Greenock, 1736; M. 5612; Elch. *Her. and Conq.* 1. It rather seems that teinds bought by a proprietor of lands went with the lands. See D. Hamilton, *supra.* Elch. *Her. and Conq.* 3. 1 M'Laren on Wills and Succ. 77. 3 Ersk. 8. § 47.

1673. Subjects which were truly heritage in the person of the deceased, 'did' not become conquest by the interposition of a conveyance in his favour (*a*).

(*a*) 2 Craig, 15. § 17. 3 Stair, 5. § 10. 3 Ersk. 8. § 15.

1674. Things which 'came' by force of destination, and 'were' taken up by service as heir of provision, 'were' not conquest, but heritage; as an estate coming to a middle brother by deed of entail (*a*).

(*a*) Boyd *v.* Boyd, 1774; M. 3070; Hailes, 577; see 2 Ill. 321. Mark the error in Brown's Synopsis, 85, *voce Her. and Conq.* See Miller *v.* Miller's Trs., 1831; 9 S. 295; aff. 7 W. & S. 1. Robison *v.* Robison, 1859; 21 D. 905. 1 M'Laren on Wills, etc., § 145.

1675. Conquest, in descending *from* the heir of conquest to his heir, 'became' heritage (*a*).

(*a*) 3 Ersk. 8. § 15.

1676. But it seems necessary to this effect that it should 'have been' *vested* in the heir of conquest by titles made up in his person; otherwise, remaining *in hæreditate jacente* of the acquirer, it 'would' go to *his* heir of conquest (*a*).

(*a*) Hope's Min. Pract. p. 770, § 47. Aitchison *v.* Aitchison, 1829; 7 S. 558; 2 Ill. 321.

1677. Rights of an Apparent Heir.—An apparent heir is the person who, after the succession has opened, is entitled to take it up as heir-at-law, but who has not yet made up his titles. Before the opening of the succession, he is only the *heir presumptive* (*a*).

'But it seems that, since the Conveyancing Act of 1874, possession as apparent heir is no longer an existing institution of the law of Scotland (*b*).'

(*a*) 3 Ersk. 8. § 54. Ragg *v.* Brown, 1708; M. 5260; 2 Ill. 322.
(*b*) See above, § 779A; but see § 1684, 2337, *infra*, and *qu.*?

1678. *Rights Vesting without Service.*—Some rights descend to, and are vested in, the apparent heir without any service; and he may enter into possession of the land, and is entitled to exercise even certain rights requiring sasine, before completing his title.

1679. Thus titles of honour and dignities require no service, but vest *ipso jure sanguinis* (*a*). 'Udal lands in Orkney and Shetland vest in the heir without service (*b*).'

(*a*) 3 Ersk. 8. § 77. See below, § 1825.
(*b*) Beatton *v.* Gaudie, 1832; 10 S. 286.

1680. Leases vest by mere apparency without service, to the effect not merely of possessing, but of transferring the right (*a*). 'The statute as to long leases does not appear to alter this rule, so far as the transmission of the right to the heir is concerned. But it provides that heirs who have been served by general or special service may complete their titles by recording in the Register of Sasines a notarial instrument, or without service by recording a writ of acknowledgment from the proprietor infeft (*b*).'

(*a*) Boyd *v.* Sinclair, 1671; M. 14,375; 2 Ill. 322. Hume *v.* Johnston, 1675; *ib.* Rattray *v.* Graham, 1623; M. 10,366; corrected by Campbell *v.* Cunningham, 1739; M. 14,375. Scott *v.* Baird, 1754; M. 14,376; 5 B. Sup. 814; aff. 6 Pat. 719. See below, § 1825. Murdoch *v.* Murdoch's Trs., 1863; 1 Macph. 330.
(*b*) 20 and 21 Vict. c. 26, § 8. 1 M'Laren on Wills, etc., § 182.

1681. Rights which run a course of future time vest without service (*a*).

(*a*) 3 Ersk. 8. § 77.

1682. *Right to Possession.*—An apparent heir may continue his ancestor's possession without a title (*a*), and cannot be disinherited of this right otherwise than by an effectual conveyance *inter vivos* or *mortis causa* (*b*). He may enter into the actual possession of the lands, etc.; may also continue the civil possession, and levy rents and interests (*c*); but he may not remove tenants deriving right from the deceased proprietor. To an effectual removing, whether under the old Act or under the Act of Sederunt, infeftment previous to decree is indispensable; the distinction having been little regarded in a recent case (*d*). His right to the rents vests *ipso jure*; so that on his death his executors take the unlevied rents or interests of the price of land sold (*e*).

(*a*) 3 Ersk. 8. § 58. Weir *v.* Drummond, 1664; M. 5244; 2 Ill. 322.
(*b*) Ross *v.* Ross, 1770; M. 5019. See below, § 1691, 1692.
(*c*) See the authorities in note (*c*); also 3 Stair, 5. § 2; 4 Stair, 26. § 4; and Ferguson *v.* Cowan, 1819; Hume, 222; and 20 D. 662, note. The L. J.-C. Inglis in Malcolm *v.* Dick, 1866, 5 Macph. 20, has been misreported.
(*d*) Ersk. *ut supra.* Paton *v.* M'Intosh, 1757; M. 5273. Sutherland *v.* Graham, 1759; M. 5276. Campbell *v.* M'Kellar, 1808; M. Apx. *Removing*, 8; 2 Ill. 213. John-

stone *v.* Martin, March 3, 1810; F. C. Scott *v.* Fisher, 1832; 10 S. 284. Mackenzie *v.* Gillanders, 1853; 16 D. 158; and above, § 1268 (*f*).

(*c*) Hamilton *v.* Hamilton, 1760; M. 5253; rev. 1767, 2 Paton, 137. L. Banff *v.* Joass, 1765; 5 B. Sup. 912. Spalding *v.* Spalding, 1792; M. 5257; Bell's Ca. 244. 3 Ersk. Pr. 8. 25, 16th ed. 1 Bell's Com. 99. 2 Hunter, L. & T. 304 sqq. E. Wemyss *v.* Campbell, 1864; 2 Macph. 461.

1683. *Power to challenge Ancestor's Deeds.*—The apparent heir 'was under the former law' entitled to challenge deeds done on death-bed (*a*). And it has been doubted whether he is not entitled to reduce any infeftment affecting the estate, to which as heir he has a right to succeed (*b*). The rule seems to be, that when the deed to be challenged is that of a former proprietor in the fee, and the heir challenges in his character of heir of provision under previous investitures, there must be a service. Where the challenge arises from the alleged inefficacy or illegality of the deed, as excluding the heir who would otherwise take, he may vindicate that right without service (*c*).

(*a*) Graham *v.* Graham, 1779; M. 3186; Hailes, 823; 2 Ill. 323. See as to Deathbed, below, § 1786.

(*b*) Cochran *v.* Ramsay, 1828; see 6 S. 773-4; 4 W. & S. 128; 2 Ill. 433.

(*c*) Rutherford *v.* Nisbet, 1830; 9 S. 3; 2 Ill. 323. Mr. Mackay (Practice of Ct. of Session, i. 286) states the principle (which is to be extracted from L. Moncreiff's note in the case cited) thus, that he may reduce deeds, and even infeftments, "where the right of challenge has first accrued to himself, and does not require to be transmitted by service to the previous proprietor." In other cases he must be infeft, or at least served in general. See 4 Stair, 20. § 14. Wilson *v.* Gilchrist's Trs., 1851; 13 D. 636. Dingwall *v.* Burns, 1871; 9 Macph. 582. See M'Andrew *v.* Reid, 1868; 6 Macph. 1063.

1684. An apparent heir may bring his ancestor's estate to judicial sale for debt, although the estate is not bankrupt (*a*).

(*a*) 1695, c. 24. See below, § 2337.

1685. *Annus Deliberandi.*—The heir is entitled to decline responsibility for his ancestor's debts; and in order to deliberate whether he shall do so, he 'was' allowed a year, computed from the ancestor's death; or from the heir's own birth if posthumous (*a*). But the term will not be prolonged on account of distance of the place in which the ancestor dies (*b*). If the apparent heir should die during the *annus deliberandi*, the next heir has the privilege of his own *annus deliberandi* from the death (*c*). During the *annus deliberandi*, the heir is not bound to answer in any action, in the defence whereof he must speak as heir (*d*), except in relation to the widow's jointure (*e*). But this privilege of deliberating is lost, 1. By service as heir; 2. By passive representation (*f*); and 3. It will not stop an action of judicial sale raised against the predecessor (*g*).

'The time of the heir's deliberation is now restricted to six months from the date of his becoming heir, so far as actions for attaching the heritable estate for debt are concerned, by the enactment that "actions of constitution and actions of constitution and adjudication against an apparent heir on account of his ancestor's debt, for the purpose of attaching the ancestor's heritable estate, and actions of adjudication against such heir on account of his own debt or obligation, may be insisted in at any time after the lapse" of that period (*h*).'

(*a*) 3 Ersk. 8. § 54. Summers *v.* Simson, 1757; M. 6882; 2 Ill. 324.

(*b*) Henderson *v.* Campbell, 1783; M. 5292; Hailes, 929.

(*c*) Stevenson *v.* Tweedie, 1649; 1 B. Sup. 422. Summers, *supra* (*a*).

(*d*) 3 Ersk. 8. § 55. Stewart *v.* Anderson, 1749; M. 6881.

(*e*) Pitcairn *v.* Welwood, 1702; M. 6876.

(*f*) Edgar *v.* Halliday, 1624; 1 B. Sup. 17. Hamilton *v.* Bonar, 1677; M. 6873. Ferguson *v.* M'Gachen, 1829; 7 S. 580.

(*g*) Campbell *v.* ——, 1708; M. 6877. Act of Sed., Nov. 23, 1711, § 5. 3 Ersk. 8. § 55.

(*h*) 31 and 32 Vict. c. 101, § 61, re-enacting 21 and 22 Vict. c. 76, § 27, and 23 and 24 Vict. c. 143, § 16. See below, § 1926.

1686. The heir must deal equally with his creditors in this matter; and the law will aid the creditors in accomplishing that object (*a*).

(*a*) Summers, *supra*, § 1685 (*a*). See Blair *v.* Brown, 1631; M. 6870. 3 Ersk. 8. § 55 *fin.* *Infra*, § 2337.

1687. Charges to enter heir cannot regularly proceed within the year. The charge may indeed be given during the year, and even the summons may be executed along with it; but no proceeding judicially can follow till the year, 'now six months, have' expired (*a*).

(*a*) Summers, *supra*, § 1685 (*a*). See M'Intosh *v.* M'Queen, 1829; 7. S. 882; 2 Ill. 325. See below, § 1858.

1688. *Exhibition ad Deliberandum* is an accessory of the right of deliberating, and entitles any apparent heir (*a*) to raise an action for exhibition of all deeds or obligations by which the state of the deceased's affairs may be explained, and so of all deeds relative to the predecessor's (*b*) land or estate, or debts owing by him. This action is not, in point of time, limited to the *annus deliberandi*, but may be raised any time before service (*c*). 'He does not seem to be entitled to delivery of the ancestor's title-deeds till he has expede a general service (*d*).'

(*a*) Crawford *v.* Crawford, 1714; M. 3986; 2 Ill. 325. Spark *v.* Barclay, 1715; M. 3988. Adair *v.* Adairs, 1787; M. 3992. See Campbell *v.* E. Breadalbane, 1868; 6 Macph. 632; aff. 1869, 7 Macph. H. L. 101.

(*b*) Fulton *v.* E. Eglinton, 1878; 5 R. 752.

(*c*) Nisbet *v.* Whitelaw, 1626; M. 3982. M'Farlane *v.* Buchanan, 1779; M. 3991; Hailes, 815.

(*d*) Smith *v.* Jackson, 1871; 10 Macph. 211.

1689. The heir may thus call (1) for deeds even in favour of strangers (*a*); (2) for deeds on which infeftment has followed (*b*); but (3) he may not call generally for all deeds, debts, etc., which may be hurtful or profitable to the heir (*c*). (4) Where the ancestor has been divested by infeftment on an entail or irredeemable disposition, the disponee is not bound to produce (*d*). (5) The ancestor is not divested by adjudication with infeftment, if the legal be not expired, and decree of declarator of expiry pronounced (*e*). 'And (6) it has been held that a disposition which leaves the formal title to the lands still in the granter's heirs, *e.g.* a general *mortis causa* disposition to trustees, is not a title which excludes the heir from inspection of his ancestor's titles (*f*).'

(*a*) Maxwell *v.* Maxwell, 1675; M. 4009; 2 Ill. 325. Buchanan *v.* M. of Montrose, 1705; M. 4010. Spark, *supra*, § 1688 (*a*).

(*b*) 4 Stair, 33. § 4. Spark, *supra*, § 1688 (*a*).

(*c*) Heron *v.* Heron, 1756; M. 4019.

(*d*) D. Hamilton *v.* Douglas, 1761; M. 3966. Cathcart *v.* E. Cassillis, 1795; M. 3993; and 1 W. & S. 240, 265. See Liddell *v.* Wilson, *infra* (*f*).

(*e*) M'Farlane, *supra*, § 1688 (*c*).

(*f*) Liddell *v.* Wilson, 1855; 18 D. 274. Douglas *v.* Holmes, 1854; 16 D. 1116. But see 31 and 32 Vict. c. 101, § 19, and M'Laren, Wills & Succn. ii. 364.

1690. *Liability of next Heir for Debts.*—'Although' the heritable estate 'did' not vest in the heir by mere survivance, yet as the possession and ostensible right of an apparent heir, when long continued, raises to him a credit as proprietor, it 'was' on equitable considerations enacted, that if such possession as apparent heir 'had' been continued for three years, his debts and onerous deeds 'should,' to the value of the estate, form a debt against the next heir who 'should' pass him over and make up titles to a previous ancestor (*a*).

(*a*) 1595, c. 24. See below, of Passive Titles, § 1929, 1914A, etc.

II. TESTATE SUCCESSION, OR BY DEED.

1691. Simple Deeds (*a*).—Succession by deed in Scotland depends, not on the nomination of an heir, but on an effectual conveyance of the heritage *intuitu mortis.* Hence the rule 'was' that in all heritable succession, 'opening by death before 31st December 1868 (*b*),' the legal descent 'took' effect, unless it 'were' altered by dispositive words of conveyance *de præsenti*, or substitution (*c*). The most clearly expressed will not only 'was' ineffectual to carry the land, but it 'was' not held to impose an obligation on the heir to implement (*d*). But a marriage contract, though containing only words of provision, and not of disposition, 'would' by force of the obligation be effectual (*e*).

(*a*) See below, § 1775, for conditional deeds of settlement.

(*b*) See below, § 1692A; Kirkpatrick, *infra* (*c*).

(*c*) 3 Ersk. 8. § 20. Henderson *v.* Henderson, 1667; M. 11,339; 2 Ill. 326. Simpson *v.* Barclay, 1752; Elch. *Test.* 12, and Notes, 486; 5 B. Sup. 794. Hamilton *v.* Douglas, 1762; M. 4368. See 2 Pat. 449–481, and 1 Ross' L. C. 10. **Ogilvie** *v.* **Mercer,** 1793; M. 3336; aff. 3 Pat. 434. Montgomery *v.* Innes & Fowlis, 1795; Bell's fol. Cases, 203. For these cases see 1 Ross' L. C. 1–16, 723 sqq. Govan *v.* Setons, Jan. 28, 1812; F. C. Reid, *infra* (*e*); 3 Ill. 760. See above, § 760. Glassford's Tr. (Howden) *v.* Glassford, 1864; 2 Macph. 1317. **Kirkpatrick** *v.* **Kirkpatrick's Trs.,** 1873; 11 Macph. 551; rev. 1874, 1 R. H. L. 37.

(*d*) Montgomery, *supra* (*c*). *Infra*, § 1692A.

(*e*) Reid *v.* Young, 1838; 16 S. 363.

1692. A proprietor cannot, 'except by force of the statutes of 1868 and 1874,' effectually dispose of Scottish heritage by will or testament (*a*); although the deed should be framed and executed in a country by the law of which real estate is disposable by will (*b*). Neither can he deprive the heir by mere words of disinherison (*c*). He must, 'apart from these statutes,' use dispositive words, either disponing the subject to himself, whom failing, to the person whom he wishes to favour; or giving it directly to that person, reserving his own liferent; or disponing and conveying the subject to another, reserving a power to alter (*d*).

The deed must either be delivered in evidence of final purpose; or it may be kept secret in the granter's repository, provided it bear a clause declaring it effectual though not delivered at his death (*e*); 'or, it seems, without such a clause, if it bear to be a *mortis causa* deed (*f*).'

It will not 'under the common law' invalidate the deed as a conveyance of heritage, if it should bear the form of a testament, provided words of conveyance *de præsenti* be made use of (*g*).

'When the heir is divested by a valid trust-disposition for purposes therein declared, or that may be declared by another writing, these purposes may, even according to the law prior to the statutes above mentioned, be declared by any writing valid by the law of the place where it is executed. If the heir be effectually excluded by the conveyance to the trustees, the question, what are the purposes, the ultimate intention, of the testator, is one of construction, not of technical conveyancing (*h*).'

An effectual conveyance *mortis causa* may be made in general terms; as "of all lands and heritage belonging to me." But such general disposition (*i*) will not carry a mere *spes successionis*, or estate which has not opened to the disponer during his life; or at least, in order to carry such right, it ought to be specially mentioned, or described and conveyed (*k*). 'The effect of the words of a general disposition depends on the presumed intention of the granter. Such a disposition does not derogate from or "evacuate" a prior special destination by the testator himself of a particular estate, unless it be clearly his intention to do so; nor does it defeat a special destination of subjects acquired by the testator after its date. But it defeats a special destination (*l*) in a deed by another man under which the granter was at the date of the general disposition vested in the fee of a particular estate, unless his contrary intention be clear. In order to ascertain his intention, evidence not only of the circumstances surrounding the maker of the deed, but also, contrary to the general rule of evidence, of subsequent deeds and dealings in respect to the property, is admissible (*m*). It prevails over a general destination to heirs and assignees in a disposition of subjects subsequently acquired by the granter (*n*); but its operation will be excluded in such a case by a special destination, or other pregnant circumstances indicating a different intention (*o*).

'Under the older form of conveyancing a *mortis causa* general disponee completed his title to the disponer's lands, where the disponer's heir refused to make up a title and convey to him, by an action of constitution and adjudication in implement (*p*). Since the passing of the Titles to Land Acts of 1858 and 1860, the general disponee records a notarial instrument in a statutory form, proceeding upon the settlement or will, or on an extract or letters of administration of it, which is equivalent to a recorded instrument of sasine in the lands contained in the instrument; and this may follow upon two or more successive general dispositions, although they do not contain an assignation of writs (*q*).'

(*a*) 3 M'Kenzie, 8. 3 Stair, 4. § 31. 3 Ersk. 8. § 20. Brand *v.* Brand, 1735; M. 15,941; 2 Ill. 327. Stewart *v.* Stewart, 1803; 1 Sandf. on Her. Suc. 62; Hume, 880. *Infra*, § 1863.

(*b*) Hendersons *v.* Murray, 1623; M. 4481. Melvil *v.* Drummond, 1634; M. 4483. Burgess *v.* Stantin, 1764; M. 4484. Crawfurds *v.* Crawfurd, 1774; M. 4486. Robertson's Crs. *v.* Mason, 1795; M. 4491. Henderson *v.* Selkrig, 1795; M. 4489. Snodgrass *v.* Buchanan, 1806; M. *Serv. of H.* Apx. 1. Ross *v.* Ross, July 4, 1809; F. C. (bonds excluding executors; 2 Ill. 328). See below, Studd *v.* Studd (Cook), § 1692A (*a*), (*d*).

(*c*) Ross, *supra* (*b*). Blackwood *v.* Dykes, 1833; 11 S. 443. See above, § 1683, 1691 (*c*).

(*d*) Mitchell *v.* Wright, 1759; M. 8082. Robertson *v.* Robertson, 1785; M. 15,947. **Ogilvie** *v.* **Mercer,** 1793; M. 3336; aff. 3 Pat. 434. Galloway, petr., 1802; M. 15,950. See above, § 1691 (*c*). A settlement of heritage may be in the form of a procuratory of resignation. 3 Stair, 2. § 8. **Renton** *v.* **Anstruther,** 1837; 16 S. 184; 1842, 6 D. 230; aff. 1843, 2 Bell's App. 214; 1 Ross' L. C. 21; 2 *ib.* 435. On the question whether an invalid settlement operates as a revocation of a previous valid deed, see cases cited *infra*, § 1810 seq., 1866, 1940; and **Kirkpatrick,** § 1691 (*c*).

(*e*) 3 Ersk. 2. § 43-4. See *supra*, § 24, and cases there. Anderson *v.* Robertson, 1867; 5 Macph. 503.

(*f*) 3 Ersk. 2. § 44. M. Bell's Convg. 109. Duff's Feud. Conv. § 20. Duff on Deeds, § 85. *Supra*, § 24.

(*g*) Douglas *v.* Allan, 1733; M. 15,940. Brown *v.* Bower, 1770; M. 5440. Welsh *v.* Cairnie, June 28, 1809; F. C. Glover *v.* Brough, Dec. 7, 1810; F. C.; 1 Ross' L. C. 98.

(*h*) **Willoch** *v.* **Auchterlony,** 1769; M. 5539; Hailes, 321; aff. 3 Pat. 659. **Cameron** *v.* **Mackie,** 1831; 9 S. 601; aff. 1834, 7 W. & S. 106; 1 Ross' L. C. 406. Richmond's Trs. *v.* Winton, 1864; 3 Macph. 95. Bankes *v.* Bankes' Trs., 1882; 9 R. 1046. See below, § 1997. As to the competent form of writings of instructions, see the cases cited, and those in § 1868, *infra*.

(*i*) A general disposition of lands is a "conveyance which, from the want of a full description of the lands, or from the want of proper feudal clauses, does not of itself constitute a sufficient warrant to the disponee to obtain infeftment directly, by recording the deed in the Register of Sasines, or by expeding and recording an instrument of sasine." *Per* L. Watson in **Studd** *v.* **Cook,** 1883; 10 R. H. L. 53; 8 App. Ca. 577. As to real burdens in a general disposition, see above, § 919 (*a*).

(*k*) Farquharsons (Mearns, etc.) *v.* Farquharson, 1756; M. 2290; aff. 1759, 6 Pat. 724. Macdowall *v.* Russell, 1824; 2 S. 682; 2 Ill. 351. Leitch's Tr. (Smith) *v.* Leitch, 1826; 4 S. 659; aff. 1829, 3 W. & S. 366. See below, of Settlements by Trust-deed, § 1991 et seq.

(*l*) Watson's Trs. *v.* Hamilton, 1894; 21 R. 451; aff. *ib.* H. L. 35; 1894, A. C. 310.

(*m*) Farquharson, *cit.* Campbell *v.* Campbell, 1740; M.

14,855; 1743, 1 Pat. 343. Thoms *v.* Thoms, 1868; 6 Macph. 704. **Glendonwyn** *v.* **Gordon,** 1870; 8 Macph. 1075; aff. 1873, 11 Macph. H. L. 33; L. R. 2 Sc. App. 320. Catton *v.* Mackenzie, 1870; 8 Macph. 1049; 1872, 10 Macph. H. L. 12. Gray *v.* Gray's Trs., 1878; 5 R. 820. Walker's Exr. *v.* Walker, 1878; 5 R. 965. Campbell *v.* Campbell, 1878; 6 R. 310; aff. 1880; 7 R. H. L. 100. Walker *v.* Galbraith, 1895; 23 R. 347. See below, § 1866.

(*n*) 3 Ersk. 8. § 47. Robson *v.* Robson, 1794; M. 14,958. Philip *v.* Philip, 1885; 13 R. 329.

(*o*) Webster *v.* Webster, 1876; 4 R. 101. Farquharson *v.* Farquharson, 1883; 10 R. 1253.

(*p*) *Supra*, § 835. Glover, and cases in note (*g*).

(*q*) 31 and 32 Vict. c. 101, § 19, re-enacting 8 and 9 Vict. c. 31, § 4; 21 and 22 Vict. c. 76, § 12; and 23 and 24 Vict. c. 143, § 6. Smith *v.* Wallace, 1869; 8 Macph. 204. 37 and 38 Vict. c. 94, § 29. 50 and 51 Vict. c. 69, § 5. See above, § 782; and below, § 1692A *fin.*

1692A. 'It is competent for any owner of heritage who was alive at or after 31st Dec. 1868, to settle the succession to it at his death not only by conveyance *de præsenti*, but also by testamentary or *mortis causa* deed. No testamentary or *mortis causa* deed or writing purporting to convey or bequeath lands, granted after that date, or even before that date by any person who survived it, is invalid as a settlement of the lands to which it applies, on the ground that the word "dispone" or other word of present conveyance has not been used. But if such a deed uses with reference to heritage language sufficient in a testament of moveables to give to the granter's executor, or grantee, or legatee, a right to claim and receive such moveables, it is equivalent, if duly executed in the manner required or permitted in the case of any testamentary writing by the law of Scotland (*a*), to a general disposition of the heritage, creating an obligation on the granter's successors to make up titles to the lands, and convey them to the grantee or legatee. The grantee completes his title to the lands in the same manner and to the same effect as if the deed or writing had been a general disposition, *i.e.* either under the conveyancing statutes by notarial instrument, or by action of constitution and adjudication in implement (*b*). Although technical words, or even words of direct conveyance or gift, are not required, there must be clear specification of what is intended to be conveyed; and the words used must not be inapplicable to lands. Thus, *e.g.*, a general bequest of "effects" does not embrace any kind of heritage (*c*). But no particular form of words is required to operate a conveyance of heritage; and although there be no direct words of gift or conveyance, it is enough if the testator's intention to convey heritage can be gathered from the whole terms of the writing (*d*). It is enacted by the Conveyancing Act of 1874 that general dispositions forming links in a series of titles are not invalid because they do not contain an assignation of writs; and that decrees, instruments, or conveyances are not invalid because they proceed on series of titles in which two or more of the links are general dispositions (*e*).'

(*a*) Therefore as a will executed abroad according to the form of the place of execution was always valid to carry moveables in Scotland, it is now sufficient, if it expresses such an intention, to carry heritable property. Connel's Trs. *v.* Connel, 1872; 10 Macph. 627. See 24 and 25 Vict. c. 114. Purvis' Trs. *v.* Purvis' Exrs., 1861; 23 D. 812. Guthrie's Savigny's International Law, 321, 323, 325.

(*b*) 31 and 32 Vict. c. 101, § 20. See *ib.* § 19; 37 and 38 Vict. c. 94, § 27. Smith *v.* Wallace, 1869; 8 Macph. 204. Robb's Trs. *v.* Robb, 1872; 10 Macph. 692. See above, § 782 *fin.*, 835.

(*c*) Pitcairn *v.* Pitcairn, 1870; 8 Macph. 604. Hardy's Trs. *v.* Hardy, 1871; 9 Macph. 736 (terms of trust conveyance held to carry a lease). Edmond *v.* Edmond, 1873; 11 Macph. 348. M'Leod's Trs. *v.* M'Leod, 1875; 2 R. 481. Urquhart *v.* Dewar, 1879; 6 R. 1026 (executor directed to divide "residue of estate," not conveyance of heritage). Farquharson *v.* Farquharson, 1883; 10 R. 1253 ("goods, gear, debts, effects, sums of money, heritable and moveable," etc., does not carry land—surrounding circumstances and subsequent actings aid in construction. See above, § 1692). Ford's Trs. *v.* Ford, 1884; 11 R. 1129.

(*d*) M'Leod's Tr. *v.* M'Luckie, 1883; 10 R. 1056 ("property wherever situated"). Aim's Tr. *v.* Aim, 1880; 8 R. 294. Campbell *v.* Campbell, 1887; 15 R. 103 ("means and estate" limited by context). Grant *v.* Morren, 1893; 20 R. 404 (ditto). Wallace's Exrs. *v.* Wallace, 1895; 23 R. 142 ("residuary legatee" in will disposing expressly of heritage and moveables, carries heritage on predecease of donee of heritage). Forsyth *v.* Turnbull, 1887; 15 R. 172 ("means and effects"). Cases in note (*c*). See § 1694 (*g*). As to a conveyance in the technical language of a foreign country, see Studd *v.* Studd (Studd *v.* Cook), 1880; 8 R. 249; aff. 1883, 10 R. H. L. 53; 8 App. Ca. 577.

(*e*) 37 and 38 Vict. c. 94, § 29. See above, § 782.

1693. Deeds with Substitutions (*a*).—Substitution is commonly indicated by the words "whom failing"; but may also be indicated by the words "then to," or by the words "and to" (*b*). The first disponee is Institute; those who are appointed to take the subject on his death are Substitutes. The dispositive words are applied provisionally to the substitutes, and to those who come in by a power of nomination, as directly as to the institute. Those words contained in the dispositive clause give the rule or law of succession to the subject conveyed (*c*). They do not, as in moveable succession, establish, 'in the absence of contrary indication, no more than' a conditional institution, to take effect only in case the institute should not take; bestowing no right on the substitute if the institute should succeed. If the institute shall take, and afterwards die, the property descends to the heirs and substitutes to whom by the deed it is destined (*d*). 'A substitution, however, in a destination of heritable estate implies a conditional institution in the event of the persons previously named predeceasing the granter (*e*).' When ambiguous, the dispositive clause may be interpreted by the precept or procuratory of the deed, or from the whole strain and purpose of it (*f*).

(*a*) See also below, § 1717 et seq.
(*b*) Richardson *v.* Stewart, 1824; 2 S. App. 149; 2 Ill. 330. Lockhart *v.* Macdonald (Largie Case), *infra*, § 1700. L. Polwarth's Case (H. of L., 1835); 2 Ill. 332. Edward *v.* Shiell, 1848; 10 D. 685.
(*c*) Shanks *v.* Kirk-Session of Ceres, 1797; M. 4295. Sutherland *v.* Sinclair, 1801; M. Apx. *Tailzie*, 8. Grahame *v.* Grahame, June 20, 1816; F. C.; aff. 1825, 1 W. & S. 353. Tinnoch *v.* M'Lewnan, Nov. 26, 1817; F. C. Richardson, *supra* (*b*). Forrester *v.* Hutchison, 1826; 4 S. 824. See below, § 1744. Young's Trs. *v.* Young, 1867; 5 Macph. 1101.
(*d*) 3 Ersk. 8. § 44. Watson *v.* Giffen, 1884; 11 R. 444. See below, § 1881.
(*e*) Colquhoun *v.* Colquhoun, 1828; 7 S. 200; rem. 1831, 5 W. & S. 32; 9 S. 911; 2 Ill. 426. **Fogo** *v.* **Fogo**, 1840; 2 D. 651; rem. 1841, 2 Rob. 440; 1842, 4 D. 1063; aff. 1843, 2 Bell's App. 195; 2 Ross' L. C. 36. Grant's Trs. *v.* Grant, 1862; 24 D. 1211. See § 1839.
(*f*) See Shanks, Sutherland, and Forrester (*c*). Miller *v.* Miller, 1831; 9 S. 295; aff. 1833, 7 W. & S. 1. Halliday *v.* Maxwell, 1802; 4 Pat. 346. Above, § 760.

1694. (1.) *Construction* (*a*).—In construing technical words used for describing the several classes of heirs, the rule is to adhere to that meaning which has been fixed on the words; and not to yield to extraneous indications of a different intention, arising either from the narrative (*b*), or from other deeds (*c*), or from parole 'or other' evidence of purpose and meaning (*d*), or from the construction deducible from the operation being for election purposes without any design of altering the succession (*e*). Nothing, in short, but an express declaration or necessary implication is admitted to alter the settled meaning of words of destination (*f*). Where technical words are not used, the question must depend on the *voluntas testatoris*, to be collected from the whole strain and purpose of the deed (*g*).

(*a*) See below, § 1871, 1879.
(*b*) Campbell *v.* Campbells, 1770; M. 14,949; 2 Ill. 332. **Hay** *v.* **Hay** (Linplum Case), 1788; M. 2315; aff. 1789, 3 Pat. 142. See L. Eldon's remarks on that case in the **Roxburghe Cause**, 6 W. & S. Apx. 62; 2 Ill. 332.
(*c*) D. Hamilton *v.* E. Selkirk, 1740; M. 14,935, 5615; 2 Ill. 333; Elch. *Her. and Conq.* 3; 5 B. Sup. 684; 1 Cr. St. & P. 271.
(*d*) D. Hamilton *v.* Douglas, 1762; M. 4369; 5 B. Sup. 467. Baillie *v.* Tennant, 1766; M. 14,941; rev. 1770, 2 Pat. 243. Murray *v.* Flint, 1774; M. 14,952. Ball *v.* Coutts, 1806; 17 F. C. 344. Blair *v.* Blair, 1849; 12 D. 97 (written instructions).
(*e*) Rose *v.* Rose, 1784; M. 14,955. Sutties *v.* Sutties, Jan. 19, 1809; F. C. Molle *v.* Riddell, Dec. 13, 1811; F. C.; aff. 1816, 6 Pat. 168; 2 Ill. 69, 334.
(*f*) **Innes** *v.* **Ker (Roxburghe Cause)**, 1807; M. *Tailzie*, Apx. 13; 1810, 5 Pat. 320; 2 Ill. 334; Sandf. on Suc. Apx.; 6 W. & S. Apx.; 2 Ill. 332, 334. Gordon *v.* Gordon's Trs., 1866; 4 Macph. 501. Braid *v.* Waddell, 1860; 22 D. 433. Connell *v.* Grierson, 1867; 5 Macph. 379. § 1692A (*d*).
(*g*) Smith *v.* Stewarts, 1830; 9 S. 180. Bryden *v.* Grierson, 1831; 9 S. 457; aff. 1835, 6 W. & S. 354. Martin *v.* Kelso, 1853; 15 D. 950. Swinton's Tr. *v.* Swinton, 1862; 24 D. 278.

1695. (2.) *Meaning of Destinations to Heirs.*—It is important to mark the proper use and meaning of the words descriptive of the several classes of heirs:

"Heirs," in a destination, is a technical expression including all those who are heirs by law; namely, heirs of Line, heirs of Conquest, and heirs of Investiture.

1696. "Heir of Line" 'might' sometimes mean the heir of conquest. It is synonymous with heir-at-law, heir-general, heir whatsoever (*a*).

(*a*) 2 Stair, 5. § 10. See above, § 1670; below, § 1701. Sillars's Trs. *v.* Stewart (Glen *v.* S.), 1872; 11 Macph. 160; aff. 1874, 1 R. H. L. 48 (heir-at-law).

1697. "Heir-male" applies only to males connected by males; exclusive of females, and also of males connected by females.

1698. "Heir-male of Line," though apparently an incongruous expression, is not so. It means the heir-male, excluding the heir of conquest (*a*).

(*a*) Sinclair *v.* E. Fife, 1766; M. 14,944; aff. April 6, 1767; 2 Ill. 366.

1699. "Heir-female" applies to the heir-at-law, male or female, failing heirs-male (*a*).

(*a*) 3 Ersk. 8. § 48. **Bargany Case (Dalrymple** *v.* **Hope)**, 1738; Elch. *Prov. to Heirs*, 2; rev. 1 Cr. St. & P. 237; 2 Ill. 336. Lyon *v.* Blair, 1739; 5 B. Sup. 663; Sandford on Entails, 64. Ewing *v.* Miller, 1747; M. 2308. See L. P. Blair's remarks on this case in Ker *v.* Ker, Nov. 13, 1810; F. C. Johnstone *v.* Johnstone, 1839; 2 D. 73. **Connell** *v.* **Grierson**, 1867; 5 Macph. 379. Innes *v.* Ker, *infra*, § 1700.

1700. "Heir-male of the Body" is to be distinguished from heir-male. He is not necessarily a son born of the person named, but must be in the direct line of descent (*a*).

(*a*) Forrester *v.* Hutchison, 1826; 4 S. 824; 2 Ill. 331. Innes *v.* Ker, *cit.* § 1694. Lockhart *v.* Macdonald (Largie Case), 1837; 15 S. 376; 1840, 2 D. 377; aff. 1842, 1 Bell's App. 202. Johnstone *v.* Johnstone, 1839; 2 D. 73. E. Eglinton *v.* Montgomerie, 1842; 4 D. 425. Braid *v.* Waddell, 1860; 22 D. 433 (heirs-male lawfully begotten).

1701. "Heirs whatsoever," or "Heirs whomsoever," seems to have been an expression first used to prevent the fee from reverting to the superior on the failure of heirs-male (*a*). At present it is useful only in limited destinations. When an antecedent limitation gives the succession to a particular order of heirs, the general word "heirs" used in a subsequent deed must be understood not of the heir-at-law, but of the heir in the former destination. But the expression "heirs whatsoever" has a different meaning, and enlarges the destination to heirs-at-law (*b*). The expression "heirs whatsoever" is a flexible term to a certain extent, with this observance always, that it is not to give way to any construction arising on *supposed* intention, but is to be bent from its natural and proper signification to a more limited sense only when that is necessary in order to give a meaning to what is not otherwise intelligible, and where it can be said to be demonstrative of intention. It may take its construction from other more specific clauses of destination (*c*).

(*a*) 2 Craig, 14. § 3.

(*b*) Correct 3 Ersk. 8. § 47, by M. Clydesdale *v.* E. Dundonald, 1727; M. 14,930; 2 Ill. 337. D. Hamilton *v.* E. Selkirk, *cit.* § 1694 (*c*). Brodies *v.* Brodie, 1749; 5 B. Sup. 466. D. Hamilton *v.* Douglas, 1762; M. 4369; 1777, 5 B. Sup. 467. Richardson *v.* Stewart, 1824; 2 S. App. 149; 2 Ill. 330.

(*c*) 3 Stair, 5. § 12. 3 Ersk. 8. § 48. Hay *v.* Crawford, 1698; M. 14,899. Greenock *v.* Greenock, 1736; M. 5612. D. Hamilton, *cit.* § 1694 (*c*). Maclauchlan *v.* Campbell, 1757; M. 2312. Richardson, *supra* (*b*). Hay *v.* Hay, 1788; M. 2315; 2 Ill. 332, note. See below, § 1723. Sillars's Trs., *supra*, § 1696. M'Gregor *v.* Gordon, 1864; 3 Macph. 148, 168 (*per* L. Cowan). Gordon *v.* Gordon's Trs., 1881; 9 R. 50; aff. 1882, *ib.* H. L. 101. E. Northesk *v.* Paul, 1882; 10 R. 77.

1702. Great care is necessary—1. In distinguishing the right character of heir, when more than one character concurs in the same person (*a*). 2. In settling which is the governing term. 3. The effect produced or pleadable, by the mingling of popular with technical language, as *daughter* used along with *heir-female*, is important (*b*).

(*a*) Dalyell *v.* Dalyell, May 30, 1809; F. C.; 2 Ill. 338. **Bargany Case (Dalrymple v. Hope)**, 1738; Elch. *Prov. to Heirs*, 2, Notes, 370; 1 Cr. St. & P. 237; 2 Ill. 336. Lyon *v.* Blair, 1739; 5 B. Sup. 663; Sandford on Entails, 64. **Lady Essex Ker v. Ker**, Nov. 13, 1810; F. C.; aff. 1812, 5 Pat. 579. M. Hastings *v.* Hastings, 1844; 7 D. 1; 1841, 6 Bell's App. 3. Fullerton *v.* Hamilton, 1824; 2 S. 698; 1825, 1 W. & S. 410.

(*b*) See cases, *supra* (*a*). Redhouse's Crs. *v.* Glass, 1743; M. 2306; aff. 1744; see Elch. Notes, 373; 1 Cr. St. & P. 372; 6 Pat. 681. Kilk. remarks on Ewing *v.* Miller, 1747; M. 2308. Ker, *supra* (*a*). Shepherd *v.* Grant, 1836; 15 S. 173; aff. 1838, 3 S. & M'L. 255. Lockhart *v.* Macdonald, *cit.* § 1700. M. Hastings, *cit.*

1703. Ambiguity in construction may arise in point of time; the effect, where one is mentioned out of the ordinary line of succession (as daughter or eldest daughter, or second son), being very different according to the point of time to which the expression refers. The general rule seems to be, that the reference is not to the time of making the deed, but to the opening of the succession (*a*).

(*a*) **Innes v. Ker (Roxburghe Case)**, *cit.* § 1694. Shepherd, *supra*, § 1702 (*b*).

1704. A destination to A. includes his heirs; but an immediate substitution of one person to another excludes the heirs of the institute (*a*), unless in deeds by parents to children. A substitution by name after heirs of another, takes effect only when the whole line of descent of the institute is exhausted; and so a destination to one and his heirs-male, followed by a substitution, brings in all the heirs-male before the substitute, and is not confined to heirs-male of the body (*b*). Such destinations may be altered gratuitously.

(*a*) Forsyth *v.* Fergusson, 1832; 10 S. 646; 2 Ill. 340. See below, § 1776, 1989. Watson *v.* Giffen, 1884; 11 R. 444.

(*b*) Baillie *v.* Tennant, 1766; M. 14,941; rev. 2 Pat. 243. See 6 W. & S. Apx. 79; 2 Ill. 333.

1705. (3.) *A Clause of Return* provides that the subject shall return to the granter and his heirs (*a*). In general, and in the line of succession, it has no stronger effect than a simple destination (*b*). It has in the construction of such a clause been conceived—1. That in a gratuitous conveyance to a stranger disponee, a clause of return is a condition; and the disponee has no power gratuitously to disappoint the return (*c*). 2. That if the deed be onerous, or the deed to heirs *alioquin successuri*, the clause of return is defeasible (*d*).

(*a*) See Watson's Trs. *v.* Hamilton, 1894; 21 R. 451; aff. *ib.* H. L. 35; 1894, A. C. 310.

(*b*) 3 Ersk. 8. § 45. D. Hamilton *v.* Douglas, 1763; M.

4358 ; 5 B. Sup. 467 ; 2 Ill. 341. M. Clydesdale *v.* E. Dundonald, 1726 ; M. 4343, 1262 ; Robertson's Ap. 564.

(*c*) D. Douglas *v.* Lockhart, 1717 ; M. 4343. See Duff *v.* Gordon, 1807 ; M. *Memb. of Parl.* Apx. No. 13. Johnston *v.* Mags. of Canongate, 1804 ; M. 15,112.

(*d*) M'Kay *v.* Campbell's Trs., 1835 ; 13 S. 246.

1706. (4.) *Power to name Heirs.*—Sometimes a branch of the destination is introduced in the shape of a power to name heirs; and if duly exercised, the nomination is effectual as part of the substitution accruing to and becoming part of the original investiture (*a*).

(*a*) **Stewart *v.* Porterfield**, 1821 ; 1 S. 9 ; 1826, 2 W. & S. 369 ; 1829, 8 S. 16 ; 1831, 5 W. & S. 515 ; 2 Ill. 342. See above, § 1693. Martin *v.* Kelso, 1853 ; 15 D. 950. E. Strathmore *v.* Strathmore's Trs., 1837 ; 15 S. 449 ; aff. 1840, 1 Rob. 189.

CHAPTER III

OF FEE AND LIFERENT

1707. Nature of Fee and Liferent.—The full and unlimited right of a proprietor is called FEE: the inferior right of usufruct during life is called LIFERENT. These rights may subsist at one and the same time in different persons existing (*a*). 'A liferent estate in land in Scotland can be granted since August 14, 1848, only in favour of a person in life at the date of the grant; and any person of full age holding any land or estate in liferent by virtue of a deed dated on or after August 1, 1848, is not, if born after the date of the deed, affected by any prohibitions, restrictions, conditions, or limitations contained in the deed, or by which the same or his interest therein may bear to be qualified; and he is deemed and taken to be the fee-simple proprietor (*i.e.* fiar) of such estate. And he may obtain and record an act and decree of the Court of Session giving effect to his right (*b*). A similar enactment relates to such persons possessing under trust-deeds (*c*) and leases tending to defeat the Entail Amendment Act (*d*).'

(*a*) See above, § 939 and 1037.
(*b*) 11 and 12 Vict. c. 36, § 48 (Rutherfurd Act). See below, § 1951.
(*c*) *Ib.* § 47. (*d*) *Ib.* § 49.

1708. The right of fee may be held jointly by more than one *pro indiviso*. The settling of the validity and effect of those several rights in different situations is of great practical importance.

1709. Conjunct Fee.—With regard to conjunct fee in strangers (*a*)—1. When a subject is conveyed in "conjunct fee" to two or more strangers, they enjoy the subject in common *pro indiviso*; the heir of each succeeding him on his death, and taking up his *pro indiviso* share along with the survivor. 2. Where the right is "in conjunct fee and liferent," the parties are joint fiars during their joint lives; but the survivor enjoys his own fee of the one half, and a liferent of the other; the heir of the predeceaser being excluded till the death of the survivor. 3. Where the right is taken to the parties "jointly, and the survivor and their heirs," the survivor has the fee; and it descends to *his* heir, not to the heirs of both by a renewal of the joint right. 4. Where the destination is to the parties, and "the heirs of one of them," that person whose heirs are preferred has the fee (*b*).

(*a*) The doctrine of conjunct fee and liferent to husband and wife, or parent and child, will be better understood in considering contracts of marriage. See below, § 1950 et seq. It seems, notwithstanding the words "in strangers" used here, that there is no authority for giving to the words "conjunct fee," in a destination to spouses, a different construction from that which would be put on them in a destination to persons not connected by marriage. *Per curiam* in Walker *v.* Galbraith, 1895; 23 R. 347.
(*b*) 2 Stair, 3. § 41. 3 Ersk. 8. § 35. Bisset *v.* Walker, 1799; M. *Deathbed*, Apx. 2.

1710. Fee in Pendente.—The law of Scotland does not recognise a fee in a pendent state, *i.e.* where there is no person alive to take it up.

1711. The principle on which this rests is, that the superior on the one hand, and the vassal on the other, must have some one to fill the feudal place of vassal or superior; and that creditors shall be able to know with whom the right of property is. The fee, therefore, is not *in pendente* merely by the death of the proprietor; for the creditors of the ancestor can affect it as *in hæreditate* *jacente*, and the heir, or anyone in his right, can take it; while in the feudal relation of superior and vassal the remedy is open to either. It is *in pendente* only when there is no one in whom it can be vested. In order to avoid the difficulty arising from the fee being thus *in pendente*, certain rules have been settled, now to be explained (*a*).

(*a*) See Newlands *v.* Newlands' Crs. and Frog's Crs. *v.* Children, and other cases in § 1712 (*d*). Williamson *v.* Cochrane, § 1713. M'Intosh *v.* M'Intosh, Jan. 28, 1812; F. C.; 3 Ross' L. C. 708. Ferguson's Trs. *v.* Hamilton, 1860; 22 D. 1442 (esp. *per* L. Wood, p. 1456); aff. 1862, 24 D. H. L. 8; 4 Macq. 397.

1712. Construction of Fee and Liferent.—Much confusion has arisen from the loose way in which the words fee and liferent have been used by conveyancers. In common language they are quite distinct: Liferent importing a life interest merely; Fee a full right of property in reversion after a liferent. But the proper meaning of the word liferent has sometimes been confounded by a combination with the word fee, so as in some degree to lose its appropriate sense, and occasionally to import a fee. This seems to have begun chiefly in destinations to "husband and wife in conjunct fee and liferent, and children in fee"; where the true meaning is, that each spouse has a joint liferent while both live, but that each has a *possible fee*, as it is uncertain which is to survive (*a*). The same confusion of terms came to be extended to the case of a destination to parent and child,—"To A. B. in liferent, and the heirs of the marriage in fee,"—where the word liferent was held to confer a fee on the parent (*b*). It gradually came to be held as the technical meaning of the words "liferent to a parent, with a fee to his children *nascituri*," 'that is to say, unnamed and (or) unborn,—children as a class (*c*),' that the word liferent meant a fee in the father (*d*). And the expression was held as strictly limited to its proper meaning of liferent by the accompanying word "allenarly," or some similar expression of restriction (*e*); or where the fee was given to children *nati* and *nominatim*, there being in that case no necessity to divert the word liferent from its proper meaning, 'the children named taking an absolute fee for themselves and a fiduciary fee for those unborn'; or (on a similar principle) where the settlement was by means of a trust created to take up the fee (*f*), 'and to *hold* for the parent in liferent and children in fee (*g*).'

Such being the progress of the professional use of those words, and the gradual clearing away of the confusion arising from a vague and loose employment of them, the following seem to be the rules of legal construction of such settlements. 'And they are applied to destinations of moveables as well as of land (*h*), but not to leases (*i*).'

(*a*) Pearson *v.* Martin, 1665; M. 4249; 2 Ill. 343. Truly it imports a liferent in the husband during the marriage, even when the property comes from the wife under an antenuptial contract. Thom *v.* Thom, 1852; 14 D. 862.

(*b*) Thomson *v.* Lawson, 1681; M. 4258. Paterson's Crs. *v.* Anderson, 1705; M. 4259.

(*c*) Lindsay *v.* Dott, *cit.* (*d*). Ferguson's Trs. *v.* Hamilton, *infra* (*h*). Porterfield *v.* Graham, *infra*, § 1714.

(*d*) Frog's Crs. *v.* His Children, 1735; M. 4262; 3 Ross' L. C. 602. Lillie *v.* Riddell, 1741; M. 4267; Elch. *Fiar*, 7. Douglas *v.* Ainslie, 1761; M. 4269. Dewar *v.* Campbell, 1825; 1 W. & S. 161; 2 Ill. 348. Lindsay *v.* Dott, 1807; M. Apx. *Fiar*, 1. **Gordon** *v.* **M'Intosh**, 1841; 4 D. 192; aff. 1845, 4 Bell's App. 124; 3 Ross' L. C. 617. Mackellar *v.* Marquis, 1840; 3 D. 172. Fulton *v.* King, 1811; Hume, 533. See the cases in 3 Ross' L. C. 602 sqq.

(*e*) Gerran *v.* Alexander, 1781; M. 4402. **Newlands** *v.* **Newlands' Crs.**, 1794; M. 4289; Bell's Ca. 54; aff. 4 Pat. 43; 3 Ross' L. C. 634; 2 Ill. 347. See Ferguson *v.* Ferguson, 1875; 2 R. 627. Thomson *v.* Thomsons, 1794; Bell's Ca. 72; 1 Dow, 417; 5 Pat. 654. Watherston *v.* Renton, 1801; M. 4297. Harvey *v.* Donald, May, 26, 1815; F. C. Dewar, *supra* (*d*). Allardice *v.* Allardice, 1795; Bell's Ca. 156. Scotts *v.* Napier (Crombie), 1826; 4 S. 454; 1827, 2 W. & S. 550. Fisher *v.* Dixon, 1833; 6 W. & S. 431. See below, § 1714. Studd *v.* Studd (Studd *v.* Cook), 1880; 8 R. 249; aff. 1883, 10 R. H. L. 53; 8 App. Ca. 577. Bryson *v.* Munro's Trs., 1893; 20 R. 986.

(*f*) Seton *v.* Seton's Crs., March 1793; M. 4219. *Infra*, § 1715, 1958. Macgowan *v.* Robb, 1861; 1 Macph. 141; 2 Macph. 943. Martin's Trs. *v.* Milliken, 1864; 3 Macph. 326. Dykes *v.* Boyd, June 3, 1813; F. C. M'Intosh *v.* M'Intosh, Jan. 28, 1812; F. C.

(*g*) Ross *v.* King, 1847; 9 D. 1327. *Infra*, § 1715. If the trustees are to *pay* to the father in liferent and children in fee, the father has a fee. Hutton's Trs. and Ferguson's Trs., *infra*, § 1713.

(*h*) Mure *v.* Mure, 1786; M. 4288. Mein *v.* Taylor, *infra*, § 1713 (*a*). M'Donald *v.* M'Lachlan, 1831; 9 S. 269. Gordon *v.* M'Intosh, 1841; 4 D. 192; aff. 1845, 4 Bell's App. 105. **Ferguson's Trs.** *v.* **Hamilton**, 1860; 24 D. 1442; aff. 1862, 4 Macq. 397; 24 D. H. L. 8. Forrest *v.* Forrest, 1863; 1 Macph. 806.

(*i*) Macalister *v.* Macalister, 1859; 21 D. 560, *supra*, § 1219. See Walker *v.* Galbraith, 1895; 23 R. 347.

1713. (1.) Under a destination "to a person named and his heirs," or "to a husband and wife in conjunct fee and liferent, and their heirs," or to them and "their children to be born of the marriage," or "to the father in liferent and the children of his marriage in fee," the fee is held to be in the parents, or in the father, and a *spes successionis* merely in the heirs or future children (*a*).

(*a*) Pearson *v.* Martin, 1665; M. 4249; 2 Ill. 343. Lamington *v.* Moore, 1675; M. 4252. Paterson's Crs. *v.* Anderson, 1705; M. 4259. Thomson *v.* Lawsons, 1681; M. 4258. Angus *v.* Ninian, 1733; Elchies, *Fiar*, 1. Frog's Crs. *v.* His Children, 1735; M. 4262. Lillie *v.* Riddel, 1741; M. 4267. Cumming *v.* Lord Advocate, 1756; M. 4268. Douglas *v.* Ainslie, 1761; M. 4269. Cuthbertson *v.* Thomson, 1781; M. 4279. Mure *v.* Mure, 1786; M. 4288. Lindsay *v.* Dott, 1807; M. *Fiar*, Apx. 1. Maxwell *v.* Gracie, 1822; 1 S. 408. Kennedy *v.* Allan, 1825; 3 S. 383. Scotts *v.* Napier (Crombie), 1826; 4 S. 454; 2 W. & S. 550. **Mein** (printed Muir) *v.* **Taylor**, 1827; 5 S. 779; aff. 4 W. & S. 22; 3 Ross' L. C. 696. Williamson *v.* Cochran, 1828; 6 S. 1035. Miller *v.* Miller, 1835; 12 S. 32. Jamieson *v.* Strachan, 1835; 13 S. 18. See Young *v.* Watson, 1835; 14 S. 85. See below, § 1952, 1957. Hutton's Trs. *v.* Hutton, 1847; 9 D. 639. Edward *v.* Shiell, 1848; 10 D. 685. Findlay *v.* M'Intyre, 1849; 12 D. 325. Ramsay *v.* Beveridge, 1854; 16 D. 764. **Ferguson's Trs.** *v.* **Hamilton**, 1860; 22 D. 1442; aff. 1862, 4 Macq. 397; 24 D. H. L. 8.

1714. (2.) In such a destination, the addition of words exclusive of a substantial fee in the liferenter still leaves in him (to satisfy the legal maxim) a fiduciary fee. Such, 'among other indications (*a*),' is the expression, "for liferent use allenarly" (*b*). But the construction which has been put on the word "allenarly," as restricting to a liferent what would otherwise be held a fee, is not so fixed that opposite indications of a fee may not prevail. Such are, a power to uplift money, a power to sell land, etc., without any obligation to reinvest (*c*), 'a direction to convey to the beneficiary, etc.; provided there be an absolute power of disposal, not a mere faculty, and it be granted, or rather reserved, to one who is *sui juris* (*d*). But while the word "allenarly" may thus be defeated by other words in the deed, it is not meant merely to protect persons favoured (*prædilectæ*) by the testator, but it restricts the right to a liferent even in favour of the liferenter's heir of line in a destination to heirs whomsoever in fee (*e*).'

(*a*) See Scott *v.* Napier, 1826; 4 S. 454; aff. 1827, 2 W. & S. 550. Hunter *v.* Hunter, 1794; Bell's Ca. 73. Ramsay *v.* Beveridge, *cit.* § 1713 (*a*) *fin.* Maule, etc. petrs., 1876; 3 R. 831. Gerran *v.* Alexander, *infra* (*b*) (liferent alimentary). Douglas *v.* Sharpe, 1811; Hume, 173 (do.). Dawson's Trs. *v.* Dawsons, 1877; 4 R. 597.

(*b*) Gerran *v.* Alexander, 1781; M. 4402; 2 Ill. 347. Newlands, Watherston, Thomson, Harvey, and Allardice, *supra*, § 1712 (*c*). Hunter *v.* Hunter's Tr., 1794; Bell's Ca. 73. Dewar, *supra*, § 1712 (*d*). Falconar *v.* Wright, 1824; 2 S. 537; 1825, 3 S. 455. Scotts, *supra*, § 1713 (*a*). Rollo *v.* Ramsay, 1832; 11 S. 132; 2 Ill. 500. Houlditch *v.* Spalding, 1847; 9 D. 1204. Emslie *v.* Fraser, 1850; 12 D. 724 (powers of fiduciary fiar,—see further, Fraser, H. & W. 1453 *sqq.*). Barstow *v.* Stewart, 1858; 20 D. 612. Snell *v.* White, 1872; 10 Macph. 745.

(*c*) Lamington, *supra*, § 1713 (*a*). Tulliallan *v.* Clackmannan, 1626; M. 4253. Drumkilbo *v.* L. Stormont, 1629; M. 4254. Dickson *v.* Dickson, 1780; M. 4269; Hailes, 865. Porterfield *v.* Graham, 1779; M. 4277; aff. 1780, 2 Pat. 537; 2 Ill. 349. Cumming *v.* Lord Advocate, 1756; M. 15,854. Baillie *v.* Clark, Feb. 23, 1809; F. C. Robertson *v.* Houston, 1858; 20 D. 989.

(*d*) Morris (Pollock) *v.* Tennant, 1853; 15 D. 716; aff. 1855, 18 D. H. L. 42; 27 S. Jur. 546. Alves *v.* Alves, 1861; 23 D. 712. Pursell *v.* Newbigging (Elder), 1856; 19 D. 71; 1865, 3 Macph. H. L. 53. See below, § 1944 (*f*), 1952, and Coltart *v.* Corie, 1853; 15 D. 606. Sprot *v.* Pennycook, 1855; 17 D. 840. Dawson's Trs., *cit.* (*a*). Boustead *v.* Gardner, 1879; 7 R. 139. Cases in § 1562 (*e*).

(*e*) Cumstie *v.* Philip, 1876; 3 R. 921.

1715. (3.) Wherever the right, though conceived as a fee, is given as a fiduciary or qualified fee, the liferent provided is not to be extended beyond its usufructuary nature, nor construed as a fee. And this also holds where a trust is constituted in another, with an interest declared of liferent to a person, and fee to his children unborn or unnamed. The trust fee satisfies the maxim, and, 'if the trust be for holding and protecting the estate and not merely for paying it over,' the liferent is construed according to the true meaning of the words (*a*); 'but if the direction to the trustees be to pay or convey during the subsistence of the marriage to the parent in liferent and the children in fee, the rule of construction above laid down receives effect (*b*).'

'In all cases of such destinations of heritage infeftment must be taken in terms of the destination in favour of each of the parties interested as individuals or as a class, in order to make their respective rights real and indefeasible, and to limit the parent's right to a liferent, if it has previously been a fee in him (*c*).'

(*a*) Turnbull *v.* Tawse, 1822; 2 S. 1; rev. 1 W. & S. 80; 2 Ill. 350. See Shaw's Bell's Com. 694 (*d*). Mein, *supra*, § 1713 (*a*). Seton *v.* Seton's Crs., 1793; M. 4219. Ewan *v.* Watt, 1828; 6 S. 1125. M'Dowal *v.* Russell, 1824; 2 S. 574. Leitch *v.* Leitch's Trs., 1826; 4 S. 665; aff. 3 W. & S. 366. **Fisher** *v.* **Dixon**, 1831; 10 S. 55; aff. 1833, 6 W. & S. 431. Thomson *v.* Scougall, 1835; 2 S. & M'L. 305. Douglas *v.* Sharpe, 1811; Hume, 173. Jamieson *v.* Strachan, 1835; 13 S. 318. Cameron *v.* Young, 1837; 15 S. 1205. See below, § 1956 (5). Ross *v.* King, 1847; 9 D. 1327; 3 Ross' L. C. 687. Ramsay *v.* Beveridge, 1854; 16 D. 764. Watson *v.* Watson, 1854; 15 D. 803. Ferguson's Trs., *infra* (*b*). Donaldson's Trs. *v.* Cuthbertson, 1863; 2 Macph. 435. Ferguson *v.* Ferguson, 1875; 2 R. 627. Mackie *v.* Gloag's Tr. (Herbertson), 1883; 10 R. 746; rev. 1884, 11 R. H. L. 10; 9 App. Ca. 303. Rait *v.* Arbuthnott, 1892; 19 R. 687 (executor — separate *bequests* of liferent and fee).

(*b*) Hutton's Trs. *v.* Hutton, 1847; 9 D. 639. M'Donald *v.* Maclachlan, 1831; 9 S. 269. Ferguson's Trs. *v.* Hamilton, 1860; 22 D. 1442; 1862, 4 Macq. 397; 34 S. Jur. 659; 24 D. H. L. 8. Alexander *v.* Alexander, 1849; 12 D. 345. Beveridges *v.* Beveridge's Trs., 1878; 5 R. 1116.

(*c*) Graham *v.* Graham, 1759; M. 6931. Falconar *v.* Wright, 1824; 2 S. 537. Houlditch *v.* Spalding, 1847; 9 D. 1204; 3 Ross' L. C. 662, 667. Stewart *v.* Rae, 1883; 10 R. 463. Fraser, H. & W. 1450.

CHAPTER IV

OF ENTAILS

1716. Nature and History.—By the law of Scotland, a conveyance of land implies a fee. There cannot be a series of liferents (*a*); and restraints on the power of a fiar can be imposed only by prohibitions and forfeitures. 'A fee may be limited by reservation (*supra*, § 861), but once vested is not defeated by any condition subsequent repugnant to the right; "for property or dominion," says Lord Stair (*b*), "passes not by conditions or provisions, but by tradition, and other ways prescribed in law."' In the first attempt to make an effectual limitation on the fee, inhibition was employed, but it was found ineffectual (*c*). Next, interdiction was resorted to, but also without effect (*d*). Then Sir Thomas Hope devised two clauses: one, to annul the deed attempted to be granted; the other, to dissolve and forfeit the right of the person making the attempt (*e*). The doubts entertained of the efficacy of this device (*f*), and the peculiar circumstances of the country, led to a statute giving the sanction of Parliament to entails (*g*), provided they should contain irritant and resolutive clauses; that they should be duly recorded by warrant of the Court of Session in a special register; and that they should be followed by sasine containing the prohibitory and irritant and resolutive clauses, recorded in the Register of Sasines. The form of an entail with such prohibitions and restrictions is not different from that of any other settlement of land; the conditions and destination, the prohibitions and the irritancies, being clearly expressed. The effect is either against heirs or against third parties. The former depends on the expression of the deed, and the principle that the acceptance of a conditional gift implies an obligation. The latter depends on due compliance with the requisites of the Act (*h*).

(*a*) Allardice *v.* Allardice, 1795; Bell's Ca. 156; 2 Ill. 349. Abernethie *v.* Forbes, 1835; 13 S. 263; 3 Ill. 356.

(*b*) 1 Stair, 14. § 5. Comp. Co. Litt. 206*a*. Mary Portington's Case, 10 Rep. 42. Hamilton *v.* M'Dowall, *infra* (*f*). White's Trs. *v.* Whyte, 1877; 4 R. 786. Kirkland *v.* Kirkland's Tr., 1886; 13 R. 786 (prohibition to assign *spes successionis*). Chaplin's Trs. *v.* Hoile, 1890; 18 R. 27 (resolutive condition not inconsistent with a liferent).

(*c*) Hope, Min. Pract. 402, § 9. Bryson *v.* Chapman, 1760; 5 B. Sup. 940.

(*d*) Balfour, 187. Cranston *v.* Cranston, 1586; M. 7125.

(*e*) Hope, Min. Pract. 402, § 9. 2 Stair, 3. § 58, 59. 3 Mackenzie, 8. § 17. V. Stormont *v.* Annandale's Crs., 1662; M. 15,475 and 13,994; 2 Ill. 355. Craig *v.* Craig, 1712; M. 15,494; Robertson's App. Ca. 110. Sharp *v.* Sharp, 1631; M. 4299.

(*f*) 1685, c. 22. 2 Stair, 3. § 58. 3 Ersk. 8. § 23. Sandford on Entails. Hamilton *v.* M'Dowall, March 3, 1815; F. C. (*per* L. Meadowbank at p. 326).

(*g*) 1685, c. 22.

(*h*) Campbell's Trs. *v.* Campbell, 1836; 14 S. 770.

1717. Substitutions with Prohibition to Alter (*a*).—Deeds containing substitutions, although accompanied by prohibitions to alter, are not entails, but defeasible; having effect only as personal contracts, with a condition annexed to the conveyance.

(*a*) See also above, § 1693; below, § 1718.

1718. Prohibitions to dispone or convey are 'at common law' effectual to prevent gratuitous deeds (*a*). 'And a deed merely prohibiting the alteration of the succession is effectual *inter hæredes* at common law (*b*). But the terms of the Rutherfurd Act are so broad as to invalidate all such entails, even though valid *inter hæredes* at common law, so that the doctrine of this section has ceased to be of practical importance, unless the deed of contravention has come into operation before the passing of that Act (*c*).'

(*a*) 1621, c. 18. E. Callander *v.* Hamilton, 1687; M. 15,477; 2 Ill. 352. Ure *v.* E. Crawford, 1756; M. 4315. See Cathcart *v.* Cathcart (Carleton), 1830; 8 S. 497; aff. 1831, 5 W. & S. 315. **Buchanan** *v.* **Carrick,** 1838; 16 S. 358; rem. 1842; 1 Bell's App. 368; aff. 1844, 4 Bell's App. 342. Lindsay *v.* Oswald's Trs., 1863; 2 Macph. 249; aff. 1867, 5 Macph. H. L. 12; L. R. 1 Sc. App. 99. See Lang *v.* Lang, 1839; M'L. & Rob. 871. Gilmour *v.* Cadell, 1838; 16 S. 1261. Syme *v.* Dickson, March 3, 1821; F. C. M'Laren on Wills, etc., § 1052.

(*b*) Cathcart, Carrick, and Lindsay, *citt.* L. Duffus' Trs. *v.* Dunbar, 1842; 4 D. 523.

(*c*) See below, § 1730A. Cunyngham *v.* Cunyngham, 1852; 14 D. 636. Dewar *v.* Dewar, 1852; 14 D. 1062. Ferguson *v.* Ferguson, 1852; 15 D. 19. Scott *v.* Scott, 1855; 18 D. 168. Rollo *v.* Rollo, 1864; 3 Macph. 78. D. Hamilton *v.* Hamilton, 1868; 7 Macph. 139; aff. 1869, 8 Macph. H. L. 48. Dempster *v.* Dempster, 1857; 3 Macq. 62. Baillie *v.* Cochrane, 1855; 17 D. 659; aff. 2 Macq. 529.

1719. But such prohibitions are not effectual against onerous deeds, and will not authorise inhibition, or stop a sale, or defeat the diligence of creditors (*a*).

They were at one time held to raise a personal obligation to indemnify those concerned (*b*); and so to relieve the estate of debts (*c*); and to restore the price, and re-employ it as before (*d*). But in the House of Lords this has been reversed (*e*), and that decision has been followed since (*f*). The essential difference between the effect of such limited deeds *inter hæredes*, and against third parties, is, that third parties are not affected by them unless the conditions of the Entail Act are complied with; while heirs 'were' at common law bound by the deed, but only according to a strict and rigorous construction (*g*).

(*a*) Young *v.* Bothwell, 1705; M. 15,482; 2 Ill. 352. Bryson *v.* Chapman, 1760; M. 15,511; 5 B. Sup. 873 and 940. See L. Kames's Arg. *ib.* 940, 941. Young *v.* Young, 1761; 5 B. Sup. 884. See the cases of Stewart, etc., below (*b*).

(*b*) Lockhart *v.* Stewart, July 11, 1811; F. C. E. Breadalbane, June 12, 1812; n. r.—referred to in Ascog Case, 5 S. Apx. **Stewart** *v.* **Fullarton,** 1827; 5 S. 419; rev. 4 W. & S. 196; 2 Ill. 353, Ascog Case. Bruce *v.* Bruce, 1827; 5 S. 822; 4 W. & S. 240. See below (*f*).

(*c*) L. Strathnaver *v.* D. Douglas, 1730; M. 15,373; aff. 1 Cr. & St. 32.

(*d*) Cuming *v.* Gordon, 1761; M. 15,513. Young *v.* Young, 1761; 5 B. Sup. 884. Sutherland *v.* Sinclair, 1801; M. *Tailzie*, Apx. 15. Lockhart, *supra* (*b*); and see 5 S. 424, note. Stewart and Bruce, *supra* (*b*).

(*e*) Stewart's and Bruce's cases, as revd. (*b*). D. Queensberry *v.* M. Queensberry, 1830; 4 W. & S. 254. So far as the grounds of the judgment of the House of Lords "can be expressed in one proposition, it seems to be this: That the deed of entail, on which alone the right of the substitute heirs was founded, gave no such remedy as an action of damages, but a remedy of quite a different sort, namely, forfeiture of the estate for the contravention; that under a complete entail no other remedy but that given by the deed is competent under the Act 1685; and that where the Act does not apply (as here, where the entail was not recorded), there is no restraint and no remedy in law, whatever obligation may be imagined in morality." 2 Ill. 355. See Buchanan *v.* Carrick, *cit.* § 1718, in H. L.; and E. Breadalbane *v.* Jamieson, 1877; 4 R. 677 (and cases there cited, *per* L. P. Inglis).

(*f*) L. Elibank *v.* Murray, 1833; 11 S. 858; aff. 1835, 1 S. & M'L. 1. Campbell *v.* M. Breadalbane, 1838; 1 D. 81; aff. 1841, 2 Rob. 109. E. Eglinton *v.* Montgomerie, 1842; 4 D. 425; aff. 1845, 2 Bell's App. 149.

(*g*) See last section *in fine*.

1719A. '**Subject of Entail.**—It is generally thought that an entail of moveables is not valid even *inter hæredes* (*a*). Rights of reversion, adjudications on which sasine has followed, though not declarator of the expiry of the legal, and it would seem, though only *inter hæredes*, heritable rights not capable of being feudalised, may be entailed (*b*). The ordinary subjects of entail are lands, including burgage subjects and houses (*c*). A *pro indiviso* share of an estate may be entailed (*d*).'

(*a*) Veitch *v.* Young, 1808; M. Apx. *Service*, 4. Baillie *v.* Grant, 1859; 12 D. 838. 1 M'Laren on Wills, etc., § 995. Kinnear *v.* Kinnear, 1875; 2 R. 765; 1876, 4 R. 705. Sandys *v.* Bain's Trs., 1898; 25 R. 261, 279. See M. Bute *v.* Mss. Bute's Trs., 1880; 8 R. 191.

(*b*) Chisholm *v.* Chisholm Batten, 1864; 3 Macph. 202. Dalyell *v.* Dalyell, Jan. 17, 1810; F. C. See M'Millan *v.* Campbell, 1831; 9 S. 551; aff. 7 W. & S. 441 (radical right under trust for creditors). See below, § 1722.

(*c*) 1 M'Laren on Wills, etc., § 994. Soutar *v.* Brown, 1870; 8 Macph. 702. 31 and 32 Vict. c. 101, § 14. 37 and 38 Vict. c. 94, § 25.

(*d*) Stirling *v.* Dun, 1827; 6 S. 272. Stewart *v.* Nicolson, 1859; 22 D. 72. Howden *v.* Rocheid, 1868; 6 Macph. 300; aff. 1869, 7 Macph. H. L. 110.

1720. Construction of Entails.—'In considering the subject of proper entails,' it is not surprising to find that much difference of opinion should have taken place relative to the construction and effect of a statute which gives sanction to so extraordinary an exercise of power over the future succession and management of land property, and authorises restraints on the successive proprietors of the land greater than are known in any other European nation of modern times. And although it is difficult to lay down any rules for reconciling these differences, the best approximation to a regular and uniform course of decision seems to be, to take the words of the statute and of the deed, according to their strict construction, as furnishing the guiding rule throughout the whole system of entails (*a*). 'Contrary to the rule of construction in contracts (§ 524 (3)), if an expression in an entail admits of two meanings, both equally technical and intelligible, that construction must be adopted which destroys the entail rather than that which supports it (*b*).'

(*a*) Speid *v.* Speid, 1837; 15 S. 618. See Rowe *v.* Monypenny, 1837; 15 S. 500. Preston *v.* Heirs of Entail of Valleyfield, 1845; 7 D. 305. Lumsden *v.* Lumsden, 1842; 2 Bell's App. 114. E. Buchan *v.* Erskine, 1842; 4 D. 1430; aff. 1845, 4 Bell's App. 22 (*per* L. Campbell). Maxwell *v.* Smith, 1860; 22 D. 1341. E. of Kintore *v.* L. Inverury, 1861; 23 D. 1105; 1863, 4 Macq. 520; 1 Macph. H. L. 32. Wauchope *v.* Wauchopes, 1884; 11 R. 424.

(*b*) Lumsden *v.* Lumsden, *cit.* (*per* L. Campbell). Wauchope *v.* Wauchopes, *cit.* (*per* Inglis, L. P.); and cases in (*a*).

1721. Requisites of an Entail.—The essential character of an entail consists in the establishment by the proprietor of land of such a destination as shall carry the land to a specified line of heirs, and guard the succession of the estate, and to a certain extent the management of it, so as to be secure not only against heirs, but also against third parties, and to defeat any attempt to dispose of it, or to carry it off for payment of debt, or from the prescribed line of succession.

For the accomplishment of these purposes, besides the external observances required by the statute (of registration of the original deed of entail in the Register of Entails, and completion of the real right by sasine duly registered in the Record of Sasines), there must be—1. A right of property in the maker; 2. A destination clearly expressed; 3. Such conditions as shall guard against the accidental disappointment of the entailer's intentions; 4. Prohibitions against sale and debt, and alteration of the destination; and, 5. Occasionally relaxation of those restraints by clauses of power.

1722. Title to make an Entail.—The same right as heritable proprietor which is required to enable one to dispose of land, is requisite to the efficacy of an entail. But it is not necessary that the maker of the entail shall be feudally infeft: a personal right will enable him to make a deed which will be effectual to compel his heir to fulfil the intention, or which will be valid on the making up of the proper titles (*a*). One who has made a trust-deed conveying his estate for the behoof of creditors, has still in him a sufficient right to make a valid entail of whatever may remain in the way of reversion (*b*).

(*a*) Livingston *v.* L. Napier, 1762; M. 15,418; 5 B. Sup. 885; Bell's Ca. p. 184, note; aff. 2 Pat. 108; 2 Ill. 383; 2 Ross' L. C. 425. Renton *v.* Anstruther, 1837; 16 S. 184; 1 Bell's App. 129; 6 D. 430; aff. 2 Bell's App. 114; 2 Ross' L. C. 435. Stirling *v.* Stirling, 1801; M. 15,455. Fogo *v.* Fogo, 1840; 2 D. 651; aff. 2 Bell's App. 195. E. Fife *v.* Duff, 1861; 23 D. 657; 24 D. 936, 942, etc.; aff. 1863, 1 Macph. H. L. 19; 4 Macq. 469. See Chisholm, *infra* (*b*).

(*b*) Campbell of Edderline *v.* Creditors, 1801; M. *Adjud.* Apx. 11; 2 Ill. 555. M'Millan *v.* Campbell, 1834; 7 W. & S. 441. So the right of reversion under a wadset may be the subject of an entail. Chisholm *v.* Chisholm Batten, 1864; 3 Macph. 202.

1723. Destination.—This must be clear and intelligible, and regulated by the principles already laid down (*a*). The person to whom the lands are first directly disponed is the institute; those to whom they are destined on failure of the institute are substitutes. The substitutes take by service either on the death of the institute, or on contravention and irritancy established by decree of declarator, or on repudiation (*b*). It has been held that the entailed destination terminates wherever females are introduced, or the succession comes to heirs-female, while no provision is made for excluding heirs-portioners, and securing that they shall succeed without division (*c*). And it is not allowed in such a case, 'in an executed entail,' to infer from the intention of the entailer an exclusion of the heirs-portioners; 'but in a trust to entail, the trustees, in executing the deed of entail, may exclude heirs-portioners, although there is no special direction to do so in the trust-deed' (*d*). A destination terminating in heirs whatsoever, if not limited to those of a particular description, is held to close the entail; 'and the last substitute under the previous part of the destination takes in fee-simple (*c*).' It has been doubted whether this is in all cases correct, or only where the destination terminates in heirs-female (*f*). But there can be no such doubt where their right as heirs-portioners is excluded. 'On the same principle (viz. that the statute of entails was intended to enable proprietors to transmit their estates in a line *different* from the legal order of succession), an immediate destination to an institute and his "heirs whatsoever," or heirs and assignees whomsoever, is not a good tailzied destination, and the institute takes in fee-simple (*g*). And the mere exclusion of heirs-portioners is not sufficient to make such a destination valid in an entail (*h*).'

When in the destination particular heirs are described as the persons to take the estate, the description must be applied to those who shall answer the description at the time the succession opens (*i*). 'A direction to make an entail is ineffectual unless a specific destination is added (*k*).'

(*a*) See above, § 1691 et seq. Macgregor *v.* Gordon, 1864; 3 Macph. 148. Gordon *v.* Gordon's Trs., 1866; 4 Macph. 501.

(*b*) Simson & Horne *v.* E. Home, 1797; M. 15,353; 2 Ill. 357. Irvine *v.* Irvine, 1723; M. 15,369. Dundas *v.* Murray, 1774; M. 15,430; Hailes, 601. Gordon's Crs. *v.* Gordon, 1749; M. 15,384; Elch. *Tailzie*, 37; 5 B. Sup. 774; and 1753; M. 10,258; Elch. *Tailzie*, 51. Stewart *v.* Denholm (Carlton Case), 1726; M. 7275. **Fullerton** *v.* **Hamilton** (Bargany Case), 1824; 2 S. 585; 1 W. & S. 410 (effect of repudiation, 2 Ill. 358). Leslie *v.* Dick, 1710; M. 15,358; 2 Ill. 358 (termination of destination). E. March *v.* Kennedy, 1760; M. 15,412; aff. 2 Pat. 49 (ditto). Henry *v.* Watt, 1832; 10 S. 644. Hunter *v.* Kelly, 1834; 13 S. 185; 2 Ill. 359 (heirs-portioners). Mure *v.* Mure, 1837; 15 S. 581; aff. 1838, 3 S. & M'L. 237.

(*c*) Farquhar *v.* Farquhar, 1838; 1 D. 131. See also Mure, *supra* (*b*), and Craig, below (*f*). Macdonald *v.* Lockhart, 1842; 5 D. 372. Hunter *v.* Kellie, 1834; 13 S. 185. See Collow's Trs. *v.* Connell, 1866; 4 Macph. 465. Connell *v.* Grierson, 1867; 5 Macph. 379.

(*d*) Mure, *supra* (*b*). 3 Ersk. 8. § 32. Sprot *v.* Sprot, 1828; 6 S. 833. Sands *v.* Sands, 1844; 6 D. 365. Forrest's Trs. *v.* Forrest, 1845; 8 D. 304. Martin *v.* Kelso, 1853; 15 D. 950; 1857, 2 Macq. 556. Gordon *v.* Mosse, 1851; 14 D. 269. Steele *v.* Coupar, 1853; 15 D. 385.

(*e*) Mure, *supra* (*b*). E. March, *supra* (*b*). Henry *v.* Watt, 1832; 10 S. 644. Colville *v.* Colville, 1843; 5 D. 861; 1845, 4 Bell's App. 248. **Gordon** *v.* **Gordon's Trs.**, 1881; 9 R. 78; aff. 1882, *ib.* H. L. 101; 7 App. Ca. 818.

(*f*) Craig *v.* M'Culloch, 1839; 1 D. 545. See below (*g*), (*h*).

(*g*) **Leny** *v.* **Leny**, 1860; 22 D. 1272. Macgregor *v.* Gordon, 1864; 3 Macph. 148. Gordon *v.* Gordon's Trs., 1866; 4 Macph. 501. Moubray's Trs. *v.* Moubray, 1896; 22 R. 801. See Collow's Trs., and Connell, *supra* (*c*). It has now been enacted that where a tailzie is invalid in respect of such a destination, the estate is to be held a fee-simple estate without declarator or judicial procedure; and that when money is invested in trust to buy lands to be entailed, or lands are directed to be entailed and the direction has not yet been carried into effect, the trust money or lands are to be dealt with as if the destination were in fee-simple. 38 and 39 Vict. c. 61, § 13.

(*h*) Primrose *v.* Primrose, 1854; 16 D. 498. Gordon and Steele, *supra* (*d*). Macgregor and Gordon, *supra* (*g*).

(*i*) Shepherd *v.* Grant, 15 S. 173; aff. 3 S. & M'L. 255; 2 Ill. 339. See Martin *v.* Kelso, 1853; 15 D. 950; aff. 2 Macq. 556. See below, § 1880–1883.

(*k*) Gordon, *supra* (*a*). Comp. Leny, *supra* (*g*). Thorburn's Trs. *v.* Maclaine, 1866; 3 Macph. 101. Gordon, *supra* (*e*). Moubray's Trs. (*g*). As to the effect and construction of executory trusts to make entails, see Sandys *v.* Bain's Trs., 1897; 25 R. 261.

1724. Conditions.—The statute authorises landowners to tailzie their lands (*a*) "with such provisions and conditions as they think fit"; requiring, as necessary to their efficacy, that "these conditions shall be recorded in the Register of Tailzies," and that they "shall be repeated in all the subsequent conveyances"; omission being declared "a contravention, but so as not to militate against creditors or other singular successors contracting *in bonâ fide*." 'These conditions are optional to the entailer; but are enforceable, like the proper and indispensable prohibitions, if duly fenced and if the entail be otherwise valid.'

(*a*) The lands must in a question with creditors be distinctly specified. King *v.* E. Stair, 1844; 6 D. 821; aff. 1846, 5 Bell's App. 82. See Dalrymple *v.* E. Stair, 1844; 6 D. 837; as to identification of lands, E. Leven and Melville *v.* Cartwright, 1861; 23 D. 1038.

1724A. 'The Rutherfurd Act dispensed with the insertion of the irritant and resolutive clauses in every deed of entail dated on or after 1st August 1848, and containing a clause authorising registration in the Register of Tailzies; and this provision was extended to the cardinal prohibitions by the Titles Acts of 1858 and 1860 (*a*). The Act of 1868, consolidating these laws, provides that "where a deed of entail contains an express clause authorising registration of the deed in the Register of Tailzies, it shall not be necessary to insert clauses of prohibition against alienation, contracting debt, and altering the order of succession, and irritant and resolutive clauses, or any of them; and such clause of registration contained in any deed of entail of lands not held by burgage tenure, dated on or after the 1st day of October 1858, or of lands held by burgage tenure, dated on or after the 10th day of October 1860, shall have in every respect the same operation and effect as if such clauses of prohibition and such irritant and resolutive clauses had been inserted in such deed of entail" (*b*).'

(*a*) 11 and 12 Vict. c. 36, § 39. 21 and 22 Vict. c. 76, § 18. 23 and 24 Vict. c. 143, § 12.
(*b*) 31 and 32 Vict. c. 101, § 14.

1724B. 'By the Lands Transference Acts, 1847 (*a*), it was made lawful in all deeds and instruments necessary to transmit, renew, or complete a title under an entail, to omit the full insertion of the conditions, provisions, and prohibitory, irritant, and resolutive clauses, provided they are specially referred to as set forth at full length in the recorded deed of entail (if it be recorded), or in any recorded instrument of sasine forming part of the progress, and that in terms provided by a schedule. The Titles to Land Acts substituted a similar reference for the full insertion of the destination of heirs in renewals of the investiture, as well as in excambions of entailed lands (*b*). The existing Act makes it unnecessary in deeds relating to entailed lands, or lands obtained by excambion in exchange for entailed lands, or purchased or acquired for the purpose of being added to an entailed estate, to insert the conditions of entail, or the destination of heirs, or the conditions, provisions, prohibitory, irritant, and resolutive clauses, or clause authorising registration in the Register of Tailzies, contained in the deed of entail; provided they are specially referred to in a statutory form, as set forth at length in such deed recorded in the Register of Tailzies, or as set forth in any deed recorded in the appropriate Register of Sasines, and forming part of the progress of title-deeds of the entailed lands. Such reference has the same effect as if these clauses had been fully inserted (*c*).'

(*a*) 10 and 11 Vict. c. 48, § 4. 10 and 11 Vict. c. 47, § 5. 10 and 11 Vict. c. 49, § 3. 10 and 11 Vict. c. 51, § 26.
(*b*) 21 and 22 Vict. c. 76, § 17. 23 and 24 Vict. c. 143, § 11, 27.
(*c*) 31 and 32 Vict. c. 101, § 9.

1725. The usual conditions are:—

(1.) *To use the Name and Arms of the Entailer.* — This injunction, sometimes the offspring of vanity, may be intended to prevent the accumulation of several entailed estates in one person, and the sinking of the name and family of the entailer. It is held an effectual and binding condition (*a*).

(*a*) Stevenson *v.* Stevenson, 1677; M. 15,475 and 17,000; 2 Ill. 359. Moir *v.* Graham, 1794; M. 15,537. Munro *v.* Munro, 1826; 4 S. 467; aff. 3 W. & S. 344. Cuming's Trs. *v.* Cuming, 1832; 10 S. 804. Hunter *v.* Weston, 1882; 9 R. 492. M. Bell's Convg. 1017.

1726. (2.) *Exclusion of the Heir on succeeding to another Estate or to a Peerage.*—This has a similar purpose and effect with one of the purposes of the condition as to name and arms; and is, *inter hæredes*, interpreted so as to give full effect to the intention of the testator. So a condition, "if he shall succeed to a peerage or estate," is held to comprehend the case of his so succeeding in the first place, and taking under the entail afterwards (*a*).

(*a*) Simson *v.* E. Home, 1697; M. 15,353; 2 Ill. 357. Lockhart *v.* Gilmour, 1755; M. 15,404; 1 Cr. St. & P. 610; 2 Ill. 360. Leslie *v.* Leslie, 1742; Elch. *Tailzie*, 15; 1 Cr. St. & P. 324. Fleming *v.* L. Elphinstone, 1804; M. 15,559. Bruce Henderson *v.* Henderson, 1790; M. 4215; 3 Pat. 686. Stirling *v.* Stirling, 1834; 12 S. 296. Cuningham Bontine *v.* Graham, 1838; 1 D. 286. See Munro *v.* Munro, 1826; 4 S. 467; aff. 1828, 3 W. & S. 34. M. Hastings *v.* Hastings, 1845; 7 D. 1; aff. 1847, 6 Bell's App. 30. E. Eglinton *v.* Hamilton (Bourtreehill Case), 1847; 9 D. 1167; aff. 6 Bell's App. 136. Lawson *v.* Imrie, 1841; 3 D. 1001. Stewart *v.* Nicolson, 1859; 22 D. 72. Vss. Hawarden *v.* Howden, 1866; 4 Macph. 343. Howden *v.* Fleeming, 1867; 5 Macph. 658; rev. 1868, 6 Macph. 113. Munro *v.* Johnstone, 1868; 7 Macph. 250. Bruce *v.* Preston's Trs., 1874; 1 R, 740 (heir whose right is subject to defeasance by this condition is entitled to disentail). Home *v.* Home, 1876; 3 R. 591. Home *v.* Logan, 1880; 7 R. 1137.

1727. (3.) *To make up Titles under the Entail, obtain Infeftment, record the Entail, and possess under the Entail only.*—These are the requisites of an effectual entail against third parties, and the neglect of these conditions is declared to infer a forfeiture of the estate. The purpose of this precaution is, that by completing the entail creditors and purchasers shall be excluded, who might otherwise be enabled to affect the estate by diligence, or to complete a right to it under a voluntary conveyance. 'The latter part of the condition, now dispensed with (§ 1724B), was' a condition conformable to the statute itself, by which, "if the provisions and irritant clauses shall not be repeated in the rights whereby any of the heirs of tailzie shall brook or enjoy the entailed estate, the said omission shall import a contravention," etc., and "the said estate shall *ipso facto* fall and devolve," etc. (*a*). The substitutes are empowered to enforce this obligation (*b*). But it has been held that the mere act of making up titles in fee-simple is not to be deemed an irritancy beyond remedy; and that the making up a title under the entail, before decree of declarator, will purge the irritancy, provided ample security be given against the claim of any singular successor who may have acquired a right to affect the estate while under fee-simple titles (*c*).

(*a*) V. Garnock *v.* Garnock, 1725; M. 15,596; 2 Ill. 373.
(*b*) See below, § 1738.
(*c*) Abernethie *v.* Forbes (Gordon), 1837; 15 S. 1167; aff. 1840, 1 Rob. 434. See above, § 1724B. M'Laren on Wills, etc., § 1069 sqq.

1728. (4.) *To pay off the Entailer's Debts, and purge or prevent Adjudications.*—The heir of entail is not, as such, bound to pay the entailer's debts, as not being his representative; but only for the interest during his possession, as the rents are bound (*a*); and he may either neglect to pay the debt, or, paying it, he may by assignation keep it up as a debt against the estate (*b*). One design, then, of this condition is to prevent the continuance of the debts as a burden on the land, and to compel the heir to pay what otherwise he might be entitled to leave a burden on future heirs. Another purpose is to avoid the danger of adjudications. Formerly the heir could not sell for payment of the entailer's debt; but by statute new powers are granted to sell entailed estates for payment of the entailer's debts, so as to save the expense of going to Parliament (*c*).

(*a*) 3 Ersk. 8. § 27. Campbell *v.* Campbell, Nov. 29, 1815; F. C.; 2 Ill. 379.
(*b*) Kerr *v.* Turnbull, 1758; M. 15,551. See below, § 1743. Caddell *v.* Caddell's Trs., 1845; 7 D. 1014.
(*c*) 6 and 7 Will. IV. c. 42, § 7 et seq. Torrance, petr., 1837; 16 S. 174. See below, § 1771. 4 and 5 Vict. c. 24; 11 and 12 Vict. c. 36, § 37.

1729. Prohibitions.—These affect the power of transference, of pledging the estate for debt, or of altering the succession (*a*). 'The heir of entail in possession is a fiar or full owner in all respects except so far as he is tied up by the entail; and not, as in England, a mere tenant for life by settlement, *eo ipso* incapable of doing anything that may extend beyond his life estate. He has therefore every power of ownership which is not expressly taken from him (*b*), and his doing an act of ownership which is not a contravention of the entail can infer no liability to the succeeding heirs of entail, as against him or his executors (*c*). Contraventions of the entail may be prevented by interdict, but the only remedy for them when committed is an action of declarator of contravention and irritancy (*d*). On the other hand, while a succeeding heir is entitled, as a third party, to challenge deeds granted in violation of the entail by his predecessor, in regard to the entailed estate he is heir and *eadem persona cum defuncto*, and thus, *e.g.*, entitled to challenge deeds obtained from the predecessor by fraud or concealment (*e*).'

The machinery by which these prohibitions are made effectual consists of two sets of clauses; the prohibitory, and the irritant and resolutive clauses.

(*a*) See below, § 1748 et seq.
(*b*) 3 Ersk. 8. § 29. E. Eglinton *v.* Montgomerie, 1843; 2 Bell's App. 149. Cases, § 1730 (*a*) *infra*.
(*c*) E. Breadalbane *v.* Jamieson, 1877; 4 R. 667.
(*d*) *Ib.*
(*e*) Cleland *v.* Morrison, 1878; 6 R. 156 (*per* L. Young, p. 173).

1730. (1.) *Prohibitory Clauses.* — These must be clear and pointed in describing the acts prohibited, and in directing the prohibition against the persons meant to be restrained. The great rule is, that restraints not expressed are not to be implied from others which are expressed; nor from one limitation is another to be inferred (*a*). But the heir is not to deal collusively and fraudulently, so as, under any omission or defect in one prohibition, to facilitate or accomplish the defeat of another; to raise, for example, a fictitious debt under an omission in the prohibition against contracting debt, for the purpose of altering the succession (*b*). The prohibitions may, to a certain extent, be imposed by reference to other deeds (*c*); 'but this statement is thought to apply only to questions *inter hæredes* (*d*); or to deeds of nomination of heirs under powers reserved in a proper deed of entail to the granter or another (*e*). The general rule is, that the restraining clauses must, in entails prior to 1848, be complete in themselves in the deed which enters the record (*f*).'

(*a*) **D. Roxburghe,** 1807; M. *Tailzie*, 13; 2 Dow, 114, 210; 5 Pat. 362. Rickart *v.* E. Hopetoun, 1734; Cr. & St. 143; 2 Ill. 361. Gilmour *v.* Cadell, 1838; 16 S. 1261. Braimer *v.* Bethune, 1839; 1 D. 383. Trotter's Trs. *v.* Gordon, 1840; 2 D. 826. Hay *v.* Hay, 1851; 13 D. 945. D. Hamilton *v.* Hamilton, 1868; 7 Macph. 139; aff. 1870, 8 Macph. H. L. 48. Cathcart *v.* Cathcart, 1863; 1 Macph. 759. Fraser *v.* Fraser, 1879; 7 R. 134; and many other cases.
(*b*) Cathcart *v.* Cathcart (Carleton Case), 1830; 8 S. 497; aff. 5 W. & S. 315.

(c) Don v. Don, 1713 ; M. 15,591 ; Robertson's Ap. 76. Lawrie v. Spalding, 1764 ; M. 15,612. Broomfield v. Paterson, 1784 ; M. 15,618 ; 1786, 3 Pat. 51 ; 2 Ill. 374. Vere v. Hope, 1833 ; 11 S. 520 ; aff. 2 S. & M'L. 817. Turnbull v. Hay Newton, 1836 ; 14 S. 1031. Cuninghame Bontine v. Grahame, 1835 ; 13 S. 905 ; aff. M'L. & Rob. 347.

(d) See *per* L. Moncreiff in Lindsay v. E. Aboyne, 1842 ; 4 D. 843, 858. Don v. Don, *cit.* Cochrane v. Baillie, and Gammell v. Cathcart, *citt. infra.*

(e) Stewart v. Porterfield, 1821 ; 1 S. 9 ; 1826, 2 W. & S. 369 ; 1831, 5 W. & S. 515. Fraser v. L. Lovat, and Gammell, *infra.*

(f) See More on Stair, Notes, 138. Fraser v. L. Lovat, 1842 ; 1 Bell's App. 105. Lindsay v. E. Aboyne, 1842 ; 4 D. 843 ; aff. 3 Bell's App. 254. Paterson v. Lindsay, 1845 ; 7 D. 950. Gammell v. Cathcart (Countesswells Case), 1847 ; 12 D. 19 ; aff. 1852, 1 Macq. 362. L. Forbes v. Gammell, 1858 ; 20 D. 917. Cochrane v. Baillie, 1855 ; 17 D. 659 ; aff. 1857, 2 Macq. 529. Munro v. Butler Johnstone, 1868 ; 7 Macph. 250. Kenny v. Taylor, 1875 ; 2 R. 636. See above, § 1724A ; and below, § 1730A, 1734.

1730A. '*Rutherfurd Act.*—By Lord Rutherfurd's Act it is enacted, that where any entail shall not be valid and effectual in terms of the Act 1685, in regard to the prohibitions against alienation and contraction of debt, and alteration of the order of succession, in consequence of defects either of the original deed of entail or of the investiture following thereon, but shall be invalid and ineffectual as regards any one of such prohibitions ; such entail is to be deemed invalid and ineffectual as regards all the prohibitions, and the estate is to be subject to the deeds and debts of the heir then in possession, and of his successors as they shall thereafter in order take under such tailzie ; and no action of forfeiture shall be competent at the instance of any heir substitute against the heir in possession by reason of any contravention of the prohibitions (a). Such entails are null without declarator, as from the date of the statute, which has not retrospective effect (b).'

(a) 11 and 12 Vict. c. 36, § 43. Cochrane v. Baillie, 1855 ; 17 D. 659 ; aff. 2 Macq. 529. Dempster v. Dempster, 1857 ; 3 Macq. 62. D. Hamilton v. Hamilton, 1868 ; 7 Macph. 139 ; aff. 8 Macph. H. L. 48. Catton v. Mackenzie, 1870 ; 8 Macph. 1049 ; alt. 1872, 10 Macph. H. L. 12.

(b) Urquhart v. Urquhart, 1851 ; 13 D. 742 ; aff. 1 Macq. 658. Russell v. Russell, 1852 ; 15 D. 192. Scott v. Scott, 1855 ; 18 D. 168. Cochrane v. Baillie (a). Ochterlony v. Ochterlony, 1877 ; 4 R. 587. This case shows that a defective deed executed by trustees being reduced, the institute or heir does not hold as fee-simple proprietor, unless he has possessed for the prescriptive period, but as a beneficiary, and that the trustees are bound to execute a new and valid entail.

1731. (2.) *Irritant and Resolutive Clauses.*—These, in order to give effect against third parties, must be distinctly pointed or applied to the particular act in question. These 'clauses' are confounded in the writings of lawyers (a) ; but, correctly, the irritant clause irritates or annuls and voids the act or deed prohibited, in so far as it may affect the estate ; and the resolutive forfeits, dissolves, or resolves the right of him who has contravened the prohibition (b).

(a) 3 Ersk. 8. § 25.

(b) 3 Ersk. 8. § 25. M'Kenzie on Tailzies, 5 Bell's Forms of Deeds, 25–27. See more fully below, § 1748 et seq. The rule stated in § 1730A applies to the irritant clauses. Scott v. Scott, 1855 ; 18 D. 168.

1732. (3.) *Construction.*—The following rules regulate these clauses:—1. That there are no *voces signatæ*, no formal and indispensable words requisite to the efficacy of these clauses ; provided the two sanctions of nullity and forfeiture be clearly expressed (a). Where a clause was defective in grammatical expression, but capable of having the syntax and plain meaning restored by means of a reference to the context, the Court sustained it ; but in the House of Lords this has been admitted only where by no possibility any other meaning or words can be introduced, and where the construction is necessary and inevitable (b). 2. That the irritant and resolutive clauses must both be clearly directed against an act prohibited, otherwise third parties are not touched by the prohibition (c). 3. That the application or pointing of these two clauses may either be generally to all the prohibitions, or specially to each (d). But great discrimination is necessary in the pointing of any general expressions, that they be not applicable to some of the prohibitions, and not to others (e) ; 'as well as in adopting the method of particularising or enumerating the things prohibited, that the clause may not fail upon the principle of defective enumeration (f).' 4. That it is by the combination of these clauses that the effect is produced, and therefore both are necessary. So the want of an irritant clause is fatal, though there should be an ample resolutive clause (g). And the want of a resolutive clause is fatal, though there should be a clear irritant clause (h). 5. That these clauses must not only be pointed clearly to the several prohibitions, but distinctly directed to the persons meant to be affected (i). And such persons, though under the clauses of prohibition, will not be liable to any claim at the instance of the heirs of entail (k). But

6. That it is not necessary that the deeds made in contravention shall be declared void as against the contravener, provided they are annulled as against the estate (*l*). 'And they must be declared null as against the estate, not merely as against the subsequent heirs (*m*).'

(*a*) Munro *v.* Munro, 1826 ; 4 S. 467 ; 3 W. & S. 344 ; 2 Ill. 364. See Sharpe *v.* Sharpe (Hoddam Case), 1832 ; 10 S. 747 ; rev. 1835, 1 S. & M'L. 612. Lindsay *v.* E. Aboyne, 1842 ; 4 D. 843 ; aff. 1844, 3 Bell's App. 254. Adam *v.* Farquharson, 1840 ; 2 D. 1162 ; aff. 1844, 3 Bell's App. 295. Anstruther *v.* Anstruther, 1840 ; 3 D. 142. Borthwick *v.* Glassford, 1853 ; 16 D. 37.

(*b*) Sharpe, *supra* (*a*). Cases above, § 1729. M'Donald *v.* M'Donald, 1874 ; 1 R. 858 ; aff. 1875, 2 R. H. L. 28. Gollan *v.* Gollan, 1862 ; 24 D. 1410 ; H. L. 1863, 1 Macph. H. L. 65 ; 4 Macq. 585. Holmes *v.* Cunningham, 1851 ; 13 D. 869.

(*c*) Stewart *v.* Fullarton (Ascog), 1830 ; 4 W. & S. 196 ; 2 Ill. 353. Gibson *v.* Gibson, 1869 ; 7 Macph. 790.

(*d*) Bruce *v.* Bruce (Tillicoultry), 1799 ; M. 15,539 ; 2 Ill. 365. Dick *v.* Drysdale (Prestonfield Case), Jan. 14, 1812 ; F. C. Lang *v.* Lang (Overton Case), 1838 ; 1 D. 98 ; 1839, M'L. & R. 871. Horne *v.* Rennie, 1837 ; 15 S. 376 ; 3 S. & M'L. 146. Scott Moncrieff *v.* Cuningham, 1804 ; 4 Pat. 652 ; 1 D. 600, note ; and 3 S. & M'L. 156, note. Speid *v.* Speid, 1837 ; 15 S. 618. Buchanan *v.* Carrick, 1838 ; 16 S. 358 ; 1844, 3 Bell's App. 342 ; 3 Ill. 160. Lumsden *v.* Lumsden, 1840 ; 3 D. 136 ; aff. 1843, 2 Bell's App. 104. E. Buchan *v.* Erskine, 1842 ; 4 D. 1430 ; 1845, 4 Bell's App. 22. Lawrie *v.* Lawrie, 1853 ; 17 D. 181. E. Kintore *v.* L. Inverury, 1861 ; 23 D. 1105 ; aff. 1863, 4 Macq. 520 ; 1 Macph. H. L. 34. Maxwell *v.* Maxwell, 1852 ; 14 D. 537. Preston *v.* Heirs of Valleyfield, 1845 ; 7 D. 305. Dingwall *v.* Dingwall, 1842 ; 4 D. 816 ; 1845, 4 Bell's App. 149. Gilmour *v.* Gordon, 1853 ; 15 D. 587. Maxwell *v.* Smith, 1860 ; 22 D. 341. Howden *v.* Rocheid, 1868 ; 6 Macph. 300 ; aff. 1869, 7 Macph. H. L. 110. Lady Hawarden *v.* Dunlop **(Howden *v.* Fleeming)**, 1865 ; 3 Macph. 748 ; aff. 4 Macph. H. L. 41. L. Wharncliffe *v.* Nairne, 1849 ; 12 D. 1 ; 1850, 7 Bell's App. 132.

(*e*) Adam *v.* Barclay, 1821 ; Hume, 877 ; 1 S. App. 24. Lang *v.* Lang, *cit.* (*d*). Sinclair *v.* Sinclair, 1841 ; 3 D. 636. Hay *v.* Hay, 1842 ; 5 D. 347. Graham *v.* Murray, 1848 ; 10 D. 380 ; aff. 1849, 6 Bell's App. 441. Baillie *v.* Baillie, 1850 ; 12 D. 1220. Cunyngham *v.* Cunyngham, 1852 ; 14 D. 636. Dewar *v.* Dewar, 1852 ; 14 D. 1062. Drummond *v.* Hay, 1872 ; 10 Macph. 451.

(*f*) Horne and Bruce, *citt.* (*d*). Lang *v.* Lang, *cit.* (*d*). Glen *v.* M'Turk, 1852 ; 14 D. 359. Fairlie *v.* Cunningham, 1857 ; 19 D. 596. Menzies *v.* Menzies, 1852 ; 14 D. 522. L. Duffus *v.* Dunbar, 1842 ; 4 D. 523. Martin *v.* Dunbar, 1844 ; 6 D. 1320. E. Kintore (*d*). Ogilvie *v.* E. Airlie, 1852 ; 15 D. 252 ; 1855, 2 Macq. 260. L. Rollo *v.* Rollo, 1865 ; 3 Macph. 78. Scott *v.* Scott, 1855 ; 18 D. 168. D. Hamilton *v.* Hamilton, 1868 ; 7 Macph. 139 ; aff. 8 Macph. H. L. 48. Wallace *v.* Wallace's Trs., 1880 ; 7 R. 902.

(*g*) 3 Ersk. 8. § 25, 29. 3 M'Kenzie, 8. § 17. V. Stormont *v.* E. Annandale's Crs., 1662 ; M. 15,472. Baillie *v.* Carmichael, 1734 ; M. 15,500 ; Elchies, *Tailzie*, 1. Gairdner *v.* Primrose, 1744 ; M. 15,501. Kempt *v.* Watt, 1779 ; M. 15,528 ; Hailes, 819. Adam *v.* Barclay, 1821 ; Hume, 877 ; 1 S. App. 24. Thomson *v.* Milne, 1839 ; 1 D. 592.

(*h*) Reidhaugh *v.* Bruce, 1707 ; M. 15,489. Craig's Crs. *v.* Craig, 1712 ; M. 15,494 ; Robertson's Ap. 110. Hepburn *v.* Hepburns (Humbie Case), 1758 ; M. 15,507 ; 5 B. Sup. 331 and 864 ; 2 Pat. 17. Bruce *v.* Bruce, 1830 ; 4 W. & S. 240. Mitchelson *v.* Atkinson, 1831 ; 9 S. 741.

(*i*) Munro, *supra* (*a*). Gordon *v.* Gordon (Carleton Case), 1749 ; M. 15,384 ; 5 B. Sup. 774. Gilmour *v.* Hunter, 1801 ; M. *Tailzie*, Apx. 18. L. Elibank *v.* Murray, 1835 ; 1 S. & M'L. 1 ; 2 Ill. 358. Morehead *v.* Morehead, 1835 ; 1 S. & M'L. 29. Douglas & Co. *v.* Glassford, 1825 ; 1 W. & S. 323. M'Gregor *v.* Brown, 1838 ; aff. 3 S. & M'L. 84. Campbell *v.* M. Breadalbane, 1838 ; 1 D. 81. Wauchope *v.* Wauchopes, 1884 ; 11 R. 424.

(*k*) Campbell, *supra* (*i*). (*l*) Munro, *supra* (*a*).

(*m*) L. Wharncliffe *v.* Nairne, 1849 ; 12 D. 1 ; aff. 1850, 7 Bell's App. 132. Gibson *v.* Gibson, 1869 ; 7 Macph. 791.

1733. Powers under Entails.—While the entailer wishes in general strictly to prohibit the sale or burdening of the estate, there may be particular occasions on which, for the benefit of all concerned, a relaxation of those restraints may be useful. This is the use of clauses of power, which are commonly directed to the following purposes:—1. A power to sell for satisfying the entailer's debts (*a*). 2. A power to excamb, or to sell and reinvest for the purpose of concentrating the estate (*b*). 3. A power to grant feus of portions of the estate, or to a certain extent, or in particular circumstances (*c*); it not being permitted, however, under such a clause substantially to defeat the entail. 4. A power to burden the estate, to a certain extent, with provisions for widows or children (*d*); and this either within prescribed limits, at a certain number of years' rent of the estate (*e*), or left discretionary (as by the term "reasonable provisions"), in which case the Court must deal with it according to equity (*f*). 5. A power to alter the destination, so as to avoid the succession of an idiot or a bankrupt (*g*); 'or to nominate heirs in the event of the succession opening to heirs-portioners (*h*).' 6. A power in particular circumstances (qualifying the clause prohibiting alienations) to grant long leases (*i*).

(*a*) Kilburney *v.* Schaw, 1669 ; M. 15,347 ; 2 Ill. 368. See above, § 1728 ; and below, § 1771.

(*b*) 6 and 7 Will. IV. c. 42. See E. Breadalbane, petr., 1830 ; 8 S. 490. See below, § 1770. Baird *v.* Baird, 1844 ; 6 D. 643 ; aff. 1847, 6 Bell's App. 7.

(*c*) D. Roxburghe *v.* Don, 1734 ; Cr. & St. 126. Shaw *v.* L. Cathcart, 1754 ; M. 15,558 ; 5 B. Sup. 816 ; aff. 1 Pat. 618. Innes *v.* D. Roxburghe, *infra*, § 1750. M. Abercorn *v.* Marnoch, Jan. 26, 1816 ; F. C.

(*d*) See below, § 1772. Erskine *v.* E. Mar, 1829 ; 7 S. 844. E. Rothes *v.* Css. Rothes, 1829 ; 7 S. 330. Cleghorn *v.* Elliot, 1833 ; 11 S. 259. See the cases in Rankine on Landownership, 588–593. A relaxation of one of the prohibitions for this purpose, even although it should give power to sell part of the estate to satisfy the provisions, is not a "defect" making the entail "invalid and ineffectual" in terms of the 43rd sec. of the Rutherfurd Act (*supra*, § 1730A). Catton *v.* Mackenzie, 1870 ; 8 Macph. 1049 ; aff. 1872, 10 Macph. H. L. 12. Rogerson *v.* Rogerson, 1872 ; 10 Macph. 698. Malcolm *v.* Kirk, 1873 ; 11 Macph. 722.

(*e*) Douglas *v.* Douglas, 1822 ; 1 S. 408. Malcolm *v.* Malcolm, 1823 ; 2 S. 514. E. Rothes, *supra* (*d*). See below, § 1751 and 1772. Gray, petr., 1870 ; 8 Macph. 990. Irving *v.* Irving, 1871 ; 9 Macph. 539. L. Lovat *v.* Fraser, 1885 ; 12 R. 1179.

(*f*) E. Mar *v.* Erskine, 1831 ; 5 W. & S. 611. Howden *v.* Porterfield, 1834 ; 12 S. 734 ; 1 S. & M'L. 739.

(g) Halket v. Wedderburn, 1762; M. 15,416. See below, § 1759.
(h) Martin v. Kelso, 1853; 15 D. 950.
(i) See 10 Geo. III. c. 51; below, § 1752 and 1764 et seq. Besides the above conventional clauses of powers, the Legislature has interfered on several occasions with statutes of power; for which see below, § 1762 et seq. As to power to redeem the land-tax, see below, § 1773.

1734. Completion of Entail.—It is required, as indispensable to an entail effectual against third parties, that the prohibitions, conditions, and irritancies shall enter the registered infeftment; and that the deed shall be recorded in the Register of Tailzies. 'By the Titles to Land Consolidation Act, an instrument of sasine is not necessary; the deed of entail itself may be recorded in the Register of Sasines (a). And in conveyances of entailed lands, or lands purchased or acquired for the purpose of being added to an entailed estate, or entailed on the heirs, or under the conditions specified in any deed of entail, it is enough specially to refer in a statutory form to the destination of heirs, or the conditions, provisions, and prohibitory, irritant, and resolutive clauses, or clause authorising registration in the Register of Tailzies, as set forth at full length in the deed of entail recorded in the Register of Tailzies, or in any deed recorded in the appropriate Register of Sasines, and forming part of the progress of titles (b).'

(a) See above, § 770A.
(b) 31 and 32 Vict. c. 101, § 9. See Mowbray's Hendry's Manual of Conveyancing, pp. 448, 449.

1735. (1.) *Sasine.*—Although the statute applies only to entails which shall be completed by sasine, and duly registered in the Record of Sasines, in which the prohibitions, conditions, and irritancies shall appear, yet certain distinctions are of importance:—

1736. While the deed of entail is not yet completed by infeftment, the conditions and prohibitions, properly guarded by irritant and resolutive clauses, will be effectual against third parties deriving right from the heir in possession, *if he has no other title but only the tailzie.* The principle of this is, that the personal right is qualified or limited by its conditions (a).

(a) **Stewart (Baillie)** v. **Denham,** 1733; M. 7275; Cr. & St. 113; 2 Ill. 371; 3 Ross' L. C. 186. Boyd v. ——, 1766; 5 B. Sup. 919 and 922. Syme v. Dewar, 1803; M. 15,619. Chisholm v. M'Donald, 1800; M. Apx. *Tailzie,* No. 6. E. Fife v. Duff, 1861; 23 D. 657; 1862, 24 D. 936; aff. 1863, 1 Macph. H. L. 19; 4 Macq. 469 (not necessary that entail constituted by conveyance of personal fee should form part of the feudal title). Comp. Howden v. Fleeming, 1867; 5 Macph. 658; rev. 1868; 6 Macph. H. L. 113.

1737. If the person in possession be also *heir-at-law* (*alioquin successurus*), his creditors may attach the estate by means of that right of succession, provided the entail shall not have been completed by sasine and registration of the entail. Or such heir *alioquin successurus*, disregarding the entail, may complete his title as heir, and effectually sell or burden the estate (a).

(a) **Douglas (Kelhead)** v. **Stewart,** 1765; M. 15,616; Bell's Ca. 168, note; 5 B. Sup. 907; 2 Ill. 372; 3 Ross' L. C. 174. Cunningham's Crs. v. Cunninghams, 1806; Hume, 872. Russell v. Pirrie, 1791; M. 10,300; Bell's Ca. 166. Dickson v. Syme, 1801; M. *Tailzie,* No. 7. Graham v. Graham's Crs., 1795; M. 15,439; Bell's Ca. 162. Mitchell v. Tarbert, Feb. 4, 1809; F. C. See Munro v. Drummond, 1831; 5 W. & S. 359. Ross v. Drummond, 1841; 3 D. 698.

1738. (2.) *Enforcement.*—The heir may, at the suit of the substitutes, be judicially compelled to complete his title under the entail, with the conditions, prohibitions, and irritant and resolutive clauses; and this not only by force of a condition in the deed to that effect, but by force also of the statute.

1739. In construing the obligation to insert the restraining clauses in the procuratories of resignation, charters, precepts, and instruments of sasine (a), it 'was' held, 'in regard to old titles,'—That a reference in the precept to the prohibitions and irritant and resolutive clauses in another part of the deed will be sufficient, provided the clauses appear in the instrument of sasine (b); that the clauses, in order to be effectual, must appear in the instrument of sasine (c); that the clauses must also be engrossed in the deed of entail itself, or at least by reference to another entail upon record (d); and that it is not sufficient that the entail shall once have been thus completed by infeftment; each succeeding heir must insert the clauses in his infeftment, in order to bind third parties (e). 'Entails invalid in regard to any of the prohibitions by reason of any defect in the investiture, are now deemed invalid as regards all the prohibitions (f). But an error in the investiture is cured, so far as the estate is not affected by the debts and deeds of former heirs, by a succeeding heir making up a correct title (g).'

(*a*) See above, § 1724B.
(*b*) Kynynmond's Crs. *v.* Kynynmond, 1744 ; M. 15,380 ; 5 B. Sup. 738 ; Elch. *Tailzie*, 26 ; 2 Ill. 373.
(*c*) Kynynmond, *supra* (*b*). V. Garnock *v.* Garnock, 1725; M. 15,596; 2 Ill. 373 and 377. Porterfield *v.* Corbett, 1842; 4 D. 23. E. Buchan *v.* Erskine, 1842 ; 4 D. 1430 ; aff. 1845, 4 Bell's App. 22.
(*d*) Broomfield *v.* Paterson, 1784 ; M. 15,618 ; 1786, 3 Pat. 50. Don *v.* Don, July 14, 1713 ; Robertson's Ap. 76 ; 2 Ill. 362. Lawrie *v.* Spalding, 1764; M. 15,612. See Vere *v.* Hope, 1833 ; 11 S. 520 ; 2 S. & M'L. 817. The fetters must be in the deed containing the disposition, and cannot be imposed by reference. See above, § 1730.
(*e*) V. Garnock, *supra* (*c*). See Holmes *v.* Cuningham, 1851 ; 13 D. 689. Cuningham's Trs. *v.* Cuningham, 1852 ; 14 D. 1065. Stirling *v.* Moray, 1845 ; 7 D. 640. Lady Hawarden *v.* Dunlop, 1865 ; 3 Macph. 748 ; aff. 4 Macph. H. L. 41.
(*f*) 11 and 12 Vict. c. 36, § 43. See above, § 1730A.
(*g*) Borthwick *v.* Glassford, 1853 ; 16 D. 37. Hamilton *v.* Lindsey Bucknall, 1869 ; 8 Macph. 323.

1740. (3.) *Recording of the Entail.*—This registration is by judicial warrant of the Court of Session, and in a register appointed for tailzies (*a*). The writ to be recorded is the original entail, not a charter proceeding on it; and although the entailer has himself sold part of the lands, the whole entail must be recorded (*b*). 'Alterations of the settlement, as by deeds of nomination of heirs, must be recorded in the Register of Tailzies (*c*); but not a deed of propulsion (*d*).'

(*a*) 1685, c. 22. Irvine *v.* E. Aberdeen, 1776 ; 5 B. Sup. 622 ; M. *Tailzie*, Apx. 1 ; aff. 2 Pat. 249 ; 2 Ill. 374. Hamilton, petr., 1777 ; 5 B. Sup. 624. An entail might thus be exposed to danger during a whole vacation, when no warrant to record could be obtained. Williamson *v.* Sharp, 1851; 14 D. 127. See 38 and 39 Vict. c. 61, § 12 (1).
(*b*) Moore, petr., Nov. 28, 1821 ; 1 S. 173. Irvine, *supra*. L. Forbes *v.* Gammell, 1858 ; 20 D. 917. E. Fife *v.* Duff, 1862; 24 D. 936 ; aff. 4 Macq. 469. Padwick *v.* Stewart, 1874 ; 1 R. 697. King *v.* E. Stair, 1844 ; 6 D. 821 ; aff. 5 Bell's App. 82 (general disposition). E. Mansfield *v.* Stewart, 1844 ; 6 D. 1073 ; aff. 5 Bell's App. 139. See 31 and 32 Vict. c. 101, § 11, permitting short descriptions and descriptions by reference.
(*c*) E. Mansfield *v.* Stewart, 1844 ; 6 D. 1073 ; aff. 5 Bell's App. 139. Montgomerie *v.* E. Eglinton, 1842 ; 4 D. 425 ; 1843, 2 Bell's App. 149. Inglis *v.* Inglis, 1851 ; 14 D. 54 ; 15 D. H. L. 44. Broomfield, *supra*, § 1739 (*d*). Padwick, *supra* (*b*).
(*d*) Turnbull *v.* Newton, 1836 ; 14 S. 1031.

1741. Recording in the Register of Tailzies is not necessary in order to render the tailzie effectual against the heirs and substitutes themselves (*a*). But without such registration the tailzie has no effect against third parties. The estate may be effectually sold (*b*), and is at all times open to the diligence of creditors who have contracted with the heir in possession before the recording of the entail (*c*).

(*a*) Willison *v.* Callendar, 1724 ; M. 15,369 ; 2 Ill. 374. Hall *v.* Cassie, 1726 ; M. 15,373. M'Gill *v.* Law, 1798 ; M. 15,451. Broomfield, *supra*, § 1739 (*d*). Turnbull *v.* Hay-Newton, 1836 ; 14 S. 1031 ; 2 Ill. 363. Norton *v.* Stirling, 1852 ; 14 D. 944 ; aff. 2 Macq. 205. King, *supra*, § 1740 (*b*). Dalrymple *v.* E. Stair, 1841 ; 3 D. 837. Montgomerie *v.* E. Eglinton, *cit.* § 1740 (*c*).
(*b*) Paterson *v.* Cuthbert, 1787 ; Hume, 869. Graham *v.* Graham, 1829 ; 8 S. 231 ; 5 W. & S. 759 ; 2 Ill. 375.
(*c*) Willison, *supra* (*a*). Napier *v.* Welsh, 1805 ; Hume, 870. Wilson *v.* Gray, 1808 ; *ib.* 873. Smollet's Crs. *v.* Smollet, 1807 ; M. *Tailzie*, Apx. 25 ; 2 Ill. 375. Ferrier *v.* D. Roxburghe, Dec. 10, 1813 ; F. C. Munro *v.* Drummond, 1828 ; 6 S. 945 ; aff. 5 W. & S. 359 ; 1836, 14 S. 453. See the following cases as to entails made before the Act 1685. Cant *v.* Borthwick, 1726 ; M. 15,554. Craig *v.* Craig, Robertson's Ap. 117, note ; 2 Ill. 356 and 377. Hepburn *v.* Hepburns, 1758 ; M. 15,507 ; 5 B. Sup. 331; aff. 2 Pat. 17 ; 2 Ill. 377. Philp *v.* E. Rothes, 1758 ; M. 15,609 ; 5 B. Sup. 365, 869. V. Garnock *v.* E. Glasgow, 1740 ; Cr. & St. App. 281 (cf. *supra*, § 1739 (*c*)). Kinnaird *v.* Hunter, 1761 ; M. 15,611 ; aff. 2 Pat. 97 ; 2 Ill. 277. E. Rosebery *v.* Baird, 1765 ; M. 15,616. Irvine *v.* E. Aberdeen, 1772 ; M. *Tailzie*, Apx. 1 ; 5 B. Sup. 622 ; aff. 2 Pat. 249 ; 2 Ill. 374.

1742. The proper party to produce the deed and apply for the recording of it as a tailzie is the maker of the entail, or the institute or heir in possession (*a*); but it may be done after the entailer's death (*b*), and by any substitute who has an interest, and can produce the original deed of entail; for which incident diligence will be granted (*c*). It would seem that an "heir whatsoever" is not entitled to apply for the recording of the entail (*d*). The application is by summary petition to the Court of Session (*e*).

(*a*) Nairne *v.* Nairne, 1757 ; M. 15,605 ; 5 B. Sup. 335. Reid, petr., 1710 ; 4 B. Sup. 794 ; 2 Ill. 378.
(*b*) L. Napier *v.* Livingstone, 1762 ; 5 B. Sup. 888. See Kilk. 5 B. Sup. 335.
(*c*) 3 Ersk. 8. § 26. Cavers *v.* Cavers, 1707 ; 4 B. Sup. 666. Spittal, petr., 1781 ; M. 15,617. Ker, petr., 1804 ; M. 14,984. Drummond *v.* Drummond, 1744 ; Elchies, *Tailzie*, 27 ; Notes, 453. See Gilmour *v.* Gilmour, 1856 ; 19 D. 134.
(*d*) Jessop, petr., 1822 ; 1 S. 273. See above, § 1723.
(*e*) More, petr., 1753 ; M. 15,602. Houston *v.* Shaw, 1715 ; M. 15,366. Nairne, *supra* (*a*) ; Kilk. 5 B. Sup. 335. Ker, *supra* (*c*).

1743. Liabilities of Heirs of Entail.—1. An heir of entail is personally liable for the entailer's debts only to a limited extent. This, after much diversity of opinion (*a*), has been fixed to be only to the amount of the value of the estate (*b*). 2. The entailed estate itself is liable, and may be adjudged or sold for those debts (*c*). 3. The heir of entail in possession is not bound to pay those debts, but may leave them, both principal and interest, as burdens on the estate, in the hands of subsequent heirs of entail (*d*); and it is to prevent this that the condition compelling the heir of entail to pay off debts and purge adjudication is so frequently inserted in entails. Sometimes leave is given to constitute the entailer's debt a burden, or to sell part of the estate for discharging it, and such condition will be effectual (*e*); and now by statute such sale is authorised to take place (*f*). The entailer's debts will be allocated rateably on two estates left by him under entails, in a question between the respective heirs (*g*). 4. The heir of entail, although not bound to pay off those debts, may, on paying them, take assignations, and keep them up against the estate (*h*), 'and will be held to have done so in the absence of evidence to the contrary (*i*). But by taking a simple discharge, an heir of entail paying a debt due by the estate is held to intend to extinguish the debt (*k*).' 5. As to the debts of preceding heirs of entail, those arising on meliorations under leases will not bind subsequent heirs (*l*), unless made effectual under the 10 Geo. III. (*m*); and debts which may lawfully be incurred under the entail will not, unless constituted as the entail prescribes, bind succeeding heirs; as, for example, aliment, mourning, etc., of the widow and family, and even funeral expenses of a preceding heir (*n*); and provisions granted in terms of the entail may be kept up against the estate (*o*).

(*a*) Maitland *v.* Maitland's Crs., 1755; 5 B. Sup. 837; 2 Ill. 378. Murray Kynynmond *v.* ——, 1748; Elch. *Tailzie*, No. 34; 5 B. Sup. 764. Gordon *v.* Maitland, 1757; M. 11,166.

(*b*) Sutherland *v.* Sinclair, 1801; M. *Tailzie*, Apx. No. 8.

(*c*) E. Lauderdale *v.* Heirs of Entail, 1730; M. 15,556.

(*d*) Campbell *v.* Campbell, Nov. 29, 1815; F. C. Dss. Richmond *v.* D. Richmond, 1837; 16 S. 172; 3 Ill. 161. But though, if he fail to pay, the interest as well as the principal affects the entailed estate, yet the heir in possession is primarily liable for the interest of such debts. Cases cited. Erskine *v.* E. Mar, 1829; 7 S. 844. Sands *v.* Brisbane, 1835; 13 S. 1040. See 11 and 12 Vict. c. 36, § 17, 18, 21.

(*e*) Vis. Strathallan *v.* Drummond, 1828; 6 S. 881.

(*f*) 6 and 7 Will. IV. c. 42, § 9. See also 4 and 5 Vict. c. 24; 11 and 12 Vict. c. 36.

(*g*) Lawrie *v.* Donald, 1830; 9 S. 147.

(*h*) Kerr *v.* Turnbull, 1758; M. 15,551. Campbell *v.* Campbell, Nov. 29, 1815; F. C. Welsh *v.* Barstow, 1837, 15 S. 537. *Supra*, § 1728. M'Donald *v.* M'Donald, 1877; 4 R. 280.

(*i*) Caddell *v.* Caddell's Trs., 1845; 7 D. 1014. Crawford, *infra* (*l*).

(*k*) Wauchope *v.* D. Roxburghe, Dec. 14, 1815; F. C.; aff. 1825, 1 W. & S. 41.

(*l*) Crawford *v.* Hotchkis, March 11, 1809; F. C. Lawrie, *supra* (*g*). Fraser *v.* Vans Agnew, 1827; 5 S. 722; aff. 5 W. & S. 69. See § 1256.

(*m*) See below, § 1764.

(*n*) Lauder *v.* Baird, 1744; M. 15,378. Campbell *v.* Campbell, Dec. 16, 1818; F. C.

(*o*) Crawford *v.* Hotchkis, March 11, 1809; F. C.

1744. Persons affected by the Fetters.—Considering an entail in its effects against third parties, the only descriptions of persons in relation to whom the effect of the limitations may be doubtful are: the Institute, 'the Conditional Institute,' and the Maker of the Entail (*a*).

(*a*) In regard to the application of the fetters to the heirs generally, see Dunbar *v.* Dunbars, 1799; M. 15,452. Munro *v.* Munro, 1826; 4 S. 467; aff. 1828, 3 W. & S. 344. Dalrymple *v.* Hunter, 1784; 6 Pat. 807. Holmes *v.* Cunningham, 1851; 13 D. 689. Wauchope *v.* Wauchopes, 1884; 11 R. 424.

1745. (1.) *Institute.*—The strict *words* of the statute do not authorise any restraint on the institute, who is a disponee, not an heir (*a*). Those words sanction "tailzies with irritant and resolutive clauses, whereby it shall not be lawful *to the heirs of tailzie* to sell," etc. And opinions have varied as to the competency of conditions or limitations directed against the institute. But at last it is settled that the institute may be placed under the conditions and prohibitions of the entail (*b*); but that he must be specifically comprehended in the prohibitory clauses, and pointed out by clear indications, not being included under the expressions "heir or member" of tailzie (*c*); and that in the irritant and resolutive clauses the institute may be included under a general term, provided the prohibitory clauses distinctly comprehend him (*d*).

(*a*) Willison *v.* Callendar, 1726; M. 15,458; 2 Ill. 374. Erskines *v.* Balfour-Hay, 1758; M. 4406; 2 Ill. 380. **Edmonston** *v.* **Edmonston** (Duntreath Case), 1769; M. 4409, 4411; Hailes, 298; in H. of Lords, 2 Pat. 255; 2 Ill. 380. See also **Gordon** *v.* **Lindsay Hay**, 1777; M. 15,462, and Apx. *Tailzie*, 2; Hailes, 761. Lord Chancellor Eldon's observations in Steel's Case, below (*c*), 5 Dow, 84.

(*b*) See the cases, *supra* (*a*), and below (*c*), *passim*.

(*c*) Steel *v.* Steel, May 12, 1814; F. C.; 5 Dow, 72; 6 Pat. 322. Baugh *v.* Murray, 1834; 12 S. 279. See Douglas & Co. *v.* Glassford, 1823; 2 S. 487; 1825, 1 W. & S. 323; 2 Ill. 368. Morehead *v.* Morehead, 1833; 11 S. 863; 1835, 1 S. & M'L. 29. Maxwell (Logan) *v.* Logan, 1836; 15 S. 291; 1839, 1 M'L. & R. 790. Brown *v.* M'Gregor, 1837; 15 S. 837; 1838, 3 S. & M'L. 84. Murray *v.* L. Elibank, 1833; 11 S. 858; 1835, 1 S. & M'L. 1. Campbell *v.* M. Breadalbane, 1838; 1 D. 81; 1841, 2 Rob. 109. Glendonwyn *v.* Gordon, 1870; 8 Macph. 1075; 1873, 11 Macph. H. L. 33. Thoms *v.* Thoms, 1868; 6 Macph. 704.

(*d*) Douglas & Co., *supra* (*c*). See Syme *v.* Dickson, 1799; M. 15,473; aff. 1803, 4 Pat. 471. Carrick Buchanan *v.* Carrick, 1838; 16 S. 358; 1844, 3 Bell's App. 342. Lindsay *v.* E. Aboyne, 1844; 3 Bell's App. 254. Seton *v.* Seton, 1854; 16 D. 658. Observe that by the definition clauses of the entail statutes of 1848, 1868, 1875, and 1882, "heir of entail" in these Acts includes the institute.

1746. (2.) *Conditional Institute.*—In distinguishing who shall be held as bound under the description of "heirs of tailzie," the person is institute to whom the first fee is directly given, whether he be maker of the tailzie (*a*); or another, named after a reserved liferent (*b*); or a conditional disponee, to whom the estate opens by the purifying of the condition (*c*). But it does not make one an institute, 'so as not to be bound by fetters directed only against heirs of tailzie,' that *ex eventu* he becomes the first holder of the estate in fee by the predecease of prior disponees; 'that is to say, the rule stated in the previous section does not apply to an heir substitute taking in virtue of the rule that a substitution implies a conditional institution' (*d*). Neither is a fiduciary fee sufficient to make the person to whom it is given institute; as, when a liferent allenarly is constituted, and the fee to persons unborn, the heir on his existence is institute (*e*). But it may be doubted whether a liferent to a father unrestricted, and a fee to children *nascituri* construed as a fee in the father, would be sufficient to characterise him as institute, so as to make the heir a substitute.

(*a*) Livingstone *v.* L. Napier, 1762; M. 15,418; 5 B. Sup. 885; 2 Pat. 108; 2 Ill. 383. Gordon *v.* M'Culloch, 1791; M. 15,465; Bell's Ca. 180. Maxwell *v.* Maxwell, 1817; Hume, 875.

(*b*) Wellwood *v.* Wellwood, 1791; M. 15,463, and see 15,466; Bell's Ca. 191. M. Titchfield *v.* Cumming, 1798; M. 15,467; aff. 4 Pat. 157. Miller *v.* Cathcart, 1799; M. 15,471. Maxwell, *supra*, § 1745 (*c*).

(*c*) 3 Ersk. 8. § 44. Menzies *v.* Menzies, 1785; M. 15,436; Hailes, 969; aff. 4 Pat. 242, and 5 Pat. 522. Stevenson *v.* Barr, 1784; M. 14,862.

(*d*) Maxwell *v.* Maxwell, 1817; Hume, 875. M'Kenzie *v.* M'Kenzie, Nov. 24, 1818; F. C.; 1 S. App. 150; 2 Ill. 383. See above, § 1693; below, § 1839.

(*e*) Maxwell (Logan) *v.* Logan, *supra*, § 1745 (*c*).

1747. (3.) *Maker of the Entail.*—One cannot by a mere act of will or of settlement remove his estate from the reach of his creditors while he retains the fee; and so the maker of a tailzie cannot gratuitously include himself within the prohibitions, to the effect of prejudicing his creditors (*a*). But by an onerous or mutual tailzie such restraints may be imposed on the maker; or the estate may be withdrawn from the diligence of creditors 'whose debts have not become real charges on the estate before infeftment and registration' (*b*).

(*a*) 3 Ersk. 8. § 24. Scott *v.* Scott, 1713; M. 15,569; Robertson's Ap. 226; 2 Ill. 387. L. Lindores *v.* Stewart, 1714; M. 7735. **Dickson** *v.* **Cunninghame**, 1786; M. 15,534; 5 W. & S. 662; 1829, 7 S. 503; aff. 1831, 5 W. & S. 657; 2 Ill. 388.

(*b*) Sharp *v.* Sharp, 1631: M. 15,562 and 4299. Houston (Schaw) *v.* Schaw, 1715; M. 15,572; Robertson's Ap. 203. **Vans Agnew** *v.* **Stewart** (Sheuchan Case), 1784; M. 15,435; rem. 1814, 6 Pat. 60; June 2, 1818, F. C.; rev. 1 S. App. 320. See below, § 1757. Paul *v.* M'Leod, 1828; 6 S. 826. Dickson, *supra* (*a*). Carmichael *v.* Carmichael, Nov. 15, 1810, F. C.; aff. 1816, 6 Pat. 155.

1748. Effect of Prohibitions.—The restraints imposed by deeds of entail 'were' of three classes:—1. Against alienation. 2. Against the contraction of debt, so as to affect the estate. 3. Against altering the order of succession (*a*). 'But only the third remains under the present law (*b*).'

(*a*) The general rules of construction applicable to these clauses have already been stated above, § 1730; in addition to which, see below, § 1760.

(*b*) 45 and 46 Vict. c. 53, § 18–28.

1749. (1.) *Prohibition to Alienate* (*a*).—The words of the statute authorising this prohibition are: "Whereby it shall not be lawful to sell, annailzie or dispone the lands, or any part thereof." This prohibition must be clear and express (*b*). It must be distinctly pointed to the person whose power of alienation is in question, or to a class of persons within which he falls (*c*). It has been doubted whether the life-interest of the heir of entail in possession can be alienated or affected by diligence without incurring an irritancy under the clauses of prohibition. But it has been settled that a sale or adjudication of the life-interest, if duly guarded against any possible effect subsequent to the right of the heir in possession, is unobjectionable (*d*). And it has been held not to prevent a conveyance to an heir-presumptive, so as to propel the estate (*e*).

(*a*) See above, § 1732.

(*b*) Hepburn *v.* Hepburns, 1758; M. 15,507; aff. 2 Pat. 17; 2 Ill. 367. See Gordon Cumming *v.* Gordon, 1761; M. 15,513. Elliot *v.* Heirs of Entail, 1803; M. 15,542. Glassford's Tr. *v.* Glassford, 1864; 2 Macph. 1317. A prohibition against selling is held not to prevent gratuitous alienation. Russell *v.* Russell, 1852; 15 D. 192. E. Eglinton *v.* Montgomerie, 1845; 7 D. 425; aff. 1847, 6 Bell's App. 136. Boswell *v.* Boswell, 1852; 14 D. 378.

(*c*) Lady Nairn *v.* Nairn, 1736; Elchies, *voce* Tailzie, 5; rev. Cr. & St. 192; 2 Ill. 389. *Supra*, § 1745, 1746.

(*d*) Scottish Union Insur. Co. *v.* Graham, 1839; 1 D. 532. Graham *v.* Hunter, 1828; 7 S. 13. Fairlie's Trs. *v.* Fairlie, 1860; 22 D. 632.

(*e*) Gordon's Crs. *v.* Gordon (Carleton Case), 1749; M. 15,384; Elch. *Tail.* 37; 5 B. Sup. 774; 2 Ill. 357. Suttie *v.* ——, 1758; 5 B. Sup. 866. Halket Craigie *v.*

Craigie, Dec. 4, 1817; F. C.; 2 Ill. 389. M'Leod *v.* Mackenzie, 1827; 6 S. 77. Dalrymple *v.* Css. Glencairn, 1783; M. 15,433; aff. 6 Pat. 807. L. Wharncliffe, petr., 1852; 24 S. Jur. 553. 16 and 17 Vict. c. 94, § 22. 31 and 32 Vict. c. 84, § 13. V. Dupplin *v.* Hay, 1871; 10 Macph. 89. Steel *v.* Buchanan, 1879; 7 R. 15.

1750. The prohibition to alienate, when clearly expressed, strikes against the granting of feus, as well as against absolute and complete conveyances for a price (*a*).

(*a*) Innes or Ker *v.* D. Roxburghe, 1807; M. *Tailzie*, Apx. No. 13; 1808, *ib.* No. 18; 1813, 2 Dow, 149; 5 Pat. 320, 609, 768; 2 Ill. 369. See M'Kie *v.* Neill, 1736; Elchies, *Glebe*, 2; 2 Ill. 389. Robertson *v.* Hrs. of Little Dunkeld, 1791; M. 5153; Bell's Ca. 235. Halket Craigie, *supra*, § 1749 (*e*). Anstruther *v.* Anstruther, 1820; 3 D. 142; aff. 2 Bell's App. 242.

1751. The general prohibition to alienate is effectual to prevent the granting of a liferent or locality to the widow beyond the amount of the terce (*a*). This requires clauses of power usual in entails, and is the groundwork of Lord Aberdeen's Act (*b*). Even the terce may be excluded; but this requires an express provision in the entail (*c*).

(*a*) 3 Ersk. 8. § 30. See Halket Craigie, *supra*, § 1749 (*e*). Cant *v.* Borthwick, 1726; M. 15,554; 2 Ill. 390. Borthwick *v.* Borthwick, 1730; M. 15,556. See above, § 1733. Rogerson *v.* Rogerson, 1872; 10 Macph. 698.

(*b*) See below, § 1772.

(*c*) Gibson *v.* Kincaid, 1795; M. 15,869. Makgill *v.* Law, 1798; M. 15,451.

1752. Leases may also fall under this prohibition, whether, in expressing the prohibition, the word alienate or the word dispone be used (*a*). Long leases are thus barred; under which description (after many doubts and conflicting decisions) all leases seem to be included which exceed the ordinary term of a fair agricultural lease, or which are not leases for the purpose of improvement (*b*). And leases granted in violation of such a prohibition are not good to any extent, nor will they be sustained even when at the time of challenge the period to run is not beyond the term permitted by the entail (*c*). Leases, whether of long or of short duration, in which, instead of the full rent, a grassum is taken, are held to fall under the prohibition against alienation (*d*). And a collusive or fraudulent lease, at a low rent, granted in circumstances to gain an advantage over the next heir, is reducible (*e*). An heir of entail may take a renunciation from a tenant and grant a new lease (*f*). But a new lease, while the old is current, will not be effectual to bind the succeeding heir of entail (*g*).

Leases of coal, marble, stone, etc., are 'not' within the prohibition against alienation (*h*). And no lease of the mansion-house and policy, or fields around the house, can, in the face of a prohibition to alienate, be granted to the prejudice of the 'next' heir of entail (*i*).

Where there is no prohibition against alienation, there is no limitation of the power to grant leases, either as to duration or as to grassum. Nor is the heir who takes a grassum in such case bound to invest it for the benefit of the substitutes (*k*).

(*a*) Elliot *v.* Pott, 1803 and 1814; rev. 1 S. App. 16 and 89; 2 Ill. 390. Stirling *v.* Walker, 1821; rev. 3 W. & S. 462. Montgomery *v.* E. Wemyss, 1817; 5 Dow, 293. Mordaunt *v.* Innes, March 9, 1819; F. C.; 1 S. App. 169. Queensberry Leases, 1807; M. Apx. *Tailzie*, 15; 1813, 5 Pat. 758; 1819, 2 Dow, 94; 1 Bligh, 339; 1 S. App. 169; 2 W. & S. 265; 6 Pat. 466; 2 Ill. 392. E. Elgin *v.* Welwood, 1821; 1 S. App. 44. Bontine *v.* Bontine, 1864; 2 Macph. 918.

(*b*) Leslie *v.* Orme, 1779; M. 15,530; Hailes, 832; aff. 2 Pat. 533; 2 Ill. 391. See 2 Dow, 112, and 1 Bligh, 510. Malcolm *v.* Henderson, 1807; M. *Tailzie*, Apx. 57; aff. 2 Dow, 285. Turner *v.* Turner, 1817; M. Apx. *Tailzie*, 16; aff. 1 Dow, 423. Queensberry Leases, *supra* (*a*). Mordaunt, *supra* (*a*). See Jordanhill's Crs. *v.* E. Crawford, 1852; Elchies, *Tack*, 18; 5 B. Sup. 797.

(*c*) D. Gordon *v.* Innes, 1822; 1 S. App. 169. Malcolm *v.* Bardner, 1823; 2 S. 366. See above, § 1182 sqq., 1194, 1195. 1 Bell's Com. 70. Forbes *v.* Wilson, 1873; 11 Macph. 454. Miller *v.* Carrick, 1867; 5 Macph. 715; aff. 1868, 6 Macph. H. L. 101. Cleland *v.* Morrison, 1878; 6 R. 156 (distinct and separate grants).

(*d*) Elliot *v.* Currie, 1798; M. 15,450. Queensberry Leases, *supra* (*a*). E. Wemyss *v.* D. Queensberry's Exrs., 1821; 1 S. 202.

(*e*) L. Elibank *v.* Hamilton, 1827; 6 S. 69. Justice *v.* Ross, 1829; 8 S. 108.

(*f*) D. Queensberry's Exrs. *v.* E. Wemyss, Nov. 15, 1815; F. C.

(*g*) Leslie, *supra* (*b*). Redhead *v.* Kerr, 1792; Bell's Ca. 202; as rev. 3 Pat. 309.

(*h*) Muirhead *v.* Young, 1855; 17 D. 875; 1858, 20 D. 592.

(*i*) L. Cathcart *v.* Stewart (Nicolson), 1755; M. 15,399; 5 B. Sup. 818; aff. Cr. & St. 618. Leslie, *supra* (*b*). See Roxburghe Case (Innes *v.* Ker), 2 Dow, 149; 5 Pat. 320. Turner *v.* Turner, Dec. 6, 1811; F. C.

(*k*) Wellwood *v.* Wellwood, 1823; 2 S. 423; 2 Ill. 394. Denham *v.* Wilson, 1761; M. 15,512.

1753. The constitution of a thirlage to a mill, not part of the estate, was under this clause held an alienation (*a*).

(*a*) Ranking of Balgair, 1763; 5 B. Sup. 622; 2 Ill. 395.

1754. An heir of entail under prohibition to alienate may cut down wood, and cannot be stopped by the substitutes (*a*). It has been attempted in various circumstances to restrain operations of this kind, as the cutting of unripe wood, of ornamental timber, of wood which it is proper in the right administration of the estate to preserve, and so forth; but in all these cases the restraint is so discretionary, and so little grounded on any settled judicial principle, as to raise great doubts whether it can be enforced (*b*). 'It has been laid down that, where there are no express provisions or prohibitions in the entail, the heir in possession may be restrained from cutting down trees which are required for the reasonable enjoyment of the mansion-house, or which are not ripe for cutting (*c*).'

(*a*) Hamilton *v.* Viscss. Oxford, 1757; M. 15,408; 2 Ill. 395.

(*b*) M'Kenzie *v.* Mackenzie, 1824; 2 S. 643. Bontine *v.* Carrick, 1827; 5 S. 811, and 6 S. 74. See Cathcart, *supra*, § 1752 (*i*). Gordon *v.* Gordon, Jan. 24, 1811; F. C. See Moir *v.* Graham, 1826; 7 S. 730. L. Elibank *v.* Renton, 1833; 11 S. 238. Boyd *v.* Boyd, 1870; 8 Macph. 637. Gordon *v.* Rae, 1883; 11 R. 67.

(*c*) Boyd *v.* Boyd, *cit.* (*b*) and cases in (*b*). See also M. Huntly's Trs. *v.* Hallyburton, 1880; 8 R. 50.

1755. General provisions against doing any deed to prejudice the succession, or infringe or innovate the entail, do not import a prohibition to sell (*a*). The prohibition will be effectual if the prohibitory and irritant and resolutive clauses are pointed against "disponing, or squandering, or putting away" the estate, or any part thereof (*b*).

(*a*) Campbell *v.* Wightman, 1746; M. 15,505; Elchies, *Tailzie*, 29; 2 Ill. 395. Sinclair *v.* Sinclair, 1749; M. 15,382; Elchies, *ib.* 36; aff. Cr. & St. 459. Scott Nisbet *v.* Young, 1763; M. 15,516; aff. 2 Pat. 98; 2 Ill. 396. Murray *v.* Murray, 1842; 4 D. 803; aff. 3 Bell's App. 100. See Hay *v.* Hay, 1842; 5 D. 372.

(*b*) Gordon Cumming *v.* Gordon, 1761; M. 15,513.

1756. (2.) *Prohibition to contract Debt.*—The words of the statute authorise clauses "whereby it shall not be lawful" "to contract debt, or do any other deed whereby the lands, or any part thereof, may be apprised, adjudged, or evicted from the other substitutes," etc. This prohibition is commonly directed against the contracting of debt so as to affect the estate; and though general against "contracting debt," it is held to mean such debt as may affect the estate, or shall be made the ground of adjudication (*a*); 'but it does not become invalid because it is limited by an exception giving heirs in possession power to make provisions for their children (*b*). In the prohibition it is necessary to use words expressly prohibiting the contraction of debt whereby the lands may be affected, or words equivalent (*c*). This prohibition does not prevent an heir from pledging his life interest in the estate (*d*).' It has been doubted whether the substitutes of an entail are barred from objecting to a deed as falling under one of the direct prohibitions, if there be no prohibition against the contraction of debt, and the deed necessarily raise a debt against the estate. And it has been held that in such case the challenge is barred, as met by the debt being effectual (*e*).

(*a*) Nairne *v.* Gray, Feb. 15, 1810; F. C.; 2 Ill. 396. M'Kenzie *v.* M'Kenzie, 1823; 2 S. 331. Denham *v.* Denham, 1737; 5 B. Sup. 200; Elch. *Tailzie*, 9. See Nisbet *v.* Moncreiff, 1823; 2 S. 381. Monro *v.* Monro, 1826; 4 S. 467; aff. 3 W. & S. 344.

(*b*) Rogerson *v.* Rogerson, 1872; 10 Macph. 698. Catton *v.* Mackenzie, 1870; 8 Macph. 1049; 1872, 10 Macph. H. L. 12.

(*c*) Cathcart *v.* Cathcart, 1830; 8 S. 497; aff. 5 W. & S. 315. Seton *v.* Seton, 1854; 16 D. 659. Martin *v.* Dunbar, 1844; 6 D. 1320. Cathcart *v.* Maclaine, 1846; 8 D. 970. Dewar *v.* Burden, 1845; 8 D. 90; aff. 1850, 7 Bell's App. 32. Lindsay *v.* E. Aboyne, 1842; 4 D. 843; aff. 1844; 3 Bell's App. 254. Cochrane *v.* Bogle & Co., 1850; 7 Bell's App. 65. Adam *v.* Farquharson, 1840; 2 D. 1163; aff. 1844; 3 Bell's App. 295. Cathcart *v.* Cathcart, 1863; 1 Macph. 759. Arbuthnot *v.* Arbuthnot, 1865; 3 Macph. 835. Howden *v.* Rocheid, 1868; 6 Macph. 300. Rogerson *v.* Rogerson, 1872; 10 Macph. 698.

(*d*) Nairne *v.* Gray, *cit.* Bontine *v.* Graham, 1837; 15 S. 711. Ferrier *v.* Gartmore Crs., 1835; 13 S. 1121. See above, § 1749.

(*e*) Oliphant *v.* Scott, 1830; 8 S. 980; 2 Ill. 388.

1757. Under this provision and prohibition it is of course implied that the entail shall be duly completed; and in questions of competition between the heirs of entail and creditors, it is settled that where the entail is onerous, or purchased by money, or a mutual entail which cannot be recalled, the heirs of entail are to be dealt with as creditors in competition; so that the right of the proper creditors if first completed by infeftment, or of the heirs of entail if first made perfect under the statute by infeftment and recording in the record of tailzies, is to be preferred (*a*). But when the entail is not onerous, the estate is liable to attachment for debts contracted prior to the completion or recording of the entail; and such debts are not excluded by the completing and recording of the entail before the diligence (*b*).

(*a*) **Vans Agnew** *v.* **Stewart** (Sheuchan Case), 1784; M. 15,435; June 12, 1812; F. C.; rev. 1822, 1 S. App. 320; 2 Ill. 387.

(*b*) Smollet *v.* Smollet, 1807; M. Apx. *Tailzie*, 25; 2 Ill. 375. Rose *v.* Drummond, June 11, 1828; F. C.; 6 S. 945. See Agnew, *supra* (*a*); 5 W. & S. 360. Ferrier *v.* D. Roxburghe, Dec. 10, 1813; F. C. Munro *v.* Drummond, 1831; 5 W. & S. 359. Grahame *v.* Grahame, 1831; 5 W. & S. 759. Munro *v.* Drummond, 1836; 14 S. 453.

1758. A prohibition against altering or infringing the entail is not a bar to the contracting of debt; but a prohibition to burden the lands is a bar. The debts, however, will be effectual to all intents, except as burdens on the estate (*a*).

(*a*) Nisbet, *supra*, § 1756 (*a*). Rogerson *v.* Rogerson, 1872; 10 Macph. 698.

1759. (3.) *Prohibition to alter the Order of Succession.*—The words of the statute relative to this matter give sanction to provisions, etc., whereby "the succession may be frustrat or interrupted." This, like the others, must be a substantive prohibition, directed against the alteration of the order of the succession (*a*). No particular words are necessary to make the prohibition effectual, provided it be clearly expressed that no alteration shall be made on the line of succession; as, that the heir shall do nothing to hurt, prejudice, or infringe the foresaid tailzie, whereby the estate may be evicted, or the hopes of succession evaded (*b*). Such words used vaguely, and in the close of any of the other prohibitions, will not be sufficient (*c*). Where there is such a prohibition, it is not competent to add to the destination; or to impose new restrictions, though fortifying rather than invalidating the entail; or to add a resolutive clause; or to supply any other defect in order to make the entail more effectually binding (*d*). 'Hence an heir possessing under a defective entail prohibiting the alteration of the order of succession, could not make a new entail with more stringent fetters excluding the diligence of creditors, even in favour of the same series of heirs (*e*). But one result of the Entail Amendment Act is, that by acquiring the estate in fee-simple, an heir in possession may more effectually re-settle the estate in strict entail (*f*).'

(*a*) Stewart *v.* Sloan, 1789; M. 15,535; 2 Ill. 396. As to this prohibition, see above, § 1718.

(*b*) Innes or Ker *v.* D. Roxburghe, 1807; M. Apx. *Tailzie*, 13; aff. 2 Dow, 149; 5 Pat. 320, 609, 768. Maclaine *v.* Maclaine, 1807; M. Apx. *Tailzie*, 14. This case overruled; see Lang *v.* Lang, *infra*. Campbell *v.* Buchan, 1839; M'L. & R. 898.

(*c*) Brown *v.* Css. Dalhousie, 1808; M. Apx. *Tailzie*, No. 19. Purves' Trs. *v.* Campbell, 1814; Hume, 873. Henderson *v.* Henderson, Nov. 21, 1815; F. C. Oliphant *v.* Oliphant, June, 7, 1816; F. C. Barclay *v.* Adams, 1821; 1 S. App. 24; 2 Ill. 366. Tytler *v.* Tytler, 1826; 4 S. 541; 2 Ill. 347. E. Fife *v.* Duff, 1828; 6 S. 698. Cathcart *v.* Cathcart, 1830; 8 S. 497; aff. 5 W. & S. 315; 2 Ill. 361. Gilmour *v.* Cadell, 1838; 16 S. 1261. Braimer *v.* Bethune, 1839; 1 D. 383. Lang *v.* Lang, 1838; 1 D. 98; rev. 1839, M'L. & R. 871. Elphinston *v.* Burnett, 1850; 12 D. 848.

(*d*) Menzies *v.* Menzies (Culdares Case), 1785; M. 15,436; Hailes, 969; rem. 4 Pat. 242; aff. 5 Pat. 522; 2 Ill. 385. Douglas *v.* Johnston, 1804; M. Apx. *Fiar Abs.* 1; 2 Ill. 515. Monro *v.* Monro, Feb. 13, 1810; F. C. M'Wharrie, June 28, 1815, and Campbell, Dec. 15, 1820, not reported, but quoted as "the Argyll cases" in Lord Fife's Case, 6 S. 698. Meldrum *v.* Maitland, 1827; 5 S. 857. See Seton *v.* Seton, 1854; 16 D. 658. Graham *v.* Stewart, 1855; 2 Macq. 295.

(*e*) Cases cited (*d*).

(*f*) Urquhart *v.* Urquhart, 1851; 13 D. 472; aff. 1853, 1 Macq. 698. Scott *v.* Scott, 1855; 18 D. 168. Cochrane *v.* Baillie, 1855; 17 D. 659; aff. 1857, 2 Macq. 529. See 11 and 12 Vict. c. 36, § 4.

1760. (4.) *General Observations.*—In relation to these several prohibitions, it is of importance to observe, That it is not enough that the act or deed in question shall substantially have the effect of defeating the intention of the testator, if not clearly and substantially prohibited: That the general expression subjoined to any particular prohibition, "nor to do any other deed whereby the entail may be defeated," or the like vague terms, will be held as having reference only to an act or deed of that particular description to which the general words are subjoined: But that it is not necessary, on the other hand, to have the prohibition set forth in a distinct and separate clause; it having been held sufficient to distinguish it as a substantive and separate prohibition, if it be set off by such words as "nor" or "nor yet" (*a*). It has been doubted, on the words of the Act as a permissive statute, whether entails are sanctioned which do not protect the estate against *all* these three classes of danger. But the House of Lords, affirming a decision of the Court of Session, fixed that this 'was' not necessary; that the entail 'was' effectual so far as it 'went,' although it 'did' not proceed to the whole extent of the Act (*b*). 'But, as we have seen, this has been altered (*c*).'

(*a*) See Innes or Ker *v.* D. Roxburghe (Roxburghe Case), 1807; M. Apx. *Tailzie*, 3; aff. 2 Dow, 149; 5 Pat. 320; 2 Ill. 396. Maclaine *v.* Maclaine, 1807; M. Apx. *Tailzie*, No. 14. See as this case, Lang *v.* Lang, *infra*. Brown *v.* Css. Dalhousie, 1808; M. Apx. *Tailzie*, 19. Henderson *v.* Henderson, Nov. 21, 1815; F. C. Rowe *v.* Moneypenny, 1837; 15 S. 500. Gilmour *v.* Cadell, 1838; 16 S. 1261. Lang *v.* Lang, 1838; 1 D. 98; rev. 1 M'L. & Rob. 871.

(*b*) Cathcart *v.* Cathcart, 1830; 8 S. 497; aff. 5 W. & S. 315. Cochrane *v.* Bogle & Co., 1848; 11 D. 908; aff. 1850, 7 Bell's App. 65. See *supra*, § 1718.

(*c*) See *ante*, § 1730A.

1761. Effect of Irritancies.—By the statute "the next heir of tailzie may, immediately on contravention, pursue declarator thereof, and serve heir to him who died last infeft in the fee, and did not contravene, without necessity any way to represent the contravener." The contraventions which thus open the succession to the next substitute are, either from neglect of the conditions, or breach of any of the prohibitions, or some act declared to be a contravention incurring irritancy. So the irritancy must be declared (*a*), 'in an action commenced during the life of the contravener (*b*), by any substitute however remote (*c*).' As the heir of entail in possession commits no contravention, and of course incurs no irritancy by burdening the lands only during his own incumbency; when he creates such burdens, and afterwards incurs an irritancy, it 'was' much doubted what 'should' be the effect of the declarator. In one case (*d*) the irritancy was declared, but the effect against creditors holding real burdens on the contravener's life-interest was left undecided; as to which, on the one hand, it 'was' argued that what has once been done legitimately in favour of a third party cannot be defeasible by any subsequent act of the debtor, and that substitutes who take by contravention can take only under the burdens lawfully constituted. On the other hand, it 'was' contended that a creditor who takes a security on an estate liable to irritancy, must receive it only as a precarious security, dependent on the personal conduct and good faith of his debtor. 'It is now, however, enacted that no irritancy committed shall affect any person, being a purchaser or *boná fide* onerous creditor prior to the execution of the summons of declarator on which decree shall proceed, provided the conveyances, deeds, or securities are not inconsistent with the provisions of the entail (*e*). The irritancy may be purged before decree, if *restitutio in integrum* can be given (*f*).'

(*a*) 3 Ersk. 8. § 32. Simpson *v.* E. Home, 1697; M. 15,353; 2 Ill. 357. Gordon *v.* L. Adv., 1750; M. 4728; Elch. *Tailzie*, 38; 5 B. Sup. 782; see Cr. & St. 558; 2 Ill. 398.

(*b*) Bontine *v.* Dunlop, 1823; 2 S. 115. Maxwell *v.* Maxwell, 1843; 6 D. 255; aff. 1845, 5 Bell's App. 165. Fullerton *v.* Dalrymple, 1825; 1 W. & S. 410. Stewart *v.* Denholm, 1726; M. 7275.

(*c*) Simpson, *cit.* Irvine *v.* Irvine, 1713; M. 15,369. Dundas *v.* Murray, 1774; M. 15,430.

(*d*) Bontine *v.* Graham, 1837; 15 S. 711; 1838, 1 D. 286; 1840, 1 Rob. 347.

(*e*) 11 and 12 Vict. c. 36, § 40.

(*f*) Abernethie *v.* Forbes (Gordon), 1835; 13 S. 263; 1837, 15 S. 1167; aff. 1 Rob. App. 434.

1762. Statutory Powers.—Many entails contain, in clauses of power, relaxations of the general prohibitions (*a*). But the omission of such provisions, or inadequate and imperfect expression of them, leaves certain evils and inconveniences, which have induced the Legislature in several respects to relax the restraints imposed in deeds of entail. This is done either by special or by general statutes. And in all operations authorised by such statutes, the precise rules prescribed must be correctly and pointedly observed, according to the legal construction of the Act (*b*).

(*a*) See above, § 1733 et seq.

(*b*) Vans Agnew *v.* Stewart, 1832; 1 S. App. 333 (and above, § 1747). Lawrie *v.* Lawrie, 1814; 2 Dow, 556. Malcolm *v.* Malcolm, 1821; 2 Ill. 400. Elliot *v.* Wilson, 1826; 3 W. & S. 61. Paget *v.* E. Galloway, 1837; 15 S. 667. See below, § 1773.

1763. (1.) *Power to sell Superiorities.*—For the enfranchising of vassals holding of subject superiors, heirs of entail are allowed to sell superiorities to the vassal; the price to be laid out in 'payment of entailer's debts or other real charges, or in buying other' lands to be settled under the limitations of the tailzie (*a*).

(*a*) 20 Geo. II. c. 50, § 14, 15, 16, 17. 20 Geo. II. c. 51, § 2, 3. Howden *v.* Fleeming, 1867; 5 Macph. 658; rev. 1868, 6 Macph. H. L. 113 (see *per* L. Westbury). Fleeming *v.* Howden, 1868; 6 Macph. 782.

1764. (2.) *Power to grant Leases.*—By two several statutes leases may be granted by heirs of entail notwithstanding prohibitions and irritancies. By the first Act (*a*), leases for thirty-one years, or for fourteen years and an existing lifetime, or for two existing lifetimes, are permitted, provided that in leases for a time certain, one-third of the land let shall be enclosed in one-third of the term, two-thirds before the expiration of two-thirds of the term, and the whole before the expiration of the term; that in leases for two lifetimes, a third shall be enclosed in ten years, two-thirds in twenty, and the whole in thirty; that not more than forty acres shall be in one enclosure, if fit for the plough; that the manor-place, offices, garden, and enclosures, usually in the owner's possession, shall not be included; that the rent shall not be lower than that of the previous lease, and without any grassum; and that the former lease shall have expired, or be within a year of expiration (*b*). By a later Act, 'the Rosebery Act' (*c*), heirs of entail in possession are empowered to grant leases not exceeding twenty-one years, without grassum or any valuable consideration except the rent, 'and of minerals for a period not exceeding thirty-one years'; but not to include the home-farm or mansion-house (*d*) in any lease beyond the granter's life.

(*a*) 10 Geo. III. c. 51, § 1–7. This (the Montgomery Act) did not apply to entails dated on or after August 1, 1848. 11 and 12 Vict. c. 36, § 12; but this enactment is now repealed, 31 and 32 Vict. c. 84, § 8.

(*b*) Muirhead *v.* Young's Trs., 1855; 17 D. 875 (minerals). Clerk *v.* Clerk, 1872; 10 Macph. 647 (minerals). E. Fife's Trs. *v.* Wilson, 1859; 22 D. 191 (shootings). Gray *v.* Skinner, 1854; 16 D. 923. Mure *v.* Mure, Dec. 22, 1808; F. C. Miller *v.* Carrick, *infra*, § 1765.

(*c*) 6 and 7 Will. IV. c. 42, § 1. It applies to all entails, whether dated before or after August 1, 1848. See 1 and 2 Vict. c. 70, as to unrecorded entails; and 11 and 12 Vict. c. 36, § 4, and 16 and 17 Vict. c. 94, § 6, as to more extensive powers of leasing. See 4 and 5 Vict. c. 24.

(*d*) Montgomerie *v.* Vernon, 1895; 22 R. 465.

1765. To encourage the building of villages and houses, leases may be granted, not exceeding ninety-nine years, of five acres, and no more, to one person; not being within three hundred yards of the mansion-house; to be void, if 'at least one dwelling'-house to the value of £10 shall not be built on each half-acre within ten years (*a*). The houses are to be kept in repair, and tenantable 'under the same nullity'; and the rent is not to be under the former rent, and without grassum (*b*).

'The recent Entail Acts authorise feuing or letting on lease, with consents as in the case of disentails, the whole or any part of the estate (*c*). The heir in possession may, formerly with the authority of the Court, now of the Sheriff (*d*), grant feus or long leases of any part of the estate, except the mansion-house and policy, for the highest rent or feu-duty that can be got; such feus or leases being now subject to no limit as to area, but not exceeding in all, under the Act of 1848, one-eighth part of the estate, and no grassum being taken (*e*). Power may now be obtained by "continuing" petition to the Court to grant feus or long leases in a general form, with minimum rates of rent or feu-duty fixed by the Court (*f*).'

(*a*) This condition infers nullity, and is not a mere irritancy purgeable before decree. Miller *v.* Carrick, 1867; 5 Macph. 715; aff. 1868, 6 Macph. H. L. 101. See Carter *v.* Lornie, 1890; 18 R. 353 (factory of greater value not = dwelling-house).

(*b*) 10 Geo. III. c. 51, § 5. D. Buccleuch *v.* Ewart, 1827; 6 S. 128; 2 Ill. 401. 3 and 4 Vict. c. 48 gives power to grant in feu or long lease sites for churches and schools, playgrounds, burying-grounds, and dwelling-houses for the ministers and schoolmasters. Power to grant feus and long leases at the sight of the Sheriff is conferred by 31 and 32 Vict. c. 84, § 3–5. See 1 Hunter, L. & T. 92. 4 and 5 Vict. c. 38. 7 and 8 Vict. c. 37, and c. 44. 12 and 13 Vict. c. 49. 14 Vict. c. 24. 31 and 32 Vict. c. 44. The Education (Scotland) Act, 1872 (35 and 36 Vict. c. 62, § 37), partly incorporates the Lands Clauses Consolidation Act.

(*c*) 11 and 12 Vict. c. 36, § 4. See below, § 1774A. Christie, 1888; 15 R. 793.

(*d*) 31 and 32 Vict. c. 84, § 3–5.

(*e*) 11 and 12 Vict. c. 36, § 24. 31 and 32 Vict. c. 84, § 3–5. Stewart *v.* Stewart, 1877; 4 R. 981; 1878, 6 R. 145. Stewart *v.* Murdoch, 1882; 9 R. 458. See 45 and 46 Vict. c. 53, § 4, 5, 6, 8, 9.

(*f*) 16 and 17 Vict. c. 94, § 6, 13.

1766. (3.) *Power to make Improvements.*—The heir in possession under an entail cannot burden the succeeding heirs with the expense of improvements, 'which, so far as unpaid by him, pass at common law as a debt against his executors' (*a*). But in order to encourage improvement, by enclosing, planting, draining, etc., it was provided by the Legislature, that any heir of entail who shall lay out money in improvements, shall be a creditor to the succeeding and subsequent heirs of entail for three-fourths of the money so expended, to the extent of four years' free rent of the entailed estate, after deducting liferents, and public burdens, and interest of debts; provided he give notice in writing to the heir of entail next after his own issue, three months before commencing his improvement, of the kind of improvement intended; that he lodge a copy with the Sheriff-Clerk; and that annually, within four months after Martinmas, he lodge with the Sheriff-Clerk an account signed by him, with the vouchers, of the money expended that year (*b*). The forms prescribed must be very punctually observed, and are attended with so many difficulties as often to defeat the purpose (*c*). 'This Act is extended to private roads through entailed estates (*d*), to cottages for labourers (*e*), and to many (or most) other kinds of improvements (*f*). Facilities for granting bonds of annualrent or bonds and dispositions in security for sums expended on permanent or on substantial and beneficial improvements, are granted by the Entail Amendment Acts (*g*).'

(*a*) Dillon *v.* Campbell, 1780; M. 15,432; Hailes, 841 and 827; 2 Ill. 205. Webster *v.* Farquhar, 1791; M. 15,439; Bell's Ca. 207. Taylor *v.* Bethune, 1791; Bell's Ca. 214. Fraser *v.* Fraser, 1825; 4 S. 73; 1827, 5 S. 673; 1830, 8 S. 409; 5 W. & S. 69. Tod *v.* Moncrieff & Skene, 1823; 2 S. 213; 1 W. & S. 217. Mackenzie *v.* Mackenzie, 1849; 11 D. 956. Runcie *v.* Lumsden's Reprs., 1857; 19 D. 965. See Jolly *v.* Graham, 1831; 5 W. & S. 280. Ross *v.*

Hawkins, 1848; 10 D. 1288. Learmonth *v.* Sinclair's Trs., 1878; 5 R. 548. Sinclair's Trs. *v.* Sinclair, 1881; 8 R. 749. Waterson *v.* Stewart, 1881; 9 R. 155. By 41 and 42 Vict. c. 28, obligations incurred by an heir of entail in possession to tenants, or under other contracts for improvements, devolve, in case of his death after the Act, upon the heirs succeeding to the estate, to the relief of his executors. See E. Breadalbane *v.* Jamieson, 1877; 4 R. 667. Macdonald *v.* Johnstone, 1883; 10 R. 959. *Supra*, § 1256.

(*b*) 10 Geo. III. c. 51, § 9–26.

(*c*) Finlayson *v.* Monro, 1821; 1 S. 196. Thomson *v.* Mowat, 1824; 3 S. 372. Campbell *v.* Douglas, 1822; 1 S. 409. Elliot's Trs. *v.* Elliot, 1793; M. 15,624. Torrance *v.* Crawford, 1826; 2 W. & S. 429. Stirling *v.* Dalrymple, Dec. 14, 1814; F. C.

(*d*) 11 and 12 Vict. c. 36, § 20.

(*e*) 23 and 24 Vict. c. 95. 31 and 32 Vict. c. 84, § 12.

(*f*) 38 and 39 Vict. c. 61.

(*g*) 11 and 12 Vict. c. 36, § 13, 18, etc. 38 and 39 Vict. c. 61, § 7 sqq. 45 and 46 Vict. c. 53, § 5, 6, 23 (7). For the numerous cases under the Rutherfurd Act and the amending Acts, see the annotated Acts in the appendix to Mr. Rankine's valuable work on Landownership. As to power granted by the Court to borrow moneys for improvement expenditure and charge on the estate, see 38 and 39 Vict. c. 61, § 7 sqq.; 41 and 42 Vict. c. 28, § 3; 45 and 46 Vict. c. 53, § 4–6. See also above, § 1256 (*i*).

1767. The heir of entail succeeding may free himself from the demand for the expense of such improvements, by assigning one-third of the free rent of the estate, to be drawn by the executors of the heir who has expended the money, until they shall be indemnified; and any balance that may remain will become a debt against the next succeeding heir, preferable upon the rents; and if the next succeeding heir shall die before the expenditure shall be reimbursed, like proceedings may be taken against his successor; and so on till the money shall be repaid (*a*).

(*a*) 10 Geo. III. c. 51, § 18. See 11 and 12 Vict. c. 36.

1768. It is provided, that for money laid out in building and repairing the mansion-house, the heir of entail who shall expend it may be declared a creditor to the next succeeding and subsequent heirs of entail for three-fourths of the money, on following out proceedings similar to those relative to improvements; and if there are more estates than one, the right to build a mansion-house on one of the estates is not barred by the existence of a mansion-house already on the other; the rent of the whole being the criterion of the expense (*a*).

(*a*) 10 Geo. III. c. 51, § 27 et seq. Stirling, *supra*, § 1766 (*c*). 38 and 39 Vict. c. 61, § 3 (7). E. Breadalbane *v.* Jamieson, 1877; 4 R. 667. See Fogo, petr., 1877; 5 R. 319. M. Ailsa, petr., 1853; 15 D. 368.

1769. (4.) *Expenses of Roads, Jails, etc.*—For the building of jails, heirs of entail may be creditors of the succeeding heirs (according to the method of the above statute) for three-fourths of the money, but limited to one year's rent (*a*). For the expense of making roads, they may, to the extent of a year's rent, burden the estate, so that the estate itself shall not be adjudged, but only diligence against the rents be competent (*b*). The heir of entail may grant leave to take ground or materials, and renounce all claim for indemnification, so as to bind succeeding heirs (*c*).

(*a*) 59 Geo. III. c. 61, § 15, 16, 17.

(*b*) 4 Geo. IV. c. 49, § 25. (*c*) *Ib.* § 26.

1770. (5.) *Power to Excamb.*—A power is given by the statute of Geo. III., at the sight of the Sheriff, and with certain precautions, to exchange ground, to the extent of 30 acres of arable, or 100 of hill, 'now to the extent of 300 acres (*a*),' lying in one place and together (*b*). But more ample powers are conferred by a later Act (*c*). After three months' notice to the five next heirs of entail or their guardians, summary application may be made to the Court of Session for an excambion of any portion of the entailed estate not exceeding one-fourth part of the whole estate, and not including the mansion-house and home-farm or policy. On proof of the relative values, and a report of skilful persons, the Court, if satisfied of the expediency of the transaction, may authorise the excambion (*d*). The transaction is to be settled by a contract of excambion at the sight and with the approbation of the Court, and recorded in the Sheriff Court books. The lands exchanged to be, the one free of the entail, the other placed under it; the excess of value on either side, if under £200, to be paid to the heir in possession, or fee-simple proprietor, as the case may be (*e*). 'With the same consents and procedure as are required in a disentail, an heir in possession may excamb the whole estate (*f*).'

(*a*) 31 and 32 Vict. c. 84, § 14.

(*b*) 10 Geo. III. c. 51, § 32–3. M'Kechnie *v.* Graham, 1821; 1 S. 116; 2 Ill. 402. Hamilton *v.* Chancellor, 1833; 12 S. 22.

(*c*) 6 and 7 Will. IV. c. 42, § 3 et seq. See 4 and 5 Vict. c. 24; 16 and 17 Vict. c. 36, § 5, 36, 37; 16 and 17 Vict. c. 94, § 11; 38 and 39 Vict. c. 61, § 6, 12; 45 and 46 Vict. c. 53, § 12.

(*d*) L. Macdonald, petr., 1838; 16 S. 1259.

(*e*) 6 and 7 Will. IV. c. 42, § 3, 4, 5, 6.

(*f*) 11 and 12 Vict. c. 36, § 5. 38 and 39 Vict. c. 61, § 5. 45 and 46 Vict. c. 53, § 12. See below, § 1774A. Hamilton, petr., 1867; 5 Macph. 324.

1771. (6.) *Sale for Entailer's Debts.*—By the same statute (*a*), power has been given to sell part of the entailed estate for payment of the debts of the entailer. This is authorised to be done by summary petition to the Court of Session. On this the Court directs due notice to be given, and an inquiry and account to be taken of the debts; and in ascertaining the value, it has been held that, besides the real worth of the land, an additional sum as the price of the advantage of gaining a portion in the heart of the entailed estate was to be taken into view (*b*). The necessity is to be ascertained, and the portion of the estate fit to be sold. The intended sale is then to be advertised; the sale is to proceed by auction on articles of roup; the lands sold are to be adjudged to the purchaser free from the entail; the price is to be lodged in one of five banks specified in the Act at the highest interest, with an annual accumulation to be added to the principal, and bear interest. The price is to be applied by order of the Court to pay off the debt; and any balance of the price exceeding £200, with accruing interest, is to be laid out in the purchase of land to be entailed as before; if under £200, to be paid to the heir of entail in possession. 'More ample powers for selling the estate for paying entailer's debts are granted by the Rutherfurd Act as amended in later statutes (*c*).'

(*a*) 6 and 7 Will. IV. c. 42, § 7–19. Torrance, petr., 1839; 16 S. 1258.

(*b*) L. Macdonald, petr., 1838; 16 S. 1259.

(*c*) 11 and 12 Vict. c. 36, § 4, 6, 25, 26, 30; 16 and 17 Vict. c. 94, § 9; and 31 and 32 Vict. c. 84, § 9–11. See Duff's Commentary, p. 86; Menzies' Lectures, p. 708. *Supra*, § 1728.

1772. (7.) *Provisions to Widows and Children.*—Power is given (*a*) 'to heirs of entail in possession, which term includes the institute (*b*),' to provide a liferent 'annuity' of one-third of the free rent (*c*), 'as at the death of the granter (*d*),' to the widow of the heir in possession, deducting public burdens, liferents, and yearly interest of debts (*e*); to provide the husband of an heiress of entail in a liferent of a half of the free rent, one-third if there be already a similar liferent; to provide children, if one, to the extent of a year's rent, two years' rent if two, three years' rent if three or more 'in such proportions as the father pleases (*f*)': such allowances, however, not being permitted to affect the fee, but only the heir in possession; with power to him to demand a discharge on assigning to a trustee, to be named by the Court of Session, one-third of the clear rent of the estate, and so that in no case he shall thus be deprived of more than two-thirds of the rent. 'Provisions under this statute (the Aberdeen Act) are not evacuated by the operation of a clause of devolution (*g*). Heirs-apparent to entailed estates, with the consent of the heir in possession, may make provision for their wives and children to the same extent as the heir in possession can do under the Aberdeen Act (*h*).'

(*a*) 5 Geo. IV. c. 87. See 31 and 32 Vict. c. 84, § 8 (entailed money). 11 and 12 Vict. c. 36, § 4. 38 and 39 Vict. c. 61, § 6. 45 and 46 Vict. c. 53, § 4, 24. By 11 and 12 Vict. c. 36, § 12, 21, 29; 16 and 17 Vict. c. 94, § 7 and 23; 31 and 32 Vict. c. 84, § 8; and 45 and 46 Vict. c. 53, § 10, powers are conferred on heirs to grant provisions to children by bond and disposition in security affecting the fee of the estate. Duff's Commentary, 83; Menzies, 703. Callendar *v.* Callendar, 1869; 7 Macph. 777. Hope Johnstone, petr., 1880; 8 R. 160. Jardine *v.* Grant, 1891; 18 R. 870. See 38 and 39 Vict. c. 61, § 10. Rankine's Land-ownership, Annotated Acts in Appendices.

(*b*) Hamilton, petr., 1857; 19 D. 723.

(*c*) Including game rents and the value of shootings though unlet, the actual rent of minerals under current leases even though nearly exhausted, and the value of minerals unlet. Macpherson *v.* Macpherson, 1843; 5 D. 651; aff. 1846, 5 Bell's App. 280. Leith *v.* Leith, 1862; 24 D. 1059. Wellwood *v.* Wellwood, 1848; 11 D. 248. Douglas *v.* Scott, 1869; 8 Macph. 360. Menzies *v.* Inland Rev., 1878; 5 R. 531. Christie *v.* Christie, 1878; 6 R. 301; and the stipulated amount of feu-duty though unpaid. Lamont Campbell *v.* Carter Campbell, 1895; 22 R. 260. L. Belhaven and Stenton, 1895; 23 R. 423 (minerals nearly exhausted—overruling Wellwood and Douglas, *citt.*, which allowed an average of yearly rents to be taken). See also Maclaine *v.* Maclaine, 1845; 8 D. 150. D. Roxburghe *v.* Russell, 1881; 8 R. 862, and the cases in Rankine's Notes, *cit.*

(*d*) But if the annuity granted exceeds this limit, it is capable of expansion on the lapse of a previous annuity. Morison *v.* Morison, 1894; 21 R. 538.

(*e*) Bonar *v.* Anstruther, 1868; 6 Macph. 910; see Morison, *cit.*

(*f*) Paterson *v.* Paterson, 1888; 15 R. 1060.

(*g*) E. Kinnoull's Trs. *v.* Drummond, 1869; 7 Macph. 576. Cf. Bruce, petr., 1874; 1 R. 740.

(*h*) 31 and 32 Vict. c. 84, § 6.

1773. (8.) *Power to redeem Land-Tax* (*a*).—Power is given to heirs of entail to redeem the land-tax, either by selling or by borrowing money. The Court of Session is empowered to adjudge, after intimations in the *Gazette*, etc., a certain part of the estate for sale, the price to be paid to a trustee, on his finding security to pay it into the Bank of England; the surplus, after reducing the land-tax, to be lodged in bank, and employed in paying off debts of the entailer, but not such as do not affect the fee. But a sale for redemption of land-tax on terms different from those in the articles of sale is null (*b*). The precautions and proofs required by the statute must be carefully observed and produced, otherwise the sale will be defeated (*c*). The Court has power to judge of the fitness of the part sold for the purpose; as superiorities (*d*). The minority of the next heir is no bar, provided the next succeeding heir is called (*e*). An error of judgment in the Court of Session in executing the Act is not fatal to the sale (*f*). A sale of part of an entailed estate, to redeem the land-tax of that and another entailed estate, is legal (*g*). The fraud of an heir in possession, in managing such a sale, will not affect a stranger purchaser if the terms of the Act shall have been observed, but otherwise it will be fatal even to a stranger (*h*).

(*a*) Anderson & Dundas, petrs., Nov. 18, 1814; F. C.; 2 Ill. 403. 42 Geo. III. c. 116, § 61 sq. 16 and 17 Vict. c. 117. Sandford on Entails, 348 sqq. Scott (Elibank's Tr.) *v.* Alnutt, 1827; 6 S. 22; aff. 5 W. & S. 416.
(*b*) Malcolm *v.* Malcolm, 1821; 1 S. 174.
(*c*) Wilson *v.* Elliot, 1826; 4 S. 435; aff. 3 W. & S. 60.
(*d*) Sir J. Colquhoun, petr., 1803; M. 15,089.
(*e*) Elliot, *supra* (*c*).
(*f*) E. Wemyss *v.* Montgomerie, 1824; 2 S. App. 1.
(*g*) Lawrie *v.* Lawrie, 1806; M. Apx. *Public Burden*, 2; aff. 2 Dow, 556; see 4 S. 56.
(*h*) Lawrie, *supra* (*g*). Elliot, *supra* (*c*). Hamilton *v.* Miller, 1830; 9 S. 165. Baird *v.* Neill, 1835; 13 S. 927. As to results of rescinding the sale, see Cleghorn *v.* Eliott, 1833; 11 S. 259; 1837, 3 D. 1, 19; aff. M'L. & Rob. 1033.

1774. (9.) *Sale for Canals and Railways.*—Among the numerous Acts for canals and railways which have of late years been passed, questions are likely to arise relative to entailed estates. In one case, where the price to be paid for opening a particular line through an estate having been ascertained, the canal company proposed to give a large sum for the proprietor's consent to another line, and in the question whether this additional sum was to be invested like the rest of the price in lands to be entailed, or paid to the heir in possession, it was held to belong to all the heirs, and not to be distinguishable from the rest of the price (*a*).

(*a*) Maitland *v.* Gibson, 1831; 9 S. 443; aff. 6 W. & S. 388. See 8 and 9 Vict. c. 19, § 7–9, 67 sq., 71 sqq. (Lands Clauses Consolidation Act). Stewart *v.* Scottish North-E. Ry. Co., 1856; 18 D. 541; 1859, 3 Macq. 382, 416. 11 and 12 Vict. c. 36, § 26 (Rutherfurd Act). 16 and 17 Vict. c. 94, § 14, 16 (see cases in Digest, and Rankine on Landownership, 924).

1774A. '(10.) *Power to Disentail.*—The power of disentailing the estate was conferred on heirs of entail in possession by virtue of the tailzie, by the Rutherfurd Act (*a*).

'*Old Entails.*—All estates held under entails made *prior to 1st August* 1848 (*b*) might, under the authority of the Court of Session, be disentailed by an instrument of disentail executed by the heir in possession born after that date, being of full age; or by an heir born before that date, with consent of the heir-apparent born after that date and twenty-one years old (or if he were the only heir in existence, and unmarried); or with consent of all the heirs, if less than three; or with consent of the three next heirs (*c*); or with consent of the heir-apparent and two of the heirs who would (including the heir-apparent) be successively heir-apparent, provided that the nearest heir were twenty-one years old; or, if such consents were not given by any heir (including, since 1882, the nearest heir for the time, whose consent must formerly have been given by himself), the Court might assess the value of the heir's interest, and dispense with his consent, on payment or security of such value.

'*New Entails.*—Estates held under entails made *on or after 1st August* 1848 might under this Act be disentailed on the application of the heir in possession born after that date and of full age; or although born before that date, with the consent of the heir-apparent under the entail born after that date and twenty-five years old (*d*). But by the Entail (Scotland) Act, 1882, the distinction between old and new entails in regard to disentailing is removed. It is lawful for the heir in possession under a new entail to disentail and acquire the estate or part of it (*e*) in fee-simple in the manner provided by the previous Acts, if he be the only heir of entail in existence, or if he obtain the consents required by sec. 3 of the Rutherfurd Act in the case of old entails (*f*). If any heir should refuse his consent, the Court is empowered to ascertain the value in money of his expectancy or interest, and on payment of or security for the value to dispense with the consent and proceed in the disentail as if it had been given, arrangements always being made for the creditors of the heir secured over his right of succession or interest prior to the Act of 1882, or his wife's and children's provisions granted under the Entail Acts (*g*). A very important provision is also made in this Act for enabling the creditors of an heir entitled to disentail to proceed against the estate as if disentailed or force a disentail (*h*).

'An heir born and holding under an entail made before 1848 might disentail if he is the only heir in existence, and unmarried (*i*); or with the consent of all the heirs, if there were less than three at the time, or of the three nearest heirs at the time, or of the heir-apparent and the heir or heirs (not being fewer than two, including such heir-apparent), who would successively be heirs-apparent. An heir in possession, whose right is liable under a resolutive condition to be extinguished by the emergence of a nearer heir, may take advantage of these provisions (*k*). Upon the recording of the instrument of disentail in the Register of Tailzies, the estate is held in fee-simple, *i.e.* free from the fetters of the entail. It remains subject to the destination in the deed of entail, till that is altered by a habile deed (*l*). After the time for appealing to the House of Lords has elapsed, judgments of disentail are, as regards third parties, acting *bonâ fide* on the faith thereof, not reducible for irregularity or non-compliance with the provisions of the Act (*m*). When an entail is set aside, every provision and condition of the entail falls with it (*n*).'

(*a*) 11 and 12 Vict. c. 36, amended by 16 and 17 Vict. c. 94, and 38 and 39 Vict. c. 61. Hepburn *v.* Davies, 1868; 6 Macph. 1094. Irving *v.* Irving, 1871; 9 Macph. 539. See cases in Duncan's Manual of Entail Procedure. V. Dupplin *v.* Hay, 1871; 10 Macph. 89. Shand, petr., 1876; 3 R. 544. Binny, petr., 1876; 3 R. 831.

(*b*) Black *v.* Auld, 1873; 1 R. 133. Riddell, petr., 1874; 1 R. 462. Riddell *v.* L. Polwarth, 1876; 3 R. 879. Blair *v.* M'Gillivray, 1877; 4 R. 308. Buchanan *v.* Jameson, 1883; 10 R. 809.

(*c*) The interest of a child *in utero* is not regarded, the consents required being those of the nearest heirs at the time. See Douglas *v.* Campbell, 1885; 12 R. 916.

(*d*) V. Fincastle *v.* E. Dunmore, 1876; 3 R. 345.

(*e*) D. Sutherland *v.* M. Stafford, 1892; 19 R. 504.

(*f*) 45 and 46 Vict. c. 53, § 3, 17.

(*g*) *Ib.* § 13. De Virte *v.* Wilson, 1877; 5 R. 328. MacDonald *v.* MacDonalds, 1879; 6 R. 521, 869; rev. 1880, 7 R. H. L. 41. Kennedy *v.* Stewart, 1889; 16 R. 421; aff. 1890, 15 App. Ca. 75; 17 R. H. L. 1. Baird *v.* Baird, 1891; 18 R. 1184. Pringle *v.* Pringle, 1892; 19 R. 926.

(*h*) *Ib.* § 18.

(*i*) Gordon *v.* Mosse, 1851; 13 D. 954; 14 D. 269.

(*k*) Bruce, petr., 1874; 1 R. 740. Home *v.* Home, 1876; 3 R. 591. Forbes *v.* Burness, 1888; 15 R. 797.

(*l*) Gray *v.* Gray's Trs., 1878; 5 R. 820.

(*m*) 16 and 17 Vict. c. 94, § 24. V. Fincastle, *cit.* Mackenzie *v.* Catton's Trs., 1877; 5 R. 313.

(*n*) Dalgleish *v.* Rudd, 1897; 25 R. 225.

1774B. 'The Acts give general power to sell and alienate, charge, etc., on the same conditions as the power to disentail (*a*).'

(*a*) 11 and 12 Vict. c. 36, § 4. 38 and 39 Vict. c. 61, § 6. 45 and 46 Vict. c. 53, § 4. Plummer, petr., 1885; 12 R. 1349.

1774C. '*General Power of Sale.*—An heir in possession, or the person entitled under a trust for entailing land, may now apply to the Court for an order of sale of the estate or part of it (*a*). The Court must be satisfied that no patrimonial interest will be injuriously affected by the sale, and in the case of married women, minors, etc., that the sale is for their benefit. The Act contains regulations for carrying out the sale, and requires the money, so far as not required for paying incumbrances, etc., to be secured for the heirs of entail and persons entitled to provisions (*b*). Money held in trust for the purchase of land to be entailed may be similarly dealt with (*c*).'

(*a*) 45 and 46 Vict. c. 53, § 19. Ballantine, petr., 1883; 10 R. 106.

(*b*) *Ib.* § 21–25.

(*c*) *Ib.* § 26.

CHAPTER V

OF CONDITIONAL SETTLEMENTS OF LAND

1775. Different Kinds of Conditions.—Settlements of land may be dependent on conditions; and these are either Implied conditions or Express conditions.

1776. Implied Conditions.—These are to be distinguished in their effect from express conditions. There is a legal presumption or implied condition (especially in a settlement of one's whole estate), that the conveyance shall be effectual only *si testator sine liberis decesserit*—if the testator shall have 'died survived by (*a*)' no lawful child (*b*). And besides the legal effect of a conveyance by a parent to a child, as implying a conditional institution of that child's issue, there is in direct substitutions after children of the testator, an implied condition that if a child should die (*c*) leaving a lawful child, the substitution is not to take effect; but only if the institute should die childless (*d*). This presumption '*si institutus sine liberis decesserit*' was borrowed from the Roman law, and was at first confined to moveables (*e*), but afterwards extended to heritable succession (*f*). 'It is extended to all *mortis causa* (*g*) deeds containing provision for descendants of the granter, and for his nephews and nieces (or their descendants), where it appears from the will itself that the testator intends to stand to them *in loco parentis* (*h*); in other words, that he was moved to make the bequest by their relationship to him, and not merely by personal favour to the legatee (*i*). This presumption is of course stronger, if, in the case of collaterals, they are called as a class (*k*); yet the omission of a member of a class does not *necessarily* prevent the operation of the rule (*l*). It does not apply in favour of children even of descendants, when called as heirs whatsoever or next of kin (*m*). In provisions with a substitution of survivors to the share of predeceasers, the issue of a predeceaser are entitled to the share of their parent, but not, it has been held, without a positive indication of the testator's intention, to any part of the "accrued" share of other predeceasers which the parent might have taken if he had survived (*n*). The condition, *si testator sine liberis decesserit* operates to give heritage to the heir and moveables to the younger children (*o*).' The presumption may be defeated by opposite presumptions or by evidence 'of facts and circumstances showing the testator's intention that the will should stand (*p*).'

(*a*) See § 1778.

(*b*) Hamilton *v.* Hamilton, 1838; 16 S. 478; 3 Ill. 162. Colquhoun *v.* Campbell, 1829; 7 S. 709. See below, § 1782. Dobie's Trs. *v.* Pritchard, 1887; 15 R. 2. 3 Ersk. 8. § 46. 1 M'Laren, Wills and Succn. 257.

(*c*) *I.e.* after the date of the settlement in which the parent is *institutus*. Sturrock *v.* Binny, 1843; 6 D. 117. Rhind's Trs. *v.* Leith, 1865; 5 Macph. 104. Low's Trs. *v.* Whitworth, 1892; 19 R. 431.

(*d*) 3 Ersk. 8. § 46. Mags. of Montrose *v.* Robertson, 1738; M. 6398; Elch. *Warrandice*, 3; 2 Ill. 403. Binning *v.* Binning, 1767; M. 13,047. Wood *v.* Aitchison, 1789; M. 13,043 (no distinction of provisions to children called *nominatim* and children *nascituris*). Roughhead *v.* Rannie, 1794; M. 6403. Wallace *v.* Wallace, 1807; M. *Clause*, Apx. 6. Neilson *v.* Baillie, 1822; 1 S. 427. Christie *v.* Patersons, 1822; 1 S. 498. Booth *v.* Black, 1831; 9 S. 406; aff. 1832, 6 W. & S. 175. Greig *v.* Malcolm, 1835; 13 S. 607. Dixon *v.* Brown (Dixon), 1836; 14 S. 938; aff. 1841, 2 Rob. 1. Wilkie *v.* Jackson, 1836; 14 S. 1121. See below, § 1990. 1 M'Laren, Wills and Succn. 669. Black *v.* Valentine, 1844; 6 D. 689. Taylor *v.* Taylor, 1884; 11 R. 423.

(*e*) See below, § 1867.

(*f*) Grant's Trs. *v.* Grant, 1862; 24 D. 1211.

(*g*) See Mags. of Montrose, *cit.* (*d*). Crichton's Tr. *v.* Howat, 1890; 18 R. 260. Also to marriage contracts; *infra*, § 1989 (*g*), but not to destinations in leases. Marquis *v.* Prentice, 1896; 23 R. 595 (2nd Div.).

(*h*) Thomson's Trs. *v.* Thomson, 1862; M'Laren on Wills,

§ 1295. Thomson's Trs. *v.* Robb, 1851; 13 D. 1326. Rhind's Trs. *v.* Leith, 1866; 5 Macph. 104. Dixon, *cit.* Thomson *v.* Scougal, 1834; 12 S. 910; aff. 1835, 2 S. & M'L. 305 (grandchildren). Robertson *v.* Houston, 1858; 20 D. 989 (do.). Walker *v.* Park, 1859; 21 D. 286 (do.). Halliday *v.* M'Callum, 1869; 8 Macph. 112. Bryce's Tr. *v.* Bryce, 1878; 5 R. 722. Grant *v.* Brooke, 1882; 10 R. 92 (descendants however remote). Tod (Berwick's Exr.) *v.* Tod, 1885; 12 R. 565. Allan *v.* Thomson's Trs., 1893; 20 R. 733. The condition applies to provisions and settlements, not to simple personal legacies founded on mere personal predilection. Douglas' Exrs. *v.* Scott, etc., 1869; 7 Macph. 504. Wauchope, etc. (Brown's Trs.) *v.* Brown's Tutors, 1882; 10 R. 441. M'Alpine *v.* M'Alpine, 1883; 10 R. 837. It does not apply to legacies in favour of cousins —Rhind's Trs., *cit.*; or to natural children—Martin's Trs. *v.* Milliken, 1864; 3 Macph. 326; or to brothers and sisters—Hall *v.* Hall, 1891; 18 R. 690 (whole Court). Comp. Blair's Exrs. *v.* Taylor, 1876; 3 R. 362. Bryce's Tr., *cit.* Berwick's Exr. *v.* Tod, 1885; 12 R. 565.

(*i*) Bogie's Trs. *v.* Christie, 1882; 9 R. 453. Waddell's Trs. *v.* Waddell, 1896; 24 R. 189.

(*k*) See Hamilton (*b*). M'Gowan's Trs. *v.* Robertson, 1869; 8 Macph. 356. Chancellor *v.* Mosman, 1872; 10 Macph. 995. Blair's Exrs., *cit.* Gillespie *v.* Mercer, 1876; 3 R. 561. Gauld's Tr. *v.* Duncan, 1877; 4 R. 691.

(*l*) Bogie and Waddell, *citt.*

(*m*) Black (*d*). Cockburn's Trs. *v.* Dundas, 1864; 2 Macph. 1185.

(*n*) E. Lauderdale *v.* Boyle's Exrs., 1830; 8 S. 771. Greig *v.* Malcolm, *cit.* (*d*). Thornhill *v.* Macpherson, 1841; 3 D. 394. Walker *v.* Park, 1859; 21 D. 286. Robertson *v.* Houston, 1858; 20 D. 989. Young *v.* Robertson, 1862; 4 Macq. 337; 24 D. H. L. 1. Graham's Tr. *v.* Graham, 1868; 6 Macph. 820. M'Nish *v.* Donald's Trs., 1879; 7 R. 96. Henderson *v.* Henderson, 1889; 17 R. 293. See, however, Lord M'Laren's doubts. M'Culloch's Trs. *v.* M'Culloch, 1892; 19 R. 777. Neville *v.* Shepherd, 1895; 23 R. 351.

(*o*) Grant's Trs. *v.* Grant, 1862; 24 D. 1211. See below, § 1867.

(*p*) Greig *v.* Malcolm, 1835; 13 S. 607. Sturrock *v.* Binny, 1843; 6 D. 117. M'Call *v.* Dennistoun, 1862; 10 Macph. 281. Douglas' Exrs., and other cases cited in note (*h*). M'Gowan's Trs., *cit.* (*k*). Bogie's Trs., *supra* (*i*), and Berwick's Exr., *supra* (*h*). Adamson's Trs. *v.* Adamson's Exrs., 1891; 18 R. 1133. Carter's Trs. *v.* Carter, 1892; 19 R. 408. Millar's Tr. *v.* Millar, 1893; 20 R. 1040. Elder's Trs. *v.* Elder, 1894; 21 R. 704. Forrester's Trs. *v.* Forrester, 1894; 21 R. 971. M'Kie's Tutor *v.* M'Kie, 1897; 24 R. 526.

1777. If a lawful child who was believed to be dead shall afterwards cast up, or if an illegitimate child shall have been made legitimate by marriage with the mother, the principle of this presumption seems to apply, and the implied revocation of the deed to take place.

1778. If the child shall not have survived the granter or the institute, the presumption of revocation or substitution will not hold. It has not the same effect with an express condition (*a*).

(*a*) Watt *v.* Jervie, 1760; M. 6401. See below, § 1782.

1779. A posthumous child will have the benefit of the presumption; for it is not a presumed *power* to revoke, implying the existence of the granter at the birth of the child, but a presumed *condition* resolutive of the settlement and operating *ipso jure* (*a*) 'And the presumption applies in favour of a child subsequently born, in a question with other children previously born, as well as with strangers (*b*).'

(*a*) Christie *v.* Christie, 1681; M. 8197; 2 B. Sup. 26; 3 *ib.* 444. Oliphant *v.* Oliphant, 1794; Bell's fo. Ca. 125; 5 B. Sup. 648. See Spalding *v.* Spalding's Trs., 1874; 2 R. 234. Findlay's Trs. *v.* Findlay, 1886; 14 R. 167.

(*b*) Elder's Trs. *v.* Elder, 1894; 21 R. 704.

1780. If the settlement be only partial, and the child have survived long enough to give the granter an opportunity of altering the destination without his having made any alteration, the presumption will not hold. But the force of the presumption is greater when it is a universal settlement (*a*).

(*a*) Yule *v.* Yule, 1758; M. 6400; 2 Ill. 406. Colquhoun *v.* Campbell, 7 S. 709; 2 Ill. 404. 3 Ersk. 8. § 46.

1781. Express Conditions.—Conditions annexed to settlements, if clear and intelligible and lawful, will be effectual against the grantee (*a*).

(*a*) See as to conditions annexed to substitutions in entails, § 1724. Wyllie *v.* Ross, 1825; 4 S. 172. Falconar Stewart *v.* Wilkie, 1892; 19 R. 630. See above, § 916.

1782. There is sometimes expressly inserted in a settlement, a condition *si sine liberis decesserit.* It has so far a different construction from the implied condition, that the mere existence of the child will make the condition effectual (*a*); unless the survivance or the actual succession of the child be specified in the condition (*b*).

(*a*) Robertson *v.* General Assembly, 1833; 11 S. 297; 2 Ill. 406. Ballantyne *v.* Scott, 1687; M. 2953. Watt *v.* Forrest, 1702; M. 2954. See above, § 1776. M'Laren on Wills, § 1134.

(*b*) L. Royston *v.* Haliburton, 1715; M. 2955.

1783. Conditions may be questionable as to effect, either from defect of power, or from being impracticable, or inconsistent with law, or *contra bonos mores.*

1784. Where the granter has no power to dispose of the estate conditionally, the condition may yet have effect by being combined in the settlement with some grant or donation, the acceptance of which will infer homologation of the condition (*a*).

(*a*) See below, of Approbate and Reprobate, § 1937 et seq.

1785. Conditions physically impossible are in settlements held *pro non scriptis.* And if unlawful, or *contra bonos mores*, they are regarded by law as impossible (*a*). In this class it has sometimes been said that restraints on marriage are to be held as unlawful. But they are so only when absolute and total, or when imposed on persons entitled to succeed independently of the settlement (*b*). Reasonable restraints (as to marry 'in minority, or within a certain age or period,' with consent of certain persons, or to marry (*c*) or not to marry (*d*) a particular person) are effectual; but those whose consent is by the condition required to the marriage, must justify their objection on reasonable grounds (*e*). 'A condition annexed to a provision to a wife (*f*), or a husband (*g*), restraining her or him from a second marriage, is valid. And a limitation, not prohibitory, of a provision to the period of the grantee's maidenhood is effectual (*h*).'

(*a*) See above, § 39. 1 Stair, 3. § 7. 3 Ersk. 3. § 85. Reid *v.* Coates, March 5, 1813; F. C.; 2 Ill. 407 (residence). Fraser *v.* Rose, 1849; 11 D. 1466 (ditto). Grant's Trs. *v.* Grant, 1898; 25 R. 929. *Infra*, § 1883. Wilkinson *v.* Wilkinson, 40 L. J. Ch. 242 (condition requiring a wife to live separate from her husband).

(*b*) Hume *v.* Tenants, 1629; M. 2964; 1 B. Sup. 298. Hamilton *v.* Hamilton, 1681; M. 2970. Foord *v.* Foord, 1682; M. 2970; 2 B. Sup. 3. Grahame *v.* Stevenson's Trs., 1774; M. 2979; Hailes, 560. Douglas *v.* Douglas' Trs., 1792; M. 2985; rev. 1796, 3 Pat. 448.

(*c*) This is said to be erroneous: M'Laren, Wills and Succn. i. 589; but it seems without sufficient reason. See as to the qualifications applicable to this case, 3 Ersk. 3. § 85. Mackrath *v.* Alexander, 1712; M. 2975. Fraser, H. & W. 474.

(*d*) Ommanney *v.* Bingham, 1796; 3 Pat. 448. Graham *v.* Graham, 1823; 1 S. App. 365.

(*e*) Foord, *supra* (*b*). Gordon *v.* Petrie, March 30, 1682; 3 B. Sup. 433. Dalziel *v.* Scotstarvet, 1688; M. 2971; 2 B. Sup. 124. Pringle *v.* Pringle, 1688; M. 2972. Buntin *v.* Buchanan, 1710; M. 2972. Wellwood's Trs. *v.* Boswell, 1851; 13 D. 1211. Forbes *v.* Forbes' Trs., 1882; 9 R. 675.

(*f*) Newton *v.* Marsden, 31 L. J. Ch. 690. Foulis *v.* Gilmours, 1672; M. 2965; 2 B. Sup. 160. Kidd *v.* Kidd, *infra*.

(*g*) Kidd *v.* Kidd, 1863; 2 Macph. 227. Allen *v.* Jackson, 1 Ch. D. 399.

(*h*) Sturrock *v.* Rankin's Trs., 1875; 2 R. 850. *Supra*, § 39. Fraser, H. & W. 464 sqq. M'Laren, Wills and Succn. 589. See 2 Wh. & Tud. L. C. 144. Bellairs *v.* Bellairs, 43 L. R. Ch. 669; L. R. 18 Eq. 510. Pollock on Contracts, 324.

CHAPTER VI

OF THE LAW OF DEATHBED

1786. Nature of the Law.—By this law, if a person, while ill of the disease of which he died, 'had' executed a deed conveying or burdening his heritable estate to the prejudice of his lawful heir, he 'was' presumed to have acted under the undue influence of importunity; and the heir 'might' have redress. And the rule 'was by statute' extended to guard wives and children against defeat of their legal provisions, and to protect minors in the nomination of curators or of tutors against exemption from the usual responsibility (*a*). 'It is not in all cases necessary, though it is generally expedient, to reduce the deathbed deed (*b*).'

'*Partial Abolition of the Law of Deathbed.*—This ancient law, which was the only (though most imperfect) protection known to the law of Scotland against the perpetual dedication of land to corporate or ecclesiastical uses by mortification (mortmain) (*c*), was abolished, or nearly abolished, in 1871, by an Act which provided that "no deed, instrument, or writing made by any person who shall die after the passing of this Act shall be liable to challenge or reduction *ex capite lecti*" (*d*). Lord Fraser has pointed out that the Act does not reach every challengeable transaction, *e.g.* the delivery of cash upon deathbed and the lending out of money on heritable securities in prejudice of the rights of relicts and bairns, the only case contemplated being apparently that of dispositions of heritage executed on deathbed (*e*). The Act of 1871 is by a blunder included among the Acts repealed by the Statute Law Revision Act of 1883; but the saving clauses in that Act amply protect the public from any doubt which may be raised as to the effect of the mistake, providing that the repeal shall not revive or restore any "right, privilege, usage, practice, procedure, or other matter or thing not now existing or in force" (*f*). As some questions of deathbed may still arise, the present tense is retained in the following sections.'

(*a*) 2 Reg. Maj. c. 18. § 7, 9. 1 Stair, 12. § 34. 4 Stair, 20. § 38. 3 Ersk. 8. § 95. Dirl., *Legit. Liber.* 1 Bell's Com. 84 sqq. Maxwell *v.* Fairley, 1629; M. 3303; 2 Ill. 407. L. Forbes *v.* Forbes, 1755; M. 3277; 5 B. Sup. 288; rev. 1756, 2 Pat. 8 (deed executed under reserved faculty). See below, § 1803.

(*b*) Thain *v.* Thain, 1891; 18 R. 1196.

(*c*) 3 Stair, 4. § 27. 4 Stair, 20. § 38. Scottish Law Review, vol. i. p. 22 (Feb. 1885).

(*d*) 34 and 35 Vict. c. 81.

(*e*) Fraser, H. & W. 1008. Hay *v.* Coutts' Trs., 1890; 18 R. 244. So, *e.g.*, alienation of fixtures, sale of wood, etc., *infra*, § 1797, 1804, etc.

(*f*) 46 and 47 Vict. c. 39.

1787. Essential Requisites.—It is essential to deathbed, as opposed to that degree of vigour which is known by the name of "liege poustie," that the deceased at the date of the deed should have been ill of the disease of which he died (*a*). And so the presumption of weakness and yielding to importunity does not hold, if a supervening disease or accident shall have terminated his life (*b*). It is not required that the disease shall be, strictly speaking, in nosological character, a mortal disease (*c*).

(*a*) Cogan *v.* Lyon, 1834; 12 S. 569; 2 Ill. 409.

(*b*) Weir *v.* Knox, 1791; Hume, 135. Thomson *v.* Thomson, 1801; *ib.* 142. Brock *v.* ——, 1813; *ib.* 137. Corsnip *v.* Sked, 1815; *ib.* 151. Spiers *v.* Mackie, 1802; *ib.* 144. Paterson *v.* Johnston, 1816; 1 Mur. 71; 2 Ill. 408. Hiddleston *v.* Goldie, 1819; 2 Mur. 120. M'Kay *v.* Davidson, 1828; 6 S. 367; aff. 5 W. & S. 210.

(*c*) 3 Stair, 4. § 28. 3 Ersk. 8. § 96. Shaw *v.* Gray, 1624; M. 3291 and 3208. Robertson *v.* Fleming, 1622; M. 3290. Dun *v.* Duns, 1668; M. 3291. Lady Scotston *v.* Drummond, 1694; M. 3297. Primrose *v.* Primrose, 1756; M. 3300; 5 B. Sup. 843. Laird *v.* Kirkwood, 1763;

M. 3315. Crawford *v.* Kincaid, 1782; Hailes, 907. Black *v.* Black, 1787; M. 3302. Robertson *v.* M'Caig, 1823; 2 S. 544.

1788. Liege Poustie.—In opposition to the presumption of deathbed, and in support of the presumed strength to resist importunity notwithstanding illness at the date of the deed, two tests have been selected. These are: 1. Survivance during sixty days; and 2. Going to kirk or market unsupported.

1789. (1.) *Survival for Sixty Days.*—To avoid the inconvenience of continuing the presumption of imbecility too long (*a*), it is enacted that "it shall be a sufficient exception to exclude the reason of deathbed, as to all bonds, dispositions, contracts, or other rights that shall be made and granted by any person after the contracting of sickness, that the person live for the space of threescore days after the making and granting of the said deeds, albeit during that time they did not go to kirk and market"; reserving a right to reduce, "if it shall be alleged and proven that the person was so afflicted by the disease at the time of the doing of the said deeds, that he was not of sound judgment and understanding" (*b*). In construing the Act, the day of making the deed is not reckoned; and survivance till the morning of the sixtieth day is sufficient, according to the maxim, *dies inceptus pro completo habetur* (*c*). The date of the deed must be proved, as well as its authenticity (*d*).

(*a*) Richardson *v.* L. Cranston, 1635; M. 3291; 2 Ill. 409. Gordon *v.* Gordon, 1696; M. 3299.
(*b*) 1696, c. 4; 10 Acta Parl. 33.
(*c*) Crawford *v.* Kincaid, 1782; Hailes, 907. See Ogilvie *v.* Mercer, 1793; M. 3336; aff. 3 Pat. 434. Mitchell *v.* Watson, 1801; M. Apx. *Deathbed*, 9.
(*d*) Merry *v.* Howie, 1801; M. Apx. *Writ*, 3; aff. 5 Pat. 101. See Gibson *v.* Pott, 1813; Hume, 150. Yeats *v.* Yeats' Tr., 1833; 11 S. 915. Campbell *v.* Fisher, 1838; 16 S. 1279. Waddell *v.* Waddell's Trs., 1845; 7 D. 605. Suttie *v.* Ross, 1838; 16 S. 429. Fairholme *v.* Fairholme's Trs., 1856; 19 D. 178. Dickson on Evidence, § 714, 715.

1790. (2.) *Going to Kirk or Market.*—By consuetude, sanctioned by the reference to it in the Act of Parliament 1696, and regulated in practice by Act of Sederunt, it is also an exception to the plea of deathbed that the granter of the deed has been at kirk or market between the date of the deed and his death (*a*).

(*a*) Maxwell *v.* Fairley, 1629; M. 3303; 2 Ill. 407. Richardson *v.* Sinclair, 1635; M. 3210; 2 Ill. 410. A. S., Feb. 29, 1692. Lockhart *v.* Lockhart, 1677; M. 3297. Pargeileis *v.* Pargeileis, 1669; M. 3304. L. Balmerino's Crs. *v.* Couper, 1671; M. 3292; 2 B. Sup. 445. Cleland *v.* Cleland, 1672; M. 3305. Crawford *v.* Brichan, 1711; M. 3315. Kyle *v.* Kyle, 1825; 3 S. 641. M'Cracken *v.* Pearson, 1821; 2 Mur. 551.

1791. It is not necessary that the granter shall be both at kirk and market (*a*).

(*a*) Balmerino, *supra*, § 1790 (*a*). Ragg *v.* Forbes, 1725; M. 3314; 2 Ill. 411.

1792. The granter must be at kirk or market without "supportation or straining of nature" (which is a question of evidence for a jury). And though not in perfect health, yet he must not be so enfeebled by his disease as to be unable to support himself (*a*).

(*a*) A. S., *supra*, § 1790 (*a*). 3 Stair, 4. § 28. 3 Ersk. 8. § 96. 3 Bankt. 4. § 41. Balmerino and Crawford, *supra*, § 1790 (*a*). Faichney *v.* Faichneys, 1776; M. 3316; and Apx. *Deathbed*, 1; 5 B. Sup. 422; 2 Ill. 411. Young *v.* Scotts, 1777; 5 B. Sup. 423; Hailes, 757. Angus *v.* Angus, 1793; Hume, 137. Harvie *v.* Reston, 1799; *ib.* 139. Ormiston *v.* Greig, May 17, 1821; F. C.; Hume, 149. Tailzeour *v.* Tailzeour, 1787; M. 3317. Cowan *v.* Cowan, 1817; Hume, 142. Rait *v.* Rait, Nov. 27, 1818; F. C.; Hume, 155. Smyth *v.* ——, June 9, 1812; F. C.; Hume, 148.

1793. It has not been settled what shall be held a market; but it rather seems requisite that it shall be a proper market for the sale of goods, commodities, cattle, etc. (*a*).

(*a*) Scotstoun *v.* Colquhoun, 1694; M. 3322; 2 Ill. 411. E. Rosebery *v.* Primrose, 1763; M. 3322; Elchies, *Deathbed*, 8. Laird *v.* Kirkwood, 1763; M. 3315; 2 Ill. 408. M'Cracken *v.* Pearson, 1821; 2 Mur. 251. Maitland *v.* Maitland, May 16, 1815; F. C. Rait, *supra*, § 1792 (*a*).

1794. Equivalents to going to kirk or market, even though indicating superior strength, will not overturn the presumption (*a*).

(*a*) Lowrie *v.* Drummond, 1671; M. 3319; 2 Ill. 412. Balmerino, *supra*, § 1790 (*a*). Mountonhall's Daughters *v.* Hamilton, 1683; M. 3320. Livingstoun *v.* Goodale, 1683; M. 3321. Keirie *v.* Craigengelt, 1687; M. 3321. Maitland, *supra*, § 1793.

1795. Fraudulent compliance with the words of the rule will not support the deed (*a*).

(*a*) Ormiston, *supra*, § 1792 (*a*). 3 Stair, 4. § 28. 3 Ersk. 8. § 96.

1796. Deeds liable to Challenge.—All deeds alienating or affecting heritage, to the prejudice of the heir, are within the rule; and the rule extends to all heirs, heirs-male or of tailzie, and heirs in personal rights to land (*a*), as well as heirs to infeftments. This prejudice may be by alienating the land, or part of it, or by creating burdens, or granting leases of extraordinary duration, or discharging debts due to the heir.

(*a*) Thain *v.* Thain, 1891; 18 R. 1197.

1797. Alienations without full consideration, or even for full consideration if spontaneous and prejudicial, may be challenged; and they will be held prejudicial not only on account of pecuniary loss, but by splitting or dismembering the estate, or depriving the heir of his rightful inheritance (*a*). This rule is not confined to land or houses, but extends to all fixtures, or what law holds to be part of the land,—as woods (*b*); and to all those things to which the heir has right, as heritable bonds, or bonds excluding executors (*c*). In reducing onerous deeds, the heir must reimburse the person to whom the deed has been made. If the heir insist on having back the estate, he must pay the price. If he reduce an assignation of a heritable bond, he must repay what has been paid for the assignation. And if in such case the price has gone to the executors, he will have his remedy against them (*d*).

(*a*) 3 Ersk. 8. § 97. Hepburn *v.* Hepburn, 1663; M. 3177; 2 Ill. 412. Richardson *v.* Sinclair, 1635; M. 3210. Maxwell *v.* Corrie, 1724; M. 3329. Lindsay *v.* Lindsay, 1819; Hume, 156. Campbell *v.* Rankine, 1805; M. Apx. *Deathbed*, 5. Fairholme *v.* Fairholme's Trs., 1856; 19 D. 178. Jack *v.* Jack, 1857; 19 D. 747. Gray *v.* Gray, 1872; 10 Macph. 854.
(*b*) Maxwell, *supra* (*a*).
(*c*) M'Kay *v.* Robertson, 1725; M. 3224. Pringle *v.* Pringle, 1688; M. 3219. Murrays *v.* Borthwick, 1797; M. 3237. Fairholme and Jack, *citt.*
(*d*) Gillespie (Irvine) *v.* Gillespie, 1802; Hume, 145. See Gray, *supra* (*a*).

1798. Burdens and securities may be challenged if the heir is not already liable (*a*); the heir, where he is not liable finally, having redress against the executors, etc. (*b*).

(*a*) Darling *v.* Hay, 1709; M. 3222; 2 Ill. 413.
(*b*) Pollocks *v.* Fairholm, 1632; M. 3209. Christison *v.* Kerr, 1733; M. 3226; Elch. *Deathbed*, 2. Bogle *v.* Bogle, 1759; M. 3235. Semple *v.* Semple, June 1, 1813; F. C.

1799. Discharge of heritable debt is good to the debtor on full payment, though on deathbed. But the heir will have his remedy against the executor; or even against the debtor, if the discharge be fraudulent or gratuitous (*a*).

(*a*) 3 Stair, 4. § 29. Brown *v.* Thomson, 1634; M. 3200. Gillespie *v.* Marshall, 1802; Hume, 145; 2 Ill. 413.

1800. Bonds of provision burdening the heir are challengeable (*a*), unless grounded on an obligation binding on the heir; the natural obligation of a parent, 'or husband, so far as the provision exceeds the terce, or if terce be excluded,' not being sufficient (*b*).

(*a*) Logan *v.* Campbell, 1757; M. 3230; 5 B. Sup. 338; 2 Ill. 413. Leslie *v.* Leslies, 1747; M. 3229. L. Cranston Riddel *v.* Richardson, 1637; M. 3212. Fowlis *v.* Fowlis, 1721; M. 3223. Hay Newton *v.* Hay Newton, 1867; 5 Macph. 1056; aff. 1870, 8 Macph. H. L. 66. Boyack *v.* Foreman's Trs., 1829; 7 S. 704.
(*b*) Edmonston *v.* Edmonston, 1706; M. 3219. Burden *v.* Oliphant, 1709; 4 B. Sup. 746.

1801. Leases beyond those of ordinary administration, and to the heir's prejudice, are challengeable (*a*).

(*a*) See above, § 1182.

1802. Deeds indirectly prejudicial to the heir are, even against third parties, reducible as far as gratuitous. So the voluntary conversion of a subject from heritable to moveable may be challenged (*a*). Moveable bonds, legacies, or provisions are reducible, in so far as prejudicial to the heir, either as debts, or as exhausting the fund for creditors, and exposing the heir to a demand (*b*). But if an obligation be already incurred in liege poustie which would bind the heir, a deed in fulfilment of it is not challengeable although made on deathbed (*c*). 'The law of deathbed does not apply to deeds executed under powers of disposal or powers to burden (*d*); nor does it invalidate a marriage or prevent legitimation by a marriage contracted on deathbed (*e*).'

(*a*) 3 Ersk. 8. § 98.
(*b*) Shaw *v.* Gray, 1624; M. 3208; 2 Ill. 414. E. Leven *v.* Montgomery, 1683; M. 3217. Cowie *v.* Brown, 1707; M. 3220.
(*c*) Anderson *v.* Anderson, 1568; M. 3208. Shaw, *supra* (*b*). Heriot *v.* Lyon, 1678; M. 3217. Pollocks *v.* Fairholm, 1632; M. 3209. Darling *v.* Hay, 1709; M. 3222. Edmonston, *supra*, § 1800 (*b*). Campbell *v.* Ranken, 1805; M. Apx. *Deathbed*, 5.
(*d*) Somervell *v.* Geddie, 1743; Elch. *Deathbed*, 16. Morris *v.* Tennant, 1853; 15 D. 716; 1855, 18 D. H. L. 42; 27 S. Jur. 546. Pringle *v.* Pringle, 1767; 2 Pat. 120. Forbes *v.* Forbes, 1756; 2 Pat. 8. Hay Newton *v.* Hay Newton, 1867; 5 Macph. 1056; aff. 1870, 8 Macph. H. L. 66.
(*e*) Lauderdale Peerage Case, 1885; 10 App. Ca. 692, 753.

1803. As to deeds not affecting the heir, a father cannot on deathbed name tutors with an exemption from responsibility for omission (*a*); nor can he name curators at all to his children, unless in liege poustie (*b*).

(*a*) 1696, c. 8. 1 Ersk. 7. § 27. Watson *v.* Watson, 1714; M. 3244; 2 Ill. 414.
(*b*) 1696, c. 8. Crawfurd *v.* Johnston, 1751; M. 3230; Elch. *Tut.* 23. Greig *v.* Greig, 1872; 11 Macph. 20.

1804. One cannot on deathbed defeat the legitim or *jus relictæ* (*a*).

(*a*) Dirleton, *Legitima Liberorum.* 3 Ersk. 9. § 16. Henderson *v.* Henderson, 1728; M. 8199; 2 Ill. 272.

1805. Various devices have been employed to evade the law of deathbed.

1806. It will not be effectual to evade this law, that a power has been given in a Crown charter, or reserved in a settlement on the heir, of disponing or contracting debt on deathbed, or "at any time in life" (*a*); 'but such a power reserved in a settlement on a stranger is effectual as a condition of the grant, and excludes challenge by the disponee or heir of provision (*b*).'

(*a*) Hepburn *v.* Hepburn, 1663; M. 3177. Douglas *v.* Douglas, 1670; M. 329. Davidson *v.* Davidson, 1687; M. 3255. Bertram *v.* Vere, 1706; M. 3258; Dirleton & Stewart, 334 and 137. Miller *v.* Marsh, 1855; 15 D. 823; aff. 2 Macq. 284. Morris *v.* Tennant, *cit.* § 1802 (*d*).

(*b*) 1 Bell's Com. 95. Livingstone *v.* Menzies, 1705; M. 3261. Coutts *v.* Crawford, 1806; 5 Pat. 95. Shaw *v.* Campbell's Trs., 1847; 9 D. 782. See Pattison *v.* Dunn's Trs., 1866; 4 Macph. 555; aff. 1868, 6 Macph. H. L. 147.

1807. It will be an effectual bar against the heir's challenge, if, in a settlement on heirs in a contract of marriage, power is reserved to make provision for younger children at any time of the father's life; or if the heir shall have accepted of a settlement, with a reservation of powers to grant some specific deed or provision (*a*).

(*a*) Forbes *v.* Forbes, 1755; M. 3277; 5 B. Sup. 288; rev. 2 Pat. 8. Pringle *v.* Pringle, 1765; M. 3290. Reids *v.* Campbell, 1728; M. 3327. Inglis *v.* Inglis (Hamilton), 1733; M. 3327.

1808. A deed executed blank cannot be filled up on deathbed (*a*).

(*a*) Pennicuik *v.* Thomson, 1687; M. 3243; 2 Ill. 415. Birnies *v.* L. Polmaise, 1678; M. 3242; 3 B. Sup. 235.

1809. The total exclusion of the heir by a deed in liege poustie, with power to alter, will bar him from challenging a deed on deathbed disposing otherwise of the succession, but not revoking the former (*a*).

(*a*) D. Roxburghe *v.* Wauchope, Dec. 13, 1816; F. C.; 2 Bligh, 630; 2 Ill. 417. E. Strathmore *v.* Strathmore's Trs., 1831; 5 W. & S. 170. Barstow *v.* Black, 1868; 6 Macph. H. L. 147; 1 Sc. App. 392.

1810. If there be two deeds on deathbed,—one a distinct and separate revocation of a liege poustie conveyance, the other a new conveyance prejudicial to the heir,—the heir's right revives by the revocation, so as to entitle him to challenge the new conveyance (*a*).

(*a*) Findlay *v.* Birkmyre, 1779; M. 3188; 2 Ill. 415. Miller *v.* Marsh, 1855; 15 D. 823; aff. 2 Macq. 284. Stewart *v.* Neilson, 1850; 22 D. 646. Erskine *v.* Erskine's Trs., 1850; 13 D. 223. Cameron *v.* West's Trs., 1864; 2 Macph. 584.

1811. Even where the revocation of the liege poustie deed and the new conveyance are contained in one deed, but the revocation is not made provisional, the heir may take the benefit of the revocation, and also challenge the new conveyance (*a*).

(*a*) Coutts *v.* Crawford, 1796; Bell's Ca. 207; M. 14,958, and Apx. 3; 1806, 2 Bligh's Ap. 655; 5 Pat. 73; 2 Ill. 415. Whitelaw *v.* Lang, 1809; 2 S. App. 13, footnote; 2 Ill. 417. Battley *v.* Small, Feb. 2, 1815; F. C. Mudie *v.* Moir, March 2, 1820; F. C.; 2 S. App. 9. Anderson *v.* Fleming, 1833; 11 S. 612. See below, § 1940. See Leith *v.* Leith, 1863; 1 Macph. 949. Cameron *v.* West's Trs., 1864; 2 Macph. 584.

1812. Where the revocation (separate or in the same deed) is declared to be provisional, to take effect only if the new deed shall stand, the heir is excluded (*a*). An *implied* revocation is held provisional (*b*).

(*a*) Coutts, *supra*, § 1811 (*a*); 2 Bligh, 686.

(*b*) Cunningham *v.* Cunningham, 5 B. Sup. 412; 2 Ill. 418. Rowand *v.* Alexander, 1775; 5 B. Sup. 423; M. 11,371; Hailes, 659; see 2 Bligh, 662, 679, 680–1, 687. D. Roxburghe, *supra*, § 1809 (*a*). Lawrie *v.* Lawrie's Trs., 1830; 8 S. 379.

1813. A liege poustie trust-deed will not enable the granter to defeat the heir's right by a testamentary direction to trustees, or other deed on deathbed, unless by the trust-deed the heir shall be effectually excluded (*a*). But if the trust-deed shall have the effect of bringing in others than the heir-at-law, in case the deathbed deed should be reduced, it will bar the heir's challenge (*b*); and if a power to alter be in such circumstances reserved to be exercised by a deed under the granter's hand, a testamentary deed will be effectual, if executed according to the form of the country where it is made (*c*).

(*a*) Willoch *v.* Auchterlony, 1769; M. 5539; Hailes, 321; aff. 3 Pat. 659; 2 Ill. 418; 1 Ross' L. C. 401. Wauchope *v.* Ker, 1806; 1812, 5 Pat. 559. Erskine *v.* Erskine's Trs., 1850; 13 D. 223. Clyne *v.* Clyne's Trs., 1837; 15 S. 911; 1839, M'L. & R. 72.

(*b*) Brack *v.* Johnston, 1827; 6 S. 113; aff. 1831, 6 W. & S. 61; 2 Ill. 419. Bellenden Ker *v.* Lady Essex Ker's Trs., 1829; 7 S. 454; 1830, 8 S. 694; aff. 5 W. & S. 713.

(*c*) Same cases.

1814. The heir's consent to a particular deed will bar his challenge; but a general obligation by the heir not to challenge on deathbed, or a renunciation obtained fraudulently, is ineffectual to bar a challenge (*a*).

(*a*) Inglis *v.* Inglis (Hamilton), 1733; M. 3327; Elch. *Deathbed*, 1; 2 Ill. 419. Murray *v.* Murray's Trs., 1826; 4 S. 374. See Richardson *v.* Richardson, 1848; 10 D. 872.

1815. Heirs entitled to Challenge.—The following persons have a title and interest sufficient to maintain the challenge:—1. The heir-at-law, whether of line or conquest (*a*). 2. The heir of investiture, even against the heir of line (*b*). 3. Even where the destination is still personal, the heir of provision has the right to challenge (*c*); but one entitled only by contract to succeed is a creditor and not an heir, and cannot plead deathbed (*d*). 4. A remoter heir may challenge a deathbed deed to his prejudice, on the immediate heir's death, even where the immediate heir was not prejudiced by it, provided the immediate heir have not already homologated (*e*). 5. An apparent heir may challenge on deathbed (*f*); and even an heir of provision, whose title is not yet completed, has been held entitled to challenge (*g*); 'but not legatees or beneficiaries under trust-deed (*h*).' But, 6. Where a service is considered necessary, a general service is not held a sufficient title to reduce on deathbed (*i*). And, 7. Creditors of the heir may exercise the faculty of challenging the deathbed deed (*k*); 'or his disponee (*l*); but not the husband of an heiress without her consent (*m*).' In all those cases, though the title to challenge may be good, the action may be met by a plea of want of interest (*n*).

(*a*) 3 Ersk. 8. § 99, 100.
(*b*) 3 Ersk. 8. § 100. Hepburn *v.* Hepburn, 1663; M. 3177; 2 Ill. 412. Porterfield *v.* Cant, 1672; M. 3179; 2 Ill. 419. Maxwell *v.* Neilson, 1722; M. 3191. Howie *v.* Merry, 1806; M. Apx. *Writ*, 3; 5 Pat. 101. Coutts *v.* Crawford, 1806; 5 Pat. 73. Cogan *v.* Lyon, 1830; 4 W. & S. 391.
(*c*) M. Clydesdale *v.* E. Dundonald, 1726; M. 3180.
(*d*) Campbells *v.* Campbells, 1738; M. 3195; 5 B. Sup. 214, 651; Elch. *Mut. Cont.* 14. See Kilk. 456. Shaw *v.* Campbell's Exrs., 1847; 9 D. 872. Wyllie *v.* M'Bride, 1890; 18 R. 218.
(*e*) Kennedy *v.* Arbuthnot, 1722; M. 3198. Craigs *v.* Glasgow Maltsters, 1739; M. 3199; Elch. *Deathbed*, 11, and *Notes*, 11, p. 116. Irvine *v.* Tait, 1808; M. Apx. *Deathbed*, 6. See Leith *v.* Leith, 1848; 10 D. 1137.
(*f*) Graham *v.* Graham, 1779; M. 3186; Hailes, 823.
(*g*) Edmonston *v.* Edmonstons, 1636; M. 16,089. Graham, *supra* (*f*).
(*h*) Shaw, *cit.* Morison *v.* Morison, 1808; Hume, 147.
(*i*) Graham, *supra* (*f*). (*k*) 3 Ersk. 8. § 100.
(*l*) Thain *v.* Thain, 1891; 18 R. 1196.
(*m*) Greenhill *v.* Ford, 1826; 4 S. 478. Aitkins *v.* Orr, 1802; M. 16,140.
(*n*) Shiells *v.* Smith, 1830; 8 S. 553. Bellenden Ker *v.* Lady Essex Ker's Trs., 1830; 5 W. & S. 718.

1816. Personal Bar.—The heir's ratification or homologation (*a*) is a bar; but it will not bar his heir, if the ratification be on deathbed (*b*). Nor will it bar creditors, if the heir be insolvent, and the ratification gratuitous (*c*); or if the ratification be executed in favour of a creditor within sixty days of bankruptcy (*d*); or collusively, to confer a preference over other creditors (*e*).

(*a*) 3 Ersk. 3. § 48. See Kennedy *v.* Kennedy, 1723; M. 9441. Leith *v.* Leith, 1848; 10 D. 1137. Richardson *v.* Richardson, 1848; 10 D. 872.
(*b*) Hedderwick *v.* Campbell, 1740; Elch. *Deathbed*, 13; 2 Ill. 420. Cleuch *v.* Leslie, 1744; M. 3182; Elch. *Deathbed*, 17. This case appears to decide the opposite of the proposition stated.
(*c*) 1621, c. 18. (*d*) 1696, c. 5.
(*e*) 1 Bell's Com. 93.

CHAPTER VII

OF ENTRY OF HEIRS BY PRECEPT OF CLARE CONSTAT, AND BY SERVICE

In order to vest the succession in the heir, he must enter as such either by service or by precept of *clare constat*; the general principles of which have been already stated, but must now be more particularly explained (*a*).

(*a*) See *ante*, § 775–82.

I. PRECEPT OF CLARE CONSTAT.

1817. Effect.—On the opening of the succession by the death of the vassal, the superior 'might,' by his precept of *clare constat*, give an effectual entry to the heir-at-law, or of investiture, or of provision (*a*). 'He is now bound to grant a precept or writ of *clare constat*, if required by an heir entitled to demand such an entry, on production of a prior charter or writ showing the *tenendas* and *reddendo* of the lands, and on tender of the duties and casualties (*b*).' If the superior be himself infeft in the superiority, his precept is a perfect warrant for infeftment; if not yet infeft, the vassal's infeftment proceeding on the precept of *clare constat* will become effectual by accretion of the superior's infeftment (*c*).

(*a*) See above, § 778A.
(*b*) 31 and 32 Vict. c. 101, § 101; re-enacting 21 and 22 Vict. c. 76, § 11.
(*c*) Dickson *v.* Syme, 1801; M. Apx. *Tailzie*, 7. 1 Bell's Com. 698 (737, M'L.'s ed.). 2 Ersk. 7. § 3. See above, § 881.

1818. Who may be entered.—In this way may be entered, one who is heir-at-law, either immediate or by failure of nearer heirs of the person last infeft; or the heir of investiture; or the heir of provision, by a deed of settlement conformable to and within the terms of the standing investiture; or the superior himself. But a disponee cannot thus enter, and does not require such a precept (*a*).

(*a*) Crichton's Crs. *v.* Christian Knowl. Socy., 1798; M. 15,115; 2 Ill. 421; 2 Ross' L. C. 280. Calderwood Durham's Trs. *v.* Graham, 1798; M. 15,118.

1819. A precept of *clare constat* is not the competent mode of entering one who is not at the time the immediate heir (*natus vel factus*) of him who died last vest and seised in the lands. And even the consent of that next heir will not make it valid (*a*).

(*a*) Landales *v.* Landale, 1752; M. 14,465; Elch. *Service*, 6; 5 B. Sup. 79; 2 Ill. 48; 2 Ross' L. C. 253. Finlay *v.* Morgan, 1770; M. 14,480; and 1774, M. 6904; Hailes, 357 and 555; 2 Ill. 422; 2 Ross' L. C. 265. See above, § 778.

1820. Heir, how described.—It is not indispensable (as 'it was before 1874' in a service) that a precept of *clare constat* shall set forth the precise description and character of heir; provided the superior is satisfied that this is the heir of investiture, and it is substantially correct, bearing reference to the necessary documents as produced to the superior (*a*).

(*a*) Reid *v.* Woods, 1788; M. 14,483; 2 Ill. 422; overruled by Fairservice *v.* Whyte, 1789; M. 14,486; and Crichton's Crs. and Durham, *supra*, § 1818. Ogilvy *v.* Ogilvy,

1817; Hume, 724. *Supra*, § 778, 779c. 37 and 38 Vict. c. 94, § 11. *Infra*, § 1830.

1821. A superior is not reinvested by the death of the vassal, so as to have it in his power to give a new charter; but in his precept of *clare constat* he may alter the investiture, and introduce new conditions, so that if the vassal's heir accept of the precept so qualified it will be effectual (*a*).

(*a*) Mags. of Edinburgh *v.* Stratton, 1777; 5 B. Sup. 612; 2 Ill. 422.

1822. Precept Personal.—A precept of *clare constat* is strictly personal. It falls 'at common law' by the death either of the superior or of the vassal, so that no effectual infeftment can thereafter be taken on it; and it is incapable of assignation (*a*). 'But by statute, it subsists during the life of the grantee, notwithstanding the death of the granter (*b*).'

(*a*) 1693, c. 35. 3 Ersk. 3. § 42.
(*b*) 10 and 11 Vict. c. 48, § 15; re-enacted by 31 and 32 Vict. c. 101, § 103.

1823. What it Imports.—A precept of *clare constat* is a title only to the lands expressed in it, and does not include a general title as heir (*a*), nor imply passive representation beyond the value of the subject (*b*). 'But the heir entering in this manner is liable, under the statute 1695, c. 24, for the debts of an apparent heir three years in possession (*c*).' And the heir's title thus made up is not protected, as a title by service is, by the vicennial prescription.

(*a*) 3 Ersk. 8. § 71. Farmer *v.* Elder, 1683; M. 14,003; 2 Ill. 422. E. Rosebery *v.* Primrose's Crs., 1766; 5 B. Sup. 927, note. See below, § 1847.
(*b*) See below, § 1914 et seq., 1922.
(*c*) Brown *v.* Henderson, 1852; 14 D. 1041.

II. SERVICE OF HEIRS.

1824. Nature and Effect of Service.—The general view of the law in requiring the proof of the heir's title by service has already been explained (*a*). Service is a judicial proceeding and *actus legitimus* for transmitting the succession, and establishes the opening of the succession, the acceptance of the *hæreditas* by the heir, the special character in which he takes, and the vesting of the succession. 'But a personal right to land now vests in the heir by his mere survivance (*b*).'

(*a*) See *supra*, § 779. (*b*) See above, § 779A.

1825. When Service necessary or not.—There are certain cases in which it is not necessary, 'even at common law,' to have either precept of *clare constat* or service to vest the succession. Honours and dignities vest *jure sanguinis* without service or possession (*a*). A *jus crediti* under a contract of marriage vests in the heir of the marriage, without service (*b*). But service is necessary where one dispones to himself in liferent and another in fee, whom failing the fiar's heirs, whom failing the disponer; even where infeftment has not followed, and the fiar has predeceased the disponer without issue (*c*). Leases vest in the heir without either service or possession, not only to the effect of his continuing his ancestor's possession, but of being entitled to assign it when that is permitted (*d*). Heirship moveables, 'before the right to them was abolished, required' no service, but 'were' vested by possession (*e*). Moveables which by settlement are made heritable, as books, furniture, pictures, destinated to pass along with an entailed estate, do not require a service to vest them, but are vested by possession. A service, however, is competent for vesting such subjects (*f*).

(*a*) 3 Ersk. 8. § 77. See Cockburn *v.* Crs. of Langton, 1747; M. 150.
(*b*) Ogilvy *v.* Ogilvy, Dec. 16, 1817; F. C.; 2 Ill. 434. See above, § 1712 sqq.; below, § 1967.
(*c*) Hay *v.* Hay, 1758; M. 14,369; 5 B. Sup. 351; 2 Ross' L. C. 568, 600. Dennistoun *v.* Crichton, 1824; 2 S. 678. See below, § 1833; and the discussion of Hay *v.* Hay, by Professor Moir, in the Notes to 3 Ersk. Pr. 8. 36.
(*d*) Rattray *v.* Graham, 1623; M. 14,374; 2 Ill. 322. Boyd *v.* Sinclair, 1671; M. 14,375. Campbell *v.* Cuningham, 1739; M. 14,375. Scott *v.* Baird, 1754; M. 14,376; 5 B. Sup. 814. Rule *v.* Hume, 1635; M. 14,374; 2 Ill. 435. See 20 and 21 Vict. c. 26, § 8.
(*e*) Ersk. *ut supra*. 31 and 32 Vict. c. 101, § 160.
(*f*) Veitch *v.* Young, May 25, 1808; F. C. See above, § 1475, 1719A.

1826. Kinds.—Service is either Special or General: the former establishing, along with the general title of heir, his specific right to enter and be infeft in particular lands; the latter establishing the general title of heir, without application to any particular subject.

1827. Special Service is used where the purpose is to have the heir infeft in the feudal right of subjects in which the ancestor died infeft.

1828. (1.) *Proceedings.*—The service is intended to establish judicially the several points on which the heir's right to demand a feudal entry from the superior depends. For establishing those several points, 'under the law in force before 1847,' a brieve 'was' issued from Chancery, directed to the Sheriff of the shire where the lands 'lay,' or if situated in several counties (or in case of a competition of brieves), to the Sheriff of Edinburgh (*a*), requiring him to impannel a jury, and have a verdict returned on seven several points: the death of the ancestor, at the faith and peace of the sovereign; the propinquity of the claimant; the claimant's lawful age (now of no use); the extent or valuation of the land; the superior; the tenure and *reddendo*; the person in whose hands the lands 'had' been by non-entry since the ancestor's death.

(*a*) 1 and 2 Geo. IV. c. 38. 1 and 2 Vict. c. 86, § 2. The forms of service are altered; see below, § 1832A.

1829. The brieve 'was' executed edictally at the market-cross of the head burgh on a market-day, and on a citation of fifteen days. The diet 'was' peremptory; and if deserted the brieve 'fell,' and 'could' not be executed to a new day. The service 'might' be opposed by one having an interest, on the ground of any irregularity in the brieve or executions; or by exceptions instantly verified; or by a retour of a special service, as an exclusive title; or by showing the fee to be full (*a*).

(*a*) 4 Stair, 3. § 17. See Sutherland *v.* Grant, 1743; M. 16,347 (nature of brieve). Innes *v.* Ker, 1807; M. *Tailzie*, Apx. 13. See below, § 1842.

1830. The heir 'set' forth in a claim, the death of the ancestor, and the precise character of heir in which he desires to be served. There must be a perfect accordance between the brieve, the claim, and the proofs. The death of the person last vest must be shown, for there can be no service if the fee be full (*a*). The particular character as heir of line, heir-male, heir of provision, in which the claimant is under the standing investitures entitled to take the fee, must 'according to the old law' be clearly made out; for a service in one character 'would' not carry a subject descendible to an heir of another description, although the same person 'might' have in him both characters (*b*). To this rule, however, there is an exception in the case of a service in a character which necessarily involves that in which the subject is to be taken up, and where the intention of taking in both characters is obvious (*c*). 'Service as heir-male general also connects the person served with all estates destined to him in that character (*d*). It is not a valid objection to any precept or writ from Chancery or of *clare constat*, or to any decree of general or special service, that the character of the heir is erroneously stated, if he is truly entitled to succeed as heir to the lands specified (*e*).' Every link in the chain of propinquity must be specified (*f*).

(*a*) 3 Stair, 5. § 34. 3 Ersk. 8. § 66. Meikle *v.* Liston, 1664; M. 16,091; 2 Ill. 423. Robertson *v.* M. Athol, 1681; M. 16,096. Cunningham *v.* Glen, Feb. 27, 1812; F. C.

(*b*) Edgar *v.* Maxwell (Elshieshiells Case), 1736; M. 3089, 4325, 14,015; Elch. *Service of Heirs*, 2; *Serv. and Conf.* 6; Cr. St. & Pat. 334; 2 Ross' L. C. 596; 2 Ill. 68. Cairns *v.* Garrioch's Crs., 1742; M. 14,438; 2 Ill. 423. See Forbes *v.* Maitland, 1753; M. 14,431; 5 B. Sup. 250; aff. Cr. St. & Pat. 570. See Elch. Notes, *Retour*, 3; 2 Ill. 431. Hay *v.* Hay, *supra*, § 1825 (*c*). Cathcart's Tr. *v.* E. Cassillis, 1802 and 1807; M. 14,447; Apx. *Serv. of Heirs*, 2; 5 Pat. 1; 1825, 1 W. & S. 239; 2 Ross' L. C. 525; 2 Ill. 431. Ogilvy *v.* Ogilvy, Dec. 16, 1817; F. C. Woodmass *v.* Hislop's Trs., 1825; 3 S. 476. As to the case of Woodmass, see 1 M'Laren on Wills, § 1205. L. Elibank *v.* Campbell, 1833; 12 S. 74.

(*c*) Livington *v.* Menzies, 1705; M. 14,004; 2 Ill. 430. E. Dalhousie *v.* Hawley, 1712; M. 14,014; 2 Ill. 423; 2 Ross' L. C. 292. Bell *v.* Carruthers, 1749; M. 14,016. Haldane *v.* Haldanes, 1766; M. 14,443; Hailes, 167; 2 Ross' L. C. 564. See Rose *v.* Rose, 1784; M. 14,955; 2 Ill. 334. D. Queensberry's Trs. *v.* E. Wemyss, 1819; Hume, 727. Colvin *v.* Alison, 1796; Hume, 723. See M. Bell's Convg. 1100. 1 M'Laren on Wills, p. 625, note. Todd *v.* Mackenzie, 1874; 1 R. 1203.

(*d*) Cathcart, *cit.* Anderson *v.* Anderson, 1832; 10 S. 696.

(*e*) *Supra*, § 779C.

(*f*) 3 Stair, 5. § 35. 3 Ersk. 8. § 66. E. Cassillis *v.* E. Wigton, 1629; M. 14,423; 2 Ill. 424. How *v.* Bryden, 1822; 1 S. 393. Galbraith *v.* Galbraith, 1826; 4 S. 734; aff. 1831, 5 W. & S. 84.

1831. The Lands—Old and New Extent.—The retour 'formerly' must contain an answer as to the "extent" of the lands (*a*). The purpose of having this returned 'was' to serve as the rule of payment of the casualties of non-entry and relief; and also in Crown holdings formerly, to serve as the criterion of qualification for the elective franchise. The valued rent appears in the roll of the county where the lands lie; the old extent is proved by retours. This is a matter involved in some obscurity. The contributions levied in Scotland in the twelfth and thirteenth centuries appear to have had reference to the value of the lands at the time, ascertained either by some general estimate, or by separate investigations, or retours of the several lands. Whether the one or the other mode of ascertaining the value was referred to, it became in process of time necessary to state the value of lands at a very different rate, in consequence of the devastation of war, which in Scotland was very great, from the prevailing policy of arresting the progress and cutting off the supplies of an invading army, by an entire and total devastation of the invaded territory. In the beginning of the fourteenth century, brieves were issued under the authority of Edward I., and retours made to Chancery, distinguishing the valuation "tempore pacis quando terræ fuerunt ædificatæ et cultæ per totum," and the valuation "nunc propter destructionem guerræ." It appears that the new valuation was, between the middle of the fourteenth and the middle of the fifteenth century, less than the old by more than one-half. Then it appears that the old and new valuation came to be pretty much on the same level; and previous to 1643, when the valued rent was introduced, the practice was adopted of estimating the new extent by adding a certain proportion to the old valuation, to compensate for the advanced improvement of the country, and for the difference in the value of money (*b*).

(*a*) 2 Craig, 17. § 35 et seq. 3 Stair, 5. § 38. 2 Ersk. 5. § 31 et seq. 10 and 11 Vict. c. 47, § 4. 31 and 32 Vict. c. 101, § 29.
(*b*) Cranston *v.* Gibson, May 16, 1818; F. C.; 2 Ill. 424.

1832. The Verdict 'was' recorded and signed by the chancellor of the jury; the Sheriff 'interposed' his authority, and 'signed' an entry in the record to that effect. The return, or retour, containing an answer to the brieve, 'was' made to Chancery; and an extract 'was' given out, which 'was' legal evidence of the heir's right in general service (*a*), and which in special service 'contained' a warrant for issuing a precept for infefting the heir, if the lands 'held' of the Crown; or for making a requisition on the superior to grant his precept for infefting, if the lands 'held' of a subject (*b*).

(*a*) Dalrymple *v.* Hope (Bargany Case), 1738; Elchies, *Retour*, 1; Cr. & St. 237; 2 Ill. 336. M'Intosh *v.* M'Intosh, 1698; M. 14,431; 2 Ill. 434.
(*b*) See as to prescription of services, below, § 2024.

1832A. 'Modern Mode of Service.—The forms of proceeding stated above were abolished by *the Service of Heirs Act*, 1847 (*a*). In place of a brieve, a petition to the Sheriff of the county, where the lands, whether held by burgage tenure or not, are situated, or to the Sheriff of Chancery (a Court created by the statute), is competent; and where they are situated in several counties, it must be presented to the latter. In the petition, which must be subscribed by the petitioner himself or by a mandatory specially authorised, the heir sets forth the death of the ancestor, the date of it, the description of the lands (which may be by reference), the ancestor's title, the claimant's propinquity, the character in which he desires to be served, and the deed, if any, under which he claims (*b*). The petition must be published in the county where the lands are situated, and edictally in Edinburgh (*c*). No proof can be led, or decree pronounced, until after the lapse of fifteen days in the usual case, twenty days as to Orkney and Shetland, and thirty days in the case of services to persons dying abroad, from the latest day of publication (*d*). The Sheriff is, without the intervention of a jury, the judge both of the fact and of the law; and his decree is declared to be equivalent to the verdict of a jury under the brieve of inquest (*e*). On the petition and decree, proof and inventories of productions, being transmitted to the Director of Chancery, an extract is issued, which is a warrant to infeft (*f*). The decree is declared to be equivalent to a disposition by the deceased in favour of the heir, with a double manner of holding where the lands contain no prohibition of subinfeudation or of an alternative holding, or, before the abolition of burgage holdings, in the case of burgage lands, with a holding in free burgage. It also vests in the heir a personal transmissible right to the lands, and makes them liable to his debts and deeds. Infeftment of the heir may be taken by registration of the decree with a warrant of registration, as if it were a disposition; and provision is made for making up the titles of his heirs and assignees (*g*). It is not now necessary to set forth in the petition and decree, as formerly, the destination or conditions of tailzie, provided they be duly referred to as set forth in any recorded writ (*h*).'

(*a*) 10 and 11 Vict. c. 47; substantially re-enacted by 31 and 32 Vict. c. 101, § 27–58.
(*b*) 31 and 32 Vict. c. 101, § 29, and Sch. Q.
(*c*) *Ib.* § 30. (*d*) *Ib.* § 33. (*e*) *Ib.*

(*f*) *Ib.* § 36, 37, 46.
(*g*) *Ib.* § 46. See Moreton's Trs. *v.* Mereton, 1854; 16 D. 1108.
(*h*) *Ib.* Sch. Q. & C. and § 9.

1833. (2.) *When Special Service required or not.*—The feudal right vested in the person last infeft can be taken out of his *hæreditas jacens* only by means of an infeftment in the person of another. This is to be accomplished either by a conveyance containing authority to infeft the disponee; or by *clare constat* or service of the heir, on the death of the person infeft. A conveyance of the subject may be completed by sasine in the person of the disponee (*a*). If there be no conveyance, the feudal right is to be taken up only by special service, either as heir-at-law or as heir of provision to the person last infeft: and a new infeftment obtained thereupon by precept from the Crown, or entry by the superior, completes the right.

On these principles depend several questions as to the completing of titles under settlements and destinations. Thus, as a disposition to one in liferent and another in fee, followed by infeftment, vests the feudal right of fee in the latter as disponee, no service is necessary on the liferenter's death; and, on the fiar's death, his heir's title is made up by special service to the fiar (*b*).

(*a*) See above, § 783 et seq.
(*b*) Ker *v.* Howison, 1708; M. 14,357; 12 Ill. 424. See above, § 1825.

1834. A disposition to the granter himself, whom failing to A. B., followed by infeftment, vests the fee in the granter; and on his death A. B. must enter by special service as heir of provision to him (*a*).

(*a*) Ker, *supra*, § 1833. 3 Ersk. 8. § 73. Cunningham *v.* Glen, Feb. 27, 1812; F. C.; 2 Ill. 425. See Livingston *v.* L. Napier, 1761; M. 15,409; 5 B. Sup. 885; aff. 1765, 2 Pat. 108. Gordon *v.* M'Culloch, 1791; Bell's Cases, 180. So even where the right remains personal. Young's Trs. *v.* Young, 1867; 5 Macph. 1101.

1835. Where, in such a case, infeftment has not followed on the disposition, service is still necessary in the person of A. B.; but there is no place for a special service to take up the right under the disposition: the right to the unexecuted procuratory or precept contained in the disposition, being personal, must be taken up by a general service. In bonds, the institute's right in such a case as this is construed as a mere liferent, and so the fee is held to be in the substitute: but this does not extend to lands (*a*).

(*a*) 3 Stair, 4. § 33. Dirleton and Stewart, *voce Heirs of Provision and Substitute*. Hamilton *v.* Hamilton, 1714; M. 14,360; rev. 1724, Robertson's Ap. 493. Livingston, *supra*, § 1834. See observations on the bench in Wilson *v.* Glen, Dec. 14, 1819; F. C. The reversal of Hamilton *v.* Hamilton has been disregarded or overruled, see Young's Trs., *supra*, § 1834, and note in 2 Ill. 425.

1836. Where the *nominatim* substitution is not *immediate* (as in a destination to A. and his heirs, whom failing to B.), the necessity of service by B. has never been doubted; and that service must be special if the institute have taken infeftment (*a*).

(*a*) Ker, *supra*, § 1833. M'Culloch *v.* M'Leod, 1731; M. 14,366; 2 Ill. 426. Gordon *v.* Gordon's Crs., 1748; M. 14,368; see 2 Ill. 426. Peacock *v.* Glen, 1826; 4 S. 742; 2 Ross' L. C. 53.

1837. Where the disposition is not to the granter himself, but to the heirs-male of the granter, whom failing to A. *nominatim*, and there are no heirs-male of the granter, this 'was formerly' not held a conditional institution of A., and he must serve heir of provision in special to the granter (*a*): 'but the service, though still expedient, will be only in *modum probationis* (*b*).'

(*a*) Peacock, *supra*, § 1836 (*a*).
(*b*) See below, § 1839. M. Bell's Convg. 846, 1109. M'Laren on Wills, etc., 622.

1838. Where one infeft in land dispones, not to himself, but to A., whom failing to B., and the deed is delivered, and A. *survives* the granter, but dies without taking infeftment, the personal right is in A.: and B. must make up his title by serving heir of provision in general to A., not in special to the granter (*a*). Where, in such a case, the deed is undelivered, and A. the institute *predeceases* the granter, it was held by a majority of the Court that nothing had vested in the institute: that the next heir was not to make up his title by serving heir to the institute: that he could not serve heir to the granter; and that the proper course was by a declarator that, as the conditional institute, he had right to the land. This was greatly doubted by the minority of the Court, on the ground chiefly that a right was vested in the institute. But there was no occasion to decide the question, and the case having gone to the House of Lords, was remitted to have the opinions of the judges on this point (*b*); when the opinion of the judges confirmed the above opinion of the majority (*c*), that the estate not having vested in the institute, a service to him was unnecessary, but still that this point was not necessary to be decided. 'It is now held that, in such circumstances, the next heir takes as a conditional institute, and may be infeft on the settlement without any service, on the principle that every substitution implies a conditional institution (*d*).'

(*a*) 3 Ersk. 8. § 73. Denniston *v.* Crichton, 1824; 2 S. 678; 2 Ill. 426.
(*b*) Colquhoun *v.* Colquhoun, 1828; 7 S. 200; 1831, 5 W. & S. 32.
(*c*) Same case, 1831; 9 S. 911.
(*d*) Colquhoun, *cit.* **Fogo** *v.* **Fogo,** 1840; 2 D. 651; 1841, 2 Rob. 440; 1842, 4 D. 1063; 1843, 2 Bell's App. 195; 2 Ross' L. C. 36. M. Bell's Convg. 1106 sqq.

1839. When the disposition is to the granter's heirs-male or heirs of his body, whom failing to A., whom failing to B., and the granter survives such heirs, and A. predeceases, it has been held that the fee is still in the granter, and that B.'s title is to be made up by service as heir of provision to the granter (*a*). 'But it has recently been explained that this section expresses the result of a special case where the Court had to construe the terms of a peculiar deed, and that "when one by *mortis causa* conveyance in the ordinary form dispones to the heirs of his body or the heirs-male of his body, whom failing to a person named, the person so named (there being no heirs of his, the granter's, body then existing) is conditional institute; and if heirs of the granter's body do not come into existence, or existing predecease him, the condition is purified, and the person named is, on the death of the granter, without qualification or condition, disponee, and as such is entitled to use the executory clauses of the disposition for feudalising his right without service or declarator" (*b*).'

(*a*) Gordon *v.* Gordon's Crs., 1748; M. 14,368; 2 Ill. 426; Falconer's report is incorrect. **Peacock** *v.* **Glen,** 1826; 4 S. 742; see L. Drummore's Note, 10 S. 701, footnote. Anderson *v.* Anderson, 1832; 10 S. 696. Murray *v.* Murray, 1833; 11 S. 629.
(*b*) Hutchison *v.* Hutchison, 1872; 11 Macph. 229 (*per curiam*). See Fogo and Colquhoun, *supra*; 1 M'Laren on Wills, etc., pp. 497, 622.

1840. When the land is duly taken out of the *hæreditas jacens* of the person last vest and seised as of fee, a special service is excluded. So, if infeftment have passed on a service which is objectionable, the infeftment must be reduced before the heir can serve (*a*); but if the infeftment have proceeded on a precept of *clare constat*, without service, this, as the mere act of the superior, will not exclude the service (*b*). A mere disposition, without infeftment, is not sufficient to exclude a special service (*c*).

(*a*) Cunningham *v.* Glen, Feb. 27, 1812; F. C.; 2 Ill. 423. See Lady Forbes *v.* Hunter, July 3, 1810; F. C.; 2 Ill. 428.
(*b*) Opinion of the Court in M'Callum *v.* Campbell, 1793; M. 16,135. See also Lord Moncreiff's opinion in Rutherford *v.* Nisbet's Trs., 9 S. 6, note.
(*c*) Suttie *v.* D. Gordon, 1733; M. 14,457. Douglas *v.* D. Hamilton, 1761; M. 14,457.

1841. Opposition and Competition.—A service may be opposed on an exclusive title; on objection to the process; on a preferable right to the character claimed (*a*).

(*a*) 3 Ersk. 8. § 60. Innes *v.* Ker (Roxburghe Cause); M. *Tailzie*, Apx. 13, *cit.* § 1694.

1842. Not only may the service be opposed by one having interest (*a*); but where there is more than one pretender to the character of heir, each may purchase a brieve 'or present a petition for service' (*b*), and they are allowed to come into competition, and meet before the same inquest.

(*a*) If a caveat be lodged with a Sheriff-clerk against any petition to be presented, he is bound to give notice of such petition. 31 and 32 Vict. c. 101, § 31.
(*b*) *Ib.* § 35 sqq.

1843. In cases of competition or difficulty, the service 'might,' on the application of the parties to the Lord Ordinary on the Bills, be advocated to the Court of Session (*a*). 'Under the present system of procedure, where the Sheriff refuses to serve a petitioner, or dismisses his petition, or repels the objection of an opposing party, an appeal to the Court of Session is competent within fifteen days. Further evidence may be taken in the appeal, with or without a jury (*b*). A petitioner may appeal for trial by jury (*c*); and provision is made for reduction of decrees of service (*d*).'

(*a*) 3 Ersk. 8. § 64. 1 and 2 Geo. IV. c. 38, § 11. Anderson *v.* Anderson, 1834; 12 S. 729. Officers of State *v.* Alexander, 1835; 13 S. 1044.
(*b*) 31 and 32 Vict. c. 101, § 42. Campbell *v.* Campbell, 1866; 4 Macph. 867. Mackintosh *v.* Ross, 1873; 11 Macph. 636. Swinton *v.* Swinton, 1862; 24 D. 833.
(*c*) *Ib.* § 41. Fenton *v.* Livingstone, 1853; 16 D. 104.
(*d*) *Ib.* § 43.

1844. Objections 'might' be stated to the brieve; or to the executions as blotted and erased, as incorrect in date, as not on the proper number of days; or other similiar objections if obvious *ex facie*, not otherwise (*a*).

(*a*) 1429, c. 114. 1503, c. 94. 3 Stair, 5. § 33. 3 Ersk. 8. § 60. Lesly *v.* Grant, 1758; 5 B. Sup. 862; 2 Ill. 428.

1845. The right of the claimant may be opposed on the merits, by exceptions instantly verified (*a*): as, that the fee is full; that either the deceased or the claimant is bastard, the presumption being for legitimacy (*b*); that there is a nearer heir, although *in utero* (*c*). But the renunciation of a nearer heir will not validate the service of one more remote (*d*).

(*a*) 3 Ersk. 8. § 60.
(*b*) 3 Ersk. 8. § 66. Crosbie *v.* Shaw, 1629; M. 2747; 2 Ill. 428. Lindsay *v.* Kerr, 1824; 2 S. App. 147. 1503, c. 94.
(*c*) 3 Stair, 5. § 50. 3 Ersk. 8. § 76. Middlemore *v.* M'Farlane's Reprs., March 5, 1811; F. C. See L. Mountstewart *v.* M'Kenzie, 1707; M. 14,903; 2 Ill. 317. M'Kinnon *v.* M'Donald, 1756; 5 B. Sup. 848; and 1765, M. 5279; 5 B. Sup. 904; aff. 2 Pat. 252. See M'Kenzie *v.* L. Mountstewart, 1709; M. 14,912. See above, § 1642.
(*d*) Hay *v.* ——, 1588; M. 14,865. Dalgleish *v.* Anderson, 1609; M. 14,866.

1846. As to the mode of opposing,—One having an interest may 'perhaps' examine witnesses, or adduce evidence of the above exceptions; or, on a competing brieve, 'in the present day, on a competing petition for service, which is the only effective mode of opposing any service (*a*),' he may contend for and prove his own preferable right; or he may reduce the service, and in such reduction the Court of Session will judge of the evidence already given, or in their discretion allow additional evidence (*b*). 'A declarator that a person is not the heir of one deceased was incompetent, but seems now to be authorised by statute (*c*).'

(*a*) See Graham's Guardians *v.* Graham, 1850; 13 D. 125, and Shaw's Bell's Com. 1040 (*b*); and below, § 1853.
(*b*) Don *v.* Don, 1712; M. 14,425. Innes *v.* Ker (Roxburghe Cause), 1807; M. *Tailzie*, Apx. 13; 2 Dow, 149. See Suttie and Douglas, *supra*, § 1840. Anderson *v.* Anderson, 1834; 12 S. 729; 2 Ill. 429. Gifford *v.* Gifford, 1837; 15 S. 592. Officers of State *v.* Alexander, 1839; 1 D. 1188. (See next note.) Barclay *v.* Barclay, 1842; 5 D. 394. Norris *v.* Gilchrist, 1847; 9 D. 466; 1852, 14 D. 919; 1 Stu. 393. *Supra*, § 1843.
(*c*) Officers of State *v.* Alexander, 1866; 4 Macph. 741; aff. 1868, 6 Macph. H. L. 54; L. R. 1 Sc. App. 276. Norris, *supra* (*b*). See 37 and 38 Vict. c. 94, § 13.

1847. Effect of the Retour or Decree.—The retour 'had' of itself no effect to vest the right to lands in which the predecessor was infeft. If the heir, though retoured, 'died' uninfeft, the retour, 'before 1868, expired' as a title to the special lands (*a*); and although it has been said that it will in this way evanish even as a general service, unless completed (*b*), that does not seem to be law, and has not in practice been so understood (*c*). The title proceeding on a retour 'was' favoured in having a shorter prescription of twenty years (*d*).

(*a*) 3 Ersk. 8. § 78.
(*b*) More's Notes, p. cccxxvi.
(*c*) 3 Ersk. 8. § 51 and 75. Drummond *v.* ——, 1676; M. 14,457. Duff's Feud. Convg. 469. See above, § 779A, 1832A; also as to the effect of service, § 782.
(*d*) 1617, c. 13. See below, of Prescription, § 2024.

1848. General Service.—The object of this form of service has already been explained, as necessary in completing the heir's title to heritable subjects not feudalised (as servitudes, bonds heritable by destination, etc.); or to personal rights in feudal subjects; or to unexecuted procuratories or precepts (*a*).

(*a*) See *ante*, § 781. For general service, *cum beneficio inventarii*, or with specification, see below, § 1926.

1849. (1.) *Proceedings.* — The brieve on which the general service 'proceeded might' be directed to any Judge Ordinary, without regard to the domicile of the deceased or of the heir, or to the local situation of the lands to which ultimately it 'might' be intended to complete a title (*a*). The brieve 'was' published at the head burgh of the jurisdiction applied to; and the verdict, and of course the retour, 'contained' an answer only to three of the heads of the brieve, viz.: 1. Whether the ancestor died at the faith and peace of the Queen (which is presumed); 2. Whether the claimant 'was' his nearest and lawful heir; and, 3. Whether the claimant is of lawful age. And so a special service, which 'answered' to these three points, necessarily includes a general in the same character (*b*), 'but now only as to the particular lands embraced in it, and it does not infer passive representation beyond their value.' The heir must be served correctly in that character to which the right to be vested belongs (*c*), or at least in a character which necessarily includes it (*d*). The heir must be served to the person in whom the personal right was last vested (*e*). If the heir's right is by deed or destination, the service must not only be in a character necessarily comprehending the description of heirs in the destination, but also as "heir of provision," the deed containing the destination being laid before the jury (*f*). It has been held that a service as heir of provision will extend to any right to which that particular description of heir of provision applies (*g*); but if the service be as heir of provision, and a deed be specified, the retour will not serve as a general title as heir of provision under any other deed.

(*a*) 3 Ersk. 8. § 64, 66. L. Caskieben, suppl., 1630; M. 14,420; 2 Ill. 429.
(*b*) See above, § 1847. 10 and 11 Vict. c. 47, § 23. 31 and 32 Vict. c. 101, § 47. 37 and 38 Vict. c. 94, § 12.
(*c*) 3 Stair, 5. § 35. 3 Ersk. 8. § 66. E. Cassillis *v.* E. Wigton, 1629; M. 14,423: 2 Ill. 424. Edgar *v.* Johnston, 1738; M. 14,015; Elchies, *Serv. and Conf.* 6; 2 Ill. 430. Coulterallers *v.* Kilbucho, 1742: 5 B. Sup. 717. Cairns *v.* Garrioch's Crs., 1742; M. 14,438.
(*d*) 3 Stair, 4. § 33. 3 Ersk. 8. § 75. Haldane *v.* Haldanes, 1766; M. 14,443; Hailes, 167; 2 Ross' L. C. 564. See above, § 1830, 779c.
(*e*) Livington *v.* Menzies, 1706; M. 14,007. Bell *v.* Carruthers, 1749; M. 14,016. Spalding *v.* Laurie, 1784; M. 14,461. Gordon *v.* Bruce, 1682; M. 15,352. Campbell *v.* Campbells, 1770; M. 14,949.
(*f*) Haldane, *supra* (*d*). Cathcart's Tr., *supra*, § 1830 (*b*). Colvin *v.* Alison, 1796; Hume, 723. Ogilvy *v.* Ogilvy, 1817; *ib.* 724. See 10 and 11 Vict. c. 47, § 4. 31 and 32 Vict. c. 101, § 29.
(*g*) Forbes, *cit.* § 1830 (*b*). Hay *v.* Hay, 1758; M. 14,369; 5 B. Sup. 351. There is no room for such a construction, as it is necessary that the petition for the service specify the deed or deeds under which the character of heir of provision is claimed. 31 and 32 Vict. c. 101, § 29.

1849A. 'The form of proceeding is now by petition to the Sheriff within whose territory the party died domiciled, or to the Sheriff of Chancery; and to the latter in all cases where the defunct was domiciled furth of Scotland. The petition is published within the county of the domicile of the deceased, and edictally. It is no longer necessary to prove more than the death of the ancestor, its date, his domicile, and that the petitioner is the nearest and lawful heir (*a*).'

(*a*) 31 and 32 Vict. c. 101, § 27–30. See above, § 1832A.

1850. (2.) *When General Service required or not.*—A general service has the double effect of establishing the character of heir, and so giving a title to pursue and reduce; and of vesting those rights which do not require infeftment. Where, therefore, an heir is excluded by an infeftment which he deems to be challengeable, he must serve in general (whether the ancestor was infeft, or held only a personal right), in order to entitle him to maintain the challenge (*a*); and this service must be in the proper character in which he would, but for the opposing deed, be entitled to the succession (*b*); and under it the person serving will be liable to all objections which, as obligations, would be incumbent on him if the title were completed (*c*).

(*a*) Horns *v.* Stevenson, 1746; M. 16,117. Carmichael *v.* Carmichael, Nov. 15, 1810; F. C.; aff. 1816, 6 Pat. 155; 2 Ill. 432. But see § 1852, note.
(*b*) M'Callum *v.* Campbell, 1793; M. 16,135.
(*c*) Carmichael, *supra* (*a*).

1851. General service is necessary to validate any proceeding or action grounded on the service (*a*). It is sufficient to vest and transmit all personal rights to heritable subjects and personal titles to lands (*b*). Therefore, although it was formerly held that there was nothing to prevent a second person from serving also as heir in general, to the effect of establishing this character, the next heir, in order to carry any personal right vested by a prior general service, must serve to the person who has thus served in general; and the Record of Retours in Chancery is in this way important in relation to the vesting of personal fees.

(*a*) M'Intosh *v.* M'Intosh, 1698; M. 14,431; 2 Ill. 434. Bargany Case (Dalrymple *v.* Hope), 1738; Elch. *Retour*, 1; 1739; Cr. St. & Pat. 237; 2 Ill. 336.
(*b*) 1693, c. 35. See above, § 779A.

1852. (3.) *Competency of a Second Service.*—It was in the Court of Session held not incompetent to serve a second time in general as heir to the deceased, although an intervening heir had already served; but this was reversed in the House of Lords (*a*). For the purpose of vesting a right to a particular subject, it has long been settled that there can be no second general service.

(*a*) Carmichael, *supra*, § 1850. Cochrane *v.* Ramsay, 1828; 6 S. 751; rev. 1830, 4 W. & S. 128. See Rutherford *v.* Nisbet's Trs., 1830; 9 S. 3; 2 Ill. 323 (heir-apparent may without service sue reduction of service and infeftment). See Young *v.* Leith, 1844; 6 D. 370. Macara *v.* Wilson, 1848; 10 D. 707. Wilson *v.* Gilchrist's Trs., 1851; 13 D. 636.

1853. Opposition and Competition.—No opposition is allowed in a general service, unless by one having a competing brieve in the specific character assumed in the claim, or on the ground of the succession not being open (*a*).

(*a*) Lady Forbes *v.* Hunter, July 3, 1810; F. C.; 2 Ill. 433. Cochrane *v.* Ramsay, June 28, 1821; F. C.; 1 S. 9. Somerville *v.* Thomson, May 19, 1815; F. C.; rev. 1818, 6 Pat. 393; 2 Ill. 316. Aitchison *v.* Aitchison, 1829; 7 S. 558. Graham's Guardians *v.* Graham, 1850; 13 D. 125; Shaw's Bell's Com. 1040 (*b*). *Supra*, § 1846.

III. CHARGES TO ENTER HEIR.

1854. General View.—The debts of a person deceased become burdens on the heir who takes his property, a certain mode being appointed by which that responsibility may be limited to the amount of the estate (*a*). To compel the heir to accept or to renounce the succession, and so to give access to creditors, it has been enacted,—that by a writ under the Signet, an heir may be charged at the instance of a creditor of the predecessor, to enter heir in the lands or other heritable subjects, after the expiration of the *annus deliberandi* (*b*), otherwise the land, etc., may be apprised (now adjudged) to the creditor as if the heir were entered (*c*); that the heir's own creditors may have a similar remedy (*d*); and that a preference shall be given to the ancestor's creditors, if they shall complete their diligence within three years (*e*).

(*a*) See § 1922 et seq. (*b*) See *ante*, § 1685.
(*c*) 1540, c. 106; 2 Acta Parl. 375, c. 24.
(*d*) 1621, c. 27; 4 Acta Parl. 627, c. 27.
(*e*) 1661, c. 24; 7 Acta Parl. 63, c. 88.

1855. Under these Acts practice improved the proceeding by the introduction of the general charge, and by distinguishing charges into special and general-special (*a*): 'all now abolished; see below, § 1858A.'

(*a*) Couper *v.* M'Martin, 1627; M. 2700. See for a similar remedy in moveable succession, below, § 1901.

1856. General Charge, 'now incompetent, was' a writ issued under the Signet, containing a warrant to charge the heir to enter within forty days as heir to the deceased, with certification that, if he 'failed,' the creditor 'should' have such action and diligence against him as if he had entered, or such as he might have had against his predecessor had he been alive. The use of this charge 'was' to fix on the heir the representation generally, or to compel him to renounce the succession. If he 'disobeyed' the charge, an action of constitution 'might' be raised, and decree and execution proceed against him; 'and this procedure remains competent, the execution of the summons in it being equivalent to the general charge (*a*).' If he compeared in the action, and refused or failed, after reasonable time allowed, to renounce, he 'incurred, under the law previous to 1874,' a passive title, and 'could' not be reponed (*b*). If he renounce the succession, an action of constitution *cognitionis causâ tantum* is raised, to the effect of enabling the creditor to proceed *contra hæreditatem jacentem* (*c*).

(*a*) Smith *v.* Oliphant's Exrs., 1807; Hume, 439.
(*b*) 3 Jurid. Styles, 362. 2 Ersk. 12. § 12. See below, § 1858A. Under the new law as to the liability of heirs, the rights of the ancestor's creditors on renunciation continue the same. 37 and 38 Vict. c. 94, § 12. *Infra*, § 1914A.
(*c*) See below, § 1858A.

1857. Special Charge, or General-Special Charge, 'followed' after the general charge, being writs also under the Signet, containing a warrant to charge the heir to enter heir in special under the proper character.

(1.) *Special Charge* 'called' on the heir to enter to the lands of A., wherein B. died last vest and seised, with certification; and the effect 'was' to enable the creditors either to adjudge the lands as if they were the heirs, or as *in hæreditate jacente* of the ancestor (*a*).

(2.) *General-Special Charge* 'was' used where the subject to be taken up 'was' a personal right either in a heritable subject not feudal, or in a feudal subject in which the ancestor was not infeft. The certification and effect 'were' the same as in a special charge (*b*).

(*a*) 3 Jurid. Styles, 369. 2 Ersk. 12. § 12.
(*b*) 3 Jurid. Styles, 373.

1858. The chief points to be observed relative to those charges are these:—The special or general-special charge must be preceded by the general charge, where the debt 'was' the ancestor's (*a*). The debt must be constituted by decree, but special charge 'might' be raised before extract (*b*). In all attempts to adjudge a tailzied estate, the charge must be directed against the heir of tailzie, not the heir of law (*c*). Although the heir 'might' be charged before the expiration of the *annus deliberandi* (*d*), and the summons executed at the same time, the action 'could' not be called till after (*e*). It 'was' not necessary to charge the heir to enter in special, if already served heir in special, although not infeft (*f*). And it 'was' not necessary to charge the heir in special to enter, where the creditor 'was' to proceed with diligence for attaching a lease (*g*).

(*a*) E. Cassillis *v.* M'Martin, 1627; M. 2167; 2 Ill. 435. Monro *v.* Crs. of Easterfearn, 1737; M. 2173. Oliphant *v.* Hamilton, 1667; M. 2171. Brodie *v.* Douglas, 1672; M. 2172.

(*b*) Catrine's Crs. *v.* Baird, 1738; M. 2173.
(*c*) Gairns *v.* Drum, 1682; 2 B. Sup. 21.
(*d*) § 1858A. 31 and 32 Vict. c. 101, § 61.
(*e*) M'Intosh *v.* M'Queen, 1829; 7 S. 882; 2 Ill. 325.
(*f*) Dickson *v.* Ker, 1629; M. 169, 2169.
(*g*) Rule *v.* Hume, 1635; M. 14,374.

1858A. 'Actions of Constitution and Adjudication.—Letters of charge are abolished: and (1) in an action of *constitution of an ancestor's debt or obligation* against his unentered heir, the execution of the summons is equivalent to a general charge (*a*). (2) In an action of *adjudication* against an unentered heir, whether for debt or in implement, following *on such decree of constitution*, or in an *adjudication* against him founded *on his own debt or obligation*, the execution of the summons is equivalent to a special charge or general-special charge, as the circumstances may require (*b*). (3) Actions of *constitution and adjudication* against an unentered heir founded *on his ancestor's debt or obligation* may be combined in one summons, whether the heir renounce or not; and the execution of the summons is equivalent to a general charge, or a general charge and a special charge, or a general charge and a general-special charge, as the circumstances may require.

'The *induciæ* of these statutory charges expire with the *induciæ* of the summonses, and infer the like certification with the appropriate charges under the law and practice before 30th Sept. 1847; and thereafter in the respective actions the procedure adopted and decrees pronounced are the same as if the summons had been preceded by the appropriate charge. The decrees are declared valid decrees of constitution, of adjudication, or of constitution and adjudication, as the case may be; and decree of constitution and adjudication may be pronounced in one and the same interlocutor (*c*). These actions may be insisted in at any time after the lapse of six months after the heir becomes apparent heir (*d*).

'The decree of adjudication (like other decrees of adjudication, except those of heritable securities) has the effect of a conveyance of the lands contained in the decree in favour of the adjudger, on which he may complete his title (*e*).'

(*a*) *Supra*, § 1856. (*b*) *Supra*, § 1857.
(*c*) 31 and 32 Vict. c. 101, § 60, re-enacting 10 and 11 Vict. c. 48, § 16, as to feudal subjects, and c. 49, § 8, as to burgage.
(*d*) *Ib.* 61.
(*e*) 37 and 38 Vict. c. 94, § 62. *Supra*, § 828A.

IV. ENTRY BY ADJUDICATION ON TRUST BOND.

1859. Nature of it.—This mode of entry is chiefly as a tentative title, for the purpose of challenging an adverse right. It is effectual as a title, and at first was held to infer no passive representation (*a*). Afterwards it was by Act of Sederunt, and subsequently by statute, made to infer representation, if intromission followed (*b*). It is now an established mode of entry (*c*).

(*a*) Glendonwyn *v.* E. Nithsdale, 1662; M. 9738; 2 Ill. 435. See above, § 834.
(*b*) Act of Sed., Feb. 28, 1662. 1695, c. 24.
(*c*) Nevoy *v.* L. Balmerino, 1676; M. 9741. Gordon *v.* Ogilvie, 1761; M. 14,070. Hepburn *v.* Scotts, 1781; M. 14,487. Craigie *v.* Innes Ker, 1808; M. *Adjud.* Apx. 16. Bellenden Ker *v.* Lady Essex Ker's Trs., 1823; 2 S. 369; aff. 1825; 1 W. & S. 381. See 5 W. & S. 718; 2 Ill. 419. Dunlop *v.* Cochrane, 1824; 2 S. App. 115. Rutherford *v.* Nisbet's Trs., 1830; 9 S. 3. Beveridges *v.* Crawford, 1793; M. 5296.

CHAPTER VIII

OF SUCCESSION IN MOVEABLES

1860. Distinction between Moveable and Heritable Succession.—Moveable succession differs from heritable in these points (*a*): that there is no preference of males; that there is no law of primogeniture; that there is 'at common law, though this has been altered by statute,' no representation of the deceased parent by the child (*b*); and that there 'never was any' distinction of conquest.

(*a*) 3 Stair, t. 8. 3 Ersk. t. 9. Robertson on Personal Successions. 2 Blackst. Com. 489 et seq. 2 Kent, Com. on Amer. Law, 408 et seq. Story's Conf. of Laws, 403 and 391. 2 Stephen's Com. 193 sqq. 1 M'Laren on Wills and Succession, 110 sqq. Savigny's Private International Law, p. 282 sqq. (2nd ed. Edinr. 1880). Westlake's Private International Law, p. 88 sqq. Bar, Das Internationale Privatrecht, § 103 sqq.

(*b*) In some of these points the English law differs materially from the Scottish, and important questions in international law arise from this difference. For these I refer to the work of Mr. Robertson on the Rules of Personal Succession.

I. INTESTATE SUCCESSION.

1861. Rules.—The whole moveable estate if the deceased die unmarried, or the dead's part if married, descends thus by law:—The free moveable estate divides among the nearest in kin at the death. The full blood excludes the half; and neither the mother nor maternal relations, 'except under the statute of 1855 after mentioned,' succeed in moveables. The lines of succession follow the same order as in heritable succession: first, descendants; next, collaterals 'in the narrower sense, *i.e.* brothers and sisters or their descendants'; finally, ascendants with their collaterals. If the heir of the deceased in his heritable estate be also one of the next of kin, and do not choose to share the heritable estate with the other next of kin, he will be entitled to no share of the moveables (*a*). The succession in moveables is regulated by the law of the domicile at the time of death (*b*), and this suggests the importance of attending to the difference in the law of personal succession in England and Scotland (*c*).

(*a*) See below, of Collation, § 1910.

(*b*) 3 Ersk. 9. § 2–4. Dirleton's Doubts, 129. Stewart, 210.

(*c*) Robertson on Personal Succession, 2 et seq. Story, Confl. of Laws, 391–403.

1861A. 'Representation in Moveables.—By the Intestate Moveable Succession Act, 1855, it is declared that in all cases of intestate moveable succession, accruing after the passing of the Act, where any person who, had he survived the intestate, would have been among his next of kin (*a*), has predeceased the intestate, the lawful child or children of the person so predeceasing shall come in the place of that person; and the issue of such child or children, or of any descendant of such child or children, who may, in like manner, have predeceased the intestate, shall come in the place of his or their parent predeceasing, and shall respectively have right to the share of the moveable estate to which the parent, if he had survived the intestate, would have been entitled. But no representation is admitted among "collaterals" after brothers' and sisters' descendants (*b*). The surviving next of kin claiming the office of executor have exclusive right thereto, in preference to the children or other descendants of any predeceasing next of kin, but such children or descendants are entitled to confirmation when no next of kin are competing for the office (*c*). The representation thus introduced applies only where some of the next of kin have predeceased the intestate, leaving children who but for the statute would have been excluded from a share in the succession. Hence, where the next of kin are nephews and nieces, the issue of different brothers or sisters, they take in their own right *per capita* and not *per stirpes* as representing their parents (*d*).'

(*a*) As to the meaning of next of kin in this Act, and in testamentary destinations since the Act, see Young's Trs. *v.* Janes, 1880; 8 R. 242. Tronsons *v.* Tronsons, 1884; 12 R. 155. Murray *v.* Gregory's Trs., 1887; 14 R. 368; revd. 1889, 14 App. Ca. 124; 16 R. H. L. 11 (as Hood *v.* Murray or Gregory's Trs. *v.* Alison); and cases below, § 1880.

(*b*) Ormiston *v.* Broad, 1862; 1 Macph. 10. See above, § 1650, note.

(*c*) 18 and 19 Vict. c. 23, § 1. See Dowie *v.* Barclay, 1871; 9 Macph. 726.

(*d*) Turner *v.* Couper, 1869; 8 Macph. 222.

1861B. 'Succession of Parents and of Brothers uterine.—If any person dying intestate predecease his father without issue, his father has right to one-half of his moveable estate, in preference to any brothers or sisters, or their descendants, who may have survived such intestate (*a*). If an intestate dying without issue, whose father has predeceased him, be survived by his mother, she is to have right to one-third of his moveable estate, in preference to his brothers and sisters, or their descendants, or next of kin of the intestate (*b*). If an intestate shall die without issue, whose father and mother have both predeceased him, and shall not leave any brother or sister german or consanguinean, nor any descendant of them, but shall leave a brother or sister uterine, or any descendant of them, these brothers and sisters uterine, and such descendants in place of their predeceasing parent, have right to one-half of his moveable estate (*c*).'

(*a*) 18 and 19 Vict. c. 23, § 4. Webster *v.* Shiress, 1878; 6 R. 102.

(*b*) *Ib.* § 4. Muir, petr., 1876; 4 R. 74.

(*c*) *Ib.* § 5.

II. TESTATE SUCCESSION.

1862. Last Will or Testament.—The dead's part may be bequeathed by last Will; to which nothing more is necessary than a clear expression of the testator's intention as to the disposal of his effects, provided it be testamentary and finally concluded (*a*). 'When on the face of the document it is doubtful whether it is testamentary (*i.e.* is the complete expression of the writer's will) extrinsic evidence of the circumstances in which it was written and found, and of the writer's conduct, etc., is admitted to show whether it was or was not his testament (*b*).' It is at the best doubtful whether, by will, a general and unlimited power of distribution after the testator's death can be given to another (*c*); but if distinct limits are appointed for the exercise of the power, it will be effectual (*d*).

(*a*) 3 Stair, 8. § 35. 3 Ersk. 9. § 5. 2 Jurid. Styles, 565. Henderson *v.* Selkrig, 1795; M. 4489; 2 Ill. 328. Robertson *v.* Mason, 1795; M. 4491, 15,950. See Robertson *v.* Robertson, Feb. 16, 1816; F. C.; 2 Ill. 436. Horsbrugh *v.* Horsbrugh, 1847; 9 D. 324. Grant (Bell's Exrs.) *v.* Stoddart, 1849; 11 D. 860; rev. 1852, 24 Sc. Jur. 555; 1 Macq. 162. **Mags. of Dundee *v.* Morris,** 1856; 19 D. 918; 1858, 3 Macq. 134. Forsyth *v.* Forsyth's Trs., 1872; 10 Macph. 616. Ritchie *v.* Whish, 1880; 8 R. 101. Whyte *v.* Hamilton, 1881; 8 R. 940; aff. 1882, 9 R. H. L. 53; 7 App. Ca. 400. See as to void Wills and Wills of accumulation, below, § 1865.

(*b*) Monro *v.* Coutts, 1813; 1 Dow, 437; 2 Ill. 441. Forsyth's Trs., *cit.* Scott *v.* Sceales, 1864; 2 Macph. 613. Lowson *v.* Ford, 1866; 4 Macph. 631. Whyte *v.* Hamilton, *cit.* Colvin *v.* Hutchison, 1885; 12 R. 947. See below, § 1869.

(c) It seems that it cannot. Kirkpatrick's Trs. v. Kirkpatrick, 1874; 1 R. H. L. 37. Sutherland's Trs., *infra*.

(d) Gellie v. Panton, 1709; M. 8061; 2 Ill. 455. Murray v. Fleming, 1729; M. 4075. Wharrie v. Wharrie, 1760; M. 6599. Brown's Trs. v. Brown, 1762; M. 2318. Hill v. Burns, 1824; 3 S. 389; aff. 2 W. & S. 80. Crichton v. Grierson, 1826; 4 S. 553; 3 W. & S. 329. Mags. of Dundee, *supra*. Ewen v. Mags. of Montrose, 1828; 6 S. 479; rev. 1830, 4 W. & S. 346 (not approved in Mags. of Dundee v. Morris, *cit.*). Black's Trs. v. Miller, 1836; 14 S. 555; aff. 1837, 2 S. & M'L. 866. Douglas v. Douglas's Trs., 1859; 21 D. 1066 (construction of alleged power to correct or alter). Sutherland's Trs. v. Sutherland's Trs., 1893; 20 R. 925. Cobb v. Cobb's Trs., 1894; 21 R. 638 (direction to trustees to pay to useful, benevolent, and charitable institutions in their discretion not void for uncertainty).

1863. A Will does carry heritage 'by the common law' (a); but a *mortis causâ* conveyance of heritage in liege poustie will not be defeated merely because it contains clauses peculiar to a testament (b). 'By 31 and 32 Vict. c. 101, § 20, heritable property may be bequeathed by all persons alive at or after 31st December 1868, by testamentary or *mortis causâ* deeds or writings, which are declared to have the effect of a general disposition, and under which the legatee's title is to be made up as provided in the statute (c).'

(a) Brand v. Brand, 1735; 5 B. Sup. 183; 2 Ill. 438.

(b) Binning v. Contie, 1742; Elchies, *Testament*, 7; 2 Ill. 438. Brown v. Bower, 1770; M. 5440; Hailes, 332; 2 Ill. 329. Robertson v. Robertson, 1785; M. 15,947. See as to the true effect of these cases, imperfectly stated in the text, M. Bell's Convg. 928 sqq.; and Oag's Cur. v. Corner, 1885; 12 R. 1162.

(c) See above, § 1692A.

1864. A Will may be made (and is presumed in law to be made) in the last moment of life (a), and so is at all times during life revocable. There is no law of deathbed, as 'there was' in heritage, to defeat a Will made in mortal sickness. To reduce the Will, proof of insanity or imbecility, or of want of a sound disposing mind, or of deception and fraud, will be required (b).

(a) Hyslop v. Maxwell, 1834; 12 S. 413. Nimmo v. Murray's Trs., 1864; 2 Macph. 1144.

(b) Towart v. Sellers, 1817; 5 Dow, 231 (lucid interval). White v. Ballantyne, 1823; 1 S. App. 472 (onus of proving intelligence where Will made by lunatic). Gillespie v. Gillespie, Feb. 11, 1817; F. C. (paralytic and weak-minded). Watson v. Noble's Trs., 1825; 4 S. 200; 2 W. & S. 468 (evidence of intelligence). M'Diarmid v. M'Diarmid, 1826; 4 S. 583 (misrepresentation). Waddel v. Waddel's Trs., 1845; 7 D. 1017. M'Kellar v. M'Kellar, 1861; 24 D. 143. Morrison v. M'Lean's Trs., 1862; 24 D. 625. Cartwright v. Cartwright, 1 Phillimore, 90. Smith v. Tebbitt, 36 L. J. Pr. & Mat. 97; L. R. 1 Pr. 398. Banks v. Goodfellow, 39 L. J. Q. B. 237; L. R. 5 Q. B. 549 (partial insanity). Harwood v. Baker, 3 Moore, P. C. C. 122. Knight v. Boughton, L. R. 3 Pr. 64; 42 L. J. Pr. 25. Parfitt v. Lawless, L. R. 2 Pr. 462; 41 L. J. Pr. 68 (rules as to undue influence different from cases of gifts or contracts *inter vivos*). Nisbet's Trs. v. Nisbet, 1871; 9 Macph. 937 (lucid intervals). Maitland's Trs. v. Maitland, 1871; 10 Macph. 79. Munro v. Strain, 1874; 1 R. 1039 (facility and circumvention). Ballantyne v. Evans, 1886; 13 R. 652 (partial insanity—delusions). Hope v. Hope's Trs., 1896; 23 R. 513; rev. 1899, A. C. 1 (general averment of unsoundness of mind—specification necessary where nothing in personal history or Will itself speaks of insanity or delusion). See below, § 2105, 2107.

1865. By uncertainty, or unintelligible complexity of purpose, a Will is void (a).

As to Wills of accumulation, there is not, by the common law of Scotland, any impediment to accumulation but inextricability (b). By statute such Wills are annulled where 'and so far as' the profits or produce of real or personal estate in England, or of moveable succession, 'or, since 1848, of heritable property (c),' in Scotland, are directed, 'expressly or by implication (d),' to be accumulated, and the beneficial enjoyment of them postponed beyond the granter's life, and twenty-one years after his death; unless such arrangement shall be for the purpose of paying debts, or raising provisions for children, or regulating the produce of timber (e). 'Accumulation is forbidden after the lapse of twenty-one years from the testator's death, even when it is directed to commence at a date which occurs long after his death (f). The proceeds of property thus illegally directed to be accumulated are, it is enacted, to "go and be received by such person or persons as would have been entitled thereto if such accumulation had not been directed." It has been decided that where there is a gift or disposition distinct and separable from the directions to accumulate, and presently operative at the end of the twenty-one years, the illegal accumulations go to the donee or beneficiary, because the rest of the Will remains unimpaired by the operation of the statute disallowing the accumulations; while if there be no such gift or disposition, but merely limitations, the accumulations are undisposed of, and go to the legal representatives of the testator as at his death, as intestate succession (g).'

(a) See § 1862. See further as to uncertainty in testamentary writings, 1 M'Laren on Wills, 318 seq.

(b) M'Nair v. M'Nair, 1791; M. 16,210; Bell's Cases, 546; 2 Ill. 456. M'Culloch v. M'Cullochs, 1752; 5 W. & S. 180, footnote. Mason v. Skinner, 1844; 16 Jur. 422. 1 Bell's Com. 38.

(c) 11 and 12 Vict. c. 36, § 41. Keith's Trs. v. Keith, 1857; 19 D. 1040.

(*d*) Lord *v.* Colvin, *infra.* Tench *v.* Cheese, 19 Beav. 324; 6 De G. M. & G. 453. M'Larty's Trs. *v.* M'Laverty, 1864; 2 Macph. 489.

(*e*) 39 and 40 Geo. III. c. 98. **Thellusson's Case** (Thellusson *v.* Woodford), 4 Vesey, jun. 227; aff. 11 Vesey, jun. 112; 8 R. R. 104; 4 R. R. 205; see 9 R. R. 175; 14 R. R. 62. E. Strathmore *v.* Strathmore's Trs., 1831; 5 W. & S. 170. 11 & 12 Vict. c. 36, § 41. **Pursell's Trs.** *v.* **Newbigging** (Elder), 1856; 19 D. 71; rev. 1865, 3 Macph. H. L. 59; 4 Macq. 992. Suttie *v.* Suttie's Trs., 1846; 18 Jur. 442. Williams *v.* Lewis, 6 H. L. Ca. 1013; 28 L. J. Ch. 505. Matthews *v.* Keble, L. R. 6 Ch. 691; 37 L. J. Ch. 657.

(*f*) Campbell's Trs. *v.* Campbell, 1891; 18 R. 992.

(*g*) Ogilvie's Trs. *v.* Kirk-Sess. of Dundee, 1846; 8 D. 1229. Keith's Trs. *v.* Keith, 1857; 19 D. 1040. **Lord** *v.* **Colvin**, 1860; 23 D. 111; 1865, 3 Macph. 1083. Pursell's Trs. *v.* Elder, *cit.* Mackenzie *v.* Mackenzie's Trs., 1877; 4 R. 962. Maxwell's Trs. *v.* Maxwell, 1877; 5 R. 249. Smyth's Trs. *v.* Kinloch, 1880; 7 R. 1176. Cathcart's Trs. *v.* Heneage's Trs., 1883; 10 R. 1205. Campbell's Trs. *v.* Campbell, *cit.* (*f*). Colquhoun *v.* Colquhoun's Trs., 1892; 19 R. 946. Logan's Trs. *v.* Logan, 1896; 23 R. 848 (conversion—heritable or moveable surplus income). Combe *v.* Hughes, 34 L. J. Ch. 344. Green *v.* Gascoyne, 34 L. J. Ch. 268.

1866. Revocation.—A clause in a Will declaring it irrevocable will not make it so (*a*); 'nor will delivery (*b*). But a defunct may be bound by contract *inter vivos* not to alter (*c*).' Various questions, difficult in point of evidence, may arise relative to revocation: whether the Will has been cancelled by accident (*d*); whether partial obliteration revokes, and to what extent; whether the revocation of a latter gives effect to a former Will (*e*); what shall be the effect of violent or fraudulent obstruction to the revocation. These are circumstantial questions, with regard to which no rule of law can be laid down *a priori* for ascertaining what is to be held as revocation (*f*). 'Cancellation or destruction of a Will is *primâ facie* evidence of revocation (*g*). It will, of course, be more easily rebutted if the document has been cancelled or destroyed under the testator's directions, out of his presence, and not by himself; but the authority or mandate to do so may be proved by parole (*h*). The effect of a general revocation or general conveyance on prior deeds is, as in heritable destinations, a question of intention (*i*).'

(*a*) Dougal's Trs. *v.* Dougal, 1789; M. 15,949; 2 Ill. 436.

(*b*) Somerville *v.* Somerville, May 18, 1819; F. C. Millar *v.* Dickson, 1825; 4 S. 822. Fernie *v.* Colquhoun's Trs., 1854; 17 D. 233.

(*c*) 3 Stair, 8. § 28–33. 3 Ersk. 9. § 6. Paterson *v.* Paterson, 1893; 20 R. 484.

(*d*) Cunningham *v.* Mouat's Tr., 1851; 13 D. 1376.

(*e*) Decided in the affirmative, Howden *v.* Crichton (Howden), June 8, 1815; F. C. Dove *v.* Smith, 1827; 5 S. 734. Ker *v.* Erskine, 1851; 13 D. 492. As to implied revocation and the question which of several testamentary writings are to be held as effectual, see Horsbrugh *v.* Horsbrugh, Grant *v.* Stoddart, and other cases in § 1862, *supra*; and 1 M'Laren, Wills and Succn. 266. Bertram's Trs. *v.* Matheson's Trs., 1888; 15 R. 572. Dalglish's Trs. *v.* Crum, 1891; 19 R. 170 ("reattestation" does not recall intermediate codicils).

(*f*) See 1 Powel on Devises, 595 et seq. Lord John Thynne's Case, 1 Addam, Eccles Rep. 52. Nasmyth *v.* Hare, 1817; rev. 1 S. App. 65; 2 Ill. 437. Howden *v.* Crichton, *cit.* Dove *v.* Smith, 1827; 5 S. 734. Walker *v.* Steel, 1825; 4 S. 323. Buchanan *v.* Paterson, 1704; M. 15,932. Bibb *v.* Thomas, 2 W. Blackst. 1043. Laing *v.* Bruce, 1838; 1 D. 59. Irving *v.* Laing, 1840; 2 D. 804. Falconer *v.* Stephen, 1848; 11 D. 220. Dow *v.* Dow, 1848; 10 D. 1465. Purvis' Trs. *v.* Purvis, 1861; 23 D. 812 (foreign will). Winchester *v.* Smith, 1863; 1 Macph. 685. Crosbie *v.* Wilson, 1865; 3 Macph. 870 (duplicate wills). Sibbald's Trs. *v.* Greig, 1871; 9 Macph. 399 (whether a later deed revokes prior testamentary writings, though it does not mention them, see also Kenmore's Trs. *v.* Kenmore, 1869; 7 Macph. 771). Stirling Stuart *v.* Stirling Crawford's Trs., 1885; 12 R. 610 (no implied revocation by subsequent invalid deed). As to "mutual settlements," see above, § 1616. Hogg *v.* Campbell, 1863; 1 Macph. 647. Brown *v.* L. Adv., 1852; 1 Macq. 72. Whyte *v.* Paul, 1879; 7 R. 321. Lang's Trs. *v.* Lang, 1885; 12 R. 1265, and cases there cited. Kay's Trs. *v.* Stalker, 1892; 19 R. 1071. M'Laren on Wills and Succn. i. 253 sqq.

(*g*) Cases in previous notes. Elder's Trs. *v.* Free Church, 1892; 20 R. 2.

(*h*) Falconer *v.* Stephen and Winchester *v.* Smith, *citt.* Bonthrone *v.* Ireland, 1883; 10 R. 779.

(*i*) See Paterson's Factor *v.* Paterson's Trs., 1897; 24 R. 499; and above, § 1692.

1867. The condition *si sine liberis decesserit* is held to qualify a Will, as well as a settlement of land (*a*). 'But it operates to the effect of restoring the legal succession, and not so as to set up a former Will, even though that provided for children *nascituri*. It appears to cut down all former settlements or Wills except such as are obligatory and matter of contract (*b*).'

(*a*) 3 Ersk. 8. § 46. Watt *v.* Jervie, 1760; M. 6401; 2 Ill. 406. Neilson *v.* Baillie, 1822; 1 S. 458; 2 Ill. 404. Colquhoun *v.* Campbell, 1829; 7 S. 709. See 1 Powel on Devises, 530. Booth *v.* Black, 1831; 9 S. 406. Dixon *v.* Brown, 1836; 14 S. 938. Hamilton *v.* Hamilton, 1838; 16 S. 478; 3 Ill. 162. See *ante*, § 1776. Grant *v.* Brooke, 1882; 10 R. 82. Brown's Trs. *v.* Millar, 1890; 20 R. 1040.

(*b*) Elder's Trs. *v.* Elder, 1895; 22 R. 505.

1868. Form of Will.—A Will must be in writing; a verbal Will being inadmissible either as the nomination of an executor, or as the recall of former Wills or bequests (*a*). 'It requires no stamp (*b*).' If the testator cannot write, his Will may be authenticated by one notary (or a clergyman) and two witnesses (*c*). It is subject to challenge, as not truly the Will of the deceased, if not read over to him (*d*): 'this, with other circumstances, being regarded as evidence that a testament executed *in extremis*, or by an uneducated person, is not the real expression of his will. But the reading over of a Will is not a necessary solemnity (*e*).' A holograph Will 'signed by the testator' is good (*f*); 'and although it was thought in some cases that if the writing appear to be otherwise complete, the granter's name *in gremio* might be held to supply the place of a signature at the end (*g*), that doctrine is negatived; and, in the absence of special circumstances showing that the writing was intended to be complete, holograph writings unsubscribed are "understood" to be incomplete (*h*). Holograph testamentary writings are now deemed to be of the dates they bear, in the absence of evidence to the contrary (*i*).' But no improbative writing will have effect as a Will or as a codicil (*k*). A writing in itself improbative may acquire force and efficacy by 'clear and distinct' reference 'or adoption' in a Will duly executed 'or holograph'; as where the testator 'writes with his own hand words clearly identifying and expressing an adoption (*l*) of what is not in his handwriting; and the testator may in a regular writing dispense with the usual forms and solemnities (*m*), or prescribe special forms (*n*) for codicils or other ancillary or occasional testamentary writings, whether past or future, as when he' declares that such bequest 'shall be paid' as shall be made in a writing under my hand, or signed by me, or by a letter signed by me. In those cases it is necessary to distinguish: "A writing under my hand" is held to mean an authentic writing only; but a "letter" has been sustained, though not formally authenticated (*o*). The Court will not interfere, after a Will is produced in judgment or recorded, to correct an error or omission in the testing clause (*p*), 'and will at no time correct or construe a Will by a paper of instructions (*q*).'

(*a*) Houston *v*. Houston, 1631; M. 12,307; 2 Ill. 438. Whiteford *v*. Aiton, 1742; M. 12,338. Smith *v*. Taylor, 1749; M. 6594. Thomson *v*. Dunlop, 1884; 11 R. 453. The writing may be in pencil, Muir's Trs. *v*. Muir, 1869; 8 Macph. 53. Simsons *v*. Simsons, 1883; 10 R. 1249. Lamont *v*. Mags. of Glasgow, 1887; 14 R. 603.

(*b*) 54 and 55 Vict. c. 39, sched., General Exemptions.

(*c*) 1584, c. 133. Bog *v*. Hepburn, 1623; M. 16,960. Trail *v*. Trail, 1805; M. 15,955. 3 Stair, 8. § 34. 3 Ersk. 2. § 13. Galletly *v*. Macfarlan, 1843; 6 D. 1. Ferrie *v*. Buchanan, 1863; 1 Macph. 291 (notary interested). See below, § 2232, and 37 and 38 Vict. c. 94, sched. I. for form of docquet.

(*d*) Young *v*. Anderson, 1688; M. 15,929. Lady Arbuthnot *v*. Burnet, 1694; *ib*. Robertson *v*. Kerr, 1742; M. 15,942–3. See Petrie *v*. Lithgow, 1735; M. 15,941; Elchies, *Testament*, 3.

(*e*) Robertson *v*. Kerr, and other cases cited. Duff on Moveable Deeds, 134.

(*f*) Pennicuick *v*. Campbell, 1709; M. 16,970–1. See 3 Ersk. 2. § 22. 1 M'Laren on Wills, etc., § 455 sqq. *Supra*, § 20; *infra*, § 2231. Dunlop *v*. Dunlop, 1839; 1 D. 913. Maitland's Trs. *v*. Maitland, 1871; 10 Macph. 79. Robb's Trs. *v*. Robb, 1872; 10 Macph. 692.

(*g*) Currence *v*. Hackett, 1688; 2 B. Sup. 121. Gillespie *v*. Donaldson's Trs., 1831; 10 S. 174. Speirs *v*. Speirs, 1879; 6 R. 1359. See Baird (Preston's Trs.) *v*. Jack, 1856; 18 D. 1246; and Weir *v*. Robertson, 1872; 10 Macph. 438. M. Bell's Convg. 82. As to signature by initials, see Speirs, *cit*. Robertson *v*. Ogilvie's Trs., 1844; 7 D. 236.

(*h*) Dunlop, *cit*. Skinner *v*. Forbes, 1883; 11 R. 88. Russell's Trs. *v*. Henderson, 1883; 11 R. 283. Goldie *v*. Shedden, 1885; 13 R. 138. Bradford *v*. Young, 1884; 11 R. 1135. Petticrew *v*. Petticrew's Trs., 1884; 12 R. 249. Burnie's Tr. *v*. Lawrie, 1894; 21 R. 1015.

(*i*) 37 and 38 Vict. c. 94, § 40.

(*k*) 3 Ersk. 2. § 23. Ker *v*. Hay, 1708; M. 16,968. Moncrieff *v*. Monypenny, 1710; M. 15,936. Crichton, petr., 1802; M. 15,952. Dundas *v*. Lowis, 1807; M. *Writ*, Apx. No. 6; Hume, 917. Rankine *v*. Reid, 1849; 11 D. 543.

(*l*) Comp. above, § 20, 889. The strongest implication has been held insufficient in the absence of express adoption, as where a printed form is carefully filled up in all particulars and signed by the intending testator. Macdonald *v*. Cuthbertson, 1890; 18 R. 101 (L. M'Laren *diss.*).

(*m*) Nasmyth *v*. Hare, 1821; 1 S. App. 65. Gillespie, *infra*.

(*n*) The decisions to this effect are questioned by M'Laren, 1 Wills and Succn. 245, as violating the statutes as to the authentication of writings.

(*o*) Dundas, *supra* (*k*). Buchan *v*. Inglis, 1828; 6 S. 864; rev. (Inglis *v*. Harper), 1831, 5 W. & S. 785. Gillespie *v*. Donaldson's Trs., 1831; 10 S. 174. Cleland *v*. M'Lellan, 1851; 13 D. 504 (docquet on envelope enclosing document insufficient to identify). Wilsone's Trs. *v*. Stirling, 1861; 24 D. 163. Young's Trs. *v*. Ross, 1864; 3 Macph. 10. Callander *v*. Callander's Trs., 1862; 2 Macph. 291. Crosbie *v*. Wilson, 1865; 3 Macph. 870. Christie's Trs. *v*. Muirhead, 1870; 8 Macph. 461. Maitland's Trs., *cit*. (*f*). Lamont *v*. Mags. of Glasgow, 1887; 14 R. 603.

(*p*) Brown, petr., March 11, 1809; F. C. See Caldwell, petr., 1871; 10 Macph. 99, and cases there referred to.

(*q*) Blair *v*. Blair, 1849; 12 D. 97.

1869. Nuncupative Will.—Under the description of Nuncupative Will are included Wills unsigned or left uncompleted at the testator's death (*a*); but mere directions to make a Will have no effect (*b*). Where one is named residuary legatee, and verbal directions are given to him, which he acknowledges, they are effectual as a condition of the trust; 'but this rule does not apply to a disposition to a trustee who has not the beneficial interest (*c*). A nuncupative legacy receives effect only to the extent of £100 Scots (*d*).'

(*a*) Shaw *v*. Lewis, 1665; M. 4494; 2 Ill. 440. Soutray's Daughters *v*. Soutray, 1670; M. 15,927. Stewart *v*. Smith, 1680; M. 15,928. Hopkins *v*. D. Athol, 1728; M. 15,940. Dempster *v*. Willison, 1799; M. 16,947. See below, § 1874. Forsyth's Trs. *v*. M'Lean, 1854; 16 D. 343. Kelly *v*. Kelly, 1861; 23 D. 703.

(*b*) M'Farquhar *v*. Calder, 1779; M. 3600. Monro *v*. Coutts, 1813; 1 Dow, 437; 2 Ill. 441. Stainton *v*. Stainton, 1828; 6 S. 363. See cases in § 1862 (*d*). Aim's Trs. *v.* Aim, 1880; 8 R. 294.

(*c*) Phin *v.* Guthrie, 1738; 5 B. Sup. 203; Elchies, *Legacy*, 5. Same case, under name of Hannah *v.* Guthrie, M. 3837. See Forsyth's Trs. *v.* M'Lean, *cit.* (*a*); and comp. Thomson *v.* Dunlop, 1884; 11 R. 453.

(*d*) Forsyth's Trs. *v.* M'Lean, and Kelly, *citt.* (*a*). *Supra*, § 1868 (*a*); *infra*, § 1874.

1870. The Nomination of an Executor is a common but no indispensable part of a Will. It is truly the appointment of a trustee to hold the executry funds, '*i.e.* the whole moveable estate, including *jus relictæ* and legitim,' for the benefit of himself and all concerned (*a*). And if none be appointed, the law supplies an executor. The executor 'was till 1855' entitled by law to a third of the dead's part, "all debts being first paid" (*b*); meaning thereby not only proper debts, but also legacies as debts under the Will (*c*). If a legacy 'were' left to the executor, it 'was' imputed towards his third. If nothing be said as to the funds after paying legacies, the executor is held a trustee for the 'widow, children, and' next of kin (*d*). 'An executor cannot be appointed by parole (*e*); but no technical language is required in the nomination (*f*).'

(*a*) See below, § 1899. 1617, c. 14. 3 Ersk. 9. § 5 and 26. Soutray's Daughters *v.* Soutray, 1670; M. 1592; 2 Ill. 440. Kemps *v.* Ferguson, 1802; M. 16,949; 2 Ill. 442. **White *v.* Finlay,** 1861; 24 D. 38, 47. Robertson *v.* Ogilvy's Trs., 1844; 7 D. 236 (settlement valid though names of trustees erased). Edinr. Infirmary *v.* L. Adv., 1861; 23 D. 1213.

(*b*) 1617, c. 14. Nasmyth *v.* Hare, Feb. 17, 1819; F. C. Grant (Bell's Exrs.) *v.* Murray, 1849; 12 D. 201; aff. 1852, 24 S. Jur. 561; 1 Stu. 1069. This right is abolished by 18 Vict. c. 23, § 8.

(*c*) 3 Ersk. 9. § 26. Moncrieff *v.* Moncrieff, 1636; 1 B. Sup. 371.

(*d*) Soutar *v.* M'Gregor, 1801; M. *Implied Will*, Apx. No. 2. Beizly *v.* Napier, 1739; M. 6591. Nasmyth, *supra* (*b*). *Infra*, § 1899. 1617, c. 14. White *v.* Finlay, *cit.*

(*e*) Thomson *v.* Dunlop, 1884; 11 R. 453.

(*f*) Dundas *v.* Dundas, 1837; 15 S. 427. Tod, petr., 1890; 18 R. 152 ("judicial factor"). Martin *v.* Ferguson's Trs., 1892; 19 R. 474 ("wish estate to be managed"). In the last-cited case the appointment was by reference to another person's Will. Comp. Jerdon *v.* Forrest, 1897; 24 R. 395.

1871. Construction of Wills.—Ambiguities in Wills are frequent and are of two kinds: either such as arise on the face of the 'deed,' and from the uncertain meaning of the words used; or such as arise from the uncertain application of the words to external circumstances. The former Lord Bacon called "ambiguitas patens"; the latter, "ambiguitas latens"; and they are to be dealt with differently. The general rule resulting from all the cases is, that a patent ambiguity can be cleared only from the context or rest of the Will; and that a latent ambiguity, as it arises from outward circumstances, may be resolved by extrinsic and parole evidence (*a*).

(*a*) See for the leading cases on this subject in England, 1 Powel on Devises, 465; 1 Roberts on Wills, 547. Comp. above, § 524, and Morton and Logans there cited, note (*c*); also cases in § 1692. Wigram on Extrinsic Evidence, § 200 sqq. Jarman on Wills, 429. Taylor on Evidence, 1011. Best's Princ. of Evid. § 226. Dickson on Evid. § 213 sqq. M'Laren on Wills, § 726 sqq.

1872. The words, "all debts, goods, gear, and sums of money," will not carry debts secured by infeftment or adjudication (*a*). "Goods and gear" will carry corporeal moveables only, not debts (*b*). "All goods and gear, whether heritable or moveable," will not carry a lease (*c*). "All my plate, and horses, and moveables whatsoever, and pay and arrears of pay due to me," 'and even the expression "whole other moveable estate," following an enumeration of corporeal moveables,' does not include a bond for borrowed money (*d*). Vague and general terms receive their construction from the words with which they stand connected (*e*). 'Thus, general words following an enumeration of particulars *ejusdem generis* are limited, as in the cases above mentioned, to things of the kind especially enumerated. If the general words precede, the enumeration of particulars does not restrict their meaning (*f*). But general words following an enumeration of subjects of a different character are construed according to their natural meaning (*g*).' "Furniture" seems to comprehend only articles for domestic use, not books nor wine. And a bequest of "all the testator's furniture and moveables lying in his house," has been held not to include gold, money, bank-notes, or moveable bonds, lying in his house at his death (*h*). '"Effects" carries only moveable estate, and seems to apply more properly to corporeal moveables (*i*). The words "estate" and "property" carry both heritage and moveables (*k*). "Cash" includes money and bank-notes, but not bonds, bills, and moveable securities (*l*). "All my money wherever deposited" has been held to include the testator's whole moveable estate not otherwise disposed of (*m*).'

Entails of moveables are regulated on the principle of implied obligation and engagement, being effectual against the heir who takes the subject with the condition annexed (*n*).

'As "it is an invariable rule that testamentary deeds shall receive the most liberal interpretation, and that which carries the presumed intention of the testator into effect (*o*)," a general deed disposing of a testator's estate is held to be a valid exercise of a power of disposal of a fund given by the settlement of another person, provided the deed and the surrounding circumstances show clearly that the granter intended thereby to exercise the power (*p*).'

(*a*) Mochrie *v.* Linn, 1736; M. 5018; Elch. *Implied Will*, No. 1; 2 Ill. 457. Galloway, petr., 1802; M. 15,950. Brown *v.* Henderson, 1805; M. *Clause*, Apx. 5. See Ross, July 11, 1809; F. C.; 2 Ill. 228. Waddel *v.* Colt, 1789; M. 5022.

(*b*) Fraser *v.* Smith, 1776; M. 2322; Hailes, 709; 2 Ill. 443. E. Fife *v.* M'Kenzie, 1795; M. 2325; aff. 1797, 3 Pat. 549.

(*c*) Paterson *v.* Fairish, 1800; Hume, 128. Sutherland *v.* Jeffrey, 1805; Hume, 133. Murdoch *v.* Murdoch Trs., 1863; 1 Macph. 330.

(*d*) Dunbar's Trs. *v.* Dunbar, 1808; Hume, 267. Carsewell's Trs. *v.* Carsewell, 1858; 20 D. 516.

(*e*) Ross *v.* Ross, 1770; M. 5019; Hailes, 346; aff. 1771, 2 Pat. 254.

(*f*) M'Laren on Wills, § 612. See Mackie *v.* Mackie's Trs., 1883; 11 R. 255.

(*g*) M'Laren, *l.c.* Glover *v.* Brough, Dec. 7, 1810; F. C. Welsh *v.* Cairnie, June 28, 1809; F. C.

(*h*) Cunningham *v.* Livingstone, 1737; M. 11,660; 5 B. Sup. 195. Ker *v.* Young, 1745; M. 2274. M'Nab *v.* Spittal, 1797; M. 2303. See Lady Rankeillor *v.* Ayton, 1709; M. 5759; 2 Ill. 458. E. Leven *v.* Montgomery, 1683; M. 5803. Reed *v.* Strathallan, 1835; 13 S. 810. Blair *v.* Blair, 1831; 9 S. 514. 1 M'Laren on Wills, § 619.

(*i*) Pitcairn *v.* Pitcairn, 1870; 8 Macph. 604. See above, § 1692A.

(*k*) Neilson *v.* Stewart, 1860; 22 D. 647. Munro *v.* Munro, 1825; 4 S. 328. Oag's Cur. *v.* Corner, 1885; 12 R. 1162. Mayor of Hamilton *v.* Hodsdon, 6 Moo. P. C. 76.

(*l*) Jarvie *v.* Pearson, 1860; 22 D. 1395.

(*m*) Easson *v.* Thomas, 1879; 7 R. 251. Dunsmure *v.* Dunsmure, 1879; *ib.* 261.

(*n*) See above, § 1719A.

(*o*) *Per* L. Corehouse in **Hyslop** *v.* **Maxwell,** 1834; 12 S. 413.

(*p*) Smith *v.* Milne, 1826; 4 S. 679. Hyslop, *cit.* Grierson *v.* Miller, 1852; 14 D. 939. Mackenzie *v.* Gillanders, 1874; 1 R. 1050 (power held not to be so exercised). Dalgleish's Trs. *v.* Young, 1893; 20 R. 904. Clark's Trs. *v.* Clark's Exrs., 1894; 25 R. 546.

1873. Legacies.—The chief purpose of the Will is the disposal and distribution of the estate by bequests or legacies. A legacy is a donation or bequest, *mortis causâ*, of a sum, or subject, or *universitas*, to be paid or delivered by the executor of the Will out of the free moveable estate of the deceased, after payment of debts, to a person named or plainly designated, called legatee or legatary (*a*). No legacy is effectual against creditors. Legacies may be bequeathed in the Will itself, or in a codicil, or, 'it was said,' by indorsing a bill, 'but the cases of this kind are rather donations *mortis causâ*' (*b*). But the granting of a bill or note 'or cheque' payable after death is not a competent mode of bestowing a legacy (*c*). 'A legacy or transference from the dead to the living may be validly made by taking the destination of a bond, debenture, or mortgage in favour of the testator and a successor (*d*).'

(*a*) 3 Ersk. 9. § 6. 3 Stair, 8. § 20. Below, § 1887.

(*b*) Anonymous, 1752; 5 B. Sup. 802. Murray *v.* Todd, 1818; Hume, 275. See Cathill *v.* Burns, 1862; 24 D. 849. L. Adv. *v.* M'Neill, 1864; 2 Macph. 626; rev. 1866, 4 Macph. H. L. 20. And the cases cited below, § 1874.

(*c*) Wright *v.* Wrights, 1761; M. 8088; 2 Ill. 442. Dowie *v.* Millie, 1786; M. 8107. Miller *v.* Miller, 1874; 1 R. 1107. Milne *v.* Grant's Exrs., 1884; 11 R. 887. Watt's Trs. *v.* Mackenzie, 1869; 7 Macph. 930 (undelivered deposit receipt). As to obligations prestable after death, see above, § 8, 64.

(*d*) Watt's Trs. *v.* Mackenzie, 1869; 7 Macph. 930. Walker's Exrs. *v.* Walker, 1878; 5 R. 965. Buchan *v.* Porteous, 1879; 7 R. 211. Connell's Trs. *v.* Connell's Trs., 1886; 13 R. 1175. Paterson's Factor *v.* Paterson's Trs., 1897; 24 R. 499. It is still the rule that such transference cannot be effected by destinations in mercantile documents undelivered, as deposit receipts and savings bank books (Dinwoodie's Ex. *v.* Carruthers' Ex., 1895; 23 R. 234); but the recent decisions in § 1874 (*g*), *infra*, tend to innovate on the rule.

1874. (1.) *A Nuncupative or Verbal Legacy* is effectual to the extent of £100 Scots (£8, 6s. 8d.); and several legacies may thus be bequeathed 'to different persons' each to that extent (*a*). But a distinction has been admitted between a legacy and a *donatio mortis causâ*; the latter, being *de præsenti*, is effectual 'to any amount; and may be proved by parole evidence, which must be unambiguous and conclusive, so as to establish the intention and desire to make a present gift' (*b*).

'A donation *mortis causâ* is a conveyance of an immoveable or incorporeal right, or a transference of corporeal moveables or money by delivery, so that the property is immediately transferred to the grantee, subject to the donor's power of revocation. When actual possession or control is given to the donee, he is said to hold for the granter so long as he lives and does not revoke (*c*), and on his death without revocation then for himself (*d*). A title taken to heritage in name of another may be altered by the purchaser; but although the purchaser so taking it retains the deed in his own possession, it is an effectual donation *mortis causâ*, if unaltered or unrevoked at his death. If delivered by the purchaser to the disponee, the donation is absolute (*e*).

In a question with creditors, a bond or policy of insurance conceived in favour of a third party at the request of the creditor or insured, but retained in his possession undelivered, confers no vested right on the grantee (*f*).

'In the case of a gift by documents giving a title, as by indorsed deposit receipts, actual delivery of the document seems not to be necessary if the intention of present donation be distinctly proved (*g*). The donation must be made in contemplation of death; but it is perhaps too strict to say that it takes effect only if death ensues from the existing illness, or that it must be made in view of immediate death or imminent peril (*h*). It is not competent to make a donation *mortis causâ* to a person, that he may administer or dispose of the gift for persons as beneficiaries, that being a parole Will or appointment of an executor (*i*).'

(*a*) Smith *v.* Taylor, 1749; M. 6594; Elch. *Testament*, 10; 2 Ill. 440. See above, § 1869.

(*b*) Mitchell *v.* Wright, 1759; M. 8082. See 3 Ersk. 8. § 20. Anon., Nov. 30, 1752; 5 B. Sup. 802. Fyfes *v.* Kedslie, 1847; 9 D. 853 (transfer of bank shares with back letter promising to pay interest and retransfer to donor if required). Brit. Lin. Co. *v.* Martin, 1849; 11 D. 1004 (deposit receipt). Kennedy *v.* Rose, 1863; 1 Macph. 1042 (deposit receipt). Bryce *v.* Young's Exr., 1866; 4 Macph. 312 (cheque). Muir *v.* Ross's Exrs., 1866; 4 Macph. 820 (deposit receipt indorsed blank and delivered). **Morris** *v.* **Riddick**, 1867; 5 Macph. 1036. M'Cubbin's Exrs. *v.* Tait, 1898; 6 Macph. 310; 40 S. Jur. 158. Robertson *v.* Taylor, 1868; 6 Macph. 917 (deposit receipt). Ross *v.* Mellis, 1871; 10 Macph. 197 (deposit receipt). Sharp *v.* Paton, 1883; 10 R. 1000. Macdonald *v.* Macdonald, 1889; 16 R. 758 (effect of destination in deposit receipt). Morrison *v.* Forbes, 1890; 17 R. 958 (deposit receipt—trustee). Cases in following notes.

(*c*) See instances of revocation in Wright's Trs. *v.* Wright, 1870; 8 Macph. 708. M'Farquhar *v.* M'Kay, 1869; 7 Macph. 766.

(*d*) Morris and other cases in note (*b*).

(*e*) Spence *v.* Ross, 1826; 5 S. 16; aff. 1829, 3 W. & S. 380. *Per* L. Curriehill in Kennedy *v.* Rose (*b*). Rust *v.* Smith, 1865; 3 Macph. 378. Cases in § 1873.

(*f*) Hill *v.* Hill, 1755; M. 11,580. Walker's Exrs. *v.* Walker, 1878; 5 R. 965. Jarvie's Tr. *v.* Jarvie's Trs., 1887; 14 R. 411.

(*g*) Gibson *v.* Hutchison, 1872; 10 Macph. 923. Crosbie's Trs. *v.* Wrights, 1881; 7 R. 823. Thomson's Exrs. *v.* Thomson, 1882; 9 R. 911 (donation *inter vivos*). L. Adv. *v.* Galloway, 1884; 11 R. 541 (distinction between donation *mortis causâ* and donation *inter vivos*). Blyth *v.* Curle, 1885; 12 R. 674. Connell's Trs. *v.* Connell's Trs., 1886; 13 R. 1175. But if these decisions are taken as laying down this rule, it is difficult to distinguish such donations *mortis causâ* from nuncupative legacies, or legacies proved by parole. *Per* L. Young in Milne *v.* Grant's Exrs., 1884; 11 R. 887. Delivery of an unindorsed deposit receipt cannot make an effectual donation *mortis causâ*. M'Nicol *v.* M'Dougall, 1889; 17 R. 25.

(*h*) Cases in previous notes. Blyth *v.* Curle, 1885; 12 R. 674.

(*i*) Thomson *v.* Dunlop, 1884; 11 R. 453. Comp. above, § 1869.

1875. (2.) *Plurality of Legacies.*—If more than one (*a*) legacy be left to the same person by different Wills, they will be payable, unless a contrary intention clearly appear (*b*); 'as, *e.g.*, if the latter Will be a general settlement plainly revising and thus revoking all previous Wills (*c*); or if, being given in the same writings, the provisions be so similar as to indicate mere repetition (*d*). An unconditional legacy merges in a subsequent gift of the residue; but not a conditional legacy (*e*).'

(*a*) A second legacy of the same specific thing is obviously a mere repetition. Edgar *v.* Hamilton's Trs., 1828; 6 S. 693. Horsbrugh and Baird, *infra* (*b*).

(*b*) M'Intyre *v.* M'Farlane, March 1, 1821; F. C.; 2 Ill. 442. Elliot *v.* E. Stair's Trs., 1823; 2 S. 250. Clark *v.* Hay's Trs., 1823; 2 S. 313. Sutherland *v.* Sutherland, 1825; 4 S. 220. Gillespie *v.* Donaldson Trs., 1831; 10 S. 174; 2 Ill. 440. Stirling *v.* Deans, 1704; M. 11,442. Macdowall *v.* Gordon, 1833; 11 S. 952. Straton's Trs. *v.* Cunningham, 1840; 2 D. 820. Grant *v.* Anderson, 1840; 3 D. 89 (provision to daughter in settlement, and same in her subsequent marriage contract, not double). Smith *v.* Common Agent of Auchinblane, 3 D. 1109 (converse of last case). **Horsbrugh** *v.* **Horsbrugh,** 1847; 9 D. 329; 1848, 10 D. 824. Grant *v.* Stoddart, 1849; 11 D. 860; rev. 1852, 1 Macq. 163. Baird (Preston's Tr.) *v.* Jaap, 1856; 18 D. 1246. Beattie *v.* Thomson, 1861; 23 D. 1163. Kippen *v.* Darley, 1856; 18 D. 1137; aff. 1858, 3 Macq. 203. Kippen *v.* Kippen's Trs., 1874; 1 R. 1171. Bryce's Trs. *v.* Bryces, 1878; 5 R. 722. Milne *v.* Scott, 1880; 8 R. 83. Arres's Trs. *v.* Mather, 1881; 9 R. 107. Free Church Trs. *v.* Maitland, 1887; 14 R. 333. Haviland *v.* Johnston, 1895; 22 R. 396.

(*c*) Beattie and Grant, *citt.* Brander's Trs. *v.* Anderson, 1883; 10 R. 1258.

(*d*) Horsbrugh and Baird, *citt.* Royal Infirmary *v.* Muir's Trs., 1881; 9 R. 352 (two legacies of the same sum). Free Church Trs. *v.* Maitland, *cit.* See Arres's Trs., *cit.* In doubt the Court has regard to the testator's circumstances at the date of the writing, but not to jottings or notes indicative of intention. Free Church Trs., *cit.*

(*e*) Somervell *v.* Somervell, 1884; 11 R. 1004.

1876. (3.) *General Legacy.*—This, which is the *legatum quantitatis*, is a legacy, not of a special article or debt, but indefinite, of so much money, or fungibles, or moveables of a particular description or class (*a*).

A general legacy confers on the legatee a personal right only of action against the executor (*b*).

General legacies abate with the inadequacy of the fund (*c*); and this rateably or *pari passu*, not according to seniority or priority of bequest.

Some general legacies, to a certain extent, partake of the nature of special; as, if a sum shall be bequeathed for a special purpose, it is held that in making the abatement as on a general legacy, what is necessary for the purpose of the bequest must be left (*d*).

(*a*) 3 Ersk. 9. § 11, 12.
(*b*) See above, § 1870; below, § 1899.
(*c*) 3 Ersk. 9. § 11, 12. Monro *v.* Scott's Exrs., 1630; M. 8048; 2 Ill. 444. See below, § 1886. As to abatement of legacies, see M'Laren, Wills and Succn. i. 396 sqq. 7 Scot. Law Rev. p. 7.
(*d*) Caldwell *v.* Caldwell, 1736; M. 8066.

1877. (4.) *Special Legacy* is of a particular subject, or debt, or sum distinguished and made specific (*a*). But it is not enough to constitute a special legacy that the testator has directed land to be sold to pay debts and legacies, the residue to be laid out in the purchase of land. On the fund proving inadequate, the direction to purchase land was found not special to defeat the legacies, but a *residuary* provision (*b*).

A special legacy has the effect of an assignation *mortis causâ* to the particular thing, and is completed by the testator's death. And although legacies have no effect to exclude creditors, yet, where creditors take in preference to a special legatee, they must assign their debts to him (*c*). The efficacy of a special legacy depends on the existence of the thing bequeathed (*d*); whereas a general legacy is effectual if there shall, after paying debts, be enough to satisfy it.

Special legacies do not abate, if there be enough besides to pay the debts and expenses (*e*).

A special legatee has an action direct against the possessor of the fund or subject, the executor being called as a party (*f*). A legacy of a discharge of everything the legatee may owe the testator at his death, is held to include only debts properly due by the legatee in his own right, not a claim for money received on the testator's account (*g*).

(*a*) 3 Ersk. 9. § 11, 12. Wauchope *v.* Wilson, 1724; M. 8063; 2 Ill. 443. Presbytery of Kirkcudbright *v.* Blair, 1742; Elch. *Legacy*, 10. Jack *v.* Lauder, 1742; M. 11,357; Elch. *Legacy*, 11. Panton *v.* Gillies, 1824; 2 S. 632, Hagart *v.* Hagart, 1834; 13 S. 35. See § 1885. Pagan *v.* Pagan, 1838; 16 S. 383. Cunninghame *v.* Vassall, 1871; 10 Macph. 49.
(*b*) Hamilton *v.* Bennet, 1832; 10 S. 330; aff. 1833, 6 W. & S. 533. See above, § 1876. Dewar *v.* Kirk-Session of Torryburn, 1864; 2 Macph. 910. This is rather what is called by English lawyers a demonstrative legacy. 1 M'Laren on Wills, § 748, 749. Chivas' Trs. *v.* M'Leod, 1881; 9 R. 86.
(*c*) Balmerino *v.* Balmerino's Crs., 1746; M. 8074.
(*d*) Hence it is revoked by the appropriation of the subject to other purposes by the testator during his life. Wauchope and Pagan, *citt.* Chalmers *v.* Chalmers, 1851; 14 D. 57. This hard and fast rule of construction, which excludes all regard to the testator's intention, has been introduced from England (2 Wh. & Tud. L. C. 291). It may lead to hardship, and in Anderson *v.* Thomson, 1877, 4 R. 1101, was followed with reluctance. See below, § 1886. It is not certain whether a specific legacy of a moveable is affected by charges created by the testator, *e.g.* a pledge. Stewart *v.* Stewart, 1891; 19 R. 310.
(*e*) *Supra*, § 1876. Greig's Trs. *v.* Greig, 1854; 16 D. 899. Fergus *v.* Fergus, 1833; 11 S. 362 (legacy of money specially secured).
(*f*) Forrester *v.* Clark, 1627; M. 2194. Gray *v.* Cockburn, 1711; M. 8062.
(*g*) Graham *v.* Denniston, 1792; M. 8108; Bell's 8vo Ca. 302. Dougall *v.* Dougall, 1789; M. 15,949.

1878. (5.) *Universal Legacy, or Residue.*—This comprehends all the testator's estate; or the reversion or residue (*a*), after satisfying expenses, debts, and other legacies (*b*). The disposal of the *universitas* of the succession is to be distinguished from legacies which are not universal (*c*). 'It is a *unum quid*, although its amount may be affected by contingencies, the residuary legatee not being a conditional institute as to contingent legacies, but being burdened with them in certain events (*d*).'

(*a*) As to the construction of a legacy of the free annual proceeds of residue, where the estate consists partly of mineral leases or a going business, see above, § 1042 *fin.*
(*b*) So when a wife claims *jus relictæ*, the burden falls upon the residue, and general and special legacies are affected only if it be insufficient. Tait's Trs. *v.* Lees, 1886; 13 R. 1104.
(*c*) 3 Ersk. 9. § 11. Cunningham *v.* Livingston, 1737; M. 11,660; 2 Ill. 443. M'Nab *v.* Spittal, 1797; M. 2303. Johnston *v.* Wilson, 1758; M. 11,364. E. Fife *v.* M'Kenzie, 1795; M. 2325. Fraser *v.* Smith, 1776; M. 2322; Hailes, 709. Comp. above, § 1872 (*h*).
(*d*) Storie's Trs. *v.* Gray, 1874; 1 R. 953.

1879. Construction of Legacies.—(1.) *Vesting.*—A legacy does not vest during the life of the testator (*a*); but on the legatee's survivance, it does vest so as to enable him to dispose of it, or his creditors to attach it, or his heirs to take it on his death. But questions of some nicety arise in legacies with a complexity of interests. Where a legacy is bequeathed to one in liferent, 'or to several liferenters,' and another, 'or to another and his heirs and successors,' in fee, the fee vests in the fiar by his survivance of the testator, though he should die before the liferenter (*b*); 'and the same rule applies to directions to trustees to pay to one in liferent and another in fee (*c*), and to bequests not to an individual, but to a class of persons (*d*).' Where one is substituted for another in a legacy, and the institute dies before the testator, the legacy vests in the substitute by his survivance of both (*e*). Where the settlement is by trust-deed, and the trustees are to hold for a liferenter and successive persons as fiars, it has been doubted whether the effect of the trust is not to suspend the vesting of the fee till the death of the liferenter, the fee vesting in the fiar then found to survive (*f*). 'But in money provisions, the creation of a trust, which is necessary to protect the interests of the fiar, does not prevent the vesting of the fee at the testator's death (*g*).'

If an express term of payment be mentioned (by date or by event that *must* happen), the legacy vests by the death of the testator; but is payable, and interest due, only from the time mentioned (*h*). 'The presumption is that legacies vest *a morte testatoris*; and the postponement of the term of payment has of itself no effect to overturn the presumption, so long as its object is only to secure an intermediate benefit to a third party, and it is not a condition annexed to the gift itself (*i*). But if a contingency be created by a "destination over" to another than the first legatee named, or, in legacies to a plurality of persons, by a clause of survivorship, vesting is postponed to the period of distribution (*k*).'

NOTE.—The modern decisions as to the construction of wills and settlements, including the subjects of destinations and vesting, are so numerous, that it is impossible, without unduly enlarging this book, to take notice of them all; or even to edit the text so as to make it perfectly consistent with the present law. Reference must be made for fuller information to Lord M'Laren's Treatise on the Law of Wills and Succession. See a useful summary of principles by Lord M'Laren in Hay's Trs. *v.* Hay, 1890; 17 R. 961.

(*a*) See Graham *v.* Hope, and Miller *v.* Milne's Trs., *infra*, § 1881 (*d*), 1880 (*n*).

(*b*) Turnbull *v.* Turnbull, 1778; M. 4248; 2 Ill. 450. Fowke *v.* Duncan, 1770; M. 8092; aff. 2 Pat. 290; 2 Ill. 452. Wallace *v.* Wallace, 1807; M. Apx. *Clause*, 6. Nisbet *v.* M'Dougal, June 27, 1809; F. C. Calder *v.* Dickson, 1842; 4 D. 1365. Maxwell, *infra*.

(*c*) *Infra*, § 1881. Maxwell *v.* Wylie, 1837; 15 S. 1005; 2 Ill. 446. Nimmo *v.* Murray's Trs. 1864; 2 Macph. 1144. Marchbanks *v.* Brockie, 1836; 14 S. 521. Cochrane *v.* Cochrane's Exrs., 1854; 17 D. 103. Douglas *v.* Douglas, 1864; 2 Macph. 1008. Miller *v.* Finlay's Trs., 1875; 2 R. H. L. 1. Snell's Trs. *v.* Morison, 1877; 4 R. 709. Taylor *v.* Gilbert's Trs., 1877; 5 R. 49; *ib.* H. L. 217. M'Alpine *v.* Steuart, 1883; 10 R. 836.

(*d*) Forbes *v.* Luckie, 1838; 16 S. 374. Matthew *v.* Scott, 1844; 6 D. 718. Douglas, *cit.* Duncan's Trs. *v.* Thomas, 1882; 9 R. 731.

(*e*) Nisbet, *supra* (*b*). Glendinning *v.* Walker, 1825; 4 S. 241. Marchbanks *v.* Brockie, 1836; 14 S. 521. See below, § 1881.

(*f*) Lord Jeffrey proposed as a test in such cases, that when directions are given to trustees destinating the fee on expiration of the liferent to one individual, it should vest as in the common case; but that when the destination is to several persons successively, the construction must be that the fee is to remain in suspense till the event of the liferenter's death. But it was held by the Court that the existence of the trust did not here suspend the vesting of the fee, and that no distinction is to be made between the cases. Marchbanks, *cit.*

(*g*) Nimmo *v.* Murray's Trs., 1864; 2 Macph. 1144. Forbes *v.* Luckie, Maxwell *v.* Wylie, *citt.* See below, § 1882, 1956.

(*h*) Turnbull, Fowke, Wallace, and Nisbet, *supra* (*b*). Jordan *v.* Dickson, 1809; Hume, 260. Johns *v.* Monro, 1833; 12 S. 146. See below, § 1885.

(*i*) Marchbanks, etc., *citt.* Jackson *v.* M'Millan, 1876; 3 R. 627. Popham's Trs. *v.* Parker's Exrs., 1883; 10 R. 888.

(*k*) See below, § 1881, 1883 *fin.*

1880. (2.) *Simple Legacies.* — These are legacies bequeathed to a certain person 'or persons' by name or description (*a*). '"*Falsa demonstratio non nocet*"; a legacy is not invalid because of a false description of the legatee or the thing bequeathed, if it be certain who or what is meant. So a false or mistaken reason (*falsa causa*) does not invalidate, unless it be so stated as to make it a condition (*b*).' A legacy to "poorest friends and relations" is held to include relations both on the father's and mother's side (*c*). A legacy to children of a person named has been held to mean immediate children only (*d*), 'and to be limited to children alive at the testator's death or period of vesting, excluding *post-nati* (*e*), and children of predeceased members of the class (*f*). A destination to a person's "issue" includes not children only but descendants of every degree *per stirpes* (*g*).' A legacy "to the personal representatives" of the testator has been extended to all his next of kin (*h*). Heir is a flexible term, to be construed according to the subject, 'and so, even when the succession is mixed, a destination to heirs and assignees carries the heritable estate to the heir-at-law, and the moveable estate to the next of kin, although it is thus necessary to give the same word two different meanings (*i*). The same construction applies when the word "successors" is used (*k*).' A legacy by description to the lawful heirs of A. has been held a legacy to those heirs of A. who are alive at the testator's death (*l*). Such legacies, '*i.e.* all legacies,' are held to be strictly personal, and with the condition of survivance (*m*); so that they do not vest in the legatee and are not assignable till the testator's death (*n*).

'There have been various cases of construction of bequests to classes of persons designated by words expressing (1) their propinquity in blood, or (2) their relation in the order of legal succession to the testator, or to a person favoured or instituted by him. The words "next of kin," and the like, are used in the former class of cases, and, it seems, are not affected by the Intestate Moveable Succession Act, but, unless the testator has impressed another meaning on them by the context (*o*), designate the class of relations entitled to succeed to moveables by the common law (*p*). In cases of the latter kind the words "personal representatives," "heirs," "heirs *in mobilibus*," "heirs and successors," "heirs or executors," or the like, are used, and in proper testamentary deeds (*q*) appear to include persons called to the succession *ab intestato* by the statute, if the testator survived its passing (*r*), but not otherwise (*s*). In cases where a testator or settlor defines the persons favoured by words commonly descriptive of a class ascertainable at the time of his own death, these words are understood, unless a different intention be indicated, to refer to the persons holding that character at that time, and not at the time of vesting, or when the bequest becomes operative (*t*). When a bequest is made to a class, as "issue" or "children," the division is presumably equal; and so, if it be to the issue of several persons (*u*), or even to one or more *nominatim* and the issue of a third (*v*), the distribution will be *per capita*; unless the intention to make the division *per stirpes* be expressed or be clearly implied, as when the fund given in fee is previously liferented by the several parents of the class on whom the fee is conferred (*w*).'

(*a*) Scott *v.* Ramsay, 1777; 5 B. Sup. 504; 2 Ill. 445.

(*b*) Inst. ii. 20. § 29–31. Dig. xxxv. 1. 17. § 1–3. 3 Ersk. 9. § 8. Scottish Missionary Soc. *v.* Home Mission Committee, 1858; 20 D. 634. L. Lovat *v.* Fraser, 1884; 11 R. 1119. As to legacies to classes *designative*, see cases in notes following; and Scott *v.* Scott, 1852; 14 D. 1057; 1855, 2 Macq. 281 (legacy to "relations" of testator or his wife not void for uncertainty). Williamson *v.* Gardner, 1865; 4 Macph. 66. Miller's Trs. *v.* Rattray, 1891; 18 R. 989 (legacy to A.'s children described as of a certain number—*post-nati*); and cases in M'Laren on Wills, etc., § 1389, as to a power of selection by trustees. Extrinsic evidence is admitted for identifying the persons or society intended by the testator. Wigram, Extr. Ev. par. 67, 133, 183. Dickson on Evid. § 1070 seq. M'Intyre *v.* Fairrie's Trs., 1863; 2 Macph. 94. Duff's Trs. *v.* Soc. of Scripture Readers, 1862; 24 D. 552. Wilson's Exrs. *v.* Scot. Soc. for Conversion of Israel, 1869; 8 Macph. 233. Bogie's Trs. *v.* Swanston, 1878; 5 R. 634. *In re* Kilvert's Trusts, L. R. 7 Ch. App. 170; 40 L. J. Ch. 703; 41 *ib.* 351. See as to marginal jottings by testator, Brown *v.* Maxwell's Exrs., 1884; 11 R. 821.

(*c*) Brown's Trs. *v.* His Relations, 1762; M. 2318.

(*d*) Wishart *v.* Grant, 1763; M. 2310. Rhind's Trs. *v.* Leith, 1866 5 Macph. 104. As to legacies to illegitimate children, see Occleston *v.* Fullalove, 43 L. J. Ch. 297, and cases there cited. See Norris *v.* Norris, 1838; 2 D. 220 (nephews and nieces of full and half blood). Buchan *v.* Porteous, 1879; 7 R. 210. Brown *v.* Maxwell's Exrs., 1884; 11 R. 821, and Maxwell's Exrs. *v.* Grant, 1886; 13 R. 854 (legacy to "servants").

(*e*) Stopford Blair's Exrs. *v.* Maxwell, 1872; 10 Macph. 760. Wood *v.* Wood, 1861; 23 D. 338. **Macdougall (Richardson or Young)** *v.* **Macdougall,** 1866; 4 Macph. 372; rev. 6 Macph. H. L. 18. Davidson's Trs. *v.* Davidson, 1871; 9 Macph. 995. Buchanan's Trs. *v.* Buchanan, 1877; 4 R. 754. Ross *v.* Dunlop, 1878; 5 R. 833 (fund distributed in different portions at different times).

(*f*) Morrison's Trs. *v.* Macdonald, 1890; 18 R. 181.

(*g*) Turner's Trs. *v.* Turner, 1897; 24 R. 619. Macdonald *v.* Hall, 1893; A. C. 642, 651; 20 R. H. L. 88.

(*h*) Stewart *v.* Stewart, 1802; M. App. *Clause*, No. 4. Manson *v.* Hutcheon, 1874; 1 R. 371. See Haldane's Trs. *v.* Sharp's Tr., 1890; 17 R. 385 (heirs *in mobilibus*). Scott's Exrs. *v.* Methven's Exrs., 1890; 17 R. 389.

(*i*) Blair *v.* Blair, 1849; 12 D. 97; and earlier authorities cited there and in 1 M'Laren, Wills and Succn. 704 sqq. Sutherland *v.* Douglas, 1865; 4 Macph. 105. White *v.* White, 1860; 22 D. 1335 (effect of direction to sell). See Sillar's Trs. *v.* Stewart, 1872; 11 Macph. 160; aff. 1874, 1 R. H. L. 48.

(*k*) Blair, *cit.* O'Reilly *v.* Sempill, 1855; 2 Macq. 288. Nimmo *v.* Murray's Trs., 1864; 2 Macph. 1144.

(*l*) Pearson *v.* Corrie, 1825; 4 S. 119.

(*m*) Rutherford *v.* Turnbull, 1821; 1 S. 37; 2 Ill. 445. Paterson *v.* Paterson, 1741; M. 8070. Fleming *v.* Martin, 1798; M. 8111. Nicholson *v.* Ramsay, 1806; M. *Legacy*, Apx. 3. Maxwell *v.* Wylie, 1837; 15 S. 1005. Hamilton *v.* Hamilton, 1838; 16 S. 478; 3 Ill. 162. *Supra*, § 1879 (*a*); *infra*, § 1881.

(*n*) Bedwells *v.* Tod, Dec. 2, 1819; F. C.; 2 Ill. 445. See Miller *v.* Milne's Trs., 1859; 21 D. 377.

(*o*) Connell *v.* Grierson, 1867; 5 Macph. 379. Scott *v.* Scott, 1852; 14 D. 1057; aff. 1855, 2 Macq. 281.

(*p*) Young's Trs. *v.* Janes, 1880; 8 R. 242. See Ferrier *v.* Angus, 1876; 3 R. 396; above, § 1861A; and Tronson *v.* Tronsons, 1884; 12 R. 155.

(*q*) Hood *v.* Murray **(Gregory's Trs.** *v.* **Alison)**, *infra.*

(*r*) Stewart and Pearson, *citt.* (*h*), (*l*). Nimmo *v.* Murray's Trs., *cit.* (*k*). Maxwell *v.* Maxwell, 1864; 3 Macph. 318. Williamson *v.* Gardiner, 1865; 4 Macph. 66. Ewart *v.* Cottom, 1870; 9 Macph. 232.

(*s*) Cockburn's Trs. *v.* Dundas, 1864; 2 Macph. 1185. See Hood *v.* Murray, *infra.*

(*t*) Hood *v.* Murray **(Gregory's Trs.** *v.* **Alison)**, 1889; 14 App. Ca. 124; 16 R. H. L. 10; rev. Murray *v.* Gregory's Trs., 1887; 14 R. 368, and virtually overruling Haldane's Trs. (Wannop) *v.* Murphy, 1881; 9 R. 269. See also Stodart *v.* Stodart's Trs., 1870; 8 Macph. 667. E. Dalhousie's Trs. *v.* Young, 1889; 16 R. 681. Mags. of Irvine *v.* Muir, 1888; 15 R. 396 ("natives of Irvine"—boundaries of royal or parliamentary burgh), and cases in note (*r*).

(*u*) M'Kenzie *v.* Holte's Legatees, 1781; M. 6602. Grant *v.* Fyfe, May 22, 1810; F. C. Rennie *v.* Crosbie, 1822; 2 S. 60. So where a mutual settlement by spouses gave their estate "to the nearest in kin of us equally." Hogg *v.* Bruce, 1887; 14 R. 887.

(*v*) M'Courtie *v.* Blackie, 1812; Hume, 270.

(*w*) Macdougall (Richardson) *v.* Macdougall, *supra* (*e*). Ramsay's Trs. *v.* Ramsay, 1876; 4 R. 243. Home's Trs. *v.* Ramsay, 1884; 12 R. 314. Cunningham's Trs. *v.* Cunningham, 1891; 18 R. 380.

1881. (3.) *Legacies with Substitutions* are bequeathed to a second or third person (by name or description), failing the first legatee. So a legacy "to A. and his heirs" does not lapse by A.'s predecease, 'the heirs of A. taking as conditional institutes' (*a*); though a different rule prevails in bonds of provision (*b*).

But where the testator plainly assumes that the legatee shall take in the first place, the legacy will lapse by the legatee's predecease (*c*). A destination "to assignees" is held to infer as a condition of its vesting the survivance of 'the date of vesting by' the legatee named (*d*). A legacy "to one and his heirs, and any to whom he shall leave it," goes to the heirs on the legatee's predecease; but he has no power of disposal before the legacy vests in him (*e*). A legacy "to A., whom failing to B.," is only a conditional institution, unless it be plainly declared otherwise; and so the right of the substituted legatee becomes extinct as soon as the legacy vests in the first legatee (*f*). 'Even where a substitution in moveables is effectually created, it is evacuated, if the institute survives the vesting period, and if there be not a trust, by his Will or general settlement (*g*).'

(*a*) Inglis *v.* Miller, 1760; M. 8084; 2 Ill. 446. See Scott *v.* Ramsay, 1777; 5 B. Sup. 504; 2 Ill. 445 (anticipation by loan). Turnbull *v.* Turnbull, 1778; M. 8099. Boston *v.* Horsburgh, 1781; M. 8099. E. Moray *v.* Stuart, 1782; M. 8103. See above, § 1879. Cochrane *v.* Cochrane's Exrs., 1854; 17 D. 103. Marchbanks *v.* Brockie, 1836; 14 S. 521. Halliburton *v.* Halliburton, 1884; 11 R. 979. Cleland *v.* Allan, 1891; 18 R. 377.

(*b*) Russell *v.* Russell, 1767; M. 6372. Findlay, *infra* (*c*). Cleland (*a*).

(*c*) Scott *v.* Carfrae, 1769; M. 8090. See Dunlop *v.* Crawford, June 2, 1812; F. C. Findlay *v.* Mackenzie, 1875; 2 R. 909 (disposition to a wife, her heirs and assignees).

(*d*) Graham *v.* Hope, 1807; M. *Leg.* Apx. 5; see Obs. on Bench. Torrie *v.* King's Remembrancer, 1832; 10 S. 597. Bell *v.* M'Intosh's Trs. (Cheape), 1845; 7 D. 614. Maxwell *v.* Maxwell, 1864; 3 Macph. 318. See next note (*e*).

(*e*) Henry *v.* Grant, 1824; 2 S. 725. Cases in previous note (*d*).

(*f*) Campbell *v.* Campbell, 1740; M. 14,055; aff. 1 Cr. & St. 343; 2 Ill. 448. Brown *v.* Coventry, 1792; M. 14,863; Bell's Ca. 310. Duncan *v.* Myles, June 27, 1809; F. C. (See Strachan *v.* Dunbar, 1714; M. 4312. Craich *v.* Craich, 1739; M. 16,342; 5 B. Sup. 667.) Johnston *v.* Greig, 1831; 9 S. 806; 6 W. & S. 406. Ramsay *v.* Ramsay, 1838; 1 D. 83. Allan *v.* Fleming, 1845; 7 D. 908. Ogilvie *v.* Cumming, 1852; 14 D. 363; aff. 1856, 19 D. H. L. 7. Paul *v.* Home, 1872; 10 Macph. 937. See above, § 1693.

(*g*) 3 Stair, 5. § 51. Fyffe *v.* Fyffe, 1841; 3 D. 1205. Dyer *v.* Carruthers, 1874; 1 R. 943. Johnston *v.* Greig, and Brown *v.* Coventry, *citt.* M'Dowall *v.* M'Gill, 1847; 9 D. 1284. Bell's Ex. *v.* Borthwick, 1897; 24 R. 1120. As to Substitutions in Moveables, see M'Laren, Wills and Succn. i. 299 sqq., 631 sqq.

1882. (4.) *Legacy to several Legatees.*—A legacy may be given to several persons, either jointly, or severally, or successively. A legacy "to A. and B. jointly" goes to them equally, or to the survivor (*a*). "Jointly and severally" has the same construction. In a legacy "to two persons equally," or "to be equally divided between them," 'or in other language of the same import, *i.e.* implying severance, the persons favoured being named or sufficiently described for identification,' the right is separately to each of one-half, without any *jus accrescendi*, and the survivor has only his own share (*b*). A legacy to "A. in liferent and B. in fee" seems to give a liferent succeeded by a fee, if both survive; or a liferent, or a fee, as the liferenter or fiar shall survive. A legacy to a parent in liferent and children *nominatim* in fee, gives a fee to the children, the father being a trustee to maintain the interest of the children (*c*). A sum bequeathed to one in liferent, and on the liferenter's death to A., vests in A. on his surviving the testator; but if there be a trust, and the trustees are to pay to A. after the liferenter's death, there is no intermediate fee vested in A. (*d*). If a legacy be left to certain persons provided they shall claim within a given time; if not, to certain other persons,—the legacy will not vest in the eventual legatees till the expiration of the time limited (*e*).

(*a*) 3 Stair, 8. § 27.

(*b*) Paterson *v.* Paterson, 1741; M. 8070; 2 Ill. 450. Rose *v.* Rose, 1782; M. 8101; Elchies, *Legacy*, 9. See above, § 1067. Torrie *v.* Munsie (King's Remembrancer), 1832; 10 S. 597. M. Breadalbane's Trs. *v.* Pringle, 1841; 3 D. 357. Wauchope *v.* Brown's Tutors, 1882; 10 R. 441. Paxton's Trs. *v.* Cowie, 1886; 13 R. 1191. In legacies to a class of persons of unascertained number, words indicating division into shares seem not to exclude accretion. See 1 M'Laren, Wills and Succn. 678–9. **Carleton** *v.* **Thomson**, 1867; 5 Macph. H. L. 151; L. R. 1 Sc. App. 241. Paul *v.* Home, 1872; 10 Macph. 937. Muir's Trs. *v.* Muir, 1889; 16 R. 954.

(*c*) Turnbull *v.* Turnbull, 1778; M. 4248, 8099. Gerran *v.* Alexander, 1781; M. 4402; 2 Ill. 347. See Williamson *v.* Cochrane, 1828; 6 S. 1035; 2 Ill. 346. Mackintosh *v.* Mackintosh, Jan. 28, 1812; F. C. The fee also vests if the bequest be to the children of the liferenter as a class. Forbes *v.* Luckie, and Matthew *v.* Scott, *supra*, § 1879 (*d*).

(*d*) Burden *v.* Smith, 1738; Elchies, *Mutual Contr.* 7; Cr. & St. 214. Nisbet *v.* M'Dougal, June 27, 1809; F. C. Glendinning *v.* Walker, 1825; 4 S. 237. Moubray *v.* Scougal, 1834; 12 S. 910; aff. 2 S. & M'L. 305. Buchanan *v.* Downie, 1830; 8 S. 516. Marchbanks *v.* Brockie, 1836; 14 S. 521. The rule here stated does not depend on the mere existence of a trust, but on the intention manifested to postpone vesting by making the interest of the fiars depend on their surviving the liferenter; a trust, unless so far as it appears to be intended to secure the ultimate beneficiaries, and not merely for administration, having little or no effect in regard to vesting. See cases in § 1879 (*c*), and **Carleton** *v.* **Thomson**, 1867; 5 Macph. H. L. 151; L. R. 1 Sc. App. 241 (*per* L. Colonsay).

(*e*) Stevenson *v.* Macintyre, 1826; 4 S. 776. Neilson *v.* Coulter, *infra*, § 1883 (*a*).

1883. (5.) *Conditional and Contingent Legacies.*—Legacies are pure and conditional, and the rules are:—1. A condition receives effect if it be a possible condition (*a*); if not, it is held *pro non scripto*. In construction, a legacy to one in the event of there being two children living at any time, was not held purified by the birth of a second child which was not heard to cry (*b*). 2. It is not a condition rendering a legacy contingent, if it be made payable on a future event that *must* happen. 3. If the legacy depend on an event uncertain as to *time* alone (as death), the *payment* is suspended, but the legacy vests. 4. If it be uncertain not only in respect of time, but of *existence* (as majority or marriage, or attaining a certain age), it is then a condition; and the vesting of the legacy is suspended 'unless there be evidence of a contrary intention of the testator; as, for instance, by a declaration that the legacy is to bear interest, or a destination over to the heirs and assignees of the legatee, or other circumstances indicating that the uncertain term is annexed to the payment only, and not to the gift (*c*).' And this is not only when the contingency is pointed to the *constitution* of the legacy, but also when annexed to the *payment*, 'provided that nothing is expressed in favour of the beneficiary except a direction to pay or convey to him (*d*).' 5. If a legacy be "to one, on failure of the children of another," it remains in suspense while the children *may* exist (*e*). 6. A legacy in consideration of future services is conditional (*f*). 7. A legacy, provided the legatee come home to claim it within a certain time, is conditional (*g*). '8. If the words of gift be clear, a mere direction as to the time of payment (which never arrives) does not import a condition (*h*). 9. A legacy or provision may vest subject to a possible divestiture, or defeasance. Thus a fund given to A.'s children and vested in his only child may be divested to the extent of a half by the birth of a second child (*supra*, § 1642); or a testator may bequeath a fund so that there is a qualified vesting in the donee subject to the power of trustees to divest it, as by restricting it to a liferent. In such cases an arrestment by creditors of the donee, which attaches his right only *tantum et tale*, does not prevent the trustees from afterwards exercising the power (*i*).

'The most common instances of contingent destinations postponing vesting are destinations over to conditional institutes, and still more clearly destinations to the survivors in legacies to a plurality of persons. When the distribution is postponed, and no period of failure is expressed, these conditions are referred to the period of distribution, such as the termination of a liferent. But in the case of a destination over, the presumption against vesting is not so strong; and vesting in the class first called will take place, if the intention appear to be merely to provide for the event of there being no persons of that class in existence at the testator's death. The existence of such persons is held to evacuate the ulterior destination (*k*).'

(*a*) Waddell *v.* Waddell, 1738; M. 6366; 2 Ill. 453. See Neilson *v.* Coulter, 1710; 4 B. Sup. 807. See above, § 49, 1785. Dunbar *v.* Scott's Trs., 1872; 10 Macph. 982.

(*b*) Roberton *v.* Roberton, 1833; 11 S. 297.

(*c*) Wood *v.* Burnet's Trs., 1813; Hume, 271. Donaldson's Trs. *v.* Macdougall, *infra* (*k*) (in Ct. of S., rev. on other points). Kennedy *v.* Crawford, 1841; 3 D. 1266. Ralston *v.* Ralston, 1842; 4 D. 1496. Clark's Exrs. *v.* Paterson, 1851; 14 D. 141. Alves's Trs. *v.* Grant, 1874; 1 R. 969. Ross's Trs. *v.* Ross, 1884; 12 R. 378.

(*d*) V. Oxenford *v.* ——, 1671; 2 B. Sup. 525. Burnet *v.* Forbes, 1783; M. 8105. Omey *v.* M'Larty, 1788; M. 6340. Sempill *v.* Sempill, 1792; M. 8108. Grindlay *v.* Merchant Company, July 1, 1814; F. C.; 2 Ill. 538. See above, § 1879; and below, § 1990. Home *v.* Home, 1807; Hume, 530. Torrie *v.* Munsie (King's Remembrancer), 1832; 10 S. 507. Matthew *v.* Scott, 1844; 6 D. 718. Mackintosh *v.* Wood, 1872; 10 Macph. 933. Bryson's Trs. *v.* Clark, 1880; 8 R. 141. See Hay's Trs. *v.* Hay, 1890; 17 R. 961. Reeve's Exrs. *v.* Reeve's Factor, 1892; 19 R. 1013.

(*e*) Carstairs *v.* Carstairs, 1672; M. 2992.

(*f*) Leckie *v.* Rennie, 1748; M. 6347; Elchies, *Tut.* 21. Lockhart *v.* Purves, 1729; M. 6366. Henderson *v.* Stuart, 1825; 4 S. 306. See Bryce *v.* Aitken, 1827; 5 S. 817. See further as to the right of executors and trustees not accepting or acting, to legacies left to them. 1 More's Notes on Stair, 37. 2 M'Laren, Wills and Succn. 207.

(*g*) Neilson, *supra* (*a*).

(*h*) Grant *v.* Cowe, 1887; 15 R. 81.

(*i*) **Chambers's Trs.** *v.* **Smith**, 1877; 5 R. 97; rev. 1878, 5 R. H. L. 151. See Snell's Trs. *v.* Morrison, 1877; 4 R. 709. Cases in Op. of L. Pr. Inglis in Haldane's Trs. (Wannop) *v.* Murphy, 1881; 9 R. 269; Murray *v.* Gregory's Trs., 1887; 14 R. 368; revd. (as Hood *v.* Murray) 1889, 14 App. Ca. 124; 16 R. H. L. 11. E. Dalhousie's Trs. *v.* Young, 1889; 16 R. 681. Logan's Trs. *v.* Ellis, 1890; 17 R. 425. Russell *v.* Bell's Trs., 1897; 24 R. 666. See as to vesting subject to defeasance, Haldane's Trs., *cit.* Steel's Trs. *v.* Steel, 1888; 16 R. 204. Turner *v.* Gow, 1894; 21 R. 563, etc.

(*k*) **Donaldson's Trs.** *v.* **Macdougall** (Richardson *v.* Donaldson's Trs.), 1859; 22 D. 1527; rev. 1862, 4 Macq. 314. **Carleton** *v.* **Thomson**, 1865; 3 Macph. 514; aff. 1867; 5 Macph. H. L. 151; L. R. 1 Sc. App. 232. Howat's Trs. *v.* Howat, 1869; 8 Macph. 337 (vesting postponed till actual receipt or conveyance—see Macdougall *v.* M'Farlane's Trs., 1890; 17 R. 761). Miller *v.* Finlay's Trs., 1875; 2 R. H. L. 1; revg. 1873, 45 S. Jur. 564.

1884. (6.) *Legatum rei alienæ.*—The rules relative to this kind of legacy are these:—1. If the testator erroneously supposed the thing bequeathed to be his own, it is no legacy (*a*). 2. If he knew it *not* to be his own, the legacy is to be made good by purchasing the thing, or satisfying the legatee (*b*). 3. If the legacy be of a subject not disposable by Will, it may still be available on the principle of approbate and reprobate; the executor or residuary legatee being bound as by implied engagement (*c*). 4. Where the testator erroneously imagined the subject to be moveable, and the executor has it not to bestow, the legacy is unavailing (*d*).

(*a*) 3 Ersk. 9. § 10.
(*b*) Falconer *v.* Dougall, 1664; M. 13,301; 2 Ill. 455.
(*c*) Ersk. *ut supra*. Drummond *v.* Drummond, 1624; M. 2261. Kinloch *v.* Lundie, 1663; M. 8052. Cranston *v.* Brown, 1674; M. 8059 (legacies of heritable subjects put on same footing as a *legatum rei alienæ*). Catto *v.* Gordons, 1748; M. 8077. Douglas's Trs. *v.* Douglas, 1862; 24 D. 1191. M'Donald *v.* M'Donald, 1876; 4 R. 45. See below, § 1940. Hewit's Trs. *v.* Lawson, 1891; 18 R. 793.
(*d*) Wardlaw *v.* Fraser, 1663; M. 5703. 3 Ersk. 9. § 10 *in fin.*

1885. (7.) *Time of Payment.*—If no term be appointed, the legacy is due, and, as it would seem, bears interest from the testator's death; but payment cannot be enforced till the expiration of six months (*a*). 'In specific legacies interest is due from the testator's death, even if the term of payment be postponed (*b*). Where the term of payment is postponed, the intermediate proceeds not being expressly disposed of, interest is due on legacies or provisions by a father to his children, or by one standing *in loco parentis*, from the testator's death (*c*). In other cases of postponed distribution, undisposed of interest seems to fall into residue (*d*). The rate of interest is 5 per cent. when the trustees are *in morâ*; in other cases what the estate has produced (*e*).'

(*a*) A. of S. Feb. 1662. M'Dowall *v.* Crichton's Crs., 1779; M. 542; 2 Ill. 452. Arbuthnot *v.* Arbuthnot, 1758; M. 539. Fowke, Wallace, and Johns, *supra*, § 1879. Interest is held to be due from the testator's death, or the date when the fund becomes productive. Duff's Trs. *v.* Scripture Readers, 1862; 24 D. 552. M'Lean's Trs. *v.* M'Leans, 1891; 18 R. 892 ("payable as at my death").
(*b*) Glasgow's Trs. *v.* Glasgow, 1830; 9 S. 87; 3 S. Jur. 45. M'Alister's Trs. *v.* M'Alister's Trs., 1836; 15 S. 170.
(*c*) Gillespie *v.* Marshall, 1802; M. Apx. *Accessorium*, 2. Campbell *v.* Reid, 1840; 2 D. 1084. Ogilvie *v.* Cumming, 1852; 14 D. 363; aff. 19 D. H. L. 7; 28 Sc. Jur. 646. Fergusson *v.* Smith, 1867; 6 Macph. 83. Payment of accruing income in anticipation of vesting was authorised in special circumstances in Duncan's Trs. *v.* Ellison, 1877; 4 R. 1093.
(*d*) Pursell *v.* Elder, 1856; 19 D. 71; aff. 1865, 3 Macph. H. L. 59; 4 Macq. 992. Sturgis *v.* Campbell, 1860; 23 D. 1128; aff. 3 Macph. H. L. 70.
(*e*) Inglis' Trs. *v.* Breen, 1891; 18 R. 487, explaining Sharpe's Trs. *v.* Kirkpatrick, 6 R. H. L. 4.

1886. Ademption of 'Special' Legacies.—Points of great nicety arise on the question, whether acts of the testator relative to particular funds mentioned in his Will shall extinguish bequests of those funds? Without entering into all the subtleties of this matter, it would seem that whenever a sum is bequeathed out of a particular fund; or when the expression of the bequest points rather to the amount of the fund than to the designation of it as a specific *corpus*; or when the bequest plainly refers to the money, not to the security; or to a preconceived intention unconnected with the investment of the money; in such cases the legacy is general, to be made good out of the general fund, although the money should have been uplifted from the investment referred to in the Will (*a*). It has sometimes been held material in this question of ademption to inquire whether the change has been compulsory or voluntary; the one indicating a change of intention or destination on the part of the testator, not the other. But this circumstance seems at best no more than a mere indication to be taken with other proofs (*b*).

(*a*) See the English cases in 2 Roberts on Wills, 111 et seq. Le Grice, 3 Merivale, 50. Pagan *v.* Pagan, 1838; 16 S. 383. Congreve's Trs. *v.* Congreve, 1874; 1 R. 1102. Mitchell's Trs. *v.* Fergus, 1889; 16 R. 903.
(*b*) Roberts, *ut supra*, 112. Pagan, *supra* (*a*). See above, § 1877. 1 M'Laren on Wills, etc., § 508, 860 sq., 875 sqq. Chalmers *v.* Chalmers, 1851; 14 D. 57.

1887. Legacy Duty.—Not only is there a tax on moveable succession (*a*), but duties are also imposed on legacies, 'and on residue accruing under a Will or under intestacy,' payable by the legatee, and rising (according to the remoteness of the relationship) from one to ten per cent. on the sum bequeathed, 'or in the case of residue, on the sum realised (*b*).' The rules generally are: That all legacies, 'and shares of residue, although not of the value' of £20 (*c*) out of 'moveable' estates 'not under' £100 (*d*), shall pay duty; that in joint legacies, parties differently rateable shall be chargeable according to their interest: and that any gift by Will, or testamentary instrument (*e*), to be satisfied out of the personal estate of the deceased; or out of 'personal' (*f*) estate which the deceased had power to dispose of, not being his own real estate; and every gift having effect as a donation *mortis causâ*, is to be held a legacy, and liable to duty (*g*). 'Where the net value of the heritable and moveable property passing on a death and subject to estate duty, and not settled otherwise than by the deceased's Will, is not over £1000, and where estate duty, fixed or graduated, has been paid, the estate is exempt from legacy duty (*h*). Legacies and residue falling to the deceased's wife or husband are exempt (*i*). It is further provided that legacies released or compounded for less than the value bear duty according to the sum taken in satisfaction (*k*). Where the legacy or residue, or part of the residue, accrues to a child or descendant of a child—or to the father or mother, or any lineal ancestor—of the deceased, the duty is £1 per cent.; but this duty is abolished wherever (as in the ordinary case) inventory or estate duty has been paid on the estate (*l*); if to a brother or sister, or any descendant of a brother or sister, £3 per cent.; if to a brother or sister of the father or mother of the deceased, or any descendant of such brother or sister, £5 per cent.; if to a brother or sister of a grandfather or grandmother of the deceased, or any descendant of such brother or sister, £6 per cent.; and if to any person in any other degree of collateral consanguinity to the deceased, or to a stranger in blood, £10 per cent. (*m*).'

It is held, in the construction of these Acts, that a sum given while the testator is still in life, in order to save the duty, 'if distinguished from a donation *mortis causâ*,' is not an illegal evasion of the duty (*n*); 'that the liability of an estate to legacy duty depends on the testator's domicile at his death (*o*)'; that the duty is payable by the legatee (*p*), unless the Will shall otherwise direct; in which case the exemption *in dubio* is extended to a substitute (*q*); that the rule of different rates according to relationship 'was' to be applied to the case of husband and wife named as joint legatees, as to a mixed case—one-half to each (*r*); 'but now a person taking a legacy or residue, if married to a nearer relative of the deceased, is liable only to the duty appropriate to the nearer relationship (*s*); and that one who acquires under the Entail Amendment Acts an absolute interest in money bequeathed to be laid out in the purchase of land, must pay duty on the whole, without deducting what he has paid for consent by substitute heirs (*t*).

'A stamp duty in lieu of legacy and other duties is laid on bodies corporate and unincorporate (*u*).'

(*a*) As to inventory duty and estate duty, see below, § 1898, 1898A; and as to succession duty, § 1898C.

(*b*) L. Adv. *v.* Pringle, 1878; 5 R. 912.

(*c*) 44 and 45 Vict. c. 12, § 42; altering the former law—as to which see Stewart's Trs. *v.* L. Adv., 1857; 20 D. 453 (distinct legacies under £20 to different schemes of the same Church not subject to duty).

(*d*) 43 Vict. c. 14, § 13.

(*e*) A Will or testamentary instrument is a writing of whatever form, which remains dormant during the life of the person executing it, if it be revocable "until his death, and if it only comes into active power at his death." Att.-Gen. *v.* Ramsay's Trs., 2 C. M. & R. 229, n. L. Adv. *v.* Trotter, 1847; 10 D. 56. Att.-Gen. *v.* Evans, 2 C. M. & R. 221. L. Adv. *v.* Reid's Exrs., 1880; 7 R. 483.

(*f*) 51 Vict. c. 8, § 21 (2).

(*g*) 36 Geo. III. c. 52, § 7; 44 Geo. III. c. 98; 45 Geo. III. c. 28, § 4; all repealed by 35 and 36 Vict. c. 63. 48 Geo. III. c. 149; and 55 Geo. III. c. 184; both partly repealed, 8 and 9 Vict. c. 76, § 4. See for a full explanation of all the cases and details under these Acts, Gwynne's Law of Duties on Legacies, 1834. See 24 and 25 Vict. c. 92. L. Adv. *v.* Trotter, 1847; 10 D. 56 (provision in ante-nuptial marriage-contract not liable). L. Adv. *v.* Oswald, 1848; 10 D. 969 (patent). L. Adv. *v.* Hill, 1862; 24 D. 808. Weir *v.* L. Adv., 1865; 3 Macph. 1006. L. Adv. *v.* Paterson's Trs., 1879; 6 R. 906. L. Adv. *v.* Miller's Trs., 1884; 11 R. 1046. Att.-Gen. *v.* Wyndham, 1 H. & C. 563; 32 L. J. Ex. 1. Att.-Gen. *v.* Brackenbury, 1 H. & C. 782. Drake *v.* Att.-Gen., 10 C. & F. 257.

(*h*) 57 and 58 Vict. c. 30, § 16 (3). See below, § 1898A.

(*i*) 55 Geo. III. c. 184, sched. part 3.

(*k*) L. Adv. *v.* Freckleton's Factor, 1894; 21 R. 743.

(*l*) 44 and 45 Vict. c. 12, § 41. 57 and 58 Vict. c. 30, § 1 and sched. 1 (5). See below, § 1898A.

(*m*) 55 Geo. III. c. 184, sched. part 3.

(*n*) Brown *v.* L. Adv., 1852; 24 S. Jur. 565; 1 Macq. 79. L. Adv. *v.* Trotter, *cit.*

(*o*) L. Adv. *v.* Thomson, 1845; 4 Bell's App. 1; 12 Cl. & F. 1. Comrs. of Inl. Rev. *v.* Gordon's Exrs., 1850; 12 D. 657. Wallace *v.* Att.-Gen., L. R. 1 Ch. 1; 35 L. J. Ch. 124. Chatfield *v.* Berchtoldt, 41 L. J. Ch. 255; L. R. 7 Ch. 192. L. Adv. *v.* Smith, 1852; 14 D. 585; aff. 1 Macq. 760. L. Adv. *v.* Hamilton, 1856; 18 D. 636.

(*p*) 36 Geo. III. c. 52. Fischer *v.* E. Seafield, 1825; 4 S. 192. See Nisbet's Trs. *v.* Learmonth, 1845; 8 D. 69. L. Adv. *v.* Miller's Trs., 1884; 11 R. 1046.

(*q*) Charteris *v.* Young, 2 Rus. Ch. Ca. 183. Bulloch *v.* Beaton, 1853; 15 D. 373.

(*r*) Att.-Gen. *v.* Bacchus, 1823; 11 Price, 547.

(*s*) 16 and 17 Vict. c. 51, § 11.

(*t*) L. Adv. *v.* Dunlop's Trs., 1892; 19 R. 461; aff. 1894, A. C. 291; 21 R. H. L. 28; and see 21 R. 348.

(*u*) 48 and 49 Vict. c. 51, § 11 sqq. See cases in § 1898B (*f*).

III. CONFIRMATION OF MOVEABLES.

1888. Jurisdiction.—The administration of the moveable estate of deceased persons having fallen into the hands of the Church, there gradually arose a jurisdiction in relation to it in the Bishop's Court. A certain share of the estate was allotted to the Bishop for his faithful administration; and this was first converted into a composition to the Commissary-clerk, and at last abolished (*a*). The Bishop's Court was, in Queen Mary's time, succeeded by the Commissary Court; consisting of the Head Court at Edinburgh, having a universal as well as diocesan jurisdiction, with twenty-three provincial Commissaries. The latter are superseded, and the duty devolved on the Sheriffs of counties (*b*). And the Commissary Court of Edinburgh has also been abolished, and its duties and powers transferred to the Sheriffs of Edinburgh (*c*).

(*a*) Scottish Prov. Councils at Perth, July 16, 1420; 6 Hailes' Annals, 22. 1540, c. 120. 1701, c. 14. 4 Geo. IV. c. 97, § 1; 2 Ill. 458.

(*b*) Balfour, Pract. 665, 667. 1669, c. 26. Dirleton, Consistorius; and Stewart's Ans. 4 Geo. IV. c. 97.

(*c*) 1 Will. IV. c. 69, § 31. 6 and 7 Will. IV. c. 41. 4 Geo. IV. c. 97. See 13 and 14 Vict. c. 50. 21 and 22 Vict. c. 56; and 39 and 40 Vict. c. 70, the last of which completes the transference of the functions of the Commissaries to the Sheriffs; and makes provision for the abolition of the separate Commissary-clerk in every county except Edinburgh.

1889. Nature of Confirmation.—Confirmation is a sentence of a Sheriff as Commissary, giving authority to an executor (or more than one) to administer, "intromit with, uplift, receive, discharge, and, if needful, to pursue"; in short, to recover and distribute, as trustee for all concerned, the moveable estate belonging to a person deceased (*a*).

'*Provident Nominations.*—By the Provident Nominations and Small Intestacies Act, 1883, payment of sums not exceeding £100 may be made without confirmation to the nominees or representatives of a deceased person, by savings banks, friendly societies, trade unions, etc. (*b*).'

(*a*) 3 Ersk. 9. § 27. Statutes, *supra*, § 1888. Confirmation in the Court of the deceased's domicile does not of itself subject executors, all of whom reside in another territory, to the jurisdiction of that Court. Halliday *v.* Halliday, 1886; 14 R. 251. But the practice in cases of caution for an executor is to make the granters of the bond of caution express themselves as subject to the jurisdiction of the confirming Court. See Kirkwood *v.* Kirkwood, 1889; 6 Sh. Ct. Rep. 43. Currie on Confirmation (2nd ed.), 181. See M'Laren on Wills and Succn. i. 49 sqq.

(*b*) 46 and 47 Vict. c. 47. See as to estates under £300, below, § 1895A.

1890. Effect of Confirmation.—Confirmation was formerly required for two purposes,—to vest the succession, and give an active title.

1891. (1.) *Vesting Succession.*—Confirmation was till recently necessary to vest the succession in the next of kin, at least where the ancestor died intestate; so that if one succeeding to the moveables of a person deceased did not confirm, or died before confirmation was completed, the right to the succession went from his children or heirs in moveables to the next in kin of the person to whom he had succeeded (*a*). But by statute this is not now required in the case of intestate succession; it being declared to vest 'in next of kin surviving the passing of the Act (*b*)' by the mere survivance of the next of kin (*c*).

In the case of testate succession, there is not, by the common law (as held to be confirmed by the statute), any necessity for confirmation to take the moveables out of the *hæreditas jacens* of the deceased (*d*).

(*a*) 3 Ersk. 9. § 30. Stewart *v.* Graeme, 1799; M. 14,407; 2 Ill. 458. See Lennox *v.* Grant, 1784; M. 15,381. Grant *v.* M'Leay, 1791; Bell's Ca. 319. Smith *v.* Grieve, 1801; M. *Substitute*, Apx. 1.

(*b*) Cuningham *v.* Farie, 1856; 18 D. 312.

(*c*) 4 Geo. IV. c. 98. Ivory's Ersk. p. 894, note 611. Robertson *v.* Gilchrist, 1828; 6 S. 446. Smith *v.* Thomas, 1830; 8 S. 468. Milligan *v.* Milligan, 1826; 4 S. 432. Frith *v.* Buchanan & Co., 1837; 15 S. 729. Mein *v.* M'Call, 1844; 6 D. 1112. Elder *v.* Watson, 1859; 21 D. 1122. See below, § 1893. Webster *v.* Shiress, 1878; 6 R. 102.

(*d*) Robertson, *supra* (*c*).

1892. (2.) *Active Title.*—Confirmation is still necessary, in general, as an active title (*a*). No debtor is bound 'or is safe' to pay without it (*b*); and the general rule is, that no diligence is effectual in competition where confirmation has not preceded it. But to this last rule there are some exceptions. So, if the testator have conveyed by his Will the thing or debt in question specially, or by general disposition referring to an inventory signed by him, and containing it, the title is good without confirmation; 'but a bare general disposition, though sufficient at common law to vest the right in the disponee, is not itself a title of administration' (*c*). Or if the debtor to the deceased have renewed or corroborated his debt by bond, etc., to the executor, no confirmation is necessary (*d*). Or if the executor have obtained actual possession, he will require, 'to the extent of the subjects possessed (*e*),' no confirmation, nor can be deprived of such possession on pretence of want of title (*f*). But doubts may arise as to what is to be held possession; whether constructive possession of moveables, for example, be sufficient; or, still more, in regard to debts, payment of the interest of which, though sufficient to vest the succession (*g*), may not be safely relied on as a title for competing diligence.

(*a*) Atkinson *v.* Learmonth, 1808; M. *Serv. and Confirm.* Apx. 3; 2 Ill. 460. Park's Crs. *v.* Maxwell, 1785; M. 14,382; 2 Ill. 458. Lennox and Grant, *supra*, § 1891 (*a*). Hinton *v.* Connell's Trs., 1883; 10 R. 1110. See below, § 1899 (*e*).
(*b*) Taylor *v.* Forbes & Co., 1827; 5 S. 782; rev. 1830, 4 W. & S. 444. Buchanan *v.* Royal Bank, 1842; 5 D. 211.
(*c*) 1690, c. 26. Dobie *v.* Oliphant, 1707; M. 14,390. 4 Geo. IV. c. 98, § 3. Lyle *v.* Lyle, 1842; 5 D. 236. Wright *v.* Turner, 1855; 17 D. 629. Robertson, *supra*, § 1891 (*c*). Christie *v.* Dun, 1809; M. Apx. *Prov. to Heirs*, 5. Bell *v.* Willison, 1831; 9 S. 266. Innerarity *v.* Gilmour, 1840; 2 D. 813.
(*d*) Watson *v.* Marshall, 1782; M. 6009.
(*e*) Richardson *v.* Shiells, 1784; M. 14,377. MacDowall *v.* MacDowall, 1784; M. 14,404. Smith's Trs. *v.* Grant, 1862; 24 D. 1142.
(*f*) M'Whirter *v.* Millar, 1744; M. 14,395. Spence *v.* Wilson, 1751; M. 14,399. Smith's Trs. *v.* Grant, *cit.*
(*g*) See Robertson, *supra*, § 1891 (*c*).

1893. Proceedings in Confirmation.—Confirmation may be applied for in several situations (*a*).

(1.) *Executor-Nominate.*—An executor appointed by Will, grounds his application on the Will which contains the nomination. It is produced, with a full inventory, seen and confirmed; and the authority is granted by decree of confirmation, 'the Sheriff being judge of the formal validity of the Will, subject to the ordinary appeal (*b*).' This is called Confirmation of a Testament-testamentar (*c*).

(*a*) An erroneous conception had arisen in practice, that no pupil or minor can be confirmed or decerned executor. This has been authoritatively denied; but the office may be conferred also on his curators on his behalf. Johnston *v.* Lowden, 1838; 16 S. 541. See below, § 1894 (*i*).
(*b*) Anderson *v.* Gill, 1850; 20 D. 1326; aff. 1858, 3 Macq. 180; 1860, 23 D. 250. Henry *v.* Reid, 1871; 9 Macph. 503. Wills bearing to be holograph do not need to be proved such. Cranston, petr., 17 R. 410. See above, § 20.
(*c*) 48 Geo. III. c. 49, § 38. 55 Geo. III. c. 184. 4 Geo. IV. c. 98. 2 Juridical Styles, 601.

1894. (2.) *Executor-Dative.*—Where there is no nomination by Will, the Commissaries, on application from anyone interested, 'issued' an edict (*a*) for citing those concerned; and if, on the expiration of the days of citation, there be a competition for the office, it is conferred according to the following order:—1. A universal disponee is preferred (*b*); 2. the next of kin (*c*), 'and that, in the absence of competition, although they should have no beneficial interest in the succession (*d*)'; 3. the widow (*e*), 'or the father and mother taking under the Intestate Moveable Succession Act; and that either alone or in conjunction with next of kin (*f*); or in like manner the husband taking under the Married Women's Property Act of 1881 (*g*)'; 4. a creditor; 5. a legatee (*h*); 6. the Procurator-fiscal of Court (*i*). The person preferred must lodge a full inventory on oath, and must find caution to an amount to be fixed by the Court (*k*). 'The right to the office belongs to those who are next of kin according to the law of the domicile of the deceased (*l*). And the administrator of one who has died domiciled in England or Ireland appointed by the Court of Probate will receive a concurring appointment in Scotland (*m*).'

(*a*) See below, § 1895A, for the modern procedure.
(*b*) 3 Ersk. 9. § 32. M'Gowan *v.* M'Kinlay, 1835; 14 S. 105.
(*c*) See above, § 1861A.
(*d*) Bones *v.* Morrison, 1866; 5 Macph. 240. See M'Pherson *v.* M'Pherson, 1855; 17 D. 358. Webster *v.* Shiress, 1878; 6 R. 102.
(*e*) The widow is really a creditor. L. Dundaff *v.* Craigie, 1612; M. 3843. Inglis *v.* Inglis, 1869; 7 Macph. 435. Compare § 1591, above.
(*f*) *Supra*, § 1861A, 1861B. Muir, petr., 1876; 4 R. 74. Webster *v.* Shiress, 1878; 6 R. 102.
(*g*) 44 and 45 Vict. c. 21, § 6; *supra*, § 1580A. Stewart *v.* Kerr, 1890; 17 R. 707. Campbell *v.* Falconer, 1892; 19 R. 563.
(*h*) This includes the assignee of a beneficiary. M'Pherson *cit.*
(*i*) A judicial factor is more commonly appointed. Where it is necessary to confirm money or moveables, a judicial factor on the estate of a beneficiary or person interested may obtain himself decerned executor-dative, "unless some other person having a title offer to confirm." A. of S. Feb. 13, 1730, § 7. See Johnston *v.* Lowden, 1838; 16 S. 541. Martin *v.* Ferguson's Trs., 1892; 19 R. 474. Pupils and minors may be decerned and confirmed in their own names, or along with their tutors and curators. Reid *v.* Turner, 1830; 8 S. 960. Keith *v.* Archer, 1836; 15 S. 116. Ferguson *v.* Dormer, 1870; 8 Macph. 426. Consuls or vice-consuls of foreign States may obtain administration of the estates of foreigners dying in Her Majesty's dominions, if there be no persons present entitled to administer their estates. 24 and 25 Vict. c. 121, § 4.
(*k*) 4 Geo. IV. c. 98, § 2. 1695, c. 41. See below, § 1895A. 21 and 22 Vict. c. 56, § 7.
(*l*) Mss. Hastings *v.* Hastings' Exrs., 1852; 14 D. 489.
(*m*) 21 and 22 Vict. c. 56, § 14. Stiven *v.* Myers, 1868; 6 Macph. 885. Whiffen *v.* Lees, 1872; 10 Macph. 797. See below, § 1895A.

1895. (3.) *Executor-Creditor.*—Creditors may apply for confirmation where no one appears to undertake the administration. Thus, a creditor of the deceased may apply for a warrant to administer to the extent of his debt. If he hold a liquid document of debt, bond, bill, etc., by the deceased, he may proceed at once to apply for an edict (*a*). If his debt be not liquid, he must proceed to constitute it by charging the nearest of kin (*b*) to confirm as executor to the deceased within twenty days; after the expiration of which time, he may have action and decree, either against the executor, or *contra hæreditatem jacentem*, if the executor should renounce (*c*); and upon this he may apply for an edict. A creditor of the next of kin may also proceed by charge, in like manner, to compel his debtor to confirm; and under the certification of the charge he may apply for an edict, as if he were creditor to the deceased,—a preference being reserved to the creditors of the deceased doing diligence within year and day of the death (*d*). The creditor who applies must swear to the verity of his debt; and the edict must be not only executed in the usual form, but advertised in the *Edinburgh Gazette*; and the administration 'may be, and in practice' is, restricted to the amount of the debt (*e*). Other creditors may 'before confirmation' insist on being conjoined (*f*). 'The diligence of executors-creditors is not excluded by a foreign title of administration unconfirmed in Scotland (*g*), nor by a decree of preference in a multiplepoinding (*h*). But it does not attach subjects specially assigned to any executor-nominate or disponee (*i*). Confirmation as executor-creditor is incompetent after the date of the first deliverance in a sequestration of the deceased debtor's estate (*k*). And confirmation as executor-creditor is of no effect (except to give the creditor a preference for the expenses of such confirmation) in competition with the trustee in any sequestration of the deceased debtor's estate occurring within seven months after his death (*l*).'

(*a*) See *supra*, § 1894 (*k*). (*b*) See below, § 1901.
(*c*) 1695, c. 41. Davidson *v.* Clark, 1867; 6 Macph. 151. Forrest *v.* Forrest, 1863; 1 Macph. 806.
(*d*) 1695, c. 41. See below, § 1934. As to the question whether, since 4 Geo. IV. c. 98, this right of personal creditors lapses where the next of kin dies unconfirmed, see Smith's Trs. *v.* Grant, 1862; 24 D. 1142; 1 M'Laren on Wills, etc., § 1680; and above, § 1891.
(*e*) 4 Geo. IV. c. 98. See Greig *v.* Christie, 1837; 15 S. 697; 2 Ill. 461. Smith's Trs., *cit.*
(*f*) 3 Ersk. 9. § 34. Gibbon *v.* Johnston, 1787; Hume, 276. Lee *v.* Donald, May 17, 1816; F. C. Wilson *v.* Fleming, 1823; 2 S. 430. Willison *v.* Smart, 1840; 3 D. 273. Morris *v.* Stewart, 1852; 14 D. 576 (on death of one of several executors-creditors a debtor is not bound to pay to the others without confirmation of his share).
(*g*) Clarke *v.* Edgar, 1810; Hume, 175. Smith's Trs. *v.* Grant, *cit.*
(*h*) Anderson *v.* Stewart, 1831; 10 S. 49.
(*i*) Bell *v.* Willison, 1831; 9 S. 266. Innerarity *v.* Gilmour, 1840; 2 D. 813.
(*k*) 19 and 20 Vict. c. 79, § 30. (*l*) *Ib.* § 110.

1895A. '*Procedure.*—The forms of procedure in obtaining confirmation are regulated by statute (*a*). Where any person is desirous of being decerned executor of a deceased person, as disponee, next of kin, creditor, or in any other character whatsoever formerly competent, or of having some other person possessed of such character decerned executor to a deceased person (*b*), instead of applying for an edict, he presents to the Sheriff (*c*), formerly to the Commissary, a petition in a statutory form (*d*) for the appointment of an executor. This petition must be subscribed by the petitioner or by his agent (*e*).

'The petition is presented to the Sheriff of the county in which the deceased died domiciled; and in the case of persons dying domiciled furth of Scotland, or without any fixed or known domicile, having personal or moveable property in Scotland, to the Sheriff of Edinburgh (*f*).

'The petition is intimated by affixing a full copy on the door of the Commissary Court-house, or in some conspicuous place of the Court, and on the door of the office of the clerk of Court; and by the Keeper of the Record of Edictal Citations inserting in a book, kept by him for that purpose, the names and designations of the petitioner and of the deceased person, the place and date of his death, and the character in which the petitioner seeks to be decerned executor. These particulars the keeper causes to be printed and published weekly, along with the abstracts of the petitions for general and special services, in a statutory form. To enable the keeper to make such publication, the clerk of Court transmits to him the above particulars; and to enable the clerk to grant the certificate after mentioned, the keeper transmits to the clerk a copy, certified by the keeper, of the printed and published particulars (*g*). The clerk, after receiving the certified copy of the printed and published particulars, certifies on the petition that the same has been intimated and published in terms of the Act, and special intimation of any subsequent petition must be made to all executors already decerned or confirmed (*h*).

'On the expiration of nine days after such certificate, the petition may be called in Court, and an executor decerned: or other procedure may take place according to the forms previously in use in edicts of executry; and decree-dative may be extracted on the expiration of three lawful days after it has been pronounced, but not sooner (*i*).

'Confirmations are in the form, or as nearly as may be, of schedules annexed to the Act; and they have the same force and effect with the like writs formerly in use (*k*).

'When any confirmation of the executor of a person who has died domiciled in Scotland, which includes, besides the personal estate situated in Scotland, personal estate situated in England or Ireland, is produced in the principal Court of Probate in England or Ireland, bearing an authenticated statement that the person died domiciled in Scotland, and a copy of it deposited with the registrar, the confirmation is sealed with the seal of the Probate Court, and returned to the person producing the same; and afterwards has the like force and effect in England or Ireland as if a probate or letters of administration (as the case may be) had been granted by the Court of Probate (*l*).

'In like manner, when any probate or letters of administration granted by the Court of Probate in England or Ireland to the executor or administrator of a person who is therein, or by any note or memorandum written thereon signed by the proper officer, stated to have died domiciled in England or in Ireland, is produced in the Commissary Court of the county of Edinburgh, and a copy of it deposited with the clerk of that Court, the clerk endorses or writes on the grant a certificate in a statutory form; and such probate or letters of administration, being duly stamped, are of the like force and effect, and have the same operation in Scotland, as if a confirmation had been granted by the Court (*m*).

'Persons paying on the faith of the above probates and confirmations are protected in so doing, notwithstanding any defect or circumstance whatsoever affecting their validity (*n*).

'*Small Estates Acts.*—A cheap form of confirmation, carried through by the clerk of Court, was provided for the representatives in whatever character of deceased persons whose estates did not exceed £300, and who died on or after 1st June 1881 (*o*); and it has been extended to estates not exceeding £500, gross heritable and moveable estate, in the case of persons who have died on or after 1st August 1894 (*p*).'

(*a*) 21 and 22 Vict. c. 56. A. S. March 19, 1859. A. S. January 15, 1890.

(*b*) Nothing in the Act is to alter or affect the course of procedure formerly in use before the Commissaries in confirmation of executors-nominate (§ 7).

(*c*) 39 and 40 Vict. c. 70, § 35.

(*d*) The form in 39 and 40 Vict. c. 70, sched. A, has superseded that in the schedule of the 1858 Act.

(*e*) 21 and 22 Vict. c. 56, § 2. (*f*) *Ib.* § 3, 8.

(*g*) *Ib.* § 4. See A. S. March 19, 1859, § 1–3.

(*h*) *Ib.* § 4. See the A. S. of 1859, § 4. 39 and 40 Vict. c. 70, § 44.

(*i*) *Ib.* § 5. (*k*) *Ib.* § 10.

(*l*) *Ib.* § 12, 13. The English Court would not seal an eik or additional confirmation. In the goods of Wingate, 2 S. & T. 625. In the goods of Hutchison, 3 S. & T. 165; 32 L. J. Pr. 167; but the enactment quoted in the text was extended to these grants by 39 and 40 Vict. c. 70, § 42. See below, § 1898A.

(*m*) *Ib.* § 14. (*n*) 22 and 23 Vict. c. 30.

(*o*) 38 and 39 Vict. c. 41 (Intestates' Widows and Children (Scotland) Act, 1875). 39 and 40 Vict. c. 24 (Small Testate Estates (Scotland) Act, 1876). 39 and 40 Vict. c. 70 (Sheriff Courts Act, 1876). 44 Vict. c. 12, § 34–36 (Customs and Inland Revenue Act, 1881). The two earlier Acts may be applied to the estates of persons dying before June 1, 1881, and where the estate is under £150.

(*p*) 57 and 58 Vict. c. 30, § 16.

1896. (4.) *Double Confirmation.*—Where one is to confirm to a person who has died unconfirmed, a double confirmation is necessary. As to testate succession, the executor (or assignee) of an executor-nominate, who has died without confirming, confirms first to the executor-nominate deceased, from whom he derives his title to take up the executry of the first defunct; giving up in his inventory the right and benefit which the deceased executor-nominate had in the first defunct's estate, and which he is to take as being in his place. And then, in the second place, he confirms to the original defunct as disponee or executor-creditor, giving up in inventory the debts or effects to which he means to make up a title. As to intestate succession, it is now in this respect on the same footing with the testate; but as the words of the statute give to such second executor or representative a right to confirm "in the same manner as the next of kin are entitled to be confirmed immediately on the intestate's death," it is, on this footing, the practice to confirm at once (*a*).

(*a*) 4 Geo. IV. c. 98, § 1. Nicoll *v.* Wilson, 1856; 18 D. 1000.

1897. (5.) *Confirmation ad Omissa.*—'Every person applying for confirmation, except executors-creditors, is bound to confirm the whole moveable estate of the deceased person known at the time; a partial confirmation being unavailing (*a*). But' if the whole succession be not given up in the inventory, the executor may have the omission corrected (*b*). Or anyone interested may apply, either to have the executor compelled to confirm the omission, or himself to have an edict to confirm it (*c*).

(*a*) 44 Geo. III. c. 98, § 23. 48 Geo. III. c. 149, § 3, 4, 38. 21 and 22 Vict. c. 56. Buchanan *v.* Royal Bank, 1842; 5 D. 211. Smith's Trs. *v.* Grant, *supra*, § 1895. Williamson *v.* Fraser, 1832; 11 S. 7. Brown *v.* Millar, 1853; 16 D. 225. Elder *v.* Watson, 1859; 21 D. 1122. Taylor *v.* Forbes & Co., 1827; 5 S. 785; rev. 4 W. & S. 444.

(*b*) 48 Geo. III. c. 149, § 38–42. 4 Geo. IV. c. 98, § 3.

(*c*) 3 Ersk. 9. § 36, 37. Lee *v.* Donald, May 17, 1816; F. C. Smith *v.* Smith, 1880; 7 R. 1013.

1898. '**Death Duties.**—There are two kinds of taxes charged on property at or about the period of the death of the person owning it or having some other interest in it—one kind (inventory or probate duty and estate duty) charged with reference to what the deceased owned or could dispose of, and varying with the amount of the estate; and the other kind (legacy duty and succession duty) charged with reference to what the deceased's successors receive as a benefit from him, and varying with their relationship to him, as well as with the amount of the estate. The legacy duty has been noticed already (*a*); the other principal duties are here shortly treated of.'

Inventory or Probate Duty.—The duties are regulated by the several Stamp Acts, aided by the statute relative to confirmations (*b*); and payment of them is secured by penalties (*c*), and by declarations of the inefficacy of the executor's title, if not duly paid. 'Assets situated abroad are not liable (*d*), nor are assets which are neither *in bonis* of the deceased nor disposable by him (*e*).' These duties are necessarily levied in a manner exceedingly inconvenient. The duty 'was' paid in the first place on the whole succession (*f*), without deduction of debts; a return being given on proof of *all* the debts (*g*) being paid; but not for funeral expenses (*h*). 'It is now, however, competent to deduct debts and funeral expenses in the inventory, and to pay duty only on the net value of the estate (*i*).' The true value only is required to be stated, and there are provisions for relief or addition, if the estimate shall have been made too high or too low. With certain precautions, power may be given to proceed in recovering the funds; and if there should be any innocent omission, an additional inventory may be lodged (*k*); but it must specify the amount of the whole succession, and must 'formerly' be written on a stamp corresponding to the whole amount; the Solicitor of Stamps being bound to repay the original duty thus twice paid (*l*). In the case above stated of a double confirmation, duties are paid on the two inventories as on two confirmations. This is the settled rule in testate succession; and it would seem also the correct rule in intestate under the statute. 'Inventory duty, when still appropriate, is charged, under the Customs and Inland Revenue Acts, 1881 and 1889, on all donations *inter vivos* made within twelve months of death, and on all donations *mortis causâ*; on all property gratuitously invested in the name of the owner and another so that it passes to that other on the owner's death; and on all property conveyed by gratuitous settlement under reservation of a liferent, or of a power to revoke and resume the property (*m*).'

(*a*) Above, § 1887.

(*b*) 48 Geo. III. c. 149. 55 Geo. III. c. 184. 4 Geo. IV. c. 98. See 23 and 24 Vict. c. 15, § 6. 23 and 24 Vict. c. 80, § 1; and 31 and 32 Vict. c. 101, § 117, etc., as to heritable securities; above, § 910A, 1485, 1895A.

(*c*) L. Adv. *v.* Meiklam, 1860; 23 D. 57.

(*d*) See L. Adv. *v.* Laidlay's Trs., 1889; 16 R. 959; rev. 1890, 17 R. H. L. 67; 15 App. Ca. 468. Comp. below, § 1898A (*h*).

(*e*) 23 Vict. c. 15, § 4. See L. Adv. *v.* Bogie, 1893; 20 R. 429; aff. 1894, 21 R. H. L. 6; A. C. 83. Drake *v.* Att.-Gen., 1840; 10 Cl. & F. 257.

(*f*) It is due on what the executor takes as personal, *e.g.* on heritable securities or heritage acquired by tutors for a pupil out of the savings of his income. L. Adv. *v.* Anstruther, 1850; 13 D. 450.

(*g*) As to the questions what provisions settled by marriage-contract are debts entitling to this drawback, see L. Adv. *v.* Hagart's Exrs., 1870; 9 Macph. 358; 1872, 10 Macph. H. L. 62. Moir's Trs. *v.* L. Adv., 1874; 1 R. 345. Marshall's Exrs. *v.* L. Adv., 1874; 1 R. 847. But see the stricter provisions of 57 and 58 Vict. c. 30, § 7, as to debts allowed against estate duty; below, § 1898A.

(*h*) 55 Geo. III. c. 184, § 51. See Regulations of Stamp Commissioners, art. 2 and 3; 2 Juridical Styles, 605 (863, 5th ed.).

(*i*) 44 Vict. c. 12, § 28.

(*k*) Brown *v.* Miller's Trs., 1853; 16 D. 225. Above, § 1897.

(*l*) 48 Geo. III. c. 149, § 40. See 2 Jur. Styles, 602 (874, 5th ed.). 4 Geo. IV. c. 98. 16 and 17 Vict. c. 59, § 8.

(*m*) 44 Vict. c. 12, § 38. 52 Vict. c. 7, § 11 (1). L. Adv. *v.* Galloway, 1884; 11 R. 541. 2 Jur. Styles, 860, 5th ed. Crossman *v.* The Queen, 18 Q. B. D. 256. L. Adv. *v.* Wilson, 1894; 21 R. 997. As to absolute transfer avoiding duty, see L. Adv. *v.* M'Court, 1893; 20 R. 488.

1898A. '*Estate Duties* (1894).—In the case of persons dying after 1st August 1894 there is payable (in lieu of inventory or probate duty, a tax on the title of the administrator) a stamp duty called *estate duty*, a tax on the principal value of all property, heritable or moveable, real or personal, which passes on the death (*a*). Property passing is not limited to what was *in bonis* of the deceased, but it includes, besides the deceased's own property, property of which he was competent to dispose (*b*) (including an entailed estate in possession of the heir or institute (*c*)), donations *mortis causâ*, gifts *inter vivos* made within twelve months of death or of which possession was not at once taken to the exclusion of the deceased, investments by the deceased on joint title, so that an interest passes by survivorship, liferents to the deceased created by himself, policies on his life kept up for a donee's benefit (*d*), and annuities (other than a single annuity of £25 or less) which the deceased provided so that a benefit accrued on his death (*e*). Property subject to terce or courtesy is not exempt (*f*). The date when the property passes may be the death, or a period ascertainable only with reference to it (*g*). Immoveable property out of the United Kingdom is exempt, as is moveable property abroad when the deceased owned it and was domiciled abroad (*h*). The exemptions also include property held by the deceased in trust (*i*), *bonâ fide* purchases (*k*), the property of common seamen, marines, or soldiers dying in their service, and sums under £100 payable without representation being required (*l*).

'All classes of property passing on the death are aggregated (*m*), and the duty is levied on a graduated scale, in respect of the principal value, after funeral expenses, debts, and incumbrances have been deducted from the moveable and heritable estates—the debts and incumbrances being limited to those created for a full consideration in money or money's worth (*n*). The scale ranges from 1 per cent. on estates valued between £100 and £500, to 8 per cent. on estates valued over £1,000,000 (*o*).

'Where property subject to estate duty is "settled," a further estate duty, called *settlement estate duty*, at 1 per cent., is levied on it in certain cases, and the settled estate is thereupon relieved of estate duty on the death of the person benefited by the settlement, and till the death of a person competent to dispose of the estate (*p*) and *sui juris* (*q*).

'An estate not exceeding £1000 net value, when property settled otherwise than by the deceased's Will is not reckoned, may be relieved from the consequences of aggregation with other property passing on the death; and on estates not exceeding £500 gross the duty may be much lightened (*r*). The duty on heritable property may be spread over eight years, on interest being added (*s*), and that property must, for the purpose of determining the aggregate estate and the rate of duty, be contained or referred to in an account annexed to the inventory of moveable estate (*t*).'

(*a*) 57 and 58 Vict. c. 30 (Finance Act, 1894), § 1; amended by 61 and 62 Vict. c. 10.

(*b*) The Act, § 2 (1) (*a*).

(*c*) The Act, § 23 (15).

(*d*) The Act, § 2 (1) (*c*). 44 and 45 Vict. c. 12, § 38. 52 and 53 Vict. c. 7, § 11. Contrast L. Adv. *v.* M'Court, 1893, 20 R. 488, with Att.-Gen. *v.* Booth, 1894; 63 L. J. Q. B. 356; Att.-Gen. *v.* Gosling, 1892; Q. B. 545 (reservation); and L. Adv. *v.* Wilson, 1894; 21 R. 997 (do.).

(*e*) The Act, § 2 (1) (*d*), 15 (1).

(*f*) The Act, § 23 (19), 2 (1) (*b*).

(*g*) The Act, § 22 (1) (*l*).

(*h*) The Act, § 2 (2). L. Adv. *v.* Thomson, *cit.* § 1887. Wallace, Campbell, and Duncan, *cit.* § 1898c (*a*).

(*i*) The Act, § 2 (3).

(*k*) The Act, § 3.

(*l*) The Act, § 8.

(*m*) The Act, § 4.

(*n*) The Act, § 7; cf. 44 Vict. c. 12, § 28 (debts and funeral expenses). The Act, § 23 (10) (incumbrances).

(*o*) The Act, § 17.

(*p*) The Act, § 5, 22 (1) (*h*) (*i*). 45 and 46 Vict. c. 38, § 2 (1).

(*q*) 61 and 62 Vict. c. 10, § 13.

(*r*) The Act, § 16.

(*s*) The Act, § 6 (8).

(*t*) The Act, § 6 (2), 4.

1898B. '*Collection.*—Inventories and relative testamentary writings may be given up and recorded in, and confirmations may be granted and issued by, any Court to which it is competent to apply in virtue of the provisions of the Act for the appointment of an executor-dative to the deceased (*a*). It is competent to include in the inventory of the estate of any person who has died domiciled in Scotland, any personal estate or effects of the deceased situated in England or in Ireland, or both; provided that the person applying for confirmation shall state in his affidavit that the deceased died domiciled in Scotland; and also that the value of the personal estate and effects in England or Ireland respectively shall be separately stated in such inventory, and such inventory shall be impressed with a stamp corresponding to the entire value of the estate and effects included therein, wheresoever situated within the United Kingdom (*b*). Whether estate is personal or not is determined by the law of its *situs* (*c*). In any of the cases where the deceased person shall be stated in or upon the probate of letters of administration to have been domiciled in England or in Ireland, such probate or letters of administration are, for the purpose of securing the payment of the stamp duties, to be deemed as being granted for the whole of the personal and moveable estate and effects of the deceased in the United Kingdom, within the meaning of the Stamp Acts, and the affidavit or inventory required in England and Ireland and in Scotland respectively to precede the grant of probate or confirmation shall include the whole personal and moveable estate of the deceased person in the United Kingdom, and the value thereof (*d*). For granting relief where too high a stamp duty has been paid on any probate or letters of administration or inventory, the provisions of the Acts relating to probates and letters of administration granted in England and in Ireland, and relating to inventories in Scotland, apply to the probates and letters of administration, and to the inventories under the Act of 1858 (*e*).

'Property held by collective bodies, whether corporate or unincorporate, is now subject to a tax of 5 per cent. on the annual value, in lieu of the probate, succession, and legacy duties which it formerly escaped (*f*).'

(*a*) 21 and 22 Vict. c. 56, § 8.

(*b*) *Ib.* § 9. 39 and 40 Vict. c. 70, § 41. See above, § 1895A (*l*). Lady Hawarden *v.* Dunlop, 2 S. & T. 340; 31 L. J. Pr. 17.

(*c*) Monteith *v.* Monteith's Trs., 1882; 9 R. 982. Above, § 1550.

(*d*) *Ib.* § 1. See above, 1895A, 1897. (*e*) *Ib.* § 16.

(*f*) 48 and 49 Vict. c. 51, § 11. Soc. of Writers to the Signet *v.* Comrs. of Inland Rev., 1886; 14 R. 34. Glasgow Tailors Incorp. *v.* Comrs. of Inland Rev., 1887; 14 R. 729.

1898C. '*Succession Duty.* — A succession duty is now levied on all beneficial interest in property, real or personal, accruing to any party upon the death, which shall have taken place after 19th May 1853, of any person dying domiciled within the United Kingdom (*a*); and on every increase of benefit accruing to any person after that day, by the determination of any charge on real or personal property, where such charge is determinable only by reference to death. Legacies payable from or charged on heritable estate bear this duty instead of legacy duty as formerly (*b*). The rate of this duty varies according to the degree of consanguinity, or the absence of consanguinity, between the party becoming beneficially entitled and the party from whom the interest is derived, and varies according to the same scale as the legacy duty (*c*), with the addition, in the case of heritable estate and when no estate duty is payable (*d*), (1) where the successor is a lineal ascendant or descendant, of ½ per cent., and (2) in other cases of 1½ per cent. duty; and there are the like exemptions of estates under £100, of estates not over £1000, and of descendants and ascendants, as in the case of legacy duty (*e*). This duty is not chargeable in *addition* to that under the Legacy Duty Acts; and successions of less than £20 value are not relieved from it (*f*), though, if the whole successions derived from the same predecessor upon any death do not amount to £100 in value, they are not chargeable (*g*). The husband or wife of the predecessor is not chargeable with duty (*h*), and a successor whose spouse is more nearly related to the predecessor than himself is charged with respect to the nearer relationship (*i*). Where the succession duty has become payable, notice must be given of it, within such period as the Act directs, to the Commissioners of Inland Revenue, under a heavy penalty in case of neglect; and a like penalty is payable every month during which the neglect continues (*k*). This duty, when charged in respect of heritable estate, was payable on the income, capitalised as an annuity for the remainder of the successor's life; but now, when the successor is competent to dispose of such estate, or it is entailed, the duty is payable on the capital value (*l*) as has been the rule with other kinds of estate.

'A stamp duty in lieu of succession, legacy, and probate duties is laid on the property of bodies incorporated and unincorporated (*m*).'

(*a*) This proposition as to domicile is subject to some qualifications and exceptions. See Dicey on Domicile, 317 sqq. Littledale's Trs. *v.* L. Adv., 1882; 10 R. 226. So succession duty is not payable on moveable estate situated in this country and passing under the Will of one domiciled abroad. Wallace *v.* Att.-Gen., L. R. 1 Ch. 1; 35 L. J. Ch. 124. Lyall *v.* Lyall, 42 L. J. Ch. 195. But on the ceasing of an annuity payable under such a settlement out of funds directed to be invested in this country, succession duty is due on the increase of benefit thereby accruing to the persons interested next in order. Att.-Gen. *v.* Campbell, 41 L. J. Ch. 611 (H. L.). Duncan's Tr. *v.* M'Cracken, 1888; 15 R. 638. See above, § 1887.

(*b*) 51 Vict. c. 8, § 21 (2). See as to conversion above, § 1493. L. Adv. *v.* Blackburn's Trs., 1847; 10 D. 166. L. Adv. *v.* Williamson, 1840; 13 D. 456; 10 Cl. & F. 1; 2 Bell's App. 89. L. Adv. *v.* Smith, 1852; 24 S. Jur. 285; aff. 1854, 1 Macq. 760. Att.-Gen. *v.* Mangles, 5 M. & W. 120. Att.-Gen. *v.* Simcox, 1 Ex. 749. Hobson *v.* Weale, 8 Ex. 368.

(*c*) Above, § 1887. (*d*) Above, § 1898A.

(*e*) Above, § 1887. (*f*) 52 Vict. c. 7, § 10 (2).

(*g*) 16 and 17 Vict. c. 51, § 18.

(*h*) *Ib.* § 18, applying 55 Geo. III. c. 184, sched., part 3.

(*i*) *Ib.* § 11.

(*k*) 16 and 17 Vict. c. 51 (Succession Duty Act), § 44, 46. 51 and 52 Vict. c. 8, § 21, 22. On the construction of this Act (with which are incorporated 36 Geo. III. c. 52, § 10–12, 14, 23), see Brown *v.* L. Adv., 1852; 24 S. Jur. 565; 1 Macq. 79. L. Adv. *v.* Roberts' Trs., 1857; 20 D. 449. L. Adv. *v.* L. Saltoun, 1858; 21 D. 124; rev. 1860, 3 Macq. 659 (heirs of entail). L. Adv. *v.* M'Culloch, 1895; 22 R. 356 (do.). L. Adv. *v.* Gordon, 1872; 10 Macph. 1015 (do.). L. Adv. *v.* Macdonald, 1862; 24 D. 1175. L. Adv. *v.* E. Fife, 1864; 3 Macph. 1172; 1866, 5 Macph. 166. L. Adv. *v.* Stevenson, 1866; 4 Macph. 322; aff. 1869, 7 Macph. H. L. 1. L. Adv. *v.* E. Glasgow, 1875; 2 R. 317. L. Adv. *v.* E. Zetland, 1876; 4 R. 199; aff. 1878, 5 R. H. L. 51. L. Adv. *v.* M'Kersies, 1881; 19 S. L. R. 438 (reservation). L. Adv. *v.* M. Ailsa, 1881; 9 R. 40 (woods). L. Adv. *v.* E. Fife, 1883; 11 R. 222. L. Adv. *v.* Murray Graham, 1884; 12 R. 318. L. Adv. *v.* Jamieson, 1886; 13 R. 737. L. Adv. *v.* D. Buccleuch, 1888; 15 R. 33 (unlet shootings liable). L. Adv. *v.* Robertson, 1895; 22 R. 568 (insurance policy assigned to and kept up by daughter). Att.-Gen. *v.* Hallet, 2 H. & N. 369. Att.-Gen. *v.* L. Middleton, 3 H. & N. 125. Att.-Gen. *v.* Sibthorp, *ib.* 424. *In re* Elwes, *ib.* 719. Att.-Gen. *v.* Baker, 4 H. & N. 10. Att.-Gen. *v.* Braybrooke, 5 H. & N. 448. Att.-Gen. *v.* Gell, 3 H. & C. 615. Att.-Gen. *v.* Gardner, 1 H. & C. 639. L. Braybrooke *v.* Att.-Gen., 9 H. L. Ca. 150. Att.-Gen. *v.* Upton, L. R. 1 Ex. 224; 35 L. J. Ex. 138. Att.-Gen. *v.* E. Sefton, 11 H. L. Ca. 257. Att.-Gen. *v.* Smythe, 9 H. L. Ca. 498. Att.-Gen. *v.* Littledale, 40 L. J. Ex. 241 (H. L.).

(*l*) 57 and 58 Vict. c. 30, § 18, 23 (15).

(*m*) 48 and 49 Vict. c. 51, § 11 sqq. See cases in § 1898B (*f*).

1899. Office, Liabilities, and Duties of an Executor. — Every executor is a trustee (*a*), though the executor-creditor, who restricts his confirmation to the amount of the debt due to him, is so only in so far as he shall be wanting in due diligence, or shall have intromitted with more than the amount of his debt. 'Co-executors act by the resolution of the majority (*b*).

'But while an executor might be called a trustee, *i.e.* to the effect of administering the estate confirmed and making it forthcoming to all having interest, the phraseology naturally used to enforce the distinction between the modern and the old law, which permitted an executor to appropriate to himself the whole or part of the goods of the deceased, is now less appropriate. To certain effects an executor is not a trustee, but rather a representative of the deceased, and as such debtor *secundum vires inventarii* to creditors, and even to legatees and next of kin. So debts and legacies due by him fall under the negative prescription, and creditors may acquire preferences against him by diligence (*c*). But the mere office of executor, and even the administration of the estate for some time for his own or the beneficiaries' interest, is not enough to make him liable, as a trustee for creditors, to account to them for more than the amount of the estate at the date of the testator's death (*d*).'

The executor is the person entitled to sue the debtors of the estate (*e*); and although the rights of the wife and of the children vest *ipso jure*, they have no direct action against the debtors to the deceased, but only against the executor (*f*). The liability of a cautioner for an executor-dative is limited to the sum in the inventory (*g*); and he cannot, in order to relieve himself of his obligation, interrupt the administration, unless by showing maladministration, or that the executor is *vergens ad inopiam* (*h*). 'Executors may be superseded by the appointment of a judicial factor, not on the ground merely that their personal interests in some respects conflict with their duty as executors, but if they have deliberately taken up a position inconsistent with the interest of the executry estate (*i*).'

(*a*) Thomson *v.* Thin's Crs., 1675; M. 5939; 2 Ill. 461. Spalding *v.* Farquharson, May 15, 1811; F. C. Pearson *v.* Wright, 1679; M. 3497. A. S., Nov. 14, 1679. Pearson *v.* Grierson, 1825; 4 S. 205.

(*b*) Mackenzies *v.* Mackenzie, 1886; 13 R. 507. **Scott** *v.* **Craig's Reprs.**, 1897; 24 R. 462. See below, § 1998 (*a*).

(*c*) Globe Ins. Co. *v.* Mackenzie, etc. (Scott's Trs.), 1849; 11 D. 618; aff. 1850, 7 Bell's App. 296. Jamieson *v.* Clark, 1872; 10 Macph. 399. See below, § 1900 (*b*); above, § 1870, 1895; below, § 1934. When executors are entrusted with duties involving continuing management, they are trustees in every sense, and may exercise the powers conferred on trustees by statute, *e.g.* of assumption. Ainslie *v.* Ainslie, 1886; 14 R. 209.

(*d*) Stewart's Tr. *v.* Stewart's Execx., 1896; 23 R. 739.

(*e*) An executor-dative or nominate has a title to sue without being confirmed, but he must be confirmed before extract. Stevenson *v.* M'Laren, 1800; Hume, 171. Chalmers' Trs. *v.* Watson, 1860; 22 D. 1060. Bones *v.* Morrison, 1866; 5 Macph. 240. Hinton *v.* Connell's Trs., 1883; 10 R. 1110. See Malcolm *v.* Dick, 1866; 5 Macph. 18. Fyffe *v.* Fergusson, 1842; 4 D. 1482. See above, § 1892. The rule applies to executors-creditors. Maitland *v.* Cockerell, 1827; 6 S. 109. Dickson *v.* Barbour, 1828; 6 S. 856. See as to suing and charging for debts valued in inventory at less than full amount, Brown *v.* Miller's Exrs., 1853; 16 D. 225.

(*f*) M'Kie *v.* Dunbar, 1628; M. 1788. See White *v.* Finlay, 1861; 24 D. 38, 47 (*per* L. Neaves and L. J.-C. Inglis).

(*g*) Napier *v.* Menzies, 1740; M. 3849; 2 Ill. 462. Murdoch *v.* M'Hardy, 1826; 4 S. 479.
(*h*) Simpson and Morrison *v.* Gardner, 1826; 4 S. 487.
(*i*) Birnie *v.* Christie, 1891; 19 R. 334.

1900. The executor as trustee is liable,—1. For his actual intromissions. 2. For the amount of the funds in the inventory, 'but not *ultra fines inventarii* (*a*)'; discharging himself by showing due diligence (*b*),—viz. denouncing the debtor, or taking decree, and showing reasonable evidence of insolvency. 3. For the due and safe investment of the funds. But he is not liable for money lost by having been left in the bank where the deceased had placed it (*c*). 4. For interest on sums bearing interest at the death; on moveables from the expiration of six months after the death; and on debts from a year after the death (*d*). 5. The executry fund is a trust fund, which may be vindicated by those having interest against the private creditors of the executor, if it be distinguishable.

The rules by which payment of debts by the executor is regulated are these:—The executor is bound to pay to the creditors on decree only (*e*). He cannot be compelled to pay to anyone till the expiration of six months from the death (*f*). He is liable to personal action if he has recovered funds; and must pay to all personal creditors of the deceased equally who have cited him 'even beyond the six months (*g*),' while the funds are still undistributed (*h*). He may be compelled by personal action to pay, and is safe in paying, *primo venienti*, after the six months (*i*). 'He is not, however, entitled to pay beneficiaries till he has provided for payment of all debts; and he must pay the debts according to the order of their legal preference (*k*).' Creditors of the deceased may proceed directly with diligence against the funds, and by their diligence may, 'at any time while funds remain in the executor's hands,' acquire preferences (*l*). The executor's confirmation, if he be also a creditor, is a diligence under which he may pay himself by retention (*m*). There are certain debts preferable, as being privileged (*n*). The creditors of the deceased have a preference over those of the next of kin, provided they do diligence within a year (*o*). The creditors of the next of kin may claim or do diligence, and after a year will be entitled to rank on the funds *pari passu* with the creditors of the deceased.

(*a*) Renton *v.* Renton, 1851; 14 D. 35. § 1922, *infra*.
(*b*) As to liability for negligence in recovering debts, see Forman *v.* Burns, 1853; 16 D. 362.
(*c*) Gibb *v.* Gibb, 1769; M. 16,363. Pearson *v.* Grierson, *supra*, § 1899 (*a*). See 2 M'Laren, Wills and Succn. 305, and Forman *v.* Burns, *cit.*
(*d*) See Howat's Trs. *v.* Howat, 1838; 16 S. 627; where it is explained that this rule does not exempt the executor from paying interest on sums in his hands, but throws on him after a year the burden of showing that he has used due diligence to recover the debts.
(*e*) Johnston *v.* Lady Kincaid, 1664; M. 3853; 2 Ill. 463. But he must not put creditors to unnecessary expense to constitute their debts. M'Gaan *v.* M'Gaan's Trs., 1883; 11 R. 249. Jackson's Trs. *v.* Black, 1832; 10 S. 597. Crawford, *infra* (*l*). 30 and 31 Vict. c. 97, § 2.
(*f*) A. S., Feb. 28, 1662; 2 Ill. 463. See 1654, c. 16 and 18. 2 Bell's Com. 86 sqq.
(*g*) Globe Ins. Co. *v.* Scott's Trs., 1849; 11 D. 618; aff. 1850, 7 Bell's App. 296.
(*h*) Russell *v.* Simes, 1791; Bell's Ca. 217. See Gray *v.* Callander, 1723; M. 3140. Græme *v.* Murray, 1738; M. 3141. M'Dowall *v.* M'Dowall, 1742; Elch. *Executor*, 9. Johnston's Crs. *v.* Dickieson, 1742; Elch. *Executor*, 10.
(*i*) Alison *v.* E. Dundonald's Trs., 1793; M. 16,211. Gardner *v.* Pearson, Nov. 28, 1810; F. C. More's Exrs. *v.* Malcolm, 1835; 13 S. 313.
(*k*) Lamond's Trs., 1871; 9 Macph. 662. Cf. Stewart's Trs., 1871; 9 Macph. 810.
(*l*) Atkinson *v.* Learmonth, 1808; M. *Serv. and Conf.* Apx. 3. Crawford *v.* Cook, 1833; 11 S. 406. Swayne *v.* Fife Bkg. Co., 1822; 1 S. 517. Globe Ins. Co. *v.* Scott's Exrs., *cit.*
(*m*) L. Napier *v.* Menzies, 1740; M. 2099. M'Dowall *v.* M'Dowall, 1744; M. 10,008. Murdoch *v.* M'Kirdy, 1826; 4 S. 479. M'Leod *v.* Wilson, 1837; 15 S. 1043. See Elder *v.* Watson, 1859; 21 D. 1122. 3 Stair, 8. § 73. 3 Ersk. 4. § 23. 2 Bell's Com. 84.
(*n*) See above, § 1402 et seq.
(*o*) See below, § 1933 et seq. 2 Bell's Com. 89 (85, M'L.'s ed.).

1901. Charge to Confirm.—Analogous to the charge to enter heir in heritage (*a*), there has been introduced a mode of reaching the *hæreditas jacens* in moveables by a similar charge with certification.

(*a*) See above, § 1854 et seq.

1902. This remedy is competent to the creditors of the defunct, and to the creditors of the next of kin. If the person charged neither renounce nor confirm within twenty days, he will incur a passive title. If he renounce, the creditors may have decree *cognitionis causâ*, and proceed against the *hæreditas jacens* (*a*).

(*a*) 1695, c. 41; 2 Ill. 465. 3 Ersk. 9. § 35. See below, § 1925. One who fails to renounce may still renounce in an action against him as a vitious intromitter, but is liable for expenses. Davidson *v.* Clark, 1867; 6 Macph. 151.

IV. HEIRSHIP MOVEABLES.

1903. Who entitled.—The heir of a baron or burgess, though excluded from the moveable succession where there are relations of the same decree who have right as executors, 'had' right to the best of certain moveables, that he 'might' not enter to his predecessor's dwelling-house quite dismantled by the executors (*a*). 'But since 1868 the right to heirship moveables is abolished (*b*).'

(*a*) Leg. Burg. c. 126. 1474, c. 54; 2 Acta Parl. 107, c. 8. Balfour, Pract. 234. Hope, Min. Pract. Apx. 3. Stair, 5. § 7, 9 et seq., and 3. 6. § 8, 9. 3 Ersk. 8. § 17.
(*b*) 31 and 32 Vict. c. 101, § 160.

1904. A Baron in this question, 'was' any feudal proprietor who at his death is vest and seised in lands, houses (whether burgage or not), or annualrents forth of land (*a*). But if divested (*b*), or if he 'held' a mere liferent (*c*) or conjunct fee (*d*), or if he 'held' only a personal right to land, he 'was' not held to be a baron in this sense (*e*).

(*a*) Scrymgeour *v.* Murrays, 1664; M. 5396; 2 Ill. 465. Jameson *v.* Waugh, 1678; M. 5398. Arbuthnot *v.* Arbuthnot, 1758; 5 B. Sup. 356. Todrig *v.* Primrose, 1615; M. 5390. Irvine *v.* Irvines, 1744; M. 2304.
(*b*) Straton *v.* Chirnside, 1636; M. 5395. See Arbuthnot, *supra* (*a*).
(*c*) Scott *v.* Muirhead, 1668; M. 5396.
(*d*) Monro *v.* Monro, 1730; M. 5400.
(*e*) Montgomery *v.* Stewart, 1666; M. 5396. Seaton *v.* Seaton, 1674; M. 5397. Cochran *v.* Dss. Hamilton, 1685; M. 5398. Cumming *v.* Cumming, 1698; M. 5399.

1905. A Burgess must be either infeft in a burgage tenement (*a*), or be a trading burgess, in order to entitle his heir to heirship moveables (*b*).

(*a*) Arbuthnot, *supra*, § 1904 (*a*).
(*b*) Dunbar *v.* Leslie 1628; M. 5392; 2 Ill. 466. Cumming, *supra*, § 1904 (*e*).

1906. Heirship moveables 'might' be claimed by the heir, although the land 'was' settled on another (*a*). Heirs-portioners (contrary to Erskine's opinion) 'divided' the heirship moveables (*b*). If the heir 'renounced' heirship moveables they 'went' to the executor (*c*).

(*a*) Crawford *v.* Crawford, 1543; M. 5389; 2 Ill. 466.
(*b*) Cruickshanks *v.* Cruickshanks, 1801; M. *Heir Portioner*, Apx. 2; 2 Ill. 466. 3 Ersk. 8. § 17.
(*c*) Pollock *v.* Pollock, 1667; M. 5403.

1907. Subjects of Heirship 'were' moveables appropriated to the person, and insight and outsight plenishing (*a*). It 'was' held that heirship 'was' not limited to the moveables left upon the lands in which the deceased was infeft (*b*); that the heir 'was' entitled not to the furniture of the *best* house, but to the *best* articles of furniture in *every* house belonging to the deceased (*c*); that farm stock, raised or fed for sale, 'was' not heirship (*d*); that in fixing the *jus relictæ*, the heirship moveables 'were' not to be deducted from the goods in communion (*e*).

(*a*) See the lists in the authorities cited, *supra*, § 1903. Knolls *v.* Halkerston, 1489; M. 5385; 2 Ill. 466. Brown *v.* Brown, 1527; M. 5386. Reid *v.* Thomson, 1611; M. 5387. A. *v.* B., 1630; M. 14,386. Hepburn *v.* Skirving 1793; M. 5387. Kincaid *v.* ——, 1650; 1 B. Sup. 458. E. Leven *v.* Montgomery, 1683; M. 5803. Leith *v.* Leith, 1863; 1 Macph. 949.
(*b*) Darg *v.* Darg, Dec. 23, 1808; F. C.
(*c*) L. Drummond *v.* Lady D., 1575; M. 5386.
(*d*) Darg, *supra* (*b*).
(*e*) Lindsay *v.* Carlyle, 1727; M. 5406; correcting Goodlet *v.* Nairn, 1668, M. 5404; and Stevenson *v.* Paul, 1680, M. 5405. See also Kilfauns *v.* Lyon, 1734; M. 11,356.

1908. The heir's right to heirship moveables 'was' protected by the law of deathbed.

1909. Vesting. — Heirship moveables 'vested' in the heir by mere possession, without the necessity of service. If not taken possession of, they 'went' to the heir of the person first deceasing (*a*).

(*a*) 3 Ersk. 8. § 77.

V. COLLATION.

1910. Nature of Collation.—Although heritage goes to the heir, and moveables to the next of kin, the heir (provided he is also one of the next of kin) may throw that heritage to which he succeeds as heir into the common stock, and insist for an equal share of the aggregate with the other next of kin. This is called "Collation." The heir is in some cases, '*e.g.* if the right of his brothers and sisters to legitim or dead's part be discharged or excluded,' entitled to claim a share without collation (*a*). 'The heir must collate as a condition of claiming legitim or executry (*b*).'

(*a*) 3 Stair, 4. § 24, and 5. § 9. 3 Ersk. 9. § 3. Murray *v.* Murray, 1678; M. 2372; 2 Ill. 467.
(*b*) Law *v.* Law, 1553; M. 2365. Murray, *cit.* Sinclair *v.* Sinclair, 1678; M. 8188. See L. Panmure *v.* Crokat, 1856; 18 D. 703, 713. Fraser, H. & W. 1045 sqq. M'Laren on Wills, etc. (3rd ed.), p. 150. Above, § 1590.

1911. Persons entitled to Collate.—This right belongs to the heir *ab intestato*, only as he is one of the next of kin, where there is both a heritable and a moveable estate. But if the heir be not one of the next of kin (as where a grandson is heir, and the executors are his uncles and aunts), he is not entitled 'at common law' to collate (*a*). If the privilege be renounced by the heir, his representatives cannot demand it in the face of such repudiation (*b*); 'and if he dies without collating, they cannot share in the moveable estate unless they can collate (*c*).' If the heir be sole executor, he is not bound to collate with the widow (*d*). A collateral heir, as well as a direct descendant, is entitled to collate (*e*). There is no collation in heritage amongst heirs-portioners 'who are sole next of kin'; so that one heir-portioner getting by settlement or marriage-contract a particular subject, is held as a singular successor, and is entitled also to her full share of the rest of the succession, whether heritable or moveable, without collation (*f*). 'But heirs-portioners must collate with the other next of kin who are not heirs in heritage; *e.g.* when nieces succeed as heirs-portioners, and children of another brother or sister of the deceased are next of kin along with them (*g*).' The privilege of collation may be excluded by the Will of the deceased.

(*a*) M'Caw *v.* M'Caw, 1787 (correcting 3 Ersk. 9. § 3); M. 2383; 2 Ill. 467. See § 1911A.
(*b*) Dick *v.* Dicks, 1698; M. 10,326.
(*c*) Newbigging's Trs. *v.* Steel's Trs., 1873; 11 Macph. 411.
(*d*) Trotter *v.* Rochead, 1681; M. 2375.
(*e*) Chancellor *v.* Chancellor, 1742; M. 2379; Elchies, *Suc.* 8.
(*f*) Jack *v.* Jacks, 1673; M. 2368. Ricart *v.* Ricarts, 1720; M. 2378.
(*g*) Balfour *v.* Scott, 1789; M. 2379; Hailes, 1032; rev. on another point, 3 Pat. 300. Anstruther *v.* Anstruther, 1836; 2 S. & M'L. 639. See § 1911A.

1911A. 'By the Intestate Moveable Succession Act of 1855, it is enacted that "where the person predeceasing would have been the heir in heritage of an intestate leaving heritable as well as moveable estate, had he survived such intestate, his child, being the heir in heritage of such intestate, shall be entitled to collate the heritage, to the effect of claiming for himself alone if there be no other issue of the predeceaser, or for himself and the other issue of the predeceaser if there be such other issue, the share of the moveable estate of the intestate which might have been claimed by the predeceaser upon collation if he had survived the intestate; and daughters of the predeceaser, being heirs-portioners of the intestate, shall be entitled to collate to the like effect. And where, in the above case, the heir shall not collate, his brothers and sisters, and their descendants in their place, have right to a share of the moveable estate equal in amount to the excess in value over the value of the heritage of such share of the whole estate, heritable and moveable, as their predeceasing parent, had he survived the intestate, would have taken on collation" (*a*).'

(*a*) 18 and 19 Vict. c. 23, § 2. Jamieson *v.* Walker, 1896; 23 R. 547. Innes *v.* Coghill, 1897; 25 R. 23.

1912. Property to be Collated.—The heir, as one of the next of kin, is not obliged to collate heritage not his by disposition of the law. Thus, 1. Where he takes as heir of provision, not being heir *alioquin successurus*, he is entitled to his share of moveables without collation (*a*). 2. He is not obliged to collate heritage which comes to him from a stranger, not from the deceased whose moveable succession is in question (*b*); 'but as an heir now acquires by mere survivance a personal right to heritage without service, it would seem that this rule does not now apply to the case of one who makes up titles to a remoter ancestor, passing over his father or other relative who has died in apparency, and that he must collate in order to share in the moveable estate of the latter (*c*).' 3. He must collate land descendible to him as heir *alioquin successurus*, although directly he takes it by deed of settlement; and so an heir of entail, if heir *alioquin successurus*, cannot share without collating (*d*). 4. He must collate heritable estate in another country in claiming a share of moveables in Scotland (*e*); but he is not bound to collate in order to claim his share of moveables under the English statute of distributions, or where the moveable succession is regulated by the law of a country which does not require collation (*f*). 5. Where the heir cannot collate, it has been questioned whether this inability deprives him of his share of the moveables. Thus, where an heir succeeds to a lease which excludes assignees and sub-tenants, or takes the land as heir of entail, he cannot give to the executors a right so exclusively his (*g*); but it is held that he must either communicate to the utmost of his power (his liferent interest, for example, in an entailed estate, the profits of his farm, 'value of his lease,' etc.), or want the benefit of his share of the moveables (*h*). And, (6). It is now finally settled that an heir succeeding under an old entail as one of a special class of heirs (*ex. gr.* as heir-male), and under the limitation of a strict tailzie, is bound to collate (*i*).

(*a*) Ricart, *supra*, § 1911 (*f*). Rae Crawford *v.* Stewart, 1794; M. 2384; 2 Ill. 468. D. Buccleuch *v.* E. Tweeddale, 1677; M. 2369.

(*b*) Spalding *v.* Farquharson, Dec. 11, 1812; 1 Bell's Com. 102. Russell *v.* Russell, 1822; 1 Bell's Com. 102, note, 1 S. 435, n. ed. Cf. Newbigging's Trs., § 1911 (*c*). But in Blair *v.* Blair, 1849, 12 D. 97, under a destination by a stranger of heritage and moveables to the heirs or successors of A., which was construed to carry the heritage to A.'s heirs and the moveables to A.'s executors, the heir was not allowed to take a share of the moveables without collating. See as to this case, Sinclair's Trs. *v.* Sinclair, 1881; 8 R. 749; and Fraser, H. & W. 1047.

(*c*) 37 and 38 Vict. c. 94, § 9, 10. Fraser, H. & W. 1049.

(*d*) Baillie *v.* Clark, Feb. 23, 1809; F. C. Murray *v.* Murray, 1678; M. 2372-4. **Little Gilmour** *v.* **Gilmour**, Dec. 13, 1809; F. C. Ricart, *supra*, § 1911 (*f*). See observations on this case in Little Gilmour's Case, *supra*. Hay Balfour *v.* Scott, 1789; M. 2379; Hailes, 1032; 6 Br. Parl. Ca. 550; 3 Pat. 300; 2 Ill. 471. See 1 Bell's Com. 103, note. Fisher *v.* Fisher's Trs., 1844; 7 D. 129.

(*e*) Robertson *v.* Robertson, Feb. 16, 1816; F. C. Robertson *v.* Macvean, Feb. 18, 1817; F. C. See Trotter *v.* Trotter, 1826; 5 S. 78; 3 W. & S. 407; 2 Ill. 496. Dundas *v.* Dundas, 1829; 1 Jur. 7.

(*f*) Hay Balfour, *supra* (*d*).

(*g*) Stewart *v.* M'Naughton, 1824; 3 S. 351.

(*h*) Little Gilmour, *supra* (*d*). *Infra*, § 1913 (*c*). Fisher's Trs. *v.* Fisher, 1850; 13 D. 245. See Napier *v.* Orr, 1868; 6 Macph. 264.

(*i*) Little Gilmour, *supra* (*d*). Anstruther *v.* Anstruther, 1833; 12 S. 140; 1835, 1 S. & M'L. 463; and on remit, 14 S. 272; aff. 2 S. & M'L. 369. M. Breadalbane *v.* Chandos, 1836; 14 S. 309; 2 S. & M'L. 377. Johnston *v.* Johnston, 1814; Hume, 290.

1913. Mode of Collation.—Where the heir is one of the next of kin, but not bound to collate, he is entitled to be confirmed as an executor; either alone, if he is the sole next of kin, or along with the others (*a*). Where the heir must collate, he is entitled, on making up his titles to the heritage and disponing to the other next of kin, to assume the character of executor. The transaction is commonly settled by private contract, the heir and executors completing their respective titles and dividing the funds. If judicial proceedings be necessary, the heir raises his action against the executors, concluding for declarator of his right, for an order on the executors to account, and (on his completing his title and disponing) for an order to deliver or pay over his share (*b*). 'The heir collating may, if he choose, retain the estate and pay over to the executors in money the value of his interest as at the opening of the succession, for distribution along with the rest of the moveable estate (*c*).'

(*a*) Macmichan *v.* Mitchell, 1852; 14 D. 318.

(*b*) 1 Bell's Com. 103, 104.

(*c*) Fisher's Trs. *v.* Fisher, 1850; 13 D. 245. But see as to the effect of collation on the succession of the next of kin, Napier *v.* Orr, 1868; 6 Macph. 264.

CHAPTER IX

OF PASSIVE REPRESENTATION

1914. General Principle.—It 'was' a ruling principle in the law of Scotland, that the heir to whom the estate and funds of a deceased person go by succession 'was' subject to his obligations or debts; and although the extent of the obligation ought naturally to be commensurate with the amount of the benefit, it 'was' held to be universal, unless certain precautions 'should' be used within a limited time, to show the true amount of the estate taken up by the heir. This doctrine may be taken under four heads:—Universal Passive Representation; Limited Representation; Representation of Apparent Heirs; and the preference given to the Creditors of the Ancestor during a certain term.

1914A. 'Limitation of Heir's Liability to Value of his Succession.—The general rule of law has been altered by the enactment in the same statute which makes estates vest in heirs without service, that "an heir shall not be liable for the debts of his ancestor beyond the value of the estate of such ancestor to which he succeeds." If an heir renounce the succession, the creditors of the ancestor have the same rights against the estate as on a renunciation under the former law. And when, before renunciation, an heir has intromitted with his ancestor's estate, he is liable for the ancestor's debts to the extent of such intromissions, but no further (*a*). The effect of this enactment is to supersede much of the law stated in this chapter.'

(*a*) 37 and 38 Vict. c. 94, § 12. See 10 and 11 Vict. c. 47, § 23 (Service of Heirs Act).

1915. Universal Passive Representation.—One who takes the *hæreditas* of a person deceased is liable for payment of his debts; and the responsibility 'was' extended universally to the full amount of the debt, for the benefit of creditors, not of heirs, in the following situations:—

1916. (1.) *Entry as Heir.*—The entry of an heir in heritage by service, special or general, whether as heir of line or of conquest, or heir-male (*a*) generally, 'inferred' (if benefit 'were' derived from it) a universal responsibility for all the debts of the deceased, the heir being held as *eadem persona cum defuncto* (*b*). And refusal or omission to renounce when charged to enter heir 'had' the same effect (*c*).

Heirs-portioners are liable each for their rateable share only; or, in so far as the co-heirs are insolvent, *in quantum lucratæ* (*d*), the rest being called into the field (*e*).

(*a*) Correct this by 1 Bell's Com. 659 (703, M'L.'s ed.). 2 M'Laren, Wills and Succn. 452. *Infra*, § 1922 (3).

(*b*) 3 Ersk. 8. § 50. Aytoun *v.* Aytoun, 1784; M. 9732; 2 Ill. 471. E. Fife *v.* Duff, 1828; 6 S. 698. M'Kay *v.*

M'Kinnon Campbell, 1835; 13 S. 246. Nisbet's Trustees v. Halket, 1835; 13 S. 497; aff. 1839, 1 Rob. 53. See § 1914A.

(c) See above, § 1856.

(d) 3 Ersk. 8. § 51 and 53. Home v. Home, 1632; M. 14,678. Jordanhill v. Edmiston, 1687; M. 14,682. Burnet v. Lepers, 1665; M. 5863. White v. Hay, 1698; M. 14,683.

(e) M'Millan v. Tait, 1775; M. 14,683. See Mackenzie v. Mackenzie, 1847; 9 D. 836.

1917. The heir will be responsible though he evade the form, if he enjoy the benefit of an entry as heir; and such evasion is called (in a more restricted sense) a passive title. Of these there are two in heritage,—*Præceptio Hæreditatis* and *Gestio pro Hærede*; and one in moveables, Vitious Intromission.

1918. (2.) *Præceptio Hæreditatis.*—If the heir shall take gratuitously a right to a heritable estate, to which he would otherwise have succeeded, it is called *præceptio hæreditatis*, and infers responsibility (*a*). But it is doubtful whether this 'was' a universal responsibility (*b*). To this passive title it is necessary that the person called on as liable shall be heir *alioquin successurus* (*c*). The responsibility is continued to the heir's representatives if, after taking possession, he die before the ancestor (*d*). The conveyance must be gratuitous, the proof of onerosity being laid on the heir (*e*). The responsibility is only for debts contracted before the sasine on the conveyance (*f*), and those which are declared burdens on the conveyance (*g*). In circumstances which would have subjected the heir if the father had died, the creditors may have recourse to reduction on the Act 1621, c. 18, during the father's life (*h*).

(*a*) 3 Stair, 7. § 1–5. 3 Ersk. 8. § 88. 1 Bell's Com. 660.

(*b*) See Burnet v. Nasmith, 1693; M. 3040; 2 Ill. 473. Henderson v. Wilson, 1717; M. 9784. 1 Bell's Com. 660. 2 M'Laren on Wills and Succn. 470.

(*c*) Forbes v. Fullerton, 1636; M. 9771. Smeaton v. Smeaton, 1639; M. 9774. Scot v. Boswell, 1665; M. 9775. Spencerfield v. Kilbrachmont, 1672; M. 9779. Hamilton v. Macfarlane, 1662; M. 9775. Harper v. Home, 1662; M. 9774. See 3 Ersk. 8. § 90, 92.

(*d*) 3 Ersk. 8. § 87, 91. Henderson, *supra* (*b*).

(*e*) Hadden v. Haliburton, 1676; M. 9794. Higgins v. Maxwell, 1678; M. 9795.

(*f*) 3 Stair, 7. § 6. 3 Ersk. 8. § 88. Smith v. Marshall, 1780; M. 2322.

(*g*) Smith, *supra* (*f*). Bruce v. Bruce, 1826; 5 S. 119.

(*h*) Lamb v. M'Donald, 1793; Hume, 428.

1919. (3.) *Gestio pro Hærede.*—Where the heir enters to, or possesses after the predecessor's death, a heritable estate, or any part of an estate, to which he would otherwise have succeeded (*a*); or buys such estate, or any right thereto, otherwise than at public lawful sale; or intromits with papers, as a charter-chest,—he 'was' held thereby to incur a universal responsibility as heir (*b*). But this 'was' saved—1. By any right in a third party taking the estate out of the ancestor's person; 2. By any singular title in the heir (*c*), or by adjudication during the ancestor's life (*d*); 3. By the insignificance of the intromission and absence of fraud (*e*); 4. By service *cum beneficio inventarii* (*f*); or, 5. By a title made up at desire of creditors to save expense (*g*).

(*a*) See Montgomerie v. Boswell, 1841; 4 D. 332.

(*b*) 3 Stair, 6. § 6, 13. 3 Ersk. 8. § 83. 1695, c. 24. See Act of Sed., Feb. 7, 1662. M'Neil v. Mathie, 1759; M. 9752; 2 Ill. 474. Ellis v. Carse, 1670; M. 9668; 2 B. Sup. 476. Scott v. L. Belhaven, 1821; 1 S. 33; Hume, 438; 2 Ill. 477. Fergusson v. M'Gachen, 1829; 7 S. 580. See § 1914A.

(*c*) Grant v. Grant, 1676; M. 9763.

(*d*) M'Neil, *supra* (*b*).

(*e*) 3 Ersk. 8. § 83–86. Jeffrey v. Blair, 1791; Bell's 8vo Ca. 482. Penman v. Penman, 1775; M. 9836.

(*f*) 3 Stair, 6. § 10, 11.

(*g*) Hall v. Buchanan, 1760; M. 9730. Blount v. Nicolson, 1783; M. 9731; 2 Ill. 472. Gordon v. Clerk, 1789; M. 9733. Jeffrey, *supra* (*e*). See below, § 1922.

1920. In the following cases there is no passive representation by *gestio*:—1. Where the succession is not open, or the intromitter is not apparent heir, there is no passive title on intromission (*a*). 2. Where the apparent heir does any ineffectual act although in the character of apparent heir, it is not held as *gestio* (*b*). 3. Intromission makes no passive title, if the property did not truly belong to the predecessor (*c*). 4. Where the intromission may fairly be ascribed to another title than the assumption of the succession, it will not infer *gestio* (*d*). 5. The assuming of a predecessor's title of honour is not *gestio* (*e*); nor the taking of an hereditary office (*f*). 6. Making up a title erroneously, for the mere purpose of redisponing a trust-estate, has been held not to infer representation (*g*). 7. Making up a title by general service, but taking nothing by it, does not infer a passive title (*h*).

(*a*) Irvine v. Monimusk, 1626; M. 9649; 2 Ill. 475. Cunningham v. Moutray, 1629; M. 9664; 2 B. Sup. 75.

(*b*) Jamieson v. Seaton, 1670; 1 B. Sup. 620. E. Middleton v. Stanfield, 1682; M. 9651.

(*c*) Farquhar v. Campbell, 1628; M. 9654. E. Gordon v. Leith, 1663; M. 9667.

(*d*) Reid v. Salmond, 1667; M. 9656. Dunbar v. Leslie, 1628; M. 9681. Webster v. Greigs, 1802; Hume, 436.

(*e*) L. Sempill *v.* Hay, 1622; M. 9706.
(*f*) Bower *v.* E. Marischal, 1682; 2 B. Sup. 18.
(*g*) Aytoun *v.* Aytoun, 1784; M. 9732; 2 Ill. 471.
(*h*) E. Fife *v.* Duff, 1828; 6 S. 698.

1921. (4.) *Vitious Intromission.* — The proper mode of entry, and the only effectual check on dishonesty in intromission with the moveable funds of a person deceased, is Confirmation; and wherever one having an opportunity of intromitting does so without confirmation, a universal responsibility is raised against him (*a*). Intromission with writings and title-deeds in a charter-chest infers responsibility, unless where the deeds have been received on inventory, or under a special deed of assignment (*b*). This passive title is not confined to those who have a right to succeed, but extends to all intromitters; 'and where there is a plurality of intromitters, the liability attaches to them jointly and severally (*c*).' Any *bonâ fide* title of intromission, or circumstances removing the suspicion of fraud and affording a check on the intromission, will relieve against the penal consequence (*d*); so, if the creditors shall have approved of the proceedings, and taken a dividend, it discharges vitious intromissions (*e*). Vitious intromission is purged by confirmation before the action, or within year and day, as executor (*f*), not as executor-creditor merely (*g*). Action grounded on vitious intromission is not relevant after the death of the party, nor effectual against the heirs of the intromitter further than in so far as *lucrati* (*h*). 'Vitious intromission may be pleaded by way of exception against an intromitter, to the effect of extinguishing a claim made by him against the succession (*i*). Being a passive title for the benefit of creditors of the deceased, vitious intromission is not a ground of action that can be maintained by a legatee, a widow, or any other who has only a right of succession to the deceased (*k*).'

(*a*) 3 Stair, 9. § 9. 3 Ersk. 9. § 49. See cases in the Dictionary and in Elch. *Vitious Intromission*; and 4 B. Sup. 374, 416, 424, 813; 5 *ib.* 838. Ritchie *v.* Bower, 1795; M. 9838; 2 Ill. 477. Campbell *v.* Campbell, 1714; M. 3156. Scott *v.* L. Belhaven, 1821; 1 S. 33; Hume, 438. Forbes *v.* Forbes, 1823; 2 S. 395. Cunningham *v.* M'Kirdy, 1827; 5 S. 315. M'Eachern *v.* M'Eachern, 1833; 11 S. 441. Montgomerie *v.* Boswell, 1841; 4 D. 332. **Simpson** *v.* **Barr,** 1854; 17 D. 33. Bremner *v.* Campbell, 1839; 1 D. 618; aff. 1842, 1 Bell's App. 280.
(*b*) Ellis *v.* Carse, 1670; M. 9668; 2 B. Sup. 476. Diggles *v.* Stewarts, 1706; M. 9676.
(*c*) Wilson *v.* Taylor, 1865; 3 Macph. 1060.
(*d*) 3 Ersk. 9. § 52. Wilson *v.* Smith, 1772; M. 9833; Hailes, 482. Tawse *v.* Findlater, 1783; M. 9837. Webster *v.* Greig, 1802; Hume, 436. Gardner *v.* Davidson, 1802; M. 9840. Rae *v.* Weir, 1803; Hume, 437. Brown *v.* Stewarts, 1824; 2 S. 739. Gardner *v.* Stevenson, 1830; 8 S. 600. Young *v.* Marshall, 1831; 9 S. 638. Thomson *v.* Miller, 1834; 13 S. 143. Dudgeon *v.* Dudgeon's Trs., 1844; 6 D. 1015. **Adam** *v.* **Campbell**, 1854; 16 D. 964.
(*e*) French *v.* Muirkirk Iron Co., 1797; Hume, 435.
(*f*) 3 Ersk. 9. § 52. Thomson *v.* Kerr, 1663; M. 9873; 2 Ill. 478. Moor *v.* Maxwell, 1712; 5 B. Sup. 85. Cochran *v.* Sturgeon, 1624; M. 9825. Bog *v.* Bailey, 1630; 1 B. Sup. 311. Barbour *v.* Kelvie, 1824; 3 S. 210.
(*g*) Watson *v.* Haliburton, 1650; 1 B. Sup. 453. See Montgomerie *v.* Boswell, *cit.*
(*h*) Cranston *v.* Wilkison, 1666; M. 10,340. Home *v.* Grierson, 1678; 3 B. Sup. 224. Couper *v.* Meek, 1694; 4 B. Sup. 200. Penman *v.* Brown, 1775; M. 9836; Hailes, 667; 2 Ill. 475.
(*i*) **Simpson** *v.* **Barr**, 1854; 17 D. 33; on this point overruling Buchanan *v.* Royal Bank, 1843; 5 D. 211.
(*k*) 3 Ersk. 9. § 54. *Supra*, § 1915.

1922. Limited Representation.—There are some titles which do not infer a universal, but only a limited responsibility.

(1.) *An Entry by Precept of Clare Constat* does not infer responsibility where the estate is carried off by reduction (*a*).

(2.) *Entry more Burgi* is limited to the estate so carried (*b*).

(3.) *An Heir of Provision* taking by a particular deed or destination is not universally liable (*c*).

'(3A.) *A gratuitous Disponee*, like an heir of provision or legatee, incurs passive liability only to the extent of his succession (*d*).'

(4.) *An Heir to a Lease excluding Assignees and Sub-tenants* would seem not to be liable on the passive titles, both as he is in the condition of an heir of provision, and as he takes what the predecessor's creditors could not avail themselves of (*e*); 'and it has been so held (*f*).'

(5.) *An Executor* does not by confirming incur a responsibility beyond the estate, his title being strictly limited (*g*).

(6.) *Entry by a Stranger as Heir*, who is not entitled to the character, does not infer passive title; and intromission in such a case makes the person only liable to account (*h*).

(*a*) Farmer *v.* Elder, 1683; M. 14,003; 2 Ill. 472. *Supra*, § 1823.
(*b*) Blount *v.* Nicolson, 1783; M. 9731.
(*c*) Dirleton, *Heirs of Tailzie*, p. 150. 3 Ersk. 8. § 51. Baird *v.* E. Rosebery, 1766; M. 14,019; 5 B. Sup. 926; aff. 3 Pat. 651; 2 Ill. 472. Maitland *v.* Maitland, 1757; 5 B. Sup. 860. See above, § 1916 (*a*). Farquhar *v.* Hamilton, 1842; 4 D. 600. Sir G. Sinclair *v.* Dunbar, 1845; 7 D. 1085. **Dewar** *v.* **Burden**, 1845; 8 D. 90; aff. 1850, 7 Bell, 32.
(*d*) Webster *v.* Greig, 1802; Hume, 436. Montgomerie *v.* Montgomerie, 1837; Elchies, *Implied Will*, 2. Wylie

v. Ross, 1825; 4 S. 172; 1827, 2 W. & S. 576. Bruce *v.* Bruce, 1826; 5 S. 119. Horne *v.* M. Breadalbane's Trs., 1835; 13 S. 296.

(*e*) See Campbell *v.* Gallanach, July 11, 1806; 1 Bell's Com. 82. Hunter, L. & T. i. 221. Comp. § 1219, above.

(*f*) Bain *v.* Mackenzie, 1896; 23 R. 528, overruling Campbell, *cit.* See More's Notes on Stair, 364.

(*g*) 3 Stair, 9. § 64. 2 Ersk. 9. § 41. Renton *v.* Renton, 1851; 14 D. 35. Legatees or beneficiaries may be sued by creditors for repetition of their shares of the succession, after discussion of the proper legal representatives; but the recipient of a legacy or provision incurs representation only to the amount of its value, and only in regard to proper creditors of the deceased. 3 Stair, 8. § 70. Grierson *v.* Wallace, 1821; 1 S. 13. Poole *v.* Anderson, 1834; 12 S. 481. Brunton *v.* Thomson, 1832; 11 S. 190. Clelland *v.* Baillie, 1845; 7 D. 461. See also Maccomie's Exrs. *v.* Strachan, 1760; M. 8087. Bruce *v.* Bruce, 1831; 9 S. 695.

(*h*) Mercer *v.* Scotland, 1745; M. 9786; Elchies, *Provisions to Heirs and Ch.* No. 8.

1923. (7.) *Trust for Creditors.*—Where an heir has intromitted at the request of creditors, and as trustee for their benefit, and with notice that no use is to be made of it but for them, he has been held not liable on the passive titles (*a*).

(*a*) Walker *v.* Home, 1827; 6 S. 204.

1924. (8.) *The Pleading of a 'peremptory' Defence* in an action brought as against an heir imports a passive title, but only as to that debt (*a*).

(*a*) 3 Ersk. 8. § 93. Carfrae *v.* Telfer, 1675; M. 9711; 2 Ill. 479. Lundie *v.* Sinclair, 1713; M. 12,064. Gilmour *v.* Campbell, 1821; 1 S. 216. Smith *v.* Drummond, 1829; 7 S. 792. Brown *v.* Stewart, 1824; 2 S. 739. Kirkpatrick *v.* Douglas, 1838; 16 S. 608; aff. 1841, 2 Rob. 471. Grieve (Dingwall) *v.* Burns, 1871; 9 Macph. 582.

1925. (9.) *Charge to enter Heir or to Confirm.*—The representation inferred from a charge to enter heir unanswered, 'or its equivalent, a summons in an action of constitution,' is limited to that particular occasion (*a*).

(*a*) 3 Ersk. 8. § 93. See *supra*, § 1854 et seq., and § 1901. Richan *v.* Hill, 1832; 11 S. 237. Graham *v.* Colquhoun, 1809; Hume, 440. Montgomerie *v.* Boswell, 1841; 4 D. 332.

1926. (10.) *Service cum Beneficio Inventarii.*—The heir entering to the *universitas* of the heritage 'might' limit his responsibility by serving heir *cum beneficio inventarii, i.e.* with reference to an inventory of the amount and value of the estate, lodged with the Sheriff-clerk of the shire where the lands lie (*a*). But the inventory must for this purpose be lodged with the Sheriff-clerk, and recorded within a year from the ancestor's death, or from the birth of a posthumous child (*b*); or if the first heir 'had' died in apparency, the next heir 'might' claim the benefit, provided he give in the inventory within a year after the succession opens to him (*c*). The form 'was' in no respect different from an ordinary service, except in being qualified by the words *cum beneficio inventarii*, and in there being a particular inventory given up on oath, and recorded, of all the predecessor's lands, houses, and heritable rights of all kinds which the heir 'meant' to take up (*d*). 'This procedure was superseded by the Service of Heirs Act (*e*).'

(*a*) See § 1914A, 1927A.

(*b*) 1695, c. 24. See Cod. lib. 6, tit. 30. l. 22, § 2, 3, 4, de Jure Deliberat. Baillie *v.* Rose, 1789; Hume, 427.

(*c*) Bruce *v.* E. Southesk, 1704; M. 5329; 2 Ill. 479.

(*d*) See 5 Bell's Forms, 557. 1 Jur. Styles, 401.

(*e*) 10 and 11 Vict. c. 47, § 25. See § 1914A, 1927A.

1927. The requisites of this form of service 'were,'—that a full and particular inventory of the heritable estate, signed by the heir before witnesses, and sworn to as correct, must, before the service 'proceeded,' be lodged with the Sheriff-clerk of every shire in which the lands lie; or of the shire where the deceased died, if the subjects 'did' not require sasine (*a*). Before the service, the inventory must be signed by the Sheriff, and recorded in his books, within the *annus deliberandi*, or at least within a year after the succession opens to the heir serving; yet the Court has allowed the inventory to be recorded after the year, where, from the heir having been abroad, or some other inevitable impediment, the registration has been too late; but this always "reserving all objections" (*b*). Within forty days after the expiration of the year, the inventory must be recorded in the books of Session, in a particular record kept for the purpose. The lodging of this inventory 'inferred,' of itself, no passive title, provided it be not followed up by service. Service 'might' proceed at any time after the inventory is recorded.

(*a*) 1695, c. 24. Jur. St. and Bell's Forms, *ut supra.* 1 Bell's Com. 662. M'Kay *v.* Sinclair, 1708; M. 5331; 2 Ill. 480. Campbell *v.* Campbell, 1709; M. 5333. Codrington *v.* Johnston, Feb. 11, 1818; F. C.; 1824, 2 S. App. 118.

(*b*) M'Kenzie, petr., 1749; M. 5353; Elch. *Heir cum Ben.* 5. Bell, petr., Nov. 17, 1818; F. C. Bell, petr., 1830; 8 S. 839. Finlayson, petr., 1838; 16 S. 1270. Anderson *v.* Bank of Scotland, 1838; 1 D. 268.

1927A. 'These forms were changed by the Service of Heirs Act of 1847; under which Act a general service might be applied for and obtained with limited liability, by annexing a specification subscribed by the petitioner or his mandatary, which inferred a liability "for the deceased's debts and deeds, only to the extent or value of the lands or other heritages contained in the relative specification." On decree being pronounced, limited to the specification, the latter was also signed by the Sheriff-clerk; whereupon the whole was transmitted to Chancery, where it was recorded, and an extract given out (*a*). But now the heir is liable, without any proceedings taken to limit his liability, only to the extent of the estate to which he succeeds (*b*).'

(*a*) 10 and 11 Vict. c. 47, § 25. 31 and 32 Vict. c. 101, § 49.
(*b*) 37 and 38 Vict. c. 94, § 12.

1928. The effects of a service *cum beneficio inventarii* 'were'—1. To make the heir personally liable for debts of the deceased, to the extent of the inventory; but not to make those debts burdens on the lands, as on a trust-estate, or to bring in the creditors *pari passu* (*a*). 2. To entitle the heir to satisfy any creditor on demand. 3. To limit the demands of creditors against him to the amount of the inventory. 4. To entitle the heir to dispose of the estate as he pleases, if not prevented by diligence. 5. To impose on the heir the duty of a trustee, to account for the estates in the inventory. And, first, the creditors 'might' insist on having the estate itself given up to them; and the heir 'might' prevent an adjudication by offering to convey the lands to the adjudger (*b*); secondly, they 'were' entitled to have the estate with any improvements which the heir 'might' have made (*c*).

(*a*) Gordon *v.* Ross, 1741; M. 5352; 2 Ill. 480. Scott *v.* Burnet, 1724; M. 5336.
(*b*) L. Ormiston *v.* Hamilton, 1711; M. 5334.
(*c*) Lawson *v.* M'Dougall's Crs., 1738; M. 5348; Elch. *Heir cum Ben.* 2. Scott, *supra* (*a*). Johnston *v.* Strachan, 1731; M. 5345. Veitch *v.* Young, 1733; M. 5345. Aikenhead *v.* Russel, 1725; M. 5342; and 1727, M. 5344. Douglas *v.* Pringle, 1724; M. 5335. Gray *v.* M'Caul, 1733; M. 5345. Murray *v.* Pringle's Crs., 1736; M. 5346. Strachan's Heirs *v.* Creditors, 1738; M. 5348. See 3 Ersk. 8. § 70.

1929. Representation of Apparent Heir Three Years in Possession.—The possession of an estate as apparent heir and proprietor naturally raises a credit with the public which it is hard and unjust to disappoint; and the Legislature, in 1695, so far sanctioned this credit, as to enact "that if any man shall serve himself heir, etc., not to his immediate predecessor, but to one remote, he shall be liable for the debts and deeds of the person interjected, to whom he was apparent heir, and who was in the possession of the lands and estate to which he is served for the space of three years, and that in so far as may extend to the value of the said lands and estate, and no further, deducting the debts already paid" (*a*).

'As possession of an estate as apparent heir is no longer known in the law of Scotland, this Act is superseded. But the deeds of the heir apparent, who now possesses the estate as absolute proprietor on a personal right, are made good against his successor, though not beyond the value of the estate to which he succeeds, by the stronger statute of 1874 (*b*).'

(*a*) 1695, c. 24; 9 Acta Parl. 427, c. 9. 3 Ersk. 8. § 93, 94. 1 Bell's Com. 664 (708, M'L.'s ed.).
(*b*) *Per* L. Pres. Inglis in M'Adam *v.* M'Adam, 1879; 6 R. 1256. 37 and 38 Vict. c. 97, § 9, 12. *Supra*, § 1914A.

1930. In the construction of the statute, it is held—1. That it applies to titles made up to a former, although not the next immediate predecessor (*a*); and although his right was only personal, he not having been infeft (*b*). 2. The interjected apparent heir must have *actually* possessed, naturally or civilly, 'not necessarily exclusively or completely'; possession being not *animi*, but *facti*, and it not being enough that the heir has done all he could to obtain possession, and found it impossible (*c*). 3. Possession by a tutor for a pupil is the possession of the heir (*d*). 4. A liferenter's possession is to be held the fiar's only where it proceeds from him (*e*). 5. On the other hand, actual possession is enough, although another might have excluded the apparent heir if he had chosen (*f*). 6. Possession by a judicial factor in a ranking at the apparent heir's instance, is not the apparent heir's possession (*g*). 7. And so of the possession of a trustee for paying off debt and settling the reversion (*h*). 8. A second apparent heir may enter as such to possession of the estate, and if he do not make up his titles he will not be passively liable; the statute attaching the responsibility only to the making up of the title (*i*). 'Entry by precept of *clare constat* brings an heir within the statute (*k*).' 9. Inhibition used against the apparent heir will not avail the inhibitor in competition with a subsequent creditor of the apparent heir, after the entry of the next heir passing by has opened the estate to their diligence (*l*). 10. It will not relieve from responsibility, to show that another had a preferable right to the apparent heir in possession; the statute requiring only possession, but not that there should be no preferable title. 11. If the possession has been otherwise than as apparent heir, it will not avail creditors. 12. The liability is only for onerous debts and deeds, and with relief against the apparent heir's representatives (*m*), unless the obligation has relation to a particular estate, in which case the relief is only against those taking that estate (*n*). 13. It is only a personal responsibility, not making the apparent heir's debts burdens on the estate (*o*). 14. The common rule by which a lease granted by one not infeft is ineffectual, seems to admit of an exception under this Act, in so far as the heir passing by is concerned; but the lease will not be effectual against creditors (*p*). 15. Although the creditors of the interjected apparent heir have no real security or preference on the subjects, it would appear that the preference provided for ancestor's creditors will be available to them (*q*). 16. The personal responsibility is subsidiary to the obligation of the apparent heir's representatives, so that the heir making up titles has the benefit of discussion, 'provided that he would have had that benefit if he had served to his immediate predecessor' (*r*); and if he should pay without pleading such benefit, he has relief against those properly liable (*s*). 17. There is no responsibility by this Act where the estate is entailed, and the debts are under the prohibitions of the entail, unless the requisites of the Entail Act have been neglected; and even then the recording of the entail will exclude the creditors of the apparent heir (*t*); or unless the debt of the apparent heir is permitted by the entail (*u*).

The debts and deeds to which the responsibility extends are such only as are onerous (*v*). But it has been held that a debt grounded on a natural obligation, 'such as a reasonable provision for wife or children,' is to be regarded as onerous (*w*).

(*a*) Hay *v.* Hay, 1775; M. 9755; Hailes, 607; 2 Ill. 481. Grieve (Dingwall) *v.* Burns, 1871; 9 Macph. 582. The statute applies to an entry by precept of *clare constat.* Brown *v.* Henderson, 1852; 14 D. 1041.

(*b*) See and correct 1 Prin. of Equity, 124.

(*c*) Yule *v.* Ritchie, 1758; M. 5299. Buchan *v.* M'Donald, 1796; M. 9822; Hume, 432. M'Caul's Crs. *v.* M'Caul, 1745; M. 9748. M'Brair *v.* Maitland, 1736; Elch. *Passive Title*, 4. See Donald *v.* Colquhoun, 1835; 13 S. 574. Corbet *v.* Porterfield, 1839; 1 D. 1038; aff. 1842, 1 Bell's App. 476. Duncan *v.* Duncan, 1859; 22 D. 180. Glen *v.* Scales's Trs., 1881; 9 R. 317.

(*d*) M'Brair, *supra* (*c*). Johnston, *infra* (*e*). Bremner *v.* Campbell, 1842; 1 Bell's App. 280.

(*e*) Johnston *v.* Steel, 1733 and 1736; M. 9809; Elch. *Pass. Title*, 3; 2 Ill. 481. Pitcairn *v.* Lundie, 1752; M. 9749. Grant *v.* Sutherland, 1749; M. 5265; Elch. *Minor*, 12; 1 Cr. & St. 416. See Knox *v.* Irvine, 1759; M. 5276; 2 Ill. 178.

(*f*) Kinminity's Heir *v.* The Creditors, 1756; 5 B. Sup. 853. Knox, *supra* (*e*).

(*g*) Buchan, *supra* (*c*).

(*h*) Donald, *supra* (*c*).

(*i*) Sinclair *v.* Sinclair, 1736; M. 9810; Elch. *Pass. Title*, 2; Notes, 317, 318. Leith *v.* L. Banff, 1741; *ib.* 5; Notes, 318. Kinminity's Crs. *v.* Heir, 1749; M. 5265; Elch. *Minor*, 12; Cr. & St. 416. Grant *v.* Sutherland, 1754; M. 9819; aff. 1 Cr. & St. 605. "It is very remarkable that in the report of this case no notice is taken of the previous decisions or of the opposite judgment of the House of Lords." 2 Ill. 482. See 1 Bell's Com. 666 (709, M'L.'s ed.). Burns *v.* Pickens, 1758; M. 5273; 5 B. Sup. 361. Murray *v.* Ramsay & Co., Jan. 17, 1811; F. C.

(*k*) Brown *v.* Henderson, 1852; 14 D. 1041.

(*l*) Sutherland *v.* Sutherland, 1786; M. 5294.

(*m*) Muirhead *v.* Muirhead, 1724; M. 9807; 2 Ill. 483. Gordon *v.* Gordon, 1742; Elch. *Pass. Title*, 7. Coulter-allers *v.* Kilbucho, 1742; 5 B. Sup. 717. M. Clydesdale *v.* E. Dundonald, 1726; M. 1262; Robertson's Ap. 564. Css. Glencairn *v.* Cunningham Graham, 1800; M. *Heir App.* Apx. 1; aff. 5 Pat. 134. Kennedy *v.* Kennedy, 1829; 7 S. 397. Adamson *v.* Inglis, 1832; 11 S. 40. Russell *v.* Russell, 1852; 15 D. 192. Taylor *v.* Hutton, 1854; 16 D. 885. See below (*v*), (*w*).

(*n*) Ogilvy *v.* Ogilvy, Dec. 16, 1817; F. C. Smyth *v.* Murray, Dec. 9, 1814; F. C. M. Annandale *v.* E. Hopetoun, 1732; Elch. *Mut. Cont.* 12; rev. 1 Cr. & St. 225.

(*o*) 3 Ersk. 8. § 94. Simpson *v.* Hamilton, 1707; M. 9807.

(*p*) Lowdon *v.* Murray, 1752; M. 5270; 2 Ill. 174. Killilung Tenants, 1760; 5 B. Sup. 877. Gordon *v.* Milne, 1780; M. 10,309; 2 Ill. 175. *Supra*, § 1181.

(*q*) See below, § 1931.

(*r*) Vint *v.* E. Dalhousie, 1712; M. 3562. 3 Ersk. 8. § 94. Morris *v.* Beveridge, 1867; 6 Macph. 60. See below, § 1935.

(*s*) M. Clydesdale, and cases *supra* (*m*) and (*n*).

(*t*) Graham *v.* Graham's Heirs, 1795; M. 15,439; 1 Bell's Com. 667; 2 Ill. 372. Dickson *v.* Syme, 1801; M. *Tailzie*, Apx. No. 7. See note in 2 Ill. 484.

(*u*) Glencairn and Kennedy, *supra* (*m*).

(*v*) Not gratuitous or *mortis causâ* deeds. Lindsay *v.* Univ. of Glasgow, 1794; Hume, 429. Erskine *v.* Erskine, 1795; Hume, 431. Absolute warrandice presumes an onerous consideration. Taylor *v.* Hutton, 1854; 16 D. 885.

(*w*) Kennedy, *supra* (*m*). Russell, *supra* (*m*). Orr *v.* Orr's Trs., 1871; 9 Macph. 500. Glen *v.* Scales's Trs. (*c*). Burness *v.* Fleming's Tutors, 1882; 9 R. 1013.

1931. Preference of the Ancestor's Creditors.—By two statutes a preference is secured to the creditors of the ancestor upon his estate, heritable or moveable, over those of his successor entering as heir to that estate. But this preference is provisional, a term being fixed within which the ancestor's creditor must complete his diligence for attaching the estate, otherwise he has no preference.

1932. (1.) *On the Heritable Estate.*—The creditors of the ancestor are, during certain terms, protected against voluntary deeds of the heir, and against the diligence of the heir's creditors.

(i.) Effect of Voluntary Deeds by Heir.—It is enacted that "no right or disposition made by the apparent heir, so far as may prejudge his predecessor's creditors, shall be valid unless made and granted a full year after the defunct's death" (*a*). In the construction of this statute it is held—1. That it comprehends all conveyances made by the heir, whether entered as heir or not (*b*). 2. Not only conveyances to creditors of the heir, but onerous deeds 'within the year' to third parties, are forbidden by this statute (*c*). 'After the year has expired, an heir in possession can grant a valid security over the estate for an instant advance, just as he can sell for an adequate price, and in good faith (*d*).' 3. A conveyance to the ancestor's creditors generally will be good (*e*), but not to one in preference over others of that class (*f*). 4. The ancestor's creditors are those whom the law is intended to protect, and they have the right to challenge, while the creditors of the heir can claim no participation. And, 5. It is thus not necessary that the ancestor's creditors should do diligence within the three years, in order to exclude the creditors of the heir (*g*).

(*a*) 1661, c. 24. 1 Bell's Com. 734 (770, M'L.'s ed.).
(*b*) Mags. of Ayr *v.* Macadam, 1780 ; M. 3135 ; 2 Ill. 485.
(*c*) Taylor *v.* L. Braco, 1747 ; M. 3133. Mags. of Ayr, *supra* (*b*). Paton *v.* Renny, 1835 ; 13 S. 509.
(*d*) Macalpine *v.* Lang, 1885 ; 12 R. 604.
(*e*) 3 Ersk. 8. § 102.
(*f*) Ersk. *ut supra.* L. Ballenden *v.* Murray, 1685 ; M. 3127. Christie *v.* Royal Bank, 1839 ; 1 D. 745 ; aff. 1841, 2 Rob. 118. Torrance *v.* Murdoch, 1842 ; 4 D. 774. Arniston *v.* Ballenden, 1685 ; 2 B. Sup. 93.
(*g*) Bell *v.* Lothian, 1773 ; M. 3134. Taylor, *supra* (*c*), especially Kilkerran's Report.

1933. (ii.) Effect of Diligence of Creditors of Heir.—It is enacted that "the creditors of the defunct shall be preferred to the creditors of the appearand heir in time coming as to the defunct's estate, providing that the defunct's creditors do diligence against the appearand heir, and the real estate belonging to the defunct, within the space of three years after the defunct's death" (*a*). In the construction of this part of the Act it is held—1. That it does not apply to moveables (*b*). 2. That the rule holds good although the ancestor's creditor is *non valens agere* during the whole or part of the three years (*c*). 3. That under the term apparent heir a *nominatim* substitute in a bond is comprehended, to the effect of giving to the creditors of the institute the statutory preference over those of the substitute (*d*). 4. That the rule applies to all heritage descending to the heir, whether *suâ naturâ* or by destination (*e*). 5. That the expression "appearand heir" does not confine the remedy to cases where the heir has not made up his titles (*f*). 6. That "doing diligence" means *completing* the diligence (*g*): and a judicial sale at the instance of the apparent heir, 'being equivalent to an adjudication for all the creditors included in the decree,' will secure the preference to the creditors of the ancestor (*h*). Sequestration also is held sufficient, if the ancestor's creditors have proved their debts under it, 'having lodged their claims' within the three years (*i*). 7. If the creditor should be delayed in proceeding with his diligence by litigation with the heir or other creditors, his preference would not be forfeited (*k*).

(*a*) 1661, c. 24. 1 Bell's Com. 729 (766, M'L.'s ed.).
(*b*) Kerr *v.* Scott, 1712 ; M. 690 ; 2 Ill. 485.
(*c*) Paterson *v.* Bruce, 1678 ; M. 3126. See, however, 1 Bell's Com. 731 (767, M'L.'s ed.).
(*d*) Graham *v.* M'Queen, 1711 ; M. 3128. Bruce *v.* Bruce, 1831 ; 9 S. 700. Boyd *v.* Boyd, 1851 ; 13 D. 1302 (heir of entail).
(*e*) M'Kay *v.* M'Kay's Reprs., 1783 ; M. 3137 ; 2 Ill. 486.
(*f*) 3 Ersk. 8. § 102. Mags. of Ayr *v.* Macadam, 1780 ; M. 3135.
(*g*) 2 Stair, 12. § 29. 3 Ersk. 8. § 101. L. Ballenden *v.* Murray, 1685 ; M. 3127. Taylor *v.* L. Braco, 1747 ; M. 3133 ; 2 Ill. 485. Inhibition is not complete diligence, and therefore does not satisfy the proviso in the statute. Menzies *v.* Murdoch, 1841 ; 4 D. 257.
(*h*) Russell *v.* Hamilton's Crs., 1760 ; M. 3134 ; 5 B. Sup. 874. Irvine *v.* Maxwell, 1748 ; M. 5264. M'Lachlan *v.* Bennet, 1826 ; 4 S. 712 ; aff. 1829, 3 W. & S. 449.
(*i*) M'Lachlan *supra* (*h*). See 19 and 20 Vict. c. 79, § 102–107. 19 and 20 Vict. c. 91, § 4.
(*k*) L. Ballenden, *supra* (*g*). 1 Bell's Com. 730, 731 (767, M'L.'s ed.).

1934. (2.) *Preference of Ancestor's Creditors on the Moveable Estate.*—By statute, '"in the case of a moveable estate left by a defunct and falling to his nearest of kin, who lies out and doth not confirm . . . ,' the creditors of the defunct doing diligence to affect the moveable estate within year and day of the debtor's decease, shall always be preferred to the diligence of the creditors of the nearest of kin" (*a*). This is grounded on the common law (*b*). Diligence in the sense of the statute must be complete: poinding, arrestment and forthcoming, confirmation as executor-creditor. Where the executor has confirmed, 'the statute does not apply, and' he is held to act as trustee for the creditors of the deceased, so as to give them their preference on the funds so long as distinguishable (*c*).

(*a*) 1695, c. 41.
(*b*) 3 Stair, 8. § 71. 3 Ersk. 9. § 43–6.
(*c*) Bell *v.* Campbell, 1781; Hailes, 893; 2 Ill. 487. Tait *v.* Kay, 1779; M. 3142. Murray Kinninmond's Crs., 1744; Elchies, *Exec.* No. 13. Russell, *supra*, § 1933 (*h*). See above, § 1899. Christie *v.* Allan's Crs., 1835; 13 S. 938.

1935. Order of Responsibility among Heirs.—Heirs, although liable universally to creditors (*a*), are yet responsible only in a particular order; and hence the doctrines of Discussion and Relief.

(1.) *Discussion of Heirs.*—The benefit of discussion pleadable by heirs is regulated thus:—1. Where in the obligation, particular heirs are bound, these are first to be called upon (*b*). 2. Where the debt is made a burden on a particular subject, the heir taking that subject is liable in the obligation (*c*); and a special and precise appointment will be required to entitle such heir to relief against executors 'or general disponees (*d*).' 3. If the debt be secured on two heritable subjects destined to different heirs, they are liable *pro ratâ* of the value of the subjects (*e*). 4. Where the obligation is general, not distinctly heritable or moveable, and not directed against any particular heir, the creditor may call either the heir or the executor as he thinks fit (*f*). But where the debt is properly heritable, the heir of line is primarily liable, and is bound totally to relieve the heir of provision or of conquest (*g*). 5. In his action against heirs the creditor must follow a certain order (*h*); taking first the heir of line (*i*), next 'under the old law' the heir of conquest (*k*), then the heirs of provision (*l*): and of them the heir-male or heir by any general character first (*m*); the heir of marriage (having right rather *obligatione* than *destinatione*) being taken last. 6. By discussion is meant, not merely calling the heir in an action, and even obtaining decree against him; but also proceeding either to personal diligence or to the adjudging of any heritable estate that can be pointed out as belonging to him (*n*).

(*a*) There is no right of discussion, though there is a right of relief (*infra*, § 1936) between heir and executor, creditors in any kind of debt being entitled to sue either heir or executor, and not being bound to call the other. 3 Ersk. 9. § 48. M'Gillivray's Exrs. (Walker) *v.* Masson, 1857; 19 D. 1099. Br. L. Co. *v.* L. Reay, 1850; 12 D. 949. Moncrieff *v.* Miln, 1856; 18 D. 1286. See below (*f*), (*g*).
(*b*) 3 Ersk. 8. § 52. Blair *v.* Anderson, 1663; M. 3571; 2 Ill. 487.
(*c*) 3 Stair, 5. § 17. 3 Ersk. 8. § 52. E. Kinghorn *v.* Leslie, 1607; M. 3574. Fairlie *v.* Blair, 1611; M. 3575. Gordon *v.* M'Dowall, 1615; *ib.* Robertson's Crs. *v.* A. Robertson's Crs., 1803; M. *Competition*, Apx. 2. Ogilvie *v.* Dundas, 1826; 2 W. & S. 214. Henderson *v.* Hamilton, 1858; 20 D. 479. Bain *v.* Reeves, 1863; 23 D. 416. 31 and 32 Vict. c. 101, § 131. As to the transmission of heritable securities against heirs and disponees of the subjects burdened, see 37 and 38 Vict. c. 94, § 47. Kippen *v.* Stewart, 1852; 14 D. 533. Reid *v.* Lamond, 1857; 19 D. 265. Carrick *v.* Rodger, Watt, & Paul, 1881; 9 R. 242; which is questioned in Wright's Trs. *v.* M'Laren, 1891; 18 R. 841. Ritchie & Sturrock *v.* Dullatur Feuing Co., 1881; 9 R. 358. Above, § 910A.
(*d*) M. Breadalbane's Trs. *v.* Dss. Buckingham, 1842; 4 D. 1259. A general direction to trustees and executors to pay all lawful debts does not relieve the heir from payment of a debt due by heritable bond of earlier date. Fraser, and M'Nicol *v.* M'Nicol, § 1936. Carrick's Trs. *v.* Moore, 1840; 2 D. 1068. M. Breadalbane's Trs., *cit.*
(*e*) Sinclair's Exrs. *v.* Fraser, 1798; Hume, 176. Rose, *infra*, § 1936 (*d*). Moncrieff *v.* Skene, 1825; 1 W. & S. 672. Stirling Crawford's Trs. *v.* Stirling Stuart, 1886; 14 R. 131.
(*f*) Baillie *v.* Henderson, 1662; M. 3564. Adam *v.* Gray, 1626; *ib.* Carnegie *v.* Knowles, 1627; *ib.* Kirkpatrick *v.* Irvine, 1838; 16 S. 608; 1841, 2 Rob. 475. See above, note (*a*).
(*g*) Walls *v.* Maxwell, 1700; M. 3561. Vint *v.* E. Dalhousie, 1712; M. 3562; 2 Ill. 484. Innes, see below (*n*); and above, § 1930 (*r*). Dundas *v.* Ogilvie, 1804; M. *Discussion*, Apx. 1; 1826, 2 W. & S. 214. Park's Curator *v.* Black, 1871; 9 Macph. 1078.
(*h*) 3 Ersk. Pr. 8. § 24. 3 Ersk. Inst. 8. § 52. 3 Stair, 5. § 17. 3 Bankt. 5. § 69. This is on the assumption that there is not a general disposition by the ancestor; for general disponees or trustees are primarily liable for debts not charged on particular estates, or on particular beneficiaries or legatees. Weir *v.* Parkhill, 1738; M. 5857. Mercer *v.* Scotland, 1745; M. 9786; Elch. *Implied Will*, 4.
(*i*) Fairlie's Crs. *v.* Heirs, 1630; M. 3559.
(*k*) Brown *v.* Brown, 1782; M. 5228. See above, § 1670.
(*l*) Forrester *v.* Fotheringham, 1649; 1 B. Sup. 429. Burnett *v.* Burnett, 1854; 16 D. 780. It is held that heirs of different estates are liable rateably according to the value of their respective inheritances. Mackenzie *v.* Mackenzie, 1847; 9 D. 836.
(*m*) Innes, see below (*n*).
(*n*) 3 Ersk. 8. § 53. Straiton *v.* E. Lauderdale, 1708; M. 3579; 2 Ill. 489. Innes *v.* Sinclair, 1773; M. 3567.

1936. (2.) *Relief among Heirs.*—Heirs who are liable only *subsidiarie*, but choose to pay the debt, are creditors of those primarily liable, and have action against them for indemnification or relief. So, 1. The heir paying a moveable, or the executor a heritable debt, has action against the person who is primarily liable (*a*). 'Only an express declaration by a testator, or an implication so strong as to be equivalent to such a declaration, suffices to invert the general rule of law that the heir is primarily liable for heritable debts, and the personal estate for general debts (*b*).' 2. The heir or executor paying a debt secured on a particular estate, or laid on a particular heir, is entitled to relief (*c*). 3. A catholic security over all the predecessor's estates, divides among the heirs taking those estates when the succession splits; and one of them paying has proportional relief (*d*).

(*a*) Carnoustie *v.* Meldrum, 1630 ; M. 5204 ; 2 Ill. 489. Robertson *v.* Baillie, 1705 ; M. 5473. Home *v.* ——, 1740 ; M. 5211. Mullo *v.* Mullos, 1758 ; M. 5221. Denham *v.* Denham, 1765 ; M. 5224. Forbes *v.* Forbes, 1766 ; Hailes, 138. Arbuthnot *v.* Arbuthnot, 1773 ; M. 5225 ; Hailes, 528. Fraser *v.* Fraser, 1804 ; M. *Heir and Exec.* Apx. 3 ; aff. 1812, 5 Pat. 642. M'Nicol *v.* M'Nicol, Jan. 16, 1814 ; and Jan. 31, 1816 ; F. C. Ross *v.* Clayton, 1824 ; 3 S. 271, and F. C. ; aff. 1826 ; 2 W. & S. 40. 3 Ersk. 9. § 48. Campbell *v.* Campbell, 1817 ; Hume, 180. Carrick's Trs. *v.* Moore, 1840 ; 2 D. 1068. Moncrieff *v.* Miln, 1856 ; 18 D. 1287. Wallace *v.* Ritchie's Trs., 1846 ; 8 D. 1038. Renton *v.* Renton, 1851 ; 14 D. 35. Bain *v.* Reeves, 1861 ; 23 D. 416. Crawford's Trs. *v.* Crawford, 1867 ; 5 Macph. 275. Douglas' Trs. *v.* Douglas, 1868 ; 6 Macph. 223. Stainton's Trs. *v.* Dawson, 1868 ; 6 Macph. 240. Mackintosh *v.* Mackintosh's Trs., 1870 ; 8 Macph. 628 ; rev. 1873, 11 Macph. H. L. 28. Park's Curator *v.* Black, 1871 ; 9 Macph. 1078.

(*b*) Fraser, M'Nicol, Carrick's Trs., Douglas' Trs., etc., cited above. Macleod's Trs. *v.* Macleod's Exrs., 1871 ; 9 Macph. 903. Duncan *v.* Duncan, 1883 ; 10 R. 1042. Bell's Tr. *v.* Bell, 1884 ; 12 R. 85. Ramsay *v.* Ramsay, 1887 ; 15 R. 25. Brand *v.* Scott's Trs., 1892 ; 19 R. 768.

(*c*) See Fergus *v.* Fergus, 1833 ; 11 S. 332. Elliot's Trs. *v.* E. Minto, 1833 ; 6 W. & S. 381. Ogilvie *v.* Dundas, *supra*, § 1935 (*c*). Stewart *v.* Campbell, 1852 ; 14 D. 443.

(*d*) Rose *v.* Rose, 1786 ; M. 5229 ; Hailes, 1011 ; rev. 3 Pat. 66. See above, § 1935 (*e*).

1937. Crown Ultimus Hæres.—Both in lands and moveables, the Crown is *ultimus hæres*, on failure of the blood of the proprietor (*a*). This right passes to the Crown as alone having a legal title. But the representation or liability of the Crown or donatary for the deceased's debts is limited to the amount of the estate (*b*).

(*a*) Halcro, 1626 ; M. 1348. See above, § 1669.

(*b*) 3 Ersk. 10. § 4.

CHAPTER X

OF APPROBATE AND REPROBATE

1938. Principle. | 1939. Express Conditions. | 1940. Implied Conditions.

1938. Principle.—It is a rule of law that no person can at once accept and reject the same deed; and on this ground, an heir or executor, by accepting under a settlement a benefit which otherwise he would not have enjoyed, may be bound by a deed which of itself would not have been effectual to bind him. The whole doctrine depends on the effect of acceptance and consequent engagement (*a*). In English law a similar doctrine is called Election; with us it is called Approbate and Reprobate. The alternative which compels the party to make an election, is raised either by an express or by an implied condition.

(*a*) 3 Ersk. 3. § 49. Kers *v.* Wauchope, 1815; Hume, 25; aff. 1819; 1 Bligh, 1; 2 Ill. 493. Martin *v.* Martin, 1795; 3 Pat. 421.

1939. Express Conditions. — Where the condition is expressly imposed in case of acceptance, the maxim "quod approbo non reprobo" directly applies (*a*). The condition must be possible and lawful (*b*). And the person imposing the condition must have power to make the settlement stated in the condition; or, at least uncontrolled power to confer or withhold the benefit conditionally bestowed (*c*).

(*a*) Turnbull *v.* Kinnear, 1711; M. 15,364; 2 Ill. 492. Cunningham *v.* Gainer, 1758; M. 617. See 1 Bligh, 27. Douglas *v.* Douglas, 1763; 5 B. Sup. 896. Gibson *v.* M'Bean, 1786; M. 620. Brodie *v.* Barry, 2 Ves. & B. 127; 13 R. R. 6, 37. See Kers, *supra*, § 1938 (*a*). Dundas *v.* Dundas, 1829; 7 S. 241; aff. 1830, 4 W. & S. 460. Bennet *v.* Bennet's Trs., 1829; 7 S. 817. Gillies *v.* Gillies' Trs., 1881; 8 R. 505.

(*b*) Arbuthnot *v.* Arbuthnot, 1792; M. 620; Bell's Ca. 161. Stewart *v.* Leslie, March 10, 1810; Sandford on Entails, 191.

(*c*) Ker, *supra*, § 1938 (*a*). Brodie, *supra* (*a*). Welby *v.* Welby, 2 Ves. & B. 187; 13 R. R. 58. *Supra*, § 1784. Douglas' Trs. *v.* Douglas, 1862; 24 D. 1191. M'Donald *v.* M'Donald, 1876; 4 R. 45.

1940. Implied Conditions. — To raise an implied condition and put the party to his election, the intention to make a condition of the acceptance must be clear beyond all doubt. There seems to be a fair inference to that effect, from a deed or deeds of settlement framed to regulate the deceased's whole succession, and of which the parts are plainly meant to stand or fall together (*a*); and an heir, 'knowing the circumstances (*b*),' can neither take under such a deed and free himself from the counterpart, nor can he on 'the ground of' deathbed challenge the deed, and under it claim a legacy or provision (*c*). But it must be on the face of the deed clearly the intention of the maker to put the party to his election; and so it was held not applicable to a case where the testator had acquired property after the date of the Will, and the words did not affect that property (*d*), 'or to a case where the disposal of English heritage was null and void under the statutes of mortmain (*e*).' It must also plainly appear, where two or more deeds are executed, that they are intended to be so combined as in the mind of the testator to form a united settlement of which the parts are conditional (*f*).

Where there is a revocation of a former conveyance unfavourable to the heir, and the declaration of a new disposition also adverse to his interest, the heir is so far favoured by the law, that his right of succession, and so of challenge on deathbed, is held to revive if the revocation be not made provisionally (*g*); and in such a case the new disposition will be considered as an independent substantive deed, and liable to the same objections as if it were so (*h*). If the disposition of the heritage is not made in such a form as to be effectual without the heir's consent, an *implied* condition of the heir's assent by acceptance will not be of force sufficient to put him to his election (*i*). But if the deed be only subject to challenge for the benefit of the heir, and not in itself null, good evidence of intention that it shall be conditional will be sufficient to compel the heir to make his choice (*k*).

'*Claim for Legitim—Equitable Compensation to Beneficiaries affected.*—On the same principle a child cannot defeat a settlement by claiming legitim, and take the benefit provided by the settlement: either, if the testator have indicated that forfeiture shall follow (as by expressly stating that the provision is in full of legitim), the provision is forfeited; or the provision is applied so far as necessary to compensate the legatees or beneficiaries disappointed by the claim made for legitim, the remainder only (if any, and if consistent with the Will) going to the person so claiming legitim (*l*). Nor can one claim a legacy under a settlement, and after thus homologating it claim legitim (*m*).'

(*a*) Css. Strathmore *v.* M. Clydesdale, 1729; M. 6377; 2 Ill. 495. Turnbull *v.* Turnbull, 1776; 5 B. Sup. 380. Loudon *v.* Loudon, 1811; Hume 23. Campbell *v.* Munro, 1836; 15 S. 310. See Dow *v.* Beith, 1856; 18 D. 820.

(*b*) If, *e.g.*, he does not know of the existence of one of two deeds forming a total settlement, he is not barred by taking under the other from challenging the former, but he must renounce and restore. E. Glasgow's Tr. *v.* E. Glasgow, 1872; 11 Macph. 218.

(*c*) Ladies Ker *v.* Wauchope, 1815; Hume, 25; aff. 1 Bligh, 1; 2 Ill. 493. Urquhart *v.* Urquhart, 1851; 13 D. 742; 1 Macq. 658. Crawford's Trs. *v.* Crawford, 1867; 5 Macph. 275.

(*d*) Wightman *v.* De Lisle, 1802; M. 4479; Hume, 24, note. Hislop *v.* Hislop, 1808; *ib.* 25. See Robertson *v.* Ogilvie's Trs., 1844; 7 D. 236. Maitland *v.* Maitland, 1843; 6 D. 244.

(*e*) Hewit's Trs. *v.* Lawson, 1891; 18 R. 793.

(*f*) Hill *v.* Hunter's Trs., 1818; Hume, 27. Stewart *v.* Stephen, 1832; 11 S. 139. Black *v.* Watson, 1841; 3 D. 522. Harveys *v.* Harveys' Trs., 1860; 22 D. 1310; 1862, 1 Macph. 345. Dow, *supra* (*a*).

(*g*) See opinions in Crawford *v.* Coutts, 2 Bligh, 664; 2 Ill. 415; 1 Ross' L. C. 617. Cunningham *v.* Whitefoord, 1748; Elchies, *Deathbed*, 19; 5 B. Sup. 234; 2 Ill. 418. Mudie *v.* Moir, 1824; 2 S. App. 9, and cases there cited; 2 Ill. 417. See above, § 1811. Cameron *v.* West's Trs., 1864; 2 Macph. 584. Ker *v.* Erskine, 1851; 13 D. 492.

(*h*) See Brodie *v.* Barry, *cit.* § 1939. Ker, *supra* (*c*).

(*i*) See Hearle *v.* Greenbank, 3 Atk. 695; 13 Vesey, jr. 223. Montgomery *v.* Foulis, 1795; Bell's Ca. 283; 2 Ill. 327. Henderson *v.* Wilson, 1797; M. 15,444; rev. 3 Pat. 316; 2 Ill. 495. Trotter *v.* Trotter, 1826; 5 S. 78; 3 W. & S. 407; Murray *v.* Smith, 1828; 6 S. 690. Dundas *v.* Dundas, 1829; 7 S. 241; aff. 4 W. & S. 460. Bennet *v.* Bennet's Trs., 1829; 7 S. 817. Hewit's Trs., *cit.* See above, § 1884.

(*k*) Paterson *v.* Spreul, 1745; M. 3333. Ker, *supra* (*c*).

(*l*) **M. Breadalbane's Trs.** *v.* **D. Buckingham,** 1840, 2 D. 731. Minto *v.* Kirkpatrick, 1842; 4 D. 1224. Davidson's Trs. *v.* Davidson, 1871; 9 Macph. 995. **Macfarlane's Trs.** *v.* **Oliver**, 1882; 9 R. 1138 (whole Court—where the doctrine of equitable compensation is fully discussed). See above, § 1587, 1890. Russell's Trs. *v.* Gardiners, 1886; 13 R. 989. Ross *v.* Ross, 1896; 23 R. 1024.

(*m*) M'Laren *v.* Howie, 1869; 8 Macph. 106. Darling's Exrs. *v.* Darling, 1869; 41 Sc. Jur. 545. See as to the application of the principle of implied will in a universal settlement to a widow claiming her legal rights, Caithness' Trs. *v.* Caithness, 1877; 4 R. 937. M'Fadyen *v.* M'Fadyen's Trs., 1882; 10 R. 285. Donaldson *v.* Tainsh's Trs., 1886; 13 R. 969. Stewart *v.* Bruce's Trs., 1898; 25 R. 965; and above, § 1591 (*k*).

CHAPTER XI

OF MARRIAGE CONTRACTS

1941. General View. — The patrimonial rights of the parties as legally affected by marriage (*a*), may be variously modified by contract (*b*): and two situations are distinguishable in considering this subject: one, where the parties are under no restraint or limitation; another, where the parties (or one of them), by former marriage contract or otherwise, are under limitations (*c*).

'When a marriage contract is entered into, it is usual that the husband's *jus mariti* be expressly renounced, or be excluded from the wife's benefits under the contract, even though the right has been abolished by statute in the case of marriages contracted since 18th July 1881 (*d*); and it is still necessary as well as usual that the husband's *jus administrationis* (*e*) be renounced or excluded expressly, seeing that the latter right is only partially affected by the Act. An ante-nuptial conveyance of the wife's estate to trustees excludes by implication the *jus mariti* from that estate; indeed, it is enough to exclude that right that the wife has by ante-nuptial contract dealt with her property in a way inconsistent with the assignation otherwise implied in marriage (*f*). Moreover, as mere exclusion of the husband's rights does not prevent the wife from intrusting her funds to him, whereby they may be subjected to his debts, it is usual to put them under the control of trustees—a device apt at the same time to secure provisions by the husband in favour of his wife and children (*g*).

'It is important to bear in mind that marriage contracts, ante-nuptial and post-nuptial, and the law relating to them, are unaffected by the Married Women's Property Act of 1881 (*h*). The capacity of entering into a contract of marriage is the same as that of marrying (*i.e.* the same as that of contracting generally (*i*)), and the woman's capacity is determined by the law of her own domicile (*k*). It is probable that the onerous and protective character of a marriage contract as ante-nuptial will not be impaired by its having been actually completed after the ceremony of marriage, if it have been finally adjusted before the ceremony, or have followed on an anterior specific obligation to execute it (*l*).'

(*a*) See above, § 1546 et seq., and 1593 et seq.
(*b*) 3 Ersk. 3. § 30, and 8. § 38–43. 1 Bell's Com. 636, 641; 2 *ib.* 188, 190. Fraser, Husband and Wife (2nd ed.), 1333 sqq. Murray, Property of Married Persons, 86 sqq. M. Bell's Convg. (3rd ed.), 850 sqq., which perhaps contains the best and clearest exposition of the subject in our law.
(*c*) Below, § 1978 sqq. (*d*) Above, § 1560D, 1561 sq.
(*e*) Above, § 1560D, 1563 sq.
(*f*) *Per* L. M'Laren in Bruce's Trs. *v.* Bruce's Tr., 1894; 21 R. 593. Above, § 1562; and comp. § 1946 (4), etc., below, as to claims on death.
(*g*) Below, § 1944, 1986, etc.
(*h*) 44 and 45 Vict. c. 21, § 1 (5), 8. Bel *v.* Bell, 1897; 25 R. 310. Above, § 1560D.
(*i*) Above, § 1506, 1523, 1537; below, § 2067 sqq., 2088 sqq.
(*k*) Cooper *v.* Cooper's Trs., *cit.*, § 1946.
(*l*) Cooper, *cit.* Brown *v.* Govan, 1 Feb. 1820; F. C.

1942. Marriage contracts are ante-nuptial or post-nuptial. These differ in a very important respect from each other (*a*). The stipulations in an *ante-nuptial* marriage contract are conditions of the marriage, and onerous (*b*); effectual not only to bind the parties themselves, but as against creditors, to raise a *jus crediti* or sustain a preference (*c*); 'effectual as against third parties donors to a spouse to override conditions of the gift, unless guarded by a trust, inconsistent with the obligations of the marriage contract (*d*). But as the parties contract merely with reference to the intended marriage and its consequences, stipulations which have no immediate relation to these presumed purposes, such as provisions or destinations in favour of strangers to the marriage, including ascendant or collateral relatives of either spouse, though in form contractual, are *primâ facie* not onerous and binding on the parties (*e*). On the other hand, those in favour not only of the wife and children, but also of the issue of children of the marriage, have this quality (*f*). There is no presumption that a marriage contract is primarily or substantially of a testamentary nature. That depends on the tenor of the deed and of its several parts; and in many cases it is important to notice—in regard, for example, to questions of vesting—that such deeds are intended to regulate the rights of parties during their lives (*g*).

'*Homologation by Marriage.*—Contrary to the rule which obtains in England under the Statute of Frauds (*h*), an informal and invalid ante-nuptial contract is confirmed by the subsequent marriage, as *rei interventus* (*i*).'

As marriage without a contract has the effect of incorporating and identifying the condition and fortunes of the wife and children with those of the husband and father, no alteration to the prejudice of creditors can be made by *post-nuptial* contract in favour of wife or children after insolvency (*k*); and even the *jus crediti* arising to children in respect to legitim by the unconditional marriage of their parents, is protected against such contracts.

(*a*) 4 Ersk. 1. § 33-4; 1 Bell's Com. 636, 641, and vol. ii. 188, 190. 1621, c. 18. Above, § 1616 sqq. Below, § 1986. M'Laren on Wills (3rd ed.), p. 656.

(*b*) Onerosity may exist though the deed be not in form mutual, but unilateral. Mercer *v.* Anstruther, 1871; 9 Macph. 618; 1872, 10 Macph. H. L. 39. Forrest *v.* Robertson, 1876; 4 R. 22, 37. See Mackenzie *v.* Mackenzie's Trs., 1878; 5 R. 1027. Onerosity as between the parties may be imported into a post-nuptial mutual deed of the spouses by that deed being made a substitute for their ante-nuptial contract, under which they are sole beneficiaries and which they can thus supersede. Croll's Trs. *v.* Alexander, 1895; 22 R. 677.

(*c*) Carphin *v.* Clapperton, 1867; 5 Macph. 797. Below, § 1944.

(*d*) Douglas' Trs. *v.* Kay's Trs., 1879; 7 R. 295; and Simson's Trs. *v.* Brown, 1890; 17 R. 581; overruling Thurburn's Trs. *v.* Maclaine, 1864; 3 Macph. 134.

(*e*) 1 Bankt. 5. § 15. 3 Ersk. 8. § 39. Sommerville *v.* Sommerville, May 18, 1819; F. C. Macleod *v.* Cunninghame, 1841; 3 D. 1288; aff. 5 Bell's App. 210. Mackie *v.* Gloag's Trs. (Herbertson), 1884; 9 App. Ca. 303; 11 R. H. L. 10. De Mestre *v.* West, 1891; A. C. 264.

(*f*) Hall's Trs. *v.* Macdonald, 1892; 19 R. 567; revd. 1893, A. C. 642; 20 R. H. L. 88. Authorities in (*a*), (*b*), (*c*). See Ferguson's Curator *v.* Ferguson's Trs., 1893; 20 R. 835.

(*g*) M'Onie *v.* Whyte, 1890; 15 App. Ca. 156; 17 R. H. L. 53.

(*h*) See, *e.g.*, Caton *v.* Caton, L. R. 2 H. L. 127; 35 L. J. Ch. 272.

(*i*) 3 Ersk. 3. § 48. Nisbet *v.* Newlands, 1630; M. 5682, 17,016, followed in Lang *v.* Lang's Trs., 1889; 16 R. 590.

(*k*) Wood *v.* Fairley, 1823; 2 S. 549; 2 Ill. 497. Jeffrey *v.* Campbell, 1825; 4 S. 32.

1943. Provisions against Premature Dissolution of Marriage. — The dissolution of marriage within the year, and without issue, 'defeated' not only the legal provisions, but also those which 'were' settled by convention between the parties, if there 'were' no stipulation to the contrary; nay, even settlements made by relations on the spouses in contemplation of the marriage 'were' thus defeated (*a*). 'But this law was altered by 18 Vict. c. 23, § 7, by which it is provided that "the whole rights of the survivor and of the representatives of the predeceaser shall be the same as if the marriage had subsisted for the period of year and day."'

It 'was' even doubted whether 'the old rule of law did' not defeat those settlements also which 'might' have been made by a father on his own son (*b*). In order to guard against these consequences, it 'was' competent and usual to provide by the contract, that notwithstanding the dissolution of the marriage within year and day, the legal provisions, or the provisions in the contract, 'should' subsist or take effect and continue in force (*c*).

(*a*) 1 Stair, 4. § 19. 1 Ersk. 6. § 38, 40. King *v.* Kerr, 1627; M. 6169; 2 Ill. 497. Guthrie *v.* Guthrie, 1672; M. 6171; 2 Ill. 277. Calder *v.* M'Intosh, 1610; M. 6167. Sommerville *v.* Bell, 1751; M. 13,045 and 6161. Cumming *v.* Gordon, 1781; M. 6165. Hunter *v.* Brown, 1766; M. 6164; Hailes, 126. See above, § 1575.

(*b*) 1 Ersk. 6. § 38 *in fin.* L. Burleigh *v.* Arnot, 1678; M. 6174. Hood *v.* Jack, 1739; M. 6178 and 6175; Elch. *Mut. Cont.* 17, and Notes, p. 303.

(*c*) Garden *v.* Stewart, 1743; M. 2271.

1944. Provisions against Insolvency of the Husband.—One great use of a marriage contract is to provide against the consequences of the future misconduct or misfortune of the husband (*a*). In order to give effect against creditors to provisions by marriage contract, they must be stipulated in an ante-nuptial or onerous contract; and, at all events, they must be reasonable in the circumstances of the parties (*b*).

Wife's Provisions.—And, 'irrespective of the provisions of the Married Women's Property Act, 1881, and previous statutes (*c*), which do not exclude or abridge the power of settlement by marriage contract,' 1. The rents of a heritable estate, or moveable funds coming to the wife from a third party, or belonging to herself, may by convention be kept separate for the wife's use. They may be settled on her with that provision by her father or other third party (*d*); or they may before marriage be placed by herself for that purpose in trust (*e*); 'but even where there is a trust, the wife has not a preference against creditors or protection against her subsequent acts, unless the right of the trustees be completed by infeftment or intimation or possession, as the case may require (*f*)'; or the husband may, by ante-nuptial contract, effectually renounce his *jus mariti* over the tocher or other fund, if clearly distinguished and separated (*g*). 2. Such a separate provision may be made from the husband's funds for the wife's use during the marriage by a deed before marriage; or even after, if the husband be solvent at the time (*h*). But it is inconsistent with such a purpose that the fund should be left under the husband's administration, 'or should be a mere right of succession (*i*). And the income of a provision payable to the husband during the marriage cannot be secured by himself against his creditors by being declared alimentary (*k*). That, however, may be done by a third party so settling or providing a fund, for he may attach what quality he pleases to his gift, if he protect it efficiently (*l*).' 3. A jointure or locality, to take effect on the husband's death, may be secured to the wife (*m*); 'and without such security, by infeftment or trust, the wife can only have a *jus crediti* for any provision, entitling her to a ranking, not a preference (*n*)'; but if made payable by half-yearly terms, though said to be for all the days of the life, there 'was, until the Apportionment Acts,' no claim for broken terms (*o*).

'*Revocation and Renunciation.*—4. When a provision for a wife, whether derived from her own or her husband's estate, is secured by an ante-nuptial contract and conveyance to trustees, or even by a post-nuptial conveyance to trustees, being reasonable in amount, she cannot during the marriage revoke the trust, which is held to have been constituted for the purpose of securing her, not only against her husband's creditors, but against his influence (*p*). On the other hand, there is no rule of law which prevents a married woman from renouncing or assigning to her husband, or to another with his consent, a provision which is only secured by infeftment, and is not vested in trustees (*q*); or from disposing freely of a fund conveyed to trustees but not settled for any matrimonial purpose in her own favour, *e.g.* if it be settled only for a liferent to her husband, which he renounces (*r*), or only for the purpose of giving her uncontrolled possession of the estate (*s*); or from revoking with consent of her husband, there being no children, a trust-deed executed by herself alone before marriage for behoof of the spouses in liferent and children in fee (*t*).'

Children's Provisions.—5. Provision may be made for the children; and if made payable 'or to bear interest' during the father's life, 'or at a period which may arrive during his life,' the children may be effectually secured in a preference, or entitled at least to rank with creditors for the amount (*u*).

(*a*) 1 Stair, 4. § 9. 1 Ersk. 6. § 14. Fraser, H. & W. 1344, 1348 sqq.

(*b*) Lady Campbell *v.* Campbell's Crs., 1744; M. 988; 2 Ill. 498. Jeffrey *v.* Campbell's Crs., 1825; 4 S. 32. M'Lachlan *v.* Campbell, 1824; 3 S. 192. Dunlop, *infra.* **Miller** *v.* **Learmonth,** 1870; 42 S. Jur. 418; L. R. 2 Sc App. 109; 1871, 10 Macph. 107; aff. 1875, 2 R. H. L. 62. Cf. Carphin *v.* Clapperton, 1867; 5 Macph. 797. Watson *v.* Cameron, 1874; 1 R. 882. Ker's Trs. *v.* Justice, 1866; 5 Macph. 4. Forrest *v.* Robertson's Trs., 1876; 4 R. 22. *Supra*, § 1942. Fraser, H. & W. 1348 sqq.

(*c*) See above, § 1560 sqq.

(*d*) Annand *v.* Chessels, 1774; M. 5844; aff. 2 Pat. 369; 2 Ill. 268.

(*e*) Murray's Trs. *v.* Dalrymple, 1745; M. 5843.

(*f*) Hyslop *v.* Small, 1821; 1 S. 137. Campbell's Trs. *v.* Whyte, 1884; 11 R. 1078. Mitchell's Trs. *v.* Gladstone, 1894; 21 R. 589 (wife's possession enough). See above, § 1317.

(*g*) M'Donald *v.* Doig, 1793; M. 5845; 2 Ill. 264. See above, § 1562.

(*h*) Dirleton, *Aliment.* Dickson *v.* Braidfoot, 1705; M.

10,396; 2 Ill. 497. This doctrine is incorrect, except so far as provision may now be made from funds coming to the wife by succession or donation, and apt to fall under the *jus mariti*. See above, § 1560A sqq. Dunlop *v.* Johnston, 1865; 3 Macph. 758; aff. 1867, 5 Macph. H. L. 22. Craig *v.* Galloway, 1860; 22 D. 1211; rev. 1861, 4 Macq. 267. **Miller** *v.* **Learmonth,** *supra.* Thomas *v.* City of Glasgow Bank, 1879; 6 R. 607. It even appears from the case of Miller, *cit.*, that post-nuptial provisions to take effect during the marriage made with mutual considerations would not now be readily sustained at common law, on the principles of § 71, above, given effect to in the cases of Woollen Manuf. of Haddington and Boswell, *ibi cit.* See the English cases in Mackay *v.* Douglas, 41 L. J. Ch. 539.

(*i*) Miller (*b*) and other cases in notes (*b*), (*p*). Grant *v.* Robertson, 1872; 10 Macph. 804. Honeyman & Wilson *v.* Robertson, 1886; 14 R. 163. *Infra*, § 1986, 1989.

(*k*) Mackenzie, *cit.*, § 1986 (*e*). **Learmonth** *v.* **Miller,** 1875; 2 R. H. L. 62. Hamilton's Trs. *v.* Hamilton, 1879; 6 R. 1216. Comp. Purdom *v.* Eliott, 1894; 21 R. 955; aff. 1895, A. C. 371; 22 R. H. L. 26 (annuity to wife for husband's behoof).

(*l*) See above, § 1562, 1942. Fraser, H. & W. 765. Lewis *v.* Anstruther, 1852; 15 D. 260. Corbet *v.* Waddell, 1879; 7 R. 200. Simson's Trs. *v.* Brown, 1890; 17 R. 581 (legacy excluding marriage trust ineffectual).

(*m*) Combe *v.* Chapman, 1826; 4 S. 513. Fraser, H. & W. 1423 sqq. Below, § 1946, 1947, 1953.

(*n*) *Infra*, § 1946. 1 Bell's Com. 637, 638 (682, 683, M'L.'s ed.). Burden *v.* Smith, 1736; Elch. *Mutual Contract*, 7; 1738, Cr. St. & Pat. 214. Mitchell *v.* Findlay, 1799; M. *Bankrupt*, Apx. 10. Wilson's Trs. *v.* Pagan, 1856; 18 D. 1096.

(*o*) Colebrook *v.* Gibson Craig, 1835; 13 S. 756. See above, § 1047, 1497A. 33 and 34 Vict. c. 35.

(*p*) **Anderson** *v.* **Buchanan,** 1837; 15 S. 1073. Pringle *v.* Anderson, 1868; 6 Macph. 982. Hope *v.* Hope's Trs., 1870; 8 Macph. 699. Ramsay *v.* Ramsay's Trs., 1871; 10 Macph. 120. **Menzies** *v.* **Murray,** 1875; 2 R. 507. Low *v.* Low's Trs., 1877; 5 R. 185 (post-nuptial). Peddie *v.* Peddie's Trs., 1891; 18 R. 491 (do.). Mackenzie *v.* Mackenzie's Trs., 1878; 5 R. 1027. Cf. Williamson *v.* Boothby, 1890; 17 R. 927 (bond of interdiction adopted by spouses). Reliance Life Ass. Co. (*s*) (wife's assignation of her whole benefit). *Secus* as to the trust for the wife involved in a policy under the M. W. Pol. of Ass. Act of 1880. Schumann *v.* Scot. Widows' Fund, 1886; 13 R. 678.

(*q*) Standard Prop. Invt. Co. *v.* Cowe, 1877; 4 R. 695. *Ante*, § 1562.

(*r*) Ramsay *v.* Ramsay's Trs., *cit.* Newlands *v.* Miller, 1882; 9 R. 1104. Laidlaws *v.* Newlands, 1884; 11 R. 481. See Fraser, H. & W. 1489 sqq.; *ante*, § 1560, 1562. See Higginbotham's Trs. *v.* Higginbotham, 1886; 13 R. 1016.

(*s*) Reliance Life Ass. Co. *v.* Halkett's Factor, 1891; 18 R. 615. Fowler's Trs. *v.* Fowler, 1898; 25 R. 1034.

(*t*) Watt *v.* Watson, 1897; 24 R. 330. See Mackenzie, *supra* (*p*), and below, § 2001. See also Eliott's Tr. *v.* Eliott, 1894; 21 R. 975. Taylor's Trs. (Murison) *v.* Dick, 1854; 16 D. 529 (revocation before marriage).

(*u*) 3 Ersk. 8. § 38, 39. See further below, § 1986. Strachan *v.* Strachan's Crs., Brown *v.* Govan, Mackenzie's Crs. *v.* Mackenzie, Cruickshank's Trs. *v.* Cruickshanks, and Goddard *v.* Stewart, *ibi citt.*

1945. Modification of Legal Provisions.—The legal provisions 'emerging at the dissolution of marriage' are not always suited to the views of the parties or to their situation, and are occasionally enlarged or restricted.

1946. (1.) *Modification of Jus Relictæ.*—The *jus relictæ* (*a*) may be modified thus:—1. A certain sum or annuity on survivance is sometimes provided, conferring a preference; or at least a *jus crediti*, which will entitle the wife to rank, on the husband's insolvency, as a contingent creditor in case of her survivance. 2. The provision is sometimes extended to her heirs; making her claim on insolvency not contingent merely, but future. 3. Sometimes the furniture, or a part of it, is provided to the wife; which, however, does not seem to give her any preference, as by retention (*b*). 4. If it be intended to give the wife a preference, it must be secured by infeftment (*c*). 5. If the wife do not discharge her *jus relictæ* (*d*), she will, in the general case, be held entitled to both that and her conventional provisions; although on summing up the conventional provisions, and comparing them with the husband's means, they may appear ample and reasonable. But where there is a plain intention by the marriage contract to regulate the whole succession, it may be inferred, as in a *quæstio voluntatis*, that a virtual discharge of the *jus relictæ* was intended (*e*). The wife may be relieved against an express or implied discharge of the provisions, on showing ignorance of her rights (*f*).

(*a*) See above, § 1591, and as to *jus relicti*, § 1580A.

(*b*) As to the construction of particular words, see above, § 1872. See as to furniture, above, § 1043, 1872. Fraser, H. & W. 1342. Tod's Trs. *v.* Finlay, 1872; 10 Macph. 422.

(*c*) See Ross *v.* Mackenzie, 1838; 16 S. 1385. Fraser, H. & W. 1355, 1423. Above, § 1944 (*n*). Below, § 1947.

(*d*) See above, § 1581.

(*e*) M'Kinnon *v.* M'Donald, 1763; M. 2278, 6451; 5 B. Sup. 894 (see note in 2 Ill. 280). Riddel *v.* Dalton, 1781; M. 6457. Tod *v.* Wemyss, 1770; M. 6451; Hailes, 384. Steuart's Trs. *v.* Steuart, 1891; 18 R. 1114. Buntine *v.* Buntine's Trs., 1894; 21 R. 714 (*jus relicti*). See above, § 1591. Fraser, H. & W. 1060 sqq.

(*f*) Hope *v.* Dickson, 1833; 12 S. 222; 2 Ill. 498. Bell *v.* Laurie, 1801; Hume, 486. Stewart *v.* Stewart, 1836; 15 S. 112; aff. M'L. & R. 401; 6 Cl. & F. 911. M'Gregor *v.* Black, March 2, 1839; F. C.; Macfarlane's Jury Ca. 266. Ross *v.* Masson, 1843; 5 D. 483. See Fraser, H. & W. 1062–1070. *Infra*, § 2100. A novel doctrine has lately been laid down, that in order to set aside an ante-nuptial renunciation of *jus relictæ* and terce on the ground of minority and lesion, a wife must prove not only ignorance, but actual patrimonial loss in respect of property actually vested in her; so that if she has no fortune of her own, it is not lesion if she merely gives away her chance of gain at the dissolution of the marriage. Cooper *v.* Cooper's Trs., 1885; 12 R. 473 (2nd Div.); rev. on a different ground, 1888, 13 App. Ca. 88; 15 R. H. L. 21.

1947. (2.) *Modification of the Terce.*—In the stipulations of a marriage contract these points are important:—1. A provision by jointure, locality, etc., if accepted, discharges the claim of terce (*a*). 2. Jointure (provided instead of terce) is an annuity secured on land, or by assignment of rents; the wife's preference depending on the completion of the real right. 3. Locality is an appropriation of certain lands to the wife in liferent; her security depending on the completion of her right by infeftment duly recorded (*b*). 4. If a jointure-house be provided, it is by a liferent infeftment, or by an obligation to pay a certain rent in place of a house (*c*). 5. If, by fault or fraud of the husband, those provisions should be left unsecured, the wife seems entitled to recur to her terce (*d*); and sometimes there is a stipulation to this effect.

(*a*) 1681, c. 10. See above, § 1596 et seq. Fraser, H. & W. 1112 sqq.
(*b*) 1 Bell's Com. 55, 637 (682, M'L.'s ed.). M. Bell's Convg. 866. Fraser, H. & W. 1425. M'Laren on Wills (3rd ed.), 661.
(*c*) 1 Jur. Styles, 188, 198, 201.
(*d*) 2 Craig, 22. § 27. Dirleton, *Terce*. 2 Stair, 6. § 16. M. Annandale *v.* Scott, 1711; M. 15,848; 2 Ill. 291. But see above, § 1597 *fin.*

1948. (3.) *Modification of Courtesy* (*a*).—Where there is an heir of the wife by a former marriage, a provision may be given to the husband instead of courtesy. No express provision made for the husband will exclude the courtesy, unless it be specially renounced.

(*a*) *Supra*, § 1605. Fraser, H. & W. 1125 sqq.

1949. (4.) *Modification of Legitim.*—The legitim may be defeated,—1. By a clause in an ante-nuptial marriage contract providing a sum in full of the children's claim of legitim (*a*). 2. It is not enough that the clause shall discharge all that the child may claim by the father's death; the legitim must be expressly discharged. 3. Without such a clause of discharge, the settlement of the stock and conquest of the parties on them and the children will not by implication discharge the legitim (*b*). 4. No provision to children in full of legitim, in a post-nuptial contract or deed of settlement, will defeat that right, unless accepted by the children (*c*); and where a provision is made to a child in liferent, and his or her children in fee, the rejection of the liferent and taking of the legitim has been held, 'in the absence of a contrary direction in the deed (*d*),' not to defeat the fee in the grandchildren (*e*). 5. The father has no power to regulate the succession to the legitim of his children, even in the case of an idiot or bankrupt (*f*).

(*a*) Stirling *v.* Luke, 1732; Elch. *Legitim*, 1; 2 Ill. 284. See above, § 1582 et seq., 1587. Fraser, H. & W. 1012 sqq.
(*b*) Burden *v.* Smith, 1736; Elch. *Mut. Cont.* 7; rev. 1738; 1 Cr. & St. 215. Nisbet *v.* Nisbet, 1726; M. 8181; rev. Robertson's Ap. 594; 2 Ill. 281. But see Home *v.* Watson, 1757; 5 B. Sup. 330. M. Breadalbane *v.* M. Chandos, 1836; 2 S. & M'L. 377; 2 Ill. 500. Collier *v.* Collier, 1833; 11 S. 912; and above, § 1587 (*c*), (*m*). Somerville's Trs. *v.* Dickson's Trs., 1887; 14 R. 770. See Rait *v.* Arbuthnott, 1892; 19 R. 687.
(*c*) 3 Ersk. 9. § 23. Johnston *v.* Paterson, 1825; 4 S. 234; 1829, 7 S. 229.
(*d*) Campbell's Trs. *v.* Campbell, 1889; 16 R. 1007.
(*e*) Fisher *v.* Dixon, 1831; 10 S. 55; 1833, 6 W. & S. 438. Jack's Trs. *v.* Marshall, 1879; 6 R. 543. Snody's Tr. *v.* Gibson's Trs., 1883; 10 R. 599.
(*f*) See above, § 1585.

1950. General Rules of Construction.—As general rules in construing the provisions and clauses of marriage contracts, it may be laid down—

1. That lands belonging to the husband, settled by marriage contract on the heirs of the marriage, are presumed to be still with the husband in fee; so that he may dispose of them for onerous causes, though not gratuitously (*a*). And they descend to the heir in heritage, unless otherwise specially destinated (*b*).

2. That the *universitas* of the fortunes of the parties is presumed to be with the husband in fee, descendible partly to the heir, partly to the executors; unless altered by special words of settlement (*c*). And the father has a discretionary power of distribution (*d*).

3. That conquest by the industry of the husband belongs still more clearly to the husband in fee, and is under his uncontrolled power of distribution (*e*).

4. That sums of money are the husband's in fee, descendible to executors, unless under special destination (*f*).

5. That the husband's fee may be restricted by special stipulation (*g*), and a more effectual and active right conferred on the children (*h*).

(*a*) Below, § 1959, 1960, 1971.
(*b*) Below, § 1964. (*c*) Below, § 1964, 1973.
(*d*) Below, § 1965 sqq., 1983, 1988.
(*e*) Below, § 1977. (*f*) Below, § 1987.
(*g*) Below, § 1978 sqq.
(*h*) Below, § 1968, 1986 sqq.

1951. Construction of Fee and Liferent. (1.) *General Rules.*—In the settlement of estates by marriage contract, the doctrine of fee and liferent is of great importance. The meaning of the terms, and the legal objection to a fee being *in pendente*, have already been explained (*a*). 'A liferent in moveable estate may be constituted or reserved only in favour of one in life at the date of the deed constituting or reserving such liferent. Where any person of full age, and born after the date of the deed, is in right of a liferent of moveable estate under any deed dated after July 31, 1868, such moveable estate belongs to him absolutely, and if held by trustees must be made over to him. The date of a testamentary deed is held, in regard to this question, to be the date of the testator's death, and that of a marriage contract to be the date of the dissolution of the marriage (*b*).'

(*a*) See above, § 1712 et seq.
(*b*) 31 and 32 Vict. c. 84, § 17. Comp. above, § 1707, 1712 *fin.*

1952. In marriage contracts,—1. The expression "conjunct fee and liferent" imports conjugal liferent only (*a*). It bestows a more ample right than an ordinary liferent, with a right to the casualties of superiority; but leaves the fee still where the former investiture placed it (*b*). 2. The simple expression "fee" implies always a right of property. 3. The simple expression "liferent" implies a mere usufruct, unless the fee is provided to persons (*c*) *nascituri*, in which case a supposed necessity implies a fee in the liferenter (*d*). 4. The addition of restrictive words, as "allenarly" confines the right to a mere usufruct, or at most to a fiduciary fee; 'and this construction applies equally to destinations of feudal and of moveable subjects' (*e*). 5. Where an 'absolute' power to dispone is expressly given, it implies a fee, or inclines the bias of construction towards a fee (*f*). And yet it is not inconsistent with a mere liferent (if that be plainly indicated), that there should be conferred a power to dispone in order to provide for particular circumstances or occasions (*g*); 'or an unlimited power to borrow (*h*).'

(*a*) During the marriage the husband alone is the liferenter. Thom *v.* Thom, 1852; 14 D. 862. Fraser, H. & W. 1435.
(*b*) 2 Stair, 6. § 11. Fergusson *v.* M'George, § 1954 (*a*). Muirhead *v.* Paterson, 1824; 2 S. 617; 2 Ill. 500. M'Gregor *v.* Forrester, § 1958 ("conjunct fee"). Madden *v.* Currie's Trs., 1842; 4 D. 749; 3 Ross' L. C. 723. Fraser, H. & W. 1429 sqq.
(*c*) The rule appears to be limited to destinations to parents and children; and a liferent to A. and B. and fee to the unborn children of B. does not import a fee in A. Ramsay *v.* Beveridge, 1854; 16 D. 764.
(*d*) See cases, *supra*, § 1712.
(*e*) **Mein** *v.* **Taylor**, 1827; 5 S. 779; aff. 1830, 4 W. & S. 22; 2 Ill. 345; printed Muir. See cases below (*f*). Gordon *v.* M'Intosh, 1845; 4 Bell's App. 105. *Supra*, § 1712 (*h*), 1714.
(*f*) Cumming *v.* L. Adv., 1756; M. 4268; 2 Ill. 244. Porterfield *v.* Graham, 1779; M. 4277; aff. 1780; 2 Pat. 537; 2 Ill. 350. Dickson *v.* Dickson, 1780; M. 4269. Baillie *v.* Clark, Feb. 23, 1809; F. C.; 2 Ill. 468. Falconer *v.* Moncrieff, 1825; 3 S. 455; 2 Ill. 527. Ramsay *v.* Cowan, 1833; 11 S. 967. Morris *v.* Tennant, 1853; 15 D. 716; aff. 1855, 18 D. H. L. 43; 27 S. Jur. 546; 30 *ib.* 493. This rule seems to apply only to liferents by reservation. A liferent by constitution, even with the widest power of disposal, is generally construed as a mere liferent. Alves *v.* Alves, 1861; 23 D. 712. Morris, *cit.* See, however, Mickel's Fr. *v.* Oliphant, 1892; 20 R. 172.
(*g*) **Wilson** *v.* **Glen**, Dec. 14, 1819; F. C.; 3 Ross' L. C. 716. Coltart *v.* Corrie, 1853; 15 D. 606. See above, § 1714.
(*h*) Boustead *v.* Gardner, 1879; 7 R. 139.

1953. (2.) *Husband, Wife, and Children.*—Where the husband has a large land estate, the standing investitures are commonly no otherwise changed than to give to the wife a jointure or locality (*a*); and to settle the succession on the heirs of the marriage, so as to confer a *jus crediti* effectual against gratuitous deeds (*b*).

(*a*) Above, § 1944 (3), 1947. Fraser, H. & W. 1423–5, 1458.
(*b*) Below, § 1966, 1971, etc. Fraser, H. & W. 1401 1467.

1954. Where the land estate is small, or the fortune of the parties in bonds, the interests of the husband and wife are commonly arranged and construed as follows:—1. If, in regard to land or bonds (as *quasi feuda*), words are used plainly indicative of a *fee*, they are held to confer a fee, provided there is power to bestow it (*a*). 2. If the right be expressly restricted to a *liferent*, this never is construed as a fee, unless where it is necessary to prevent the fee being *in pendente*, and then the fee is only fiduciary (*b*). 3. Where the words are so ambiguous, or so unskilfully used, as neither distinctly to confer a fee nor to restrict to a liferent, the fee goes according to the former destination, or the nature of the subject (*c*). 4. Where the fee is neither clearly disposed of nor left on the former destination, it is held *in dubio* to be with the husband as head of the family; leaving to the children *nascituri* only a *spes successionis* (*d*).

(*a*) *E.g.* a destination to the husband and wife and the longest liver and *their* heirs, etc., in fee. **Fergusson** *v.* **M'George**, 1739; M. 4202; Elch. *Fiar*, 5; 5 B. Sup. 664; 2 Ill. 500. See also Riddells *v.* Scott, 1747; M. 4203, 14,874; Elchies, *Fiar*, 8. Fraser, H. & W. 1435.
(*b*) See cases above, § 1952 and 1712. Fraser, H. & W. 1444.

(*c*) Livingston *v.* L. Napier, 1762; Bell's Ca. 184; 5 B. Sup. 885; 2 Ill. 425. Muirhead *v.* Paterson, 1824; 2 S. 617.
(*d*) Gordon *v.* Sutherland, 1748; M. 4398; 1751, 1 Cr. & St. 493. Fraser, H. & W. 1428–9.

1955. Where the property is derived from the wife, and given expressly or tacitly as tocher, the husband is fiar, if there be no clear destination to the contrary (*a*).

(*a*) Elliot's Crs. *v.* Elliot, 1720; M. 4244; 2 Ill. 502. Angus *v.* Ninian, 1733; M. 4244; Elch. *Fiar*, 1. Watson *v.* Johnston, 1766; M. 4288; Hailes, 82; 5 B. Sup. 927. Cameron *v.* Young, 1837; 15 S. 1205. Bruce Henderson *v.* Henderson, 1790; M. 4215; aff. 3 Pat. 686. Blairs *v.* Bell, 1782; M. 2280. Anderson *v.* Laidlaw, 1816; Hume, 218. See Dr. Mowbray's note in Hendry's Manual of Convg. (4th ed.), p. 390.

1956. In general, with regard to lands, where the words are restrictive, the rules are:—1. If the property (though the wife's) be settled on the parties "in conjunct fee and liferent, for *her* liferent only, and the heirs of the marriage in fee," the fee is with the husband (*a*). 'It is so also if the destination be to them in conjunct fee and liferent and the longest liver, and the heirs of the marriage in fee (*b*); and even though the fee should be destined to the children *nominatim*, that being a mere substitution (*c*).' 2. If a settlement which, conceived in simple terms, would give a fee to the husband, conveys to him the subjects "for *his liferent alimentary*," or "*liferent allenarly*, the fee to the heirs or children *nascituri*," there arises by legal necessity a fiduciary fee in the father, the real fee being in the children (*d*), 'and vesting in them immediately on birth, so as to transmit to their representatives without service or declarator, the children being disponees and not heirs of the fiduciary fiar (*e*).' 3. If the wife's heritable property 'or property coming from her father' be settled on the parties "in conjunct fee and liferent for *their* liferent only, and the children of the marriage in fee, whom failing, the heirs whatsoever of the parties equally," 'or the heirs whomsoever of the longest liver,' and if there are no heirs of the marriage, the fee is untransferred, and still in the wife (*f*). 4. If the subject be not one belonging to the wife, and be taken to the husband and wife and the longest liver in liferent, for their liferent use allenarly, and to their children *nominatim* in fee, the surviving wife is entitled to the liferent, notwithstanding any conveyance of the husband (*g*). 5. Where an estate or fund is vested in trust "for the parents in liferent, and the children in fee" (*h*), or where there is any other clear indication of the parent's right being a *mere liferent*, the fee is in the children (*i*). '6. It has been settled that a destination to the husband and wife in conjunct fee and liferent, and the longest liver and their heirs and assignees in fee, imports a fee to the survivor, even although the wife should survive (*k*); and the same effect is given even if the destination bear to be "in conjunct liferent" merely (*l*). But if instead of "*their* heirs" the fee be given in such a destination to the heirs of the marriage, the surviving spouse has only a liferent, and the fee remains where it was, there being no room for making the liferent by construction into a fee (*m*).'

(*a*) **Wilson** *v.* **Glen**, Dec. 14, 1819; F. C.; 2 Ill. 501; 3 Ross' L. C. 716. Comp. Livingston *v.* Napier, 1763; M. 15,418, 15,461; aff. 2 Pat. 108. Gordon *v.* M'Culloch, 1791; M. 15,465; Bell's 8vo Ca. 180.
(*b*) **Madden** *v.* **Currie's Trs.**, 1842; 4 D. 749; 3 Ross' L. C. 723.
(*c*) Wilson *v.* Glen, *cit.* Forrest *v.* Forrest, 1863; 1 Macph. 806.
(*d*) Gerran *v.* Alexander, 1781; M. 4402; 2 Ill. 347. **Newlands** *v.* **Newlands' Crs.**, 1794; M. 4289 and 4294; Bell's Ca. 54; 4 Pat. 43; 3 Ross' L. C. 634. Thomson *v.* Thomsons, 1794; Bell's Ca. 72; 1 Dow, 417; 5 Pat. 654. Harvey *v.* Donald, May 26, 1815; F. C. Falconar *v.* Moncrieff, 1825; 3 S. 455. Observe Dewar *v.* Campbell, 1825; 1 W. & S. 161; 3 Ross' L. C. 607. See Gibson's Trs. *v.* Ross, 1877; 4 R. 1038.
(*e*) Maxwell *v.* Logan, 1836; 15 S. 291; aff. 1839, M'L. & Rob. 790. Douglas *v.* Thomson, 1870; 8 Macph. 374. Otto *v.* Weir, 1871; 9 Macph. 660. If the fee be destined not to children but to the liferenter's "heir" or "the heirs of the marriage," it is uncertain who is fiar, and there is no vesting till the uncertainty is purified by death of the liferenter or dissolution of the marriage. Ferguson *v.* Ferguson, 1875; 2 R. 627. Maule, petr., 1876; 3 R. 831.
(*f*) Reid *v.* Reid, 1827; 6 S. 198; 2 Ill. 504. Cameron *v.* Young, 1837; 15 S. 1205. Myles *v.* Calman, 1857; 19 D. 408. Mackellar *v.* Marquis, 1840; 3 D. 172; 3 Ross' L. C. 741. Brough *v.* Adamson, 1887; 14 R. 858.
(*g*) Paterson *v.* Foreman, 1824; 2 S. 619. Gordon *v.* Baddon, 1848; 10 D. 1385.
(*h*) Seton *v.* Seton's Crs., 1793; M. 4219; 3 Ross' L. C. 685. It is so only when the trust is for preservation of the liferent funds till emergence of the fee. See above, § 1715, 1879.
(*i*) Bushby *v.* Rennie, 1825; 4 S. 110; 2 Ill. 505. Scotts *v.* Napier (Crombie), 1826; 4 S. 454; aff. 2 W. & S. 550; 2 Ill. 346. Cunningham *v.* Thomson, 1827; 5 S. 814. Ewan *v.* Watt, 1828; 6 S. 1125. Contrast Williamson *v.* Cochran, 1828; 6 S. 1035. See above, § 1715.
(*k*) Fergusson *v.* M'George, *supra*, § 1954 (*a*). Riddells, *ib.* Burrowes *v.* M'Farquhar's Trs., 1842; 4 D. 1484. See Scott *v.* Maxwell, 1850; 12 D. 932; aff. 2 Macq. 282. It is said that in moveable subjects the husband's and wife's heirs succeed equally under such a destination. 3 Ersk. 8. § 36 *fin.*
(*l*) M'Gregor *v.* Forrester, § 1958 (*a*).
(*m*) Mackellar *v.* Marquis, *cit.* (*f*). Cases in note (*f*).

1957. Where the settlement of feudal subjects or of bonds is not thus restricted, but conceived "to the husband and wife in conjunct fee and liferent" (or "in liferent"), "and the children of the marriage unnamed or unborn in fee"; or "to the husband (or to the wife) in liferent, and the children unborn or unnamed in fee"; there is construed to be only a *spes successionis* to the children, and the fee is held to be with the parent (*a*);—a construction 'of the latter form of destination,—in liferent,—' which, although it must now be adhered to, is so little justified by any real necessity, that it will not be extended (*b*).

(*a*) Watson *v.* Johnston, 1766; M. 4288; Hailes, 82; 2 Ill. 503. Ayton *v.* Jamieson, 1609; M. 4198; 2 Ill. 505. Johnston *v.* Cunningham, 1667; M. 4199; 2 B. Sup. 431. Allardice *v.* Smart, 1721; Robertson's Ap. 399. Neilson *v.* Murray, 1732; 1 Cr. St. & P. 65. Fulton *v.* King, 1811; Hume, 533. Dewar *v.* M'Kinnon, 1825; 1 W. & S. 161; 2 Ill. 348. Cases above, § 1713.

(*b*) **Mein** *v.* **Taylor,** 1827; 5 S. 779; aff. 1830, 4 W. & S. 22; 2 Ill. 345; printed Muir. Seton, *supra*, § 1956 (*h*).

1958. Where the fee is not left on the former investiture, but is *nominatim* given to one or other of the parties, or to the survivor, or to a child *nominatim*, this rules the fee (*a*).

(*a*) M'Intosh *v.* M'Intosh, Jan. 28, 1812; F. C.; 2 Ill. 506. Cannan *v.* Greig, 1794; M. 12,005. See Dykes *v.* Boyd, June 3, 1813; F. C. M'Gregor *v.* Forrester, 1831; 9 S. 675; aff. 1835, 1 S. & M'L. 441; 3 Ross' L. C. 733. Burrowes *v.* M'Farquhar's Trs., 1842; 4 D. 1484. Scott *v.* Maxwell, 1850; 12 D. 932. *Supra*, § 1712 (*e*).

1959. Where, in absence of other indications, the right is given to the heirs of either of the parties, it is a simple settlement *in obligatione*; giving so far a fee to the person whose heirs are favoured, that *onerous* deeds will be effectual, but not *gratuitous* deeds (*a*). Where the settlement gives a fee to the husband and a liferent to the wife, but restricts that liferent in the event of children of the marriage, the restriction is for behoof of the children only, and does not accresce to the fee, so as to be available to the creditors of the husband (*b*).

(*a*) Craig, 22. § 6. 3 Stair, 5. § 51. Cranston *v.* Wilkison, 1667; M. 4227; 2 Ill. 507. Elliot's Crs. *v.* Elliot, 1720; M. 4244; 2 Ill. 502. Angus *v.* Ninian, 1733; M. 4244. Blairs *v.* Bell, 1782; M. 2280. Fead *v.* Maxwell, 1709; M. 4240. See below, § 1964, 1950 (1). Gordon *v.* Mackintosh, 1841; 4 D. 192; aff. 1845, 4 Bell, 105. Reid *v.* Reid, § 1956 (*f*). Watson *v.* Johnston, *cit.* § 1957.

(*b*) Blairs, *supra* (*a*). Duff on Deeds, 195. The wife ranks for her whole jointure, and the provision is held to be made by her.

1960. Where, in land estates, the previous destination is not clearly changed, or where the subject comes as a tocher, a child, though named in the destination, has not the fee, but only *spes successionis in obligatione* (*a*). But where words are used which defeat the right that in either of these cases is presumed to be in the father, the fee is held then to be either in children named or born, or in the father as a fiduciary holder for children unborn (*b*).

(*a*) Livingston *v.* Napier, 1757; 5 B. Sup. 885; Bell's Ca. 184; 2 Ill. 425. Wilson *v.* Glen, Dec. 14, 1819; F. C.; 2 Ill. 501.

(*b*) Dykes *v.* Boyd, June 3, 1813; F. C.; 2 Ill. 506.

1961. Where the fund is moveable (as a legacy left to the wife), and it is settled on the spouses "in conjunct fee and liferent for the liferent use allenarly of the husband," or "of the survivor," and the wife survives, the wife is entitled, in so far as the fund is extant, to exclude creditors; and if it be used and consumed, she may claim as a creditor on the husband's estate (*a*).

(*a*) Rollo *v.* Ramsay, 1832; 11 S. 132; 2 Ill. 500.

1962. Provisions to Heirs and Children.—A destination to heirs-male of the marriage, with a provision, failing them, of a sum to daughters, will be available to the daughters though a son should exist, if he predecease the father (*a*).

(*a*) 3 Ersk. 8. § 38. Fraser, H. & W. 1456.

1963. Moveable funds go by law equally to all the younger children; and this rule prevails, unless the words distinctly change this disposition. Therefore a settlement of moveables on the "heirs or children of the marriage," or on the "bairns of the marriage," leaves the rule of law to operate (*a*).

(*a*) M'Doual *v.* M'Doual, 1727; M. 12,844; 2 Ill. 508. See Dallas *v.* Dallas, 1743; 5 B. Sup. 728; as qualified by Watson *v.* Scott, 1760; M. 985. Robertson *v.* Robertson, 1766; Hailes, 87. Comp. Blair *v.* Blair, 1849; 12 D. 97. Irvine *v.* Irvine, 1851; 13 D. 1367; *infra*, § 1964.

1964. A mixed succession of funds, both heritable and moveable, divides, according to the legal rule, between heir and executor. Therefore a settlement on "heirs," or on "heirs and children," or on "heirs and bairns," leaves that rule undisturbed, the estate going *seriatim* to the children, with the lawful preference of sex and age (*a*); or subject to construction, as in a *quæstio voluntatis* (*b*). But the expression is very different in effect when the flexible term heir is dropped, and the settlement is on "bairns and children of the marriage." By this destination *all* the children are included, and the preferable right of the heir *as such* is excluded, while he is comprehended as one of the children (*c*). A settlement on "bairns or children" implies in the father a power of distribution (*d*); but he cannot under that power give the estate to one (*e*). 'A destination to "issue" (a flexible term) includes all descendants, unless some limitation is suggested by the deed (*f*).' A distinction is to be observed between the construction of popular language in money provisions, and the same terms used in destinations of land (*g*).

(*a*) Wilson *v.* Wilson, 1769; M. 12,845; Hailes, 313; 2 Ill. 508. Lamond *v.* Lamond, 1776; M. 12,991; *Prov. to Heirs*, Apx. 1; Hailes, 710. Fairservice *v.* White, 1789; M. 2317, 14,486. Dollar *v.* Dollar, 1792; M. 13,008. Reid *v.* Woods, 1788; M. 14,483; 2 Ill. 422. Herries *v.* Herries, 1806; Hume, 528. Bowie *v.* Bowie, Feb. 23, 1809; F. C. Above, § 1950 (1), (2).

(*b*) Duncan *v.* Robertson, Feb. 9, 1813; F. C. Scott's Crs. *v.* Scott, 1760; M. 985. Rankine *v.* Rankine, 1736; M. 14,931; Elch. *Mut. Cont.* 4. Scott *v.* Scott, 1684; M. 12,842. Grant's Trs. *v.* Grant, 1862; 24 D. 1211.

(*c*) Duncan, *supra* (*b*). Hay *v.* Morison, 1663; M. 12,839. Carnegie *v.* Clark, 1677; M. 12,840. Kinloch *v.* Kinloch, 1678; M. 12,841; 3 B. Sup. 218. Herries, *cit.* Wilson *v.* Wilson, 1811; Hume, 534. Kibble *v.* Stevenson, 1832; 10 S. 341. Jardine *v.* Jardine, 1850; 12 D. 504.

(*d*) Lamond and Herries, *supra* (*a*). See also Hume, 530, note. Wight *v.* Wight, 1818; Hume, 539. Fraser, H. & W. 1365.

(*e*) It is said that the Court will correct an inadequate or illusory division. But "there is no case in which it has been successfully pleaded." *Per* L. Benholme in Smith's Trs. *v.* Graham, 1873; 11 Macph. 630. See Crawcour *v.* Graham, 1844; 6 D. 589; and Marder's Trs. *v.* Marder, 1853; 15 D. 633. Mackie *v.* Mackie's Trs., 1885; 12 R. 1230, 1239. Absolute exclusion of one of the objects of the power does not now avoid the appointment. 37 and 38 Vict. c. 37. Mackie, *cit.* Best's Trs. *v.* Reid, 1885; 13 R. 121. See Wight, *cit.* Watson *v.* Marjoribanks, 1837; 15 S. 586. *Infra*, § 1977 (*h*), and 1988.

(*f*) Macdonald, § 1965 (*a*). Turner's Trs. *v.* Turner, 1897; 24 R. 619. Bowie's Trs. *v.* Black, Feb. 25, 1899; 26 S. L. R. 475, and cases cited there.

(*g*) Redhouse's Crs. *v.* Glass, 1743; M. 2306; Elch. *Prov. to Heirs*, 7; aff. 1744, 1 Cr. & St. 372; 2 Ill. 339. Ewing *v.* Miller, 1747; M. 2308; Elch. Notes, 373; 2 Ill. 337. See § 1695 et seq.

1965. Where the destination of a marriage contract is "to heirs of the marriage," 'or "children of the marriage and their issue" (*a*),' or "to sons," or "to sons in their order," or "to heirs-portioners"; or where the father is bound at a certain time to take the investitures in such terms; the right of the children is a *spes successionis in obligatione* (*b*). 'Such a destination leaves to the father the fullest power of administration and even dilapidation during his life, subject only to the obligation to leave the estate to his children at his death, according to the rules stated in the following sections (*c*). The heir of provision taking under it will be subject to his father's debts, including provisions to younger children duly constituted (*d*).'

(*a*) Macdonald *v.* Hall, 1892; 19 R. 567; rev. 1893, A. C. 642; 20 R. H. L. 88. Cf. below, § 1989 (7).

(*b*) 3 Stair, 5. § 19. 3 Ersk. 8. § 38. Home *v.* French, 1608; M. 12,886. Dykes *v.* Dykes, Feb. 9, 1811; F. C.; 2 Ill. 526. Hyslop *v.* Maxwell, June 1, 1804; quoted in Dykes' Case. Cunningham *v.* Hathorn, Dec. 20, 1810; F. C.; 2 Ill. 511. E. Wemyss *v.* E. Haddington, Feb. 28, 1815; F. C.; aff. 1818, 6 Pat. 390.

(*c*) Cunningham and E. Wemyss, *citt.* **Arthur & Seymour** *v.* **Lamb,** 1870; 8 Macph. 928; 42 S. J. 542. Greenoak *v.* Greenoak, 1870; 8 Macph. 386. Cases above, § 1562. The effect of such a destination is not altered, even if it end in a destination to "his or their assignees." E. Glasgow's Trs. *v.* E. Glasgow, 1872; 11 Macph. 218.

(*d*) Macleod *v.* Leslie, 1868; 6 Macph. 445. See Bain *v.* Mackenzie, 1896; 23 R. 528.

1966. The right in the heir or children of a marriage, under a marriage contract so conceived as to confer a *jus crediti*, is not that of an heir, but of a proper creditor, 'subject to any conditions involved in the contract or presumed by law as to the vesting of the rights (*a*).'

(*a*) Below, § 1986, 1989. Blackburn, *cit.* § 1989.

1967. It requires no service, therefore, in the heir of a marriage to vest in him a right so conceived, or even to transmit it to his heir (*a*).

(*a*) 3 Ersk. 8. § 73. Ogilvy *v.* Ogilvy, Dec. 16, 1817; F. C.; 2 Ill. 434. Gordon's Trs. *v.* Harper, 1821; 1 S. 175; 2 Ill. 516. See above, § 1825; below, § 1987 *in fin.*

1968. The husband binding himself to lay out and secure money on land, etc., for the wife and children, may be compelled by action to do so; but (in the case of tenants particularly) so as not to ruin himself, leaving the efficacy in regard to the wife and children for subsequent question (*a*). The effect is, that to the wife the security will not be available against onerous, but only against gratuitous deeds (*b*); that the children cannot oppose onerous creditors (*c*); that, if the wife and children be disappointed by onerous deed, the father, his cautioners and representatives, are bound to indemnify (*d*); and that the father has, in regard to such sums 'given to children as a class,' a discretionary power of division among the children (*e*).

(*a*) See Granton *v.* Collington, 1628; M. 12,974; 2 Ill. 518. Smith *v.* Henderson, 1750; M. 6564. See below, § 1987. Wilson's Trs. *v.* Pagan, 1856; 18 D. 1056. The wife's desertion of her husband is no defence to her action for implement of an ante-nuptial contract. Smith *v.* Smith, 1866; 4 Macph. 279.

(*b*) Laws *v.* Tod, 1697 ; M. 4236, 12,899. Dalrymple *v.* Sinclair, 1748 ; M. 13,035. See Fraser, H. & W. 1355 ; and above, § 1946.
(*c*) Graham *v.* Rome, 1677 ; M. 12,887 ; 3 B. Sup. 131. Marjoribanks *v.* Marjoribanks, 1682 ; M. 12,891. Murray *v.* Murray, 1686 ; M. 12,895. Napier *v.* Irvine, 1696 ; M. 12,898.
(*d*) M'Intosh *v.* M'Intosh, 1717 ; M. 12,883. Fraser *v.* Fraser, 1677 ; M. 12,859. Fotheringham *v.* Fotheringham, 1734 ; M. 12,929, 12,941. See below, § 1971 (*a*).
(*e*) Edmonstone *v.* Edmonstone, 1706 ; M. 3193, 3219, 13,002. See above, § 1964 ; below, § 1971, 1977. Fraser, H. & W. 1365.

1969. Where lands are settled by marriage contract on the heir of the marriage, and afterwards much improved, the meliorations do not make a debt against the heir 'in favour of younger children on whom the moveable estate is settled' (*a*).

(*a*) Hyslop's Trs. *v.* Hyslop, Jan. 18, 1811 ; F. C. ; 2 Ill. 520.

1970. Father's Powers.—The effects of the rights above mentioned are important, in conferring powers on the father, or in leaving his ordinary powers unimpaired, or in laying him under limitations (*a*).

(*a*) See above, § 1964, 1968 ; and below, § 1977, 1988.

1971. 1. Where there is a fee in him, he may sell, or burden, or exhaust the subject; but under a personal obligation to indemnify at his death to the amount of the price received (*a*). 2. He cannot gratuitously alienate (*b*) ; and so can neither defeat the right of the heir, nor bestow the subject on a younger son (*c*) ; nor prefer a second son to the children of the eldest (*d*) ; nor cut off daughters of the marriage (or of a son of the marriage), preferring his own sons by another (*e*) ; nor select one out of the legal order of succession (*f*) ; nor sell and distribute, 'directly or by trust-deed,' to the disappointment of the heir of the marriage (*g*) ; nor make such additions to provisions as to compel a sale (*h*) ; 'nor purchase for his own behoof the interest of one of the children in an apportionable subject (*i*).' 3. Among the doubts entertained on this point, the safe rule is to hold that a father has no discretionary powers of substitution, distribution, etc., under settlements in marriage contracts, unless specially conferred (*k*). 4. The father has no power to limit, by entail or otherwise, those heirs who have right under the contract of marriage unqualified (*l*). And, 5. If there be power stipulated to entail the estate, the exercise of such power must be within the terms reserved (*m*).

(*a*) Cunningham *v.* Cunningham, 1804 ; M. 13,029 ; 2 Ill. 511. Cunningham *v.* Hathorn, Dec. 20, 1810 ; F. C. E. Wemyss *v.* E. Haddington, Feb. 28, 1815 ; F. C.; aff. 6 Pat. 390. Fulton *v.* King, 1811 ; Hume, 533. *Supra*, § 1968 (*d*).
(*b*) Home *v.* Home, 1708 ; M. 12,900 ; aff. Robertson's Ap. 47.
(*c*) Riddell *v.* Riddell, 1766 ; M. 13,019. Dykes *v.* Dykes, Feb. 9, 1811 ; F. C. ; 2 Ill. 526. Miller *v.* Miller, 1834 ; 12 S. 708. Haig *v.* Haig, 1857 ; 19 D. 449.
(*d*) Douglas *v.* Douglas, 1751 ; Elchies, *Tailzie*, 43 ; M. 12,989.
(*e*) Strang *v.* Strang, 1751 ; M. 12,988 ; Elch. *Tailzie*, 42. Graham *v.* Coltrain, 1743 ; M. 13,010 ; see Kilk. note, 5 B. Sup. 222. Speirs *v.* Dunlop, 1778 ; M. 13,026 ; Hailes, 806. Ormiston *v.* Ormiston, 1809 ; Hume, 531.
(*f*) Stewart *v.* Graham, 1743 ; M. 13,010 ; Elch. *Mut. Cont.* 20 ; 1 Cr. & St. 364. See as to altering order of succession so as to pass over idiot or bankrupt, 3 Ersk. 8. § 39, 49. Douglas *v.* Douglas, 1724 ; M. 13,002. Dicks *v.* Lindsay, *infra*, § 1973. Speirs *v.* Dunlop, *cit.* (*e*). Halket *v.* Halket, 1761 ; 5 B. Sup. 625 ; M. 15,416 ; 2 Pat. 231. Stewart, *infra* (*k*).
(*g*) Farquhar Gordon *v.* Gordon's Trs., 1790 ; M. 13,028. Hyslop *v.* Maxwell, 1804 ; F. C. for 1810, p. 192. M'Pherson, *infra* (*l*).
(*h*) Campbell *v.* M'Neill, 1766 ; M. 4287 ; 5 B. Sup. 933 ; Hailes, 154. Dykes, *supra* (*c*).
(*i*) M'Donald *v.* M'Gregor, 1874 ; 1 R. 817.
(*k*) 3 Ersk. 8. § 49, also § 39. Douglas *v.* Douglas, 1724 ; M. 13,002. Stewart *v.* Stewart, March 2, 1815 ; F. C. Thomson *v.* Thomsons, 1762 ; M. 13,018. "A very doubtful decision. See next case" ; 2 Ill. 514. Speirs, *supra* (*e*). Ponton *v.* Ponton, 1837 ; 15 S. 544. See Moir's Trs. *v.* Warner's Trs., 1871 ; 9 Macph. 848 ; Gillon's Trs., § 1988 (*n*), as to the distinction between a power reserved by an owner settling his estate in a marriage contract, and a mere power given to one who has no previous or other connection with the fund. Above, § 1968 ; below, § 1977.
(*l*) Watson *v.* Pyot, 1801 ; M. *Prov. to Heirs*, Apx. No. 4. Monro *v.* Monro, Feb. 13, 1810 ; F. C. Douglas *v.* Johnston, 1804 ; M. *Fiar Absol.* Apx. 1. M'Neil *v.* M'Neil's Trs., 1826 ; 4 S. 393. M'Pherson *v.* M'Pherson's Trs., 1827 ; 5 S. 826 ; 1831, 5 W. & S. 77. M'Donald's Trs. *v.* M'Donald, 1874 ; 1 R. 794 ; rev. 1875, 2 R. H. L. 125. Gillon's Trs., § 1988 (*n*).
(*m*) M'Neil, *supra* (*l*). M'Leod *v.* M'Leod, 1828 ; 6 S. 1043. Fleming *v.* Fleming, 1782 ; 2 Pat. 588. Cf. § 1988 (4) below.

1972. The concurrence of the heir of the marriage, having *jus crediti*, may render valid deeds otherways beyond the father's power ; for if the father should implement his obligation under the contract, the heir has then the absolute right to dispose of the subject as he chooses. The father and son concurring accomplish the same purpose by a single act which separately they may do (*a*). And the rule is not different where the heir of the marriage predeceases the father (*b*). 'So subsequent heirs under the destination are bound by the act of the heir first called, who is considered the favoured person, in accepting a conveyance, or homologating an entail, which is *ultra vires* of the father (*c*). It is otherwise if the heir under the contract be expressly forbidden to alter the destination (*d*).' But although the heir is thus held entitled to discharge his right by anticipation, there is nothing in him to transmit by assignation (*e*).

(*a*) Traill *v.* Traill, 1737; M. 12,985; to be corrected by Elch. *Mut. Cont.* No. 5; 2 Ill. 516; 1 Sandford on Entails, 247. Fothringham *v.* Ogilvie, 1797; M. 12,991.

(*b*) See Moodie *v.* Stewart, 1728; 1 Cr. & St. 20. Ranken *v.* Rankens, 1736; M. 14,931. **Routledge** *v.* **Carruthers**, May 22, 1812; F. C.; 1816, 4 Dow, 392; Dec. 16, 1819; F. C.; aff. 1820, 2 Bligh, 692; 6 Pat. 597. See as to this anomaly, *per* LL. Watson and Shand in Hall's Trs. *v.* Macdonald, 1893, A. C. 642; 20 R. H. L. 88.

(*c*) Bonar *v.* Arnot, 1683; M. 12,976; 2 B. Sup. 33. Elliot *v.* Elliot, 1803; M. 15,542. Routledge and Moodie, *citt.* See Baillie *v.* Cochrane, 1855; 17 D. 659; aff. 1857, 2 Macq. 529.

(*d*) Haig *v.* Haig, 1857; 19 D. 449.

(*e*) M'Conochie *v.* Greenlee, 1780; M. 13,040; 2 Ill. 518.

1973. A settlement generally of all lands, bonds, etc., which shall belong to the husband at his death, refers entirely to the actual state of his property at that time, leaving him the power of rational settlement (*a*), 'and of disposing *inter vivos* (*b*).'

(*a*) Dicks *v.* Lindsay, 1776; M. *Prov. to Heirs and Children*, 4; 5 B. Sup. 420; Hailes, 739; 2 Ill. 521. Champion *v.* Duncan, 1867; 6 Macph. 17.

(*b*) Hagart's Tr. *v.* Hagart, 1895; 22 R. 625 (wife's power to make gifts). Cf. § 1976 *fin.*, below.

1974. Provision of Conquest.—*Subjects.*—The provisions regarding conquest exhibit considerable varieties of expression. The word "conquest," used substantively in marriage contracts, comprehends whatever is acquired, whether heritable or moveable, during the marriage, by industry, economy, purchase or donation (*a*); but not what comes by succession, or legacy, or accession to a subject already acquired (*b*).

(*a*) As to donation, see *contra*, Fraser, H. & W. 1339, quoting Mercer, *cit.* (*b*). 1 Bankt. p. 109, and Kames' Eluc. art. 6, p. 41.

(*b*) 3 Stair, 5. § 52. 3 Ersk. 8. § 43. M'Laren, Wills (3rd ed.), 662. Stewart *v.* Stewart, 1678; M. 3052; 2 Ill. 522. Mercer *v.* Mercer, 1730; M. 3054. Rae *v.* Rae, Jan. 23, 1810; F. C. (legacies). Css. Dunfermline *v.* E. Dunfermline, 1628; 1 B. Sup. 252. Wauchope *v.* Wauchope, 1683; M. 12,948. Hunter's Trustees *v.* Macan, 1839; 1 D. 817.

1975. The word conquest is also sometimes used as a verb—"what we shall conquest or acquire": or its meaning is qualified by descriptive words; and the extent varies with the expression. But it may be observed that words generally descriptive of conquest are taken as extensively as if the single word conquest were employed. When the clause of conquest is special, it is strictly interpreted; so that conquest of lands and annualrents will not include leases; or conquest of lands, goods, and gear, will not carry debts; and so forth (*a*). 'So a provision of "estate and effects to be acquired" does not carry life interests and annuities (*b*).' The clause may be extended to what the husband may succeed to during the marriage; but this must be specially stipulated. 'But this meaning will more readily be given to a conveyance to trustees by the wife, of what she may "conquest or acquire" during the marriage (*c*).'

(*a*) 3 Stair, 5. § 52. Css. Dunfermline, *supra*, § 1974 (*b*), as reported by Durie; M. 3048. Robson *v.* Robson, 1673; M. 3050; 2 Ill. 521. Aiken *v.* ——, 1682; M. 3053. Young *v.* Young, 1696; M. 3054. Oliphant *v.* Finnie, 1629; M. 3066; contrasted with Knox *v.* Brown, 1625; M. 3065. Prestongrange *v.* Craigleith, 1682; M. 3054. Duncan *v.* Rae, Feb. 15, 1810; F. C. Paterson *v.* Farish, 1800; Hume, 128.

(*b*) Boyd's Trs. *v.* Boyd, 1877; 4 R. 1082. Young's Trs. *v.* Hally's Trs., 1885; 12 R. 968. Neilson's Trs. *v.* Henderson, 1897; 24 R. 1135.

(*c*) Diggens *v.* Gordon, 1865; 3 Macph. 609; aff. 1867; 5 Macph. H. L. 75. See Napier *v.* Orr, 1864; 3 Macph. 57.

1976. *Time of Acquisition.*—In questions relative to conquest during the marriage, doubts may arise as to the time at which the acquisition takes place; and this in special clauses of conquest is commonly settled. 'In a provision by a wife of all that belongs to her at the inception, or that shall belong to her during the subsistence of her marriage, is *primâ facie* included all she acquires while the marriage endures (*a*). The conquest as a provision to children is ascertainable at the death of the parent making it (*b*).'

(*a*) Young's Trs. *v.* Young's Trs., 1892; 20 R. 22. Contrast Wyllie's Trs. *v.* Boyd, 1891; 18 R. 1121 ("now or at my decease"); and see Dowie *v.* Hagart, 1894; 21 R. 1052.

(*b*) Anderson, Cruickshanks, and Russell, below, § 1977 (*f*), (*h*). 3 Ersk. 8. § 43.

1977. *Effect.*—These points seem to be fixed:—1. If provision be made in favour of the wife, of a direct liferent of the conquest, or by allotting to her a share of the conquest, the husband will have power over it or not, according to the force of the expression. But, generally, it may be observed that, unless excluded, he has an implied power (saving always a competency to the wife) of providing rationally either for children of a former marriage (*a*), or for children of a subsequent marriage (*b*). 2. A provision of conquest to the children may be variously conceived: as, to heirs and bairns; to the heir of the marriage; to heirs of the marriage; to bairns or children of the marriage. And these are construed as already stated (*c*). 3. A provision of conquest gives no *jus crediti* during marriage or the father's life (*d*). 4. The father, 'although he cannot (it seems) defeat the destination by purely gratuitous deeds (*e*),' has power of onerous and rational disposal, under a provision of the *universitas* of conquest (*f*). 5. Children have no action against their father to ascertain the extent of the conquest, even on dissolution of the marriage; nor are they entitled to use inhibition against him (*g*). 6. Not only has the father full power of onerous and rational disposal of the conquest, but his obligation under such clauses is only to the family, and he has an ample power of distribution, though not of exclusion (*h*).

(*a*) Robson, *supra*, § 1975 (*a*). Anderson *v.* Bruce, 1680; M. 12,890; 2 Ill. 523.
(*b*) Anderson, *supra* (*a*). See below, § 1981.
(*c*) See above, § 1694 et seq., 1964.
(*d*) Fraser *v.* Fraser, 1677; M. 12,859; 2 Ill. 520. Arthur & Seymour *v.* Lamb, 1870; 8 Macph. 928.
(*e*) *Infra*, cases in note (*h*). Fraser, H. & W. 1413. *Supra*, § 1971.
(*f*) 3 Ersk. 8. § 43. Murray *v.* Murray, 1677; M. 12,944. Mitchell *v.* Littlejohn, 1676; M. 3190. Gibson *v.* Thomson, 1679; M. 12,946. Gordon *v.* Gordon, 1693; 4 B. Sup. 51, 260. Oliphant *v.* Oliphant, 1693; *ib.* 74. Anderson *v.* Anderson, 1684; M. 12,960. Cruickshanks *v.* Cruickshanks, 1685; M. 12,964. M'Conochie *v.* Greenlee, 1780; M. 13,040; 2 Ill. 518. Ormiston *v.* Ormiston, 1809; Hume, 531. Cowan and Champion, *infra*. Cf. Hagart's Trs. *v.* Hagart, 1895; 22 R. 625. Above, § 1950 (3).
(*g*) Lawson *v.* Kennedy, 1694; 4 B. Sup. 154. Carnegie *v.* Smith, 1677; M. 12,888. Leslie *v.* Leslie's Crs., 1710; M. 1018. 3 Ersk. 8. § 38, 39.
(*h*) Dowie *v.* Dowie, 1727; M. 13,004. Russells *v.* Russell, 1779; M. 3072; Hailes, 833. Campbells *v.* Campbells, 1738; M. 6849, 4076, 13,004; 5 B. Sup. 214, 651, 683, 720; Elch. *Mut. Cont.* 14. Lamond *v.* Lamond, 1776; M. 12,991, and *Prov. to Heirs and Children*, Apx. 1; Hailes, 710; 2 Ill. 509. Cuming *v.* Kennedy, 1699; M. 6443, 12,959. Ormiston, *supra* (*f*). Wilson *v.* Wilson, 1811; Hume, 534. Cowan *v.* Young, 1669; M. 12,942. Champion *v.* Duncan, 1867; 6 Macph. 17, 22 (*per* L. Curriehill). See above, § 1964.

1978. Effect of Marriage Contracts under first and subsequent Marriages (*a*).—The rights of existing children have influence on those of the issue of a subsequent marriage; and parties about to enter into marriage, or to settle provisions on each other or on children, may be restrained by previous marriage contracts or limitations.

(*a*) Fraser, H. & W. 1361, 1415, 1502.

1979. The right of children of a former marriage may be prejudicial to that of the children of a subsequent marriage; the children of the husband by a former marriage being entitled to partake of the legitim, as it may turn out at his death (*a*); while children of the wife by a former marriage will partake of her *jus relictæ*. And stipulations may be required in a second marriage contract, either to extend or to limit the right of the prior children (*b*). 'So the children of a former marriage may be treated in a marriage contract along with those to be procreated of the intended marriage as a single class, and at once take a vested interest in the settled estate (*c*).'

(*a*) See Bishop's Trs. *v.* Bishop, 1894; 21 R. 728.
(*b*) Balmain *v.* Graham, 1721; M. 8199; 2 Ill. 526.
(*c*) Mackie *v.* Gloag's Tr. (Herbertson), 1883; 10 R. 746; rev. 1884, 11 R. H. L. 10; 9 App. Ca. 303. Correct Fraser, H. & W. 1410.

1980. By marriage contract, the father's or mother's power of settling by subsequent contract the heritable or moveable estate may be abridged.

1981. In marriage contracts relating to land, it is held that, notwithstanding a former contract, in which the land has been settled simply on the children *nascituri*, or on the heirs of the marriage, the father has still a power of granting rational provisions to his subsequent wife or children, should he have no other fund out of which to provide them, 'and the same principle is applicable where the settlement or obligation relates to moveable estate' (*a*). But it will bar such power of subsequent provision, if, under the first marriage contract, a real right of fee shall have been constituted in the children; or such proper *jus crediti* created in them as will support an inhibition (*b*).

(*a*) 3 Ersk. 8. § 40, 42. Dykes *v.* Dykes, Feb. 9, 1811; F. C.; 2 Ill. 526 (provision of jointure to wife of younger son). See M'Culloch *v.* M'Culloch, 1763; 5 B. Sup. 895. Bruce *v.* Bruce, 1761; M. 13,036. Miller *v.* Miller, 1822; 1 S. App. 308. Guthrie *v.* Cowan, 1846; 9 D. 124. Wilson's Trs. *v.* Pagan, 1856; 18 D. 1097. Cumming *v.* Cumming, 1858; 20 D. 1280. Arthur & Seymour *v.* Lamb, 1870; 8 Macph. 928. Walkinshaw's Trs. *v.* Walkinshaw, 1872; 10 Macph. 763. Haldane *v.* Hutchison, 1885; 13 R. 179. See above, § 1971.
(*b*) Falconar *v.* Moncrieff, 1825; 3 S. 455. Erskine *v.* Erskine, 1826; 4 S. 357. Thomson *v.* Gourlay, 1824; 2 S. App. 183. See also Douglas *v.* Douglas, 1724; M. 12,910. Marjoribanks' Crs. *v.* Marjoribanks, 1682; M. 12,891; 2 Ill. 519. Wood *v.* Fairley, 1823; 2 S. 477; 2 Ill. 497. Douglas *v.* Johnston, 1804; M. *Fiar Absol.* Apx. 1. Monro *v.* Monro, Feb. 13, 1810; F. C.

1982. When bonds have been granted to, or obligations undertaken to lay out money for, children of a former marriage, these, according to the conception of them, will either confer a preference or give a ground of action in favour of the former children (*a*).

(*a*) 3 Ersk. 8. § 40. Miller *v.* Cunningham, 1793; Hume, 527. Mackie *v.* Gloag's Tr. (Herbertson), *supra*, § 1979 (*c*).

1983. *Universitas settled on children* leaves in the father the power of rational provision for subsequent children (*a*).

(*a*) See cases cited above, § 1981.

1984. A father may be restrained from granting subsequent provisions, by becoming a party to the marriage contract of his son; the degree of restraint depending on the stipulation undertaken (*a*).

(*a*) Miller *v.* Miller, 1822; 1 S. App. 308; 2 Ill. 528. Grant *v.* Grant, 1712; 5 B. Sup. 86.

1985. Effect of Money Provisions to Heirs and Children.—In the granting of such provisions two objects are proposed: either, 1. Absolute security to the child or children against the future misfortunes of the father; or, 2. A reasonable security against capricious and gratuitous alienations to their prejudice. The former requires the investment of money with special destination; or the constitution of a trust for the children; or bonds of provision conferring a *jus crediti*; or at least an obligation to invest the money (*a*). The latter requires only a simple destination in a bond; or the providing of a sum to the children, payable at the father's death; or in the marriage contract a provision of money to the heirs, or to the children or bairns of the marriage. The effects of such provisions are to be viewed either as in a question with creditors, or as in a question with the father and his representatives.

(*a*) 1 Bell's Com. 640 (685, M'L.'s ed.). **Goddard** *v.* **Stewart,** 1844; 6 D. 1018, 1024. Herries, Farquhar, & Co. *v.* Brown, *infra*, § 1986 (*c*). Beattie's Trs. *v.* Cowper's Trs., 1862; 24 D. 519. Walkinshaw's Trs. *v.* Walkinshaw, 1872; 10 Macph. 763. An unfulfilled obligation to provide and secure does not give the security as stated. Goddard, *cit.*, and next section (*b*).

1986. (1.) *Effect in a Question with Creditors.*—In such provisions it is material to observe whether the marriage contract be ante-nuptial or post-nuptial, attending to the distinction of effect already stated (*a*).

In ante-nuptial contracts, the effect of money provisions, as against creditors, depends mainly on their being made payable during the father's life, so as to form a debt against him. If so made payable, the *jus crediti* will either be preferable, or will rank *pari passu* with creditors, according as there is an accompanying real security, or only a personal obligation (*b*). If the provision be not payable till after the father's death, it cannot compete with creditors (*c*), unless the provision has been made for an onerous consideration (*d*). Where the provision is to children *nascituri*, it is effectual to confer a *jus crediti*, if a term be fixed, 'although only for payment of interest,' which, although contingent, *may* happen during the father's life (*e*). It was in some cases held that, although the provision was secured heritably, this was not sufficient to give a *jus crediti*, effectual in competition with creditors, if the provision was payable only on the father's death; the security, as accessory, being held to have no greater extent than the principal (*f*). But the whole Court has found the *jus crediti* to be fully established by such security, 'or by intimated assignation, whatever may be the term of payment, where there is an express or constructive trust for the children, as, if the father's right be strictly limited to a liferent' (*g*).

In post-nuptial contracts (and in *mortis causâ* settlements by a father), the provisions to the wife and children will receive effect only where the husband was solvent at the time of making the deed; or, if payable on his death, where he has died solvent, leaving sufficient to pay both his debts and the provisions (*h*).

(*a*) See above, § 1942.

(*b*) 3 Ersk. 8. § 40. Cases, *infra* (*c*). Fraser, H. & W. 1356 sqq., 1379. Above, § 1944 (4).

(*c*) Strachan *v.* Strachan's Crs., 1754; M. 13,053, also 998; 5 B. Sup. 814–15, and *ib.* p. 274 for Kilkerran's Report; Elch. *Adjud.* 41; *Aliment*, 14; 2 Ill. 528. Blackburn *v.* Oliver, May 29, 1816; F. C.; 2 Ill. 532; and Wilson *v.* Wight, 1816; Hume, 537 (see 18 D. 1103). Brown *v.* Govan, Feb. 1, 1820; F. C.; 2 Ill. 530. **Herries, Farquhar, & Co.** *v.* **Brown,** 1838; 16 S. 948. *Supra*, § 1944 (*g*). Browning *v.* Hamilton, 1837; 15 S. 999. Goddard *v.* Stewart, 1844; 6 D. 1018. Cruickshanks' Trs. *v.* Cruickshanks, 1853; 16 D. 7. Jameson *v.* Strachan, 1835; 13 S. 318.

(*d*) Garden *v.* Stirling, Nov. 26, 1822; F. C.; 2 S. 34; 2 Ill. 532; see L. Moncreiff's Note, 11 S. 371. Gordon *v.* Murray, 1833; 11 S. 368. Thomson *v.* Gourlay, 1824; 2 S. App. 183.

(*e*) Lyon *v.* Crs. of Easter Ogle, 1724; M. 8150. Ballingall *v.* Henderson, 1759; M. 12,919. M'Tavish *v.* Creditors, 1787; M. 12,922. See 1 Bell's Com. 641, note. Mackenzie's Crs. *v.* Mackenzie, 1792; M. 12,924; and

Prov. to Heirs, Apx. 3; Bell's 8vo Ca. 404; 3 Pat. 409. Goddard, *cit.* Wilson *v.* Pagan, 1856; 18 D. 1134. Cruickshanks, *cit.*

(*f*) Brown, *supra* (*c*). Goddard *v.* Stewart, Wilson *v.* Wight, and Wilson *v.* Pagan, *citt.* A trust coming into effect at the truster's death is unavailing. Forrest *v.* Robertson's Trs., 1876; 4 R. 22.

(*g*) **Herries, Farquhar, & Co.**, *supra* (*c*), and cases therein cited. Poole *v.* Anderson, 1834; 12 S. 481. M'Gregor *v.* M'Donald, 1843; 5 D. 888. Rollo *v.* Ramsay, 1832; 11 S. 132.

(*h*) Cult's Crs. *v.* Children, 1783; M. 974. Grierson *v.* Wallace, 1821; 1 S. 9. Remington & Co. *v.* Bruce, 1826; 5 S. 119, and 1829, 8 S. 215; 1 Ill. 76. See 2 Bell's Com. 192. *Supra*, § 1944.

1987. (2.) *Effect in a Question with the Father's Representatives.*—The effect of such provisions is very different in a question with the representatives of the father, from their effect against creditors. 1. Where the fee is in the father, and the right of the children a mere *spes successionis,* there is no action or diligence to the children against the father. 2. Where the father has a mere liferent, or is bound to infeft the children at a particular term, or is bound not to contract debt so as to defeat the provision, action and diligence are competent to the children (*a*). 3. Where the father has bound himself to the children, they are creditors, with different remedies in different circumstances. Thus, where the obligation is to pay or invest during the marriage, the children require no service as a title to pursue, and have remedy by inhibition or under the Act 1621 (*b*). Where the obligation is not prestable during the father's life, the children, although they have no *jus crediti* against onerous creditors of the father, may pursue the father's representative for implement (*c*), and challenge gratuitous deeds as *contra fidem tabularum nuptialium* (*d*). And even where the terms are so general as to give no *jus crediti* in relation to creditors, action will lie against the father's cautioner (*e*). 4. Where the father has invested the money, or settled the stipulated sum, on the heirs of the marriage, a service is necessary; for the relation is no longer as debtor and creditor, but the children have only *spes successionis* (*f*).

(*a*) 3 Ersk. 8. § 40. Fraser, H. & W. 1363; *supra*, § 1968.

(*b*) Wallace *v.* Wallace, 1665; M. 12,857; 2 Ill. 533. Panton *v.* Irvine, 1684; M. 12,860. Fraser *v.* Fraser, 1677; M. 12,859; 2 Ill. 520. Hay *v.* E. Tweeddale, 1676; M. 12,857. Cairns *v.* Cairns, 1705; M. 12,862. Douglas *v.* Douglas, 1724; M. 12,910. Anderson *v.* Shiell's Heirs, 1747; M. 12,868. Monro *v.* Duff, 1733; M. 12,886. Gibson *v.* Arbuthnot, 1726; M. 12,885. Oliphant *v.* Oliphant, 1704; M. 12,966. Moncreiff *v.* Moncreiff's Crs., 1759; M. 12,871. 3 Ersk. 8. § 38 *in fin.*

(*c*) Borthwick *v.* Borthwick, 1731; Cr. & St. 53. Dundas *v.* Dundas, 1839; 1 D. 731. Wilson *v.* Wilson, 1811; Hume, 534. Kibble *v.* Stevenson, 1832; 10 S. 341.

(*d*) Marshall's Crs. *v.* Children, 1709; M. 12,907; 2 Ill. 535. Lockhart's Crs. *v.* Lockhart, 1741; M. 12,914. Strachan *v.* Strachan's Crs., 1754; M. 13,053; 2 Ill. 528.

(*e*) Dickson *v.* Mill, 1707; M. 12,940–1. Fotheringham *v.* Fotheringham, 1734; M. 12,941; correcting Crawford *v.* Kennoway, Nov. 23, 1677; M. 12,934. Fraser, H. & W. 1381.

(*f*) Anderson, *supra* (*b*). See Campbell *v.* Duncan, 1732; M. 12,885. Christie *v.* Dunn, 1806; M. *Prov. to Heirs and Chil.* 5. Moncreiff *v.* Crs., 1765; 5 B. Sup. 909. See M. 12,871. Cameron *v.* Robertson, 1784; M. 12,879; Hailes, 953. See below, § 1989. Fraser, H. & W. 1475.

1988. *Implement.*—1. The obligation must be fulfilled according to its true import. So, an obligation to settle lands on the *heirs* of the marriage is not implemented by a disposition to children equally (*a*); nor is it duly implemented by a deed, whereby part of the estate is otherwise disposed of (*b*); nor by a settlement in which additional provisions are given gratuitously to younger children, or so as to compel the heir to sell the estate (*c*); nor by a deed in which unfavourable conditions are imposed on the heir (*d*). But, 2. Provided the full right is given, there may be substitutions not impairing the right (*e*); or there may be reservations of the father's liferent (*f*). 3. Onerous or ante-nuptial provisions are not revocable (*g*); but post-nuptial or gratuitous provisions may be revoked by a second marriage contract (*h*). But a disposition of lands to the eldest son under the burden of debts is not a revocation (*i*). 4. In exercising a reserved or implied power of division, it must appear that there was truly an intention to exercise the faculty (*k*). 'Such a power may be exercised from time to time by several appointments (*l*); and it may be executed in a will which deals also with other estate of the testator immixed with the fund to be divided (*m*). But it must be exercised according to the terms of the deed by which it is given or reserved, not (*e.g.*) conferring benefits on persons who are strangers to the power, or altering the quality of the estate given, as by limiting it to a liferent (*n*). The appointment may not be valid as to part, and void so far as it is *ultra vires*; for it is impossible to know what the appointer might have have done if he had known that what he attempted was inept (*o*).'

(*a*) Hyslop *v.* Maxwell, June 1, 1804; F. C. for 1810, p. 192; 2 Ill. 514.
(*b*) Watson *v.* Pyot, 1801; M. *Prov. to H. and Ch.* Apx. No. 4.
(*c*) Riddell *v.* Riddell, 1766; M. 13,019. Campbell *v.* M'Neil, 1766; M. 4287; 5 B. Sup. 917, 933; Hailes, 152. Dykes *v.* Dykes, Feb. 9, 1811; F. C.
(*d*) Douglas *v.* Douglas' Trs., 1792; M. 2985; 2 Ill. 537. *Supra*, § 1971.
(*e*) Nisbet *v.* Nisbet, 1738; M. 12,986; Elch. *Mut. Cont.* 9. Trail *v.* Trail, 1737; M. 12,985; Elch. *ib.* 5. Craik *v.* Craik, 1728; M. 12,984. See Bonar *v.* Arnot, Feb. 1683; M. 12,976. As to the effect of such substitutions and the institute's power of defeating them, see Fraser, H. & W. 1410, 1411, 1419, 1420. *Supra*, § 1972 (*c*).
(*f*) Paton *v.* Urquhart, 1698; 4 B. Sup. 400.
(*g*) Above, § 1944 (4), and cases there cited.
(*h*) Mitchelson *v.* Mitchelson, Nov. 15, 1820; F. C.
(*i*) Thom *v.* Lunn, 1779; M. 2292.
(*k*) Sievwright *v.* Dallas, 1824; 2 S. 643. Mercer *v.* Anstruther's Trs., 1872; 10 Macph. H. L. 39; in C. of S., 7 Macph. 689; 8 Macph. 1013; 9 Macph. 619. Jardine, *infra* (*n*).
(*l*) Anstruther's Trs., *supra*. Murray's Trs. *v.* Murray, 1872; 10 Macph. 778.
(*m*) Milne *v.* Milne, 1826; 4 S. 679. Mackie *v.* Mackie's Trs., 1885; 12 R. 1230.
(*n*) Fraser, H. & W. 1368. Greenock Bank *v.* Smith, 1844; 6 D. 1340. Brodie *v.* Mowbray, 1840; 3 D. 31. Ormiston *v.* Ormiston, 1809; Hume, 531. Baikie's Trs. *v.* Oxley, 1862; 24 D. 589. M'Donald *v.* M'Donald, 1874; 1 R. 794; rev. 1875, 2 R. H. L. 125 (condition annexed null). Jardine *v.* Jardine, 1850; 12 D. 504. Whyte *v.* Murray, 1888; 16 R. 95. Gillon's Trs. *v.* Gillon, 1890; 17 R. 435 (*per* L. Rutherfurd Clark).
(*o*) Baikie and Gillon's Trs., *citt.* Eccles *v.* Hunter, 1856; 18 D. 778. V. Strathallan *v.* D. Northumberland, 1840; 2 D. 840. See M'Donald, *cit.* (*n*); and above, § 1964, 1971.

1989. Vesting and Lapsing of Provisions (*a*).—Here the distinction between *jus crediti* and *spes successionis* is important (*b*). And, 1, If the provision be given to the children as successors of the father, the fee being still in him, they take as heirs, and there is no transmission of the right without service. 2. A proper *jus crediti* vests and transmits; but the presumption, 'it was said,' is that the father means the provision to affect his heir only, and not himself (*c*); and strong expressions are required to counteract it (*d*). 'It has been laid down, however, by very high authority that the presumption (if there be a presumption) has in later times been reversed (*e*).' 3. Where the provision is to heirs of the marriage, and not a *jus crediti*, there must be a service to transmit to the child's heir (*f*). 4. Where the provision is to a child or children *nominatim*, no service is required. '5. An obligation in favour of children expressed in general terms is presumed to be prestable at the dissolution of the marriage (*g*).' 6. Where the child or heir of the marriage dies before the term of payment, or before the father, the provision lapses (*h*). But, 7. The lawful issue of such child will succeed to the provision (*i*), 'according to the condition *si sine liberis* (*k*).' 8. The father may, during the child's life, transact and obtain a discharge (*l*); 'but all such discharges are construed strictly against the father (*m*); and if obtained to the child's lesion, and when he was ignorant of his legal rights, will be ineffectual (*n*). 9. The exercise of a power of appointment by a spouse during life has been found not to accelerate the vesting, where the appointer's death was the period designated by the contract (*o*); and exercise of such a power at the appointer's death likewise leaves the vesting unaffected, where the death of his surviving spouse is the stipulated period (*p*).'

(*a*) Fraser, H. & W. 1370 sqq.
(*b*) See above, § 1965 et seq.
(*c*) 3 Ersk. 8. § 40 *in fin.* Wilson *v.* Sellars, 1757; M. 5184; 2 Ill. 538. Wilson *v.* Niblie, 1825; 2 S. 430. See Somerville's Trs. *v.* Dickson, 1865; 3 Macph. 602; aff. 1867, 5 Macph. H. L. 69.
(*d*) Clerk *v.* His Sisters, 1682; M. 12,881. L. Braxfield in Cameron *v.* Robertson, 1784; M. 12,879; Hailes, 953; 2 Ill. 536. Wilson, *supra* (*c*). 3 Ersk. 8. § 40. M'Tavish *v.* Creditors, 1787; M. 12,922; 1 Bell's Com. 641, note.
(*e*) Herries, Farquhar, & Co. *v.* Brown, 1838; 16 S. 948, 969.
(*f*) Anderson *v.* Shiells' Heirs, 1747; M. 12,868; 2 Ill. 534. See above, § 1987 (*f*).
(*g*) *Per* L. M'Laren in Blackburn, *infra*. Fraser, H. & W. 1371.
(*h*) M'Conochie *v.* Greenlee, 1780; M. 13,040; 2 Ill. 518. Ainslie *v.* Elliot, 1749; M. 13,044. Russell *v.* Russell, 1769; M. 13,049. M'Intosh *v.* M'Intosh, 1716; M. 12,881. Grindlay *v.* Merchant Co., July 1, 1814; F. C.
(*i*) See *supra*, § 1704, 1776. Wood *v.* Aitchison, 1789; M. 13,043; 2 Ill. 404. Binning *v.* Binning, 1767; M. 13,047; 2 Ill. 403. Montrose Mags. *v.* Robertson, 1733; M. 6398. Rattray *v.* Blair, 1790; Hume, 526. Edwardes *v.* Hughes, 1892; A. C. 583; 19 R. H. L. 33 (revg. 18 R. 319), and authorities cited.
(*k*) Stewart *v.* Graham, and M'Leod, *supra*, § 1971 (*f*), (*m*). Arthur, § 1965 (*c*). Macdonald *v.* Hall, 1892; 19 R. 567; rev. 1893, A. C. 642; 20 R. H. L. 88.
(*l*) Routledge *v.* Carruthers, May 22, 1812; F. C.; 1816, 4 Dow, 392; Dec. 16, 1819; F. C.; aff. 1820, 2 Bligh, 692; 6 Pat. 597; 2 Ill. 517. Trail *v.* Trail, 1737; Elch. *Mut. Cont.* 5. Monro *v.* Gordon, 1769; 5 B. Sup. 880. See Mercer's Trs. *v.* Anstruther's Trs., 1871; 9 Macph. 618; 1872, 10 Macph. H. L. 39. Whyte *v.* Robertson, 1896; 17 R. 708.
(*m*) Ewen *v.* Ewen's Trs., 1825; 1 W. & S. 595; 4 W. & S. 346.
(*n*) See above, § 11 *fin.*, 14 (*s*). Gordon *v.* Glendonwyn, 1835; 13 S. 882; aff. 1838; 3 S. & M'L. 57 (fair discharge sustained).
(*o*) Cuming's Tr. *v.* Cuming, 1896; 24 R. 153.
(*p*) Blackburn's Trs. *v.* Blackburn, 1896; 23 R. 698.

1990. *Conditions.*—1. Although provisions to children in marriage contracts which do not give a *jus crediti* prestable during the father's life, lapse by the child's predecease without lawful issue (*a*), a provision payable at a day certain does not lapse by predecease, but transmits to the representatives of the child (*b*); and the same rule applies where the payment is made to depend on any event which must arrive; as the death of any person (*c*). 2. A provision payable at a contingent term falls by predecease (*d*), and does not vest by the father's predecease, unless the child shall survive the contingent term (*e*). 3. It signifies not whether the contingency is applied to the payment of the money or to the provision itself (*f*). 4. Where there is an inconsistency in the condition, it is a *quæstio voluntatis* with a bias in favour of the provision (*g*). 5. A provision depending on an uncertain event is suspended, and vests no right, while the event is uncertain,—as a provision to daughters on failure of heirs-male (*h*); but if the condition be annexed only to the *payment*, a trust being created to sustain the right till payment shall be exigible, the right vests, and payment may be demanded when the condition seems to be reasonably fulfilled (*i*).

(*a*) See above, § 1775, as to conditions. Bell *v.* Davidson, 1730; M. 6342; 2 Ill. 539. Gordon *v.* Ross, 1757; M. 6343. Arbuthnot *v.* Arbuthnot, 1816; Hume, 536; and see *supra*, § 1989.

(*b*) Campbell *v.* Pollock, 1717; M. 6342.

(*c*) Home *v.* Home, 1807; Hume, 530.

(*d*) Edgar *v.* Edgar, 1665; M. 6325, 12,854. Clerk *v.* His Sisters, 1682; M. 6330. Bell *v.* Mason, 1749; M. 6332; Elch. Notes, p. 112. Omey *v.* M'Larty, 1788; M. 6340; 2 Ill. 454. Home, *supra* (*c*).

(*e*) Grindlay *v.* Merchant Co., July 1, 1814; F. C.

(*f*) See above, § 1883.

(*g*) M'Kays *v.* L. Reay, 1790; Bell's Ca. 394. Fraser, H. & W. 1373.

(*h*) Carstairs *v.* Carstairs, 1672; M. 2992–3 and 13,049; 2 B. Sup. 637; 2 Ill. 454.

(*i*) Scheniman *v.* Wilson, 1828; 6 S. 1019; 2 Ill. 540. Shaw *v.* Shaw, 1828; 6 S. 1149 (condition of failure of issue); see Blackwood *v.* Blackwood, 1833; 11 S. 699. Craigie *v.* Gordon, 1837; 15 S. 1157. Primrose, petr., 1850; 12 D. 917. Massy *v.* Cunninghame, 1872; 11 Macph. 173.

CHAPTER XII

OF TRUST-DEEDS

1991. Nature and Object of Trust-Deeds.—Conveyancers provide for many of the difficulties which arise in the settlement of estates on marriage by means of deeds of trust. This also is a very convenient device for securing estates to unknown, or unborn, or very numerous parties; or for distributing in shares, or dividing among creditors, the property or price of lands. The whole doctrine and practice depends on these principles: 1. That a full legal estate is created in the person of the trustee, to be held by him against all adverse parties and interests, for the accomplishment of certain ends and purposes. 2. That the uses and purposes of the trust operate as qualifications of the estate in the trustee, and as burdens on it preferable to all who may claim through him. 3. That those purposes and uses are effectually declared by directions in the deed, or by a reservation of power to declare in future, and a declaration made accordingly. 4. And that the reversionary right, so far as the estate is not exhausted by the uses and purposes, remains with the truster, available to him, his heirs and creditors.

1992. Constitution of the Trust.—In order to make an available trust, the subject of it must be legally vested in the trustee; and the purposes of the investment, and the powers necessary for accomplishing them, plainly and intelligibly declared in the deed of trust, or reserved to be declared afterwards.

1993. Nomination, Acceptance, Failure, and Assumption of Trustees.—The number of trustees differs according to the purpose of the trust. And,

1. For settling an insolvency or bankruptcy a single trustee is most eligible; the object of the trust being the immediate recovery of the funds, and settlement of the debts.

2. In cases of continued and prospective management (as in family settlements, or in trusts for the arrangement and extrication of the truster's affairs), it is desirable to unite the discretion and other trustworthy qualities of several trustees. 'It was formerly thought that' the presumption is, that the trustees are meant to act jointly, and the confidence of the truster to be reposed in them only while they continue together; and so in such a case it would seem that if one dies, the nomination falls. It certainly is so, '*i.e.* the nomination of all falls by the death of one,' if the nomination be 'expressly (*a*)' joint. 'But it has been settled that, in a testamentary deed containing a simple nomination of trustees; an appointment of the survivors is implied, on the principle that the truster prefers that any one of the trustees nominated should manage the estate rather than a judicial factor. The truster's intention is the rule (*b*).' Where a certain number is appointed a quorum, that number must accept, survive, act, and concur, in order to fulfil the trust (*c*). Where one is named *sine quo non*, he must concur in all acts, and his death dissolves the nomination (*d*).

The nomination commonly is to the acceptors or survivors, in which case the trust subsists while any survive and have accepted (*e*).

Where a nomination of trustees is defeated by unlooked-for failure of some of the nominees, the Court of Session will not authorise the diminished number to proceed (*f*). But they give effect to the trust by naming a factor. Formerly they named a trustee (*g*); now they interpose by the appointment of a judicial factor, responsible under the precautions of an Act of Sederunt providing for security, and the observance of certain rules in the execution of the office (*h*). But although this be the general rule, the Court has power in cases of necessity to supply a nomination of a trustee (*i*). The Court will not appoint a new trustee, or authorise one of several to act where discretionary powers are to be exercised (*k*).

'The Court exercised at common law the power of authorising a trustee or trustees to act alone where their number was reduced by the death, non-residence, or incapacity of the others (*l*). And doubts which existed have been removed by the Administration of Trusts Act, 1867, which applied only to trusts in which the trustees act gratuitously (*m*), but has since been extended to all trusts as defined in the Trusts Amendment Act, 1884 (*n*), and provides that, when trustees cannot be assumed under any trust-deed (*o*), or when a sole acting trustee has become insane or incapable of acting from physical or mental disability, the Court may appoint a trustee or trustees. Upon such appointment the former trustee ceases to be a trustee under the trust-deed (*p*); and trustees so appointed have no power to assume new trustees, unless it is expressly conferred upon them by the Court.'

3. No one can, without his consent and acceptance, be named a trustee, to the effect of compelling him to act. But if infeftment should be taken in his name without his knowledge, he may be compelled either to act or to denude, on being relieved of all consequences; or at least he may be denuded by a declarator or reduction (*q*).

4. One accepting as trustee is not afterwards entitled to decline acting, when his concurrence is necessary for extricating the trust (*r*), and he will be liable for the consequences of his refusal (*s*). 'But, with the consent of the beneficiaries, a trustee might competently resign (*t*); or upon cause shown, might obtain leave to resign from the Court (*u*). By statute, every gratuitous trust-deed not expressing the contrary is held to include an absolute (*v*) power of resignation,—a rule which applies to deeds executed prior to the date of the Act, if the trusts thereby constituted are afterwards in operation (*w*). By a later statute, regulations are introduced with regard to the resignation of trustees (*x*). Unless it is expressly permitted by the trust-deed, no trustee can resign to whom a legacy or bequest is expressly given on condition of his accepting the office of trustee (*y*).'

5. Among the various forms of nomination, the effect seems to be that while all those who are named are alive, and accept, they act by the majority, or by a quorum if such be named (*z*); that not the presence merely, but the concurrence also, of any one named as *sine quo non* is requisite; and that the non-acceptance, death, or incapacity of any of those named jointly, or of those necessary to form a quorum, or of the *sine quo non*, will defeat the nomination (*aa*), leaving the radical right or beneficial interest in the trust-estate to be made effectual by the Court of Session (*bb*). Trust is regarded in law as under the contract of mandate and gratuitous, and so it was held at one time even as to trusts for creditors (*cc*); but this would probably now be held only as to family trusts.

6. Sometimes trustees are empowered to assume others into the trust, or to devolve it on others; 'and now in every trust a sole trustee, or the quorum of trustees, has power to assume new trustees, unless the contrary be expressed in the trust-deed (*dd*)'; and this power, if exercised in lawful form, and strictly in terms of the power, 'was, and is,' effectual, even although executed on deathbed (*ee*). Or if that trust fails before the purposes are accomplished, the Court of Session, in its equitable jurisdiction, will interpose, or will authorise the person having the radical right to enter by a declaratory adjudication (*ff*).

(*a*) 1 Stair, 12. § 13. 3 Ersk. 3. § 34. Young *v.* Watson, 1740; M. 16,346.

(*b*) See 2 M'Laren on Wills, § 1723 sqq. Halley *v.* Gowans, 1840; 2 D. 623. Findlay, petr., 1855; 17 D. 1014. Gordon's Trs. *v.* Eglinton, 1851; 13 D. 1381. Seton *v.* Seton, 1855; 18 D. 117. Oswald's Trs. *v.* City of Glasgow Bank, 1879; 6 R. 461. Dalgleish *v.* Land Feuing Co., 1885; 13 R. 221. See Dawson *v.* Stirton, 1863; 2 Macph. 196. Miles *v.* N. B. Ry. Co., 1867; 5 Macph. 402.

(*c*) Freen *v.* Beveridge, 1832; 10 S. 727; 2 Ill. 542. Mr. Shaw says: This seems to apply to trusts *inter vivos*, not to those *mortis causâ*. Shaw's Bell's Com. 847 (*c*). But the distinction is hardly warranted by principle or authority. See 2 M'Laren, Wills and Succn. 177. Blisset''s Trs. *v.* Hope's Trs., 1854; 16 D. 482. Laird *v.* Miln, 1833; 12 S. 187. Shanks *v.* Aitken, 1830; 8 S. 639. Halley *v.* Gowans, *cit.* (*b*).

(*d*) See Vere *v.* Vere's Tutors, 1791; Bell's 8vo Ca. 554. Forbes *v.* E. Galloway's Trs., Feb. 2, 1808; F. C.; aff. 5 Pat. 226. 2 M'Laren, Wills and Succn. 180. *Infra*, note (*aa*).

(*e*) See above (*b*).

(*f*) Nisbet *v.* Fraser, 1835; 13 S. 384; 2 Ill. 545.

(*g*) Hepburn *v.* Ctess. Tarras, 1699; M. 7428. Campbell *v.* L. Monzie, 1752; M. 16,203. Grant, petr., 1790; M. 7454. See King's Coll. of Aberdeen, petrs., 1741; Elch. *Trust*, 11; *Jurisd.* 21; Notes, p. 215; 2 Ill. 543. Wotherspoon, petr., 1775; Hailes, 665. Littlejohn *v.* Hamilton, 1834; 7 W. & S. 380; 2 Ill. 544.

(*h*) See below, § 2117, 2121.

(*i*) Alexander, petr., 1824; 2 S. 745. Moir, petrs., 1826; 4 S. 801. Sheriffs *v.* Boyd, 1829; 7 S. 314. Smith, petrs., 1832; 10 S. 531. Lacy *v.* Lacy, 1836; 14 S. 1112. L. Melville *v.* Lady Baird Preston, 1838; 16 S. 457; H. L. 2 Rob. 45; 8 C. & F. 16. Miller *v.* Black's Trs., 1836; 14 S. 555; aff. 2 S. & M'L. 889. M'Aslan, petrs., 1841; 3 D. 1263; and other cases in 2 M'Laren, Wills and Succn. 220 sqq. Aikman, petr., 1881; 9 R. 213.

(*k*) Ireland *v.* Glass, 1833; 11 S. 626. Nisbet, *supra* (*f*). See Allan *v.* Mackay & Ewing, 1869; 8 Macph. 139. Simsons, petrs., 1883; 10 R. 540.

(*l*) Fraser, petr., 1837; 15 S. 692; 2 Ill. 545. Millar, petr., 1854; 16 D. 358. Watt, petr., 1854; 16 D. 952. 2 M'Laren on Wills, etc., § 1805, 1806.

(*m*) Mackenzie, petrs., 1872; 10 Macph. 749. It does not apply to an English trust, even when part of the trust-estate consists of heritable property in Scotland. Brockie, petrs., 1875; 2 R. 923. See below, § 1998B.

(*n*) 47 and 48 Vict. c. 63, § 2. Royal Bank, petrs., 1893; 20 R. 741.

(*o*) This applies to the case of a lapsed trust. Zoller, petr., 1868; 6 Macph. 577.

(*p*) 30 and 31 Vict. c. 97, § 12, where provision is also made for the completion of the title of the new trustee. See 37 and 38 Vict. c. 94, § 43–45.

(*q*) Dallas *v.* Leishman, 1710; M. 16,191. See Royal Infirmary *v.* L. Adv., 1861; 23 D. 1213, 1221.

(*r*) L. Lynedoch *v.* Ochterlony, 1827; 5 S. 358; 1830, 4 W. & S. 148. See Carstairs, petr., 1776; Hailes, 678. Davidson *v.* Mackenzie, 1835; 13 S. 1802.

(*s*) L. Lynedoch *v.* Ochterlony, 1832; 11 S. 60.

(*t*) Hill *v.* Mitchell, 1846; 9 D. 239.

(*u*) Hill, *cit.* Gordon, petr., 1854; 16 D. 884. Dick's Trs., petrs., 1855; 17 D. 835. Scott *v.* Muir's Trs., 1894; 22 R. 78.

(*v*) M'Connell's Trs., 1897; 25 R. 330.

(*w*) 24 and 25 Vict. c. 84, § 1. 26 and 27 Vict. c. 115. Reid, petr, 1863; 1 Macph. 774. Blair's Trs. *v.* Blair, 1863; 2 Macph. 284. Maxwell's Trs. *v.* Maxwell, 1874; 2 R. 71. Dalgleish *v.* Land Feuing Co., 1885; 13 R. 223.

(*x*) 30 and 31 Vict. c. 97, § 2, 9, 10, 18. 54 and 55 Vict. c. 44, § 7. Sinclair *v.* City of Glasg. Bk., 1879; 6 R. 571. Mitchell *v.* City of Glasg. Bk., 1878; 6 R. 439; aff. 1879, *ib.* H. L. 60. Fullarton's Trs. *v.* James, 1895; 23 R. 104 (revocation of resignation).

(*y*) *Ib.* § 1. See Orphoot, petr., 1897; 24 R. 871 (repayment of legacy).

(*z*) See L. Lynedoch, *supra* (*r*). Blisset's Trs. *v.* Hope's Trs., 1854; 16 D. 482. M'Culloch *v.* Wallace, 1846; 9 D. 32. Darling *v.* Darling, 1898; 25 R. 747 (duty of majority to dissenting minority). See as to executors, M'Target *v.* M'Target, 1829; 7 S. 591. Torrance *v.* Bryson, 1841; 4 D. 71. If no quorum be expressed, a majority of accepting and surviving trustees is a quorum. 24 and 25 Vict. c. 84, § 1.

(*aa*) Dick *v.* Ferguson, 1758; M. 7440. Stodart *v.* Rutherford, June 30, 1812; F. C. *Supra* (*d*).

(*bb*) Campbell, *supra* (*g*). Gavin *v.* Kirkpatrick, 1826; 4 S. 629; aff. 4 W. & S. 48. Hepburn, *supra* (*g*). M'Dowal *v.* M'Dowal, 1789; M. 7453. Busby, petr., 1823; 2 S. 176. Alexander, Sheriffs, and Smith, *supra* (*i*).

(*cc*) Johnston's Trs. *v.* Creditors, 1738; Elch. *Trust*, 6; M. 13,047. See 21 D. 1383. L. Gray *v.* Dundas, 1856; 19 D. 1. Lauder *v.* Miller, 1859; 21 D. 1353. Goodsir *v.* Carruthers, 1858; 20 D. 1141. Scott *v.* Handyside's Trs., 1868; 6 Macph. 753. *Infra*, § 1998 (*gg*).

(*dd*) 24 and 25 Vict. c. 84, § 1. 26 and 27 Vict. c. 115. 30 and 31 Vict. c. 97, § 11. Allan's Trs. *v.* Hairstens, 1878; 5 R. 576. Ainslie *v.* Ainslie, 1886; 14 R. 209 (executors). Malcolm *v.* Goldie, 1895; 22 R. 968. See above, par. 2 *fin.*

(*ee*) Roughhead *v.* Hunter, 1833; 11 S. 516; 2 Ill. 548. Ferrie *v.* Baird, 1834; 12 S. 672. Nisbet, *supra* (*f*). As to the mode of assuming trustees and completing title, see Mackilligin *v.* Mackilligin, 1855; 18 D. 96. Kelland *v.* Douglas, 1863; 2 Macph. 150. Bell *v.* City of Glasg. Bk., 1879; 6 R. 548; aff. *ib.* H. L. 55. Dalgleish *v.* Land Feuing Co., 1885; 13 R. 223. Murray's Trs. *v.* Young, 1887; 14 R. 574. 30 and 31 Vict. c. 97, § 11–13. Trustees to be assumed cannot be also tutors nominate, a father having no power to delegate the appointment of tutors. Walker *v.* Stronach, 1874; 2 R. 120. The power of assuming new trustees must be exercised with deliberation, regularity, and fairness (Reid *v.* Maxwell, 1852; 14 D. 449. Ferrie *v.* Baird, 1834; 12 S. 672. Davidson *v.* Mackenzie, 1835; 13 S. 1082); and an assumption without notice to a co-trustee is invalid (Wyse *v.* Abbott, 1881; 8 R. 983). The Court will not lightly interfere with the power to assume. Neilson *v.* Neilson, 1885; 12 R. 670.

(*ff*) Drummond *v.* M'Kenzie, 1758; M. 16,206. Dalziel *v.* Dalziel, 1756; M. 16,204. Sheriffs, *supra* (*i*). See above, No. 2; and above, § 835 (*h*).

1994. Vesting of the Estate in the Trustees.—This completes the constitution of the trust, with purpose to preserve it as a separate estate in the person of the trustees for the uses and purposes intended; guarding it at once against the truster himself, and his creditors or representatives, and against the trustee and his creditors. The estate must, in order to make the trust effectual, be vested either in all the trustees, or in some one to be held subject to the acts and directions of the others; and this vesting must be either by sasine, 'or by its modern equivalent, registration of the trust-deed, or a notarial instrument thereon,' or in such other mode already pointed out as may be requisite in completing conveyances. It may be conveyed to the trustees either *ex facie* absolutely, with an obligation or back-bond, in writing or otherwise, to fulfil the purposes of the trust; or it may be expressly conveyed in trust. It is convenient to have the estate absolute and *ex facie* unqualified in the trustees, as facilitating sales and transactions with third parties; but it exposes the estate to the creditors of the trustee, 'while the back-bond remains unrecorded' (*a*). Where the trust is made an express condition of the conveyance, it is an effectual qualification while the right continues personal; it is only a personal obligation if not recorded in the Register of Sasines and Reversions (*b*). If duly recorded, the trust is an inherent condition of the conveyance.

'A truster cannot, after the deed has passed beyond his control, revoke a deed, though gratuitous, truly intended, not to be testamentary, but to divest himself and confer an indefeasible and immediate right on the persons indicated by the words declaring the trusts (*c*).'

(*a*) See Jeffrey *v.* Paul, 1835; 1 S. & M'L. 767. Dalrymple *v.* Ranken, 1836; 15 S. 306; 2 Ill. 548. As to the completion of trustees' titles, see 37 and 38 Vict. c. 94, § 43–46.

(*b*) 1459, c. 27. 1617, c. 16. Keith *v.* Maxwell, 1795; M. 1163; Bell's fol. Ca. 234; 2 Ill. 106.

(*c*) See above, § 23. Tennent *v.* Tennent's Trs., 1869; 7 Macph. 936. Spalding *v.* Spalding's Trs., 1874; 2 R. 237, and Mackie *v.* Gloag's Trs., 1883; 10 R. 746; rev. 1884, 11 R. H. L. 10; 9 App. Ca. 303, and cases therein cited. Robertson *v.* Robertson's Trs., 1892; 19 R. 849. Shedden *v.* Shedden's Trs., 1895; 23 R. 228. Byres' Trs. *v.* Gemmell, 1895; 23 R. 332. See also § 1981, 1986 sqq.

1995. Proof of Trust.—Where the estate is conveyed in terms absolute, the qualification of trust must be established by writ or oath of the trustee. By the statute 1696, "no action of declarator of trust shall be sustained as to any deed of trust made for hereafter, except upon a declaration or back-bond of trust lawfully subscribed by the person alleged to be trustee, and against whom or his heirs or assignees the declarator shall be intended; or unless the same be referred to the oath of party *simpliciter*" (*a*). But to this rule there are exceptions, in distinguishing which two situations are to be marked. And,

(1.) *As between the Truster and his Heirs, and the Trustee and his Heirs*, the statute gives the rule, that the only evidence to be relied on is the writ or oath of the trustee. At one time a distinction was made between the effect of a deed of trust and the trust arising from professional employment and breach of mandate (*b*). But this was afterwards rejected, and the rule of the statute applied (*c*). It is not held necessary (notwithstanding the words of the Act) that the writing shall be a probative deed, provided it be subscribed by the party (*d*). Where the trust arises by *negotiorum gestio*, or where pupils are concerned, and where there is no opportunity of requiring a back-bond, other evidence will be received (*e*); 'so also where the defender's possession of the property sought to be recovered may be referred not to a distinct "deed of trust" establishing a right of property in him (*f*), but to transactions in the execution of a distinct and separate contract; such, for example, as may occur in questions between partners or joint obligants (*g*), or under an alleged mandate or employment (*h*), or where a life insurance policy truly belongs to a firm of which the insured is a member (*i*)'; or where the declaration of trust has been destroyed by fraud, or has perished by mischance (*k*). 'In short, the statute applies only where, for some reason of convenience and by agreement of parties, the documents of title to some property have been taken in the name of the trustee, though the beneficial right is really in the other party to the arrangement (*l*).' It is not indispensable that the deed or back-bond shall contain a positive, clear, and simple acknowledgment of trust; it is enough if it sufficiently evince or import a trust (*m*). 'And when the trust is proved by writ, the extent of the trustee's obligation may be cleared by parole (*n*).'

(2.) *As between the Truster's Creditors and the Trustee, 'or any third person who was not a party to the constitution of the Trust, but who has an interest in proving it, and the Trustee,'* the rule of the Act 1696 is not to be strictly applied, otherways frauds would be inscrutable by creditors (*o*). An acknowledgment of the trust by the representatives of the trustee is effectual to establish the trust (*p*).

(*a*) 1696, c. 25.

(*b*) Tweedie *v.* Loch, and Maxwell *v.* Maxwell (undated), 5 B. Sup. 630.

(*c*) Alison *v.* Forbes, 1771; M. 12,760; 2 Ill. 547. **Duggan** *v.* **Wight,** 1797; M. 12,761; aff. 3 Pat. 610. Mackay *v.* Ambrose, 1829; 7 S. 699. Macfarlane *v.* Fisher, 1837; 15 S. 978. L. Strathnaver *v.* Macbeath, 1731; M. 12,757; and Jackson *v.* Monro, M. 16,197, are not to be relied on. Leckie *v.* Leckie, 1854; 17 D. 77. Seth *v.* Hain, 1855; 17 D. 1117 (interest in lease). See **Marshall** *v.* **Lyell,** 1859; 21 D. 514. Walker *v.* Buchanan, Kennedy, & Co., 1857; 20 D 259. M'Vean *v.* M'Vean, 1864; 2 Macph. 1150 (interest in lease). Currer *v.* Dickson, 1857; 19 D. 99. Chalmers *v.* Chalmers, 1845; 7 D. 870. Gordon's Trs. *v.* E. Fife's Exrs., 1862; 34 Jur. 232. Dickson on

Evid. § 576. Evans *v.* Craig, 1871; 9 Macph. 801. Thomson *v.* Lindsay, 1873; 1 R. 73.

(*d*) Watson *v.* Forrester, 1708; M. 12,755. Taylor *v.* Crawford, 1833; 12 S. 39. Macfarlane, *cit.* (*c*). Seth *v.* Hain, and Walker, *citt.*

(*e*) Spreul *v.* Crawford, 1741; Elch. *Trust*, No. 1; M. 16,201. As to this case, see Marshall *v.* Lyell, 1859; 21 D. 514, 521.

(*f*) Laird & Co. *v.* Laird & Rutherfurd, 1884; 12 R. 294.

(*g*) Hume *v.* Middlemass, 1836; 15 S. 30. Kilpatrick *v.* Kilpatrick, 1841; 4 D. 109. Knox *v.* Martin, 1850; 12 D. 719. Lindsay *v.* Barmcotte, 1851; 13 D. 718. M. Queensberry *v.* Scottish Union Ins. Co., 1839; 1 D. 1203; aff. 1842; 1 Bell's App. 183. Laird & Co., *cit.*

(*h*) Horne *v.* Morrison, 1877; 4 R. 977. Pant Mawr Quarry Co. *v.* Fleming, 1883; 10 R. 457. See Lyell *v.* Kennedy, 1889; 14 App. Ca. 437, as to position of such a trustee and the application of limitations or prescription.

(*i*) Forrester *v.* Robson's Trs., 1875; 2 R. 755.

(*k*) Kennoway *v.* Ainslie, 1752; Elch. *Trust*, No. 15. See Chalmers and Walker, *citt.* (*c*). Watson *v.* Johnston, 1848; 6 Bell's App. 245. Church of Engl. Ins. Co. *v.* Wink, 1857; 19 D. 1079.

(*l*) Boswell *v.* Selkrig, 1811; Hume, 350. Horne *v.* Morrison, *cit.* Laird *v.* Laird & Rutherfurd, *cit.* (*f*). I have not altered the text in consequence of Dunn *v.* Pratt, 1898; 25 R. 461,—a case which depends on a fine distinction between trust and mandate, and in which Lord Kinnear dissented.

(*m*) Ramsay *v.* Butchers of Perth, 1748; M. 12,757. Stewart's Exrs. *v.* Stewart, 1777; 5 B. Sup. 631. See Watson, *supra* (*d*). Macfarlane, *supra* (*c*). Taylor *v.* Crawford, 1833; 12 S. 39. Mackay, *supra* (*c*). See cases cited above (*c*).

(*n*) Wood, Small, & Co. *v.* Spence, 1833; 12 S. 32. Miller *v.* Oliphant, 1843; 5 D. 836.

(*o*) L. Elibank *v.* Hamilton, 1827; 6 S. 69. Scott *v.* Miller, 1832; 11 S. 21. Lindsay *v.* Barmcotte, 1851; 13 D. 718. Middleton *v.* Rutherglen, 1861; 23 D. 526. Wink *v.* Speirs, 1867; 6 Macph. 77. Univ. of Aberdeen *v.* Mags. of Aberdeen, 1876; 3 R. 1087, 1101; aff. 4 R. H. L. 48. Hastie *v.* Steel, 1886; 13 R. 843. But the cases cited are not to be held as negativing the distinction between cases in which it is averred that rights have been taken as both the parties intended, to which the statute applies, and those in which the trust is said to have arisen by the act of the trustee alone. See Dickson on Evid. § 576.

(*p*) Montgomery's Exrs., petrs., Feb. 7, 1811; F. C.

1996. Beneficial Interest under the Trust.—This is in its nature a *jus crediti*, and has preference over the private creditors of the trustee, while it is effectual against the truster's creditors by the real right vested in the trustee for behoof of those entitled to the benefit of the trust. This *jus crediti* may be transferred to the trustee himself, in consequence of advances or engagements undertaken (*a*); or it may be in any number of persons, or in future or possible persons, or with any variety of conditions calculated to get quit of the technical difficulties of conveyancing. This *jus crediti* gives a personal action against the trustee. It may be conveyed by settlement (*b*) or by assignation (*c*). It is heritable or moveable, as the obligation is to transfer subjects, or to account for funds to the person favoured; and it may be attached accordingly '*tantum et tale* as it exists in the person of the beneficiary (*d*)' by adjudication or by arrestment (*e*). If the trust be for creditors enumerated in the trust-deed as recorded, the security is real. Whether a trust-deed will give preference to creditors whose names are not enumerated, and the amount of their debts recorded, is a question not yet settled (*f*).

(*a*) Fraser *v.* M'Naughton, 1829; 8 S. 104; 2 Ill. 559. See 2 M'Laren on Wills, 551; and *supra*, § 1453; *infra*, § 1998 (10).

(*b*) Gordon's Trs. *v.* Harper, 1821; 1 S. 221; 2 Ill. 516. 2 M'Laren on Wills, 127.

(*c*) M'Dowal *v.* Russell, 1824; 2 S. 682; 2 Ill. 351. 2 M'Laren on Wills, etc., 122.

(*d*) Weller *v.* Ker's Trs., 1864; 2 Macph. 371; aff. 1866, 4 Macph. H. L. 8; L. R. 1 Sc. App. 11. Smith *v.* Chambers' Trs., 1877; 5 R. 97; rev. 1878, *ib.* H. L. 151. See Trappes *v.* Meredith, 1871; 10 Macph. 38 (effect of sequestration in bankruptcy).

(*e*) See above, § 1474, 1482.

(*f*) L. Elibank *v.* Dornoch's Crs., 1765; 5 B. Sup. 906. See 2 Bell's Com. 490 (385 M'L.'s ed.). Ettles *v.* Robertson, 1833; 11 S. 397; 7 W. & S. 176. Hawkins *v.* Hawkins, 1843; 5 D. 1035. 2 M'Laren, Wills and Succn. 408.

1997. Purposes of the Trust, and Reversionary Interest.—(1.) *The Purposes*, if clearly expressed either in the trust-deed or in a separate lawful deed, give the law of the trust. The declaration of uses and purposes receives interpretation and effect according to the fair meaning (*a*). What is necessary to the rational interpretation and purposes of the trust is implied (*b*). The purposes may be declared in a deed or Will at any time, when power so to declare is reserved in the deed. The only difficulty 'arose' from the law of deathbed,—as to which the rule 'was,' that no such declaration of purpose on deathbed 'would' carry land, unless the heir 'were' effectually excluded in liege poustie. Where the declaration of purposes 'was' not within the law of deathbed, it 'proved' no fatal objection to it that it 'was' in the form of a Will (*c*).

(2.) *The Reversionary Interest* in the truster, 'if not disposed of by the trust-deed so as to divest the truster,' stands on the footing of his original titles, 'the radical right remains with him, the trust being merely a burden on the fee'; and so it is adjudgeable by his creditors (*d*), and the truster may make an effectual entail of the reversionary estate (*e*).

Where a person has the beneficial interest of an annuity, with a provision of a capital to be laid out for securing it, those having the reversionary right have been found not entitled, 'except with the annuitant's consent,' to divide the fund on purchasing an annuity (*f*).

The whole estate being vested in the trustees, the residue, after the purposes are fulfilled, if not otherwise appropriated, may be adjudged or disposed of by deed of settlement or otherwise, or, on the death of the truster, will go to the heir-at-law (*g*).

(*a*) Sprot *v.* Sprot's Trs., 1828; 6 S. 833; 1830, 8 S. 712; 2 Ill. 553. Martin *v.* Kelso, 1853; 15 D. 950; aff. 1856, 2 Macq. 556. As to charitable trusts and the doctrine of *cy près* or approximation, see Young's Trs. *v.* Deacons of Perth Trades, 1893; 20 R. 778.

(*b*) Robertson (Glasgow's Trs.) *v.* Allan, 1832; 10 S. 438; rev. 2 S. & M'L. 333.

(*c*) Fordyce *v.* Cockburn, 1827; 5 S. 897; 2 Ill. 554. Brack *v.* Hog, 1827; 6 S. 113; and cases cited; 2 Ill. 419. Cameron *v.* M'Kie, 1831; 9 S. 601; aff. 1834, 7 W. & S. 106. The law of deathbed is abolished, 34 and 35 Vict. c. 81; *supra*, § 1786.

(*d*) **Campbell** *v.* **Campbell of Edderline's Crs.**, 1801; M. Apx. *Adjudication*, 11; 1 Ross' L. C. 458; 2 Ill. 555. Barbour *v.* M'Minn, 1826; 4 S. 806. Renton *v.* Girvan, 1833; 12 S. 266. Turnbull *v.* Tawse, 1825; 1 W. & S. 80. Lindsay *v.* Giles, 1844; 6 D. 771. Herries, Farquhar, & Co. *v.* Burnett, 1846; 9 D. 111. Herries, Farquhar, & Co. *v.* Brown, 1838; 16 S. 948. Globe Ins. Co. *v.* Murray, 1854; 17 D. 217. See Professor Moir in notes to Erskine's Principles, B. iii. tit. ix. Note A, pp. 567, 568 (16th ed.).

(*e*) M'Millan *v.* Campbell, 1831; 9 S. 551; aff. 1833, 7 W. & S. 441; 1 Ross' L. C. 466. Stirling *v.* Stirling's Trs., 1838; 1 D. 130. Williams and James *v.* Maclaine's Trs., 1872; 10 Macph. 362.

(*f*) Wilson *v.* Beveridge, 1833; 11 S. 343; aff. 7 W. & S. 457. Forsyth *v.* Kilgour, 1854; 17 D. 208.

(*g*) Cathcart *v.* Cathcart, 1830; 8 S. 803. See 1 M'Laren on Wills, etc., 400 sq. Williams and James, *supra* (*e*).

1998. Administration of the Trust, and Powers of the Trustees.—'Trustees act, in matters of ordinary administration, by the resolution of a majority (*a*); and in the trusts falling within the scope of the recent Acts a majority of the trustees accepting and surviving is a quorum, unless the contrary be expressed in the trust-deed (*b*).'

The powers of the trustees, where not expressed, must correspond with the object of their appointment (*c*). 1. Whatever is essential to the accomplishment of the purposes of the trust, is implied as a power in the trustees, —as to sell for payment of debt (*d*), 'or to carry out the purposes of the trust' (*e*), to lay out money in building a mansion-house on land which they are directed to purchase and entail (*f*). No power to sell a fee-simple estate in order to purchase land to be entailed can be implied, but requires the most clear directions (*g*). 2. Trustees to recover and distribute funds may pursue actions, recover payment, and discharge the debtor; and when empowered to sell, may borrow money to pay debts (*h*). Under sequestration the trustee has power, with the aid of commissioners, to *submit*, *compromise*, and *agree to compositions* (*i*); and even in ordinary cases trustees seem to have such power when necessary in the fair and reasonable management of the affairs (*k*). 'Trustees seem not to have had power at common law to submit or refer. But that power is now given to all trustees, where it is not inconsistent with the terms or purposes of the trust (*l*). A reference or submission by trustees in that character does not fall by the death of one or more of them (*m*).'

3. In selling property, they may use their discretion in disposing of it to the best advantage; and they will be bound by sales made by their factor duly authorised to sell (*n*). 'Sellers must satisfy themselves as to the trustees' power to sell, having no claim, if the sale is set aside, against the trust-estate (*o*).'

4. *Paying Debts, Beneficiaries, etc.*—In trusts for family purposes or economical arrangements, the trustees are, like the truster himself, entitled to pay off debts, etc., as they are demanded (*p*); 'and all trustees may now "pay debts due by the truster or the trust-estate, without requiring the creditors to constitute such debts, if they are satisfied that the debts are the proper debts of the trust" (*q*).' 5. When judicially called upon to pay a debt, they are not safe preferably to answer a similar demand without having funds to pay both (*r*). 6. When called on by creditors, though extrajudicially, if there be a manifest shortcoming, they are not safe to pay without a multiplepoinding. 'They will not be personally liable for a debt afterwards emerging, if they have, in ignorance and in good faith, paid away the whole estate to beneficiaries (*s*); but it was held, where the trustees were aware of a debt to become due, and believed that it was amply secured by the estate remaining in their hands, that they paid beneficiaries at their own risk (*t*).' 7. When trustees are named to pay debts, and entail a certain part of the estate, they will be authorised to sell the part specified, if the rest be inadequate to the discharge of the

debts (*u*). 8. Where trustees are directed to purchase land to be entailed, it is only the principal, not the interest or rents of the trust-estate, which is to be so bestowed. The heir who is to take the estate as institute, and the others in their order as they succeed, are entitled, 'unless there be a direction to accumulate,' to the intermediate interests or proceeds (*v*).

9. *Accounting.*—The trustees must be able to account strictly for their intromissions, keeping exact accounts (*w*), taking credit only for actual payments, communicating for the benefit of the trust whatever "eases" they may have had in paying, and giving up to those interested all acquisitions made by them in the course of their administration (*x*). 'Not only are trustees liable in interest if they unduly delay to pay or put the beneficiaries in possession of the funds or property after the date of distribution (*y*); but in all cases they are subjected in penal interest if they retain money in their own hands (beyond what is reasonably required for the administration of the trust), instead of investing it in proper securities, or placing it in a separate bank account (*z*).' They are not to avail themselves of any rights purchased by them, although such as might otherwise have come into competition with those concerned in the trust (*aa*). 'A trustee of any kind, *e.g.* a director, may be compelled to make over to his constituents any advantage obtained to himself personally in the execution of the trust; and if he acquires any benefit as ostensible owner of the trust property, he cannot retain it, but must surrender it to the beneficiaries (*bb*).'

10. *Advances and Indemnification.*—When a trustee has made advances, he cannot be compelled to denude till indemnified; and if he has a power of sale, and has from his own funds paid debts, he may sell, unless immediately relieved (*cc*). 'But, without power given expressly or by implication in the trust-deed, or special power obtained from the Court, trustees cannot borrow money on the security of the trust-estate, or so as to bind it for repayment (*dd*).'

11. When the trustees hold mixed funds, to which several claimants make pretension, it is competent to raise a multiplepoinding in their name (*ee*).

12. *Factors.*—Trustees 'were' generally empowered to name a factor, 'and have now this power by statute;' and even when they are not, as theirs is a gratuitous office, they seem to have such power (*ff*). But they cannot supersede a factor appointed by the truster (*gg*).

13. Trustees 'cannot be *auctores in rem suam*, that is to say, they are personally disqualified from contracting in any way with the trust-estate (*hh*). Thus they' cannot be purchasers at a sale of the trust-estate (*ii*), 'or borrowers from it even on heritable security (*kk*)'; and commissioners in a mercantile sequestration have not been allowed to purchase outstanding debts (*ll*). 'Nor can a trustee receive remuneration for work done professionally for the trust, unless it be authorised by the constitution of the trust (*mm*).'

14. Trustees infeft in trust, with power to sell, have power to enter vassals (*nn*). 15. When a trustee is empowered to sell and divide the trust-estate, no person interested is entitled to interrupt him by inhibitions; but the remedy is by bill of suspension and interdict (*oo*).

'16. When the truster confers on trustees a discretion or power of disposal, or power to regulate the interest of a beneficiary, they are bound to exercise it, and cannot by anticipation deprive themselves of it, or abandon it (*pp*).

'17. The *expenses* of administering and executing a trust are generally to be charged against capital (*qq*).'

(*a*) Campbell *v.* M'Intyre, 1824; 3 S. 126. Cases in § 1993 (*z*), (*aa*), *supra*.

(*b*) 24 and 25 Vict. c. 84, § 1.

(*c*) Campbell *v.* Campbell, 1852; 15 D. 27. Kinloch, petr., 1859; 22 D. 174.

(*d*) Erskine *v.* Wemyss, 1829; 7 S. 594; 2 Ill. 553. Henderson *v.* Somerville, 1841; 3 D. 1049. Graham *v.* Graham's Trs., 1850; 13 D. 420. Meiklam's Trs. *v.* Meiklam's Trs., 1852; 15 D. 159. L. Adv. *v.* Smith, 1852; 14 D. 585; 1 Macq. 760. See Glasgow's Trs. *v.* Allan, *supra*, § 1997 (*b*).

(*e*) Thomson's Trs. *v.* Thomson, 1898; 25 R. 19.

(*f*) Sprot's Trs. *v.* Sprot, 1830; 8 S. 712. Some doubt was thrown on this case in the Second Division, in Paterson's Case. Winter Session, 1838.

(*g*) Robertson (Glasgow's Trs.) *v.* Allan, *supra*, § 1997 (*b*).

(*h*) Dewar *v.* Ross, 1792; Bell's Ca. 541; 2 Ill. 556. 2 M'Laren on Wills, etc., 244, 253, 254.

(*i*) 2 and 3 Vict. c. 41, § 98. 19 and 20 Vict. c. 79, § 176.

(*k*) Kennedy *v.* Kennedy, 1843; 6 D. 40. Mackintosh *v.* Williamson, 1849; 11 D. 1246. Watson *v.* Morrison, 1848; 10 D. 1414. City of Glasgow Bank *v.* Geddes' Trs., 1880; 7 R. 731.

(*l*) Thomson's Trs. *v.* Muir, 1867; 6 Macph. 145. 30 and 31 Vict. c. 97, § 2.

(*m*) Alexander's Trs. *v.* Dymock's Trs., 1883; 10 R. 1189.

(*n*) Thomas *v.* Walker's Trs., 1829; 7 S. 828. Mitchell *v.* Mackinlay, 1842; 4 D. 634. Clelland *v.* Brodie, 1844; 7 D. 147. 2 M'Laren, Wills and Succn. 252, 330.

(*o*) Mags. of Airdrie *v.* Smith, 1850; 12 D. 1222. Mitchell *v.* Major, 1856; 19 D. 30. See above (*d*). As to the warrandice to be given by trustees to purchasers from them of heritage, see Forbes' Trs. *v.* Mackintosh, 1822; 1 S. 497. Kelly *v.* Macindoe, 1858; 20 D. 773. Bald *v.* Globe Ins. Co., 1847; 10 D. 289.

(*p*) Rankine *v.* Gardner, 1741; M. 16,201. Alison *v.* E. Dundonald's Trs., 1793; M. 16,211. See cases in (*s*).

(*q*) 30 and 31 Vict. c. 97, § 2.

(*r*) See cases (*p*). Lamond's Trs. *v.* Croom, 1871; 9 Macph. 662. See below, § 2001 (*g*).

(*s*) Stewart's Trs. *v.* Evans, 1871; 9 Macph. 810. Beith *v.* Mackenzie, 1875; 3 R. 185.

(*t*) Herit. Sec. Invt. Ass. *v.* Miller's Trs., 1893; 20 R. 675 (L. M'Laren, *diss.*, and holding that the measure of their responsibility is that they are to make the estate forthcoming in a due course of administration).

(*u*) Erskine and Henderson, *supra* (*d*). Robertson, *supra* (*g*). Campbell's Trs. *v.* Campbell, 1838; 1 D. 153.

(*v*) Templer (Graham) *v.* Templer, 1828; 3 W. & S. 47. E. Stair *v.* Stair's Trs., 1827; 2 W. & S. 414 and 614. Howat's Trs. *v.* Howat, 16 S. 622. Campbell's Trs. *v.* Campbell, 1838; 16 S. 1251. Macpherson's Exrs. *v.* Macpherson, 1850; 12 D. 486; as revd. 1 Macq. 243. Dickson's Tutors *v.* Scott, 1853; 16 D. 1. And see M'Laren on Wills, etc., chap. 65, § 2.

(*w*) Gourlay *v.* Dumbreck, 1710; M. 16,192. Home *v.* Home, 1712; Robertson's Ap. 47. As to assumed trustees, see Somerville's Trs. *v.* Wemess, 1854; 17 D. 151. Nicol *v.* Wilson, 1856; 18 D. 1000.

(*x*) E. Crawford *v.* Hepburn, 1767; M. 16,208; and cases of Maxwell, Rae, and Sinclair there cited. Chalmers *v.* Cunningham, 1735; Elch. *Trust*, 3 and 7. See the cases cited, notes (*ii*), (*ll*), (*bb*).

(*y*) L. Lynedoch *v.* Ochterlony, 1832; 11 S. 60.

(*z*) Wellwood's Trs. *v.* Boswell, 1856; 19 D. 187. *Supra*, § 32 *fin.*

(*aa*) Wright *v.* Wright, 1712; M. 16,193. Anderson *v.* Lauder, 1740; Elch. *Trust*, 10. See Cochrane *v.* Black, 1855; 17 D. 321. Laird *v.* Laird, 1855; 17 D. 984. Hamilton *v.* Wright, 1839; 1 D. 668; rev. 1842, 1 Bell's App. 574. Thorburn *v.* Martin, 1853; 15 D. 845.

(*bb*) **Huntington Copper Co. *v.* Henderson**, 1877; 4 R. 294; aff. 5 R. H. L. 1. Cases below, notes (*ii*), (*kk*), (*ll*); and above, § 222 (*c*), (*d*). Univ. of Aberdeen *v.* Mags. of Aberdeen, 1876; 3 R. 1087; aff. 1877, 4 R. H. L. 48. Laird *v.* Laird, 1858; 20 D. 981. 2 M'Laren, Wills and Succn. 112 (chap. xliv.).

(*cc*) Elliot's Trs. *v.* Elliot, 1828; 6 S. 1058. Sheriffs *v.* Boyd, 1829; 7 S. 314. Innes *v.* Innes, 1829; 7 S. 206. See as to trustees' right of retention, 2 Bell's Com. 123 (117, M'L.'s ed.). Henderson *v.* Norrie, 1866; 4 Macph. 691. Robinson *v.* Fraser's Trs., 1880; 7 R. 694; rev. 1881, 8 R. H. L. 127; 6 App. Ca. 855 (indemnity for calls where funds severed for investment for separate beneficiaries). *Supra*, § 1453, 1996. As to their claim to be indemnified for expenses of litigation, etc., see 2 M'Laren, Wills and Succn. 550; *infra*, § 2000 (*a*).

(*dd*) 2 Bell's Com. 84. Dewar *v.* Ross, 1792; Bell's 8vo Ca. 541. *Infra*, § 1998B. Lawson *v.* Walker, 1845; 8 D. 232. M'Millan *v.* Armstrong, 1848; 11 D. 191. Ralston *v.* M'Intyre's Factor, 1882; 10 R. 72. Binnie (Broom, etc.) *v.* Binnie's Trs., 1888; 15 R. 417; rev. 1889, 14 App. Ca. 576; 16 R. H. L. 23. See above (*n*), and below, § 1998B. But the trust-estate will be liable so far as the money borrowed was required for the uses of the trust and so applied. M'Millan and Ralston, *citt.*

(*ee*) Dixon *v.* Dixon, 1833; 11 S. 517. See Kyd *v.* Waterson, 1880; 7 R. 884. Robb's Trs. *v.* Robb, 1880; *ib.* 1049. See below, § 2000 (1).

(*ff*) Sym *v.* Charles, 1830; 8 S. 741. 30 and 31 Vict. c. 97, § 2. Home *v.* Pringle, 1837; 16 S. 142; aff. 1841, 2 Rob. 384. Home *v.* Menzies, 1845; 7 D. 1010. Thomson *v.* Campbell, 1838; 16 S. 560. Cameron *v.* Anderson, 1844; 7 D. 92. Hay *v.* Binnie, 1861; 23 D. 594. Edmond *v.* Blaikie, 1866; 4 Macph. 1011.

(*gg*) Fulton *v.* Macalister, 1831; 9 S. 442. M'Cuaig *v.* M'Aulay, 1836; 14 S. 318.

(*hh*) York Bdgs. Co. and Aberdeen Ry. Co., *citt. infra.* Hamilton *v.* Wright, 1842; 1 Bell's App. 574; 9 Cl. & F. 111. Buckner *v.* Jopp's Trs., 1887; 14 R. 1006 (transaction with legatees—*mora*). It seems that sales cannot be set aside on this ground at the instance of a third party having an interest, the beneficiaries being satisfied. Aberdein *v.* Stratton's Trs., 1867; 5 Macph. 726. Comp. cases in § 2000 (*y*) *fin.*, and above, notes (*z*) and (*aa*).

(*ii*) **York Bdgs. Co. *v.* Mackenzie**, 1793; M. 13,367; rev. 8 Br. Par. Ca. 42; 3 Pat. 378; see also 4 Dow, 380. Smith *v.* Roberton, 1826; 4 S. 442. Drew *v.* Paterson, 1825; 4 S. 259. Jeffrey *v.* Aiken, 1826; 4 S. 722; 2 Ill. 97. Taylor *v.* Watson, 1846; 8 D. 1406. Gillies *v.* Maclachlan's Reprs., 1846; 8 D. 487. Fraser *v.* Hankey, 1847; 9 D. 415. Brown *v.* Burt, 1848; 11 D. 388. Thorburn *v.* Martin, 1853; 15 D. 845. **Aberdeen Railway Co. *v.* Blaikie**, 1854; 1 Macq. 461. Elias *v.* Black, 1856; 18 D. 1225. Morrison *v.* Rennie, 1847; 9 D. 1483; rev. 1849, 6 Bell's App. 422. Fleming *v.* Imrie, 1868; 6 Macph. 363. Paterson *v.* Portobello Town Hall Co., 1866; 4 Macph. 726. Mackie's Trs. *v.* Mackie, 1875; 2 R. 312. Univ. of Aberdeen, *supra* (*bb*). Dunn *v.* Chambers, 1897; 25 R. 247 (purchase of shares by company of which curator is director).

(*kk*) Perston *v.* Perston's Trs., 1863; 1 Macph. 245. Baird *v.* Mags. of Dundee, 1865; 4 Macph. 65. Crosskery *v.* Gilmour's Trs., 1890; 17 R. 697.

(*ll*) M'Kellar *v.* Balmain, March 6, 1817; F. C. Drew *v.* Paterson, *cit.* (*ii*). 19 and 20 Vict. c.79, § 120.

(*mm*) Home *v.* Pringle, 1841; 2 Rob. App. 384. Aitken *v.* Hunter, 1871; 9 Macph. 756. L. Gray *v.* Dundas, and cases in § 1993 (*cc*), *supra*. *Infra*, § 2087.

(*nn*) Ker *v.* Russel, 1838; 1 D. 179.

(*oo*) Hay *v.* Morrison, 1838; 16 S. 1273. See M'Laren's Wills and Succn. 132, 570 sqq.

(*pp*) Weller *v.* Ker's Trs., 1864; 2 Macph. 371; aff. 1871, 4 Macph. H. L. 8; L. R. 1 Sc. App. 11. Smiths *v.* Chambers' Trs., 1877; 5 R. 97; rev. 1878, *ib.* H. L. 151. M'Nicol's Exr. *v.* M'Nicol, 1893; 20 R. 386. See as to undue delay barring trustees from exercising such a power to the prejudice of an assignee or creditor of the beneficiary, Adam *v.* Forsyth's Trs., 1867; 6 Macph. 31.

(*qq*) Smith *v.* Bennie, 1890; 18 R. 44. This is usually a direction in the deed of trust.

1998A. '*Statutory Powers.*—In all trusts constituted by virtue of any deed or by private or local Act of Parliament, or by resolution of any corporation or public or ecclesiastical body (*a*), the trustees (including a tutor, curator or judicial factor) (*b*) have power to do the following acts, where they are not at variance with the terms or purposes of the trust:—1. To appoint factors and law-agents, and to pay them a suitable remuneration. 2. To discharge trustees who have resigned, and the representatives of trustees who have died. 3. To grant leases of the heritable estate of a duration not exceeding twenty-one years for agricultural lands, and thirty-one years for minerals, and to remove tenants (*c*). 4. To uplift, discharge, or assign debts due to the trust-estate. 5. To compromise, or to submit and refer all claims connected with the trust-estate. 6. To grant all deeds necessary for carrying into effect the powers vested in the trustees. 7. To pay debts due by the truster or by the trust-estate, without requiring the creditors to constitute such debts, where the trustees are satisfied that the debts are proper debts of the trust (*d*). 8. To make abatement or reduction, temporary or permanent, of the rent of lands let for agricultural and for pastoral occupation, and to accept renunciations of leases of such subjects (*e*).'

(*a*) Def. in 47 and 48 Vict. c. 63, § 1. (*b*) *Ib.*
(*c*) As to accepting the renunciation of a lease, see Berwick, etc., petrs., 1874 ; 2 R. 90.
(*d*) 30 and 31 Vict. c. 97, § 2.
(*e*) 50 and 51 Vict. c. 18.

1998B. '*Special Powers.*—Contrary to some earlier opinions and practice, it was held that the Court of Session had not at common law jurisdiction, by the exercise of its *nobile officium*, to grant special powers to trustees, in cases of necessity, beyond the powers conferred expressly or by implication by the trust-deed (*a*). By statute, however, the Court, on the petition of the trustees, may grant authority to them, being trustees for the administration of a Scotch trust (*b*), to do any of the following acts, on being satisfied that it is expedient for the execution of the trust, and not inconsistent with the intention thereof:—1. To sell the trust-estate, or any part of it (*c*). 2. To grant feus or long leases of the heritable estate or any part of it (*d*). 3. To borrow money on the security of the trust-estate or any part of it. 4. To excamb any part of the trust-estate which is heritable.

'If all the beneficiaries in existence at the date of presenting such petition are of full age and capable of acting, they may, by deed of consent, grant authority to the trustees to do any of these acts, if not inconsistent with the intention of the trust; and such acts are then equally valid and effectual as if the authority of the Court had previously been obtained (*e*).

'Powers of sale conferred on trustees by the trust-deed, or under the Act of 1867, may be exercised either by public roup or private bargain, unless otherwise directed in the trust-deed, or by the Court, or deed of consent; and heritable estate may in such sales be sold subject to a feu-duty or ground-annual, at rates and under conditions to be agreed on; and in all sales and feus, mines and minerals may be reserved (*f*).'

(*a*) Kinloch, petr., 1859 ; 22 D. 174. Robertson (Glasgow's Trs.) *v.* Allan, 1832 ; 10 S. 438 ; 1835, 2 S. & M'L. 333.
(*b*) Carruthers' Trs., 1896 ; 24 R. 238. Cf. *supra*, § 1993 (*m*). Allan's Trs., 1897 ; 24 R. 718.
(*c*) Hay's Trs. *v.* Hay Miln, 1873 ; 11 Macph. 694. Weir's Trs., petrs., 1877 ; 4 R. 876. Downie, petr., 1879 ; 6 R. 1013.
(*d*) Anderson, petr., 1876 ; 3 R. 639. Birkmyre, petr., 1881 ; 8 R. 477. Campbell's Trs. *v.* Campbell, 1882 ; 9 R. 725 ; 10 R. H. L. 65 (unworked minerals). Molleson *v.* Hope, 1888 ; 15 R. 665 (liferenter's and fiar's interests in conflict). Trustees in permanent trusts for charitable purposes have at common law power to feu the mortified lands. Mercht. Co. of Edinr. *v.* Heriot's Hosp., 1767 ; M. 5750. Mags. of Elgin *v.* Morrison, 1882 ; 10 R. 342.
(*e*) 30 and 31 Vict. c. 97, § 3. (*f*) *Ib.* § 4.

1998C. '*Investments.*—Unless the contrary be expressly provided in the constitution of the trust, trustees, tutors, curators or judicial factors may invest the trust-funds in any of the Government stocks, public funds, or securities of the United Kingdom, stock of the Bank of England, securities the interest of which is guaranteed by Parliament, debenture stock of railways in Great Britain, certain railway and municipal stocks or annuities, East India stock, and colonial stock, approved by the Court of Session (*a*), feu-duties and ground-annuals; or may lend them on the security of such stocks or funds, or of heritable property in Great Britain, or on certain railway, municipal, (*b*) or Indian railway stock or debentures; and may at their discretion vary any such investment or loan. But they do not become subject as defendants or respondents to the jurisdiction of any court of law or equity in England or Ireland by reason of such investment or loan. These statutory powers of investment, which are nearly what trustees possess at common law, do not restrict or control any powers of investment expressly contained in any trust-deed (*c*).'

(*a*) M'Lean's Tr., petr., 1884 ; 12 R. 529. Accountant of Court *v.* Crumpton's Curator, 1886 ; 14 R. 55.
(*b*) Annan *v.* Hutton, 1897 ; 24 R. 851 ; aff. 1898, A. C. 289 ; 25 R. H. L. 23. Cowan's Trs. and other cases in § 2000 (*s*).
(*c*) 30 and 31 Vict. c. 97, § 5, 6. 47 and 48 Vict. c. 63, § 3. See as to debentures of railways and other companies, 33 and 34 Vict. c. 27. See a convenient list of trust investments in Parliament House Book, Div. D. *ad fin.*

1998D. '*Advances to Minors.*—The Court may, under such conditions as it sees fit, authorise trustees to advance any part of the capital of a fund destined, either absolutely or contingently, to minor descendants of the truster, being beneficiaries having a vested interest in such fund, if the income of the fund is insufficient or not applicable to, and if such advance is necessary for, the maintenance or education of such beneficiaries. This must not be expressly prohibited by the trust-deed, and the rights of parties other than the heirs or representatives of such minor beneficiaries must not be thereby prejudiced (*a*). The Court may authorise trustees to apply the whole or part of trust-funds directed to be invested in the purchase of heritage, to the payment or redemption of debts or burdens affecting heritable property destined to the same series of heirs, and subject to the same conditions as are by the trust-deed made applicable to the heritable property directed to be purchased, if such application is not inconsistent with the other provisions of the trust-deed (*b*).'

(*a*) 30 and 31 Vict. c. 97, § 7, 8. Pattison *v.* Pattison's Trs., 1870; 8 Macph. 575. Christie *v.* Christie's Trs., 1877; 4 R. 620. Latta, petr., 1880; 7 R. 881. Thomson *v.* Miller's Trs., 1883; 11 R. 401. Webster's *v.* Miller's Trs., 1887; 14 R. 501. Ross' Trs., 1894; 21 R. 995 (vesting in children as a class).

(*b*) *Ib.*

1999. Responsibility of Trustees.—Trustees may be liable either as trustees to the amount of the estate or funds, or as individuals.

(1.) *As Trustees.*—They are, as trustees, responsible to the extent of the trust-funds for the faithful execution of the trust, for payment of the debts of the trust, for denuding of the trust-estates, and accounting for their intromissions (*a*); for fulfilment of the obligations undertaken by themselves or their factor duly authorised (*b*), and for expenses found due to third parties in litigation with the trust-estate (*c*); and a trustee for creditors is not entitled to enter into litigation, under a protest not to be liable for the expense (*d*). Road trust funds 'were for some time held' not liable for injuries from negligence (*e*).

(*a*) D. Hamilton *v.* D. Hamilton's Crs., 1740; M. 16,201; Elch. *Trust*, 9, 13; aff. Cr. St. & P. 447. Anderson *v.* Small, 1833; 11 S. 382; 2 Ill. 562. As to jurisdiction in the case of foreigners' trustees in a Scotch trust, see M'Gennis *v.* Rooney, 1891; 18 R. 817.

(*b*) Thomas *v.* Walker's Trs., 1829; 7 S. 828; 2 Ill. 556. Lamond's Trs. *v.* Croom, 1871; 9 Macph. 662. *Supra*, § 1998 (3), (12).

(*c*) Dickson *v.* Bonar's Trs., 1829; 8 S. 99. See next section. Even when a trustee declines to sist himself, the bankrupt estate is liable to a ranking for the expenses of an action against the bankrupt depending at the date of the sequestration. Miller *v.* M'Intosh, 1884; 11 R. 729. Trust-estate may also be made liable. Stewart *v.* Forbes, 1888; 15 R. 383 (adjudication of trust-estate).

(*d*) Buchanan *v.* Corbet, 1827; 5 S. 805. Below, § 2000 (1).

(*e*) See, however, § 2031.

2000. (2.) *As Individuals.*—Trustees may become responsible as individuals beyond the amount of the trust-estate, and in their own persons and fortunes in the following cases:—

'*Liability to Third Parties.*'—1. Wherever, under cover of their character as trustees, they have occasioned damage to third parties, they must be so liable; and so for the expense of litigation conducted in *malâ fide*, or improperly and oppressively (*a*); and a trustee for creditors will be liable even for such litigation as he has maintained in the character of trustee, where he is aware, without disclosing it, that there are no funds out of which to indemnify the antagonist for his expenses (*b*). 'But the liability of trustees for the expenses of litigation must be stated still more broadly; for it is settled that trustees litigating are in all cases personally liable to the opposite party under an unqualified finding of expenses in his favour (*c*).

'Where there is no improper conduct on their part, they have relief against the trust-estate; but it is not necessarily a good defence or excuse to them that the trust-funds are exhausted so that they cannot be reimbursed (*d*). And they are generally, but not always, entitled to be indemnified by the trust-estate, or by the beneficiaries, for the expenses of defending an invalid trust-deed in their favour (*e*). In questions with persons claiming under the settlement, trustees are entitled to take at least the expenses of raising an action for distribution and of getting exoneration out of the trust-estate; but not if the litigation is made necessary by their fault (*f*). It is fault making trustees personally liable, or at least it bars them from pleading that they have not assets to meet an obligation of the trust-estate, if they inequitably or negligently dispose of the trust-funds which they were bound to make forthcoming to the creditors of the truster and the trust-estate (*g*). Indeed, the cases referred to show that a creditor is entitled to raise any question of negligence or breach of duty against a trustee which can be raised by a beneficiary; and thus the following sub-sections as to beneficiaries apply also to creditors.'

'*Liability to Beneficiaries.*'—2. Where trustees resist the execution of their duty, or are guilty of *culpa lata* in neglecting their duty, they will be personally liable 'to the beneficiaries so injured (*h*). When the breach of trust is an absolutely illegal act, *e.g.* the lending of trust-funds to one of themselves, they are liable *in solidum*, and every one of them may be sued as for a delict or quasi delict (*i*). The general rules in judging of negligence are, that a trustee does his duty if he follows the ordinary course of business that would be pursued by a prudent man, and that he is liable only for such diligence as such a man would use in his own affairs (*k*). This is quite consistent with another principle, namely, that clear abuse of a power, or failure in a duty, belonging to or incumbent on him as a trustee, infers liability to those who suffer thereby (*l*). It involves personal liability, and even removal from office, if trustees lend trust money on personal security (*m*), or on insufficient heritable security (*n*), or to one of themselves (*o*), or invest money in trading companies (*p*). The law now gives a certain protection to a trustee lending trust-funds on heritable security which turns out to be insufficient on certain conditions as to valuation, and restricts his liability to the excess of the sums so lent above what would have been at the time a proper investment (*q*).' 3. Where trustees have exceeded their powers, they will be personally responsible to those interested in the trust, 'whether as beneficiaries or creditors' (*r*).

4. Where trustees give a bill or other liquid obligation for a trust-debt, 'or, without limiting the responsibility to the trust-estate, enter into a contract on account of the trust, adopt a lease, or engage in trade or partnership (including the holding of shares in joint-stock companies) for the benefit of the trust,' they give assurance of funds, and pledge themselves to retain sufficient to answer the debt, '—in effect, bind themselves personally (*s*). In ordinary trusts for administration, realisation, and distribution, trustees are not at liberty, if there be no express direction or power given to them (*t*), to invest funds in trade or shares of trading companies; and they will even be personally liable if they retain an investment of this kind selected by the testator himself after it can with reasonable diligence be realised and reinvested or distributed (*u*). In borrowing on heritable security, trustees having power to do so and obliging themselves specially in their character of trustees, do not incur personal liability except to make the trust-estate forthcoming (*v*). In selling land, trustees are only bound to warrant the conveyance from their own facts and deeds, binding the truster or beneficiaries according to the circumstances (*w*).'

5. For their intromissions they will be answerable, in so far as they cannot discharge their responsibility, according to the principles of a trustee's accounting; as where they have paid to one not entitled to receive the payment (*x*). 6. In this responsibility 'it was said that' they will be jointly liable, unless in so far as the truster, for himself and for those on whom he has bestowed the beneficial interest, shall have dispensed with this responsibility, and limited each trustee's obligation to the amount of his own actual intromissions (*y*). As trust is gratuitous, and too often a troublesome and a thankless office, trust-deeds generally contain, as an inducement to undertake it, a clause exempting the trustees from liability for omissions, and restricting their responsibility to their own actual intromissions (*z*). Such a clause, even where a small sum is bequeathed to the trustees, is effectual to discharge their responsibility when the expressions are clear, and the act in question distinctly falls within them. 'But the statement in this passage as to joint liability has been questioned, and there is much reason for saying that the indemnity clause referred to is only declaratory of the common law (*aa*). It has been enacted that all trusts constituted by deed or local Act of Parliament, under which gratuitous trustees are nominated, shall be held to include, unless the contrary be expressed, a provision that each such trustee shall only be liable for his own acts and intromissions, and shall not be

liable for the acts and intromissions of co-trustees, and shall not be liable for omissions (*bb*). Homologation by beneficiaries of unauthorised investments may not suffice to relieve trustees from responsibility (*cc*).'

Difficulties sometimes arise in point of construction as to the distinction between intromission and mere omission; and, (1.) Where trustees expressly authorise money to be drawn or received, and disposed of in such a way as to incur loss, this is held not a mere omission, but a positive act (*dd*). (2.) Where there is a mere negligence of superintendence, the exemption will free the trustees (*ee*). (3.) Where neglect of superintendence amounts to *culpa lata*, the exempting clause will be no protection (*ff*). (4.) Where the neglect is a positive breach of the truster's order, 'or the intromission takes place after the appointment has been effectually recalled (*gg*),' the clause will not protect (*hh*). (5.) A trustee ratifying the assumption of a new trustee is exempt by the clause from liability for his acts; and trustees electing a factor reputed responsible and fit for the office under the express or implied powers in the trust, are exempt from liability for that factor's acts or deficiencies, if merely negligent in superintending his proceedings (*ii*). 'Money awaiting investment must not be deposited in the factor's name or mixed with his funds (*kk*).'

(*a*) Dickson *v.* Bonar's Trs., 1829; 8 S. 99; 2 Ill. 562. Fleming *v.* Little, 1829; 8 S. 172.

(*b*) Scott *v.* Paterson, 1826; 5 S. 172. See Torbet *v.* Borthwick, 1849; 11 D. 694. Muir *v.* Tay Insurance Co., 1843; 5 D. 579. Davidson's Trs. *v.* Carr, 1850; 12 D. 1069.

(*c*) Kay *v.* Wilson's Trs., 1850; 12 D. 845. Buchanan *v.* Corbet, 1827; 5 S. 805. Sandeman *v.* Shepherd, 1835; 13 S. 1037. A finding of expenses against them "as trustees" negatives personal liability. Craig *v.* Hogg, 1896; 24 R. 6. Stewart *v.* Forbes, 1897; 24 R. 1112.

(*d*) Clyne's Trs. *v.* Alison, 1840; 2 D. 554. Young *v.* Nith Comrs., 1876; 3 R. 991. Gibson *v.* Caddall's Trs., 1895; 22 R. 889.

(*e*) Graham *v.* Marshall, 1860; 23 D. 41. Chalmers *v.* Scott, 1830; 8 S. 961. Morrison *v.* Morrison's Trs., 1848; 11 D. 279. Munro *v.* Strain, 1874; 1 R. 1039. Watson *v.* Watson's Trs., 1875; 2 R. 344.

(*f*) Hill *v.* Hill, 1856; 18 D. 316. Kirkland *v.* Crighton, 1842; 4 D. 613. Cameron *v.* Anderson, 1844; 7 D. 92 (incidence on funds of expenses found due to one entitled under trust-deed, and see Scott *v.* Ross, 1821; 1 S. 448). *Supra*, § 1998 (11). On this subject and the responsibility of trustees for creditors for the expenses of litigation, see 2 M'Laren, Wills and Succn. 562; 2 Mackay's Practice, 571; and comp. above, § 1999.

(*g*) Young *v.* Johnston's Trs., 1841; 3 D. 1020. Cruickshanks' Trs. *v.* Cruickshanks, 1845; 4 Bell's App. 179. Aitken *v.* Glasgow Road Trs., 1829; 7 S. 390. Bon Accord Ins. Co., *infra* (*s*); and cf. Lucas *v.* Beresford's Trs., 1892; 19 R. 943.

(*h*) Morrison *v.* Miller, 1827; 5 S. 322. Stark *v.* Moncrieff, 1838; 16 S. 1014. Forman *v.* Burns, 1853; 15 D. 362 (neglecting to get in debts). Heggie *v.* Heggie, 1858; 20 D. 823 (do.). As to jurisdiction, see § 1999 (*a*).

(*i*) Crosskery *v.* Gilmour's Trs., 1890; 17 R. 697; and cases in § 59.

(*k*) 1 Stair, 12. § 10. Seton *v.* Dawson, 1841; 4 D. 310. Kennedy *v.* Kennedy, 1884; 12 R. 275. Speight *v.* Gaunt, 9 App. Ca. 1. Learoyd *v.* Whiteley, 12 App. Ca. 727. Rae *v.* Meek, 1888; 15 R. 1033; revd. 1889, 14 App. Ca. 558; 16 R. H. L. 31. Carruthers *v.* Cairns, 1890; 17 R. 769. It was held to be a breach of this rule to let trust-funds lie for years in bank on deposit receipt instead of investing permanently, and that the trustees were bound to make good the difference between bank interest and the higher interest that might have been obtained. Melville *v.* Noble's Trs., 1896; 24 R. 243 (2nd Div.).

(*l*) Millar's Trs. *v.* Polson, 1897; 24 R. 1038.

(*m*) Anderson *v.* Small, 1833; 11 S. 382. Moffat *v.* Robertson, 1834; 12 S. 369. Blain *v.* Paterson, 1836; 14 S. 361. Watson *v.* Crawcour, 1843; 5 D. 1182. Ross *v.* Allan's Trs., 1850; 13 D. 44. Trustees are not in general removed where there is good faith, and no malversation. Gilchrist's Trs *v.* Dick, 1883; 11 R. 22. Harris *v.* Howie's Tr., 1893; 21 R. 16. The Court will remove a trustee for a breach of trust, although it may not involve a "moral delinquency"; but this phrase seems not to be quite accurately used. M'Whirter *v.* Latta, 1889; 17 R. 68. Fleming *v.* Craig, 1863; 1 Macph. 850. As to the practice in removal of trustees and sequestration of trust-estates, see M'Laren, Wills and Succn. ii. 449. Butchart *v.* Butchart, 1857; 13 D. 1358. Morris *v.* Bain, 1858; 20 D. 716. Dryburgh *v.* Walker's Trs., 1873; 1 R. 31. Hope *v.* Hope, 1884; 12 R. 27. Foggo, petr., 1892; 20 R. 273. Henderson *v.* Henderson, 1893; 20 R. 536. Whittle *v.* Carruthers, 1896; 23 R. 775 (sequestration in bankruptcy).

(*n*) Acct. of Court *v.* Forsyth, 1853; 15 D. 345. Millar's Factor *v.* Knox, etc., 1886; 14 R. 22; aff. (nom. Knox *v.* Mackinnon) 1888; 13 App. Ca. 753; 15 R. H. L. 83. Guild *v.* Glasg. Educ. Endowment Board, 1887; 14 R. 944 (judicial factor—buildings in course of erection). Crabbe *v.* Whyte, 1891; 18 R. 1065 (do.). Maclean *v.* Soady's Tr., 1888; 15 R. 966. Rae *v.* Meek, *cit.* Learoyd *v.* Whiteley, 12 App. Ca. 727. See above, § 1998 (*kk*).

(*o*) *Supra*, § 1998 (13).

(*p*) See above, cases in § 403c (*k*). Laird *v.* Laird, 1855; 17 D. 984; 1858, 20 D. 972. Cochrane *v.* Black, 1855; 17 D. 321. *Infra* (*t*), (*u*). As to disregarding instructions to invest in particular securities, see Sym *v.* Charles, 1830; 8 S. 741. Pollexfen *v.* Stewart, 1841; 4 D. 224.

(*q*) 54 and 55 Vict. c. 44, § 4, 5.

(*r*) Cases in (*g*) and (*h*). Bon Accord Ins. Co. (creditors), and cases cited below (*s*). *E.g.* in making unauthorised investments. Douglas *v.* Douglas' Trs., 1864; 2 Macph. 1379; 1867, 5 Macph. 827. Laird, Cochrane, in (*p*), and other cases in (*s*).

(*s*) Thomson *v.* M'Lachlan, 1829; 7 S. 787; 2 Ill. 564. Higgins *v.* Livingstone, 1816; 6 Pat. 244. Jeffrey *v.* Brown, 1822; 1 S. 102; aff. 1824; 2 S. App. 349; Eaton, Hammond, & Co. *v.* M'Gregor's Exrs., 1837; 15 S. 1012 (bills). Findlay, Bannatyne, & Co. *v.* Ord, 1846; 8 D. 1089 (do.). Carswell *v.* Irvine, 1850; 12 D. 462 (bond). Anderson *v.* M'Dowal, 1865; 3 Macph. 727 (bills). Bon Accord Ins. Co. *v.* Souter's Trs., 1850; 12 D. 1010; 13 D. 295 (shares). Lumsden *v.* Buchanan, 1863; 2 Macph. 695; rev. 1865, 3 Macph. H. L. 89; 4 Macq. 950 (bank stock). Grant *v.* Baillie, 1869; 8 Macph. 77 (do.). Breatcliff *v.* Bransby's Trs., 1886; 14 R. 307 (railway mortgage—real security); and see other cases as to shares in companies, *supra*, 403c; also Cowan's Trs. *v.* Ferrie's Cur., 1897; 24 R. 590 (Greenock Harbour Trust rates)). Laird and Cochrane, *supra* (*p*). Stead *v.* Cox, 1835; 13 S. 280 (adoption of lease by tenant's trustee, cf. *supra*, § 1212 (*f*)). Dundas *v.* Kirkaldy's Trs., 1853; 15 D. 752; 1857, 20 D. 225 (do.). Bertram *v.* Guild, 1880; 7 R. 1122 (do. by landlord's trustee in sequestration). Ralston *v.* M'Intyre's

Factor, 1882; 10 R. 72 (borrowing money). Personal liability will not readily be inferred in favour of an agent or factor, who has often better means of knowing the condition of the trust-estate than the trustees. Cullen *v.* Baillie, 1846; 8 D. 511. Manson *v.* Baillie, 1855; 2 Macq. 80. Brodie *v.* M'Farlan's Crs., 1846; 8 D. 537. While trustees are thus liable, however, for their own acts, they are not, without homologation, responsible for the acts of their co-trustees beyond the execution of the trust, *e.g.* in making personal obligations. Higgins, *cit.*

(*t*) Robinson *v.* Fraser's Trs., 1880; 7 R. 694; rev. 1881, 8 R. H. L. 127; 6 App. Ca. 855. Curror *v.* Loudon, 1879; 7 R. 289. Cuninghame *v.* Montgomerie, 1879; 6 R. 1333.

(*u*) Cochrane and Laird, *supra* (*p*) and § 1998 (*bb*). Brownlie *v.* Brownlie's Trs., 1879; 6 R. 1233. Ritchie *v.* Ritchie's Trs., 1888; 15 R. 1086. *Supra*, note (*r*).

(*v*) Campbell *v.* Gordon, 1840; 2 D. 639; aff. 1842, 1 Bell's App. 428. As to the effect of warrandice, see Horsburgh's Trs. *v.* Welch, 1886; 14 R. 67.

(*w*) Forbes' Trs. *v.* M'Intosh, 1822; 1 S. 497. Duff's Feudal Convg. p. 90. M. Bell's Lectures, 637. *Supra*, § 894.

(*x*) Donaldson *v.* Kennedy, 1833; 11 S. 740; 1 Ill. 334. Mags. of Airdrie *v.* Smith, 1850; 12 D. 1222. Macpherson *v.* Tytler, 1850; 12 D. 486.

(*y*) Dalrymple *v.* Murray, 1784; M. 16,210. Sym *v.* Charles, 1830; 8 S. 741. Wallace *v.* Taylor, 1832; 10 S. 364.

(*z*) See E. Traquair's Trs. *v.* Henderson, 1835; 13 S. 417. Carruthers *v.* Cairns, *cit.* (*k*).

(*aa*) 2 M'Laren, Wills and Succn. 529, 535, referring to 3 Ersk. 3. § 36. Thomson *v.* Campbell, 1838; 16 S. 560, etc. Duff on Deeds, 172.

(*bb*) 24 and 25 Vict. c. 84, § 1. 26 and 27 Vict. c. 115. And see 1696, c. 8, as to tutors-nominate.

(*cc*) Sanders *v.* Beveridge, 1879; 7 R. 157. Robinson *v.* Fraser's Trs., *cit.* (*t*). City of Glasgow Bk. *v.* Gillespie, 1880; 7 R. 749. See Aberdein *v.* Stratton's Trs., *supra*, § 1998 (*hh*); and Spence *v.* Boyd, 1888; 15 R. 376.

(*dd*) Moffat *v.* Robertson, 1834; 12 S. 369. Seton *v.* Dawson, 1841; 4 D. 310 (liability incurred by signing receipts. See Blain, *infra* (*hh*)).

(*ee*) E. Traquair's Trs., *supra* (*z*). Urquhart *v.* Brown, 1843; 5 D. 1142. Ainslie *v.* Cheape, 1835; 13 S. 417. Seton, *cit.* (*dd*). Kennedy *v.* Kennedy, 1884; 12 R. 275.

(*ff*) Home *v.* Pringle, 1837; 16 S. 142; aff. 1841, 2 Rob. App. 384. Thomson *v.* Campbell, 1838; 16 S. 560. Seton, *cit.* Home *v.* Menzies, 1845; 7 D. 1010. M'Millan *v.* Armstrong, 1848; 11 D. 191. Western Bk. *v.* Baird, 1862; 24 D. 859. Carruthers *v.* Cairns, *cit.* (*k*). As to liability for factors, see, further, cases in § 1998 (*gg*).

(*gg*) Edmond *v.* Blaikie, 1866; 4 Macph. 1011.

(*hh*) Blain *v.* Paterson, 1836; 14 S. 361. See above, note (*p*); and Carruthers *v.* Carruthers' Trs., 1895; 22 R. 775; rev. 1896, A. C. 659; 23 R. H. L. 55.

(*ii*) E. Traquair, *supra* (*z*). Home and Thomson, *supra* (*ff*). Cases in note (*ee*).

(*kk*) Ferguson *v.* Paterson, 1898; 25 R. 697.

2001. Termination of the Trust.—Trust is at an end, by the death of the trustee; or by his bankruptcy, in so far as it incapacitates the trustee from acting (*a*). It is also terminated by recall of the trust; but this must be taken under these qualifications: That if the trust be for the benefit of creditors, it cannot be so recalled but by consent of all concerned; and that where the trustee has made advances or undertaken engagements under the trust, it cannot be recalled till he is reimbursed or relieved (*b*). 'Under a similar limitation, and where no special circumstances exist, a beneficiary having a vested right, who is the only party interested in the trust-estate or a distinct portion of it, may require the trustees to cede possession of it to him, and so bring the trust to an end (*c*), but this only if the truster's intention can be carried out, and the beneficiaries' interest protected, as effectually as by maintaining the trust (*d*); or the same result may be effected by arrangement among beneficiaries, as where a liferenter renounces that the fee may be conveyed at once to the fiar (*e*).'

The trustees, in order to be formally divested of such part of the estate as remains after accomplishing the purposes of the trust, or for finally executing those purposes, are bound to grant the proper conveyances (*f*); but this obligation they cannot be compelled to fulfil without full exoneration, which they may obtain judicially by an action of multiplepoinding and exoneration (*g*). When the trust is at an end, the trustees may be compelled to denude by an action of declarator of trust and adjudication; or if the trust-fund is personal or moveable property, an ordinary action will be sufficient. 'Persons continuing to act after the recall of the trust are liable for the slightest negligence (*h*).'

Trust-estates are generally vested either in the trustees and their heirs, or in the trustees without mention of heirs. If the trustees have died, the trust-estate must be restored in one or other of these methods: viz. if heirs have been mentioned in the trust-conveyance, the heir-at-law makes up his title (*i*), and dispones to other trustees, or to those having the radical right; or, if he will not spontaneously do so, a declarator of trust and adjudication directed against the heir of the trustee will accomplish the same purpose (*k*). If heirs have not been mentioned, there is greater difficulty, as the trust terminates with the trustee's death, and there is nothing in the heir. But the trust-estate is *in hæreditate jacente* of the deceased trustee, and his heir has an interest to prevent it from being taken out of it, without payment of advances, and indemnification for engagements undertaken, etc.; and so in this case also there is a sufficient ground for calling the heir in a declarator of trust and adjudication in implement (*l*). 'The appointment of a judicial factor with power to make up titles, or of new trustees, is in general the simplest way of extricating a trust when all the trustees are dead (*m*). A beneficiary entitled to the possession, for his own absolute use, of property the title to which is taken in the name of a trustee, judicial factor, or other person who has died or become incapable of acting without having conveyed it, may, by petition to the Court of Session, obtain authority to make up a title to it in his own name (*n*).'

(*a*) M'Dowal *v.* M'Dowal, 1789; M. 7453; 2 Ill. 565. See *per* L. Moncreiff in Cowan *v.* Crawford, 1837; 15 S. 404. Smyth, etc., petrs., 1832; 10 S. 531; 2 Ill. 544. See 2 M'Laren on Wills, etc., 445.

(*b*) Renton *v.* Campbell, 1831; 10 S. 38. Barnet's Trs. *v.* Barnet, 1872; 10 Macph. 730; *supra*, § 1998 (*cc*). See as to indemnity to trustees and executors having power to carry on the testator's business, and doing so with consent of creditors, Dowse *v.* Gorton, 1891; A. C. 190.

(*c*) Martin *v.* Bannatyne, 1861; 23 D. 705. Gordon *v.* Gordon's Trs., 1866; 4 Macph. 501. Tod *v.* Tod's Trs., 1871; 9 Macph. 728. Kippen *v.* Kippen's Trs., 1871; 10 Macph. 134. Spens *v.* Monypenny's Trs., 1875; 3 R. 50. Dow *v.* Kilgour's Trs., 1877; 4 R. 403. **Miller's Trs.** *v.* **Miller,** 1890; 18 R. 301

(*d*) Smith *v.* Campbell, 1873; 11 Macph. 639. Cosens *v.* Stevenson, 1873; 11 Macph. 761. Menzies *v.* Murray, 1875; 2 R. 507. White's Trs. *v.* Whyte, 1877; 4 R. 786 (alimentary annuitant cannot discharge it). Montgomerie's Trs. *v.* Montgomerie, 1888; 15 R. 369. Haldane's Trs. *v.* Haldane, 1895; 23 R. 276. Eliott's Trs. *v.* Eliott, 1894; 21 R. 975. Hughes *v.* Edwardes, 1890; 18 R. 319; rev. 1892, A. C. 583; 19 R. H. L. 33.

(*e*) Rainsford *v.* Maxwell, 1852; 14 D. 450. Pretty *v.* Newbigging, 1854; 16 D. 362. Foulis *v.* Foulis, 1857; 19 D. 362. M'Lean's Trs. *v.* M'Lean, 1878; 5 R. 679. Louson's Trs. *v.* Dicksons, 1886; 13 R. 1003. M'Murdo's Trs. *v.* M'Murdo, 1897; 24 R. 458.

(*f*) Allan *v.* M'Crae, 1791; Bell's Ca. 538.

(*g*) Elliot's Trs. *v.* Elliot, 1828; 6 S. 1058. See Watt *v.* Greenfield's Trs., 1825; 3 S. 544. Dallas *v.* Leishman, 1710; M. 16,191. Scheniman *v.* Willison's Trs., 1832; 10 S. 759.

(*h*) Edmund *v.* Blaikie, 1866; 4 Macph. 1011.

(*i*) This may be done by service as heir of provision.

(*k*) Dalziel *v.* Dalziel, 1756; M. 16,204; 2 Ill. 549. See Gardner *v.* Trinity House of Leith, 1848; 7 D. 293. Gordon's Trs. *v.* Eglinton, 1851; 13 D. 1381. Ferguson *v.* Marjoribanks, 1853; 15 D. 637. M'Leish's Trs. *v.* M'Leish, 1841; 3 D. 914. 2 M'Laren on Wills, etc., § 1828 seq.

(*l*) Drummond *v.* Mackenzie, 1758; M. 16,206. See 2 Ill. 548. See Gordon's Trs. *v.* Harper, 1821; 1 S. 199; 2 Ill. 516.

(*m*) See 30 and 31 Vict. c. 97, § 12, 15; 31 and 32 Vict. c. 101, § 24; 37 and 38 Vict. c. 94, § 43, 44, 45; and *supra*, § 724. As to charitable and educational trusts, see 13 Vict. c. 13.

(*n*) 30 and 31 Vict. c. 97, § 14.

CHAPTER XIII

OF POSITIVE PRESCRIPTION

2002. General Nature; and Statutes.—Referring to what has been already explained, of the distinction between negative prescription, as a discharge and abandonment of an obligation, and positive prescription, as a method of confirming and consolidating defective titles to property (*a*); the more particular consideration of the latter now demands attention. By one statute, the possession of lands or annualrents for forty years on charter and sasine freed the possessor from the necessity of showing his procuratories and instruments of resignation, precepts of *clare constat*, or precepts of sasine; provided the charter bore resignation to have been made, and that the instrument of sasine made mention of the precept (*b*). By a subsequent statute, a more perfect remedy was given against insecurity in the enjoyment of property in land. It was enacted, that persons having brooked (or possessed) "by themselves, their tenants, or others having their rights, their lands, baronies, annualrents, and other heritages, by virtue of their heritable infeftments made to them by His Majesty, or others their superiors and authors, for the space of forty years continually and together, following and ensuing the date of their said infeftments, and that peaceably, without any lawful interruption made to them therein during the said space of forty years; that such persons, their heirs and successors, shall never be troubled, pursued, nor inquieted in the heritable right and property of the said lands and heritages foresaid, by His Majesty or others their superiors and authors, their heirs and successors, nor by any other person pretending right to the same by virtue of prior infeftments, public or private, nor upon no other ground, reason, or argument competent of law, except for falsehood; provided they be able to show and produce a charter of the said lands and others foresaid, granted to them or their predecessors by their said superiors and authors, preceding the entry of the said forty years' possession, with the instrument of sasine following thereupon; or, where there is no charter extant, that they show and produce instruments of sasine, one or more, continued and standing together for the said space of forty years, either proceeding upon retours or upon precepts of *clare constat*" (*c*). But a provision was added, that "in the course of the said forty years' prescription, the years of minority and lessage shall noways be counted, but only the years during which the parties against whom the prescription is used and objected were majors, and past twenty-one years of age" (*d*).

(*a*) See *ante*, § 605.
(*b*) 1594, c. 214; 4 Acta Parl. 68, c. 24.
(*c*) 1617, c. 12; 4 Acta Parl. p. 543, c. 12. 2 Stair, 12. 3 Ersk. 7. Kames, Elucid. art. 33.
(*d*) See below, § 2022.

2003. Subjects.—The proper subjects of the positive prescription are (1) Feudal subjects vested by infeftment (*a*); (2) Subjects which do not admit of sasine, or which may be transmitted without it (*b*): so tacks (*c*), teinds (*d*), tacks of teinds (*e*), patronages (*f*), servitudes (*g*), are comprehended under the word "heritages" in the statute (*h*).

(*a*) 2 Stair, 12. § 22, 23. 3 Ersk. 7. § 3.
(*b*) See Stair and Ersk. *ut supra*.
(*c*) Maule *v.* Maule, 1829; 7 S. 527, and Apx. for opinions; 2 Ill. 566 and 572.
(*d*) Ferguson *v.* Hers. of Kingarth, 1671; M. 10,775; 1 B. Sup. 624. Maxwell *v.* Maxwell, 1699; 4 B. Sup. 462. Solr. of Teinds *v.* Budge, 1797; Hume, 455. E. Fife *v.* Innes, 1809; Hume, 468. L. Adv. *v.* Balfour, 1860; 23 D. 147.
(*e*) Muir *v.* Hers. of Dunlop, 1746; M. 10,820; 2 Ill. 566.
(*f*) F. Home *v.* Officers of State, 1758; M. 10,777; 5 B. Sup. 365, 867; aff. as to this point, 2 Pat. 25. Mags. of Peebles *v.* Officers of State, 1800; Hume, 457. L. Adv. *v.* L. Dundas, 1830; 8 S. 755; aff. 5 W. & S. 723. See below, § 2006, 2013.
(*g*) E. Breadalbane *v.* Menzies, 1740; Elch. *Presc.* 21; 5 B. Sup. 700. Muir, *supra* (*e*). Porteous *v.* Allan, 1773; M. 14,512; Hailes, 280; 5 B. Sup. 598; 2 Ill. 128. See Officers of State *v.* E. Haddington, 1826; 2 W. & S. 468; 2 Ill. 14. See above, § 993.
(*h*) See below, § 2013.

2004. Requisite Possession.—Possession is required by the statute to give effect to the prescription (*a*). It implies the detention or occupation of the subject by an owner, or one having reasonable grounds to believe himself owner, with the purpose of holding the subject as his own. This includes right, or the rational belief of it—in other words *bona fides*; and the fact of continued possession (*b*). 'But the language of Mr. Bell here, in regard to *bona fides*, is not consistent with principle or authority, and has not been accepted as an accurate statement of the law. Where there is a title "not chargeable with falsehood," *bona fides* is presumed *præsumptione juris et de jure* (*c*). The possession must be in virtue of the titles founded on, and not inconsistent with them (*d*).'

(*a*) M'Kerrell *v.* Keith, 1801; Hume, 458. Anderson *v.* Low, 1863; 2 Macph. 100.
(*b*) Younger *v.* Johnston, 1665; M. 10,924; 2 Ill. 566. Murray *v.* M'Lellan, 1713; M. 10,934. Wilson *v.* Campbell, 1765; M. 10,924; 5 B. Sup. 543, 916, 930; rev. 2 Pat. 193; 2 Ill. 567. M'Lean *v.* D. Argyle, 1777; *ib.* 544.
(*c*) 3 Ersk. 7. § 15. 3 Ersk. Pr. 7. § 12. 2 Stair, 12. § 5 sq. 3 Mackenzie, 7. § 5. Napier, Prescription, 51–57. D. Buccleuch *v.* Cunningham, *infra*, § 2009 (*a*). See below, § 2010, cases there in notes (*b*), (*c*); and above, § 612.
(*d*) **L. Adv.** *v.* **Hunt**, 1865; 3 Macph. 426; rev. 1867, 5 Macph. H. L. 1, and authorities cited there and in § 738. 2008 (*b*), 2020 (*i*). Rankine on Landownership, 40–43. Scott *v.* Napier, 1869; 7 Macph. H. L. 35. Dalrymple *v.* E. Stair, 1841; 3 D. 837. King *v.* E. Stair, 1844; 6 D. 821; aff. 1846, 5 Bell's App. 82, 100. See above, § 738, as to bounding charters.

2005. (1.) *Nature of Possession.*—The possession may be either natural or civil; in which sense the liferenter's possession has been admitted as the fiar's (*a*), and the possession of a disponee as that of his author (*b*). But it must be of a description clearly indicative of the right; so, fishing of salmon by angle, spear, and wand, was not held sufficient for salmon-fishing (*c*); 'and it must be coextensive with the right to be established, for *tantum præscriptum, quantum possessum* (*d*).'

The possession, 'which must always be judged of *secundum subjectam materiam* (*e*),' must be 'exclusive (*f*), and lawful in respect of the right which it is setting up or explaining (*g*), as well as' continually and together for forty years (*h*); and so, if abandoned, the possession is interrupted and the term of prescription broken (*i*). 'But in actions commenced on or after 1st Jan. 1879, prescription may be pleaded on an *ex facie* valid irredeemable title recorded in the appropriate Register of Sasines, and possession following thereon for the space of TWENTY years continually and together, and that peaceably without any interruption made during the said space of twenty years. Such possession is declared to be equivalent for all the purposes of the Act 1617, c. 12, to possession for forty years by virtue of heritable infeftments for which charters and instruments of sasine or other sufficient titles are shown and produced according to the provisions of the Act. This enactment does not alter or affect the law as to the character or period of the possession, use, or enjoyment necessary to constitute or prove the existence of a servitude or of any public right of way or other public right; provided that possession for any space of time prior to the specified date shall have no effect for the purposes of the new enactment, unless such space of time immediately preceded and was continuous up to the said first day of January (*k*).'

(*a*) Younger and Wilson, *supra*, § 2004 (*b*). Neilson *v.* Erskine, 1823; 2 S. 247 (6 D. 483, n.); 2 Ill. 567. See **Shepherd** *v.* **Grant's Trs.**, 1844; 6 D. 464; aff. 1847, 6 Bell's App. 153.
(*b*) Dickson *v.* Miller, 1766; M. 10,937; 5 B. Sup. 919; Hailes, 1. Crawford *v.* Durham, June 2, 1826; F. C.; 4 S. 665; 3 Ross' L. C. 438; 2 Ill. 568, 572.
(*c*) Forbes *v.* Udny, 1701; M. 10,929. See above, § 1112. E. Fife's Trs. *v.* Cumming, 1830; 9 S. 386.
(*d*) *Supra*, § 993. 2 Ersk. 9. § 4. L. Adv. *v.* Cathcart, 1871; 9 Macph. 744.
(*e*) M'Donnell *v.* D. Gordon, 1828; 6 S. 600. E. Fife's Trs. *v.* Sinclair, 1849; 12 D. 223. Forbes, below, § 2006. Murray *v.* Peddie, 1880; 7 R. 804 (one tide's fishing of salmon yearly). L. Adv. *v.* L. Lovat, 1880; 7 R. H. L. 122. Ogston *v.* Stewart's Trs., *infra* (*k*) (salmon fishing).

(*f*) E. Fife's Trs. *v.* Sinclair, *cit.* Wallace *v.* Dundee Police Comrs., 1875; 2 R. 565.

(*g*) Mackenzie *v.* Renton, 1840; 2 D. 1078 (illegal mode of fishing). Cf. Ramsay, *infra* (*h*). An illegal *mode* of possession may, however, be strong evidence of the existence of a legal right. L. Adv. *v.* L. Lovat (*e*).

(*h*) See Wilson *v.* Wilson, 1843; 6 D. 7. Christison *v.* Hope, 1847; 10 D. 119. (Road): M. Breadalbane *v.* M'Gregor, 1846; 9 D. 210; and 7 Bell's App. 43. Crawford *v.* Menzies, 1849; 11 D. 1127. (Bleaching ground): Home *v.* Young, 1846; 9 D. 286. (Fishings): Ramsay *v.* D. Roxburghe, 1848; 10 D. 661; aff. 1850, 7 Bell's App. 248. (Harbour Dues): Mags. of Campbelton *v.* Galbraith, 1845; 7 D. 482. Dundee Harbour Trs. *v.* Dougall, 1848; 11 D. 6; aff. 1 Macq. 317. Greig *v.* Mags. of Kirkcaldy, 1851; 13 D. 975. Macpherson *v.* Mackenzie, 1881; 8 R. 706. (Superiority): E. Fife's Trs. *v.* Sinclair, *cit.* Possession being proved for forty years back, it is presumed to have continued from time immemorial to the effect of connecting it with an earlier habile title. L. Adv. *v.* Sinclair, 1865; 3 Macph. 981; aff. 1867, 5 Macph. H. L. 97. L. Adv. *v.* M'Culloch, 1874; 2 R. 27. Cf. Cuthbertson *v.* Young, 1851; 14 D. 300; 1 Macq. 455.

(*i*) 3 Ersk. 7. § 42.

(*k*) 37 and 38 Vict. c. 94, § 34. Buchanan *v.* L. Adv., 1882; 9 R. 1218. Geils *v.* Do., *ib.* See Brodie *v.* Mann, 1884; 11 R. 925; rev. 1885, 10 App. Ca. 378; 12 R. H. L. 52. Ogston *v.* Stewart's Trs., 1896, A.C. 120; 23 R. H. L. 16. See below, § 2012, 2022, etc.

2006. Peculiarities occur in the possession of coal and of patronage.

As to coal, the rule seems to be, that slight acts of working at intervals will not be enough; but that it must be reasonably continuous and adverse, allowing for inundations, troubles, etc. The working of one of several fields, all in the same charter and under one *reddendo*, will be sufficient for the whole, 'but not if two parcels are granted as separate subjects, though in one charter for convenience (*a*).'

As to patronage, in which, 'while it remained,' the acts of possession 'were' necessarily at intervals, 'it was said that' continuous possession 'seemed' to require at least two acts without intermediate interruption (*b*); after which possession 'was' presumed till interrupted. The incumbent's possession, after one exercise of the right, 'was' not enough for the patron, as being held entirely independent of the patron (*c*).

(*a*) Forbes *v.* Livingston, 1822; 1 S. 282; 1 W. & S. 657; and 1827, 6 S. 167; 2 Ill. 568. Crawford *v.* Durham, 1826; 4 S. 665. See 20 Dec. 1822; 21 F. C. 69.

(*b*) 4 Stair, 40. § 20; and 4. 45. § 17. M'Donnell *v.* D. Gordon, 1828; 6 S. 600. See § 2003, 2013.

(*c*) Same case.

2007. (2.) *Interruption of Possession* may be extrajudicial, *viâ facti* (*a*); by demanding and obtaining, or effectually assuming possession (*b*), or by notarial protest. But protest is an interruption only *to* the protester and *against* the possessor; not affecting or available to singular successors, unless an instrument shall be extended and recorded, 'formerly' in a particular register, 'now in the General Register of Sasines' (*c*). Or interruption may be judicial, by citation by a messenger-at-arms, on a summons under the signet, containing the grounds of interruption, and recorded within sixty days, in order to have effect against singular successors (*d*); the citation being either personal or at the dwelling-place, or at the Record of Citations if the party is abroad (*e*). Interruption by citation, not followed by an action, requires to be renewed every seven years. If, after citation, the summons is called, and the action brought into Court, the interruption no longer rests on mere citation, but endures as an interruption for forty years (*f*).

(*a*) 3 Ersk. 7. § 39, 42. As to interruptions in the case of public rights of way, see Rodgers *v.* Harvie, 1826; 4 Mur. 25; 1827, 5 S. 917; aff. 1828, 3 W. & S. 251. **Mags. of Elgin** *v.* **Jenkins,** 1862; 24 D. 301, 788; 2 Macph. 1162; 5 Macph. H. L. 27; 6 Macph. 951; 7 *ib.* 739. Brodie *v.* Mann, 1884; 11 R. 925; rev. 1885, 12 R. H. L. 52; 10 App. Ca. 378.

(*b*) Brown *v.* Town of Kirkcudbright, 1680; M. 11,294; 2 Ill. 569. Home *v.* Linthill, 1684; M. 11,253. It may be, apparently, by formal acknowledgments by the possessor, see *per* L. Curriehill and L. Deas in Fleeming *v.* Howden, 1868; 6 Macph. 794, 795.

(*c*) 1696, c. 19; 10 Acta Parl. p. 60, c. 19. 31 and 32 Vict. c. 64, § 15. (*d*) *Ib.*

(*e*) 1669, c. 10; 7 Acta Parl. p. 561, c. 15. 6 Geo. IV. c. 120.

(*f*) 3 Ersk. 7. § 43. Wilson *v.* Innes, 1705; M. 10,974, 11,330. Wallace *v.* E. Eglinton, 1830; 8 S. 1018. See 19 and 20 Vict. c. 79, § 109; and above, § 620, 2005.

2008. Title for Prescription.—In order to ground prescription, there must be a title, and such as to imply *bona fides* (*a*). It is not requisite to a prescriptive title that it should be a disposition in chief; a clause of part and pertinent is sufficient (*b*). So a title to a barony will serve to prescribe a subject as part and pertinent (*c*). So a consuetudinary right may be acquired by prescription, 'if it be truly a customary right annexed to the title' (*d*). It is necessary, however, that the right shall be conferred absolutely in the dispositive clause (*e*); any limitation imposed, and appearing in the sasine or record, being perpetuated (*f*).

'The Conveyancing Act of 1874, adapting the law of prescription to the modernised system of Titles to Land, provides that in any action commenced after 1st January 1879, "any *ex facie* valid irredeemable title to an estate in land recorded in the appropriate Register of Sasines shall be a sufficient foundation for prescription" (*g*). This appears to make no change in substance on the former law, as now to be stated.'

The words of the Act describing the title are confined to the case of subjects with feudal titles; but practice having extended the construction to all heritages, distinctions must be made as to title.

(*a*) See above, § 2004.
(*b*) 3 Ersk. 7. § 4. E. Fife's Trs. *v.* Cumming, 1830; 8 S. 326; and 1831, 9 S. 336; 2 Ill. 40 and 155. See § 738. Mackenzie *v.* Mackenzie, 1818; 6 Pat. 376. Dalrymple *v.* E. Stair, 1841; 3 D. 837. Carnegie *v.* M'Tier, 1844; 6 D. 932, 1381. Baird *v.* Fortune, 1859; 21 D. 848; 1861, 4 Macq. 127; 23 D. H. L. 5. L. Advocate *v.* Hunt, 1865; 3 Macph. 426; rev. 1867, 5 Macph. H. L. 1; L. R. 1 Sc. Ap. 85.
(*c*) Mags. of Perth *v.* E. Wemyss, 1829; 8 S. 82; 2 Ill. 40. D. Montrose *v.* MacIntyre, 1848; 10 D. 896 (ferry). Dss. Sutherland *v.* Watson, 1868; 6 Macph. 199 (mussel scalps). See § 748, 750.
(*d*) Officers of State *v.* E. Haddington, 1823; 2 S. 420; 2 W. & S. 468; 5 W. & S. 479; 2 Ill. 14; see 2 Ill. 573. Macpherson *v.* Mackenzie, 1881; 8 R. 706 (burgh harbour dues).
(*e*) Agnew *v.* Mags. of Stranraer, 1822; 2 S. 42; 2 Ill. 573.
(*f*) Elliot *v.* Maxwell, 1727; M. 10,977. "This decision is not law. See Scott *v.* Bruce Stewart, 1776; 5 B. S. 542; Hailes, 811." 2 Bell's Ill. 573. 3 Ross' L. C. 464 sqq. 3 Ersk. 7. § 10 *fin.* *Infra*, § 2017 (*l*). Monro *v.* Monro, May 19, 1812; F. C. Geddes *v.* Miller, May 28, 1819; F. C. Chambers *v.* Law, 1823; 2 S. 366.
(*g*) 37 and 38 Vict. c. 94, § 34. *Infra*, § 2012.

2009. (1.) *Feudal Subjects.*—It is requisite as a title to such subjects, that there shall be produced an infeftment proceeding on a regular charter or disposition; or, alternatively, on a retour or precept of *clare constat*, one or more, for forty years; the rule being, that in relation to feudal subjects, prescription requires the possessor to connect himself with a sasine (*a*). 'By the former law, as by the late statute, the title must be *ex facie* valid (*b*).' But it is not necessary, in prescribing a right to the lands by a feudal superior, that he should have a title flowing from the vassal; his own title to the superiority, being *ex facie* a title to the land, is sufficient (*c*). The question of title may arise in relation to a purchaser, an heir, or a creditor.

(*a*) D. Buccleuch *v.* Cunningham, 1826; 5 S. 57; 2 Ill. 570. Walker *v.* Grieve, 1827; 5 S. 469; 2 Ill. 17. Bruce *v.* Bruce Carstairs, 1770; M. 10,805; Hailes, 378; aff. 1772, 2 Pat. 258; 2 Ill. 17. Harvey *v.* Wilson, 1822; 1 S. 366; 2 Ill. 570. Crawford, *supra*, § 2006 (*a*). Neilson *v.* Erskine, 1823; 2 S. 247. The rule is, that there can be no prescription without a sasine; *nulla sasina nulla terra.* 2 Stair, 3. § 16. Napier on Prescr. 105.
(*b*) See below, § 2010 (*c*), (*d*). **Shepherd** *v.* **Grant's Trs.**, 1844; 6 D. 464; aff. 1847, 6 Bell's App. 153. Glen *v.* Scales' Trs., 1881; 9 R. 317.
(*c*) Campbell of Otter *v.* Wilson, 1765; 5 B. Sup. 916; 2 Ill. 54. E. Dunmore *v.* Middleton, 1774; M. 10,944; 5 B. Sup. 614; Hailes, 587; see 2 Ill. 17. **Robertson** *v.* **D. Athol**, 1808; Hume, 463; 1815, 3 Dow, 114; 1 Ross' L. C. 208. L. Elibank *v.* Campbell, 1833; 12 S. 74; 3 Ross' L. C. 534. **Bontine** *v.* **Graham**, 1837; 15 S. 711; aff. 1840, 1 Rob. 347. Wilson *v.* Pollock, 1839; 2 D. 139. See above, § 689, 821; below, § 2017 (*c*), 2320.

2010. In regard to a purchaser, the infeftment, '*i.e.* the instrument of sasine and its warrants, including all connecting links,' is an indispensable point of the prescriptive title in feudal subjects (*a*). It has been held in one case, that an extract from the register is not sufficient to supply the place of the sasine (*b*); but this has been doubted. The law of prescription looks to the title as the ground of *bona fides*; and although, under the statute, reduction—improbation is competent, when the sasine itself must be produced, the extract is, on a fair construction of the statute, said to be effectual for all other purposes.

An infeftment with its warrant (a charter, disposition, or procuratory of resignation) is a perfect title of prescription, although proceeding *a non domino*, and although the title be subject to a latent nullity (*c*); nay, it has been held good even where the title bore evidence *in gremio* of the objection, but the ground of that objection was to be collected extraneously (*d*). Where a mediate title only is shown (as an obligation to infeft), with sasine following, it is doubtful whether, in a question with singular successors, that be sufficient (*e*). In sasine *propriis manibus* no precept is necessary (*f*). This is the rule also in burgage holdings, where the warrant and the act of taking infeftment are recited in one instrument (*g*).

(*a*) Fraser *v.* Hog, 1679; M. 10,784; 3 B. Sup. 533; 2 Ill. 570. Officers of State *v.* Ochterlony, 1823; 2 S. 437; aff. 1 W. & S. 533. Maconochie *v.* Trinity Hospital, 1852; 14 D. 813. Glen *v.* Scales' Trs., 1881; 9 R. 317.
(*b*) Cuming *v.* Irvine, 1680; M. 10,785. M. Bell's Convg. 657. Duff's Feud. Convg. § 121.
(*c*) 2 Stair, 12. § 20. 3 Ersk. 7. § 4. Scott *v.* Bruce Stewart, 1779; M. 13,519. Purdie *v.* L. Torphichen, 1739; M. 10,796. Fraser *v.* L. Lovat, 1898; 25 R. 603. Hilson *v.* Scott, 1895, 23 R. 241.
(*d*) D. Buccleuch, *supra*, § 2009 (*a*). Forbes, *supra*, § 2006 (*a*). L. Adv. *v.* Graham, 1844; 7 D. 183. Tayport Land Co. *v.* Dougall's Trs., 1895; 23 R. 287.
(*e*) 2 Stair, 3. § 19, and *ut supra.* 2 Bankt. 160. § 20. Ersk. *ut supra.* Cuming, *supra* (*b*).
(*f*) See above, § 765.
(*g*) Heriot's Hospital *v.* Hepburn, 1695; M. 10,787. Ker *v.* Abernethy, 1705; M. 10,813.

2011. For an heir's title, a sasine grounded on a retour, or proceeding on a precept of *clare constat* (*a*), or on entry by hasp and staple (*b*), with possession for forty years, or a series of sasines grounded on retours successively following each other (*c*), or connected by the uninterrupted possession of apparent heirs (*d*), will form a good title of prescription without production of the original charter.

(*a*) Bruce *v.* Bruce Carstairs, 1770; M. 10,805; 2 Ill. 17.
(*b*) Ker *v.* Abernethy, 1805; M. 10,813; 2 Ill. 571.
(*c*) 2 Stair, 12. § 15. Monro *v.* Monro, May 19, 1812; F. C. Purdie *v.* L. Torphichen, 1739; M. 10,797. M'Neill *v.* M'Neal, 1858; 20 D. 735. Fraser *v.* L. Lovat, *cit.*
(*d*) 3 Ersk. 7. § 5, to be corrected. E. Marchmont *v.* E. Home, 1724; M. 10,797. Caitcheon *v.* Ramsay, 1791; M. 10,810. Neilson *v.* Erskine, 1823; 2 S. 247. Waddel *v.* Pollock, 1828; 6 S. 999. Crawford *v.* Durham, Dec. 20, 1822; F. C. E. Glasgow *v.* Boyle, 1887; 14 R. 419.

2012. An adjudication with sasine is a good title to ground prescription in favour of a creditor; and if followed by forty years' possession, it confers an effectual and irredeemable right. But the *terminus a quo* is the expiry of the legal (*a*). 'As an adjudication with sasine is not an *ex facie* irredeemable title, the period of prescription on a decree of adjudication followed by infeftment is still forty years (*b*).'

(*a*) Caitcheon, *supra*, § 2011 (*d*). **Robertson** *v.* **D. Athol**, 1808; Hume, 463; 1815, 3 Dow, 114; 1 Ross' L. C. 208. See above, § 831, below, § 2302; 1 Bell's Com. 706; and Napier on Prescr. 133 et seq. 1 Ross' L. C. 222. Thomson *v.* Stewart, 1840; 2 D. 564 (necessity of sasine). Cf. 1 Bell's Com. 707, note (746, M'L.'s ed.).
(*b*) See above, § 2008. Hinton *v.* Connell's Trs., 1883; 10 R. 1110.

2013. (2.) *Subjects not Feudal.*—To such subjects the words of the Act cannot be applied, but the analogy may. So, in teinds, a tack is a good title of prescription (*a*), or an adjudication or disposition without infeftment (*b*), 'but not apparently the *jus coronæ* (*c*).' A grant of patronage 'was' a good title of prescription, but not if there 'were' a reservation of the right to present (*d*).

(*a*) E. Leven *v.* Hers. of Kennoway, 1696; M. 10,818; 2 Ill. 572. Muir *v.* Hers. of Dunlop, 1746; M. 10,820; 2 Ill. 566. See Speirs *v.* Officers of State, 1858; 20 D. 525. See above, § 837.
(*b*) Gordon *v.* Kennedy, 1758; M. 10,825; 5 B. Sup. 358; 2 Ill. 63. Irvine *v.* Burnet, 1764; M. 10,830. See L. Adv. *v.* Balfour, 1860; 23 D. 147.
(*c*) Cheape *v.* L. Adv., 1871; 9 Macph. 377, 395, 396.
(*d*) See § 2003. L. Adv. *v.* E. Mansfield, 1830; 8 S. 765. L. Adv. *v.* Graham, 1844; 7 D. 183.

2014. A lease or tack is a good title of prescription to a tenant (*a*); and, of course, the connection with the original lease may be continued without any retour, as no service is required in a lease. In servitudes, a right to lands, houses, or other dominant tenement is a good title (*b*). Commonty requires a clause "cum communio," or "with commonty," or "with pertinents" (*c*).

(*a*) See Maule *v.* Maule, 1829; 7 S. 527 and Appendix; 2 Ill. 566 and 572. It was here agreed that the "positive" prescription had come to be applied to leases; but Mr. Napier (pp. 289–343) shows that there is ground for holding that in cases of personal rights, such as leases, only the negative prescription had properly been allowed to operate. See Carlyle *v.* Baxter, 1869; 41 S. Jur. 342.
(*b*) 2 Ersk. 9. § 3. See § 2003 (*g*); also Servitudes, § 993. Beaumont *v.* L. Glenlyon, 1843; 5 D. 1337. Carnegie *v.* M'Tier, 1844; 6 D. 932, 985, 1381. Cameron *v.* Gunn, 1848; 10 D. 446. (Walking): Dyce *v.* Hay, 1849; 11 D. 1266; aff. 1852, 1 Macq. 305. (Road): Torrie *v.* D. Athol, 1849; 12 D. 329; aff. 1 Macq. 65. (Ferry): Greig *v.* Mags. of Kirkcaldy, 1851; 13 D. 975. (Curling): Harvey *v.* Lindsay, 1853; 15 D. 768. Thirlage, § 1022; Pasturage, § 1013.
(*c*) See above, § 1089. As to a ferry, D. Montrose *v.* MacIntyre, 1848; 10 D. 896.

2015. Objections cut off by Prescription.—Prescription is a good defence against objections to the titles, grounded either on nullities in those titles which are not required to be produced (*a*); or on latent nullities or extrinsic objections, as an error in the ceremony of sasine (*b*); but it is no defence against intrinsic nullities (*c*). 'Prescription explains the effect or extent of an ambiguous title; so, even, as to exclude reference to prior or contemporaneous titles. For example, where a description in a charter and sasine could be construed as embracing either the whole or a part of an estate, the whole of which was possessed for the prescriptive period, that possession was held to protect the possessor against one holding an express title of earlier date, whether to the whole or part of the lands (*d*).'

(*a*) 3 Ersk. 7. § 9. 3 Ersk. 7. § 4. Purdie *v.* L. Torphichen, 1739; M. 10,796; 2 Ill. 570. Ged *v.* Baker, 1740; M. 10,789; 2 Ill. 574; 1 Ross' L. C. 200.
(*b*) Scott *v.* Bruce Stewart, 1776; M. 13,519; Hailes, 811 and 730; 5 B. S. 542. Kinloch *v.* Bell, 1867; 5 Macph. 360. See above, § 610; and below, § 2016, 2017; and cases, § 2016 (*a*).
(*c*) 3 Ersk. 7. § 9. Shaw Stewart *v.* Houston, 1823; 2 S. 300. Shepherd *v.* Grant's Trs., 1844; 6 D. 464; aff. 6 Bell's App. 153. Kinloch, *cit.*
(*d*) Auld *v.* Hay, 1880; 7 R. 663. Cf. Cooper's Trs. *v.* Stark's Trs., 1898; 25 R. 1160.

2016. Negative Prescription as connected with Positive.—Negative prescription extinguishes debts, and is established by one clause in the Act of 1617, as applicable to heritable bonds, reversions, etc., as well as to personal debts; but there is no law introducing negative prescription, or any length of abandonment, as an extinction of property. It is by positive prescription alone that a right of property can be established, however long the true proprietor may have neglected his right. And so the negative prescription is insufficient to extinguish any 'objection or burden affecting a' right or claim of property, unless there be an opposite right 'at least' in the course of being confirmed at the same time (*a*).

(*a*) 3 Ersk. 7. § 8. Paton *v.* Drysdale, 1725; M. 10,709; 2 Ill. 574. Presby. of Perth *v.* Mags. of Perth, 1728; M. 10,723; 1 Cr. St. & P. 39. Paul *v.* Reid, Feb. 8, 1814; F. C.; 1 Ross' L. C. 182. Shaw Stewart *v.* Houston, 1823; 2 S. 300. M'Donnell *v.* D. Gordon, 1828; 6 S. 601; 2 Ill. 569. **Cubbison *v.* Hyslop,** 1837; 16 S. 112; 3 Ross' L. C. 316–337. See above, § 607 sqq. E. Dundonald *v.* Boyes, 1836; 14 S. 737. **Chisholm *v.* Chisholm-Batten,** 1864; 2 Macph. 202 (*per* L. Deas, p. 225). Wauchope *v.* York Bdgs. Co., 1781; M. 10,706; aff. 2 Pat. 595. Officers of Ordnance *v.* Mags. of Edin., 1859; 22 D. 219; aff. 1862, 4 Macq. 447. The text is here corrected by § 2018, *infra*, the cases cited, especially Cubbison and Dundonald, and Napier on Prescr. *passim*.

2017. But negative prescription is not without effect in fortifying a title, for it extinguishes and gets rid of various objections otherwise competent, which do not appear *ex facie* of the titles (*a*). It will 'not, as the author stated,' extinguish an original tenure, 'although it cuts off the superior's right to arrears of feu-duties and casualties, and by positive prescription a vassal may effect a change of tenure (*b*). Professor Bell's statement that the negative prescription will extinguish' a base right in favour of the superior possessing on his title of superiority (*c*), 'has also been criticised; and it seems that in the cases cited, consolidation (see § 2020) or extinction of the limited title was effected by positive prescription (*d*). It has been held that the negative prescription will extinguish' the limitations of an entail (*e*); an adjudication not followed by possession (*f*); a *jus crediti* in land rights,—as an obligation to entail lands (*g*), 'or to create a real burden (*h*),' or to lay out certain funds in purchasing lands to be entailed (*i*), or a destination in a marriage-contract (*k*); or an objection grounded on latent defects in titles, as in a sasine (*l*); a power of redemption not repeated in the title (*m*); 'an objection to a decree of valuation of teinds (*n*); a right of real warrandice (*o*).' But it will not extinguish a right *meræ facultatis* (*p*).

(*a*) Cubbison, M'Donnell, and Paul, *citt.* § 2016. It does not obviate an *ex facie* nullity, *e.g.* an erasure *in essentialibus*. **Shepherd *v.* Grant's Trs.,** 1844; 6 D. 464; aff. 1847; 6 Bell's App. 153.

(*b*) D. Buccleuch *v.* Officers of State, 1768; M. 10,711; Hailes, 237, 303, 333; 2 Ill. 574. See Napier on Prescr., p. 558 sqq., 591–2. M'Kerrel *v.* L. Keith, 1801; Hume, 458. Hamilton *v.* Scotland, 1807; Hume, 461. See **D. Montrose *v.* Bontine,** 1840; 2 D. 1186; 3 Ross' L. C. 405. Wallace *v.* Crawford's Exrs., 1838; 1 D. 162. D. Buccleuch *v.* Boyd, 1890; 18 R. 1.

(*c*) Walker *v.* Grieve, 1827; 5 S. 569; 2 Ill. 17. Bruce *v.* Bruce Carstairs, 1770; M. 10,805; Hailes, 378; aff. 1772, 2 Pat. 258. Harvey *v.* Wilson, 1822; 1 S. 306; 2 Ill. 570.

(*d*) Napier on Prescr., p. 563 sq. Comp. Dalrymple *v.* E. Stair, 1841; 3 D. 837, 863. **Robertson *v.* D. Athol,** 1808; Hume, 463; 1815, 6 Pat. 108; 3 Dow, 114; 1 Ross' L. C. 208. L. Elibank *v.* Campbell, 1833; 12 S. 74; 3 Ross' L. C. 534. Bontine *v.* Graham, 1837; 15 S. 711; aff. 1840, 1 Rob. 347. Wilson *v.* Pollock, 1839; 2 D. 159. See 2 Ross' L. C. 581. See above, § 689, 821, 2009; below, § 2020. E. Glasgow *v.* Boyle, 1887; 14 R. 419.

(*e*) L. Belhaven *v.* Hamilton, 1761; M. 10,681; 2 Ill. 575. Douglas *v.* Douglas, 1753; M. 4350 and 10,955; aff. Cr. St. & P. 553. Scott *v.* Bruce Stewart, 1776; 5 B. Sup. 542; Hailes, 811. Paterson *v.* Campbell, 1823; 1 S. App. 401. D. Buccleuch *v.* Cuningham, 1826; 5 S. 57; 2 Ill. 570. D. Hamilton *v.* Westenra, 1827; 6 S. 44. Montgomerie *v.* E. Eglinton, 1843; 2 Bell's App. 149. Stewart *v.* Stewart, 1844; 6 D. 1073; aff. 5 Bell's App. 139. Baillie *v.* Cochrane, 1855; 17 D. 659; aff. 1857, 2 Macq. 529.

(*f*) Anderson *v.* Nasmith, 1758; M. 10,676; 2 Ill. 576; 1 Ross' L. C. 152. Robertson *v.* Robertson, 1770; M. 10,694; Hailes, 362, 707. Ross *v.* M'Kenzie, 1776; M. 5176; 5 B. Sup. 543. See 3 Pat. 676. Napier on Prescr., 567–581. Campbell *v.* Scotland, 1794; 1 Ross' L. C. 155, 163.

(*g*) Porterfield *v.* Porterfield, 1771; M. 10,698. Paul *v.* Reid, Feb. 8, 1814; F. C. E. Eglinton *v.* E. Eglinton, etc., 1861; 23 D. 1369. Paterson *v.* Wilson, 1859; 21 D. 322. Stewart, *cit.* (*e*).

(*h*) Pearson *v.* Malachi, 1892; 20 R. 167.

(*i*) Kinloch *v.* Rocheid, 1800; M. *Presc.* Apx. 8 and 18; 1805, 5 Pat. 35. Barns *v.* Barns' Trs., 1857; 19 D. 626.

(*k*) **Routledge *v.* Carruthers,** Dec. 16, 1819; F. C.; 2 Bligh, 692; 6 Pat. 597. Macdonald *v.* Lockhart, 1842; 5 D. 372; 3 Ross' L. C. 367. In these cases, however, there was positive as well as negative prescription.

(*l*) **Scott *v.* Bruce Stewart,** 1779; M. 13,519; 5 B. Sup. 542, 588; Hailes, 811; 2 Ill. 83; 3 Ross' L. C. 464. This differs from 3 Ersk. 7. § 10. See Agnew *v.* Mags. of Stranraer, 1822; 2 S. 42. *Supra*, § 874 *fin.*

(*m*) Monro *v.* Monro, May 19, 1812; F. C.; 3 Ross' L. C. 373. Chambers *v.* Law, 1823; 2 S. 366.

(*n*) L. Torphichen *v.* Hers. of Calder, 1743; M. 15,740. M'Intyre *v.* M'Lean, March 7, 1828; 3 F. C. 794; S. Td. Ca. 160. Deans of Chapel Royal *v.* Johnstone, 1867; 5 Macph. 414, 455, etc.; aff. 1869; 7 Macph. H. L. 19.

(*o*) Gardner *v.* Scott, 1839; 2 D. 185; rev. 1843, 2 Bell's App. 129.

(*p*) Crawford *v.* Bethune, 1821; 1 S. 111. See Crawford *v.* Durham, Dec. 12, 1822; 21 F. C. 69; and 1826, 4 S. 665; 2 Ill. 568. Leck *v.* Chalmers, 1859; 21 D. 408. Gellatly *v.* Arrol, 1863; 1 Macph. 592. Smith *v.* Stewart, 1884; 11 R. 921. Mitchell *v.* Brown, 1888; 5 Sh. Ct. Rep. 9. *Supra*, § 999, 1112. "Res meræ facultatis sunt quæ non actu quæsita, verum semper in potentia sunt ut constituantur et acquirantur." Huber, Prælect. vol. iii. 64 (ad Dig. 24. 6. 11); correcting Grot. de J. B. et P. ii. 4. 15; a definition hardly wide enough, perhaps, to include all the things which Scotch lawyers include under the term. Their learning on the subject is probably derived from such passages as J. Voet. Pand. xliv. 3. 11, and xiii. 7. 7, and Vinn. Sel. Qu. ii. 6. See also Kames' Eluc., art. 33 (pp. 238, 246, 275).

2018. In order to be entitled to plead the negative prescription, it is necessary either to have a right of property, or such a right at least as shall give the direct benefit of the extinction (*a*). 'Such rights as levying customs, port dues, and other privileges of royal burghs, may be lost by the negative prescription, though the exercise of the right at one point preserves it over the whole territory to which the grant applies. On the other hand, immunity may be established, *i.e.* dereliction may be set up, on the principle of the negative prescription, by possession for forty years by positive acts inconsistent with the subsistence of the right in whole or in part; and such dereliction or negative prescription appears to be pleadable against the grantees without any written title (*b*).'

(*a*) Shaw Stewart *v.* Houston, 1823; 2 S. 300. Paul *v.* Reid, Feb. 8, 1814; F. C.; 2 Ill. 574; 1 Ross' L. C. 182. E. Dundonald *v.* Boyes's Trs., 1836; 14 S. 737; 2 Ill. 577; and other cases, cited *supra*, § 2016 (*a*).

(*b*) See above, § 655 (*h*); and Miller *v.* Storie, 1757; M. 10,738. Mags. of Linlithgow *v.* Mitchell, 1822; 1 S. 515.

2019. Prescription on Double Titles.—One may have in his person various titles, namely, as disponee, as heir-at-law, as heir of a marriage, as heir of tailzie; some limited, others unlimited. And two questions may arise: first, The effect of possessing on one title in extinguishing the others; and second, The effect to third parties interested in any of those titles, of a possession on the other.

2020. The rules on this subject are, that a person having different titles in his person, is to be held as possessing on them all, to the effect of preserving his own right in each. Where the titles are equally beneficial, the law presumes the possession to proceed on that which he is under an obligation to adopt (*a*). Where one title is more beneficial than another, possession *in dubio* is to be ascribed to the more beneficial title (*b*). In order to prescribe on an unlimited against a limited title, there must be a choice made of the former, by an indication so clear as to create an independent and separate title capable of being fortified by possession (*c*). Where such choice is made, and a title is made up on an unlimited, adversely to a limited title, and possession for forty years uninterruptedly has taken place on it, the limited title will be extinguished, and the fee disburdened, although the heir so possessing should have both titles in his person (*d*). Where the possession is on apparency, by one having the character both of heir-at-law and heir of a limited title (as an entail), it must be ascribed to the limited title, if it ever have been completed, so as to form the standing investiture; and even where it has not been feudalised, the entail will be held the governing title, and the possession ascribed to the personal right under it, as well as to the other (*e*). Not only where there are two titles (one as heir-at-law, the other by destination, but not entailed nor guarded by prohibitions against altering), the heir possessing on apparency does not prescribe against the destination; but this holds good even where he makes up a title as heir-at-law; for there being no prohibition to alter, those interested to challenge are *non valentes agere cum effectu* (*f*). But where, instead of merely possessing, the heir grants a conveyance altering the destination, 'or obtains a new investiture (*g*),' prescription will run against the deserted title (*h*). There can be no prescription inconsistent with the terms of the title (*i*). Where the subject is not feudal, but a personal though heritable right, as a lease, there is no room for this prescription on double titles (*k*).

(*a*) **Smith & Bogle** *v.* **Gray**, 1751 and 1752; M. 10,803; Elch. *Prov. to Heirs*, 12; 5 B. Sup. 790; 1 Pat. 334; 2 Ross' L. C. 577; 2 Ill. 578. Durham *v.* Durham, 1802; M. 11,229; aff. 1811, 5 Pat. 482. Snodgrass *v.* Buchanan, 1806; M. Apx. *Service of Heirs*, 1. Ogilvie *v.* Erskine, 1837; 15 S. 1037. *Supra*, § 851 sqq.

(*b*) **M'Dougal** *v.* **M'Dougal**, 1739; M. 10,947; Elch. *Presc.* 20; 5 B. Sup. 674; 3 Ross' L. C. 510. L. Reay *v.* Mackay, 1823; 2 S. 520; aff. 1 W. & S. 306. D. Hamilton *v.* Westenra, 1827; 6 S. 44; 2 Ill. 576. Smith, *supra*; Bruce, *infra*. Dalrymple *v.* E. Stair, 1841; 3 D. 837.

(*c*) **Welsh Maxwell** *v.* **Welsh Maxwell**, 1808; M. *Prescription*, Apx. 8; aff. 6 Pat. 65; 2 Ill. 579; 3 Ross' L. C. 522. Lumsdaine *v.* Balfour, June 13, 1811; F. C.; aff. 6 Pat. 150; 2 Ill. 580. D. Hamilton *v.* Westenra, 1824; 3 S. 24; and 1827, 6 S. 44. See Maule *v.* Maule, 1782; M. 10,963; Hailes, 899. L. Elibank *v.* Campbell, § 2017 (*d*).

(*d*) 3 Ersk. 7. § 6. M'Dougal, *supra* (*b*). Douglas *v.* Douglas, 1753; M. 10,955; Elchies, *Prov. to Heirs*, 19; aff. Cr. & St. 553; 2 Ill. 575. Ayton *v.* Monypenny, 1756; M. 10,956; rev. Cr. & St. 500. See 2 Ill. 580. D. of Hamilton *v.* Douglas, 1762; M. 10,962. Bruce *v.* Bruce Carstairs, 1770; M. 10,805; Hailes, 378; 2 Ill. 170; aff. 2 Pat. 258. Maule, *supra* (*c*). Scott *v.* Bruce Stewart, 1776; M. 13,519; 5 B. Sup. 542. Gordon (Auchindachy's Crs.) *v.* Byres, *infra*, § 2022. Majendie (Routledge), *cit. supra*, § 2017 (*k*). Stewart *v.* Stewart, 1844; 6 D. 1073; aff. 1846, 5 Bell's App. 139. E. of Glasgow *v.* Boyle, 1887; 14 R. 419. See above, § 821.

(*e*) Welsh Maxwell and Lumsdaine, *supra* (*c*). Maule *v.* Maule, 1829; 7 S. 527.

(*f*) Smith and Durham, *supra* (*a*).
(*g*) Zuille, *cit. infra*. Molle *v.* Riddell, Dec. 13, 1811; aff. 1816; 6 Pat. 168.
(*h*) Zuille *v.* Morrison, March 4, 1813; F. C. **Edgar** *v.* **Maxwell**, 1736; M. 3090; Elch. *Serv.* 6; aff. 1742; 1 Pat. 334. *Supra*, § 854.
(*i*) Dalziel *v.* Dalziel, Jan. 17, 1810; F. C. Murray Oliphant *v.* Ramsay & Co., Jan. 17, 1811; F. C. Cf. *supra*, § 2004 (*d*).
(*k*) See Maule, *supra* (*c*).

2021. Exceptions to Prescription.—There are two cases in which prescription does not take place; one statutory, the other by common law.

2022. (1.) *Minority.*—This exception declared by the statute applies to the positive as well as to the negative prescription (*a*). But it extends no further than to the person who is in the actual right (*b*), 'and not therefore to the minority of substitutes in entails. The person whose minority is to be deducted must be the *verus dominus*, having a vested right in the estate, though not necessarily infeft (*c*). And since 1st January 1879, if possession on an *ex facie* valid irredeemable title duly recorded has continued for thirty years, the possession for any period prior to that date having been continuous, no deduction is to be made for the years of minority or legal disability (*d*).'

(*a*) Kames' Eluc., art. 33. 3 Ersk. 7. § 35. Blair *v.* Shedden, 1754; M. 11,156; 5 B. Sup. 725; 2 Ill. 582. **Fullarton** *v.* **Dalrymple**, 1798; 3 Pat. 691; 4 Pat. 175; 1 Ross' L. C. 484; 1 W. & S. Apx. See *ante*, § 625. "The doubts on this question rested—1. On legal grounds, from the analogy of the Roman law; and 2. On grounds of expediency strongly fortifying those doubts, as tending to render property insecure against the policy of the statute of positive prescription, and rendering the records less perfect by giving effect to objections not appearing on the record. . . . The point was, by the judges in Scotland, held to be fixed by Hamilton Blair's case and Ayton's in the House of Lords, that minority is to be deducted from the course of the positive prescription. And Lord Thurlow and Lord Loughborough, Chancellor, concurred in this. Lord Thurlow said 'that he had considered the Act 1617 with as much attention as he could; and if it had fallen to him to decide the question, he should have held that the last clause in the Act, relative to the deduction of minority, had a reference only to the negative prescription,—not only because the grammatical construction required such an interpretation, but because the exception is contrary to the nature of the positive prescription; but as this point was decided differently a long time ago, and as it is not impossible to interpret the statute so as to justify that decision, it would be dangerous to bring the matter into question now.'" 2 Ill. 582. Buchanan *v.* Boyle, 1847; 9 D. 686. Craufurd *v.* Menzies, 1849; 11 D. 1127 (right of way). Grieve (or Dingwall) *v.* Burns, 1871; 9 Macph. 582.
(*b*) **M'Dougal** *v.* **M'Dougal**, *cit.* § 2020. Ayton *v.* Monypenny, 1756; M. 10,956; rev. 1 Cr. & St. 650. Gordon *v.* Gordon, 1784; M. 10,968; Hailes, 960. **Gordon**, etc. (Auchindachy's Crs.) *v.* **Grant**, 1792; M. 10,971; Bell's 8vo Ca. 199; 1 Ross' L. C. 481; aff. 1794, 3 Pat. 317. Fullarton, *supra* (*a*). D. of Buccleuch *v.* Cuningham, 1826; 5 S. 57; 2 Ill. 570. Maule *v.* Maule, 1829; 7 S. 527; 2 Ill. 566 and 572. Kinloch *v.* Rocheid, 1800; M. Apx. *Prescription*, 8 and 18; 1805, 5 Pat. 35.
(*c*) Black *v.* Mason, 1881; 8 R. 497.
(*d*) 37 and 38 Vict. c. 94, § 34.

2023. (2.) *Non Valens Agere.*—It is a rule, not of statute, but of common law, that 'the negative (*a*)' prescription does not operate against one who cannot effectually resist it. 'But the rule does not (except in prescription upon double titles, § 2020) apply to the positive prescription, which runs in favour of the person acquiring under it, even when there is no existing person who can object (*a*). Former editions, therefore, were erroneous in stating that the positive prescription' will not be pleadable in the following cases: If one is barred from prosecuting his right, or incapable (*b*); or if he be hindered *vi majori* (*c*); or if a woman have a right, and her husband is the 'adverse' party (*d*); or if the person who pleads prescription could derive no benefit from the challenge (*e*). But in a land estate the fiar cannot plead *non valens agere* merely because a liferenter is in possession (*f*), though it is different as to a bond (*g*). 'In general, there must be a legal incapacity to sue, not merely a difficulty in doing so (*h*). But since 1st January 1879 the exception does not apply in cases where there has been possession for thirty years (*i*).'

(*a*) M'Neill *v.* M'Neal, 1858; 20 D. 735. Innes *v.* Innes, 1695; M. 11,612. Millar *v.* Dickson, 1766; M. 10,937. Wilson *v.* Campbell, 1766; 5 B. Sup. 915, 926; 1777, 2 Pat. 193.
(*b*) Dirleton and Stewart, 374. D. Lauderdale *v.* E. Tweeddale, 1678; M. 11,193; 2 Ill. 584. See *ante*, § 627.
(*c*) D. Lauderdale, *supra* (*b*). Robertson *v.* King's Adv., 1758; M. 11,280; 5 B. Sup. 357; 1 Ill. 365.
(*d*) Hamilton *v.* Sinclair, 1622; M. 10,717. M'Kie *v.* Shaw, 1665; M. 11,204.
(*e*) Innes *v.* Innes, 1695; M. 11,212. Elliot *v.* Aitchison, 1724; M. 11, 209. See M'Dougal, *supra*, § 2022 (*b*).
(*f*) Neilson *v.* Erskine, 1823; 2 S. 247; 2 Ill. 567. See, however, Shepherd *v.* Grant's Trs., 1844; 6 D. 464, 475, 483; and Rankine on Landownership, 35, 36.
(*g*) See 5 B. Sup. 915.
(*h*) Graham *v.* Watt, 1843; 5 D. 1368; aff. 1846, 5 Bell's App. 172.
(*i*) 37 and 38 Vict. c. 94, § 34.

2024. Prescription of Services.—There is a special prescription established by the Act of 1617 in the case of services, by which a retour is not subject to challenge after twenty years (*a*). In the construction of this Act, it has been doubted whether it is necessary to the heir who pleads it to show possession, as under the Act 1617, c. 12. But although in one case possession was held requisite (*b*), this does not seem to be law. It rather appears that the expiration of the twenty years will be an absolute protection to the retour against all challenge 'not proceeding on a stronger title than that of mere heirship' (*c*), which does not appear *ex facie* of the retour (*d*). The protection afforded by this Act, however, is only to the title as a retour, without interfering with the rest of the Act 1617, c. 12, further than an unexceptionable retour has effect in the circumstances. 'This prescription applies to retours of heirs of provision, as well as of heirs *jure sanguinis* (*e*).'

(*a*) 1617, c. 13. Mackenzie's Observations. See Mackenzie's Works, i. 379, 443.
(*b*) Wrights of Elgin *v.* Hutcheson, 1794; Bell's Cases, 7; 2 Ill. 584. Drummond *v.* Drummond, 1793; M. 6936; aff. 1797, 3 Pat. 557.
(*c*) Neilson *v.* Cochrane's Reprs., 1837; 16 S. 365; 2 Ill. 585; aff. 1840, 1 Rob. 82; 3 Ross' L. C. 583.
(*d*) Fullerton *v.* Hamilton, 1824; 2 S. 698; aff. 1 W. & S. 410. Rocca *v.* Catto's Trs., 1876; 4 R. 70 (pleadable by singular successors. Cf. Neilson (*c*)).
(*e*) Campbell *v.* Campbell, 1848; 10 D. 461; 3 Ross' L. C. 595.

2024A. 'The necessity of service to transmit a personal right to land having been removed by the Conveyancing Act of 1874, it is provided that the right of any person to an estate in land acquired by succession after 1st October 1874 can only be challenged within twenty years of his infeftment as heir and his entering into possession, by anyone who would have been entitled to challenge the decree of service had a service been expede under the previous law. In the absence of evidence to the contrary, the date of infeftment is for the purpose of this limitation deemed to be the date of entering into possession. The challenge may be made by action to negative or set aside the alleged right of succession, or to reduce any title expede in virtue of it (*a*). But nothing in the Act cited is to prejudice or affect previously existing remedies of a person having lawful title and interest to prevent another from taking possession as heir, or to remove him, the interim possession being regulated as a question apart from the title (*b*).'

(*a*) 37 and 38 Vict. c. 94, § 13. (*b*) *Ib.* § 14.

2025. Prescription against the Crown, Church, etc. — The positive prescription is effectual against the Crown, by the express words of the Act (*a*).

With regard to the Church, communities, and hospitals, there is no exception to the rule of the Act (*b*).

(*a*) 1617, c. 12. 2 Stair, 3. § 33. 3 Ersk. 7. § 31. E. Leven *v.* Balfour, 1711; M. 10,930; 2 Ill. 585. Comrs. of Anxd. Estates *v.* Menzies, 1773; M. 7860. See L. Adv. *v.* Hunt, 1865; 3 Macph. 426; rev. 1867, 5 Macph. H. L. 1; L. R. 1 Sc. Ap. 85; and see as to Negative, Deans of Chapel Royal *v.* Johnstone, 1867; 5 Macph. 414; aff. 1869, 7 Macph. H. L. 19.
(*b*) 2 Stair, 8. § 29. 3 Ersk. 7. § 32. Crawford *v.* Maxwell, 1724; M. 10,819. Magdalen Chapel *v.* Drysdale, 1671; M. 11,148. College of Aberdeen *v.* E. Northesk, 1675; M. 7230.

BOOK FOURTH

OF RIGHTS OF THE PERSON

CHAPTER I

OF PROTECTION OF PERSON AND CHARACTER.

2026. Classification of Rights of Persons.—The rights of persons may be distinguished, as those which belong to individuals in their private character and relations; or those which belong to persons, individual or corporate, in public or political relations.

2027. The rights which belong to persons in their individual capacity may be distinguished as absolute or relative; the former having reference to the condition of the person in respect of safety, freedom, and reputation; the latter having reference to the relation in which they stand with other individuals.

I. PROTECTION OF PERSON.

2028. Personal Safety.—Everyone who lives under the protection of the law has an absolute right to the safety of his person; and wherever this right is invaded, there is in civil law a provision for redress of the injury, as well as in penal law a punishment for the crime (*a*).

(*a*) See *ante*, § 543 et seq.

2029. Reparation or Assythment for Homicide.—The law takes cognisance of the loss and suffering of the family of a person killed, and gives assythment, both as indemnification and as *solatium* (*a*). 'In practice the action of assythment has given place to the action of damages for personal injuries (*actio injuriarum*) (*b*). The action of assythment is distinguished from this mainly in respect that it is applicable only when a crime has been committed by the defender (*c*).' This (assythment) was formerly taxed by the Barons of Exchequer, but in more modern times it is matter for the jurisdiction of the Court of Session. The rules are: That capital punishment of a murderer, with forfeiture of his moveables, is a satisfaction at once of public justice and of private vengeance, and no assythment is due (*d*): That if the criminal be not condemned to death, but to a lesser punishment, the sentence is held to include a judgment for assythment if the prosecution is by the private party; and not to exclude the demand where the public prosecutor pursues: That a pardon is granted only under condition of paying the assythment; and so to plead a pardon is to admit the assythment, the amount of which may thereupon be taxed (*e*): That a general indemnity by Parliament does not discharge the assythment (*f*): That where the criminal has been outlawed, assythment is due (*g*): That assythment is a *solatium*, as well as indemnification for damage (*h*). And the right of action is with the wife and family of the deceased; the division being like that of the goods in communion (*i*).

(*a*) 8 Stair, 9. § 7. 4 Ersk. 4. § 105. Kames' Law Tracts. Foster's Crown Law. 1 Hume, Crim. Law, 284: 2. 124.

(*b*) See § 544 sqq., 2030.

(c) See Eistens v. N. B. Ry. Co., 1870; 8 Macph. 981; and Horn v. N. B. Ry. Co., 1878; 5 R. 1055.
(d) M'Harg v. Campbell, 1767; M. 12,541; Hailes, 192; see 3 Ill. 1.
(e) 1457, c. 74. 1528, c. 7. 1592, c. 155. 1593, c. 174. 4 Ersk. 4. § 105. 1 Hume, 286.
(f) 4 Ersk. 4. § 106.
(g) Leithhall v. E. Fife, 1768; M. 13,904; Hailes, 206.
(h) Moodie v. Stewart, 1741; 5 B. Sup. 709. Stewart v. Story, 1768; 5 B. Sup. 646.
(i) Guild v. Home, 1605; M. 13,903. See Eistens v. N. B. Ry. Co., etc., *supra*, § 546.

2030. Reparation for Injuries by Negligence (a).—The law protects personal safety, not only against malice and crime, but also against negligence and gross disregard of the safety and interests of others. And to this class of cases jury trial has been declared to be peculiarly applicable, as furnishing the best means for deciding whether damages ought to be given, and to what amount (b). 'But in the greater number of such cases evidence is now taken and recorded in shorthand before the Sheriffs or the Lord Ordinary, who are judges both of facts and law, subject to the ordinary right of appeal to superior Courts (c).'

(a) See *ante*, § 543 et seq.
(b) As to the effect of *mora* in such claims, see Cook v. N. B. Ry. Co., 1872; 10 Macph. 513.
(c) 29 and 30 Vict. c. 112, § 4. 37 and 38 Vict. c. 64. Mackay's Practice, ii. 14. Dove Wilson, Sheriff Court Practice, 53.

2031. These questions, 'when Professor Bell wrote,' chiefly 'arose' from the injuries so frequently caused by rapid travelling by land or water (a). The cause of action is, insufficiency of the vehicle, or negligence, or overloading, or furious driving. The presumption is against the coach proprietor, and so the *onus probandi* lies upon him (b). 'But the carrier is not liable for the acts or negligence of persons not in his employment or subject to his control, and therefore not for injuries caused by third parties, or even by fit and proper contractors performing operations for himself. He is entitled to assume that such persons doing work not in itself extremely and unusually hazardous to the passengers will take the proper precautions to prevent accidents (c).' The remedy extends not merely to reparation for loss sustained, but includes a *solatium* for pain and distress (d).

'*Contributory Negligence.*—When the contract between the parties is not such as to affect the question of liability, the burden of proof is on the person injured and complaining. He has to prove negligence on the part of the defender, and that that negligence was the direct or proximate cause of the accident (e). Hence the claim is excluded by "contributory negligence" on the part of the person injured; *i.e.* fault materially contributing to bring about the accident or occurrence by which the damage is caused. In other words, the plaintiff cannot recover if he could have avoided the injury or loss caused by the defender's fault by using ordinary care; in short, and more properly, if his own negligence is the *proximate* cause of the harm he has suffered (f). If the injured person by his *subsequent* negligence aggravates or increases the loss, that only affects the amount of damages (g).

'A different defence is that founded on the principle, *volenti non fit injuria*. A person takes a risk on himself when, with full knowledge and assent, he exposes himself to danger, as by engaging in a dangerous game (h); or continuing a party to a combined work or organisation where accidents may be expected (i). Mere knowledge of danger is not sufficient to infer assent to taking a risk (k); but it depends not only on the nature of the risk and the injured person's connection with it, but on the whole circumstances of the case (l).'

Reparation is demandable not only against the servant by whose fault the injury happens, but against the master who employs him, provided the injury arises from the manner of doing the master's work, not from some cause unconnected, or some licence used by the servant (m). So the tacksman of a quarry was held liable for injury done by his workmen incautiously blasting a rock (n).

Difficulties 'were' raised regarding the liability of police commissioners for damages occasioned by their officers, and it 'was' held that the commissioners of police under the Act of 3 Geo. IV. c. 78 'were' liable not only for acts of their officers proceeding under their immediate order, but for oppression or damage done by them in acting as police officers (o); and that in libelling an action for such damage, the commissioners 'might' be called by their clerk, and 'were' sufficiently charged with what substantially is wilful corruption or oppression, though not in the precise words of the Act (*p*).

Similar difficulties 'were' raised as to the responsibility of road trustees for acts or negligence of workmen employed by them or their surveyors and contractors; and they 'were' held liable in Scotland, while the matter 'was' viewed otherwise in England (*q*). 'It was afterwards held for many years, in consequence of the judgment of the House of Lords in Duncan *v.* Findlater, in 1839, that trustees or a corporation holding funds for special statutory purposes could not be made liable in damages for the fault or negligence of themselves or their servants in the execution of their duties, so as to affect these funds held on trust and in which they had no beneficial interest (*r*). But the case on which that view was founded appears to have been misunderstood, or to have gone too far; and the general rule is now fixed, that statutory trustees and local authorities, unless the statutes under which they act provide otherwise, are liable to make good in their corporate capacity and out of their public funds, the damage caused by their own or their servants' fault, in the same way as individuals (*s*). The magistrates of a burgh, being charged with the duty of keeping the streets in good order, are liable in damages to persons injured by their being in an unsafe condition (*t*).' Under the Act of 3 Geo. IV. c. 33, § 10, action, 'which must be brought within a month,' has been sustained against the town-clerk of a burgh for damage done by a riotous mob (*u*).

'A lessor may make himself liable for wrong done to a third party by his lessee, if he authorises the wrong-doing, or if in the ordinary course of business such wrong is the result of the letting, *e.g.* if he lets ground on a stream for the establishment of such a work as naturally tends to pollute it to the damage of riparian owners (*v*), or lets minerals under land which is not his, or which he has given off to feuars, who are injured by subsidence due to the ordinary and proper working of the mines (*w*).'

(*a*) The statutes made for punishing such injuries do not preclude the civil claim for reparation. See above, § 170 (*r*).

(*b*) Lyon *v.* Lamb, 1838; 16 S. 1188. See § 164, 170 (*y*).

(*c*) Daniel *v.* Metr. Ry. Co., 37 L. J. C. P. 280; 40 L. J. C. P. 121 (H. L.); L. R. 3 C. P. 591; 5 H. L. 25. Carty *v.* Nicoll, 1878; 6 R. 194.

(*d*) Black *v.* Cadell, 1804; M. 13,905; aff. 5 Pat. 567; 1 Ill. 331. Smith *v.* Milne, March 8, 1810; F. C.; 2 Dow, 390; 1 Ill. 553. Brown *v.* M'Gregor, Feb. 26, 1813; F. C. Elder *v.* Croall, 1849; 11 D. 1040. Dow *v.* Brown & Co., 1844; 6 D. 534.

(*e*) Metr. Ry. Co. *v.* Jackson, 3 App. Ca. 193; 47 L. J. C. P. 303.

(*f*) Macnaughton *v.* Cal. Ry. Co., 1858; 21 D. 160. Watson *v.* M'William, 1866; 38 Jur. 365. Grant *v.* Cal. Ry. Co., 1870; 9 Macph. 258. Waite *v.* N.-E. Ry. Co., E. B. & E. 719; 28 L. J. Q. B. 258 (as to which, see Mills *v.* Armstrong, 12 App. Ca. 1). Lumsden *v.* Russel, 1856; 18 D. 468. Traill *v.* Small & Boase, 1873; 11 Macph. 888. Gibb *v.* Crombie, 1875; 2 R. 886. Campbell *v.* Ord & Maddison, 1873; 1 R. 149. Adams *v.* G. & S.-W. Ry. Co., 1875; 3 R. 215. Jardine *v.* Stonefield Laundry Co., 1887; 14 R. 839 (driving over man in street). Wilson *v.* Wishaw Coal Co., 1883; 10 R. 1021. Pirie *v.* Cal. Ry. Co., 1890; 17 R. 1157 (putting head out of carriage window). Tuff *v.* Warman, 5 C. B. N. S. 573; 27 L. J. C. P. 322. **Radley** *v.* **L. & N.-W. Ry. Co.**, 44 L. J. Ex. 73; 46 *ib.* 573; L. R. 10 Ex. 100; 1 App. Ca. 754. Wakelin *v.* L. & S.-W. Ry. Co., 12 App. Ca. 41 (onus of proving contributory fault is on defender). See above, § 547A, note (*e*), 547B (*h*), (*i*). As to contributory negligence by or in regard to children injured, see Lumsden, Grant, Traill, Campbell, *citt.* Auld *v.* M'Bey, 1881; 8 R. 495. Greer *v.* Stirlingshire Road Trs., 1882; 9 R. 1069. Frasers *v.* Edinr. Street Tramways Co., 1882; 10 R. 264. M'Gregors *v.* Ross & Marshall, 1883; 10 R. 725. Adams *v.* Mags. of Aberdeen, 1884; 11 R. 852. Morran *v.* Waddell, 1883; 11 R. 44. Findlay *v.* Angus, 1886; 14 R. 312. Martin *v.* Ward, 1887; 14 R. 814 (public street). Morrison *v.* M'Ara, 1896; 23 R. 564 (do.). Clarke *v.* Chambers, 3 Q. B. D. 327. Macmullin *v.* Thomson & Currie, 1889; 5 Sh. Ct. R. 318. As to trespass in questions of reparation, see Lumsden, *cit.* Balfour *v.* Baird, 1857; 20 D. 238. Galloway *v.* King, 1872; 10 Macph. 788. Black *v.* Cadell, 1804; M. 13,905; aff. 5 Pat. 567. Hislop *v.* Durham, 1842; 4 D. 1158. Fraser *v.* Younger & Sons, 1867; 5 Macph. 861. The contributory negligence of a third party, *e.g.* of a contractor or tradesman employed by the injured person, or of a railway company using the same line as that on which he is carried by the defenders, is no bar to his recovering damages against one with whom he has a contract, and who fails to perform it. Burrows *v.* March Gas Co., L. R. 5 Ex. 67; 7 Ex. 96; 39 L. J. Ex. 33; 41 *ib.* 46.

(*g*) Moffat *v.* Park, 1877; 4 R. 13. Shearman on Negligence, § 25.

(*h*) Reid *v.* Mitchell, 1885; 12 R. 1129. Pollock on Torts, 142.

(*i*) Cases cited above, § 547A (*e*), 547B (*f*), (*g*), (*h*), (*i*).

(*k*) See Thrussell *v.* Handyside, 20 Q. B. D. 359. For an important discussion of the brocard, see Membery *v.* G. W. Ry. Co., 1889; 14 App. Ca. 179.

(*l*) See above, § 547A. **Smith** *v.* **Baker**, 1891, A. C. 325. Forsyth *v.* Ramage & Ferguson, 1890; 18 R. 21 (ship under repair or being built—manhole). Webster *v.* Brown, 1892; 19 R. 765 (landlord and tenant—worn steps). Smith *v.* Forbes & Co., 1897; 24 R. 699.

(*m*) Allan *v.* M'Leish, 2 Mur. 158. Gunn *v.* Gardiner, 1820; *ib.* 194. Baird *v.* Hamilton, 1826; 4 S. 790. See above, § 547, 554.

(*n*) Sword *v.* Cameron, 1839; 1 D. 493 (explained in **Smith** *v.* **Baker**, *cit.*, *per* LL. Herschell and Watson). See cases, *supra* (*m*). Grant *v.* Drysdale, 1883; 10 R. 1159.

(*o*) Mitchell *v.* Stuart, 1838; 16 S. 409; rev. 1 Rob. 162. See below (*q*); and observe that the reversal proceeded on the same grounds mainly as that in Findlater *v.* Duncan, *infra* (*q*).

(*p*) Kelly *v.* Stuart, 1833; 11 S. 287; aff. 1834, 7 W. & S. 343.

(*q*) Dauney *v.* Maxwell, 1836; 14 S. 1037; 3 Ill. 2. Findlater *v.* Duncan, 1838; 16 S. 1150; rev. 1839, M'L. & Rob. 911. See Ainslie *v.* Stewart, 2 D. 140, f. n. New Clyde Shipping Co. *v.* Clyde Trs., 1842; 4 D. 1521. Barclay *v.* Barclay, 1854; 16 D. 714. Beckett *v.* Campbell & Hutchison, 1864; 2 Macph. 482; aff. 1866, 4 Macph. H. L. 6. Kinloch *v.* Clark, 1865; 4 Macph. 107.

(*r*) Findlater and other cases cited (*q*).

(*s*) **Gibbs** *v.* **Mersey Docks and Harbour Board**, and Penhallow *v. eosd.*, 27 L. J. Ex. 321; 30 L. J. Ex. 320; 35 L. J. Ex. 225 (H. L.); L. R. 1 E. & I. App. 93; 11 H. L. Ca. 686. **Virtue** *v.* **Alloa Police Comrs.**, 1873; 1 R. 285. Holman *v.* Irvine Harbour Comrs., 1877; 4 R. 406. Young *v.* Nith Comrs., 1876; 3 R. 991. Thomson *v.* Greenock Harbour Trs., 1876; 3 R. 1194. Kennedy *v.* Police Comrs. of Fort-William, 1877; 4 R. 302 (wrongous interdict by Comrs.). Buchanan *v.* Clyde Lighthouse Trs., 1884; 11 R. 531 (Harbour Trustees—buoys).

(*t*) Innes *v.* Mags. of Edinbr., 1798; M. 13,189. Dargie *v.* Mags. of Forfar, 1855; 17 D. 730. Keir *v.* Mags. of Stirling, 1858; 21 D. 169. Stephen *v.* Thurso Police Comrs., 1876; 3 R. 535 (liability for contractors). M'Fee *v.* Police Comrs. of Broughty Ferry, 1890; 17 R. 764 (railway bridge too low). Edwards *v.* Par. Bd., 1891; 18 R. 867 (sanitary authority — statutory protection under Public Health Act—*ultra vires*). Strachan *v.* Aberdeen County Coun., 1894; 21 R. 915.

(*u*) Johnston *v.* Kerr, 1837; 16 S. 104. By the Act the sum decerned for is leviable by assessment on the real rent. In counties such actions are directed against the clerk of supply, and the damages levied on the valued rent. The Act, § 10-16.

(*v*) Dunn *v.* Hamilton, 1837, 15 S. 853; aff. 1838, 3 S. & M'L. 356 (see *per* L. C. p. 379).

(*w*) Thomson *v.* Wilson's Trs., 1895; 22 R. 867. Comp. Stewart's Hospital *v.* Waddell, 1890; 17 R. 1077, and notes to Vicars *v.* Wilcocks in 2 Smith's L. C.

2032. Reparation for Assault. — Personal violence is so direct and gross an invasion of the right now under review, as to require reparation wherever there is no justification on account of official duty (*a*), or absolute necessity, or self-defence (*b*), 'or rather private defence (*c*)'; or the defence of one's wife, or child, or property; or excuse by unavoidable accident. Verbal injury is no justification, 'but will mitigate the damages' (*d*). The civil claim of damage is not merely for damage sustained, but in *solatium* for affront and insult (*e*). It is not discharged by the interposition of the penal law; and the demand is for indemnification of the injury, not for punishment (*f*).

(*a*) Muckarsie *v.* Dickson, 1848; 11 D. 4 (schoolmaster). Ewart *v.* Brown, 1882; 10 R. 163 (ditto). Scorgie *v.* Lawrie, 1883; 10 R. 610 (ditto). Wallace *v.* Mooney, 1885; 12 R. 810 (police-officer removing a convicted person from race-stand). Reekie *v.* Norrie, 1842; 5 D. 368 (shipmaster—justification). As to railway and omnibus companies' servants removing passengers and the like, see Seymour *v.* Greenwood, 7 H. & N. 355; 30 J. L. Ex. 327. Bayley *v.* Man. Sheff. & Linc. Ry. Co., 42 L. J. C. P. 78; L. R. 8 C. P. 148. Menzies *v.* Highland Ry. Co., 1878; 5 R. 887. Apthorpe *v.* Edinr. Tram. Co., 1882; 10 R. 344. Gillespie *v.* Hunter, 1898; 25 R. 916. Maxwell *v.* Cal. Ry. Co., 1898; *ib.* 550.

(*b*) Hallowell *v.* Niven, 1843; 5 D. 759. As to *compensatio injuriarum*, see Dick *v.* Small, 1834; 13 S. 1134; and below, § 2057 (*b*) *ad fin.*

(*c*) Indian Penal Code.

(*d*) Thom *v.* Graham, 1835; 13 S. 1129; 3 Ill. 2. Falconer *v.* Cochrane, 1837; 15 S. 891. Fraser *v.* Berkley, 2 Mood. & Rob. 3. Gordon *v.* Stewart, 1843; 5 D. 8.

(*e*) Cruikshank *v.* Forsyth, 1747; M. 4043. Anderson *v.* Marshall, 1835; 13 S. 1130.

(*f*) Hyslop *v.* Miller, 1 Mur. 43; and see *ib.* 148, 249, 410, 422. Beatson *v.* Drysdale, 1819; 2 Mur. 151, 505; 3 Mur. 23, 408; 4 Mur. 82. Seymour *v.* M'Laren, 1828; 6 S. 969. Anderson *v.* Barr & Cavens, 1847; 9 D. 929 (two assailants). As to what constitutes assault, see Hyslop, 1816; 1 Mur. 53. Armstrong, 1823; 3 Mur. 315. Lang *v.* Lillie, 1826; 4 Mur. 82. Ewing *v.* Earl of Mar, 1851; 14 D. 314, 330.

2033. Reparation for Seduction. — The seduction of an unmarried woman, although an injury in some degree proceeding with her consent, yet by the law of Scotland entitles her to damages for the consequences of that wrong by means of which the injury is accomplished (*a*). 'It may be combined with a claim for breach of promise of marriage (*b*).' A husband may also competently sue the seducer of his wife, on the grounds of loss of her society and of domestic happiness, and of injury to his family. It is no answer in law that the husband was unfaithful, or that the parties lived separate; though these circumstances will no doubt weigh with a jury in assessing damages. The action is not, on the one hand, barred by the husband having afterwards obtained decree of divorce (*c*); nor is it necessary (as sometimes supposed) that a decree of divorce should precede the claim (*d*). But if the husband, after knowledge of the injury, continue to cohabit with his wife, he seems to have no action against the adulterer for damages (*e*); 'or rather he may be held to have, as a matter of fact, sustained no loss. But condonation of adultery does not *per se* bar the husband from suing the paramour for *solatium* and damages (*f*).

'*Seduction of Servants and Workmen.*—In like manner a master has a legal right and interest in the services of workmen who have contracted to serve him, and anyone who maliciously entices or seduces them to break their engagement and desert his employment (*g*), or to reveal secrets connected with his trade (*h*), is answerable to him in damages. Special damage must be averred and proved.'

(*a*) Hyslop *v.* Ker, 1697; M. 13,908; 3 Ill. 2. Linning *v.* Hamilton, 1748; M. 13,909. Buchanan *v.* M'Nab, 1785; M. 13,918. Stewart *v.* Menzies, 1837; 15 S. 1198 (the seductive arts must be averred). M'Candy *v.* Turpy, 1826; 4 S. 520. Walker *v.* M'Isaac, 1857; 19 D. 340. Paton *v.* Brodie, 1858; 20 D. 258. Kay *v.* Wilson's Trs., 1850; 12 D. 845. Forbes *v.* Wilson, 1868; 7 Macph. 770. Gray *v.* Brown, 1878; 5 R. 971. In England the woman has no action for seduction. A father or master has action for loss of service; and juries are uniformly directed, in awarding damages, to have regard to the wounded feelings of the party. See Irwin *v.* Dearman, 11 East, 23; 10 R. R. 423. Pollock on Torts, 193-202. 2 Selw. Nisi Prius, 1066. 3 Steph. Com. 556.

(*b*) Paton and Forbes, *citt. Supra*, § 25, 1508.

(*c*) Stedman *v.* Stedman, 1744; M. 13,909; Elch. *Adult.* 1 The paramour may be made a party to the action of divorce, to the effect of being made liable in the expenses of the process. 24 and 25 Vict. c. 86, § 7. *Supra*, § 1530.

(*d*) Maxwell *v.* Montgomery, 1787; M. 13,919. Paterson *v.* Bone, 1803; M. 13,920. Glover *v.* Samson, 1856; 18 D. 609.

(*e*) Aitken *v.* M'Crae, Feb. 6, 1810; F. C.; 2 Ill. 251.

(*f*) Macdonald *v.* Macdonald, 1885; 12 R. 1327.

(*g*) Dickson *v.* Taylor, 1816; 1 Mur. 141. Rutherford *v.* Boak, 1836; 14 S. 732. Couper & Sons *v.* Macfarlane, 1879; 6 R. 683. Lumley *v.* Gye, 2 E. & B. 217; 22 L. J. Q. B. 217, 463. Bowen *v.* Hall, 6 Q. B. D. 333. See Pollock on Torts, 269, 450 sqq.

(*h*) Kerr *v.* D. Roxburghe, 1822; 3 Mur. 126, 141. Rutherford, *supra* (*g*). Roxburgh *v.* M'Arthur, 1841; 3 D. 556.

2034. Reparation for Wrongous Imprisonment.—The right to the enjoyment of absolute freedom of the person may be lawfully abridged for debt; and for crime, either in order to trial or for punishment. Wrongous imprisonment may proceed by abuse of the criminal law or of the civil, as well as by an act of private violence and detention.

2035. (1.) *Wrongous Imprisonment under the Act* 1701, *c.* 6.—The Scottish statute of 1701, "for preventing wrongous imprisonment, and for preventing undue delays in trials," is analogous to the English Act of Habeas Corpus (*a*). The amount of bail was at one time placed in the discretion of the Court of Justiciary in cases of sedition (*b*). But that discretionary power is now taken away (*c*). By the Act 1701, under certain exceptions (as taking security for keeping the peace, imprisoning for indignities to judges, for thieving and pickeries, etc.), it is necessary to a lawful imprisonment for a criminal cause, that there shall be a written and signed warrant, specifying by name or description the person against whom it is directed, and the particular cause of imprisonment; that this shall proceed on an information of a precise criminal charge (not merely of suspicion), signed by the informer (*d*); and that the person accused shall have a copy of the warrant. 'It is a general rule that no one is to be deprived of his liberty without the warrant of a magistrate; but to this there are several well-defined exceptions. Thus Police Acts, general and local, give powers to constables to apprehend, without a warrant, persons who are committing certain offences, or even persons whom they suspect of an intention to commit crime. And the law and common sense permit, if they do not require, not only constables, but anyone who is present, to detain in custody those who are taken *in flagranti delicto*, as when a thief is caught with his hand in a pocket or a till, or the like. But after a lapse of time such apprehension is generally unlawful, unless authorised by a regular warrant (*e*).'

Bail.—In bailable offences, *i.e.* in all cases 'of crimes and offences, except murder and treason (*f*),' the prisoner is entitled to be released instantly on bail being found. 'Formerly bail had to be found' as fixed by law, at £1200 for a nobleman; £600 for a landed gentleman; £300 for any other gentleman, burgess, or householder; and £60 for an inferior person (*g*). 'But the Act cited is repealed, and any magistrate having jurisdiction to try the offence charged, or to commit the accused for trial (defined to mean the Sheriff or Sheriff-substitute), may at his discretion, after hearing the prosecutor, admit to bail or refuse to do so. The statutory limit of bail is abolished, and the magistrate fixes the bail at such amount as he may consider sufficient to ensure the appearance of the accused. There is an appeal to the Court of Justiciary (*h*).' To prevent undue detention and delay by trial, it is enacted, that in crimes 'bailable' on a written application to the Judge-committer, or Lords of Justiciary, or to any judge competent to try the crime, the prisoner's 'application shall be disposed of' within twenty-four hours, 'failing which the prisoner shall be forthwith' liberated (*i*).

Running the Letters.—It 'was' also provided 'by the Act 1701, c. 6, now repealed,' that, on petition by one in custody in order to trial, accompanied by production of the warrant, whether the crime be bailable or not, a precept 'should' be issued within twenty-four hours, for the Lord Advocate, Procurator-fiscal, or private prosecutor, to fix within sixty days a day for trial; the person to be instantly liberated if no day of trial 'should' be so fixed; and an application to this effect 'could' not be defeated by setting the man at liberty (*k*). It 'was' doubted whether the application 'was' competent by one not in confinement; but it rather seems the prevailing opinion that in such case it 'was' not competent (*l*); 'and the analogous procedure substituted by the Criminal Procedure Act of 1887 for that here narrated, is competent only to a prisoner who is in prison on a commitment (*m*).' The prisoner, however, 'was' not even thus assured that the trial 'should' take place within the sixty days; for in the last moment of that term a day of trial 'might' be fixed at the distance of forty days if before the Justiciary, or thirty days before an inferior judge. But when a day 'was' so fixed, if no trial 'were' brought within twenty-four hours after the expiration of the term so appointed, the prisoner must be liberated; and there 'could' then be no new trial. If a trial 'had' commenced, it 'was' doubted whether the diet 'might' not be deserted, and a new warrant of imprisonment granted and a new indictment brought. But if so, it must at least proceed and be concluded within forty days from the new imprisonment (*n*). 'By the Criminal Law Procedure Act, 1887, provision for the prevention of delay in trials has been made in imitation of the statute above summarised (*o*). But even if its terms were susceptible of lucid condensation, it would not be desirable to state them here.'

The breach of any of these rules, whether by magistrates or by individuals (*p*), 'was' wrongous imprisonment. Action for the penalties 'under the repealed Act was' limited to three years (*q*); but this does not apply to the common law action for damages on account of injury (*r*).

(*a*) 31 Ch. II. c. 2. See also 1 Will. and Mary, stat. 2. c. 2.

(*b*) 1701, c. 6. 39 Geo. III. c. 49.

(*c*) 6 Geo. IV. c. 47, § 5. 2 Hume's Crim. Law, 90. 2 Alison's Practice of Crim. Law, 167.

(*d*) Peacock *v.* Mags. of Stirling, 1704; M. 17,085; 3 Ill. 3. See M'Kenzie *v.* E. Marchmont, 1704; 4. B. Sup. 595. Strachan *v.* Nairn, 1706; *ib.* 655. Campbell *v.* Ramsay, 1736; M. 17,067; Elch. *Wrongful Imp.* 1. Neill *v.* Miller, 1739; *ib.* 5; 5 B. Sup. 565. Mure *v.* Sharp, July 10, 1811; F. C. Anderson *v.* Smith, Nov. 26, 1814; F. C.; 3 Ill. 7.

(*e*) See General Police Act, 55 and 56 Vict. c. 55. Leask *v.* Burt, 1893; 21 R. 32 (*per* L. Young). As to actions against police constables and their employers or superiors, see Young *v.* Mags. of Glasgow, 1891; 18 R. 625. Girdwood *v.* Joint Committee of Midlothian, 1894; 22 R. 11. The case of Peffers *v.* Countess of Lindsay, 1895, 22 R. 84, is very odd. If a policeman apprehends a man at the "order" of a private individual who makes no charge, is not the wrong done by the policeman, who ought not to obey the "order"? *Causa proxima*, etc. See Malcolm *v.* Duncan, 1897; 24 R. 747. Peggie *v.* Clark, 1868; 7 Macph. 89.

(*f*) 51 and 52 Vict. c. 36, § 2 (Bail (Scotland) Act, 1888).

(*g*) 39 Geo. III. c. 49; amended as to bail for sedition by 6 Geo. IV. c. 47, § 5.

(*h*) 51 and 52 Vict. c. 36.

(*i*) L. Adv. *v.* Cameron, 1754; M. 11,742. Andrew *v.* Murdoch, 1814; 2 Dow, 401; see 2 S. 399. Arbuckle *v.* Taylor, 1815; 3 Dow, 160. See 51 and 52 Vict. c. 36.

(*k*) M'Donald *v.* Young, 1832; 2 Alison, 185; 3 Ill. 5.

(*l*) Same case.

(*m*) 50 and 51 Vict. c. 35, § 43.

(*n*) See Smith, 1842; 1 Broun, 134. Arcus, 1844; 2 Broun, 239. Balfour, 1850; 1 J. Shaw, 377. Hinchy, 1864; 4 Irv. 561. Molyson, 1862; 4 Irv. 180.

(*o*) 50 and 51 Vict. c. 35, § 43.

(*p*) Paterson *v.* Anderson, 1736; M. 17,069; Elch. *Wrongous Imp.* 2. Sutherland *v.* Sinclair, 1737; Elch. *ib.* 4. Ramsay *v.* Coulter & Sprott, 1799; M. *Wrong. Imp.* Apx. 1.

(*q*) 1701, c. 6. 2 Hume, Crim. Law. Mure *v.* Sharp, July 10, 1811; F. C. Andrew, *supra* (*i*).

(*r*) Sinclair *v.* Sinclair, 1742; Elch. *Wrongous Imp.* 7. M'Christie *v.* Fisher, 1831; 9 S. 312 (not to action for imprisonment for civil debt).

2036. (2.) *Wrongous Imprisonment at Common Law.*—The Statute of 1701, imperfect even within its own range, would be still more so if it superseded the remedy at common law. It 'did' not apply to criminal prosecutions before the Court of Session (*a*); or to imprisonment for further examination, which must at common law be terminated within a reasonable time (*b*); or to oppression not within its words, which is left to common law (*c*); or to imprisonment for debt, against the abuses of which 'before its abolition' the common law 'gave' remedy (*d*).

(*a*) L. Advocate *v.* Renny, 1737; M. 6782; 3 Ill 5. Rogers *v.* Renny, 1737; Elch. *Wrongful Imp.* 3. Kerr *v.* Orr & Fulton, *ib.* 8. Stark *v.* Burnet, 1748; M. 3442. Blacklaw, petr., 1777; 5 B. Sup. 507. Duncan *v.* L. Adv., 1825; 1 W. & S. 608.

(*b*) Fife *v.* Ogilvie, 1762; M. 11,750. Andrew *v.* Murdoch, 1806; M. *Wrongous Imp.* Apx. 3; Buch. Ca. 1; 2 Dow, 401; 2 S. 399. Arbuckle *v.* Taylor, 1815; 3 Dow, 160.

(*c*) Campbell *v.* Ramsay, 1736; M. 17,067; Elch. *Wrongous Imp.* 1; 3 Ill. 3.

(*d*) Gordon *v.* Hope, 1705; M. 17,066. Robertson *v.* Pedison, 1705; M. 17,067.

2037. The right of action on the statute 'was' allowed to be assigned, and the conclusions to comprehend damages instead of the penalties (*a*). But action 'was' not competent both for the penalties of the statute, and for damages at common law (*b*); nor 'did' a summons libelled on the Act 1701 support a conclusion for damages at common law (*c*).

(a) Sinclair, *supra*, § 2035 (r). —— v. Sheriff of Sutherland, 1739; 5 B. Sup. 674; 3 Ill. 6. Philp v. Mags. of Anstruther, 1748; M. 17,071.
(b) Gibson v. Murdoch, June 18, 1817; F. C.
(c) Millar v. Mills, 1831; 9 S. 625.

2038. A magistrate or clerk will be liable on proof of malice 'and want of probable cause' in his proceedings 'in granting a warrant' (*a*). But he will also be liable if there be gross irregularity in imprisonment, though no malice can be shown (*b*). Slight irregularity will not, however, be sufficient to dispense with proof of malice 'and want of probable cause' (*c*).

(a) Anderson v. Hill, 1837; 15 S. 481. Watt v. Thomson & Ligertwood, 1869; 6 Macph. 1112; aff. 1870; 8 Macph. H. L. 77. Watt v. Ligertwood, 1871; 11 Macph, 960; rev. 1874, 1 R. H. L. 22. As to the protection of justices and inferior magistrates under the "Twopenny Acts," see 43 Geo. III. c. 141; 9 Geo. IV. c. 29, § 26; 1 Will. IV. c. 37, § 13. Gibsons v. Murdoch & Eaton, June 18, 1817; F. C. Malonie v. Walker, 1841; 3 D. 418. M'Kellar v. M'Lachlan, 1841; 4 D. 287.
(b) Leitch v. Farie, 1711; M. 13,946; 3 Ill. 6. Wishart v. Bowie, 1698; 4 B. Sup. 409. Bell v. Maxwell, 1743; M. 17,070. Pitcairn v. Deans, 1715; M. 13,948. Laing v. Watson, 1790; M. 8555; aff. 3 Pat. 219. Anderson v. Smith, Nov. 26, 1814; F. C. Strachan v. Stodart, 1828; 7 S. 4. Pollock v. Clark, 1829; 8 S. 7. Richardson v. Williamson, 1832; 10 S. 607. M'Crone v. Sawers, 1835; 13 S. 243. Orr v. Currie, 1839; 1 D. 551.
(c) M'Gregor v. Wright, 1826; 3 Ill. 8. Milhollan v. Bertram, 1826; 5 S. 170.

2039. It is not necessary to an action of damages against an individual 'for apprehension on a warrant as *in meditatione fugæ* (*a*),' to prove malice, or even gross irregularity. And action of damages 'lay' against an individual for the improper use of diligence 'against the person'; or for diligence proceeding upon irregular warrants in civil cases, 'though not for diligence proceeding upon a decree regularly obtained, whether *in foro* or in absence, on the allegation that the decree was open to some objection (*b*); or for diligence on a small debt decree on grounds involving review of the decree or the procedure leading to it (*c*). An action of damages will lie, for imprisonment wrongously on a criminal charge or on a false charge, the proceeding always being *periculo petentis*. 'But a private individual making a criminal charge to an officer of the law, is not liable if he acts in good faith; and the rule is, except (it has been said) in extreme cases, where the conduct of an informer is patently unjustifiable, that a party against whom a criminal charge is made in the proper way has no claim of damages, unless he avers and proves malice and want of probable cause (*d*).'

(a) Marshall v. Dobson, 1844; 7 D. 232. M'Meekin v. Russel & Tudhope, 1881; 8 R. 587. *Supra*, § 553 (4).
(b) Fullerton v. E. Kilmarnock, 1715; M. 13,949; 3 Ill. 6. Anderson v. Ormiston, 1750; M. 13,955; 3 Ill. 7. Lesly v. Pringle, 1761; *ib.* Murray v. Bissett, May 15, 1810; F. C. (no decree enforceable by summary imprisonment, but only by horning and caption). Bryson v. Hamilton, March 10, 1812; F. C. Dougal v. Commercial Bank, 1829; 8 S. 275. See M'Gregor v. Wright, 1826; 4 S. 434. Swayne v. Fife Bank, 1835; 13 S. 103. Richmond v. Thomson, 1838; 16 S. 995. *Supra*, § 553. **Aiken** v. **Finlay,** 1837; 15 S. 683. Bell v. Gunn, 1859; 21 D. 1008; and cases above, § 553 (*u*). Sturrock v. Welsh & Forbes, 1890; 18 R. 109.
(c) Crombie v. M'Ewan, 1861; 23 D. 333. Gray v. Smart, 1892; 19 R. 692.
(d) Munro v. Taylor, 1845; 7 D. 506. Shepperd v. Fraser, 1849; 11 D. 446. Callendar v. Milligan, 1849; 11 D. 1174. M'Pherson v. Cattanach, 1850; 13 D. 287. Carne v. Manuel, 1851; 13 D. 1253. Smith v. Green, 1853; 15 D. 549; 1854, 16 D. 429. Urquhart v. Dick, 1865; 3 Macph. 932. Thomson v. Adam, 1865; 4 Macph. 29. See above, § 2035; below, § 2045, 2054A, and cases there cited.

2040. The mere failure of an accusation will not infer damages against the accuser, if the circumstances justify his suspicion (*a*). 'And a procurator-fiscal or public prosecutor cannot be made liable in damages without averment and proof of malice and want of probable cause (*b*), the facts being averred from which malice is to be inferred (*c*), or at least of gross and culpable irregularity in procedure (*d*).'

(a) Jamieson v. Napier, 1747; M. 17,070; 3 Ill. 9. Henderson v. Scott, 1793; M. 17,072. Craig v. Peebles, 1876; 3 R. 441. See below, § 2045.
(b) Mains v. M'Lullich, 1861; 23 D. 1258. Nelson v. Black & Morrison, 1866; 4 Macph. 328. Mone v. Anderson, 1842; 4 D. 786.
(c) Beaton v. Ivory, 1887; 14 R. 1057; cf. *infra*, § 2051 (*a*), 2054A (*d*).
(d) Bell v. Black & Morrison, 1865; 3 Macph. 325.

2041. Messengers and their cautioners are liable for oppression or abuse of diligence, 'or for blunders in the diligence under which one is incarcerated (*a*).'

(a) M'Donell v. Bank of Scotland, 1834; 13 S. 701. Brock v. Kemp, 1844; 6 D. 709.

2042. The groundless confinement of a person in a lunatic asylum will give a good foundation for an action of damages (*a*).

(a) See M'Cosh v. M'Cosh, 1832; 10 S. 579. Strang v. Strang, 1849; 11 D. 378. Mackintosh v. Fraser, 1859; 21 D. 783; 22 D. 421; 1 Macph. H. L. 37. Mackintosh v. Smith and Lowe, 1864; 2 Macph. 389, 1261; aff. 1865, 3 Macph. H. L. 6; 4 Macq. 913. Mackintosh v. Weir, 1875; 2 R. 877.

II. PROTECTION OF CHARACTER.

2043. Reparation for Injuries to Character.—The chief remedy formerly against attacks on reputation was by action before the Commissary Court, or Court of Session, for fine, palinode, and imprisonment, proceeding on the expediency of preventing breaches of the peace, and combining with punishment an acknowledgment or retraction of the calumny (*a*). But the modern and more frequent remedy is by action for damages and reparation, 'which' in the Court of Session 'is generally' tried by jury (*b*). In this action there are two points,—viz. the injury or loss suffered, actual or probable, for which reparation is sought; and the insult and offence to the individual (*c*), for which a *solatium* is due. In this last respect a material distinction is to be observed between the Scottish and the English law, 'which gives no damages for wounded feelings. Hence in Scotland an action lies for a slander contained in an unpublished letter sent to the pursuer (*d*), or uttered to himself when no other person is present (*e*). But words which would found an action, if addressed to a third person, may not do so when addressed to the party himself who complains of them (*f*).

'Even when a statement is not slander in the proper sense, it founds an action of damages if it be false, if it be intended to injure, and has injured the person regarding whom it is made (*g*).

'In actions of damages for slander, the words used, the time and place when they were uttered, and some at least of the persons in "whose presence and hearing" they were uttered, must be distinctly specified in the condescendence; and an issue or proof will not be allowed unless the Court is of opinion that the words are slanderous (*h*). Nor will damages be recovered if it be shown that the words complained of were not used in a defamatory sense, *e.g.* if they were capable of bearing and were intended in an innocent sense (*i*), or were merely intemperate expressions of dissent or dispute (*rixa*) not imputing any characteristic vice (*k*).

'If the words used are not obviously slanderous, they may be pointed in the pleadings and issue by an *innuendo*, *i.e.* an averment by the pursuer of the meaning actually conveyed. That the words did actually convey this meaning must be proved by the pursuer; or sometimes may be inferred from the words themselves and the surrounding circumstances (*l*). When the words are in their natural and obvious sense not actionable, and the pursuer undertakes to prove that they were used in a non-natural sense, he is bound to state on record the extrinsic facts from which the inference is to be drawn. Where a non-natural sense is not ascribed to the words, but it is merely alleged that the writing or statement, though ambiguous, is truly a libel, it is enough for him to aver the libellous meaning he attaches to it (*m*). The Court will not allow an *innuendo*, unless the alleged libel will reasonably bear the construction put upon it (*n*); though it is the business of the jury to determine whether the alleged libel is false and calumnious.

'When the defence of *veritas convicii* is set up in a case of this kind, it does not seem to be in all cases necessary for the defender to prove the whole of the *innuendo* to be true: he must prove the substantial truth of the statement actually uttered; but it is a question of circumstances how far his justification requires proof of the truth of the pursuer's construction of it (*o*). The falsehood of the charge being of the essence of an action of slander, the mere addition of an *innuendo* will not give relevancy to a statement which admits the alleged slander to be true (*p*).'

(*a*) 4 Ersk. 4. § 80–1; and 1 Ersk. 5. § 30. Cruickshanks *v.* Forsyth, 1747; M. 4034. Hamilton *v.* Arbuthnot, 1750; Elchies, *Reparation*, 6; 3 Ill. 9. Warrand *v.* Falconar, 1771; M. 13,933; 5 B. Sup. 445. Memis *v.* Managers of Aberdeen Infirmary, 1776; 5 B. Sup. 576. 3 Ill. 9.

(*b*) 6 Geo. IV. c. 120, § 28. Tullis *v.* Glenday, 1834; 13 S. 698. As to the expenses where nominal damages are given, see 31 and 32 Vict. c. 100, § 40. Craig *v.* Jex Blake, 1871; 9 Macph. 973. As to the jurisdiction of the Sheriff in regard to slander by foreigners uttered within the jurisdiction, see Kermick *v.* Watson, 1871; 9 Macph. 984. As to slander uttered abroad by Scot against Scot, M'Larty *v.* Steele, 1881; 8 R. 435. As to slander by incorporated companies, see Brit. Legal Life Ass. Co. *v.* Pearl Life Ass. Co., 1887; 14 R. 818; and below, § 2044; by a football club, Murdison *v.* Scot. Football Union, 1896; 23 R. 449.

(*c*) Caldwell *v.* Monro, 1872; 10 Macph. 717.

(*d*) Hutchison *v.* Naismith, Bryson *v.* Inglis, Kennedy *v.* Baillie, Mackay *v.* M'Cankie, etc., *citt. infra*, § 2056.

(*e*) Mackay *v.* M'Cankie, 1883; 10 R. 537. M'Fadyen *v.* Spencer & Co., 1891; 19 R. 350.

(*f*) Kennedy *v.* Baillie, 1855; 18 D. 138. Stuart *v.* Moss, 1885; 13 R. 299.

(*g*) Paterson *v.* Welch, 1893; 20 R. 744; and cases in § 2055 (*b*). Waddell *v.* Roxburgh, 1894; 21 R. 883 (specific averments necessary). Burns *v.* Diamond, 1896; 23 R. 507.

(*h*) Jameson *v.* Bonthrone, 1873; 11 Macph. 703. Capital and Counties Bank *v.* Henty, 7 App. Ca. 741.

(*i*) M'Neill *v.* Forbes, 1883; 10 R. 867.

(*k*) Watson *v.* Duncan, 1890; 17 R. 404; and cases as

to *rixâ*, below, § 2057 (*d*). Turnbull & Oliver, 1891; 19 R. 154.

(*l*) Walker *v.* Cumming, 1868; 6 Macph. 318. Broomfield, *infra*. Grant *v.* Fraser, 1870; 8 Macph. 1011. Mackay *v.* M'Cankie, *cit.* Capital and Counties Bank, *cit.*

(*m*) Sexton *v.* Ritchie & Co., 1890; 17 R. 680 (*per* L. P. Inglis, referring to Brydone and Broomfield, *infra*); aff. 1891, 18 R. H. L. 20.

(*n*) Godfrey *v.* Thomson, 1890; 17 R. 1109. Archer *v.* Ritchie & Co., 1891; 18 R. 719. Broomfield, *cit.* Brydone *v.* Brechin, 1881; 8 R. 697. Dun *v.* Bain, 1877; 4 R. 317. Macfarlan *v.* Black & Co., 1887; 14 R. 870. Fraser *v.* Morris, 1888; 15 R. 454. Macrae *v.* Sutherland, 1890; 16 R. 476. Cockburn *v.* Reekie, 1890; 17 R. 568. See also as to *innuendos*, Rodgers *v.* M'Ewan, 1848; 10 D. 882. Scouller *v.* Gunn, 1852; 14 D. 920. M'Culloch *v.* Litt, 1850; 13 D. 334.

(*o*) Broomfield *v.* Greig, 1868; 6 Macph. 563. Torrance *v.* Weddell, 1868; 7 Macph. 243. Ogilvie *v.* Paul, 1873; 11 Macph. 776. M'Iver *v.* M'Neill, *ib.* 777. Beattie *v.* Mather, 1860; 22 D. 952. Bertram *v.* Pace, 1885; 12 R. 798. Milne *v.* Walker, 1893; 21 R. 155.

(*p*) Campbell *v.* Ferguson, 1882; 9 R. 467.

2044. Malice, actual or implied, is an ingredient in the action for redress of injuries of this kind; 'indeed, it is the foundation of an action of defamation; and' malice is implied in all cases of insult and injury, except in those called privileged cases, where the law gives either absolute protection against such actions, or presumes what is complained of to proceed from the impulse of duty, and requires malice to be averred and proved. 'And malice has in practice been required and allowed to be proved as an element of an action for "privileged slander" against a company or partnership (*a*).'

(*a*) Gordon *v.* British and Foreign Metaline Co., 1886; 14 R. 75, and cases cited there and in § 224B, 2043 (*b*), *supra*. Macaulay *v.* North Uist School Board, 1887; 15 R. 99. See, however, *per* L. Bramwell in Abrath *v.* N.-E. Ry. Co., 11 App. Ca. 247.

2045. Privileged Cases.—Cases are privileged where the due conduct of national or judicial inquiries, or course of private duty, requires an exemption from the strict responsibility attendant on spontaneous interference with the conduct and character of others, and where injury alone does not imply malice. 'A defamatory statement may be made in such circumstances that the malice which is essential to slander is not to be inferred merely from the statement itself; and this is all that is meant by the word privilege. "Implied" malice merely signifies the absence of just cause or excuse; and it can be re-dargued only by establishing such an excuse, or by the failure of the pursuer's proof (*a*).

'The question whether privilege exists is always for the determination of the Court, not of the jury (*b*). If it arises on the facts of the case as averred by the pursuer, under the existing system of pleading and issues, malice must be averred and put in issue. Although malice and want of probable cause be not in the issue, yet if, in the opinion of the judge, privilege is proved at the trial, the pursuer, if he has averred them in his record, is allowed to prove them to meet the defence of privilege (*c*). The privilege or immunity is "absolute" or unqualified in the cases of Parliament and proceedings in courts of justice, mentioned in the following sections. In other cases, with one or two still doubtful exceptions, it is qualified; a party aggrieved being entitled to recover damages if he avers and proves that the statement was made maliciously.

'There are two classes of cases not separated by a very definite line of distinction, in one of which a general allegation of malice is sufficient, while in the other the pursuer must set forth facts and circumstances from which malice is to be inferred (*d*). In the latter class are relevant or even not impertinent statements by litigants (*e*), and statements made by public officials in the performance of their duty (*f*).

'*Proof of Malice.*—When privilege exists it is reasonable to hold that there must be affirmative proof of malice. It is submitted, notwithstanding a recent judgment of the Second Division, that merely to bring forward such evidence of the untruth of a statement made on a privileged occasion as with the other evidence makes the case "evenly balanced," does not afford proof of malice; and that a verdict for the pursuer in such a case is contrary to evidence, and a new trial should be allowed (*g*).'

(*a*) Capital and Counties Bank *v.* Henty, 7 App. Ca. 787. Nelson *v.* Irving, 1897; 24 R. 1054. Smyth *v.* Mackinnon, *ib.* 1086.

(*b*) Dunbar *v.* Stoddart, *infra*. Urquhart *v.* Dick, 1865; 3 Macph. 932.

(*c*) Fenton *v.* Currie, 1843; 5 D. 705. Dunbar *v.* Stoddart, 1849; 11 D. 587. Graham *v.* M'Lachlan, 1853; 15 D. 889. M'Kellar *v.* D. Sutherland, 1859; 21 D. 222. Macbride *v.* Williams, 1869; 7 Macph. 427. Craig *v.* Peebles, 1876; 3 R. 441. See Ritchie & Sons *v.* Barton, 1883; 10 R. 813 (privilege disclosed at trial — malice proved though not averred—defender barred by acquiescence from afterwards objecting). Scott *v.* Johnston, 1885; 12 R. 1022.

(*d*) Innes *v.* Adamson, 1889; 17 R. 11 (*per* L. Pres. Inglis).

Laidlaw *v.* Gunn, 1890 ; 17 R. 394. Farquhar *v.* Neish, 1890, 17 R. 716 (2nd Div.), seems to extend the latter class further than any other authority. Cf. Reid *v.* Moore, 1893 ; 20 R. 712 ; and Ingram *v.* Russell, 1893 ; 20 R. 771.

(*e*) Scott *v.* Turnbull, 1884 ; 11 R. 1131, and cases there cited.

(*f*) M'Murchy *v.* Campbell, 1887 ; 14 R. 725. Innes *v.* Adamson (*d*).

(*g*) Martin & Stark *v.* Cruickshanks, 1896 ; 23 R. 874. In England the jury would probably have been directed in this case that there was no evidence of malice ; for it cannot prove malice that there is as much evidence against the truth of the privileged statement as there is in favour of its truth. See Pollock on Torts, 234. Addison on Torts, and the cases there cited, esp. Clark *v.* Molyneux, 3 Q. B. D. 237 ; 42 L. J. Q. B. 230. Guthrie Smith on Repn. 270.

2046. Of this 'privilege' there are several examples :—

(1.) *Parliament.*—It is an important privilege of Parliament, declared in the Bill of Rights as essential to the liberties of England, that there shall be absolute freedom of speech (*a*). The exception is, that no member is entitled to publish out of his place in Parliament what may affect the character of another (*b*), '*i.e.* to publish a single speech with the intention or effect of injuring an individual ; but such a publication seems to be privileged if *bonâ fide* published by a member of Parliament for the information of his constituents (*c*).' But an extraordinary question has arisen : How far the publication, under the order of the House of Commons, of reports of committees involving libellous matter are privileged ? The Court of Queen's Bench has correctly held that the authority of the House of Commons is no justification of the bookseller (*d*). 'A faithful report in a newspaper of a debate in Parliament, containing matter disparaging to the character of an individual spoken in the debate, and articles commenting on it, are not actionable (*e*).'

(*a*) William and Mary, stat. 2. c. 2.

(*b*) King *v.* L. Abingdon, 1 Esp. 226 ; 3 Ill. 9 ; 5 R. R. 733. King *v.* Creevey, 1 M. & S. 273 ; 3 Ill. 10 ; 14 R. R. 427.

(*c*) See Davidson *v.* Duncan, 7 E. & B. 232 ; 26 L. J. Q. B. 107. See Wason *v.* Walter, *infra.*

(*d*) The King *v.* Wright, 8 T. R. 293 ; 4 R. R. 649. Stockdale *v.* Hansard, 2 Mood. & Rob. 9 ; confirmed, 9 Ad. & El. 1 et seq. ; 3 Ill. 10. The House of Commons has declared such actions a breach of privilege, which seems an effectual bar against any of them in future.

(*e*) Wason *v.* Walter, 38 L. J. Q. B. 34 ; L. R. 4 Q. B. 73 ; 8 B. & S. 671. As to authorised publication of Parliamentary papers, etc., see 3 Vict. c. 9.

2047. (2.) *General Assembly of the Church of Scotland.*—There is no privilege in this Assembly as in Parliament, but only as a court of justice (*a*).

(*a*) See Porteous *v.* Izatt, 1781 ; M. 13,937 ; 3 Ill. 11.

2048. (3.) *Courts of Justice.*—In Courts there is, on the part of the judge, of the parties, and of their advisers, an 'absolute' privilege to state whatever is pertinent to the inquiry.

2049. This privilege protects a judge, and the dignity and independence of his place. It 'was erroneously stated by Mr. Bell that it' is forfeited by malice. In an action against a judge, therefore, malice, 'he says,' must be libelled and proved. And the proof must be by other evidence than the mere construction of the words used (*a*) ; and this without distinguishing whether the words spoken be strictly within the case (*b*). 'It is more correct to say that the privilege of a judge absolutely excludes an action of damages for words said in his judicial capacity, even though it be averred that they were malicious and irrelevant, provided only they relate in some way to the matter before the Court (*c*). The same privilege extends to a military court of inquiry (*d*), and a Select Committee of Parliament (*e*).'

(*a*) Hagart's Tr. *v.* Hope, June 1, 1821 ; F. C. ; 2 Sh. App. 125 ; 3 Ill. 11. Gibb *v.* Scott, 1740 ; Elch. *Public Officer*, 9. Hamilton *v.* Anderson, 1856 ; 18 D. 1006 ; aff. 3 Macq. 363. Watt *v.* Thomson & Ligertwood, 1868 ; 6 Macph. 1112 ; aff. 1870, 8 Macph. H. L. 77.

(*b*) Robertson *v.* Allardice, 1829 ; 7 S. 601 ; rev. 4 W. & S. 102 ; 5 Mur. 326. See Adam on Jury Trial, 349 sqq. ; 3 Bell's Ill. 12. See Oliphant *v.* M'Neill, 1776 ; 5 B. Sup. 573 ; 3 Ill. 11. Sinclair *v.* Justices of Caithness, 1767 ; 5 B. Sup. 574.

(*c*) Hagart's Tr., Hamilton, and Watt, *citt.* Harvey *v.* Dyce, 1877 ; 4 R. 265. Scott *v.* Stansfield, L. R. 3 Ex. 220 ; 37 L. J. Ex. 155.

(*d*) Dawkins *v.* L. Rokeby, L. R. 8 Q. B. 255 ; 7 H. L. 744 ; 45 L. J. Q. B. 8. Dawkins *v.* Prince Edward of Saxe Weimar, 1 Q. B. D. 499 ; 45 L. J. Q. B. 567. Smith *v.* L. Adv., 1898 ; 25 R. 112. It has been held that no action can be maintained against a military officer, even on the allegation of malice and want of probable cause, for statements in an official report, inasmuch as such questions are purely of military cognisance. Dawkins *v.* Paulet, 39 L. J. Q. B. 52 ; L. R. 5 Q. B. 94.

(*e*) Goffin *v.* Donnelly, 6 Q. B. D. 307.

2050. A judge, in checking the misconduct of practitioners, has the same privilege as in deciding a cause (*a*).

(*a*) Hagart, *supra*, § 2049 (*a*). Hamilton and Watt, *ib.*

2051. Parties 'litigants' are privileged in the statement of whatever they believe to be true, and which is relevant to the cause, unless malice be proved (*a*) ; and counsel have the same privilege, provided their statement be within their instructions (*b*). 'But the latter statement is too narrow, for the general rule has been fixed, that whatever is said or written in the course of judicial proceedings by those engaged in them, whether as judges, counsel, witnesses, or jurors, is absolutely privileged, however false, malicious, or irrelevant it may be, provided only it be said or done relative to the matter in question (*c*).

'The publication of reports of public proceedings in courts of justice is privileged, if proved to be fair and accurate (*d*).' But the privilege does not extend to the '*ex parte* or unfair' publication of those statements '(*i.e.* of counsel), or of the proceedings generally in public courts (*e*).'

(*a*) Cullen *v.* Ewing, 1830; 9 S. 31; rev. 1833, 6 W. & S. 566. **M'Kellar *v.* D. Sutherland,** 1859; 21 D. 222; 24 D. 1124. Nelson *v.* Black & Morrison, 1866; 4 Macph. 328. M'Intosh *v.* Flowerdew, 1851; 13 D. 726; 14 D. 116. Bayne *v.* Macgregor, 1862; 24 D. 1126. Scott *v.* Turnbull, 1884; 11 R. 1131 (specification required of circumstances inferring malice). Gordon *v.* British, etc., Metaline Co., 1886; 14 R. 75 (do.). Selbie *v.* Saint, 1890; 18 R. 88 (do.). Cf. *supra*, § 2040.

(*b*) Graham *v.* Robertson, 1815; 3 Dow, 273; 3 Ill. 12. Davidson *v.* Megget, 1821; 1 S. 3. Taylor *v.* Swinton, 1824; 2 S. App. 245. Ewing *v.* M'Kenzie, 1833; 6 W. & S. 566. Gray *v.* Walker, 1837; 15 S. 6. Hodgson *v.* Scarlett, 1 B. & Ald. 232. See Moodie *v.* Henderson, 1800; M. 360.

(*c*) Forteath *v.* E. Fife, Nov. 18, 1819; F. C.; 1821, 2 Mur. 1463. Bayne *v.* Macgregor, 1862; 24 D. 1126; 1 Macph. 615. Williamson *v.* Umfray and Robertson, 1890; 17 R. 905. Rome *v.* Watson, 1898; 25 R. 733. Authorities in **Munster *v.* Lamb,** 11 Q. B. D. 588. Bigelow on Torts, 95. Pollock on Torts, 99, 225. As to judges, see § 2049. As to witnesses, see Revis *v.* Smith, 18 C. B. 126. Henderson *v.* Broomland, 4 H. & N. 569. Fitzjohn *v.* Mackintosh, 9 C. B. N. S. 505; 30 L. J. C. B. 257. M'Lellan *v.* Miller, 1832; 11 S. 187. Mackintosh *v.* Weir, 1875; 2 R. 877.

(*d*) Drew *v.* Mackenzie, 1862; 24 D. 649. Lewis *v.* Levy, E. B. & E. 537; 27 L. J. Q. B. 282. Usill *v.* Hales, 3 C. P. D. 309; 47 L. J. C. P. 323. Stevens *v.* Sampson, 5 Ex. D. 53; 49 L. J. Ex. 120. Lawrie *v.* Campbell, 1800; Hume, 606. Riddell *v.* Clydesdale Horse Soc., 1885; 12 R. 976. Ross *v.* M'Kittrick, 1886; 14 R. 255. Macdougall *v.* Knight & Son, 17 Q. B. D. 636; aff. 1889; 14 App. Ca. 194. Wright & Greig *v.* Outram, 1890; 16 R. 1004; 17 R. 596. Crabbe & Robertson *v.* Stubbs, 1895; 22 R. 860. The privilege does not extend to the publication of papers or writs lodged in process, but not published or referred to in open court. Richardson *v.* Wilson, 1879; 7 R. 237. Macleod *v.* Lewis Justices, 1892; 20 R. 218. As to the publication of the names of debtors and defenders appearing in the Registers of Protested Bills and the decrees in absence in the Act Books of Courts of Law, see Fleming *v.* Newton, and Reid *v.* Outram, *infra*, § 2054A (*g*); and as to reports of Parliamentary proceedings, *supra*, § 2046.

(*e*) Porteous *v.* Izatt, 1781; M. 13,937; 3 Ill. 11.

2052. (4.) *Clergymen.* — Although the clergy have cognisance of the morals of their parishioners in general, and even of individuals, for private admonition, they, '*i.e.* individual clergymen and Church courts,' are not privileged (except in the regular course of Church censure) in expressing against individuals public reprehension (*a*), far less in printing their censure (*b*).

(*a*) Scotland *v.* Thomson, 1775; M. Apx. *Delinquency*, 3; 5 B. Sup. 575; Hailes, 669, 716; 3 Ill. 13. Dudgeon *v.* Forbes, 1833; 11 S. 1013. See M'Lean *v.* Fraser, 1823; 3 Mur. 353. M'Dougal *v.* Campbell, 1828; 6 S. 742 (elder). Adam *v.* Allan, 1841; 3 D. 1058. Cooper *v.* Greig, 1813; Hume, 648. Auchincloss *v.* Black, 1793; Hume, 595. Dunbar *v.* Stoddart, 1849; 11 D. 587. Dunbar *v.* Skinner, 1851; 13 D. 1217. Sturrock *v.* Greig, 1849; 11 D. 1220 (minute of kirk-session). Edwards *v.* Begbie, 1850; 12 D. 1134 (vestry). Lockhart *v.* Cumming, 1852; 14 D. 452. Thallon *v.* Kinninmont, 1855; 18 D. 27 (kirk-session). Lang *v.* Presby. of Irvine, 1864; 2 Macph. 823. Caldwell *v.* Munro, 1872; 10 Macph. 717. Rankine *v.* Roberts, 1873; 1 R. 225 (kirk-session). Inglis *v.* Croucher, 1889; 16 R. 774. Macmillan *v.* Free Church, 1862; 24 D. 1382. It was held that no action lies against a kirk-session or other court of the Church of Scotland, as such, for a sentence or other judicial act, even if malice and want of probable cause be averred (Sturrock *v.* Greig, *cit.*); while the members of such bodies or of the sessions or presbyteries or other "courts" of dissenting Churches may be sued for what they do either beyond their proper functions or maliciously (Sturrock, Auchincloss, Edwards, Rankine, and other cases cited).

(*b*) Snodgrass *v.* Wotherspoon, 1776; 5 B. Sup. 573.

2053. (5.) *Corporations.*—A member of a corporation 'or club or society (*a*)' is privileged in relevant inquiries into, 'and statements made to the proper domestic authority regarding,' the conduct of members over whom the body have cognisance; and, to ground damages, malice must be proved. 'The same rule applies to statements as to conduct of fellow-servants made to the proper superior officer (*b*); and to statements pertinently made by an elector during an election, *e.g.* of a county or town councillor, regarding a candidate (*c*).'

(*a*) Murdison *v.* Scot. Football Union, 1896; 23 R. 449.

(*b*) Hamilton *v.* Hope, 1827; 5 S. 569; 4 Mur. 222; 3 Ill. 13. Newlands *v.* Shaw, 1833; 12 S. 550. Fraser *v.* Wilson, 1850; 13 D. 289. See § 2054, 2054A. Fosdick *v.* N. B. Ry. Co., 1850; 13 D. 281 (complaint to railway manager by one official against another). Blackett *v.* Lang, 1854; 16 D. 989 (one post office clerk against another). Macbride *v.* Williams, 1869; 7 Macph. 427 (one professor against another). Auld *v.* Shairp, 1875; 2 R. 940 (do.). Milne *v.* Bauchope, 1867; 5 Macph. 1114 (one teacher against another). M'Murchy *v.* Campbell, 1887; 14 R. 725.

(*c*) Bruce *v.* Leisk, 1892; 19 R. 482. Anderson *v.* Hunter, 1891; 18 R. 467.

2054. (6.) *Private Persons* are privileged, when called on in self-defence, or by duty, to state what may be offensive or injurious. So a master, in giving the character of a servant, is privileged (*a*). A creditor, in discussing 'with other creditors or persons concerned' the bankruptcy of his debtor, is privileged (*b*); 'and confidential commercial communications, not needlessly divulged, to a friend who asks for them with a view to dealing with an individual, are privileged (*c*).' A near relation is privileged to give information of misconduct which may have influence on an intended marriage (*d*). And a merchant in one case was held privileged in stating in the long room of the Custom House the misconduct of a broker to a foreign shipmaster (*e*).

(*a*) Christian *v.* Kennedy, 1818; 1 Mur. 419. Anderson *v.* Wishart, 1818; *ib.* 429; 3 Ill. 13. Matheson *v.* M'Kinnon, 1832; 10 S. 825. Ewing *v.* M'Kenzie, 1833; 6 W. & S. 566; 3 Ill. 12. Watson *v.* Burnet, 1862; 24 D. 494. Laidlaw *v.* Gunn, 1890; 17 R. 394. Farquhar *v.* Neish, 1890; 17 R. 716 (volunteered letter to keeper of register office). See as to a medical man, White *v.* Smith, 1851; 14 D. 177.

(*b*) Stein *v.* Marshall, 1804; M. 12,443; Apx. *Proof*, 1; 3 Ill. 14. Torrance *v.* Leafe & Co., 1834; 13 S. 72 and 1146. Spill *v.* Maule, L. R. 4 Ex. 232; 38 L. J. Ex. 138.

(*c*) Couseland *v.* Cuthill, 1830; 5 Mur. 148. Kennedy *v.* Baillie, 1856; 18 D. 138. See Lockhart *v.* Cumming, 1852; 14 D. 452. Swift *v.* Winterbotham, 42 L. J. Q. B. 111; 43 *ib.* 56; L. R. 8 Q. B. 244; 9 Q. B. 301.

(*d*) Todd *v.* Hawkins, 1837; 3 Ill. 14. See Henderson *v.* Henderson, 1855; 17 D. 348; and see as to a statement in answer to inquiry by elders of Free Kirk as to the conduct of a member, Gibb *v.* Barron, 1859; 21 D. 1099. See Rankine *v.* Roberts, 1873; 1 R. 225; above, § 2053.

(*e*) Mitchell *v.* Thomson, 1829; 7 S. 458. See Stewart *v.* Swinton, 1825; 3 Ill. 14.

2054A. 'Litigants and persons making criminal charges to a proper official, as to a policeman or procurator-fiscal, are privileged, whatever their motives may be, if they have reasonable grounds for believing the statement (if pertinent) made by them to be true, although it is proved to be false; *i.e.* one suing them for damages must aver and prove both malice and want of probable cause (*a*). Persons making formal complaints to the proper department of the Government as to the conduct of magistrates and persons in the public service are privileged (*b*); or in some cases to employers as to the conduct of their servants (*c*). And public officials (including members of public boards) are privileged in regard to all pertinent statements made by them in the performance of their proper functions (*d*).

'In short, wherever a clear moral duty to make the statement complained of is shown to have been incumbent on the defender (*e*); or where he has in self-protection replied, in relevant and reasonable terms, to an attack upon himself (*f*), he is privileged, in the sense that the burden lies on the pursuer to prove that the defender was actuated by malice.

'Public registers being open to the public, the publication of a list of persons who have dishonoured their bills, as they appear on the Register of Protests, is not libellous, if it be strictly accurate in every particular (*g*). And the same rule applies to decrees of courts of law accurately copied or abstracted from the books of court. In estimating damages in cases of wrongful use of diligence and the like, the publication of decrees in absence, protests, etc., in Black Lists, is now regarded as a natural result of the wrong done (*h*).'

(*a*) **Arbuckle** *v.* **Taylor,** 1815; 3 Dow, 160. Young *v.* Leven, 1822; 1 S. App. 179. Dallas *v.* Mann, 1853; 15 D. 746. Cameron *v.* Hamilton, 1855; 18 D. 426 (the technical words must be used—"groundlessly" not equivalent to "without probable cause"). Marianski *v.* Henderson, 1841; 3 D. 1036. **Bayne** *v.* **Macgregor,** 1864; 1 Macph. 615. M'Intosh *v.* Flowerdew, 1851; 14 D. 116. Ferguson *v.* Colquhoun, 1862; 24 D. 1428. Davies & Co. *v.* Brown & Lyell, 1867; 5 Macph. 842. **Green** *v.* **Chalmers,** 1878; 6 R. 318. Lightbody *v.* Gordon, 1882; 9 R. 934. Hassan *v.* Paterson, 1885; 12 R. 1164. Urquhart *v.* M'Kenzie, 1886; 14 R. 18. See above, § 2039, 2051. Want of probable cause may be in law as well as in fact. Craig *v.* Peebles, 1876; 3 R. 441. A repetition of the charge at a different time to unofficial persons is not privileged. Walker *v.* Cumming, 1868; 6 Macph. 318; comp. Ferguson and Hassan, *citt.*

(*b*) Thomson *v.* Gillie, May 16, 1810; F. C. Young *v.* Leven, 1822; 1 S. App. 179. Harrison *v.* Bush, 5 E. & B. 344; 25 L. J. Q. B. 25. Proctor *v.* Webster, 16 Q. B. D. 112.

(*c*) M'Fadyen *v.* Spencer & Co., 1892; 19 R. 350.

(*d*) Boyd *v.* Reid, 1801; Hume, 610. Vass *v.* Board of Customs, Feb. 20, 1818; F. C.; rev. 1822, 1 S. App. 229. Blackett *v.* Lang, 1854; 16 D. 989. Fenton *v.* Currie, 1843; 5 D. 705. Nelson *v.* Black & Thomson, 1866; 4 Macph. 328. Mackay *v.* Chalmers, 1860; 21 D. 443. Newlands *v.* Shaw, 1833; 12 S. 550. Rae *v.* M'Lay, 1852; 14 D. 988; 1 Stu. 986. Fraser *v.* Wilson, 1850; 13 D. 289. Wallace *v.* Mooney, 1885; 12 R. 710 (police constable). M'Murchy *v.* Campbell, 1887; 14 R. 725 (specification required of grounds of allegation of malice). Macaulay *v.* N. Uist School Board, 1887; 15 R. 99. Shaw *v.* Morgan, 1888; 15 R. 865 (town councillor). Neilson *v.* Johnston, 1890; 17 R. 442. As to a law agent acting for a client, see Wilson *v.* Purvis, 1890; 18 R. 72.

(*e*) Durham *v.* Mair, 1796; Hume, 599. Grieve *v.* Smith, 1808; Hume, 637. Lockhart *v.* Cumming, 1852; 14 D. 452. Fraser and Blackett, *citt.* (*d*). Gibb *v.* Barron, 1859; 21 D. 1099. Milne *v.* Bauchope, 1867; 5 Macph. 1114. Urquhart *v.* Grigor, 1864; 3 Macph. 283. Macbride *v.* Williams, 1869; 7 Macph. 427, 790. Auld *v.* Shairp, 1875; 2 R. 940. Inglis *v.* Croucher, 1889; 16 R. 774. Hill *v.* Thomson, 1892; 19 R. 377. Jenoure *v.* Delmege, P. C., 1891; A. C. 73. Davies *v.* Snead, L. R. 5 Q. B. 608; 39 L. J. Q. B. 202.

(*f*) Laughton *v.* Bishop of Sodor and Man, L. R. 4 P. C. 495; 42 L. J. P. C. 11. Gray *v.* Soc. for Prevn. of Cruelty, 1890; 17 R. 1185.

(*g*) Fleming *v.* Newton, 1848; 6 Bell's App. 175. Reid *v.* Outram, 1852; 14 D. 577. Andrews *v.* Drummond & Graham, 1887; 14 R. 568. Taylor *v.* Rutherford, 1888; 15 R. 608. Crabbe & Robertson *v.* Stubbs, 1895; 22 R. 860.

(*h*) Gibson & Co. *v.* Anderson & Co., 1897; 24 R. 556.

2055. (7.) *The Press* is free; but the party who publishes (*a*) is responsible for any libel or defamation of which he may be guilty (*b*). 'It has been fixed that when a newspaper takes the responsibility of a libellous letter published in it, the newspaper cannot be compelled to disclose the name of the writer. Its proprietors take the place of the writer, and the pursuer could take no benefit, the newspaper company being solvent, by the disclosure (*c*). There are, however, exceptions to the rule, and it may in many cases be doubted whether the rule is well grounded (*d*).

'Even where there is no slander in the proper sense, a continuous series of articles, holding up the pursuer to public hatred, contempt, and ridicule, has been held actionable (*e*).' The conduct of a public man (a member of the Government, a functionary under Government, or a member of Parliament) is open to animadversion and censure; but that must be confined to his public character (*f*). A person attending as a member of a public meeting, and taking part in the proceedings, is subject to the same animadversion on his public conduct, and has the same protection of his private character (*g*). An author is liable to criticism and animadversion in his capacity as an author, but protected as other men are in his private character (*h*); 'and criticism ceases to be "fair" when under pretence of criticising an author's work it attacks his personal character, or ascribes to him vicious sentiments which he has not written (*i*).'

(*a*) It seems that sale and circulation in Scotland of a newspaper published by persons residing in England does not subject them to the jurisdiction of Scotch Courts. Opinions in Longworth *v.* Hope, 1865; 3 Macph. 149. Parnell *v.* Walter, 1889; 16 R. 917.

(*b*) See Mackie *v.* Lawson, 1851; 13 D. 725. Scouller *v.* Gunn, 1852; 24 Jurist, 552. M'Douall *v.* Guthrie, 1853; 15 D. 778. Faulks *v.* Park, 1854; 17 D. 247. Drew *v.* Mackenzie & Co., 1862; 24 D. 649. Johnston *v.* Dilke, 1875; 2 R. 836. Fletcher *v.* Wilson, 1885; 12 R. 683 (slight mistake apologised for—not necessary to prove real damage when man branded as a thief). See as to reports of legal proceedings, § 2051, 2054A (*g*). On the question whether it is competent to interdict the publication of libellous matter as such, see Fleming *v.* Newton, *cit.* Riddell *v.* Clydesdale Horse Soc., 1885; 12 R. 976, and authorities there.

(*c*) Lowe *v.* Taylor, 1843; 5 D. 1261. Brims *v.* Reid, 1885; 12 R. 1016. Morrison *v.* Smith & Co., 1897; 24 R. 471.

(*d*) Cunningham *v.* Duncan & Jamieson, 1889; 16 R. 383; and *per* Lord Young in Morrison *v.* Smith & Co., *cit.*

(*e*) Sherriff *v.* Wilson, 1855; 17 D. 528. Cunningham *v.* Phillips, 1868; 6 Macph. 926. M'Laren *v.* Ritchie, 1856, in Glegg on Repn. 497. M'Laughlan *v.* Orr, Pollock, & Co., 1894; 22 R. 38. See above, § 2043 (*g*).

(*f*) The King *v.* Cobbet, Holt, 114; 3 Ill. 14. L. A. Hamilton *v.* Stevenson, 1822; 2 Mur. 81. Alexander *v.* Macdonald, 1826; 4 Mur. 94; 3 Ill. 16. Shepstone *v.* Davis, 11 App. Ca. 187. It has been said that every man has a right to discuss freely, if he does it honestly and without malice, any subject in which the public are generally interested. Henwood *v.* Harrison, 41 L. J. C. P. 206; L. R. 7 C. P. 606, and cases cited there; but see **Campbell** *v.* **Spottiswoode**, 3 B. & S. 769; 32 L. J. Q. B. 185.

(*g*) Aiton *v.* M'Culloch, 1823; 3 Mur. 284. Archer *v.* Ritchie, 1891; 18 R. 719.

(*h*) Carr *v.* Hood, 1 Camp. 355. Talbot *v.* Tipps, 1 Camp. 305. Leslie *v.* Blackwood, 3 Mur. 157. Davis *v.* Miller, 1855; 17 D. 1050, 1166. The question, what is fair criticism, is for the jury. Campbell *v.* Spottiswoode, *cit.* Merivale *v.* Carson, 20 Q. B. D. 275. As to a professor in a university or college, see Alexander, *cit.* Macbride *v.* Williams, 1869; 7 Macph. 427, 790. Craig *v.* Jex Blake, 1871; 9 Macph. 973. Auld *v.* Shairp, 1874; 2 R. 191.

(*i*) Campbell *v.* Spottiswoode, and Merivale *v.* Carson, *citt.*

2056. (8.) *Private Letters.*—Libellous or defamatory matter contained in a private letter is actionable (*a*).

(*a*) M'Candies *v.* M'Candie, 1827; 4 Mur. 197. Lovi *v.* Wood, 1814; Hume, 613. Hutchison *v.* Naismith, 1808; M. Apx. *Delinquency*, 4. Brown *v.* Wason, 1838; M'F. 38. Bryson *v.* Inglis, 1844; 6 D. 363. M'Neill *v.* Rorison, 1847; 10 D. 15. Aird *v.* Kennedy, 1851; 13 D. 775. Kennedy *v.* Baillie, 1855; 18 D. 138. Stephen *v.* Paterson, 1865; 3 Macph. 571. Mackay *v.* M'Cankie, 1883; 10 R. 537. Stuart *v.* Moss, 1885; 13 R. 299. See above, § 2043.

2057. Veritas Convicii may be a defence (*a*) in a civil action of damages, though not in a criminal action. It is in the ordinary case an answer to *implied* malice, and so pleadable in justification, provided it be set forth as such 'specifically, with time, place, and person, so as to show the pursuer what is brought against him (*b*),' in circumstances to call for the statement, and an issue taken on the point; and where the circumstances do not call for the statement, it will in general 'not be allowed to be proved (*c*) merely to' mitigate the damages (*d*). 'The general rule is that the circumstances in which the slander or libel was uttered, including the defender's state of mind, may be proved, for the purpose either of aggravating or mitigating damages (*e*). Evidence of provocation is admitted without a separate action or issue, to the effect of entitling the defender to *absolvitor* where the pursuer has been equally abusive in a squabble or altercation (*in rixâ*) (*f*). But the defender making a similar claim of damages against the pursuer (*compensatio injuriarum*) must bring a separate action (*g*).'

(*a*) Even when the defender denies the slander. Burnet *v.* Gow, 1896, 24 R. 156, explaining on this point Harkes *v.* Mowat, *cit.* Mason *v.* Tait, *cit.*

(*b*) Scott *v.* M'Gavin, *infra.* M'Rostie *v.* Ironside, 1849; 12 D. 74. Fraser *v.* Wilson, 1850; 13 D. 289. Mason *v.*

Tait, 1850; 13 D. 1347. Harkes *v.* Mowat, 1862; 24 D. 701. Paul *v.* Jackson, 1884; 11 R. 460, etc. Adam on Jury Trial, 102.

(*c*) Lowe *v.* Taylor, 1844; 7 D. 117. M'Neill *v.* Rorison, 1847; 10 D. 15. Craig *v.* Jex Blake, 1871; 9 Macph. 973. Torrance *v.* Weddell, 1868; 7 Macph. 243. Paul *v.* Jackson, *cit.* Brown *v.* Macfarlane, 1889; 16 R. 368. The opposite was laid down in previous editions on the authority of Ogilvie, *infra.* See as to pleading justification generally, *supra,* § 2043 *fin.* Lowe and Harkes, *citt.* Brownlie *v.* Thomson, 1859; 21 D. 480. Rankin *v.* Simpson, 1859; 21 D. 1057. Carmichael *v.* Cowan, 1862; 1 Macph. 204. Ogilvie *v.* Paul, 1873; 11 Macph. 776. M'Iver *v.* M'Neill, 1873; 11 Macph. 777.

A prevailing rumour against the pursuer may, it appears, be proved in mitigation of damages. Scott *v.* M'Gavin, 1821; 2 Mur. 497. M'Culloch *v.* Litt, 1851; 13 D. 960. Rose *v.* Robertson, 1803; Hume, 614. Gardner *v.* Marshall, 1803; Hume, 620. Aitken *v.* Reid, 1819; 2 Mur. 159. Such a defence should be pleaded. Bryson *v.* Inglis, 1844; 6 D. 363. Brodie *v.* Blair, 1834; 12 S. 941; See, however, as to this point, Macpherson *v.* Daniels, 10 B. & C. 273. Watkin *v.* Hall, L. R. 3 Q. B. 396; 37 L. R. Q. B. 125. Addison on Torts, 776, 805, 817. Folkard on Libel, 278.

(*d*) Sinclair *v.* Justices of Caithness, 1767; 5 B. Sup. 574. Hamilton *v.* Aitken, 1771; M. 13,924; Hailes, 439; 5 B. Sup. 574; 3 Ill. 16. Chalmers *v.* Douglas, 1785; M. 13,939. See 3 Ill. 17. Peat *v.* Smith, 1793; M. 13,941. Thomson *v.* Gillie, May 16, 1810; F. C. M'Donald *v.* M'Donald, June 2, 1813; F. C. Dyce *v.* Kerr, July 4, 1816; F. C. "The above-mentioned cases were decided while jury trial was not yet fully established. The following cases show the maturing of this plea of justification in the jury court." Note in 3 Ill. 17. Scott *v.* M'Gavin, 1821; 2 Mur. 486, 503. Walker *v.* Robertson, 1821; *ib.* 512. Denham *v.* Ogilvie, 1827; 4 Mur. 195; 3 Ill. 17. Tytler *v.* M'Intosh, 1823; 3 Mur. 236. Brodie *v.* Blair, 1836; 14 S. 267. Ogilvie *v.* Scott, 1836; 14 S. 729. See Taylor *v.* Anderson, 1844; 6 D. 1026. White *v.* Clough, 1847; 10 D. 332. Burnaby *v.* Robertson, 1848; 10 D. 855. Aird, *supra,* § 2056 (*a*). Balfour *v.* Wallace, 1853; 15 D. 913. Mackellar *v.* D. Sutherland, 1859; 21 D. 222. M'Donald *v.* Begg, 1862; 24 D. 685. Brownlie *v.* Thomson, 1859; 21 D. 480. Blaikie *v.* Duncan, 1857; 19 D. 983. Rankin *v.* Simpson, 1859; 21 D. 1057.

(*e*) See all the authorities in Cunningham *v.* Duncan & Jamieson, 1889; 16 R. 383. See above, § 545.

(*f*) Robertson *v.* Falconer, 1789; Hume, 603. Lovi *v.* Wood, 1814; Hume, 613. Forbes *v.* Young, 1805; Hume, 627. M'Crae *v.* Stevenson, 1806; Hume, 631. M'Guffie *v.* M'Donell, 1809; *ib.* 638 (see Allan *v.* Douglas, *ib.* 639). Brown *v.* Fernie, 1810; *ib.* 643. Hyslop *v.* Miller, 1816; 1 Mur. 54. Goddard & Co. *v.* Haddaway, 1816; 1 Mur. 156. Edwards *v.* Macintosh, 1824; 3 Mur. 386. Bryson *v.* Inglis, 1844; 6 D. 363.

(*g*) Tullis *v.* Crichton, 1850; 12 D. 867. Bertram *v.* Pace, 1885; 12 R. 798.

CHAPTER II

OF BASTARDS

2058. Rights of Bastards.—The rights of lawful children (*a*) are denied to bastards. 'Unless legitimated (*infra*, § 2064), a bastard has by law no place in the family of either of his parents, and no patrimonial rights or obligations, as of succession, exist between him and either of them (§ 2063). Hence he has no title to sue for solatium or damages for the death of either, nor can even his mother sue such an action for his death (*b*).' But still out of the relation of parent and child, although not by marriage, arise certain more confined rights and duties of which the law takes cognisance.

(*a*) See above, § 1624 et seq.
(*b*) Weir *v.* Coltness Iron Co., 1889 ; 16 R. 614. Clarke *v.* Carfin Coal Co., 1891 ; A. C. 412 ; 18 R. H. L. 63. See above, § 546.

2059. The description of bastardy is the converse of that of a legitimate birth.

2060. Proof of Paternity.—Law has here to deal with what, though not punishable as a crime, is secret and industriously concealed. And to detect the skulking paramour, in justice to the unhappy mother, the rule of evidence, 'though altered by modern legislation,' is 'still perhaps' stretched beyond the common extent. 'In Scotland the ordinary jurisdiction of the Courts has been found sufficient for this class of cases; while in England "bastardy orders" are obtained under a statutory jurisdiction conferred on Justices of Peace and other courts of summary jurisdiction. In Scotland, actions of filiation (or affiliation) and aliment are invariably, though not necessarily, brought in the Sheriff Court. This Court, and courts of summary jurisdiction in England, have, under a recent Act of Parliament, jurisdiction in such matters against persons "within the jurisdiction of the Court" . . . "notwithstanding that such person ordinarily resides, or the child has been born, or the mother of it ordinarily resides, where the Court is English, in Scotland, or, where the Court is Scotch, in England, in like manner as the Court has jurisdiction in any other case." Provision is made for enforcing this jurisdiction and for citing witnesses in England and Scotland respectively (*a*).

(*a*) 44 and 45 Vict. c. 24, § 4, 6 (Summary Jurisdiction Process Act, 1881). Berkley *v.* Thomson, 10 App. Ca. 45.

2061. What 'was' called a *semiplena probatio* 'gave' admission, 'so long as parties were held to be inadmissible as witnesses,' to the mother's oath in supplement (*a*). 'Since the Evidence Act of 1853, however, the woman is examined (as well as the alleged father) as a witness in the cause, and the Court considers the evidence as a whole; the question no longer being whether there is a *semiplena probatio, i.e.* such evidence short of complete evidence as induces a reasonable suspicion, and justifies the admission of the mother as a witness, but whether the whole evidence taken together proves the paternity (*b*). The difference is one rather of procedure than of substance, and the following practical rules for weighing the evidence laid down in the earlier editions are still valid, though stated in phraseology which has been superseded.' To this *semiplena probatio* it is necessary, either that intercourse shall be proved with the mother of the bastard child at the time corresponding with the gestation; and to such proof in this respect it is no relevant answer that others (*c*) also have had intercourse. Or, previous 'or subsequent' intercourse, with opportunity of further intercourse corresponding to the time of gestation, will raise a *semiplena probatio*, to be completed by the woman's oath (*d*). Or gross familiarity and indecency, with actual or possible opportunity, is construed as a *semiplena probatio* (*e*). But opportunity alone (*f*) is not sufficient (*g*).

It is essential that the facts established for *semiplena probatio* shall correspond and combine with the woman's oath as to the particular circumstances of the connection (*h*).

(*a*) 1 Ersk. 6. § 51. Dykes *v.* Findlay, 1836; 14 S. 815; 3 Ill. 20. M'Laren *v.* M'Culloch, 1844; 6 D. 1133.

(*b*) 16 and 17 Vict. c. 20. § 3. Scott *v.* Chalmers, 1856; 19 D. 119. M'Bayne *v.* Davidson, 1860; 22 D. 739 (narrowest case on record). Ross *v.* Fraser, 1863; 1 Macph. 783. M'Kinven *v.* M'Millan, 1892; 19 R. 369. Young *v.* Nicol, 1893; 20 R. 768.

(*c*) Caldwell *v.* Stewart, *infra* (*g*). Hagart *v.* Croll; 1836; 14 S. 852. Lawson *v.* Eddie, 1861; 23 D. 876. Scrimgeour *v.* Stewart, 1864; 2 Macph. 667.

(*d*) Wightman, Hunter *v.* Hunter, Humphrey, and Robertson, *citt. infra* (*g*). Brown *v.* Smith, 1799; Elliot *v.* Scott, 1800, and other cases in Hume, 32 sqq. Ross, *cit.* (*b*). Lawson *v.* Eddie, 1861; 23 D. 876. M'Donald *v.* Glass, 1833; 11 R. 57. Scott *v.* Dawson, 1884; 11 R. 518 (intercourse three years after birth and not averred on record admitted to proof).

(*e*) Lawson, *cit.* (*c*). Bertram (*g*), etc.

(*f*) Bowie *v.* Robertson, Dec. 1. 1808; F. C. Kirkpatrick *v.* Donaldson, 1843; 5 D. 1104. Gray *v.* Marshall, 1875; 2 R. 907. Burton *v.* Loudon, 2 Sel. Sh. Ct. Ca. 369.

(*g*) Lyon *v.* Grant, 5 B. Sup. 556; 3 Ill. 18. Liddel *v.* Heugh, 1779; 5 B. S. 553. Caldwell *v.* Stewart, 1773, 1777; 5 B. S. 390, 555. Wightman *v.* Tomlinson, 1807; M. *Proof*, Apx. 10; Hume, 33. Craig *v.* Crichton, June 14, 1809; F. C. Hunter *v.* Watson, June 15, 1811; F. C. "This decision went a great deal too far"; 3 Ill. 18. Hunter *v.* Hunter, May 24, 1814; F. C. Humphrey *v.* Aitken, 1822; 1 S. App. 111. Robertson *v.* Petrie, 1825; 4 S. 333. Bertram *v.* Steel, 1829; 7 S. 434. Fraser on Par. & Child, 131 sqq. As to the period of gestation, see Boyd *v.* Kerr, 1843; 5 D. 1213 (protracted). Gibson *v.* M'Fagan, 1874; 1 R. 853 (do.). Fraser, P. & C. 11 sqq. Henderson *v.* Somers, 1876; 3 R. 997 (do.). Cook *v.* Rattray, 1880; 8 R. 217 (do.). Whyte *v.* Whyte, 1884; 11 R. 710 (do.). Ritchie *v.* Cunningham, 1857; 20 D. 35 (early birth). As to delay in raising action, see Ruddiman *v.* Bruce, 1863; 2 Macph. 70. Scott *v.* Dawson, *cit.* (*d*).

(*h*) Greig *v.* Morrice, 1833; 15 S. 338, 1132. M'Naughton *v.* Glass, 1838; 16 S. 614, 1103. M'Millan *v.* Tait, 1875, n. r. (a *cause célèbre*). Folley *v.* Douglas, 1848; 10 D. 1424. Mann *v.* Forrest, 1850; 12 D. 1090 (woman's character).

2062. Aliment.—The father and mother are both liable for aliment to the child; and the father, while concealing himself, is debtor to the mother for his share, and she has all the remedies of a creditor (*a*). 'The debt transmits against the father's representatives (*b*). Mr. Bell says that' the amount and period of aliment are regulated by the *condition* of the parties, and the child's ability to subsist itself (*c*). 'But in this, as in most other claims for aliment, the rank of the parties is not now considered, and only what is necessary for subsistence is allowed (*d*). The amount allowed against the father, as his half, varies slightly in different districts. In Glasgow it is £8 per annum. Refusal by father or mother to aliment a bastard, whereby it becomes chargeable to the parish, is punishable by fine and imprisonment (*e*).' The mother has the custody till seven in males, ten in females (*f*); after which, if the father is to 'assist to' maintain the child longer, he may, 'unless the welfare of the child forbids (*g*),' make his own arrangements for it (*h*). If the child be insane, or otherwise incapable of providing for itself, the obligation of the parents will continue during life (*i*). The father's obligation to aliment lasts in the common case till puberty, with such differences as circumstances fairly justify (*k*). 'In one case it was decided by a majority of the Second Division that a bastard is bound, if able, to support his indigent mother (*l*); but that judgment was examined and overruled by the House of Lords (*m*). The mother of a bastard being the proper custodier of her child, may sue in the Sheriff Court or Court of Session for delivery of it (*n*); but she cannot appoint a guardian to it (*o*).'

(*a*) A. B. *v.* C. D., 1842; 4 D. 670. **Thomson** *v.* **Westwood,** 1842; 4 D. 833. **Corrie** *v.* **Adair,** 1860; 22 D. 900. Buie *v.* Steven, 1863; 2 Macph. 223. Westlands *v.* Pirie, 1887; 14 R. 763 (presumed discharge and *mora*).

(*b*) Gairdner *v.* Munro, 1848; 10 D. 650. Clarkson *v.* Fleming, 1858; 20 D. 1224. Downs *v.* Wilson's Tr., 1886; 13 R. 1101. Oncken's Factor *v.* Reimers, 1892; 19 R. 519.

(*c*) 1 Ersk. 6. § 56.

(*d*) **Maule** *v.* **Maule,** 1825; 1 W. & S. 266. See Fraser, P. & C. 126.

(*e*) 8 and 9 Vict. c. 83, § 80.

(*f*) Goadby *v.* Macandys, July 7, 1815; F. C.; 3 Ill. 20. Baxter *v.* Dougal's Trs., 1825; 4 S. 139. Weepers *v.* Hers. of Kennoway, 1844; 6 D. 1173. Buie, *supra* (*a*). Macpherson *v.* Leishman, 1887; 14 R. 780 (retractation of arrangement by mother). Sutherland *v.* Taylor 1887; 15 R. 224 (do.—mother's petition refused for special reasons).

(*g*) Brown *v.* Halbert, 1896; 23 R. 733.

(*h*) Kay *v.* Watson, 1826; 4 S. 706. Pott *v.* Pott, 1833; 12 S. 183. Corrie *v.* Adair, 1860; 22 D. 900. Grant *v.* Yuill, 1872; 10 Macph. 511. Hardie *v.* Leith, 1878; 6 R. 115. Dunnet *v.* Campbell, 1883; 11 R. 280. Fraser, P. & C. 129 sqq. His liability after the age of seven or ten continues until he offers to take and provide for the child. Shearer *v.* Robertson, 1877; 5 R. 263. The petition in an action of filiation and aliment ought to conclude not for aliment till the age of seven or ten, but till such age, "or until the child is able to maintain himself," or the like, so that a second action may be unnecessary.

(*i*) Finlayson *v.* Gown, July 7, 1809; F. C. Pott, *supra* (*h*). Anderson *v.* Lauder, 1848; 10 D. 961. Clarkson *v.* Fleming, 1858; 20 D. 1224.

(*k*) Glendinning *v.* Flint, 1782; M. 442. Paterson *v.* Spiers, 1782; M. 445. Graham *v.* Kay, 1740; M. 441. Scott *v.* Oliver, 1778; M. 445; 5 B. Sup. 390. Burges *v.* Halliday, 1758; M. 1357. Short *v.* Donald, 1765; M. 442, 1358. Dunnet *v.* Campbell, *cit.* (*h*).

(*l*) Samson *v.* Davie, 1886; 14 R. 113.

(*m*) Clarke *v.* Carfin Coal Co., *cit.* § 2058.

(*n*) Brand *v.* Shaws, 1888; 15 R. 449. Mackenzie *v.* Keillor, 1892; 19 R. 963 (jurisdiction—grounds for refusing mother's demand for custody). See as to mother's rights of control over bastard, Barnardo *v.* M'Hugh, 1891; A. C. 388.

(*o*) *Ib.* and Brand *v.* Shaws, 1888; 16 R. 315. The Guardianship of Infants Act, 1886, does not apply to bastards; *ib.*

2063. Succession.—There is no succession to or from a bastard, except in the case of his having lawful issue (*a*). He has no father recognised in law (*b*), and of course no relations to whom his property can go, unless where he himself is the father of lawful children. But he may dispose of his property *inter vivos* without control. He may dispose of his land *mortis causâ* in liege poustie. And he may by testament dispose of his moveables (*c*).

(*a*) 4 Stair, 12. § 1. 3 Ersk. 10. § 8.

(*b*) Weepers *v.* Hers. and Kirk-session of Kennoway, 1844; 6 D. 1166, 1173. Corrie, *supra*, § 2062 (*h*).

(*c*) 6 Will. IV. c. 22.

2064. Legitimation.—Legitimation may be either absolute, by the subsequent intermarriage of the parents (*a*); or by royal letters of legitimation. But this last species of legitimation is limited. It only dispenses with the Queen's right of succession. It confers the power to convey the Queen's right to the bastard's agnates. But in this last case the letters of legitimation must bear a special clause to that effect. It has no effect in restoring the bastard to the right of succession in prejudice of lawful children. By letters of legitimation, those who would have succeeded if the bastard had been legitimate, may acquire a right to take his succession as if legal heirs (*b*).

(*a*) See *ante*, § 1627–8.

(*b*) 3 Stair, 3. § 45. 3 Ersk. 10. § 7. Ramsay *v.* Goudie, 1758; M. 1359; 3 Ill. 21. Hunter *v.* Hunter, 1784; M. 1362; Hailes, 942. Fraser on Par. & Ch. 43.

CHAPTER III

OF GUARDIANSHIP OF PUPILS, MINORS, AND PERSONS MENTALLY INCAPABLE

2065. General View.—The law provides guardians for the weak in intellect, whether from defect of age, or from disease, or from natural imbecility (*a*).

(*a*) See English cases on this subject, 3 Ill. 22 et seq.

2066.—Twenty-one is the age of presumed legal capacity in either sex. Until arrival at that age, a person is in law a minor; the term being divided into pupillarity, and minority strictly so called. Guardianship is a gratuitous office (*a*). But a factor for tutors, and even one of the guardians acting as such 'under a power conferred by the nomination (*b*),' is entitled to remuneration (*c*).

(*a*) Scotstarvet *v.* E. Buccleuch, 1642; M. 16,266; 3 Ill. 26. Scott *v.* Strachan, 1736; M. 13,433, 16,341; Elchies, *Tutor*, 4. Muschet *v.* Doig, 1739; M. 9456. L. M'Donald *v.* Muir, 1780; M. 16,437. M'Donald *v.* M'Donald, 1854; 16 D. 1023.

(*b*) Home *v.* Pringle, and other cases below (*c*).

(*c*) Lady Montgomerie *v.* Wauchope, 1822; 1 S. 491. Home *v.* Pringle, 1837; 16 S. 142; aff. 1841; 2 Rob. 384. Cullen *v.* Baillie, 1846; 8 D. 511. Bon Accord Ins. Co. *v.* Souter's Trs., 1850; 12 D. 1010. Fegan *v.* Thomson, 1855; 17 D. 1146. See 30 and 31 Vict. c. 97, § 2; and above, § 1998 (12), 1998A, 2000, etc.

I. TUTORY, OR GUARDIANSHIP OF PUPILS.

2067. Definition and Effect of Pupillarity.—Pupillarity is, in contemplation of the law, a state of absolute incapacity (*a*); the period of this incapacity extending from birth to fourteen in males, and twelve in females. No act done by the pupil, or action raised in his name, has any effect without the interposition of a guardian; while a decree in an action against him, without the appearance of his tutors, is a decree in absence, and as such reducible, but not null and void (*b*). The tutors are lawfully cited when the pupil is duly cited, and edictally "his tutors, if he any has," 'if he has no known tutors; but if known, the tutors should be cited *nominatim* (*c*). If there be no tutor or father, a curator *ad litem* ought to be appointed after an action by or against the pupil is brought into court (*d*).'

The guardianship is either that of the father 'or mother' or that of a tutor.

(*a*) 1 Ersk. 1. § 1.

(*b*) Sinclair *v.* Stark, 1828 ; 6 S. 336 ; 3 Ill. 26. Dick *v.* M'Ilwham, 1828 ; 6 S. 798 ; 1829, 7 S. 364. See note in 3 Ill. 26. M'Kenzie *v.* Sinclair, 1834 ; 12 S. 822. Keith *v.* Archer, 1836 ; 15 S. 116. Sinclair *v.* Brown, 1835 ; 13 S. 594 ; rem. 2 S. & M'L. 103 ; 1837, 15 S. 770 ; 1841, 3 D. 871. **E. Craven** *v.* **L. Elibank's Trs.**, 1854 ; 16 D. 811. Grieve (or Dingwall) *v.* Burns, 1871 ; 9 Macph. 582.

(*c*) Sinclair *v.* Stark, *cit.* Thomson's Trs. *v.* Livingston, 1864 ; 2 Macph. 114. E. Craven, *cit.*

(*d*) Agnew *v.* E. Stair, 1822 ; 1 S. App. 333, 357 sqq. E. Craven, *cit.* Authorities in Fraser, P. & C. 156, 162.

2068. Father Administrator in Law.—A father, 'and after his death a surviving mother, subject to the provisions of the Act of 1886 (*a*),' is the natural guardian of his infant offspring. 1. He is *ipso jure* administrator in law, requiring no appointment or judicial authority to give validity to his acts; and, in the ordinary case, he is not obliged to find security (*b*). But, 2. Where there is danger from the father's intromission, and the interests of the child require it, the Court of Session may interfere, and compel him to find security; or they may appoint a factor *loco tutoris* (*c*); 'but they will not remove him from the office of administrator in law (*d*).' 3. The father must authorise all actions or diligence by the pupil (*e*); 'or more correctly he sues such actions as tutor and administrator. He is personally liable for expenses in such actions (*f*).' 4. He may, under the above precaution, uplift and discharge debts due to his child in pupillarity (*g*). 5. But he cannot be *auctor in rem suam* (*h*). 6. The father has the custody and direction of the residence and education of his child during pupillarity (*i*). And, 7. Although unquestionably the Supreme Court has jurisdiction to superintend and control, and even to supersede, the exercise of a father's guardianship, where it manifestly tends to the injury of the child, or of property held independently of the father, yet it is a power to be exercised only under the pressure of extreme necessity, and with a very cautious and delicate reserve. In England, when a fortune is bestowed on an infant, the Lord Chancellor seems to be considered as guardian; and the infant, as a ward of Chancery, is not only under protection directly as to the estate, but indirectly in regard to the marriage of the child, and the education fit for its condition (*k*). But no such principle is recognised in Scotland, and the power of the Supreme Court is, 'or before the Guardianship of Infants Act was (*l*),' limited to the redress or prevention of actual injury sustained or threatened (*m*).

(*a*) See below, § 2069A, 2077A, 2083, etc.

(*b*) 1 Ersk. 6. § 54. See Fraser, P. & C. 65 sqq. The Court will grant him special powers, as to a tutor, in some cases. See L. Clinton, petr., 1875 ; 3 R. 62 (to feu). Logan, petr., 1898 ; 25 R. 51 (to sell); and below, § 2084.

(*c*) Govan *v.* Richardson, 1633 ; M. 16,263 ; 3 Ill. 27. Wilkie *v.* L. Dalziel, 1688 ; M. 16,311. Graham *v.* Duff, 1794 ; M. 16,383 (absent from Scotland). Johnston *v.* Wilson, 1822 ; 1 S. 558. See cases cited below, (*i*) and (*m*). Stevenson's Trs. *v.* Dumbreck, 1859 ; 19 D. 462 ; 1861, 4 Macq. 86. M'Nab *v.* M'Nab, *infra*, § 2092. Cochrane, petr., 1891 ; 18 R. 456.

(*d*) Robertson, petrs., 1865 ; 3 Macph. 1077. See Graham, petr., 1881 ; 8 R. 996 (tutor-dative appointed to lunatic on father's application, father being aged).

(*e*) Fleming *v.* Dickson, 1545 ; M. 16,221. Keith *v.* Archer, 1836 ; 15 S. 116.

(*f*) White *v.* Steel, 1894 ; 21 R. 649.

(*g*) Boswell *v.* ——, 1747 ; M. 16,353. Stevenson *v.* Dumbreck, *cit.* (*c*).

(*h*) Crawford *v.* Cordiners of Canongate, 1694 ; M. 16,315. Bontine *v.* Graham, Dec. 20, 1838 ; F. C. ; 1839, 1 D. 286 ; 2 D. 27. See above, § 1998 (13).

(*i*) See M'Farlane *v.* M'Farlane, 1847; 9 D. 904. A. B. *v.* C. D., 1847; 10 D. 229. M'Iver *v.* M'Iver, 1859; 21 D. 1103. Nicolson *v.* Nicolson, 1869 ; 7 Macph. 1118. Steuart *v.* Steuart, 1870 ; 8 Macph. 821. Lilley *v.* Lilley, 1877 ; 4 R. 397. Pagan *v.* Pagan, 1883 ; 10 R. 1072 (father abroad). Ross *v.* Ross, 1885 ; 12 R. 1351 (mother hiding children, or out of jurisdiction). Leys *v.* Leys, 1886 ; 13 R. 1223. Delaney *v.* Colston, 1890 ; 16 R. 753 ; 1891, 19 R. 8. Hutchison *v.* Hutchison, 1890 ; 18 R. 237. Mackellar *v.* Mackellar, 1898 ; 25 R. 883. Cases cited below, (*m*). See below, § 2083.

(*k*) Cruise *v.* Hunter, 2 Br. Chan. Cases, 500 ; 3 Ill. 58. De Manneville *v.* De Manneville, 10 Vesey, jun. 52. Whitfield *v.* Hales, 12 Ves. 492. Shelley *v.* Westbrook, Jacob, 267. Wellesley *v.* Beaufort, 2 Russell, 1 ; aff. 2 Bligh, 124. *In re* Besant, 11 Ch. D. 508.

(*l*) This Act modifies the severity of the Scotch law. See below, § 2083 (*g*). Stevenson *v.* Stevenson, 1894 ; 21 R. 430 ; alt. *ib.* H. L. 96 ; A. C.

(*m*) Morrison *v.* Morrison, 1716 ; M. 410 ; 2 Ill. 311. The last subdivision of this section is transferred by Mr. Shaw from another place (§ 2122). In the previous edition the power of the Court in Scotland to control the father is limited to the case where "the child is in danger from manifest cruelty, oppression, or contamination." See Harvey *v.* Harvey, 1860 ; 22 D. 1198. Robertson, petrs., *cit.* (*d*). Wardrop *v.* Gossling, 1869 ; 7 Macph. 532. Lang *v.* Lang, 1869 ; 7 Macph. 445. Ketchen *v.* Ketchen, 1870 ; 8 Macph. 952. Beattie *v.* Beattie, 1883 ; 11 R. 85. Markey *v.* Colston, 1888 ; 15 R. 921. Cases cited above, (*c*) and (*i*) ; and 24 and 25 Vict. c. 86, § 9 (Conjugal Rights Act). *Supra*, § 1540A.

2069. There is no such power of legal administration in the grandfather (*a*).

(*a*) L. Lamington *v.* Jolly, 1685 ; M. 16,306 ; 3 Ill. 28. See Flannigan *v.* Inspr. of Bothwell, *infra*, § 2090.

2069A. '*Mother as Guardian or Tutrix.*—On the father's death the surviving mother is now the guardian of an infant, either alone when no guardian has been appointed by the father, or jointly with any guardian or tutor appointed by the father as after-mentioned (§ 2070 sqq.). Failing a guardian appointed by the father, the Court of Session, or Sheriff

Court of the district in which the respondents or any of them reside, may, if it shall think fit, from time to time appoint a tutor or tutors to act jointly with the mother (*a*).'

(*a*) 49 and 50 Vict. c. 27, § 2 (Guardianship of Infants Act, 1886). Campbell *v.* Maquay, 1888; 15 R. 784 (mother not disqualified by second marriage). Martin *v.* Stewart, 1888; 16 R. 185. Willison, 1890; 18 R. 228.

2070. Appointment of Tutors.—Tutors are either named by the father; or they take the office by legal title; or are appointed by the sovereign's paternal power.

2071. (1.) *Tutor-Nominate.* — The father alone can 'at common law' nominate tutors by Will (*a*). In doing so he delegates his own power of administration; and all other tutors must yield to his (*b*). One nominated by any other person is only a special guardian, in the character of trustee of special property left to the pupil; and so far the power of the tutor-nominate may be superseded by the appointment of a special guardian in the settlement of a particular estate, for conducting the management of it; the guardian so appointed having the full power of acting with respect to that property (*c*). A tutor-nominate has the same general guardianship, both of estate and person, which the father himself has by whom he is named. A natural child has no recognised father, and so his reputed father cannot appoint tutors, though he may, as a stranger, appoint a special guardian for property left to the pupil (*d*).

(*a*) 1 Ersk. 7. § 2, 3. The King *v.* Oliphant, 1528, and Murray *v.* Marshall, 1555; M. 16,216; 3 Ill. 28. Forbes *v.* Bishop of Caithness, 1613; M. 16,241. See Fraser, P. & C. 174; and below, § 2077A.

(*b*) Auchterlony *v.* Oliphant, 1631; M. 16,258.

(*c*) Scott *v.* Kennedy, 1675; M. 8970, 16,291. Kilpatrick *v.* M'Alpine, 1793; M. 16,381, is doubted. See 3 Ill. 28.

(*d*) Johnston *v.* Clark, 1785; M. 16,374.

2072. The father may name tutors, one or more, in any authentic deed, and may exempt them from liability for omissions, or for others. The nomination may be in a last Will. But the father is thus far under restraint, that he cannot give exemption from the usual responsibility, except in liege poustie; and even then only in relation to estates descending from himself (*a*).

(*a*) 1696, c. 8; 3 Ill. 29. *Infra*, § 2081, 2085. *Supra*, § 1803, 2000 *fin.*, and cases there.

2073. Anyone may be named as tutor who is of the lawful age of twenty-one, except a married woman, who, being herself under the curatory of her husband, cannot act as tutor during the subsistence of her marriage (*a*). 'This disqualification does not extend to a surviving mother becoming tutrix under the Guardianship of Infants Act, 1886 (*b*).' One residing in England may be appointed (*c*).

(*a*) 1 Ersk. 7. § 4 and 12.

(*b*) See above, § 2069A.

(*c*) Bell *v.* Henderson, 1784; M. 16,374; 3 Ill. 31. Robb *v.* Robb, Dec. 22, 1814; F. C. Sandilands *v.* Tenants, 1569; M. 16,231; 3 Ill. 29. E. Wemyss *v.* Charters, 1733; M. 14,702. See Stoddart *v.* Rutherford, June 30, 1812; F. C.; 2 Ill. 298; and Fraser, P. & C. 171, 172. *Infra*, § 2078 (*d*).

2074. If more than one be named, their powers may be regulated so that the nomination shall subsist, or the tutors act, jointly; or by a majority: or with a *sine quo non*; or by a quorum; or by the acceptors or survivors (*a*). Where the nomination is simple, any of those named who accept 'and survive' are tutors entitled to act, and liable *singuli in solidum* (*b*). A joint nomination falls if anyone die or refuse to accept (*c*). If a quorum be named, and the number fall below that of a quorum, the nomination was at one time held not vacated (*d*); but that is not law (*e*). A *sine quo non* has a negative on the acts of the rest (*f*); and the non-acceptance or death of the *sine quo non* vacates the nomination (*g*), unless there be plain indication to the contrary (*h*).

(*a*) 1 Ersk. 7. § 30. Aikenhead *v.* Durham, 1703; M. 14,701; 3 Ill. 30.

(*b*) Ellis *v.* Scott, 1672; M. 14,695; 3 Ill. 29. Young *v.* Watson, 1740; M. 16,346; Elch. *Tutory*, 13. Scott *v.* Stewart, 1834; 7 W. & S. 237. Findlay, etc., petrs., 1855; 17 D. 1014. See Dawson *v.* Stirton, 1863; 2 Macph. 196. *Supra*, § 1993, 2000.

(*c*) M. Montrose *v.* Tutors, 1688; M. 14,697. A case of two *sine quibus non*. But in a joint nomination, as to which see many authorities in Fraser, P. & C. 178, each tutor is a *sine quo non*.

(*d*) Watt *v.* Scrymgeour, 1692; M. 14,700. Css. Callender *v.* E. Linlithgow, 1693; M. 14,701.

(*e*) L. Drumore *v.* Somerville, 1742; M. 14,703. See above, § 1993.

(*f*) Vere *v.* E. Hyndford, 1791; M. 16,378; Bell's Ca. 554.

(*g*) L. Drumore, *supra* (*e*).

(*h*) Same case. Scott *v.* Scott, June 1775; 5 B. Sup. 633; Hailes, 752.

2075. The favour for the father's nomination is so great, that clear indication of an intention to prefer any of those who may be named to the tutor-at-law, will be effectual (*a*).

(*a*) See cases in § 2073 (*b*); and *supra*, § 2074 (*c*). Fairside *v.* Adamson, 1609; M. 14,692; 3 Ill. 29. Young *v.* Watson, 1740; M. 16,346; Elch. *Tut. & Cur.* 13.

2076. Where the nomination has taken effect, it will fall by the death or incapacity of any one of those who are held indispensable in the nomination. But where a father names advisers, with whom his widow or other specially named tutor is to consult, the death or non-acceptance of these persons does not annul the nomination (*a*).

(*a*) Clark *v.* Bakers, 1696 ; M. 16,316 ; 3 Ill. 31.

2077. The father may name a factor along with the tutors; and such factor will have preference to one named by the tutors. He may empower them to appoint one to conduct the affairs (*a*); and, indeed, there is an implied power in this gratuitous office of tutor-nominate to appoint factors to carry on the business necessary. Where persons are appointed trustees, and also named as tutors, and act indiscriminately, they are bound in the character of tutors to make up inventories; and unless exempted, are responsible *singuli in solidum* (*b*). 'But a father cannot appoint trustees that may be assumed to be tutors along with the original trustees; for "tutor incertus dari non potest" (*c*).'

(*a*) Straiton's Tutor *v.* Gray, 1743 ; M. 16,348 ; 3 Ill. 31.
(*b*) Mollison *v.* Murray, 1833 ; 12 S. 237.
(*c*) Walker *v.* Stronach, 1874 ; 2 R. 120.

2077A. '*Appointment of Tutors by Mother.*—By the Guardianship of Infants Act, 1886, the mother may, by deed or will, appoint guardians of her infant after the death of herself and the father (if the infant be then unmarried); and guardians appointed by both parents act jointly (*a*).

'By deed or will she may provisionally appoint guardians to act after her death jointly with the father; and the Court of Session, or Sheriff Court, may, after her death, confirm the appointment, if it be shown that the father is for any reason unfitted to be the sole guardian of his children; or make such other order in respect of the guardianship as it deems right (*b*).'

(*a*) 49 and 50 Vict. c. 27, § 3 (1).
(*b*) *Ib.* § 3 (2).

2078. (2.) *Tutor-at-Law.*—Failing an effectual appointment of tutors-nominate, the child falls to the guardianship of a tutor-at-law. The next male agnate of twenty-five years of age (or of male agnates equally near he who is heir-at-law) is entitled to the office of tutor, if there shall be no effectual nomination by the father (*a*). And a more remote agnate cannot be served while the nearest agnate is not in a situation to claim or accept the office (*b*). He is held to be the best guardian of the pupil's estate, the worst of his person; which is therefore given to the mother or nearest cognate (*c*). One who claims this office ought to be within the jurisdiction of the Court of Session; but it is not settled that this is indispensable (*d*). There is not, as in the Roman law, a plurality of tutors-at-law; only one person can be appointed to that office (*e*).

(*a*) 1 Ersk. 7. § 4, 5. 1474, c. 51 ; 3 Ill. 31. Sinclair *v.* Gordon, 1563 ; M. 16,221. Ruthven *v.* —, 1611 ; M. 16,240. See Fraser, P. & C. 183.
(*b*) Ramsay *v.* Dalhousie, 1688 ; M. 16,313.
(*c*) 1 Ersk. 7. § 7. Higgins *v.* Boyd, 1821 ; 1 S. 49 ; 3 Ill. 35.
(*d*) Hadden *v.* Barr, 1822 ; 1 S. 397. See Ramsay, *supra* (*b*). Bell *v.* Henderson, 1784 ; M. 16,374. Robb *v.* Robb, Dec. 22, 1814 ; F. C. See 3 Ill. 32, and Fenwick *v.* Hannah's Trs., 1893 ; 20 R. 848. *Supra*, § 2073.
(*e*) 1 Ersk. 7. § 5.

2079. The entry of tutor-at-law is by brieve and service, as of right. These points are to be answered by the inquest:—Who is the next agnate of the lawful age of twenty-five, fit to manage his own affairs, and able to give security? Whether he is next heir? And if the nearest agnate be the next heir, who is the nearest cognate (*a*)? The brieve is directed to any judge ordinary. The jury return their verdict on a claim (*b*). A bond of caution to the satisfaction of the clerk to the service (*c*) must be lodged, and the cautioner must be a person within the jurisdiction of the Court of Session (*d*). The brieve is retoured to Chancery, and the extract of the retour is a warrant for a letter of tutory under the quarter-seal, which vests the office; it is the tutor's authority for acting, and finally binds the cautioner, whose bond will otherwise be ineffectual (*e*).

(*a*) 1 Ersk. 7. § 6.
(*b*) It may be advocated or appealed. Godwin *v.* Sawers, 1841 ; F. C. ; 3 D. 996 ; 4 D. 1451. 1 and 2 Vict. c. 86 ; 31 and 32 Vict. c. 100, § 64 sqq.
(*c*) Liddel *v.* Ure, 1748 ; M. 13,965 ; 3 Ill. 32. See § 10 and 26 of 12 and 13 Vict. c. 51.
(*d*) Hadden *v.* Barr, 1822 ; 1 S. 397.
(*e*) 3 Bell's Forms, 258–9. See Liddel, *supra* (*c*).

2080. (3.) *Tutor-Dative* (*a*).—Failing tutors-nominate, and a tutor-at-law, the royal authority is granted in Exchequer, 'now by the Court of Session as the Court of Exchequer,' to a person or persons to act for the pupil as tutors-dative (*b*). The application is by signature presented in Exchequer, with consent of the two next of kin, after a year (*c*) allowed to the tutor-at-law to deliberate whether to enter; or by a summons, the next of kin being cited to appear (*d*). A warrant for a gift of tutory is issued under the condition of finding caution (*e*). There may be more than one tutor-dative, and with various modifications of a quorum, *sine quo non*, etc. (*f*); and a woman may be named (*g*). The authority of tutors-dative, when two or more are appointed, terminates by the death of one of them; and the cautioner for a factor named by them is not liable for his subsequent acts (*h*).

(*a*) See Fraser, P. & C. 190.
(*b*) 2 Will. IV. c. 54. 2 and 3 Vict. c. 36, § 4. 19 and 20 Vict. c. 56, § 19. 20 and 21 Vict. c. 57. The nearest male agnate may be appointed tutor-dative. Urquhart, petr., 1860; 22 D. 932. Simpson, petr., 1861; 23 D. 1292.
(*c*) Martin, petr., 1859; 22 D. 45. Simpson, petr., *cit.*
(*d*) 1672, c. 2.
(*e*) See 12 and 13 Vict. c. 51, § 26. Grant, petr., 1848; 10 D. 1052.
(*f*) 1 Stair, 6. § 14. Stewart *v.* Baikie & Scott, 1829; 7 S. 330; and 10 S. 392; 3 Ill. 32; rev. 1834, 7 W. & S. 211.
(*g*) A. *v.* B., 1548; M. 16,222.
(*h*) Stewart, *supra* (*f*), as reversed. See Fraser, P. & C. 192.

2081. Administration of Tutors.—There is some difference to be observed, as to the mode of entering on the administration of their office, between tutors of different classes.

(1.) *Caution and Inventories.*—A tutor-nominate is entitled to enter on his duties immediately, and without finding caution; a tutor-at-law, or dative, only after finding caution, and the issuing of the letter or gift (*a*).

In all cases 'formerly, but since the Pupils Protection Act (1849), in the case of tutors-nominate only,' inventories must be made up, as a check on the administration of the tutor (*b*). When this is neglected, the tutors have no legal power to act, and debtors are not bound to pay to them; they are not allowed any expenses (however necessary or profitable) of legal proceedings or diligence; are not entitled to charge against the estate or pupil any expenditure, except for the pupil's maintenance, or the repairs of houses or occasions of the estate; nor sums lent out, and lost by failure of the debtor or of security; and they forfeit the benefit of any exemption which may have been granted from responsibility for omissions, and are liable *singuli in solidum* (*c*). In the proceeding for making up inventories, the next of kin on both sides are called, unless they shall be abroad (*d*); a person is appointed by the judge to examine the correctness of the inventory; three copies are lodged with the judge ordinary of the place of the pupil's residence, subscribed by the tutors,—one for the next of kin on either side, and one for recording. On the judge's sanction, the inventories are recorded, and an act is extracted bearing the names of the subscribers, and of the persons in whose custody the copies are left. The inventories must specify the lands, bonds, debts, and moveables; and no debtor is bound to pay whose debt is not there stated. Where additional property is acquired, it must be added or *eiked* to the inventory after a similar course of proceeding. 'If the parent was illegitimate, the proceeding will be authorised at sight of the relations on the mother's side (*e*).'

(*a*) See Pupils Prot. Act, 12 and 13 Vict. c. 51, § 26.
(*b*) See below, § 2081A.
(*c*) 1672, c. 2; 3 Ill. 32. Act of Sed., Feb. 28, 1693; 3 Ill. 33. Murray *v.* Strachan, 1832; 10 S. 276; 1833, 11 S. 663. Mollison *v.* Murray, 1833; 12 S. 237.
(*d*) Cruickshank, etc., petrs., Feb. 11, 1819; F. C. Hobbs, etc., petrs., 1831; 9 S. 841. Shields' Trs., petrs., 1832; 10 S. 282. Thomson, petr., 1855; 18 D. 193.
(*e*) Auchincloss, etc., petrs., 1831; 9 S. 300; 3 Ill. 33. Wilson *v.* Alexander, 1859; 21 D. 736. Kyle, petr., 1861; 23 D. 1104.

2081A. 'Since the passing of the Pupils Protection Act (1849), tutors-at-law, tutors-dative, and judicial factors, instead of making up inventories, are required, within six months after their bond of caution is received, to lodge with the Accountant of the Court of Session a detailed rental of all lands under their management, a list of all moneys and funds belonging and debts due to the estate, specifying the securities, vouchers, etc., and an inventory of furniture, farm-stocking, and goods belonging to the estate. They are bound also to recover and produce to the Accountant all writings and documents of importance. The rental, list, and inventory, when adjusted and approved by the Accountant, are signed by him and the tutor, and form a ground of charge against the tutor, being declared equivalent to the tutorial inventory under the statute. Additions must be made if new claims or property are discovered, and these are equivalent to an *eik*. Tutors-at-law and tutors-dative cannot enter upon their office till the rental, list, and inventory are lodged (*a*).'

(*a*) 12 and 13 Vict. c. 51, § 3, 25, 30. A. of S., Dec. 11, 1849; and Feb. 1, 1850. 52 Vict. c. 39, § 6, and see below, § 2117, etc.

2082. (2.) *Actions.*—Tutors act alone, the pupil having no legal person. But all proceedings ought to be in the pupil's name, as well as in that of the tutor; and in all actions the pupil ought to be called as a party (*a*).

(*a*) See **E. Craven** *v.* **L. Elibank's Trs.**, 1854; 16 D. 811. *Supra*, § 2067.

2083. (3.) *Custody and Education of the Pupil.*—In their powers over the person there is a distinction among tutors. The tutor-nominate, having the entire confidence of the father, is entrusted with the care of the person after seven years of age; but not if he be next heir, or has made a purchase of the succession (*a*). This care of the person entitles the tutor to direct the education and place of residence (*b*), but subject to the control of the Court of Session (*c*). The mother has the custody of an infant pupil till seven; unless she be unfit for the charge, as on account of a second marriage, having had a natural child, or the health or nurture of the child forbid it (*d*); the superintendence of education being with the tutor. Failing the mother, the custody is with the tutor-nominate; or even the tutor-at-law, if not heir; or with the nearest cognate if there be no tutor-nominate (*e*).

'The Court of Session or Sheriff Court may, on the mother's application (*f*), make such order as it may think fit regarding the custody of an infant and the right of access thereto of either parent, having regard to the welfare of the infant, the conduct of the parents, and to the wishes of the mother as well as the father; and may alter, vary, or discharge such order on the application of either parent, or of a tutor under the Act of 1886, after the death of either parent; and in every case may make an order regarding the mother's costs and the father's liability for them (*g*). The Court will, it seems, interfere on the application of other relatives of pupil children, if a case for its interference be alleged and made out; but it is by no means clearly defined what such a case is (*h*).

'The Custody of Children Act, 1891, makes certain provisions as to the powers and duties of the Court of Session when a parent applies for the production of a child, particularly when the child is being brought up by another person, or parochial board; and as to the religious education of such children (*i*).

'The Court, which pronounces a decree of judicial separation or of divorce, may thereby declare the parent by reason of whose misconduct the decree is made, to be unfit to have the custody of the children; and in such case that parent is not, on the death of the other, entitled as of right to the custody or guardianship of the children (*k*). The statutory provision scarcely enlarges or affects the inherent powers of the Court (*l*).

'Under the Criminal Law Amendment Act, a Court before which it is proved that certain offences committed against girls under sixteen years of age have been caused, encouraged, or favoured by the father, mother, or other guardian, may appoint another guardian to such girl (*m*).'

(*a*) Edgar *v.* Inglis, 1606; M. 16,237; 3 Ill. 34. Chalmers *v.* L. Gadgirth, 1611; M. 16,239. Gibson *v.* Dunnett, 1824; 3 S. 249. This was the old rule; but in modern practice the child will not be separated from the mother even after that age without some valid reason. Campbell, *cit.* (*d*). See Johnston *v.* Otto, 1848; 11 D. 718. A. B. *v.* C. D., 1850; 12 D. 1297. Fraser, P. &. C. 218. See Borthwick *v.* Dundas, 1845; 8 D. 318. Morton *v.* Thorburn, *infra* (*d*).

(*b*) Scott *v.* Scott, 1759; M. 16,361. Walker *v.* Walker, 1824; 2 S. 788.

(*c*) Reoch *v.* Robb, Nov. 19, 1817; F. C. See Borthwick, *cit.* Speirs, petr., 1854; 17 D. 289. Stuart *v.* Moore (M. Bute's Case), 1860; 22 D. 1504; 1861, 23 D. 51, 446; rev. 4 Macq. 1; 23 D. 902; 23 D. 779. Fenwick *v.* Hannah's Trs., 1893; 20 R. 848.

(*d*) Walker, *supra* (*b*). Fisher *v.* Fletcher, 1827; 6 S. 270. Morton *v.* Thorburn, 1835; 13 S. 640. Campbell *v.* Campbell, 1833; 11 S. 544. Paul, petr., 1838; 16 S. 822. Borthwick *v.* Dundas, 1845; 8 D. 318. Kennedy *v.* Steele, 1841; 4 D. 12. Denny *v.* M'Nish, 1863; 1 Macph. 268. M'Callum *v.* M'Donald, 1853; 15 D. 535. Muir *v.* Milligan, 1868; 6 Macph. 1125. Gulland *v.* Henderson, 1878; 5 R. 768. Couper *v.* Riddell, 1872; 44 S. Jur. 484.

(*e*) Higgins, petr., 1821; 1 S. 50. Robertson *v.* Elphinston, May 28, 1814; F. C. Stuart *v.* Moore, *cit.*

(*f*) Stevenson *v.* Stevenson, 1894; 21 R. H. L. 96.

(*g*) 49 and 50 Vict. c. 27, § 5. Maquay *v.* Campbell, 1888; 15 R. 606. Beedie *v.* Beedie, 1889; 16 R. 648.

(*h*) Morrison *v.* Quarrier, 1894; 21 R. 889, 1071, and cases cited there. Reilly *v.* Quarrier, 1895 ; 22 R. 879. Kincaid *v.* Quarrier, 1896 ; 23 R. 676 (*mora*).

(*i*) 54 Vict. c. 3. Campbell *v.* Croall, 1895 ; 22 R. 869. Soutar *v.* Carrie, 1894 ; 21 R. 1050 (repayment of costs of upbringing).

(*k*) 49 and 50 Vict. c. 27, § 7.

(*l*) See above, § 1540. As to the jurisdiction of the Sheriff Court in a mother's application for the custody of a bastard, see Brand *v.* Shaws, 1888 ; 15 R. 449 ; and above, § 2062.

(*m*) 48 and 49 Vict. c. 69, § 12.

2084. (4.) *Estate and Funds.* — In this respect all tutors are on the same footing. 1. Tutors may intromit with, sue, receive, or discharge debts due to the pupil.

2. *Leases.*—They 'might at common law' grant leases to continue during their office (*a*), but not at an under value. The Court of Session, however, authorised a tutor-testamentary, on his making it manifest that rents would fall on a short or precarious lease, to let farms by roup for nineteen years (*b*). 'Leases of ordinary administration are now authorised by the Court, not only under the Pupils Protection Act, in the case of tutors-at-law, tutors-dative, and judicial factors, but also on the application of tutors-nominate.' Tutors have also been authorised to renounce a lease to which the pupil has succeeded, when it threatened to become ruinous to the child (*c*). The proper form is a declarator, with the report of persons of skill; but it has been done on a summary application (*d*). It would seem justifiable, if not a necessary 'common law' power of administration in tutors, to grant abatements of rent to tenants, when required by the state of the country (*e*); 'and by the Pupils Protection Act, provisions are made for judicial factors applying to the Court of Session, where "there is a strong expediency," for granting abatement of rent, renewing or granting a lease for a period of years, for draining or otherwise improving the estate (*f*).'

3. Tutors may enter vassals. 4. They may implement the ancestor's obligations, in order to save the expense of an adjudication of the pupil's estate (*g*).

5. *Selling or Burdening the Estate.*—They have no power to sell or burden (*h*) the heritable estate, except in cases of absolute necessity, either from the nature of the subject (*i*), or on account of debt (*k*), 'or for the maintenance of the pupil (*l*).' But to show this, an action of cognition and sale is competent, and 'was, under the earlier practice,' necessary before the Court of Session, in which heirs and creditors must be called (*m*). 'But powers to tutors and similar officers are now regularly given upon application by summary petition (*n*).'

6. They may purchase land with the pupil's money, but not in their own name (*o*). 7. They may change securities, but not to the effect of altering the pupil's succession (*p*). 8. When in an entail an alternative is given to choose between two estates, there must be a power to make election; but this seems to require the authority of the Court of Session (*q*). 9. They may transact or compromise claims which are doubtful or intricate (*r*). 10. They may submit to arbitration (*s*). 11. They cannot engage the pupil in copartnership 'or place, or even, where the business is hazardous, leave his funds in trade' (*t*). 12. No tutor can be *auctor in rem suam* (*u*); a rule which in England has been carried farther than hitherto in Scotland, and on principles recognised in both (*v*). 13. Tutors may not in general encroach on the pupil's capital, for the pupil's maintenance or education; but circumstances may justify this (*w*). 14. They are not entitled to take titles to land in their own name, and were in one case held bound, having done so, to denude simply, without being allowed to retain for security of the pupil on her marriage (*x*).

(*a*) Hallows, petr., 1794 ; M. 14,981 ; 3 Ill. 36. L. Reay *v.* Anderson, 1800 ; M. 16,385. Ross *v.* Ross, March 9, 1820 ; F. C. See above, § 1184.

(*b*) Forbes, petr., 1838 ; 1 D. 355. See above, § 1184. 12 and 13 Vict. c. 51, § 7. Fraser, P. & C. 257.

(*c*) Cockburn's Tutors *v.* Cockburn, 1825 ; 3 S. 642. Meikle *v.* Meikle, 1823 ; 2 S. 242 ; 3 Ill. 53. Turner, petr., 1862 ; 24 D. 694.

(*d*) Carrick, petr., 1829 ; 7 S. 848 ; 8 S. 208. Brown's Tutors, petrs., 1867 ; 5 Macph. 1046.

(*e*) Annand *v.* Grant, March, 7, 1817 ; F. C. See Grant's Cur., petr., 1880 ; 7 R. 1011.

(*f*) 12 and 13 Vict. c. 51, § 7. Grant's Cur., *cit.* Sinclair *v.* Wemyss, 1882 ; 9 R. 1131 (power refused to build mansion). Semple *v.* Tennent, 1888 ; 15 R. 810 (cost of new mansion disallowed in curator's accounts).

(*g*) E. Aberdeen *v.* Laird, 1823 ; 2 S. 527 ; 2 Ill. 92. Fraser, P. & C. 253.

(*h*) Scott's Trs. *v.* Scott, 1887 ; 14 R. 1043.

(*i*) Plummer *v.* Plummer, 1757 ; M. 16,358.

(*k*) Colt *v.* Colt, 1800 ; M. 16,387. Vere *v.* Dale, 1804 ; M. 16,389. Finlayson *v.* Finlayson, Dec. 22, 1810 ; F. C. Bellamy, petr., 1854 ; 17 D. 115. Mackenzie, petr., 1855 ; 17 D. 314. White, petr., 1855 ; 17 D. 599. Fraser, P. & C. 248 sqq. Parrot *v.* Fraser, 1810 ; Hume, 889. Grant, petr., 1889 ; 16 R. 365 (to pay provisions). Special power to feu as a necessary act of administration was granted to a father as administrator-in-law in L. Clinton, petr., 1875 ; 3 R. 62 ; and to a tutor-nominate in Campbell, petr., 1880 ; 7 R. 1032.

(*l*) Mackenzie, petr., 1866 ; 5 Macph. 158. Here power

to sell was granted to a tutor-nominate, but a *curator bonis* was appointed to receive the money. See below (*w*). The rule in Colt's Case, adopted by the L. Pr. (Inglis) in L. Clinton, *cit.*, is—"The Court may with propriety sanction an alienation of a pupil's heritage, when the sale is necessary for payment of debt, for the pupil's aliment, and in case of urgency to avoid loss. But the Court ought not to interfere merely from views of procuring future advantage to the minor."

(*m*) Beatson, petr., Feb. 24, 1810; F. C., and Colt, *cit.* (*k*). See Fraser, P. & C. 493 sq.

(*n*) See 12 and 13 Vict. c. 51. 20 and 21 Vict. c. 56, § 4. Mackay's Practice of the Court of Session, ii. 351 sqq. Fraser, P. & C., *l.c.*

(*o*) L. Kennedy *v.* Innes, 1823; 2 S. 375. Lambe *v.* Chapman, 1835; 12 S. 775.

(*p*) Ross *v.* Ross' Trs., 1793; M. 5545; 2 Ill. 225. Graham *v.* E. Hopetoun, 1798; M. 5599. Morton *v.* Young, Feb. 11, 1813; F. C.; 2 Ill. 283. L. Adv. *v.* Anstruther, 1843; 13 D. 450. Moncrieff *v.* Miln, 1856; 18 D. 1286. *Supra*, § 1486, 1487, etc.

(*q*) Cuningham Bontine *v.* Graham, 1838; 1 D. 286.

(*r*) Aikenhead *v.* Aikenhead, 1711; M. 16,331. Balfour *v.* Forbes, 1700; M. 16,318; 3 Ill. 37. *Quære* as to claims affecting heritage? Bell on Arbitration, 101. Fraser, P. & C. 24[illegible].

(*s*) Aiton *v.* Scott, 1711; M. 16,331. See Aberdeen Town and County Bank *v.* Dean & Son, 1871; 9 Macph. 842. *Supra*, § 1998 (2), 1998A.

(*t*) See 2 Bell's Com. 624. Accountant of Court *v.* Baird, 1858; 20 D. 1176. Lumsden *v.* Buchanan, 1866; 5 Macph. 34. Bontine's Curator, petr., 1870; 8 Macph. 976. Fraser, P. & C. 266. *Supra*, § 2000 (4).

(*u*) Wilson *v.* Wilson, 1789; M. 16,376. Elphinston *v.* Robertson, May 28, 1814; F. C. Fraser, P. & C. 279 sqq. See above, § 1998.

(*v*) See in England the general principle, in Wright *v.* Proud, 13 Ves. 135, and other cases cited. Lyles *v.* Terry, 1895; 2 Q. B. 685. Hylton *v.* Hylton, 2 Ves. sen. 547.

(*w*) Sandilands *v.* Telfer, 1680; M. 16,300; Blair *v.* Mitchell, 1802; M. 16,388. Dss. Gordon *v.* L. Adv., 1755; M. 16,356; 3 Ill. 43. *Supra* (*l*). Kennedy *v.* Rutherglen, 1860; 22 D. 567. Milne, petr., 1888; 15 R. 437. As to expenditure where the pupil's income is large, *e.g.* on allowance to his mother, etc., see Munnoch *v.* Munnoch, 1836; 15 S. 302. Munnoch *v.* M'Ewan, 1842; 4 D. 662.

(*x*) L. Kennedy, *supra* (*o*).

2084A. '*Application to Court for Direction.*—In the event of guardians being unable to agree upon a question affecting the welfare of a pupil, any of them may apply to the Court of Session, or the Sheriff Court, for its direction, and the Court may make such orders regarding the matters in difference as it shall think proper (*a*).'

(*a*) 49 and 50 Vict. c. 27, § 3 (3).

2085. Responsibility of Tutors.—Tutors seem in general, 'according to one case,' not to be liable *singuli in solidum*, but each only for his own intromissions (*a*). 'But the authorities rather show that they are all liable for each other, without the benefit of discussion or division (*b*); with relief *inter se* according to their actual intromissions (*c*).' At least it is a legitimate and effectual qualification in a nomination of tutors, that they shall not be liable for each other: in which case, the Court on a petition will dispense with calling as defenders those not directly liable (*d*). In the construction of the statute and Act of Sederunt, the neglect of inventories renders the tutor *suspect*, as well as chargeable with omissions, and liable to forfeiture of expenses debursed (*e*). But this, as being a penalty, does not transmit against heirs (*f*).

(*a*) M'Murdoch *v.* Findlay, 1699; M. 3509.

(*b*) 1 Stair, 6. § 23. 1 Ersk. 7. § 27. Fraser, P. & C. 303, 372. More's Notes on Stair, 38. Murray *v.* Murray, 1833; 11 S. 661. Logan *v.* Meiklejohn, 1843; 5 D. 1072. See above, § 1999.

(*c*) Guthrie *v.* Guthrie, 1630; M. 14,640. Rose *v.* Lockhart, 1829; 1 S. Jur. 369. Fraser, P. & C. 305.

(*d*) See above, § 2000.

(*e*) Thomson *v.* Waddell, June 16, 1812; F. C. Gibson & Thomson *v.* Sharp, Dec. 21, 1811; F. C. Austin *v.* Wallace, 1826; 5 S. 177. See cases of Gibson, Kennedy, Cathcart, Turnbull, Guthrie—M. 16,299, 16,319. Henderson *v.* Henderson, 1788; M. 16,375; aff. 3 Pat. 283. Rob *v.* Rob, Dec. 22, 1814; F. C. 1672, c. 2. But neglect to make up inventories or the equivalent under the Act does not *per se* infer fraud. Morrison *v.* Morrison, 1841; 4 D. 337. See 12 and 13 Vict. c. 51, § 3, 14, 21, 25, etc.; and on the general subject of the responsibility of tutors, Seton *v.* Dawson, 1841; 4 D. 310. Miller's Trs. *v.* Miller, 1848; 10 D. 765. Stevenson's Trs. *v.* Dunbreck, 1857; 19 D. 462. Thomson *v.* Christie, 1852; 1 Macq. 236. Urquhart *v.* Brown, 1843; 5 D. 1142. Murray *v* Murray, 1833; 11 S. 663. Scott *v.* Gray, 1862; 1 Macph. 57.

(*f*) Lady C. Graham *v.* E. Hopetoun, 1798; M. 5599. M'Turk *v.* Greig, 1838; 8 S. 995.

2086. Expiration of Office.—Tutors once accepting cannot renounce. The office expires by the death of either tutor or pupil, and is terminated by puberty; after which the tutor cannot act, and is not bound to answer as tutor (*a*). His acts subsequently are null, and his discharge for money paid is ineffectual to the debtor (*b*). Tutors 'might under the earlier practice' be removed as suspect, by action in the Court of Session; not by summary complaint; 'but in later cases it has been done upon summary petition (*c*); and by the Pupils Protection Act, all guardians appointed after its date, except testamentary tutors and a few others, are placed under the superintendence of the Accountant of the Court of Session, who may proceed against them by summary complaint (*d*). Still wider powers of removing tutors, and of appointing others in place of those removed, are conferred on the Court of Session by the Guardianship of Infants Act, 1886 (*e*).'

(*a*) A. *v.* B., 1533; M. 16,218; 3 Ill. 38. Cass *v.* Ellies, 1672; M. 1625.

(*b*) Lockhart *v.* Trotter (M'Kenzie), 1826; 5 S. 136; aff. 3 W. & S. 481.

(*c*) Butchart *v.* Butchart, 1851; 13 D. 1258. But see Dewar, petr., 1853; 16 D. 163, 489. Fleming *v.* Craig,

1863; 1 Macph. 850. Mitchell, petr., 1864; 2 Macph. 1378. Any near relative of the pupil has a title to sue in such proceedings. 1 Stair, 6. § 26. Austin *v.* Wallace, 1826; 5 S. 177. Welsh *v.* Welsh, 1778; M. 16,373; Hailes, 778; 5 B. S. 634.

(*d*) 12 and 13 Vict. c. 51, § 25, 31.

(*e*) 49 and 50 Vict. c. 27, § 6.

2087. Mutual Actions.—(1.) *Actions by Pupils against the Tutors.*—These actions are against the tutor and his cautioner for an account of intromissions, and for delivery of deeds to the pupil. The rules of accounting are,—to charge the tutors according to the inventory (*a*): to charge them with the interest which has been or might have been made upon the funds by depositing them in bank (*b*), 'as well as with all profits actually made by the employment of the funds (*c*)'; to require them to communicate all "eases" which they have received in settling transactions, and to give the benefit of all improvements or rights acquired to the pupil (*d*).

'*The accounts* must be brought to an annual balance, and bank interest allowed *de die in diem* to the end of the year, the balance above expenditure being lent out on heritable or other permitted security, if possible, within three months from the end of the year. Bank interest is chargeable against the tutor on such balances before, and the interest obtainable on heritable security after, the three months (*e*).'

The pupil will also have an action of damages against his tutors on account of any transaction or deed on their part to his hurt and injury, and against which he cannot obtain redress by action of restitution. But this action must be brought, or the privilege of minority for restitution resorted to, within the *quadriennium utile* (*f*); the elapse of which time without challenge will operate as homologation (*g*).

Judicial Discharge.—'**A discharge obtained from the Court of Session by a tutor falling within the scope of the Pupils Protection Act is final and conclusive against all parties concerned, though pronounced in absence, unless it shall be opened up as a decree in absence in the Court of Session within the time limited for appealing to the House of Lords, or shall be appealed against within that time (*h*).**'

(2.) *Actions by Tutors against Pupil.*—An action also lies at the instance of the tutors against the pupil, for reimbursement of money laid out for him, 'with interest at five per cent. on advances (*i*)'; for relief of engagements undertaken; for discharge of accounts of intromission, in which, however, there must be no charge for trouble or remuneration of risk (*k*), unless the tutor be law agent or professional accountant for the other tutors 'under a special power to that effect' (*l*). The action prescribes in ten years (*m*). And it has been held that the tutor does not lose the benefit of 'the decennial' prescription 'of tutorial accounts' by omitting to make up inventories (*n*).

(*a*) *Supra*, § 2081. The inventory puts the *onus* on the tutor of accounting for its contents; but it is not conclusive either against him or to show that the pupil had not other property. See Fraser, P. & C. 321. Butchart *v.* Butchart. 1863; 1 Macph. 1123.

(*b*) Lady Montgomerie *v.* Wauchope, June 4, 1822: F. C.; 1 S. 491; 4 Dow, 110; 1 Ill. 40. *Infra*, § 2117.

(*c*) Laird *v.* Laird, 1855; 17 D. 984. Guthrie, petr., 1853; 16 D. 214. Cochrane *v.* Black, 1855; 17 D. 321; 1857, 19 D. 1019. *Supra*, § 1999.

(*d*) Cochran *v.* Cochran, 1732: M. 16,339; 3 Ill. 39. Wilsons *v.* Wilson, 1789; M. 16,376. V. Oxenford *v.* Curators, 1671; M. 4417. Fraser, P. & C. 289, 322, 324, etc.

(*e*) L. Montgomerie, *cit.* Haldane, petr., 1848; 11 D. 286. Accountant of Court *v.* Geddes, 1858; 20 D. 1174. A. B., petr., 1854; 16 D. 1004. Morison, petr., 1856; 19 D. 132. As to tutors-dative and tutors-at-law, see 12 and 13 Vict. c. 51, § 5, 15–17, 33, 37, etc.

(*f*) See below, § 2099.

(*g*) Cuningham *v.* Curators, 1727; M. 16,338; 3 Ill. 44. See § 2099.

(*h*) 12 and 13 Vict. c. 51, § 34.

(*i*) Condie *v.* M'Donald, 1834; 13 S. 61. Stuart *v.* Stevenson, 1828; 6 S. 591.

(*k*) M'Donald *v.* Muir, 1780; M. 13,437; and above, § 2066.

(*l*) Lady Montgomerie, *supra* (*b*). See above, § 2066. Observe that while at common law a discharge can be obtained only by way of ordinary action as here stated (Marjoribanks, petr., 1816; 9 D. 168), tutors and factors falling under the Pupils Protection Act obtain discharge on a summary petition. *Supra* (*h*); *infra*, § 2119.

(*m*) See *supra*, § 635.

(*n*) 1696, c. 9. Mercer *v.* Irvine, 1736; M. 10,996; 3 Ill. 34. Gowans *v.* Oswald, 1831; 10 S. 144.

II. CURATORY, OR GUARDIANSHIP OF MINORS.

2088. Definition and Effect of Minority.—**Minority is a state, not of total incapacity like pupillarity, but of limited capacity; in which the minor is held capable of consent, but of inferior judgment or discretion, requiring the protection of the law (*a*). The rules are: That a minor or his representatives have redress against any deed attended with lesion; that where curators have been named or are chosen as guardians of the minor, all**

deeds '*inter vivos* affecting his property' are null which have not their assent (*b*); that the appointment of guardians, while to a certain extent it protects the minor, is not conclusive to bar a challenge where lesion can be proved (*c*).

(*a*) Koehler *v.* Neidrick, 1772: M. 8975; 3 Ill. 25. 1 Stair, 6. § 44. 1 Ersk. 7. § 34. Harvey *v.* Harvey, 1860; 22 D. 1198. Hill *v.* City of Glasgow Bk., 1879; 7 R. 68.

(*b*) 1 Ersk. 7. § 34. Kincaid *v.* Johnston, 1561; M. 8979; 3 Ill. 40. Bruce *v.* Bruce, 1569; M. 16,231. Robertson *v.* Oswald, 1584; M. 8980. Hamilton *v.* Hamilton, 1587; M. 8981. Paterson *v.* Wishart, 1613; M. 16,241. Bell *v.* Crawford, 1687; M. 16,310. Harvie *v.* Gordon, 1726; M. 5712. Bell *v.* Sutherland, 1728; M. 8985. Fraser, P. & C. 385. Thomson *v.* Stewart, 1840; 2 D. 564 (effect of long prescription as against the plea of nullity). Manuel *v.* Manuel, 1853; 15 D. 284.

(*c*) 1 Stair, 6. § 44. 1 Ersk. 7. § 34, *in fin.* Clerk's Crs. *v.* Gordon, 1699; M. 3668. Thomson *v.* Stevenson, 1666; M. 8982. See below, § 2098.

2089. While the last Will of a minor is as effectual as that of a major (*a*), a disposition or settlement of land *mortis causâ* by a minor is null (*b*). So also are all acts by a minor having curators, without their concurrence (*c*).

(*a*) Stevenson *v.* Allans, 1680; M. 8949; 3 Ill. 40. Yorkston *v.* Shiells, 1697; M. 8950. See Waddell *v.* Waddell, 1739; M. 8965; Elch. *Prov. to Heirs.* 1 Ersk. 7. § 33.

(*b*) M. Clydesdale *v.* E. Dundonald, 1726; M. 8964 and 1265; Robertson's App. 564. Hunter *v.* ——, 1728; M. 8964. M'Culloch *v.* M'Culloch, 1731; M. 8965. Cunyngham *v.* Whitefoord, 1797; M. 8966. Irvine *v.* Tait, 1808; M. Apx. *Deathbed,* 6. It is said that this rule does not apply to what is only heritable by destination. Brand's Trs. *v.* Brand's Trs., 1874; 2 R. 258.

(*c*) But this is not without qualification, *e.g.* if the minor be engaged in trade; and an ante-nuptial marriage contract is reducible only on proof of lesion. Bruce *v.* Hamilton, 1854; 17 D. 265. *Infra,* § 2100, *in fin.*; *supra,* 2088 (*a*), (*b*).

2090. Minor's Person.—A minor's person is not subject to the control of curators (*a*). '*Tutor datur personæ, curator rei* (*b*).'

(*a*) Kincaid *v.* Johnston, 1561; M. 16,228; 3 Ill. 40. Scot *v.* Kennedy, 1675; M. 16,291; 1 B. Sup. 747. Anstruther *v.* Murray, 1694; 4 B. Sup. 159. Graham *v.* Graham, 1780; M. 8934; Hailes, 860; 5 B. Sup. 635. Harvey *v.* Harvey, 1860; 22 D. 1207. See Flannigan *v.* Inspr. of Bothwell, 1892; 19 R. 909 (application by a grandmother for custody of a pauper *minor pubes* refused).

(*b*) 4 Inst. 1. § 14 (*qui testam.*). 1 Ersk. 7. § 14. Fraser, P. & C. 143, 363. Savigny, vom Beruf unserer Zeit für Gesetzgebung, etc., 101–106.

2091. Evidence of Minority.—This depends on the proof of the time of birth, and 'minority' extends from the age of 14 in males, or of 12 in females, to 21 (*a*).

(*a*) Wilson *v.* Aitken. 1626; M. 12,700; 3 Ill. 40. Bell *v.* Wilson, 1639; M. 8493. Thomson *v.* Stevenson, 1667; M. 12,701. Hay *v.* Bantin, 1683; M. 9045. Sutherland *v.* Morson, 1825; 3 S. 449, a plea of personal bar by representations—comp. Gibb *v.* Crombie, 1875; 2 R. 886. See below, § 2100 *fin.*

2092. Father Legal Administrator.—As the father is *ipso jure* tutor to his infant child, so is he curator to the minor; and this to the effect of annulling deeds granted without the father's concurrence, or in which he is *auctor in rem suam* (*a*).

(*a*) 1 Ersk. 6. § 54, 55. M'Kenzie *v.* Fairholm, 1666; M. 8961; 3 Ill. 41. M'Gibbon *v.* M'Gibbon, 1852; 14 D. 605. Stevenson *v.* Adair, 1872; 10 Macph. 919. See below, § 2098. If the father declines to concur in an action by the minor, or has an adverse interest, or the minor has no curators, a curator *ad litem* will be appointed; but the omission to do so does not invalidate the proceedings; lesion must be proved. M'Connochie *v.* Bennie, 1847; 9 D. 791. Cunningham *v.* Smith, 1880; 7 R. 424. See as to the father's power over minor children, Harvey *v.* Harvey, 1860; 22 D. 1198. Edgar *v.* Fisher, 1893; 21 R. 59, 325, 1076; and as to the remedy when his conduct is injurious to the ward's interests, above, § 2068 (2).

2093. Curators named by the Father.—As he has the nomination of tutors during pupillarity, the father may also, in liege poustie (*a*), name curators to his child, and thus delegate his right of administration during minority (*b*). Curators so named supersede or bar a nomination of curators by the minor (*c*); but it was held in one case that the father's nomination could not, under the statute, compel his son to act with the persons named (*d*). The father in liege poustie may exempt curators from omissions. The guardianship extends over the whole concerns of the minor (*e*).

(*a*) Greig *v.* Greig, 1872; 11 Macph. 20.

(*b*) 1696, c. 8; 10 Acta Parl. p. 34, c. 8. As to the acceptance of such curators, see Bruce *v.* Hamilton, 1854; 17 D. 265.

(*c*) Primrose *v.* E. Rosebery, 1715; M. 16,335; 3 Ill. 41. Pitcairns *v.* Curators, 1731; M. 16,339. Bruce, *cit.*

(*d*) L. Drumore *v.* Murray, 1744; M. 16,349. See below, § 2096.

(*e*) 1696, c. 8. 1 Ersk. 7. § 11.

2094. Curators named by a Stranger.—One who gives or leaves an estate to the minor may appoint a special curator for managing it during minority, as he may appoint a special tutor during pupillarity; but this 'curator is merely a trustee or factor, and his' guardianship is limited to the estate or subject (*a*).

(*a*) 1 Ersk. 7. § 13. Scot *v.* Kennedy, 1675; M. 8970, 16,291; 1 B. Sup. 747; 3 Ill. 41. Wilson *v.* Campbell, March 10, 1819; F. C. (bastard). See Fraser, P. & C. 174, 354.

2095. Curators named by the Minor.—A minor may name curators, according to a certain proceeding pointed out by statute (*a*).

An edict is issued by the Sheriff on the minor's application; or he raises a summons before the Court of Session, in either of which there is a warrant to cite two of the nearest of kin on either side, who are within the kingdom at the time (*b*). Where the minor is a natural child, or where there are no next of kin in Scotland, the Court has authorised 'him to choose' curators, after intimation in the minute-book (*c*). The minor, either personally in court or by deed, names curators (*d*). 'He cannot name a married woman (*e*).' They accept and find caution (*f*); and the Court sanctions the appointment, and decerns the persons chosen to be curators. An inventory is made up and recorded; and an act of curatory is extracted, containing the inventory, which is the curator's title to act. The minor cannot in his nomination of curators give them the same exemption from omissions which the statute authorises a father to declare (*g*). In order to prevent as much as possible the minor from being unduly influenced or compelled in the election of curators, the Court of Session will, on application, place him in neutral custody (*h*).

(*a*) 1555, c. 35; 3 Ill. 41. 1 Ersk. 7. § 11. As to the appointment of a *curator bonis* to minors, see the cases in Fraser, P. & C. 457.

(*b*) Wallace *v.* Kennedy, 1674; M. 290. See as to procedure, Fraser, P. & C. 354. 2 Mackay's Practice, 293 sqq. Dove Wilson's Sh. Ct. Practice, 502.

(*c*) Young, petr., Feb. 19, 1818; F. C. Cruickshank, petr., Feb. 11, 1819; F. C.; 3 Ill. 33. See Wilson *v.* Campbell, March 10, 1819; F. C.

(*d*) The Court will not sanction the nomination of persons domiciled out of Scotland without necessity. Ferguson *v.* Dormer, 1870; 8 Macph. 425.

(*e*) Chalmers' Trs. *v.* Sinclair, 24 R. 1047.

(*f*) Grant, petr., 1848; 10 D. 1052.

(*g*) Watson *v.* Rae, 1773; M. 16,369. 1 Ersk. 7. § 27.

(*h*) Bargany *v.* Hamilton, 1702; M. 16,319. Wilson, *supra* (*c*). See Harvey *v.* Harvey, 1860; 22 D. 1207. Grant *v.* Innes, 1844; 7 D. 226.

2096. Administration. — The curator is guardian of the estate, not of the person (*a*). The minor acts, but with a presumed imperfectness of judgment, which the curator, as his adviser and the consenter to his deeds, supplies. Deeds done by the curator alone are null; both he and the minor must concur (*b*). But the minor cannot be compelled to act with his curators (they being only advisers and curators), unless in so far as other parties refuse to act with him alone. If the minor be obstinate in resisting what is proper to be done, the curator may apply to be discharged of his office; but he cannot supersede the minor, nor compel him to concur (*c*). The powers of administration, where minor and curators concur, are larger than in tutory. Leases (*d*) may be granted to endure beyond the years of minority; sales of land may be made, and heritable burdens created; and the Court will not lessen the responsibility, by interfering to authorise what the minor and curator have full power to do (*e*).

(*a*) See cases, *supra*, § 2090.

(*b*) Foster *v.* Foster, 1610; M. 16,238; 3 Ill. 43. M'Intosh *v.* Fraser, 1675; M. 16,290. Drumore, *infra* (*c*). Allan *v.* Walker, 1812; Hume, 586. Stirling *v.* Campbell, 1816; 6 Pat. 238. See Stark *v.* Tennant, 1843; 5 D. 542; 1846, 8 D. 1001. Pentland *v.* Murray, 1831; 5 W. & S. 28. See Jamieson *v.* Spottiswoode's Trs., Dec. 6, 1808; F. C. M'Kirdy *v.* M'Lauchlan, May 26, 1840; F. C. Andrew *v.* Colquhoun, 1852; 14 D. 164. Fraser, P. & C. 369, 378.

(*c*) L. Drumore *v.* Murray, 1744; M. 8930, 16,349; Elch. *Min.* 10; 5 B. Sup. 737.

(*d*) See 1 Ersk. 7. § 16. 1 Bell's Com. 134. Fraser, P. & C. 376. Alexander *v.* Thomson, 1813; Hume, 44.

(*e*) Hamilton *v.* Sharp, 1630; M. 8981. Wallace *v.* Wallace, March 8, 1817; F. C.; 1 Bell's Com. 134. Ogilvie *v.* Traill, 1824; 3 S. 124. Campbell *v.* Campbell, 1738; M. 8930. Harkness *v.* Graham, 1832; 11 S. 760; 1836, 14 S. 1015.

2097. Expiration of Office.—The termination of the office, and the reciprocal actions, are analogous to those of tutors (*a*).

(*a*) *Supra*, § 2086.

2098. Restitution on Minority and Lesion. — Every deed in nonage, whether during pupillarity or minority, and whether with or without consent of tutors or curators, is liable to reduction on proof of lesion. The distinction chiefly to be observed is, that deeds null (*a*) may be challenged at any time; while those which are duly authorised 'or rather, granted,' by tutors, or by a minor without curators, or by a minor with his curators concurring, not only require to an effectual challenge a proof of lesion, but they must be challenged, 'on the ground of minority and lesion,' within four years after majority, called the "quadriennium utile" (*b*).

(*a*) *I.e.* in regard to this question, deeds granted by a pupil; and by a minor having curators, without their consent (*supra*, § 2087, 2088. Fraser, P. & C. 391), or gratuitous deeds by a minor in favour of his curators. Thomson *v.* Pagan, 1781; M. 8985; and Manuel and M'Gibbon, *infra*.

(*b*) 1 Ersk. 7. § 34, 39, 42. M. Montrose *v.* Buchanan, 1697; M. 9046; 3 Ill. 44. See above, § 2087 (1). M'Gibbon *v.* M'Gibbon, 1852; 14 D. 605. Manuel *v.* Manuel, 1853; 15 D. 284. Stevenson *v.* Adair, 1872; 10 Macph. 919 (cautioner for minor acting without his curators is bound).

2099. Mere revocation within the *quadriennium utile* is not sufficient. The deeds against which the minor is entitled to be restored must also be challenged by an action of reduction, 'at the instance of the minor, his heirs (*a*), or his creditors (*b*),' in the Court of Session within that term (*c*).

(*a*) 1 Stair, 6. § 44. 1 Ersk. 7. § 42. 1 Bell's Com. 134.

(*b*) 1 Stair, 6. § 44. 1 Bell's Com. 135. Harkness *v.* Graham, 1833 ; 11 S. 760.

(*c*) Stewart *v.* Snodgrass, 1860 ; 23 D. 187. Fraser, P. & C. 427.

2100. The grounds of restitution are, minority and lesion (*a*). Minority must be proved by the date of birth (*b*). Lesion, 'which must be "enorm," *i.e.* not inconsiderable (*c*) as at the time of the transaction (*d*),' must be shown in point of fact; as the settlement of extravagant provisions to the husband or wife in a contract of marriage (*e*). But there is a presumption to aid the proof of lesion in donations; in cautionary obligations (*f*); in loans of money to a minor (*g*); even in payments to a minor (*h*). These presumptions of lesion may be counteracted by showing the lesion to be subsequent, and the result of mismanagement; or by proving that the character of trader, or of majority, was assumed in the transaction; or by homologation after majority (*i*). The minor is entitled only to be replaced in his former state, not to derive an advantage which he could not otherwise have enjoyed (*k*). But he will not be entitled to redress against lesion arising in consequence of payment by debtors, if with consent of curators (*l*).

There are two exceptions, however, to a minor's right to restitution. In the marriage of a minor, the interests of others are so deeply implicated, that he cannot be restored against the marriage, although he may have restitution against hurtful provisions in a conventional marriage contract (*m*). And where the minor has engaged in trade, 'or' (*n*) held himself out as major, so as to deceive the party with whom he deals, he is not entitled to restitution (*o*).

(*a*) 1 Ersk. 7. § 36.

(*b*) See above, § 2091.

(*c*) 1 Ersk. 7. § 36.

(*d*) Auth. in **Cooper** *v.* **Cooper's Trs.**, 1885 ; 12 R. 473, 486. It may be doubted whether it properly follows from this principle that restitution is not competent against a discharge in an ante-nuptial contract of contingent rights brought into existence by the marriage itself, as held in Cooper, *cit.*, but not decided in the H. of L. 1888, 13 App. Ca. 88 ; 15 R. H. L. 21. See above, § 1946.

(*e*) Carmichael *v.* Castlehill, 1698 ; M. 8938 ; 3 Ill. 44. See Montgomery *v.* E. Leven, 1683 ; M. 8992. Byres *v.* Reid, 1708 ; M. 8995. Chalmers *v.* Lyon's Crs., 1710, and Lyon's Crs. (Gray) *v.* Stewart, 1714 ; M. 6059, 8996. Anderson *v.* Abercrombie's Trs., 1824 ; 2 S. 662 ; 1 Bell's Com. 134. Bruce *v.* Hamilton, 1854 ; 17 D. 265.

(*f*) 1 Stair, 6. § 44. 1 Bell's Com. 135. Fraser, P. & C. 407.

(*g*) **Harkness** *v.* **Graham**, 1833 ; 11 S. 760. Ferguson *v.* Yuill, 1835 ; 13 S. 886.

(*h*) In opposition to 1 Ersk. 7. § 36 ; and to Koehler *v.* Neidrick, 1772 ; M. 8975 ; 3 Ill. 25. See Hay *v.* Grant, 1749 ; M. 8973. Kirkman *v.* Pym, 1782 ; M. 8977 ; Hailes, 909. See Fraser, P. & C. 338, 410. The case last cited, and Jack *v.* N. B. Ry. Co., 1886, 14 R. 263, show that a minor can validly receive and discharge interest or rents,—ordinary acts of administration,—but not a capital sum for investment, so as to be safe against future challenge. In the enumerated classes of cases the minor may state the objection by exception. Harkness *v.* Graham, *cit.* (*g*). Crawford *v.* Bennet, *infra* (*o*). Fraser, P. & C. 407, 427. See Dennistoun *v.* Mudie, *infra* (*i*). As to "necessaries" sold and delivered to minors, confusion or difficulty may arise from the Sale of Goods Act, 56 and 57 Vict. c. 71, § 2. But it is not clear, as Mr. R. Brown suggests in his monograph, p. 15, that the law of Scotland differs from that of England as to the burden of proof on the seller. Mr. Brown seems to rest this on one old case, which is contrary to the current of practice and authority. Fraser, P. & C. 96, 416 ; Brodie's Stair, p. 45, note. See above, cases in § 1630 (*a*).

(*i*) Melville *v.* Arnot, 1782 ; M. 8998. Roberton *v.* Roberton, 1831 ; 9 S. 865. Dennistoun *v.* Mudie, 1850 ; 12 D. 613. M'Michael *v.* Barbour, 1840 ; 3 D. 279. Harkness (*g*). Dempster *v.* Potts, 1837 ; 15 S. 364. Kyle *v.* Allan, 1832 ; 11 S. 87.

(*k*) Gray *v.* Purves, 1816 ; Hume, 411. Fraser, P. & C. 415, 430.

(*l*) Fraser, P. & C. 229, 410.

(*m*) *Supra*, § 1523. 1 Ersk. 7. § 38. Lyon's Crs. (Gray) *v.* Stewart, 1714 ; M. 6059 (wife not limited to *anni utiles*). Davidson *v.* Hamilton, 1632 ; M. 8988. Bruce *v.* Hamilton, 1854 ; 17 D. 265. Arbuthnot *v.* Morison, 1716 ; M. 9487 ; 1 Cr. & St. 7. Anderson (*e*). Taylor's Trs. (Murison) *v.* Dick, 1854 ; 16 D. 529 (revocation before marriage). See Cooper *v.* Cooper's Trs., 1885 ; 12 R. 473 (where it was held that restitution may be granted to a minor on the ground of lesion against a conveyance of property *intuitu matrimonii*, but not against a discharge in an ante-nuptial contract of the contingent rights arising by the marriage, *i.e. jus relictæ* and terce). See above, § 1946 *fin.*, and § 11.

(*n*) In previous editions, "and." Correct by 1 Bell's Com. 135.

(*o*) Ersk. *ut supra.* Heddel *v.* Duncan, June 5, 1810 ; F. C. Sutherland *v.* Morson, 1825 ; 3 S. 449. Crawford *v.* Bennet, 1827 ; 2 W. & S. 608. See above, § 2091. Wilkie *v.* Dunlop, 1834 ; 12 S. 506. Dennistoun *v.* Mudie, *cit.* (*i*). Pollock on Contracts, 55, 75 (3rd ed.).

2101. Privileges of Minors.—They have the privilege of not being compellable to defend the validity of their paternal ancestor's rights to their lands, when vested in the ancestor by sasine, against one claiming preferably (*a*). 'But the rule, *minor non tenetur placitare super hæreditate*, was said nearly a hundred years ago to be among the antiquities of the law (*b*). It does not apply to *ex facie* nullity, which may always be pleaded, there being no *hæreditas* (*c*); nor when the action has been commenced against the ancestor in his lifetime (*d*).'

(*a*) 1 Stair, 6. § 45. 1 Ersk. 7. § 43, 44. Kello *v.* Pringle, 1665; M. 9063. Douglas *v.* Inglis, 1744; 5 B. Sup. 738. Macfarlan *v.* Hume, 1797; M. 9086. Fraser, P. & C. 439.

(*b*) Macfarlan, *cit.*

(*c*) Donaldson *v.* Donaldson, 1749; 5 B. Sup. 236: M. 9080; Elch. *Blank Writ*, 2. Tomison *v.* Tomison, 1840; 12 S. Jur. 382. There were other limitations, see Ersk. *l.c.*

(*d*) Fraser, P. & C. 446.

III. PRO-TUTORS AND PRO-CURATORS (*a*).

2102. Nature of their Office.—Pro-tutors and pro-curators are persons who assume the office of guardian; and the whole doctrine relative to them depends on the principles of *negotiorum gestio* (*b*). They have no recognised powers; and they may be called to account at any time (*c*). They are entitled to reimbursement and relief; but, as excluding others, they are responsible for exact diligence—for omissions as well as intromissions (*d*); 'and their discharge is not valid, unless it be shown that the money paid was applied for the minor's benefit (*e*).'

(*a*) See below for Factors loco Tutoris, Curators Bonis, etc., § 2114 et seq.

(*b*) *Supra*, § 540. Dunbar *v.* Wilson & Dunlop's Tr., 1887; 15 R. 210 (law-agent for pro-curator). It is not, however, everyone who manages or intromits with the affairs of a minor who is subjected to the liabilities of a pro-tutor or pro-curator, but only one who does so under the character of tutor when he is not. *Per* L. Kilkerran in Fowler *v.* Campbell, *cit. infra.* Fulton *v.* Fulton, 1864; 2 Macph. 893.

(*c*) Paterson *v.* Greig, 1861; 24 D. 1370.

(*d*) 1 Ersk. 7. § 28. Act of Sed. June 10, 1665; 3 Ill. 43. Cass *v.* Ellies, 1671; M. 16,285. Muir *v.* Crawford, 1676; M. 16,316. Fowler *v.* Campbell, 1739; M. 16,343; Elchies, *Tut.* 11. See Allan *v.* Hamilton, July 1715; M. 5654.

(*e*) Lockhart *v.* M'Kenzie's Trs., 1826; 5 S. 136; aff. 3 W. & S. 481.

IV. GUARDIANSHIP OF PERSONS MENTALLY INCAPABLE.

2103. Total Incapacity.—Incapacity not proceeding from defect of age is either total or partial.

Total incapacity cannot, like the defect of years, be regulated by any general criterion, but must in each case be established either by the verdict of a jury, under a brieve from Chancery, directed 'formerly' to the judge ordinary of the territory in which the person to be cognosced resides, 'now to the Lord President of the Court of Session (*a*)'; or by an action directed to the annulling of a particular deed. The presumption of the law is for sanity (*b*); which is overcome in either of these modes of proceeding. The presumption from a verdict of insanity is to be overcome only by an action and proof *pro re natâ*, to establish sanity in a particular instance, or to reduce the verdict.

(*a*) 30 and 31 Vict. c. 100, § 101. A. of S. Dec. 3, 1868. It is tried before a special jury.

(*b*) Lindsay *v.* Watson, 1843; 5 D. 1194.

2104. Incapacity is reducible to two classes: Furiosity and Idiocy. The trial may be either by inquest and verdict; or, in relation to a particular deed or transaction, by reduction. The former comprehends a period retrospective and prospective; the latter is directed, in point of time, to the date of the deed. In the former, the person into whose state of mind the inquiry is to be proved must be before the jury; in the latter, this is not indispensable. The former can proceed only while the person is alive, and is intended as necessary to guardianship; the latter may proceed after the death of the party (*a*).

'But the inquiry in the modern form of cognition is always the same, namely, "whether the person sought to be cognosced is insane"; and "such person shall be deemed insane if he be furious, or fatuous, or labouring under such unsoundness of mind as to render him incapable of managing his affairs" (*b*).'

(*a*) Loch *v.* Dick, 1638; M. 6278; 3 Ill. 47. Christie *v.* Gibb, 1700; M. 6283. Alexander *v.* Horner, 1632; M. 6278. Lindsay *v.* Trent, 1683; M. 6285. Watson *v.* Noble's Trs., 1827; 2 W. & S. 648. M'Diarmid *v.* M'Diarmid, 1826; 4 S. 583; 1828, 3 W. & S. 37. Blair *v.* Blair, 1748; M. 6293. Waddel *v.* Waddel's Trs., 1845; 7 D. 605, 1017.

(*b*) 31 and 32 Vict. c. 100, § 101.

2105. (1.) *Furiosity or Insanity.*—The brieve 'was' directed to inquire "si sit incompos mentis, prodigus, et furiosus, viz. qui nec tempus nec modum impensarum habet, sed bona dilaceranda profundit" (*a*). The points to be made out in the cognition 'were': the existence of unsound mind; the particular character of the furiosity, as admitting of lucid intervals or otherwise; the period of retrospect (*b*). 'But under the present Act the sole heads of inquiry are whether the person sought to be cognosced "is insane, who is his nearest agnate, and whether such agnate is of lawful age" (*c*); and the points here dealt with are material chiefly in inquiries into the validity of particular deeds.'

The question of insanity presents many difficulties. One important distinction is between partial, and intermittent insanity with lucid intervals. Wherever there is delusion with partial insanity, it seems to be a case for guardianship, on account of the uncertainty to what extent the delusion goes; the partial insanity being held as general for the person's own safety and that of his relations, as of one unfit to deal with human affairs according to the sober estimate and standard of reason, and unsafe to be trusted to the accidental occurrence of the train of association which excites his malady. Another important distinction is between insanity with delusion excited by a particular train of associations, and monomania; in which a man is insane on one point only, and, during the prevalence even of the fit, sane on all other points. The rule seems to be, that where there is a distinct interruption or lucid interval, an act done in that interval is not null (*d*); and that even in monomania, while such acts as are traceable to the delusion are null, whatever is done uninfluenced by the delusion is effectual (*e*). 'At least the existence of a delusion on some extraneous point unconnected with the subject-matter of the deed will not necessarily be fatal to a deed (*f*).' As to lucid interval, there seems to be one species of it which marks the disease as intermittent. But it does not appear that the law will always require this sort of case to be made out; and that proof of lucid interval in point of fact, as established by the act itself, rational in its own character, and rationally done, will be sufficient to sustain a deed (*g*).

(*a*) See Colquhoun's Report of the case of Yoolow.

(*b*) 1 Ersk. 7. § 51. Blair *v.* Blair, 1748; M. 6293; 3 Ill. 47. Pollock *v.* Paterson, Dec. 10, 1811; F. C. Dew *v.* Clark, 3 Hag. Eccl. Ca. 311; 3 Addams, 40; 3 Ill. 46. See above, § 2103, note.

(*c*) 31 and 32 Vict. c. 100, § 101.

(*d*) Neill *v.* Morley, 9 Ves. jun. 478. Currie *v.* Jardine, 1827; 5 S. 838.

(*e*) Dew, *supra* (*b*). Fraser *v.* Fraser, 1834; 13 S. 703. Laing *v.* Bruce, 1838; 1 D. 59. Forsyth, petr., 1862; 24 D. 1435.

(*f*) Cases cited. Morrison *v.* M'Lean's Trs., 1862; 24 D. 625. Ballantyne *v.* Evans, 1886; 13 R. 652. Nisbet's Trs. (*g*).

(*g*) Cartwright *v.* Cartwright, 1 Phillim. Eccl. Cases, 90. See Nichols *v.* Binns, 1 S. & T. 239. Smith *v.* Tebbitt, 36 L. J. Pr. 97; L. R. 1 Pr. 398. Banks *v.* Goodfellow, 39 L. J. Q. B. 237; L. R. 5 Q. B. 549. Morrison, *cit.* Nisbet's Trs., § 2107 (*b*) (deed executed in lunatic asylum held valid). Ballantyne, *cit.*

2106. The person, as already said, must be before the jury (*a*), and the cognition will be ordered to proceed at a place where this may be possible (*b*). The points in the verdict were: 1. The present state; 2. The time at which the malady commenced (*c*),—the effect of this being only to overturn the presumption of sanity, not to prevent an investigation in any particular case; and, 3. Lucid intervals. A verdict showing lucid interval on a particular day, is not conclusive to bar reduction of a deed made on that day (*d*).

(*a*) Dewar *v.* Dewar & Reid, Feb. 25, 1809; F. C.; 3 Ill. 48. See Fraser, P. & C. 530.

(*b*) Falconer, petr., 1709; 4 B. Sup. 742.

(*c*) 1475, c. 67; 2 Acta Parl. p. 112, c. 8.

(*d*) Currie *v.* Jardine, 1827; 5 S. 838.

2107. The verdict is not conclusive. It may be reduced, and a new brieve directed (*a*). If a lucid interval can be proved at the point of time when a deed was made, or a contract entered into, the retrospect of the verdict will not be held to preclude the inquiry in the shape of a reduction and declarator of lucid interval, or as a plea in a reduction of the deed. Reconvalescence may be established by a declaratory action, or the person cognosced may resume his administration, taking care to preserve evidence of sanity in any important transaction (*b*).

(*a*) Dewar, § 2106 (*a*). Gray *v.* Gray, 1738; Elch. *Idiotry*, 1. See Matthew *v.* Wighton, 1843; 6 D. 305.

(*b*) Inglis *v.* His Tutor, 1701; 4 B. Sup. 517; 5 B. Sup. 5. Bryce *v.* Graham, 1828; 6 S. 425; aff. 1828, 3 W. & S. 323. Lockhart, petr., 1862; 24 D. 1086. Nisbet's Trs. *v.* Nisbet, 1871; 9 Macph. 937. Banks *v.* Goodfellow, *supra*, § 2105 (*g*).

2108. (2.) *Idiocy.*—The distinction is 'or was' important between the character of incapacity in idiocy and in furiosity; unremitting in the one, subject to remission or capable of cure in the other (*a*).

(*a*) See authorities in § 2196. Also Carstairs *v.* Carstairs, 1672; M. 13,049; 3 Ill. 45.

2109. The brieve 'was' to try, "si sit incompos mentis, fatuus et naturaliter idiota, sic quod timetur de alienatione tam terrarum suarum quam aliarum rerum mobilium." The character here is that of total incapacity without interval, and without cure.

2110. Guardianship.—The title to institute proceedings for a verdict and guardianship is with the next of kin (*a*) 'or any near relation (*b*).'

(*a*) M'Allister *v.* Somerville, 1798; 6 S. 440, note; 3 Ill. 48.
(*b*) Larkin *v.* M'Grady, 1874; 2 R. 170.

2111. The right of guardianship rests with the nearest male agnate. If he be unfit, or under age, or unwilling to serve, the verdict is limited to the state of mind; and a tutor-dative is applied for (*a*). There is no power in the father to name testamentary tutors to an insane person to continue after his majority (*b*). Nor would it be safe to enter into a transaction with such tutor after the insane person attains majority. 'The husband of a married woman is her curator when insane, to the exclusion of her nearest agnate (*c*).'

(*a*) Stewart *v.* Spreul, 1663; M. 6279; 3 Ill. 48. Moncrieff *v.* Maxwell, 1710; M. 6286. Bryce *v.* Graham, 1828; 6 S. 425; aff. 1828, 3 W. & S. 323. Young *v.* Rose, 1839; 1 D. 1242. See Larkin *v.* M'Grady, *supra*, § 2110 (*b*).
(*b*) D. Athole's Curators, 1831; 3 S. Jur. 419. Crawford *v.* Ballantyne, 1828; 6 S. 749. 1 Ersk. 7. § 49.
(*c*) Haliburton *v.* Maxwell, 1791; M. 16,379; Bell's Ca. 155. See Fraser, P. & C. 434. *Infra*, § 2114.

2112. The guardian of an insane person is bound to settle accounts with him on convalescence (*a*); and the recurrence of the malady will not reinvest the curator in his office (*b*).

(*a*) Millar, petr., May 15, 1819; F. C.; 3 Ill. 50. See as to his bond of caution, 12 and 13 Vict. c. 51, § 26.
(*b*) Edderline's Tutor, 1740; Elch. *Tutor*, No. 12.

2113. Imbecility, or Partial Incapacity.—There are many cases which require protection, and yet in which no remedy by cognition and curatory can be obtained. The power of interposing in such cases (one of the most delicate that can be committed to a judge) is vested in the Supreme Court (*a*). The occasions for its exercise are, 'generally, those where the incapacity is not quite clearly permanent, but "for the time" (*b*),'—Imbecility from age (*c*); from natural facility of temper; from organic affection (*d*): Temporary incapacity, as delirium: Absence abroad: The interval before a cognition can take place. In these cases, the judicial remedies applied are, the appointment of a judicial factor or *curator bonis*. 'Where a lunatic's property is not properly applied for his benefit, the Lunacy Board or the Accountant of Court may report the matter to the Court, who will appoint a judicial factor, or take other necessary measures (*e*).'

(*a*) This branch of jurisdiction is now exercised in almost all cases by the Junior Lord Ordinary. 20 and 21 Vict. c. 56, § 4.
(*b*) A. of S. Feb. 13, 1730. Bryce *v.* Graham, *cit.* § 2111. A. B. *v.* C. D., 1890; 18 R. 90; aff. 1891, *ib.* H. L. 40; A. C. 616. See Irving *v.* Swan, 1868; 7 Macph. 86.
(*c*) See Mackie *v.* Mackie, 1866; 5 Macph. 60.
(*d*) See Kirkpatrick, petr., 1853; 15 D. 734 (deaf and dumb). Mark, petr., 1845; 7 D. 882 (deaf and blind). Allan *v.* Yoolow, 1852; 14 D. 1009.
(*e*) 20 and 21 Vict. c. 71, § 81.

2114. (1.) *Factor loco Tutoris* (*a*).—This office is not conferred as a matter of course. It is competent to be applied for where a father, or a tutor already named, is incapable of acting; or during the year allowed to the nearest agnate to deliberate (*b*); or where the tutor cannot interfere (*c*). But not where a wife is insane and the husband alive; even though separated by voluntary contract (*d*).

'All judicial factors, *i.e.* as defined by the Acts, factors *loco tutoris*, factors *loco absentis*, and *curatores bonis* (*e*), and all other persons appointed by any Court in Scotland to hold, administer, or protect any property or funds belonging to any persons or estates in Scotland, are subject to the rules of the Pupils Protection Act, 1849, and the Judicial Factors Act, 1889, and are under the superintendence of the Accountant of Court (*f*). Judicial factors, *i.e.* factors *loco tutoris* and *curatores bonis*, may now be appointed by the Sheriff, where the estate does not exceed £100 in yearly value (*g*).'

(*a*) 1 Ersk. 7. § 10. Act of Sederunt, Feb. 13, 1730; Dec. 11, 1849; March 11, 1851. Fraser, P. & C. 400.
(*b*) Morrison, petr., 1770; Hailes, 359; 3 Ill. 51.
(*c*) Anstruther *v.* Anstruther, March 3, 1818; F. C. Donaldson, petrs., 1770; M. 16,364. Weir *v.* Prentice, 1829; 7 S. 805.
(*d*) Haliburton *v.* Maxwell, 1791; M. 16,379; 3 Ill. 48. See above, § 2111.
(*e*) See Accountant of Court *v.* Morrison, 1857; 19 D. 504.
(*f*) 12 and 13 Vict. c. 51. 52 and 53 Vict. c. 39. Executors-dative and trustees appointed by the Court under the Trusts Acts, the Entail Act, 1882, or under any other power, may apply for a superintendence order as to the investment and distribution of the estate under their care. *Ib.* § 18. See A. of S. March 13, 1889, as to fees payable to Accountant.
(*g*) 43 and 44 Vict. c. 4. A. of S. Jan. 14, 1881. Penny *v.* Scott, 1894; 22 R. 5 (minor).

2115. Not more than one person is ever appointed, 'either jointly or in succession,' to the office (*a*); nor anyone who is entitled to be tutor-at-law, if not willing to act gratuitously (*b*); nor a bankrupt, if he has any interested object in the appointment (*c*); 'nor, in modern practice, women, although they are not incompetent (*d*).' A clergyman of the Church of Scotland is never appointed (*e*), though a seceding clergyman may be named to the office (*f*). But although one entitled to be tutor-at-law will not be appointed unless he agree to act gratuitously, the office is not necessarily gratuitous. If a stranger be appointed, and comply with all points of his duty, he is entitled to commission and professional emoluments or expenditure, under the equitable control of the Court (*g*). 'But a law agent appointed factor cannot act as law agent for the ward, except on condition of doing so gratuitously (*h*).'

(*a*) Brown, petr., Feb. 1, 1815; F. C.; 3 Ill. 51. Small, petr., 1822; 1 S. 106. Pettigrew, petr., 1839; 1 D. 543. Sloane, petr., 1844; 7 D. 227. Dow, petr., 1847; 9 D. 616. See Kirk, petr., 1836; 14 S. 814; 3 Ill. 57.

(*b*) Jackson, petr., 1821; 1 S. 210. Robertson, petr., 1830; 8 S. 307, 435. See M'Donald, petr., 1854; 16 D. 1023.

(*c*) Dixon *v.* Watson, 1832; 10 S. 209.

(*d*) Thorburn, petr., 1846; 8 D. 1000. Bethune, petr., 1851; 14 D. 11. Lindsay, petr., 1855; 17 D. 321. Fraser, P. & C. 460.

(*e*) Whitson, petr., 1833; 10 S. 268. Thomson, petr., 1829; 8 S. 12. Bisset, petr., 1836; 15 S. 4. See *contra*, Campbell, petr., 1849; 12 D. 913.

(*f*) Hall, petr., 1830; 8 S. 553. Smith, petr., 1850; 13 D. 951. Forbes, petr., 1853; 16 D. 109.

(*g*) Cranstoun *v.* Scott, 1826; 5 S. 62.

(*h*) Morrison *v.* Rennie, 1847; 9 D. 1483; 1849, 6 Bell's App. 422. Flowerdew, petr., 1855; 17 D. 263. Kennedy *v.* Rutherglen, 1860; 22 D. 567.

2116. The application is intimated on the walls of the Court and in the minute-book, and served on the next of kin on the father's and mother's side (*a*). And in case of undue keenness in competition, the Court will appoint a neutral person (*b*). The person applying must in his petition state the ground of necessity or expediency for the appointment, and suggest the person to be appointed, that both may be intimated with the petition. In cases of urgency, the Court will, during intimation, make an interim appointment (*c*). The authority is conferred and the power vested in the factor only by the extracted act and warrant, the finding of caution being a condition precedent of the extract; and payment to a factor *loco tutoris* before extract is unavailing, and at the risk of the person who pays (*d*). 'The appointment falls if the factor fail to find caution within such time after his appointment as the Court shall direct (*e*).'

(*a*) Cowans, petrs., 1788; M. 7452; 3 Ill. 52. Heatley *v.* Logan, 1828; 6 S. 477. Fowlds *v.* Hodges, 1836; 15 S. 244.

(*b*) Urquhart *v.* Scott, 1824; 2 S. 789. Cochrane *v.* M'Aslan, 1849; 12 D. 147. Menteath, petr., 1840; 2 D. 1234. Grant *v.* Murray, 1847; 10 D. 194. Brown, petr., 1848; 11 D. 102. M'Intosh, petr., 1849; 11 D. 1029.

(*c*) Kirk, petr., 1827; 5 S. 564. A. B., petr., 1829; 8 S. 89. Davidson, petr., 1830; 8 S. 1027. Weir *v.* Prentice, 1829; 7 S. 805.

(*d*) Donaldson *v.* Kennedy, 1833; 11 S. 740. See further, as to caution, 12 and 13 Vict. c. 51, § 2, 11, 27; 20 and 21 Vict. c. 71, § 84. Fraser, P. & C. 515 sqq. M'Kinnon, petr., 1884; 11 R. 676; 12 R. 184 (power of Court to fix amount—Guarantee Society). Calver *v.* Howard, Baker, & Co., 1894; 22 R. 1 (action raised by curator before extract).

(*e*) 12 and 13 Vict. c. 51, § 2, 11, 27. A. of S. Jan. 14, 1881, § 5 (Sheriff Courts).

2117. The powers of such a guardian are not distinguishable from those of a tutor in regard to the estate (*a*). He may enter into submissions (*b*). Administration and responsibility are regulated by Act of Sederunt (*c*) 'and the Pupils Protection Act, passed in 1849 (*d*)'; and the Court is most justly averse to interfere in sanctioning any act of the factor, but leaves him to act on his own responsibility (*e*). In cases in which judicial authority is necessary, the Court will interfere to empower the factor to act (*f*); and the cases of necessity are,—where a loss is to be guarded against; where an obvious advantage is to be secured; where there is danger of the estate being torn in pieces by the diligence of creditors proceeding or threatening to proceed with adjudication, etc.; where the interest of third parties, as superiors or vassals, requires something to be done; or where for the subsistence of a pupil a fund must be provided (*g*). Even in other cases, where there is danger of the factor injuring the person whom he is appointed to protect, from too great dread of responsibility, and leaving useful acts unperformed, the Court will interfere (*h*). Such special powers must be specially applied for (*i*); 'and are now obtained under the provisions of the Pupils Protection Act, not only by petition as formerly (*k*), but by a note to the Junior Lord Ordinary accompanied by a report by the Accountant of Court (*l*).' The salutary reserve or aversion on the part of the Court to interfere has sometimes been relaxed of late years '(1839),' perhaps to a dangerous extent. But whether the Court authorise the act or not, the application is so far a protection to the factor, that the statement and evidence laid before the Court are useful in establishing the facts in the event of any future challenge or inquiry.

The factor is held liable for interest on the interest of sums which he has neglected to recover (*m*), 'and is subject to a severe penalty for keeping more than £50 belonging to the estate in his own hands for more than ten days (*n*).' And he will not be held entitled to commission if he neglect the rules of the Act of Sederunt. 'His liability for the expenses of litigation appears to be the same as that of trustees (*o*).'

The factor has no power over the person of the pupil (*p*).

(*a*) Robertson *v.* Elphinston, May 28, 1814; F. C.; 3 Ill. 52. See above, § 2081 sqq. See § 2121, note (*b*).
(*b*) Brown *v.* Scoular, 1758; M. 16,359. Falconar *v.* Thomson, 1792; M. 16,380.
(*c*) A. S. Feb. 13, 1730.
(*d*) 12 and 13 Vict. c. 51. See above, § 2081A.
(*e*) Craigie, petr., 1758; M. 16,361. Home, petr., 1793; M. 16,382. Henderson, petr., 1803; M. 14,982. Hay *v.* Thomson, June 20, 1811; F. C. Meikle *v.* Meikle, 1823; 2 S. 274.
(*f*) Meikle, *supra* (*c*). Cockburn *v.* Cockburn, 1825; 2 S. 642; 3 Ill. 37 and 53.
(*g*) Somerville, petr., 1836; 14 S. 451. M'Gruther, petr., 1835; 13 S. 569. Finlayson *v.* Kidd, 1835; 13 S. 861. Miller, petr., 1836; 15 S. 147; 3 Ill. 54; and other cases, 3 Ill. 53–4.
(*h*) Carrick, petr., 1829; 7 S. 848; 8 S. 208; 3 Ill. 37. Mark, petr., 1829; 8 S. 195. Slade, petrs., 1831; 10 S. 167. Morrison, petr., 1832; 10 S. 204; and cases of Pedie, Robertson, and Bushby there cited. See as to factor's powers, and the cases in which special authority is generally asked, above, § 2084; Fraser, P. & C. 480 sqq., 492 sqq., and cases there cited.
(*i*) A. B., petr., 1829; 7 S. 327.
(*k*) Mackenzie, petr., 1862; 24 D. 844.
(*l*) 12 and 13 Vict. c. 51, § 7. 20 and 21 Vict. c. 56, § 4.
(*m*) Cranston *v.* Scott, 1826; 5 S. 62. A. of S. Feb. 13, 1730. 3 Ersk. 3. § 37. Lambe *v.* Ritchie, 1837; 16 S. 219. 12 and 13 Vict. c. 51, § 3. *Supra*, § 2087.
(*n*) 12 and 13 Vict. c. 51, § 5, 32, 37. M'Donald *v.* M'Donald, 1854; 16 D. 1123. Maxwell's Trs. *v.* Jeffs, 1862; 24 D. 1181.
(*o*) Craig *v.* Hogg, 1896; 24 R. 6. *Supra*, § 1999, 2000.
(*p*) Robertson *v.* Elphinston, *cit.* (*a*). Bryce *v.* Graham, 1828; 3 W. & S. 323. See § 2081, and Denny, *ibi cit.*

2118. The duties are generally prescribed in the Act of Sederunt, 13th Feb. 1730; and in particular, the factor is ordered regularly to lodge annual factor accounts, under certain penalties; and those penalties the Court rigorously exacts (*a*). 'The investment of factorial funds is not strictly limited to heritable securities, Government deposits, and bank deposits (*b*). The Accountant of Court examines the factor's accounts and considers the investments (*c*); but his passing the accounts does not relieve the factor from responsibility for improper investments (*d*).'

(*a*) Lambe *v.* Ritchie, 1837; 16 S. 219; 3 Ill 55. See 12 and 13 Vict. c. 51, § 4, 13, etc.; and above, § 2117 (*n*). Nairne, petr., 1863; 1 Macph. 515. Fisher *v.* Tod, 1865; 3 Macph. 889. Morrison *v.* Dryden, 1890; 17 R. 704.
(*b*) Grainger's Curator, compearer, 1876; 3 R. 479 (loans to trustees under statutory trusts approved). Acct. of Court *v.* Crumpton's Cur., 1886; 14 R. 55.
(*c*) 12 and 13 Vict. c. 51, § 13.
(*d*) Annan (Hutton) *v.* Annan's Cur., 1897; 24 R. 851; aff. 1898, A. C. 289; 25 R. H. L. 23.

2119. The office expires in the same way with tutory, or by the serving of a tutor-at-law (*a*). In order to exoneration, the curator must call a proper contradictor; 'under the existing Act, all persons interested in the estate, so far as known (*b*).'

(*a*) Bell *v.* Henderson, 1784; M. 16,374. Young *v.* Rose, 1839; 1 D. 1242. As to resignation, see M'Ewan *v.* Drummond, 1857; 19 D. 936.
(*b*) M'Gavin, petr., 1821; 1 S. 78; 3 Ill. 55. See 12 and 13 Vict. c. 51, § 34. *Supra*, § 2057. Campbell *v.* Grant, 1869; 8 Macph. 227.

2120. (2.) *Factor loco Absentis.* — This appointment proceeds strictly on the principles of interdict and sequestration, and for the purpose of preventing waste and preserving the estate of a person while abroad (*a*).

(*a*) White *v.* Thomson, 1829; 7 S. 555; 3 Ill. 55. M'Lean, petr., 1828; 6 S. 1018.

2121. (3.) *Curator Bonis* (*a*).—In cases not marked by any infallible criterion of incapacity, and definite and acknowledged necessity for interference, the appointment of a stranger to supersede one's own management of his affairs is a delicate and difficult exercise of judicial power. But the remedy sanctioned by long usage in Scotland is not properly a judicial curatory of a permanent character, as sometimes has been supposed; it is intermediate only. As such, if the application is sanctioned by all those who are naturally interested in the person to be protected, it is a very convenient and beneficial proceeding. 'The ward's estate is not transferred to the curator, but only the administration of it, and hence the ward's name may be used in legal proceedings (*b*).' Where there is opposition by the person himself whose capacity is in question, or by another having interest, the question of judicial interference becomes exceedingly delicate; and perhaps the proper limit of jurisdiction in such cases is that which the principle of interdiction supplies, for the intermediate preservation of property in danger of being dissipated, abused, or encroached upon (*c*). The proper case for such interference is incapacity of a kind in which no verdict of insanity will be returned, while yet the person is unfit to do those acts which may be essentially necessary. And the points of inquiry for such a remedy are: 1. The degree of incapacity, to be cleared by the visitation and evidence of physicians; and, 2. The necessity for interference (*d*).

(*a*) See *ante*, § 2114 (1). Fraser, P. & C., etc. 523.
(*b*) Yule *v.* Alexander, 1891, 19 R. 167, citing this section. *Qu.* whether the doctrine does not apply to judicial factors also, under § 2113 sqq.?
(*c*) Bryce *v.* Graham, 1826; 2 W. & S. 481; 6 S. 425; 3 W. & S. 323; 3 Ill. 55. See Gordon *v.* Gunn, 1832; 10 S. 742. Lockhart, petr., 1857; 19 D. 1075. Allan, petr., 1852; 14 D. 1009.
(*d*) Gordon, *supra* (*c*). Dewar *v.* Dewar, 1834; 12 S. 345. Howden *v.* Sibbald, 1833; 11 S. 561. Dalrymple *v.* Ranken, 1836; 14 S. 1011. Speirs, petr., 1851; 14 D. 11. Irving *v.* Swan, 1868; 7 Macph. 86. Facility from age and undue influence tending to defeat the expectations of persons claiming an interest under settlements were held not to be sufficient grounds for a judicial factory. Dowie *v.* Hagart, 1894; 21 R. 1052.

2122. The power of appointing such temporary guardians belongs properly to the Court itself; and they 'formerly did' not delegate the authority to the Lord Ordinary on the Bills (*a*). But when the occasion has arisen during vacation, the Ordinary on the Bills 'might' make an interim appointment (*b*). The Court will not give authority to the curator to bring a reduction of a deed, leaving it to his own responsibility (*c*); nor to carry on a manufactory (*d*). And, on the whole, the general rule is, not to grant special powers; yielding only in cases of obvious necessity (*e*). 'The effect of the appointment is practically the same as that of cognition, the ward being held incapable of managing his affairs (*f*).'

(*a*) Bremner, petr., 1833; 11 S. 551; 3 Ill. 26. See above, § 2113 (*a*).
(*b*) Ellis, petr., 1836; 15 S. 262.
(*c*) Howie, petr., 1826; 5 S. 55; 3 Ill. 54. Blaikie *v.* Milne, 1838; 1 D. 18. As to election between legal and testamentary provisions, see above, § 1587 *fin.*
(*d*) Philip, petr., 1827; 6 S. 103. Gilray (Robertson's Curator), compearer, 1872; 10 Macph. 715.
(*e*) Drummond, petr., 1832: 10 S. 216. Borthwick, petr., 1832; 10 S. 620. Campbell, petr., 1829; 7 S. 296. Pulteney, petr., 1832; 10 S. 362. Gilray (Robertson's Curator), petr., 1876; 3 R. 619. Facilities for obtaining special powers in certain cases are provided by 12 and 13 Vict. c. 51, § 7. As to power to compromise, see Scott *v.* Craig's Reprs., 1897; 24 R. 462; and above, § 2117.
(*f*) Bryce *v.* Graham, *cit.* Mitchell & Baxter *v.* Cheyne, 1891; 19 R. 324.

2123. Interdiction.—Interdiction is a restraint laid on those who are in danger of suffering by their profusion or facility of temper; disabling them from signing any deed to their prejudice, without the consent of their interdictors. The case for which this remedy is provided, as described in the modern summons, is that of a person "lavish and prodigal; of weak and facile disposition; easily imposed on, and liable to be concussed to do deeds to his lesion or prejudice." The protection thus afforded proceeds on the general right to redress against all attempts to take advantage of avowed imbecility; and thus it becomes an indispensable part of the protection, that the restraint shall be published.

2124. Interdiction is either judicial or voluntary.

2125. (1.) *Judicial Interdiction.*—This is an adverse proceeding. It is pursued by the next of kin, or presumptive heir, by summons in the Court of Session; or *ex proprio motu* it may be ordered by a judge. There is a judgment finding and declaring the person to be of a weak and facile disposition; interdicting him to A., B., C., etc.; discharging and prohibiting him from selling his lands or other heritage; from contracting debts, entering into cautionary obligations, or doing any deed, direct or indirect, whereby the rights of his lands, etc., may be adjudged; and declaring all deeds so entered into void and null, and of no force, etc. Letters of publication are issued on that decree; and they are executed at the market-cross of the jurisdiction. The interdiction is recorded in the Register of Inhibitions of the county in which any lands lie which are to be protected (*a*). At one time private knowledge of the interdiction was not held sufficient to ground a challenge, but this was afterwards altered (*b*).

(*a*) 1581, c. 19; 3 Acta Parl. p. 223, c. 24. 1 Ersk. 7. § 54–6. 2 Ersk. 11. § 45. Seaton *v.* Aitchison's Crs., 1628; M. 7128; 3 Ill. 59. Robertson *v.* Gray, 1681; M. 7134 (interdiction by Court *ex proprio motu*). Thomson *v.* Thomson, 1776; 5 B. Sup. 488 (ditto). There is now only one General Register of Inhibitions, etc. 31 and 32 Vict. c. 64, § 16.
(*b*) Tenants *v.* Spreul, 1725; M. 7165. This doctrine is stated more broadly than the case cited warrants. It applies only to deeds in favour of the interdictor. See Fraser, P. & C. 558.

2126. (2.) *Voluntary Interdiction.*—This is a proceeding not older than the beginning of the seventeenth century. It proceeds by consent of the party himself, expressing in a bond or other writing his consciousness of facility, and binding himself to certain persons that he shall not, without their consent, grant any deed. Letters of publication follow, which are published as in the judicial interdiction, and then registered in the Record of Inhibitions, without which the whole is unavailing (*a*).

(*a*) 1 Ersk. 7. § 54. 2 Ersk. 11. § 45. Stewart *v.* Hay, 1676; M. 7132; 3 Ill. 59. Richardson *v.* Michie, 1685; M. 6147 (interdiction of wife in marriage-contract). Row *v.* Monro, 1703; M. 7162. Napier *v.* Houston, 1706; 4 B. Sup. 633. Braimer, Feb. 13, 1789; 3 Ill. 59.

2127. Effect of Interdiction. — This proceeding has the effect, — 1. To restrain the person interdicted from alienating or burdening lands, or contracting debts to affect his heritage within the shire where it is published and registered (*a*). But, 2. It has no effect on deeds relative to moveables (*b*). 3. It affects acts or deeds, not so as to annul, but only to reduce them so far as prejudicial, not defeating onerous or rational deeds (*c*). And even a sale to one of the interdictors has been sustained (*d*). 4. A Will is not defeated by it; but it is said a settlement of heritage is, like a minor's deed, ineffectual, though, 'said Professor Bell,' this may be doubted (*e*); 'and it has been decided that interdiction does not affect deeds of mere succession (*f*). It has been said that the consent of the interdictors makes the ward's deeds unchallengeable, even for gross lesion; but this has been doubted (*g*).'

(*a*) Ramsay *v.* M'Lellan, 1662; M. 7131; 3 Ill. 59.
(*b*) Davidson *v.* Town of Edinburgh, 1684; M. 7142. Erskine *v.* Marjoribanks, 1694; 4 B. Sup. 231. Arbuthnot *v.* Arbuthnot, 1724; M. 7144.
(*c*) A. *v.* B., 1672; M. 7149; 1 B. Sup. 655.
(*d*) Kyle *v.* Kyle, 1826; 5 S. 128. See Fraser *v.* Fraser, 1827; 5 S. 301. Rankin *v.* Russell, 1868; 7 Macph. 126.
(*e*) See 1 Ersk. 7. § 58. Correct this by Gray *v.* Smith, 1751; M. 10,803; Elch. *Prov. to Heirs and Children*, 14; 5 B. Sup. 790.
(*f*) Mansfield *v.* Stuart, 1841; 3 D. 1103.
(*g*) See Brown *v.* Shortt, 1807; cited in Fraser, P. & C. 565.

2128. Termination of Interdiction. — This may take place,—1. By death of the interdictors 'or of a quorum of them' (*a*). 2. By sentence of a judge recalling the interdiction, on proof of rationality and strength of mind, or of the interdiction having been improperly obtained (*b*). 3. By consent of the interdictors.

(*a*) Hepburn *v.* Hepburn, 1708; M. 7154; 3 Ill. 60. Only voluntary interdictions are terminated by the death or consent of the interdictors.
(*b*) Gichen *v.* Davidson, 1623; M. 7160; 3 Ill. 60. A. *v.* B., 1618; M. 7158. Wilkie *v.* ——, 1666; M. 7160. Hunter *v.* Hunter, 1698; M. 7161. As to the removal of an interdictor for misconduct, see Cameron, petr., Dec. 12, 1810; F. C.

CHAPTER IV

OF SUBJECT AND ALIEN; PEERAGE AND COMMONS

2129. Persons in their Public Relations.—Without entering on constitutional questions here, there are several relations in which individuals stand to each other, and to society generally, so intimately connected with the rules of private jurisprudence, that they require to be explained.

2130. There are now few distinctions remaining among the people, in respect to their political rights, arising from religious divisions (*a*); and the only distinction material to be taken notice of here is that of Subject and Alien.

(*a*) 10 Geo. IV. c. 7. 2 and 3 Will. IV. c. 115. 3 and 4 Will. IV. c. 49, and c. 82. Resolution of House of Commons, April 18, 1833, in relation to persons professing the Jewish religion. 21 and 22 Vict. c. 48 and 49, removing disabilities of Jews; 10 Geo. IV. c. 7, those of Roman Catholics.

I. SUBJECT AND ALIEN.

2131. Natural born Subjects are those born within the British dominions. By this they are placed at once under the protection of the Crown, and under an implied original and virtual allegiance. And this applies not only to children so born of the Queen's subjects, but also to those of aliens (not being enemies) born within the realm. The oath of allegiance may enforce this tie by the addition of perjury, but it does not create it.

2132. The description is extended by particular statutes. The children of all natural born subjects, though born out of the allegiance of the Queen, are declared to be natural born subjects (*a*). Children so born of fathers who at the time of the birth are natural born subjects (not attainted of high treason or felony, or in the service of a foreign prince at enmity), are natural born subjects (*b*). But children of British mothers and alien fathers are not within the rule (*c*). Grandchildren, *i.e.* children of fathers so naturalised, are also held natural born subjects (*d*). By a Scottish statute for erecting the Bank of Scotland, it was provided "that all foreigners who shall join as partners of this bank shall thereby become naturalised Scotsmen to all intents and purposes whatever" (*e*). But this has been held to apply only to the original partners (*f*).

(*a*) 7 Anne, c. 5.
(*b*) 4 Geo. II. c. 21, § 1. The child, if born where legitimation *per subsequens matrimonium* is not the law of the land, must, in order to be within this statute, be legitimate at birth. Shedden *v.* Patrick, 1854; 1 Macq. 535.
(*c*) Doe *v.* Jones, 4 T. R. 300; 2 R. R. 390.
(*d*) 13 Geo. III. c. 21, § 1. Dundas *v.* Dundas, 1839; 2 D. 31.
(*e*) Act, July 19, 1695.
(*f*) Macao *v.* The Officers of State, Nov. 14, 1820; F. C.; 1 S. App. 138.

2132A. 'It has been enacted with regard to the national status of women and children,—1. That a married woman is deemed to be a subject of the State of which her husband is for the time being a subject. 2. A natural born British woman who has become an alien by marriage, or anyone who has become an alien in another recognised way, may, when she becomes a widow, obtain a certificate of readmission to British nationality. 3. Where the father becomes an alien, or the mother, being a widow, becomes an alien, their children becoming resident in infancy in the country where the father or mother is naturalised, and being naturalised by the law of that country, are deemed subjects of that country, and not British subjects. 4. The children of a father or widow who has been readmitted to British nationality, becoming resident in the British dominions with their parent, resume the position of British subjects to all intents. 5. The children of a father or of a mother, being a widow, who obtains a certificate of naturalisation, becoming resident with such parent in the United Kingdom, are deemed naturalised British subjects (*a*).'

(*a*) 33 and 34 Vict. c. 14, § 10 (Naturalisation Act, 1870). 58 and 59 Vict. c. 43. See below, § 2133 (*a*); and also 33 and 34 Vict. c. 102 (oath). 35 and 36 Vict. c. 39.

2133. Allegiance is natural or local.

(1.) *Natural Allegiance* is that of natural born subjects, whom the sovereign is at all times bound to protect; and this allegiance 'was' held not to be dissoluble without the royal consent. 'But provision is made by the existing Naturalisation Act for natural born and naturalised subjects renouncing their allegiance, and also for persons being readmitted to British nationality (*a*).' Such consent was given by the declaration of the independence of America; and this had the effect of dissolving the allegiance of natural born subjects adhering to America, so that one continuing in America forfeited the character of natural born subject to his children not subjects; and of depriving subjects of Great Britain, adhering to the Crown, of the right of inheriting lands in America (*b*).

(2.) *Local Allegiance* is temporary. It is such as is due from an alien or stranger born while he continues within the British dominions and protection.

(*a*) 33 and 34 Vict. c. 14, § 4, 6–8.
(*b*) Doe *v.* Acklam, 2 B. & Cr. 779. See American cases in Wheaton's Rep. 535. See Lady Nisbet *v.* Nisbet's Trs., 1834; 12 S. 293. Dundas *v.* Dundas, 1839; 2 D. 31. Stewart, petr., 1857; 19 D. 430.

2134. Aliens are persons born beyond the dominions of the Queen (*a*), of parents who are not themselves natural born subjects. 'An alien has no legal right enforceable by action to land in this country or the colonies, and restrictions on the immigration of certain aliens (*e.g.* Chinese) have been enacted by certain colonies (*b*).' They are, while in this country, entitled to protection; but the effects of the revolutionary war of France introduced many special regulations as to aliens, which have only of late been relaxed (*c*). By the most recent statute on the subject, the regulations of the 7th George IV. are repealed; and from 1st July 1836, masters of ships are to declare, under a penalty, what aliens they bring into the country. All aliens are on arrival to enter their name and show their passport, under a penalty of £2; the registration of their name and description is to be transmitted to the Secretary of State, and a certificate granted without fee. On leaving the realm, the alien is to return his certificate, to be sent to the Secretary of State. And these regulations are not to affect foreign ministers, or aliens who have been in the country for three years, or persons under fourteen years of age (*d*).

(*a*) The definition includes persons born in Hanover while it was under the same sovereign as Great Britain. Isaacson *v.* Durant, 17 Q. B. D. 54.
(*b*) Musgrove *v.* Chun Teeong Toy, 1891; A. C. 272. See 33 and 34 Vict. c. 14, § 16.
(*c*) 33 Geo. III. c. 4. 38 Geo. III. c. 50 and 77. 42 Geo. III. c. 92. 43 Geo. III. c. 155. 58 Geo. III. c. 97. 7 Geo. IV. c. 54.
(*d*) 6 and 7 Will. IV. c. 11.

2135. Aliens are either friendly or hostile. Friendly aliens, under allegiance to a government at peace with Great Britain, 'were' yet incapable of acquiring heritage either by purchase or succession (*a*). 'By recent legislation, however, aliens are enabled to take, acquire, hold, and dispose of real and personal property of every description in all respects as natural born subjects, and to transmit a title to such property. But this relaxation of the law does not qualify them for any office, or any municipal, parliamentary, or other franchise, or confer any right as a British subject other than those above expressed in regard to property; nor does it affect any estate or interest to which any person has become entitled mediately or immediately, in possession or expectancy, under a disposition made before the Act, or by devolution by law on the death of anyone dying before the passing of the Act.' And an alien woman marrying a landholder in Scotland seems, 'according to Mr. Bell and the earlier cases,' to have no right to terce (*b*), nor an alien husband to courtesy. 'But this is altered by the statute (*c*).' An alien 'could' not hold even a lease for years, but 'might' hire a house for habitation (*d*). He cannot exercise the elective franchise (*e*), or be a peer or member of Parliament. He may trade as freely as a subject, and acquire property in goods, money, and moveable estate, and make a Will, and sue for personal debts. 'He cannot own a British ship (*f*).' Alien enemies have no right or title to pursue for debt in this country, unless by the Queen's special licence (*g*). But their right to debts due to them before the war is only suspended, not forfeited. The assignee of an alien enemy is in the same condition as to the recovery of debt with himself (*h*).

(*a*) 3 Ersk. 10. § 10. Leslie *v.* Forbes, 1749; M. 4636. See Dundas, *supra*, § 2133 (*b*). 7 and 8 Vict. c. 66, § 5.
(*b*) See Stewart *v.* Hoome, 1792; M. 4649. Nisbet *v.* Nisbet's Trs., *cit.* § 2133.
(*c*) 33 and 34 Vict. c. 14, § 2, 10. *Supra*, § 2132A.
(*d*) This statement of the common law of Scotland is disputed by Mr. Hunter, Landl. and Tenant, i. 192.
(*e*) Wight, 291. 33 and 34 Vict. c. 14, § 2.
(*f*) 33 and 34 Vict. c. 14, § 14. 57 and 58 Vict. c. 60, § 1.
(*g*) Carron *v.* Cowan & Co., Nov. 28, 1809; F. C. See *supra*, § 43.
(*h*) Johnston & Wight *v.* Goldsmid, Feb. 15, 1809; F. C.

2136. The disabilities of aliens may to a certain extent be relaxed, but not to the effect of identifying them with natural born subjects.

2137. Aliens may be naturalised by Act of Parliament to all intents and purposes, except the capacity of holding a seat in the Privy Council or in Parliament, and the power of holding offices of trust, or receiving grants from the Crown (*a*). And certain privileges of British subjects may be conferred by denization, which is by letters patent issued by the Queen. Thus a denizen may purchase lands, or take them by deed, and transmit them to his heirs born after the grant, not to heirs born before the grant, till which time he had no inheritable blood; but he cannot take by inheritance. He cannot be a member of the Privy Council or of Parliament, nor hold any office of trust, nor take a grant of lands from the Crown (*b*). 'A certificate of naturalisation, giving a right to all the privileges of a British subject, unless when the party receiving it is within the limits of the State of which he was previously a subject, and has not ceased by its laws or by treaty to be a subject of it, may now be obtained from the Secretary of State by persons who have lived five years in the United Kingdom, or served for five years under the Crown, and who intend when naturalised to live in the United Kingdom or serve under the Crown (*c*).'

(*a*) 12 Will. III. c. 2. 1 Geo. I. c. 4. 14 Geo. III. c. 84. 58 Geo. III. c. 97. 7 Geo. IV. c. 54. 1 Blackst. 374. See 33 and 34 Vict. c. 14.
(*b*) 3 Ersk. 10. § 10. 12 and 13 Will. III. c. 2. See above, § 2135.
(*c*) 33 and 34 Vict. c. 14, § 7. See as to the United States and renunciation of nationality, 35 and 36 Vict. c. 39.

II. PEERAGE.

2138. Classes of Peers.—The peerage is a privileged order of the people having precedence in the intercourse of society; distinguished by their titles; exempt from personal diligence of imprisonment; and members, either in their own right or by election, of the House of Lords. They are either,—1. Scottish Peers; or, 2. Peers of Great Britain raised to that dignity since the Union.

2139. Scottish Peerage.—The ancient records of our peerage are in a very imperfect state. While there are some peerages on the ancient rolls of Parliament of which the creation is not to be traced, it is certain that before the reign of James VI. titles of honour were conferred on the erection of lands into earldoms and lordships, and descended according to the destination in the titles of the land. Frequently they were resigned with the lands, and a new charter and descent settled; and, since the time of James VI., honours were granted by patents containing a destination of descent, some of those patents being connected with particular entails of land, while others bore a descent to such persons as the grantee might name to succeed to the peerage (*a*). 'In the absence of contrary limitation a peerage is presumed to descend to heirs-male and not to heirs general, and this presumption cannot be rebutted by inferential deduction (*b*).' At the Union, the Scottish peerage was fixed so that there could be no subsequent augmentation of it; and after that event a return was made to the House of Lords by the Lord Clerk Register of Scotland of one hundred and fifty-four peers (*c*); and afterwards, in 1740, another list was made up by the Lords of Session of the subsisting peerages (*d*).

(*a*) Report by the Lords of Session to the House of Peers in 1740. See Berkeley Peerage, 8 H. L. Ca. 21. Crawford and Lindsay Peerages, 2 H. L. Ca. 534.
(*b*) Herries Peerage, 3 Macq. 585; 2 H. L. Sc. 258. Mar Peerage, 1 App. Ca. 1.
(*c*) Journals of the Lords, 618, p. 468. Robertson on Scottish Peerage.
(*d*) Roll or List and Report in Wight's Apx.; Bell's Apx.; and Connell's Apx.; also Wood's Peerage, Apx. No. 5, vol. ii. p. 697.

2140. By the Act ratifying the treaty of Union, all peers of Scotland, and the successors to their honours and dignities, are to be peers of Great Britain. They are to have rank and precedency next after the peers of the like orders and degrees in England at the time of the Union, and before all peers of Great Britain of the like orders and degrees created after the Union. They are to be tried as peers of Great Britain, and enjoy all privilege of peers as fully as the peers of England, except that they are not to enjoy the right and privilege of sitting in the House of Lords, and the privileges depending thereon, and particularly the right of sitting on the trial of peers (*a*).

(*a*) 1707, c. 7.

2141. The Scottish Peerage is represented in the House of Lords by sixteen peers. The election is regulated by the Act passed after the conclusion of the treaty of Union (*a*); the representative peers are elected only for the Parliament for which they are chosen, not (like the Irish representative peers) for life. Scottish peers (of twenty-one years of age) alone can vote or be elected (*b*); but the vote of a Scottish peer is not destroyed by his holding an English peerage or a British peerage (*c*). There is now no disqualification to vote or sit in Parliament on account of Popery, provided the oath prescribed shall be taken (*d*). No alien, although naturalised, can be a representative peer, or vote in the election (*e*). Peers may vote by proxy (no peer, however, holding more than two proxies at a time), or by a signed list (*f*); but a peeress cannot vote (*g*). If a vote be objected to, a protest is the only competent proceeding at the election meeting (*h*). The Clerks of Session are bound to give effect to any resolution of the House of Lords, of which they have notice by order of the House (*i*). In case of equality there is no casting vote.

(*a*) 1707, c. 8. See as to the mode of election, 10 and 11 Vict. c. 52; 14 and 15 Vict. c. 87.
(*b*) 1707, c. 8.
(*c*) Resolution, Jan. 1709. Duke of Hamilton's Case, 1711; and again in 1782, in 1787, and June 6, 1793. Robertson's Proceedings, 42, 154, 441. Journals of House of Lords, c. 39, 693, 726–8. See Bell's Dict. (Ross' ed.), p. 315.
(*d*) 10 Geo. IV. c. 7, § 2 and 5. See 21 and 22 Vict. c. 48.
(*e*) 12 and 13 Will. III. c. 2. 1 Geo. I. c. 4. See Nicolson's Election Law, 8. 33 and 34 Vict. c. 14.
(*f*) 1707, c. 3, 8, and 23. See 15 and 16 Vict. c. 35.
(*g*) Herries Peerage, *cit.*
(*h*) E. Stirling *v.* Smith, 1836; 14 S. 221. See Breadalbane Peerage, 2 H. L. Sc. 269.
(*i*) Resolution, April 21, 1788.

2142. British Peerage.—Since the Union, peers created by the Crown are either British or Irish peers (limited in number), not English or Scottish. British peers sit in the House of Lords in their own right. Creation is by writ or patent.

2143. (1.) *Creation by Writ.*—This is effected by the sovereign's summons to attend the House of Peers, followed by actually taking seat in the House of Lords (*a*). The dignity thus conferred inures to the peer and his heirs descending from his body, although there be no such words in the writ (*b*).

(*a*) 1 Blackst. 400.
(*b*) *Ib.* 401. Devon Peerage, 5 Bligh, N. S. 313.

2144. (2.) *Creation by Patent.*—It would appear that in England, down to the time of Henry VII., parliamentary consent was required to the creation of a peer by patent; but this has been long abandoned. The patent may be personal, and is adjudged to be so, if there be no words of inheritance; as to heirs general or limited. 'But such a patent, even with the usual writ of summons to the House, does not enable the grantee to sit and vote in Parliament (*a*).'

(*a*) *Ib.* 401. See as to peerages for life, Resolution of the Committee of Privileges, Feb. 22, 1856. The Wensleydale Peerage, 5 H. L. Ca. 958; 2 Macq. 579. See as to Lords of Appeal in Ordinary (Life), 39 and 40 Vict. c. 59, and later Acts.

2145. **The Privileges of the Peerage** are these:—They are, as a personal, not a parliamentary privilege, exempt from imprisonment for a civil cause, even when Parliament is not sitting (*a*); and this is extended to peeresses by marriage, but forfeited in widowhood on marrying a commoner. They are privileged to be tried by their peers in treason, and felony, and misprision; but in other crimes, like a commoner, by a jury. They give verdict on trial of peers on their honour; but in giving evidence, even in the House of Lords, as well as on ordinary occasions, they are put upon oath. Scottish peers who are not elected as representative peers, and hold no British peerage, are excluded from Parliament; for they cannot, like Irish peers not elected, sit for English or Irish counties or burghs, although their eldest sons may (*b*). 'Peers of Parliament cannot vote at elections of members of the House of Commons; and are therefore not entitled to be placed on the register of voters (*c*).'

(*a*) D. Newcastle *v.* Morris, L. R. 4 H. L. 661; 40 L. J. Bkr. 4 (effect of bankruptcy statute applying to persons having privilege of Parliament). Peers who become bankrupt are disqualified from sitting in Parliament, 34 and 35 Vict. c. 50; 46 and 47 Vict. c. 52, § 32.

(*b*) Bryson & Henderson *v.* D. Athole, 1710; M. 10,029. E. Winton's Case, 1711; M. 10,028–9. D. Montrose *v.* M'Auley, 1711, *ib.* Erskine *v.* E. Kincardine, 1712; 4 B. Sup. 897. E. Breadalbane *v.* Innes, 1736; 1 Cr. & St. 181. Campbell *v.* Css. Fife, 1772; M. 9404. 2 and 3 Will. IV. c. 65, § 37.

(*c*) E. Beauchamp *v.* Madresfield Overseers, L. R. 8 C. P. 245; 42 L. J. C. P. 32; 2 Hopw. & C. 41. L. Rendlesham *v.* Haward, L. R. 9 C. P. 252; 43 L. J. C. P. 33; 2 Hopw. & C. 175.

2146. Although peers themselves are a privileged order, their families are in all senses commoners; except that the lady of a peer (but not the husband of a peeress) enjoys the privilege of nobility during her marriage and widowhood (*a*); that the eldest son of a duke, marquis, or earl, enjoys by courtesy a title of nobility; and that the eldest son of a Scottish peer, by the former law, could not elect or be elected a member to the Commons House of Parliament for a Scottish county or burgh (*b*); but may now, by the Act to amend the representation of the people in Scotland (*c*).

(*a*) M'Donald *v.* Widow of a Peer, 1756; M. 10,031.

(*b*) L. Daer *v.* Stewart, 1792; M. 8692; Apx. 16 (aff. 3 Pat. 293). See Connell on Elections, 260, note.

(*c*) 2 and 3 Will. IV. c. 65.

2147. **Descent of Peerages.**—The title and privileges descend according to the destination of the patent. Patents may be to the female as well as to the male line. Where the patent is lost, or the original so destroyed that the line of descent cannot be read, it was in one case held that the descent is to the heir of line, though a female; but this is said to have been afterwards adjudged otherwise (*a*). There is no occasion for service to vest the right. Many instances appear to have occurred before the Union of resignations of titles of honour along with estates; and charters on such resignations were held to carry the title as well as the land, provided the signature was superscribed by the King (*b*). It was also not unusual to grant honours to heirs of entail, and even to give a power of altering or nominating heirs. But although the two former practices might be lawful, the latter was by our best lawyers held unlawful, and the nomination under the power null and void. When the title to the peerage is contested, it seems that the proper tribunal is the House of Lords. It undoubtedly is a correct and legitimate proceeding for one who claims a Scottish peerage to apply to the Queen to have his title recognised; and Her Majesty may refer it to the House of Peers as her commissioners and great council. The question of right may be raised on the election of a representative peer, in consequence of an objection to the vote of one claiming his right to elect: and it rests with the House of Lords to determine the objection (*c*). But it seems to be correctly held, that in a strict judicial inquiry as to the point of title, and where no patrimonial interest is in question, the jurisdiction as to peerage is in the House of Lords, and not in a court of law subject to appeal to the House of Lords (*d*). 'The Court of Session refuses even to entertain an action of exhibition *in modum probationis* of writings relating to a claim to a peerage (*e*).'

(*a*) Oliphant *v.* Oliphant, 1633; M. 10,027, 14,866. L. Lovat's Case, 1729; M. 14,866. The presumption is that a peerage was limited to heirs-male. Kennedy *v.* E. Ruglen, 1762; 2 Pat. 55. Glencairn Peerage, 1797; 1 Macq. 444. Crawford and Lindsay Peerage, *infra*. Herries Peerage, 1858; 3 Macq. 585, 600; L. R. 2 Sc. App. 258.

(*b*) Crawford and Lindsay Peerage, 2 H. L. Ca. 534. Herries Peerage, 3 Macq. 585.

(*c*) Wight, 125.

(*d*) 1707, c. 8, § 19. Oliphant *v.* Oliphant, 1633; M. 10,027. Bruce *v.* E. Kincardine, 1707; M. 3167. Lovat, 1729; M. 14,866; and July 3, 1730. See resolutions of the Lords, May 2, 1822; Journal of House of Lords. Campbell *v.* Craufurd, 1824; 2 S. 737; 2 W. & S. 440. Montrose Peerage, 1853; 1 Macq. 401. Roxburghe Peerage, 1812; 5 Pat. 601. Huntly Peerage, 5 C. & F. 349. E. Waterford's Claim, 6 C. & F. 133.

(*e*) Campbell *v.* Craufurd, *cit.* Campbell *v.* Campbell, 1869; 7 Macph. 759. Barclay Allardice *v.* D. Montrose, 1872; 10 Macph. 774.

2148. Extinction of Peerages.—Peerage is extinguished only by death, or attainder (*a*), or degradation by Act of Parliament.

(*a*) Perth Peerage, 2 H. L. Ca. 865. Southesk Earldom, 2 H. L. Ca. 908.

III. COMMONS.

2149. Members of Parliament.—An extensive department of law has been rendered obsolete by the passing of the Acts for "amending the representation of the people in Scotland" (*a*). By those Acts there 'were' fifty-three representatives or members of Parliament for Scotland to the House of Commons, instead of forty-five. Of these, thirty are the representatives of counties, and twenty-three for burghs and towns. There is a combination of certain counties with each other, or with parts of other counties; and a combination of certain burghs and towns, together with a description of the boundaries of the several towns (*b*). 'By the Reform Act, 1868, seven additional members were given to Scotland; three to counties, two to burghs, and two to the universities (*c*). The Redistribution of Seats Act, 1885, gives Scotland 39 county and 31 burgh members, besides the two university representatives (*d*).' Members of Parliament have certain privileges. They enjoy freedom from arrest for debt 'while Parliament is sitting, and also' during forty days before the meeting of Parliament, and forty days after its prorogation (*e*); and privilege of speech in Parliament.

(*a*) 2 and 3 Will. IV. c. 65; 4 and 5 Will. IV. c. 88; and 6 and 7 Will. IV. c. 78.

(*b*) 2 and 3 Will. IV. c. 65, § 1–4, and Schedules B, E, M.

(*c*) See 31 and 32 Vict. c. 48, § 9, 10.

(*d*) 48 and 49 Vict. c. 23.

(*e*) 10 Geo. III. c. 50. 4 Geo. III. c. 33. Cassidy *v.* Steuart, 2 M. & Gr. 169. 2 Scott, N. R. 432. Goudy *v.* Duncombe, 1 Ex. 430; 17 L. J. Ex. 76. A person who has been adjudged bankrupt is disqualified for being elected to or sitting or voting in the House of Commons or any Committee thereof. 46 and 47 Vict. c. 52, § 32. See *ex p.* Pooley, L. R. 7 Ch. 519; 41 L. J. Bkr. 67.

2150. Representation of Counties. — The representation is regulated, as to those entitled to vote in counties; as to the mode of registration; and as to the mode of election.

2151. (1.) *Persons entitled or not to Vote.*—Persons entitled to vote require personal qualification, and qualification by property.

2152. No person subject to legal incapacity can be registered to vote; as Scottish peers (*a*), minors, lunatics, idiots, women (*b*), aliens; nor sheriffs, sheriff-substitutes, sheriff-clerks, and town-clerks, in their respective counties. A disqualification which existed under the former law is now removed: the eldest son of a Scottish peer may be registered or elected (*c*).

(*a*) See above, § 2145.

(*b*) Brown *v.* Ingram, 1868; 7 Macph. 281.

(*c*) 2 and 3 Will. IV. c. 65, § 7, 37. The disability of persons engaged in the collection or management of taxes is removed by 31 and 32 Vict. c. 73.

2153. If not disqualified, the following persons may be registered and vote, viz.:—Those who on 17th July 1832 were lawfully on the roll of freeholders of any shire in Scotland, or entitled so to be; or who, previous to March 1831, had become owners or superiors of lands affording the qualification for being so enrolled, so long as they retain such qualification; and under this rule there is an alternative vote to a liferenter and fiar so qualified (*a*).

Every person not subject to legal incapacity, who, when the Sheriff proceeds to consider his claim of registration, has been, for not less than six calendar months previous to the last day of July in that year, the owner (though not infeft) of any lands, houses, feu-duties, or other heritable subjects (except debts heritably secured) within the shire, of the yearly value of £10, actually yielding or capable of yielding that value to the claimant, after deducting feu-duty, ground-annual, or other consideration which he is bound to pay or account for as a condition of his right; provided he be in actual possession of the subject, or in receipt of the profits and issues thereof to the extent of £10, although payable at longer intervals than once a year.

Every person to whom by inheritance, marriage, marriage settlement, or *mortis causâ* disposition, or by appointment to place or office, such property comes within the six months before the last day of July, is entitled at the first registration after such acquisition to be enrolled. Each joint proprietor is entitled to vote, if his interest is worth £10 a year.

Liferenters may be registered and vote, not fiars.

Husbands are entitled to vote on the property of their wives, or on their own possession under courtesy.

Tenants in lands, houses, or other heritable subjects are entitled to be registered, if, when the Sheriff proceeds to consider their claim, they have held for not less than twelve months previous to the last day of July, on a fifty-seven years' lease, missive, or other written title, exclusive of breaks, or on a liferent lease, subjects in which their interest is of the clear yearly value of £10, after payment of rent and other consideration; or on a lease of not less than nineteen years, subjects of clear yearly value to the tenant, after payment of rent, of £50 a year; or where the rent is £50, and the tenant in the personal occupancy; or where the tenant has paid a grassum of not less than £300 (the value of grain rents to be estimated by the average fiar prices of the county for the three preceding years, or the average market prices for three years where payable in other produce). Tenants succeeding to a lease of the above description within the six months are entitled to registration. But no sub-tenant or assignee to any fifty-seven or nineteen years' lease is entitled to be registered, unless in actual occupation of the premises (*b*).

(*a*) See 5 and 6 Will. IV. c. 78, § 10.
(*b*) 2 and 3 Will. IV. c. 65, § 7, 8, 9.

2153A. '*The Reform Act of* 1868 added certain new franchises, but did not take away any of those above stated. In counties, it provides that every man shall be entitled to be registered as a voter, who, when the Sheriff proceeds to consider his right to be registered or to be retained on the register, is of full age and not subject to any incapacity, and who has been for six calendar months before the last day of July the proprietor, though not infeft, of lands and heritages, the yearly value of which, as appearing from the valuation roll of the county, is £5 or upwards, after deducting feu-duty, ground-annual, or other annual consideration which he may be bound to pay or give or account for as a condition of his right, and after deducting any annuity, liferent, or other such annual burden (*a*).

'The tenancy qualification belongs to every man who, when the Sheriff proceeds to consider his right to be inserted or retained on the roll, is of full age and subject to no incapacity, and has been for twelve calendar months before the last day of July in the actual personal occupancy, as tenant, of lands and heritages within the county of the annual value of £14 or upwards, as appearing on the valuation roll. Exemption from payment of poor-rates on the ground of poverty, failure to pay poor-rates due in respect of the lands occupied, or receipt of parochial relief within the said period of twelve months, disqualifies (*b*). A provision is added for successive occupancy, which is applicable also to £50 tenants claiming under the former Reform Act (*c*).

'The provisions as to liferenters and fiars, husbands of owners, and joint owners and joint occupants, are similar to those under the former Act. But only two persons can be registered as joint owners or joint tenants and occupants of the same lands and heritages, unless their shares have come to them by marriage or succession, or they are *bonâ fide* engaged in business on the same (*d*).'

(*a*) 31 and 32 Vict. c. 48, § 5. (*b*) *Ib.* § 6.
(*c*) *Ib.* § 13. (*d*) *Ib.* § 14.

2153B. '*The Representation of the People Act of* 1884 extended to counties the franchises introduced in burghs by the statute of 1868 just recited. (See below, § 2157A.) It enacts that "a uniform household franchise and a uniform lodger franchise at elections shall be established in all counties and boroughs throughout the United Kingdom, and every man possessed of a household qualification or a lodger qualification shall, if the qualifying premises be situate in a county in England or Scotland, be entitled to be registered as a voter, and when registered to vote at an election for such county" (*a*). The disqualification, introduced by judicial decisions, of persons occupying a dwelling-house by virtue of any office, service, or employment, is removed by the same statute in cases where the employer does not inhabit the dwelling-house (*b*). It also contains certain prohibitions against the multiplication of votes (*c*). And in regard to the occupation qualification, it is provided that, " Every man occupying any land or tenement in a county or borough in the United Kingdom of a clear yearly value of not less than ten pounds shall be entitled to be registered as a voter, and, when registered, to vote at an election for such county or borough in respect of such occupation, subject to the like conditions respectively as a man is, at the passing of the Act, entitled to be registered as a voter and to vote at an election for such county in respect of the county occupation franchise, and at an election for such borough in respect of the borough occupation franchise " (*d*).'

(*a*) 48 Vict. c. 2. (*b*) *Ib.* § 3.
(*c*) *Ib.* § 4. (*d*) *Ib.* § 5.

2154. (2.) *Mode of Registration.*—No one can vote unless he be registered. In the case of those on the old roll of freeholders, this registration takes place by transference of their names by the Sheriff-clerk to his list or register of voters on the new constituency, without requiring any claim to be made (*a*).

'The provisions of the Act of 1832 as to registration, formerly stated here, have been repealed, and new regulations introduced, in which the machinery introduced for the valuation of lands (*b*) has been made available for the registration of voters. In counties (*c*), the assessor under the Lands Valuation Act prepares and advertises each year before the 25th August a list of changes on the register. Claimants must send their claims to him, and objectors must give notice of their objection to him and the claimant or party on the roll, by 4th September. Lists of claims and objections are advertised by the assessor by 11th September, and copies of these and of the corrected register and list of changes are sent by him to the Sheriff-clerk. The Sheriff must hold his Registration Courts between 11th September and 11th October. When the Sheriff has revised the register, the Sheriff-clerk must enter it in a book before 31st October, the voters' names being numbered and arranged alphabetically in parishes. It is then printed in polling districts.

'An appeal lies from the Sheriff's judgment in the Registration Court to the Registration Appeal Court, which consists of three judges of the Court of Session. This appeal is in the form of a special case prepared by the Sheriff, and stating only the facts of the case and his decision (*d*). This Court may direct the Sheriff to make alterations on the register, which then becomes from the 31st October conclusive evidence that the persons therein named have the right to vote. Such persons are not required to take the oath of possession (*e*).'

(*a*) 2 and 3 Will. IV. c. 65, § 20.
(*b*) See above, § 1136B.
(*c*) 24 and 25 Vict. c. 83 (County Voters Act). 48 Vict. c. 16.
(*d*) 31 and 32 Vict. c. 48, § 23.
(*e*) *Ib.* § 54.

2155. (3.) *Mode of Election* (*a*).—After proclamation of the writ at the market-cross of the county town, if there 'were' only one candidate, the Sheriff, on a show of hands, 'proclaimed' the candidate duly elected. 'There is now no show of hands, public nominations being abolished. If there is only one candidate for each vacancy, the Sheriff declares him duly elected an hour after the time fixed for the election (*b*).' If there be more than one, and a poll is demanded, the Sheriff orders it to proceed within 'not less than' two 'nor more than six' days (*c*). Certain polling places (*d*) are appointed by the Sheriff, where, under the superintendence of the Sheriff or '" presiding officers "' named by him, and proper clerks, every person whose name is on the registration list being properly identified on oath (*e*) if necessary, gives his vote 'by secretly making a cross opposite the name of each candidate for whom he votes on a ballot paper, and depositing the paper in a ballot box in presence of the presiding officer (*f*)'; or anyone rejected may vote under protest. The poll 'was' not to be kept open for more than two days, from nine till four the first day, and from eight till four the second. 'But it is now open only for one day, from eight o'clock in the forenoon till eight o'clock in the afternoon, except in Orkney and Shetland (*g*).' The polling books being sealed up, the seals 'were' on the next day but one after closing the poll broken by the Sheriff, who is to make the return to the writ, the numbers cast up, and the state of the poll openly declared, and proclamation made of the member chosen. The return is made to the Clerk of the Crown in England under the hand and seal of the Sheriff,—a double return being made in case of equality. 'Under the present law the ballot boxes and election documents are sealed up and returned to the Sheriff or returning officer, who counts the votes as soon as practicable in presence of the candidates' agents. If the votes are equal, the Sheriff has a casting vote; or if he prefers, he may make a double return (*h*).'

(*a*) 2 and 3 Will. IV. c. 65, § 26, 27, 28, 29, 32, 33. As to the appointment and announcement of day and place of election, see 17 and 18 Vict. c. 102, § 11; 18 and 19 Vict. c. 24, § 1. The most important statute on the subject is now the Ballot Act, 35 and 36 Vict. c. 33. See Crichton's Analysis of the Ballot Act. Haswell *v.* Stewart, 1874; 1 R. 925.
(*b*) 35 and 36 Vict. c. 33, § 1, etc.
(*c*) *Ib.* Sch. I. Rule 14.
(*d*) See 16 Vict. c. 28, § 2, 3; 31 and 32 Vict. c. 48, § 26. Crichton's Analysis, p. 80.
(*e*) By declaration, 24 and 25 Vict. c. 83, Sch. D. Nicolson on Elections, 178. Crichton, p. 22.
(*f*) 35 and 36 Vict. c. 33. Sch. I. Rules 24, 25.
(*g*) 16 Vict. c. 28. 48 Vict. c. 10.
(*h*) 35 and 36 Vict. c. 33, § 2, and Sch. I. Rule 32 sqq.

2156. Representation of Burghs (*a*).—The great principles are the same on which this election is regulated, but necessarily with certain differences in detail.

(*a*) See below, § 2163, for the election of town councils.

2157. (1.) *Persons entitled or not to Vote.*—The election is no longer in town councils or burghs, but in individual voters. The claimant, not being subject to legal incapacity, nor being town-clerk or depute town-clerk (*a*) of the burgh, nor having been in the receipt of parochial relief within twelve calendar months, must have been, when the Sheriff proceeds to consider his claim of registration, for not less than twelve calendar months previous to the last day of July in the occupancy as proprietor, tenant, or liferenter of any house, warehouse, counting-house, shop, or other building within the limits of the burgh or town, which separately is of the value of £10 yearly, or which, taken jointly with any other house, shop, or other building, is of that value; or shall, previous to the 31st July, be the true owner of such premises, though not occupant of premises of the necessary value; or the husband of the owner. He must, on or before the 20th day of July, have paid all assessed taxes payable in respect of such premises previous to 6th April then preceding. And he must have resided (*b*) for six calendar months previous to the last day of July within the city, burgh, or town, or within seven miles of it. It is enough for the title of occupancy, if the voter have been, during the twelve months requisite, in possession of different premises in succession, provided he have paid the assessed taxes for them all. And where the premises are of the yearly value of £20 or more, joint occupants, provided each share shall be of the yearly value of £10, are entitled to vote (*c*). 'One of two or more joint owners may be registered, if he reside within seven miles (*d*).'

(*a*) Johnstone *v.* M'Muldrow, 1868; 7 Macph. 281.
(*b*) See 48 Vict. c. 9 (letting house furnished).
(*c*) 2 and 3 Will. IV. c. 65, § 11, 12.
(*d*) 48 and 49 Vict. c. 3, § 4. Roughead, 1885; 13 R. 75.

2157A. 'In burghs, besides those possessing the qualification stated in the foregoing section, every man is entitled to vote at elections of a member of Parliament, who, when the Sheriff considers his claim to be inserted or retained on the roll, is of full age and subject to no incapacity, and (1) has been for not less than twelve months, previous to the last day of July, an inhabitant occupier (not a joint occupier), as owner or tenant, of any dwelling-house within the burgh; provided that he has not during the said period been exempted from payment of poor-rates on the ground of inability to pay, nor has failed to pay poor-rates, nor has received parochial relief within said period (*a*); or (2) has occupied as a lodger in the same burgh, separately and as sole tenant, for the twelve months preceding the last day of July, lodgings of a clear yearly value, if let unfurnished, of £10 or upwards, has resided in such lodgings for the said twelve months, and has claimed to be registered as a voter (*b*). The same rule as to successive occupancy applies both in counties and burghs (*c*).'

(*a*) 31 and 32 Vict. c. 48, § 3.
(*b*) *Ib.* § 4. (*c*) *Ib.* § 13.

2158. (2.) *Mode of Registration.*—'The clauses of the first Reform Act as to registration in burghs, formerly stated here, have been repealed, and a new method introduced similar to that in use in counties (*a*). The town-clerk acts instead of the Sheriff-clerk. The new list of voters must be advertised by 15th September, notices of claims and objections given by 21st September, and the lists of such notices advertised by 25th September. The Registration Courts are held between 25th September and 15th October. Thereafter the town-clerk prints the revised lists of voters, arranged in wards and polling districts, which is conclusive evidence for the ensuing year of the right of those named in it to vote, and they are not required to take the oath of possession. The Court of Appeal and rules for appeal are the same as in counties (*b*).'

(*a*) See above, § 2154.
(*b*) 19 and 20 Vict. c. 58. 31 and 32 Vict. c. 48, § 20, 22. 48 Vict. c. 16.

2159. (3.) *Mode of Election.*—The mode of election is, with the necessary differences, the same in burghs and towns as in counties. The Sheriff, 'on the day of or day' after receiving the writ for towns or burghs, is to announce a day of election, not less than four, 'now three,' nor more than ten, 'now six clear days, except in the case of the Wick District of Burghs, where the Sheriff, under the old law, must fix a day not less than ten or more than sixteen days,' after receipt of the writ (*a*). 'The day of nomination must now be not later than the fourth, or in a district of burghs the ninth, day after the receipt of the writ. The polling day must be not less than two and not more than six clear days after the nomination in the case of a district of burghs, and not more than three days in an ordinary burgh.' He is to arrange the polling places so that not more than 300 shall be apportioned to each, or even to a greater extent, the candidate paying the expense. And the poll for cities is to be kept open for one day only, with power to adjourn it if interrupted by riot or violence (*b*).

(*a*) Ballot Act, Sch. I. Rules 2, 14.
(*b*) 5 and 6 Will. IV. c. 78. 17 and 18 Vict. c. 102, § 11. 28 and 29 Vict. c. 92. 31 and 32 Vict. c. 48, § 44. See the Ballot Act, 35 and 36 Vict. c. 33.

2159A. '*The Universities* of Aberdeen and Glasgow return one member of Parliament, and those of Edinburgh and St. Andrews another. The franchise belongs to the chancellor, members of the University Court, professors and registered members of the General Councils of the respective universities (*a*).

'*Registration.*—Annually, on 1st December, the registrar of the university begins to prepare a new register. This must be completed within fifteen days, is then revised by the registrar and two assistant registrars appointed by the University Court, and authenticated by the vice-chancellor on or before 31st December. An appeal is competent against undue omission or insertion of names for ten days thereafter. Appeals are heard by the University Court before 30th January. The register is conclusive evidence of the right to vote for the year from 1st January to 31st December (*b*). The election in universities is by means of voting papers, and in the manner prescribed by the Act of 1868 (*c*).'

(*a*) 31 and 32 Vict. c. 48, § 27, 28.
(*b*) *Ib.* § 29–36. (*c*) *Ib.* § 37–40.

2160. Clergy.—The clergy, at one time a privileged and distinct body, are now in all respects, except what pertains to their clerical functions, on the same footing with the laity. From the time of the Reformation and full establishment of the present system of Church government in Scotland, a clergyman, after due presentation or call, and act of admission by the presbytery, and ordination as a presbyter, has full right to his benefice as minister of the parish, and is thenceforward a constituent member of the Church judicatories, and subject in all spiritual matters to the jurisdiction of the Church courts; but in all other respects he is, like the laity, subject to the civil magistrate, and ordinary courts of law, civil and criminal, and holds no privilege or exemption beyond other subjects (*a*).

(*a*) 1560. 1567, c. 2. 1592, c. 116. 1597, c. 231. 1606, c. 3. 1690, c. 5.

CHAPTER V

OF BURGHS AND CORPORATIONS

I. BURGHS.

2161. General View.—The early history of cities and towns forms a very interesting feature in the progress of Europe from barbarism to civilisation. That of the cities and towns of Scotland is very obscure. One class of burghs, belonging to the royalty (as Edinburgh, Stirling, Dumbarton, etc.), seems to have grown up in the neighbourhood of the King's castles; acquiring privileges and immunities in return for subsidies and benevolences, contributed from the growing wealth of the inhabitants. Another class of burghs, analogous to these, grew up within the regality around the castles of nobles (as Dunbar, Thirlestane, Doune, etc.), with similar privileges for like aids. The former are the Royal Burghs (*a*); the latter are Burghs of Regality and of Barony (*b*).

A new constitution has been provided for royal burghs, and also for those burghs, not being royal burghs, which have a right of sending or contributing to send a member to Parliament (*c*). And provision has also been made for enabling all burghs in Scotland, whether royal burghs or burghs of regality or barony, 'and all populous places now known as "police burghs,"' to establish a general system of police, 'and for extending their boundaries' (*d*).

(*a*) See above, § 839.
(*b*) See above, § 848.
(*c*) 3 and 4 Will. IV. c. 76 and 77. See above, § 2156 et seq.
(*d*) 3 and 4 Will. IV. c. 46. 10 and 11 Vict. c. 39. 13 and 14 Vict. c. 33 (General Police Act of 1850). 16 and 17 Vict. c. 93. 23 and 24 Vict. c. 96. 25 and 26 Vict. c. 101 (General Police Act, 1862). 31 and 32 Vict. c. 102. 39 Vict. c. 12 (Burgesses Act, 1876). 40 and 41 Vict. c. 22. 41 and 42 Vict. c. 30. 45 and 46 Vict. c. 6. 52 and 53 Vict. c. 51; all repealed by the General Police Act, 1892, 55 and 56 Vict. c. 55, § 6, Sch. 1, except so far as they are incorporated by reference in unrepealed local Acts.

2162. Royal Burghs.—The royal burghs became important, as bearing a regular share of the public burdens. Called only occasionally at first to conventions for the purpose of imposing taxes, they were at last recognised as one of the estates of the realm. The royal burghs were sixty-six in number.

2163. Constitution of Royal Burghs.—(1.) *Ancient.*—The royal burghs derive their existence and constitution from royal charter, either express, or which is presumed to have existed, and by the accidents of war and time to have perished. The right of electing the common councils and magistrates was in ancient times in large classes of the inhabitants, merchants, and craftsmen. By statute in the fifteenth century (*a*), a constitution was established in the royal burghs; but by deviations in the several burghs, and gradual abrogation, the system of election lost its former free and popular form, and at last a close and exclusive plan of power and rotatory election was established in the persons of the leading members of corporations.

(*a*) 1424, c. 39. 1469, c. 30.

2164. (2.) *Modern.*—This close system has, by a statute following up the spirit of the

Acts for reforming the representation of the people in Parliament, been abolished, and the ancient free constitution substantially restored (*a*). The election of the town council of every royal burgh (with nine exceptions) (*b*) is placed in such owners and occupants of premises (*c*), 'including women, whether married or not (*d*),' within the royalty of the burgh as shall be qualified to vote in the election of a member of Parliament for such burgh by the Act of 2 and 3 William IV. c. 65, 'or 31 and 32 Vict. c. 48,' and who shall have resided, 'in the case of persons qualified under the first-mentioned Act,' six months previous to 30th June preceding the election, within the royalty or within seven miles thereof; 'and in that of persons possessed of the qualifications which would make them parliamentary voters, if their premises, being within the municipal boundaries, are not beyond the parliamentary boundaries of the burgh.' Provision is made for enrolling persons entitled to vote in such burghs as were not at the date of the Act entitled to send members to Parliament, and for deciding on their claims, and keeping lists of their names. Lists of persons entitled to vote in both these classes of burghs are to be kept by the town-clerk. The burghs of Edinburgh, Glasgow, Aberdeen, Dundee, Perth, Dunfermline, Dumfries, and Inverness are to be divided into wards by commissioners, to be appointed (and who have accordingly made such division) for the purpose of choosing a certain number of councillors for each ward, so as to make up the whole number required (*e*). Each royal burgh, on the first Tuesday of November, chooses 'by ballot, formerly' by open poll, in one day, from those qualified to elect, such a number of councillors as by the sett or constitution of each burgh constitutes the common council of the burgh, or the smallest number authorised by the sett. The polling lists, sealed up and transmitted to the provost or head magistrate (*f*), 'were, before the Ballot Act,' by him publicly opened, summed up, and the result declared (*g*). No one is entitled to be a councillor unless he shall be a burgess of the burgh, to which he shall be admitted on payment of the ordinary fees, no merely honorary burgess being admissible. 'He may pay the burgess dues after his election as a councillor, but before his induction (*h*). No one who has been "adjudged bankrupt," *i.e.* "whose estates are sequestrated, or who is under a decree of *cessio bonorum*," can be elected to or hold or exercise the office of councillor (*i*).' Each succeeding year, a new election of a third of the council takes place, —a third of the old council going out of office; those who had the smallest number of votes at the election going out first, but being capable of re-election (*k*). On the third day after the election of the council the councillors elect from their number the provost and bailies, and other officers: the provost continuing for three years in his office 'after his appointment, his tenure of office not being affected by the date of his election as councillor (*l*).'

(*a*) 3 and 4 Will. IV. c. 76. See 4 Will. IV. c. 19, § 3. 4 and 5 Will. IV. c. 86 and 87. 15 and 16 Vict. c. 32. 31 and 32 Vict. c. 108. 33 and 34 Vict. c. 92. 35 and 36 Vict. c. 33 (Ballot Act).

(*b*) Dornoch, New Galloway, Culross, Lochmaben, Bervie, Wester Anstruther, Kilrenny, Kinghorn, and Kintore. This exception is repealed by 31 and 32 Vict. c. 108, § 3.

(*c*) Generally "such persons as are qualified in respect of any premises within the royalty, whether original or extended, of such burgh," including therefore lodgers. 31 and 32 Vict. c. 108, § 3.

(*d*) 44 and 45 Vict. c. 13, § 23. 57 and 58 Vict. c. 58, § 11, 55, Sch. 1.

(*e*) Power to rearrange wards, and to divide into wards burghs not already divided, is given by 31 and 32 Vict. c. 108, § 16, 17. 39 and 40 Vict. c. 25.

(*f*) Mags. of Musselburgh, petrs., 1881; 9 R. 78. Mags. of Peebles, petrs., 1881; 9 R. 80.

(*g*) In royal burghs not enumerated in any of the lists above given, the election of councillors was by signed lists.

(*h*) 23 and 24 Vict. c. 47.

(*i*) 46 and 47 Vict. c. 52, § 32, 34. 47 and 48 Vict. c. 16, § 5. Thom *v.* Mags. of Aberdeen, 1885; 12 R. 701.

(*k*) This rule was applicable only to the two years immediately following the passing of the Act, and ever since the third going out of office consists of the councillors who have been longest in office, the number of votes becoming the test only where less than a third of the council have been three years in office. Scott *v.* Mags. of Edinr., 1838; 1 D. 347. Thomson *v.* Mags. of Rutherglen, 1876; 3 R. 451, 458. See 33 and 34 Vict. c. 92, § 5.

(*l*) 3 and 4 Will. IV. c. 76, § 24. 3 and 4 Will. IV. c. 77, § 22. Whyte *v.* Scott, 1851; 14 D. 105. Thomson, *supra* (*k*). Dunlop *v.* Fleming, 1837; 16 S. 254. As to the bailies, see Marwick's Law and Practice of Municipal Elections, § 163. See as to null elections, Kidd *v.* Anstruther Wester, 1852; 15 D. 257. 16 and 17 Vict. c. 26; and as to the case where all the magistrates are included in the retiring third of the council, 15 and 16 Vict. c. 32, § 5. Ogilvie *v.* Guthrie, 1865; 3 Macph. 588. Mags. of Renfrew, 1897; 25 R. 18. The election of a provost and magistrates is a statutory duty to be enforced by the Supreme Court. Herron *v.* Town Council of Renfrew, 1880; 7 R. 497.

2165. While the rights of the guildry, trades, etc., to elect their own deacons, dean of guild, etc., are preserved, these are in most of the burghs no longer recognised as official and constituent members of the town council; and the functions of those officers are now performed by a member of the council, elected by the majority of councillors. But the Dean of Guild and Deacon Convener of Trades in Edinburgh and Glasgow, and the Deans of Guild in Aberdeen, Dundee, and Perth, elected as formerly, are continued as constituent members of the council to perform all the functions of those offices (*a*).

(*a*) 3 and 4 Vict. c. 76, § 19, 22. 31 and 32 Vict. c. 108, § 10. Marwick's Municipal Elections, § 142, 238. As to the jurisdiction and powers of the Dean of Guild and magistrates in regard to buildings, see 2 Ersk. 9. § 9. Scouller *v.* Pollok, 1832; 10 S. 241. Milne *v.* Melville, 1841; 4 D. 111. Smellie *v.* Thomson, 1868; 6 Macph. 1024. Lang *v.* Bruce, 1873; 11 Macph. 377. More *v.* Bradford, 1873; 1 R. 208. Lammond *v.* Cumming, 1875; 2 R. 784. Tainsh *v.* Mags. of Hamilton, 1877; 4 R. 315. Crawfurd *v.* Mags. of Paisley, 1870; 8 Macph. 693 (*per* L. Deas). Pitman *v.* Burnett's Trs., 1881; 8 R. 914; 1882, 9 R. 444. Speed *v.* Philip, 1883; 10 R. 795. Colville *v.* Carrick, 1883; 10 R. 1241. Mitchell *v.* Dean of Guild of Edinr., 1885; 12 R. 844. Johnston *v.* Edinr. Gaslight Co., 1885; 12 R. 974. Manson *v.* Forrest, 1887; 14 R. 802 (*qu.* whether he has jurisdiction as to nuisances?). Robertson *v.* Thomas, 1887; 14 R. 822 (ditto). Kirkwood's Trs. *v.* Leith & Bremner, 1888; 16 R. 255. Walker & Dick *v.* Park, 1888; 15 R. 477 (building restrictions in titles). Somerville *v.* M'Gregor, 1889; 17 R. 46. Paisley Prov. Co-op. Soc. *v.* Buchanan, 1889; 17 R. 66. Eglinton Chem. Co. *v.* M'Jannet, 1890; 18 R. 34 (buildings entirely within and not touching the boundaries of the owner building). Walker *v.* Lang, 1891; 18 R. 928 (appeal—record). Lawrie *v.* Jackson, 1894; 18 R. 1154 (appeal—party not immediately adjoining). Somerville *v.* L. Adv., 1893; 20 R. 1050 (Crown not subject to jurisdiction of D. of G.). Greenock Police Board *v.* Shaw Stewart, 1896; 23 R. 776. Macgregor *v.* Mags. of Leith, 1897; 24 R. 971 (alteration—valuation—B. P. Act, § 167). Saltoun *v.* Mags. of Edinr., 1897; 23 R. 956; 24 R. 832.

2166. The burgh, acting according to its reformed sett or constitution, has the power of making by-laws (not inconsistent with the laws of the land) for the good government of the burgh, the management of its funds, and the regulation of its corporations.

2167. Privileges of Burgesses.—The burgesses and guild-brethren 'had' within the limits of the burgh a monopoly of trade and manufacture unless on market days, when the sale 'was' open to dealers and manufacturers in the country, or unfreemen in town, to sell their wares. 'All exclusive privileges of trading within burghs were abolished by 9 and 10 Vict. c. 17, but the guilds and corporations still exist, with power to elect their own deacons and officers for managing their own affairs (*a*).'

(*a*) See 3 and 4 Will. IV. c. 76, § 21. Thomson *v.* Candlemakers of Edinr., 1855; 17 D. 765. Wrights of Leith, petrs., 1856; 18 D. 981 (incompetent to divide funds directly or indirectly). Guildry of Arbroath, petrs., 1856; 18 D. 1207. Anderson *v.* Wrights of Glasgow, 1862; 1 Macph. 152; aff. 1865, 3 Macph. H. L. 1. Morris *v.* Guildry of Dunfermline, 1866; 4 Macph. 457. Masons and Wrights of Haddington, petrs., 1881; 8 R. 1029 (application of funds on decline of Society). Muir *v.* Rodger, 1881; 9 R. 149 (ditto).

2168. Finances of Royal Burghs. — To remedy disorders in the revenues of royal burghs, it was formerly enacted that certified accounts should be annually deposited with the town-clerk, to remain for thirty days open to inspection and complaint in writing to the Exchequer; the power of feuing was regulated and checked; and the power of contracting debt was limited (*a*). The annual account is now ordered on a better footing, by the Act for reforming the constitution of burghs (*b*).

Annually, on the 15th October, a state of the affairs, funds, properties, and revenues, and all transactions regarding them, is to be made up and lodged with the town-clerk, open to the inspection of the electors; no magistrates or councillors being, as such, personally responsible for the debts of the burgh, or acts of his predecessors, otherwise than as a burgess or inhabitant.

(*a*) 3 Geo. IV. c. 91 (Sir Wm. Rae's Act). Mags. of Renfrew *v.* Murdoch, 1892; 19 R. 823.
(*b*) 3 and 4 Will. IV. c. 76, § 32, 33; c. 77, § 31.

2169. The burgh bears a share of the public taxes allocated among the burghs by the Convention of Royal Burghs, and levied by stenting and assessment.

2170. The expense of general and local prisons 'was' to be borne by burghs, assessed according to rules laid down in statute. 'The prison assessment was afterwards laid on lands and heritages in each county and the burghs therein, according to their value as appearing on the valuation roll; but the expenses of prisons are now defrayed by Parliament (*a*).'

(*a*) 2 and 3 Vict. c. 42, § 46 et seq. 23 and 24 Vict. c. 105. 28 and 29 Vict. c. 84, repealed by the Prisons (Scotland) Act, 1877, 40 and 41 Vict. c. 53.

2171. Property of Royal Burghs. — The burgh as a corporation holds its property and privileges without sasine, of the Crown, for the services of watching and warding. The several holders of burgage property are also

Crown vassals, entering with the magistrates as commissioners of the Crown (*a*).

(*a*) See above, § 839 et seq.

2172. Convention of Royal Burghs.—The royal burghs having a common interest in matters of trade were accustomed to meet occasionally at Edinburgh. This convention appears to have been at first a court under the direction of the Chamberlain, called the "Court of the Four Burghs"; that officer being assisted by delegates from Edinburgh, Stirling, Berwick, and Roxburgh. In the fifteenth century, delegates were directed to come to the meeting from all the burghs, to treat of their common interests (*a*). The Chamberlain seems to have ceased to hold those courts, but the delegates formed a convention which gradually assumed a regular and systematic constitution. The records of this assembly commence in the sixteenth century; and annually, for a long series of years, the convention has regularly met at Edinburgh by delegates from every royal burgh, with two from Edinburgh. The convention was held entitled to regulate the setts of the several burghs.

(*a*) 1487, c. 111. Cunningham *v.* Convention of Royal Burghs, 1839; 1 D. 1077.

2173. Parliamentary Burghs not being Royal Burghs. — Certain burghs, not being royal burghs, have been admitted to the privilege of sending, or contributing to send, members to Parliament, and a new constitution has been conferred on them by an Act (*a*) analogous to that made for regulating royal burghs. These are: Paisley, Greenock, Leith, Kilmarnock, Falkirk, Hamilton, Peterhead, Musselburgh, Airdrie, Port Glasgow, Cromarty, Portobello, and Oban. For each of these burghs a certain number of councillors is appointed to be chosen; the election to be with the persons qualified to vote for a member of Parliament. 'All municipal elections are conducted in the manner prescribed by the Ballot Act (*b*).' A third of the council to go out and others to be elected every year; and the provost and magistrates to be chosen by the council from their own number.

(*a*) 3 and 4 Will. IV. c. 77. 4 and 5 Will. IV. c. 86 and 87. See 31 and 32 Vict. c. 108.
(*b*) 35 and 36 Vict. c. 33, § 20.

2174. Burghs of Regality and Barony.—These burghs, deriving their privileges as corporations from royal charters, hold of subjects, and are governed by magistrates elected by the lord of regality or baron, or by the inhabitants of the town. Their only privilege is that of trade and manufacture within the burgh (*a*). But sometimes a power is granted to the burgh to erect corporations in crafts, analogous to royal burghs (*b*). The general law of incorporations applies to those burghs (*c*). They have power to administer their common good, to elect officers, to make by-laws; and the burgesses are entitled to challenge the alienation of the burgh's property (*d*).

(*a*) Town of Edinburgh *v.* Town of Leith, 1630; M. 1823. Burgh of Kelso *v.* Hutchison, 1739; M. 1829. Feuars of Kelso *v.* D. Roxburghe, 1755; M. 1830, 10.737. See above, § 849. Exclusive privileges of trading were abolished by 9 and 10 Vict. c. 17.
(*b*) Fleshers of Canongate *v.* Town of Edinr., 1677; M. 1824. Kelso, *supra* (*a*).
(*c*) See below, § 2176 et seq.
(*d*) Wilson *v.* Story, 1775; 5 B. Sup. 629. Stewart *v.* Mags. of Paisley, Jan. 22, 1822; F. C.

2175. As to jurisdiction, there is a distinction between such burghs as had a local magistracy depending on the superior, and those held independent of him; the former being abolished with other heritable jurisdictions, the latter preserved (*a*). And, by statute, means are provided for establishing in all burghs of regality and barony, as well as in royal burghs, a general system of police (*b*).

(*a*) 20 Geo. IV. c. 43. Walkinshaw *v.* Bailies of Greenock, 1794; Bell's Ca. 15; M. 7714.
(*b*) 3 and 4 Will. IV. c. 46. 13 and 14 Vict. 33. 25 and 26 Vict. c. 101. 55 and 56 Vict. c. 55 (1892).

2175A. 'Populous Places under the General Police Acts. — Seven householders of any "populous place" containing above seven hundred inhabitants, may apply to the Sheriff to fix its boundaries for the purposes of the General Police Act (*a*). Householders for this purpose are occupiers of lands or premises whose occupancy would qualify them to vote for a member of Parliament for a burgh, and include female occupiers entitled to vote at municipal elections (*b*). The Sheriff directs intimation by advertisement of the application, nominates a person to report on the population of the place, and, after hearing parties, determines what area, if any, is in substance a town, and defines its boundaries. He must find the place to be a burgh, if its population exceeds 2000. He also fixes whether the burgh is to be in wards, and the limits of the wards. His deliverance, unless appealed against, is final, and is recorded along with the application in his Court Books (*c*). If the Sheriff does not declare the place a burgh, another application is not competent for two years (*d*). The Sheriff is next furnished by the Assessor under the Valuation Acts with a list of the householders of the new burgh, and conducts an election (*e*) by ballot (*f*) of police commissioners (the number varying according to population (*g*)). The commissioners first elected choose out of their number the magistrates, viz.: a provost and bailies (*h*). Vacancies occurring during the year, and deficiencies at elections, are filled up by the remaining commissioners (*i*). The future annual elections of commissioners are conducted as the elections of town councillors in burghs (*k*), one-third of the commissioners retiring from office annually, but the provost always remaining in office for three years after his election as such (*l*). The magistrates are *ex officio* justices of peace and commissioners of supply of the county (*m*). They have, where no dean of guild court is established, a jurisdiction similar to that of the dean of guild in regard to buildings within the "police burgh" (*n*); but, while they can try offences against the Public Houses Acts, the jurisdiction in licensing remains with the county justices (*o*).'

(*a*) 55 & 56 Vict. c. 55 (Burgh Police (Scotland) Act, 1892), § 9 (1), 4 (26).
(*b*) *Ib.* § 4 (14). (*c*) *Ib.* § 9, 29.
(*d*) *Ib.* § 16. (*e*) *Ib.* § 25, 26.
(*f*) *Ib.* § 26. 35 & 36 Vict. c. 33, § 20. See Hamilton *v.* Dunoon Police Commissioners, 1875; 2 R. 299.
(*g*) *Ib.* § 29. (*h*) *Ib.* § 35, 36. (*i*) *Ib.* § 28, 32.
(*k*) *Ib.* § 32. See above, § 2164.
(*l*) *Ib.* § 37. See above, § 2164 (*k*).
(*m*) 33 and 34 Vict. c. 37.
(*n*) 55 and 56 Vict. c. 55, § 201 sqq. See Michie's Trs. *v.* Grant, 1872; 11 Macph. 51. Fort-William Police Comrs. *v.* Kennedy, 1877; 4 R. 266. Tainsh *v.* Mags. of Hamilton, 1877; 4 R. 315. Robertson *v.* Greenock Police Board, 1883; 11 R. 304. See above, § 2165.
(*o*) 55 and 56 Vict. c. 55, § 38. Tennent *v.* Mags. of Partick, 1894; 21 R. 735.

II. CORPORATIONS.

2176. Nature and Kinds.—A corporation may be described as an ideal and legal person, intended to perpetuate the enjoyment of certain rights and privileges for the public benefit. In former times, the erection of corporations for the advancement of religion, learning, and commerce, formed an important department of public policy. The object was to maintain a perpetual succession, and carry on to maturity, from generation to generation, institutions liable to fall into decay on the death of individuals. For this purpose, many persons were united into one society by the royal authority, with particular privileges,—a power to hold property; to make by-laws for regulating their community; a course of succession; and on many occasions a monopoly in trade, in manufactures, or in teaching. Such are the royal burghs of Scotland; the guildry and corporations of which they consist: and universities (*a*). With the same view of perpetuating the interest and continuing the right from generation to generation, another kind of corporation is known in law, called by English lawyers a corporation *sole*; of which the highest example is the sovereign, and almost the only other example in Scotland, the minister of a parish.

(*a*) See below, § 2182 et seq. See 1 Ersk. 7. § 64. Grant on Corporations. Clark on Partnership and Joint-Stock Companies, 32 sqq.

2177. Constitution.—There can be no corporation in Scotland without a charter from the Crown, express or implied (*a*). Many implied grants are to be found in burghs whose charters of erection are not now extant, but are by the law supposed to have perished (*b*). Express grants of corporate privileges are either by the royal authority, with consent of Parliament; or by royal charter, without legislative interposition. An Act of Parliament is necessary wherever the corporation is invested with a monopoly; for the power of granting monopolies was taken from the Crown in James VI.'s time (*c*). The Crown has the power of creating a corporation, and this either directly or indirectly: directly, by grant of corporation privileges; indirectly, by giving a delegation of authority to make inferior corporations, as in a burgh. By statute, it may in such charters be provided that the members of the corporation shall be individually liable in their persons and property for debts, contracts, and engagements of such corporation, to such extent, and subject to such regulations and restrictions, as may be thought fit and proper, and as shall be declared and limited in and by such charter (*d*).

(*a*) Univ. of Glasgow *v.* Faculty of Physicians and Surgeons, 1834; 13 S. 9; 1835, 2 S. & M'L. 275; 1837, 15 S. 736; aff. 1840, 1 Rob. 397.

(*b*) Dempster *v.* Masters and Seamen of Dundee, 1831; 9 S. 313.

(*c*) 21 James I. c. 3. 1641, c. 76.

(*d*) 6 Geo. IV. c. 91 (The "Bubble Companies" Act), repealed S. L. Revn. Act, 1873.

2178. Powers. — The incidents to a corporation are these:—As a legal person, the corporation has *persona standi in judicio.* It may sue or be sued, grant and receive, by its corporate name. It has a power of electing officers to represent the community; and to elect new members, unless by the charter, or by any by-law made under the powers which it confers, this right be limited or regulated. It may purchase and hold lands, and be infeft by its corporate name and title: and has perpetual succession (*a*). It has power, for the better government of the corporation, to make by-laws or private statutes binding upon the corporation and its members, unless contrary to the laws of the land. The act of the majority, 'within the powers of the corporation (*b*),' is the act of the whole, unless it shall be otherwise appointed in a charter, or ruled by a by-law. The sovereign is by law visitor or head of all corporations. But the jurisdiction which is vested in the Supreme Court is not of a visitorial nature, nor in any degree discretionary, being strictly judicial (*c*).

(*a*) Hence arises, in relation to the feudal superior when lands are purchased, the difficulty already explained, § 722.

(*b*) Gray *v.* Smith, 1836; 14 S. 1062. Howden *v.* Incorporation of Goldsmiths, 1840; 2 D. 996. Rodgers *v.* Tailors of Edinr., 1842; 5 D. 295. Balfour's Trs. *v.* Edinr. and Northern Ry. Co., 1848; 10 D. 1240. Wedderburn *v.* Scottish Central Ry. Co., 1848; 10 D. 1317. Clouston *v.* Edinr. and Glasgow Ry. Co., 1865; 4 Macph. 207. Galloway *v.* Ranken, 1864; 2 Macph. 1199. Pollock on Contracts, 122–143, 656 sqq. 1 Smith's L. C. 411 sqq.

(*c*) See Kesson *v.* Aberdeen Wrights' Incorpn., 1898; 1 F. 36.

2179. Extinction.—A corporation may be extinguished in one or other of the following modes:—By expiration of time, if of limited duration; by Act of Parliament, when the powers or privileges of a corporation are deemed fit to be recalled; by inability to fulfil the purposes of its institution, as by insolvency of a chartered trading company: by forfeiture of its privileges, as by abuse of its powers, and breach of the implied condition of its existence.

2180. The effect of a dissolution of a corporation is, to entitle the Crown, or other donor of lands to the body corporate, to resume them; to entitle the creditors of the corporation to insist for sale and distribution of its property in payment of its debts; but not to expose the members to personal responsibility beyond the amount of their stock.

2181. Corporations in Burghs.—The burgh, as a corporation for the advancement of trade and manufactures, consists of several inferior corporations. The rights of those corporations are preserved by the Act for reforming the constitution of royal burghs (*a*).

(*a*) 3 and 4 Will. IV. c. 76, § 21. The exclusive privilege of trading in burghs was abolished by 9 and 10 Vict. c. 17. See above, § 2167.

2182. (1.) *Merchant Guild.* — This great mercantile corporation is recognised in our old laws and deeds under the name of the Guild. By an Act in the sixteenth century, the jurisdiction of the dean of guild is declared in all causes between merchant and merchant, and merchant and mariner; but this jurisdiction has gone into oblivion. Guild-brethren must be burgesses; and the privilege of the guild 'was, until the abolition of all privileges of exclusive trading in burghs,' that of trade within the burgh. Under this privilege, none but a guild-brother 'could' import for sale in the burgh, except on market days; inhabitants 'might' buy beyond the burgh, and bring the commodities so bought for consumption within it; craftsmen 'might' import the rude materials of their manufactures to be worked up for sale; craftsmen and inhabitants 'might' export the produce of their labour; and the members of guild 'might' buy from unfree craftsmen and sell within the burgh (*a*).

(*a*) 1593, c. 184. 1690, c. 12. 1693, c. 31. 1698, c. 19. Buchanan *v.* Incorporation of St. Mary's Chapel, 1695; 4 B. Sup. 239. Guildry of Stirling *v.* Deacon Convener, 1697; M. 1916. Goldsmiths of Edinburgh *v.* Cunningham, 1802; M. *Burgh Royal*, Apx. 10.

2183. (2.) *Crafts.*—These are manufacturing corporations, erected either by Crown charter; or by a seal of cause or grant from the magistrates, as delegates from the Crown; or by prescription, implying a charter now supposed to be lost (*a*).

(*a*) 1555, c. 52. M'Kenzie, Obs. 6 Parl. Mary, c. 52.

2184. The privilege of the crafts 'was' a monopoly of the combined right of manufacture and sale within burgh. Inhabitants 'might' manufacture for their own consumption, or for exportation out of the burgh; or they 'might' sell on market days. They 'might' import the manufactures of the craft bought out of burgh for their own use; and the guild 'might' buy, import, and sell work done out of the burgh. It 'was' a fraud on the privileges to combine collusively to defeat the monopoly called "packing and peeling."

2185. (3.) *Freedom, how acquired.* — The freedom of those corporations may be acquired either by apprenticeship, or by services as a soldier or sailor.

2186. In England, by a general law, an apprentice serves during seven years for a universal privilege over all England. In Scotland, an apprentice 'gained' only the freedom of his corporation within the burgh of which it forms an integral part. The obligation of the apprentice is to be faithful, punctual, and obedient; that of the master is to teach his calling to the apprentice, and to be reasonable in his requisitions of service and obedience within the fair line of the contract and usage of the trade (*a*).

(*a*) See Fraser on Master and Servant.

2187. The freedom acquired by military or naval service extends over the whole country. By statutes passed on the termination of successive wars, officers, mariners, soldiers, marines, and militiamen called out into actual service, 'were,' after a certain period of service (and after their death, their wives and children), allowed to exercise such trade as they are apt and able for in any part of Great Britain or Ireland (*a*). But this 'did' not entitle one to exercise a plurality of trades. And the privilege 'was' not communicable; so that a soldier's daughter marrying 'did' not confer it on her husband.

(*a*) 3 Geo. III. c. 8. 24 Geo. III. c. 6. 37 Geo. III. 42 Geo. III. c. 69. 52 Geo. III. c. 68, § 122, 179. 54 Geo. III. c. 19. 56 Geo. III. c. 67. See *supra*, § 1281 (*a*).

2188. Universities are corporations; and whether they are directly corporations under the Crown, or, like the corporations of a burgh subordinate to the magistrates or founder, the law of corporations is generally applicable to them (*a*).

(*a*) College of Aberdeen *v.* Town of Aberdeen, 1669; M. 2533; 1678, M. 2536. Park *v.* Univ. of Glasgow, 1675; M. 2535. Halden *v.* Rhymer, 1707; M. 2387. Burnett *v.* Simpson, 1711; M. 2389. Gordon *v.* Black, 1712; M. 2397. Leechman *v.* Trail, 1770; M. *College*, Apx. 1. Arnot *v.* Hill, 1807; *ib.* 3; remitted by House of Lords; 1809, 5 Pat. 256. Muirhead *v.* Glassford, May 16, 1809; F. C. Mags. of Edinburgh *v.* Principal and Professors, 1829; 7 S. 255. Univ. of Glasgow *v.* Kirkwood, 1872; 10 Macph. 1000 (poor-rates). Jex Blake *v.* Univ. of Edinr., 1873; 11 Macph. 784 (women's right to study and graduate). The government of the universities is now regulated by 21 and 22 Vict. c. 83.

CHAPTER VI

OF SCHOOLS; AND OF THE RELIEF OF THE POOR

I. SCHOOLS.

2189. Non-Parochial Schools (*a*). — Of schools not parochial, a distinction is admitted between public schools or academies, and schools strictly private.

(1.) *Burgh Schools.*—The schools established in burghs by the magistrates, not being parochial, 'were' held, 'even before they were brought under the care of the school boards,' to be public, and the schoolmasters public officers holding a *munus publicum*; their offices, 'however, not (*b*)' being *ad vitam aut culpam* (*c*).

(2.) *Academies, etc.*—As to academies and schools established by royal charter (*d*), the directors have no power to elect a schoolmaster to hold the office at pleasure, or to dismiss him when duly elected, without just cause shown. But there may be special powers conferred by the charter; and among others, that of making by-laws; under which, provided they are consistent with the chartered constitution, the schoolmaster may be more in the discretionary power of the directors (*e*).

(3.) *Private Schools* established under settlements or trusts are on a different footing from public schools. The schoolmaster has no *munus publicum*; his office is at the discretionary will of those who have the management, 'unless the contract bear to the contrary'; and the deed of constitution and contract of the parties give the rule of their respective rights and powers (*f*). It is to be observed as to private schools, that they 'were and' are not under the superintendence of the presbytery; and that, by a statute of George II. (*g*), no one, 'until 1871, could' keep a private school in a parish for teaching English, Latin, Greek, or any part of literature, until the description of the school 'had' been registered, and the master 'had' qualified himself by taking the oath to Government.

'By the Educational Endowments (Scotland) Act, 1882, a commission was appointed to reorganise educational endowments given previously to the Education Act of 1872, or by a testator who died before the date of that Act, excepting endowments administered by or in the gift of the universities, and endowments for theological instruction or belonging to theological institutions. This commission has wide powers to prepare schemes, subject to the approval of the Scottish Education Department, and to the control of the Court of Session under a case stated on point of law, for the government and management of educational endowments, altering within limits stated in the Act the conditions and provisions of the endowments (*h*). It has been laid down that an alteration on the scheme of an endowment will not be sanctioned when it does not further the purpose of the foundation, that purpose being one which has been made a duty of the ratepayers (*e.g.* free education), but merely relieves the ratepayers (*i*).'

(*a*) See as to parochial schools, *ante*, § 1132–4.

(*b*) See above, § 1132 (*p*), and cases in (*a*).

(*c*) Mags. of Montrose *v.* Strachan, 1710; M. 13,118. Hastie *v.* Campbell, 1769; M. 13,132; rev. 1772, 2 Pat. 277. Gordon *v.* Bell's Trs., 1843; 6 D. 222. Presby. of

Elgin *v.* Mags. of Elgin, 1861; 23 D. 287. 24 and 25 Vict. c. 107, § 22. *Supra*, § 1132 *fin.*, 1134 (*c*).

(*d*) Adam *v.* Directors of Inverness Academy, July 7, 1815; 14 S. 714, note. A. B. *v.* Directors of Ayr Academy, 1825; 4 S. 63. Gibson *v.* Tain Academy Directors, 1836; 14 S. 710. A. *v.* B. (Weir), 1844; 6 D. 1238; aff. 6 Bell's App. 112 (appointment *ad vitam aut culpam* by private directors—their right of inquiry and dismissal for *culpa*). Murray *v.* Lindsay, 1833; 11 S. 856.

(*e*) Gibson *v.* Directors of Tain Academy, 1837; 16 S. 301. Gordon, *cit.* (*c*).

(*f*) Mason *v.* Scott's Trs., 1836; 14 S. 343. Bell *v.* Mylne, 1838; 16 S. 1136; aff. 2 Rob. 286. Gordon, *cit.* (*c*). Trs. of Woodside Instn. *v.* Kiellar, 1865; 4 Macph. 9. Douglas' Trs. *v.* Milne, 1884; 12 R. 141.

(*g*) 19 Geo. II. c. 39; and 21 Geo. II. c. 34, § 12, repealed by 34 and 35 Vict. c. 48.

(*h*) 45 and 46 Vict. c. 59. Forrest's Trs. *v.* Educational Endowments Commrs., 1884; 11 R. 719.

(*i*) Kirk-Session of Prestonpans *v.* School Board of Prestonpans, 1891; 19 R. 193. Jonathan Anderson's Trust, petrs., 1896; 23 R. 592.

II. RELIEF OF THE POOR.

2190. Principle and Policy.—The principle and policy of the Scottish poor law is to provide a compulsory fund only for the diseased and impotent poor, and in that proportion only which is found to be necessary to supply to the admitted claimants the deficiency of the church-door and other contributions: the able-bodied being left to the resources of private charity. Referring to what has already been said of the assessments imposed for the levying of the compulsory provision from the heritors and inhabitants of parishes (*a*), it is now to be considered who are comprehended within the description of poor entitled to relief.

(*a*) See *ante*, § 1135 et seq.

2191. Who entitled to Relief.—Generally, under this description, are included all poor persons of seventy years (*a*), if unable to gain a livelihood by their work; and all (even foreigners), 'whether' possessed of a settlement in any parish 'or not (*b*),' who by infancy, mental or corporeal weakness, disability or permanent 'or other' disease, are unable to earn their subsistence by labour (*c*), and who have no separate means of subsistence (*d*).

(*a*) But see below, § 2193 *fin.*

(*b*) See below, § 2195 *fin.*

(*c*) 1661, c. 38. 1672, c. 18. 1 Ersk. 7. § 63. Dunlop's Parochial Law, 357 et seq. Com. of Supply of Wigtownshire *v.* St. Quivox, 1823; 2 S. 236. *Id.* *v.* Officers of State, 5 S. 767 (criminal lunatic to be supported by Crown). Scott *v.* Thomson, Nov. 13, 1818; F. C. Higgins *v.* Barony Parish, 1824; 3 S. 239. Petrie *v.* Meek, 1859; 21 D. 614. Knox *v.* Hewat, 1870; 8 Macph. 397 (bedridden child above puberty of able-bodied man). Isdale *v.* Jack, 1864; 2 Macph. 978; aff. 1866, 4 Macph. H. L. 1; L. R. 1 Sc. App. 1.

(*d*) Hers. of Ettrick *v.* Sword, 1824; 2 S. 715.

2192. It has been doubted whether a woman, who in her own person is not within the above description, is brought within the class of poor entitled to relief by having the burden of children. And in one case the Court has refused to interfere with the allowance given by the heritors and kirk-session, or to authorise a rate of aliment till the children attained an age able to assist the mother (*a*): in another, the Court remitted for further investigation (*b*). Such a person is entitled only to temporary aid, not permanent supply, when her father-in-law is able to support the children, and she has an action depending against him for aliment (*c*). 'Parochial boards may obtain relief of their past (*d*) advances to paupers against any persons who are, by relationship or by representation, bound and able to support them. See § 1629 sqq. But there is no such right of relief against a pauper himself if he should afterwards succeed to property, unless he has granted a disposition *omnium bonorum* (*e*).'

(*a*) Robert *v.* Fife, 1825; 3 S. 500.

(*b*) Watson *v.* Hers. of Ancrum, 1828; 6 S. 736. See below, § 2193.

(*c*) Watson *v.* Hers. of Ancrum, 1829; 7 S. 495. See § 2193 (*b*).

(*d*) Den *v.* Lumsden, 1891; 17 R. 77. Gillies *v.* M'Dougall, 1871; 1 Guthrie's Sel. S. C. Ca. 27.

(*e*) M'Lauchlan *v.* Kirk-Session of Stevenston, 1828; 6 S. 443. Henderson *v.* Alexander, 1857; 29 S. Jur. 559. Inspr. of Kilmartin *v.* Macfarlane, 1885; 12 R. 713 (lunatics). See 1 Stair, 8. § 3. 3 Ersk. 3. § 92. Guthrie Smith, Poor Law, 270. *Supra*, § 533.

2193. The great difficulties of the poor laws have arisen from temporary distress by dearth, stagnation of trade, discharge of workmen from great manufactories, etc. But it seems to be law, 'said Mr. Bell in 1839,' that persons who are able-bodied and fit to labour for subsistence, are not entitled to the benefit of this relief (*a*): 'and it is now fixed that parochial boards have not power to give able-bodied men relief, although destitute and unable to obtain employment (*b*). The question whether a person is able-bodied and able to maintain himself is to be solved by inquiry into his condition and circumstances, and not merely by reference to age (*c*).'

(*a*) 1 Ersk. 7. § 63. 1 Bankt. 2. § 60. Dunlop, 362. Pollock *v.* Darling, 1804; M. 10,591. See remarks on this case, and the opinion of Sir Ilay Campbell, in Dunlop's

Parochial Law, p. 366, f. n. 8 and 9 Vict. c. 83, § 68. M'William *v.* Adam, 1849; 11 D. 719; aff. 1 Macq. 120.

(*b*) **Isdale** *v.* **Jack,** 1864; 2 Macph. 978; aff. 1866, 4 Macph. H. L. 1; L. R. 1 Sc. App. 1. An able-bodied widow or deserted wife with three, or even one or two, children, is not in practice within this rule. See above, § 2192. Hay *v.* Doonan, 1851; 13 D. 1223. Mackay *v.* Baillie, 1853; 15 D. 971. Petrie *v.* Meek, 1859; 21 D. 614. If she has no children, she must support herself. Scott *v.* Beattie, 1880; 7 R. 1047. Nor an able-bodied man with a lunatic wife or child, Palmer *v.* Russell, 1871; 10 Macph. 185. See below, § 2197, 2202, and 20 and 21 Vict. c. 71, § 75. Hay *v.* Paterson, 1857; 19 D. 332. Beattie *v.* Adamson, 1866; 5 Macph. 47. Wallace *v.* Turnbull, 1872; 10 Macph. 675. Milne *v.* Henderson, 1879; 7 R. 317. Beattie *v.* Crozier, 1881; 8 R. 787.

(*c*) Beattie *v.* M'Culloch, 1880; 7 R. 902.

2194. Those who do not fall within the description of chargeable poor, are by law left to private charity and voluntary arrangements for relief.

2195. Parish Settlement.—The poor entitled to relief are by law chargeable only on the parish in which they have a settlement, and this depends on residence, parentage, birth, or marriage. 'A settlement once acquired is not affected by the transfer of the pauper's birthplace or place of residence into the territory of a different parish (*a*). But all destitute persons must be relieved by the parish in which they are found, until their parish of settlement be ascertained and their claim on it admitted or established, or until they are removed (*b*).'

(*a*) Galashiels Inspr. *v.* Melrose, 1892; 19 R. 758, explaining or correcting Borthwick *v.* Temple, 1891; 18 R. 1190. The decision rests on the general rule that laws are not retroactive. See Savigny Syst. § 383 sqq. Guthrie's Savigny, pp. 343, 354, 361, etc. (2nd ed.).

(*b*) 8 and 9 Vict. c. 83, § 70. Taylor *v.* Strachan, 1864; 3 Macph. 34. M'Caig *v.* Sinclair, 1888; 14 R. 539. Robertson *v.* Dempster, 1889; 17 R. 272 (foreign pauper's voluntary change of residence while receiving relief).

2196. (1.) *Settlement by Residence.*—The rule universally applicable to all persons above fourteen (*a*), and not of the class of chargeable poor, and to foreigners as well as natives, is that mere residence within a parish, "haunting and resorting" (*b*) for three years continuously (*c*), 'without having recourse to common begging (*d*) by themselves or their families, or receiving or applying for parochial relief (*e*),' without interruption of any one year (*f*), and though not possessed of house, land, hiring, or service, within the parish (*g*), will confer a right of settlement. 'Pupils, minors not forisfamiliated, married women, and lunatics, do not acquire settlements in their own right by residence (*h*). The question whether a pauper has a settlement in a parish does not, like the question of domicile, depend on his intention, for the statute regards the *fact* of residence as the test (*i*); but while mere intention not indicated by action can have no effect, the circumstances attending an interruption of residence in a parish are to be considered, in order to see whether they indicate a severance of the pauper's connection with it, or a temporary or accidental absence (*k*). And in exceptional cases (*e.g.* sailors and fishermen), it is now fixed, after some conflict of judicial opinion, that a constructive settlement may be acquired by the residence of wife and children, by one who has lived but occasionally and for comparatively brief periods at his home (*l*).'

(*a*) See as to forisfamiliation, Fraser *v.* Robertson, 1867; 5 Macph. 819. Dempster *v.* M'Whannell, 1879; 7 R. 276. M'Lennan *v.* Waite, 1872; 10 Macph. 908. Lees *v.* Kemp, 1891; 19 R. 6. Mackay *v.* Munro, 1892; 19 R. 396. Guthrie Smith, Poor Law, 300.

(*b*) Higgins *v.* Barony Parish, 1821; 3 S. 239. Inveresk *v.* Tranent, 1757; M. 10,571; 5 B. Sup. 334. Gladsmuir *v.* Preston, 1806; M. *Poor*, Apx. 5. Howie *v.* Kirk-Session of Arbroath, 1800; *ib.* 1. Pennicuik *v.* Hers. of Duddingston, March 3, 1813; F. C. Hers. of Cockburnspath, petrs., June 9, 1809; F. C. See as to residence prior to 1845, Thomson *v.* Knox, 1850; 12 D. 1112. Hay *v.* Thomson, 1856; 18 D. 510, etc.

(*c*) From 1846 (8 and 9 Vict. c. 83, § 76), the time required for acquiring a settlement was *five* years. That section was repealed and the former rule restored by 61 and 62 Vict. c. 21, § 1, as from October 1, 1898.

(*d*) Blantyre *v.* Rutherglen, 1897; 24 R. 695.

(*e*) 8 and 9 Vict. c. 83, § 76. 61 and 62 Vict. c. 21, § 1. See Kirk-Session of Crieff *v.* Foulis Wester, 1842; 4 D. 1538 (complete period). Hay *v.* Cumming, 1851; 13 D. 683. Hay *v.* Ferguson, 1852; 14 D. 352; 15 D. 62. Webster *v.* Mackenzie, 1853; 15 D. 399. Porteous *v.* Blair, 1856; 19 D. 181 (no interruption by casual relief to wife, husband being absent in search of work—see also Cochran *v.* Kyd, 1871; 9 Macph. 836; and Wallace *v.* Turnbull, 1872; 10 Macph. 675). Greig *v.* Chisholm, 1857; 20 D. 339. Johnston *v.* Black, 1859; 21 D. 1293. Simpson *v.* Allan, 1859; 21 D. 1363. Hamilton *v.* Kirkwood, 1863; 2 Macph. 117 (relief fraudulently given to prevent acquisition of settlement; see Petrie *v.* Meek, 1859; 21 D. 614. Jack *v.* Thom, 1860; 23 D. 173). Wallace *v.* Dempster, 1880; 8 R. 27 (interruption by small medical relief).

(*f*) Dunse *v.* Edrom, 1645; M. 10,553. Crailing *v.* Roxburgh, 1767; M. 10,573; Hailes, 198. Hutton *v.* Coldstream, 1770; M. 10,574; Hailes, 389. Waddel *v.* Hutton, 1781; M. 10,583. Runciman *v.* Heritors of Mordington, 1784; M. 10,583.

(*g*) Dalmellington *v.* Irvine, 1800; M. *Poor*, Apx. 2.

(*h*) See as to pupils, etc., *infra*, § 2199; as to married women, *infra*, § 2202; and as to lunatics, Gladsmuir, *cit.* (*b*). Melville *v.* Flockhart, 1857; 20 D. 341. Watt *v.* Hannah, 1857; 20 D. 342; overruled by **Crawford** *v.* **Petrie & Beattie,** 1862; 24 D. 357. Milne *v.* Henderson, 1879; 7 R. 317. Mere weakness of intellect, or incapacity to earn a livelihood, or being deaf and dumb, does not prevent the acquisition of a settlement. Greig *v.* Ross, 1877; 4 R. 465. Watson *v.* Caie & Macdonald, *infra* (*k*). Allan *v.* Higgins, 1868; 6 Macph. 358. Walker *v.* Russel, 1870; 8 Macph.

893. Boyd & Beattie *v.* Dempster, 1882; 9 R. 1091. Cassels *v.* Somerville & Scott, 1885; 12 R. 1155. Nixon *v.* Rowand, 1885; 15 R. 191.

(*i*) **Crawford** *v.* **Petrie & Beattie,** 1862; 24 D. 357.

(*k*) Hutchison *v.* Fraser, 1858; 20 D. 545. Hay *v.* Beattie & Hardie, 1857; 20 D. 146. Hamilton *v.* Kirkwood, 1863; 2 Macph. 117. Watson *v.* Caie & Macdonald, 1878; 6 R. 202. Harvey *v.* Rogers, 1878; 6 R. 446. Beattie *v.* Stark, 1879; 6 R. 956. Dempster, *supra* (*a*). Greig *v.* Simpson, 1888; 16 R. 18. Welsh *v.* Lowden, 1894; 22 R. 7. The cases upon acquisition of settlement and continuity of residence are too numerous for citation here, and reference must be made to the special treatises, especially Guthrie Smith's Digest of the Poor Law, and Reid's Poor Law Digest.

(*l*) Greig *v.* Miles, 1867; 5 Macph. 1132. Moncrieff *v.* Ross, 1869; 7 Macph. 331. Milne *v.* Ramsay, 1872; 10 Macph. 731. Beattie *v.* Smith & Paterson, 1876; 4 R. 19. Cruickshank *v.* Greig, 1877; 4 R. 267. See Aberdeen Infirmary *v.* Watt, 1858; 21 D. 117 (sailor lodging). Jackson *v.* Robertson, 1874; 1 R. 342 (ditto). Wallace *v.* Beattie & Highet, 1881; 8 R. 345. Deas *v.* Nixon, 1884; 11 R. 945. See below, § 2197 (*f*).

2197. A settlement once obtained by residence 'could' be lost only by acquiring a new settlement in another parish (*a*); that parish in which the pauper last resided during the three 'or five' years immediately previous to his application being the parish of his settlement. A woman's settlement by residence is suspended, not discharged by her marriage (*b*). 'By the Poor Law Amendment Act, 1845, and Act of 1898, a settlement is lost if, during any subsequent period of five (since 1st October 1898, of four) years, the pauper shall not have resided in the parish for at least one year and a day. That is to say, absence for three years extinguishes his settlement (*c*). It seems not to be different when the absence is involuntary (*e.g.* by a lunatic, or by confinement in a lunatic asylum out of the parish) (*d*); and a soldier has no privilege of retaining a constructive settlement, unless he has a wife and family remaining in the parish of his residence (*e*).'

(*a*) Brown *v.* Kirk-Session of Mordington, 1806; M. *Poor*, Apx. 4. Crailing and Hutton, *supra*, § 2196 (*f*).

(*b*) Pennicuik, *supra* (*b*). See below, § 2200. Reid *v.* Edmiston, 1890; 18 R. 25. See Kirkwood *v.* Manson, etc., in § 2202 (*a*), *infra*.

(*c*) 61 and 62 Vict. c. 21, § 1. Hay *v.* Morrine, 1851; 13 D. 628. Johnstone *v.* Black, 1859; 21 D. 1293. Cochrane *v.* Kyd, 1871; 9 Macph. 836. Inverkip *v.* Greenock, 1893; 21 R. 64 (parochial relief during the absence does not prevent loss).

(*d*) 20 and 21 Vict. c. 71, § 75, 95. Crawford *v.* Petrie & Beattie, 1862; 24 D. 357. Lindsay *v.* Mackenzie, 1866; 4 Macph. 1037. Kirkwood *v.* Lennox, 1869; 7 Macph. 1027. Thomson *v.* Kidd, 1881; 9 R. 37.

(*e*) Hay *v.* Croll & Beattie, 1858; 20 D. 507. Mason *v.* Greig, 1865; 3 Macph. 707. Beeby *v.* Caldwell, 1884; 12 R. 257. See above, § 2196 (*l*).

2198. A parish in which a pauper requiring immediate aid is found must advance an interim aliment,—having relief against the parish of settlement 'for expenditure incurred after written notice to the inspector of poor of that parish (*a*), including a proportion of the management expenses of poorhouse or asylum and of current interest on debt for buildings (*b*). But even after notice given, that right may be cut off by *mora* (*c*).'

(*a*) Scott *v.* Thomson, Nov. 13, 1818; F. C. Inveresk *v.* Tranent, 1737; M. 10,552. 8 and 9 Vict. c. 83, § 70, 71. Anderson *v.* Mackenzie, 1864; 3 Macph. 353. Dinwoodie *v.* Graham, 1870; 8 Macph. 436; 42 Jur. 209. Wallace *v.* Turnbull, 1872; 10 Macph. 675. Anderson *v.* Paterson, 1878; 5 R. 904.

(*b*) Beattie *v.* Muir, 1892; 19 R. 417. Hay *v.* Melville, 1858; 20 D. 480 (not including expense of inspector, etc.).

(*c*) Brown *v.* Lemon, 1864; 2 Macph. 454. Jack *v.* Simpson, 1864; 2 Macph. 1221. Beattie *v.* Wood, 1866; 4 Macph. 427. Guthrie Smith on the Poor Law, p. 280 sqq. An admission of liability by one parish to another cannot be retracted on the ground of error (Beattie *v.* Greig & Arbuckle, 1875; 2 R. 330. Young *v.* Gow, 1877; 4 R. 448. Dempster *v.* Lemon, 1878; 6 R. 278) in a question with that parish. Beattie *v.* Brown, 1883; 11 R. 250.

2199. (2.) *Settlement by Birth and Marriage.*—A child 'unforisfamiliated' has a settlement in the settlement of the parent 'however acquired,' without regard to the child's residence, lawful children following the father's, illegitimate the mother's (*a*). 'After the death or desertion of the father, pupil children follow the mother's settlement, for she is the pauper (*b*), and his desertion, while it subsists, is equivalent to his death (*c*); but the settlement derived from the father revives if she dies during their pupillarity (*d*). Imbecile and lunatic children are and continue to be chargeable to the parish of the parent's settlement, whether that be acquired by the parent's residence or birth (*e*). For all pupils have only a derivative settlement, taking a settlement in their own birth parish (in default of another) only on attaining puberty (*f*). A child born in a poorhouse is deemed, so far as regards any question of liability for maintenance, to have been born in the parish by which the mother was sent (*g*).'

(*a*) **Inveresk** *v.* **Tranent,** 1757; M. 10,571; 5 B. Sup. 334. Guthrie *v.* Arbroath, 1777; 5 B. Sup. 539; Hailes, 772. Coldingham *v.* Dunse, 1779; M. 10,582; 5 B. Sup. 539. Howie *v.* Arbroath, *supra*, § 2196 (*b*). Rescobie *v.* Aberlemno, 1801; M. 10,589. Gladsmuir *v.* Preston, *supra*, § 2196 (*b*). Kirk-Session of Edinburgh *v.* Brown, June 11, 1806; F. C.; M. Apx. *Poor*, 5. Kirk-Session of Lasswade *v.* St. Cuthbert's, 1844; 6 D. 956. Hay & Thomson *v.* Murray, 1856; 18 D. 510. **Barbour** *v.* **Adamson,** 1851; 13 D. 1279; rev. 1853, 1 Macq. 376. Greig *v.* Young, 1878; 5 R. 977 (bastard of Irishwoman having no Scotch settlement: cf. Caldwell *v.* Dempster, *infra* (*f*). Primrose *v.* Milne, 1890; 17 R. 512 (bastard)).

(*b*) Greig *v.* Adamson, 1865; 3 Macph. 575. Carmichael *v.* Adamson, 1863; 1 Macph. 453. M'Lennan *v.* Waite, 1872; 10 Macph. 908.

(*c*) Cases in (*b*). Hunter *v.* Henderson, 1895; 22 R. 331.

(*d*) Beattie *v.* M'Kenna, 1878; 5 R. 737. See Gibson *v.* Murray, 1854; 16 D. 926. Henry *v.* Mackison, 1880; 7 R. 458. A minor forisfamiliated acquires a residential settlement only by his own industrial residence, not by piecing together his parents' residence, while he was in family, with his own subsequent residence, so as to make a period of five years. M'Lennan *v.* Waite, 1872; 10 Macph. 908.

(*e*) Gladsmuir, *cit.* Hay *v.* Paterson, 1857; 19 D. 329. Lawson *v.* Gunn, 1874; 4 R. 151. Milne *v.* Ross, 1883; 11 R. 273.

(*f*) Craig *v.* Greig, 1863; 1 Macph. 1172. M'Lennan *v.* Waite, *cit.* Ferrier *v.* Kennedy, 1873; 11 Macph. 402. Caldwell *v.* Dempster, 1883; 10 R. 1263. Greig *v.* Young, *cit.* (*a*).

(*g*) 49 and 50 Vict. c. 51, § 5.

2200. This derivative settlement is lost beyond revival by the acquisition of a settlement by residence, or by the marriage of a female (*a*) 'The father being dead, a pupil's settlement in the father's birth parish is lost by the attainment of puberty (*b*), except in the case of idiots (*c*); but his settlement derived from his father's residence, or a widow's derived from her husband's residence, continues till lost by three years' non-residence after the removal of the family (*d*).'

(*a*) 1 Ersk. 6. § 54. 1 Bankt. 6. § 13. *Arg. ex* Howie, Gladsmuir, Cockburnspath, *supra*, § 2196 (*b*); and Inveresk, *supra*, § 2199 (*a*). Dunlop, 382. See Gibson *v.* Murray, 16 D. 926. Hay *v.* Thomson & Manson, 1854; 16 D. 994. Craig *v.* Greig & M'Donald, 1863; 1 Macph. 1172. M'Crorie *v.* Cowan, *infra*, § 2202.

(*b*) Cases in § 2199, notes (*b*) and (*f*), *supra*. Ferrier, § 2201 (*b*). Greig *v.* Ross, 1877; 4 R. 465. So also their chargeability (§ 2199) on the mother's settlement. Shotts *v.* Bathgate and Rutherglen, 1896; 24 R. 169.

(*c*) Lawson *v.* Gunn, 1876; 4 R. 151.

(*d*) Allan *v.* Higgins, 1864; 3 Macph. 309. St. Cuthbert's *v.* Cramond, 1873; 1 R. 174. Jackson *v.* Ireland, 1879; 6 R. 605. Simpson *v.* Miles, 1883; 10 R. 928. Caldwell *v.* Glass, 1887; 15 R. 166. Wallace *v.* Caldwell, 1894; 22 R. 43 (bastard—mother's residential settlement).

2201. Failing other grounds of settlement, one is entitled to relief from the parish of 'actual (*a*)' birth (*b*). 'But a parish relieving one whose settlement by parentage or marriage is in England or Ireland has no remedy except by removal; and if removal be impracticable, has not recourse against the birth parish of the pupil or wife whom it has relieved (*c*).'

(*a*) Russell *v.* Greig & Craig, 1881; 8 R. 440.

(*b*) 1579, c. 74. 1672, c. 18. Dunlop, 387. Hume *v.* Pringle & Halliday, 1849; 12 D. 411. Barbour *v.* Adamson, *cit.* § 2199. Gibson *v.* Murray, *cit.* Keay *v.* Stewart, 1858; 21 D. 89. Aberdeen Infirmary *v.* Watt, 1858; 21 D. 117. See above, § 2199. Ferrier *v.* Kennedy, 1873; 11 Macph. 402, and cases there cited. As to proof of the parish of birth, see Hay *v.* Murdoch, 1854; 16 D. 364. Beattie *v.* Nish, 1878; 5 R. 775. Lemon *v.* Wallace, 1887; 15 R. 92.

(*c*) M'Crorie *v.* Cowan, 1862; 24 D. 723. Greig *v.* Young, 1878; 5 R. 977. Caldwell *v.* Dempster, 1883; 10 R. 1263.

2202. A woman by marriage acquires the settlement of the husband, retains it (her own being suspended) during the marriage, and seems, even on the dissolution of the marriage by death of the husband, to enjoy it during her widowhood (*a*), 'until lost by non-residence or a second marriage (*b*). In one case a woman may have a different settlement from her husband, viz. where she has become chargeable as a lunatic pauper, and he afterwards acquires a settlement in a different parish, her support as a lunatic continuing to be incumbent on the parish of settlement at the time relief was first given (*c*). A deserted wife may during the desertion acquire a settlement for herself and children as if the husband were dead (*d*).'

(*a*) Pennicuik, *supra*, § 2196 (*b*). Dunlop, 382. Gray *v.* Fowlie, 1847; 9 D. 811. Hay *v.* Skene, 1850; 12 D. 1019; 1852, 15 D. 62. Hay *v.* Waite & Carse, 1860; 22 D. 872. Kirkwood *v.* Manson, 1871; 9 Macph. 693. Palmer *v.* Russell, 1871; 10 Macph. 185. Reid *v.* Edmiston, 1890; 18 R. 25. Cases in § 2199 (*b*). By marriage it seems that a Scotchwoman's settlement is lost, even though her husband be a foreigner (an Irishman), with no settlement in Scotland. M'Crorie *v.* Cowan, 1862; 24 D. 723. Johnston *v.* Wallace, 1873; 11 Macph. 699 (lunatic deserted wife). Cases, *supra*, § 2200. A widow cannot acquire a settlement by combining her husband's residence before his death with her own subsequent residence so as to make up a period of five years. Kirkwood *v.* Wylie, 1865; 3 Macph. 398.

(*b*) 8 and 9 Vict. c. 83, § 76. Kirkwood *v.* Manson, *cit.*

(*c*) 20 and 21 Vict. c. 71, § 75, 95. Palmer, *cit.* Coupar-Angus *v.* Murroes, 1894; 21 R. 583 (lunatic child).

(*d*) Mason *v.* Greig, 1865; 3 Macph. 707. Beattie *v.* Greig, 1875; 2 R. 923. Greig *v.* Simpson & Craig, 1876; 3 R. 642. See Johnston *v.* Wallace, *cit.*

2203. Removal of Paupers.—Paupers becoming chargeable may be removed to the parish of their settlement, 'subject since 1898 to an appeal by the pauper, if he has resided for a year in the relieving parish, to the Local Government Board'; the expense to be borne in the first place 'by the relieving parish,' with relief against the settlement parish. No one who does not beg can be removed from a parish in which no settlement has yet been acquired, merely from apprehension of becoming chargeable (*a*). 'Parishes on which English and Irish paupers become chargeable, and in which they have not acquired settlement, may, with the authority of the Sheriff, remove them compulsorily to England, Ireland, or the Isle of Man, under certain regulations (*b*). But since 1898 five years' residence in Scotland, without begging or applying for parochial relief, of which one has been continuously in the relieving parish, makes an English or Irish pauper irremoveable. And all removals are now subject to the supervision of the Local Government Board (*c*).'

(*a*) 1579, c. 74. Proclamation, Aug. 11, 1692. 8 and 9 Vict. c. 85, § 72. 61 and 62 Vict. c. 21, § 3. See Guthrie Smith, Poor Law, 87, 287. Hay *v.* Melville, 1858; 20 D. 480. M'Intosh *v.* Welch, 1860; 20 D. 1423.

(*b*) 8 and 9 Vict. c. 86, § 77. 8 and 8 Vict. c. 117. 10 and 11 Vict. c. 33. 24 and 25 Vict. c. 76. 25 and 26 Vict. c. 113 (the governing statute). 26 and 27 Vict. c. 89. Beattie *v.* Mahone, 1861; 23 D. 412. M'Crorie *v.* Cowan, 1862; 24 D. 723. Guthrie Smith, 274.

(*c*) 61 and 62 Vict. c. 21, § 5 sqq.

2204. Making up the Lists.—It 'was' by the law of Scotland wisely ordered, that the application of those who desire relief shall be subject to the cognisance of a tribunal, combining those who have an interest to restrain the relief within the narrowest limits, with the humane spirit of a neutral body, and subject to the control of courts of justice. This tribunal 'was' composed of the ministers, elders, and heritors of the parish (*a*); the heritors being entitled to vote by proxy (*b*). This, however, 'was' only in landward parishes; the jurisdiction in relation to the poor being with the magistrates in royal burghs, entitled (and in use) to take the aid of the heritors and kirk-session in investigating the circumstances of claimants (*c*). The meetings of the ministers, elders, and kirk-session 'were' ordered to be held twice a year; and they 'might' meet at any other time when occasion 'called.' The right of determining in the first instance on all claims for aid 'was' with this tribunal (*d*); and it 'was' the peculiar duty of the kirk-session to investigate each claim, and report to the general body (*e*). The name and surname of each person admitted in the list, with the age and condition, 'were' entered in a register book (*f*). This tribunal 'was' properly judicial and inquisitorial; but the heritors and kirk-session 'were' not liable to paupers for relief, with a right to be indemnified against the parish. They 'might' be complained of to the Court of Session if they 'refused' a remedy, as other judicatories may for failure in the execution of their duties (*g*). 'The management was from 1846 vested in elective parochial boards for the management of the poor, and is now transferred to Parish Councils and the Local Government Board. When relief is wrongly refused, the remedy is by a summary application to the Sheriff (*h*).'

(*a*) 1672, c. 18. Proclamations, Aug. 11, 1692: Aug. 29, 1693; March 3, 1699; and statute, 1695, c. 43. 1696, c. 29. 1698, c. 21. Hers. of Humbie *v.* Minister, 1751; M. 10,555; Elch. *Poor*, 3. E. Galloway *v.* Kirk-Session of Dalry, Feb. 22, 1810; F. C.

(*b*) Robertson *v.* Murdoch, 1830; 8 S. 587. See as to proxies, Lawrie *v.* Thomson, 1874; 1 R. 402. Thompson *v.* Muir, 1871; 10 Macph. 178; aff. 1876, 3 R. H. L. 1.

(*c*) Proclam. Aug. 11, 1692. 1672, c. 18.

(*d*) Hers. of Paisley *v.* Richmond, 1821; 1 S. 212. Higgins *v.* Barony Heritors, 1824; 3 S. 239.

(*e*) 1672, c. 18. (*f*) *Ib.* See also 1579, c. 74.

(*g*) Telford *v.* Ancrum, 1826; 4 S. 545. Hers. of Glassford *v.* Orr, 1827; 5 S. 921.

(*h*) See above, § 1136 sqq.

BOOK FIFTH

OF THE EVIDENCE AND ENFORCEMENT OF RIGHTS

CHAPTER I

OF EVIDENCE (*a*)

(*a*) The third edition of this work contains a statement of the principles of the law of judicial procedure. This was omitted in the fourth edition, the last issued in Professor Bell's life, on the ground, as stated in an introductory note prefixed to this Book of the "Principles," that "the subject of judicial proceedings has become of late years so complicated, and the decisions on points of practice so numerous, that it will require and be the subject of a separate work."

2205. General View.—Those rights which have already been explained are, when brought into question, inquired into, and established by the judicial process of an action; in which the person who seeks to enforce his right states the extent and nature of his demand, and must be ready to establish it to the satisfaction of a judge or a jury, by the exhibition of such evidence as the law requires. The rules by which that evidence is regulated, and proofs of particular kinds admitted or rejected, are now to be stated. Judicial evidence, taken in its full extent, consists of Written Evidence; Parole Evidence; Presumptive Evidence; and Evidence by Confession, on application to the conscience of the party.

I. WRITTEN EVIDENCE.

2206. Kinds of Written Evidence.—Written proofs (*a*) are either such as are preconcerted by the parties, with a view to prevent future question; or such as happen casually to furnish evidence, on the occurrence of a dispute.

(*a*) See above, § 18.

2207. Proofs of the former class are intended not only to establish that a particular act or contract has passed or been agreed to, but to set forth the precise nature and import of the agreement or transaction itself, so as to remove all the doubts which might otherwise arise from the confusion or forgetfulness of witnesses as to the words made use of, and to leave no ambiguity but that which proceeds from the imperfection or careless use of language. This class of proofs consists of public and judicial records, or of private records, deeds, and contracts.

2208. Acts of Parliament are records written on the rolls of Parliament; and which from the numerous checks against falsehood interposed by the forms of Parliament, form the highest of all kinds of written evidence, and are not allowed to be questioned. 'They may be contradicted in regard to matters which they do not enact (*a*).'

(1.) *Public Acts.*—These concern the public generally, and, strictly speaking, are held to be known, and require only to be suggested to the memory by referring to the Act. Any dispute as to the words is determined by the production of a copy printed by the Queen's printers 'or under the superintendence or authority of H.M. Stationery Office (*b*). The rubric is not part of the statute (*c*).'

(2.) *Local and Personal Acts* relate to a particular class of men, or to individuals, or to some local interest or concern; but when declared by special clauses to be public Acts, they are, 'even if passed before 1851,' proved in the same way as public Acts.

(3.) *Private Acts*, when directed to be printed by the Queen's printer, and copies so printed to be evidence, are so made evidence. But private Acts, although declared generally to be public, must be proved by a copy sworn to have been examined with the Parliament Roll (*d*). 'Every Act of Parliament passed after 4th February 1851 is to be deemed and judicially taken notice of as a public Act, unless the contrary be expressly declared (*e*).'

(*a*) R. *v.* Greene, 6 Ad. & E. 548. As to a codifying Act as evidence of the law before its passing, see *per* L. Blackburn in M'Lean *v.* Clydesdale Bank, 1883; 11 R. H. L. 1; 9 App. Ca. 95.

(*b*) 41 Geo. III. c. 90, § 9. 45 and 46 Vict. c. 9, § 2.

(*c*) Farquharson *v.* Whyte, 13 R. Justy. 29. Sutton *v.* Sutton, 22 Ch. D. 513.

(*d*) Brett *v.* Beales, 1 M. & M. 421; 3 Ill. 61. These rules are settled in England. With us, the matter is more loosely dealt with. In daily practice in the Court of Session, printed copies of private Acts are received without objection. But this must be referred to acquiescence; for if an objection were made, the *onus probandi* would be determined according to the rules above mentioned. And in a jury trial an objection to the copy of a private Act would be disposed of according to those rules.

(*e*) 13 and 14 Vict. c. 21, § 7. Stephen *v.* Aiton, 1875; 2 R. 470; aff. 1876, 3 R. H. L. 4; 1 App. Ca. 456 (private Acts). As to the effect of statements in private Acts as against third parties, see also Dickson on Evid. § 1108.

2209. Official Records.—Official records are of various kinds:—

(1.) *Gazette.*—The London Gazette is evidence of public acts of Government, published by authority of the Queen; *ex. gr.* proclamations and orders in Council, as passing the Great Seal before they can be entered in the Gazette (*a*). But the Gazette is not evidence of a commission in the army (*b*). It is evidence of advertisements and notices authorised to be there published, as of sequestrations, discharges of bankrupts, and so forth (*c*). 'The Documentary Evidence Act, 1868, makes the London, Edinburgh, and Dublin Gazettes *primâ facie* evidence of orders and proclamations by certain departments of Government; and provides further for evidence of official documents (*d*).'

But when brought as evidence of other notices not so authorised (as of dissolutions of partnerships), the perusal, or at least the possession, of the paper by the party must be proved (*e*). And a distinction is observed in matters of evidence, between the fact of notice made and the truth of what is stated in the notice.

(*a*) The King *v.* Holt, 5 T. R. 439; 3 Ill. 61. General Picton's Case, 30 Howell's State Trials, 493. 1 Phillips on Evidence, 387, and cases cited. Attorney-General *v.* Theakstone, 8 Price, 89; 22 R. R. 716.

(*b*) Kirwan *v.* Cockburn, 5 Esp. 233; 8 R. R. 849. The King *v.* Gardner, 2 Camp. 513; 11 R. R. 784.

(*c*) 2 and 3 Vict. c. 41. 19 and 20 Vict. c. 79, § 48. It is not strictly evidence of the fact of bankruptcy. See Dickson on Evid. § 1113. And as to English bankruptcies, see Reg. *v.* Levi, 10 Cox C. C. 110; 34 L. J. Mag. Ca. 174. Reg. *v.* Robinson, 10 Cox C. C. 467; 36 L. J. Mag. Ca. 78; L. R. 2 C. C. 80.

(*d*) 31 and 32 Vict. c. 37. 45 and 46 Vict. c. 9. 58 and 59 Vict. c. 9.

(*e*) Jenkins *v.* Blizard, 1 Starkie, N. P. 420; 18 R. R. 792. Harratt *v.* Wise, 9 B. & Cr. 712. 6 Geo. IV. c. 16, § 83. 46 and 47 Vict. c. 52, § 132 (Engl. Bkrptcy. Acts).

2210. (2.) *Journals of Parliament.*—The journals of the House of Lords and of the House of Commons are evidence of their proceedings, though not properly records; but not of the facts stated in the resolutions. An unstamped copy of the minutes of a judgment of the House of Lords, without more of the proceedings, is evidence (*a*).

(*a*) Jones *v.* Rendal, Cowp. 17; 3 Ill. 61. See 8 and 9 Vict. c. 113, § 3, 5, admitting copies printed by the Queen's printer; which, however, does not extend to Scotland.

2211. (3.) *The Records of Public Offices*—the War Office, Navy Office, Excise and Customs, Bank of England, etc.—are proof of the facts which are regularly recorded there; but the books themselves must, if required, be produced when removable, or at least a copy sworn to by the clerk who made it, or by a witness as having examined it (*a*).

(*a*) Dunbar *v.* Harvie, July 5, 1815; rev. 2 Bligh, 351; 3 Ill. 61. Paris *v.* Smith, 1823; 3 Mur. 336. Kay *v.* Roger, 1832; 10 S. 831. Dickson on Evid. § 1163 sqq. (1205 sqq. 3rd ed.).

2212. (4.) *Parish Registers* were formerly kept with such irregularity in Scotland, that they were not much to be relied on (*a*). In many parishes they are now kept with exemplary correctness; and it is not improbable—'1839'—that there may be soon a legislative regulation for the due keeping of parish registers, as furnishing an important class of facts in marriage, legitimacy, succession, minority, etc. A record of burials is no evidence of the age of the person, though mentioned in the record (*b*). 'The value of such records depends on the manner in which they were kept; and therefore the original ought to be produced (*c*).'

(*a*) Wilson *v.* Aitken, 1626; M. 12,700; 3 Ill. 62. Thomson *v.* Stevenson, 1667; M. 12,701. Dickson on Evid. § 1126–1135 (1168–1178, 3rd ed.).
(*b*) Watson *v.* Watson, 1836; 14 S. 734; 1837, 15 S. 753.
(*c*) See Hay *v.* Murdoch, 1854; 16 D. 364. Beattie *v.* Nish, 1878; 5 R. 775. Lemon *v.* Wallace, 1887; 15 R. 92. Kennedy *v.* Lyell, 1889; 14 App. Ca. 437 (effect in England).

2212A. 'The registers of births, deaths, and marriages throughout Scotland are since 1854 (*a*) under the charge of a Registrar-General for Scotland. In each parish or district there is a registrar, appointed by the parochial board in rural parishes (*b*), and by the Town Council in burghs. At stated periods the parish or district registers are transmitted to the General Register for preservation. Provisions are made to secure uniformity and accuracy. Extracts of entries in these registers, duly authenticated and signed by the Registrar-General or the local registrar, according as the particular register is kept at the General Register Office or the local office, are "admissible as evidence in all parts of Her Majesty's dominions, without any other or further proof of such entry" (*c*). They afford *primâ facie* evidence of the facts they purport to record, and may be inpugned for error.'

(*a*) 17 and 18 Vict. c. 80. 18 and 19 Vict. c. 29. 23 and 24 Vict. c. 85. 37 and 38 Vict. c. 88. 48 and 49 Vict. c. 61.
(*b*) Laurie *v.* Thomson, 1874; 1 R. 402.
(*c*) 17 and 18 Vict. c. 80, § 58.

2213. This distinction is to be observed, that when a record is kept by a person authorised to do so, it will be received, and a copy sworn to as examined will be admitted. But where it is a private register, it must be produced, and can be received only with the credit and inferences attending it which the jury in the circumstances may think it entitled to (*a*).

(*a*) See Mathers *v.* Laurie, 1849; 12 D. 433 (minutes or records of dissenting congregation). Hay *v.* Murdoch, 1854; 16 D. 364. As to the removal of public registers for proof to England or out of Scotland, see Kennedy, petr., 1880; 7 R. 1129. E. of Euston, petr., 1883; 11 R. 235, and reporters' note.

2214. (5.) *Certificate of Ship Registry, and Log-Book.*—A certificate of registry of a ship is evidence to negative ownership (*a*); but it is not necessarily proof of ownership (*b*). A distinction may be observed between the log-book of a man-of-war acting as convoy, and such log-book (or that of a merchant ship) relating to the ship's proceedings (*c*). 'Entries in official log-books made in manner provided by the Merchant Shipping Act are admissible in evidence (*d*).'

(*a*) Camden *v.* Anderson, 5 T. R. 709; 3 Ill. 62. Marsh *v.* Robinson, 4 Esp. 98; 3 R. R. 617. See above, § 1327.
(*b*) Tinkler *v.* Walpole, 14 East, 226. Fraser *v.* Hopkins, 2 Taunt. 15; 1 Ill. 418. Pirie *v.* Anderson, 4 Taunt. 652. Scott *v.* Miller, 1832; 11 S. 21; 3 Ill. 149.
(*c*) D'Israeli *v.* Jowett, 1 Esp. 427. See above, § 496. Heathcote's Divorce Bill, 1 Macq. 277. Dickson on Evid. § 1164. 1 Bell's Com. 612 (658 M'L.'s ed.).
(*d*) 57 and 58 Vict. c. 60, § 239.

2215. Judicial Records.—These consist either of the written proceedings before the Court; or of deeds, warrants, etc., registered by the proper officers.

(1.) *Judgments.*—In evidence of the fact of a judgment having been pronounced, or of the right or other consequence established by that judgment (*a*), an extract by the clerk, according to the settled rules, is evidence (*b*). But it is not the sole evidence; the original record read by the clerk is also evidence (*c*). It is not evidence of any fact involved in the judgment (*d*). So, conviction for assault is evidence of the conviction, to the effect of punishing, or of saving from a second prosecution or punishment. But it will not prove the assault to support an action of damages.

(*a*) Macharg *v.* Campbell, 1767; M. 12,541; Hailes, 192.
(*b*) 50 Geo. III. c. 112, § 1, 10. 1 and 2 Vict. c. 118. Dickson on Evid. § 1286 sqq.

(*c*) Baillie *v.* Bryson, 1818; 1 Mur. 327; 3 Ill. 63.
(*d*) Mackintosh *v.* Smith & Lowe, 1864; 2 Macph. 1261; aff. 1865, 3 Macph. H. L. 6; 4 Macq. 913.

2216. (2.) *Verdicts* are proved by the record, so far as to show the existence of the verdict; but as to the fact found by the verdict, although it is on grounds of public policy conclusive between the same parties and their representatives (*a*), it is not so against others who were not parties; nor even against one who was truly a party, but where the present adversary was not a party; or where he who objects to it was restrained in his opposition by the limited purpose for which the verdict was meant; though a verdict may be referred to in explanation (*b*). So a verdict in a criminal case will not be conclusive evidence in a civil; nor a verdict in a civil, evidence in a criminal case; nor a cognition of insanity conclusive in reduction. But in such cases they may serve as *primâ facie* proofs (*c*).

(*a*) Van Wart, 1 Ry. & Moo. 4; 3 Ill. 63. See 2 Smith's L. C. 803 sqq. (736 sqq. 10th ed.).
(*b*) Dalziel *v.* D. Queensberry's Exrs., 1825; 4 Mur. 13. Mackintosh *v.* Smith & Lowe, *cit.* § 2215.
(*c*) E. Fife *v.* E. Fife's Trs., 1816; 1 Mur. 126. See Fraser *v.* Hill, 1854; 16 D. 789. Dickson on Evid. § 1082 sqq. Andersons *v.* Jeffrey, 1826; 4 Mur. 99.

2217. (3.) *Recorded Deeds and Warrants.*—Of these, an extract, certified by the signature of the proper officer of Court, is probative in all the Courts of Scotland (*a*). But when it is indispensable to produce the original, either in a reduction improbation in a Scottish Court or in an English Court, warrant will, on due precautions, be granted for having the original transmitted (*b*). In bankruptcy, extracts are effectual abroad, if fortified by the seal of the Court of Session (*c*).

(*a*) Morton *v.* Lord Clerk Register, 1831; 10 S. 162; 3 Ill. 63. See Clark *v.* Thomson, 1816; 1 Mur. 163, 178.
(*b*) Bloxham *v.* E. Rosslyn, 1825; 3 S. 428. Annandale *v.* Lord Clerk Register, 1828; 6 S. 657. See as to production in a Scotch Court, A. of S., Feb. 16, 1841. Mackay's Practice of C. of Sess. i. 451, ii. 42. Maclean *v.* Maclean's Trs., 1861; 23 D. 1262; and in regard to applications for production of such deeds abroad, which are granted with great difficulty, Dunlop, petr., 1861; 24 D. 107. Jolly, petr., 1864; 2 Macph. 1288. Young, petr., 1866; 4 Macph. 344. Western Bank, petrs., 1868; 6 Macph. 656. Macdonald, petr., 1877; 5 R. 44. Inglis, petr., 1882; 9 R. 761.
(*c*) See as to the act and warrant confirming a trustee, 19 and 20 Vict. c. 79, § 73.

2218. (4.) *Pleadings.*—There is still much doubt as to the effects of pleadings, condescendences, answers, etc., regarded as evidence. In the Court of Session, the practice 'was' extremely loose; and the case often argued and decided on the statements in papers of an argumentative nature. But the rules of evidence seem to be these: that direct admissions specifically made are evidence against the party making them, 'and bind him in the action in which they are made'; that specific statements made on the record are evidence against him who makes them; that mere inferences from statements not contradicted, are not to be relied on as evidence; and generally that admissions and statements, 'at least when founded on in different proceedings (*a*),' require to have been known to, and authorised by, the party (*b*). 'There is not the same distinction between intrinsic and extrinsic qualifications when the admissions of a party are founded on, as in an oath on reference. The admissions, if taken alone, must be taken with the qualifications annexed to them; but the other party may prove his own case in the ordinary way, and may disprove these qualifications, so as to take advantage of the admission, if he has not barred himself from doing so (*c*).'

(*a*) See Marianski *v.* Cairns, 1854; 1 Macq. 766. Aitchison *v.* Aitchison, 1877; 4 R. 899, 921. In modern practice it would require pregnant proof of want of authority to relieve a party from the effect of an explicit admission in his pleadings.
(*b*) E. Fife *v.* E. Fife's Trs., 1817; 1 Mur. 137. White *v.* Clark, 1817; 1 Mur. 422. Grub *v.* Mackenzie, 1818; 2 Mur. 3. Allen *v.* M'Leish, 1819; *ib.* 159. Miller *v.* Moffat, 1820; *ib.* 322. Smith *v.* Puller, 1820; *ib.* 342. Ballantyne *v.* Ross, 1821; *ib.* 533. Anderson *v.* Jeffrey, 1826; 4 Mur. 100. See Dickson on Evid. § 1386, 1434, 1485. 6 Geo. IV. c. 120, § 2, 8, 10, 13, etc. Wauchope *v.* N. B. Ry., 1860; 23 D. 191.
(*c*) **Milne** *v.* **Donaldson,** 1852; 14 D. 849. Campbell *v.* M'Cartney, 1843; 14 D. 1087. **Picken** *v.* **Arundale,** 1872; 10 Macph. 987. Gelstons *v.* Christie, 1875; 2 R. 983. Kerr's Trs. *v.* Ker, 1883; 11 R. 108. As to the effect of qualified admissions, see also Couper *v.* Young, 1849; 12 D. 190. Dowdy *v.* Graham, 1859; 22 D. 181 (letters). Robertson & Co. *v.* Bird & Co., 1897; 24 R. 1076 (counter allegation irrelevant).

2219. Public Instruments.—These comprehend executions of messengers and notarial instruments.

2220. (1.) *Messenger's Executions.*—Citations, charges, etc., can be proved only by the written execution or return of the messenger (*a*), 'except in small debt cases, where they may be proved either by the officer's oath or by written execution (*b*).' Executions, when signed by the messenger and one witness, are *primâ facie* evidence of the citation, charge, etc. (*c*), but may be redargued (*d*).

(*a*) Hay *v.* L. Ballegerno, 1680 ; M. 3790, 12,268 ; 3 Ill. 63. M'Calla *v.* Mags. of Ayr, 1679 ; M. 12,632. Haswell *v.* Mags. of Jedburgh, 1714 ; M. 12,270. Hog. *v.* M'Lellan, 1797 ; M. 8346. Henderson *v.* Richardson, 1848 ; 10 D. 1035 (amended execution). Allan *v.* Miller, 1848 ; 10 D. 1060 (do.). Stewart *v.* Macdonald, 1860 ; 22 D. 1514. Hamilton *v.* Monkland Iron Co., 1863 ; 1 Macph. 676.

(*b*) 6 Geo. IV. c. 48, § 3. 1 Vict. c. 41, § 3. Citations of witnesses and jurors might be proved by oath. 1 Will. IV. c. 37, § 7. 55 Geo. III. c. 42, § 22. Now the certificate of the Sheriff-clerk is the proper evidence of citation of jurors, which is made by registered post letters. 31 and 32 Vict. c. 100, § 47.

(*c*) 1 and 2 Vict. c. 114, § 32 ; c. 119, § 23. 9 and 10 Vict. c. 67, § 1. 13 and 14 Vict. c. 36, § 20, Sch. B. 16 and 17 Vict. c. 80, Schs. F and I.

(*d*) This must be in a reduction improbation, where the challenge is on the ground of fraud or falsehood in the messenger or witnesses. M'Vitie *v.* Barbour, 1838 ; 16 S. 1184. Balfour *v.* Robertson, 1839 ; 1 D. 458 ; but obvious irregularities might be pleaded *ope exceptionis*, Stewart *v.* Macdonald, *cit.* (*a*). The latter course can rarely now be adopted, since a party who appears is not allowed to state any objection to the regularity of the execution or service as against himself. 31 and 32 Vict. c. 100, § 21 (Court of Session). 39 and 40 Vict. c. 70, § 12 (2) (Sheriff Courts). As to executions in Sheriff Courts, see A. of S., 1839, § 91. Dickson on Evidence, § 1243, 1246.

2221. (2.) *Notarial Instruments.*—Notarial instruments, when *actus legitimi*, are good evidence of the act which it is the province of a notary to perform, but not of extraneous facts recited in the instrument (*a*). But when produced only as proofs of notice or intimation, their effect is limited to the fact of the *notice*, and can be evidence of the *statement* only by inference from acquiescence (*b*). Notarial copies are evidence only by admission (*c*).

(*a*) Clark's Trs. *v.* Hill, 1827 ; 4 Mur. 205. Thomson *v.* Bisset, 1823 ; 3 Mur. 297. Hosie *v.* Baird, 1828 ; 4 Mur. 417, 431. Brown *v.* Cuthill, 1828 ; 4 Mur. 475. 4 Ersk. 2. § 5. See of the notarial instrument as a title to land, § 774B, etc.

(*b*) D. Roxburghe *v.* Ker, 1822 ; 1 S. App. 157, and cases there cited ; 3 Ill. 64.

(*c*) Williamson *v.* Fraser, 1834 ; 12 S. 466.

2222. (3.) *Minutes of Public Meetings.*—These are received as evidence of what took place there (*a*). 'This doctrine applies, however, only to the minutes of meetings of bodies recognised by the law as having a public function or status, such as parochial boards, kirk-sessions of the Church of Scotland, town councils, etc. (*b*). The minutes of persons who meet to deliberate about some common project, as of a provisional committee, or of a body of creditors (except in a statutory sequestration, which are the proper *primâ facie* evidence of the proceedings), are conclusive evidence only against the parties who have signed them ; but when duly proved they are admissible as adminicles of evidence (*c*). The minutes of companies incorporated under the Companies Act, 1862, purporting to be signed by the chairman, are by statute evidence in regard to the proper business of the company, to be received in all legal proceedings (*d*) ; and so, also, are the notes or minutes of certain orders, appointments, etc., of companies under the Companies Clauses Act, 1845 (*e*).'

(*a*) Hamilton *v.* Hope, 1827 ; 4 Mur. 239. Wilson *v.* Jamieson, 1827 ; *ib.* 366. Lea *v.* Landale, 1828 ; 6 S. 350 ; 3 Ill. 64. Oswald *v.* Laurie, 1828 ; 5 Mur. 8. See Inglis *v.* Cunningham, 1826 ; 4 Mur. 77.

(*b*) Arneill *v.* Robertson, 1843 ; 5 D. 400 (a Secession Presbytery). Mathers *v.* Laurie, 1849 ; 12 D. 433 (Free Kirk-Session). Hill *v.* Lindsay, 1847 ; 10 D. 78. Ivison *v.* Edinr. Silk Yarn Co., 1846 ; 9 D. 1039. Forbes *v.* Morrison, 1851 ; 14 D. 134. Ferguson *v.* Hers. of Kirkpatrick-Durham, 1850 ; 12 D. 1145 ; aff. 1 Macq. 232. A. *v.* B., 1858 ; 20 D. 407. Beattie *v.* Mackay, 1863 ; 1 Macph. 279. Such minutes are properly authenticated by the signature of the chairman of the meeting (see G. N. Ry. Co. *v.* Inglis, *infra* ; Ivison *v.* Silk Yarn Co., *supra*, and other cases cited). In practice they are generally proved or identified by the evidence of some official or his clerk producing them ; and it rather appears that this is, strictly speaking, necessary, unless in cases within the clause of the Companies Act, 1862, cited below. See also Marwick, Law and Practice of Municipal Elections, etc., 482.

(*c*) Macartney *v.* Mackenzie, 1831 ; 5 W. & S. 504. Johnston *v.* Scott, 1860 ; 22 D. 393.

(*d*) 25 and 26 Vict. c. 89, § 67. Liqrs. of City of Glasgow Bank, petrs., 1880 ; 7 R. 1196, 1199.

(*e*) 8 and 9 Vict. c. 17, § 101. Great Northern Ry. Co. *v.* Inglis, 1851 ; 13 D. 1315 ; aff. 1852, 1 Macq. 112 ; 24 Sc. Jur. 434.

2223. (4.) *The Sederunt Book of a Sequestration* is not evidence of the date of sequestration, or of the bankrupt's discharge (*a*).

(*a*) Smith *v.* M'Kay, 1835 ; 13 S. 323 ; 3 Ill. 64. Mansfield *v.* Maxwell, 1835 ; 13 S. 731. *Quære?* Dickson on Evid. § 1216. The case of Mansfield decided only that it is not evidence *in favour* of the trustee or bankrupt.

2224. (5.) *Official Reports*, and other proofs in writing, must be lodged for jury trial in due time before the trial (*a*).

(*a*) Donaldson *v.* Manchester Assur. Co., 1833 ; 11 S. 570. As to this matter of procedure, see 2 Mackay's Practice, 40, etc.

2225. Private Deeds and Writings (*a*).—The requisites of solemn attested deeds, holograph deeds, and privileged deeds, are settled partly by statute, partly by consuetudinary law, partly by mercantile usage. Where these requisites are duly complied with, the writing is said to be probative—there is a presumption of truth and authenticity; and it is not necessary, as in England, to prove the signature, etc., of the writing (*b*). But it has been a great object in the laws relative to those requisites, to supply to those interested the means of invalidating or checking the authenticity of the deed, and so of challenging and reducing it if false; and this by requiring, in solemn attested deeds, the names and description of the witnesses, the name and description of the writer, to which at common law is added the place and date, which, however, are not essential in point of authenticity.

'It is not now absolutely necessary to the validity of a formal deed that all the solemnities should be exactly observed. For it is enacted by the Conveyancing Act of 1874, that no writing subscribed by the granter, and "bearing to be attested by two witnesses subscribing, and whether relating to land or not, shall be deemed invalid or denied effect according to its legal import because of any informality of execution"; but the burden of proving that it was so subscribed by the granter and by the witnesses shall lie on the party using or upholding it. Such proof may be led either in any proceeding in which the deed is founded on, or in a special petition to the Court of Session or Sheriff of the defender's domicile (*c*).'

(*a*) See as to stamps, above, § 22.

(*b*) As to the effect of admission of signature, see M'Farlane *v.* Grieve, 1790; M. 17,057, 8459; Hailes, 1080. Smith *v.* Bank of Scotland, Jan. 25, 1821: F. C.; aff. 1824; 2 S. App. 265. *Supra*, cases in § 249 (*a*) and (*b*). Brown *v.* Duncan, 1888; 15 R. 511 (signing on erasure).

(*c*) 37 and 38 Vict. c. 94, § 39. In M'Laren *v.* Menzies, 1876, 3 R. 1151, and Brown, petr., 1883, 11 R. 400, deeds of several sheets signed only on last page were set up under this section; in Thomson's Trs. *v.* Easson, 1878, 6 R. 141, one which wanted the designations of the witnesses; and in Tener's Trs. *v.* Tener's Trs., 1879, 6 R. 1111, a deed in which one witness subscribed after the granter's death. Richardson's Trs. *v.* Rankine, 1891; 18 R. 1131 (blundered testing clause). Geddes *v.* Reid, 1891; 18 R. 1186 (in this case it is said that although the proof of the witnesses' due subscription and attestation fails, the deed will be valid if the granter's signature be proved). Thomson *v.* Clarkson's Trs., 1892; 20 R. 59 (subscription of witnesses *ex intervallo*). Nisbet, 1897; 24 R. 411.

2226. (1.) *Attested Deeds* (*a*).—In authenticating these deeds, the general rules are, that the party must himself subscribe without the aid or tracing of the letters by another (*b*). Subscription by a mark is improbative, but by initials good, if admitted or proved by the instrumentary witnesses to be genuine, and the usual mode of signing (*c*). The party must either subscribe in presence of witnesses who know him, or acknowledge to them his subscription (*d*). Witnesses, 'who' may be women (*e*), and are not disqualified in testamentary writings by taking benefit under them (*f*),' capable of identifying the deed must sign the deed (*g*), and 'till 1874 had to' be named and designed in the testing clause (*h*). 'It is now enough if the designations of the witnesses are, before recording or production in any court, appended to or follow their subscriptions, whether written by themselves or not (*i*).' The writer of the deed must, 'according to the former law,' be designed in the testing clause (*k*); but the writer of the testing clause need not be mentioned (*l*). 'Since 1874 it is no objection that the writer or printer of a deed is not named or designed (*m*).' The testing clause may be filled up at any time before being 'recorded or' produced in judgment,—a very dangerous practice (*n*). Where the party cannot write, the deed must, 'according to the older law and practice,' be subscribed by two notaries, before four subscribing witnesses, all present at the time, and by mandate of the party expressed in the 'holograph (*o*)' docquet of the notaries (*p*).

'Any deed may now be validly executed after being read over to a party who cannot write from any cause, permanent or temporary, by one notary (*q*) or justice of peace subscribing in his presence and by his authority, without the necessity of touching the pen according to the old practice, all before two witnesses. The holograph (*o*) docquet, for which there is a statutory form, sets forth the granter's giving authority, and that it was read over to him before the witnesses. It is no longer an objection that the number of pages is not specified (*r*).

'One who grants and delivers an *ex facie* regularly executed, onerous deed, with the intention that the grantee shall act upon it, is barred by doing so from challenging it for a latent technical objection, *e.g.* that a witness did not see it signed or hear the subscription acknowledged (*s*).'

(*a*) See above, § 19.

(*b*) Moncrieff *v.* Monypenny, 1710; M. 15,936; Robertson's Ap. 26; 3 Ill. 65. Robertson *v.* Young, 1744; Elch. *Writ*, 18. Crosbie *v.* Pickans, 1749; M. 16,814; Elch. *Writ*, 25 (copy put before granter). Falconer *v.* Arbuthnot, 1751; M. 16,817; Elch. *Writ*, 26. Wilson *v.* Raeburn, 1800; Hume, 912 (copy). Ballingall *v.* Robertson, 1806; Hume, 916. Shaw *v.* Shaw, 1809; Hume, 922. Wilson *v.* Pringles, 1814; *ib.* 923. E. Fife, *infra* (*d*). Reid *v.* Reid's Trs., 1835; 13 S. 1063; 1837, 16 S. 273 (blind). Noble *v.* Noble, 1875; 3 R. 74 (attempted distinction by Second Div. between "leading" and "supporting" the hand). Stirling Stuart *v.* Stirling Crawford's Trs., 1885; 12 R. 610 (signing by stamp invalid—retouching—proof).

(*c*) Thomson *v.* Shiels, 1729; M. 16,810. M'Ilwraith *v.* M'Miken, 1785; M. 16,820; Hailes, 970; 1 Ill. 229. Cockburn *v.* Gibson, Dec. 8, 1815; F. C. (mark—cf. Din *v.* Gillies, 1812, f. n. in Cockburn, *cit.*). Weirs *v.* Ralston, June 22, 1813; F. C. Monro *v.* Monro, 1820; Hume, 81. Graham *v.* Macleod, 1848; 11 D. 173 (mark). Crosbie *v.* Wilson, 1865; 3 Macph. 870 (do.).

(*d*) Campbell *v.* Robertson, 1698; M. 16,887. Walker *v.* Adamson, 1716; M. 16,896. Forbes *v.* Reid, 1698; 4 B. Sup. 404. Sim *v.* Donaldson, 1708; M. 16,891. Young *v.* Glen, 1770; M. 16,905; Hailes, 364. Condie *v.* Buchan, 1823; 2 S. 432. Duff *v.* E. Fife, 1823; 3 Mur. 497; 1 S. App. 498; 4 S. 335; 2 W. & S. 166; 3 Ill. 75. Hogg *v.* Campbell, 1864; 2 Macph. 848 (acknowledgment not necessarily to both witnesses at same time). Morrison *v.* M'Lean's Trs., 1862; 24 D. 625; 1863, 1 Macph. 304. Cumming *v.* Skeoch's Trs., 1879; 6 R. 963 (whether indirect acknowledgment).

(*e*) 31 and 32 Vict. c. 101, § 139. Hannay, petr., 1873; 1 R. 246.

(*f*) Simson *v.* Simsons, 1883; 10 R. 1247.

(*g*) As to time of the witnesses' subscribing, see Thomson *v.* Clarkson's Trs., 1892; 20 R. 59; and Condie *v.* Buchan, and Hogg *v.* Campbell, *citt.* (*d*). Arnott *v.* Burt, 1872; 11 Macph. 62. *Supra*, § 2226 (*c*).

(*h*) Grant *v.* Keir, 1698; M. 16,913; 3 Ill. 67. Abercromby *v.* Innes, 1707; M. 17,022. Halden *v.* Kerr, 1714; M. 16,924; 1 Cr. & St. 56. Hepburn *v.* Hepburn, 1736; Elch. *Writ*, 3. Wallace *v.* Campbell, 1749; M. 16,900. Archibalds *v.* Marshall, 1787; M. 16,907; Hailes, 1035. Douglas, Heron, & Co. *v.* Clark, 1787; M. 16,908. Wemyss *v.* Hay, 1825; 1 W. & S. 140. L. Blantyre, petr., 1850; 13 D. 40. It is enough if the witnesses be designed, though not named, if the designation along with the subscription suffice for identification. M'Dougall *v.* M'Dougall, 1875; 2 R. 814.

(*i*) 37 and 38 Vict. c. 94, § 38. Thomson's Trs. *v.* Easson, 1878; 6 R. 141.

(*k*) Kirkpatrick *v.* Ferguson, 1704; M. 17,022, 12,061. Duncan *v.* Scrymgeour, 1706; M. 16,914. Logie *v.* Ferguson, 1710; M. 17,026. Dronnan *v.* Montgomerie, July 26, 1716; M. 16,869. Ewing *v.* Semple, 1739; 5 B. Sup. 211; M. 1352. D. Gordon *v.* Gordon, 1761; M. 16,870. M'Farlane *v.* Grieve, 1790; M. 17,057, 8459; Hailes, 1080. Lockhart *v.* Kay, Feb. 16. 1815; F. C. Callander *v.* Callander's Trs., 1863; 2 Macph. 591. Laurie *v.* Laurie, 1859; 21 D. 240. Macpherson *v.* Macpherson, 1855; 17 D. 357. Johnston *v.* Pettigrew, 1865; 3 Macph. 954. Mitchell *v.* Scott's Trs., 1874; 2 R. 162.

(*l*) Watsons *v.* Scott, 1682; M. 16,860, *note*. Gray *v.* Scott, 1703; M. 12,602. Andrews *v.* Thomson, 1836; 14 S. 598. Lindsay *v.* Giles, 1844; 6 D. 771. See as to deeds partly written, partly printed, 21 and 22 Vict. c. 76, § 34; 23 and 24 Vict. c. 143, § 20; 31 and 32 Vict. c. 101, § 149.

(*m*) 37 and 38 Vict. c. 94, § 38.

(*n*) Dury *v.* Dury, 1753; M. 16,936; Elch. *Writ*, 27. Bank of Scotland *v.* Telfer's Creditors, 1790; M. 16,909. Brown, petrs., March 11, 1809; F. C. Blair *v.* E. Galloway, 1827; 6 S. 51. Reid *v.* Kedder, 1834; 12 S. 781; 3 Ill. 69. See 13 S. 619; aff. 1840; 1 Rob. 183. Rait *v.* Primrose, 1859; 21 D. 965. Shaw *v.* Shaw, 1851; 13 D. 877. M'Neillie *v.* Cowie, 1858; 20 D. 1229. Hill *v.* Arthur, 1870; 9 Macph. 223. Caldwell *v.* L. Clerk Register, 1871; 10 Macph. 99. See 37 and 38 Vict. c. 94, § 38, 39. Addison, petrs., 1875; 2 R. 457. Veasey *v.* Malcolm's Trs., 1875; 2 R. 748. Millar *v.* Birrell, 1876; 4 R. 87. Stewart *v.* Burns, 1877; 4 R. 427 (where the witnesses also had signed after an interval, and after one of the parties had repudiated the bargain). As to the effect of declarations inserted in the testing clause relating to matters not appropriate to that clause, see Dunlop *v.* Greenlees's Trs., 1863; 2 Macph. 1; aff. 1865, 3 Macph. H. L. 46; 37 S. Jur. 470. Chambers' Trs. *v.* Smith, 1877; 5 R. 97; 1878, 5 R. H. L. 151. Barbour *v.* Chalmers & Co., 1891; 18 R. 610.

(*o*) Henry *v.* Reid, 1871; 9 Macph. 503; Irvine *v.* M'Hardy, 1892; 19 R. 458. Campbell *v.* Purdie, 1895; 22 R. 443.

(*p*) Phillip *v.* Cheap, 1667; M. 16,835; 3 Ill. 70. Birrell *v.* Moffat, 1745; M. 16,846; Elch. *Writ*, 19. Yorkston *v.* Grieve, 1794; M. 16,856. Duff *v.* E. Fife, *supra* (*d*). 1579, c. 80. 1681, c. 5. Graeme *v.* Graeme's Trs., 1868; 7 Macph. 14. 37 and 38 Vict. c. 94, § 41. Atchison's Trs. *v.* Atchison, 1876; 3 R. 388. Watson *v.* Beveridge, 1883; 11 R. 40.

(*q*) The notary must not be personally interested in the deed. Ferrie *v.* Ferrie's Trs., 1863; 1 Macph. 291 (trust-disponee). Lang *v.* Lang's Trs., 1889; 16 R. 590.

(*r*) 37 and 38 Vict. c. 94, § 38. Watson *v.* Beveridge, 1883; 11 R. 40.

(*s*) Baird's Tr. *v.* Murray, 1883; 11 R. 153. See Stirling-Stuart *v.* Stirling-Crawford's Trs., 1885; 12 R. 610.

2227. The tests by which the authenticity of a deed is to be judged of when challenged are the following:—*Comparatio literarum*; the examination of the instrumentary witnesses; the examination of the writer.

2228. *Comparatio literarum* is a kind of proof the most doubtful and least to be relied on. In almost every trial where the opinions have been taken of engravers, post-office clerks, and others professing a discriminating knowledge of handwriting, the numbers are found equal on either side. And it seems to be only where persons well acquainted with the handwriting, and who have seen the person write, concur with the result of the professional testimony, that any reliance is to be placed on it (*a*).

(*a*) See Renton *v.* E. Leven, 1662; M. 12,652. And the trial of Mr. Justice Johnson, 29 State Trials, 475; and Bishop Atterbury's Case, 16 State Trials, 323. Greig *v.* Clark, 1829; 7 S. 773. Paul *v.* Harper, 1832; 10 S. 486, 491. Bryson *v.* Crawford, 1834; 12 S. 937. Turnbull *v.* Doods, 1844; 6 D. 896, 902. Gellatley *v.* Jones, 1851; 13 D. 961. Forster *v.* Forster, 1869; 7 Macph. 797. See Best's Pr. of Evid. § 232-248.

2229. An obvious objection to the evidence of an instrumentary witness who admits his subscription to be genuine is, that he comes at a distance of time, when his memory may play him false, and under circumstances which may *ex eventu* influence his recollection or judgment, to contradict what by his written testimony he has solemnly asserted. But the only effect of this is to cast suspicion on the witness's testimony, not to render him inadmissible, and to require the clearest evidence to invalidate the deed (*a*).

(*a*) 3 Ersk. 2. § 22 et seq. Tait on Evidence, 56 et seq. Bell on Testing of Deeds, 254. Frank *v.* Frank, 1793; M. 16,822; and 1795, M. 16,824; aff. 5 Pat. 278; Bell on Testing, 254; 3 Ill. 73. Swany *v.* Bank of Scotland, 1807; M. *Writ*, Apx. 7. Richardson *v.* Newton, Feb. 28, 1811; F. C. Condie *v.* Buchan, 1823; 2 S. 432; 3 Ill. 66. Smith *v.* Bank of Scotland, 1824; 2 S. App. 256. Duff *v.* E. Fife, 1823; 1 S. App. 498; 1826, 2 W. & S. 166. Wemyss *v.* Hay, 1825; 1 W. & S. 140; 3 Ill. 67. Cleland *v.* Cleland, 1838; 1 D. 254. Donaldson *v.* Stewart, 1842; 4 D. 1215. Morrison *v.* Maclean's Trs., 1862; 24 D. 629; 1863, 1 Macph. 304.

2230. There is not the same objection to the examination of the writer of the deed as to that of the instrumentary witnesses; and the Legislature has been anxious to secure the evidence of one so intimately connected with the framing and execution of the deed, by requiring his name and description to be inserted, under the pain of nullity. The principle of this rule should require also the name and designation of the writer of the testing clause; but it has not been so held; 'and it is not now necessary to name the writer of the deed in the testing clause (*a*).'

(*a*) *Supra*, § 2226.

2231. (2.) *Holograph Deeds* are probative for twenty years, after which time they must be proved by the writing or oath of the granter, or of his heir after his death, admitting the authenticity of the writing, and of the subscription (*a*).

(*a*) 1669, c. 9. Ellis *v.* Ellis, 1630; 1 B. Sup. 312; 3 Ill. 71. Inglis *v.* M'Cubbin, 1631; M. 16,962. Wauchope *v.* Niddry, 1662; M. 12,605 (postscript of letter). Currence *v.* Halket, 1688; 2 B. Sup. 121 (unsigned). Buchanan *v.* Dennistoun & Co., 1831; 9 S. 557 (holograph of firm). See Miller *v.* Farquharson, 1835; 13 S. 838 (co-obligants). See above, § 20, 590, 1868.

2232. (3.) *Privileged Writings* are, mercantile writings—bills, notes, bank cheques, orders, mandates, guarantees, letters *in re mercatoriâ*. These require nothing but the genuine subscription of the party (*a*). 'And subscription by mark is sustained in some such documents, *e.g.* bills, notes, receipts, and some kinds of mandates, provided it is proved or admitted to be genuine and to be the granter's usual manner of signing (*b*). Initialled entries in a bank pass-book are *primâ facie* evidence that the sums entered have been paid in, but may be redargued (*c*).'

(4.) *Last Wills* must be regularly attested, or holograph, if not executed by notarial interposition; but one notary is sufficient to sign for the party, or in absence of a notary a clergyman. 'The author said' the clergyman of the parish 'in which the testator lives' is not required; 'but this statement seems to be erroneous, except perhaps where the minister is absent and the minister of a neighbouring parish is called in (*d*).'

(*a*) Ramsay *v.* Pyronon, 1632; M. 16,963; 3 Ill. 72. E. Northesk *v.* V. Stormont, 1671; M. 16,967. Goodlet Campbell *v.* Lennox, 1739; M. 16,979.

See, as to writings not *in re mercatoriâ*, and the distinction in regard to acknowledgment of subscription between cases where writing is *de solemnitate* and those where the obligation may be otherwise proved, Fogo *v.* Milligan, 1746; M. 16,979. Walker *v.* Duncan, 1785; Hailes, 985. Wallace *v.* Wallace, 1782; M. 17,056; Hailes, 912. Edmonstone *v.* Lang, 1786; M. 17,057; compared with Brown *v.* Campbell, 1794; Bell's fol. Ca. 115. Sinclair *v.* Sinclair, 1795; Bell's Ca. 140. Robertson & Co. *v.* Galloway, 1821; 1 S. 191; 1 Ill. 175; and above, § 249.

See above, § 21, 1868. 1 Bell's Com. 325 (342, M'L.'s ed.). Rhind *v.* Comml. Bank, 1857; 19 D. 519; rem. 1860, 32 S. Jur. 283; 3 Macq. 643. Paterson *v.* Wright, Jan. 30, 1810; F. C.; aff. 1814, 6 Pat. 38; 1 Ill. 176. Hamilton *v.* Struthers, 1858; 21 D. 51 (acknowledgment of loan). Thoms *v.* Thoms, 1867; 6 Macph. 174 (back letter relating to a bill). Purvis *v.* Dowie, 1869; 7 Macph. 764 (ditto). Stewart & Macdonald *v.* M'Call, 1869; 8 Macph. 544 (contract of service). M'Laren *v.* Howie, 1869; 8 Macph. 106 (receipt for legacy). Haldane (Speirs' Factor) *v.* Speirs, 1872; 10 Macph. 537 (effect of a cheque in proof of loan). As to "fitted accounts," see the doubtful case of M'Adie *v.* M'Adie's Exrx., 1883; 10 R. 741.

(*b*) Bell's Com. i. p. 343 (M'L.'s ed.). Ker *v.* Riddel, 1803; Hume, 50. Cockburn *v.* Gibson, Dec. 8, 1815; F. C. Kennedy *v.* Watson, May 25, 1816; F. C. Bryan *v.* Murdoch, 1824; 3 S. 282; aff. 2 W. & S. 568. Craigie *v.* Scobie, 1832; 10 S. 570. Graham *v.* M'Leod, 1848; 11 D. 173. Rose *v.* Johnston, 1878; 5 R. 600. Thomson *v.* Muir, 1871; 10 Macph. 178; aff. 1876, 3 R. H. L. 1.

(*c*) Rhind's Trs. *v.* Comml. Bank, 1857; 19 D. 519; rem. 1860, 32 Jur. 283; 3 Macq. 643. Couper's Trs. *v.* Natl. Bank, 1889; 16 R. 412.

(*d*) Hepburn *v.* L. Wauchton, 1606; M. 16,827. Duff's Feudal Convg. p. 14. Menzies's Lect. 136. M. Bell's Convg. 39, 45, 78. The docquet given in 37 and 38 Vict. c. 94, Sched. I, implies that the power is limited to the minister of the parish. See Act 1584, § 133. The minister of a *quoad sacra* parish is probably competent. Murrie *v.* M'Donald, 1853; 16 D. 325. 7 and 8 Vict. c. 44, § 8.

2233. (5.) *Books and Letters* of one of the parties not communicated to the other, are to be received against the person who keeps them (*a*): against others, 'business books, but not in general private books and diaries, are admitted' only as circumstances which, by the concurrence of other proofs, may become evidence (*b*). Books of a company afford proof against a partner (*c*). 'The effect of books depends on circumstances. Thus an entry in a private note-book of the debtor irregularly kept and of old date, while it proves the fact that money passed, does not prove that the debt is subsisting and unpaid. But, on the other hand, such a presumption may arise from the state of books which profess to keep a complete record of a man's transactions (*d*). By statute, proved excerpts from bankers' books are accepted as *primâ facie* evidence, in lieu of the books (*e*).'

(*a*) Pentland *v.* Bell & Co., 1822; 1 S. 426; 3 Ill. 76. Anderson *v.* Clouston, 1824; 2 S. 620. Blair *v.* Russel, 1828; 6 S. 836. Bell *v.* Murray, 1833; 12 S. 554. Ivison *v.* Edinr. Silk Yarn Co., 1846; 9 D. 1039. Couper *v.* Young, 1849; 12 D. 190. Thom *v.* North Br. Bkg. Co., 1850; 13 D. 134. British Linen Bank *v.* Thomson, 1853; 15 D. 314. As to private plans in questions of boundaries, see Place *v.* E. Breadalbane, 1874; 1 R. 1202. Reid *v.* Haldane's Trs., 1891; 18 R. 744; and above, § 738.

(*b*) Forbes & Co. *v.* Hudson, 1822; 3 Mur. 46. Smith *v.* Mitchell, 1826; 5 S. 32; aff. 4 W. & S. 47. Hatton *v.* Buckmaster, 1853; 15 D. 574. B. L. Bank, *cit.* (*a*). Hogg *v.* Campbell, 1864; 2 Macph. 1158. Catto, Thomson, & Co. *v.* Thomson, 1867; 6 Macph. 54 (private books of a partner not the writ of the firm).

(*c*) Smith, *supra* (*b*). Kenney *v.* Walker, 1836; 14 S. 803; 3 Ill. 76. Knox *v.* Martin, 1850; 12 D. 719.

(*d*) Waddel *v.* Waddel, 1790; 3 Pat. 188. Wink *v.* Speirs, 1868; 6 Macph. 657. Storeys *v.* Paxton, 1878; 6 R. 293. Dickson on Evid. § 1183.

(*e*) 42 Vict. c. 11.

2234. In contradistinction to preconcerted evidence, that which *ex post facto* is found to exist may competently be brought in proof of circumstances or contracts which are past. Such are letters, notes, jottings (*a*); with regard to which three points are of importance: the proof of the authenticity of the writ; the fact of its having been sent or communicated; and the inference from its tenor (*b*). Among these may be included writings or entries by third parties having knowledge of the fact, and no interest to falsify it. Such are the books of a law agent, midwife, physician, or surgeon (*c*); in regard to which it is necessary only to guard against fraud (*d*) and against negligence.

(*a*) See Kid *v.* Bunyan, 1842; 5 D. 193. Pollok *v.* Morris, 1845; 7 D. 973.

(*b*) Stewart *v.* Buchanan, 1816; 1 Mur. 40; 3 Ill. 77. Whyte *v.* Clark, 1817; *ib.* 241. Houldsworth *v.* Walker, 1819; 2 *ib.* 82. Toosey *v.* Williams, 1 M. & Malk. 129. M'Kenzie *v.* Roy, 1830; 5 Mur. 263. Taylor *v.* Crawford, 1833; 12 S. 39. M'Farlane *v.* Fisher, 1837; 15 S. 978. Wright *v.* Tatham, 4 Bing. 489. Smith *v.* Mackay, 1835; 13 S. 323. Robertson *v.* Gamack, 1835; 14 S. 139. Hogg *v.* Campbell, 1865; 3 Macph. 1018. Letters written by living persons are not evidence of the facts stated in them, although they may be used against the writer, if a party, or for the purpose of refreshing a witness's memory or testing his evidence. Livingston *v.* Dinwoodie, 1860; 22 D. 1333. Steven *v.* Nicoll, 1875; 2 R. 292. County Coun. of Fife *v.* Thoms, 1898; 24 R. 1097.

(*c*) Doe *v.* Robertson, 15 East, 31.

(*d*) Fraud may not be in the particular note, but in some other requiring a conformity of entries to fortify it.

2235. Usage is admissible to construe contracts (*a*); 'and even to make or modify the law which rules the relations of persons between whom no contract exists (*b*). But the custom must be reasonable and consistent with law, a saying which really means (1) that a custom which is not reasonable is not proved, for custom is "mos consensu utentium comprobatus," and if not reasonable that such practice as exists must be ascribed to compulsion or some cause other than assent of those who practise it; and (2) that it must not be opposed to public policy or morality, or grounded on a mere mistake as to a fundamental or absolute rule of law. It is not allowed to *contradict* a written contract (*c*).'

(*a*) Robertson *v.* French, 4 East, 135; 7 R. R. 535. Smith *v.* Wilson, 3 B. & Ad. 728 (see 20 R. R. 337). Haynes *v.* Holiday, 7 Bing. 587. Blacket *v.* R. E. Ass. Co., 2 Cr. & J. 249. Ld. Hardwicke in Baker's Case, 1 Ves. 459.

(*b*) See, *e.g.*, as to whale-fishing, above § 1289.

(*c*) Savigny, Syst. § 25 and vol. i. Beyl. ii. Donell. i. cap. 10. 1 Smith's L. C. 534–560. Ersk. i. 1. 44. *Supra*, § 524 et al. Bruce *v.* Smith, 1890; 17 R. 1000. Anderson *v.* M'Call, 1866; 4 Macph. 765.

II. PAROLE AND PRESUMPTIVE EVIDENCE.

2236. General View.—Parole is the great source of evidence, not only in those unforeseen circumstances which form the object of inquiry in criminal law, or which are the subject of redress in actions of damages, but also in the daily transactions of life, or interruptions and embarrassments in the course of the fulfilment of contracts. One great benefit of jury trial is, that it requires less (*a*) the exclusion of any kind of evidence; leaving the collected materials to be disposed of on the footing of credibility, by an impartial tribunal of men accustomed to judge of the ordinary transactions of life. But still there are certain technical rules of exclusion of testimony, in which what may be called the *law* of parole evidence consists. The questions on all such matters are two: 1. What is *admissible* testimony? 2. What is *sufficient* evidence?—the former being matter of law for the Court; the latter, matter of deliberation and decision for the jury, but still with some aid from the law as to what shall not in particular cases be held sufficient evidence.

(*a*) It is not invariably so.

2237. Who are Admissible Witnesses.—The exclusion of witnesses depends on two principles: the danger of trusting a Court or jury with certain descriptions of evidence; and of perjury, or extreme hardship on witnesses, in allowing or requiring them to give testimony in particular cases.

2238. The general rule, 'when Mr. Bell wrote, was,' that all persons 'were' competent witnesses, who, not being convicted of a crime inferring infamy, have the use of reason, and such religious belief as to feel the obligation of an oath: and who are not influenced by interest, or connected with the party for whom they are called by near relationship, or biassed in his favour by confidential connection or communication, or actuated by hostility against the adverse party. Even this general statement differs materially from the statement of the older law; and the prevailing tendency 'was' to convert some of these disqualifying circumstances (as relationship, confidential connection, and hostility) into matter of credit with the jury, rather than exclusion of the witnesses.

'The law of parole evidence has been greatly changed by the statutes 3 and 4 Vict. c. 59, 15 and 16 Vict. c. 27, and 16 and 17 Vict. c. 20. With few exceptions, it may be stated that all persons are now admissible as witnesses who are not disqualified by incapacity. The changes thus made will be hereafter noticed.'

2239. Disqualification by Incapacity.—Incapacity must be marked by plain and palpable characters,—pupillarity, insanity, idiocy.

2240. (1.) *Pupils* are not admitted, if they are incapable of the obligation of an oath, or unfit to comprehend the subject of inquiry. As to the oath, it is 'said to have been' the practice of Courts of justice to examine the infant, and to put the oath only if it be understood. 'But in the present day, those who are in pupillarity are not sworn, but admonished to tell the truth.' In point of intelligence, a child is admitted (with reservation of credibility) in facts of injury and crime, but not in matters of civil contract (*a*). And as witnesses to facts happening during pupillarity, they are admissible after they have passed that age (*b*).

(*a*) 4 Stair, 43. § 7. 4 Ersk. 2. § 22. Tait, 356. 2 Hume, p. 2. Burnet, 391. 6. Davidson *v.* Charteris, 1738; M. 16,899; Elch. *Wit.* 12; 3 Ill. 78. 3 and 4 Vict. c. 59. Purves, 1841; 2 Swin. 531. Steuart, 1855; 2 Irv. 166. Thomson, 1857; 2 Irv. 747. Macbeth, 1867; 5 Irv. 353. Miller, 1870; 1 Coup. 430.

(*b*) Douglas *v.* Graham, 1694; 4 B. Sup. 180; 3 Ill. 78. Ballantine *v.* Charteris, 1705; *ib.* 620.

2241. *Insanity and Idiocy* of course disqualify, unless when the fact and the examination both occur within a lucid interval of the insane person (*a*).

(*a*) 4 Stair, 43. § 7. Tait, 357. See Murray, 1866; 5 Irv. 232. Sheriff, 1866; 5 Irv. 226. Coupland, 1863; 4 Irv. 370; R. *v.* Hill, 5 Cox, Cr. Ca. 259; 20 L. J. Mag. Ca. 222. Tosh *v.* Ogilvy, 1873; 1 R. 254.

2242. Disqualification by Defect of Religious Belief.—Law 'trusted' not to the mere sense of honour, or regard to character, or dread of punishment; it 'required' also the sanction of religion. But whatever the sect or form of religion of the witness may be, if he 'believed,' or 'professed' to believe, in the existence of God and a future state; or 'was' willing to take the oath,—acknowledging it as an appeal to God binding on his conscience,—he 'was' admissible; certain indulgences in form being given to Quakers, Moravians, and Separatists (*a*). 'Subsequent legislation has altered these rules, and virtually forbids religious belief to be made a test of the competency of witnesses. By 1 and 2 Vict. c. 105, it is enacted that all persons are to be held bound by the oath administered to them in any Court in the United Kingdom, provided the same shall be in such form and with such ceremonies as such persons may declare to be binding; and they are liable to be convicted of perjury for wilful false swearing. After various statutes had been passed on the subject, the Act 28 and 29 Vict. c. 9 was enacted, whereby a form of affirmation is provided for persons called as witnesses in any Court of civil or criminal jurisdiction in Scotland, or required to make an affidavit or deposition in any proceeding, civil or criminal, who shall refuse or be unwilling from alleged conscientious motives to be sworn. Such affirmation is equivalent to an oath, and infers the penalties attaching to perjury (*b*).'

(*a*) 1 Phillips, 20. Tait, 359. 53 Geo. III. c. 127, § 23. 9 Geo. IV. c. 32. 3 and 4 Will. IV. c. 49, and c. 82. 1 Vict. c. 15. Menzies *v.* Morrison, Jan. 19, 1712; M. 16,732; 3 Ill. 78. Nicolson *v.* Nicolson, 1770; M. 16,770; Hailes, 371; aff. 3 Pat. 655. M'Farlane *v.* Young, 1821; 3 Mur. 411. As to the incompetency of witnesses for want of belief, see Omichund *v.* Barker, Willes, 538; 1 Atk. 21. Maden *v.* Catanach, 7 H. & N. 360; 31 L. J. Ex. 118. White, 1842; 1 Br. Just. Rep. 228. Henry, 1842; *ib.*

221. Rice, 1864; 4 Irv. 493. Clarke *v.* Bradlaugh, 9 Q. B. D. 38; 51 L. J. Q. B. 1.

(*b*) See 4 Ersk. 2. § 23, and notes. Taylor on Evid. § 1252, etc. Best's Pr. of Ev. § 134, 161, etc. Dickson on Evid. § 1688 sqq.

2243. Disqualification by Infamy.—Infamy may be *infamia facti* or *infamia juris*: the former resulting from a depraved and infamous course of life and abandoned character; the latter from conviction of a crime.

(1.) *Infamia Facti* goes only to credibility (*a*). But even to the effect of credibility, the law of Scotland does not admit any inquiry into the conduct and character of a witness (*b*), 'further than by asking the witness himself whether he has committed a crime which affects his credibility,—a question which the witness may decline to answer (*c*).' Nor 'was' it permitted to affect the credibility by proving that the witness had formerly given a different account of the matter (*d*). 'It is now, however, competent to ask any witness whether he has on any specified occasion (not being a criminal precognition) made a statement on any matter pertinent to the issue different from the evidence he has given, and to adduce evidence to prove such different statement on the occasion specified (*e*).'

(2.) *Infamia Juris* alone 'could' exclude, 'until the exclusion was abolished by 15 and 16 Vict. c. 27, § 1, reserving the right to examine with regard to credibility, as to such convictions.' The infamy must 'have been' by conviction or sentence of the Supreme Court (*f*). It must 'have been' conviction of an infamous crime, *i.e.* either in its nature inferring a disregard to truth and honesty,—as perjury, forgery, theft, robbery; or a crime to which the punishment of infamy is specially annexed (*g*). A reversal of the conviction 'removed' the exclusion (*h*). A pardon also 'discharged' the objection, leaving the effect on credibility (*i*); but not if the infamy 'were' a part of the punishment imposed by the law. Suffering the punishment 'discharged' the infamy, except in perjury and subornation (*k*).

(*a*) L. Milton *v.* Lady Milton, 1671; M. 16,674; 3 Ill. 78. Anderson and Fogharty, 1822; 2 Hume on Cr. 352; S. Just. Ca. 22. Tennant *v.* Tennant, 1883; 10 R. 1187 (evidence of prostitutes).

(*b*) E. Fife *v.* E. Fife's Trs., 1816; 1 Mur. 131. Baillie *v.* Bryson, 1818; *ib.* 320.

(*c*) Burke and Macdowall, 1828; Syme, 364; Dickson on Evid. § 1796. King *v.* King, 1842; 4 D. 530.

(*d*) Hislop *v.* Miller, 1 Mur. 49. Auchmutie *v.* Ferguson, *ib.* 212. M'Kenzie *v.* Henderson, 2 Mur. 218. Wight *v.* Liddell, 1827; 4 Mur. 328. Walker *v.* Ritchie, 1836; 14 S. 1128.

(*e*) 15 Vict. c. 27, § 3. O'Donnell, 1855; 2 Irv. 236. Pritchard, 1865; 5 Irv. 88. Luke, 1866; 5 Irv. 293. Emslie *v.* Alexander, 1862; 1 Macph. 209 (precognition). Inch *v.* Inch, 1856; 18 D. 997 (ditto). See also O'Donnell, 1855; 2 Irv. 236. Robertson, 1873; 2 Couper, 495. Dickson on Ev. § 1808. Gall *v.* Gall, 1870; 9 Macph. 177. Robertson *v.* Stewart, 1874; 1 R. 530. See below, § 2259.

(*f*) 2 Hume, 354. Armstrong *v.* Leith Bkg. Co., 1834; 12 S. 440. Aitchison *v.* Patrick, 1836; 15 S. 360; 3 Ill. 79.

(*g*) 4 Ersk. 2. § 33. Hume, *ut supra*. Tait, 358. Burnet, 396. Thomson, 1842; 1 Broun, 413.

(*h*) Lord Lovat's Case, Howel's State Trials, vol. xviii. 1004, 1011.

(*i*) 2 Starkie, 720, and cases cited. Hume, *ut supra*. Johnstone, 1845; 2 Broun, 401.

(*k*) 9 Geo. IV. c. 32. 1 Will. IV. c. 37, § 9.

2244. Disqualification by Interest.—No one 'could formerly' be a witness in his own cause; and interest in the event of the suit 'made' him a party. The necessity of proceeding on general rules, and the consideration that a Court has no scales fine enough to detect the preponderance of self-interest in its effect on testimony, led to an indiscriminate exclusion of all witnesses interested in the cause, however trifling the interest 'might' be (*a*).

'The objection of interest is abolished (*b*); and it is enacted that in civil cases "it shall be competent to adduce and examine as a witness in any action or proceeding, any party to such action or proceeding" (*c*). Certain exceptions in *Consistorial Actions* remained (*d*) till 1874: but these are now entirely removed, even in regard to actions instituted in consequence of adultery; with the sole provision that no witness, whether a party to the suit or not, is liable to be asked or bound to answer any question tending to show that he or she has been guilty of adultery, unless he or she has already given evidence in the same proceeding in disproof of his or her alleged adultery (*e*). No change is made in regard to the proof of promise of marriage in declarators of marriage founded on promise *cum subsequente copulá* (*f*).'

(*a*) The authorities referred to here and afterwards in support of the old law have been omitted, as was the case in Mr. Shaw's edition. They will be found in the fourth edition, and the Illustrations, vol. iii. p. 79 et seq.

(*b*) 15 and 16 Vict. c. 27, § 1. Anderson *v.* Gill, 1850; 20 D. 1326; aff. 1858, 3 Macq. 180.

(*c*) 16 and 17 Vict. c. 20, § 1. See below, § 2263. The respondent in a complaint for breach of interdict may be adduced. Miller *v.* Bain, 1879; 6 R. 1215.

(*d*) *Ib.* § 4.

(*e*) 37 and 38 Vict. c. 64, § 1, 2. Cook *v.* Cook, 1876; 4 R. 78. Kirkwood *v.* Kirkwood, 1875; 3 R. 235. Bannatyne *v.* Bannatyne, 1886; 13 R. 619. As to a judicial examination of parties in consistorial cases, see Surtees *v.* Wotherspoon, 1872; 10 Macph. 355, 866; and *infra*, § 2262.

(*f*) *Ib.* § 3.

2245. The interest must, in order to disqualify, 'have been' present, certain, and immediate, either in the question put as it affects the result of the cause, or as the verdict or judgment may serve as an instrument of evidence or other occasion of benefit to the witness himself; otherwise it 'went' only to credibility. And so, when one 'was' not immediately concerned in the cause, and 'had' no interest in the event in support of which the verdict in that cause 'might' be given in evidence by him in any other proceeding instituted by or against him, he 'was' a competent witness.

2246. Pecuniary interest to the smallest amount 'disqualified.' So a creditor on an estate, in a cause for establishing the right to it, 'was' rejected; so one having a servitude over ground, the boundaries of which 'were' in question; and a legatee under a testament, in a reduction of it; and a cautioner in the suspension of a bill, when called as witness in a reduction improbation of it; and office-bearers in a chartered bank holding shares; and witnesses in many similar cases.

2247. A creditor has a direct pecuniary interest in the increase or diminution of his debtor's estate; and a bankrupt has a similar interest to enlarge his funds. They 'were' not admissible in cases having such effect.

Interest in the event of the suit 'disqualified'; as, if the witness 'were' to share the sum awarded; or if he 'were' promised an advantage by the gaining of the suit, as a lease on an estate in question; or if he 'were' bound to pay money on the failure of the party by whom he 'was' called. If the verdict 'was' to be available as an instrument of evidence to the witness in another case, the interest 'was' held to be direct. But this in England 'was' altered by a statute making such a verdict or judgment unavailing to the witness (*a*).

(*a*) 3 and 4 Will. IV. c. 42, 26.

2248. It 'was' not a disqualifying interest that the witness 'had' a wish for the success of the party who 'called' him, or a strong bias in his favour, or some other eventual prospect or hope of advantage in the issue. These, though they 'might' influence his testimony, 'went' to his credibility only. Nor 'was' it enough that the witness 'had' a similar case to maintain, if the verdict or judgment 'could' not be used in his favour; nor that one 'had' an impression or apprehension of an interest, though this 'might' affect his credit. And it 'was' not a disqualification if the interest 'were' uncertain.

2249. Protective interest 'disqualified,' where clear and certain, as much as pecuniary interest. Interest is protective where the witness is called on to save character or avoid punishment. A witness may decline to answer what may criminate himself, 'or tend to show that he has committed adultery' (*a*), or expose him to any penalty or forfeiture; but he cannot plead such exemption to avoid liability in civil matters (*b*).

(*a*) See 16 and 17 Vict. c. 20, § 3. *Supra*, § 2244. *Infra*, § 2251A. Dickson on Evid. § 2016.

(*b*) 46 Geo. III. c. 37. See § 2251A, below.

2250. Exceptions to the rule of disqualification from interest 'were' admitted in the following cases:—

Shipmasters, and mariners for their owners; and agents, factors, carriers, clerks, servants, for their principal, 'were and' are admissible witnesses; a rule in some degree necessary to the common intercourse of trade. The interest which they may have in establishing a contract, or in the delivering of articles, etc., goes to their credit.

Where the interest 'was' discharged, the witness 'was' admissible. This, of course, still 'left' the question of credibility. And often there are such palpable manifestations of preparing evidence in this way, that the case is open to observations seriously affecting the credibility of the witness. The interest may be taken away by a discharge of any responsibility of the witness arising out of the matter or cause; by a general discharge of responsibility for anything which has happened previous to the date of the discharge; by the witness discharging all demands that may accrue to him from the effect of the judgment; by previously paying the witness what, as legatee or creditor, or otherwise, he could gain by his testimony. And it 'was' held that neither 'was' the adverse party entitled to prevent a discharge of the witness's interest, nor 'was' the witness entitled to persist in his disqualification, by refusing to accept of a discharge or satisfaction. But there 'were' interests which 'could' not be discharged, and the witness must continue disqualified.

2251. Disqualification by Relationship.—This vestige of a rule of evidence, suited to a tribunal which does not see the witness, ought now, 'said Mr. Bell, before its abolition by statute,' to go to credibility only. It 'was' a disqualification grounded on the presumed identification of the witness with the party with whom he 'stood' related, and not capable, like interest, of being discharged. The witness must be related to one of the actual parties in the suit; the nearest relationship to one who is only interested (however deeply) in the suit 'did' not disqualify. The same degree of relationship which 'disqualified' as a judge (parent and child; brother and sister even by affinity; uncle and nephew, or aunt and niece, if by consanguinity) 'disqualified' a witness. But the tendency 'was' to admit the witness, reserving all objections to credit. A bastard (after much vacillation of opinion) 'was' held not within the rule, leaving the connection to go to credit. The same relationship to both parties 'was' held not to neutralise the witness. A parent 'might' decline to give testimony against his child in a criminal cause.

'It is now "no objection to the admissibility of any witness, that he or she is the father or mother, or son or daughter, or brother or sister by consanguinity or affinity, or uncle or aunt, or nephew or niece by consanguinity, of any party adducing such witness in any action, cause, prosecution, or other judicial proceeding, civil or criminal; nor shall it be competent to any witness to decline to be examined and give evidence on the ground of any such relationship" (*a*). And it has been made "competent to adduce and examine as a witness in any action or proceeding any party to such action or proceeding, or the husband or wife of any party, whether he or she shall be individually named in the record or proceeding or not." But this is not to "render any person, or the husband or wife of any person, who in any criminal proceeding is charged with the commission of any indictable offence, or any offence punishable on summary conviction, competent or compellable to give evidence for or against himself or herself, his wife or her husband, excepting in so far as the same may be at present competent by the law and practice of Scotland" (*b*); nor "render any person compellable to answer any question tending to criminate himself or herself," nor "any husband competent or compellable to give against his wife evidence of any matter communicated by her to him during the marriage, nor any wife competent or compellable to give against her husband evidence of any matter communicated by him to her during the marriage" (*c*). The adducing of a party as a witness by the adverse party has not the effect of a reference to oath; but one who has adduced his opponent as a witness cannot afterwards refer the cause, or any part of it, to his oath (*d*).'

(*a*) 3 and 4 Vict. c. 59, § 1. 16 and 17 Vict. c. 20, § 3.
(*b*) See Dickson on Evid. § 1717. 2 Hume, Cr. Law, 349. And above, § 2244.
(*c*) 16 and 17 Vict. c. 20, § 3.
(*d*) 16 Vict. 20, § 5.

2252. Disqualification by Malice.—Enmity must, in order to prevail as an objection to admissibility, be deep and serious, and clearly proved (*a*). 'In practice, proof of enmity is adduced only to affect the witness's credibility.'

(*a*) M'Kenzie *v.* Roy, 1830; 5 Mur. 259. Thomas *v.* Pinkston, 1796; Hume, 894. King *v.* King, 1841; 4 D. 124. Greig, 1842; 1 Broun, 259. Rose *v.* Junor, 1846; 9 D. 12.

2253. Disqualification by Agency and Partial Counsel.—This 'was' in our practice extended beyond professional agency, to that spontaneous adoption of another's cause which gratuitously supplies advice, suggestions, aid, in carrying it on. Professional agency 'disqualified,' while it 'continued,' as to all matters of the cause. Even after one 'had' ceased to be agent, he 'was' not admissible in regard to such matters as he 'had' himself conducted in that capacity. Partial counsel 'disqualified, consisting' in the instigating of the prosecution; being present at consultations, corresponding about the cause, suggesting witnesses, pleas, or inquiries, examining witnesses, and collecting information; the tendency, however, now being to leave all this to credit. Being intentionally present at the precognition of other witnesses, or having the depositions of others sent to him, 'was' an objection to the witness. Accidental perusal of papers in the cause 'was' not enough to disqualify the witness. The objection grounded on the witness ultroneously coming forward 'is' limited to credit.

2253A. 'By the Act of 1852, it was enacted that no witness should be excluded from giving evidence "by reason of agency or of partial counsel, or by reason of having appeared without citation, or by reason of having been precognosced subsequently to the date of citation; but every person so adduced, who is not otherwise by law disqualified from giving evidence, shall be admissible as a witness, and shall be admitted to give evidence as aforesaid, notwithstanding of any objections offered on the above-mentioned grounds." This does not "affect the right of any party in the action or proceeding in which such witness shall be adduced, to examine him on any point tending to affect his credibility" (*a*). By this statute the agent in the action was excluded from being a witness, "excepting in so far as the same may be competent by the existing law and practice of Scotland" (*b*); but this was repealed in the following year (*c*).'

(*a*) 15 and 16 Vict. c. 27, § 1. (*b*) *Ib.*
(*c*) 16 and 17 Vict. c. 20, § 2. 37 and 38 Vict. c. 64, § 1 (repealing a clause excluding law agents' evidence in consistorial actions).

2254. Disqualification by Confidentiality.—This entitles the *party* to object to a betraying of the confidence reposed in a counsel or law agent, 'with reference to actual or contemplated legal proceedings,' and the witness is bound to respect this privilege (*a*). But the objection extends no further (*b*). So the witness cannot waive the privilege (*c*); but if the party should waive it, the witness cannot refuse his testimony (*d*). 'A party calling his agent as a witness waives all objections on the ground of confidentiality (*e*).' A party cannot insist for the production of letters by a client to his agent, nor a memorial for an opinion by counsel (*f*). 'A husband or a wife cannot be allowed or compelled to disclose communications made by the one to the other during the marriage, except in causes concerning the conduct of the spouses towards each other (*g*), or in examination under the Bankruptcy Act (*h*).'

(*a*) 1 Phillips, 131. Cromack *v.* Heathcote, 2 B. & B. 4; 3 Ill. 86; 22 R. R. 638. M'Leod *v.* M'Leod, 1744; M. 16,744. Bower *v.* Russel, May 26, 1810; F. C. Lady Bath's Exrs. *v.* Johnston, Nov. 12, 1811; F. C. Lumsdain *v.* Balfour, 1828; 7 S. 7. Gavin *v.* Montgomerie, 1830; 9 S. 213. Hay *v.* Edin. and Glas. Bank, 1858; 20 D. 701. Inglis *v.* Gardner, 1843; 5 D. 1029. Wark *v.* Bargaddie Coal Co., 1855; 17 D. 526; aff. 1859, 3 Macq. 488. See as to communications between co-defenders, Rose *v.* Medical Invalid Ins. Socy., 1847; 10 D. 156.
(*b*) Wilson *v.* Rastall, 4 T. R. 753; 2 R. R. 515. Bramwell *v.* Lucas, 2 B. & Cr. 745. Stewart *v.* Miller, 1834; 14 S. 837. M'Donald *v.* M'Donalds, 1881; 8 R. 357. See as to priests and clergymen, M'Lachlan *v.* Douglas, 1863; 4 Irv. 273.
(*c*) Kerr *v.* D. Roxburghe, 1822; 3 Mur. 13.
(*d*) Forteith *v.* E. Fife, 1821; 2 Mur. 467.
(*e*) 15 and 16 Vict. c. 27, § 1.
(*f*) Gavin, Wilson, and Stewart, *supra* (*a*) and (*b*). Lumsdain *v.* Balfour, 1828; 7 S. 7. E. Fife *v.* E. Fife's Trs., 1816; 1 Mur. 103. Clark *v.* Spence, 1824; 3 Mur. 455. The privilege is not pleadable when fraud or crime is in question. M'Cowan *v.* Wright, 1852; 15 D. 229, 494. M'Leod, *cit.* (*a*). Morrison *v.* Somerville, 1860; 23 D. 232. A bankrupt's law agent must answer all lawful questions as to the bankrupt's affairs. 19 and 20 Vict. c. 79, § 90, 91. A. B. *v.* Binny, 1858; 20 D. 1058. Paul *v.* Robb, 1855; 17 D. 457.
(*g*) 16 Vict. c. 20, § 3.
(*h*) 19 and 20 Vict. c. 79, § 90. Sawers *v.* Balgarnie, 1858; 21 D. 153. *Supra*, § 2251.

2255. Disqualification by Presence in Court.—A party is 'entitled to be present in Court during the trial of his cause; but a witness is' not allowed to be present in Court during the examination of other witnesses, unless when as a professional man he is called to the construction of testimony.

'The law in this respect has been altered to this effect: "That in any trial before any judge of the Court of Session or Court of Justiciary, or before any Sheriff or Steward, it shall not be imperative on the Court to reject any witness against whom it is objected that he or she has, without the permission of the Court, and without the consent of the party objecting, been present in Court during all or any part of the proceedings; but it shall be competent for the Court in its discretion, to admit the witness where it shall appear to the Court that the presence of the witness was not the consequence of culpable negligence or criminal intent, and that the witness has not been unduly instructed or influenced by what took place during his or her presence, or that injustice will not be done by his or her examination" (*a*).'

(*a*) 3 and 4 Vict. c. 59, § 3.

2256. Exceptions from the Rules of Exclusion.—These exceptions are 'or were' introduced from necessity, to the effect of reducing the objection from disqualification to credibility. Such is the case in *penuria testium*. This is confined chiefly to criminal acts, where secrecy is studied; or to domestic occurrences, which necessarily exclude the presence of strangers; or to the case of witnesses necessary to the act in question (*a*).

(*a*) 4 Stair, 43. § 8, 19. 4 Ersk. 2. § 26. Tait on Evidence, 383. Boyd *v.* Gibb, 1770; M. 16,770. Nicolson *v.* Nicolson, 1770; M. 16,770; Hailes, 371, 418; aff. 3 Pat. 655. Laings, petrs., Nov. 16, 1814; F. C. Martin *v.* Maxwell, Feb. 8, 1816; F. C. Brown *v.* Winton, 1821; 2 Mur. 455. Young *v.* Allison, 1820; *ib.* 229. Wilkie *v.* Jackson, 1834; 12 S. 520. Stewart *v.* Menzies, 1835; 13 S. 408. Murray *v.* Sinclair, 1847; 9 D. 598. Surtees *v.* Wotherspoon, 1872; 10 Macph. 866.

2257. Legal Evidence. — It is the undoubted province of the jury alone to weigh the evidence; but still this has been placed under the restraint of certain rules in regard to what shall in particular circumstances amount to legal evidence.

(1.) *Incompetency of Parole.*—Written evidence alone is competent in bargains and conveyance of land (*a*), and in proof of trust (*b*). But to these rules there are exceptions, as when *rei interventus* bars *locus pœnitentiæ* (*c*); 'when the party founding on a written contract admits that it gives an untrue account of the facts (*d*); when it is challenged for fraud or error (*e*)'; and when the question of trust is between the trustee and third parties. Parole is not sufficient, and so is excluded, as proof to establish a loan (*f*), 'advance, or payment (*g*)' of money 'above the sum of £100 Scots,' or simple promise (*h*), or qualification of a document of debt (*i*), or alteration of a written agreement (*i*), or acceptance of a bill, 'or innominate (?) contracts of a very unusual kind (*k*).' And non-onerosity of a bill 'was, till 1882,' proveable only by writ or oath (*l*).

(2.) *A Single Witness is not sufficient to prove a Fact* (*m*).—This rule in England is confined to cases of treason and perjury, and equity cases (*n*). But still there is a certain practical approximation to the same principle in the laws of England and of Scotland; one witness being enough in Scotland, if corroborated by circumstances, or if several acts going to the same result are proved by different witnesses (*o*).

(*a*) See *ante*, § 889. (*b*) See *ante*, § 1995.

(*c*) See *ante*, § 26.

(*d*) Hotson *v.* Paul, 1831; 9 S. 685. Miller *v.* Oliphant, 1843; 5 D. 856. Grant's Trs. *v.* Morrison, 1875; 2 R. 377.

(*e*) Steuart's Trs. *v.* Hart, 1875; 3 R. 192; and cases in § 11, 13, 14.

(*f*) Annand's Trs. *v.* Annand, 1869; 7 Macph. 526. **Haldane (Speirs' Factor)** *v.* **Speirs**, 1872; 10 Macph. 537. Duncan's Trs. *v.* Shand, 1873; 11 Macph. 255. Paterson *v.* Paterson, 1897; 25 R. 144. See as to I O U's and other acknowledgments, above, § 202A, 310. Williamson *v.* Allan, 1882; 9 R. 859. Neilson *v.* Neilson's Trs., 1883; 11 R. 119. Laidlaw *v.* Shaw, 1886; 13 R. 724 (writ of agent—deposit-receipt).

(*g*) Mackenzie *v.* Brodie, 1859; 21 D. 1048. White *v.* Arthur, 1864; 2 Macph. 1154. Except payment of a ready-money sale or other transaction; Tod *v.* Flockhart, 1799; Hume, 499. Shaw *v.* Wright, 1877; 5 R. 245. Stewart *v.* Gordon, 1831; 9 S. 466. Except also, it would seem, payment of a bill or note; 45 and 46 Vict. c. 61, § 100. But there is room for doubt as to the effect of this enactment. When money is proved to have passed as by the indorsation on a cheque, parole is allowed to show the relation of the parties as debtor and creditor (Nicoll *v.* Reid, 1878; 6 R. 216), agent and principal (Robb *v.* Robb's Trs., 1884; 11 R. 881), etc.,—a rule analogous to that which holds in regard to donation, but which may be thought not quite consistent in principle with Haldane *v.* Speirs; see above, § 1874 (*b*), 202A (*e*), 566 (*e*). Williamson *v.* Allan, 1882; 9 R. 859 (*per* Lord Shand). See further as to proof of payment, above, § 566.

(*h*) See above, § 8.

(*i*) Mackenzie *v.* Dunlop, 1853; 16 D. 129. **Wark** *v.* **Bargaddie Coal Co.,** 1856; 18 D. 772; rev. 1858; 3 Macq. 467. Macpherson *v.* Haggart, 1881; 9 R. 306. Sutherland *v.* Montrose Shipbuilding Co., 1860; 22 D. 665. Ritchie *v.* Ritchie, 1858; 20 D. 1093. Law *v.* Gibson, 1835; 13 S. 396 (agreement to abate rent under written lease). Turnbull *v.* Oliver, 1891; 19 R. 154 (do.). See above, § 27. In executory contracts, or contracts for work to be done, when parties stipulate that alterations are not to be made or extras charged without written authority, *quære* whether that does not exclude evidence even of *rei interventus* in support of alterations or modifications of the contract by verbal orders, fraud not being averred? See above, § 25, 26. M'Elroy *v.* Tharsis Sulphur Co., 1877; 5 R. 161; rev. 1878, *ib.* H. L. 181. Spencer & Co. *v.* Dobie & Co., 1879; 7 R. 396.

(*k*) **Edmonston** *v.* **Edmonston,** 1861; 23 D. 995. Johnston *v.* Goodlet, 1868; 6 Macph. 1067. Thomson *v.* Fraser, 1868; 7 Macph. 39. Dobie *v.* Lauder's Trs., 1873; 11 Macph. 749. **Taylor** *v.* **Forbes,** 1853; 24 D. 19 (law agent's agreement to act gratuitously; and see cases in § 36 (2) (*d*), *supra*). Forbes *v.* Caird, 1877; 4 R. 1141. Stewart & Craig *v.* Phillips, 1882; 9 R. 501 (interest under lease of shootings). Downie *v.* Black, 1885; 13 R. 271. Reid *v.* Reid Bros., 1887; 14 R. 789. Garden *v.* E. Aberdeen, 1893; 20 R. 896. Proof of compromise or transaction, at least regarding moveables, may be by parole. Jaffray *v.* Simpson, 1835; 13 S. 1122. Thomson *v.* Fraser, 1868; 7 Macph. 39. Love *v.* Marshall, 1872; 10 Macph. 795. Dewar *v.* Ainslie, 1892; 20 R. 203.

(*l*) See Young *v.* Bell, 1837; 15 S. 1202. M'Ewen *v.* Graham, 1833; 12 S. 110. Hunter *v.* George's Trs., 1834; 7 W. & S. 333. See above, § 333B. Little *v.* Smith, 1845; 8 D. 265. Dougall *v.* Hamilton, 1863; 1 Macph. 1142.

(*m*) 4 Stair, 43. § 1, 2, 3. Tait on Evidence, 435. Thomson *v.* Stevenson, 1682; M. 16,886; 3 Ill. 89. Blair *v.* Peddie, 1684; M. 13,942. Dougal *v.* Dougal, 1833; 11 S. 1020. Cleland *v.* Paterson, 1837; 15 S. 1246.

(*n*) 1 Ed. VI. c. 12, § 22. 7 and 8 Will. III. c. 3, § 2, 4. See 36 Geo. III. c. 7, § 1. 11 and 12 Vict. c. 12, § 4.

(*o*) Tait, 435. Landales *v.* Gray, 1816; 1 Mur. 81. Ramsay *v.* Nairn, 1833; 11 S. 1033. Wilson *v.* Weir,

1861; 24 D. 67. Murray *v.* Murray, 1847; 9 D. 1556. Thomson's Exr. *v.* Thomson, 1882; 9 R. 911.

2258. (3.) *The best Evidence alone can be relied on:* That is to say, in point of law (as well as in just reasoning), no evidence is to be received which necessarily implies, '*e.g.* as parole adduced to prove the contents of existing writings,' the existence of better evidence (*a*). 'Thus, when a contract is embodied in a formal writing, the intention is to be gathered from the writing alone, which supersedes and excludes all preliminary negotiations or communings whether oral or in letters. But in construing the words of the deed or contract, it is proper to take into consideration the facts and circumstances with regard to which they were used (*b*).'

(*a*) 1 Phillips, 206. 1 Starkie, 103, 389, 396. Bryson *v.* Crawford, 1834; 12 S. 937. Clark *v.* Clark's Trs., 1861; 23 D. 74 (rule applied to proof of contents of improbative deed validated *rei interventu*). Thom *v.* North Br. Bkg. Co., 1850; 13 D. 134. Maconochie *v.* Stirling, 1864; 2 Macph. 1104.

(*b*) See above, § 524 (7) (9), and **Inglis** *v.* **Buttery,** *ibi cit.*; also § 1692 (*l*). Maclean *v.* Maclean, 1873; 11 Macph. 506. Lee *v.* Alexander, 1882; 10 R. 230; on app. 1883, *ib.* H. L. 91; 8 App. Ca. 853 (missives of sale not admissible to explain ambiguous conveyance, although it refers to them).

2259. (4.) *Hearsay is in general not admissible;* partly because it is not on oath, partly on the principle which requires the best evidence, partly because no opportunity is afforded of cross-examinations (*a*). But where the person is dead, his evidence, 'whether contained in a written document or proved by living witnesses (*b*),' may thus be given at second-hand, provided he had no interest at the time he spoke (*c*); 'or as it has been expressed in recent cases, since the objection of interest has been abolished, provided there be nothing in the statement or the circumstances to raise a suspicion of bad faith, or that it was a coloured or partial version of the truth (*b*), which seems after all to mean that the Court will, when it is without a jury, weigh the evidence. And to a certain extent hearsay is allowed in questions of pedigree (*d*).' Where a person examined on an interim warrant, 'or in previous litigation between the same parties,' has become incapable of testimony, the same rule applies (*e*); but not where merely he cannot attend: at least there must be a new examination for the trial (*f*).

(*a*) 1 Phillips, 218 et seq. 1 Starkie, 40, 47. Tait on Evid. 429 et seq. E. Fife *v.* E. Fife's Trs., 1816; 1 Mur. 95; 3 Ill. 90. Christian *v.* Kennedy, 1818; *ib.* 424. Dickson on Evid. § 83 sqq.

(*b*) Dysart Peerage Case, 6 App. Ca. 489. Lauderdale Peerage Case, 10 App. Ca. 692. Comp. Tennent *v.* Tennent, 1890; 17 R. 1205.

(*c*) E. Fife, *supra* (*a*). Cochran *v.* Wallace, 1820; 2 Mur. 298. Smith *v.* Bank of Scotland, 1826; 5 S. 98. Watson *v.* Watson, 1836; 14 S. 734; 1837, 15 S. 753. See as to interest, § 2244.

(*d*) Alexander *v.* Officers of State, 1868; 6 Macph. H. L. 54; L. R. 1 Sc. App. 276. Macpherson *v.* Duncan, 1876; 4 R. 132; aff. 1877, *ib.* H. L. 87.

(*e*) Tait on Evidence, 438.

(*f*) Gunn *v.* Gardiner, 1820; 2 Mur. 197. Aitchison *v.* Patrick, 1836; 15 S. 360. Watson, *supra* (*c*). Bell *v.* Reid, 1862; 24 D. 1428. Geils *v.* Geils, 1855; 17 D. 404.

2260. Presumptive Evidence.—Presumptions are legal rules to exclude, or to abridge, or to aid the inquiry by regulating the *onus probandi.* A presumption of fact is an inference from circumstances; a presumption of law is a rule of exclusive, or inclusive, or *primâ facie* proof. There are some cases in which the law has settled certain presumptions of force sufficient to guide the jury in weighing evidence.

(1.) *Præsumptio juris et de jure* is absolute, and must be so received by the jury (*a*). Such is the negative prescription (*b*), deathbed (*c*), fraudulent preference in bankruptcy (*d*).

(2.) *Præsumptio juris* is not an absolute, but a *primâ facie* proof, yielding to evidence. Such is the presumption of life (*e*), of *præpositura* (*f*), of property in moveables from possession (*g*), and many others.

(3.) *Circumstantial Evidence* is not the same with presumptive proof, except in so far as an inference may be called a presumption.

(*a*) 4 Ersk. 2. § 35. Tait, 447.

(*b*) *Supra*, § 606. (*c*) *Supra*, § 1786.

(*d*) 1696, c. 5. 2 and 3 Vict. c. 41. 19 and 20 Vict. c. 79.

(*e*) 4 Ersk. 2. § 36; *ante*, § 1640.

(*f*) *Supra*, § 1565. (*g*) § 1313.

III. CONFESSION OR OATH OF PARTY.

2261. General Rule.—It is competent to apply to the conscience of the party,—1. For a confession or denial of such facts as he must necessarily be acquainted with; and 2. By reference to his oath, to peril on his answer the whole matter in contest.

2262. Judicial Examination.—The Court may call upon either party, where a statement is made of a suspicious nature, to confess or deny the fact by solemn declaration. This 'was' frequently done, 'when the examination of the parties to the cause was incompetent,' in the Inferior Court (*a*), and it is not competent to apply against such an order by advocation (*b*); and by statute it 'was under a former Small Debt Act' made a competent and final mode of disposing of small causes before the Sheriff (*c*). The same course is also occasionally followed in the Court of Session; but it is entirely discretionary to the judge, and not what either party has a right to demand (*d*). The cases in which it is proper are those in which there is a suspicion of fraud or concealment (*e*).

(*a*) Act of Sederunt, July 11, 1839, § 66.
(*b*) Turner *v.* Gibb, 1826; 4 S. 449; 3 Ill. 90.
(*c*) 6 Geo. IV. c. 24.
(*d*) 4 Ersk. 2. § 22. Tait, 303. Act of Sederunt, Feb. 1, 1715.
(*e*) Goodfellow *v.* Madder, 1785; M. 1483; 3 Ill. 90. Campbell *v.* Turner, 1826; 5 S. 54. Fell *v.* Lyon, 1830; 8 S. 543. Wilson *v.* Beveridge, 1831; 9 S. 485. Barrie *v.* Tait, 1843; 6 D. 102. A. *v.* B., 1843; 6 D. 342 and 932. Mackenzie *v.* Stewart, 1848; 10 D. 611. Couper *v.* Leslie, 1847; 9 D. 909. Mackellar *v.* Scott, 1862; 24 D. 499. Sceales *v.* Sceales, 1866; 4 Macph. 575. Steuart *v.* Steuart, 1870; 8 Macph. 821. Surtees *v.* Wotherspoon, 1872; 10 Macph. 355, 866. See above, § 2244.

2263. Reference to Oath.—This is competent as to the last resource of a party who fails in, or despairs of, any other evidence. And it is ultimate and conclusive, it not being competent to refute the oath, in so far as that cause is concerned. It is a transaction by which the party who refers places the cause on the sole issue of his antagonist's oath, and agrees to stand by it as decisive (*a*). This mode of proof may competently be resorted to at any stage of the proceedings, even after verdict or judgment (*b*); 'but after judgment the reference must be of the whole cause, or of a separate and distinct part of the cause (*c*).'

It is not competent in crimes, nor is anyone bound to swear where his guilt or innocence of a crime, or his liability to punishment or penalty may follow (*d*), with certain exceptions in the Justice of Peace Acts (*e*); nor where writing is *de solemnitate* required, as in transferences and bargains relative to land. And it is not competent to refer to the oath of an agent, by whom an alleged contract was made for the party, the terms of the contract (*f*). 'For a reference must be made to a party having interest (*g*). Hence, in general, reference is made to the oaths of all the partners of a firm, although the effect of the deposition of one of them may be to bind all (*e.g.* in regard to the constitution of a debt within the ordinary authority of a partner), or to liberate all, as when he swears in a reference of resting owing that the debt has been paid (*h*). On the same principle, in a question with an assignee under an intimated assignation, it is incompetent for the debtor to refer to the oath of the cedent, who is no longer the party having interest (*i*), or in a question with the trustee in a sequestration to refer to the oath of the bankrupt (*k*).' Nor is it competent to refer a matter of law to oath (*l*). 'Under the existing law, reference to oath is excluded where the party has already been competently examined as a witness upon the same subject (*m*).'

It is in the equity of the Court to admit the reference, 'with or without imposing conditions,' and to judge whether truth is likely to be obtained by such an examination, 'and whether it may not tend to a perversion of justice' (*n*). But the reference may be retracted before the oath is sworn, 'with the permission of the Court, and' on paying the expenses occasioned by it (*o*). The party referred to is entitled to insist that his antagonist shall declare that he has no other, at least no written evidence, to which to refer (*p*).

(*a*) Yule *v.* Robertson, 1788; M. 9419; 3 Ill. 91. Elliotts *v.* Ainslie, 1749; M. 9363. Waddell *v.* Graham, 1806; Hume, 416. **Pattinson *v.* Robertson,** 1846; 9 D. 226 (*per* L. Moncreiff). Adam *v.* M'Lachlan, 1847; 9 D. 560.
(*b*) Clark *v.* Hyndman, Nov. 20, 1819; F. C. Campbell *v.* Turner, 1822; 1 S. 538. Law *v.* Lundin, 1747; M. 12,158. Dalziel *v.* Richmond, 1792; M. 9407. Aitchison *v.* M'Donald, 1823; 2 S. 329. M'Lennan *v.* Imray, 1826; 4 S. 781. Young *v.* Paton, 1826; 5 S. 161. Shirreff *v.* Shirreff's Trs., 1836; 15 S. 115. Fleming *v.* Simpson & Kay, 1798; Hume, 412. Gray *v.* Leny, 1801; Hume, 414. Binnie *v.* Willox, 1844; 6 D. 520. A. *v.* B., 1843; 16 S. Jur. 84. M'Donald *v.* Cooper, 1848; 10 D. 740 (Bill Chamber). Brown *v.* Ferguson, 1852; 24 Jur. 486. Anstruther and Kirkpatrick *v.* Bell, *infra* (*l*). **Longworth *v.* Yelverton**, 1865; 3 Macph. 645; 5 Macph. H. L. 144. Aikman *v.* Aikman's Trs., 1868; 6 Macph. 277. A reference to oath seems to be incompetent after a cause has been judicially referred. M'Larens *v.* Shore, 1883; 10 R. 1067.
(*c*) Sinclair *v.* M'Beath, 1869; 7 Macph. 934. *Infra*, § 2265.
(*d*) Conacher *v.* Conacher, 1859; 21 D. 597. Longworth, *cit.* M'Callum *v.* M'Call, 1825; 3 S. 551.
(*e*) 46 Geo. III. c. 37. But see Cameron *v.* Paul, 1853; 1 Irv. 316.

(*f*) Kirkwood *v.* Wilson, 1823; 2 S. 425. Mackay *v.* Ure, 1849; 11 D. 982. Sawers *v.* Clark, 1892; 19 R. 1090.

(*g*) *Per* L. Medwyn in M'Nab, *infra.* Mein and Adam, *infra*, etc. Farquhar *v.* Farquhar, 1886; 13 R. 596. A husband is not affected by his wife's oath in regard to an ante-nuptial debt. 4 Ersk. 2. § 10. Morrice *v.* Monro, 1829; 8 S. 156.

(*h*) Nisbett's Trs. *v.* Morrison, 1829; 7 S. 307. Easton *v.* Johnston, 1831; 9 S. 440. M'Nab *v.* Lockhart, 1843; 5 D. 1014. Broom & Co. *v.* Edgeley, 1843; 5 D. 1087. Neill & Co. *v.* Campbell & Hopkirk, 1849; 11 D. 979; 1850, 12 D. 618. Cleland *v.* M'Lellan, 1854; 13 D. 504. See the older cases in 3 Ill. 97–99. As to references to officers of corporations, see White *v.* Cal. Ry. Co., 1869; 7 Macph. 583. References to oath under the sexennial and triennial prescriptions are by the statutes expressly limited to the oath of the "debtor" and the "party" respectively. (See above, § 594, 599, 628, 632.) Certain *dicta* and one or two decisions support the view that where a whole business is entrusted or delegated to a factor, agent, or manager, reference may be made to his oath or to that of the person who has entire charge of the particular department. Gow *v.* M'Donald, 1827; 5 S. 445. Dickson *v.* Ker, 1830; 9 S. 125. M'Nab *v.* Lockhart, *cit.* Clark on Partnership, 281 sq. Dickson on Evid. § 1590. It seems reasonable that some such rule should obtain in the case of companies and incorporations, which can act only by directors and agents; but the point does not seem to have been formally settled, and is left open, in regard to cases not under the statutes of limitation, by the judgment in Bertram & Co. *v.* Stewart, 1874; 2 R. 255. An exception to the general principle appears to exist in the case of wives, *supra*, § 1566.

(*i*) 3 Stair, 1. § 18. 3 Ersk. 5. § 9, 10; 3 Ersk. 6. § 16. Lang *v.* Hislop, 1854; 16 D. 908. Campbell *v.* Campbell, 1860; 23 D. 159.

(*k*) Mein *v.* Towers, 1829; 7 S. 902; 3 Ill. 99. Adam *v.* M'Lachlan, 1847; 9 D. 560. Thomson *v.* Duncan, 1855; 17 D. 1089.

(*l*) Taylor *v.* Hall, 1829; 7 S. 565; 3 Ill. 99. See Lawson *v.* Murray, 1829; 7 S. 380. Conachar *v.* Robertson, 1829; 8 S. 141. Grub *v.* Porteous, 1835; 13 S. 603. Anstruther *v.* Wilkie, 1856; 18 D. 405. Kirkpatrick *v.* Bell, 1864; 2 Macph. 1369; 1864, 3 Macph. 252. Phœnix Fire Office, *infra*, § 2265, 2267. Savigny, Syst. vol. vii. p. 86 (§ 314).

(*m*) 16 Vict. c. 20, § 5. Dewar *v.* Pearson, 1866; 4 Macph. 493. Swanson *v.* Gallie, 1870; 9 Macph. 208. See above, § 2244. M'Leay *v.* Campbell, 1876; 3 R. 999.

(*n*) Ritchie *v.* Mackay, 1825; 4 S. 534; 3 W. & S. 484. **Pattinson** *v.* **Robertson,** 1846; 9 D. 226. Muirhead *v.* M'Ewan, 1852; 15 D. 16. Conacher, *cit.* (*d*). Aikman, *supra* (*b*). M'Leay *v.* Campbell, *cit.* **Longworth** *v.* **Yelverton,** *supra* (*b*), where a reference was refused on the ground that the reference involved the interests of third parties, viz. the status of the wife and children of the defender in a declarator of marriage. Robertson *v.* Mackay's Trs., 1894; Sh. Ct. of Lanarksh.

(*o*) Chalmers *v.* Jackson, Feb. 11, 1813; F. C. Bennie *v.* Mack, 1832; 10 S. 255. Jameson *v.* Wilson, 1853; 15 D. 414. Dick *v.* Hutton, 1876; 3 R. 448. Galbraith, *infra*, § 2264.

(*p*) 4 Stair, 44. § 2. 4 Ersk. 2. § 8. When a proof by writ or oath of party has been allowed, it is the universal practice to find that proof by writ has failed or been renounced before reference to oath is sustained; but the principle above stated does not seem to operate in the present day further than this.

2264. He may *defer* or refer back to the referrer where the case suggests that he must have better knowledge of the fact; yet a party cannot thus escape from swearing to a fact well known to him (*a*).

(*a*) 4 Stair, 44. § 13. 4 Ersk. 2. § 8. Tait, 241. Galbraith *v.* M'Neill, 1828; 7 S. 63.

2265. Effect.—As a reference to oath is a transaction, it follows that the whole cause, 'or question referred,' must be perilled on the oath (*a*), that the oath is conclusive, and that no conviction of falsehood and perjury will alter the effect of the oath on the cause (*b*). 'After the oath is taken, the only point to be inquired into is the import of it, not what is true, but what has been sworn (*c*).' It is not, however, a bar to a trial and conviction and punishment for perjury.

(*a*) Ogle *v.* Smith & Co., 1825; 3 S. 629; 3 Ill. 92. Butter *v.* Loch, 1830; 8 S. 843. Phœnix Fire Office *v.* Young, 1834; 12 S. 921. See above, § 2263. Lawson *v.* Murray, 1829; 7 S. 380. Sinclair *v.* M'Beath, 1869; 7 Macph. 934.

(*b*) Kincaid *v.* Dickson, 1673; M. 12,143. Thomson *v.* D. of Hamilton, 1688; 2 B. Sup. 121. Wyllie *v.* Latta, 1832; 11 S. 151.

(*c*) 4 Ersk. 2. § 8. "Non aliud quæritur quam an juratum sit," l. 5, § 2, D. de jurej. 12. 2, etc. In other words, the oath of party, like judicial admissions, and the judicial sentence itself (*res judicata*), merely establishes *formal* truth, a fiction of truth,—"pro veritate accipitur" (l. 207, D. de Reg. J. 50. 17). The practice of Scotland in regard to the oath of party is founded on the Roman law; and although the rules have been altered in many particulars, it is instructive to consult the exposition of Savigny, Syst. vol. vii. p. 47 sqq. (§ 309–314), and especially the statement of the modern practice of countries which observe the Roman law, p. 84 sqq.

2266. As a transaction between the parties, the oath affects them only. Co-obligants are not bound by the result, or at least not by an affirmative oath, though they seem to have the benefit of the negative (*a*).

(*a*) See 3 Ersk. 2. § 10, and the cases as to partners cited above, § 2263 (*h*). It is fixed that the oath of a partner after dissolution of the firm cannot affect the former partners, who are then merely *correi debendi.* And the oath of a joint adventurer—even of a ship's husband who is also a joint-owner—does not bind the other joint-adventurers. Duncan *v.* Forbes, 1831; 9 S. 540.

2267. Construction of the Oath.—The construction of the oath gives rise to difficult questions, which are for the Court, not for a jury (*a*). The answer must be special, and to fact, not inference; the referrer being entitled to put questions in minute detail, so as to expose any falsehood, or any assumed legal inference (*b*). 'Documents referred to in the deposition must be produced, the deponent's narrative or construction of them being ignored (*c*). Even when produced, they are available only so far as expressly examined on and made part of the deposition (*d*).'

(*a*) See Allan *v.* Thomson, 1822; 3 Mur. 3; 3 Ill. 94.

(*b*) Callander *v.* Wallace, 1709; M. 9416. A. *v.* B., 1757; M. 12,475. Swan *v.* Swan, 1786; M. 9418; Hailes, 998. Heddle *v.* Baikie, 1841; 3 D. 370. Crichton *v.* Campbell, 1857; 19 D. 661.

(*c*) Hunter *v.* Geddes, 1835 ; 13 S. 369. See Jackson *v.* Cochrane, 1873 ; 11 Macph. 475

(*d*) Gordon *v.* Pratt, 1860 ; 22 D. 903. Broatch *v.* Dodds, 1892 ; 19 R. 855.

2268. Intrinsic and Extrinsic Qualities.—The chief questions relate to qualifications adjected to oaths. A qualified oath is one in which the deponent acknowledges what is referred to his oath to be true, but adds what he affirms to be necessary to a complete answer for determining the cause. And the difficulty is to ascertain whether such addition be truly necessary to the complete answer, and such as the party referring is bound to take as part of the answer to his reference. In that case it is called an *intrinsic quality.* If it be unnecessary and superfluous, so that the referrer is not bound to admit it into the answer, the deponent having the *onus probandi*, in that case it is called an *extrinsic quality* (*a*).

(*a*) 4 Stair, 44. § 11. 4 Ersk. 2. § 11, 12, 13. Dirleton, *voce* Oath Qualified. Howe *v.* Wyllie, 1765 ; 5 B. Sup. 914 ; 3 Ill. 95. Brown *v.* M'Intyre, 1828 ; 6 S. 1022 ; 3 Ill. 96. Grant *v.* Wishart, 1845 ; 7 D. 274. Stewart *v.* Robertson, 1852 ; 15 D. 12. Gifford *v.* Rennie, 1853 ; 15 D. 451. Thomson *v.* Duncan, 1855 ; 17 D. 1081.

2269. It is of importance to mark the effect of the party who refers placing his whole cause upon the oath. In the ordinary case, the pursuer proves his libel, the defender his exception ; the pursuer his reply, the defender his duply. But where the oath alone is relied on, every point essential and necessarily implied in the case of the referrer is put to the test of that oath, and every quality in the oath which goes to the essence of the case of the referrer is intrinsic. So the pursuer who refers resting owing to the defender, must admit *payment* as an intrinsic quality in the answer, although in the ordinary case, where he could prove the debt *aliundè*, this would be an exception to be proved by the defender (*a*). In the same way, where he refers a libel grounded on a contract of sale, a condition in the contract is intrinsic (*b*). The defender also who refers to oath, must admit as an answer whatever goes to the essence of his defence (*c*). But the deponent is not entitled to relieve himself from the *onus probandi* where his case depends on a ground not necessarily involved in, or connected with, the matter referred. So a counter-claim of compensation, 'not being part of the original bargain,' is extrinsic, not to be proved by the defender's oath (*d*) ; 'unless it also bear that the creditor agreed to the discharge of the debt in this way (*e*).'

(*a*) 4 Ersk. 2. § 11, to be corrected. Campbell *v.* Douglas, 1676 ; M. 13,203 ; 3 Ill. 94. Trotter *v.* Clark, 1687 ; M. 13,204 ; and cases M. 13,025–6, 13,225. Campbell *v.* Scotland, 1778 ; M. 9530 ; Hailes, 812. Douglas *v.* Grierson, 1794 ; M. 11,116 ; Bell's Ca. 97 ; 1 Ill. 370. Robertson *v.* Thomson, 1824 ; 3 S. 186. Donald *v.* Minty; 1824 ; 3 S. 394. Carnegy *v.* Carnegy, 1825 ; 3 S. 566. See Anderson *v.* Rintoul, 1827 ; 5 S. 744. Brown *v.* M'Intyre, 1828 ; 6 S. 1022. Robertson *v.* Thomson, 1830 ; 8 S. 810. Stewart *v.* Walpole, 1804 ; Hume, 416. Young *v.* Sheridan, 1837 ; 15 S. 664. Johnstone *v.* Law, 1843 ; 6 D. 201. Galloway *v.* Moffat, 1845 ; 7 D. 1088. Heddle *v.* Baikie, 1847 ; 9 D. 1254. Mackay *v.* Ure, 1849 ; 11 D. 982. Hamilton's Exrs. *v.* Struthers, 1858 ; 21 D. 51. Newlands *v.* M'Kinlay, 1885 ; 13 R. 353.

(*b*) Howie *v.* Wylie, *cit.* (*a*). Forbes *v.* Craigie's Debtors, 1711 ; M. 13,212. Greig *v.* Boyd, 1830 ; 8 S. 382. Thomson *v.* Duncan, *infra* (*d*).

(*c*) 4 Ersk. 2. § 12. Burnet *v.* Morrow, 1864 ; 2 Macph. 929. Galbraith *v.* Cuthbertson, 1866 ; 4 Macph. 295.

(*d*) Learmonth *v.* Russel, 1664 ; M. 13,241 ; 3 Ill. 94 ; and cases M. 13,234, 13,210, 13,220, 13,221 ; Hailes, 995 ; M. 13,245. Halliday *v.* Halliday, 1826 ; 5 S. 116. Brown *v.* M'Intyre, 1828 ; 6 S. 1022. Hepburn *v.* Hepburn, 1806 ; Hume, 419. Hunter *v.* Kinnaird's Trs., 1830; 9 S. 154. Wright *v.* M'Farlane, 1837 ; 16 S. 67. Stevenson *v.* Stevenson, 1838 ; 16 S. 1088. Stewart *v.* Robertson, 1852 ; 15 D. 12. Thomson *v.* Duncan, 1855 ; 17 D. 1081. Wilson *v.* Wilson, 1871 ; 9 Macph. 920. If the oath bears that the creditor had actually agreed to take payment in goods, or to hold the debt compensated by a counter-claim, or otherwise discharged, that is intrinsic in a reference under the Act 1597, c. 83 (triennial prescription), because the Act requires the creditor after three years to prove both constitution and resting owing by his debtor's oath. Dickson on Evid. § 1646 sqq. Wilson *v.* Wilson, *cit.* Cooper *v.* Marshall, 1877 ; 5 R. 258. Coubrough *v.* Robertson, 1879 ; 6 R. 1301. So also in other cases where the subsistence of the debt is within the reference. Wilson *v.* Wilson, *cit.* Galbraith *v.* Cuthbertson, *cit.* (*c*).

(*e*) Thomson *v.* Duncan, and Coubrough *v.* Robertson, *citt.*

CHAPTER II

OF DILIGENCE AGAINST MOVEABLES

2270. General View.—The diligences proper to moveables for the enforcing of decrees are: 1. Arrestment and Forthcoming; 2. Poinding; 3. Writ of Extent; and, 4. Confirmation as Executor-Creditor (*a*).

(*a*) The subject of confirmation as executor-creditor has already been explained; see *ante*, § 1895. Besides these diligences, there is Sequestration, which is a universal diligence (see below, § 2341); *Cessio bonorum* (see below, § 2321); and the Landlord's Sequestration, which is peculiar to landlords. See *ante*, § 1233 et seq.

2271. Every decree of a Court (unless in declaratory actions) contains a warrant, on which execution may proceed.

The extracts of decrees of the Court of Session contain a warrant for charging the debtor to pay; for arresting, poinding, and registering, to the effect of denouncing the debtor, on which a warrant for imprisonment may proceed in the Bill Chamber (*a*).

Extracts of the decrees of Inferior Courts contain a direct warrant or precept under which they may be executed by the officers of the Court. Moveables within the shire or burgh may be attached or arrested, and thereafter, by sentence of the Court, adjudged to the creditor; or they may be poinded, and access got by opening lockfast places; and by order of the judge sold, and the price adjudged to the creditor. The person 'might' also, 'until 1880,' be imprisoned after registration of the unanswered charge on a warrant issued by the Sheriff-clerk. The same execution may proceed against the moveables in other sheriffdoms, by means of concurring warrants (*b*).

(*a*) 1 and 2 Vict. c. 114, § 1–8.
(*b*) 1 and 2 Vict. c. 114, § 9–15. See as to arrestments under the Small Debt and Debts Recovery Acts, 1 Vict. c. 41, § 3, 6, 13; and 30 and 31 Vict. c. 96, §, 3, 5, 6.

I. ARRESTMENT AND FORTHCOMING.

2272. Nature of this Diligence.—The operation of this diligence depends on the combined effect of an immediate attachment with a subsequent adjudication; and it is accordingly divisible into two parts, the one called "Arrestment," the other "Forthcoming" (*a*).

(*a*) 4 Stair, 50. § 26 et seq. 3 Ersk. 6. § 2. 2 Bell's Com. 65.

2273. Arrestment is the attaching of a pecuniary fund or of a moveable, so to remain till the debt be satisfied. It may proceed (1) at the instance of a creditor in a debt actually due; or (2) at the instance of a creditor in a future or contingent debt, or of a claimant whose *jus crediti* is not yet established by decree. In the former case, the arrestment is intended for immediate execution; in the latter, it is an arrestment in security.

'Arrestment *jurisdictionis fundandæ causâ* belongs to the law of procedure. There is a question whether it imposes any *nexus* on the subject arrested. If it does impose a *nexus*, that comes to an end when the owner finds caution *judicio sisti*, or enters appearance without objecting to the jurisdiction (*a*).'

(*a*) Carlberg *v.* Borjesson, 1877; 5 R. 188. Malone & M'Gibbon *v.* Cal. Ry. Co., 1884, 11 R. 853, where the authorities are cited. Stewart *v.* North, 1889; 16 R. 927; aff. 1890, 15 App. Ca. 452; 17 R. H. L. 60. Lindsay *v.* L. & N. W. Ry. Co., 1860; 22 D. 571. The opinions in Stewart *v.* North are not quite in harmony as to this point with those in Craig *v.* Brunsgaard & Co., 1896; 23 R. 500.

2274. Arrestment for Execution.—This proceeds in execution of a decree pronounced in an action, or a decree of registration; or without decree, on a liquid document of debt (*a*). The warrant to arrest on a decree, whether of the Superior or of an Inferior Court, is contained in the extract. It gives authority "lawfully to fence and arrest all and sundry moveable goods and gear, debts and sums of money, and other moveable effects, all to remain under sure fence and arrestment, at the complainer's instance, aye and until he be completely satisfied and paid." Where the groundwork is a liquid debt, but without decree, the arrestment is "to remain till sufficient caution be found to be made forthcoming to the complainer in terms of law." Upon such arrestment in either form the forthcoming follows, to make the arrested fund effectual to the creditor (*b*); 'and arrestments are unavailing unless they can be followed by a decree transferring the common debtor's right against the arrestee to the arresting creditor (*c*).'

(*a*) See below, § 2297, as to arrestment for Crown debts.
(*b*) Stair and Ersk. *ut supra*. 2 Bell's Com. 66. 3 Jurid. Styles, 547 et seq. 1 and 2 Vict. c. 114, § 2, 4, 9, 13, 16, 21. See below, § 2283. 40 and 41 Vict. c. 40, § 1–3 (Registered Writs Execution Act).
(*c*) Lucas's Trs. *v.* Campbell & Scott, 1894; 21 R. 1096.

2275. Arrestment for Security.—A creditor may arrest the debt or moveables of his debtor, in security of a debt for which he has raised an action, or which is not yet due (*a*). This may be done by a warrant contained in the summons, or separate (*b*). The arrestment may proceed on a summons containing an alternative conclusion *ad factum præstandum*, and for damages (*c*); 'but not on a summons of declarator or reduction or other summons containing no pecuniary conclusion except one for expenses (*d*).' The warrant in such cases "is to arrest, etc., to remain under sure fence and arrestment, aye and until sufficient caution be found that the same shall be made forthcoming to the complainer, as accords of the law." In this case, as in the other, as soon as the term of payment arrives, or when decree on the dependence (*e*) has been obtained, the action of forthcoming may proceed, and the fund or subject arrested may be adjudged to the creditor (*f*). 'Even without a decree of forthcoming, arrestment on the dependence, if there have been no undue delay in following it up, confers the same preference as another arrestment, in a sequestration or liquidation of the defender's estates (*g*).' When an arrestment has been used on a summons, or on letters of arrestment raised on a summons, the warrant of citation must be executed within twenty days after the date of the arrestment, and the summons called in Court within twenty days of the day of compearance, or on the first sederunt day after, if in vacation; otherwise the arrestment will be unavailing (*h*).

(*a*) Arrestment in security for a future or contingent debt is competent only when the debtor is *vergens ad inopiam*, or perhaps for other exceptional reasons. 3 Ersk. 6. § 10. 2 Bell's Com. 73 (69, M'L.'s ed.). Symington *v.* Symington, 1875; 3 R. 205. Smith *v.* Cameron, 1879; 6 R. 1107. Burns *v.* Burns, 1879; 7 R. 355. James *v.* James, 1886; 13 R. 1153. See below, § 2280; *supra*, § 46 (*b*).
(*b*) 3 Ersk. 6. § 2. 2 Bell's Com. 67. 1 and 2 Vict. c. 114, § 16, 17, 19. See as to Sheriff Court summonses, 39 and 40 Vict. c. 70, sch. A (ordinary court); 1 Vict. c. 41, § 8 (Small Debt Act); 30 and 31 Vict. c. 96, § 3, etc. (Debts Recovery Act).
(*c*) More *v.* Stirling & Sons, 1822; 1 S. 547.
(*d*) Ketchen *v.* Grant, 1871; 9 Macph. 966. Stafford *v.* M'Laurin, 1875; 3 R. 148. As to consistorial actions, see Fraser, H. & W. 579; and correct by Symington and Burns, *citt.* (*a*).
(*e*) *I.e.* in the depending action. The expense of arresting on the dependence cannot be recovered by the pursuer in the depending action. Taylor *v.* Taylor, Jan. 25, 1820; F. C. Symington *v.* Symington, 1874; 1 R. 1006. Black *v.* Jehangeer Framjee & Co., 1887; 14 R. 678 (arr. of ship).
(*f*) Oliphant *v.* Campbell, 1750; M. 677.
(*g*) Mitchell *v.* Scott, 1881; 8 R. 875. Benhar Coal Co. *v.* Turnbull, 1883; 10 R. 558. See Queensland Merc., etc. Co. *v.* Australas. Inv. Co., 1888; 15 R. 935.
(*h*) 1 and 2 Vict. c. 114, § 17.

2276. What may be arrested, and in whose hands.—The debtor's funds are equally liable to be attached for execution or for security. Personal debts and moveables in the possession (*a*) of another man than the 'common' debtor, are the proper subjects of arrestment (*b*). A sum due 'directly to the arrestor's debtor' is held as in possession of a debtor 'of his'; and in his hands, or in those of persons identified with him, arrestment is to be used, not in the hands of those indebted to such debtor (*c*). 'In order to the validity of an arrestment there must be direct personal obligation of the arrestee to deliver or pay to the common debtor (*d*). Arrestment cannot be used in the hands of one identified with the common debtor, as a servant or his wife.'

A trustee 'or judicial factor' is a debtor in this sense, 'in whose hands arrestments may be laid,' or anyone who is bound to account (*e*). And arrestment in a trustee's hand is competent, although the fund be not turned into money, 'provided the common debtor's interest in the trust-fund be moveable' (*f*). Arrestment of a trust-fund must be made in the hands of such trustees as are by the trust-deed entitled to act, '*i.e.* of a quorum, etc.' (*g*).

Debts by bill are not arrestable (*h*). Goods or money specially appropriated cannot be arrested (*i*). The subject must be already in possession of the arrestee (*k*), with the exception of an insurance broker for premiums (*l*); and a trustee, or one under obligation to do diligence and account (*m*). Rents, interests, and annuities may be arrested *currente termino*, '*i.e.* after the expiry of the whole of the previous term-day' (*n*). Alimentary funds '"expressly constitute and not exceeding the measure of aliment"' (*o*), are not arrestable (*p*); 'but the arrears not uplifted, being plainly in excess of the amount of reasonable aliment, are not preferable, except so far as they may be required to meet alimentary debts, and they may be arrested, and compensation may be pleaded against them (*q*). And the Court may restrict an exorbitant alimentary provision, having regard to the station and circumstances of the beneficiary (*r*).' But the salary of an extractor in the Court of Session was held arrestable (*s*); 'so also ministers' stipends (*t*). Fees, salaries, and pensions payable by the Crown are not arrestable (*u*). Wages of labourers and manufacturers, so far as necessary for their subsistence, are, at common law and by statute, not arrestable. All arrestments of wages on the dependence of small-debt summonses are illegal. The wages of all labourers, farm-servants, manufacturers, artificers, and workpeople are now exempted from arrestment, except so far as they exceed 20s. a week. But this exemption does not apply to debts contracted before January 1, 1871, alimentary debts, or rates and taxes imposed by law (*v*).'

(*a*) Young *v.* Aktiebolaget Ofverums Bruk, 1890; 18 R. 163. Brown *v.* Duff's Trs., 1850; 13 D. 149. Kellas *v.* Brown, 1856; 18 D. 1089 (shipmaster—owners).

(*b*) 3 Stair, 1. § 25. 3 Ersk. 6. § 5. 2 Bell's Com. 73 (70, M'L.'s ed.). Appine's Crs., 1760; M. 749. Cunningham *v.* Home, 1760; M. 747. Davidson *v.* Murray, 1784; M. 761. Glendinning's Crs. *v.* Montgomerie, 1745; M. 2573. In the case of companies and corporations, arrestment should be made in the same way as intimations of assignations. See above, § 1464A. Sinclair *v.* Staples, 1860; 22 D. 600. Ewing *v.* M'Lelland, 1860; 33 Jur. 1. Mags. of Dundee *v.* Taylor, 1863; 1 Macph. 701. Graham *v.* M'Farlan & Co., 1869; 7 Macph. 640. Hay *v.* Dufourcet & Co., 1880; 7 R. 972. Macdonald *v.* Reid, 1881; 9 R. 211 (police commissioners). See as to seller's power to attach goods sold in his own hands by arrestment or poinding, 19 and 20 Vict. c. 60, § 3, and Sale of Goods Act, 1893, § 40, 60. *Supra*, § 1300A sqq.

(*c*) 3 Ersk. 6. § 4. Campbell *v.* Faikney, 1752; M. 742. Henderson *v.* Stewart, 1796; M. 5534.

(*d*) Young, *cit.* Heron *v.* Winfields, 1894; 22 R. 183.

(*e*) Cross & Bogle *v.* Moir, 1775; M. 757; Hailes, 615. Wilson *v.* Smart, May 31, 1809; F. C. Ramsay *v.* Grierson, 1780; M. 759; Hailes, 855. Douglas *v.* Mason, 1796; M. 16,213. Lothian *v.* M'Cree, 1828; 7 S. 72. Cameron *v.* M'Ewen, 1830; 8 S. 440. Todd *v.* Smith, 1851; 13 D. 1371. Hume *v.* Baillie, 1852; 14 D. 821 (guest's horses not arrestable). Donaldson *v.* Ord, 1855; 17 D. 1053. Mitchell *v.* Scott, 1881; 8 R. 875. Cases in note (*f*).

(*f*) Kyle's Trs. *v.* White, 1827; 6 S. 40. Ramsay and Douglas, *citt.* Learmont *v.* Shearer, 1866; 4 Macph. 540. Comp. *supra*, § 1482, 1883, 1996. Smiths *v.* Chambers' Trs., 1877; 5 R. 97; rev. *ib.* H. L. 151.

(*g*) Black *v.* Scott, 1830; 8 S. 367.

(*h*) 2 Bell's Com. 71, 72 (68, M'L.'s ed.). Thomson on Bills, 318. More *v.* Paxton, 1766; M. 12,259, and the other cases there cited. Dick *v.* Goodall, June 1, 1815; F. C.

(*i*) Baillie *v.* Naismith, 1674; M. 703. Souper *v.* Smith's Crs., 1756; M. 744; 5 B. Sup. 308. Stalker *v.* Aiton, 1759; M. 745. 2 Bell's Com. 12, 75 (71, M'L.'s ed.). Wight's Trs. *v.* Allan, 1840; 3 D. 243. Mags. of Dundee, *supra* (*b*). Mackenzie & Co. *v.* Finlay, 1868; 7 Macph. 27. Trowsdale's Trs. *v.* Forcett Ry. Co., 1870; 9 Macph. 88.

(*k*) Stalker, *supra* (*i*). Hunter *v.* Lees, 1733; M. 736. Brown *v.* Duff's Trs., 1850; 13 D. 149. Stuart *v.* Cowan & Co., 1883; 10 R. 581. See as to consigned money, Pollock *v.* Scott, 1844; 6 D. 1297. Rennie *v.* Sang & Adam, 1847; 10 D. 223. Campbell *v.* Lothians, 1858; 21 D. 63. As to money and valuables in the hands of police officers, procurators-fiscal, or Sheriff-clerks for public purposes, see Stuart *v.* Cowan & Co., *cit.*

(*l*) Pitcairn & Scott *v.* Adair, Feb. 7, 1809; F. C. As to arrestment of future and conditional debts, Strachan *v.* M'Dougle, 1835; 13 S. 954. Smith & Kinnear *v.* Burns, 1847; 9 D. 1344 (annuity). Marshall *v.* Nimmo & Co., 1847; 10 D. 328 (instalment contract). Whittall *v.* Christie, 1894; 22 R. 91 (interest in policy assigned to debtor's m. c. trustees).

(*m*) See Kyle, *supra* (*f*).

(*n*) Wright *v.* Cunningham, 1802; M. 15,919. Handyside *v.* Corbyn, Jan. 15, 1813; F. C. Smith & Kinnear, *cit.*

(*o*) 3 Stair, 1. § 37.

(*p*) 3 Ersk. 6. § 7. 1 Bell's Com. 129 (124, M'L.'s ed.) et seq. See Irvine *v.* M'Laren, 1829; 7 S. 317. Harvey *v.* Calder, 1840; 2 D. 1095. Bell *v.* Innes, 1855; 17 D. 778. Craig *v.* Ferguson, 1884; 11 R. 1038 (expense of apprehending dangerous lunatic not chargeable on alimentary fund).

(*q*) Drew *v.* Drew, 1870; 9 Macph. 163. Muirhead *v.* Miller, 1877; 4 R. 1139. See Reid *v.* Bell, 1884; 12 R. 178.

(*r*) Stair, *cit.* 1 Bell's Com. 128 (124 M'L.'s ed.). Livingstone *v.* Livingstone, 1886; 14 R. 43. See cases in note (*q*); and above, § 1560.

(*s*) Miller *v.* Wilson, 1827; 5 S. 926. *Sed quære?* See

note (*u*). This case seems to have been overruled by Syme *v.* Forbes & Mason, Dec. 20, 1841 ; n. r. (Ct. of Exch.).

(*t*) Hale *v.* Creditors, 1796 ; M. 711. Smith *v.* E. Moray, Dec. 13, 1815 ; F. C. Learmonth *v.* Paterson, 1858 ; 20 D. 418. Reasonable aliment will be reserved in this and similar cases. Murray *v.* Bell, 1833 ; 11 S. 599. Moinet *v.* Hamilton, 1833 ; 11 S. 348.

(*u*) A. of S., June 11, 1613. 2 Stair, 1. § 18. 3 Stair, 1. § 37. 1 Bell's Com. 128 (124, M'L.'s ed.).

(*v*) 1 Vict. c. 41, § 7. Shanks *v.* Thomson, 1838 ; 16 S. 1353. 8 and 9 Vict. c. 39. 33 and 34 Vict. c. 63. M'Murchy *v.* Emslie, 1888 ; 15 R. 375. As to seamen's wages, see § 451B *fin.*

2277. Formalities.—The warrant to arrest is executed by leaving in the arrestee's hands, if within Scotland, a schedule or short copy, and returning indorsed on the warrant, or separately, an execution bearing that the arrestment was duly executed. If the arrestee is forth of Scotland, the arrestment is executed by delivery of a schedule at the Record Office of Citations in the Court of Session ; 'but in this case the arrestee is not interpelled from paying to the common debtor, unless he or those having authority to act for him were previously in the knowledge of the arrestment having been used' (*a*). If the warrant be from the Sheriff, and the arrestee is not in his sheriffdom, the arrestment may be executed in another sheriffdom, by a concurring warrant from the Sheriff, 'now upon endorsement by the Sheriff-clerk,' of that shire (*b*).

An arrestment must be executed at the domicile, or personally ; not at the counting-house of a company of which the arrestee is a partner (*c*). By statute it is required, that in the execution the messenger and the witness shall be named and described, and shall sign the execution ; otherwise the execution is null (*d*). At common law, it is required that the execution shall describe all that is essential to the execution ; and by statute, that the copy delivered shall be signed by the messenger, and shall bear the date of the execution, and the name and description of the witness ; but there is no declaration of nullity (*e*). In construing these requisites, it has been held that, although in summonses where the party appears, less strictness is to be exacted (*f*), in arrestments and all such diligences, the omission of anything essential in the execution, the incorrect description of the debt (*g*), or a disregard of the requisites of the Act 1681 (*h*), will be fatal ; but the omission of the requisites of the Act 1693 respecting short copies will not annul the diligence (*i*). An erroneous or faulty return of execution may be replaced by a correct one, before being produced in judgment (*k*).

(*a*) 1 and 2 Vict. c. 114, § 18. See 19 and 20 Vict. c. 91, § 1. The inevitable ignorance of the arrestee excuses him even if he be in Scotland. Laidlaw *v.* Smith, 1838 ; 16 S. 367 ; aff. 1841, 2 Rob. 490.

(*b*) *Ib.* § 19. Act of S., July 10, 1839, § 155.

(*c*) Sharp, Fairlie, & Co. *v.* Garden, 1822 ; 1 S. 337. As to service on corporations, see Campbell *v.* Watson's Tr., 1898 ; 25 R. 690.

(*d*) 1681, c. 5. See 9 and 10 Vict. c. 67.

(*e*) 1693, c. 12.

(*f*) 2 Ersk. 5. § 55. Stewart *v.* Brown, 1824 ; 3 S. 56. See 39 and 40 Vict. c. 70, § 12.

(*g*) Montgomery *v.* Fergushill, 1632 ; M. 3749. Crichton's Crs. *v.* Dickson, 1684 ; M. 3750. Wight *v.* Wight, 1822 ; 1 S. 424. Scott *v.* Fisher, 1825 ; 4 S. 261. Opinion of judges in Holmes *v.* Reid, 1829 ; 7 S. 535, 541.

(*h*) *Ib.*

(*i*) Holmes, *supra* (*g*). Thomson *v.* Gavin, 1830 ; 8 S. 921.

(*k*) May *v.* Malcolm, 1825 ; 4 S. 76. Hog *v.* Maclelland, 1797 ; M. 8346.

2278. Effect of the Arrestment. — The arrestment confers a preference while the thing arrested remains with the arrestee, and subjects the arrestee to a claim for the value if he part with it ; but it creates no further real right, so as to entitle the creditor to follow and vindicate it from third parties acquiring it in *bonâ fide* (*a*). Arrestment on a depending action remains in force notwithstanding a decree of *absolvitor*, where an appeal is entered (*b*). It covers not the principal only, but also the interest of the debt pursued for, and the expense of the action (*c*). A trustee, after arrestment in his hands, is not entitled to make advances to the truster (*d*). There are differences between the effect of arrestment for execution and arrestment for security. The former subsists for three years from the date of arrestment ; the latter 'for three, formerly' for five, years from the time at which the debt is due or constituted. 'Both "prescribe" "if not pursued or insisted on within that time"' (*e*). 'Arrestments on a future or contingent debt prescribe in three years from the time when the debt becomes due and the contingency is purified.' A creditor arresting for a future debt ranks with other creditors, with an abatement of interest ; a contingent creditor, only for a dividend to be deposited.

(*a*) See on this point Mr. G. Stewart's Treatise on Diligence, p. 126, where the authorities are cited.

(*b*) Css. Haddington *v.* Richardson, 1822 ; 1 S. 433.

(*c*) M'Donald *v.* Wingate, 1825 ; 3 S. 494. May *v.* Malcolm, 1825 ; 4 S. 76.

(*d*) Bank of Scotland *v.* Macdonell, 1826 ; 4 S. 804.

(c) 1669, c. 9, 2; altered by 1 and 2 Vict. c. 114, § 22. Jameson v. Sharp, 1887; 14 R. 643 (furthcoming or multiplepoinding required).

2278A. '*Ranking of Arrestments*.—Arrestments are preferable according to their date, when their effect is not modified by the special rules that obtain in bankruptcy (*a*). Creditors arresting within sixty days preceding or four months after the notour bankruptcy of the debtor, or any creditor producing in a process relative to the subject of the arrestment liquid grounds of debt or decree of payment within such period, are to be ranked *pari passu* as if they had arrested of the same date, subject to payment of the expenses of the arrestment; but arresters after the four months are to be ranked on the reversion of the subject according to the rules of law (*b*). Arrestments or poindings on or after the sixtieth day prior to sequestration or judicial liquidation, or after sequestration or judicial liquidation, are ineffectual to create a preference to the arresting creditor in competition with the trustee or liquidator, the right to enforce the arrestments being transferred to the trustee, subject in the former case to a claim for the expenses (*c*).'

(*a*) 2 Bell's Com. 69.
(*b*) 19 and 20 Vict. c. 79, § 12.
(*c*) *Ib.* § 108. Mackenzie v. Campbell, 1894; 21 R. 904. Dobbie & Co. v. Nisbet, 1854; 16 D. 881. Rough's Trs. v. Miller, 1857; 19 D. 305. Bank of Scotland v. Robertson, 1870; 8 Macph. 391. Mitchell v. Scott, 1881; 8 R. 875. 49 Vict. c. 23.

2279. Recall and Loosing of Arrestment.—An arrestment for execution can be loosed only on payment of the debt, unless where the decree or obligation is brought under suspension (*a*). Arrestment in security may be recalled without caution, or loosed on caution, in the following cases:—

(*a*) 3 Ersk. 6. § 12. White, petr., 1741; M. 802; Elch. *Arrest.* 17. See 1 Mackay's Practice, 67.

2280. (1.) *Recall.*—Where arrestment in security is used oppressively, and even where used nimiously (*i.e.* where it is a superfluous and vexatious precaution), 'or where the arrestment has been effected or made possible by the fraud or wrong of the arrester,' the Lord Ordinary in the cause, or the Sheriff, when the arrestment is on the dependence, or the Lord Ordinary on the Bills, may recall or restrict it, or grant warrant for loosing on caution, or without caution (*a*). This remedy may be applied in a future or contingent debt where there is no change in the debtor's credit, or where the creditor is already secured by diligence, caution, lien, etc., and there is no ground to suspect the security (*b*). 'But questions involving the validity of the arrestment, *e.g.* whether the debt is due, or a subject arrested belongs to the common debtor, are properly tried in a forthcoming, not in a petition for recall (*c*).'

(*a*) Maule v. Maule, 1828; 6 S. 790. Eliott v. Cleghorn, 1828; 6 S. 1097. Maule v. Maule, 1829; 7 S. 639. 1 and 2 Vict. c. 114, § 20, 21. Farrell v. Willox, 1849; 11 D. 565. Marsh v. Miller, 1849; 12 D. 172. Clark v. Loos, 1855; 17 D. 306. Hamilton v. Bruce's Trs., 1857; 19 D. 745. Neilson v. Stewart, 1862; 24 D. 956. Cullen v. Buchanan, 1862; 24 D. 1280. Carlberg v. Borjesson, 1877; 5 R. 390 (legal wrong). Rintoul & Co. v. Bannatyne, 1862; 1 Macph. 137 (do.). Heron, *cit.* § 2276 (*d*). Ketchen v. Grant, 1871; 9 Macph. 966. Stevens v. Campbell, 1873; 11 Macph. 772. Wilson v. Mackie, 1875; 3 R. 18. Symington v. Symington, 1875; 3 R. 205. Buchanan v. Black, 1882; 9 R. 926. See 1 Vict. c. 41, § 8. 30 and 31 Vict. c. 96, § 5. As to the use of the old form of loosing arrestments where the forms under the Personal Diligence Act are inapplicable, see Smith v. Mackintosh, 1848; 10 D. 455. Ballinten v. Connon, 1848; 11 D. 26. As to expenses of recall, see Clark, *cit.* Dobbie v. Duncanson, 1872; 10 Macph. 810. Roy v. Turner, 1891; 18 R. 717.
(*b*) Jolly v. Grahame, 1830, 8 S. 361. See above, § 2275. Mags. of Dundee v. Taylor & Grant, 1863; 1 Macph. 701.
(*c*) Vincent v. Lindsay, 1877; 5 R. 43. Brand v. Kent, 1892; 20 R. 29.

2281. (2.) *Loosing on Caution.*—When the arrestment is loosed on caution, the arrestee may deliver up the subject or pay the debt (*a*). The proceeding is either for a special loosing of some particular arrestment, or for a general loosing of all arrestments used or to be used by the creditor (*b*).

(*a*) 1617, c. 17.
(*b*) Act of Sederunt, July 11, 1826. See Paterson v. Cowan, 1826; 4 S. 477. 2 Bell's Com. 69, 70 (67, M'L.'s ed.). Macdougall's Tr. v. Law, 1864; 3 Macph. 68. Cases in § 2280 (*a*).

2282. The caution is received by the clerk of Court, and he must satisfy himself of its sufficiency (*a*). The cautioner's obligation is to make the goods, etc., forthcoming while unremoved and extant, or to give up the effects in as good condition as at first (*b*), or to pay the arrester's debt, to the amount of the value of the arrested goods (*c*). While the goods remain, the arrester's preference continues. 'A cautioner in the loosing of arrestments on the dependence remains liable, after the cause is referred, for the sum decerned for in terms of the award (*d*).'

(*a*) 1617, c. 17.
(*b*) Middlemas v. Brown, 1828; 6 S. 511.

(c) 2 Bell's Com. 70 (67, M'L.'s ed.). Anderson, Child, & Co. v. Pott, 1826; 3 S. 498.

(d) Potter v. Bartholomew, 1847; 10 D. 97. Stewart v. Hickman, 1843; 6 D. 151. Macdougall's Tr. v. Law, *cit.*

2283. Forthcoming.—This is an accessory action of adjudication of moveables, the parties being the arrester, the arrestee, and the debtor. The points of the action are: to ascertain precisely the subject, or the reality and extent of debt arrested (*a*); and to adjudge the debt to the arrester, or so much of it as may pay his debt; or where the subject is corporeal, not a debt, to authorise a sale and payment out of the proceeds (*b*). This sentence establishes judicially in the purchaser a right to the subject arrested (*c*). 'When there is a competition of arrestments, the appropriate action is a multiplepoinding.'

(*a*) 3 Ersk. 6. § 16. The arrestee has no interest to object to the arrester's debt, but he may insist as against the arrester in all objections competent to him as against the common debtor. Houston v. Aberdeen Town and County Bank, 1849; 11 D. 1490. See London v. Young, 1856; 18 D. 856. The remedy of an arrestee charged on a decree obtained by the common debtor against him is not a multiplepoinding, but a suspension. Mitchell v. Strachan, 1869; 8 Macph. 154. Caw, Prentice, & Clapperton v. Creighton, 1898; 25 R. 518.

(*b*) Stevenson v. Paul, 1684; M. 5405.

(*c*) Muirhead v. Corrie, 1735; M. 687. Stevenson v. Grant, 1767; M. 2762. Sinclair v. Staples, 1860; 22 D. 600 (shares in company).

II. POINDING.

2284. Nature of Poinding.—Poinding is an adjudication and judicial sale of moveables for the payment of debt, and is either real or personal.

2285. Real Poinding, or Poinding of the Ground, is for a debt forming a real burden on the land (*a*). This diligence proceeds by summons either in the Court of Session or before the Sheriff (*b*). The title to pursue is the feudal right of the superior, or the completed right of one holding a real burden, or *debitum fundi* (*c*); 'but the pursuer may connect himself by a personal title with the original infeftment constituting the *debitum fundi* (*d*). The remedy of poinding of the ground is not competent to persons possessing as proprietors, *e.g.* adjudgers (*e*); nor even to creditors whose security is in the form of an absolute disposition with a back-bond (*f*).'

The parties to be called are the vassal, where the debt is the feu-duty due to the superior, and in all cases the tenants and possessors of the ground. The conclusion of the summons is not personal, but only for a warrant to messengers-at-arms to pass and seek for, fence, arrest, comprise, poind, and distrain all the moveable goods on the lands (*g*); but in so far as the moveables there belong to the tenants, only to the amount of the rent due by them (*h*). 'It does not attach goods belonging to strangers (*i*).

'A poinding of the ground is not so much a diligence as a declaratory real action. The real right on which it is founded already affects not only the land, but the moveables on it as accessories; and it does not confer a preference, but only gives effect to one already existing, and is ranked according to the priority of the pursuer's infeftment. The service of the summons declaring the creditor's right in the moveables puts a "nexus" on them, and prevents other rights from being acquired over them by diligence or otherwise (*k*). But the validity of that "nexus," and of the creditor's preference, depends on the due and timeous execution of the statutory procedure for completing the diligence by sale, and it is still a question whether the property in the poinded goods passes at service or after the report of sale is lodged (*l*).' The decree of poinding of the ground is in terms of the conclusions, and thereupon is issued a warrant for poinding, and the diligence is completed by the messenger's execution (*m*). There is no occasion for a previous charge, as in personal poinding, before proceeding to poind, there being no personal conclusion in the summons (*n*).

'It was enacted by two of the Bankruptcy Acts, that' a creditor holding a security preferable to the trustee in sequestration, 'might' proceed to poind the ground, 'or obtain a decree of maills and duties, but only' for the interest of the present term and one year's arrears, 'no poinding of the ground not carried out by sale of the effects sixty days before sequestration having any further avail in competition with the trustee (*o*). But this limitation of the rights of heritable creditors was repealed, and a heritable creditor having a right preferable to the trustee might, as formerly, attach the moveables for his whole debt even after sequestration (*p*); until the Legislature again interfered to restore the law which existed between 1839 and 1874, limiting the rights of heritable creditors in competition with the trustee in bankruptcy (*q*) and the liquidator in a winding up (*r*). It was held that this limitation did not operate in favour of the trustee in an English bankruptcy (*s*), or of the general creditors in a liquidation under the Companies Act, 1862 (*t*), nor against creditors of the bankrupt's ancestor (*u*); but the Legislature has made it apply to "all poindings of the ground by which moveables forming part of or belonging to a bankrupt estate, whether administered in Scotland or furth thereof, are sought to be attached or affected, and that whether the debts or securities in respect of which such poindings of the ground shall be brought shall have been constituted or granted by the bankrupt, or by any ancestor or predecessor of the bankrupt, or by any other person" (*v*).'

(*a*) See above, § 699, 914, 922.
(*b*) Kennedy *v.* Buick, 1852; 14 D. 513. 1 and 2 Vict. c. 114, § 9.
(*c*) 4 Ersk. 1. § 11. Wilson *v.* Fraser, 1822; 1 S. 350; aff. 2 S. App. 162. Stewart *v.* Gibson's Tr., 1880; 8 R. 270 (poinding in security of current interest). Douglas *v.* Tait, 1884; 12 R. 10 (joinder of two separate bondholders?). Bell's Trs. *v.* Copeland, 1896; 23 R. 650 (ground-annual).
(*d*) Tweedie *v.* Beattie, 1836; 14 S. 337. Jeffray *v.* M. Ailsa, 1859; 21 D. 492.
(*e*) But see *contra*, Stewart on Diligence, p. 496.
(*f*) Ersk. *l.c.* Garthland *v.* L. Jedburgh, 1832; M. 10,545. Scott. Her. Sec. Co. *v.* Allan & Co., 1876; 3 R. 333. Henderson *v.* Wallace, 1875; 2 R. 272. See Scot. Union Ins. Co. *v.* James, 1886; 13 R. 928. Luke *v.* Wallace, 1896; 23 R. 634 (not to holder of bond over registered lease).
(*g*) Thomson *v.* Scoular, 1882; 9 R. 430. Urquhart *v* M'Leod's Tr., 1883; 10 R. 991.
(*h*) 1469, c. 36. 4 Stair, 23. § 10, 14. 2 Ersk. 8. § 23. 4 Ersk. 1. § 12. See Brown *v.* Scott, 1859; 22 D. 273. Royal Bank *v.* Dixon, 1868; 6 Macph. 995. Lang *v.* Hislop, 1854; 16 D. 908.
(*i*) Nelmes & Co. *v.* Gillies, 1883; 10 R. 880 (hired furniture). Thomson *v.* Scoular, 1882; 9 R. 430.
(*k*) Campbell's Trs. *v.* Paul, 1835; 13 S. 237. Barstow *v.* Mowbray, 1856; 18 D. 846. Lyons *v.* Anderson, 1880; 8 R. 24. It does not interfere with the priority given to public rates and taxes. N. B. Prop. Inv. Co. *v.* Paterson, 1888; 15 R. 885.
(*l*) Henderson *v.* Grant, 1896; 23 R. 659. Turner *v.* Mitchell and Rae, 1884; 2 Sel. Sh. Ct. Ca. 152. The words "by litigiosity" in § 699, *supra*, seem to show that Mr. Bell had no longer the view expressed in 2 Com. 64 (M'L. 61).
(*m*) See Kennedy *v.* Buick, 1852; 14 D. 513. 1 and 2 Vict. c. 114, § 9.
(*n*) 4 Ersk. 1. § 12.
(*o*) 2 and 3 Vict. c. 41, § 95. 19 and 20 Vict. c. 79, § 118. See Budge *v.* Brown's Trs., 1872; 10 Macph. 958; above, § 914.
(*p*) 37 and 38 Vict. c. 94, § 55 (Conveyancing Act). Royal Bank *v.* Bain, 1877; 4 R. 985. Dick's Trs. *v.* Whyte's Trs., 1879; 6 R. 586. See Campbell's Trs. *v.* Paul, and Barstow *v.* Mowbray, *citt.* (*k*). As to the wrongful (?) removal of goods to disappoint the diligence of a heritable creditor, see Urquhart *v.* M'Leod's Tr., *cit.* (*g*).
(*q*) 42 and 43 Vict. c. 40, § 3.
(*r*) 49 Vict. c. 23, § 3 (4) (Companies Act, 1886).
(*s*) Athole Hydropathic Co. *v.* Scott. Prov. Ass. Co., 1886, 13 R. 818; corrected by 49 Vict. c. 23, § 3 (4).
(*t*) Scot. Union, etc. Ins. Co. *v.* James, 1886; 13 R. 928.
(*u*) Millar's Trs. *v.* Miller & Son's Tr., 1886; 13 R. 543.
(*v*) 50 and 51 Vict. c. 69, § 2. These statutes seem not to affect superiors. See above, § 699.

2286. Personal Poinding is the direct diligence for transferring to the creditor in personal obligations, moveables in possession of his debtor or of another (*a*). It proceeds either under the extracted decree of the Sheriff, where the moveables are within his territory, or under letters of horning and poinding, by warrant of the Court of Session, or on the warrant contained in the extracted decree of that Court (*b*). But in no case, 'except when the debtor has been personally present at the pronouncing of judgment in the Sheriff's Small Debt Court (*c*),' till the debtor has been regularly charged to pay the debt, and the days of the charge have expired, can this poinding be executed (*d*).

(*a*) By § 3 of 19 and 20 Vict. c. 60, superseded by Sale of Goods Act, 1893, § 40, 60, it is competent for the seller of goods, while still in his own possession, and when they have been sold by the buyer to a third party, to poind them for payment of the price.
(*b*) 1 and 2 Vict. c. 114, § 1, 4, 9. 40 and 41 Vict. c. 40, § 1-3.
(*c*) 1 Vict. c. 41, § 13.
(*d*) 1 and 2 Vict. c. 114, § 4.

2287. The messenger has by the warrant, whether of the Court of Session or of the Sheriff, authority to open lockfast places (*a*). He, with two sworn (*b*) appraisers, values the things poinded, proclaims the value, offers the goods to the debtor at the appraised value, and, on the debtor's refusal, adjudges them to belong to the creditor in payment of his debt (*c*). He leaves them, with a signed note of the value, in the debtor's hands, 'except in poindings at the instance of the Crown (*d*),' and reports his execution of poinding to the Sheriff (*e*). The rest of the proceeding is judicial. If any stranger claims the goods, his remedy is before the Sheriff (*f*). Any person carrying off or intromitting with the goods to disappoint the poinding, is liable, 'on a summary complaint to the Sheriff, to be imprisoned till he restore the effects, or pay' double the appraised value (*g*). The debtor may, on cause shown, be deprived of the possession. A report is made to the Sheriff within eight days, specifying the diligence, the debt, the name of the creditor, the effects, their value, the names and designations of the valuators, and the person in whose hands the goods were left (*h*). The Sheriff directs a sale to be made within twenty days, but not sooner than eight days after notice of the day of sale (*i*). And a note of the sale being lodged with the Sheriff-clerk, the nett sum is paid to the poinding creditor (*k*).

(*a*) In poindings in the old form, and under the Small Debt Act till 1889 (52 and 53 Vict. c. 26, § 7), a special warrant to open shut and lockfast places must be obtained upon an execution setting forth the fact that the goods were within lockfast places. Scott *v.* Letham, 1846; 5 Bell's App. 126.

(*b*) Leconte *v.* Douglas, 1880; 8 R. 175.

(*c*) He may poind for the expenses of the poinding. M'Neill *v.* M'Murchy, 1841; 3 D. 554. The appraisement is an essential part of the proceedings, being a protection against excessive poinding; and while a critical valuation is not required, the appraisers must use their best skill and judgment to give a true idea of the value of the poinded articles. Leconte *v.* Douglas, *cit.* As to Small Debt procedure, see 1 Vict. c. 41, § 20.

(*d*) 19 and 20 Vict. c. 56, § 32. 43 and 44 Vict. c. 19, § 97 (Taxes Management Act).

(*e*) 1 and 2 Vict. c. 114, § 24.

(*f*) Scotland *v.* Lawrie, 1828; 6 S. 961. Clark *v.* Clark, 1824; 3 S. 143. In practice this is generally by interdict, though the claimant may appear in the poinding and vindicate his right. See Stewart on Diligence, p. 351.

(*g*) 1 and 2 Vict. c. 114, § 30. Brown *v.* Stephenson, 1849; 11 D. 1083. Wilson *v.* M'Kellar, 1896; 24 R. 254 (concurrence of P. F. not necessary).

(*h*) 1 and 2 Vict. c. 114, § 25.

(*i*) See M'Neill, *supra* (*c*). Thom *v.* Stewart, 1842; 5 D. 369. A specified day and place must be fixed for the sale. Kewly *v.* Andrew, 1843; 5 D. 860. M'Vicar *v.* Kerr, 1857; 19 D. 948. M'Kinnon *v.* Hamilton, 1866; 4 Macph. 852.

(*k*) 1 and 2 Vict. c. 114, § 27, 28. See 1 Vict. c. 41, § 13, 20. 30 and 31 Vict. c. 96, § 6, 16. Crombie *v.* M'Ewan, 1861; 23 D. 333. As to poindings within the sixty days previous to bankruptcy, see above, § 2278A.

2288. Poinding is not competent within the palace of Holyrood House (*a*).

(*a*) E. Strathmore *v.* Laing, 1821; 1 S. 134; rev. 2 W. & S. 1. 1 and 2 Vict. c. 114, § 23.

2289. Subjects of Poinding.—These are,—moveables, 'except plough-goods in time of labouring, if the tenant has any other poindable goods (*a*), and except also tools or implements absolutely necessary for the earning of the debtor's livelihood, if he be a labouring man (*b*).' But doubts have been raised as to such moveables as are not marketable, as a man's shop books, to the effect of levying his book-debts, or bonds, bills, bank-notes, or money not separated and made specific. The general rule is, that only things corporeally valuable, and capable of being sold by the Sheriff's warrant, are poindable. Debts must be arrested. The competency of poinding bank-notes, or money in a man's pocket, or the ring on his finger, has not yet been expressly decided (*c*). The things poinded may be in the custody of others, or in the possession of the debtor; 'or of the creditor (*d*). By statute the rolling stock and plant used or provided by a railway company for the purpose of the traffic on their railway or of their stations and workshops, is not, after the railway or any part of it is open for public traffic, liable to be attached by diligence; but in lieu thereof, the creditor in a decree against the company may obtain the appointment of a judicial factor, who not only applies and distributes all the monies he receives in payment of the debts of the company under direction of the Court, and according to the rights and priorities of the persons for the time being interested therein (*e*), but has the sole and exclusive management of the undertaking (*f*).'

(*a*) 1503, c. 98. 3 Ersk. 6. § 22.

(*b*) Gassiot, Nov. 12, 1814; F. C. 2 Bell's Com. 486. See Macmillan *v.* Barrie, 1890; 6 Sh. C. R. 103.

(*c*) Ross on Conveyancing, vol. i. Hamilton *v.* Bailie of Holyrood, 1741; Elchies, *Abbey*, No. 2 and Notes, 5; 5 B. Sup. 708. Alexander *v.* M'Lay, 1826; 4 S. 439. In poinding by the Crown the debtor's "whole moveable effects without exception" may be attached, "including bank-notes, money, bonds, bills, crop, stocking, and implements of husbandry of all kinds." 19 and 20 Vict. c. 56, § 32. Corn growing may be poinded (Ballantine *v.* Watson, 1709; M. 10,526), but not if merely brairded (Elder *v.* Allan, 1833; 11 S. 902); not goods in which the debtor has only a joint interest (Fleming *v.* Twaddle, 1828; 7 S. 92), or of which he is only liferenter (Scott *v.* Price, 1837; 15 S. 916). As to debts due to the Crown, see below, § 2297.

(*d*) See above, § 2286. Lochhead *v.* Graham, 1883; 11 R. 201.

(*e*) 30 and 31 Vict. c. 127. 8 Vict. c. 17, § 56, 57.

(*f*) Haldane *v.* Girvan and Portpatrick Ry. Co., 1881; 8 R. 669.

2290. Conjunction of Poindings.—Other creditors 'holding warrants to poind' may concur, and insist on being conjoined in the poinding; in which case the appraisement, adjudication, and report proceed for all the debts jointly, and all the concurring creditors share in the proceeds of the sale (*a*).

(*a*) See 1 and 2 Vict. c. 114, § 23, 27. 19 and 20 Vict. c. 79, § 7, 12.

III. DILIGENCE FOR CROWN DEBTS.

2291–2296. 'In former editions an explanation was given of the English law for the recovery of debts due to the Crown, which was introduced into Scotland *per aversionem* by 6 Ann. c. 25. It is unnecessary to retain what was said as to Writs of Extent, Extent in Chief, Extent in Aid, and Writ of

Diem Clausit Extremum, which were also treated of in Bell's Com. (vol. ii. p. 41 sqq.). Other forms of execution were substituted by the Exchequer Act of 1856, by which and the Taxes Management Act, 1880, the whole subject is now governed.'

2297. '**New Forms.**—By the Court of Exchequer Act, 1856, a form of process by *subpœna*, information, special case, etc., is established for obtaining before a judge of the Court of Session decrees for debts due to the Crown. These decrees, as well as registered decrees proceeding upon bonds or other obligations to the Crown, are to be extracted by the extractor of the Court of Session: the extracts are to contain a warrant to Sheriffs to execute diligence in terms specified; and they are to be sufficient warrants to messengers-at-arms or Sheriff-officers to execute, charge, arrest, and poind (*a*). It is the duty of the Sheriff to whom any extract shall be entrusted for execution by any public officer on behalf of the Crown, to enforce implement of the warrant by arrestment in ordinary form, which has the effect of transferring to the Crown preferably the arrested fund; and the arrestee is in safety to pay to the Sheriff the fund to the extent of the Crown debt, interest and expenses, without a forthcoming (*b*). The Sheriff is also, after a charge, to cause poind the debtor's moveable effects, including bank-notes, money, bonds, bills, crop, stocking, and implements of husbandry; and the poinding is to be carried through in ordinary form, except that the officer may take possession of the poinded effects (*c*). The Sheriff may seize books of accounts, papers, etc., in order to discover funds (*d*). Proceedings may also be taken in the usual form for imprisoning the debtor (*e*). And provisions are made for arresting and poinding the moveable effects of a deceased debtor (*f*).'

(*a*) 19 and 20 Vict. c. 56, § 28.
(*b*) *Ib.* § 28, 29.
(*c*) *Ib.* § 31, 32.
(*d*) *Ib.* § 35.
(*e*) *Ib.* § 33, 34.
(*f*) *Ib.* § 36.

CHAPTER III

OF DILIGENCE AGAINST HERITABLE ESTATES

2298. Different Kinds. — Lands may be attached either in execution or in security: the former by adjudication in execution; the latter by adjudication in security, or by inhibition.

I. ADJUDICATION IN EXECUTION (*a*).

2299. Nature of Adjudication.—Adjudication is an action of execution, following upon a decree or liquid document of debt not prescribed, and not contingent. The object of it is to transfer to the creditor the land or other heritable estate of the debtor in security and satisfaction of his debt, with a power of redemption to the debtor by payment within a certain time. It may by a certain proceeding be converted into an absolute right of property in the creditor after the term of redemption has expired. Adjudication, although a diligence by an individual creditor, is capable of combination with other adjudications, as a complex diligence for the use of many (*b*).

(*a*) See above, § 823 et seq.; and for Adjudication in Implement, see § 835.

(*b*) 1672, c. 19. M'Kenzie's Obs. 2 Par. Char. II. Sess. 3. c. 17. 3 Stair, 2. § 14 et seq. 2 Ersk. 12. § 39. 1 Bell's Com. 701 (740, M'L.'s ed.). Fergusson *v.* Robertson, Feb. 20, 1816; F. C. Scott *v.* Brown, 1828; 7 S. 192. See Wallwood *v.* Seton, 1693; 4 B. Sup. 89. A *spes successionis* is not adjudgeable. Kirkland *v.* Kirkland's Tr., 1886; 13 R. 798.

2300. Proceedings. (1.) *Summons.*—The summons 'contained, until 1847,' an alternative conclusion for special or general adjudication. Though special adjudication 'was even then' never made use of to any good purpose, the debtor 'was' called upon by one conclusion to produce the titles to his lands; to concur in a fair valuation and appropriation of as much as will satisfy the debt; and to consent to a transference of it, redeemable within five years. If the debtor 'did' not thus concur, the next conclusion 'was' for a general adjudication of all the debtor's lands and estate in satisfaction of the debt, redeemable in ten years; 'and this conclusion alone is now in use (*a*).'

(2.) *Intimation.*—The first step of proceeding is a judicial intimation to all other creditors. In consequence of this, such creditors as hold a decree, or liquid ground of debt, may move to be conjoined in the adjudication (*b*).

(3.) *Decree.*—The decree of general adjudication adjudges particular lands, by name and description, with all right and interest competent to the debtor concerning the same; and generally decerns and declares them to pertain and belong to the pursuer, and his heirs, heritably, for payment and satisfaction of the debt, interest, etc.; and it 'was till 1847' decerned and ordained that the pursuer shall be infeft, etc., to be held of the superior; and there 'was' also a warrant for letters of horning to charge the superior to enter the adjudgers (*c*).

(4.) *Abbreviate and Recording.*—The decree is extracted with an abbreviate, and is recorded in the Register of Abbreviates of Adjudication, 'now united with the Register of Inhibitions,' within sixty days after the date of the decree (*d*).

(*a*) 10 and 11 Vict. c. 48, § 18; and c. 49, § 10. 31 and 32 Vict. c. 101, § 59.
(*b*) 54 Geo. III. c. 137, § 9. 19 and 20 Vict. c. 91, § 5.
(*c*) See above, § 825, 828A. (*d*) See above, § 826.

2301. Completion of the Creditor's Right.—If the subject be heritable, but not such as to require sasine, the decree duly recorded gives the complete right as from its date. If it consist of a proper feudal subject, the creditor's title 'was formerly' completed by a charter of adjudication and infeftment, 'now by infeftment on the decree without charter (*a*).'

(*a*) Stair and Ersk. *ut supra.* 1 Bell's Com. 705, 718 (743, 756, M'L.'s ed.), and cases cited. See above, § 825 sqq.

2302. Expiry of the Legal.—The right of an adjudger in a general adjudication is redeemable within ten years. But the expiration of the term, and the penal effect of a conversion into an irredeemable right, must, in order to be effectual, be declared by a decree of declarator of expiry of the legal; it being in the action competent to the debtor to call on the creditor to account for his intromission (*a*). The same effect is produced if the creditor shall have completed his feudal investiture by sasine, and this shall have been followed by forty years' possession from the date of expiration of the legal (*b*).

(*a*) 1 Bell's Com. 705 (743, M'L.'s ed.). Campbell, Ormiston, Stewart, Robertson, all cited above, § 830, 831.
(*b*) Johnston, Spence, and Robertson, cited § 831. See and contrast with § 831 and § 2012.

2303. Adjudication of Estates to which the Debtor has succeeded.—If the debtor have entered heir, and completed his titles, adjudication proceeds as against his own original estate. If not, he may be compelled to enter, or to leave the estate to his creditors. This 'was' done by charges to enter heir, 'now unnecessary, the summons of constitution, or of adjudication, being made equivalent to the charges formerly required' (*a*); after which, if unanswered, the adjudication proceeds as if the heir were entered.

(*a*) See above, § 1854 et sqq.

2304. Adjudication of the Debtor's Property after Death.—This diligence proceeds either against a representative of the deceased, or against his *hæreditas jacens*; the debt being constituted by action against the heir in the former case, or against the *hæreditas jacens* in the latter. There is required a title in the heir to the estate to be adjudged; or a renunciation, so that access may be had to the *hæreditas jacens.* Hence a general charge, 'now unnecessary,' and decree of constitution form the first step of this diligence; the constitution being either against the heir if he do not renounce, or against the *hæreditas jacens* if he do (*a*). The special charge 'was' the next step; and being in execution of the decree of constitution, it 'could' proceed only after that decree (*b*). And on the heir's entry, or on the certification of that charge, the adjudication 'proceeded' against the estate as vested in the heir; or, on renunciation, *contra hæreditatem jacentem.*

This species of adjudication was competent before the introduction of adjudication in the ordinary case, and may still proceed before the Sheriff, while the other is competent only to the Court of Session.

(*a*) 1540, c. 106. 3 Ersk. 8. § 93. 1 Bell's Com. 711 (749, M.L.'s ed.). See for the alterations on this mode of proceeding, *ante*, § 1858A.
(*b*) E. Cassilis *v.* M'Martin, 1627; M. 2167. Catrine's Crs. *v.* Baird, 1738; M. 2173. Maxwell *v.* Paterson, 1751; M. 176.

II. ADJUDICATION IN SECURITY.

2305. Nature of it.—This differs from the common adjudication, in being intended only for those cases in which the creditor is not yet entitled to have execution for satisfaction. In point of form, there is no essential difference. The power of redemption or Legal does not expire. It is a remedy given only where there is impending insolvency, or an accidental loss of security, or the likelihood of being cut off from competing with other adjudgers (*a*).

(*a*) 2 Ersk. 12. § 42. See *ante*, § 832.

III. INHIBITION.

2306. Object, Nature, and Execution.—A creditor may be secured against the alienation of his debtor's heritable estate to the disappointment of his diligence, not only by adjudication in security, but by Inhibition. This is a writ passing under the signet, prohibiting the debtor from alienating any part of his estate, and from contracting debt by means of which it may be carried off, to the prejudice of the creditor inhibiter; and interdicting third parties from taking conveyances of the heritage. In form, it is directed against the whole estate, but it has force only against heritage (*a*). To make this diligence effectual, it is necessary to execute it against the debtor; 'formerly' to publish it edictally against third parties, at the head burgh of the county, 'not' where the lands lie, 'but where the debtor resides (*b*)'; and to record it in the Register of Inhibitions within forty days of its publication (*c*). 'No publication to the lieges is now required except registration in the General Register of Inhibitions. The inhibition takes effect from the date of its registration, or of the registration of a notice of inhibition, which may be recorded before execution, provided the inhibition itself be recorded within twenty-one days after the notice (*d*).'

(*a*) *Infra*, § 2310. 2 Bell's Com. 142. The new form introduced by 31 and 32 Vict. c. 101, § 156, is directed only against lands and heritages.

(*b*) See 2 Ersk. 11. § 4. 3 Jurid. Styles, 528. Cooke, *infra*.

(*c*) 4 Stair, 50. 2 Ersk. 11. Dirleton and Stewart, *Inhibition*. 2 Bell's Com. 142 (134, M'L.'s ed.). Scott (Langton's Crs.) *v*. Coutts, 1750; M. 6988. Oliphant *v*. Irving, 1703; M. 5562. See Malcolm *v*. Mansfield, 1846; 8 D. 1201; 1849, 6 Bell's App. 359. Cooke *v*. Falconer's Reps., 1850; 13 D. 157. Walker *v*. Hunter, 1853; 16 D. 226. As to inhibition against holder of bond and disposition in security or wadset, see A. of S., Feb. 19, 1680. Mackintosh's Trs. *v*. Davidson & Garden, 1898; 25 R. 554. The register of inhibitions is regulated by 31 and 32 Vict. c. 64.

(*d*) 31 and 32 Vict. c. 101, § 155. 31 and 32 Vict. c. 100, § 18.

2307. Grounds.—Inhibition may proceed on any liquid ground of debt, although the term of payment should be future or contingent, 'but in this case only if the debtor is *vergens ad inopiam*' (*a*); or on an action of constitution upon production of the summons duly executed (*b*), or at any time prior to the final decision in the House of Lords (*c*).

(*a*) 2 Ersk. 11. § 3. 2 Bell's Com. 144 (136, M'L.'s ed.). See Campbell *v*. Cullen, 1848; 10 D. 1496. Dove *v*. Henderson, 1865; 3 Macph. 339. Ketchen *v*. Grant, 1871; 9 Macph. 966; and above, § 2275 (*a*).

(*b*) Rosehill's Crs. *v*. Thomson's Crs., 1714; M. 6968. Milne *v*. Cockburn, 1698; M. 8158. Ranking of Tofts, 1722; M. 6970. See Ivory's Ersk. p. 526, note 322. See Hawkins *v*. Wedderburn, 1842; 4. D. 924. Fordyce *v*. Bridges, 1842; 4 D. 1334. Seton *v*. Hawkins, 1842; 5 D. 396. Inhibition is not competent upon a small debt or debts recovery summons; Lamont, complr., 1867; 6 Macph. 84. Warrants for inhibition may now be inserted in the wills of summonses, and executed either when the summons is served or at any time thereafter. 31 and 32 Vict. c. 100, § 18.

(*c*) Heron *v*. Heron, 1774; M. 7007.

2308. Recall.—Inhibition may be recalled, if nimious or oppressive, where the debt is future, contingent, or not yet constituted: not where the debt is already due (*a*).

(*a*) See 2 Ersk. 11. § 8, notes. 2 Ersk. Pr. 11. § 3. 2 Bell's Com. 144, 146 (137–8, M'L.'s. ed.). Blackwood *v*. Marshall, 1749; M. 6982; Elchies, *Inhibition*, 10. Royal Bank *v*. Bank of Scotland, 1728; M. 875; rev. 1729, Cr. St. & P. 14. As to interdict of threatened inhibition, see Beattie & Son *v*. Pratt, 1880; 7 R. 1171.

2309. Effect.—Inhibition is merely prohibitory. It is only by an accompanying adjudication that a real right is constituted. The inhibition gives no preference as by a transference, but still it has important effects. As a prohibition of alienation, while it annuls a subsequent sale in so far as prejudicial to the inhibiter, it leaves it untouched and valid in all other respects; the consequence of which is, that it enables the inhibiter to acquire by reduction *ex capite inhibitionis*, followed by adjudication, a preference in which no other creditor posterior to the sale can participate (*a*). As a prohibition of burdens, it excludes creditors holding voluntary securities granted subsequent to the date (*b*). As a prohibition of debts prejudicial to the inhibiter, it entitles the inhibiter, in competition with adjudgers, to a preference over those whose debts were contracted after the inhibition (*c*). But inhibition is no bar to what the debtor is already bound specifically to do; and so sasine on a deed already granted, or a conveyance taken in implement of a minute of sale, will not fall by the inhibition (*d*). 'Neither does it interrupt the dealings under a cash credit heritable bond executed prior to the recording of the inhibition (*e*).' As inhibition is no bar to adjudication by those creditors whose debts are not affected by it, and will not entitle the inhibiter to compete with such adjudication, the inhibition will not even give security against such debts, though future or contingent, without also adjudging, where such creditors proceed to adjudge.

(*a*) Horne *v.* Kay, 1824; 3 S. 81. Carlyle *v.* Mathison's Crs., 1739; M. 6971. Munro *v.* Gordon's Crs., 1777; M. *Inhib.* Apx. 1; 2 Bell's Com. 147 (139, M'L.'s ed.). M'Lure *v.* Baird, 1807; M. *Competition*, Apx. 3. Lennox *v.* Robertson, 1790; Hume, 243. Campbell *v.* Gordon, 1841; 3 D. 629; rev. 1 Bell's App. 563. Baird & Brown, *cit. infra.*

(*b*) 4 Stair, 35. § 21; 50. § 23, note. 2 Ersk. 9. § 71. 2 Bell's Com. 149 (141, M'L.'s ed.).

(*c*) Watson *v.* Marshall, 1782; M. 7009. M'Math *v.* M'Kellar, 1791; Bell's Ca. 22. Campbell *v.* Gordon, *cit.* Baird & Brown *v.* Stirrat's Tr., 1872; 10 Macph. 414. Inhibition has now no effect against lands acquired after the date of registration, unless destined at that date to the person inhibited by an indefeasible title such as an entail. 31 and 32 Vict. c. 101, § 157.

(*d*) Livingstone *v.* M'Farlane, 1842; 5 D. 1.

(*e*) Campbells' Tr. *v.* De Lisle's Exrs., 1870; 9 Macph. 252.

2310. By the 'old' form of letters of inhibition, the debtor is prohibited from alienating his moveables or contracting any debt (*a*). But it has been long settled that it affects not moveables; and that no debt is objectionable on the ground of inhibition, unless it be shown to be injurious to the inhibiter, as directly or indirectly an alienation of the heritage.

(*a*) See above, § 2306 (*a*).

2310A. '**Prescription of Inhibitions.**—All inhibitions subsisting at 1st October 1874 prescribe not later than five years after that date. Inhibitions recorded since that date prescribe five years after the date on which they take effect. The inhibiters, or their heirs or assignees, may again record them or a memorandum in a certain form, before the expiry of the five years, to the effect of giving them force for an additional period of five years after the re-recording, and so forth for periods of five years thereafter. But inhibitions existing at 1st October 1874 are not by this enactment made effectual for any longer period than they would otherwise have been (*a*).'

(*a*) 37 and 38 Vict. c. 94, § 42.

CHAPTER IV

OF DILIGENCE AGAINST THE PERSON

2311. Imprisonment for Debt, formerly requiring the authority of the Court of Session, by signet letters of horning and caption, 'was afterwards' made competent directly on a warrant from the Court of Session or Sheriff Court (*a*). And though formerly competent for debt of any amount, it 'was' abolished 'in 1835' as a mode of execution for debts of 'less than' the amount of £8, 6s. 8d. (*b*); 'and was entirely abolished, except as a mode of execution for taxes, fines, and penalties due to Her Majesty, for rates and assessments, and for sums decerned (*c*) for aliment, by the Debtors (Scotland) Act, 1880 (*d*). The Act does not affect or prevent apprehension or imprisonment under a *meditatio fugæ* warrant, or under any decree or obligation *ad factum præstandum* (*e*). As, however, by the common law a *meditatio fugæ* warrant is incompetent where the remedy of imprisonment is not available to the creditor for recovery of his debt (*f*), such warrants are now competent only in the cases excepted from the operation of the Act (*g*). This remarkable statute required amendment in each of the two following years; and the Civil Imprisonment Act of 1882 further provided that no one should be apprehended or imprisoned on account of his failure to pay any sum decerned for aliment (*h*), except on proof of wilful default in any application to the Sheriff (*i*); and that no one should, for failure to pay rates and assessments, be imprisoned for a longer period than six weeks (*k*). The Act of 1880 had already provided that no person should be imprisoned in the cases excepted from the operation of that Act for a longer period than twelve months (*l*).' The old warrant of horning and caption is still competent 'in the excepted cases,' but under this condition, that the debtor shall not be liable for the expense of such diligence (*m*).

'The following sections, as they treat of a subject for which this book will rarely be referred to, are printed as in former editions; and the reader will bear in mind that imprisonment is not now, except in rare cases, a remedy to which creditors can have recourse.'

(*a*) 1 and 2 Vict. c. 114, § 6, 7, 11, 12, 14, 15, 35.

(*b*) 5 and 6 Will. IV. c. 70, § 1 and 5. This Act (now repealed, S. L. R. Act, 1891), did not affect obligations *ad facta præstanda*, taxes and rates, fines and forfeitures imposed by law (Lawson *v.* Jopp, 1853; 15 D. 392), and sums decerned for aliment, including inlying expenses and expenses of process. Cheyne *v.* M'Gungle, 1860; 22 D. 1490.

(*c*) A decree of registration upon an agreement to pay aliment is not within the Act. Purdon *v.* Purdon, 1884; 28 J. of J. 500; 2 Sel. Sh. Ct. Ca. 160 (Sh. Ct. of Lanarkshire).

(*d*) 43 and 44 Vict. c. 34.

(*e*) *Ib.* § 4. Mackenzie *v.* Balerno Paper Co., 1883; 10 R. 1147 (decree of consignation is a decree *ad. f. pr.*).

(*f*) Kidd *v.* Hyde, 1882; 9 R. 803. Marshall *v.* Dobson, 1844; 7 D. 232.

(*g*) Hart *v.* Anderson's Trs., 1890; 18 R. 169. See Pascoe *v.* Simpson, 1883; 2 Sel. Sh. Ct. Ca. 138.

(*h*) Tevendale *v.* Duncan, 1883; 10 R. 852 (exception is not available to parochial board suing for relief of sums already expended). But a mother holding a decree of aliment for her bastard may imprison for arrears. Cain *v.* M'Colm, 1892, 19 R. 813, where Tevendale *v.* Duncan is distinguished and considered. See A. *v.* B., 1884; 2 Sel. Sh. Ct. Ca. 157 (*per* Dove Wilson).

(*i*) Strain *v.* Strain, 1886; 13 R. 1029 (Sheriff's refusal to grant warrant to imprison is not appealable). Cook *v.* Wallace & Wilson, 1889; 16 R. 565.

(*k*) 45 and 46 Vict. c. 42.

(*l*) 43 and 44 Vict. c. 34, § 1. Walker *v.* Bryce, 1881; 9 R. 249.

(*m*) 1 and 2 Vict. c. 114, § 8.

2312. Warrant from the Court of Session.—The extract of a decree *in foro*, or of registration, contains a warrant to charge the debtor to pay within a certain number of days, under the pain of poinding and imprisonment 'so far as competent' (*a*). And on expiration of the days of charge, and within year and day, the execution of charge may be registered in the Register of Hornings at Edinburgh, to the effect of denouncing the debtor as rebel, and of accumulating the debt and interest into a principal or capital sum to bear interest (*b*). The warrant for caption 'when competent' is on this applied for by a minute signed by a Writer to the Signet, presented in the Bill Chamber, on which the clerk of the Bills enters a "fiat," which authorises imprisonment as on a caption (*c*). And when the diligence is sued out by an assignee, on the assignation being produced with an accompanying minute, the warrant is granted in his name (*d*).

(*a*) 1 and 2 Vict. c. 114, § 1.
(*b*) *Ib.* § 5, and Act of Sed., Dec. 24, 1838, § 1.
(*c*) *Ib.* § 6. (*d*) *Ib.* § 7.

2313. Warrant from the Sheriff Court.—A warrant to imprison may now be issued from the Sheriff Court. The extract of the decree bears a warrant of charge to pay, under the pain of poinding and imprisonment 'so far as competent.' And on expiration of the days of charge, the execution of charge may be recorded in a Register of Hornings kept by the Sheriff-clerk, to the effect of denunciation, as in the case of the Court of Session diligence (*a*). Thereupon the creditor himself, or a procurator of Court, may, 'when competent,' by a minute subscribed, apply for a warrant of imprisonment, which is granted by a "fiat" written out and signed by the Sheriff-clerk (*b*). And if the debtor is beyond the sheriffdom, a warrant of concurrence may be obtained on application to the Sheriff within whose shire execution is required (*c*).

(*a*) 1 and 2 Vict. c. 114, § 10.
(*b*) *Ib.* § 11, 12. (*c*) *Ib.* § 13, 14, 15.

2314. Act of Warding.—Decrees of magistrates of burghs 'might' be followed by an act of warding, which authorises the town-officers, after due search for the goods of the debtor (*a*), to take his person, and keep him in sure ward until he shall make payment of the debt, if above £8, 6s. 8d (*b*).

(*a*) See Marshall *v.* Lamont, 1803; M. Apx. *Burgh Royal*, 14.
(*b*) 5 and 6 Will. IV. c. 70.

2315. Sanctuary.—The spirit of the law of Scotland is mild in regard to the imprisonment of debtors, while it is sufficiently vigilant to prevent fraudulent absconding.

2316. Every man's house is his sanctuary in Scotland against an act of warding, but not against a warrant for imprisonment from the Court of Session or Sheriff. The Abbey of Holyrood House is a sanctuary, not as an ancient religious establishment, but as a royal residence (*a*). It is a sanctuary to a debtor, but not to a criminal (*b*), nor to one under diligence for performance of a fact within his power (*c*), nor to a debtor of the Queen (*d*). And imprisonment may take place within the Abbey for debts contracted within the sanctuary (*e*), or on *meditatio fugæ* warrants (*f*).

(*a*) Dirleton, 52. E. Strathmore *v.* Laing, 1826; 2 W. & S. 1.
(*b*) 1535, c. 23. Park & Brown *v.* Bennet, Feb. 10, 1787; M. 7 (fraudulent bankrupt).
(*c*) Turner *v.* Ross, 1709; M. 11,802.
(*d*) 4 Ersk. 3. § 25. Munro *v.* M'Millan, 1736; Elch. *Abbey*, 1.
(*e*) Cockburn, supplicant, 1708; M. 2877. Berry *v.* Bowes, Feb. 24, 1820; F. C.
(*f*) Scudamore *v.* Lechmere, 1797; M. 8559.

2317. The benefit of sanctuary is attained by merely entering within the precincts. But this protection lasts only for twenty-four hours, after which the debtor must have his name entered in the record of the Abbey Court, on which a certificate of protection is given to him (*a*).

(*a*) See 2 Bell's Com. 572 (463, M'L.'s ed.). Grant *v.* Donaldson, 1779; M. 5; Hailes, 816. M'Kellar *v.* Livingston & Co., 1861; 23 D. 1269.

2318. Meditatio Fugæ Warrant.—No debtor can be arrested for debt in Scotland till the expiration of the days of charge. But a warrant of imprisonment against the debtor as *in meditatione fugæ* is competent, on proof of just ground to suspect the debtor of an intention to abscond.

The creditor who applies for such warrant must swear to his debt, and his belief of an intention on his debtor's part to abscond, and he must justify his belief by the statement of the grounds on which it rests. Before a warrant to imprison is granted, the debtor must be brought up for examination. The magistrate must look to any collateral evidence that may be offered. And if, after due inquiry, it appear that the debtor is not merely going to another part of Scotland, or to the sanctuary, or in the course of his duty as a soldier or sailor, but that he is about to leave Scotland, warrant will be granted to imprison him until he shall find caution *de judicio sisti* (*a*). 'The Act which abolishes imprisonment for debt does not affect or prevent the apprehension or imprisonment of any person under a warrant against him as being *in meditatione fugæ*. A warrant of this kind cannot to any effect be executed, even with indorsation of an English magistrate, after the debtor has left the territory of Scotland (*b*).'

(*a*) See 2 Bell's Com. 557 (448, M'L.'s ed.) et seq. See above, § 274, 2311.
(*b*) Adam *v.* Crowe, 1887 ; 14 R. 800.

2319. Bill of Health.—In a case of a prisoner's sickness and danger of life, he may, on a certificate from a physician, surgeon, apothecary, or minister of the gospel, apply to the magistrates for liberty to reside out of prison during the continuance of his sickness; and this, on calling the creditor, the magistrates are empowered to grant, under such precautions as may seem just (*a*). 'Where a prisoner's health suffers from confinement, he may apply to the Sheriff for temporary removal (*b*).

(*a*) A. of S., June 14, 1671. 2 Bell's Com. 548 (440, M'L.'s. ed.). Gillies, petr., 1843 ; 5 D. 572.
(*b*) 23 and 24 Vict. c. 105, § 72 (not repealed by the Prisons (Scotland) Act, 1877, 40 and 41 Vict. c. 53).

2320. Act of Grace.—A prisoner for debt, if unable to maintain himself in prison, is entitled to call upon his creditor to aliment him. And although this was intended directly as a relief only to magistrates, it operates indirectly to give greater mildness to the law of imprisonment. The original Act is much improved by a 'subsequent' statute (*a*). Under these laws, the creditor, at incarcerating his debtor, must deposit ten shillings, to be returned in thirty days if the prisoner do not apply, etc., or to be applied to the prisoner's aliment if necessary. The debtor applies by petition, and the creditor must be called. If there be no appearance for the creditor, or if he shall not settle an aliment on the debtor, the prisoner is to be liberated on the expiration of ten days. The debtor, on his being thus liberated, grants a disposition *omnium bonorum* for behoof of all his creditors (*b*).

(*a*) 1696, c. 32. 6 Geo. IV. c. 62. 45 and 46 Vict. c. 42 § 8.
(*b*) 2 Bell's Com. 553 (445, M'L.'s ed.). Brechin *v.* Taylor, 1842 ; 4 D. 909. Pender *v.* M'Arthur, 1846 ; 8 D. 408. Smith *v.* Nicholson, 1853 ; 15 D. 697 (imprisonment on decree *ad factum præstandum*). L. Adv. *v.* Mags. of Inverness, 1856 ; 18 D. 356 (imprisonment for Crown debt). White *v.* Robertson, 1858 ; 21 D. 28. Thomson *v.* Mags. of Kirkcudbright, 1878 ; 5 R. 561.

2321. Cessio Bonorum. — This process, formerly a remedy to the debtor against the evils of imprisonment only, has of late, 'and still more under the legislation of 1880–1882 above referred to,' been made also to supply the place of sequestration in small bankruptcies. The great objects have been to reduce the expense and lessen delays, to prevent the necessity of protracted imprisonment, to bring the debtor and his creditors together before the judge for a strict investigation into the state of his affairs, and to make the surrender by the bankrupt available to the creditors.

On receiving a charge for payment, a debtor 'might' apply by petition to the Sheriff of his domicile for the benefit of *cessio*. 'Under the present law the petition for *cessio* may be presented by any debtor who is notour bankrupt (*a*), or any creditor of such a debtor (*b*).' His creditors, 'whether in the country or abroad (*c*),' are either cited or called by letter accompanied by a Gazette notice, to appear in Court within thirty days. The debtor may then, on producing his books and instructions of his debt, apply for protection or liberation; and appearing personally in Court to undergo an examination in presence of his creditors, the merits of his case 'were' disposed of by the judge, either by the refusal of the *cessio*, or the granting of it unconditionally, or qualified by a certain term of exposure to personal diligence. The decree of *cessio* 'vested' his creditors with a full right to all his moveables, and he 'was' bound to grant a conveyance of his heritage (*d*). The judgment of the Sheriff is subject to the review of the Court of Session (*e*). 'Under the present law the Sheriff, after the bankrupt's examination or on his wilfully failing to appear on citation at any diet, may in his discretion grant *cessio*, refuse it *in hoc statu*, or make such order as the justice of the case requires, taking into account the conduct of the bankrupt, and all the circumstances, including the amount or existence of estate for distribution (*f*). *Cessio* may be granted, as under the former law, with a condition annexed, *e.g.* that the debtor assign to his creditors a proportion of his income (*g*), or the condition may be imposed when he applies for discharge (*h*). There is provision for the nomination of a trustee by the creditors, or by the Sheriff if they fail to agree; and until the debtor executes a disposition *omnium bonorum* in his favour, the Sheriff's decree ordering him to do so operates as an assignation of his existing moveables in favour of the trustee (*i*). Provision is made for distribution of the estate, and a discharge of the bankrupt on the expiration of six months from the date of the decree of *cessio*, subject to the same provisions as in sequestrations in bankruptcy (*k*). The decree of *cessio* has not the effect of a sequestration as a universal diligence in favour of the trustee, and does not prevent poinding creditors from selling, subject, however, to the equalising clause of the Bankruptcy Act (*l*). Nor until the debtor has obtained his discharge are prior creditors prevented from doing diligence against property acquired by the debtor after the date of the decree (*m*).

'Actions of *cessio* can now be instituted only in the Sheriff Court. Under the bankruptcy statute, a majority in number and value of the creditors of a sequestrated bankrupt whose estate is not likely to yield a free fund of more than £100, may resolve that he shall only be entitled to obtain a decree of *cessio*, which may be granted in the sequestration, and shall have no right to a discharge. Trustees in *cessio* are subject to the supervision of the Accountant in Bankruptcy (*n*).'

(*a*) M'Nab *v.* Clarke, 1889; 16 R. 610.
(*b*) 43 and 44 Vict. c. 34, § 7, 8.
(*c*) Kennedy *v.* Ker, 1838; 16 S. 990.
(*d*) 6 and 7 Will. IV. c. 56, and A. of S., June 6, 1839.
(*e*) *Ib.* § 8, 9, 10. See 39 and 40 Vict. c. 70, § 26. 43 and 44 Vict. c. 34, § 9 (4). Taylor's Tr. *v.* Paul, 1888; 15 R. 313.
(*f*) Reid *v.* Anderson's Tr., 1890; 17 R. 757. Mackenzie *v.* Ewart, 1891; 18 R. 925. Sproul *v.* M'Cusker, 1892; 19 R. 539.
(*g*) Calderhead *v.* Freer, 1890; 17 R. 1098.
(*h*) Sproul *v.* M'Cusker, *cit.*
(*i*) 43 and 44 Vict. c. 34, § 9. Gray *v.* Gray's Tr., 1895; 22 R. 326. See as to the effect of the order in preventing preferences to creditors, Shaw's Tr. *v.* Stewart & Bissett, 1887; 15 R. 32.
(*k*) 44 and 45 Vict. c. 22. A. of S., Dec. 22, 1882, which provides the machinery for distribution omitted in the recent Acts of Parliament. See Taylor's Tr. *v.* Paul, *cit.*
(*l*) Simpson *v.* Jack, 1888; 16 R. 131. See also Henderson *v.* Robb, 1889; 16 R. 341.
(*m*) Reid *v.* Graham, 1894; 21 R. 935.
(*n*) 39 and 40 Vict. c. 70, § 26. 19 and 20 Vict. c. 79, § 168. *Ib.* § 167.

CHAPTER V

OF INSOLVENCY, AND EQUALISATION OF DILIGENCE

2322. General View.—While a debtor is solvent, his creditors proceed each in his course of diligence to compel payment or satisfaction either against the estate or by constraint of the person. But with insolvency commences a species of common interest in the debtor's estate, and a humane consideration of the debtor's condition; which the law has interfered to regulate according to the principles of equity and humanity suitable to such a case. This interposition of the law has, with respect to the estate, the great object in view of introducing a perfect equality among all those creditors who have not, previous to the debtor's insolvency, acquired by voluntary grant or legal diligence a preferable right over the rest; and in respect to the debtor's person, he is admitted to freedom, or even obtains a discharge in certain cases. For the attainment of these objects, there are laws directed against voluntary preferences, and to the regulation of diligence (*a*).

(*a*) See Shaw's Bell's Com. 1117 et seq. 2 M'Laren's Bell's Com. 152 sqq.

2323. Gratuitous and Confidential Conveyances.—The statutes by which the Legislature has endeavoured to prevent or annul fraudulent preferences, were enacted in the seventeenth century, and have lately received some improvements.

2324. No one is permitted, after insolvency (*a*), to convey gratuitously and by direct or indirect means, to relations or confidential friends, the funds which truly belong to his creditors. And by statute (as construed by decisions), deeds of conveyance are presumed to be fraudulent, and so null, if gratuitous, and made after the contracting of debt, and in favour of a near relation (conjunct person) or confidential friend (*b*); 'and such deeds may be set aside by way either of action or exception (*c*).'

(*a*) See below, § 2325 (*c*).
(*b*) 1621, c. 18, with an ample commentary by Sir George Mackenzie. And 2 Bell's Com. 183 et seq. Goudy on Bankruptcy, ch. v. See above, § 64.
(*c*) 19 and 20 Vict. c. 79, § 10, 11. 20 and 21 Vict. c. 19, § 9. Dickson *v.* Murray, 1866; 4 Macph. 797. Moroney & Co. *v.* Muir & Sons, 1867; 6 Macph. 7.

2325. Illegal Preferences after Bankruptcy.—To prevent a debtor on the eve of bankruptcy from unduly favouring particular creditors, it has been enacted that all deeds conferring preferences (*a*) on particular creditors, to the exclusion of the rest, not completed till within sixty days (*b*) of bankruptcy or after that event, are null, as legal frauds. And bankruptcy to this effect is ascertained by the fact of imprisonment; or by the debtor resisting the officer, or absconding, or taking sanctuary after a charge to pay, in order to avoid caption; or by sequestration (*c*). Where a debtor is abroad, or not subject to imprisonment by reason of privilege or personal protection, arrestment unloosed for fifteen days, or a poinding, or decree of adjudication, together with an expired charge for payment, completes the bankruptcy (*d*). 'Notour bankruptcy is now constituted—

(1) by sequestration, or adjudication of bankruptcy in England or Ireland; or (2) by insolvency—*i.e.* inability to meet current obligations, although the debtor's assets may ultimately suffice to pay his debts (*e*)—concurring with (A) a charge for payment, followed by imprisonment where competent, or by apprehension, flight, absconding, retreat to the sanctuary, or forcible defending of the debtor's person against diligence; or, where imprisonment is incompetent or impossible, by arrestment not loosed or discharged for fifteen days, poinding, or adjudication for payment or in security; or (B) with sale of his effects under a poinding or sequestration for rent, or with his retiring to the sanctuary for twenty-four hours, or making application for *cessio bonorum*. Notour bankruptcy of a company is constituted in any of these ways, or by a partner being made notour bankrupt for a company debt. Under the Debtors (Scotland) Act, 1880, notour bankruptcy is constituted in the cases in which that Act makes imprisonment incompetent, by insolvency concurring with a charge for payment, followed by the expiry of the days of charge without payment, or if a charge is not necessary or not competent, by insolvency concurring with an extract decree for payment without payment being made before the lapse of the days intervening prior to execution (*f*).' Securities for prior debts not completed sixty days before a debtor's death are of no effect in a sequestration awarded within seven months of that event (*g*).

(*a*) Spier *v.* Dunlop, 1826; 2 W. & S. 253. Gibson *v.* Forbes, 1833; 11 S. 929. Mansfield *v.* Walker's Trs., 1833; 11 S. 813; aff. 1835, 1 S. & M'L. 203. Ferguson *v.* Welsh, 1869; 7 Macph. 592. Matthew's Tr. *v.* Matthew, 5 Macph. 957. M'Cowan *v.* Wright, 1853; 15 D. 494. Taylor *v.* Farrie, 1855; 17 D. 639. Lindsay *v.* Shield, 1862; 24 D. 821. Rose *v.* Falconer, 1868; 6 Macph. 960. Laurie's Tr. *v.* Beveridge, 1867; 6 Macph. 85. M'Farlane *v.* Robb & Co., 1870; 9 Macph. 370. Stiven *v.* Scott & Simson, 1871; 9 Macph. 923. Gourlay *v.* Hodge, 1875; 2 R. 738. Walker (Paterson's Tr.) *v.* Paterson's Trs., 1891; 19 R. 91. Cowdenbeath Coll. Co. *v.* Clydesdale Bank, 1895; 22 R. 682.

(*b*) Ivory's Ersk. B. iv. note 26. 2 Bell's Com. 178 (167, M'L.'s ed.). Scott *v.* Rutherfurd, 1839; 2 D. 206. And see 19 and 20 Vict. c. 79, § 6. *Supra*, § 46.

(*c*) 1696, c. 5. 1 and 2 Vict. c. 114, § 6, 7, 8, 11, 35. 2 and 3 Vict. c. 41, § 25. See 2 Bell's Com. 197 sqq.

(*d*) 54 Geo. III. c. 137, § 1. Nicolson *v.* Johnston and Wright, 1872; 11 Macph. 179. 19 and 20 Vict. c. 79, § 7, 8, 9.

(*e*) 1 Bell's Com. 163 (154, M'L.'s ed.). Goudy, Bkrptcy. 18. Teenan's Tr. *v.* Teenan, 1886; 13 R. 833. M'Nab *v.* Clarke, 1889; 16 R. 610. In some other questions, as under the Act of 1621, absolute insolvency seems to be required. See Bell's Com. and Goudy, *citt.*

(*f*) 43 and 44 Vict. c. 34, § 6. Black *v.* Watson, 1881; 9 R. 167.

(*g*) 2 and 3 Vict. c. 41, § 74. 19 and 20 Vict. c. 79, § 110.

2326. In order to prevent the evasion of the statute, dispositions, etc., for relief or security of debts to be contracted for the future, are declared to be of no force as to what shall be contracted after sasine on the conveyance (*a*). But this law has so far been relaxed as to give sanction to securities for cash-accounts on particular conditions (*b*).

(*a*) 1696, c. 5. See 2 Bell's Com. 205 (191, M'L.'s ed.) et seq., 233 (218, M'L.'s ed.) et seq.

(*b*) 54 Geo. III. c. 137, § 14. 19 and 20 Vict. c. 91. 21 and 22 Vict. c. 19. *Supra*, § 46, 299, 911.

2327. Title to Object.—The remedy introduced by these statutes is competent only to a prior creditor, 'or a trustee in a sequestration representing such a creditor (*a*), but not to a trustee under a private deed merely as such (*b*). The effect of the nullity is to restore the alienated subject to its former position, so that it becomes part of the bankrupt's assets, and is open to the diligence of all creditors, and subject to the preferences they may be able to establish in a sequestration or otherwise. The Act does not *per se* give him a title to recover the subject for himself or other creditors (*c*).' The challenge must be of a preference, directly or indirectly conferred by means of a conveyance, security, or obligation, in favour of one who is already a creditor; payment in money not being challengeable (*d*); 'nor transactions in the ordinary course of trade, and *nova debita* (*e*); nor, it seems, a mere acknowledgment of an existing debt, entitling the creditor to an ordinary ranking, even although the creditor would have been unable to prove his debt without it (*f*); nor an act which is the specific implement of an obligation contracted before the sixty days (*g*). It is a universal rule that a man cannot put his money or estate beyond the reach of his creditors while he retains his own right to it, and to the beneficial use of it (*h*).'

(*a*) Edmond *v.* Grant, 1853; 15 D. 703. 19 and 20 Vict. c. 79, § 10, 11. These sections do not deprive an individual creditor of his right to reduce preferences to his prejudice. Brown & Co. *v.* M'Callum, 1890; 18 R. 311.

(*b*) Fleming's Trs. *v.* M'Hardy, 1892; 19 R. 542. Cook *v.* Sinclair & Co. *infra.* M'Laren's Tr. *v.* Nat. Bk., 1897; 25 R. 920.

(*c*) Brown & Co. *v.* M'Callum, *cit.* Cook *v.* Sinclair & Co., 1896; 23 R. 925.

(*d*) Thomas *v.* Thomson, 1865; 3 Macph. 358. Nicol *v.* M'Intyre, 1882; 9 R. 1097. Carter *v.* Johnstone, 1886; 13 R. 698 (indorsed cheques). Coutts' Tr. *v.* Webster, 1886; 13 R. 1112. Shaw's Tr. *v.* Stewart & Bissett, 1887; 15 R. 32. Jones' Tr. *v.* Jones, 1888; 15 R. 328. Dawson *v.* Thorburn, 1888; 15 R. 891. M'Dougall's Tr. *v.* Gibbon, 1889; 16 R. 740.

(*e*) Loudon Brothers *v.* Reid, 1877; 5 R. 293, 298, and cases cited there. Horsbrugh *v.* Ramsay & Co., 1885; 12 R. 1171.

(*f*) Matthew's Tr. *v.* Matthew, 1867; 5 Macph. 957. See Stiven *v.* Watson, 1874; 1 R. 412, and 2 Bell's Com. 213 (198, M'L.'s ed.). Wallace *v.* Sharp, 1888; 12 R. 687.

(*g*) Lindsay *v.* Adamson & Ronaldson, 1880; 7 R. 1036, and authorities there cited.

(*h*) **Miller** *v.* **Learmonth**, 1875; 10 Macph. 107; aff. 2 R. H. L. 72. Mackenzie *v.* Campbell, 1894; 21 R. 904.

2328. Equalisation of Diligence.—It is consistent with equity that all creditors who come at the same time to demand satisfaction of the debtor's personal obligation, should be made equal in the division of his inadequate fund. And this has served as the groundwork of several legislative measures, respecting both the moveable and heritable estate.

2329. Equalisation of Diligence against the Moveable Estate. (1.) *Creditors of a Deceased Debtor.*—Confirmation as an executor-creditor can take place only after notice in the Gazette to all other creditors to appear and take their share (*a*).

(*a*) 4 Geo. IV. c. 98. See above, § 1895 and 1895A.

2330. (2.) *Creditors insisting against the Executor.*—A period of six months after death has been appointed, within which the executor cannot be compelled, and is not safe, to pay to any creditors of the deceased (*a*).

(*a*) Act of Sederunt, Feb. 28, 1662. See above, § 1900.

2331. (3.) *Creditors Poinding or Arresting.*—By statute it is enacted, that in all cases creditors who shall arrest or poind the moveables of their debtor within sixty days preceding his bankruptcy, or four months after it, shall be equal: arresters to rank *pari passu* as if all their arrestments were of the same date; poinders being bound to communicate to all having liquidated grounds of debt, or decrees for payment, and summoning the poinders, or judicially producing the same in a process of competition (*a*). In sequestration, no arrestment or poinding executed on or after the sixtieth day prior to the sequestration, or executed after the sequestration, is effectual; but the subject is to be taken into the general fund; the expense of such diligence, if done in *bonâ fide*, being paid out of the fund (*b*). 'This subject is now dealt with by 19 and 20 Vict. c. 79, § 12. Arrestments and poindings executed within the period above mentioned are ranked *pari passu.* Arrestments on the dependence (*c*) or for illiquid debts must be completed without undue delay; creditors judicially producing liquid grounds of debt or decree of payment during said period in a process (*d*) relative to the subject of the arrestment or poinding, are ranked as if they had executed arrestment or poinding; creditors obtaining payment during said period are bound to account to others entitled to rank *pari passu*; and arrestments used after the four months are not to compete with those used before, but may rank according to law on any reversion.'

(*a*) 54 Geo. III. c. 137, § 2. 2 and 3 Vict. c. 41, § 83. Nicolson *v.* Johnston & Wright, 1872; 11 Macph. 179. Wood *v.* Cranston & Elliot, 1891; 18 R. 382.

(*b*) 2 and 3 Vict. c. 41, § 83. 19 and 20 Vict. c. 79, § 108.

(*c*) See above, § 2275 (*g*).

(*d*) Clark *v.* Hinde, Milne, & Co., 1884; 12 R. 347.

2332. Equalisation of Diligence against the Heritable Estate. Adjudications.—The first statutes for equalising adjudications, and preventing accidental and undue preferences, were confined to a *pari passu* preference of all creditors who should adjudge within a year and day from the date of the decree pronounced in the adjudication first made effectual by sasine, or a charge to the superior (*a*). The next step in the progress was to require notice by the first adjudger, to enable every creditor ready to adjudge to be conjoined in the first adjudication, instead of adjudging separately (*b*). The last step has been to introduce and improve the processes of ranking and sale and sequestration; and to declare these proceedings to be equally available to every creditor, superseding all separate adjudications.

(*a*) 1661, c. 62. 1672, c. 19. See 1 Bell's Com. 717 (754, M'L.'s ed.).

(*b*) 23 Geo. III. c. 18. 33 Geo. III. c. 74, § 10. 54 Geo. III. c. 137, § 9. 19 and 20 Vict. c. 91. As to the preferences between adjudgers and others, see the authorities in 1 Ross' L. C. 202–286. 2 Bell's Com. 508 sqq. (402, M'L.'s ed.).

2333. Judicial Sale and Ranking.—This process may be regarded as the most complete and perfect of the diligences against land, where there are several creditors, and an inadequate fund of payment. It is, in respect of the ranking, a process of competition; in respect of the sale, a diligence against the land. It is of two kinds: one by creditors; the other by the proprietor himself, before he has completed his title. 'It is now superseded in practice by the provisions of the Bankruptcy Act of 1856.'

2334. (1.) *Judicial Sale by Creditors.*—This action proceeds at the instance of a creditor holding a real right, the creditors being in possession of the estate; and concludes that, on proof of insolvency, the estate shall be sold by authority of the Court of Session, and irredeemably adjudged to the purchaser, and the superior ordained to enter him; and that the price shall be divided in the process of ranking. The decree of sale being an adjudication by all the creditors (*a*).

(*a*) 1681, c. 17. 1690, c. 20. 54 Geo. III. c. 137, § 10. 2 Bell's Com. 254 sqq. (232 M'L.'s ed.). 19 and 20 Vict. c. 91. *Supra*, § 833.

2335. The pursuer must be a creditor holding a real right, and the creditors must be in possession either actually, or by decree of maills and duties, or by sequestration of the rents; and the whole estate must be included (*a*).

(*a*) 1681, c. 17. 2 Bell's Com. 250 (236, M'L.'s ed.).

2336. The Court of Session fixes the upset price, and the day and place of sale; and certain notices being given, the sale proceeds on articles of roup in presence of the Lord Ordinary, before whom the process of sale depends. The price is secured by caution and consignation for the purpose of division in the ranking; and the purchaser's title is an irredeemable decree of sale and adjudication, fortified by assignations to the debts and securities of the creditors holding real rights over the estate (*a*).

(*a*) 2 Bell's Com. 270 (251, M'L.'s ed.), and cases there cited.

2337. (2.) *Judicial Sale by an Apparent Heir.*—It is made competent to the apparent heir of the debtor to bring his predecessor's estate to a judicial sale, whether there be insolvency or not (*a*). Apparency alone is a sufficient title. 'And the right is not lost by behaviour as heir (*b*), nor by renunciation in an action of constitution (*c*).' But where the heir is actually entered, he cannot thus sell the estate (*d*). The apparent heir is regarded as a trustee for all the creditors; and so the sale is an adjudication for them all (*e*). But in this respect both kinds of judicial sale are now on the same footing; the decree of sale being held as an adjudication for all concerned, as at the date of the first calling of the process of sale, and all separate adjudications are discharged.

(*a*) 1695, c. 24.

(*b*) Blair *v.* Stewart, 1733; M. 5247. 2 Ersk. 12. § 61. 2 Ersk. Pr. 12. § 27. *Supra*, § 1919.

(*c*) Belshier's Crs. *v.* Heir, 1776; 5 B. Sup. 561; Hailes, 693. Smith *v.* Harris, 1854; 16 D. 727. See above, § 1686.

(*d*) 3 Ersk. 8. § 69. 2 Bell's Com. 259 (241, M'L.'s ed.).

(*e*) Irvine *v.* Maxwell, 1748; M. 5264. Haldane *v.* Palmer, 1791; M. 5299. Massey *v.* Smith, 1785; M. 8377.

2338. Sequestration of Land Estate.—Before the introduction of judicial sale, the only method of making the estate available to several creditors was by sequestration. At present, sequestration is an intermediate and preservative proceeding, for collecting and accounting for the rents. It is competent wherever the estate is in competition, and an action of sale in dependence (*a*). It is a summary proceeding by petition; a factor is appointed on the recommendation of the creditors, accountable according to fixed rules (*b*).

(*a*) Elliot *v.* Scott, 1843; 5 D. 1075. Russell *v.* M'Inturner, 1847; 9 D. 989. Munro *v.* Graham, 1849; 11 D. 1202. Watson *v.* Shand, 1849; 12 D. 394. Gilmour *v.* Gilmour's Trs., 1850; 12 D. 1266. Campbell *v.* Campbell, 1863; 1 Macph. 991; aff. 1864, 2 Macph. H. L. 41; 4 Macq. 711. Thoms *v.* Thoms, 1865; 3 Macph. 776. Padwick *v.* Steuart, 1871; 9 Macph. 793. Catton *v.* Mackenzie, 1870; 8 Macph. 713.

(*b*) Act of Sederunt, Jan. 17, 1756. See 2 Bell's Com. 262 (244, M'L.'s ed.) et seq.

2339. The creditors, assembled according to certain rules, elect a person to attend to the common interest of all, in conducting the sales, and receiving the claims, and arranging the ranking, so as to have the rights and interests of the creditors fairly discussed (*a*).

(*a*) Act of Sederunt, July 11, 1794.

2340. A committee for superintendence and advice is named by the creditors from their own number (*a*).

(*a*) Act of Sederunt, July 11, 1794.

CHAPTER VI

OF STATUTORY SEQUESTRATION

2341. General View.—This process includes the whole estates, heritable and moveable, of merchants and manufacturers, and has been by a late statute greatly reformed (*a*). It may be sufficient to present a very slight and general idea of this system of proceeding, the details of which require a very anxious study of the statute.

(*a*) 2 and 3 Vict. c. 41.

2341A. 'The existing statute is 19 and 20 Vict. c. 79, with an amending Act, 20 and 21 Vict. c. 19 (*a*). Generally speaking, the provisions are the same as those in the statute 2 and 3 Vict. c. 41. The most important differences are,—1*st*, That sequestration is not confined to the estates of merchants, but is extended to those of all persons; and 2*nd*, That sequestration may be awarded by the Sheriff Courts as well as by the Court of Session. Another statute, 19 and 20 Vict. c. 91, re-enacted *verbatim* certain provisions in the Act of 54 Geo. III. c. 137, relative to arrestments, poindings, judicial sales, adjudications, and securities for cash credits.'

(*a*) A full exposition of the Sequestration Statute is given by Mr. Shaw in his edition of Bell's Commentaries, p. 1186 et seq., and is reprinted with additional matter in Lord M'Laren's edition, vol. ii. p. 281 et seq. See also Goudy on Bankruptcy.

2342. Title to Sequestrate.—It 'was' competent to a creditor having a debt of a certain extent to apply to the Lord Ordinary on the Bills for sequestration of the estates of his debtor, if a merchant or manufacturer in Scotland, or a company within that description, and bankrupt in terms of the Act 1696 (*a*): or having retired to and remained in the sanctuary for twelve months (*b*). The debtor himself, though not bankrupt, 'might' apply for sequestration to the same effect; and the estate of a person deceased who 'gave' a mandate to that effect, or died notour bankrupt, or after having been for sixty days in the sanctuary, 'might' be sequestrated (*c*). The proceedings which formerly were conducted in the Court of Session, 'were' sent to the Sheriff; his orders and judgments being subject to the review of the Court of Session (*d*).

'Sequestration may now be awarded of the estates of any living debtor subject to the jurisdiction of the Supreme Courts (*e*), on his own petition, with the concurrence of a creditor or creditors to a certain amount; or on the petition of a creditor or creditors duly qualified (*f*), provided the debtor be notour bankrupt, and have within a year before the date of the presentation of the petition resided or had a dwelling-house or place of business in Scotland; or in the case of a company being notour bankrupt, if it have within such time carried on business in Scotland, and any partner have so resided or had a dwelling-house, or if the company have had a place of business, in Scotland. Sequestration may also be awarded of the estates of a deceased debtor who at the date of his death was subject to the jurisdiction of the Supreme Courts, on the petition of a mandatary to whom he had granted a mandate to apply for sequestration; or on the petition of a creditor or creditors duly qualified. The statutory conditions being complied with, sequestration must be awarded, and the Court has no discretion: it must exercise its ministerial duty and grant sequestration (*g*).'

(*a*) 1696, c. 5. 2 and 3 Vict. c. 41, § 5 and 6.
(*b*) *Ib.* § 7. (*c*) *Ib.* § 5. (*d*) *Ib.* § 13 et seq.
(*e*) See Joel *v.* Gill, 1859; 21 D. 929; 22 D. 6. By 22 and 23 Vict. c. 34, a sequestration may be recalled if three-fourths in number and value of the bankrupt's creditors reside in England or Ireland, and it shall appear to the Court of Session more expedient that his affairs should be wound up there. Cooper *v.* Baillie, 1878; 5 R. 564. A royal burgh may have its estates sequestrated. Wotherspoon *v.* Mags. of Linlithgow, 1863; 2 Macph. 348. A foreign sequestration gives the trustee or assignee a title to deal with the bankrupt's moveable estate in Scotland, and the Court will generally refuse to grant a second sequestration in Scotland. Strother *v.* Read, M. *Forum Comp.* 4. Goetze *v.* Aders, 1874; 2 R. 150. See Phosphate Sewage Co. *v.* Lawson & Son's Tr., 1878; 5 R. 1125; but it does not necessarily avoid a subsequent Scotch sequestration. Gibson *v.* Munro, 1894; 21 R. 840.
(*f*) 2 M'Laren's Bell's Com. 288 sqq.
(*g*) Joel *v.* Gill, *cit.* Stuart & Stuart *v.* Macleod, 1891; 19 R. 223.

2343. Trustee and Commissioners.—The trustee is elected by the creditors, under superintendence of the Sheriff, and he proceeds with advice of three commissioners, and of the creditors themselves, to have the estate and effects sold and realised, and the proceeds divided (*a*).

(*a*) Shaw's Bell's Com. 1211 et seq. 2 M'Laren's Bell's Com. 302 et seq.

2344. Vesting and Sale of the Estate.—Confirmation of the trustee's election vests him, 'as at the date of the sequestration, which is in all questions the date of the first deliverance in the petition for sequestration,' with the heritable estate in Scotland, as by absolute and irredeemable adjudication in implement, 'as well as a decree of adjudication for payment and in security of debt, subject to no legal reversion, and as if a decree of poinding of the ground had then been executed,' and also with estates in other countries under certain observances. He has thereby right also to future acquisitions of the bankrupt 'before his discharge,' and to all his moveable estate (*a*); 'but not to a mere expectancy or *spes successionis* (*b*). On the other hand, a bankrupt cannot, before he gets his discharge, alienate or discharge a *spes successionis* to the possible prejudice of his creditors (*c*).' The general adjudication operates as such to all the creditors, accumulating their debts as at the date of the first deliverance, and ranking with any prior effectual adjudication within year and day. The creditors may direct the estate thus vested in the trustee to be sold by the old process of judicial sale, or by public voluntary sale on articles of roup. The price is lodged in bank, subject to division in the sequestration (*d*). 'The Bankruptcy Act contains no prohibition of actions by creditors against the bankrupt for debts incurred before the sequestration. In general, creditors must establish their disputed debts by claiming in the sequestration, and appealing to the Sheriff or the Supreme Court if the trustee rejects their claims (*e*). It is doubtful whether in exceptional circumstances actions may not be raised against the bankrupt (*f*).'

(*a*) 19 and 20 Vict. c. 79, § 102, 103. See above, § 1468 (*g*). Jackson *v.* M'Kechnie, 1875; 3 R. 130. Barron *v.* Mitchell, 1881; 8 R. 933. By allowing an undischarged bankrupt to keep his estate or acquire new stock by trading as if independent, and by lapse of time, creditors may be barred from insisting in their right to after acquired property to the exclusion of new creditors. Christie *v.* Lowden, 1835; 14 S. 191. Taylor *v.* Charteris & Andrew, 1879; 7 R. 128. Abel *v.* Watt, 1883; 11 R. 149. See Drybrough *v.* Macdonald, 1893; 20 R. 396 (appointment of new trustees after nineteen years' delay and acquiescence).
(*b*) Reid *v.* Morrison, 1893; 20 R. 510.
(*c*) Obers *v.* Paton's Trs., 1897; 24 R. 719.
(*d*) Shaw's Bell's Com. 1246 et seq. 2 M'Laren's Bell's Com. 335 et seq.
(*e*) Phosphate Sewage Co. *v.* Molleson, 1874; 1 R. 840 (*per* L. Shand).
(*f*) See Goudy on Bankruptcy, 361, and the cases cited. M'Kinnon *v.* Monkhouse, 1881; 9 R. 394, 401 (*per* L. P. Inglis). Fraser *v.* Robertson, 1881; 8 R. 347. Swan *v.* Craig, 1874; 1 Sel. Sh. Ct. Ca. 51. Melvin *v.* Campbell, 1876; *ib.* 54. M'Kellar *v.* Stark, 1888; 4 Sh. C. R. 404, where the cases are reviewed.

2345. Proof of Debts.—It is necessary to produce such accounts and vouchers of his debt in the creditor's possession as are necessary to prove the debt, and also to swear to the verity of the debt, specifying in his oath all his securities; and in order to vote respecting any of the questions in the sequestration 'or to rank,' he is required to deduct such securities and collateral obligations as afford a right of relief to the bankrupt. Those proofs undergo a certain scrutiny in case of contested elections or disputed resolutions. And in preparing for payment of a dividend, it is the duty of the trustee to examine and judge of the admissibility of the several claims, his judgment being subject to the review of the Sheriff or the Lord Ordinary on the Bills, and finally to the judgment of the Inner House of the Court of Session and House of Lords (*a*).

(*a*) Shaw's Bell's Com. 1213 et seq. 2 M'Laren's Bell's Com. 304, 309, 331.

2346. Payment of Dividends.—The dividends are to be paid, the first at the end of 'six' months, the second at the end of 'ten' months, and the subsequent dividends at the end of every 'three' months (*a*).

(*a*) Shaw's Bell's Com. 1277 et seq. 2 M'Laren's Bell's Com. 365.

2347. Composition. — It is competent, at the meeting for electing a trustee, or at any meeting called for the purpose after the examination of the bankrupt, to propose the payment of a composition to the creditors on the whole debts; which being intimated by Gazette notice, and by letter to each creditor, if accepted by a majority in number and nine-tenths in value, 'or, if made at a subsequent meeting, if accepted by a majority in number and four-fifths in value,' and caution found to the satisfaction of the creditors, shall be confirmed, and the bankrupt discharged (*a*).

(*a*) Shaw's Bell's Com. 1264 et seq. 2 M'Laren's Bell's Com. 348 sqq. When the offer has been accepted there is a completed contract, and neither bankrupt nor cautioner can withdraw except on cause shown. Lee *v.* Stevenson's Tr., 1883; 11 R. 26.

2348. Person of the Bankrupt.—Where a debtor has failed by innocent misfortune, and gives up to his creditors for their satisfaction all his means of payment, it is equitable, and consistent with humanity and good policy, that his person should be freed from imprisonment. This 'was' done in sequestration, 'before the practical abolition of imprisonment for debt,' either as an intermediate proceeding, or as a final discharge, or by *cessio bonorum* (*a*).

(*a*) See *ante*, § 2321.

2349. (1.) *Protection.* — At awarding the sequestration, the Sheriff 'was' empowered to grant an interim protection against arrest or imprisonment for civil debt, or a warrant of liberation until the meeting of creditors for the election of a trustee. And the protection 'might' be renewed on the resolution of a majority 'in number and value' of the creditors 'present at the statutory meetings or at a meeting called for the purpose' to that effect (*a*).

(*a*) Shaw's Bell's Com. 1206 et seq. 2 M'Laren's Bell's Com. 298.

2350. (2.) *Allowance to the Bankrupt.* — The creditors at the meeting for choosing a trustee, or 'at the meeting held after the' examination of the bankrupt, or when called for the purpose, may, by a majority of four-fifths in value of those present, grant an allowance to the bankrupt of 'not more than' three guineas per week till the time of paying the second dividend (*a*). 'At any time afterwards, if a majority express an opinion that a special allowance to the bankrupt is for the benefit of the estate, and if the Accountant of Court report in its favour, the Lord Ordinary or the Court of Session, on the application of the trustee, may award such allowance.'

(*a*) Shaw's Bell's Com. 1235. 2 M'Laren's Bell's Com. 323.

2351. Discharge.—The bankrupt, after he has undergone his examinations, 'and upon a report by the trustee (*a*),' may apply for a discharge with the unanimous consent of the creditors who have produced their oaths; or on the expiration of 'six' months from the sequestration, he may apply with consent of a majority in number and four-fifths in value; 'on the lapse of twelve months, he may apply with consent of a majority in number and two-thirds in value; at the expiration of eighteen months, he may apply with concurrence of a majority in number and value; and on expiration of two years, he may apply without any concurrence.' In twenty-one days after a Gazette notice, the Lord Ordinary or Sheriff shall determine on any objections that may be stated in opposition to the demand, and either grant the discharge or refuse it, or allow it under certain conditions, certain precautions being provided against collusive and undue discharges (*b*). 'But no bankrupt is at any time entitled to a discharge, unless it is proved to the Lord Ordinary or the Sheriff either (1) that a dividend or composition of five shillings in the pound out of the estate or security for payment thereof has been found to the satisfaction of the creditors; or (2) that the failure to do so has arisen from circumstances for which (in the opinion of the Lord Ordinary or the Sheriff) the bankrupt cannot justly be held responsible (*c*).'

(*a*) White *v.* White's Tr., 1879; 6 R. 854. Mather *v.* M'Kittrick, 1881; 8 R. 952.

(*b*) Shaw's Bell's Com. 1284 et seq. 2 M'Laren's Bell's Com. 367 sqq.

(*c*) 44 and 45 Vict. c. 22, § 6. Clarke *v.* Crockatt & Co., 1883; 11 R. 246. Boyle, petr., 1885; 12 R. 1147. Alison *v.* Robertson's Trs., 1890; 18 R. 212.

INDEX OF MATTERS

The figures refer to the section—not to the page.

B

D

I

S

TABLE

Showing the Numbers of the Sections in this Edition which correspond with the Numbers of the Sections in the Fourth (or preceding) Edition, in so far as the former Numbers were altered by Mr. Shaw. In many of these, part *only of a Section in the Fourth has been transferred to or embraced in another Section in this Edition. This is marked by a circumflex.*

Sects. in the Fourth Edition.	Corresponding Sects. in this Edition.
152	151
246	247
248	246 248
308	306 307
313	306
314	313
329	325
381	382
382	381
392	400
393	392
395	396
396	393
418	419
467 472	466
560	559
561	560 561
632	630
648	651
651	652
692 693	692
694	693
695	693 694
704 705	705
718 727	728
726 728	726 727
734	730
735	736
749	750
799	798
825	826
826	827
827	825
864	865
865	866
866	867
869	864
870	870
871	869
872	870 871 872
879	889
975	976
976	977
977	978

Sects. in the Fourth Edition.	Corresponding Sects. in this Edition.
978	975
980	979
979 983	980
1033	1034
1034	1033
1035	1036
1036	1035
1042 1044	1044
1043	1042 1043
1169	1171
1170	1169
1171	1170
1179	1178
1269	1270
1270	1269
1324	1325
1325	1324
1356	1357
1357	1358
1358	1359
1359	1360
1360	1361
1361	1360
1410 1411	1410
1461	1462
1467	1460
1514	1515
1516 1517	1517
1519	1516
1544	1541
1549	1552
1551	1553
1552	1549
1553	1551
1652	1653 1654
1653	1652
1670 1676	1671
1671	1670
1675	1675 1676
1708 1710	1707
1711	1710
1716	1717
1717	1718
1718 1719	1719
1720	1716

Sects. in the Fourth Edition.	Corresponding Sects. in this Edition.
1721	1720
1722	1721
1723	1722
1724	1723
1748	1756 1760
1825	1826
1826	1827
1827	1826 1828
1828	1829
1829	1830
1830	1831
1831	1832
1832	1842
1833	1843
1834 1835	1833
1836	1834
1837	1835
1838	1836
1839	1837
1840	1838
1841	1839
1842	1841
1843	1840
1850 1851	1850 1852
1853	1851
1854	1825
1855	1854
1863	1864
1864	1866
1865	1867
1866	1863
1867	1868
1868	1869 1874
1869	1870
1870 1871 1871	1873 1875
1872	1878
1873 1875 1875	1876 1880
1874 1875	1877
1876	1886
1877	1880
1878	1881
1879	1882
1880	1879
1881	1883
1882	1884

Sects. in the Fourth Edition.	Corresponding Sects. in this Edition.
1883	1862
1884	1865
1885	1871, 1872
1886, 1887, 1888	1887
1902	1901
1816, 1922	1922
1937	1938
1939	1940
1940	1937
1950	1952, 1951
1951	1952
1960	1961
1961	1962
1962	1963
1963	1964
1964	1960
1966	1970
1967	1971
1968	1966
1969	1967
1970	1972
1971	1968
1994	1995
1995	1993
1996	1997
2008, 2015	2008
2013	2009
2014	2013, 2014
2016	2015
2017	2016, 2017
2059	2058
2060	2059
2061	2060, 2061
2081	2085
2085	2086
2086	2087
2087	2088
2088	2100
2089	2090
2090	2089
2093	2092
2094	2093, 2094
2098	2102
2106	2109
2107	2108
2108	2110
2109	2111
2110	2106
2111	2107
2121	2121, 2122
2122	2068
2147	2148
2148	2149
2150	2160
2151	2189
2152	2190
2153	2191
2154	2192
2155	2193
2156	2194
2157	2195
2158	2196
2159	2197
2160	2198
2161	2199
2162	2200
2163	2201
2164	2202
2165	2203
2166	2204
2167	2176
2168	2177
2169	2178
2170	2179
2171	2189
2173	2161
2174	2162
2175	2172
2176	2163, 2164, 2165, 2168
2177	2166
2178	2167
2179	2169
2180	2170
2181	2171
2182	2168
2183	2181
2184	2182
2185	2183
2186	2184
2187	2185
2188	2186
2189	2187
2190	2173
2191	2174
2192	2175
2193	2188
2194	2149
2195	2150
2196	2151
2197	2152
2198	2153
2199	2154
2200	2155
2201	2156
2202	2157
2203	2158
2204	2159
2264	2263, 2265
2265	2266
2266	2264
2271	2270
2270	2271
2289	2288
2288	2289
2294	2295
2297	2296
2300	2301
2301	2302
2302	2303
2303, 2304	2304
2327	2326
2326	2327
2339	2336
2336	2338
2337	2339
2338	2340
2340	2337
2347	2348
2348	2349
2349	2350
2350	2351
2351	2347
2352, 2353, 2354	2321

Howden on Trusts and Trustees.

Trusts, Trustees, and the Trusts Acts in Scotland. With a Chapter on Executors. By CHARLES R. A. HOWDEN, M.A., Advocate. 8vo, price 15s. net.

SUMMARY OF CONTENTS :—Constitution and Proof of Trust.—Classification.—Resulting and Constructive Trusts.—The Office of Trustee Gratuitous.—Truster, Trustee, and Beneficiary.—Estate in Truster, Trustee, and Beneficiary.—Trust Purposes.—Nomination of Trustees.—Acceptance of Office.—Assumption of New Trustees.—Appointment by Court.—Removal of Trustee by Court.—Resignation.—Termination of Trust, and Exoneration and Discharge of Trustee.—Executors.—Confirmation and Probate Act, 1858.—Powers.—Special Powers.—Liability as between Trustees and Beneficiaries.—Liability to Third Parties.—Liability for Expenses.—Charitable Trusts.—Foreign Law and Jurisdiction.—APPENDIX.—INDEX OF CASES CITED.—INDEX OF SUBJECTS.

'Mr. Howden's treatise will be found comprehensive and complete, in a highly creditable degree, within the branch of the law with which it deals. His scheme of arrangement is good, and renders the work convenient for reference. . . . Altogether, the work, in our opinion, is a successful one, and is certain to prove itself genuinely useful both to practitioners and to trustees and executors.'—*Scots Law Times.*

Smith on Expenses.

The Law of Expenses in the Supreme and Sheriff Courts of Scotland. By R. E. MONTEITH SMITH, M.A., LL.B., Advocate. In demy 8vo, price 18s.

SUMMARY OF CONTENTS :—Practice of Court in Granting, Refusing, Modifying, and Reserving Expenses.—Caution for Expenses.—Sisting a Mandatary.—Poor's Roll.—Effect of Tender upon Expenses.—Expenses in course of an ordinary Action.—In Jury Trials.—Parties liable in and entitled to Expenses.—Expenses affecting Agents.—In particular Actions. — Under particular Statutes.—In Teind, Justiciary, and Registration Courts.—In Appeals to House of Lords.—In Sheriff and Small Debt Courts.—Audit and Taxation of Accounts.—APPENDICES.—INDICES.

'The needs of practising lawyers are so well understood, and so carefully consulted, that the treatise will at once have a high reputation. Exactness, comprehensiveness, good arrangement, and an elaborate and accurate apparatus of reference, are the best qualities of a digest of this kind, and they are present in every part of the book. The work leaves no department of its large subject untouched, and is always clear and succinct in its statements of rules and exceptions.'—*Scotsman.*

Smith on Damages. *Second Edition.*

The Law of Damages: A Treatise on the Reparation of Injuries, as administered in Scotland. By JOHN GUTHRIE SMITH, Sheriff of Aberdeen, Kincardine, and Banff. Second Edition. In demy 8vo, price 20s.

CONTENTS :—CHAP. I. Grounds of Responsibility. II. Delict and Contract. III. The Limitations of Responsibility. IV. The Church and the Civil Law. V. Trespass to Person and Property. VI. Road and Railway Accidents. VII. Collisions at Sea. VIII. Fraud. IX. Injuries to Land. X. Defamation. XI. Abuse of Legal Process. XII. Infringement of Copyright, Patents, and Trade Marks. XIII. Master and Servant. XIV. The Measure of Damages. Appendix.

'This work, touching every province of human life or experience, could have been written only by one who had pronounced many decisions and turned over many law books. It bears the stamp of long industry and wide erudition in domestic and foreign jurisprudence.'—*The Juridical Review.*

Bell's Commentaries.

Seventh Edition.

Commentaries on the Law of Scotland, and on the Principles of Mercantile Jurisprudence. By GEORGE JOSEPH BELL, Professor of the Law of Scotland in the University of Edinburgh. Seventh Edition. Being a republication of the Fifth Edition, with additional Notes, adapting the work to the present state of the Law, and comprising abstracts of the more recent English authorities illustrative of the Law of Scotland. By the Hon. Lord M'LAREN. In Two Volumes, demy 4to, price £5, 5s.

Dickson on Evidence.

A Treatise on the Law of Evidence in Scotland. By WILLIAM GILLESPIE DICKSON, Advocate. Re-cast, adapted to the present state of the Law, and in part rewritten, by P. J. HAMILTON GRIERSON, B.A. Oxon., Advocate. In Two Volumes, royal 8vo, price 42s.

'"Dickson on Evidence" has no rival.'—*Scottish Law Review.*

'The editorial work has been excellently done. . . . The highest praise that can be given to Mr. Grierson is that many, if not all, of his additions have so much the character and accurate induction of the original work that they cannot be distinguished from "Dickson" without looking at the older editions, or the date of the authority cited.'—*Glasgow Herald.*

Coldstream's Procedure in the Court of Session.

Fourth Edition.

By JOHN P. COLDSTREAM, W.S., Lecturer in the University of Edinburgh on Civil and Criminal Procedure. Fourth Edition, Enlarged and Revised. In demy 8vo, price 18s.

'The rapidity with which the work has gone through so many editions since its first appearance is the best evidence of its value. Written originally as a text-book for students, it has come to be largely used by the legal profession as a guide and aid in practice.'—*Scotsman.*

'A Fourth Edition has been published of Mr. Coldstream's "Procedure in the Court of Session." For thoroughness and handiness combined, Mr. Coldstream's work is by far the best manual extant of the forms of procedure in our Supreme Court. . . . For the Law Agent's examination in especial it is the recognised preparative. The present edition has been carefully revised and largely added to, so as to bring it abreast with the latest reforms of the law.'—*Scottish Leader.*

Fraser on Husband and Wife. *Second Edition.*

Treatise on Husband and Wife, according to the Law of Scotland. By the late Hon. LORD FRASER, LL.D. In Two Volumes, royal 8vo, Second Edition, price £4.

'Still more conspicuously in its new than in its old form, the book furnishes proof of the learning, the industry, and the expository power of its author, and it is not likely to lose its place among the very highest authorities on the vast and complex subject with which it deals.'—*Scotsman.*

'It is a book that will be necessary to every practising lawyer, to every student of Scotch history, and to every one who attempts to meddle with the marriage laws of Scotland in parliamentary or popular discussion.'—*Glasgow Herald.*

'One of the most complete legal monographs that has ever been written.'—*Journal of Jurisprudence.*

Fraser on Master and Servant. *Third Edition.*

Treatise on Master and Servant, Employer and Workman, and Master and Apprentice. Third Edition. By WILLIAM CAMPBELL, M.A., Advocate. In One Volume, royal 8vo, price 36s.

This Edition embodies the whole changes effected in the law in recent years as to Employers' Liability; Factories; Miners, Seamen, and other workmen; together with Forms of Procedure in actions relative to Masters and Servants at Common Law, and under the various statutes applicable to workmen. It also contains the 'Summary Jurisdiction (Scotland) Act, 1881,' and the 'Summary Jurisdiction (Process) Act, 1881,' with a Commentary and Notes.

'There can be no question that Lord Fraser has been very fortunate in his editor, and that Mr. Campbell has given great labour and research to the successful discharge of his task. . . . The book is a good book, which has been well edited, and its best praise is, that it is worthy in its present form to take the place beside Lord Fraser's own edition of "Husband and Wife." There is an excellent general index, as befits a standard work for practical use.'—*Scotsman.*

Renton's Criminal Procedure.

Procedure and Appeal in Summary Criminal Cases in Scotland, with Appendix containing Forms of Complaints and Appeals, and Statutes. By R. W. RENTON, S.S.C., Procurator-Fiscal of Fifeshire. In demy 8vo, price 7s. 6d.

'This book is a new departure, and supplies a want in the profession. . . . We heartily recommend it for its clearness, point, and practical usefulness.'—*The Juridical Review.*

'Mr. Renton's book will be welcome to practitioners in the Inferior Courts as a concise and well-arranged digest of the rules of the statutes and decisions which regulate the manner of conducting prosecutions.'—*Scotsman.*

'It is a thoroughly good piece of workmanship. Not only is the matter clearly and orderly arranged, but concise digests of "illustrative cases" are sandwiched between the sections of the expository text. The usefulness of such a manual is not confined to those actually engaged in the work of summary criminal courts: it provides also a short cut for the consulting lawyer in cases of difficulty to arrive at the sources of the law on a necessarily technical subject.'—*Scots Observer.*

Stewart on Fishing. *Second Edition.*

A Treatise on the Law of Scotland relating to Rights of Fishing. Comprising the Law affecting Sea Fishing, Salmon Fishing, Trout Fishing, Oyster and Mussel Fishing, etc. With an Appendix of Statutes and Bye-Laws. By CHARLES STEWART, Advocate. Second Edition. Edited by J. C. SHAIRP, Advocate, Sheriff-Substitute, Inveraray. In demy 8vo, price 20s.

'The standard authority on the subject. . . . We cordially recommend the second edition of Mr. Stewart's treatise, as containing a clear, full, and accurate account of the Law of Scotland relating to Rights of Fishing.'—*Field.*

'With so far-reaching and careful a revision, the work will rise high in the estimation of the legal profession and become a standard book of reference on the subject.'—*Scotsman.*

Irvine's Game Laws. *Third Edition.*

Treatise on the Game Laws of Scotland; with Appendix containing the principal Statutes and Forms. By ALEXANDER FORBES IRVINE, Advocate. Third Edition. Price 12s. 6d.

'This work may well claim to be *the* authority on the Game Laws of Scotland, not only on account of the exhaustive method in which the subject is treated, but also on account of the clear and learned manner in which the law has been laid down and expounded.'—*Glasgow Herald.*

Johnston's Crofters' Act.

The Crofters' Holdings (Scotland) Acts, 1886, 1887, and 1888. With an Introduction and Notes, and an Appendix containing the Rules of Procedure, Forms for use under the Acts, the Table of Fees, etc. By CHRISTOPHER N. JOHNSTON, M.A., Advocate. Second Edition. In demy 8vo, price 5s.

'The book, which is well indexed, is altogether a very creditable piece of work, and thoroughly analyses our latest "new departure" on the legislative line.'—*Scotsman.*

Steele's Landed Estates.

Handbook on the Management of Landed Estates and the Law relating thereto. With Appendix. By W. H. STEELE, Solicitor. In demy 8vo, price 5s.

'It will, without doubt, prove useful to factors, landlords, and tenants, as bringing them a plain definition of their position in law.'—*Scotsman.*

'In a concise and simple manner the author has produced a *vade mecum* for landlords, their agents and tenants, by the use of which they will be enabled to thoroughly comprehend the various clauses of an agricultural lease, and their respective rights and privileges under the same.'—*Estates Gazette.*